Mediterranean Europe

Tom Brosnahan
Stefano Cavedoni
Steve Fallon
Kate Galbraith
Helen Gillman
Paul Hellander
Charlotte Hindle
John King

Jeanne Oliver
Corinne Simcock
Damien Simonis
Dorinda Talbot
Sally Webb
Julia Wilkinson
David Willett
Neil Wilson

LONELY PLANET PUBLICATIONS
Melbourne • Oakland • London • Paris

MEDITERRANEAN EUROPE

Mediterranean Europe
4th edition – January 1999
First published – January 1993

Published by
Lonely Planet Publications Pty Ltd A.C.N. 005 607 983
192 Burwood Rd, Hawthorn, Victoria 3122, Australia

Lonely Planet Offices
Australia PO Box 617, Hawthorn, Victoria 3122
USA 150 Linden St, Oakland, CA 94607
UK 10a Spring Place, London NW5 3BH
France 1 rue du Dahomey, 75011 Paris

Front cover photograph
Simon Bracken, Lonely Planet Images
Images are available for licensing from Lonely Planet Images.
email: lpi@lonelyplanet.com.au

ISBN 0 86442 619 4

Contents – Text

ITALY

MACEDONIA

MALTA

MOROCCO

4 Contents – Text

Contents – Maps

MAP LEGEND – SEE BACK PAGE

The Authors

Tom Brosnahan

Tom wrote the Turkey chapter. He was born in Pennsylvania, went to college in Boston, then set out on the road. He first went to Turkey as a US Peace Corps volunteer, teaching English and learning Turkish. He studied Ottoman Turkish history and language for eight years, but abandoned the writing of his PhD dissertation in favour of writing guidebooks. Tom is also an author of Lonely Planet guides to Turkey, Istanbul, Guatemala, Belize & Yucatán: La Ruta Maya, Mexico, Central America, New England, the Turkish phrasebook, and other Lonely Planet guides. His email address is tbros@infoexchange.com.

Steve Fallon

Steve was the coordinating author and updated most of the introductory chapters. Born in Boston, Massachusetts, he can't remember a time when he was not obsessed with travel, other cultures and languages. As a teenager he worked an assortment of jobs to finance trips to Europe and South America, and he graduated from Georgetown University with a Bachelor of Science in modern languages. The following year he taught English at the University of Silesia near Katowice, Poland. After working several years for a Gannett newspaper and obtaining a Master's degree in journalism, his fascination with the 'new' Asia took him to Hong Kong, where he lived and worked for 13 years for a variety of publications and was editor of *Business Traveller* magazine. In 1987, he opened Wanderlust Books, Asia's only travel bookshop. Steve lived in Budapest for 2½ years from where he wrote *Hungary* and *Slovenia* before moving to London in 1994. He has written or contributed to a number of other Lonely Planet titles.

Helen Gillman & Stefano Cavedoni

Helen and Stefano updated the Italy chapter. Helen worked as a journalist in Australia (where she was born) for many years before moving to Italy in 1990. Helen is the coordinating author of Lonely Planet's *Italy* guide and of the new *Walking in Italy* guide. Stefano is an actor and writer. He was a member of the successful Italian rock band Skiantos in the 1970s and later wrote and performed his own humorous one-man shows. He has recently made his first documentary for Italian television. Stefano wrote several chapters in the *Walking in Italy* guide and also helped update the *Italy* guide.

Kate Galbraith

Kate worked on the Bosnia chapter. Kate fell in love with Bosnia in 1996, when she worked for a local news agency in Sarajevo. She has been astounded by the changes the city has undergone since then, from the development of inter-entity bus lines to the introduction of a Versace gallery in Sarajevo centre. Before settling back into Bosnia for Lonely Planet, she made a grand tour of Eastern Europe as a freelance writer. She suspects that she may forever be a wanderer.

Paul Hellander

Paul updated the Albania, Macedonia and Yugoslavia chapters. Paul has never really stopped travelling since he was born in England to a Norwegian father and English mother. He arrived in Australia in 1977, via Greece and 30 other countries, taught Modern Greek and trained interpreters and translators for thirteen years and then threw it all away for a life as a travel writer. Paul joined Lonely Planet in 1994 and wrote LP's *Greek phrasebook* before being assigned to the *Greece* and *Eastern Europe* books. Paul also updated the information on Singapore for *Singapore, Malaysia, Singapore & Brunei* and *South-East Asia*. He was last seen heading for Israel, but can always be reached at paul@planetmail.net.

Charlotte Hindle

Charlotte updated the Cyprus chapter. Born in Caerphilly, Wales, she studied art history at Leicester University. She au-paired in France, worked in a Swiss ski resort and sold theatre tickets in London before travelling to Australia. In 1988 Charlotte joined Lonely Planet and worked at the head office in Melbourne for 3½ years. In 1991 she returned to London to set up and run Lonely Planet's London office.

Jeanne Oliver

Jeanne updated the Croatia chapter. Born in New Jersey, she eventually moved to New York City where she got a job at the Village Voice newspaper and then earned a law degree. Her legal practice was interrupted by ever more frequent trips to Central and South America, Europe, and the Middle East. Finally she took down her shingle and headed east through Africa, India and Southeast Asia before finally landing in Paris. She now makes a living as a travel writer, covering France and other European destinations. In 1998, Jeanne wrote the first edition of Lonely Planet's guidebook to Croatia and can be reached in cyberspace at j-oliver@worldnet.fr.

Corinne Simcock

Corinne helped to update the Greece chapter. Born in London, she spent the first 10 years of her career as a sound engineer in the music industry. In 1988, sick of spending 18 hours a day in a basement listening to people who can't play, she chucked it all in to become a journalist, writing for national newspapers and magazines about everything from travel and crime to business and personal finance. She has travelled through more than 30 countries and her passion in life is deserts.

Damien Simonis

Damien updated the Andorra and Spain chapters. Following a degree in languages and several years' reporting and sub-editing on several Australian newspapers (including *The Australian* and *The Age*), Sydney-born Damien left Australia in 1989. He has lived, worked and travelled extensively throughout Europe, the Middle East and North Africa. Since 1992, he has been kept busy by Lonely Planet's *Jordan & Syria, Egypt & the Sudan, Morocco, North Africa, Italy, Spain* and *The Canary Islands*. He was last seen in Barcelona writing Lonely Planet's forthcoming guide to that city. When not on the road, Damien resides in splendid Stoke Newington, in deepest north London.

Dorinda Talbot

Dorinda updated the Morocco chapter. Born in Melbourne, she began travelling at the age of five months – to visit her grandparents in Blighty – and has since visited several other far flung corners of the globe. After studying journalism at Deakin University in Geelong, Dorinda worked as a reporter in Alice Springs and a sub-editor in Melbourne before travelling across South-East Asia to London. She worked as a journalist (and sometime fruiterer) in London for several years before hauling on her walking boots to update Lonely Planet's *Canada* guide (the flat bits as it turned out). Dorinda also updated Lonely Planet's guides to Morocco and Samoa and has contributed to *Western Europe* and *Africa*.

Sally Webb

Sally updated the Malta chapter. She was born and brought up in Melbourne but has spent many years living in both Britain and Italy and has travelled extensively throughout Europe, the USA and Asia. After a few years as an art historian, she decided it was time for a career change and became a journalist and travel writer instead. Sally moved to Italy in 1994 (in search of the perfect 'tiramisu') and currently lives in the heart of Rome where she works as a writer and editor.

Julia Wilkinson & John King

Julia and John updated the Portugal chapter. Julia has been a travel junkie ever since she donned her first backpack at the age of four. After university, she headed for Australia but got sidetracked in Hong Kong, where she worked in publishing and radio before becoming a writer and photographer. Since then she has travelled throughout Asia, writing for international publications and contributing to various guidebooks. In addition to helping update the Portugal chapters of *Western Europe* she has also authored Lonely Planet's *Lisbon City Guide* and co-authored Lonely Planet's *Portugal* guide with her husband John King.

John grew up in the USA, and in earlier 'incarnations' has been a university physics teacher and an environmental consultant. In 1984 he headed off to China, and ended up living there for half a year. During that time he and Julia crossed paths in Lhasa, the Tibetan capital. After surviving a three-month journey across China and Pakistan they decided anything was possible, and in 1988 John took up travel writing, starting with the 1st edition of Lonely Planet's *Karakoram Highway*. He is also co-author of Lonely Planet's *Central Asia; Russia, Ukraine & Belarus; Pakistan; Czech & Slovak Republics*; and the *Prague City Guide*.

After two decades in Hong Kong, Julia and John are now based in south-west England, with their son Kit and daughter Lia.

David Willett

David worked on the Greece chapter. He is a freelance journalist based near Bellingen on the mid-north coast of New South Wales, Australia. He grew up in Hampshire, England, and wound up in Australia in 1980 after working on newspapers in Iran (1975-78) and Bahrain. He spent two years as a sub-editor on Melbourne's *Sun* newspaper before trading a steady job for a warmer climate. David has travelled extensively in Europe, the Middle East and Asia.

Neil Wilson

Neil updated the France chapter using research done by Nicola Williams, Steve Fallon, Daniel Robinson and Teresa Fisher. After working as a petroleum geologist in Australia and the North Sea and doing research at Oxford University, Neil gave up the rock business for the more precarious life of a freelance writer and photographer. Since 1988 he has travelled in five continents and written some 25 travel and walking guides for various publishers. Born in Glasgow, Neil defected to the east at the age of 18 and still lives in Edinburgh. This is his first project for Lonely Planet.

FROM THE AUTHORS

Tom Brosnahan Thanks to Pat Yale, co-author of Lonely Planet's *Turkey*; Mr Selami Karaibrahimgil of the Turkish Tourism Office in New York; Mr Bülent Erdemgil, Press Counsellor in the Turkish Embassy in Washington; Mr Ersan Atsür and Ms Ebru Akkale of Orion-Tour in İstanbul; Mr Süha Ersöz of the Esbelli Evi in Ürgüp; and Ms Ann Nevens of the Hotel Empress Zoe in İstanbul for her help, hospitality and friendship.

Steve Fallon Special thanks to Črtomir Šoba for his assistance in whipping the Slovenia chapter into shape and much, much more. Thanks also to Charlotte Hindle and the staff at the Lonely Planet office in London for throwing me a lifeline (in this case, a desk) when I was adrift at sea. Caroline Birch and Pat Read, who loves paprika, did that too, and it is much appreciated.

Helen Gillman & Stefano Cavedoni Many thanks to Stefano's Sicilian friends Sandro Privitera and Ugo Esposito for their great support and hospitality. Thanks also to Paolo and Isabella Ciarchi in Milano, to Luca and Battina Tassara and Paolo Parodi in Liguria, to Beppe, Daniele, Ermanno, Norma and Filippo in Torino, to Ivrea in Piemonte, and to Riccardo Held and Rita Degli Esposti in Venezia. Thanks also to the various tourism offices in Italy for their help, in particular to ENIT (Ente Nazionale del Turismo), Lara Fantoni (Firenze APT), Aldo Cianci (Napoli APT), Rag. Pinna and Sig.Nardi (ESIT Sardegna), Dott. Sciacca and Sig.a Zappalà (Catania AAPIT), Arch. Sortino and Dott.ssa Salfi (Palermo APT), Dott. Butera, Sig.a Geraci and Paolo Sciortino (Trapani APT), Dott. Riggi (Comando Ripartimentale Foreste – Catania), Azienda Promozione Turistica Dolomiti, and Alto Adige Promozione Turismo.

Kate Galbraith In Sarajevo and Banja Luka, thanks to the respective tourist bureaus. In Banja Luka, thanks to Zagatha and her family for the special tour. In Mostar, *sretno* to Michael and Mladi Most, the unofficial bar/hotel/cinema/junk food restaurant. And David B, your support and history wisdom helped enormously.

And finally, as always, special thanks to my wonderful family.

Paul Hellander Thanks to Graham Witt (Melbourne); Geoff Harvey of DriveAway (Sydney); Mirko Apostolov (Ohrid); Marilyn-Rath Ivanovska, Steven Nicholas, Beti Banovska (Skopje); the Belgrade Tourism Office; Venera Ćoćolli (Tirana); Alekos and Valentini Papadopoulos (Thessaloniki), and Demetres Dounas (Athens) for providing a home and office away from home. Finally I must thank Stella for putting up with two overseas trips in short succession. My work, as ever, is dedicated to my sons Marcus and

Byron in Ioannina, Greece who may one day take inspiration from their father's peripatetic life.

Charlotte Hindle Charlotte would like to thank her father, Tom Hindle, who accompanied her on the research trip. She would also like to thank Andreas Christodoulides from the Cyprus Tourism Organisation, and Yilmaz Kalfaoglu from the North Cyprus Tourism Centre, both in London.

Jeanne Oliver A special thanks to the indefatigable Mirjana Žilić of the Croatian National Tourism Office for her patient support. Zdravko Kufrin and Damir Foršek of Adriatic Travel worked hard to make sure my trip went smoothly. Marie-Rose Kordić in Rab was exceptionally hospitable and makes a respectable French wine from her Rab vineyard. Thanks to the prizewinning Stanka Kraljević in Korčula for her outstanding dedication and to Aljoša Milat for his invaluable help. Vesna Jovićić in Pula is informative, insightful and went far out of her way to extend a warm welcome. Other tourism workers whose help I appreciate include Majda Šale in Baška, Gordana Perić in Zadar, Zdravko Banović in Split, and Antonjeta-Nives Miloš and Dubravka Vrenko in Dubrovnik. Hvala to all.

Corinne Simcock A huge thank you to everyone who helped with information, especially the following: Francesco, Maria, Archie and Henrik from Francesco's (Ios), Moraig and Stratos from Rhapsody bar (Mykonos), Debbie and Stratos from Café Picasso (Naxos); George and Stella from Olga's Pension (Rethymno); Andreas, Dimitri and Josette from Pension Andreas; also Jean, Danielle, Beatrice and Sara (Rhodes); Anna from Dakoutros Travel (Santorini); Jane from the Sunflower sandwich and salad bar (Symi); Christofis Ilias from Hotel Irini; and Pete Plumbley from Laskarina Holidays (Tilos). Thanks also to Mario Camerini from Postermap in Milan for his stunningly artistic and incredibly accurate aerial maps.

Damien Simonis People all over the place have helped me in many different ways. In Madrid, Debby, Gary and Alex Luhrman rolled out the welcome mat and allowed me free run of their home. As usual, a gaggle of friends in Madrid made my time there not only productive, but fun (maybe too much fun). They include Bàrbara Azcona, David Ing, Arancha Lamela Ruiz, Diane Palumbo, Àngeles Sànchez Caballero, Jean-Marc Simon, and Luis Soldevila. Geoff Leaver Heaton and Lola down in Màlaga gave Gnomo the valiant Renault 5 a temporary home while I was not thrashing the poor beasty. Up in Barcelona, I owe a lot to Susana Pellicer, Susan Kempster and the gang from Carrer de Sant Pere més alt (Michael, Paloma, Natalia).

Dorinda Talbot In Tangier, sincere thanks to Jack Adelmann ('Juan Capacha') for his charming company and invaluable help with research; thanks also to Abdesselom and all the staff at the Hôtel Continental. Many thanks to Alami Abdelafi for expert guidance through the old city of Fès and to Aziz Ihrouren of Casablanca for his homemade tajines and thoughtful medical assistance (not connected). In Marrakesh, a big round of applause to Fatima Outizal and all the other wonderful staff at the Hôtel Sherazade; to Khalida Hilm for an enjoyable tour through the souks, and to the many fellow travellers (Guy from Canada, Joannie and Bruce from Rome, Nicholas from Argentina, Patrick and Lucie from Marseille, Paul from Zimbabwe, the crew from Berkeley, Madelaine Murray, Alyssa Banta and the boys from Florence) who contributed to this update in some way.

Sally Webb Special thanks to Marika Doublet at the national Tourism Organisation Malta for her invaluable assistance. Thanks also to NTOM's Louis Azzopardi, James Azzopardi and Tessie Agius, and to Carmelj Caruana at the NSTS. In Rome, thanks to Helen Gillman and Stefano Cavedoni for their advice, to Mary, Maggie and Sabina for covering for me, and to Orla and Sari for cups of tea and pasta dinners respectively.

Julia Wilkinson & John King Our thanks first to Pilar Pereira of ICEP (Portugal's tourism organisation) in London for logistical support and patient responses to many queries. We are indebted, too, to Miguel Gonzaga of Lisbon's Visitors & Convention Bureau and to the formidable troika of Marco Oliveira, Maria José Braga and Joana Firmino at Porto's municipal turismo. The turismo staff at Aveiro, Beja, Bragança, Coimbra, Estremoz, Évora Faro, Sintra, Tavira and Vila Real also deserve a big obrigado. For first-rate help, we're grateful to Peter Mills of Rail Europe; Sue Copper of Eurolines; Pieter Beelen of Eurail; Paul Gowen at the RAC; and staff of several STA travel offices around the world. Finally, a toast of the best vintage port to John Hole for the memorable balloon flight over Castelo Branco (and the even more memorable landing!).

David Willett I'd like to thank my partner, Rowan, and our son, Tom, who accompanied me on my trip to Tunisia. Thanks also to the Grar family (Larbi, Nejia, Kamel, Lamia and Anis) for their hospitality. In Greece, I'd like to thank Tolis, Kevin and Lisa for their hospitality in Athens; special thanks go to my mate Iris for her dedication to bar and restaurant research.

Neil Wilson Many thanks to Steve Fallon, Nicola Williams, Daniel Robinson and Teresa Fisher for prompt replies to pedantic queries.

This Book

Many people helped create this 4th edition of *Mediterranean Europe*. Among the major contributors to past editions were Mark Armstrong, Mark Balla, Colin Clement, Adrienne Costanzo, Geoff Crowther, Rob van Driesum, Richard Everist, Hugh Finlay, Frances Linzee Gordon, Rosemary Hall, John Noble, Daniel Robinson, David Stanley, Robert Strauss, Gary Walsh, Tony Wheeler and Pat Yale.

This edition was updated by Tom Brosnahan, Steve Fallon, Kate Galbraith, Helen Gillman & Stefano Cavedoni, Paul Hellander Charlotte Hindle, Jeanne Oliver, Corinne Simcock, Damien Simonis, Dorinda Talbot, Sally Webb, Julia Wilkinson & John King, David Willett and Neil Wilson. Mark Honan updated the Getting Around chapter.

Mediterranean Europe is part of Lonely Planet's Europe series, which includes *Eastern Europe*, *Central Europe*, *Scandinavian & Baltic Europe* and *Western Europe*. Apart from these titles Lonely Planet also produces *Europe on a shoestring* which features 40 countries and publishes phrasebooks to these regions.

From the Publisher

The editing of this edition of *Mediterranean Europe* was coordinated by Rowan McKinnon and the cartography was coordinated by Jane Hart. The book was laid out by Rachel Black. They were very ably assisted by Janet Austin, Carolyn Bain, Vicki Beale, Simon Bracken, Miriam Cannell, Bethune Carmichael, Ada Cheung, Paul Clifton, Katie Cody, Piotr Czajkowski, Tony Fankhauser, Liz Filleul, Jane Fitzpatrick, Quentin Frayne, Ron Gallagher, Marcel Gaston, Paul Harding, Ann Jeffree, David Kemp, Chris Lee Ack, Dan Levin, Clay Lucas, Nicholas Lynagh-Banikoff, Craig MacKenzie, Anne Mulvaney, Mary Neighbour, Anthony Phelan, Helen Rowley, Jacqui Saunders, Andrew Tudor, Rebecca Turner, Tim Uden, Tamsin Wilson and Chris Wyness.

THANKS
Many thanks to the travellers who used the last edition and wrote to us with helpful hints, advice and interesting anecdotes. Your names appear in the back of this book.

Foreword

ABOUT LONELY PLANET GUIDEBOOKS

The story begins with a classic travel adventure: Tony and Maureen Wheeler's 1972 journey across Europe and Asia to Australia. Useful information about the overland trail did not exist at that time, so Tony and Maureen published the first Lonely Planet guidebook to meet a growing need.

From a kitchen table, then from a tiny office in Melbourne (Australia), Lonely Planet has become the largest independent travel publisher in the world, an international company with offices in Melbourne, Oakland (USA), London (UK) and Paris (France).

Today Lonely Planet guidebooks cover the globe. There is an ever-growing list of books and there's information in a variety of forms and media. Some things haven't changed. The main aim is still to help make it possible for adventurous travellers to get out there – to explore and better understand the world.

At Lonely Planet we believe travellers can make a positive contribution to the countries they visit – if they respect their host communities and spend their money wisely. Since 1986 a percentage of the income from each book has been donated to aid projects and human rights campaigns.

Updates Lonely Planet thoroughly updates each guidebook as often as possible. This usually means there are around two years between editions, although for more unusual or more stable destinations the gap can be longer. Check the imprint page (following the colour map at the beginning of the book) for publication dates.

Between editions up-to-date information is available in two free newsletters – the paper *Planet Talk* and email *Comet* (to subscribe, contact any Lonely Planet office) – and on our Web site at www.lonelyplanet.com. The *Upgrades* section of the Web site covers a number of important and volatile destinations and is regularly updated by Lonely Planet authors. *Scoop* covers news and current affairs relevant to travellers. And, lastly, the *Thorn Tree* bulletin board, and *Postcards* section of the site carry unverified, but fascinating, reports from travellers.

Correspondence The process of creating new editions begins with the letters, postcards and emails received from travellers. This correspondence often includes suggestions, criticisms and comments about the current editions. Interesting excerpts are immediately passed on via newsletters and the Web site, and everything goes to our authors to be verified when they're researching on the road. We're keen to get more feedback from organisations or individuals who represent communities visited by travellers.

> Lonely Planet gathers information for everyone who's curious about the planet – and especially for those who explore it first-hand. Through guidebooks, phrasebooks, activity guides, maps, literature, newsletters, image library, TV series and web site we act as an information exchange for a worldwide community of travellers.

Research Authors aim to gather sufficient practical information to enable travellers to make informed choices and to make the mechanics of a journey run smoothly. They also research historical and cultural background to help enrich the travel experience and allow travellers to understand and respond appropriately to cultural and environmental issues.

Authors don't stay in every hotel because that would mean spending a couple of months in each medium-sized city and, no, they don't eat at every restaurant because that would mean stretching belts beyond capacity. They do visit hotels and restaurants to check standards and prices, but feedback based on readers' direct experiences can be very helpful.

Many of our authors work undercover, others aren't so secretive. None of them accept freebies in exchange for positive write-ups. And none of our guidebooks contain any advertising.

Production Authors submit their raw manuscripts and maps to offices in Australia, USA, UK or France. Editors and cartographers – all experienced travellers themselves – then begin the process of assembling the pieces. When the book finally hits the shops some things are already out of date, we start getting feedback from readers, and the process begins again....

WARNING & REQUEST

Things change – prices go up, schedules change, good places go bad and bad places go bankrupt – nothing stays the same. So, if you find things better or worse, recently opened or long since closed, please tell us and help make the next edition even more accurate and useful. We genuinely value all the feedback we receive. Julie Young coordinates a well-travelled team that reads and acknowledges every letter, postcard and email and ensures that every morsel of information finds its way to the appropriate authors, editors and cartographers.

Everyone who writes to us will find their name in the next edition of the appropriate guidebook. They will also receive the latest issue of *Planet Talk*, our quarterly printed newsletter, or *Comet*, our monthly email newsletter. Subscriptions to both newsletters are free. The very best contributions will be rewarded with a free guidebook.

Excerpts from your correspondence may appear in new editions of Lonely Planet guidebooks, the Lonely Planet Web site, *Planet Talk* or *Comet*, so please let us know if you *don't* want your letter published or your name acknowledged.

Send all correspondence to the Lonely Planet office closest to you:

Australia: PO Box 617, Hawthorn, Victoria 3122
UK: 10A Spring Place, London NW5 3BH
USA: 150 Linden St, Oakland CA 94607
France: 1 rue du Dahomey, Paris 75011

Or email us at: talk2us@lonelyplanet.com

For news, views and updates see our web site: www.lonelyplanet.com

HOW TO USE A LONELY PLANET GUIDEBOOK

The best way to use a Lonely Planet guidebook is any way you choose. At Lonely Planet we believe the most memorable travel experiences are often those that are unexpected, and the finest discoveries are those you make yourself. Guidebooks are not intended to be used as if they provide a detailed set of infallible instructions!

Contents All Lonely Planet guidebooks follow the same format. The Facts about the Country chapters or sections give background information ranging from history to weather. Facts for the Visitor gives practical information on issues like visas and health. Getting There & Away gives a brief starting point for researching travel to and from the destination. Getting Around gives an overview of the transport options when you arrive.

The peculiar demands of each destination determine how subsequent chapters are broken up, but some things remain constant. We always start with background, then proceed to sights, places to stay, places to eat, entertainment, getting there and away, and getting around information – in that order.

Heading Hierarchy Lonely Planet headings are used in a strict hierarchical structure that can be visualised as a set of Russian dolls. Each heading (and its following text) is encompassed by any preceding heading that is higher on the hierarchical ladder.

Entry Points We do not assume guidebooks will be read from beginning to end, but that people will dip into them. The traditional entry points are the list of contents and the index. In addition, however, there is a complete list of maps and an index map illustrating map coverage.

There's also a colour map that shows highlights. These highlights are dealt with in greater detail in the Facts for the Visitor chapter, along with planning questions and suggested itineraries. Each chapter covering a geographical region begins with a locator map and another list of highlights. Once you find something of interest in a list of highlights, turn to the index.

Maps Maps play a crucial role in Lonely Planet guidebooks and include a huge amount of information. A legend is printed inside the back cover. We seek to have complete consistency between maps and text, and to have every important place in the text captured on a map. Map key numbers start in the top left corner.

Although inclusion in a guidebook usually implies a recommendation we cannot list every good place. Exclusion does not necessarily imply criticism. In fact there are reasons why we'll exclude an outstanding place – sometimes because it would be inappropriate to encourage an influx of travellers.

Introduction

Mediterranean Europe evokes images of beautiful beaches, the brilliant blue of the Mediterranean Sea, spectacular landscapes dotted with olive and citrus groves, outdoor cafés, wonderful food, friendly local people, exuberant festivals and a relaxed way of life. It *is* all this – and even more.

This book offers an insight into the many different countries of the region, their peoples and cultures, and provides practical information to help you get the most out of your time and money. It covers the area from Portugal and Morocco in the west to Cyprus and Turkey in the east. Although Portugal is not on the Mediterranean, and Morocco, Tunisia and most of Turkey are not part of Europe, these countries have been included because of their proximity and accessibility as well as their historical ties to the region.

Given the exceptional diversity of the countries and cultures in Mediterranean Europe, the choice of things to see and do is almost limitless. Some of Europe's earliest and most powerful civilisations flourished around the Mediterranean, and traces of them remain in the many archaeological sites and in the monuments, architecture, art, writings and music they created. There are countless churches, galleries and museums with works of art ranging from the Renaissance masters to 20th-century innovators. The region features architectural masterpieces as diverse as the Parthenon in Athens, Chartres' cathedral in France, the Hagia Sofia in Istanbul, St Peter's Basilica in Rome, the Alhambra in Granada and Gaudí's extraordinary creations in Barcelona.

When museums and churches begin to overwhelm you, turn to the many outdoor pursuits Mediterranean Europe has to offer. There is skiing or trekking in the Alps, Apennines, Pyrenees and Atlas Mountains; island-hopping in Greece; or you can simply laze on a beach anywhere along the coast. The food of the Mediterranean region is one of its principal delights, not to mention the wine of Burgundy, Tuscany and elsewhere. There are even places where you can escape from other travellers, as relatively few tourists have made their way to Albania or to many parts of eastern Turkey and southern Italy.

Mediterranean Europe includes much practical information on how to get there and how to get around once you've arrived, whether it's by road, rail or ferry. There are extensive details on what to see, when to see it and how much it all costs. The thousands of recommendations about places to stay range from *domatia* (rooms to rent) in Greece to cheap hotels in the medinas (old towns) of Morocco. Restaurant recommendations include outdoor cafés in France, trattorias in Italy and *gostilne* in Slovenia. If shopping appeals, the Mediterranean area offers outlets ranging from chic boutiques in Paris and Istanbul's Grand Bazar to flea markets.

It's 3000km from the Strait of Gibraltar to the Turkish coast – a huge region with a huge number of attractions waiting to be enjoyed. To experience them, all you have to do is go.

Facts for the Visitor

There are those who say that Mediterranean Europe is so well developed that you don't have to plan a thing before your trip since anything can be arranged on the spot. As any experienced traveller knows, the problems you worried about at home often turn out to be irrelevant or sort themselves out once you're on the move.

This is fine if you've decided to blow the massive inheritance sitting in your bank account, but if your financial status is somewhat more modest, a bit of prior knowledge and careful planning can make your budget stretch further than you thought it would. You'll also want to make sure that the things you plan to see and do will be possible at the particular time of year you'll be travelling.

HIGHLIGHTS
The Top 10
There is so much to see and do in Mediterranean Europe that compiling a top 10 is next to impossible. But we asked the authors involved in this book to list their personal highlights. The results are as follows:

1. Paris
2. Rome
3. The Alps
4. Florence
5. Epiros in north-west Greece
6. Venice
7. Istanbul
8. Morocco's High Atlas Mountains
9. Tuscany
10. Dalmatian coast

Other nominations included Greek island-hopping, Barcelona, Umbria, Provence, the Pyrenees, Corsica, Andalucía, Seville, Lisbon, the wine cellars of Oporto, Cappadocia and camel trekking in the Sahara.

The Bottom 10
The writers were also asked to list the 10 worst 'attractions' of the region:

1. Spain's Costa del Sol
2. The Greek island of Kos

3. Albufeira on Portugal's Algarve
4. Disneyland Paris
5. Palma de Mallorca
6. France's far northern coast
7. Milan
8. Monte Carlo's casino
9. Agios Nikolaos on Crete
10. Bullfights in Spain

PLANNING
When to Go
Any time can be a good time to visit Mediterranean Europe, depending on what you want to do. Summer lasts roughly from June to September in the northern half of Europe and offers the most pleasant climate for outdoor pursuits. Along the Mediterranean coast, on the Iberian Peninsula and in southern Italy and Greece, where the summers tend to be hotter and longer, you can extend that period by one or even two months either way, when temperatures may also be more agreeable. The best time to visit most of Tunisia and Morocco is spring and autumn.

You won't be the only tourist during the summer months in Mediterranean Europe – everyone in France, Spain and Italy, for instance, goes on holiday in August. Prices can be high, accommodation fully booked and the sights packed. You'll find much better deals – and far fewer crowds – in the shoulder seasons either side of summer; in April and May, for instance, flowers are in bloom and the weather can be surprisingly mild, and Indian summers are common in Mediterranean Europe in September and October.

On the other hand, if you're keen on winter sports, resorts in the Alps and the Pyrenees begin operating in November or early December and move into full swing after the New Year, closing down again when the snows begin to melt in March or April.

The Climate & When to Go sections under Facts for the Visitor in the individual country chapters explain what to expect and when to expect it, and the Climate Charts in Appendix I in the back of the book will help you compare the weather in different destinations. The temperate climate along the Atlantic

World Heritage List

UNESCO keeps a list of 'cultural and natural treasures of the world's heritage', including the following places in Mediterranean Europe:

ALBANIA
Ancient ruins of Butrint

CROATIA
Dubrovnik's old city

Plitvice Lakes National Park

Poreč's Euphrasian Basilica

Split's historic centre with Diocletian's Palace

Trogir's old town

CYPRUS
Ancient capital of Paphos

Painted churches of Troodos Massif

FRANCE
Amiens Cathedral

Arc-et-Senans' royal saltworks

Arles' Roman and Romanesque monuments

Avignon's historic centre

Bourges Cathedral

Carcassonne

Canal du Midi

Chambord's chateau and estate

Chartres Cathedral

Corsica's Cape Girolata, Cape Porto, Les Calanche and Scandola Natural Reserve

Fontenay's Cistercian abbey

Lascaux and other caves in the Vézère Valley

Mont Saint Michel and its bay

Place Stanislas, Place de la Carrière and Place d'Alliance in Nancy

Pont du Gard roman aqueduct near Nîmes

Roman theatre and triumphal arch at Orange

Notre Dame and banks of the Seine in Paris

Abbey of St Rémi and Tau Palace at Reims

Church of Saint Savin sur Gartempe

Grande Île section of Strasbourg

Chateau of Versailles and gardens

Vézelay's basilica

GREECE
The Acropolis in Athens

Mount Athos

Temple of Apollo Epicurios at Bassae

Monasteries of Daphni, Hossios, Luckas and Nea Moni at Chios

Delos

Delphi archaeological site

Meteora

Mystras

Olympia's archaeological site

Medieval city of Rhodes

Pythagorio and Hereon at Samos

Thessaloniki's early Christian and Byzantine monuments

Vergina's archaeological site

ITALY
Agrigento archaeological area

Caserta's Royal Palace with the park, aqueduct of Vanvitelli and the San Leucio complex

Castel del Monte

Cinque Terre, Portvenere and islands

Costiera Amalfitana

Crespi d'Adda

The Renaissance city of Ferrara

The historic centre of Florence

World Heritage List

ITALY (continued)

The sassi (traditional stone houses) of Matera

Milan's Church of Santa Maria delle Grazie and convent including *The Last Supper* by Leonardo da Vinci

Modena's cathedral, Torre Civica and Piazza Grande

The historic centre of Naples

Padua's Botanical Garden

Pienza's historic centre

Pisa's Piazza del Duomo

Archaeological areas of Pompei and Herculaneum

Ravenna's early Christian monuments and mosaic

Rome's historic centre

The historic centre of San Gimignano

Siena's historic centre

Su Nuraxi fortress at Barumini

Valle Camonica's rock carvings

Vatican City

Venice and its lagoon

Villa Romana del Casale

Vincenza and its Palladian villas

MACEDONIA

Ohrid and its lake

MALTA

Hypogeum prehistoric temples at Paola

Valetta

MOROCCO

Kasbah of Aït Benhaddou

The medina at Fès

The medina at Marrakesh

Meknès

The medina at Tetouan Volubilis archaeological site

PORTUGAL

Monastery of Alcobaça

The central zone of Angra do Heroism in the Azores

Batalha Monastery

Lisbon's Monastery of the Hieronymites and Tower of Belém

Évora's historic centre

Oporto's historic centre

The cultural landscape of Sintra

Convent of Christ in Tomar

SLOVENIA

Škocjan Caves

SPAIN

Altamira Cave

Churches of the Asturias kingdom

The old town section of Ávila

Güell park and palace and Casa Mila in Barcelona

Burgos cathedral

The old town section of Cáceres

Historic centre of Córdoba

Cuenca's walled city

Doñana National Park

Garajonay National Park

La Alhambra, El Generalife summer palace and Albaicín Moorish quarter of Granada

El Escorial near Madrid

Archaeology Mérida

Poblet Monastery

Salamanca's old town

Royal Monastery of Santa María de Guadeloupe

Santiago de Compostela's old town and route

The old town and aqueduct of Segovia

Sevilla's cathedral, Alcázar Archivo de Indias

Mudejar architecture of Teruel

Toledo's historic centre

Valencia's La Lonja de la Seda

World Heritage List

TUNISIA

Carthage archaeological site	Carthaginian site and necropolis of Kerkouane	The medina at Sousse
Ichkeul National Park		Tunis' medina
The amphitheatre at El Jem	The walled city of Kairouan	

TURKEY

Divrigi's Great Mosque and hospital	Walled city of Hattuşaş	Safranbolu and its traditional timber houses
Göreme National park and Cappadocia	Hierapolis-Pamukkale	Xanthos-Letoön
	Istanbul's historic areas	
	Nemrut Dag	

YUGOSLAVIA

Durmitor National Park	Stari Ras and Sopoćani Monastery	Studenica Monastery
Kotor and its gulf		

seaboard is relatively wet all year, with moderate extremes in temperature; the Mediterranean coast is hotter and drier, with most rainfall occurring during the mild winter; and the continental climate in eastern France and the Alps has greater extremes in weather between summer and winter.

What Kind of Trip?

Travelling Companions If you decide to travel with others, keep in mind that travel can put relationships to the test like few other experiences can. Many a long-term friendship has collapsed under the strain of constant negotiations about where to stay and eat, what to see and where to go next. But many friendships also become closer than ever before. You won't find out until you try, but make sure you agree on itineraries and routines beforehand and try to remain flexible about everything – even in the heat of an August afternoon in Rome or Madrid. Travelling with someone else also has financial benefits as a single room is more expensive per person than a double in most countries.

If travel is a good way of testing established friendships, it's also a great way of making new ones. Hostels and camping grounds are good places to meet fellow travellers, so even if you're travelling alone, you need never be lonely.

The Getting Around chapter has information on organised tours.

Move or Stay? 'If this is Tuesday, it must be Barcelona.' Though often ridiculed, the mad dash that crams six countries into a month does have its merits. If you've never visited Mediterranean Europe before, you won't know which areas you'll like, and a quick 'scouting' tour will give an overview of the options. A rail pass that offers unlimited travel within a set period of time is the best way to do this.

But if you know where you want to go, or find a place you like, the best advice is to stay put for a while, discover some lesser known sights, make a few local friends and settle in. It's also cheaper in the long run.

For information on working in Mediterranean Europe, see the Work section later in this chapter.

Maps

Good maps are easy to come by once you're in Europe, but you might want to buy a few beforehand to plan and track your route. The maps in this book will help you get an idea of where you might want to go and will be a useful first reference when you arrive in a city. However, if you're driving or cycling proper road maps are essential.

You can't go wrong with Michelin maps and, because of their soft covers, they fold up easily so you can stick them in your pocket. Some people prefer the meticulous maps produced by Freytag & Berndt, Kümmerly & Frey and Hallwag. As a rule, maps published by European automobile associations (the AA in Britain, the ADAC and AvD in Germany etc) are excellent and sometimes free if membership of your local association gives you reciprocal rights. Some of the best city maps are produced by Falk; RV Verlag's EuroCity series is another good bet. Tourist offices are often another good source for (usually free and fairly basic) maps.

What to Bring

It's very easy to find almost anything you need in Mediterranean Europe and, since you'll probably buy things as you go along, it's better to start with too little rather than too much.

A backpack is still the most popular method of carrying gear as it is convenient, especially for walking. On the down side, a backpack doesn't offer too much protection for your valuables, the straps tend to get caught on things and some airlines may refuse to accept responsibility if the pack is damaged or tampered with.

Travelpacks, a combination backpack/shoulder bag, are very popular. The backpack straps zip away inside the pack when they are not needed, so you almost have the best of both worlds. Some packs have sophisticated shoulder-strap adjustment systems and can be used comfortably even on long hikes. Backpacks or travelpacks can be made reasonably theft-proof with small padlocks. Another alternative is a large, soft zip bag with a wide shoulder strap so it can be carried with relative ease. Forget suitcases unless you're travelling in style, but if you do take one, make sure it has wheels to allow you to drag it along behind you.

As for clothing, the climate will have a bearing on what you take along. Remember that insulation works on the principle of trapped air, so several layers of thin clothing are warmer than a single thick one (and will be easier to dry). You'll also be much more flexible if the weather suddenly turns warm. Be prepared for rain at any time of year.

Bearing in mind that you can buy virtually anything on the spot, a minimum packing list could include:

- underwear, socks and swimming gear
- a pair of jeans and maybe a pair of shorts or a skirt
- a few T-shirts and shirts
- a warm sweater
- a solid pair of walking shoes
- sandals or thongs for showers
- a coat or jacket
- a raincoat, waterproof jacket or umbrella
- a medical kit and sewing kit
- a padlock
- a Swiss Army knife
- soap and towel
- toothpaste, toothbrush and other toiletries

A padlock is useful to lock your bag to a luggage rack in a bus or train; it may also be needed to secure your hostel locker. A Swiss Army knife comes in handy for all sorts of things. *Any* pocketknife is fine, but make sure it includes such essentials as scissors, a bottle opener and strong corkscrew! Soap, toothpaste and toilet paper are readily obtainable, but you'll need your own supply of paper in many public toilets and those at camping grounds. Tampons are available at pharmacies and supermarkets in all but the most remote places. Condoms, both locally made and imported, are widely available in Mediterranean Europe.

A tent and sleeping bag are vital if you want to save money by camping. Even if you're not camping, a sleeping bag is still very useful. Get one that can be used as a quilt. A sleeping sheet with pillow cover (case) is necessary if you plan to stay in hostels – you may have to hire or purchase one if you don't bring your own. In any case, a sheet that fits into your sleeping bag is easier to wash than the bag itself. Make one yourself out of old sheets (include a built-in pillow cover) or buy one from your hostel association.

Other optional items include a compass, a torch (flashlight), a pocket calculator for currency conversions, an alarm clock, an adapter plug for electrical appliances (such as a cup or immersion water heater to save on expensive tea and coffee), a universal bath/sink plug (a film canister sometimes works), portable short-wave radio, sunglasses, a few clothes pegs and premoistened towelettes or a large cotton handkerchief that you can soak in fountains and use to cool off while touring cities in the hot summer months. During city sightseeing, a small daypack is better than a shoulder bag at deterring thieves (see Theft in the Dangers & Annoyances section of this chapter).

Also, consider using plastic carry bags or bin liners inside your backpack to keep things separate but also dry if the pack gets soaked.

Appearances & Conduct

Most Mediterranean countries attach a great deal of importance to appearance, so your clothes may well have some bearing on how you're treated, especially in Spain, Portugal, Italy and Greece.

By all means dress casually, but keep your clothes clean and ensure sufficient body cover (trousers or a knee-length dress) if your sightseeing includes churches, monasteries, mosques or synagogues. Wearing shorts away from the beach is not very common among men in Mediterranean Europe. Also keep in mind that in most Muslim countries, such as Morocco, western women *or* men in shorts or sleeveless shirts are virtually in their underwear in the eyes of the more conservative locals. Many nightclubs and fancy restaurants refuse entry to anyone wearing jeans, or a tracksuit and sneakers (trainers); men might consider packing a tie as well, just in case.

On the beach, nude bathing is generally limited to restricted areas, but topless bathing is common in many parts of Mediterranean Europe. Nevertheless, women should be wary of sunbathing topless in more conservative countries or untouristed areas. If nobody else seems to be doing it, you should not do it either.

You'll soon notice that Europeans shake hands and even kiss when they greet one another. Don't worry about the latter with those you don't know well, but get into the habit of shaking hands with virtually everyone you meet. In some parts of Mediterranean Europe, it's also customary to greet the proprietor when entering a shop, café or quiet bar, and to say goodbye when you leave.

VISAS & DOCUMENTS
Passport

Your most important travel document is your passport, which should remain valid until well after you return home. If it's just about to expire, renew it before you go. This may not be easy to do overseas, and some countries insist your passport remain valid for a specified period (usually three months beyond the date of your departure from that country).

Applying for or renewing a passport can take anything from an hour to several months, so don't leave it till the last minute. Bureaucratic wheels usually turn faster if you do everything in person rather than relying on the post or agents, but check first what you need to take with you: photos of a certain size, birth certificate, population register extract, signed statements, exact payment in cash etc.

Australian citizens can apply at a post office or the passport office in their state capital; Britons can pick up application forms from major post offices, and the passport is issued by the regional passport office; Canadians can apply at regional passport offices; New Zealanders can apply at any district office of the Department of Internal Affairs; US citizens must apply in person (but may usually renew by mail) at a US Passport Agency office or at some courthouses and post offices.

Once you start travelling, carry your passport at all times and guard it carefully (see the following Photocopies section for advice about carrying copies of your passport and other important documents). Camping grounds and hotels sometimes insist that you hand over your passport for the duration of your stay, which is very inconvenient, but a driving licence or Camping Card International usually solves the problem.

Citizens of the European Union (EU) and those from certain other European countries (eg Switzerland) don't need a valid passport to travel to another EU country or even some non-EU countries; a national identity card is sufficient. But if you want to exercise this option, check with your travel agent or the embassies of the countries you plan to visit.

Visas

A visa is a stamp in your passport or on a separate piece of paper permitting you to enter the country in question and stay for a specified period of time. Often you can get the visa at the border or at the airport on arrival, but not always – check first with the embassies or consulates of the countries you plan to visit – and note that visas are seldom issued on trains.

There's a wide variety of visas, including tourist, transit and business ones. Transit visas are usually cheaper than tourist or business visas, but they only allow a very short stay (one or two days) and can be difficult to extend. Most readers of this book, however, will have very little to do with visas. With a valid passport you'll be able to visit most of the countries around the Mediterranean for up to three months (sometimes even six), provided you have some sort of onward or return ticket and/or 'sufficient means of support' (ie money).

In line with the Schengen Agreement there are no longer passport controls at the borders between Germany, France, Spain, Portugal, the Benelux countries (Belgium, Netherlands and Luxembourg), Italy and Austria. A national identity card should suffice, but it's always safest to carry your passport. The other EU countries (Britain, Denmark, Finland, Greece, Ireland and Sweden) are not yet full members of Schengen and still maintain low-key border controls over traffic from other EU countries.

Border procedures between EU and non-EU countries can still be fairly thorough, though citizens of Australia, Canada, Israel, Japan, New Zealand, Norway, Switzerland

Visa Requirements – Country of Origin

	Aust	Can	Ire	NZ	UK	USA	SA
Albania	+	+	+	+	+	+	✓
Andorra	–	–	–	–	–	–	–
Bosnia-Hercegovina	✓	–	–	✓	✓	✓	✓
Croatia	–	–	–	–	–	–	✓
Cyprus	–	–	–	–	–	–	–
France	–	–	–	–	–	–	✓
Greece	–	–	–	–	–	–	✓
Italy	–	–	–	–	–	–	✓
Macedonia	✓	✓	✓	✓	✓	✓	✓
Malta	–	–	–	–	–	–	✓
Morocco	–	–	–	–	–	–	✓
Portugal	*	–	–	*	*	*	✓
Slovenia	–	–	–	–	–	–	✓
Spain	–	–	–	–	–	–	✓
Tunisia	–	–	–	✓	–	–	✓
Turkey	–	–	✓	–	✓	✓	+
Yugoslavia	✓	✓	✓	✓	✓	✓	✓

✓ tourist visa required
+ 30-day maximum stay without visa
* 60-day maximum stay without visa

and the USA do not need visas for tourist visits to any Schengen country.

All non-EU citizens visiting a Schengen country and intending to stay for longer than three days or to visit another Schengen country from there are supposed to obtain an official entry stamp in their passport either at the point of entry or from the local police within 72 hours. But this is very loosely enforced. In general registering at a hotel will be sufficient.

For those who do require visas, it's important to remember that these will have a 'use-by' date, and you'll be refused entry after that period has elapsed. Your visa may not be checked when entering these countries overland, but major problems can arise if it is requested during your stay or on departure and you can't produce it.

Visa requirements can change, and you should always check with the individual embassies or a reputable travel agent before travelling. It's generally easier to get your visas as you go along, rather than arranging them all beforehand. Carry spare passport photos (you may need from one to four every time you apply for a visa). The accompanying table lists visa requirements for some nationalities.

Photocopies
The hassles created by losing your passport can be considerably reduced if you have a record of its number and issue date or, even better, photocopies of the relevant data pages. A photocopy of your birth certificate can also be useful.

Also add the serial numbers of your travellers cheques (cross them off as you cash them) and photocopies of your credit cards, airline ticket and other travel documents. Keep all this emergency material separate from your passport, cheques and cash, and leave extra copies with someone you can rely on back home. Add some emergency money (eg US$50 to US$100 in cash) to this separate stash as well. If you do lose your passport, notify the police immediately to get a statement, and contact your nearest consulate.

Travel Insurance
A travel-insurance policy to cover theft, loss and medical problems is a good idea. The policies handled by STA Travel and other student-travel organisations are usually good value. Some policies offer lower and higher medical expense options; the higher ones are chiefly for countries like the USA that have extremely high medical costs. There is a wide variety of policies available so check the small print.

Some policies specifically exclude 'dangerous activities', which can include scuba diving, motorcycling and even trekking. Some even exclude entire countries – like Bosnia and Yugoslavia. A locally acquired motorcycle licence is not valid under some policies.

You may prefer a policy that pays doctors or hospitals directly rather than you having to pay on the spot and claim later. If you have to claim later make sure you keep all documentation. Some policies ask you to call back (reverse charges) to a centre in your home country where an immediate assessment of your problem is made.

Check that the policy covers ambulances or an emergency flight home.

International Driving Permit
Many non-European drivers' licences are valid in Europe, but it's still a good idea to bring along an International Driving Permit (IDP), which can make life much simpler, especially when hiring cars and motorcycles. Basically a multilingual translation of the vehicle class and personal details noted on your local driver's licence, an IDP is not valid unless accompanied by your original licence. An IDP can be obtained for a small fee (eg £4 in Britain) from your local automobile association – bring along a passport photo and a valid licence.

Camping Card International
The Camping Card International (CCI; formerly the Camping Carnet) is a camping ground ID that can be used instead of a passport when checking into a camping ground and includes third-party insurance for damage you may cause. As a result, many camping grounds offer a small discount if you sign in with one. CCIs are issued by automobile associations, camping federations and sometimes on the spot at camping grounds. In the UK, the AA issues them to its members for UK£4.50.

Hostel Card

A hostelling card is useful – if not always mandatory – for those staying at hostels. Some hostels in Mediterranean Europe don't require that you be a hostelling-association member, but they often charge less if you have a card. Many hostels will issue one on the spot or after a few stays, though this might cost a bit more than getting it in your home country. See Hostels in the Accommodation section later in this chapter.

Student & Youth Cards

The most useful of these is the International Student Identity Card (ISIC), a plastic ID-style card with your photograph, which provides discounts on many forms of transport (including airlines and local public transport), cheap or free admission to museums and sights, and inexpensive meals in some student cafeterias and restaurants.

There is a worldwide industry in fake student cards, and many places now stipulate a maximum age for student discounts or, more simply, they've substituted a 'youth discount' for a 'student discount'. If you're aged under 26 but not a student, you can apply for a GO25 card issued by the Federation of International Youth Travel Organisations (FIYTO) or the Euro<26 card, which go under different names in various countries. Both give much the same discounts and benefits as an ISIC.

All these cards are issued by hostelling organisations, student unions or youth-oriented travel agencies. They do not automatically entitle you to discounts, and some companies and institutions refuse to recognise them altogether, but you won't find out until you flash the card.

Seniors' Cards

Museums and other sights, public swimming pools and spas and transport companies frequently offer discounts to retired people, old age pensioners and those over 60 (slightly younger for women). Make sure you bring proof of age; that suave *signore* in Italy or that polite Parisian *mademoiselle* is not going to believe you're a day over 39.

European nationals aged over 60 can get a Rail Europe Senior (RES) Card. For more information see Cheap Tickets under Train in the Getting Around chapter.

International Health Certificate

You'll need this yellow booklet only if you're arriving in Europe from certain parts of Asia, Africa and South America, where diseases such as yellow fever are prevalent. See Immunisations in the Health section for more information on jabs.

EMBASSIES & CONSULATES

See the individual country chapters for information on embassies and consulates.

Getting Help From Your Embassy

As a tourist, it's important to realise what your own embassy – the embassy of the country of which you are a citizen – can and can't do.

Generally speaking, it won't be much help in emergencies if the trouble you're in is remotely your own fault. Remember that you are bound by the laws of the country you are visiting. Your embassy will not be sympathetic if you end up in jail after committing a crime locally, even if such actions are legal in your own country.

In genuine emergencies you might get some assistance, but only if other channels have been exhausted. For example, if you need to get home urgently, a free ticket home is exceedingly unlikely – the embassy would expect you to have insurance. If you have all your money and documents stolen, it might assist with getting a new passport, but a loan for onward travel is almost always out of the question.

Embassies used to keep letters for travellers or have a small reading room with home newspapers, but these days the mail holding service has been stopped and even newspapers tend to be out of date.

CUSTOMS

Throughout much of Mediterranean Europe, the usual allowances on tobacco (eg 200 cigarettes), alcohol (2L of wine, 1L of spirits) and perfume (50g) apply to duty-free goods purchased at the airport or on ferries. From June 1999, however, duty-free goods will no longer be sold to those travelling from one EU country to another.

Do not confuse these with duty-paid items (including alcohol and tobacco) bought at normal shops and supermarkets in one EU country and brought into another, where certain goods might be more expensive. (Cigarettes in France, for example, are cheaper than they are in Italy.) Then the allowances are more than generous: 800 cigarettes, 200 cigars, or 1kg of loose tobacco; 10L of spirits (more than 22% alcohol by volume), 20L of fortified wine or aperitif, 90L of wine or 110L of beer; unlimited quantities of perfume.

Customs inspections among EU countries have now all but ceased. At most border crossings and airports elsewhere they are pretty cursory but don't be lulled into a false sense of security. When you least expect it ...

MONEY
Costs

The secret to budget travel in Mediterranean Europe is cheap accommodation. Europe has a highly developed network of camping grounds and hostels, some of them quite luxurious, and they're great places to meet people.

Other money-saving strategies include preparing your own meals and avoiding alcohol; using a student card (see the earlier Visas & Documents section) and buying any of the various rail and public transport passes (see the Getting Around chapter). Also remember that the more time you spend in any one place, the lower your daily expenses are likely to be as you get to know your way around.

Including transport, but not private motorised transport, your daily expenses could work out to around US$35 to US$40 a day if you're operating on a rock-bottom budget. This means camping or staying in hostels, eating economically and using a transport pass. In Greece, Portugal, Spain and especially Turkey, you could probably get the daily cost down below that.

Travelling on a moderate budget, you should be able to manage on about US$40 to US$50 in the cheaper countries and US$60 to US$80 a day elsewhere in the region. This would allow you to stay at cheap hotels or guesthouses. You could afford meals in economical restaurants and even a few beers. Again Greece and Portugal would be somewhat cheaper, while France and Italy would be pricier.

A general warning about all the prices listed in this book: they're likely to change, usually moving upward, but if last season was particularly slow they may remain the same or even come down. Nevertheless, relative price levels should stay fairly constant – if hotel A costs twice as much as hotel B, it's likely to stay that way.

Cash

Nothing beats cash for convenience, or risk. If you lose it, it's gone forever and very few travel insurers will come to your rescue. Those that will, limit the amount to somewhere around US$200 to US$300. For tips on carrying your money safely, see Theft in the Dangers & Annoyances section later in this chapter.

It's still a good idea to bring some local currency in cash, if only to tide you over until you get to an exchange facility or find an automatic-teller machine (ATM). The equivalent of US$50 should usually be enough. Some extra cash in an easily exchanged currency (eg US dollars or Deutschmarks) is also a good idea.

Travellers Cheques

The main idea of carrying travellers cheques rather than cash is the protection they offer from theft, though they are losing their popularity as more travellers – including those on tight budgets – deposit their money in their bank at home and withdraw it as they go along through ATMs.

American Express, Visa and Thomas Cook travellers cheques are widely accepted and have efficient replacement policies. If you're going to remote places, it's worth sticking to American Express since small local banks may not always accept other brands.

When you change cheques, don't just look at the exchange rate; ask about fees and commissions as well. There may be a service fee per cheque, a flat transaction fee or a percentage of the total amount irrespective of the number of cheques. Some banks charge fees (often exorbitant) to cash cheques and not cash; others do the reverse.

Plastic Cards & ATMs

If you're not familiar with the options, ask your bank to explain the workings and relative merits of credit, credit/debit, debit, charge and cash cards.

A major advantage of credit cards is that they allow you to pay for expensive items (eg airline tickets) without your having to carry great wads of cash around. They also allow you to withdraw cash at selected banks or from the many ATMs that are linked up internationally. However, if an ATM in Europe swallows a card that was issued outside Europe, it can be a major headache. Also, some credit cards aren't hooked up to ATM networks unless you specifically ask your bank to do this.

Cash cards, which you use at home to withdraw money directly from your bank account or savings account, can be used throughout Europe at ATMs linked to international networks like Cirrus and Maestro.

Credit and credit/debit cards like Visa and MasterCard are widely accepted. MasterCard (also known as Access in the UK) is linked to Europe's extensive Eurocard system, and Visa (sometimes called Carte Bleue) is particularly strong in France and Spain. However, these cards often have a credit limit that is too low to cover major expenses like long-term car rental or airline tickets and can be difficult to replace if lost abroad. Also when you get a cash advance against your Visa or MasterCard credit-card account, your issuer charges a transaction fee and/or finance charge. With some issuers, the fees can reach as high as US$10 *plus* interest per transaction, so check with your card issuer before leaving home and compare rates.

Charge cards like American Express and Diners Club have offices in the major cities of most countries that will replace a lost card within 24 hours. However, charge cards are not widely accepted off the beaten track.

The best advice is not to put all your eggs in one basket. If you want to rely heavily on bits of plastic, go for two different cards – an American Express or Diners Club, for instance, along with a Visa or MasterCard. Better still is a combination of credit or cash card and travellers cheques so you have something to fall back on if an ATM swallows your card or the banks in the area are closed.

A word of warning: in Europe, as elsewhere, fraudulent shopkeepers have been known to quickly make several charge slip imprints with your credit card when you're not looking, and then simply copy your signature from the one that you authorise. Try not to let your card out of sight, and always check your statements upon your return.

International Transfers

Telegraphic transfers are not very expensive but, despite their name, can be quite slow. Be sure to specify the name of the bank and the name and address of the branch where you'd like to pick it up.

It's quicker and easier to have money wired via an American Express office (US$60 for US$1000). Western Union's Money Transfer system (available at post offices in some countries) and Thomas Cook's MoneyGram service are also popular.

Guaranteed Cheques

Guaranteed personal cheques are another way of carrying money or obtaining cash. Eurocheques, available if you have a European bank account, are guaranteed up to a certain limit. When cashing them (eg at post offices), you will be asked to show your Eurocheque card bearing your signature and registration number, and perhaps a passport or ID card. Your Eurocheque card should be kept separately from the cheques. Many hotels and merchants refuse to accept Eurocheques because of the relatively large commissions.

Currency Exchange

By the year 2002, the EU will have a single currency called the euro (see boxed text called Europe's New Currency). Until then francs, lire, pesetas, escudos and drachmas remain in place or share equal status with the euro in the five EU countries covered in this guide.

In general, US dollars, Deutschmarks, pounds sterling, and French and Swiss francs are the most easily exchanged currencies in Europe, followed by Italian lire and Dutch guilders, but you may well decide that other currencies suit your purposes better. You lose out through commissions and customer exchange rates every time you change money, so if you only visit Portugal, for example, you may be better off buying escudos straight away if your bank at home can provide them.

The importation and exportation of certain currencies (eg Moroccan dirham, Tunisian dinar and Cypriot pounds) is restricted or banned entirely so get rid of any local currency before you leave the country. Try not to have too many leftover Portuguese escudos or Maltese lire, and definitely get rid of any Yugoslav dinar as it is impossible to change them back into hard currency. More and more banks and *bureaux de change* will

Europe's New Currency

Don't be surprised if you come across two sets of prices for goods and services in Mediterranean Europe. From 1 January 1999 Europe's new currency – the euro – is legal tender here along with the local monetary unit.

It's all part of the harmonisation of the EU. Along with national boarders, venerable currencies like the franc and escudo have been phased out. Not all EU members have agreed to adopt the euro, but the franc and lira will be among the first of 11 currencies to go the way of the dodo.

No actual coins or banknotes will be issued until 1 January 2002; until then, the euro will in effect be 'paperless'. Prices can be quoted in euros, but there won't actually be any euros in circulation. Companies will use the new European currency for their accounting, banks can offer euro accounts and credit-card companies can bill in euros. Essentially, the euro can be used anytime it is not necessary to hand over hard cash.

This can lead to confusion, and travellers should be forewarned that the scheme is open to abuse. For instance, a restaurant might list prices in both francs and euros or escudos and euros. Check your bill carefully – the total might have the amount in francs or escudos, your credit card may bill you in the euro equivalent.

Things will probably get worse during the first half of 2002. There is a six-month period when countries can use both their old currencies and the newly issued euro notes and coins.

The euro will have the same value in all member countries of the EU; the €5 note in France is the same €5 note you will use in Italy and Portugal. The official exchange rates were set on 1 January 1999.

Coins and notes have already been designed. The banknotes come in denominations ranging from €5 to €500. All bills feature a generic 'European' bridge on one side and a vaguely familiar but unidentifiable 'European' arch on the reverse. Each country is permitted to design coins with one side standard for all euro coins and the other bearing a national emblem.

Rates of exchange of the euro and foreign currencies against local currencies are given in the country chapters.

Currency Exchange

Australia	A$1	=	€0.57
Canada	C$1	=	€0.62
France	1FF	=	€0.15
Germany	DM1	=	€0.51
Ireland	IR£1	=	€1.27
Italy	L1000	=	€0.51
Japan	¥100	=	€0.66
Netherlands	f1	=	€0.45
New Zealand	NZ$1	=	€0.48
Spain	100pta	=	€0.59
South Africa	R1	=	€0.15
UK	UK£1	=	€1.50
USA	US$1	=	€0.92

now exchange Croatian kuna and Slovenian tolar but usually in neighbouring countries just over the border.

Most airports, central train stations, some fancy hotels and many border posts have banking facilities outside working hours, sometimes open on a 24-hour basis. Post offices in Europe often perform banking tasks, tend to have longer opening hours, and outnumber banks in remote places. Be aware that while they always exchange cash, they might not be prepared to change travellers cheques unless they're denominated in the local currency.

The best exchange rates are usually at banks. *Bureaux de change* usually – but not always by any means – offer worse rates or charge higher commissions. Hotels are almost always the worst places to change money. American Express and Thomas Cook offices usually do not charge commissions for changing their own cheques, but they may offer a less favourable exchange rate than banks.

Tipping

In many European countries it's common (and the law in France) for a service charge to be added to restaurant bills, in which case no tipping is necessary. In others, simply rounding up the bill is sufficient. See the individual country chapters for details.

Taxes & Refunds

A kind of sales tax called value-added tax (VAT) applies to most goods and services in many European countries; it's 20.6% in France, 20% in Italy and Slovenia, 18% in Greece and 16% in Spain. In most countries, visitors can claim back the VAT on purchases that are being taken out of the country. Those actually *residing* in one EU country are not entitled to a refund on VAT paid on goods bought in another EU country. Thus an American citizen living in London is not entitled to a VAT rebate on items bought in Paris while an EU passport holder residing in New York is.

The procedure for making the claim is fairly straightforward, though it may vary somewhat from country to country, and there are minimum-purchase amounts imposed (eg in France you must be over 15, spend less

than six months in the country and purchase goods worth at least 1200FF). First of all make sure the shop offers duty-free sales (often identified with a sign reading 'Tax-Free for Tourists'). When making your purchase, ask the shop attendant for a VAT-refund voucher (sometimes called a Tax-Free Shopping Cheque) filled in with the correct amount and the date. This can either be refunded directly at international airports on departure or stamped at ferry ports or border crossings and mailed back for refund.

POST & COMMUNICATIONS
Post

From major European centres, air mail typically takes about five days to North America and a week to Australasian destinations. Postage costs vary from country to country, and so does post office efficiency – the Italian post office is notoriously unreliable (Lonely Planet manuscripts sent special-delivery air mail have taken up to two months to reach Australia). The postal systems in Greece and Tunisia are also less than reliable.

You can collect mail from poste restante sections at major post offices. Ask people writing to you to print your name clearly and underline your surname. When collecting mail, your passport may be required for identification and you may have to pay a small fee (eg 3FF to 4FF in France, depending on the weight of the letter). If an expected letter is not awaiting you, ask to check under your given name; letters commonly get misfiled. Post offices usually hold mail for about a month, but sometimes less. Unless the sender specifies otherwise, mail will always be sent to the city's main post office.

You can also have mail (but not parcels) sent to you at American Express offices so long as you have an American Express card or are carrying American Express travellers cheques. When you buy the cheques, ask for a booklet listing all the American Express offices worldwide.

Telephone

You can ring abroad from almost any phone box in Europe. Public telephones accepting stored-value phonecards, available from post offices, telephone centres, newsstands or

CHANGING PHONE NUMBERS

Over the next few years, as EU countries come into line with EU rules on the deregulation of local telecommunications industries, local telephone numbers are going to change. Where changes are imminent there's information in the Post & Communications sections of the individual country chapters.

retail outlets, are virtually the norm now; in some countries, coin-operated phones are difficult to find. The card solves the problem of finding the correct coins for calls (or lots of correct coins for international calls) and come in various denominations.

Without a phonecard, you can ring from a booth inside a post office or telephone centre and settle your bill at the counter. Reverse-charge (collect) calls are often possible, but not always. From many countries, however, the Home Country Direct system lets you phone home by billing the long-distance carrier you use at home. The numbers can often be dialled from public phones without even inserting a phonecard.

Fax & Telegraph
You can send faxes, telegrams and telexes from most main post offices in Mediterranean Europe.

INTERNET RESOURCES
Email & Internet Access
Travelling with a portable computer is a great way to stay in touch with life back home but, unless you know what you're doing, it's fraught with potential problems. A good investment is a universal AC adaptor for your appliance, so you can plug it in anywhere without frying the innards, if the power supply voltage varies. You'll also need a plug adaptor for each country you visit, often easiest bought before you leave home.

Secondly, your PC-card modem may or may not work once you leave your home country – and you won't know for sure until you try. The safest option is to buy a rep-

utable 'global' or 'world' modem before you leave home, or buy a local PC-card modem if you're spending an extended time in any one country. Keep in mind that the telephone socket in each country you visit will probably be different from that at home, so ensure that you have at least a US RJ-11 telephone adaptor that works with your modem. You can almost always find an adaptor that will convert from RJ-11 to the local variety. For more information on travelling with a portable computer, see www.teleadapt.com or www.warrior.com.

Major Internet service providers (ISPs) such as AOL (www.aol.com), CompuServe (www.compuserve.com) and IBM Net (www.ibm.net) have dial-in nodes throughout Europe; it's best to download a list of the dial-in numbers before you leave home. If you access your Internet email account at home through a smaller ISP or your office or school network, your best option is either to open an account with a global ISP, like those mentioned above, or to rely on cybercafés and other public access points to collect your mail.

If you do intend to rely on cybercafés, you'll need to carry three pieces of information with you so you can access your Internet mail account: your incoming (POP or IMAP) mail server name, your account name, and your password. Your ISP or network supervisor will give you these. Armed with this information, you should be able to access your Internet mail account from any net-connected machine in the world, provided it runs some kind of email software (remember that Netscape and Internet Explorer both have mail modules). It pays to become familiar with the process for doing this before you leave home. A final option to collect mail through cybercafés is to open a free Web-based email account like HotMail (www .hotmail.com) or Yahoo! Mail (mail.yahoo .com). You can then access your mail from anywhere in the world from any net-connected machine running a standard Web browser.

You'll find cybercafés throughout Europe: check out the country chapters in this book, and see www.netcafeguide.com for an up-to-date list. You may also find public net access in post offices, libraries, hostels, hotels, universities and so on.

Useful Sites

The World Wide Web is a rich resource for travellers. You can research your trip, hunt down bargain air fares, book hotels, check on weather conditions or chat with locals and other travellers about the best places to visit (or avoid!).

The following Web sites offer useful general information about Mediterranean Europe, its cities, transport systems, currencies etc.

Lonely Planet
There's no better place to start your Web explorations than the Lonely Planet Web site (www.lonelyplanet.com). Here you'll find succinct summaries on travelling to most places on earth, postcards from other travellers and the Thorn Tree bulletin board, where you can ask questions before you go or dispense advice when you get back. You can also find travel news and updates to many of our guidebooks, and the subWWWay section links you to the most useful travel resources elsewhere on the Web.

Tourist Offices
www.mbnet.mb.ca/lucas/travel – lists tourist offices at home and around the world for most countries

Rail Information
www.raileurope.com – train fares and schedules on the most popular routes in Europe, including information on rail and youth passes

Airline Information
www.travelocity.com – information on which airlines fly where, when and for how much

Airline Tickets
www.priceline.com – name the price you're willing to pay for an airline seat and if an airline has an empty seat for which it would rather get something than nothing, US-based Priceline lets you know

NEWSPAPERS & MAGAZINES

In larger towns and cities you can buy the excellent *International Herald Tribune* on the day of publication, as well as the colourful but superficial *USA Today*. Among other English-language newspapers widely available are the *Guardian*, the *Financial Times* and *The Times*. The *European* weekly newspaper is also readily available, as are *Newsweek*, *Time* and the *Economist*.

RADIO & TV
Radio

You can pick up a mixture of the BBC World Service and BBC for Europe on medium wave at 648kHz AM and on short wave at 6195, 9410, 11955, 12095 (a good daytime frequency) and 15575kHz, depending on the time of day. BBC Radio 4 broadcasts on long wave at 198kHz.

The Voice of America (VOA) can usually be found at various times of the day on 7170, 9535, 9680, 9760, 9770, 11805, 15135, 15205, 15255, 15410 and 15580kHz. There are also numerous English-language broadcasts (or even BBC World Service and VOA re-broadcasts) on local AM and FM radio stations.

TV

Cable and satellite TV have spread across Europe with much more gusto than radio. Sky TV can be found in many upmarket hotels throughout Mediterranean Europe, as can CNN, BBC Prime and other networks. You can also pick up many cross-border TV stations, including British stations close to the Channel.

VIDEO SYSTEMS

If you want to record or buy video tapes to play back home, you won't get a picture if the image registration systems are different. Europe generally uses PAL (SECAM in France), which is incompatible with the North American and Japanese NTSC system. Australia also uses PAL.

PHOTOGRAPHY

Mediterranean Europe is extremely photogenic, but the weather and where you'll be travelling will dictate what film to use. In places like northern France where the sky can often be overcast, photographers should bring high-speed film (200 or 400 ASA), but for most of the sunny Mediterranean, slower film is the answer.

Film and camera equipment are available everywhere in the region, but obviously shops in the larger towns and cities will have a wider selection. Avoid buying film at tourist sites in Europe – eg at the kiosks below the Leaning Tower of Pisa or at the entrance to the Acropolis. It may have been stored badly or have reached its sell-by date. It will certainly be more expensive.

TIME

Most of the countries covered in this book are on Central European Time (GMT/UTC plus one hour), the same time used from Spain to Poland. Morocco is on GMT/UTC (all year) while Greece, Turkey and Cyprus are on East European Time (GMT plus two hours).

Clocks are advanced for daylight-saving time in most countries on the last Sunday in March and set back one hour on the last Sunday in September. At that time Central European Time is GMT/UTC plus two hours and East European Time (GMT plus two hours).

ELECTRICITY
Voltage & Cycle

Most of Europe runs on 220V, 50Hz AC. The exceptions are the UK and Malta, which have 240V, and Spain and Andorra, which usually have 220V but sometimes still the old 125V depending on the network (some houses can have both). Some old buildings and hotels in Italy, including Rome, might also have 125V. All EU countries were supposed to have been standardised at 230V by now, but like everything else in the EU, this is taking longer than anticipated.

Check the voltage and cycle (usually 50Hz) used in your home country. Most appliances set up for 220V will handle 240V without modifications (and vice versa); the same goes for 110 and 125V combinations. It's always preferable to adjust your appliance to the exact voltage if you can (some modern battery chargers and radios will do this automatically). Just don't mix 110/125V with 220/240V without a transformer (which will be built into an adjustable appliance).

Several countries outside Europe (such as the USA and Canada) use 60Hz AC, which will affect the speed of electric motors even after the voltage has been adjusted to European values, so CD and tape players (where motor speed is all-important) will be useless. But things like electric razors, hair dryers, irons and radios will be fine.

Plugs & Sockets

Cyprus and Malta use a design like the one in the UK and Ireland: three flat pins (two for current and one for earth). The rest of Mediterranean Europe uses the 'europlug' with two round pins. Many europlugs and some sockets don't have provision for earth, since most local home appliances are double-insulated. When provided, earth usually consists of two contact points along the edge, although Italy and Greece use a third round pin. In Greece the standard two-pin plug still fits the sockets, but this is not always so in Italy.

If your plugs are of a different design, you'll need an adapter. Get one before you leave, since the adapters available in Europe usually go the other way. If you find yourself without one, however, a specialist electrical-supply shop should be able to help.

HEALTH

Travel health depends on your predeparture preparations, your daily health care while travelling and how you handle any medical problem that does develop.

Predeparture Planning

Immunisations Jabs are not really necessary for Mediterranean Europe, but they may be an entry requirement if you're coming from an infected area – yellow fever is the most likely requirement. If you're going to Europe with stopovers in Asia, Africa or South America, check with your travel agent or with the embassies of the countries you plan to visit. There are, however, a few routine vaccinations that are recommended whether you're travelling or not, and this Health section assumes that you've had them: polio (usually administered during childhood), tetanus and diphtheria (usually administered together during childhood, with a booster shot every 10 years) and measles. See your physician or nearest health agency about these. You might also consider having an immunoglobulin or hepatitis A vaccine (Havrix) before extensive travels in southern Europe; a tetanus booster; an immunisation against hepatitis B before travelling to Malta; or a rabies (pre-exposure) vaccination.

Medical Kit Check List

Consider taking a basic medical kit including:

☐ **Aspirin** or **paracetamol** (acetaminophen in the US) – for pain or fever.

☐ **Antihistamine** (such as Benadryl) – a decongestant for colds and allergies, eases the itch from insect bites or stings and helps prevent motion sickness. Antihistamines may cause sedation and interact with alcohol, so care should be taken when using them; take one you know and have used before, if possible.

☐ **Antibiotics** – useful if you're travelling well off the beaten track, but they must be prescribed; carry the prescription with you.

☐ **Lomotil** or **Imodium** – to treat diarrhoea; prochlorperazine (eg Stemetil) or metaclopramide (eg Maxalon) is good for nausea and vomiting.

☐ **Rehydration mixture** – to treat severe diarrhoea; particularly important when travelling with children.

☐ **Antiseptic**, such as povidone-iodine (eg Betadine) – for cuts and grazes.

☐ **Multivitamins** – especially useful for long trips when dietary vitamin intake may be inadequate.

☐ **Calamine lotion** or **aluminium sulphate spray** (eg Stingose) – to ease irritation from bites or stings.

☐ **Bandages** and **Band-aids**

☐ **Scissors, tweezers** and a **thermometer** – (note that mercury thermometers are prohibited by airlines).

☐ **Cold** and **flu tablets** and **throat lozenges** – Pseudoephedrine hydrochloride (Sudafed) may be useful if flying with a cold to avoid ear damage.

☐ **Insect repellent, sunscreen, Chapstick** and **water purification tablets**

☐ **A couple of syringes** – in case you need injections in a country with medical hygiene problems. Ask your doctor for a note explaining why they have been prescribed.

All vaccinations should be recorded on an International Health Certificate (see that entry in the Visas & Documents section). Don't leave this till the last minute, as the vaccinations may have to be staggered over a period of time.

Health Insurance Make sure that you have adequate health insurance. See Travel Insurance in the Visas & Documents section for details.

Other Preparations If you're healthy before you start travelling you'll have a lot less problems. If you are going on a long trip make sure your teeth are OK. If you wear glasses take a spare pair and your prescription.

If you require a particular medication take an adequate supply, as it may not be available locally. Take part of the packaging showing the generic name, rather than the brand, which will make getting replacements easier. It's a good idea to have a legible prescription or letter from your doctor to show that you legally use the medication to avoid any problems.

Basic Rules

Care in what you eat and drink is the most important health rule in North Africa and the more remote parts of Turkey and southern Europe; stomach upsets are the most likely travel health problem here but most of these upsets will be relatively minor.

Food Salads and fruit should be safe throughout Europe, but elsewhere they should be washed with purified water or peeled where possible. Ice cream is usually OK, but beware of street vendors in North Africa and Turkey, and of any ice cream that has melted and been refrozen.

Take great care with fish or shellfish (eg cooked mussels that haven't opened properly can be dangerous), and avoid undercooked meat. In general, places that are packed with either travellers or locals (or both) should be fine. Always be wary of an empty budget restaurant.

Picking mushrooms is a favourite pastime in some parts of Europe as autumn approaches, but make sure that you don't eat any mushrooms that haven't been positively identified as safe. Many cities and towns set up inspection tables at markets or at entrances to national parks to separate the good from the deadly.

Water Tap water is almost always safe to drink in Europe, but be wary of water taken directly from rivers or lakes unless you can be sure that there are no people or cattle upstream. Run-off from fertilised fields is also a concern. Tap water is usually *not* safe to drink in North Africa or Turkey (though probably OK in Istanbul), so stick to bottled water and avoid ice cubes and even fruit juice, as water may have been added to it. In these areas, use purified water rather than tap water to brush your teeth.

Dairy products are fine throughout Europe, but should be treated with suspicion in North Africa and Turkey because milk is often unpasteurised. Boiled milk is fine if it is kept hygienically, and yoghurt is always good.

Water Purification If you're going to spend some time in North Africa or Turkey, or are planning extended hikes where you have to rely on water from rivers or streams, you'll need to know about water purification. The simplest way of purifying water is to boil it thoroughly. Vigorously boiling should be satisfactory though at high altitude water boils at a lower temperature, so germs are less likely to be killed. Boil it for longer in this situation.

Consider purchasing a water filter for a long trip. There are two main kinds of filter. Total filters take out all parasites, bacteria and viruses, and make water safe to drink. They are often expensive, but they can be more cost effective than buying bottled water. Simple filters (which can even be a nylon mesh bag) take out dirt and larger foreign bodies from the water so that chemical solutions work much more effectively; if water is dirty, chemical solutions may not work at all.

It's very important when buying a filter to read the specifications so that you know exactly what it removes from the water and what it doesn't. Simple filtering will not remove all dangerous organisms so if you cannot boil water it should be treated chemi-

cally. Chlorine tablets (Puritabs, Steritabs or other brand names) will kill many pathogens, but not some parasites like giardia and amoebic cysts. Iodine is more effective in purifying water and is available in tablet form (eg Potable Aqua). Follow the directions carefully and remember that too much iodine can be harmful.

Medical Problems & Treatment

Local pharmacies or neighbourhood medical centres are good places to visit if you have a small medical problem and can explain what the problem is. Hospital casualty wards will help if it's more serious. Major hospitals and emergency numbers are mentioned in the various country chapters of this book and sometimes indicated on the maps. Tourist offices and hotels can put you on to a doctor or dentist, and your embassy or consulate will probably know one who speaks your language.

Environmental Hazards

Altitude Sickness Lack of oxygen at high altitudes (over 2500m) effects most people to some extent. The affect may be mild or severe and occurs because less oxygen reaches the muscles and the brain at high altitude, requiring the heart and lungs to compensate by working harder. Symptoms of Acute Mountain Sickness (AMS) usually develop during the first 24 hours at altitude but may be delayed up to three weeks. Mild symptoms include headache, lethargy, dizziness, difficulty sleeping and loss of appetite. AMS may become more severe without warning and can be fatal. Severe symptoms include breathlessness, a dry, irritating cough (which may progress to the production of pink, frothy sputum), severe headache, lack of coordination and balance, confusion, irrational behaviour, vomiting, drowsiness and unconsciousness. There is no hard-and-fast rule as to what is too high: AMS has been fatal at 3000m, although 3500 to 4500m is the usual range.

Fungal Infections Fungal infections occur more commonly in hot weather and are usually found on the scalp, between the toes or fingers, in the groin and on the body (ringworm). You get ringworm (which is a fungal infection, not a worm) from infected animals or other people. Moisture encourages these infections.

To prevent fungal infections wear loose, comfortable clothes, avoid artificial fibres, wash frequently and dry carefully. If you do get an infection, wash the infected area at least daily with a disinfectant or medicated soap and water, and rinse and dry well. Apply an antifungal cream or powder like tolnaftate (Tinaderm). Try to expose the infected area to air or sunlight as much as possible and wash all towels and underwear in hot water, change them often and let them dry in the sun.

Heat Exhaustion Dehydration and salt deficiency can cause heat exhaustion. Take time to acclimatise to high temperatures, drink sufficient liquids and do not do anything too physically demanding.

Salt deficiency is characterised by fatigue, lethargy, headaches, giddiness and muscle cramps; salt tablets may help, but adding extra salt on your food is better.

Heatstroke This serious, occasionally fatal condition can occur if the body's heat-regulating mechanism breaks down and the body temperature rises to dangerous levels. Long, continuous periods of exposure to high temperatures and insufficient fluids can leave you vulnerable to heatstroke.

The symptoms are feeling unwell, not sweating very much (or at all) and a high body temperature (39°C to 41°C or 102°F to 106°F). Where sweating has ceased the skin becomes flushed and red. Severe, throbbing headaches and lack of coordination will also occur, and the sufferer may be confused or aggressive. Eventually the victim will become delirious or convulse. Hospitalisation is essential, but in the interim get victims out of the sun, remove their clothing, cover them with a wet sheet or towel and then fan continually. Give fluids if they are conscious.

Hypothermia Too much cold can be just as dangerous as too much heat. Be prepared for cold, wet or windy conditions even if you're just out walking or hitching.

Hypothermia occurs when the body loses heat faster than it can produce it and the core temperature of the body falls. It is surprisingly easy to progress from very cold to dangerously cold due to a combination of wind, wet clothing, fatigue and hunger, even if the air temperature is above freezing. It is best to dress in layers; silk, wool and some of the new artificial fibres are all good insulating materials. A hat is important, as a lot of heat is lost through the head. A strong, waterproof outer layer (and a 'space' blanket for emergencies) are essential. Carry basic supplies, including food containing simple sugars to generate heat quickly and fluid to drink.

Symptoms of hypothermia are exhaustion, numb skin (particularly toes and fingers), shivering, slurred speech, irrational or violent behaviour, lethargy, stumbling, dizzy spells, muscle cramps and violent bursts of energy. Irrationality may take the form of sufferers claiming they are warm and trying to take off their clothes.

To treat mild hypothermia, first get the person out of the wind and/or rain, remove their clothing if it's wet and replace it with dry, warm clothing. Give them hot liquids – not alcohol – and some high-kilojoule (calorie), easily digestible food. Do not rub victims; instead allow them to slowly warm themselves. This should be enough to treat the early stages of hypothermia. The early recognition and treatment of mild hypothermia is the only way to prevent severe hypothermia, which is a critical condition.

Jet Lag A person experiences jet lag when travelling by air across more than three time zones (each time zone usually represents a one-hour time difference). It occurs because many of the functions of the human body (such as temperature, pulse rate and emptying of the bladder and bowels) are regulated by internal 24-hour cycles. When we travel long distances rapidly, our bodies take time to adjust to the 'new time' of our destination, and we may experience fatigue, disorientation, insomnia, anxiety, impaired concentration and loss of appetite. These effects will usually be gone within three days of arrival, but to minimise the impact of jet lag:

- Rest for a couple of days prior to departure.
- Try to select flight schedules that minimise sleep deprivation; arriving late in the day means

you can go to sleep soon after you arrive. For very long flights, try to organise a stopover.

- Avoid excessive eating (which bloats the stomach) and alcohol (which causes dehydration) during the flight. Instead, drink plenty of non-carbonated, non-alcoholic drinks such as fruit juice or water.
- Avoid smoking (if allowed on board).
- Make yourself comfortable by wearing loose-fitting clothes and perhaps bringing an eye mask and ear plugs to help you sleep.
- Try to sleep at the appropriate time for the time zone you are travelling to.

Motion Sickness Eating lightly before and during a trip will reduce the chances of motion sickness. If you are prone to motion sickness try to find a place that minimises movement – near the wing on aircraft, close to midships on boats, near the centre on buses. Fresh air usually helps; reading and cigarette smoke do not. Commercial motion-sickness preparations, which can cause drowsiness, have to be taken *before* the trip commences. Ginger (available in capsule form) and peppermint (including mint-flavoured sweets) are natural preventatives.

Prickly Heat Prickly heat is an itchy rash caused by excessive perspiration trapped under the skin. It usually strikes people who have just arrived in a hot climate. Keeping cool, bathing often, drying the skin and using a mild talcum or prickly-heat powder or resorting to air-conditioning may help.

Sunburn You can get sunburned surprisingly quickly, even through cloud cover. Use a sunscreen, hat and barrier cream for your nose and lips. Calamine lotion or Stingose are good for mild sunburn. Protect your eyes with good quality sunglasses, particularly if you will be near water, sand or snow.

Infectious Diseases

Diarrhoea Simple things like a change of water, food or climate can all cause a mild bout of diarrhoea, but a few rushed toilet trips with no other symptoms is not indicative of a major problem.

Dehydration is the main danger with any diarrhoea, particularly in children or the elderly, as dehydration can occur quite quickly. Under all circumstances fluid replacement (at least equal to the volume being lost) is the most important thing to remember. Weak black tea with a little sugar, soda water or soft drinks allowed to go flat and diluted 50% with clean water are all good. With severe diarrhoea a rehydrating solution is preferable to replace minerals and salts lost. Commercially available oral rehydration salts (ORS) are very useful; add them to boiled or bottled water. In an emergency you can make up a solution of six teaspoons of sugar and half a teaspoon of salt to a litre of boiled or bottled water. You need to drink at least the same volume of fluid that you are losing in bowel movements and vomiting. Urine is the best guide to the adequacy of replacement – if you have small amounts of concentrated urine, you need to drink more. Keep drinking small amounts often. Stick to a bland diet as you recover.

Viral Gastroenteritis This is caused not by bacteria but, as the name suggests, by a virus. It is characterised by stomach cramps, diarrhoea, and sometimes by vomiting and/or a slight fever. All you can do is rest and drink lots of fluids.

Hepatitis Hepatitis is a general term for inflammation of the liver. It is a common disease worldwide. The symptoms are fever, chills, headache, fatigue, feelings of weakness and aches and pains, followed by loss of appetite, nausea, vomiting, abdominal pain, dark urine, light-coloured faeces, jaundiced (yellow) skin and the whites of the eyes may turn yellow. **Hepatitis A** is transmitted by contaminated food and drinking water. You should seek medical advice, but there is not much you can do apart from resting, drinking lots of fluids, eating lightly and avoiding fatty foods. People who have had hepatitis should avoid alcohol for some time after the illness, as the liver needs time to recover.

There are almost 300 million chronic carriers of **Hepatitis B** in the world. It is spread through contact with infected blood, blood products or body fluids, for example through sexual contact, unsterilised needles and blood transfusions, or contact with blood via small breaks in the skin. Other risk situations include having a shave, tattoo, or having your body pierced with contaminated equipment.

The symptoms of type B may be more severe and may lead to long-term problems.

HIV & AIDS HIV, the Human Immunodeficiency Virus, develops into AIDS, Acquired Immune Deficiency Syndrome, which is a fatal disease. HIV is a major problem in many countries. Any exposure to blood, blood products or body fluids may put the individual at risk. The disease is often transmitted through sexual contact or dirty needles – vaccinations, acupuncture, tattooing and body piercing can be potentially as dangerous as intravenous drug use. HIV/AIDS can also be spread through infected blood transfusions; some developing countries cannot afford to screen blood used for transfusions.

If you do need an injection, ask to see the syringe unwrapped in front of you, or take a needle and syringe pack with you.

Fear of HIV infection should never preclude treatment for serious medical conditions.

Sexually Transmitted Diseases Gonorrhoea, herpes and syphilis are among these diseases; sores, blisters or rashes around the genitals, discharges or pain when urinating are common symptoms. In some STDs, such as wart virus or chlamydia, symptoms may be less marked or not observed at all especially in women. Syphilis symptoms eventually disappear completely but the disease continues and can cause severe problems in later years. While abstinence from sexual contact is the only 100% effective prevention, using condoms is also effective. The treatment of gonorrhoea and syphilis is with antibiotics. The different sexually transmitted diseases each require specific antibiotics. There is no cure for herpes or AIDS.

Cuts, Bites & Stings

Bedbugs & Lice Bedbugs live in various places, but particularly in dirty mattresses and bedding, evidenced by spots of blood on bedclothes or on the wall. Bedbugs leave itchy bites in neat rows. Calamine lotion or Stingose spray may help.

All lice cause itching and discomfort. They make themselves at home in your hair (head lice), your clothing (body lice) or in your pubic hair (crabs). You catch lice through direct contact with infected people or by sharing combs, clothing and the like. Powder or shampoo treatment will kill the lice and infected clothing should then be washed in very hot, soapy water and left in the sun to dry.

Insect Bites & Stings Mosquitoes can be a nuisance in southern Europe, particularly around lakes and rivers or, for example, on the Camargue delta in southern France. Fortunately, mosquito-borne diseases like malaria are for the most part unknown in Mediterranean Europe. Most people get used to mosquito bites after a few days as their bodies adjust, and the itching and swelling will become less severe. An antihistamine cream may help alleviate the symptoms. For some people, a daily dose of vitamin B will keep mosquitoes at bay.

Cuts & Scratches Wash well and treat any cut with an antiseptic such as povidone-iodine. Where possible avoid bandages and Band-aids, which can keep wounds wet.

Mosquitoes Mosquitoes can be a nuisance in southern Europe, particularly around lakes and rivers or, for example, in the Camargue delta area in southern France. Fortunately, mosquito-borne diseases like malaria are for the most part unknown in Mediterranean Europe. Most people get used to mosquito bites after a few days as their bodies adjust, and itching and swelling will become less severe. An antihistamine cream may help alleviate the symptoms. For some people, a daily dose of vitamin B will keep mosquitoes at bay.

Ticks You should always check all over your body if you have been walking through a potentially tick-infested area as ticks can cause skin infections and other more serious diseases. If a tick is found attached, press down around the tick's head with tweezers, grab the head and gently pull upwards. Avoid pulling the rear of the body as this may squeeze the tick's gut contents through the attached mouth parts into the skin, increasing the risk of infection and disease. Smearing chemicals on the tick will not make it let go and is not recommended.

Lyme disease is a tick-transmitted infection that may be acquired in parts of southern Europe. The illness usually begins with a spreading rash at the site of the tick bite and is accompanied by fever, headache, extreme fatigue, aching joints and muscles, and mild neck stiffness. If untreated, these symptoms usually resolve over several weeks but over subsequent weeks or months disorders of the nervous system, heart and joints may develop. Treatment works best early in the illness. Medical help should be sought.

Rabies Rabies is a fatal viral infection found in many countries. Many mammals can be infected (such as dogs, cats, bats and monkeys) and it is their saliva which is infectious. Any bite, scratch or even lick from a warmblooded, furry animal should be cleaned immediately and thoroughly. Scrub with soap and running water, and then apply alcohol or iodine solution. Medical help should be sought promptly to receive a course of injections to prevent the onset of symptoms and death.

Snakes To minimise your chances of being bitten always wear boots, socks and long trousers when walking through undergrowth where snakes may be present. Don't put your hands into holes and crevices, and be careful when collecting firewood.

Snake bites do not cause instantaneous death and antivenenes are usually available. Immediately wrap the bitten limb tightly, as you would for a sprained ankle, and then attach a splint to immobilise it. Keep the victim still and seek medical help, if possible with the dead snake for identification. Don't attempt to catch the snake if there is a possibility of being bitten again. Tourniquets and sucking out the poison are now comprehensively discredited.

Women's Health
Gynaecological Problems Sexually transmitted diseases are a major cause of vaginal problems. Symptoms include a smelly discharge, painful intercourse and sometimes a burning sensation when urinating. Male sexual partners must also be treated. Medical attention should be sought and remember in addition to these diseases

HIV or hepatitis B may also be acquired during exposure. Besides abstinence, the best thing is to practise safe sex using condoms.

Antibiotic use, synthetic underwear, sweating and contraceptive pills can lead to fungal vaginal infections when travelling in hot climates. Maintaining good personal hygiene, and loose-fitting clothes and cotton underwear will help to prevent these infections.

Fungal infections, characterised by a rash, itch and discharge, can be treated with a vinegar or lemon-juice douche, or with yoghurt. Nystatin, miconazole or clotrimazole pessaries or vaginal cream are the usual treatment.

WOMEN TRAVELLERS
Women are more likely to experience problems in rural Spain, southern Italy (especially Sicily), Morocco, Turkey and Tunisia, where many men still think that staring at or calling out to a passing woman is to pay her a flattering compliment. Slightly conservative dress can help to deter lascivious gazes and wolf whistles and sunglasses may prevent unwanted eye contact. Marriage is highly respected in the region, and a wedding ring (on the left ring finger) sometimes helps, along with talk about 'my husband'.

In Muslim countries, a western woman without a male companion will have a trying time coping with constant attention from males. The average Muslim woman is still bound to very strict codes of behaviour and dress, so it's not surprising that her western counterpart is seen as being free from moral or sexual constraints. Although head cover is not compulsory in these countries, it's a good idea to wear a headscarf if you're visiting mosques and so on. Hitching alone in these areas is definitely asking for trouble.

GAY & LESBIAN TRAVELLERS
Mediterranean Europe lists contact addresses and gay and lesbian venues in the individual country chapters; look in the Facts for the Visitor and Entertainment sections.

The *Spartacus International Gay Guide* (Bruno Gmünder, Berlin; US$32.95) is a good male-only international directory of gay entertainment venues in Europe and elsewhere. It's best when used in conjunction with listings in local gay papers, usually distributed for free at gay bars and clubs.

For lesbians, *Women's Travel in Your Pocket* (Ferrari Publications, London; UK£8.99) is a good international guide.

DISABLED TRAVELLERS

If you have a physical disability, get in touch with your national support organisation (preferably the 'travel officer' if there is one) and ask about the countries you plan to visit. Such organisations often have complete libraries devoted to travel, and can put you in touch with travel agencies that specialise in tours for the disabled.

The British-based Royal Association for Disability & Rehabilitation (RADAR) publishes a useful guide entitled *European Holidays & Travel Abroad: A Guide for Disabled People* (UK£5), which gives a good overview of facilities for disabled travellers in Europe (published in even-numbered years) and one to places farther afield called *Long-Haul Holidays* (in odd-numbered years). The *Accessible Holidays in the British Isles* (£7.50) also includes Ireland. Contact RADAR (☎ 0171-250 3222; fax 0171-250 0212) at 12 City Forum, 250 City Rd, London EC1V 8AF.

SENIOR TRAVELLERS

Senior citizens are entitled to many discounts in Europe on things like public transport and museum admission fees, provided they show proof of their age. In some cases they might need a special pass. The minimum qualifying age is generally 60 or 65 for men and slightly younger for women.

In your home country, a lower age may already entitle you to all sorts of interesting travel packages and discounts (eg on car hire) through organisations and travel agents that cater for senior travellers. Start hunting at your local senior citizens advice bureau. European residents over 60 are eligible for the Rail Europe Senior Card; see Cheap Tickets under Train in the Getting Around chapter for details.

TRAVEL WITH CHILDREN

Successful travel with young children requires planning and effort. Don't try to overdo things; even for adults, packing too much into the time available can cause problems. And make sure the activities include the kids as well – balance that day at the Louvre with a day at Disneyland Paris. Include children in the trip planning; if they've helped to work out where you will be going, they will be much more interested when they get there. Lonely Planet's *Travel with Children* by Maureen Wheeler is a good source of information.

Most car-rental firms in Europe have children's safety seats for hire at a nominal cost, but it is essential that you book them in advance. The same goes for highchairs and cots (cribs); they're standard in most restaurants and hotels, but numbers are limited. The choice of baby food, infant formulas, soy and cow's milk, disposable nappies (diapers) and the like is as great in the supermarkets of most European countries as it is at home, but the opening hours may be quite different. Run out of nappies on Saturday afternoon and you're facing a very long and messy weekend.

DANGERS & ANNOYANCES

On the whole, you should experience few problems travelling in Mediterranean Europe – even alone – as the region is well developed and relatively safe. But do exercise common sense.

Whatever you do, don't leave friends and relatives back home worrying about how to get in touch with you in case of emergency. Work out a list of places where they can contact you. Better still, phone home now and then or email.

Theft

Theft is definitely a problem in Mediterranean Europe, and nowadays you also have to be wary of other travellers. The most important things to guard are your passport, papers, tickets and money – in that order. It's always best to carry these next to your skin or in a sturdy leather pouch on your belt. Train station lockers or luggage storage counters are useful places to store your bags (but *never* valuables) while you get your bearings in a new town. Be very suspicious about people who offer to help you operate your locker. Carry your own padlock for hostel lockers.

You can lessen the risks further by being careful of snatch thieves. Cameras or shoulder bags are an open invitation for these people, who sometimes operate from motorcycles or scooters and expertly slash the strap before you have a chance to react. A small daypack is better, but watch your rear. Be very careful at cafés and bars; loop the strap around your leg while seated.

Pickpockets are most active in dense crowds, especially in busy train stations and on public transport during peak hours. A common ploy is for one person to distract you while another zips through your pockets. Beware of gangs of kids – both dishevelled-looking *and* well dressed – waving newspapers and demanding attention. In the blink of an eye, a wallet or camera can go missing.

Be careful even in hotels; don't leave valuables lying around in your room. Parked cars are prime targets for petty criminals in most cities, and cars with foreign number plates and/or rental-agency stickers in particular. Remove the stickers (or cover them with local football club stickers or something similar), leave a local newspaper on the seat and generally try to make it look like a local car. Don't ever leave valuables in the car, and remove all luggage overnight, even if it's in a parking garage. In some places, freeway service centres have become unsafe territory: in the time it takes to drink a cup of coffee or use the toilet, your car can be broken into and cleared out.

Another ploy is for muggers to pull up alongside your car and point to the wheel; when you get out to have a look, you become one more robbery statistic. While driving in cities, beware of snatch thieves when you pull up at the lights – keep doors locked and windows rolled up high. In case of theft or loss, always report the incident to the police and ask for a statement. Otherwise your travel-insurance company won't pay up.

Drugs

Always treat drugs with a great deal of caution. There are a lot of drugs available in Mediterranean Europe, but that doesn't mean they are legal. Even a little harmless hashish can cause a great deal of trouble in some places.

Don't even think about bringing drugs home with you either. With what they may consider 'suspect' stamps in your passport (eg Morocco), energetic customs officials could well decide to take a closer look.

ACTIVITIES

Mediterranean Europe offers countless opportunities to indulge in more active pursuits than sightseeing. The varied geography and climate supports the full range of outdoor pursuits: windsurfing, fishing, trekking, cycling, mountaineering and skiing – you name it, Europe will have several great places to do it. For more local information, see the individual country chapters.

Windsurfing & Surfing

After swimming and fishing, windsurfing could well be the most popular of the many water sports on offer in Europe. It's easy to rent sailboards in many tourist centres, and courses are usually available for beginners.

Believe it or not, you can also go surfing in Europe. While the calm Mediterranean is not the best place for the sport, there can be excellent surf (and an accompanying surfer scene) along the Atlantic coast of France and Portugal, and along the north and south-west coasts of Spain. The Atlantic seaboard of Morocco, too, has some excellent waves and deserted beaches.

Boating

The Mediterranean itself is not the only body of water with opportunities for boating. The region's many lakes, rivers and other coastlines offer a variety of boating options unmatched anywhere in the world. You can kayak down rapids in Slovenia, charter a yacht in the Aegean, row on a peaceful Alpine lake, rent a sailing boat on the Côte d'Azur, cruise the canals of France – the possibilities are endless. The country chapters have more details.

Hiking

Keen hikers can spend a lifetime exploring Europe's many exciting trails. Probably the most spectacular are in the Alps and Italian

Dolomites which are crisscrossed with well-marked trails, and food and accommodation are available along the way in season. The equally sensational Pyrenees are less developed, which can add to the experience as you often rely on remote mountain villages for rest and sustenance. Hiking areas that are less well known but nothing short of stunning can be found in Corsica, Sardinia, Crete, Croatia and northern Portugal while the High Atlas Mountains in Morocco offer a mind-blowing experience through tumbledown Berber villages in untamed country. The Picos de Europa range in Spain is also rewarding.

The Ramblers' Association (☎ 0171-339 8500) is a London charity that promotes long-distance walking and can help with maps and information. The British-based Ramblers Holidays (☎ 01707-331 133) in Hertfordshire offers hiking-oriented trips in Europe and elsewhere.

Every country in Europe has national parks and other interesting areas that may qualify as a trekker's paradise, depending on your preferences. Guided treks are often available for those who aren't sure about their physical abilities or who simply don't know what to look for. Read the Hiking information in the individual country chapters in this book and take your pick.

Cycling

Along with hiking, cycling is the best way to really get close to the scenery and the people, while keeping yourself fit in the process. It's also a good way to get around many cities and towns.

Much of Europe is ideally suited to cycling. In the north-west, the flat terrain ensures that bicycles are a popular form of everyday transport, though strong headwinds often spoil the fun. In the rest of the continent, hills and mountains can make for heavy going, but this is offset by the dense concentration of things to see. Cycling is a great way to explore many of the Mediterranean islands, though the heat can get to you after a while (make sure you drink enough fluids).

Popular cycling areas include the coastal areas of Sardinia (around Alghero) and Apulia, and the hills of Tuscany and Umbria in Italy, anywhere in the Alps (for those fit enough), and the south of France.

If you are arriving from outside Europe, you can often bring your own bicycle along on the plane (see Bicycle in the Getting Around chapter). Alternatively, this book lists many places where you can hire one (make sure it has plenty of gears if you plan anything serious), though apart from in Ireland the bike-hire proprietors might take a dim view of rentals lasting more than a week.

See the introductory Getting Around chapter for more information on bicycle touring, and the Getting Around sections in the individual country chapters for rental agencies and tips on places to visit.

Skiing

In winter, Europeans flock to the hundreds of resorts in the Alps and Pyrenees for downhill skiing and snowboarding, though cross-country is very popular in some areas.

Skiing is quite expensive due to the costs of ski lifts, accommodation and the inevitable après-ski drinking sessions. Equipment hire (or even purchase), on the other hand, can be relatively cheap if you follow the tips in this book, and the hassle of bringing your own skis may not be worth it. As a rule, a skiing holiday in Europe will work out twice as expensive as a summer holiday of the same length. Cross-country skiing costs less than downhill since you don't rely as much on ski lifts.

The skiing season generally lasts from early December to late March, though at higher altitudes it may extend an extra month either way. Snow conditions can vary greatly from one year to the next and from region to region, but January and February tend to be the best (and busiest) months. During the snow season, the Thursday and Friday editions of the *International Herald Tribune* have a weekend ski report on snow conditions at every major ski resort in Europe.

Ski resorts in the French Alps offer great skiing and facilities but are also among the most expensive in Europe. Prices in the French Pyrenees and Italian Alps and Apennines are slightly cheaper (with upmarket exceptions like Cortina d'Ampezzo), and can work out to be relatively cheap with the right package. Cheaper still are the Julian Alps in Slovenia, which are luring skiers away from the flashier resorts just across the border in Austria and Italy.

Possibly the cheapest skiing in Europe can be found in the Pyrenees in Spain and Andorra, and in the Sierra Nevada mountain range in the south of Spain. Greece also boasts a growing ski industry, and skiing there is good value. See the individual country chapters for more information.

COURSES

If your interests are more cerebral, you can enrol in courses in Mediterranean Europe on anything from language to alternative medicine. Language courses are available to foreigners through universities or private schools, and are justifiably popular since the best way to learn a language is in the country where it's spoken. But you can also take courses in art, literature, architecture, drama, music, cooking, alternative energy, photography and organic farming, among other subjects.

The individual country chapters in this book give pointers on where to start looking. In general, the best sources of information are the cultural institutes maintained by many European countries around the world; failing that, try their national tourist offices or embassies. Student-exchange organisations, student-travel agencies, and organisations like the YMCA/YWCA and Hostelling International (HI) can also put you on the right track. Ask about special holiday packages that include a course.

WORK

European countries aren't keen on handing out jobs to foreigners with unemployment rates what they are in some areas. Officially, an EU citizen is allowed to work in any other EU country, but the paperwork isn't always straightforward for long-term employment. Other country/nationality combinations require special work permits that can be almost impossible to arrange, especially for temporary work. That doesn't prevent enterprising travellers from topping up their funds occasionally by working in the hotel or restaurant trades at beach or ski resorts or teaching a little English, and they don't always have to do this illegally either.

The UK, for example, issues special 'working holiday' visas to Commonwealth citizens aged between 17 and 27 valid for two years. In France you can get a visa for work as an au pair if you are going to follow a recognised course of study (eg a French-language course) and complete all the paperwork before leaving your country. Your national student-exchange organisation may be able to arrange temporary work permits to several countries through special programs. For more details on working as a foreigner, see Work in the Facts for the Visitor sections of the individual country chapters.

If one of your parents or a grandparent was born in an EU country, you may have certain rights you never knew about. Get in touch with that country's embassy and ask about dual citizenship and work permits – if you go for citizenship, also ask about any obligations, such as military service and residency. Ireland is particularly easy-going about granting citizenship to people with an Irish parent or grandparent, and with an Irish passport, the EU is your oyster. Be aware that your home country may not recognise dual citizenship.

If you do find a temporary job, the pay may be less than that offered to local people. The one big exception is teaching English, but these jobs are hard to come by, at least officially. Other typical tourist jobs (picking grapes in France, washing dishes in Alpine resorts) often come with board and lodging, and the pay is little more than pocket money, but you'll have a good time partying with other travellers.

Work Your Way Around the World by Susan Griffith gives good, practical advice on a wide range of issues. Its publisher, Vacation Work, has many other useful titles, including *Summer Jobs Abroad*, edited by David Woodworth. *Working Holidays*, published by the Central Bureau for Educational Visits & Exchanges in London, is another good source.

If you play an instrument or have other artistic talents, you could try working the streets. As every Peruvian pipe player (and his fifth cousin) knows, busking is fairly common in major cities of Mediterranean Europe, especially in France, Spain and Italy. Beware though: many countries require municipal permits that can be hard to obtain. Talk to other buskers first.

Selling goods on the street, apart from at flea markets, is generally frowned upon and can be tantamount to vagrancy. It's also a hard way to make money if you're not selling something special. Most countries require permits for this sort of thing. It's fairly common, though officially illegal, in Spain.

ACCOMMODATION

The cheapest places to stay in Europe are camping grounds, followed by hostels and accommodation in student dormitories. Cheap hotels are virtually unknown in the northern half of Europe, but guesthouses, pensions and private rooms often offer good value. Self-catering flats and cottages are worth considering with a group, especially if you plan to stay somewhere for a while.

See the Facts for the Visitor sections in the individual country chapters for an overview of the local accommodation options. During peak holiday periods, accommodation can be hard to find, and unless you're camping, it's advisable to book ahead. Even camping grounds can fill up, especially in or around big cities.

Reservations

Cheap hotels in popular destinations (eg Paris, Rome and Madrid), especially the well-run ones in desirable or central neighbourhoods, fill up quickly. It's a good idea to make reservations as many weeks ahead as possible – at least for the first night or two. A three-minute international phone call to reserve a room (followed, if necessary, by written confirmation and/or deposit) is a lot cheaper than wasting your first day in a city looking for a place to stay.

If you arrive in a country by air and without a reservation, there is often an airport accommodation-booking desk, although it rarely covers the lower strata of hotels. Tourist offices often have extensive accommodation lists, and the more helpful ones will go out of their way to find you something suitable. In most countries the fee for this service is very low and if accommodation is tight it can save you a lot of running around. This is also an easy way to get around any language problems. Agencies offering private rooms can be good value. Staying with a

local family doesn't always mean that you'll lack privacy, but you'll probably have less freedom than in a hotel.

Sometimes people will come up to you on the street offering a private room or a hostel bed. This can be good or bad, there's no hard-and-fast rule – just make sure it's not way out in a dingy suburb somewhere and that you negotiate a clear price. As always, be careful when someone offers to carry your luggage: they might carry it off altogether.

Camping

Camping is immensely popular in Mediterranean Europe (especially among German and Dutch tourists) and provides the cheapest accommodation. There's usually a charge per tent or site, per person and per vehicle. National tourist offices should have booklets or brochures listing camping grounds for their country. See the earlier Visas & Documents section for information on the Camping Card International.

In large cities, most camping grounds will be some distance from the centre. For this reason, camping is most popular with people who have their own transport. If you're on foot, the money you save by camping can quickly be eaten up by the bus or train fares spent on commuting to and from a town centre. You may also need a tent, sleeping bag and cooking equipment, though not always. Many camping grounds hire bungalows or cottages accommodating from two to eight people.

Camping other than on designated camping grounds is difficult because the population density of Europe makes it hard to find a suitable spot to pitch a tent away from prying eyes. It is also illegal without permission from the local authorities (the police or local council office) or from the owner of the land (don't be shy about asking – you may be pleasantly surprised by the response).

In some countries (eg France), free camping is illegal on all but private land, and in Greece it's illegal altogether. This doesn't prevent hikers from occasionally pitching their tent for the night, and they'll usually get away with it if they have only a small tent, are discreet, stay only one or two nights, take the tent down during the day and do not light a campfire or leave rubbish. At worst, they'll be woken up by the police and asked to move on.

Hostels

Hostels offer the cheapest (secure) roof over your head in Europe, and you don't have to be a youngster to use them. Most hostels are part of the national youth hostel association (YHA), which is affiliated with what was formerly called the IYHF (International Youth Hostel Federation) and has been renamed Hostelling International (HI) in order to attract a wider clientele and move away from the emphasis on youth. The situation remains slightly confused, however. Some countries, such as the USA and Canada, immediately adopted the new name, but many European countries will take a few years to change their logos. In practice it makes no difference: IYHF and HI are the same thing and the domestic YHA almost always belongs to the parent group.

Technically, you're supposed to be a YHA or HI member to use affiliated hostels, but you can often stay by paying an extra charge and this will usually be set against future membership. Stay enough nights as a nonmember and you're automatically a member.

To join the HI, ask at any hostel or contact your local or national hostelling office. The offices for English-speaking countries appear below. Otherwise, check the individual country chapters for addresses.

Australia
  Australian Youth Hostels Association (☎ 02-9565 1699; fax 02-9565 1325; yha@yha.org.au) Level 3, 10 Mallett St, Camperdown, NSW 2050
Canada
  Hostelling International Canada (☎ 613-237 7884; fax 613-237 7868) 205 St Catherine St, Suite 400, Ottawa, Ontario K2P C3
England & Wales
  Youth Hostels Association, Trevelyan House (☎ 01727-855 215; fax 01727-844 126; YHA-CustomerServices@compuserve.com) 8 St Stephen's Hill, St Albans, Herts AL1 2DY
Ireland
  An Óige (Irish Youth Hostel Association; ☎ 01-830 4555; 01-830 5808; anoige@iol.ie) 61 Mountjoy St, Dublin 7
New Zealand
  Youth Hostels Association of New Zealand (☎ 03-379 9970; fax 03-365 4476; info@yha .org.nz) PO Box 436, Union House, 193 Cashel St, 3rd Floor, Christchurch

Northern Ireland
  Youth Hostel Association of Northern Ireland (☎ 01232-315 435; fax 01232-439 699) 22-32 Donegall Rd, Belfast BT12 5JN
Scotland
  Scottish Youth Hostels Association (☎ 01786-891 400; fax 891 333; admin@syha.org.uk) 7 Glebe Crescent, Stirling FK8 2JA
South Africa
  Hostelling International South Africa (☎ 021-424 2511; fax 021-424 4119; info@hisa.org.za) PO Box 4402, St George's House, 73 St George's Mall, Cape Town 8001
USA
  Hostelling International/American Youth Hostels (☎ 202-783 6161; fax 202-783 6171; hiayhserv@hiayh.org) 733 15th St NW, Suite 840, Washington DC 20005

At a hostel, you get a bed for the night, plus use of communal facilities, which often include a kitchen where you can prepare your own meals. You are usually required to have a sleeping sheet – simply using your sleeping bag is not permitted. If you don't have your own approved sleeping sheet, you can usually hire or buy one. Hostels vary widely in character, but the growing number of travellers and the increased competition from other forms of accommodation, particularly private 'backpacker hostels', have prompted many hostels to improve their facilities and cut back on rules and regulations. Increasingly, hostels are open all day, curfews are disappearing and the 'warden' with a sergeant-major mentality is an endangered species. In some places you'll even find hostels with single and double rooms. Everywhere the trend has been towards smaller dormitories with just four to six beds.

There are many hostel guides with listings available, including the *HI Europe* (£7). Many hostels accept reservations by phone or fax, but usually not during peak periods, and they'll often book the next hostel you're heading to for a small fee. You can also book hostels through national hostel offices. Popular hostels can be heavily booked in summer and limits may even be placed on how many nights you can stay.

University Accommodation

Some university towns rent out student accommodation during holiday periods. This is very popular in France (see the France chapter for details). Accommodation will sometimes be in single rooms (more commonly in doubles or triples) and may have cooking facilities. Enquire at the college or university, at student information services or at local tourist offices.

Guesthouses & Hotels

There's a huge range of accommodation above the hostel level. In some countries private accommodation may go under the name of pension, guesthouse, *chambre d'hôte*, *domatia* and so on. Although the majority of guesthouses are simple affairs, there are more expensive ones where you will find attached bathrooms and other luxuries.

Above this level are hotels which, at the bottom of the bracket, may be no more expensive than guesthouses, but at the other extreme extend to luxury five-star properties with price tags to match. Although categorisation depends on the country, the hotels recommended in this book will generally range from no stars to one or two stars. You'll often find inexpensive hotels clustered around the bus and train station areas – always good places to start hunting.

Check your hotel room and the bathroom before you agree to take it, and make sure you know what it's going to cost – discounts are often available for groups or for longer stays. Ask about breakfast: sometimes it's included but at other times it may be obligatory and you'll have to pay extra for it. If the sheets don't look clean, ask to have them changed right away. Check where the fire exits are.

If you think a hotel room is too expensive, ask if there's anything cheaper. (Often, hotel owners may have tried to steer you into more expensive rooms.) In southern Europe in particular, hotel owners may be open to a little bargaining if times are slack. In France it is now common practice for business hotels (usually rated higher than two stars) to slash their rates by up to 40% on Friday and Satur-

day nights when business is slow. Save your big hotel splurge for the weekend here.

FOOD

Few regions in the world offer such a variety of cuisines in such a small area as Mediterranean Europe. Dishes are completely different from one country (and even region) to the next, and sampling the local food can be one of the most enjoyable aspects of travel. The Facts for the Visitor sections in the individual country chapters contain details of local cuisines, and the Places to Eat sections list many suggestions.

Restaurant prices vary enormously. The cheapest places for a decent meal are often the self-service restaurants in department stores. University restaurants are dirt cheap, but the food tends to be bland and you may not be allowed in if you're not a local student. Kiosks often sell cheap snacks that can be as much a part of the national cuisine as the fancy dishes.

Self-catering – buying your ingredients at a shop or market and preparing them yourself – can be a cheap and wholesome way of eating. Even if you don't cook, a lunch on a park bench with a half a loaf of fresh bread, some local cheese and salami and a tomato or two, washed down with a bottle of local wine, can be among the highlights of your trip. It also makes a nice change from restaurant food.

If you have dietary restrictions – you're a vegetarian or you keep kosher, for example – tourist organisations may be able to advise you or provide lists of suitable restaurants. We list some vegetarian and kosher restaurants in this book.

In general, vegetarians needn't worry about going hungry in Mediterranean Europe; many restaurants have one or two vegetarian dishes, and southern European menus in particular tend to contain many vegetable dishes and salads. Some restaurants will prepare special dishes on request, but you should approach them about this in advance.

Getting There & Away

Step one of your trip is actually getting to Mediterranean Europe and, in these days of severe competition among airlines, there are plenty of opportunities to find cheap tickets to a variety of gateway cities.

Forget shipping, unless by that you mean the many ferry services between southern Europe and North Africa. Only a handful of ships still carry passengers across the Atlantic; they don't sail often and are very expensive, even compared with full-fare air tickets. The days of ocean liners as modes of transport are well and truly over, but if you're still keen, see the Sea section at the end of this chapter for more details.

Some travellers still arrive or leave overland – the options being Africa, the Middle East, Asia, and what used to be the Soviet Union. The Trans-Siberian and Trans-Mongolian express trains could well begin to carry more people to and from Europe as Russia and the Central Asia republics open up to tourism. See the Land section later in this chapter for more information.

For information on online transport and booking services see the Internet Resources section in the Facts for the Visitor chapter.

AIR

Always remember to reconfirm your onward or return bookings by the specified time – at least 72 hours before departure on international flights. Otherwise there's a real risk that you'll turn up at the airport only to find that you've missed your flight because it was rescheduled, or that you've been reclassified as a 'no show' and 'bumped' (see the Air Travel Glossary in this chapter).

Buying Tickets

Your plane ticket will probably be the single most expensive item in your travel budget, and it's worth taking some time to research the current state of the market. Start early: some of the cheapest tickets have to be bought well in advance, and some popular flights sell out early. Have a talk to recent

travellers, look at the ads in newspapers and magazines and watch for special offers.

Cheap tickets are available in two distinct categories: official and unofficial. Official ones have a variety of names including advance purchase tickets, advance purchase excursion (Apex) fares, super-Apex and simply budget fares.

Unofficial tickets are simply discounted tickets that the airlines release through selected travel agents (usually not sold by the airline offices themselves). Airlines can, however, supply information on routes and timetables and make bookings; their low season, student and seniors' fares can be quite attractive. Also, normal, full-fare airline tickets sometimes include one or more side trips in Europe free of charge, which can make them good value.

Return (round-trip) tickets usually work out cheaper than two one-way fares – often *much* cheaper. Be aware that immigration officials often ask for return or onward tickets, and that if you can't show either, you'll have to provide proof of 'sufficient means of support', which means you have to show a lot of money or, in some cases, valid credit cards.

Round the world (RTW) tickets can also work out to be no more expensive or even cheaper than an ordinary return ticket. The official airline RTW tickets are usually put together by a combination of two or more airlines, and permit you to fly anywhere you want on their route systems so long as you don't backtrack. Other restrictions are that you (usually) must book the first sector in advance and cancellation penalties apply. There may be restrictions on how many stops (or kilometres/miles) you are permitted, and usually the tickets are valid for from 90 days up to a year. Prices start at about UK£800, A$1700 or US$1300, depending on the season and length of validity. An alternative type of RTW ticket is one put together by a travel agent using a combination of discounted tickets. These can be much cheaper than the official ones, but usually carry a lot of restrictions.

Air Travel Glossary

Baggage Allowance This will be written on your ticket and usually includes one 20kg item to go in the hold, plus one item of hand luggage.

Bucket Shops These are unbonded travel agencies specialising in discounted airline tickets.

Bumped Just because you have a confirmed seat doesn't mean you're going to get on the plane (see Overbooking).

Cancellation Penalties If you have to cancel or change a discounted ticket, there are often heavy penalties involved; insurance can sometimes be taken out against these penalties. Some airlines impose penalties on regular tickets as well, particularly against 'no-show' passengers.

Check-In Airlines ask you to check in a certain time ahead of the flight departure (usually one to two hours on international flights). If you fail to check in on time and the flight is overbooked, the airline can cancel your booking and give your seat to somebody else.

Confirmation Having a ticket written out with the flight and date you want doesn't mean you have a seat until the agent has checked with the airline that your status is 'OK' or confirmed. Meanwhile you could just be 'on request'.

Courier Fares Businesses often need to send urgent documents or freight securely and quickly. Courier companies hire people to accompany the package through customs and, in return, offer a discount ticket which is sometimes a phenomenal bargain. In effect, what the companies do is ship their freight as your luggage on regular commercial flights. This is a legitimate operation, but there are two shortcomings – the short turnaround time of the ticket (usually not longer than a month) and the limitation on your luggage allowance. You may have to surrender all your allowance and take only carry-on luggage.

Full Fares Airlines traditionally offer 1st class (coded F), business class (coded J) and economy class (coded Y) tickets. These days there are so many promotional and discounted fares available that few passengers pay full economy fare.

ITX An ITX, or 'independent inclusive tour excursion', is often available on tickets to popular holiday destinations. Officially it's a package deal combined with hotel accommodation, but many agents will sell you one of these for the flight only and give you phoney hotel vouchers in the unlikely event that you're challenged at the airport.

Lost Tickets If you lose your airline ticket an airline will usually treat it like a travellers cheque and, after inquiries, issue you with another one. Legally, however, an airline is entitled to treat it like cash and if you lose it then it's gone forever. Take good care of your tickets.

MCO An MCO, or 'miscellaneous charge order', is a voucher that looks like an airline ticket but carries no destination or date. It can be exchanged through any International Association of Travel Agents (IATA) airline for a ticket on a specific flight. It's a useful alternative to an onward ticket in those countries that demand one, and is more flexible than an ordinary ticket if you're unsure of your route.

No-Shows No-shows are passengers who fail to show up for their flight. Full-fare passengers who fail to turn up are sometimes entitled to travel on a later flight. The rest are penalised (see Cancellation Penalties).

On Request This is an unconfirmed booking for a flight.

Air Travel Glossary

Onward Tickets An entry requirement for many countries is that you have a ticket out of the country. If you're unsure of your next move, the easiest solution is to buy the cheapest onward ticket to a neighbouring country or a ticket from a reliable airline which can later be refunded if you do not use it.

Open Jaw Tickets These are return tickets where you fly out to one place but return from another. If available, this can save you backtracking to your arrival point.

Overbooking Airlines hate to fly empty seats and since every flight has some passengers who fail to show up, airlines often book more passengers than they have seats. Usually excess passengers make up for the no-shows, but occasionally somebody gets bumped. Guess who it is most likely to be? The passengers who check in late.

Point-to-Point Tickets These are discount tickets that can be bought on some routes in return for passengers waiving their rights to a stopover.

Promotional Fares These are officially discounted fares, available from travel agencies or direct from the airline.

Reconfirmation At least 72 hours prior to departure time of an onward or return flight, you must contact the airline and 'reconfirm' that you intend to be on the flight. If you don't do this the airline can delete your name from the passenger list and you could lose your seat.

Restrictions Discounted tickets often have various restrictions on them – such as needing to be paid for in advance and incurring a penalty to be altered. Others are restrictions on the minimum and maximum period you must be away, such as a minimum of 14 days or a maximum of one year.

Round-the-World Tickets RTW tickets give you a limited period (usually a year) in which to circumnavigate the globe. You can go anywhere the carrying airlines go, as long as you don't backtrack. The number of stopovers or total number of separate flights is decided before you set off and they usually cost a bit more than a basic return flight.

Stand-by This is a discounted ticket where you only fly if there is a seat free at the last moment. Stand-by fares are usually available only on domestic routes.

Travel Agencies Travel agencies vary widely and you should choose one that suits your needs. Some simply handle tours, while full-services agencies handle everything from tours and tickets to car rental and hotel bookings. If all you want is a ticket at the lowest possible price, then go to an agency specialising in discounted tickets.

Transferred Tickets Airline tickets cannot be transferred from one person to another. Travellers sometimes try to sell the return half of their ticket, but officials can ask you to prove that you are the person named on the ticket. This is less likely to happen on domestic flights, but on an international flight tickets are compared with passports.

Travel Periods Ticket prices vary with the time of year. There is a low (off-peak) season and a high (peak) season, and often a low-shoulder season and a high-shoulder season as well. Usually the fare depends on your outward flight – if you depart in the high season and return in the low season, you pay the high-season fare.

Generally, you can find discounted tickets at prices as low as, or lower than, advance purchase or budget tickets. Phone around the travel agencies for bargains. You may discover that those impossibly cheap flights are 'fully booked, but we have another one that costs a bit more ...' Or that the flight is on an airline notorious for its poor safety record and will leave you for 14 hours in the world's least-favourite airport, where you'll be confined to the transit lounge unless you get an expensive visa ... Or the agent may claim that the last two cheap seats until next autumn will be gone in two hours. Don't panic – keep ringing around.

If you are travelling from the USA or South-East Asia, you will sometimes find that the cheapest flights are being advertised by obscure agencies whose names have yet to reach the telephone directory. Many such firms are honest and solvent, but there are a few rogues who will take your money and run, only to reopen elsewhere a month or two later under a new name.

If you feel suspicious about a firm, don't give them all the money at once – leave a deposit of 20% or so and pay the balance when you get the ticket. If they insist on cash in advance, go somewhere else or be prepared to take a very big risk. And once you have the ticket, ring the airline to confirm that you are booked on the flight.

You may decide to pay more than the rock-bottom fare by opting for the safety of better known travel agents. Firms such as STA Travel (www.sta-travel.com or www.statravel.co.uk), which has offices worldwide, Council Travel (www.counciltravel.com) in the USA and elsewhere or Travel CUTS (www.travelcuts.com) in Canada offer good prices to most destinations, and won't disappear overnight leaving you clutching a receipt for a nonexistent ticket.

Use the fares quoted in this book as a guide only. They are approximate and based on the rates advertised by travel agents at the time of research. Most are likely to have changed by the time you read this.

Travellers with Special Needs

If you have special needs of any sort – you're vegetarian or require a special diet, you're travelling in a wheelchair, taking a baby, terrified of flying etc – let the airline people know as soon as possible so that they can make the necessary arrangements. Remind them when you reconfirm your booking (at least 72 hours before departure) and again when you check in at the airport. It may also be worth ringing around the airlines before you make your booking to find out how they can handle your particular needs.

In general, children under the age of two travel for 10% of the standard fare (or, on some carriers, for free) as long as they don't occupy a seat. They don't get a luggage allowance either. Skycots, baby food, formula, nappies (diapers) etc should be provided by the airline if requested in advance. Children aged between two and 12 can usually occupy a seat for half to two-thirds of the full fare and do get a standard baggage allowance.

The USA

The flight options across the North Atlantic, the world's busiest long-haul air corridor, are bewildering. The *Chicago Tribune*, *LA Times*, *New York Times* and *San Francisco Chronicle* all have weekly travel sections in which you'll find any number of travel agents' ads. Council Travel and STA have offices in major cities nation-wide. You should be able to fly from New York to London and back for US$400 to US$500 in the low season and US$550 to US$700 in the high season. Equivalent fares from the West Coast are US$100 to US$300 higher.

On a stand-by basis, one-way fares can work out to be remarkably cheap. New York-based Airhitch (☎ 212-864 2000; www.airhitch.org) specialises in this sort of thing and can get you to/from Europe for US$175/225/255 each way from the East Coast/Midwest/West Coast.

An interesting alternative to the boring New York-London flight is offered by Icelandair (☎ 800-223 5500), which has competitive year-round fares to many European destinations with a three-night stopover in Iceland's capital, Reykjavík – a great way to spend a few days in an unusual country that's otherwise hard to get to.

Another option is a courier flight. A New York-London return ticket can be had for as little as US$300 in the low season. You may also be able to fly one way. The drawbacks are that your stay in Europe may be limited to one or two weeks; your luggage is usually restricted to hand luggage (the courier company uses your checked luggage allowance to send its parcels); there is unlikely to be more than one courier ticket available for any given flight; and you may have to be a local resident and apply for an interview before they'll take you on.

You can find out more about courier flights from the International Association of Air Travel Couriers (☎ 561-582 8320; fax 561-582 1581; www.courier.org; iaatc@courier.org), As You Like It Travel (☎ 212-679 6949; fax 212-779 9674; www.asulikeit. com) or Now Voyager Travel (☎ 212-431 1616; fax 212-334 5243; www.nowvoyagertravel.com).

Canada

Travel CUTS (☎ 1-888 838 CUTS) has offices in all major cities. You might also scan the budget travel agents' ads in the *Globe & Mail, Montreal Gazette,* the *Toronto Star* and the *Vancouver Sun.*

See the previous section for general information on courier flights. Airhitch (see the USA section) has stand-by fares to/from Toronto, Montreal and Vancouver.

Australia

STA and Flight Centres International are major dealers in cheap air fares. Saturday's travel sections in the *Sydney Morning Herald* and Melbourne's *The Age* have many ads offering cheap fares to Europe, but don't be surprised if they happen to be 'sold out' when you call: they're usually low-season fares on obscure airlines with conditions attached. With Australia's large and well organised ethnic populations, it pays to check special deals in the ethnic press.

Airlines like Malaysian have fares to London and Paris from about A$1500 (low season) to A$1800 (high season). Airlines like Thai, Qantas and Singapore have fares to London and Paris starting from about A$1500 (low season) up to A$2500. All have frequent promotional fares so it pays to check daily newspapers. Flights to/from Perth are a couple of hundred dollars cheaper. Another option for travellers wanting to go to Britain between November and February is to hook up with a charter flight returning to Britain. These low-

season, one-way fares do have restrictions, but may work out to be considerably cheaper. Ask your travel agent for details.

New Zealand

As in Australia, STA and Flight Centres International are popular travel agents in New Zealand. The cheapest fares to Europe are routed through Asia. An RTW ticket could be cheaper than a return ticket. An RTW with Air New Zealand and Lufthansa in the low season is about NZ$2300.

From Auckland to Rome or Paris via Asia the low season fare is NZ$1185 one way and NZ$2049 return. From Auckland to Paris or Milan via the USA the low season fares are NZ$1265 one way and NZ$2299 return.

Africa

Nairobi is probably the best place in Africa to buy tickets to Europe, thanks to the many bucket shops and the lively competition between them. Several West African countries offer cheap charter flights to France and London. Charter fares from Morocco and Tunisia can be quite cheap if you're lucky enough to find a seat.

From South Africa, Air Namibia has particularly cheap return youth fares to London from as low as R3840. The big carriers' return fares average about R6820. Student Travel Centre (☎ 011-447 5551) in Johannesburg, and the Africa Travel Centre (☎ 021-235 555) in Cape Town are worth trying for cheap tickets.

Asia

Singapore and Bangkok are the discount airfare capitals of Asia. Shop around for fares and ask the advice of other travellers. STA has branches in Hong Kong (Sincerity Travel), Tokyo, Singapore, Bangkok, Jakarta and Kuala Lumpur.

Mumbai and Delhi are the air transport hubs in India. In Delhi check out the bucket shops around Connaught Place, but check with other travellers about their current trustworthiness.

The UK

If you're looking for a cheap way into or out of central Europe, London is the Continent's major centre for discounted fares. In the low season you should be able to fly to any of the major cities of Mediterranean Europe (Paris, Rome, Madrid etc) for between UK£100 (sometimes even less) and UK£150.

For longer journeys, you can sometimes find air fares that beat overland travel alternatives in terms of cost, depending on the season. Return air fares from London to Paris, for example, start at about UK£80 (higher in summer and other peak periods), whereas a two-month return by rail and ferry from London is UK£159. From Athens, you can get good deals to elsewhere in Mediterranean Europe; typical one-way fares are UK£87 to Rome, UK£94 to Milan and UK£116 to Madrid. Depending on the season, there are cheap charter flights from London, Paris and Madrid to Morocco and Tunisia.

The following are addresses of some of the best agencies to contact for discounted tickets in London:

Campus Travel
   (☎ 0171-730 7285; tube: Victoria) 52 Grosvenor Gardens, London SW1W OAG
Council Travel
   (☎ 0171-287 3337; www.counciltravel.com; tube: Oxford Circus) 28A Poland St, London W1V 3DB
STA Travel
   (☎ 0171-361 6262; www.sta-travel.com or www.statravel.co.uk; tube: High Street Kensington) Priory House, 6 Wrights Lane W8 6TA
Trailfinders
   (☎ 0171-937 5400 for trans-Atlantic flights, ☎ 0171-938 3939 for long-haul ones; tube: High Street Kensington) 194 Kensington High St, London W8 7RG

The entertainment listings weekly *Time Out*, the weekend newspapers and the *Evening Standard* carry ads for cheap fares. Also look out for the free magazines and newspapers widely available in London, especially *TNT* and *Southern Cross*. You can often pick them up outside main train and tube stations.

Make sure the agent is a member of some sort of traveller-protection scheme, such as that offered by the Association of British Travel Agents (ABTA). If you have paid for your flight to an ABTA-registered agent who then goes out of business, ABTA will guarantee a refund or an alternative. Unregistered bucket shops are riskier but usually cheaper.

Continental Europe

Though London is the travel discount capital of Europe, there are several other cities in the region where you'll find a wide range of good deals, particularly Amsterdam, Athens and even Paris. See the country chapters for details.

Many travel agents in Europe have ties with STA Travel, where cheap tickets can be purchased and STA tickets can often be altered free of charge the first time around. Outlets in important transport hubs include: NBBS Reizen (☎ 020-624 0989), Rokin 38, Amsterdam; Voyages Wasteels (☎ 01 43 43 46 10), 2 Rue Michel Chasles, 75012 Paris; SRID Reisen (☎ 069-703 035), Bockenheimer Landstrasse 133, 60325 Frankfurt; and International Student & Youth Travel Service (ISYTS), ☎ 01-322 1267), Nikis 11, 2nd floor, 10557 Athens.

LAND

Bus

Eurolines, Europe's largest network of buses, has seven circular explorer routes, always starting and ending in London. For details, see Bus in the Getting Around chapter. On ordinary return trips with Eurolines, youth (under 26) fares are about 10% less than the adult full fare, eg a London-Madrid return ticket costs UK£148 for adults or UK£134 for those under 26. The adult/youth fares to Rome from London are UK£135/£122. All tickets are valid for six months.

Train

UK There are two distinctly different services under the Channel via the Channel Tunnel: the Eurostar passenger service and Le Shuttle, the vehicle-carrying service. Eurostar operates between London and Paris; the two other Eurostar stops in France, Calais-Fréthun and Lille, are via Ashford. In winter Eurostar Ski Trains link London with the Alps.

Le Shuttle goes only between Folkestone and just beyond Calais carrying cars, motorcycles and bicycles with their passengers or riders. Train-boat-train connections are possible but scarcely worth considering.

Eurostar The highly civilised Eurostar passenger train service through the Channel Tunnel takes three hours (not including the one-hour time change) to get from London's Waterloo station to the Gare du Nord in Paris. Passport and customs checks take place on board or very cursorily on arrival.

The regular 2nd-class fare is £120/220 one way/return or £179/305 if you want to travel 1st class. A 2nd-class Leisure Return ticket costs £119 return (£199 in 1st) and requires that you stay away either three nights or a Saturday night. Changes to date and time of travel can be made before each departure, and full refunds are available before the outward trip. A 2nd-class Excursion return ticket must include a Saturday overnight; it costs £99 and although changes to date and time of travel can be made before the departure of each train, it is nonrefundable. The 2nd-class Mid Week Travel ticket is the cheapest (£79) but carries a lot of restrictions: it must be purchased seven days in advance; it is valid for travel on Tuesday, Wednesday and Thursday only in each direction; your visit must include a Saturday night away; the ticket cannot be changed and is nonrefundable.

The Youth Return ticket (£85) available to those under 26 can be booked at any time. Changes can be made but, if you cancel your trip, a 50% refund is available only before departure of the outward trip. The same rules apply to Senior Return tickets (£99), available to those over 60.

Children's one-way/return fares, available for those aged four to 11 years, are £69/119 in 1st class and £37/65 in 2nd. There are often special deals on offer (eg day returns, weekend trips etc), so it pays to phone Eurostar or its agents for the latest information.

Eurostar tickets are available from some travel agents, at Waterloo station, from Victoria station's Eurostar ticket office, from international ticket offices at many of the UK's mainline train stations, from SNCF's French Railways House (☎ 0171-803 3030 or 0990-300 003; tube Piccadilly Circus) at 179 Piccadilly, London W1V 0BA; they also sell all other SNCF tickets. To book by phone you can ring Eurostar on ☎ 0990-186 186. The number to ring in Paris is ☎ 08 36 35 35 39.

Tickets, for which you pay by credit card, can be either sent to you by post or picked up at Waterloo station.

You can have a bicycle sent on Eurostar as registered luggage (UK£20).

Le Shuttle Le Shuttle, the train service through the Channel Tunnel between Folkestone and Coquelles (5km south-west of Calais), takes cars, motorcycles and, on some services, bicycles with their passengers or riders. Fares on Le Shuttle vary with the time of year, the day of the week, the time of the day and a variety of other competitive pressures. The normal one-way/return fare for a car with driver and all passengers is £95/120, but there are promotional fares as low as £12 (late departure and late return on the same day) and prices increase substantially in peak periods. A motorcycle and rider costs £45 for a same day return or £85 return for longer stays.

Bicycles can be taken on Le Shuttle but only on two trips per day and they must be booked 24 hours in advance on ☎ 01303-270 111. The cost is £15 for bicycle and rider.

For information and reservations, contact a travel agent or call Le Shuttle in the UK (☎ 0990-353 535) or in France (☎ 08 00 12 71 27; Minitel 3615 LE SHUTTLE).

Le Shuttle runs 24 hours a day, every day of the year, with up to four departures an hour during peak periods. During the 35-minute crossing, passengers can sit in their cars or walk around the air-conditioned, sound-proofed rail carriage. The entire process, including loading and unloading, should take about an hour.

Train-Boat-Train There are train-boat-train combos in association with Hoverspeed (☎ 0990-240 241 or ☎ 01304-240 241 in Dover; ☎ 03 21 46 14 14 in Calais; www. hoverspeed.co.uk) and others from London's Charing Cross station to Paris' Gare du Nord that take between seven and eight hours and cost £44 one way for adults, £33 for children aged 12 to 15 and £22 for kids four to 11. The round-trip fares are £59/48/32. It's obviously cheaper than Eurostar but takes a lot longer, and you've got to mess around transferring by bus between the train station and the ferry terminal on both sides.

Africa & Asia Morocco and most of Turkey lie outside Europe, but the rail systems of both countries are still covered by Inter-Rail (see the Getting Around chapter). The price of a cheap return train ticket from London to Morocco compares favourably with equivalent bus fares.

It *is* possible to get to central Europe by rail from central and eastern Asia, though count on spending at least eight days doing it. You can choose from four different routes to Moscow: the Trans-Siberian (9297km from Vladivostok), the Trans-Mongolian (7860km from Beijing) and the Trans-Manchurian (9001km from Beijing), which all use the same tracks across Siberia but have different routes east of Lake Baikal; and the Trans-Kazakhstan, which runs between Moscow and Urumqi in north-western China. Prices vary enormously, depending on where you buy the ticket and what is included – advertised 2nd-class fares include US$490 from Vladivostok and US$282 from Beijing. Details are available from the Russian National Tourist Office (www.interknowledge. com/russia/trasib.01.htm) and Finnsov (www .finnsov.fi/fs–trsib.html).

There are countless travel options between Moscow and the rest of Europe. Most people will opt for the train, usually to/from Berlin, Helsinki, Munich, Budapest or Vienna. The *Trans-Siberian Handbook* (Trailblazer) by Bryn Thomas is a comprehensive guide to the route as is *The Trans-Siberian Rail Guide* (Compass Star) by Robert Strauss & Tamsin Turnbull. Lonely Planet's *Russia, Ukraine & Belarus* has a separate chapter on trans-Siberian travel.

Overland Trails

Asia In the early 1980s, the overland trail to/from Asia lost much of its popularity as the Islamic regime in Iran made life difficult for most independent travellers, and the war in Afghanistan closed that country off to all but the foolhardy. Now that Iran seems to be rediscovering the merits of tourism, the Asia route has begun to pick up again, though unsettled conditions in Afghanistan, southern Pakistan and north-west India could prevent the trickle of travellers turning into a flood for the time being.

A new overland route through what used to be the Soviet Union could become important over the next decade. At this stage the options are more or less confined to the four lines to/from Moscow listed in the previous Train section, but other modes of transport are likely to become available beyond the Urals as the newly independent states open up to travellers.

Africa Discounting the complicated Middle East route, going to/from Africa involves a Mediterranean ferry crossing (see the following Sea section). Due to unrest in Africa, the most feasible overland routes through the continent have all but closed down.

Travelling by private transport beyond Europe requires plenty of paperwork and other preparations. A detailed description is beyond the scope of this book, but the following Getting Around chapter tells you what's required within Europe.

SEA
Channel Ferries

Several different ferry companies compete on all the main Channel ferry routes. The resulting service is comprehensive but very complicated. The same ferry company can have a host of different prices for the same route, depending upon the time of day or year, the validity of the ticket, or the length of your vehicle. Vehicle tickets include the driver and often up to five passengers free of charge. It is worth planning (and booking) ahead where possible as there may be special reductions on off-peak crossings and advance purchase tickets. On Channel routes, apart from one-day or short-term excursion returns, there is little price advantage in buying a return ticket as against two singles.

The shortest cross-Channel routes between England and France (Dover to Calais or Folkestone to Boulogne) are also the busiest, though there is now great competition from the Channel Tunnel. P&O Stena handle the short-hop Newhaven-Dieppe and Dover-Calais routes. P&O European and Brittany Ferries sail direct between England and northern Spain, taking 24 to 35 hours.

Rail-pass holders are entitled to discounts or free travel on some lines (see the earlier

Train section), and most ferry companies give discounts to disabled drivers. Food on ferries is often expensive (and lousy), so it is worth bringing your own when possible. It is also worth knowing that if you take your vehicle on board, you are usually denied access to it during the voyage.

Mediterranean Ferries

There are many ferries across the Mediterranean between Africa and Europe. The ferry you take will depend on your travels in Africa, but options include: Spain-Morocco, Italy-Tunisia and France-Morocco and France-Tunisia. There are also ferries between Greece and Israel via Cyprus. Ferries are often filled to capacity in summer, especially to/from Tunisia, so book well in advance if you're taking a vehicle across. See the relevant country chapters.

Passenger Ships & Freighters

Regular, long-distance passenger ships disappeared with the advent of cheap air travel and were replaced by a small number of luxury cruise ships. Cunard's *Queen Elizabeth 2* sails between New York and Southampton 20 times a year; the trip takes six nights each way and costs around UK£1400 for the return trip, though there are also one-way and 'fly one-way' deals. The bible for passenger ships and sea travel is the *OAG Cruise & Ferry Guide* published by the UK-based Reed Travel Group (☎ 01582-600 111), Church St, Dunstable, Bedfordshire LU5 4HB.

A more adventurous alternative is as a paying passenger on a freighter. Freighters are far more numerous than cruise ships and there are many more routes from which to choose. With a bit of homework, you'll be able to sail between Europe and just about anywhere else in the world, with stopovers at exotic ports that you may never have heard of. The previously mentioned *OAG Cruise & Ferry Guide* is the most comprehensive

source of information though *Travel by Cargo Ship* (Cadogan) is also a good source.

Passenger freighters typically carry six to 12 passengers (more than 12 requires a doctor on board) and, though less luxurious than dedicated cruise ships, give you a real taste of life at sea. Schedules tend to be flexible and costs vary, but seem to hover around US$100 a day; vehicles can often be included for an additional fee.

LEAVING MEDITERRANEAN EUROPE

Some countries charge you a fee for the privilege of leaving from their airports. Some also charge port fees when departing by ship. Such fees are *usually* included in the price of your ticket, but it pays to check this when purchasing it. If not, you'll have to have the fee ready when leaving. Details of departure taxes are given at the end of the Getting There & Away sections of individual country chapters.

WARNING

This chapter is particularly vulnerable to change – prices for international travel are volatile, routes are introduced and cancelled, schedules change, special deals come and go, and rules and visa requirements are amended. Airlines seem to take a perverse pleasure in making price structures and regulations as complicated as possible; you should check directly with the airline or travel agent to make sure you understand how a fare (and ticket you may buy) works.

In addition, the travel industry is highly competitive and there are many schemes and bonuses. The upshot of this is that you should get opinions, quotes and advice from as many airlines and travel agents as possible before you part with your hard-earned cash. The details given in this chapter should be regarded as pointers and are not a substitute for careful, up-to-date research.

Getting Around

Travel within most of the EU, whether by air, rail or car, has been made easier following the Schengen Agreement, which abolished border controls between signed-up states. Countries within this agreement are Austria, Belgium, France, Germany, Italy, Luxembourg, the Netherlands, Portugal, Spain and Greece (though the latter has signed but not yet ratified the agreement).

AIR

Air travel is best viewed as a means to get you to the starting point of your itinerary rather than as your main means of travel, since it lacks the flexibility of ground transport. Also, if you start taking flights for relatively short hops it gets extremely expensive, particularly as special deals are not as common on domestic flights as they are on international ones.

But for longer journeys, you can sometimes find air fares that beat overland alternatives in terms of cost, depending on the season. Return air fares from London to Paris, for example, start from about UK£80 (higher in summer and other peak periods), whereas a two-month return by rail and ferry from London is UK£159. From Athens, you can get good deals to elsewhere in Mediterranean Europe; typical one-way fares are UK£87 to Rome, UK£94 to Milan and UK£116 to Madrid. Depending on the season, there are cheap charter flights from London, Paris and Madrid to Morocco and Tunisia.

Since 1997 air travel within the EU has been deregulated. An 'open skies' policy allows greater flexibility in routing, and potentially greater competition and lower prices. Air travel is still dominated by the large state-run and private carriers, but these have been joined by a new breed of no-frills small airlines, such as the UK-based Go (a subsidiary of British Airways) and EasyJet, which sell budget tickets directly to the customer.

Refer to the Air Travel Glossary in the earlier Getting There & Away chapter for information on types of air tickets. London, Amsterdam and Athens are good centres for picking up cheap, restricted-validity tickets through bucket shops. The individual country chapters list places where you can buy cheap tickets.

So-called open-jaw returns, by which you can travel into one city and exit from another, are worth considering, though they sometimes work out more expensive than simple returns. In the UK, Trailfinders (☎ 0171-937 5400) and STA Travel (☎ 0171-361 6161) can give you tailor-made versions of these tickets. Your chosen cities don't necessarily have to be in the same country. Lufthansa has Young Europe Special (YES) flights, which allow travel around Europe by air for UK£39, UK£59 or UK£79 per flight (minimum four flights, maximum 10). Britain is the starting point, and the offer is open to students under 31 years of age and anybody under 26. Alitalia's Europa Pass is a similar deal.

If you are travelling alone, courier flights are a possibility. You get cheap passage in return for accompanying a package or documents through customs and delivering it to a representative at the destination airport. EU integration and electronic communications mean there's increasingly less call for couriers, but you might find something. British Airways, for example, offers courier flights through the Travel Shop (☎ 0181-564 7009). Sample return fares from London are UK£80 to Barcelona or Lisbon.

Getting between airports and city centres is no problem in Europe thanks to good public-transport networks.

BUS
International Buses

International bus travel tends to take second place to train travel. The bus has the edge in terms of cost, sometimes quite substantially, but is generally slower and less comfortable. Europe's biggest network of international buses is provided by a group of companies operating under the name Eurolines.

Eurolines representatives include:

Deutsche Touring (☎ 069-790 32 40), Am Romerhof 17, Frankfurt

Eurolines Austria (☎ 01-712 0453), Autobusbahn-
hof Wien-Mitte, Landstrasser Hauptstrasse 1/b,
1030 Vienna

Eurolines France (☎ 01-49 72 51 51), Gare
Routière Internationale, 28 Ave du Général de
Gaulle, 75020 Paris

Eurolines Italy (☎ 06-440 4009), Ciconvallazione
Nonentana 574, Lato Stazione Tiburtina, Rome

Eurolines Nederland (☎ 020-560 87 87), Rokin 10,
1012 KR Amsterdam

Eurolines Peninsular (☎ 93-490 4000), Estació
d'Autobuses de Sants, Calle Viriato, Barcelona

Eurolines UK (☎ 0990-143 219), 52 Grosvenor
Gardens, London SW1W 0AU

These companies may also be able to advise
you on other bus companies and deals.

Eurolines has seven circular explorer
routes, always starting and ending in London.
The popular London-Amsterdam-Paris route
costs UK£69 (no youth reductions). Eurolines also offers passes, but they're neither as
extensive nor as flexible as rail passes. They
cover 30 European cities as far apart as
London, Barcelona, Rome, Budapest and
Copenhagen, and cost UK£229 for 30 days
(UK£199 for youths and senior citizens) or
UK£279 for 60 days (UK£249). The passes
are cheaper off peak (1st October to 14 June).

On ordinary return trips, a youth (under
26) fare is about 10% less than an adult full
fare, eg a London-Madrid return ticket costs
UK£148 for adults or UK£134 for those
under 26. The adult/youth fares to Rome
from London are UK£135/122. Explorer or
return tickets are valid for six months.

Busabout operates buses that complete set
circuits round Europe, stopping at major
cities. The Eurobus company, which used to
offer a similar service, went out of business
in 1998. There are three interlocking circuits.
The North Zone, or Zone 1, runs from Paris
through Brussels and Amsterdam to Copenhagen, Berlin and Prague. It continues to
Munich, where it links up with the South
Zone, or Zone 2, (to Italy and southern
France) and, in winter, the Snow Zone around
the Alps. Zone 3 links Paris, Berne,
Barcelona and Madrid. There are also connections to London and Athens.

Pick up points are usually convenient for
hostels, budget hotels and camping grounds
and departures are every second day. You get
unlimited travel per sector and can 'hop-on,
hop-off' at any scheduled stop, then resume
with a later bus. Each circuit costs UK£109
(UK£99 for youth and student card-holders)
for two weeks, with the add-on from London
to Paris an extra UK£30 return. The Bed-
about scheme gives you 10 nights
accommodation in tents for UK£70.

Tickets are available in many countries
worldwide. In Britain you can buy them
direct from the company (☎ 0181-936 784
2815; www.busabout.com) or from suppliers
such as Usit Campus and STA Travel.

The Moroccan national bus line, CTM
(Compagnie des Transports Marocains), operates buses from France, Belgium and
northern Italy to most of the large Moroccan
towns. The once-weekly Eurolines service
between Paris and Tangier takes at least 9½
hours, including the ferry crossing.

See the individual country chapters for
more information about long-distance buses.

National Buses

Domestic buses provide a viable alternative
to the rail network in most countries. Again,
compared to trains they are usually slightly
cheaper and, with the exception of Spain,
Portugal and Greece, somewhat slower.

Buses tend to be best for shorter hops such
as getting around cities and reaching remote
villages. They are often the only option in
mountainous regions where railway tracks
don't exist. Advance reservations are rarely
necessary. On many city buses you usually
buy your ticket in advance from a kiosk or
machine and cancel it on boarding.

See the individual country chapters and
city sections for more details on local buses.

TRAIN

Trains are a popular way of getting around:
they are comfortable, frequent and generally
on time. The Channel Tunnel makes it possible to get from Britain to Continental
Europe using the Eurostar service (see the
France Getting There & Away section). In
some countries, such as Italy, Spain and Portugal, fares are subsidised; in others,

European rail passes make travel more affordable. Supplements and reservation costs are not covered by passes, and pass-holders must always carry their passport for identification purposes.

If you plan to travel extensively by train, it might be worth getting hold of the *Thomas Cook European Timetable*, which gives a complete listing of train schedules and indicates where supplements apply or where reservations are necessary. It is updated monthly and is available from Thomas Cook outlets in the UK and Australia, and in the USA from Rail Europe Inc, c/o Forsyth Travel Inc (☎ 800-367 7984; fax 914 681 7251), 226 Westchester Ave, White Plains NY 10604. If you are planning to do a lot of train travel in one or a handful of countries – Spain and Portugal, say – it might be worthwhile getting hold of the national timetables published by the state railways. The *European Planning & Rail Guide* is an informative annual magazine; send US$1 (US$3 from outside the USA; MasterCard and Visa card accepted) to BETS (☎ 734-668 0529; fax 665 5986), 2557 Meade Court, Ann Arbor, MI 48105-1304, USA.

In Mediterranean Europe, Paris and Milan are important hubs for international rail connections; see the relevant city sections for details and budget ticket agents. Some approximate 2nd-class fares are Paris-Milan US$82 (under seven hours) and Lisbon-Madrid US$50 (10 hours).

Note that European trains sometimes split en route in order to service two destinations, so even if you know you're on the right train, make sure you're in the correct carriage as well.

Express Trains

Fast trains or those that make few stops are identified by the symbols EC (Eurocity) or IC (InterCity). The French TGV and Spanish AVE are even faster. Supplements can apply on fast trains, and it is a good idea (sometimes obligatory) to make seat reservations at peak times and on certain lines.

Overnight Trains

Overnight trains will usually offer a choice of couchette or sleeper if you don't fancy sleeping in your seat with somebody else's head on your shoulder. Again, reservations are advisable as sleeping options are allocated on a first-come, first-served basis.

Couchettes have four bunks per compartment in 1st class and six in 2nd class. They are comfortable enough, if lacking a bit in privacy. A bunk costs around US$28 for most international trains, irrespective of the length of the journey.

Sleepers are the most comfortable option, offering beds for one or two passengers in 1st class, and two or three passengers in 2nd class. Charges vary depending upon the journey, but they are significantly more expensive than couchettes. Most long-distance trains have a dining or buffet (café) car; or an attendant who wheels a snack trolley through carriages. Food prices tend to be steep.

Security

Stories occasionally surface about train passengers being gassed or drugged and then robbed, though bag-snatching is more of a worry. Sensible security measures include not letting your bags out of your sight (especially when stopping at stations), chaining them to the luggage rack, and locking compartment doors overnight.

Rail Passes

Shop around, as pass prices can vary between different outlets. Once purchased, take care of your pass, as it cannot be replaced or refunded if lost or stolen. European passes get reductions on Eurostar through the Channel Tunnel and on certain ferries.

Eurail These passes can only be bought by residents of non-European countries, and are supposed to be purchased before arriving in Europe. However, Eurail passes can be purchased within Europe, so long as your passport proves you've been there for less than six months, but the outlets where you can do this are limited, and the passes will be more expensive than getting them outside Europe. Rail Europe in London (see under Cheap Tickets later in the train section) is one such outlet. If you've lived in Europe for more than six months, you are eligible for an Inter-Rail pass, which is a better buy.

Eurail passes are valid for unlimited travel on national railways and some private lines in Austria, Belgium, Denmark, Finland, France (including Monaco), Germany, Greece, Hungary, Ireland, Italy, Luxembourg, the Netherlands, Norway, Portugal, Spain, Sweden and Switzerland (including Liechtenstein). The UK is not covered.

Eurail is also valid on some ferries between Italy and Greece and between Sweden and Finland. Reductions are given on some other ferry routes and on river/lake steamer services in various countries.

Eurail passes offer reasonable value to people aged under 26. A Youthpass gives unlimited 2nd-class travel within a choice of five validity periods: 15/22 days (US$376/489) or one/two/three months (US$605/857/1059). The Youth Flexipass, also for 2nd class, is valid for freely chosen days within a two-month period: 10 days for US$458 or 15 days for US$603. Overnight journeys commencing after 7 pm count as the following day's travel. The traveller must fill out in ink the relevant box in the calendar before starting a day's travel; not validating the pass in this way earns a fine of US$50, plus the full fare. Tampering with the pass (eg using an erasable pen and later rubbing out earlier days) costs the perpetrator the full fare plus US$100, and confiscation of the pass.

For those aged over 26, the equivalent passes provide 1st-class travel. The standard Eurail pass costs US$538/698 for 15/22 days or US$864/1224/1512 for one/two/three months. The Flexipass costs US$634/836 for 10/15 days within two months. Two people travelling together can get a 'saver' version of either pass, saving about 15%. Eurail passes for children are also available.

Europass Also for non-Europeans, the Europass gives unlimited travel on freely chosen days within a two-month period. Youth (aged under 26) and adult (solo, or two sharing) versions are available, and purchasing requirements and sales outlets are as for Eurail passes. The Europass is cheaper than the Eurail pass as it covers only France, Germany, Italy, Spain and Switzerland. The youth/adult price is US$216/326 for five travel days, plus US$29/42 for each additional travel day (maximum 10 days extra). For a small additional charge each or all of Austria, Belgium (including Luxembourg and the Netherlands), Greece (including ferries from Italy) and Portugal can be added onto the basic pass.

Inter-Rail Inter-Rail passes are available to European residents of at least six months standing (passport identification is required). Terms and conditions vary slightly from country to country, but in the country of origin there is a discount of around 50% on normal fares.

The Inter-Rail pass is split into zones. Zone A is Ireland (and Britain if purchased in Continental Europe); B is Sweden, Norway and Finland; C is Denmark, Germany, Switzerland and Austria; D is the Czech Republic, Slovakia, Poland, Hungary and Croatia; E is France, Belgium, the Netherlands and Luxembourg; F is Spain, Portugal and Morocco; G is Italy, Greece, Turkey, Slovenia and Italy-Greece ferries; H is Bulgaria, Romania, Yugoslavia and Macedonia.

The normal Inter-Rail pass is for people under 26, though travellers over 26 can get the Inter-Rail 26+ version. The price for any one zone is UK£159 (UK£229 for 26+) for 22 days. Multizone passes are valid for one month: two zones is UK£209 (UK£279), three zones is UK£229 (UK£309), and all zones is UK£259 (UK£349).

Euro Domino There is a Euro Domino pass (called a Freedom pass in Britain) for each of the countries covered by the Inter-Rail pass, except Macedonia. Adults (travelling 1st or 2nd class) and youths under 26 can choose from three, five or 10 days validity within one month. Examples of adult/youth prices for 10 days in 2nd class are UK£182/140 for Italy and UK£227/£182 for Spain.

National Rail Passes If you intend to travel extensively within one country, check which national rail passes are available. These can sometimes save you a lot of money; details can be found in the Getting Around sections in the individual country chapters. You need to plan ahead if you intend to take this option, as some passes can only be purchased prior to arrival in the country concerned.

Cheap Tickets

European rail passes are only worth buying if you plan to do a reasonable amount of intercountry travelling within a short space of time. Some people tend to overdo it and spend every night they can on the train, ending up too tired to enjoy sightseeing the next day.

When weighing up options, consider the cost of other cheap ticket deals. Travellers aged under 26 can pick up BIJ (Billet International de Jeunesse) tickets which can cut fares by up to about 30%. Unfortunately, you can't always bank on a substantial reduction. Paris to Rome return is UK£117, saving just UK£7 on the standard fare, whereas Paris to Madrid return for UK£141 saves UK£35. Various agents issue BIJ tickets in Europe, eg Wasteels (☎ 0171-834 7066) in London's Victoria station and Voyages Wasteels (☎ 01-43 43 46 10) at 2 Rue Michel Chasles, Paris. Rail Europe (☎ 0990-848 848) sells BIJ tickets and Eurail and Inter-Rail passes. It has London offices at 179 Piccadilly and in Victoria station.

Special circular tickets are sometimes available, such as Explorer tickets, formerly sold under the name Eurotrain. Alternatively, normal international tickets are valid for two months, and you can make as many stops as you like en route; make your intentions known when purchasing, and inform the train conductor how far you're going before they punch your ticket.

For a small fee, European residents aged over 60 can get a Rail Europe Senior Card as an add-on to their national rail senior pass. It entitles the holder to reduced European fares. The percentage saving varies according to the route.

TAXI

Taxis in Europe are metered and rates are high. There might also be supplements (depending on the country) for things like luggage, the time of day, the location from which you were picked up, and extra passengers. Good bus, rail and underground railway networks make taxis all but unnecessary for most travellers, but if you need one in a hurry taxi ranks can usually be found near train stations or outside big hotels. Lower fares make taxis more viable in some countries, such as Spain, Greece and Portugal.

CAR & MOTORCYCLE

Travelling with your own vehicle is the best way to get to remote places and it gives you the most flexibility. Unfortunately, the independence you enjoy does tend to isolate you from the local people. Also, cars are usually inconvenient in city centres, where it is generally worth ditching your vehicle and relying on public transport. Various car-carrying trains can help you avoid long, tiring drives.

Paperwork & Preparations

Proof of ownership of a private vehicle should always be carried (Vehicle Registration Document for British-registered cars) when touring Europe. An EU driving licence is acceptable for driving throughout Europe. However, old-style green UK licences are no good for Spain or Italy, and should be backed up by a German translation in Austria. If you have any other type of licence it is advisable, or may be necessary, to obtain an International Driving Permit (IDP) from your motoring organisation (see Visas & Documents in the Facts for the Visitor chapter earlier). An IDP is recommended for Turkey even if you have a European licence.

Third-party motor insurance is a minimum requirement in Europe. Most UK motor insurance policies automatically provide this for EU countries and some others. Get your insurer to issue a Green Card (which may cost extra) – an internationally recognised proof of insurance – and check that it lists all the countries you intend to visit. You'll need this in the event of an accident outside the country where the vehicle is insured. Also ask your insurer for a European Accident Statement form, which can simplify things if the worst happens. Never sign statements you can't read or understand – insist on a translation and sign that only if it's acceptable.

If you want to insure a vehicle you've just purchased (see Purchase & Leasing later in this chapter) and have a good insurance record, you might be eligible for considerable discounts if you can show a letter to this effect from your insurance company back home.

Taking out a European motoring assistance policy, such as the AA Five Star Service or the RAC Eurocover Motoring Assistance, is a good investment. Expect to pay about UK£54 for 14 days cover with a small discount for association members. With the Five Star Service you can request a bail bond for Spain (which will ensure the payment of bail if you are imprisoned), which is less necessary nowadays than in the past, but could be worth having.

Non-Europeans might find it cheaper to arrange international coverage with their national motoring organisation before leaving home. Ask your motoring organisation for details about free and reciprocal services offered by affiliated organisations around Europe.

Every vehicle travelling across an international border should display a sticker showing its country of registration (see the International Country Abbreviations appendix at the back of this book). A warning triangle, to be used in the event of breakdown, is compulsory almost everywhere. Recommended accessories are a first-aid kit (compulsory in Austria, Slovenia, Croatia, Yugoslavia and Greece), a spare bulb kit (compulsory in Spain), and a fire extinguisher (compulsory in Greece and Turkey). In the UK, contact the RAC (☎ 0800-550 055) or the AA (☎ 0990-500 600) for more information.

Road Rules

With the exception of Malta and Cyprus, driving is on the right in Mediterranean Europe. Vehicles brought over from the UK or Ireland, where driving is on the left, should have their headlights adjusted to avoid blinding oncoming traffic at night (a simple solution on older headlight lenses is to cover up a triangular section of the lens with tape). Priority is usually given to traffic approaching from the right in countries that drive on the right-hand side. The RAC publishes the annual *European Motoring Guide*, which gives an excellent summary of regulations in each country, including parking rules. Motoring organisations in other countries have similar publications.

Take care with speed limits, as they vary from country to country. You may be surprised at the apparent disregard for traffic regulations in some places (particularly in Italy and Greece), but as a visitor it is always best to be cautious. Many driving infringements are subject to an on-the-spot fine in most European countries. Always ask for a receipt.

European drink-driving laws are particularly strict. The blood-alcohol concentration (BAC) limit when driving is generally between 0.05% and 0.08%, though it is 0% in Gibraltar. See the introductory Getting Around sections in the country chapters for more details on traffic laws.

Roads

Conditions and types of roads vary across Europe, but it is possible to make some generalisations. The fastest routes are four or six-lane dual carriageways/highways (ie two or three lanes either side) called *autoroutes*, *autostrade* etc. These tend to skirt cities and plough through the countryside in straight lines, often avoiding the most scenic bits. Some of these roads incur tolls, which are often quite hefty (eg in Italy, France and Spain), but there will always be an alternative route you can take. Motorways and other primary routes are generally in good condition.

Road surfaces on minor routes are not so reliable in some countries (eg Morocco and Greece) although normally they will be more than adequate. These roads are narrower and progress is generally much slower. To compensate, you can expect much better scenery and plenty of interesting villages along the way.

Rental

The big international firms – Hertz, Avis, Budget Car, Eurodollar and Europe's largest rental agency, Europcar – will give you reliable service and a good standard of vehicle. Usually you will have the option of returning the car to a different outlet at the end of the rental period.

Unfortunately, if you walk into an office and ask for a car on the spot, you will pay more, even allowing for special weekend deals. If you want to rent a car and haven't prebooked, look for national or local firms, which can often undercut the big companies by up to 40%. Nevertheless, you need to be wary of dodgy deals such as where they take your money and point you towards some clapped-out wreck, or where the rental agreement is bad news if you have an accident or the car is stolen – a cause for concern if you can't even read what you sign.

Prebooked and prepaid rates are always cheaper, and there are fly-drive combinations and other programs that are worth looking into. Holiday Autos (☎ 0990-300 400) in the UK has a lowest price guarantee. It has branches in Europe, and its USA office is Kemwel Holiday Autos (☎ 800-678 0678) in Harrison, New York. Sometimes there are restrictions about driving rental cars across country borders.

No matter where you rent, make sure you understand what is included in the price (unlimited or paid kilometres, tax, injury insurance, collision damage waiver etc) and what your liabilities are. We recommend taking the collision damage waiver, though you can probably skip the injury insurance if you and your passengers have decent travel insurance.

The minimum rental age is usually 21 or even 23, and you'll probably need a credit card. Note that prices at airport rental offices are usually higher than at branches in the city centre.

Motorcycle and moped rental is common in Italy, Spain, Greece and the south of France, but it is all too common to see inexperienced riders leap on bikes and very quickly fall off them again.

Purchase & Leasing

The purchase of vehicles in some European countries is illegal for nonresidents of that country. The UK is probably the best place to buy: second-hand prices are good and, whether buying privately or from a dealer, the absence of language difficulties will help you to establish exactly what you are getting and what guarantees you can expect in the event of a breakdown. Remember that you will be getting a car with the steering wheel on the right in the UK. If you want left-hand drive and can afford to buy new, prices are reasonable in the Netherlands and Greece (without tax), in France and Germany (with tax), and in Belgium and Luxembourg (regardless of tax). Paperwork can be tricky wherever you buy, and many countries have compulsory roadworthiness checks on older vehicles.

Leasing a vehicle has none of the hassles of purchasing and can work out considerably cheaper than hiring over longer periods. The Renault Eurodrive Scheme provides new cars for non-EU residents for a period of between 17 and 170 days. Under this scheme, a Renault Clio 1.2 for 30 days, for example, would cost FF4745 (if picked up/dropped off in France), including insurance and roadside assistance. Other companies with comparable leasing programs include Peugeot and Citroën. Check out the options before leaving home. In the USA, Kemwel Holiday Autos (☎ 800-678 0678) arranges European leasing deals.

Camper Van

A popular way to tour Europe is for three or four people to band together to buy or rent a camper van. London is the usual embarkation point. Look at the advertisements in London's free magazine *TNT* if you wish to form or join a group. *TNT* is also a good source for purchasing a van, as is the *Loot* newspaper and the Van Market in Market Rd, London N7 (near the Caledonian Rd tube station), where private vendors congregate on a daily basis. Some second-hand dealers offer a 'buy-back' scheme for when you return from the Continent, but buying and reselling privately should be more advantageous if you have the time.

One reader recommended Down Under Insurance (☎ 0171-402 9211) for European camper van cover.

Camper vans usually feature a fixed hightop or elevating roof and two to five bunk beds. Apart from the essential camping gas cooker, professional conversions may include a sink, fridge and built-in cupboards. You will need to spend at least UK£2000 (US$3200) for something reliable enough to get you around Europe for any length of time. Getting a mechanical check (about UK£30) is a good idea before you buy. An eternal favourite for budget travellers is the VW Kombi; they aren't made any more but the old ones seem to go on forever, and getting spare parts isn't a problem. Once on the road you should be able to keep budgets lower than backpackers using trains, but don't forget to set some money aside for emergency repairs.

The main advantage of going by camper van is flexibility: with transport, eating and sleeping requirements all taken care of in one unit, you are tied to nobody's timetable but your own.

A disadvantage of camper vans is that you are in a confined space for much of the time. (Four adults in a small van can soon get on each other's nerves, particularly if the group has been formed at short notice.) Another drawback is that they're not very manoeuvrable around town, and you'll often have to leave your gear unattended inside (many people bolt extra locks onto the van). They're also expensive to buy in spring and hard to sell in autumn. As an alternative, consider a car and tent.

Motorcycle Touring

Mediterranean Europe is made for motorcycle touring, with good-quality winding roads, stunning scenery and an active motorcycling scene.

The wearing of helmets for both rider and passenger is compulsory everywhere in Europe. Croatia, Portugal, Slovenia, Spain and Yugoslavia (plus Austria, Belgium, France, Germany, Luxembourg and some eastern nations) also require that motorcyclists use headlights during the day.

On ferries, motorcyclists rarely have to book ahead as they can generally be squeezed in. Take note of local custom about parking motorcycles on pavements (sidewalks). Though this is illegal in some countries, the police usually turn a blind eye so long as the vehicle doesn't obstruct pedestrians.

Fuel

Fuel prices can vary enormously from one country to the next, and may bear little relation to the general cost of living, eg fuel in Spain is cheaper than it is Portugal, and Gibraltar and Andorra are cheaper still. France and Italy have Europe's most expensive petrol.

Unleaded petrol is now widely available throughout Europe (except in Morocco) and is usually slightly cheaper than super (premium grade, the only 'leaded' choice in some countries). Diesel is usually significantly cheaper.

BICYCLE

A tour of Europe by bike may seem a daunting prospect, but one organisation that can help in the UK is the Cyclists' Touring Club (CTC; ☎ 01483-417 217; cycling@ctc.org. uk), Cotterell House, 69 Meadrow, Godalming, Surrey GU7 3HS. It can supply information to members on cycling conditions in Europe as well as detailed routes, itineraries, maps and cheap specialised insurance. Membership costs UK£25 per annum, UK£12.50 for students and people under 18, or UK£16.50 for senior citizens. Michelin maps indicate scenic routes, which can help you construct good cycling itineraries.

A primary consideration on a cycling tour is to travel light, but you should take a few tools and spare parts, including a puncture repair kit and an extra inner tube. Panniers are essential to balance your possessions on either side of the bike frame. A bike helmet is also a very good idea. Take a good lock and always use it when you leave your bike unattended.

Seasoned cyclists can average 80km a day, but there's no point in overdoing it. The slower you travel, the more local people you are likely to meet. If you get tired of pedalling or simply want to skip a boring transport section, you can put your feet up on the train. On slower trains, bikes can usually be transported as luggage, subject to a small supplementary fee. Fast trains can rarely accommodate bikes: they might need to be sent as registered luggage and may end up on a different train from the one you take. This is often the case in France and Spain. Eurostar (the train service through the Channel Tunnel) charges UK£20 to send a bike as registered luggage on its routes. You can also transport your bicycle with you on Le Shuttle through the Channel Tunnel. With a bit of tinkering and dismantling (eg removing wheels), you might be able to get your bike into a bag or sack and take it on a train as hand luggage.

The European Bike Express (☎ 01642-251 440) is a coach service where cyclists can travel with their bicycles. It runs in the summer from north-eastern England to France, Italy and Spain, with pick-up/drop-off points en route. The maximum return fare is UK£160 (£10 off for CTC members).

For more information about cycling, see Activities in the Facts for the Visitor chapter and in the individual country chapters.

Rental

It is not as easy to hire bikes in Mediterranean Europe as it is elsewhere on the Continent, but where available they are hired out on an hourly, half-day, daily or weekly basis. It is sometimes possible to return the bike to a different outlet so you don't have to retrace your route. Many train stations have bike-rental counters. See the country chapters for more details.

Purchase

For major cycling tours, it's best to have a bike you're familiar with, so consider bringing your own (see the following section) rather than buying on arrival. There are plenty of places to buy in Europe (shops sell new and second-hand bicycles or you can check local papers for private vendors), but you'll need a specialist bicycle shop for a machine capable of withstanding European touring. CTC can provide a leaflet on purchasing. European prices are quite high (certainly higher than in North America), but non-Europeans should be able to claim VAT on the purchase.

Bringing Your Own

If you want to bring your own bicycle to Europe, you should be able to take it along with you on the plane relatively easily. You can either take it apart and pack everything in a bike bag or box, or simply wheel it to the check-in desk, where it should be treated as a piece of luggage. You may have to remove the pedals and turn the handlebars sideways so that it takes up less space in the aircraft's hold; check all this with the airline well in advance, preferably before you pay for your ticket. If your bicycle and other luggage exceed your weight allowance, ask about alternatives or you may suddenly find yourself being charged a fortune for excess baggage.

HITCHING

Hitching is never entirely safe in any country in the world, and we don't recommend it. Travellers who decide to hitch should under-

stand that they are taking a small but potentially serious risk. People who do choose to hitch will be safer if they travel in pairs and let someone know where they plan to go.

Hitching can be the most rewarding and frustrating way of getting around. Rewarding, because you get to meet and interact with local people and are forced into unplanned detours that may yield unexpected highlights off the beaten track. Frustrating, because you may get stuck on the side of the road to nowhere, with nowhere (or nowhere cheap) to stay.

That said, hitchers can end up making good time, but obviously your plans need to be flexible in case a trick of the light makes you appear invisible to passing motorists. A man and woman travelling together is probably the best combination. Two or more men must expect some delays; two women together will make good time and should be relatively safe. A woman hitching on her own is taking a big risk, particularly in parts of southern Europe, Turkey and North Africa.

Don't try to hitch from city centres: take public transport to suburban exit routes. Hitching is usually illegal on motorways (freeways) – stand on the slip roads, or approach drivers at petrol stations and truck stops. Look presentable and cheerful and make a cardboard sign indicating your intended destination in the local language. Never hitch where drivers can't stop in good time or without causing an obstruction. At dusk, give up and think about finding somewhere to stay. If your itinerary includes a ferry crossing (from mainland France to Corsica, for instance), it's worth trying to score a ride before the ferry rather than after, since vehicle tickets sometimes include a number of passengers free of charge. This also applies to Le Shuttle, the vehicle-carrying train through the Channel Tunnel.

It is sometimes possible to arrange a lift in advance: scan student notice boards in colleges, or contact car-sharing agencies. Such agencies are particularly popular in France (eg Allostop Provoya, Auto-Partage).

BOAT
Mediterranean Ferries

There are many ferries across the Mediterranean between southern Europe and North Africa, including ones from Spain to Morocco, Italy to Tunisia, and France to Algeria, Morocco and Tunisia. There are also ferries between Italy and Greece (eg Brindisi or Bari to Corfu, Igoumenitsa or Patras), and between Greece and Israel. Ferries are often filled to capacity in summer, especially to/from Tunisia, so book well in advance if you're taking a vehicle across.

The Greek islands are connected to the mainland and each other by a spider's web of routings; the excellent *Thomas Cook Guide to Greek Island Hopping* gives comprehensive listings of ferry times and routes, as well as information on sightseeing. Ferries also link other islands in the Mediterranean with mainland ports: Corsica with Nice, Marseille and Toulon (France) and Genoa, La Spezia, Piombino and Livorno (Italy); Sicily and Sardinia with Genoa and Naples (among other Italian ports) as well as Tunis; and Malta with Sicily and Naples. See the relevant country chapters in this book for more details.

ORGANISED TOURS

Tailor-made tours abound; see your travel agent or look in the small ads in newspaper travel pages. Specialists include Ramblers Holidays (☎ 01707-331 133; ramhols@dial .pipex.com) in Britain and CBT Bicycle Tours (☎ 800-736-BIKE or 773-404 1710) in the USA.

Young revellers can party on Europewide bus tours. An outfit called Acacia offers budget coach/camping tours for under US$40 per day, plus contributions to a food fund. It has a London office (☎ 0171-937 3028; acacia@afrika.demon.co.uk) and is represented in Australia and New Zealand by Adventure World; in North America, call ☎ 800-233 6046.

Contiki (☎ 0181-290 6422; travel@contiki .co.uk) and Top Deck (☎ 0171-370 4555; s+m.topdeck@dial.pipex.com) offer camping or hotel-based bus tours, also for the 18 to 35 age group. The latter's 42-day 'Marrakesh Express' costs from UK£859 plus your UK£230 food fund. Both have offices or representatives in North America, Australasia and South Africa.

For people aged over 50, Saga Holidays (☎ 0800-300 500), Saga Building, Middelburg Square, Folkestone, Kent CT20 1AZ, offers holidays ranging from cheap coach tours to luxury cruises (and has cheap travel insurance). Saga operates in the USA as Saga International Holidays (☎ 800-343 0273), 222 Berkeley St, Boston, MA 02116, and in Australia as Saga Holidays Australasia (☎ 02-9957 4266), Level One, 110 Pacific Highway, North Sydney 2060, NSW.

National tourist offices in most countries offer organised trips to points of interest. These may range from one-hour city tours to several-day circular excursions. They often work out more expensive than going it alone, but are sometimes worth it if you are pressed for time. A short city tour will give you a quick overview of the place and can be a good way to begin your visit.

Albania

Until 1990 a closed communist country, Albania caught world attention in November of that year as the last domino to tumble in Eastern Europe's sudden series of democratic revolutions. Yet the changes date back to 1985 and the death of Enver Hoxha, Albania's Stalinist leader since 1944. The statues of Stalin and Hoxha toppled, and the non-communist opposition was elevated to power in March 1992, putting Albania at a crossroads. Its first years of attempted democracy have been troubled by economic chaos, shady elections and outright social anarchy.

Long considered fair prey by every imperialist power, Albania chose a curious form of isolation. Blood vendettas and illiteracy were replaced by what some claimed was the purest form of communism. Right up until December 1990, monuments, factories, boulevards and towns were dedicated to the memory of Joseph Stalin. Although Hoxha's iron-fisted rule did save Albania from annexation by Yugoslavia after WWII, it's unlikely that you'll find many in Albania with much good to say about him. On the contrary, most blame him for the country's present problems.

Politics aside, few European countries have the allure of the mysterious Republika e Shqipërisë. Albanians call their country the 'Land of the Eagle'. Albania is Europe's last unknown, with enchanting classical ruins at Apollonia, Butrint and Durrës, the charming 'museum towns' of Gjirokastra and Berat, vibrant cities like Tirana, Shkodra, Korça and Durrës, colourful folklore and majestic landscapes of mountains, forests, lakes and sea. You can see a great number of things in a pocket-sized area and the Albanians are extremely friendly and curious about their handful of visitors.

In the capital, Tirana, and the port of Durrës people are already quite used to seeing foreigners, but almost everywhere else you'll be an object of curiosity. Things have greatly improved since the collapse of the old system in 1992 – trains are back on the rails, increasing numbers of private buses are plying the roads, private rooms are becoming

AT A GLANCE

Capital	Tirana
Population	3.3 million
Area	28,750 sq km
Official Language	Albanian (Tosk)
Currency	1 lekë (L) = 100 qintars
GDP	US$4.4 billion (1996)
Time	GMT/UTC+0100

more readily available in the towns, fine restaurants have opened up, travel agencies are in operation and all areas of the country are now accessible to travellers. As Albania slowly opens up to the world, visitors have the chance to meet the people in a way that's almost impossible elsewhere in Europe.

Facts about Albania

HISTORY

In the 2nd millennium BC, the Illyrians, ancestors of today's Albanians, occupied the western Balkans. The Greeks arrived in the

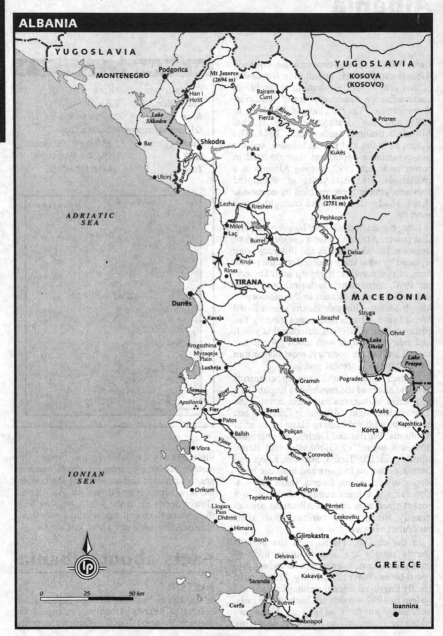

ALBANIA

YUGOSLAVIA

MONTENEGRO

Podgorica

Han i
Hotit

Mt Jezerce
(2694 m)

Bajram
Curri

Fierza

YUGOSLAVIA

KOSOVA
(KOSOVO)

Prizren

Lake
Shkodra

Bar

Shkodra

Puka

Kukës

Drin

River

Ulcinj

Buna River

Lezha   Rreshen

Mt Korab
(2751 m)

Peshkopi

ADRIATIC
SEA

Milot
Laç

Burrel

Kruja   Klos

Debar

Drin

River

Rinas

TIRANA

Durrës

Kavaja

Librazhd

Struga

MACEDONIA

Lake
Ohrid

Ohrid

Rrogozhina
Myzaqeja
Plain
Lushnja

Elbasan

Lake
Prespa

Seman

Apollonia

Fier

River

Osum

Patos

Ballsh

Vlora

Vjose

Berat

Gramsh

Poliçan

Çorovoda

Devoll

River

Pogradec

Maliq

Korça

Kapshtica

IONIAN
SEA

Orikum

Memaliaj

River

Tepelena

Kelçyra

Erseka

Llogara
Pass
Dhërmi

Himara

Borsh

Drino

Gjirokastra

River

Përmet

Leskoviku

GREECE

Delvina

Saranda

Kakavija

Corfu

Butrint

Ioannina

Konispol

0   25   50 km

7th century BC to establish self-governing colonies at Epidamnos (now Durrës), Apollonia and Butrint. They traded peacefully with the Illyrians, who formed tribal states in the 4th century BC. The south became part of Greek Epirus.

In the second half of the 3rd century BC, an expanding Illyrian kingdom based at Shkodra came into conflict with Rome, which sent a fleet of 200 vessels against Queen Teuta (who ruled over the Illyrian Ardian kingdom) in 228 BC. In 214 BC, after a second Roman naval expedition in 219 BC, Philip V of Macedonia came to the aid of his Illyrian allies. This led to a long war which resulted in the extension of Roman control over the entire Balkans by 167 BC.

Like the Greeks, the Illyrians preserved their own language and traditions despite centuries of Roman rule. Under the Romans, Illyria enjoyed peace and prosperity, though the large agricultural estates were worked by slave labour. The main trade route between Rome and Constantinople, the Via Egnatia, ran from Durrës to Thessaloniki. In 285 AD, a provincial reorganisation carried out by the Roman emperor Diocletian (an Illyrian himself) broke Illyria up into four provinces: Epirus Vetus (capital Ioannina), Épirus Nova (capital Durrës), Praevalitana (capital Shkodra) and Dardania (today the Kosova region of Yugoslavia).

When the Roman Empire was divided in 395 AD, Illyria fell within the Eastern Roman Empire, later known as Byzantium. Invasions by migrating peoples – Visigoths, Huns, Ostrogoths and Slavs – continued through the 5th and 6th centuries and only in the south did the ethnic Illyrians survive. Prior to the Roman conquest, Illyria had stretched north to the Danube. In the 11th century, control of this region passed back and forth between the Byzantines, the Bulgarians and the Normans.

The feudal principality of Arbëria was established at Kruja in 1190. Other independent feudal states appeared in the 14th century and towns then developed. In 1344 Albania was annexed by Serbia, but after the defeat of Serbia by the Turks in 1389 the whole region was open to Ottoman attack. The Venetians occupied some coastal towns, and from 1443 to 1468 the national hero Skanderbeg (George Kastrioti) led Albanian resistance to the Turks from his castle at Kruja. Skanderbeg (Skënderbeg in Albanian) won all 25 battles he fought against the Turks, and even Sultan Mehmet-Fatih, conqueror of Constantinople, could not take Kruja.

Albania was not definitively incorporated into the Ottoman empire until 1479. It remained there until 1912, the most backward corner of Europe. In the 15th and 16th centuries thousands of Albanians fled to southern Italy to escape Turkish rule and over half of those who remained converted to Islam so as to become first-class citizens of the theocratic Ottoman empire. In the late 18th century, the Albanian nobles Karamahmut Pasha Bushatlli of Shkodra and Ali Pasha Tepelena of Ioannina (Janina) established semi-independent pashaliks (military districts), but Ottoman despotism was reimposed in the early 19th century.

In 1878 the Albanian League at Prizren (in present-day Kosova, Yugoslavia) began a struggle for autonomy that was put down by the Turkish army in 1881. Uprisings between 1910 and 1912 culminated in a proclamation of independence and the formation of a provisional government led by Ismail Qemali at Vlora in 1912. These achievements were severely compromised by the London ambassador's conference, which handed Kosova, nearly half of Albania, over to Serbia in 1913. In 1914 the Great Powers (Britain, France, Germany, Italy, Austria-Hungary and Russia) imposed a German aristocrat named Wilhelm von Wied on Albania as head of state but an uprising soon forced his departure. With the outbreak of WWI, Albania was occupied by the armies of Greece, Serbia, France, Italy and Austria-Hungary in succession.

In 1920 the Congress of Lushnja denounced foreign intervention and moved the capital from Durrës to less vulnerable Tirana. Thousands of Albanian volunteers converged on Vlora and forced the occupying Italians to withdraw. In May 1924, Bishop Fan Noli established a fairly liberal government which was overthrown on Christmas Eve that year by Ahmet Zogu, who represented the landed aristocracy of the lowlands and the tribal chieftains of the highlands. Zogu ruled with Italian support, declaring himself King Zog I in 1928, but his close collaboration with Italy backfired in April 1939 when Mussolini ordered an invasion of Albania. Zog fled to Britain and used gold looted from the Albanian treasury to rent a floor at London's Ritz Hotel.

On 8 November 1941 the Albanian Communist Party was founded with Enver Hoxha (pronounced Hodja) as first secretary, a position he held until his death in April 1985. The communists led the resistance against the Italians and, after 1943, against the Germans. A provisional government was formed at Berat in October 1944, and by 29 November the Albanian Army of National Liberation had crushed the 'Balli Kombetar', a grouping of tribal quislings in the north, and pursued the last Nazi troops from the country. Albania was the only Eastern European country where the Soviet army was not involved in these operations. By tying down some 15 combined German-Italian divisions, Albania made an important contribution to the final outcome.

The Rise of Communism

After the fighting died down, the communists consolidated power. In January 1946 the People's Republic of Albania was proclaimed, with Enver Hoxha as president. In February a program of socialist construction was adopted and all large economic enterprises were nationalised. By 1952 seven years of elementary education had become mandatory (this was raised to eight years in 1963) and literacy was increased from just 15% before WWII to 72% in 1995.

In October 1946 two British warships struck mines in the Corfu Channel, causing the loss of 44 lives. The British government blamed Albania and demanded £843,947 compensation. To back their claim they impounded 1574 kg of gold (now worth £10 million) which the fascists had stolen from Albania and which had passed into British hands at the end of WWII. Albania has never accepted responsibility for the incident, nor has it agreed to pay damages. The stubborn British are still holding Albania's gold, despite agreeing in principle in 1992 to return it, less reparations. It is now widely believed that Yugoslavia placed the mines. Good relations with Tito were always important to the British, whereas Albania was expendable.

In September 1948, Albania broke off relations with Yugoslavia, which had hoped to incorporate the country into the Yugoslav Federation. Instead, Albania allied itself with Stalin's USSR and put into effect a series of Soviet-style economic plans, the first a two-year plan, and then five-year plans beginning in 1951. After WWII there were British and US-backed landings in Albania by right-wing émigrés. One British attempt in 1949 was thwarted when Stalin passed to Hoxha a warning he had received from double agent Kim Philby.

Albania collaborated closely with the USSR until 1960, when a heavy-handed Khrushchev demanded a submarine base at Vlora. With the Soviet alliance becoming a liability, Albania broke off diplomatic relations with the USSR in 1961 and reoriented itself towards the People's Republic of China.

From 1966 to 1967 Albania experienced a Chinese-style cultural revolution. Administrative workers were suddenly transferred to remote areas and younger cadres were placed in leading positions. The collectivisation of agriculture was completed and organised religion banned. Western literary works were withdrawn from circulation and a strong national culture firmly rooted in socialist ideals was carefully cultivated.

After the Soviet invasion of Czechoslovakia in 1968, Albania left the Warsaw Pact and embarked on a self-reliant defence policy. Today, some 750,000 igloo-shaped concrete bunkers and pillboxes with narrow gun slits are strung along all borders, both terrestrial and maritime, as well as the approaches to all towns. The highway from Durrës to Tirana is one bunker after another for 35km. The amount of time and materials employed in creating these defences must have been tremendous and the bunkers still occupy much agricultural land today.

With the death of Mao Zedong in 1976 and the changes in China after 1978, Albania's unique relationship with China came to an end. In 1981 there was a power struggle within the Albanian Party of Labour (as the Communist Party had been called since November 1948) and former partisan hero and prime minister Mehmet Shehu 'committed suicide' after being accused of being a 'polyagent' (multiple spy).

Shehu had wanted to expand Albania's foreign contacts, an orientation which brought him into direct conflict with Hoxha. Until 1978 Albania had thrived on massive Yugoslav, Soviet and Chinese aid in succession, but building socialism alone, without foreign loans or credit, proved to be difficult. Because its exports didn't earn sufficient hard currency to pay for the import of essential equipment, the country fell far behind technologically.

Post-Hoxha

Hoxha died after a long illness in April 1985 and his longtime associate Ramiz Alia assumed leadership of the 147,000-member Party of Labour. Aware of the economic decay caused by Albania's isolation, Alia began a liberalisation program in 1986 and broadened Albania's ties with foreign countries. Travellers arriving in Albania at this time no longer had their guidebooks confiscated and their beards and long hair clipped by border barbers, and short skirts were allowed.

By early 1990 the collapse of communism in most of Eastern Europe had created a sense of expectation in Albania and in June some 4500 Albanians took refuge in Western embassies in Tirana. After a brief confrontation with police and the Sigurimi (secret police) these people were allowed to board ships to Brindisi, Italy, where they were granted political asylum.

After student demonstrations in December 1990, the government agreed to allow opposition parties. The Democratic Party, led by heart surgeon Sali Berisha, was formed. Further demonstrations won new concessions, including the promise of free elections and independent trade unions. The government announced a reform program and party hardliners were purged.

In early March 1991, as the election date approached, some 20,000 Albanians fled to Brindisi by ship, creating a crisis for the Italian government, which had begun to view them as economic refugees. Most were eventually allowed to stay. In the run-up to the 31 March 1991 elections, Alia won the support of the peasants by turning over state lands

and granting them the right to sell their produce at markets. This manoeuvre netted the Party of Labour 169 seats in the 250-member People's Assembly, which promptly re-elected Alia president for a five-year term.

In mid-May a general strike forced the renamed Socialist Party (formerly the Party of Labour) to form a coalition with the opposition Democrats in preparation for fresh elections the following year. As central economic planning collapsed, factories ceased production and the food distribution network broke down. In August another 15,000 young male Albanians attempted to take refuge in Italy, but this time they were met by Italian riot police and quickly deported. By late 1991 mass unemployment, rampant inflation and shortages of almost everything were throwing Albania into chaos and in December food riots began. Fearful of another refugee crisis, the European Union stepped up economic aid and the Italian army established a large military base just south of Durrës, ostensibly to supervise EU food shipments.

The March 1992 elections ended 47 years of communist rule as the Democratic Party took 92 of the 140 seats in a revamped parliament. After the resignation of Ramiz Alia, parliament elected Sali Berisha president in April. In their campaign, the Democrats promised that their victory would attract foreign investors and gain Western immigration quotas for Albanian workers. When these failed to materialise, the socialists bounced back to win the municipal elections of July 1992.

In September 1992 Ramiz Alia was placed under house arrest after he wrote articles critical of the Democratic government, and in January 1993 the 73-year-old widow of Enver Hoxha, Nexhmije Hoxha, was sentenced to nine years imprisonment for allegedly misappropriating government funds between 1985 and 1990. In August 1993 the leader of the Socialist Party, Fatos Nano, was also arrested on corruption charges. He was sentenced to 12 years imprisonment in April 1994.

By mid-1992 Albania had signed a military agreement with Turkey, and followed that in December by joining the Islamic Conference Association. This reorientation towards the Islamic world stems from practical security considerations. Greek politicians have made territorial claims to southern Albania (which they call Northern Epiros) and the alliance with Turkey was seen as a balance. In mid-1993 relations with Greece hit a new low following the deportation from Albania of a hardline Greek bishop who had attempted to organise the Greek minority in Albania for political ends. In retaliation, Athens ordered the expulsion of 20,000 of the 150,000 Albanian immigrants in Greece.

Meanwhile, private pyramid investment schemes – widely thought to have been supported by the government – collapsed spectacularly in late 1996 leading to nationwide disturbances and violence, and ultimately to the call for new elections which were won by the Socialist Party under Fatos Nano. Since taking power prime minister Nano has restored a large degree of security within the country and a certain amount of investor confidence and foreign business people are once more active in the capital.

Tension over the Albanian-speaking region of Kosova (Kosovo) Yugoslavia's southern province has meant that relations with the Milošević régime in Belgrade were stretched to the limit and by mid-1998 all-out war with Yugoslavia was only just being averted.

GEOGRAPHY & ECOLOGY

Albania's strategic position between Greece, Macedonia, Yugoslavia and Italy has been important throughout its history. Vlora watches over the narrow Strait of Otranto, which links the Adriatic Sea to the Ionian Sea. For decades Albania has acted as a barrier separating Greece from the rest of Europe. The Greek island of Corfu is only a few kilometres from Albania in the Ionian Sea.

Over three-quarters of this 28,748-sq-km country (a bit smaller than Belgium) consists of mountains and hills. There are three zones: a coastal plain, a mountainous region and an interior plain. The coastal plain extends over 200km from north to south and up to 50km inland. The 2000m-high forested mountain spine that stretches along the entire length of Albania culminates at Mt Jezerce (2694m) in the north. Although Mt Jezerce is the highest mountain entirely within the country,

Albania's highest peak is Mt Korab (2751m), on the border with Macedonia. The country is subject to destructive earthquakes, such as the one in 1979 which left 100,000 people homeless.

The longest river is the Drin River (285km), which drains Lake Ohrid. In the north the Drin flows into the Buna, Albania's only navigable river, which connects shallow Lake Shkodra to the sea. Albania shares three large tectonic lakes with Yugoslavia, Macedonia and Greece: Shkodra, Ohrid and Prespa respectively. Ohrid is the deepest lake in the Balkans (294m), while Lake Prespa, at 853m elevation, is one of the highest. The Ionian littoral, especially the 'Riviera of Flowers' from Vlora to Saranda, offers magnificent scenery. Forests cover 40% of the land, and the many olive trees, citrus plantations and vineyards give Albania a true Mediterranean air.

Large parts of the country were subjected to ecological vandalism during the communist years particularly near the Fier oil fields in central Albania and from industrial fallout in the Elbasan valley from the enormous Chinese-built steel mill. This communist quest for higher production was carried out with little or no consideration for the environment and today's industrial wastelands are scenes of utter desolation far beyond anything else in Europe. You'll see ponds covered with a slick of oil leaking from a nearby oil well and large buildings with every window broken and the walls collapsing. Many Albanians treat their country like a giant rubbish dump, the aluminium cans, chocolate wrappers and other debris joining the tens of thousands of broken concrete bunkers and dozens of derelict factories. Albanians are turning their attention to cleaning up their act, but more pressing issues still take precedence such as rebuilding roads and modernising the basic housing infrastructure.

GOVERNMENT & POLITICS

Albania has a parliamentary democracy with a president (currently Rexhap Mejdani) and prime minister, Fatos Nano of the Socialist Party. Opposition parties include the Democratic Party, the Democratic Alliance and the Social Democrats. Elections were last held in 1997 and are due to be held again in 2000.

The Current Situation

In mid-1998 the situation in Albania had quietened down considerably following the widespread civil disturbances of early 1997. The disturbances had broken out after the virtual collapse of the economic and banking system which was brought about after most people in the country had sunk their savings into fradulent pyramid savings schemes.

These ill-conceived schemes subsequently collapsed leaving many people in dire financial straits. Anarchy and violence ensued throughout most of the country, particularly in the south, and travel to any part of Albania during 1997 was extremely dangerous due to armed gangs and rebels.

At the time this book went to print foreigners were once again able to visit Albania. Tirana, Durrës and Kruja were safe to visit and more intrepid travellers could visit other parts of the country with the possible exception of the north. However, accommodation and restaurant infrastructure outside of Tirana may still not be up to scratch given that much was destroyed and looted during the civil disturbances.

For this edition of *Mediterranean Europe* only Tirana, Durrës and Kruja were visited and conditions described for other parts of the country may differ from what you will find.

ECONOMY

Albania stuck to strict Stalinist central planning and wage and price controls longer than any other Eastern European country. Under communism two-thirds of the national income was directed towards consumption and social benefits, and the rest was used for capital investment. Industrial development was spread out, with factories in all regions. Unfortunately, much of the technology used is now thoroughly outdated and the goods produced are unable to compete on world markets. Between 1990 and 1992 industrial production fell 60%; huge investments, now gradually entering the economy, will be required to turn the situation around.

Albania is rich in natural resources such as crude oil, natural gas, coal, copper, iron, nickel and timber and is the world's third-largest producer of chrome, accounting for about 10% of the world's supply. The Central Mountains yield minerals such as copper (in the north-east around Kukës), chromium (farther south near the Drin River), and iron nickel (closer to Lake Ohrid). There are textiles industries at Berat, Korça and Tirana. Oil was discovered in Albania in 1917 and the country was until recently supplying all its own petroleum requirements. Oil and gas from Fier also enabled the production of chemical fertilisers.

There are several huge hydroelectric dams on the Drin River in the north. Albania obtains 80% of its electricity from such dams and by 1970 electricity had reached every village in the country. From 1972 to 1990 Albania exported hydroelectricity to Yugoslavia and Greece. The dams were built with Chinese technical assistance.

Under communist central planning Albania grew all its own food on collective farms, with surpluses available for export. About 20% of these farms were state farms run directly by the government, and the rest were cooperatives. The main crops were corn, cotton, potatoes, sugar beet, tobacco, vegetables and wheat. Lowland areas were collectivised in the 1950s, mountain areas during the 1967 Cultural Revolution.

Following the breakdown of authority in 1991, peasants seized the cooperatives' lands, livestock and buildings and terminated deliveries to the state distribution network, leading to widespread food shortages. After a period of neglect in the agricultural sector, farmers have begun the long task of rebuilding the rural infrastructure. Land is once more heavily cultivated and farms are once again providing produce for the markets.

Considering the country's small size, self-sufficiency was a real challenge, yet before 1990 Albania was one of the few countries in the world with no foreign debt (in 1976 a provision was included in its constitution forbidding any overseas loans). By 1994, however, the government had accumulated an estimated US$920 million foreign debt and must seek new loans just to cover interest on the existing loans.

After the breaks with the USSR and China, Albania's foreign trade had to be completely redirected. Until 1990 Albania's main trading partners were Bulgaria, Czechoslovakia, Hungary, Italy and Yugoslavia, which purchased Albanian food products, asphalt, bitumen, chromium, crude oil and tobacco. Minerals, fuels and metals accounted for 47% of Albania's exports. Today Albania still trades with its Balkan neighbours, but also with Italy and Greece. A new east-west trading route is slowly taking shape from Turkey, Bulgaria, Macedonia and Albania to Italy called the 8th Corridor – an envisioned new Via Egnatia. Other new highways and railways are on the drawing board and investments of US$2.5 billion are envisioned over the next 10 years. Foreign investors are once back in Albania after the 1997 disturbances and a cautious optimism among the business community is apparent.

POPULATION & PEOPLE

The Albanians are a hardy Mediterranean people, physically different from the more Nordic Slavs. Although the Slavs and Greeks look down on the Albanians, the Albanians themselves have a sense of racial superiority based on their descent from the ancient Illyrians, who inhabited the region before the coming of the Romans. The country's name comes from the Albanoi, an ancient Illyrian tribe.

Approximately 3.3 million Albanians live in Albania and a further two million suffer Serbian oppression in Kosova (regarded by Albanians as part of greater Albania), in Yugoslavia. (While in Albania you'll avoid offence by calling the region Kosova instead of Kosovo.) A further 400,000 are in western Macedonia. Harsh economic conditions in Albania have unleashed successive waves of emigration: to Serbia in the 15th century, to Greece and Italy in the 16th century, to the USA in the 19th and 20th centuries and to Greece, Italy and Switzerland today. The Arbereshi, longtime Albanian residents of 50 scattered villages in southern Italy, fled west in the 16th century to escape the Turks. As many as two million ethnic Albanians live in Turkey, emigrants from Serb-dominated Yugoslavia between 1912 and 1966. Since 1990 some 300,000 Albanians – 10% of the population – have migrated to Western Europe (especially Greece and Italy) to escape the economic hardships at home. Minorities inside Albania include Greeks (3% of the population) and Vlachs, Macedonians and Roma (comprising a further 2% of the population).

Tirana, the capital, is the largest city, with 444,000 inhabitants, followed by Durrës, Shkodra, Elbasan, Vlora, Korça, Fier and Berat. The apartment buildings which house a high percentage of the population may look decrepit on the outside but inside they're quite attractive. If you travel around the country much you'll most likely be invited to visit one.

The Shkumbin River forms a boundary between the Gheg cultural region of the north and the Tosk region in the south. The people in these regions still vary in dialect, musical culture and traditional dress.

ARTS
Music

Polyphony, the blending of several independent vocal or instrumental parts, is a southern Albanian tradition that dates back to ancient Illyrian times. Peasant choirs perform in a variety of styles, and the songs, usually with epic-lyrical or historical themes, may be dramatic to the point of yodelling or slow and sober, with alternate male or female voices combining in harmonies of unexpected beauty. Instrumental polyphonic *kabas* are played by small Roma ensembles usually led by a clarinet. Improvisation gives way to dancing at colourful village weddings. One well-known group which often tours outside Albania is the Lela Family of Përmet.

An outstanding recording of traditional Albanian music is the compact disc *Albania, Vocal and Instrumental Polyphony* (LDX 274 897) in the series 'Le Chant du Monde' (Musée de l'Homme, Paris).

The folk music of the Albanian-speaking villages founded five centuries ago in southern Italy has been popularised by Italian singer Silvana Licursi. Although Licursi sings in the Albanian language, her music bears a strong Italian imprint.

Literature

Prior to the adoption of a standardised orthography in 1909, very little literature was produced in Albania, though Albanians resident elsewhere in the Ottoman empire and in Italy did write works. Among these was the noted poet Naim Frashëri (1846-1900), who lived in Istanbul and wrote in Greek. Around the time of independence (1912), a group of romantic patriotic writers at Shkodra wrote epics and historical novels.

Perhaps the most interesting writer of the interwar period was Fan Noli (1880-1965). Educated as a priest in the USA, Fan Noli returned there to head the Albanian Orthodox Church in America after the Democratic government of Albania, in which he served as premier, was overthrown in 1924. Although many of his books are based on religious subjects, the introductions he wrote to his own translations of Cervantes, Ibsen, Omar Khayyám and Shakespeare established him as Albania's foremost literary critic.

Fan Noli's contemporary, the poet Migjeni (1911-38), focused on social issues until his early death from tuberculosis. In his 1936 poem, *Vargjet e lira* (Free Verse), Migjeni seeks to dispel the magic of the old myths and awaken the reader to present injustices.

Albania's best-known contemporary writer is Ismail Kadare, born in 1935, whose 15 novels have been translated into 40 languages. Unfortunately the English editions are sometimes disappointing as they are translated from the French version rather than the Albanian original. *The Castle* (1970) describes the 15th century Turkish invasion of Albania, while *Chronicle in Stone* (1971) relates wartime experiences in Kadare's birthplace, Gjiro-kastra, as seen through the eyes of a boy. *Broken April* deals with the blood vendettas of the northern highlands before the 1939 Italian invasion. Among Kadare's other novels available in English are *The General of the Dead Army* (1963), *The Palace of Dreams* (1981) and *Doruntina* (1988). Although Kadare lived in Tirana throughout the Hoxha years and even wrote a book, *The Great Winter* (1972), extolling Hoxha's defiance of Moscow, he sought political asylum in Paris in October 1990. His latest book, *Printemps Albanais* (Fayard, Paris, 1990), tells why.

Cinema

A recent film worth checking out is *Lamerica*, a brilliant and stark look at Albanian post-communist culture. Despite its title, it is about Albanians seeking to escape to Bari, Italy, in the immediate post-communist era. The title is a symbol for ordinary Albanians seeking a better and more materially fulfilling life in the west. Woven loosely around a plot concerning a couple of Italian scam artists, the essence of the film is the unquenchable dignity of ordinary Albanians in the face of adversity.

SOCIETY & CONDUCT

Traditional dress is still common in rural areas, especially on Sunday and holidays. Men wear embroidered white shirts and knee trousers, the Ghegs with a white felt skullcap and the Tosks with a flat-topped white fezes. Women's clothing is brighter than that of the men. Along with the standard white blouses with wide sleeves, women from Christian areas wear red vests, while Muslim women wear baggy pants tied at the ankles and coloured headscarves. Older Muslim women wear white scarves around the neck; white scarves may also be a sign of mourning.

The *Kanun* is an ancient social law outlining most aspects of social behaviour including the treatment of guests. This has meant that Albanians can be hospitable in the extreme and will often offer travellers lodging and food free of charge. Travellers must be wary of exploiting this tradition and while payment may well be acceptable in some cases, a small gift of a book or a momento from home will often suffice.

Observe respect when visiting mosques – remove your shoes and avoid visits during prayer times.

RELIGION

From 1967 to 1990 Albania was the only officially atheist state in Europe. Public religious services were banned and many churches were converted into theatres or cinemas. In mid-1990 this situation ended and in December of that year Nobel Prize-winner Mother Teresa of Calcutta, an ethnic Albanian from Macedonia, visited Albania and met President Alia. Traditionally,

Albania has been 70% Sunni Muslim, 20% Albanian Orthodox (mostly in the south) and 10% Roman Catholic (mostly in the north). Albania is the only country in Europe with an Islamic majority. The spiritual vacuum left by the demise of communism is being filled by US evangelical imperialists. New churches and mosques are springing up all over the country as evidence of the revival of traditional spiritual customs.

LANGUAGE

Albanian (Shqipja) is an Indo-European dialect of ancient Illyrian, with many Latin, Slavonic and (modern) Greek words. The two main dialects of Albanian diverged over the past 1000 years. In 1909 a standardised form of the Gheg dialect of Elbasan was adopted as the official language, but since WWII a modified version of the Tosk dialect of southern Albania has been used. Outside the country, Albanians resident in former Yugoslavia speak Gheg, those in Greece speak Tosk, whereas in Italy they speak another dialect called Arberesh. With practice you can sometimes differentiate between the dialects by listening for the nasalised vowels of Gheg. The Congress of Orthography at Tirana in 1972 established a unified written language based on the two dialects which is now universally accepted.

Italian is the most useful foreign language to know in Albania, with English a strong second. Some of the older people will have learnt Italian in school before 1943; others have picked it up by watching Italian TV stations or through recent trips to Italy (as is the case with many of the young men).

An excellent teach yourself course of Albanian called *Colloquial Albanian* by Isa Zymberi is available from Routledge Publications (11 New Fetter Lane, London EC4P 4EE, UK) or ordered from your bookseller. The book-and-cassette-tape package has 24 well-structured language units, easy to follow grammar tables and an English-Albanian-English vocabulary and would have to be the best modern guide to the Albanian language on the market. Lonely Planet's *Mediterranean Europe phrasebook* contains a helpful list of translated Albanian words and phrases.

Many Albanian place names have two forms because the definite article is a suffix. In this book we use the form most commonly used in English, but Tirana actually means *the* Tiranë. On signs at archaeological sites, *p.e. sonë* means BC, and *e sonë* means AD. Public toilets may be marked *burra* for men and *gra* for women or may simply show a man's or a woman's shoe or the figure of a man or woman. Albanians, like Bulgarians, shake their heads to say yes and nod to say no.

See the Language Guide at the back of the book for pronunciation guidelines and useful words and phrases.

Facts for the Visitor

HIGHLIGHTS

The Onufri Museum in Berat Citadel houses real masterpieces of medieval icon painting. The National Museum of History in Tirana and the historical museum in Kruja Citadel are excellent. The museum town of Gjirokastra is worth a couple of days visit as is the archaeological site of Butrint.

LOWLIGHTS

Broken-down and abandoned factories that litter the countryside. Abysmal roads and chaotic driving conditions. The one million Kalashnikov rifles that have been taken by one in four residents of Albania. Former state-run hotels. The 'Steel of the Party' factory in Elbasan.

SUGGESTED ITINERARIES

Depending on the length of your stay, you might want to see and do the following things in Albania:

Two days
    Visit Gjirokastra, Saranda and Butrint.
One week
    Visit Gjirokastra, Fier/Apollonia, Berat, Durrës, Tirana and Pogradec or Korça.
Two weeks
    Visit Gjirokastra, Fier/Apollonia, Berat, Durrës, Tirana, Kruja, Lezha, Shkodra and Kukës.
One month
    Visit every place included in this chapter.

PLANNING

Climate & When to Go

Albania has a warm Mediterranean climate. The summers are hot, clear and dry, and the winters, when 40% of the rain falls, are cool, cloudy and moist. In winter the high interior plateau can be very cold as continental air masses move in. Along the coast the climate is moderated by sea winds. Gjirokastra and Shkodra receive twice as much rain as Korça, with November, December and April being the wettest months. The sun shines longest from May to September and July is the warmest month, but even April and October are quite pleasant. The best month to visit is September, as it's still warm and fruit and vegetables are abundant. Winter is uncomfortable as most rooms are unheated and tap water is ice-cold.

Books & Maps

Previously, one of the best travel guidebooks to Albania was *Nagel's Encyclopedia-Guide Albania* (Nagel Publishers, 5-7, Rue de l'Orangerie, 1211 Geneva 7, Switzerland), published in English and German editions in 1990. It's seldom found in bookshops, however, so consider ordering a copy through mail order. Nagel's provides no practical hotel or restaurant information but it's good on historical background up to 1990.

High Albania by Edith Durham, first published in 1909, is an Englishwoman's account of the tribes of northern Albania based on seven years of travel in the area.

In *Albania, The Search for the Eagle's Song*, June Emerson gives a picture of what it was like to visit Albania just before 1990. Untainted by hindsight, her book is an unwitting snapshot of a time that has vanished forever.

The Artful Albanian: The Memoirs of Enver Hoxha, edited by Jon Halliday, contains selected passages from the 3400 pages of Hoxha's six volumes of memoirs. Chapters like 'Decoding China' and 'Battling Khrushchev' give an insight into the mind of this controversial figure.

Anton Logoreci's political and factual narrative *Albanians* is a well-balanced and readable account of Albanian history up to 1987, while *Albania and the Albanians* by

Derek Hall is a comprehensive political history of Albania published in 1994.

Biografi by New Zealand writer Lloyd Jones is a fanciful but very readable tale set in immediate post-communist Albania involving the search for Enver Hoxha's alleged double, Petar Shapallo.

Probably the best overall country map is the *Albania – EuroMap* with maps of five towns and a handy distance chart.

What to Bring

Most essential items found in Western Europe are available in Tirana. If you are planning to spend some time in the country, bring all your personal toiletries and medications. A universal sink plug is about the most practical commodity you can take to Albania.

TOURIST OFFICES

There are no tourist information offices in Albania, but hotel receptionists will sometimes give you directions. The moribund state tourism authority Albturist may eventually be reincarnated in privatised form, but don't count on it just yet. You can buy city maps of Tirana, but in most other towns they're unobtainable. In addition, many streets lack signs and the buildings have no numbers! Some streets don't seem to have any name at all. Most of the towns are small enough for you to do without such things.

The Albania Society of Britain (☎ 0181-540 6824), 7 Nelson Road, London SW19 1HS, England, exists 'to promote contacts between Albania and Britain, to offer factual information concerning Albania and to foster cultural and social bonds between the two peoples'. The Society's quarterly journal *Albanian Life* carries a good range of interesting, readable articles, and membership (£8 in the UK, £12 overseas) includes a subscription.

In Australasia write to FG Clements, The Albania Society, PO Box 14074, Wellington, New Zealand.

In the USA, Jack Shulman (☎ 718-633 0530), PO Box 912, Church Street Station, New York, NY 10008, sells Albanian books, maps, videos and folk-music cassettes by mail order. Jack also carries English translations of Ismail Kadare's best novels.

In Germany you can contact the Deutsch-Albanische Freundschaftsgesellschaft (☎/fax 040-511 1320), Bilser Strasse 9, D-22297 Hamburg, Germany, which publishes the quarterly magazine *Albanische Hefte*.

An excellent source of rare and out-of-print books on Albania is Eastern Books (☎/fax 0181-871 0880; info@easternbooks .com), 125a Astonville St, Southfields, London SW18 5AQ, England, UK. Write for its 24-page catalogue of books about Albania, or check its Web page (www.easternbooks .com). Also try Oxus Books (☎/fax 0181-870 3854), 121 Astonville St, London SW18 5AQ, England, UK.

VISAS & EMBASSIES

No visa is required from citizens of Australia, Bulgaria, Canada, Iceland, New Zealand, Norway, Switzerland, Turkey, the USA and EU countries. Travellers from other countries can obtain their Albanian visa at the border for a price equivalent to what an Albanian would pay for a tourist visa in those countries. Those who don't need a visa must still pay an 'entry tax' of US$5. Citizens of the USA do not have to pay the US$5 entry tax. Land border authorities may try to take anything up to US$20 from you. Insist on $5 and ask for a receipt.

Upon arrival you will fill in an arrival and departure card. Keep the departure card with your passport and present it when you leave.

Albanian Embassies Abroad

Albanian embassies are found in the following cities: Ankara, Athens, Beijing, Belgrade, Bonn, Brussels, Bucharest, Budapest, Cairo, Geneva, Havana, Istanbul, London, New York, Paris, Prague, Rome, Skopje, Sofia, Stockholm, Vienna, Warsaw and Washington. Listed below are some of the main addresses. For other Eastern Europe embassies, see under the relevant country.

France
   (☎ 01-45 53 51 32) 13 rue de la Pompe, Paris 75016
Greece
   (☎ 01-723 4412; fax 723 1972) Karahristou 1, 115 21 Athens
Netherlands
   (☎ 070-427 2101) Koninginnegracht 12, 2514 AA, The Hague

UK
   (☎ 0171-730 5709; fax 730 5747) 38 Grosvenor Gardens, London SW1 0EB
USA
   (☎ 202-223 4942; fax 628 7342) 1511 K Street NW, Washington, DC 20005

Foreign Embassies in Albania

Bulgaria
   (☎ 33 155; fax 38 937) Rruga Skënderbeg 12; Monday, Wednesday & Friday 10.30 am to noon
Hungary
   (☎ 32 238; fax 33 211) Rruga Skënderbeg; Monday and Wednesday 9 to 11 am
Macedonia
   (☎ 30 909; fax 32 514) Lekë Dukagjini 2; Monday to Friday, 10 am to noon
UK
   (☎/fax 34 973) Rruga Skënderbeg; Tuesday to Friday, 9 am to noon
USA
   (☎ 32 875; fax 32 222) Rruga Elbasanit 103; Monday to Friday, 8.30 am to 4.30 pm
Yugoslavia
   (☎ 32 089; fax 23 042) Rruga Durrësit 192-196; Monday to Friday, 10 am to noon

MONEY

Albanian banknotes come in denominations of 100, 200, 500 and 1000 lekë. There are 5, 10, 20 and 50 lekë coins. Notes issued after 1997 are smaller and contain a sophisticated watermark to prevent forgery. In 1964 the currency was revalued 10 times and prices are often still quoted at the old rate. Thus if people tell you that a ticket costs 1000 lekë, they may really mean 100 lekë, so take care not to pay 10 times more! Conversely, a taxi driver who quotes a fare of 1000 lekë may actually mean 1000 new lekë, so watch out. This situation can be very confusing.

In mid-1998, US$1 got you about 155 lekë. Everything can be paid for with lekë; hotel and transport prices in this book are usually quoted in dollars or Deutschmarks, but you can pay in lekë at the current rate. Although Albania is an inexpensive country for foreigners, for Albanians it's different as the average monthly wage is less than US$100, though this is changing quickly.

The private Banka e Kursimeve is usually the most efficient when it comes to changing travellers cheques and they keep longer hours than the National Bank. Some banks will change US dollar travellers cheques into US dollars cash without commission. Travellers cheques in small denominations may be used when paying bills at major hotels but cash is preferred everywhere. Credit cards are only accepted in larger hotels and travel agencies. There are no ATMs in Albania yet.

Every town has its free currency market which usually operates on the street in front of the main post office or state bank. Look for the men standing with pocket calculators in hand. Such transactions are not dangerous and it all takes place quite openly, but make sure you count their money twice before tendering yours. The rate will be about the same as at a bank. The advantages with changing money on the street are that you avoid the 1% commission, save time and don't have to worry about banking hours. Unlike the banks, private moneychangers never run out of currency notes.

Deutschmarks are preferred in Yugoslavia but in Albania US dollars are the favourite foreign currency; you should bring along a supply of dollars in small bills as they can be used to bargain for everything from hotel rooms to curios and taxi rides. Greek drachmas are often quite acceptable. The import and export of Albanian currency is prohibited, but there's no reason to do either. Conversion rates for major currencies in mid-1998 are listed below:

Exchange Rates

Australia	A$1	=	95 lekë
Canada	C$1	=	103.8 lekë
euro	€1	=	172.9 lekë
France	1FF	=	26 lekë
Germany	DM1	=	87.5 lekë
Japan	¥100	=	109.6 lekë
UK	UK£1	=	258 lekë
USA	US$1	=	156 lekë

For the most recent currency rates of the Albanian lek, point your Web browser at: www.gopher://gopher.undp.org:70/00/uncurr /exchrates.

Tipping

Albania is a tip-conscious society. You should round up the bill in restaurants. However, with taxi drivers you will normally agree on a fare beforehand so an extra tip will not be considered necessary.

POST & COMMUNICATIONS
Post

Sending Mail Postage is inexpensive and the service surprisingly reliable, but always use air mail. There are no public mailboxes in Albania; you must hand in your letters at a post office in person. Leaving letters at hotel reception for mailing is unwise, although the Rogner Hotel in Tirana has a reliable postal service. Mail your parcels from the main post office in Tirana to reduce the amount of handling. Letters to the USA, Australia and Canada cost 100 lekë and within Europe 50 lekë.

Receiving Mail Mail sent to Poste Restante, Tirana, Albania should reach you OK. However, Albania is not a good country for receiving mail as letters to Albania may be opened.

Telephone

Long-distance telephone calls made from main post offices are cheap, costing about 150 lekë a minute to Western Europe. The cost of a three-minute call to the USA is 840 lekë. In 1997 Albania introduced public cardphones which makes calling home a lot easier. Cards are available from the post office and street kiosks in versions of 50 units (520 lekë), 100 units (910 lekë) and 200 units (1700 lekë).

Getting through to Albania (country code ☎ 355) may require some persistence. Currently 16 towns have direct-dial access and the relevant codes are listed under each town. For other towns call ☎ 10 for the operator.

Albania also has a mobile phone network covering at present the central plains from Shkodra in the North to Vlora in the South. Check with your home provider for possible roaming agreements. Local mobile phone numbers are in the format 038 123 4567.

Albania's international access code is ☎ 00.

Fax

Faxing can be done fairly easily from the main post office in Tirana, or from major hotels, though they will charge more. Sending a one-page fax from the post office to the USA should cost around 390 lekë.

INTERNET RESOURCES

Albania is linked to the Internet, but there is currently only one Internet Centre providing public access. (See Cybercafés in the Tirana section). Useful Web sites to point your browser at are: www.albanian.com (the Albanian WWW Home Page) or www.tirana.al which was the first Web site established in Albania and set up by the United Nations Development Project.

NEWSPAPERS & MAGAZINES

Some 18 newspapers are published in Tirana, up from seven in 1989. Many are sponsored by political parties, such as *Zëri i Popullit* (The People's Voice), organ of the Socialist Party; *RD* (Democratic Renaissance), the Democratic Party's paper; *Alternativa*, the Social Democratic Party's paper; and *Republika*, the Republican Party's paper. *Koha Jonë* is the paper with the widest readership.

The *Albanian Daily News* (adn@icc.al .eu.org) is a fairly dry English-language publication with nonetheless useful insights into events in the country including a press review of the major Albanian-language papers. It is available from major hotels, or you can read it online – www.AlbanianNews.com.

RADIO & TV

There are many TV channels available in Albania including the state TV service TVSH, the private station TVA and, among others, BBC, CNN, Euronews, Eurosport, several Italian channels and a couple of French ones to boot.

The BBC World Service can be picked up in and around Tirana on 103.9 FM.

PHOTOGRAPHY & VIDEO

Tirana has several good one-hour developing and printing services. In the country it's considered rude to take pictures of people without asking permission, but this will almost never be refused. If you promise to send prints to local people, be sure to honour those promises. As a photographer you'll arouse a lot of friendly curiosity. Do not take photographs of any military or government establishments. Bring your own video paraphernalia – batteries and tapes etc – even though these are now available in Tirana.

TIME

Albania is one hour ahead of GMT/UTC, the same as Yugoslavia, Macedonia and Italy, but one hour behind Greece. Albania goes on summer time at the end of March, when clocks are turned forward an hour. At the end of September, they're turned back an hour.

ELECTRICITY

The electric current is 220V, 50Hz, and plugs have two round pins.

WEIGHTS & MEASURES

Albania uses the metric system.

TOILETS

Public toilets should be used in dire circumstances only! There are only three in the whole of Tirana. Use hotel or restaurant toilets whenever you can. The ones in the main hotels in Tirana are very clean and modern. Plan your 'rest' stops carefully when travelling in the country.

HEALTH

Health services are available to tourists for a small fee at state-run hospitals, but service and standards are not crash hot. You are better off taking out health insurance and using the private clinics where available.

WOMEN TRAVELLERS

While women are not likely to encounter any predictable dangers, it is recommended that you travel in pairs or with male companions, in order to avoid unwanted attention – particularly outside Tirana. Bear in mind that Albania is a predominantly Muslim country. Dress should be conservative.

GAY & LESBIAN TRAVELLERS

Gay sex became legal in Albania early in 1995, however attitudes towards homosexuality are still highly conservative. The Gay Albania Society (Shoqata Gay Albania) is at PO Box 104, Tirana, Albania.

DISABLED TRAVELLERS

Getting around Tirana and Albania in general will be problematic for travellers in wheelchairs since few special facilities exist. There are toilets for disabled people in the Tirana International and the Europapark (Rogner) Hotel in Tirana.

DANGERS & ANNOYANCES

Beware of pickpockets on crowded city buses and don't flash money around! Walking around the towns is safe during the day, even in small streets and among desolate apartment blocks, but at night you must beware of falling into deep potholes in the unlit streets, and occasional gangs of youths. Be aware of theft generally, but don't believe the horror stories you hear about Albania in Greece and elsewhere.

Take special care if accosted by Roma women and children begging, as they target foreigners and are very pushy. If you give them money once, they'll stick to you like glue. When accosted, do not respond and avoid eye contact. Just keep walking and they will soon give up. Head for the nearest hotel if they haven't given up in five minutes. They will soon scarper.

Corrupt police may attempt to extort money from you by claiming that something is wrong with your documentation, or on another pretext. Strongly resist paying them anything without an official receipt. If they threaten to take you to the police station, just go along for the experience and see things through to the end. Always have your passport with you.

Hepatitis B is prevalent in Albania. Get a vaccination before arriving and take care swimming near built-up areas and drinking tap water.

BUSINESS HOURS

Most shops open at 7 am and close for a siesta from noon to 4 pm. They open again until 7 pm and some also open on Sunday. In summer the main shops stay open one hour later but private shops keep whatever hours they like. State banks will change travellers cheques from 7.30 to 11 am only.

Albanian museums don't follow any pattern as far as opening hours go. Museums in small towns may only open for a couple of hours a week. You may find them inexplicably closed during the posted hours or simply closed with no hours posted. Since state subsidies have been slashed, foreigners must pay 100 to 300 lekë admission to major museums.

PUBLIC HOLIDAYS & SPECIAL EVENTS

Public holidays in Albania include New Year's Day (1 January), Easter Monday (March/April), Labour Day (1 May), Independence & Liberation Day (28 November) and Christmas Day (25 December).

Ramadan and Bajram, variable Muslim holidays, are also celebrated.

ACCOMMODATION

Many of the large tourist hotels are still owned by the State Bureau for Tourism, Albturist, though many are being privatised. Most Albturist hotels are in pretty bad shape, so it's always a good idea to check your room first. Albturist itself is barely hanging on in the changing tourist market, so don't depend on it for too much advice on places to stay.

Accommodation is undergoing a rapid transformation in Albania with the opening up of new custom-built private hotels, and the conversion of homes or villas into so-called private hotels. For budget travellers, these are without doubt the best way to go.

New custom-built hotels tend to have Western European prices, ie US$40 to $50 per person per night and upwards, but these are modern, well-appointed establishments – a far cry from the state-run hotels of old – and they usually include breakfast.

In this book we have tended to provide advice on private accommodation and on state accommodation when that is the only option. You can often find unofficial accommodation in private homes by asking around. You may even get a meal or two thrown in as well.

There are no camping grounds but free camping is possible in emergencies. For security, camp out of sight of the road and never leave your tent unattended. Don't camp in the same area more than one night, unless you have permission to camp next to someone's house (even then you risk losing things). Expect to arouse considerable curiosity.

FOOD

Lunch is the main meal of the day though eating out in the evening is very common in Tirana. The quality of restaurants in the capital has improved greatly. In the country and other towns things are also getting much better, so you should have no problem getting a decent meal.

State-owned hotel restaurants are cheaper but the standards are low and they're also poor value. Everywhere beware of waiters who refuse to bring the menu, pad your bill with extras and 'forget' to bring your change. The many hamburger stands in the towns are a much better deal, but choose one that is patronised by a lot of people.

Albanian cuisine, like that of Serbia, has been strongly influenced by Turkey. Grilled meats like *shishqebap* (shish kebab), *romstek* (minced meat patties) and *qofte* (meat balls) are served all across the Balkans. Some local dishes include *çomlek* (meat and onion stew), *fërges* (a rich beef stew), *rosto me salcë kosi* (roast beef with sour cream) and *tavë kosi* (mutton with yoghurt). Lake Shkodra carp and Lake Ohrid trout are the most common fish dishes. Try the ice cream (*akullore*), which is very popular everywhere.

DRINKS

Albanians take their coffee both as *kafe turke* (Turkish coffee) and *kafe ekspres* (espresso). If you ask for *kafe surogato* you will get what is the closest to filter coffee. Any tourist or resident expatriate will tell you not to drink the water, but Albanians do so all the time with no consequences. It all depends on what your stomach is acclimatised to. Avoid unbottled, ungassed drinks as they may be questionable.

Albanian white wine is better than the vinegary red. However the red *Shesi e Zi* from either Librazhd or Berat is an excellent drop. Most of the beer consumed in Albania is imported from Macedonia or Greece, but draught Austrian or Italian beer is available in the posher joints in Tirana. *Raki* (a clear brandy distilled from grapes) is taken as an apéritif. There's also *konjak* (cognac), *uzo* (a colourless aniseed-flavoured liqueur like Greek ouzo) and various fruit liqueurs. *Fërnet* is a medicinal apéritif containing herbal essences, made at Korça.

Public bars and cafés patronised mostly by local men are very sociable and if you enter one for a drink with an Albanian always try to pay. Nine times out of 10 your money will be refused and by having the opportunity to insist on paying your host will gain face in front of those present. The favourite Albanian drinking toast is *gëzuar!*

ENTERTAINMENT

Check the local theatre for performances. These are usually advertised on painted boards either in front of the theatre or on main streets. Ask someone to direct you to the venue if it's not clear. Football is played at local stadiums on Saturday and Sunday afternoons. As a foreigner, you may need someone to help you obtain tickets.

THINGS TO BUY

Most hotels have tourist shops where you can buy Albanian handicrafts such as carpets, silk, ornaments (made from silver, copper and wood), embroidery, handmade shoes, shoulder bags, picture books, musical instruments, and records and cassettes of folk music.

Getting There & Away

AIR

Rinas airport is 26km north-west of Tirana. Taxis and a bus ply the route to Tirana. The airport phone number is ☎ 042-62 620

Ada Air arrives from Bari, Athens and Skopje; Adria Airways from Ljubljana; Albanian Airlines from Rome, Zürich, Munich and Vienna; Alitalia from Rome; Arbëria

Airlines from New York; Hemus Air from Sofia; Lufthansa from Frankfurt and Munich; Malév Hungarian Airlines from Budapest; Olympic Airlines from Athens via Ioannina or Thessaloniki and Swissair from Zürich.

These expensive flights are used mostly by business people or Albanians resident abroad and are of little interest to budget travellers, who can come more cheaply by land or sea. An exception is Malév Hungarian Airlines' service three times a week from Budapest to Tirana, which is usually good value and saves you from having to transit Yugoslavia.

Unfortunately, the Italian government requires its state airline flying between Italy and Albania to charge business class fares for one-way tickets, which makes Italy a poor gateway. For example, with Alitalia, Tirana-Bari is US$318 one way, Tirana-Rome US$462 one way. However, Alitalia does do weekend return specials to/from Rome for US$339. In comparison to flying to Rome, it is cheaper to fly further on Albanian Airlines (☎/fax 42 857), a joint venture with a Kuwaiti concern, which has flights to Zürich (twice weekly, US$388 one way), Munich (three times a week, US$395 one way) and Vienna (three times a week, US$370 one way). Return flights to/from Rome or Bologna with Albanian Airlines cost US$296.

Before investing in any of the above fares, compare them with the price of a cheap flight to Athens or Thessaloniki, from where Albania is easily accessible by local bus with a change of bus at the border; you could also look at the cost of a charter flight to Corfu, from where you can take a ferry to Saranda in southern Albania. Flying to Tirana from Thessaloniki will cost around 23,500 drachmas (US$78) one way.

LAND
Bus

The simplest way to get into Albania by bus is from Greece. For Tirana or Gjirokastra there is a bus from Athens via Ioannina. This bus leaves Athens at 9 pm daily (except Friday) and passes through Ioannina at about 7 am the following day on its way to Tirana. This bus leaves Tirana for Athens (732km, 6000 lekë) daily at 6 am from the Axhensi

bus office on a side street near the art gallery in Tirana. Alternatively, nine local buses a day run from Ioannina, Greece, to the Albanian border at Kakavija (one hour, 1100 dr). You must arrive at the border before 11 am to connect with a local bus on to Gjirokastra (26km) or Tirana (263km).

Alternatively, it's fairly easy to cover the 93km from Korça to Florina, Greece, via Kapshtica (see the Korça section in this chapter for details). There are two buses a day from the Greek border to Florina (1½ hours, 1000 dr), otherwise you will need to take a taxi (6000 dr). Unscheduled local buses from Tirana to Kakavija and Korça to Kapshtica leave throughout the day. There is also a direct bus from Korça to Thessaloniki six times a week. To/from Athens you're better off going via Kakavija, to/from Thessaloniki via Kapshtica.

If you're Macedonia-bound, take the daily bus at 6 am to either Ohrid (15 DM) or Tetovo (20 DM) from the Axhensi bus office. From Tetovo you can take a frequent local bus to Skopje. Tickets can also be bought from Esterida Bus Services behind the Palace of Culture.

Buses for Sofia (505km, US$30 – payable only in US dollars) depart on Tuesday and Wednesday at 10 am from Albtransport on Rruga Mine Peza in Tirana.

Although Shkodra is linked to Podgorica, Yugoslavia, by rail there's no passenger service.

Car & Motorcycle

In the recent past, bringing a car to Albania was a risky business. Today there is no real reason why you should not travel by car through Albania – if we ignore the security problems in the North still prevailing by mid-1998.

Travel is slow because of the poor condition of the roads and the arterial infrastructure cannot yet properly support the marked increase in vehicular traffic that Albania has recently experienced. Apart from an 8km stretch of 'freeway' between Tirana and Durrës there has been no visible improvement in the roads since the days of communism. See the following Getting Around section for further information on local driving conditions.

It should be possible to transit the country from Hani i Hotit on the Montenegran border to the Kakavija border with Greece (or vice versa) in about eight or nine hours, though Tirana makes for a convenient overnight stop. The following highway border crossings are open to both motorists and persons on foot or bicycle.

Yugoslavia Crossing from Yugoslavia may now be extremely difficult if not impossible due to the 1998 border tensions with Kosova (Kosovo). You can in theory cross at Han i Hotit (between Podgorica and Shkodra) and at Morina (between Prizren and Kukës). For information about crossing at Morina, see the Kukës section in this chapter and Prizren in the Yugoslavia chapter. A new border crossing was planned at Muriqan, between Shkodra and Ulcinj in Montenegro, but to date no opening date has been announced.

Macedonia Cross at Tushemisht (near Sveti Naum, 29km south of Ohrid), Qafa e Thanës (between Struga and Pogradec) and Maqellare (between Debar and Peshkopi). See the Pogradec section of this chapter for information about crossing at Tushemisht.

Greece The border crossings are Kapshtica (between Florina and Korça) and Kakavija (between Ioannina and Gjirokastra). A new EU-funded border crossing between Sagiada and Konispol, south of Saranda, is planned but no opening date has yet been announced.

Warning Travel conditions in mid-1998 for private cars are still not favourable or even possible given the threat of banditry in the North and the likelihood of the Albanian/ Yugoslav border posts being closed.

SEA

The Italian company Adriatica di Navigazione offers ferry services to Durrës from Bari (220km, nine hours), Ancona (550km, 20 hours) and Trieste (750km, 25 hours) several times a week. The routes are served by 272-vehicle, 1088-passenger ships of the *Palladio* class. The food aboard ship is good.

Deck fares are US$70 Bari-Durrës,

US$100 Ancona-Durrës and US$120 Trieste-Durrës. Pullman (airline-style) seats cost US$80 Bari-Durrës, US$110 Ancona-Durrës, and US$135 Trieste-Durrës. Cabins for the Trieste-Durrës trip vary in price from US$155 for a bed in a four-bed C-class cabin to US$195 for an A-class cabin.

These are high-season fares, applicable eastbound from 4 July to 15 August, westbound from 2 August to 2 September. During other months it's about 25% cheaper. The cost of a return fare is double the one-way fare. Meals are not included and a port tax of 5000 lire is charged on departures from Italy and US$4 from Albania. Bicycles are carried free.

In Trieste ferry tickets are available from Agenzia Marittima 'Agemar' (☎ 040-363 737), Via Rossini 2, right on the old harbour five blocks from Trieste railway station. The booking office is closed from noon to 3 pm and on weekends. In Bari the agent is 'Agestea' (☎ 080-331 555), Via Liside 4. In Ancona it's Maritime Agency Srl (☎ 071-204 915), Via XXIX Settembre 2/0. In Albania tickets are sold at the harbour in Durrës or from Albania Travel & Tours (☎ 042-32 983; fax 33 981) in Tirana.

Transeuropa Lines runs a service twice a week between Bari in Italy and Durrës. One-way deck prices are quoted at 90,000 lire with a 25% discount on the return ticket. In Durrës contact Shpresa Agency (☎/fax 052-22 423) and in Bari contact Morfimare (☎/fax 080-524 0139).

Illyria Lines SA in Durrës (☎/fax 052-23 723), in Vlora (☎/fax 063-25 533) and in Brindisi (☎ 0831-562 043; fax 562 005) runs two ferries between these three ports. Prices are US$69 for a deck ticket or US$83 for an aircraft-type seat.

The fastest ferry connection between Bari and Durrës is the 315-passenger catamaran *La Vikinga* (3½ hours, US$112, VIP class US$125). This high-speed vessel departs Durrës daily at 9.30 am and Bari at 4 pm and travels at speeds of up to 90km/h. The Bari agent is Morfimare (☎/fax 080-524 0139), Corso de Tullio 36/40.

The shortest and least expensive ferry trip to/from Italy is the Otranto-Vlora link (100km, three times a week, US$45). Tickets are available from Biglietteria Linee Lauro

(☎ 0836-806 061; fax 806 062), at the port in Otranto, or Albania Travel & Tours (☎ 042-32 983) in Tirana.

Travellers from Corfu are advised to look for the ticket vendors (from any of the three ferry companies) who hang around the New Harbour before the ferries depart. The *Kamelia* departs Corfu at 10 am, the *Oleg Volvać* at 10.30 am and the *Harikla* at 3 pm. Tickets prices at last count were around US$10, one way. (These times and services may have changed, so check before making concrete plans.)

ORGANISED TOURS

Several companies offer package tours to Albania which include transport, accommodation, meals, admission fees and guides, but not visa fees, airport taxes, or alcohol with the meals. Single hotel rooms also cost extra. As always, group travel involves a trade-off: lack of control over the itinerary and the obligation to wait around for slower group members. Tours also tend to isolate you from the everyday life of Albania, though the trekking tours bring you more into contact with people and places.

The companies to contact are:

Alumni Travel
   (☎ 02-9290 3856; fax 9290 3857) 100 Clarence St, Sydney, NSW 2001, Australia
Exodus
   (☎ 0181-675 5550; fax 673 0779; sales@exodustravels.co.uk) 9 Weir Rd London SW12 0LT, UK
ITS
   (☎ 0161-839 2222; fax 839 0000; all@its-travel.u-net.co.uk) 546-550 Royal Exchange, Old Bank Street, Manchester M2 7EN, UK
Regent Holidays
   (☎ 0117-921 1711; fax 925 4866; 106041.1470@compuserve.com) 15 John St, Bristol BS1 2HR, UK
Kutrubes Travel
   (☎ 617-426 5668; fax 426 3196) 328 Tremont St, Boston, MA 02116 USA
Intertrek BV
   (☎ 070-363 6416) Postbus 18760, NL-2502 ET Den Haag, Netherlands
Scope Reizen
   (☎ 077-735 533) Spoorstraat 41, NL-5931 PS Tegelen, Netherlands

Skënderbeg-Reisen GmbH
   (☎ 0234-308 686) Postfach 102204, D-44722 Bochum, Germany
Egnatia Tours
   (☎ 0222-406 97 32) Piaristengasse 60, A-1082 Vienna, Austria

Regent Holidays has a five-day bus tour of central Albania four times a year at £508, return flight from London included. ITS offers eight-day tours of 'Classical Albania' for £799, covering most of the major sights. Kutrubes Travel offers a 10-day bus tour of southern Albania every two weeks from May to October at US$2260, including return air fare from Boston. Northern Albania is offered once in July and again in August (US$2367).

Exodus offers 15-day hiking and discovery tours between May and September. Its free brochure is quite informative.

LEAVING ALBANIA

Airport departure tax is US$10, which is payable in dollars or lekë. Departure tax from Albanian ports is US$2. Private cars departing from Albania pay US$5 road tax per day for each day spent in the country.

Getting Around

BUS

Most Albanians travel around their country in private minibuses or state-owned buses. These run fairly frequently throughout the day between Tirana and Durrës (38km) and other towns north and south. Buses to Tirana depart from towns all around Albania at the crack of dawn. Tickets are sold by a conductor on board, and for foreigners the fares are low. Although old, the buses are usually comfortable enough, as the number of passengers is controlled by police.

TRAIN

Before 1948, Albania had no railways, but the communists built up a limited north-south rail network based at the port of Durrës, with daily passenger trains leaving Tirana for Shkodra (98km, 3½ hours), Fier (4¼ hours), Ballsh (five hours), Vlora (5½ hours) and

Pogradec (seven hours). Seven trains a day make the 1½-hour trip between Tirana and Durrës. In August 1986 a railway was completed from Shkodra to Podgorica, Yugoslavia, but this is for freight only.

Albanian railways use mostly old Italian rolling stock seconded as a form of aid. There's still only one type of train ticket, so you can sit in 1st or 2nd class for the same price. Train fares are about a third cheaper than bus fares, but both are very cheap by European standards.

Train travel is really only useful between Tirana and Durrës. All trains to southern Albania call at Durrës, a roundabout route that makes them much slower than bus. The bus to Shkodra in the north is also much faster. Still, travelling by train is an interesting way to see the country and meet the people. But be warned: many trains don't have toilets and the carriages can be very decrepit, with broken windows.

CAR & MOTORCYCLE

Albania has only just acquired an official road traffic code and most motorists have only learned to drive in the last few years. The road infrastructure is poor and the roads badly maintained, but the number of cars on the road is growing daily. There are petrol stations in the cities, but they are few and far between in the country. Very few Albanians ride motorcycles and the poor road conditions are a concern for foreign motorcyclists. You can hire a car, but timid drivers might prefer hiring a car and a driver.

Hazards include pedestrians who use the roads as an extension of the footpaths; animals being herded along country roads; gaping potholes; a lack of road warnings and signs and occasionally reckless drivers. Security is also an issue. Park your vehicle in a secure location, such as hotel grounds, or in a guarded parking lot. Store removables like hubcaps inside the car when parked. An immobiliser alarm is a good idea.

Modern petrol stations are opening up all over the country so fuel is no longer a problem. Unleaded fuel may only be available closer to Tirana, so fill up when you can. A litre of unleaded petrol costs 145 lekë.

BICYCLE

Cycling around Albania, while not unheard of, is still a novelty. A number of foreign cyclists, including solo riders, have written of interesting and hassle-free trips through the country, though some caution should still be exercised. If you are planning to cycle into the country, it is preferable to do so in groups of two or more for security – primarily for your belongings on the bike. Facilities outside Tirana, while improving, are not very sophisticated. You will need to be as self-sufficient as possible. Car drivers may not show much respect for cyclists, so ride defensively. Keep a look out for potholes. Mountain bikes are hardier than road bikes.

HITCHING

With buses so cheap, hitching will probably only be an emergency means of transport. You can afford to be selective about the rides you accept as everyone will take you if they possibly can. Truck drivers usually refuse payment from foreigners for lifts (even if Albanian passengers must pay). Never accept rides in cars containing three or more excited young men as they will drive wildly and possibly crash the car.

You can get an indication of where a vehicle might be going from the letters on the licence plate: Berat (BR), Durrës (DR), Elbasan (EL), Fier (FR), Gjirokastra (GJ), Korça (KO), Kruja (KR), Lezha (LE), Pogradec (PG), Saranda (SR), Shkodra (SH), Tirana (TR), Vlora (VL).

LOCAL TRANSPORT

Shared minibuses run between cities. They usually cost about five times the bus fare but for foreigners they're still relatively cheap. Ask locals what they think the fare should be and then bargain for something approaching that.

City buses operate in Tirana, Durrës and Shkodra (pay the conductor). Watch your possessions on crowded city buses.

There are two types of taxis: the older private taxis, which are usually found around the market or at bus and train stations, and the shiny Mercedes tourist taxis parked outside the Rogner and Tirana International hotels (which quote fares in US dollars but also take lekë). Taxi fares are set at approximately 60 lekë per kilometre. Work out the price in your head before getting in and make sure you reach an agreement with the driver before setting off. Car rentals with or without a company driver are available in Tirana.

Don't trust truck drivers who enthusiastically offer to give you a lift somewhere the following day as their plans could change and all the morning buses may have left before you find out about it.

Tirana

☎ 042

Tirana (Tiranë), a pleasant city of 444,000 people (compared with 30,000 before WWII, but now unofficially 650,000), lies almost exactly midway between Rome and Istanbul. Mt Dajti (1612m) rises to the east. Founded by a Turkish pasha (military governor) in 1614, Tirana developed into a craft centre with a lively bazar.

In 1920 the city was made capital of Albania and the bulky Italianate government buildings went up in the 1930s. In the communist era, larger-than-life 'palaces of the people' blossomed around Skënderbeg Square and along Bulevardi Dëshmorët e Kombit (Martyrs of the Nation Blvd). You'll see Italian parks and a Turkish mosque, but the market area on the east side of Tirana is also worth exploring. The city is compact and can be explored on foot.

Orientation

Orientation is easy in Tirana since the whole city revolves around central Skenderbeg Square. Running south from the square is Bulevardi Dëshmorët e Kombit which leads to the three-arched university building. Running north the same street leads to the train station. Coming from the airport (26km) you will enter the city along Rruga Durrësit. Buses from neighbouring countries will drop you off close to Skënderbeg Square. Most major services and hotels are within a few minutes walk of Skënderbeg Square.

Information

Money The State Bank of Albania (Banka e

Shtetit Shqiptar) on Skënderbeg Square (open weekdays from 8.30 am to noon) changes travellers cheques for 1% commission.

A free currency market operates directly behind the State Bank near the post office. One of the men with a pocket calculator in hand will take you aside. A number of small kiosks here will also change your cash for a similar rate.

The Unioni Financiar Tiranë Exchange just south of the post office is a good place to send and receive money electronically and to cash your money as well.

Post & Communications The telephone centre (Telekomi Shqiptar) is on Bulevardi Dëshmorët e Kombit, diagonally opposite Hotel Arbëria and a little towards Skënderbeg Square. It's open 21 hours a day and calls go straight through. This is also the cheapest place to send a fax.

Cybercafés Though not quite an Internet Café (yet) the Open Internet Center (ilirz@soros.al), Rruga Themistokli Germenji 3/1, is a great place to check mail and surf for free. It's open from 2 pm to 5 pm on weekdays. Visit its Web page: www.soros.al/oic.

Travel Agencies The American Express representative is World Travel (☎/fax 27 908), Mine Peza 2. It can cash and supply travellers cheques, provide air and ferry tickets and arrange private or group tours around Albania.

Albania Travel & Tours (☎ 32 983; fax 33 981), Rruga Durrësit 102, sells tickets for the ferry from Vlora to Otranto, Italy (three a week, US$45), perhaps the cheapest way across the Adriatic. Skanderbeg Travel, a few blocks north-west up the same street, is good about providing general information.

Newspapers & Magazines Foreign newspapers and magazines are sold at all major hotels and at many street kiosks. The UK *Guardian* arrives in Tirana at about 6 pm on the day it is published. Major Sunday papers arrive on Wednesday.

Medical & Emergency Services Hospital services at the Policlinic will cost you a minimum fee of about 1000 lekë, but if you

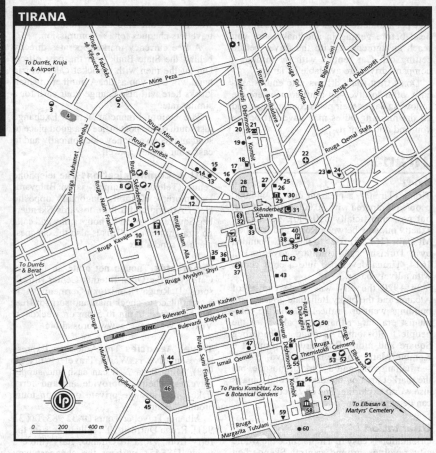

TIRANA

have travel insurance you would probably be better off heading for the new and private Poliklinika at Luigji Monti on Rruga Kavajes. The phone number for the public Hospital No 1 in Tirana is ☎ 62 620 and for Hospital No 2 it is ☎ 62 641.

The emergency phone number for an ambulance is ☎ 17 and for the police ☎ 19.

Things to See & Do

Most visits to Tirana begin at **Skënderbeg Square**, a great open space in the heart of the city.

Beside the 15-storey Tirana International hotel (the tallest building in Albania), on the north side of the square, is the **National Museum of History** (1981), the largest and finest museum in Albania (open Thursday to Saturday only from 9 am to 3 pm, admission 300 lekë). A huge mosaic mural entitled *Albania* covers the façade of the museum building (the rooms describing the communist era are closed). Temporary exhibits are shown in the gallery on the side of the building facing the Tirana International Hotel (admission free).

TIRANA

PLACES TO STAY					
12	Hotel California	5	Yugoslav Embassy	37	Unioni Financiar Tiranë
20	Hotel Arbëria	6	Hungarian Embassy		Exchange
26	Hotel Miniri	7	Bulgarian Embassy	38	Teatri Kombetar
27	Tirana International	8	UK Embassy	39	Axhensi Bus Office
35	Hotel Klodiana	9	Poliklinika at Luigji Monti	40	Guarded Parking
36	Europa International Hotel	10	Orthodox Church	41	Parliament
43	Hotel Dajti	11	Cathedral of St Anthony	42	Art Gallery
54	Hotel Europapark (Rogner)	13	World Travel	45	Southern Bus Station
		14	Skanderbeg Travel	46	Selman Stërmasi Stadium
		15	Albtransport	47	Former Residence of
PLACES TO EAT		16	Albania Travel & Tours		Enver Hoxha
17	Piazza Restaurant; Piano Bar	18	London Bar	48	Former Central Committee
24	Qendra Stefan	19	Philatelic Bureau		Building
25	Restorant Popullor	21	Telephone Centre	49	Former Enver Hoxha Museum
30	Berlusconi Restaurant		(Telekomi Shqiptar)	50	Macedonian Embassy
44	Ujvara Restaurant	22	Policlinic	51	US Embassy
59	Bar Artisti	23	Market	52	Romanian Embassy
		28	National Museum of History	53	Open Internet Centre
OTHER		29	Palace of Culture	55	Italian Embassy
1	Train Station	31	Mosque of Ethem Bey	56	Palace of Congresses
2	Kruja Bus Station	32	State Bank of Albania	57	Qemal Stafa Stadium
3	Northern Bus Station	33	Teatri I Kukallave	58	Archaeological Museum
4	Asllan Rusi Stadium	34	Main Post Office	60	Tirana University

To the east is another massive building, the **Palace of Culture**, which has a theatre, restaurant, cafés and art galleries. Construction of the palace began as a gift from the Soviet people in 1960 and was completed in 1966, after the 1961 Soviet-Albanian split. The entrance to the **National Library** is on the south side of the building. Opposite this is the cupola and minaret of the **Mosque of Ethem Bey** (1793), one of the most distinctive buildings in the city. Enter to see the beautifully painted dome. Tirana's **clock tower** (1830) stands beside the mosque.

On the west side of Skënderbeg Square is the State Bank of Albania, with the main post office behind it. The south side of the square is taken up by the massive ochre-coloured buildings of various government ministries. In the middle of the square is an equestrian statue (1968) of Skënderbeg himself looking straight up Bulevardi Dëshmorët e Kombit (formerly Bulevardi Stalin and before that, Bulevardi Zog I), north towards the train station.

A massive statue of Enver Hoxha used to stand on the high marble plinth between the National Museum of History and the State Bank but it was unceremoniously toppled after the return to democracy. A small fairground now occupies the central part of the square.

Behind Skënderbeg's statue extends Bulevardi Dëshmorët e Kombit, leading directly south to the three arches of **Tirana University** (1957). As you stroll down this tree-lined boulevard, you'll see Tirana's **art gallery** (closed Monday), a one-time stronghold of socialist realism, with a significant permanent collection that has been exhibited here since 1976.

Continue south on Bulevardi Dëshmorët e Kombit to the bridge over the Lana River. On the left just across the river are the sloping white-marble walls of the **former Enver Hoxha Museum** (1988), used as a disco and on weekends as a giant slide for hoards of children. The museum closed down at the start of 1991 and the brilliant red star was removed from the pyramid-shaped building's tip. Just beyond, on the right, is the four-storey former **Central Committee building** (1955) of the Party of Labour, which now houses various ministries.

Follow Rruga Ismail Qemali, the street on the south side of the Central Committee building, a long block west to the **former**

residence of Enver Hoxha (on the north-west corner of the intersection). Formerly it was forbidden to walk along these streets, since many other party leaders lived in the surrounding mansions. When the area was first opened to the general public in 1991, great crowds of Albanians flocked to see the style in which their 'proletarian' leaders lived.

On the left, farther south on Bulevardi Dëshmorët e Kombit, is the ultramodern **Palace of Congresses** (1986), next to which is the **Archaeological Museum** (closed while this book was being researched). There are no captions but a tour in English is usually included in the 300 lekë admission price.

Some 1800 selected objects from prehistoric times to the Middle Ages are on display and it's interesting to note how the simple artefacts of the Palaeolithic and Neolithic periods give way to the weapons and jewellery of the Copper and Bronze ages, with evidence of social differentiation. Although Greek and Roman relics are well represented, evidence of the parallel Illyrian culture is present throughout, illustrating that the ancestors of the present Albanians inhabited these lands since time immemorial.

Behind the museum is the **Qemal Stafa Stadium** (1946) where football matches are held every Saturday and Sunday afternoon, except during July and August. The boulevard terminates at the university, with the Faculty of Music on the right.

Beyond the university is **Parku Kombëtar** (National Park), a large park with an open-air theatre (Teatri Veror) and an artificial lake. There's a superb view across the lake to the olive-coloured hills. Cross the dam retaining the lake to **Tirana Zoo**. Ask directions to the excellent **botanical gardens** just west of the zoo. If you're keen, you can hire a rowing boat and paddle on the lake.

About 5km south-east on Rruga Elbasanit is the **Martyrs' Cemetery** (Varrezat e Dëshmorëve), where some 900 partisans who died during WWII are buried. Large crowds once gathered here each year on 16 October, Enver Hoxha's birthday, since this is where he and other leading revolutionaries such as Gog Nushi, Qemal Stafa and Hysni Kapo were formerly interred. (In May 1992 Hoxha's lead coffin was dug up and reburied in a common grave in a public cemetery on the other side

of town.) The hilltop setting with a beautiful view over the city and mountains is subdued, and a great white figure of Mother Albania (1972) stands watch. Nearby, on the opposite side of the highway, is the **former palace of King Zog**, now a government guesthouse.

West of Tirana's centre on Rruga Kavajes is the Catholic **Cathedral of St Anthony**, which served as the Rinia Cinema from 1967 to 1990. Many foreign embassies are situated along Rruga Skënderbeg just beyond the cathedral. Since the rush of refugees into these in 1991, access for Albanians is restricted.

Organised Tours
World Travel on Mine Peza 2 can arrange individual or group tours around Albania, depending on demand and requirements.

Places to Stay
Private Rooms Staying in private rented apartments or with local families is the best budget accommodation in Tirana. The formerly cheap (and often dire) state-owned hotels have either closed or been renovated, with accordingly higher prices. Newer private hotels are similarly high priced.

Albania Travel & Tours, Rruga Durrësit 102 (weekdays 8 am to 7 pm), has private rooms at around 2500 lekë per person. It can also organise private rooms or hotels in Gjirokastra, Korça, Vlora and Durrës.

Skanderbeg Travel (☎/fax 23 946), Rruga Durrësit 5/11, a couple of blocks west of Albania Travel & Tours (weekdays 8.30 am to 1.30 pm and 4.30 to 7.30 pm), arranges private apartments with TV and fridge for between 4000 and 4500 lekë.

Hotels The 96 rooms at the state-run, six-storey *Hotel Arbëria* (☎ 60 813) on Bulevardi Dëshmorët e Kombit, to the north of Skënderbeg Square, cost 2500/3500 lekë for a single/double with bath. Check your room as some have broken windows and no running water, and the hotel is unheated in winter.

The *Hotel Klodiana* (☎ 27 403) has just a few private rooms but is OK. A single/double costs 3000/4000 lekë. It is just back from Rruga Myslym Shyri and shares the same phone number as the Europa International Hotel.

The ageing and somewhat old-fashioned

Hotel Dajti (☎ 33 326; fax 31 691) on Bulevardi Dëshmorët e Kombit was erected in the 1930s by the Italians. The 90 rooms with bath are US$55/65 for singles/doubles.

A pleasant private hotel is the *Europa International Hotel* (☎/fax 27 403), which has very modern singles/doubles for US$60/70. Look for the sign on Rruga Myslym Shyri. Just off Rruga Durrësit, at Rruga Mihal Duri 2/7, is the nifty *Hotel California* (☎ 32 228; fax 31 691). Clean rooms with mini-bar and TV cost US$55/65 for singles/doubles.

To the right of the Tirana International is the newer but smaller *Hotel Miniri* (☎ 30 930; fax 33 096) at Rruga e Dibres 3. Singles/doubles with phone and TV are US$60/100.

The high-rise *Tirana International* (☎ 34 185; fax 34 188) on Skënderbeg Square is now Italian-run. Rooms cost US$140/190 for well-appointed singles/doubles. The price includes breakfast.

Finally, the newest and best hotel in Tirana is the *Hotel Europapark* (☎ 35 035; fax 35 050) at Blvd Dëshmorët e Kombit 1, run by the Rogner group. Singles/doubles are a pricey US$200/250 per night.

Places to Eat

There is no shortage of small restaurants and snack bars on and around Skënderbeg Square and Blvd Dëshmorët e Kombit, and small, stylish bars have mushroomed everywhere. Here are some places that you might not easily stumble across.

You can enjoy tasty kebabs, salad and beer at the convenient and economical *Restorant Popullor*, close to Hotel Miniri on Rruga e Dibres.

Check out the *Bar Artisti* cafeteria at the Institute of Art if you want to have a coffee and snack and mingle with Tirana's arty set. If you fancy a cuppa and a sandwich – or even a pizza or nachos – call into *Qendra Stefan*, a friendly, no-smoking American-run place. Lunchtime specials are posted on a blackboard outside. It's near the fruit-and-vegetable market.

The *Berlusconi* bar and restaurant is a trendy Italian-influenced place hidden away behind the Palace of Culture. Pasta and pizza are the main fare and prices are very reasonable.

The *Ujvara* restaurant on the south side of the river near the southern bus station is another alternative spot for an evening meal. Ignore the apparent squalor of the neighbourhood; the restaurant and food is top-notch.

The *Piazza Restaurant* is a tastefully designed and well-appointed establishment just north of Skënderbeg Square. The food and service are excellent and prices, for what you get, are reasonable. The adjoining *Piano Bar* is a relaxing place to unwind with a pre-dinner drink.

Entertainment

As soon as you arrive, check the *Palace of Culture* on Skënderbeg Square for opera or ballet performances. Most events in Tirana are advertised on placards in front of this building. The ticket window opens at 5 pm and most performances begin at 7 pm.

The *Teatri i Kukallave*, beside the State Bank on Skënderbeg Square, presents puppet shows for children on Sunday at 10 and 11 am all year round. During the school year there are also morning shows on certain weekdays (ask when you get there).

Pop concerts and other musical events often take place in the *Qemal Stafa Stadium* next to the university. Look out for street banners bearing details of upcoming events.

The *London Bar* at Blvd Dëshmorët e Kombit 51 (near the Hotel Tirana International) is a mixed gay and straight bar.

Things to Buy

Tirana's public market, just north of the Sheshi Avni Rustemi roundabout several blocks east of the clock tower, is at its largest on Thursday and Sunday. A few shops here sell folkloric objects such as carved wooden trays, small boxes, wall hangings and bone necklaces.

The Philatelic Bureau (Filatelia), on Bulevardi Dëshmorët e Kombit, north-west of Hotel Tirana International, charges 40 times the face value of the stamps but they're still not too expensive by western standards and there is a good selection.

Getting There & Away

Air For information about routes and fares of flights to/from Rinas airport see the Getting There & Away section earlier in this chapter.

Many of the airline offices are on Rruga Durrësit, just off Skënderbeg Square. Here you'll find Ada Air, Adria Airways, Arbëria Airlines, Albanian Airlines, Croatia Airlines, Hemus Air and Malév Hungarian Airlines. Alitalia (☎ 30 023) has an office on Skënderbeg Square behind the National Museum of History and Swissair (☎ 32 011) is at Hotel Europapark. Olympic Airways (☎ 28 960), is in the Ve-Ve Business Centre on Deshmorët e Kombit behind the Tirana International Hotel.

Bus Both private and state-owned buses operate between Tirana and most towns. There's no one central bus station in Tirana and pick-up venues may change, so check for the latest departure points. Service to/from Durrës (38km, 40 lekë) is fairly frequent, leaving from the block adjacent to the train station.

Buses to Berat (122km), Elbasan (54km), Fier (113km), Gjirokastra (232km), Kakavija (263km), Korça (181km), Lushnja (83km), Pogradec (140km), Saranda (284km) and Vlora (147km) leave from southern bus station, on the west side of Selman Stërmasi Stadium. From about 6 am every day you can get buses to almost anywhere south and east from here: they leave when full throughout the day. As late as 5 pm you'll still find some to Berat, Elbasan, Fier and perhaps further.

Buses to Kruja (32km) leave from Rruga Mine Peza, at the beginning of the highway to Durrës.

North-bound buses to Lezha (69km), Shkodra (116km), Kukës (208km) and other places leave from a station out on the Durrës highway just beyond the Asllan Rusi Stadium. Buses to Shkodra leave throughout the day but those to Kukës leave at 4 and 5 am only.

Information on all bus services out of Tirana can be obtained by calling ☎ 26 818.

Train The train station is at the north end of Bulevardi Dëshmorët e Kombit. Seven trains a day go to Durrës, a one-hour journey (36km). Trains also depart for Ballsh (four hours, daily), Elbasan (four hours, three daily), Pogradec (seven hours, twice daily), Shkodra (3½ hours, twice daily), Fier (4¼ hours, daily) and Vlora (5½ hours, daily).

Getting Around

To/From the Airport The bus to Rinas airport leaves from in front of the Albtransport office, Rruga Durrësit (26km, 50 lekë; pay the driver). Buses to the airport leave at 6, 8 and 10 am, and 12.30 and 3.05 pm. Buses to Tirana from the airport leave at 2.30, 4 and 5.30 pm. A taxi to/from the airport should cost a flat US$20, 40 DM or 5000 drachmas – depending on what currency you have in your pocket.

Car & Motorcycle There are two guarded parking lots, both charging 300 lekë a night. One is on Rruga Myslym Shyri, around the corner from Hotel Dajti, and the other is behind the Hotel Tirana International.

World Travel, Mine Peza 2, rents out cars at 5500 lekë daily without a driver, 7500 lekë daily with a driver/guide. As you may expect, they feel more comfortable with their own employee behind the wheel.

Taxi Local taxis park on the south side of the roundabout at the market. These are much cheaper for excursions out into the countryside than the Mercedes taxis parked at Hotel Tirana International, but the drivers don't speak English so take along someone to bargain and act as interpreter.

AROUND TIRANA
Durrës
☎ 052

Unlike Tirana, Durrës (Durazzo in Italian) is an ancient city. In 627 BC the Greeks founded Epidamnos (Durrës) whose name the Romans changed to Dyrrhachium. It was the largest port on the eastern Adriatic and the start of the Via Egnatia (an extension of the Via Appia) to Constantinople. The famous Via Appia (Appian Way) to Rome began 150km southwest of Durrës at Brindisi, Italy.

Durrës changed hands frequently before being taken by the Turks in 1501, under whom the port dwindled into insignificance. A slow revival began in the 17th century and from 1914 to 1920 Durrës was the capital of Albania. Landings here by Mussolini's troops on 7 April 1939 met fierce though brief resistance and those who fell are regarded as the first martyrs in the War of National Liberation.

Today, Roman ruins and Byzantine fortifications embellish this major industrial city and commercial port, which lies 38km west of Tirana. Durrës is Albania's second-largest city, with 85,000 inhabitants. On a bay south-east of the city are long, sandy beaches where all the tourist hotels are concentrated. In 1991 the city saw desperate mobs attempting to escape by ship to Italy and there's now a heavy Italian military presence in the area. Car ferries from Italy dock on the east side of the port. The entry/exit point is even further east. Look for road signs to the ferry quay when departing.

Information The National Bank near the port (open weekdays from 8 to 11 am) changes travellers cheques for a commission of 100 lekë per cheque, as does the Banka e Kursimeve up the street, half-way between the port and the large mosque (open Monday to Saturday from 9 am to 2 pm). Unofficial currency exchange is carried out on the street around the main post office in town.

The post office and phone centre are located one block west of the train and bus stations. Look for the big Telekom sign.

Things to See A good place to begin your visit to Durrës is the **Archaeological Museum** (open 9 am to 1 pm, closed Monday, 100 lekë admission), which faces the waterfront promenade near the port. Its two rooms are small but each object here is unique and there's a large sculpture garden outside. Behind the museum are the 6th-century Byzantine **city walls**, built after the Visigoth invasion of 481 and supplemented by round Venetian towers in the 14th century.

The impressive **Roman amphitheatre**, built between the 1st and 2nd centuries AD, is on the hillside just inside the walls. Much of the amphitheatre has now been excavated and you can see a small built-in 10th-century Byzantine church decorated with wall mosaics. Follow the road just inside the walls down towards the port and you'll find the **Sultan Fatih Mosque** (1502) and the **Moisiut Ekspozita e Kulturës Popullore**, with ethnographic displays housed in the former home of actor Alexander Moisiu (1879-1935). It's open in the morning only.

The former **palace of King Ahmet Zog** is on the hill top west of the amphitheatre. The soldiers guarding the palace will expect you to buy a ticket from them to wander around. In front of the palace is a statue of Skënderbeg and huge radar disks set up by the Italian army. The next hill beyond bears a **lighthouse** which affords a splendid view of Albanian coastal defences, Durrës and the entire coast.

As you're exploring the centre of the city, stop to see the **Roman baths** directly behind Aleksandër Moisiu Theatre, on the central square. The large **mosque** on the square was erected with Egyptian aid in 1993, to replace one destroyed during the 1979 earthquake. At the western end of Rruga Dëshmorevë is the **Martyrs' Cemetery**, guarded by half-a-dozen decrepit bunkers.

Places to Stay Durrës offers cheap private rooms and a few hotels.

In Town You may be able to scrounge a room at the rather run-down four-storey *Hotel Durrësi*, next to the main post office in town. Expect to pay about 1000 lekë. The amenities are pretty basic.

The Romeo Harizi family, left along the waterfront from the tower, a block beyond the Archaeological Museum, rents out private rooms very cheaply. There's a sign outside in English.

There is not much choice these days in Durrës town. The best hotel is *Hotel Pameba* (☎/fax 24 149), about 400m up the hill from the port entrance. Singles/doubles with TV are US$50/70, including breakfast.

At the Beach One traveller reported getting a room in a private *villa* near the beach just south-east of Hotel Adriatik for 1500 lekë, so it pays to look around.

The main tourist hotel used to be the Stalin-era *Adriatik* (☎ 23 612 or 23 001), on the sandy beach 5km south-east of Durrës. The 60 rooms in this stark, neo-classical building prior to the troubles were US$43/46 for a single/double, with bath and breakfast included. It closed down in mid-1997 and may or may not have reopened by the time you read this.

Nearby are the *Durrësi*, *Apollonia*, *Butrinti* and *Kruja* hotels, all in some kind

ALBANIA

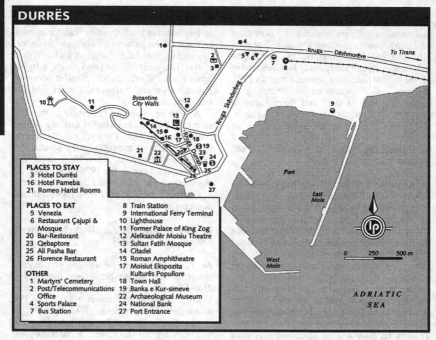

DURRËS

PLACES TO STAY
3 Hotel Durrësi
16 Hotel Pameba
21 Romeo Harizi Rooms

PLACES TO EAT
5 Venezia
6 Restaurant Çajupi & Mosque
20 Bar-Restorant
23 Qebaptore
25 Ali Pasha Bar
26 Florence Restaurant

OTHER
1 Martyrs' Cemetery
2 Post/Telecommunications Office
4 Sports Palace
7 Bus Station
8 Train Station
9 International Ferry Terminal
10 Lighthouse
11 Former Palace of King Zog
12 Alelksandër Moisiu Theatre
13 Sultan Fatih Mosque
14 Citadel
15 Roman Amphitheatre
17 Moisiut Ekspozita Kulturës Popullore
18 Town Hall
19 Banka e Kur-simeve
22 Archaeological Museum
24 National Bank
27 Port Entrance

Rruga – Dëshmorëve
To Tirana

Byzantine City Walls
Rruga Skënderbeg

Port
East Mole
West Mole

ADRIATIC SEA

0   250   500 m

of renovation or privatisation process. Prices, once the work is complete, can be expected to be higher than those of the Adriatik.

Places to Eat There's a modern restaurant/bar called *Florence* opposite the port entrance.

On Rruga Durrah, the main street, is a fairly modern and clean nameless kebab place. Look for the *Qebaptore* sign outside. Almost opposite is another decent restaurant simply called *Bar-Restorant*. Look out for the Löwenbräu sign. The *Hotel Pameba* also has a small restaurant.

Restorant Çajupi, west across the square from the train station, is a private restaurant serving rich beef soup. Just behind the Çajupi is the *Venezia*, with good coffee and ice cream. Unfortunately neither place has a menu so get the staff to write down the prices before ordering.

Entertainment Visit the *Aleksandër*

Moisiu Theatre in the centre of Durrës and the *Sports Palace* on Rruga Dëshmorevë to see if anything is on.

There are any number of new bars and cafeterias opening up on and around the main street. There is a disco and even a poker machines joint. Try the pleasant outdoor *Ali Pasha* bar, very close to the port entrance, for a relaxing drink.

Getting There & Away Albania's 720km railway network centres on Durrës. There are seven trains a day to Tirana (1½ hours), two to Shkodra, one to Elbasan, two to Pogradec, one to Vlora and one to Ballsh. The station is beside the Tirana Highway, conveniently close to central Durrës. Tickets are sold at the 'Biletaria Trenit' office below the apartment building nearest the station or at a similar office below the next building. Buses to Tirana and elsewhere leave from in front of the train station and service is fairly frequent.

Ferry Agjencia Detare Shteterore per Adriatica at the entrance to the port sells tickets for car ferries to Trieste, Ancona and Bari. Shpresa Transeuropa (☎ 22 423) in a kiosk nearby handles the ferries between Durrës and a number of destinations.

The ticket office of the fast catamaran *La Vikinga* (☎ 22 555) from Durrës to Bari is on Rruga Durrah, the street from the port to the mosque.

Some of the agencies require payment in Italian lira which you must purchase on the black market. If you have a valid ISIC student card always try for a student discount.

Ferries arrive in Durrës several times a week from Bari, Otranto, Ancona and Trieste in Italy. If boarding a ferry at Durrës allow plenty of time, as it can be a long, complicated process, especially at night.

Getting Around There's a bus service on the main highway from the Adriatik Hotel into Durrës. For the return journey, look for the bus near the main post office in Durrës. Pay the conductor.

Northern Albania

A visit to northern Albania usually takes in only the coastal strip, but a journey into the interior is well worthwhile for the marvellous scenery. Between Puka and Kukës the road winds through 60km of spectacular mountains.

Shkodra, the old Gheg capital near the lake of the same name, is a pleasant introduction to Albania for those arriving from Montenegro. South of here is Lezha and Skënderbeg's tomb. Kruja is 6.5km off the main road but is often visited for its crucial historical importance and striking location 608m up on the side of a mountain.

Other than to Kruja, visits to northern Albania should perhaps be avoided until the security situation has stabilised since there have been reports, up to mid-1998, of sporadic banditry and violence.

KRUJA
☎ 0532

In the 12th century, Kruja was the capital of the Principality of Arberit, but this hilltop town attained its greatest fame between 1443 and 1468 when national hero George Kastrioti (1405-68), also known as Skënderbeg, made Kruja his seat.

At a young age, Kastrioti, son of an Albanian prince, was handed over as a hostage to the Turks, who converted him to Islam and gave him a military education at Edirne. There he became known as Iskënder (after Alexander the Great) and Sultan Murat II promoted him to the rank of bey (governor), thus the name Skënderbeg.

In 1443 the Turks suffered a defeat at the hands of the Hungarians at Niš, giving the nationally minded Skënderbeg the opportunity he had been waiting for to abandon Islam and the Ottoman army and rally his fellow Albanians against the Turks. Among the 13 Turkish invasions he subsequently repulsed was that led by Murat II himself in 1450. Pope Calixtus III named Skënderbeg 'captain general of the Holy See' and Venice formed an alliance with him. The Turks besieged Kruja four times. Though beaten back in 1450, 1466 and 1467, they took control of Kruja in 1478 (after Skënderbeg's death) and Albanian resistance was suppressed.

Things to See & Do
Set below towering mountains, the **citadel** that Skënderbeg defended still stands on an abrupt ridge above the modern town. In 1982 an excellent **historical museum** (open from 9 am to 1 pm and 3 to 6 pm, Thursday 9 am to 1 pm, closed Monday, admission 100 lekë) opened in the citadel. The saga of the Albanian struggle against the Ottoman empire is richly told with models, maps and statuary. The museum was designed by Pranvera Hoxha, Enver's daughter, who attempted to portray Hoxha and Skënderbeg as parallel champions of Albanian independence. Like Hoxha, Skënderbeg was something of a social reformer. He abolished the blood vendetta (*gjakmarrje*) but the feuds began afresh soon after his death.

In an old house opposite the main citadel museum is an **ethnographical museum** (open from 9 am to 3 pm, Thursday 9 am to 1 pm and 3 to 6 pm, closed Wednesday).

Hidden in the lower part of the citadel are the Teqja e Dollmës or **Bektashi Tekke** (1773), place of worship of a mystical Islamic sect, and the 16th-century **Turkish baths** (*hammam*), which are just below the tekke.

Between the citadel and Hotel Skënderbeu is Kruja's 18th-century **Turkish bazar**, which was later destroyed but has now been fully restored and made into a workplace for local artisans and craftspeople.

It's possible to climb to the top of the mountain above Kruja in an hour or so and it's even possible to hike back to Tirana along a path that begins near the citadel entrance.

Places to Stay & Eat

The four-storey *Hotel Skënderbeu* (☎ 23 29) is next to the equestrian statue of Skënderbeg near the terminus of the buses from Tirana. The 33 rooms are US$20 for a single/double without bath and US$25 with bath. A speciality of the hotel restaurant is a mixed plate with skallop (beef in sauce), kanellane (mince wrapped in pastry) and qofte (a long, mince patty).

The *Pestiqe* restaurant in the main street of the artisans' quarter is very good value for money and does ample meals in comfortable traditional surroundings, with chairs covered in woollen rugs.

The *Karakteristik* restaurant, just up the hill from the museum in the citadel, is also very cosy, but a little more expensive.

Getting There & Away

It's possible to visit Kruja by local bus as a day trip from Tirana (32km). If there's no direct bus to Kruja, get one to Fush-Kruja where you'll find several going to Kruja; for example, the Laç bus stops at Fush-Kruja. In the afternoon it's much easier to get back to Tirana from Kruja than vice versa.

LEZHA

☎ 10 (operator)

It was at Lezha (Alessio) in March 1444 that Skënderbeg succeeded in convincing the Albanian feudal lords to unite in a League of Lezha to resist the Turks. Skënderbeg died of fever here in 1468 and today his tomb may be visited among the ruins of the Franciscan **Church of St Nicholas**. Reproductions of his helmet and sword grace the gravestone and along the walls are 25 shields bearing the names and dates of battles he fought against the Turks.

Near the tomb, beside the grey apartment blocks, is the **Ethnographical Museum**, and on the hill top above is the medieval **Lezha Citadel**. Much of old Lezha was destroyed by an earthquake on 15 April 1979.

Places to Stay & Eat

The only real option is the state-run but still cosy *Hotel Gjuetisë*, commonly known as the Hunting Lodge – some 5km off the main road at Ishull i Lezhës, a lagoon popular for bird-watching. Doubles here should go for around US$50 including breakfast. There is also a reasonable, folksy-decorated restaurant. The only disadvantage is the surly, state-appointed staff who seem to treat guests as annoyances.

Getting There & Away

There's a bus from Tirana to Lezha.

SHKODRA

☎ 0224

Shkodra (also Shkodër and, in Italian, Scutari), the traditional centre of the Gheg cultural region, is one of the oldest cities in Europe. In 500 BC an Illyrian fortress already guarded the strategic crossing just west of the city where the Buna and Drin rivers meet and all traffic moving up the coast from Greece to Montenegro must pass. These rivers drain two of the Balkans' largest lakes: Shkodra, just north-west of the city, and Ohrid, far up the Drin River, beyond several massive hydroelectric dams. The route inland to Kosova also begins in Shkodra. North of Shkodra, line after line of cement bunkers point the way to the Han i Hotit border crossing into Montenegro (33km). Tirana is 116km south.

Queen Teuta's Illyrian kingdom was centred here in the 3rd century BC. Despite wars with Rome in 228 and 219 BC, Shkodra was not taken by the Romans until 168 BC. Later the region passed to Byzantium before becoming the capital of the feudal realm of the Balshas in 1350. In 1396 the Venetians occupied Shkodra's Rozafa Fortress, which they held against Suleiman Pasha in 1473 but lost to Mehmet Pasha in 1479. The Turks lost 14,000 men in the first siege and 30,000 in the second.

As the Ottoman empire declined in the late 18th century, Shkodra became the centre of a semi-independent pashalik, which led to a blossoming of commerce and crafts. In 1913, Montenegro attempted to annex Shkodra (it succeeded in taking Ulcinj, but this was not recognised by the international community and the town changed hands often during WWI. Badly damaged by the 1979 earthquake, Shkodra was subsequently repaired and now, with a population of 81,000, is Albania's fourth-largest city.

Even by mid-1998 Shkodra was considered still risky for individual travellers to visit, so it might be better to give the area a miss until the situation clarifies.

Orientation & Information

From the Migjenit Theatre on the Five Heroes Roundabout, Rruga Marin Barleti (formerly Bulevardi Stalin) runs south-east past Hotel Rozafa and the post office. The post office faces north-east up Bulevardi 13 Dhjetori, a delightful old street lit by antique lamps in the evening and lined with harmonious buildings, many of which are now shops selling Albanian handicrafts. The train station is at the far south-east end of Rruga Marin Barleti, 1.5km from the centre of town, whereas buses leave from around Migjenit Theatre.

Money Two adjacent banks on Bulevardi 13 Dhjetori change travellers cheques for 1% commission (open weekdays 7 am to 1 pm). Otherwise look for moneychangers along the street between these banks and the post office.

Post & Communications The post office on Rruga Marin Barleti, across the square from the Rozafa Hotel, is open Monday to Saturday from 7 am to 2 pm, Sunday 8 am to noon. The telephone centre here operates around the clock.

Things to See

Shkodra's skyline is dominated by the brand new and impressive **Sheik Zamil Abdullah Al-Zamil mosque**, completed in 1995. It stands next to the Muzeo Popullor on the corner of Rruga Marin Barleti and Bulevardi 13 Dhjetori. Its pastel façade and silver domes are very striking.

The **Muzeu Popullor**, in the eclectic

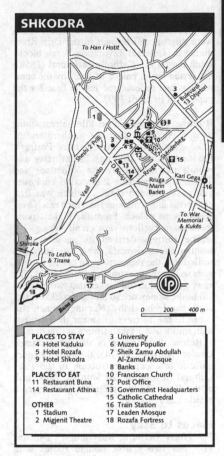

palace (1860) of an English aristocrat opposite Hotel Rozafa, contains recent paintings and historic photos upstairs, and an excellent archaeological collection downstairs.

Shkodra was the most influential Catholic city of Albania, with a large cathedral and Jesuit and Franciscan monasteries, seminaries and religious libraries. From 1967 to 1990 the **Franciscan Church** on Rruga Ndre Mjeda off Bulevardi 13 Dhjetori was used as an auditorium but now it's a church again. Just inside is a photo exhibit of Shkodra priests who died in communist prisons. Note especially the

---

SHKODRA

To Han i Hotit

To War Memorial & Kukës

To Shiroka

To Lezha & Tirana

Buna R.

0   200   400 m

PLACES TO STAY	3 University
4 Hotel Kaduku	6 Muzeu Popullor
5 Hotel Rozafa	7 Sheik Zamu Abdullah
9 Hotel Shkodra	Al-Zamul Mosque
	8 Banks
PLACES TO EAT	10 Franciscan Church
11 Restaurant Buna	12 Post Office
14 Restaurant Athina	13 Government Headquarters
	15 Catholic Cathedral
OTHER	16 Train Station
1 Stadium	17 Leaden Mosque
2 Migjenit Theatre	18 Rozafa Fortress

photos of Catholic poet Gjergj Fishta (1871-1940), formerly buried here but whose bones were dug up and thrown in the Drin River during the Cultural Revolution. A few blocks south-east is the **Catholic cathedral** (1858), converted into a palace of sport by the communists and rededicated just in time for the papal visit in April 1993.

Rozafa Fortress Two kilometres south-west of Shkodra, near the southern end of Lake Shkodra, is the Rozafa Fortress, founded by the Illyrians in antiquity and rebuilt much later by the Venetians and Turks. Upon entering the second enclosure you pass a ruined church (which was first converted into a mosque) and then reach a restored stone palace. From the highest point there's a marvellous view on all sides.

The fortress derived its name from a woman named Rozafa, who was allegedly walled into the ramparts as an offering to the gods so that the construction would stand. The story goes that Rozafa asked that two holes be left in the stonework so that she could continue to suckle her baby. Nursing women still come to the fortress to smear their breasts with milky water taken from a spring here.

Below the fortress is the many-domed **Leaden Mosque** (1774), the only Shkodra mosque to escape destruction in the 1967 Cultural Revolution. At **Shiroka**, 7km north of the Buna Bridge, there's a pleasant café beside Lake Shkodra.

Places to Stay

The *Hotel Shkodra*, Bulevardi 13 Dhjetori 114, has two sparse double rooms with shared bath at 500 lekë per person and three five-bed dormitories at 500 lekë per person. The old people who run this place in their old home are very friendly.

The ramshackle *Hotel Kaduku* (☎ 22 16) can be hard to find but it's adequate and clean enough. It's right next to the Hotel Rozafa; look for the 'Dentist' sign. The owner Hasan Kaduku charges US$15 per person.

The city's main tourist hotel, where all tourists were required to stay until 1991, is the *Hotel Rozafa* (☎ 27 67), a nine-storey building on the Five Heroes Roundabout. Rooms are US$20/40 for singles/doubles with bath, breakfast included.

Places to Eat

Restaurant Buna, close to the big mosque, is an OK kind of choice and a little more convenient to reach if you don't feel like walking.

Shkodra's best restaurant is the *Restaurant Athina*, a little way from the older part of town. The food is nominally Greek and is reasonably good value. The toilet has an electronic soap dispenser!

Around sunset half the population of Shkodra go for a stroll along the lakeside promenade towards the Buna Bridge and there are several small restaurants where you can have fried fish, tomato salad and beer while observing the passing parade.

Getting There & Away

Buses to Tirana (frequent, 116km, 110 lekë) and Durrës (infrequent, 124km, 100 lekë) depart from near Migjenit Theatre, most reliably around 7 am and also at 1 pm.

Two direct daily trains from Shkodra to Tirana depart at 5 am and 1.15 pm (3½ hours, 100 lekë). These trains don't pass Durrës. The train station is on the south-east side of town. Bus travel is more convenient, though perhaps less picturesque.

KUKËS

☎ 10 (operator)

Kukës has perhaps the most beautiful location of any town in Albania, set high above Lake Fierza below the bald summit of Mt Gjalica (2486m). Old Kukës formerly stood at the junction of two important rivers, the White Drin from Kosova and the Black Drin from Lake Ohrid, but from 1962 the town was moved to its present location when it was decided that the 72-sq-km reservoir of the 'Light of the Party' hydroelectric dam would cover the old site. It's a pleasant place to get in tune with Albania if you've just arrived from Kosova, and a good stop on your way around the country.

Information

Cash changes hands among the trees at the market, not far from the bus stop.

Places to Stay & Eat

Cheapest is the *Hotel Gjalica*, an unmarked

three-storey building on the nameless main street in the centre of town, opposite a place with the large yellow sign 'Fruta Perime'. A simple but adequate room with washbasin and lumpy, smelly bed will be US$16 per person.

For a room with private bath the price jumps to 2000 lekë per person at the four-storey *Hotel Drini* overlooking the lake on the same street as the post office.

One of Albania's finest hotels is the *Hotel Turizmi* (☎ 452), a five-storey cubist edifice on a peninsula jutting out into the lake, a five-minute walk from town. Rooms here are 3000 lekë per person – better value than the Drini.

All three hotels have restaurants but forget the wretched one at the Gjalica. The terrace at the Turizmi is great for a drink and their restaurant is the best in town. A few basic places near the market serve lunch.

Getting There & Away

Minibuses to Kukës from Tirana leave from the minibus stand near the guarded parking lot. The fare is 500 lekë per person and the trip takes 6½ hours with meal stops. Look for the KU license plates or ask.

Several buses to Tirana (208km, 300 lekë) leave Kukës around 6 am. Getting to Shkodra (129km, 200 lekë) is problematic; if you can't find a direct bus it's best to take the Tirana bus to Puka (60km) and look for an onward bus from there.

Occasional buses run the 17km from Kukës to the Yugoslav border at Morina. The Albanian and Yugoslav border posts are adjacent but have been closed on occasion since March 1997 and crossing may be problematic if not impossible.

Southern Albania

The south of the country is rich in historical and natural beauty. Apollonia and Butrint are renowned classical ruins, while Berat and Gjirokastra are museum towns and strongholds of Tosk tradition. Korça is the cultural capital of the south, whereas Pogradec and Saranda, on Lake Ohrid and the Ionian Sea respectively, are undeveloped resort towns.

South-east of the vast, agricultural Myzaqeja plain, the land becomes extremely mountainous, with lovely valleys such as those of the Osum and Drino rivers, where Berat and Gjirokastra are situated. The 124km of Ionian coast north from Saranda to Vlora are stunning, with 2000m mountains falling directly to the sea and not a hotel in sight.

The 115km road from Tepelena to Korça is one of the most scenic in Albania. About 60km from Tepelena it takes a sharp turn north at a small village and from here to Erseka there are many switchbacks. There are through buses from Korça to Gjirokastra and Saranda in the early morning. Because of the relatively light traffic this is one road that is in reasonable shape, though winter driving is not advised. You may be stopped by curious police on this section, probably more out of boredom than anything else. Bring your own food supplies since the towns along the way are not used to travellers.

FIER & APOLLONIA
☎ 0642

Fier is a large town by the Gjanica River at a junction of road and rail routes, 89km south of Durrës. Albania's oil industry is centred at Fier, with a fertiliser plant, an oil refinery and a thermal power plant fuelled by natural gas. Fier has a pleasant riverside promenade.

Things to See

Visitors first reach Fier's imposing 13th-century Orthodox **Monastery of St Mary**. The icons in the church, the capitals in the narthex and the Byzantine murals in the adjacent refectory are outstanding. The monastery now houses an extremely rich **archaeological museum** (admission 100 lekë) with a large collection of ceramics and statuary from the ruins of Apollonia. Near the post office is a **historical museum** with well-presented exhibits covering the district's long history.

By far the most interesting sight in the vicinity is the ruins of ancient **Apollonia** (Pojan), 12km west of Fier, set on a hill top surrounded by impressive bunkers. Apollonia was founded by Corinthian Greeks in 588 BC and quickly grew into an important city-state, minting its own currency. Under the Romans the city became a great cultural centre with a famous school of philosophy. Julius Caesar rewarded Apollonia with the title 'free city' for supporting him against Pompey the Great during a civil war in the 1st century BC and sent his nephew Octavius, the future Emperor Augustus, to complete his studies there. After a series of military disasters, the population moved south to present-day Vlora (the ancient Avlon), and by the 5th century only a small village with its own bishop remained at Apollonia.

Only a small part of ancient Apollonia has so far been uncovered. The first ruin to catch the eye is the roughly restored 2nd-century **bouleuterion**, or Hall of the Agonothetes. In front of it is the 2nd-century **odeon** (a small theatre). To the west of this is a long, 3rd-century BC **portico** with niches that once contained statues.

Apollonia's **defensive walls** are nearby. The lower portion of these massive walls, which are 4km long and up to 6.5m high, date back to the 4th century BC.

Places to Stay & Eat

The *Hotel Apollonia* (☎ 21 11), was once a somewhat run-down four-storey hotel in the main square offering basic singles/doubles for 1600 lekë. This place may well have bitten the dust after the disturbances. The six-storey *Hotel Fieri* (☎ 23 94), by the river, has 50 rooms, with prices ranging from US$20/25 to US$50/55 for singles/doubles, depending on the facilities provided.

Hotel Fieri has a clean restaurant. The *Restorant Kosova* on the main square near Hotel Fieri is basic but OK. If you want a pizza or a hamburger, try the *Llapi*, also on the main square.

Getting There & Away

All buses between Tirana and Vlora or Gjirokastra pass this way and other buses run from Fier to Berat (42km). There's also a daily train to/from Tirana (4¼ hours).

Getting Around

There are village buses from Fier direct to Apollonia in the morning. You can also get there on the Seman bus but you'll have to walk 4km from the junction to the ruins. In Fier the Seman bus leaves from a place called Zogu i Zi near the Historical Museum, or from the train station.

VLORA
☎ 063

Vlora (Vlorë), the main port of southern Albania, sits on lovely Vlora Bay just across an 80km strait from Otranto, Italy. Inexpensive ferries run between these towns three times a week, making Vlora a useful gateway to/from southern Italy. This is probably the only real reason to come here as Vlora's own attractions don't warrant a special trip.

Money

Moneychangers hang around the corner between Hotel Sazani and the post office. The Banka e Shtetit Shqiptar is a long block away, if you have travellers cheques and are there on a weekday morning.

Things to See & Do

The **archaeological museum** is across the street from Hotel Sazani, and a house museum dedicated to the Laberia Patriotic Club (1908) is nearby.

In the park behind Hotel Sazani is a large stone **monument** commemorating the proclamation of an independent Albania at Vlora in 1912. A block south of this monument is the well-preserved **Murad Mosque** (1542). In 1480 and 1536 the Turks used Vlora as a base for unsuccessful invasions of Italy.

A **war cemetery** on the hillside directly opposite the 1912 monument overlooks the town and from the cemetery a road winds around to the Liria Café, on a hill top with a sweeping view of the entire vicinity – a good place for a drink at sunset. A stone stairway descends directly back to town from the café.

You can take a bus from the 1912 monument down Vlora's main street to the south end of the **city beach** every half-hour.

Places to Stay & Eat

Accommodation choices in Vlora are limited. The very run-down three-storey *Hotel Sazani* (☎ 23 548), near the post office and market in the centre of town, will start off asking 1000 lekë per person for a basic room with shared bath, but try bargaining. The buffet at the Sazani serves reasonable meals (with beer).

Hotel Meeting on Rruga Jonaq Kilica, opposite the Halim Dhelo school, has been recommended by one traveller who was charged 1200 lekë for a double room without bath.

The best option is the *Kompleksi Turistik VEFA* (☎ 24 179), on the beach about 8km south of Vlora. This modern complex provides motel-style rooms and has a modern restaurant and guarded parking. Prices are US$30 per person including breakfast.

There are a number of very pleasant restaurants in and around the central area near Hotel Sazani, as well as any number of beachside restaurants on the south side of town.

Getting There & Away
There are daily trains to Tirana (5½ hours) and Durrës but buses are more frequent and convenient. Unfortunately, no bus travels the full length of the spectacular 124km Riviera of Flowers – you can only get as far as Himara, from where you will need to take a taxi. The early morning bus to Saranda takes a roundabout 190km route through Fier, Tepelena and Gjirokastra.

If you're interested in taking the Linee Lauro ferry to Otranto, Italy (three times a week, 100km, US$45), pick up tickets beforehand at Albania Travel & Tours in Tirana. The Otranto agent is listed in the introductory Getting There & Away section earlier this chapter. This is probably the cheapest way to cross the Adriatic.

SARANDA
☎ 10 (operator)
Saranda (Sarandë) is an animated town on the Gulf of Saranda, between the mountains and the Ionian Sea, 61km south-west of Gjirokastra. An early Christian monastery dedicated to 40 saints (Santi Quaranta) gave Saranda its name. This southernmost harbour of Albania was once the ancient port of Onchesmos. Saranda's pebble beach is nothing special although the setting of the town is quite appealing. Today, Saranda's main attractions are its sunny climate and the nearby ruins of Butrint. It is also a very convenient entry and exit point for travellers arriving in Albania via Corfu in Greece.

Orientation & Information
Saranda is spread out around a bay. Most tourist accommodation and eating places are on the south side of the bay. The main bus station is right in the centre of town, about 200m back from the waterfront. Taxis congregate on the main square in front of the town hall, which is 200m south of the bus station. The ferry terminal is at the north end of the bay.

Money There are two banks on the main street, but the simplest and best way to change money is to use the money changers behind the town hall on the main square.

Post & Communications The most efficient way to call home from Saranda is to use the informal cellular phone entrepreneurs who congregate around the little boat harbour. A quick and easy-to-make call to the USA or Australia will cost you 300 lekë a minute. Calls are routed via Greece.

Things to See
Saranda's palm-fringed waterfront promenade is attractive and is gradually livening up, with new restaurants and bars opening every month. In the centre of town are some ancient ruins with a large mosaic covered with sand. Ask around town if you are interested in seeing the recently discovered **catacombs** of the Church of the Forty Saints.

The **Blue Eye spring**, 15km east of Saranda, to the left off the Gjirokastra road and before the ascent over the pass to the Drino valley, is definitely worth seeing. Its iridescent blue water gushes from the depths of the earth and feeds the Bistrica River. French divers have descended to 70m, but the spring's actual depth is still unknown.

Places to Stay & Eat
The *Halyl Hyseni* hotel (really just private rooms) on Rruga Ade Sheme has very comfortable singles/doubles for 4000/4500 lekë, with private bathroom and TV. It is about 150m inland from the waterfront. The rooms suffer from some street noise.

The rooms of *Panajot Qyro* (☎ 25 64), also on Rruga Adem Sheme, are basic but clean and have a modern communal bathroom. Single/double rates are 500/1000 lekë. Look for the blue railings of the electricity sub-station. The rooms are right opposite.

About 500m south of Hotel Butrinti is the

attractively sited *Hotel Delfini,* with rooms overlooking the water. Rates are 3500 lekë per room. The Delfini also has a very pleasant restaurant. Just 100m north of the Hotel Butrinti is the attractive but pricey *Kaoni Villa.* Single/double rates here are 4500/6000 lekë for spacious rooms with shared bathroom. Look for the big green gates.

The seven-storey, state-run *Hotel Butrinti* (☎ 417), overlooking the harbour just south of town, has singles/doubles for 3000/4500 lekë. Like most state-run hotels, the place is run-down and not all that appealing.

The *Paradise Restaurant* close to Hotel Butrinti has excellent food and the service is top notch. The *Three Roses* restaurant in the middle of Saranda is another good place to eat. It is set back from the waterfront on the 2nd floor of a big building. Look for the prominent sign.

Getting There & Away

Buses to Saranda from both Tirana and Vlora follow an interior route via Gjirokastra; unfortunately, no buses connect Saranda with Himara, north along the coast. A taxi to Himara should cost about 3000 lekë one way or 4000 lekë return. From Himara there is a daily bus to Vlora. Several buses to Gjirokastra (62km) and Tirana (289km) leave Saranda in the morning.

Three daily passenger ferries cross between Corfu and Saranda. One of the ferries takes up to five cars. The *Harikla* leaves Saranda at 10 am; the *Oleg Volvaç* goes at 1 pm; the car-carrying *Kamelia* leaves at 2 pm. The crossing takes 60 to 90 minutes. One-way fares cost 1600 lekë. Taking a car costs 4000 lekë. Check these times before making plans since schedules may have changed since the disturbances.

BUTRINT

The ancient ruins of Butrint, 18km south of Saranda, are surprisingly extensive and interesting. Virgil claimed that the Trojans founded Buthroton (Butrint), but no evidence of this has been found. Although the site had been inhabited long before, Greeks from Corfu settled on the hill in Butrint in the 6th century BC. Within a century Butrint had become a fortified trading city with an acrop-

olis. The lower town began to develop in the 3rd century BC and many large stone buildings existed when the Romans took over in 167 BC. Butrint's prosperity continued throughout the Roman period and the Byzantines made it an ecclesiastical centre. Then the city declined; it was almost abandoned when Italian archaeologists arrived in 1927 and began carting off any relics of value to Italy until WWII interrupted their work. In recent years the Italian government has returned some important Butrint sculptures to Albania. These are now in Tirana's National Museum of History.

There are two buses daily to Butrint, leaving Saranda at 6.30 am and noon.

Things to See

The site (open daily 7 am to 2 pm, 200 lekë, but check first) lies by a channel connecting salty Lake Butrint to the sea. A triangular **fortress** erected by warlord Ali Pasha Tepelena in the early 19th century watches over the ramshackle vehicular ferry that crosses the narrow channel.

In the forest below the acropolis is Butrint's 3rd-century BC **Greek theatre**, which was also in use during the Roman period. Nearby are the small **public baths**, which have geometrical mosaics. Deeper in the forest is a wall covered with crisp Greek inscriptions, and a 6th-century palaeo-Christian **baptistry** decorated with colourful mosaics of animals and birds. The mosaics are covered by protective sand. Beyond a 6th-century basilica stands a massive **Cyclopean wall** dating from the 4th century BC. Over one gate is a splendid relief of a lion killing a bull, symbolic of a protective force vanquishing assailants.

In a crenellated brick building on top of the acropolis is a **museum** (if it is open) full of statuary from the site. Reports suggest that the contents of the museum may have been looted in the civil disturbances of 1997.

GJIROKASTRA
☎ 0726

This strikingly picturesque museum town, midway between Fier and Ioannina, is like an Albanian eagle perched on the mountainside with a mighty citadel for its head. The fortress surveys the Drino Valley above the three and four-storey tower houses clinging to the slopes. Both buildings and streets are made of the same white-and-black stone. For defence purposes during blood feuds, these unique stone-roofed houses (*kulla*) had no windows on the ground floor, which was used for storage, and the living quarters above were reached by an exterior stairway.

The town's Greek name, Argyrokastro, is said to refer to a Princess Argyro, who chose to throw herself from a tower rather than fall into the hands of enemies, though it's more likely to be derived from the Illyrian Argyres tribe which inhabited these parts.

Gjirokastra was well established by the 13th century, but the arrival of the Turks in 1417 brought on a decline. By the 17th century Gjirokastra was thriving again with a flourishing bazar where embroidery, felt, silk and the still-famous white cheese were traded. Ali Pasha Tepelena took the town in the early 19th century and strengthened the citadel. Today all new buildings must conform to a historical preservation plan.

Gjirokastra really took the brunt of the 1997 troubles and many building were smashed and looted. Things were getting better at last reports.

Things to See

Above the **Bazar Mosque** (1757) in the centre of town is the **Mëmëdheu ABC Monument**, commemorating the renaissance of Albanian education around the turn of the century. The monument, which you may have to ask directions to find, affords an excellent view of the town.

Dominating the town is the 14th-century **citadel**, now a Museum of Armaments (8 am to noon and 4 to 7 pm, closed Monday and Tuesday, 200 lekë), with a collection of old cannons and guns and a two-seater US reconnaissance plane that made a forced landing near Berat in 1957. During the 1920s the fortress was converted into a prison and the Nazis made full use of it during their stay in 1943-44. Definitely visit the prison: the water torture cells are particularly grim.

A National Folk Festival used to be held every five years in the open-air theatre beside the citadel but the last one was in 1988 and

now the festival rotates round various cities in the country.

Enver Hoxha was born in 1908 in his family home, among the narrow cobbled streets of the Palorto quarter, up Rruga Bashkim Kokona beyond the Gjimnazi Asim Zeneli. The original house burned down in 1916, but the building was reconstructed in 1966 as a Museum of the National Liberation War and now houses the **Ethnographic Museum** (100 lekë).

The 17th-century **Turkish baths** are below the Çajupi Hotel in the lower town, near the polyclinic. The remnants of the **Mecate Mosque** are nearby. Gjirokastra has a lively Sunday market. The town was severely effected by the civil disturbances of 1997 and basic facilities may still be struggling to recover.

Places to Stay & Eat

Two cheap hotels are always worth a try. The *Argjiro Hotel* is right next to the Çajupi. A very basic single/double costs 700/1400 lekë with shared, smelly toilets. Across the street is the *Hotel Sapoti* with similarly basic singles/doubles for 600/1200 lekë.

The *Çajupi Hotel* (☎ 23 26) is another run-down former state enterprise. It is located prominently on the main taxi square, just before the old town. Singles/doubles with bath cost 2500/3500 lekë, but the hotel may have been closed because of the civil disturbances.

By far the most accommodating place to stay is the rooms of *Haxhi Kotoni*. Very cosy singles/doubles cost 2000/3000 lekë, including breakfast. The 'Bing Crosby' suite is a sight to behold. To reach the rooms, bear left by the mosque and after 50m take a sharp right turn downwards. You will find a sign on the wall on your left after about another 50m.

Eating places are thin on the ground in Gjirokastra. The *Argjiro Restaurant* next to the hotel of the same name is about as cheap and convenient as you will get. On the hill high above the town is the *Tourist Restaurant* with a great view but higher prices. Follow the road past the Kotoni rooms to walk to it in about 20 minutes.

Getting There & Away

Gjirokastra is on the main bus route from Tirana to Kakavija and Saranda. Most through buses stop on the main highway below Gjirokastra though some buses depart from the Çajupi Hotel below the citadel, including one to Tirana at 5 am.

BERAT
☎ 062

Although not as enchanting as Gjirokastra, Berat deserves its status as Albania's second most important museum town. Berat is sometimes called the 'city of a thousand windows' for the many openings in the white-plastered, red-roofed houses on terraces overlooking the Osum River. Along a ridge high above the gorge is a 14th-century citadel that shelters small Orthodox churches. On the slope below this, all the way down to the river, is Mangalem, the old Muslim quarter. A seven-arched stone bridge (1780) leads to Gorica, the Christian quarter.

In the 3rd century BC an Illyrian fortress called Antipatria was built here on the site of an earlier settlement. The Byzantines strengthened the hill-top fortifications in the 5th and 6th centuries, as did the Bulgarians 400 years later. The Serbs, who occupied the citadel in 1345, renamed it Beligrad, or 'White City', which has become today's Berat. In 1450 the Ottoman Turks took Berat. The town revived in the 18th and 19th centuries as a Turkish crafts centre specialising in woodcarving. For a brief time in 1944, Berat was the capital of liberated Albania. Today, most of Albania's crude oil is extracted from wells just north-west of the city, but Berat itself is a textile town with a mill once known as Mao Zedong.

Things to See
On the square in front of Hotel Tomori is a white hall where the National Liberation Council met from 20 to 23 October 1944 and formed a Provisional government of Albania, with Enver Hoxha as prime minister. It is now a billiard hall. Beyond this is the **Leaden Mosque** (1555), named for the material covering its great dome. Under the communists it was turned into a museum of architecture, but it is now a mosque again.

Follow the busy street north towards the citadel and, after a few blocks, behind the market building, you'll reach the **King's Mosque** (1512), formerly the Archaeological

Museum. Inside is a fine wooden gallery for female worshippers and across the courtyard is the **Alveti Tekke** (1790), a smaller shrine where Islamic sects such as the Dervishes were once based.

By the nearby river is the Margarita Tutulani Palace of Culture, a theatre worth checking for events. Beyond this is the **Bachelor's Mosque** (1827), now a folk-art museum (open Tuesday and Thursday only). A shop downstairs sells cassettes of Albanian folk music.

Continue on towards the old stone bridge (1780) and you'll see the 14th-century **Church of St Michael** high up on the hillside, below the citadel. In Mangalem, behind the Bachelor's Mosque, is the **Muzeu i Luftes** (closed Monday), which is worth seeing as much for its old Berati house as for its exhibits on the partisan struggle during WWII. Beyond the bank on the stone road leading up towards the citadel is the **Muzeu Etnografik** (open Wednesday and Friday only) in another fine old building.

After entering the **citadel** through its massive gate, continue straight ahead on the main street and you will see the sign to the **Muzeu Onufri** (open daily from 9 am to 3 pm, 200 lekë). The Museu Onufri and the **Orthodox Cathedral of Our Lady** (1797) are both within the monastery walls. The wooden iconostasis (1850) and pulpit in the cathedral are splendid. The museum has a large collection of icons, including many by the famous mid-16th century artist after whom the museum is named. Onufri's paintings are more realistic, dramatic and colourful than those of his predecessors.

Other churches in the citadel include the 14th-century **Church of the Holy Trinity** (Shen Triadhes), on the west side near the walls. Its exterior is impressive but the frescoes inside are badly damaged. The 16th-century **Church of the Evangelists** is most easily found by following the eastern citadel wall. At the south end of the citadel is a rustic **tavern** and battlements offering splendid views of Gorica and the modern city.

Places to Stay
The basic *Hotel Dyrmo* has three rooms with bath. They charge 500/1000 lekë for a single/double. It is just back from the west

end of the main street. Ask at the restaurant if no one is around.

The *Hotel Gega* was being renovated but should have reopened by the time you read this. It's a couple of hundred metres east of the Leaden Mosque along the main street.

The five-storey *Hotel Tomori* (☎ 32 462) is named after Mt Tomori (2416m), which towers above Berat to the east. The hotel is by the river on the east side of town. It has no lift but the balcony views of the riverside park compensate for the climb. The 56 rooms are US$32/50 for a single/double with bath and breakfast included. The hotel sign lacks the word 'Tomori'.

Places to Eat

The *Iliri Restorant* alongside the river has good food and an upstairs balcony with a view over the street. The atmosphere, however, can get a little rowdy at times. The cosy little *Onufri Restorant*, very close to the Onufri Museum in the citadel, is very good value for money.

Getting There & Away

The bus station is next to the Leaden Mosque near Hotel Tomori. A bus from Tirana to Berat (122km) takes three hours, a little long for a day trip. Buses to Fier (47km) and Tirana are fairly frequent and some buses run from Berat direct to Gjirokastra (120km). Minibus taxis also run from here to Fier, Tirana and Gjirokastra, and to places south of Berat.

ELBASAN

☎ 0545

Elbasan is on the Shkumbin River, midway between Durrës and Pogradec and 54km south-east of Tirana. It has been prominent since 1974, when the Chinese built the mammoth 'Steel of the Party' steel mill. It also has a cement factory and burgeoning pollution, though the old town retains a certain charm. With 83,000 inhabitants, Elbasan is Albania's third-largest city, having more than doubled in size since 1970.

The Romans founded Skampa (Elbasan) in the 1st century AD as a stopping point on the Via Egnatia. Stout stone walls with 26 towers were added in the 4th century to protect against invading barbarians. The Byzantines

continued this trend, also making Skampa the seat of a bishopric. In 1466, Sultan Mohammed II rebuilt the walls as a check against Skënderbeg at Kruja and renamed the town El Basan ('The Fortress' in Turkish). Elbasan was an important trade and handicrafts centre throughout the Turkish period.

Elbasan can be visited as a day trip from Tirana and the drive across the mountains is spectacular. Look out for the Citadel of Petrela, which stands on a hill top above the Erzen River.

Things to See

The 17th-century **Turkish baths** are in the centre of town, beside Hotel Skampa. Directly across the park on the other side of the hotel is Sejdini House, a typical 19th-century Balkan building, now the **Ethnographical Museum**.

Opposite the hotel are the **city walls**, erected by the Turks and still relatively intact on the south and west sides. Go through the **Bazar Gate** near the clock tower and follow a road directly north past the 15th-century **King's Mosque** to **St Mary's Orthodox Church**, which has a fine stone arcade on each exterior side and a gilded pulpit and iconostasis inside. This church is usually locked to prevent theft but it's worth asking around for the person with the key (who will expect a tip). Visible from behind St Mary's is a large Catholic church (closed). On the west city wall is a museum dedicated to the partisan war.

Places to Stay & Eat

The eight-storey *Hotel Skampa* (☎ 22 40) has 112 rooms at US$21/38 for a single/double with bath. It also has an OK restaurant downstairs.

The *Restaurant Universi*, about 200m west of Hotel Skampa, is another eating option. It is clean and prices are low. Failing that there are any number of snack bars or hamburger stands along or opposite the city walls nearby.

Getting There & Away

All buses to/from Pogradec (86km) pass through here but they arrive full. Getting a bus to Tirana is easier and there are also minibus taxis, departing from the parking lot next to the Skampa Hotel.

The train station is about five blocks from the Skampa Hotel. There are trains to Tirana and Durrës three times a day.

POGRADEC

☎ 10 (operator)

Pogradec is a pleasant beach resort at the southern end of Lake Ohrid, 140km southeast of Tirana. The 700m elevation gives the area a brisk, healthy climate and the scenery is beautiful. Pogradec is much less developed than the Macedonian lake towns of Ohrid and Struga. The nearby border crossing at Sveti Naum makes Pogradec a natural gateway to/from Macedonia.

Places to Stay & Eat

The eight-storey *Guri i Kuq Hotel* (☎ 414), opposite the post office, is named after the 'red-stone' mountain on the west side of the lake where nickel and chrome ore are extracted. It was last reported to be gutted and closed down, but it may reopen.

A much cheaper place to stay is the old, privately operated *Hotel Turizmi i Vjetar* on the beach about 180m west of the Guri i Kuq.

The *Hotel Koço Llakmani* is essentially private rooms above a restaurant/bar of the same name. It is on the little square 100m west of the Guri i Kuq Hotel. Just round the corner is the *Greek Taverna* which has very little Greek about it but serves excellent Ohrid trout at one third of the price you'd pay in Ohrid.

Getting There & Away

The train station, with two daily services to Tirana (seven hours) and Durrës, is near the mineral-processing factory, about 4km from the Guri i Kuq Hotel. Buses run to Tirana (140km), Korça (46km) and other towns.

Macedonia It's fairly easy to hitch the 6km east from Pogradec to the Tushemisht border post with Macedonia. Halfway is Drilon, a well-known tourist picnic spot, then the lakeside road goes through Tushemisht village and along the hillside to the border crossing. On the Macedonian side is the monastery of Sveti Naum, where there is a bus to Ohrid (29km); and a boat service in summer.

Tushemisht is a much better crossing for pedestrians and private cars than the Qafa e Thanës border crossing on the west side of the lake, which is used mostly by trucks and other commercial vehicles.

KORÇA

☎ 0824

The main city of the south-eastern interior, Korça sits on a 869m-high plateau west of Florina, Greece, 39km south of Lake Ohrid. Under the Turks, Korça was a major trading post and carpet-making town – it's still Albania's biggest carpet and rug-producing centre. Although it is in the heart of a rich agricultural area, Korça saw hard times in the late 19th and early 20th centuries and became a centre of emigration. Albanians abroad often regard Korça as home and quite a few still come back to retire here. Moneychangers work the street just west of Hotel Iliria.

Things to See

The **Muzeu Historik** is in the old two-storey building on Bulevardi Themistokli Gërmenji behind Hotel Iliria. Further up the boulevard on the left is the **Muzeu i Arsimit Kombëtar**, or Education Museum, housed in the first school to teach in the Albanian language (in 1887). (both museums are apparently closed indefinitely). Nearby at the top of the boulevard is the **statue of the National Warrior** (1932) by Odhise Paskali.

Delve into the small streets behind this statue and veer left to find the former **Muzeu i Artet Mesjetar Shqiptar** (Museum of Albanian Medieval Art), once the most important of Korça's museums, with several icons by Onufri. In a striking reversal of roles, Orthodox Albanians have recently taken over the modern museum building and turned it into a church to replace their original place of worship, which was destroyed by the communists.

Much of the old city centre was gouged out by urban renewal after devastating earthquakes in 1931 and 1960 which toppled the minarets and flattened the churches. Some of the colour of old Korça still remains in the Oriental-style **bazar area** west of Hotel Iliria.

Walk the crumbling cobbled streets lined with quaint old shops and swing south to the **Mirahorit Mosque** (1485), one of the oldest in Albania.

Places to Stay & Eat

Rozetta Qirjako and her husband Niko are a friendly couple and will take people in for about 1000 lekë per person. Their address is Rruga Dhori Lako L1, No 8. Niko is also a mechanic.

Among Korça's hotels catering mostly to Albanians is the friendly *Hotel Pallas*, on Bulevardi Themistokli Gërmenji just up from Hotel Iliria. On the opposite side of the same building is the *Hotel Gramosi* (it has no sign, so just ask). The prices asked of foreigners at these places varies, but for Albanians it's considerably cheaper.

The eight-storey *Hotel Iliria* (☎ 31 68) costs US$16/26 for a single/double without bath, US$30/48 with bath. Breakfast is included.

The *Alfa Restaurant* close to the above hotels is a good place to eat, otherwise Hotel Iliria has a restaurant. *Dolce Vita* on Bulevardi Republike offers fine Italian food and a surreal ambience. It's open until 11 pm.

Getting There & Away

There are buses to/from Tirana (179km) via Elbasan. Korça is a gateway to Albania for anyone arriving from Florina, Greece, via the Kapshtica border crossing 28km east. Buses to Kapshtica leave when full throughout the day from near Skënderbeg Stadium at the east end of Bulevardi Republike. From Krystallopigi on the Greek side of the border it's 65km to Florina (two buses daily, 1000 dr; taxi 7000 dr), a major Greek city with good connections to/from Thessaloniki. There is also a direct bus to Korça to/from Thessaloniki (5100 drachmas) which leaves from the forecourt of the Thessaloniki train station at 8 am every day except Sunday.

Andorra

The princedom of Andorra, covering just 464 sq km, is nestled between France and Spain in the midst of the Pyrenees. Although it *is* tiny, this political anomaly is at the heart of some of the most dramatic scenery in Europe.

Once a real backwater, Andorra has developed since the 1950s as a skiing centre and duty-free shopping haven, bringing not only wealth and foreign workers but also some unsightly development around the capital, Andorra la Vella. Until 1993 the country was a 'co-princedom' with its sovereignty invested in two 'princes': the Catholic bishop of the Spanish town of La Seu d'Urgell and the French president (who inherited the job from France's pre-Revolutionary kings). This arrangement dated back seven centuries. Now Andorra has a constitution that puts full control in the hands of its people, although the two 'princes' remain the joint heads of state. The elected parliament, the Consell General (General Council), has 28 members, four from each parish. Although not a member of the European Union (EU), Andorra entered the United Nations in 1993 and the Council of Europe in 1994.

Andorrans form only about a quarter of Andorra's total population (65,000) and are outnumbered by Spaniards. The official language is Catalan, which is related to both Spanish and French. Most people speak a couple of these languages, sometimes all three.

Facts for the Visitor

VISAS & EMBASSIES

You do not need a visa to visit Andorra, but you must carry your passport or national identity card. Andorra does not have any diplomatic missions abroad, but Spain and France have embassies in Andorra la Vella.

MONEY

Andorra uses the Spanish peseta and the French franc. Prices are usually given in pesetas, except in Pas de la Casa on the French border. It's best to use pesetas: the exchange rate for francs in shops and restaurants is seldom in your favour. See the France and Spain chapters for exchange rates.

1FF   = 25.20 ptas
100 ptas = 3.93FF

Andorra's low tax regime has made it a famous duty-free bazaar for electronic goods, cameras, alcohol etc. Today prices for these things no longer justify a special trip, but if you're prepared to shop around you can find

AT A GLANCE

Capital	Andorra la Vella
Population	64,000
Area	450 sq km
Official Language	Catalan
Currency	1 French franc (FF) = 100 centimes; 1 peseta (Ptas) = 100 centimos
GDP	US$1.2 billion (1996)
Time	GMT/UTC+0100

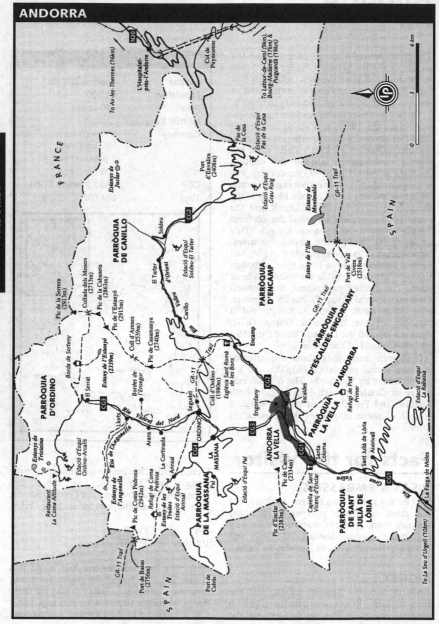

ANDORRA

To Ax-les-Thermes (16km)

N20

L'Hospitalet-près-l'Andorre

Col de Puymorens

To Latour-de-Carol (9km), Bourg-Madame (17km) & Puigcerdà (19km)

6 km

3

0

FRANCE

Port d'Envalira (2408m)

Estanys de Juclar

Pas de la Casa

Estació d'Esquí Pas de la Casa

Estació d'Esquí Grau Roig

Estany de Montmalús

GR-11 Trail

SPAIN

PARRÒQUIA DE CANILLO

CG2

Soldeu

El Tarter

Estació d'Esquí Soldeu-El Tarter

Estany de l'Illa

Pic de la Serrera (2913m)

Collada dels Meners (2713m)

Pic de la Cabaneta (2863m)

d'Orient

Port de Vall Civera (2518m)

PARRÒQUIA D'ENCAMP

Estany de l'Estanyó (2339m)

Pic de l'Estanyó (2915m)

Coll d'Arenes (2539m)

Valira

Canillo

GR-11 Trail

Borda de Sorteny

Coll de Casamunya (2740m)

Riu

Encamp

PARRÒQUIA DE DESCALDES-ENGORDANY

PARRÒQUIA D'ORDINO

El Serrat

Estanys de l'Estanyó

Bordes de l'Ensegur

GR-11 Trail

Església Sant Romà de les Bons

Estació d'Esquí La Rabassa

Estanys de Tristaina

Restaurant La Coma Altitude

Estació d'Esquí Ordino-Arcalís

Riu de l'Angonella

Estanys de l'Angonella

Llorts

Riu Valira del Nord

Segudet

Coll d'Ordino (1980m)

CG2

D'ESCALDES-ENGORDANY

Escaldes

D'ENCAMP PRAT

Refugi de Prat Primer

Pic de Coma Pedrosa (2942m)

Refugi de Coma Pedrosa

Ansalonga

ORDINO

Engordany

Pal

Sispony

ANDORRA LA VELLA (1034m)

PARRÒQUIA LA VELLA

Estació d'Esquí Arinsal

Estació les Trulles

Arans

La Cortinada

Anisal

LA MASSANA

CG3

Santa Coloma

Sant Julià de Lòria

Capella de Sant Vicenç d'Enclar

PARRÒQUIA DE LA MASSANA

Estació d'Esquí Pal

Pic de Carroi (2334m)

Aixirivall

PARRÒQUIA DE SANT JULIÀ DE LÒRIA

GR-11 Trail

Port de Baiau (2755m)

Pic d'Enclar (2383m)

Valira

Gran

La Farga de Moles

Port de Cabús

To La Seu d'Urgell (10km)

SPAIN

some cameras or electronic goods about 20% or 30% cheaper than in France or Spain. There are limits on what you can take out of Andorra duty-free – tourist offices have details.

POST & COMMUNICATIONS
Post
Andorra has no postal system of its own; France and Spain each operate separate systems with their own Andorran stamps. Andorran stamps of both types are valid only for mail posted in Andorra and are needed only for international mail – letters within the country are free and do not need stamps. Regular French and Spanish stamps cannot be used in Andorra.

Postal rates are the same as those of the issuing country, with the French tariffs slightly cheaper. You are better off routing all international mail (except letters to Spain) through the French postal system. Poste restante mail to Andorra la Vella goes to the French post office there.

Telephone
To call Andorra from any other country, dial the international access code, then ☎ 376, then the six-digit local number. To call other countries from Andorra, dial ☎ 00, then the country code, area code and local number.

Public telephones take pesetas (francs in Pas de la Casa) or an Andorran *teletarja*, which works like a phonecard in most European countries. Teletarges (plural) worth 500 and 900 ptas are sold at post offices, tourist offices and some shops. Andorra does *not* have reverse-charge (collect) calling facilities.

A three-minute call to the USA at normal rates costs 330 ptas.

TIME & ELECTRICITY
Andorra is one hour ahead of GMT/UTC in winter and two hours ahead from the last Sunday in March to the last Sunday in September. Electric current is either 220V or 125V, both at 50Hz.

HEALTH
Medical care has to be paid for. For emergency medical help, call ☎ 116; for the police ☎ 110.

BUSINESS HOURS
Shops in Andorra la Vella are open daily from 9.30 am to 1 pm and 3.30 to 8 pm, except (in most cases) Sunday afternoon.

ACTIVITIES
Above the main valleys, where most people live, is plenty of high, attractive, lake-dotted mountain country, good for skiing in winter and walking in summer. Some peaks remain snowcapped until July or later. Tourist offices give out a useful English-language booklet, *Sport Activities*, describing numerous walking and mountain-bike routes. In summer, reasonably good quality mountain bikes can be rented at several places for around 2500 ptas a day.

Skiing
Andorra has the best inexpensive skiing and snowboarding in the Pyrenees. The season lasts from December to April (snow cover permitting). For information on the five downhill ski areas *(estaciós d'esquí)*, ask at one of the capital's tourist offices or contact Ski Andorra (☎ 864389). The largest and best resorts are Soldeu-El Tarter and Pas de la Casa/Grau Roig, but the others – Ordino-Arcalís, Arinsal and Pal – are a bit cheaper. Ski passes cost 2600 to 3900 ptas a day, depending on the location and season; ski-gear rental is around 1500 ptas a day.

Hiking
There are some beautiful hiking areas in the north and north-west of Andorra (see the Parròquia d'Ordino section for more information). Several long-distance walking routes, including the Spanish GR11 and the (mainly French) Haute Randonnée Pyrenéenne, which both traverse the Pyrenees from the Mediterranean to the Atlantic, cross the country. The best time for hiking is from June to September, when temperatures climb well into the 20s in the day, although they drop to around 10°C at night. June can be wet.

A 1:25,000-scale *mapa topogràfic* of the country costs 1200 ptas in bookshops and tourist offices. Maps at 1:10,000 are also available. Hikers can sleep for free in more than two-dozen *refugi* (mountain huts).

ANDORRA

ACCOMMODATION

There are no youth hostels, but plenty of camping grounds, hotels and cheaper *pensiós*, *residèncias* etc. Prices in many places are the same year-round, although some go up in August and/or at Christmas, Easter and the height of the ski season.

The 26 mountain refuges have bunks and fireplaces, and all except one are free. Nearly all have drinking water. Tourist offices have more information, and maps indicating their locations.

Getting There & Away

The only way into Andorra is by road. If you're coming from France, you won't soon forget Port d'Envalira (2408m), the highest pass in the Pyrenees. The municipal tourist office in Andorra la Vella has bus timetables and knows ticket office hours.

From France, by public transport you need to approach by train and then get a bus for the final leg. The nearest station is L'Hospitalet, two hours from Toulouse by four daily trains. The two daily buses between L'Hospitalet and Plaça de Guillemó bus stop in Andorra la Vella (1½ to 2¼ hours, 925 ptas) connect with trains.

From Barcelona, Alsina Graells runs five buses daily to Andorra la Vella's Estació d'Autobusos on Carrer de Bonaventura Riberaygua (four hours, 2505 ptas). Other services include: Tarragona daily (four hours, 1800 ptas); Zaragoza and Madrid's Estación Sur (8½ hours, 4700 ptas), three per week; and Burgos, Valladolid and Tuy, two per week. There are five or more buses daily between La Seu d'Urgell and Plaça de Guillemó (30 minutes, 340 ptas).

The nearest Spanish train station to Andorra is Puigcerdà. The early morning trains from Barcelona get you to Puigcerdà in time to reach Andorra la Vella (with a change of bus at La Seu d'Urgell) the same day – a trip of about 6½ hours in total for about 2000 ptas. Or you can stay on the train as far as Latour-de-Carol on the French side of the border and pick up the 1 pm bus for Andorra la Vella there (1125 ptas). If you miss it, you could get the 3.32 pm bus from Latour-de-

Carol for L'Hospitalet (30 minutes), from where there are two or three daily buses with La Hispano Andorrana (☎ 821372 in Andorra) to Andorra la Vella (which take a little less than two hours). One leaves at 5.20 pm or 6.05 pm. Otherwise, there's another at 7.35 am the next day. On Saturday there are as many as five buses to Pas de la Casa.

Getting Around

BUS

Cooperativa Interurbana (☎ 820412) runs eight bus lines along the three main highways from Andorra la Vella. Autobus Parroquial de La Massana i d'Ordino operates a few services from La Massana. The municipal tourist office in Andorra la Vella has timetables. Destinations from Andorra la Vella include Ordino (130 ptas), daily every 20 or 30 minutes from 7 am to 9 pm; Arinsal (185 ptas) three times daily; Soldeu (340 ptas) hourly from 9 am to 8 pm; and Pas de la Casa (590 ptas) at 9 am. Buses to all these places leave from the Plaça del Príncep Benlloch stop in Andorra la Vella.

CAR & MOTORCYCLE

With all the twists and turns it's almost impossible to reach the inter-hamlet speed limit of 90km/h. The biggest problems are Andorra la Vella's traffic jams and the ever-vigilant parking officers. If you don't buy a coupon (available from machines everywhere) and place it on the dashboard, you will be fined for sure.

Petrol in Andorra is about 15% cheaper than in Spain and 25% cheaper than in France.

Andorra la Vella

Andorra la Vella (Vella is pronounced 'VEY-yah'; population 22,000) is in the Riu Valira valley at an elevation of just over 1000m. The town is given over almost entirely to retailing of electronic and luxury goods. With its mountains, constant din of jackhammers and 'mall' architecture, travellers familiar with Asia may be reminded of Hong Kong.

The only differences seem to be the snow-capped peaks and lack of noodle shops!

Orientation

Andorra la Vella is strung out along the main drag, called Avinguda de Meritxell in the east and Avinguda del Príncep Benlloch in the west. The tiny historic quarter (Barri Antic) lies south-west of Plaça del Príncep Benlloch. The town merges with the once-separate villages of Escaldes and Engordany to the east and Santa Coloma to the south-west.

Information

Tourist Offices The helpful municipal tourist office (Oficina d'Informació i Turisme; ☎ 827117) on Plaça de la Rotonda has maps, all sorts of brochures, stamps and phonecards. It's open daily from 9 am to 1 pm and 4 to 8 pm (7 pm on Sunday). In July and August, it's open from 9 am to 9 pm (7 pm on Sunday).

The national tourist office (Sindicat d'Iniciativa Oficina de Turisme; ☎ 820214) is on Carrer del Doctor Vilanova just down from Plaça de Rebés; it's open Monday to Saturday from 10 am (9 am from July to September) to 1 pm and 3 to 7 pm, and on Sunday morning.

Money Banks are open weekdays from 9 am to 1 pm and 3 to 5 pm and on Saturday to noon. There are banks every 100m or so along Avinguda de Meritxell and Avinguda del Príncep Benlloch in the town centre, most with ATMs. American Express is represented by Viatges Relax (☎ 822044) at Carrer de Mossén Tremosa 2. It doesn't change money but can replace American Express cards and travellers cheques, and sell travellers cheques against card-holders' personal cheques.

Post & Communications The main French post office (La Poste) is at Carrer de Pere d'Urg 1. It is open weekdays from 8.30 am to 2.30 pm and Saturday from 9 am to noon. During July and August, weekday hours are 9 am to 7 pm. Payment is in French francs only.

The main Spanish post office (Correus i Telègrafs) is nearby at Carrer de Joan Maragall 10. It's open weekdays from 8.30 am to 2.30 pm and Saturday from 9.30 am to 1 pm, and only accepts pesetas. You can make international telephone calls from street pay phones.

Medical Services The main hospital is the modern Hospital Nostra Senyora de Meritxell (☎ 871000) at Avinguda de Fiter i Rossell 1-13, about 1.5km east of Plaça de Guillemó.

Things to See & Do

Casa de la Vall Built in 1580 as a private home, Casa de la Vall, on Carrer de la Vall in the Barri Antic, has been the seat of Andorra's parliament and its forerunners for almost three centuries. Downstairs is the Sala de la Justicia, the only courtroom in the whole country. Free guided tours (sometimes in English) are given about once an hour on weekdays from 9 am to 1 pm and 3 to 7 pm: you should book a week ahead to ensure a place, but individuals can sometimes join a group at the last minute.

Caldea Caldea (☎ 800999) in Escaldes is an enormous spa complex of pools, hot tubs and saunas fed by thermal springs, all enclosed in what looks like a futuristic cathedral. Three-hour tickets (2500 ptas) are available from the tourist offices. Caldea is just east of Avinguda de Fiter i Rossell, a 2km walk from Plaça de Guillemó.

Places to Stay

Camping About 1.5km south-west of Plaça de Guillemó on Avinguda de Salou, *Camping Valira* (☎ 822384) charges 525 ptas per person and the same for a tent and for a car. It's open all year, and has a heated covered swimming pool.

Hotels – Plaça de Guillemó & Barri Antic At Carrer de la Llacuna 21, just off Plaça de Guillemó, *Residència Benazet* (☎ 820698) has large, serviceable rooms with washbasin and bidet at 1300 ptas per person. *Hotel Les Arcades* (☎ 821355) at Plaça de Guillemó 5 has singles/doubles with shower and toilet from 2000/3000 ptas to 3000/5000 ptas depending on the season.

In the Barri Antic, the nondescript rooms at *Pensió La Rosa* (☎ 821810) at Antic Carrer Major 18 are 1700/3000 ptas. Quiet *Hostal Calones* (☎ 821312), at No 8, has

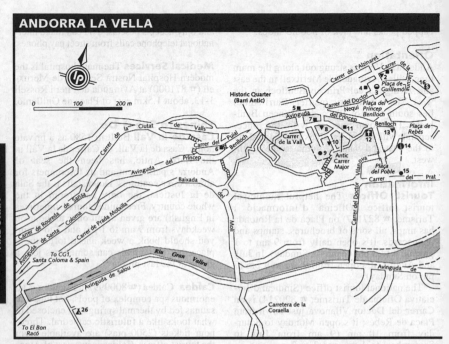

ANDORRA LA VELLA

PLACES TO STAY
1 Residència Benazet
4 Hotel Les Arcades
5 Hôtel Pyrénées
6 Habitacions Baró
7 Pensió La Rosa
11 Hostal Calones
18 Hotel Costa
20 Hotel Residència
    Albert
26 Camping Valira

PLACES TO EAT
2 El Timbaler del Bruch
8 Restaurant Can Benet
10 Restaurant Ca La Conxita
13 Pans & Company
21 Pans & Company

OTHER
3 Plaça Guillemó Bus Stop
9 Casa de la Vall
12 Església de Sant Esteve

14 National Tourist Office
15 Public Lift to Plaça del
    Poble
16 American Express
17 Pyrénées Department Store
19 Municipal Tourist
    Office
22 Spanish Post Office
23 French Post Office
24 Police Station
25 Estació d'Autobusos

better rooms with big bathrooms for 2800/
3700 ptas. *Habitacions Baró* (☎ 821484),
Carrer del Puial 21 – up the steps opposite
Avinguda del Príncep Benlloch 53 – has
rooms for 1300/2400 ptas.

Hotel Pyrénées (☎ 860006; fax 820265),
Avinguda del Príncep Benlloch 20, has a
tennis court, swimming pool and all mod

cons, and is priced accordingly at 5000/8000
ptas to 5750/9300 ptas.

Hotels – Farther East At Avinguda de
Meritxell 44, *Hotel Costa* (☎ 821439) has
basic but clean rooms for 1600/3000 ptas.
Bathrooms are shared. *Hotel Residència
Albert* (☎ 820156), Avinguda del Doctor

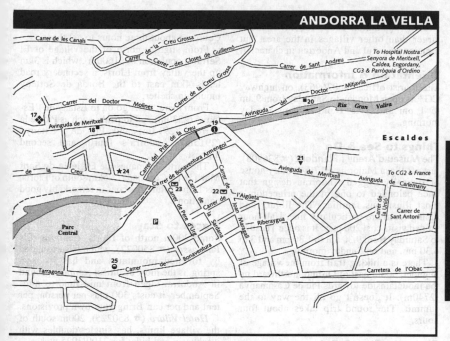

ANDORRA LA VELLA

Mitjavila 16, has singles/doubles with shower for 1500/3000 ptas.

Places to Eat

El Timbaler del Bruch, on Plaça de Guillemó, does good, generous torrades (open toasted sandwiches) from 375 ptas. *Pans & Company*, at Plaça de Rebés 2 and Avinguda de Meritxell 91, is good for hot and cold baguettes with a range of fillings (350 to 500 ptas).

In the Barri Antic, *Restaurant Ca La Conxita*, Placeta de Monjó 3, is a busy little family business where you can watch them preparing your hearty meal. You eat well for around 2500 ptas. Virtually around the corner at Carrer Major 9, *Restaurant Can Benet* is a little more pricey but also delightful.

The best place for real Catalan cooking is the upmarket *El Bon Racó* at Avinguda de Salou 86 in Santa Coloma, about 1km west of

Camping Valira. Meat – especially xai (lamb) – roasted in an open hearth is the speciality, but you might also try escudella, a Catalan stew of chicken, sausage and vegetables. Expect to part with close to 3000 ptas for a full meal with wine.

Getting There & Around

See the Getting There & Away and Getting Around sections at the start of this chapter for international and domestic transport options to/from Andorra la Vella.

Parròquia d'Ordino

The mountainous parish of Ordino, north of Andorra la Vella, is arguably the country's most beautiful region, with slate and field-stone farmhouses, rushing streams and picturesque stone bridges. Virtually everything of interest is along the 35km highway CG3.

ORDINO

Ordino (population 1000; 1300m) is much larger than other villages in the area, but remains peaceful and Andorran in character.

Orientation & Information

The tourist office (☎ 836963), on highway CG3, is open Monday to Saturday from 9 am to 1 pm and 3 to 7 pm and on Sunday morning.

Things to See & Do

The Museu d'Areny i Plandolit (☎ 836908), just off Plaça Major, is a 17th-century house of typically rugged Andorran design that once belonged to one of the princedom's most illustrious families. The library and dining room are particularly fine. Half-hour guided visits cost 200 ptas. It is open Tuesday to Saturday from 9.30 am to 1.30 pm and 3 to 6.30 pm, and on Sunday morning.

There is a hiking trail from the village of Segudet, 500m east of Ordino, northward up the mountainside towards Pic de Casamanya (2740m). It doesn't go all the way to the summit. The round trip takes about four hours.

Places to Stay & Eat

Just off Plaça Major, in the alley behind the Crèdit Andorrà bank, is the *Hotel Quim* (☎ 835013). Doubles with shower cost up to 4500 ptas. Much more expensive is the *Hotel Santa Bàrbara de la Vall d'Ordino* (☎ 837100), on Plaça Major, which has singles/doubles for as much as 7000/8500 ptas.

Restaurant Ricard on Plaça Major has a menú of mainly Catalan dishes for 1700 ptas. *Restaurant Armengol*, nearby, has a less imaginative menú for 1500 ptas.

LLORTS

The tiny mountain hamlet of Llorts (1413m), on the CG3 6km north of Ordino, has traditional architecture set amid tobacco fields and near-pristine mountains. With only 100 people living here, this is one of the most unadulterated spots in the principality.

Things to See & Do

Llorts is a good area for hiking trails. One leads west from the village up the Riu de l'Angonella valley to a group of lakes, Estanys de l'Angonella, at about 2300m. Count on about three hours to get there.

From slightly north of the village of El Serrat (population 60; 1600m), which is 3km up the valley from Llorts, a secondary road leads 4km east to the Borda de Sorteny mountain shelter.

From there, trails go on to Estany de l'Estanyó (2339m) and to peaks such as Pic de la Serrera (2913m) and Pic de l'Estanyó (2915m), Andorra's fourth and second highest.

The partly Romanesque Església de Sant Martí in La Cortinada, 2.5km south of Llorts, has 12th-century frescoes in remarkably good condition.

Places to Stay

Some 200m north of Llorts, *Camping Els Pardassos* (☎ 850022), which is surrounded by forested mountains and has its own spring, is the most beautiful camping ground in Andorra. Open from mid-June to mid-September, it costs 300 ptas per person, per tent and per car. Bring your own provisions.

Hotel Vilaró (☎ 850225), 200m south of the village limits, has singles/doubles with washbasin and bidet for 2100/3925 ptas.

Getting There & Away

The 1 and 8.30 pm buses from Andorra la Vella to El Serrat stop at Llorts, as do the handful of daily buses from Ordino to Arcalís.

ESTACIÓ D'ESQUÍ ORDINO-ARCALÍS

The Ordino-Arcalís ski area (☎ 850121) lies in the north-west corner of Andorra. In winter, 12 lifts operate (mostly tow lines) and there are 24km of pistes of all levels of difficulty. In summer, this beautiful mountainous area has some of Andorra's most rewarding hiking trails. The nearest accommodation is in El Serrat or Llorts.

Restaurant La Coma Altitude, at 2200m near the third car park, is a useful landmark. It is open daily from December to early May and, except on Monday, from the end of June to early September. The long Telecadira La Coma chair lift rises opposite.

Things to Do

The souvenir kiosk opposite the Telecadira La Coma's lower station rents mountain bikes from late June to early September (daily from 10 am to 6 pm; closed Monday in June and July).

The trail behind Restaurant La Coma Altitude leads eastward across the hill then north over the ridge to a group of beautiful lakes, Estanys de Tristaina. You can also start walking from the top of Telecadira La Coma (2700m), which operates daily from late June to early September from 10 am to 6 pm.

Getting There & Away

There are a few buses daily from Ordino, through Llorts and El Serrat.

Bosnia-Hercegovina

Sandwiched between Croatia and Yugoslavia, the small mountainous country of Bosnia-Hercegovina has been a meeting point of east and west for nearly two millennia. Here the realm of Orthodox Byzantium mingled with Catholic Rome, and the 15th-century swell of Turkish power settled among the Slavs. This unique history created one of the most fascinating cultures in Europe, with a heterogeneous population of Croats, Serbs and Slavic converts to Islam.

In the 20th century Bosnia-Hercegovina has had more than its share of strife. WWI was sparked in Sarajevo when a Serb nationalist assassinated an Austrian aristocrat, and much of the bitter partisan fighting of WWII took place in this region. Forty-five years of peace ensued, with Bosnia-Hercegovina as the third-largest republic in Yugoslavia. This ended soon after Bosnia declared independence in October 1991. Six months later Bosnian Serb ultranationalists, assisted by Yugoslavia's federal army, began a campaign of ethnic cleansing intended to bring Bosnia-Hercegovina into Belgrade's orbit.

When the three-way war ended in 1995, it left the country physically devastated and ethnically divided. Out of a prewar population of five million, over two million fled their former homes. Peace is currently enforced by 34,000 NATO troops, and a large international civilian presence is working to reintegrate and rebuild the country. Progress since peace has been substantial, but as a destination for visitors Bosnia-Hercegovina itself is unalterably changed.

Facts about Bosnia-Hercegovina

HISTORY

The ancient inhabitants of this region were Illyrians, followed by the Romans who settled around the mineral springs at Ilidža near Sarajevo. When the Roman Empire was divided in 395 AD, the Drina River, today the border between Bosnia-Hercegovina and Yugoslavia, became the line that divided the Western Roman Empire from Byzantium.

The Slavs arrived in the late 6th and early 7th centuries. In 960 the area became independent of Serbia, only to pass through the hands of other conquerors: Croatia, Byzantium, Duklja (modern-day Montenegro), and Hungary. The first Turkish raids came in 1383 and by 1463 Bosnia was a Turkish province with Sarajevo as its capital. Hercegovina is named after Herceg (Duke) Stjepan Vukčić, who ruled the southern portion of the

AT A GLANCE

Capital	Sarajevo
Population	3.2 million
Area	51,233 sq km
Official Language	Croatian/Serbian (Bosnian)
Currency	1 dinar = 100 para; 1 kuna = 100 lipas
GDP	US$1.9 billion (1996)
Time	GMT/UTC+0100

The Two 'Entities' of Bosnia-Hercegovina p124

BOSNIA-HERCEGOVINA

present republic from his mountaintop castle at Blagaj near Mostar until the Turkish conquest in 1468.

During the 400-year Turkish period, Bosnia-Hercegovina was completely assimilated and became the boundary between the Islamic and Christian worlds. Wars with Venice and Austria were frequent. One Christian heretic sect, the Bogomils, converted to Islam, and the region still forms a Muslim enclave deep within Christian Europe.

As the Ottoman Empire weakened in the 16th and 17th centuries, the Turks strength-

ened their hold on Bosnia-Hercegovina as an advance bulwark of their empire. The national revival movements of the mid-19th century led to a reawakening among the South Slavs, and in 1875-76 there were peasant uprisings against the Turks in Bosnia-Hercegovina and Bulgaria. In 1878 Turkey suffered a crushing defeat by Russia in a war over Bulgaria, and it was decided at the Congress of Berlin that same year that Austria-Hungary would occupy Bosnia-Hercegovina. However, the population desired autonomy and had to be brought under Habsburg rule by force.

Resentment against foreign occupation intensified in 1908 when Austria annexed Bosnia-Hercegovina outright. The assassination of the Habsburg heir Archduke Franz Ferdinand by a Bosnian Serb at Sarajevo on 28 June 1914 led Austria to declare war on Serbia one month later. When Russia supported Serbia, and Germany came to the aid of Austria, the world was soon at war.

Following WWI, Bosnia-Hercegovina was taken into the Serb-dominated Kingdom of the Serbs, Croats, and Slovenes (renamed Yugoslavia in 1929). In 1941 the Axis powers annexed Bosnia-Hercegovina to the fascist Croatian state, but the area's mountains quickly became a wartime partisan stronghold. A conference in 1943 in Jajce laid the ground for postwar Yugoslavia, and after the war Bosnia-Hercegovina was granted republic status within Yugoslavia.

In the republic's first free elections in November 1990, the communists were easily defeated by nationalist Serb and Croat parties and by a predominantly Muslim party favouring a multiethnic Bosnia-Hercegovina.

The Croat and Muslim parties united against the Serb nationalists and independence from Yugoslavia was declared on 15 October 1991. Serb parliamentarians withdrew and set up a government of their own at Pale, the village 20km east of Sarajevo where the 1984 Winter Olympics took place. Bosnia-Hercegovina was recognised internationally and admitted to the UN, but this over-hasty recognition caused talks between the parties to break down.

The War

War broke out in April 1992, shortly after Bosnian Serb snipers in the Sarajevo Holiday Inn opened fire on unarmed civilians demonstrating for peace in Sarajevo, killing a dozen people.

The Serbs had inherited almost the entire arms stock of the Yugoslav National Army (JNA). As had been done in Croatia they began seizing territory with the support of some of the 50,000 JNA troops in Bosnia-Hercegovina. Sarajevo came under siege by Serb irregulars on 5 April 1992 and shelling by Serb artillery began soon after. Directed from nearby Pale, the brutal siege was to leave over 10,000 civilians dead and the city ravaged before it ended in summer 1995.

Serb forces began a campaign of 'ethnic cleansing', brutally expelling the Muslim population from northern and eastern Bosnia to create a 300km corridor joining Serb ethnic areas in the west of Bosnia and in Serbia proper. Villages were terrorised and looted, and homes were destroyed to prevent anyone from returning. Crowning their campaign of ethnic cleansing, the Serbs set up concentration camps for Muslims and Croats and initiated the mass atrocities which were a devastating feature of this war.

In August 1992 the UN Security Council authorised the use of force to deliver humanitarian relief supplies and by September 7500 UN troops were in Bosnia-Hercegovina. However, this UN Protection Force (UNPROFOR) was notorious for its impotence, which was dramatically displayed in January 1993 when the vice-premier of Bosnia-Hercegovina, Hakija Turajlić, was pulled out of a UN armoured personnel carrier at a Serb checkpoint and executed in front of French peacekeepers.

By mid-1993, with Serb 'ethnic cleansing' almost complete, the UN proposed setting up 'safe areas' for Muslims around five Bosnian cities, including Sarajevo. The Serbs, confident that the west would not intervene, continued their siege of Sarajevo.

The Vance-Owen peace plan, which would have divided Bosnia-Hercegovina into 10 ethnically based provinces, was rejected by Serb leaders in 1993. Nonetheless, the plan's formulation seemed to confirm to all sides that Bosnia's fate lay in ethnic partition.

The Croats wanted their own slice of Bosnia-Hercegovina. The Croatian Community of Herceg-Bosna was set up in July 1992, and in March 1993 fighting erupted between Muslims and Croats. The Croats instigated a deadly mini-siege of the Muslim quarter of Mostar, which culminated in the destruction of Mostar's historic old bridge in 1993.

In May 1993 Croatian president Franjo Tudjman made a bid for a 'Greater Croatia' by making a separate deal with the Bosnian Serbs to carve up Bosnia-Hercegovina between themselves. This was foiled by the renewed strength of the Bosnian army, and fighting between Muslims and Croats intensified.

NATO finally began taking action against the Bosnian Serbs. After a Serb mortar attack on a Sarajevo market in February 1994 left 68 dead and 200 injured, NATO's threatened air strikes cowed the Bosnian Serbs into withdrawing their guns temporarily from around the city.

US fighters belatedly began enforcing the no-fly zone over Bosnia by shooting down four Serb aircraft in February 1994 (the first actual combat in NATO's 45-year history). Two months later NATO aircraft carried out their first air strikes against Bosnian Serb ground positions after the Serbs advanced on a UN 'protected area'. When a British plane was shot down, the NATO raids quickly ceased.

Meanwhile, at talks held in Washington in March 1994, the US pressured the Bosnian government to join the Bosnian Croats in a federation. Worried about Serb enclaves on its own soil, Croatia went on the offensive in May 1995 and rapidly overran Croatian Serb positions and towns in western Slavonia, within Croatia.

With Croatia now heavily involved, a pan-Balkan war seemed closer than ever. Again, Bosnian Serb tanks and artillery attacked Sarajevo, again UN peacekeepers requested NATO air strikes. When air strikes to protect Bosnian 'safe areas' was finally authorised, the Serbs captured 300 UNPROFOR peacekeepers and chained them to potential targets to keep the planes away.

In July 1995 Bosnian Serbs attacked the safe area of Srebrenica, slaughtering an estimated 6000 Muslim men as they fled through the forest. This was the largest massacre in the war, and highlighted the futility of the UN presence.

Nonetheless, the twilight of Bosnian Serb military dominance was at hand. European leaders called loudly for strong action not just to try once more to defend the Bosnians but to defeat the Bosnian Serbs. Croatia renewed its own internal offensive, expelling Serbs from the Krajina region.

With Bosnian Serbs finally on the defensive and battered by two weeks of NATO air strikes in September 1995, US president Bill Clinton's proposal for new peace talks was accepted.

The Dayton Accord

The peace conference in Dayton, Ohio, USA, began in November 1995 and the final agreement was signed in Paris in December.

The Dayton agreement stated that the country would retain its prewar external boundaries, but would be composed of two parts or 'entities'. The Federation of Bosnia-Hercegovina (the Muslim and Croat portion) would administer 51% of the country, including Sarajevo, and the Serb Republic of Bosnia-Hercegovina 49%. The latter is commonly referred to as the Republika Srpska (RS). Eastern and western portions of the RS would be linked together by the narrow Posavina Corridor in the northeast. The town of Brčko, situated in the narrowest part of the corridor, was so contentious that its final fate was left up to international arbitration, which has subsequently postponed a decision.

The agreement also emphasised the rights of refugees to return to their prewar homes. This was relevant for both the 1.2 million people who sought refuge in other countries (including Yugoslavia and Croatia), and the one million people who were displaced

The Two Entities of Bosnia-Hercegovina

- ⬤ ZAGREB

Muslim-Croat Federation
Republika Srpska

Prijedor • Posavina Corridor
• Bihać Sanski Most • Banja Luka • Brčko
Tuzla
Travnik
CROATIA SARAJEVO ⬤ • Pale
• Split Goražde
Mostar
• Medugorje
ADRIATIC SEA YUGOSLAVIA
0   50   100 km   Dubrovnik
ALBANIA

within Bosnia-Hercegovina during the ethnic cleansing process.

A NATO-led peace implementation force, IFOR, was installed as the military force behind the accords. IFOR's 60,000 international troops gave way in January 1997 to the 30,000-strong Stabilisation Force (SFOR), whose current mandate has no definite time limit.

The Dayton accords also emphasised the powers of the War Crimes Tribunal in the Hague, which had been established in 1993. NATO was given the authority to arrest indicted war criminals. Thus far, 74 people have been publicly indicted, but only 27 have been brought to the Hague and the most-wanted war criminals, Bosnian Serb leader Radovan Karadžić and his military henchman Ratko Mladić, remain at large.

After Dayton

In early 1996 Bosnian, Serb and Croat forces withdrew to the agreed lines, and NATO-led IFOR took up positions between them. Karadžić stepped down from the RS presidency in July 1996, after the international community threatened to reintroduce sanctions against the Serbs if he did not quit public office. Seemingly unfazed, Karadžić continued to wield behind-the-scenes influence, even as his successor Biljana Plavšić took over as the RS president.

Bosnia-Hercegovina's first post-war national elections in September 1996 essentially shored up the existing leadership. Municipal elections scheduled for the same time were postponed for one year while the international community, which supervised the elections, ironed out the logistics of allowing people to vote in their prewar municipalities. When municipal elections finally took place in September 1997, exile leaders were elected in several towns, notably Muslims in Serb-controlled Srebrenica and Prijedor and Serbs in Croat-controlled Drvar.

Meanwhile Plavšić, wooed by western support and ostensibly concerned about corruption, split from the hardline Karadžić during summer 1997. The RS itself seemed to be splintering along these lines, with the Pale-based eastern RS backing Karadžić and Plavšić's domain in Banja Luka-based western RS becoming more open. Banja Luka emerged

triumphant from the struggle and took over from Pale as the RS capital in January 1998.

Western hopes were given a further boost in January 1998 when a new, relatively liberal Bosnian Serb Prime Minister Milorad Dodik came to power. Dodik quickly pushed several measures through the RS parliament aimed at compliance with Dayton, including a common license plate (that would no longer be entity-specific), common passports and a new common currency called the convertible mark. A new national flag was approved just in time for the 1998 Winter Olympic Games.

Bosnia-Hercegovina today remains deeply divided along ethnic lines. Muslim-Croat tensions have ebbed, but few people dare to cross between the RS and the Federation. Many of the country's towns are physically destroyed, although a US$5.1 billion reconstruction program is underway.

GEOGRAPHY

Bosnia-Hercegovina is a mountainous country of 51,129 sq km on the west side of the Balkan Peninsula, almost cut off from the sea by Croatia. Most of the country's rivers flow north into the Sava; only the Neretva cuts south from Jablanica through the Dinaric Alps to Ploče on the Adriatic Sea. Bosnia-Hercegovina contains over 30 mountain peaks from 1700 to 2386m high.

GOVERNMENT & POLITICS

The Dayton Accords stipulate that the central government be headed by a rotating three-person presidency, with one elected by the Serb Republic and the others, a Muslim and a Croat, by the Federation. The House of Peoples is selected from the legislatures of the two entities and a House of Representatives directly elected by each entity. Two-thirds of each house is from the Federation, one-third from the Serb Republic, and a Council of Ministers is responsible for carrying out government policies and decisions.

Despite ideals of a central government in Sarajevo, each division of Bosnia-Hercegovina maintains an essentially separate administration. Few of the ethnically joint institutions called for by the Dayton agreement are functioning, even between Muslims and Croats within the Federation.

In lieu of local cooperation, Bosnia-Hercegovina is essentially ruled by the west, which has taken an increasingly firm hand in forcing the parties to come to decisions together. The international community's High Representative received stronger powers at a conference in Bonn in December 1997 and began dismissing obstructionist officials.

ECONOMY

Bosnia-Hercegovina was one of the poorest regions of Yugoslavia, its economy driven by mining, hydroelectricity and timber. War brought virtually all activity to a halt, but the situation has improved remarkably during peacetime. The unemployment rate has shot down from 50% at the end of 1995 to about 30% in early 1998. And the new figure does not even reflect the country's most popular occupations – working as a translator or driver for the well-paying international organisations.

The Republika Srpska, which until recently received less international assistance, is significantly poorer than the Federation.

POPULATION & PEOPLE

Before the war, Bosnia-Hercegovina's population stood at around four million. In 1991 the largest cities were Sarajevo (525,980), Banja Luka (195,139), Zenica (145,577), Tuzla (131,861) and Mostar (126,067). The massive population shifts have changed the size of many cities, swelling the population of Banja Luka to 220,000 and shrinking Sarajevo (347,901) and Mostar (108,265).

Bosnia-Hercegovina's prewar population was incredibly mixed, but ethnic cleansing has concentrated Croats in Hercegovina (to the south), Muslims in Sarajevo and central Bosnia, and Serbs in areas adjacent to Yugoslavia.

Serbs, Croats and Bosnian Muslims are all South Slavs of the same ethnic stock. Physically the three peoples are indistinguishable.

ARTS

Bosnia's best known writer is Ivo Andrić (1892-1975), winner of the 1961 Nobel Prize for Literature. His novels *Travnik Chronicles* and *Bridge on the Drina*, both written during WWII, are fictional histories which deal with the intermingling of Islamic and Orthodox societies in the small Bosnian towns of Travnik and Višegrad.

SOCIETY & CONDUCT

Removing one's shoes is customary in Muslim households; the host family will provide slippers. The Bosnian people are incredibly friendly, but when the subject turns to politics, the best strategy is listening. People are eager to talk about the war but are generally convinced that their side is right.

RELIGION

Before the war, Bosnia-Hercegovina's population was 43% Muslim Slavs, 31% Orthodox Serbs and 17% Catholic Croats. Of the current population of 2.8 million, approximately 42% are Muslim, 37% Serb, and 15% Croat. The current proportions are roughly the same despite the population shifts. In each part of Bosnia-Hercegovina, churches and mosques are being built (or rebuilt) at lightning speed. This phenomenon is more a symptom of nationalism than of religion, since most people are fairly secular.

LANGUAGE

Dialects notwithstanding, the people of Bosnia-Hercegovina speak the same language. However, that language is referred to as 'Bosnian' in the Muslim part of the Federation, 'Croatian' in Croat-controlled parts, and 'Serbian' in the RS. The Federation uses the Latin alphabet but the RS uses Cyrillic. See the Croatian, Serbian, & Bosnian section of the Language chapter at the back of the book for pronunciation guidelines and useful words and phrases.

Facts for the Visitor

HIGHLIGHTS

Sarajevo is a major historic site, simultaneously vibrant and shockingly destroyed. Beautiful Mostar deserves a visit for its cobbled old town and former Stari Most.

Driving or taking the bus through the ravaged countryside of Bosnia-Hercegovina is an unforgettable experience.

SUGGESTED ITINERARIES

Two days
    Visit Sarajevo
One week
    Visit Sarajevo and Mostar
Two weeks
    Visit Sarajevo, Travnik and Banja Luka

PLANNING
Climate & When to Go

Since Bosnia-Hercegovina is a mountainous country, it gets hot in the summer but quite chilly in the winter, and snowfall can last until April. The best time to visit is spring or summer. Don't worry about a seasonal crush of tourists just yet.

Books & Maps

Noel Malcolm's book *Bosnia: A Short History* is a good country-specific supplement to Rebecca West's mammoth classic *Black Lamb and Grey Falcon*, which exhaustively describes her trip through Yugoslavia in the late 1930s. For a detailed account of the recent war, try *The Death of Yugoslavia* by Laura Silber and Allan Little, or *The Fall of Yugoslavia* by Misha Glenny.

What to Bring

It's a myth that Bosnia suffers from shortages. Shops sell goods imported from the rest of Europe, but bring plenty of Deutschmarks, since you'll be paying in cash.

VISAS & EMBASSIES

No visas are required for citizens of the USA, Canada, Ireland, the UK, and most other EU countries. Citizens of other countries can obtain a tourist visa in advance by sending a personal cheque or money order for US$35, your passport, a copy of a round-trip plane ticket, an invitation letter, and an application to the nearest embassy. According to passport control in the Sarajevo airport, visitors flying into Sarajevo can obtain a visa for DM90 but it may involve some paperwork.

Those entering Bosnia-Hercegovina by land may not need a visa on the border, particularly if you are passing into Hercegovina from Croatia or the RS from Yugoslavia.

RS border officials have been known to charge illegal DM60 'transit visas' to travellers crossing into Yugoslavia.

Tourists in Bosnia are required to register with the local police. A hotel or accommodations agency will do this for you, but foreigners staying in private houses must do this themselves (in Sarajevo, go to Zmaja od Bosne 9, room 3).

Bosnian Embassies Abroad

Bosnia-Hercegovina has embassies and/or consulates in the following countries; check the web page www.bosnianembassy.org/bih/dipoffi.htm for further listings.

Australia
    (☎ (02) 6239 5955; fax (02) 6239 5793) 15 State Circle, Forrest ACT 2603
France
    (☎ 01-426 734 22; fax 01-405 385 22) 174 Rue de Courcelles, 75017 Paris
Croatia
    (☎ 01-276 776 or 425 899; fax 01-455 6177) Torbarova 9, 41000 Zagreb
Slovenia
    (☎ 061-132 2214; fax 061-132 2230) Likozarjeva 6 Ljubljana
UK
    (☎ 0171-255 3758; fax 0171-255 2760) 320 Regent St, London W1R 5AB
US
    (☎ 202-833 3612; fax 202-337 1502) 2109 E St NW, Washington DC 20037
    (☎ 212-751 9015/9016; fax 212-751 9019) (Consulate) 866 UN Plaza, Suite 580, New York NY 10017

Foreign Embassies in Bosnia-Hercegovina

These embassies are in Sarajevo:

Bulgaria
    (☎ 071-668 191; fax 071-668 182) Trampina 12/II
Canada
    (☎ 071-447 900; fax 071-447 901) Logavina 3b
Croatia
    (☎ 071-444 330; fax 071-472 434) 16 Mehmeda Spahe
Czech Republic
    (☎/fax 071-447 525) Potoklinica 6

Slovenia
   (☎ 071-447 660; fax 071-447 659) Bentbaša 7
UK
   (☎ 071-444 429; fax 071-666 131) Tina Ujevića 8
USA
   (☎ 071-659 969 or 445 700; fax 071-659 722)
   Alipašina 43

MONEY
Currency
The 'convertible mark' has been approved as
Bosnia's official common currency, to be tied
to the Deutschmark at a rate of KM1 to DM1.
However, the KM was not yet introduced at
the time of writing, although many menus in
Sarajevo already list prices in 'KM.' In
theory, the convertible mark will be used
throughout Bosnia-Hercegovina. In practice,
it may take quite a while.

Bosnia-Hercegovina's currency situation
mirrors the country's divisions. Sarajevo and
other Muslim parts of the Muslim-Croat Federation use Deutschmarks interchangeably
with tattered paper notes called Bosnian
dinars, which are fixed at a rate of BHD100
to DM1. In Croat-controlled parts of the Federation, Croatian kuna are widely used, and in
the Republika Srpska prices are in Serbian
dinars (different from Bosnian dinars!). The
good news is that Deutschmarks are accepted everywhere in Bosnia-Hercegovina.

Changing Money
ATMs are unavailable. Travellers cheques
can be exchanged at banks in most cities;
however, commissions are generally 3% and
above, on top of poor exchange rates. Converting to the local currency (Bosnian dinars,
Croatian kuna, Serbian dinars) is cheaper
than making the extra conversion to
Deutschmarks. If you're stuck with large
Deutschmark bills, which are difficult to
break at markets or shops, go to a bank and
ask nicely for smaller bills.

Credit Cards
The Sarajevo offices of some western airlines
(Swissair and Austrian Airlines) accept major
credit cards, along with a smattering of hotels
in Hercegovina. A few banks can give credit
card advances, but otherwise the rule is cash
cash cash.

Tipping
Tipping is customary at nice restaurants –
just leave DM5 or 10 on the table, or round
up the bill. Taxi fares can be treated the same
way.

POST & COMMUNICATIONS
Post
Bosnia's postal system works, but poste
restante is unavailable except at the post
office in west Mostar.

Telephone & Fax
To call Bosnia-Hercegovina from abroad,
dial the international access code ☎ 387 (the
country code for Bosnia-Hercegovina), the
area code (without the initial zero) and the
number. If you are calling the Republika
Srpska, you may have more luck dialing
through Yugoslavia (☎ 381, then city code).

To make an international call from Bosnia-
Hercegovina, it's cheapest to go to the post
office. Dial the international access number
(☎ 00 from the Muslim part of the Federation, ☎ 99 from elsewhere), then the country
code and number. A three-minute call to the
USA costs DM6.

Telephone cards, useful for local or short
international calls, can be purchased at post
offices. Note however that cards issued in
Serb, Croat, and Muslim-controlled areas are
not interchangeable.

Some important telephone numbers are
☎ 901 (international operator), ☎ 988 for
local directory information, ☎ 92 for police,
☎ 93 for the fire department, and ☎ 94 for
emergency assistance.

Faxes can be sent from most post offices,
though machines may be slow and prices
consequently high.

INTERNET RESOURCES
For general background on the country take
a 'Bosnia Virtual Fieldtrip' at (http://geog
.gmu.edu/gess/jwc/bosnia/bosnia.html). You
can always visit the web site of the Office of
the High Representative (http://www.ohr.int)
to get detailed news updates.

Although email is so far unavailable
publicly in Bosnia-Hercegovina, it can be accessed cheaply and easily from the university
in Sarajevo.

NEWSPAPERS & MAGAZINES

All parts of Bosnia-Hercegovina have different papers. Sarajevo's independent daily *Oslobođenje* functioned throughout the war. *Dani*, the popular and outrageous biweekly magazine, keeps the Sarajevo government on its toes with colourful covers and entertaining political satire.

RADIO & TV

Studio 99 is both a television and a radio station; the latter carries some Radio Free Europe broadcasting. Radio Zid has some Voice of America news. Serb Radio Television (SRT) is broadcast out of Banja Luka.

PHOTOGRAPHY & VIDEO

Kodak and Fuji film is available in larger cities for DM10 and up to DM14 a roll. It is quite common to take photographs of war damage, but use prudence and sensitivity.

TIME

Bosnia-Hercegovina is on Central European Time, which is GMT/UTC plus one hour. Daylight savings time in late March sets clocks forward one hour, but in late November clocks are turned back one hour.

ELECTRICITY

Electricity is 220V, 50Hz AC, with the standard three-pronged European plugs.

WEIGHTS & MEASURES

Measurements in Bosnia-Hercegovina fall under the metric system.

HEALTH

Clinics with western doctors serve only international organisations. Visiting a Bosnian doctor costs about DM10 to 30. Make sure that your medical insurance plan does not exclude evacuation from Bosnia-Hercegovina.

WOMEN TRAVELLERS

Women travelling alone should feel no particular anxiety. Indeed, people will be surprised that you are alone and may offer help.

DANGERS & ANNOYANCES

Always look into local political conditions before undertaking a journey. Use particular caution when travelling in the Republika Srpska, where anti-western sentiments are generally higher than in the Federation.

Mines

Over one million land mines are estimated to be in Bosnia-Hercegovina. These were laid mostly in conflict zones. All of Sarajevo's suburbs are heavily mined, as are areas around Travnik and Mostar. The most frightening statistic is that only about half of Bosnia-Hercegovina's minefields are in known locations. The Mine Action Centre in Sarajevo (☎ 071-201 298 or 299; fax 071-667 311) runs valuable 1½-hour mine information briefings which are open to visitors.

Unexploded ordinances (UXOs, mortars, grenades, and shells) also pose a huge danger around former conflict areas.

The golden rule for mines and UXOs is to stick to asphalt surfaces. Abandoned-looking areas are avoided for a reason. Do not drive off the shoulder of roads, do not poke around in abandoned villages or damaged houses, do not get curious about shiny metal objects on the grass, and regard every centimetre of ground as suspicious.

PUBLIC HOLIDAYS

Bosnia-Hercegovina observes Independence Day (1 March), May Day (1 May), Day of the Republic (25 November) and two Muslim religious holidays of Bajram, which will fall in January and March in the years 1999 and 2000.

ACCOMMODATION

The year-round presence of international officials on expense accounts has jump-started Bosnia-Hercegovina's hotel industry. Sarajevo and Mostar have some pleasant new hotels, but in general prices are much higher than the typical socialist-style buildings warrant. Except in a few hotels in west Mostar and Međugorje, payment is in cash only. Deutschmarks are always accepted, and usually US dollars.

Pansions and private accommodation agencies have sprouted in Sarajevo, but elsewhere (except for Međugorje, where every house is

BOSNIA-HERCEGOVINA

a pansion) there are few. The situation is changing quickly, so inquire at the tourist office. Or ask locals at the market or shops.

Private accommodation is usually very pleasant. Likely as not, your host will ply you with coffee, pull out old pictures of Tito (depending on his politics), and regale you with tales of Bosnia-Hercegovina's past glory.

Most accommodations charge tax (DM2 to 5), which is included in the prices listed in this chapter.

FOOD & DRINKS

Bosnia's Turkish heritage is savoured in its grilled meats such as *bosanski lonac* (Bosnian stew of cabbage and meat). When confronted with the ubiquitous *burek* (a layered meat pie sold by weight), vegetarians can opt for *sirnica* (cheese pie) or *zeljanica* (spinach pie). *Ćevapčići*, another favourite, is lamb and beef rolls tucked into a half-loaf of spongy somun bread. For sugar-soaked deserts, try baklava or *tufahije*, an apple cake topped with walnuts and whipped cream.

Good wines from Hercegovina include Žilavka (white) and Blatina (red). These are best sampled in the region's wineries. A meal can always be washed down with a shot of *šlivovica* (plum brandy) or *loza* (grape brandy).

Getting There & Away

AIR

Airlines serving Sarajevo include Croatia Airlines, Crossair (the partner of Swissair), Lufthansa, and Austrian Airlines. Air Bosna, a tiny new airline which has leased a few planes from Ukraine, flies to Turkey and Germany.

Yugoslav National Airlines (JAT) has service to Banja Luka from Belgrade. The Mostar airport is not yet open to commercial traffic.

LAND

In the absence of international train lines, buses are an excellent, safe way to enter Bosnia-Hercegovina, and to see the countryside. Stowing luggage costs up to DM5,

depending on the route. Buses usually run on time, although they are slow due to windy roads and occasional stops for drivers and passengers to eat and smoke.

Bus travel between Croatia and the Muslim-Croat Federation of Bosnia-Hercegovina is routine. Two daily buses travel between Sarajevo and Zagreb (417km) and Sarajevo and Split. The Sarajevo-Dubrovnik bus makes one trip each day via Mostar, and buses from Sarajevo go to Germany several times a week. The Republika Srpska is closely connected by bus to Yugoslavia. Buses run every hour between Banja Luka and Belgrade, and a different bus runs from the Serb-held Sarajevo suburb of Lukavica to Belgrade. A daily bus goes between Zagreb and Banja Luka, though you change buses at the border (the other bus will be waiting).

LEAVING BOSNIA-HERCEGOVINA

There is a DM20 departure tax from the Sarajevo airport.

Getting Around

Trains are essentially useless, as they run only from Sarajevo to Zenica and a few other small cities. Trains from Banja Luka have a similarly limited radius within the RS.

Within each entity (the Federation and the RS), Bosnia's bus network is quite comprehensive. Inter-entity travel has become less of a problem since the 1998 introduction of two daily buses between Sarajevo and Banja Luka.

Plenty of rent-a-car places have sprung up, particularly in Sarajevo, Mostar, and Medugorje. However, renting a car does not give you clearance to drive anywhere in Bosnia. License plates are badges of identity. Cars with Sarajevo plates will not be welcome in the Republika Srpska and vice-versa (though the Muslim and Croat-controlled parts of the Federation are compatible). Ask if the rental car agencies use the new common license plates which should facilitate trans-entity travel.

As elsewhere in the Balkans, people drive like maniacs, passing even on sharp curves.

Around the Country

SARAJEVO
☎ 071

Sarajevo, tucked in a valley beside the Miljacka River, is the capital of Bosnia-Hercegovina. Before the war, the city was also an ethnic microcosm of Yugoslavia. For hundreds of years it was where Muslims, Serbs, Croats, Turks, Jews and others peacefully coexisted.

From the mid-15th century until 1878, Turkish governors resided in Sarajevo. The city's name comes from *saraj*, Turkish for 'palace'. Sarajevo is one of the most Oriental cities in Europe, retaining the essence of its rich history in its mosques, markets and the picturesque old Turkish bazaar called Baščaršija. When the Turks finally withdrew, half a century of Austro-Hungarian domination began, culminating in the assassination of Archduke Franz Ferdinand and his wife Sophie by a Serbian nationalist in 1914. In 1984 Sarajevo again attracted world attention by hosting the 14th Winter Olympic Games.

Sarajevo's heritage of six centuries was pounded into rubble by Bosnian Serb artillery during the siege of 1992 to 1995, when Sarajevo's only access to the outside world was via a 1km tunnel under the airport. Over 10,500 Sarajevans died and 50,000 were wounded by Bosnian Serb sniper fire and shelling. The endless new graveyards near Koševo stadium leave a silent record of the terrible years.

Despite the highly visible scars of war, Sarajevo is again bursting with energy. Colourful trams run down the road once called 'Sniper's Alley', innumerable cafés blast pop music into the streets, and locals spend leisurely evenings strolling down the main pedestrian street, Ferhadija. A large international presence made up of government officials and humanitarian aid workers is also altering the face of the city. Large UN jeeps and camouflage SFOR vehicles melt into the rest of the traffic. The energy poured into Bosnia-Hercegovina's recovery has rendered Sarajevo the fastest-changing city in Europe.

Orientation

Surrounded by mountains, Sarajevo is beside the peaceful Miljacka River near the geographic centre of Bosnia-Hercegovina. From the airport 13km to the west, the main road runs through Novo Sarajevo, then past the turn-off to the bus and train stations and into the town centre. Baščaršija is on the east end of town.

Information

The Tourist Information Bureau (☎ 532 606; fax 532 281), ul Zelenih Beretki 22, keeps good tabs on the changes in Sarajevo and can answer most questions about the city. It has a good supply of books and maps and is open weekdays from 8 am to 3 pm and Saturday from 9 am to 2 pm.

Money Most banks will exchange travellers cheques for a hefty commission or poor rates. The Central Profit Banka (☎ 533 582), ul Zelenih Beretki 24 with other branches around town, exchanges travellers cheques for 3% commission (1.5% if you want dinars). Receiving wired money is also possible (1% commission), as are Diner's Club and American Express cash advances (bring personal American Express cheques along). Shed excess kuna at Gospodarska Banka, the Croatian bank on ul Maršala Tita 56.

Post & Communications A post office just behind the eternal flame on Ferhadija sends letters and faxes and sells phonecards. To make a lengthy international call, head to the post office at Obala Kulina Bana 8 (open Monday to Saturday from 8 am to 3 pm; telephones only).

Internet Resources Internet access is available in the University of Sarajevo building on Obala Kulina Bana 7. Go to the top floor and turn right, following the signs to Interlink Computer Centre. The pricing system is odd but thankfully cheap: DM10 for 15 hours. Across the river, the university building on ul Skenderija 70 has computers with free Internet access in room 12.

You can register for an account on the local server (BIHNET) at the post office on Zmaja od Bosne 100, four tram stops past the Holiday Inn. Register between 9 and 10 am at window 16 or 17. It costs DM15 a month plus 1 to 2DM per hour.

Bookshop & Library Šahinpašić, ul Mula Mustafe Bašekije 1 near the eternal flame, sells English-language newspapers, maga-

SARAJEVO

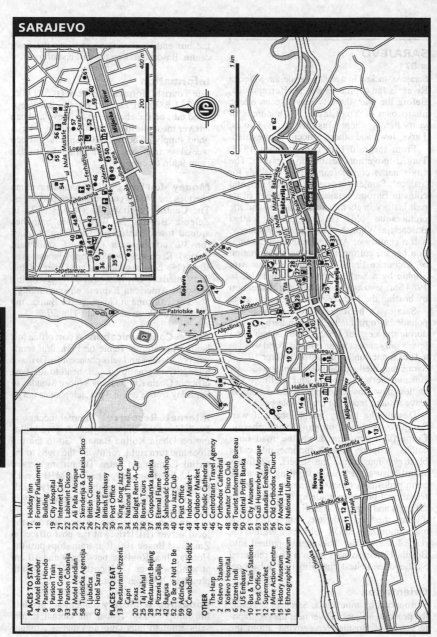

BOSNIA-HERCEGOVINA

PLACES TO STAY
4   Motel Belveder
5   Pansion Hondo
8   Pansion Train
9   Hotel Grand
33 Pansion Cobanija
54 Motel Meridian
58 Turistička Agencija
     Ljubačica
62 Hotel Saraj

PLACES TO EAT
13 Restaurant-Pizzeria
     Capri
20 Texas
25 Taj Mahal
28 Restaurant Beijing
32 Pizzeria Galija
42 Ragusa
52 To Be or Not to Be
59 Aščinica
60 Ćevabdžinica Hodžić

17 Holiday Inn
18 Former Parliament
     Building
19 City Hospital
21 Internet Cafe
22 Labiwrint Disco
23 Ali Paša Mosque
24 Skenderija & Galaxia Disco
26 British Council
27 Marquee
29 British Embassy
30 Post Office
31 King Kong Jazz Club
34 National Theatre
35 Budget Rent-A-Car
36 Bosnia Tours
37 Gospodarska Banka
38 Eternal Flame
39 Šahinpašić bookshop
40 Clou Jazz Club
41 Post Office
44 Outdoor Market
43 Indoor Market

OTHER
1   The Harp
2   Koševo Stadium
3   Koševo Hospital
6   Pizzeria Indi
7   US Embassy
10 Bus & Train Stations
11 Post Office
12 Supermarket
14 Mine Action Centre
15 History Museum
16 Ethnographic Museum
45 Catholic Cathedral
46 Centrotrans Travel Agency
47 Orthodox Cathedral
48 Senator Disco Club
49 Tourist Information Bureau
50 Central Profit Banka
51 City Museum
53 Gazi Husrevbey Mosque
55 Canadian Embassy
56 Old Orthodox Church
57 Morića Han
61 National Library

zines, and cheap Penguin classics. Don't miss the Survival Map (DM10), a striking cartoon-like depiction of wartime Sarajevo, with helpful English-language explanations on the back. The British Council Library (☎ 200 895) is at Obala Kulina Bana 4.

Medical Services Try Koševo Hospital, ul Bolnička 25 (☎ 666 620) or the City Hospital (☎ 664 724), ul Kranjčevića 12. The US embassy can provide a list of private doctors.

Things to See
The cobbled **Baščaršija** (the Turkish Quarter), where bronze artisans ply their trade, is the heart of Sarajevo. This is the only spot in the city where most cafés serve real Turkish coffee in a *džežva*, as opposed to espresso. **Morića Han**, now a café along Sarači, used to be a tavern and stable when Sarajevo was an important crossroads between east and west.

The graceful Austro-Hungarian **National Library** lies on the east end of town along the river at the end of Baščaršija. The building was destroyed by an incendiary shell on 25 August 1992, 100 years after construction began. It has since gotten a new dome courtesy of Austria but is still not open to visitors.

Austrian Archduke Franz Ferdinand and his wife Sophie paused at the National Library (then the town hall) on 28 June, 1914, then rode west along the riverside in an open car to the second bridge. It was here that they were shot, an event which led to WWI. A plaque bearing the footprints of the assassin, Gavrilo Princip, was ripped out of the pavement during the recent war because Princip was a Bosnian Serb. The one-room **City Museum**, where ul Zelenih Beretki meets the river, now stands on 'Princip's corner'.

In the city centre, the **eternal flame** commemorates WWII. Places of worship for four different religions – Catholic, Orthodox, Muslim, and Jewish – lie in close vicinity to one another, as Sarajevans still very proudly point out. These include the large Catholic church on Ferhadija (which has an English-language service on Sunday at noon); the old Orthodox Church on ul Mula Mustafe Bašekija (which predates the yellow and brown Orthodox cathedral); the Gazi-Husrevbey Mosque (1531), built by masons from Dubro-

vnik; and the old Jewish synagogue (now closed) along ul Mula Mustafe Bašekija.

The three-year siege made Sarajevo itself a stunning sight. The road into the city from the airport (now Zmaja od Bosne) was dubbed **'Sniper's Alley'** during the war because Serb snipers in the surrounding hills picked off civilians crossing the road. The bright yellow **Holiday Inn** was the wartime home to international journalists, as the city's only functioning wartime hotel. The side facing Sniper's Alley was heavily damaged, but the hotel has since been given a massive facelift. Across from the Holiday Inn is the **National Museum**, which is closed to the public while it temporarily houses the Bosnia-Hercegovina parliament. A **History Museum** just up the road shows old photographs of Bosnia-Hercegovina and has rotating exhibits, some of which pertain to the recent war.

A **treeline** still rings the city, demarcating the former front line. Residents cut down trees and burned benches for heat during the siege. Watch the pavement for **Sarajevo roses**, which are skeletal hand-like indentations where a shell exploded. Many of these are symbolically filled in with red rubber.

Special Events
In late August, internationally produced films are shown at the annual Sarajevo Film Festival (☎ 668 186; fax 664 547; sff@soros.org.ba). The Winter Festival in February and March features theatre and musical performances.

Places to Stay
Finding a room in Sarajevo is no longer difficult, since hotels and private rooms have sprung up to house visiting international officials. However, prices remain very high, and reservations are wise. Private accommodation is a relative bargain at DM40 to 50 per person, but some rooms may not be near the centre. Wherever you stay, be sure to ask about the water situation, since parts of the city have running water only during certain times of day.

Private Rooms *Bosnia Tours* (☎535 829; fax 202 206/207), ul Maršala Tita 54, near the eternal flame, has plenty of good rooms near the centre for DM40 a person (DM70 for two people). If you don't like the room, they'll gladly show you another. The agency is closed Sunday.

Turistička Agencija Ljubačica (☎/fax 232 109), ul Mula Mustafa Bašekije 65 in Baščaršija, has a handful of rooms near the centre and more rooms further out. Prices are DM30 to 55, depending on location and room quality; you may be able to bargain. If you arrive after 10 pm, call their mobitel (☎ 090 121 813).

Ask at the *Motel Meridian* (☎ 446 177; ☎/fax 446 176), Jaroslava Černija 3 off ul Mula Mustafa Bašekija, about its five private rooms which are pleasanter and much cheaper than the motel itself. The rooms, a 10-minute walk uphill from the cathedral, are all in a spacious, two-storey flat with soft pink walls, a kitchen, and satellite TV (DM63/106 for one or two people).

Pansions The cheapest place in town is the bizarre *Pansion Train* (☎ 200 517), Halida Kajtaza 11, where beds in a stationary train sleeper car cost DM33/40 for a single/double. Besides novelty and price, however, it's a bit cramped, and the showers and toilets are not the cleanest. From the bus station, take the road to Hotel Grand. Turn left at the gas station, and follow the big sign to the pansion.

The cosy *Pansion Hondo*, ul Zaima Šarca 23 (☎ 666 564; ☎/fax 469 375), is a 20-minute walk uphill from the centre. Rooms cost DM80/120 a single/double, with breakfast included. Head straight up ul Pehlivanuša, behind the cathedral. It will turn into ul Zaima Šarca.

Pansion Čobanija (☎ 441 749; ☎/fax 203 937), ul Čobanija 29, just past Pizzeria Galija on the south side of the river, has rooms with nice marbled private baths, cable TV, and a fax machine available for guests' use. Request an upstairs room, and enjoy proximity to the large sitting room. Prices are DM80/120 for a single/double.

Hotels & Motels At DM150 to 300 a night, hotels are not cost-effective. *Hotel Saraj* (☎ 472 691; fax 447 703), ul Nevjestina 5, is the white building visible on the hill behind the National Library. Singles/doubles

begin at DM150/200. Rooms with a view of Sarajevo are more expensive, but all rooms are pleasant, with satellite TV and breakfast included. Another quality option is *Hotel Grand* (☎ 205 444; fax 204 745), on ul Muhameda ef Pandže 7 behind the train station, which has singles/doubles with breakfast for DM182/284.

The aqua-green *Motel Belveder* (☎ 664 877; fax 206 470), on ul Višnjik 2 near Koševo hospital, has plain but comfortable rooms with satellite TV, phone, and shower for DM120/150 a single/double, including breakfast. Call for airport pick-ups.

Places to Eat

Sarajevo's restaurants are the domain of internationals, since Bosnians socialise over coffee and eat at home. Most restaurant menus are in English, and main meals usually cost DM10 to 15.

Ragusa, Ferhadija 10b, serves tasty Bosnian cuisine to diners relaxing at wood tables. Be sure to wash down dinner with a traditional shot of *rakija*. *To Be or Not to Be*, Čizmedžiluk 5 in Baščaršija, has deep, colourful salads in a candlelit setting. Vegetarians can opt for an omelette or spaghetti, while others can enjoy the classic Bosnian steaks. A short way beyond the city centre in Grbavica, the upmarket *Restaurant-Pizzeria Capri*, ul Hamdije Čemerlić 45, has delicious main meals for slightly higher prices (DM20 to 30). Try the salmon, or go for the cheaper pasta and pizza.

Sarajevo's roster of new ethnic restaurants is crowned by *Restaurant Beijing*, ul Maršala Tita 38, a delicious place which actually dares to offer tofu. Main meals are DM13 to 20. Spicy Indian dishes at *Taj Mahal*, ul Hamdije Kreševljakovića 6, are slightly less expensive. Or fill up on hearty burritos at *Texas*, ul Vladmira Perića 4 near the Internet Café.

The most popular pizza spots include *Pizzeria Galija*, ul Čobanija 20 across the river, and *Pizzeria Indi*, at the corner of ul Gabelina and ul Koševo.

For a quick meal, ćevapi, burek, and 'Fast Food' joints are ubiquitous, but *Ćevabdžinica Hodžić*, ul Bravadžiluk 34 near the National Library, is a ćevapi star. It's just up the street from *Aščinican*, ul Bravadžiluk 28, where you can choose what you want from the array of salads, vegetables and meats.

Self-Catering Sarajevo's only sizeable supermarket is a bright, unmistakable yellow building four tram stops beyond the Holiday Inn along Zmaja od Bosne. A year-round outdoor market, behind the cathedral on ul Mule Mustafa Bašekija, has a good selection of fruits and vegetables. Its indoor counterpart, with dairy products and meats, is across the street in the sandy-coloured building.

Entertainment
Theatre The tourist office keeps a monthly list of concerts, ballets, and performances at the National Theatre on ul Zelenih Beretki, the Sarajevo War Theatre (in the same building as Ragusa restaurant), and Kamerni Theater, upstairs on ul Maršala Tita 56.

Discos The king of Sarajevo's disco world is *Senator*, on ul Strossmayerova near the cathedral (open Thursday to Saturday from 10pm; DM10 cover). Other options are *Labiwrint*, ul Jezero 1, not far from the US Embassy (closed Monday; DM5 cover), and *Galaxia*, across the river in the Skenderija complex (no cover).

Pubs & Jazz Clubs Sarajevo's best-known bar is unquestionably the *Internet Café*, ul Maršala Tita 5, near the intersection with ul Alipašina. Although Internet access is a myth, the café has live music some weekends and Czech Budweiser on tap, which can be consumed for half-price at happy hour (5 to 7 pm). *The Harp*, on ul Patriotske lige, is an Irish bar with Guinness and other native brews on tap. Head up ul Koševo, which turns into ul Patriotske lige bb. The pub is at the triangular intersection, a 25-minute walk from the centre. The crowded *Marquee*, Obala Kulina Bana 5, plays rock music.

For occasional live jazz, try *Clou*, ul Mula Mustafe Bašekija 5 (open from 6 pm), and *King Kong*, ul Hamdije Kreševljakovića 17.

Cinema Many cinemas play American movies with subtitles. *Oslobođendje*, Sarajevo's daily paper, has daily cinema listings under the 'Kina' column.

Things to Buy
Metalworking craft shops line ul Kazandžiluk, at the end of Baščaršija. Turkish coffee sets and snazzy plates aside, the trendiest souvenirs are engraved shell cases (that's shell as in cartridge). Small ones sell for around DM10. Bargaining is possible, indeed necessary, in these shops.

Getting There & Away
Bus Two buses a day run to Sarajevo from Zagreb, and two from Split and one from Dubrovnik. Two daily buses also go to and from Banja Luka. Buses run from the Serb-controlled Sarajevo suburb of Lukavica to various parts of the RS and Belgrade. Explain to a taxi driver that you want to go to the bus station in Lukavica, and he will take you to a spot on the RS border near the airport, where you can switch cabs or walk 150m to the bus station and buy a ticket.

Getting Around
An efficient but often crowded tram network runs east-west between Baščaršija and Illidža. Tram 4 from Baščaršija peels off at the bus station; tram 1 goes between the bus station to Illidža. Buy tickets (DM1) at kiosks near tram stations. Buses and trolleybuses also cost DM1 (punch your ticket on board); purchase bus tickets from the driver.

To/From the Airport One under-utilised bus goes sporadically to and from the airport, about 13km west of the city centre. Call ☎ 447 955 for departure times or ask at the tourist office. A taxi should cost about DM15.

Taxi Sarajevo's ubiquitous taxis all have meters that begin at DM2 and cost DM1 per kilometre. Call ☎ 970 for Radio Taxi.

Car Budget (☎/fax 206 640), ul Branilaca Sarajeva 21, also has an office at the airport (☎ 463 598); Diner's Club and American Express cards are accepted. ASA Rent has offices at ul Branilaca Sarajeva 20 (☎/fax 445 209/210) and at the airport (☎ 463 598).

AROUND SARAJEVO
Twenty-five kilometres south-east of Sarajevo, the deserted slopes of **Mount Jahorina**,

the site of the 1984 Winter Olympics, still offer some of the best skiing in Europe at extremely cheap prices. Unfortunately, Jahorina lies in Bosnian Serb territory just above the politically hardline town of Pale, so getting there is problematic. The British-based firm Harlequin Leisure (☎ 445 076; in the UK 0044-370-694 069; harlequin–sport@ hotmail.com) knows the ropes and ferries travellers up to Jahorina in sturdy Land Rovers. It can arrange accommodation (DM30 to 70 per night) and ski rental (DM15 to 25; lift tickets DM10; lessons DM15). Skiing on Jahorina is safe from mines.

MOSTAR
☎ 088

Mostar, the main city in Hercegovina, is a beautiful medieval town set in the valley of the aqua-green Neretva River. Its name derives from the 16th-century Turkish bridge which used to arc over the river; *mostari* means keepers of the bridge. Sadly, the town was the scene of intense Muslim-Croat fighting during the recent war, which left many buildings destroyed or scarred. Even the bridge was destroyed by Croat shelling in November 1993. Once divided only by the Neretva River, Mostar is now segregated into Muslim and Croat sectors. Nonetheless, visitors are slowly drifting back to enjoy the old medieval buildings, cobbled streets, and Turkish souvenir shops that give Mostar its charm.

Orientation

Mostar is a divided city. Though there are no physical barriers, Croats live on the west side of the Neretva River and Muslims on the east (though Muslims also control a small strip on the river's west bank).

Information

Tourist Office Atlas Travel Agency (☎/fax 318 771), in the same building as Hotel Ero, has useful suggestions and a rough map of the west side. The tourist agency on the east side beside the bus station speaks no English and has sparse information.

Money Prices on the east side are in Bosnian dinars or Deutschmarks, and prices on the west side are in kuna (though Deutschmarks

are accepted). Hrvatska Banka, adjacent to Hotel Ero, changes travellers cheques to any currency except dinars for 1.5% commission.

Post & Communications The large, modern post office on the west side, around the corner from Hotel Ero, is the only place in Bosnia for poste restante mail (held for one month; pick-up is at window 12). Address mail to Name, Poste Restante, 88000 Mostar (Zapadni), Bosnia-Hercegovina.

Inquire at the new Training Centre (Centar za Obuku; ☎ 551 127), ul Oneščukova 24 about 60m west of Stari Most, about public Internet access.

Things to See

Stari Most (old bridge) is still the heart of the old town, though it is now replaced by a swinging metal bridge. The small **Crooked Bridge**, built a few years before Stari Most and possibly used as a model, spans a Neretva tributary nearby.

The cobbled old town itself, called **Kujundžiluk**, extends on both sides of Stari Most. It is still pleasantly awash with small shops selling Turkish-style souvenirs. Along the east side, the most famous mosque in Mostar is the **Karadžozbeg Mosque** (1557). The top of its minaret was blown off in the recent war. Not far away, the 350-year-old **Turkish House**, on ul Biščevića, has colourful rugs and furniture in old Turkish style.

The dramatic **front line**, which now essentially divides the town between Muslims and Croats, runs along the street behind Hotel Ero, then jogs one street west to the main boulevard.

Places to Stay

Mostar's three hotels are expensive, but a few pleasant pansions offer relief. All pansion rooms have multiple beds. Reserve a week in advance, because groups occasionally fill the space. The 12-bed *Pansion Zlatni Liljan* (☎ 551 353), ul Sehovina 6, costs DM20, with breakfast DM25. Past the Pavarotti Music Centre, swing left and follow the cobblestone road that starts by the mosque. The 10-bed *Vila Ossa* (☎ 578 322), Gojka Vokovića 40, is on the other side of the river. The price for one/two people is DM30/40, with breakfast DM35/50. *Pansion Ćorić* (☎ 219 560; fax 219 559), ul Matije Gupca

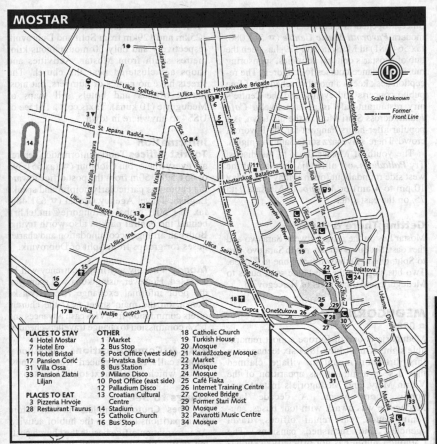

MOSTAR

PLACES TO STAY	OTHER	
4 Hotel Mostar	1 Market	18 Catholic Church
7 Hotel Ero	2 Bus Stop	19 Turkish House
11 Hotel Bristol	5 Post Office (west side)	20 Mosque
17 Pansion Ćorić	6 Hrvatska Banka	21 Karadžozbeg Mosque
31 Villa Ossa	8 Bus Station	22 Market
33 Pansion Zlatni	9 Milano Disco	23 Mosque
Liljan	10 Post Office (east side)	24 Mosque
	12 Palladium Disco	25 Café Fiaka
PLACES TO EAT	13 Croatian Cultural	26 Internet Training Centre
3 Pizzeria Hrvoje	Centre	27 Crooked Bridge
28 Restaurant Taurus	14 Stadium	29 Former Stari Most
	15 Catholic Church	30 Mosque
	16 Bus Stop	32 Pavarotti Music Centre
		34 Mosque

Scale Unknown

Former Front Line

125A, is about a 20-minute walk directly west of Stari Most. Beds cost DM50 including breakfast, and the proprietors speak German but not English.

Hotel Ero (☎ 317 166/167; fax 314 394), on ul Ante Starčevića directly across the river from the bus station, has polished rooms with porches for DM72/124 for a single/double (American Express cards accepted). The newly reopened *Hotel Bristol* (☎ 550 082/083/084; fax 550 081), on ul Mostarskog Bataljona on the river's west bank, has singles/doubles for DM81.5/177. *Hotel Mostar*, Kneza Domagoja

bb (☎ 322 679; fax 315 693), has similar prices but is the most cramped of the lot.

Places to Eat
Čevapi spots are ubiquitous, and restaurants with divine views of the river cluster along the western riverbank near Stari Most. Tables on a covered porch at *Restaurant Taurus* offer a lovely view of Crooked Bridge; the food is hearty and traditional.

For a big salad or good pizza, try *Restaurant-Pizzeria Hrvoje*, Kralja Tomislava (☎ 321 385), in west Mostar.

Entertainment

Since it opened in December 1997, the large modern *Pavorotti Music Centre* (☎ 564 080; fax 564 081) ul Maršala Tita 179, has been the hub of Mostar's cultural activities, sponsoring music and dance courses for children. The reception desk keeps a monthly schedule of free public concerts and events, and the Centre's airy restaurant-café is always lively. *Café Fiaka*, across Stari Most in the old town, is a popular after-hours hangout for the Pavorotti crowd. There's live jazz some Saturday nights.

The youth of Mostar flock to the discos. Try *Palladium*, off ul Kralja Tvrtka near the west side roundabout (open Friday to Sunday 10 pm to 4 am) or *Milano*, ul Maršala Tita 75, on the east side.

Getting There & Away

Mostar lies on the route between Sarajevo and the coast. Six buses per day run to Sarajevo, two to Split, one to Dubrovnik, and one to Zagreb. Two bus stops on the west side send buses to Međugorje and other parts of Hercegovina.

MEĐUGORJE
☎ 088

Međugorje is one of Europe's most remarkable sights. On 24 June 1981 six teenagers in this dirt-poor mountain village claimed they'd seen a miraculous apparition of the Virgin Mary, and Međugorje's instant economic boom began. A decade later Međugorje was awash with tour buses, souvenir stands, car rental offices, travel agencies, and furnished pansions. The Catholic Church has not officially acknowledged the apparitions (the first in Europe since those of Lourdes, France, in 1858 and Fatima, Portugal, in 1917), but 'religious tourism' has been developed as if this were a beach resort.

After a wartime hiatus, the busloads of package pilgrims are returning with renewed fervour. Tourist facilities are fully intact, since the front line did not reach Međugorje – some locals attribute this to divine protection. Crowds are especially heavy around Easter, the anniversary of the first apparition (June 24), the Assumption of the Virgin (15 August) and the Nativity of the Virgin (8 September).

Orientation

Međugorje lies in the heart of Hercegovina, 125km and 129km from Split and Dubrovnik respectively and only 30 mountainous kilometres south from Mostar. Activities and shops are clustered near the church. The streets have no names or numbers, but most tourist offices and hotels sell maps of Međugorje (10 kuna). Taxis cost a flat fee of US$4 to anywhere in town.

Information

Tourist Offices Tourist information centres are everywhere, but Globtour (☎/fax 651 393 or 651 593), 50m from the post office toward the church, is particularly helpful and speaks English. Travel Agency Global (☎ 651 489; fax 651 501; global-medjugorje@int.tel.hr), behind the central park is also worth trying. Both can arrange accommodation and charter buses for groups from Split or Dubrovnik.

Money Virtually any major currency will be accepted. However, using kuna will spare you the poor informal exchange rate. Hrvatska Banka, on the main street near the church, offers commission-free Visa cash advances and 1.5% commission to change travellers cheques.

Post & Communications International phone calls can be placed from the post office, which is right next to the bus stop.

Things to See

St James' Church, completed in 1969 before the apparitions began, is the hub of activity. An information office beside the church posts the daily schedule, as well as polylingual printouts of the Virgin's latest message.

Apparition Hill, where the Virgin was first spotted on 24 June 1981, is near the hamlet Podbrdo south-west of town. A blue cross marks the place where the Virgin was supposedly seen with a cross in the background, conveying a message of peace. It is a place for silence and prayer. To reach Apparition Hill, take the road curving left (east) from the centre of town, and follow the signs to Podbrdo (about 3km).

Cross Mountain (Mt. Križevac) lies about 1.5km south-west of town. The 45-minute hike to the top leads to a white cross planted there in 1934 to commemorate the

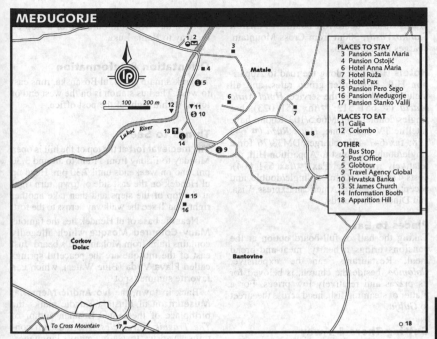

MEĐUGORJE

PLACES TO STAY
3 Pansion Santa Maria
4 Pansion Ostojić
6 Hotel Anna Maria
7 Hotel Ruža
8 Hotel Pax
15 Pansion Pero Šego
16 Pansion Međugorje
17 Pansion Stanko Valilj

PLACES TO EAT
11 Galija
12 Colombo

OTHER
1 Bus Stop
2 Post Office
5 Globtour
9 Travel Agency Global
10 Hrvatska Banka
13 St James Church
14 Information Booth
18 Apparition Hill

Matale

Lukoč River

Corkov Dolac

Bantovine

To Cross Mountain

0   100   200 m

1900th anniversary of Christ's death. Pilgrims stop to say the rosary at crosses along the trail. Wear sturdy shoes, as the path is extremely rocky. Candles are forbidden due to fire danger. After the hike, knock on the door of Pansion Stanko Vasilj, 300m from the base of Cross Mountain, and relax with a cool glass (DM1) of the town's best home-made wine.

Places to Stay

With 17,000 rooms, Međugorje has more space than the rest of Bosnia combined. Reduced tourism means that accommodation is easy to find, except around major holidays. Larger pansions and hotels can fill unpredictably with large tour groups, so book in advance. Most pansion rooms look the same, though rooms around the church are the most expensive. Friendly proprietors usually offer the choice of bed and breakfast, half-board, and full-board. Home-made meals are often rounded out with a bottle of *domaći vino*

(home-made wine). Tourist offices can also arrange accommodation, but this is more expensive than contacting the pansion directly. Tour groups can find reduced rates.

The city's few hotels are blander and more expensive than the pansions, and the rooms are not much better.

Pansions The 49-bed *Pansion Ostojić* (☎ 651 562; fax 651 095), not far from the post office, has rooms for DM20/35/45 (breakfast/half-board/full-board). Inquire in the Café Santa Fe, just in front of the pansion.

About 100m behind Ostojić, the white-washed *Pansion Santa Maria* (☎ 651 523; fax 651 723) charges DM26.5/36.5/45.5 for bed and breakfast/half-board/full-board. Reserve early, as it is often filled with groups.

The road to Cross Mountain yields some gems. The *Pansion Pero Šego* costs DM21.5/31.5 for bed and breakfast/half-board. Further on, the homy 25-bed Pansion Međugorje (☎ 651 315; fax 651 452), is a steal at DM15/30/45 a person for bed and breakfast/half-board/full-board. *Pansion Stanko Vasilj*, 300m from Cross Mountain, charges DM25/35/45.

Hotels Hotels lie along the road to Apparition Hill. Most offer group rates, and all include breakfast in the service. *Hotel Anna Maria* (☎ 651 512; ☎/fax 651 023), has singles/doubles for DM66.5/103. Rooms have satellite TV and phone. *Hotel Ruža* (☎ 643 118; fax 647 431) charges DM38/76 for a single/double. Closest to Apparition Hill, the relatively ritzy Hotel Pax (☎/fax 651 604), costs DM61.5/130 for a single/double and accepts MasterCard, American Express, Visa, and Diner's Club cards.

Places to Eat

Taking the half or full-board option at the pansions brings a hearty, meat-and-bread meal. Restaurants can be expensive. *Colombo*, beside the church, is beloved for its pizzas and relatively low prices. For a platter of steaming fish, head across the street to *Galija*.

Getting There & Away

Most visitors come to Međugorje from Croatia. Two buses run daily from Split (3½ hours), one from Dubrovnik (3 hours), and one from Zagreb (9 hours). Buses also go twice a week to and from Germany. Many international bus lines are run by Globtour; ask there for a schedule. A handful of buses run daily between Međugorje and Mostar. There's no posted schedule, so inquire at the post office about times.

TRAVNIK
☎ 072

Tucked into a narrow valley only 90km north-west of Sarajevo, Travnik served as the seat of Turkish viziers who ruled Bosnia from 1699 to 1851. The town grew into a diplomatic crossroads, and earned fame more recently as the birthplace of Bosnia's best-known writer Ivo Andrić.

Though fighting between Muslims and Croats went on in the surrounding hills, it mostly spared the town itself. With its lovely medieval castle and pristine natural springs, the town, in Muslim hands today, is well worth a day trip from Sarajevo or a stop on the way to Banja Luka.

Orientation & Information

Travnik's main street, ul Bosanska, runs east to west. The bus station is on the west end of town, within sight of the post office.

Things to See

The **medieval fort** at the top of the hill is open Monday to Friday from 11 am to around 3.30 pm, and on weekends until 7.30 pm. Head up ul Hendek on the east side of town, turn right at the top of the steps and then take another right; you'll see the walkway across to the fort.

Near the base of ul Hendek lies the famous **Many-Coloured Mosque** which allegedly contains hairs from Mohammed's beard. Just east of the mosque are the peaceful springs called **Plava Voda** (Blue Water), which is a favorite summer spot.

Back in town, the **Ivo Andrić Memorial Museum** on ul Mustafa Kundić marks the birthplace of the famed Bosnian author of *The Travnik Chronicles*. The museum contains Andrić texts in many languages, photographs of the 1961 Nobel Prize ceremonies, and a model 19th-century bedroom. Don't be fooled, though: the museum was reconstructed in 1974 and is not the original birth house. Ask at Restaurant Divan downstairs for someone with the key.

Places to Stay & Eat

The *Hotel Orient* (☎/fax 814 888), ul Bosanska 29, is not far from the bus station. Singles and doubles cost DM82/104. It's best to book in advance.

The much nicer *Hotel Slon* (☎/fax 811 008), ul Fatmić 11, hosted Princess Diana shortly before her death. The spacious, clean rooms have satellite TV. Singles/doubles cost DM90/120. The reception may also have ideas about private rooms.

The best food in town is at *Restaurant Divan*, on ul Mustafa Kundić, directly below the Ivo Andrić museum. Coming from the bus station, turn left on ul Zenjak and go one block. Patio seating is available in summer.

Getting There & Away

Buses go almost hourly to Sarajevo and two per day go to Banja Luka.

BANJA LUKA

☎ 078 (☎ 058 from Sarajevo)

This important crossroads on the Vrbas River in north-western Bosnia is now known to the world as the capital of the Republika Srpska. Banja Luka was never much of a tourist centre and in 1993 local Serbs made sure it never would be by blowing up all 16 of the city's mosques, complementing the damage previously done by WWII bombings and a 1969 earthquake. While not otherwise damaged during the recent war, the city is economically depressed and flooded with Serb refugees from the Bosnian Federation and the Croatian Krajina. Even as the RS leadership in Banja Luka opens slowly to the west, the city's transportation, banking, and communication networks remain closely tied to Belgrade.

Orientation

Banja Luka lies beside the river Vrbas in the north-west Bosnia-Hercegovina, only 184km from Zagreb, 235km from Sarajevo, and 316km from Belgrade. Many of Banja Luka's streets, including the main street Kralja Petra, have been renamed since the war and locals may not recognise the new names.

Information

Tourist Office The surprisingly helpful and well-equipped Turistički Savez (☎/fax 12 323; ☎ 18 022) is at ul Kralja Petra 175. It sells maps of Banja Luka and can give advice; inquire about new accommodation options. Some English is spoken.

Money Commission-free visa cash advances into Serbian dinars are available at Vojvodjanska Banka, ul Kralja Petra 87. Bank Kristal, on Franje Jukića 4 near the town hall, will change travellers cheques to Deutschmarks or dinars (1 to 1.5% commission).

Post & Communications The main post office, ul Kralja Petra 93, has numerous telephone booths and sells phonecards. Getting through to Sarajevo is extremely difficult.

Things to See

The large 16th-century **fort** along the Vrbas river is an interesting place to explore. Note the overgrown amphitheatre, whose benches were burned for fuel during the war.

War is the main theme of Banja Luka's sights. Atop the Šehitluci hill south-east of town stands a huge white stone **WWII memorial**. This solitary and impressive slab affords a great view of the city.

In the city centre is the **presidential palace**, which has been the seat of government since January 1998. It faces the town hall. If you come across a bare patch of land in Banja Luka, most likely it used to be one of the city's 16 destroyed mosques. The most famous of these was **Ferhadija** (1580), built with the ransom money for an Austrian count. Ferhadija used to be across ul Kralja Petra from the tourist office.

Places to Stay

The 200-room *Hotel Bosna* (☎ 41 355 or 31 418; fax 44 536) is situated smack in the centre of town. Functional rooms, all with phone, cable TV, and bath tubs (a novelty in these parts), go for DM120/180 a single/double; breakfast is included. Reserve a week in advance, as this hotel is residually full of international officials. *Hotel Slavija*, ul Kralja Petra 85, has shabby rooms for DM40/50 a single/double.

Places to Eat

Restaurant Tropik Klub is tucked inside the castle walls in the former prison (*kazamat*). It serves excellent traditional food (mains DM11 to 13) and has outdoor seating overlooking the Vrbas river in summer. The best place for fish is *Alas,* Braće Mažar 47, off the transit road between Zagreb and Sarajevo. *Lanaco* is a popular pizza joint, with live bands on weekends. Follow the signs off ul Kralja Petra into Stojanovića Park.

Getting There & Away

Banja Luka airport, 35km north of the city, has flights only to Belgrade on JAT. The train and bus stations lie roughly 3km north of the town centre; a taxi should cost DM3.5. Buses (information ☎ 45 355) run twice a day to Zagreb and Sarajevo, and no less than 23 times to Belgrade (seven hours).

BOSNIA-HERCEGOVINA

Croatia

Croatia (Hrvatska) extends in an arc from the Danube River in the east to Istria in the west and south along the Adriatic coast to Dubrovnik. Roman Catholic since the 9th century, and under Hungary since 1102, Croatia only united with Orthodox Serbia in 1918. Croatia's centuries-long resistance to Hungarian and Austrian domination was manifested in 1991 in its determined struggle for nationhood. Yet within Croatia, cultural differences remain between the Habsburg-influenced Central European interior and the formerly Venetian Mediterranean coast.

Croatia's capital, Zagreb, is the country's cultural centre, while coastal towns such as Poreč, Rovinj, Pula, Mali Lošinj, Krk, Rab, Zadar, Šibenik, Trogir, Split, Hvar, Korčula and Dubrovnik all have well-preserved historic centres with lots to see. Before 1991 the strikingly beautiful Mediterranean landscapes of this country attracted nearly 10 million foreign visitors a year.

Traditionally, tourism has been focused along the Adriatic coast, with its unsurpassed combination of history, natural beauty, good climate, clear water and easy access. Seaside resorts are numerous, the swimming is good, and the atmosphere is relaxed – there are few rules about behaviour and few formalities. Since 1960 nudism has been promoted and Croatia is now *the* place to go in Europe to practise naturism.

When Yugoslavia split apart in 1991, no less than 80% of the country's tourist resorts ended up in Croatia. Istria and the lovely Adriatic islands were largely untouched by the fighting and remained peaceful and safe even during the dark days when Osijek, Vukovar and Dubrovnik were world headlines.

The publicity brought tourism almost to a standstill but Croatia is slowly regaining its balance. In July and August, Istria and Krk are filled to capacity and much of Dalmatia is busy as well but outside the peak season all is quiet and, south of Krk in particular, you'll have some beautiful places all to yourself.

AT A GLANCE

Capital	Zagreb
Population	4.7 million
Area	56,538 sq km
Official Language	Serbo-Croatian
Currency	1 Croatian kuna (KN) = 100 lipas
GDP	US$21.4 billion (1996)
Time	GMT/UTC+0100

Facts about Croatia

HISTORY

In 229 BC the Romans began their conquest of the indigenous Illyrians, establishing a colony at Salona (near Split) in Dalmatia. Emperor Augustus extended the empire and created the provinces of Illyricum (Dalmatia and Bosnia) and Pannonia (Croatia). In 285 AD, Emperor Diocletian decided to retire to his palace fortress in Split, today the greatest Roman ruin in Eastern Europe. When the empire was divided in 395, what is now

CROATIA (HRVATSKA)

Slovenia, Croatia and Bosnia-Hercegovina stayed with the Western Roman Empire, while present-day Serbia, Kosovo and Macedonia went to the Eastern Roman Empire, later known as the Byzantine Empire. Visigoth, Hun and Lombard invasions marked the fall of the Western Roman Empire in the 5th century.

Around 625, Slavic tribes migrated from present-day Poland. The Serbian tribe settled in the region that is now south-western Serbia and extended their influence southward and westward. The Croatian tribe moved into

what is now Croatia and occupied two former Roman provinces: Dalmatian Croatia along the Adriatic and Pannonian Croatia to the north.

By the early part of the ninth century, both settlements had accepted Christianity but the northern Croats fell under Frankish domination while Dalmatian Croats came under the nominal control of the Byzantine Empire. The Dalmatian duke Tomislav united the two groups in 925 in a single kingdom which prospered for nearly 200 years.

Late in the 11th century, the throne fell

vacant and a series of ensuing power struggles weakened central authority and split the kingdom. The northern Croats, unable to agree upon a ruler, united with Hungary in 1102 for protection against the Orthodox Byzantine Empire.

In 1242 a Tatar invasion devastated both Hungary and Croatia. In the 14th century the Turks began pushing into the Balkans, defeating the Serbs in 1389 and the Hungarians in 1526. Northern Croatia in 1527 turned to the Habsburgs of Austria for protection against the Turks and remained under their influence until 1918. To form a buffer against the Turks, in the 16th century the Austrians invited Serbs to settle the Vojna Krajina (military frontier) along the Bosnian border. The Serbs in the borderlands had an autonomous administration under Austrian control and these areas were not reincorporated into Croatia until 1881.

The Adriatic coast fell under Venetian influence as early as the 12th century although Hungary continued to struggle for control of the region. Some Dalmatian cities changed hands repeatedly until Venice imposed its rule on the Adriatic coast in the early 15th century and occupied it for nearly four centuries. Only the Republic of Ragusa (Dubrovnik) maintained its independence. The Adriatic coast was threatened, but never conquered, by the Turks and, after the naval Battle of Lepanto in 1571, when Spanish and Venetian forces wiped out the Turkish fleet, this threat receded.

After Venice was shattered by Napoleonic France in 1797, the French occupied southern Croatia, entering Ragusa (Dubrovnik) in 1808. Napoleon's merger of Dalmatia, Istria and Slovenia into the 'Illyrian provinces' in 1809 stimulated the concept of South Slav ('Yugoslav') unity. After Napoleon's defeat at Waterloo in 1815, Austria-Hungary moved in to pick up the pieces along the coast.

A revival of Croatian cultural and political life began in 1835. In 1848 a liberal democratic revolution led by Josip Jelačić was suppressed, but serfdom was abolished. An 1868 reform transferred northern Croatia from Austria to Hungary, united the territory with Hungarian Slavonia and granted a degree of internal autonomy. Dalmatia remained under Austria. In the decade before the outbreak of WWI, some 50,000 Croats emigrated to the USA.

With the defeat of the Austro-Hungarian empire in WWI, Croatia became part of the Kingdom of Serbs, Croats & Slovenes (called Yugoslavia after 1929), which had a centralised government in Belgrade. This was strongly resisted by Croatian nationalists, who organised the Paris assassination of King Alexander I in 1934. Italy had been promised the Adriatic coast as an incentive to join the war against Austria-Hungary in 1915 and it held much of northern Dalmatia from 1918 to 1943.

After the German invasion of Yugoslavia in March 1941, a puppet government dominated by the fascist Ustaša movement was set up in Croatia and Bosnia-Hercegovina under Ante Pavelić (who fled to Argentina after the war). At first the Ustaša tried to expel all Serbs from Croatia to Serbia. But when the Germans stopped this because of the problems it was causing, the Ustaša launched an extermination campaign which surpassed even that of the Nazis in scale, brutally murdering some 350,000 ethnic Serbs, Jews and Roma (gypsies). The Ustaša program called for 'one-third of Serbs killed, one-third expelled and one-third converted to Catholicism'.

Not all Croats supported these policies, however. Maršal Tito was himself of Croat-Slovene parentage and tens of thousands of Croats fought bravely with his partisans. Massacres of Croats conducted by Serbian Četniks in southern Croatia and Bosnia forced almost all antifascist Croats into the communist ranks, where they joined the numerous Serbs trying to defend themselves from the Ustaša. In all, about a million people died violently in a war which was fought mostly in Croatia and Bosnia-Hercegovina.

Recent History

Postwar Croatia was granted republic status within the Yugoslav Federation. During the 1960s Croatia and Slovenia moved far ahead of the southern republics economically, leading to demands for greater autonomy. The 'Croatian Spring' of 1971 caused a backlash and purge of reformers, and increasing economic inertia due to a cumbersome system of 'self-management' of state enterprises by employees. After Tito died in 1980 the paralysis spread to government; the federal presidency began rotating annually among the republics.

In 1989 severe repression of the Albanian majority in Serbia's Kosovo province sparked renewed fears of Serbian hegemony and heralded the end of the Yugoslav Federation. With political changes sweeping Eastern Europe, many Croats felt the time had come to end more than four decades of communist rule and attain complete autonomy into the bargain. In the free elections of April 1990 Franjo Tudj-man's Croatian Democratic Union (Hrvatska Demokratska Zajednica) easily defeated the old Communist Party. On 22 December 1990 a new Croatian constitution was promulgated, changing the status of Serbs in Croatia from that of a 'constituent nation' to a national minority.

The constitution's failure to guarantee minority rights, and mass dismissals of Serbs from the public service, stimulated the 600,000-strong ethnic Serb community within Croatia to demand autonomy. In early 1991 Serb extremists within Croatia staged provocations designed to force federal military intervention. A May 1991 referendum (boycotted by the Serbs) produced a 93% vote in favour of independence but, when Croatia declared independence on 25 June 1991, the Serbian enclave of Krajina proclaimed its independence from Croatia.

Heavy fighting broke out in Krajina (the area around Knin north of Split), Baranja (the area north of the Drava River opposite Osijek) and Slavonia (the region west of the Danube). The 180,000-member, 2000-tank Yugoslav People's Army, dominated by Serbian communists, began to intervene on its own authority in support of Serbian irregulars under the pretext of halting ethnic violence. After European Community (EC) mediation, Croatia agreed to freeze its independence declaration for three months to avoid bloodshed.

In the three months following 25 June, a quarter of Croatia fell to Serbian militias and the federal army. In September the Croatian government ordered a blockade of 32 federal military installations in the republic, lifting morale and gaining much-needed military equipment. In response, the Yugoslav navy blockaded the Adriatic coast and laid siege to the strategic town of Vukovar on the Danube.

In early October 1991 the federal army and Montenegrin militia moved against Dubrovnik to protest against the ongoing blockade of their garrisons in Croatia. On 7 October the presidential palace in Zagreb was hit by rockets fired by Yugoslav air-force jets in an unsuccessful assassination attempt against President Tudjman. Heroic Vukovar finally fell on 19 November when the army culminated a bloody three-month siege by concentrating 600 tanks and 30,000 soldiers there. During six months of fighting in Croatia 10,000 people died, hundreds of thousands fled and tens of thousands of homes were deliberately destroyed.

In early December the United Nations special envoy, Cyrus Vance, began successful negotiations with Serbia over the deployment of a 14,000-member UN Protection Force (UNPROFOR) in the Serbian-held areas of Croatia. Beginning on 3 January 1992, a 15th cease-fire was generally held. The federal army was allowed to withdraw from its bases inside Croatia without having to shamefully surrender its weapons and thus tensions diminished.

When the three-month moratorium on independence expired on 8 October 1991, Croatia declared full independence. To fulfil a condition for EC recognition, in December the Croatian parliament belatedly amended its constitution to protect minority and human rights. In January 1992 the EC, succumbing to strong pressure from Germany, recognised Croatia. This was followed three months later by US recognition and in May 1992 Croatia was admitted to the United Nations.

The UN peace plan in Krajina was supposed to have led to the disarming of local Serb paramilitary formations, the repatriation of refugees and the return of the region to Croatia. Instead it only froze the existing situation and offered no permanent solution.

In January 1993 the Croatian army suddenly launched an offensive in southern Krajina, pushing the Serbs back as much as 24km in some areas and recapturing strategic points such as the site of the destroyed Maslenica bridge, Zemunik airport near Zadar and the Perućac hydroelectric dam in the hills between Split and Bosnia-Hercegovina. The

Krajina Serbs vowed never to accept rule from Zagreb and in June 1993 they voted overwhelmingly to join the Bosnian Serbs (and eventually Greater Serbia).

The self-proclaimed 'Republic of Serbian Krajina' held elections in December 1993 which no international body recognised as legitimate or fair. Meanwhile continued 'ethnic cleansing' left only about 900 Croats in the Krajina out of an original population of 44,000. Although no further progress was made in implementing the Vance Peace Plan, the Krajina Serbs signed a comprehensive cease-fire on 29 March 1994 which substantially reduced the violence in the region and established demilitarised 'zones of separation' between the parties.

While the world's attention turned to the grim events unfolding in Bosnia-Hercegovina, the Croatian government quietly began procuring arms from abroad. On 1 May 1995, the Croatian army and police entered occupied western Slavonia, east of Zagreb, and seized control of the region within days. The Krajina Serbs responded by shelling Zagreb in an attack that left seven people dead and 130 wounded. As the Croatian military consolidated its hold in western Slavonia, some 15,000 Serbs fled the region despite assurances from the Croatian government that they were safe from retribution.

Belgrade's silence throughout this campaign made it clear that the Krajina Serbs had lost the support of their Serbian sponsors, encouraging the Croats to forge ahead. At dawn on 4 August the military launched a massive assault on the rebel Serb capital of Knin, pummelling it with shells, mortars and bombs. Outnumbered by two to one, the Serb army fled towards northern Bosnia, along with 150,000 civilians whose roots in the Krajina stretched back centuries. The military operation ended in days, but was followed by months of terror. Widespread looting and burning of Serb villages, as well as attacks upon the few remaining elderly Serbs, seemed designed to ensure the permanence of this massive population shift.

The Dayton agreement signed in Paris in December 1995 recognised Croatia's traditional borders and provided for the return of eastern Slavonia, a transition that was completed in January 1998.

Although stability has returned to the country, a key provision of the agreement was the promise by the Croatian government to allow the return of Serbian refugees, a promise that is far from being fulfilled. Housing, local industry and agriculture in Slavonia and the Krajina were devastated by the war, making resettlement both costly and complicated. To the frustration of the international community, the government has clearly manifested more enthusiasm for resettling Croatian refugees while Serbian refugees face a tangle of bureaucratic obstacles and a political environment they fear may be less than welcoming.

Since regional peace depends upon the return of refugees, international pressure upon the Croatian government has been unrelenting. Threats to withdraw the life support of international loans and bar the government from participation in international organisations have been taken seriously by a government that is determined to extract the country from Balkan misery and enter 'civilised' Europe.

GEOGRAPHY & ECOLOGY

Croatia is half the size of present-day Yugoslavia in area (56,538 sq km) and population. The republic swings around like a boomerang from the Pannonian plains of Slavonia between the Sava, Drava and Danube rivers, across hilly central Croatia to the Istrian Peninsula, then south through Dalmatia along the rugged Adriatic coast.

The narrow Croatian coastal belt at the foot of the Dinaric Alps is only about 600km long as the crow flies, but it's so indented that the actual length is 1778km. If the 4012km of coastline around the offshore islands is added to the total, the length becomes 5790km.

Most of the 'beaches' along this jagged coast consist of slabs of rock sprinkled with naturists – don't come expecting to find sand. Beach shoes are worth having along the rocky, urchin-infested shores. Officially there are no private beaches in Croatia, but you must pay to use 'managed' beaches. The waters are sparkling clean, even around large towns.

Croatia's offshore islands are every bit as beautiful as those in Greece. There are 1185 islands and islets along the tectonically sub-merged Adriatic coastline, 66 of them inhabited. The largest are Cres, Krk, Mali Lošinj, Pag and Rab in the north; Dugi otok in the middle; and Brač, Hvar, Korčula, Mljet and Vis in the south. Most are barren and elongated from north-west to south-east, with high mountains that drop right into the sea.

When the Yugoslav Federation collapsed, seven of its finest national parks ended up in Croatia. Brijuni near Pula is the most careful-ly cultivated park, with well-preserved Mediterranean holm oak forests. Mountain-ous Risnjak National Park near Delnice, east of Rijeka, is named after one of its inhabitants – the *ris*, or lynx. Dense forests of beech trees and black pine in Paklenica National Park near Zadar are home for a number of endemic insects, reptiles and birds, as well as the en-dangered griffon vulture. The abundant plant and animal life, including bears, wolves and deer, in Plitvice National Park between Zagreb and Zadar has put it onto UNESCO's list of world natural heritage sites. Both Plitvice and Krka National Park near Šibenik feature a dramatic series of cascades. The 101 stark and rocky islands of the Kornati Archi-pelago and National Park make it the largest in the Mediterranean. The island of Mljet near Korčula also contains a forested national park.

GOVERNMENT & POLITICS

Croatia is a parliamentary democracy with a strong presidency. In 1997 Franjo Tudjman was re-elected to a second five-year term as president in an election that foreign observers characterised as free but not fair. State control of the media, especially television, strongly favoured and continues to favour the ruling party, Croatian Democratic Union or HDZ.

Since the election, support for the ruling party may have eroded amid widespread al-legations of corruption and cronyism, particularly in the privatisation of state-owned assets. The imposition of the 22% value-added tax is widely perceived as an unfair burden upon an increasingly impover-ished population while the ruling elite continues to enrich themselves at taxpayers' expense.

The opposition is too fractured to mount a serious challenge to HDZ leadership but the former communists, refashioned as the Social Democratic Party, may benefit from wide-spread discontent in the next legislative elections.

ECONOMY

The years since independence have present-ed the government with some formidable challenges. As a new country, the govern-ment must switch from a state-controlled to a privatised economy while rebuilding its infrastructure after a devastating war, re-housing returning refugees and finding new markets for its products after losing markets in the southern regions of former Yugoslavia. Vital transfusions of money from the Inter-national Monetary Fund and the World Bank have kept the economy functioning as the government searches for long-term solutions.

The former communist government of Yu-goslavia emphasised heavy industry, especially in aluminium, chemicals, petro-leum and shipbuilding. The shipyards of Pula, Rijeka and Split made Croatia the world's third-largest shipbuilder. The chemi-cal industry was concentrated at Krk, Rijeka, Split and Zagreb; machine-tool manufacture at Karlovac, Slavonski Brod and Zagreb; heavy electrical engineering at Zagreb; and textiles at Zagreb and in north-western Croatia. Unfortunately, many of these indus-tries have stagnated since the war, their problems compounded by large debts that have inhibited necessary restructuring. Growth in industrial output has been slow, hampered by an overvalued kuna that pe-nalises exports while making imports cheap.

In the past, one-third of Croatia's national income came from tourism, but between 1991 and 1995 tourist numbers fell dramatically. Dalmatia was the hardest hit and has yet to recover while Istria and Krk have begun to rebound with an influx of Germans, Austrians, Italians and Czechs. It may be years before tourism reaches prewar levels, however, and attracting tourism requires capital outlays. Many hotels along the coast require costly renovation after years of sheltering refugees. Investment in air, road and boat connections along the coast are also necessary if tourism is to be the cornerstone of the Croatian economy.

Unlike the trade and industrial sectors, agriculture has been in private hands since the failure of collectivisation just after WWII. Private farmers with small plots continue to work most of the land. The interior plains produce fruit, vegetables and grains (especially corn and wheat), while olives and grapes are cultivated along the coast. The return of fertile eastern Slavonia should eventually give the economy a boost once the war damage is repaired.

Perhaps the most troublesome task facing the government is reform of the banking sector. Too many banks made too many bad loans under circumstances that are cloudy at best. Poor management has made restructuring a lengthy process despite the government's efforts to recapitalise and rehabilitate weaker banks.

For the average Croatian, life is difficult with no gleaming light at the end of the tunnel. The average wage is less than 2500KN (US$400) a month and a high percentage of the population is unemployed (17.6% in 1997). Although inflation is low (3.6% in 1997), the recent imposition of the 22% value-added tax has eroded purchasing power, particularly for pensioners on fixed incomes. There's a widespread perception that the standard of living has fallen since the prewar years and the social safety net has been abruptly snatched away. A middle class faced with growing insecurity could eventually pose a serious threat to further economic reform.

POPULATION & PEOPLE

Before the war, Croatia had a population of nearly five million, of which 78% were Croats and 12% were Serbs. Now it's around 4.7 million, but with a constant flow of refugees in both directions, reliable statistics since the war have been difficult to compile. It's estimated that only 5% of the Serbian population remains. Small communities of Slavic Muslims, Hungarians, Slovenes, Italians, Czechs and Albanians complete the mosaic. The largest cities in Croatia are Zagreb (1 million), Split (300,000), Rijeka (225,000), Osijek (175,000) and Zadar (150,000).

ARTS

The work of sculptor Ivan Meštrović (1883-1962) is seen in town squares all around

Croatia. Besides creating public monuments, Meštrović designed imposing buildings such as the circular Croatian Historical Museum in Zagreb. Both his sculpture and architecture display the powerful classical restraint he learnt from Rodin. Meštrović's studio in Zagreb and his retirement home at Split have been made into galleries of his work.

Music

Croatian folk music bears many influences. The *kolo*, a lively Slavic round dance in which men and women alternate in the circle, is accompanied by Roma-style violinists or players of the *tambura*, a three or five-string mandolin popular throughout Croatia. The measured guitar-playing and rhythmic accordions of Dalmatia have a gentle Italian air.

A recommended recording available locally on compact disc (DD-0030) is *Narodne Pjesme i Plesovi Sjeverne Hrvatske* (Northern Croatian Folk Songs and Dances) by the Croatian folkloric ensemble Lado. The 22 tracks on this album represent nine regions, with everything from haunting Balkan voices reminiscent of Bulgaria to lively Mediterranean dance rhythms.

SOCIETY & CONDUCT

Croats take pride in keeping up appearances. Despite a fragile economy money can usually be found to brighten up the town centre with a fresh coat of paint or to repair a historic building. Even as their bank accounts diminish most people will cut out restaurants and movies to afford a shopping trip to Italy for some new clothes. The tidy streets and stylish clothes are rooted in the Croats' image of themselves as Western Europeans, not Yugoslavs, a word that makes Croats wince. Dressing neatly will go a long way towards gaining a traveller acceptance.

Because of the intense propaganda surrounding the recent war, Croats are inclined to see themselves as wholly right and the other side as wholly wrong. Comments questioning this assumption are not particularly appreciated. People who have had their lives disrupted, if not shattered, by war are generally uninterested in the political niceties of their situation.

CROATIA

RELIGION

Croats are overwhelmingly Roman Catholic, while virtually all Serbs belong to the Eastern Orthodox Church. In addition to various doctrinal differences, Orthodox Christians venerate icons, allow priests to marry and do not accept the authority of the Roman Catholic pope. Long suppressed under communism, Catholicism is undergoing a strong resurgence in Croatia; churches have strong attendances every Sunday. Muslims make up 1.2% of the population and Protestants 0.4%, with a tiny Jewish population in Zagreb.

LANGUAGE

As a result of history, tourism and the number of returned 'guest workers' from Germany, German is the most commonly spoken second language in Croatia. Many people in Istria speak Italian and English is popular among young people.

Croatian is a South Slavic language, as are Serbian, Slovene, Macedonian and Bulgarian. Prior to 1991 both Croatian and Serbian were considered dialects of a single language known as Serbo-Croatian. As a result of the civil war in former Yugoslavia, the local languages are being revised, so spellings and idioms may change.

The most obvious difference between Serbian and Croatian is that Serbian is written in Cyrillic script and Croatian in Roman script. There are also a number of variations in vocabulary.

Geographical terms worth knowing are *aleja* (walkway), *cesta* (road), *donji* (lower), *gora* (hill), *grad* (town), *jezero* (lake), *krajina* (frontier), *luka* (harbour), *malo* (little), *novo* (new), *obala* (bank, shore), *otok* (island), *planina* (mountain), *polje* (valley), *prolaz* (strait), *put* (path), *rijeka* (river), *selo* (village), *šetalište* (way), *stanica* (station, stop), *stari* (old), *šuma* (forest), *sveti* (saint), *toplice* (spa), *trg* (square), *ulica* (street), *veliko* (big), *vrata* (pass), *vrh* (peak) and *zaljev* (bay).

Two words everyone should know are *ima* (there is) and *nema* (there isn't). If you make just a small effort to learn a few words, you'll distinguish yourself from the packaged tourists and be greatly appreciated by the local people.

Lonely Planet's *Mediterranean Europe phrasebook* includes a useful chapter on the Serbian and Croatian languages, with translations of key words and phrases from each appearing side by side, providing a clear comparison of the languages. For a basic rundown on travellers' Croatian and Serbian, see the Language Guide at the end of this book.

Facts for the Visitor

HIGHLIGHTS
Museums & Galleries

Art museums and galleries are easier for a foreign visitor to enjoy than historical museums, which are usually captioned in Croatian only. In Zagreb the Museum Mimara contains an outstanding collection of Spanish, Italian and Dutch paintings as well as an archaeological collection, exhibits of ancient art from Asia and collections of glass, textiles, sculpture and furniture. The Strossmayer Gallery, also in Zagreb, is worthwhile for its exhibits of Italian, Flemish, French and Croatian paintings.

The Meštrović Gallery in Split is worth a detour to see and in Zagreb the Meštrović Studio gives a fascinating insight into the life and work of this remarkable sculptor.

Castles

The palace of the Roman emperor Diocletian in Split has been named a world heritage site by UNESCO. Despite a weathered façade, this sprawling imperial residence and fortress is considered the finest intact example of classical defence architecture in Europe.

Just outside Zagreb is an impressive circle of castles. To the north is Veliki Tabor, a fortified medieval castle in the process of restoration but the most impressive is Trakošćan, beside a long lake. Medvedgrad, west of Zagreb, was built by bishops in the 13th century. The square baroque castle of Lukavec lies in the picturesque Turopolje region south-east of Zagreb. The Varaždin Castle in northern Croatia has recently been restored and hosts an annual music festival. Trsat Castle in Rijeka offers a stunning view of the Kvarner Gulf.

Historic Towns

All along the Adriatic coast are white-stone towns with narrow, winding streets enclosed by defensive walls. Each town has its own flavour. Hilly Rovinj looks out over the sea, while the peninsula of Korčula town burrows into it. Zadar retains echoes of its original Roman street plan while Hvar and Trogir are traditional medieval towns. None can match the exquisite harmony of Dubrovnik, with its blend of elements of medieval and Renaissance architecture.

SUGGESTED ITINERARIES

Depending on the length of your stay, you might want to see and do the following things:

Two days
    Visit Dubrovnik.
One week
    Visit Zagreb, Split and Dubrovnik.
Two weeks
    Visit Zagreb and all of Dalmatia.
One month
    Visit all the areas covered in this chapter.

PLANNING
Climate & When to Go

The climate varies from Mediterranean along the Adriatic coast to continental inland. The high coastal mountains help to shield the coast from cold northerly winds, making for an early spring and late autumn. In spring and early summer a sea breeze called the *maestral* keeps the temperature down along the coast. Winter winds include the cold *bura* from the north and humid *široko* from the south.

The sunny coastal areas experience hot, dry summers and mild, rainy winters, while the interior regions are cold in winter and warm in summer. Because of a warm current flowing north up the Adriatic coast, sea temperatures never fall below 10°C in winter and are as high as 26°C in August. You can swim in the sea from mid-June until late September. The resorts south of Split are the warmest.

May is a nice month to travel along the Adriatic coast, with good weather and few tourists. June and September are also good, but in July and August all of Europe arrives and prices soar. September is perhaps the best

month since it's not as hot as summer, though the sea remains warm, the crowds will have thinned out as children return to school, off-season accommodation rates apply and fruit such as figs and grapes will be abundant. In April and October it may be too cool for camping, but the weather should still be fine along the coast and private rooms will be plentiful and inexpensive.

Books & Maps

For a comprehensive account of the personalities and events surrounding the collapse of ex-Yugoslavia it would be hard to surpass *The Death of Yugoslavia* by Laura Silber & Allan Little, based on the 1995 BBC television series of the same name. Richard Holbrooke's *To End a War* is a riveting account of the personalities and events surrounding the Dayton peace agreement. *Café Europa* is a series of essays by a Croatian journalist, Slavenka Drakulić, that provides an inside look at life in the country since independence. Rebecca West's 1937 travel classic, *Black Lamb & Grey Falcon*, contains a long section on Croatia as part of her trip through Yugoslavia. Robert Kaplan's *Balkan Ghosts* touches on Croatia's part in the tangled web of Balkan history.

Kimmerley & Frey's map *Croatia & Slovenia* (1:500,000) is detailed and depicts the latest borders. Most tourist offices in the country have local maps, but make sure the street names are up to date.

TOURIST OFFICES

Municipal tourist offices and any office marked 'Turist Biro' will have free brochures and good information on local events. These offices are found in Dubrovnik, Pula, Rijeka, Split and Zagreb. Most towns also have an office selling theatre and concert tickets.

Tourist information is also dispensed by commercial travel agencies such as Atlas, Croatia Express, Generalturist, Kompas and Kvarner Express, which also arrange private rooms, sightseeing tours etc.

Keep in mind that these are profit-making businesses, so don't be put off if you're asked to pay for a town map etc. The agencies often sell local guidebooks, which are excellent

CROATIA

value if you'll be staying for a while. Ask if they have the schedule for coastal ferries.

Croatian Tour Companies Abroad

The Croatian Ministry of Tourism has few offices abroad, but the tour companies listed here specialise in Croatia and will gladly mail you their brochures containing much information on the country:

Germany
(☎ 069-25 20 45) Kroatische Zentrale für Tourismus, Karlsluher Strasse 18, D-60329 Frankfurt am Main
Netherlands
(☎ 020-405 7066) Kroatische Centrale voor Tourisme, Schipholboulevard 205 WTC, 1118 BH Luchthaven Schiphol
UK
(☎ 0181-563 7979) Phoenix Holidays, 2 The Lanchesters, 162-164 Fulham Palace Rd, London W6 9ER
USA
(☎ 201-428-0707) Croatian National Tourist Office, 300 Lanidex Plaza, Parsippany, NJ 07054

VISAS & EMBASSIES

Visitors from Australia, Canada, New Zealand, the UK and the USA no longer require a visa for stays less than 90 days. For other nationalities, visas are issued free of charge at Croatian consulates. Croatian authorities require foreigners to register with local police when they first arrive in a new area of the country, but this is a routine matter which is normally handled by the hotel, hostel, camp site or agency securing private accommodation.

Croatian Embassies Abroad

Croatian embassies and consulates around the world include the following:

Australia
(☎ 02-6286 6988) 14 Jindalee Crescent, O'Malley, ACT 2601
(☎ 03-9699 2633) 9-24 Albert Rd, South Melbourne, Victoria 3205
(☎ 02-9299 8899) 379 Kent St, Level 4, Sydney, NSW 2000
(☎ 09-321 6044) 68 St George's Terrace, Perth, WA 6832

Canada
(☎ 613-230 7351) 130 Albert St, Suite 1700, Ottawa, Ontario K1P 5G4
(☎ 905-277 9051) 918 Dundas St E, Suite 302, Mississauga, Ontario L4Y 2B8
New Zealand
(☎ 09-836 5581) 131 Lincoln Rd, Henderson, Box 83200, Edmonton, Auckland
UK
(☎ 0171-387 0022) 21 Conway St, London W1P 5HL
USA
(☎ 202-588-5899) 2343 Massachusetts Ave NW, Washington, DC 20008

For the addresses of Croatian embassies in Bucharest, Budapest, Ljubljana, Prague and Sofia, turn to the sections of this book relating to those cities.

Foreign Embassies in Croatia

All the following addresses are in Zagreb unless otherwise noted:

Albania
(☎ 01-48 10 679) Jurišiaeva 2a
Australia
(☎ 01-45 77 433) Mihanovićeva 1
Bosnia-Hercegovina
(☎ 01-46 83 767) Torbarova 9
Bulgaria
(☎ 01-45 52 288) Novi Goljak 25
Canada
(☎ 01-45 77 905) Mihanovićeva 1
Czech Republic
(☎ 01-61 15 914) Savska 41
Hungary
(☎ 01-422 654) Krležin Gvozd 11a
Poland
(☎ 01-278 818) Krležin Gvozd 3
Romania
(☎ 01-23 36 091) Srebrnjak 150a
Slovakia
(☎ 01-48 48 941) Prilaz Gjure Deželića 10
Slovenia
(☎ 01-61 56 945) Savska 41
UK
(☎ 01-45 55 310) Vlaška 121, Zagreb 21000
(☎ 021-341 464) Obala hrvatskog narodnog preporoda 10, Split 21000
(☎ 020-412 916) Pile 1, Dubrovnik 20000
USA
(☎ 01-45 55 500) Andrije Hebranga 2
Yugoslavia
(☎ 01-46 80 553) Mesićeva 19

MONEY

Currency

In May 1994 the Croatian dinar was replaced by the kuna, which takes its name from the marten, a fox-like animal whose pelt was a means of exchange in the Middle Ages. You're allowed to import or export Croatian banknotes up to a value of around 2000KN but there's no reason to do either.

Exchange Rates

Australia	A$1	=	3.90KN
Canada	C$1	=	4.25KN
euro	€1	=	7.13KN
France	1FF	=	1.08KN
Germany	DM1	=	3.6KN
Japan	¥100	=	4.44KN
New Zealand	NZ$1	=	3.29KN
UK	UK£1	=	10.50KN
USA	US$1	=	6.43KN

Changing Money

There are numerous places to change money, all offering similar rates; ask at any travel agency for the location of the nearest exchange. Banks and exchange offices keep long hours. Exchange offices may deduct a commission of 1% to change cash or travellers cheques but some banks do not. Kuna can be converted into hard currency only at a bank and if you submit a receipt of a previous transaction. Hungarian currency is difficult to change in Croatia.

Credit Cards

Visa cards are accepted for cash advances in Croatia only at Splitska Banka. (American Express, MasterCard and Diners Club cards are more easily accepted.) Cirrus cards can be used for cash withdrawals and you get the best rate. Diners Club cards can also be used for cash withdrawals in many places. Major cities have ATM machines but many of the islands are not yet hooked up to the system. Make sure you have a four-digit PIN.

Costs

The government deliberately overvalues the kuna to obtain cheap foreign currency. Hotel prices are set in Deutschmarks and thus are fairly constant, though you pay in kuna calculated at the daily official rate. Accommodation is more expensive than it should be for a country trying to lure more tourism and real budget accommodation is in short supply. Transport, concert and theatre tickets, and food are reasonably priced for Europe.

Average accommodation prices per person are around 90KN for a private room, 25KN for a meal at a self-service restaurant and 25 to 45KN for an average intercity bus fare. It's not that hard to survive on 200KN daily if you stay in hostels or private rooms and you'll pay less if you camp and self-cater, sticking to things like bread, cheese, tinned fish or meat, yoghurt and wine (cooking facilities are seldom provided).

Your daily expenses will come down a lot if you can find a private room to use as a base for exploring nearby areas. Coastal towns which lend themselves to this include Rovinj, Krk, Rab, Split, Korčula and Dubrovnik. You will also escape the 30 to 50% surcharge on private rooms rented for less than four nights.

Tipping

If you're served fairly and well at a restaurant, you should round up the bill as you're paying. (Don't leave money on the table.) If a service charge has been added to the bill no tip is necessary. Bar bills and taxi fares can also be rounded up. Tour guides on day excursions expect to be tipped.

POST & COMMUNICATIONS

Post

Mail sent to Poste Restante, 10000 Zagreb, Croatia, is held at the post office next to the Zagreb railway station, which is open 24 hours. A good coastal address to use is c/o Poste Restante, Main Post Office, 21000 Split, Croatia.

If you have an American Express card, you can have your mail addressed to Atlas travel agency, Trg Nikole Zrinjskog 17, 10000 Zagreb, Croatia, or Atlas travel agency, Trg Braće Radić, 21000 Split, Croatia.

Telephone

To call Croatia from abroad, dial your international access code, ☎ 385 (the country code for Croatia), the area code (without the initial zero) and the local number.

CROATIA

To make a phone call from Croatia, go to the main post office – phone calls placed from hotel rooms are much more expensive. As there are no coins you'll need tokens or a phonecard to use public telephones.

Phonecards are sold according to units (*impulsa*) and you can buy cards of 50, 100, 200 and 500 units. These can be purchased at any post office and most tobacco shops and newspaper kiosks. Many new phone boxes have button on the upper left with a flag symbol. Press the button and you get instructions in English. A three-minute call from Croatia will cost around 20KN to the UK and 23KN to the USA or Australia. The international access code is ☎ 00. Some other useful numbers are ☎ 92 for the police, ☎ 93 for fire, ☎ 94 for emergency medical assistance and ☎ 901 to place an operator-assisted call.

INTERNET RESOURCES

Croatia has blasted into cyberspace with the speed of the Starship Enterprise. Web sites relating to businesses and organisations are proliferating with a mad pace even as home computers remain out of reach for the average Croatian. America Online has access numbers in Zagreb, Split and Rijeka but most Croatians connect through the post office, which offers a connection at 33600bps with unlimited Internet access for 70KN a month plus a 35KN subscription fee. The only cybercafé is in Zagreb but that is bound to change soon.

NEWSPAPERS & MAGAZINES

The most respected daily newspaper in Croatia is *Vjesnik* but the most daring is the satirical newsweekly *Feral Tribune*. Its investigative articles and sly graphics target increasingly unamused political parties, who have responded with taxes, libel suits and general harassment. German and Italian newspapers are widely available and a daily newspaper in Italian, *La Voce del Popolo*, is published in Rijeka. American, British and French newspapers and magazines can be hard to find outside large cities.

RADIO & TV

The three national television stations in Croatia fill a lot of air time with foreign programming, usually American and always in the original language. For local news, residents of Zadar, Split, Vinkovci and Osijek turn to their regional stations. Croatian Radio broadcasts news in English four times daily (8 am, 10 am, 2 pm, 11 pm) on FM frequencies 88.9, 91.3 and 99.3.

TIME

Croatia is on Central European Time (GMT/UTC plus one hour). Daylight saving comes into effect at the end of March, when clocks are turned forward an hour. At the end of September they're turned back an hour.

ELECTRICITY

Electricity is 220V, 50Hz AC. Croatia uses the standard European round-pronged plugs.

WEIGHTS & MEASURES

The metric system is used. Like other Continental Europeans, Croats indicate decimals with commas and thousands with points.

LAUNDRY

Self-service laundrettes are virtually unknown outside of Zagreb. Most camping grounds have laundry facilities, hotels will wash clothes for a (hefty) fee or you could make arrangements with the proprietor if you're staying in private accommodation.

HEALTH

Everyone must pay to see a doctor at a public hospital (*bolnica*) or medical centre (*dom zdravcja*) but the charges are reasonable. Travel insurance is important, especially if you have a serious accident and have to be hospitalised. Medical centres often have dentists on the staff, otherwise you can go to a private dental clinic (*zubna ordinacija*).

WOMEN TRAVELLERS

Women face no special danger in Croatia although women on their own may be harassed and followed in large coastal cities. Some of the local bars and cafés seem like private men's clubs; a woman alone is likely to be greeted with sudden silence and cold stares. Topless sunbathing is considered acceptable;

in fact, judging from the ubiquitous photos of topless women in tourist brochures it seems almost obligatory.

GAY & LESBIAN TRAVELLERS

Homosexuality has been legal in Croatia since 1977 and is generally tolerated, if not welcomed with open arms. Public displays of affection between members of the same sex may meet with hostility, however, especially outside major cities. A small lesbian and gay community is developing in Zagreb but not to the extent of many western European cities. For further information contact LIGMA (Lesbian and Gay Men Action; PO Box 488, 10001 Zagreb).

DANGERS & ANNOYANCES

Land mines left over from the recent war in Croatia pose no threat to the average visitor but it's important to be aware that certain areas of the country are still dangerous. Although the government moved with lightning speed to remove mines from any area even remotely interesting to tourists, the former confrontation line between Croat and federal forces is still undergoing de-mining operations. Eastern Slavonia was heavily mined and, outside of the main city of Osijek, de-mining is not yet completed. Main roads from Zagreb to the coast that pass through Karlovac and Knin are completely safe but it would be unwise to stray into fields or abandoned villages. As a general rule, you should avoid any area along this route in which shattered roofs or artillery-pocked walls indicate that rebuilding and, possibly, de-mining has not yet occurred. If a place is abandoned, there may be a reason.

Personal security and theft are not problems in Croatia. The police and military are well disciplined and it's highly unlikely you'll have any problems with them in any of the places covered in this chapter.

See Post & Communications for emergency telephone numbers.

BUSINESS HOURS

Banking hours are from 7.30 am to 7 pm on weekdays and 8 am to noon on Saturday. Many shops open from 8 am to 7 pm on weekdays and 8 am to 2 pm on Saturday. Along the coast, life is more relaxed; shops and offices frequently close around 1 pm for an afternoon break. Croats are early risers and by 7 am there will be lots of people on the street and many places will already be open.

PUBLIC HOLIDAYS & SPECIAL EVENTS

Public holidays are New Year's Day (1 January), Easter Monday (March/April), Labour Day (1 May), Bleiburg and Way of the Cross Victims Day (15 May), Statehood Day (30 May), Day of Antifascist Struggle (22 June), Homeland Thanksgiving Day (5 August) Feast of the Assumption (15 August), All Saints' Day (1 November) and Christmas (25 and 26 December). Statehood Day marks the anniversary of the declaration of independence in 1991, while Day of Antifascist Struggle commemorates the outbreak of resistance in 1941.

In July and August there are summer festivals in Dubrovnik, Opatija, Split and Zagreb. Mardi Gras celebrations that mark the beginning of Lent have recently been revived in many towns with the attendant parades and festivities. The many traditional annual events held around Croatia are included under Special Events in the city and town sections.

ACTIVITIES
Kayaking

There are countless possibilities for anyone carrying a folding sea kayak, especially among the Elafiti Islands (take the daily ferry from Dubrovnik to Lopud) and the Kornati Islands (take the daily ferry from Zadar to Sali). See Organised Tours in the Getting Around section for information on sailing and kayaking tours.

Hiking

Risnjak National Park at Crni Lug, 12km west of Delnice between Zagreb and Rijeka, is a good hiking area in summer. Buses run from Delnice to Crni Lug near the park entrance about three times daily, and there's a small park-operated hotel (☎ 051-836 133) at Crni Lug, with rooms at around 120KN per person including breakfast. Because of the likelihood of heavy snowfalls, hiking is only advisable from late spring to early autumn. It's a 9km, 2½-hour climb from the park entrance at Bijela Vodica to Veliki Risnjak (1528m).

The steep gorges and beech forests of Paklenica National Park, 40km north-east of Zadar, also offer excellent hiking. Starigrad, the main access town for the park, is well connected by hourly buses from Zadar. Hotels and private accommodation are available in Starigrad, as well as a camping ground, Paklenica (☎ 023-369 236), open May to September.

For a great view of the barren coastal mountains, climb Mt Ilija (961m) above Orebić, opposite Korčula.

Scuba Diving

The clear waters and varied underwater life of the Adriatic have led to a flourishing dive industry along the coast. Most dive shops offer certification courses for about 2124KN and one dive with rented equipment for 227 to 268KN. Cave diving is the real speciality in Croatia; night diving and wreck diving are also offered and there are coral reefs in some places but in rather deep water. You must get a permit to dive but this is easy: go to the harbour captain in any port with your passport, certification card and 70KN. Permission is valid for a year in any dive spot in the country. The fee is slated for the preservation of underwater life. In Hvar, try Divecentre Hvar (☎ 021-761 026) at Hotel Jadran, Jelsa) and Dive and Watersportcentre, (☎ 021-742 490) at Hotel Amphora, Hvar. On Krk, there's Delphin (☎ 051-656 126), Emilia Geistlicha 48, Baška. On Rab, there's Mirko (☎ 051-721 154), Barbat 710, Rab, and Rab-ek-O (☎ 051-6776 272), Kampor, Rab. Diving Center Hidra (☎ 264 474) is in Lumbarda on Korčula Island.

COURSES

The Croatian Heritage Foundation (Hrvatska matica iseljenika; ☎ 01-61 15 116; fax 01-45 50 700; www.matis.hr/odjeli.htm), Trg Stjepana Radića 3, Zagreb, runs a series of programs on Croatian language and culture during July and August (exact dates an-

nounced the preceding February). Though designed for people of Croatian descent living abroad, everyone is welcome.

The Faculty of Arts at the University of Zagreb (founded in 1669) organises a more intensive, academically oriented four-week course. Students sit an exam at the end of the course and those who pass receive a certificate of merit.

Contact the Croatian Heritage Foundation in Zagreb for application information. Also ask about regular semester courses offered throughout the academic year.

WORK

The Croatian Heritage Foundation also organises summer 'taskforces' of young people from around the world, often of Croatian descent, to assist in war reconstruction. Often these programs have an ecological or archaeological slant, such as repairing the bridges in Plitvice National Park or restoring a damaged church. For details, contact the foundation.

Suncokret (☎ 01-211 104; fax 01-222 715; suncokret@public.srce.com), Seferova 10, 10000 Zagreb, accepts summer volunteers to do unpaid relief work among women, children and the elderly traumatised by the war in Croatia. Preference is given to teachers, social workers, counsellors and applicants with prior experience in the helping professions.

ACCOMMODATION

Along the coast, accommodation is priced according to three seasons, which vary from place to place. Generally April, May and October are the cheapest months, June and September are mid-priced, but count on paying top price in July and August, especially in the peak period from mid-July to mid-August. Prices quoted in this chapter are for the peak period and do not include 'residence tax' of 7.60KN in peak season, 5KN in June, the beginning of July and September and 4.30KN at other times. Deduct about 20% if you come in June, the beginning of July and September, about 30% for May and October and about 40% for all other times. Prices for rooms in Zagreb are constant all year.

Accommodation is generally cheaper in Dalmatia than in Kvarner or Istria but in July and August you should make arrangements in advance wherever you go.

This chapter provides the phone numbers of most accommodation facilities. Once you know your itinerary it pays to go to a post office, buy a telephone card and start calling around to check prices, availability etc. Most receptionists speak English.

Camping

Nearly 100 camping grounds are scattered along the Croatian coast. Most operate from mid-May to September only, although a few are open in April and October. In May and late September, call ahead to make sure the camping ground is open before beginning the long trek out. The opening and closing dates in travel brochures and this book are only approximate and even local tourist offices can be wrong.

Many camping grounds are expensive for backpackers because the prices are set in dollars or Deutschmarks per person and include the charge per tent, caravan, car, electric hook-up etc. This is fine for people with mobile homes which occupy a large area but bad news for those with only a small tent. If you don't have a vehicle, you're better off at camping grounds which have a much smaller fee per person and charge for the extras.

Germans are the leading users of Croatian camping grounds. Unfortunately, many grounds are gigantic 'autocamps' with restaurants, shops and row upon row of caravans. Nudist camping grounds (marked FKK) are among the best because their secluded locations ensure peace and quiet. Freelance camping is officially prohibited.

Hostels

The Croatian YHA (☎ 01-422 953; fax 01-48 41 269; www.nncomp.com/hfhs/hfhs.html), Dežmanova 9, Zagreb, operates summer youth hostels in Dubrovnik, Šibenik and Zadar and year-round hostels at Zagreb and Pula. Bed and breakfast costs about 65KN for YHA members in May, June, September and October and 75KN in July and August. Non-members pay an additional 12KN per person daily for a welcome card; six stamps on the card then entitles you to a membership. The Zagreb hostel has higher prices.

Private Rooms

The best accommodation in Croatia is private rooms in local homes, the equivalent of small private guesthouses in other countries. Such rooms can be arranged by travel agencies, which add a lot of taxes and commission to your bill, so you'll almost always do better dealing directly with proprietors you meet on the street or by knocking on the doors of houses with 'sobe' or 'zimmer' (meaning 'rooms') signs. This way you avoid the residence tax and four-night minimum stay, but you also forgo the agency's quality control. Hang around coastal bus stations and ferry terminals, luggage in hand, looking lost, and someone may find you. Otherwise, go to town and see if anyone in a local café can help.

If the price asked is too high, bargain. Be sure to clarify whether the price agreed upon is per person or for the room. Tell the proprietor in advance how long you plan to stay or they may try to add a surprise 'supplement' when you leave after a night or two. At the agencies, singles are expensive and scarce but, on the street, sobe prices are usually per person, which favours the single traveller. Showers are always included.

It may be worthwhile to take half-board. Most families on the coast have a garden, a vineyard and access to the sea. You could begin with a home-made aperitif and progress to a garden-fresh salad, home-grown potatoes and grilled fresh fish, washed down with your host's very own wine.

Although renting an unofficial room is common practice along the Adriatic coast, be discreet, as technically you're breaking the law by not registering with the police. Don't brag to travel agencies about the low rate you got, for example.

If you stay less than four nights, the agencies add a 20 to 30% surcharge. Travel agencies have classified rooms as either category I, II or III, which will soon change to a star system. The most expensive rooms will be three-star and include a private bathroom. In a two-star room, the bathroom is shared with one other room; in a one-star room, the bathroom is shared with two other rooms. If you're travelling in a small group, it may be worthwhile to get a small apartment with

CROATIA

cooking facilities, which are widely available along the coast.

At the time of writing, accommodation rates were fixed with no variance from agency to agency but that system is changing and, by the time of your trip, it may be worthwhile to compare prices.

Hotels

There are few cheap hotels in Croatia – prices generally average around 350KN a double in the summer along the coast, dropping to around 250KN in late spring or early autumn. Still, if you're only staying one night and the private room agency is going to levy a 50% surcharge, you might consider getting a hotel room. In the off season, when most rooms are empty, you could try bargaining for a more realistic rate.

Hotels are classified as A, B, C and (rarely) D but the country is moving towards a star system which may be in place by the time of your visit. Category A hotels are the most luxurious (satellite TV, direct-dial phones and minibars in rooms that are often air-conditioned); there may be a swimming pool or two, a fitness centre and a nightclub. The vast majority of hotels are category B and equipped with TV, telephones and a hotel restaurant. Category C hotels have a private bathroom but no TV or telephone, while rare category D hotels will have shared bathrooms.

Most hotels along the coast were built to accommodate package tourists and have the sort of blandness that will delight lovers of concrete. Every so often you'll run across faded but elegant older hotels that recall the days when the Austrian aristocracy took holidays on the Adriatic. Unfortunately these solidly built structures were often the ones used to house refugees during the recent war and are now waiting for a Prince Charming to come along with enough money to rescue them from slow decay.

FOOD

A restaurant (restauracija) or pub may also be called a gostionica and a café is a kavana. Self-service cafeterias are quick, easy and inexpensive, though the quality of the food varies. If the samples behind glass look cold or dried out, ask them to dish out a fresh plate for you. Better restaurants aren't that much more expensive if you choose carefully. In most of them the vegetables, salads and bread cost extra and some deluxe restaurants add a 10% service charge (not mentioned on the menu). Fish dishes are often charged by weight, which makes it difficult to know how much a certain dish will cost. Ice-cream cones are priced by the scoop.

Restaurants in Croatia can be a hassle because they rarely post their menus outside, so to find out what they offer and charge, you have to walk in and ask to see the menu. Then if you don't like what you see, you must walk back out and appear rude. Always check the menu, however, and if the price of the drinks or something else isn't listed, ask, otherwise you'll automatically be charged the 'tourist price'.

Breakfast is difficult in Croatia as all you can get easily is coffee. For eggs, toast and jam you'll have to go somewhere expensive, otherwise you can buy some bread, cheese and milk at a supermarket and picnic somewhere. Throughout ex-Yugoslavia the breakfast of the people is burek, a greasy layered pie made with meat (mesa) or cheese (sira) and cut on a huge metal tray.

A load of fruit and vegetables from the local market can make a healthy, cheap picnic lunch. There are plenty of supermarkets in Croatia – cheese, bread, wine and milk are readily available and fairly cheap. The person behind the meat counter at supermarkets will make a big cheese or bologna sandwich for you upon request and you only pay the regular price of the ingredients.

Regional Dishes

Italian pizza and pasta are a good option in Istria and Dalmatia, costing about half of what you'd pay in Western Europe. The Adriatic coast excels in seafood, including scampi, prstaci (shellfish) and Dalmatian brodet (mixed fish stewed with rice), all cooked in olive oil and served with boiled vegetables or tartufe (mushrooms) in Istria. In the Croatian interior, watch for manistra od bobića (beans and fresh maize soup) or štrukle (cottage cheese rolls). A Zagreb speciality is štrukli (boiled cheesecake).

DRINKS

It's customary to have a small glass of brandy before a meal and to accompany the food with one of Croatia's fine wines. Ask for the local regional wine. Croatia is also famous for its plum brandies (*šljivovica*), herbal brandies (*travarica*), cognacs (*vinjak*) and liqueurs such as maraschino, a cherry liqueur made in Zadar, or herbal *pelinkovac*. Italian-style espresso is popular in Croatia.

Zagreb's Ožujsko beer (*pivo*) is very good but Karlovačko beer from Karlovac is better. You'll want to practise saying *živjeli!* (cheers!).

ENTERTAINMENT

Culture was heavily subsidised by the communists and admission to operas, operettas and concerts is still reasonable. The main theatres offering musical programs are listed in this chapter, so note the location and drop by some time during the day to see what's on and purchase tickets. In the interior cities, winter is the best time to enjoy the theatres and concert halls. The main season at the opera houses of Rijeka, Split and Zagreb runs from October to May. These close for holidays in summer and the cultural scene shifts to the many summer festivals. Ask at municipal tourist offices about cultural events in their area.

Discos operate in summer in the coastal resorts and all year in the interior cities but the best way to mix with the local population is to enjoy a leisurely coffee or ice cream in a café. With the first hint of mild weather, Croatians head for an outdoor terrace to drink, smoke and watch the passing parade.

The cheapest entertainment in Croatia is a movie at a *kino* (cinema). Admission fees are always low and the soundtracks are in the original language. The selection leans towards popular American blockbusters and the last film of the day is usually hard-core pornography. Check the time on your ticket carefully, as admission is not allowed once the film has started.

THINGS TO BUY

Among the traditional handicraft products of Croatia are fine lace from Pag Island, hand-made embroidery, woodcarvings, woollen and leather items, carpets, filigree jewellery, ceramics, national costumes and tapestries.

Getting There & Away

AIR

Croatia Airlines (☎ 01-45 51 244), ulica Teslina 5, Zagreb, has flights from Zagreb to Amsterdam, Berlin, Brussels, Copenhagen, Dublin, Düsseldorf, Frankfurt, London, Moscow, Mostar, Munich, Paris, Prague, Rome, Sarajevo, Skopje, Stuttgart, Tirana, Vienna and Zürich. Note that all batteries must be removed from checked luggage for all Croatia Airlines flights.

LAND

Bus

Austria Eurolines (☎ 01-712 0453), Landstrasser Hauptstrasse 1b, A-1030 Vienna, runs two buses a week from Vienna to Rijeka, Split and Zadar (312KN) and a daily bus to Zagreb (157KN).

Benelux Budget Bus/Eurolines (☎ 020-520 8787; Rokin 10, Amsterdam) offers a weekly bus all year to Zagreb (26 hours, 781KN one way, 1218KN return) and another bus to Rijeka and Split with an extra weekly bus to both destinations during summer. All buses change at Frankfurt. Reductions are available for children under 13, but not for students or seniors. Eurolines (☎ 02-203 0707) rue du Progres 80, Brussels, operates a twice-weekly service all year from Brussels to Zagreb, changing in Munich and another twice weekly bus to Rijeka and the Dalmatian coast, changing in Frankfurt. On all Dutch and Belgian services you will be charged DM5 per piece of luggage. An advance reservation (19KN) is recommended.

Germany Because Croatia is a prime destination for Germans, the bus service is good and the buses of the Deutsche Touring GmbH (☎ 069-79 03 50), Am Romerhof 17, Frankfurt, are cheaper than the train. There are buses from Berlin, Cologne, Dortmund, Frankfurt/Main, Mannheim, Munich, Nuremberg, Stuttgart and other cities to Zagreb and three buses a week to Dubrovnik. There's a weekly bus to Istria from Frankfurt and two buses a week from Munich. The Dalmatian coast is also served by daily buses from German cities and there's a twice weekly bus direct from Berlin to Rijeka and on to Split. Baggage is DM5 extra per piece. Information is available at bus stations in the cities just mentioned.

Hungary Frequent connections between Nagykanizsa (145km, twice daily, 55KN) and Barcs (202km, five daily, 30KN), going on to Pécs. From Barcs there are frequent trains to Pécs (67km) and then less-frequent buses to Szeged (188km), where there are trains and buses to Subotica (47km) in Vojvodina (Yugoslavia). Nagykanizsa is more convenient if you're travelling to/from Budapest.

Yugoslavia Buses leave hourly between 5 am to 1 pm from Zagreb to Belgrade (six hours, 180KN). At Bajakovo on the border, a Yugoslav bus takes you on to Belgrade.

Train
Austria The *Ljubljana* express travels daily from Vienna to Rijeka (eight hours), via Ljubljana, and the EuroCity *Croatia* from Vienna to Zagreb (6½ hours, 304KN); both travel via Maribor.

Germany InterCity 296/297 goes overnight nightly from Munich to Zagreb (nine hours, 443KN) via Salzburg and Ljubljana. Reservations are required southbound but not northbound. The EuroCity *Mimara* between Berlin and Zagreb (1110KN), stopping at Leipzig and Munich, travels by day.

Hungary To go from Budapest to Zagreb (6½ hours, US$28) you have a choice of four trains daily. A daily train links Zagreb to Pécs (four hours, 105KN), leaving Pécs in the early morning and Zagreb in the afternoon, connecting through Osijek. As well as the international express trains, there are unreserved local trains between Gyékényes (Hungary) and Koprivnica (20 minutes) three times daily, with connections in Gyékényes to/from Nagykanizsa, Pécs and Kaposvár. Two unreserved trains daily travel between Varaždin and Nagykanizsa (1½ hours).

Italy Railway fares in Italy are relatively cheap so, if you can get across the Italian border from France or Switzerland, it won't cost an arm and a leg to take a train on to Trieste, where there are frequent bus connections to Croatia via Koper. Between Venice and Zagreb (226KN) there are the *Simplon* and *Venezia* express trains via Trieste and Ljubljana (seven hours). Between Trieste and Zagreb, there's the daily *Kras* via Ljubljana (five hours).

Romania There are no direct trains between Bucharest and Zagreb but there are two daily trains that connect in Budapest with trains to Zagreb (18 to 26 hours).

Yugoslavia Two trains daily connect Zagreb with Belgrade (6½ hours, 220KN).

Car & Motorcycle
The main highway entry/exit points between Croatia and Hungary are Goričan (between Nagykanizsa and Varaždin), Gola (23km east of Koprivnica), Terezino Polje (opposite Barcs) and Donji Miholjac (7km south of Harkány). There are 29 crossing points to/from Slovenia, too many to list here. There are 23 border crossings into Bosnia-Hercegovina and 10 into Yugoslavia, including the main Zagreb to Belgrade highway. Major destinations in Bosnia-Hercegovina, such as Sarajevo, Mostar and Međugorje, are accessible from Zagreb, Split and Dubrovnik.

SEA
Regular boats connect Croatia with both Italy and Greece. The Croatian Jadrolinija line, the Italian Adriatica Navigazione and the Croatian company Lošinjska Plovidba all serve the Adriatic coast. Five or six Jadrolinija ferries run a week year-round between Ancona and Split (10 hours, 249KN), stopping twice a week in July and August at Stari Grad on Hvar Island. Adriatica Navigazione connects Ancona and Split three times a week in summer for the same price and twice a week in winter.

Other Jadrolinija lines in the summer from Ancona stop at Zadar (four times a week, 224KN), Šibenik, Vis Island and Vela Luka on Korčula Island (weekly, 249KN).

From Bari, Adriatica Navigazione runs a ferry to Dubrovnik once a week all year and Jadrolinija connects the two cities twice a week in summer and once a week in winter. The eight-hour trip costs about 249KN.

Both Adriatica Navigazione and Lošinjska Plovidba connect Italy with the Istrian coast in summer. From May to September Adriatica Navigazione runs the *Marconi* between Trieste and Rovinj (3½ hours; L30,000), stopping at the Brijuni Islands six times a week and stopping twice a week in July and August at Poreč. In Trieste, contact Agemar (☎ 040-363 737), Piazza Duca degli Abruzzi, 1a. Lošinjska Plovidba's *Marina* connects Venice with Zadar (14½ hours; L87,000) twice a week from late June to September, stopping at Pula and Mali Lošinj. In Venice, contact Agenzia Favret (☎ 041-257 3511), Via Appia 20. Payment must be made in Italian lire and the prices include departure tax.

From May to September, the Atlas travel agency runs a fast boat between Zadar and Ancona (three hours, 340KN) and there's a new Croatian company, SEM (☎ 021-589 433), that runs a daily boat between Split, Trieste and Ancona; the Split-Ancona trip costs 234KN.

During the summer, Jadrolinija runs a ferry twice a week between Dubrovnik and Igoumenitsa, stopping in Bari (17½ hours, 265KN). Unless the ferry service to Albania resumes, there is no choice but to connect via Ancona or Bari. Both the Jadrolinija line to Bari and the Adriatica Navigazione line to Ancona connect well to other Adriatica Navigazione ferries to Durrës, Albania. From Ancona and Bari it is also possible to catch the Anek Lines boats to Igoumenitsa, Patrasso and Corfu.

Prices given above are for deck passage in the summer season. Prices are about 10% less in the off season and there's a 25% reduction for a return ticket on Jadrolinija ferries. A couchette on an overnight boat costs about an extra 90 to 100KN.

LEAVING CROATIA

The airport departure tax is 37KN. There is no port tax if you leave the country by boat.

Getting Around

AIR

Croatia Airlines has daily flights from Zagreb to Dubrovnik (620KN), Pula (414KN) and Split (556KN). Its twice-weekly flight to Skopje is very expensive at 715KN one way.

BUS

Bus services in Croatia are excellent. Fast express buses go everywhere, often many times a day, and they'll pick up passengers at designated stops anywhere along their route. Prices vary slightly between companies and depend on the route taken but the prices in this book should give you an idea of costs. Because the price is per kilometre it's possible to pay more for a slow local bus than a fast express. Luggage stowed in the baggage compartment under the bus costs extra (5KN a piece, including insurance). If your bag is small you could carry it onto the bus, although the seats are often placed close together, making this impossible on crowded buses.

At large stations, bus tickets must be purchased at the office, not from drivers; try to book ahead to be sure of a seat. Lists of departures over the various windows at the bus stations tell you which one has tickets for your bus. Tickets for buses that arrive from somewhere else are usually purchased from the conductor. On Croatian bus schedules, *vozi svaki dan* means 'every day', *ne vozi nedjeljom ni praznikom* means 'not Sundays and public holidays'.

Some buses travel overnight, saving you having to pay for a room. Don't expect to get much sleep, however, as the inside lights will be on and music will be blasting the whole night. Take care not to be left behind at meal or rest stops and beware of buses leaving 10 minutes early.

TRAIN

Train travel is about 15% cheaper than bus travel and often more comfortable, if slower. Baggage is free. Local trains usually have only unreserved 2nd-class seats but they're rarely crowded. Reservations may be required on express trains. 'Executive' trains have only 1st-class seats and are 40% more expensive than local trains. No couchettes are available on any domestic services. Most train stations have left-luggage offices charging about 10KN apiece (passport required).

There are two daily trains from Zagreb to Zadar and Split stopping at Knin where you can change to Šibenik. Other trains include Zagreb to Osijek (288km, five hours), Koprivnica (92km, 1½ hours, local), Varaždin (110km, three hours, local), Ljubljana (160km, three hours, local), Rijeka (243km, five hours, local) and Pula. There are also trains from Rijeka to Ljubljana (155km, 2½ hours, local).

On posted timetables in Croatia the word for arrivals is *dolazak* and for departures it's *odlazak* or *polazak*. Other terms you may encounter include *poslovni* (executive train), *brzi* or *ubrazni* (fast train), *putnički* (local train), *rezerviranje mjesta obvezatno* (compulsory seat reservation), *presjedanje* (change of trains), *ne vozi nedjeljom i blagdanom* (no service Sundays and holidays) and *svakodnevno* (daily).

CAR & MOTORCYCLE

Motorists require vehicle registration papers and the green insurance card to enter Croatia. Two-way amateur radios built into cars are no problem but must be reported at the border.

Petrol is either leaded super, unleaded (*bezolovni*) or diesel. You have to pay tolls on the motorways around Zagreb, to use the Učka tunnel between Rijeka and Istria, and for the bridge to Krk Island.

Along the coast, the spectacular Adriatic highway from Italy to Albania hugs the steep slopes of the coastal range, with abrupt drops to the sea and a curve a minute. You can drive as far south as Vitaljina, 56km southeast of Dubrovnik.

Motorists can turn to the Hrvatski Autoklub (HAK) or Croatian Auto Club for help or advice. Addresses of local HAK offices are provided throughout this chapter and the nationwide HAK road assistance (*vučna služba*) number is ☎ 987.

Unless otherwise posted, the speed limits for cars and motorcycles are 60km/h in built-up areas, 90km/h on main highways and 130km/h on motorways. Police systematically fine motorists exceeding these limits. On any of Croatia's winding two-lane highways, it's illegal to pass long military convoys or a whole line of cars caught behind a slow-moving truck. Drive defensively, as local motorists lack discipline.

Rental

The large car-rental chains represented in Croatia are Avis, Budget, Europcar and Hertz, with Budget (offices in Opatija, Split and Zagreb) generally the cheapest and Hertz the most expensive. Avis, Budget and Hertz have offices at Zagreb and Split airports. Throughout Croatia, Avis is allied with Autotehna, while Hertz is often represented by Kompas. Independent local companies are often much less expensive than the international chains, but Avis, Budget, Europcar and Hertz have the big advantage of offering one-way rentals which allow you to drop the car off at any one of their many stations in Croatia free of charge. Some local companies offer this service but have fewer stations.

The cheapest cars include the Renault 5, Peugeot 106, Opel Corsa and Fiat Uno. Prices at local companies begin at around 80KN a day plus 0.80KN per kilometre (100km minimum) or 225KN a day with unlimited kilometres. Shop around as deals vary widely and 'special' discounts and weekend rates are often available. Third-party public liability insurance is included by law, but make sure your quoted price includes full collision insurance, called collision damage waiver (CDW). Otherwise your responsibility for damage done to the vehicle is usually determined as a percentage of the car's value beginning at around 1000KN. Full CDW begins at 45KN a day extra (compulsory for those aged under 25), theft insurance at 15KN a day and personal accident insurance is another 10KN a day. Add 22% value-added tax to all charges.

The minimum age to rent a car is 21 and some companies require that you have a licence for at least a year. If you're paying by cash, the amount of the cash deposit is usually based upon the type of car and the length of the rental.

Sometimes you can get a lower car-rental rate by booking the car from abroad. Tour companies in Western Europe often have fly-drive packages which include a flight to Croatia and a car (two-person minimum).

BOAT

Jadrolinija Ferries

Year-round big, white and blue international Jadrolinija car ferries operate along the Rijeka-Dubrovnik coastal route, stopping at Zadar, Split, and the islands Rab, Hvar, Vis Korčula, and Mljet. Service is almost daily to the big cities during the summer but is greatly reduced in the winter. The most scenic section is Split to Dubrovnik, which all Jadrolinija ferries cover during the day. Rijeka to Split (13 hours) is usually an overnight trip in either direction.

Ferries are a lot more comfortable than buses, though considerably more expensive. From Rijeka to Dubrovnik the deck fare is 152KN but is at least 10% cheaper from October to May and there's a 25% reduction if you buy a return ticket. On certain boats there is a surcharge of 10% on weekends to and from Rijeka. With a through ticket, deck passengers can stop at any port for up to a week, provided you notify the purser beforehand and have your ticket validated. This is much cheaper than buying individual sector tickets. Cabins should be booked a week ahead, but deck space is usually available on all sailings.

Deck passage on Jadrolinija is just that: reclining seats (*poltrone*) are about 26KN extra and four-berth cabins (if available) begin at 329KN (Rijeka to Dubrovnik). Cabins can be arranged at the reservation counter aboard ship, but advance bookings are recommended if you want to be sure of a place. Deck space is fine for passages during daylight hours and when you can stretch out a sleeping bag on the upper deck in good weather, but if it's rainy you could end up sitting in the smoky cafeteria which stays open all night. During the crowded midsummer season, deck class can be unpleasant in wet weather.

Meals in the restaurants aboard Jadrolinija ships are about 80KN for a set menu. All the cafeteria offers is ham-and-cheese sandwiches for 18KN. Coffee is cheap in the cafeteria but wine and spirits tend to be expensive. Breakfast in the restaurant is about 30KN.

It's best to bring some food and drink with you.

Other Ferries

Local ferries connect the bigger offshore islands with each other and the mainland. The most important routes are Baška on Krk Island to Lopar on Rab Island (two daily from May to September), Zadar to Preko on Ugljan Island (nine daily), Split to Stari Grad on Hvar Island (three daily), Split to Vela Luka on Korčula Island via Hvar (daily), Orebić to Korčula Island (10 daily) and Dubrovnik to Sobra on Mljet Island (two daily). On most lines, service is increased from May to September.

Taking a bicycle on these services incurs an extra charge. Some of the ferries operate only a couple of times a day and, once the vehicular capacity is reached, remaining motorists must wait for the next service. In summer the lines of waiting cars can be long, so it's important to arrive early. Foot passengers and cyclists should have no problem getting on.

Travel agencies such as Atlas run fast hydrofoils up and down the coast in the summer, especially between Rijeka and Zadar, with Rab and Hvar also served (Rijeka-Zadar is 3½ hours, 210KN). Stop in any Atlas office and ask for the summer schedule.

HITCHING

Hitchhiking in Croatia is undependable. You'll have better luck on the islands but in the interior you'll notice that cars are small and usually full. Tourists never stop. Unfortunately, the image many Croats have of this activity is based on violent movies like *The Hitcher*.

LOCAL TRANSPORT

Zagreb has a well-developed tram system as well as local buses but in the rest of the country you'll only find buses. Buses in major cities such as Rijeka, Split, Zadar and Dubrovnik run about every 20 minutes, less often on Sunday. Small medieval towns along the coast are generally closed to traffic and have infrequent links to outlying suburbs.

CROATIA

ORGANISED TOURS

The Atlas travel agency offers 'adventure' tours which feature birdwatching, canoeing, caving, cycling, diving, fishing, hiking, riding, sailing, sea kayaking and white-water rafting in both Croatia and Slovenia. The eight-day tours cost from about US$700 to $900 (all-inclusive) and you join the group in Croatia. These tours allow you to combine the advantages of group and individual travel. Travel agents in North America book through Atlas Ambassador of Dubrovnik (☎ 202-483 8919), 1601 18th St NW, Washington, DC 20009.

The Croatian-owned Dalmatian and Istrian Travel (☎ 081-749 5255; fax 081-740 4432), 21 Sawley Road, London W12 0LG, offers independent packages in accommodation ranging from luxury hotels to camping as well as discounts on boat travel and outdoor activities. A typical package that includes a return London-Dubrovnik air fare and a week's stay in private accommodation costs £320 high season.

An interesting alternative for sailing enthusiasts is Katarina Line (☎ 051-272 110) at the Hotel Admiral, Opatija, which offers week-long cruises from Opatija to Krk, Rab, Pag, Mali Lošinj and Cres. Prices start at 1800KN a week and include half-board.

Zagreb

☎ 01

Zagreb, an attractive city of over a million inhabitants, has been the capital of Croatia since 1557. Spread up from the Sava River, Zagreb sits on the southern slopes of Medvednica, the Zagreb uplands. Medieval Zagreb developed from the 11th to the 13th centuries in the twin towns of Kaptol and Gradec. Kaptol grew around St Stephen's Cathedral and Gradec centred on St Mark's Church. Clerics established themselves in Kaptol as early as 1094, whereas Gradec was the craftspeople's quarter.

Much of medieval Zagreb remains today, although the stately 19th-century city between the old town and the train station is the present commercial centre. There are many fine parks, galleries and museums in both the upper and lower towns. Zagreb is Croatia's main centre for primitive or naive art. Finding a place to stay at a reasonable price remains the biggest problem for a traveller in this calm and graceful city.

Orientation

As you come out of the train station, you'll see a series of parks and pavilions directly in front of you and the twin neo-Gothic towers of the cathedral in the distance. Trg Jelačića, beyond the northern end of the parks, is the main city square. The bus station is 1km east of the train station. Tram Nos 2, 3 and 6 run from the bus station to the train station, with No 6 continuing to Trg Jelačića.

Information

Tourist Offices The tourist office (☎ 48 14 051), Trg Jelačića 11, is open weekdays from 8.30 am to 8 pm, Saturday from 10 am to 6 pm and Sunday from 10 am to 2 pm. A City Walks leaflet is available free and provides a good introduction to Zagreb's sights.

The Croatian Auto Club (HAK) has two travel offices in Zagreb: a smaller office (☎ 431 142) at Draškovićeva ulica 46 and a main information centre (☎ 46 40 800) six blocks east at Derenčinova 20.

Plitvice National Park maintains an information office (☎ 46 13 586) at Trg Tomislava 19. It also has information on other national parks around Croatia.

Money Exchange offices at the bus and train stations change money at the bank rate with 1% commission. Both the banks in the train station (open 7 am to 9 pm) and the bus station (open 6 am to 8 pm) accept travellers cheques.

The American Express representative is Atlas travel agency (☎ 61 24 389), Trg Zrinjskoga 17. It will hold clients' mail.

Post & Communications Any poste-restante mail is held (for one month) in the post office on the eastern side of the train station which is open 24 hours (except on Sunday morning). Have your letters addressed to Poste Restante, 10000 Zagreb, Croatia.

This same post office is also the best place to make long-distance telephone calls. Public telephones in Zagreb use phonecards.

Cybercafé Zagreb's first and only cybercafé is Sublink (☎ 48 11 329; sublink@sublink.hr) Teslina 12, open Monday to Friday from noon to 10 pm and weekends from 3 to 10 pm. 'Membership' with an email address and 30 minutes of Internet time costs 10KN.

Travel Agencies Dali Travel (☎ 422 953), Dežmanova 9, the travel branch of the Croatian YHA, can provide information on HI hostels throughout Croatia and make advance bookings. It also sells ISIC student cards (40KN), requiring proof of attendance at an educational institution. It's open weekdays from 8 am to 4 pm.

Bookshops Algoritam in the Hotel Dubrovnik on Trg Jelačića has the widest selection of English-language books. Antik- varijat, next to the Atlas travel agency, has some paperbacks in English as well as several excellent (though expensive) maps.

Laundry Predom, across the street from HAK on Draškovićeva 31, is open Saturday morning and weekdays from 7 am to 7 pm. Jeans and shirts cost 6KN each to wash and press. Underwear and socks are washed for 1KN each.

Left Luggage Left-luggage offices in both the bus and train stations are open 24 hours. The price posted at the left-luggage office in the bus station is 1.20KN *per hour*, so be careful. At the train station you pay a fixed price of about 10KN per day.

Medical & Emergency Services If you need to see a doctor, your best bet is the Emergency Centar (☎ 46 00 911), Draskovića 19. It's open all the time and charges 200KN for an examination. The police station for foreigners with visa concerns is at Petrinjska 30.

Things to See

Kaptol Zagreb's colourful **Dolac vegetable market** is just up the steps from Trg Jelačića and continues north along Opatovina. It's open daily, with especially large gatherings on Friday and Saturday. The twin neo-Gothic spires of **St Stephen's Cathedral** (1899), now renamed the Cathedral of the Assump-

tion of the Blessed Virgin Mary, are nearby. Elements from the medieval cathedral on this site, destroyed by an earthquake in 1880, can be seen inside, including 13th-century frescoes, Renaissance pews, marble altars and a baroque pulpit. The baroque **Archiepiscopal Palace** surrounds the cathedral, as do 16th-century fortifications constructed when Zagreb was threatened by the Turks.

Gradec From ulica Radićeva 5, off Trg Jelačića, a pedestrian walkway, stube Ivana Zakmardija, leads to the **Lotršćak Tower** and a funicular railway (1888), which connects the lower and upper towns (2KN). The tower has a sweeping 360° view of the city (closed Sunday). To the right is the baroque **St Catherine's Church**, with Jezuitski trg beyond. The **Gallerija Fortezza**, Jezuitski trg 4 (closed Monday), is Zagreb's premier exhibition hall where superb art shows are staged. Farther north and to the right is the 13th-century **Stone Gate**, with a painting of the Virgin which escaped the devastating fire of 1731.

The colourful painted-tile roof of the Gothic **St Mark's Church** on Markov trg marks the centre of Gradec. Inside are works by Ivan Meštrović, Croatia's most famous modern sculptor, but the church is only open for mass twice daily on weekdays and four times on Sunday. On the eastern side of St Mark's is the **Sabor** (1908), Croatia's National Assembly.

To the west of St Mark's is the 18th-century **Banski Dvori Palace**, the presidential palace with guards at the door in red ceremonial uniform. From April to September there is a guard-changing ceremony on weekends at noon.

At Mletačka 8 nearby is the former **Meštrović Studio**, now a museum which is open weekdays from 9 am to 2 pm. Other museums in this area include the **Croatian Historical Museum** (open for temporary exhibitions), Matoševa 9, the **Gallery of Naive Art**, Čirilometodska 3 (closed Monday), and the **Natural History Museum**, Demetrova 1 (closed Monday). More interesting is the recently renovated **City Museum**, Opatićeka 20 (closed Monday), with a scale model of old Gradec. Summaries in English and German are in each room of the museum, which is in the former Convent of St Claire (1650).

CROATIA

Lower Town Zagreb really is a city of museums. There are four on the parks between the train station and Trg Jelačića. The yellow **exhibition pavilion** (1897) across the park from the station presents changing contemporary art exhibitions. The second building north, also in the park, houses the **Strossmayer Gallery** of the Academy of Arts & Sciences, with old master paintings. It's closed on Monday, but you can enter the interior courtyard to see the Baška Slab (1102) from the island of Krk, one of the oldest inscriptions in the Croatian language.

The **Archaeological Museum** at Trg Nikole Zrinjskog 19 used to display prehistoric to medieval artefacts, as well as Egyptian mummies, but has been closed for several years and plans for its reopening are uncertain. Behind the museum is a garden of Roman sculpture that has been turned into a pleasant open-air café in the summer.

West of the Centre The **Museum Mimara** at Rooseveltov trg 5 (closed Monday) is one of the finest art galleries in Europe. In a neo-Renaissance former school building (1883), this diverse collection shows the loving hand of Ante Topić Mimara, a private collector who donated over 3750 priceless objects to his native Zagreb, even though he spent much of his life in Salzburg, Austria. The Spanish, Italian and Dutch paintings are the highlight, but there are also large sections of glassware, sculpture and Oriental art.

Nearby on Trg Maršala Tita is the neo-baroque **Croatian National Theatre** (1895), with Ivan Meštrović's sculpture *Fountain of Life* (1905) in front. The **Ethnographic Museum** (closed Monday) at Trg Mažuranića 14 has a large collection of Croatian folk costumes with English explanations. South is the Art-Nouveau **National Library** (1907). The **Botanical Garden** on ulica Mihanovićeva (closed Monday; free) is attractive for the plants and landscaping as well as its restful corners.

North of the Centre A 20-minute ride north on bus No 106 from the cathedral takes you to **Mirogoj**, one of the most beautiful cemeteries in Europe. One wag commented that the people here are better housed in death

than they ever were in life. The English-style landscaping is enclosed by a long 19th-century neo-Renaissance arcade.

Organised Tours

Within Zagreb, the tourist office organises walking tours for 45KN per person (minimum four people) and minibus tours every Wednesday morning leaving from the InterContinental and Esplanade hotels for about 80KN.

Special Events

In odd years in April there's the Zagreb Biennial of Contemporary Music, since 1961 Croatia's most important music event. Zagreb also hosts a festival of animated films every other year in June. Croatia's largest international fairs are the Zagreb spring (mid-April) and autumn (mid-September) grand trade fairs. In July and August the Zagreb Summer Festival presents a cycle of concerts and theatre performances on open stages in the upper town.

Places to Stay

Budget accommodation is in short supply in Zagreb. An early arrival is recommended, since private room-finding agencies are an attractive alternative and usually refuse telephone bookings.

Camping There's a camping area outside the Motel Plitvice (☎ 65 30 444) which is not in Plitvice at all but near the town of Lučko on the Obilazinica highway south-west of Zagreb. The motel sometimes runs a minibus from Savski Most. Call to find out if and when their service is operating. Otherwise, take tram 7 or 14 to Savski Most and then the Lučko bus to Lučko village from which the motel/camp site is about a 10-minute walk. The price is 23KN per person and 20KN per tent and there's a lake and a sports centre nearby.

Hostels The noisy 215-bed *Omladinski Hotel*, actually a youth hostel, (☎ 48 41 261; fax 48 41 269), Petrinjska 77, near the train station is open all year and charges 210KN for a double without bath, 280KN with bath, including tax; it has no singles. Some of the six-bed dormitories (73KN per person) may

ZAGREB

PLACES TO STAY
28 Hotel Dubrovnik
32 Hotel Jadran
47 Hotel Sheraton
48 Omladinski Hotel
   (Youth Hostel) &
   Hotel Astoria
55 Intercontinental
   Hotel
59 Hotel Esplanade
60 Central Hotel

PLACES TO EAT
21 Market
22 Delikatese
23 Pizzicato
25 Restaurant Split
31 Mimiće
33 Melong
35 Hard Rock Café
58 Studentski Centar

OTHER
1 Polish Embassy
2 City Museum
3 Natural History Museum
4 Meštrović Studio
5 Historical Museum
  of Croatia
6 Banski Dvori Palace
7 St Mark's Church
8 Sabor (Parliament)
9 Stone Gate
10 Komedija Theatre
11 Gallery of Naive Art
12 Muzejski Prostor
13 Lotršćak Tower
14 St Catherine's Church
15 Dolac Market
16 St Stephen's Cathedral
17 Funicular Railway
18 British Council
19 Nama Department Store
20 Croatian YHA/
   Dali Travel
24 Academy of Music
26 Trg Petra Preradovića
27 Blagasija Oktogon
29 Tourist Office
30 Post Office/
   Telephone Centre
34 Archaeological Museum
36 Sublink
37 Embassy of Slovakia
38 Arts & Crafts Museum
39 Croatian National Theatre
40 Atlas Travel Agency
41 US Embassy
42 Gallery of Modern Art
43 Strossmayer Gallery
44 Emergency Centar
45 Croatian Auto
   Club (HAK)
46 Predom
49 Exhibition Pavilion
50 Puppet Theatre
51 Plitvice National
   Park Office
52 Pivnica Tomaslav
53 Ethnographic Museum
54 Museum Mimara
56 National Library
57 Technical Museum
61 Post Office
62 Train Station
63 City Hall
64 Vatroslav Lisinski
   Concert Hall

still be occupied by war refugees but most rooms remain available. The 5KN YHA discount is only available to people under 27 sleeping in the dormitory. You must check out by 9 am and you can't occupy the room until 2 pm.

The **Studenthotel Cvjetno Naselje** (☎ 61 91 240), off Slavonska avenija in the south of the city, charges 219/287KN for a single/double, breakfast included. The rooms are good, each with private bath, and the staff are friendly. There's no student discount, although showing your ISIC and pleading

poverty occasionally works. There's a self-service student restaurant here where a filling meal with a Coke will cost 30KN. The Cvjetno Naselje is available to visitors only from mid-July to the end of September – the rest of the year it's a student dormitory. Take tram Nos 4, 5, 14, 16 or 17 south-west on Savska cesta to 'Vjesnik'. Opposite the stop is a tall building marked 'Vjesnik'. The student complex is just behind it.

In July and August head straight for the **Studentski dom Stjepan Radić** (☎ 334 255), Jarunska ulica 3, off Horvaćanska ulica in the

CROATIA

south of the city near the Sava River (tram Nos 5 or 17). Rooms in this huge student complex cost 200/250KN for a single/double and one of Zagreb's more popular discos, The Best, is across the street.

Private Rooms Try not to arrive on Sunday if you intend to stay in a private apartment as most of the agencies are closed. You'll notice that prices are surprisingly high but little of the money actually goes to your host. Taxes bite off a chunk and the agency takes nearly half the money with barely a quarter left for the host.

The Turističko Društvo Novi Zagreb (☎ 65 52 047; fax 65 21 523), Trnsko 15e, has private rooms in apartment buildings in the Novi Zagreb neighbourhood south of the Sava River (tram Nos 7, 14 or 16 to Trnsko) for 200/260KN a single/double, plus tax, with a 30% surcharge for one-night stays. The office is open weekdays from 8 am to 6 pm and Saturday from 9 am to 1 pm.

Lina Gabino (☎ 39 21 27) on Petračićeva, just west of the town centre, rents out both two-bedroom apartments (400/420KN a single/double) and private rooms (265/350KN plus tax). Prices are about 10% cheaper if you stay more than one night. Her office is open weekdays from 9 am to 5 pm and Saturday from 9 am to 2 pm.

Evistas (☎ 429 974 or 48 19 133; fax 431 987), Šenoina 28, between the bus and train station, also rents out apartments, beginning at 350KN for two people and rising to 675KN for five with a minimum stay of three nights. Private rooms are also available in the town centre for 170/230KN a single/double (145/190KN for people under 25). The office is open weekdays from 9 am to 1.30 pm and 5 to 8 pm and Saturday from 9.30 am to 5 pm.

If you're new to Croatia, don't be put off by these high prices. Along the coast, especially from Rab south, private rooms cost less than half as much.

Hotels There aren't any cheap hotels in Zagreb. Most of the older hotels have been renovated and the prices raised to B category.

If you can't arrange a morning arrival and afternoon departure to avoid spending the night in Zagreb, be prepared to bite the bullet

and pay a lot more for a place to sleep than you would elsewhere in Croatia. The only easy escape is to book an overnight bus to Split or Dubrovnik.

The best deal is the brand new and friendly *Hotel Ilica* (☎ 37 77 522; fax 37 77 722), Ilica 102, two stops from Trg Jelačića, which offers 12 quiet, pleasant rooms with bath and breakfast for 251/380KN a single/double and 441KN for a double with two beds.

The 110-room *Central Hotel* (☎ 484 11 22; fax 48 41 304), Branimirova 3 opposite the train station, is blandly modern and charges 308/446KN a single/double, including bath, breakfast and tax.

The six-storey *Hotel Jadran* (☎ 414 600; fax 46 12 151), Vlaška 50 near the city centre, charges 362/432KN with shower and breakfast.

For a memorable splurge, stay at the five-star *Hotel Esplanade* (☎ 45 66 666; fax 45 77 907) next to the train station (890/1200KN a single/double plus tax with a buffet breakfast). There's a 30% discount for weekend stays. This six-storey, 215-room hotel erected in 1924 is truly majestic and has one of the best restaurants in Zagreb.

Places to Eat

One of the most elegant places in town is undoubtedly the *Paviljon* in the yellow exhibition pavilion across the park from the train station. Main courses with an Italian flavour start at 70KN. The fresh fish and local wines at *Restaurant Split*, Ilica 19, also make a delicious treat. For regional dishes and lots of local colour, dine in one of the outdoor restaurants along ulica Tkalčićeva, up from Trg Jelačića, on summer evenings.

Pizza places are everywhere, but it would be hard to do better than the delicious, freshly made pies at *Pizzicarto* Gundilićeva 4 near the Academy of Music. Prices start at 18KN and the menu is translated into English. Vegetarians should head to *Melong*, Petrinjska 9 near Ilica. The menu is in Croatian and the staff speaks limited English but whatever you order is bound to be tasty. *Mimiće*, Jurišićeva 21 has been a local favourite for decades, turning out plates of fried fish that cost from 9KN for 10 sardines and a hunk of bread.

Delikatese, Ilica 39, is a good place to pick up cheese, fruit, bread, yoghurt and cold meat for a picnic. Next door is a *grocery store* that sells whole roasted chicken and an assortment of prepared salads. Further along Ilica at Trg Britanski, there's a daily fruit and vegetable *market* open every day until 3 pm which sells farm fresh produce. Don't hesitate to bargain.

Cafés & Bars The *Rock Forum Café*, Gajeva ulica 13, occupies the rear sculpture garden of the Archaeological Museum (open in summer only) and across the street is the *Hard Rock Café*, full of 1950s and 1960s memorabilia. Farther back in the passageway from the Hard Rock is the *Art Café Thalia* which really tries to live up to its name. A couple of other cafés and music shops share this lively complex at the corner of Teslina and Gajeva streets. Check out the *BP Club* in the complex basement for jazz, blues and rock bands.

Zagreb's most pretentious cafés are *Gradska Kavana* on Trg Jelačića and *Kazališna Kavana* on Trg Maršala Tita opposite the Croatian National Theatre. *Models* café next door to *Kazališna Kavana* is adorned with photos of the superstar models the café is evidently trying (and, so far, failing) to attract.

Entertainment

Zagreb is a happening city. Its theatres and concert halls present a great variety of programs throughout the year. Many (but not all) are listed in the monthly brochure *Zagreb Events & Performances*, which is usually available from the tourist office.

Bars & Clubs The liveliest scene in Zagreb is along Tkalčićeva, north off Trg Jelačića, where crowds spill out of cafés onto the street, drinks in hand. Farther up on Kozarska ulica the city's young people cluster shoulder to shoulder. Trg Petra Preradovića, Zagreb's flower-market square attracts street performers in mild weather and occasional bands. The *Pivnica Tomislav*, Trg Tomislava 18, facing the park in front of the train station, is a good local bar with inexpensive draught beer.

Kulušić, Hrvojeva 6 near the Hotel Sheraton (open Thursday to Sunday from 10 pm to 4 am; entry 30KN) is a casual, funky disco

that offers occasional live bands, fashion shows and record promos as well as standard disco fare.

Sokol klub, across the street from the Ethnographic Museum (open Wednesday to Sunday from 10 pm to 4 am; entry 30KN) is more polished and admits women free before midnight. Live rock concerts are presented every Sunday.

Gay & Lesbian Venues Gays are generally welcome in Zagreb's bars and discos but the city's only exclusively gay bar is *Bacchus* bar on Tomislava near the train station. At the moment the bar attracts mostly men with a sprinkling of women. *Gjuro*, Medveščak 58, in north Kaptol is a disco that attracts a gay and straight crowd.

Cinemas There are 18 cinemas in Zagreb which show foreign movies in their original language with subtitles. Posters around town advertise the programs. Kinoteca, Kordunska 1, shows classic foreign movies on weekdays at 6:30 pm.

Theatre It's worth making the rounds of the theatres in person to check their programs. Tickets are usually available, even for the best shows. A small office marked 'Kazalište Komedija' (look for the posters) in the Blagasija Oktogon, a passage connecting Trg Petra Preradovićeva to Ilica near Trg Jelačića, also sells theatre tickets.

The neobaroque *Croatian National Theatre* (☎ 48 28 532), Trg Maršala Tita 15, was established in 1895. It stages opera and ballet performances and the box office is open weekdays from 10 am to 1 pm and 5 to 7.30 pm and Saturday from 10 am to 1 pm as well as for a half-hour before performances on Sunday. You have a choice of orchestra (parket), lodge (lože) or balcony (balkon) seats.

The *Komedija Theatre* (☎ 433 209), Kaptol 9 near the cathedral, stages operettas and musicals.

The ticket office of the *Vatroslav Lisinski Concert Hall* (☎ 61 21 166) just south of the train station, is open weekdays from 9 am to 8 pm and Saturday from 9 am to 2 pm.

Concerts also take place at the *Croatian Music Institute* (☎ 424 533), Gundulićeva 6a, off Ilica.

CROATIA

There are performances at the *Puppet Theatre*, ulica Baruna Trenka 3, on Saturday at 5 pm and Sunday at noon.

Spectator Sport

Basketball is popular in Zagreb, and from October to April games take place at the Cibona Centar, Savska cesta 30 opposite the Technical Museum, usually on Saturday at 7.30 pm. Tickets are available at the door.

Soccer games are held on Sunday afternoon at the Maksimir Stadium, Maksimirska 128 on the eastern side of Zagreb (tram Nos 4, 7, 11 or 12 to Bukovačka). If you arrive too early for the game, Zagreb's zoo is just across the street.

Things to Buy

Ilica is Zagreb's main shopping street. Get in touch with Croatian consumerism at the Nama department store on Ilica near Trg Jelačića.

Folk-music compact discs are available from Fonoteca at Nama. Rokotvorine, Trg Jelačića 7, sells traditional Croatian handicrafts such as red and white embroidered tablecloths, dolls and pottery.

The shops, fast food outlets and grocery stores in the mall under the tracks beside the train station have long opening hours.

Getting There & Away

Bus Zagreb's big, modern bus station has a large, enclosed waiting room where you can stretch out while waiting for your bus (but there's no heating in winter). Buy most international tickets at window Nos 11 and 12, and change money (including travellers cheques) at A Tours open daily from 6 am to 8 pm. The left-luggage office is always open (take care – the charge is 1.20KN *per hour*).

Buses depart from Zagreb for most of Croatia, Slovenia and places beyond. Buy an advance ticket at the station if you're travelling far.

The following domestic buses depart from Zagreb: Dubrovnik (713km, eight daily, 140KN), Krk (229km, three daily, 95KN), Ljubljana (135km, five daily, 60KN), Plitvice (140km, 19 daily), Poreč (264km, six daily), Pula (283km, 13 daily, 100KN), Rab (211km, daily), Rijeka (173km, 21 daily 70KN), Rovinj (278km, eight daily, 110KN), Split (478km, 27 daily, 100KN), Varaždin

(77km, 20 daily, 43KN), Mali Lošinj (298km, daily, 120KN) and Zadar (320km, 20 daily, 80KN).

Bus services to Yugoslavia have resumed. From 5 am to 1 pm there are hourly buses to Belgrade, changing at the border town, Bajakovo, for a local bus. The six-hour trip costs 180KN. There are two buses daily to Sarajevo (417km, 362KN) and four to Međugorje (420km, 153KN).

There's buses to Nagykanizsa (145km, twice daily 55KN) and Barcs (202km, five daily, 90KN) in Hungary. Nagykanizsa is preferable if you're bound for Budapest or Balaton Lake, while Barcs is better for Pécs or Yugoslavia.

Other international buses worth knowing about are to Vienna (twice daily, 157KN), Munich (576km, twice daily, 285KN) and Berlin (twice daily, DM190 – payment in Deutschmarks only). Luggage is DM5 per piece.

Train The *Venezia* and *Maestral* express trains depart from Zagreb for Budapest (seven hours, 181KN) every morning. The *Avas* leaves early afternoon and the *Kvarner* late afternoon. A ticket from Zagreb to Nagykanizsa, the first main junction inside Hungary, costs 72KN. A useful daily train runs between Zagreb and Pécs, Hungary (five hours, 105KN).

Zagreb is on both the Munich-Ljubljana and Vienna-Maribor main lines. There are trains twice daily between Munich and Zagreb (nine hours, 443KN) via Salzburg. Two trains daily arrive from Venice (seven hours, 226KN).

Four trains daily run from Zagreb to Osijek (4½ hours, 68KN), six to Koprivnica (two hours), 13 to Varazdin (three hours, 33KN), seven to Ljubljana (160km, 62KN), four to Rijeka (five hours, 58KN), two to Pula (5½ hours, 145KN) and three or four to Split (nine hours, 91KN). Both daily trains to Zadar (11 hours, 80KN) stop at Knin. Reservations are required on some trains, so check.

Getting Around

Public transport is based on an efficient but overcrowded network of trams, although the city centre is compact enough to make them unnecessary. Tram Nos 3 and 8 don't run on weekends.

Buy tickets (4.50KN) at newspaper kiosks. You can use your ticket for transfers within 90 minutes but only in one direction.

A *dnevna karta* (day ticket), valid on all public transport until 4 am the next morning, is available for 12KN at most Vjesnik or Tisak news outlets.

To/From the Airport The Croatia Airlines bus to Pleso airport, 17km south-east of Zagreb, leaves from the bus station every half-hour or hour from about 4 am to 8.30 pm, depending on flights, and returns from the airport on about the same schedule (20KN).

Car Of the major car rental companies, Budget Rent-a-Car (☎ 45 54 936) in the Hotel Sheraton often has the lowest rates (325KN a day with unlimited kilometres). Other companies are Europcar (☎ 65 54 003) at the airport, Avis Autotehna (☎ 48 36 296) at the InterContinental Hotel and Hertz (☎ 48 47 222), Kračićeva 9a near the InterContinental Hotel. Local companies usually have lower rates. Try Niva Rent-a-Car (☎ 61 59 280), Miramarska 22 near the Hotel Esplanade, and, at the airport, Mack (☎ 442 222) and Uni Rent (☎ 65 25 006).

Taxi Zagreb's taxis all have meters which begin at a whopping 15KN and then ring up 6KN a kilometre. On Sunday and nights from 10 pm to 5 am there's a 20% surcharge. Waiting time is 40KN an hour. The baggage surcharge is 2KN per suitcase.

PLITVICE

Plitvice Lakes National Park lies midway between Zagreb and Zadar. The 19.5 hectares of wooded hills enclose 16 turquoise lakes which are linked by a series of waterfalls and cascades. The mineral-rich waters carve new paths through the rock, depositing tufa in continually changing formations. Wooden footbridges follow the lakes and streams over, under and across the rumbling water for an exhilaratingly damp 18km. Swimming is allowed in several lakes. Park admission is 60KN (students 30KN) but is valid for the entire stay.

Places to Stay

Camping *Korana* (☎ 053-751 015) is about 1km north of the entrance along the main road to Zagreb and charges 25KN per person and 18KN per tent.

Hotels *Hotel Bellevue* (☎ 053-751 700; fax 053-751 965) offers rustic accommodation within the park for 252/396KN a single/double but at the hotels *Plitvice* (☎ 053-751 100) and *Jezero* (☎ 053-751 400) you'll pay about 50% more. Three kilometres north of the entrance along the main road to Zagreb is the *Motel Grabovac* (☎ 053-751 999), which has singles/doubles for 252/366KN.

Check at the Plitvice National Park office in Zagreb for information on private accommodation.

Getting There & Away

Buses run hourly from Zagreb to Plitvice (140km) and then continue to Zadar or Split. It is possible to visit Plitvice for the day on the way to or from the coast but be aware that buses will not pick up passengers at Plitvice if they are full. Luggage can be left at the tourist information centre (open daily from 8 am to 6.30 pm) at the first entrance to the park.

Istria

Istria (Istra to Croatians), the heart-shaped 3600-sq-km peninsula just south of Trieste, Italy, is named after the Illyrian Histri tribe conquered by the Romans in 177 BC.

Istria has been a political basketball. Italy took Istria from Austria-Hungary in 1919, then had to give it to Yugoslavia in 1947. A large Italian community lives in Istria and Italian is widely spoken. Tito wanted Trieste (Trst) as part of Yugoslavia too, but in 1954 the Anglo-American occupiers returned the city to Italy so that it wouldn't fall into the hands of the 'communists'. Today the Koper-Piran strip belongs to Slovenia while the rest is held by Croatia.

The 430km Istrian Riviera basks in the Mediterranean landscapes and climate for which the Adriatic coast is famous. The long summer season from May to October attracts large crowds. Mercifully, Istria was spared the fighting that occurred elsewhere in former Yugoslavia and it's a peaceful place to visit. Industry and heavy shipping are concentrated along the northern side of Istria around Koper and Izola, and Umag is a scattered, characterless resort you could easily skip. Novigrad is nicer, but the farther south you go in Istria the quieter it gets, with cleaner water, fewer visitors and cars and less industry. See Piran quickly, then move south to Rovinj, a perfect base from which to explore Poreč and Pula.

Getting There & Away

Bus Koper and Rijeka are the main entry/exit points, with buses to most towns on Istria's west coast every couple of hours. Train services in Istria are limited, so plan on getting around by bus.

Boat For information on connections between Istria and Italy see the Getting There & Away section at the beginning of this chapter.

In Istria, travel agencies such as Kvarner Express or Atlas should know the departure times and prices of all international boats although tickets may only be available on board. All boats connecting Istria with Italy or the Dalmatian coast depart from the landings marked 'Customs Wharf' on the maps in this book; schedules are sometimes posted there. It's an exciting way to travel.

POREČ
☎ 052

Poreč (Italian: Parenzo), the Roman Parentium, sits on a low, narrow peninsula about halfway down the west coast of Istria. The ancient Dekumanus with its polished stones is still the main street. Even after the fall of Rome, Poreč remained important as a centre of early Christianity, with a bishop and a famous basilica. The town is now the centre of a region packed with tourist resorts but vestiges of earlier times and a quiet, small-town atmosphere make it well worth a stop or at least a day trip from Rovinj. There are many places to swim in the clear water off the rocks north of the old town.

Orientation
The bus station (with a left-luggage office open from 6 am to 8 pm daily, except Sunday, when it closes at 5 pm) is directly opposite the small-boat harbour just outside the old town.

Information
The tourist office (☎ 451 293) is at Zagrebačka 8. The Atlas travel agency (☎ 434 983) at Eufrazijeva 63 represents American Express. There's another office (☎ 432 273) at Boze Milanovića 11.

The Auto-Klub Poreč (☎ 431 665), Partizanska bb (no street number), is in a large white building visible across the field north of the market.

The telephone centre in the main post office, Trg Slobode 14, is open Monday to Saturday from 7 am to 9 pm and Sunday from 9 am to noon.

Things to See
The many historic sites in the old town include the ruins of two **Roman temples**, between Trg Marafor and the western end of the peninsula. Archaeology and history are featured in the four-floor **Regional Museum** (open daily year-round) in an old baroque palace at Dekumanus 9 (captions in German and Italian).

The main reason to visit Poreč, however, is to see the 6th-century **Euphrasian basilica**, a world heritage site which features wonderfully preserved Byzantine gold mosaics. The capitals, sculpture and architecture are remarkable survivors of that distant period. Entry to the church is free and for a small fee you may visit the 4th-century mosaic floor of the adjacent Early Christian basilica.

From May to mid-October there are passenger boats (12KN return) every half-hour to **Sveti Nikola**, the small island opposite Poreč Harbour, departing from the new wharf on Obala Maršala Tita.

Special Events
Annual events include the Folk Festival (June), the Inter Folk Fest (August), the Annual Art Exhibition (June until late August) and the Musical Summer (May to September). Ask about these at the tourist office.

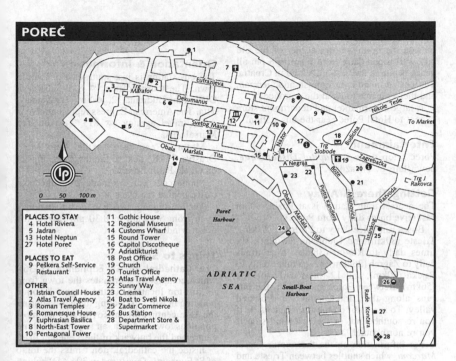

POREČ

```
0    50   100 m
```

PLACES TO STAY
4 Hotel Riviera
5 Jadran
13 Hotel Neptun
27 Hotel Poreč

PLACES TO EAT
9 Peškera Self-Service
   Restaurant

OTHER
1 Istrian Council House
2 Atlas Travel Agency
3 Roman Temples
6 Romanesque House
7 Euphrasian Basilica
8 North-East Tower
10 Pentagonal Tower

11 Gothic House
12 Regional Museum
14 Customs Wharf
15 Round Tower
16 Capitol Discotheque
17 Adriatikturist
18 Post Office
19 Church
20 Tourist Office
21 Atlas Travel Agency
22 Sunny Way
23 Cinema
24 Boat to Sveti Nikola
25 Zadar Commerce
26 Bus Station
28 Department Store &
   Supermarket

Places to Stay

Accommodation in Poreč is tight and the camping grounds are far from the town centre, so you might want to stop off only for the day on your way south or north.

Camping There are two camping grounds at Zelena Laguna, 6km south of Poreč. Both *Autocamp Zelena Laguna* (☎ 410 541) and *Autocamp Bijela Uvala* (☎ 410 551) are open from April to mid-October and charge around 24KN per person, 14KN per tent. Take the 'Plava Laguna' bus which runs hourly from the bus station and get off at Zelena Laguna resort. Both camping grounds are a short walk away.

Private Rooms There are very few private rooms available in Poreč and nearly none outside the main season. In the town centre, try Kompas-Istra (☎ 451 200; fax 451 114), Obala Marsala Tita 16 across from the Hotel Neptun. Around Trg Rakovca, there's Kvarner Express (☎ 451 600). Expect to pay about 90/132KN for a single/double with a shared bath in July and August. Make sure to arrive early in the day outside the main May to September tourist season as many agencies close around noon.

Hotels One of the following hotels in the town centre is open year-round but it changes from year to year. Try the modern, five-storey *Hotel Poreč* (☎ 451 811). In July and August a single/double with bath, breakfast and dinner costs 333/556KN. *Hotel Neptun* (☎ 452 711; fax 431 531), Obala M. Tita 15, overlooks the harbour. A single/double with bath and breakfast costs 227/387KN in the peak season.. Near the bus station is the *Jadran* (☎ 451 422), Obala Marsala Tita 431-236, which has rooms for 212/366KN.

All prices assume a four-night minimum stay and drop about 50% during May, June, September and October.

CROATIA

Places to Eat

The *Peškera Self-Service Restaurant*, just outside the north-western corner of the old city wall (open daily from 9 am to 8 pm all year), is one of the best of its kind in Croatia. The posted menu is in English and German, and there's a free toilet at the entrance.

A large supermarket and department store is next to Hotel Poreč near the bus station.

Entertainment

Poreč's top disco is *Capitol Discotheque*, downstairs at V Nazor 9.

Getting There & Away

The nearest train station is at Pazin, 30km east (five buses daily from Poreč).

Buses run twice daily to Portorož (54km), Trieste (89km) and Ljubljana (176km); six times daily to Rovinj (38km); nine times daily to Zagreb (264km), seven times daily to Rijeka (80km); and 12 times daily to Pula (56km). Between Poreč and Rovinj the bus runs along the Lim Channel, a drowned valley. To see it, sit on the right-hand side if you're southbound, or the left-hand side if you're northbound.

For information on the fast motor vessel *Marconi,* which shuttles between Trieste and Poreč (2¾ hours; L27,000) inquire at the Sunny Way agency (☎ 452 021), Alda Negrija 1 and see the Getting There & Away section at the beginning of this chapter.

The cheapest price for car rental is at Zadar Commerce (☎ 434 103), Istarskog razvoda 11.

ROVINJ
☎ 052

Relaxed Rovinj (Italian: Rovigno), its high peninsula topped by the great 57m-high tower of massive St Euphemia Cathedral, is perhaps the best place to visit in Istria. Wooded hills punctuated by low-rise luxury hotels surround the town, while the 13 green offshore islands of the Rovinj archipelago make for pleasant, varied views. The cobbled, inclined streets in the old town are charmingly picturesque. Rovinj is still an active fishing port, so you see local people going about their day-to-day business. There's a large Italian community here.

Friendly Rovinj is just the place to rest before your island-hopping journey farther south.

Orientation & Information

The bus station is just south-east of the old town. The tourist office (☎ 811 566) is at Obala Pina Budicina 12, just off Trg Maršala Tita. The American Express representative is Atlas travel agency (☎ 811 241) on Trg Maršala Tita.

Motorists can turn to the Auto Moto Društva (HAK) next to the large parking lot on Obala Palih Boraca.

Phone calls can be made from the post office behind the bus station.

The left-luggage office at the bus station is open from 5.15 am to 8.30 pm (ask at the ticket window).

Things to See

The **Cathedral of St Euphemia** (1736), which completely dominates the town from its hill-top location, is the largest baroque building in Istria, reflecting the period during the 18th century when Rovinj was the most populous town in Istria, an important fishing centre and the bulwark of the Venetian fleet.

Inside the cathedral, don't miss the tomb of St Euphemia (martyred in 304 AD) behind the right-hand altar. The saint's remains were brought from Constantinople in 800. On the anniversary of her martyrdom (16 September) devotees congregate here. A copper statue of her tops the cathedral's mighty tower.

Take a wander along the winding narrow backstreets below the cathedral, such as ulica Grisia, where local artists sell their work. Rovinj has developed into an important art centre and each year in mid-August Rovinj's painters stage a big open-air art show in town.

The **Regional Museum** on Trg Maršala Tita (closed Monday) contains an unexciting collection of paintings and a few Etruscan artefacts found in Istria. These might attract some interest if the captions were in something other than Croatian and Italian. The **Franciscan convent**, up the hill at E de Amicis 36, also has a small museum.

Better than either of these is the **Rovinj Aquarium** (1891) at Obala Giordano Paliaga 5 (open daily but closed mid-October to Easter; 10KN). It exhibits a good collection

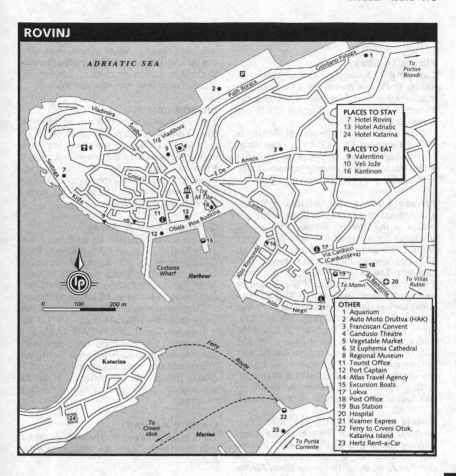

ROVINJ

ADRIATIC SEA

Vladimira
Trg Vladibora
Svalbe
Grisia
Svetoga
Križa
Obala Pina Budicina
Palih Boraca
Giordano Paliaga
Amicis
E De
Carera
Alzo Rismondo
Via Carducci (Carduccijeva)
M Benussija
To Monvi
Aldo
Negri
Customs Wharf
Harbour
To Porton Biondi
To Villas Rubin

0   100   200 m

Katarina

To Crveni otok
Marina
To Punta Corrente

PLACES TO STAY
7 Hotel Rovinj
13 Hotel Adriatic
24 Hotel Katarina

PLACES TO EAT
9 Valentino
10 Veli Jože
16 Kantinon

OTHER
1 Aquarium
2 Auto Moto Društva (HAK)
3 Franciscan Convent
4 Gandusio Theatre
5 Vegetable Market
6 St Euphemia Cathedral
8 Regional Museum
11 Tourist Office
12 Port Captain
14 Atlas Travel Agency
15 Excursion Boats
17 Lokva
18 Post Office
19 Bus Station
20 Hospital
21 Kvarner Express
22 Ferry to Crveni Otok, Katarina Island
23 Hertz Rent-a-Car

of local marine life, from poisonous scorpion fish to colourful anemones.

When you've seen enough of the town, follow the waterfront southwards past the Park Hotel to **Punta Corrente Forest Park**, which was afforested in 1890 by Baron Hütterodt, an Austrian admiral who kept a villa on Crveni otok. Here you can swim off the rocks, climb a cliff or just sit and admire the offshore islands.

Organised Tours

Delfin Agency (☎ 813 266), near the ferry

dock for Crveni otok, runs half-day scenic cruises to the **Lim Channel** (70KN) or you can take the hourly ferry to Crveni otok (Red Island; 15KN return). There's a frequent ferry to nearby **Katarina Island** (10KN) from the same landing and you get tickets on the boat. These boats operate from May to mid-October only.

Special Events

The city's annual events include the Rovinj-Pesaro Regata (early May), the 'Rovinj Summer' concert series (July and August),

CROATIA

the Rovinj Fair (August) and the ACI Cup Match Yacht Race (September).

Places to Stay

Camping The camping ground closest to Rovinj is *Porton Biondi* (☎ 813 557), less than a kilometre from the town (on the Monsena bus), which charges 15KN per person and 9KN per tent.

Five kilometres south-east of Rovinj is *Polari Camping* (☎ 813 441), open from May to mid-October. Get there on the Villas Rubin bus. All these camping grounds charge about 20KN per person including a tent.

Private Rooms Many offices in Rovinj offer private rooms costing from 72KN per person in the summer season, with a 50% surcharge for a stay of less than four nights and a 100% surcharge for a one-night stay. The only agency that doesn't impose surcharges is Lokva (☎ 813 365), Via Carducci 4 opposite the bus station. If they're out of rooms, try Marco Polo (☎ 816 955) also opposite the bus station, or Generalturist (☎ 811 402; fax 813 324) and Kompas (☎ 813 211; fax 813 478), both on Trg Maršala Tita in the centre. There's also Kvarner Express (☎ 811 155) on the harbour near the bus station. Get to town early, as most agencies close from 2 to 6 pm. Pula and Poreč are within easy commuting distance from Rovinj, so having to stay four nights may not be such a problem.

Hotels *Hotel Rovinj* (☎ 811 288) has a splendid location on Svetoga Križa overlooking the sea; it charges 245/410KN a single/double for a four-night stay. The cheapest hotel is the 192-room *Hotel Monte Mulin* (☎ 811 512; fax 815 882), on the wooded hillside overlooking the bay just beyond Hotel Park. It's about a 15-minute walk south of the bus station and is open year-round. Bed and breakfast is 198/310KN a single/double (20% lower in spring and autumn).

Places to Eat

Most of the fish and spaghetti places along the harbour cater to well-heeled tourists but *Kantinon*, 18 obala Alzo Rismondo, sells fresh grilled fish beginning at 20KN to a local crowd. *Veli Jože*, Svetoga Križa 1, is some-

what more expensive but is a good place to try Istrian dishes in an interior crammed with knick-knacks or at tables outside. Picnickers can pick up supplies at the *supermarket* next to the bus station or in one of the kiosks selling burek near the vegetable market.

Entertainment

The best show in town is watching the sunset from *Valentino*, Santa Croce 28. At 20KN for a glass of wine it's not cheap but sitting on the rocks next to the sea with a view of Katarina Island is worth the splurge. For a night out, head down to the huge *Zabavni* entertainment complex at Monvi for discos, cabarets and restaurants.

Getting There & Away

There's a bus from Rovinj to Pula (34km) every hour or so; there's seven daily to Poreč (38km), seven daily to Rijeka (84km), eight daily to Zagreb (278km), two daily to Koper (81km) and Split (509km) and one daily to Dubrovnik (744km) and Ljubljana (190km).

The closest train station is Kanfanar, 19km away on the Pula-Divača line.

Eurostar Travel (☎ 813 144), Obala Pina Budicina 1, has information about the *Marconi* which shuttles between Rovinj and Trieste and may have tickets (which must be paid in Italian lire). Otherwise try asking the port captain on the opposite side of the same building.

Getting Around

Local buses run every two hours from the bus station north to Monsena and south to Villas Rubin.

PULA
☎ 052

Pula (the ancient Polensium) is a large regional centre with some industry, a big naval base and a busy commercial harbour. The old town with its museums and well-preserved Roman ruins is certainly worth a visit and nearby are rocky wooded peninsulas overlooking the clear Adriatic waters, which explains the many resort hotels and camping grounds.

Orientation

The bus station is on ulica Carrarina in the

centre of town. One block south is Giardini, the central hub, while the harbour is just north of the bus station. The train station is near the water about 1km north of town.

Information

The Tourist Association of Pula at ulica Istarska 11 (open weekdays from 9 am to 1 pm and 5 to 8 pm) will have the latest city map. The American Express representative is Atlas travel agency (☎ 214 172; ulica Starih Statuta 1, Pula 52100).

Long-distance telephone calls may be placed at the main post office at Danteov Trg 4 (open till 8 pm daily).

Jadroagent (☎ 22 568), Riva 14, and the adjacent Kvarner Express office (☎ 22 519) sell ferry tickets.

The bus station has a left-luggage office open daily from 5 am to 10 pm, except for two half-hour breaks. The train station's left-luggage service is open from 9 am to 4 pm but closed on Sunday.

Things to See

Pula's most imposing sight is the 1st-century **Roman amphitheatre** overlooking the harbour and north-east of the old town. At 14KN admission, the visit is expensive, but you can see plenty for free from outside. Around the end of July a Croatian film festival is held in the amphitheatre, but there are cultural events all summer.

The **Archaeological Museum** (10KN; open daily in summer, closed weekends in winter) is on the hill opposite the bus station. Even if you don't get into the museum be sure to visit the large sculpture garden around it, and the **Roman Theatre** behind. The garden is entered through 2nd-century twin gates.

Along the street facing the bus station are **Roman walls** which mark old Pula's eastern boundary. Follow these walls south and continue down Giardini to the **Triumphal Arch of Sergius** (27 BC). The street beyond the arch winds right around old Pula, changing names several times as it goes. Follow it to where you'll find the ancient **Temple of Augustus** and the **old town hall** (1296). Above this square is the **Franciscan church** (1314), with a museum in the cloister (entry from around the other side) containing paintings, medieval frescoes and a Roman mosaic.

The **Museum of History** (open daily) is in the 17th-century Venetian citadel on a high hill in the centre of the old town. The meagre exhibits deal mostly with the maritime history of Pula but the views of Pula from the citadel walls are good.

Places to Stay

Camping The closest camping ground to Pula is *Autocamp Stoja* (☎ 24 144; open mid-April to mid-October), 3km south-west of the centre (take bus No 1 to the terminus at Stoja). There's lots of space on the shady promontory, with swimming possible off the rocks and it's open all year. The two restaurants at the camping ground are good. There are more camping grounds at Medulin and Premantura, coastal resorts south-east of Pula.

Hostels The *Ljetovalište Ferijalnog Saveza Youth Hostel* (☎ 210 002; fax 212 394), is 3km south of central Pula in a great location overlooking a clean pebble beach. Take the No 2 or the No 7 Verudela bus to the 'Piramida' stop and walk back to the first street, turn left and look for the sign. Bed and breakfast is 75KN per person and camping is allowed (56KN including breakfast). The hostel is now heated and open all year. You can sit and sip cold beer on the terrace, where a rock band plays on some summer evenings. Ask about Disco Piramida or the Disco Fort Bourguignon nearby. If the youth hostel is full and you have a tent, it's only a 10-minute walk to *Autocamp Ribarska Koliba* (☎ 22 966), open from June to August.

Private Rooms Arenatours (☎ 34 355), Giardini 4, a block south of the bus station, and Kvarner Express (☎ 22 519; fax 34 961) have private rooms year-round for 54KN per person, with an additional 50% surcharge for one-night stays and 25% surcharge if you stay less than four nights. Brijuni Turist Biro (☎ 22 477), ulica Istarska 3, beside the bus station and Atlas travel agency also have rooms at the same rates.

Hotels There are no cheap hotels but for a little luxury, try the elegant *Hotel Riviera* (☎ 211 166; fax 211 166), Splitska ulica 1, overlooking the harbour. Erected in 1908, it offers large, comfortable rooms for 190/320KN a single/double with shared bath (215/363KN with private bath), breakfast included. From October to May prices are about 25% lower. Compare the price of a room with half and full board when you check in.

Hotel Omir (☎ 22 019), Dobricheva 6, just off Zagrebačka ulica near Giardini, is a private hotel with 11 rooms for 235/375KN single/double with bath and breakfast. If you're willing to pay that, you're better off at the Riviera.

Places to Eat

For grilled meats and local dishes such as goulash, smoked ham and squid risotto, try *Varaždin*, Istarska 30. It's a little expensive, but reasonable if you order carefully. *Delfin*, Kandlerova 17 has a pleasant terrace and an excellent selection of Istrian dishes, especially seafood. Locals rave about the home cooking at *Vodnjanka*, Vitežića 4. It's cheap and casual but open for lunch only. To get there, walk south on Radićeva to Vitežića.

Platak Self-Service, Narodni trg 5 opposite the vegetable market (open daily from 9.30

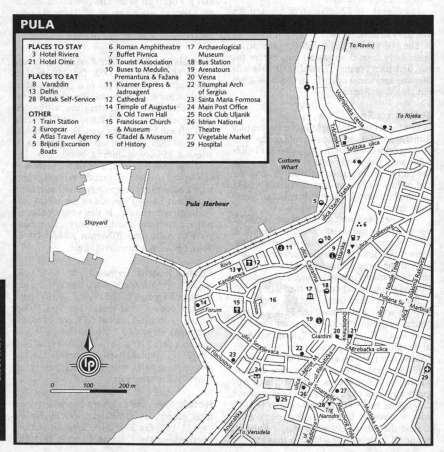

PULA

PLACES TO STAY
3 Hotel Riviera
21 Hotel Omir

PLACES TO EAT
8 Varaždin
13 Delfin
28 Platak Self-Service

OTHER
1 Train Station
2 Europcar
4 Atlas Travel Agency
5 Brijuni Excursion Boats
6 Roman Amphitheatre
7 Buffet Pivnica
9 Tourist Association
10 Buses to Medulin, Premantura & Fažana
11 Kvarner Express & Jadroagent
12 Cathedral
14 Temple of Augustus & Old Town Hall
15 Franciscan Church & Museum
16 Citadel & Museum of History
17 Archaeological Museum
18 Bus Station
19 Arenaturs
20 Vesna
22 Triumphal Arch of Sergius
23 Santa Maria Formosa
24 Main Post Office
25 Rock Club Uljanik
26 Istrian National Theatre
27 Vegetable Market
29 Hospital

Customs Wharf

To Rovinj

To Rijeka

Pula Harbour

Shipyard

0   100   200 m

CROATIA

am to 8:45 pm), is easy since you see what you're getting and pay at the end of the line.

The people at the cheese counter in *Vesna*, next to Kino Istra on Giardini, prepare healthy sandwiches while you wait. They're open Monday to Saturday from 6.30 am to 8 pm.

Entertainment

Posters around Pula advertise live performances. *Rock Club Uljanik*, Jurja Dobrile 2, is great whenever something's on. You can dance there.

Buffet Pivnica in the back courtyard at Istarska 34 near the Roman amphitheatre (open daily from 8 am to 4 pm) is one of the least expensive places in Pula to get a draught beer, glass of wine or espresso and all prices are clearly listed. No food is available but there's a convenient free toilet.

Although most of the nightlife is out of town in Verudela, in mild weather the cafés along the pedestrian streets, Flanatička and Sergijevaca are lively people-watching spots.

Two cinemas on Giardini are the *Zagreb* at No 1 and *Pula* at No 12. Quality art films are shown at the *Istrian National Theatre* a couple of times a week.

Getting There & Away

Bus The 20 daily buses to Rijeka (110km, 1½ hours) are sometimes crowded, especially the eight which continue to Zagreb, so reserve a seat a day in advance. Going from Pula to Rijeka, be sure to sit on the right-hand side of the bus for a stunning view of the Gulf of Kvarner.

Other buses from Pula include 18 daily to Rovinj (42km); 12 to Poreč (56km); 11 to Zagreb (292km); three to Zadar (333km); two each to Postojna (161km), Trieste (124km) and Split (514km); and one each to Portorož (90km), Koper (104km), Ljubljana (211km) and Dubrovnik (749km).

Train Ever since Pula was the main port of the Austro-Hungarian empire, the railway line in Istria has run north towards Italy and Austria instead of east into Croatia but there are two daily trains to Ljubljana (four hours, 92KN) and two to Zagreb (6½ hours, 145KN).

Boat The fast boat *Marina* connects Pula and Venice (L57,000) and Zadar (75KN) in the

summer. See the Getting There & Away section at the beginning of this chapter. The ferry to Mali Lošinj (28KN) and Zadar (54KN) runs once a week all year. Ask at Jadroagent or Kvarner Express on the harbour.

Getting Around

The only city buses of use to visitors are bus No 1 which runs to the camping ground at Stoja and bus Nos 2 and 7 to Verudela which pass the youth hostel and Pension Ribarska Koliba. Frequency varies from every 15 minutes to every 30 minutes, with service from 5 am to 11.30 pm daily. Tickets are sold at newsstands for 8KN and are good for two trips.

AROUND PULA
Brijuni Islands

The Brijuni (Italian: Brioni) island group consists of two main pine-covered islands and 12 islets off the coast of Istria and just north-west of Pula. Each year from 1949 until his death in 1980, Maršal Tito spent six months at his summer residences on Brijuni in a style any western capitalist would admire. In 1984 Brijuni was proclaimed a national park. Some 680 species of plants grow on the islands, including many exotic subtropical species planted at Tito's request.

You may only visit Brijuni National Park with a group. Instead of booking an excursion with one of the travel agencies in Pula, Rovinj or Poreč, which costs 200KN, you can take a public bus from Pula to Fažana (8km), then sign up for a tour (145KN) at the Brijuni Tourist Service (☎ 525 883) office near the wharf. It's best to book in advance, especially in summer.

Also check along the Pula waterfront for excursion boats to Brijuni. The five-hour boat trips from Pula to Brijuni may not actually visit the islands but only sail around them. Still, it makes a nice day out.

Gulf of Kvarner

The Gulf of Kvarner (Italian: Quarnero) stretches 100km south from Rijeka, between the Istrian Peninsula on the west and the Croatian littoral on the east. The many elongated islands are the peaks of a submerged

CROATIA

branch of the Dinaric Alps, the range which follows the coast south all the way to Albania. Krk, Cres and Pag are among the largest islands in Croatia.

Rijeka, a bustling commercial port and communications hub at the northern end of the gulf, is well connected to Italy and Austria by road and rail. The railway built from Budapest to Rijeka in 1845 gave Hungary its first direct outlet to the sea. Big crowds frequent nearby Opatija, a one-time bathing resort of the Habsburg elite, and Krk Island, now linked to the mainland by bridge. Historic Rab, the jewel of the Gulf of Kvarner, is much harder to reach; with some difficulty it can be used as a stepping stone on the way south.

RIJEKA
☎ 051

Rijeka (Italian: Fiume), 126km south of Ljubljana, is such a transportation hub that it's almost impossible to avoid. The network of buses, trains and ferries that connect Istria and Dalmatia with Zagreb and points beyond all seem to pass through Rijeka. As Croatia's largest port, the city is full of boats, cargo, fumes, cranes and the kind of seediness that characterises most port cities.

Although Rijeka is hardly a 'must see' destination, the city does have a few saving graces, such as the pedestrian mall, Korzo, stately 19th century buildings and a tree-lined promenade along the harbour. Because there is so little to interest tourists, accommodation, information and resources for visitors are scarce. The assumption seems to be that everyone will either leave the area as fast as possible or base themselves in Opatija.

Orientation

The bus station is on Trg Žabica below the Capuchin Church in the centre of town. The Jadrolinija ferry wharf (no left-luggage section) is just a few minutes east of the bus station. Korzo runs east through the city centre towards the fast-moving Rječina River.

Information
Tourist Offices Try Kvarner Express (☎ 213 808), Trg Jadranski near the bus

station, or the Turistički Savez Općine Rijeka (☎ 335 882) at Užarska 14. The Auto-Klub Rijeka (☎ 621 824), Preluk 6, assists motorists.

Money You can change money at Croatia Express on platform No 1 at the train station Monday to Friday from 8 am to 9 pm and weekends from 9 am to 1 pm and 5 to 9 pm.

There's an exchange counter in the main post office, opposite the old city tower on Korzo.

The telephone centre in the main post office on Korzo is open from 7 am to 9 pm daily.

Post & Communications Kvarner Express, Trg Jadranski 3, changes money, finds private accommodation and sells excursions.

Jadroagent (☎ 211 276; fax 335 172), at Trg Ivana Koblera 2, is an excellent source of information on all ferry sailings from Croatia.

Left Luggage If the left-luggage office in the bus station (open daily from 5.30 am to 10.30 pm) is full, there's a larger *garderoba* (cloakroom) in the train station (open from 7.30 am to 9 pm), a seven-minute walk west on ulica Krešimirova.

Things to See
The **Modern Art Gallery** (closed Sunday and Monday) is at Dolac 1, upstairs in the scientific library across from Hotel Bonavia. The **Maritime Museum** and the **National Revolution Museum** (both closed Sunday and Monday) are adjacent at Žrtava fašizma 18, above the city centre. Worth a visit if you have time is the 13th-century **Trsat Castle** (closed Monday) on a high ridge overlooking Rijeka and the canyon of the Rječina River.

Places to Stay
The closest camping ground is listed in the Opatija section.

Kvarner Express (☎ 213 808), Trg Jadranski 3, has private rooms for 100/140KN a single/double but only in the summer. Singles are seldom available and frequently all rooms are full.

The A-category *Hotel Bonavia* (☎ 333 744), Dolac 4, is central and has singles/doubles with bath for 348/476KN. The C-category

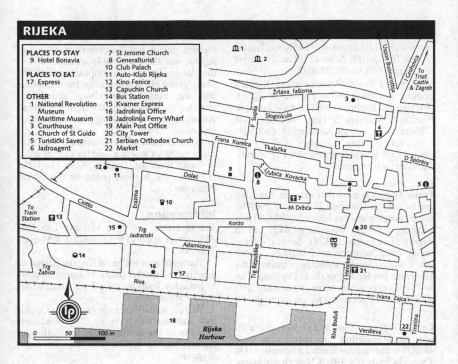

RIJEKA

PLACES TO STAY
9 Hotel Bonavia

PLACES TO EAT
17 Express

OTHER
1 National Revolution Museum
2 Maritime Museum
3 Courthouse
4 Church of St Guido
5 Turistički Savez
6 Jadroagent
7 St Jerome Church
8 Generalturist
10 Club Palach
11 Auto-Klub Rijeka
12 Kino Fenice
13 Capuchin Church
14 Bus Station
15 Kvarner Express
16 Jadrolinija Office
18 Jadrolinija Ferry Wharf
19 Main Post Office
20 City Tower
21 Serbian Orthodox Church
22 Market

Hotel Neboder (☎ 217 355), Strossmayerova 1, and the B-category *Hotel Kontinental* (☎ 216 477), Andrije Kašića Miočaca, are a block apart in an uninspiring neighbourhood north-east of the town centre. Single/double rooms with bath cost 249/311KN at Neboder and 271/333KN at Kontinental. For those prices you might as well pay more and stay in Opatija.

Places to Eat

Restoran Index, at ulica Krešimirova 18 between the bus and train stations, has a good self-service section (samoposluzi). *Express*, 14 Riva, near the Jadrolinija office, is another self-service open daily from 7 am to 9 pm. There's a large *supermarket* between the bus and train station on ulica Krešimirova.

Entertainment

Performances at the *Ivan Zajc National Theatre* (1885) are mostly dramas in Croat-

ian, though opera and ballet are sometimes offered. The ticket office is open weekdays.

Club Palach, in the back alley accessible through a small passageway next to the Riječka Banka on Trg Jadranski, opens at 8 pm daily. It's a good, noncommercial place to drink and dance.

Getting There & Away

Bus There are 13 buses daily between Rijeka and Krk (1½ hours, 27KN), using the huge Krk Bridge. Buses to Krk are overcrowded and a seat reservation in no way guarantees you a seat. Don't worry – the bus from Rijeka to Krk empties fairly fast so you won't be standing for long.

Other buses depart from Rijeka for Baška, also on Krk Island (76km, six daily, 39KN), Dubrovnik (639km, three daily, 230KN), Koper (86km), Ljubljana (128km, once daily, 58KN), Mali Lošinj (122km, four daily), Poreč (91km, nine daily), Pula (110km,

CROATIA

17 daily), Rab (115km, two daily), Rovinj (105km, seven daily), Split (404km, seven express and 11 local daily, 145KN), Trieste (70km, five daily), Zadar (228km, 14 daily) and Zagreb (3½ hours, 23 daily).

There's a bus to Vienna every Sunday evening and buses twice a week to Zürich (801km) and Berlin, as well as daily buses to Frankfurt, Munich (571km) and Stuttgart (786km). The bus to Amsterdam (740KN) runs every Sunday. Luggage is DM5 per piece on all international services (Deutschmarks in cash required).

Train There's a train that runs on Saturday and Sunday to Budapest (11 hours, 296KN) and an evening train to Munich (439KN) and Salzburg (283KN). Four trains daily run to Zagreb (five hours, 58KN). Several of the seven daily services to Ljubljana (three hours, 44KN) require a change of trains at the Slovenian border and again at Postojna. The *poslovni* (executive) trains have only 1st-class seats and reservations are compulsory.

Car ATR Rent a Car (☎ 337 544), Riva 20 near the bus station, has rental cars from 480KN a day with unlimited kilometres. On a weekly basis it's 1980KN with unlimited kilometres. Also try Kompas Hertz (☎ 215 425), Zagrebačka 21.

Boat Jadrolinija (☎ 211 444), Riva 16, has tickets for the large coastal ferries that run all year between Rijeka and Dubrovnik. Southbound ferries depart from Rijeka at 6 pm daily.

Fares are 116KN to Split (13 hours), 140KN to Korčula (18 hours) and 152KN to Dubrovnik (17 to 24 hours). Fares are lower in winter. Berths to Dubrovnik are 329KN per person in a four-bed cabin, 399KN in a double or 479KN in a double with private bath.

Since the Jadrolinija ferries travel between Rijeka and Split at night, you don't get to see a lot so it's probably better to go from Rijeka to Split by bus and enjoy excellent views of the Adriatic coast. In contrast, the ferry trip from Split to Dubrovnik is highly recommended.

OPATIJA
☎ 051

Opatija, just a few kilometres due west of Rijeka, was *the* fashionable seaside resort of the Austro-Hungarian empire until WWI. Many grand old hotels remain from this time and the elegant waterfront promenade stretches for 12km along the Gulf of Kvarner. Although you get a passing glance of Opatija (meaning 'abbey') from the Pula bus, the graceful architecture and stunning coastline make the town worth a stop for at least a day or two. West of Opatija rises Mt Učka (1396m), the highest point on the Istrian Peninsula.

Information

The tourist office is at Maršala Tita 101. Atlas travel agency (☎ 271 032) is at Maršala Tita 116.

The main post office, at Eugena Kumičića 2 behind the market (*tržnica*), opens Monday to Saturday from 8 am to 7 pm and Sunday from 9 am to noon.

There's no left-luggage facility at Opatija bus station, which is on Trg Vladimira Gortana in the town centre, but Autotrans Agency at the station will usually watch luggage.

Places to Stay

Preluk Autokamp (☎ 621 913), beside the busy highway between Rijeka and Opatija, is open from May to September. City bus No 32 stops near the camping ground.

For private rooms, try the following places along Maršala Tita: Kvarner Express (☎ 711 070) at No 128, Generalturist (☎ 271 613; fax 271 345) next to the Hotel Paris and GIT (☎/fax 271 967) at No 65. All have rooms for 70KN per person plus a 50% surcharge for single-room occupancy, a 30% surcharge for stays less than four nights and 20KN for breakfast.

There are no cheap hotels in Opatija but the most reasonable are the elegant *Hotel Paris* (☎ 271 911; fax 711 823), 198 Maršala Tita, and the sprawling *Jadran* (☎ 271 700; fax 271 519), Maršala Tita 109 on the sea. Both have rooms for 205/338KN a single/double for a four-night stay in the high season, including bath and breakfast.

Places to Eat

Maršala Tita is lined with decent restaurants offering pizza, grilled meat and fish. There's a *supermarket/deli* at Maršala Tita 80 and a *burek stand* down the stairs next to No 55 on Stubište Tomaševac.

Getting There & Away

Bus No 32 stops in front of the train station in Rijeka (11km, 11KN) and runs right along the Opatija Riviera west from Rijeka to Lovran every 20 minutes until late in the evening.

KRK ISLAND

☎ 051

Croatia's largest island, 409-sq-km Krk (Italian: Veglia) is barren and rocky. In 1980 Krk was joined to the mainland by the massive Krk Bridge, the largest concrete arch bridge in the world, with a span of 390m. Since then, Krk has suffered from too-rapid development – Rijeka airport and some industry at the northern end of Krk, and big tourist hotels in the middle and far south. Still, the main town (also called Krk) is rather picturesque and Baška has an impressive setting. You can easily stop at Krk town for a few hours of sightseeing, then catch a bus to Baška and Krk's longest beach.

Krk Town

From the 12th to the 15th centuries, Krk town and the surrounding region remained semi-independent under the Frankopan Dukes of Krk, an indigenous Croatian dynasty, at a time when much of the Adriatic was controlled by Venice. This history explains the various medieval sights in Krk town, the ducal seat.

Orientation & Information The bus from Baška and Rijeka stops by the harbour, a few minutes walk from the old town of Krk. There's no left-luggage facility at Krk bus station.

Things to See The 14th-century **Frankopan Castle** and lovely 12th-century Romanesque **cathedral** are in the lower town near the harbour. In the upper part of Krk town are three old monastic churches. The narrow streets of Krk are worth exploring.

Places to Stay There is a range of accommodation options in and around Krk, but many places only open for the summer.

The closest camping ground is *Autocamp Ježevac* (☎ 221 081) on the coast, a 10-minute walk south-west of Krk town. The rocky soil makes it nearly impossible to use tent pegs, but there are lots of stones to anchor your lines. There's good shade and places to swim.

Camping Bor (☎ 221 581) is on a hill inland from Ježevac. *Politin FKK* (☎ 221 351) is a naturist camp south-east of Krk, just beyond the large resort hotels.

From mid-June to September youth hostel accommodation is available at the *Ljetovalište Ferialnog Saveza* (☎ 854 037; fax 434 962) at Punat, between Krk town and Baška. All buses to Baška stop here.

Kvarner Express (☎ 221 403; fax 221 035) on the main square at Krk has private rooms for 90/130KN a single/double plus a 30% surcharge for stays of less than four nights. Similar rooms can be booked from Autotrans (☎ 221 111) at the bus station and Adriatours (☎ 221 666) in the old town. Prices are about 10% cheaper in May and June and about 20% less at other times. Ask for the brochure with pictures of the accommodation.

Getting There & Away About 14 buses a day travel between Rijeka and Krk town (1½ hours), of which six continue on to Baška (one hour). One of the Rijeka buses is to/from Zagreb (229km). To go from Krk to the island of Mali Lošinj, change buses at Malinska for the Lošinj-bound bus that comes from Rijeka but check the times carefully as the connection only works once or twice a day.

Baška

Baška, at the southern end of Krk Island, is a popular resort with a 2km-long pebbly beach set below a high ridge. The swimming and scenery are better than at Krk and the old town has a lot of charm. This is a good base for hiking and you can pick up a map of hiking routes from the tourist office.

Orientation & Information The bus from Krk stops at the top of a hill on the edge of the old town, between the beach and the harbour. The main street is Zvonimirova,

CROATIA

which has exchange offices, travel agencies and restaurants.

The tourist office (☎ 856 817) is at Zvonimirova 114, just down the street from the bus stop.

Places to Stay

During July and August, it is essential to arrange accommodation well in advance as the town swarms with Austrian, German and Czech tourists. By late spring, hotels are booked solid for the summer season and accommodation is tight in the shoulder season as well.

Camping There are two camping options at Baška. *Camping Zablaće* (☎ 856 909), open from May to September, is on the beach south-west of the bus stop (look for the rows of caravans). In heavy rain you risk getting flooded here.

A better bet is *FKK Camp Bunculuka* (☎ 856 806), open from May to September. A naturist camping ground over the hill east of the harbour (a 15-minute walk), it's quiet, shady and conveniently close to town.

Private Rooms The places to try for private-room bookings are Guliver (☎ 656 004) and Primaturist (☎ 856 132; fax 856 971), both at Zvonimira 98 in the town centre; at the Hotel Corinthia, try Kvarner Express (☎/fax 856 895), Kompas (☎ 856 460) or Ara (☎ 856 298). Expect to pay at least 90/130KN a single/double plus a 30% surcharge for stays of less than four nights.

If you come in July or August, you may find it impossible to rent a room for less than four nights, impossible to rent a single room, impossible to rent a room near town or just plain impossible. Plan ahead.

Hotels The choice of hotels is not outstanding. The cheapest rooms are at the *Hotel Zvonimir* or *Adria*, where you can find singles/doubles for 234/396KN. Next up in price is the *Corinthia II*, which has rooms for 277/486KN. Head of the pack is the *Hotel Corinthia* (☎ 656 111; fax 856 584), with rooms for 366/612KN a single/double. The hotels are all part of the same modern complex on the edge of town right next to the beach. Bookings for these places are made through the Hotel Corinthia.

Getting There & Away

The ferry from Baška to Lopar on Rab Island (23KN) operates up to five times daily from June to September but between October and May there's no service and you will be forced to backtrack to Rijeka to get farther south. To reach the Lopar ferry, follow the street closest to the water through the old town, heading south-east for less than 1km.

RAB ISLAND

Rab (Italian: Arbe), near the centre of the Kvarner Island group, is one of the most enticing islands in the Adriatic. The north-eastern side is barren and rocky, whereas the south-west is green with pine forests and dotted with sandy beaches and coves. High mountains protect Rab's interior from cold north and east winds.

Rab Town
☎ 051

Medieval Rab town is built on a narrow peninsula which encloses a sheltered harbour. The old stone buildings climb from the harbour to a cliff overlooking the sea. For hundreds of years Rab was an outpost of Venice until the Austrians took over in the 19th century. Today it is a favourite destination of German tourists, which is not surprising considering the beauty of the town and island. Rab would be the perfect stepping stone between Krk and Zadar if only the transport connections were more convenient.

Orientation The bus station is at the rear of a new commercial centre and around the corner from the Merkur department store, a five-minute walk from the old town. The large Jadrolinija ferries tie up on the south-eastern tip of the peninsula.

Information There are two tourist offices. One is around the corner from the bus station opposite the Merkur department store and the other (☎ 771 111) is on Arba Municipium, across from Café Revelin. There is a post office in the commercial centre and another on Arba Municipium. Both post offices are open Monday to Saturday from 7 am to 8 pm. The Atlas travel agency (☎ 724 585) is on Arba Municipium and opposite the post office. Despite a sign at the bus station advertising a garderoba, the left-luggage service is not operational because the station is only open for limited hours.

Things to See Four tall church towers rise above the red-roofed mass of houses on Rab's high peninsula. If you follow Rade Končara north from the **Monastery of St Anthony** (1175), you soon reach the Romanesque **cathedral**, alongside a pleasant terrace with a view overlooking the sea. Farther along, beyond a tall **Romanesque tower** and another convent, is a second terrace and **St Justine Church**, now a small museum of religious art. Just past the next chapel, look for a small gate giving access to a park with the foundations of Rab's oldest church and the fourth tower (which you can climb).

Rade Končara ends at the north city wall, which affords a splendid view of the town, harbour, sea and hill. The scene is especially beautiful just after sunset. North of the wall is the extensive **city park** with many shady walkways.

Special Events Annual events to ask about include the Rab Fair (25 to 27 July) and the Rab Music Evenings (June to September).

Places to Stay Everything from camping to expensive hotels can be found in and around Rab town.

Camping To sleep cheaply, carry your tent south along the waterfront for about 25 minutes to *Autocamp Padova* (☎ 724 355) at Banjol (14KN per person, 13KN per tent). Farther out of town at Kampor is a small camping ground with a large beach, *Halović* (☎ 776 087).

Private Rooms Several agencies rent out private rooms, including Turist Biro Mila (☎ 725 499) on the south-eastern corner of the bus station and Turist Biro Kristofor (☎ 725 543), on the north-western corner. In town, try Numero Uno (☎ 724 688; fax 724 688) next to Merkantours, Arba Kompas (☎ 724 484; fax 724 284) on Donya ulica 4 and Atlas. Prices are more or less the same, beginning at 54KN per person, 7KN for breakfast and a 30% surcharge for stays less

than three nights. Some agencies forgo the surcharges when things are slow. You could be approached by women at the bus station or at the Lopar ferry offering private rooms.

Hotels The *Hotel International* (☎ 711 266; fax 724 206) on Obala kralja Petra Krešimira IV, facing the harbour, has the cheapest rooms at 241/396KN a single/double with bath and breakfast in peak season. It's a pleasant place if you don't mind the price.

Places to Eat One of the few restaurants in Rab which posts a menu outside is *Alibaba* on ulica Ivana Lole Ribara in the old town. It's not cheap but it does have a good selection of seafood. *Pizza Paradiso*, ulica Radića 2, serves pizza for 40KN in a touristy but attractive enclosed terrace. For fast food, head to *Buffet Buza*, ulica Ugalje near Arba Municipium, where you can eat a plate of fried squid for 20KN. There's a good *supermarket* in the basement at the Merkur department store for picnic supplies.

Getting There & Away All the local travel agencies have bus and ferry schedules posted in their offices.

Bus The most reliable way to travel is on one of the two daily buses between Rab and Rijeka (115km, 62KN). In the tourist season there are two direct buses from Zagreb to Rab (211km, five hours). These services can fill up, so book ahead if possible.

There's no direct bus from Rab to Zadar but there are two daily buses that connect at Senj with Rijeka buses to Zadar (five hours, 94KN). To avoid backtracking from Senj to Jablanac and also save some kuna, you can take the bus to the highway at Jablanac, wait for about an hour and a half and catch the Rijeka bus as it heads to Zadar.

Boat In addition to the summer ferry between Baška on Krk Island and Lopar, there's the weekly Jadrolinija ferry but sometimes it doesn't call at Rab if there's 'fog' (ie not enough passengers to drop off or pick up).

In summer, tourist agencies offer day excursions to Mali Lošinj (130KN return) or Pag Island (70KN return) once or twice a week.

CROATIA

Lopar

The bus from Rab town to Lopar stops in front of Pizzeria Aloha, opposite the small-boat harbour about 300m ahead of the Lopar ferry landing. The stop is unmarked, so ask. There's a bus every hour or two to Rab town (12km). Several houses around here have 'sobe' signs. *Camping San Marino* is about 3km south of the Lopar ferry landing, across the peninsula. It has a long sand beach and the same prices as the *Autocamp Padova* (see above).

Dalmatia

Dalmatia (Dalmacija) occupies the central 375km of Croatia's Adriatic coast, from the Gulf of Kvarner in the north to the Bay of Kotor in the south, including offshore islands. The rugged Dinaric Alps form a 1500m-high barrier separating Dalmatia from Bosnia, with only two breaks: the Krka River canyon at Knin and the Neretva Valley at Mostar, both of which have railway lines.

After the last Ice Age, part of the coastal mountains were flooded, creating the same sort of long, high islands seen in the Gulf of Kvarner. The deep, protected passages that lie between these islands are a paradise for sailors and cruisers.

Historical relics abound in towns like Zadar, Trogir, Split, Hvar, Korčula and Dubrovnik, framed by a striking natural beauty of barren slopes, green valleys and clear water. The ferry trip from Split to Dubrovnik is one of the classic journeys of Eastern Europe. The vineyards of Dalmatia supply half of Croatia's wine. A warm current flowing north up the coast keeps the climate mild – dry in summer, damp in winter. Dalmatia is noticeably warmer than Istria or the Gulf of Kvarner and it's possible to swim in the sea right up until the end of September. This is the Mediterranean at its best.

ZADAR

☎ 023

Zadar (the ancient Zara), the main city of northern Dalmatia, occupies a long peninsula which separates the harbour on the east from the Zadar Channel on the west. The city of Iader was laid out by the Romans,

who left behind considerable ruins. Later the area fell under the Byzantine Empire, which explains the Orthodox churches with their central domes. In 1409 Venice took Zadar from Croatia and held it for four centuries. Dalmatia was part of the Austro-Hungarian empire during most of the 19th century, with Italy exercising control from 1918 to 1943. Badly damaged by Anglo-American bombing raids in 1943-44, much of the city had to be rebuilt. Luckily, the original street plan was respected and an effort was made to harmonise the new with what remained of old Zadar.

In November 1991, Zadar seemed to be re-living history as Yugoslav rockets ploughed into the old city, damaging the cathedral. For the next three months the city's inhabitants were under siege, unable to leave their homes for fear of being hit. Although the Serb gunners were pushed back by the Croatian army during its January 1993 offensive, this experience has embittered many residents and people may be suspicious of you until they know who you are.

Few war wounds are visible, however. Zadar's narrow, traffic-free stone streets are again full of life and the tree-lined promenade along Obala kralja Petra Krešimira IV is perfect for a lazy stroll or a picnic. Tremendous 16th-century fortifications still shield the city on the landward side and high walls run along the harbour. Museums and monuments have recently been repaired and reopened, in an attempt to lure tourists from the beaches and camp sites at nearby Borik. Zadar can be a fascinating place to wander around and, at the end of the day, you can sample Zadar's famous maraschino cherry liqueur.

Orientation

The train and bus stations are adjacent and a 15-minute walk south-east of the harbour and old town.

From the stations, Zrinsko-Frankopanska ulica leads north-west past the main post office to the harbour. Buses marked 'Poluotok' run from the bus station to the harbour. Narodni trg is the heart of Zadar.

Information

The official tourist office is Turistička Zajednica, (☎ 212 412), Smiljanića 4. The

American Express representative is the Atlas travel agency (☎ 314 206), Branimirova Obala 12, across the footbridge over the harbour, just north-east of Narodni trg. Croatia Express (☎ 211 660) is on Široka ulica.

Telephone calls can be made from the main post office at Zrinsko-Frankopanska ulica 8 (open from 7 am to 8 pm daily).

There is one left-luggage office for both the train and bus stations, open 24 hours a day.

Things to See

The main things to see are near the circular **St Donatus Church**, a 9th-century Byzantine structure built over the Roman forum. Slabs for the ancient forum are visible in the church and, on the north-western side is a pillar from the Roman era. In summer, ask about musical evenings here (Renaissance and early baroque music). The outstanding **Museum of Church Art** (open daily, except Sunday evening, from 10 am to 12.30 pm and 6 to 7.30 pm) in the Benedictine monastery opposite offers a substantial display of reliquaries and religious paintings. The obscure lighting deliberately re-creates the environment in which the objects were originally kept.

The 13th-century Romanesque **Cathedral of St Anastasia** nearby never really recovered from WWII destruction; the **Franciscan Monastery** a few blocks away is more cheerful. The large Romanesque cross in the treasury behind the sacristy is worth seeing.

Other museums include the **Archaeological Museum** (closed Sunday), across from St Donatus, and the **Ethnological Museum** in the Town Watchtower (1562) on Narodni trg. The latter should reopen as soon as renovations are completed. More interesting is the **National Museum** on Poljana Pape Aleksandra III just inside the Sea Gate. This excellent museum features scale models of Zadar from different periods and old paintings and engravings of many coastal cities. The same admission ticket will get you into the local **art gallery** on Smiljanića. Unfortunately, the captions in all Zadar's museums are in Croatian. Notable churches include the 12th-century St Krševan church, St Simun with a 14th-century gold chest and St Petar Stari with Roman-Byzantine frescoes.

Organised Tours

Any of the many travel agencies around town can supply information on the tourist cruises to the beautiful Kornati Islands (250KN, including lunch and a swim in the sea or a salt lake). As this is about the only way to see these 101 barren, uninhabited islands, islets and cliffs it's worthwhile if you can spare the cash. Check with Kvarner Express (☎/fax 212 215), Kraljice Elizabete Kotromanić 3, Kompas (☎/fax 433 380) on Široka ulica and Croatia Express across the street. Also ask about excursions to Krka National Park which is inaccessible to individual travel. Although there are too few tourists in the region to run the excursion regularly, if there's a group going you can tag along.

Special Events

Major annual events include the town fair (July and August), the Dalmatian Song Festival (July and August), the musical evenings in St Donatus Church (August) and the Choral Festival (October).

Places to Stay

Staying in town is nearly impossible. Most visitors head out to the 'tourist settlement' at Borik, 3km north-west of Zadar, on the Puntamika bus (every 20 minutes from the bus station, 6KN) where there are hotels, a hostel, a camp site and numerous 'sobe' signs; you can arrange a private room through an agency in town. If you arrive in the off season, try to arrange accommodation in advance since hotels, hostels and camp sites will be closed.

Camping *Zaton* (☎ 264 303) is 16km north-west of Zadar on a sandy beach and should be open from May to September but call first. There are 12 buses marked 'Zaton' leaving daily from the bus station. Nearer to Zadar is *Autocamp Borik* (☎ 332 074), only steps away from Borik beach.

Hostels Also near the beach at Borik is the *Borik Youth Hostel* (☎ 331 145; fax 331 190), Obala Kneza Trpimira 76, which is open from May to September. Bed and breakfast costs 70KN and full board is 100KN.

Private Rooms Agencies finding private accommodation include Kompas, Kvarner

ZADAR

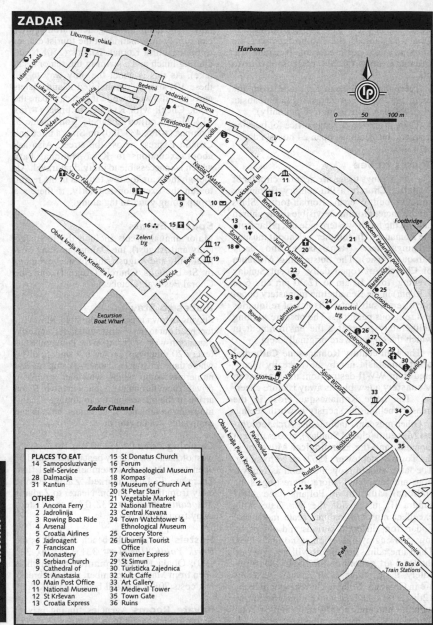

0   50   100 m

Liburnska obala

Harbour

Footbridge

Zeleni trg

Excursion Boat Wharf

Zadar Channel

Narodni trg

To Bus & Train Stations

PLACES TO EAT
14 Samoposluzivanje Self-Service
28 Dalmacija
31 Kantun

OTHER
1   Ancona Ferry
2   Jadrolinija
3   Rowing Boat Ride
4   Arsenal
5   Croatia Airlines
6   Jadroagent
7   Franciscan Monastery
8   Serbian Church
9   Cathedral of St Anastasia
10 Main Post Office
11 National Museum
12 St Krševan
13 Croatia Express

15 St Donatus Church
16 Forum
17 Archaeological Museum
18 Kompas
19 Museum of Church Art
20 St Petar Stari
21 Vegetable Market
22 National Theatre
23 Central Kavana
24 Town Watchtower & Ethnological Museum
25 Grocery Store
26 Liburnija Tourist Office
27 Kvarner Express
29 St Simun
30 Turistička Zajednica
32 Kult Caffe
33 Art Gallery
34 Medieval Tower
35 Town Gate
36 Ruins

CROATIA

Express or Marlin Tours (☎/fax 313 194), around the corner from Atlas at Jeretova 3. Liburnija tourist office (☎ 211 039) next to Kvarner Express also might have rooms. Prices vary so check around. Expect to pay around 120KN per person with a 30% surcharge for stays less than three nights. Breakfast is an extra 6KN.

Hotels There are no budget hotels in town and only one regularly operating hotel, the *Hotel Kolovare* (☎ 203 200), Bože Peričića 14, which is being transformed into a luxury establishment. The best bet is to head out to nearby Borik on the Puntamika bus. The B-category *Novi Park* (☎ 206 100) *Zadar* (☎ 332 184), and *Donat* (☎ 332 184), all at Majstora Radovana 7, offer rooms but you must take half-board for 224/369KN a single/double.

Places to Eat

Dalmacija at the end of Kraljice Elizabete Kotromanić is a good place for pizza, spaghetti, fish and local specialities. *Kantun*, Stomarica 6, serves plates of fried fresh fish for 25KN. The newly renovated *Samoposluzivanje* is a self-service restaurant in the passage off Nikole Matafara 9 which has hot dishes starting at 25KN.

Central Kavana on Široka ulica is a spacious café and hang-out with live music on weekends. *Kult Caffe* on Stomarica draws a young crowd to listen to rap music indoors or relax on the large shady terrace outside. In summer the many cafés along Varoška and Klaića place their tables on the street; it's great for people-watching. There's a *grocery store* on the corner of Grisogona and Barakovića that sells bread and cold cuts for sandwiches and you'll find a number of *burek stands* around the vegetable market.

Entertainment

The National Theatre box office on Široka ulica has tickets to the cultural programs advertised on posters outside. Zadar's most popular disco is *Saturnus*, in Zaton near Zadra. It's the largest disco in Croatia.

Getting There & Away

Bus & Train There are buses to Rijeka (228km), Split (158km), Mostar (four daily, 301km), Dubrovnik (393km, seven daily, 114KN) and Sarajevo (twice daily, 93KN). There are two daily trains to Zagreb (11 hours, 80KN) that change at Knin. The bus to Zagreb (320km, 70KN) is quicker.

The Croatia Express travel agency sells bus tickets to many German cities, including Munich (366KN), Frankfurt (576KN), Cologne (666KN) and Berlin (720KN).

Boat From late June to September the fast boat *Marina* runs from Venice to Zadar twice a week and from Pula to Zadar four times a week, stopping at Mali Lošinj. There are weekly local ferries all year (four times a week in summer) between Mali Lošinj and Zadar (six hours, 30KN) and between Pula and Zadar (eight hours, 58KN). The Jadrolinija coastal ferry from Rijeka to Dubrovnik calls at Zadar four times a week (116KN).

For information on connections to Italy see the Getting There & Away section at the beginning of this chapter and contact Jadroagent (☎ 211 447) on ulica Natka Nodila just inside the city walls. Jadrolinija (☎ 212 003), Liburnska obala 7 on the harbour, has tickets for all local ferries.

On Tuesday and Thursday there's a ferry to Zaglav on Dugi otok island (11KN), which is a good day trip (on other days there's no connection to return to Zadar).

TROGIR

☎ 021

Trogir (formerly Trau), a lovely medieval town on the coast and just 20km west of Split, is well worth a stop if you're coming south from Zadar. A day trip to Trogir from Split can easily be combined with a visit to the Roman ruins at Salona (see the Salona section later in this chapter).

The old town of Trogir occupies a tiny island in the narrow channel between Čiovo Island and the mainland, and is just off the coastal highway. There's many sights on the 15-minute walk around this island. The nearest beach is 4km west at the Medena Hotel.

Orientation

The heart of the old town is a few minutes walk from the bus station. After crossing the small bridge near the station, go through the North Gate. Trogir's finest sights are around Narodni trg, slightly left and ahead.

Information

The tourist office (☎ 881 554) opposite the cathedral sells a map of the area. There's no left-luggage office in Trogir bus station, so you'll end up toting your bags around town if you only visit on a stopover.

Things to See

The glory of the three-naved Venetian **Cathedral of St Lovro** on Narodni trg is the Romanesque portal of Adam and Eve (1240) by Master Radovan, which you can admire for free at any time. Enter the building through an obscure back door to see the perfect Renaissance Chapel of St Ivan and the choir, pulpit, ciborium and treasury. You can even climb the cathedral tower, if it's open, for a delightful view. Also on Narodni trg is the **town hall**, with an excellent Gothic staircase and Renaissance loggia.

Places to Stay

Vranića Camping (☎ 894 141) is just off the highway to Zadar and about 5km west of Trogir by bus 24. *Seget* (☎ 880 394), 2km west of Trogir, is reliably open from June to September.

The Turist Biro (☎/fax 881 554) opposite the cathedral has private rooms for 150/288KN a single/double plus a 30% surcharge for stays less than three nights. Prices are lower in the off season.

Three kilometres west of Trogir there is the C-category *Hotel Jadran* (☎ 880 008; fax 880 401), which offers rooms for 180/364KN and, a little farther, the B category *Hotel Medena* (☎ 880 588; fax 880 019), with rooms for 252/366KN. Both hotels are on the route of numerous local buses.

Getting There & Away

Southbound buses from Zadar (130km) will drop you off in Trogir. Getting buses north can be more difficult, as they often arrive full from Split.

City bus No 37 runs between Trogir and Split (28km) every 20 minutes throughout the day with a stop at Split airport en route. In Split bus No 37 leaves from the local bus station. If you're making a day trip to Trogir also buy your ticket back to Split, as the ticket window at Trogir bus station is often closed. Drivers also sell tickets if you're stuck.

There's also a ferry once a week between Trogir and Split.

SPLIT
☎ 021

Split (Italian: Spalato), the largest Croatian city on the Adriatic coast, is the heart of Dalmatia. The old town is built around the harbour, on the southern side of a high peninsula sheltered from the open sea by many islands. Ferries to these islands are constantly coming and going. The entire western end of the peninsula is a vast, wooded mountain park, while industry, shipyards, limestone quarries and the ugly commercial-military port are mercifully far enough away on the northern side of the peninsula. High coastal mountains set against the blue Adriatic provide a striking frame to the scene.

Split achieved fame when the Roman emperor Diocletian (245-313 AD), noted for his persecution of early Christians, had his retirement palace built here from 295 to 305. After his death the great stone palace continued to be used as a retreat by Roman rulers. When the nearby colony of Salona was abandoned in the 7th century, many of the Romanised inhabitants fled to Split and barricaded themselves behind the high palace walls, where their descendants live to this day.

First Byzantium and then Croatia controlled the area, but from the 12th to the 14th centuries medieval Split enjoyed a large measure of autonomy, which favoured its development. The western part of the old town around Narodni trg, which dates from this time, became the focus of municipal life, while the area within the palace walls proper continued as the ecclesiastical centre.

In 1420 the Venetians conquered Split, which led to a slow decline. During the 17th century, strong walls were built around the city as a defence against the Turks. In 1797 the Austrians arrived and remained until

1918, with only a brief interruption during the Napoleonic wars.

Since 1945, Split has grown into a major industrial city with large apartment-block housing areas. However, much of old Split remains, which combined with its exuberant nature makes it one of the most fascinating cities in Europe. It's also the perfect base for excursions to many nearby attractions, so settle in for a few days.

Orientation

The bus, train and ferry terminals are adja-cent on the eastern side of the harbour, a short walk from the old town. Obala hrvatskog narodnog preporoda, the waterfront promenade, is your best central reference point in Split.

Information

Tourist Office The turistički biro (☎/fax 342 142) is at Obala hrvatskog narodnog preporoda 12.

Money The American Express representative, Atlas travel agency (☎ 343 055), is at Trg Braće Radića.

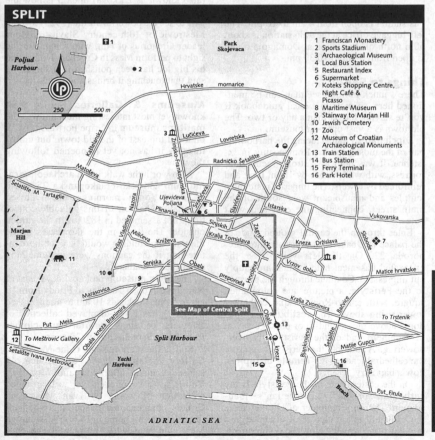

SPLIT

1 Franciscan Monastery
2 Sports Stadium
3 Archaeological Museum
4 Local Bus Station
5 Restaurant Index
6 Supermarket
7 Koteks Shopping Centre, Night Café & Picasso
8 Maritime Museum
9 Stairway to Marjan Hill
10 Jewish Cemetery
11 Zoo
12 Museum of Croatian Archaeological Monuments
13 Train Station
14 Bus Station
15 Ferry Terminal
16 Park Hotel

Poljud Harbour

Park Skojevaca

Hrvatske mornarice

0   250   500 m

Lučićeva
Lovretska
Radničko Šetalište

Zrinsko-frankopanska

Kačturska
Matoševa
Šetalište M Tartaglie

Ujevićeva Poljana
Plinarska

Nazora
Pula Vladimira
Milićeva
Kniževa

Senjska

Marasovica

Put Meja
To Meštrović Gallery
Šetalište Ivana Meštrovića

Marjan Hill

Sinjskih
Kralja Tomislava
Obala preporoda

Slavićeva
Istarska
Zagrebačka
Hrvojeva

Vukovarska
Kneza Drislava
Vrzov dolac

Kralja Zvonimira
Bačvice
To Trstenik
Matice hrvatske

See Map of Central Split

Split Harbour

Yacht Harbour

Obala kneza Branimira

Obala kneza Domagoja

Bankinjeva
Šetalište
Matije Gupca
Put Firula
Beach
Viška

ADRIATIC SEA

Post & Communications Poste-restante mail can be collected at window No 7 at the main post office, Kralja Tomislava 9. The post office is open weekdays from 7 am to 8 pm and Saturday from 7 am to noon. The telephone centre here is open daily from 7 am to 9 pm. On Sunday and in the early evening there's always a line of people waiting to place calls, so it's better to go in the morning.

Bookshops Steps away from the Peristyle at Polyana Grgura Ninskog 7, the bookstore Tamaris has a wide selection of English language paperbacks. Look for the sign 'Antikvariyat Grgur'.

Left Luggage The garderoba kiosk at the bus station is open from 4 am to 10 pm. The left-luggage office at the train station is about 50m north of the station at Domagoja 6 and is open from 5 am to 10.30 pm.

Things to See

There's much more to see than can be mentioned here, so pick up a local guidebook if you're staying longer than a day or two. The old town is a vast open-air museum.

Diocletian's Palace, facing the harbour, is one of the most imposing Roman ruins in existence. It was built as a strong rectangular fortress, with walls 215m by 180m long and reinforced by towers. The imperial residence, temples and mausoleum were south of the main street, connecting the east and west gates.

Enter through the central ground floor of the palace at Obala hrvatskog narodnog preporoda 22. On the left you'll see the excavated basement halls, which are empty but impressive. Continue through the passage to the **Peristyle**, a picturesque colonnaded square, with a neo-Romanesque cathedral tower rising above. The **vestibule**, an open dome above the ground-floor passageway at the southern end of the Peristyle, is overpowering. A lane off the Peristyle opposite the cathedral leads to the **Temple of Jupiter**, now a baptistry.

On the eastern side of the Peristyle is the **cathedral**, originally Diocletian's mausoleum. The only reminder of Diocletian in the cathedral is a sculpture of his head in a circular stone wreath below the dome directly above the baroque white-marble altar. The Romanesque wooden doors (1214) and stone pulpit are worth noting. You may climb the tower for a small fee.

The west palace gate opens onto medieval Narodni trg, dominated by the 15th-century Venetian Gothic **old town hall**. Trg Braće Radića, between Narodni trg and the harbour, contains the surviving north tower of the 15th-century Venetian garrison castle, which once extended to the water's edge. The east palace gate leads into the market area.

In the Middle Ages the nobility and rich merchants built residences within the old palace walls; the Papalic Palace at Papalićeva (also known as Žarkova) ulica 5 is now the town museum. Go through the north palace gate to see the powerful **statue** (1929) by Ivan Meštrović of 10th-century Slavic religious leader Gregorius of Nin, who fought for the right to perform Mass in Croatian. Notice that his big toe has been polished to a shine; it's said that touching it brings good luck.

Museums & Galleries Split's least known yet most interesting museum was the **maritime museum** in Gripe Fortress (1657), on a hill top east of the old town, but unfortunately it has not yet re-opened following the war.

Also worth the walk is the **archaeological museum**, Zrinjsko-Frankopanska 25, north of town (open mornings only, closed Monday). The best of this valuable collection, first assembled in 1820, is in the garden outside. The items in the showcases inside the museum building would be a lot more interesting if the captions were in something other than Croatian.

The **town museum** on Papalićeva, east of Narodni trg (open Tuesday to Friday from 10 am to 5 pm, weekends 10 am to noon, closed Monday), has a well-displayed collection of artefacts, paintings, furniture and clothes from Split. Captions are in Croatian.

Split's finest art museum is the **Meštrović Gallery**, Šetalište Ivana Meštrovića 46 (closed Sunday afternoon and Monday). You'll see a comprehensive, well-arranged collection of works by Ivan Meštrović, Croatia's premier modern sculptor, who built the gallery as his home in 1931-39. Although Meštrović intended to retire here, he emigrated to the USA soon after WWII. Bus No 12 passes the gate infrequently. There are beaches on the southern side of the peninsula below the gallery.

From the Meštrović Gallery it's possible to hike straight up **Marjan Hill**. Go up ulica Tonča Petrasova Marovića on the western side of the gallery and continue straight up the stairway to Put Meja ulica. Turn left and walk west to Put Meja 76. The trail begins on the western side of this building. Marjan Hill offers trails through the forest, lookouts, old chapels and the local zoo.

Organised Tours

Atlas runs excursions to Krka waterfalls once a week (215KN). It also offers a canoe picnic on the Cetina River (275KN, including lunch) and a fast boat to Bol beach on Brać every Sunday (120KN return).

Special Events

The Split Summer Festival (mid-July to mid-August) features opera, drama, ballet and concerts on open-air stages. There's also the Feast of St Dujo (7 May), a flower show (May) and the four-day Festival of Popular

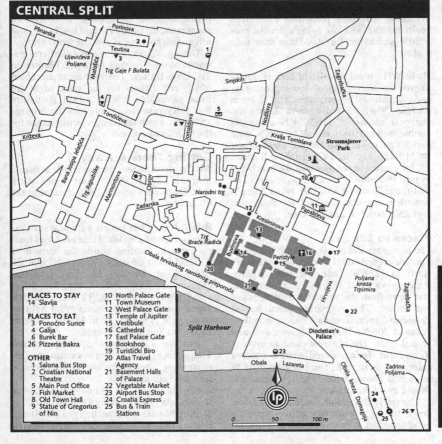

CENTRAL SPLIT

PLACES TO STAY
14 Slavija

PLACES TO EAT
3   Ponoćno Sunce
4   Galija
6   Burek Bar
26 Pizzeria Bakra

OTHER
1   Salona Bus Stop
2   Croatian National Theatre
5   Main Post Office
7   Fish Market
8   Old Town Hall
9   Statue of Gregorius of Nin
10 North Palace Gate
11 Town Museum
12 West Palace Gate
13 Temple of Jupiter
15 Vestibule
16 Cathedral
17 East Palace Gate
18 Bookshop
19 Turistički Biro
20 Atlas Travel Agency
21 Basement Halls of Palace
22 Vegetable Market
23 Airport Bus Stop
24 Croatia Express
25 Bus & Train Stations

Split Harbour

Diocletian's Palace

0   50   100 m

CROATIA

Music (end of June). The traditional February Carnival has recently been revived and from June to September a variety of evening entertainment is presented in the old town.

Places to Stay

Camping The nearest camp site used to be *Autocamp Trstenik* (☎ 521 971), 5km east of the city centre near the beach, but it has been closed for several years. Call to find out if it has reopened. See Trogir for more reliable camping alternatives.

Private Rooms In the summer, you may be met at the bus station by women offering zimmer. Otherwise, you'll need to head for the Turistički biro (☎/fax 342 142), Obala hrvatskog narodnog preporoda 12. Prices begin at 130/158KN for a single/double, plus a 30% surcharge for stays less than four nights.

Hotels The hotel situation in Split is slowly improving after years of housing refugees and international peacekeepers. The 32-room *Slavija* (☎ 47 053), Buvinova 3, has the cheapest rooms at 170/220KN a single/double without bath and 211/260KN with bath. You could also try the *Park Hotel* (☎ 515 411; fax 591 247), Šetalište Bačvice 15, for a resort experience near the beach and to pay 390/500KN for a single/double. The mid-range *Zenta* (☎ 357 229), Ivana Zajca 2, is farther east than the Park Hotel. Rooms cost 250/360KN a single/double.

Places to Eat

The best pizza in town is served at *Galija* on Tončićeva (daily until 11 pm), where the pies start at 22KN, but *Pizzeria Bakra*, Radovanova 2, off ulica Sv Petra Starog and just down from the vegetable market, is not bad either. The vegetarian salad bar at *Ponoćno Sunce*, Teutina 15, is an excellent value at 30KN. They also serve pasta and grilled meat. The cheapest place in town is *Restaurant Index*, a self-service student eatery at Svačićeva 8. You can get a plate of meat and cabbage for 19KN. Vegetarians should avoid this place.

The spiffy *Burek Bar*, Domaldova 13, just down from the main post office, serves a good breakfast or lunch of burek and yoghurt

for about 12KN. The vast *supermarket/delicatessen* at Svačićeva 1 has a wide selection of meat and cheese for sandwiches and nearly everything else you might want for a picnic. You can sit around the fountain and eat your goodies.

Entertainment

In summer everyone starts the evening at one of the cafés along Obala hrvatskog narodnog preporoda, Ujevićeva Poljana or around the cathedral before heading to a disco. *Night Café* is popular. You'll find it in the Koteks shopping centre, a huge white complex a 10-minute walk east of the old town beyond the Maritime Museum. It is the largest of its kind in Dalmatia and includes a supermarket, department store, boutiques, a couple of restaurants, the trendy *Picasso* bar, banks, post office, two bowling alleys and sports centre.

During winter, opera and ballet are presented at the *Croatian National Theatre* on Trg Gaje Bulata. The best seats are about 60KN and tickets for the same night are usually available. Erected in 1891, the theatre was fully restored in 1979 in the original style; it's worth attending a performance for the architecture alone.

Getting There & Away

Air Croatia Airlines operates one-hour flights to/from Zagreb up to four times daily (568KN in peak season, 50% cheaper in the off season).

Bus Advance bus tickets with seat reservations are recommended. There are buses from the main bus station beside the harbour to Zadar (158km, 26 daily), Zagreb (478km, 26 daily), Rijeka (404km, 14 daily), Ljubljana (532km, one daily), Pula (514km, four daily) and Dubrovnik (235km, 12 daily, 70KN). There are seven daily buses from Split to Međugorje (156km), 11 to Mostar (179km) and six to Sarajevo (271km).

Bus No 37 to Solin, Split airport and Trogir leaves from a local bus station on Domovinskog, 1km north-east of the city centre (see the Split map).

Croatia Express (☎ 342 645), near the bus station, has buses to many German cities, including Munich (912km, daily, 378KN) and Berlin (Saturday and Sunday, 738KN).

CENTRAL DALMATIA FERRY ROUTES

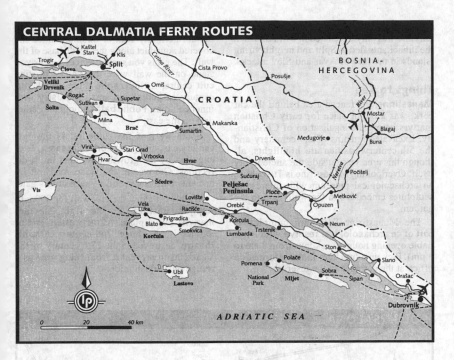

Agencija Touring (☎ 361 797) at the bus station also has many buses to Germany and a weekly bus to Amsterdam (810KN).

Train There are three or four trains daily between Split and Zagreb (nine hours, 91KN), and two trains daily between Split and Šibenik (74km, 25KN).

Boat Jadrolinija (☎ 355 399), in the large ferry terminal opposite the bus station, handles services to Hvar Island, which operate three or four times a week year-round but the local ferry is cheaper (23KN) and calls at Vela Luka on Korčula Island (25KN) daily.

For information on connections to Italy see the Getting There & Away section at the beginning of this chapter and get the schedule and tickets from Jadroagent in the ferry terminal (open daily from 8 am to 1.30 pm and 5 to 8 pm in the off season; it doesn't close in summer).

Getting Around

The bus to Split airport (20KN) leaves from Obala Lazareta 3, a five-minute walk from the train station. This bus leaves 90 minutes before flight times. You can also get there on bus No 37, as described in Getting There & Away (two-zone ticket).

You can buy a 7KN ticket from a kiosk which is good for two trips but if you buy a ticket from the driver you pay 5KN for only one trip. Validate the ticket once aboard, one end at a time for a two-trip ticket.

SOLIN

The ruins of the ancient city of Solin (Roman: Salona), among the vineyards at the foot of mountains 5km north-east of Split, are about the most interesting archaeological site in Croatia. Today surrounded by noisy highways and industry, Salona was the capital of the Roman province of Dalmatia from the time Julius Caesar elevated it to the status of colony. Salona held out against the barbarians and was only evacuated in 614 AD when the inhabitants fled to Split and neighbouring islands in the face of Avar and Slav attacks.

Things to See

Manastirine, the fenced area behind the car park, was a burial place for early Christian martyrs before the legalisation of Christianity. Excavated remains of the cemetery and the 5th-century basilica are highlights, although this area was outside the ancient city itself. Overlooking Manastirine is **Tusculum**, an archaeological museum with interesting sculptures embedded in the walls and in the garden.

The Manastirine-Tusculum complex is part of an **archaeological reserve** with unreliable opening hours (weekdays from 8 am to 3 pm). Pick up a brochure in the information office at the entrance to the reserve.

A path bordered by cypresses runs south to the northern **city wall** of Salona. Notice the covered aqueduct along the inside base of the wall. The ruins you see in front of you as you stand on the wall were the Early-Christian cult centre, including the three-aisled 5th-century **cathedral** and small **baptistry** with inner columns. **Public baths** adjoin the cathedral on the east.

South-west of the cathedral is the 1st-century east city gate, **Porta Caesarea**, later engulfed by the growth of Salona in all directions. Grooves in the stone road left by ancient chariots can still be seen at this gate.

Walk west along the city wall for 500m to **Kapljuc Basilica** on the right, another martyrs' burial place. At the western end of Salona is the huge 2nd-century **amphitheatre**, destroyed in the 17th century by the Venetians to prevent it from being used as a refuge by Turkish raiders.

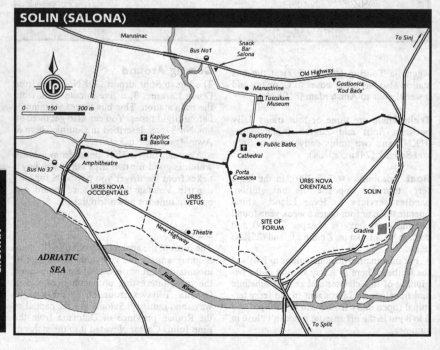

SOLIN (SALONA)

Getting There & Away

The ruins are easily accessible on Split city bus No 1 direct to Salona every half-hour from opposite Trg Gaje Bulata.

From the amphitheatre at Solin it's easy to continue to Trogir by catching a westbound bus No 37 from the nearby stop on the adjacent new highway. If, on the other hand, you want to return to Split, you can use the underpass to cross the highway and catch an eastbound bus No 37 (buy a four-zone ticket in Split if you plan to do this).

HVAR ISLAND

☎ 021

Called the 'Croatian Madeira', Hvar is said to receive more sunshine than anywhere else in the country, 2724 hours each year. Yet the island is luxuriantly green, with brilliant patches of lavender, rosemary and heather. The fine weather is so reliable that hotels give a discount on cloudy days and a free stay if you ever see snow.

Hvar Town

Medieval Hvar lies between protective pine-covered slopes and the azure Adriatic, its Gothic palaces hidden among narrow backstreets below the 13th-century city walls. A long seaside promenade winds along the indented coast dotted with small, rocky beaches. The traffic-free marble avenues of Hvar have an air of Venice; under Venetian rule that Hvar grew rich exporting wine, figs and fish.

Orientation & Information The big Jadrolinija ferries drop you off in the centre of old Hvar. The barge from Split calls at Stari Grad, 20km east.

The tourist office (☎ 741 059) is in the arsenal building on the corner of trg Sv Stjepana.

The Atlas travel agency (☎ 741 670) facing the harbour, represents American Express. Public telephones are in the post office (open Monday to Friday from 7 am to 8 pm and Saturday from 7 am to 5 pm) on the waterfront. A curious feature of Hvar is its lack of street names. You may stumble across a faded name on a plaque every so often but, in a small town where everyone knows

everyone, street names seem superfluous to the residents.

The attendant at the public toilets beside the market adjoining the bus station holds luggage for 6KN apiece, but the toilets are only open during market hours, so check the closing time carefully.

Things to See The full flavour of medieval Hvar is best savoured on the backstreets of the old town. At each end of Hvar is a monastery with a prominent tower. The **Dominican monastery** at the head of the bay was destroyed by Turks in the 16th century and the local **archaeological museum** is now housed among the ruins. If the museum is closed (as it usually is), you'll still get a good view of the ruins from the road just above, which leads up to a stone cross on a hill top offering a picture-postcard view of Hvar.

At the south-eastern end of Hvar is the 15th-century Renaissance **Franciscan monastery**, with a fine collection of Venetian paintings in the church and adjacent museum, including *The Last Supper* by Matteo Ingoli.

Smack in the middle of Hvar is the imposing Gothic **arsenal**, its great arch visible from afar. The local commune's war galley was once kept here. Upstairs off the arsenal terrace is Hvar's prize, the first **municipal theatre** in Europe (1612), which was rebuilt in the 19th century. Try to get inside to appreciate its delightful human proportions.

On the hill top high above Hvar town is a **Venetian fortress** (1551), well worth the climb for the sweeping panoramic views. Inside is a tiny collection of ancient amphoras recovered from the sea bed. The fort was built to defend Hvar from the Turks, who sacked the town in 1539 and 1571.

The best beach in Hvar is in front of the Hotel Amphora, around the western corner of the cove, but most people take a launch to the naturist islands of Jerolim and Stipanska, just offshore.

Places to Stay A recent fire on the northern part of the island destroyed the only camp site convenient to Hvar town but there are frequent buses to Jelsa, where you can pitch a tent at *Grebišće* (☎ 761 191) or *Mina* (☎ 761 227).

CROATIA

For private accommodation, try *Mengola Travel* (☎/fax 21 450; mengola-hvar@ st.tel.hr), a right-hand turn from Sv Stjepana along the harbour, or *Pelegrini* (☎/fax 742 250), next to where the Jadrolinija ferries tie up. Expect to pay 100/158KN a single/ double, with a 30% surcharge for stays less than three nights. Outside of the peak season (last week in July through August), you can negotiate a much better price.

The cheapest hotels are the *Dalmacija* (☎/fax 741 120) and the *Delfin* (☎/fax 741 168) on either side of the harbour and charging 270/460KN a single/double with a 20% surcharge for a stay less than four nights. Both hotels open in mid-June. The *Slavija* (☎ 741 820; fax 741 147) is open all year and charges only about 10KN more per person.

Places to Eat The pizzerias along the harbour offer the most predictable but inexpensive eating. For good quality fish, pasta and grilled meat, try *Bounty*, next to the Mengola agency, *Hannibal* on the southern side of trg Sv Stjepana and *Paradies Garden* up some stairs on the northern side of the cathedral. Expect to pay about 45 to 65KN for a meal.

The *grocery store* on Trg Sv Stjepana is your best alternative to a restaurant, and there's a nice park in front of the harbour just made for picnics.

Entertainment Hvar has a lively nightlife when the tourist season is in full swing. On summer evenings there's live music on the terrace of the *Hotel Slavija*, just as you would expect to see in Venice. The disco *Veneranda*, above the Hotel Delfin, provides a reliably good time if you like techno. Otherwise, *Max*, a club outside of town is a good bet; there may be shuttle buses operating between the town and the club.

Getting There & Away The Jadrolinija ferries between Rijeka and Dubrovnik call at Hvar three or four times a week all year, stopping in Hvar Town in winter and Stari Grad in summer before continuing to Korčula. The Jadrolinija agency (☎ 741 132) beside the landing sells tickets.

The local ferry from Split calls at Stari Grad (23KN) three times daily and connects Hvar town with Vela Luka on Korčula Island in the afternoon.

It's possible to visit Hvar on a (hectic) day trip from Split by catching the morning Jadrolinija ferry to Stari Grad, a bus to Hvar town, then the last ferry from Stari Grad directly back to Split.

Stari Grad

Stari Grad (Old Town), 20km east of Hvar and on the island's north coast, is quite picturesque, though somewhat of a disappointment after Hvar. Stari Grad was the capital of the island until 1331 when the Venetians shifted the administration to Hvar. This explains the extensive medieval quarter still at Stari Grad. The palace of the Croat poet Petar Hektorović (1487-1572) is worth a visit to see the fish pond and garden.

Places to Stay Just off the harbour and in the centre of Stari Grad is *Kamp Jurjevac* (☎ 765 555), open from June to early September. There's no sign, so ask for directions.

Private-room proprietors are less likely to meet the buses and ferries here than in Hvar town and at last report there was no agency renting rooms, so you'll just have to ask around.

Getting There & Away Besides the local ferries that run from Split to Stari Grad, there's a weekly Jadrolinija car-ferry from Stari Grad to Ancona, Italy (244KN), stopping at Split. Buses meet all ferries that dock at Stari Grad.

There are five buses daily from Stari Grad to Hvar town in the summer season (13KN) but services are reduced on Sunday and in the off season.

KORČULA ISLAND
☎ 020

Korčula is the largest island in an archipelago of 48 islets. Rich in vineyards and olive trees, the island was named Korkyra Melaina (Black Korčula) by the original Greek settlers because of its dense woods and plant life. The southern coast is dotted with quiet coves and small beaches linked to the interior by winding, scenic roads.

Korčula Town

The town of Korčula (Italian: Curzola), at the north-eastern tip of the island, hugs a small, hilly peninsula jutting into the Adriatic Sea. With its round defensive towers and compact cluster of red-roofed houses, Korčula is a typical medieval Dalmatian town. In contrast to Turkish cities like Mostar and Sarajevo, Korčula was controlled by Venice from the 14th to the 18th century. Venetian rule left its mark, especially on Cathedral Square. It's a peaceful little place (population 3000), with grey-stone houses nestling between the deep-green hills and gunmetal-blue sea. There are rustling palms all around.

There's lots to see and do, so it's worth planning a relaxed four-night stay to avoid the 30% surcharge on private rooms. Day trips are possible to Lumbarda, Vela Luka, Orebić on the Pelješac Peninsula and the islands of Badija and Mljet.

Orientation The big Jadrolinija car-ferry drops you off below the walls of the old town of Korčula. The passenger launch from Orebić is also convenient, terminating at the old harbour, but the barge from Orebić goes to Bon Repos in Dominče, several kilometres south-east of the centre.

Information The Turist Biro (☎ 711 067) is near the old town. Atlas travel agency (☎ 711 231) is the local American Express representative and there's a Jadrolinija office (☎ 711 101) about 25m up from the harbour.

The post office (with public telephones) is rather hidden next to the stairs up to the old town.

There's no left-luggage office at the bus station.

Things to See Other than following the circuit of the former city walls or walking along the shore, sightseeing in Korčula centres on Cathedral Square. The Gothic **Cathedral of St Mark** features two paintings by Tintoretto (*Three Saints* on the altar and *Annunciation* to one side).

The **treasury** in the 14th-century Abbey Palace next to the cathedral is worth a look; even better is the **town museum** in the 15th-century Gabriellis Palace opposite. The exhibits of Greek pottery, Roman ceramics

and home furnishings have explanations in English. It's said that Marco Polo was born in Korčula in 1254; for a small fee, you can climb the tower of what is believed to have been his house. There's also an **icon museum** in the old town. It isn't much of a museum, but visitors are let into the beautiful old **Church of All Saints**.

In the high summer season, water taxis at the Jadrolinija port collect passengers to visit various points on the island as well as **Badija Island**, which features a 15th-century Franciscan monastery (now a D-category hotel) and a naturist beach.

Organised Tours Marko Polo Tours (☎ 715 400; fax 715 800; marko-polo-tours@ du.tel.hr) and Atlas travel agency offer tours to Mljet Island (122KN) and guided tours of Korčula Island (105KN), as well as a half-day boat trip around the surrounding islands (74KN).

Places to Stay Korčula offers quite a range of accommodation, though prices are high in July and August.

Camping The *Autocamp Kalac* (☎ 711 182) is behind Hotel Bon Repos, near a beach, and charges 21KN a person and 14KN a tent.

Private Rooms The Turist Biro (☎ 711 067) and Marko Polo Tours (facing the East Harbour) arrange private rooms, charging 72/108KN for a single/double, except in peak season, when prices increase from 20 to 50%, depending on the period. There are few category II rooms and there is usually a 30% surcharge for stays less than four nights. You may get a better deal from the private operators who meet the boats, but check with the agencies first, since they're only steps from the harbour.

Hotels The B-category *Hotel Bon Repos* (☎ 711 102), overlooking a small beach outside town, and *Hotel Park* (☎ 726 004) in town have the same rates: 280/421KN a single/double with bath and breakfast, except in July and August when prices increase about 22%. You could try the D-category *Badija* (☎ 711 115; 711 746) on Badija Island which has a pool, beach, handball courts and other sports facilities. Singles/doubles are 162/281KN with full board.

Places to Eat Just around the corner from Marco Polo's house, *Adio Mare* has a charming maritime décor and a variety of fresh fish. Restaurant-grill *Planjak*, between the supermarket and the Jadrolinija office in town, is popular with a local crowd which appreciates the fresh, Dalmatian dishes as much as the low prices. A 20-minute walk outside town on the road to Lombarda takes you to another local favourite, *Gastrionica Hajuk*, for delicious, inexpensive food. The shady terrace at *Hotel Korčula* is a nice place for a coffee.

Entertainment In July and August, there's moreška sword dancing by the old town gate every Thursday at 8.30 pm. Tickets (50KN) can be purchased from the Turist Biro or Marko Polo Tours.

Getting There & Away Connections to Korčula are good. There's a daily bus service from Dubrovnik to Korčula (113km, 42KN) as well as a daily bus to Zagreb (150KN) and two buses a week to Sarajevo (145KN).

Six daily buses link Korčula town to Vela Luka at the west end of the island (1½ hours, 15KN). Buses to Lumbarda run about hourly in the morning (7km, 5KN). No bus runs to Lumbarda on Sunday and service to Vela Luka are sharply reduced on weekends.

Boat Getting to Korčula is easy, as all the Jadrolinija ferries between Split and Dubrovnik tie up at the landing next to the old town. If it's too windy in the east harbour, this ferry moors at the west harbour in front of Hotel Korčula. Once a week from June to September Jadrolinija runs a car-ferry between Korčula and Ancona, Italy (16 hours, 249KN) stopping at Split and Vis. Buy car-ferry tickets at the Jadrolinija office (☎ 715 410).

From Orebić, look for the passenger launch (15 minutes, four times daily year-round except weekends, 8KN one way) which will drop you off at the Hotel Korčula right below the old town's towers. This is best if you're looking for a private room, but if you want to camp or stay at the hotel take the car-ferry to Bon Repos in Dominče

(6.80KN, 15 minutes). The car-ferry is the only alternative on weekends. On Saturday, it connects with the bus from Lumbarda but on Sunday there is only one bus in the morning from Korčula to Orebić and one late afternoon bus returning.

Lumbarda

Just 15 minutes from Korčula town by bus, Lumbarda is a picturesque small settlement, known for its wine, near the south-eastern end of Korčula Island. A good ocean beach (Plaza Pržina) is on the other side of the vineyards beyond the supermarket.

The *Bebić* pension (☎ 712 183) and restaurant has a breathtaking view over the coast and serves good food. A double room or apartment is 200KN with bath and breakfast or 234KN per person with half-board.

The Turist Biro (☎/fax 712 023) arranges private accommodation and there are several small, inexpensive camp sites up the hill from the bus stop.

Vela Luka

Vela Luka, at the western end of Korčula, is the centre of the island's fishing industry because of its large sheltered harbour. There isn't a lot to see and there's no real beaches, so if you're arriving by ferry from Split or Hvar you might jump straight on the waiting bus to Korčula town and look for a room there.

Places to Stay Six kilometres north-west of Vela Luka (no bus service) is *Camping Mindel* (☎ 812 494). The Turist Biro (☎ 812 042), open in summer only, arranges private rooms. It is beside the Jadran Hotel (☎ 812 036) on the waterfront 100m from the ferry landing.

If the Turist Biro is closed your next best bet is the *Pansion u Domaćinstva Barćot* (☎ 812 014), directly behind the Jadran Hotel. This attractive 24-room guesthouse is open all year and its prices are just a little above what you'd pay for private rooms. Some rooms on the 3rd floor have balconies.

Getting There & Away Ferries from Split land at the western end of the harbour and buses to Korčula town meet all arrivals. There's at least one boat daily from Vela Luka to Split (25KN), calling at Hvar five times a week throughout the year. It leaves Vela Luka very early in the morning, so you might want to spend the night if you'll be catching it, although a bus from Korčula does connect with it.

OREBIĆ

Orebić, on the south coast of the Pelješac Peninsula between Korčula and Ploče, offers better beaches than those found at Korčula, 2.5km across the water. The easy access by ferry from Korčula makes it the perfect place to go for the day and a good alternative place to stay.

Things to See & Do

Orebić is great for hiking so pick up a map of the hiking trails from the tourist office. A trail leads up from Hotel Bellevue to an old **Franciscan monastery** on a ridge high above the sea. A more daring climb is to the top of **Mt Ilija** (961m), the bare grey massif that hangs above Orebić. Your reward is a sweeping view of the entire coast.

Places to Stay

The helpful Turist Biro (☎ 713 014; open April to September), next to the post office near the ferry landings, rents out private rooms (50/137KN a single/double) and can provide a town map. If the office is closed, try Orebić Tours (☎ 713 367), Jelačića 84a, or just walk around looking for 'sobe' signs – you'll soon find something.

The best beach in Orebić is Trstenica cove, a 15-minute walk east along the shore from the port. The *Hauptstrand* (☎ 713 399) and *Trstenica* (☎ 713 348) camping grounds overlook the long, sandy beach. The latter rents out rooms with a shared bathroom for 72KN per person, not including breakfast.

Getting There & Away

In Orebić the ferry terminal and the bus station are adjacent. If you're coming from the coast, there are four daily ferries (six in summer) from Ploče to Trpanj which connects with a bus to Orebić. Korčula buses to Dubrovnik, Zagreb and Sarajevo stop at Orebić. See Korčula for additional bus and ferry information.

MLJET ISLAND

Created in 1960, **Mljet National Park** occupies the western third of the green island of Mljet (Italian: Meleda), between Korčula and Dubrovnik. The park centres around two saltwater lakes surrounded by pine-clad slopes. Most people visit on day trips from Korčula but it's possible to come by regular ferry from Dubrovnik, stay a few days and go hiking, biking and boating.

Orientation

Tour boats from Korčula arrive at Pomena wharf at Mljet's western end, where a good map of the island is posted. Jadrolinija ferries arrive at Sobra on the eastern end and are met by a local bus for the 1½-hour ride to Pomena.

Things to See & Do

From Pomena it's a 15-minute walk to a jetty on **Veliko jezero**, the larger of the two lakes. Here the groups board a boat to a small lake islet and are served lunch at a 12th-century **Benedictine monastery**, now a restaurant.

Those who don't want to spend the rest of the afternoon swimming and sunbathing on the monastery island can catch an early boat back to the main island and spend a couple of hours walking along the lakeshore before catching the late-afternoon excursion boat back to Korčula. There's a small landing opposite the monastery where the boat operator drops off passengers upon request. It's not possible to walk right around the larger lake as there's no bridge over the channel connecting the lakes to the sea.

Mljet is good for cycling; the hotels rent out bicycles (60KN a half-day).

Organised Tours

The Atlas travel agency (☎ 711 060) in Korčula offers day trips to Mljet Island twice a week from May to mid-October. The tour lasts from 8.30 am to 6 pm (122KN per person, including the 48KN park entry fee). The boat trip from Korčula to Pomena takes at least two hours, less by hydrofoil. Lunch isn't included in the tour price and meals at the hotels on Mljet are very expensive, so it's best to bring a picnic lunch.

Places to Stay

There's no camping in the national park but there's a small camping ground (☎ 745 071) in Ropa, about a kilometre from the park, open from June to September. The tourist office in Polace (☎ 744 086) arranges private accommodation at 148KN a double room in peak season but it is essential to make arrangements before arrival. Don't count on 'sobe' signs. The only hotel is the luxury *Odisej* in Pomena with rooms at 361KN per person in July and August with half-board, 50% less in the off season.

Getting There & Away

A regular ferry (daily except Sunday; 21KN) leaves from Dubrovnik at 2 pm and goes to Sobra. The return ferry leaves from Sobra at 5:30 am, which means a very early morning departure by local bus from the national park. There are additional ferries in both directions in July and August. The big Jadrolinija coastal ferries also stop at Mljet twice a week in summer and once a week during the rest of the year.

Dubrovnik

☎ 020

Founded 1300 years ago by refugees from Epidaurus in Greece, medieval Dubrovnik (Ragusa until 1918) was the most important independent city-state on the Adriatic after Venice. Until the Napoleonic invasion of 1806, it remained an independent republic of merchants and sailors.

Like Venice, Dubrovnik's fortunes now depend upon its tourist industry. Stari Grad, the perfectly preserved old town, is unique because of its marble-paved squares, steep cobbled streets, tall houses, convents, churches, palaces, fountains and museums, all cut from the same light-coloured stone. The intact city walls keep motorists at bay and the southerly position between Split and Albania makes for an agreeable climate and lush vegetation.

For those who watched the shelling of Dubrovnik on TV in late 1991, here's a bit of good news: the city is still there, as beautiful as ever, with few visible reminders of its recent trauma. Some buildings on the back

streets are still damaged but you won't see it as the shutters will be down and the windows closed. The eight-month siege by the federal army from October 1991 to May 1992 tore through the town's distinctive honey-coloured clay roofs, however. Replacing them with matching tiles was extremely problematic and you'll notice a patchwork of colours as you walk around the city walls. The most severe blow to Dubrovnik was in the catastrophic decline of tourism which left its residents feeling abandoned and apprehensive. The city has recently begun to climb back and in July and August the streets are again crowded with visitors. Whatever the time of year the magical interlay of light and stone is as enchanting as ever. Don't miss it.

Orientation

The Jadrolinija ferry terminal and the bus station are a few hundred metres apart at Gruž, several kilometres north-west of the old town. The camping ground and most of the luxury tourist hotels are on the leafy Lapad Peninsula, west of the bus station.

Information

Tourist Offices The tourist office (☎ 426 354) is on Placa, opposite the Franciscan monastery in the old town. The American Express representative is the Atlas travel agency (☎ 442 222; 411 100) on Brsalje 17, outside Pile gate next to the old town; but mail is held at another office (☎ 432 093) across from Fort Revelin at Frana Supila 2. There's also an office in the harbour at Gruz (☎ 418 001) and another in Lapad at Lisinskog 5 (☎ 442 555).

Post & Communications The main post office is at Ante Starčevića 2, a block from Pile Gate (open Monday to Saturday from 7 am to 8 pm and Sunday from 8 am to 2 pm). Place international telephone calls here. There's another post office-telephone centre at Lapad near Hotel Kompas.

Left Luggage Left-luggage at the bus station is open from 4.30 am to 10 pm. The bus service into town is fairly frequent.

Things to See

You'll probably begin your visit at the city bus stop outside **Pile Gate**. As you enter the city, Placa, Dubrovnik's wonderful pedestrian promenade, extends before you all the way to the clock tower at the other end of town. Just inside Pile Gate is the huge **Onofrio Fountain** (1438) and the **Franciscan monastery**, with the third-oldest functioning pharmacy (since 1391) in Europe by the cloister.

In front of the clock tower at the eastern end of Placa, you'll find the **Orlando Column** (1419) – a favourite meeting place. On opposite sides of Orlando are the 16th-century **Sponza Palace** (now the State Archives) and **St Blaise's Church**, a lovely Italian baroque building.

At the end of the broad street beside St Blaise, Pred Dvorom, is the baroque **cathedral** and, between the two churches, the Gothic **Rector's Palace** (1441), now a museum with furnished rooms, baroque paintings and historical exhibits. The elected rector was not permitted to leave the building during his one-month term without the permission of the senate. The narrow street opposite this palace opens onto Gundulićeva Poljana, a bustling morning market. Up the stairway at the southern end of the square is the imposing **Jesuit monastery** (1725).

Return to the cathedral and take the narrow street in front to the **aquarium** in Fort St John. Through an obscure entrance off the city walls, above the aquarium, is the **Maritime Museum**. If you're 'museumed out' you can safely give these two a miss.

By this time you'll be ready for a leisurely walk around the **city walls**. Built between the 13th and 16th centuries and still intact, these powerful walls are the finest in the world and Dubrovnik's main claim to fame. They enclose the entire city in a curtain of stone over 2km long and up to 25m high, with two round towers, 14 square towers, two

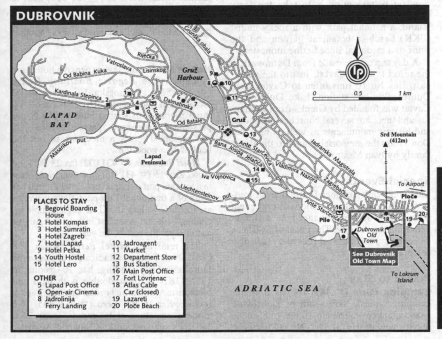

DUBROVNIK

Gružka obala
Rijećka
Vatroslava   Lisinskog
Od Babina Kuka
Kardinala Stepinca
Gruž Harbour
Dalmatinska
Kralja Tomislava
LAPAD BAY
Od Batale
Gruž
Bana Josipa Jelačića
Masarikov put
Lapad Peninsula
Iva Vojnovića
Liechtensteinov put
Vladimira Nazora
Jadranska Magistrala
Zagrebačka
Ante Starčevića

Srd Mountain (412m)

0   0.5   1 km

To Airport
Ploče
Ante Starčevića
Pile
Dubrovnik Old Town
See Dubrovnik Old Town Map
To Lokrum Island
ADRIATIC SEA

PLACES TO STAY
1 Begović Boarding House
2 Hotel Kompas
3 Hotel Sumratin
4 Hotel Zagreb
7 Hotel Lapad
9 Hotel Petka
14 Youth Hostel
15 Hotel Lero

OTHER
5 Lapad Post Office
6 Open-air Cinema
8 Jadrolinija Ferry Landing

10 Jadroagent
11 Market
12 Department Store
13 Bus Station
16 Main Post Office
17 Fort Lovrjenac
18 Atlas Cable Car (closed)
19 Lazareti
20 Ploče Beach

CROATIA

corner fortifications and a large fortress. The views over the town and sea are great – this walk could be the high point of your visit.

Whichever way you go, you'll notice the large **Dominican monastery** in the north-eastern corner of the city. Of all Dubrovnik's religious museums, the one in the Dominican monastery is the largest and most worth paying to enter.

Dubrovnik has many other sights, such as the unmarked **synagogue** at ulica Žudioska 5 near the clock tower (open from 10 am to noon on Friday and from 5 to 7 pm on Tuesday). The uppermost streets of the old town below the north and south walls are pleasant to wander along.

Beaches   The closest beach, Ploče, to the old city is just beyond the 17th-century **Lazareti** (former quarantine station) outside Ploče Gate. There are also 'managed' hotel beaches on the **Lapad Peninsula**, but you could be charged admission unless they think you're a guest.

A far better option is to take the ferry which shuttles hourly in summer to **Lokrum Island**, a national park with a rocky nudist (FKK) beach, a botanical garden and the ruins of a medieval Benedictine monastery.

A day trip can be made from Dubrovnik to the resort town of **Cavtat**, just to the south-east. Bus No 10 runs often to Cavtat from Dubrovnik's bus station. Like Dubrovnik, Cavtat was founded by Greeks from Epidaurus and there are several churches, museums and historic monuments as well as beaches. Don't miss the memorial chapel to the Račić family by Ivan Meštrović.

Special Events

The Dubrovnik Summer Festival from mid-July to mid-August is a major cultural event with over 100 performances at different venues in the old city. The Feast of St Blaise (3 February) and carnival (February) are also celebrated.

Places to Stay

Camping *Porto* (☎ 487 078) is a small, camping ground, 8km south of Dubrovnik near a quiet cove. The No 10 bus to Srebeno leaves you nearly at its gate. Otherwise,

there's the much larger *Zaton* (☎ 280 280), about 15km west of the city.

Hostels   The *YHA hostel*, (☎ 423 241; fax 412 592) up Vinka Sagrestana from Bana Josipa Jelačića 17, is newly opened and completely refurbished. A bed in a room for four with breakfast is 75KN. Lunch and dinner can be arranged but the hostel is on one of the liveliest streets in Lapad, full of bars, cafés and pizzerias.

Private Rooms   The easiest way to find a place to stay is to accept the offer of a sobe from one of the women who may approach you at the ferry terminal. Their prices are lower than those charged by the room-finding agencies and, unless you arrive in July or August, they are open to bargaining.

Officially, there are no single rooms but in the off season you may be able to knock 20% off the price of a double room, which begins at 108KN in May, June and September. Agencies that handle private accommodation include Atlas, Gulliver (☎ 411 088) next to Jadroagent, and Globtour (☎ 428 144; fax 426 322) on Placa. The tourist office on Placa opposite the Franciscan monastery is another place to try.

Hotels   Most of the less expensive hotels are in Lapad. The *Begović Boarding House* (☎ 428 563), Primorska 17, a couple of blocks from Lapad post office (bus No 6), has three rooms with shared bath at 70KN per person and three small apartments for 90KN per person. There's a nice terrace out the back with a good view.

Hotel Sumratin (☎ 431 031; fax 23 581) and *Hotel Zagreb* (☎ 431 011) are near each other in a tranquil part of Lapad but Hotel Zagreb has more of a traditional European flavour. Prices are the same at 190/320KN a single/double including bath and breakfast in July and August and cheaper the rest of the year.

The renovated *Hotel Petka* (☎/fax 418 058), Obala Stjepana Radića 38, opposite the Jadrolinija ferry landing, has 104 rooms at 198/342KN a single/double with bath and breakfast. Along a busy road through Lapad, Iravojnovica, *Hotel Lero* (☎ 411 455) is a modern structure with rooms from 263/373KN a single/double in July and August.

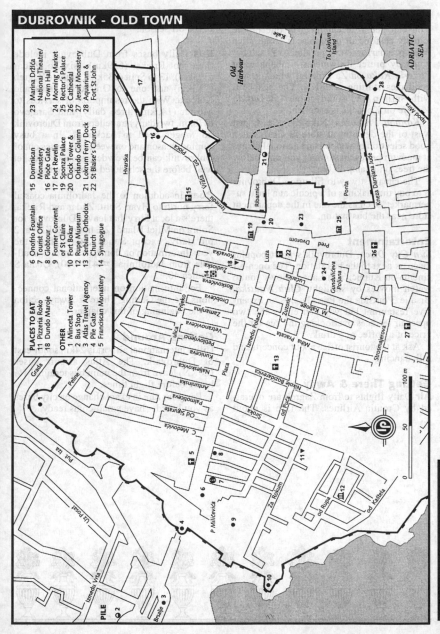

DUBROVNIK - OLD TOWN

PLACES TO EAT
11 Pizzeria Roko
18 Dundo Maroje

OTHER
1 Mlinceta Tower
2 Bus Stop
3 Atlas Travel Agency
4 Pile Gate
5 Franciscan Monastery
6 Onofrio Fountain
7 Tourist Office
8 Globtour
9 Former Convent of St Claire
10 Fort Bokar
12 Rupe Museum
13 Serbian Orthodox Church
14 Synagogue
15 Dominican Monastery
16 Ploce Gate
17 Fort Revelin
19 Sponza Palace
20 Clock Tower & Orlando Column
21 Lokrum Ferry Dock
22 St Blaise's Church
23 Marina Držića National Theatre/ Town Hall
24 Morning Market
25 Rector's Palace
26 Cathedral
27 Jesuit Monastery
28 Aquarium & Fort St John

ADRIATIC SEA

Old Harbour

Kaše

To Lokrum Island

PILE

CROATIA

Places to Eat

You can get a decent meal at one of the touristy seafood or pasta places along ulica Prijeko, a narrow street parallel to Placa, but you may prefer the quieter atmosphere at *Pizzeria Roko* on Za Rokum, which serves good pies starting at 28KN. The spaghetti with shrimp and squid risotto at *Dundo Maroje* on Kovačka is excellent.

Konoba Primorka, Nikole Tesle 8, just west of the department store in Gruž, has a good selection of seafood and national dishes at medium prices. In summer you dine below the trees on a lamp-lit terrace.

The cheapest way to fill up in Dubrovnik is to buy the makings of a picnic at a local supermarket, such as the one in the department store near the bus station.

Entertainment

Sun City Disco, Dubrovnik's most popular disco, is next to the bus station. The open-air cinema on Kumičića in Lapad allows you to watch movies by starlight. *Club Nautika*, Brsalje 3 outside the Pile Gate, is an expensive restaurant but you can enjoy the two open-air terraces overlooking the sea for the price of a coffee or a drink.

Ask at the tourist office about concerts and folk dancing.

Getting There & Away

Air Daily flights to/from Zagreb are operated by Croatia Airlines. The fare is about 620KN one way in the summer but much less in the off season.

Bus Daily buses from Dubrovnik include three to Rijeka (639km), six to Zadar (393km), 13 to Split (235km), eight to Zagreb (713km) and one to Orebić (113km) and Korčula. With the resumption of services to Mostar (143km, three daily) and Sarajevo (278km, two daily) travellers from Dubrovnik no longer need to backtrack. In a busy summer season and on weekends, buses out of Dubrovnik can be crowded, so book a ticket well before the scheduled departure time.

Boat In addition to the Jadrolinija coastal ferry north to Hvar, Split, Zadar and Rijeka, there's a local ferry that leaves Dubrovnik for Sobra on Mljet Island (2½ hours, 21KN) at 2 pm daily, except Sunday, throughout the year. Information on domestic ferries is available from Jadrolinija (☎ 418 000), Obala S Radića 40.

For information on international connections see the Getting There & Away section at the beginning of this chapter.

Getting Around

Čilipi international airport is 24km south-east of Dubrovnik. The Atlas airport buses (20KN) leave from the main bus terminal 1½ hours before flight times.

Pay your fare in exact change on city buses as you board – have small coins ready.

Cyprus

Cyprus, the Mediterranean's third-largest island, is the legendary birthplace of Aphrodite. Close to Greece, Turkey, Jordan, Israel and Egypt, it is a useful stepping stone for those travelling between east and west.

Cyprus presents an infinite variety of natural and architectural delights. Two high mountain ranges tower above a fertile plain. Landscapes are dotted with ancient Greek and Roman ruins, Orthodox monasteries and crusader castles.

There's an easy-going lifestyle on the island, the crime rate is low and the sun shines a lot. All of this makes Cyprus sound like a paradise, and perhaps it would be, were it not for the Turkish invasion of 1974 and subsequent partition of the island. Despite this, its people are friendly, relaxed and hospitable.

Facts about Cyprus

HISTORY

Cyprus' position in the eastern Mediterranean has meant that since ancient times it has been an important trading post, and consequently, has a history fraught with battles and conquest.

Inhabited since the Neolithic period, Cyprus has been colonised by the Mycenaeans, Phoenicians, Egyptians, Assyrians and Persians. In 295 BC, Ptolemy I, one of Alexander's generals who became king of Egypt, won control of the island. His dynasty ruled Cyprus until it was annexed by Rome in 58 BC.

As part of the Roman Empire, Cyprus enjoyed relative peace and prosperity, it came to be torn between the warring Byzantine and the Islamic empires, and from the 7th to the 11th century it changed hands at least 11 times.

Richard the Lionheart conquered the island in 1191 during the Third Crusade, but when the Cypriots rebelled, he sold the island to the Knights Templar. They in turn sold it to Guy de Lusignan, the deposed king of Jerusalem, whose French dynasty ruled Cyprus for the next three centuries. This was a period of prosperity but also oppression of Cypriot culture and Greek Orthodoxy.

AT A GLANCE

Capital	Lefkosia (formerly Nicosia)
Population	911,000 (inc 175,000 people in North Cyprus)
Area	9,250 sq km (3,355 sq km in the Turkish area)
Official Languages	Greek, Turkish in North Cyprus
Currency	1 Cypriot pound (CY£) = 100 cents; 1 Turkish lira (TL) = 100 kurus
GDP	US$8.8 billion (1996)
Time	GMT/UTC+0200

By the late 14th century the Lusignanians were in decline and the Venetians took control in 1489. They strengthened the island's fortifications, but in 1570 the Turks attacked, killing some 2000 people, and began 300 years of Ottoman rule.

CYPRUS

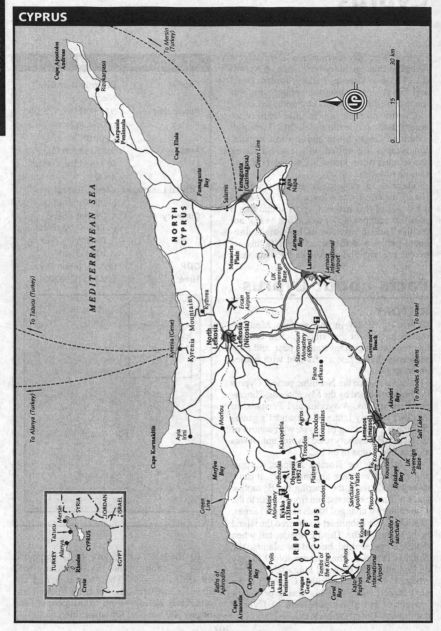

CYPRUS

In 1878 the administration of Cyprus was ceded to Britain. This was done out of fear of Russia's expansionist policy, with Britain promising in return to aid Turkey in the event of a Russian attack.

In 1925 Cyprus became a UK crown colony. By now, Cypriots were deeply frustrated by their lack of self-determination, and the first stirrings of the *enosis* movement (which wanted union with Greece) were felt. This led to intercommunal riots between Greeks and Turks. The latter (18% of the population) opposed enosis, believing that it would lead to even greater oppression. By the late 1940s, the Cypriot Orthodox Church openly supported enosis, and a 1951 plebiscite showed that 96% of Greek Cypriots were also in favour.

In 1954 Britain prepared a new constitution for Cyprus which was accepted by the Turkish population, but not the extremist National Organisation of Cypriot Freedom Fighters (EOKA) which wanted enosis and began guerilla activities against the British administration, causing much suffering and many deaths.

In August 1960 the UK granted independence to Cyprus. Archbishop Makarios became president, with a Turk, Fasal Kükük, as vice president. In December 1963 Makarios proposed constitutional amendments which would have given the Greeks greater control. The Turkish government rejected these and threatened military intervention, but was restrained by international pressure. Intercommunal violence increased significantly and in 1964 the United Nations sent in a peacekeeping force.

In 1967 a military junta seized power in Greece and the demands for enosis ceased – nobody wanted union with such a repressive regime. However, on 15 July 1974, Greece overthrew Makarios in a coup d'état. When he escaped assassination and fled the country, Greece put ex-guerilla leader Nicos Samson in power. The Turks responded by invading Cyprus, and the Greek junta realised the magnitude of the mistake. Samson was removed and the Greek offensive collapsed. The Turkish troops continued to advance until they occupied the northern third of the island, forcing some 180,000 Greek Cypriots to flee their homes for the safety of southern Cyprus. Neither the UK nor the USA intervened.

Cyprus remains a divided island. From time to time violence between the two sides erupts, like that which occurred in August 1996. Unsuccessful peace talks, mostly under the auspices of the UN, have been held sporadically. During recent years Richard Holbrooke, the US diplomat who had done much to end the war in Bosnia, has attempted to effect a reconciliation, but as yet to no avail.

There is some hope of reunification because both sides want to join the EU. However, as of June 1998 tension has returned to the area due to the Republic's plans to install Russian-built S-300 anti-aircraft missiles; the year has been marked by tit-for-tat airforce manoeuvres.

GEOGRAPHY & ECOLOGY

There are two mountain ranges: the Kyrenia Mountains in North Cyprus and the Troodos Massif in the centre of the Republic in the south. Between them is the Mesaoria Plain.

Much of southern Cyprus' coastline has been spoilt by tourism, so most of the island's impressive range of flora and fauna (especially birds) is restricted to the well-managed areas of the Troodos Mountains and the Akamas Peninsula, near Polis. Diverse wildlife is found all over North Cyprus, particularly on the relatively unexplored Karpasia Peninsula.

GOVERNMENT & POLITICS

In 1960 Cyprus was declared an independent sovereign republic with a presidential system of government. It is currently ruled by the National Unity Party led by Glafkos Clerides.

In November 1983, Rauf Denktash declared northern Cyprus the independent Turkish Republic of Northern Cyprus, with himself as president. Only Turkey recognises this self-styled nation. Denktash leads a coalition of the National Unity Party and the Democrat Party.

ECONOMY

Partition had a devastating effect on the Cypriot economy. The Republic (southern Cyprus), with its own currency, has made a steady recovery and tourism is now its biggest source of income. The north uses the Turkish lira, tying the area's economy to Turkey's high inflation; agriculture and a developing tourist industry provide most of the income.

POPULATION & PEOPLE

Since partition, the vast majority of Greek Cypriots live in the Republic, while Turkish Cypriots and colonists live in the north. Cyprus' total population is 911,000 with 175,000 living in the north.

ARTS

Reminders of Cyprus' history include ancient Greek temples, Roman mosaics and 15th-century church frescoes. Building on a rich and varied tradition, the visual arts are very much alive today. Many villages specialise in one or another, whether it be pottery, silver and copperware, basket-weaving, tapestry work, or the famous lace from Lefkara.

SOCIETY & CONDUCT

Since the island's split, Greek Cypriots have become more culturally defined. An example of this is the Republic's decision to change some of its place names, making them more Cypriot than English. In the north, the Turks have succeeded in imbuing the region with an all-pervasive Turkishness. They have changed the Greek place names to Turkish ones and embraced culture of Turkey.

On both sides of the Green Line, the people are friendly, honest and law-abiding (there is hardly any crime or vandalism anywhere). Family life, marriage and children still play a central role in society, as does religion. Greek and Turkish Cypriots are fiercely patriotic.

RELIGION

Most Greek Cypriots belong to the Greek Orthodox Church and most Turkish Cypriots are Sunni Muslims.

LANGUAGE

Most Cypriots in the Republic speak English and many road signs are in Greek and English. In North Cyprus this is not the case outside the touristy areas and you'll have to brush up your Turkish. In both areas, the spelling of place and street names varies enormously.

Since mid-1995 the Republic has converted all place names into Latin characters according to the official system of Greek transliteration. As a result, Nicosia has become Lefkosia, Limassol is now Lemesos, Famagusta is Ammochostos, and Kyrenia is Keryneia. Throughout this chapter the new names are given since the old ones are being phased out on all tourist maps and road signs. The new Greek names for Famagusta and Kyrenia in North Cyprus have not been used.

The Turkish names for North Lefkosia, Famagusta, Kyrenia are Lefkoşa, Gazimağusa, and Girne.

See the Turkish and Greek language guides at the back of the book for pronunciation guidelines and useful words and phrases.

Facts for the Visitor

HIGHLIGHTS
Republic of Cyprus

Nine of the frescoed Byzantine churches in the Troodos Massif are on UNESCO's World Heritage List and they really are special. The Tombs of the Kings, dating back to the 3rd century BC, are a lot more fun than the famous Paphos Mosaics, and only half as crowded.

North Cyprus

With the castle at one end, Kyrenia's waterfront must be one of the most beautiful in the Mediterranean. Some people are a bit disappointed by the archaeological site at Salamis, but the number of well-preserved upright columns in the gymnasium is incredible.

SUGGESTED ITINERARIES
Republic of Cyprus

Depending on the length of your stay, you might want to see and do the following things:

One week
    Allow two days for Lefkosia, two days for Paphos, one day for exploring the ancient coastal sites between Paphos and Lemesos, and the rest in the Troodos Massif.
Two weeks
    As above but make two trips into North Cyprus, add Polis and the Akamas Peninsula (beaches and walks) and have a steam and/or massage at the Hammam in Lemesos.

North Cyprus

One week

Allow one day for North Lefkosia, one day for Famagusta, half a day for Salamis, and spend the rest staying in Kyrenia and visiting the castles in the Kyrenia Mountains.

Two weeks

As above but have a Turkish bath in North Lefkosia and spend some time exploring the near-deserted Karpasia Peninsula and its archaeological sites.

PLANNING
Climate & When to Go

Cyprus has a typical Mediterranean climate. April/May and September/October are the most pleasant times to visit.

Books & Maps

Bitter Lemons by Lawrence Durrell and *Journey into Cyprus* by Colin Thubron are both worth reading. The free tourist maps are adequate for most purposes.

TOURIST OFFICES

The Cyprus Tourism Organisation (CTO) has offices in major towns in the Republic. Its leaflets and maps are excellent.

In North Cyprus there are tourist offices in North Lefkosia, Famagusta and Kyrenia which have free country and town maps plus an increasing number of brochures.

Tourist Offices Abroad

The CTO has branches in most European countries, the USA, Russia, Israel and Japan.

North Cyprus tourist offices can be found in the UK, Belgium, the USA, Pakistan and Turkey; otherwise inquiries are handled by Turkish tourist offices.

VISAS & EMBASSIES

In both the Republic and North Cyprus, nationals of the USA, Australia, Canada, Japan, New Zealand, Singapore and EU countries can enter and stay for up to three months without a visa.

If you have a North Cyprus stamp in your passport you can still visit the Republic, but it will be deleted by customs on entry, and this will not prevent you from visiting Greece, either. Despite this, it is advisable to get immigration to stamp a separate piece of paper instead of your passport when entering North Cyprus.

Cypriot Diplomatic Missions Abroad

The Republic of Cyprus has diplomatic representation in 26 countries, including:

Australia

(☎ 02 6281 0832), 30 Beale Crescent, Deakin, ACT 2600

Germany

(☎ 228 363 336), Kronprinzenstrasse 58, D-53173 Bonn

Greece

(☎ 1 723 2737), Irodotou 16, 10675, Athens

Israel

(☎ 3 525 0212), 50 Dizengoff St, 14th floor, Top Tower, Dizengodd Centre, 64322 Tel Aviv

UK & Ireland

(☎ 0171 499 8272), 93 Park St, London W1Y 4ET

USA

(☎ 202 462 5772), 2211 R St North West, Washington, DC, 20008

The Turkish Republic of Northern Cyprus has offices in:

Canada

(☎ 905 731 4000), 328 Highway 7 East, Suite 308, Richmond Hill, Ontario LB4 3P7

Germany

(☎ 02683 32748), Auf Dem Platz 3, 53577 Neustadt Wied-Neschen

Japan

(☎ 03 203 1313), 4th Floor, 6th Arai Blog-1-4, Kabohi-Cho, Shinytku-Ku, Tokyo 160

Turkey

(☎ 312 437 6031), Rabat Sokak No 20, Gaziosmanpasa 06700, Ankara

UK

(☎ 0171 631 1920), 26 Bedford Sq, London WC1B 3EG

USA

(☎ 212 687 2350), 821 United Nations Plaza, 6th floor, New York, NY 10017

Diplomatic Missions in Cyprus

Countries with diplomatic representation in the Republic of Cyprus include:

Australia

(☎ 02 473001), 4 Gonia Leoforos Stassinou & Annis Komninis St, 2nd Floor, 1060 Lefkosia

Canada
  (☎ 02 451630), Office 403, 15 Themistokli
  Dervi St, Lefkosia
Germany
  (☎ 02 444362), 10 Nikitara St, 1080 Lefkosia
Greece
  (☎ 02 441880), Leoforos Vyronos 8-10, PO Box
  1799, 1513 Lefkosia
Israel
  (☎ 02 445195), Grypari 4, PO Box 1049, 1500
  Lefkosia
UK
  (☎ 02 473131), Alexandrou Palli St, PO Box
  1978, 1587 Lefkosia
USA
  (☎ 02 476100), Gonia Metochiou & Ploutar-
  chou Sts, 2406 Egkomi, Lefkosia

Countries with diplomatic representation in
North Cyprus include:

Australia
  (☎ 227 1115), Saray Hotel, Attaturk Square,
  North Lefkosia
Turkey
  (☎ 222 72314; fax 222 82209) Bedreddin
  Demirel Caddesi, North Lefkosia, KKTC,
  Mersin 10, Turkey
UK
  (☎ 227 1938), 23 Mehmet Akif Sokak, North
  Lefkosia
USA
  (☎ 227 2443), 20 Güner Türkmen Caddesi,
  North Lefkosia

CUSTOMS

Items which can be imported duty-free into
the Republic are 250g of tobacco or the
equivalent in cigarettes, 2L of wine or 1L of
spirits, and one bottle of perfume not exceeding 600ml. In North Cyprus it is 500g of
tobacco or 400 cigarettes, and 1L or spirits or
1L of wine.

MONEY
Currency

The Republic's unit of currency is the Cyprus
pound (CY£), divided into 100 cents. There
is no limit on the amount of Cyprus pounds
you can bring into the country, but foreign
currency equivalent to US$1000 or above
must be declared. You can leave Cyprus with
either CY£100 or the amount with which you
entered. The unit of currency in North Cyprus

is the Turkish lira (TL), and there are no restrictions.

Banks throughout Cyprus will exchange
all major currencies in either cash or travellers cheques. Most shops, hotels etc in
North Cyprus accept CY£ and other hard currencies.

In the Republic you can get a cash advance
on Visa, MasterCard, Diners Club, Eurocard
and American Express at one or more banks,
and there are plenty of ATMs. In North
Cyprus cash advances are given on Visa
cards at the Vakiflar and Kooperatif banks in
North Lefkosia and Kyrenia; major banks in
large towns will have ATMs.

Exchange Rates

Australia	A$1	=	CY£0.32
Egypt	£E1	=	CY£0.15
euro	€1	=	CY£0.58
France	1FF	=	CY£0.09
Germany	1DM	=	CY£0.29
Greece	100Dr	=	CY£0.17
Israel	100NIS	=	CY£0.14
Japan	¥100	=	CY£0.37
New Zealand	NZ$1	=	CY£0.27
UK	UK£1	=	CY£0.88
USA	US$1	=	CY£0.53

Exchange rates for the Turkish lira have not
been given because of the high inflation rate
(80% in 1996). All prices quoted in the North
Cyprus section are in UK pounds.

Costs

Cyprus is a cheaper place to visit than most
European countries, and in North Cyprus
costs are slightly lower still. Living frugally,
you could just get by on CY£14 a day, or live
quite adequately on CY£30. Accommodation
costs tend to go up between April and November, peaking during July and August.

If not free, admission to all museums and
sites is between CY£1 to CY£2, and so are
not detailed in the text.

Tipping & Bargaining

In both parts of the island a 10% service
charge is sometimes added to a restaurant
bill, but if not, then a tip of similar percentage is expected. Taxi drivers and hotel

porters always appreciate a small tip. It is not normal to bargain for goods in markets.

POST & COMMUNICATIONS

In the Republic, postal rates for cards and letters are between 25 and 41 cents. There are poste restante services in Lefkosia, Larnaca, Paphos and Lemesos.

In North Cyprus, rates are between UK£0.39 and UK£0.45. There are poste restante services in North Lefkosia, Kyrenia and Famagusta. All mail must be addressed to Mersin 10, Turkey, *not* North Cyprus.

In the Republic, you can make overseas calls from all telephone boxes but they only take phonecards available from newsagents, some banks or the Republic's telephone company (CYTA). At peak times, a three minute call to the USA will cost CY£2.90, and 21 cents during off-peak (10 pm to 8 am, and Sunday). The Republic's country code is ☎ 357.

In North Cyprus most public telephone boxes only take phonecards bought at a Turkish Telecom administration office; the old system of tokens (*jetonlar*) has almost been phased out. A peak three minute call to the USA will set you back UK£1.35 and off-peak UK£0.90. To call North Cyprus from abroad dial ☎ 90 (Turkey), the country code ☎ 392, and then the area code and the number. Area codes also must be used when calling locally (codes have been incorporated into all phone numbers in the North Cyprus section)

In both regions most people now use mobile phones, but if you have an international one it won't work in North Cyprus.

In the south you can send faxes from the post office, and in the north from the Turkish Telecom administration offices, or from high street shops in both regions.

INTERNET RESOURCES

There are Internet cafés in all main towns in southern Cyprus and several in the north. The majority open late, close in the early hours of the morning and have become real social centres. They all charge in the region of CY£2.50 for the first hour and CY£1 for subsequent hours. Despite this, practically no tourist facilities (accommodation, restaurants, etc) have email addresses.

The Internet has lots of interesting information Cyprus, and the most comprehensive site on North Cyprus is at www.cypnet.com /cyradise/cyradise.html

NEWSPAPERS & MAGAZINES

The Republic's English-language papers are the *Cyprus Mail* and the *Cyprus Weekly*. The North Cyprus publications are the *Turkish Daily News* and *Cyprus Today*.

RADIO & TV

CyBC (Cyprus Broadcasting Corporation) has programs and news bulletins in English on Radio 2 (FM 91 to 1MHz) at 10 am, 2 and 8 pm. BFBS (British Forces Broadcasting Services) broadcasts 24 hours a day in English, and the BBC World Service is easily picked up.

CyBC TV has news in English at 8 pm on Channel 2. Satellite dishes are very common, so many hotels have CNN, BBC, SKY or NBC.

TIME

Cyprus is two hours ahead of GMT/UTC. Clocks go forward one hour on the last weekend in March and back one hour on the last weekend in October.

ELECTRICITY

The electric current is 240V, 50Hz. Plugs are large with three square pins as in the UK.

WEIGHTS & MEASURES

Cyprus uses the metric system.

LAUNDRY

There are plenty of dry-cleaners and laundrettes can be found in all main towns, but they are not common. Most hotels have a laundry service.

TOILETS

There are public toilets in the main towns and at tourist sites. They are invariably clean and western-style, although in North Cyprus you sometimes come across dirtier ones or those of the squat variety.

HEALTH

Tap water is safe to drink everywhere. The greatest health risk comes from the sun, so take care against sunstroke, heat exhaustion and dehydration.

Foreigners do not receive free health care in either part of the island.

WOMEN TRAVELLERS

Women travellers will encounter little sexual harassment, although it is worth steering clear of any red-light areas and some of the cheaper hotels because they may be brothels.

GAY & LESBIAN TRAVELLERS

Homosexuality is legal in the Republic and the Gay Liberation Movement can be contacted at PO Box 1947, Lefkosia (☎ 02 443346).

In North Cyprus homosexuality is still illegal.

DISABLED TRAVELLERS

Any CTO can send you the *What the Disabled Visitor Needs to Know about Cyprus* factsheet, which lists some useful organisations. The Republic's airports have truck-lifts for arriving or departing disabled travellers. Some of the hotels have facilities for the disabled, but there's little help at sites or museums. In North Cyprus there are few facilities for the disabled visitor.

SENIOR TRAVELLERS

Older visitors will find travelling around both the Republic and North Cyprus fairly easy. In general, no concessions exist for seniors.

DANGERS & ANNOYANCES

For locals and tourists alike, Cyprus is a safe place to travel.

BUSINESS HOURS

Opening hours vary according to whether it is winter, spring or summer.

During summer, banks in the Republic are open from 8.15 am to 12.30 pm Monday to Friday, and from 3.15 to 4.45 pm on Monday; some large banks offer a tourist service on other afternoons. In North Cyprus banks are open from 8 am to noon and in winter from 2 to 4 pm also.

In summer, shops are open from 8 am to 1 pm and 4 to 7.30 pm Monday to Saturday, closing at 2 pm on Wednesday and Saturday. In North Cyprus they are open from 4 to 7 pm every afternoon Monday to Saturday.

PUBLIC HOLIDAYS & SPECIAL EVENTS

Holidays in the Republic are the same as in Greece, with the addition of Greek Cypriot Day (1 April) and Cyprus Independence Day (1 October). Easter is the most important religious festival and just about everything stops. Fifty days earlier this is carnival time. A useful publication is the *Diary of Events* available from any CTO.

North Cyprus observes Muslim holidays, including the month of Ramadan, which means the north can sometimes shut down for periods of up to a week. It also has Turkish Cypriot Resistance Day (1 August) and the Proclamation of the Turkish Republic of Northern Cyprus (15 November).

WORK

In the Republic, work permits can only be obtained through a prospective employer applying on your behalf. The best place to look for jobs is in the *Cyprus Weekly*. During the tourist season you can sometimes pick up bar or café work in return for bed and board, payment is rare (if you don't have a permit).

If you want to work in North Cyprus, apply to the Immigration department of the Turkish Republic of Northern Cyprus (TRNC) authorities for a work permit. Your application will be considered on its merits.

ACCOMMODATION
Camping

There are seven licensed camping grounds in the Republic, mostly with limited opening times. They are all equipped with hot showers, a minimarket and a snack bar, and charge around CY£1.50 a day for a tent space and CY£1 per person per day. In the North there are two camping grounds.

Hostels

There are four HI hostels in the Republic; these are slightly cheaper if you are a member. The Cyprus Youth Hostel Association (☎ 442027) is at PO Box 1328, 1506 Lefkosia. There are no HI hostels in North Cyprus.

Hotels

Hotels in the Republic are classified from one to five stars and prices for a double room range from CY£18 to CY£112. Guesthouses cost between CY£14 and CY£22. Prices are negotiable in winter. In North Cyprus these prices are slightly lower.

Other Accommodation

In southern Cyprus you can sometimes stay overnight in a monasteries, ostensibly for free, but a donation is expected.

FOOD

Cypriot food is a combination of Greek and Turkish cuisine, based primarily on meat, salad and fruit. The local cheese is *halloumi*. The barbecue is a very popular way of cooking meat and fish, and a *meze* is a traditional meal consisting of around 20 different small dishes.

DRINKS

Cypriot wine, made in the villages of the Troodos, is excellent and Greek/Turkish coffee and instant coffee (called Nescafé) are widely available. Raki is widely available in North Cyprus, but ouzo is less frequently drunk.

ENTERTAINMENT

Restaurants sometimes have live music and there are cinemas, clubs and Internet cafés open until 2 am or later in most major towns and tourist areas.

THINGS TO BUY

Good buys include local wine and spirits, most leather items and the crafts mentioned in the Arts section.

Getting There & Away

AIR

The Republic's airports are at Larnaca and Paphos. There are scheduled and charter flights from most European cities and the Middle East (around UK£230 return from London, including tax), with discounts for students, but they are heavily booked in the high season. From Cyprus there are daily flights to Greece (CY£95), and frequent services to Israel (CY£82), Egypt (CY£94), Jordan (CY£80), Lebanon (CY£64) and Syria (CY£69) – prices include taxes.

Ercan airport in North Cyprus is not recognised by the international airline authorities, so you can't fly there direct. Turkish airlines touch down in Turkey and then continue on to North Cyprus (around UK£315 from London, including tax) and other airlines can fly you to Turkey, where you change planes.

SEA

The Republic's passenger ferry port is in Lemesos. In summer there are regular boats to Greece (CY£47) and Israel (CY£40) – prices include taxes but are deck-only. Student reductions are available. In summer there is sometimes a ferry which goes to Rhodes, Crete and Piraeus (Greece). See the Lemesos section for cruise details.

From North Cyprus there are three routes to mainland Turkey: Famagusta to Mersin (UK£9), Kyrenia to Taşucu (from UK£15.60) and, during peak season, to Alanya.

LEAVING CYPRUS

In the Republic, departure tax is CY£15-18 when leaving by sea, and CY£7 by air. In North Cyprus it is UK£3.60 by sea and UK£3.50 by air. In both areas it's normally included in the cost of your ticket.

Getting Around

You can usually make a day trip into North Cyprus from the Republic (see the Lefkosia section). It is impossible to travel in the opposite direction.

BUS

Urban and long-distance buses run Monday to Saturday and are operated by a host of private companies. There are no services on Sunday. Buses between major towns are frequent and efficient, charging around CY£1.50 for most journeys.

SERVICE TAXI

Service taxis, which take up to eight people, are run by a number of private firms and you'll usually find at least one of them operating on a Sunday. You can get to most places in the Republic, but often not direct. The fixed fares are still competitive with bus travel. Either go to the taxi office, or telephone to be picked up at your hotel.

North Cyprus only has service taxis between Kyrenia and North Lefkosia. There are also normal (more expensive) taxis everywhere.

CAR & MOTORCYCLE

Cars and 4WD vehicles are widely available for hire and cost between CY£12 and CY£50 a day. You can also rent motorbikes (from CY£9) or mopeds (CY£5) in some towns. Driving is on the left and international road signs are used.

In the Republic, children under five must not sit in the front seat and you are advised against travelling due west in the late afternoon because of the sun's glare. The blood alcohol limit is 0.09%. Any car or motorcycle license is valid in the Republic, but you must be over 21 years of age to drive a car; if you're over 18 you can ride a motorcycle of 50cc and above, and 17-year-olds can ride a motorcycle of less than 49cc. In North Cyprus you can drive from the age of 18. Officially, you need either a British or an international driving license. Both of these laws also apply to motorcycles.

Parking is cheap. Super and low-lead petrol cost 38 cents for 1L, regular costs 35 cents and diesel just 13 cents.

The Cyprus Automobile Association (☎ 313233) is at 12 Chr Mylona St, Lefkosia.

BICYCLE

Bicycles can be hired in most areas but particularly in the Troodos. Rates start from around CY£2.50 a day.

HITCHING

Hitching is easy but not common.

The Republic of Cyprus

In the Republic, which comprises 63% of the island, you'll find a real mix of Greek, eastern and western cultures. The British legacy lives on in the island's two UK military bases – at Akrotiri near Lemesos, and Dhekelia near Larnaca.

LEFKOSIA
☎ 02

Lefkosia (formerly Nicosia), is the capital, bisected by the Green Line separating the Republic from North Cyprus. According to the sign at UN-patrolled barrier at Lidras St, this is 'the last divided Capital', and a visit is essential to appreciate the island's plight. Being inland, it attracts far fewer visitors, and so is much more genuinely Cypriot than the coastal towns.

Orientation

The old town is inside the 16th-century Venetian wall and is the most interesting area for visitors; the new town sprawls without. Reduced in height and dissected by wide thoroughfares, the wall is hardly visible in places. The city centre is Plateia Eleftherias on the south-western edge of the wall. The UN crossover point (Ledra Palace Hotel checkpoint) is at the far west and Famagusta Gate is to the east. At the base of the wall there are car parks and municipal gardens.

Information

Tourist Office The CTO (☎ 444264) in the old town is in Laiki Yitonia, a fairly touristy, restored area. It is open from 8.30 am to 4 pm Monday to Friday and from 8.30 am to 2 pm on Saturday. The CTO head office (☎ 337715; fax 331644; cytour@cto.org.cy) is in the new town at 19 Leoforos Lemesou.

CYPRUS

LEFKOSIA (NICOSIA)

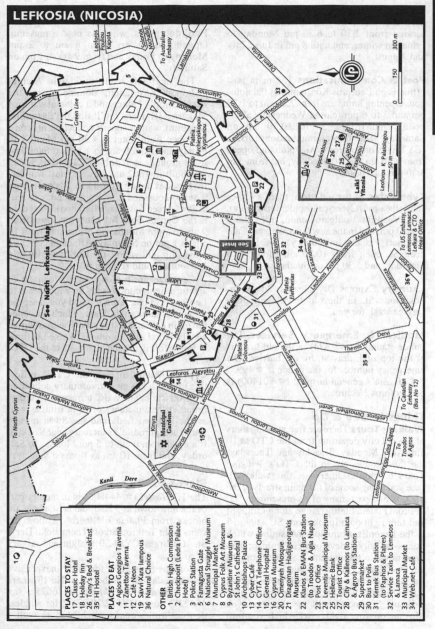

PLACES TO STAY
17 Classic Hotel
18 Holiday Inn
26 Tony's Bed & Breakfast
35 HI Hostel

PLACES TO EAT
4 Agios Georgios Taverna
11 Zanettos Taverna
12 Café Neon
19 Savvi Kara Iampous
36 Natural Choice

OTHER
1 British High Commission
2 Checkpoint (Ledra Palace Hotel)
3 Police Station
5 Famagusta Gate
6 National Struggle Museum
7 Municipal Market
8 Cyprus Folk Art Museum
9 Byzantine Museum &
   St John's Cathedral
10 Archbishops Palace
13 Cyber Café
14 CYTA Telephone Office
15 General Hospital
16 Cyprus Museum
20 Omeriyeh Mosque
21 Dragoman Hadjigeorgakis Museum
22 Klarios & EMAN Bus Station
   (to Troodos & Agia Napa)
23 Post Office
24 Leventis Municipal Museum
25 Hellenic Bank
27 Tourist Office
28 City & Kallenos (to Larnaca
   & Agros) Bus Stations
29 Supermarket
30 Bus to Polis
31 Kemek Bus Station
   (to Paphos & Platres)
32 Service Taxis to Lemesos
   & Larnaca
33 Municipal Market
34 Web.net Café

Money The Hellenic Bank, 1A Solonos St, near the CTO, has an afternoon tourist service from 2.30 to 6.30 pm Monday to Friday in winter, and until 8 pm in June, July and August.

Post & Communications The main post office is on Leoforos Konstantinou Palaiologou. Opening hours are from 7.30 am to 1.30 pm and 3 to 6 pm (closed Wednesday afternoon), and from 8.30 to 10.30 am on Saturday. The telecommunications office (CYTA) is on Leoforos Aigyptou and opens from 7.30 am to 1.30 pm daily, but from 3 to 5.30 pm on Tuesday.

Cybercafés In the old town, there's Cyber Café (theatro@Cyber-cafe.spidernet.com.cy), 15A Vasiliou Voulgaroctonou, open daily from 3 pm; and in the new town Web.net Café (webnet1@ dial.cylink.com.cy), 10C Stasandrou St, open from 10.30 am Monday to Saturday, and 5.30 pm on Sunday.

Laundry Express Dry-Cleaners at 49 Ippokratous St, in the old town, will do a service wash for you.

Medical & Emergency Services The police station (☎ 477434) in the old town is at the top of Lidras St, by the barrier. The emergency number for the police is ☎ 199.

Lefkosia's general hospital (☎ 801400) is on Leoforos Nechrou.

Things to See & Do

Walking Tours There are free walking tours of the old city departing from the CTO at 10 am every Monday, Tuesday and Thursday; the three routes are in the CTO's *Walking Tours* brochure. Otherwise, this walk will take you along some of the main streets of the old city and past many of its museums.

From Plateia Eleftherias go along Lidras St and turn right onto Ippokratous St. At No 17 is the **Leventis Municipal Museum**, which traces the city's development from prehistoric times to the present. It's open from 10 am to 4.30 pm Tuesday to Sunday.

Continue to the end of Ippokratous St, turn left onto Thrakis St and take the dogleg onto Trikoupi St. Soon you'll see the Omeriyeh Mosque on your right, after which you turn

right onto Patriarchou Grigoriou St. On the right is the 18th-century house of **Dragoman Hadjigeorgakis**, which is now a museum. Opening times are from 8 am to 2 pm Monday to Friday and from 9 am to 1 pm on Saturday.

The next left leads to Plateia Archiepiskopou Kyprianou, dominated by the **Archbishop's Palace** and a colossal statue of Makarios III. Here you'll find the **Byzantine Museum**, with a superb collection of icons. It's open from 9 am to 4.30 pm Monday to Friday and from 9 am to 1 pm on Saturday. In its grounds is **St John's Cathedral**, which was built in 1662 and has the most wonderful frescoes dating from 1736. It's open from 9 am to noon and 2 to 4 pm Monday to Saturday (closed Saturday afternoon). Next door is the **Cyprus Folk Art Museum**, open from 9 am to 5 pm Monday to Friday and from 10 am to 1 pm on Saturday. Although currently closed for renovation, the **National Struggle Museum** should re-open in 1999.

Continue north along Agiou Ioannou St and turn right onto Thiseos St, which leads to Leoforos N Foka. Turn left and you'll see the imposing **Famagusta Gate**, which was once the main entrance to the city. The most direct way back to Laiki Yitonia is to take Leoforos N Foka, following the signposts to the CTO.

Cyprus Museum Near the CYTA office, this museum has an extraordinary collection of 2000 7th-century BC terracotta figurines found at the sanctuary of Ayia Irini, as well as the original Leda and the Swan mosaic found at Aphrodite's sanctuary near Kouklia. It's open from 9 am to 5 pm Monday to Saturday, and from 10 am to 1 pm on Sunday.

Places to Stay

The HI *Hostel* (☎ 444808) is in a quiet part of the new town at 5 Hadjidakis St, about six blocks from Plateia Eleftherias. Follow the signs from Tefkrou St, off Themistokli Dervi St. It charges CY£4.50 a night and is very pleasant.

Solonos St is good for fairly inexpensive accommodation. The best is at No 13 where *Tony's Bed & Breakfast* (☎ 466752; fax 454225) costs CY£12/20/27/32 for singles/doubles/triples/quads, slightly more with a bathroom. Tony also has cheaper rooms for self-catering stays of a week or more.

Most of the more expensive hotels are found in the new town, but inside the walls at 90 Rigainis St is the three-star *Classic Hotel* (☎ 464006; fax 360072) where singles/doubles are CY£26/36, including breakfast. This option has a lot more character than the *Holiday Inn* (☎ 475131; fax 473337), 70 Rigainis St, where room-only rates are CY£65/89 single/double.

Places to Eat
For a drink during the day or in the evenings try the characterful *Café Neon* (name in Greek script), just by the Faneromeni Church. For a huge meze which only costs CY£4.50, head for *Zanettos Taverna* at 65 Trikoupi St. Also worth checking out is *Savvi Xara Iampous* (name in Greek) at 65 Solonos St and the *Agios Georgios Taverna* on the north side of the market.

In the new town, about 2km from the HI hostel, is *Natural Choice*, 11 Chytron St, where you can get excellent vegetarian food. It's open from 8.30 am to 5.30 pm.

In the old city, the *municipal market* is on Diogenous St, and in the new town there's one on the corner of Leoforos Evgenias Kai Antoniou Theodotou and Digeni Akrita St. Both open in the mornings and on Wednesday and Saturday afternoons. There's a decent *supermarket* on Plateia Solomou.

Getting There & Away
North Cyprus Depending on diplomatic relations, you're usually allowed into North Cyprus for one day, but check at the CTO first. The border crossing at the Ledra Palace Hotel is open from 8 am to 1 pm, returning at 5 pm. You simply walk to the Turkish checkpoint and pay CY£3.55 for an entry permit. Private cars can be taken over the border, but not hired ones. There is no limit to the number of times you can do this.

Air Lefkosia's international airport is in the UN buffer zone and is no longer a passenger airport.

Bus There are lots of private companies operating out of Lefkosia.

Kemek, at 3 Omirou St, off Leonidou St,

has five buses a day to Lemesos (CY£1.35; fewer on Saturday), one to Paphos (CY£2.70) and one to Platres (CY£2) at 12.15 pm. Kallenos operates from Plateia Solomou and has five or six buses a day to Larnaca (CY£1.50). Also from Plateia Solomou is a direct bus to Polis (C£Y4) at noon.

Klarios goes to Troodos (CY£1.50) once a day at 11.30 am and much more frequently to Kakopetria (CY£1.10). EMAN goes to Agia Napa (CY£2) daily at 3pm, departing from the Constanza car park.

Service Taxi Just outside the city walls near Laiki Yitonia are A Makris (☎ 466201) and Kypros (☎ 464811) at 11 and 9 Leoforos Stasinou respectively; both service Larnaca (CY£2.10) and Lemesos (CY£3).

Getting Around
The city bus station is at Plateia Solomou; Nicosia Buses operates numerous routes to and from the city and suburbs.

Also at Plateia Solomou is A Petsas & Sons (☎ 462650) where you can hire cars. To hire motorcycles ring Geofil on ☎ 466349.

There are no bicycles for rent in or around the old city.

LARNACA
☎ 04
Larnaca is a coastal resort built over the ancient city of Kition. It has a city beach, a new waterfront promenade, an old Turkish area and a fort. North of the fort, touristy cafés line the seafront, but the other side is less spoilt and much quieter.

The CTO (☎ 654322) is on Plateia Vasileos Pavlou, two blocks west of the Sun Hall Hotel. It's open from 8.15 am to 2.30 pm and 3 to 6.30 pm Monday to Friday, but is closed on Wednesday and Saturday afternoons. There is also a CTO at the airport.

There are around four Internet cafés in town. The first one was Web Café (webcafe@webcafe.com.cy) at 54, Lordou Vyronos St, a seven-minute walk south-west from the CTO.

Things to See
The site of ancient **Kition** is about 1.5km outside Larnaca. It dates back to the 13th

century BC but was completely rebuilt by the Phoenicians in the 9th century BC after an earthquake. The city walls are impressive, otherwise it's not that thrilling.

En route is the **District Archaeological Museum** where artefacts found at Kition are on display. Both Kition and the museum are open from 9 am to 2.30 pm Monday to Friday, and sometimes on a Thursday afternoon. Both are signposted from the town centre.

On Agiou Lazarou, the ornate Byzantine church of **St Lazaros** and its museum are worth a visit, as is the **medieval fort**.

Places to Stay & Eat

The nearest camping ground is *Forest Beach Camping* (☎ 644514), 8km along the beach road towards Agia Napa, but it's a bit rundown. To get there take the tourist bus from the north side of the Sun Hall Hotel.

The HI *Hostel* (☎ 621188), 27 N Rossou St, is just east of St Lazaros church and charges CY£3.50 a night; nothing to write home about. At 17 Onisillos St, about 500m west of the fort, in a very quiet part of town, is the friendly two-star *Onisillos Hotel* (☎ 651100; fax 654468). Singles/doubles with bathroom cost C£25/33, including breakfast.

North-east from here towards the sea is an area called Laiki Geitonia, where you'll find some nice bars, and a newly opened *Hard Rock Café*. South, beside the mosque, is *Prasino Amaxoudi* where you'll get good-value, freshly prepared souvlaki, doner kebab or halloumi pitta sandwiches.

South of the fort on the waterfront is *Militzis Restaurant* where all the locals eat. At the other end of town, near the CTO at 6 Stasinou St, is *1900 Art Café*. It's an art gallery, a bookshop and also a restaurant with an ever-changing menu of home-cooked Cypriot dishes for CY£3.50.

The *municipal market* is at the northern end of N Rossou St.

Getting There & Away

Bus The bus stop for Lefkosia (CY£1.50), Lemesos (CY£1.70) and Agia Napa (CY£2) is almost opposite the Dolphin Café Restaurant on the waterfront. On Sunday there is only a service to Agia Napa.

Service Taxi Acropolis (☎ 655555), opposite the police station on Leoforos Archiepiskopou Makariou III, and A Makris (☎ 652929), on the north side of the Sun Hall Hotel, operate to Lefkosia (CY£2.10) and Lemesos (CY£2.60).

Getting Around

To/From the Airport Bus No 19 from St Lazaros church goes near the airport, which is 6km away. The first bus is at 6.20 am and the last at 7 pm in summer, 5.45 pm in winter. A private taxi costs CY£3.

Bus A Makris buses run every 30 minutes from the north side of the Sun Hall Hotel to the tourist hotel area, 8km along the coast towards Agia Napa (CY£0.80 return).

Car & Motorcycle Thames (☎ 656333), next door to A Makris, rents cars, and there are also car-rental booths at the airport. You can hire motorcycles or mopeds from Anemayia (☎ 645619) on the Larnaca to Dhekelia road; ring for free delivery.

Bicycle Bicycles can be hired at Anemayia.

AGIA NAPA
☎ 03

On the coast 35km east of Larnaca is Agia Napa. Once a small fishing village with a coastline of beautiful beaches, it is now Cyprus' main package-tourist resort. As a result, it is very crowded in summer and accommodation, if not booked in advance with a tour operator, is scarce, especially since the hostel closed. (See the Larnaca and Lefkosia sections for transport details.)

LEMESOS
☎ 05

Lemesos (Limassol) is Cyprus' second-largest city and the main passenger and cargo port. Bland apartments and public gardens line the waterfront; behind these to the west is the more attractive old town with crumbling houses, a mosque, old-fashioned artisans' shops and a castle. Behind the old section sprawls the new town.

The CTO (☎ 362756) is at 15 Spyros Araouzou St on the waterfront near the old harbour. It keeps the same hours as the CTO in Larnaca.

Currently, there are about 14 Internet cafés in Lemesos. The most successful is CyberNet (cafeinfo@zenon.logos.cy.net) at 79 Eleftherias St, a couple of blocks behind the CTO. On weekdays it doesn't open until 1pm.

Things to See
The main attraction is the well-restored **castle** where Richard the Lionheart married Berengaria of Navarre in 1191 and which now houses the **Medieval Museum**. Close by, near the mosque, is a newly restored **hammam** where for CY£5 you can get a steam and sauna or a massage. It is open daily from 2 to 10 pm and all sessions are mixed.

Lemesos has a number of other museums but of greater interest are the sites to the west. Fourteen kilometres on the road to Paphos is **Kolossi Castle**, and a further 5km away are the extensive remains of **Kourion** and the nearby **Sanctuary of Apollon Ylatis.**

Places to Stay & Eat
The nearest camping ground is *Governor's Beach Camping* (☎ 632300 or 632878), 20km east of town.

The cheapest hotels are clustered in the old town, to the east of the castle. A good one with large, clean rooms is the *Luxor Guest House* (☎ 362265), 101 Agiou Andreou St, which charges CY£5 per person, no breakfast.

Otherwise, the two-star *Continental Hotel* (☎ 362530; fax 373030) on the waterfront at 137 Spyrou Araouzou St, has very pleasant singles/doubles with bathroom for CY£15/25, including breakfast.

Phylacton Arcade is a very nice spot for a drink; for an evening meal try *Mikph Mapia*, 3 Ankara St, to the left of the castle, where the 24-dish meze costs CY£5. A good place to lunch or snack is the unlikely *Richard & Berengaria* café, just by the castle.

The *municipal market* is at the northern end of Saripolou St.

Getting There & Away
Bus Kemek has frequent daily services to Lefkosia (CY£1.50) and Paphos (CY£1.50) from the corner of Enoseos and Eirinis Sts, north of the castle. From here there is also a weekday bus at noon to Agros (CY£1.50) in the Troodos Mountains.

Kallenos goes to Larnaca (CY£1.70) from the old port or from outside the CTO. From Monday to Saturday, the Kyriakos/Karydas service-taxi company has a minibus which goes to Platres (CY£1.50) at 11.30 am from its office.

Service Taxi Close to the CTO at 65 Spyros Araouzou St, Acropolis Taxis (☎ 366766) has taxis every half-hour to Lefkosia (CY£3), Larnaca (CY£2.60) and Paphos (CY£2.30). Kyriakos/Karydas (☎ 364114), at 21 Thessalonikis St, travels the same routes.

Ferry You can buy ferry tickets from any travel agency or direct from Salamis Tours Ltd (☎ 355555) or Poseidon Lines (☎ 745666). The port is 5km south-west of town. See the Getting There & Away section at the start of this chapter.

Getting Around
The city bus station is on A Themistokleous St, close to the municipal market. Bus No 1 goes to the port, bus No 16-17 goes to Kolossi and bus No 30 goes north-east along the seafront. Frequent buses also run from the castle to Kourion and its beach. From April to October there's a daily Governor's Beach bus which leaves from the CTO 9.50 am, returning at 4.30 pm.

Lipsos Rent-a-Car (☎ 365295) is at 6 Richard & Berengaria St (opposite the castle). The Oceanic Supermarket at 232 Oktovriou 28 St rents mopeds and bicycles.

Cruises Two and three-day cruises depart from Lemesos all year. They go to Haifa (Israel), Port Said (Egypt), a selection of Greek islands, and sometimes (in summer) to Lebanon. You can book at any travel agent, but these are not designed for one-way travel.

TROODOS MASSIF
☎ 05
The mountains of the Troodos region are beautiful with their secluded Byzantine monasteries, 15th-century frescoed churches, small wine-making villages, pine forests and numerous walking trails. In summer the area

offers some respite from the heat, and in winter there's enough snow to ski.

The CTO (☎ 421316) in the square at Platres is open from 9 am to 3.30 pm Monday to Friday and from 9 am to 2.30 pm on Saturday. There's enough in this area to keep you busy for at least a week.

Things to See & Do

The **Kykkos Monastery**, 20km west of Pedhoulas, is the best known but also the most touristy of the monasteries. Although it dates from the 12th century, it has been completely renovated and all the mosaics, frescoes and stonework are new. It also has a museum containing priceless religious icons and relics.

In Pedhoulas is the small, World Heritage-listed **Church of Archangelos**, with frescoes dating from 1474. The key to the church is at the house with the light-green door, to the right of the church as you face the entrance. Another fine church is **St Nicholaos of the Roof**, near Kakopetria, open from 9 am to 4 pm Tuesday to Saturday, and from 11 am to 4 pm on Sunday.

Omodos is in the wine-growing region, almost directly south of Pedhoulas, with local wine available for sale and tastings. You can also visit **Socrates' Traditional House**, a 500-year-old house with a wine cellar and period distillery. Also in Omodos is the **Stavros Monastery,** more intimate than the larger, more renowned ones.

The walking in this area is superb and well marked; ask at the CTO for details.

Places to Stay & Eat

Even though there are hotels or rooms in almost all the villages, there aren't enough so in July and August you'd be wise to book. Outside these months, you can negotiate on prices.

The only reason to stay in Troodos itself, more a touristy hill station than a village, is the walks. Two kilometres north, in a pine forest, there is a *camping ground* (☎ 421624) which is open from May to October. The Troodos HI *Hostel* (☎ 422400) is usually open from April to October (depending on the weather) and charges CY£5 for the first night and CY£4 thereafter. Rather more luxurious is the three-star *Troodos Hotel*

(☎ 421635; fax 422500), where singles/doubles cost CY£27/38, including breakfast.

A good regional base is Platres. The *Pafsilypon Hotel* (☎ 421738) is a lovely old place, very cheap, but open irregularly. More reliable is the Swiss-style *Petit Palais* (☎ 421723; fax 421065), where en suite rooms with breakfast cost CY£19/32 in high season. These hotels, and others, are signposted.

The best restaurant in Platres is the good-value *Kalidonia*. Just outside Platres on the road to Troodos is the *Psilo Dendro* lunch restaurant and trout farm, where fresh trout costs CY£4.40.

Getting There & Away

There's a daily bus at 5 am from Platres to Lefkosia (CY£2) via Pedhoulas and a number of other villages, and a daily minibus at 7 am from Platres to Lemesos (CY£1.50). At 7 am there's a daily bus from Troodos to Lefkosia (CY£1.50), and from Agros to Lemesos (CY£1.50). From Kakopetria there are about 12 daily buses to Lefkosia (CY£1.10). Otherwise, there are service taxis in the main square at Platres.

PAPHOS
☎ 06

Once the capital of Cyprus, Paphos has always been historically and mythologically important. Today it consists of Kato (lower) Paphos on the coast, where you'll find most of the places of interest, and Paphos, which is 1km inland. Kato Paphos is full of huge hotels and expensive bars and eateries which spoil the old harbour and port area. Paphos itself is much more pleasant, with an authentic life of its own.

The tourist office (☎ 253341) is at 3 Gladstonos St, just down from Paphos' main square. Its opening hours are the same as Larnaca's CTO, although in July and August it often closes at 3.45 pm. There's another tourist office at the airport.

The most central Internet café is Surf Café (surfcafe@cytanet.com.cy) at 1 Glastonos St, very close to the CTO.

Things to See

There is lots to see in Paphos but most renowned are the **Paphos Mosaics,** well-preserved (if dusty) floors from the villas of 3rd-century AD Roman nobles. They mostly depict mythological themes, emphasising the exploits of Dionysos, the uninhibited God of Wine. The site is open daily, closing at 7.30 pm in summer and 5 pm in winter. On the way to the mosaics you pass the remains of a **Byzantine castle** and an **odeon**.

About 2km north of Kato Paphos, on the coastal road to Polis, are the **Tombs of the Kings** which date from the 3rd century BC. These underground tombs are fascinating to explore and the site opens the same hours as the Paphos Mosaics.

Places to Stay & Eat
The nearest camping ground is *Zenon Gardens* (☎ 242277), 5km south of Kato Paphos and behind the summer cinema. It is close to the beach and you camp in the shade of trees.

The HI *Hostel* (☎ 232588) is quite a way north of Paphos at 37 Leoforos Eleftheriou Venizelou. To get there, walk up Leoforos Evagora Pallikaridi and it is off on the right. The hostel is unkempt and costs CY£4.50.

At the top of Gladstonos St is Leoforos Archiepiskopou Makariou III where, at No 91, the one-star *Kiniras* (☎ 241604; fax 242176) provides bed and breakfast for CY£15 per person. All rooms have private facilities and there's a very pleasant garden at the back. At 2 Eves Malioti St, is the friendly two-star *Axiothea Hotel* (☎ 232866; fax 245790) where singles/doubles with breakfast cost CY£23/31.50. On the high ground to the south of the CTO, it has a glass-fronted bar and reception with wonderful views of the sea – perfect for sunset watching.

A highly recommended restaurant in Paphos is *Fettas Corner* at 33 Iannis Agrotis St, not far from the Axiothea Hotel. It is where the locals eat and a large meal for two with wine will cost around CY£13. In Kato Paphos try the family-owned *Ifigenia* at 2 Agamemnonos St, opposite the Sofianna Hotel.

The *municipal market* is near the covered bazaar area, not far from the Kiniras.

Getting There & Away
Bus The Amaroza and Kemek bus companies operate to Polis, Lemesos and Lefkosia.

Their office is at 79 Leoforos Evagora Pallikaridi, north of Paphos' main square; there are around 10 buses a day to Polis (CY£1) and one to Lemesos, which continues to Lefkosia at 2.30 pm. Alepa Ltd (☎ 231755) also has daily buses to Lemesos (CY£2) and Lefkosia (CY£4). If you book in advance they'll pick you up from your hotel; otherwise they leave from the urban bus station, and outside the municipal market.

Service Taxi Karydas/Kyriakos (☎ 232424) at 9 Leoforos Evagora Pallikaridi and A Makris (☎ 246802) at 2 Grammou St, opposite the police station, have service taxis to Lemesos (CY£2.30) every half-hour.

Getting Around
There are no buses or service taxis to/from the airport; a normal taxi costs CY£7.

The urban bus station is at Karavella Parking, behind the Amaroza bus company office. Bus No 1 goes to Geroskipou Tourist Beach, 9km north of Paphos; bus No 11 goes to Kato Paphos; and bus No 10 goes to Coral Bay. They all stop at the municipal market.

D Antoniades Ltd (☎ 233301), 111-113 Leoforos Evagora Pallikaridi, rents mountain bikes, motorcycles and mopeds.

POLIS
☎ 06
In the heart of Chrysochou Bay, near the wild, remote hiking region of the Akamas Peninsula, is the large village of Polis. At present it isn't half as spoilt by tourism as Cyprus' other coastal towns. However, an enormous five-star hotel has just been built at the gateway to the protected Akamas area, and others look to follow so Polis' charm and serenity is under threat.

The new CTO (☎ 322468) at 2 Agiou Nikolaou is very central and opens from 9 am to 1 pm and 2.30 to 5.30 pm Monday to Saturday, but closes Wednesday and Saturday afternoons. There are plenty of mountain bike, motorcycle and car-rental companies.

Things to See & Do
The **Akamas Peninsula** is a rugged patchwork of barren rock and lush vegetation, with a wide variety of flora and fauna, including

some rare species. A network of paths criss-cross the peninsula, making it ideal for walkers.

At the start of these trails are the famous and much-visited **Baths of Aphrodite**, 10km west of Polis. According to one legend, the goddess bathed there to renew her virginity after encounters with her many lovers.

In the village, Byzantine frescoes have recently been uncovered in the church of **Agios Andronikos**. The key is held at the CTO.

Places to Stay & Eat

About 1km north of Polis towards the sea is a *camping ground* (☎ 321526), surrounded by eucalyptus trees; it is signposted from the town centre. Many houses have rooms to rent from CY£7, and there are plenty of apartments for hire. Otherwise, a good hotel is the *Akamas* (☎ 321521; fax 321561), on the main street, where smallish rooms (mostly with wonderful views) cost CY£5 a night. The hotel has a good restaurant too.

There are now lots of cafés and restaurants, but the most popular eatery remains the *Arsinoe Fish Tavern* where you can get a delicious fish meze for CY£5.50, and other fresh fish dishes.

Getting There & Away

The New Amaroza bus company office is on Kyproleontos St, beside the Old Town Restaurant. It runs 10 buses a day to Paphos (CY£1) and in summer also has services to Latsi (35 cents) and the Baths of Aphrodite (50 cents). At 9.30 am there's also a daily bus from the main square to Lefkosia (CY£4).

North Cyprus

The Turkish Republic of Northern Cyprus (TRNC) occupies 37% of the island. Almost completely unspoilt by tourism, it has some of the island's best beaches, as well as awe-inspiring monasteries, archaeological sites and castles.

In this section, Greek place names are used with the Turkish in brackets.

NORTH LEFKOSIA (LEFKOŞA)

North Lefkosia, the capital of North Cyprus, is a quiet city with some good examples of

Gothic and Ottoman architecture. Although it can sometimes seem populated only by soldiers, if you wander the backstreets of the old town you'll find lots of locals toiling away in small workshops, making or mending a whole variety of everyday articles.

Orientation

The city centre is Atatürk Square in the old city. Girne Caddesi is the main thoroughfare which runs north from Atatürk Square to the well-preserved Girne Gate. To the east of the square is the Selimiye quarter, where you'll find most of the interesting places.

Information

Inside Girne Gate there's a new tourist office with all the relevant maps and brochures for North Cyprus. There's also a new tourist office (☎ 22 79112; fax 22 85625) at the Ministry of Tourism, about 2km north on Bedrettin Demirel Caddesi in the new town. The Girne tourist office is closed on Sunday, but the other one is open.

The main post office is on Sarayönü Sokak, just west of Atatürk Square. The telecommunications office is on Kizilay Sokak, in the new town, west of the telecom tower; it's open daily from 8 am to midnight.

In an emergency ring ☎ 112 for the hospital, ☎ 155 for the police or ☎ 199 for the fire station.

Cybercafés The easiest to find is Super Computer Internet Café (info@super-cyprus .com), 19 Galleria Muhtar Yusuf, to the north of the long-distance bus terminal.

Things to See & Do

The **Turkish Museum** is at the northern end of Girne Caddesi in a 17th-century Islamic monastery which was used by 19th-century dervishes (Muslim ascetics), and now displays dervish artefacts. Extending from the museum is a long, thin mausoleum containing the tombs of 16 sheikhs. The museum is open from 8 am to 5 pm Monday to Friday.

The old quarter east of Atatürk Square is dominated by the **Selimiye Mosque**, which was originally a cathedral built between 1209 and 1326. Next door is the **Bedesten**, a building comprising two churches, which became an Ottoman bazaar.

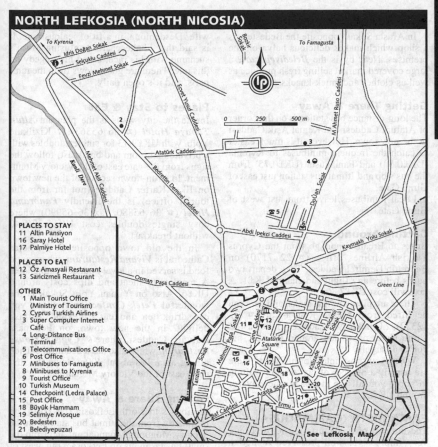

NORTH LEFKOSIA (NORTH NICOSIA)

To Kyrenia
Idris Doğan Sokak
Selçuklu Caddesi
Fevzi Mehmet Sokak
To Famagusta
Bedir Sokak

Evvet Yusuf Caddesi
M Ahmet Ruso Caddesi

0   250   500 m

Atatürk Caddesi

Mehmet Akif Caddesi
Kenti Dere

Bedrettin Demirel Caddesi

Doğan Sokak

Abdi İpekci Caddesi

Kaymaklı Yolu Sokak

PLACES TO STAY
11 Altin Pansiyon
16 Saray Hotel
17 Palmiye Hotel

PLACES TO EAT
12 Öz Amasyali Restaurant
13 Saricizmeli Restaurant

OTHER
1   Main Tourist Office
    (Ministry of Tourism)
2   Cyprus Turkish Airlines
3   Super Computer Internet
    Café
4   Long-Distance Bus
    Terminal
5   Telecommunications Office
6   Post Office
7   Minibuses to Famagusta
8   Minibuses to Kyrenia
9   Tourist Office
10 Turkish Museum
14 Checkpoint (Ledra Palace)
15 Post Office
18 Büyük Hammam
19 Selimiye Mosque
20 Bedesten
21 Belediyepuzari

Osman Pasa Caddesi

Green Line

Girne Caddesi
Tenarmi Sokak
Atatürk Square
Mahmut Paşa Sokak
Tanzim Sokak
Kızılzade Sokak
Araşta Sokak
Ermu Caddesi
Baf Caddesi

See Lefkosia Map

The **Büyük Hammam**, by the Antalya Pansiyon, is a world-famous Turkish bath frequented by locals and tourists of both genders. A steam bath and a massage (male masseurs only) costs UK£7.80.

Places to Stay & Eat

Most of the budget hotels are around the Selimiye Mosque area and in the streets east of Girne Caddesi. They all have dormitory-style rooms where a bed costs around UK£3, but are pretty dire places.

Better is the *Palmiye Hotel* (☎ 22 87733) on Mecidiye Sokak, where rooms costs UK£3.25/6.50 for singles/doubles. Also passable is the *Altin Pansiyon* (☎ 22 85049), 63 Girne Caddesi, which costs UK£5.20/7.80 for singles/doubles without breakfast. The best hotel in the old town is the three-star *Saray* (☎ 22 83115; fax 22 84808) on Atatürk Square charging UK£18.60/30 for singles/doubles, with breakfast.

On Girne Caddesi there are two friendly restaurants, *Saricizmeli* and *Öz Amasyali*, which are open all day. A substantial plate of mixed fare will cost around UK£3 in either. There's also a restaurant in the *Saray Hotel*.

In Arasta Sokak, opposite the Bedesten, is a shop which makes delicious halva on the premises. Near by is the *Belediyepazari*, a large covered market selling fresh produce as well as clothes and knick-knacks.

Getting There & Away

The long-distance bus station is on the corner of Atatürk Caddesi and Kemal Aşik Caddesi in the new town. However, it is much easier to catch the frequent minibuses to Kyrenia (UK£0.50) and Famagusta (UK£0.75) from the bus stop and Itimat bus station just east of Girne Gate.

Local minibuses leave from just west of Girne Gate.

Getting Around

Buses to Ercan airport go from the Cyprus Turkish Airlines office (☎ 22 7170) on Bedrettin Demirel Caddesi. They depart two hours before any flight and charge UK£1. A taxi will cost UK£7.80.

There are plenty of taxi ranks, and cars can be hired from Memo Rent-a-Car (☎ 22 72322), 2 Cumhuriyet Caddesi, to the east of Girne Gate; prices are around UK£25, but you can bargain.

When you cross into North Cyprus there are usually a number of taxi drivers waiting to show you all the sights in one day for around UK£52.

FAMAGUSTA (GAZIMAĞUSA)

The old part of Famagusta is enclosed by a very impressive, well-preserved Venetian wall. The tourist office (☎ 36 62864) is on Fevzi Cakmak Caddesi outside the wall, about 300m east of the **Victory Monument** (a huge black monstrosity depicting soldiers in battle) on the right.

Things to See

Famagusta's **St Nicholas Cathedral**, now the Mustafa Pasha Mosque, is the finest example of Cypriot Gothic architecture. Rather incongruously, a small minaret perches on top of one of its ruined towers.

Othello's Castle, part of the city walls and battlements, was built by the Lusignans in the 13th century. According to legend, it was

here that Christophore Moro (Venetian governor of Cyprus from 1506 to 1508) killed his wife, Desdemona, in a fit of jealous rage. It is said that Shakespeare, confusing Moro's surname with his race, based his tragedy on this tale. There are good views from the ramparts, and it's open daily.

Places to Stay & Eat

Inside the city walls is the pleasant *Altun Tabaya Hotel* (☎ 36 65363), 7 Kizilkule Yolu, with UK£9/13 for singles/doubles with a private bathroom and breakfast; follow the signs from the gate east of the Victory Monument. In a run-down section of the new town on Ilker Karter Caddesi (not far from the tourist office) is the friendly *Panorama Hotel* (☎ 36 65880; fax 36 65990) where cosy singles/doubles cost UK£5.20/5.40 without breakfast.

In the old town opposite St Nicholas Cathedral is *Viyana Restaurant,* where good food is served in a lovely outside eating area. A meal with meat and dips costs around UK£6. Also on Yiman Yolu Sokak is the wonderful *Petek Confectioner* where you can drink tea and eat cake and Turkish delight. In the new town, on Polatpaşa Bulvari Caddesi, there's *Cyprus House Restaurant* which also has a beautiful outside dining area. It's about 400m down the first right east of the Victory Monument.

Getting There & Away

Minibuses to North Lefkosia (UK£0.75) go frequently from the Itimat bus station on the Victory Monument roundabout and from the small bus terminus on Lefkoşa Yolu, west of the Monument. Also from here minibuses for Kyrenia leave every half hour or so (UK£0.90).

Ferries to Mersin in Turkey leave on Tuesday, Thursday and Friday from the port behind Canbulat Yolu. They take eight hours and the trip costs about UK£9 one way. You can buy tickets from 3 Bulent Ecevit Bulvari (☎ 36 65995; fax 36 67840)

SALAMIS

Nine kilometres north of Famagusta is the huge site of Cyprus' most important classical city. Among many other remains, there is a fully restored Roman amphitheatre, a gymnasium still surrounded by the majority of its marble columns with adjacent baths, and some mosaics. The site is open daily from 8 am to 6 pm in summer. There is a bar/restaurant (with very clean western-style toilets) in the car park by the ticket office.

Allow at least half a day here as there is also a long sandy beach next to the site, and a camping ground. There are no buses to Salamis and a return taxi will cost UK£8.

KYRENIA (GIRNE)

Kyrenia is a very attractive town built around a horseshoe-shaped harbour dominated on one side by an impressive Byzantine castle. Behind the harbour is Hürriyet Caddesi which runs from the town hall roundabout westward; at the very far end on the left you'll find the tourist office (☎ 81 52145). The waterfront is lined with lovely outdoor cafés and restaurants where it is delightful to sit and watch the boats.

At No 10 on Ecevit Caddesi, running south from the roundabout, you'll find Café Online (cafeonline@cc.emu.edu.tr).

Things to See

The star attraction of the castle is the **Shipwreck Museum**, which houses the world's oldest shipwreck and its cargo. The ship is believed to have sunk in a storm near Kyrenia around 3000 BC. The castle was built by the Byzantines as a defence against marauding Arabs. Both the castle and the museum are open from 8 am to 5 pm daily.

Places to Stay & Eat

There's lots of accommodation in Kyrenia, with much of the cheaper options along Ecevit Caddessi and between Hürriyet Caddesi and the harbour. The *Bingöl Guest House* (☎ 81 52749) on the main roundabout is good and central and costs UK£7.80/13 for singles/doubles with bathroom and breakfast; they also have triples and quads. At the same price is the *New Bristol Hotel* (☎ 81 56570; fax 81 57365), 42 Hürriyet Caddesi, which is a really pleasant place to stay. If you want a sea view and old-fashioned charm, the *Girne Harbour Lodge Motel* (☎ 81 57392; fax 81 53744) at the west end of the harbour charges UK£13/21 singles/doubles with bathroom and breakfast.

Little Arif's Restaurant, on the same side of the road as the New Bristol Hotel, is very good value; turn right into a cul-de-sac opposite the European Travel Services office. You can't really go wrong with any of the restaurants and cafés on the harbour, and they all have such a picturesque view. Try the *Set Fish Restaurant* where a fresh seafood dinner costs UK£8.

Getting There & Away

The long-distance bus station is on Ecevit Caddesi in the south of the new town. Minibuses to Famagusta (UK£0.90) and North Lefkosia (UK£0.50), as well as shared taxis to North Lefkosia (UK£0.50), all depart from the roundabout in front of the town hall.

There are express boats to Taşucu in Turkey daily at 9.30 am, taking three hours. There's also a daily ferry which takes about seven hours. One-way tickets cost UK£21 and UK£15.60 respectively; tickets can be bought from the passenger lounge at the port or from Fergün Shipping Co Ltd (☎ 81 52344) in front of the town hall. During peak season there is sometimes also a ferry to Alanya in Turkey.

France

France's most salient characteristic is its exceptional diversity. The largest country in Western Europe, France stretches from the rolling hills of the north to the seemingly endless beaches of the south; from the wild coastline of Brittany to the icy crags of the Alps, with cliff-lined canyons, dense forest and vineyards in between. France's towns and cities also hold many charms. Whether strolling along grand boulevards, sitting at a café terrace or picnicking in the beautiful public parks, it's easy to sense the famous *joie de vivre* of the country. Outstanding museums and galleries are also a nationwide phenomenon.

Over the centuries, France has received more immigrants than any other country in Europe. From the ancient Celtic Gauls and Romans to the more recent arrivals from France's former colonies in Indochina and Africa, these peoples have introduced new elements of culture, cuisine and art, all of which have contributed to France's unique and diverse civilisation.

At one time, France was on the western edge of Europe. Today, as Europe moves towards unification of one sort or another, it is at the crossroads: between England and Italy, Belgium and Spain, North Africa and Scandinavia. Of course, this is exactly how the French have always regarded their country – at the very centre of things.

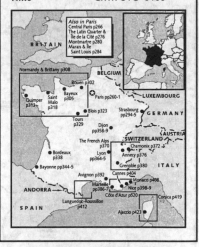

Facts about France

HISTORY
Prehistory

Human presence in France is known to date from the middle Palaeolithic period, about 90,000 to 40,000 years ago. Around 25,000 BC the Stone Age Cro-Magnon people appeared on the scene and left their mark in the form of cave paintings and engravings. The most visible evidence of France's Neolithic age are the menhirs and dolmens dating from 4000 to 2500 BC. With the dawning of the Bronze Age, and the demand for copper and tin for bronze, trade began to develop between France and the rest of Europe around 2000 BC.

Ancient & Medieval History

The Celtic Gauls moved into what is now France between 1500 and 500 BC. By about 600 BC, they had established trading links with the Greeks, whose colonies on the Mediterranean coast included Massilia (Marseille). After several centuries of conflict between Rome and the Gauls, Julius Caesar's legions took control of the territory around 52 BC, when a revolt led by the Gallic chief Vercingétorix was crushed. Christianity was introduced to Roman Gaul early in the 2nd century AD.

FRANCE

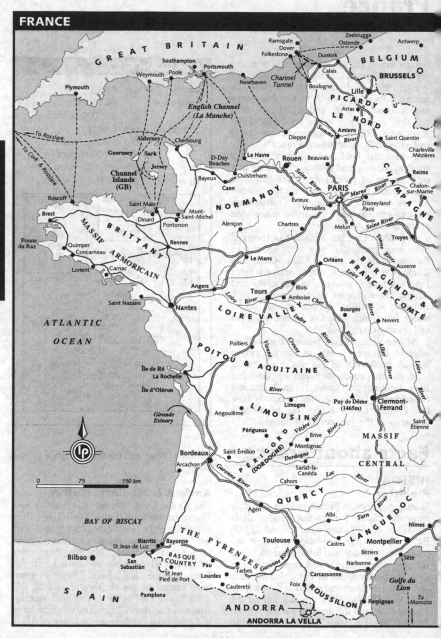

FRANCE

FRANCE

France remained under Roman rule until the 5th century, when the Franks (thus 'France') and other Germanic groups overran the country. These peoples adopted important parts of Gallo-Roman civilisation – including Christianity – and their eventual assimilation resulted in a fusion of Germanic, Roman and Celtic cultures.

Two Frankish dynasties, the Merovingians and the Carolingians, ruled from the 5th to the 10th century. The Frankish tradition by which the king was succeeded by all of his sons led to power struggles and the eventual disintegration of the kingdom into a collection of small, feudal states. In 732, Charles Martel defeated the Moors at Poitiers, thus ensuring that France would not follow Spain and come under Muslim rule.

Charles Martel's grandson, Charlemagne, significantly extended the power and boundaries of the kingdom and was crowned Holy Roman Emperor (Emperor of the West) in 800. But during the 9th century, the Scandinavian Vikings (also known as the Normans, ie Northmen) began raiding France's western coast. They eventually settled in the lower Seine Valley and formed the Duchy of Normandy in the early 10th century.

The Capetian dynasty was founded in 987, when the nobles elected Hugh Capet as their king. At the time, the king's domains were quite modest, consisting mostly of small pieces of land around Paris and Orléans.

Under William the Conqueror, the Duke of Normandy, Norman forces occupied England in 1066, making Normandy – and later, Plantagenet-ruled England – a formidable rival of the kingdom of France. A further third of France came under the control of the English Crown in 1154, when Eleanor of Aquitaine married Henry of Anjou (later King Henry II of England). The subsequent battle between France and England for control of Aquitaine and the vast English territories in France lasted for three centuries.

The struggle between the Capetians and the English king Edward III (a member of the Plantagenet family) over the powerful French throne set off the Hundred Years' War, which was fought on and off from 1337 to 1453. The Black Death ravaged the country in 1348, killing about a third of the population, but the plague only briefly interrupted the fighting.

FRANCE

In 1415, French forces were defeated at Agincourt; in 1420, the English took control of Paris, and two years later King Henry IV of England became king of France. Just when it seemed that the Plantagenets had pulled off a dynastic union of England and France, a 17-year-old peasant girl known to history as Jeanne d'Arc (Joan of Arc) surfaced in 1429 and rallied the French troops at Orléans. She was captured, convicted of heresy by a court of French ecclesiastics and burned at the stake two years later, but her efforts helped to turn the war in favour of the French. With the exception of Calais, the English were expelled from French territory in 1453.

The Renaissance

The ideals and aesthetics of the Italian Renaissance arrived in France towards the end of the 15th century, introduced in part by the French aristocracy returning from military campaigns in Italy. The influence was most evident during the reign of François I, and the chateaux of Fontainebleau, near Paris, and Chenonceau in the Loire are good examples of Renaissance architectural style.

The Reformation

By the 1530s the position of the Protestant Reformation sweeping Europe had been strengthened in France by the ideas of the Frenchman John Calvin, an exile in Geneva. The Edict of January (1562), which afforded the Protestants certain rights, was violently opposed by ultra-Catholic nobles, whose fidelity to their religion was mixed with a desire to strengthen their power base in the provinces.

The Wars of Religion (1562-98) involved three groups: the Huguenots (French Protestants); the Catholic League, led by the House of Guise; and the Catholic monarchy. The fighting severely weakened the position of the king and brought the French state close to disintegration. The most outrageous massacre took place in Paris in 1572, when some 3000 Huguenots who had come to Paris to celebrate the wedding of Henry of Navarre were slaughtered in the Saint Bartholomew's Day Massacre (24 August).

Henry of Navarre, a Huguenot who had embraced Catholicism, eventually became King Henry IV. In 1598, he promulgated the Edict of Nantes, which guaranteed the Huguenots freedom of conscience and many civil and political rights. It was revoked by Louis XIV less than 100 years later.

Louis XIV & the Ancien Régime

Le Roi Soleil (the Sun King) ascended the throne in 1643 at the age of five and ruled until 1715. Throughout his long reign, he sought to extend the power of the French monarchy – bolstered by claims of divine right – both at home and abroad. He involved France in a long series of costly wars that gained it territory but nearly bankrupted the treasury. Louis XIV was not known for his parsimony domestically either, and poured huge sums of money into building his extravagant palace at Versailles.

His successor, Louis XV (ruled 1715-74), was followed by the incompetent – and later universally despised – Louis XVI. As the 18th century progressed, new economic and social circumstances rendered the old order (ancien régime) dangerously at odds with the needs of the country. The regime was further weakened by the anti-establishment and anti-clerical ideas of the Enlightenment, whose leading lights included Voltaire, Rousseau and Montesquieu. But entrenched vested interests, a cumbersome power structure and royal lassitude delayed reform until it was too late.

The Seven Years' War (1756-63), fought by France and Austria against Britain and Prussia, was one of a series of ruinous wars pursued by Louis XV, culminating in the loss of France's flourishing colonies in Canada, the West Indies and India to the British. It was in part to avenge these losses that Louis XVI sided with the colonists in the American War of Independence. But the Seven Years' War cost a fortune and, even more disastrous for the monarchy, it helped to disseminate in France the radical democratic ideas which the American Revolution had thrust onto the world stage.

The French Revolution

By the late 1780s, Louis XVI and his queen, Marie Antoinette, had managed to alienate virtually every segment of society – from enlightened groups to conservatives. When the king tried to neutralise the power of the more reform-minded delegates at a meeting of the Estates General in 1789, the urban masses took to the streets and, on 14 July, a Parisian mob stormed the Bastille prison – the ultimate symbol of the despotism of the ancien régime.

At first, the Revolution was in the hands of relative moderates. France was declared a constitutional monarchy and various reforms were made, including the adoption of the Declaration of the Rights of Man. But as the masses armed themselves against the external threat to the Revolution posed by Austria, Prussia and the many exiled French nobles, patriotism and nationalism melded with revolutionary fervour, thereby popularising and radicalising the Revolution. It was not long before the moderate, republican Girondists (Girondins in French) lost power to the radical Jacobins, led by Robespierre, Danton and Marat who established the First Republic in 1792, after Louis XVI proved unreliable as a constitutional monarch. In January 1793, Louis was guillotined in what is now Place de la Concorde in Paris. In March, the Jacobins set up the notorious Committee of Public Safety. This body had virtually dictatorial control over the country during the Reign of Terror (September 1793 to July 1794), which saw religious freedoms revoked and churches desecrated.

By autumn, the Reign of Terror was in full swing, and by the middle of 1794 some 17,000 people had been beheaded. In the end, the Revolution turned on its own, and many of its leaders, including Robespierre, followed their victims to the guillotine.

Napoleon

In the resulting chaos, the leaders of the French military began disregarding instructions from the increasingly corrupt and tyrannical Directory (the executive power in Paris), pursuing instead their own ambitions on the battlefield. One dashing young general by the name of Napoleon Bonaparte was particularly successful in the Italian campaign of the war against Austria, and his victories soon turned him into an independent political force. In 1799, when it appeared that the Jacobins were again on the ascendancy in the legislature, Napoleon overthrew the discredited Directory and assumed power himself.

At first, Napoleon took the title of First Consul. In 1802, a referendum declared him 'consul for life' and his birthday became a national holiday. By 1804, when he had himself crowned Emperor of the French by Pope Pius VII at Notre Dame Cathedral in Paris, the scope and nature of Napoleon's ambitions were obvious to all. But to consolidate and legitimise his authority, Napoleon needed more victories on the battlefield. So began a seemingly endless series of wars in which France came to control most of Europe. But in 1812, in an attempt to do away with his last major rival on the continent, Tsar Alexander I, Napoleon invaded Russia. Although his Grande Armée (Grand Army) captured Moscow, it was wiped out shortly after by the brutal Russian winter. Prussia and Napoleon's other enemies quickly recovered from their earlier defeats, and less than two years after the fiasco in Russia, the Allied armies entered Paris. Napoleon abdicated and left France for his tiny Mediterranean island-kingdom of Elba.

At the Congress of Vienna (1814-15), the Allies restored the House of Bourbon to the French throne, installing Louis XVI's brother as Louis XVIII (Louis XVII, Louis XVI's son, had died in exile in 1795). But in March 1815, Napoleon escaped from Elba, landed in southern France and gathered a large army as he marched northward towards Paris. His 'Hundred Days' back in power ended when his forces were defeated by the English at Waterloo in Belgium. Napoleon was exiled to the remote South Atlantic island of Saint Helena, where he died in 1821.

Although reactionary in some ways – slavery was re-established in the colonies, for instance – Napoleon instituted a number of important reforms, including a reorganisation of the judicial system and the promulgation of a new legal code, the Code Civil (or Napoleonic Code), which forms the basis of the French legal system (and many others in Europe) to this day. More importantly, he preserved the essence of the changes wrought by the Revolution. Napoleon is therefore remembered by the French as a great hero.

The 19th Century

The 19th century was a chaotic one for France. Louis XVIII's reign (1815-24) was dominated by the struggle between extreme monarchists, who wanted a return to the ancien régime, and those who saw the changes wrought by the Revolution as irreversible. Charles X (ruled 1824-30) handled the struggle between reactionaries and liberals with great ineptitude and was overthrown in the July Revolution of 1830. Louis-Philippe (ruled 1830-48), an ostensibly constitutional monarch of upper bourgeois sympathies and tastes, was then chosen by parliament to head what became known as the July Monarchy.

Louis-Philippe was in turn overthrown in the February Revolution of 1848, in whose wake the Second Republic was established. In presidential elections held that year, Napoleon's undistinguished nephew Louis-Napoleon Bonaparte was overwhelmingly elected. A legislative deadlock led Louis-Napoleon to lead a coup d'état in 1851, after which he was proclaimed Napoleon III, Emperor of the French.

The second empire lasted from 1852 until 1870. During this period, France enjoyed significant economic growth. But as his uncle had done, Napoleon III embroiled France in a number of conflicts, including the disastrous Crimean War (1853-56). It was the Prussians, however, who ended the second empire. In 1870, the Prussian prime minister Bismarck goaded Napoleon III into declaring war on Prussia. Within months the thoroughly unprepared French army had been defeated and the emperor taken prisoner.

When news of the debacle reached the French capital, the Parisian masses took to the streets and demanded that a republic be declared. The Third Republic began as a provisional government of national defence – the Prussians were, at the time, advancing on Paris. But in the Assemblée Nationale (National Assembly) elections of February 1871 (required by the armistice which had been signed after a four-month siege of Paris by the Prussians), the republicans, who had called on the nation to continue resistance, lost to the monarchists, who had campaigned on a peace platform.

As expected, the monarchist-controlled National Assembly ratified the Treaty of Frankfurt (1871). However, when ordinary Parisians heard of its harsh terms – a five

billion franc war indemnity and surrender of the provinces of Alsace and Lorraine – they revolted against the government. The Communards, as the supporters of the Paris Commune were known, took over the city but were slowly pushed back in bloody fighting in which several thousand rebels were killed. A further 20,000 or so Communards, mostly from the working class, were summarily executed.

The greatest moral and political crisis of the Third Republic was the infamous Dreyfus Affair, which began in 1894 when a Jewish army officer named Captain Alfred Dreyfus was framed as a German spy, court-martialled and sentenced to life imprisonment. Despite bitter opposition from the army command, right-wing politicians and many Catholic groups, the case was eventually reopened and Dreyfus vindicated. The affair greatly discredited both the army and the Church. The result was more rigorous civilian control of the military and, in 1905, the legal separation of church and state.

WWI

Central to France's entry into WWI was the desire to regain Alsace and Lorraine, lost to Germany in 1871. This was achieved but at immense human cost: of the eight million French men who were called to arms, 1.3 million were killed and almost one million crippled. The war was officially ended by the Treaty of Versailles in 1919, whose severe terms (Germany was to pay US$33 billion in reparations) were heavily influenced by the uncompromising French prime minister Georges Clemenceau.

WWII

During the 1930s the French, like the British, did their best to appease Hitler, but two days after the 1939 German invasion of Poland, the two countries reluctantly declared war on Germany. By June of the following year, France had capitulated. The British expeditionary force sent to help the French barely managed to avoid capture by retreating to Dunkirk and crossing the English Channel in small boats. The hugely expensive Maginot Line, a supposedly impregnable wall of fortifications along the Franco-German border, had proved useless; the German armoured divisions had simply outflanked it by going through Belgium.

The Germans divided France into a zone under direct German occupation (in the north and along the west coast) and a puppet state based in the spa town of Vichy, which was led by the ageing WWI hero, General Philippe Pétain. Both Pétain's collaborationist government (whose leaders and supporters assumed that the Nazis were Europe's new masters and had to be accommodated) and French police forces in German-occupied areas were very helpful to the Nazis in rounding up French Jews and other targeted groups for deportation to concentration camps.

After the capitulation, General Charles de Gaulle, France's undersecretary of war, fled to London and set up a French government-in-exile. He also established the Forces Françaises Libres (Free French Forces), a military force dedicated to continuing the fight against Germany. The underground movement known as the Résistance, which included no more than perhaps 5% of the population (the other 95% either collaborated or did nothing), engaged in such activities as railway sabotage, collecting intelligence for the Allies, helping Allied airmen who had been shot down, and publishing anti-German leaflets.

The liberation of France began with the US, British and Canadian landings in Normandy on D-Day (6 June 1944). On 15 August, Allied forces also landed in southern France. After a brief insurrection by the Résistance, Paris was liberated on 25 August by an Allied force spearheaded somewhat superficially by Free French units.

The Fourth Republic

De Gaulle soon returned to Paris and set up a provisional government, but in January 1946 he resigned as its president, miscalculating that such a move would create a popular outcry for his return. A few months later, a new constitution was approved by referendum. The Fourth Republic was a period of unstable coalition cabinets that followed one another with bewildering speed (on average one every six months). It was characterised by slow economic recovery helped by massive US aid (the Marshall Plan), an un-

successful war to reassert French colonial control of Indochina and an uprising by Arab nationalists in Algeria, whose population included over one million French settlers.

The Fifth Republic

The Fourth Republic came to an end in 1958, when extreme right-wingers, furious at what they saw as defeatism in dealing with the uprising in Algeria, began conspiring to overthrow the government. De Gaulle was brought back to power to prevent a military coup and even civil war. He soon drafted a new constitution that gave considerable powers to the president at the expense of the National Assembly.

The Fifth Republic (which continues to this day) was rocked in 1961 by an attempted coup staged in Algiers by a group of right-wing military officers. When it failed, the Organisation de l'Armée Secrète (OAS; a group of French settlers and sympathisers opposed to Algerian independence) turned to terrorism, trying several times to assassinate De Gaulle. In 1962, de Gaulle negotiated an end to the war in Algeria. Some 750,000 *pieds noirs* ('black feet' – as Algerian-born French people are known in France) flooded into France. In the meantime, almost all of the other French colonies and protectorates in Africa had demanded and achieved independence. Shrewdly, the French government began a program of economic and military aid to its former colonies in order to bolster France's waning international importance.

The crisis of May 1968 took the government, and much of the country, by total surprise. A seemingly insignificant incident, in which police broke up yet another protest by university students, sparked a violent reaction on the streets of Paris: students occupied the Sorbonne, barricades were erected in the Latin Quarter and unrest spread to other universities. Workers then joined in the protests. About nine million people participated in a general strike, virtually paralysing the country. But just when the country seemed on the brink of revolution, de Gaulle defused the crisis by successfully appealing to people's fear of anarchy. With stability restored, the government made a number of important changes, including a reform of the higher education system.

In 1969, de Gaulle was succeeded as president by the Gaullist leader Georges Pompidou, who was in turn succeeded by Valéry Giscard d'Estaing in 1974. François Mitterrand, a Socialist, was elected president in 1981 and re-elected for a second seven-year term in 1988. In the 1986 parliamentary elections, the right-wing opposition led by Jacques Chirac won a majority in the National Assembly. For the next two years, Mitterrand was forced to work with a prime minister and cabinet from the opposition, an unprecedented arrangement which became known as *cohabitation*.

Cohabitation was again the order of the day after the 1993 parliamentary elections, in which a centre-right coalition took 480 of 577 seats in the National Assembly and Édouard Balladur of Chirac's party was named prime minister. The closely contested presidential election of May 1995 resulted in Chirac winning the mandate with 52% of the vote. More surprising was the considerable success of the extreme-right Front National (FN) led by Jean-Marie Le Pen. In the presidential elections, this party took 15% of votes in the first round.

Chirac earned credit for decisive words and actions in matters relating to the EU and the war in former Yugoslavia, but on the home front his moves to restrict welfare payments led to the largest protests and strikes since 1968. In the 1997 election Chirac remained president but his party lost support to a coalition of Socialists, Communists and Greens, led by Lionel Jospin, who became prime minister. France had once again entered into a period of cohabitation – with Chirac on the other side this time around. As president, Chirac retains the power to dissolve parliament after two years of a government's mandate (ie mid-1999) has elapsed. But with the fractious right unable to agree on whether or not to opt for economic liberalism and the absence of a uniting leader, this appears unlikely.

GEOGRAPHY & ECOLOGY

France covers an area of 551,000 sq km and is the largest country in Europe after Russia and Ukraine. It's shaped like a hexagon bordered by either mountains or water except for the relatively flat, north-east frontier which abuts Germany, Luxembourg and Belgium.

France has a rich variety of flora and fauna, including some 113 species of mammals (more than any other country in Europe). Unfortunately, intensive agriculture, the draining of wetlands, the encroachment of industry and the expansion of the tourism infrastructure are among the problems threatening some species. The proportion of protected land is relatively low in France, but animal reintroduction programs, such as storks bred in Alsace, have met with some success. France is home to nearly two million hunters; the 1979 *Directive de Bruxelles*, introduced to protect wild birds and their habitats, was signed by the French government, but has yet to become part of French law.

France's nuclear energy industry continues to thrive and about three-quarters of the country's electricity is produced in this way. Since 1960, France has also maintained an independent arsenal of nuclear weapons. In 1992, the French government finally agreed to suspend nuclear testing on the Polynesian island of Mururoa and a nearby atoll, and this decision was reaffirmed in 1994. In 1995, however, Jacques Chirac decided to conduct one last round of tests before supporting a worldwide test ban treaty. The tests were concluded in January 1996, and France signed the treaty in April 1998.

GOVERNMENT & POLITICS

Despite a long tradition of highly centralised government, the country remains linguistically and culturally heterogeneous, and in some areas there's less than complete acceptance of control by Paris. There are even groups in the Basque Country, Brittany and Corsica demanding complete independence from France.

France has had 11 constitutions since 1789. The present one, which was instituted by de Gaulle in 1958, established what is known as the Fifth Republic (see the previous History section). It gives considerable power to the president of the republic.

The 577 members of the National Assembly are directly elected in single-member constituencies for five-year terms. The 321 members of the rather powerless Sénat, who serve for nine years, are indirectly elected. The president of France is elected directly for a seven-year term. The voting age is 18 and women were given the franchise in 1944.

Executive power is shared by the president and the Council of Ministers, whose members, including the prime minister, are appointed by the president but are responsible to parliament. The president, who resides in the Palais de l'Élysée in Paris, makes all major policy decisions.

France is one of the five permanent members of the UN Security Council. It withdrew from NATO's joint military command in 1966.

Local Administration

Before the Revolution, the country consisted of about two dozen regions. Their names are still widely used, but for administrative purposes the country has been divided into units called *départements* since 1790. At present, there are 96 departments in metropolitan France and another five overseas. The government in Paris is represented in each department by a *préfet* (prefect). A department's main town, where the departmental government and the prefect are based, is known as a *préfecture*.

ECONOMY

The recession hit France especially hard in the early 1990s; the French economy has now recovered somewhat and is growing at around the EU average. This sluggish rise in annual gross domestic product – predicted at just under 3% in 1999 – will keep France's relatively high unemployment near 12% (over 3 million people), a figure that has not budged in years.

The government has long played a significant interventionist (*dirigiste*) role in managing and running the French economy, which during the 1950s was one of the most tariff-protected and government-subsidised in Europe. Under direct government control is the world-famous Renault car works and most of the major banks. Although privatisation has been embraced in some sectors and is accelerating under Chirac, the lack of competition in other areas can mean poor service.

Union activity is strongest in the public sector where strike action is often a daily occurrence. But only about 15% of the French workforce is unionised – among the lowest rates in the EU – despite the fact that France is one of the most industrialised nations in the world, with around 40% of the workforce employed in the industrial sector. France is also the largest agricultural producer and exporter in the EU. Nearly one in 10 workers is engaged in agricultural production, which helps to account for the attention given by the government to French farmers during their periodic protests against cheaper imports.

POPULATION & PEOPLE

France has a population of 58.3 million, more than 20% of whom live in the Paris greater metropolitan area. The number of French people living in rural and mountain areas has been declining since the 1950s. For much of the last two centuries, France has had a considerably lower rate of population growth than its neighbours.

On the other hand, during the last 150 years France has received more immigrants than any other European country (4.3 million between 1850 and 1945), including significant numbers of political refugees. During the late 1950s and early 1960s, as the French colonial empire collapsed, more than one million French settlers returned to metropolitan France from Algeria, Morocco, Tunisia and Indochina.

In recent years, there has been a racist backlash against France's non-white immigrant communities, especially Muslims from North Africa. The extreme-right FN party has fanned these racist sentiments in a bid to win more votes. In 1993, the French government tightened its immigration laws, making it harder for immigrants to get French citizenship, and in January 1997 the National Assembly approved by a large margin new legislation that legitimised the status of some illegal immigrants but also implemented measures that made it easier to locate and repatriate others.

ARTS
Architecture

A religious revival in the 11th century led to the construction of a large number of Romanesque churches, so called because their architects adopted many elements (eg vaulting) from

FRANCE

Gallo-Roman buildings still standing at the time. Romanesque buildings typically have round arches, heavy walls that let in very little light and a lack of ornamentation bordering on the austere.

The Gothic style originated in the mid-12th century in northern France, whose great wealth enabled it to attract the finest architects, engineers and artisans. Gothic structures are characterised by ribbed vaults, pointed arches and stained-glass windows, with the emphasis on space, verticality and light. The invention of the flying buttress (a structural support which conducts the thrust of the building down through a series of arches to the ground) meant that greater height and width were now possible. This new technology subsequently spread to the rest of Europe. By the 15th century, decorative extravagance led to the Flamboyant Gothic style, so named because its wavy stone carving was said to resemble flames.

Painting

An extraordinary flowering of artistic talent took place in France during the late 19th and early 20th centuries. The impressionists, who dealt with colour as a property of light (rather than of objects) and endeavoured to capture the ever-changing aspects of reflected light, included Édouard Manet, Claude Monet, Edgar Degas, Camille Pissarro and Pierre-Auguste Renoir. They were followed by a diverse but equally creative group of artists known as the postimpressionists, among whose ranks were Paul Cézanne, Paul Gauguin and Georges Seurat. A little later, the Fauves (literally, 'wild beasts'), the most famous of whom was Henri Matisse, became known for their radical use of vibrant colour. In the years before WWI Pablo Picasso, who was living in Paris, and Georges Braque pioneered cubism, a school of art which concentrated on the analysis of form through abstract and geometric representation.

Music

When French music comes to mind, most people hear accordions and chansonniers (cabaret singers) like Édith Piaf. But they're only part of a much larger and more complex picture. At many points in history France has been at the centre of musical culture in Europe.

In the 17th and 18th centuries, French baroque music greatly influenced European musical output. Composers such as François Couperin (1668-1733), noted for his harpsichord studies, and Jean Phillipe Rameau (1683-1764), a key figure in the development of modern harmony, were two major contributors. The opulence of the baroque era is reflected also in the art and architecture of the time.

France's two greatest classical composers of the 19th century were the Romantic Hector Berlioz, the founder of modern orchestration, and César Franck. Berlioz's operas and symphonies and Franck's organ compositions sparked a musical renaissance in France that would produce such greats as Gabriel Fauré and the impressionists Claude Debase and Maurice Ravel.

Jazz hit Paris in the 1920s and has remained popular ever since. France's contribution to the world of jazz includes the violinist Stéfane Grappelli and, in the 1950s, Claude Luter and his Dixieland Band.

Popular music has come a long way since the yéyé (imitative rock) of the 1960s sung by Johnny Halliday – though you might not think so listening to middle-of-the-roaders Vanessa Paradis and Patrick Bruel. Watch out for rappers MC Solaar, Reg'lyss and I Am from Marseille. Evergreen balladeers/folk singers include Francis Cabrel and Julien Clerc. Some people like the new age space music of Jean-Michel Jarre; others say his name fits his sound.

France's claim to fame over the past decade has been sono mondial (world music) – from Algerian raï (Cheb Khaled, Zahouania) and Senegalese mbalax (Youssou N'Dour) to West Indian zouk (Kassav, Zouk Machine). La Mano Negra and Négresses Vertes are two bands that combine many of these styles – often with outstanding results.

Literature

To get a feel for France and its literature of the 19th century, you might pick up a translation of any novel by Victor Hugo (Les Misérables or The Hunchback of Notre Dame), Stendahl (The Red and the Black), Honoré de Balzac (Old Goriot), Émile Zola (Germinal) or Gustave Flaubert (A Sentimental Education or Madame Bovary).

After WWII, existentialism, a significant literary movement, emerged. Based upon the philosophy that people are self-creating beings, it placed total moral responsibility upon individuals to give meaning to their existence. The most prominent figures of the movement – Jean-Paul Sartre (*Being and Nothingness*), Simone de Beauvoir, and Albert Camus (*The Plague*) – stressed the importance of the writer's political commitment. De Beauvoir, author of the ground-breaking study *The Second Sex*, has had a profound influence on feminist thinking.

In the late 1950s, some younger novelists began to experiment with the novel in an attempt to show different aspects of reality. Critics began to speak of the *nouveau roman* (new novel), referring to the works of Alain Robbe-Grillet, Nathalie Sarraute, Michel Butor and Claude Simon among others. Although these writers did not form a school, they all rejected the traditional novel with its conventions of plot, linear narrative and identifiable characters. Other authors who enjoy a wide following are Marguerite Duras, Françoise Sagan, Patrick Modiano, Pascal Quignard and Denis Tillinac.

Cinema

Film has always been taken very seriously as an art form in France, and as such has attracted artists, intellectuals and theorists. Some of the most innovative and influential film makers of the 1920s and 1930s were Jean Vigo, Marcel Pagnol and Jean Renoir.

After WWII, a new generation of directors burst onto the scene with experimental films that abandoned such constraints as temporal continuity and traditional narrative. Known as the *nouvelle vague* (new wave), this genre includes many disparate directors such as Jean-Luc Godard, François Truffaut, Claude Chabrol, Alain Resnais, Agnès Varda and Eric Rohmer, whose main tenet was that a film should be the conception of the film maker – not the product of a studio or a producer.

Despite the onslaught of American films in Europe, France is still producing commercially viable (albeit subsidised) films. Contemporary directors of note include Bertrand Blier (*Trop belle pour toi*), Jean-Jacques Beineix (*Betty Blue*) and Jacques

Rivette (*Jeanne la Pucelle*). The French film industry's main annual event is the Cannes Film Festival held in May, when the coveted Palme d'Or is awarded to French and foreign films.

SOCIETY & CONDUCT

Some visitors to France conclude that it would be a lovely country if it weren't for the French. As in other countries, however, the more tourists a particular town or neighbourhood attracts, the less patience the locals tend to have for them. The following tips might prove useful when interacting with the French:

Never address a waiter or bartender as '*garçon*' (boy); '*s'il vous plaît*' is the way it's done nowadays. Avoid discussing money, keep off the manicured French lawns (signs read '*Pelouse Interdite*'), and resist handling produce in markets; trust the shopkeeper to choose for you.

Perhaps the easiest way to improve the quality of your relations with the French is always to address people as *Monsieur/Madame/Mademoiselle*.

Monsieur means 'sir' and can be used with any male person who isn't a child. Madame is used where 'Mrs' would apply in English; Mademoiselle is equivalent to 'Miss' and is used when addressing unmarried women. When in doubt, use 'Madame'.

Finally, when you go out for the evening, it's a good idea to follow the local custom of being relatively well dressed, particularly in a restaurant. If invited to someone's home or a party, always bring some sort of gift, such as good wine.

RELIGION

Some 80% of French people say they are Catholic, but although most have been baptised very few attend church – especially among the middle classes. The French Catholic church is generally progressive and ecumenically minded.

Protestants, who were severely persecuted during much of the 16th and 17th centuries, now number about one million. They are concentrated in Alsace, the Jura, the southeastern part of the Massif Central and along the Atlantic coast.

France now has between 4 and 5 million Muslims, making Islam the second-largest religion in the country. The vast majority are immigrants (or their offspring) who came from North Africa during the 1950s and 1960s.

There has been a Jewish community in France almost continuously since the Roman period. About 75,000 Jews resident in France were killed during the Holocaust. The country's Jewish community now numbers some 650,000.

LANGUAGE

Around 122 million people worldwide speak French as their first language; it is an official language in Belgium, Switzerland, Luxembourg, Canada and over two dozen other countries, most of them former French colonies in Africa. It's also spoken in the Val d'Aosta region of north-western Italy. Various forms of creole are used in Haiti, French Guiana and parts of Louisiana. France has a special government ministry (Ministère de la Francophonie) to deal with the country's relations with the French-speaking world.

The French tend to assume that all human beings should speak French; it was the international language of culture and diplomacy until WWI. Your best bet is always to approach people politely in French, even if the only words you know are *'Pardon, Monsieur/Madame/Mademoiselle, parlez-vous anglais?'* ('Excuse me Sir/Madam/Miss, do you speak English?').

See the Language Guide at the back of the book for pronunciation guidelines and useful words and phrases.

Facts for the Visitor

HIGHLIGHTS
Beaches

The Côte d'Azur – the French Riviera – has some of the best known beaches in the world, but you'll also find lovely beaches farther west on the Mediterranean coast as well as on Corsica, along the Atlantic coast (eg at Biarritz) and even along the English Channel (eg Dinard).

Museums

Every city and town in France has at least one museum, but a good number of the country's most exceptional ones are in Paris. In addition to the rather overwhelming Louvre, Parisian museums not to be missed include the Musée d'Orsay (late 19th and early 20th-century art), the Pompidou Centre (modern and contemporary art), the Musée Rodin, and the Musée National du Moyen Age (Museum of the Middle Ages) at the Hôtel de Cluny. Other cities known for their museums include Nice, Bordeaux, Strasbourg and Lyon.

Chateaux

The royal palace at Versailles is the largest and most grandiose of the hundreds of chateaux located all over the country. Many of the most impressive ones, including Chambord, Cheverny, Chenonceau and Azay-le-Rideau, are in the Loire Valley around Blois and Tours.

Cathedrals

The cathedrals at Chartres, Strasbourg and Rouen are among the most beautiful in France.

SUGGESTED ITINERARIES

Depending on the length of your stay, you might want to consider the following options:

Two days
    Paris – the most beautiful city in the world.
One week
    Paris plus a nearby area, such as the Loire Valley, Champagne, Alsace or Normandy.
Two weeks
    As above, plus one area in the west or south, such as Brittany, the Alps or Provence.
One month
    As above, but spending more time in each place and visiting more of the west or south – Brittany, say, or the Côte d'Azur.
Two months
    In summer, hiking in the Pyrenees or Alps; hanging out at one of the beach areas on the English Channel, Atlantic coast or the Mediterranean; spending some time in more remote areas (eg the Basque Country or Corsica).

PLANNING
Climate & When to Go
Weather-wise, France is at its best in spring, though wintry relapses are not unknown in April and the beach resorts only begin to pick up in mid-May. Autumn is pleasant, too, but later on (late October) it gets a bit cool for sunbathing. Winter is great for snow sports in the Alps and Pyrenees, but Christmas, New Year and the February/March school holidays create surges in domestic and foreign tourism that can make it very difficult to find accommodation. On the other hand, Paris always has all sorts of cultural activities during its rather wet winter.

In summer, the weather is warm and even hot, especially in the south, which is one reason why the beaches, resorts and camping grounds are packed to the gills. Also, millions of French people take their annual month-long holiday (*congé*) in August. Resort hotel rooms and camp sites are in extremely short supply, while in the half-deserted cities – only partly refilled by the zillions of foreign tourists – many shops, restaurants, cinemas, cultural institutions and even hotels simply shut down. If at all possible, avoid travelling in France during August.

Books
There are many excellent histories of France in English. Among the best is Fernand Braudel's two-volume *The Identity of France* (*History and Environment* and *People and Production*). *Citizens*, a very readable work by Simon Schama, looks at the first few years of the French Revolution. *France Today* by John Ardagh provides excellent insights into the way French society has evolved since WWII.

Paul Rambali's *French Blues* is a series of uncompromising yet sympathetic snapshots of modern France, while *Paris Notebooks* by veteran journalist Mavis Gallant reviews the years 1968 to 1985. Patrick Howarth's *When the Riviera Was Ours* traces the lives of expatriates who frequented the Mediterranean coast during the two centuries up to WWII. *A Year in Provence* by Peter Mayle is an irresistible account of country life in southern France. *Toujours Provence* is its witty sequel.

France has long attracted expatriate writers from the UK, North America and Australasia, many of whom spent at least part of their stay writing in the country. *A Moveable Feast* by Ernest Hemingway portrays Bohemian life in 1920s Paris. Henry Miller also wrote some pretty dramatic stuff set in the French capital of the 1930s, including *Tropic of Cancer* and *Tropic of Capricorn*. Gertrude Stein's *The Autobiography of Alice B Toklas* is an entertaining account of Paris' literary and artistic circles from WWI to the mid-1930s, featuring such figures as Picasso, Matisse and Apollinaire.

Travel Guides Lonely Planet's *France* guide has comprehensive coverage of France and includes chapters on Andorra and Monaco.

Maps
For driving, the best road map is Michelin's *Motoring Atlas France*, which covers the whole country in 1:200,000 scale (1cm = 2km). If you'll only be in one or several regions of France, you might prefer to use Michelin's yellow-jacketed 1:200,000 scale sheet maps.

Éditions Didier & Richard's series of 1:50,000 scale trail maps are adequate for most hiking and cycling excursions. The Institut Géographique National (IGN) publishes maps of France in both 1:50,000 and 1:25,000 scale. Topoguides are little booklets for hikers that include trail maps and information (in French) on trail conditions, flora, fauna, villages en route etc.

Abbreviations commonly used on city maps include: *R* for *rue* (street); *Boul* or *Bd* for boulevard; *Av* for avenue; *Q* for *quai* (quay); *C* or *Cr* for *cours* (avenue); *Pl* for *place* (square); *Pte* for *porte* (gate); *Imp* for *impasse* (dead-end street); and *St* and *Ste* for saint (masculine and feminine, respectively). The street numbers 14 bis (14 twice) or 92 ter (92 thrice) are the equivalent of 14A or 92B.

What to Bring
English-language books, including used ones, cost about 50% more in France than in the UK (double North American prices), so voracious readers might want to bring along a supply. A pocketknife (penknife) and eating utensils are invaluable for picnicking. Bikini tops are not used much in France; you might

FRANCE

leave them at home! And, of course, bring as much money as you can afford – France can be an expensive (and a very tempting) place to visit.

TOURIST OFFICES
Local Tourist Offices
Virtually every French city, town and one-chateau village has some sort of tourist office. See Information under each town or city for details.

Tourist Offices Abroad
French Government Tourist Offices are located in the following countries and can provide brochures and tourist information.

Australia
   (☎ 02-9231 5244; fax 02-9221 8682; frencht@ozemail.com.au) 25 Bligh St, 22nd floor, Sydney, NSW 2000
Canada
   (☎ 416-593 4723; fax 416-979 7587; french.tourist@sympatico.ca) 30 Saint Patrick St, Suite 700, Toronto, Ont M5T 3A3
UK
   (☎ 0891-244 123; fax 0171-493 6594; piccadilly@mdlf.demon.co.uk) 178 Piccadilly, London W1V OAL
USA
   (☎ 212-838-7800; fax 212-838-7855; info@francetourism.com) 444 Madison Ave, New York, NY 10020-2452

VISAS & EMBASSIES
Citizens of the USA, Canada, Australia, New Zealand, most European countries and a handful of other nations can enter France for up to three months without a visa. South Africans, however, must have visas, even as tourists (to avoid delays, apply for a French visa before leaving home). Visas can not be obtained at border crossing points. The usual length of a tourist visa is three months.

If you plan to stay in France for over three months to study or work, apply to the French consulate nearest where you live for the appropriate sort of long-stay visa. If you're not an EU citizen, it is extremely difficult to get a work visa; one of the few exceptions is the provision that people with student visas can apply for permission to work part-time. For any sort of long-stay visa, begin the paperwork several months before you leave home. By law, everyone in France, including tourists, must carry identification with them. For visitors, this means a passport. A national identity card is sufficient for EU citizens.

Visa Extensions
Tourist visas *cannot* be extended. If you qualify for an automatic three-month stay upon arrival, you'll get another three months if you exit and then re-enter France. The fewer French entry stamps you have in your passport, the easier this is likely to be.

French Embassies Abroad
Australia
   (☎ 02-6216 0100) 6 Perth Ave, Yarralumla, ACT 2600
Canada
   (☎ 613-789 1795) 42 Sussex Drive, Ottawa, Ontario K1M 2 C9
Germany
   (☎ 0228-955 6000) An der Marienkapelle 3, 53179 Bonn
Italy
   Consulate: (☎ 06-68 80 64 37) Via Giulia 251, 00186 Rome
New Zealand
   (☎ 04-472 0200) Robert Jones House, 1-3 Willeston St (PO Box 1695), Wellington
Spain
   Consulate: (☎ 91-319 7188) Calle Marques de la Enseñada 10, 28004 Madrid
UK
   Consulate: (☎ 0171-838 2051; 0891-887 733 for general information on visa requirements) 6A Cromwell Place, London SW7
USA
   (☎ 202-944 6000) 4101 Reservoir Rd, NW Washington, DC, 20007-2185

Foreign Embassies in France
Australia
   (☎ 01 40 59 33 00) 4 Rue Jean Rey, 15e; metro Bir Hakeim
Canada
   (☎ 01 44 43 29 00) 35 Ave Montaigne, 8e; metro Alma Marceau or Franklin D Roosevelt
New Zealand
   (☎ 01 45 00 24 11) 7 ter Rue Léonard de Vinci, 16e; metro Victor Hugo
Spain
   (☎ 01 44 43 18 00) 22 Ave Marceau, 8e; metro Alma Marceau

FRANCE

UK
    Consulate: (☎ 01 44 51 31 00 or, 24 hours a day in an emergency, ☎ 01 42 66 29 79) 16 Rue d'Anjou, 8e; metro Concorde
USA
    Consulate: (☎ 01 43 12 23 00 for a recording, ☎ 01 43 12 49 48 in an emergency, 24 hours) 2 Rue Saint Florentin, 1er; metro Concorde

MONEY

Generally you'll get a better exchange rate for travellers cheques than for cash. The most useful travellers cheques are those issued by American Express in US dollars or French francs, which can be exchanged at many post offices.

Do not bring travellers cheques in Australian dollars as they are hard to change, especially outside Paris. US$100 bills are also difficult to change because there are so many counterfeits around; many Banque de France branches refuse them.

Visa (Carte Bleue in France) is more widely accepted than MasterCard (Eurocard). Visa card-holders with a 'PIN' number can get cash advances from banks and automatic teller machines nationwide – even in remote Corsican towns. American Express cards are not very useful except to get cash at American Express offices in big cities or to pay for things in upmarket shops and restaurants. To have money sent from abroad, have it wired to either Citicorp's Paris office (see Money in the Paris section) or to a specific branch of a French or foreign bank. You can also have money easily sent via American Express.

Currency

One French franc (FF) equals 100 centimes. French coins come in denominations of five, 10 and 20 centimes and half, one, two, five, 10 and 20FF (the last two are two-tone). Banknotes are issued in denominations of 20, 50, 100, 200 and 500FF. The higher the denomination, the larger the bill. It can be difficult to get change for a 500FF bill.

Exchange Rates

Australia	A$1	=	3.70 FF
Canada	C$1	=	4.10 FF
euro	€1	=	6.60 FF
Germany	DM1	=	3.35 FF
Japan	¥100	=	4.30 FF
New Zealand	NZ$1	=	3.15 FF
Spain	100 pta	=	3.95 FF
UK	UK£1	=	9.80 FF
USA	US$1	=	6 FF

Banque de France, France's central bank, offers the best exchange rates, especially for travellers cheques, and it does not charge any commission (except 1% for travellers cheques in French francs). There are Banque de France bureaus in the prefectures of each department.

Many post offices make exchange transactions at a very good rate. They accept banknotes in a variety of currencies as well as American Express travellers cheques, but *only* if the cheques are in US dollars or French francs.

In large cities, *bureaux de change* (currency exchange offices) are faster, easier, have longer opening hours and often give better rates than the banks, but are not beyond milking clueless tourists. As always, your best bet is to compare the rates offered by various banks, which charge at least 20 to 30FF per transaction, and exchange bureaus, which are not allowed to charge commission.

If your American Express travellers cheques or credit card are lost or stolen, call ☎ 01 47 77 70 00 or ☎ 01 47 77 72 00, both staffed 24 hours a day. For lost or stolen Visa cards, call ☎ 01 42 77 11 90 in Paris, 02 54 42 12 12 in the provinces.

Costs

If you stay in hostels (or, if there are two or more of you, the cheapest hotels) and buy provisions from grocery stores rather than eating at restaurants, it is possible to tour France on as little as US$35 a day per person (US$45 in Paris). Eating out, lots of travel or treating yourself to France's many little luxuries can increase this figure dramatically.

Discounts Museums, cinemas, the SNCF, ferry companies and other institutions offer all sorts of price breaks to people under the age of either 25 or 26; students with ISIC cards (age limits may apply); and *le troisième age* (seniors, ie people over 60 or, in some cases, 65.) Look for the words *demi-tarif* or *tarif réduit* (half-price tariff or reduced rate) on rate charts and then ask if you qualify.

FRANCE

Tipping

It's not necessary to leave a tip (*pourboire*) in restaurants, hotels etc; under French law, the bill must already include a 15% service charge. Some people leave a few francs on the table for the waiter, but this is not expected (especially for drinks). At truly posh restaurants, however, a more generous gratuity will be anticipated. For a taxi ride, the usual tip is about 2 or 3FF no matter what the fare.

Consumer Taxes

France's VAT (value-added tax, ie sales tax) is known in French as TVA (*taxe sur la valeur ajoutée*). The TVA is 20.6% on the purchase price of most goods (and for non-commercial vehicle rental). Prices that include TVA are often marked TTC (*toutes taxes comprises*), which means 'all taxes included'.

It's possible (though rather complicated) to get a reimbursement for TVA if you meet several conditions: 1) You are not an EU national and are over 15 years of age; 2) you have stayed in France less than six months; 3) you are buying more than 1200FF worth of goods (not more than 10 of the same item); and 4) the shop offers duty-free sales (*vente en détaxe*).

To claim a TVA, you fill out the proper export sales invoice (*bordereau de vente*) at the time you make your purchase. This is then stamped at your port of exit, thereby proving that you have taken the goods out of the country. The shop then reimburses you – by mail or bank transfer within 30 days – for the TVA you've paid.

POST & COMMUNICATIONS

Post

Postal Rates Postal services in France are fast, reliable and expensive. Postcards and letters up to 20g cost 3FF within the EU, 4.40FF to the USA and Canada and 5.20FF to Australasia. Aerograms cost 5FF to all destinations. All overseas packages are now sent by air only, which is very expensive.

Receiving Mail All mail to France *must* include the area's five-digit postcode, which begins with the two-digit number of the de-partment. In Paris, all postcodes begin with 750 and end with the arrondissement number, eg 75004 for the 4th arrondissement, 75013 for the 13th. The local postcode appears in each destination in this book under Information or Post.

Poste restante mail is held alphabetically by family name, so make sure your last name is written in capital letters. Poste restante mail not addressed to a particular branch post office ends up at the town's main post office (*recette principale*). In Paris, this means the central post office (☎ 01 40 28 20 00) at 52 Rue du Louvre (1er; metro Sentier or Les Halles). See Post in the Paris section for details. There's a 3FF charge for every poste restante claimed.

It's also possible to receive mail care of American Express offices, although if you do not have an American Express card or travellers cheques there's a 5FF charge each time you check to see if you have received any mail.

Telephone

Public Telephones You can dial direct from any phone in France to almost anywhere in the world. Almost all public phones now require phonecards (*télécartes*), which are sold at post offices, tobacconists' shops (*tabacs*), Paris metro ticket counters and supermarket check-out counters. Cards worth 50/120 units cost 40.60/97.50FF. Each unit is good for one three-minute local call. Rates for calls abroad vary according to the time of day, so you will need to ask the French operator (see International Dialling below). To make a call with a phonecard, pick up the receiver, insert the card and dial when the LCD screen reads 'Numérotez'.

All telephone cabins can take incoming calls, so if you want someone to call you back, give them the new 10-digit number (see Domestic Dialling below) written after the words '*ici le*' on the information sheet next to the phone.

Domestic Dialling France is divided into five telephone zones and all telephone numbers, no matter where you are calling from in France, are 10-digit. Paris and Île de France numbers begin with 01. The other codes are: 02 for areas in the north-west; 03

for the north-east; 04 for the south-east; and 05 for the south-west.

Toll-free numbers (*numéros verts*) begin with 0800. For directory assistance (*service des renseignements*), dial ☎ 12.

International Dialling To call France from abroad, first dial the international access code, then ☎ 33 (France's country code), but omit the 0 at the beginning of the new 10-digit number (see Domestic Dialling above).

Direct-dial calls to almost anywhere in the world can be placed using a phonecard. Just dial ☎ 00, wait for the second tone, and then add the country code, area code and local number. If the country code is not on the information sheet posted in phone cabins, consult a phone book or dial ☎ 12 (directory assistance). A three-minute call to the USA costs 9/7FF peak/off-peak.

To make a reverse-charge (collect) call (*en PCV*) or person-to-person (*avec préavis*) from France to other countries, dial ☎ 00 (the international operator), wait for the second tone and then dial ☎ 33 plus the country code of the place you're calling. If you're using a public phone, you must insert a phonecard (or, in the case of coin telephones, deposit 1FF) first.

For directory inquiries outside France, dial ☎ 00, and when the second tone sounds, dial 33, then 12, and finally the country code. For information on home-country direct calls, see the Telephones Appendix in the back of this book.

Minitel Minitel is a telephone-connected, computerised information service. Though useful, it can be expensive to use and is now competing against the Internet. Minitel numbers consist of four digits (eg 3611, 3614, 3615 etc) and a string of letters. Most of the terminals in post offices are free for directory inquiries (though some require a 1 or 2FF coin), and many of them let you access pay-as-you-go on-line services.

Fax & Telegrams
Virtually all French post offices can send and receive domestic and international faxes (*télécopies* or *téléfaxes*), telexes and telegrams. It costs around 20/80FF to send a one-page fax within France/to the USA.

INTERNET RESOURCES
Email can be sent and received at cybercafés (see Cybercafés in the Information section for individual cities).

At the time of going to print, La Poste was setting up Internet access centres at 1000 post offices around France where 90FF will buy three hours' access. France Telecom, meanwhile, has been sponsoring 'Internet stations' including one in Paris called Cyber Espace at 35 Rue du Cherche Midi (6e) on the corner of Blvd Raspail. These are not cybercafés as such but high-tech centres where people can surf the Internet, send emails and take free beginners' courses on how to use the Net. Access rates are cheaper than commercial cybercafés: 20/30FF for a half-hour/hour.

Useful Web sites in English include:

Paris tourist office Web site
 www.paris-promotion.fr
Information about selected regions in France
 www.guideweb.com

NEWSPAPERS & MAGAZINES
The excellent *International Herald Tribune* is sold at many news kiosks throughout France for 10FF. Other English-language papers you can find include two British papers with European editions, the *Guardian* and the *Financial Times*; the *European*; and the colourful *USA Today*. *Newsweek*, *Time* and the *Economist* are also widely available.

RADIO & TV
The BBC World Service can be picked up on 195kHz AM and 6195kHz, 9410kHz, 9760kHz and 12095kHz short wave. In northern France, BBC for Europe is on 648kHz AM. Upmarket hotels often offer cable TV access to CNN, BBC TV and other networks. Canal+ (pronounced 'ka-NAHL pluce'), a French subscription TV station available in many mid-range hotels, sometimes screens undubbed English movies.

PHOTOGRAPHY & VIDEO
Be prepared to have your camera and film forced through the ostensibly film-safe x-ray machines at airports and when entering sensitive public buildings such as any Palais de

Justice (Law Courts) or Banque de France branch. The most you can do is ask that they hand-check your film, if not your whole camera. Film is widely available, and costs 37/48FF for a 36-exposure roll of 100ASA print/slide film, excluding processing.

Note that French videotapes cannot be played on British, Australian or American video cassette recorders or TVs unless they are equipped with SECAM.

TIME

France is one hour ahead of GMT/UTC in winter and two hours ahead in summer. Daylight Saving Time runs from the last Sunday in March till the last Sunday in September. The 24-hour clock is widely used in France – even informally. Thus 14.30 (or 14h30) is 2.30 pm, 00.15 (00h15) is 12.15 am and so on.

ELECTRICITY

The electric current in France is 220V, 50Hz. Plugs have two round pins.

WEIGHTS & MEASURES

France uses the metric system, which was invented by the French Academy of Sciences and adopted by the French government in 1795. For a chart of metric equivalents, see the inside back cover of this guide.

LAUNDRY

To find a self-service laundrette (*laverie libre service*), ask at the front desk of your hotel or hostel. Costs are generally 18 to 20FF a load and around 2FF for five minutes of drying. Bring lots of coins; few laundrettes have change machines.

TOILETS

Public toilets (*toilettes* or *wc*) are scarce, though small towns often have one near the town hall (*mairie*). In Paris, you're more likely to come upon one of the tan, self-disinfecting toilet pods. Get your change ready as many public toilets cost 2FF or even 2.50FF. Except in the most tourist-filled areas, café owners are usually amenable to your using their toilets provided you ask politely (and with just a hint of urgency).

HEALTH
Public Health System

France has an extensive public health care system. Anyone who is sick can receive treatment in the emergency room (*service des urgences*) of any public hospital. Such treatment costs much less in France than in many other countries, especially the USA. Hospitals usually ask that foreigners settle their account right after receiving treatment.

Condoms

Many pharmacies have 24-hour automatic condom (*préservatif*) dispensers near the door. Some brasseries and nightclubs also have condom-vending machines.

WOMEN TRAVELLERS

In general, women need not walk around in fear of passers-by – women are rarely physically attacked on the street. However, you are more likely to be left alone if you have about you a purposeful air that implies that you know exactly where you're going – even if you haven't a clue!

If you are subject to catcalls or are hassled in any way while walking down the street, the best strategy is usually to carry on and ignore the macho lowlife who is disrupting your holiday. Making a cutting retort is ineffective in English and risky in French if your slang isn't extremely proficient.

France's national rape crisis hotline, which is run by a women's organisation called Viols Femmes Informations, can be reached toll-free by dialling ☎ 0800 05 95 95. It's staffed by volunteers Monday to Friday from 10 am to 6 pm.

GAY & LESBIAN TRAVELLERS

Most of France's major gay organisations are based in Paris. Centre Gai et Lesbien (CGL; ☎ 01 43 57 21 47), 3 Rue Keller (11e; metro Ledru Rollin) 500m east of Place de la Bastille, serves as a headquarters for lots of organisations that hold a variety of meetings and activities each week. The bar, library etc are open Monday to Saturday from 2 to 8 pm; the Sunday activities (2 to 7 pm) are mainly for people who are HIV positive. Paris Pride is held on the last weekend in June.

Gay publications include the monthlies *3 Keller*, *Action* and *Gay*. The weekly *e.m@le* has interviews, gossip and articles (in French), with the best listings of gay clubs, bars and associations and personal classifieds. The monthly *Lesbia* gives a rundown of what's happening around the country. Web sites worth checking out include: www.france.qrd.org – the Queer Resources Directory for gay and lesbian travellers; and www.gaipied.fr – a good online guide to the whole of France.

DISABLED TRAVELLERS

France is not particularly well equipped for disabled people (*handicapés*): kerb ramps are few and far between, older public facilities and bottom-end hotels often lack lifts, and the Paris metro, most of it built decades ago, is hopeless. But the physically disabled who would like to see France can overcome these problems. For instance, most hotels with two or more stars are equipped with lifts, and Michelin's *Guide Rouge* indicates hotels with lifts and facilities for disabled people. Details of train travel for wheelchair users is available in SNCF's booklet *Guide du Voyageur à Mobilité Réduite*. You can also contact SNCF Accessibilité toll-free on ☎ 0800 15 47 53.

Hostels in Paris that cater to disabled travellers include the Foyer International d'Accueil de Paris Jean Monnet and the Centre International de Séjour de Paris Kellermann (see Hostels & Foyers under Places to Stay in the Paris section).

SENIOR TRAVELLERS

People aged over 60 are eligible for a reduction of up to 50% on 1st and 2nd-class train travel with a Carte Senior (see Train in the Getting Around section). Entry to most museums and monuments in France is half-price for people over 60 – always check the tariff rules to see if you are eligible for a reduction. Senior citizens are usually offered a reduction on cinema tickets during the week. Some hostels, particularly in Paris, only offer accommodation to 'young' people; again, check the rules if you're thinking of hostelling.

DANGERS & ANNOYANCES

The biggest crime problem for tourists in France is theft – especially of and from cars. Never, *ever* leave anything in a parked motor vehicle or you'll learn the hard way. Pickpockets are a problem, and women are a common target because of their handbags. Be especially careful at airports and on crowded public transport in cities.

France's laws regarding even small quantities of drugs are very strict. Thanks to the Napoleonic Code, the police have the right to search anyone they want at any time, whether or not there is probable cause, and they have been known to stop and search charter buses coming from Amsterdam.

If stopped by the police for any reason, your best course of action is to be polite and to remain calm. It is a very bad idea to be overly assertive, and being rude or disrespectful is asking for serious trouble. Emergency telephone numbers in use all over France include:

Ambulance (SAMU)	☎ 15
Fire Brigade	☎ 18
Police	☎ 17

The rise in support for the extreme right-wing National Front in recent years reflects the growing racial intolerance in France, particularly against Muslim North Africans and, to a lesser extent, blacks from sub-Saharan Africa and France's former territories in the Caribbean. In many parts of France, especially in the south (eg Provence and the Côte d'Azur), entertainment places such as bars and nightclubs are, for all intents and purposes, segregated: owners and their ferocious-looking bouncers make it quite clear who is 'invited' to use their public facilities and who is not.

BUSINESS HOURS

Most museums are closed on either Monday or Tuesday and on public holidays (*jours fériés*), though during the summer some stay open seven days a week. Most small businesses are open from 9 or 10 am to 6.30 or 7 pm daily, except Sunday and perhaps Monday, with a break between noon and 2 pm or 1 and 3 pm. In the south, midday closures are more like siestas and may continue until 3.30 or even 4 pm.

FRANCE

Many food shops are open daily, except Sunday afternoon and Monday. As a result, Sunday morning may be your last chance to stock up on provisions until Tuesday. Most restaurants are open only for lunch (noon to 2 or 3 pm) and dinner (6.30 to about 10 or 11 pm); outside Paris, very few serve meals throughout the day. All are closed at least one full day per week and sometimes at lunchtime as well. In August, lots of establishments simply close so that owners and employees alike can take their annual month-long holiday. With most museums and other sights closed at midday and lunch menus cheaper than dinner ones, it pays to take your main meal at lunch and picnic at night.

Banque de France branches throughout France are open Monday to Friday from around 8.45 am to 12.15 pm and 1.30 to 3.30 pm. The opening hours of other banks vary. The main post office in towns and cities, and all branches in Paris, are open weekdays from 8 am to 6.30 or 7 pm and on Saturday to noon. Branches outside Paris are generally open from 8.30 am to noon and 1.30 or 2 to 5.30 or 6.30 pm weekdays, and also on Saturday morning.

PUBLIC HOLIDAYS & SPECIAL EVENTS

National public holidays in France include New Year's Day, Easter Sunday and Monday, May Day (1 May), 1945 Victory Day (8 May), Ascension Thursday (40th day after Easter), Pentecost Sunday and Whit Monday (seventh Sunday and Monday after Easter), Bastille Day (14 July), Assumption Day (15 August), All Saints' Day (1 November), 1918 Armistice Day (11 November) and Christmas Day.

Most French cities have at least one major cultural festival each year. Some of the biggest and best events in France are listed here. For more details about what's on and when (dates change from year to year), contact the main tourist office in Paris or a French Government Tourist Office abroad.

Festival d'Avignon

This world-famous event takes place between early July and early August, when some 300 shows involving music, drama and dance are staged every day. There's a simultaneous fringe event, the Festival Off.

Fête Nationale (Bastille Day)

This annual celebration on 13 and 14 July is marked in Paris by a huge military procession and fly-past along the Avenue des Champs-Élysées and a firework display at the Eiffel Tower or the Invalides. Many other French cities also stage fireworks and other festivities.

Francofolies

Huge crowds of young people attend this six-day festival in La Rochelle, held annually in mid-July. Performances by singers, dancers and musicians from all over the French-speaking world are supplemented by a fringe festival and a gospel and blues festival.

Festival Interceltique

For 10 days in early August the Breton town of Lorient is given over to a celebration of Celtic music, literature and dance, with artists from Brittany, Ireland, Wales, Cornwall and Scotland.

Biennale de la Danse/d'Art Contemporain

In even-numbered years from mid-September to October, Lyon hosts a month-long dance festival. In odd-numbered years, the city holds a festival of contemporary art over the same period.

Carnaval de Nice

This carnival, held every spring around Mardi Gras (Shrove Tuesday), fills the streets with colourful floats and musicians.

ACTIVITIES
Skiing

The French Alps have some of the finest (and priciest) skiing in Europe, but there are cheaper, low-altitude ski stations in the Pyrenees; www.skifrance.fr provides information in English about ski resorts, services, conditions etc.

Surfing

The best surfing in France (and some of the best in all of Europe) is on the Atlantic coast around Biarritz.

Hiking

France has thousands of kilometres of hiking trails in every region of the country and through every kind of terrain. These include *sentiers de grande randonnée*, long-distance hiking paths whose alphanumeric names begin with the letters GR and are sometimes hundreds of kilometres long (as in Corsica).

Canoeing

The Fédération Française de Canoë-Kayak (☎ 01 45 11 08 50) at 87 Quai de la Marne, 94340 Joinville-le-Pont, can supply information on canoeing and kayaking clubs around the country. The sports are very popular in the Périgord (Dordogne) area. See Getting Around for information about houseboats and canal boats.

COURSES

For details on language and cooking courses, see Courses in the Paris section. For water sports courses see Courses in Bayonne.

Information on studying in France is available from French consulates and French Government Tourist Offices abroad. In Paris, you might also contact the Ministry of Tourism-sponsored International Cultural Organisation (ICO; ☎ 01 42 36 47 18; fax 01 40 26 34 45; metro Châtelet) at 55 Rue de Rivoli (1er), BP 2701, 75027 Paris CEDEX.

WORK

Getting a *carte de séjour* (temporary residence permit), which in most cases lets you work in France, is almost automatic for EU citizens; contact the Préfecture de Police in Paris or, in the provinces, the *mairie* (town hall) or nearest prefecture. For anyone else it's almost impossible, though the government does seem to tolerate undocumented workers helping out with some agricultural work, especially the apple and grape harvests in autumn. It's hard work and you are usually put up in barracks, but it's paid.

Working as an au pair – a kind of mother's helper – is very common in France, especially in Paris. Single young people – particularly women – receive board, lodging and a bit of money (500FF per week is the going rate) in exchange for taking care of the kids and doing light housework. Knowing at least a bit of French may be a prerequisite. Even US and other non-EU citizens can become au pairs, but they must be studying something (eg a recognised language course) and have to apply for an au pair's visa three months *before* leaving home.

For information on au pair placement, contact a French consulate or the Paris tourist office. Most private agencies charge the au pair 650 to 800FF and collect an additional fee from the family. Some agencies check the family and the living conditions they are offering; others are less thorough. In any case, be assertive in dealing with the agency to make sure you get what you want.

ACCOMMODATION

More and more cities and towns in France are instituting a *taxe de séjour*, which is a tax on each night you stay in a hotel and sometimes even hostels or camping grounds. In Paris, the tax ranges from 1 to 7FF per person per night but is usually included in the quoted price.

Camping

France has thousands of seasonal and year-round camping grounds, many of which are situated near streams, rivers, lakes or the ocean. Facilities and amenities, which are reflected in the number of stars the site has been awarded, determine the price. At the less fancy places, two people with a small tent should expect to pay 25 to 55FF a night. Another option in some rural areas is farm camping (*camping à la ferme*). Tourist offices will have details.

Camping grounds near cities and towns covered in this guide are detailed under Places to Stay for each city or town. For information on other camping grounds, inquire at a tourist office or consult the *Guide Officiel Camping/Caravaning* or Michelin's *Camping/Caravaning France*. Both are updated annually.

Campers who arrive at a camping ground without a vehicle can usually get a spot, even late in the day, but not in July and especially not in August, when most are packed with families on their annual holiday.

If you're backpacking, remember that in national and regional parks camping is permitted only in proper camping grounds. Camping elsewhere (*camping sauvage*) is tolerated to varying degrees (but not at all in Corsica); you probably won't have any problems with the police if you're not on private land, have only a small tent, are discreet, stay only one night and are at least 1500m from a camping ground.

Refuges & Gîtes d'Étape

Refuges (mountain huts or shelters) are basic dorm rooms operated by national park authorities, the Club Alpin Français and other private organisations along trails in uninhabited mountainous areas frequented by hikers and mountain climbers. They are marked on hiking and climbing maps. Some are open all year, others only during the warm months.

In general, refuges are equipped with mattresses and blankets but not sheets, which you have to bring yourself. Charges average 50 to 70FF per night per person. Meals, prepared by the *gardien* (attendant), are sometimes available. Most refuges are equipped with a telephone, so it's a good idea to call ahead and make a reservation. For details on refuges, contact a tourist office near where you'll be hiking.

Gîtes d'étape, which are usually better equipped and more comfortable than refuges (some even have showers), are found in less remote areas, often in villages. They also cost around 50 to 70FF per person. *Les Gîtes d'Étape* published annually by Fivedit covers the whole of France and should be available in bookshops or at newsstands.

Hostels

In the provinces, hostels (*auberges de jeunesse*) generally charge from 50FF (for out-of-the-way places with basic facilities) to 70FF for a bunk in a single-sex dorm room. A few of the more comfortable places that aren't officially auberges de jeunesse charge from 70 to 90FF, usually including breakfast. In Paris, expect to pay 95 to 120FF a night, including breakfast. In the cities, especially Paris, you will also find *foyers*, student dorms used by travellers in summer. Information on hostels and foyers is available from tourist offices. Most of France's hostels belong to one of three Paris-based organisations:

Fédération Unie des Auberges de Jeunesse (FUAJ; ☎ 01 44 89 87 27; fax 01 44 89 87 10) 27 Rue Pajol, 18e; metro La Chapelle. FUAJ has 190 hostels in France and is the only group affiliated with Hostelling International (HI)

Ligue Française pour les Auberges de la Jeunesse (LFAJ; ☎ 01 44 16 78 78; fax 01 45 44 57 47) 67 Rue Vergniaud, 13e; metro Glacière

Union des Centres de Rencontres Internationales de France (UCRIF; ☎ 01 40 26 57 64; fax 01 40 26 58 20) 27 Rue de Turbigo, 2e; metro Étienne Marcel

Hotels

Staying in an inexpensive hotel often costs less than a hostel when two or more people share a room. Unless otherwise indicated, prices quoted in this chapter refer to rooms in unrated or one-star hotels equipped with a washbasin (and usually a bidet, too) but without a toilet or shower. Most doubles, which generally cost the same or only marginally more than singles, have only one bed. Doubles with two beds usually cost a little more. Taking a shower (*douche*) in the hall bathroom can be free or cost between 10 and 25FF.

Reservations If you'll be arriving after noon (or after 10 am during peak tourism periods), it's a good idea to call ahead and make reservations; it will save you a lot of time and hassle in the long run. For advance reservations, most hotels require that you send them a deposit by post. But if you call on the day you'll be coming and sound credible, many hotels will hold a room for you until a set hour (rarely later than 6 or 7 pm). At small hotels, reception is usually closed on Sunday morning or afternoon. Local tourist offices will also make reservations for you, usually for a small fee.

FOOD

A fully fledged traditional French dinner – usually begun about 8.30 pm – has quite a few distinct courses: an apéritif or cocktail; a first course (*entrée*); the main course (*plat principal*); salad (*salade*); cheese (*fromage*); dessert (*dessert*); fruit (*fruit*); coffee (*café*); and a *digestif*.

France has lots of restaurants where several hundred francs get you excellent French cuisine, but inexpensive French restaurants are in short supply. Fortunately, delicious and surprisingly cheap ethnic cuisine is available from the many restaurants specialising in dishes from France's former colonies in Africa, Indochina, India, the Caribbean and the South Pacific. One of the most delicious of the North African dishes is *couscous*, steamed semolina eaten with vegetables and some sort of meat: lamb shish kebab, *merguez* (North African sausage), *mechoui* (lamb on the bone) or chicken.

Restaurants & Brasseries
There are two principal differences between restaurants and brasseries: restaurants usually specialise in a particular cuisine while brasseries – which look very much like cafés – serve quicker meals of more standard fare (eg steak and chips/French fries, omelettes etc). Restaurants are usually open only for lunch and dinner; brasseries, on the other hand, serve meals (or at least something solid) throughout the day.

Most restaurants offer at least one fixed-price, multicourse meal known in French as a *menu*, *menu à prix fixe* or *menu du jour*. In general, *menus* cost much less than ordering each dish separately (*à la carte*), but some may only be available at lunch. When you order the *menu*, you usually get to choose a first course, a main meat or fish dish and a cheese or dessert course. A *formule* usually allows you to choose two of the three courses. Drinks (*boissons*) cost extra unless the menu says *boisson comprise* (drink included), which usually means a quarter litre of wine.

Cafés
Sitting in a café to read, write or talk with friends is an integral part of everyday life in France. People use cafés as a way to keep in touch with their neighbourhood and friends, and to generally participate in the social life of their town or city.

A café located on a grand boulevard (such as Blvd du Montparnasse or the Champs-Élysées in Paris) will charge considerably more than a place that fronts a side street. Once inside, progressively more expensive tariffs apply at the counter (*comptoir*), in the café itself (*salle*) and outside on the *terrasse*. The price of drinks goes up at night, usually after 8 pm, but the price of a cup of coffee (or anything else) earns you the right to sit for as long as you like.

Self-Catering
France is justly renowned for its extraordi-nary chefs and restaurants, but one of the country's premier culinary delights – especially for vegetarians, who will find France's restaurants obsessed with meat and seafood – is to stock up on fresh breads, cheeses, fruit, vegetables, prepared dishes etc and have a picnic. Although prices are likely to be much higher than you're used to, you will find that the food is of excellent quality.

While supermarkets (*supermarchés*) and slightly more expensive grocery shops (*épiceries*) are more and more popular with working people in cities, many people still buy their food from small neighbourhood shops, each with its own speciality. The whole setup is geared towards people buying fresh food each day, so it's completely acceptable to purchase very small quantities – a few slices (*tranches*) of sliced meat or a few hundred grams of salad.

Fresh *baguettes* and other breads are baked and sold at a *boulangerie*. It may also sell sandwiches, quiches and small (very ordinary) pizzas. Mouthwatering pastries are available from a *pâtisserie*. For chocolate and sweets, look for a *confiserie*. (These three shops are often combined.) For a selection of superb cheeses, such as *chèvre* (goat's-milk cheese) and a half-round of perfectly ripe Camembert, go to a *fromagerie* (also called a *crémerie*). Fruit and vegetables are sold by a *marchand de legumes et de fruits*. Wine is sold by a *marchand de vin*.

A general butcher is a *boucherie*, but for specialised poultry you have to go to a *marchand de volaille*, and a *boucherie chevaline* will sell you horsemeat, still popular in France all these years after the war. Fish is available from a *poissonnerie*. A *charcuterie* is a delicatessen offering pricey but delicious sliced meats, seafood salads, pâtés and ready-to-eat main dishes. Most supermarkets have a charcuterie counter. The word *traiteur* (caterer) means the establishment sells ready-to-eat take-away dishes.

In most towns and cities, most foods are available one or more days a week at open-air markets (*marchés découverts*) or their covered equivalents (*marchés couverts* or *halles*).

DRINKS

Nonalcoholic Drinks

There's no medical reason to buy expensive bottled water; the tap water in France is perfectly safe. Make sure you ask for *une carafe d'eau* (a jug of water) or *de l'eau du robinet* (tap water) or you may get costly mineral water (*eau de source*).

A small cup of espresso is called *un café*, *un café noir* or *un express*. You can also ask for a large (*grand*) version. *Un café crème* is espresso with steamed cream. *Un café au lait* is espresso served in a large cup with lots of steamed milk. Decaffeinated coffee is *un café décaféiné* or simply *un déca*.

Other hot drinks that are popular include: tea (*thé*), but if you want milk you ask for '*un peu de lait frais*'; herbal tea (*tisane*); and usually excellent hot chocolate (*chocolat chaud*).

Alcohol

The French almost always take their meals with wine – red (*rouge*), white (*blanc*) or *rosé*, chosen to complement what's being eaten. The least expensive wines cost less per litre than soft drinks. Wines that meet stringent regulations governing where, how and under what conditions the grapes are grown, fermented and bottled, bear the abbreviation AOC (*Appellation d'Origine Contrôlée*, which means 'mark of controlled place of origin'). The cheapest wines have no AOC certification and are known as *vins ordinaires* or *vins de table* (table wines). They sell for as little as 5FF a litre in wine-producing areas and closer to 9 or 13FF a litre in supermarkets, but spending 5 or 10FF per bottle can make all the difference.

Alcoholic drinks other than wine include apéritifs, such as *kir* (dry white wine sweetened with *cassis* – blackcurrant liqueur), *kir royale* (champagne with cassis), and *pastis* (anise-flavoured alcohol drunk with ice and water); and *digestifs* such as brandy or Calvados (apple brandy). Beer is usually either from Alsace or imported. A *demi* (about 250ml) is cheaper on draught (*à la pression*) than from a bottle.

ENTERTAINMENT

If you don't fancy seeing your favourite actors lip-synching in French, look in the film listings and on the theatre marquee for the letters 'VO' (*version originale*) or 'VOST' (*version originale sous-titrée*), which mean the film retains its original foreign soundtrack but has been given French subtitles. If there's no VO or if you see 'VF' (*version française*), the film has been dubbed.

THINGS TO BUY

France is renowned for its luxury goods, including *haute couture* fashion, expensive accessories (eg Hermès scarves), perfume and such alcoholic beverages as champagne and brandy. Purchases of over 1200FF by people who live outside the EU are eligible for a rebate of the value added tax (TVA) on most goods. See Consumer Taxes under Money earlier in this section.

Getting There & Away

AIR

Air France and scores of other airlines link Paris with every part of the globe. Other French cities with direct international air links include Nice, Lyon and Marseille. For details on agencies selling discount international tickets in Paris, see Travel Agencies in the Paris section. For information on Paris' two international airports, Orly and Roissy-Charles de Gaulle, see Getting There & Away in the Paris section. Information on how to get from the airports into Paris (and vice versa) is given under Getting Around in the Paris section.

Britain

Flights between London and Paris are sometimes available for as little as 500FF return; Air France offers one-way youth fares for 390FF. You must stay over a Saturday night. In Paris contact Nouvelles Frontières (☎ 08 03 33 33 33) at 66 Blvd Saint Michel (6e; metro Luxembourg). Look Voyages (☎ 01 53 43 13 13 or ☎ 08 36 68 01 20) has information on round-trip packages; on Minitel, key in 3615 SOS CHARTER.

Elsewhere in Europe

One-way discount charter fares available for

flights from Paris start at 580FF to Rome; 920FF to Athens; 730FF to Dublin; 940FF to Istanbul; and 710FF to Madrid. Contact a travel agent or call SOS Charters for more information.

LAND
Britain

The highly civilised Eurostar passenger train service through the Channel Tunnel began operating between Paris' Gare du Nord and London's Waterloo Station in late 1994. The three parallel, concrete-lined tunnels – two rail tunnels and one for servicing them – were bored between Folkestone and Calais through a layer of impermeable chalk marl 25 to 45m below the floor of the English Channel. The journey takes about three hours (20 minutes through the tunnel) and will be shortened when Britain completes its portion of high-speed track at the end of the decade. The full one-way/return fare between Paris and London is 820/1590FF, but if you travel during the week and spend more than three nights away you can get a return fare for as little as 990FF.

Le Shuttle, which also began operating in 1994, whisks buses and cars (and their passengers) on single and double-deck wagons from near Folkestone to Coquelles just west of Calais in 35 minutes. Actual travel time from *autoroute* (the A26 to/from Paris) to motorway (the M20 to/from London) is closer to an hour, though. The regular one-way fare for a car and its passengers is 645FF. Shuttles run round the clock, and no bookings are required.

The Eurostar and Le Shuttle office in Paris (☎ 08 36 35 35 39) is in the Maison de la Grande Bretagne at 19 Rue des Mathurins (9e; metro Havre Caumartin), north-west of Place de l'Opéra. Information is also available on Minitel 3615 SNCF/Le Shuttle, and www.eurotunnel.com.

Elsewhere in Europe

Bus For bus services between France and other parts of Europe, see Getting There & Away in the Paris section.

Train Paris, France's main rail hub, is linked with every part of Europe. Depending on

where you're coming from, you may have to transit through Paris to get to the provinces. For details on Paris' six train stations, each of which handles traffic to/from different parts of France and Europe, see Trains under Getting There & Away in the Paris section.

BIJ (Billet International Jeunes) tickets, which are available to people under 26, cost about 20 to 25% less than regular tickets on international 2nd-class train travel started during off-peak periods. See Discounts under Trains in the following Getting Around section for details. BIJ tickets are not sold at train station ticket windows; you have to go to an office of Transalpino, Frantour Tourisme or Voyages Wasteels. There's usually one in the vicinity of a major train station.

SEA
Britain & the Channel Islands

The hovercraft (*aéroglisseur*) takes 30 minutes to cross the Channel. Hoverspeed (☎ 0800 90 17 77 in France, ☎ 0990-240 241 in the UK) runs both giant catamarans (SeaCats) and hovercraft from Calais to Dover (Douvres), Boulogne to Dover and Boulogne to Folkestone. For a one-way Calais-Dover trip or a return completed in less than five days, Hoverspeed charges pedestrians 150FF. A car with five passengers is charged 590 to 890FF one way, 10% to 25% more for five-day return, depending on the season.

SeaFrance Sealink (☎ 01 44 94 40 40 in Paris, ☎ 03 21 34 55 00 in Calais and ☎ 0990-711 711 in Dover), in Paris' Maison de la Grande Bretagne at 19 Rue des Mathurins (9e; metro Havre Caumartin), runs car ferries from Calais to Dover (1½ hours). One-way fares for passengers and cyclists start at 200FF. Cars cost from 560 to 960FF one way.

P&O Stena (☎ 01 44 51 00 51), 38 Ave de l'Opéra (2e; metro Opéra), operates car ferries and catamarans (from 230FF one way for pedestrians; 555 to 1330FF for a car with two passengers) from Dieppe to Newhaven. Brittany Ferries (☎ 08 03 82 88 28) sail from Roscoff to Plymouth daily from mid-March to mid-November (150 to 260FF one way for pedestrians; 670 to 1230FF for a car and driver). There is only one sailing a week in winter.

P&O European Ferries (☎ 08 03 01 30 13 in France, ☎ 0990-980 555 in the UK), in the same building as Sealink in Paris, runs car ferries from Le Havre to Portsmouth (5¾ hours) and Cherbourg to Portsmouth (3¾ hours).

Ireland

Irish Ferries (☎ 01 42 66 90 90) links Roscoff and Cherbourg with Rosslare. The trip takes about 20 hours. There are only two or three ferries a week from October to March but daily runs the rest of the year. Passengers pay from 315 to 650FF one way, depending on when they travel, and students get a small discount. Irish Ferries' Paris office is at 32 Rue du 4 Septembre (2e; metro Opéra). Eurail passes are valid on some of these ferry services.

Italy

For information on ferry services between Italy and Corsica, see Getting There & Away in the Corsica section. You can purchase tickets from many French travel agents.

North Africa

The Société Nationale Maritime Corse Méditerranée (SNCM) and its Algerian counterpart, Algérie Ferries, operate ferry services from Marseille to the Algerian ports of Algiers (Alger), Annaba, Bejaia, Skikda and Oran. SNCM also has services from Marseille to Tunis in Tunisia (from 915FF) and Porto Torres in Sardinia. For details, see Ferry under Getting There & Away in the Marseille section.

The Compagnie Marocaine de Navigation (☎ 04 67 46 68 00) runs ferries from Sète (near Montpellier) to the Moroccan cities of Tangier (Tanger) and Nador. The trip takes about 36 hours.

Getting Around

AIR

Air France (including Air Inter; ☎ 0 802 802 802; Minitel: 3615 AF) handles most domestic passenger flights. Flying within France is quite expensive, but people under 25 (and students under 27) can get discounts of 50% and more on certain Air Inter flights. The most heavily discounted flights may be cheaper than long-distance rail travel. Details are available from travel agents.

BUS

Because the French train network is state-owned and the government prefers to operate a monopoly, the country has only a limited intercity bus service. Buses are widely used, however, for short-distance intra-departmental routes, especially in rural areas with relatively few train lines (eg Brittany and Normandy).

Costs

In some areas (eg along the Côte d'Azur), you may have the choice of going by either bus or train. For longer trips, buses tend to be much slower but slightly cheaper than trains. On short runs they are slower and usually more expensive.

TRAIN

France's excellent rail network, operated by the Société Nationale des Chemins de Fer (SNCF), reaches almost every part of the country. Places not served by train are linked with major railheads by SNCF buses. France's most important train lines fan out from Paris like the spokes of a wheel, making rail travel between certain provincial towns and cities infrequent and rather slow. In some cases, you have to transit through Paris, which may require transferring from one of Paris' six train stations to another (see Train under Getting There & Away in the Paris section for details).

The pride and joy of the SNCF is the world-famous TGV (*train à grande vitesse*), which means 'high-speed train'. There are three TGV lines: the TGV Sud-Est, which links Paris' Gare de Lyon with Lyon, Valence and – due for completion in late 1999 – Marseille; the TGV Atlantique, which runs from Paris' Gare Montparnasse to the Loire Valley, Bordeaux and the south-west; and the TGV Nord Europe, which goes from Paris' Gare du Nord to Calais and London. Although it usually travels at 300km/h, the TGV Atlantique has, in test runs, reached over 515km/h, the world speed record for trains. Going by TGV costs the same as travelling on regular trains except that you must pay a reservation fee (see Costs & Reservations below) of 20 to 90FF, depending on when you travel.

Most larger SNCF stations have a left-luggage office (*consigne manuelle*) which charges 30FF per bag (35FF for a bicycle) for 24 hours.

Information

Most train stations have both ticket windows (*guichets*) and an information and reservation office or desk. SNCF now has a nationwide telephone number (☎ 08 36 35 35 35 in French, ☎ 08 36 35 35 39 in English, cost 2.23FF a minute) for all rail inquiries and reservations.

Formalities

Before boarding the train on each leg of your journey, you must validate your ticket *and* your reservation card by time-stamping them in one of the *composteurs*, orange postbox-like machines that are located somewhere between the ticket windows and the tracks. Eurail passes and France Railpasses *must* be time-stamped before you begin your first journey to initiate the period of validity.

Costs & Reservations

Train fares consist of two parts: the cost of passage, which is calculated according to the number of kilometres you'll be travelling, and a reservation fee. The reservation fee is optional unless you travel by TGV or want a couchette or special reclining seat. In addition, on especially popular trains (eg on holiday weekends) you may have to make advance reservations in order to get a seat. Eurail-pass holders should bear in mind that they must pay any applicable reservation fees. Since some overnight trains are equipped only with couchettes – eg most of the overnight trains on the Paris-Nice run – there's no way Eurail-pass holders can avoid the reservation fee except by taking a day train with a supply of unreserved seats.

Discounts

For the purpose of granting discounts, SNCF now divides train travel into two periods: blue (*bleue*), when the largest discounts are available, and white (*blanche*), when there

are far fewer bargains. To be eligible for the discount, your journey must begin during a period of the appropriate colour. For a chart of blue and white periods, ask for a *Calendrier Voyageurs* at any SNCF information counter.

Discounts for Non-EU Citizens The France Vacances Pass (called the France Railpass in North America) allows unlimited travel by rail in France for three to nine days over the course of a month. The pass can be purchased in France (from Gare du Nord, Gare de Lyon, Gare Saint Lazare and the two airports in Paris, and the main train stations in Nice and Marseille only) but will be more expensive than buying it before you leave home. In the USA, the three-day 2nd-class version costs US$165; each additional day is US$30. The France Youthpass, available to people who have not reached their 26th birthday on the first day of travel, costs US$150 for four days of travel over two months; additional days (up to a maximum of 10 in total) cost US$25. These passes are available through travel agents anywhere outside Europe and from a limited number of places within Europe. In North America, Rail Europe (☎ 1-800-438 7245) has all the information.

Discounts Available in France Discounts of 25% on one-way or return travel within France are available at train station ticket windows for certain groups of travellers, subject to availability. Just show the ticket agent proof of eligibility, and you'll get the reduction on the spot. If you're over 12 but have not yet reached your 26th birthday on the date of travel, you are eligible for a Découverte 12/25 fare, which replaces the old BSE tickets. One to four adults travelling with a child aged four to 11 qualify for the Découverte Enfant Plus fare. People over 60 enjoy a fare called Découverte Senior.

In addition, any two people who are travelling together qualify for a Découverte Deux fare, which gives you a 25% reduction in 1st or 2nd class, but only on return travel. On Thalys trains to Belgium, Holland and Cologne, people aged 12 to 25 get 50% off the full fare; seniors get a 30% discount.

No matter what age you are, the Découverte Séjour excursion fare gives you a 25%

reduction for return travel within France if you meet two conditions: the total length of your trip is at least 200km; and you'll be spending a Saturday night at your destination.

TAXI

France's cities and larger towns all have 24-hour taxi service. French taxis are always equipped with meters; prices range from 3.50FF per kilometre in Paris to as high as 10FF in Corsica. Tariffs are quite a bit higher after 7 pm and on Sunday and public holidays. There are often surcharges (5 or 6FF) for each piece of heavy luggage or if you are picked up or dropped off at a train station or airport. Passengers always sit in the back seat.

CAR & MOTORCYCLE

There's nothing like exploring the back roads of the Loire Valley or the Alps on your own, free of train and bus schedules. Unfortunately, travelling around France by car or motorcycle is expensive; petrol is costly and tolls can reach hundreds of francs a day if you're going cross-country in a hurry. Three or four people travelling together, however, may find that renting a car is cheaper than taking the train. Throughout France, you must use a meter to park. Buy a ticket from the machine you'll see on every block and display it *inside* the car on the dashboard.

Road Rules

To drive in France, you must carry a passport or EU national identity card, a valid driver's licence, proof of insurance and car-ownership papers.

Unless otherwise posted, speed limits are 130km/h (110km/h in the rain) on the *autoroutes* (dual carriageways/expressways whose alphanumeric names begin with A); 110/90km/h on the *routes nationales* (highways whose names begin with N); and 90km/h on the *routes départementales* (rural highways whose names start with D). The moment you pass a sign indicating that you've entered the boundaries of a town, village or hamlet, the speed limit automatically drops to 50km/h (or less as posted) and stays there until you pass an identical sign with a red bar across it.

The maximum permissible blood-alcohol level in France is 0.5 grams per litre (0.05%).

Expenses

Petrol prices in France can vary by half a franc or more per litre depending on the station – it pays to shop around. Unleaded (*sans plomb*) petrol with an octane rating of 98 costs around 6.40FF a litre. Diesel fuel (*gasoil* or *gazole*) is about 4.60FF a litre. Fuel is most expensive at the rest stops along the autoroutes.

Tolls are another major expense: expect to pay around 40FF per 100km.

Rental

Renting a car in France is expensive, especially if you do it through one of the international car-hire companies. In the Getting Around sections for many cities, the Car & Motorcycle entry supplies details on the cheapest places to rent cars.

If you get into a minor accident, fill out a Constat Aimable d'Accident Automobile (joint car accident report) – there should be one in the glove compartment – with the other driver. You both sign and each of you gets a copy. If you were not at fault, make sure all the facts reflecting this are included on the form which, unless your French is really fluent, should be filled out with the assistance of someone who can translate all the French automobile terms.

Purchase-Repurchase Plans

If you'll be needing a car in France for between 24 and 180 days it's *much* cheaper to 'purchase' one from the manufacturer and then 'sell' it back than it is to rent one. In reality, you only pay for the number of days you use the vehicle, but the purchase-repurchase (*achat-rachat*) aspect of the paperwork, none of which is your responsibility, lets you save France's whopping 20.6% VAT on noncommercial car rentals. Only non-EU residents are eligible.

Both Renault and Peugeot have excellent-value purchase-repurchase plans – contact the dealer in your country. It can be up to 35% cheaper arranging your purchase-repurchase car abroad, where various discounts are available, than in France. You usually have to book and pay about a month before you pick up the car.

Automobile Associations

In Paris, the Automobile Club de l'Île de France (☎ 01 40 55 43 00; metro Argentine) at 14 Ave de la Grande Armée (17e) sells insurance coverage and, if you stop by the office, can supply you with basic maps and suggestions for itineraries. The Automobile Club National no longer exists.

BICYCLE

Most large towns have at least one cycling shop that hires out bikes by the hour, day or week. You can still get low-tech one and three-speeds or 10-speeds (*vélos à 10 vitesses*), but in some areas such antiquated contrivances are going the way of the penny-farthing. A growing number of shops only have mountain bikes (*vélos tout-terrain* or VTTs), which generally cost 60 to 100FF a day. Most places, especially those renting expensive mountain bikes, require a deposit of 1000 to 2000FF (though a passport will often suffice).

BOAT

Travelling through some of France's 7500km of navigable waterways on a houseboat or canal boat is a unique and relaxing way to see the country. For a brochure listing boat-rental companies around France, contact the Paris-based Syndicat National des Loueurs de Bateaux de Plaisance (☎ 01 44 37 04 00) at Port de Javel Haut (15e; metro Javel).

HITCHING

Hitching in France is more difficult than almost anywhere else in Europe. (See the Hitching section in the introductory Getting Around chapter for general information.) Getting out of big cities like Paris, Lyon and Marseille or travelling around the Côte d'Azur by thumb is well nigh impossible. Remote rural areas are your best bet, but few cars are likely to be going farther than the next large town. Women should not hitch alone.

It's an excellent idea to hold up a sign with your destination followed by the letters *s.v.p.* (for *s'il vous plaît* – 'please'). Some people have reported good luck hitching with truck drivers from truck stops. It's illegal to hitch on autoroutes and other major expressways, but you can stand near the entrance ramps.

In Paris, Allostop-Provoya (☎ 01 53 20 42 42; metro Cadet) at 8 Rue Rochambeau (9e) can put you in touch with a driver who is going your way. If you are not a member (180FF for up to eight journeys over two years), there's a per-trip fee of between 30FF (for distances under 200km) and 70FF (for distances over 500km). In addition, you have to pay the driver 0.22FF per kilometre for expenses.

ORGANISED TOURS

Though independent travel is usually far more rewarding then being led from coach to sight and back to coach, some areas in France are difficult to visit on your own unless you have wheels. Tour options are mentioned under Organised Tours in sections where they are relevant (eg Loire Valley, the D-Day Beaches in Normandy, the Vézère Valley in Périgord). A number of Paris-based companies have tours of various lengths into the hinterland (Champagne, Burgundy, the Loire Valley, Normandy) including Cityrama (☎ 01 44 55 61 00; metro Palais Royal) at 4 Place des Pyramides (1er). The tourist office in Paris has a complete list.

Paris

☎ 01

Paris (population 2.2 million; metropolitan area 10.5 million) has almost exhausted the superlatives that can reasonably be applied to a city. Notre Dame and the Eiffel Tower – at sunrise, at sunset, at night – have been described ad nauseam, as have the Seine and the subtle (and not-so-subtle) differences between the Left and Right banks. But what writers have been unable to capture is the grandness and even the magic of strolling along the city's broad avenues – a legacy of the 19th century – which lead from impressive public buildings and exceptional museums to parks, gardens and esplanades. Paris is enchanting at any time, in every season. You too may find yourself humming that old Cole Porter favourite as you walk the streets: 'I love Paris in the springtime, I love Paris in the fall ...'

Orientation

In central Paris (which the French call Intra-Muros – 'within the walls'), the Rive Droite (Right Bank) is north of the Seine, while the Rive Gauche (Left Bank) is south of the river. For administrative purposes, Paris is divided into 20 *arrondissements* (districts), which spiral out clockwise from the centre of the city. Paris addresses always include the arrondissement number. In this section, these numbers are listed in parentheses immediately after the street address, using the usual French notation. For example, 1er stands for *premier* (1st), 4e for *quatrième* (4th) and 19e for *dix-neuvième* (19th). When an address includes the full five-digit postal code, the last two digits indicate the arrondissement: 75001 for the 1st, 75014 for the 14th etc.

As there is nearly always a metro station within 500m, you can whiz around under the traffic and pop up wherever you choose. To help you find your way, we've included the station nearest each hotel, museum etc, immediately after the telephone or arrondissement number.

Maps The best map of Paris is Michelin's 1:10,000 scale *Paris Plan*. It comes both in booklet (*Paris Plan 11*) and sheet form (*Paris Plan 10*) and is available in bookshops, stationery stores and kiosks around the city.

Information

Tourist Offices Paris' main tourist office (☎ 01 49 52 53 54, or ☎ 01 44 29 12 12 for info in English; fax 01 49 52 53 00; metro Charles de Gaulle-Étoile) is 100m east of the Arc de Triomphe at 127 Ave des Champs-Élysées (8e). It's open every day of the year, except 1 May and 25 December, from 9 am to 8 pm (11 am to 6 pm on Sunday in winter). This is the best source of information on the city's museums, concerts, expositions, theatre performances and the like. Information on other parts of France is also available. For a small fee and a deposit, the office can find you a place to stay in Paris for that night or in the provinces up to eight days in advance.

There are tourist office annexes open Monday to Saturday from 8 am to 8 pm (9 pm in summer) in all of Paris' train stations except Gare Saint Lazare. From May to September, the tourist office annexe (☎ 01 45 51 22 15) at the Eiffel Tower (7e) is open from 11 am to 6 pm.

Many French regions and departments such as Périgord, Pyrénées and Hautes-Alpes have tourist outlets (Maisons du Tourisme) in Paris. Ask at the main tourist office for a list.

Money All of Paris' six major train stations have exchange bureaus open seven days a week until at least 7 pm, but the rates are not very good. The exchange offices at Orly (Orly-Sud terminal) and Roissy-Charles de Gaulle (both Aérogares) are open until 11 pm. Unless you want to get about 10% less than a fair rate, avoid the big exchange-bureau chains like Chequepoint and ExactChange.

Banque de France By far the best rate in town is offered by Banque de France, France's central bank, whose headquarters (☎ 01 42 92 22 27; metro Palais Royal-Musée du Louvre) is three blocks north of the Louvre at 31 Rue Croix des Petits Champs (1er). The exchange service is open Monday to Friday from 9.30 am to 12.30 pm and 1.30 to 4 pm. The Banque de France branch (☎ 01 44 61 15 30; metro Bastille) at 5 Place de la Bastille (4e), which is opposite the new Opéra-Bastille, is open weekdays from 9 to 11.45 am and 1.30 to 3.30 pm.

American Express Paris' landmark American Express office (☎ 01 47 77 77 07; metro Auber or Opéra) at 11 Rue Scribe (9e) faces the west side of Opéra Garnier. Exchange services, cash advances, refunds and poste restante are available Monday to Saturday from 8.30 am to 6.30 pm (10 am to 5 pm on Sunday for exchange only). You can get slightly better exchange rates elsewhere and the office is usually jammed.

Citibank Money wired from abroad by or to Citibank usually arrives at its head office (☎ 01 49 06 10 10; metro Grande Arche de la Défense) in the suburb of La Défense, which is west of the Arc de Triomphe. The address is 19 Le Parvis, and it's open Monday to Friday from 10 am to 5.30 pm.

Notre Dame (4e & 5e) Le Change de Paris (☎ 01 43 54 76 55; metro Saint Michel) at 2 Place Saint Michel (6e) has some of the best rates in all of Paris. It's open daily from 10 am to 7 pm. There's another exchange bureau (☎ 01 46 34 70 46; metro Saint Michel) with good rates one block south of Place Saint Michel at 1 Rue Hautefeuille (6e); it's open daily from 9 am to 9 pm.

Panthéon (5e) The Banque Nationale de Paris (☎ 01 43 29 45 50; metro Luxembourg) at 7 Rue Soufflot exchanges foreign currency Monday to Friday from 9 am to 5 pm.

Champs-Élysées (8e) Thanks to fierce competition, the Champs-Élysées is an excellent place to change money. The *bureau de change* (☎ 01 42 25 38 14; metro Franklin D Roosevelt) at 25 Ave des Champs-Élysées is open every day of the year from 9 am to 8 pm.

Montmartre (18e) There's a *bureau de change* (☎ 01 42 52 67 19; metro Abbesses) at 6 Rue Yvonne Le Tac, two blocks east of Place des Abbesses. It's open Monday to Saturday from 10 am to 6.30 pm (6 pm weekends; closed Sunday October to April).

Post & Communications Paris' main post office (☎ 01 40 28 20 00; metro Sentier or Les Halles) at 52 Rue du Louvre (1er) offers all the usual services every day round the clock. Foreign exchange is only available during regular post office hours – on weekdays from 8 am to 7 pm and Saturday from 8 am to noon. All poste-restante mail not specifically addressed to a particular branch post office ends up here.

At the post office (☎ 01 42 56 13 71; metro George V) at 71 Ave des Champs-Élysées (8e), you can place telephone calls with phonecards, pick up poste-restante mail and send letters, telegrams and faxes Monday to Saturday from 8 am to 10 pm and on Sunday and public holidays from 10 am to noon and 2 to 8 pm. See Orientation for an explanation of Paris postcodes.

Cybercafés Café Orbital (☎ 01 43 25 76 77; metro Odéon) at 13 Rue de Médicis (6e) is open daily from 10 am to 10 pm. Internet access costs 55FF per hour, 200/300FF for five/10 hours; a student discount is available.

The Web Bar (☎ 01 42 72 66 55; webbar@webbar.fr; metro Filles du Calvaire) is at 32 Rue de Picardie (3e), off Rue des Archives. It charges 40FF per hour or 250FF for 10 hours; it's open daily from 11.30 am to 2 am.

Travel Agencies Nouvelles Frontières (☎ 08 03 33 33 33; Minitel 3615 NF; www.nouvelles-frontieres.com; metro Luxembourg) specialises in discount long-distance air fares and has 13 outlets around the city, including one at 66 Blvd Saint Michel (6e), open Monday to Saturday from 9 am to 7 pm. Council Travel (☎ 01 44 55 55 44; metro Pyramides) has its main Paris office at 22 Rue des Pyramides (1er). It's open Monday to Friday from 9.30 am to 6.30 pm and on Saturday from 10 am to 5.30 pm.

Bookshops Paris' famous English-language bookshop Shakespeare & Company (☎ 01 43 26 96 50; metro Saint Michel) is at 37 Rue de la Bûcherie (5e), which is across the Seine from Notre Dame Cathedral. The shop has a varied collection of new and used books in English, but even the second-hand stuff doesn't come cheap. There's a library/ reading room on the 1st floor. Shakespeare & Company is generally open daily from noon to midnight.

The largest English-language bookshop in the city, WH Smith (☎ 01 44 77 88 99; metro Concorde) at 248 Rue de Rivoli (1er), is a block east of Place de la Concorde. It's open Monday to Saturday from 9.30 am to 7 pm and on Sunday from 1 to 7 pm. At 29 Rue de la Parcheminerie (5e), the mellow, Canadian-run Abbey Bookshop (☎ 01 46 33 16 24; metro Cluny-La Sorbonne) has an eclectic, though somewhat limited, selection of titles. It's open daily from 10 am to 7 pm (10 pm Wednesday to Saturday in the summer).

Lonely Planet books and other travel guides are available from Ulysse (☎ 01 43 25 17 35; metro Pont Marie) at 26 Ave St Louis en L'Île (4e); from FNAC Librairie Internationale (☎ 01 44 41 31 50; metro Cluny-La Sorbonne) at 71 Blvd Saint Germain (5e); and from L'Astrolabe Rive Gauche (☎ 01 46 33 80 06; metro Cluny-La Sorbonne) at 14 Rue Serpente (6e).

PARIS

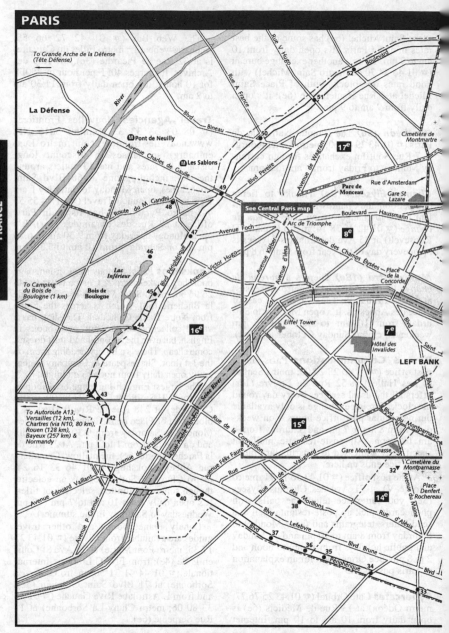

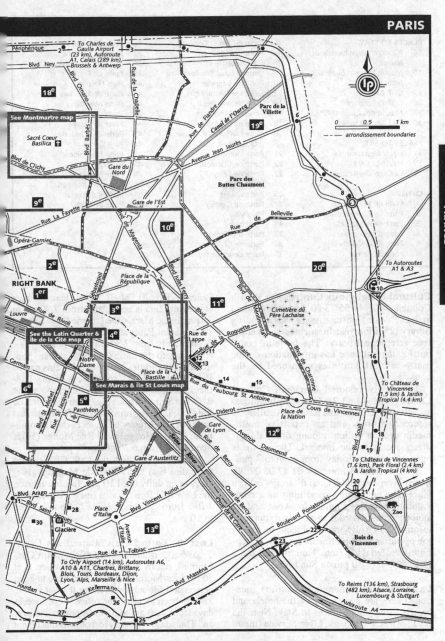

Périphérique
2
Blvd Ney
To Charles de
Gaulle Airport
(23 km), Autoroute
A1, Calais (289 km),
Brussels & Antwerp
3
4
5

18e

See Montmartre map

Sacré Coeur
Basilica
Blvd Barbès
Rue de la Chapelle
Ave de Flandre
Canal de l'Ourcq
Parc de la
Villette
19e
6

Blvd Ornano
Blvd de Clichy
Gare du
Nord
Avenue Jean Jaurès
7

0   0.5   1 km
- · - arrondissement boundaries

9e
Rue La Fayette
Gare de l'Est
Parc des
Buttes Chaumont
8

Opéra-Garnier
Blvd de Magenta
10e
Rue   de   Belleville

2e
Blvd de Sébastopol
Place de la
République
Blvd Jules Ferry
20e
To Autoroutes
A1 & A3
10

RIGHT BANK
1er
Rue de Rivoli
3e
11e
Blvd de Ménilmontant
Cimetière du
Père Lachaise
16

Louvre
4e
Rue de
Lappe
Rue de la Roquette
Blvd Voltaire
Blvd de Charonne
To Château de
Vincennes
(1.5 km) & Jardin
Tropical (4.4 km)

Germain
Notre
Dame
Place de la
Bastille
11
12
13
Rue du Faubourg St Antoine
14
15
Place de
la Nation
Cours de Vincennes
17

6e
Blvd St Michel
Rue St Jacques
5e
Panthéon
See the Latin Quarter &
Île de la Cité map
See Marais & Île St Louis map
Diderot
Blvd
Gare
de Lyon
Avenue   Daumesnil
18
19
To Château de
Vincennes
(1.6 km), Park Floral (2.4 km)
& Jardin Tropical (4 km)

Seine   River
Gare d'Austerlitz
12e
Rue de Bercy
Blvd Soult
20
21
Zoo

29
Blvd St Marcel
Quai de Bercy
Quai de la Gare
Boulevard Poniatowski
22
Bois de
Vincennes

Blvd Arago
31
Blvd Saint Jacques
28
Place
d'Italie
Blvd Vincent Auriol
Blvd de l'Hôpital
Avenue
d'Italie

30
Glacière
13e
23

Rue de Tolbiac
To Orly Airport (14 km), Autoroutes A6,
A10 & A11, Chartres, Brittany,
Blois, Tours, Bordeaux, Dijon,
Lyon, Alps, Marseille & Nice
Jourdan
Blvd Kellermann
26
27
25
Blvd Masséna
24
To Reims (136 km), Strasbourg
(482 km), Alsace, Lorraine,
Luxembourg & Stuttgart
Autoroute A4

PARIS

	PLACES TO STAY		7	Porte du Pré St Gervais		36	Porte Brancion
14	Auberge Internationale des Jeunes		8	Porte des Lilas		37	Porte de la Plaine
			9	Gare Routière Internationale		38	Lost Property Office
15	Maison Internationale des Jeunes			(International Bus Terminal)		39	Porte de Sèvres
			10	Porte de Bagnolet		40	Paris Heliport
19	CISP Ravel		12	Le Balajo Discothèque		41	Porte de St Cloud
26	CISP Kellermann		16	Porte de Montreuil		42	Porte Molitor
28	Maison des Clubs UNESCO		17	Porte de Vincennes		43	Porte d'Auteuil
30	FIAP Jean Monnet		18	Porte de St Mandé		44	Porte de Passy
			20	Musée des Arts d'Afrique et		45	Porte de la Muette
	PLACES TO EAT			d'Océanie		46	Paris Cycles
11	Ethnic Restaurants		21	Porte Dorée		47	Porte Dauphine
13	Havanita Café		22	Porte de Charenton		48	Paris Cycles
32	La Cagouille Restaurant		23	Porte de Bercy		49	Porte Maillot
			24	Porte d'Ivry		50	Porte de Champerret
	OTHER		25	Porte d'Italie		51	Porte d'Asnières
1	Porte de Saint Ouen		27	Porte de Gentilly		52	Porte de Clichy
2	Porte de Clignancourt		29	Paris Vélo			
3	Porte de la Chapelle		31	Catacombs			
4	Porte d'Aubervilliers		33	Porte d'Orléans			
5	Porte de la Villette		34	Porte de Châtillon			
6	Porte de Pantin		35	Porte de Vanves			

Cultural & Religious Centres The British Council (☎ 01 49 55 73 00; metro Invalides) at 9-11 Rue de Constantine (7e) has a lending library (250FF a year for membership) and a free reference library. The bulletin board outside the entrance has information on the many cultural activities sponsored by the council.

The newly restored Canadian Cultural Centre (☎ 01 44 43 21 31; metro Invalides) at 5 Rue de Constantine has an art gallery, a reference library and an extensive multi-media section which, among other things, offers access to the Internet. The centre is open Monday to Friday from 9 am to 7 pm.

The American Church (☎ 01 47 05 07 99; metro Invalides) at 65 Quai d'Orsay (7e) is a place of worship and something of a community centre for English speakers, and its announcement board is an excellent source of information on all sorts of subjects, including job openings and apartments for rent. Reception is staffed daily from 9 am to 1 pm and 2 to 10.30 pm (7.30 pm on Sunday).

Laundry The laundrettes (*laveries*) mentioned here are near many of the hotels and hostels listed under Places to Stay. Near the BVJ hostels, the Laverie Libre Service (metro Louvre Rivoli) at 7 Rue Jean-Jacques Rousseau (1er) is open daily from 7.30 am to 10 pm. In the Marais, the Laverie Libre Service (metro Saint Paul) at 25 Rue des Rosiers (3e) is open daily from 7.30 am to 10 pm.

Thanks to the Latin Quarter's student population, laundrettes are plentiful in this part of Paris. Three blocks south-west of the Panthéon, the laundrette (metro Luxembourg) at 216 Rue Saint Jacques (5e), near the Hôtel de Médicis, is open from 7 am to 10.30 pm. Just south of the Arènes de Lutèce, the Lavomatique (metro Monge) at 63 Rue Monge (5e) is open daily from 6.30 am to 10 pm.

Near Gare de l'Est, the Lav' Club (metro Gare de l'Est) at 55 Blvd de Magenta (10e) stays open daily until 10 pm. In Montmartre, the Laverie Libre Service (metro Blanche) at 4 Rue Burq (18e) is open daily from 7.30 am to 10 pm.

Lost & Found Paris' Bureau des Objets Trouvés (Lost and Found Office; metro Convention), run by the Préfecture de Police, is at 36 Rue des Morillons (15e). You have to go in person and fill out forms to see if what you've lost has been located. The office is open weekdays from 8.30 am to 5 pm (8 pm on Tuesday and Thursday). The only lost objects that do not make their way here are those found in SNCF train stations; these are taken to the *objets trouvés* bureau – usually attached to the left-luggage office – of the relevant train station.

Medical & Emergency Services Paris has about 50 *Assistance Publique* (public health service) hospitals. An easy one to find is the Hôtel Dieu hospital (☎ 01 42 34 82 34; metro Cité), on the northern side of Place du Parvis Notre Dame (4e), the square in front of the cathedral. The emergency room (*service des urgences*) is open 24 hours a day.

Dangers & Annoyances For its size, Paris is a safe city, but you should always use common sense; for instance, avoid the large Bois de Boulogne and Bois de Vincennes parks after nightfall. Although it's fine to use the metro until it stops running at about 12.45 am, some stations are best avoided late at night, especially if alone. These include Châtelet (1er) and its many seemingly endless tunnels to the Les Halles and Châtelet-Les Halles stops; Château Rouge in Montmartre (18e); Gare du Nord (10e); Strasbourg-Saint Denis (2e and 10e); Réaumur-Sébastopol (2e); and Montparnasse-Bienvenüe (6e and 15e).

Things to See
Museum Hours & Discounts Paris has more than 100 museums of all sizes and types; a comprehensive list is available from the tourist office for 10FF. Government-run museums (*musées nationaux*) in Paris and the Île de France (eg the Louvre, the Musée Picasso) are open daily, except Tuesday. The only exceptions are the Musée d'Orsay, Musée Rodin and Versailles, which are closed Monday. Entry to most of the national museums is free for people 17 or younger and half-price for those aged 18 to 25 or over 60. Paris' municipal museums are open daily, except Monday, and are free on Sunday.

The Carte Musées et Monuments museum pass gets you into some 75 museums and monuments in Paris and the surrounding region without having to queue for a ticket. The card costs 80/160/240FF for one/three/five consecutive days and is on sale at the museums and monuments it covers, at some metro ticket windows and at the tourist office.

Things to See – Left Bank
Île de la Cité (1er & 4e) Paris was founded sometime during the 3rd century BC, when members of a tribe known as the Parisii set up a few huts on Île de la Cité. By the Middle Ages, the city had grown to encompass both banks of the Seine, but Île de la Cité remained the centre of royal and ecclesiastical power.

Notre Dame Paris' cathedral (☎ 01 42 34 56 10; metro Cité or Saint Michel) is one of the most magnificent achievements of Gothic architecture. Its construction was begun in 1163 and completed around 1345. Exceptional features include the three spectacular rose windows, especially the one over the west façade, and the window on the north side of the transept, which has remained virtually unchanged since the 13th century. One of the best views of Notre Dame is from the lovely little park behind the cathedral, where you can see the mass of ornate flying buttresses that encircle the chancel and hold up its walls and roof. (While there, have a look at the haunting **Mémorial des Martyrs de la Déportation** in memory of the more than 200,000 people deported by the Nazis and French fascists during WWII.)

Notre Dame is open daily from 8 am to 6.45 pm (7.45 pm at weekends). There is no entrance fee. Free concerts are held every Sunday at 5.30 pm. The **Trésor** (Treasury) at the back of the cathedral, which contains precious liturgical objects, is open Monday to Saturday from 9.30 to 6.30 pm; admission is 15FF (10FF for students). The **North Tower**, from which you can view many of the cathedral's most ferocious-looking gargoyles and a good deal of Paris, can be climbed via long spiral steps. It's open daily from 9.30 am to 6.45 pm during summer; 10 am to 4.45 pm in winter. Entry is 32FF (21FF reduced rate).

The **Crypte Archéologique** (☎ 01 43 29 83 51) under the square in front of the cathedral displays Gallo-Roman and later remains found on the site. Entrance costs the same as the North Tower; a combined ticket for crypt and tower is 40FF.

Sainte Chapelle The gem-like upper chapel of Sainte Chapelle (☎ 01 53 73 78 51; metro Cité), illuminated by a veritable curtain

FRANCE

of 13th-century stained glass, is inside the **Palais de Justice** (Law Courts) at 4 Blvd du Palais (1er). Consecrated in 1248, Sainte Chapelle was built in only 33 months to house a crown of thorns (supposedly worn by the crucified Christ) and other relics purchased by King Louis IX (later Saint Louis) earlier in the 13th century. From October to March, it's open daily from 10 am to 5 pm; the rest of the year, from 9.30 am to 6.30 pm. Tickets cost 32FF (21FF reduced rate). A ticket valid for both Sainte Chapelle and the nearby Conciergerie costs 50FF. The high-security visitors' entrance to the Palais de Justice is opposite 7 Blvd du Palais (1er).

Conciergerie The Conciergerie (☎ 01 53 73 78 50; metro Cité) was a luxurious royal palace when it was built in the 14th century – the **Salle des Gens d'Armes** (Cavalrymen's Room) is the oldest medieval hall in Europe – but was later transformed into a prison and continued as such until 1914. During the Reign of Terror (1793-94), the Conciergerie was used to incarcerate 'enemies' of the Revolution before they were brought before the tribunal, which met next door in what is now the Palais de Justice. Among the almost 2600 prisoners held here before being bundled off to the guillotine were Queen Marie Antoinette and the Revolutionary radicals Danton and Robespierre. The Conciergerie has the same hours and entry fees as the Sainte Chapelle; guided visits in French leave every half-hour. The entrance is at 1 Quai de l'Horloge (1er).

Île Saint Louis (4e) Île Saint Louis, the smaller of Paris' two islands, is just east of Île de la Cité. The 17th-century houses of grey stone and the small-town shops that line the streets and quays impart an almost provincial feel, making this quarter a great place for a quiet stroll. If circumnavigating the island makes you hungry, you might want to join the line in front of Berthillon at 31 Rue Saint Louis en l'Île (4e; metro Pont Marie), which is reputed to have Paris' best ice cream. On foot, the shortest route between Notre Dame and the Marais passes through Île Saint Louis.

Latin Quarter (5e & 6e) This area is known as the Quartier Latin because, up till the Revolution, all communication between students and their professors here took place in Latin. The 5e has become increasingly touristy but still has a large population of students and academics affiliated with the University of Paris and other institutions. Shop-lined **Blvd Saint Michel**, known as the 'Boul Mich', runs along the border of the 5e and the 6e.

Panthéon (5e) The Latin Quarter landmark now known as the Panthéon (☎ 01 43 54 34 51; metro Luxembourg or Cardinal Lemoine), which is at the eastern end of Rue Soufflot, was commissioned as an abbey church in the mid-18th century. In 1791, the Constituent Assembly converted it into a mausoleum for the 'great men of the era of French liberty'. Permanent residents include Victor Hugo, Émile Zola, Voltaire and Jean-Jacques Rousseau. Much of the Panthéon's ornate marble interior and colonnaded dome will be closed for some time during a massive renovation. From October to March, the Panthéon is open daily from 10 am to 6.15 pm (9.30 am to 6.30 pm the rest of the year when there are guided visits). Entrance costs 32FF (21FF reduced rate).

Sorbonne (5e) Paris' most famous university was founded in 1253 as a college for 16 poor theology students. After serving for centuries as France's major theological centre, it was closed in 1792 by the Revolutionary government but reopened under Napoleon. Today, the Sorbonne's main campus complex (bounded by Rue Victor Cousin, Rue Saint Jacques, Rue des Écoles and Rue Cujas) and other buildings nearby house several of the 13 autonomous universities created when the University of Paris was reorganised in 1968. **Place de la Sorbonne** links Blvd Saint Michel with **Église de la Sorbonne**, the university's domed 17th-century church.

Jardin du Luxembourg (6e) When the weather is warm, Parisians flock to the Luxembourg Gardens (metro Luxembourg) in their thousands to sit and read, write, relax, talk and sunbathe while their children sail little boats in the fountains. The gardens' main entrance is across the street from 65 Blvd Saint Michel. The **Palais du Luxembourg**, fronting

Rue de Vaugirard at the northern end of the Jardin du Luxembourg, was built for Maria de' Medici (Marie de Médicis in French), queen of France from 1600 to 1610. It now houses the Sénat, the upper house of the French parliament.

Musée National du Moyen Age (5e)

The Museum of the Middle Ages (☎ 01 53 73 78 00; metro Cluny-La Sorbonne), also known as the Musée de Cluny, houses one of France's finest collections of medieval art. Its prized possession is a series of six late 15th-century tapestries from the southern Netherlands known as *La Dame à la Licorne* (The Lady and the Unicorn). The museum is housed in two structures: the frigidarium (cold room) and other remains of Gallo-Roman baths from around 200 AD, and the late 15th-century residence of the abbots of Cluny. The museum's entrance is at 6 Place Paul Painlevé, and is open from 9.15 am to 5.45 pm daily, except Tuesday. Entry is 30FF (20FF reduced rate). On Sunday, everyone pays 20FF.

Paris Mosque (5e)

Paris' central mosque (☎ 01 45 35 97 33; metro Monge) at Place du Puits de l'Ermite was built between 1922 and 1926 in an ornate Moorish style. There are tours from 9 am to noon and 2 to 6 pm daily, except Friday. The mosque complex includes a small souk (marketplace), a *salon de thé* (tearoom), an excellent couscous restaurant and a public bath (*hammam*). The hammam (☎ 01 43 31 18 14) is open from 10 am to 9 pm on Monday, Wednesday, Thursday, Friday and Saturday for women and from 2 to 9 pm on Tuesday and 10 am to 9 pm on Sunday for men. It costs 85FF. The entrance is at 39 Rue Geoffroy Saint Hilaire.

The mosque is opposite the western end of the **Jardin des Plantes** (Botanical Gardens), which includes a small **zoo** (☎ 01 40 79 37 94) as well as the recently renovated **Musée d'Histoire Naturelle** (☎ 01 40 79 30 00; metro Monge). It's open weekdays, except Tuesday, from 10 am to 6 pm (until 10 pm on Thursday). Entrance is 40FF (30FF reduced rate).

Institut du Monde Arabe (5e)

Established by 20 Arab countries to showcase Arab and Islamic culture and to promote cultural contacts, this institute (☎ 01 40 51 38 38; metro Jussieu) at 1 Rue des Fossés Saint Bernard occupies one of the most graceful and highly praised modern buildings in Paris. The 7th-floor **museum** (buy your tickets on the ground floor) of 9th to 19th-century Muslim art and crafts is open daily, except Monday, from 10 am to 6 pm and costs 25FF (20FF reduced rate).

Catacombes (14e)

In 1785, it was decided that the hygiene problems posed by Paris' overflowing cemeteries could be solved by exhuming the bones and storing them in the tunnels of three disused quarries. One such ossuary is the Catacombes (☎ 01 43 22 47 63; metro Denfert Rochereau), in which the bones and skulls of millions of Parisians from centuries past are neatly stacked along the walls. During WWII, these tunnels were used by the Résistance as headquarters. The route through the Catacombes begins from the small green building at 1 Place Denfert Rochereau. The site is open Tuesday to Friday from 2 to 4 pm and on weekends from 9 to 11 am and 2 to 4 pm. Tickets cost 27FF (19FF reduced rate).

Musée d'Orsay (7e)

The Musée d'Orsay (☎ 01 40 49 48 14; metro Musée d'Orsay), along the Seine at 1 Rue de Bellechasse, exhibits paintings, sculptures, *objets d'art* and other works of art produced between 1848 and 1914, including the fruits of the impressionist, postimpressionist and Art Nouveau movements. It thus fills the chronological gap between the Louvre and the Musée d'Art Moderne at the Centre Pompidou. The Musée d'Orsay is spectacularly housed in a former train station built in 1900 and re-inaugurated in its present form in 1986. It's open daily, except Monday, from 10 am (9 am on Sunday mid-June to August) to 6 pm (9.45 pm on Thursday). Entrance costs 39FF (27FF reduced rate).

Musée Rodin (7e)

The Musée Auguste Rodin (☎ 01 47 05 01 34; metro Varenne) at 77 Rue Varenne is one of the most pleasant museums in Paris. Rodin's extraordinarily vital bronze and marble sculptures (look for *The Kiss*, *Cathedral* and, of course, *The*

FRANCE

CENTRAL PARIS

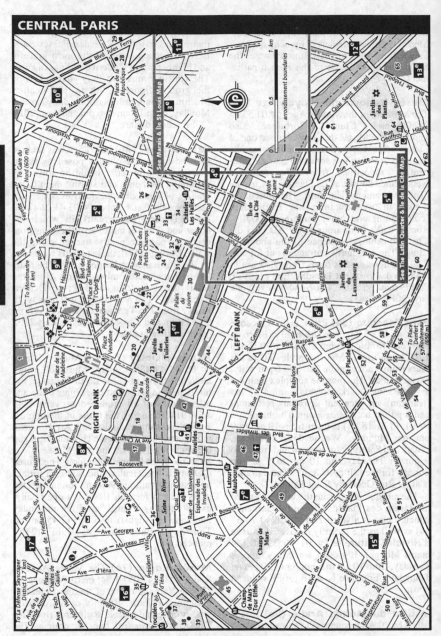

CENTRAL PARIS

PLACES TO STAY
29 Auberge de Jeunesse Jules Ferry
32 Centre International BVJ Paris-Louvre & Laundrette
50 Three Ducks Hostel
51 Aloha Hostel

PLACES TO EAT
14 Chartier Restaurant
15 Le Drouot Restaurant
26 Le Loup Blanc
55 Rue d'Odessa Crêperies
56 Mustang Café
58 Le Caméléon Restaurant
59 CROUS Restaurant Universitaire (6e)
60 CROUS Restaurant Universitaire Bullier
62 Founti Agadir

OTHER
1 Gare Saint Lazare
2 Gare de l'Est
3 Arc de Triomphe
4 Main Tourist Office
5 Post Office
6 Bureau de Change
7 La Madeleine Church
8 Au Printemps (Department Store)
9 Galeries Lafayette (Department Store)
10 Galeries Lafayette
11 Eurostar & Ferry Offices
12 American Express
13 Opéra-Garnier
16 Canadian Embassy
17 Grand Palais
18 Musée du Petit Palais
19 US Embassy
20 WH Smith Bookshop
21 Food Shops
22 Council Travel
23 Musée de l'Orangerie
24 Banque de France
25 Main Post Office
27 Rue Saint Denis Sex District
28 Cinémathèque
30 Louvre Museum
31 Change du Louvre (Currency Exchange)
33 Église Saint Eustache
34 Forum des Halles (Shopping Mall & Park)
35 Musée Guimet
36 Bateaux Mouches (Boat Tours)
37 Cinémathèque
38 Palais de Chaillot
39 Jardins du Trocadéro
40 American Church
41 Aérogare des Invalides (Buses to Orly)
42 Palais Bourbon (National Assembly Building)
43 British Council
44 Musée d'Orsay
45 Eiffel Tower
46 Hôtel des Invalides
47 Église du Dôme
48 Musée Rodin
49 École Militaire
52 FNAC Store & Ticket Outlet
53 Montparnasse Tower
54 Gare Montparnasse
57 Cimetière du Montparnasse
61 Institut du Monde Arabe
63 Paris Mosque & Hammam
64 Museum of Natural History
65 Gare d'Austerlitz

Thinker) are on display both inside the 18th-century Hôtel Biron and in the delightful gardens at the back. The Musée Rodin is open from 9.30 am to 5.45 pm (4.45 pm during winter) daily except Monday. From Tuesday to Saturday, entrance costs 28FF (18FF reduced rate); on Sunday, everyone gets in for 18FF. The gardens cost 5FF.

Invalides (7e) The Hôtel des Invalides (metro Invalides for the Esplanade, metro Varenne or Latour Maubourg for the main building) was built in the 1670s by Louis XIV to provide housing for 4000 disabled veterans (*invalides*). The building also served as the headquarters of the military governor of Paris, and was used to store weapons and ammunition. On 14 July 1789, the Paris mob forced its way into the building and, after fierce fighting, took 28,000 firearms before heading for the Bastille prison.

The **Église du Dôme** was built between 1677 and 1735 and is considered one of the finest religious edifices erected under Louis

XIV. The church was initially a mausoleum for military leaders in 1800, and in 1861 received the remains of Napoleon, encased in six concentric coffins.

The buildings on either side of the **Cour d'Honneur** (Main Courtyard) house the **Musée de l'Armée** (☎ 01 44 42 37 67), a huge military museum. The Musée de l'Armée and the light and airy **Tombeau de Napoléon 1er** (Napoleon's Tomb) are open daily from 10 am to 4.45 pm (5.45 pm in summer). Entrance costs 37FF (27FF reduced rate).

Eiffel Tower (7e) The Tour Eiffel (☎ 01 44 11 23 23; metro Champ de Mars-Tour Eiffel) faced massive opposition from Paris' artistic and literary elite when it was built for the 1889 Exposition Universelle (World's Fair), held to commemorate the Revolution. It was almost torn down in 1909 but was spared for practical reasons – it proved an ideal platform for newfangled transmitting antennae. The Eiffel Tower is 318m high, including the television antenna at the very tip. This figure can vary by as much as 15 cm as the tower's 7000 tonnes of steel, held together by 2.5 million rivets, expand in warm weather and contract when it's cold.

There are three levels open to the public. The lift (west and north pillars) costs 20FF for the 1st platform (57m above ground), 42FF for the 2nd (115m) and 57FF for the 3rd (276m). Walking up the stairs (south pillar) to the 1st or 2nd platforms costs 14FF. The tower is open every day from 9.30 am to 11 pm (9 am to midnight in summer). You can walk up from 9 am to 6.30 pm (9 pm in May and June, 11 pm in July and August).

Champ de Mars (7e)
The Champ de Mars, the grassy park around the Eiffel Tower, was originally a parade ground for the École Militaire (France's military academy), the huge, 18th-century building at the south-eastern end of the lawns.

Things to See – Right Bank

Jardins du Trocadéro (16e)
The Trocadéro gardens (metro Trocadéro), whose fountain and nearby sculpture park are grandly illuminated at night, are across the Pont d'Iéna from the Eiffel Tower. The colonnaded **Palais de Chaillot**, built in 1937, houses four museums but two of them – the Musée du Cinéma Henri Langlois (Henri Langlois Cinema Museum; ☎ 01 45 53 74 39) and the Musée des Monuments Français (French Monuments Museum; ☎ 01 44 05 39 10) – will be closed until late 1999. The other two, both closed on Tuesday, are the Musée de l'Homme (Museum of Mankind; ☎ 01 44 05 72 72; 30/20FF reduced price), and the Musée de la Marine (Maritime Museum; ☎ 01 53 65 65 69; 38/25FF reduced price).

Musée Guimet (16e)
The Guimet museum (☎ 01 47 23 88 11; metro Iéna) at 6 Place d'Iéna, about midway between the Eiffel Tower and the Arc de Triomphe, displays a fabulous collection of antiquities and works of art from throughout Asia. Large sections of the museum, however, will be closed for renovation until sometime in 1999. It's open daily, except Tuesday, from

9.45 am to 5.45 pm. Entrance costs 16FF (12FF reduced rate and on Sunday for all).

Louvre (1er)
The Louvre Museum (☎ 01 40 20 53 17, or ☎ 01 40 20 51 51 for a recorded message; metro Palais Royal-Musée du Louvre), constructed around 1200 as a fortress and rebuilt in the mid-16th century as a royal palace, became a public museum in 1793. The paintings, sculptures and artefacts on display have been assembled by French governments over the past five centuries and include works of art and artisanship from all over Europe as well as important collections of Assyrian, Egyptian, Etruscan, Greek, Coptic, Roman and Islamic art. The Louvre's most famous work is undoubtedly Leonardo da Vinci's *Mona Lisa*. Since it takes several serious visits to get anything more than the briefest glimpse of the offerings, your best bet – after seeking out a few things you really want to see (eg masterpieces such as the *Winged Victory of Samothrace* and *Venus de Milo*) – is to choose a period or section of the museum and pretend the rest is somewhere across town.

The Louvre's entrance is covered by a glass pyramid designed by American architect IM Pei. Commissioned by François Mitterrand and completed in 1990, the design generated bitter opposition but is now generally acknowledged as a brilliant success.

The Louvre is open daily, except Tuesday, from 9 am to 6 pm (until 9.45 pm on Monday and Wednesday). Ticket sales end 45 minutes before closing time. The entry fee is 45FF (26FF reduced rate), but on Sunday and every day after 3 pm everyone pays just 26FF. Entry is free for all on the first Sunday of every month.

Free brochures with rudimentary maps of the museum are available at the information desk in Hall Napoléon, where you can also get details on guided tours. Cassette tours in six languages can be rented for 30FF on the mezzanine level beneath the pyramid. Detailed explanations in a variety of languages, printed on heavy plastic-coated pages, are stored on racks in each display room.

Place Vendôme (1er)
The elegant Place Vendôme (metro Tuileries) and its arcaded buildings were designed in the 17th century to display a giant statue of Louis XIV that

was later destroyed during the Revolution. The present 44m column in the middle of the square consists of a stone core wrapped in a spiral of bronze made from 1250 cannons captured by Napoleon at the Battle of Austerlitz (1805). The shops around the square are among the most fashionable – and expensive – in Paris.

Musée de l'Orangerie (1er) The Musée de l'Orangerie (☎ 01 42 97 48 16; metro Concorde), which is in the south-east corner of Place de la Concorde, displays important impressionist works, including a series of Monet's spectacular *Nymphéas* (Water Lilies) and paintings by Cézanne, Matisse, Modigliani, Picasso and Renoir. It's open daily, except Tuesday, from 9.45 am to 5.15 pm. The entry fee is 30FF (20FF reduced rate and on Sunday for all).

Place de la Concorde (8e) This vast, cobbled square, set between the Jardin des Tuileries and the eastern end of the Champs-Élysées, was laid out between 1755 and 1775. Louis XVI was guillotined here in 1793 – as were another 1343 people over the next two years including his wife, Marie Antoinette, and Robespierre. The 3300-year-old Egyptian **obelisk** in the middle of the square was given to France in 1829 by the ruler of Egypt, Mohammed Ali.

La Madeleine (8e) The church of Saint Mary Magdalene (metro Madeleine) is 350m north of Place de la Concorde along Rue Royale. Built in the style of a Greek temple, it was consecrated in 1842 after almost a century of design changes and construction delays. The front porch affords a superb view of the square and, across the river, the 18th-century **Palais Bourbon** (now the home of the National Assembly) whose façade dates from the early 19th century.

Fauchon (☎ 01 47 42 60 11; metro Madeleine) at 26 Place de la Madeleine, is Paris' most famous gourmet food shop and is open daily, except Sunday, from 9.40 am to 7 pm.

Champs-Élysées (8e) The 2km-long Ave des Champs-Élysées links Place de la Concorde with the Arc de Triomphe. Once popular with the aristocracy as a stage on which to parade their wealth, it has, in recent decades, been partly taken over by fast-food restaurants and overpriced cafés. The nicest bit is the park with the Petit Palais and the Grand Palais between Place de la Concorde and Rond Point des Champs-Élysées.

Musée du Petit Palais (8e) The Petit Palais (☎ 01 42 65 12 73; metro Champs-Élysées-Clemenceau), built for the 1900 Exposition Universelle, is on Ave Winston Churchill, which runs between Ave des Champs-Élysées and the Seine. Its museum specialises in medieval and Renaissance porcelain, clocks, tapestries, drawings and 19th-century French painting and sculpture. It's open daily, except Monday, from 10 am to 5.40 pm (8 pm Thursday). The entry fee is 27FF (14.50FF reduced tariff). Temporary exhibitions usually cost 35FF extra (25FF if you qualify for the reduction).

The **Grand Palais** (☎ 01 44 13 17 17), which is across Ave Winston Churchill from the Petit Palais on Square Jean Perrin, was also built for the 1900 World's Fair. It's now used for temporary exhibitions.

Arc de Triomphe (8e) The Arc de Triomphe (☎ 01 43 80 31 31; metro Charles de Gaulle-Étoile), Paris' second most famous landmark, is a couple of kilometres north-west of Place de la Concorde in the middle of Place Charles de Gaulle. Also called Place de l'Étoile, this is the world's largest traffic roundabout and the meeting point of 12 avenues. The Arc de Triomphe was commissioned in 1806 by Napoleon to commemorate his imperial victories but remained unfinished when he started losing battles and then entire wars. It was finally completed in the 1830s. An Unknown Soldier from WWI is buried under the arch, his fate and that of countless others like him commemorated by a memorial flame that is lit with ceremony each evening at around 6.30 pm.

The platform atop the arch (lift up, steps down) is open April to September from 9.30 am to 11 pm daily except on public holidays. Winter hours are 10 am to 10 pm. It costs 35FF (23FF reduced rate), and there's a small **museum** with a short videotape. The only

FRANCE

sane way to get to the base of the arch is via the underground passageways from its perimeter; trying to cross the traffic on foot is suicidal.

The **Voie Triomphale** (Triumphal Way) stretches another 4.5km north-west from the Arc de Triomphe along Ave de la Grande Armée, and beyond to the new skyscraper district of **La Défense**. Its best known landmark, the **Grande Arche** (Grand Arch), is a hollow cube (112m to a side) completed in 1989.

Centre Georges Pompidou (4e) This centre (☎ 01 44 78 12 33; metro Rambuteau or Châtelet-Les Halles), also known as the Centre Beaubourg, is dedicated to displaying and promoting modern and contemporary art. Thanks in part to its outstanding temporary exhibitions it's by far the most frequented sight in Paris but is undergoing a massive renovation that will not be completed until late 1999, though the escalator with its spectacular views remains open. **Place Igor Stravinsky** and its crazy fountains south of the centre and the large square to the west attract street artists, mimes, musicians, jugglers and 'artisans' who will write your name on a grain of rice.

The design of the Centre Pompidou has attracted wide-eyed gazes and critical comment since it was built between 1972 and 1977. In order to keep the exhibition halls as spacious and uncluttered as possible, the architects put the building's 'insides' on the outside.

The Centre Pompidou consists of six floors and several sections. The **Musée National d'Art Moderne**, which displays the national collection of modern and contemporary art on the 4th floor, is open daily, except Tuesday, from noon (10 am on weekends and public holidays) to 10 pm. Entrance costs 30FF (22FF reduced rate), but everyone gets in for free on Sunday from 10 am to 2 pm. The free **Bibliothèque Publique d'Information**, with the same opening hours, is a huge, nonlending library equipped with the latest high-tech information retrieval systems. The entrance is on the 2nd floor.

Les Halles (1er) Paris' central food market, Les Halles, occupied this site from the 12th century until 1969, when it was moved out to the suburb of Rungis. A huge underground shopping mall (Forum des Halles) was built in its place and has proved highly popular with Parisian shoppers. Just north of the grassy area on top of Les Halles is one of Paris' most attractive churches, the mostly 16th-century **Église Saint Eustache**, noted for its wonderful pipe organ.

Hôtel de Ville (4e) Paris' city hall (☎ 01 42 76 40 40; metro Hôtel de Ville) at Place de l'Hôtel de Ville was burned down during the Paris Commune of 1871 and rebuilt in the neo-Renaissance style between 1874 and 1882. There are guided tours in French every first Monday of the month at 10.30 am, and the small **museum** has imaginative exhibits on Paris. The visitors' entrance is at 29 Rue de Rivoli.

Marais Area (4e) The Marais, the part of the 4e east of the Centre Pompidou and north of Île Saint Louis, was a marsh (*marais*) until the 13th century, when it was converted to agricultural use. During the 17th century this was the most fashionable part of the city, and the nobility erected luxurious but discreet mansions known as *hôtels particuliers*. When the aristocracy moved to trendier pastures, the Marais was taken over by ordinary Parisians. By the time renovation was begun in the 1960s, the Marais had become a poor but lively Jewish neighbourhood centred around **Rue des Rosiers**. In the 1980s the area underwent serious gentrification and is today one of the trendiest neighbourhoods to live and shop in. It's also something of a gay quarter.

Place des Vosges (4e) In 1605, King Henri IV decided to turn the Marais into Paris' most fashionable district. The result of this initiative, completed in 1612, was the Place Royale – now Place des Vosges (metro Chemin Vert) – a square ensemble of 36 symmetrical houses with ground-floor arcades, steep slate roofs and large dormer windows north of Rue Saint Antoine. Duels were once fought in the elegant park in the middle. Today, the arcades around Place des Vosges are occupied by upmarket art galleries, antique shops and salons de thé.

The **Maison de Victor Hugo** (☎ 01 42 72 10 16), where the author lived from 1832 to

1848, is open daily, except Monday, from 10 am to 5.40 pm. The entry fee is 27FF (19FF reduced rate).

Musée Picasso (3e) The Picasso Museum (☎ 01 42 71 25 21; metro Saint Sébastien-Froissart), housed in the mid-17th century Hôtel Salé, is a few hundred metres northeast of the Marais at 5 Rue de Thorigny. Paintings, sculptures, ceramic works, engravings and drawings donated to the French government by the heirs of Pablo Picasso (1881-1973) to avoid huge inheritance taxes are on display, as is Picasso's personal art collection (Braque, Cézanne, Matisse, Rousseau etc). The museum is open daily, except Tuesday, from 9.30 am to 6 pm (5.30 pm in the winter). The entry fee is 30FF (20FF reduced rate).

Bastille (4e, 11e & 12e) The Bastille is the most famous nonexistent monument in Paris; the notorious prison was demolished shortly after the mob stormed it on 14 July 1789 and freed all seven prisoners. Today, the site where it stood is known as Place de la Bastille; the 52m **Colonne de Juillet** in the centre was erected in 1830. The new (and rather drab) **Opéra Bastille** (☎ 01 44 73 13 99 or ☎ 08 36 69 78 68; metro Bastille) at 2-6 Place de la Bastille (12e) is another grandiose project initiated by President François Mitterrand.

Opéra Garnier (9e) Paris' better known opera house (☎ 01 40 01 22 63; metro Opéra) at Place de l'Opéra was designed in 1860 by Charles Garnier to display the splendour of Napoleon III's France and is one of the most impressive monuments erected during the second empire. The extravagant **entrance hall**, with its grand staircase, is decorated with multicoloured marble and a gigantic chandelier. The **ceiling** of the auditorium was painted by Marc Chagall in 1964. The building also houses the **Musée de l'Opéra**, open from 10 am to 5 pm daily. Entrance is 30FF (20FF reduced rate).

Montmartre (18e) During the 19th century – and especially after 1871, when the Communard uprising began here – Montmartre's Bohemian lifestyle attracted artists and writers, whose presence turned the area into Paris' most vibrant centre of artistic and literary creativity. In English-speaking countries, Montmartre's mystique of unconventionality has been magnified by the notoriety of the **Moulin Rouge** (☎ 01 53 09 82 82; metro Blanche) at 82 Blvd de Clichy, a nightclub founded in 1889 and known for its twice-nightly *revue* (at 10 pm and midnight) of nearly naked chorus girls. Today it's an area of mimes, buskers, tacky souvenir shops and commercial artists.

Basilique du Sacré Cœur Perched at the very top of Butte de Montmartre, the Basilica of the Sacred Heart (metro Lamarck Caulaincourt) was built to fulfil a vow taken by many Parisian Catholics after the disastrous Franco-Prussian War of 1870-71. On warm evenings, groups of young people gather on the steps below the church to contemplate the view, play guitars and sing. Although the basilica's domes are a well-loved part of the Parisian skyline, the architecture of the rest of the building, which is typical of the style of the late 19th century, is not very graceful.

The basilica is open daily from 7 am to 11 pm. The entrance to the **dome** and the **crypt**, which costs 15FF (8FF for students), is on the west side of the basilica. Both are open daily from 9 am to 6 pm; they say you can see for 30km on a clear day from the dome. The recently rebuilt funicular up the hill's southern slope costs one metro/bus ticket each way. It runs from 6 am to 12.45 am.

The **Musée d'Art Naïf** (Museum of Naive Art) in Halle Saint Pierre (☎ 01 42 58 72 89; metro Anvers), south-west of the basilica at 2 Rue Ronsard, is worth a visit (40FF; 30FF for students).

Place du Tertre Just west of **Église Saint Pierre**, the only building left from the great abbey of Montmartre, Place du Tertre is filled with cafés, restaurants, portrait artists and tourists and is always animated. But the real attractions of the area, apart from the view, are the quiet, twisting streets and shaded parks. Look for the two **windmills** west on Rue Lepic and the last **vineyard** in Paris on the corner of Rue des Saules and Rue Saint Vincent.

Pigalle (9e & 18e) Pigalle, only a few blocks south-west of the tranquil, residential areas of Montmartre, is one of Paris' major sex districts. Although the area along Blvd de Clichy between the Pigalle and Blanche metro stops is lined with sex shops and striptease parlours, the area has plenty of legitimate nightspots too, including La Locomotive discothèque (see Entertainment later in the Paris section) and several all-night cafés.

The new **Musée de l'Érotisme** (Museum of Eroticism; ☎ 01 42 58 28 73; metro Blanche) at 72 Blvd de Clichy tries to raise erotic art both antique and modern to a loftier plane – but we know why we've come here. The museum is open daily from 10 am to 2 am. Entry is 40FF (30FF reduced rate).

Cimetière du Père Lachaise (20e) Père Lachaise Cemetery (☎ 01 43 70 70 33; metro Père Lachaise), final resting place of such notables as Chopin, Proust, Oscar Wilde, Édith Piaf and Sarah Bernhardt, may be the most visited cemetery in the world. The best known tomb (and the one most visitors come to see) is that of 1960s rock star Jim Morrison, lead singer for the Doors, who died in 1971. It's in Division 6. Maps indicating the graves' locations are posted around the cemetery.

The cemetery is open weekdays from 8 am to 5.30 pm (Saturday from 8.30 am, Sunday from 9 am). From mid-March to early November, the cemetery closes at 6 pm. Admission is free. There are five entrances; the main one is opposite 23 Blvd de Ménilmontant.

Bois de Vincennes (12e) This large English-style park, the 9.29-sq-km Bois de Vincennes, is in the far south-eastern corner of the city. Highlights include the **Parc Floral** (Floral Garden; metro Château de Vincennes) on Route de la Pyramide; the Parc Zoologique de Paris (Paris Zoo; ☎ 01 44 75 20 10) at 53 Ave de Saint Maurice (metro Porte Dorée); and, at the park's eastern edge, the **Jardin Tropical** (Tropical Garden; RER stop Nogent-sur-Marne) on Ave de la Belle Gabrielle.

Château de Vincennes (12e) The Château de Vincennes (☎ 01 48 08 31 20;

metro Château de Vincennes), at the northern edge of the Bois de Vincennes, is a bona fide royal chateau complete with massive fortifications and a moat. You can walk around the grounds for free, but to see the Gothic **Chapelle Royale**, built between the 14th and 16th centuries, and the 14th-century **donjon** (keep) with its small historical museum, you must take a guided tour (32FF; 21FF reduced rate). Daily opening hours are from 10 am to 5 pm (6 pm in summer). The main entrance, which is opposite 18 Ave de Paris in the inner suburb of Vincennes, is right next to the Château de Vincennes metro stop.

Musée des Arts d'Afrique et d'Océanie (12e) This museum (☎ 01 44 74 84 80; metro Porte Dorée) at 293 Ave Daumesnil specialises in art from Africa and the South Pacific. It's open weekdays, except Tuesday, from 10 am to noon and 1.30 to 5.30 pm (12.30 to 6 pm on weekends). The entry fee is 30FF (20FF reduced rate).

Bois de Boulogne (16e) The 8.65-sq-km Bois de Boulogne, located on the western edge of the city, is endowed with meandering trails, gardens, forested areas, cycling paths and *belle époque*-style cafés. Rowing boats can be rented at the **Lac Inférieur** (metro Ave Henri Martin), the largest of the park's lakes.

Paris Cycles (☎ 01 47 47 76 50) rents city and mountain bicycles at two locations: on Route du Mahatma Gandhi (metro Les Sablons), opposite the Porte des Sablons entrance to the Jardin d'Acclimatation amusement park; and near the Pavillon Royal (metro Ave Foch) at the northern end of the Lac Inférieur. Charges are 30FF an hour or 80FF a day. From mid-April to mid-October, bicycles are available daily from 10 am to sundown. During the rest of the year, you can rent them on Wednesday, Saturday and Sunday only.

Courses
Language Courses The Alliance Française (☎ 01 45 44 38 28; metro Saint Placide) at 101 Blvd Raspail (6e) has month-long French courses beginning the first week of each month. The registration office is open Monday to Friday from 9 am to 5 pm. French courses with the same schedule offered by the

Accord Language School (☎ 01 42 36 24 95; metro Les Halles) at 52 Rue Montmartre (1er) get high marks from students. A one-month course costs 1800FF in winter (eight hours a week) and 2700FF in summer (15 hours a week).

Cooking Courses Several cooking schools offer courses of various lengths including the famed École Ritz Escoffier (☎ 01 43 16 30 50; metro Concorde) at 38 Rue Cambon (1er) and École Le Cordon Bleu (☎ 01 53 68 22 50; metro Vaugirard) at 8 Rue Léon Delhomme (15e). Fees range from US$200 to $500 a day.

Organised Tours

Bus The cheapest way to see Paris on wheels between mid-April and late September is to hop aboard RATP's Balabus which follows a 50-minute route from the Gare de Lyon to the Grande Arche de la Défense and back, passing many of the city's most famous sights. Details are available at metro counters. ParisBus (☎ 01 42 88 69 15) offers a longer (2¼ hours) tour with English and French commentary year-round on red double-decker buses. There are nine stops (including the Eiffel Tower and Notre Dame) and you can get on and off as you wish over two days. Tickets, available on the bus, are 125FF (60FF for children under 12).

Bicycle Paris Vélo (☎ 01 43 37 59 22; metro Censier Daubenton) at 2 Rue du Fer à Moulin (5e) runs well reviewed bicycle tours of Paris and its major monuments for between 120 and 180FF. To reserve a place, phone a day ahead Monday to Saturday from 10 am to 12.30 pm and 2 to 6 pm (in summer from 10 am to 2 pm and 5 to 7 pm). It also rents bicycles for 90/420FF a day/week.

Boat In summer, the Batobus river shuttle (☎ 01 44 11 33 99) stops at half a dozen places along the Seine, including Notre Dame and the Musée d'Orsay. The boats come by every 35 minutes and cost 20FF per journey or 60FF for the whole day. The Bateaux Mouches company (☎ 01 42 25 96 10; metro Alma Marceau), which is based on the north bank of the Seine just east of Pont de l'Alma (8e), runs the biggest tour boats on the river.

The cost for a 1¼-hour cruise with commentary is 40FF (no student discount). Vedettes du Pont Neuf (☎ 01 46 33 98 38; metro Pont Neuf), whose home port is on the western tip of Île de la Cité (1er) near the Pont Neuf, operates one-hour boat circuits day and night for 50FF (25FF for children under 12).

Places to Stay

Accommodation Services Accueil des Jeunes en France (AJF) can always find anyone accommodation in a hostel, hotel or private home, even in summer. It works like this: you come in on the day you need a place to stay and pay AJF for the accommodation, plus a 10FF fee, and you get a voucher to take to the establishment. The earlier in the day you come the better, as the convenient and cheap places always go first. Prices start at 120FF per person (excluding 10FF fee). AJF's main office (☎ 01 42 77 87 80; metro Rambuteau) is at 119 Rue Saint Martin (4e), just west of the Centre Pompidou's main entrance. It's open Monday to Friday from 10 am to 6.45 pm, 5.45 on Saturday. Be prepared for long queues during the summer.

The main Paris tourist office (☎ 01 49 52 53 54) can also find you accommodation in Paris for the evening of the day you visit its office. For information on the tourist office and its annexes, see Tourist Offices under Information at the start of the Paris section.

Camping The only camping ground actually within the Paris city limits, *Camping du Bois de Boulogne* (☎ 01 45 24 30 00) on Allée du Bord de l'Eau (16e), is along the Seine at the far western edge of the Bois de Boulogne. In summer, two people with a tent pay around 60 to 77FF or 89 to 118FF with a car. From April to September, privately operated shuttle buses (fare 11FF) from the Porte Maillot metro stop (16e and 17e) run daily from 8.30 am to 1 pm and 5 pm to sometime between 11 pm and 1 am. During July and August, the shuttles run every half-hour from 8.30 am to 1 am. Throughout the year, you can take either bus No 244 from Porte Maillot or bus No 144 from the Pont de Neuilly metro stop from 6 am to about 8.30 pm.

Hostels & Foyers Many hostels allow guests to stay for only three nights maximum, especially in summer. Places that have age limits (eg up to 30) tend not to enforce them very rigorously. Only official hostels require that guests present Hostelling International cards. Curfews at Paris hostels tend to be 1 or 2 am, though some are earlier. Few hostels accept reservations by telephone; those that do are noted in the text. Some hostels have a 15FF rental charge for sheets if you don't bring your own sheet sleeping bag.

Louvre Area (1er) The *Centre International BVJ Paris-Louvre* (☎ 01 53 00 90 90; metro Louvre-Rivoli) at 20 Rue Jean-Jacques Rousseau is only a few blocks north-east of the Louvre. Bunks in single-sex rooms cost 120FF, including breakfast.

Marais (4e) The Maison Internationale de la Jeunesse et des Étudiants, better known as MIJE, runs three hostels (☎ 01 42 74 23 45 for all) in attractively renovated 17th and 18th-century residences in the Marais. A bed in a single-sex dorm with shower costs 125FF, including breakfast. The nicest of the three, *MIJE Fourcy*, is at 6 Rue de Fourcy (metro Saint Paul), 100m south of Rue de Rivoli. *MIJE Fauconnier* is two blocks away at 11 Rue du Fauconnier (metro Pont Marie). *MIJE Maubisson* is at 12 Rue des Barres (metro Hôtel de Ville). Individuals can make reservations for all three hostels, up to seven days in advance, by dropping in at MIJE Fourcy.

Panthéon Area (5e) The clean and friendly *Y&H Hostel* (☎ 01 45 35 09 53; young@youngandhappy.fr; metro Monge) is at 80 Rue Mouffetard, a hopping, happening street known for its restaurants and pubs. A bed in a cramped room with a sink costs 97FF plus 15FF for sheets. Reservations can be made only if you leave a deposit for the first night. Reception is open all hours.

11e Arrondissement At 8 Blvd Jules Ferry is the *Auberge de Jeunesse Jules Ferry* (☎ 01 43 57 55 60; metro République). This hostel is a bit institutional but the atmosphere is fairly relaxed but and – an added bonus – it doesn't accept large groups. A bed costs 113FF, including breakfast. For 5FF you can surf the Web on the computer in reception.

The *Auberge Internationale des Jeunes* (☎ 01 47 00 62 00; fax 01 47 00 33 16; aij@aijparis.com; metro Ledru Rollin) at 10 Rue Trousseau (11e) is a clean and very friendly hostel, 700m east of Place de la Bastille – walk along Rue du Faubourg Saint Antoine until you come to Rue Trousseau on your left. It attracts a young, international crowd and is very full in summer. Beds in dorms for two to six people cost just 81FF from November to February, 91FF from March to October, including breakfast. Rooms are closed for cleaning between 10 am and 3 pm. You can book in advance, and they'll hold a bed for you if you call from the train station.

The *Maison Internationale des Jeunes* (☎ 01 43 71 99 21; metro Faidherbe Chaligny) at 4 Rue Titon is about 1km east of Place de la Bastille. A bed in a spartan dorm room for two, three, five or eight people costs 110FF, including breakfast. Telephone reservations are accepted only for the day you call.

12e Arrondissement The *Centre International de Séjour de Paris (CISP) Ravel* (☎ 01 44 75 60 00; metro Porte de Vincennes) is on the south-eastern edge of the city at 4-6 Ave Maurice Ravel. A bed in a 12-person dormitory is 113FF. Rooms for two to five people cost 138FF per person, and singles are 181FF. All prices include breakfast. Reservations are accepted from individuals no more than two days in advance.

13e & 14e Arrondissements The *Foyer International d'Accueil de Paris (FIAP) Jean Monnet* (☎ 01 45 89 89 15; metro Glacière) is at 30 Rue Cabanis, a few blocks south-east of Place Denfert Rochereau. A bed costs 131/161/184FF (including breakfast) in modern rooms for eight/four/two people. Singles cost 281FF. Rooms specially outfitted for disabled people (*handicapés*) are available.

The *Centre International de Séjour de Paris (CISP) Kellermann* (☎ 01 44 16 37 38; metro Porte d'Italie) is at 17 Blvd Kellermann (13e). A bed in an attractive dorm for eight costs 113FF, and staying in a double or quad will cost 138FF per person. Singles are 156FF (186FF with toilet and shower). All prices include sheets and breakfast. This place also has facilities for disabled people on the 1st floor. Telephone reservations are accepted up to 48 hours in advance.

The rather institutional *Maison des Clubs UNESCO* (☎ 01 43 36 00 63; girardin@fiap.asso.fr; metro Glacière) is at 43 Rue de la Glacière (13e), midway between Place Denfert Rochereau and Place d'Italie. A bed in a large, unexceptional room for three or four people is 125FF; singles/doubles cost 165/145FF per person.

15e Arrondissement The friendly, helpful *Three Ducks Hostel* (☎ 01 48 42 04 05; metro Commerce), a favourite with young backpackers, is at 6 Place Étienne Pernet. A bunk bed costs 97FF (87FF from November to April), and telephone reservations are accepted. The *Aloha Hostel* (☎ 01 42 73 03 03; metro Volontaires) at 1 Rue Borromée, about 1km west of Gare Montparnasse, is run by the same people and has the same prices.

Hotels A rash of renovations, redecorations and other improvements has turned many of Paris' best budget hotels into quaint and spotless two-star places where the sheets are changed daily and the minibar is full. But there are still bargains to be had.

Marais (4e) One of the best deals in town is the friendly *Hôtel Rivoli* (☎ 01 42 72 08 41; metro Hôtel de Ville) at 44 Rue de Rivoli. Room rates range from 160FF (for singles without shower) to 250FF (for doubles with bath and toilet). The front door is locked at 2 am. The *Hôtel Le Palais de Fès* (☎ 01 42 72 03 68; fax 01 42 60 49 33; metro Hôtel de Ville) at 41 Rue du Roi de Sicile has fairly large, modern doubles for 200FF with washbasin, 250FF with shower and 280FF with shower and toilet. Singles start at 150FF. Hall showers are 15FF. Reception is in the Moroccan restaurant on the ground floor.

The *Hôtel Moderne* (☎ 01 48 87 97 05; metro Saint Paul) at 3 Rue Caron has basic singles/doubles for 130/160FF, 190FF with shower and 220FF with shower and toilet. The *Hôtel Pratic* (☎ 01 48 87 80 47; metro Saint Paul) is just around the corner at 9 Rue d'Ormesson. Singles/doubles cost 180/245FF with washbasin; double rooms cost 290FF with shower, 340FF with bath and toilet.

One of the most attractive medium-priced hotels in the area is the *Hôtel de Nice* (☎ 01 42 78 55 29; fax 01 42 78 36 07; metro Hôtel de Ville), a comfortable oasis at 42 bis Rue de Rivoli. Doubles/triples/quads with shower and toilet are 450/550/650FF and many of the rooms have balconies. The completely overhauled *Grand Hôtel Malher* (☎ 01 42 72 60 92; fax 01 42 72 25 37; metro Saint Paul) is at 5 Rue Malher. Singles/doubles with everything start at 475/605FF (580/730FF in summer).

Notre Dame Area (5e) The run-down *Hôtel du Centre* (☎ 01 43 26 13 07; metro Saint Michel) at 5 Rue Saint Jacques has very basic singles/doubles starting at 100/150FF. Doubles with shower cost from 180FF. Hall showers are 20FF. Reservations are not accepted, but reception is open 24 hours a day.

Because of its location at 4 Rue Saint Julien le Pauvre directly across the Seine from Notre Dame, the *Hôtel Esmerelda* (☎ 01 43 54 19 20; metro Saint Michel) is everybody's favourite. Its three simple singles (160FF) are almost always booked up months in advance – other singles/doubles (with shower and toilet) start at 320FF.

Panthéon Area (5e) The *Hôtel de Médicis* (☎ 01 43 54 14 66; metro Luxembourg) at 214 Rue Saint Jacques is just what a dilapidated Latin Quarter dive for impoverished travellers should be like. Very basic singles start at 85FF, but the cheapest rooms are usually occupied. Basic doubles/triples are 160/230FF and hall showers are 10FF.

A much better deal is the *Grand Hôtel du Progrès* (☎ 01 43 54 53 18; metro Luxembourg) at 50 Rue Gay Lussac. Singles with washbasin start at 150FF and there are larger rooms with fine views of the Panthéon for 240FF. Hall showers are free. There are also large old-fashioned singles/doubles with shower and toilet for 310/330FF. A cut above, the *Hôtel Gay Lussac* (☎ 01 43 54 23 96; metro Luxembourg) at No 29 on the same street has small singles/doubles with washbasin for 200/260FF; doubles/quads with shower and toilet are 360/500FF.

The clean, well managed *Résidence Monge* (☎ 01 43 26 87 90/54 47 25) at 55 rue

FRANCE

THE LATIN QUARTER & ÎLE DE LA CITÉ

FRANCE

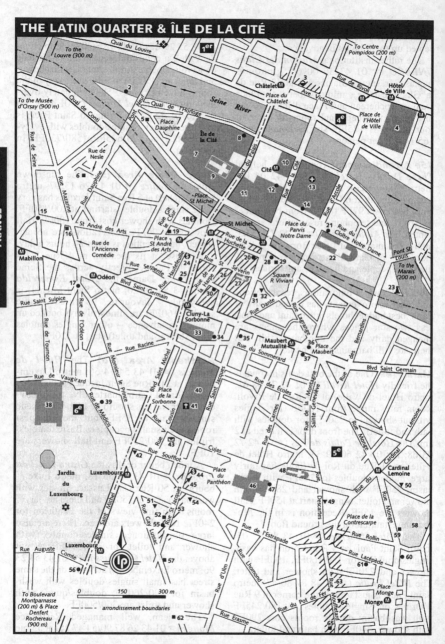

THE LATIN QUARTER & ÎLE DE LA CITÉ

PLACES TO STAY
5 Hôtel Henri IV
6 Hôtel de Nesle
16 Hôtel Petit Trianon
19 Hôtel Saint Michel
29 Hôtel Esmerelda
31 Hôtel du Centre, Le Cloître
    Pub & Polly Maggoo Pub
52 Hôtel de Médicis
57 Hôtel Gay Lussac
59 Résidence Monge
62 Grand Hôtel du Progrès
65 Y & H Hostel

PLACES TO EAT
26 Restaurants ('Bacteria Alley')
32 Chez Maï
42 McDonald's
45 Perraudin
49 Savannah Café
50 Le Petit Légume
51 Douce France Sandwich Bar
54 Tashi Delek Tibetan
    Restaurant
63 Restaurants
64 Crêpe Stand

OTHER
1 Samaritaine
   (Department Store)
2 Vedettes du Pont Neuf
   (Boat Tours)
3 Noctambus (All-Night Bus)
   Stops
4 Hôtel de Ville (City Hall)
7 Palais de Justice &
   Conciergerie
8 Conciergerie Entrance
9 Sainte Chapelle
10 Flower Market
11 Préfecture de Police
12 Préfecture Entrance
13 Hôtel Dieu (Hospital)
14 Hospital Entrance
15 Food Shops
17 Carrefour de l'Odéon
18 Le Change de Paris
20 Caveau de la Huchette Jazz
    Club
21 Notre Dame Tower Entrance
22 Notre Dame Cathedral
23 WWII Deportation Memorial
24 Bureau de Change
25 L'Astrolabe Rive Gauche
    Travel Bookshop

27 Église Saint Séverin
28 Shakespeare & Co Bookshop
30 Abbey Bookshop
33 Musée du Moyen Age
    (Thermes de Cluny)
34 Musée du Moyen Age
    Entrance
35 Eurolines Bus Office
36 Food Shops
37 Fromagerie (Cheese Shop)
38 Palais du Luxembourg
    (French Senate Building)
39 Café Orbital
40 Sorbonne (University of
    Paris)
41 Église de la Sorbonne
43 Post Office
44 Banque Nationale de Paris
46 Panthéon
47 Panthéon Entrance
48 Église Saint Étienne du Mont
53 Food Shops
55 Laundrette
56 Nouvelles Frontières
    (Travel Agency)
58 Arènes de Lutèce
60 Laundrette
61 Ed l'Épicier Supermarket

FRANCE

Monge is right in the thick of things. It's an expensive choice if you're alone (singles 380 to 480FF) but a good deal if you've got a companion or two; doubles and triples start at 450FF.

Saint Germain des Prés (6e) The wonderfully eccentric *Hôtel de Nesle* (☎ 01 43 54 62 41; metro Odéon or Mabillon) at 7 Rue de Nesle, with its frescoed rooms and cool garden out the back, is a favourite with students and young people from all over the world. Singles cost 250FF, and a bed in a double is 150FF. Doubles with shower and toilet are 400FF. The only way to get a place here is to book in person in the morning. The nearby *Hôtel Petit Trianon* (☎ 01 43 54 94 64; metro Odéon) at 2 Rue de l'Ancienne Comédie also attracts lots of young travellers. Singles start at 170FF. Doubles with shower are 350FF.

The well-positioned *Hôtel Henri IV* (☎ 01 43 54 44 53; metro Pont Neuf) is at 25 Place Dauphine (1er), a quiet square at the western end of Île de la Cité near Pont Neuf. Perfectly adequate singles without toilet or shower are 116 to 250FF, doubles are 200 to 270FF, and hall showers are 15FF. This place is usually booked up months in advance.

The *Hôtel Saint Michel* (☎ 01 43 26 98 70; metro Saint Michel) is a block west of Place Saint Michel and a block south of the Seine at 17 Rue Gît le Cœur. Comfortable, soundproofed rooms start from 190FF, from 285FF for rooms with shower but no toilet, and from 325 to 370FF for rooms with shower and toilet. The hall shower costs 12FF.

Montmartre (18e) The metro station Abbesses is convenient for the hotels that follow. The *Idéal Hôtel* (☎ 01 46 06 63 63) at 3 Rue des Trois Frères has simple but acceptable singles/doubles starting at 125/180FF. A hall shower is 20FF; rooms with showers are 250FF. The *Hôtel Audran*

(☎ 01 42 58 79 59) is on the other side of Rue des Abbesses at 7 Rue Audran. Singles/doubles start at 120/160FF with showers costing 10FF. A cut above is the renovated *Hôtel des Arts* (☎ 01 46 06 30 52; fax 01 46 06 10 83) at 5 Rue Tholozé. This two-star place has singles/doubles with shower and toilet starting at 340/460FF. Breakfast is 30FF extra.

The *Hôtel de Rohan* (☎ 01 46 06 82 74; metro Château Rouge) at 90 Rue Myrha has basic, tidy singles/doubles for 110/140FF. Doubles/triples with shower are 170/200FF. Showers in the hall cost 20FF.

Places to Eat

Restaurants Except for those in touristy areas (Notre Dame, Louvre, Champs-Élysées), most of the city's thousands of restaurants are pretty good value for money. Intense competition tends to rid the city quickly of places with bad food or prices that are out of line. Still, you can be unlucky. Study the posted menus carefully and check to see how busy the place is before entering.

Forum des Halles The *Mélodine Cafeteria* (☎ 01 40 29 09 78; metro Rambuteau) at 2 Rue Brantôme, across from the north side of the Centre Pompidou (4e) is a huge, self-service cafeteria. The food is better than you might expect, and main dishes cost only 27 to 40FF. Pizzas are 27 to 36FF and salads are available. It's open daily from 11 am to 10 pm. *Le Loup Blanc* (☎ 01 40 13 08 35; metro Étienne Marcel) at 42 Rue Tiquetonne (2e) is billed as a techno restaurant (though it's hard to see or hear exactly why). It does offer some decent main courses, though, like Thai-style prawns and squid with anise (57 to 85FF). It's open daily from 8 pm to 12.30 am and brunch is available on Sunday from noon to 5 pm.

Opéra Area (2e & 9e) On the 1st floor at 103 Rue de Richelieu (2e), 500m east of Opéra Garnier, is *Le Drouot* (☎ 01 42 96 68 23; metro Richelieu Drouot), whose décor and ambience haven't changed much since the late 1930s. A three-course traditional French meal with wine costs only 100FF. Le Drouot is open daily for lunch and dinner. *Chartier* (☎ 01 47 70 86 29; metro Rue

Montmartre) at 7 Rue du Faubourg Montmartre (9e), under the same management, is famous for its ornate, late 19th-century dining room. Prices, fare and hours are similar to those at Le Drouot, but it closes a little earlier (10 pm).

Marais (4e) The heart of the old Jewish neighbourhood, Rue des Rosiers (metro Saint Paul), has quite a few kosher (*kascher*) and kosher-style restaurants but most of them are European-orientated. If you're after kosher couscous and kebabs, check out the restaurants along Blvd de Belleville (11e and 20e; metro Belleville or Couronnes).

Chez Rami et Hanna (☎ 01 42 78 23 09; metro Saint Paul) at 54 Rue des Rosiers (4e) serves Israeli dishes, including the assiette royale (a plate of seven salads; 60FF), daily from 11 am to 2 am. Paris' best known Jewish restaurant, founded in 1920, is *Restaurant Jo Goldenberg* (☎ 01 48 87 20 16) at 7 Rue des Rosiers. The food (main dishes about 80FF) is Jewish but not kosher. Jo Goldenberg is open from 8.30 am until about midnight daily except on Yom Kippur.

Minh Chau (☎ 01 42 71 13 30; metro Hôtel de Ville) at 10 Rue de la Verrerie (4e) is a tiny but welcoming Vietnamese place where you can enjoy tasty main dishes (such as grilled chicken with lemon grass, roast duck) for only 26 to 32FF. It's open Monday to Saturday from 11.30 am to 3 pm and 5.30 to 11 pm.

Aquarius (☎ 01 48 87 48 71; metro Rambuteau) at 54 Rue Sainte Croix de la Bretonnerie is a good bet for vegetarian food. It has a calming, airy atmosphere and is open Monday to Saturday from noon to 10 pm. The plat du jour is available only at lunch and dinner times. The two-course/three-course *menu* costs 62/92FF.

Bastille (4e, 11e & 12e) Lots of ethnic restaurants line Rue de la Roquette and Rue de Lappe (11e), which intersects Rue de la Roquette 200m north-east of Place de la Bastille, include Chinese, North African, Tex Mex and Japanese places. The Cuban-inspired *Havanita Café* (☎ 01 43 55 96 42; metro Bastille) at 11 Rue de Lappe (11e) is not as trendy as it used to be but still worth a look. Draught beers are 20 to 24FF, cocktails

40 to 48FF, starters 34 to 78FF and the excellent main courses 58 to 160FF. It's open daily from noon to 3 pm and 5 pm to 2 am. Happy hour – when cocktails are 15 to 20FF cheaper – is from 5 to 8 pm.

Latin Quarter (4e, 5e & 6e) The Greek, North African and Middle Eastern restaurants in the area bounded by Rue Saint Jacques, Blvd Saint Germain, Blvd Saint Michel and the Seine attract mainly foreign tourists, who are unaware that some people refer to Rue de la Huchette and its nearby streets as 'bacteria alley' because of the high incidence of food poisoning at restaurants there. But the takeaway kebab and shwarma sandwiches (20FF) aren't bad.

The Moroccan *Founti Agadir* (☎ 01 43 37 85 10; metro Censier Daubenton) at 117 Rue Monge (5e) has some of the best couscous, grills and tajines (70 to 85FF) on the Left Bank. There's a *menu* – with or without couscous – for 84FF. It's open daily, except Monday. For cheap and tasty food try *Chez Maï* (☎ 01 43 54 05 33; metro Maubert Mutualité) at 65 Rue Galande (5e), a hole-in-the-wall Vietnamese place that's open daily from noon to 3 pm and 7 to 11 pm. Main dishes (including excellent shrimp ones) cost only 25 to 30FF; soup is 20FF and salads and omelettes from 20FF.

Perraudin (☎ 01 46 33 15 75; metro Luxembourg) at 157 Rue Saint Jacques (5e) is a reasonably priced traditional French restaurant that hasn't changed much since the turn of the century. Main courses cost 59FF, and at lunchtime there's a *menu* for 63FF; a quarter litre of wine is 10FF. It's open from noon to 2.15 pm and 7 to 11.15 pm (closed Saturday at noon and all day Sunday).

A good place for a quick vegetarian lunch is *Le Petit Légume* (☎ 01 40 46 06 85; metro Cardinal Lemoine) at 36 Rue des Boulangers (5e). Dinner *menus* are 50, 64 and 75FF.

The area around Rue Mouffetard is filled with dozens of places to eat and is especially popular with students. Some of the best discount crêpes in Paris are sold from a little stall across the street from 68 Rue Mouffetard between 11 am and 2 am. They start at 11FF. For Tibetan food, a good choice is the friendly *Tashi Delek* (☎ 01 43 26 55 55; metro Luxembourg) – that's 'bon jour' in Tibetan –

at 4 Rue des Fossés Saint Jacques. Tashi Delek is open for lunch and dinner from Monday night to Saturday. Lunch/dinner *menus* start at 65/105FF.

The food served at the *Savannah Café* (☎ 01 43 29 45 77; metro Cardinal Lemoine) at 27 Rue Descartes (5e) is as eclectic as the carnival-like decorations strewn around the place. Tabouli mixes with tortellini and fromage blanc with baklava. At lunch, *menus* cost either 75FF or 134FF; at dinner, only the 134FF *menu* is available. À la carte entrées are 37 to 60FF, main courses 76 to 84FF and pasta dishes from 72 to 76FF. It's open for lunch and dinner till 11.30 pm Tuesday to Saturday; on Monday it opens at midday, and on Sunday it's closed.

Montparnasse (6e & 14e) Somewhat pricey, but a real 'find' in this area is *Le Caméléon* (☎ 01 43 20 63 43; metro Vavin) at 6 Rue de Chevreuse (6e), which has never-to-be-forgotten lobster ravioli (82FF) on its menu. Bookings are essential.

There are several *crêperies* at 20 Rue d'Odessa and several more around the corner on Rue du Montparnasse. *Mustang Café* (☎ 01 43 35 36 12; metro Montparnasse-Bienvenüe) at 84 Blvd du Montparnasse (14e) has passable Tex-Mex (platters and chilli from 45FF; fajitas 98FF) available to 5 am.

Montmartre (9e & 18e) There are dozens of cafés and restaurants around Place du Tertre but they tend to be touristy and overpriced. An old Montmartre favourite is *Refuge des Fondus* (☎ 01 42 55 22 65) at 17 Rue des Trois Frères (18e), whose speciality is fondues. For 87FF, you get wine and a good quantity of either cheese fondue Savoyarde or meat fondue Bourguignonne (minimum of two). It's open daily from 7 pm to 2 am and is very popular, so book. *Le Mono* (☎ 01 46 06 99 20) at 40 Rue Véron (18e) serves West African dishes (Togolese to be exact) priced from 25 to 70FF. It's open every night except Wednesday. Get off at metro station Abbesses for the above restaurants.

Il Duca (☎ 01 46 06 71 98; metro Abbesses) at 26 Rue Yvonne le Tac (18e) is a neat and intimate Italian restaurant with good, straightforward food including a lunchtime

FRANCE

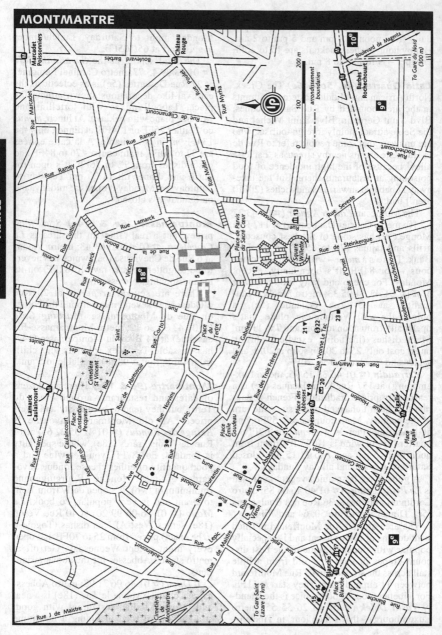

MONTMARTRE

MONTMARTRE

PLACES TO STAY	OTHER		
7 Hôtel des Arts	1 Vineyard	13	Museum of Naive Art
10 Hôtel Audran	2 Moulin de la Galette	15	La Locomotive Discothèque
14 Hôtel Rohan	(Windmill)	16	Moulin Rouge Nightclub
23 Idéal Hôtel	3 Moulin Radet (Windmill)	17	Musée de l'Érotisme
	4 Église Saint Pierre	18	Pigalle Sex & Entertainment
PLACES TO EAT	5 Crypt & Dome Entrance		District
9 Le Mono African Restaurant	6 Sacré Cœur Basilica	20	Post Office
19 Il Duca	8 Laundrette	22	Bureau de Change
21 Refuge des Fondus	11 Food Shops		
Restaurant	12 Funicular Railway		

menu for 69FF and main courses at 70 to 82FF. Home-made pasta dishes are 45 to 75FF.

University Restaurants The Centre Régional des Œuvres Universitaires et Scolaires, or CROUS (☎ 01 40 51 36 00), runs 15 student cafeterias (*restaurants universitaires*) in the city. Tickets (on sale at meal times) cost 23FF for ISIC holders and 27.90FF for others. Some of the restaurants also have à la carte brasseries. In general, CROUS restaurants have rather confusing opening times that change according to rotational agreements among the restaurants and school holiday schedules (eg most are closed on weekends and during July and August).

Restaurant Universitaire Bullier (metro Port Royal) is on the 2nd floor of the Centre Jean Sarrailh at 39 Rue Bernanos (5e). Lunch and dinner are served Monday to Friday and, during some months, on weekends as well. The ticket window, which is up one flight of stairs, is open from 11.30 am to 2 pm and 6.15 to 8 pm. One of the nicest CROUS restaurants in town is on the 7th floor of the Faculté de Droit et des Sciences Économiques (Faculty of Law and Economics; metro Vavin), which is south of the Jardin du Luxembourg at 92 Rue d'Assas (6e). It's open weekdays from 11.30 am to 3 pm. The ticket window is on the 6th floor.

Self-Catering Buying your own food is one of the best ways to keep down costs. Supermarkets are always cheaper than small grocery shops. The *Monoprix* supermarket

(opposite metro Pyramides) at 21 Avenue de l'Opéra is convenient for the Louvre district, and is open 8.30 am to 8 pm Monday to Saturday. In the Latin Quarter, try Ed l'Épicier (metro Monge) at 37 Rue Lacépède, open 9 am to 7.30 pm Monday to Saturday.

For sandwiches to take to the Jardin du Luxembourg, try the popular hole-in-the-wall ***Douce France*** at 7 Rue Royer Collard (metro Luxembourg), where the lunchtime line of Sorbonne students confirms the quality of their sandwiches (including vegetarian options; 13.50FF), coffee (3FF) and fruit juices (6FF). It's open weekdays from 11 am to 4 pm.

Food Markets The freshest and best quality fruits, vegetables, cheeses and meats at the lowest prices in town are on offer at Paris' neighbourhood food markets. The city's dozen or so covered markets are open from 8 am to sometime between 12.30 and 1.30 pm and from 3.30 or 4 to 7.30 pm daily, except Sunday afternoon and Monday. The open-air markets – about 60 scattered around town – are set up two or three mornings a week in squares and streets like Rue Mouffetard (5e) and Rue Daguerre (14e) and are open from 7 am to 1 pm.

Notre Dame Area (4e & 5e) On Île Saint Louis, there are boulangeries, fromageries and fruit and vegetable shops on Rue Saint Louis en l'Île and Rue des Deux Ponts (4e; metro Pont Marie). There's a cluster of food shops in the vicinity of Place Maubert (5e; metro Maubert-Mutualité), which is 300m south of Notre Dame, and on Rue Lagrange. On

FRANCE

Tuesday, Thursday and Saturday from 7 am to 1 pm, Place Maubert is transformed into an outdoor produce market. There's an excellent fromagerie (metro Maubert-Mutualité) at 47 Blvd Saint Germain (5e).

Saint Germain des Prés (6e) The largest cluster of food shops in the neighbourhood is one block north of Blvd Saint Germain around the intersection of Rue de Buci and Rue de Seine. There are also food shops along Rue Dauphine and the two streets that link it with Blvd Saint Germain, Rue de l'Ancienne Comédie and Rue de Buci.

Panthéon Area (5e) There are several food shops (metro Luxembourg) along Rue Saint Jacques between Nos 172 and 218 (the area just south of Rue Soufflot).

Marais (4e) There are quite a few food shops on Rue de Rivoli and Rue Saint Antoine around the Saint Paul metro stop. *Flo Prestige* (metro Bastille) at 10 Rue Saint Antoine (4e) has picnic supplies and, more importantly, some of the most delectable pastries and baked goods in Paris. It's open daily from 8 am to 11 pm.

Louvre Area (1er) You'll find a number of food shops one block north of where the western part of the Louvre meets the eastern end of Jardin des Tuileries.

Montmartre (18e) Most of the food shops in this area are along Rue des Abbesses, which is about 500m south-west of Sacré Cœur, and Rue Lepic.

Entertainment

Information in French on cultural events, music concerts, theatre performances, films, museum exhibitions, festivals, circuses etc is listed in two publications that come out each Wednesday: *Pariscope* (3FF), which includes an eight-page English section, and *L'Officiel des Spectacles* (2FF). They are available at most news kiosks.

Tickets Reservations and ticketing for all sorts of cultural events are handled by the ticket outlets in the FNAC stores at 136 Rue de Rennes (☎ 01 49 54 30 00; metro Saint Placide;

6e) and at the 3rd underground level of the Forum des Halles shopping mall (☎ 01 40 41 40 00; metro Châtelet-Les Halles) at 1-7 Rue Pierre Lescot (1er); and in the Virgin Megastores at 52-60 Ave des Champs-Élysées (☎ 01 49 53 50 00; metro Franklin D Roosevelt; 8e) and 99 Rue de Rivoli (☎ 01 49 53 50 00; metro Franklin D Roosevelt; 1er).

Pubs At 19 Rue Saint Jacques (5e), *Le Cloître* (☎ 01 43 25 19 92; metro Saint Michel) is an unpretentious, relaxed place with mellow background music which seems to please the young Parisians who congregate there. It's open daily from 3 pm to 2 am. Informal, friendly *Polly Maggoo* (☎ 01 46 33 33 64; metro Saint Michel) up the street at 11 Rue Saint Jacques was founded in 1967 and still plays music from that era. It's open daily from 1 pm to the wee hours.

Café Oz (☎ 01 43 54 30 48; metro Luxembourg) at 18 Rue Saint Jacques is a casual, friendly Australian pub with Foster's on tap. It's open daily from 4 pm to 2 am. In the Marais, *Stolly's* (☎ 01 42 76 06 76; metro Hôtel de Ville) at 16 Rue de la Cloche Percée (4e), just off Rue du Rivoli, is an Anglophone bar that is always crowded, particularly during the 5 to 8 pm happy hour. It's open daily, there are chairs on the pavement and a demi/pint of Guinness is 20/35FF. A 1.6L pitcher of cheap *blonde* (house lager) is 50FF.

Discothèques The discothèques – not really 'discos' as we know them but any place where there's music and dancing – favoured by the Parisian 'in' crowd change frequently, and many are officially private, which means that the gorilla-like bouncers can refuse entry to whomever they don't like the look of. Single men, for example, may not be admitted simply because they're alone and male. Women, on the other hand, get in free on some nights. Expect to pay at least 50FF on weekdays and 100FF on weekends.

Le Balajo (☎ 01 47 00 07 87; metro Bastille), a mainstay of the Parisian dance-hall scene since the time of Édith Piaf, is at 9 Rue de Lappe (11e), two blocks north-east of Place de la Bastille. It offers accordion music on Saturday and Sunday afternoons from 3 to 7 pm and dancing on Thursday, Friday and

Saturday nights from 11.30 pm to 5 am. On Saturday and Sunday afternoon admission costs 50FF. At night admission is 100FF and includes one drink. Wednesday is mambo night – entrance costs 80FF.

La Locomotive (☎ 01 53 41 88 88; metro Blanche) at 90 Blvd de Clichy (18e), which is in Pigalle next to the Moulin Rouge nightclub, occupies three floors, each offering a different ambience and kind of music. It's open nightly from 11 pm (from midnight on Monday) until 6 am (7 am weekends). Entrance costs 70FF on weekdays and 100FF on Friday and Saturday nights, including one drink. Women get in free before 12.30 am and on Sunday.

Jazz For the latest on jazz happenings in town, check the listings (see the beginning of this section). *Caveau de la Huchette* (☎ 01 43 26 65 05; metro Saint Michel) at 5 Rue de la Huchette (5e) is a favourite with live jazz. It's open every night from 9.30 pm to 2 am (4 am Saturday, Sunday and holiday nights). From Sunday to Thursday, entry costs 60FF (55FF for students) and 70FF on Friday and Saturday.

Classical Music & Opera Paris has all sorts of orchestra, organ and chamber music concerts, including free organ concerts held at Notre Dame every Sunday at 5.30 pm. The Opéra National de Paris now splits its performances between its old home *Opéra Garnier* (☎ 01 44 73 13 99; metro Opéra) at Place de l'Opéra (9e) and *Opéra-Bastille* (☎ 01 44 73 13 99; metro Bastille) at 2-6 Place de la Bastille (12e), which opened in 1989. Opera tickets cost 145 to 635FF. Ballets cost 70 to 280FF (45FF for the cheapest seats). Concerts are 85 to 240FF (45FF for the least expensive seats). If there are unsold tickets, people under 25 or over 65 and students can get excellent seats for about 100FF only 15 minutes before the curtain goes up. Ask for the *tarif spécial*.

Cinemas The fashionable cinemas on Blvd du Montparnasse (6e and 14e; metro Montparnasse Bienvenüe) show both dubbed (VF) and original (VO) feature films. There's another cluster of cinemas at Carrefour de l'Odéon (6e; metro Odéon) and lots more movie theatres along the Ave des Champs-Élysées (8e; metro George V) and Blvd Saint Germain (6e; metro Saint Germain des Prés).

The *Cinémathèque Française* (☎ 01 47 04 24 24, or ☎ 01 45 53 21 86 for a recorded message) usually leaves foreign films undubbed. Screenings take place almost every day at two locations: in the far eastern tip of the Palais de Chaillot on Ave Albert de Mun (16e; metro Trocadéro or Iéna) and at 18 Rue du Faubourg du Temple (11e; metro République). Tickets cost 28FF (17FF reduced rate).

Parisian movie-going is rather pricey. Expect to pay around 45FF for a ticket. Students and people under 18 and over 60 usually get discounts of about 25% except on weekend nights. On Monday and/or Wednesday most cinemas give everyone a discount.

Things to Buy

Fashion For fashionable clothing and accessories, some of the fanciest shops in Paris are along Ave Montaigne (8e), Rue Saint Honoré (1er and 8e), Place Vendôme (1er) and Rue du Faubourg Saint Honoré (8e). Rue Bonaparte (6e) offers a good choice of mid-range boutiques.

Department Stores Right behind Opéra Garnier are two of Paris' largest department stores. Au Printemps (☎ 01 42 82 50 00; metro Havre Caumartin) is at 64 Blvd Haussmann (9e) and Galeries Lafayette (☎ 01 42 82 36 40; metro Auber or Chaussée) at 40 Blvd Haussmann (9e) is housed in two adjacent buildings linked by a pedestrian bridge. The third of Paris' 'big three', Samaritaine (☎ 01 40 41 20 20; metro Pont Neuf), consists of four buildings between Pont Neuf and Rue de Rivoli. There is an amazing 360° view of the city from the 10th-floor terrace of Building 2 at 19 Rue de la Monnaie. Take the lift to the 9th floor and walk up the narrow staircase. All three stores are open Monday to Saturday from 9.30 am to 7 pm (10 pm on Thursday).

Getting There & Away

Air Paris has two major international airports. Aéroport d'Orly is 14km south of central Paris. For flight and other information, call ☎ 01 49 75 15 15. Aéroport Charles de Gaulle (☎ 01 48 62 22 80), also known as Roissy-Charles de Gaulle in the suburb of Roissy, is 23km north-east of central Paris.

FRANCE

MARAIS & ÎLE SAINT LOUIS

FRANCE

Telephone numbers for information at Paris'
airline offices are:

Air France	☎ 0802 802 802
Air Inter	☎ 01 45 46 90 00
Air Liberté	☎ 08 03 80 58 05
Air UK	☎ 01 44 56 18 08
American Airlines	☎ 08 01 872 872
British Airways	☎ 08 02 80 29 02
Continental Airlines	☎ 08 00 25 31 81
Northwest Airlines	☎ 01 42 66 90 00
Qantas Airways	☎ 01 44 55 52 00
Singapore Airlines	☎ 01 45 53 90 90
Thai Airways	☎ 01 44 20 70 80

Tower Air	☎ 01 55 04 80 80
United Airlines	☎ 01 41 40 30 30

Bus Eurolines runs buses from Paris to cities
all over Europe. The company's terminal,
Gare Routière Internationale (☎ 01 49 72 51
51; metro Gallieni), is at Porte de Bagnolet
(20e) on the eastern edge of Paris. Its ticket
office in town (☎ 01 43 54 11 99; metro
Cluny-La Sorbonne) at 55 Rue Saint Jacques
(5e) is open Tuesday to Friday from 9.30 am
to 1 pm and 2.30 to 7 pm and on Monday and
Saturday to 6 pm.

MARAIS & ÎLE SAINT LOUIS

PLACES TO STAY
11 Grand Hôtel Mahler
12 Hôtel Pratic
13 Hôtel Moderne
15 Hôtel Rivoli
17 Hôtel de Nice
18 Hôtel Le Palais de Fés
20 MIJE Maubisson
22 MIJE Fourcy
23 MIJE Fauconnier

PLACES TO EAT
2 Mélodine Cafeteria
5 Aquarius Vegetarian
    Restaurant
7 Chez Rami et Hanna

9 Restaurants
10 Restaurant Jo Goldenberg
16 Minh Chau
26 Ethnic Restaurants
27 Flo Prestige
35 Berthillon Ice Cream

OTHER
1 Web Bar
3 Accueil des Jeunes en France
    (AJF)
4 Centre Pompidou
6 Musée Picasso
8 Laundrette
14 Hôtel de Ville (City Hall)
19 Stolly's

21 Memorial to the Unknown
    Jewish Martyr
24 Food Shops
25 Victor Hugo's House
28 Banque de France
29 Colonne de Juillet
30 Entrance to Opéra-Bastille
31 Opéra-Bastille
32 Port de Plaisance de Paris
    Arsenal
33 Notre Dame
34 WWII Deportation Memorial
36 Food Shops
37 Ulysse Bookshop

Cities served include Amsterdam (270FF one way, 7½ hours), London (280FF, nine hours), Madrid (590FF, 17 hours) and Rome (600FF, 23 hours). People under 26 and over 60 get a discount of about 10%. Because the French government prefers to avoid competition with the state-owned rail system and regulated domestic airlines, there is no domestic, intercity bus service to or from Paris.

Train Paris has six major train stations (*gares*), each handling traffic to different parts of France and Europe. For information in English call ☎ 08 36 35 35 39; the switchboards are staffed from 7 am to 10 pm. All the stations have exchange bureaus, and there is a tourist information office at each one except Gare Saint Lazare. The metro station attached to each train station bears the same name as the *gare*. Paris' major train stations are:

Gare d'Austerlitz
(13e) Quai d'Austerlitz (metro Gare d'Austerlitz) – trains to the Loire Valley, Spain and Portugal and non-TGV trains to south-western France (Bordeaux, the Basque Country)
Gare de l'Est
(10e) Place du 11 Novembre 1918 (metro Gare de l'Est) – trains to parts of France east of Paris (Champagne, Alsace, Lorraine), Luxembourg, parts of Switzerland (Basel, Lucerne, Zürich), southern Germany (Frankfurt, Munich) and Austria

Gare de Lyon
(12e) Place Louis Armand (metro Gare de Lyon) – regular and TGV Sud-Est trains to points south-east of Paris, including Dijon, Lyon, Provence, Côte d'Azur, Alps, parts of Switzerland, Italy and Greece
Gare Montparnasse
(15e) Blvd de Vaugirard (metro Montparnasse Bienvenüe) – trains to Brittany and places on the way (Chartres, Angers, Nantes); and the TGV Atlantique, which serves Tours, Bordeaux and other places in south-western France
Gare du Nord
(10e) Rue de Dunkerque (metro Gare du Nord) – trains to northern France (Lille, Calais), the UK via the Channel Tunnel (TGV Nord), Belgium, Netherlands, northern Germany, Scandinavia, Moscow etc
Gare Saint Lazare
(8e) Rue Saint Lazare (metro Saint Lazare) – trains to Normandy and, via the Channel ports, ferries to England.

Getting Around

RATP, Paris' public transit system, is one of the most efficient in the world and one of the biggest urban transport bargains (see Metro/ Bus Tickets). Free metro/RER/bus maps are available at the ticket windows of most stations and at tourist offices. For 24-hour information in English on metros and RER commuter trains and buses, call ☎ 08 36 68 41 14.

To/From Orly Airport Orly Rail is the quickest way to get to the Left Bank and the

16e. Take the free shuttle bus to the Pont de Rungis-Aéroport d'Orly RER (commuter rail) station, which is on the C2 line, and get on a train (30FF) heading into the city. Another fast way into town is to hop on the Orlyval shuttle train (57FF); it stops near Orly-Sud's Porte F and links Orly with the Antony RER station, which is on line B4. Orlybus (30FF or six bus/metro tickets), takes you to the Denfert-Rochereau metro station (14e).

Air France buses charge 40FF to take you to Ave du Maine at the Gare Montparnasse (15e) or the Aérogare des Invalides, which is next to Esplanade des Invalides (7e). RATP bus No 183 (three tickets or 24FF) goes to Porte de Choisy (13e) but is very slow. Jetbus, the cheapest option, links both terminals with the Villejuif-Louis Aragon metro stop, costs 24FF and takes 20 minutes. All the services between Orly airport and Paris run every 15 minutes or so (less frequently late at night) from early in the morning (sometime between 5.30 and 6.30 am) to 11 or 11.30 pm.

Taking a taxi from Orly airport costs 110 to 150FF plus 6FF per heavy bag, and can work out cheaper per person if there are four people to share it.

To/From Charles de Gaulle Airport
The fastest way to get to/from the city is by Roissy Rail. Free shuttle buses take you from the airport terminals to the Roissy-Charles de Gaulle RER (commuter rail) station. You can buy tickets to Charles de Gaulle (CDG) at RER stations for 47FF. If you get on at an ordinary metro station you can buy a ticket when you change to the RER or pay at the other end or on the train (with a fine) if you get caught.

Air France bus No 2 will take you to Porte Maillot (16e and 17e; metro Porte Maillot) and the corner of Ave Carnot near the Arc de Triomphe (17e) for 55FF; bus No 4 to Blvd de Vaugirard at the Gare Montparnasse (15e) cost 65FF. Roissybus (RATP bus No 352) goes to the American Express office (9e) near Place de l'Opéra and costs 45FF. RATP bus No 350 goes to Gare du Nord (10e) and Gare de l'Est (10e). Until 9.15 pm (heading into the city) and 8.20 pm (towards the airport), RATP bus No 351 goes to Ave du Trône (11e and 12e), on the eastern side of Place de la Nation. Both RATP buses require six tickets or 48FF.

Unless otherwise indicated, the buses and trains from CDG to Paris run from sometime between 5 and 6.30 am until 11 or 11.30 pm.

Bus Paris' extensive bus network tends to get overlooked by visitors, in part because the metro is so quick, efficient and easy to use. Bus routes are indicated on the free RATP maps No 1, *Petit Plan de Paris*, and No 3, *Grand Plan Île de France*.

Short trips cost one bus/metro/RER ticket (see Underground/Bus Tickets below), while longer rides require two. Travellers without tickets can purchase them from the driver. Whatever kind of ticket (*coupon*) you have, you must cancel it in the little machine next to the driver. The fines are hefty if you're caught without a ticket or without a cancelled ticket. If you have a Carte Orange, Formule 1 or Paris Visite pass (see the following Metro & RER section), just flash it at the driver – do not cancel your ticket.

After the metro shuts down at around 12.45 am, the Noctambus network, whose symbol is a black owl silhouetted against a yellow moon, links the Châtelet-Hôtel de Ville area (4e) with lots of places on the Right Bank (lines A to H) and a few on the Left Bank (lines J and R). Noctambuses begin their runs from the even-numbered side of Ave Victoria (4e), which is between the Hôtel de Ville and Place du Châtelet, every hour on the half-hour from 1.30 to 5.30 am. A ride requires three tickets (four tickets if your journey involves a transfer).

Metro & RER Paris' underground rail network consists of two separate but linked systems: the Métropolitain, known as the metro, which has 13 lines and over 300 stations, many marked by Hector Guimard's famous noodle-like Art Nouveau entrances with the red 'eyes', and the suburban commuter rail network, the RER which, along with certain SNCF lines, is divided into eight concentric zones. The term 'metro' is used in this chapter to refer to the Métropolitain and any part of the RER system within Paris. The whole system has been designed so that no point in Paris is more than 500m from a metro stop; in fact, some places in the city centre are within a few hundred metres of up to three stations. (A new high-speed line called the Météor and linking the Madeleine stop with the Bibliothèque Nationale de France (13e) and RER line C will probably have opened by the time you read this.)

You may be able to reduce the number of transfers you'll have to make by going to a station a bit farther on from your destination. For metro stations to avoid late at night, see Dangers & Annoyances earlier in the Paris section.

How it Works Each metro train is known by the name of its terminus; trains on the same line have different names depending on which direction they are travelling in. On lines that split into several branches and thus have more than one end-of-the-line station, the final destination of each train is indicated on the front, sides and interior of the train cars. In the stations, white-on-blue *sortie* signs indicate exits and black-on-orange *correspondance* signs show how to get to connecting trains. The last metro train sets out on its final run at 12.30 am. Plan ahead so as not to miss your connection. The metro starts up again at 5.30 am.

Metro/RER/Bus Tickets The same green 2nd-class tickets are valid on the metro, the bus and, for travel within the Paris city limits, the RER's 2nd-class carriages. They cost 8FF if bought separately and 48FF for a booklet (*carnet*) of 10. For children aged four to nine a carnet costs 24FF. One ticket lets you travel between any two metro stations, including stations outside of the Paris city limits, no matter how many transfers are required. You can also use it on the RER commuter rail system for travel within Paris (within zone 1).

For travel on the RER to destinations outside the city, purchase a special ticket *before* you board the train or you won't be able to get out of the station and could be fined. Always keep your ticket until you reach your destination and exit the station; if you're caught without a ticket, or with an invalid one, you'll be fined.

The cheapest and easiest way to travel the metro is to get a Carte Orange, a bus/metro/RER pass whose accompanying magnetic coupon comes in weekly and monthly versions. You can get tickets for travel in up to eight urban and suburban zones; unless you'll be using the suburban commuter lines an awful lot though, the basic ticket – valid for zones 1 and 2 – is probably sufficient.

The weekly ticket costs 75FF for zones 1 and 2 and is valid from Monday to Sunday. Even if you'll be in Paris for only three or four days, it may very well work out cheaper than purchasing a carnet – you'll break even at 16 rides – and it will certainly cost less than buying a daily Mobilis or Paris Visite pass. The monthly Carte Orange ticket (255FF for zones 1 and 2) begins on the first day of each calendar month. Both are on sale in metro and RER stations from 6.30 am to 10 pm and at certain bus terminals.

To get a Carte Orange, bring a small photograph of yourself to any metro or RER ticket counter (four photos for about 25FF are available from automatic booths in the train stations and certain metro stations). Request a Carte Orange (which is free) and the kind of coupon you'd like. To prevent tickets from being used by more than one person, you must write your surname (*nom*) and given name (*prénom*) on the Carte Orange, and the number of your Carte Orange on each weekly or monthly coupon you buy (next to the words Carte No).

The rather pricey Mobilis and Paris Visite passes, designed to facilitate bus, metro and RER travel for tourists, are on sale in many metro stations, the train stations and international airports. The Mobilis card (and its *coupon*) allows unlimited travel for one day in two to eight zones. The version valid for zones 1 and 2 costs 30FF. Paris Visite passes, which allow the holder discounts on entries to certain museums and activities as well as transport, are valid for one/two/three/five consecutive days of travel in either three, five or eight zones. The one to three-zone version costs 50/85/120/170FF for one/two/three/five days. Children aged four to 11 pay half-price. They can be purchased at larger metro and RER stations, at SNCF bureaus in Paris and at the airports.

Taxi Paris' 15,000 taxis have a reputation for paying little heed to riders' convenience. Another common complaint is that it can be difficult to find a taxi late at night (after 11 pm) or in the rain. The flag fall is 13FF; within the city, it costs 3.45FF per kilometre between 7 am and 7 pm Monday to Saturday. On nights, Sunday and holidays, it's 5.70FF per kilometre. Animals, a fourth passenger and heavy luggage cost extra. Tips are not obligatory, but no matter what the fare is, usual tips range from 2FF to a maximum of 5FF.

The easiest way to find a taxi is to walk to the nearest taxi stand (*tête de station*), of which there are 500 scattered around the city and marked on any of the Michelin 1:10,000 maps. Radio-dispatched taxis include Taxis Bleus (☎ 01 49 36 10 10), G7 Taxis (☎ 01 47 39 47 39), Alpha Taxis (☎ 01 45 85 85 85), Taxis-Radio 7000 (☎ 01 42 70 00 42) and Artaxi (☎ 01 42 41 50 50). If you order a taxi by phone, the meter is switched on as soon as the driver gets word of your call – wherever that may be (but usually not too far away).

Car & Motorcycle Driving in Paris is nerve-wracking but not impossible, though having a car in the city is often more of a hindrance than a help. The fastest way to get across Paris is usually the Périphérique (M1) – the ring road or beltway that encircles the city.

In many parts of Paris you have to pay 10FF an hour to park your car on the street. Large municipal parking garages usually charge from 12 to 15FF an hour or, for periods of 12 to 24 hours, 80 to 130FF. Parking fines are usually 75 or 200FF. Parking attendants dispense them with great abandon (some say glee), but Parisians appear simply to ignore them.

Renting a small car (eg a Peugeot 106) for one day with 400km, plus insurance and taxes, costs about 350FF but there are better deals from smaller agencies from as low as 199FF a day or 549FF for a three-day weekend with 800km. Rent A Car (☎ 01 43 45 15 15), has offices at 79 Rue de Bercy (12e; metro Bercy) and 84 Ave de Versailles (16e; metro Mirabeau). Avis (☎ 01 46 10 60 60) has offices at all six train stations, both airports and several other locations in the Paris area. Europcar (☎ 01 30 43 82 82) has bureaus at both airports and almost 20 other locations. Hertz (☎ 01 47 88 51 51) also has offices at the airports and at many other places around Paris.

For information on purchase/repurchase plans, see the Getting Around section at the start of this chapter.

Bicycle With its heavy traffic and impatient drivers Paris has never been a cyclist's paradise. But the city now has almost 100km of bicycle lanes – with another 50km planned by the year 2000 – that run north-south and east-west through the city; for information ring ☎ 01 40 28 73 73. They're not particularly attractive or safe, but cyclists may be fined about 250FF for failing to use them. The tourist office distributes a free brochure-map produced by the mayor's office called *100km pour Vivre Paris à Vélo*.

Maison du Velo (☎ 01 42 81 24 72) at Rue Fénélan (10e; metro Gare du Nord) has bicycles available for 90 to 150FF per day, 260FF per weekend and 575FF per week.

Cyclic (☎ 01 43 25 63 67) at 19 Rue Mange (5e; metro Cardinal Lemoine) rents bikes by the hour (20FF), day (100FF) and week (300FF).

See the sections on Bois de Boulogne (Things to See) and Bicycle (Organised Tours) for more information.

Around Paris

The region surrounding Paris is known as the Île de France (Island of France) because of its position between four rivers: the Aube, Marne, Oise and Seine. It was from this relatively small area that, starting around 1100, the kingdom of France began to expand. Today, the region's proximity to Paris and a number of remarkable sights make it an especially popular day-trip destination for people staying in Paris.

DISNEYLAND PARIS

It took US$4.4 billion to turn beet fields 32km east of Paris into the much heralded Disneyland Paris, which opened in 1992 amid much fanfare and controversy. Although it struggled financially for the first few years, what was then known as EuroDisney is now in the black, and the park has become the most popular tourist attraction in Europe, with 12.6 million visitors in 1997.

Disneyland Paris is open 365 days a year from 10 am to 6 pm (8 pm on Saturday and some Sundays). In July and August the hours are 9 am to 11 pm daily. Admission costs 200FF (155FF for children aged three to 11) from late March to October. The rest of the year, except during the Christmas holidays, prices drop to 160/130FF. To get there, take RER line A4 to the terminus (Marne-la-Vallée Chessy), but check the destination boards to ensure your train goes all the way to the end. Trains, which take 35 minutes from the Nation metro stop on Place de la Nation (12e), run every 10 or 15 minutes or so and cost 39FF.

VERSAILLES

The site of France's grandest and most famous chateau, Versailles (population 95,000) served as the country's political capital and the seat of the royal court from 1682 until 1789, when Revolutionary mobs massacred the palace guard and dragged Louis XVI and Marie Antoinette off to Paris, where they were later guillotined. After the Franco-Prussian War of 1870-71, the victorious Prussians proclaimed the establishment of the German empire from the chateau's Galerie des Glaces (Hall of Mirrors). In 1919 the Treaty of Versailles was signed in the same room, officially ending WWI and imposing harsh conditions on a defeated Germany, Austria and Hungary.

Because Versailles is on most travellers' 'must-see' lists, the chateau can be jammed with tourists, especially on weekends, in summer and most especially on summer Sundays. The best way to avoid the lines is to arrive early in the morning.

Information

The tourist office (☎ 01 39 50 36 22) is at 7 Rue des Réservoirs, just north of the chateau. From mid-September to April, it's open Monday to Saturday from 9 am to 12.30 pm and 1.30 to 6 pm (on Saturday to 5 pm). During the rest of the year, it's open daily from 9 am to 7 pm.

Château de Versailles

The enormous Château de Versailles (☎ 01 30 84 74 00) was built in the mid-17th century during the reign of Louis XIV (the Sun King). Among the advantages of Versailles was its distance from the political intrigues of Paris; out here, it was much easier for the king to contain and keep an eye on his scheming nobles. The plan worked brilliantly, all the more so because court life turned the nobles into sycophantic courtiers who expended most of their energy vying for royal favour à la Les Liaisons Dangereuses.

The chateau essentially consists of four parts: the main palace building, which is a classical structure with innumerable wings, sumptuous bedchambers and grand halls; the vast 17th-century gardens, laid out in the formal French style; and two out-palaces, the late 17th-century Grand Trianon and the mid-18th century Petit Trianon.

Opening Hours & Tickets The main building is open daily, except Monday and public holidays, from 9 am to 5.30 pm (6.30 pm from May to September). Entrance to the **Grands Appartements** (State Apartments), including the 73m-long **Galerie des Glaces** (Hall of Mirrors) and the **Appartement de la Reine** (Queen's Suite), costs 45FF (35FF reduced rate). Everyone pays 35FF on Sunday. Tickets are on sale at Entrée A (Entrance A), which is off to the right from the equestrian statue of Louis XIV as you approach the building. You won't be able to visit other parts of the main palace unless you take one of the guided tours (see Guided Tours below). Entrée H has facilities for the disabled, including a lift.

The **Grand Trianon**, which costs 25FF (15FF reduced rate), is open daily, except Monday. From October to April, opening hours are 10 am to 12.30 pm and 2 to 5.30 pm (10 am to 5.30 pm on weekends). During the rest of the year, hours are 10 am to 6.30 pm. The **Petit Trianon**, open the same hours as the Grand Trianon, costs 15FF (10FF reduced rate).

The gardens are open daily from 7 am to nightfall. Entry is free, except on Sunday from May to early October when the baroque fountains 'perform'. The **Grandes Eaux** show takes place from 3.30 to 5 pm and costs 25FF.

Guided Tours Several different guided tours are available in English. A one-hour tour costs 25FF in addition to the regular entry fee. To buy tickets and make advance reservations go to entrées C or D. Cassette-guided tours lasting 80 minutes are available at entrée A for 30FF.

Other Attractions
The town of Versailles is filled with beautiful buildings from the 17th and 18th centuries. The tourist office has a brochure of historic walks (*promenades historiques*) pinpointing more than two dozen of these structures. They include: the **Jeu de Paume** (check the opening hours with the tourist office) on Rue du Jeu de Paume, where the representatives of the Third Estate constituted themselves as a National Assembly in June 1789; the **Musée Lambinet** (☎ 01 39 50 30 32) at 54 Blvd de la Reine (open Tuesday and Friday from 2 to 5 pm, Wednesday and Thursday from 1 to 6 pm and on Saturday and Sunday from 2 to 6 pm); and the mid-18th century **Cathédrale Saint Louis** at Place Saint Louis, renowned for its enormous pipe organ.

Getting There & Away
Bus Bus No 171 takes you from the Pont de Sèvres metro stop in Paris all the way to Place d'Armes, right in front of the chateau.

Train Versailles, 23km south-west of central Paris, has three train stations: Versailles-Rive Gauche, Versailles-Chantiers and Versailles-Rive Droite. Each is served by one of the three rail services that link Versailles with Paris.

RER line C5 takes you from Paris' Gare d'Austerlitz and various other RER stations on the Left Bank (including Saint Michel and Champ de Mars-Tour Eiffel) to Versailles-Rive Gauche, which is 700m south-east of the chateau on Ave Général de Gaulle. Check the electronic destination lists on the platform to make sure you take a train that goes all the way there.

SNCF trains go from Paris' Gare Montparnasse to Versailles-Chantiers, which is 1.3km south-east of the chateau just off Ave de Sceaux. SNCF trains also run from Paris' Gare Saint Lazare to Versailles-Rive Droite, 1.2km north-east of the chateau. Many of the trains from Gare Montparnasse to Versailles

continue on to Chartres. Eurail-pass holders can travel free on the SNCF trains but not on those operated by the RER.

CHARTRES
The indescribably beautiful 13th-century cathedral of Chartres (population 40,000) rises abruptly from the corn fields 88km south-west of Paris. Crowned by two soaring spires – one Gothic, the other Romanesque – it dominates the attractive medieval town clustered around its base. The present cathedral has been attracting pilgrims for eight centuries, but the city has been a site of pilgrimage for over two millennia: the Gallic Druids may have had a sanctuary here, and the Romans apparently built a temple dedicated to the Dea Mater (mother goddess).

Orientation
The medieval sections of Chartres are situated along the Eure River and the hillside to the west. The cathedral, which is visible from almost everywhere, is about 500m east of the train station.

Information
Tourist Office The tourist office (☎ 02 37 21 50 00) is across Place de la Cathédrale from the cathedral's main entrance. From April to September it's open Monday to Saturday from 9 am to 7 pm and on Sunday from 9.30 am to 5.30 pm. During the rest of the year, the Monday to Saturday hours are 10 am to 6 pm and the Sunday hours are from 10 am to 1 pm and 2.30 to 4.30 pm. Hotel reservations cost 10FF (plus a 50FF deposit).

Money & Post The Banque de France at 32 Rue du Docteur Maunoury is open Monday to Friday from 8.45 am to 12.30 pm and 1.50 to 3.35 pm. The main post office at Place des Épars is open Monday to Friday from 8.30 am to 7 pm and on Saturday from 8.30 am to noon. Chartres postcode is 28000.

Things to See & Do
Cathédrale Notre Dame Chartres' cathedral (☎ 02 37 21 75 02) was built in the first quarter of the 13th century and, unlike so many of its contemporaries, it has not been significantly modified since then. Built to

replace an earlier structure devastated by fire in 1194, the construction of this early Gothic masterpiece took only 25 years, which is why the cathedral has a high degree of architectural unity. It was almost torn down during the Reign of Terror and managed to survive WWII bombing raids unscathed.

The cathedral is open daily from 7.30 am (8.30 am on Sunday) to 7.15 pm. From April to November (and sometimes in winter), Englishman Malcolm Miller gives fascinating tours (30FF) of what he calls 'this book of stained glass and sculpture' at noon and 2.45 pm every day, except Sunday.

The 105m Clocher Vieux (old bell tower), the tallest Romanesque steeple still standing, is to the right as you face the Romanesque Portail Royal (the main entrance). The Clocher Neuf (new bell tower) has a Gothic spire dating from 1513 and can be visited daily, except Sunday morning, from 9.30 or 10 to 11.30 am and 2 to 4 or 5 pm (November to February) or 6 pm (May to August). The fee is 20FF.

Inside, the cathedral's most exceptional feature is its extraordinary stained-glass windows, most of which are 13th-century originals and are slowly being cleaned at great expense. The three exceptional windows over the main entrance date from around 1150. The strange labyrinth on the nave floor in dark and light stone was used by medieval pilgrims while praying. The trésor (treasury) displays a piece of cloth given to the cathedral in 876 said to have been worn by the Virgin Mary. From April to October it's open 10 am to noon and 2 to 6 pm from Tuesday to Sunday (closed Sunday morning); in winter it closes at 4.30 pm (5 pm on Sunday and holidays).

The early 11th-century Romanesque crypt, the largest in France, can be visited by a half-hour guided tour in French for 11FF. Tours depart from the cathedral's gift shop, La Crypte, which is outside the south entrance at 18 Rue du Cloître Notre Dame, every day between 11 am and 4.15 pm. From mid-June to mid-September there's an additional tour at 5.15 pm.

Centre International du Vitrail The International Centre of Stained Glass Art (☎ 02 37 21 65 72), partly housed in a 13th-century underground storehouse north of the cathedral at 5 Rue du Cardinal Pie, has exhibits on stained-glass production, restoration, history and symbolism; it's not a bad idea to stop by here before visiting the cathedral if you read French. The centre is open daily from 9.30 am to 12.30 pm and 1.30 to 6 pm. The entry fee is 20FF (12FF reduced rate).

Musée des Beaux-Arts The fine arts museum (☎ 02 37 36 41 39), which is behind (north of) the cathedral at 29 Rue du Cloître Notre Dame, is housed in the 17th and 18th-century Palais Épiscopal (Bishop's Palace). Its collections include paintings from the 16th to 19th centuries, wooden sculptures from the Middle Ages, a number of 17th and 18th-century harpsichords and some tapestries. The museum is open daily, except Sunday morning and Tuesday, from 10 am to noon and 2 to 5 pm (10 am to 6 pm from April to October). Entrance is 10FF (5FF reduced rate).

Old City During the Middle Ages, the city of Chartres grew and developed along the banks of the Eure River. Among the many buildings remaining from that period are private residences, stone bridges, tanneries, wash houses and a number of churches. Streets with buildings of interest include Rue de la Tannerie, which runs along the Eure, and Rue des Écuyers, which is midway between the cathedral and the river. Église Saint Pierre at Place Saint Pierre has a massive bell tower dating from around 1000 and some fine (and often overlooked) medieval stained-glass windows.

Walking Tour Self-guided cassette-tape tours of the old city can be rented at the tourist office for 35/40FF for one or two people (plus 100FF deposit).

Places to Stay

Camping About 2.5km south-east of the train station on Rue de Launay is *Les Bords de l'Eure* camping ground (☎ 02 37 28 79 43), which is open from April to early September. To get there from the train station take bus No 8 to the Vignes stop.

Hostel The pleasant and calm *Auberge de*

Jeunesse (☎ 02 37 34 27 64) at 23 Ave Neigre is about 1.5km east of the train station via the ring road (Blvd Charles Péguy and Blvd Jean Jaurès). By bus, take line No 3 from the train station and get off at the Rouliers stop. Reception is open daily from 2 to 10 pm (11 pm in summer). A bed costs 65FF, including breakfast.

Hotels The *Hôtel de l'Ouest* (☎ 02 37 21 43 27), a two-star place opposite the train station at 3 Place Pierre Sémard, has somewhat dingy, carpeted doubles/triples for 120/170FF (with washbasin and bidet), 140/240FF (with shower) and 210/260FF (with shower and toilet). You might also try the eight-room *Hôtel Au Départ* (☎ 02 37 36 80 43) at 1 Rue Nicole where doubles/triples with washbasin and bidet are 110/170FF. Reception (at the bar) is closed on Sunday.

A lovely two-star choice is *Hôtel de la Poste* (☎ 02 37 21 04 27; fax 02 37 36 42 17), north-west of Place des Épars at 3 Rue du Général Koening, with singles from 230FF with shower (330FF with shower and toilet). Triples/quads with shower cost 370/440FF.

Places to Eat

The plat du jour at *Café Serpente* (☎ 02 37 21 68 81), a brasserie and salon de thé across from the south porch of the cathedral at 2 Rue du Cloître Notre Dame, will cost you 98FF; there also are salads for 35 to 42FF. It's open daily from 10 am to 1 pm. At *La Vesuvio* (☎ 02 37 21 56 35) at 30 Place des Halles, pizzas (35 to 60FF), salads (42 to 48FF) and light meals are served daily from noon to 3 pm and 7 to 11 pm. The *Monoprix* supermarket at 21 Rue Noël Ballay north-east of Place des Épars is open Monday to Saturday from 9 am to 7.30 pm.

Getting There & Around

Train The train station is at Place Pierre Sémard. The trip from Paris' Gare Montparnasse (71FF one way) takes 50 to 70 minutes. The last train back to Paris leaves Chartres just after 9 pm on weekdays, 7.40 pm on Saturday and 10 pm on Sunday and holidays. There is also direct rail service to/from Nantes, Quimper, Rennes and Versailles.

Alsace

Alsace, the easternmost part of northern France, is nestled between the Vosges Mountains and, about 30km to the east, the Rhine River, marking the Franco-German border. The area owes its unique language, architecture, cuisine and atmosphere to both sides of this river.

Most of Alsace became part of France in 1648, although Strasbourg, the region's largest city, retained its independence until 1681. But more than two centuries of French rule did little to dampen 19th and early 20th-century German enthusiasm for a foothold on the west bank of the Rhine, and Alsace was twice annexed by Germany: from the Franco-Prussian War (1871) until the end of WWI and again between 1939 and 1944.

Language

The Alsatian language, a Germanic dialect similar to that spoken in nearby parts of Germany and Switzerland, is still used by many Alsatians, especially older people in rural areas. Alsatian is known for its singsong intonations, which also characterise the way some Alsatians speak French.

STRASBOURG

The cosmopolitan city of Strasbourg (population 423,000), just a couple of kilometres west of the Rhine, is Alsace's great metropolis and its intellectual and cultural capital. Towering above the restaurants, pubs and *bars à musique* of the lively old city is the cathedral, a medieval marvel in pink sandstone near which is clustered one of the finest ensembles of museums in France. Strasbourg's distinctive architecture, including the centuries-old half-timbered houses, and its exemplary orderliness impart an unmistakably Alsatian ambience.

When it was founded in 1949, the Council of Europe (Conseil de l'Europe) decided to base itself in Strasbourg. The organisation's huge headquarters, the Palais de l'Europe, is used for one week each month (except in summer) by the European Parliament, the legislative branch of the EU.

Orientation

The train station is 400m west of the old city, which is an island delimited by the Ill River to the south and the Fossé du Faux Rempart to the north. The main public square in the old city is Place Kléber, 400m north-west of the cathedral. The quaint Petite France area is in the old city's south-west corner.

Information

Tourist Office The main tourist office (☎ 03 88 52 28 28; fax 03 88 52 28 29; otsr@strasbourg.com; www.strasbourg.com) at 17 Place de la Cathédrale is open from 9 am to 6 pm (7 pm June to September).

There's a tourist office annexe (☎ 03 88 32 51 49) in the underground complex beneath the Place de la Gare in front of the train station. It's open from 8.30 am to 12.30 pm and 1.45 to 6 pm (closed on Sunday from November to Easter). From June to early October, daily hours are 9 am to 7 pm. This is a good place to pick up bus tickets. The office also sells the Strasbourg Pass (58FF, valid for three days) which gets you free/reduced tours and museum admissions.

Money The Banque de France is at 3 Place Broglie. The Banque CIAL bureau in the train station is open weekdays from 9 am to 1 pm and 2 to 7.30 pm and weekends from 9 am to 8 pm. The commission is 15FF on weekdays and 26FF on weekends. There's a 24-hour exchange machine outside the CCF bank at Place Gutenberg. The new American Express bureau (☎ 03 88 21 96 59) at 19 Rue des Francs Bourgeois is open on weekdays from 8.45 am to noon and 1.30 to 6 pm.

Post The main post office at 5 Ave de la Marseillaise is open weekdays from 8 am to 7 pm and on Saturday till noon. The branch post office to the left of the train station keeps the same hours. Both offer currency exchange.

Cybercafés The Best Coffee Shop (☎ 06 80 46 43 15 by cellular phone) at 10 Quai des Pêcheurs charges 35FF an hour for Internet access. Opening hours are 11 am (2 pm on Saturday) to 1 am; it's closed Sunday.

Things to See & Do

Walking Tour Strasbourg is a great place for an aimless stroll. The bustling **Vieille Ville** (old town) is filled with pedestrian malls, upmarket shopping streets and lively public squares. There are river views from the quays and paths along the Ill River and the Fossé du Faux Rempart, and in **La Petite France,** half-timbered houses line the narrow streets and canals. The city's parks – **Parc de l'Orangerie** and **Place de la République** particularly – provide a welcome respite from the traffic and bustle. Guided tours of the town (38FF) are organised by the tourist office. They begin daily at 10.30 am and 8.30 pm in July and August, several times a week the rest of the year.

Cathédrale Notre Dame Strasbourg's impossibly lacy Gothic cathedral was begun in 1176 after an earlier cathedral had burnt down. The west façade was completed in 1284, but the spire (its southern companion was never built) was not in place until 1439. Following the Reformation and a long period of bitter struggle, the cathedral came under Protestant control and was not returned to the Catholic Church until 1681. Many of the statues decorating the cathedral are copies – the originals can be seen in the Musée de l'Œuvre Notre-Dame (see the Museums section).

The cathedral is open from 7 to 11.40 am and 12.35 to 7 pm daily, except during masses. The 30m-high Gothic and Renaissance contraption just inside the south entrance is the **horloge astronomique**, a 16th-century clock (the mechanism dates from 1842) that strikes every day at precisely 12.30 pm. There is a 5FF charge to see the carved wooden figures do their thing.

The 66m-high platform above the façade (from which the tower and its spire soar another 76m) can be visited daily – if you don't mind the 330 steps to the top. It's open from 9 am (8.30 am in July and August) to 4.30 pm (November to February), 5.30 pm (March and October), 6.30 pm (April to June and September) or 7 pm (July and August). The entrance is at the base of the tower that was never built. Tickets cost 20FF (10FF for students).

STRASBOURG

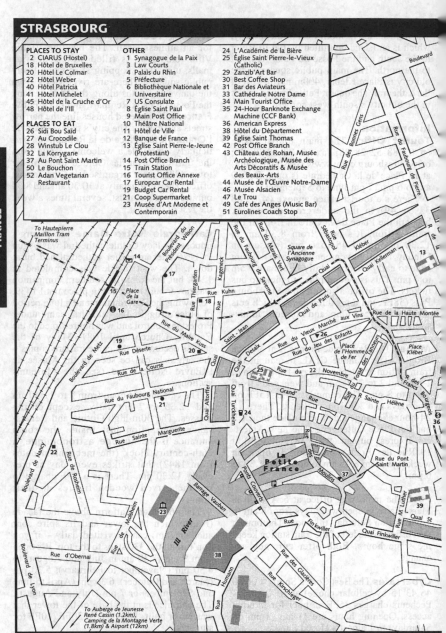

PLACES TO STAY
2 CIARUS (Hostel)
18 Hôtel de Bruxelles
20 Hôtel Le Colmar
22 Hôtel Weber
40 Hôtel Patricia
41 Hôtel Michelet
45 Hôtel de la Cruche d'Or
48 Hôtel de l'Ill

PLACES TO EAT
26 Sidi Bou Saïd
27 Au Crocodile
28 Winstub Le Clou
32 La Korrygane
37 Au Pont Saint Martin
50 Le Bouchon
52 Adan Vegetarian
    Restaurant

OTHER
1 Synagogue de la Paix
3 Law Courts
4 Palais du Rhin
5 Préfecture
6 Bibliothèque Nationale et
   Universitaire
7 US Consulate
8 Église Saint Paul
9 Main Post Office
10 Théâtre National
11 Hôtel de Ville
12 Banque de France
13 Église Saint Pierre-le-Jeune
   (Protestant)
14 Post Office Branch
15 Train Station
16 Tourist Office Annexe
17 Europcar Car Rental
19 Budget Car Rental
21 Coop Supermarket
23 Musée d'Art Moderne et
   Contemporain

24 L'Académie de la Bière
25 Église Saint Pierre-le-Vieux
   (Catholic)
29 Zanzib'Art Bar
30 Best Coffee Shop
31 Bar des Aviateurs
33 Cathédrale Notre Dame
34 Main Tourist Office
35 24-Hour Banknote Exchange
   Machine (CCF Bank)
36 American Express
38 Hôtel du Département
39 Église Saint Thomas
42 Post Office Branch
43 Château des Rohan, Musée
   Archéologique, Musée des
   Arts Décoratifs & Musée
   des Beaux-Arts
44 Musée de l'Œuvre Notre-Dame
46 Musée Alsacien
47 Le Trou
49 Café des Anges (Music Bar)
51 Eurolines Coach Stop

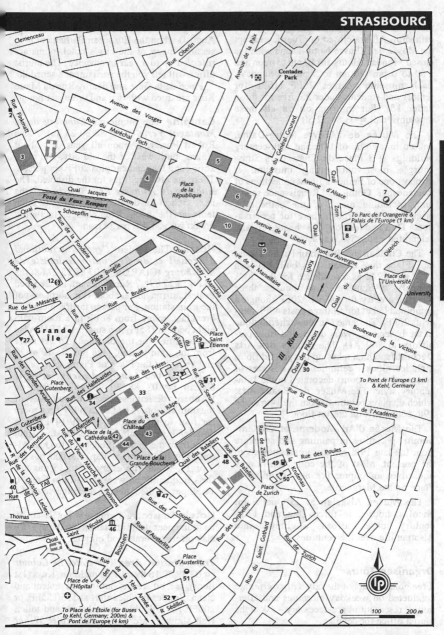

FRANCE

Museums Strasbourg's most important museums are in the immediate vicinity of the cathedral. All are closed on Tuesday except the Musée de l'Œuvre Notre-Dame which is closed Monday. Hours are 10 am to noon and 1.30 to 6 pm (10 am to 5 pm on Sunday). Each museum charges 20FF (10FF for seniors and students under 25, free for those under 15). For information on all these museums, call ☎ 03 88 52 50 00.

The **Musée de l'Œuvre Notre-Dame**, housed in a group of 14th and 15th-century buildings at 3 Place du Château, is Strasbourg's most outstanding museum. It displays one of France's finest collections of Romanesque, Gothic and Renaissance sculpture, including many of the cathedral's original statues, brought here for preservation. Don't overlook the beautiful and celebrated statue *Synagoga*.

The **Château des Rohan** or Palais Rohan, at 2 Place du Château, was built between 1732 and 1742 as a residence for the city's princely bishops. It now houses three museums; entry for each is 20FF though a combined ticket for all three costs 40FF (students 20FF). The large **Musée Archéologique** in the basement covers the period from pre-history to 800 AD. The **Musée des Arts Décoratifs**, which takes up the ground floor, includes clocks, ceramics and a series of episcopal state rooms decorated in the 18th-century style. The **Musée des Beaux-Arts**, which displays paintings from the 14th to the 19th century, is on the 1st floor.

The **Musée d'Art Moderne et Contemporain** specialises in painting and sculpture from the late 19th-century impressionists to the present. Most of the collection is now housed in an impressive new building at Place Sainte Marguerite.

The **Musée Alsacien** at 23 Quai Saint Nicolas, housed in three 16th and 17th-century houses, affords a glimpse into Alsatian life over the centuries.

Organised Tours

Free guided tours of the city's *brasseries* are conducted on weekday mornings and afternoons; reservations are necessary – ask at the tourist office for details.

Places to Stay

During the one week each month (except August) when the European Parliament is in session, many of the city's hotel rooms are reserved up to a year in advance. The tourist office will tell you the parliament's schedule.

Place de la Gare and nearby Rue du Maire Kuss are lined with two and three-star hotels.

Camping The municipal *Camping de la Montagne Verte* (☎ 03 88 30 25 46), 2 Rue Robert Forrer, is open all year. It's about 2.5km south-west of the old city, and costs 26FF for a tent and car plus 20FF per person. There are also facilities for the disabled. The *Auberge de Jeunesse René Cassin* (see the next section for details) has a place to pitch tents at the back. The charge, including breakfast, is 42FF per person.

Hostels The modern *Centre International d'Accueil et de Rencontre Unioniste de Strasbourg* (CIARUS; ☎ 03 88 15 27 88; fax 03 88 15 27 89), 7 Rue Finkmatt, is a 285-bed Protestant-run hostel about 1km north-east of the train station. Per person tariffs, including breakfast, range from 86FF in a room with eight beds to 185FF in a single. CIARUS also has facilities for the disabled. To get there from the train station, take bus No 10 or 20 and get off at the Place de Pierre stop.

The 286-bed *Auberge de Jeunesse René Cassin* (☎ 03 88 30 26 46), 9 Rue de l'Auberge de Jeunesse, is 2km south-west of the train station. A bed costs 69FF (in a room for four to six people) and 99/149FF in a double/single, including breakfast. To get there from the train station, walk to Quai Altorffer by the river (see map) and take bus No 3 or 23, which run every 10 to 15 minutes (less frequently on weekends) from 6 am to 11.30 pm, to the Auberge de Jeunesse stop.

Hotels Strasbourg's cheapest hotels are to be found near the train station but the old city also offers several good options.

Train Station Area The *Hôtel Le Colmar* (☎ 03 88 32 16 89), 1 Rue du Maire Kuss (1st floor), is a bit sterile, but it's convenient and clean. Singles/doubles start at 135/155FF, or 200FF for a double with shower and toilet. Hall showers are 15FF. The *Hôtel Weber*

(☎ 03 88 32 36 47), 22 Blvd de Nancy, is on the grim side, but it's cheap and convenient if you arrive by train. Decent doubles start at 130FF; doubles/triples with shower and toilet are 220/310FF. Hall showers are 12FF.

The two-star *Hôtel de Bruxelles* (☎ 03 88 32 45 31; fax 03 88 32 06 22), 13 Rue Kuhn, has clean and fairly large doubles with washbasin for 145FF. Rooms with shower and toilet are 250/320/350FF for doubles/triples/quads.

Old City The small, family-run *Hôtel Michelet* (☎ 03 88 32 47 38), 48 Rue du Vieux Marché aux Poissons, offers simple singles/doubles starting at 140/165FF (201/250FF with shower and toilet). Hall showers are free. The *Hôtel Patricia* (☎ 03 88 32 14 60), 1a Rue du Puits, a few blocks farther west, has very ordinary singles/doubles with washbasin for 170FF; doubles with shower and toilet are 220FF. The hall shower costs 12FF.

The pleasant two-star *Hôtel de l'Ill* (☎ 03 88 36 20 01; fax 03 88 35 30 03), 8 Rue des Bateliers, across the river from the cathedral, has comfortable singles/doubles with shower for 180/240FF, and with shower and toilet for 245/280FF.

More expensive is the two-star *Hôtel de la Cruche d'Or* (☎ 03 88 32 11 23; fax 03 88 21 94 78), 6 Rue des Tonneliers, south-west of the cathedral. Singles/doubles with shower and toilet start at 170/290FF. An extra bed is 60FF.

Places to Eat

Local specialities can be sampled at two uniquely Alsatian kinds of eating establishments. Winstubs ('VEEN-shtub') serve both wine and typically hearty Alsatian fare such as choucroute (sauerkraut) and baeckeoffe (pork, beef and lamb marinated in wine for one to two days before being cooked with vegetables in a baeckeoffe, or baker's oven). Some places serve baeckeoffe only on certain days (eg Friday).

Bierstubs ('BEER-shtub') primarily serve beer – the selection may include dozens, scores, even hundreds! Although they do have food (such as tarte flambée, a pastry base with cream, onion and bacon), they don't usually serve multicourse meals (see also Entertainment).

Restaurants In La Petite France, *Au Pont Saint Martin* (☎ 03 88 32 45 13), 15 Rue des Moulins, specialises in Alsatian dishes, including choucroute (70FF) and baeckeoffe (88FF). Vegetarians can order the fricassée de champignons (48FF). Meals are served every day from noon to 2.30 pm and 6.30 to 11 pm.

Adan (☎ 03 88 35 70 84), 6 Rue Sédillot, is a popular self-service vegetarian restaurant. Lunch is served from 11.45 am to 2 pm (closed on Sunday and in the evenings) and *menus* start at 59FF.

Le Bouchon (☎ 03 88 37 32 40), 6 Rue Sainte Catherine, offers Lyonnaise specialities at reasonable prices. It's open Monday to Saturday from 7 pm to 2 am (11.30 pm on Monday). The owner is a *chansonnière* (singer) of local repute and performs most nights at about 11 pm.

For Breton crêpes in a relaxed environment, try *La Korrygane* (☎ 03 88 37 07 34), 12 Place du Marché Gayot, off Rue des Frères (open daily). Crêpes and galettes range from 17 to 49FF. On the Grande Île, *Sidi Bou Saïd* (☎ 03 88 32 35 88), 22 Rue du Vieux Marché aux Vins, offers North African food, including hearty helpings of couscous for 55 to 70FF.

For all-out indulgence, head for the three-Michelin-star *Au Crocodile* (☎ 03 88 32 13 02), 10 Rue de l'Outre, east of Place Kléber. On offer are dishes such as truffle-flavoured pig's trotters and ears, and foie gras set in Gewürztraminer jelly. The four-course *menus* start at a mere 295/395FF for lunch/dinner. Au Crocodile is closed on Sunday and Monday and during the last three weeks of July.

Winstubs The *Winstub Le Clou* (☎ 03 88 32 11 67), 3 Rue du Chaudron (a tiny alley north of the cathedral), is a warm, authentic Alsatian eatery; diners are seated together at long tables. Specialities include baeckeoffe (97FF) and wädele braisé au pinot noir (ham knuckles in wine; 86FF). Meals are served from 11.45 am to 2.15 pm and 5.30 pm to 12.30 am (closed Wednesday at midday and on Sunday and holidays).

FRANCE

Self-Catering The *Coop supermarket*, 19 Rue du Faubourg National (near the train station), is open Monday to Friday from 8 am to 12.30 pm and 3 to 7 pm and on Saturday from 8 am to 6 pm. There is an all day *food market* at Place Broglie on Wednesday and Friday.

Entertainment
Live Music The mellow, informal *Café des Anges* (☎ 03 88 37 12 67), 5 Rue Sainte Catherine, has dancing to jazz, soul, R&B, funk and acid in the cellar, while on the ground floor the bods move to salsa and assorted other types of music. This place is open from 9 pm to 4 am (closed Sunday and Monday except on holidays), but things only really get going around 11 pm. There's no entry fee; drinks start at 15 or 20FF.

Bars The lively *Bar des Aviateurs* (☎ 03 88 36 52 69), 12 Rue des Sœurs, whose poster-covered walls and long wooden counter impart a 1940s sort of atmosphere, is open daily from 8 pm to 4 am. The friendly, laid-back *Zanzib' Art Bar* (☎ 03 88 37 91 81), 1 Place Saint Étienne, is open daily from 11 am until as late as 4 am. Beers start at 10FF (15FF after 9 pm).

Bierstubs Housed in a vaulted brick cellar at 5 Rue des Couples, *Le Trou* (☎ 03 88 36 91 04) is open daily from 8 pm to 4 am. Prices for a demi (33ml) on tap start at 15FF (10FF from 8 to 9 pm). At the friendly *Académie de la Bière* (☎ 03 88 32 61 08), 17 Rue Adolphe Seyboth, you can choose from among 70 beers; prices start at 12FF (17FF after 9 pm). It's open daily from 9 am to 4 am.

Getting There & Away
Bus Eurolines (☎ 03 88 22 73 74) coaches arrive and depart from Place d'Austerlitz. Strasbourg's city bus No 21 goes from Place Gutenberg to the Stadthalle in Kehl across the Rhine in Germany.

Train For information on trains call ☎ 08 36 35 35 39. There is always at least one ticket counter at the train station open every day from 5 am to 9 pm. Strasbourg is well connected by rail with Paris (210FF; four hours; at least 10 trains a day), Colmar (56FF; 30 to 50 minutes), Basel (Bâle; 102FF; 1½ hours),

and Frankfurt (215FF; three hours). There are also daily trains to Amsterdam (417FF), Lyon (253FF) and Nice (463FF). Certain early evening trains to/from Paris require payment of a supplement.

Car Near the train station, Budget (☎ 03 88 52 87 52), 14 Rue Déserte, is open Monday to Saturday from 8 am to noon and 2 to 6 pm (closed Saturday afternoon and Sunday). Europcar (☎ 03 88 22 18 00), 16 Place de la Gare, opens Monday to Saturday from 8 am to noon and 2 to 7 pm (5 pm on Saturday, closed Sunday).

Getting Around
Bus and tram tickets (7FF) or a Multipass (31/62FF) good for five/10 trips are available from the tourist office and the CTS office in the train station. Tourpasses (20FF) are valid for 24 hours of travel from the moment you time-stamp them. Buses from Strasbourg's city centre run until about 11.30 pm.

Strasbourg's futuristic tram line connects various places in the city centre, including the train station, Place de l'Homme de Fer, Place Kléber and Place de l'Étoile. Tickets can be bought from the machines at each stop.

There are taxi ranks at the train station and Place de la République. To order a cab, call Taxi Treize on ☎ 03 88 36 13 13.

COLMAR
Colmar (population 65,000), an easy day trip from Strasbourg, is famous for the typically Alsatian architecture of its older neighbourhoods and the unparalleled *Issenheim Altarpiece* in the Musée d'Unterlinden.

Orientation
Ave de la République stretches from one block in front of the train station to the Musée d'Unterlinden; the streets of the old city are to the south-east. Petite Venise, a neighbourhood of old, half-timbered buildings, runs along the Lauch River at the southern edge of the old city.

Information
Tourist Office The efficient tourist office (☎ 03 89 20 68 92) is opposite the museum at 4 Rue d'Unterlinden. It's open Monday to Saturday from 9 am to noon and 2 to 6 pm

(no midday closure from April to October; open until 7 pm in July and August). Sunday hours are 10 am to 2 pm.

Money & Post The Banque de France is at 46 Ave de la République. The main post office, 36 Ave de la République, also has exchange services.

Things to See

Musée d'Unterlinden This museum (☎ 03 89 20 15 50) is home to the famous *Issenheim Altarpiece* (*Retable d'Issenheim*), acclaimed as one of the most dramatic and moving works of art ever created. The gilded wooden figures of this reredos (ornamental screen) were carved by Nicolas of Hagenau in the late 15th century; the wooden wings – which originally closed over each other to form a three-layered panel painting – are the work of Matthias Grünewald, and were painted between 1512 and 1516. The museum's other displays include an Alsatian wine cellar, 15th and 16th-century armour and weapons, pewterware and Strasbourg faïence.

From November to March, the museum is open from 9 am to noon and 2 to 5 pm (closed Tuesday); from April to October, it's open daily from 9 am to 6 pm. Tickets cost 32FF (22FF for children and students under 26).

Musée Bartholdi This museum (☎ 03 89 41 90 60) at 30 Rue des Marchands – once the home of Frédéric Auguste Bartholdi (1834-1904), creator of New York's *Statue of Liberty* – displays some of the sculptor's work and personal memorabilia. The museum is open daily, except Tuesday, from 10 am to noon and 2 to 6 pm. Admission is 20FF (15FF for students).

Église des Dominicains This desanctified church at Place des Dominicains is known for its 14th and 15th-century stained glass and the celebrated triptych *La Vierge au Buisson de Roses* (The Virgin and the Rosebush), painted by Martin Schongauer in 1473. It's open daily from 10 am to 1 pm and 3 to 6 pm (closed from January to late March). Entrance costs 8FF (6FF for students under 30).

Old City The medieval streets of the old city, including **Rue des Marchands** and much of **Petite Venise**, are lined with half-timbered buildings. **Maison Pfister**, opposite 36 Rue des Marchands, was built in 1537 and is remarkable for its exterior decoration (frescoes, medallions and a carved wooden balcony). The **Maison des Têtes** at 19 Rue des Têtes is known for its façade covered with all manner of carved stone heads and faces; it was built in 1609.

Places to Stay

Camping The *Camping de l'Ill* (☎ 03 89 41 15 94) is 4km from the train station in Horbourg-Wihr. It's open from February to November, and costs 19FF for a tent and car plus 17FF per person. Take bus No 1 from the train station.

Hostels The *Maison des Jeunes et de la Culture* (MJC; ☎ 03 89 41 26 87) is five minutes walk south of the train station at 17 Rue Camille Schlumberger. A bed costs 46FF; breakfast is 20FF extra. The *Auberge de Jeunesse Mittelhart* (☎ 03 89 80 57 39), 2 Rue Pasteur, is just over 2km north of the station. You can take bus No 4 from here or from the Unterlinden stop and get off at the Pont Rouge stop. Reception is open before 10 am or after 5 pm. A bed costs 66FF including breakfast. Curfew is at midnight.

Hotels The one-star *Hôtel La Chaumière* (☎ 03 89 41 08 99), 74 Ave de la République, is Colmar's cheapest hotel with simple rooms for 150 to 180FF. Singles/doubles with shower and toilet are 220/240FF. The two-star *Hôtel Rhin et Danube* (☎ 03 89 41 31 44), 26 Ave de la République, has old-fashioned, shower-equipped doubles for 170FF; doubles with shower and toilet are 240 to 260FF, depending on the season.

The *Hôtel Primo* (☎ 03 89 24 22 24), 5 Rue des Ancêtres, is two blocks from the Musée d'Unterlinden. It has motel-type rooms with washbasin for up to three people for 159FF. Hall showers are free. Rooms with shower and toilet for one/two/three/four people cost 269/329/349/399FF.

Places to Eat

Reasonably priced restaurants are not Colmar's forte, but one good bet is *La Maison Rouge* (☎ 03 89 23 53 22), 9 Rue des

Écoles, which specialises in Alsatian cuisine, including ham on the bone cooked on a spit (57FF). The two-course Alsatian *menu* costs 85FF. It's open from noon to 2 pm and 6.30 to 9.30 or 10 pm (closed on Sunday evening and Wednesday). The cheapest *menus* at the Vietnamese restaurant *Les Gourmets d'Asie* (☎ 03 89 41 75 10), 20b Rue d'Alspach, cost 65 and 75FF; the plat du jour is 39FF. It's closed Monday.

There is a *Monoprix* supermarket (closed Sunday) across the square from the Musée d'Unterlinden. *Fromagerie Saint Nicolas*, 18 Rue Saint Nicolas, sells fine, traditionally made cheeses. It's closed all day Sunday and Monday morning.

Getting There & Around

The train trip to/from Strasbourg takes 30 to 50 minutes and costs 58FF each way.

All nine of Colmar's bus lines – which operate Monday to Saturday until sometime between 6 and 8 pm – serve the Unterlinden (Point Central) stop next to the tourist office and the Musée d'Unterlinden. To get to the museum from the train station, take bus No 1, 2, 3, 4 or 5. Service is drastically reduced on Sunday.

ROUTE DU VIN

The Route du Vin (Wine Route) winds its way some 120km south from Strasbourg to Thann, south of Colmar. This area is famous for its excellent Alsatian wines and its picturesque villages of half-timbered houses set amid vine-covered hills and overlooked by hilltop castles. The tourist office in Colmar has brochures on the wine route and information about tours.

Riquewihr and Ribeauvillé are perhaps the most attractive villages – and the most visited. Less touristy places include Mittelbergheim, Eguisheim and Turkheim, all of which can be seen on a day trip from Colmar. If you have your own transport, visit the imposing chateau of Haut-Koenigsbourg, rebuilt early this century by Emperor William II. The wine route is also where you're most likely to see some of Alsace's few remaining storks.

Normandy

The one-time duchy of Normandy (Normandie) derives its name from the Norsemen (or Vikings) who took control of the area in the early 10th century.

Often compared with the countryside of southern England, Normandy is the land of the *bocage*, farmland subdivided by hedges and trees. Set amid this lush, pastoral landscape are Normandy's cities and towns. Rouen, the region's capital, is especially rich in medieval architecture, including a spectacular cathedral. Bayeux is home to the 11th-century Bayeux Tapestry and is only about 12km from the D-Day landing beaches. In Normandy's south-western corner is one of France's greatest attractions, the island abbey of Mont Saint Michel. Because of its proximity to Paris, the Normandy coastline is lined with beach resorts, including the fashionable twin towns of Deauville and Trouville. Rural Normandy is famed for its cheeses and other dairy products, apples and cider brandy (Calvados).

Getting Around

Given rural Normandy's beauty and its limited public transport, renting a car will add more to your visit here than almost anywhere else in France.

ROUEN

The city of Rouen (population 105,000), for centuries the farthest point downriver where you could cross the Seine by bridge, is known for its many spires and church towers. The old city is graced with over 800 half-timbered houses, a renowned Gothic cathedral and a number of excellent museums. The city can be visited on an overnight or even a day trip from Paris.

Orientation

The train station (Gare Rouen-Rive Droite) is at the northern end of Rue Jeanne d'Arc, the major thoroughfare running south to the Seine. The old city is centred around Rue du Gros Horloge between the Place du Vieux Marché and the cathedral.

Information

Tourist Office The tourist office (☎ 02 32 08 32 40) is in an early 16th-century building at 25 Place de la Cathédrale. It's open Monday to Saturday from 9 am to 6.30 pm and Sunday from 10 am to 1 pm. From May to September, opening hours are Monday to Saturday from 9 am to 7 pm and on Sunday and holidays from 9.30 am to 12.30 pm and 2.30 to 6 pm. In summer, guided tours of the city (33FF) depart from the tourist office daily at 10.30 am and 3 pm.

Money & Post The Banque de France is at 32 Rue Jean Lecanuet. The *bureau de change* near the cathedral at 9 Rue des Bonnetiers offers good rates. It's open from 10 am to 7 pm daily, except Sunday.

Rouen's main post office, which also has exchange services, is at 45 bis Rue Jeanne d'Arc.

Things to See

Old City Rouen's old city suffered enormous damage during WWII but has since been painstakingly restored. The main street, **Rue du Gros Horloge**, runs from the cathedral to **Place du Vieux Marché**, where 19-year-old Joan of Arc was burned at the stake for heresy in 1431. The striking **Église Jeanne d'Arc** marking the site was completed in 1979; you'll learn more about her life from its stained-glass windows than at the tacky **Musée Jeanne d'Arc** across the square at No 33.

The pedestrians-only Rue du Gros Horloge is spanned by an early 16th-century gatehouse holding aloft the **Gros Horloge**, a large medieval clock with only one hand. The late 14th-century belfry above it will be under renovation until 2000 and is currently closed to visitors.

The incredibly ornate **Palais de Justice** (law courts) was left a shell at the end of WWII, but has since been restored to its early 16th-century Gothic glory. The courtyard, which is entered through a gate on Rue aux Juifs, is well worth a look for its spires, gargoyles and statuary. Under the courtyard is the **Monument Juif**, a stone building used by Rouen's Jewish community in the early 12th century.

Cathédrale Notre Dame Rouen's cathedral, which was the subject of a series of paintings by the impressionist painter Claude Monet, is considered a masterpiece of French Gothic architecture. Built between 1201 and 1514, it suffered extensive damage during the war and has been undergoing restoration and cleaning for decades. The Romanesque **crypt** was part of a cathedral completed in 1062 and destroyed by fire in 1200. There are several guided visits (10FF) a day to the crypt, ambulatory (containing Richard the Lion-Heart's tomb) and **Chapel of the Virgin** during Easter, July and August, but only on weekends the rest of the year. The cathedral is open Monday to Saturday from 8 am to 7 pm (6 pm on Sunday).

Museums Dedicated to the blacksmith's craft, the **Musée Le Secq des Tournelles** (☎ 02 35 71 28 40) displays 12,000 locks, keys, scissors, tongs and other wrought-iron utensils made between the 3rd and 19th centuries. Located on Rue Jacques Villon (opposite 27 Rue Jean Lecanuet), it's open from 10 am to 1 pm and 2 to 6 pm daily, except Tuesday. Entry is 13FF (9FF for students).

The **Musée de la Céramique** (☎ 02 35 07 31 74), whose speciality is 16th to 19th-century Rouen ceramics, is north of Square Verdrel up some stairs at 1 Rue du Faucon. Entry costs 13FF (9FF for students). The **Musée des Beaux-Arts** (☎ 02 35 71 28 40) facing the square at 26 bis Rue Jean Lecanuet features some major paintings from the 16th to 20th centuries, including some of Monet's cathedral series. Entry is 20FF (13FF for students). Both museums keep the same hours as the Musée Le Secq des Tournelles.

Aître Saint Maclou Behind the Gothic **Église Saint Maclou** at 186 Rue Martainville is the *aître* (ossuary), a rare surviving example of a medieval burial ground for plague victims. The curious ensemble of 16th-century buildings that surrounds the courtyard is decorated with macabre carvings of skulls, crossbones, grave-diggers' tools and hourglasses. It's open every day from 8 am to 8 pm, and entry is free.

La Tour Jeanne d'Arc This tower (☎ 02 35 98 16 21) in Rue du Donjon south of the train station is the only one left of the eight that once ringed the chateau built by Philippe

FRANCE

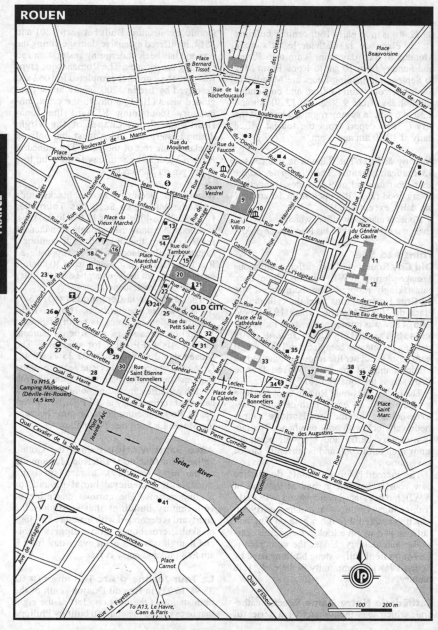

ROUEN

PLACES TO STAY		OTHER		24	Banks
2	Hôtel de la Rochefoucauld	1	Gare Rouen-Rive Droite	25	Gros Horloge (Medieval
4	Hôtel Normandya		(Train Station)		Clock)
5	Hôtel Sphinx	3	La Tour Jeanne d'Arc	26	Rouen Cycles
6	Hostellerie du Vieux Logis	7	Musée de la Céramique	27	Bus Station
13	Hôtel des Flandres	8	Banque de France	29	Métrobus (Local Bus Infor-
22	Hôtel Le Palais	9	Musée des Beaux-Arts		mation)
28	Hôtel Viking	10	Musée Le Secq des Tour-	30	Théâtre des Arts
35	Hôtel de la Cathédrale		nelles	32	Tourist Office
		11	Hôtel de Ville	33	Cathédrale Notre Dame
PLACES TO EAT		12	Église Saint Ouen	34	Bureau de Change
15	Pascaline	14	Main Post Office	36	Alimentation Générale
17	Les Maraîchers	16	Covered Food Market		Supermarket
23	Chez Pépé	18	Église Jeanne d'Arc	37	Église Saint Maclou
31	Gourmand'grain	19	Musée Jeanne d'Arc	38	Aître Saint Maclou
39	Kim Ngoc	20	Palais de Justice	41	Prefecture
40	Chez Zaza	21	Palais de Justice Courtyard &		
			Monument Juif		

FRANCE

Auguste in the early 13th century. Joan of Arc was imprisoned here before her execution. The tower and its two exhibition rooms are open from 10 am to noon and 2 to 5 pm daily, except Tuesday. Entrance is 10FF (free for students).

Places to Stay

Camping The *Camping Municipal* (☎ 02 35 74 07 59) in the suburb of Déville-lès-Rouen is 5km north-west of the train station on Rue Jules Ferry. From the Théâtre des Arts on Rue Jeanne d'Arc or the nearby bus station, take bus No 2 and get off at the *mairie* (town hall) of Déville-lès-Rouen. Two people with a tent are charged 56FF. It's open all year.

Hostel Rouen's *Auberge de Jeunesse* closed recently but there are plans for a new one to open soon. Contact the tourist office for the latest news.

Hotels The spotless and friendly *Hôtel Normandya* (☎ 02 35 71 46 15), 32 Rue du Cordier, is on a quiet street 300m south-east of the train station. Singles (some with shower) are 110 to 140FF, and doubles are 10 to 20FF more; a hall shower is 10FF. The welcoming *Hôtel de la Rochefoucauld* (☎ 02 35 71 86 58), opposite the Saint Romain church in Rue de la Rochefoucauld, offers

simple singles/doubles from 120/150FF including breakfast. Showers cost 15FF.

The *Hôtel Sphinx* (☎ 02 35 71 35 86), 130 Rue Beauvoisine, is a cosy, friendly place with some timbered rooms. Doubles range from 90 to 100FF; an additional bed is 60FF. Showers cost 10FF.

The very French *Hostellerie du Vieux Logis* (☎ 02 35 71 55 30), 5 Rue de Joyeuse (almost 1km east of the train station), has a relaxed and pleasantly frayed atmosphere with a lovely little garden out the back. Singles/doubles start at 100FF, two-bed triples cost 150FF. Showers are free.

The *Hôtel des Flandres* (☎ 02 35 71 56 88), 5 Rue des Bons Enfants, has doubles for 125FF with washbasin and bidet, 140FF with shower and 160FF with shower and toilet. The *Hôtel Le Palais* (☎ 02 35 71 41 40), 12 Rue du Tambour, between the Palais de Justice and the Gros Horloge, has singles and doubles with shower for 120FF. The somewhat pricier *Hôtel Viking* (☎ 02 35 70 34 95), 21 Quai du Havre, near the bus station, has singles/doubles with shower overlooking the river for 270/285FF.

If you're going flush, the *Hôtel de la Cathédrale* (☎ 02 35 71 57 95; fax 02 35 70 15 54) sits in the shadow of Rouen's cathedral in a 17th-century house at 12 Rue Saint Romain. Rooms are from 270 to 415FF. Ask for a room looking onto the courtyard.

Places to Eat

The bistro-style *Les Maraîchers* (☎ 02 35 71 57 73), 37 Place du Vieux Marché, is definitely the pick of the Vieux Marché's many restaurants, with its lively pavement terrace and varied *menus* from 69FF.

Chez Pépé (☎ 02 35 15 01 50), 19 Rue du Vieux Palais, is a pizzeria open from 11.30 am to 2 pm and 7 to 11.30 pm daily. *Gourmand'grain* (☎ 02 35 98 15 74), behind the tourist office at 3 Rue du Petit Salut, is a lunchtime vegetarian café with good salads and health-food *menus* for 45 and 69FF.

Near Église Saint Maclou, *Chez Zaza* (☎ 02 35 71 33 57), 85 Rue Martainville, specialises in couscous (from 45FF) and is open daily for lunch and dinner. *Kim Ngoc* (☎ 02 35 98 76 33), nearby at No 168, is one of Rouen's many Vietnamese restaurants with *menus* for 69 and 90FF. It's open daily, except Monday.

For a splurge, the old-fashioned bistro *Pascaline* (☎ 02 35 89 67 44), 5 Rue de la Poterne, has two/three-course *menus* for 59/97FF. It's open daily for lunch and dinner.

Dairy products, fish and fresh produce are on sale from 6 am to 1.30 pm daily, except Monday, at the *covered food market* at Place du Vieux Marché. The *Alimentation Générale* supermarket, 78 Rue de la République, is open daily from 8 am to 10.30 pm.

Getting There & Away

Bus Buses to Dieppe (66FF; 2 hours; three a day) and Le Havre (84FF; three hours; five a day) are slower and more expensive than the train. The bus station (☎ 02 35 52 92 00) is at 25 Rue des Charrettes near the Théâtre des Arts.

Train There are 24 trains a day to and from Paris' Gare Saint Lazare (102FF; 70 minutes). The last leaves at about 9 pm for Paris and 10 pm for Rouen. The information office at Rouen's train station (☎ 08 36 35 35 39) is open Monday to Saturday from 8.30 am to 7.45 pm.

Getting Around

Bus & Metro TCAR operates Rouen's local bus network as well as its metro line. The metro links the train station with the Théâtre des Arts before crossing the Seine into the southern suburbs, and runs between 5 am (6 am on Sunday) and 11.30 pm daily. Bus tickets cost 8FF, or 59FF for a magnetic card good for 10 rides, and the Carte Découverte costs 20/30/40FF for one/two/three days unlimited travel. They can be purchased at the Métrobus counters in the train station, in front of the Théâtre des Arts and in the Place du Général de Gaulle near the Hôtel de Ville.

Bicycle Rouen Cycles (☎ 02 35 71 34 30), 45 Rue Saint Éloi, rents mountain bikes and 10-speed bicycles for 120FF a day (2000FF deposit needed). The shop is open Tuesday to Saturday from 8.30 am to 12.15 pm and 2 to 7.15 pm.

BAYEUX

Bayeux (population 15,000) is celebrated for two trans-Channel invasions: the conquest of England by the Normans under William the Conqueror in 1066 (an event chronicled in the Bayeux Tapestry) and the Allied D-Day landings of 6 June 1944, which launched the liberation of Nazi-occupied France. Bayeux was the first town in France to be freed.

Bayeux is an attractive – though fairly touristy – town with several excellent museums. It also serves as a base for visits to the D-Day beaches (see that section for details).

Orientation & Information

The cathedral, the major landmark in the centre of Bayeux and visible throughout the town, is 1km north-west of the train station. The tourist office (☎ 02 31 51 28 28) is at Pont Saint Jean just off the northern end of Rue Larcher. It's open Monday to Saturday from 9 am to noon and 2 to 6 pm. During July and August, it opens on Sunday from 9.30 am to 12.30 pm and 2.30 to 6.30 pm.

Money & Post Banks are open Tuesday to Saturday from 8.30 am to noon and from about 2 to 5 pm. There is a Société Générale at 26 Rue Saint Malo and a Caisse d'Épargne at No 59 on the same street. The main post office, at 14 Rue Larcher opposite the Hôtel de Ville, also has exchange facilities.

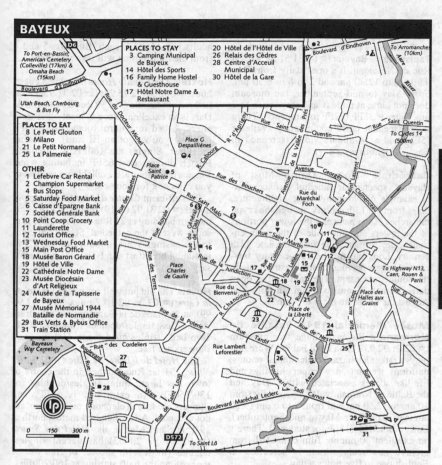

BAYEUX

PLACES TO STAY
3 Camping Municipal de Bayeux
14 Hôtel des Sports
16 Family Home Hostel & Guesthouse
17 Hôtel Notre Dame & Restaurant
20 Hôtel de l'Hôtel de Ville
26 Relais des Cèdres
28 Centre d'Acceuil Municipal
30 Hôtel de la Gare

PLACES TO EAT
8 Le Petit Glouton
9 Milano
21 Le Petit Normand
25 La Palmeraie

OTHER
1 Lefebvre Car Rental
2 Champion Supermarket
4 Bus Stops
5 Saturday Food Market
6 Caisse d'Épargne Bank
7 Société Générale Bank
10 Point Coop Grocery
11 Launderette
12 Tourist Office
13 Wednesday Food Market
15 Main Post Office
18 Musée Baron Gérard
19 Hôtel de Ville
22 Cathédrale Notre Dame
23 Musée Diocésain d'Art Religieux
24 Musée de la Tapisserie de Bayeux
27 Musée Mémorial 1944 Bataille de Normandie
29 Bus Verts & Bybus Office
31 Train Station

FRANCE

Things to See

A multipass ticket (*billet jumelé*) valid for both museums listed here (plus two others – the Musée Diocésain d'Art Religieux and the Musée Baron Gérard) costs 38FF (22FF for students).

Bayeux Tapestry The world-famous Bayeux Tapestry – actually a 70m-long strip of coarse linen decorated with woollen embroidery – was commissioned by Odo, bishop of Bayeux and half-brother to William the Conqueror, for the consecration of the cathedral in Bayeux in 1077. The tapestry, which was probably made in England, recounts the dramatic story of the Norman invasion of 1066 and the events that led up to it – from the Norman perspective. The story is told in 58 panels presented like a modern comic strip, with action-packed scenes following each other in quick succession. The events are accompanied by a written commentary in dog Latin. The scenes themselves are filled with depictions of 11th-century Norman and Saxon dress, food, cooking, weapons and tools. Halley's Comet, which passed through our part of the solar system in 1066, also makes an appearance.

The tapestry is housed in the **Musée de la Tapisserie de Bayeux** (☎ 02 31 51 25 50), on Rue de Nesmond. It's open daily from 9 or 9.30 am to 12.30 pm and 2 to 6 or 6.30 pm. From May to mid-September, the museum does not close at midday and stays open to 7 pm. Entry is 38FF (22FF for students). There is an excellent taped commentary available (5FF) and a 14-minute video (screened in English eight times a day).

Cathédrale Notre Dame Most of Bayeux's spectacular cathedral, an exceptional example of Norman-Gothic architecture, dates from the 13th century, though the crypt, the arches of the nave and the lower portions of the towers on either side of the main entrance, are Romanesque from the late 11th century. Look out for the 15th-century frescoes of angels playing musical instruments in the southern transept. The cathedral is open daily from 8.30 am to 6 pm. In July and August the hours are 8 am to 7 pm.

Musée Mémorial 1944 Bataille de Normandie Bayeux's huge war museum (☎ 02 31 92 93 41) on Blvd Fabien Ware displays a rather haphazard collection of photos, uniforms, weapons, newspaper clippings and life-like scenes associated with D-Day and the Battle of Normandy. It's open daily from 10 am to 12.30 pm and from 2 to 6 pm (9.30 am to 6.30 pm from May to mid-September). Entry costs 31FF (15FF for students). There's an excellent 30-minute film compiled from archive newsreels which is screened in English two to five times a day.

The **Bayeux War Cemetery**, a British cemetery on Blvd Fabien Ware a few hundred metres west of the museum, is the largest of the 18 Commonwealth military cemeteries in Normandy. It contains the graves of 4868 soldiers from 11 countries, including 466 Germans. Many of the headstones are inscribed with poignant epitaphs.

Places to Stay

Camping The *Camping Municipal de Bayeux* (☎ 02 31 92 08 43) is 2km north of the town centre, just south of Blvd d'Eind-

hoven. It's open from mid-March to mid-November. A tent site costs from 8.40FF and adults pay 16.20FF each. Bus Nos 5 and 6 from the train station will take you there.

Hostels The *Family Home* hostel and guesthouse (☎ 02 31 92 15 22; fax 02 31 92 55 72) in three old buildings at 39 Rue du Général de Dais is an excellent place to meet other travellers. A bed in a dorm room costs 100FF (90FF if you've got an HI card), including breakfast. Singles are 160FF. Multicourse French dinners cost 65FF including wine. Vegetarian dishes are available on request or you can cook for yourself.

The efficient *Centre d'Accueil Municipal* hostel (☎ 02 31 92 08 19) is housed in a large, modern building at 21 Rue des Marettes, 1km south-west of the cathedral. Sterile but comfortable singles are good value at 92FF, including breakfast. An HI card is not necessary.

Hotels The old but well maintained *Hôtel de la Gare* (☎ 02 31 92 10 70; fax 02 31 51 95 99), at 26 Place de la Gare (opposite the train station) has singles/doubles from 85/140FF. Two-bed triples/quads are 160FF and showers are free.

The *Hôtel de l'Hôtel de Ville* (☎ 02 31 92 30 08), 31 ter Rue Larcher, in the centre of town has large, quiet singles/doubles for 130/150FF. An extra bed is 50FF, and showers are free. Telephone reservations are not accepted. A few hundred metres north at 19 Rue Saint Martin, the *Hôtel des Sports* (☎ 02 31 92 28 53) has decent singles/doubles (most with shower or free use of those along the hall) starting at 160/200FF.

The *Relais des Cèdres* (☎ 02 31 21 98 07), somewhat fussily done up in 'French country' style, is in an old mansion at 1 Blvd Sadi Carnot. Doubles cost 150 to 220FF, or 250FF with shower and toilet. Hall showers are free.

If you can afford something more upmarket, you might try *Hôtel Notre Dame* (☎ 02 31 92 87 24; fax 02 31 92 67 11), 44 Rue des Cuisiniers, a one-star place opposite the western façade of the cathedral. Doubles are 250 to 260FF with shower or bath, but they have half a dozen cheaper rooms for 160FF. Hall showers cost 20FF.

Places to Eat

Le Petit Normand (☎ 02 31 22 88 66), 35 Rue Larcher, specialises in traditional Norman food. Simple fixed-price *menus* start at 58FF. The restaurant is open every day, except Wednesday and Sunday evenings.

For couscous (from 55FF), try *La Palmeraie* (☎ 02 31 92 72 08) near the Bayeux Tapestry Museum at 62-64 Rue de Nesmond. It's open for lunch and dinner every day, except Monday and midday on Saturday. *Milano* (☎ 02 31 92 15 10), 18 Rue Saint Martin, serves very good pizza. It's open for lunch and dinner Monday to Saturday, and daily from 11.30 am to 10 pm from June to August.

The food at the *Hôtel Notre Dame* restaurant (☎ 02 31 92 87 24) is Norman at its best; count on 60FF for a lunch *menu* and 90FF per person at dinner. From November to March it's closed Sunday lunch and all day Monday.

There are lots of takeaway places and food shops along or near Rue Saint Martin and Rue Saint Jean, including *Le Petit Glouton* at 42 Rue Saint Martin and the *Point Coop* grocery at 25 Rue du Maréchal Foch, open Tuesday to Saturday from 8.30 am to 12.15 pm and 2.30 to 7.15 pm and on Sunday from 9 am to noon. There are *food markets* in Rue Saint Jean on Wednesday morning and in Place Saint Patrice on Saturday morning. The *Champion* supermarket across the road from the Camping Municipal is open Monday to Saturday from 9 am to 8 pm.

Getting There & Away

The train station (☎ 02 31 92 80 50) is open daily from about 7 am to 8.45 pm. Trains serve Paris' Gare Saint Lazare (via Caen), Cherbourg, Rennes and points beyond.

Getting Around

The local bus line, Bybus (☎ 02 31 92 02 92), which shares an office with Bus Verts (across from the train station), has four routes traversing Bayeux, all of which end up at Place G Despallières. From the train station, take bus No 3. See the D-Day Beaches section for information on car rental and transport to places in the vicinity of Bayeux.

Taxis can be ordered 24 hours a day by calling ☎ 02 31 92 92 40.

D-DAY BEACHES

The D-Day landings were the largest military operation in history. Early on the morning of 6 June 1944, swarms of landing craft – part of a flotilla of almost 7000 boats – hit the beaches, and tens of thousands of soldiers from the USA, UK, Canada and elsewhere began pouring onto French soil. Most of the 135,000 Allied troops stormed ashore along 80km of beaches north of Bayeux codenamed (from west to east) Utah, Omaha, Gold, Juno and Sword. The landings on D-Day – *Jour J* in French – were followed by the 76-day Battle of Normandy that began the liberation of Europe from Nazi occupation.

Things to See

Arromanches In order to unload the vast quantities of cargo necessary for the invasion, the Allies established two prefabricated ports. The remains of one of them, Port Winston, can still be seen at Arromanches, a seaside town 10km north-east of Bayeux. Over 140 massive cement caissons were towed over from England and sunk to form a semicircular breakwater. In the three months after D-Day, 2½ million men, four million tonnes of equipment and 500,000 vehicles were unloaded here. At low tide you can walk out to many of the caissons.

The **Musée du Débarquement** (Landing Museum; ☎ 02 31 22 34 31) explains the logistics and importance of Port Winston and makes a good first stop before visiting the beaches. Museum hours are 9 am to 6 pm in April, 9 am to 7 pm from May to September, and 9.30 to 5 pm from October to December and from February to March. It's closed Monday and January. Entrance is 35FF (20FF for students). The last guided tour (in French, with a written text in English) leaves 45 minutes before closing time.

Omaha Beach The most brutal combat of 6 June was fought 20km west of Arromanches at Omaha Beach, where a memorial marks the site of the first US military cemetery on French soil. Today, Omaha Beach is lined with holiday cottages and is popular with swimmers and sunbathers. Little evidence of the war remains except the bunkers and munitions sites of a German fortified point to the west (look for the tall obelisk on the hill).

FRANCE

FRANCE

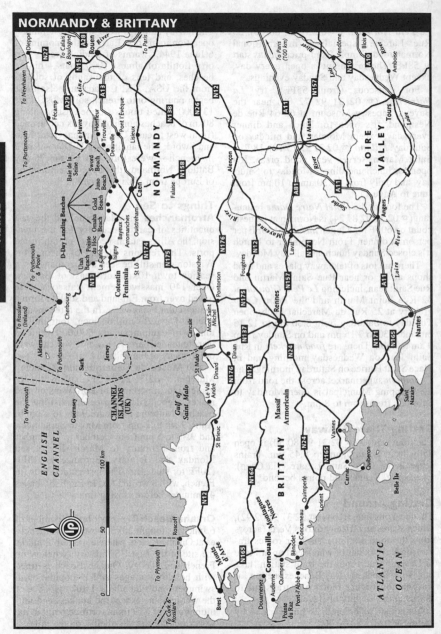

NORMANDY & BRITTANY

American Military Cemetery The remains of the Americans who lost their lives during the Battle of Normandy were either sent back to the USA or buried in the American Military Cemetery (☎ 02 31 51 62 00) at Colleville-sur-Mer. The cemetery contains the graves of 9386 American soldiers and a memorial to 1557 others whose bodies were never found. The huge expanse of white crosses and Stars of David, set on a hill overlooking Omaha Beach, testifies to the extent of the killing which took place around here in 1944; there's a large colonnaded memorial, a reflecting pond and a chapel for silent meditation. The cemetery is open from 8 am to 5 pm (9 am to 6 pm from about mid-April to mid-October). From Bayeux, it can be reached by Bus Verts' line No 70, but service is infrequent.

Commonwealth Military Cemeteries By tradition, Commonwealth soldiers were buried close to where they fell. As a result, the 18 Commonwealth military cemeteries in Normandy follow the line of advance of British and Canadian troops. The Canadian cemetery at Bény-sur-Mer is 18km east of Bayeux near Juno Beach. See the Bayeux section for information on the mostly British Bayeux War Cemetery. The cemeteries are permanently open.

Organised Tours
Tours of the D-Day beaches are offered by Bus Fly (☎ 02 31 22 00 08), who have an office on the D13 in Les Sablons (Vaucelles) west of Bayeux, but reservations are most easily made through the Family Home hostel (see Places to Stay in Bayeux). An afternoon tour to major D-Day sites costs 160FF (140FF for students with an HI card), including museum entry fees.

Getting There & Away
Bus Bus No 70 run by Bus Verts (☎ 02 31 92 02 92), goes westward to the American cemetery at Colleville-sur-Mer and Omaha Beach. Bus No 74 serves Arromanches, and Gold and Juno beaches. During July and August only, Bus No 75 goes to Caen via Arromanches, Gold, Juno and Sword beaches and the port of Ouistreham. The Bus Verts office, opposite the train station in Bayeux, is open

weekdays from 10 am to noon and 3 to 6 pm. It's closed during most of July. There are timetables posted in the train station and at Place G Despallières.

Car & Motorcycle For three or more people, renting a car can actually be cheaper than a tour. Lefebvre Car Rental (☎ 02 31 92 05 96) on Blvd d'Eindhoven in Bayeux charges 320FF per day with 200km free (about the distance of a circuit to the beaches along coastal route D514). The office is open every day from 8 am to 8 pm.

Bicycle The Family Home hostel in Bayeux has one-speeds for 60FF a day (plus 200FF deposit). Cycles 14 (☎ 02 31 92 27 75) on Blvd Winston Churchill, to the north-east of town, rents mountain bikes for 70FF a day or 340FF a week (plus 1500FF deposit). It's open daily, except Sunday, from 9 am to 12.15 am and 2 to 7 pm.

MONT SAINT MICHEL
It's difficult not to be impressed by your first sighting of Mont Saint Michel. Covering the summit of the rocky island is a massive abbey, a soaring ensemble of buildings in a hotchpotch of architectural styles. Topping the abbey – 80m above the sea – is a slender spire, at the tip of which is a gilded copper statue of the Archangel Michael slaying a dragon. Around the base are the ancient ramparts and a jumble of buildings that house the 120 people who still live there.

At low tide, Mont Saint Michel looks out over bare sand stretching for many kilometres into the distance. At high tide – only about six hours later – this huge expanse of sand is under water. Depending on the phase of the moon the difference between the level of the sea at low and high tides can reach 13m – one of the world's biggest tidal ranges – but only the very highest tides cover the 900m causeway that connects the islet to the mainland.

History
In 708 AD, Saint Michael appeared to Aubert, Bishop of Avranches, and told him to build a devotional chapel on the island, which was a sacred Celtic site. In 966, Richard I,

Duke of Normandy, transferred Mont Saint Michel to the Benedictines, who built an abbey which became an important centre of learning and pilgrimage. In the 13th century, the Mont became something of an ecclesiastical fortress, with a military garrison at the disposal of the abbot and the king.

In the early 15th century, during the Hundred Years' War, the English blockaded and besieged Mont Saint Michel three times. But the fortified abbey withstood these assaults; it was the only place in all of western and northern France not to fall into English hands. After the French Revolution, Mont Saint Michel was turned into a prison. In 1966 the abbey was symbolically returned to the Benedictines as part of the celebrations marking its millennium.

Orientation

There is only one opening in the ramparts: Porte de l'Avancée, immediately to the west as you walk down the causeway. The single street within the walls (Grande Rue), for pedestrians only, is lined with restaurants, a few hotels, souvenir shops and entrances to some rather tacky exhibits in the crypts below. **Pontorson**, the nearest town, is 9km south and the base for most travellers. Route D976 from Mont Saint Michel runs right into Pontorson's main thoroughfare, Rue du Couësnon.

Information

Tourist Office The tourist office (☎ 02 33 60 14 30) is up the stairs to the left as you enter Porte de l'Avancée. It's open every day, except Sunday, from 9 am to noon and 2 to 5.45 pm (1 to 6.30 pm from Easter to September). In July and August hours are from 9 am to 7 pm daily. If you are interested in what the tide will be doing during your visit, look for the *horaire des marées* posted outside. A detailed map of the Mont is available at the tourist office for 16FF. There is another tourist office in Pontorson, open Tuesday to Friday from 9.30 am to noon and 2.30 to 5 pm (to 7.30 pm daily from mid-June to mid-September).

Money & Post There are several places to change money in Mont Saint Michel, but better rates are offered at the CIN bank, 98

Rue du Couësnon, in Pontorson. It's open weekdays from 8.30 to noon and from 2 to 5.30 pm and on Saturday morning.

The Pontorson post office is on the east side of the Place de l'Hôtel de Ville.

Things to See & Do

Abbaye du Mont Saint Michel The Mont's major attraction is the renowned abbey (☎ 02 33 89 80 00), at the top of the Grande Rue, up the stairway. It's open daily from 9.30 am to 4.30 pm. From mid-May to September, it's open from 9 am to 5.30 pm, and there are also night-time tours of the abbey (60FF) every evening, except Sunday, starting at 9 or 10 pm. Visitors explore the illuminated and music-filled rooms at their own pace.

During the day, it's worth taking the guided tour included in the ticket price of 36FF (22FF for students and 18 to 25s, 10FF for children). One-hour tours in English depart three to eight times a day.

In the 11th century the Romanesque **Église Abbatiale** (Abbey Church) was built on the rocky summit of the Mont over its 10th-century predecessor, now the underground chapel of **Notre Dame de Sous Terre**. When the choir collapsed in 1421, a new one was built in Flamboyant Gothic style, supported by vaults with vast load-bearing columns. The church is famous for its mixture of architectural styles.

In the early 13th century a monastery called **La Merveille** (literally 'the wonder' or 'marvel') was built on three levels and added to the church's north side. Considered a Gothic masterpiece, it was completed in only 16 years. The famous **cloître** (cloister) is surrounded by a double row of delicately carved arches resting on slender marble pillars, and is a good example of the Anglo-Norman style. The early 13th-century **réfectoire** (dining hall) is illuminated by a wall of recessed windows, a remarkable arrangement given that the sheer drop-off precluded the use of flying buttresses. The High Gothic **salle des hôtes** (guest hall), which dates from 1213, has two giant fireplaces.

The French government is currently spending US$86 million restoring Mont Saint Michel to its former glory, so don't be surprised if you find it covered in scaffolding.

Places to Stay

Camping The *Camping du Mont Saint Michel* (☎ 02 33 60 09 33) is on the road to Pontorson (D976), 2km from the Mont. It's open from mid-February to mid-November and charges 22FF per person, and 20FF for a tent and car. Bungalows for two people with shower and toilet are also available for 220FF. There are several other camping grounds a few kilometres farther towards Pontorson.

Hostel *Centre Duguesclin* (☎ 02 33 60 18 65) in Pontorson operates as a 10-room hostel from Easter to mid-September. A bed in a three-bunk room costs 41FF a night, but you must bring your own sheets. There are kitchen facilities. The hostel is closed from 10 am to 6 pm, but there is no curfew. The hostel is about 1km west of the train station on Rue du Général Patton, which runs parallel to the Couësnon River north of Rue du Couësnon. The hostel is on the left side in an old three-storey stone building opposite No 26.

Hotels Mont Saint Michel has about 15 hotels but almost all are expensive. *La Mère Poulard* (☎ 02 33 60 14 01; fax 02 33 48 52 31), the first hotel on the left as you walk up the Grande Rue, has twins with shower from 250FF.

Your best bet is to stay in Pontorson. Across Place de la Gare from the train station, there are a couple of cheap hotels. The *Hôtel de l'Arrivée* (☎ 02 33 60 01 57), 14 Rue du Docteur Tizon, has doubles for 87FF with washbasin, 110FF with washbasin and toilet and 155FF with shower. Triples/quads with washbasin or toilet are 160/180FF. Hall showers are 15FF. The *Hôtel Le Rénové* (☎ 02 33 60 00 21), nearby at 4 Rue de Rennes, has doubles for 150FF (with washbasin) and 180FF (with shower). Triples or quads cost 250FF. Hall showers are free.

The *Hôtel La Tour de Brette* (☎ 02 33 60 10 69), 8 Rue du Couësnon, has an excellent deal. Its singles and doubles – all with shower and TV – are 149FF to 220FF.

Places to Eat

The tourist restaurants around the base of the Mont have lovely views but they aren't bargains; *menus* start at about 90FF. A few places along the Grande Rue sell sandwiches, quiches and the like.

In Pontorson, *La Squadra* (☎ 02 33 68 31 17), 102 Rue Couësnon, has decent pizzas from 36FF, salads and pasta and is open daily, except Monday. For crêpes and savoury galettes (20FF), try *La Crêperie du Couësnon* (☎ 02 33 60 16 67), 21 Rue du Couësnon. *La Tour de Brette* (☎ 02 33 60 10 69), across from the river at 8 Rue du Couësnon, has very good *menus* from 56FF.

The nearest supermarket to the Mont is next to the Camping du Mont Saint Michel on the D976. It's open from mid-February to October daily (except Sunday) from 8 am to 8 pm (10 pm in July and August).

Getting There & Away

Bus Bus No 15 run by STN (☎ 02 33 58 03 07 in Avranches) goes from Pontorson train station to Mont Saint Michel. There are nine buses a day in July and August (six on weekends and holidays) and three or four during the rest of the year. Most of the buses connect with trains to/from Paris, Rennes and Caen.

For information on buses to/from Saint Malo, 43km to the west, see Getting There & Away in the Saint Malo section. The Pontorson office of Courriers Bretons buses (☎ 02 33 60 11 43) is 50m west of the train station at 2 Rue du Docteur Tizon. It's open weekdays from 10.30 to noon and 5.45 to 7 pm.

Train There are trains to the Pontorson train station (☎ 08 36 35 35 39) from Caen (via Folligny) and Rennes (via Dol). From Paris, take the train to Caen (from Gare Saint Lazare), Rennes (from Gare Montparnasse) or direct to Pontorson via Folligny (Gare Montparnasse).

Bicycle Bikes can be rented at Pontorson train station (55FF per day plus 1000FF deposit) and from E Videloup (☎ 02 33 60 11 40), 1 bis Rue du Couësnon, which charges 35/70FF per day for one-speeds/mountain bikes. E Videloup is open from 8.30 am to 12.30 pm and 2 to 7 pm from Monday afternoon to Saturday.

Brittany

Brittany (Bretagne in French, Breizh in Breton), the westernmost region of France, is famous for its rugged countryside and wild coastline. The area is also known for its many colourful religious celebrations (*pardons*). Traditionàl costumes, including extraordinarily tall headdresses of lace worn by the women, can still be seen at some of these and other local festivals, including night-time dance meets called *fest-noz*.

Breton customs are most in evidence in Cornouaille, the area at the south-western tip of the Breton peninsula, whose largest city is Quimper. Saint Malo is a popular tourist destination and seaside resort on Brittany's north coast.

Breton Identity
The early inhabitants of Brittany, driven from their homes in what is now Great Britain by the Anglo-Saxon invasions, migrated across the English Channel in the 5th and 6th centuries, bringing with them their Celtic language and traditions. For centuries a rich and powerful duchy, Brittany became part of France in 1532. To this day, many Bretons have not abandoned the hope that their region will one day regain its independence or at least a greater degree of autonomy.

Language
The indigenous language of Brittany is Breton, a Celtic language related to Welsh and, more distantly, to Irish and Scottish Gaelic. Breton – which, to the untrained ear, sounds like Gaelic with a French accent – can sometimes still be heard in western Brittany and especially in Cornouaille, where perhaps a third of the population understands it. However, only a tiny fraction of the people speak Breton at home.

Getting Around
Brittany's lack of convenient, intercity public transport and the appeal of exploring out-of-the-way destinations make renting a car or motorcycle worth considering here. Brittany – especially Cornouaille – is an excellent area for cycling, and bike-rental places are never hard to find.

QUIMPER
Situated at the confluence (*kemper* in Breton) of two rivers, the Odet and the Steïr, Quimper (which is pronounced 'cam-PAIR'; population 60,000) has managed to preserve its Breton architecture and atmosphere and is considered by many to be the cultural and artistic capital of Brittany. Some even refer to the city as the 'soul of Brittany'.

The Festival de Cornouaille, a showcase for traditional Breton music, costumes and culture, is held here every year between the third and fourth Sundays in July.

Orientation
The old city, largely pedestrianised, is to the west and north-west of the cathedral. The train and bus stations are just under 1km east of the old city. Mont Frugy overlooks the city centre from the south bank of the Odet River.

Information
Tourist Office The tourist office (☎ 02 98 53 04 05; fax 02 98 53 31 33) at Place de la Résistance is open Monday to Saturday from 9 am to 12.30 pm and 1.30 to 6.30 pm. In July and August, the hours are from 9 am to 7 pm. From May to mid-September, the office is also open on Sunday from 10 am to 1 pm and 3 to 7 pm.

Money & Post The Banque de France is 150m from the train station at 29 Ave de la Gare, and is open Monday to Friday from 8.45 am to noon and 1.30 to 3.30 pm. The Crédit Lyonnais in Place Saint Corentin is open Tuesday to Saturday from 8 am to noon and 1.50 to 5 pm. The main post office is at 37 Blvd Amiral de Kerguélen.

Things to See
Walking Tour Strolling the quays that flank both banks of the Odet River is a fine way to get a feel for the city. The old city is known for its centuries-old houses, which are especially in evidence on **Rue Kéréon** and around **Place au Beurre**. To climb 72m-high **Mont Frugy**, which offers great views of the city, follow the switchback path **Promenade du Mont Frugy** next to the tourist office.

Cathédrale Saint Corentin Built between 1239 and 1515 (with spires added in

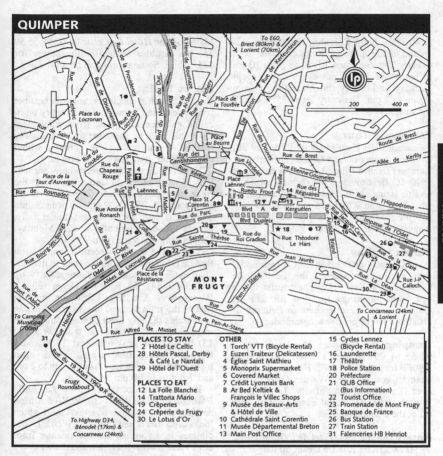

QUIMPER

FRANCE

PLACES TO STAY	OTHER	
2 Hôtel Le Celtic	1 Torch' VTT (Bicycle Rental)	15 Cycles Lennez
28 Hôtels Pascal, Derby	3 Euzen Traiteur (Delicatessen)	(Bicycle Rental)
& Café Le Nantaïs	4 Église Saint Mathieu	16 Launderette
29 Hôtel de l'Ouest	5 Monoprix Supermarket	17 Théâtre
	6 Covered Market	18 Police Station
PLACES TO EAT	7 Crédit Lyonnais Bank	20 Préfecture
12 La Folle Blanche	8 Ar Bed Keltiek &	21 QUB Office
14 Trattoria Mario	François le Villec Shops	(Bus Information)
19 Crêperies	9 Musée des Beaux-Arts	22 Tourist Office
24 Crêperie du Frugy	& Hôtel de Ville	23 Promenade de Mont Frugy
30 Le Lotus d'Or	10 Cathédrale Saint Corentin	25 Banque de France
	11 Musée Départemental Breton	26 Bus Station
	13 Main Post Office	27 Train Station
		31 Faïenceries HB Henriot

the 1850s), Quimper's newly cleaned cathedral incorporates many Breton elements, including – on the western façade between the spires – an equestrian statue of King Gradlon, the city's mythical 5th-century founder. The early 15th-century nave is out of line with the choir, built two centuries earlier. The cathedral's patron saint is Saint Corentin, who was Quimper's first bishop. The loaf of bread you'll see in the south transept in front of a relic of Saint Jean Discalcéat (1279-1349) was left by one of the faithful asking for a blessing. The really poor

– not you – are entitled to it. Mass in Breton is said on the first Sunday of every month.

Museums The **Musée Départemental Breton** (☎ 02 98 95 21 60), next to the cathedral in the former bishop's palace on Place Saint Corentin, houses exhibits on the history, furniture, costumes, crafts and archaeology of the area. It opens from 9 am to noon and 2 to 5 pm daily, except Sunday morning and Monday. From June to September it's open daily from 9 am to 6 pm. Entry is 20FF (10FF for students) but rises to

25/12FF in summer. The **Musée des Beaux-Arts** (☎ 02 98 95 45 20), in the Hôtel de Ville at 40 Place Saint Corentin, has a wide collection of European paintings from the 16th to early 20th centuries. It's open from 10 am to noon and 2 to 6 pm every day, except Tuesday, in July and August daily from 10 am to 7 pm. The entry fee is 25FF (15FF for students).

Faïencerie Tour

Faïenceries HB Henriot (☎ 02 98 90 09 36) has been turning out the famous Quimper (or Kemper) faïence (glazed earthenware) since 1690. It offers tours of the factory, which is on Rue Haute south-west of the cathedral, on weekdays from 9 to 11.15 am and 2 to 4.15 pm on weekdays (5.15 pm in July and August). The cost is 20FF.

Places to Stay

It is extremely difficult to find accommodation in Quimper during the Festival de Cornouaille in late July. The tourist office can make bookings for you for 2FF in Quimper, and 5FF elsewhere in Brittany. It also has a list of private accommodation.

Camping The *Camping Municipal* (☎ 02 98 55 61 09) charges 17.70FF per person, 3.90FF for a tent and 6.70FF for a car, and is open all year. It's on Ave des Oiseaux just over 1km west of the old city. To get there from the train station, take bus No 1 and get off at the Chaptal stop.

Hotels The spotless *Hôtel de l'Ouest* (☎ 02 98 90 28 35), 63 Rue Le Déan, up Rue Jean-Pierre Calloch from the train station, has large, pleasant singles/double rooms from 100/150FF and triples/quads from 220/250FF. Singles/doubles with shower are 180/190FF. Hall showers are 15FF. The *Hôtel Pascal* (☎ 02 98 90 00 81) at 17 bis Ave de la Gare has a few doubles for 120FF, but most singles/doubles have showers and cost from 155/180FF.

The *Hôtel Derby* (☎ 02 98 52 06 91; fax 02 98 53 39 04), 13 Ave de la Gare, has singles/doubles with shower, toilet and TV from 150/200FF. The *Hôtel Café Le Nantaïs* (☎ 02 98 90 07 84), 23 Ave de la Gare, has simple singles/doubles from 118FF.

Much closer to the action at 13 Rue Douarnenez (100m north of Église Saint Mathieu), the *Hôtel Le Celtic* (☎ 02 98 55 59 35) has doubles without/with shower for 125/165FF. Some rooms can be a bit noisy.

Places to Eat

Crêpes, a Breton speciality, are your best bet for a cheap and filling meal. Savoury ones, called galettes, are made from wholemeal flour (blé noir or sarrazin) and are usually washed down with cidre (cider), which comes either doux (sweet) or brut (dry).

You'll find crêperies everywhere, particularly along Rue Sainte Catherine, across the river from the cathedral. The *Crêperie du Frugy* (☎ 02 98 90 32 49), 9 Rue Sainte Thérèse, is open for lunch and dinner daily, except Sunday lunchtime and Monday. Crêpes range in price from 7 to 32FF.

You'll find several decent restaurants on Rue Le Déan not far from the train station, including the Vietnamese *Le Lotus d'Or* (☎ 02 98 53 02 54), 53 Rue Le Déan, (closed Wednesday). Ave de la Libération, running east of the train station, has a strip of ethnic restaurants ranging from Chinese and Indian to Italian. *Trattoria Mario* (☎ 02 98 95 42 15) behind the post office at 35 Rue des Réguaires specialises in pizza and is open from Tuesday to Sunday from 11 am to 2 pm and 7 pm to 11.30 pm.

If you want to splurge, try *La Folle Blanche* (☎ 02 98 95 76 76), 39 Blvd Amiral de Kerguélen, an attractive restaurant which looks onto part of the Jardin l'Évêché. It specialises in Lyonnais cuisine (*menus* from 80FF) and is open for lunch and dinner every day but Sunday.

The delicatessen *Euzen Traiteur*, 10 Rue du Chapeau Rouge, sells a good selection of meats, patés, savouries and prepared dishes. It's open from 8 am to 7.30 pm daily, except Sunday. The *Monoprix* supermarket on Quai du Port au Vin (near the covered market) is open from 9 am to 7 pm daily, except Sunday.

Things to Buy

Ar Bed Keltiek (☎ 02 98 95 42 82), 2 Rue du Roi Gradlon, has a wide selection of Celtic books, music, pottery and jewellery. The shop is open Tuesday to Saturday from 9 am to 1 pm and 2 to 7 pm. During July and August it's open every day from 8 am to 8 pm. For good-quality faïence (pottery) and textiles decorated with traditionally inspired designs, go next door to the shop of François le Villec (☎ 02 98 95 31 54) at No 4. It's open Monday to Saturday from 9.30 am to 12.30 pm and 2 to 7 pm (daily with no midday break in summer).

Getting There & Away

Bus The bus station (☎ 02 98 90 88 89) is in the modern building to the right as you exit the train station. It serves half a dozen bus companies and has information and timetables for all. The office is open from 7.15 am to 12.30 pm and 1 to 7.15 pm on weekdays, to 5 pm on Saturday and from 5 pm to 7.30 pm on Sunday. There is reduced service on Sunday and during the off season. Bus destinations include Brest, Pointe du Raz (France's westernmost point), Roscoff (from where there are ferries to Plymouth, England), Concarneau and Quimperlé. For information on SNCF buses to Douarnenez, Camaret-sur-Mer, Concarneau and Quiberon, inquire at the train station.

Train The train station (☎ 02 98 98 31 26 or ☎ 08 36 35 35 39) is east of the city centre on Ave de la Gare. The information counters are open daily from 8 am to 7.15 pm, except Friday and Sunday (8 am to 7 pm in July and August). A one-way ticket on the TGV to Paris' Gare Montparnasse costs 368FF (4½ hours). You can also reach Saint Malo by train via Rennes. The station has luggage lockers (15 to 30FF).

Getting Around

Bus QUB (☎ 02 98 95 26 27), which runs the local buses, is opposite the tourist office at 2 Quai de l'Odet. It's open weekdays from 8 am to 12.15 pm and 1.30 to 6.30 pm and on Saturday from 9 am to noon and 2 to 6 pm. Tickets are 6FF each or 45FF for a carnet of 10. Buses stop running around 7 pm and do not operate on Sunday (except No 8). To reach the old city from the train station, take bus No 1 or 6.

Taxi Radio taxis can be reached on ☎ 02 98 90 21 21.

Bicycle Torch' VTT (☎ 02 98 53 84 41), 58 Rue de la Providence, rents mountain bikes for 90/65FF a day/half day (70/45FF from October to April). The shop, which is open from 9.30 am to 12.30 pm and 2 to 7 pm daily, except Sunday and Monday morning, is a good source of information on cycling routes. Cycles Lennez (☎ 02 98 90 14 81) just west of the train station at 13 Rue Aristide Briand has road bikes for 69/95/125FF for one/two/three days. Lennez also rents *cyclos* and scooters for 150FF and 200FF a day.

CONCARNEAU

Concarneau (Konk-Kerne in Breton; population 18,500), 24km south-east of Quimper, is France's third most important trawler port. Much of the tuna brought ashore here is caught in the Indian Ocean and off the coast of Africa; you'll see handbills announcing the size of the incoming fleet's catch all around town. Concarneau is slightly scruffy and at the same time a bit touristy, but it's refreshingly unpretentious and is near several decent beaches.

Orientation & Information

Concarneau curls around the busy fishing port, the Port de Pêche, with the two main quays running north-south along the harbour. The tourist office (☎ 02 98 97 01 44; fax 02 98 50 88 81) is on Quai d'Aiguillon, 200m north of the main (west) gate to the Ville Close. It's open Monday to Saturday from 9 am to 12.30 pm and from 1.45 to 7 pm. From May to June, it keeps Sunday hours from 9.30 am to 12.30 pm, and in July and August it's open daily from 9 am to 8 pm.

Money & Post The Société Générale, 10 Rue du Général Morvan, half a block west of the tourist office, is open weekdays from 8.10 am to noon and from 1.35 to 5.10 pm. Caisse d'Épargne on Rue Charles Linement, which runs parallel two streets south, opens Tuesday to Saturday from 8.45 am till noon and 1.30 to 5.30 pm (4 pm on Saturday). The main post office, which has exchange facilities, is at 14 Quai Carnot.

Things to See & Do

The **Ville Close** (walled city), built on a small

island measuring 350 by 100m and fortified between the 14th and 17th centuries, is reached from Place Jean Jaurès by a footbridge. As you enter, note the sundial warning us all that 'Time passes like a shadow'. The Ville Close is packed with shops and restaurants, and there are nice views of the town, the port and the bay from the **ramparts**, which are open daily from 10 am to 6 pm, 9 am to 7 pm in summer. The ticket office is up the stairs to the left just inside the main gate.

The **Musée de la Pêche** (☎ 02 98 97 10 20), on Rue Vauban just beyond the gate, has four aquariums and interesting exhibits on everything you could possibly want to know about fish and the fishing industry over the centuries. It's open daily from 10 am to noon and 2 to 6 pm (9.30 am to 7 pm in July and August). Prices are 30/20FF for adults/under 16s.

The more serious **Marinarium** (☎ 02 98 97 06 59) next to the hostel at Quai de la Croix has aquariums as well as exhibits dealing with oceanography and marine biology. It's open Easter to September daily from 2 to 6.30 pm. Prices are 20/12FF for adults/children.

Plage des Sables Blancs (White Sands Beach) is 1.5km north-west of the tourist office on Baie de la Forêt; to get there, take bus No 2. **Plage du Cabellou**, several kilometres south of town, can be reached by bus No 2.

From April to September, three companies offer excursions to the **Îles de Glénan**, nine little islands about 20km south of Concarneau with an 18th-century fort, sailing and scuba-diving schools, a bird sanctuary and a few houses. Vedettes Glenn (☎ 02 98 97 10 31), 17 Ave du Docteur Nicolas, and Vedette Taxi (☎ 02 98 97 25 25; based in Quimper) charge 100FF return (50FF for children).

Places to Stay

Camping Concarneau's half a dozen camping grounds include *Camping Moulin d'Aurore* (☎ 02 98 50 53 08), 600m south-east of the Ville Close at 49 Rue de Trégunc. It's open from April to September and costs 20FF per person and 19FF for a tent and car. To get there take bus No 1 or 2 and get off at Le Rouz, or the little ferry from Ville Close

to Place Duquesne and walk south along Rue Mauduit Duplessis.

Hostel The *Auberge de Jeunesse* (☎ 02 98 97 03 47; fax 02 98 50 87 57) is right on the water at Quai de la Croix, next to the Marinarium. To get there from the tourist office, walk south to the end of Quai Peneroff and turn right. A bed is 46FF, and breakfast 19FF. Reception is open from 9 am to noon and 6 to 8 pm only.

Hotels The *Hôtel Les Voyageurs* (☎ 02 98 97 08 06), 9 Place Jean Jaurès, has slightly overpriced doubles for 175FF with washbasin and bidet, and 200FF with shower. Hall showers are free. If you can afford a bit more, *Hôtel des Halles* (☎ 02 98 97 11 41; fax 02 98 50 58 54), just around the corner from Hôtel Les Voyageurs on Place de l'Hôtel de Ville, charges 220FF for a double with shower and TV, and 290FF with shower, TV and toilet. Or try the *Hôtel Modern* (☎ 02 98 97 03 36; fax 02 98 97 84 04), north of the port at 5 Rue du Lin, a quiet backstreet. It has singles/doubles with washbasin for 200FF and with shower from 280FF. Use of the private garage costs 40FF.

About 1km out of town, the friendly *Bonne Auberge* is situated on the beach at Le Cabellou and surrounded by gardens. Singles/doubles start from 120/150FF with washbasin and 200/240FF with shower.

Places to Eat

A number of eateries north of the fishing port offer good value for money. *L'Escale* (☎ 02 98 97 03 31), 19 Quai Carnot, is particularly popular with local Concarnois – a hearty lunch or dinner *menu* (available daily except Saturday night and all day Sunday) costs just 51FF. Next door at No 20, the similar *Le Chalut* (☎ 02 98 97 02 12) (closed Friday and Saturday nights) has a 50FF *menu*.

For excellent home-style crêpes, try the unpretentious little crêperie called *Crêperie du Grand Chemin* (☎ 02 98 97 36 57), 17 Ave de la Gare. Your basic crêpe au beurre (buttered crêpe) costs only 7FF – and there's a big discount if you order them by the pair. More extravagant varieties are 15 to 23FF.

The *covered market* on Place Jean Jaurès is open to 1 pm daily, except Sunday. The

Rallye Super supermarket on Quai Carnot next to the post office is open Monday to Saturday from 8.45 am to 7.30 pm. During most of July and August, it's also open on Sunday from 9.30 am to 12.30 pm.

Getting There & Away
The bus station is in the parking lot north of the tourist office. Caoudal (☎ 02 98 56 96 72) runs up to four buses a day (three on Sunday) between Quimper and Quimperlé (via Concarneau and Pont Aven). The trip from Quimper to Concarneau costs 24.50FF and takes 30 minutes.

Getting Around
Bus Concarneau's three bus lines run by Busco operate between 7.20 am and 7.20 pm daily, except Sunday. All of them stop at the bus terminal next to the tourist office and tickets are 5FF (45FF for a 10-ticket carnet). For information, consult the Busco office (☎ 02 98 60 53 76) in the covered market on Place Jean Jaurès. It's open from 10 am to noon and 2 to 5 pm on weekdays, except Tuesday.

Taxi For taxis in Concarneau call ☎ 02 98 97 06 06.

Boat A small passenger ferry links the Ville Close and Place Duquesne on Concarneau's eastern shore year-round. From mid-June to August, sailings are between 7.30 am and 10 pm. Off season, they start an hour later, take a lunch break and finish at 6.20 pm (7.20 pm at the weekend). One way is 3FF (20FF for 10 tickets).

SAINT MALO
The Channel port of Saint Malo (population 48,000) is one of the most popular tourist destinations in Brittany – and with good reason. Situated at the mouth of the Rance River, it's famed for its walled city and nearby beaches. The Saint Malo area has one of the biggest tidal ranges in the world – during spring tides (which occur twice a month), the high-water level can be up to 13m or more above low water.

Saint Malo is an excellent base from which to explore the Côte d'Émeraude, the northern

'Emerald Coast' of Brittany between Cancale and Le Val André. Mont Saint Michel (see Normandy, earlier) can be visited easily as a day trip from Saint Malo.

Saint Malo reached the height of its importance during the 17th and 18th centuries, when it was one of France's most active ports for both merchant ships and privateers, whose favourite targets were, of course, the English.

Orientation
Saint Malo consists of the resort towns of Saint Servan, Saint Malo, Paramé and Rothéneuf. The old city, signposted as Intra-Muros ('within the walls') and also known as the Ville Close, is connected to Paramé by the Sillon Isthmus. The train station is 1.2km east of the old city.

Information
Tourist Office Saint Malo's tourist office (☎ 02 99 56 64 48; fax 02 99 40 93 13) is just outside the old city on Esplanade Saint Vincent. It's open Monday to Saturday from 9 am to noon and 2 to 6 pm. From April to June and in September, it stays open to 7 pm and keeps Sunday hours from 10 am to noon and 2 to 6 pm. In July and August, it's open Monday to Saturday from 8.30 am to 8 pm and on Sunday from 10 am to 7 pm.

Money & Post There are half a dozen banks near the train station, along Blvd de la République and at Place de Rocabey. All are open on weekdays and keep about the same hours: 8.30 am to noon and 1.30 to 4.30 pm. In the old city, the *bureau de change* at 2 Rue Saint Vincent gives a horrible rate, but it's open daily from mid-March to mid-November from 10 am to 7 pm (9 am to 10 pm from June to September).

The main post office is near Place de Rocabey at 1 Blvd de la Tour d'Auvergne. Currency exchange services are available. In the old city, there's a branch at 4 Place des Frères Lamennais.

Things to See & Do
Old City During the fighting of August 1944, which drove the Germans from Saint Malo, 80% of the old city was destroyed. After the war, the principal historical monuments were

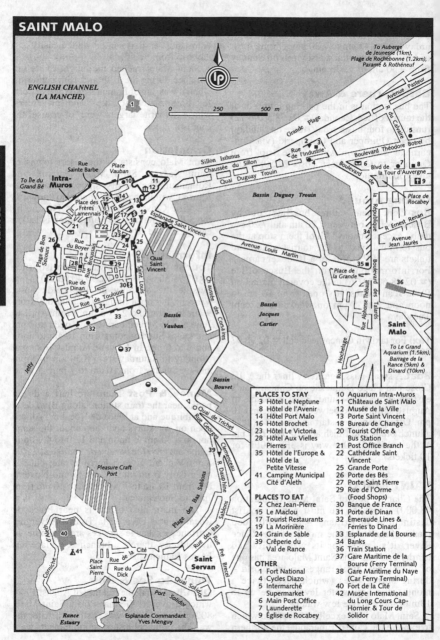

SAINT MALO

*ENGLISH CHANNEL
(LA MANCHE)*

0   250   500 m

To Auberge
de Jeunesse (1km),
Plage de Rochebonne (1.2km),
Paramé & Rothéneuf

Avenue Pasteur

R. du Calvaire

Grande Plage

Rue
de l'Industrie

Boulevard Théodore Botrel

Blvd de
la Tour d'Auvergne

Place de
Rocabey

R. Ernest Renan

Avenue
Jean Jaurès

Sillon Isthmus

Chaussée du Sillon

Quai Duguay Trouin

Rue
Sainte Barbe

Place
Vauban

Intra-
Muros

To l'île du
Grand Bé

Place des
Frères
Lamennais

Rue
du Boyer

Rue Broussais

Plage de Bon
Secours

Rue de
Dinan

Rue
du Boyer

Rue
de Toulouse

Esplanade Saint Vincent

Bassin Duguay Trouin

Avenue Louis Martin

Quai Saint Louis

Quai
Saint Vincent

Ch. aussée des Corsaires

Place de
la Grande

Boulevard des Talards

Saint
Malo

Rue Alphonse Thébault

Bassin
Vauban

Bassin
Jacques
Cartier

Rue Hochelage

To Le Grand
Aquarium (1.5km),
Barrage de la
Rance (5km) &
Dinard (10km)

Jetty

Bassin
Bouvet

Quai de Trichet

Rue Georges Clemenceau

R. Dauphine

Pleasure Craft
Port

Plage des Bas Sablons

Rue des Bas
Sablons

Rue du Pré Bréc el

Saint
Servan

Corniche d'Aleth

Fort de la Cité

Place
Saint Pierre

Rue de la Cité

Rue du
Dick

Quai Solidor

Port Solidor

Rance
Estuary

Esplanade Commandant
Yves Menguy

PLACES TO STAY
3 Hôtel Le Neptune
8 Hôtel de l'Avenir
14 Hôtel Port Malo
16 Hôtel Brochet
23 Hôtel Le Victoria
28 Hôtel Aux Vielles
    Pierres
35 Hôtel de l'Europe &
    Hôtel de la
    Petite Vitesse
41 Camping Municipal
    Cité d'Aleth

PLACES TO EAT
2 Chez Jean-Pierre
15 Le Maclou
17 Tourist Restaurants
19 La Morinière
24 Grain de Sable
39 Crêperie du
    Val de Rance

OTHER
1 Fort National
4 Cycles Diazo
5 Intermarché
    Supermarket
6 Main Post Office
7 Launderette
9 Église de Rocabey

10 Aquarium Intra-Muros
11 Château de Saint Malo
12 Musée de la Ville
13 Porte Saint Vincent
18 Bureau de Change
20 Tourist Office &
    Bus Station
21 Post Office Branch
22 Cathédrale Saint
    Vincent
25 Grande Porte
26 Porte des Bés
27 Porte Saint Pierre
29 Rue de l'Orme
    (Food Shops)
30 Banque de France
31 Porte de Dinan
32 Émeraude Lines &
    Ferries to Dinard
33 Esplanade de la Bourse
34 Banks
36 Train Station
37 Gare Maritime de la
    Bourse (Ferry Terminal)
38 Gare Maritime du Naye
    (Car Ferry Terminal)
40 Fort de la Cité
42 Musée International
    du Long Cours Cap-
    Hornier & Tour de
    Solidor

FRANCE

faithfully reconstructed but the rest of the area was rebuilt in the style of the 17th and 18th centuries. **Cathédrale Saint Vincent**, begun in the 11th century, is noted for its medieval stained-glass windows. The striking modern altar in bronze reveals a Celtic influence.

The **ramparts**, built over the course of many centuries, survived the war and are largely original. They afford superb views in all directions: the freight port, the interior of the old city and the English Channel. There is free access to the **ramparts walk** at Porte de Dinan, the Grande Porte, Porte Saint Vincent and elsewhere. The remains of the 17th-century **Fort National**, for many years a prison, are just beyond the northern stretch.

The **Musée de la Ville** (☎ 02 99 40 71 57), in the Château de Saint Malo at Porte Saint Vincent, deals with the history of the city and the Pays Malouin (the area around Saint Malo). It's open daily from 10 am to noon and 2 to 6 pm (closed on Monday in winter). Entry is 25FF (12.50FF for students).

The **Aquarium Intra-Muros** (☎ 02 99 40 91 86), with over 100 tanks, is built into the walls of the old city next to Place Vauban. It's open daily from 10 am to 7 pm (10 pm in July and August). Prices for adults/students are 30/20FF. **Le Grand Aquarium Saint Malo** (☎ 02 99 21 19 02) on Ave Général Patton, 1.5km south of the train station, is Europe's first circular aquarium. From mid-June to September it's open from 9 am to 9 pm and costs 50/44FF for adults/students. The rest of the year it's open from 9.30 am to 6 pm and costs 44/30FF for adults/students. To get there take bus No 5 from the train station and hop off at La Madelaine stop.

Île du Grand Bé You can reach the Île du Grand Bé, where the 18th-century writer Chateaubriand is buried, on foot at low tide via the Porte des Bés and the nearby old city gates. Be warned: when the tide comes in (and it comes in fast), the causeway remains impassable for about six hours.

Saint Servan Saint Servan's fortress, **Fort de la Cité**, was built in the mid-18th century and served as a German base during WWII. The German pillboxes of thick steel flanking the fortress walls were heavily scarred by Allied shells in August 1944.

The **Musée International du Long Cours Cap-Hornier** (☎ 02 99 40 71 58) is housed in the 14th-century **Tour de Solidor** on Esplanade Menguy and it displays nautical instruments, ship models and other exhibits relating to the sailors who sailed around Cape Horn between the early 17th and early 20th centuries. There is a great view from the top of the tower. The museum is open from 10 am to noon and 2 to 6 pm daily (closed Monday from October to April). Tickets cost 20FF (10FF for students); a combined ticket which includes entry to the Musée de la Ville is 30/15FF.

Beaches Just outside the old city walls to the west is **Plage de Bon Secours**. Saint Servan's **Plage des Bas Sablons** is popular with older sunbathers. The **Grande Plage**, which stretches north-eastward from the Sillon Isthmus, is spiked with tree trunks that act as breakers. **Plage de Rochebonne** is 1km or so to the north-east.

Places to Stay

Camping The *Camping Municipal Cité d'Aleth* (☎ 02 99 81 60 91), next to Fort de la Cité in Saint Servan, is open all year and charges 18.50FF per person and 26FF for a tent and car. In summer, take bus No 1. During the rest of the year, your best bet is bus No 6.

Hostel The *Auberge de Jeunesse* (☎ 02 99 40 29 80; fax 02 99 40 29 02), 37 Ave du Père Umbricht (in Paramé), is a bit under 2km north-east of the train station. A bed in a four or six-person room costs from 64 to 69FF, doubles are from 77 to 82FF per person, and singles with wash-basin are 70FF, all including breakfast. From the train station, take bus No 5.

Hotels It can be difficult finding a hotel room in Saint Malo during July and August. Among the cheaper places, the noisy and charmless hotels near the train station are the first to fill up. If you're looking for a bargain, the hotels around Place de Rocabey are probably your best bet, though there are also a few good deals in the old city.

Place de Rocabey The small *Hôtel de l'Avenir* (☎ 02 99 56 13 33), 31 Blvd de la

Tour d'Auvergne, has singles and doubles for 120FF (150FF with shower). Hall showers cost 15FF. Close to the Grande Plage, *Hôtel Le Neptune* (☎ 02 99 56 82 15), 21 Rue de l'Industrie, is an older, family-run place. Adequate doubles with washbasin cost from 120FF. Doubles with shower and toilet cost 190FF. Hall showers are 15FF.

Train Station Area The *Hôtel de l'Europe* (☎ 02 99 56 13 42), 44 Blvd de la République, is across the roundabout from the train station. Modern, nondescript doubles start at 160FF (170FF from mid-April to August). Shower-equipped rooms without/with toilet are 190/200FF (230/260FF from May to August). There are no hall showers. Like other places in this area, it's somewhat noisy. The *Hôtel de la Petite Vitesse* (☎ 02 99 56 01 93) next door at No 42 has good-sized but noisy doubles from 160FF (190FF with shower) and two-bed quads from 290FF. Hall showers are 25FF. Telephone reservations are not accepted in summer.

Old City The friendly, family-run *Hôtel Aux Vieilles Pierres* (☎ 02 99 56 46 80) is in a quiet part of the old city at 4 Rue des Lauriers. Singles/doubles start at 130FF (160FF with shower); hall showers are free. The *Hôtel Le Victoria* (☎ 02 99 56 34 01), 4 Rue des Orbettes, is more in the thick of things. It has doubles from 150FF (167FF in summer). Hall showers are free.

The *Hôtel Port Malo* (☎ 02 99 20 52 99; fax 02 99 40 29 53), 150m from Porte Saint Vincent at 15 Rue Sainte Barbe, has singles/doubles with shower and toilet for 145/175FF (175/220FF in July and August). The *Hôtel Brochet* (☎ 02 99 56 30 00) due south at 1 Rue de la Corne de Cerf has singles/doubles with shower and TV from 200FF (250FF in summer).

Places to Eat

The old city has lots of tourist restaurants, crêperies and pizzerias in the area between Porte Saint Vincent, the cathedral and the Grande Porte; if you're after better food, and better value, avoid this area completely.

As good as any for seafood is *La Morinière* (☎ 02 99 40 85 77), 9 Rue Jacques Cartier, with *menus* at 70 and 90FF (closed Wednesday). Or try the more intimate *Grain de Sable* (☎ 02 99 56 68 72), on the same street at No 2, which serves an excellent fish soup. For takeaway sandwiches available until 1 am daily (closed from 2.30 to 5.30 pm), head for *Le Maclou* (☎ 02 99 56 50 41), 22 Rue Sainte Barbe.

Chez Jean-Pierre (☎ 02 99 40 40 48), popular for pizza and pasta (from 50FF), has an enviable location across from the Grande Plage at 60 Chaussée du Sillon. It's open daily. Near Plage des Bas Sablons in Saint Servan, *Crêperie du Val de Rance* (☎ 02 99 81 64 68), 11 Rue Dauphine, serves Breton-style crêpes and galettes (8 to 35FF) all day. Order a bottle of Val de Rance cider and drink it, as they do here, from a teacup.

In the old city, you'll find a number of food shops along Rue de l'Orme, including the excellent *cheese shop* at No 9 (closed Sunday and Monday), a *fruit and vegetable shop* (closed Sunday) at No 8 and two *boulangeries*. A large *Intermarché* supermarket is two blocks from Place de Rocabey on Blvd Théodore Botrel.

Getting There & Away

Bus The bus station, which several bus companies operate from, is at Esplanade Saint Vincent. Many of the buses departing from here also stop at the train station.

Les Courriers Bretons (☎ 02 99 56 79 09) has regular services to Cancale (20.50FF), Fougères (48FF, Monday to Saturday only) and Mont Saint Michel (50FF, one hour). The daily bus to Mont Saint Michel leaves at 11.10 am and returns around 5.30 pm. During July and August, there are five return trips a day. The Courriers Bretons office is open Monday to Friday from 8.30 am to 12.15 pm and 2 to 6.15 pm and Saturday morning (all day in summer).

Tourisme Verney (☎ 02 99 40 82 67), with identical opening hours, has buses to Cancale (20FF), Dinan (33.50FF), and Rennes (54.50FF). Buses to Dinard run about once an hour until around 6 pm (to Saint Malo) and 7 pm (to Dinard); they leave Esplanade Saint Vincent in Saint Malo and pick up passengers at the train station before continuing to Dinard. The fare (one way) is 19FF.

Voyages Pansart (☎ 02 99 40 85 96),

whose office is open Monday to Saturday (daily in July and August), offers various excursions. All day tours to Mont Saint Michel (115/103.50/55FF for adults/students/children) operate twice a week from April to October, and three times a week in July and August.

Train The train station (☎ 02 99 56 04 40 or ☎ 08 36 35 35 39) is 1km east of the old city along Ave Louis Martin. The information counters are open Monday to Friday from 5.30 am to 8 pm (Saturday 6 am, Sunday 7.30 am). There is a direct service to Paris' Gare Montparnasse (290FF; 4¼ hours) in July and August only. During the rest of the year, you have to change trains at Rennes. There are local services to Dinan (44FF) and Quimper (206FF).

Ferry Ferries link Saint Malo with the Channel Islands, Weymouth and Portsmouth in England. There are two ferry terminals: hydrofoils, catamarans and the like depart from Gare Maritime de la Bourse; car ferries leave from the Gare Maritime du Naye. Both are south of the walled city. Shuttles to Dinard (see the Dinard section for details) depart from just outside the old city's Porte de Dinan.

From Gare Maritime de la Bourse, Condor (☎ 02 99 20 03 00) has catamaran and jetfoil services to Jersey (275FF one-day excursion) and Guernsey (315FF) from mid-March to mid-November and to Sark and Alderney (525FF three-day excursion) up to mid-September. Condor's service to Weymouth (579FF one way; 5½ hours) operates daily from late April to October.

Émeraude Lines (☎ 02 99 40 48 40) has ferries to Jersey, Guernsey and Sark. Service is most regular between late March and mid-November. Car ferries to Jersey run all year long, except in January.

Between mid-March and mid-December, Brittany Ferries (☎ 02 99 40 64 41) has boats to Portsmouth once or twice a day leaving from the Gare Maritime du Naye. One-way fares are 180 to 260FF for foot passengers, and 580 to 1370FF for a car, including driver. In winter, ferries sail four or five times a week.

The Bus de Mer ferry (run by Émeraude

Lines) links Saint Malo with Dinard from April to September. The trip costs 20/30FF one way/return and takes 10 minutes. In Saint Malo, the dock (☎ 02 99 40 48 40) is just outside the Porte de Dinan; the Dinard quay (☎ 02 99 46 10 45) is at 27 Ave George V. There are eight to 16 trips a day from 9.30 or 10 am to around 6 or 7 pm. In July and August there are three or four evening sailings.

Getting Around

Bus Saint Malo Bus has seven lines, but line No 1 runs only in summer. Tickets cost 7FF and can be used as transfers for one hour after they're time-stamped; a carnet of 10 costs 49FF and a one-day pass is 20FF. In summer, Saint Malo Bus tickets are also valid on Courriers Bretons buses for travel within Saint Malo. Buses run until about 7.30 pm, but in summer certain lines keep running until about midnight. The company's information office at Esplanade Saint Vincent (☎ 02 99 56 06 06) is open from 8.30 or 9 am to noon and 2 to 6.15 or 6.30 pm daily in summer, and from 2.15 to 6 pm from September to June.

Esplanade Saint Vincent is linked with the train station by bus Nos 1, 2, 3 and 4.

Taxi Taxis can be ordered by phoning ☎ 02 99 81 30 30.

Bicycle Cycles Diazo (☎ 02 99 40 31 63), 47 Quai Duguay Trouin, is open Monday to Saturday from 9 am to noon and 2 to 6 pm. Three-speeds cost 55FF and mountain bikes are 85FF a day.

AROUND SAINT MALO
Dinard

While Saint Malo's old city and beaches are oriented towards middle-class families, Dinard (population 10,000) attracts a well heeled clientele – especially from the UK – who have been coming here since the town first became popular with the English upper classes in the mid-19th century. Indeed, Dinard has the feel of a turn-of-the-century English beach resort, especially in summer, with its candy-cane bathing tents, beachside

FRANCE

FRANCE

carnival rides and spiked-roof *belle époque* mansions perched above the waters.

Beautiful seaside trails extend along the coast in both directions from Dinard. The famous **Promenade du Clair de Lune** (Moonlight Promenade) runs along the Baie du Prieuré, which is south-west of the Embarcadère at the Place du Général de Gaulle.

Perhaps the town's most attractive walk is the one which links the Promenade du Clair de Lune with Plage de l'Écluse via the rocky coast of **Pointe du Moulinet**, from where Saint Malo's old city can be seen across the water. This trail continues to the west running along the coast, passing Plage de Saint Énogat en route to Saint Briac, some 14km away. Bikes are not allowed on the trail. If you are in the mood for a bit of a hike, you can take the bus or ferry over from Saint Malo and walk the 12km back via the Barrage de la Rance hydroelectric dam.

The tourist office (☎ 02 99 46 94 12; fax 02 99 88 21 07) is in a round, colonnaded building at 2 Blvd Féart. It's open Monday to Saturday from 9 am to noon and 2 to 6 pm (to 7.30 pm with no midday break in July and August). Staying in Dinard can be a bit hard on the budget, but since the town is just across the Rance Estuary from Saint Malo, a day trip by bus or boat is an easy option. See Getting There & Away under Saint Malo for transport details.

Loire Valley

From the 15th to 18th centuries, the Loire Valley (Vallée de la Loire) was the playground of kings, princes, dukes and nobles who expended family fortunes and the wealth of the nation to turn it into a vast neighbourhood of lavish chateaux. Today, the region is a favourite destination of tourists seeking architectural testimony to the glories of the Middle Ages and the Renaissance.

The earliest chateaux in the Loire Valley were medieval fortresses (*châteaux forts*), some constructed hastily in the 9th century as a defence against the marauding Vikings. These structures were built on high ground and, from the 11th century, when stone came

into widespread use, were often outfitted with fortified keeps, massive walls topped with battlements, loopholes (arrow slits) and moats spanned by drawbridges.

As the threat of invasion diminished – and the cannon (in use by the mid-15th century) rendered castles almost useless for defence – the architecture of new chateaux (and the new wings added to older ones) began to reflect a different set of priorities, including aesthetics and comfort. Under the influence of the Italian Renaissance, with its many innovations introduced to France at the end of the 15th century, the defensive structures so prominent in the early chateaux metamorphosed into whimsical, decorative features such as can be seen at Azay-le-Rideau, Chambord and Chenonceau. Instead of being built on isolated hilltops, the Renaissance chateaux were placed near a body of water or in a valley and proportioned to harmonise with their surroundings. Most chateaux from the 17th and 18th centuries are grand country houses built in the neoclassical style and set amid formal gardens.

BLOIS

The medieval town of Blois (population 49,000), whose name is pronounced 'blwah', was a major centre of court intrigue between the 15th and 17th centuries, and during the 16th century served as something of a second capital of France. A number of dramatic events, involving some of the most important kings and other personages of French history (Louis XII, François I and Henri III among them), took place inside the city's outstanding attraction, the Château de Blois. The old city, seriously damaged by German attacks in 1940, retains its steep, twisting medieval streets. Several of the most rewarding chateaux in the Loire Valley, including Chambord and Cheverny, are within a 20km radius of the city.

Orientation

Blois, lying on the north bank of the Loire River, is a compact town and almost everything is within walking distance of the train station. The old city is both south and east of the Château de Blois, which towers over Place Victor Hugo.

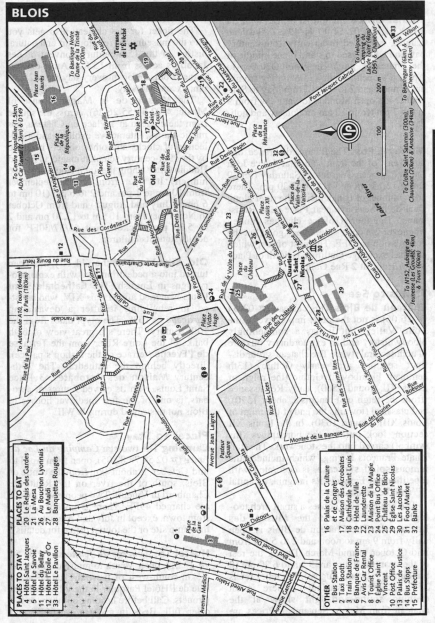

BLOIS

PLACES TO STAY
4   Hôtel Saint Jacques
5   Hôtel Le Savoie
11 Hôtel du Bellay
12 Hôtel l'Étoile d'Or
33 Hôtel Le Pavillon

PLACES TO EAT
20 Le Relais des Gardes
21 La Mesa
26 Au Bouchon Lyonnais
27 Le Maïdi
28 Banquettes Rouges

OTHER
1   Bus Station
2   Taxi Booth
3   Train Station
6   Banque de France
7   Avis Car Rental
8   Tourist Office
9   Point Bus Office
    Vincent
10 Post Office
13 Palais de Justice
14 Bus Stops
15 Préfecture
16 Palais de la Culture
    et de Congrès
17 Maison des Acrobates
18 Cathédrale Saint Louis
19 Hôtel de Ville
22 Launderette
23 Maison de la Magie
24 Point Bus Office
25 Château de Blois
29 Église Saint Nicolas
30 Les Jacobins
31 Food Market
32 Banks

FRANCE

Information

Tourist Office The tourist office (☎ 02 54 90 41 41; fax 02 54 90 41 49), 3 Ave Jean Laigret, is housed in an early 16th-century pavilion which used to stand in the middle of the chateau's gardens. From October to April, it's open Monday to Saturday from 9 am to noon and 2 to 6 pm. From May to September it's open Monday to Saturday from 9 am to 7 pm (from 10 am on Sunday and holidays).

Money & Post The Banque de France, one block east of the train station at 4 Ave Jean Laigret, is open Tuesday to Saturday from 9 am to 12.15 pm and 1.45 to 3.30 pm. There are a number of banks facing the river along Quai de la Saussaye near Place de la Résistance. The tourist office changes money whenever it's open – the rate is good but the commission is 33FF. The post office, which also has exchange facilities, is north of Place Victor Hugo at 2 Rue Gallois.

Things to See

Château de Blois This chateau (☎ 02 54 74 16 06) is not the most impressive in the Loire Valley, but it has a compellingly bloody history and an extraordinary mixture of architectural styles. The chateau's four distinct sections are: early Gothic (13th century); Flamboyant Gothic (the reign of Louis XII around 1500); early Renaissance (from the reign of François I, about 1520); and classical (towards the end of the reign of Louis XIII, around 1630). In the Louis XII section, look out for the porcupines (his symbol) carved into the stonework. The Italianate François I wing, which includes the famous **spiral staircase**, is decorated with repetitions of François I's insignia, a capital 'F' and the salamander.

The chateau also houses a small **archaeological museum** and the **Musée des Beaux-Arts**. The Château de Blois is open daily from 9 am to noon and 2 to 5 pm from mid-October to mid-March. During the rest of the year, the hours are 9 am to 6.30 pm (8 pm during July and August). The entry fee is 35FF (25FF for students). There is an evening **sound-and-light show** at the chateau from May to September. Prices are 60/30FF. For show times, check with the tourist office.

The ticket for the chateau also gets you into the museums of religious art and natural history in the 15th-century convent of **Les Jacobins** across from 15 Rue Anne de Bretagne. Both are open every day from 2 to 6 pm, except Monday.

The **Maison de la Magie** (House of Magic; ☎ 02 54 55 26 26), across the square from the chateau at 1 Place du Château, has magic shows, interactive exhibits and a collection of clocks and other objects invented by the 19th-century scientist/magician Robert Houdin (after whom the great Houdini named himself). It's open from June to September from 10 am to 1 pm and 2 to 6 pm (10 am to 6 pm in July and August) and from October to November from 10 am to 12.30 pm and 2 to 5.30 pm. Tickets cost 43/37/30FF for adults/students/children.

Old City Much of the old city has been turned into a pedestrian area with explanatory signs in English. The **Cathédrale Saint Louis** is named after Louis XIV, who assisted in rebuilding it after a devastating hurricane in 1678. The crypt dates from the 10th century. There's a great view of both banks of the Loire River from the **Terrasse de l'Évêché** (terrace of the bishop's palace), directly behind the cathedral. The 15th-century **Maison des Acrobates**, 3 Place Saint Louis, with its carved figures of acrobats, is one of the few medieval houses in Blois not destroyed during WWII.

Places to Stay

Camping The two-star *Camping du Lac de Loire* (☎ 02 54 78 82 05), open from April to mid-October, is about 4km from the centre of Blois, south of the river on the Route de Chambord in Vineuil. Two people with a tent are charged 49FF. There is no bus service from town, except in July and August (phone the camp site or the tourist office for details).

Hostel The *Auberge de Jeunesse* (☎ 02 54 78 27 21), open March to mid-November, is 4.5km south-west of the train station at 18 Rue de l'Hôtel Pasquier in the village of Les Grouëts. Call before heading out there as it's often full. Beds in a dorm are 60FF and breakfast (optional) is 19FF. The hostel is closed from 10 am to 6 pm. To get there, take bus No 4, which runs until 7 or 7.30 pm, from Place de la République.

Hotels Near the train station, your best bet is the friendly *Hôtel Saint Jacques* (☎ 02 54 78 04 15; fax 02 54 78 33 05), 7 Rue Ducoux. Basic doubles start at 125FF; with shower, toilet and TV they're 190 to 215FF. Just opposite at No 6-8, the family-run *Hôtel Le Savoie* (☎ 02 54 74 32 21) has well kept singles/doubles with shower, toilet and TV for 230/280FF.

North of the old city, the *Hôtel du Bellay* (☎ 02 54 78 23 62; fax 02 54 78 52 04), 12 Rue des Minimes, has doubles for 135 to 160FF; hall showers are free. Doubles with bath and toilet are 185FF. Nearby, the *Hôtel L'Étoile d'Or* (☎ 02 54 78 46 93), 7 Rue du Bourg Neuf, has doubles from 150FF (220FF with shower and toilet). Hall showers are free.

Across the river from the old city, the *Hôtel Le Pavillon* (☎ 02 54 74 23 27), 2 Ave Wilson, has ordinary doubles with washbasin and high ceilings for 120 to 150FF; hall showers cost 15FF (free if you stay more than one night, depending on the season). Doubles/quads with shower and toilet are 150/260FF.

Places to Eat

Le Maïdi (☎ 02 54 74 38 58), a North African restaurant in the old city at 42 Rue Saint Lubin, serves excellent couscous and has *menus* from 65FF. Hours are noon to 2 pm and 6.30 to 10 pm (midnight in summer); closed on Thursday (open on Thursday evening in July and August and holiday weekends). *La Mesa* (☎ 02 54 78 70 70) is a pleasant place at 11 Rue Vauvert, up the alleyway from 44 Rue Foulerie. It serves good pizzas and salads, and you can eat al fresco in the courtyard. *Menus* are 75 and 130FF. It's open Monday to Saturday (daily from July to September) from noon to 2 pm and 7 to 11 pm.

For something a bit more upmarket, try the local favourite *Au Bouchon Lyonnais* (☎ 02 54 74 12 87), 25 Rue des Violettes (above Rue Saint Lubin), where *menus* are 115 and 165FF. The restaurant is open daily, except Sunday and Monday (but opens Sunday evening in July and August). Another good bet is *Banquettes Rouges* (☎ 02 54 78 74 92), an old-fashioned bistro at 16 Rues des Trois Marchands, with *menus* at 99, 105 and 145FF. *Le Relais des Gardes*, 52 Rue Foulerie, (☎ 02 54 74 36 56), is a stone, stucco and wood-beamed place that specialises in crêpes (12 to 38FF), gallettes (29 to 48FF) and cider. It's closed at midday Sunday and on Monday. A 65FF *menu* is available.

In the old city, there's a *food market* along Rue Anne de Bretagne, off Place Louis XII, on Tuesday, Thursday and Saturday until 1 pm.

Getting There & Away

The train station (☎ 08 36 35 35 39) is at the western end of Ave Jean Laigret. The information office is open from 9 am to 6.30 pm daily, except Sunday. The journey between Blois and Paris' Gare d'Austerlitz takes about 1½ hours. Bordeaux (240FF) is four hours by direct train (less if you change to a TGV at Saint Pierre des Corps near Tours).

Getting Around

Bus Buses within Blois – run by TUB – operate from Monday to Saturday until 8 or 8.30 pm. On Sunday, service is greatly reduced. All buses except No 4 stop at the train station. Tickets cost 6FF or 41FF for a carnet of 10. For information, consult the Point Bus office (☎ 02 54 78 15 66) at 2 Place Victor Hugo (beneath the chateau).

Taxi Taxis (☎ 02 54 78 07 65) can be hired for trips into the Loire Valley (see Getting There & Away in the Blois Area Chateaux section).

Car See Getting There & Away in the Blois Area Chateaux section for rental information.

BLOIS AREA CHATEAUX

The Blois area is endowed with some of the finest chateaux in the Loire Valley, including the spectacular Château de Chambord, the magnificently furnished Château de Cheverny, the beautifully situated Château de Chaumont (also accessible from Tours) and the modest but more personal Beauregard. The town of Amboise (see the Tours Area Chateaux section) can also be reached from Blois. Don't try to visit too many though; you'll soon find yourself 'chateau-saturated'.

Organised Tours

Without your own wheels, the best way to see more than one chateau in one day is with an organised tour. The regional TLC bus company (same office as Point Bus; ☎ 02 54 78 55 61) in Blois offers two Circuits Châteaux itineraries (prices do not include admission fees): Chambord and Cheverny (65FF return; 50FF for students) and Chaumont and Chenonceau (110/90FF). Both operate daily from mid-June to mid-September.

Getting There & Away

Bus TLC runs limited bus services to destinations in the vicinity of Blois. All times quoted here are approximate and should be verified with the company first. Buses depart from Place Victor Hugo (in front of the Point Bus office) and from the bus station to the left of the train station as you exit.

Taxi At the taxi booth (☎ 02 54 78 07 65) in front of the Blois train station, it's possible to hire a taxi or a minibus with space for eight passengers. A return trip (including a one-hour stop at each destination) costs 240FF to Cheverny, 260FF to Chambord and 425FF to Chenonceau; Sunday and holiday rates are 340, 365 and 640FF respectively. Various chateaux combinations are possible.

Car Avis (☎ 02 54 74 48 15), 6 Rue Jean Moulin, is open Monday to Saturday from 8 am to noon and 2 to 7 pm.

Bicycle The countryside around Blois, with its quiet country back roads, is perfect for cycling. Unfortunately, Chambord, Cheverny and Chaumont are each about 20km from Blois. An excursion to all, which are 20km apart, is a 60km proposition – quite a bit for one day if you're not in shape. A 1:200,000 scale Michelin road map or a 1:50,000 scale IGN is indispensable to find your way around the rural back roads.

Château de Chambord

The Château de Chambord (☎ 02 54 50 50 02), begun in 1519 by François I (1515-47), is the largest and most visited chateau in the Loire Valley. Its Renaissance architecture and decoration, grafted onto a feudal ground plan, may have been inspired by Leonardo da Vinci who, at the invitation of the king, lived in Amboise (45km south-west of here) from 1516 until his death three years later.

Chambord is the creation of François I, whose emblems – a royal monogram of the letter F and a salamander of a particularly fierce disposition – adorn many parts of the building. Though forced by liquidity problems to leave his two sons unransomed in Spain and to help himself to both the treasuries of his churches and his subjects' silver, the king kept 1800 workers and artisans at work on Chambord for 15 years. At one point he even demanded that the Loire River be rerouted so that it would pass by Chambord; eventually, a smaller river, the Cosson, was diverted instead (you can still see a bridge spanning dry land on the road from Blois). Molière first staged two of his most famous plays at Chambord to audiences that included Louis XIV.

The chateau's famed **double-helix staircase**, attributed by some to Leonardo, consists of two spiral staircases that wind around the same central axis but never meet. The rich ornamentation is in the style of the early French Renaissance. Of the chateau's 440 rooms, only about 10 are open to the public. Watch out for the **tapestries** in the lovely chapel, the **Comte de Chambord bedroom** (a late 19th-century pretender to the throne) and the fine collection of **Dresden tiles** on the 1st floor.

The royal court used to assemble on the Italianate **rooftop terrace** to watch military exercises, tournaments and the hounds and hunters returning from a day of stalking deer. As you stand on the terrace (once described as resembling an overcrowded chessboard), you will see all around you the towers, cupolas, domes, chimneys, dormers and slate roofs with geometric shapes that create the chateau's imposing skyline.

Tickets to the chateau are on sale daily from 9.30 to 4.45 pm (October to March), 5.45 pm (April to June and September) or

6.30 pm (July and August). Guests already in the chateau can stay there for three-quarters of an hour after ticket sales end. The entrance fee is 40FF (25FF if you're aged 12 to 25 on production of a student card). A brochure in English (30FF) is available, but there are good multilingual explanatory signs posted in the major rooms.

The Centre d'Information Touristique (☎ 02 54 20 34 86) is at Place Saint Michel, the parking lot surrounded by tourist shops. It's open daily from early April to September from 9.30 or 10 am to 6 or 7 pm with a break usually between 12.30 and 1.30 pm.

Getting There & Away Chambord is 16km east of Blois and 18km north-east of Cheverny. During the school year, TLC bus No 2 averages three daily return trips from Blois to Chambord (18.50FF one way). The first bus out to Chambord leaves Blois at 12.10 pm Monday to Saturday. The last bus back to Blois leaves Chambord at 6.40 pm (5.10 pm on weekends and holidays). During July and August, your *only* bus option is TLC's tourist bus (see Organised Tours at the beginning of the Blois Area Chateaux section).

Getting Around Bicycles are available from the Centre d'Information Touristique for 25FF an hour, 35FF for two hours and 80FF a day.

Château de Cheverny

The Château de Cheverny (☎ 02 54 79 96 29), the most magnificently furnished of the Loire Valley chateaux and still privately owned, was completed in 1634. After entering the building through its finely proportioned neoclassical façade, visitors are treated to some 17 sumptuous rooms outfitted with the finest of period appointments: canopied beds, tapestries (note the *Abduction of Helen* in the **Salle d'Armes**, the former armoury), paintings, mantelpieces, parquet floors, painted ceilings and walls covered with embossed Córdoba leather. The pamphlet provided is extremely useful. Don't miss the three dozen panels illustrating the story of *Don Quixote* in the 1st-floor dining room.

On exiting the chateau, you can visit the **Salle des Trophées** – exhibiting the antlers

of almost 2000 stags – and the kennels where a pack of some 80 hounds is still kept.

Cheverny is open daily from 9.15 or 9.30 am to noon and 2.15 to 5 pm (November to February), to 5.30 pm (October and March), to 6 pm (the last half of September) or 6.30 pm (April and May). From June to mid-September, the chateau stays open every day from 9.15 am to 6.45 pm. The entry fee is 33FF (25FF for students).

Getting There & Away Cheverny is 15km south-east of Blois. TLC bus No 4 from Blois to Romorantin stops at Cheverny (13.80FF one way). Buses leave Blois Monday to Saturday at 6.45 am and 12.15 pm. Heading back to Blois, the last bus leaves Cheverny at 6.50 pm (Monday to Friday), 8.15 pm (Sunday and holidays) or 12.50 pm (Saturday).

Château de Beauregard

Beauregard (☎ 02 54 70 40 05), the closest chateau to Blois, is relatively modest in size and a bit scruffy on the outside, which somehow adds to its charm. Built in the early 16th century as a hunting lodge for François I and enlarged 100 years later, it is set in the middle of a large park which is now being converted (with EU assistance) to what will be one of the largest gardens (70 hectares) in Europe. The count and countess who own the place still live in one wing, which is why only five rooms are open to the public.

Beauregard's most famous feature is the **Galerie des Portraits** on the 1st floor, featuring 327 portraits of 'who was who' in France from the 14th to 17th centuries. The floor is very unusual also, covered with 17th-century Dutch tiles.

From April to September, Beauregard is open daily from 9.30 am to noon and 2 to 6.30 pm; there is no closure at midday during July and August. During the rest of the year (except from early January to mid-February, when it's closed), the chateau is open from 9.30 am to noon and 2 to 5 pm (closed Wednesday). Entry is 40FF (30FF for students under 25 and children).

Getting There & Away The Château de Beauregard, only 6km south of Blois, makes a good destination for a short bike ride. There is road access to the chateau from both the D765 (the Blois-Cheverny road) and the D956 (turn left at the village of Cellettes).

TLC bus No 5 from Blois to Saint Aignan stops at the village of Cellettes, 1km southwest of the chateau, on Wednesday, Friday and Saturday. The first one leaves Blois at noon. Unfortunately, there is no afternoon bus back except the one operated by Transports Boutet (☎ 02 54 34 43 95), which passes through Cellettes at about 6.30 pm from Monday to Saturday and at about 6 pm on Sunday (except during August).

Château de Chaumont

The Château de Chaumont (☎ 02 54 51 26 26), set on a bluff overlooking the Loire, looks as much like a feudal castle as any chateau in the area. Built in the late 15th century, it served as a 'booby prize' for Diane de Poitier when her lover, Henry II, died in 1559, and hosted Benjamin Franklin several times when he served as ambassador to France after the American Revolution. The luxurious **écuries** (stables) are Chaumont's most famous feature, but the **Salle du Conseil** (Council Chamber) on the 1st floor with its majolica tile floor and tapestries, and **Catherine de' Medici's bedroom** overlooking the chapel are also remarkable.

Tickets are on sale daily from 9.30 am to 6 pm (10 am to 4.30 pm from October to mid-March); the chateau itself closes half an hour later. The entrance fee is 31FF (21FF if you're aged 12 to 25). The park around the chateau, with its many cedar trees, is open daily from 9 am to 5 pm (7 pm from April to September).

Wine Tasting There are many wine cellars in the area offering tastings; consult the tourist office (☎ 02 54 20 91 73) just below the chateau on Rue du Maréchal Leclerc as times vary. From around Easter to September, for example, there is free tasting in the small building 50m up Rue du Village Neuf from the start of the path up to the chateau.

Getting There & Away The Château de Chaumont is 20km south-west of Blois and 15km north-east of Amboise in the village of Chaumont-sur-Loire. The path leading up to

the park and the chateau begins at the intersection of Rue du Village Neuf and Rue Maréchal Leclerc (route D751). By rail, you can take a local train from Blois on the Orléans-Tours line and get off at Onzain (18FF), which is a 2km walk across the river from the chateau.

TOURS

While Blois remains essentially medieval in layout and small-townish in atmosphere, Tours (population 270,000) has the cosmopolitan and bourgeois air of a real French provincial city. Tours was devastated by German bombardment in June 1940; much of it has been rebuilt since WWII. It is said that the French spoken in Tours is the purest in all of France.

Orientation

Tours' focal point is Place Jean Jaurès, where the city's major thoroughfares (Rue Nationale, Blvd Heurteloup, Ave de Grammont and Blvd Béranger) join up. The train station is 300m to the east along Blvd Heurteloup. The old city, centred around Place Plumereau, is about 400m west of Rue Nationale.

Information

Tourist Office The tourist office (☎ 02 47 70 37 37; fax 02 47 61 14 22) is at 76 Rue Bernard Palissy opposite the new Centre International de Congrès (International Convention Centre). It's open Monday to Saturday from 10 am to 12.30 pm and 2.30 to 5 pm, and on Sunday and holidays from 10 am to 1 pm. From May to September, weekday and Saturday hours are 8.30 am to 6.30 pm (7 pm from June to August); on Sunday and holidays it's open from 10 am to 12.30 pm and 3 to 6 pm.

Money & Post Most banks in Tours are closed on Sunday and Monday. The Banque de France branch at 2 Rue Chanoineau has its exchange service through the door marked 'Bureaux'. It's open Monday to Friday from 8.45 am to noon and 1.20 to 3.30 pm.

The main post office is 200m west of Place Jean Jaurès at 1 Blvd Béranger. It also offers currency exchange.

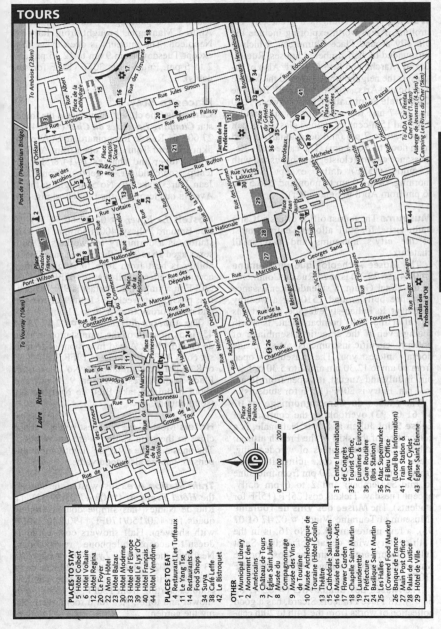

TOURS

PLACES TO STAY
5   Hôtel Colbert
6   Hôtel Voltaire
12 Hôtel Regina
20 Le Foyer
22 Mon Hôtel
23 Hôtel Balzac
30 Hôtel Moderne
33 Hôtel de l'Europe
39 Hôtel Le Lys d'Or
40 Hôtel Français
44 Hôtel Vendôme

PLACES TO EAT
4   Restaurant Les Tuffeaux
11 Le Yang Tse
14 Restaurants & Food Shops
34 Surya
38 Café Leffe
42 Le Bistroquet

OTHER
1   Municipal Library
2   Monument des Americains
3   Château de Tours
7   Église Saint Julien
8   Musée du Compagnonnage
9   Musée des Vins de Touraine
10 Musée Archéologique de Touraine (Hôtel Gouin)
13 Théâtre
15 Cathédrale Saint Gatien
16 Musée des Beaux-Arts
17 Flower Garden
18 Chapelle Saint Martin
19 Launderette
21 Préfecture
24 Basilique Saint Martin
25 Les Halles (Covered Food Market)
26 Banque de France
27 Main Post Office
28 Palais de Justice
29 Hôtel de Ville
31 Centre International de Congrès
32 Tourist Office, Eurolines & Europcar
35 Gare Routière (Bus Station)
36 Atac Supermarket
37 Fil Bleu Office (Local Bus Information)
41 Train Station & Amster Cycles
43 Église Saint Étienne

To Amboise (23km)

Pont de Fil (Pedestrian Bridge)

To Vouvray (10km)

Pont Wilson

Loire River

Old City

To ADA Car Rental, Cher River (1.5km) & Auberge de Jeunesse (4km) & Camping Les Rives du Cher (5km)

Things to See

Walking Tour Tours is a great city for strolling. Areas worth exploring include the **old city** around Place Plumereau, which is surrounded by half-timbered houses, **Rue du Grand Marché** and **Rue Colbert**. Also of interest is the neighbourhood around the Musée des Beaux-Arts, where you will find the **Cathédrale Saint Gatien**, built between 1220 and 1547 and renowned for its spectacular 13th and 15th-century stained glass. It's open from 9 am to 7 pm (and occasionally closed from noon to 2 or 3 pm). The cathedral's Renaissance **cloître** (cloister) can be visited with a guide (15FF) daily, except Sunday morning, from 10 am to noon and 2 to 5 pm (6 pm from April to September).

Museums The tourist office offers a 'Carte multi-visite' for 50FF allowing entry to most of the city's museums and two small chateaux.

The **Musée Archéologique de Touraine** (☎ 02 47 66 22 32) is at 25 Rue du Commerce in the Hôtel Goüin, a splendid Renaissance residence built around 1510 for a wealthy merchant. Its Italian-style façade, all that was left after the 1940 bombardment, is worth seeing even if the eclectic assemblage of pottery, scientific instruments, art etc inside doesn't interest you. The museum is open from 10 am to 12.30 pm and 2 to 5.30 or 6.30 pm; in July and August, it's open from 10 am to 7 pm. Entry is 20FF (12FF for students).

The **Musée du Compagnonnage** (☎ 02 47 61 07 93) overlooking the courtyard of **Église Saint Julien** at 8 Rue Nationale, is a celebration of the skill of the French artisan; exhibits include examples of woodcarving, metalwork and even cake-icing. It's open from 9 am to noon (12.30 pm from mid-June to mid-September) and 2 to 6 pm daily, except Tuesday. Tickets cost 25FF (15FF for students). The **Musée des Vins de Touraine** (Museum of Touraine Wines; ☎ 02 47 61 07 93), a few metres away at No 16, is in the 13th-century wine cellars of Église Saint Julien. Hours are the same as those for the Musée du Compagnonnage. Entry costs 15FF (10FF for students).

The **Musée des Beaux-Arts** (☎ 02 47 05 68 73), 18 Place François Sicard, has a good collection of works from the 14th to 20th centuries but is especially proud of two 15th-. century altar paintings by the Italian painter Andrea Mantegna, brought from Italy by Napoleon. The museum is open every day, except Tuesday, from 9 am to 12.45 pm and 2 to 6 pm. Entry costs 30FF (15FF for students).

Places to Stay

Camping The closest camp site is the three-star *Camping Les Rives du Cher* (☎ 02 47 27 27 60), 61 Rue de Rochpinard, in St Avertin, 5km south of Tours. It's open from April to mid-October and charges 14/14/8/8FF per tent/person/child/car. To get there from Place Jean Jaurès, take bus No 5 straight to the St Avertin bus terminal, then follow signs.

Hostels *Le Foyer* (☎ 02 47 60 51 51), 16 Rue Bernard Palissy, 400m north of the train station, is a dormitory for workers of both sexes aged 16 to 25. If they have space (availability is best from June to August), they accept travellers of all ages for 65FF a person (70FF in a single). Breakfast is 9FF. Check-in is possible on weekdays from 9 am to 6 pm and on Saturday from 8.30 to 11 am.

The *Auberge de Jeunesse* (☎ 02 47 25 14 45) is 5km south of the train station in Parc de Grand Mont. A bed in a room of four or six costs 47FF; breakfast is 19FF. Until 8.30 or 8.45 pm, you can take bus No 1 or 6 from Place Jean Jaurès; between 9.20 pm and about midnight, take Bleu de Nuit bus N1 (southbound).

Hotels Most of the cheapest hotels – those close to the train station – are pretty basic. The ones near the river are slightly more expensive but are also good value.

Train Station Area Just west of the station, the *Hôtel Français* (☎ 02 47 05 59 12), 11 Rue de Nantes, has simple doubles/triples/quads for 120/150/170FF (190/220/250FF with shower). Hall showers cost 10FF. It doesn't accept telephone reservations. Nearby is the *Hôtel Le Lys d'Or* (☎ 02 47 05 33 45; fax 02 47 64 19 00), 21-23 Rue de la Vendée, with quiet, comfortable singles/doubles starting from 120FF, or 185FF with shower and toilet. Ask for a room overlooking the garden.

An excellent choice a bit farther from the station to the south-west is *Hôtel Vendôme* (☎ 02 47 64 33 54), 24 Rue Roger Salengro. This cheerful place, run by a very friendly couple, has simple but decent singles/doubles starting at 120/130FF. A triple with shower is 200FF. Hall showers are free. *Mon Hôtel* (☎ 02 47 05 67 53), 500m north of the train station at 40 Rue de la Préfecture, can provide singles/doubles with an oversized bed starting at 100/115FF (170/200FF with shower and toilet). Showers are 15FF.

If you can afford a bit more, the *Hôtel de l'Europe* (☎ 02 47 05 42 07; fax 02 47 20 13 89), 12 Place du Maréchal Leclerc, has high ceilings and carpeted hallways that give it a sort of *belle époque* ambience. Large rooms with shower and toilet are 250/300/350FF a single/double/triple. The warm, family-run *Hôtel Moderne* (☎ 02 47 05 32 81; fax 02 47 05 71 50), 1-3 Rue Victor Laloux, has decent doubles from 245FF; similar rooms without toilet are 194FF.

River Area The *Hôtel Voltaire* (☎ 02 47 05 77 51) is 900m north of the train station at 13 Rue Voltaire. Comfortable but rather noisy singles/doubles start at 100FF, or 130FF with shower. The *Hôtel Regina* (☎ 02 47 05 25 36) is due south at 2 Rue Pimbert. Well maintained singles/doubles start at 110/120FF, or 135/150FF with shower and toilet. Hall showers cost 15FF.

A cut above in this area is the *Hôtel Colbert* (☎ 02 47 66 61 56; fax 02 47 66 01 55), 78 Rue Colbert, with large singles/doubles with shower, toilet and TV for 230/270FF. Slightly farther from the river, the centrally placed *Hôtel Balzac* (☎ 02 47 05 40 87), 47 Rue de la Scellerie, has 18 comfortable rooms (most with shower and toilet) from 220FF.

Places to Eat
In the old city, Place Plumereau and Rue du Commerce are filled with bars, cafés, crêperies, pâtisseries and restaurants.

Near Place Plumereau at 83 bis Rue du Commerce is *Le Yang Tse* (☎ 02 47 61 47 59), a hole-in-the-wall Chinese/Vietnamese restaurant which has main dishes from 30 to 35FF. It's open daily from noon till 11 pm. *Surya* (☎ 02 47 64 34 04), 65 Rue Colbert, is

a North Indian restaurant open from noon to 2.30 pm and 7 to 11 pm (closed Monday at midday). The weekday lunch *menu* costs 59FF.

Along or just off Rue Colbert, there are plenty of places to splurge, including *Restaurant Les Tuffeaux* (☎ 02 47 47 19 89), 19-21 Rue Lavoisier, which is open from noon to 1.30 pm and 7.30 to 9.30 pm (closed Monday lunch and Sunday). The innovative *cuisine gastronomique* is made with lots of fresh local produce. *Menus* are 110 to 200FF, and reservations are a good idea on weekends. Another good place – more relaxed and much cheaper with *menus* from 45FF – is *Le Bistroquet* (☎ 02 47 05 12 76), 17 Rue Blaise Pascal. Its speciality is paella. It's open from noon to 1.30 pm and 7 to 9.15 pm (closed Saturday and Sunday).

Café Leffe (☎ 02 47 61 48 54), near the train station at 15 Place Jean Jaurès, is open daily from 7 am to 2 am; brasserie meals are served from noon to 3 pm and 7 to 11.30 pm. *Moules marinières* (mussels cooked with white wine and onions) and chips cost 49FF.

Les Halles covered market, 500m west of Rue Nationale at Place Gaston Pailhou, is open daily until 7 pm (until 1 pm on Sunday). The *Atac* supermarket in front of the train station at 5 Place du Maréchal Leclerc is open Monday to Saturday from 8.30 am to 8 pm and on Sunday from 9.30 am to 12.30 pm.

Getting There & Away
Bus Eurolines (☎ 02 47 66 45 56) has a ticket office next to the tourist office at 76 Rue Bernard Palissy. It's open Monday to Saturday from 9 am to noon and 1.30 to 6.30 pm.

Train The train station (☎ 08 36 35 35 39) is off Blvd Heurteloup at Place du Maréchal Leclerc. The information office is open Monday to Saturday from 8.30 am to 6.30 pm. Paris' Gare Montparnasse is about 70 minutes away by TGV (201FF). There is also a service to Paris' Gare d'Austerlitz, Bordeaux (217FF; 2½ hours) and Nantes (147FF; two hours). Some of the chateaux around Tours can be reached by train or SNCF bus, both of which accept Eurail passes. See the Getting There & Away section under Tours Area Chateaux for details.

FRANCE

Car Europcar (☎ 02 47 64 47 76), next to the tourist office at 76 Blvd Bernard Palissy, is open from 8 am to noon and 2 to 6.30 pm Monday to Saturday.

Getting Around

Bus Fil Bleu is the bus network serving Tours and its suburbs. Almost all lines stop near Place Jean Jaurès. Three Bleu de Nuit lines operate about every hour from around 9.30 pm to just after midnight. Tickets (6.50FF) are valid for one hour after being time-stamped; a carnet of five/10 tickets is 32/59FF.

Fil Bleu has an information office (☎ 02 47 66 70 70) in the Jean Jaurès centre at 5 bis Rue de la Dolve, 50m west of Place Jean Jaurès. It's open daily, except Sunday, from 7.30 am to 7 pm (9 am to 5.30 pm on Saturday).

Taxi Call Taxi Radio (☎ 02 47 20 30 40) to order a cab 24 hours a day.

Bicycle See the Getting There & Away section under Tours Area Chateaux for information on renting a bike.

TOURS AREA CHATEAUX

Tours makes a good base for visits to some of the Loire chateaux, including Chenonceau (which you can also visit on a tour from Blois), Azay-le-Rideau, Amboise (also accessible from Blois) and Chaumont (listed under Blois Area Chateaux). If you have a Eurail pass, more chateaux can be reached from Tours than from any other railhead in the region.

Organised Tours

Several companies offer English-language tours of the chateaux. Reservations can be made at the Tours tourist office or you can phone the company directly. Prices often include entrance fees or entitle you to discounts (such fees are a major expense if you go on your own).

Half-day tours with Acco-Dispo (☎ 02 47 57 67 13) are 130FF, and 170FF for a full day, exclusive of entry fees (open all year except January). Touraine Évasion (☎ 02 47 63 25 64) runs half-day/day trips by eight-

person minibus for 95/170FF, not including entry fees (April to mid-November). Services Touristiques de Touraine (☎ 02 47 05 46 09), based at the train station, has coach tours from 185 to 200FF for a half-day and 290FF for a full day, including entry fees (April to October).

Getting There & Away

Bus CAT runs limited bus services to the area around Tours every day, except Sunday and holidays, departing from the Gare Routière (bus terminal) in front of the Tours train station. Schedules are posted. The information desk (☎ 02 47 05 30 49) is open Monday to Saturday from 7.30 am to noon and 2 to 6.30 pm. Tickets are sold on board. It's possible to visit Chenonceau and Amboise in a day using CAT bus No 10 (study the schedules carefully).

Train Many of the chateaux (including Amboise, Azay-le-Rideau, Chenonceau and Chaumont) can be reached from Tours by train or SNCF bus. In summer, certain lines allow you to take a bicycle free of charge, which makes it possible to cycle either there or back. For up-to-date schedules, ask for the brochure *Les Châteaux de la Loire en Train* at the Tours train station.

Bicycle From May to September, Amster Cycles (☎ 02 47 61 22 23) has a rental point 30m right of the main entrance to the train station. For an 18-speed/tandem the price is 80/160FF per day (cheaper for longer periods). It can also lend you maps.

Château de Chenonceau

With its stylised (rather than defensive) moat, drawbridge, towers and turrets straddling the Cher River, 16th-century Chenonceau (☎ 02 47 23 90 07) is everything you imagine a fairy-tale castle to be. The chateau's interior, however, filled with period furniture, tourists, paintings, tourists, tapestries and more tourists, is of only moderate interest.

One of the series of remarkable women who created Chenonceau, Diane de Poitiers, mistress of King Henri II, planted the garden to the left (east) as you approach the chateau down the avenue of plane trees. After Henri's death in 1559, she was forced to give up her beloved Chenonceau by the vengeful Catherine de' Medici, Henri's wife. Catherine then applied her own formidable energies to the chateau and, among other works, laid out the garden to the west (Diane's is prettier).

The 60m-long **Galerie**, spanning the Cher River, was built by Catherine de' Medici and was converted into a hospital during WWI. Between 1940 and 1942, the demarcation line between Vichy-ruled France and the German-occupied zone ran down the middle of the Cher. For many people trying to escape to Vichy, this room served as a crossing point. Two other must-see rooms are Catherine's lovely little **library** on the ground floor with the oldest original ceiling (1521) in the castle, and the **bedroom** where Louise de Lorraine lived out her final days after the assassination of her husband, Henri III, in 1589. Macabre illustrations of bones, skulls, shovels and teardrops adorn the walls.

Chenonceau is open all year from 9 am until sometime between 4.30 pm (mid-November to January) and 7 pm (mid-March to mid-September). The entrance fee is 45FF (30FF for students and children). You'll be given an easy-to-follow tour brochure in English as you enter.

Getting There & Away The Château de Chenonceau is 34km east of Tours, 10km south-east of Amboise and 40km south-west of Blois. Local trains on the Tours-Vierzon line stop at Chisseaux, 2km east of Chenonceaux. There may also be two or three trains a day from Tours to Chenonceaux station (33FF), which is only 500m from the chateau. CAT bus No 10 leaves Tours at 10 am Monday to Saturday, and arrives at Chenonceaux about an hour later; the return bus leaves Chenonceaux at 4.45 pm. The one-way/return fare is 39.40/69.90FF.

Château d'Azay-le-Rideau

Azay-le-Rideau (☎ 02 47 45 42 04), built on an island in the Indre River and surrounded by a quiet pool and lovely park, is one of the most harmonious and elegant of the Loire chateaux. It's adorned with stylised fortifications and turrets intended both as decoration and to indicate the owners' rank. But only seven rooms are open to the public, and their contents are disappointing (apart from a few 16th-century Flemish tapestries). The self-guiding brochure is a bit sketchy.

From April to October, the chateau is open daily from 9.30 am to 6 pm (until 7 pm in July and August). The rest of the year, hours are 9.30 am to 12.30 pm and 2 to 5.30 pm. The park stays open a half-hour later. Tickets cost 32FF (21FF for under 25s).

Getting There & Away Azay-le-Rideau is 26km south-west of Tours. SNCF has a year-round service two or three times a day from Tours to Azay (the station is 2.5km from the chateau) by either train or bus for 28FF one way. The train is faster, but the bus goes direct to the chateau. The last train/bus back to Tours leaves Azay at about 6 pm (just after 8 pm on Sunday).

Amboise

The picturesque hillside town of Amboise (population 11,000), an easy day trip from Tours, is known for its chateau which reached the pinnacle of its importance around the turn of the 16th century.

Tourist Office The tourist office (Accueil d'Amboise; ☎ 02 47 57 09 28; fax 02 47 57 14 35), along the river opposite 7 Quai Général de Gaulle, is open Monday to Saturday from 9 am to 12.30 pm and 2 pm to 6.30 pm; from mid-June to August, hours are 9 am to 8.30 pm. It's also open on Sunday morning (10 am to noon) from Easter to October and on Sunday afternoon (4 to 7 pm) from mid-June to August.

Château d'Amboise The rocky outcrop overlooking the town has been fortified since Gallo-Roman times, but the Château d'Amboise (☎ 02 47 57 00 98), which now lies atop it, began to take form in the 11th and 12th centuries. King Charles VIII, who grew up here, began work to enlarge it in 1492 after a visit to Italy, whose artistic creativity and luxurious lifestyle had deeply impressed him. François I lived here during the first few years of his reign, a wild period marked by balls, masquerade parties and tournaments.

The chateau's ramparts and open gallery afford a panoramic view of the town, the Loire Valley and – on a clear day – Tours.

The most notable features of the chateau are the **Tour des Chevaliers**, with a vaulted spiral ramp once used to ride horses in and out of the castle, and the Flamboyant Gothic **Chapelle Saint Hubert**, with a curious spire decorated with antlers. The remains of Leonardo da Vinci (1452-1519), who lived in Amboise for the last three years of his life, are supposedly under the chapel's northern transept. Exit the chateau via the souvenir shop; the side door leads to the 15th-century **Tour Hurtault**, whose interior consists of a circular ramp decorated with sculptured faces, animals and angels.

The entrance to the chateau is a block east of Quai Général de Gaulle. In winter, it's open daily, except Christmas and New Year's days, from 9 am to noon and 2 to 5 or 5.30 pm; from April to October, hours are 9 am to 6.30 pm (7.30 pm in July and August). The entrance fee is 37FF (30FF for students, 18FF for children aged seven to 14).

Le Clos Lucé Leonardo da Vinci came to Amboise at the invitation of François I in 1516. Until his death at the age of 67 three years later, Leonardo lived and worked in Le Clos Lucé (☎ 02 47 57 62 88), a 15th-century brick manor house 500m south-east of the chateau on Rue Victor Hugo. The building now contains restored rooms and scale models of some 40 of Leonardo's inventions – including a proto-automobile, armoured tank, parachute and hydraulic turbine. It's a fascinating place with a lovely garden, watchtower and recorded Renaissance music – infinitely more evocative of the age than the chateau. Le Clos Lucé is open daily from 9 am to 7 pm from March to December (except July and August when it's open until 8 pm) and in winter from 9 am to 6 pm (10 am to 5 pm in January). The entry fee is a steep 38FF (28FF for students). The road to Le Clos Lucé passes several troglodyte dwellings – caves in the limestone hillside in which local people still live (with all mod cons and a mortgage, of course).

Wine Tasting The Caveau de Dégustation (☎ 02 47 57 23 69) opposite 14 Rue Victor Hugo (in the base of the south side of the chateau), run by local *viticulteurs* (wine-growers), is open daily from early May to late September; hours are 10 am to 7 pm. The tasting is free but you have to pay 1FF to use the toilets next door.

Getting There & Away Amboise is 23km east of Tours and 35km west of Blois. Several trains a day between Tours and Blois stop at Amboise (28FF one way from Tours, 33FF from Blois). The last train back to Tours departs around 9.30 pm. From Tours, you can also take the CAT bus No 10 (25.30/45.50FF one way/return).

South-Western France

The south-western part of France includes a number of diverse regions, ranging from the Bordeaux wine-growing area near the beach-lined Atlantic seaboard to the Basque Country and the Pyrenees mountains in the south. There is convenient rail transport from this region to Paris, Spain and the Côte d'Azur.

LA ROCHELLE

La Rochelle (population 100,000) is a lively city midway down France's Atlantic coast and is popular with middle-class French families and students on holiday. The ever-expanding Université de La Rochelle, opened in 1993, has added to the city's attraction for young people. The quays of La Rochelle are lined with pleasant cafés and bars, and the nearby Île de Ré is surrounded by tens of kilometres of fine-sand beaches.

La Rochelle was one of France's most important seaports between the 14th and 17th centuries, and it was here that Protestantism first took root in France, incurring the wrath of Catholic authorities during the Wars of Religion in the latter half of the 16th century. In 1628 this Huguenot stronghold surrendered to Louis XIII's forces but 5000 of its 28,000 residents had starved to death during a 15-month siege orchestrated by Cardinal Richelieu, the principal minister to Louis XIII. There was a German submarine base here during WWII; Allied attacks on it devastated La Rochelle.

Orientation

The old city is at the northern end of Quai Valin, which runs more or less north-south along the Vieux Port (old port). Quai Valin is linked to the train station – 500m south-east – by Ave du Général de Gaulle. To get to Place du Marché, with its covered market and lots of restaurants, walk 250m north along Rue des Merciers from the old city's Hôtel de Ville. Rue du Palais, with its arcades and 18th-century merchants' homes, is the main shopping street.

Information

The tourist office (☎ 05 46 41 14 68; fax 05 46 41 99 85) is in Le Gabut, the area due west of where Quai Valin and Ave du Général de Gaulle meet. It's open Monday to Saturday from 9 am to 12.30 pm and 2 to 6 pm, and on Sunday from 10.30 am to 12.30 pm. From June to September, opening hours are Monday to Saturday from 9 am to 7 pm (8 pm in July and August) and Sunday from 11 am to 5 pm.

The Banque de France is at 22 Rue Réaumur. The main post office is to the north-east on Place de l'Hôtel de Ville.

Things to See & Do

Old City To protect the harbour at night and defend it in times of war, a chain used to be stretched between the two 14th-century stone towers at the harbour entrance. Visitors can climb to the top of the 36m **Tour Saint Nicolas** (☎ 05 46 41 74 13), and visit the **Tour de la Chaîne** (☎ 05 46 34 11 81), which houses a rather corny exhibition called 'La Rochelle in the Middle Ages'. West along the old city wall is **Tour de la Lanterne** (☎ 05 46 41 56 04), which was used for a long time as a prison and now houses a museum. The English-language graffiti you'll see on the walls was written by English privateers held here during the 18th century. All three towers are open daily from 10 am to 12.30 pm and 2 to 5.30 pm; from April to September, hours are 10 am to 7 pm. Entry to each costs 25FF (15FF for people aged 12 to 25); a ticket for all three is 45FF.

Parts of the **Tour de la Grosse Horloge**, the imposing clock tower on Quai Duperré, were built in the 13th century but most of it

dates from the 18th century. There's an excellent view of the city from the roof.

The **Hôtel de Ville** (Town Hall; ☎ 05 46 41 14 68) at Place de l'Hôtel de Ville in the old city was begun in the late 15th century and still houses the municipal government. Guided tours of the interior (17FF; 11FF for students) take place on Saturday and Sunday at 3 pm and daily at 3 and 4 pm in July and August.

Musée Maritime Neptunea This maritime museum (☎ 05 46 28 03 00) at Bassin des Chalutiers, soon to be the permanent home of Jacques Cousteau's research ship *Calypso*, occupies what was once the city's wholesale fish market. In the **wind pool**, radio-controlled model sailing ships demonstrate the principles of navigating under sail (eg tacking into the wind). The entry fee (45FF; 30FF for under 16s and students) includes tours of a *chalutier* (fishing trawler) and the frigate *France I*. It's open daily from 10 am to 7 pm (ticket sales end at 6 pm). From November to January or February it may be open only from 2 to 6 pm.

Île de Ré & Beaches The Île de Ré, a 30km-long island whose eastern tip is 9km west of La Rochelle's centre, is reached by a 3km toll bridge. In summer, the island's many beaches are a favourite destination for families with young children. The island is accessible from Quai Valin and the train station by Autoplus bus No 1, which goes to Sablanceaux (the narrow bit of the island nearest La Rochelle). The entire island is served by Rébus (☎ 05 46 09 20 15 in Saint Martin de Ré) from Place de Verdun and the train station. Eight buses a day go to both Saint Martin de Ré (28FF one way) and La Flotte (23.50FF). If you decide to drive, be prepared for the 110FF bridge toll from June to September (60FF at other times).

Places to Stay

During July and August, most places in La Rochelle are full by noon and prices are higher than during the rest of the year.

Camping In summer, many camping grounds open up in the La Rochelle area, especially on the Île de Ré. The closest to La

Rochelle is *Camping du Soleil* (also known as Camping Municipal Les Minimes; ☎ 05 46 44 42 53) on Ave des Minimes about 1.5km south of the city centre. It's open from mid-May to mid-September and is often full. Two people with a tent and car are charged 60FF. From Quai Valin or the train station, take bus No 10.

Hostel The *Centre International de Séjour-Auberge de Jeunesse* (☎ 05 46 44 43 11) is 2km south-west of the train station on Ave des Minimes. A dorm bed/double room costs 72/179FF, including breakfast. To get there take bus No 10, which runs until about 7.30 pm (later from June to September).

Hotels The *Hôtel Henri IV* (☎ 05 46 41 25 79; fax 05 46 41 78 64), near the Vieux Port at 31 Rue des Gentilshommes, has doubles from 160FF (205FF with shower and toilet). Hall showers are free. Just south, the *Hôtel de Bordeaux* (☎ 05 46 41 31 22; fax 05 46 41 24 43), 43 Rue Saint Nicolas, has pleasant doubles from 165FF (210FF from May to September). For something a little more up-market, try the extremely pleasant *Hôtel de Paris* (☎ 05 46 41 03 59; fax 05 46 41 03 24), 18 Rue Gargoulleau, which has clean and tidy doubles/triples/quads with shower and toilet from 190/240/280FF (November to March) to 310/370/430FF (July to September).

A number of cheap hotels can be found in the vicinity of Place du Marché, 250m north of the old city. The unremarkable *Hôtel Printania* (☎ 05 46 41 22 86), 9 Rue du Brave Rondeau, has doubles from 150FF (195FF with shower and toilet). Hall showers cost 10FF. The *Hôtel de la Paix* (☎ 05 46 41 33 44; fax 05 46 50 51 28), housed in an 18th-century building at 14 Rue Gargoulleau, has a few doubles with shower and toilet from 180FF (260FF from April to September). A huge, old-fashioned room for five with fireplace is 390FF (450FF in season).

One of the nicest hotels in La Rochelle and convenient to the Place du Marché is the *Hôtel François 1er* (☎ 05 46 41 28 46; fax 05 46 41 35 01) at tranquil 13-15 Rue Bazoges. It has decent but smallish doubles for 390 to 475FF (less in winter) plus a couple of rooms with washbasin for 215FF. Several French

kings stayed in this building in the 15th and 16th centuries.

Places to Eat

Classical French cuisine is available at the elegantly rustic *La Galathée* (☎ 05 46 41 17 06), 45 Rue Saint Jean du Perot, where *menus* cost 80, 120 and 180FF. It's open daily, except Tuesday evening and Wednesday (daily except Wednesday in July and August). The elegant *Bistrot l'Entracte* (☎ 05 46 50 62 60), 22 Rue Saint Jean du Perot, specialises in fish. The four course *menu* costs 155FF. Hours are 12.15 to 1.45 pm and 9.15 to 9.45 pm (closed Sunday).

At *Café de la Paix* (☎ 05 46 41 39 79), 54 Rue Chaudrier (Place de Verdun), you can sip beer (15FF) and dine on brasserie food (49 to 76FF for mains) amid gilded pilasters and turn-of-the-century marble, mouldings and mirrors.

Pizzeria La Provençale (☎ 05 46 41 43 68), 15 Rue Saint Jean du Perot, has pizzas (40 to 65FF), meat mains (50 to 70FF) and three *menus* (for 69, 89 and 120FF). It's closed Sunday for most of the year, but from July to September it's open every day. It's also open public holidays.

The ethnic places in Le Gabut include *Loan Phuong* (☎ 05 46 41 90 20), on Quai du Gabut, which has an all-you-can-eat Chinese-Vietnamese lunch/dinner buffet for 69/75FF (39/45FF for youngsters under 12). The weekday lunch *menu* costs just 40FF.

There's a lively *covered market* at Place du Marché, open daily from 7 am to 1 pm. In the old city, the *Prisunic* supermarket across from 55 Rue du Palais is open Monday to Saturday from 8.30 am to 8 pm. In July and August it's open on Sunday morning until 12.30 pm.

Getting There & Away

Bus Eurolines (☎ 05 46 50 53 57) reservations can be made at the Citram office at 30 Cours des Dames.

Train La Rochelle's train station (☎ 08 36 35 35 39) is at the southern end of Ave du Général de Gaulle. The information office is open Monday to Saturday from 9 am to 7 pm. From Paris you can take a TGV from Gare Montparnasse to La Rochelle (305 to 365FF;

three hours) or a non-TGV from Gare d'Austerlitz (256FF; five hours), which usually requires a change at Poitiers. Other destinations served by direct trains include: Bordeaux (131FF; two hours); Nantes (126FF; two hours); and Toulouse (246FF; 4½ hours).

Getting Around

Bus The innovative local transport system, Autoplus (☎ 05 46 34 02 22), has its main terminus and information kiosk (open Monday to Saturday from 6.45 am to 7.30 pm) at Place de Verdun. Most lines run until sometime between 7.15 and 8 pm. A single ride ticket, valid for 45 minutes after it's timestamped, costs 8FF; a seven ride ticket is 39.20FF. A bus pass valid for 24 hours after it's time-stamped costs 24FF; a three-day pass is 58FF.

Electric Car Bright yellow electric cars and scooters are available for rent from the Autoplus bus company at Place de Verdun. The cars are good for 50km and cost 60/100FF per half-day/day; scooters need to be recharged after 35km and cost 40/70FF. Both require a 2500FF cash or credit card deposit.

Bicycle The Autoplus bus company runs an unusual bicycle rental service called Les Vélos Autoplus (☎ 05 46 34 02 22); bikes are available year round at Place de Verdun, and from May to September opposite 11 Quai Valin. An adult's or child's bike (lock included) is free for the first two hours; after that the charge is 6FF per hour (there's a 60FF charge for keeping the bike overnight). The Place de Verdun outlet is open daily from 7.30 am (1 pm on Sunday) to 7 pm; the hours at Quai Valin are 9 am to 12.30 pm and 1.30 to 7 pm (no midday closure in July and August).

Boat Autoplus' Bus de Mer links the Vieux Port with the beach at Les Minimes. From April to September boats leave from the pier just north of Tour de la Chaîne every hour from 9 or 10 am to 7 pm (10 or 11FF one way). In July and August departures are increased to two per hour until 11.30 pm. In winter the Bus de Mer runs only at weekends.

BORDEAUX

Bordeaux (population 700,000) is known for its neoclassical architecture, wide avenues, colossal statues and well tended public squares and parks. The city's ethnic diversity (there are three universities here with 60,000 students, many from developing countries), excellent museums and untouristy atmosphere make it much more than just a convenient stop between Paris and Spain.

Bordeaux was founded by the Romans in the 3rd century BC. From 1154 to 1453, it prospered under the rule of the English, whose fondness for the region's red wines (known as claret across the Channel) gave impetus to the local wine industry. The marketing and export of Bordeaux wine remains the single most important economic activity.

Orientation

Cours de la Marne stretches from the train station to Place de la Victoire, which is linked to Place de la Comédie by the pedestrians-only Rue Sainte Catherine. The city centre lies between Place Gambetta and the Garonne River. Cours de l'Intendance is the city's main shopping street. Rue de la Porte Dijeaux is also a pedestrian mall.

Information

Tourist Office The very efficient main tourist office (☎ 05 56 00 66 00; fax 05 56 00 66 01; otb@bordeaux-tourisme.com; www.bordeaux-tourisme.com), 12 Cours du 30 Juillet, is open Monday to Saturday from 9 am to 7 pm and on Sunday from 9.45 am to 4.30 pm. From May to September, it's open until 8 pm (7 pm on Sunday). The free city map (with English text) suggests a walking tour itinerary. Hotel reservations in the Bordeaux area are free.

The tourist office annexe at the train station is open Monday to Saturday from 9 am to 6 pm. From May to September, it's open daily until 7 pm. For information on the Gironde region, visit the Maison du Tourisme de la Gironde (☎ 05 56 52 61 40; fax 05 56 81 09 99) at 21 Cours de l'Intendance.

Money & Post The Banque de France is around the corner from the tourist office at 13 Rue Esprit des Lois; it's open weekdays from

FRANCE

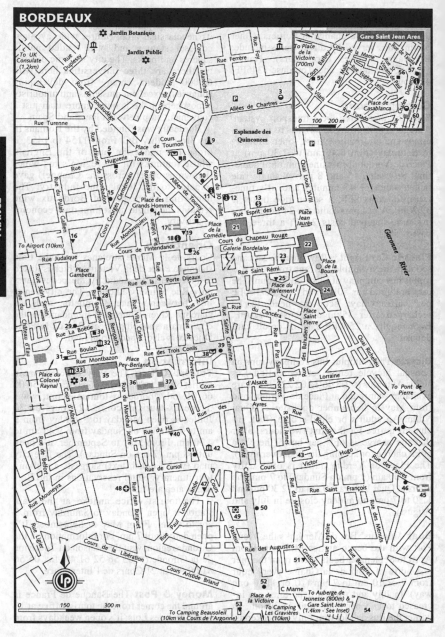

BORDEAUX

Jardin Botanique

Jardin Public

Gare Saint Jean Area

To UK
Consulate
(1.2km)

Rue Duplessy

Rue de Fondaudège

Rue Turenne

Rue Lafaure de Monbadon

Rue du Palais Gallien

To Airport (10km)

Rue Judaïque

Place Gambetta

Rue Saint Sernin

Rue du Château d'Eau

Rue de Belfort

Rue Mouneyra

Rue Ligier

Cours du Maréchal Foch

Cours de Verdun

Rue Ferrère

Rue Foy

Place de Tourny

Cours de Tournon

Huguerie

Rue JJ Rousseau

Allées de Tourny

Rue Georges Clemenceau

Place des Grands Hommes

Rue Montesquieu

Rue Vauban

Cours de l'Intendance

Rue de la Porte Dijeaux

Rue de Grassi

Rue Vital Carles

Allées de Chartres

Esplanade des Quinconces

Cours du 30 Juillet

Rue Esprit des Lois

Place de la Comédie

Cours du Chapeau Rouge

Galerie Bordelaise

Place Jean Jaurès

Quai Louis XVIII

Garonne River

Rue Saint Rémi

Place de la Bourse

Place du Parlement

Place Saint Pierre

Rue Margaux

Rue Sainte Catherine

Rue du Cancéra

Rue du Pas Saint Georges

Rue des Bahutiers

Quai Richelieu

Rue Bouffard

Rue La Boëtie

Rue Boulan

Rue Montbazon

Place Pey-Berland

Rue des Trois Conils

Cheverus

et
d'Alsace
Lorraine

To Pont de Pierre

Place du Colonel Raynal

Cours d'Albret

Rue du Maréchal Joffre

Cours

Ayres

Rue Saint James

Bouquière

Rue Hugo

Rue des Faures

Rue du Hâ

Rue Sainte

Rue Sainte Catherine

Rue Saint François

Rue des Menuts

Rue de Cursol

Rue Paul Louis Lande

Cours Victor

Rue du Mirail

Rue Leyteire

Rue Bergeret

Rue Jean Burguet

Cours Pasteur

Rue des Augustins

R Cravilot

To Auberge de Jeunesse (800m) &
Gare Saint Jean
(1.4km - See Inset)

Cours de la Libération

Cours Aristide Briand

Place de la Victoire

C Marne

To Camping Beausoleil
(10km via Cours de l'Argonne)

To Camping
Les Gravières
(10km)

To Place de la Victoire (700m)

Cours Barbey

Cours de la Marne

Rue de Tauzia

Rue St Vincent de Paul

Rue Charles Domercq

Cours Mabec

Rue Eugène Leroy

Rue Vilaris

Place de Casablanca

Rue Furado

0   100   200 m

0   150   300 m

BORDEAUX

PLACES TO STAY		3	Bus Station	34	Jardin de la Mairie
6	Hôtel Touring & Hôtel Studio	4	Launderette	35	Hôtel de Ville
8	Hôtel de Sèze & Hôtel Royal	7	Post Office Branch	36	Cathédrale Saint André
	Médoc	9	Monument des Girondins	37	Tour Pey-Berland
20	Hôtel Blayais	10	Bordeaux Magnum (Wine	38	Post Office Branch
28	Hôtel Bristol		Shop)	39	Place Saint Projet
30	Hôtel La Boètie	11	Maison du Vin de Bordeaux	41	Cyberstation
31	Hôtel Boulan	12	Tourist Office & Vinothèque	42	Musée d'Aquitaine
55	Auberge de Jeunesse		de Bordeaux (Wine Shop)	43	Porte de la Grosse Cloche
56	Hôtel Les Deux Mondes	13	Banque de France	44	Porte des Salinières
		14	Marché des Grands Hommes	45	Église Saint Michel
PLACES TO EAT			(Food Market)	46	Tour Saint Michel
5	Restaurant Baud et Millet	15	Launderette	48	Hôpital Saint André
16	Restaurant Agadir	17	Église Notre Dame	49	Synagogue
19	La Chanterelle	18	Maison du Tourisme de la	50	Champion Supermarket
23	Chinese Restaurants		Gironde	52	Porte d'Aquitaine
25	Chez Édouard	21	Grand Théâtre	54	Marché des Capucins
40	Ethnic Restaurants	22	Bourse du Commerce		(Wholesale Food Market)
47	La Fournaise	24	Hôtel de la Douane	57	Thomas Cook
51	La Dakaroise		(Customs)	58	SNCF Information Office
53	Cassolete Café	26	American Express	59	Bus Stops
		27	Porte Dijeaux	60	Gare Saint Jean (Train
OTHER		29	Launderette		Station)
1	Musée d'Histoire Naturelle	32	Musée des Arts Décoratifs		
2	Musée d'Art Contemporain	33	Musée des Beaux-Arts		

9 am to noon and 1 to 3.30 pm. American Express (☎ 05 56 00 63 33), 14 Cours de l'Intendance, is open Monday to Friday from 8.45 am to noon and 1.30 to 6 pm. The Thomas Cook bureau in the train station is open until 5.30 pm (6.30 pm in the summer; closed on Sunday from November to April).

The branch post office at Place Saint Projet (on Rue Sainte Catherine) is open until 6.30 pm (noon on Saturday). The post office at 29 Allées de Tourny is open until 6 pm (noon on Saturday), with a break from 12.30 pm to 2 pm.

Cybercafés Cyberstation (☎ 05 56 01 15 15; info@cyberstation.fr), 23 Cour Pasteur (across the street from the Musée d'Aquitaine), is open from 11 am to 2 am (from 2 pm to midnight on Sunday).

Laundry The laundrette at 5 Rue de Fondaudège, near Place de Tourny, is open seven days a week from 7 am to 8.30 pm. Two blocks south-west, the laundrette at 3 Rue Lafaurie de Monbadon is open from 7 am to 9 pm.

Things to See

The most prominent feature of the **Esplanade des Quinconces**, laid out in 1820, is a towering fountain-monument to the Girondins, a group of moderate, bourgeois legislative deputies during the French Revolution, 22 of whom were executed in 1793 for alleged counter-revolutionary activities. The **Jardin Public**, an 18th-century 'English park', is along Cours de Verdun. It includes Bordeaux's **botanical garden** and **Musée d'Histoire Naturelle** (Natural History Museum).

The much-praised, neoclassical **Grand Théâtre** at Place de la Comédie was built in the 1770s. Lovely **Place de la Bourse**, flanked by the old Hôtel de la Douane (customs house) and the Bourse du Commerce (stock exchange), was built between 1731 and 1755. The riverside area nearby is run-down and fairly lifeless.

Porte Dijeaux, which dates from 1748 and is one of the few city gates still standing, leads to **Place Gambetta**, a beautiful garden by a pond. Today it is an island of calm in the midst of the urban hustle and bustle, but during the Reign of Terror a guillotine was used here to sever the heads of 300 people.

Cathédrale Saint André in the Place Pey-Berland was where the future King Louis VII married Eleanor of Aquitaine in 1137. The cathedral's 15th-century belfry, **Tour Pey-Berland**, stands behind the choir, whose chapels are nestled among the flying buttresses. The cathedral is open from 7.30 to 11.30 am (12.30 pm on Sunday) and 2 to 6 or 6.30 pm (closed on Sunday afternoon except perhaps in summer).

Bordeaux's Moorish **synagogue** (☎ 05 56 91 79 39), inaugurated in 1882, is just west of Rue Sainte Catherine on Rue du Grand Rabbin Joseph Cohen. During WWII, the interior was ripped apart by the Nazis, who turned the complex into a prison. Visits are possible Monday to Thursday from 5 to 6 or 6.30 pm – ring the bell marked *gardien* at 213 Rue Sainte Catherine.

Museums The outstanding **Musée d'Aquitaine** (☎ 05 56 01 51 00), 20 Cours Pasteur, illustrates the history and ethnography of the Bordeaux area from prehistory to the 19th century by means of exceptionally well designed exhibits.

At 20 Cours d'Albert, the **Musée des Beaux-Arts** (☎ 05 56 10 16 93) occupies two wings of the 18th-century Hôtel de Ville, which frame an attractive public garden called Jardin de la Mairie. The museum houses a large collection of paintings, including 17th-century Flemish, Dutch and Italian works and a major painting by Delacroix.

At 39 Rue Bouffard, the **Musée des Arts Décoratifs** (☎ 05 56 00 72 50) specialises in porcelain, silverware, glassware, furniture and so on. The excellent **Musée d'Art Contemporain** (☎ 05 56 44 16 35) at 7 Rue Ferrère hosts changing exhibits by contemporary artists on three floors. The museum is housed in the Entrepôts Lainé, built in 1824 as a warehouse for the exotic products of France's colonies: coffee, cocoa, peanuts, vanilla etc.

Bordeaux's museums are open from 11 am (2 pm on Sunday for the Arts Décoratifs) to 6 pm daily, except Monday and holidays (daily except Tuesday and holidays for the Beaux-Arts and Arts Décoratifs). On Wednesday, the Art Contemporain stays open until 8 pm. Admission to each museum costs 20FF (10FF for seniors; free for students and, on the first Sunday of each month, for everyone).

Places to Stay

Camping *Camping Beausoleil* (☎ 05 56 89 17 66) is open all year, and charges 60FF for two people and tent (85FF with a car). It's about 10km south-west of the city centre at 371 Cours du Général de Gaulle (route N10) in Gradignan. To get there, take bus G from Place de la Victoire to Gradignan Beausoleil and get off at the terminus.

Camping Les Gravières (☎ 05 56 87 00 36), also open all year, charges 22FF for a tent plus 19FF per person; it's an extra 30FF for a car. It's 10km south-east of central Bordeaux at Place de Courréjean in Villenave d'Ornon. Take bus B from Place de la Victoire to Courréjean and get off at the terminus.

Hostels The charmless *Auberge de Jeunesse* (☎ 05 56 91 59 51; fax 05 56 94 02 98), 22 Cours Barbey, is 650m west of the train station. A bed in a utilitarian, eight-bed room is only 62FF (72FF if you don't have an HI card). The 1st floor (women's section) and the 2nd floor (men's section) are reached by separate staircases. There's an 11 pm curfew, but have a word with the manager in advance if you'll be staying out late. The reception is open daily from 8 to 10 am and 4 to 11 pm. The hostel will be closed for renovations during part of 1999.

Hotels Hotels in the area around the train station are convenient for rail passengers, but the neighbourhood is rather seedy. In terms of both price and value, you're much better off staying around the tourist office, Place de Tourny or Place Gambetta.

Tourist Office Area The old-fashioned *Hôtel Blayais* (☎ 05 56 48 17 87; fax 05 56 52 47 57), east of the baroque Église Notre Dame at 17 Rue Mautrec, has fairly large singles/doubles with shower and toilet for 190/200FF.

Place de Tourny The best inexpensive choice here is the two-star *Hôtel Touring* (☎ 05 56 81 56 73; fax 05 56 81 24 55), 16

Rue Huguerie, which has gigantic, spotless singles/doubles for 120/140FF (200/220FF with shower and toilet). The *Hôtel Studio* (☎ 05 56 48 00 14; fax 05 56 81 25 71; studio@hotel-bordeaux.com; www.hotel-bordeaux.com) nearby at No 26 is the headquarters of Bordeaux's cheap hotel empire – the family owns three other inexpensive places on the same street, all of them offering small but serviceable singles doubles with flimsy showers, toilets, mini-fridges and cable TV for 98/120FF; slightly larger rooms are 135FF. Rooms for three to five people go for 180 to 250FF.

The best choice in a higher price range in this area is the three-star, 45 room *Hôtel Royal Médoc* (☎ 05 56 81 72 42; fax 05 56 51 74 98) at 3 Rue de Sèze. It offers comfortable, sound-proofed singles/doubles/triples for 220/250/310FF. Next door at No 7, the *Hôtel de Sèze* (☎ 05 56 52 65 54; fax 05 56 44 31 83) has similar prices.

Place Gambetta There are several excellent deals in the area between Place Gambetta and the Musée des Beaux-Arts. The quiet *Hôtel Boulan* (☎/fax 05 56 52 23 62), 28 Rue Boulan, has pleasant singles/doubles with high ceilings for 100/110FF (120/140FF with shower). Hall showers cost 10FF.

Hôtel La Boëtie (☎ 05 56 81 76 68; fax 05 56 51 24 06; bristol@hotel-bordeaux.com), 4 Rue La Boëtie, features modern singles/doubles/quads with toilet and shower from 120/135/200FF.

The excellent *Hôtel Bristol* (☎ 05 56 81 85 01; fax 05 56 51 24 06; bristol@hotel-bordeaux.com), 2 Rue Bouffard, has cheerful singles/doubles with 4m-high ceilings, a bathroom, toilet and TV from 210/290FF.

Train Station Area The choice around here is limited in both quality and quantity. The 14 room *Hôtel Les Deux Mondes* (☎ 05 56 91 63 09; fax 05 56 92 12 11), 10 Rue Saint Vincent de Paul, has unexciting singles/doubles/triples with shower and toilet for 120/165/210FF.

Places to Eat

The inexpensive cafés and restaurants around Place de la Victoire, popular with students, include the *Cassolette Café* (☎ 05 56 92 94 96) at No 20 which serves family-style French food in a unique way – each small/large *cassolette* (terra cotta plate) that you order costs 11/33FF. It's open from noon to 2.30 pm and 6 to 11.30 pm (closed Sunday).

The very popular *Chez Édouard* (☎ 05 56 81 48 87), 16 Place du Parlement, purveys French bistro-style meat and fish dishes. *Menus* cost 57.50FF (weekday lunches), 79.50, 125 and 139.50FF. It's open daily from noon to 2.15 pm and 7.15 to 11.15 pm. *Restaurant Baud et Millet* (☎ 05 56 79 00 77), 19 Rue Huguerie, serves cheese-based cuisine (most dishes are vegetarian), including all-you-can-eat meals of raclette (110FF) and fondue Savoyarde (95FF); the *menus* cost 140 to 170FF. The basement buffet has 100 to 150 kinds of cheese. This place is open Monday to Saturday from 11 am to 11 pm.

Bordeaux is a multicultural city and its restaurants reflect that. Around Place de La Victoire, *La Dakaroise* (☎ 05 56 92 77 32), 9 Rue Gratiolet, specialises in West African dishes like yassa poisson (fish cooked with lime) and maffé (beef in a peanut sauce); the fixed *menu* is 55FF. It's open Tuesday to Saturday from 7.30 pm to 2 am. *La Fournaise* (☎ 05 56 91 04 71), 23 Rue de Lalande, serves the cuisine of Réunion, which has strong Indian, Chinese, Basque and Breton elements. The *menus* cost 55FF (weekday lunches only), 75, 95 and 130FF (closed Sunday and Monday).

The richly ornamented *Restaurant Agadir* (☎ 05 56 52 28 04), 14 Rue du Palais Gallien, has Moroccan couscous and tajines for 60 to 80FF; *menus* are 60FF (lunch), 100 and 150FF. It's open daily from 11.30 am to 2.30 pm and 6.30 to 11.30 pm (12.30 am on Friday and Saturday nights). Near the Musée d'Aquitaine, there are several ethnic restaurants (Vietnamese, Indian, Lebanese) on Rue du Hâ. There are half a dozen Chinese restaurants along Rue Saint Rémi, a block north of Place du Parlement.

If price is no object, eat at *La Chanterelle* (☎ 05 56 81 75 43), one of the best restaurants in Bordeaux with *menus* costing 90 to 150FF (65 and 70FF at lunch). It's at 3 Rue Martignac (heading east, Rue Martignac is left off Cours de l'Intendance, just after Place de la Comédie) and is closed on Wednesday night and Sunday.

The modern, mirrored *Marché des Grands Hommes* at Place des Grands Hommes, 100m north of Cours de l'Intendance, has stalls in the basement selling fruit, vegetables, cheese, bread, pastry and sandwiches. It's open Monday to Saturday from 7 am to 7.30 pm. The *Champion* supermarket at 190 Rue Sainte Catherine is open from 8.30 am to 8 pm daily, except Sunday.

Things to Buy

Bordeaux wine in all price ranges is on sale at several speciality shops near the main tourist office, including Vinothèque de Bordeaux at 8 Cours du 30 Juillet and Bordeaux Magnum at 3 Rue Gobineau.

Getting There & Away

Bus Buses to places all over the Gironde and nearby departments leave from the bus station on Allée de Chartres, north-east of Place de Tourny. The information office (☎ 05 56 43 68 43) is open weekdays from 6 to 8.30 am and 1 to 8.30 pm; on Saturday from 9 am to 12.30 pm and 5 to 8.30 pm; and on Sunday from 8.30 to 10.30 am and 5 to 8.30 pm. There's a year-round service to the medieval vineyard town of Saint Émilion. See the Bordeaux Vineyard Visits section for fares and frequencies.

Train Bordeaux's train station, Gare Saint Jean (☎ 08 36 35 35 39), is about 3km south-east of the city centre at the end of Cours de la Marne. It is one of France's major rail transit points. The station's information office is open Monday to Saturday from 9 am to 7 pm. If you take the TGV Atlantique, Bordeaux is only about three hours from Paris' Gare Montparnasse (337 to 387FF). Non-TGV trains use the Gare d'Austerlitz.

Getting Around

Bus Single tickets on Bordeaux's urban bus network, CGFTE (☎ 05 57 57 88 88), cost 7.50FF and are *not* valid for transfers. Ten-ticket carnets (54FF), available at tabacs, come with two *talons* (coupons) bearing the same serial number as the tickets – you may be asked to show one of the coupons when transferring. You can transfer up to three times after your initial ride but don't forget to time-stamp your ticket each time you board.

The last time-stamping must be done less than 60 minutes after the first. Carte Bordeaux Découverte allows unlimited bus travel for one day (23.50FF) to six days (77FF).

Bus information bureaus on Place Gambetta and at the southern end of the train station have user-friendly route maps. Bus Nos 7 and 8 link the train station with the city centre.

Taxi To order a taxi in central Bordeaux, call ☎ 05 56 91 47 05.

BORDEAUX VINEYARD VISITS

The Bordeaux wine-producing region is subdivided into 57 production areas called *appellations*, whose climate and soil impart distinctive characteristics to the wines produced there. The majority of the region's diverse wines (reds, rosés, sweet and dry whites, sparkling wines) have earned the right to include the abbreviation AOC on their labels, indicating that the contents have been grown, fermented and aged according to strict regulations. In 1997, the region produced 855 million bottles of wine.

Bordeaux has over 5000 *châteaux* (also known as *domaines*, *crus* and *clos*) – not castles, but properties where grapes are grown, fermented and matured into wine. Some of their names may be familiar: Graves, Sauternes, Pommarol, Saint Émilion. The smaller chateaux often accept walk-in visitors year round, except in August, but many of the larger and better known ones (eg Château Mouton-Rothschild) accept visitors only by appointment. Each vineyard has different rules about tasting – at some it's free, others make you pay, and others do not serve wine at all. As you drive around, look for signs that say *dégustation* (wine tasting), *en vente directe* (direct sales) or *vin à emporter* (wine to take away/to go).

Information

Opposite Bordeaux's main tourist office, the Maison du Vin de Bordeaux (☎/fax 05 56 00 22 66; civb@vins-bordeaux.fr; www.vins-bordeaux.fr), has lots of information on visiting vineyards. First decide which growing area you would like to visit (use the maison's colour-coded map of *appellations*); the staff will give you the address of the local *maison du vin* (a sort of tourist office for wine-growing areas), which has details on which chateaux are open and when.

The Maison du Vin de Bordeaux is open weekdays from 8.30 am to 5.30 or 6 pm. From mid-June to mid-October it's also open on Saturday from 9 am to 4 pm. There is free wine tasting here at 11 am and (sometimes) at 3 pm in summer.

Organised Tours

The Bordeaux tourist office runs half-day bus tours in French and English to local chateaux on Wednesday and Saturday (daily from May to October) at 1.15 pm. The cost is 160FF (140FF for students and seniors over 65).

Saint Émilion

One easily accessible wine-producing area to visit on your own is Saint Émilion, a medieval gem of a village 39km east of Bordeaux and famous for its full-bodied, deeply coloured reds. The local tourist office (☎ 05 57 55 28 28) at Place des Créneaux is open daily. From Bordeaux, Saint Émilion is accessible by train, with departures at 7.10 am (9.10 am on Sunday) and 1.30 pm, and last train back at 6.30 pm (43FF one way). CITRAM buses go there and back about five times a day (there may be a transfer at Libourne). If you're driving take route D89 east to D670.

Virtually every shop in Saint Émilion sells wine (which you can also sample) but stick with the professionals. Maison du Vin (☎ 05 57 55 50 55) around the corner from the tourist office on Place Pierre Meyrat has an enormous selection and one-hour introductory wine-tasting courses (100FF) in summer.

If you get hungry in Saint Émilion, *L'Envers du Décor* (☎ 05 57 74 48 31) next to the tourist office on Rue Clocher has excellent plats du jour for around 50FF and vintage wine by the glass from 15 to 40FF. *Restaurant Dominique* (☎ 05 57 24 71 00) on Rue de la Petite Fontaine, which serves a variety of regional specialities, has *menus* for 68, 89 and 130FF (38FF for youngsters). It's open from noon to 2.30 pm and 7 to 10 pm (closed Monday except from June to September); it's

closed over December and January. Macaroons – soft cookies made from almond flour, egg whites and sugar – are a speciality of Saint Émilion. Fabrique de Macarons Matthieu Mouliérac on Tertre de la Tente has the best.

BAYONNE

Bayonne (population 40,000) is the most important city in the French part of the Basque Country (Euskadi in Basque, Pays Basque in French), a region straddling the French-Spanish border with its own unique language, culture, history and identity. Unlike the upmarket beach resort of Biarritz a short bus ride away, Bayonne retains much of its Basqueness: the riverside buildings with their green, red and white shutters are typical of the region and you'll hear almost as much Euskara (Basque language) as French. Most of the graffiti you'll see around town – like *Amnistia!* in bold letters on the massive Château Neuf – is the work of nationalist groups seeking an independent Basque state.

Bayonne's most important festival is the annual Fête de Bayonne, which begins on the first Wednesday in August. The festival includes a 'running of the bulls' like the one in Pamplona except that here they have cows rather than bulls and usually it's the people – dressed in white with red scarves around their necks – who chase the cows rather than the other way around. The festival also includes Basque music, bullfighting, a float parade and rugby matches (a favourite sport in south-west France).

Orientation

The Adour and Nive rivers split Bayonne into three parts: Saint Esprit, the area north of the Adour, where the train station is located; Grand Bayonne, the oldest part of the city, on the west bank of the Nive; and the very Basque Petit Bayonne to the east. The suburban area of Anglet is sandwiched between Bayonne and the beach resort of Biarritz, 8km to the west.

Information

Tourist Office The tourist office (☎ 05 59 46 01 46; fax 05 59 59 37 55) is on Place des Basques just north of Grand Bayonne. It's

BAYONNE

PLACES TO STAY
2 Hôtel Paris-Madrid
5 Hôtel Monte Carlo
6 Hôtel Adour
7 Hôtel Frantour Loustau
11 Hôtel Côte Basque
23 Hôtel des Arceaux
35 Hôtel des Basques
41 Hôtel des Basses Pyrénées

PLACES TO EAT
8 Bistrot Saint Cluque
9 Restaurant Koskera
31 Auberge du Cheval Blanc
36 Restaurant Euskalduna
39 Restaurant Dacquois
42 Crêperie de la Rade de Brest

OTHER
1 Train Station
3 Bus Station
4 Taxi Rank
10 STAB Bus Stops
12 Distillerie de la Côte Basque
13 Launderette
14 Post Office
15 STAB Bus Information Office
16 Hôtel de Ville
17 Tourist Office
18 Post Office
19 ATCRB Bus Stops
20 Banque de France
21 War Memorial
22 Château Vieux
(Closed Military Area)
24 Cazenave Chocolate Shop
25 Police Station
26 Musée Bonnat
27 Monoprix Supermarket
28 Cathédrale Sainte Marie
29 Cloître
30 Les Halles (Food Market)
32 Église Saint André
33 Porte de Mousserolles
34 Château Neuf
(Closed Military Area)
37 Zabal Elkar Bookshop
38 Alice Springs Boutique
40 Porte d'Espagne
43 Arsenal

To Main Post Office (1km)
& Biarritz (8km)

Avenue des Allées Marines

Jardin
Public

Avenue Léon Bonnat

To Arènes
(bullfights)
(400m)

Avenue du Maréchal Foch

Place des Basques

Cité
Administrative

Rue Jules Labat

Rue du 49ème Régiment d'Infanterie

Rue Lormand

Rue Albert 1er

Rue Thiers

Allées Paulmy

Avenue du 11 Novembre

Grand
Bayonne

Rue Port Neuf

Rue
Orbe

Rue

Château
22

Rue des Gouverneurs

Place
Monseigneur
Vansteenberghe

Rue de la Monnaie

Place
Louis
Pasteur

Rue de la
Salie

Avenue des

Rue du Rempart Lachepaillet

Rue des Faures

Douer

Rue Montaut

Rue de Luc

28

Place
Montaut

Rue d'Espagne

Rue
Poissonnerie

Rue du Maréchal Lautrec

P

To Anglet (4km), Biarritz (8km),
Auberge de Jeunesse d'Anglet (10km)
& Camping de Parme (10km)

Ave du Maréchal Soult

Avenue

de Pampelune

Place
des
Victoires

41

40

Rue

Tour de

Sault

Rue Gosse

38

39

42

43

Rue des Basques

Quai Amiral Jauréguiberry

Pont
du Génie

Ave R des Martres

To Centre Hospitalier (600m)

FRANCE

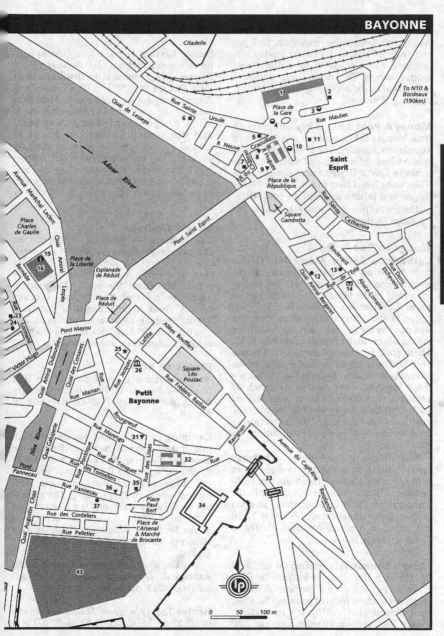

BAYONNE

Citadelle

To N10 &
Bordeaux
(190km)

Rue Sainte

Rue Sainte

Quai de Lesseps

Place de
la Gare

1

2

3

6

Ursule

Rue Maubec

11

R. Neuve

Graouillats

5

R. Hugues

8

10

Saint
Esprit

7

R. Au Château

9

Place de la
République

Rue Sainte Catherine

Adour River

Square
Gambetta

Pont Saint Esprit

Boulevard

Avenue Maréchal Leclerc

Place
Charles
de Gaulle

Quai Amiral Lespès

Place de
la Liberté

13

Rue de l'Este

Rue Denis Etcheverry

15

16

12

Quai Amiral Bergeret

Alsace-Lorraine

Esplanade
de Réduit

14

Bernède

Rue Lormand

Place de
Réduit

23

24

Rue

Victor Hugo

Pont Mayou

Quai Amiral Dubourdieu

Allées Boufflers

Lafitte

25

Quai des Corsaires

Rue Jacques

26

Square
Léo
Pouzac

Rue Frédéric Bastiat

Petit
Bayonne

Rue Marsan

Nive River

Quai Galuperie

Bourgneuf

Rue Marengo

31

Avenue du Capitaine

Ravignan

Rue

Pont
Pannecau

Rue Pontrique

Rue du Trinquet

Rue des Lisses

32

Resplandy

Rue des Tonneliers

36

35

33

Rue Pannecau

37

Place
Paul Bert

34

Quai Augustin Chao

Rue des Cordeliers

Place de
l'Arsenal &
Marché
de Brocante

Rue Pelletier

43

0   50   100 m

open weekdays from 9 am to 6.30 pm and on Saturday from 10 am to 6 pm. In July and August, it's open daily from 9 am to 7 pm and from 10 am to 1 pm on Sunday. Its brochure *Fêtes* is useful for cultural and sporting events. The freebie *Guide Loisirs* is indispensable for organising hiking, biking, climbing, diving etc.

Money & Post Banks in Bayonne are open from Monday to Friday; those in Anglet open Tuesday to Saturday. The Banque de France is at 18 Rue Albert 1er, and there are more banks in Grand Bayonne near the Hôtel de Ville, along Rue Thiers and on Rue du 49ème Régiment d'Infanterie east of the post office.

The post office at 11 Rue Jules Labat has exchange facilities.

Things to See & Do

Cathédrale Sainte Marie This Gothic cathedral is on Rue de la Monnaie at the southern end of the Rue du Port Neuf pedestrian mall in the heart of the oldest part of town. Construction of the cathedral was begun in the 13th century, when Bayonne was ruled by the English, and completed after the area came under French control in 1451. These political changes are reflected in the ornamentation on the vaulted ceiling of the nave, which includes both the English arms – three leopards – and that most French of emblems, the *fleur de lis*. Some of the stained glass dates from the Renaissance but many of the statues that once graced the church's very crumbly exterior were smashed during the Revolution.

Sainte Marie is open Monday to Saturday from 10 am to noon and 3.30 to 6 pm; from 3 to 6 pm on Sunday. The beautiful 13th-century **cloître** (cloister), south of the cathedral on Place Louis Pasteur, is open daily, except Saturday, from 9.30 am to 12.30 pm and 2 to 5 pm (6 pm from Easter to October). Entry is free.

Musée Bonnat This museum (☎ 05 59 59 08 52) at 5 Rue Jacques Laffitte in Petit Bayonne has a diverse collection of works, including a whole room of paintings by Peter Paul Rubens (1577-1640). It's open daily, except Tuesday, from 10 am to noon and 2.30

to 6.30 pm (to 8.30 pm on Friday). The entry fee is 20FF (10FF for children and students).

Izarra Tasting Izarra, a local liqueur supposedly distilled from '100 flowers of the Pyrenees', is produced at the **Distillerie de la Côte Basque** (☎ 05 59 55 07 48) at 9 Quai Amiral Bergeret in Saint Esprit. Half-hour tours of the plant and the little museum – with a tasting at the end – take place on weekdays from April to October from 9 to 11.30 am and 2 to 4.30 pm (to 6 pm from mid-July to August and on Saturday as well). Admission for anyone over 18 years of age is 15FF – about the price of a small glass of the green or yellow-coloured firewater at any café or bar.

Sports Courses

The Auberge de Jeunesse d'Anglet (see Places to Stay) offers very popular one-week courses (*stages*) in surfing, body-boarding (*morey boogie*), scuba diving and horse riding throughout the year. The courses, which are in French (though the instructors usually speak a little English), last from Sunday evening to Saturday afternoon and cost between 2395 and 2800FF, including accommodation, meals and equipment.

Places to Stay

Accommodation is most difficult to find from mid-July to mid-August, especially during the five-day Fête de Bayonne in August.

Camping In southern Anglet, on the south side of the airport (Aérogare de Parme), the three-star *Camping de Parme* (☎ 05 59 23 03 00) on Route de l'Aviation is open all year. Charges are 22FF per adult and 35FF per tent site, including parking. The nearest bus stop (Parme-Aéroport) is a bit over 1km to the north-west – it's near the airport end of line No 6. The Biarritz-La Négresse train station is 1.5km south-west of the camping ground.

You can also pitch a tent in the yard of the *Auberge de Jeunesse d'Anglet* (see Hostel) for about 45FF per person.

Hostel The *Auberge de Jeunesse d'Anglet* (☎ 05 59 58 70 00; fax 05 59 58 70 07) is at

19 Route des Vignes in Anglet. It's open all year except mid-December to mid-January and charges 80 FF for a bed, including breakfast (71FF in winter). To get there from the Bayonne train station, take bus No 4 towards Biarritz and get off at the Auberge de Jeunesse stop. From the Biarritz-La Négresse train station, take bus No 2 (direction Bayonne) to the Hôtel de Ville stop where you change to bus No 4.

Hotels There are a number of hotels right around the train station in Saint Esprit. The *Hôtel Paris Madrid* (☎ 05 59 55 13 98; fax 05 59 55 07 22) is to the left (east) as you exit the station. The cheapest singles cost 90FF. Big, pleasant singles and doubles without/ with shower cost 120/145FF. Doubles with shower and toilet are 165FF. The *Hôtel Monte Carlo* (☎ 05 59 55 02 68), opposite the train station at 1 Rue Sainte Ursule, has singles/doubles from 90FF (150FF with shower). Hall showers are free.

The *Hôtel Adour* (☎ 05 59 55 11 31; fax 05 59 55 86 40), 13 Rue Sainte Ursule, has singles/doubles with shower from 195/ 240FF. The *Hôtel Côte Basque* (☎ 05 59 55 10 21; fax 05 59 55 39 85), opposite the station at 2 Rue Maubec, has large doubles with shower, toilet and TV for 295FF.

Saint Esprit's nicest hotel is the *Hôtel Frantour Loustau* (☎ 05 59 55 08 08; fax 05 59 55 69 36) facing the Adour River on Quai de Lesseps (the actual address is 1 Place de la République) in an 18th-century building. Doubles/triples with shower and toilet are 410/455FF (360/430FF in winter).

In the centre of Grand Bayonne, the *Hôtel des Arceaux* (☎ 05 59 59 15 53), 26 Rue du Port Neuf, has doubles with bath, toilet and TV from 230FF. Doubles/triples with washbasin start at 130/170FF. The two-star *Hôtel des Basses Pyrénées* (☎ 05 59 59 00 29; fax 05 59 59 42 02), close to the Porte d'Espagne on Place des Victoires, has doubles/triples/ quads with shower and toilet from 280/ 350/400FF. There are a few simple rooms with washbasin from 150 to 190FF.

The least expensive hotel in the colourful Petit Bayonne quarter is the *Hôtel des Basques* (☎ 05 59 59 08 02), which is next to 3 Rue des Lisses on Place Paul Bert. Large, pleasant singles/doubles start at 130FF (one

bed) and 210FF (two beds). Hall showers cost 10FF. The hotel is closed from mid-October to early November.

Places to Eat

You can sample Basque cuisine in Petit Bayonne at the *Restaurant Euskalduna* (☎ 05 59 59 28 02), near the Hôtel des Basques at 61 Rue Pannecau. It offers a Basque *menu* at 60FF and main dishes from 35 to 50FF. It's open Monday to Friday for lunch only. Across the river, *Restaurant Koskera* (☎ 05 59 55 20 79), south of the train station at 3 Rue Hugues, has inexpensive Basque plats du jour and *menus* at 70 and 95FF. It's open Monday to Saturday (and Sunday in the summer) from noon to 2 pm and 8 to 10.30 pm; from October to mid-June it opens for lunch only. Also in Saint Esprit is the *Bistrot Sainte Cluque* (☎ 05 59 55 82 43) at 9 Rue Hugues. Its speciality is paella (55FF) and there are *menus* from 55FF. It's open daily from 12 to 2 pm and from 7 to 11pm.

In Grand Bayonne, a good bet is the unpretentious *Restaurant Dacquois* (☎ 05 59 59 29 61), 48 Rue d'Espagne, open Monday to Saturday from 8 am to 8.30 pm for breakfast, lunch and dinner. Sandwiches cost from 12FF and the 65FF *menu* provides a choice of main dishes and hors d'œuvres. For a selection of crêpes, stop by the *Crêperie de la Rade de Brest* (☎ 05 59 59 13 62), 7 Rue des Basques. It's open Tuesday to Saturday from noon to 2 pm and 7 to 10 pm (11 pm on Friday and Saturday). From May to September it's also open on Monday.

If your budget can stand it, some of the most creative dishes in town can be had at the elegant French *Auberge du Cheval Blanc* (☎ 05 59 59 01 33), 68 Rue Bourgneuf, in Petit Bayonne. It boasts a Michelin star and is closed Sunday evening and Monday (open daily in July and August). *Menus* cost 118, 185 and 260FF.

The central market *Les Halles* is in a wonderful building on the west quay (Quai Amiral Jauréguiberry) of the Nive River and is open every morning, except Sunday. The *Monoprix* supermarket at 8 Rue Orbe is open Monday to Saturday from 8 or 8.30 am to 7 pm.

FRANCE

Spectator Sports

Bullfights *Corrida*, Spanish-style bullfighting in which the bull is killed, has its devotees all over the south of France, including Bayonne. Tournaments are held about half a dozen times each summer. Advance reservations are usually necessary – information is available at the tourist office.

Pelote Pelote Basque or pelota is the name given to several games native to the Basque Country which are played with a *chistera* (a curved leather and wicker racquet strapped to the wrist) and a *pelote* (a hard ball with a rubber centre). The best known variety of pelota in the Basque Country is cesta punta, the world's fastest ball game, played in a covered court with three walls. For information on matches, which take place in Bayonne, Biarritz, Saint Jean de Luz and elsewhere year-round, inquire at one of the area's tourist offices. See the Biarritz section for information on pelota lessons.

Things to Buy

Bayonne is famous throughout France for its ham and chocolate. Buy the former at Charcuterie Brouchican (✆ 05 59 59 27 18), 20 Quai Augustin Chao, in Petit Bayonne; the latter at the very traditional *chocolaterie* Cazenave (✆ 05 59 59 03 16) at 19 Rue Port Neuf.

Zabal Elkar (✆ 05 59 25 43 90) at 52 Rue Pannecau has a large selection of cassettes and CDs of Basque music. It also carries lots of books (a few in English) on Basque history and culture and hiking in the Basque Country. The shop is open from 9.15 am to 12.30 pm and 2.30 to 7.30 pm daily, except Monday morning and all day Sunday.

Homesick Aussies should check out Alice Springs (✆ 05 59 59 13 72), a *boutique australienne* at 25 Rue Poissonnerie open weekdays from 10 am to 7 pm.

Getting There & Away

Bus The tiny bus station (✆ 05 59 55 17 59) is in front of the train station at Place de la Gare. The information office is open weekdays from 9 am to 12.15 pm and 2 to 5.30 pm. RDTL serves destinations in Les Landes, the department to the north, including Dax, Léon and Vieux Boucau. To get to the beaches along the coast north of Bayonne such as Mimizan and Moliets, take the bus heading for Vieux Boucau (37FF; 1¼ hours).

Buses run by ATCRB (✆ 05 59 26 06 99 in Saint Jean de Luz) serve Saint Jean de Luz (20FF; 40 minutes), Hendaye (33.50FF), and San Sebastián in Spain (40.50FF). They leave from the bus stop at 9 Rue du 49ème Régiment d'Infanterie.

Train The train station (✆ 08 36 35 35 39) is in Saint Esprit at Place de la Gare. The information office is open Monday to Saturday from 9 am to noon and 2 to 6.30 pm (daily from 9 am to 7.30 pm in July and August). The TGV to/from Paris' Gare Montparnasse takes five hours (413FF). Other Paris-bound trains take about eight hours and stop at Gare d'Austerlitz (371FF). There are also trains to Bordeaux (142FF; 1½ hours), Lourdes (104FF; 1¾ hours), Pau (81FF; 1¼ hours), Saint Jean de Luz (26FF; 20 minutes) and Saint Jean Pied de Port (46FF; one hour).

Getting Around

Bus The bus network serving the BAB metropolitan area – Bayonne, Anglet and Biarritz – is called STAB. Single tickets cost 7.50FF (62FF for a carnet of 10) and remain valid for an hour after they are time-stamped.

In Grand Bayonne, STAB has an information office (✆ 05 59 59 04 61) in the Hôtel de Ville. It's open Monday to Friday from 8 am to noon and 1.30 to 6 pm. Bus No 1 links Bayonne's train station with the centre of Biarritz (Hôtel de Ville stop) via Anglet. Bus No 2 starts at Bayonne's train station and passes through the centre of Biarritz before continuing to the Biarritz-La Négresse train station. Bus No 4 links the train station in Bayonne and the centre of Biarritz via the Anglet coast and its beaches. No 9 is a scenic – if slow – way to get from Bayonne to Biarritz.

Taxi To order a taxi, call ✆ 05 59 59 48 48. There's a large rank in front of the train station.

BIARRITZ

The classy coastal town of Biarritz (population 30,000 – but four times that in summer),

8km west of Bayonne, got its start as a resort in the mid-19th century when Emperor Napoleon III and his Spanish-born wife, Eugénie, began coming here. In later decades, Biarritz became popular with wealthy Britons and was visited by Queen Victoria and King Edward VII, both of whom have streets named in their honour. These days, Biarritz is known for its fine beaches and some of the best surfing in Europe.

Biarritz can be a real budget-buster; consider making it a day trip from Bayonne.

Information

Tourist Office The tourist office (☎ 05 59 22 37 10; fax 05 59 24 97 80) is one block east of Ave Édouard VII at 1 Square d'Ixelles. It's open daily from 9 am to 6.45 pm. From June to September it's open from 8 am to 8 pm when there's also an annexe at the train station open from 8.30 am to 7.30 pm.

Money & Post There are lots of commercial banks around Place Clemenceau. The Bureau de Change Atollíssimo (☎ 05 59 22 27 27) at 27 Place Clemenceau offers some of the best rates in town and is open from 9 am to 6.30 pm from Monday to Saturday (daily from 9 am to 8 pm from mid-June to mid-September).

The main post office is between Place Clemenceau and Ave Jaulerry on Rue de la Poste.

Things to See & Do

The **Grande Plage**, lined in season with striped bathing tents, stretches from the Casino Bellevue to the grand old Hôtel du Palais, built in the mid-19th century as a villa for Napoleon III and Empress Eugénie. North of the Hôtel du Palais is **Plage Miramar**, bounded on the north by **Pointe Saint Martin** and the **Phare de Biarritz** (lighthouse), erected in 1834. There are 4km of beaches north of Pointe Saint Martin in Anglet.

Heading southward from the Grande Plage, you can walk along the coast past the old fishing port and around the mauve cliffs of **Rocher de la Vierge**, a stone island topped with a white statue of the Virgin Mary and reached by a footbridge. There's a small beach just south of Rocher de la Vierge at **Port Vieux**. The long **Plage de la Côte des Basques** begins a few hundred metres farther down the coast.

The **Musée de la Mer** (☎ 05 59 24 02 59), Biarritz's sea museum, is on the esplanade near the Rocher de la Vierge footbridge. It has a 24-tank aquarium, exhibits on commercial fishing, and seal and shark pools. The museum is open daily from 9.30 am to 12.30 pm and 2 to 6 pm. From mid-July to August the museum stays open till midnight. Entry is 45FF (30FF for students).

Introductory one/two hour **pelota lessons** are available for 100/180FF per person (including equipment) for a minimum of four people. For information, contact Fronton Couvert Plaza Berri (☎ 05 59 22 15 72) at 42 Ave du Maréchal Foch. You will probably need to book a few days in advance.

Places to Stay

Camping *Biarritz Camping* (☎ 05 59 23 00 12), 28 Rue d'Harcet, is 3km south-west of the centre and 1.5km east of Biarritz-La Négresse train station. It's open from late April to late September and costs 100FF for two adults with a tent or caravan and car. To get there, take bus No 9 to the Biarritz Camping stop.

Hostel A new *Auberge de Jeunesse* (☎ 05 59 41 76 00; fax 05 59 41 76 07) has recently opened in Biarritz at 8 Rue Chiquito de Cambo next to the train station, with prices from 76FF per night (plus 25FF for sheets) or 105FF for half-pension. It's run by the same people as the Auberge de Jeunesse in Anglet.

Hotels Most hotels in Biarritz are packed to the gills in July and August, when they raise their rates substantially, sometimes by almost 100%.

The friendly *Hôtel Berthouet* (☎ 05 59 24 63 36), near the market at 29 Rue Gambetta, is a good deal, offering clean singles/doubles for 110/130FF with washbasin and 180/210FF with shower. Hall showers are 20FF.

One of the most attractive – and quietest – hotels in Biarritz is the *Hôtel Etche-Gorria* (☎ 05 59 24 00 74), 21 Ave du Maréchal Foch. Situated in an old villa with a terrace and charming garden, it has doubles with washbasin and bidet from 180FF, and with shower and toilet from 290FF.

Places to Eat

There are quite a few decent little restaurants scattered around Les Halles. *Le Croque en Bouche* (☎ 05 59 22 06 57), 5 Rue du Centre, serves high-quality regional cuisine in an elegant dining room. Starters/main courses/desserts start from 65/75/35FF or you can choose a *menu* at 90 or 145FF. The restaurant is closed Sunday evening, Monday and the second half of January. A few blocks east, the restaurant at the *Hôtel Le Bistroye* has delicious hot dishes starting from 48FF. It's closed Wednesday evening and all day Sunday.

Pizzeria Les Princes (☎ 05 59 24 21 78), 13 Rue Gambetta, has pizzas for 40 to 50FF and pasta from 38 to 50FF. It's open for lunch and dinner (to 11.30 pm) daily, except Monday lunch and all day Sunday.

Les Halles, the large food market south along Rue Gambetta, is open seven days a week from 7 am to 1.30 pm.

Getting There & Away

Bus For information on STAB buses to/from Bayonne and Anglet, see Getting Around in the Bayonne section. The STAB information office in Biarritz (☎ 05 59 52 59 52) is across Square d'Ixelles from the tourist office. It's open Monday to Saturday from 8 am to noon and 1.30 to 6 pm.

Train The Biarritz-La Négresse train station (☎ 08 36 35 35 39) is 3km south of the centre at the southern end of Ave du Président John F Kennedy (the continuation of Ave du Maréchal Foch). SNCF has a downtown office (☎ 05 59 24 00 94) at 13 Ave du Maréchal Foch. It's open Monday to Friday from 9 am to noon and 2 to 6 pm.

Getting Around

Taxi To order a taxi, call ☎ 05 59 03 18 18 or ☎ 05 59 63 17 17.

Bicycle Two-wheeled conveyances of all sorts can be rented from Sobilo (☎ 05 59 24 94 47), 24 Rue Peyroloubilh, which is south of Place Clemenceau where Rue Gambetta becomes Ave Beaurivage. Mountain bikes cost 50FF a day (plus 1000FF deposit).

AROUND BIARRITZ

Saint Jean de Luz

The seaside town of Saint Jean de Luz (Donibane Lohitzun in Basque; population 13,000), 15km south of Biarritz, is an attractive beach resort with a colourful history of whaling and piracy. It's still an active fishing port and is celebrated for its fine Basque linen.

The richly decorated (and almost windowless) **Église Saint Jean Baptiste**, a mid-17th century church built in the traditional Basque style on Rue Gambetta, was the scene in 1660 of the marriage of King Louis XIV to the Spanish princess Marie-Thérèse, only an infant at the time. Don't miss the exceptional 17th-century **altar screen** with gilded wooden statues.

The tourist office (☎ 05 59 26 03 16) is south of the Église Saint Jean Baptiste on Place du Maréchal Foch and is open Monday to Saturday from 9 am to 12.30 pm and 2 to 6.30 pm. During July and August it's open Monday to Saturday from 9 am to 8 pm and on Sunday and holidays from 10 am to 1 pm and from 3 to 7 pm.

If you want to spend the night (Saint Jean de Luz is an easy day trip from Bayonne or Biarritz), one of the nicest – if not cheapest – places is the two-star *Hôtel Ohartzia* (☎ 05 59 26 00 06; fax 05 59 26 74 75), a few steps from the ocean at 28 Rue Garat. Doubles with shower and TV start at 330FF (390FF in summer).

For a meal, *Restaurant Muscade* (☎ 05 59 26 96 73) nearby at 20 Rue Garat specialises in savoury tartes (28 to 60FF) and mixed salads (41 to 98FF). The speciality at *La Vieille Auberge* (☎ 05 59 26 19 61), 22 Rue Tourasse (the street running parallel to the west), is *ttoro* (Basque fish soup). *Menus* start at 75FF.

Frequent trains and buses link Saint Jean de Luz with Bayonne and Biarritz (see Getting There & Away and Getting Around in the Bayonne section). Buses leave from Place du Maréchal Foch. The train station is 200m south.

Saint Jean Pied de Port

The walled Pyrenean town of Saint Jean Pied de Port (Donibane Garazi in Basque; population 1400), 53km south-east of Bayonne, was once the last stop in France for pilgrims on their way south to the Spanish city of Santiago de Compostela, the most important Christian pilgrimage site after Jerusalem and Rome in the Middle Ages. Today the town, which is in a hilly rural area, retains much of its Basque character. The views from the 17th-century **Citadelle** are picture-postcard perfect.

The tourist office (☎ 05 59 37 03 57), at 14 Place Charles de Gaulle just north of the Nive River, is open from 9 am to noon and 2 to 7 pm weekdays (to 6 pm on Saturday). From mid-June to mid-September it's also open on Sunday and holidays from 10.30 am to 12.30 pm and 3 to 6 pm. The office sells useful maps of hiking and cycling routes.

The *Camping Municipal Plaza Berri* (☎ 05 59 37 11 19) on Ave du Fronton occupies a lovely, riverside site with lush grass and thick tree cover. It's open from May to September. Tariffs are 15/10FF per adult/child, 8FF for a tent or caravan site and 8FF to park. One of the cheapest hotels in town is the *Hôtel des Remparts* (☎ 05 59 37 13 79) south of the Nive at 16 Place Floquet. Singles/doubles with shower are 195/200FF.

For more comfort, head north from the tourist office to the *Hôtel Itzalpea* (☎ 05 59 37 03 66; fax 05 59 37 33 18), 5 Place du Trinquet, which has doubles with shower and toilet from 200FF. It also has a restaurant with hearty regional cuisine and *menus* from 58FF. For a real splurge, try the *Restaurant des Pyrénées* (☎ 05 59 37 01 01), which boasts two Michelin stars. *Menus* cost from 230 to 500FF.

There's an all-day *food market* every Monday at Place Charles de Gaulle, and a *Unimarché* grocery close to the tourist office at 3 Place du Trinquet, open daily, except Saturday and Sunday afternoons, from 8 am to 12.30 pm and 3 to 7.30 pm.

Half the reason for coming to Saint Jean Pied de Port is the scenic train trip (three to five a day) from Bayonne, which takes about an hour. The cost from Bayonne is 45FF one way.

LOURDES

Lourdes (population 17,000) was just a sleepy market town on the edge of the snow-capped Pyrenees in 1858 when Bernadette Soubirous, a 14-year-old peasant girl, saw the Virgin Mary in a series of 18 visions that took place in a grotto near the town. The girl's account was eventually investigated by the Vatican, which confirmed them as bona fide apparitions. Bernadette, who lived out her short life as a nun and died in 1879, was canonised as Saint Bernadette in 1933.

These events set Lourdes on the path to becoming one of the world's most important pilgrimage sites. Some five million pilgrims from all over the world converge on Lourdes annually, including many sick people seeking cures. But accompanying the fervent, almost medieval piety of the pilgrims is an astounding display of commercial exuberance that can seem unspeakably tacky. Wall thermometers, shake-up snow scenes and plastic statues of the Virgin are easy to mock; just remember that people have spent their life savings to come here and for many of the Catholic faithful Lourdes is as sacred a place as Mecca, the Ganges, or the Wailing Wall in Jerusalem.

Orientation
Lourdes' two main east-west streets are Rue de la Grotte and, 300m north, Blvd de la Grotte. Both lead to the Sanctuaires Notre Dame de Lourdes, but Blvd de la Grotte takes you to the main entrance at Pont Saint Michel. The principal north-south thoroughfare, known as Chaussée Maransin where it passes over Blvd de la Grotte, connects Ave de la Gare and the train station with Place Peyramale.

Information
Tourist Office The horseshoe-shaped glass and steel tourist office (☎ 05 62 42 77 40; fax 05 62 94 60 95) at Place Peyramale is open Monday to Saturday from 9 am to noon and 2 to 6 pm (7 pm from Easter to mid-October when it's also open on Sunday). From June to September, there is no midday closure. The office sells a pass called Visa Passeport Touristique for 159FF (80FF for children under 12) allowing entry to five museums in Lourdes.

Money & Post The Crédit Lyonnais at 11 Rue Saint Pierre is open weekdays from 8.20 am to noon and 1.10 to 4.40 pm. There are several other banks nearby. The main post office, east of the tourist office at 1 Rue de Langelle, has a foreign exchange service.

Things to See

The huge religious complex that has grown around the cave where Bernadette saw the Virgin, **Sanctuaires Notre Dame de Lourdes**, is west of the city centre across the small Gave de Pau River. The grounds can be entered 24 hours a day via the Entrée des Lacets, which is on Place Monseigneur Laurence at the end of Rue de La Grotte. The Pont Saint Michel entrance is open from 5 am to midnight.

The more noteworthy sites in the complex include the **Grotte de Massabielle**, where Bernadette had her visions and which today is hung with the crutches of cured cripples; the nearby **pools** in which 400,000 people seeking to be healed immerse themselves each year; and the **Basilique du Rosaire** (Basilica of the Rosary), which was built at the end of the 19th century in an overwrought pseudo-Byzantine style. Proper dress is required within the complex (don't wear shorts, short skirts or sleeveless shirts) and smoking is prohibited.

From the Sunday before Easter to at least mid-October, there are solemn **torch-lit processions** nightly at 8.45 pm from the Grotte de Massabielle. The **Procession Eucaristique** (Blessed Sacrament Procession), in which groups of pilgrims carrying banners march along the esplanade, takes place daily during the same period at 4.30 pm.

Other attractions in Lourdes include the **Musée Grévin** wax museum (☎ 05 62 94 33 74) at 87 Rue de la Grotte, where you can see life-size dioramas of important events in the lives of both Jesus Christ and Bernadette Soubirous, and the **Musée de Lourdes** (☎ 05 62 94 28 00), with similar exhibits a few steps south in the Parking de l'Égalité. The museums are open from 9 to 11.40 am and 1.30 to 6.30 pm (and from 8.30 to 10 pm in July and August). Admission to the Musée Grévin is 35FF (18FF reduced rate), and 30/20FF to the Musée de Lourdes.

Sites directly related to the life of Saint Bernadette include: her birthplace, the **Moulin de Boly** (Boly Mill), down the alley next to 55 Blvd de la Grotte (12 Rue Bernadette Soubirous); the **Cachot**, the former prison where the impoverished Soubirous family was forced to move in 1857, at 15 Rue des Petits Fossés; and **Bernadette's school** in the Centre Hospitalier Général west of the train station on Chaussée Maransin. Visits to all three are free and self-guided.

The eyrie-like medieval **Château Fort**, whose buildings date mainly from the 17th or 18th centuries, houses the **Musée Pyrénéen**. The entrances to the chateau (opposite 42 Rue du Fort and off Rue du Bourg) are open daily from 9 am to noon and 2 to 6 pm.

Places to Stay

Lourdes has over 350 hotels, more than any city in France except Paris; even in winter, when many places close, it is no problem finding a relatively cheap room.

Camping The camping ground nearest the town centre is *Camping de la Poste* (☎ 05 62 94 40 35), 26 Rue de Langelle, a few blocks east of the main post office. It's open from April to late October and charges 19FF for a tent plus 14FF per person. It also has double/quad rooms with washbasin and bidet for 130/180FF in a nearby building.

Hotels Near the train station, the friendly *Hôtel d'Annecy* (☎ 05 62 94 13 75), 13 Ave de la Gare, is open from the week before Easter to late October. Plain singles/doubles cost 90/145FF with washbasin and 135/185FF with shower and toilet. Hall showers are 10FF. The tidy *Hôtel Saint Sylve* (☎ 05 62 94 63 48) in the town centre at 9 Rue de la Fontaine has large singles/doubles with washbasin for 70/130FF. With shower, they're 100/160FF. The Saint Sylve is open from April to October.

A much more stylish place (and priced accordingly) is the *Hôtel de la Grotte* (☎ 05 62 94 58 87; fax 05 62 94 20 50), 66 Rue de la Grotte, with balconies and a pretty garden. Singles/doubles with all mod cons start at 345/370FF (370/390FF in summer) at this fin-de-siècle hotel.

Places to Eat

Most hotels offer pilgrims half or full-board; some even require guests to stay on those terms. It usually works out cheaper than eating elsewhere, but the food is seldom very inspiring. Restaurants close early in this pious town; even *McDonald's* at 7 Place du Marcadal is slammed shut at 10 pm.

The *Restaurant Saint Yves-Croix du Périgord* (☎ 05 62 94 26 65), 13-15 Rue Basse, just west of the tourist office, serves up steak frites and a salad at lunch for only 45FF; pasta dishes start at 30FF and cassoulet is 50FF. *La Rose des Sables* (☎ 05 62 42 06 82) across from the tourist office at 8 Rue des Quatre Frères Soulas specialises in couscous (from 58FF) and is open for lunch and dinner every day, except Monday.

Les Halles, the covered market on Place du Champ Commun south of the tourist office, is open Monday to Saturday (daily from Easter to October) from 7 am to 1 pm. There's a *Prisunic* supermarket across the square, open Monday to Saturday from 8.30 am to 7.30 pm.

Getting There & Away

Bus The bus station (☎ 05 62 94 31 15), down Rue Anselme Lacadé from the covered market, has services to regional towns including Pau (36.50FF; 1¼ hours). SNCF buses to the Pyrenean towns of Cauterets (36FF; one hour) and Luz Saint Sauveur (38FF; one hour) leave from the train station parking lot.

Train The train station (☎ 08 36 35 35 39) is 1km east of the Sanctuaires on Ave de la Gare. Trains connect Lourdes with many cities including Bayonne (104FF; 1¼ hours), Bordeaux (178FF; three hours) and Marseille (327FF; eight hours). There are three slow trains daily to Paris' Gare d'Austerlitz (487FF; nine hours) and several TGVs to Gare Montparnasse (439FF; 5½ hours). Local buses link the train station with the Grotte de Massabielle from Easter to mid-October.

AROUND LOURDES

The resort town of **Cauterets** (population 1200), 30km south of Lourdes and accessible from there by SNCF bus, makes an excellent base for exploring the Parc National des Pyrénées, which stretches for about 100km along the Franco-Spanish border.

Cauterets (altitude 930m) is in a valley surrounded by mountains of up to 2800m, which offer some of the best skiing in the Pyrenees (at **Cirque du Lys** and **Pont d'Espagne**). The École de Ski Français (☎ 05 62 92 55 06) at Place Georges Clemenceau gives group and individual lessons. Other activities include taking the waters in the **Thermes César** (☎ 05 62 92 51 60) hot springs at 3 Place de la Victoire or hiking in the park. For information and maps, contact the Maison du Parc National des Pyrénées (☎ 05 62 92 52 56) at Place de la Gare.

There are a number of camping grounds slightly north of town along Ave du Mamelon Vert, including *Les Bergeronnettes* (☎ 05 62 92 50 69) and *Le Mamelon Vert* (☎ 05 62 92 51 56). You can also pitch a tent at the Centre UCJG Cluquet (☎ 05 62 92 52 95) on Ave Docteur Domer, which has tent and dorm beds for 40 to 55FF. It's open mid-June to mid-September.

The helpful tourist office (☎ 05 62 92 50 27; fax 05 62 92 59 12) at Place du Maréchal Foch can book hotel rooms, but the cheapest places in town are the *Hôtel du Béarn* (☎ 05 62 92 53 54), around the corner at 4 Ave du Général Leclerc, and the friendly *Hôtel Le Grum* (☎ 05 62 92 53 01) at 4 Rue de l'Église. Both have simple rooms from 110 to 140FF; doubles with shower and toilet start at 190FF.

Périgord (Dordogne)

Although the name Périgord dates from pre-Roman times, the region is better known in English-speaking countries as the Dordogne, referring both to the department that covers most of the area and one of Périgord's seven rivers.

Périgord was one of the cradles of human civilisation. A number of local caves, including the world-famous Lascaux, are adorned with extraordinary prehistoric paintings, and there have been major finds here of the remains of Neanderthal and Cro-Magnon people. Périgord is also justly renowned for its cuisine, which makes ample use of those very French products, *truffes du Périgord* (black truffles – subterranean fungi with a very distinct aroma and taste) and *foie gras*, the fatty liver of force-fed geese, served on its own or used in preparing the finest *pâté*.

PÉRIGUEUX

Founded over 2000 years ago on a curve in the gentle Isle River, Périgueux (population 30,000) rests these days on its two laurels: its proximity to the prehistoric sites of the Vézère Valley to the south-east and its status as the capital of one of France's true gourmet regions.

Orientation

The medieval and Renaissance old city (Puy Saint Front) lies on the hillside between Blvd Michel Montaigne and the Isle River. To the south-west is the older Gallo-Roman quarter (La Cité), whose centre is a ruined 2nd-century amphitheatre. The train station area and its cheap hotels are about 1km north-west of the old city.

Information

The tourist office (☎ 05 53 53 10 63; fax 05 53 09 02 50), 26 Place Francheville, next to the 15th-century Tour Mataguerre, is open from 9 am to 12.15 pm and 1.30 to 6 pm (closed Sunday and holidays). From mid-June to mid-September, daily hours are 9 am to 7 pm (10 am to 6 pm Sunday and holidays). For regional information, contact the Espace Tourisme Périgord (☎ 05 53 35 50 24) at 25 Rue du Président Wilson, which is open weekdays from 8.30 am to 12.30 and 2 to 5 pm.

The Banque de France is on Place Franklin Roosevelt. Other banks line Place Bugeaud. The main post office is 150m south-east at Rue du 4 Septembre.

Things to See & Do

The most appealing part of Périgueux is the **Puy Saint Front** quarter around the cathedral. When viewed at sunset, the five-domed **Cathédrale Saint Front** looks like something transported from Istanbul. Originally Romanesque, the massive church (the largest in south-western France) was almost totally rebuilt in mock-Byzantine style in the mid-19th century. The interior is noteworthy only for the spectacularly carved 17th century baroque **retable** (altar screen) in the choir.

The **Musée du Périgord** (☎ 05 53 06 40 70), north of the cathedral at 22 Cours Tourny, is France's second-most important prehistoric museum after the one at Les Eyzies de Tayac (see that section). It's open daily, except Tuesday, from 10 am to 6 pm. Admission is 20FF (10FF for students).

Places to Stay

Camping The *Barnabé Plage* camp site (☎ 05 53 53 41 45) is about 2.5km east of the train station along the Isle River. Open all year, it charges 15.50FF for a tent plus 16FF per adult and 10FF for parking. To get there take bus No D from Place Michel Montaigne to the Rue des Bains stop.

Hostel The small *Foyer Des Jeunes Travailleurs* (☎ 05 53 53 52 05) south of the Puy Saint Front quarter is open all year and charges 73FF a night, including breakfast. Reception is open from 5 pm. Bus No G from Place Montaigne goes to the nearby Lakanal stop.

Hotels One of the cheapest places near the train station is the *Hôtel des Voyageurs* (☎ 05 53 53 17 44), 26 Rue Denis Papin, with basic doubles without/with shower for 80/100FF. The *Hôtel du Midi et Terminus* (☎ 05 53 53 41 06; fax 05 53 08 19 32), on the same street at No 18-20, is a huge, amiable place with basic singles/doubles from 140/145FF and doubles with shower from 170FF. Quads with two beds plus shower go for 215FF.

Near the old city, *Le Lion d'Or* (☎ 05 53 53 49 03; fax 05 53 35 19 62), 17 Cours Fenelon, has large singles/doubles for 100/160FF. A much more pleasant option is the two-star *Hôtel de l'Univers* (☎ 05 53 53 34 79), 18 Cours Michel Montaigne. It has three small attic doubles without shower (hall showers are free) for 180FF and larger rooms with shower from 220FF.

Places to Eat

In Puy Saint Front, there are a number of eateries on Rue Éguillerie and the streets that branch off it. *La Grignotière* (☎ 05 53 53 86 91), 6 Rue du Puy Limogeanne, specialises in salads (48 to 65FF) and has *menus* from 58FF to 95FF. *Le Saint Louis* (☎ 05 53 53 53 90), a bar-brasserie at 26 bis Rue Éguillerie, serves tasty sandwiches at lunchtime and three-course *menus* in the evening from 55FF. It's open daily from 7 am to 2 am (8 pm from October to Easter, when it's closed on Sunday).

The *Monoprix* on Place Bugeaud has a huge grocery section upstairs and is open Monday to Saturday from 8.30 am to 8 pm.

Getting There & Away

Bus The bus station (☎ 05 53 08 91 06) is on Place Francheville south-west of the tourist office. Except on Sunday and holidays, there are buses to Montignac (34FF), Bergerac (40FF) and Sarlat (49.50FF).

Train Périgueux's train station (☎ 08 36 35 35 39) is on Rue Denis Papin, about 1km north-west of the tourist office. It's connected to Place Montaigne by bus Nos A and C. There are connections from here to Bordeaux (97FF; 1½ hours), Bergerac (74FF; 1½ hours), Sarlat (73FF; 1½ hours) and Les Eyzies de Tayac (39FF; 40 minutes).

VÉZÈRE VALLEY

Périgord's most important prehistoric caves are in the Vézère Valley south-east of Périgueux. Stretching from Le Bugue, near where the Vézère and Dordogne rivers meet, north to Montignac, the valley's centre is the village of Les Eyzies de Tayac, 45km from Périgueux. Another 22km south-east is Sarlat-la-Canéda, a lovely Renaissance town and the most pleasant base from which to explore the valley by car. Those without their own transport might consider a day tour (see Organised Tours in the Sarlat-la-Canéda section), as bus and train services in the valley are very limited.

Les Eyzies de Tayac

As one of the world's major prehistoric sites, this tiny village (population 850) at the confluence of the Vézère and Beune rivers attracts a great many tourists. Most come to see some of the oldest art works in the world at the **Musée National de la Préhistoire** (☎ 05 53 06 45 45) or visit the **Musée de l'Abri Pataud** (☎ 05 53 06 92 46), an im-

pressive Cro-Magnon rock shelter towering above the town. From mid-November to March, the museum is open daily, except Tuesday, from 9.30 am to noon and 2 to 5 pm (6 pm the rest of the year with no midday closure in July and August). Entry is 22FF (15FF for students and free for those under 18). The rock shelter is open from 10 to noon and 2 to 6 pm (closed in the morning in November and December; closed in January). July and August hours are 10 am to 7 pm. Entry costs 28FF (14FF for students).

Two caves, **Grotte de Font de Gaume** and **Grotte des Combarelles**, are 1km and 3km respectively north-east of Les Eyzies de Tayac on Route D47 (Route de Sarlat). Combarelles has thousands of animal engravings dating back some 15,000 years, and the narrow passages of Font de Gaume are covered with lifelike paintings of bison, reindeer, woolly rhinoceros and wolves in red, brown, white and black. Each cave costs 35/23FF for adults/students and both are open year round. Tours start from 9 or 10 am to noon and 2 to 6 pm (5.30 pm in October and March; 5 pm from November to February). Combarelles is closed on Wednesday, Font de Gaume on Tuesday. Because the number of visitors is limited, you must book ahead on site or by phone (☎ 05 53 06 90 80).

Les Eyzies de Tayac's tourist office (☎ 05 53 06 97 05; fax 05 53 06 90 79) is on the main street and open weekdays (and weekends from April to October) from 9 or 10 am to noon and from 2 to 5 or 6 pm (8 pm in July and August, when there's no midday break).

Montignac

Montignac (population 2900), picturesquely situated on the Vézère River, is near Lascaux Cave and its replica Lascaux II. The tourist office (☎ 05 53 51 82 60) is at 22 Rue du Quatre Septembre, next to the 14th-century Église Saint Georges le Prieuré.

Lascaux Cave About 2.5km south of Montignac off route D704 is the world-famous Lascaux Cave, discovered by four teenage boys in 1940 and sometimes called 'the Sistine Chapel of prehistoric art'. The cave was closed to visitors in 1960 when it was discovered that carbon dioxide and condensation from human breath were damaging the

17,000-year-old paintings. Today the cave is kept at a constant 12°C and 98% humidity. Visitors are allowed in at a rate of only five a day, three times a week, and the waiting list is more than two years long.

But everyone can visit **Lascaux II** (☎ 05 53 51 95 03), a meticulous copy of the most important section of the original cave. The reproductions of the bison, horses and reindeer are so vivid and alive that the paintings in the real caves may be a disappointment! Lascaux II can handle 2000 people a day in groups of 40; in the high season tours begin every 10 or 15 minutes.

Lascaux II is open daily from 9 am to 7 pm from April to October (closed Monday in October); 10 am to 12.30 pm and 1.30 to 5.30 pm from November to March (closed Monday and for three weeks starting mid-January). Tickets cost 48FF (20FF for kids aged 6 to 12), and are sold at the entrance, except in July and August when they *must* be purchased in Montignac, next to the tourist office (get there early as queues are long). If you're in a large group, ie more than 10 of you, you may need a reservation.

Tickets also allow entry into **Le Thot** (☎ 05 53 50 70 44), a prehistoric theme park with a museum, mock-ups of Palaeolithic huts and living examples of some of the animals seen in the cave paintings. It's all very *Flintstones*. Le Thot is just off scenic route D706 about 4km south of Lascaux II and has the same opening hours.

Sarlat-la-Canéda

Despite centuries of war and conflagration, this beautiful Renaissance town (population 10,000) north of the Dordogne River has managed to retain most of its 16th and 17th-century limestone buildings.

Orientation & Information The town stretches northward for 2km from the train station to the Auberge de Jeunesse. The main drag linking the two is known as Rue de la République where it slices the heart-shaped old town almost in half. Three lovely squares – Place du Marché aux Oies, Place de la Liberté and Place du Peyrou – are in the restored eastern half.

The tourist office (☎ 05 53 59 27 67; fax 05 53 59 19 44) is in the beautiful Hôtel de

Maleville on Place de la Liberté. It's open Monday to Saturday from 9 am to noon and 2 to 6 pm (7 pm from June to September, when it's also open on Sunday from 10 am to noon and 2 to 6 pm). There's no midday break in July and August.

Things to See & Do The **Cathédrale Saint Sacerdos** on Place du Peyrou was originally part of a 9th-century Benedictine abbey but has been extended and rebuilt in a mixture of styles over the centuries. To the east is the **Jardin des Pénitents**, Sarlat's medieval cemetery, and the beehive-shaped **Lanterne des Morts** (Light of the Dead), a 12th-century tower dedicated to Saint Bernard. There's a colourful **Saturday market** on Place de la Liberté chock-full with truffles, mushrooms, geese and parts thereof.

Organised Tours HEP! Excursions (☎ 05 53 28 10 04) runs various tours to regional destinations, including the southern Vézère Valley (180FF).

Places to Stay The closest camping ground to Sarlat is the expensive *Les Périères* (☎ 05 53 59 05 84), about 800m to the north-east along route D47 towards Sainte Nathalène. It charges 115FF for two people including tent and is open from April to September. Tents can also be pitched at the Auberge de Jeunesse (see Hostel).

Hostel Sarlat's *Auberge de Jeunesse* (☎ 05 53 59 47 59), 77 Ave de Selves, is open from mid-March to mid-November. Charges are 45FF a night or 25FF for those who want to camp in the tiny backyard. It's just over 2km from the train station, but the minibus stops close by at the Cimetière stop.

Hotels One of the cheaper places in this relatively expensive town is the friendly *Hôtel les Récollets* (☎ 05 53 31 36 00; fax 05 53 30 32 62), 4 Rue Jean-Jacques Rousseau. It has attractive rooms with washbasin and bidet for 180FF, with toilet and shower for 220FF. Near the tourist office, the *Hôtel de la Mairie* (☎ 05 53 59 05 71), 13 Place de la Liberté, has fairly basic doubles/triples with shower from 220/260FF.

Rooms with shower, toilet and TV at the

large, chateau-like *Hôtel La Couleuvrine* (☎ 05 53 59 27 80; fax 05 53 31 26 83), 1 Place de la Bouquerie, start at 295FF.

Places to Eat *Pizzeria Romane* (☎ 05 53 59 23 88), 3 Côte de Toulouse, has pizzas, spaghetti and a Périgord-style *menu* (80FF) that includes confit de canard. It's closed on Sunday at midday and on Monday. *Napoli Pizza* (☎ 05 53 31 26 93), a rustic, informal place at 2 Blvd Eugène Le Roy, has pizzas for 35 to 60FF, pasta for 30 to 51FF and red meat dishes for 50 to 90FF. It's generally open for lunch and dinner, but closed Sunday lunchtime and all day Monday.

For more salubrious surroundings, head for the *Restaurant Rossignol* (☎ 05 53 31 02 30), 15 Rue Fénelon, which has *menus* from 87 to 290FF; dishes on offer include fish. It's open from noon to 1.30 pm and 7 to 8.30 pm (closed Wednesday).

Getting There & Away Buses to Périgueux via Montignac (25.50FF; 25 minutes) leave from Place de la Petite Rigaudie at 6 am (8.25 am in July and August); the return bus leaves Montignac at 7.15 pm (1 pm on Saturday; 4.35 pm in July and August). The information office (☎ 05 53 59 01 48) is at 31 Rue de Cahors halfway between the old town and the train station.

Sarlat's tiny train station (☎ 08 36 35 35 39) is just over 1km south of town at the end of Ave de la Gare. Trains go to Périgueux (74FF; 1½ hours), Les Eyzies de Tayac (46FF; 50 minutes), and Bordeaux (116FF; 2½ hours).

Getting Around Peugeot Cycles (☎ 05 53 28 51 87), north of the train station at 36 Ave Thiers, rents bicycles for 70FF a day.

Burgundy & the Rhône Region

The Duchy of Burgundy (Bourgogne), situated on the great trade route between the Mediterranean and northern Europe, was wealthier and more powerful than the kingdom of France during the 14th and 15th centuries. These days, the region and its capital, Dijon, are known for their superb wines, haute cuisine and rich architectural heritage.

By far the most important urban centre in the Rhône region (which lies south of Burgundy) is Lyon. Centuries of commercial and industrial prosperity, made possible by the mighty Rhône River and its tributary the Saône, have created an appealing city with superb museums, an attractive centre, shopping to rival that of Paris, and a flourishing cultural life.

DIJON

Dijon (population 230,000), the prosperous capital of the dukes of Burgundy for almost 500 years, is one of France's most appealing provincial cities, its centre graced by elegant medieval and Renaissance residences. Despite its long history, Dijon has a distinctly youthful air, in part because of the major university situated there. The city is a good starting point for visits to the vineyards of the Côte d'Or, arguably the greatest wine-growing region in the world.

Orientation

Dijon's main thoroughfare runs eastward from the train station to Église Saint Michel. Ave Maréchal Foch links the train station with the tourist office. Rue de la Liberté, the principal shopping street, runs between Porte Guillaume (a triumphal arch erected in 1788) and the Palais des Ducs. The social centre of Dijon is Place François Rude, a popular hang-out in good weather.

Information
Tourist Office The tourist office (☎ 03 80 44 11 44; fax 03 80 42 18 83; infotourisme@ ot-dijon.fr; www.ot-dijon.fr), 300m east of the train station at Place Darcy, is open daily from mid-October to April from 9 am to 1 pm and 2 to 7 pm. During the rest of the year, hours are 9 am to 9 pm. The tourist office annexe at 34 Rue des Forges, opposite the north side of the Palais des Ducs, is open from 10 am to 6 pm (closed Sunday and holidays and, except from May to mid-October, on Saturday).

Money & Post The Banque de France is at 2 Place de la Banque (just north of the

DIJON

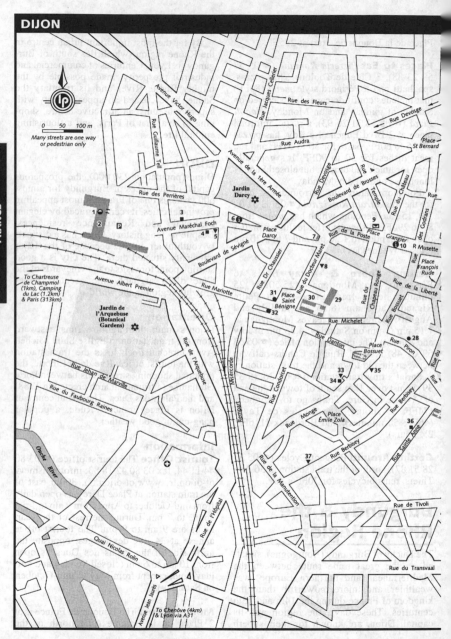

0   50   100 m

Many streets are one way
or pedestrian only

To Chartreuse
de Champmol
(1km), Camping
du Lac (1.2km)
& Paris (313km)

Avenue Victor Hugo

Rue des Fleurs

Rue Devosge

Place
St Bernard

Rue Jacques Cellerier

Rue Guillaume Tell

Rue des Perrières

Avenue de la 1ère Armée

Rue Audra

Rue Devosge

Jardin
Darcy

Boulevard de Brosses

Rue du Château

Rue Temple

Rue

Avenue Maréchal Foch

1

2

P

3

6

Place
Darcy

7

9

Place
Grangier

10   R Musette

Rue de la Poste

des Godrans

Place
François
Rude

4   5

Boulevard de Sévigné

Rue Dr Chaussier

Rue du Docteur Maret

8

Rue de la Liberté

Avenue Albert Premier

Rue Mariotte

31   Place
Saint
Bénigne

30

29

Rue du Chapeau Rouge

Rue Bossuet

Jardin de
l'Arquebuse
(Botanical
Gardens)

32

Rue Michelet

Rue Danton

Place
Bossuet

Rue Piron

28

Rue de l'Arquebuse

33

34

35

Rue Jehan de Marville

Rue du Faubourg Raines

Rampart

Miséricorde

Rue Condorcet

Rue Monge

Place
Émile Zola

Rue Berbisey

36

Rue Sainte Anne

Oche River

Rue Berbisey

37

Rue de la Manutention

Rue de Tivoli

Quai Nicolas Rolin

Rue de l'Hôpital

Rue du Transvaal

Avenue Jean Jaurès

To Chenôve (4km)
& Lyon via A31

DIJON

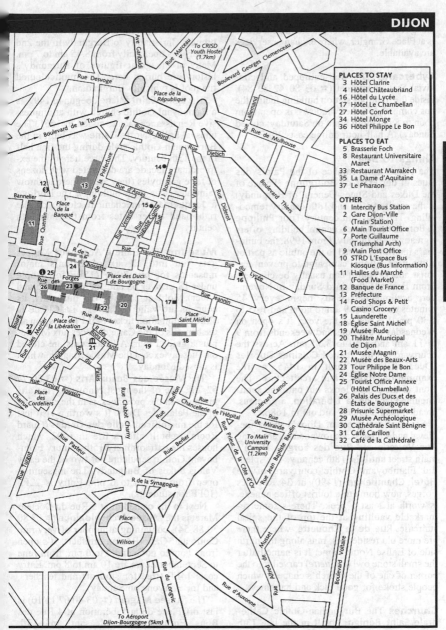

PLACES TO STAY
3 Hôtel Clarine
4 Hôtel Châteaubriand
16 Hôtel du Lycée
17 Hôtel Le Chambellan
27 Hôtel Confort
34 Hôtel Monge
36 Hôtel Philippe Le Bon

PLACES TO EAT
5 Brasserie Foch
8 Restaurant Universitaire Maret
33 Restaurant Marrakech
35 La Dame d'Aquitaine
37 Le Pharaon

OTHER
1 Intercity Bus Station
2 Gare Dijon-Ville (Train Station)
6 Main Tourist Office
7 Porte Guillaume (Triumphal Arch)
9 Main Post Office
10 STRD L'Espace Bus Kiosque (Bus Information)
11 Halles du Marché (Food Market)
12 Banque de France
13 Préfecture
14 Food Shops & Petit Casino Grocery
15 Launderette
18 Église Saint Michel
19 Musée Rude
20 Théâtre Municipal de Dijon
21 Musée Magnin
22 Musée des Beaux-Arts
23 Tour Philippe le Bon
24 Église Notre Dame
25 Tourist Office Annexe (Hôtel Chambellan)
26 Palais des Ducs et des États de Bourgogne
28 Prisunic Supermarket
29 Musée Archéologique
30 Cathédrale Saint Bénigne
31 Café Carillon
32 Café de la Cathédrale

FRANCE

covered market). There are quite a few banks along Rue de la Liberté. The main post office is at Place Grangier, where exchange services are available.

Cybercafés The well-equipped and convivial Station Internet (☎ 03 80 42 89 84), inside the train-bus station building facing the bus company's ticket windows, is open from noon to 8 pm (until 5 pm on Saturday; closed Sunday). A half-hour online costs 20FF.

Things to See

The classical appearance of the **Palais des Ducs et des États de Bourgogne** (Palace of the Dukes and States-General of Burgundy) is the result of 17th and 18th-century remodelling. The mid-15th century **Tour Philippe le Bon**, in the palace's central building, offers a great view of the city. From 1998, the building's interior is closed to the public as part of a two-year national campaign to prevent terrorist attacks, but it can usually be climbed. From Easter to the third Sunday in November, accompanied visits begin every 45 minutes or so from 9 am to noon and 1.45 to 5.30 pm; the rest of the year, it's open on Wednesday afternoons and weekends from 9 to 11 am and 1.30 to 3.30 pm. Across the courtyard are the vaulted **Cuisines Ducales** (Ducal Kitchens) built in 1445, a fine example of Gothic civic architecture. The front of the palace looks out onto the semicircular **Place de la Libération**, a gracious, arcaded public square laid out in 1686.

Some of the finest of Dijon's many medieval and Renaissance townhouses are along **Rue Verrerie** and **Rue des Forges**, Dijon's main street until the 18th century. The splendid Flamboyant Gothic courtyard of the **Hôtel Chambellan** (1490) at 34 Rue des Forges, now home to a tourist office annexe, is worth at least a peek. There's some remarkable vaulting at the top of the spiral staircase. **Rue de la Chouette**, where there are more old residences, runs along the north side of Église Notre Dame. It is named after the small stone owl (*chouette*) carved into the corner of one of the church's chapels, which people stroke for good luck and happiness.

Churches The Burgundian-Gothic **Cathédrale Saint Bénigne**, built in the late 13th century over what may be the tomb of St Benignus (who by tradition is believed to have brought Christianity to Burgundy in the 2nd century), is open daily from 8.45 am to 7 pm. Many of the great figures of Burgundy's history are buried here. The multicoloured tile roof is typically Burgundian.

The **Église Saint Michel**, begun in 1499, is a flamboyant Gothic church with an impressive Renaissance façade added in 1661. The unusual **Église Notre Dame** was built in the Burgundian-Gothic style during the first half of the 13th century. The three tiers of the extraordinary façade are decorated with dozens of false gargoyles (they aren't there to throw rainwater clear of the building). The **Horloge à Jacquemart** (mechanical clock) on the right-hand tower dates from the late 14th century.

Museums The Carte d'Accès aux Musées gets you into all six of Dijon's major museums for just 30FF (15FF for people under 18 or over 65 and for students 25 and under). Sold at each of the museums, its coupons are valid for a year. La Clé de la Ville combination ticket (45FF) gives you all the benefits of the Carte d'Accès aux Musées plus a guided tour. All museums are closed on Tuesday except the Musée Magnin, which is closed Monday.

The **Musée des Beaux-Arts** (☎ 03 80 74 52 70), one of the most renowned fine arts museums in the provinces, is in the east wing of the Palais des Ducs. It's worth a visit just for the magnificent **Salle des Gardes** (Guard Room), rebuilt after a fire in 1502, which houses the extraordinary 15th-century Flamboyant Gothic sepulchres of two of the early Valois dukes of Burgundy. The museum is open from 10 am to 6 pm. Entry is 22FF (10FF for students).

Next to the cathedral at 5 Rue du Docteur Maret is the **Musée Archéologique** (☎ 03 80 30 88 54), containing a number of very rare Celtic and Gallo-Roman artefacts. It's open from 9 am to noon and 2 to 6 pm; from June to September hours are 10 am to 8 pm. Entry costs 14FF (free for students and teachers, and for everyone on Sunday).

The **Musée Magnin** (☎ 03 80 67 11 10) is just off Place de la Libération at 4 Rue des Bons Enfants. This pleasant, mid-17th century residence contains a collection of 2000 assorted works of art assembled by Jeanne Magnin and her brother Maurice around the turn of the century. It's open from 10 am to noon and 2 to 6 pm (closed Monday). From June to September, it does not close at midday. Admission is 18FF (12FF for students).

Places to Stay

Camping The *Camping du Lac* (☎ 03 80 43 54 72) at 3 Blvd Chanoine Kir is 1.4km west of the train station, behind the psychiatric hospital. It's open from April to mid-October and charges 16/12/8FF per person/tent/car. From the train station, take bus No 12 and get off at the Hôpital des Chartreux stop.

Hostels The *Centre de Rencontres Internationales et de Séjour de Dijon* (CRISD; ☎ 03 80 72 95 20; fax 03 80 70 00 61), Dijon's large, institutional hostel, is 2.5km north-east of the town centre at 1 Blvd Champollion. A bed in a dorm costs 71FF including breakfast; a triple with shower and toilet is 144FF (breakfast extra). Guests without either a student card or an HI card pay 8FF extra for the first four nights. The hostel is open 24 hours. To get to CRISD, take bus No 5 (towards Épirey) from Place Grangier. At night take a Line A bus to the Épirey Centre Commercial stop.

Hotels The *Hôtel Confort* (☎ 03 80 30 37 47; fax 03 80 30 03 43) is right in the centre of town at 12 Rue Jules Mercier, an alley off Rue de la Liberté. Decent singles/doubles with shower cost from 160/165FF. The friendly *Hôtel Monge* (☎ 03 80 30 55 41; fax 03 80 30 30 15), 20 Rue Monge, has singles/doubles starting at 125/135FF (200/210FF with shower, toilet and TV). Hall showers are 15FF.

The *Hôtel du Lycée* (☎ 03 80 67 12 35; fax 03 80 63 84 69), 28 Rue du Lycée, has ordinary rooms from 120 to 175FF; hall showers are free. The two-star *Hôtel Le Chambellan* (☎ 03 80 67 12 67; fax 03 80 38 00 39), 92 Rue Vannerie, occupies a 17th-century building and has a rustic feel. Comfortable doubles start at 120FF (170FF with shower, 220FF with shower and toilet).

There are several two and three-star hotels

along Ave Maréchal Foch. The *Hôtel Châteaubriand* (☎ 03 80 41 42 18; fax 03 80 59 16 28) at No 3 (1st floor) has doubles for 165 to 182FF or 206 to 251FF with shower and toilet. For something a little more luxurious, try the 45-room *Hôtel Clarine* (☎ 03 80 43 53 78; fax 03 80 42 84 17) at No 22 which has huge, comfortable one or two-bed doubles for 290FF; an extra bed costs 50FF. Even more upmarket is the 30-room *Hôtel Philippe le Bon* (☎ 03 80 30 73 52; fax 03 80 30 95 51), a three-star place at 18 Rue Sainte Anne, which has modern singles/doubles with cable TV from 370/450FF.

Places to Eat

You'll find a number of reasonably priced brasseries along Ave Maréchal Foch, including *Brasserie Foch* (☎ 03 80 41 27 93) at No 1 bis open 11.30 am to 10 pm (closed Sunday). *Restaurant Marrakech* (☎ 03 80 30 82 69), 20 Rue Monge, has huge portions of excellent couscous starting at 60FF. Food is served from noon to 2.30 pm and 7 pm to 11 pm (midnight on Friday and Saturday; closed Monday at midday).

Le Pharaon (☎ 03 80 30 11 36), one of France's few Egyptian restaurants (Lebanese fare is also on offer), is at 116 Rue Berbisey. The *menus* cost 58FF (weekday lunches only), 70FF (vegetarian), 75, 90 and 110FF. Hours are noon to 1.30 pm and 7 to 11 pm (closed Sunday at midday and Monday). For a serious splurge, try the Burgundian and south-western French cuisine at *La Dame d'Aquitaine* (☎ 03 80 30 45 65), 23 Place Bossuet, housed beneath the soaring arches of a 13th century crypt. The *menus*, served to the accompaniment of classical music, cost 138FF (lunch only; includes wine) to 245FF. It's open daily from noon to 1.30 pm and 7 to 11 pm.

The *Restaurant Universitaire Maret* (☎ 03 80 40 40 34), 3 Rue du Docteur Maret (next to the Musée Archéologique), has cheap cafeteria food for students. Except during July and August (when the university restaurant on the campus takes over), it's open on weekdays and one weekend a month. Lunch is served from 11.40 am to 2 pm and dinner from 6.40 to 8 pm. Tickets (14.10FF for students) are sold on the ground floor at lunchtime.

The cheapest place to buy picnic food is the *Halles du Marché*, a 19th-century covered market 150m north of Rue de la Liberté. It's open Tuesday, Friday and Saturday from 6 am to 1 pm. North of the Palais des Ducs, there's a cluster of boulangeries and food shops along Rue Jean-Jacques Rousseau, including a *Petit Casino* grocery at No 16 (closed Sunday afternoon and Monday morning). The *Prisunic* supermarket (closed Sunday) south of Rue de la Liberté at 11-13 Rue Piron has a food section upstairs.

Entertainment

The *Café Au Carillon* (☎ 03 80 30 63 71), opposite the cathedral at 2 Rue Mariotte, is extremely popular with young locals. Also popular is the *Café La Cathédrale* (☎ 03 80 30 42 10), across the street at 4 Place Saint Bénigne. Both are open Monday to Saturday from 6.30 am to 1 am or 2 am; the latter is also open on Sunday until 8 or 9 pm.

Getting There & Away

Bus The bus station (☎ 03 80 42 11 00) is next to the train station at the end of Ave Maréchal Foch. Buses run from here to points all over the department of Côte d'Or, including Beaune. The Transco information counter is open weekdays from 7.30 am to 6.30 pm and on Saturday morning until 12.30 pm.

Train The train station (☎ 08 36 35 35 39), Gare Dijon-Ville, was built to replace an earlier structure destroyed in 1944. The information office is open from 9 am to 7 pm (6 pm on Saturday; closed Sunday). Going to/from Paris' Gare de Lyon by TGV (217 to 267FF) takes about 1¾ hours. There are non-TGV trains to Lyon (131FF; two hours) and Nice (from 368FF; eight hours).

Getting Around

Dijon's extensive urban bus network is run by STRD (☎ 03 80 30 60 90). Single tickets (valid for transfers) cost 5.20FF; various bus passes are available, including a day ticket (16FF) and a 12-trip ticket (42.50FF). Seven different bus routes stop along Rue de la Liberté and five more stop at Place Grangier. Most STRD buses run Monday to Saturday from 6 am to 8 pm, and on Sunday from 1 to 8 pm. Six lines (A to F) run from 8 pm to

12.15 am. STRD's L'Espace Bus Kiosque (information office) in the middle of Place Grangier is open Monday to Saturday from 6.30 am to 7.15 pm.

VINEYARDS AROUND DIJON

Burgundy's finest vintages come from the vine-covered Côte d'Or, the eastern slopes of the limestone escarpment running for about 60km south from Dijon. The northern section is known as the Côte de Nuits and the southern section as the Côte de Beaune. The tourist offices in Dijon, Beaune and nearby towns can provide details of wine cellars (*caves*) that offer tours and wine tasting (*dégustation*).

For detailed information on the region's wines, get a copy of *The Wines of Burgundy* (ninth edition; 75FF) by Sylvain Pitiot and Jean-Charles Servant, on sale at the Beaune tourist office. The tourist office can also book you onto an organised minibus tour of the vineyards. The trips last two hours and start at 180FF per person, including a guide and some wine tasting.

North of Beaune are the picturesque wine-making villages of Nuits Saint Georges, Vosne-Romanée, Clos de Vougeot and Gevrey-Chambertin, which are known for their fine reds and offer excellent wine tasting opportunities. South of Beaune you can visit the *Château de Pommard* (☎ 03 80 22 12 59 or ☎ 03 80 22 07 99), where a 25-minute guided tour of the early 18th century chateau, including a glass of wine, costs 25FF (free for children under 16). From April to late November, tours begin daily from 9 am to 5.30 or 5.45 pm.

Beaune

The attractive town of Beaune (population 21,300), a major wine-making centre about 40km south of Dijon, makes an excellent day trip. Its most famous historical site is the Hôtel-Dieu, France's most opulent medieval charity hospital. The tourist office (☎ 03 80 26 21 30) is at Rue de l'Hôtel-Dieu, opposite the entrance to the Hôtel-Dieu.

The **Hôtel-Dieu**, founded in 1443 by Nicolas Rolin, is built in Flemish-Burgundian Gothic style and features a distinctive multi-coloured tile roof. Of particular interest are the hospice's **Hall of the Poor** and the **Apothecary**, with a vast array of china and glass jars full of herbal potions. Don't miss the extraordinary polyptych of *The Last Judgment*, a medieval masterpiece by Roger van der Weyden. You'll find it in the darkened room off the hall. The Hôtel-Dieu is open from the week before Easter to mid-November from 9 am to 6.30 pm; the rest of the year, hours are 9 to 11.30 am and 2 to 5.30 pm. Entry is 32FF (25FF for students). Make sure you pick up the informative brochure (in English) at the ticket counter.

For wine tasting in Beaune, you can visit the **Marché aux Vins** at Rue Nicolas Rolin, where you can sample 18 wines for 50FF. **Patriarche Père et Fils** at 6 Rue du Collège has one of the largest wine cellars in Burgundy, containing several million bottles. You can taste 13 wines for 40FF. It's open daily from 9.30 to 11.30 am and 2 to 5.30 pm.

Places to Eat As one of France's prime gastronomic centres, Beaune is a great place to indulge your taste buds. The town's abundant restaurants include the elegant *Restaurant Bernard & Martine Morillon* (☎ 03 80 24 12 06), 31 Rue Maufoux, with one Michelin star and *menus* from 180FF (closed Tuesday at midday and Monday), and *Caves Madeleine* (☎ 03 80 22 93 30), a cosy wine bar at 8 Rue du Faubourg Madeleine, which serves at least a dozen wines by the glass (from 13.30FF) and family-style Burgundian *menus* for 69 and 89FF. It's open Monday to Saturday. Another good choice is *Restaurant Maxime* (☎ 03 80 22 17 82), 3 Place Madeleine, where *menus* cost 78, 96 and 148FF; à la carte, bœuf bourguignon is 65FF. It's open from noon to 2 pm and 7 to 10 pm (closed Monday and during February).

The city also has a fantastic collection of food shops – if you want to prepare a gourmet picnic, this is the place to do it. There are several *food shops* along the Rue Carnot pedestrian mall, including *Le Tast' Fromage*, a fromagerie at the intersection of Rue Carnot and Rue Monge. On Wednesday morning, the covered market hosts a *marché gourmand* (gourmet market).

Getting There & Away You can get from Dijon to Beaune by train (37FF; about 25 minutes) or bus (38.40FF; one hour). Trains also stop at various villages along the way,

including Gevrey-Chambertin, Vougeot and Nuits Saint Georges but services are limited in winter. Transco bus No 44 is a good bet if you want to stop along the way as there are vineyards at virtually every stop. Service is greatly reduced on Sunday.

LYON

The grand city of Lyon, with a population of 415,000, is part of a prosperous urban area of almost two million people, the second-largest conurbation in France. Founded by the Romans over 2000 years ago, it has spent the last 500 years as a commercial, industrial and banking powerhouse. Lyon is endowed with outstanding museums, a dynamic cultural life, an important university, upmarket shops, lively pedestrian malls and excellent cuisine – it is, after all, one of France's gastronomic capitals, even for people on a budget.

Lyon, founded in 43 BC as the Roman military colony of Lugdunum, served as the capital of the Roman territories known as the Three Gauls under Augustus. The 16th century marked the beginning of the city's extraordinary prosperity. Banks were established, great commercial fairs were held and trade flourished. Printing arrived before the end of the 15th century; within 50 years Lyon was home to several hundred printers. The city became Europe's silk-weaving capital in the mid-1700s. The famous *traboules*, a network of covered passageways in Croix Rousse and Vieux Lyon, originally built to facilitate the transport of silk during inclement weather, proved very useful to the Resistance during WWII.

Orientation

Lyon's city centre is on the Presqu'île, a long, thin peninsula bounded by the Rhône and Saône rivers. The elevated area north of Place des Terreaux is known as Croix Rousse. Place Bellecour is 1km south of Place des Terreaux and 1km north of Place Carnot, which is next to one of Lyon's train stations, Gare de Perrache. The city's other train station, Gare de la Part-Dieu, is 2km east of the Presqu'île in a huge, modern commercial district known as La Part-Dieu. Vieux Lyon (the old city) is on the west bank of the Saône River between the city centre and Fourvière hill.

LYON

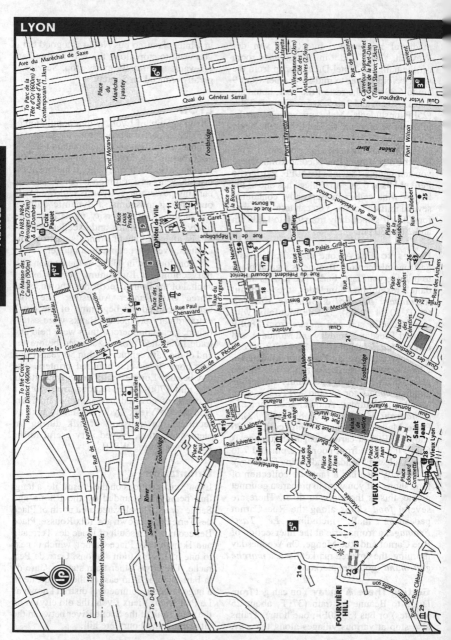

LYON

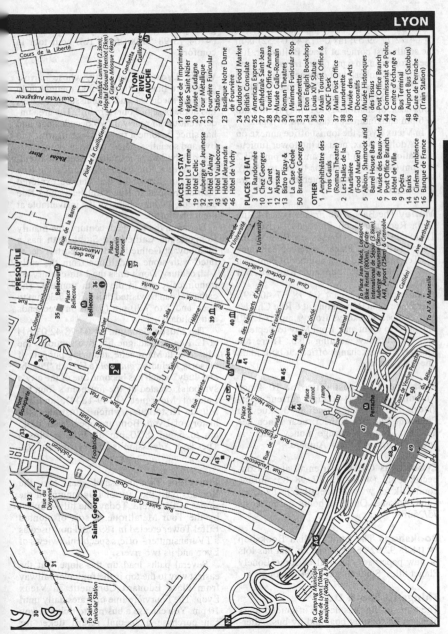

PLACES TO STAY
4   Hôtel Le Terme
19 Hôtel Celtic
32 Auberge de Jeunesse
41 Hôtel d'Ainay
43 Hôtel Vaubecour
45 Hôtel Alexandra
46 Hôtel de Vichy

PLACES TO EAT
10 La Randonnée
11 Chez Georges
12 Le Garet
13 Bistro Pizay &
     Alyssaar
     La Case Créole
50 Brasserie Georges

OTHER
1   Amphithéâtre des
     Trois Gauls
     (Roman Theatre)
2   Les Halles de la
     Martinière
     (Food Market)
5   Albion, Shamrock and
     Barrel House Bars
6   Musée des Beaux-Arts
7   Post Office Branch
8   Hôtel de Ville
9   Opéra
14 Banks
15 Cinéma Ambience
16 Banque de France
17 Musée de l'Imprimerie
18 église Saint Nizier
20 Musée Gadagne
21 Tour Métallique
22 Fourvière Funicular
     Station
23 Basilique Notre Dame
     de Fourvière
24 Outdoor Food Market
25 American Express
26 British Consulate
27 Cathédrale Saint Jean
28 Tourist Office Annexe
29 Musée Gallo-Romain
30 Roman Theatres
31 Minimes Funicular Stop
33 Launderette
34 Louis XIV Statue
35 Eton English Bookshop
36 Main Tourist Office &
     SNCF Desk
37 Main Post Office
38 Launderette
39 Musée des Arts
     Décoratifs
40 Musée Historiques
     des Tissus
42 Post Office Branch
44 Commissariat de Police
47 Centre d'échange &
     Bus Terminal
48 Airport Bus (Satobus)
49 Gare de Perrache
     (Train Station)

FRANCE

Information

Tourist Offices The main tourist office (☎ 04 72 77 69 69; fax 04 78 42 04 32) is in the south-east corner of Place Bellecour. It's open from 9 am to 6 pm (7 pm from mid-June to mid-September), and on weekends until 5 pm (6 pm in summer). The same building houses an SNCF information and reservations desk, open Monday to Friday from 9 am to 6 pm and Saturday from 9 am to 5 pm.

In Vieux Lyon, the tourist office annexe on Ave Adolphe Max, next to the lower funicular station, is open from 9 am to 1 pm and 2 to 6 pm (Saturday from 9 or 10 am to 5 pm). From mid-June to mid-September, hours are 10.30 am to 7.30 pm.

Money The Banque de France is at 14 Rue de la République on Place de la Bourse. There are plenty of banks on Rue Victor Hugo just north of Place Ampère. Near Place des Terreaux, there are a number of banks on Rue de la République and Rue du Bât d'Argent.

American Express (☎ 04 78 37 40 69), near Place de la République at 6 Rue Childebert, is open weekdays from 9 am to 12.30 pm and 2 to 6 pm and, from May to September, on Saturday morning also. There are Thomas Cook exchange offices at both main line train stations.

Post The main post office at 10 Place Antonin Poncet has foreign currency services. The branch office at 3 Rue du Président Édouard Herriot, near Place des Terreaux, can also change money. There is another office at 8 Place Ampère.

Cybercafés Check your email at the Connectik Café (☎ 04 72 77 98 85; info@connectik.fr; www.connectik.fr), 19 Quai Saint Antoine. One/five hours online costs 75/250FF.

Bookshops The Eton English Bookshop (☎ 04 78 92 92 36) at 1 Rue du Plat has lots of new paperbacks as well as some Lonely Planet titles. Students get a 5% discount.

Things to See & Do

The tourist office has details of guided tours of Lyon on foot, by boat and by bus. Alternatively you can hire a set of head phones to guide yourself round the city, or hop on a bus (☎ 04 78 98 56 00) for a two-hour tour in comfort.

Vieux Lyon The old city, whose narrow streets are lined with over 300 meticulously restored medieval and Renaissance houses, lies at the base of Fourvière hill. The area underwent urban renewal two decades ago and has since become a trendy place in which to live and socialise. Many of the most interesting old buildings are along Rue du Bœuf, Rue Juiverie, Rue des Trois Maries and Rue Saint Jean. Traboules that can be explored include those at 26 Rue Saint Jean and 1 Rue du Bœuf; a comprehensive list is available at the tourist office.

Begun in the late 12th century, the mainly Romanesque **Cathédrale Saint Jean** has a Flamboyant Gothic façade and portals decorated with stone medallions from the early 14th century. Don't miss the 14th-century astronomical clock in the north transept. The cathedral can be visited daily from 7.30 am to noon and 2 to 7.30 pm (5 pm on weekends and holidays).

The **Musée Gadagne** (☎ 04 78 42 03 61) at 12 Rue de Gadagne has two sections: the Musée de la Marionette, featuring puppets of all sorts, including *guignol* (a French 'Punch-and-Judy' which has become one of the city's symbols), created by the museum's founder, Laurent Mourguet (1769-1844); and the Musée Historique, which illustrates the history of Lyon. Both are open from 10.45 am to 6 pm (8.30 pm on Friday; closed Tuesday). Admission is 25FF (15FF for students).

Fourvière Two thousand years ago, the Romans built the city of Lugdunum on the slopes of Fourvière. Today, the hill – topped by the Tour Métallique, a sort of stunted Eiffel Tower erected in 1893 and now used as a TV transmitter – offers spectacular views of Lyon and its two rivers.

Several paths lead up the slope, but the easiest way to the top is the funicular railway from Place Édouard Commette in Vieux Lyon. The Fourvière line operates daily until 10 pm. You can use a bus/metro ticket or you can purchase a special return ticket for

12.50FF, which is valid all day for one trip up and one trip down.

The exceptional **Musée Gallo-Romain** (☎ 04 72 38 81 90), 17 Rue Cléberg (south of the Fourvière funicular station), is well worth seeing even if you don't consider yourself a fan of Roman history. Among the museum's extraordinary artefacts, almost all of which were found in the Rhône Valley area, are the remains of a four-wheeled vehicle from around 700 BC, several sumptuous mosaics and lots of Latin inscriptions, including the bronze text of a speech made by the Lyon-born Roman emperor Claudius in 48 AD. The two rebuilt Roman theatres next to the museum are still used for concerts in June. The museum is open from 9.30 am to noon and 2 to 6 pm (closed Monday and Tuesday). Admission is 20FF (10FF for students).

Like Sacré Cœur in Paris, the **Basilique de Notre Dame de Fourvière**, completed in 1896, was built by subscription to fulfil a vow taken by local Catholics during the disastrous Franco-Prussian War (1870-71). If overwrought marble and mosaics are not your cup of tea, the panoramic view from the nearby terrace still merits a visit. It's open from 6 am to 7 pm.

Presqu'île In the middle of the **Place des Terreaux** there is a monumental 19th-century fountain by Bartholdi, sculptor of New York's *Statue of Liberty*. The four horses represent the four major French rivers galloping seaward. Fronting the square is the **Hôtel de Ville**, built in 1655 but given its present façade in 1702. To the south, there are upmarket shops along and around **Rue de la République**, known for its 19th-century buildings; it's a pedestrian mall, as is Rue Victor Hugo, which runs southward from 17th-century **Place Bellecour**, one of the largest public squares in Europe.

The Lyonnais are especially proud of their **Musée Historique des Tissus** (Textiles Museum; ☎ 04 78 37 15 05) at 34 Rue de la Charité. Its collection includes extraordinary Lyonnais silks and fabrics from around the world. The museum is open from 10 am to 5.30 pm (closed Monday and holidays). Entry is 28FF (15FF for students). The ticket also gets you into the nearby **Musée des Arts Décoratifs**, at No 30, which closes between noon and 2 pm.

The history of printing, a technology that had firmly established itself in Lyon in the 1480s (less than 40 years after its invention) is illustrated by the **Musée de l'Imprimerie** (☎ 04 78 37 65 98) at 13 Rue de la Poulaillerie. Among the exhibits are some of the first books ever printed, including a page of a Gutenberg Bible (1450s) and several incunabula (books printed before 1500). The museum is open from 9.30 am to noon and 2 to 6 pm (all day Friday), closed Monday and Tuesday. The entry fee is 25FF (15FF for students).

Lyon's outstanding fine arts museum, the **Musée des Beaux-Arts** (☎ 04 72 10 17 40), whose 90 rooms house sculptures and paintings from every period of European art, is at 20 Place des Terreaux. It's open from 10.30 am to 6 pm (closed Monday and Tuesday). Entry is 25FF (15FF for students).

Set up by the Guild of Silk Workers (called *canuts* in French), the **Maison des Canuts** (☎ 04 78 28 62 04) at 10-12 Rue d'Ivry (300m north of the Croix Rousse metro stop) traces the history of Lyon's silk-weaving industry. Weavers are usually on hand to demonstrate the art of operating traditional silk looms. It's open weekdays from 8.30 am to noon and 2 to 6.30 pm and Saturday from 9 am to noon and 2 to 6 pm. Tickets cost 15FF (10FF for students).

Other Attractions The Musée d'Art Contemporain (☎ 04 72 69 17 17) is housed in the Cité Internationale, 81 Quai Charles de Gaulle, and specialises in work produced after 1960. It is only open during exhibitions (the tourist office has details).

The **Institut Lumière** (☎ 04 78 78 18 95) at 25 Rue du Premier-Film has a permanent exhibition on the work of the motion picture pioneers Auguste and Louis Lumière. The institute is open daily, except Monday, from 2 to 7 pm, and tickets cost 25FF (20FF for students). The old workshop opposite the institute is being restored to house a cinema which is scheduled to open in late 1998. On summer evenings, open-air films are screened for free in the square in front of the institute.

Places to Stay

Camping The *Camping Municipal Porte de Lyon* (☎ 04 78 35 64 55), about 10km north of Lyon in Dardilly, is open year-round. This attractive and well-equipped camping ground (with facilities for the disabled) charges 66FF for two people with a tent and car. Bus No 19 (towards Ecully-Dardilly) from the Hôtel de Ville metro station stops right in front of it.

Hostels The *Auberge de Jeunesse* (☎ 04 78 76 39 23) is about 5km south-east of Gare de Perrache at 51 Rue Roger Salengro in Vénissieux. Dorm beds cost 48FF and reception is open from 7.30 am to 12.30 am. To get there from the Presqu'île, take bus No 35 from Place Bellecour (get off at the Georges Lévy stop); from Gare de Perrache take bus No 53 (alight at the États-Unis-Viviani stop). A new auberge de jeunesse was due to open at 40-45 Montée du Chemin Neuf in Vieux Lyon in June 1998.

The *Centre International de Séjour* (☎ 04 78 76 14 22) is about 4km south-east of Gare de Perrache, behind 101 Blvd des États-Unis. A bed in a quad/double/single costs 82/104/130FF (78/93/123FF on weekends) per person, including breakfast. From the train stations, take the same buses as for the Auberge de Jeunesse.

Hotels The neighbourhood around Place Carnot, just north of Gare de Perrache, is a bit on the seedy side, but the hotels here are convenient if you're travelling by train. Close to the station is the *Hôtel Alexandra* (☎ 04 78 37 75 79; fax 04 72 40 94 34), 49 Rue Victor Hugo, which has rooms for one or two people with shower/bath for 190/249FF. One of the most affordable places in town is the nearby *Hôtel de Vichy* (☎ 04 78 37 42 58) at 60 bis Rue de la Charité (1st floor), with rock-bottom rooms for 135/145FF for one/two people.

In the area north of the train station, the spotless *Hôtel Vaubecour* (☎ 04 78 37 44 91; fax 04 78 42 90 17), 28 Rue Vaubecour, has basic singles/doubles from 110/140FF, and triples/quads with washbasin and bidet at 199FF. Hall showers are 15FF. The friendly, family-run *Hôtel d'Ainay* (☎ 04 78 42 43 42), 14 Rue des Remparts d'Ainay (2nd floor) just off Place Ampère, has singles/

doubles from 139/175FF (208/218FF with shower, 225/235FF with shower and toilet). Hall showers are 15FF.

The *Hôtel Le Terme* (☎ 04 78 28 30 45; fax 04 78 27 38 29), 7 Rue Sainte Catherine, is in a lively area a few blocks north-west of the Hôtel de Ville. It has simply furnished singles/doubles/triples with washbasin and bidet for 130/180/200FF. Doubles with shower are 250FF. The *Hôtel Celtic* (☎ 04 78 28 01 12; fax 04 78 28 01 34) at 10 Rue François Vernay in Vieux Lyon has clean singles/doubles with shared shower for 130/160FF. A private shower is 30FF extra.

Places to Eat

There are two *bouchons* – small, friendly, unpretentious restaurants that serve traditional Lyonnais cuisine – near Place des Terreaux. One is *Chez Georges* (☎ 04 78 28 30 46) at 8 Rue du Garet. The other is the cosy *Le Garet* (☎ 04 78 28 16 94) at 7 Rue du Garet, which is popular with locals and has a 56FF plat du jour. Both are open Monday to Friday. *Alyssaar* (☎ 04 78 29 57 66), 29 Rue du Bât d'Argent, is a Syrian restaurant with *menus* at 78, 87 and 105FF. It's open Monday to Saturday from 7.30 pm until midnight.

The *Bistro Pizay* (☎ 04 78 28 37 26), 4 Rue Verdi, has a terrace around the back in summer and serves unusual lasagne de foie gras aux pommes (duck liver pâté lasagne with apples). *Menus* are 72 or 98FF and it is open until 11.30 pm (closed all day Monday and Tuesday lunchtime). A young and trendy crowd inhabits *La Case Créole* (☎ 04 78 29 41 70), a Creole place at 4 Rue Verdi. *Menus* start at 68FF and it's open until 11 pm (closed all day Tuesday and Wednesday lunchtime). The cheap and cheerful *La Randonnée* (☎ 04 78 27 86 81), 4 Rue Terme, has a vegetarian plate for 30FF, a *rapide buffet* for 25FF, and evening *menus* from 49FF. It's closed Sunday lunchtime and all day Monday.

For a splurge, you might try *Brasserie Georges* (☎ 04 72 56 54 54) at 30 Cours de Verdun Perrache by the train station. It has been serving food in its vast Art Deco dining room since 1836 and has become a bit of an institution. It's open from 7 am to 12.15 am, with live music on Saturday nights.

Fresh fruit, veg, olives, cheese and bread are sold at the *outdoor food market* held each morning, except Monday, on Quai Saint Antoine. In the northern Presqu'île, the covered market *Halle de la Martinière* at 24 Rue de la Martinière is open from 6.30 am to 12.30 pm and 4 to 7.30 pm (closed Sunday afternoon and Monday). There is a giant *Carrefour* supermarket in the Part Dieu Centre (closed Sunday).

Entertainment
Ask at the tourist office for the free fortnightly publication *Le Petit Bulletin*. It gives the latest on Lyon's lively cultural life, which includes theatre, opera, dance, classical music, jazz, variety shows, sporting events and films.

The *Albion* at 12 Rue Sainte Catherine, and its near neighbours the *Shamrock* and the *Barrel House*, are three of the city's most popular late night hang-outs. All are open until 3 am on weekends. *Kafé Myzik* (☎ 04 72 07 04 26) is a hole-in-the-wall bar-cum-club at 20 Montée St Sébastien which often hosts live bands. Admission costs a token 1FF.

Getting There & Away
Air Aéroport Lyon-Satolas (☎ 04 72 22 76 91) is 25km east of the city.

Bus Most intercity buses (of which there are relatively few) depart from the bus terminal under the Centre d'Échange (the building next to Gare de Perrache). Timetables are available from the TCL information office (☎ 04 78 71 70 00; www.tcl.fr), which is on the lower level of the Centre d'Échange. Tickets are sold by the driver. Buses for destinations west of Lyon (information ☎ 04 78 43 40 74) leave from outside the Gorge de Loup metro station.

Train Lyon has two train stations: Gare de Perrache and Gare de la Part-Dieu (☎ 08 36 35 35 39 for both). You can travel between the stations by metro (change at Charpennes), but if there happens to be an SNCF train going from one station to the other you can take it without buying an additional ticket.

The complex that includes Gare de Perrache consists of two main buildings: the

Centre d'Échange, the inside of which serves as a bus terminal and metro station; and, southward over the pedestrian bridge, the SNCF station itself. In the latter, the information office on the lower level is open weekdays from 9 am to 7 pm (6.30 pm Saturday, closed Sunday). Gare de la Part-Dieu is 2km east of Place de la République. The information office (same opening hours as Perrache) is beside the Sortie Vivier-Merle exit.

Lyon has direct rail links to all parts of France and Europe. Trains to/from Paris (232 to 304FF by TGV) use the capital's Gare de Lyon. Following the completion of the new high-speed rail tracks to the south of the city (see the Getting Around section at the start of this chapter), Lyon will have direct TGV links to Avignon, Marseille and Montpellier.

Getting Around
To/From the Airport Satobus buses to Aéroport Lyon-Satolas run daily from 5 am to 9 pm (later if there are incoming flights), departing every 20 minutes. They cost 46FF and take about 45 minutes from Gare de Perrache (near the taxi stand), and 35 minutes from Gare de la Part-Dieu.

Bus & Metro Lyon's metro system, run by TCL, has four lines (A to D) which operate between 5 am and midnight. Tickets, which cost 8FF, are valid for one-way travel on buses, trolleybuses, the funicular and the metro for one hour after time-stamping. A carnet of 10 tickets is 68FF. The Ticket Liberté (24FF), good for a day of unlimited travel, can be bought at some metro ticket machines, on buses and at TCL information offices.

TCL (☎ 04 78 71 70 00) has information offices on the middle level of the Centre d'Échange; at 43 Rue de la République; underground at Place Bellecour at the entrance to metro line A; at Vieux Lyon next to the entrance to metro line D; and at 19 Blvd Marius Vivier-Merle (near Gare de la Part-Dieu).

Taxi Taxi Lyonnais (☎ 04 78 26 81 81) operates 24 hours a day.

The French Alps

The French Alps, where craggy, snowbound peaks soar above fertile, green valleys, is without doubt one of the most awe-inspiring mountain ranges in the world. In summer, visitors can take advantage of hundreds of kilometres of magnificent hiking trails and engage in all sorts of warm-weather sporting activities. In winter, the area's fine ski resorts attract enthusiasts from around the world.

If you're going to ski or snowboard, expect to pay at least 250FF a day (including equip-ment hire, lifts and transport) at low-altitude stations, which usually operate from Decem-ber to March. The larger, high-altitude stations cost 350 to 450FF a day. The cheap-est time to go skiing is in January, between the school holiday periods. Tourist offices have up-to-the-minute information on ski conditions, hotel availability and prices.

CHAMONIX

The town of Chamonix (population 9700; 1037m) sits in a valley surrounded by the most spectacular scenery in the French Alps.

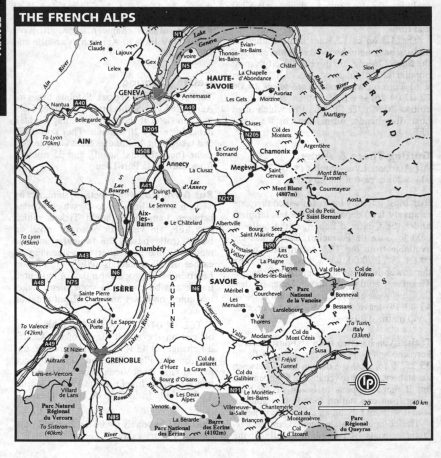

THE FRENCH ALPS

The area is almost Himalayan in its awesomeness: deeply crevassed glaciers many kilometres long ooze down the valleys between the icy peaks and pinnacles around Mont Blanc, which soars almost four vertical kilometres above the valley floor. In late spring and summer, the high-altitude snow and glaciers serve as a glistening white backdrop for meadows and hillsides rich in wild flowers, shrubs and pine woods.

There are some 330km of hiking trails in the Chamonix area. In winter, the valley offers superb skiing, with dozens of ski lifts and over 200km of downhill and cross-country ski runs.

Climate Weather changes rapidly in Chamonix. Bulletins from the meteorological service (*la météo*) are posted in the window of the tourist office and at the Maison de la Montagne. It's a good idea to bring warm clothing as even in summer it can get pretty cool at night.

Orientation
To the east of the Chamonix Valley rise the Aiguilles de Chamonix mountain range and Mont Blanc (4807m), the highest mountain in the Alps. The almost glacier-free Aiguilles Rouges range – its highest peak is Le Brévent (2525m) – runs along the western side of the valley.

Information
Tourist Office The tourist office (☎ 04 50 53 00 24; fax 04 50 53 58 90; info@chamonix .com; www.chamonix.com) at Place du Triangle de l'Amitié (opposite Place de l'Église) is open daily from 8.30 am to 12.30 pm and 2 to 7 pm (closed Sunday). Useful brochures on ski-lift hours and costs, refuges, camping grounds and parapente schools are available. In winter it sells a range of ski passes, valid for bus transport and all the ski lifts in the valley (except Lognan-Les Grands Montets).

Maison de la Montagne The Maison de la Montagne, near the tourist office at 109 Place de l'Église, houses the Office de Haute Montagne (2nd floor; ☎ 04 50 53 22 08), which has information and maps for walkers and mountaineers. It's open from 9 am to 12.30 pm and 2.30 to 6.30 pm (closed Sunday).

Money There are quite a few places to change money in the area between the tourist office and the post office. Le Change at 21 Place Balmat offers a decent rate. Outside is a 24-hour exchange machine that accepts banknotes in any of 15 currencies. The exchange service at the tourist office is open on weekends and bank holidays and, in July and August, every day. No commission is charged.

Post The post office at Place Balmat is open weekdays from 8 am to noon and 2 to 6 pm and on Saturday from 8 am to noon. During July and August, weekday hours are 8 am to 7 pm.

Cybercafés Mont Blanc Online (☎ 04 50 53 23 19; fax 04 50 53 87 21; chamonix@ montblanconline.fr), 85 Rue des Moulins, charges 30/55FF for 30 minutes/one hour online and is open from 9 am to 7 pm (closed Sunday).

Things to See & Do
Aiguille du Midi The Aiguille ('needle'; pronounced 'eh-gwee') du Midi (3842m) is a lone spire of rock 8km from the summit of Mont Blanc. The *téléphérique* (cable car) from Chamonix to the Aiguille du Midi is the highest cable car in the world, crossing glaciers, snowfields and rocky crags; the views in all directions are truly breathtaking and should not be missed. In general, visibility is best early in the morning.

Between April and September, you can take a second cable car from the Aiguille du Midi across the glacier to **Pointe Helbronner** (3466m) and down to the Italian ski resort of **Courmayeur**. Return tickets to the Aiguille du Midi cost 194FF; it's an extra 96FF return to Pointe Helbronner. One-way prices are only 20% less. A ride from Chamonix to the cable car's halfway point, Plan de l'Aiguille (2308m) – an excellent place to start hikes in summer – costs 64FF one way.

The téléphérique operates all year from 8 am to 3.45 pm (6 am to 4.45 pm in July and August). To avoid the long queues, try to arrive as early as possible, preferably before 9.30 am when the buses start to arrive. You can make advance reservations 24 hours a day by calling ☎ 04 50 53 40 00.

FRANCE

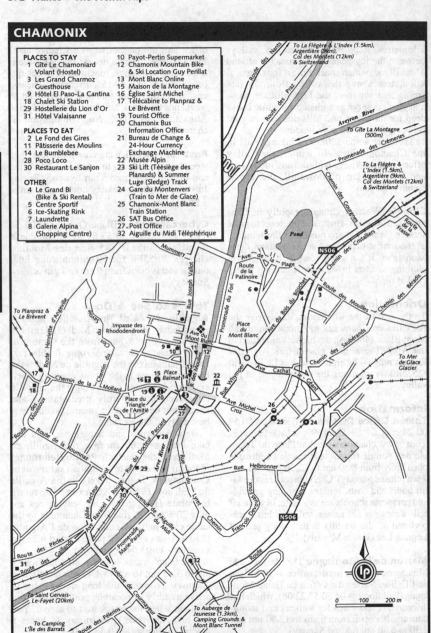

CHAMONIX

PLACES TO STAY
1 Gîte Le Chamoniard Volant (Hostel)
3 Les Grand Charmoz Guesthouse
9 Hôtel El Paso-La Cantina
18 Chalet Ski Station
29 Hostellerie du Lion d'Or
31 Hôtel Valaisanne

PLACES TO EAT
2 Le Fond des Gires
11 Pâtisserie des Moulins
14 Le Bumblebee
28 Poco Loco
30 Restaurant Le Sanjon

OTHER
4 Le Grand Bi (Bike & Ski Rental)
5 Centre Sportif
6 Ice-Skating Rink
7 Laundrette
8 Galerie Alpina (Shopping Centre)
10 Payot-Pertin Supermarket
12 Chamonix Mountain Bike & Ski Location Guy Perillat
13 Mont Blanc Online
15 Maison de la Montagne
16 Église Saint Michel
17 Télécabine to Planpraz & Le Brévent
19 Tourist Office
20 Chamonix Bus Information Office
21 Bureau de Change & 24-Hour Currency Exchange Machine
22 Musée Alpin
23 Ski Lift (Téésiège des Planards) & Summer Luge (Sledge) Track
24 Gare du Montenvers (Train to Mer de Glace)
25 Chamonix-Mont Blanc Train Station
26 SAT Bus Office
27 Post Office
32 Aiguille du Midi Téléphérique

To La Flégère & L'Index (1.5km), Argentière (9km), Col des Montets (12km) & Switzerland

Route des Nants

Route du Praz

Aveyron River

To Gîte La Montagne (500m)

Promenade des Crémeries

To La Flégère & L'Index (1.5km), Argentière (9km), Col des Montets (12km) & Switzerland

Route de la Frasse

Chemin des Cristalliers

Pond

N506

Chemin des Bérards

Chemin des Mouilles

Route des Mouilles

Mummery

Ave de la Plage

Route de la Patinoire

Route du Bois du Bouchet

Chemin des Sauberands

Rue Joseph Vallot

Promenade du Fori

Place du Mont Blanc

Ave du Bois du Bouchet

To Mer de Glace Glacier

To Planpraz & Le Brévent

Route Henriette d'Angeville

Clos du Savoie

Impasse des Rhododendrons

Ave du Mont Blanc

Chemin des Moulins

Ave Cachat - le Géant

Chemin de la J Mollard

Place Balmat

Rue Whymper

Ave Michel Croz

Place du Triangle de l'Amitié

Route des Moussoux

Route de la Roumnaz

Rue du Docteur Paccard

Arve River

Rue Ravanel Le Rouge

Allée Recteur Payot

Avenue de l'Aiguille du Midi

Rue du Lyret

Promenade Marie-Paradis

Rue Helbronner

Blanche

Rue François Devouassoux

N506

Route des Pèches

Route des Gaillands

To Saint Gervais-Le-Fayet (20km)

To Camping L'Île des Barrats

Route des Pèlerins

Avenue de Courmayeur

To Auberge de Jeunesse (1.3km), Camping Grounds & Mont Blanc Tunnel

0   100   200 m

LP

Le Brévent Le Brévent (2525m), the highest peak on the west side of the valley, is known for its great views of Mont Blanc and the Aiguilles de Chamonix. It can be reached from Chamonix by a combination of *télécabine* (gondola) and téléphérique (☎ 04 50 53 13 18) for 55FF one way (80FF return). Service begins at 9 am (8 am in summer) and stops at 5 pm (an hour or so earlier in winter). Quite a few hiking trails, including various routes back to the valley, can be picked up at Le Brévent or at the cable car's midway station, Planpraz (1999m; 46FF one way).

Mer de Glace The heavily crevassed Mer de Glace (Sea of Ice), the second-largest glacier in the Alps, is 14km long, 1950m across at its widest point and up to 400m deep. It has become a popular tourist destination thanks to a *crémaillère* (cog-wheel railway) which has an upper terminus at an altitude of 1913m.

The train, which runs all year (weather permitting), leaves from Gare du Montenvers (☎ 04 50 53 12 54) in Chamonix. A one-way/return trip costs 56/67FF. A combined ticket valid for the train, the gondola to the ice cave (Grotte de la Mer de Glace; 15FF return) and entry to the cave (14FF) costs 105FF. There are often long queues for the train during July and August. The ride takes 20 minutes each way.

The Mer de Glace can also be reached on foot from Plan de l'Aiguille (take the Grand Balcon Nord – see Activities below) and from Chamonix. The uphill trail, which takes about two or 2½ hours, begins near the summer bobsleigh track. Traversing the glacier, with its many crevasses, without a guide and proper mountaineering equipment is extremely dangerous.

Musée Alpin This museum (☎ 04 50 53 25 93), at 89 Ave Michel Croz in Chamonix, displays artefacts, lithographs and photos illustrating the history of mountain climbing and other alpine sports. From June to mid-October, it's open daily from 2 to 7 pm; between Christmas and Easter, hours are 3 to 7 pm. It's closed the rest of the year. The entry fee is 20FF.

Activities
Skiing & Snowboarding The Chamonix area has 160km of marked ski runs, 42km of cross-country trails and 64 ski lifts of all sorts.

Many sports shops around Chamonix rent skis and snowboards. Count on paying around 39/220FF a day/week for regular skis or boots. Ski Location Guy Perillat (☎ 04 50 53 54 76) at 138 Rue des Moulins is open daily and also rents out snowboards (99/148FF a day without/with boots or 590/690FF a week). Cross-country skis are available from Le Grand Bi (☎ 04 50 53 14 16) at 240 Ave du Bois du Bouchet.

Hiking In late spring and summer (mid-June to October), the Chamonix area has some of the most spectacular hiking trails anywhere in the Alps. In June and July there is enough light to hike until at least 9 pm.

The Most Beautiful Hikes for Everyone (Editions Aio; 25FF) maps out easy day hikes in the Mont Blanc region. It includes lots of trails and the locations of refuges. The best map of the area is the 1:25,000 scale IGN map (No 3630OT) entitled *Chamonix-Massif du Mont Blanc* (58FF).

The fairly level **Grand Balcon Sud** trail, which traverses the Aiguilles Rouges (western) side of the valley at about 2000m, offers great views of Mont Blanc and the glaciers to the east and south. If you'd prefer to avoid 1km of hard uphill walking, take either the Planpraz (46FF one way) or La Flégère lift (43FF one way).

From Plan de l'Aiguille (64FF one way), the midway point on the Aiguille du Midi cable car, the **Grand Balcon Nord** takes you to the Mer de Glace, from where you can hike down to Chamonix. There are a number of other trails from Plan de l'Aiguille.

There are also trails to **Lac Blanc** (2350m), a turquoise lake surrounded by mountains, from either La Flégère, or the top of Les Praz-L'Index cable car (61FF one way).

Cycling Many of the trails around the valley are perfect for mountain biking (although the well-known Petit Balcon Sud is no longer open to cyclists during July and August). See Getting Around in this section for information on bike rentals.

Parapente Parapente (paragliding) is an air sport in which you launch yourself from a mountain top suspended beneath a wing-shaped, steerable canopy that allows you to catch thermal updraughts and stay airborne for anything up to several hours. An initiation flight (*baptême de l'air*) with an instructor costs 500FF. A five-day beginners' course (*stage d'initiation*) costs around 3000FF. For information, contact the tourist office.

Places to Stay

Camping There are some 13 camp sites in the Chamonix region. In general, camping costs 25FF per person and 12 to 26FF for a tent site. Open from May to September, *L'Île des Barrats* (☎ 04 50 53 51 44) is near the base of the Aiguille du Midi cable car. The three-star *Camping Les Deux Glaciers* (☎ 04 50 53 15 84) on the Route des Tissières in Les Bossons, 3km south of Chamonix, is open all year except from mid-November to mid-December. To get there, take the train to Les Bossons or Chamonix Bus to the Tremplin-le-Mont stop. There are a number of camping grounds a couple of kilometres south of Chamonix in the village of Les Pélerins (near the turn-off to the Mont Blanc Tunnel).

Refuges Most mountain refuges, which cost 90 to 100FF a night, are accessible to hikers, though a few can be reached only by climbers. They are generally open from mid-June to mid-September.

The easier-to-reach refuges include one at Plan de l'Aiguille (☎ 04 50 53 55 60) at 2308m, the intermediate stop on the Aiguille du Midi cable car, and another at La Flégère (☎ 04 50 53 06 13) at 1877m. It's advisable to call ahead to reserve a place, especially in July and August. For information on other refuges, contact the Maison de la Montagne.

Hostels The *Chalet Ski Station* (☎ 04 50 53 20 25) is a gîte d'étape at 6 Route des Moussoux in Chamonix (next to the Planpraz/Le Brévent télécabine station). Beds cost 60FF a night, there's a 15FF charge for sheets, and showers are 5FF. It's closed from 10 May to 20 June and from 20 September to 20 December.

The semi-rustic *Gîte Le Chamoniard*

Volant (☎ 04 50 53 14 09) is on the north-eastern outskirts of town at 45 Route de la Frasse. A bunk in a cramped, functional room of four, six or eight beds costs 66FF; sheets are 20FF, and an evening meal is available for 66FF. The nearest bus stop is La Frasse.

The *Auberge de Jeunesse* (☎ 04 50 53 14 52; fax 04 50 55 92 34; chamonix@ wanadoo.fr) is a couple of kilometres south-west of Chamonix at 127 Montée Jacques Balmat in Les Pélerins. By bus, take the Chamonix-Les Houches line and get off at the Pélerins École stop. Beds in rooms of four or six cost 74FF. The hostel is closed from October to mid-December.

Hotels At 468 Chemin des Cristalliers next to the railway tracks, *Les Grands Charmoz Guesthouse* (☎ 04 50 53 45 57) has doubles for 184FF. The lively *Hôtel El Paso-La Cantina* (☎ 04 50 53 64 20; fax 04 50 53 64 22), 37 Impasse des Rhododendrons, has comfortable doubles with shared bath for 166/224FF in the low/high season; triples are 236/306FF and quads are 288/358FF. In summer a bed in a dorm costs 70FF. Some rooms can be a bit noisy as there's a lively bar downstairs.

The *Hôtel Valaisanne* (☎ 04 50 53 17 98) is a small, family-owned place at 454 Ave Ravanel Le Rouge, about 1km south of the town centre. Low/high season prices for a double room are 165/266FF. At the *Hostellerie du Lion d'Or* (☎ 04 50 53 15 09), 255 Rue du Docteur Paccard, singles/doubles start at 150/220FF. Reception is in the ground floor restaurant or the bar next door.

Places to Eat

Le Sanjon (☎ 04 50 53 56 44), 5 Ave Ravanel le Rouge, is a picturesque wooden chalet restaurant serving raclette and fondue (69F). A favourite is pierrade – three different meats that you prepare yourself on a small grill, accompanied by six sauces (98FF).

Le Fonds des Gires (☎ 04 50 55 85 76), a self-service restaurant on the north side of town at 350 Route du Bois du Bouchet, is a favourite with people staying at the nearby gîtes. It's open for lunch all year (except January) every day and for dinner until 9 pm in July and August.

Countless restaurants offering pizza,

burgers, fondue etc can be found in the centre of town. *Poco Loco* (☎ 04 50 53 43 03), 47 Rue du Docteur Paccard, has pizzas from 33 to 45FF and *menus* from 50FF. It also serves great hot sandwiches (from 23FF), sweet crêpes (from 8FF), and burgers to eat in or take away. *Le Bumblebee*, 67 Rue Moulins, specialises in good old British food, while the nearby *Pâtisserie des Moulins* (☎ 04 50 53 58 95) at No 95 has the best cakes, pastries and hot chocolate in town; it also offers a lunchtime *menu* for 50FF. *La Cantina*, the Tex-Mex restaurant attached to Hôtel El Paso, has generous main dishes from 55 to 110FF.

The *Payot-Pertin* supermarket, 117 Rue Joseph Vallot, is open 8.15 am to 7.30 pm (8.15 am to 12.45 pm on Sunday in winter only).

Getting There & Away

Bus Chamonix's bus station is next to the train station. SAT Autocar (☎ 04 50 53 01 15) has buses to Annecy (95.30FF), Courmayeur in Italy (53FF; 40 minutes), Geneva (165FF; two hours), Grenoble (157FF) and Turin (138FF, three hours).

Train The narrow-gauge train line from Saint Gervais-Le Fayet (20km west of Chamonix) to Martigny, Switzerland (42km north of Chamonix), stops at 11 towns in the Chamonix Valley. There are nine to 12 return trips a day. You have to change trains at Châtelard or Vallorcine on the Swiss border. From Saint Gervais there are trains to destinations all over France.

Chamonix-Mont Blanc train station (☎ 04 50 53 00 44) is on the east side of town. Ticket counters are staffed from 6 am to 8 pm. The left luggage counter is open from 6.45 am to 8.45 pm (20FF for the first piece of luggage; 10FF for each additional piece). Major destinations include Paris' Gare de Lyon (374FF; six to seven hours), Lyon (184FF; four to 4½ hours) and Geneva (93FF; two to 2½ hours via Saint Gervais).

Getting Around

Bus Bus transport in the valley is handled by Chamonix Bus (☎ 04 50 53 05 55), whose stops are marked by black-on-yellow roadside signs. From mid-December to mid-May, there are 13 lines to all the ski lifts in the area;

during the rest of the year, there are only two (south to Les Houches and north to Argentière and Col des Montets), both of which leave from Place de l'Église and pass by the Chamonix Sud stop. Buses stop running at about 7 pm (6 or 6.30 pm in June and September).

The Chamonix Bus information office at Place de l'Église (opposite the tourist office) is open daily in winter from 8 am to 7 pm. The rest of the year, hours are from 8 am to noon and 2 to 6.30 pm (7 pm from June to August).

Taxi There is a taxi stand (☎ 04 50 53 13 94) outside the train station.

Bicycle Between April and October, Le Grand Bi (☎ 04 50 53 14 16), 240 Ave du Bois du Bouchet, has three and 10-speeds for 65FF a day and mountain bikes for 100FF. It's open from 8.30 am to noon and 2 to 7 pm (closed Sunday).

Chamonix Mountain Bike (☎ 04 50 53 54 76), 138 Rue des Moulins, is open from 9 am to noon and 2 to 7 pm (no midday break during summer and winter holidays). The tariff is 50/95FF for two hours/one day.

ANNECY

Annecy (population 50,000; 448m), situated at the northern tip of the incredibly blue Lac d'Annecy, is the perfect place to spend a relaxing holiday. Visitors in a sedentary mood can sit along the lake and feed the swans or mosey around the geranium-lined canals of the old city. Museums and other sights are limited, but for the athletically inclined, the town is an excellent base for water sports, hiking and biking.

Orientation

The train and bus stations are 500m northwest of the old city, which is centred around the canalised Thiou River. The modern town centre is between the main post office and the Centre Bonlieu complex. The lake town of Annecy-le-Vieux is just east of Annecy.

Information

In the Centre Bonlieu north of Place de la Libération is the tourist office (☎ 04 50 45 00 33;

ANNECY

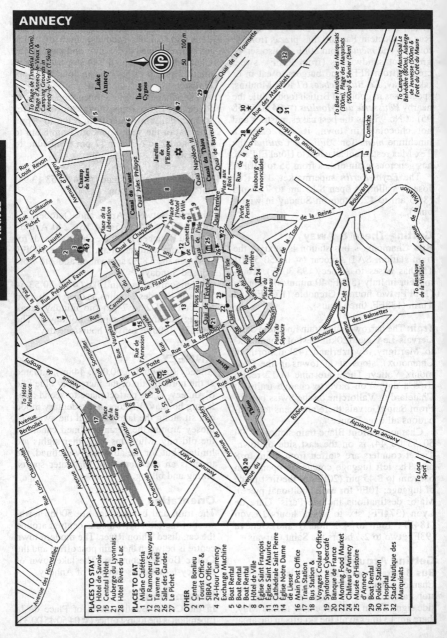

To Plage de l'Impérial (700m),
Plage d'Annecy-le-Vieux &
Camping Grounds in
Annecy-le-Vieux (1.5km)

Lake
Annecy

Île des
Cygnes

Champ
de Mars

Jardins
de l'Europe

Place de
la Libération

Place de
l'Hôtel
de Ville

Place aux
Bois

Faubourg des
Annonciades

Place du
Château

Porte du
Sépulcre

Faubourg

Place de
la Gare

Hôtel
Plaisance

Place du
Château

To Basilique
de la Visitation

To Camping Municipal le
Belvédère (800m), Auberge
de Jeunesse (500m) &
Forêt du Crêt du Maure

To Base Nautique des Marquisats
(300m), Plage des Marquisats
(500m) & Sévrier (5km)

To Loca
Sport

PLACES TO STAY
10 Hôtel de Savoie
15 Central Hôtel
21 Auberge du Lyonnais
28 Hôtel Rives du Lac

PLACES TO EAT
1 Midine Cafétéria
12 Le Ramoneur Savoyard
23 Taverne du Freti
26 Salle des Gardes
27 Le Pichet

OTHER
2 Centre Bonlieu
3 Tourist Office &
   SIBRA Office
4 24-Hour Currency
   Exchange Machine
5 Boat Rental
6 Boat Rental
7 Boat Rental
8 Hôtel de Ville
9 Église Saint François
11 Église Saint Maurice
13 Cathédrale Saint Pierre
14 Église Notre Dame
   de Liesse
16 Main Post Office
17 Train Station
18 Bus Station &
   Voyages Crolard Office
19 Syndrome Cybercafé
20 Banque de France
22 Morning Food Market
24 Château d'Annecy
25 Musée d'Histoire
   d'Annecy
29 Boat Rental
30 Police Station
31 Hospital
32 Stade Nautique des
   Marquisats

fax 04 50 51 87 20; ancytour@cyberaccess.fr; www.lac-annecy.com). It's open Monday to Saturday from 9 am to noon and 1.45 to 6.30 pm (closed Sunday). In July and August it does not close at midday and from mid-May to mid-October it's open on Sunday from 9 am to noon and 1.45 to 6 pm.

The Banque de France, 9 bis Ave de Chambéry, is open weekdays from 8.45 am to noon and 1.45 to 3.45 pm. There's a 24-hour currency exchange machine in the Crédit Lyonnais, Centre Bonlieu, that accepts 15 different currencies.

The main post office is at 4 bis Rue des Glières. Foreign exchange services are available.

Cybercafés At 3 bis ve de Chevêne the Syndrome Cybercafé (☎ 04 50 45 39 75; fax 04 50 45 85 65; infos@syndrome.com; www .syndrome.com) is open from 9 am to midnight (closed Monday and Tuesday). One hour online costs 40FF.

Things to See & Do
Walking Tour Just walking around, taking in the lake, flowers, grass and quaint buildings, is the essence of a visit to Annecy.

Just east of the old city, behind the Hôtel de Ville, are the flowery **Jardins de l'Europe**, shaded by giant Californian redwoods. There's a pleasant stroll from the Jardins de l'Europe along Quai de Bayreuth and Quai de la Tournette to the Base Nautique des Marquisats and beyond. Another fine promenade begins at the **Champ de Mars**, across the Canal du Vassé from the redwoods, and goes eastward around the lake towards Annecy-le-Vieux.

Old City The Vieille Ville, an area of narrow streets on either side of the Canal du Thiou, retains much of its 17th-century appearance despite recent 'quaintification'. On the island in the middle, the Palais de l'Isle (a former prison) houses the **Musée d'Histoire d'Annecy et de la Haute-Savoie** (☎ 04 50 33 87 31), which is open daily, except Tuesday, from 10 am to noon and 2 to 6 pm (daily from June to September with no midday closure). Entry costs 20FF (5FF for students).

Château d'Annecy The **Musée d'Annecy** (☎ 04 50 33 87 30), housed in the 13th to 16th-century chateau overlooking the town, puts on innovative temporary exhibitions and has a permanent collection of local craftwork and miscellaneous objects relating to the region's natural history. It keeps the same hours as Musée d'Histoire d'Annecy et de la Haute-Savoie. Entry is 30FF (10FF for students). The climb up to the chateau is worth it just for the view.

Beaches A kilometre north-east of the Champ de Mars there is a free beach, **Plage d'Annecy-le-Vieux**. A beach slightly closer to town, next to the casino, is the **Plage de l'Impérial**, which costs 18FF and is equipped with changing rooms, sporting facilities and other amenities. Perhaps Annecy's most pleasant stretch of lawn-lined swimming beach is the free **Plage des Marquisats**, 1km south of the old city along Rue des Marquisats. The beaches are officially open from June to September.

Activities
Hiking The Forêt du Crêt du Maure, the forested area south of the old city, has lots of trails, but there are nicer hiking areas in and around two nature reserves: **Bout du Lac** (20km from Annecy at the southern tip of the lake) and **Roc de Chère** (10km from town on the east coast of the lake). Both can be reached by Voyages Crolard buses (see Getting There & Away).

Cycling & Inline Skating There is a bike path (also suitable for inline skating) along the western side of the lake. It starts 1.5km south of Annecy (off Rue des Marquisats) and goes all the way to the lakeside town of Duingt, about 14km to the south.

Bikes can be rented from Loca Sports (☎ 04 50 45 44 33), south-west of the Vieille Ville at 37 Ave de Loverchy. Sévrier Sport Location (☎ 04 50 52 42 68), 65 Place de la Mairie (also known as the Place de l'Hôtel de Ville), rents tandems, mountain bikes and inline skates.

Boating From late March to late October, pedal boats and small boats with outboard motors can be hired at the lakeside near the mouths of the Canal du Thiou and Canal du Vassée. Various clubs at the Base Nautique des Marquisats, 800m south of the old city, rent kayaks, canoes, sailboats, and sailboards.

Swimming The Stade Nautique des Marquisats (☎ 04 50 45 39 18), 29 Rue des Marquisats, has three outdoor swimming pools and plenty of lawn. From 1 May to 1 September, the complex is open from 9 am (10 am on Sunday and holidays) to 7 pm (7.30 pm from July to early September). The entrance fee is 19FF (15FF for under 18s).

Parapente Col de la Forclaz, the huge ridge overlooking Lac d'Annecy from the east, is a perfect spot from which to descend by parapente (see the Chamonix section for an explanation of the sport). For details of parapente and hang-gliding (*delta-plane*) schools, contact the tourist office in Annecy.

Places to Stay

Camping The *Camping Municipal Le Belvédère* (☎ 04 50 45 48 30; fax 04 50 45 55 56) is 2.5km south of the train station in the Forêt du Crêt du Maure. From mid-June to early September you can take bus No 91 (Ligne des Vacances) from the train station. Charges are 23FF for a tent site and 25FF per person. There are several other camping grounds near the lake in Annecy-le-Vieux.

Hostels The *Auberge de Jeunesse* (☎ 04 50 45 33 19; fax 04 50 52 77 52) is 1km south of town at 4 Route du Semnoz in the Forêt du Semnoz. From mid-June to early September, bus No 91 goes there. Beds cost 68FF including breakfast. Sheets are an extra 17FF.

Hotels The *Hôtel Plaisance* (☎ 04 50 57 30 42), 17 Rue de Narvik, has simple but bright singles/doubles from 130/140FF and triples for 235FF. Rooms with shower are 180FF. Hall showers are 11FF and breakfast is 25FF. The small *Hôtel Rives du Lac* (☎ 04 50 51 32 85; fax 04 50 45 77 40), superbly located near the Vieille Ville and the lake at 6 Rue des Marquisats, has one or two-bed rooms with shower for 136FF. Breakfast is 24FF.

One of the cheapest places close to the Vieille Ville is the *Central Hôtel* (☎ 04 50 45 05 37) in a quiet courtyard at 6 bis Rue Royale. Doubles start at 160FF. Triples/quads cost 220/230FF. In the heart of the old

city, the *Auberge du Lyonnais* (☎ 04 50 51 26 10; fax 04 50 51 05 04), 9 Rue de la République (on the corner of Quai de l'Évêché), enjoys an idyllic setting next to the canal. Singles/doubles with toilet are 160/200FF. Rooms with shower and toilet are 240/290FF. It only has 10 rooms so get here quick.

One of the most oddly placed hotels in Savoy – if not all of France – is the *Hôtel de Savoie* (☎ 04 50 45 15 45; fax 04 50 45 11 99; hotel.savoie@dotcom.fr) at 1 Place de Saint François, with its entrance on the left side of a (still functioning) church. Spooky. Simple singles/doubles with washbasin are 150/220FF.

Places to Eat

In the old city, there are a number of cheap, hole-in-the-wall sandwich shops along Rue Perrière and Rue de l'Isle, including a couple of good crêperies. Cheap and cheerful dishes are served at *Midine Cafétéria*, a speedy buffet-style eatery at 23 Rue Sommeiller. Tartiflette and salad is 36FF, mussels are 40FF and there is a children's *menu* for 25FF. It's open from 11 am to 9.30 pm (weekends until 10 pm).

The popular *Le Ramoneur Savoyard* (☎ 04 50 51 99 99), 7 Rue de Grenette, has reasonably priced regional dishes, with *menus* from 71 to 155FF. It's open daily for lunch and dinner. *Le Pichet* (☎ 04 50 45 32 41), 13 Rue Perrière, has three-course *menus* for 62 and 74FF. The rather touristy *Salle des Gardes* (☎ 04 50 51 52 00), Quai des Vieilles Prisons, facing the old prison, has Savoyard specialities such as fondue and tartiflette – as does the *Taverne du Freti* (☎ 04 50 51 29 52), 12 Rue Sainte Claire. Its authentic raclette is well worth every centime at 68FF per person. Book a table in advance.

In the old city, there is a *food market* along Rue Sainte Claire on Sunday, Tuesday and Friday from 6 am to 12.30 pm.

Getting There & Away

Bus The bus station, Gare Routière Sud, is on Rue de l'Industrie next to the train station. Voyages Crolard (☎ 04 50 45 08 12) is open from 6.15 am to 12.30 pm and 1.15 to 7.30 pm (closed Sunday). The company has regular services to Roc de Chère on the eastern shore of Lac d'Annecy and Bout du Lac at the far southern tip, as well as to Albertville and Chamonix.

Autocars Frossard (☎ 04 50 45 73 90), open from 7.45 am to 12.30 pm and 1.45 to 7 pm (closed Sunday), sells tickets to Geneva, Grenoble, Nice and elsewhere. Autocars Francony (☎ 04 50 45 02 43) has buses to Chamonix. Its office at the bus station is open weekdays from 7.15 to 11 am and 2.15 to 6.15 pm.

Train The train station (☎ 08 36 35 35 39) is a modernistic structure at Place de la Gare. The information desks are open from 9 am to noon and 2 to 7 pm. The ticket windows are open from 6.10 am to 9.20 pm (9.10 am to 8 pm on weekends). There are frequent trains to Paris' Gare de Lyon (360FF by TGV; 3¾ hours), Nice (340FF via Lyon, 353FF via Aix-les-Bains; eight to nine hours), Lyon (110FF; two hours), Chamonix (104FF; 2½ to three hours) and Aix-les-Bains (39FF; 30 to 45 minutes).

Getting Around

Bus The local bus company SIBRA (☎ 04 50 51 72 72) has an information bureau (☎ 04 50 51 70 33) across the covered courtyard from the tourist office. It's open from 9 am to 7 pm (closed Sunday). Tickets cost 7FF each or 37.50FF for a carnet of eight. Annecy's buses run Monday to Saturday from 6 am to 8 pm. On Sunday, 20-seat minibuses provide limited service. Ligne des Vacances bus No 91 runs only from mid-June to early September.

Taxi Taxis based at the bus station can be ordered by calling ☎ 04 50 45 05 67.

GRENOBLE

Grenoble (population 155,000) is the intellectual and economic capital of the French Alps. Set in a broad valley surrounded by spectacular mountains, this spotlessly clean city has a Swiss feel to it.

Orientation

The old city is centred around Place Grenette, with its many cafés, and Place Notre Dame. Both are about 1km east of the train and bus stations.

Information

Tourist Office The Maison du Tourisme at 14 Rue de la République houses the tourist office (☎ 04 76 42 41 41; fax 04 76 51 28 69), an SNCF train information counter and an information desk for the local bus network (TAG). The first two are open from 9 am to 12.30 pm and 1.30 to 6 pm (closed Sunday). From June to mid-September, the tourist office is also open on Sunday from 10 am to noon. The TAG counter is open from 8.30 am to 6.30 pm (Saturday from 9 am to 6 pm; closed Sunday).

Money & Post The Banque de France on the corner of Blvd Édouard Rey and Ave Félix Viallet is open weekdays from 8.45 am to 12.15 pm and 1.30 to 3.30 pm. The branch post office next door to the tourist office is open weekdays from 8 am to 6.30 pm (closed Sunday and Monday) and Saturday until noon.

Cybercafés You can surf the net and collect email at Cybernet (☎ 04 76 51 73 18; fax 04 76 03 20 33; services@neptune.fr; www .neptune.fr/CyberNetCafe), 3 Rue Bayard. A 30-minute/one-hour online session costs 30/47FF. It's open from noon to 2 pm and 10 pm to 1 am.

Things to See

Built in the 16th century to control the approaches to the city (and expanded in the 19th), **Fort de la Bastille** sits on the north side of the Isère River, 263m above the old city. The fort affords superb views of Grenoble and the surrounding mountain ranges, including Mont Blanc on clear days. A sign near the disused Mont Jalla chair lift (300m beyond the arch next to the toilets) indicates the hiking trails that pass by here. To reach the fort you can take the téléphérique (☎ 04 76 44 33 65) from Quai Stéphane Jay, which costs 22/33FF one way/return (17/26FF for students). Several hiking trails lead up the hillside to the fort.

Housed in a 17th-century convent at 30 Rue Maurice Gignoux (at the foot of the Fort de la Bastille hill), the **Musée Dauphinois** (☎ 04 76 85 19 01) has displays on the history of the Dauphiné region. It's open from 10 am to 7 pm (6 pm from November to April;

GRENOBLE

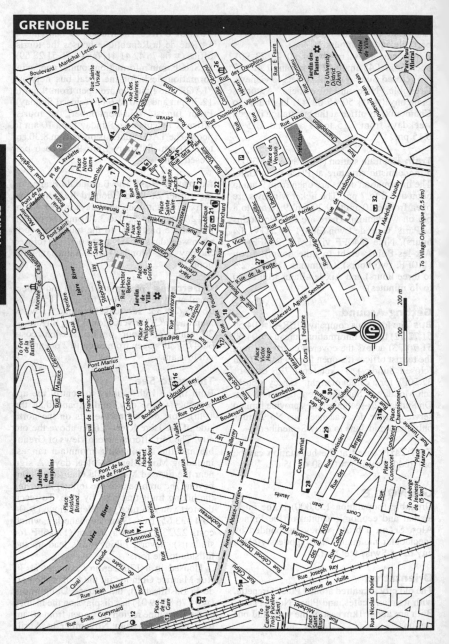

GRENOBLE

PLACES TO STAY		11	Restaurant Universitaire	13	Train Station
3	Foyer de l'Étudiante	17	Les Archers	14	Post Office Branch & Gare
15	Hôtel Alizé	25	La Panse		Europole Tram Stop
24	Hôtel du Moucherotte			16	Banque de France
27	Hôtel de la Poste	**OTHER**		18	Église Saint Louis
28	Hôtel des Doges	1	Musée Dauphinois	19	Prisunic Supermarket
29	Hôtel Victoria	2	Musée de Grenoble	20	Post Office Branch
30	Hôtel Beau Soleil	5	Cathédrale Notre Dame &	21	Maison du Tourisme
31	Hôtel Lakanal		Bishop's Palace	22	Laundrette
		6	Cybernet Cybercafé	23	Les Halles Sainte Claire
PLACES TO EAT		9	Téléphérique to Fort de la		Market
4	La Galerie Rome		Bastille	26	Musée de la Résistance
7	Le Tonneau de Diogène	10	Mountain Bike Grenoble	32	Main Post Office
8	Restaurant des Montagnes	12	Bus Station		

closed Tuesday). Tickets cost 20FF (10FF for students and seniors).

Grenoble's fine arts museum, the **Musée de Grenoble** (☎ 04 76 63 44 44), 5 Place de Lavalette, is known for its fine collection of paintings and sculpture, including a well regarded modern section that features pieces by Matisse, Picasso and Chagall. The museum is open from 11 am to 7 pm (10 pm on Wednesday; closed Monday and Tuesday). Admission costs 25FF (15FF for students).

The **Musée de la Résistance et de la Déportation** (☎ 04 76 42 38 53) at 14 Rue Hébert examines the region's role in the Resistance, and the deportation of Jews from Grenoble to Nazi concentration camps. It's open daily, except Tuesday, from 9 am till noon and 2 to 6 pm. Tickets cost 20FF (10FF for students).

The **Cathédrale Notre Dame** and the adjoining 14th-century Bishop's Palace on Place Notre Dame have recently had complete facelifts and now contain three museums: the **Crypt Archéologique**, with its Roman-era walls and baptistery dating from the 4th to 10th century; the **Musée d'Art Sacré**, containing liturgical and other religious objects; and the **Centre Jean Achard**, with exhibits of art from the Dauphiné region.

Activities

Skiing & Snowboarding Downhill skiing (*ski de piste*), cross-country skiing (*ski de fond*) and snowboarding are available at a

number of inexpensive, low-altitude ski stations near Grenoble including Col de Porte and Le Sappey (north of the city) and Saint Nizier du Moucherotte, Lans-en-Vercors, Villard-de-Lans and Méaudre (west of the city). The tourist office has comprehensive information, including accommodation lists, for all of Grenoble's surrounding ski resorts.

Summer skiing, which is relatively expensive, is possible in June and July (and even into August) at several high-altitude ski resorts east of Grenoble including Alpe d'Huez (tourist office ☎ 04 76 11 44 44), and Les Deux Alpes (see Around Grenoble).

Hiking A number of beautiful trails can be picked up in Grenoble or nearby (eg from Fort de la Bastille). The northern part of the Parc Naturel Régional du Vercors (☎ 04 76 94 38 26 for the park headquarters) is just west of town.

The place to go for hiking information is Info-Montagne (☎ 04 76 42 45 90), on the first floor of the Maison du Tourisme. It also has information on climbing, mountain biking and every other imaginable mountain activity (except skiing). It sells hiking maps and has detailed info on gîtes d'étape and refuges. The office is open from 9 am to noon and 2 to 6 pm (from 10 am on Saturday; closed Sunday).

Places to Stay

Camping The *Camping Les Trois Pucelles* (☎ 04 76 96 45 73; open all year) is at 58 Rue des Allobroges, one block west of the Drac

River, in Grenoble's western suburb of Seyssins. To get there from the train station, take the tram towards Fontaine and get off at the Maisonnat stop. Then take bus No 51 to Mas des Îles and walk east on Rue du Dauphiné. A place to camp and park costs 30/43FF for one/two people.

Hostel The *Auberge de Jeunesse* (☎ 04 76 09 33 52; fax 04 76 09 38 09; grenoble.echirolles@wanadoo.fr), 10 Ave du Grésivaudan, is in Échirolles, 5.5km south of the train station. To get there from Cours Jean Jaurès, take bus No 8 (direction Pont de Claix, which runs until about 9 pm) and get off at the Quinzaine stop – look for the Casino supermarket. Reception is open from 7.30 am to 11 pm, and a bed costs 67FF, including breakfast.

The friendly and central *Foyer de l'Étudiante* (☎ 04 76 42 00 84), 4 Rue Sainte Ursule, accepts travellers of both sexes from the end of June to the end of September. Singles/doubles cost 90/130FF a day and, for those who want to stay put, 400/600FF a week.

Hotels Near the train station, the *Hôtel Alizé* (☎ 04 76 43 12 91; fax 04 76 47 62 79), 1 Place de la Gare, has modern singles/doubles with washbasin for 126/150FF and doubles with shower for 182FF.

There are lots of inexpensive hotels in the Place Condorcet area, about 800m south-east of the train station. One of the best is the *Hôtel Lakanal* (☎ 04 76 46 03 42), off Place Championnet at 26 Rue des Bergers. It attracts a young and friendly crowd and has simple singles/doubles with toilet for just 100/120FF. Rooms with shower and toilet cost 140/180FF. Hall showers are 15FF and breakfast is 20FF. The noisy *Hôtel des Doges* (☎ 04 76 46 13 19; fax 04 76 47 67 95), 29 Cours Jean Jaurès, has basic singles/doubles from 100/120FF and ones with shower from 160FF. Hall showers cost 15FF and breakfast is 25FF.

The *Hôtel Victoria* (☎ 04 76 46 06 36), a quiet, well-maintained place at 17 Rue Thiers, has comfortable singles/doubles with shower and TV for 170/190FF. The *Hôtel Beau Soleil* (☎ 04 76 46 29 40), 9 Rue des Bons Enfants, has simple singles/doubles from 130/140FF, and from 155/170FF with shower. Hall showers are 16FF, and breakfast is 22FF.

The *Hôtel du Moucherotte* (☎ 04 76 54 61 40; fax 04 76 44 62 52), in the city centre at 1 Rue Auguste Gaché, has huge, well kept singles/doubles with shower from 145/194FF; triples/quads with showers start at 218/256FF. The pleasant and friendly *Hôtel de la Poste* (☎ 04 76 46 67 25), 25 Rue de la Poste, has basic singles/doubles for 100/160FF. Showers are free, and a traditional English fry-up for breakfast is 30FF.

Places to Eat

The *Restaurant Universitaire*, 5 Rue d'Arsonval, is open weekdays between mid-September and mid-June from 11.20 am to 1.15 pm and 6.20 to 7.50 pm. Tickets (about 15/30FF for students/nonstudents) are sold at lunchtime only.

For good French food at reasonable prices, try *Le Tonneau de Diogène* (☎ 04 76 42 38 40), 6 Place Notre Dame, which attracts a young, lively crowd. The plat du jour is 55FF, salads are 15 to 38FF, and it's open daily from 8.30 am to 1 am. *La Panse* (☎ 04 76 54 09 54), 7 Rue de la Paix, offers traditional French cuisine daily, except Sunday. The 85FF lunch *menu* and 100FF dinner *menu* are good value.

For fondue and tartiflette try the *Restaurant des Montagnes*, 5 Rue Brocherie. Salads start at 34FF, and fondues at 42FF per person. It's open from 7 am to midnight. *Les Archers* (☎ 04 76 46 27 76), 2 Rue Docteur Bailly, is a brasserie-style restaurant with great outside seating in summer. The plat du jour is 57FF, huîtres (oysters) are 106FF a dozen, and it's open from 10 am to 10 pm. Taking more of a modern approach is *La Galerie Rome*, housed inside a smart art gallery on the corner of Rue du Vieux Temple and Rue Très Cloîtres. It's open from 10 am to 10 pm (closed Sunday and Monday). *Menus* cost 58 and 90FF.

Les Halles Sainte Claire food market near the tourist office is open daily, except Monday, from 6 am to 1 pm. The *Prisunic* supermarket (closed Sunday) at 22 Rue Lafayette, a block west of the tourist office, has a supermarket in the basement.

Getting There & Away

Bus The bus station (☎ 04 76 87 90 31) is next to the train station at Place de la Gare. VFD (☎ 04 76 47 77 77) has services to Geneva

(143FF), Nice (293FF), Annecy (93FF), Chamonix (152FF), and many places in the Isère region, including a number of ski resorts. Intercars (☎ 04 76 46 19 77) handles long-haul destinations such as Madrid (540FF), London (550FF) and Venice (260FF).

Train The train station (☎ 08 36 35 35 39) is served by both tram lines (get off at the Gare Europole stop). The information office is open daily from 9 am to noon and 2 to 5.30 pm. The station and at least one ticket window are open from 4 am to 2 am. The trip to Paris' Gare de Lyon (from 348FF) takes about 3½ hours by TGV. There are three trains a day to Turin (201FF) and Milan (240FF) in Italy, and two trains a day to Geneva (115FF), and regular services to Lyon, Nice and Monaco.

Getting Around

Bus & Tram TAG (☎ 04 76 20 66 66), the local bus company, has an information desk inside the tourist office building and an office next to the post office outside the train station. Buses and trams take the same tickets (7.50FF, or 53FF for a carnet of 10, or 23/70FF for a daily/weekly pass), which are sold by bus (but not tram) drivers and by ticket machines at tram stops. They remain valid for transfers within one hour of time-stamping, but not for return trips. Most buses stop running between 6.30 and 9 pm, while the trams run from 5 am till midnight.

Taxi Radio taxis can be ordered by calling ☎ 04 76 54 42 54.

Bicycle Mountain Bike Grenoble (☎ 04 76 47 58 76), 6 Quai de France, has mountain bikes for 55/90FF for a half/full day, 160FF for two days then 70FF a day thereafter. A 2000FF deposit is required. The shop also stocks an excellent range of maps, biking and hiking guides, and is open from 10 am to noon and 2 to 7 pm (closed Sunday and Monday).

AROUND GRENOBLE
Les Deux Alpes

Les Deux Alpes (1650m) is a popular winter resort 77km south-east of Grenoble, and also

has the largest summer skiing area in Europe. The main skiing area lies below La Meije (3983m), one of the highest peaks in the Parc National des Écrins. There's some 200km of marked pistes, 20km of cross-country trails, and a snowpark with a half-pipe and jumps for snowboarders. The ESF (☎ 04 76 79 21 21; fax 04 76 79 22 07) and the more expensive École de Ski International St Christophe (☎ 04 76 79 04 21; fax 04 76 79 29 14), close to Place des Deux Alpes on Ave de la Muzelle, offer ski and snowboarding lessons.

The Maison des Deux Alpes on Place des Deux Alpes houses the tourist office (☎ 04 76 79 22 00), the accommodation service and the Bureau des Guides, which can arrange guided skiing, climbing and rafting trips.

Accommodation is available at the *Auberge de Jeunesse Les Brûleurs de Loups* (☎ 04 76 79 22 80; fax 04 76 79 26 15; fuaj.les.deux.alpes@wanadoo.fr) in the heart of the resort at Ave de Muzelle. A bed in a room for up to six people costs 49FF per person in summer. Only weekly packages are available in winter, including seven days accommodation, food and a lift pass. Prices start at 2180/2680FF in the low/high season. The accommodation service (☎ 04 76 79 24 38; fax 04 76 79 01 38; www.les2alpes.com) inside the Maison des Deux Alpes takes bookings for all types of accommodation. Two-person studios and apartments can be found from 1150/2600FF a week in the low/high season. All reservations should be made well in advance.

VFD (☎ 04 76 47 77 77) runs buses from Grenoble (99FF; 1¾ hours) to Les Deux Alpes.

Provence

Provence stretches along both sides of the Rhône River from just north of the town of Orange down to the Mediterranean and along France's southern coast from the Camargue salt marshes in the west to Marseille in the east. The spectacular Gorges d'Ardèche, created by the often torrential Ardèche River, are west of the Rhône, and to the east are the region's famous upland areas: Mt Ventoux (1909m), the Vaucluse Plateau, the Lubéron Range and the chain of hills known as the

Alpilles. East of Marseille is the Côte d'Azur and its hinterland, which, though part of Provence, is covered in the following section.

Provence was settled by the Ligurians, the Celts and the Greeks, but it was after its conquest by Julius Caesar in the mid-1st century BC that the region really began to flourish. Many exceptionally well-preserved amphitheatres, aqueducts and other buildings from the Roman period can still be seen in Arles, Nîmes (see Languedoc-Roussillon section) and Orange. During the 14th century, the Catholic Church, then led by a series of French-born popes, moved its headquarters from feud-riven Rome to Avignon, thus beginning the most resplendent period in that city's history.

Language

A thousand years ago, *oïl* and *oc* were the words for 'yes' in what is now northern and southern France respectively. As Paris-based influence and control spread, so did the Langue d'Oïl, gradually supplanting the Langue d'Oc (the language of Provence). The Provençal language is not spoken much these days, but it has left the world a rich literary legacy – the Langue d'Oc was used by the medieval troubadours, whose melodies and poems were motivated by the ideal of courtly love.

Climate

Provence's weather is bright and sunny for much of the year, and the extraordinary light has attracted a number of painters, including Van Gogh, Cézanne and Picasso. The cold, dry winds of the mistral, which gain surprising fury as they career down the Rhône Valley, can turn a fine spring day into bonechilling winter with little warning.

MARSEILLE

The cosmopolitan and much maligned port of Marseille (population 800,000), France's second-largest city and third-most populous urban area (1.23 million), is not in the least bit prettified for the benefit of tourists. Its urban geography and atmosphere are a function of the diversity of its inhabitants, the majority of whom are immigrants (or their descendants) from the Mediterranean basin, West Africa and Indochina. Although Marseille is notorious for organised crime and racial tensions (the extreme right polls about 25% here), the city has more to reward the visitor who likes exploring on foot than almost any other city in France.

Orientation

The city's main street, La Canebière, stretches eastward from the Vieux Port. The train station is north of La Canebière at the top of Blvd d'Athènes. The city centre is around Rue Paradis, which becomes more fashionable as you move south.

Information

Tourist Office The tourist office (☎ 04 91 13 89 00; fax 04 91 13 89 20; www.marseilles .com or www.visitprovence.com), next to the Vieux Port at 4 La Canebière, is open Monday to Saturday from 9 am to 7 pm and on Sunday from 10 am to 5 pm. From June to September, opening hours are 8.30 am to 8 pm daily. The tourist office annexe (☎ 04 91 50 59 18) at the train station is open weekdays only from 10 am to 1 pm and 1.30 to 6 pm (Monday to Saturday 9 am to 7 pm in July and August).

Foreign Consulates There is a UK consulate (☎ 04 91 15 72 10) at 24 Ave du Prado (near Place Castellane and the Castellane metro stop). The US consulate (☎ 04 91 54 92 00) is across from the préfecture building at 12 Blvd Paul Peytral.

Money The Banque de France is at Place Estrangin Pastré, a block west of the préfecture. There are a number of banks and exchange bureaux on La Canebière near the tourist office.

American Express (☎ 04 91 13 71 21), 39 La Canebière, is open weekdays from 8 am to 6 pm and on Saturday from 8 am to noon and 2 to 5 pm.

Post The main post office, 1 Place de l'Hôtel des Postes, is open from 8 am to 7 pm (Saturday until noon; closed Sunday). Exchange services are available.

Cybercafés The Internet Café (☎ 04 91 42 09 37; cafe@icr.internetcafe.fr), 25 Rue de

Village, charges 30/50FF for 30 minutes/one hour of access. It's open from 10 am to 8 pm (until 4.30 pm on Friday and from 2.30 pm on Sunday).

Laundry The Laverie des Allées at 15 Allées Léon Gambetta is close to many of the hotels mentioned under Places to Stay and is open seven days a week from 8 am to 9 pm.

Dangers & Annoyances Despite its fearsome reputation for underground crime, Marseille is probably no more dangerous than other French cities. As elsewhere, street crime such as bag-snatching and pickpocketing is best avoided by keeping your wits about you and your valuables hard to get at. Guard your luggage very carefully, especially at the train station, and *never* leave anything inside a parked vehicle. One Lonely Planet researcher did just that – and lost all his clothes!

At night, it's best to avoid the Belsunce area, the poor, immigrant neighbourhood south-west of the train station bounded by La Canebière, Cours Belsunce/Rue d'Aix, Rue Bernard du Bois and Blvd d'Athènes.

Things to See & Do

Walking Tour Marseille grew up around the **Vieux Port**, where Greeks from Asia Minor established a settlement around 600 BC. The quarter north of Quai du Port (around the Hôtel de Ville) was blown up by the Germans in 1943 and rebuilt after the war. The lively **Place Thiars** pedestrian zone, with its many late-night restaurants and cafés, is south of the Quai de Rive Neuve (you can walk through the traffic-clogged Tunnel Saint Laurent, but it's noisy and noxious and not recommended). Also worth a stroll is the more fashionable **6e arrondissement**, especially the area between La Canebière and the préfecture building, and the Rue Saint Ferréol pedestrian mall.

Corniche Président John F Kennedy runs along the coast from 200m west of the **Jardin du Pharo**, a park with good harbour views, to the Plages Gaston Defferre, 4.5km to the south. Along its entire length, the corniche is served by bus No 83, which goes to the Quai des Belges (the old port) and the Rond-Point du Prado metro stop.

If you like great panoramic views or overwrought mid-19th century architecture, consider a walk up to the **Basilique Notre Dame de la Garde**, which is on a hilltop (154m) 1km south of the Vieux Port – the highest point in the city. The basilica and the crypt are open from 7 am to 7 pm (7 am to 10 pm in summer). Bus No 60 will get you back to the Vieux Port.

Museums All the museums listed here charge 12/18FF for admission to their permanent/temporary exhibitions; all admit students for half-price. If you intend visiting lots of museums, consider buying a *passeport pour les musées*, which costs 50/25FF for adults/students, is valid for 15 days, and allows you unlimited entry to all the city's museums.

The **Centre de la Vieille Charité** (☎ 04 91 56 28 38), which used to be a charity centre and is housed in a hospice built between 1671 and 1745, is home to Marseille's Museum of Mediterranean Archaeology and Museum of African, Oceanic and American Indian Art. It has superb permanent exhibits on ancient Egypt and Greece and all sorts of temporary exhibitions. It is in the mostly North African Panier quarter (north of the Vieux Port) at 2 Rue de la Charité. The centre is open from 9 am to noon and 1.30 to 4.45 pm (closed on weekends).

The **Musée Cantini** (☎ 04 91 54 77 75), off Rue Paradis at 19 Rue Grignan, has changing exhibitions of modern and contemporary art. It's open from 10 am to noon and 2 to 6 pm (closed on weekends).

Roman history buffs should visit the **Musée d'Histoire de Marseille** (☎ 04 91 90 42 22) on the ground floor of the Centre Bourse shopping mall (just north of La Canebière). Its exhibits include the remains of a merchant ship that plied the waters of the Mediterranean in the late 2nd century AD. It's open from noon to 7 pm (closed Tuesday). The remains of Roman buildings uncovered during construction of the shopping mall can be seen nearby in the **Jardin des Vestiges**, which is entered via the museum.

Château d'If Château d'If (☎ 04 91 59 02 30), the 16th-century island fortress-turned-prison made infamous by Alexandre Dumas'

FRANCE

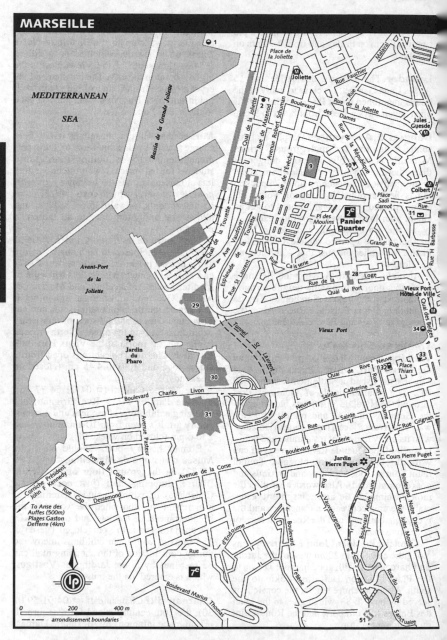

MARSEILLE

MEDITERRANEAN

SEA

Bassin de la Grande Joliette

Avant-Port
de la
Joliette

Jardin
du Pharo

Place de
la Joliette

Joliette

Rue Fauchier

Rue de la Joliette

Jules
Guesde

Quai de la Joliette

Rue de Mazenod

Avenue Robert Schuman

Boulevard

des

Dames

Rue de la République

Colbert

Rue de l'Évêche

Place
Sadi
Carnot

Rue

Quai de la Tourette

Ave Vaudoyer

Esplanade de la Tourette

Rue St Laurent

Rue de la Tourette

Pl des
Moulins

2e
Panier
Quarter

Grand' Rue

Rue Ca is serie

Rue H Barbusse

Rue de la
Loge

28

Vieux Port
Hôtel de Ville

Quai du Port

Quai des Belges

34

Tunnel St Laurent

Vieux Port

Neuve

Place
Thiars

33

32

Quai de Rive

Rue Fort N Dame

Boulevard Charles Livon

Rue Neuve Sainte Catherine

Rue Sainte

Rue Grignan

Avenue Pasteur

Rue Neuve

Rue Sainte

Boulevard de la Corderie

Jardin
Pierre Puget

Cours Pierre Puget

Corniche Président
John F Kennedy

Ave de la Corse

Rue Cap Dessemond

Avenue de la Corse

Rue Vauvenargues

Boulevard André Aune

Boulevard Notre Dame

Boulevard Jules Moulet

To Anse des
Auffes (500m)
Plages Gaston
Defferre (4km)

Rue d'Endoume

Boulevard Tellène

Rue

Rue du Fort Sanctuaire

7e

Boulevard Marius Thomas

51

0   200   400 m

------ arrondissement boundaries

MARSEILLE

PLACES TO STAY
14 Hôtel Beaulieu-Glaris
15 Hôtel d'Athènes &
    Hôtel Little Palace
17 Hôtel Gambetta
18 Hôtel Ozea &
    Hôtel Pied-à-Terre
19 Hôtel de Nice
21 Hôtel Sphinx
22 Cheap Hotels
49 Hôtel Béarn

PLACES TO EAT
10 Roi du Couscous
24 Takeaway Restaurants
33 Le Mérou Bleu
37 Restaurant Antillais
38 La Caucase &
    Le Resto Provençal
39 Ethnic Restaurants

OTHER
1   Passenger Ferry Terminal
2   SNCM Ferries Office
3   Bus Station
4   Taxi Stand
5   Post Office
6   Gare Saint Charles
7   Nouvelle Cathédrale
8   Ancienne Cathédrale
    de la Major
9   Centre de la Vieille
    Charité
11 Main Post Office
12 Jardin des Vestiges
    (Roman Ruins)
13 Musée d'Histoire de
    Marseille
16 Launderette
20 Drag Queen Café
23 Marché des Capucins
    (Food Market)
25 American Express
26 Espaces Infos RTM (Bus
    & Metro Information)
27 Nouvelles Galeries
    Supermarket
28 Hôtel de Ville
29 Fort Saint Jean
30 Bas Fort Saint Nicolas
31 Fort d'Entrecasteaux &
    Fort Saint Nicolas
32 O'Malleys Irish Bar
34 Boats to Château d'If &
    Îles du Frioul
35 Tourist Office
36 Opéra
40 La Maison Hantée
    (Music Bar)
41 SNCF Office
42 Musée Cantini
43 Law Courts
44 Préfecture de Police
45 Préfecture
46 US Consulate
47 Banque de France
48 Fruit & Vegetable Market
50 Internet Café (Cybercafé)
51 Basilique Notre Dame
    de la Garde

The Count of Monte Cristo, can be visited daily from 9 am until 7 pm (9.15 am to 5.15 pm, closed Monday, from October to March). Entry is 22FF. Boats (50FF return; 20 minutes each way) depart from Quai des Belges in the Vieux Port near the GACM office (☎ 04 91 55 50 09) and continue to the nearby Îles du Frioul (50FF return, or 80FF for both the chateau and islands).

Beaches The city's most attractive beach, the **Plages Gaston Defferre** (commonly known as the Plage du Prado), is 4km south of the city centre. To get there, take bus No 19, 72 or 83 from the Rond-Point du Prado metro stop or bus No 83 from the Quai des Belges. You can walk there along the Corniche Président John F Kennedy.

Places to Stay

Camping Tents can usually be pitched on the grounds of the *Auberge de Jeunesse de Bois Luzy* (see Hostels) for 26FF per person.

Hostels The *Auberge de Jeunesse de Bonneveine* (☎ 04 91 73 21 81; fax 04 91 73 97 23), 47 Ave Joseph Vidal, is about 4.5km south of the Vieux Port. To get there, take bus No 44 from the Rond-Point du Prado metro stop and get off at Place Louis Bonnefon. A bed in a room for six is 72FF including breakfast. The hostel is closed in January.

There's another hostel, the *Auberge de Jeunesse de Bois Luzy* (☎ 04 91 49 06 18; fax 04 91 49 06 18), Allées des Primevères, 4.5km east of the city centre in the Montolivet neighbourhood. To get there, take bus No 6 from near the Canebière-Réformés metro stop or bus No 8 from La Canebière. Beds are 44FF and breakfast is 17FF. An HI card is mandatory.

Hotels Marseille has some of France's cheapest hotels; you can still find rooms for 50FF a night but most are filthy dives in unsafe areas which rent out rooms by the hour. All of the places listed by name in this section are reputable and relatively clean.

Train Station Area The one-star *Hôtel Beaulieu-Glaris* (☎ 04 91 90 70 59; fax 04 91 56 14 04), 1-3 Place des Marseillaises, has poorly maintained singles with washbasin

from 126FF and similar doubles from 180FF. Hall showers are 15FF. The two-star *Hôtel d'Athènes* (☎ 04 91 90 12 93), 37-39 Blvd d'Athènes, has average but well kept singles/doubles with shower and toilet from 190/270FF. Rooms in its adjoining one-star annexe called the *Hôtel Little Palace* cost 120/140/220FF for singles/doubles/triples.

There are several other one and two-star hotels nearby and a cluster of small, extremely cheap hotels of less-than-pristine reputation along Rue des Petites Maries.

Around La Canebière The *Hôtel Gambetta* (☎ 04 91 62 07 88; fax 04 91 64 81 54), 49 Allées Léon Gambetta, has singles without shower for 95FF and singles/doubles with shower from 130/160FF. Hall showers are 15FF.

The *Hôtel Ozea* (☎ 04 91 47 91 84), 12 Rue Barbaroux, is across Square Léon Blum from the eastern end of Allées Léon Gambetta. This place, which welcomes new guests 24 hours a day (if you arrive late at night just ring the bell), has clean, old-fashioned doubles without/with shower for 120/150FF. There are no hall showers. Nearby, the *Hôtel Pied-à-Terre* (☎ 04 91 92 00 95) at No 18 has singles/doubles without/with shower for 120/150FF.

There are lots of rock-bottom hotels around Rue Sénac de Meilhan and Rue du Théâtre Français and a number of one-star hotels along Rue des Feuillants. The *Hôtel Sphinx* (☎ 04 91 48 70 59), 16 Rue Sénac de Meilhan, has simple but well kept singles/doubles from 70/120FF, or 130/160FF with shower. Hall showers are 17FF. Another possibility is the *Hôtel de Nice* (☎ 04 91 48 73 07) on the same street at No 11. Doubles without/with showers are 100/120FF; hall showers cost 20FF.

Préfecture Area The quiet *Hôtel Béarn* (☎ 04 91 37 75 83), 63 Rue Sylvabelle, has comfortable singles/doubles with shower for 100/120FF and singles/doubles with shower and toilet from 180/210FF. Reception closes at 11 pm.

Places to Eat

There are lots of cheap takeaway places selling pizza and Middle Eastern sandwiches of various sorts on Rue des Feuillants, which intersects La Canebière just east of Cours Saint Louis. Cours Belsunce is lined with inexpensive food kiosks.

Restaurants along and near the pedestrianised Cours Julien, a few blocks south of La Canebière, offer an incredible variety of cuisines: Antillean, Pakistani, Thai, Lebanese, Tunisian, Italian and more. *La Caucase* (☎ 04 91 48 36 30) at No 62 specialises in Armenian dishes. It's open for dinner seven nights a week from about 6 pm and has *menus* from 88FF. If you'd rather have something French, try *Le Resto Provençal* (☎ 04 91 48 71 89) at No 64. There are pleasant outdoor tables and it has a *menu* offering regional fare for 110FF, a plat du jour for 43FF and a good value lunchtime *menu* for 65FF. It's closed Sunday and Monday. Nearby, the West Indian *Restaurant Antillais* (☎ 04 91 94 25 55) at No 10 has starters from 20FF, main dishes from 40FF, and a 100FF *menu* which includes a pichet of house wine.

Roi du Couscous (☎ 04 91 91 45 46), 63 Rue de la République, is just a short distance north of the Panier Quarter. The 'King of Couscous' has dishes for 35 to 60FF, while a three-course lunchtime *menu* is just 50FF, including a quarter-litre of wine. The King holds court from noon to 2.30 or 3 pm and 7 to 10.30 pm (closed Monday).

Countless sandwich shops, cafés and restaurants line the pedestrian streets around Place Thiars, which is on the south side of the Vieux Port. Though many offer bouillabaisse, the rich fish stew for which Marseille is famous, it's difficult to find the real thing. Try *Le Mérou Bleu* (☎ 04 91 54 23 25), 32-36 Rue Saint Saëns, a popular seafood restaurant with a lovely terrace, which has bouillabaisse (89 to 135FF), other seafood dishes (72 to 125FF), pasta etc. Avoid the touristy restaurants on the Quai de Rive Neuve.

For a serious splurge, head for the chic *Chez Fonfon* (☎ 04 91 52 14 38), 140 Vallon des Auffes, overlooking the harbour of Anse des Auffes to the west of the city. Fish dishes are the house speciality with bouillabaisse du pêcheur costing 250FF per person and langoustine priced at 100FF per 100g. Reservations are advised.

There is a *supermarket*, open Monday to Saturday, in the Nouvelles Galeries department store a block north of La Canebière in the Centre Bourse shopping centre. Fresh fruit and veg are sold at the *Marché des Capucins* one block south of La Canebière on Place des Capucins, and at the *fruit and vegetable market* on Cours Pierre Puget. Both are closed Sunday.

Entertainment

Listings appear in the monthly *Vox Mag* and weekly *Taktik* and *Sortir*, all distributed for free at the tourist office, cinemas and box offices. Comprehensive listings are also contained in the weekly *L'Officiel des Loisirs* (2FF in newspaper kiosks).

Marseille's Irish pub, *O'Malleys*, overlooks the old port on the corner of Rue de la Paix and Quai de Rive Neuve. Camper than camp and full of fun is the lively *Drag Queen Café* (☎ 04 91 94 21 41), 2 Rue Sénac de Meilhan, which hosts live bands and is open until 5.30 am at weekends. For rock, reggae, country and other live music, try *La Maison Hantée* (☎ 04 91 92 09 40), 10 Rue Vian, a very hip street between Cours Julien and Rue des Trois Rois.

Getting There & Away

Air The Aéroport de Marseille-Provence (☎ 04 42 14 14 14) is 28km north-west of the city.

Bus The bus station (☎ 04 91 08 16 40) at Place Victor Hugo, 150m to the right as you exit the train station, offers services to Aix-en-Provence, Avignon, Cannes, Nice, Nice airport and Orange, among others. The information counter and the left-luggage office are open Monday to Saturday from 7 am to 6 pm and on Sunday from 9 am to noon and 2 to 6 pm. Tickets are sold on the bus.

Eurolines (☎ 04 91 50 57 55) has buses to Spain, Italy, Morocco, the UK and other countries. Its counter in the bus station is open from 8 am to noon and 2 to 6 pm (7.30 am to noon and 1 to 5 pm on Saturday; closed Sunday).

Train Marseille's passenger train station, Gare Saint Charles (☎ 08 36 35 35 39), is served by both metro lines. Trains from here go everywhere, including Paris' Gare de Lyon (367 to 447FF; 4¼ hours), Bordeaux (355FF; six hours), Toulouse (235FF; four hours) and Nice (145FF; 1½ to two hours). The information office, one floor under the platforms, is open Monday to Saturday from 9 am to 8 pm. There's an SNCF office at 17 Rue Grignan, off Rue St Ferréol a couple of blocks north of the préfecture. It's open weekdays from 9 am to 4.30 pm.

Ferry The Société Nationale Maritime Corse-Méditerranée (SNCM; ☎ 08 36 67 95 00; fax 04 91 56 35 86; www.sncm.fr) runs ferries from the passenger ferry terminal (*gare maritime*) at the foot of Blvd des Dames to Corsica (Corse), Sardinia (Sardaigne) and Tunisia. (Services to Algeria are prone to disruption because of the political troubles there.)

The SNCM office, 61 Blvd des Dames, is open weekdays from 8 am to 6 pm and on Saturday from 8.30 am to noon and 2 to 5.30 pm. It also handles ticketing and reservations for the Tunisian and Moroccan ferry companies, Compagnie Tunisienne de Navigation (CTN) and Compagnie Marocaine de Navigation (COMANAV; ☎ 04 67 46 68 00). COMANAV ferries depart from 4 Quai d'Alger in Sète (see Sea in the Getting There & Away section at the beginning of this chapter).

Getting Around

To/From the Airport TRPA buses from Gare Saint Charles go to the Marseille-Provence airport every 20 minutes from 5.30 am to 9.50 pm. From the airport, they go to the train station from 6.30 am to 10.50 pm. The trip takes about 30 to 60 minutes and costs 45FF.

Bus & Metro Marseille has two easy-to-use metro lines, a tram line and an extensive bus network, which operate from 5 am to 9pm. Night buses (*autobus de nuit*) and tram No 68 run from 9 pm to 12.30 am.

Tickets (9FF each, 42FF for a carnet of six) are valid for travel on bus, tram and metro for one hour after they have been time-stamped (no return trips). Tram stops have modern blue ticket distributors that should be used to time-stamp your ticket before you board.

For more information, visit the Espace Infos RTM (☎ 04 91 91 92 10), 6-8 Rue des Fabres, which is open weekdays from 8.30 am to 6 pm (9 am to 5.30 pm on Saturday).

Taxi Marseille Taxi (☎ 04 91 02 20 20) and Taxis France (☎ 04 91 49 91 00) will dispatch taxis 24 hours a day.

AIX-EN-PROVENCE

One of the most appealing cities in Provence, Aix (population 124,000) owes its lively atmosphere to the large number of students, who make up over 20% of the population. The city is renowned for its *calissons*, almond-paste confectionery made with candied melon, and for being the birthplace of the postimpressionist painter Cézanne. Aix hosts the Festival International d'Art Lyrique each July.

The mostly pedestrianised old city is a great place to explore, with its maze of tiny streets full of ethnic restaurants, specialist food shops and designer boutiques, intermixed with elegant 17th and 18th-century *hôtels particuliers* (private mansions) mossy fountains and crowded outdoor cafés which give the city a relaxed, friendly atmosphere.

Aix also has several interesting museums, the finest of which is the **Musée Granet** (☎ 04 42 38 14 70) at Place Saint Jean de Malte. The collection includes Italian, Dutch and French paintings from the 16th to 19th centuries as well as some of Cézanne's lesser known paintings. Admission is 10FF (free for students), and the museum is closed Tuesday. The **Musée des Tapisseries** (☎ 04 42 23 09 91), in the former bishop's palace at 28 Place des Martyrs de la Résistance, is worth visiting for its tapestries and sumptuous costumes. Entry is 15FF, and it's closed Sunday.

Atelier Paul Cézanne (☎ 04 42 21 06 53), 9 Ave Paul Cézanne, was the painter's last studio and has been left as it was when he died in 1906. It's open daily, except Tuesday, and entry is 16FF (10FF for students).

The tourist office (☎ 04 42 16 11 61) is on Place Général de Gaulle. Numerous cafés, brasseries and restaurants can be found in the heart of the city on Place des Cardeurs and Place de l'Hôtel de Ville. The *Mondial Café*, overlooking Les Rotundes at the south end of

Cours Mirabeau, specialises in shellfish dishes and super-sized salads (from 48FF), while *L'Arbre à Pain* (π 04 42 96 99 95), 12 Rue Constantin, is a vegetarian place which prides itself on its low calorie, full-flavoured dishes. A colourful morning *fruit and vegetable market* is held on Place Richelme.

Frequent trains run between Marseille and Aix (37FF; 35 minutes).

AVIGNON

Avignon (population 87,000) acquired its ramparts and its reputation as a city of art and culture during the 14th century, when Pope Clement V and his court, fleeing political turmoil in Rome, established themselves here. From 1309 to 1377 huge sums of money were invested in building and decorating the popes' palace and other important church edifices. Even after the pontifical court returned to Rome amid bitter charges that Avignon had become a den of criminals and brothel-goers, the city remained an important cultural centre.

Today, Avignon maintains its tradition as a patron of the arts, most notably through its annual performing arts festival. The city's other attractions include a bustling (if slightly touristy) walled town and a number of interesting museums, including several across the Rhône in Villeneuve-lès-Avignon. Avignon is a good base for day trips to other parts of Provence.

The world-famous Festival d'Avignon, held every year during the last three weeks of July, attracts many hundreds of performers (actors, dancers, musicians etc) who put on some 300 performances of all sorts each day. Even bigger crowds are expected in the year 2000, when Avignon will be European Capital of Culture.

Orientation

The walled city's main avenue runs northward from the train station to Place de l'Horloge; it's called Cours Jean Jaurès south of the tourist office and Rue de la République north of it. Place de l'Horloge is 200m south of Place du Palais, which is next to the Palais des Papes. The island that runs down the middle of the Rhône between Avignon and Villeneuve-lès-Avignon is known as Île de la Barthelasse.

Information

Tourist Office The tourist office (π 04 90 82 65 11; fax 04 90 82 95 03; information@ ot-avignon.fr; www.ot-avignon.fr) is 300m north of the train station at 41 Cours Jean Jaurès. It's open from 9 am to 1 pm and 2 to 6 pm (5 pm on Saturday; closed Sunday). In July and August weekday hours are 10 am to 7 pm. From mid-April to mid-August it opens on Sunday from 10 am to 5 pm. The tourist office annexe at the Pont Saint Bénézet (Pont d'Avignon) is open from 9 am to 1 pm and 2 to 7 pm (closed Monday).

Money & Post There's a Banque de France at the northern end of Place de l'Horloge, and a 24-hour banknote exchange machine at the Lyonnais de Banque, 13 Rue de la République. The main post office is on Cours Président Kennedy, which is through Porte de la République from the train station. It has currency exchange services.

Cybercafés On Rue Guillaume, Cyberdrome (π 04 90 16 05 15; fax 04 90 16 05 14; cyberdrome@cyberdrome.fr), charges 25FF for 30 minutes of online access and is open from 7 to 1 am.

Laundry Laverie La Fontaine, 66 Place des Corps Saint, is open Monday to Saturday from 7 am to 8 pm.

Things to See

Avignon's most interesting areas are within the walled city (*intra-muros*). The ramparts were restored during the 19th century but the original moats were not re-excavated, leaving the crenellated fortifications looking rather less imposing than they did originally.

Palais des Papes Avignon's leading tourist attraction is the fortified Palace of the Popes (π 04 90 27 50 74) at Place du Palais, built during the 14th century. The seemingly endless halls, chapels, corridors and staircases were once sumptuously decorated with tapestries, paintings etc but these days they are nearly empty except for a few damaged frescoes. As a result, the palace is of interest more for the dramatic events that took place here than for its inherent beauty.

The palace is open daily from 9.30 am to

FRANCE

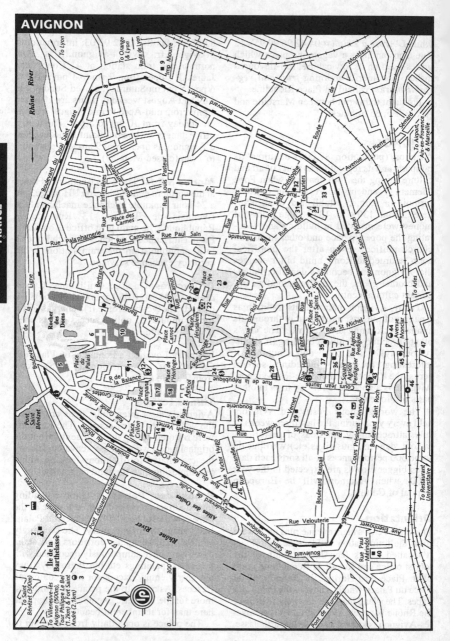

AVIGNON

AVIGNON

PLACES TO STAY
2 Camping Bagatelle & Auberge Bagatelle
9 Avignon Squash Club (Hostel)
14 Hôtel Mignon
29 Hôtel Innova
36 Hôtel Splendid
37 Hôtel du Parc
40 Hôtel Saint Roch
47 Hôtel Monclar

PLACES TO EAT
16 Natural Café & La Fourchette
19 Le Belgocargo
20 Restaurant Song Long
31 Sindabad
34 Wooloomooloo

OTHER
1 Municipal Swimming Pool
3 La Barthelasse Bus Stop
4 Entrance to Pont Saint Bénézet & Tourist Office Annexe
5 Musée du Petit Palais
6 Cathédrale Notre Dame des Doms
7 Cinéma Utopia
8 Porte Saint Lazare
10 Palais des Papes
11 Conservatoire de Musique
12 Banque de France
13 Porte de l'Oulle
15 Casino Grocery
17 Opéra d'Avignon
18 Hôtel de Ville
21 TCRA Bus Information Office
22 Synagogue
23 Les Halles (Food Market)
24 24-Hour Banknote Exchange Machine
25 Porte Sainte Dominique
26 Musée Louis Voland
27 Musée Calvet
28 Musée Lapidaire
30 Tourist Office
32 Cyberdrome (Cybercafé)
33 Cycles Peugeot
35 Launderette
38 Hospice Saint Louis
39 Porte Saint Roch
41 Main Post Office
42 Porte de la République
43 TCRA Bus Information Office
44 Bus Station
45 Car Rental Agencies
46 Train Station

FRANCE

5.45 pm (9 am to 7 pm from April to November; until 8 pm from 4 August to 30 September). Entry to the palace's interior is 40FF (32FF for students and seniors), which includes a very user-friendly audioguide in English.

Around Place du Palais At the far northern end of Place du Palais, the **Musée du Petit Palais** (☎ 04 90 86 44 58) houses an outstanding collection of 13th to 16th-century Italian religious paintings. It's open from 9.30 am to noon and 2 to 6 pm (closed Tuesday); in July and August hours are 10 am to 6 pm. Tickets cost 30FF (15FF for students and seniors). Just up the hill is **Rocher des Doms**, a delightful park that offers great views of the Rhône, Pont Saint Bénézet, Villeneuve-lès-Avignon and the Alpilles.

Pont Saint Bénézet (☎ 04 90 85 60 16) was built in the 12th century to link Avignon with Villeneuve-lès-Avignon. Yes, this is the Pont d'Avignon mentioned in the French nursery rhyme. Originally 900m long, the bridge was repaired and rebuilt several times until all but four of its 22 spans were washed away in the mid-1600s – there are plans to rebuild the bridge to celebrate the millennium. Entry to the bridge is 15FF (7FF for students and seniors). It's open Tuesday to

Sunday from 9 am to 1 pm and 2 to 5 pm (from April to September, daily from 9 am to 6.30 pm).

Synagogue The synagogue (☎ 04 90 85 21 24), 2 Place Jérusalem, was established on this site in 1221. A 13th-century oven used to bake unleavened bread for Passover is still in place, but the rest of the present dome-topped, neoclassical structure dates from the 19th century. You can visit the synagogue from 10 am to noon and 3 to 5 pm (closed Friday afternoon and weekends). Visitors should be modestly dressed, and men must cover their heads.

Museums Housed in an 18th century mansion, the **Musée Calvet** (☎ 04 90 86 33 84), 65 Rue Joseph Vernet, has a collection of ancient Egyptian, Greek and Roman artefacts as well as paintings from the 16th to 20th centuries. Admission is 30FF (15FF for students and seniors). Its annexe, the **Musée Lapidaire** (☎ 04 90 85 75 38), 27 Rue de la République, houses sculpture and statuary from the Gallo-Roman, Romanesque and Gothic periods. It's open from 10 am to noon and 2 to 6 pm (closed Tuesday). Entry is 10FF (free for students and seniors).

At 17 Rue Victor Hugo, the **Musée Louis**

Vouland (☎ 04 90 86 03 79) exhibits a fine collection of faïence (ceramics) and some superb 18th-century French furniture. It's open Tuesday to Saturday from 2 to 6 pm (also 10 am to noon from June to September). Entry costs 20FF (10FF for students and seniors).

Villeneuve-lès-Avignon Avignon's picturesque sister city also has a few interesting sights. The **Chartreuse du Val de Bénédiction** (☎ 04 90 15 24 24), 60 Rue de la République, was once the largest and most important Carthusian monastery in France. It's open daily from 9.30 am to 5.30 pm (9 am to 6.30 pm from April to September). Entry is 32FF (21FF for students and seniors). You can also buy a 45FF combined ticket which allows you to visit all of the town's major sights.

The **Musée Pierre de Luxembourg** (☎ 04 90 27 49 66) on Rue de la République has a fine collection of religious paintings, many of them from the 15th to the 17th centuries. The museum is open 10 am to 12.30 pm and 3 to 7 pm (10 am to noon and 2 to 5.30 pm from April to September; closed Monday and February). Admission is 20FF (12FF for students and seniors).

The **Tour Philippe le Bel** (☎ 04 90 27 49 68), a defensive tower built in the 14th century at what was then the north-western end of Pont Saint Bénézet, has great views of Avignon's walled city, the river and the surrounding countryside. Entry is 10FF. Another Provençal panorama can be enjoyed from the 14th-century **Fort Saint André**, which is open daily from 10 am to noon and 2 to 5 pm (9.30 am to 12.30 pm and 2 to 6 pm from April to September). Entry is 25FF (15FF for students and seniors).

From Avignon, Villeneuve can be reached by bus No 10 from the main post office. Unless you want to take the grand tour of the Avignon suburb of Les Angles, take a bus marked 'Villeneuve puis (then) Les Angles' (rather than 'Les Angles puis Villeneuve').

Places to Stay

Camping The attractive, shaded *Camping Bagatelle* (☎ 04 90 85 78 45; open all year) is on Île de la Barthelasse, slightly north of Pont Édouard Daladier. Charges are 17.80FF per adult, 8.50FF to pitch a tent and 6.50FF to park a car. To get there take bus No 10 from the main post office and get off at La Barthelasse stop.

Hostels The 210-bed *Auberge Bagatelle* (☎ 04 90 85 78 45; fax 04 90 27 16 23) and its many amenities are part of a large, park-like area on Île de la Barthelasse that includes Camping Bagatelle. A bed costs 59FF. See the Camping section for bus directions.

The friendly *Avignon Squash Club* (☎ 04 90 85 27 78), 32 Blvd Limbert, offers bunks in a converted squash court for only 58FF. Reception is open from 9 am to 10 pm (closed Sunday from September to June; open 8 to 11 am and 5 to 11 pm in July and August). Take bus No 7 from the train station and get off at the Université stop.

Hotels During the festival in July, it is nearly impossible to find accommodation in Avignon unless you've booked months in advance.

Walled City The *Hôtel du Parc* (☎ 04 90 82 71 55), 18 Rue Agricol Perdiguier, only 300m from the train station, has singles/doubles without shower for 140/ 160FF and with shower for 180/195FF. Hall showers are 5FF. Across the street at No 17 the friendly *Hôtel Splendid* (☎ 04 90 86 14 46; fax 04 90 85 38 55) has singles/doubles with shower for 130/200FF and rooms with shower and toilet for 170/280FF. The busy *Hôtel Innova* (☎ 04 90 82 54 10; fax 04 90 82 52 39), 100 Rue Joseph Vernet, has bright, comfortable and well soundproofed doubles without/with shower for 140/150FF; rooms for two/ three/four people with shower and toilet cost 200/240/260FF. Hall showers are free and breakfast is 25FF.

The *Hôtel Mignon* (☎ 04 90 82 17 30; fax 04 90 85 78 46), 12 Rue Joseph Vernet, has spotless singles/doubles with shower for 150/185FF, and doubles with shower and toilet for 220FF. Take bus No 10 from the main post office and get off at the Porte de l'Oulle.

Outside the Walls The family-run *Hôtel Monclar* (☎ 04 90 86 20 14; fax 04 90 85 94 94) is across the tracks from the train station at 13 Ave Monclar. Eminently serviceable doubles start at 165FF with sink and bidet. The pleasant *Hôtel Saint Roch* (☎ 04 90 82 18 63; fax 04 90 82 78 30), 9 Rue Paul Mérindol, has airy doubles with shower, toilet and TV for 250FF; triples and quads are 330FF.

Places to Eat

The *Restaurant Universitaire*, south-west of the train station on Ave du Blanchissage, is open from October to June except during university holidays. Meals are served from 11.30 am to 1.30 pm and 6.30 to 7.30 pm (closed Saturday evening and Sunday). People with student cards can buy tickets (about 15 or 30FF) at the CROUS office (☎ 04 90 82 42 18), 29 Blvd Limbert, just east of the walled city. It's open Monday, Tuesday, Wednesday and Friday from 10.30 am to 12.30 pm.

Restaurant Song Long (☎ 04 90 86 35 00), 1 Rue Carnot (next to Place Carnot), offers a wide variety of Vietnamese dishes, including vegetarian soups, salads, first courses and main dishes. *Menus* start at 55FF (lunch) and 78FF (dinner). *Le Belgocargo* (☎ 04 90 85 72 99), tucked behind the Eglise Saint Pierre at 7 Rue Armand de Pontmartin, serves mussels 16 different ways for 49 to 68FF and waterzooi de volaille (a creamy Belgian stew of chicken, leeks and herbs) for 58FF.

For hearty, healthy fodder in a rustic setting (tree trunks for benches etc) try the *Natural Café* (☎ 04 90 85 90 82), behind the opera house at 17 Rue Racine (closed Sunday and Monday). Adjoining it is the more conventional *La Fourchette* (☎ 04 90 85 20 93), a Michelin-recommended place with *menus* for 150FF (closed weekends).

On the other side of town, a good choice is *Woolloomooloo* (☎ 04 90 85 28 44), 16 bis Rue des Teinturiers. This lively, informal restaurant is open Tuesday to Saturday from noon to 2 pm and 7.30 pm to 1 am. *Menus* are around 60FF and vegetarian and Antillean dishes are on offer. The small, bohemian *Sindabad* (☎ 04 90 14 69 45), nearby at 53 Rue des Teinturiers, offers good Tunisian, oriental and Provençal home cooking. It has a 50FF plat du jour and is open for lunch and dinner (closed Sunday).

Near Place de l'Horloge, there's a *Casino* grocery at 22 Rue Saint Agricol (closed on Sunday). *Les Halles* food market is open from 7 am to 1 pm in Place Pie (closed Monday). Avignon's fanciest food shops are along Rue Joseph Vernet and Rue Saint Agricol.

Entertainment

Cinéma Utopia (☎ 04 90 82 65 36), 4 Rue des Escaliers Sainte Anne (follow the 'Promenade des Papes' signs east from Place du Palais), is a student entertainment/cultural centre with a jazz club, café and four cinemas screening undubbed films (30FF).

The *Opéra d'Avignon* (☎ 04 90 82 23 44), Place de l'Horloge, housed in an imposing structure built in 1847, stages operas, plays, concerts and ballet from October to June. The box office is open from 11 am to 6 pm (closed Sunday).

Getting There & Away

Bus The bus station (☎ 04 90 82 07 35) is down the ramp to the right as you exit the train station. The information window is open Monday to Friday from 8 am to noon and 1.30 to 6 pm (Saturday until noon only; closed Sunday). Tickets are sold on the buses, which are run by about 20 different companies.

Places you can get to by bus include Aix-en-Provence (86FF; one hour), Arles (37.50FF; 1½ hours), Nice (165FF), Nîmes (40FF), and Marseille (89FF; 35 minutes). Service on Sunday and during winter is less frequent.

Train The train station (☎ 08 36 35 35 39) is across Blvd Saint Roch from Porte de la République. The information office is open from 9 am to 6.15 pm (closed Sunday and holidays). There are frequent trains to Arles (33FF; 25 minutes), Nice (180FF; four hours), Nîmes (44FF; 30 minutes) and Paris (400FF).

Car Most car rental agencies are signposted from the train station: Europcar (☎ 04 90 85 01 40) is in the Ibis building; Budget (☎ 04 90 27 34 95) is down the ramp to the right as you exit the station; and Hertz (☎ 04 90 82 37 67) is at 4 Blvd Saint-Michel.

Getting Around

Bus TCRA municipal buses operate from 7 am to about 7.40 pm (8 am and 6 pm and less frequent on Sunday). Tickets cost 6.50FF each if bought from the driver; a carnet of five tickets (good for 10 rides) costs 48FF from TCRA offices in the walled city at Porte de la République and at Place Pie (closed Sunday).

Bicycle Cycles Peugeot (☎ 04 90 86 32 49), 80 Rue Guillaume Puy, has three-speeds and 10-speeds for 60/130/240FF for a day/three days/a week (plus 1000FF deposit). The Hôtel Splendid (see Hotels section) has mountain bikes to rent for 100/180/650FF a day/weekend/week (plus 2500FF deposit).

AROUND AVIGNON
Arles

Arles (population 52,000), set on the northern edge of the Camargue alluvial plain, began its ascent to prosperity and political importance in 49 BC when Julius Caesar, to whom the city had given its support, sacked Marseille, which had backed the Roman general Pompey. It soon became a major trading centre, the sort of place that, by the late 1st century AD, needed a 20,000-seat amphitheatre and a 12,000-seat theatre. Now known as the **Arènes** and the **Théâtre Antique** respectively, the two structures still stage bullfights and cultural events.

Arles is also known for its **Église Saint Trophime** and **Cloître Saint Trophime**; significant parts of both date from the 12th century and are in the Romanesque style. But the city is probably best known as the place where Van Gogh painted some of his most famous works, including *The Sunflowers*. The tourist office (☎ 04 90 18 41 20) is on Esplanade des Lices.

There are regular bus services to Marseille (82FF; 2½ hours), Aix-en-Provence (65FF; 1¾ hours) and Avignon (37.50FF; 1½ hours).

Côte d'Azur

The Côte d'Azur, which includes the French Riviera, stretches along France's Mediterranean coast from Toulon to the Italian border. Many of the towns here – Saint Tropez, Cannes, Antibes, Nice, Monaco – have become world-famous thanks to the recreational activities of the tanned and idle

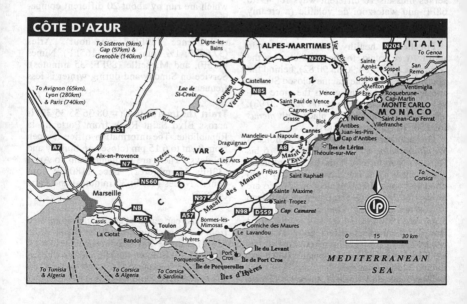

rich. The reality is rather less glamorous, but the Côte d'Azur still has a great deal to attract visitors: sunshine, 40km of beaches, all sorts of cultural activities and, sometimes, even a bit of glitter.

Unless you'll be camping or hostelling, your best bet is to stay in Nice, which has a generous supply of cheap hotels, and make day trips to other places.

Dangers & Annoyances

Theft from backpacks, pockets, cars and even laundrettes is a serious problem along the Côte d'Azur. To avoid unpleasantness, keep a sharp eye on your bags, especially at train and bus stations, and use left luggage lockers if you plan to sleep outside (say, on the beach). Again, *never* leave anything in a parked vehicle.

Getting Around

Trains run between Ventimiglia (just across the border in Italy) and Saint Raphaël via Menton, Monaco, Nice, Antibes, Cannes and many smaller towns, from early morning until late at night. See Getting There & Away in the Nice section for details.

The Côte d'Azur is notorious for its traffic jams, so if you plan to drive along the coast, especially in summer, be prepared for slow going. Around Saint Tropez, for instance, it can sometimes take hours to move just a few kilometres, which is why some of the truly wealthy have taken to reaching their seaside properties by helicopter.

NICE

Known as the capital of the Riviera, the fashionable yet relaxed city of Nice (population 342,000) makes a great base from which to explore the entire Côte d'Azur. The city, which did not become part of France until 1860, has plenty of relatively cheap accommodation and is only a short train or bus ride away from the rest of the Riviera. Nice's beach may be nothing to write home about, but the city is blessed with a fine collection of museums.

Orientation

Ave Jean Médecin runs from near the train station to Place Masséna. The Promenade des Anglais follows the curved beachfront from the city centre all the way to the airport, 6km to the west. Vieux Nice is the area delineated by the Quai des États-Unis, Blvd Jean Jaurès and the 92m hill known as Le Château. The neighbourhood of Cimiez, home to several very good museums, is north of the town centre.

Information

Tourist Office The main tourist office (☎ 04 93 87 07 07; fax 04 93 16 85 16; otc@nice.coteazur.org; www.nice.coteazur.org) at the train station is open daily from 8 am to 7 pm (until 8 pm July to September). The tourist office annexe (☎ 04 92 14 48 00) at 5 Promenade des Anglais is open Monday to Saturday from 8 am to 6 pm.

Money There's a Banque de France at 14 Ave Félix Faure. The Banque Populaire de la Côte d'Azur at 17 Ave Jean Médecin has a 24-hour currency exchange machine. Le Change at 17 Ave Thiers (to the right as you exit the train station) offers less-than-optimal rates but is open every day of the year from 7 am to midnight.

American Express (☎ 04 93 16 53 53), 11 Promenade des Anglais, is open Monday to Friday from 9 am to 9 pm and on Saturday till 1 pm (October to April hours are 9 am to noon and 2 to 6 pm, closed weekends).

Post The main post office, which will exchange foreign currency, is at 23 Ave Thiers, one block to the right as you exit the train station. There are branch post offices at 4 Ave Georges Clemenceau, on the corner of Rue de Russie, and in the old city at 2 Rue Louis Gassin.

Cybercafés The Web Store (☎ 04 93 87 87 99; info@webstore.fr), 12 Rue de Russie, charges 30/50FF for 30 minutes/one hour online. It's open from 10 am to noon and 2 to 7 pm (closed Sunday).

Laundry The laundrette at 16 Rue d'Angleterre, not far from the railway station, is open seven days a week from 7 am to 9 pm; the one at 39 Rue de la Buffa, near Place Grimaldi, is open the same hours. There are plenty of others around town.

FRANCE

NICE

PLACES TO STAY
10 Hôtel Darcy
11 Backpackers Hotel &
    Faubourg Montmartre
    Restaurant
13 Hôtel Idéal Bristol
14 Hôtel du Piemont
15 Hôtel Belle Meunière
19 Hôtel Les Orangers
23 Le Petit Louvre
27 Centre Hébergement
    Jeunesse (Summer Hostel)
33 Hôtel Les Mimosas

41 Hôtel Little Masséna
53 Hôtel Meublé Genevois
60 Hôtel au Picardie
61 Hôtel Saint FranÇois

PLACES TO EAT
7 Flunch Cafétéria
9 Cafétéria Casino
12 Restaurant Le Toscan
44 La Nissarda
45 Le Bistrot Saint Germain
65 Chez Thérésa
67 Nissa Socca

Boulevard Joseph Garnier Place Rue Raiberti
                                   Général
To Blvd Auguste Reynaud   de Gaulle
& Autoroute A8

Rue Clément – Roassal

Rue Vernier

Rue Trachel

Blvd Imperial
du Parc

Rue Nicholas II

Boulevard du Tzaréwich

Avenue Thiers

Rue de Châteauneuf

Rue F Passy

Caffarelli

Avenue des Fleurs

Ave des Orangers

Rue Bottero

Rue Dante

Avenue Gambetta

Boulevard Gambetta

Boulevard François Grosso

Rue de France

To Cannes

To Musée d'Art Naïf (1.5km)
& Airport (5km)

Rue de la Buffa

Rue de France

Promenade des Anglais

Beach Baie des Anges (Bay of Angels) Beach

Rue d'Alsace - Lorraine

Avenue Durante

Rue Georges

Clemenceau

Rue Rossini

Rue Verdi

Rue du Maréchal Joffre

Place
Grimaldi

Ave de Suède

OTHER
1 Gare du Sud
   (Trains to Digne-les-Bains)
2 Fruit & Vegetable Market
3 Musée Chagall
4 Russian Orthodox Cathedral
5 Gare Nice Ville
   (Main Train Station)
6 Main Tourist Office
8 Nicea Location Rent
   (Bike/Motorcycle Rental)
16 Rent-A-Car System
17 Le Change
    (Currency Exchange)
18 Main Post Office
20 Laundrette

21 Église Notre Dame
22 Web Store (Cybercafé)
24 Prisunic Supermarket
25 Nice étoile Shopping Mall
26 Police Headquarters
28 Airport Buses
30 Airport Buses
31 Musée Masséna
32 Cinéma Rialto
34 Laundrette
35 American Express
36 Tourist Office Annexe
37 English-American Library
38 Anglican Church
39 US Consulate

40 Cycles Arnaud
    (Bike Rental)
42 UK Consulate
43 24-Hour Currency
    Exchange Machine
46 Banque de France
47 Sun Bus
    (Local Bus Information)
48 Station Centrale
    (Local Bus Terminus)
49 Théâtre de Nice
50 Musée d'Art Moderne et
    d'Art Contemporain
51 Cinéma Nouveau Mercury
52 Opéra de Nice
54 Post Office Branch

55 Flower Market
56 Palais de Justice
57 Chez Wayne's
58 Boulangerie
59 Intercity Bus Station
62 William's Pub
63 Jonathan's Live Music Pub
64 Cathédrale Sainte
    Réparate
66 Église Saint Jacques
    le Majeur
68 Fruit & Vegetable Market
69 Buses to City Centre
70 Tour Bellanda & Lift
71 Ferry Terminal &
    SNCM Office

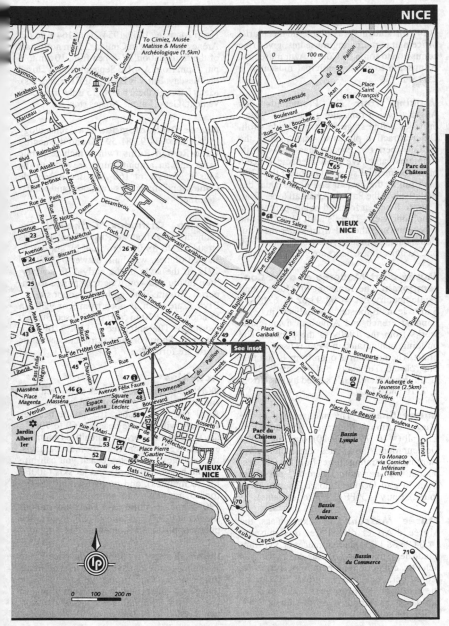

NICE

FRANCE

FRANCE

Things to See

An excellent-value museum pass (140FF; 70FF for students), available at the tourist office and participating museums, gives free admission to some 60 Côte d'Azur museums. Admission to most municipal museums is 25/15FF.

Walking Tour The **Promenade des Anglais**, which runs along Baie des Anges, provides a fine stage for a beachside stroll. Other attractive places to walk include the Jardin Albert 1er, Espace Masséna (with its fountains) and Ave Jean Médecin (Nice's main commercial street). On top of the 92m-high hill at the eastern end of the Quai des États-Unis is the **Parc du Château** (open from 7 am to 8 pm), a forested public park with a panoramic view. There's a lift (3.50/5FF one way/return) up the hill from under the Tour Bellanda. In summer it runs from 9 am to 7.50 pm. At other times, hours are 9 am to 5.50 pm.

Musée d'Art Moderne et d'Art Contemporain The Museum of Modern and Contemporary Art (☎ 04 93 62 61 62), Ave Saint Jean Baptiste, specialises in eye-popping French and American avant-garde works from the 1960s to the present. The building, inaugurated in 1990, is itself a work of art. The museum is open from 10 am to 6 pm (closed Tuesday). Admission is 25FF (15FF for students). It's served by bus Nos 3, 5, 7, 16 and 17.

Musée Chagall The main exhibit of the Musée National Message Biblique Marc Chagall (☎ 04 93 53 87 20), opposite 4 Ave Docteur Ménard, is a series of incredibly vivid paintings illustrating stories from the Old Testament. It's open from 10 am to 5 pm (6 pm from July to October; closed Tuesday year round). Entry is 30FF (20FF for students).

Musée Masséna Also known as the Musée d'Art et d'Histoire, this museum (☎ 04 93 88 11 34) has entrances at 35 Promenade des Anglais and 65 Rue de France. The eclectic collection of paintings, furniture, icons, ceramics and religious art can be viewed from 10 am to noon and 2 to 6 pm daily, except Monday. Admission is 25FF (15FF for students).

Musée Matisse This museum (☎ 04 93 81 08 08), with its fine collection of works by Henri Matisse (1869-1954), is at 164 Ave des Arènes de Cimiez in Cimiez, 2.5km north-east of the train station. It's open from 10 am to 5 pm (6 pm from April to September). It's closed on Tuesday. Entry is 25FF (15FF for students). Many buses go there but No 15 is the most convenient. Get off at the Arènes stop.

Musée Archéologique The Archaeology Museum (☎ 04 93 81 59 57) and the nearby **Gallo-Roman Ruins** (which include public baths and an amphitheatre) are next to the Musée Matisse at 160 Ave des Arènes de Cimiez, and share the same hours and admission fees.

Russian Orthodox Cathedral The Cathédrale Orthodoxe Russe Saint Nicolas (☎ 04 93 96 88 02), crowned by six onion-shaped domes, was built between 1903 and 1912 in the style of the early 17th century. Step inside and you'll be transported to Imperial Russia. The cathedral, opposite 17 Blvd Tzaréwitch, is open from 9 or 9.30 am to noon and 2.30 to 5.30 pm (closed Sunday morning). The entry fee is 12FF (10FF for students). Shorts or short skirts and sleeveless shirts are forbidden.

Activities

Water Sports Nice's beach is covered with smooth pebbles, not sand. Between mid-April and mid-October, free public beaches alternate with private beaches (60 to 70FF a day) offering all sorts of amenities (mattresses, showers, changing rooms, parasols, security etc). Along the beach you can hire paddle boats, sailboards and jet skis (300FF for 30 minutes), and go parasailing (200FF for 15 minutes) and water-skiing (100 to 130FF for 10 minutes). There are indoor showers (12FF) and toilets (2FF) open to the public opposite 50 Promenade des Anglais.

Inline Skates City Sport, in the Nice Etoile shopping centre on Ave Jean Médecin, rents inline skates (and protective kneepads for those not too proud to don something so uncool) for 30/50/80FF for a half day/day/two days.

Places to Stay

In summer, lots of young people sleep on the beach. Technically this is illegal, but the Nice police usually look the other way.

Hostels The *Auberge de Jeunesse* (☎ 04 93 89 23 64; fax 04 92 04 03 10) is 5km east of the train station on Route Forestière du Mont Alban. Beds cost 66FF, including breakfast. There's a midnight curfew, and it's often full so call ahead. Take bus No 14 from the Station Centrale terminus on Square Général Leclerc, which is linked to the train station by bus Nos 15 and 17.

From mid-June to mid-September the *Centre Hébergement Jeunes* (☎ 04 93 86 28 75) serves as a hostel. It's at 31 Rue Louis de Coppet, half a block north from 173 Rue de France. A bed in a six-person room costs only 50FF. There is a midnight curfew. Bags must be stored in the luggage room during the day, which costs 10FF a day.

Hotels There are quite a few cheap hotels near the train station and lots of places in a slightly higher price bracket along Rue d'Angleterre, Rue d'Alsace-Lorraine, Rue de Suisse, Rue de Russie and Rue Durante, also near the station. There are plenty more to the east of the station, clustered around Rue Assalit and Rue Pertinax. In summer the inexpensive places fill up by late morning – drop by or call ahead by 10 am.

Train Station Area The *Hôtel Belle Meunière* (☎ 04 93 88 66 15), 21 Ave Durante, a clean, friendly place that attracts lots of young people, is an excellent bet. Dorm beds are 76FF, including breakfast. It also has large doubles/triples from 182/243FF (with shower and toilet). This hotel is closed in December and January. Across the street at No 10 bis, the *Hôtel Les Orangers* (☎ 04 93 87 51 41; fax 04 93 87 51 41) has dorm beds for 85FF, and great doubles and triples with shower, fridge, hotplate and balcony for 210FF. The cheerful owner speaks excellent English, the result of dealing with backpackers for the past 17 years.

The *Hôtel Darcy* (☎ 04 93 88 67 06), 28 Rue d'Angleterre, has singles/doubles/triples for 125/150/195FF (210/255/300FF with shower and toilet). The dreary *Hôtel Idéal*

Bristol (☎ 04 93 88 60 72), 22 Rue Paganini, has basic doubles from 145FF (180FF with shower and toilet), and quads with shower and toilet for 425FF. It also has a 5th-floor terrace where guests can sunbathe and picnic.

The popular 20-bed *Backpackers' Hotel* (☎ 04 93 80 30 72), 32 Rue Pertinax, is above the Faubourg Montmartre restaurant. A dorm bed is 70FF a night, there's no curfew or lock-out, and cheery Patrick who runs the place is great at directing party-mad backpackers to the hot spot of the moment.

Rue d'Alsace-Lorraine is dotted with more upmarket two-star hotels. One of the cheapest is the *Hôtel du Piemont* (☎ 04 93 88 25 15) at No 19 which has bargain singles/doubles/triples with washbasin from 110/130/190FF. Singles/doubles with shower start at 130/160FF, while rooms with shower and toilet cost from 180/200FF. Triples/quads are 225/300FF.

Vieux Nice The *Hôtel Saint François* (☎ 04 93 85 88 69; fax 04 93 85 10 67), 3 Rue Saint François, has singles/doubles/triples for 130/168/237FF. Showers cost 15FF. Reception is open until 10 pm. The *Hôtel Au Picardie* (☎ 04 93 85 75 51), 10 Blvd Jean Jaurès, has singles/doubles from 120/140FF; pricier rooms include toilet and shower. Hall showers are 10FF.

The *Hôtel Meublé Genevois* (☎ 04 93 85 00 58), in an unmarked building at 11 Rue Alexandre Mari (3rd floor), has 1950s-style singles/doubles with kitchenette from 130/180FF. Large studios with shower and toilet cost 180 to 240FF for two people. If no-one answers the *sonnerie* (bell), push the little red button.

Elsewhere in Town The friendly *Hôtel Little Masséna* (☎ 04 93 87 72 34) is right in the centre of things at 22 Rue Masséna. Reception, open until 8 pm, is on the 5th floor (there's a lift). Doubles with hot plate and fridge are 140/180/220FF with washbasin/shower/toilet. The relaxed, family-style *Hôtel Les Mimosas* (☎ 04 93 88 05 59), 26 Rue de la Buffa (2nd floor), has good-sized, utilitarian singles/doubles for 120/190FF. Showers are 10FF.

Between the train station and the beach is the colourful *Le Petit Louvre* (☎ 04 93 80 15 54;

fax 04 93 62 45 08), 10 Rue Emma Tiranty. A faceless Mona Lisa greets guests as they enter and corridors are adorned with an eclectic bunch of paintings. Singles/doubles with shower, washbasin, fridge and hotplate are 171/205FF, singles/doubles with shower and toilet are 191/230FF and triples cost 249FF. Breakfast is 25FF.

Places to Eat

Cheap places near the train station include the *Flunch Cafétéria* (☎ 04 93 88 41 35), which is to the left as you exit the station building and is open daily from 11 am to 10 pm and, across the street at 7 Ave Thiers, the *Cafétéria Casino* (☎ 04 93 82 44 44), which is open from 8 am to 9.30 pm.

In the same vicinity, *Restaurant Le Toscan* (☎ 04 93 88 40 54; closed Sunday), a family-run Italian place at 1 Rue de Belgique, offers large portions of home-made ravioli. There are lots of Vietnamese and Chinese restaurants on Rue Paganini, Rue d'Italie and Rue d'Alsace-Lorraine. Nearby, *Le Faubourg Montmartre* (☎ 04 93 62 55 03), 32 Rue Pertinax (beneath the Backpackers' Hotel), is always crowded. The house speciality is bouillabaisse (120FF for two), and there's a 68FF *menu*. It's open from noon and from 5.30 pm.

La Nissarda (☎ 04 93 85 26 29), 17 Rue Gubernatis, has specialities from Nice and Normandy. The *menus* are reasonably priced at 60FF (lunch only), 78, 98 and 138FF (closed Sunday and in August). Nearby, *Le Bistrot Saint Germain* (☎ 04 93 13 45 12), 9 Rue Chauvain, has walls decorated with photos of famous Parisian scenes. It offers fresh, seasonal food at affordable prices.

In the old city, a perennial favourite with locals is *Nissa Socca* (☎ 04 93 80 18 35), 5 Rue Sainte Reparate. Its Niçois specialities include socca (chick pea rissoles), farcis (stuffed vegetables) and ratatouille. It's closed in January and June. The nearby streets, such as Rue de l'Abbaye, are lined with restaurants. *Chez Thérésa* (☎ 04 93 85 00 04) serves home-made socca from a little hole in the wall at 28 Rue Droite from 8 am to 1 pm (closed Monday).

The *Prisunic* supermarket opposite 33 Ave Jean Médecin is open 8.30 am to 8.30 pm (closed Sunday). In Vieux Nice, there's a *fruit and vegetable market* in front of the préfecture in Cours Saleya from 6 am to 5.30 pm (closed Sunday afternoon and Monday). The no-name *boulangerie* at the south end of Rue du Marché is the best place for cheap sandwiches, pizza slices, michettes (traditional savoury bread stuffed with cheese, olives, anchovies and onions) and other local breads.

Entertainment

William's Pub (☎ 04 93 85 84 66), 4 Rue Centrale, has live music every night starting around 9 pm (but not on Sunday). The pub itself is open 6 pm to 2.30 am, and there's pool, darts and chess in the basement. *Jonathan's Live Music Pub* (☎ 04 93 62 57 62), another bar à musique at 1 Rue de la Loge, has live music (country, boogie-woogie, Irish folk etc) every night in summer. *Chez Wayne's* (☎ 04 93 13 46 99), 15 Rue de la Préfecture, hosts a bilingual quiz on Tuesday, a ladies' night on Wednesday, karaoke on Sunday and live bands on Friday and Saturday. It's open from 3 pm to midnight (later on weekends). Happy Hour is until 9 pm.

Getting There & Away

Air The Aéroport International Nice-Côte d'Azur (☎ 04 93 21 30 30), is 6km west of the centre of town.

Bus The intercity bus station, opposite 10 Blvd Jean Jaurès, is served by some two dozen bus companies. The information counter (☎ 04 93 85 03 90) is open Monday to Saturday from 8 am to 6.30 pm. There are slow but frequent services every day until about 7.30 pm to Cannes (32FF; 1½ hours), Antibes (25FF; 1¼ hours), Monaco (17FF return; 45 minutes), and Menton (24FF return; 1¼ hours).

Train Nice's main train station, Gare Nice Ville, is on Ave Thiers, 1200m north of the beach. The information office (☎ 08 36 35 35 39) is open from 8 am to 6.30 pm (closed Sunday). There is fast, frequent service (up to 40 trains a day in each direction) to points all along the coast, including Monaco (40FF; 20 minutes), Antibes (17FF; 25 minutes) and Cannes (32FF; 40 minutes). The two or three TGVs that link Nice with Paris' Gare de

Lyon (467FF; seven hours) are infrequent, and you may find it more convenient to go via Marseille.

Ferry The fastest and least expensive ferries from mainland France to Corsica depart from Nice (see Getting There & Away in the Corsica section). The SNCM office (☎ 04 93 13 66 66) at the ferry port on Quai du Commerce is open from 8 am to 7 pm (until 11.45 am on Saturday; open two hours before a scheduled departure on Sunday). SNCM tickets can also be purchased at many travel agencies. To get to the ferry port from Ave Jean Médecin, take bus No 1 or 2 and get off at the Port stop.

Getting Around
To/From the Airport Sunbus bus No 23 (8FF), which runs every 20 or 30 minutes from about 6 am to 8 pm, can be picked up at the train station or on Blvd Gambetta, Rue de France or Rue de la Californie. From the intercity bus station or Promenade des Anglais, you can also take the yellow ANT bus (21FF; every 20 or 30 minutes). Buses also make the run from the train station.

Bus Local buses, run by Sunbus, cost 8/68FF for a single ticket/carnet of 10. Bus information and one, five and seven-day passes are available from the Sunbus information office (☎ 04 93 16 52 10) at the Station Centrale on Ave Félix Faure, open from 6.15 am to 7.30 pm. To go from the train station to Vieux Nice and the bus station, take bus No 2, 5 or 17. Bus No 12 links the train station with the beach.

Taxi Call ☎ 04 93 13 78 78 to order a taxi.

Car & Motorcycle Rent a Car Systeme (☎ 04 93 88 69 69), in the same building as Budget car rental opposite the train station at 38 Ave Aubert (corner of Ave Thiers), offers the best rates.

Nicea Location Rent (☎ 04 93 82 42 71), 9 Ave Thiers, rents mopeds from 250FF a day (extra for petrol and a helmet), 50cc scooters for 390FF a day and 125cc motorcycles for 465FF a day. The office is open from 9 am to 6 pm (closed Sunday).

Bicycle Bicycles (80FF a day) can be rented from Nicea Location Rent (see Car & Motorcyle above). Cycles Arnaud (☎ 04 93 87 88 55), 4 Place Grimaldi, has mountain bikes for 100/180FF a day/weekend. It's open 9 am to noon and 2 to 4 pm (closed Monday morning and Sunday).

ANTIBES
Across the Baie des Anges from Nice, Antibes (population 70,000) has beautiful, sandy beaches, 16th-century ramparts that run along the shore, an attractive pleasure-boat harbour (Port Vauban) and an old city with narrow, winding streets and lovely flower-bedecked houses. The tourist office (☎ 04 92 90 53 00) is at 11 Place de Gaulle.

The Château Grimaldi, set on a spectacular site overlooking the sea, now serves as the **Musée Picasso** (☎ 04 92 90 54 20). This outstanding museum is open from 10 am to noon and 2 to 6 pm (no midday break from mid-June to mid-September; closed Monday year round). Entry is 20FF (10FF for students).

For accommodation, there is a *Relais International de la Jeunesse* (☎ 04 93 61 34 40; open from mid-March to mid-November), 60 Blvd de la Garoupe, at Cap d'Antibes. Dorm beds are 70FF a night. The *Hôtel Caméo* (☎ 04 93 34 24 17), 62 Rue de la République, just off Place Nationale, has rooms with shower from 280FF. Nearby, the small and welcoming, one-star *Auberge Provençale* (☎ 04 93 34 13 24; fax 04 93 34 89 88), 61 Place Nationale, charges 240/250FF for a single/double with all *conforts* (mod cons).

The bus station (☎ 04 93 34 37 60) is at Place Guynemer, just off Rue de la République. The train station is on Ave Robert Soleau; call ☎ 08 36 35 35 39 for information. There are frequent trains from Nice (17FF; 25 minutes) and Cannes (17FF; 15 minutes).

CANNES
The harbour, the bay, Le Suquet hill, the beachside promenade, and the bronzed sun-worshippers on the beach provide more than enough natural beauty to make Cannes (population 69,500) worth at least a day trip. It's also fun watching the rich drop their money with such fashionable nonchalance.

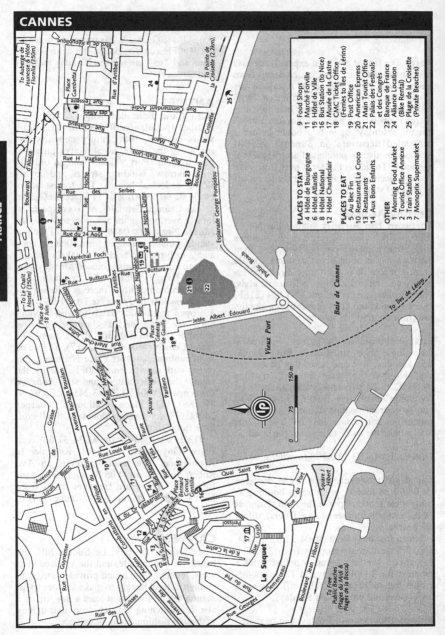

CANNES

PLACES TO STAY
4 Hôtel de Bourgogne
6 Hôtel Atlantis
8 Hôtel National
12 Hôtel Chanteclair

PLACES TO EAT
5 Au Bec Fin
10 Restaurant Le Croco
13 Restaurants
14 Aux Bons Enfants

OTHER
1 Morning Food Market
2 Tourist Office Annexe
3 Train Station
7 Monoprix Supermarket
9 Food Shops
11 Marché Forville
15 Hôtel de Ville
16 Bus Station (to Nice)
17 Musée de la Castre
18 CMC Ticket Office
   (Ferries to Îles de Lérins)
19 Post Office
20 American Express
21 Main Tourist Office
22 Palais des Festivals
   et des Congrès
23 Banque de France
24 Alliance Location
   (Bike Rental)
25 Plage de la Croisette
   (Private Beaches)

Cannes is renowned for its many festivals and cultural activities, the most famous being the International Film Festival, which runs for two weeks in mid-May. People come to Cannes all year long, but the main tourist season runs from May to October. During the off season, however, local people are more inclined to be friendly, prices are lower and there are no crowds to contend with.

Orientation

Rue Jean Jaurès, which runs in front of the train station, is four or five blocks north of the huge Palais des Festivals et des Congrès, to the west of which is the Vieux Port. Place Bernard Cornut Gentille (formerly Place de l'Hôtel de Ville), where the bus station is located, is on the north-western corner of the Vieux Port. Cannes' most famous promenade, the magnificent, hotel-lined Blvd de la Croisette, begins at the Palais des Festivals and continues eastward around the Baie de Cannes to Pointe de la Croisette.

Information

Tourist Office The main tourist office (☎ 04 93 39 24 53; fax 04 92 99 84 23; www.cannes-on-line.com) is on the ground floor of the Palais des Festivals. It's open from 9 am to 6.30 pm (closed Sunday). Daily hours in July and August are 9 am to 7.30 pm. The tourist office annexe (☎ 04 93 99 19 77) at the train station is open from 9 am to 7 pm (Saturday until 1 pm; closed Sunday). Turn left as you exit the station building and walk up the stairs next to Frantour Tourisme.

Money & Post The Banque de France, 8 Blvd de la Croisette, is open from 8.30 am to noon and 1.30 to 3.30 pm. There are more banks along Rue d'Antibes (two blocks towards the beach from Rue Jean Jaurès) and on Rue Buttura (across Blvd de la Croisette from the main tourist office). American Express (☎ 04 93 38 15 87), 8 Rue des Belges, two blocks north-east of the Palais des Festivals, is open Monday to Friday from 9 am to 6 pm and on Saturday from 9 am to 1 pm.

The main post office at 22 Rue Bivouac Napoléon, two blocks inland from the Palais des Festivals, also exchanges foreign currency.

Things to See & Do

Walking Tour Not surprisingly, the best places to walk are close to the water. Some of the largest yachts you'll ever see are likely to be sitting in the **Vieux Port**, a fishing port now given over to pleasure craft. The streets around the old port are particularly pleasant on a summer's evening, when the many cafés and restaurants – overflowing with well-heeled patrons – light up the whole area with coloured neon.

The hill just west of the Vieux Port, **Le Suquet**, affords magnificent views of Cannes, especially in the late afternoon and on clear nights. The pine and palm-shaded walkway along **Blvd de la Croisette** is probably the classiest promenade on the whole Riviera.

Musée de la Castre This museum (☎ 04 93 38 55 26), housed in a chateau atop Le Suquet, has a diverse collection of Mediterranean and Middle Eastern antiquities as well as objects of ethnographic interest from all over the world. It's open from 10 am to noon and 2 to 5 pm (closed Tuesday). From April to June afternoon hours are 2 to 6 pm; in July and August, they're 3 to 7 pm. Admission is 10FF (free for students).

Beaches Each of the fancy hotels that line Blvd de la Croisette has its own private section of the beach. Unfortunately, this arrangement leaves only a small strip of sand near the Palais des Festivals for the bathing pleasure of the masses. Free public beaches, the **Plages du Midi** and **Plages de la Bocca**, stretch for several kilometres westward from the old port along Blvd Jean Hibert and Blvd du Midi.

Îles de Lérins The eucalyptus and pine-covered **Île Sainte Marguerite**, where the Man in the Iron Mask (made famous in the novel by Alexandre Dumas) was held captive during the late 17th century, lies just over 1km from the mainland. The island, which measures only 3.25 by 1km, is crisscrossed by many trails and paths. The smaller **Île Saint Honorat** was the site of a renowned and powerful monastery founded in the 5th century. Today it's home to Cistercian monks who welcome visitors to their monastery and the seven small chapels dotted around the island.

FRANCE

CMC (Compagnie Maritime Cannoise; ☎ 04 93 38 66 33) runs ferries to Île Saint Honorat (45FF return; 20 minutes) and Île Sainte Marguerite (40FF return; 15 minutes). Both islands can be visited for 60FF. The ticket office, at the Vieux Port near the Palais des Festivals, is open from 8.30 am to 12.30 pm and 1.30 to 6.30 pm (open later in July and August).

Places to Stay

Hotel prices in Cannes fluctuate wildly according to seasonal demand. Tariffs can be up to 50% higher in July and August – when you'll be lucky to find a room at any price – than in winter. During the film festival, all the hotels are booked up to a year in advance.

Hostels Cannes' *Auberge de Jeunesse* (☎/fax 04 93 99 26 79), in a small villa at 35 Ave de Vallauris about 400m north-east of the train station, has beds in dorm rooms for four to six people for about 80FF, though you must have an HI card (available for 70/100FF for those under/over 26). Reception is open from 8 am to 12.30 pm and 2.30 to 10.30 pm (3 to 10 pm on weekends); curfew is at midnight (1 am at weekends).

The very pleasant private hostel *Le Chalit* (☎ 04 93 99 22 11; fax 04 93 39 00 28), 27 Ave du Maréchal Galliéni, is about five minutes walk north-west of the station. It charges 80FF for a bed in rooms for four to eight people. Sheets are extra. There are two kitchens. Le Chalit is open year-round and there is no curfew, but you must leave a deposit to get a key.

Hotels Heading towards the Auberge de Jeunesse, you pass the excellent value but little known *Hôtel Florella* (☎ 04 93 38 48 11), 55 Blvd République. Rooms for one/two people with washbasin cost 140/170FF; doubles with shower and TV are 190FF.

The large *Hôtel Atlantis* (☎ 04 93 39 18 72; fax 04 93 68 37 65) is south of the train station at 4 Rue du 24 Août. Despite its two-star rating, it has singles/doubles with TV for only 145/180FF during the low season. The price jumps to 340/395FF during festival periods and in July and August. At No 13 on the same street, the *Hôtel de Bourgogne* (☎ 04 93 38 36 73; fax 04 92 99 28 41) has singles/doubles for 160/180FF in the off season and 170/220FF in summer. Showers are free. Singles or doubles with shower, toilet and TV are 200FF (220 to 250FF in summer).

The *Hôtel National* (☎ 04 93 39 91 92), 8 Rue Maréchal Joffre, has singles/doubles from 150/220FF. Doubles/triples with shower and toilet are 250/350FF. The *Hôtel Chanteclair* (☎/fax 04 93 39 68 88), 12 Rue Forville, is a favourite with backpackers, and has simple singles/doubles for 130/150FF (mid-October to mid-April) and 160/190FF (peak periods). Two-wheeled conveyances can be parked in the courtyard.

Places to Eat

There are a few cheap restaurants around the Marché Forville (a block north of Place Bernard Cornut Gentille) and many small (but not necessarily cheap) restaurants along Rue Saint Antoine, which runs north-west from Place Bernard Cornut Gentille.

Near the train station, *Au Bec Fin* (☎ 04 93 38 35 86), 12 Rue du 24 Août, is often filled with regulars. You can choose from two excellent plats du jour for 45 to 60FF, or *menus* at 79, 85 or 99FF. This place is closed on Saturday evening and Sunday. Another good choice is the popular *Aux Bons Enfants*, 80 Rue Meynadier. It offers regional dishes like aïoli garni and mesclun (a rather bitter salad of dandelion greens and other roughage); the *menu* is 94FF. It's open for lunch and dinner on weekdays and for lunch on Saturday.

One of the cheapest restaurants in Cannes is *Restaurant Le Croco* (☎ 04 93 68 60 55), Rue Louis Blanc. Pizzas, grilled meat and fish and shish kebabs are the main items on the menu. The plat du jour is 49FF and *menus* are 59FF (lunch) and 89FF.

There's a *Monoprix* supermarket (closed Sunday) on the corner of Rue Buttura and Rue Jean Jaurès, half a block towards the beach from the train station. A morning *food market* is held on Place Gambetta and at the *Marché Forville*, north of Place Bernard Cornut Gentille, from Tuesday to Sunday (daily in summer). There are quite a few food shops along Rue Meynadier, a pedestrian mall two blocks inland from the old port.

Getting There & Away

Bus Buses to Nice (30FF; 1½ hours), Nice airport (70FF; 45 minutes) and other destinations, most of them operated by Rapides Côte d'Azur, leave from Place Bernard Cornut Gentille. The information office (☎ 04 93 39 11 39) is open 7 am to 7 pm (closed Sunday).

Train The train station (☎ 08 36 35 35 39) is 300m north of the Palais des Festivals on Rue Jean Jaurès. The information office (on the 1st floor over the left-luggage office) is open Monday to Saturday from 8.30 am to 6 pm. Opening hours are 8.30 am to 7 pm from mid-July to mid-September. Rail destinations include Antibes (13FF; 10 minutes), Nice (32FF; 40 minutes) and Marseille (150FF; two hours).

Getting Around

Bus Bus Azur serves Cannes and destinations up to 7km from town. Its office (☎ 04 93 39 18 71) at Place Bernard Cornut Gentille, in the same building as Rapides Côte d'Azur, is open Monday to Saturday from 7 am to 7 pm. Tickets cost 7.50FF and a carnet of 10 is 49FF.

Taxi Call ☎ 04 93 38 91 91 to order a taxi.

Bicycle Alliance Location (☎ 04 93 38 62 62), 19 Rue des Frères, rents mountain bikes for 80FF a day.

MENTON

Menton (population 29,000), reputed to be the warmest spot on the Côte d'Azur, is encircled by mountains which protect it from the mistral. The town is renowned for its production of lemons and holds a two-week Fête du Citron that begins every year sometime between mid-February and early March. The helpful tourist office (☎ 04 93 57 57 00) is in the Palais de l'Europe at 8 Ave Boyer.

It's very pleasant to wander around the narrow, winding streets of the old city and up to the cypress-shaded **Cimetière du Vieux Château**. The graves of English, Irish, North Americans, New Zealanders and other foreigners who died here during the 19th century can be seen in the south-west corner, but the view alone is worth the climb.

Église Saint Michel, the grandest baroque church in this part of France, sits perched in the centre of the **Vieille Ville**, with its many narrow and winding passageways. The ornate interior is Italian in inspiration. The **Musée Jean Cocteau** (☎ 04 93 57 72 30) is near the old city on Quai de Monléon and features the artist's drawings, tapestries and ceramics. It's open from 10 am to noon and 2 to 6 pm (closed Tuesday); afternoon hours are 3 to 7 pm from mid-June to mid-September. Entry is free.

The **beach** along the Promenade du Soleil is public and, like Nice's, is carpeted with smooth pebbles. The better, private beaches lie east of the old city in the pleasure port area, the main one being **Plage des Sablettes**.

You can pitch a tent at *Camping Saint Michel* (☎ 04 93 35 81 23; open from April to mid-October), 1km north-east of the train station up on Plateau Saint Michel. It costs 16/16/17FF per person/tent/car. The *Auberge de Jeunesse* (☎ 04 93 35 93 14) is next to Camping Saint Michel. Bed and breakfast is 66FF. It's closed from 10 am to 5 pm; curfew is at midnight. The walk from the train station is quite a hike uphill and there are lots of steps.

There are places to eat – at any time of day – along Ave Félix Faure and its pedestrianised continuation, Rue St Michel, where takeaway crêpes or gauffres (waffles) are available for between 10 and 25FF, depending on the topping. Cheaper restaurants, including pizzerias, line Quai de Monléon in the Vieille Ville.

The bus station (☎ 04 93 28 43 27) has services to Monaco (12FF return; 30 minutes), Nice (28FF return; 1¼ hours) and, just across the border in Italy, Ventimiglia (Vintimille in French; 12FF; 30 minutes).

Monaco

The Principality of Monaco, a sovereign state whose territory covers only 1.95 sq km, has been ruled by the Grimaldi family for most of the period since 1297. Prince Rainier III (born in 1923), whose sweeping constitutional powers make him far more than a figurehead, has reigned since 1949. The citizens of Monaco (Monégasques), of whom

FRANCE

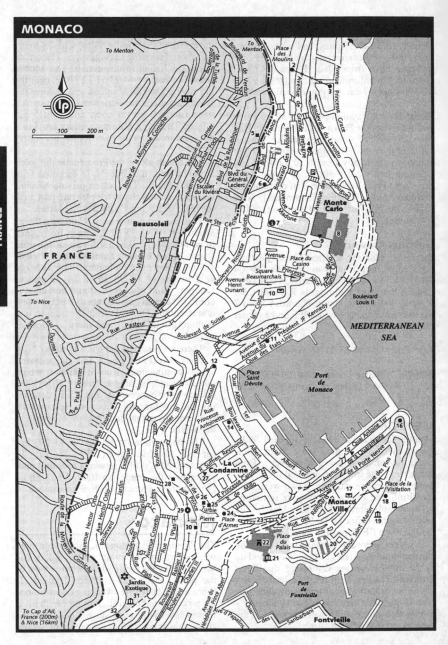

MONACO

PLACES TO STAY		OTHER		17	Post Office
5	Hôtel Cosmopolite (Beausoleil)	1	Plages de Larvotto	18	Public Lift to Parking Pêcheurs
25	Hôtel Helvetia	2	Public Lift Entrance	19	Musée Océanaographique
26	Hôtel Cosmopolite & Hôtel de France	3	Public Lift Entrance	20	Cathédrale de Monaco
28	Centre de la Jeunesse Princesse Stéphanie (Hostel)	4	Public Lift	21	Musée des Souvenirs Napoléoniens
30	Hôtel Terminus & Post Office	6	American Express	22	Palais du Prince
		7	Tourist Office	23	Rampe Major (Path to Palais de Prince)
PLACES TO EAT		8	Casino de Monte Carlo	24	Food Market
9	Café de Paris	10	Main Post Office	29	Train Station
15	Stars 'n' Bars Restaurant & Cybercafé	11	CAM Office (Local Bus Information)	31	Musée d'Anthropologie Préhistorique
27	Le Texan	12	Public Lift Entrance	32	Public Lift
		13	Public Lift Entrance		
		14	Monaco Market Supermarket		
		16	Fort Antoine		

there are only 5000 out of a total population of 30,000, pay no taxes. The official language is French, although efforts are being made to revive the country's traditional dialect, and the official religion is Roman Catholicism. There are no border formalities and Monaco makes a perfect day trip from Nice.

Orientation

Monaco consists of four principal areas: Monaco Ville, also known as the old city or the Rocher de Monaco, perched atop a 60m-high crag overlooking the Port de Monaco; Monte Carlo, famed for its casino and its Grand Prix motor race, north of the harbour; La Condamine, the flat area around the harbour; and Fontvieille, an industrial area south-west of Monaco Ville and the Port de Fontvieille. The French town of Beausoleil is just north of Monte Carlo.

Information

Tourist Office The Office National de Tourisme (☎ 92 16 61 66; fax 92 16 60 00; mgto@monaco1.org; www.monaco.mc), 2a Blvd des Moulins, is across the public gardens from the casino. It's open Monday to Saturday from 9 am to 7 pm, and Sunday from 10 am to noon. From mid-June to mid-September, several tourist office kiosks are set up around the principality, including one at the train station, one next to the Jardin Exotique and another on the Quai des États-Unis, on the north side of the port.

Money The currency of Monaco is the French franc. Both French and Monégasque coins are in circulation, but the latter are not widely accepted outside the principality.

In Monte Carlo, you'll find lots of banks in the vicinity of the casino. In La Condamine, try Blvd Albert 1er. American Express (☎ 93 25 74 45), 35 Blvd Princesse Charlotte, near the tourist office, is open weekdays from 9 am to noon and 2 to 6 pm, and on Saturday till noon.

Post & Communications Monégasque stamps are valid only within Monaco, and postal rates are the same as in France. The main post office is in Monte Carlo at 1 Ave Henri Dunant (inside the Palais de la Scala). It does not exchange foreign currency. Other post offices are at Place de la Mairie in Monaco Ville, near the Musée Océanographique, and near the train station (look for the sign of the Hôtel Terminus).

Telephone numbers in Monaco have only eight digits. Calls between Monaco and the rest of France are treated as international calls. When calling Monaco from the rest of France or abroad, dial 00 followed by Monaco's country code (377). To call France from Monaco, dial 00 and France's country code (33). This applies even if you are only making a call from the east side of Blvd de France (in Monaco) to its west side (in France)!

Online Services There is a 'cybercorner' inside the bar and restaurant Stars 'n' Bars

(☎ 93 50 95 95; info@starsnbars.com; www .isp-riviera.com/starsnbars), at 6 Quai Antoine 1er, open from 11 am to midnight (40FF for 30 minutes online).

Things to See & Do

Palais du Prince The changing of the guard takes place outside the Prince's Palace (☎ 93 25 18 31) every day at exactly 11.55 am. From June to October about 15 state apartments are open to the public daily from 9.30 am to 6.20 pm. Entry is 30FF (15FF for students). Guided tours (35 minutes) in English leave every 15 or 20 minutes. A combined ticket for entry to the **Musée des Souvenirs Napoléoniens** – a display of Napoleon's personal effects in the south wing of the palace – is 40/20FF.

Musée Océanographique If you're going to go to one aquarium on your whole trip, the world-famous Oceanographic Museum (☎ 93 15 36 00), with its 90 seawater tanks, should be it. This is also one of the few aquariums in the world to display living coral. Upstairs are all sorts of exhibits on ocean exploration. The museum, which is on Ave Saint Martin in Monaco Ville, is open daily from 9 am to 7 pm (8 pm in July and August). The entry fee – brace yourself – is 60FF (30FF for students).

Cathédrale de Monaco The unspectacular cathedral (1875) on 4 Rue Colonel has one major attraction: the grave of Grace Kelly (1929-1982). Her plain tombstone, inscribed with the Latin words 'Gratia Patricia Principis Rainerii III', lies on the west side of the cathedral choir. The Hollywood star married Prince Rainier III in 1956, but was killed in a car crash. The remains of other members of the royal family, buried in the church crypt since 1885, rest behind Princess Grace's tomb.

Walking Tour The touristy streets and alleys facing the Palais du Prince are surrounded by beautiful, shaded gardens offering great views of the entire principality (as well as a good bit of France and some of Italy).

Jardin Exotique The steep slopes of the wonderful Jardin Exotique are home to some 7000 varieties of cacti and succulents from all over the world. The spectacular view is worth at least half the admission fee of 37FF (18FF for students), which also gets you into the **Musée d'Anthropologie Préhistorique** and includes a half-hour guided visit to the **Grottes de l'Observatoire**, a system of caves 279 steps down the hillside. The garden is open daily from 9 am to 6 or 7 pm. From the tourist office, take bus No 2 to the terminus.

Casino The drama of watching people risk their money in Monte Carlo's ornate casino (☎ 92 16 21 21), built between 1878 and 1910, makes a visit to the gaming rooms almost worth the stiff entry fees: 50FF for the Salon Ordinaire (which has French roulette and trente-quarante) and 100FF for the Salons Privés (baccarat, blackjack, craps, American roulette etc). You must be at least 21 to enter. Shorts are forbidden in the Salon Ordinaire, and men must wear a tie and jacket after 9 pm in the Salons Privés. Income from gambling accounts for 4.31% of Monaco's total state revenues.

Places to Stay

There are no cheap places to stay in Monaco, and less expensive accommodation is scarce and often full. Over 75% of Monaco's hotel rooms are classified as 'four-star deluxe'.

Hostels Monaco's HI hostel, the *Centre de la Jeunesse Princesse Stéphanie* (☎ 93 50 83 20; fax 93 25 29 82), 24 Ave Prince Pierre, is 120m up the hill from the train station. You must be aged between 16 and 31 to stay here. It costs 70FF per person, including breakfast and sheets. Stays are usually limited to three nights during summer. Beds are given out each morning on a first-come first-served basis – numbered tickets are distributed from 8 am or thereabouts and registration begins at 11 am.

Hotels Close to the train station in La Condamine, the *Hôtel Cosmopolite* (☎ 93 30 16 95), 4 Rue de la Turbie, has decent singles/doubles with shower for 288/322FF and doubles without shower for 240FF. Next door, the *Hôtel de France* (☎ 93 30 24 64), 6 Rue de la Turbie, has singles/doubles with shower, toilet and TV starting at 350/360FF, including breakfast.

The *Hôtel Terminus* (☎ 92 05 63 00; fax 92 05 20 10), Ave Prince Pierre, and *Hôtel Helvetia* (☎ 93 30 21 71; fax 92 16 70 51), 1 bis Rue Grimaldi, are also close to the station and are both cheapies (by Monaco standards). Rooms at both are around 350 to 450FF.

Another (unrelated) *Hôtel Cosmopolite* (☎ 04 93 78 36 00), 19 Blvd du Général Leclerc, is up the hill from the casino in Beausoleil. It has rooms with shower and TV for 195FF (270/290FF with toilet for one/two people). When calling this hotel from Monaco (eg from the train station), dial 00 33 then the 10-digit number (dropping the first 0). The nearest bus stop is Crémaillère, served by bus Nos 2 and 4.

Places to Eat

There are a few cheap restaurants in La Condamine along Rue de la Turbie. Lots of touristy restaurants of more or less the same quality can be found in the streets leading off from Place du Palais. The terrace of the *Café de Paris* (☎ 92 16 23 00) on Place du Casino is a great place to sit and people-watch, but a beer and a sandwich will cost you more than 70FF!

The flashy *Stars 'n' Bars* (☎ 93 50 95 95), 6 Quai Antoine 1er, overlooks the port and yacht club and is open from noon to 3 am (closed Monday); the restaurant closes at midnight. Billed as a blues bar and restaurant, it offers main dishes in American-sized portions and excellent salads (60 to 70FF). There's live music on Thursday, Friday and Saturday nights in the upstairs nightclub. The Texan businessman who owns it also runs *Le Texan* (☎ 93 30 34 54), 4 Rue Suffren Reymond.

In La Condamine, there's a *food market* at Place d'Armes and a *Monaco Market* supermarket, Blvd Albert 1er, open from 8.45 am to 12.30 pm and 2.45 to 7.30 pm (no break on Friday or Saturday; closed Sunday). Summer hours are 8.30 am to 8 pm (closed Sunday).

Getting There & Away

Bus There is no single bus station in Monaco – intercity buses leave from various points around the city.

Train The train station, which is part of the French SNCF network (☎ 08 36 35 35 39), is on Ave Prince Pierre. The station's information office is open daily from 9.30 am to noon and 2.30 to 6.30 pm. There are frequent trains eastward to Menton (12FF; 10 minutes) and the first town across the border in Italy, Ventimiglia (Vintimille in French; 19FF; 25 minutes). For trains to Nice and connections to other towns, see Getting There & Away in the Nice section.

Getting Around

Bus Monaco's bus system has six lines. Line No 2 links Monaco Ville with Monte Carlo and then loops back to the Jardin Exotique. Line No 4 links the train station with the tourist office, the casino and the Larvotto district. A ticket costs 8.50FF, and magnetic cards (on sale from bus drivers and vending machines) good for four/eight rides cost 19/30FF. A one-day tourist pass is 21FF. Buses run until 7 or 9 pm. The bus company office (CAM; ☎ 93 50 62 41), 3 Ave Président John F Kennedy, is on the north side of the port.

Taxi Taxis can be ordered by calling ☎ 93 15 01 01 or ☎ 93 50 56 28.

Lift Around 15 public lifts (*ascenseurs publics*) ease passage up and down Monaco's steep hills. Most of them operate 24 hours.

Languedoc-Roussillon

Languedoc-Roussillon (created in the 1960s by the merging of two historic provinces), stretches in an arc along the Mediterranean coast from Provence to the Pyrenees and north to the Massif Central. The region has many attractions for the traveller, including the vibrant capital Montpellier, the old Roman town of Nîmes, and the fairy-tale walled city of Carcassonne.

Languedoc, the northern part of the region, takes its name from the *langue d'oc*, a language closely related to modern-day Catalan but quite distinct from the *langue d'oïl*, the forerunner of modern French spoken north of the Loire. (The words *oc* and *oïl* meant 'yes'.) While Languedoc has a Provençal feel, Roussillon, to the south, was for many centuries a part of Spanish Catalonia until it was handed over to France in 1659.

LANGUEDOC-ROUSSILLON

MONTPELLIER

Montpellier (population 211,000) is one of France's fastest-growing cities. Nearly a quarter of its population is made up of students, and the university is celebrated for its science, law, literature and especially medical faculties; Europe's first medical school was founded here early in the 12th century.

Though there is little in Montpellier that would qualify as a 'must-see', the old city – with its stone arches, fine *hôtels particuliers* and general decaying splendour – remains charming, while the beach is only 12km away.

Orientation

The heart of Montpellier is Place de la Comédie, an enormous pedestrianised square lined with distinguished buildings, in the middle of the teardrop-shaped Centre Historique. West of Place de la Comédie is the city's oldest quarter, a web of pedestrianised lanes that weave between Rue Foch, Rue de la Loge and Grand Rue Jean Moulin.

Information

Montpellier's central tourist office (☎ 04 67 60 60 60; fax 04 67 60 60 61) is behind the Pavillion de l'Hôtel de Ville at the south end of Esplanade Charles de Gaulle. It's open weekdays from 9 am to 1 pm and 2 to 6 pm, Saturday from 10 am, and Sunday from 10 am to 1 pm and 2 to 5 pm. Between 15 June and 15 September, Sunday afternoon hours are 3 to 6 pm.

The Banque de France, 6 Blvd Ledru-Rollin, is open from 8.30 am to noon and 1.30 to 3 pm (closed on weekends). The main post office, 13 Place Rondelet, is open from 8 am to 7 pm (Saturday until noon; closed Sunday).

Things to See

After strolling around the **Centre Historique**, pay a visit to the **Musée Fabre** (☎ 04 67 14 83 00), 39 Blvd Bonne Nouvelle, home to one of France's richest collections of French, Italian, Flemish and Dutch works from the 16th century onward. It's open year round from 9 am to 5.30 pm (on weekends from 9.30 am to 5 pm; closed Monday). Admission is 20/10FF for adults/students. The **Musée Languedocien** (☎ 04 67 52 93 03), 7 Rue Jacques Cœur, focuses on the region's archaeological finds as well as *objets d'art* and furniture from the 17th to 19th centuries. It's open from 2 to 5 pm (6 pm in July and August; closed Sunday). Admission is 20/10FF for adults/students.

The closest **beach** is at Palavas-les-Flots, 12km south of the city and backed by a nasty concrete skyline. However, it's easy to reach by local bus (No 17 or 28). About 20km south-east of Montpellier is **La Grande Motte**, a resort famous for its wacky, futuristic architecture.

Places to Stay

Camping The closest camp sites are some 4km south of the city centre. *L'Oasis Palavasienne* (☎ 04 67 15 11 61; fax 04 67 15 10 62), Route de Palavas is open from April to September and charges 88FF for two people with a tent or caravan. Take bus No 17 from Montpellier bus station to the Lattes stop.

Hostels The *Auberge de Jeunesse* (☎ 04 67 60 32 22; fax 04 67 60 32 30), 2 Impasse de la Petite Corraterie, is ideally located in the old city. A bed costs just 65FF a night. Reception closes at midnight and an HI card (available there) is mandatory. Take bus No 2, 4, 5 or 6 from the station to the Ursulines stop. Le Rabelais night buses stop here too.

Hotels A two-minute walk from the train station is the two-star *Hôtel Colisée Verdun* (☎ 04 67 58 42 63; fax 04 67 58 98 27), 33 Rue de Verdun, which has singles/doubles with toilet and bidet from 145/155FF. Doubles/triples with shower start at 210/300FF. The chaotically run *Hôtel des Touristes* (☎ 04 67 58 42 37; fax 04 67 92 61 37), 10 Rue Baudin, is popular with travellers. It has good-sized rooms, all with showers. Singles/doubles/triples start at 120/150/220FF.

Places to Eat

Eating places abound in Montepellier's crammed old quarter. Through the stone arch at 20 Rue Jacques Cœur is *Tripti Kulai* (☎ 04 67 66 30 51), a popular vegetarian place with salads from 49FF and a *menu* for 69FF. It's open from noon to 9.30 pm (closed Sunday). The brasserie-style *Restaurant Cerdan* (☎ 04 67 60 86 96), 8 Rue Collot, has five different *menus* of mostly local fare ranging from 71 to 190FF. It's open until 11.30 pm (closed Sunday).

The *Crêperie les Blés Noirs* (☎ 04 67 60 43 03), just off Rue du Petit Saint Jean at 5 Rue Four des Flammes, is a cosy spot with sarrasin (buckwheat) crêpes from 20 to 51FF and seafood or vegetarian salads from 32 to 43FF. The *Factory Café* at the north end of Rue de Verdun is a hard-core café with a terrace in the shade.

Food markets operating daily until about noon include one on Place Jean Jaurès, the adjoining *Halles Castellane*, and another in the car park-like *Halles Laissac* on Place Laissac. *Monoprix*, Place de la Comédie, has a ground-floor grocery section open from 8.30 am to 8 pm (closed Sunday).

Getting There & Away

Bus Montpellier's bus station (☎ 04 67 92 01 43), Place du Bicentenaire, is to the left as you exit the train station. There is an hourly bus to La Grande Motte (22FF; 40 minutes).

FRANCE

FRANCE

Train The train station (☎ 08 36 35 35 39), Place Auguste Gibert, is 500m south of Place de la Comédie. The information office is open from 8 am to 8 pm (closed Sunday). Connections from Montpellier include: Paris' Gare de Lyon (312FF via TGV; four to five hours), Carcassonne (120FF; 1½ hours), Perpignan (120FF; two hours) via Narbonne, and Nîmes (66FF; 30 minutes).

Getting Around
Bus City buses are run by SMTU (☎ 04 67 22 87 87), whose office at 27 Rue Maguelone is open from 7 am to 7 pm (closed Sunday). Individual bus tickets cost 7FF; a day pass is 20FF and a 10-ticket carnet 53FF.

Taxi Taxis wait outside the train station or can be ordered by calling TRAM (☎ 04 67 58 10 10) or Taxi 2000 (☎ 04 67 03 45 45).

Bicycle The very efficient Vill' à Vélo (☎ 04 67 92 92 67), next to the Linebus office in the bus station, rents bicycles for 5/15/25FF an hour/half day/full day and tandems for 50/80FF for a half/full day.

NÎMES
The city of Nîmes (population 133,000) has some of the best preserved Roman structures in all of Europe.

Things to See
The **Arènes** (amphitheatre), which, unlike its counterpart at Arles, retains its upper storey, dates from around 100 AD and could once seat 24,000 spectators. Throughout the year the Arènes, which is covered by a high-tech removable roof from October to April, is used for theatre performances, music concerts and bullfights. Unless there's something on, it's open from 9 am to 12.30 pm and 2 to 6 pm (9 am to 6.30 pm in summer). Admission costs 26/20FF for adults/students and children.

The rectangular **Maison Carrée**, a Roman temple in Corinthian style, is one of the best preserved Roman temples in the world. Built around 5 AD to honour Augustus' two nephews, it survived the centuries as a meeting hall (during the Middle Ages), a private residence, a stable (in the 17th century), a church and, after the Revolution, an archive.

Nîmes' three **férias** – the three-day Féria Primavera (Spring Festival) in February, the five-day Féria de Pentecôte (Pentecost Festival) in June, and the three-day Féria des Vendanges to mark the start of the grape harvest on the third weekend in September – are celebrated with bullfights and concerts in the Arènes and parades and music in the streets. The helpful tourist office (☎ 04 66 67 29 11) is at 6 Rue Auguste. There is an annexe (☎ 04 66 84 18 13) at the train station.

Places to Stay & Eat
You can camp at **Domaine de la Bastide** (☎ 04 66 38 09 21) on Route de Générac, about 4km south of town on the D13 heading toward Générac. Two people with a tent pay about 60FF and the site is open all year. The **Auberge de Jeunesse** (☎ 04 66 23 25 04; fax 04 66 23 84 27) is on Chemin de la Cigale, 3.5km north-west of the train station. A bed costs 47FF. Sheets are an extra 17FF and breakfast an extra 19FF.

Surprisingly, Nîmes has plenty of cheap, decent hotels, many of which are conveniently situated in the old city. The friendly **Hôtel de la Maison Carrée** (☎ 04 66 67 32 89; fax 04 66 76 22 57), 14 Rue de la Maison Carrée, has singles with washbasin at around 115FF; singles/doubles/triples/quads with shower are 125/180/270/330FF. The **Hôtel Concorde** (☎ 04 66 67 91 03), 3 Rue des Chapeliers has small but adequate singles/doubles from 110/115FF and ones with shower for 135/140FF.

Le Portofino Brasserie Italienne (☎ 04 66 36 16 14), 3 Rue Corneille, serves great home-made pasta dishes, and offers breakfast/lunchtime *menus* for 19/55FF. Just west of Place des Arènes is the packed **Les Olivades** (☎ 04 66 21 71 78), 18 Rue Jean Reboul, which has *menus* for 65 (lunch only), 85 and 120FF. The **Café de Columbia**, on the corner of Rue de l'Etoile and Rue Maubet, is a cheap and cheerful joint touting a 47FF *menu* which includes a glass of wine.

Getting There & Away
Bus Nîmes' bus station is just behind the train station on Rue Sainte Félicité. Destinations served include Pont du Gard (32FF; 35 minutes), Avignon (41FF; 1¼ hours) and Arles (31FF; one hour).

Train The train station (☎ 08 36 35 35 39) is at the south-eastern end of Ave Feuchères. The information office is open from 8 am to 6.30 pm (closed Sunday). The left luggage room is open from 8 am to 8 pm.

Major destinations include Paris' Gare de Lyon (328FF by TGV; five hours), Arles (61FF; 30 minutes), Avignon (65FF; 30 minutes), Marseille (114FF; 1¼ hours) and Montpellier (66FF; 30 minutes).

AROUND NÎMES
Pont du Gard

Built by the Roman general Agrippa around 19 BC, the mighty Pont du Gard is not to be missed. This aqueduct, which spans the Gard River, is 275m long and 49m high. Apart from admiring the Romans' handiwork from a distance, you can also walk inside the aqueduct, where the water once flowed.

The Maison de Tourisme (☎ 04 66 37 00 02) near the aqueduct on the southern side (right bank) is only open from June to September from 9 am to 7 pm. Otherwise the closest one is 4km south-east in Remoulins (☎ 04 66 37 22 34; fax 04 66 37 22 02). Plans for 1999 and the year 2000 include a massive new tourist centre on the site of the present car park on the north side (left bank) of the river.

The Pont du Gard is 23km north-east of Nîmes and 26km west of Avignon. Buses from Avignon and Nîmes stop 1km north of the bridge.

CARCASSONNE

From afar, Carcassonne looks like a fairy-tale medieval city. Bathed in late-afternoon sun and highlighted by dark clouds, the Cité (as the old walled town is known) is truly breathtaking.

But it should be pointed out that in July and August Carcassonne can be an overcrowded tourist hell. The American actor/director Kevin Costner might well have deemed it the perfect location for his film *Robin Hood, Prince of Thieves* in 1991, but for history buffs Carcassonne's 'medieval' Cité is slightly disappointing – the impressive fortifications were extensively renovated and rebuilt in the late 19th century.

Orientation & Information The Aude River separates the Ville Basse (lower town) from the Cité, which is on a hill 500m to the south-east. The train station is on the northern edge of the Ville Basse, just over the Canal du Midi from the northern end of the pedestrianised Rue Georges Clemenceau.

The main tourist office (☎ 04 68 10 24 30; fax 04 68 10 24 38; www.tourisme .fr/carcassonne) is in the Ville Basse opposite Square Gambetta, about halfway between the train station and the Cité. It's open from 9 am to noon and 1.45 to 6.30 pm (closed Sunday).

The Banque de France, 5 Rue Jean Bringer, is open from 8.30 am to 12.30 pm and 1.50 to 3.50 pm (closed on weekends). The central post office, 40 Rue Jean Bringer, is open from 8 am to 7 pm (until noon on Saturday; closed Sunday). In the Cité, there's a branch opposite 17 Rue Porte d'Aude.

Things to See

Carcassonne's main attraction is the **Cité**. The 1.7km-long double ramparts, spiked with 52 towers (and spectacularly floodlit at night), enclose a maze of narrow, medieval streets. However, only the lower parts of the fortifications are original – most of what you see is a restoration project that was completed in 1910. Within the walls is the 12th-century **Château Comtal** (Count's Castle; ☎ 04 68 25 01 66), which can be visited by guided tour only (32/21FF for adults/students). In July and August, an excellent English-language tour departs several times a day, usually at 11 am and again at 2 and 3 pm. The castle is open from June to September from 9 am to 7 pm (7.30 pm in July and August). From October to May, it's open from 9.30 or 10 am to 12.30 pm and 2 to 5 or 6 pm.

Near the chateau on Rue du Grand Puits is the **Musée de l'Inquisition** (☎ 04 68 71 44 03) which exhibits various torture instruments and other gruesome delights dating from the 13th to 18th centuries. Opposite is the more light-hearted **Musée des Dessins Animés** (Cartoon Museum). The sets of Walt Disney's *Sleeping Beauty* (1959) are said to have been inspired by Carcassonne's Cité. Both museums are open from 10 am to 6 pm. One ticket covering admission to both is 40/30/25FF for adults/students/children.

Places to Stay

Camping *Camping de la Cité* (☎ 04 68 25 11 77), about 3.5km south of the main tourist office on Route de Saint Hilaire, charges around 65/90FF for two people with a tent or caravan depending on the season. It's open between March and early October. Take bus No 5 (hourly until 6.40 pm) from Square Gambetta to the Route de Cazilhac stop.

Hostels In the heart of the Cité, the very pleasant and friendly 120-bed *Auberge de Jeunesse* (☎ 04 68 25 23 16; fax 04 68 71 14 84), Rue Vicomte Trencavel, has dorm beds for 70FF, including breakfast. Sheets are 14FF. The hostel is open from 7 am to 11.30 pm (closed 10 December to the end of January). Take bus No 4 (last one at 6.50 pm) from the train station to La Cité stop.

Hotels Just a five-minute walk from the train station is the highly recommended *Hôtel Astoria* (☎ 04 68 25 31 38; fax 04 68 71 34 14), 18 Rue Tourtel. It has immaculate, renovated rooms – basic singles/doubles with basin and bidet cost 110/130FF. A hall shower is 10FF. A few blocks to the south, the *Hôtel Bonnafoux* (☎ 04 68 25 01 45), 40 Rue de la Liberté, has basic singles/doubles from 100/120FF or with shower for 140/146FF. A hall shower is 15FF.

In the vicinity of the Cité, hotel rooms start at around 250FF. Inside the walls, the *Hôtel des Remparts* (☎ 04 68 71 27 72; fax 04 68 72 73 26), 3-5 Place du Grand Puits, has a lovely stone façade that hides quite garish modern rooms (from 300/330FF). Just across the river in the Ville Basse is the *Relais du Square* (☎ 04 68 72 31 72; fax 04 68 25 01 08), 51 Rue du Pont Vieux, with a good selection of large rooms. A double costs 140FF, a double with shower is 170FF, and two-bed triples are 230FF.

Places to Eat

In the Cité, *Le Château* (☎ 04 68 25 05 16), 4 Place du Château, is an upmarket place with *menus* from 88FF. Next door is the more casual *Auberge de Dame Carcas* (☎ 04 68 71 23 23).

Possibly the cheapest *menu* in town can be found at the *Relais du Square* hotel (see Places to Stay). It has two restaurants: the more upmarket, street-front *Le Gargantua* with *menus* from 78FF and the unpretentious, nameless diner out back, which has a bargain 54FF *menu du jour*.

If you want to escape other tourists, head for *Le Canigou* (☎ 04 68 25 22 01), 97 Blvd Barbés, or *L'Écurie* (☎ 04 68 72 04 04), 1 Rue d'Alembert, in the Ville Basse. Both serve hearty local cuisine at heart-warming prices.

Fresh fruit and veg are sold in abundance at the morning *food market* held on Place Carnot on Tuesday, Thursday and Saturday. The *Monoprix* supermarket, Rue Georges Clemenceau, is open from 8.30 am to 7 pm (closed Sunday).

Getting There & Away

Bus The bus station (☎ 04 68 25 12 74) is on Blvd de Varsovie, up the steps at the western end of Rue du 4 Septembre, about 500m south-west of the train station. Eurolines, whose buses mainly serve Spain and Portugal, drops off and picks up passengers at the bus station.

Train The train station (☎ 08 36 35 35 39) is at the end of Rue Georges Clemenceau, 1km north of the main tourist office and 2km from the Cité. The information office is open from 9 am until noon and 1.30 to 6.20 pm (closed Sunday). The luggage room is open between 5.30 am and 11 pm.

Carcassonne is on the main line linking Toulouse with Béziers. There are trains from Carcassonne to Perpignan (110FF; 1½ hours) and Montpellier (120FF; 1½ hours).

Getting Around

Bus Local buses are run by CART (☎ 04 68 47 82 22), which has an information kiosk on Square Gambetta, the central bus hub. Bus No 4 runs every half-hour between the train station, Square Gambetta and Rue Gustave Nadaud near the Cité's main gate. Single tickets/carnet of 10 cost 5.30/46FF.

Taxi Taxis loiter outside the train station. Alternatively, call one on ☎ 04 68 71 50 50.

PERPIGNAN

More Catalan than French, Perpignan (Perpinyà in Catalan; population 110,000) was the capital of the kingdom of Majorca, whose mainland territory extended north to Montpellier, from 1278 to 1344. Perpignan developed into an important commercial centre in the following centuries, and it is still the second-largest Catalan city after Barcelona.

Although Perpignan is not the most attractive city in southern France, it makes a great base for day trips into the mountains or along the Côte Vermeille.

Orientation & Information

The heart of the old town, encircled by boulevards and partly pedestrianised, lies around Place de la Loge and Place de Verdun. The crystal-clear Basse River, lined on either side with immaculate gardens, runs through the city centre.

The tourist office (☎ 04 68 66 30 30; fax 04 68 66 30 26) is in the Palais des Congrès, Place Armand Lanoux, at the north-eastern edge of Promenade des Platanes. It's open from 8.30 am to noon and 2 to 6.30 pm (closed Sunday). From June to September it's open from 9 am to 7 pm (Sunday from 9 am to noon and 2 to 5 pm).

There are several banks on Blvd Clemenceau across the Basse River from the old town. Most ATMs dispense Spanish pesetas as well as French francs. The main post office is on Rue du Docteur Zamenhof, west of the old town.

Things to See

The **Casa Païral**, a museum of Roussillon and Catalan folklore (☎ 04 68 35 42 05) is in the 14th-century red-brick town gate known as **Le Castillet** on Place de Verdun. Once a prison, it now houses bits and pieces of everything Catalan, including traditional women's bonnets and Catalan lace mantillas, liturgical objects, painted furniture and a complete 17th-century kitchen. The terrace at the top affords great views of the old city and, to the south, the citadel. It's open from 9 am to 6 pm (closed Tuesday). Between June and mid-September, hours are 9.30 am to 7 pm. Admission is 25FF (10FF for students).

The **Palais des Rois de Majorque** (Palace of the Kings of Majorca; ☎ 04 68 34 48 29), entered via Rue des Archers, sits on a small hill to the south of the old city. Built in 1276 for the ruler of the newly founded kingdom, it was once surrounded by extensive fig and olive groves and a hunting reserve. These grounds were lost when the palace was enclosed by the formidable walls of the **Citadelle**. The palace is open between May and September from 10 am to 6 pm. From October to April, hours are 9 am to 5 pm. Admission costs 20/10FF for adults/students.

Places to Stay

Camping *La Garrigole* (☎ 04 68 54 66 10), 2 Rue Maurice Lévy, is 1.5km west of the train station and charges 60FF for two people with a tent (closed in December).

Hostel The *Auberge de Jeunesse* (☎ 04 68 34 63 32; fax 04 68 51 16 02) is a villa-like place at the end of Rue Claude Marty. Beds in dorms or four-person rooms cost 68FF, including breakfast. The hostel is closed between 10 am and 4 pm and from 20 December to 20 January.

Hotels There's a string of hotels near the train station along Ave du Général de Gaulle. The *Hôtel L'Express* (☎ 04 68 34 89 96) at No 3 has small but functional rooms for one or two people with/without shower for 114/94FF. Triples with shower cost 184FF. About 400m farther along from the station, the friendly *La Méditerranée* (☎ 04 68 34 87 48) at No 62 bis has nicer but still basic singles/doubles (a few with private terrace) from 120/150FF. Use of the hall shower costs 15FF. Singles/doubles/triples with shower start at 170/200/240FF.

In the town centre, the *Hôtel Bristol* (☎ 04 68 34 32 68), 5 Rue des Grandes Fabriques, is a cavernous place with rooms for one or two people with shower for 190FF.

Getting There & Away

Bus The bus station (☎ 04 68 35 67 51) is on Ave Général Leclerc. Bus No 44 goes to Collioure (45 minutes), Port Vendres and Banyuls. Eurolines buses (☎ 04 68 34 11 46) leave from outside the office to the left as you exit the train station.

Train Perpignan's small train station (☎ 08 36 35 35 39) is the last major stop before entering Spain at Cerbère/Portbou. It's at the end of Ave Général de Gaulle, about 2km from the tourist office (take bus No 3 to the Palais des Congrès stop). The information office is open daily from 5.45 am to 9.45 pm.

Major destinations include Paris (443FF; 12 to 15 hours), Montpellier (120FF; two hours), Carcassonne (110FF; two hours), and Barcelona in Spain (101FF; 4½ hours). Closer to home is Collioure (28FF; 25 minutes).

AROUND PERPIGNAN
Côte Vermeille
Towards the Spanish border, where the Pyrenees foothills reach the sea, lies the Côte Vermeille (Vermilion Coast, named after the red colour of its soil), a rugged littoral riddled with small, rocky bays and little ports that once engaged in sardine and anchovy fishing but now have economies based on tourism.

One such village is the picturesque **Collioure**, whose small harbour is filled with fishing boats (though the coast is more dramatic farther south and ports like Port Vendres and Banyuls are far less touristy). Collioure found fame early this century when it inspired the Fauvist art of Matisse and Dérain. The port's castle, **Château Royal** (☎ 04 68 82 06 43) was the summer residence of the kings of Majorca and is now a museum. The tourist office (☎ 04 68 82 15 47), opposite the castle at Place 18 Juin on the waterfront, can provide all the details.

For information on getting to Collioure, see Bus under Perpignan's Getting There & Away section.

Corsica

Corsica (Corse in French) is the most mountainous and geographically diverse of all the islands of the Mediterranean. Though measuring only 8720 sq km, in many ways Corsica resembles a miniature continent, with 1000km of coastline, soaring granite mountains that stay snowcapped until July, a huge national park (the Parc Naturel Régional de Corse), flatland marshes (along the east coast), an uninhabited desert (the Désert des Agriates) in the north-west and a 'continen-tal divide' running down the middle of the island. Much of the island is covered with the typically Corsican form of vegetation called *maquis*, whose low, dense shrubs provide many of the flavourings used in Corsican cooking. During WWII, the French Résistance became known as Le Maquis because the movement was so active in Corsica.

Corsica was ruled by Genoa from the 13th century until the Corsicans, led by the extraordinary Pasquale Paoli, declared the island independent in 1755. But its independence was short-lived. France took over in 1769 and has ruled Corsica ever since – except for a period in 1794-96, when it was under English domination, and during the German and Italian occupation of 1940-43.

Despite only 14 years of self-government, the people of Corsica (who number about 250,000) have retained a fiercely independent streak. Though few support the Front de Libération National de la Corse (FLNC) and other violent separatist organisations whose initials and slogans are spray-painted on walls and road signs all over the island, they remain very proud of their language, culture and traditions.

The symbol of a black head wearing a bandanna that you will see everywhere in Corsica is the Tête de Maure (Moor's Head), the island's emblem, which dates back to the time of the Crusades. The Corsicans, like the Irish, have a long tradition of emigration. Many of the settlers in France's colonies were Corsican émigrés, and many young people still leave the island in search of better opportunities.

Climate & When to Go
The best time of year to visit Corsica is in May and June (avoid July and August when the island is overrun with mainly Italian and German holiday-makers). Outside of these months there are fewer visitors but also a reduced tourist infrastructure (many hotels etc operate only seasonally).

Language
The Corsican language (Corsu), which was until recently almost exclusively oral, is more closely related to Italian than to French. It's an important component of Corsican identity and there is a movement afoot to ensure its

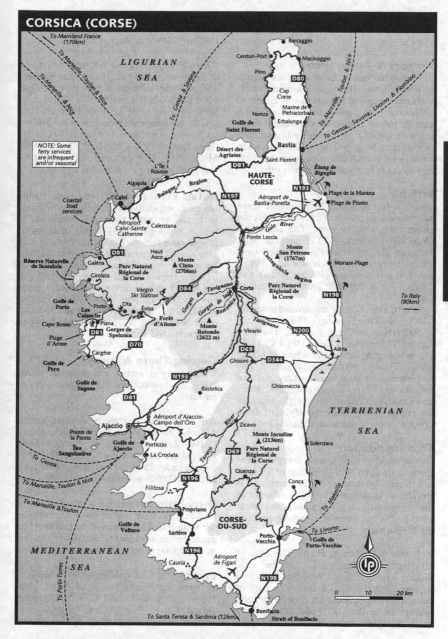

CORSICA (CORSE)

FRANCE

To Mainland France (170km)

To Marseille, Toulon & Nice

To Marseille & Nice

To Genoa & Savona

To Marseille, Toulon & Nice

To Genoa, Savona, Livorno & Piombino

LIGURIAN SEA

Barcaggio
Centuri-Port
Macinaggio
Pino
D80
Cap Corse
Nonza
Marine de Pietracorbara
Erbalunga

NOTE: Some ferry services are infrequent and/or seasonal

Golfe de Saint Florent

L'Île Rousse

Désert des Agriates

D81

Saint Florent

Bastia

Algajola

Balagne Region

HAUTE-CORSE

Étang de Biguglia

Plage de la Marana

N193

Calvi

N197

Aéroport de Bastia-Poretta

Plage de Pineto

Coastal boat services

Aéroport Calvi-Sainte Catherine

Calenzana

Golo River

Ponte Leccia

Réserve Naturelle de Scandola

D81

Galéria

Haut Asco

Monte Cinto (2706m)

Monte San Petrone (1767m)

Moriani-Plage

Castagniccia

Girolata

Parc Naturel Régional de la Corse

Vergio Ski Station

D84

Gorges du Tavignano

Corte

Parc Naturel Régional de la Corse

N198

Golfe de Porto

Les Calanche

Porto

Ota

Évisa

Gorges de l'Inzecca

Restonica

To Italy (80km)

Capo Rosso

Piana

Forêt d'Aïtone

Monte Rotondo (2622 m)

Tavignano

Vivario

N200

Tavignano River

Plage d'Arone

D81

Gorges de Spelunca

Aléria

Cargèse

D70

Ghisoni

D344

Golfe de Pero

N193

Ghisonaccia

Golfe de Sagone

D81

Bastelica

TYRRHENIAN SEA

Ajaccio

Aéroport d'Ajaccio-Campo dell'Oro

River

Monte Incudine (2136m)

Solenzara

Pointe de la Parata

Îles Sanguinaires

Golfe de Ajaccio

Porticcio

La Crociata

D69

Parc Naturel Régional de la Corse

Taravo

Zicavo

To Genoa

To Marseille, Toulon & Nice

N196

Quenza

Conca

To Marseille &Toulon

Filitosa

To Marseille

Golfe de Valinco

Propriano

CORSE-DU-SUD

To Livorno

MEDITERRANEAN SEA

Sartène

Porto-Vecchio

Golfe de Porto-Vecchio

N196

To Porto Torres

Cauria

Aéroport de Figari

N198

0   10   20 km

To Porto Torres

Bonifacio

To Santa Teresa & Sardinia (12km)

Strait of Bonifacio

survival (notably at the university in Corte). Street signs are often bilingual or exclusively in Corsican.

Dangers & Annoyances

When Corsica makes the newspapers around the world, it's usually because separatist militants have engaged in some act of violence, such as bombing a public building, robbing a bank or blowing up a vacant holiday villa. But such attacks, which in 1994 included over 400 bombings and some 40 murders, are *not* targeted at tourists and there is no reason for visitors to fear unduly for their safety.

Activities

Corsica's superb hiking trails include three *mare à mare* (sea-to-sea) trails that cross the island from east to west. The legendary GR20, also known as Frà Li Monti (literally, 'between the mountains'), stretches over 160km from Conca (20km north of Porto-Vecchio) to Calenzana (10km south-east of Calvi), and is passable from mid-June to October.

Some 600km of trails are covered in the invaluable *Walks in Corsica* (120FF), published by Robertson McCarta, London. The Parc Naturel Régional de la Corse (☎ 04 95 21 56 54), based in Ajaccio, sells a host of hiking guides (French only) for the region. It also distributes a series of free brochures entitled *Balades en Corse – Sentiers de Pays*, which map out shorter hikes (one to eight hours) in the region; many conveniently start from Corsica's remote mountain train stations.

Accommodation

Camping Most of Corsica's many camping grounds are open only from June to September. *Camping sauvage* (wild camping) is prohibited, in part because of the danger of fires (especially in the maquis). In remote areas hikers can bivouac in *refuge* grounds for 20FF a night.

Refuges & Gîtes d'Étape The Maison d'Informations Randonnées of the Parc Naturel Régional de la Corse (see Ajaccio – Information) provides hikers with lists of mountain *refuges* and gîtes d'étape (hiker's cabins) along the GR20 and other hiking trails. A night's accommodation in a park

refuge is 50FF. Nightly rates in gîtes d'étape are 40 to 80FF; most offer half-board too (145 to 185FF a night).

Gîtes If you're staying put for a while and there are several of you, *gîtes ruraux* (country cottages) can be a good deal, ranging from 1000 to 3000FF a week from October to May; prices double or triple between June and September when most places are booked up months in advance. In Ajaccio, Relais des Gîtes Ruraux (☎ 04 95 51 72 82; fax 04 95 51 72 89), 1 Rue du Général Fiorella, provides information on available cottages.

Hotels Corsica's bottom-end hotel rooms are more expensive than mainland counterparts and virtually nothing is available for less than 140FF. Many hotels in all price ranges raise their tariffs considerably in July and August (in some cases by over 200%!), but unless you make reservations months in advance (or arrive early in the morning and get lucky) you probably won't find a room anyway. On the other hand, winter visitors will find that outside of Bastia and Ajaccio, most hotels shut down completely between November and Easter.

Getting There & Away

Visitors pay an arrival *and* departure tax of 30FF; this is usually added into your ferry or air fare.

Air Corsica's four main airports are at Ajaccio, Bastia, Figari (near Bonifacio) and Calvi. Return airfares to Corsica from Nice/Marseille/Paris cost 700/800/1200FF. People under 25 or over 60 may qualify for a 600/700/800FF return fare.

Ferry During the summer – especially from mid-July to early September – reservations for vehicles and couchettes (berths) must be made well in advance (several months for the most popular routes).

France Car and passenger ferry services between the French mainland (Nice, Marseille and Toulon) and Corsica (Ajaccio, Bastia, Calvi, L'Île Rousse, Propriano and Porto-Vecchio) are handled by the Société

National Maritime Corse-Méditerranée, or SNCM (☎ 08 36 67 95 00 in Marseille; www.sncm.fr). Schedules and fares are comprehensively listed in the SNCM pocket timetable, freely distributed at tourist offices, some hotels and SNCM offices.

For a one-way passage, individuals pay 210FF (240FF from late June to early September) to/from Nice and 256FF (292FF in summer) to/from either Marseille or Toulon. Daytime crossings take about six and a half hours. For overnight trips, the cheapest couchette/most comfortable cabin costs an additional 66/288FF. For people under 25, one-way passage costs 184/210FF in winter/summer for all sailings to/from Nice and 224/256FF to/from Marseille and Toulon.

Corsica Ferries and SNCM also run an express NGV (*navire à grande vitesse*) service from Nice to Calvi (2¾ hours) and Bastia (3½ hours). Fares on these zippy NGVs, which carry 500 passengers and 148 vehicles, are similar to those for passage on the regular ferries.

Italy Corsica Ferries (☎ 04 95 32 95 95 in Bastia; ☎ 019-216 0041 in Savona; ☎ 0586-88 13 80 in Livorno; www.corsicaferries.com) has year-round car ferry services from Bastia to Savona and Livorno (four to five hours, or overnight). From mid-May to mid-September, the company also runs ferries between Savona and L'Île Rousse. Depending on route and timing, individuals pay 124 to 180FF.

From mid-April to October, Mobylines (☎ 04 95 34 84 90 in Bastia; ☎ 0586-82 68 23/82 68 25 in Livorno; www.elbalink.it/mobylines) links Bastia with Genoa and Livorno. From July to early September, their ferries also sail from Bastia to Piombino. One-way fares between Genoa and Bastia range from 110 to 195FF.

Between April and September, Corsica Marittima (☎ 04 95 54 66 66 in Bastia; 10-589 595 in Genoa; 0586-210 507 in Livorno; www.corsica-marittima.com) runs express NGV ferries from Bastia to Genoa (3¼ hours) and Livorno (1¾ hours). For information on ferries from Sardinia to Bonifacio, see Getting There & Away in the Bonifacio section.

Getting Around

Bus Bus transport around the island is slow, infrequent, relatively expensive and handled by a complicated network of independent companies. On longer routes, most of which are operated by Eurocorse, there are only one or two and at most four runs a day. Except during July and August, only a handful of intercity buses operate on Sunday and holidays.

Train Chemins de Fer de la Corse, Corsica's metre-gauge, single-track rail system, has more in common with the Kalka-Simla line through the Himalayan foothills of northern India than it does with the TGV. The two and four-car trains make their way unhurriedly through the stunning mountain scenery, stopping at tiny rural stations and, when necessary, for sheep and cows. The two-line, 232km network links Ajaccio, Corte, Bastia, Ponte Leccia and Calvi and is definitely the most interesting (and comfortable) way to tour the island.

Corsica's train system does *not* accept Eurail passes or give any discounts except to holders of Inter-Rail passes, who get 50% off. Single fares are 121FF Ajaccio-Bastia, 64FF Ajaccio-Corte and 92FF Bastia-Calvi. Taking a bicycle is 73FF extra. Leaving luggage and bikes at the stations' ticket offices costs a flat 20FF.

Car There's no doubt that a car is the most convenient way to get around Corsica. It's also the most stressful. Many of the roads are spectacular but narrow and serpentine (particularly the D81 between Calvi and Porto and N196 from Ajaccio to Bonifacio). Count on averaging 50km/h. A good road map (such as Michelin's 1:200,000 map No 90) is indispensable. Car-rental agencies in Corsica are listed under Getting There & Away in the Ajaccio and Bastia sections.

AJACCIO

The port city of Ajaccio (Aiacciu in Corsican; population 60,000), birthplace of Napoleon Bonaparte (1769-1821), is a great place to begin a visit to Corsica. This pastel-shaded, Mediterranean town is a fine place for strolling, but time spent here can also be educational. The many museums and statues

FRANCE

dedicated to Bonaparte (who, local people will neglect to mention, never returned to Corsica after becoming emperor) speak volumes – not about Napoleon himself, but about how the people of his native town prefer to think of him.

Orientation

Ajaccio's main street is Cours Napoléon, which stretches from Place du Général de Gaulle northward to the train station and beyond. The old city is south of Place Foch.

Information

Tourist Office The tourist office (☎ 04 95 51 53 03; fax 04 95 51 53 01; w3.corsenet .com), 1 Place Foch, is open from 8.30 am to 6 pm (Saturday from 9 am to noon). From July to mid-September, daily hours are 7 or 8 am to 8 pm. At the airport, the information desk (☎ 04 95 23 56 56) is open daily from 6 am to 10.30 pm.

Money & Post The Banque de France is at 8 Rue Sergent Casalonga. The main post office, which has an exchange service, is at 13 Cours Napoléon.

Hiking The Maison d'Informations Randonnées (☎ 04 95 51 79 10; fax 04 95 21 88 17), 2 Rue Major Lambroschini, provides information on the Parc Naturel Régional de la Corse and its hiking trails. It's open from 8.30 am to 12.30 pm and 2 to 6 pm (5 pm on Friday; closed on weekends).

Things to See & Do

Museums The house where Napoleon was born and raised, the **Maison Bonaparte** (☎ 04 95 21 43 89) on Rue Saint Charles in the old city, was sacked by Corsican nationalists in 1793 but rebuilt (with a grant from the government in Paris) later in the decade. It's open from 9 am (10 am from October to April) to 11.45 am and 2 to 5.45 pm (4.45 pm from October to April), closed Sunday afternoon and Monday morning. The entry fee of 22FF (15FF for students and seniors) includes a guided tour in French.

The sombre **Salon Napoléonien** (☎ 04 95 21 90 15), on the 1st floor of the Hôtel de Ville at Place Foch, exhibits memorabilia of the emperor. It's open 9 am to 11.45 am and

2 to 4.45 pm (closed on weekends). Between 15 June and 15 September it's open until 5.45 pm and on Saturday. Entry is 5FF and visitors must be properly dressed. The **Musée A Bandera** (☎ 04 95 51 07 34), 1 Rue Général Lévie, deals with Corsican military history and costs 20FF (10FF for students). It's open Monday to Saturday from 9 am to noon and from 2 to 6 pm.

The **Musée Fesch** (☎ 04 95 21 48 17), 50 Rue du Cardinal Fesch, has a fine collection of Italian primitive art (14th to 19th centuries) and yet another collection of Napoleonia in the basement. Between September and mid-June it's open from 9.15 am to 12.15 pm and 2.15 to 5.15 pm (closed Sunday and Monday); from mid-June to mid-September it's open from 10 am to 5.30 pm (Friday night from 9.30 pm to midnight; closed Tuesday). Entry costs 25FF (15FF for students and seniors). There is a separate fee of 10/5FF to get into the Renaissance **Chapelle Impériale**, the Bonaparte family sepulchre built in 1857.

Cathédrale Ajaccio's Venetian Renaissance cathedral is in the old city on the corner of Rue Forcioli Conti and Rue Saint Charles. Built in the late 1500s, it contains Napoleon's marble baptismal font, which is to the right of the entrance, and the painting *La Vierge au Sacré Cœur* (Virgin of the Sacred Heart) by Eugène Delacroix (1798-1863), to the left.

Pointe de la Parata This wild, black granite promontory is 12km west of the city on Route des Sanguinaires (route D111). It's famed for its sunsets, which can be enjoyed from the base of a crenellated, early 17th-century Genoese watchtower. Take bus No 5 from Ajaccio, or walk along the **Sentier du Bois des Anglais**.

The **Îles Sanguinaires**, a group of small islands visible offshore, can be visited from April to October on two to three-hour boat excursions which cost 100FF (120FF during July and August). Boats leave from the quayside opposite Place Foch.

Beaches Ajaccio's beaches are nothing special. Plage de Ricanto, popularly known as Tahiti Plage, is about 5km east of town on the way to the airport and can be reached on

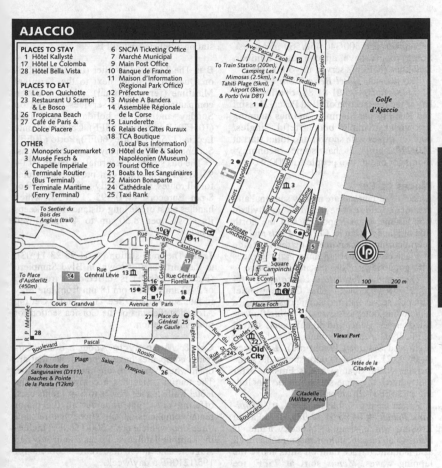

AJACCIO

PLACES TO STAY
1 Hôtel Kallysté
17 Hôtel Le Colomba
28 Hôtel Bella Vista

PLACES TO EAT
8 Le Don Quichotte
23 Restaurant U Scampi
   & Le Bosco
26 Tropicana Beach
27 Café de Paris &
   Dolce Piacere

OTHER
2 Monoprix Supermarket
3 Musée Fesch &
   Chapelle Impériale
4 Terminale Routier
   (Bus Terminal)
5 Terminale Maritime
   (Ferry Terminal)
6 SNCM Ticketing Office
7 Marché Municipal
9 Main Post Office
10 Banque de France
11 Maison d'Information
   (Regional Park Office)
12 Préfecture
13 Musée A Bandera
14 Assemblée Régionale
   de la Corse
15 Launderette
16 Relais des Gîtes Ruraux
18 TCA Boutique
   (Local Bus Information)
19 Hôtel de Ville & Salon
   Napoléonien (Museum)
20 Tourist Office
21 Boats to Îles Sanguinaires
22 Maison Bonaparte
24 Cathédrale
25 Taxi Rank

bus No 1. The smaller, segmented and more attractive beaches between Ajaccio and Pointe de la Parata (Ariane, Neptune, Palm Beach and Marinella) are served by bus No 5.

Places to Stay

Camping The *Camping Les Mimosas* (☎ 04 95 20 99 85; fax 04 95 10 01 77), open from April to October, is about 3km north of the town centre on Route d'Alata. Take bus No 4 to the roundabout at the western end of Cours Jean Nicoli and walk up Route d'Alata for

about 1km. A tent site and a place to park cost 11FF each, plus 28FF per person.

Hotels The best deal in town is the central *Hôtel Le Colomba* (☎ 04 95 21 12 66), 8 Ave de Paris, opposite Place du Général de Gaulle. It has clean, pleasant singles/doubles from 140/200FF; doubles with shower are 180FF. Reservations (by phone or post) must be in French. The friendly *Hôtel Kallysté* (☎ 04 95 51 34 45; fax 04 95 21 79 00), 51 Cours Napoléon, has spotless and charming singles/doubles/triples/quads with shower and toilet for 200/250/325/400FF in low season; 220/275/365/455 in June, July and September; and 300/340/450/560 in August. Some rooms have air-con and minibar. Breakfast (35FF) is served in your room.

The two-star *Hôtel Bella Vista* (☎ 04 95 51 71 00; fax 04 95 21 81 88) overlooks the bay at the intersection of Blvd Pascal Rossini and Rue Prosper Merimée, and has stunning sea views. Simple but tasteful singles/doubles/triples with shower and toilet start at 210/220/280FF. It has some 'economy' rooms for one or two people for 200FF.

Places to Eat

Ajaccio's restaurants are mostly seasonal and mediocre. Cafés can be found along Blvd du Roi Jérôme, Quai Napoléon and the north side of Place de Gaulle. *Café de Paris* and the neighbouring *Dolce Piacere*, on the west side of Place de Gaulle, both have giant terraces with good views of the sea and the square.

The popular *Restaurant U Scampi* (☎ 04 95 21 38 09), at 11 Rue Conventionnel Chiappe, serves fish and Corsican specialities – including octopus stew – on a fine flower-filled terrace. Lunch and dinner *menus* start at 85FF. It is open year round (closed Friday night and Saturday lunchtime). *Le Bosco* (☎ 04 95 21 25 06) next door shares the same terrace as the Scampi and seems to offer pretty much the same sort of *menus*, including a 195FF shellfish platter.

For an unsurpassable sea view, try *Tropicana Beach* (☎ 04 95 51 12 98), Blvd Pascal Rossini, which, despite its tacky name, is home to an elegant indoor restaurant as well as a fantastic terrace built on stilts above the lapping waves. *Menus* start at 75FF; ice creams and light snacks are served on the verandah. *Le Don Quichotte* (☎ 04 95 21 27 30), in Rue des Halles, has pizzas from 40 to 50FF and *menus* from 73FF.

On Square Campinchi, the **Marché Municipal** open-air food market operates until 1 pm (closed Monday except between June and September). The *Monoprix* supermarket opposite 40 Cours Napoléon is open Monday to Saturday from 8.30 am to 7.15 pm.

Getting There & Away

Air Aéroport d'Ajaccio-Campo dell'Oro (☎ 04 95 23 56 56) is 8km east of the city.

TCA bus No 1 (or, late at night, the No 6) links the airport with Ajaccio train and bus stations; tickets cost 20FF.

Bus The Terminal Routier (bus terminal) is on Quai l'Herminier next to the Terminal Maritime (ferry terminal). About a dozen companies have daily services (except on Sunday and public holidays) to Bastia (105FF), Bonifacio (105FF), Calvi via Ponte Leccia (125FF), Corte (60FF), Porto (70FF), Sartène (64FF) and many other destinations.

The bus station's information booth (☎ 04 95 51 55 45), which can provide schedules for all routes, is open daily from 7 am to 7 or 8 pm. Eurocorse (☎ 04 95 21 06 30), which handles most of the long-distance lines, keeps its kiosk open 8.30 am to 4 pm (closed Sunday).

Train The train station (☎ 04 95 23 11 03), at the north end of town on Blvd Sampiero (Place de la Gare), is staffed daily from 6.15 or 7.30 am to 6.30 pm (8 pm from late May to late September). See Train under Getting Around at the start of the Corsica section for more information.

Car & Motorcycle About a dozen car-rental companies have airport desks that are open whenever there are incoming flights. The tourist office has a complete list. The Hôtel Kallisté (see Places to Stay) rents cars, offering rates that undercut all the major rental companies. A day's/week's hire for a three-door vehicle costs 300/1560FF, including unlimited mileage. Prices rise in July and August. The hotel also rents scooters for 195/1210FF a day/week.

Ferry The Terminal Maritime is on Quai l'Herminier next to the bus station. SNCM's ticketing office (☎ 04 95 29 66 99), across the street at 3 Quai l'Herminier, is open from 8 to 11.45 am and 2 to 6 pm (closed Saturday afternoon and Sunday). For evening ferries, the SNCM bureau in the ferry terminal opens two or three hours before the scheduled departure time.

Getting Around

Bus Local bus maps and timetables can be picked up at the TCA Boutique (☎ 04 95 51

43 23), 2 Ave de Paris, open from 8 am to noon and 2.30 to 6 pm (closed Sunday). Single tickets/a carnet of 10 cost 7.50/58FF.

Taxi There's a taxi rank on the east side of Place du Général de Gaulle, or you can order one from Radio Taxis Ajacciens (☎ 04 95 25 09 13).

Bicycle The Hôtel Kallisté (see Places to Stay) rents mountain bikes for 80FF a day and 470FF a week. Prices are lower between October and April.

BASTIA

Bustling Bastia (population 37,800), Corsica's most important business and commercial centre, has rather an Italian feel to it. It was the seat of the Genoese governors of Corsica from the 15th century, when the *bastiglia* (fortress) from which the city derives its name was built. Though it's a pleasant enough place, there's not all that much to see or do, and most travellers simply pass through. Bastia does, however, make a good base for exploring **Cap Corse**, the wild, 40km-long peninsula to the north.

Orientation

The focal point of the town centre is 300m-long Place Saint Nicolas. Bastia's main thoroughfares are the east-west Ave Maréchal Sébastiani, which links the ferry terminal with the train station, and the north-south Blvd Paoli, a fashionable shopping street one block west of Place Saint Nicolas.

Information

The tourist office (☎ 04 95 31 00 89) at the northern edge of Place Saint Nicolas is open daily from 8 am to noon and 2 to 6 pm (closed Sunday afternoon). In July and August daily hours are 8 am to 8 pm. It has information on companies offering day trips to Cap Corse.

The Banque de France is at 2 bis Cours Henri Pierangeli, half a block south of Place Saint Nicolas. The main post office is on the even-numbered side of Ave Maréchal Sébastiani, a block west of Place Saint Nicolas. Exchange services are available.

Things to See & Do

Bastia's **Place Saint Nicolas**, a palm and plane tree-lined esplanade as long as three football pitches, was laid out in the late 19th century. The narrow streets and alleyways of **Terra Vecchia**, which is centred around Place de l'Hôtel de Ville, lie just south. The 16th-century **Oratoire de l'Immaculée Conception**, opposite 3 Rue Napoléon, was decorated in richly baroque style in the early 18th century.

The picturesque, horseshoe-shaped **Vieux Port** is between Terra Vecchia and the **Citadelle**; you can reach the latter by climbing the stairs through the **Jardin Romieu**, the hillside park on the south side of the port. Inside the Citadelle, built by the Genoese in the 15th and 16th centuries, stands the mustard-coloured **Palais des Gouverneurs** (Governors' Palace). It houses a rather dull anthropology museum, but the views from the gardens behind the submarine conning tower (which saw active service during WWII) are worth the climb.

Église Sainte Marie, whose entrance is on Rue de l'Évêché, was rebuilt in 1604 on the site of a much earlier church. Much more interesting is the **Église Saint Croix** down the alley to the right (south) of Sainte Marie. It's older (1543), the gilded coffered ceiling is Renaissance and the chapel to the right of the main altar contains a miraculous black statue of the crucified Christ found by two fishermen in the early 15th century.

Objectif Nature (☎/fax 04 95 32 54 34), 3 Rue Notre Dame de Lourdes, organises a host of outdoor activities including kayaking expeditions (250FF a day), hiking, mountaineering, horse riding (350FF a day including lunch), and diving (180FF for a first-time dive). Its office is open from 9 am to 6 pm (closed Sunday).

Places to Stay

Camping In Miomo, about 5km north of Bastia, you'll find *Camping Casanova* (☎ 04 95 33 91 42), which is open from mid-May to October and charges 12FF for a tent and 24FF per person. Take the bus to Sisco from opposite the tourist office.

Hotels One of the most convenient (but least salubrious) hotels in Bastia is the *Hôtel de*

FRANCE

l'Univers (☎ 04 95 31 03 38), 3 Ave Maréchal Sébastiani. Less-than-spotless singles/doubles/triples cost 150/180/220FF (190/210/250FF with shower, 230/270/310FF with shower and toilet).

The one-star *Hôtel La Riviera* (☎ 04 95 31 07 16; fax 04 95 34 17 39), 1 bis Rue du Nouveau Port, is 100m north of Place Saint Nicolas. It has doubles with shower and toilet for 200/250FF in the low/high season.

If your budget can handle it, the very central, upmarket *Hôtel Napoléon* (☎ 04 95 31 60 30; fax 04 95 31 77 83), 43 Blvd Paoli, has small but comfortable doubles equipped with all amenities for around 300FF to 450FF. Prices rise precipitously from early July to early September.

Places to Eat

There are plenty of restaurants around the Vieux Port, especially on the north side. For a cheap and cheerful approach, head straight for the fun-loving *Café Wha* (☎ 04 95 34 25 79) which also has a terrace facing the water. It serves a range of fast-food Mexican dishes and is always packed. *Le Passe Temps* (☎ 04 95 31 72 13) is another recommended place on the old port's north side. It has *menus* for 130, 150 and 195FF. In the new town, *La Voûte* (☎ 04 95 32 47 11), 6 bis Rue Luce de Casabianca, is the most inspiring option, offering some French cuisine but mainly pizzas, under brick vaults and on a terrace overlooking the port. Mains cost 65 to 99FF and the *menu* is 125FF.

A bustling *food market* is held at Place de l'Hôtel de Ville in Terra Vecchio every morning except Monday, and there is a large *Spar* supermarket on the corner of Rue César Campinchi and Rue Capanelle.

Getting There & Away

Air France's fifth-busiest airport, Aéroport de Bastia-Poretta (☎ 04 95 54 54 54), is 20km south of the town. Municipal buses to the airport (48FF) depart from the roundabout in front of the préfecture building (opposite the train station) about an hour before each flight's departure (nine or 10 times a day). A timetable is available at the tourist office.

Bus Rapides Bleus (☎ 04 95 31 03 79), 1 Ave Maréchal Sebastiani, has buses to Porto-Vecchio and Bonifacio (via Porto-Vecchio) and handles tickets for the Eurocorse service to Corte and Ajaccio. The afternoon bus to Calvi run by Les Beaux Voyages (☎ 04 95 65 02 10) leaves from outside the train station. Rue du Nouveau Port, just north of the tourist office, has been turned into a bus terminal for short-haul buses serving villages south and west of Bastia. Buses to Cap Corse (eg Sisco) leave from Ave Pietri, across the street from the tourist office.

Train The train station (☎ 04 95 32 60 06) is at the northern end of Ave Maréchal Sébastiani. See Getting Around at the start of the Corsica section for information on the train system.

Car There are a handful of rental agencies at the airport.

Ferry The ferry terminal is at the eastern end of Ave Pietri. SNCM's office (☎ 04 95 54 66 81) is across the roundabout; it handles ferries to mainland France and is open from 8 to 11.45 am and 2 to 5.45 pm daily (closed Sunday, and Saturday afternoon). The SNCM counter in the ferry terminal itself is open two hours before each sailing (three hours on Sunday).

If you're headed for Italy, Mobylines' office (☎ 04 95 34 84 94), 4 Rue du Commandant Luce de Casabianca, is 200m north of Place Saint Nicolas. It's open from 8 am to noon and 2 to 6 pm (until noon Saturday; closed Sunday). The company's bureau in the ferry terminal is open two hours before each sailing.

Corsica Ferries (☎ 04 95 32 95 95), 7 Blvd Général de Gaulle, is open from 8.30 am to noon and 2 to 6.30 pm (closed on Sunday and, except in summer, on Saturday afternoon); there's no midday closure from mid-June to mid-September. See Ferry under Getting There & Away at the start of the Corsica section for more information.

Getting Around

Bicycle Objectif Nature (see Things to See & Do above) rents mountain bikes for 100FF a day (80FF per person for groups of four or more). Weekend rental costs 150FF. It's open year round from 9 am to noon and 2 to 5 pm (closed Sunday).

CALVI

Calvi (population 4800), where Admiral Horatio Nelson lost his eye, serves both as a military town and a rather downmarket holiday resort. The Citadelle, garrisoned by a crack regiment of the French Foreign Legion, sits atop a promontory at the western end of a beautiful half-moon shaped bay.

Orientation

The Citadelle – also known as the Haute Ville (upper town) – is north-east of the port. Blvd Wilson, the main thoroughfare in the Basse Ville (lower town), is up the hill from Quai Landry and the marina.

Information

The tourist office (☎ 04 95 65 16 67; fax 04 95 65 14 09) is at the marina on the upper floor of the Capitainerie (harbour master's office). It's open Monday to Saturday from 9 am to noon and 2 to 6 pm.

The Crédit Lyonnais opposite 10 Blvd Wilson is open until 4.30 pm (closed on weekends). The main post office is about 100m to the south on the same street.

Things to See & Do

The **Citadelle**, set atop an 80m-high granite promontory and enclosed by massive Genoese ramparts, affords great views of the surrounding area. **Église Saint Jean Baptiste** was built in the 13th century and rebuilt in 1570; inside is yet another miraculous ebony icon of Christ. West of the church, a marble plaque marks the site of the house where, according to local tradition, Christopher Columbus was born. The imposing **Palais des Gouverneurs** (Governors' Palace), built in the 13th century and enlarged in the mid-16th century, is above the entrance to the citadel. Now known as Caserne Sampiero, it serves as a barracks and mess hall for officers of the French Foreign Legion.

Beaches Calvi's 4km-long beach begins just south of the marina and stretches around the Golfe de Calvi. There are a number of other nice beaches, including one at **Algajola**, west of town. The port and resort town of L'Île Rousse (Red Island) east of Calvi is also endowed with a long, sandy beach with some of the cleanest water in the Mediterranean.

Between late April and October, many of the beaches between Calvi and L'Île can be reached by shuttle train (see Getting There & Away for details).

Places to Stay

Camping & Studios The *Camping Les Castors* (☎ 04 95 65 13 30), open from April to September, is 800m south-east of the centre of town on Route de Pietra Maggiore. Campers pay 29FF per adult, 15FF for a tent site (in July and August these prices increase to 34 and 19FF). Small studios for two people with shower, toilet and kitchenette cost 1150FF a week in the low season and 2550FF in summer.

A hundred metres farther along Route de Pietra Maggiore, the two-star *Camping La Clé des Champs* (☎ 04 95 65 00 86), open from April to October, is slightly cheaper.

Hostel The friendly, 133-bed *BVJ Corsotel* hostel (☎ 04 95 65 14 15; fax 04 95 65 33 72), open from late March to October, is on Ave de la République, 70m to the left as you exit the train station. Beds in rooms for two to eight people cost 120FF per person, including breakfast. An HI card is not necessary.

Hotels The *Hôtel du Centre* (☎ 04 95 65 02 01), in an airy old building at 14 Rue Alsace-Lorraine (parallel to and one block down the hill from Blvd Wilson), is open from early June to mid-October. Basic doubles without/ with shower are 180/200FF and rise to 250/280FF in the middle of summer. *Hôtel Le Belvédère* (☎ 04 95 65 01 25; fax 04 95 65 33 20), Place Christophe Colomb, is open all year. Small doubles with shower, toilet and TV cost 200 to 250FF (300FF in July, 350FF in August). The *Hôtel du Centre* (☎ 04 95 65 02 01), in an airy old building at 14 Rue Alsace-Lorraine (parallel to and one block down the hill from Blvd Wilson), has similar rates and is open from June to mid-October.

Hôtel Le Rocher (☎ 04 95 65 20 04; fax 04 95 65 29 26), across Blvd Wilson from the post office, has mini-apartments with kitchenettes, fridges, air-con, etc for two/four people from 355/550FF to 740/980FF, depending on the season. From November to early April, when reception is unstaffed, ring ☎ 04 95 65 11 35 a day or two ahead.

FRANCE

Places to Eat

Calvi's attractive marina is lined with restaurants and cafés, and there are several budget places on Rue Clemenceau, which runs parallel to Blvd Wilson. *Best Of*, at the south end of the street, sells a huge variety of sandwiches (around 25FF) including some with Corsican fillings.

Quai Landry's line-up of waterfront cafés and restaurants includes *Île de Beauté* (☎ 04 95 65 00 46), which specialises in fish and Corsican cuisine and has *menus* for 100 and 150FF. A couple of doors away is *Le Cyranos*, recommended locally for its fish dishes (65 to 120FF).

The tiny *Marché Couvert* near Église Sainte Marie Majeure is open from 8 am to noon (closed Sunday). In complete contrast, the massive *Super U* supermarket is south of the town centre on Ave Christophe Colomb.

Getting There & Away

Air Aéroport Calvi-Sainte Catherine (☎ 04 95 65 88 88) is 7km south-east of Calvi. There is no bus service from Calvi to the airport; taxis (☎ 04 95 65 03 10) to the centre of town cost between 70 and 100FF (depending on the time of day).

Bus Buses to Bastia and Calenzana are run by Les Beaux Voyages (☎ 04 95 65 15 02), Place de la Porteuse d'Eau. From mid-May to mid-October, an Autocars SAIB (☎ 04 95 26 13 70) bus serves the island's spectacular north-west coast from Calvi's Monument aux Morts (war memorial) to Galéria (1¼ hours) and Porto (three hours).

Train Calvi's train station (☎ 08 36 35 35 39) is between the marina and Ave de la République. From mid-April to mid-October, one-car shuttle trains (*navettes*) run by Tramways de la Balagne make 19 stops between Calvi and L'Île Rousse. The line is divided into three sectors, and it costs one ticket (10FF) for each sector you travel in. The navettes run on Sunday and holidays only in summer.

Ferry SNCM ferries (☎ 04 95 65 20 09) sail to Calvi from Nice, Marseille and Toulon, but during winter they can be very infrequent. Between mid-May and mid-September, Corsica Ferries links Calvi with Genoa. See Ferries under Getting There & Away at the start of the Corsica section for more information.

PORTO

The pleasant seaside town of Porto, nestled among huge outcrops of red granite and renowned for its sunsets, is an excellent base for exploring some of Corsica's natural wonders. **Les Calanche** (Les Calanques de Piana in French), a truly spectacular mountain landscape of red and orange granite outcrops resembling humans, animals, fortresses etc, towers above the azure waters of the Mediterranean slightly south of Porto along route D81. The **Gorges de Spelunca**, Corsica's most famous river gorge, stretches almost from the town of Ota, 5km east of Porto, to the town of Evisa, 22km away.

Orientation & Information

The marina is about 1.5km down the hill from Porto's pharmacy – the local landmark – on the D81. The area, known as Vaïta, is spread out along the road linking the D81 to the marina. The Porto River just south of the marina is linked by an arched pedestrian bridge to a fragrant eucalyptus grove and a small, pebble beach.

The tourist office (☎ 04 95 26 10 55; fax 04 95 26 14 25) is built into the wall that separates the marina's upper and lower parking lots and is open from 9.30 am to noon and 2.30 to 6.30 pm Monday to Friday (9 am to 8 pm Monday to Saturday in July and August). Just around the corner is a Parc Naturel Régional de Corse office, open in summer only.

Things to See & Do

A short trail leads to the 16th-century **Genoese tower** on the outcrop above the town. It's open from April to October between 10 am and 6 pm (10FF).

From April to mid-October, the Compagnie des Promenades en Mer (☎ 04 95 26 15 16) runs **boat excursions** (170FF) to the fishing village of Girolata (passing by the Scandola Nature Reserve), and occasionally to Les Calanche in the evenings (80FF). There are also glass-bottomed boat excursions during July and August. Keep a look out for dolphins following the boat.

Motorboats for up to seven people can be rented on the Porto River near the bridge leading to the pebble beach.

Places to Stay
Camping The friendly *Funtana al' Ora* (☎ 04 95 26 11 65; fax 04 95 26 15 48), 2km east of Porto on the road to Évisa, charges 28FF per person and 11FF for a tent or car. It's open from May to November.

Hostels There are two hostels in the nearby village of Ota. *Gîte d'Étape Chez Félix* (☎ 04 95 26 12 92) and *Gîte d'Étape Chez Marie* (☎ 04 95 26 11 37) are both open all year and charge 50/60FF respectively for a bed in a dormitory room. Chez Félix has doubles/triples for 200/240FF and Chez Marie has doubles for 120FF.

Hotels There are plenty of hotels in Vaïta and at the marina. One of the best deals, with great views of the marina, is the *Hôtel du Golfe* (☎ 04 95 26 13 33), which charges 180FF for shower-equipped doubles with toilet (add 20FF per person in summer). *Hôtel Monte Rosso* (☎ 04 95 26 11 50; fax 04 95 26 12 30) nearby has doubles with shower and toilet for 240FF (300FF in July and August). If you're not staying, at least have a cup of coffee at its lovely terrace café.

Getting There & Away
Autocars SAIB (☎ 04 95 22 41 99) has two buses a day linking Porto and nearby Ota with Ajaccio (2½ hours). From mid-May to mid-October the company also runs a bus from Porto to Calvi (three hours).

CORTE
When Pasquale Paoli led Corsica to independence in 1755, one of his first acts was to make Corte (Corti in Corsican; population 5700), a fortified town at the geographical centre of the island, the country's capital. To this day, the town remains a potent symbol of Corsican independence. In 1765, Paoli founded a national university there, but it was closed when his short-lived republic was taken over by France in 1769. The Università di Corsica Pasquale Paoli was reopened in 1981 and now has about 3000 students, making Corte the island's liveliest and least touristy town.

Ringed with mountains, snowcapped until as late as June, Corte is an excellent base for hiking; some of the island's highest peaks rise west of the town.

Information
The tourist office (☎ 04 95 46 26 70), 15 Quartier des Quatre Fontaines, is open from 9 am to noon and from 2 to 5 pm (closed on weekends). In July and August it's open from 9 am to 8 pm. From 15 June to September, the Parc Naturel Régional de Corse has an information office (☎ 04 95 46 27 44) just inside the Citadelle gate.

There are several banks and ATMs on Cours Paoli, the main street which runs north-south through the town. The main post office is just off the northern end on Ave du Baron Mariani.

Things to See & Do
The **Citadelle**, built in the early 15th century and largely reconstructed during the 18th and 19th centuries, is perched on top of a hill, with the steep and twisted alleyways and streets of the **Ville Haute** and the Tavignanu and Restonica river valleys below. The **Château** – the highest part, also known as the Nid d'Aigle (Eagle's Nest) – was built in 1419 by a Corsican nobleman and was considerably expanded by the French during the 18th and 19th centuries.

The impressive **Museu di a Corsica** (Musée de la Corse; ☎ 04 95 45 25 45; www.sitec.fr/museu) houses an outstanding exhibition on Corsican folk traditions, agriculture, economy, crafts and anthropology. Captions are in French and Corsican. The museum is open from 10 am to 8 pm in July and August (between April and June until 6 pm, closed Monday); between September and March until 5 pm (closed Sunday and Monday). Admission (20/15FF for adults/students) includes a visit to the chateau, accessed from a side door inside the museum.

The **Palazzu Naziunale** (National Palace), down the hill from the Citadelle, was the governmental seat of the short-lived Corsican republic. It contains temporary exhibitions. **Università di Corsica Pasquale Paoli**,

Corsica's only university, is east of the town centre on Ave Jean Nicoli, on the way to the train station.

The **Gorges de la Restonica**, a deep valley cut through the mountains by the Restonica River, is a favourite with hikers. The river passes Corte, but some of the choicer trails begin about 16km south-west of town at the Bergeries Grotelle sheepfolds. The trails are indicated on the free town map available at the tourist office.

Places to Stay

Camping The *Camping Alivetu* (☎ 04 95 46 11 09; open from Easter to early October), is in Faubourg Saint Antoine just south of Pont Restonica, the second bridge on Allée du Neuf Septembre. It costs 15FF per tent and per car and 30FF per person.

Hostel The quiet and very rural *Gîte d'Étape U Tavignanu* (☎ 04 95 46 16 85), which is open all year, charges 80FF per person including breakfast. To get there from Pont Tavignanu (the first bridge on Allée du Neuf Septembre), walk westward along Chemin de Baliri and follow the signs (almost 1km).

Hotels The 135-room *HR Hôtel* (☎ 04 95 45 11 11; fax 04 95 61 02 85), 6 Allée du Neuf Septembre, housed in a complex of converted apartment blocks, is 300m to the left (south-west) as you exit the train station. Utilitarian singles/doubles cost 135/145FF (180/195FF with shower and toilet) and triples are 290FF.

The *Hôtel de la Poste* (☎ 04 95 46 01 37), 2 Place du Duc de Padoue, is a few blocks north of the centre of town. Spacious, simply furnished doubles/triples with shower cost 170/220FF or 230/250FF with toilet and shower. Some rooms don't have much of a window. The *Hôtel Colonna* (☎ 04 95 46 01 09), 3 Ave Xavier Luciani, in the centre just north of the main square (Place Paoli), has doubles with shower and toilet for 180 to 250FF. Reception is usually at the bar.

Places to Eat

The *Restaurant Universitaire* on the main campus of the Università di Corsica on Ave Jean Nicoli, in Résidence Pasquale Paoli, is open from October to June from 11.30 am to 1.30 pm and 6.30 to 9 pm (closed on weekends). Meal tickets are sold from 11 am to 1 pm.

Le Bip's (☎ 04 95 46 06 26), down the steps and behind 14 Cours Paoli, is a cellar restaurant specialising in Corsican cuisine. The daily *menu* costs 80FF and is good value. Fish dishes are 50 to 120FF. Heading uphill to the citadel, there is the *Restaurant U Museu* which has a great range of local fare including yummy delice à la châtaigne (chestnut cake) and fiadone (Corsican cake); and *Le Gaffory* (☎ 04 95 61 05 58), Place Gaffory, which has 60FF lunchtime *menus*.

There are a number of student-oriented sandwich and pizza takeaways on Place Paoli and along Cours Paoli. *Bar L'Oriente* (☎ 04 95 61 11 17), opposite the university on Ave Jean Nicoli, is a popular student hangout; its terrace café is particularly pleasant.

Supermarkets in Corte include the *Eurospar* on Ave Xavier Luciani and a *Rallye Super* Supermarket on Allée du Neuf Septembre (opposite the hospital). Corte's top *boulangerie* is inside the main train station building – and does a roaring trade as a result!

Getting There & Away

Corte is served by Eurocorse's twice-daily (except Sunday) bus service in each direction between Bastia and Ajaccio. The stop is in front of the Hôtel Colonna (3 Ave Xavier Luciani).

The train station (☎ 04 95 46 00 97) is about 1km south-east of the town centre along Ave Jean Nicoli. For more information see Trains under Getting Around at the start of the Corsica section.

SARTÈNE

The town of Sartène (Sartè in Corsican; population 3500), whose unofficial slogan is 'the most Corsican of Corsica's towns', is a delightful place to spend a morning or afternoon. Local people chatting in Corsican gather in **Place de la Libération**, the town's main square, where you'll find **Église Sainte Marie** – which contains a huge and very heavy wooden cross carried by a penitent every year on the eve of Good Friday – and the Hôtel de Ville, once the Genoese governor's palace. The **Musée de la Préhistoire Corse** (☎ 04 95 77 01 09) is up the hill. It's open Monday to Friday from 10 am to noon and 2 to 5 or 6 pm depending on the season. The tourist office (☎ 04 95 77 15 40), 6 Rue Borgo, is open from 3 to 6 pm (closed on weekends). In July and August it's open until 7 pm (closed Sunday); from October to April it's open mornings only.

Camping U Farrandu (☎ 04 95 73 41 69), open year round, is in a quiet, shaded gully a few kilometres towards Ajaccio, and charges 40FF per person. The only hotel actually in Sartène is the two-star *Hôtel Les Roches* (☎ 04 95 77 07 61), just off the northern end of Ave Jean Jaurès. From April to October, singles/doubles with shower and toilet cost 240/260FF; those with a valley view are 250/280FF. Prices rise in July and August.

A popular restaurant in Sartène is *La Chaumière* (☎ 04 95 77 07 13) at 39 Rue Médecin-Capitaine Louis Bénédetti, 200m south of the tourist office. Its evening *menu* is 90FF.

Sartène, on the bus line linking Ajaccio (86km) with Bonifacio (53km), is served by at least two buses in each direction; Sunday buses run in July and August only.

BONIFACIO

The famed **Citadelle** of Bonifacio (Bunifaziu in Corsican; population 2700) sits 70m above the translucent, turquoise waters of the Mediterranean, atop a long, narrow and eminently defensible promontory sometimes called 'Corsica's Gibraltar'. On all sides, limestone cliffs sculpted by the wind and the waves – topped in places with precariously perched apartment houses – drop almost vertically to the sea. The north side of the promontory looks out on 1.6km-long Bonifacio Sound, at the eastern end of which is Bonifacio's **marina**. The southern ramparts of the citadel afford views of the coast of Sardinia, 12km away.

Bonifacio was long associated with the Republic of Genoa. The local dialect – unintelligible to other Corsicans – is Genoese and many local traditions (including cooking methods) are Genoa-based.

Information

The tourist office (☎ 04 95 73 11 88; fax 04 95 73 14 97; www.planetepc.fr/bonifacio; www.corsenet.fr) is in the old town at Place de l'Europe – go in through the ground-floor entrance on the eastern side of the Hôtel de Ville. It's open from 9 am to 12.30 pm and 1.30 to 5.30 pm (closed on weekends). In May and June it's open from 9 or 10 am to noon and 2 to 6 pm (until 4 pm on Saturday; closed Sunday). In July and August it's open from 9 am to 8 pm.

In the port area, there's a Société Générale at 38 Rue Saint Erasme and several *bureaux de change* along the marina. The main post office is in the old town, up the hill south of the tourist office, in Place Correga.

Things to See & Do

Walking around the old town and looking down the dramatic cliffs to the sea is a delight; the best views are to be had from **Place du Marché** and from the walk west towards and around the cemetery. Don't miss **Porte de Gênes**, which is reached by a tiny 16th-century drawbridge, or the Romanesque **Église Sainte Marie Majeure**, the oldest building in Bonifacio. **Rue des Deux Empereurs** (Street of the Two Emperors) is so-called because both Charles V and Napoleon slept there; look for the plaques at Nos 4 and 7. The **Foreign Legion Monument** east of the tourist office was brought back from Algeria in 1963 when that country won its independence.

Places to Stay

The olive-shaded *Camping Araguina* (☎ 04 95 73 02 96), open from mid-March to October, is 400m north of the marina on Ave Sylvère Bohn. It charges 31/34FF per person in the low/high season, 11FF for a tent and 11FF to park a car.

Your best bet for budget hotel accommodation is the *Hôtel des Étrangers* (☎ 04 95 73 01 09; fax 04 95 73 16 97), Ave Sylvère Bohn, 100m up the hill from the camping ground. It's open from April to October. Plain doubles with shower and toilet cost 220FF; from July to September, prices are 280 to 390FF.

In the citadel, the two-star *Hôtel Le Royal* (☎ 04 95 73 00 51; fax 04 95 73 04 68), 8 Rue

Fred Scamaroni, has singles/doubles for 190/250FF (prices double in July and August).

Places to Eat

In the Citadelle, the *Pizzeria-Grill de la Poste* (☎ 04 95 73 13 31), 5 Rue Fred Scamaroni, has Corsican dishes as well as pizza and pasta (45 to 50FF). *A Manichella* (☎ 04 95 73 12 75), Place du Marché, is a pleasant snack bar offering light lunches and fine panoramic sea views. There are lots of touristy restaurants along the south side of the marina – the waterside *Le Volier* (☎ 04 95 73 07 06), Quai Jérôme Comparetti, has a tempting 'island of beauty' *menu* for 110FF, a seafood *menu* for 190FF and a good-value 'Citadelle' *menu* for 65FF.

There's a *Simoni* supermarket beside the marina at 93 Quai Jérôme Comparetti which is open from 8 am to 12.30 pm and 3.30 to 7.30 pm (closed Sunday afternoon). Local products, including a mouthwatering range of saucisses Corse (Corsican sausages), can

be found in abundance at *L'Aliméa*, also on Quai Jérôme Comparetti.

Getting There & Away

Bus Eurocorse (☎ 04 95 70 13 83 in Porto-Vecchio) has buses to Ajaccio via Sartène. To get to Bastia, change buses at Porto-Vecchio, which is served by two buses daily (four in summer). All buses leave from the parking lot next to the Eurocorse kiosk (open in summer only) at the east end of the marina.

Ferry Saremar (☎ 04 95 73 00 96) offers a year-round car ferry service every day from Bonifacio's ferry port to Santa Teresa in Sardinia. One-way pedestrian passage costs 58 to 70FF depending on the season, including the 10FF departure tax (see Getting There & Away at the start of the Corsica section). Fares are similar at the competition, Moby Lines (☎ 04 95 73 00 29), although they have more frequent sailings than Saremar.

Greece

The first travel guide to Greece was written 1800 years ago by the Greek geographer and historian Pausanias, so the tourism industry isn't exactly in its infancy. In the 19th century, wealthy young European aristocrats made it part of their Grand Tour; in this century it has become a mecca for sun and sea worshippers.

The country's enduring attraction is its archaeological sites; those who travel through Greece journey not only through the landscape but also through time, witnessing the legacy of Europe's greatest ages – the Mycenaean, Minoan, classical, Hellenistic and Byzantine.

You cannot wander far in Greece without stumbling across a broken column, a crumbling bastion or a tiny Byzantine church, each perhaps neglected and forgotten but still retaining an aura of former glory.

Greece is much more than beaches and ancient monuments. Its culture is a unique blend of east and west, inherited from the long period of Ottoman rule and apparent in its food, music and traditions. The mountainous countryside is a walker's paradise crisscrossed by age-old donkey tracks leading to stunning vistas.

The magnetism of Greece is also due to less tangible attributes – the dazzling clarity of the light, the floral aromas which permeate the air, the spirit of place – for there is hardly a grove, mountain or stream which is not sacred to a deity, and the ghosts of the past still linger.

And then again, many visitors come to Greece simply to get away from it all and relax in one of Europe's friendliest and safest countries.

Facts about Greece

HISTORY

Greece's strategic position at the crossroads of Europe and Asia has resulted in a long and turbulent history.

During the Bronze Age, which lasted from 3000 to 1200 BC in Greece, the advanced

Cycladic, Minoan and Mycenaean civilisations flourished. The Mycenaeans were eventually swept aside by the Dorians in the 12th century BC. The next 400 years are often referred to as the 'age of darkness' (1200-800 BC), which sounds a bit unfair for a period that saw the arrival of the Iron Age and emergence of geometric pottery. Homer's *Odyssey* and *Iliad* were composed at this time.

By 800 BC, when Homer's works were first written down, Greece was undergoing a cultural and military revival with the evolution of the city-states, the most powerful of

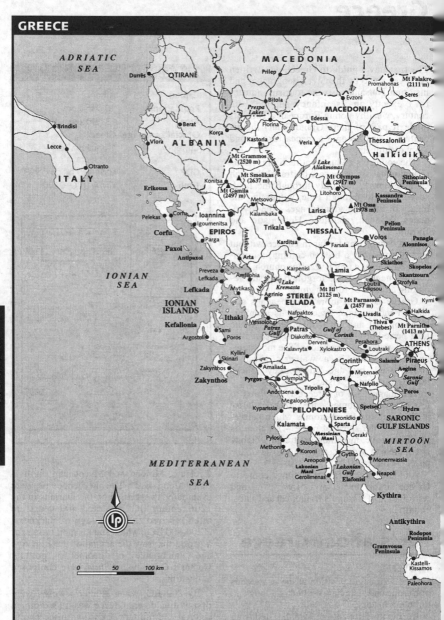

GREECE

GREECE

BULGARIA — Smolyan, Drama, Xanthi, Komotini, Edirne — TURKEY — Didymotiho — Evros — İstanbul — Izmit — BLACK SEA

Kavala — THRACE — Alexandroupolis — THRACIAN SEA — Thasos — SEA OF MARMARA — Bandırma — Bursa

Samothraki — Gökçeada — Galipoli — Çanakkale — Balıkesir

Karyes — Mt Athos (2033 m) — Athos Peninsula — Myrina — Limnos — NORTH-EASTERN AEGEAN ISLANDS — Uşak

Kyra — SPORADES — Gioura — Piperi — Agios Efstratios — Lesvos — Ayvalık — Mytilini — Manisa — İzmir

Skyros — Psara — Inousses — Chios — Çeşme — TURKEY

EVIA — AEGEAN SEA — Chios — Aydın — Denizli

Nea Styra — Karystos — Andros — Samos — Kuşadası

Gavrio — Kea — Gyaros — Tinos — Ikaria — Fourni Islands — Agathonisi — Arki — Lipsi — Farmako — Milas

Syros — Renia — Delos — Mykonos — Patmos — Bodrum — Marmaris

Kythnos — Naxos — Donoussa — Leros — Kos — Datça

Serifos — Sifnos — Paros — Naxos — Kalymnos — Astypalea — Symi

Kimolos — Antiparos — Iraklia — Kos — Nisyros — Rhodes

Sikinos — Ios — Amorgos — Sirna — Tilos — Alimia — Rhodes

Milos — Folegandros — Anafi — Halki — Lindos — Kastellorizo

CYCLADES — Thirasia — Santorini (Thira) — DODECANESE ISLANDS — Katavia

Saria

SEA OF CRETE — Karpathos — Pigadia

Hania — CRETE — Kassos

Rethymno — Iraklio — Agios Nikolaos — Sitia

Hora Sfakion — Mt Ida (2456 m) — Matala — Ierapetra

Gavdos

GREECE

which were Athens and Sparta. Greater Greece – Magna Graecia – was created, with south Italy as an important component. The unified Greeks repelled the Persians twice, at Marathon (490 BC) and Salamis (480 BC). The period which followed was an unparalleled time of growth and prosperity, resulting in what is called the classical (or golden) age.

The Golden Age

In this period, the Parthenon was commissioned by Pericles, Sophocles wrote *Oedipus the King*, and Socrates taught young Athenians to think. At the same time, the Spartans were creating a military state. The golden age ended with the Peloponnesian War (431-404 BC) in which the militaristic Spartans defeated the Athenians. So embroiled were they in this war that they failed to notice the expansion of Macedonia to the north under King Philip II, who easily conquered the war-weary city-states.

Philip's ambitions were surpassed by those of his son Alexander the Great, who marched triumphantly into Asia Minor, Egypt, Persia and what are now parts of Afghanistan and India. In 323 BC he met an untimely death at the age of 33, ostensibly from food poisoning. (Today's Greeks prefer to attribute his death to the more 'exotic' disease of syphilis.) After his death, his generals divided his empire between themselves.

Roman Rule & the Byzantine Empire

Roman incursions into Greece began in 205 BC, and by 146 BC Greece and Macedonia had become Roman provinces. In 330 AD Emperor Constantine chose Byzantium as the new capital of the Roman Empire and renamed the city Constantinople. After the subdivision of the Roman Empire into Eastern and Western empires in 395 AD, Greece became part of the Eastern Roman Empire, leading to the illustrious Byzantine age.

In the centuries that followed, Venetians, Franks, Normans, Slavs, Persians, Arabs and, finally, Turks took their turns to chip away at the Byzantine Empire.

The Ottoman Empire & Independence

The end came in 1453 when Constantinople fell to the Turks. Most of Greece soon became part of the Ottoman Empire. Crete was not captured until 1670, leaving Corfu the only island never occupied by the Turks. By the 19th century the Ottoman Empire had become the 'sick man of Europe'. The Greeks, seeing nationalism sweep Europe, fought the War of Independence (1821-32). The great powers – Britain, France and Russia – intervened in 1827, in which year Ioannis Kapodistrias was elected the first Greek president.

In 1831 Kapodistrias was assassinated and in the ensuing anarchy the European powers stepped in again and declared that Greece should become a monarchy. In January 1833 Otho of Bavaria was installed as king. His ambition, called the Great Idea, was to unite all the lands of the Greek people to the Greek motherland. In 1862 he was peacefully ousted and the Greeks chose George I, a Danish prince, as king.

In WWI, Prime Minister Venizelos allied Greece with France and Britain. King Constantine (George's son), who was married to the Kaiser's sister Sophia, disputed this and left the country.

Smyrna & WWII

After the war, Venizelos resurrected the Great Idea and, underestimating the new-found power of Turkey under the leadership of Atatürk, sent forces to occupy Smyrna (the present-day Turkish port of İzmir) which had a large Greek population. The army was repulsed and many Greeks were slaughtered. This led to the brutal population exchange between the two countries in 1923, the aim of which was to eliminate the main reason behind Greece's territorial claims.

In 1930 George II, Constantine's son, was reinstated as king and he appointed the dictator General Metaxas as prime minister. Metaxas' grandiose ambition was to take the best from Greece's ancient and Byzantine past to create a Third Greek Civilisation, though what he actually created was more a Greek version of the Third Reich. His chief claim to fame is his celebrated *okhi* (no) to Mussolini's request to allow Italian troops to traverse Greece in 1940. Despite Allied help, Greece fell to Germany in 1941, after which followed carnage and mass starvation. Resistance movements sprang up, eventually polarising into royalist and communist factions. A bloody civil war resulted, lasting until 1949 and leaving the country in chaos. More people were killed in the civil war than in WWII and 250,000 people were left homeless. The sense of despair that followed became the trigger for a mass exodus. Almost a million Greeks headed off in search of a better life elsewhere, primarily to Australia, Canada and the USA. Villages – whole islands even – were abandoned as people gambled on a new start in cities such as Melbourne, Toronto, Chicago and New York. While some have drifted back, the majority have stayed away.

The Colonels

Continuing political instability led to the colonels' coup d'état in 1967. King Constantine (son of King Paul, who succeeded George II) staged an unsuccessful counter coup, then fled the country. The colonels' junta distinguished itself by inflicting appalling brutality, repression and political incompetence upon the people. In 1974 they attempted to assassinate Cyprus' leader, Archbishop Makarios. When Makarios escaped, the junta replaced him with the extremist Nikos Samson, a convicted murderer. The Turks, who comprised 20% of the population, were alarmed at having Samson as leader. Consequently, mainland Turkey sent in troops and occupied North Cyprus, the continued occupation of which is one of the most contentious issues in Greek politics today. The junta, by now in a shambles, had little choice but to hand back power to civilians. In November 1974 a plebiscite voted 69% against restoration of the monarchy, and Greece became a republic. An election brought the right-wing New Democracy (ND) party into power.

The Socialist 1980s

In 1981 Greece entered the EC (European Community, now the EU). Andreas Papandreou's Panhellenic Socialist Movement (PASOK) won the next election, giving Greece its first socialist government. PASOK promised removal of US air bases and withdrawal from NATO, which Greece had joined in 1951.

Six years into government these promises remained unfulfilled, unemployment was high and reforms in education and welfare had been limited. Women's issues had fared better however – the dowry system was abolished, abortion legalised, and civil marriage and divorce were implemented. The crunch for the government came in 1988 when Papandreou's affair with air stewardess Dimitra Liana (whom he subsequently married) was widely publicised and PASOK became embroiled in a financial scandal involving the Bank of Crete.

In July 1989 an unprecedented conservative and communist coalition took over to implement a *katharsis* (campaign of purification) to investigate the scandals. It ruled that Papandreou and four ministers should stand trial for embezzlement, telephone tapping and illegal grain sales. It then stepped down in October 1990, stating that katharsis was completed.

The 1990s

The tough economic reforms that Prime Minister Konstantinos Mitsotakis was forced to introduce to counter a spiralling foreign debt soon made his government deeply unpopular. By late 1992, allegations began to emerge about the same sort of government corruption and dirty tricks that had brought Papandreou unstuck. Mitsotakis himself was accused of having a secret horde of Minoan art. He was forced to call an election in October 1993 after his foreign minister, Antonis Samaras, quit ND to found the Political Spring party.

Greeks again turned to PASOK and the ageing, ailing Papandreou, who had eventually been cleared of all the charges levelled in 1990. He marked his last brief period in power with a conspicuous display of the cronyism that had become his trademark. He appointed his wife as chief of staff, his son Giorgos as deputy foreign minister and his personal physician as minister of health.

He had little option but to continue with the same austerity program begun by Mitsotakis, quickly making his government equally unpopular.

Papandreou was finally forced to hand over the reins in January 1996 after a lengthy spell in hospital. He was replaced by Costas Simitis, an experienced economist and lawyer. Simitis came to power committed to further economic reform in preparation for involvement in the new Europe.

The reforms, which included a radical overhaul of the country's taxation system, have been predictably unpopular with the electorate. They have been popular in Brussels, however, and at the time of writing Greece was expecting to be admitted to the single European currency in mid-1999.

Foreign Policy

Greece's foreign policy is dominated by its extremely sensitive relationship with Turkey, its giant Muslim neighbour to the east. The two uneasy NATO allies have repeatedly come close to blows, most recently after Turkish journalists symbolically replaced the Greek flag on the tiny rocky outcrop of Imia (Kardak to the Turks) in February 1996. Both sides poured warships into the area before being persuaded to calm down.

The break-up of former Yugoslavia and the end of the Stalinist era in Albania have given Greece two new issues to worry about. The attempt by the former Yugoslav republic of Macedonia to become independent Macedonia prompted an emotional outburst from Greece, which argued that the name 'was, is, and always will be' Greek. Greece was able to persuade its EU partners to recognise Macedonia only if it changed its name. That's how the independent acronym of FYROM (Former Yugoslav Republic of Macedonia) came into being.

Greece is also at odds with Albania over that country's treatment of its significant Greek-speaking minority and the influx of refugees from the poverty stricken nation.

GEOGRAPHY & ECOLOGY

Greece consists of the southern tip of the Balkan peninsula and about 2000 islands, only 166 of which are inhabited. The land mass is 131,900 sq km and Greek territorial waters cover a further 400,000 sq km.

Most of the country is mountainous. The Pindos Mountains in Epiros are the southern extension of the Dinaric Alps, which run the length of former Yugoslavia. The range continues down through central Greece and the Peloponnese, and re-emerges in the mountains of Crete. Less than a quarter of the country is suitable for agriculture.

The variety of flora is unrivalled in Europe. The wild flowers are spectacular. They continue to thrive because much of the land is too poor for agriculture and has escaped the ravages of modern fertilisers. The best places to see the amazing variety are the mountains of Crete and the southern Peloponnese.

You won't encounter many animals in the wild, mainly due to the macho male habit of blasting to bits anything that moves. The brown bear, Europe's largest mammal, survives in very small numbers in the Pindos Mountains, as does the grey wolf. Lake Mikri Prespa in Macedonia has the richest colony of fish-eating birds in Europe, while the Dadia Forest Reserve in Thrace numbers such majestic birds as the golden eagle and the giant black vulture among its residents.

Looking at the harsh, rocky landscapes of the 20th century, it's hard to believe that in ancient times Greece was a fertile land with extensive forests. The change represents an ecological disaster on a massive scale. The main culprit has been the olive tree. In ancient times, native forest was cleared on a massive scale to make way for a tree whose fruit produced an oil that could be used for everything from lighting to lubrication. Much of the land cleared was hill country that proved unsuitable for olives. Without the surface roots of the native trees to bind it, the topsoil quickly disappeared. The ubiquitous goat has been another major contributor to ecological devastation.

The news from the Aegean Sea is both good and bad. According to EU findings, it is Europe's least polluted sea – apart from areas immediately surrounding major cities. Like the rest of the Mediterranean, it has been overfished.

GOVERNMENT & POLITICS

Since 1975, democratic Greece has been a parliamentary republic with a president as head of state. The president and parliament, which has 300 deputies, have joint legislative power. Prime Minister Simitis heads a 41-member cabinet.

Administratively, Greece is divided into regions and island groups. The mainland regions are the Peloponnese, Central Greece (officially called Sterea Ellada), Epiros, Thessaly, Macedonia and Thrace. The island groups are the Sporades, North-Eastern Aegean, Saronic Gulf, Cyclades, Dodecanese, and the Ionian, which is the only group not in the Aegean. The large islands of Evia and Crete do not belong to any group.

ECONOMY

Traditionally, Greece has been an agricultural country, but the importance of agriculture in the economy is declining. Greece has the second-lowest income per capita in the EU (Portugal's is lowest). Tourism is by far the biggest industry; shipping comes next.

POPULATION & PEOPLE

The population of Greece is 10.6 million. Women outnumber men by more than 200,000. Greece is now a largely urban society, with 68% of people living in cities. By far the largest is Athens, with more than 3.7 million in the greater Athens area – which includes Piraeus (171,000). Other major cities are Thessaloniki (750,000), Patras (153,300), Iraklio (127,600), Larisa (113,000) and Volos (110,000). Less than 15% of people live on the islands. The most populous are Crete (537,000), Evia (209,100) and Corfu (105,000).

Contemporary Greeks are a mixture of all of the invaders who have occupied the country since ancient times. There are a number of distinct ethnic minorities – about 300,000 ethnic Turks in Thrace; about 100,000 Britons; about 5000 Jews; Vlach and Sarakatsani shepherds in Epiros; Gypsies; and lately, a growing number of Albanians.

ARTS

The arts have been integral to Greek life since ancient times. In summer, Greek dramas are staged in the ancient theatres where they were originally performed.

The visual arts follow the mainstream of modern European art, and traditional folk arts such as embroidery, weaving and tapestry continue.

The *bouzouki* is the most popular musical instrument, but each region has its own speciality of instruments and sounds. *Rembetika* music, with its themes of poverty and suffering, was banned by the junta, but is now enjoying a revival.

Architecture in the classical, Hellenistic and Roman periods was based on three column orders – simple, clear Doric; slender Ionic, topped with a scroll; and the more ornate Corinthian, surmounted by a flowery burst of elaboration.

The blind bard Homer composed the narrative poems *Odyssey* and *Iliad*. These are tales of the Trojan war and the return to Greece of Odysseus, King of Ithaki, linking together the legends sung by bards during the dark age. Plato was the most devoted pupil of Socrates, writing down every dialogue he could recall between Socrates, other philosophers and the youth of Athens. His most widely read work is the *Republic*, which argues that the perfect state could only be created with philosopher-rulers at the helm.

The Alexandrian, Constantine Cavafy (1863-1933), revolutionised Greek poetry by introducing a personal, conversational style. He is considered the TS Eliot of Greek literary verse. Nikos Kazantzakis, author of *Zorba the Greek* and numerous other novels, plays and poems, is the most famous of 20th-century Greek novelists.

SOCIETY & CONDUCT

Greece is steeped in traditional customs. Name days (celebrated instead of birthdays), weddings and funerals all have great significance. On someone's name day there is an open house and refreshments are served to well-wishers who stop by with gifts. Weddings are highly festive, with dancing, feasting and drinking sometimes continuing for days.

If you want to bare all, other than on a designated nude beach, remember that Greece is a conservative country, so take care not to offend the locals.

GREECE

RELIGION

About 97% of Greeks nominally belong to the Greek Orthodox Church. The rest of the population is split between the Roman Catholic, Protestant, Evangelist, Jewish and Muslim faiths. While older Greeks and people in rural areas tend to be deeply religious, most young people are decidedly more interested in the secular.

LANGUAGE

Greeks are naturally delighted if you can speak a little of their language, but you don't need to be able to speak Greek to get around. English is almost a second language, especially with younger people. You'll also find many Greeks have lived abroad, usually in Australia or the USA, so even in remote villages there are invariably one or two people who can speak English. If you arrive in such a place and make your presence known, the local linguist will soon be produced.

See the Language Guide at the back of this book for pronunciation guidelines and useful Greek words and phrases.

Transliteration

Travellers in Greece will frequently encounter confusing, seemingly illogical English transliterations of Greek words. Transliteration is a knotty problem – there are six ways of rendering the vowel sound 'ee' in Greek, and two ways of rendering the 'o' sound and the 'e' sound. This book has merely attempted to be consistent within itself, not to solve this long-standing difficulty.

As a general rule, the Greek letter gamma (γ) appears as a 'g' rather than a 'y'; thus *agios*, not *ayios*. The letter delta (δ) appears as 'd' rather than 'dh', so *domatia*, not *dhomatia*. The letter phi (φ) can be either 'f' or 'ph'. Here, we have used the general rule that classical names are spelt with a 'ph' and modern names with an 'f' – Phaestos (not Festos), but Folegandros, not Pholegandros. Please bear with us if signs in Greek don't agree with our spelling. It's that sort of language.

Facts for the Visitor

HIGHLIGHTS

Islands

Many islands are overrun with tourists in summer. For tranquillity, try lesser-known islands such as Kassos, Sikinos, Anafi, Koufonisi, Donoussa, Shinoussa, Iraklia and Kastellorizo. (See the sections on the Cyclades and the Dodecanese islands for more information.) If you enjoy mountain walks, then Naxos, Crete, Samothraki and Samos are all very rewarding. If you prefer the beach, try Paros.

Museums & Archaeological Sites

There are three museums which should not be missed. The National Archaeological Museum in Athens houses Heinrich Schliemann's finds from Mycenae and temporarily the Minoan frescoes from Akrotiri on Santorini (Thira). The Thessaloniki Museum contains exquisite treasures from the graves of the Macedonian royal family, and the Iraklio Museum houses a vast collection from the Minoan sites of Crete.

Greece has more ancient sites than any other country in Europe. It's worth seeking out some of the lesser lights where you won't have to contend with the crowds that pour through famous sites like the Acropolis, Delphi, Knossos and Olympia.

The Sanctuary of the Great Gods on Samothraki is one of Greece's most evocative sites, and it's off the package-tourist circuit because there's no airport and there are no boats from Piraeus.

Museums and sites are free for card carrying students and teachers from EU countries. An International Student Identification Card (ISIC) gets non-EU students a 50% discount.

Historic Towns

Two of Greece's most spectacular medieval cities are in the Peloponnese. The ghostly Byzantine city of Mystras, west of Sparta, clambers up the slopes of Mt Taygetos, its winding paths and stairways leading to deserted palaces and churches. In contrast, Byzantine Monemvassia is still inhabited, but equally dramatic and full of atmosphere.

There are some stunning towns on the islands. Rhodes is the finest surviving example of a fortified medieval town, while Naxos' *hora* (main village) is a maze of narrow, stepped alleyways of whitewashed Venetian houses, their tiny gardens ablaze with flowers. Pyrgi, on Chios, is visually the most unusual village in Greece – the exterior walls of the houses are all decorated with striking black-and-white geometrical patterns.

SUGGESTED ITINERARIES

Depending on the length of your stay, you might want to see and do the following things:

Two days
  Spend both days in Athens seeing its museums and ancient sites.
One week
  Spend two days in Athens, four days in either Epiros or the Peloponnese, or four days visiting the Cycladic islands.
Two weeks
  Spend two days in Athens, three days each in Epiros and the Peloponnese and four days on the Cycladic islands, allowing two days' travelling time.
One month
  Spend two days in Athens, four days in Epiros, a week in the Peloponnese, six days on the Dodecanese and North-Eastern Aegean islands and four days each in Crete and the Cyclades.

PLANNING
Climate & When to Go

The climate is typically Mediterranean with mild, wet winters followed by hot, dry summers. Spring and autumn are the best times to visit. Winter is pretty much a dead loss, unless you're coming to Greece to take advantage of the cheap skiing. Most of the tourist infrastructure goes into hibernation between late November and early April, particularly on the islands. Hotels and restaurants close up, and buses and ferries operate on drastically reduced schedules.

The cobwebs are dusted off in time for Easter, and conditions are perfect until the end of June. Everything is open, public transport operates normally, but the crowds have yet to arrive. From July until mid-September, it's on for young and old as northern Europe heads for the Mediterranean en masse. If you want to party, this is the time to go. The flip side is that everywhere is packed out, and rooms can be hard to find.

The pace slows down again by about mid-September, and conditions are ideal once more until the end of October.

Book & Maps

The 3rd edition of Lonely Planet's *Greece* contains more comprehensive information on all the areas covered by this book as well as coverage of less-visited areas, particularly in central and northern Greece. Lonely Planet's *Trekking in Greece* is recommended for anyone considering any serious walking. Both books are strong on maps.

There are numerous books to choose from if you want to get a feel for the country. *Zorba the Greek* by Nikos Kazantzakis may seem an obvious choice, but read it and you'll understand why it's the most popular of all Greek novels translated into English. *A Traveller's History of Greece* by Timothy Boatswain & Colin Nicholson covers Greek history from Neolithic times to the present day.

Mythology was such an intrinsic part of life in ancient Greece that some knowledge of it will enhance your visit to the country. *The Greek Myths* by Robert Graves is very thorough, if a bit academic. Homer's *Odyssey*, translated by EV Rien, is arguably the best translation of this epic.

Unless you are going to trek or drive, the free maps given out by tourist offices will probably suffice. The best motoring maps are produced by local company Road Editions, newcomers on the mapping scene whose maps are produced with the cooperation of the Hellenic Army Geographic Service. Trekkers can find detailed – although somewhat outdated – ordnance survey maps at the Athens Statistical Service (☎ 01-325 9302), Lykourgou 14; take your passport. Stanfords, 12 Long Acre, London WC2E 9LP, also stocks them.

What to Bring

In summer, bring light cotton clothing, a sun hat and sunglasses; bring sunscreen too, as it's expensive in Greece. In spring and autumn, you will need light jumpers (sweaters) and thicker ones for the evenings.

In winter, thick jumpers and a raincoat are essential. You will need to wear sturdy walking shoes for trekking in the country, and comfortable shoes are a better idea than sandals for walking around ancient sites. An alarm clock for catching early-morning ferries, a torch (flashlight) for exploring caves, and a small backpack for day trips will also be useful.

TOURIST OFFICES

The Greek National Tourist Organisation (GNTO) is known as EOT in Greece. There is either an EOT office or a local tourist office in almost every town of consequence and on many islands. Most do no more than give out brochures and maps. Popular destinations have tourist police, who can often help in finding accommodation.

Local Tourist Offices

The EOT head office (☎ 01-321 0561/2; fax 325 2895; gnto@eexi.gr) is at Amerikis 2, Athens 105 64. Other tourist offices include:

Patras
    (☎ 061-420 303/4) Iroön Polytehniou 110
Piraeus
    (☎ 01-413 5716) EOT Building, Zea Marina
Thessaloniki
    (☎ 031-271 888) Plateia Aristotelous 8

Tourist Offices Abroad

Australia
    (☎ 02-9241 1663) 51 Pitt St, Sydney, NSW 2000
Canada
    (☎ 416-968 2220) 1300 Bay St, Toronto, Ontario M5R 3K8
    (☎ 514-871 1535) 1233 Rue de la Montagne, Suite 101, Montreal, Quebec H3G 1Z2
France
    (☎ 01-42 60 65 75) 3 Ave de l'Opéra, Paris 75001
Germany
    (☎ 69-237 735) Neue Mainzerstrasse 22, 6000 Frankfurt
    (☎ 89-222 035) Pacellistrasse 2, W 8000 Munich 2
    (☎ 40-454 498) Abteistrasse 33, 2000 Hamburg 13
    (☎ 30-217 6262) Wittenplatz 3A, 10789 Berlin 30

Italy
    (☎ 06-474 4249) Via L Bissolati 78-80, Rome 00187
    (☎ 02-860 470) Piazza Diaz 1, 20123 Milan
Japan
    (☎ 03-350 55 911) Fukuda Building West, 5F 2-11-3 Akasaka, Minato-ku, Tokyo 107
UK
    (☎ 0171-499 9758) 4 Conduit St, London W1R ODJ
USA
    (☎ 212-421 5777) Olympic Tower, 645 5th Ave, New York, NY 10022
    (☎ 312-782 1084) Suite 160, 168 North Michigan Ave, Chicago, Illinois 60601
    (☎ 213-626 6696) Suite 2198, 611 West 6th St, Los Angeles, California 92668

VISAS & EMBASSIES

Nationals of Australia, Canada, EU countries, Israel, New Zealand and the USA are allowed to stay in Greece for up to three months without a visa. For longer stays, apply at a consulate abroad or at least 20 days in advance to the Aliens Bureau (☎ 01-770 5711), Leoforos Alexandros 173, Athens. Elsewhere in Greece apply to the local police authority. Singapore nationals can stay in Greece for 14 days without a visa.

In the past, Greece has refused entry to people whose passport indicates that they have visited Turkish-occupied North Cyprus, though there are reports that this is less of a problem now. To be on the safe side, however, ask the North Cyprus immigration officials to stamp a piece of paper rather than your passport. If you enter North Cyprus from the Greek Republic of Cyprus, no exit stamp is put in your passport.

Greek Embassies Abroad

Greece has diplomatic representation in the following countries:

Australia
    (☎ 02 6273 3011) 9 Turrana St, Yarralumla, Canberra, ACT 2600
Canada
    (☎ 613-238 6271) 76-80 Maclaren St, Ottawa, Ontario K2P 0K6
France
    (☎ 01 47 23 72 28) 17 Rue Auguste Vaquerie, 75116 Paris

Germany
   (☎ 228-83010) Koblenzer St 103, 5300 Bonn 2
Italy
   (☎ 06-854 9630) Via S Mercadante 36, Rome 00198
Japan
   (☎ 03-340 0871/0872) 16-30 Nishi Azabu, 3-chome, Minato-ku, Tokyo 106
New Zealand
   (☎ 04-473 7775) 5-7 Willeston St, Wellington
South Africa
   (☎ 21-24 8161) Reserve Bank Building, St George's Rd, Cape Town
Tunisia
   (☎ 01-288 411) 9 Impasse Antelas, Tunis 1002
Turkey
   (☎ 312-446 5496) Ziya-ul-Rahman Caddesi 9-11, Gazi Osman Pasa 06700, Ankara
UK
   (☎ 0171-229 3850) 1A Holland Park, London W11 3TP
USA
   (☎ 202-667 3169) 2221 Massachusetts Ave NW, Washington, DC, 20008

Foreign Embassies in Greece

The following countries have diplomatic representation in Greece:

Australia
   (☎ 01-644 7303) Dimitriou Soutsou 37, Athens 115 21
Canada
   (☎ 01-725 4011) Genadiou 4, Athens 115 21
France
   (☎ 01-339 1000) Leoforos Vasilissis Sofias 7, Athens 106 71
Germany
   (☎ 01-728 5111) Dimitriou 3 & Karaoli, Kolonaki 106 75
Italy
   (☎ 01-361 7260) Sekeri 2, Athens 106 74
Japan
   (☎ 01-775 8101) Athens Tower, Leoforos Messogion 2-4, Athens 115 27
New Zealand (honorary consulate)
   (☎ 01-771 0112) Semitelou 9, Athens 115 28
South Africa
   (☎ 01-680 6645) Kifissias 60, Maroussi, Athens 151 25
Tunisia
   (☎ 1-671 7590) Ethnikis Antistasseos 91, 15231 Halandri, Athens
Turkey
   (☎ 01-724 5915) Vasilissis Georgiou B 8, Athens 106 74

UK
   (☎ 01-723 6211) Ploutarhou 1, Athens 106 75
USA
   (☎ 01-721 2951) Leoforos Vasilissis Sofias 91, Athens 115 21

CUSTOMS

Duty-free allowances in Greece are the same as for other EU countries. Import regulations for medicines are strict; if you are taking medication, make sure you get a statement from your doctor before you leave home. It is illegal, for example, to take codeine into Greece. The export of antiques is prohibited. You can bring as much foreign currency as you like, but if you want to leave with more than US$1000 in foreign banknotes the money must be declared on entry. It is illegal to bring in more than 100,000 dr, and to leave with more than 20,000 dr.

MONEY

Banks will exchange all major currencies, in either cash or travellers cheques and also Eurocheques. All post offices have exchange facilities and charge less commission than banks. Most travel agencies also change money, but check the commission charged.

All major credit cards are accepted, but only in larger establishments. If you run out of money, you can get a cash advance on a Visa card at the Greek Commercial Bank and on Access, MasterCard and Eurocard at the National Bank, or you can find a major bank and ask them to cable your home bank for money (see Money in the Facts for the Visitor chapter at the start of this book).

American Express card-holders can draw cash from Credit Bank automatic teller machines.

Currency

The Greek unit of currency is the drachma (dr). Coins come in denominations of five, 10, 20, 50 and 100 dr. Banknotes come in 50, 100, 500, 1000, 5000 and 10,000 dr denominations.

At the time of writing, however, the drachma's days appeared to be numbered. Greece was expected to adopt the single European currency, the euro, in mid-1999. Travellers can expect to find prices quoted in

GREECE

both drachma and euros from the beginning of 1999 in preparation for the changeover.

Exchange Rates

Australia	A$1	=	176.83 dr
Canada	C$1	=	193.84 dr
euro	€1	=	326.44 dr
France	1FF	=	49.41 dr
Germany	DM1	=	165.60 dr
Italy	L1000	=	167.90 dr
Japan	¥100	=	201.55 dr
New Zealand	NZ$1	=	149.99 dr
UK	UK£1	=	480.26 dr
USA	US$1	=	294.97 dr

Costs

Greece is still a cheap country by European standards, especially after recent devaluations of the drachma. A rock-bottom daily budget would be about 7000 dr, which would mean staying in hostels, self-catering and seldom taking buses or ferries. Allow at least 12,000 dr per day if you want your own room and plan to eat out regularly, as well as travelling and seeing the sites. If you want a real holiday – comfortable rooms and restaurants all the way – reckon on at least 15,000 dr per day.

Tipping & Bargaining

In restaurants the service charge is included on the bill, but it is the custom to leave a small tip – just round off the bill. There are plenty of opportunities to practise your bargaining skills. If you want to dive in the deep end, try haggling with the taxi drivers at Athens airport after a long flight! Accommodation is nearly always negotiable outside peak season, especially if you are staying more than one night. Souvenir shops are another place where substantial savings can be made. Prices in other shops are normally clearly marked and non-negotiable.

Consumer Taxes

The value-added tax (VAT) varies from 15 to 18%. A tax-rebate scheme applies at a restricted number of shops and stores; look for a Tax Free sign in the window. You must fill in a form at the shop and present it with the receipt at the airport on departure. A cheque will (hopefully) be sent to your home address.

POST & COMMUNICATIONS
Post

Postal rates for cards and small air-mail letters (up to 20g) are 140 dr to EU destinations, and 170 dr elsewhere. The service is slow but reliable – five to eight days within Europe and about 10 days to the USA, Australia and New Zealand.

Post offices are usually open from 7.30 am to 2 pm. In major cities they stay open until 8 pm and also open from 7.30 am to 2 pm on Saturday. Do not wrap up a parcel until it has been inspected at the post office.

Mail can be sent poste restante to any main post office and is held for up to one month. Your surname should be underlined and you will need to show your passport when you collect your mail. Parcels are not delivered in Greece – they must be collected from a post office.

Telephone

The phone system is modern and efficient. All public phone boxes use phonecards, sold at OTE telephone offices and *periptera* (kiosks). Three cards are available: 100 units (1700 dr), 500 units (7000 dr) and 1000 units (11,500 dr). A local call costs one unit for three minutes. The 'i' at the top left hand of the dialling panel on public phones brings up the operating instructions in English. Some periptera have metered phones. On the islands, you can often use the phones at travel agents, but they add a hefty surcharge.

Direct-dial long-distance and international calls can also be made from public phones. Many countries participate in the Home Country Direct scheme, which allows you to access an operator in your home country for reverse-charge calls. A three-minute call to the USA costs 708 dr.

If you're calling Greece from abroad, the country code is ☎ 30. If you're making an international call from Greece, the international access code is ☎ 00.

Fax

Main city post offices have fax facilities.

INTERNET RESOURCES

Greece has been a bit slow off the mark in embracing the wonders of the Internet, but is now striving to make up for lost time. Internet cafés are springing up everywhere, and are listed under the Information section for cities and islands where available.

NEWSPAPERS & MAGAZINES

The most widely read Greek newspapers are *Ethnos*, *Ta Nea* and *Apoyevmatini*, all of which are dailies.

Newspapers printed in English include the daily *Athens News* (250 dr) and the weekly *Hellenic Times* (300 dr). *Atlantis* (750 dr) is a quality monthly magazine with articles on politics and the arts. Foreign newspapers are widely available, although only between April and October in smaller resort areas. The papers reach Athens (Syntagma) at 4 pm on the day of publication on weekdays and 7 pm at weekends. They are not available until the following day in other areas.

RADIO & TV

There are plenty of radio stations to choose from, especially in Athens, but not many broadcast in English. Athens International Radio (107.1 FM) broadcasts the BBC World Service live 24 hours a day, interspersed with occasional Greek programs. If you have a short-wave radio, the best frequencies for the World Service are 618, 941 and 1507MHz.

The nine TV channels offer nine times as much rubbish as one channel. You'll find the occasional American action drama in English (with Greek subtitles). News junkies can get their fix with CNN and Euronews.

PHOTOGRAPHY & VIDEO

Major brands of film are widely available, but quite expensive outside major towns. In Athens, a 36-exposure role of Kodak Gold ASA 100 costs about 1500 dr, and a 30-minute VHS high-grade video cassette goes out for about 1800 dr. You'll pay at least 30% more on the islands.

Never photograph military installations or anything else with a sign forbidding pictures. Greeks usually love having their photos taken, but ask first. Because of the brilliant sunlight in summer, it's a good idea to use a polarising lens filter.

TIME

Greece is two hours ahead of GMT/UTC, and three hours ahead on daylight-saving time, which begins at 12.01 am on the last Sunday in March, when clocks are put forward one hour. Clocks are put back an hour at 12.01 am on the last Sunday in September.

Out of daylight-saving time, at noon in Greece it is also noon in Istanbul, 10 am in London, 11 am in Rome, 2 am in San Francisco, 5 am in New York and Toronto, 8 pm in Sydney and 10 pm in Auckland. These times do not make allowance for daylight saving in the other countries.

ELECTRICITY

The electric current is 220V, 50Hz, and plugs have two round pins. All hotel rooms have power points, and most camping grounds have power.

WEIGHTS & MEASURES

Greece uses the metric system. Liquids are sold by weight rather than volume – 950g of wine, for example, is equivalent to 1000ml. Like other Continental Europeans, Greeks indicate decimals with commas and thousands with points.

LAUNDRY

Large towns and some islands have laundrettes. Most charge about 2000 dr to wash and dry a load, whether you do it yourself or leave it to them. Hotels can normally provide you with a wash tub.

TOILETS

You'll find public toilets at all major bus and train stations, but they are seldom very pleasant. You will need to supply your own paper. In town, a café is the best bet, but the owner won't be impressed if you don't buy something.

A warning: Greek plumbing cannot handle toilet paper; always put it in the bin provided.

HEALTH

Tap water is generally safe to drink in Greece. The biggest health risk comes from the sun, so take care against sunburn, heat exhaustion and dehydration. Mosquitoes can be troublesome but coils and repellents are widely available.

Watch out for sea urchins around rocky beaches; if you get some of their needles embedded in your skin, olive oil will help to loosen them. Beware also of jellyfish; although the Mediterranean species are not lethal, their sting can be painful. Greece's only poisonous snake is the adder, but they are rare. They like to sunbathe on dry-stone walls, so it's worth having a look before climbing one.

Greece's notorious sheepdogs are almost always all bark and no bite, but if you are going to trek in remote areas, you should consider having rabies injections. There is at least one doctor on every island in Greece and larger islands have hospitals or major medical clinics. Pharmacies are widespread – in cities, at least one is rostered to be open 24 hours. All pharmacies have a list of all-night pharmacies on their doors. Remember that codeine is banned in Greece, and ensure that you carry a statement from your doctor if you have prescribed drugs with you.

The number to ring throughout Greece for advice on first aid is ☎ 166. (See the Health section in the Facts for the Visitor chapter at the start of this book for more details on travel health.)

WOMEN TRAVELLERS

Many foreign women travel alone in Greece. Hassles occur, but they tend to be a nuisance rather than threatening. Violent offences are very rare. Women travelling alone in rural areas are usually treated with respect. In rural areas it's a good idea to dress conservatively, although it is perfectly OK to wear shorts, short skirts etc in touristy places.

GAY & LESBIAN TRAVELLERS

In a country where the church still plays a major role in shaping society's views on issues such as sexuality, it should come as no surprise that homosexuality is generally frowned upon. Although there is no legislation against homosexual activity, it is wise to be discreet and to avoid open displays of togetherness.

This has not prevented Greece from becoming a popular destination for gay travellers. Athens has a busy gay scene, but most people head for the islands – Mykonos and Lesvos in particular. Paros, Rhodes, Santorini and Skiathos also have their share of gay hang-outs. The monthly magazine *To Kraximo* has information about the local scene.

On the Internet, a site called Roz Mov (www.geocities.com.westhollywood/2225/ind ex.html) has travel information as well as details of local events. Another site to check out is www. users.hol.gr/~ulman/. It has a gay guide to Athens, and guides to Athens, Thessaloniki, Mykonos and Lesvos can be ordered on-line.

DISABLED TRAVELLERS

If mobility is a problem, the hard fact is that most hotels, museums and ancient sites are not wheelchair accessible. Lavinia Tours (☎ 031-23 2828), Egnatia 101 (PO Box 11106), Thessaloniki 541 10, has information for disabled people coming to Greece.

SENIOR TRAVELLERS

Elderly people are shown great respect in Greece. There are some good deals available for EU nationals. For starters, those over 60 qualify for a 50% discount on train travel plus five free journeys per year. Take your ID card or passport to a Greek Railways (OSE) office and you will be given a Senior Card. Pensioners also get a discount at museums and ancient sites.

DANGERS & ANNOYANCES

Greece has the lowest crime rate in Europe. Athens (see Athens section) is developing a bad reputation for petty theft and scams, but elsewhere crimes are most likely to be committed by other travellers. Drug laws are strict. There's a minimum seven-year sentence for possession of even a small quantity of dope.

BUSINESS HOURS

Banks are open Monday to Thursday from 8.30 am to 2.30 pm, and Friday from 8.30 am to 2 pm. Some city banks also open from 3.30 to 6.30 pm and on Saturday morning. Shops open from 8 am to 1.30 pm and 5.30

to 8.30 pm on Tuesday, Thursday and Friday, and from 8 am to 2.30 pm on Monday, Wednesday and Saturday, but these times are not always strictly adhered to. Periptera (kiosks) are open from early morning to midnight. All banks and shops, and most museums and archaeological sites, close during holidays.

PUBLIC HOLIDAYS & SPECIAL EVENTS

Public holidays are as follows:

New Year's Day	1 January
Epiphany	6 January
First Sunday in Lent	February
Greek Independence Day	25 March
Good Friday - Easter Sunday	March/April
Spring Festival/Labour Day	1 May
Feast of the Assumption	15 August
Okhi Day	28 October
Christmas Day	25 December
St Stephen's Day	26 December

Easter is Greece's most important festival, with candle-lit processions, feasting and firework displays. The Orthodox Easter is 50 days after the first Sunday in Lent.

A number of cultural festivals are also held during the summer months. The most important is the Athens Festival, when plays, operas, ballet and classical music concerts are staged at the Theatre of Herodes Atticus. The festival is held in conjunction with the Epidaurus Festival, which features ancient Greek dramas at the theatre at Epidaurus. Ioannina, Patras and Thessaloniki also host cultural festivals.

ACTIVITIES
Windsurfing
Sailboards are widely available for hire at about 2500 dr an hour. The top spots for windsurfing are Hrysi Akti on Paros, and Vasiliki on Lefkada – reputedly one of the best places in the world to learn.

Skiing
Greece offers some of the cheapest skiing in Europe. There are 16 resorts dotted around the mainland, most of them in the north. They have all the basic facilities and are a pleasant alternative to the glitzy resorts of northern Europe. What's more, there are no package tours. More information is available from the Hellenic Ski Federation (☎ 01-524 0057), PO Box 8037, Omonia, Athens 100 10, or from the EOT.

Hiking
The mountainous terrain is perfect for trekkers who want to get away from the crowds. Lonely Planet's *Trekking in Greece* is an in-depth guide to Greece's mountain trails. The popular routes are well marked and well maintained, including the E4 and E6 trans-European treks, which both end in Greece.

If you want someone to do the organising for you, Trekking Hellas, Filellinon 7, Athens 10557 (☎ 01-325 4548; fax 01-325 1474) offers a range of treks and other adventure activities throughout the country.

LANGUAGE COURSES
If you are serious about learning Greek, an intensive course at the start of your stay is a good way to go about it. Most of the courses are in Athens. The Athens Centre (☎ 01-701 2268; fax 01-701 8603), Archimidous 48, has a good reputation.

There are also courses on the islands in summer. The Athens Centre runs courses on Spetses in June and July, while the Hellenic Culture Centre (☎/fax 01-647 7465, 0275-61 482) has courses on the island of Ikaria from June to October.

More information about courses is available from EOT offices and Greek embassies.

WORK
Your best chance of finding work is to do the rounds of the tourist hotels and bars at the beginning of the season. The few jobs available are hotly contested, despite the menial work and dreadful pay. EU nationals don't need a work permit, but everyone else does.

ACCOMMODATION
There is a range of accommodation in Greece to suit every taste and pocket. All places to stay are subject to strict price controls set by the tourist police. By law, a notice must be displayed in every room, which states the

GREECE

category of the room and the price for each season. If you think you've been ripped off, contact the tourist police.

Many places – especially in rural areas and on the islands – are closed from the end of October until mid-April.

Camping

Greece has almost 350 camping grounds. Prices vary according to facilities, but reckon on about 1000 dr per person and about 900 dr for a small tent. Most sites are open only from April to October. Freelance camping is officially forbidden, but often tolerated in remoter areas.

Refuges

Greece has 55 mountain refuges, which are listed in the booklet *Greece Mountain Refuges & Ski Centres*, available free of charge at EOT and EOS offices.

Hostels

You'll find youth hostels in most major towns and on half a dozen islands. The only place affiliated to Hostelling International (HI) is the excellent Athens International Youth Hostel (☎ 01-523 4170).

Most hostels are run by the Greek Youth Hostel Organisation (☎ 01-751 9530), Damareos 75, 11633 Athens. There are affiliated hostels in Athens, Mycenae, Patras and Thessaloniki on the mainland, and on the islands of Corfu, Crete, Ios, Naxos, Santorini (Thira) and Tinos. There are six on Crete – at Iraklio, Malia, Myrthios, Plakias, Rethymno and Sitia.

Other hostels belong to the Greek Youth Hostels Association (☎ 01-323 4107), Dragatsaniou 4, 105 59 Athens. It has hostels on the islands Crete (Hersonisos and Iraklio) and Santorini.

Both organisations appear equally underfunded and their facilities are often fairly primitive, but the hostels are mostly very casual places. Their rates vary from 1500 to 2000 dr.

Athens has a number of private hostels catering to budget travellers. Standards vary enormously – from clean, friendly places to veritable fleapits. Most charge from 1500 to 2500 dr for dorm beds.

There is a YWCA hostel (XEN in Greek) for women in Athens.

Domatia

Domatia are the Greek equivalent of the British bed and breakfast, minus the breakfast. Once upon a time, domatia consisted of little more than spare rooms that families would rent out in summer to supplement their income. Nowadays many domatia are purpose-built appendages to the family house. Rates start at about 4000/6000 dr for singles/doubles, rising to 6000/9000 dr.

Hotels

Hotels are classified as deluxe, A, B, C, D or E class. The ratings seldom seem to have much bearing on the price, but expect to pay 6000/9000 dr for singles/doubles in D and E class, and about 10,000/15,000 dr in a decent C-class place.

Some places are classified as pensions and rated differently. Both are allowed to levy a 10% surcharge for stays of less than three nights, but they seldom do. It normally works the other way – you can often bargain if you're staying more than one night. Prices are about 40% cheaper between October and May.

Apartments

Self-contained family apartments are available in some hotels and domatia. There is also a number of purpose-built apartments, particularly on the islands, which are available for either long or short-term rental.

Traditional Settlements

Traditional settlements are old buildings of architectural merit that have been renovated and turned into tourist accommodation. They are terrific places to stay if you can afford between 10,000 to 15,000 dr for a double. EOT has information on the settlements.

Houses & Flats

For long-term rental accommodation in Athens, check the advertisements in the English-language newspapers. (See also Places to Stay in the Athens section.) In rural areas, ask around in tavernas.

FOOD

If Greek food conjures up an uninspiring vision of lukewarm *moussaka* collapsing into a plate of olive oil, take heart – there's a lot more on offer.

Snacks

Greece has a great range of fast-food options for the inveterate snacker. Foremost among them are the *gyros* and the *souvlaki*. The gyros is a giant skewer laden with slabs of seasoned meat that grills slowly as it rotates, the meat being steadily trimmed from the outside. Souvlaki are small, individual kebabs. Both are served wrapped in pitta bread with salad and lashings of *tzatziki* (a yoghurt, cucumber and garlic dip). Other snacks are pretzel rings, *spanakopitta* (spinach and cheese pie) and *tyropitta* (cheese pie). Dried fruits and nuts are also very popular.

Starters

Greece is famous for its appetisers, known as *mezedes*, (literally, 'tastes'). Standards include tzatziki, *melitzanosalata* (aubergine dip), *taramasalata* (fish-roe dip), *dolmades* (stuffed vine leaves), *fasolia* (beans) and *oktapodi* (octopus). A selection of three or four represents a good meal and can be a good option for vegetarians. Most dishes cost between 500 dr and 1000 dr.

Main Dishes

You'll find moussaka (layers of aubergine and mince, topped with béchamel sauce and baked) on every menu, alongside a number of other taverna staples. They include *moschari* (oven-baked veal and potatoes), *keftedes* (meatballs), *stifado* (meat stew), *pastitsio* (macaroni with mince meat and béchamel sauce, baked) and *yemista* (either tomatoes or green peppers stuffed with mince meat and rice). Most main courses cost between 1000 dr and 1500 dr.

The most popular fish are *barbouni* (red mullet) and *ksifias* (swordfish), but they don't come cheap. Prices start at about 2500 dr for a serve. *Kalamaria* (fried squid) are readily available and cheap at about 1400 dr for a decent serve.

Fortunately for vegetarians, salad is a mainstay of the Greek diet. The most popular is *horiatiki salata*, normally listed on English menus as Greek or country salad. It's a mixed salad of cucumbers, peppers, onions, olives, tomatoes and feta (white sheep or goat's-milk cheese).

Desserts

Turkish in origin, most Greek desserts are variations on pastry soaked in honey. Popular ones include *baklava* (thin layers of pastry filled with honey and nuts) and *kadaifi* (shredded wheat soaked in honey). Delicious thick yoghurt (*yiaourti*) and rice pudding (*rizogalo*) are also available.

Restaurants

There are several varieties of restaurants. An *estiatoria* is a straightforward restaurant with a printed menu. A taverna is often cheaper and more typically Greek, and you'll probably be invited to peer into the pots. A *psistaria* specialises in charcoal-grilled dishes. *Ouzeria* (ouzo bars) often have such a good range of mezedes that they can be regarded as eating places.

Kafeneia

Kafeneia are the smoke-filled cafés where men gather to drink coffee, play backgammon and cards and engage in heated political discussion. They are a bastion of male chauvinism that Greek women have yet to break down. Female tourists tend to avoid them too, but those who venture in invariably find they are treated courteously.

Self-Catering

Buying and preparing your own food is easy in Greece as there are well-stocked grocery stores and fruit and vegetable shops everywhere. In addition, villages and each area of a town hold a once or twice-weekly *laiki agora* (street market) where goods are sold. These markets are great fun to stroll around, whether or not you are cooking for yourself.

DRINKS

Nonalcoholic Drinks

The tap water is safe to drink, but many people prefer bottled mineral water. It's cheap and available everywhere, as are soft drinks and packaged juices.

Greeks are great coffee drinkers. Greek coffee (known as Turkish coffee until the words became unspeakable after the 1974 invasion of Cyprus) comes three main ways. Greeks like it thick and sweet (*glyko*). If you prefer less sugar, ask for *metrio*; *sketo* means without sugar. Instant coffee is known as Nescafé, which is what it usually is. If you want milk with your coffee, ask for *Nescafé me ghala*.

Alcohol

Greece is traditionally a wine-drinking society. If you're spending a bit of time in the country, it's worth acquiring a taste for retsina (resinated wine). The best (and worst) flows straight from the barrel in the main-production areas of Attica and central Greece. Tavernas charge from 800 to 1000 dr for 1L. Retsina is available by the bottle everywhere. Greece also produces a large range of non-resinated wines from traditional grape varieties.

Amstel is the cheapest of several northern European beers produced locally under licence. Expect to pay about 200 dr in a supermarket, or 400 dr in a restaurant. The most popular aperitif is the aniseed-flavoured ouzo.

ENTERTAINMENT

The busy nightlife is a major attraction for many travellers. Nowhere is the pace more frenetic than on the islands in high season; Ios and Paros are famous for their raging discos and bars. Discos abound in all resort areas. If you enjoy theatre and classical music, Athens and Thessaloniki are the places to be.

Greeks are great film-goers. You'll find cinemas everywhere. They show films in the original language (usually English) with Greek subtitles.

SPECTATOR SPORT

Greek men are football mad, both as spectators and participants. If you happen to be eating in a taverna on a night when a big match is being televised, expect indifferent service. Basketball is another boom sport.

THINGS TO BUY

Greece produces a vast array of handicrafts, including woollen rugs, ceramics, leather work, hand-woven woollen shoulder bags, embroidery, copperware and carved-wood products. Beware of tacky imitations in tourist areas.

Getting There & Away

AIR

There are no less than 16 international airports, but most of them handle only summer charter flights to the islands. Athens handles the vast majority of international flights, including all intercontinental flights. Athens has regular scheduled flights to all the European capitals, and Thessaloniki is also well served. Most flights are with the national carrier, Olympic Airways, or the flag carrier of the country concerned.

Europe

Flying is the fastest, easiest and cheapest way of getting to Greece from northern Europe. What's more, the scheduled flights are so competitively priced that it's hardly worth hunting around for charter cheapies.

For example, Olympic Airways, British Airways and Virgin Atlantic all offer 30-day return tickets from London for about UK£220 (midweek departures) in high season, and Olympic and British Airways both offer returns to Thessaloniki for about UK£210.

At the time of writing, the cheapest fares were being offered by new airline EasyJet (☎ 0870 6 000 000), which was offering London (Luton) to Athens for just UK£69 one way.

Charter flights from London to Athens are readily available for UK£99/189 one way/ return in high season, dropping to UK£79/ 129 in low season. Fares are about UK£109/ 209 to most island destinations in high season. Similar deals are available from charter operators throughout Europe.

There is one important condition for charter-flight travellers (only) to bear in mind. If you travel to Greece on a return ticket, you will invalidate the return portion if you visit Turkey. If you turn up at the airport for your return flight with a Turkish stamp in your passport, you will be forced to buy another ticket.

Athens is a good place to buy cheap air tickets. Examples of one-way fares include London (25,000 dr), Madrid (56,000 dr), Paris (52,000 dr) and Rome (44,000 dr). These fare don't include the international departure tax of 6200 dr.

The USA & Canada

New York has the most direct scheduled flights to Athens. Delta Airlines and Olympic both have daily flights. The fare on Olympic Airways is US$1070 one way. Apex fares range from US$960 to US$1550, depending on the season and how long you want to stay away.

Boston is the only other east-coast city with direct flights to Athens. Fares are the same as from New York. There are no direct flights to Athens from the west coast. Delta has daily flights via New York for US$1750.

Olympic also has two flights a week from Toronto via Montreal. Apex fares start at C$1098.

Australia

Olympic flies to Athens twice a week from Sydney via Melbourne. Fares range from A$1799 to A$2199.

LAND
Northern Europe

Overland travel between northern Europe and Greece is virtually a thing of the past. Buses and trains can't compete with cheap air fares, and the turmoil in former Yugoslavia has cut the shortest overland route. All bus and train services now go via Italy and take the ferries over to Greece.

Bus If you're travelling by bus from London to Athens, it makes sense to use one of the companies that allows you to stop and check the scenery along the way. One such company is Busabout, which operates services from London to Athens (UK£140 one way) every two days between April 1 and the end of October, travelling via Paris, Stuttgart,

Munich, Innsbruck and Venice. The trip takes five days, including overnight stops in Paris and Munich. The return journey goes via Venice, Rome, Florence, Antibes, Interlaken, Bern, Strasbourg and Paris.

For more information and tickets, contact Busabout's London office (☎ 0181-784 2815; fax 0181-784 2824), 26-28 Paradise Rd, Richmond, Surrey TW9 1SE. In Athens, contact Siva Travel (☎ 01-729 1066), 7 Ravine St, Athens 115 21 – just north of the Hilton Hotel.

Train Unless you have a Eurail pass, travelling to Greece by train is prohibitively expensive. Greece is part of the Eurail network, and passes are valid on ferries operated by Adriatica di Navigazione and Hellenic Mediterranean Lines from Brindisi to Corfu, Igoumenitsa and Patras.

Neighbouring Countries

Bus The Hellenic Railways Organisation (OSE) has a bus from Athens to Istanbul (22 hours; 21,800 dr) at 7 pm every day except Wednesday. It also has a daily service to the Albanian capital of Tirana (20 hours, 12,600 dr), leaving at 9 pm. Both services use the Peloponnese train station in Athens.

Train There are daily trains between Athens and Istanbul for 19,900 dr, leaving Athens at 11.15pm. The trip takes 23 hours.

Car & Motorcycle The crossing points into Turkey are at Kipi and Kastanies; the crossings into the Former Yugoslav Republic of Macedonia (FYROM) are at Evzoni and Niki; and the Bulgarian crossing is at Promahonas. All are open 24 hours a day. The crossing points to Albania are at Kakavia and Krystallopigi.

Hitching If you want to hitchhike to Turkey, look for a through-ride from Alexandroupolis because you cannot hitchhike across the border.

SEA
Italy

The most popular crossing is from Brindisi to Patras (18 hours), via Corfu (nine hours) and

Igoumenitsa (10 hours). There are numerous services. Deck-class fares start at about 7000 dr one way in low season, 10,000 dr in high season. Eurail pass-holders can travel free with both Adriatica di Navigazione and Hellenic Mediterranean. You still need to make a reservation and pay port taxes – L8000 in Italy, and 1800 dr in Greece.

There are also ferries to Patras from Ancona, Bari, Trieste and Venice, stopping at either Corfu or Igoumenitsa on the way. In summer there are also ferries from Bari and Brindisi to Kefallonia, and from Otranto to Igoumenitsa.

Turkey

There are five regular ferry services between the Greek islands and Turkey: Lesvos-Ayvalık, Chios-Çeşme, Samos-Kuşadası, Kos-Bodrum and Rhodes-Marmaris. All are daily services in summer, dropping to weekly in winter. Tickets must be bought a day in advance and you will be asked to hand over your passport. It will be returned on the boat.

Cyprus & Israel

Salamis Lines operates a weekly, year-round service from Piraeus to the Israeli port of Haifa, travelling via Rhodes and Lemessos (formerly Limassol) on Cyprus. The service leaves Piraeus at 8 pm on Thursday and Rhodes at 5 pm on Friday, reaching Lemessos at 11 am on Saturday and Haifa at 7 am on Sunday. Deck-class fares from Piraeus are 16,800 dr to Lemessos and 24,000 dr to Haifa. Given the amount of time you'll be spending on board, it's worth getting a cabin – 24,000 dr to Lemessos and 33,100 dr to Haifa. Port tax costs an additional 5000 dr.

Students and travellers aged under 30 qualify for a 20% discount on the above fares.

Poseidon Lines operates on the same route in summer, leaving Piraeus at 7 pm on Monday.

LEAVING GREECE

An airport tax of 6200 dr for international flights is included in air fares. Port taxes are 1800 dr to Italy and 5000 dr to Turkey, Cyprus and Israel.

Getting Around

AIR

Most domestic flights are operated by Olympic Airways and its offshoot, Olympic Aviation. They offer a busy schedule in summer with flights from Athens to 24 islands and a range of mainland cities. Sample fares include Athens-Iraklio for 21,600 dr, Athens-Rhodes for 24,600 dr and Athens-Thessaloniki for 21,700 dr. There are also flights from Thessaloniki to the islands. It is advisable to book at least two weeks in advance, especially in summer. Services to the islands are fairly skeletal in winter. Air Greece provides competition on a few major routes, such as Athens-Iraklio (19,100 dr).

All the above fares include the 3100-dr tax on domestic flights, paid when you buy your ticket.

BUS

Buses are the most popular form of public transport. They are comfortable, they run on time and there are frequent services on all the major routes. Almost every town on the mainland (except in Thrace) has at least one bus a day to Athens. Local companies can get you to all but the remotest villages. Reckon on paying about 1200 dr per hour of journey time. Sample fares from Athens include 8000 dr to Thessaloniki (7½ hours) and 3500 dr to Patras (three hours). Tickets should be bought at least an hour in advance in summer to ensure a seat.

Major islands also have comprehensive local bus networks. In fact, every island with a road has a service of some sort, but they tend to operate at the whim of the driver.

TRAIN

Trains are generally looked on as a poor alternative to bus travel. The main problem is that there are only two main lines: to Thessaloniki and Alexandroupolis in the north and to the Peloponnese. In addition there are a number of branch lines, such as Pyrgos-Olympia and the spectacular Diakofto-Kalavryta mountain railway.

If there are trains going in your direction, they are a good way to travel. Be aware though that there are two distinct levels of service: the painfully slow, dilapidated trains that stop at all stations and the faster, modern intercity trains.

The slow trains represent the cheapest form of transport. It may take five hours to crawl from Athens to Patras, but the 2nd-class fare is only 1580 dr. Intercity trains do the trip in just over three hours for 2580 dr – still cheaper than the bus.

Inter-Rail and Eurail passes are valid in Greece, but you still need to make a reservation. In summer, make reservations at least two days in advance.

CAR & MOTORCYCLE

Car is a great way to explore areas that are off the beaten track. Bear in mind that roads in remote regions are often poorly maintained. You'll need a good road map.

EU nationals need only their normal licence; others need an International Driving Permit. You can bring a vehicle into Greece for four months without a carnet – only a Green Card (international third-party insurance) is required.

Average prices for fuel are 210 dr per litre for super, 195 dr for unleaded and 140 dr for diesel.

Most islands are served by car ferries, but they are expensive. Sample fares for small cars from Piraeus include 19,570 dr to Crete and 23,950 dr to Rhodes. If you are going to take your car island-hopping, do some research first – cars are useless on some of the smaller islands.

Road Rules

Greek motorists are famous for ignoring the road rules, which is probably why the country has one of the highest road fatality rates in Europe. No casual observer would ever guess that it was compulsory to wear seat belts in the front seats of vehicles, nor that it was compulsory to wear a crash helmet on motorcycles of more than 50cc – always insist on a helmet when renting a motorcycle.

The speed limit for cars is 120km/h on toll roads, 90km/h outside built-up areas and 50km/h in built-up areas. For motorcycles, the speed limit outside built-up areas is 70km/h. Speeding fines start at 30,000 dr.

Drink-driving laws are strict – a blood alcohol content of 0.05% incurs a penalty and over 0.08% is a criminal offence.

All cars are required to have a first-aid kit, a fire extinguisher and triangular warning sign (in case of a breakdown).

Rental

Car hire is expensive, especially from the multinational hire companies. Their high-season weekly rates with unlimited mileage start at about 105,000 dr for the smallest models, dropping to 85,000 dr in winter – and that's without tax and extras. You can generally do much better with local companies. Their advertised rates are 25% lower and they're often willing to bargain.

Mopeds, however, are cheap and available everywhere. Most places charge about 3000 dr per day.

Warning If you're planning to hire a motorcycle or moped, check that your travel insurance covers you for injury resulting from a motorbike accident. Many policies don't.

Lonely Planet receives a lot of letters complaining about companies hiring out poorly maintained machines. Most insurance policies won't pay out for injuries caused by defective machines.

Automobile Association

The Greek automobile club, ELPA, offers reciprocal services to members of other national motoring associations. If your vehicle breaks down, dial ☎ 104.

BICYCLE

People do cycle in Greece, but you'll need strong leg muscles to tackle the mountainous terrain. You can hire bicycles, but they are not nearly as widely available as cars and motorcycles. Prices range from about 1000 to 3000 dr. Bicycles are carried free on most ferries.

HITCHING

The farther you are from a city, the easier hitching becomes. Getting out of major cities can be hard work, and Athens is notoriously difficult. In remote areas, people may stop to offer a lift even if you aren't hitching.

BOAT

Ferry

Every island has a ferry service of some sort. They come in all shapes and sizes, from the state-of-the-art 'superferries' that run on the major routes to the ageing open ferries that operate local services to outlying islands.

The hub of the vast ferry network is Piraeus, the main port of Athens. It has ferries to the Cyclades, Crete, the Dodecanese, the Saronic Gulf islands and the North-Eastern Aegean islands. Patras is the main port for ferries to the Ionian islands, while Volos and Agios Konstantinos are the ports for the Sporades.

Some of the smaller islands are virtually inaccessible in winter, when schedules are cut back to a minimum. Services start to pick up in April and are running at full steam from June to September.

Fares are fixed by the government. The small differences in price you may find between ticket agencies are the result of some agencies sacrificing part of their designated commission to qualify as a 'discount service'. The discount seldom amounts to

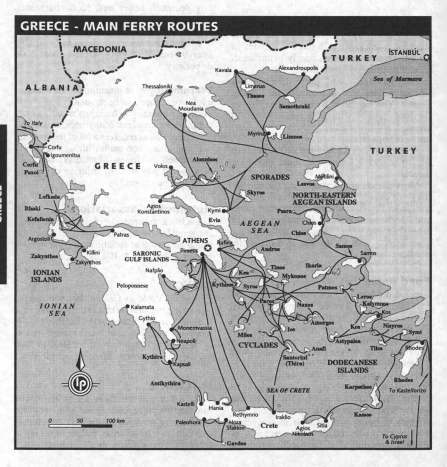

GREECE - MAIN FERRY ROUTES

more than 50 dr. Tickets can be bought at the last minute from quayside tables set up next to the boats. Prices are the same, contrary to what you will be told by agencies. Unless you specify otherwise, you will automatically be sold deck class, which is the cheapest fare. Sample fares from Piraeus include 4800 dr to Mykonos and 5400 dr to Santorini (Thira).

Hydrofoil

Hydrofoils operate competing services on some of the most popular routes. They cost about twice as much as the ferries, but get you there in half the time.

Yacht

It's hardly a budget option, but *the* way to see the islands is by yacht. There are numerous places to hire boats, both with and without crew. If you want to go it alone, two crew members must have sailing certificates. Prices start at about US$1300 per week for a four-person boat. A skipper will cost an extra US$700 per week.

Individuals can sign up with one of the companies that offer fully catered yachting holidays. Prices start at about US$900 a week in high season.

LOCAL TRANSPORT

You'll find taxis almost everywhere. Flag fall is 200 dr, followed by 58 dr per kilometre in towns and 113 dr per kilometre outside towns. The rate doubles from midnight to 5 am. There's a surcharge of 300 dr from airports and 150 dr from ports, bus stations and train stations. Luggage is charged at 55 dr per item. Taxis in Athens and Thessaloniki often pick up extra passengers along the way (yell out your destination as they cruise by; when you get out, pay what's on the meter, minus what it read when you got in, plus 200 dr).

In rural areas taxis don't have meters, so make sure you agree on a price with the driver before you get in.

Large cities have bus services which charge a flat rate of 100 dr. See the Athens section for details of buses, trolleybuses and the metro.

ORGANISED TOURS

Greece has many companies which operate guided tours, predominantly on the mainland, but also on larger islands. The major operators include CHAT, Key Tours and GO Tours, all based in Athens. It is cheaper to travel independently – tours are only worthwhile if you have extremely limited time.

STREET NAMES

Odos means street, *plateia* means square and *leoforos* means avenue. These words are often omitted on maps and other references, so we have done the same throughout this chapter, except when to do so would cause confusion.

Athens Αθήνα

☎ 01

Ancient Athens ranks alongside Rome and Jerusalem for its glorious past and its influence on western civilisation, but the modern city is a place few people fall in love with.

However inspiring the Acropolis might be, most visitors have trouble coming to terms with the surrounding urban sprawl, the appalling traffic congestion and the pollution.

The city is not, however, without its redeeming features. The Acropolis is but one of many important ancient sites, and the National Archaeological Museum has the world's finest collection of Greek antiquities.

Culturally, Athens is a fascinating blend of east and west. King Otho and the middle class that emerged after independence may have been intent on making Athens a European city, but the influence of Asia Minor is everywhere – the coffee, the kebabs, the raucous street vendors and the colourful markets.

History

The early history of Athens is so interwoven with mythology that it's hard to disentangle fact from fiction.

According to mythology, the city was founded by a Phoenician called Cecrops, who came to Attica and decided that the Acropolis was the perfect spot for a city. The gods of Olympus then proclaimed that the city should be named after the deity who could produce

GREECE

the most valuable gift to mortals. Athena and Poseidon contended. Poseidon struck the ground with his trident and a magnificent horse sprang forth, symbolising the warlike qualities for which he was renowned. Athena produced an olive tree, the symbol of peace and prosperity, and won hands down.

According to archaeologists, the Acropolis has been occupied since Neolithic times. It was an excellent vantage point, and the steep slopes formed natural defences on three sides. By 1400 BC the Acropolis was a powerful Mycenaean city.

Its power peaked during the so-called golden age of Athens in the 5th century BC, following the defeat of the Persians at the Battle of Salamis. It fell into decline after its defeat by Sparta in the long-running Peloponnesian War, but rallied again in Roman times when it became a seat of learning. The Roman emperors, particularly Hadrian, graced Athens with many grand buildings.

After the Roman Empire split into east and west, power shifted to Byzantium and the city fell into obscurity. By the end of Ottoman rule, Athens was little more than a dilapidated village (the area now known as Plaka).

Then, in 1834, Athens became the capital of independent Greece. The newly crowned King Otho, freshly arrived from Bavaria, began rebuilding the city along neoclassical lines, featuring large squares and tree-lined boulevards with imposing public buildings. The city grew steadily and enjoyed a brief heyday as the 'Paris of the Mediterranean' in the late 19th and early 20th centuries.

This came to an abrupt end with the forced population exchange between Greece and Turkey that followed the Treaty of Lausanne in 1923. The huge influx of refugees from Asia Minor virtually doubled the population overnight, forcing the hasty erection of the first of the concrete apartment blocks that dominate the city today. The belated advent of Greece's industrial age in the 1950s brought another wave of migration, this time of rural folk looking for jobs. This trend continues.

Olympic Games

After the bitter disappointment of 1992 when Athens lost out to Atlanta in the bid to stage the 1996 Olympic Games, Athenians are overjoyed by the International Olympic Committee's decision to award the 2004 Games to Athens. Shopkeepers are already cashing in, with Olympic memorabilia on sale everywhere. You can check out the latest Olympic news on the official Web site (www.athens2004.gr).

Orientation

Although Athens is a huge, sprawling city, nearly everything of interest to travellers is located within a small area bounded by Omonia Square (Plateia Omonias) to the north, Monastiraki Square (Plateia Monastirakiou) to the west, Syntagma Square (Plateia Syntagmatos) to the east and the Plaka district to the south. The city's two major landmarks, the Acropolis and Lykavittos Hill, can be seen from just about everywhere in this area.

Syntagma is the heart of modern Athens; it's flanked by luxury hotels, banks and expensive coffee shops and dominated by the old royal palace – home of the Greek parliament since 1935.

Omonia is decidedly sleazy these days. It's more of a transport hub than a square. The major streets of central Athens all meet here. Panepistimiou (El Venizelou) and Stadiou run parallel south-east to Syntagma, while Athinas leads south from Omonia to the market district of Monastiraki. Monastiraki is in turn linked to Syntagma by Ermou – home to some of the city's smartest shops – and Mitropoleos.

Mitropoleos skirts the northern edge of Plaka, the delightful old Turkish quarter which was virtually all that existed when Athens was declared the capital of independent Greece. Its labyrinthine streets are nestled on the north-eastern slope of the Acropolis, and most of the city's ancient sites are close by. It may be touristy, but it's the most attractive and interesting part of Athens and the majority of visitors make it their base.

Streets are clearly signposted in Greek and English. If you do get lost, it's very easy to find help. A glance at a map is often enough to draw an offer of assistance. Anyone you ask will be able to direct you to Syntagma (say SYN-tag-ma).

Information

Tourist Offices The main EOT tourist office (☎ 331 0561-2; fax 325 2895; gnto@eexi.gr) is close to Syntagma at Amerikis 2. It has a useful free map of Athens, which has most of the places of interest clearly marked and also shows the trolleybus routes. It also has information about public transport prices and schedules from Athens, including ferry departures from Piraeus. The office is open Monday to Friday from 9 am to 7 pm, and on Saturday from 9.30 am to 2 pm.

The EOT office (☎ 961 2722) at the East airport terminal is open Monday to Friday from 9 am to 7 pm, and Saturday from 11 am to 5 pm.

The tourist police (☎ 902 5992) are open 24 hours a day at Dimitrakopoulou 77, Veïkou. Take trolleybus Nos 1, 5 or 9 from Syntagma. They also have a 24-hour information service (☎ 171).

Money Most of the major banks have branches around Syntagma, open Monday to Thursday from 8 am to 2 pm, and Friday from 8 am to 1.30 pm. The National Bank of Greece and the Credit Bank, on opposite sides of Stadiou at Syntagma, have 24-hour automatic exchange machines.

American Express (☎ 324 4975), Ermou 2, Syntagma, is open Monday to Friday from 8.30 am to 4 pm, and Saturday from 8.30 am to 1.30 pm. Thomas Cook (☎ 322 0155) has an office at Karageorgi Servias 4, open Monday to Friday from 8.30 am to 8 pm, Saturday from 9.30 am to 4 pm and Sunday from 10 am to 4 pm.

In Plaka, Acropole Foreign Exchange, Kydathineon 23, is open from 9 am to midnight every day. The banks at both the East and West airport terminals are open 24 hours a day, although you may have trouble tracking down the staff late at night.

Post & Communications The main post office is at Eolou 100, Omonia (postcode 102 00), which is where mail addressed to poste restante will be sent unless specified otherwise. If you're staying in Plaka, it's best to get mail sent to the Syntagma post office (postcode 103 00). Both are open Monday to Friday from 7.30 am to 8 pm, Saturday from 7.30 am to 2 pm, and Sunday from 9 am to 1.30 pm. Parcels over 2kg going abroad must be posted from the parcels office at Stadiou 4 (in the arcade). They should not be wrapped until they've been inspected.

The OTE telephone office at 28 Oktovriou-Patission 85 is open 24 hours a day. There are also offices at Stadiou 15, Syntagma, and Athinas 50, Omonia office. They are open daily from 7 am to 11.30 pm.

Cybercafés If you want to send email, or surf the Internet, check out the Cybercave at the Student & Travellers' Inn (ccave1@mail.otenet.gr), Kydathineon 16, Plaka. You can also access the Internet at the Satnet Internet Cafe (info@satnet.gr), opposite the National Archaeological Museum at Marni 1.

Travel Agencies Most of the travel agencies are around Syntagma and Omonia, but only those around Syntagma deal in discount air fares. There are lots of them south of the square on Filellinon, Nikis and Voulis.

The International Student & Youth Travel Service (☎ 01-323 3767), 2nd floor, Nikis 11, is the city's official youth and student-travel service. It also issues student cards.

Bookshops There are three good English-language bookshops in Athens. The biggest is Eleftheroudakis, which has branches at Panepistimiou 17 and Nikis 4. The others are Pantelides Books, Amerikis 11, and Compendium Books, Nikis 28. Compendium also has second-hand books.

Cultural Centres The British Council (☎ 363 3215), Plateia Kolonaki 17, and the Hellenic American Union (☎ 362 9886), Massalias 22, hold frequent concerts, film shows, exhibitions etc. Both have libraries.

Laundry Plaka has a convenient laundry at Angelou Geronta 10, just off Kydathineon near the outdoor restaurants.

Medical & Emergency Services For emergency medical treatment, ring the tourist police (☎ 171) and they'll tell you where the nearest hospital is. Don't wait for an ambulance – get a taxi. Hospitals give free emergency treatment to tourists. For hospitals with outpatient departments on duty, ring ☎ 106.

GREECE

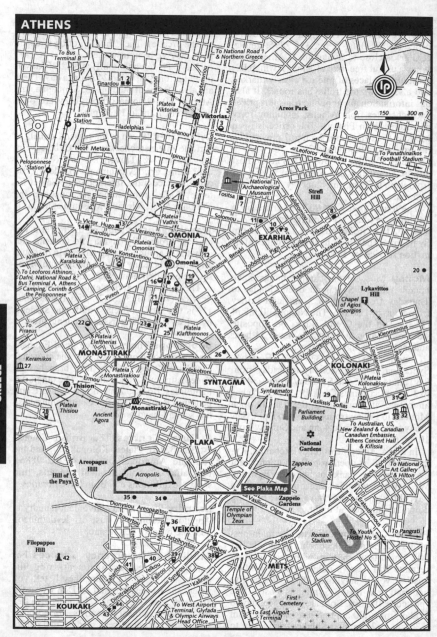

ATHENS

To Bus Terminal B

Einardou

1 2

Larisis Station

Plateia Viktorias

Viktorias

3

Lissiou

Aharnon

S Septemvriou

Mavromateon

Areos Park

0   150   300 m

To National Road 1 & Northern Greece

Filadelfias

Ioulianou

Ipirou

Leoforos Alexandras

To Panathinaikos Football Stadium

Peloponnese Station

Neof Metaxa

4

28 Oktovriou (Pattision)

National Archaeological Museum

Tositsa

7

Strefi Hill

Delfiniou

Patron

Kerameou

Ahilleos

Victor Hugo

13

14

Karolou

Plateia Karaïskaki

Agiou Konstantinou

Plateia Vathis

Plateia Omonias

OMONIA

Veranzerou

Marni

Solomou

11

10

9

EXARHIA

Kalidromiou

Themistokleous

5

6

Levidou

Deligeorgi

15

Omonia

Emmanouil Benaki

Zoödohou Pigis

Mavromihali

Harilaou Trikoupi

Ippokratous

8

20

Lykavittos Hill

Pireos

16

17

18

19

Eolou

21

22

Plateia Eleftherias

MONASTIRAKI

23

24

25

Athinas

Plateia Klafthmonos

Stadiou

Chapel of Agios Georgios

Kleomenous

Keramikos

27

26

Plateia Monastirakiou

Ermou

Kolokotroni

SYNTAGMA

Plateia Syntagmatos

Kanaris

Plateia Kolonakiou

KOLONAKI

29

30

31

32

Thision

Ermou

Mitropoleos

Vasilissis Sofias

Plateia Thisiou

28

Ancient Agora

Monastiraki

PLAKA

Niki's

Filellinon

Amalias

Parliament Building

National Gardens

To Australia, US, New Zealand & Canadian Canadian Embassies, Athens Concert Hall & Kifissia

Apostolou Pavlou

Areopagus Hill

Hill of the Pnyx

Kydathineon

Zappeio

See Plaka Map

To National Art Gallery & Hilton

Acropolis

35

34

Dionysiou Areopagitou

Temple of Olympian Zeus

Zappeio Gardens

Vasilissis Olgas

Roman Stadium

To Pangrati

To Youth Hostel No 5

Filopappos Hill

42

Rovertou Galli

36

VEÏKOU

Hatzihristou

Lembesi

38

Arditou

METS

Zaharitsa

41

40

39

Veïkou

Falirou

Syngrou

Kallirois

Voulgareos

First Cemetery

KOUKAKI

43

44

To West Airport Terminal, Glyfada & Olympic Airways Head Office

To East Airport Terminal

GREECE

PLACES TO STAY		OTHER			
1	Hostel Aphrodite	2	Atlantik Supermarket	24	Rembetika Stoa Athanaton
7	Museum Hotel	3	Mavromateon Bus Terminal	26	Vasilopoulou Delicatessen
13	Athens International	5	Rodon Club	27	Keramikos Museum
	Youth Hostel	6	Satnet Internet Café	28	Stavlos Bar
41	Art Gallery Pension	8	Supermarket	29	Benaki Museum
44	Marble House Pension	11	Plateia Exarchion	30	Goulandris Museum of
		12	AN Club & Rembetika Boemissa		Cycladic & Ancient Greek Art
PLACES TO EAT		14	Laundrette	31	UK Embassy
4	O Makis Psistaria	15	Bus 051 to Bus Terminal A	32	War Museum
9	Taverna Barbargiannis	16	Bus 049 to Piraeus	33	Byzantine Museum
10	Ouzeri I Gonia	17	Marinopoulos Supermarket	34	Ancient Theatre of Dionysos
25	Meat Market Tavernas	18	Bus 091 to Airport	35	Theatre of Herodes Atticus
36	Socrates Prison Taverna	19	Main Post Office	37	Lamda Club
43	Gardenia Restaurant	20	Lykavittos Theatre	38	Granazi Bar
		21	OTE	39	Porta Bar
		22	Bus A16 to Dafni	40	Hellaspar Supermarket
		23	Fruit & Vegetable Market	42	Monument of Filopappos

For first-aid advice, ring ☎ 166. You can get free dental treatment at the Evangelismos Hospital, Ipsilandou 45.

Dangers & Annoyances Athens has its share of petty crime.

Pickpockets Pickpockets have become a major problem in Athens. Their favourite hunting grounds are the metro system and the crowded streets around Omonia, particularly Athinas. The Sunday market on Ermou is another place where it pays to take extra good care of your valuables.

Taxi Touts Taxi drivers working in league with some overpriced C-class hotels around Omonia are a problem. The scam involves taxi drivers picking up late-night arrivals, particularly at the airport and Bus Terminal A, and persuading them that the hotel they want to go to is full. The taxi driver will pretend to phone the hotel of choice, announce that it's full and suggest an alternative. You can ask to speak to your chosen hotel yourself, or insist on going where you want.

Taxi drivers frequently attempt to claim commissions from hotel owners even if they have just gone where they were told. If the taxi driver comes into the hotel, make it clear to hotel staff that the driver is there on his own accord.

Bar Scams Lonely Planet receives a steady flow of letters warning about bar scams, particularly around Syntagma. The most popular version runs something like this: friendly Greek approaches solo male traveller and discovers that the traveller knows little about Athens; friendly Greek then reveals that he, too, is from out of town. Why don't they go to this great little bar that he's just discovered and have a beer? They order a drink, and the equally friendly owner then offers another drink. Women appear, more drinks are provided and the visitor relaxes as he realises that the women are not prostitutes, just friendly Greeks. The crunch comes at the end of the evening when the traveller is presented with an exorbitant bill and the smiles disappear. The conmen who cruise the streets playing the role of the friendly Greek can be very convincing: some people have been taken in more than once.

Things to See
Walking Tour The following walk starts and finishes at Syntagma Square and takes in most of Plaka's best-known sites. Without detours, it will take about 45 minutes. The route is marked with a dotted line on the Plaka map.

From Syntagma, walk along Mitropoleos and take the first turning left onto Nikis. Continue along here to the junction with Kydathineon, Plaka's main thoroughfare, and

GREECE

turn right. Opposite the church is the **Museum of Greek Folk Art**, which houses an excellent collection of embroidery, weaving and jewellery. It is open Tuesday to Sunday from 10 am to 2 pm; admission is 500 dr. After passing the square with the outdoor tavernas, take the second turning left onto Adrianou. A right turn at end of Adrianou leads to the small square with the **Choregic Monument of Lysicrates**, erected in 334 BC to commemorate victory in a choral festival.

Turn left and then right onto Epimenidou; at the top, turn right onto Thrasilou, which skirts the Acropolis. Where the road forks, veer left into the district of **Anafiotika**. Here the little white cubic houses resemble those of the Cyclades, and olive-oil cans brimming with flowers bedeck the walls of their tiny gardens. The houses were built by the people of Anafi, who were used as cheap labour in the rebuilding of Athens after independence.

The path winds between the houses and comes to some steps on the right, at the bottom of which is a curving pathway leading downhill to Pratiniou. Turn left onto Pratiniou and veer right after 50m onto Tholou. The yellow-ochre Venetian building with brown shutters at No 5 is the old university, now the **Museum of the University**. It is open Monday and Wednesday from 2.30 to 7 pm, and Tuesday, Thursday and Friday from 9.30 am to 2.30 pm. Admission is free.

At the end of Tholou, turn left onto Panos. At the top of the steps on the left is a restored 19th-century mansion which is now the **Paul & Alexandra Kanellopoulos Museum**, open Tuesday to Sunday from 8 am to 2.30 pm; admission 500 dr. Retracing your steps, go down Panos to the ruins of the **Roman Agora**, then turn left onto Polygnotou and walk to the crossroads. Opposite, Polygnotou continues to the **Ancient Agora**. At the crossroads, turn right and then left onto Poikilis, then immediately right onto Areos. On the right are the remains of the **Library of Hadrian** and next to it is the **Museum of Traditional Greek Ceramics**, open every day, except Tuesday, from 10 am to 2 pm. Admission is 500 dr. The museum is housed in the **Mosque of Tzistarakis**, built in 1759. After independence it lost its minaret and was used as a prison.

Ahead is Monastiraki Square, named after the small church. To the left is the metro station and the **flea market**. Monastiraki is Athens at its noisiest, most colourful and chaotic; it's teeming with street vendors.

Turn right just beyond the mosque onto Pandrossou, a relic of the old Turkish bazar. At No 89 is Stavros Melissinos, the 'poet sandalmaker' of Athens who names the Beatles, Rudolph Nureyev and Jackie Onassis among his customers. Fame and fortune have not gone to his head – he still makes the best sandals in Athens, costing from 2400 dr per pair.

Pandrossou leads to Plateia Mitropoleos and the **Athens Cathedral**. The cathedral was constructed from the masonry of over 50 razed churches and from the designs of several architects. Next to it stands the much smaller, and far more appealing, old **Church of Agios Eleftherios**. Turn left after the cathedral, and then right onto Mitropoleos and back to Syntagma.

Acropolis Most of the buildings now gracing the Acropolis were commissioned by Pericles during the golden age of Athens in the 5th century BC. The site had been cleared for him by the Persians, who destroyed an earlier temple complex on the eve of the Battle of Salamis.

The entrance to the Acropolis is through the **Beule Gate**, a Roman arch that was added in the 3rd century AD. Beyond this is the **Propylaia**, the monumental gate that was the entrance in ancient times. It was damaged by Venetian bombing in the 17th century, but it has since been restored. To the south of the Propylaia is the small, graceful **Temple of Athena Nike**, which is not accessible to visitors.

Standing supreme over the Acropolis is the monument which more than any other epitomises the glory of ancient Greece: the **Parthenon**. Completed in 438 BC, this building is unsurpassed in grace and harmony. To achieve perfect form, its lines were ingeniously curved to counteract unharmonious optical illusions. The base curves upwards slightly towards the ends, and the columns become slightly narrower towards the top, with the overall effect of making them both look straight.

Above the columns are the remains of a

PLAKA

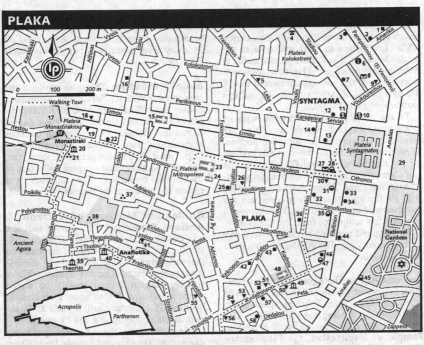

PLAKA

PLACES TO STAY

1	XEN (YWCA) Hostel
16	Hotel Tempi
42	Hotel Nefeli
43	Acropolis House Pension
46	Festos Youth & Student Guest House
52	Student & Travellers' Inn

PLACES TO EAT

5	Orient Restaurant
9	Brazil Coffee Shop
18	Savas
19	Thanasis
26	Peristeria Taverna
30	Neon Café
41	Eden Vegetarian Restaurant
50	Taverna Saita
51	The Cellar
53	Byzantino
54	Plaka Psistaria
55	Ouzeri Kouklis
56	Pantelides Damigos

OTHER

2	Books
3	Eleftheroudakis Books
4	OTE
6	Tourist Office (EOT)
7	Athens Festival Box Office
8	Parcel Post Office
10	Credit Bank
11	National Bank of Greece
12	Thomas Cook
13	American Express
14	Eleftheroudakis Books
15	Church of Kapnikarea
17	Flea Market
20	Museum of Traditional Greek Ceramics
21	Library of Hadrian
22	Centre of Hellenic Tradition
23	Athens Cathedral
24	Church of Agios Eleftherios
25	National Welfare Organisation
27	Syntagma Post Office

28	Buses to Airport
29	Parliament
31	Bus 040 to Piraeus
32	International Student & Youth Travel Service
33	Flying Dolphin Office
34	Olympic Airways
35	Buses to Cape Sounion
36	Compendium Books
37	Tower of the Winds
38	Roman Agora
39	Paulo Alexandra Kanellopoulos Museum
40	Museum of the University
44	OSE Office (Train Tickets)
45	Bus 024 to Bus Terminal B
47	Trolley Stop for Plaka
48	Church of Metamorphosis
49	Museum of Greek Folk Art
57	Acropole Foreign Exchange
58	Laundrette

GREECE

Doric frieze, which was partly destroyed by Venetian shelling in 1687. The best surviving pieces are the famous Elgin Marbles, carted off by Lord Elgin in 1801 and now in the British Museum. The Parthenon, dedicated to Athena, contained an 11m-tall gold-and-ivory statue of the goddess completed in 438 BC by Phidias of Athens (only the statue's foundations exist today).

To the north is the **Erechtheion** with its much-photographed Caryatids, the six maidens who support its southern portico. These are plaster casts – the originals (except for the one taken by Lord Elgin) are in the site's museum. The Erechtheion was dedicated to Athena and Poseidon and supposedly built on the spot where they competed for possession of ancient Athens. The Acropolis Museum has sculptures from the temples.

The site and museum are open every day from 8 am to 8 pm. The combined admission fee is 2000 dr.

Ancient Agora The Agora was the marketplace of ancient Athens and the focal point of civic and social life. Socrates spent much time here expounding his philosophy. The main monuments are the well-preserved **Temple of Hephaestus**, the 11th-century **Church of the Holy Apostles** and the reconstructed **Stoa of Attalos**, which houses the site's museum.

The site is open Tuesday to Sunday from 8 am to 8 pm (5 pm in winter); admission is 1200 dr.

Changing of the Guard Every Sunday at 11 am a platoon of traditionally costumed *evzones* (guards) marches down Vasilissis Sofias, accompanied by a band, to the Tomb of the Unknown Soldier in front of the parliament building on Syntagma. Some find the costumes (skirts and pom-pom shoes) and marching style comic, but the ceremony is colourful and entertaining.

National Archaeological Museum This is the most important museum in the country, with finds from all the major sites. The crowd-pullers are the magnificent, exquisitely detailed gold artefacts from Mycenae and the spectacular **Minoan frescoes** from Santorini (Thira), which are here until a suitable

museum is built on the island. The museum is at 28 Oktovriou-Patission 44, open Tuesday to Sunday from 8.30 am to 8 pm and on Monday from noon to 8 pm; admission is 2000 dr.

Benaki Museum This museum, on the corner of Vasilissis Sofias and Koumbari, houses the collection of Antoine Benaki, the son of an Alexandrian cotton magnate named Emmanual Benaki. The collection includes ancient sculpture, Persian, Byzantine and Coptic objects, Chinese ceramics, icons, two El Greco paintings and a superb collection of traditional costumes. The museum was closed for repairs at the time of writing.

Goulandris Museum of Cycladic & Ancient Greek Art This private museum was custom-built to display a fabulous collection of Cycladic art, with an emphasis on the early Bronze Age. Particularly impressive are the beautiful marble figurines. These simple, elegant forms, mostly of naked women with arms folded under their breasts, inspired 20th-century artists such as Brancusi, Epstein, Modigliani and Picasso.

It's at Neofytou Douka 4 and is open every day except Tuesday and Sunday from 10 am to 4 pm; admission is 400 dr.

Lykavittos Hill Pine-covered Lykavittos is the highest of the eight hills dotted around Athens. From the summit there are all-embracing views of the city, the Attic basin and the islands of Salamis and Aegina – pollution permitting.

The southern side of the hill is occupied by the posh residential suburb of Kolonaki. The main path to the summit starts at the top of Loukianou, or you can take the funicular railway from the top of Ploutarhou (400 dr).

National Gardens Formerly named the Royal Gardens, these offer a welcome shady retreat from the summer sun, with subtropical trees, peacocks, water fowl, ornamental ponds and a botanical museum.

Language Courses

The Athens Centre (☎ 701 2268; fax 701 8603), Archimidous 48, has courses covering five levels of proficiency from beginners' to advanced. It runs five immersion courses a year for beginners.

Organised Tours

Key Tours (☎ 923 3166), Kallirois 4; CHAT Tours (☎ 322 3137), Stadiou 4; and GO Tours (☎ 322 5951), Voulis 31-33, are the main operators. You'll see their brochures everywhere, offering identical tours and prices. They include a half-day bus tour (9300 dr), which does no more than point out the major sights.

Special Events

The Athens Festival is the city's most important cultural event, running from mid-June to the end of September, with plays, ballet and classical-music concerts. Performances are held in the Theatre of Herodes Atticus and begin at 9 pm. Information and tickets are available from the Festival Box Office, Stadiou 4.

Places to Stay

Camping The closest camping ground is *Athens Camping* (☎ 581 4114, 581 1562/ 63), 7km west of the city centre at Athinon 198 – on the road to Corinth. There are several camping grounds south-east of Athens on the coast road to Cape Sounion.

Hostels There are a few places around town making a pitch for the hostelling market by tagging 'youth hostel' onto their name. There are some dreadful dumps among them.

There are only a couple of youth hostels worth knowing about. They include the excellent HI-affiliated *Athens International Youth Hostel* (☎ 523 4170), Victor Hugo 16. Location is the only drawback, otherwise the place is almost too good to be true. The spotless rooms, each with bathroom, sleep two to four people. Rates are 1500 dr per person for HI members. If you're not a member, you can either pay 3600 dr to join or 600 dr for a daily stamp.

The *YWCA* (XEN, ☎ 362 4291; fax 362 2400), Amerikis 11, is an option for women only. It has singles/doubles with shared bathroom for 6000/9000 dr, or 7000/9500 dr with private bathroom.

Hotels Athens is a noisy city and Athenians keep late hours, so an effort has been made to select hotels in quiet areas. Plaka is the most popular place to stay, and it has a good choice of accommodation right across the price spectrum. Rooms fill up quickly in July and August, so it's wise to make a reservation.

Plaka The *Student & Travellers' Inn* (☎ 324 4808; fax 321 0065; students-inn@ ath.forthnet.gr), right in the heart of Plaka at Kydathineon 16, is hard to look past. It's a well-run place with beautiful polished floors and spotless rooms. Prices start at 3000 dr for bunk beds in four-person dorms, or 3500 dr for single beds. Singles/doubles/ triples are 7000/9500/12,000 dr with shared bathroom. All the rooms have central heating.

The *Festos Youth & Student Guest House* (☎ 323 2455), Filellinon 18, has been a popular place with travellers for a long time despite its situation on one of the busiest streets in Athens. Dorm beds are 3000 dr, or you can pay 2000 dr to sleep out on the roof in summer. Double/triple rooms are 7000/ 10,500 dr.

The friendly, family-run *Hotel Tempi* (☎ 321 3175; fax 321 4179), Eolou 29, occupies a quiet pedestrian mall near Monastiriki square. The rooms at the front have balconies overlooking a little square with a church and a flower market. Rates are 5500/8000 dr with shared bathroom, or 9500 dr for doubles with private bathroom. Credit cards are accepted here – unusual for a budget hotel.

The *Acropolis House Pension* (☎ 322 2344; 322 6241), Kodrou 6-8, is a beautifully preserved 19th-century house. Singles/ doubles with shared bathroom are 12,700/ 14,600 dr, or 14,300/17,150 dr with private bathroom. There's a 20% discount for stays of more than two days. All rooms have central heating.

Just around the corner from the Acropolis House is the *Hotel Nefeli* (☎ 322 8044; fax 322 5800), Iperidou 16, a modern place with air-con singles/doubles for 15,000/18,000 dr, including breakfast.

Veïkou & Koukaki There are a few good places to stay in this pleasant residential area just south of the Acropolis. The *Marble House Pension* (☎ 923 4058), Zini 35A,

GREECE

Koukaki, is a quiet place tucked away on a small cul-de-sac. Rates for the singles/doubles are 5500/9000 dr with shared bathroom or 6500/10,500 dr with private bathroom. Special weekly and monthly rates are available in winter.

The *Art Gallery Pension* (☎ 923 8376; fax 923 3025; ecotec@otenet.gr) Erehthiou 5, Veïkou, is a comfortable family-run place with singles/doubles for 12,000/14,400 dr with balcony and private bathroom.

Both these places are just a short ride from Syntagma on trolleybus Nos 1, 5, 9 or 18. Coming from Syntagma, they travel along Veïkou. Get off at the Drakou stop for the Art Gallery Pension, and at Zini for the Marble House. The trolleybuses return to Syntagma along Dimitrakopoulou.

Omonia & Surrounds There are dozens of hotels around Omonia, but most of them are either bordellos masquerading as cheap hotels or uninspiring, overpriced C-class hotels. Only a couple of places are worth a mention.

They include the excellent *Hostel Aphrodite* (☎ 881 0589; fax 881 6574; hostel-aphrodite@ath.forthnet.gr), Einardou 12, 10 minutes from the train stations. Nowhere in Athens is better set up for budget travellers. It is very clean, with dazzling white walls and good-sized rooms, many with balconies. It has dorm beds for 2500 dr, singles/doubles/triples with shared bathroom for 5000/7000/9000 dr and with private bathroom for 6000/8000/10,000 dr. It seems to be party time every night at the downstairs bar, where the action continues until the wee small hours. The hostel also offers Internet access.

The long-established *Museum Hotel* (☎ 380 5611; fax 380 0507), Bouboulinas 16, is behind the National Archaeological Museum. The rooms are comfortable and reasonably priced at 6500/9800 dr for singles/doubles with private bathroom.

Rental Accommodation For long-term rentals, check out the classifieds of the English-language newspapers and magazines. Another possibility is to look at the notice board outside Compendium Books, Nikis 28.

Places to Eat

Plaka For most people, Plaka is the place to be. It's hard to beat the atmosphere of dining out beneath the floodlit Acropolis.

You do, however, pay for the privilege – particularly at the outdoor restaurants around the square on Kydathineon. The best of this bunch is *Byzantino*, which prices its menu more reasonably and is popular with Greek family groups. One of the best deals in the Plaka is the nearby *Plaka Psistaria*, Kydathineon 28, with a range of gyros and souvlakia to eat there or take away.

Ouzeri Kouklis, Tripodon 14, is an old-style ouzeri with an oak-beamed ceiling, marble tables and wicker chairs. It serves only mezedes, which are brought round on a large tray for you to take your pick. They include flaming sausages – ignited at your table – and cuttlefish for 1100 dr, as well as the usual dips for 500 dr. The whole selection, enough for four hungry people, costs 9600 dr.

Vegetarian restaurants are thin on the ground in Athens. The *Eden Vegetarian Restaurant*, Lyssiou 12, is one of only three. The Eden has been around for years, substituting soya products for meat in tasty vegetarian versions of moussaka (1500 dr) and other Greek favourites.

With such an emphasis on outdoor eating in summer, it's no great surprise that the three cellar restaurants on Kydathineon are closed from mid-May until October. They are also three of Plaka's cheaper places, charging about 1500 dr for a main dish washed down with half a litre of retsina. The best of them is the *Taverna Saita* at No 21, near the Museum of Greek Folk Art. The others are *The Cellar* at No 10 and *Damigos* at No 41.

Peristeria Taverna, Patroou 5, is a good, basic taverna that is open all year.

Monastiraki There are some excellent cheap places to eat around Monastiraki, particularly for gyros and souvlaki fans. *Thanasis* and *Savas*, opposite each other at the bottom end of Mitropoleos, are the places to go.

The best taverna food in this part of town is at the *meat market*, on the right 400m along Athinas from Monastiraki Square. The place must resemble a vegetarian's vision of hell, but the food is great and the tavernas are open 24 hours, except Sunday. They serve traditional meat dishes such as patsas (tripe soup), podarakia (pig-trotter soup) as well as regular dishes like stifado and meatballs. Soups start at 800 dr and main dishes cost from 1000 dr.

Syntagma The *Neon Café*, opposite the post office, has spaghetti or fettucine with a choice of sauces for 980 dr, moussaka for 1450 dr and roast turkey for 1500 dr. It is probably the only eating place in Athens with a no-smoking area.

Anyone suffering from a surfeit of Greek salad and souvlakis should head for *Orient Restaurant*, Leka 26. It has an extensive menu of Cantonese, Korean and Szechwan dishes. The spicy Szechwan pork (2400 dr) is highly recommended.

Follow your nose to the *Brazil Coffee Shop* on Voukourestiou for the best coffee in town.

Veïkou & Koukaki The *Gardenia Restaurant*, Zini 31 at the junction with Dimitrakopoulou, claims to be the cheapest taverna in Athens; it has moussaka for 700 dr, large beers for 350 dr and 1L of draught retsina for 450 dr. What's more, the food is good and the service is friendly.

Socrates Prison, Mitseon 20, is not named after the philosopher, but after the owner (also called Socrates) who reckons the restaurant is his prison. It's a stylish place with an imaginative range of mezedes from 600 dr and main dishes from 1500 dr.

Exarhia There are lots of ouzeria and tavernas to choose from in the lively suburb of Exarhia, just east of Omonia. Prices here are tailored to suit the pockets of the district's largely student clientele.

Emmanual Benaki, which leads from Panepistimiou to the base of Strefi Hill, is the place to look. The *Ouzeri I Gonia*, at the corner of Emmanual Benaki and Arahovis, has a good range of tasty mezedes priced between 600 and 1400 dr. The *Taverna Barbargiannis*, farther up the hill on the corner of Emmanual Benaki and Dervenion, is another good place. It does a delicious bean

soup for 800 dr as well as a selection of meat dishes for around 1500 dr.

Around the Train Stations Wherever you choose to eat in this area you will find the lack of tourist hype refreshing. The *O Makis Psistaria*, at Psaron 48 opposite the church, is a lively place serving hunks of freshly grilled pork or beef, plus chips, for 1500 dr.

Self-Catering Supermarkets are few and far between in central Athens. Those that do exist are marked on the main Athens map. *Vasilopoulou*, Stadiou 19, is an excellent delicatessen with a good selection of cold meats and cheeses. For the best range of fresh fruit and vegetables, head for the markets on Athinas.

Entertainment

Discos & Bars Discos operate in central Athens only between October and April. In summer, the action moves to the coastal suburbs of Glyfada and Ellinikon.

The highest concentration of music bars is in Exarhia, particularly around Plateia Exarhion. Thision is another good area to look. *Stavlos*, Iraklidon 10, occupies an amazing old rabbit warren of a building. It has a rock bar playing mainly alternative British music, and more mellow sounds in the café/brasserie outside.

Gay Bars The greatest concentration of gay bars is to be found on the streets off Syngrou, south of the Temple of Olympian Zeus. Popular spots include the long-running *Granazi Bar*, Lembesi 20, and the more risque *Lamda Club*, Lembesi 15. Lesbians can try the *Porta Bar*, nearby at Falirou 10. It's not worth going until after midnight.

Rock & Jazz The *Rodon Club* (☎ 524 7427) at Marni 24 hosts touring international rock bands, while local bands play at the *AN Club* on Solomou in Exarhia. The *Hellenic Times* has listings.

Greek Folk Dances The *Dora Stratou Dance Company* performs at its theatre on Filopappos Hill at 10.15 pm every night from mid-May to October, with additional shows at 8.15 pm on Wednesday. Tickets are 1500 dr. Filopappos Hill is west of the Acropolis, off Dionysiou Areopagitou. Bus No 230 from Syntagma will get you there.

Cinemas Athenians are avid film-goers and there are cinemas everywhere. The *Athens News* and the *Hellenic Times* have listings. Admission is about 1500 dr.

Sound-and-Light Show Athens' endeavour at this spectacle is not one of the world's best. There are shows in English every night at 9 pm from the beginning of April until the end of October at the theatre on the Hill of the Pnyx (☎ 322 1459). Tickets are 1500 dr. The Hill of the Pnyx is opposite Filopappos Hill, and the show is timed so that you can cross to the folk dancing.

Rembetika Clubs Rembetika is the music of the working classes and has its roots in the sufferings of the refugees from Asia Minor in the 1920s. Songs are accompanied by bouzouki, guitar, violin and accordion. By the 1940s it had also become popular with the bourgeoisie. It was banned during the junta years, but has since experienced a resurgence, especially in Athens.

Rembetika Stoa Athanaton, Sofokleous 19 (in the meat market), is the best venue to check out. The main problem is that is closes during summer (mid-May until the end of September). For the rest of the year, it's open every day except Sunday from 3 to 7.30 pm and from midnight to 6 am. *Boemissa*, Solomou 19, Exarhia, operates all year. It's open every day except Monday from 11 pm to 4 am. Neither place charges for admission, but drinks are expensive.

Spectator Sport

Soccer is the most popular sport in Greece. Almost half of the 18 teams in the Greek first division are based in Athens or Piraeus. The most popular are Olympiakos (Piraeus) and Panathinaikos (Athens). First division matches are played on Sunday, and cup matches on Wednesday. Admission starts at 1500 dr for the cheapest terrace tickets. Fixtures and results are listed in the *Athens News*.

Things to Buy

The National Welfare Organisation shop, on the corner of Apollonos and Ipatias, Plaka, is a good place to go shopping for handicrafts. It has top-quality goods and the money goes to a good cause – the organisation was formed to preserve and promote traditional Greek handicrafts.

The Centre of Hellenic Tradition, Pandrossou 36, Plaka, has a display of traditional and modern handicrafts from each region of Greece. Most of the items are for sale.

Getting There & Away

Air Athens' dilapidated airport, Ellinikon, is 9km south of the city. There are two main terminals: West for all Olympic Airways flights, and East for all other flights. The airport's old military terminal is dusted off for charter flights in peak season.

Facilities are equally dreadful at all the terminals. Nothing is likely to change, however, until the new international airport at Spata (21km east of Athens) is completed. It is due to open in 2001.

The Olympic Airways head office (☎ 926 7251/4) is at Syngrou 96. More convenient is the office at Filellinon 13, near Syntagma.

Bus Athens has two main intercity bus stations. The EOT gives out comprehensive schedules for both with departure times, journey times and fares.

Terminal A is north-west of Omonia at Kifissou 100 and has departures to the Peloponnese, the Ionian islands and western Greece. To get there, take bus No 051 from the junction of Zinonos and Menandrou, near Omonia. Buses run every 15 minutes from 5 am to midnight.

Terminal B is north of Omonia off Liossion and has departures to central and northern Greece as well as to Evia. To get there, take bus No 024 from outside the main gate of the National Gardens on Amalias. EOT misleadingly gives the terminal's address as Liossion 260, which turns out to be a small workshop. Liossion 260 is where you should get off the bus. Turn right onto Gousiou and you'll see the terminal at the end of the road.

Buses for Attica leave from the Mavromateon terminal at the junction of Alexandras and 28 Oktovriou-Patission.

Train Athens has two train stations, located about 200m apart on Deligianni, which is about 1km north-west of Omonia. Trains to the Peloponnese leave from the Peloponnese station, while trains to the north leave from Larisis station – as do all the international trains.

Trolleybus No 1 stops 100m from Larisis station at the junction of Deligianni and Neofiliou Metaxa. Plaka residents can catch it from the southern end of the National Gardens on Amalias. Peloponnese station is across the footbridge at the southern end of Larisis Station.

Services to the Peloponnese include 14 trains a day to Corinth. The Peloponnese line divides at Corinth, with nine trains heading along the north coast to Patras, and five going south. Three of these go to Kalamata via Tripolis, while two head for Nafplio.

Services from Larisis station include nine trains a day to Thessaloniki, five of which are intercity express services. The 7 am service from Athens is express right through to Alexandroupolis, arriving at 7 pm. There are also trains to Volos and Halkida, Evia.

Tickets can be bought at the stations or at the OSE offices at Filellinon 17, Sina 6 and Karolou 1.

Car & Motorcycle National Rd 1 is the main route north from Athens. It starts at Nea Kifissia. To get there from central Athens, take Vasilissis Sofias from Syntagma and follow the signs. National Rd 8, which begins beyond Dafni, is the road to the Peloponnese. Take Agiou Konstantinou from Omonia.

The northern reaches of Syngrou, just south of the Temple of Olympian Zeus, are packed solid with car-rental firms. Local companies offer much better deals than their international rivals.

Hitching Athens is the most difficult place in Greece to hitchhike from. Your best bet is to ask the truck drivers at the Piraeus cargo wharves. Otherwise, for the Peloponnese, take a bus from Panepistimiou to Dafni, where National Rd 8 begins. For northern Greece, take the metro to Kifissia, then a bus to Nea Kifissia and walk to National Rd 1.

Ferry See the Piraeus section for information on ferries to/from the islands.

Getting Around

To/From the Airport There is a 24-hour express-bus service (No 91) between central Athens and both the East and West terminals, also calling at the special charter terminal when in use.

The buses leave Stadiou, near Omonia, every 20 minutes from 6 am to 9 pm, every 40 minutes from 9 pm until 12.20 am, and then hourly through the night. They stop at Syntagma (outside the post office) five minutes later. The trip takes from 30 minutes to an hour, depending on traffic. The fare is 200 dr (400 dr from midnight to 6 am), and you pay the driver. There are also express buses between the airport and Plateia Karaïskaki in Piraeus.

A taxi from the airport to Syntagma should cost from 1500 to 3000 dr depending on the time of day.

Bus & Trolleybus You probably won't need to use the normal blue-and-white suburban buses. They run every 15 minutes from 5 am to midnight and charge a flat rate of 100 dr. Route numbers and destinations, but not the actual routes, are listed on the free EOT map.

The map does, however, mark the routes of the yellow trolleybuses, making them easy to use. They also run from 5 am to midnight and cost 100 dr.

There are special green buses that operate 24 hours a day to Piraeus. Bus No 040 leaves from the corner of Syntagma and Filellinon, and No 049 leaves from the Omonia end of Athinas. They run every 20 minutes from 6 am to midnight, and then hourly.

Tickets can be bought from ticket kiosks and periptera. Once on a bus, you must validate your ticket by putting it into a machine; the penalty for failing to do so is 1500 dr.

Metro Central Athens is dotted with construction sites for its new metro line, which is due to open in 2000. Until then, there is just one metro line, running from Piraeus in the south to Kifissia in the north. The line is divided into three sections: Piraeus-Omonia, Omonia-Perissos and Perissos-Kifissia. The fares are 100 dr for travel within one or two sections, and 150 dr for three sections. Monastirakiou is the closest stop to Plaka.

Taxi Athenian taxis are yellow. Flagfall is 200 dr, with a 160 dr surcharge from ports, train and bus stations and 300 dr from airports. After that the day rate (tariff 1 on the meter) is 58 dr per kilometre. Rates double between midnight and 5 am.

In theory, most trips around the city centre shouldn't cost more than about 400 dr on tariff 1, but Athenian taxi drivers are notorious for pulling every scam in the book. If a taxi driver refuses to use the meter, try another – and make sure it's set on the right tariff.

To hail taxis, stand on the edge of the street and shout your destination as they pass. They will stop if they are going your way even if the cab is already occupied. Take a note of the meter reading when you get in, and pay the difference when you get out – plus 200 dr flagfall.

Radio taxis are useful if you have to get somewhere on time. Operators include Athina (☎ 921 7942), Kosmos (☎ 493 3811), Parthenon (☎ 581 4711), Ermis (☎ 411 5200), Proodos (☎ 643 3400) and Enossi (☎ 644 3345).

Bicycle You'll rarely see anyone riding a bicycle in central Athens, and you'd need to have a death wish to attempt it.

Around Athens

PIRAEUS Πειραιάς
☎ 01

Piraeus has been the port of Athens since classical times. These days it's little more than an outer suburb of the space-hungry capital, linked by a mish-mash of factories, warehouses and apartment blocks. The streets are every bit as traffic-clogged as Athens, and behind the veneer of banks and shipping offices most of Piraeus is pretty seedy. The only reason to come here is to catch a ferry or hydrofoil.

Orientation & Information
Piraeus consists of a peninsula surrounded by harbours. The most important of them is the Great Harbour. All ferries leave from here, and it has excellent connections to Athens. There are dozens of shipping agents around the harbour, as well as banks and a post

office. Zea Marina, on the other side of the peninsula, is the port for hydrofoils to the Saronic Gulf islands (except Aegina). Northeast of here is the picturesque Mikrolimano (small harbour), lined with countless fish restaurants. There's a useless EOT office (☎ 413 5716) at Zea Marina.

Getting There & Away
Bus There are two 24-hour green bus services between central Athens and Piraeus. Bus No 049 runs from Omonia to the Great Harbour, and bus No 040 runs from Syntagma to the tip of the Piraeus peninsula. This is the service to catch for Zea Marina – get off at the Hotel Savoy on Vasileos Konstantinou. Leave plenty of time – the trip can take over an hour if the traffic is bad.

There are express buses to Athens airport from Plateia Karaïskaki between 5 am and 8.20 pm, and between 6 am and 9.25 pm in the other direction. The fare is 200 dr. Blue bus No 110 runs from Plateia Karaïskaki to Glyfada and Voula every 15 minutes (100 dr). It stops outside the West terminal.

There are no intercity buses to or from Piraeus.

Metro The metro offers the fastest and most convenient link between the Great Harbour and Athens. The station is close to the ferries, at the northern end of Akti Kalimassioti. There are metro trains every 10 minutes from 5 am to midnight.

Train All services to the Peloponnese from Athens start and terminate at Piraeus, although some schedules don't mention it. The station is next to the metro.

Ferry If you want to book a cabin or take a car on a ferry, it is advisable to buy a ticket in advance in Athens. Otherwise, wait until you get to Piraeus; agents selling ferry tickets are thick on the ground around Plateia Karaïskaki.

The following information is a guide to departures between June and mid-September. Schedules are similar in April, May and October, but are radically reduced in winter – especially to small islands. The Athens EOT has a reliable schedule, updated weekly.

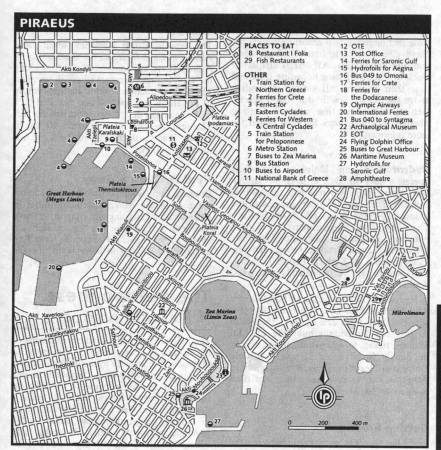

PIRAEUS

PLACES TO EAT
8 Restaurant I Folia
29 Fish Restaurants

OTHER
1 Train Station for
   Northern Greece
2 Ferries for Crete
3 Ferries for
   Eastern Cyclades
4 Ferries for Western
   & Central Cyclades
5 Train Station
   for Peloponnese
6 Metro Station
7 Buses to Zea Marina
9 Bus Station
10 Buses to Airport
11 National Bank of Greece

12 OTE
13 Post Office
14 Ferries for Saronic Gulf
15 Hydrofoils for Aegina
16 Bus 049 to Omonia
17 Ferries for Crete
18 Ferries for
   the Dodacanese
19 Olympic Airways
20 International Ferries
21 Bus 040 to Syntagma
22 Archaeolgical Museum
23 EOT
24 Flying Dolphin Office
25 Buses to Great Harbour
26 Maritime Museum
27 Hydrofoils for
   Saronic Gulf
28 Amphitheatre

GREECE

Cyclades

There are daily ferries to Kythnos, Serifos, Sifnos, Milos, Kimolos, Syros, Mykonos, Paros, Naxos, Ios and Tinos; two or three ferries a week to Iraklia, Shinoussa, Koufonisi, Donoussa, Amorgos, Folegandros, Sikinos, and Anafi; and one ferry a week to Andros.

Dodacanese

There are daily ferries to Rhodes, Kos, Kalymnos, Leros and Patmos; and two or three a week to Astypalea, Karpathos, and Kassos.

North-East Aegean

There are daily ferries to Chios, Lesvos (Mytilini),

Ikaria and Samos; and two or three a week to Limnos.

Saronic Gulf Islands

There are daily ferries to Aegina, Poros, Hydra and Spetses all year.

Crete

No island has better ferry connections. There are two boats a day to Iraklio year-round, and daily services to Hania and Rethymno. There are also two or three ferries a week to Kastelli-Kissamos (via Monemvassia, Neapoli, Gythio, Kythira and Antikythira) and one a week to Agios Nikolaos.

The departure points for the various ferry destinations are shown on the map of Piraeus. Note that there are two departure points for Crete. Check where to find your boat when you buy your ticket. All ferries display a clock face showing their departure time and have their ports of call written in English above their bows. See Boat in this chapter's Getting Around section and the Getting There & Away sections for each island for more information.

Hydrofoil Flying Dolphin hydrofoils operate a busy schedule around the Saronic Gulf between early April and the end of October. There are frequent services to the islands of Aegina, Poros, Hydra and Spetses. They also call at a range of ports on the Peloponnese, including Leonidio, Nafplio, Monemvassia and Neapoli. Occasional services continue to Kythira. Flying Dolphins also travel to the Cycladic islands of Kea and Kythnos.

Hydrofoils to Aegina leave hourly from Akti Tzelepi at the Great Harbour; all other services leave from Zea Marina. Tickets to Aegina can be bought quayside at Akti Tzelepi; tickets to other destinations should be bought in advance. There are Flying Dolphin offices at Filellinon 3 (Syntagma) in Athens, and overlooking the maritime museum at Zea Marina.

Getting Around

Local bus Nos 904 and 905 run between the Great Harbour and Zea Marina. They leave from the bus stop beside the metro at Great Harbour, and drop you by the maritime museum at Zea Marina.

DAFNI Δαφνί

The **Dafni Monastery**, 10km west of Athens, is Attica's most important Byzantine monument. Its church contains some of Greece's finest mosaics. The monastery is open Tuesday to Sunday from 8 am to 2.30 pm and entry is 800 dr. Blue Athens bus A16 from Plateia Eleftherias, north of Monastiraki, runs to Dafni every 20 minutes.

SOUNION & THE APOLLO COAST

The Apollo Coast stretches south from Athens to Cape Sounion, the southern tip of Attica. There are some good beaches along the way, but they are packed out in summer. The main attraction is the stunning **Temple of Poseidon** at Cape Sounion, perched on a rocky headland that plunges 65m into the sea. The temple is open daily from 10 am to sunset. Sunset is the best time to be there. Admission is 800 dr.

Getting There & Away

Buses to Cape Sounion (two hours, 1150 dr) leave from the Mavromateon terminal in Athens. Services using the coast road leave hourly on the half-hour and stop on Filellinon about 10 minutes later. Services travelling inland via Marcopoulo leave hourly on the hour.

The Peloponnese
Η Πελοπόννησος

The Peloponnese is the southern extremity of the rugged Balkan peninsula. It's linked to the rest of Greece only by the narrow Isthmus of Corinth, and this has long prompted people to declare the Peloponnese to be more an island than part of the mainland. Its name – Peloponnisos in Greek – translates as Island of Pelops, the mythological father of the Mycenaean royal family. It technically became an island after the completion of the Corinth Canal across the isthmus in 1893, and it is now linked to the mainland only by road and rail bridges.

The Peloponnese is an area rich in history. The principal site is Olympia, birthplace of the Olympic Games, but there are many other sites worth seeking out. The ancient sites of Epidaurus, Corinth and Mycenae in the north-east are all within easy striking distance of the pretty Venetian town of Nafplio.

In the south are the magical old Byzantine towns of Monemvassia and Mystras. The rugged Mani peninsula is famous for its spectacular wild flowers in spring, as well as for the bizarre tower settlements that dot its landscape. The beaches south of Kalamata are some of the best in Greece.

PATRAS Πάτρα
☎ 061

Patras is Greece's third-largest city and the principal port for ferries to Italy and the Ionian islands. It's not particularly exciting and most travellers hang around only long enough for transport connections.

Orientation & Information

The city is easy to negotiate and is laid out on a grid stretching uphill from the port to the old *kastro* (castle). Most services of importance to travellers are to be found along the waterfront, known as Othonos Amalias in the middle of town and Iroön Politehniou to the north. All the various shipping offices are to be found along here. The train station is right in the middle of town on Othonos Amalias, and the bus station is close by. Customs and the EOT office (☎ 361 653) are clustered together inside the port fence off Iroön Politehniou.

Money The National Bank of Greece on Plateia Trion Symahon has a 24-hour automatic exchange machine. American Express is represented by Albatros Travel (☎ 220 993), Othonos Amalias 48.

Post & Communications The post office, on the corner of Zaïmi and Mezonos, is open Monday to Friday from 7.30 am to 8 pm and Saturday from 7.30 am to 2 pm. There is also a mobile post office outside customs.

The main OTE office, on the corner of Dimitriou Gounari and Kanakari, is open 24 hours. There are also OTE offices at customs and on Agiou Andreou at Plateia Trion Symahon.

Medical & Emergency Services There is a first-aid centre (☎ 27 7386) on the corner of Karolou and Agiou Dionysiou.

The tourist police (☎ 220 902), opposite the EOT at the port, are open 24 hours.

Things to See & Do

There are great views of Zakynthos and Kefallonia from the Venetian **kastro**, which is reached by the steps at the top of Agiou Nikolaou.

Places to Stay & Eat

The nearest camping ground is *Kavouri Camping* (☎ 428 066), 2km north of town. Take bus No 1 from Agios Dionysios church.

It's hard to recommend the *YHA hostel* (☎ 427 278), Iroön Politehniou 62, following a string of complaints from female travellers. The hostel is 1.5km north of the town centre – take bus No 1 from Agios Dionysios church. Dorm beds are 1700 dr.

It's equally hard to get enthusiastic about the budget hotels, most of which double as brothels. Most travellers wind up at *Pension Nicos* (☎ 623 757), at Patreos 3 on the corner of Agiou Andreou. It has singles/doubles with shared facilities for 4000/5500 dr, and doubles with bathroom for 7500 dr.

You're better off attempting to negotiate a deal at the C-class *Hotel Rannia* (☎ 229 114; fax 220 537), Riga Fereou 24. It has been known to offer substantial discounts on its official rates of 14,000/19,000 dr for good, clean singles/doubles with bathroom.

Nicolaros Taverna, Agiou Nikolaou 50, and the nameless *restaurant* at Michalakopoulou 3 both serve good traditional food.

Getting There & Away

Many first-time visitors to Greece assume that the best way to get from Patras to Athens is by bus. Not true. The bus is faster, but it's more expensive and drops you off a long way from the centre of Athens at Terminal A on Kifissou. There's no public transport from the bus station after midnight, so you'll be up for a taxi fare of at least 1500 dr. The train, free for holders of Eurail passes, takes you close to the city centre – within easy walking distance of good accommodation.

Bus Buses to Athens (three hours, 3500 dr) run every 30 minutes, with the last at 9.45 pm. There are also 10 buses a day to Pyrgos (for Olympia) and two a day to Kalamata.

Train There are nine trains a day to Athens. Four are slow trains (five hours, 1580 dr) and five are express intercity trains (3½ hours, 2580 dr). The last intercity train leaves at 6 pm. Trains also run south to Pyrgos and Kalamata.

PATRAS

PLACES TO STAY
24 Hotel Rannai
30 Pension Nicos

PLACES TO EAT
14 Restaurant
28 Nicolaros Taverna

OTHER
2 Boats to Italy
3 EOT
4 Tourist Police
5 Customs
6 Buses to Lefkada
7 Church of Agios
   Dionysos
9 Boats to Ionian Islands
13 First-Aid Centre
15 Main Bus Station
18 Olympic Airways
19 Post Office
20 Archaeological Museum
21 Laundrette
22 Train Station
23 National Bank of Greece
25 Albatros Travel
   (American Express)
27 English-Language Books
29 Buses to Zakynthos
31 Municipal Theatre
32 Supermarket
33 Kastro

FERRY LINES
1 Hellenic Mediterranean
   Line
8 Minoan Lines
10 Adriatica
11 Superfast
12 Med Link
16 ANEK
17 Vergina Ferries
26 Marlines

Ferry There are daily ferries to Kefallonia (four hours, 3250 dr), Ithaki (six hours, 3450 dr) and Corfu (10 hours, 5800 dr). Services to Italy are covered in the Getting There & Away section at the start of this chapter. Ticket agents line the waterfront.

DIAKOFTO-KALAVRYTA RAILWAY

This spectacular rack-and-pinion line climbs up the deep gorge of the Vouraikos River from the small coastal town of Diakofto to the mountain resort of **Kalavryta**, 22km away. It is a thrilling journey, with dramatic scenery all the way. The trains leave Diakofto at 7.35, 10.05 and 11.30 am, and 1.35, 3.30 and 5.25 pm, returning at 8.48 and 11.25 am, and 1.30, 3.25, 5.20 and 7.10 pm. Kalavryta is 45 minutes east of Patras by bus or train.

Kalavryta has some good hotels, but it can be hard to find a room at weekends and during the ski season. The *Hotel Paradissos* (☎ 22 303) on Kallimani has spotless singles/doubles with bathroom for 9000/14000 dr, dropping to 4000/7000 dr outside peak times. To get there, cross the road from the train station and walk up Syngrou, then turn right onto Kallimani at the Hotel Maria.

Kalavryta has five buses a day to Patras and two to Athens.

CORINTH
☎ 0741

Modern Corinth is an uninspiring town which gives the impression that it has never quite recovered from the devastating earthquake of 1928. It is, however, a convenient base from which to visit nearby ancient Corinth.

Places to Stay & Eat
Corinth Beach Camping (☎ 27 967) is about 3km west of town. Buses to ancient Corinth can drop you there.

Corinth's budget hotels are a grim bunch. The least awful of them is the *Hotel Apollon* (☎ 22 587), near the train station at Pirinis 18, even though it doubles as a brothel. From the outside the place looks to be on the verge of collapse, but the rooms have been redecorated and are reasonable value at 4000/6000 dr for singles/doubles with bathroom.

If you can afford it, head for the friendly family-run *Hotel Ephira* (☎ 24 021; fax 24 514), Ethnikis Antistaseos 52. It charges 8500/13,000 dr for clean air-con singles/doubles with bathroom.

The *Taverna O Theodorakis*, near the port on the side street next to the Hotel Corinthos, is a lively place specialising in fish.

Getting There & Away
Bus Corinth has two main bus stations. There are buses to Athens (1½ hours, 1500 dr) every 30 minutes from the bus station on the corner of Ermou and Koliatsou, on the southeastern side of the park in the city centre. Buses to other parts of the Peloponnese leave from the station at the junction of Ethnikis Antistaseos and Aratou. There are hourly buses to ancient Corinth (20 minutes, 240 dr) from the bus stop on Koliatsou to the northwest of the central park.

Train There are 14 trains a day to Athens, five of them intercity services. There are also trains to Kalamata, Nafplio and Patras.

ANCIENT CORINTH & ACROCORINTH
The sprawling ruins of ancient Corinth lie 7km south-west of the modern city. Corinth (Κόρινθος) was one of ancient Greece's wealthiest and most wanton cities. When Corinthians weren't clinching business deals, they were paying homage to Aphrodite in a temple dedicated to her, which meant they were frolicking with the temple's sacred prostitutes. The only ancient Greek monument remaining here is the imposing **Temple of Apollo**; the others are Roman. Towering over the site is Acrocorinth, the ruins of an ancient citadel built on a massive outcrop of limestone.

Both sites are open daily from 8 am to 6 pm. Admission is 1200 dr for ancient Corinth and free for Acrocorinth.

NAFPLIO Ναύπλιο
☎ 0752

Nafplio ranks as one of Greece's prettiest towns. The narrow streets of the old quarter are filled with elegant Venetian houses and neoclassical mansions.

Information
The municipal tourist office (☎ 24 444) is on 25 Martiou opposite the OTE office and is open from 9 am to 1.30 pm and 4.30 to 9 pm daily. The bus station is on Syngrou, the street which separates the old town from the new.

Palamidi Fortress
There are terrific views of the old town and the surrounding coast from this ruined hilltop fortress. The climb is strenuous – there are almost 1000 steps – so start early and take water with you. The easy way out is to catch a taxi from town for about 1000 dr. The fortress is open Monday to Friday from 8 am to 4.30 pm, and on weekends from 8 am to 2.30 pm; admission is 800 dr.

Places to Stay & Eat
There are *camping grounds* galore along Tolo Beach, 9km east of town.

The youth hostel has finally closed after years of zero maintenance. All is not lost, however. The *Hotel Economou* (☎ 23 955), opposite the ex-hostel at Argonafton 22, has set up two rooms as dorms. Beds are 2500 dr per person. The hotel is in the new town off Argous, which is the road to Argos. The walk from the bus station takes about 15 minutes.

Most people prefer to stay in the old part of town, where there are numerous signs for domatia. Most charge about 5000/8000 dr for singles/doubles.

The best place in town is the stylish *Hotel Byron* (☎ 22 351; fax 26 338; byronhotel@ otenet.gr), Platanos 2. It has beautifully furnished singles for 12,000 dr and doubles from 15,000 to 18,000 dr.

The *Taverna Ellas* on the old town's main square, Plateia Syntagmatos, is a good place for people-watching as you tuck into tasty staples like chicken in tomato sauce or artichoke stew, both 1100 dr.

Getting There & Away
There are hourly buses to Athens (2½ hours, 2450 dr), as well as services to Argos (for Peloponnese connections), Mycenae, Epidaurus, Corinth and Tolo.

From May to September, there are hydrofoils to Piraeus every day except Sunday. Buy tickets from Yannopoulos Travel on Plateia Syntagmatos in the old town.

EPIDAURUS Επίδαυρος
The crowd-puller at this site is the huge and well-preserved **Theatre of Epidaurus**, but don't miss the more peaceful **Sanctuary of Asclepius** nearby. Epidaurus was regarded as the birthplace of Asclepius, the god of healing, and the sanctuary was once a flourishing spa and healing centre. The setting alone would have been enough to cure many ailments.

The site is open Tuesday to Sunday from 8 am to 4.30 pm, and on Monday from noon until 4.30 pm; admission is 1500 dr.

You can enjoy the theatre's astounding acoustics first hand during the **Epidaurus Festival** from mid-June to mid-August.

Getting There & Away
There are two buses a day from Athens (2½ hours, 2250 dr), as well as three a day from Nafplio (40 minutes, 600 dr). During the festival, there are excursion buses from Nafplio and Athens.

MYCENAE Μυκήνες
Mycenae was the most powerful influence in Greece for three centuries until about 1200 BC. The rise and fall of Mycenae is shrouded in myth, but the site was settled as early as the sixth millennium BC. Historians are divided as to whether the city's eventual destruction was due to outsiders or internal conflict between the various Mycenaean kingdoms. Described by Homer as 'rich in gold', Mycenae's entrance, the **Lion Gate**, is Europe's oldest monumental sculpture.

Excavations have uncovered the palace complex and royal tombs, shaft graves and extraordinary beehive-shaped tombs. The six shaft graves known as the **First Royal Grave Circle** were uncovered by Heinrich Schliemann in 1873.

The gold treasures he found in these graves, including the so-called **Mask of Agamemnon**, are among the world's greatest archaeological finds. They are now displayed in the National Archaeological Museum in Athens.

The site is open daily from 8 am to 7 pm; admission is 1500 dr.

Getting There & Away
There are buses from Argos and Nafplio.

SPARTA Σπάρτη
☎ 0731
The bellicose Spartans sacrificed all the finer things in life to military expertise and left no monuments of any consequence. Ancient Sparta's forlorn ruins lie amidst olive groves at the northern end of town. Modern Sparta is a neat, unspectacular town, but it's a convenient base from which to visit Mystras.

Orientation & Information
Sparta is laid out on a grid system. The main streets are Paleologou, which runs north-south through the town, and Lykourgou, which runs east-west. The EOT office (☎ 24 852) is in the town hall on the main square, Plateia Kentriki. It's open Monday to Friday from 8 am to 2.30 pm.

Places to Stay & Eat
Camping Mystras (☎ 22 724), on the Sparta-Mystras road, is open year-round.

There's a good choice of hotels in town. Most travellers head for the friendly *Hotel Cecil* (☎ 24 980), at Paleologou 125, which has cosy singles/doubles with bathroom for 6500/9000 dr. If it's full, try the *Hotel Lakonia* (☎ 28 951), Paleologou 61.

The *Diethnes Restaurant*, Paleologou 105, does good traditional food and has garden seating in summer.

Getting There & Away

There are frequent buses to Mystras (30 minutes, 240 dr) from Lykourgou, two blocks west of the main square. The main bus terminal is at the eastern end of Lykourgou. There are 10 buses a day to Athens (four hours, 3600 dr), three to Monemvassia and two to Kalamata.

MYSTRAS Μυστράς

Mystras, 7km from Sparta, was once the shining light of the Byzantine world. Its ruins spill from a spur of Mt Taygetos, crowned by a mighty fortress built by the Franks in 1249. The streets of Mystras are lined with glorious palaces, monasteries and churches, most of them dating from the period between 1271 and 1460, when the town was the effective capital of the Byzantine Empire. The buildings are among the finest examples of Byzantine architecture in Greece and contain many superb frescoes. Don't miss the **Church of Perivleptos**, whose walls are decorated with incredibly detailed paintings.

The site is open every day from 8 am to 7 pm. Admission is 1200 dr, which includes entrance to the museum (closed Monday). You'll need a whole day to do this vast place justice. Take a taxi or hitch a ride to the upper Fortress Gate and work your way down. Take some water.

MONEMVASSIA Μονεμβασία
☎ 0732

Monemvassia is no longer an undiscovered paradise, but mass tourism hasn't lessened the impact of one's first encounter with this extraordinary old town – nor the thrill of exploring it.

There's no EOT office but the staff at Malvasia Travel (☎ 61 752), near the bus station, are helpful.

Things to See

Monemvassia occupies a great outcrop of rock that rises dramatically from the sea opposite the village of Gefyra. It was separated from the mainland by an earthquake in 375 AD and access is by a causeway from Gefyra. From the causeway, a road curves around the base of the rock for about 1km until it comes to a narrow L-shaped tunnel in the massive fortifying wall. You emerge, blinking, in the **Byzantine town**, hitherto hidden from view.

The cobbled main street is flanked by stairways leading to a complex network of stone houses with tiny walled gardens and courtyards. Steps (signposted) lead to the ruins of the **fortress** built by the Venetians in the 16th century. The views are great, and there is the added bonus of being able to explore the Byzantine **Church of Agia Sophia**, perched precariously on the edge of the cliff.

Places to Stay & Eat

The nearest camping ground is *Camping Paradise* (☎ 61 123), 3.5km to the north. There is no budget accommodation in Monemvassia, but there are domatia in Gefyra as well as cheap hotels.

The basic *Hotel Akrogiali* (☎ 61 360), opposite the National Bank of Greece, has singles/doubles with shower for 5500/8000 dr.

If your budget permits, treat yourself to a night in one of the beautifully restored traditional settlements in Monemvassia. The pick of them is *Malvasia Guest Houses* (☎ 61 113; fax 61 722), with singles/doubles for 10,000/13,500 dr, which includes a generous breakfast.

Taverna Nikolas is the place to go for a hearty meal in Gefyra, while *To Kanoni*, on the right of the main street in Monemvassia, has an imaginative menu.

Getting There & Away

Bus There are between two and four buses a day to Athens (six hours, 5350 dr), depending on the season. They travel via Sparta, Tripolis and Corinth. In summer, there is a daily bus to Gythio (1½ hours, 1500 dr).

Ferry In July and August, there are at least two hydrofoils a day to Piraeus via the Saronic Gulf islands.

GREECE

GYTHIO Γύθειο
☎ 0731

Gythio, once the port of ancient Sparta, is an attractive fishing town at the head of the Lakonian Gulf. It is the gateway to the rugged Mani peninsula to the south.

The main attraction at Gythio is the picturesque islet of **Marathonisi**, linked to the mainland by a causeway. According to mythology, it is ancient Cranae, where Paris (a prince of Troy) and Helen (the wife of Menelaus of Sparta) consummated the love affair that sparked the Trojan War. An 18th-century tower on the islet has been turned into a **museum** of Mani history.

Places to Stay & Eat
Gythio's *camping grounds* are dotted along the coast south of town and can be reached on any bus heading to Areopoli.

There are numerous *domatia* on the waterfront near the main square. The *Saga Pension* (**☎** 23 220), between the square and the causeway, has immaculate singles/doubles with bathroom for 7000/9000 dr. The *Hotel Kranai* (24 394), Akti Vasileos Pavlou 17, charges 7000/11,000 dr for large singles/doubles with bathroom.

The nameless *farotaverna* (fish taverna) next to the Hotel Kranai is the pick of the waterfront restaurants. A large plate of kalamari costs 1200 dr and there's fresh fish by the kilogram.

Getting There & Away
Bus There are four buses a day to Athens (4½ hours, 4350 dr), and four a day to Kalamata. Two of these services go via the Mani, calling at Areopoli, Itilo, Kardamyli and Stoupa, and two go via Sparta. In summer, there is a daily bus to Monemvassia.

Services to the Inner Mani include three buses a day to the Diros Caves, two to Gerolimenas and one to Vathia – all via Areopoli.

Ferry In summer, there are two ferries a week to Kastelli-Kissamos on Crete. For information and ferry tickets, contact Rozakis Travel (**☎** 22 207) opposite the port.

THE MANI
The Mani is divided into two regions, the Lakonian (inner) Mani in the south and Messinian (outer) Mani in the north-west below Kalamata.

Lakonian Mani
☎ 0733

The Lakonian Mani is wild and remote, its landscape dotted with the dramatic stone tower houses that are a trademark of the region. They were built as refuges from the clan wars of the 19th century. The best time to visit is in spring, when the barren countryside briefly bursts into life with a spectacular display of wild flowers.

The region's principal village is **Areopoli**, about 30km south-west of Gythio. There are a number of fine towers on the narrow, cobbled streets of the old town.

Just south of here are the magnificent **Diros Caves**, where a subterranean river flows. The caves are open 8 am to 5.30 pm from June to September and 8 am to 2.30 pm from October to May. Admission is 3500 dr.

Gerolimenas, 20km farther south, is a tiny fishing village built around a sheltered bay. **Vathia**, a village of towers built on a rocky peak, is 11km south-east of Gerolimenas. Beyond Vathia, the coastline is a series of rocky outcrops sheltering pebbled beaches.

Places to Stay
There are no official camping grounds in the Lakonian Mani.

Areopoli The cheapest accommodation in Areopoli is at *Perros Bathrellos Rooms* (**☎** 51 205) on Kapetan Matapan, the main street of the old town, above the *Taverna Barbar Petros*. Singles/doubles are 4000/6000 dr with shared bath.

Tsimova Rooms (**☎** 51 301), signposted off Kapetan Matapan, offers beautiful doubles in a renovated tower house for 10,000 dr.

Gerolimenas & Vathia The *Hotel Akrogiali* (**☎** 54 204), overlooking the beach in Gerolimenas, has comfortable singles/doubles with bathroom for 5000/7500 dr. It also has an excellent restaurant. If you feel like a treat, check out the superb rooms at *Vathia Towers* (**☎** 55 244). Doubles are 14,000 dr with breakfast.

Getting There & Away There are direct buses to Gythio and Sparta from both Areopoli and Gerolimenas. Getting to Kalamata involves changing buses in Itilo, 11km north of Areopoli.

Getting Around Areopoli is the focal point of the local bus network. There are three buses a day to Itilo, two a day to the Diros Caves and Gerolimenas, and occasional buses to Vathia.

Hitching in the Mani is fairly easy. An asphalt road skirts the coast, and minor roads lead to isolated churches and villages.

Messinian Mani
☎ 0721
The Messinian Mani runs north along the coast from Itilo to Kalamata. The beaches here are some of the best in Greece, set against the dramatic backdrop of the Taygetos mountains.

Itilo, the medieval capital of all the Mani, is split by a ravine that is the traditional dividing line between inner and outer Mani.

The picturesque coastal village of **Kardamyli**, 37km south of Kalamata, is the starting point for walks up the **Taygetos Gorge**. It takes about 2½ hours to walk to the deserted **Monastery of the Saviour**. Strong footwear is essential and take plenty of water.

Stoupa, 10km south of Kardamyli, has a great beach and is a popular package destination in summer.

Places to Stay There are about half a dozen *camping grounds* along the coast between Kardamyli and Stoupa.

Kardamyli There are numerous domatia, but nowhere cheap. *Olivia Koumounakou* (☎ 73 326), opposite the post office, has immaculate doubles with private bathroom for 7500 dr. *Lela's Taverna & Rooms* (☎ 73 541) occupy a charming stone building overlooking the sea. It has stylish doubles with private bathroom for 10,000 dr.

Stoupa Accommodation is monopolised by package operators in summer. The *Hotel Stoupa* (☎ 54 308), on the road into town, has good doubles with bathroom for 11,000 dr.

Alternatively, seek out Bob Barrow at Thomeas Travel (☎ 77 689), who can advise on vacancies around town.

The *Taverna Akrogiali* has a great setting at the southern end of the main beach – and good food, if their fish soup (950 dr) is any guide.

Getting There & Away Itilo, Kardamyli and Stoupa are all on the bus route between Kalamata and Gythio. There are two buses a day in each direction.

OLYMPIA Ολυμπία
☎ 0624
The site of ancient Olympia lies just half 500m beyond the modern town, surrounded by the green foothills of Mt Kronion. There is an excellent tourist office on the main street, open from 9 am to 9 between June and September, and from 11 am to 2 pm and 5 to 8 pm for the rest of the year. It will also change money.

Things to See
In ancient times, Olympia was a sacred place of temples, priests' dwellings and public buildings, as well as being the venue for the quadrennial Olympic Games. The first Olympics were staged in 776 BC, reaching the peak of their prestige in the 6th century BC. The city-states were bound by a sacred truce to stop fighting for three months and compete.

The site is dominated by the immense, ruined **Temple of Zeus**, to whom the games were dedicated. The site is open Monday to Friday from 8 am to 7 pm, and on weekends from 8.30 am to 3 pm. Admission is 1200 dr. There's also a **museum** north of the archaeological site. It keeps similar hours and admission is also 1200 dr. Allow a whole day to see both.

Places to Stay & Eat
There are three good camping grounds to choose from. The most convenient is *Camping Diana* (☎ 22 314), 250m west of town. It has excellent facilities and a pool.

The *youth hostel* (☎ 22 580), Praxitelous Kondyli 18, has dorm beds for 1500 dr, including hot showers.

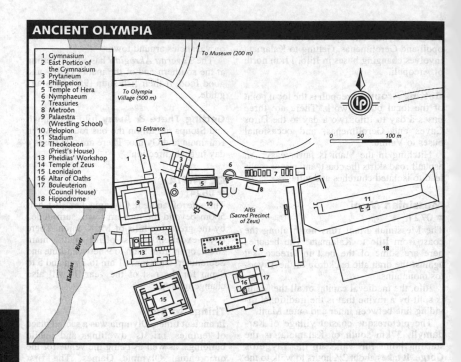

ANCIENT OLYMPIA

1 Gymnasium
2 East Portico of
   the Gymnasium
3 Prytaneum
4 Philippeion
5 Temple of Hera
6 Nymphaeum
7 Treasuries
8 Metroön
9 Palaestra
   (Wrestling School)
10 Pelopion
11 Stadium
12 Theokoleon
   (Priest's House)
13 Pheidias' Workshop
14 Temple of Zeus
15 Leonidaion
16 Altar of Oaths
17 Bouleuterion
   (Council House)
18 Hippodrome

To Museum (200 m)

To Olympia
Village (500 m)

Entrance

Altis
(Sacred Precinct
of Zeus)

Kladeos River

The *Pension Achilleys* (☎ 22 562), Stefanopoulou 4, has singles/doubles with shared bathroom for 3000/6000 dr.

The *Taverna Praxitelous*, behind the tourist office, is a favourite with locals.

Getting There & Away

There are four buses a day to Olympia from Athens (5½ hours, 5450 dr). There are also regular buses and trains to Olympia from Pyrgos, 24km away on the coast.

Central Greece

Central Greece has little going for it in terms of attractions – with the notable exception of Delphi and surroundings.

DELPHI Δελφοί
☎ 0265

Like so many of Greece's ancient sites, the setting at Delphi – overlooking the Gulf of Corinth from the slopes of Mt Parnassos – is stunning. The Delphic oracle is thought to have originated in Mycenaean times when the earth goddess Gaea was worshipped here.

By the 6th century BC, Delphi had become the Sanctuary of Apollo and thousands of pilgrims came to consult the oracle, who was always a peasant woman of 50 years or more. She sat at the mouth of a chasm which emitted fumes. These she inhaled, causing her to gasp, writhe and shudder in divine frenzy. The pilgrim, after sacrificing a sheep or goat, would deliver a question, and the priestess' incoherent mumblings were then translated by a priest. Wars were fought, voyages embarked upon, and business transactions undertaken on the strength of these prophecies.

Orientation & Information

The bus station, post office, OTE, National

Bank of Greece and tourist office (☎ 82 900) are all on modern Delphi's main street, Vasileon Pavlou. The tourist office, at No 44, is open Monday to Friday from 7.30 am to 2.30 pm. The ancient site is 1.5km east of modern Delphi.

Sanctuary of Apollo

The **Sacred Way** leads up from the entrance of the site to the **Temple of Apollo**. It was here that the oracle supposedly sat, although no chasm, let alone vapour, has been detected. The path continues to the theatre and stadium. Opposite this sanctuary is the **Sanctuary of Athena** (free admission) and the much-photographed **tholos**, which is a columned rotunda of Pentelic marble. It was built in the 4th century BC and is the most striking of Delphi's monuments, but its purpose and to whom it was dedicated are unknown.

The site is open from Monday to Friday from 7.30 am to 7.15 pm, and on weekends and public holidays from 8.30 am to 2.45 pm. The museum is open similar hours, except on Monday when it's open only from noon until 6.15 pm. Entry to each is 1200 dr.

Places to Stay & Eat

The nearest camping ground to Delphi is **Apollon Camping** (☎ 82 750), 1.5km west of modern Delphi.

The **Pension Delphi** (☎/fax 82 268), Apollonos 31, has singles/doubles for 5000/8000 dr. It's open from March to November and on Friday and Saturday in winter.

There are hotels in Delphi to suit every budget. The **Hotel Athina** (☎ 82 239), on the corner of Vasileon Pavlou and Frederikis, has singles/doubles with bathroom that go for 8000/9500 dr.

The food is good value at **Taverna Vakhos**, next to the Pension Delphi.

Getting There & Away

There are five buses a day to Delphi from Athens (three hours, 2850 dr).

Northern Greece

Northern Greece covers the regions of Epiros, Thessaly, Macedonia and Thrace. It includes some areas of outstanding natural beauty, such as the Zagoria region of northwestern Epiros.

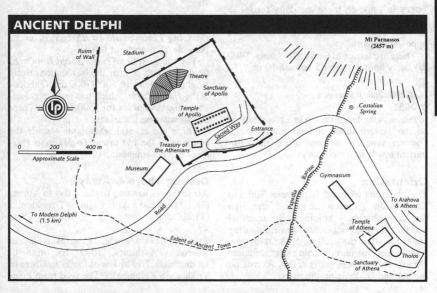

ANCIENT DELPHI

Mt Parnassos (2457 m)

Ruins of Wall

Stadium

Theatre

Sanctuary of Apollo

Temple of Apollo

Castalian Spring

Sacred Way

Entrance

Treasury of the Athenians

Museum

0   200   400 m
Approximate Scale

To Modern Delphi (1.5 km)

Road

Papadia Ravine

Gymnasium

To Arahova & Athens

Temple of Athena

Extent of Ancient Town

Tholos

Sanctuary of Athena

IGOUMENITSA Ηγουμενίτσα
☎ 0665
Igoumenitsa, opposite the island of Corfu, is the main port of north-western Greece. Few people stay any longer than it takes to buy a ticket out. The bus station is on Kyprou. To get there from the ferries, follow the waterfront (Ethnikis Antistasis) north for 500m and turn up El Venizelou. Kyprou is two blocks inland and the bus station is on the left.

Places to Stay & Eat
If you get stuck for the night, the *Hotel Egnatias* (☎ 23 648), centrally located at Eleftherias 1, has singles/doubles with bathroom for 7000/11,500 dr.

To Astron Restaurant, El Venizelou 9, and *Restaurant Martinis-Bakalis*, on the corner of 23 Fevrouariou and Gregoris Lambraki, both have main courses priced from 1100 dr.

Getting There & Away
Bus Services include nine buses a day to Ioannina (two hours, 1850 dr), and four a day to Athens (8½ hours, 8050 dr).

Ferry In summer, there are daily ferries to the Italian ports of Brindisi and Bari, and occasional boats to Otranto. Ticket agents are opposite the port.

There are ferries to Corfu (1½ hours, 1400 dr) every hour between 5 am and 10 pm.

IOANNINA Ιωάννινα
☎ 0651
Ioannina is the largest town in Epiros, sitting on the western shore of Lake Pamvotis. In Ottoman times, it was one of the most important towns in the country.

Orientation
The main bus terminal is between Sini and Zossimadon. To reach the town centre, find the large pharmacy adjoining the terminal and take the road opposite. Turn right at the Hotel Egnatias, then left onto 28 Oktovriou, which meets Ioannina's main street at Plateia Dimokratias. The street is called Averof on the left and Dodonis on the right.

Information
The helpful EOT office (☎ 25 086) is 100m along Dodonis, set back on a small square at Napoleon Zerva 2. It's open Monday to Friday from 7.30 am to 2.30 pm and from 5.30 to 8.30 pm, and on Saturday from 9 am to 1 pm. Robinson Travel (☎ 29 402), 8th Merarhias Gramou 10, specialises in treks in the Zagoria region.

Cybercafés The Internet café (☎ 77 925), Napoleon Zerva 4-6, is the place to go.

Things to See
The **old town** juts out into the lake on a small peninsula. Inside the impressive fortifications lies a maze of winding streets flanked by traditional Turkish houses.

The **Nisi** (island) is a serene spot in the middle of the lake, with four monasteries set among the trees. Ferries to the island leave from just north of the old town. They run half-hourly in summer and hourly in winter. The fare is 180 dr.

The **Perama Cave**, 4km from Ioannina, has a mind-boggling array of stalactites and stalagmites. It's open from 8 am to 8 pm in summer and 8 am to 6 pm in winter; admission is 1000 dr.

Places to Stay & Eat
Camping Limnopoula (☎ 25 265) is on the lakeside 2km north of town.

The cheapest hotel is the *Agapi Inn* (☎ 20 541), Tsirigoti 6, near the bus station. Basic singles/doubles cost 5000/7000 dr. Next door is the *Hotel Paris*, which has more comfortable singles/doubles for 5500/8000 dr. There are *domatia* on the island.

There are several restaurants outside the entrance to the old town. *To Manteio Psistaria* is recommended.

Getting There & Away
Air Ioannina has two flights a day to Athens (18,100 dr) and a daily flight to Thessaloniki (11,800 dr).

Bus Services include 12 buses a day to Athens (7½ hours, 7000 dr), nine to Igoumenitsa, five to Thessaloniki and three to Trikala via Kalambaka. The road from Ioannina to Kalambaka across the Pindos mountains is one of Greece's most spectacular drives.

ZAGORIA & VIKOS GORGE
☎ 0653

The Zagoria (Ζαγώρια) region covers a large expanse of the Pindos mountains north of Ioannina. It's a wilderness of raging rivers, crashing waterfalls and deep gorges. Snowcapped mountains rise out of dense forests. The remote villages that dot the hillsides are famous for their impressive grey-slate architecture.

The fairytale village of **Monodendri** is the starting point for treks through the dramatic **Vikos Gorge**, with its awesome sheer limestone walls. It's a strenuous 7½-hour walk from Monodendri to the twin villages of **Megalo Papingo** and **Mikro Papingo**. The trek is very popular and the path is clearly marked. Ioannina's EOT office has information.

Other walks start from **Tsepelovo**, near Monodendri.

Places to Stay & Eat
There are some excellent places to stay, but none of them come cheap. The options in Monodendri include the lovely, traditional *Monodendri Pension & Restaurant* (☎ 71 300). Doubles are 8000 dr. The *Pension Gouris* (☎ 81 214) in Tsepelovohas is a delightful place with doubles for 9000 dr. The owner, Alexis, also runs a shop and restaurant and can advise on treks.

Xenonas tou Kouli (☎ 41 138) is one of several options in Megalo Papingo. Rates start at 10,000 dr for doubles. The owners are official EOS guides. The only rooms in Mikro Papingo are at *Xenonas Dias* (☎ 41 257), a beautifully restored mansion with doubles for 10,500 dr. It has an excellent restaurant specialising in charcoal grills.

Getting There & Away
Buses to the Zagoria leave from the main bus station in Ioannina. There are buses to Monodendri on weekdays at 6 am and 4.15 pm; to Tsepelovo on Monday, Wednesday and Friday at 6 am and 3 pm; and to the Papingo villages on Monday, Wednesday and Friday at 5.30 am and 2.30 pm.

TRIKALA Τρίκαλα
Trikala is a major transport hub, but otherwise has little of interest. Eight buses a day run between Trikala and Athens, (5½ hours, 5200 dr). There are also six buses a day to Thessaloniki, two to Ioannina and hourly buses to Kalambaka (for Meteora).

METEORA Μετέωρα
☎ 0432

Meteora is an extraordinary place. The massive, sheer columns of rock that dot the landscape were created by wave action millions of years ago. Perched precariously atop these seemingly inaccessible outcrops are monasteries that date back to the late 14th century.

Meteora is just north of the town of Kalambaka, on the Ioannina-Trikala road. The rocks behind the town are spectacularly floodlit at night. **Kastraki**, 2km from Kalambaka, is a charming village of red-tiled houses just west of the monasteries.

Things to See
There were once monasteries on each of the 24 pinnacles, but only five are still occupied. They are Megalou Meteorou (Metamorphosis, open from 9 am to 1 pm and 3 to 6 pm, closed Tuesday and Wednesday), Varlaam (open from 9 am to 1 pm and 3.30 to 6 pm, closed Friday), Agiou Stefanou (open daily from 9 am to 1 pm and 3 to 5 pm), Agias Triados (open daily from 9 am to 1 pm), Agiou Nikolaou (open daily from 9 am to 6 pm) and Agias Varvaras Rousanou (open from 9am to 1 pm and from 3.30 to 5 pm, closed Wednesday). Admission is 400 dr for each monastery; free for Greeks.

Meteora is best explored on foot, following the old paths where they exist. Allow a whole day to visit all of the monasteries and take food and water. Women must wear skirts that reach below their knees, men must wear long trousers, and arms must be covered.

Places to Stay & Eat
Kastraki is the best base for visiting Meteora. *Vrachos Camping* (☎ 22 293), on the edge of the village, is an excellent site.

There are dozens of *domatia* in town, charging from 4000/6000 dr for singles/doubles. The

GREECE

METEORA

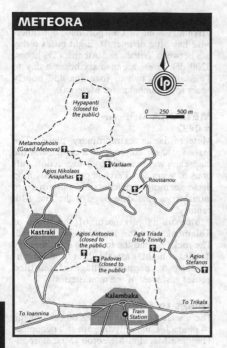

Hypapanti
(closed to
the public)

0   250   500 m

Metamorphosis
(Grand Meteora)

Varlaam

Agios Nikolaos
Anapafsas

Roussanou

Kastraki

Agios Antonios
(closed to
the public)

Agia Triada
(Holy Trinity)

Padovas
(closed to
the public)

Agios
Stefanos

Kalambaka

To Ioannina

To Trikala

Train
Station

Hotel Sydney (☎/fax 23 079), on the road into town from Kalambaka, has very comfortable doubles with bathroom for 9000 dr.

In Kalambaka, *Koka Roka Rooms* (☎ 24 554), at the beginning of the path to Agia Triada, is a popular travellers' place. Doubles with bath are 8000 dr; the taverna downstairs is good value. Telephone for a lift from the bus or train station.

Getting There & Away
Kalambaka is the hub of the transport network. There are frequent buses to Trikala and two a day to Ioannina. Local buses shuttle constantly between Kalambaka and Kastraki; five a day continue to Metamorphosis.

You can also get to Kalambaka by train. The town is the western terminus of the narrow-gauge line to Volos. There are connections with trains from Athens and Thessaloniki at Paleofarsalos (1¼ hours, 720 dr).

THESSALONIKI Θεσσαλονίκη
☎ 031
Thessaloniki, also known as Salonica, is Greece's second-largest city. It's a bustling, sophisticated place with good restaurants and a busy nightlife. It was once the second city of Byzantium, and there are some magnificent Byzantine churches, as well as a scattering of Roman ruins.

Orientation
Thessaloniki is laid out on a grid system. The main thoroughfares – Tsimiski, Egnatia and Agiou Dimitriou – run parallel to Nikis, on the waterfront. Plateias Eleftherias and Aristotelous, both on Nikis, are the main squares. The city's most famous landmark is the White Tower (no longer white) at the eastern end of Nikis.

The train station is on Monastiriou, the westerly continuation of Egnatia beyond Plateia Dimokratias, and the airport is 16km to the south-east. The old Turkish quarter is north of Athinas.

Information
Tourist Office The EOT office (☎ 271 888), at Plateia Aristotelous 8, is open Monday to Friday from 8 am to 8 pm, and Saturday from 8 am to 2 pm.

Money The National Bank of Greece and the Commercial Bank have branches on Plateia Dimokratias. American Express (☎ 269 521) has an office at Tsimiski 19.

Post & Communications The main post office is at Tsimiski 45 and the OTE telephone office is at Karolou Dil 27.

Cybercafés The most convenient of the city's several Internet cafés is the Cyber City Centre (☎ 532 311), near the port at Kalopothraki 12. An alternative is the Globus Internet Café (☎ 232 901), near the Roman Agora at Amynta 12.

Laundry Bianca Laundrette, just north of the Arch of Galerius on Antoniadou, charges 1400 dr to wash and dry a load.

Medical & Emergency Services There is a first-aid centre (☎ 530 530) at Navarhou Koundourioti 6. The tourist police (☎ 554 871) are at Dodekanisiou 4 on the 5th floor, open every day from 7.30 am to 11 pm.

Things to See
The **archaeological museum**, at the eastern end of Tsimiski, houses a superb collection of treasures from the royal tombs of Philip II. It is open on Monday from 12.30 to 8 pm, Tuesday to Friday from 8 am to 8 pm (5 pm in winter) and on weekends from 8 am to 7 pm; admission is 1500 dr.

The outstanding **Folkloric & Ethnological Museum of Macedonia**, at Vasilissis Olgas 68, includes traditional household utensils and northern Greek costumes. It's open every day, except Monday, from 8 am to 2.30 pm; admission is 200 dr.

Places to Stay
The *youth hostel* (☎ 225 946), Alex Svolou 44, has dorm beds for 2000 dr. The dorms are locked from 11 am to 6 pm, and there's a midnight curfew. An HI card is not required, but card-holders qualify for a 10% discount. To get there, take bus No 10 from outside the railway station to the Kamara stop.

The best budget hotel in town is the friendly, family-run *Hotel Acropol* (☎ 536 170), on Tantalidou, a quiet side street off Egnatia. The clean singles/doubles with shared bath are listed at 6000/9000 dr, but most of the time it charges a bargain 5000 dr per room. The *Hotel Atlantis* (☎ 540 131), Egnatia 14, has singles/doubles with shared bathroom for 6500/8000 dr. The rooms are tiny but clean.

The *Hotel Atlas* (☎ 537 046), Egnatia 40, has singles/doubles with shared bathroom for 6000/9000 dr and good doubles with bath for 12,000 dr. The rooms at the front get a lot of traffic noise. Just around the corner from the Atlas is the quiet *Hotel Averof* (☎ 538 498), Leontos Sofou 24. Pleasant singles/doubles with shared bath are 5000/8000 dr.

Rooms can be hard to find during the international trade fair in September.

Places to Eat
Ta Nea Ilysia, opposite the Hotel Averof on Leontos Sofou, is a popular place with main dishes priced from 1050 dr.

A place full of local colour is the lively *O Loutros Fish Taverna*, which occupies an old Turkish hammam near the flower market on Komninon. Most dishes cost from 2000 to 3000 dr. The place is always packed and there are often spontaneous renderings of rembetika.

Entertainment
Young people frequent the many bars along the waterfront before hitting the clubs. From October to May, the action is in town. You will find live bouzouki and folk music every night at *Show Avantaz*, opposite the Turkish consulate at Agiou Dimitriou 156. It opens at 11 pm.

A good area to check out is Ta Ladadika, near the ferry quay, where former shipping warehouses have been converted into numerous trendy cafés, bars and restaurants.

Getting There & Away
Air The airport is 16km to the south-east. There are six flights a day to Athens (21,7000 dr) and daily flights to Ioannina (11,800 dr), Lesvos (20,600 dr) and Limnos (14,900 dr). Other destinations include Iraklio and Rhodes. Olympic Airways (☎ 230 240) is at Nav Koundouriti 3. See the Getting There & Away section at the start of this chapter for information on international flights.

Bus There are several bus terminals, most of them near the train station. Buses to Athens, Igoumenitsa and Trikala leave from Monastiriou 65 & 67; buses to Alexandroupolis leave from Koloniari 17 – behind the train station; and buses to Olympia leave from Promitheos 10. Buses to the Halkidiki peninsula leave from Karakasi 68 (off the map in the eastern part of town; it's marked on the free EOT map). To reach the Halkidiki terminal, take local bus No 10 to the Botsari stop, near Odos Markou Botsari. The OSE has two buses a day to Athens from the train station, as well as international services to Istanbul, Sofia (Bulgaria) and Korça (Albania).

Train There are eight trains a day to Athens and five to Alexandroupolis. All international

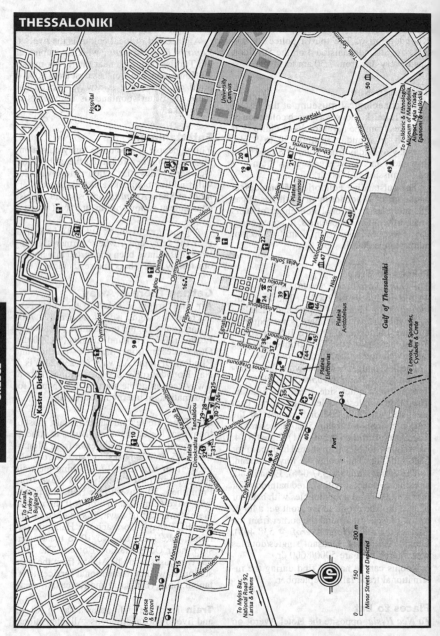

THESSALONIKI

Hospital

University Campus

Angelaki

To Folkloric & Ethnological
Museum of Macedonia,
Alipoti, Agia Triada,
Epanomi & Halkidiki

Ethnikis Amynis

Nik Germanou

Tris Septem...

50

49

48

47

21

Plateia
Navarinou

Syngrou

20

19

5
6

4

Athinas

Agiou Dimitriou

Iasonidou

Egnatia

Mitropoleos

Niki

Svolou

Agias Sofias

22

17

18

8

Olymbou

16

Filippou

Karolou Dil

24
23

39

Egnatia

Ermou

El Venizelou

Aristotelous

Komninon

45

46

Plateia
Aristotelous

Plateia
Eleftherias

Gulf of Thessaloniki

9

3

Olympiados

Plateia
Dimokratias

Tsimiski

37

44

36

35

Plateia
Eleftherias

To Levos, the Sporades,
Cyclades & Crete

Langada

Lagkada & Dimitriou

Tsimiski

Ionos Dragoumi

Tantalidou

25

29 28

30 27 26

31

32

Dodekanisou

Karipi

10

Monastiriou

33

34

Navarchou Koundourioti

Polytechniou

26 Oktovriou

To Kavala,
Turkey &
Bulgaria &
Evzoni

To Edessa
& Evzoni

Anagennisios

11

12

15

13

14

40

41

42

43

Port

St

To Mylos Bar,
National Road 92,
Larisa & Athens

Minor Streets not Depicted

0   150   300 m

Kastra District

GREECE

PLACES TO STAY		8	Church of Agios Dimitrios	31	Tourist Police
21	Youth Hostel	9	Ministry of Macedonia &	32	National Bank of Greece
25	Hotel Atlas		Thrace	33	Buses to Katerini & Litihoro
26	Hotel Averof	10	Church of the Dodeka	34	Olympic Airways
28	Hotel Atlantis		Apostoli	36	Molho English-Language
30	Hotel Acropol	11	Buses to Alexandroupolis		Bookshop
		12	Train Station	37	American Express
PLACES TO EAT		13	Airport Buses	39	Post Office
27	Ta Nea Ilysia	14	Buses to Ioannina	40	Hydrofoil Quay
35	Ta Ladadika	15	Buses to Athens, Igoumenitsa	41	Nomikos Lines
38	O Loutros Fish Taverna		& Trikala	42	First-Aid Centre
		16	Roman Agora	43	Ferry Quay
OTHER		17	Globus Internet Café	44	UK Consulate
1	Monastery of Vlatadon	18	Church of Panagia Ahiropitos	45	Cyber City Centre
2	Church of Osios David	19	Arch of Galerius	46	Tourist Office (EOT)
3	Church of Agia Ekaterini	20	Bianca Laundrette	47	Museum of the Macedonian
4	Church of Nikolaos Orfanos	22	Church of Agia Sofia		Struggle
5	Atatürk's House	23	OTE	48	US Consulate
6	Turkish Consulate	24	OSE Ticket Office	49	White Tower
7	Show Avantaz	29	Police Station	50	Archaeological Museum

trains from Athens stop at Thessaloniki. You can get more information from the OSE office at Aristotelous 18 or from the train station.

Ferry & Hydrofoil There's a Sunday ferry to Lesvos, Limnos and Chios throughout the year. In summer there are three ferries a week to Iraklio (Crete), stopping in the Sporades and the Cyclades on the way. Get your tickets from Nomikos Lines (☎ 524 544), Navarhou Koundourioti 8 – by the port. In summer there are hydrofoils most days to Skiathos, Skopelos and Alonnisos. Tickets can be bought from Egnatias Tours (☎ 223 811), Kambouniou 9.

Getting Around

To/From the Airport There is no bus service from the Olympic Airways office to the airport. Take bus No 78 from the train station (150 dr). A taxi from the airport costs about 2000 dr.

Bus There is a flat fare of 100 dr on city and suburban buses, paid either to a conductor at the rear door or to coin-operated machines on driver-only buses.

HALKIDIKI Χαλκιδική

Halkidiki is the three-pronged peninsula south-east of Thessaloniki. It's the main resort area of northern Greece, with superb sandy beaches right around its 500km of coastline. **Kassandra**, the south-western prong of the peninsula, has surrendered irrevocably to mass tourism. **Sithonia**, the middle prong, is not as over the top and has some spectacular scenery.

Mt Athos

Halkidiki's third prong is occupied by the all-male Monastic Republic of Mt Athos (also called the Holy Mountain), where monasteries full of priceless treasures stand amid an impressive landscape of gorges, wooded mountains and precipitous rocks.

To acquire a four-day visitor's permit to Mt Athos you must be male and have a letter of recommendation from your embassy or consulate. You take it to either the Ministry of Foreign Affairs, Zalokosta 2, Athens, or the Ministry of Macedonia & Thrace (☎ 257 010), Plateia Diikitirio, Thessaloniki, between 11 am and 1.45 pm, Monday to Friday. Thessaloniki's UK consulate (☎ 278 006), which also represents Australian, Canadian and New Zealand citizens, is at El

Venizelou 8, and the US consulate (☎ 242 905) is at Nikis 59. For more details, inquire at the EOT office. Armed with your permit, you can explore, on foot, the 20 monasteries and dependent religious communities of Mt Athos. You can stay only one night at each monastery.

MT OLYMPUS Ολυμπος Ορος
☎ 0352

Mt Olympus is Greece's highest and mightiest mountain. The ancients chose it as the abode of their gods and assumed it to be the exact centre of the Earth. Olympus has eight peaks, the highest of which is Mytikas (2917m). The area is popular with trekkers, most of whom use the village of **Litohoro** as a base. Litohoro is 5km inland from the Athens-Thessaloniki highway.

The EOS office (☎ 81 944) on Plateia Kentriki has information on the various treks and conditions. The office is open Monday to Friday from 9 am to 1 pm and 6 to 8.30 pm, and on Saturday from 9 am to 1 pm.

The main route to the top takes two days, overnighting at one of the refuges on the mountain. Good protective clothing is essential, even in summer.

Places to Stay & Eat
The cheapest rooms are at *Hotel Markesia* (☎ 81 831), Dionyssou 5, near Plateia Kentriki. It has clean singles/doubles with bathroom for 5500/6500 dr. It's open from June to October. At other times, try the cheery *Hotel Enipeas* (☎ 81 328) on Plateia Kentriki, where you'll find singles/doubles for 8000/10,000 dr. The *Olympos Taverna* on Agiou Nikolaou, serves standard fare at reasonable prices.

There are four *refuges* on the mountain at altitudes ranging from 270m to 930m. They are open from May to September.

Getting There & Away
There are eight buses a day to Litohoro from Thessaloniki and three from Athens (six hours, 7000 dr). There are frequent buses between Litohoro and the coastal village of Katerini.

ALEXANDROUPOLIS
Αλεξανδρούπολη
☎ 0551

Dusty Alexandroupolis doesn't have much going for it, but if you're going to Turkey or Samothraki, you may end up staying overnight here. There's a tourist office (☎ 24 998) in the town hall on Dimokratias.

Places to Stay & Eat
The nearest camping ground, *Camping Alexandroupolis* (☎ 28 735), is on the beach 2km west of town. Buses to Makri from Plateia Eleftherias, opposite the port, can drop you there. The *Hotel Lido* (☎ 28 808), one block north of the bus station at Paleologou 15, is a great budget option. Singles/doubles are 3500/4500 dr, or 6000/6500 dr with private bathroom. The *Hotel Okeanis* (☎ 28 830), almost opposite the Lido, has large, comfortable singles/doubles for 10,000/ 15,000 dr.

The *Neraida Restaurant*, on Kyprou, has a good range of local specialities priced from 1600 dr. Kyprou starts opposite the pier where ferries leave for Samothraki.

Getting There & Away
There is at least one flight a day to Athens (18,300 dr) from the airport 7km west of town. There are five trains (3000 dr) and five buses (5400 dr) a day to Thessaloniki. There's also a daily train and a daily OSE bus to Istanbul, as well as daily buses to Plovdiv and Sofia in Bulgaria.

In summer there are at least two boats a day to Samothraki (two hours, 2200 dr), dropping to one in winter. There are also hydrofoils to Chios, via Lesvos and Limnos.

Saronic Gulf Islands
Νησιά του Σαρωνικού

The Saronic Gulf islands are the closest island group to Athens. Not surprisingly they are a very popular escape for residents of the congested capital. Accommodation can be hard to find between mid-June and September, and on weekends all year round.

Getting There & Away

Ferries to all four islands, and hydrofoils to Aegina, leave from the Great Harbour in Piraeus. Hydrofoils to the other islands run from Zea Marina in Piraeus.

AEGINA Αίγινα
☎ 0297

Aegina is the closest island to Athens and a popular destination for day-trippers. Many make for the lovely **Temple of Aphaia**, a well-preserved Doric temple 12km east of Aegina town. It is open on weekdays from 8.15 am to 7 pm (5 pm in winter) and on weekends from 8.30 am to 3 pm. Admission is 800 dr. Buses from Aegina town to the small resort of **Agia Marina** can drop you at the site. Agia Marina has the best beach on the island, which isn't saying much.

Most travellers prefer to stay in Aegina town, where the *Hotel Plaza* (**☎** 25 600) has singles/doubles overlooking the sea for 4500/7500 dr.

POROS Πόρος

Poros is a big hit with the Brits, but it's hard to work out why. The beaches are nothing to write home about and there are no sites of significance. The main attraction is pretty Poros town, draped over the Sferia peninsula. Sferia is linked to the rest of the island, known as Kalavria, by a narrow isthmus. Most of the package hotels are here. There are a few *domatia* in Poros town, signposted off the road to Kalavria.

The island lies little more than a stone's throw from the mainland, opposite the Peloponnesian village of Galatas.

HYDRA Ύδρα
☎ 0298

Hydra is the island with the most style and is famous as the haunt of artists and jet-setters. Its gracious stone mansions are stacked up the rocky hillsides that surround the fine natural harbour. The main attraction is peace and quiet. There are no motorised vehicles on the island – apart from a garbage truck and a few construction vehicles.

Accommodation is expensive, but of a high standard. The cheapest rooms are at *Pension Theresia* (**☎** 53 983), which has quaint rooms around a leafy courtyard for 5000/8000 dr.

SPETSES Σπέτσες

Pine-covered Spetses is perhaps the most beautiful island in the group. It also has the best beaches, so it's packed with package tourists in summer. The **old harbour** in Spetses town is a delightful place to explore. The travel agents on the waterfront can organise accommodation.

Cyclades Κυκλάδες

The Cyclades, named after the rough circle they form around Delos, are quintessential Greek islands with brilliant white architecture, dazzling light and golden beaches.

Delos, historically the most important island of the group, is uninhabited. The inhabited islands of the archipelago are Mykonos, Syros, Tinos, Andros, Paros, Naxos, Ios, Santorini (Thira), Anafi, Amorgos, Sikinos, Folegandros and the tiny islands of Koufonisi, Shinoussa, Iraklia and Donoussa, which lie east of Naxos. The remaining six – Kea, Kythnos, Serifos, Sifnos, Kimolos and Milos – are referred to as the Western Cyclades.

Some of the Cyclades, like Mykonos, Paros and Santorini, have vigorously embraced the tourist industry, filling their coastlines with discos and bars, and their beaches with sun lounges, umbrellas and water-sports equipment for hire. But others, like Anafi, Sikinos and the tiny islands east of Naxos, are little more than clumps of rock, each with a village, a few secluded coves – and very few tourists.

To give even the briefest rundown on every island is impossible in a single chapter. The following gives information on a cross section of the islands, from those with packed beaches and a raucous nightlife, to those off the tourist circuit, where tranquillity and glimpses of a fast-dying, age-old way of life await the visitor.

History

The Cyclades enjoyed a flourishing Bronze Age civilisation (3000 to 1100 BC), more or less concurrent with the Minoan civilisation.

GREECE

By the 5th century BC, the island of Delos had been taken over by Athens, which kept its treasury there.

Between the 4th and 7th centuries AD, the islands, like the rest of Greece, suffered a series of invasions and occupations. During the Middle Ages they were raided by pirates – hence the labyrinthine character of their towns, which was meant to confuse attackers. On some islands the whole population would move into the mountainous interior to escape the pirates, while on others they would brave it out on the coast. This is why on some islands the hora (main town) is on the coast and on others it is inland.

The Cyclades became part of independent Greece in 1827.

Orientation & Information

The islands lie in the central Aegean, southeast of Athens and north of Crete. In July, August and September the Cyclades are prone to the *meltemi*, a ferocious north-easterly wind which sends everything flying and disrupts ferry schedules.

Getting There & Away

Air Mykonos and Santorini have international airports that receive charter flights from northern Europe. There are daily flights from Athens to Milos, Naxos, Paros, Mykonos and Santorini. In addition there are direct flights between Santorini and Mykonos. Both islands have direct connections with Rhodes.

Boat Most islands are served by daily boats from Piraeus, but in winter, services are severely curtailed. A daily ferry travels between Mykonos, Paros, Naxos, Ios and Santorini. In summer, hydrofoils and catamarans link Paros, Naxos, Syros, Tinos, Ios, Santorini and Crete. Bear in mind, particularly if you're visiting a remote island, that ferries are prone to delays and cancellations.

Getting Around

Most islands have buses that link the port with villages on the island. On many islands *caïques* (fishing boats) connect the port with popular beaches.

Santorini, Paros, Naxos, Ios, Milos and Mykonos have car-rental firms. Most islands

have motorcycle and moped-rental places, and some also have bicycles for rent.

Most islands are crisscrossed by donkey tracks, which are great to walk along.

NAXOS Νάξος
☎ 0285

Naxos is the island where Theseus disloyally dumped Ariadne after she helped him to slay the Minotaur (half-bull, half-man) on the island of Crete. She gave him the thread that enabled him to find his way out of the Minotaur's labyrinth once he had killed the monster.

Naxos, the greenest and most beautiful island of the archipelago, is popular but big enough to allow you to escape the hordes.

Orientation & Information

Naxos town, on the west coast, is the island's capital and port. There is no EOT, but the privately owned Naxos Tourist Information Centre (☎ 24 358; fax 25 200) opposite the quay makes up for this, thanks to the inimitable English-speaking Despina. Luggage storage is 400 dr, and the office is open daily from 8 am to midnight. To find the OTE, turn right from the quay and it's on the waterfront, 150m past the National Bank of Greece. The post office is three blocks further on.

Things to See

Naxos Town The winding alleyways of Naxos town, lined with immaculate white-washed houses, clamber up to the crumbling 13th-century kastro walls. The well-stocked archaeological museum is here, housed in a former school where Nikos Kazantzakis was briefly a pupil. The museum is open Tuesday to Sunday from 8.30 am to 3 pm; admission is 600 dr.

Beaches After the town beach of Agios Georgios, sandy beaches – which become progressively less crowded – continue southwards as far as Pyrgaki Beach.

Apollonas On the north coast, Apollonas has a rocky beach and a pleasant sheltered bay. If you're curious about the *kouros* statues, you can see the largest one, 10.5m long, just outside of Apollonas, lying aban-

NAXOS & THE MINOR ISLANDS

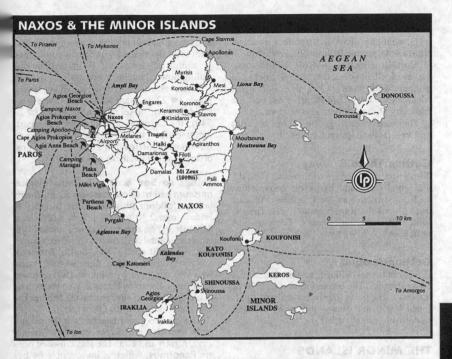

doned and unfinished in an ancient marble quarry. There are two more in the Melanes region.

It's worth taking the bus or driving from Naxos town to Apollonas for the spectacular scenery. The road winds its way through the Tragaea, gradually climbing through increasingly dramatic mountainscapes before descending to the lush valley of Apollonas.

Tragaea This gorgeous region is a vast Arcadian olive grove with Byzantine churches and tranquil villages. **Filoti**, the largest settlement, perches on the slopes of **Mt Zeus** (1004m). It takes three hours to climb the trail to the summit.

Filoti is also a good base from which to explore the region. A new asphalt road leads from the village to the picturesque and isolated hamlets of **Damarionas** and **Damalas**. From Damalas it is a short walk to the village

of **Halki**, where another dirt road leads to the twin hamlets of **Khimaros** and **Tsikalario**.

Another village, **Apiranthos**, has many old houses of uncharacteristically bare stone, and some of the women who live here still weave on looms and wear traditional costumes.

Places to Stay & Eat

Naxos' three camping grounds are *Camping Naxos* (☎ 23 500), 1km south of Agios Georgios beach; *Camping Maragas* (☎ 24 552), Agia Anna beach; and *Camping Apollon* (☎ 24 417), 700m from Agios Prokopios beach. All are open from May to October.

Dionyssos Youth Hostel (☎ 26 123) is the best budget choice, with dorm beds for 1500 dr, doubles/triples with private bath for 4000/5000 dr and cooking facilities for guests. It is signposted from Agiou Nikodemou, also known as Market Street. Book through Naxos Tourist Information Centre. The pleasant *Hotel Anixis* (☎/fax 22 112), close by, has doubles/triples with private bath for 9000/10,000 dr. The *Okeanis Hotel* (☎ 22 931), near the quay, has spotless doubles/triples with private bath for 7000/8000 dr.

Manolis Garden, just off Nikodemou, serves excellent Greek fare such as chicken in yoghurt and wine (1300 dr). For great Mexican food, try *Café Picasso*, just past the cemetery at the southern end of town.

There are bakeries, grocery shops and fruit and vegetable shops on Market St.

Getting There & Away

Naxos has daily ferries to Piraeus (4700 dr) and good ferry and hydrofoil connections with most islands in the Cyclades. At least once a week there are boats to Crete, Thessaloniki, Rhodes and Samos. For the port police, call ☎ 22 300.

Getting Around

Buses run to most villages and the beaches as far as Pyrgaki. The bus terminal is in front of the quay. There are four buses daily to Apollonas (1050 dr). Naxos has many car and motorcycle-rental outlets.

THE MINOR ISLANDS

The Minor Islands are a string of tiny islands off the east coast of Naxos. Of the seven, only Koufonisi, Donoussa, Shinoussa and Iraklia are inhabited. They see few tourists, and have few amenities, but each has some domatia. They are served by two or three ferries a week from Piraeus via Naxos, some of which continue to Amorgos.

MYKONOS & DELOS

It is difficult to imagine two islands less alike than Mykonos and Delos, yet the two are inextricably linked.

Mykonos Μύκονος
☎ 0289

Many visitors to Mykonos wouldn't know a Doric column from an Ionic column and couldn't care less, for Mykonos has become the St Tropez of Greece, the most visited island, and the one with the most sophisticated – and most expensive – nightlife.

Orientation & Information The capital and port is Mykonos town – an elaborate tableau of chic boutiques, chimerical houses with brightly painted wooden balconies, and geraniums, clematis and bougainvillea cascading down dazzling white walls.

There is no tourist office. The tourist police (☎ 22 482) are at the port, in the same building as the hotel reservation office (☎ 24 540), the association of rooms and apartments office (☎ 26 860), and the camping information office (☎ 22 852). The post office is at the southern end of town.

Things to See & Do The archaeological museum and nautical museum are mediocre, but the folklore museum (open Monday to Friday from 2.30 to 9.30 pm, Saturday from 4.30 to 9.30 pm; free entry) is well stocked with local memorabilia. Exhibits include reconstructions of traditional homes, and a somewhat macabre stuffed pelican, the erstwhile Petros, who was run over by a car in 1985. He was hastily supplanted by Petros II, who you will no doubt meet if you loiter around the fish market. The museum is near the Delos quay.

The most popular beaches are the mainly nude Paradise and Super Paradise (mainly gay), Agrari and Elia. The less crowded ones are Panormos, which is inaccessible by bus or caïque but can be walked to from the inland village of Ano Mera, and Kato Livadi, which you can walk to from Elia Beach.

Places to Stay *Paradise Beach Camping* (☎ 22 852; fax 24 350; Paradise@paradise .myk.forthnet.gr) charges 1700 dr per person and 1000 dr per tent. Two-person beach cabins with shared facilities are available for 9000 dr; cabins for four with private bath cost 18,000 dr. There is another camping ground, *Mykonos Camping* (☎ 24 578), near Platys Gialos beach. Minibuses meet the ferries and there are regular buses into town.

Rooms fill up quickly in summer, so it's prudent to succumb to the first domatia owner who accosts you.

The D-class *Hotel Carboni* (☎ 22 217), on Andronikou Matogianni, has doubles/triples with private bath for 10,000/13,000 dr. Close by, *Rooms Chez Maria* (☎ 22 480) has attractive doubles/triples with private bath for 12,000/15,000 dr.

MYKONOS

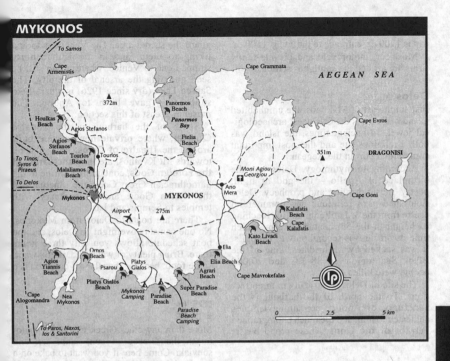

Places to Eat *Niko's Taverna*, near the Delos quay, and *Ta Kiopia*, opposite, are both popular. *Sesame Kitchen*, next to the maritime museum, serves a variety of vegetarian dishes. For great fajitas have a splurge at *La Mexicana*.

Entertainment The *Down Under* bar, run by Australian Theo, is the cheapest, with beers at 500 dr. The nearby *Scandinavian Bar* is also popular. *Rhapsody* in Little Venice plays jazz and blues. Next door, *Montparnasse Piano Bar* plays classical music at sunset.

Club Paradiso, 300m above Paradise Beach, has all-night raves starting at 3 am. Entry is 5000 dr.

Gay & Lesbian Venues *Porta*, *Kastro Bar*, *Icaros* and *Manto* are popular gay and lesbian haunts. *Pierro's* is the place for late-night dancing.

Getting There & Away Flights from Mykonos to Athens cost 18,800 dr, to Santorini 15,100 dr, and to both Rhodes and Crete 22,600 dr. The Olympic Airways office (☎ 22 490) is on Plateia Louka, by the south bus station.

There are many ferries daily to Mykonos and onwards from Piraeus (4800 dr) and Rafina (3990 dr). From Mykonos there are weekly services to Crete, the North-Eastern Aegean and the Dodecanese. For the port police, call ☎ 22 218.

Getting Around The north bus station is near the port, behind the OTE office. It serves Agios Stefanos, Elia, Kalafatis and Ano Mera. The south bus station serves Agios Yiannis, Psarou, Platys Gialos and Paradise Beach.

Super Paradise, Agrari and Elia beaches are served by caïque from Mykonos town, but easier access to these and Paradise Beach is by caïque from Platys Gialos.

GREECE

Excursion boats leave for Delos between 8 and 10 am daily except Monday. The round-trip is 1700 dr; entrance to the site is 1500 dr.

Most car, motorcycle and bicycle-rental firms are around the south bus station.

Delos Δήλος

Just south-east of Mykonos, the uninhabited island of Delos is the Cyclades' archaeological jewel. In ancient times, the island was both a religious site and the most important commercial port in the Aegean.

According to mythology, Delos was the birthplace of Apollo – the god of light, poetry, music, healing and prophecy. Delos flourished as a religious and commercial centre from the 3rd millennium BC, reaching its height in the 5th century BC, by which time its oracle was second only to Delphi's. It was sacked by Mithridates, king of the Black Sea region, in 88 BC and 20,000 people were killed.

The site of Delos is basically in three sections. To the north of the harbour is the **Sanctuary of Apollo**, containing temples dedicated to him, and the much photographed **Terrace of the Lions**. These proud beasts were carved in the 4th century BC from marble from Naxos, and their function was to guard the sacred area. The Venetians took a liking to them, and in the 17th century shipped one to Venice, where it can still be seen guarding the arsenal of the city. The **Sacred Lake** (dry since 1926) is where Leto supposedly gave birth to Apollo. The museum is east of this section.

South of the harbour is the **Theatre Quarter**, where private houses were built around the **Theatre of Delos**. East of here, towards Mt Kynthos, are the **Sanctuaries of the Foreign Gods**, containing a shrine to the Samothracian Great Gods, the sanctuary of the Syrian Gods, and a sanctuary with temples to Serapis and Isis.

There are boats to Delos from Mykonos. No one can stay overnight on Delos, and the boat schedule allows you only three hours there. Bring plenty of water and, if you want, some food, because the island's cafeteria is a rip-off.

IOS Ιος
☎ 0286

More than any other Greek island, Ios epitomises the Greece of sun, sand, sex and souvlaki. Come here if you want to bake on a beach all day and drink all night. Young people hang out in the village, where the nightlife is. The older set tends to stay in the port.

Places to Stay & Eat

Far Out Camping (☎ 91 468), on Milopotas beach, is a seriously slick operation, attracting up to 2000 people a night in summer. It costs 1200 dr per person a site; tents can be hired for 400 dr. Basic bungalows with mattresses cost 2500 dr per person; bungalows with double and single beds cost 3500 dr per person. There are email facilities for guests.

There is a wonderful view of the bay from *Francesco's* (☎/fax 91 223; fragesco@ otenet.gr), in the village. Dorm beds cost 2300 dr; doubles/triples with private bath are 6000/8000 dr. It's a lively meeting place with a bar and terrace.

Zorba's Restaurant, *Taverna Lord Byron*, *Pithari Taverna*, and *Pinocchios* – all located in the village – are the most popular eateries.

DELOS

To Stadium

Gymnasium

To Mykonos

AEGEAN SEA

Sacred Lake

Ekati

Museum

Mt Kynthos (113m)

Renia

Sacred Harbour

Sanctuary of Apollo

Delos

Commercial Harbour

To Mykonos

Sanctuaries of the Foreign gods

Theatre Quarter

Harbour Quarter

Mt Kynthos (113m)

0   100   200 m

0   1   2 km

IOS

AEGEAN
SEA

Cape Karatza

Plakotos

417m

Homer's
Tomb

514m

Agia
Theodoti
Beach

Koumbara
Beach

Paleokastro
Ruins

Psathí
Beach

Gialos

Steps to
Village

Valmas
Beach

Ios

IOS

Moni
Kalamou

Cape
Pountas

Milopotas
Beach

713m

To Naxos
Paros, Sifnos
& Piraeus

Kolitzani
Beach

Plakes
Bay

Klima
Bay

Kalamos
Beach

To Sikinos

Cape
Fidias

Cape Achlades

Manganari
Beach

0   2   4 km

To Santorini & Crete

Getting There & Away

Ios has daily connections with Piraeus (5400
dr) and there are frequent hydrofoils and
ferries to the major Cycladic islands. For the
port police call ☎ 91 381.

PAROS Πάρος
☎ 0284

Physically, Paros is 16km from Naxos, but
metaphysically it hovers somewhere between
Ios and Mykonos. It's popular with backpackers who crave style but can't afford
Mykonos. Like Mykonos, it's also popular
with gay travellers. Paros is famous for its
pure white marble – no less than the *Venus de
Milo* herself was created from it.

Paros is an attractive island, although less
dramatically so than Naxos. Its softly con-
toured and terraced hills culminate in one
central mountain, Profitis Ilias. It has some of
the finest beaches in the Cyclades.

The small island of Antiparos (Αντίπαρος)
lies 1km east of Paros. The two were originally joined, but were split by an earthquake
many millennia ago.

Orientation & Information

Paros' main town and port is Parikia, on the
west coast. The OTE is on the south-west
waterfront; turn right from the ferry pier. The
post office is also on the waterfront, but to the
north of the pier.

There is a cybercafé on Market Street, the
main commercial thoroughfare running
south-west from the main square, Plateia
Mavrogenous.

Things to See & Do

One of the most notable churches in Greece
is Parikia's **Panagia Ekatontapyliani**, which
features a beautiful, highly ornate interior.

Petaloudes, 8km from Parikia, is better
known as the Valley of the Butterflies. In
summer, huge swarms of the creatures almost
conceal the copious foliage.

The charming village of **Naoussa**, filled
with white houses and labyrinthine alleyways, is still a working fishing village,
despite an enormous growth in tourism over
the last few years.

Parikia's beaches are disappointing. Take
a caïque to a nearby beach or try Naoussa,
which has good beaches served by caïque.
Most popular are **Kolimvythres**, with bizarre
rock formations, **Monastiri**, a mainly nude
beach, and **Santa Maria**, which is good for
windsurfing.

Paros' longest beach, **Hrysi Akti** (Golden
Beach) on the south coast, is popular with
windsurfers.

The picturesque villages of **Lefkes**,
Marmara and **Marpissa** are all worth a visit.
The Moni Agiou Antoniou (Monastery of St
Anthony), on a hill above Marpissa, offers
breathtaking views. From Lefkes, an ancient
Byzantine path leads in one hour of easy
walking to the village of Prodromos, from
where it is a short walk to either Marmara or
Marpissa.

Antiparos This small island, less than 2km
from Paros, has superb beaches, but is becoming too popular for its own good. The
permanent inhabitants live in an attractive
village (also called Antiparos), but it's hidden
by all the tourist accommodation.

One of the chief attractions in Antiparos is
the cave, considered one of Europe's most
beautiful (open from 10 am to 4 pm daily in

GREECE

PAROS & ANTIPAROS

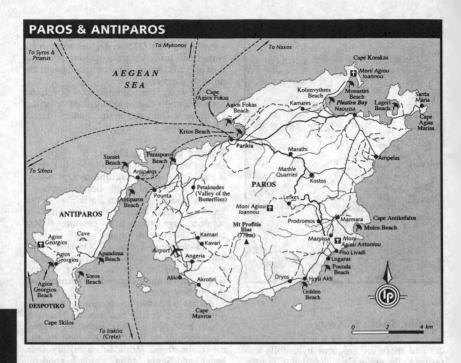

summer only). Despite indiscriminate looting of stalagmites and stalactites in times gone by, it still has a profusion of them. Entry is 500 dr.

Places to Stay

Paros has five camping grounds. *Koula Camping* (☎ 22 081), *Parasporas* (☎ 22 268) and *Krios Camping* (☎ 21 705) are near Parikia. *Naoussa Camping* (☎ 51 595) and *Surfing Beach* (☎ 52 013) are near Naoussa.

Antiparos has one camping ground, *Antiparos Camping* (☎ 61 221), on Agios Giannis Theologos Beach.

Rooms Mike (☎ 22 856) is deservedly popular with backpackers. Doubles/triples cost 7000/9000 dr, with use of a small kitchen and a roof terrace. To get there, walk 50m left from the pier and you'll find it next to the Memphis bar. Around the corner, above Taverna Parikia, Mike also has self-contained studios for 8000/10,000 dr. *Hotel Kypreou*

(☎ 21 383) has doubles/triples with private bath for 7000/10,000 dr; turn left from the pier and it's on the first street to the right.

Places to Eat

No matter how late you arrive, *To Proto*, 50m to the right from the pier, is usually open, serving fast food from 400 dr. *Taverna Parikia* has excellent daily specials at very reasonable prices.

Getting There & Away

Flights from Athens cost 18,600 dr. Paros is a major transport hub for ferries. Daily connections with Piraeus take seven hours and cost 4700 dr. There are frequent ferries to Naxos, Ios, Santorini and Mykonos, and less frequent ones to Amorgos and Astypalea, then across to the Dodecanese and the North-Eastern Aegean. In summer there are hourly excursion boats to Antiparos. For the port police call ☎ 21 240.

Getting Around

The bus station is 100m north of the tourist office. There are frequent buses to Aliki, Naoussa, Lefkes, Piso Livadi and Hrysi Akti. For Petaloudes take the Aliki bus.

There are many car and motorcycle-rental outlets.

FOLEGANDROS & SIKINOS

☎ 0286

Of these two sparsely populated islands, Sikinos (Σίκινος) is the less visited – you could be the only visitor during the low season. The port of Alopronia and the capital, Sikinos town, both have domatia and tavernas. The island also has several good beaches.

Folegandros (Φολέγανδρος) has become too popular in recent years and is no longer an island where you can get away from it all. Even so, it is considerably quieter than the major islands in the Cyclades and has a dramatic landscape, with the hora perched precariously on top of a sheer cliff. *Livadi Camping* (☎ 41 204) on Livadi Beach has good facilities. *Pavlos' Rooms* (☎ 41 232), are comfortable converted stables on the hora's main road. Doubles with/without private bath are 13,000/10,000 dr.

Getting There & Away

There are three ferries a week between Sikinos (6000 dr), Folegandros (5200 dr) and Piraeus, either via Milos, Kythnos and Serifos or via Santorini, Ios, Paros and Naxos. At least once a week there is a hydrofoil service. For the port police on Sikinos, call ☎ 51 222. On Folegandros, call ☎ 41 249.

SANTORINI (THIRA)

Σαντορίνη (Θήρα)

☎ 0286

Around 1450 BC, the volcanic heart of Santorini exploded and sank, leaving an extraordinary landscape. Today the startling sight of the malevolently steaming core almost encircled by sheer cliffs remains. It's possible that the catastrophe destroyed the Minoan civilisation, but neither this theory nor the claim that the island was part of the lost continent of Atlantis have been proven.

Since ancient times the Atlantis legend has fired the imaginations of writers, scientists and mystics, all of whom depict it as an advanced society destroyed by a volcanic eruption. Egyptian papyruses have been found which tell of a cataclysmic event which destroyed such a civilisation, but they place it farther west than the Aegean. Solon, the 6th-century BC Athenian ruler, related that on his visit to Egypt he was told of a continent destroyed 9000 years before his birth. Believers say he merely made a mathematical error and that he meant 900 years, which would correspond with the Santorini eruption. Plato firmly believed in the existence of Atlantis and depicted it as a land of art, flowers and fruit, and the frescoes from Akrotiri bear this out.

Orientation & Information

The capital, Fira, perches on top of the caldera on the west coast. The port of Athinios is 12km away. There is no EOT or tourist police, but the exceptionally helpful Dakoutros Travel Agency (☎ 22 958; fax 22 686) gives advice, sells boat tickets, arranges accommodation and changes currency. It is open from 9 am to 9 pm every day. Facing north, turn right at the Commercial Bank on the main square (Plateia Theotokopoulou).

Things to See & Do

Fira The commercialism of Fira has not reduced its all-pervasive dramatic aura. The **Megaron Gyzi Museum**, behind the Catholic monastery, houses local memorabilia, including fascinating photographs of Fira before and immediately after the 1956 earthquake. It's open Monday to Saturday from 10.30 am to 1 pm and from 5 to 8 pm; Sunday from 10.30 am to 4.30 pm. Admission is 400 dr. The **archaeological museum**, opposite the cable-car station, houses finds from ancient Akrotiri and ancient Thira. Opening times are Tuesday to Sunday from 8.30 am to 3 pm; admission is 800 dr.

Ancient Sites Excavations in 1967 uncovered the remarkably well preserved Minoan settlement of **Akrotiri**. There are remains of two and three-storey buildings, and evidence of a sophisticated drainage system. The site is

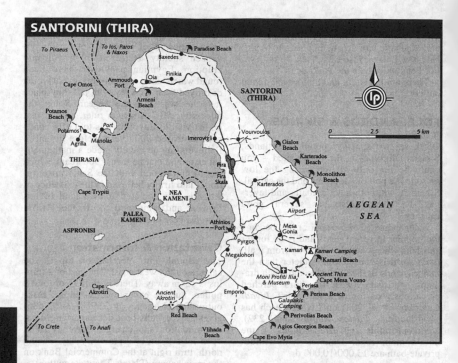

SANTORINI (THIRA)

open Tuesday to Sunday from 8.30 am to 3 pm; admission is 1200 dr.

Less impressive than Akrotiri, the site of **ancient Thira** is still worth a visit for the stunning views. The **Moni Profiti Ilia**, built on the island's highest point, can be reached along a path from ancient Thira.

Beaches Santorini's beaches are of black volcanic sand which becomes unbearably hot, making a beach mat essential. Kamari and Perissa get crowded, whereas those near Oia and Monolithos are quieter.

Other Attractions From Imerovigli, just north of Santorini, a 12km coastal path leads to the picturesque village of **Oia**. On a clear day there are breathtaking views of Folegandros and Sikinos. Oia is built on a steep slope of the caldera, and many of its traditional white Cycladic houses nestle in niches hewn from the volcanic rock.

Of the surrounding islets, only **Thirasia** is inhabited. At Palia Kameni you can bathe in hot springs, and on Nea Kameni you can clamber around on volcanic lava.

Places to Stay

Beware of the aggressive accommodation owners who meet boats and buses and claim that their rooms are in Fira when in fact they're in Karterados. Ask to see a map.

Camping Santorini (☎ 22 944), 1km east of the main square, has many facilities including a restaurant and swimming pool. The cost is 1300 dr per person and 800 dr per tent.

There are plenty of rooms to rent near the main square and on the road running east towards Camping Santorini, but they are best avoided by non-partygoers. The massive *Thira Hostel* (☎ 23 864), 200m north of the square, is a great place to meet people and sleeps as many as 145. It has a variety of small dorms with up to 10 beds for 2000 dr per person, plus doubles/triples with private bath for 6000/8000 dr. It also has a very cheap restaurant.

Rooms to Let Theoni (☎ 25 143), has a stunning view of the caldera and there's a real bargain to be had with the seven-person dorm for 25,000 dr. Doubles/triples cost 12,000/15,000 dr. To find it, walk to the caldera from the square, bear right until you pass the *Tropical* bar, hang an immediate left and look for the blue staircase.

A short walk north-east of the centre of town will take you to a quiet rural area with plenty of domatia. *Rena Kavallari Rooms* charges 10,000/12,000 dr for doubles/triples, *Pension Horizon* charges 11,000/13,000 and *Villa Gianna* – which has a pool – charges 14,000/16,800. All have private bath and balcony. To book, ring Dakoutros Travel (see Orientation and Information).

The same agent has properties in Oia on its books; most are in traditional houses with fine views. Double studios cost from 18,000 dr; a house for four from 35,000 dr.

Places to Eat

The Toast Club, on the square, is a fast-food operation and a favourite with backpackers. For the best American breakfast in town, head 125m north to *Mama's Café*. A *Mama's Special* costs 1150 dr. At night it becomes the *Cylades* restaurant, with serious portions of exceptionally good food from 1200 dr. *Restaurant Stamna*, towards the square from Dakoutros Travel, has daily specials for 1500 dr including a Greek salad.

There's a supermarket just north of the square.

Getting There & Away

Air Flights cost 21,900 dr to Athens, 15,100 dr to Mykonos and Crete and 22,600 dr to Rhodes. The Olympic Airways office (☎ 22 493) is 200m south of the hospital.

Ferry The daily ferries to Piraeus cost 5870 dr and take 10 hours. There are frequent connections with Crete, Ios, Paros and Naxos. Ferries travel less frequently to/from Anafi, Sikinos, Folegandros, Sifnos, Serifos, Kimolos, Milos, Karpathos and Rhodes. For the port police call ☎ 22 239.

Getting Around

There are daily boats from Athinios and the old port to Thirasia and Oia. The other islands surrounding Santorini can only be visited on excursions from Fira; volcano tours start from 1500 dr. A full-day Akrotiri tour costs around 5500 dr and sunset tours around 3500 dr. Check out the *Calypso*; one of only two glass-bottom boats in Greece.

Large ferries use Athinios port, where they are met by buses. Small boats use Fira Scala, which is served by donkey or cable car from Fira (800 dr each); otherwise it's a clamber up 600 steps. The cable car runs every 20 minutes from 6.40 am to 9 pm.

The bus station is just south of the main square. Buses go to Oia, Kamari, Perissa, Akrotiri and Monolithos frequently. Port buses leave Fira, Kamari and Perissa 90 minutes before ferry departures.

Car & Motorcycle Fira has many car and motorcycle-rental firms.

ANAFI Ανάφη
☎ 0286

Tiny Anafi, lying east of Santorini, is almost entirely overlooked by travellers – the island's amenities are limited and its ferry links with other islands are tenuous. It's a pristine island untainted by concessions to tourism. If you visit, be aware that the island has limited resources. The few tavernas will prevent you from starving but don't expect a wide choice. Take some food along and go easy with the water.

One or two boats a week from Piraeus (6670 dr) call in at Anafi via Paros, Naxos, Ios and Santorini.

Crete Κρήτη

Crete, Greece's largest island, has the dubious distinction of playing host to a quarter of all visitors to Greece. You can escape the hordes by visiting the undeveloped west coast, going into the rugged mountainous interior, or staying in one of the villages of the Lassithi Plateau which, when the tour buses depart, return to rural tranquillity.

GREECE

Blessed with an auspicious climate and fertile soil, Crete is Greece's cornucopia, producing the country's widest variety of crops.

As well as water sports, Crete has many opportunities for superb trekking and climbing. It is also the best place in Greece for buying high-quality, inexpensive leather goods.

History

The island was the birthplace of Minoan culture, Europe's first advanced civilisation, which flourished from 2800 to 1450 BC. The palace of Knossos, discovered at the beginning of this century, gives clues to the advanced nature of Minoan culture. They were literate – their first script resembled Egyptian hieroglyphs, which progressed to a syllable-based script called Linear A (still undeciphered).

In the ruins, archaeologists also found clay tablets with Linear B inscriptions, the form of writing used by the Mycenaeans, which suggests that Mycenaean invaders may have conquered the island, perhaps around 1500 BC.

Later, Crete passed from the warlike Dorians to the Romans, and then to the Genoese, who in turn sold it to the Venetians. Under the Venetians, Crete became a refuge for artists, writers and philosophers who fled Constantinople after it fell to the Turks. Their influence inspired the young Cretan painter Domenikos Theotokopoulos, who moved to Italy and there won immortality as the great El Greco.

The Turks finally conquered Crete in 1670. It became a British protectorate in 1898 after a series of insurrections and was united with independent Greece in 1913. There was fierce fighting during WWII when a German airborne invasion defeated Allied forces in the 10-day Battle of Crete. An active resistance movement drew heavy reprisals from the German occupiers.

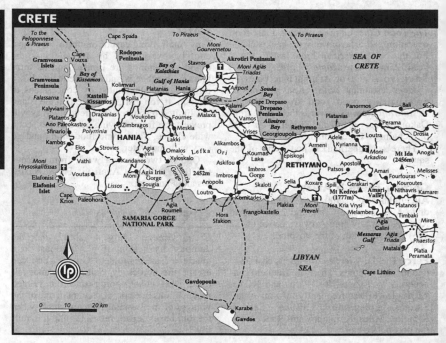

Orientation & Information

Crete is divided into four prefectures: Hania, Rethymno, Iraklio and Lassithi. All of Crete's large towns are on the north coast, and it's here that the package tourist industry thrives. Most of Crete's towns have tourist offices.

Getting There & Away

Air The international airport is at Iraklio, Crete's capital city. Hania and Sitia have domestic airports. There are several flights a day from Athens to Iraklio and Hania, and in summer there are three a week to Sitia. From Thessaloniki there are daily flights to Iraklio and two a week to Hania. There are daily flights to Rhodes from Iraklio and several flights a week in high season to Mykonos and Santorini. In summer, Kassos and Karpathos are served by one flight a week from Sitia.

Ferry Kastelli-Kissamos, Rethymno, Hania, Iraklio, Agios Nikolaos and Sitia have ferry ports. Ferries travel most days to Piraeus from Hania (5800 dr), Rethymno and Iraklio (6750 dr); less frequently from Agios Nikolaos and Sitia (7400 dr). There are at least three boats a week from Iraklio to Santorini

Regular ferries from Iraklio serve the Cyclades. There's at least one ferry a week to Rhodes (6200 dr) via Kassos and Karpathos and in season at least two a week from Agios Nikolaos to Rhodes via Sitia, Kassos and Karpathos. In summer, a weekly boat sails from Iraklio to Cyprus via Rhodes and on to Israel.

Hydrofoil At the time of writing, the hydrofoil service linking Iraklio with Santorini, Ios, Naxos and Paros had ceased.

Getting Around

Frequent buses run between towns on the north coast, and less frequently to the south coast and mountain villages. Parts of the

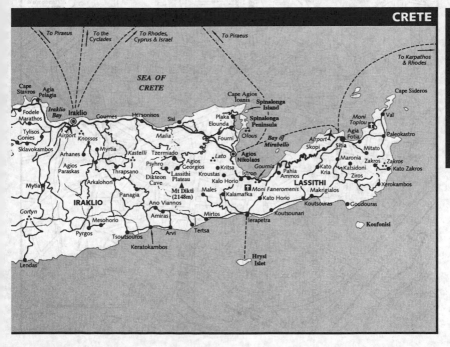

south coast are without roads, so boats are used to connect villages.

IRAKLIO Ηράκλειο
☎ 081
Iraklio, Crete's capital, lacks the charm of Rethymno or Hania, its old buildings swamped by modern apartment blocks. Yet its neon-lit streets do exude a certain dynamism.

Orientation & Information
Iraklio's two main squares are Venizelou and Eleftherias. Dikeosynis and Dedalou run between them, and 25 Avgoustou is the main thoroughfare leading from the waterfront to Venizelou. The EOT (☎ 22 8225), open weekdays from 8 am to 2.30 pm, and Olympic Airways (☎ 22 9191) are on Plateia Eleftherias. There is a laundrette and left-luggage storage at Handakos 18 (☎ 28 0858), open from 7.30 am to 9 pm. Lockers cost 400 dr per person.

Money Most of the city's banks are on 25 Avgoustou, but none open in the afternoon or on weekends. The American Express representative is at 25 Avgoustou 23.

IRAKLIO

SEA OF CRETE

To Fort

Old Harbour

New Harbour

Quay

To Camp Sites at Hersonisos & Agios Nikolaos

El Greco Park

Plateia Venizelou

To Hania Gate, Buses to Western Crete, University Hospital at Voutes, Rethymno & Hania

Plateia Eleftherias

To Airport

Plateia Kornarou

Plateia Kiprou

To Air Greece Office & Knossos

0   125   250 m

Post & Communications The central post office is on Plateia Daskalogiani, and opening hours are Monday to Friday from 7.30 am to 8 pm. The OTE, on Theotoko-poulou, just north of Plateia El Greco, is open daily from 6 am to 11 pm.

Medical & Emergency Services The University Hospital (☎ 39 111) at Voutes, 5km south of Iraklio, is the city's best equipped medical facility. The tourist police (☎ 28 3190) are at Dikeosynis 10.

Things to See

Don't leave Iraklio until you have seen the **archaeological museum's** magnificent collection. Opening times are Tuesday to Sunday from 8 am to 7 pm and Monday from 12.30 to 7 pm. Admission is 1500 dr.

You can pay homage to the great writer Nikos Kazantzakis by visiting his grave. To get there, walk south on Evans and turn right onto Plastira.

Places to Stay

Beware of taxi drivers who tell you that the pension of your choice is dirty, closed or has a bad reputation. They're paid commissions by the big hotels.

Rent Rooms Hellas (☎ 28 8851), a youth hostel at Handakos 24, is popular with backpackers despite the number of draconian rules posted in the rooftop reception and bar. Singles/doubles/triples are 5000/6500/8000 dr; dorm beds are 1600 dr. **Hotel Lena** (☎ 22 3280), Lahana 10, is one of the nicer budget hotels. Singles/doubles with shared facilities

cost 5500/7000 dr; doubles with private bath cost 7500 dr. If you don't mind surly service, **Vergina Rooms** (☎ 24 2739), 32 Hortatson, is a turn-of-the-century house with a bit of character. Doubles/triples/quads are 6000/7000/8000 dr.

If you truly can't afford anything else, there is a **youth hostel** (☎ 28 6281) at Vyronos 5, off 25 Avgoustou. Basic doubles/triples cost 4000/5000 dr. Dorms and roof beds are 1500 dr, but don't even think about the roof beds. There is a midnight curfew.

Places to Eat

The **Ippocampos Ouzeri**, on the waterfront just west of 25 Avgoustou, offers a huge range of mezedes from 450 dr. Go early to get a table. It's closed from 3.30 pm and 7 pm.

For international fast food and a beer, head for **Goody's**, on Idis. Hamburgers cost from 460 dr to 1240 dr. For Mexican, try **El Azteca**, Psaromingou 32; open from 8 pm. Tacos/burritos/enchiladas cost 1200/1500/1700 dr.

The bustling, colourful **market** is on Odos 1866.

Getting There & Away

For air and ferry information, see Getting There & Away at the start of the Crete section. For the port police, call ☎ 24 4912.

Iraklio has two bus stations. Bus station A, just inland from the new harbour, serves Agios Nikolaos, Ierapetra, Sitia, Malia and the Lassithi Plateau. Bus station B, 50m beyond the Hania Gate, serves Phaestos, Matala, Anoghia and Fodele. The Hania/Rethymno terminal is opposite bus station A.

IRAKLIO

PLACES TO STAY		OTHER			
3	Hotel Lena	2	Historical Museum of Crete	16	Venetian Loggia
4	Vergina Rooms	5	OTE	17	National Bank of Greece
6	Youth Hostel	7	American Express	18	Morosini Fountain
12	Rent Rooms Hellas		Representative	20	Tourist Police
		8	Buses to Hania & Rethymno	21	EOT
PLACES TO EAT		9	Buses to Knossos & Airport	22	Archaeological Museum
1	Ippocampos Ouzerie	10	Buses to Eastern Crete	23	Agios Minos Cathedral
11	El Azteca	13	Laundrette/Left luggage	24	Post Office
19	Goody's	14	Planet Bookstore	25	Buses to airport
		15	Buses to Knossos	26	Olympic Airways
				27	Grave of Nikos Kazantzakis

GREECE

Getting Around

Bus No 1 goes to/from the airport every 15 minutes between 6 am and 1 am; it stops at Plateia Eleftherias adjacent to the archaeological museum (150 dr). Local bus No 2 goes to Knossos every 15 minutes from bus station A and also stops on 25 Avgoustou.

Car and motorcycle-rental firms are mostly along 25 Avgoustou.

KNOSSOS Κνωσσός

The most famous of Crete's Minoan sites, Knossos, is 8km south-east of Iraklio. It inspired the myth of the Minotaur.

According to legend, King Minos of Knossos was given a bull to sacrifice to the god Poseidon, but instead decided to keep it. This enraged Poseidon, who punished the king by causing his wife Pasiphae to fall in love with the animal. The result of this bizarre union was the Minotaur – half-man and half-bull – who lived in a labyrinth beneath the king's palace, feeding on youths and maidens.

Theseus, an Athenian prince, posed as a sacrificial youth in order to kill the monster. He fell in love with Ariadne, King Minos' daughter, who gave him a ball of wool to unwind, so that he could find his way out of the labyrinth. Theseus killed the monster and fled with Ariadne, only to later dump her on Naxos.

In 1900 the ruins of Knossos were uncovered by Arthur Evans, who spent a fortune reconstructing some of the buildings. The site consists of an immense palace, courtyards, public reception rooms, private apartments, baths, storage vaults and stairways. Although archaeologists tend to disparage Evans' reconstruction, the buildings do give the layperson a good idea of what a Minoan palace may have looked like.

Very little is known of Minoan civilisation, which came to an abrupt end around 1450 BC, possibly destroyed by Santorini's volcanic eruption. The delightful frescoes depict plants and animals, as well as people participating in sports, ceremonies and festivals, and generally enjoying life, in contrast to the battle scenes found in the art of classical Greece.

A whole day is needed to see the site, and a guidebook is immensely useful – one of the best is *The Palaces of Minoan Crete* by Gerald Cadogan (paperback), which is not always available on Crete. From April to October the site is open daily from 8 am to 7 pm; entry is 1500 dr. Arrive early to avoid the crowds.

PHAESTOS & OTHER MINOAN SITES

Phaestos (Φαιστός), Crete's second-most important Minoan site, is not as impressive as Knossos but worth a visit for its stunning views of the plain of Mesara. The palace was laid out on the same plan as Knossos, but excavations have not yielded a great many frescoes. The site is open daily from 8 am to 5 pm; entry is 1200 dr.

Crete's other important Minoan sites are **Malia**, 34km to the east of Iraklio, where there is a palace complex and adjoining town, and **Zakros**, 40km from Sitia. This was the smallest of the island's palatial complexes. The site is rather remote and overgrown, but the ruins are on a more human scale than at Knossos, Phaestos or Malia.

HANIA Χανιά
☎ 0821

Hania, the old capital of Crete, has a harbour with crumbling, softly hued Venetian buildings. It oozes charm; unfortunately it also oozes package tourists.

Orientation & Information

Hania's bus station is on Kydonias, two blocks south-west of Plateia 1866, the town's main square. Halidon runs from here to the old harbour. The fortress separates the old harbour from the new.

The EOT office (☎ 92 943) is at Kriari 40, 20m from Plateia 1866. It is open weekdays from 8 am to 3 pm. The central post office is at Tzanakaki 3 and the OTE is next door. Hania's port is at Souda, 10km from town.

Things to See

The **archaeological museum** at Halidon 21 is housed in the former Venetian Church of San Francesco; the Turks converted it into a mosque. Opening hours are Tuesday to Sunday from 8.30 am to 3 pm. Admission is 500 dr.

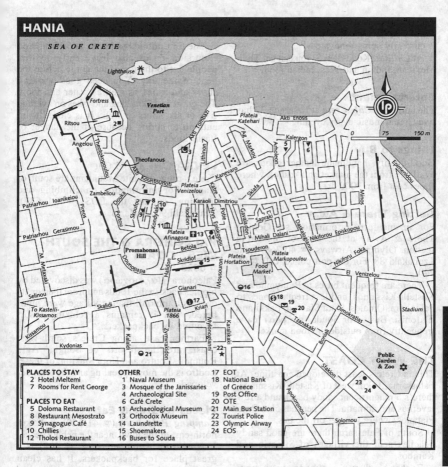

HANIA

SEA OF CRETE

PLACES TO STAY	OTHER	17 EOT
2 Hotel Meltemi	1 Naval Museum	18 National Bank
7 Rooms for Rent George	3 Mosque of the Janissaries	of Greece
	4 Archaeological Site	19 Post Office
PLACES TO EAT	6 Café Crete	20 OTE
5 Doloma Restaurant	11 Archaeological Museum	21 Main Bus Station
8 Restaurant Mesostrato	13 Orthodox Museum	22 Tourist Police
9 Synagogue Café	14 Laundrette	23 Olympic Airway
10 Chillies	15 Shoemakers	24 EOS
12 Tholos Restaurant	16 Buses to Souda	

GREECE

Places to Stay & Eat

The nearest camping ground is *Camping Hania* (☎ 31 138), 3km west of town, on the beach. Take a Kalamaka bus from Plateia 1866.

The most interesting rooms are in the ancient Venetian buildings around the old harbour. *Hotel Meltemi* (☎ 92 802), next to the fortezza, has great character and is superb value, with doubles from 5000 dr. *Rooms for Rent George* (☎ 88 715), Zambeliou 30, has singles/doubles/triples for 4000/6000/8000 dr. Turn left from Halidon onto Zambeliou

one block from the waterfront; the pension is on the right.

The central *food market* is a lively place to go and eat; there are two inexpensive tavernas. *Doloma Restaurant*, at the western end of Kalergon, is popular with students.

For interesting al fresco dining, try *Restaurant Mesostrato*, Zambeliou 31, in the remains of an ancient Venetian clubhouse, or the lovingly preserved ruins at the seriously classy *Tholos Restaurant*, Agion Deka 36. Both serve excellent Greek cuisine at reasonable prices. Similarly, the *Synagogue Café*, just off Kondylaki, is worth checking out. Next door is Crete's only synagogue, which is currently being renovated.

At *Chillies*, Kondylaki 5, you can get Thai, Mexican, Indian and West Indian food.

Entertainment

The authentic *Café Crete* at Kalergon 22 has live Cretan music every evening.

Things to Buy

Good-quality, handmade leather goods are available from the market on Skridlof, where shoes cost from 9000 dr.

Getting There & Away

For air and ferry information, see Getting There & Away at the start of the Crete section. Olympic Airways (☎ 40 268) is at Tzanakaki 88. For the port police, call ☎ 89 240.

There are frequent buses to Rethymno and Kastelli-Kissamos, and less frequent ones to Paleohora, Omalos, Hora Sfakion, Lakki and Elafonisi. Buses for Souda (the port) leave frequently from outside the food market.

THE WEST COAST

This is Crete's least developed coastline. At Falassarna, 11km west of Kastelli-Kissamos, there's a magnificent sandy beach and a few tavernas and domatia. The beach is 5km from Platanos, where you get off the bus.

South of Falassarna there are good sandy beaches near the villages of Sfinario and Kambos.

Farther south you can wade out to more beaches on Elafonisi islet. Travel agents in Hania and Paleohora run excursions to the area.

SAMARIA GORGE Φαράγγι της Σαμαριάς

It's a wonder the rocks underfoot haven't worn away completely as so many people trample through the Samaria Gorge. But it is one of Europe's most spectacular gorges, and worth seeing. You can do it independently by taking a bus to Omalos from Hania, returning by boat to Hora Sfakion, and then returning

by bus to Hania. Or you can join one of the daily excursions from Hania.

The first public bus leaves at 6.15 am and excursion buses also leave early so that people get to the top of the gorge before the heat of the day. You need good walking shoes and a hat, as well as water and food. The gorge is 16km long and takes on average five or six hours to walk. It is closed from autumn to spring because of the danger of flash floods.

LEVKA ORI Λευκά Ορι

Crete's rugged White Mountains are south of Hania. For information on climbing and trekking, contact the EOS (☎ 24 647), Tzanakaki 90, in Hania.

PALEOHORA & THE SOUTH-WEST COAST
☎ 0823

Paleohora (Παλαιοχώρα) was discovered by hippies back in the 1960s and from then on its days as a tranquil fishing village were numbered. But it remains a relaxing resort favoured by backpackers.

Farther east, along Crete's south-west coast, are the resorts of Sougia, Agia Roumeli, Loutro and Hora Sfakion; of these, Loutro is the most appealing and the least developed.

Places to Stay & Eat

Camping Paleohora (☎ 41 120) is 1.5km north-east of the town, near the pebble beach.

Homestay Anonymous (☎ 41 509) is a great place for backpackers. It has clean rooms set around a small courtyard; singles/doubles/triples are 4000/5000/5500 dr and there is a communal kitchen. The *Lissos Hotel* (☎ 41 266), El Venizelou 12, opposite the bus stop, has doubles from 5500 dr. *Oriental Bay Rooms* (☎ 41 076), at the northern end of the pebble beach, has comfortable singles/doubles with private bath for 4500/6500 dr.

Getting There & Away

There is no road linking the coastal resorts, but they are connected by boats from Paleohora in summer. Twice weekly the boat goes to Gavdos Island. Coastal paths lead from Paleohora to Sougia and from Agia Roumeli to Loutro (make sure you take plenty of water, because you'll be walking in full sun). There are five buses a day from Paleohora to Hania.

GAVDOS ISLAND Νήσος Γαύδος

The small rocky island of Gavdos, off Crete's southern coast, has some good beaches, a few domatia and tavernas, and as yet, is little visited. Freelance camping is usually tolerated.

RETHYMNO Ρέθυμνο
☎ 0831

Although similar to Hania in its Venetian and Turkish buildings (not to mention its package tourists), Rethymno is smaller and has a distinct character.

The EOT (☎ 29 148) is on the beach side of El Venizelou and is open Monday to Friday from 8 am to 3 pm. The post office is at Moatsou 21 and the OTE is at Pavlou Kountouriotou 28.

There is a cybercafé, Galero, beside Rimondi fountain.

RETHYMNO

SEA OF CRETE

0   150   300 m

PLACES TO STAY
7   Rent Rooms Garden
10 Olga's Pension;
    Stella's Kitchen
11 Youth Hostel

PLACES TO EAT
5   Taverna Kyria Maria
6   Gounakis Restaurant
    & Bar

OTHER
1   Entrance to Fortress
2   Archaeological Museum
3   Galero
    Cybercafé
4   Rimondi Fountain
8   Historical and Folk Art
    Museum
9   Nerandjes Mosque
12 The Happy Walker
13 Ellotia Tours
14 EOT
15 Bus Station
16 Olympic Airways
17 Post Office
18 OTE
19 National Bank of
    Greece

GREECE

Things to See & Do

The imposing **Venetian fortress** is open daily except Monday from 8 am to 7 pm; entry is 700 dr. The **archaeological museum** opposite the fortress entrance is open Tuesday to Sunday from 8.30 am to 3 pm: entry is 500 dr. The **historical & folk art museum** at Mesologiou 28 has a well-presented display of Cretan crafts. Its opening hours are Monday to Saturday from 9 am to 1 pm; entry is 500 dr.

The Happy Walker (☎ 52 920), Tombazi 56, has a program of daily walks in the countryside costing from 6500 dr per person.

Places to Stay

The nearest camping ground is *Elizabeth Camping* (☎ 28 694) on Myssiria beach, 3km east of town.

The *youth hostel* (☎ 22 848), Tombazi 41, is a friendly place with a bar; beds are 1500 dr in dorms or on the roof. The tranquil *Rent Rooms Garden* (☎ 28 586), Nikiforou Foka 82, is an old Venetian house with a delightful grape-arboured garden; doubles/triples are 8000/10,000 dr with private bath. *Olga's Pension* (☎ 53 206; fax 29 851), in the heart of town at Souliou 57, is spectacularly funky, with a wide choice of rooms spread about in clusters off a network of terraces bursting with greenery. Prices range from basic singles for 6000 dr up to doubles/triples with private bath for 9000/12,000 dr.

Places to Eat

Stella's Kitchen, beneath Olga's Pension, is terrific value, with staples from 1000 dr. *Taverna Kyria Maria*, Diog Mesologiou 20, tucked behind the Rimondi fountain, is a cosy family-run taverna.

Gounakis Restaurant & Bar, Koroneou 6, has live Cretan music every evening and reasonably priced food.

Getting There & Away

There are frequent buses to Iraklio and Hania, and less frequent ones to Agia Galini, Arkadi Monastery and Plakias.

For ferries, see Getting There & Away at the start of the Crete section. Ellotia Tours (☎ 51 981; elotia@ret.forthnet.gr), Arkadiou 161, is particularly helpful. For the port police, call ☎ 28 971.

AGIOS NIKOLAOS Αγιος Νικόλαος
☎ 0841

The manifestations of package tourism gather momentum as they advance eastwards, reaching their ghastly crescendo in Agios Nikolaos, or Ag Nik in package-tourist jargon.

If you don't take the first bus out, you'll find the municipal tourist office (☎ 22 357) next to the bridge between the lake and the harbour; follow the signs from the bus station and pick up a map. The tourist police (☎ 26 900) are at Kontogianni 34.

Places to Stay & Eat

The nearest camping ground is *Gournia Moon Camping* (☎ 0842-93 243), 19km from Ag Nik and almost opposite the Minoan site of Gournia. Buses to Sitia can drop you off right outside.

In town, the ramshackle *Green House* (☎ 22 025), Modatsou 15, is popular with backpackers; singles/doubles are 4000/5500 dr. Walk up Kapetan Tavla from the bus station and look for the sign.

Christina Pension (☎ 23 984), on the waterfront overlooking Ammoudi beach, has singles/doubles for 4000/6500 dr.

The *Sunbeam* hotel (☎ 25 645), Ethnikis Antistaseos 23, is outstanding; immaculate singles/doubles/triples with private bath cost 4500/6500/7500 dr. Breakfast is included and there is a bar. To find it, walk up Paleologou and hang a left six blocks after the lake.

The waterfront tavernas are expensive – head inland for better value. *Taverna Itanos*, Kyprou 1, is good value and popular with locals. *Taverna Pine Tree*, next to the lake at Paleologou 18, specialises in charcoal-grilled food, such as a plate of king prawns for 1800 dr. *Aouas Taverna*, at Paleologou 44, has traditional décor, a lovely garden and very reasonable prices.

Things to See & Do

The **archaeological museum**, on Paleologou, is open daily except Monday from 8.30 am to 2.30 pm. Admission is 500 dr. The **folk museum** next to the tourist office is open daily except Saturday from 10 am to 3 pm. Admission is 250 dr.

Getting There & Away

There are frequent buses from Agios Nikolaos to Iraklio, Malia, Ierapetra and Sitia, and
two a day to Lassithi.

For boats, see Getting There & Away at
the start of the Crete section. For the port
police, call ☎ 22 312.

LASSITHI PLATEAU

Οροπέδιο Λασιθίου

The first view of this mountain-fringed
plateau, laid out like an immense patchwork
quilt, is breathtaking. The plateau, 900m
above sea level, is a vast expanse of orchards
and fields, dotted by some 7000 metal windmills with white canvas sails.

Things to See

The **Dikteon Cave**, on the side of Mt Dikti,
is not as festooned with stalactites and stalagmites as some of Greece's other caves, but
it's still worth a visit. Here, according to
mythology, the Titan Rhea hid the newborn
Zeus from Cronos, his offspring-gobbling
father. It's open Monday to Saturday from
10.30 am to 5 pm in summer; 8.30 am to 3
pm in winter. Entry is 800 dr.

Places to Stay & Eat

Psychro is the best place to stay: it's near the
cave and has the best views. The *Zeus Hotel*
(☎ 0844-31 284) has singles/doubles with
private bath for 5000/8000 dr. On the main
street, the *Stavros* and *Platanos* tavernas
serve decent food at similar prices.

Getting There & Away

From Psychro two buses a day go to Iraklio
and Agios Nikolaos, and one to Malia.

SITIA Σητεία
☎ 0843

Back on the north coast the tourist overkill
dies down considerably by the time you reach
Sitia. Skirting a commanding hotel-lined bay
with a long sandy beach (more than can be
said of Ag Nik), Sitia is an attractive town.

The post office is on Therissou, off El
Venizelou, and the OTE is on Kapetan Sifis,
which runs inland from Plateia El Venizelou;
the main square. In summer there is a mobile
tourist office in the square. There are several
travel agents in town along El Venizelou, but
be warned – at the time of writing there was
nowhere to buy tickets at the port, though the
area is being redeveloped and this may
change. The ferry port is a bit of a hike; it is
signposted from the main square.

Places to Stay & Eat

There are no camping grounds near Sitia, but
it is possible to camp in the grounds of the
youth hostel (☎ 22 693) at Therissou 4, on
the road to Iraklio, for 1200 dr. Dorm beds
cost 1400 dr; doubles with shared facilities
are 4000 dr.

There is no shortage of domatia behind the
waterfront. The immaculate *Hotel Arhontiko*
(☎ 28 172), Kondilaki 16, has singles/
doubles/triples for 4500/5500/6500 dr. To
find it, walk towards the ferry dock along El
Venizelou, turn left up Filellinon and then
right into Kondylaki.

The *Kali Kardia Taverna*, Foundalidhou
20, is excellent value and popular with locals,
though the home-cooked food at the quayside
taverna is very hard to beat. There are many
grocery shops on Thoyntaladou, one block
south of Plateia Agonostos.

Getting There & Away

For air and ferry information, see Getting
There & Away at the start of the Crete
section. To contact the port police, call ☎ 22
310. There are at least five buses daily to Ierapetra and six to Iraklio via Agios Nikolaos.
In summer there are two or three buses daily
to Vaï and Zakros.

AROUND SITIA

The reconstructed **Toplou Monastery**, 15km
from Sitia, houses some beautifully intricate
icons and other fascinating relics.

Vaï Beach, famous for its palm tree forest,
gets pretty crowded, but it's a superb beach
and well worth a visit.

For Toplou Monastery, get a Vaï bus from
Sitia, get off at the fork for the monastery and
walk the last 3km.

Dodecanese
Δωδεκάνησα

More verdant and mountainous than the Cyclades and with comparable beaches, the islands of the Dodecanese offer more than natural beauty, for here more than anywhere else you get a sense of Greece's proximity to Asia. Ancient temples, massive crusader fortifications, mosques and imposing Italian-built neoclassical buildings stand juxtaposed, vestiges of a turbulent past. Even now, prox-imity to Turkey makes the islands a contentious issue whenever hostility between the two countries intensifies.

There are 16 inhabited islands in the group; the most visited are Rhodes, Kos, Patmos and Symi.

RHODES Ρόδος

According to mythology, the sun god Helios chose Rhodes as his bride and bestowed light, warmth and vegetation upon her. The blessing seems to have paid off, for Rhodes

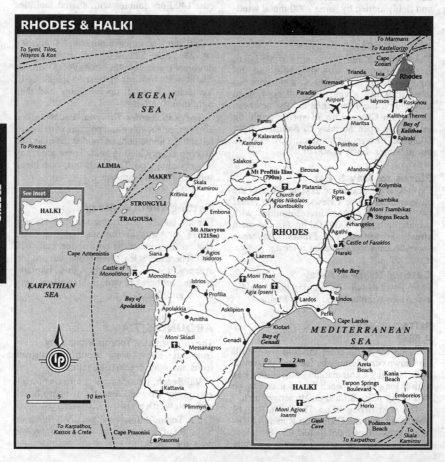

RHODES & HALKI

produces flowers in profusion and enjoys more sunny days than most Greek islands.

The ancient sites of Lindos and Kamiros are legacies of Rhodes' importance in antiquity.

In 1291 the Knights of St John, having fled Jerusalem under siege, came to Rhodes and established themselves as masters. In 1522 Süleyman I, sultan of the Ottoman Empire, staged a massive attack on the island and took Rhodes city. The island, along with the other Dodecanese, then became part of the Ottoman Empire.

In 1912 it was the Italians' turn and in 1944 the Germans took over. The following year Rhodes was liberated by British and Greek commandos. In 1948, Rhodes, along with the other Dodecanese, became part of Greece.

Rhodes City
☎ 0241

Rhodes' capital and port is Rhodes city, on the northern tip of the island. Almost everything of interest in the city lies within its walls. The main thoroughfares are Sokratous, Pythagora, Agiou Fanouriou and Ipodamou, with mazes of narrow streets between them. Many parts of the old town are prohibited to cars, but there are car parks around the periphery.

The new town to the north is a monument to package tourism, with ghettos devoted to different national groups. The town has two bus stations: one on Plateia Rimini, and the other next to the New Market.

The main port is east of the old town, and north of here is Mandraki Harbour, supposed site of the Colossus of Rhodes, a giant bronze statue of Apollo (built in 292-280 BC) – one of the Seven Wonders of the World. The statue stood for a mere 65 years before being toppled by an earthquake. It lay abandoned until 653 AD when it was chopped up by the Saracens, who sold the pieces to a merchant in Edessa. The story goes that after being shipped to Syria, it took 980 camels to transport it to its final destination.

Information The EOT office (☎ 23 255; eot-rodos@otenet.gr) is on the corner of Makariou and Papagou. It's open Monday to Friday from 7.30 am to 3 pm. The tourist police (☎ 27 423) are next door. The main post office is on Mandraki and the OTE telephone office is at Amerikis 91.

There is a cybercafé, Rock Style, at Dimokratias 7, just south of the old town.

Things to See & Do In the old town, the 15th-century Knights' Hospital is a splendid building. It was restored by the Italians and is now the **archaeological museum**, housing an impressive collection of finds from Rhodes and the other Dodecanese islands. Particularly noteworthy is the exquisite statue of *Aphrodite of Rhodes*, which so entranced Lawrence Durrell that he named his book about the island, *Reflections on a Marine Venus*, after it. Opening times are Tuesday to Sunday from 8.30 am to 3 pm. Admission is 800 dr.

Odos Ippoton – the Avenue of the Knights – is lined with magnificent medieval buildings, the most imposing of which is the **Palace of the Grand Masters**, restored, but never used, as a holiday home for Mussolini. It is open Tuesday to Sunday from 8.30 am to 3 pm. Admission is 1200 dr.

The old town is reputedly the world's finest surviving example of medieval fortification. The 12m-thick walls are closed to the public, but you can take a **guided walk** along them on Tuesday and Saturday, starting at 2.45 pm in the courtyard at the Palace of the Grand Masters (1200 dr).

The 18th century **Turkish bath** offers a rare opportunity to have a Turkish bath in Greece. It's open on Tuesday from 1 pm to 6 pm, on Wednesday, Thursday and Friday from 11 am to 6 pm and on Saturday from 8 am to 6 pm. Entry is 500 dr.

Places to Stay Freelance camping is forbidden on Rhodes. *Faliraki Camping* (☎ 85 358), 2km north of Faliraki Beach, has a restaurant, bar, minimarket and pool, and charges 1200 dr per person and 600 dr per tent. Take a bus from the east-side bus station.

The old town is well supplied with accommodation so even in high season you should be able to find somewhere to stay. The unofficial *Rodos Youth Hostel* (☎ 30 491), Ergiou 12, is very popular and has a lovely garden. Dorm beds/doubles with shared facilities cost 1500 dr per person; doubles with private bath

GREECE

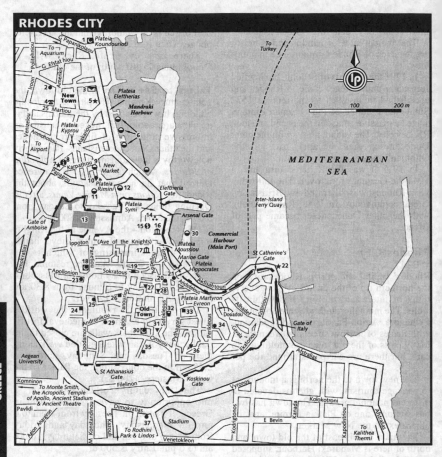

RHODES CITY

are 4000 dr. There is a kitchen available for self-caterers and during the summer there are barbecue facilities.

Pension Sunlight (☎ 21 435), above *Stavro's Bar* at Ipodamou 32, has singles/doubles/triples with private bath for 5000/7000/10,000 dr. All rooms have a fridge and a filter coffee machine.

The newly refurbished *Hotel Via-Via* (☎ 27 895), Pythagora 45, has doubles with shared facilities for 6500 dr, doubles with private bath and kitchenette for 10,500 dr. The exceptionally friendly *Pension Andreas*

(☎ 34 156; fax 74 285), Omirou 28D, has a terrace bar with terrific views. Clean, pleasant doubles with shared bathroom cost 8000 dr, triples/quads with private bath are 13,000/15,000 dr. Both places have email facilities for guests.

Most of Rhodes' other villages, including Genadi and Plimmyri, have hotels or a few domatia.

Places to Eat One of the cheapest places to eat in the old town is *Taverna Mike's*, which has excellent seafood. Find Castellania Foun-

RHODES CITY

PLACES TO STAY		OTHER			14	Temple of Aphrodite
24	Pension Sunlight	1	Mosque of Murad Reis		15	Commercial Bank of Greece
26	Rodos Youth Hostel	2	Olympic Airways Office		16	Byzantine Museum
33	Hotel Via-Via	3	Post Office		17	Archaeological Museum
35	Pension Andreas	4	OTE Telephone Office		18	Mosque of Süleyman
		5	Port Police		20	Castellania Travel Service
PLACES TO EAT		6	Excursion Boats & Hydrofoils		21	Castelliana Fountain
19	Kafekopteion	7	Tourist Police		22	Port police
27	Restaurant Two Sisters	8	EOT Office		23	Turkish Library
28	Yiannis Taverna	9	Bus Station (west side)		25	Turkish bath
31	Popeye Bar & Grill	10	Luggage storage		29	Folk Dance Theatre
32	Café Besara	11	Bus Station (east side)		30	Mosque of Retjep Pasha
36	Le Bistrot de L'Auberge	12	Taxi Rank		34	Waterhoppers Diving Centre
		13	Palace of the Grand Masters		37	Rock Style Cybercafé

tain and Mike's is in the tiny street running parallel south of Sokratous. *Yiannis Taverna*, on Platanos, is highly popular and very good value (closed over Easter); *Restaurant Two Sisters*, tucked away at the western end of Platanos, is also good. South of the old town, *To Steno*, Agion Anargiron 29, near the church, is popular with locals.

If you're sick of Greek food, *Le Bistrot de L'Auberge* (☎ 34 292), in a beautifully restored medieval house at Praxitelous 21, serves terrific French dishes, with main courses costing around 1800 dr (evenings only, closed Monday). Indian food freaks should make a beeline for the new town's *India Restaurant* (☎ 38 395), Konstantopedos 16 , directly opposite *Kringlans Swedish Bakery* on Dragoumi (evenings only, closed Monday). At 2700 dr for a vindaloo it's certainly not cheap, but it's the best you're likely to find in Greece.

The cheapest and most happening bar in town is *Café Besara*, on Sofokleous, run by Australian expat Sara. Open daily from 10 am until around 2 am, it does great breakfasts and light meals for around 900 dr.

Popeye Bar & Grill, Plateia Sofokleous, is particularly popular with divers now that it's been taken over by the Waterhoppers Diving Centre (☎/fax 38 146). On Sunday afternoon you can get barbecued meat or veggie burger with jacket potato, salad and a glass of punch for 2000 dr.

For the best Greek coffee in town and a game of backgammon or chess, try *Kafekopteion* at Sokratous 76.

Bakeries and minimarkets are dotted around the old town.

Entertainment There is a distinctly average *sound-and-light show* at the Palace of the Knights, depicting the Turkish siege. A noticeboard outside gives the times for performances in different languages, or you can check the schedule with the EOT. Admission is 1000 dr.

The *Greek Folk Dance Theatre* (☎ 29 085) on Andronikou gives first-rate performances. Admission is 3500 dr.

For live rock music, try the late-night *Sticky Fingers*, in the new town at Zervou 6.

Lindos Λίνδος
☎ 0244

The imposing **Acropolis of Lindos**, Rhodes' most important ancient city, shares a rocky outcrop with a **crusader castle**. Down below it there are labyrinths of winding streets with whitewashed, elaborately decorated houses which are undeniably beautiful but extremely touristy. The site of Lindos is open Tuesday to Friday from 8 am to 7 pm; Saturday and Sunday from 8.30 am to 3 pm. Admission is 1200 dr.

Kamiros Κάμειρος

The extensive ruins of this ancient Doric city on the west coast are well preserved, with the remains of houses, baths, a cemetery, a temple and a stoa. But the site should be visited as much for its lovely setting on a gentle hillside overlooking the sea.

GREECE

Beaches

Between Rhodes city and Lindos the beaches are crowded. If you prefer isolation, venture south to the bay of Lardos. Even farther south, between Genadi and Plimmyri, you'll find good stretches of deserted sandy beach.

On the west coast, beaches tend to be pebbly and the sea is often choppy.

Getting There & Away

Air There are daily flights from Rhodes to Athens (Olympic Airways 24,700 dr; Air Greece 23,200 dr), at least three a week to Karpathos and four a week to Crete. In summer there are regular services to Mykonos, Santorini, Kassos, Kastellorizo, Thessaloniki and Kos. The Olympic Airways office (☎ 24 571/2) is at Ierou Lohou 9.

For information and efficient service, Castellania Travel Service (☎ 75 861; castell@otenet.gr), just off the old town's Plateia Hippocrates at Evripidou 1-3, is hard to beat. For the port police, call ☎ 28 666.

Ferry There are daily ferries from Rhodes to Piraeus (8700 dr). Most sail via the Dodecanese north of Rhodes, but at least once a week there is a service via Karpathos, Kassos, Crete and the Cyclades. The EOT gives out a schedule. There are daily excursion boats to Symi (4000 dr return).

Between April and October there are regular boats from Rhodes to Marmaris (Turkey); one-way tickets cost 10,000 dr by hydrofoil (14,000 dr return) or 9000 dr by ferry, including the 3000 dr port tax.

In summer there are regular ferries to Israel (from 31,000 dr) via Cyprus (19,000 dr).

Getting Around

To/From the Airport There are frequent buses to/from the airport from the west-side bus station (400 dr). A taxi to the airport costs about 3000 dr. For a radio taxi, phone ☎ 64 712/34.

Bus The west-side bus station serves the west coast, Embona and Koskinou; the east-side station serves the east coast and inland southern villages. The EOT has a schedule.

Car & Motorcycle You'll be tripping over independent car and motorcycle-rental outlets in Rhodes city's new town, particularly on and around 28 Oktovriou. Try several and bargain even in season because the competition is fierce.

SYMI Σύμη
☎ 0241

Symi town is outstandingly attractive and so easily accessible by boat from Rhodes that it would be a shame to give it a miss, though obviously you'll have more fun if you stay over when the day-trippers have gone. *Hotel Glafkos* (☎ 71 358), *Aigli Rooms* (☎ 71 454) and *Rooms to Let Helena* (☎ 71 931) are the best budget choices. *O Meraklis* and *Taverna Neraida* are cheap and cheerful eateries; at night, the *Sunflower* sandwich and salad bar turns into an excellent vegetarian restaurant.

KARPATHOS Κάρπαθος
☎ 0245

The picturesque, elongated island of Karpathos, lies midway between Crete and Rhodes.

Orientation & Information

The main port and capital is **Pigadia**, and there's a smaller port at **Diafani**. There's no EOT, but the friendly tourist police (☎ 22 218) are next door to the post office and there's a helpful travel agency, Karpathos Travel (☎ 22 148) on Dimokratias.

Things to See & Do

Karpathos has glorious beaches, particularly at Apella and Kira Panagia. The northern village of **Olymbos** is like a living museum and is endlessly fascinating to ethnologists. Young women wear brightly coloured and embroidered skirts, waistcoats and headscarves and goatskin boots. The older women's apparel is more subdued but still distinctive. Interiors of houses are decorated with embroidered cloth and their façades with brightly painted moulded-plaster reliefs. The inhabitants speak a dialect which retains some Doric words, and the houses have wooden locks of the kind described by Homer. A two-hour uphill trail leads from Diafani to Olymbos.

Places to Stay & Eat

There's plenty of accommodation and owners meet the boats. The E-class *Hotel Avra* (☎ 22 388), 28 Oktovriou, has comfortable doubles with/without private bath for 7000/6000 dr. *Harry's Rooms* (☎ 22 188), just off 28 Oktovriou, has spotless singles/doubles with shared bathroom for 4500/5500 dr. Further along 28 Oktovriou, just beyond the Arts Centre, *To Kanaki Rooms* (☎ 22 908) has pleasant doubles with private bath for 6500 dr. Accommodation is also available at Diafani, Olymbos and several other villages.

For delectable mezedes, try the atmospheric *Kalimera Ellas Ouzeri*, near the quay.

Getting There & Away

Air Karpathos has an international airport that receives charter flights from northern Europe.

There are daily flights to Rhodes (12,500 dr) and three a week to Kassos (6600 dr) and Athens (25,700 dr). In summer there is a weekly flight to Sitia on Crete (11,500 dr).

Ferry There are two ferries a week from Rhodes and from Piraeus (6340 dr) via the Cyclades and Crete. In bad weather, ferries do not stop at Diafani. For the port police, call ☎ 22 227.

KASSOS Κάσσος
☎ 0245

On the map, Kassos looks like a bit of Karpathos that has broken away; it's rocky and barren with a couple of sandy beaches, and it's a good choice if you yearn for isolation. Kassos has air connections with Sitia, Karpathos and Rhodes and the same ferry connections as Karpathos, but if the weather is bad the ferries give it a miss. For the port police, call ☎ 41 288.

Hotel Anagennisis (☎ 41 495) has singles/doubles with shared facilities for 4500/6500 dr.

KOS Κως
☎ 0242

Kos is renowned as the birthplace of Hippocrates, father of medicine. Kos town manifests the more ghastly aspects of mass tourism, and the beaches are horrendous, with wall-to-wall sun lounges and beach umbrellas.

Orientation & Information

Kos town, on the north-east coast, is the main town and port. The municipal tourist office (☎ 24 460), Vasileos Georgiou 3, is near the hydrofoil pier. It is open daily from 8 am to 9 pm. The post office is at El Venizelou 16, one block from the OTE, on the corner of Vironos and Xanthou.

Things to See

Kos Town Before you beat a hasty retreat, check out the 13th-century **fortress** and the **archaeological museum**, open Tuesday to Sunday from 8.30 am to 3 pm. Entry is 800 dr. At the entrance to the castle is the **Hippocrates Plane Tree** beneath which, according to the EOT brochure, the great man taught – although plane trees don't usually live for more than 200 years. The **ancient agora** and the **odeion** are also worth seeing.

Asclepion On a pine-clad hill, 4km from Kos town, stand the extensive ruins of the renowned healing centre of Asclepion. The site is open Tuesday to Sunday from 8.30 am to 3 pm; admission is 800 dr.

Around the Island The villages in the **Asfendion** region of the Dikeos Mountains are reasonably tranquil. **Paradise** on the southeast coast is the most appealing beach, but don't expect to have it to yourself.

Places to Stay & Eat

Kos Camping (☎ 23 910) is 3km along the eastern waterfront. In summer its minibus meets most boats, including the 4 am ferry from Piraeus.

Otherwise, your best bet is to head straight for the convivial *Pension Alexis* (☎ 28 798, 25 594), close to the harbour, at Irodotou 9 (the entrance is in Omirou). Singles/doubles/triples with shared bath cost 4000/6500/8000 dr. The friendly English-speaking Alexis usually meets the boats and promises never to turn anyone away. He is also the owner of the tastefully furnished *Hotel Afendoulis* (☎ 25 321), Evripilou 1, where singles/doubles/triples with private bath cost 6000/9000/11,0000 dr.

Taverna Hirodion, just around the corner from Hotel Afendoulis at Artemisias 27, serves good food at reasonable prices. *Theodoras Taverna*, on Pindou, and *Filoxenia Taverna*, on the corner of Pindou and Alikarnassou, are both popular with locals.

The *food market* is on Plateia Eleftherias.

Getting There & Away

Air Apart from European charter flights, there are daily flights from Kos to Athens (21,100 dr) and three a week to Rhodes (14,100 dr). The Olympic Airways office (☎ 28 330) is at the southern end of Vasileos Pavlou.

Ferry There are frequent ferries from Rhodes which continue on to Piraeus (7500 dr) via Kalymnos, Leros and Patmos. There are less frequent connections to Nisyros, Tilos, Symi, Samos and Crete. Daily excursion boats also go to Nisyros, Kalymnos and Rhodes.

Ferries travel daily in summer to Bodrum in Turkey (13,000 dr return including port tax). For the port police, call ☎ 28 507.

Getting Around

Buses for Asclepion leave from opposite the town hall on the harbour; all other buses leave from behind the Olympic Airways office. Motorcycles, mopeds and bicycles are widely available for hire.

NISYROS & TILOS Νίσυρος & Τήλος
☎ 0242 & 0241

Volcanic Nisyros' caldera obligingly bubbles, hisses and spews – you must wear solid shoes as it gets very hot underfoot. Dramatic moonscapes combine with lush vegetation, and after the day-trippers from Kos depart, Nisyros reverts to its peaceful, unspoilt self.

Tilos is less visited than Nisyros and has gentle and enfolding hills offering many opportunities for walking, as well as some of the finest beaches in the Dodecanese.

For the port police on Nisyros, call ☎ 31 222; on Tilos call ☎ 44 350.

PATMOS Πάτμος
☎ 0247

Starkly scenic Patmos is where St John wrote his book of Revelations. It gets crowded in summer, but manages to remain remarkably tranquil.

Orientation & Information

The tourist office (☎ 31 666, open summer only), post office and police station are all in the white Italianate building at the island's port and capital of Skala.

Things to See & Do

The **Monastery of the Apocalypse**, on the site where St John wrote the Revelations, is between the port and the hora. The attraction here is the cave in which the saint lived and dictated his revelations. Opening times are 8 am to 1 pm daily and from 4 to 6 pm on Tuesday, Thursday and Sunday.

The hora's whitewashed houses huddle around the fortified **Monastery of St John**, which houses a vast collection of monastic treasures, including embroidered robes, ornate crosses and chalices, Byzantine jewellery and early manuscripts and icons. It's open the same hours as the Monastery of the Apocalypse. Admission to the monastery is free, but it costs 1000 dr to see the treasury.

Patmos' indented coastline provides numerous secluded coves, mostly with pebble beaches.

Places to Stay & Eat

Stefanos Camping (☎ 31 831), on the beach 2km north-east of Skala, charges 1400 dr per person and 700 dr per tent.

There are so many rooms for rent that you'll be fending off the owners at the port. *Pension Sofia's* (☎ 31 876), 250m up the hora road, has doubles/triples with private bath for 4500/6500 dr. Further up, *Pension Maria Paskeledi* (☎ 32 152) has singles/doubles/triples with shared bathroom for 3500/6000/8000 dr.

Pension Akteon (☎ 31 187) has immaculate self-contained studios at 4000/8000/9600 dr for singles/doubles/triples. To find it, turn right from the harbour and it's 200m up on the left.

O Pantelis Taverna, behind the waterfront Café Bar Arion, and the *Grigoris Taverna*, opposite the cafeteria/passenger-transit building, are the two most popular eateries. The food market is well signposted from the waterfront.

Getting There & Away

Frequent ferries travel between Patmos and Piraeus (6700 dr), and to Rhodes (5500 dr) via Leros, Kalymnos and Kos. There are also frequent boats to Samos. For the port police, call ☎ 34 131.

Getting Around

Skala, Hora, Grikos and Kambos are connected by buses which depart from the port. In summer there are frequent excursion boats to the various beaches and to the islets of Arki and Marathi.

KASTELLORIZO Καστελλόριζο (MEGISTI)

☎ 0241

Tiny Kastellorizo lies 116km east of Rhodes, its nearest Greek neighbour, and only 2.5km from the southern coast of Turkey. Its **Blue Grotto** is spectacular and comparable to its namesake in Capri. The name derives from the blue appearance of the water in the grotto, caused by refracted sunlight. Fishermen will take you to the cave in their boats, and also to some of the surrounding islets, all of which are uninhabited. The island's remoteness is drawing a steady trickle of visitors, but as yet it remains pristine. There are plenty of rooms for rent from 5000 dr a double. Three flights (10,600 dr) and two ferries a week operate between Rhodes and Kastellorizo. For the port police, call ☎ 49 270.

North-Eastern Aegean Islands

These islands are less visited than the Cyclades and the Dodecanese. There are seven major islands in this group: Chios, Ikaria, Lesvos, Limnos, Samos, Samothraki and Thasos.

Offshore oil – albeit not high quality – has been found around Thasos, leading to Turkey casting a covetous eye upon the whole group. The Turks claim that as this part of the Aegean lies off their coast, they should have a share of whatever it yields. But on the basis of the 1982 Law of the Sea the Aegean belongs to Greece. Turkey has not ratified this law and is pressing for negotiations. The dispute has necessitated a heavy military presence.

SAMOS Σάμος

☎ 0273

Samos was an important centre of Hellenic culture and is reputedly the birthplace of the philosopher and mathematician Pythagoras. Lush and humid, its mountains are skirted by pine, sycamore and oak-forested hills, and its air is permeated with floral scents.

Orientation & Information

Samos has three ports: Vathy (Samos town) and Karlovasi on the north coast, and Pythagorio on the south-east coast. Vathy's municipal tourist office (☎ 28 530) is in a little side street just north of Plateia Pythagora (open summer only). The post office is on Smyrnis, four blocks from the waterfront. The OTE is on Plateia Iroön, behind the municipal gardens.

Things to See & Do

Very little is left of the **ancient city** of Samos, on which the town of Pythagorio now stands. The Sacred Way, once flanked by 2000 statues, has now metamorphosed into the airport's runway.

The extraordinary **Evpalinos Tunnel** is the site's most impressive surviving relic. It was built in the 6th century BC by Evpalinos who was the chief engineer of the tyrant Polycrates. The 1km tunnel was dug by political prisoners and used as an aqueduct to bring water from the springs of Mt Ampelos. Part of it can still be explored. It's 2km north of Pythagorio and is open daily except Monday from 8.30 am to 3 pm. Entry is 800 dr.

Vathy's **archaeological museum** is outstanding, with an impressive collection of statues, votives and pottery. It is open daily except Monday from 8.30 am to 3 pm. Admission is 800 dr (400 dr for students).

The villages of **Manolates** and **Vourliotes** on the slopes of Mt Ampelos are excellent walking territory, as there are many marked pathways.

Quiet beaches can be found on the southwest coast in the Marathokampos area.

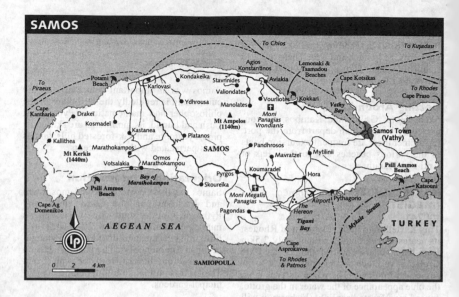

SAMOS

Places to Stay & Eat

Pythagorio, where you'll disembark if you've come from Patmos, is touristy and expensive.

Vathy, 20 minutes away by bus, is cheaper. The friendly *Pension Vasso* (☎ 23 258) is open all year round and has singles/doubles/triples for 3000/5000/6000 dr with private bath. To get there from the quay, turn right onto the waterfront, left into Stamatiadou and walk up the steps. The owners also have a charming three-bed country cottage for rent, right by the sea in the unspoilt village of Livadaki, on the north coast. It costs 8000/10,000/12,000 dr a day for two/four/six people.

Back in Vathy, *Pension Avli* (☎ 22 939), a former convent girls' school, has doubles for 7000 dr. It's on Kalomiri, close to the port, two blocks back from the waterfront. Nearby, *Hotel Ionia* (☎ 28 782) is cheap, with singles/doubles for 2500/3500 dr with shared bathroom and doubles/triples for 4000/5000 dr with private bath.

The popular *Taverna Gregory*, near the post office, serves good food at reasonable prices. On some nights three locals – the Tris Manolis – sing for their supper.

Getting There & Away

Air Samos has an international airport receiving European charter flights. There are also daily flights to Athens (17,100 dr).

Ferry There are ferries twice a week to Chios and at least twice a week to Piraeus (6000 dr); some go via Paros and Naxos, others via Mykonos. Avoid being hustled onto an excursion boat to Patmos. The normal ferry (2800 dr) is a quarter of the price.

There are daily boats to Kuşadası (for Ephesus) in Turkey, costing 11,000 dr one way and 14,000 dr return, plus port tax. For the port police call ☎ 61 225.

Getting Around

To get to Vathy's bus station, turn left onto Lekadi, 250m south of Plateia Pythagora. Buses run to all the island's villages.

CHIOS Χίος
☎ 0271

'Craggy Chios', as Homer described it, is less visited than Samos and almost as riotously fertile. Chios is famous for its mastic trees, which produce a resin used in chewing gum, and arrack, a liquor distilled from grain.

In 1822 an estimated 25,000 inhabitants of the island were massacred by the Turks.

Orientation & Information

The main town and port is Chios town, which is strident and unattractive; only the old Turkish quarter has any charm. It is, however, a good base from which to explore the island.

The municipal tourist office (☎ 44 389) is on Kanari, the main street running from the waterfront to Plateia Vounakiou in the town centre. The OTE is opposite the tourist office, and the post office is on Rodokanaki, a block back from the waterfront.

Things to See

The **Philip Argenti Museum**, near the cathedral in Chios town, contains exquisite embroideries and traditional costumes. It's open from 8 am to 2 pm Monday to Thursday, 5 to 7 pm on Friday and 8 am to 12.30 pm on Saturday. Admission is free.

The **Nea Moni** (New Monastery), 14km west of Chios town, houses some of Greece's most important mosaics. They date from the 11th century and are among the finest examples of Byzantine art in Greece. It's open daily from 8 am to 1 pm and 4 to 8 pm; entry is free.

Pyrgi, 24km from Chios town and the centre of the mastic-producing region, is one of Greece's most beautiful villages. The façades of its dwellings are decorated with intricate grey and white geometric patterns. **Emboreios**, 6km south of Pyrgi, is an attractive, uncrowded black-pebble beach.

Places to Stay

Rooms Alex (☎ 26 054), Livanou 29, is the best of the low budget accommodation. Rooms cost 6000/5500 dr with/without private bath, and there's a relaxing roof terrace. It's one block back from the waterfront, about 500m south of the quay. *Hotel Filoxenia* (☎ 26 559), signposted from the waterfront, has simple singles/doubles from 5000/6000 dr.

Places to Eat

Right opposite the ferry disembarkation point on Neorion is *Ouzeri Theodosiou*, a popular old-style establishment. For the freshest possible fish, try *Iakovos Taverna* on the northern arm of the harbour by the fish terminal.

Getting There & Away

There are daily flights from Chios to Athens (15,500 dr) and twice-weekly flights to Thessaloniki (22,100 dr).

Ferries sail at least twice a week to Samos (2800 dr) and Piraeus (5600 dr) via Lesvos, and once a week to Thessaloniki via Lesvos and Limnos. There are three boats a week to the small island of Psara, west of Chios, and two a week to the even smaller island of Inousses. In summer daily boats travel to Çeşme in Turkey; tickets cost 11,000 dr one way and 14,000 dr return. For the port police call ☎ 44 432.

Getting Around

The bus station is on Plateia Vournakio. Blue buses go to Vrontados, Karyes and Karfas, all near Chios town. Green buses go to Emboreios, Pyrgi and Mesta.

LESVOS (MYTILINI) Λέσβος (Μυτιλήνη)

Lesvos, the third-largest island in the North-Eastern Aegean, has always been a centre of artistic and philosophical achievement and creativity. Sappho, one of the greatest poets of ancient Greece, lived here and today the island is visited by many lesbians paying homage to her. Lesvos was also the birthplace of the composer Terpander and the poet Arion – an influence on both Sophocles and Euripides – and boasted Aristotle and Epicurus among the teachers at its school of philosophy. It remains to this day a spawning ground for innovative ideas in the arts and politics.

Mytilini
☎ 0251

Mytilini, the capital and port of Lesvos, is a large workaday town built around two harbours. All passenger ferries dock at the southern harbour. The EOT and the tourist police (☎ 22 776) share the same office at the entrance to the quay. The post office is on Vournazon, west of the southern harbour, and the OTE is in the same street.

Things to See Mytilini's imposing **castle**, built in early Byzantine times and renovated in the 14th century, opens daily except Monday from 8.30 am to 3 pm. The **archaeological museum**, one block north of the quay, is open Tuesday to Sunday from 8.30 am to 2.30 pm. Don't miss the **Theophilos Museum**, which houses the works of the prolific primitive painter Theophilos; it's open Tuesday to Sunday from 9 am to 1 pm and 4.30 pm to 8 pm. Entry to each costs 500 dr.

Places to Stay & Eat Domatia owners belong to a cooperative called *Sappho Self-Catering Rooms in Mytilini*. Most of these domatia are in little side streets off Ermou, near the northern harbour. Nearest to the quay is *Iren* (☎ 22 787), Komninaki 41, where clean but simple doubles/triples cost 5500/6750 dr. *Thalia Rooms* (☎ 24 640), Kinikiou 1, has doubles/triples for 6000/7200 dr with private bathroom. *Salina's Garden Rooms* (☎ 42 073), Fokeas 7, has doubles from 6000 dr.

The ramshackle but delightfully atmospheric *Ermis Ouzeri* has yet to be discovered by the tourist crowd. It's at the north end of Ermou on the corner with Kornarou. *Restaurant Averof*, in the middle of the southern waterfront, is a no-nonsense traditional eatery serving hearty Greek staples. The small, friendly *Ta Stroggylia*, at Komninaki 9, has wine barrels and good food.

Around the Island

Northern Lesvos is best known for its exquisitely preserved traditional town of **Mithymna** (otherwise known as Molyvos). Its neighbouring beach resort of **Petra**, 6km south, is affected by low-key package tourism, while the villages surrounding **Mt Lepetymnos** are authentic, picturesque and worth a day or two of exploration.

Western Lesvos is a popular destination for lesbians who come on a kind of pilgrimage in honour of the poet Sappho. The beach resort of **Skala Eresou** is built over ancient Eresos, where she was born in 628 BC.

Southern Lesvos is dominated by the 968m **Mt Olympus**. Pine forests decorate its flanks, though in recent years large sections have been ravaged by fires. **Plomari**, a large traditional coastal village, is popular with visitors, and the picturesque village of **Agiasos** is a favourite day-trip destination with some fairly genuine artisan workshops.

Getting There & Away

Air There are three flights a day from Lesvos to Athens (15,800 dr), one a day to Thessaloniki (19,600 dr) and Limnos (12,700 dr) and two a week to Chios (7100 dr). The Olympic Airways office (☎ 28 659) is at Kavetsou 44.

Ferry In summer there are daily boats to Piraeus (12 hours, 6800 dr), some via Chios. There are three a week to Kavala (6300 dr) via Limnos and two a week to Thessaloniki (8100 dr). Ferries to Turkey cost 16,000 dr. The port police (☎ 28 827) are next to Picolo Travel on Pavlou Kountouriotou.

Getting Around

There are two bus stations in Mytilini, both by the harbour. The one for long-distance buses is just beyond the south-western end of Pavlou Kountouriotou. For local villages go to the northernmost section. There are many car and motorcycle-rental firms.

SAMOTHRAKI Σαμοθράκη
☎ 0551

Until a decade ago, Samothraki was Greece's best kept secret, visited only by archaeologists and a few adventurers. But inevitably this wild, alluring island has been discovered by holiday-makers. Most people stick to the resorts of Kamariotissa, Loutra (Therma) and Pahia Ammos, leaving the rest of the island untouched.

Orientation & Information

Samothraki's port is Kamariotissa on the north-west coast. The island's capital, the hora (also called Samothraki), is 5km inland. There is no EOT office or tourist police and the regular police are in the hora. The bus station is on the waterfront just east of the quay.

Things to See & Do

Sanctuary of the Great Gods This hushed, ancient site at Paleopolis is shrouded in mystery. No one knows quite what went on here, only that it was a place of initiation into the cult of the Kabeiroi, the gods of fertility. They were believed to help seafarers, and to be initiated into their mysteries was seen as a safeguard against misfortune and in particular against shipwreck. Its winding pathways lead through lush shrubbery to extensive ruins.

The famous Winged Victory of Samothrace, which now has pride of place in the Louvre, was taken from here in the last century. Both the site and its little museum are open Tuesday to Sunday from 8.30 am to 3 pm. Admission to each is 500 dr (free on Sunday and public holidays).

Mt Fengari Legend tells that it was from the summit of Mt Fengari (1611m) that Poseidon, god of the sea and of earthquakes, watched the progress of the Trojan War. A difficult climb, Mt Fengari should only be tackled by experienced trekkers. Guides can be hired in Loutra.

Walks The island is a walker's paradise. The glorious scenery combines the jagged rocks of Mt Fengari's slopes with shady groves of plane trees, bubbling waterfalls, gentle undulating hills and meadows ablaze with wild flowers.

From the kastro ruin in the hora, a dirt track leads to Paleopolis. The walk takes about an hour.

Samothraki's only sandy beach, **Pahia Ammos**, can be reached by walking along an 8km dirt track from Lakoma.

Places to Stay & Eat

There are two private camping grounds at Loutra, and you will probably be able to camp (unofficially) at Pahia Ammos.

Otherwise, the most pleasant place to stay is the hora. Its Turkish-era houses are built in amphitheatre fashion on two adjacent mountain slopes and the town is totally authentic. There are no hotels, just rooms in private houses.

Cheap eateries line Kamariotissa's waterfront. In the hora, the *psistaria* on the square

where the bus stops and *Taverna Kastro* on the central square both serve good local food.

Getting There & Around

See Getting There & Away under Alexandroupolis in the Northern Greece section. In summer there are usually five departures a week between Kavala and Samothraki. The port police (☎ 41 305) are on the eastern waterfront.

Buses run from Kamariotissa to the hora and Loutra via Paleopolis, and to Profitis Ilias via Lakoma. In summer, caïques sail between Kamariotissa and Pahia Ammos. There is a motorcycle-rental outlet opposite the harbour.

Sporades Σποράδες

The Sporades group comprises the lush, pine-forested islands of Skiathos, Skopelos and Alonnisos, south of the Halkidiki Peninsula, and far-flung Skyros, off Evia.

Getting There & Away

Air Skiathos receives lots of charter flights from northern Europe. In summer there are daily flights from Athens to both Skiathos (16,400 dr) and Skyros (13,900 dr). There's also the odd flight between the two (9100 dr).

Ferry Skiathos, Skopelos and Alonnisos have frequent ferry services to the mainland ports of Volos and Agios Konstantinos, as well as one or two a week to Kymi (Evia), via Skyros.

In summer, three hydrofoils a week connect Skyros with other islands in the Sporades.

SKIATHOS Σκίαθος
☎ 0247

Skiathos is tagged the Mykonos of the Sporades, which means it's crowded and expensive. If you decide to go, however, the tourist police (☎ 23 172) on Papadiamanti 8, the port's main street, will help you to find accommodation. Ferries dock at Skiathos town.

SKOPELOS Σκόπελος
☎ 0424

Skopelos is less commercialised than Skiathos, but following hot on its trail. Skopelos town is an attractive place of white houses built on a hillside, with mazes of narrow streets and stairways leading up to the kastro. **Glossa**, the island's other town, lying inland in the north, is similarly appealing with fewer concessions to tourism. There is no tourist office or tourist police. The post office is signposted from the port, as is the OTE, although both are well hidden in the labyrinth of alleyways behind the waterfront.

Things to See
Four kilometres from Skopelos town, **Staphylos** is a decent beach that gets very crowded; over a headland is **Velanio**, the island's designated nudist beach.

The 2km stretch of tiny pebbles at **Milia**, 10km farther on, is considered the island's best beach.

Places to Stay & Eat
The island has no camping ground, but in Skopelos town there are plenty of rooms in family houses.

Pension Soula (☎ 22 930) has doubles/triples with private bath for 8000/10,000 dr, a communal kitchen and garden. To find it, turn left at the Hotel Amalia and follow the road, bearing right after about 200m. You will find the house on the right.

Kyr Sotos (☎ 22 805), in a lovely old building in the middle of the waterfront, has doubles/triples for 8800/14,600 dr, a communal kitchen and courtyard.

For a cheap, basic and popular restaurant, try *O Platanos*, on the way to the post office. To find it, walk up the road opposite the bus station, take the first left, the first right, the first left again, and it's on the right.

Getting There & Away
There are frequent ferries to Volos (2820 dr) and Agios Konstantinos (3480 dr). These boats also call at Alonnisos and Skiathos. Many hydrofoil services to Skopelos also call at Loutraki, the port for Glossa.

Getting Around
There are frequent buses from Skopelos town to Glossa, stopping at the beaches on the way.

The car and motorcycle-rental outlets are mostly at the eastern end of the waterfront.

ALONNISOS Αλόννησος
☎ 0424

Alonnisos is the least visited of these three islands. In 1965 the island suffered a major earthquake which devastated the inland *hora* (town centre), and villagers were forced to move to the harbour town of Patitiri.

Things to See & Do
One of the best beaches is **Kokkinokastro** (red castle), so named because the earth around here is red. Other good beaches line the coast. Alonnisos is an ideal island for walking. A winding path starting from just beyond Pension Galini in Patitiri leads within 40 minutes to the hora. **Gialia Beach**, on the west coast, is a 20-minute walk from the hora.

Places to Stay & Eat
There are two camping grounds: *Camping Rocks* (☎ 65 410) in Patitiri and *Ikaros Camping* (☎ 65 258) on the east coast at Steni Vala beach. There is a Rooms to Let service (☎ 65 577) opposite the quay.

Pension Galini (☎ 65 573) is a good budget choice: doubles/triples cost 8000/9500 dr with private bath. Spacious, well-equipped apartments for five/six people are also available for 14,000/17,000 dr. The pension is on the left, 400m up Pelasgon.

For imaginatively prepared local cuisine, try *To Kamaki Ouzeri*, on the left side of Ikion Dolopon.

Getting There & Away
There are frequent ferries to Volos (3700 dr) and Agios Konstantinos (4330 dr) via Skiathos and Skopelos.

Getting Around
In summer, caïques take passengers to the east-coast beaches.

Ionian Islands
Τα Επτάνησα

The Ionian islands stretch down the west coast of Greece from Corfu in the north to remote Kythira, off the southern tip of the Peloponnese.

Getting There & Away
Air There are lots of charter flights to Corfu from Northern Europe in summer, as well as a few flights to Kefallonia and Zakynthos. Olympic has daily flights from Athens to Corfu, Zakynthos and Kefallonia.

Ferry Most ferries between Italy and Patras call at Corfu. In summer, there are also direct services from Brindisi and Bari to Kefallonia.

For interisland ferries and ferries to the mainland, see the Getting There & Away sections under the respective islands.

CORFU Κέρκυρα
Corfu is the most important island in the group, with a population of more than 100,000.

Corfu Town
☎ 0661
The old town of Corfu, wedged between two fortresses, occupies a peninsula on the island's east coast. The narrow alleyways of high shuttered tenements in mellow ochres and pinks are an immediate reminder of the town's long association with Venice.

Orientation & Information The town's old fortress (Palaio Frourio) stands on an eastern promontory, separated from the town by an area of parks and gardens known as the Spianada. The new fortress (Neo Frourio) lies to the north-west. Ferries dock at the new port, just west of the new fortress. The long-distance bus station is on Avrami, just inland from the port.

The EOT office (☎ 37 520) is on Rizospaston Voulefton, between the OTE and the post office, and the tourist police (☎ 30 265) are at Samartzi 4. All the major Greek banks are in town, including the National Bank on the corner of Voulgareos and Theotoki. American Express is represented by Greek Skies Tours (☎ 30 883), Kapodistriou 20A.

The Corfu General Hospital (☎ 45 811) is on Polithroni Kostanda.

Things to See The **archaeological museum**, Vraili 5, houses a collection of finds from Mycenaean to classical times. The star attraction is the pediment from the Temple of Artemis, decorated with gorgons. Opening times are Tuesday to Saturday from 8.45 am to 3 pm and Sunday from 9.30 am to 2.30 pm; admission is 800 dr.

The **Church of Agios Spiridon**, Corfu's most famous church, has an elaborately decorated interior. Pride of place is given to the remains of St Spiridon, displayed in a silver casket; four times a year they are paraded around the town.

Places to Stay & Eat *Camping Kontokali Beach* (☎ 91 202), 5km north-west of town, is the closest of the island's six camping grounds. Take bus No 7 from Plateia San Rocco.

There are no decent budget places in town. A lot of people wind up at the *Hotel Europa* (☎ 39 304), but only because it's close to the port – signposted off Xenofondos Stratigou. It charges 5500/6000 dr for singles/doubles.

The cheapest reasonable rooms are at the *Hotel Ionian* (☎ 30 268), also near the port at Xenofondos Stratigou 46. It charges 8500/11,000 for singles/doubles with bathroom. A step up from this is the C-class *Hotel Constantinopolis* (☎ 48 716/717), Zavitsianou 3. Once a shabby, backpacker favourite, it has been reborn as a splendid Art Nouveau hotel with singles/doubles for 12,500/18,600 dr.

If you want to splurge, the *Cavelieri* (☎ 39 041; fax 39 283), Kapodistriou 4, is an elegant A-class hotel with singles/doubles for 28,000/31,000 dr.

Gistakis Restaurant, Solomou 20, serves excellent Corfiot regional food. Main dishes are priced from 900 dr.

Around the Island
There's hardly anywhere in Corfu that hasn't made its play for the tourist dollar, but the

CORFU

GREECE

north is totally over the top. The only attraction is the view from the summit of **Mt Pantokrator** (906m), Corfu's highest mountain. There's a road to the top from the village of **Strinila**.

The main resort on the west coast is **Paleokastritsa**, which is built round a series of pretty bays. Farther south, there are good beaches around the small village of **Agios Gordios**. Between Paleokastritsa and Agios Gordios is the hill-top village of **Pelekas**, supposedly the best place on Corfu to watch the sunset.

Places to Stay

Accommodation on Corfu is dominated by package groups. Most backpackers head straight for the *Pink Palace* (☎ 53 103/4; fax 53 025; pink-palace@ker.forthnet.gr), a huge complex of restaurants, bars and budget rooms that tumbles down a hillside outside Agios Gordios. It charges 6000 dr per day for bed, breakfast and dinner. Debauchery is the main item on a menu designed for young travellers who want to party hard. The place is open from April to November, and staff meet the boats. It has Internet access.

CORFU TOWN

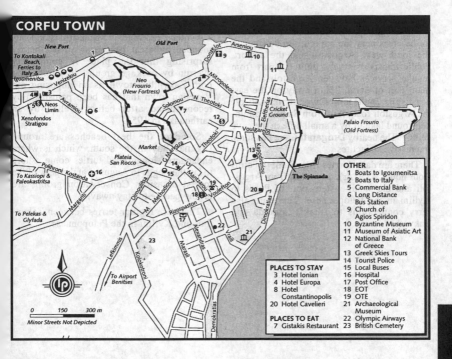

OTHER
1 Boats to Igoumenitsa
2 Boats to Italy
5 Commercial Bank
6 Long Distance Bus Station
9 Church of Agios Spiridon
10 Byzantine Museum
11 Museum of Asiatic Art
12 National Bank of Greece
13 Greek Skies Tours
14 Tourist Police
15 Local Buses
16 Hospital
17 Post Office
18 EOT
19 OTE
21 Archaeological Museum
22 Olympic Airways
23 British Cemetery

PLACES TO STAY
3 Hotel Ionian
4 Hotel Europa
8 Hotel Constantinopolis
20 Hotel Cavelieri

PLACES TO EAT
7 Gistakis Restaurant

Minor Streets Not Depicted
0   150   300 m

Getting There & Away

Air Olympic Airways flies to Athens (20,400 dr) at least three times a day and to Thessaloniki (20,600 dr) twice a week. The Olympic Airways office (☎ 38 694) is at Polila 11 in Corfu town.

Bus There are daily buses to Athens and Thessaloniki from the Avrami terminal in Corfu town. The fare of 9300 dr to Athens includes the ferry to Igoumenitsa. The trip takes 11 hours.

Ferry There are hourly ferries to Igoumenitsa (1½ hours, 1400 dr) and a daily ferry to Paxoi. In summer, there are daily services to Patras (10 hours, 5800 dr) on the international ferries that call at Corfu on their way from Italy. (See Getting There & Away at the start of the Ionian Islands section.)

Getting Around

Buses for villages close to Corfu town leave from Plateia San Rocco. Services to other destinations leave from the bus terminal on Avrami. The EOT gives out a schedule.

ITHAKI Ιθάκη

Ithaki is the fabled home of Odysseus, the hero of Homer's *Odyssey*, who pined for his island during his journeys to far-flung lands. It's a quiet place with some isolated coves. From the main town of Vathy you can walk to the **Arethusa Fountain**, the fabled site of Odysseus' meeting with the swineherd Eumaeus on his return to Ithaki. Take water with you, as the fountain dries up in summer.

Ithaki has daily ferries to the mainland ports of Patras and Astrakos, as well as daily services to Kefallonia and Lefkada.

KEFALLONIA Κεφαλλονιά

Tourism remains relatively low-key on

mountainous Kefallonia, the largest island of the Ionian group. Resort hotels are confined to the areas near the capital, the beaches in the south-west, Argostoli and the airport. Public transport is very limited, apart from regular services between Argostoli and the main port of Sami, 25km away on the east coast. The **Melissani Cave**, signposted off the Argostoli road 4km from Sami, is an underground lake lit by a small hole in the cave ceiling. The nearby **Drogarati Cave** has some impressive stalactites.

There are daily ferries from Sami to Patras (four hours, 3250 dr), as well as from Argostoli and the south-eastern port of Poros to Kyllini in the Peloponnese. There are also ferry connections to Ithaki, Lefkada and Zakynthos.

ZAKYNTHOS Ζάκυνθος

Zakynthos, or Zante, is a beautiful island surrounded by great beaches – so it's hardly surprising that the place is completely overrun by package groups. Its capital and port, Zakynthos town, is an imposing old Venetian town that has been painstakingly reconstructed after being levelled by an earthquake in 1953.

Some of the best beaches are around **Laganas Bay** in the south, which is where endangered loggerhead turtles come ashore to lay their eggs in August – at the peak of the tourist invasion. Conservation groups are urging people to stay away.

There are regular ferries between Zakynthos and Kyllini in the Peloponnese.

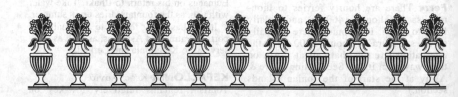

Italy

A unified nation only for the past century, Italy is a magnificently complex, if unevenly woven, tapestry.

After the collapse of the empire, Rome continued to exercise extraordinary power and attract exuberant wealth as seat of the Catholic Church, but its hold over the rest of the peninsula was far from complete. City-states to the north and feudal kingdoms to the south shared control and together left a legacy of unparalleled diversity. To travel from Bolzano to Palermo is to cross from the rim of the Germanic universe to a realm of near North African languor.

Centuries ago, well-to-do northern Europeans were drawn to the Mediterranean light, and so the Grand Tour (of Europe) was born. What they found in Italy was an extraordinary cocktail: next to the awe-inspiring artistic wealth of Rome, Venice and Florence they often encountered squalid decadence, poverty and spivs on the make.

The economic miracles of the past decades have transformed the country, but beneath all the style, fine food and delicious wine, there remains, happily, a certain chaotic air. Not everything is wonderful – expanding industry, poor urban planning, unchecked resort construction and what at times seems like an almost wilful indifference to the nation's art treasures have too often blighted the cities and countryside.

You could not hope to experience all the wonders of the country in even a year's nonstop travel. From the grandeur of the Dolomites to the rainbow-coloured sea of Sardinia, there is much more to the country than St Peter's and the Uffizi.

Facts about Italy

HISTORY

Italy's strategic position in the Mediterranean made it a target for colonisers and invaders over thousands of years. But it also gave the Romans an excellent base from which to expand their empire. Italy's history is thus a patchwork of powerful empires and foreign

AT A GLANCE

Capital	Rome
Population	57.8 million
Area	301,278 sq km (inc San Marino & Vatican City)
Official Language	Italian
Currency	1 Italian lira (L) = 100 centesimi
GDP	US$1.12 trillion (1996)
Time	GMT/UTC+0100

domination. Its people have a diverse ethnic background, and from the fall of the Roman Empire until the Risorgimento (the Italian unification movement) in 1860, the country was never a unified entity.

The traditional date for the founding of Rome by Romulus is 753 BC, but the country had been inhabited for thousands of years. Palaeolithic Neanderthals lived in Italy during the last Ice Age more than 20,000 years ago, and by the start of the Bronze Age, around 2000 BC, the peninsula had been settled by several Italic tribes.

ITALY (ITALIA)

The Etruscans

From about 900 BC, or possibly earlier, the Etruscan civilisation developed until these mysterious people, whose origins are still controversial, dominated the area between the Arno and Tiber valleys.

After the foundation of Rome, Etruscan civilisation continued to flourish and three of the seven kings who ruled Rome before the republic were Etruscan, known as the Tarquins. By the end of the 3rd century BC the Romans had overwhelmed the last Etruscan city.

The Roman Republic

The new Roman republic, after recovering from the invasion of the Gauls in 390 BC, began its expansion into the south of Italy. The Greeks had colonised this area, which they called Magna Grecia, as early as the 8th century BC, and they had established cities such as Syracuse, which rivalled Athens in power.

By about 265 BC Rome had taken the south from Greece, and Sicily was held by Carthage. Rome claimed Sicily following the First Punic War, and although the Romans were defeated by Hannibal at Lago Trasimeno after his legendary crossing of the Alps during the Second Punic War, Rome eventually defeated and destroyed Carthage in 202 BC. Within another few years Rome also claimed Spain and Greece within the empire.

Expansion & Empire

In the 1st century BC, Rome had conquered Gaul, invaded Britain, and established a series of client kingdoms in the Middle East. After Caesar's assassination on the Ides of March in 44 BC, a power struggle began between Mark Antony and Octavius, Caesar's great-nephew whom he had adopted as his heir, leading to the deaths of Antony and Cleopatra in Egypt in 31 BC. Octavius took the title of Augustus and he became, in effect, the first emperor. Augustus ruled for 45 years, and this was a period of political stability which produced great advancements in engineering, architecture, administration and literature.

The Eastern & Western Empires

By the end of the 3rd century, the empire had grown to such an extent that Emperor Diocletian divided it between east and west for administrative purposes. His reign was also noted for the persecution of Christians. His eventual successor, Constantine, declared religious freedom for Christians and moved the seat of the empire to the eastern capital, Byzantium, which he renamed Constantinople. During the 4th century, Christianity was declared the official state religion and grew in power and influence; at the same time Rome was under constant threat of barbarian invasion.

By the early 5th century, German tribes had entered Rome, and in 476 the Western Roman Empire ended when the German warrior, Odoacer, deposed the emperor and declared himself ruler.

While the Eastern Roman Empire continued to exist and even retook part of the country for Byzantium in 553, this was the period of the Dark Ages during which Italy became a battleground of barbarians fighting for control. The south and Sicily were dominated by Muslim Arabs until the Normans invaded in 1036 and established a kingdom there.

With a view to re-establishing the Western Roman Empire, Pope Leo II crowned the Frankish king, Charlemagne, emperor in 800 AD. However, the empire again declined under Charlemagne's successors, culminating in the foundation of the Holy Roman Empire in 962 by the German king Otto I, who also declared himself emperor.

The City-States

The Middle Ages in Italy were marked by the development of powerful city-states in the north, while in the south the Normans were busily imposing a severe feudal system on their subjects. After the mid-12th century, when Frederick Barbarossa was crowned emperor, conflict between Pope Alexander III and the emperor reached the point where Italy again became a battleground as cities became either Guelph (supporters of the pope) or Ghibelline (supporters of the emperor). The factional struggles died gradually, but did not prevent a period of great economic, architectural and artistic development. This was the time of Dante, Petrarch and Boccaccio, Giotto, Cimabue and Pisano. The city-states flourished under the rule of

ITALY

powerful families and the papal states were established, even though a rival papacy had been established in Avignon.

The Renaissance

It was not until the 15th century and the arrival of the Renaissance that Italy rediscovered its former glory. This period was marked by savage intercity wars, internal feuding and French invasions, but the Renaissance, which began in Florence, also spread throughout the country, fostering genius of the likes of Brunelleschi, Donatello, Bramante, Botticelli, da Vinci, Masaccio, Lippi, Raphael and, of course, Michelangelo.

By the early 16th century, the Reformation had arrived in Italy and by 1559 much of the country was under Spanish rule. This lasted until 1713 when, following the War of Spanish Succession, control of Italy passed to the Austrians. The powerful states of the country's north, however, continued to grow in power. It was not until after the invasion by Napoleon in 1796 that, for the first time since the fall of the Roman Empire, a degree of unity was introduced into the country. The Congress of Vienna in 1815, which restored power to the nobles and revived the old territorial divisions in Italy, created great discontent among the people and led directly to the Risorgimento, the movement to unite the country under one rule.

The Risorgimento

Under the leadership of Garibaldi, Cavour and Mazzini, the unification movement gained momentum until Garibaldi and his Expedition of One Thousand (also known as the Redshirts) took Sicily and Naples in 1860. The kingdom of Italy was declared in 1861 and Vittorio Emanuele was proclaimed king. Venice was wrested from Austria in 1866 and Rome from the papacy in 1870. However, the new government had great difficulty achieving national unity. As Cavour noted before his death in 1861: 'To harmonise north and south is harder than fighting with Austria or struggling with Rome'.

Mussolini & WWII

In the years after WWI, Italy was in turmoil and in 1921 the Fascist Party, formed by Benito Mussolini in 1919, won 35 of the 135 seats in parliament. In October 1921, after a period of considerable unrest and strikes, the king asked Mussolini to form a government, and he became the prime minister with only 7% representation in parliament.

The Fascists won the 1924 elections, following a campaign marked by violence and intimidation. By the end of 1925 Mussolini had become head of state, expelled opposition parties from parliament, gained control of the press and trade unions and reduced the voting public by two-thirds. He formed the Rome-Berlin axis with Hitler in 1936 and Italy entered WWII as an ally of Germany in June 1941. After a series of military disasters and an invasion by the Allies, in 1943 the King decided to support an armistice. He led a coup against Mussolini and had him arrested. After being rescued by the Germans, Mussolini tried to govern in the north, but was fiercely opposed by Italian partisans, who finally shot him and his mistress, Clara Petacci, in April 1945.

The Italian Republic

In 1946, following a referendum, the constitutional monarchy was abolished and the republic established.

Italy was a founding member of the European Economic Community in 1957 and was seriously disrupted by terrorism in the 1970s following the appearance of the Red Brigades, who kidnapped and assassinated the Christian Democrat prime minister, Aldo Moro, in 1978.

In the decades that followed WWII, Italy's national government was dominated by the centre-right Christian Democrats, usually in coalition with other parties (excluding the Communists). Italy enjoyed significant economic growth in the 1980s, but the 1990s heralded a new period of crisis for the country, both economically and politically. Against the backdrop of a severe economic crisis, the very foundations of Italian politics were shaken by a national bribery scandal.

The 1990s

The *tangentopoli* ('kickback-ville') scandal broke in Milan in early 1992 when a functionary of the Socialist Party was arrested on charges of accepting bribes in exchange for public works contracts. Investigations eventually implicated thousands of politicians, public officials and businesspeople, and left the main parties in tatters, effectively demolishing the centre of the Italian political spectrum.

National elections in March 1994 saw Italy move decisively to the right. A new right-wing coalition known as the Freedom Alliance (which includes the former Fascist National Alliance), led by billionaire media magnate Silvio Berlusconi, won the elections. Berlusconi, who had entered politics only three months before the elections, was appointed prime minister, but his government fell after only nine months. The last elections, held in April 1996, resulted in a centre-left coalition, led by economist Romano Prodi, winning the majority of votes. The win by the Olive Tree coalition represents a historic moment in Italian politics: for the first time since the establishment of the republic, the communists are participating in governing the country. In May 1998, when Italy was included in the first group of countries to join Europe's economic and monetary union (EMU), Prodi fulfilled one of his two main promises to the Italian people. The fact that the Olive Tree coalition has managed to remain in government for more than two years, with no serious signs of instability, indicates that he might also manage to realise his other promise: to serve a full five-year term (which would be a first in Italian postwar politics).

The Mafia

The 1990s have also seen Italy moving more decisively against the Sicilian Mafia, prompted by the 1992 assassinations of two prominent anti-Mafia judges. A major offensive in Sicily, plus the testimonies of several *pentiti* (informers or supergrasses), led to several important arrests – most notably of the Sicilian godfather, Salvatore 'Toto' Riina, who is now serving a life sentence. The man believed to have taken power after Riina's arrest, Giovanni Brusca, was arrested in May 1996 and implicated in the murders of anti-Mafia judges, Giovanni Falcone and Paolo Borsellino, as well as in the bombings in Florence, Milan and Rome in 1993, which damaged monuments and works of art and

killed several people. Brusca's various trials continue, as do both trials of former prime minister Giulio Andreotti. Andreotti is currently on trial in Palermo for alleged links with the Mafia, and in Perugia for alleged complicity in the 1979 murder of Carmine Pecorelli.

GEOGRAPHY & ECOLOGY

Italy's boot shape makes it one of the most recognisable countries in the world. The country, incorporating the islands of Sicily and Sardinia, is bound by the Adriatic, Ligurian, Tyrrhenian and Ionian seas, which all form part of the Mediterranean Sea. About 75% of the Italian peninsula is mountainous, with the Alps dividing the country from France, Switzerland and Austria, and the Apennines forming a backbone which extends from the Alps into Sicily. There are four active volcanoes: Stromboli and Vulcano (in the Aeolian Islands), Vesuvius (near Naples) and Etna (Sicily).

The countryside can be dramatically beautiful, but the long presence of humans on the peninsula has had a significant impact on the environment. Aesthetically the result is not always displeasing – much of the beauty of Tuscany, for instance, lies in the interaction of olive groves with vineyards, fallow fields and stands of cypress and pine. Centuries of tree clearing, combined with illegal building have also led to extensive land degradation and erosion. In May 1998, heavy rains caused a massive mudslide which engulfed a number of towns near Naples, killing more than 200 people. Many blamed erosion and poor planning for the disaster.

The alteration of the environment, combined with the Italians' passion for hunting (*la caccia*), has led to many native animals and birds becoming extinct, rare or endangered. Under laws progressively introduced this century, many animals and birds are now protected.

There are numerous national parks in Italy. Among the most important are the Parco Nazionale del Gran Paradiso and the Parco Nazionale dello Stelvio, both in the Alps, and the Parco Nazionale d'Abruzzo.

Central and southern Italy are sometimes subject to massive earthquakes. A series of

ITALY

quakes devastated parts of the Appenine areas of Umbria and the Marche in September 1997. There was an earthquake after four days of tremors in central Italy in April 1998.

GOVERNMENT & POLITICS

For administrative purposes Italy is divided into 20 regions, each of which have some degree of autonomy. The regions are then subdivided into provinces and municipalities.

The country is a parliamentary republic, headed by a president who appoints the prime minister. The parliament consists of a senate and chamber of deputies, both of which have equal legislative power. The seat of national government is in Rome. Until reforms were introduced in 1994, members of parliament were elected by what was probably the purest system of proportional representation in the world. Two-thirds of both houses are now elected on the basis of who receives the most votes in their district, basically the same as the first-past-the-post system in the UK. The old system generally produced unstable coalition governments – Italy had 53 governments in the 48 years between the declaration of the republic and the introduction of electoral reforms.

ECONOMY

Italy has the fifth-largest economy in the world, thanks to some spectacular growth in the 1980s. However, the severe economic crisis of 1992-93 prompted a succession of governments to pull the economy into line with draconian measures such as the partial privatisation of the country's huge public sector. The Olive Tree coalition worked hard to meet the Maastricht criteria for entry into the European Monetary Union (EMU), cutting the budget deficit and lowering inflation in time to be included in the first intake of countries in May 1998.

Despite years of effort and the expenditure of trillions of lire, a significant economic gap still exists between Italy's northern and southern regions. The fact remains that Italy's richest regions (Piedmont, Lombardy, Veneto and Emilia-Romagna) are all northern, and its poorest (Calabria, Campania and Sicily) are all southern.

POPULATION & PEOPLE

The population of Italy is 57.8 million. The country has the lowest birthrate in Europe – a surprising fact considering the Italians' preoccupation with children and family. Foreigners may like to think of Italy as a land of passionate, animated people who gesticulate wildly when speaking, love to eat, drive like maniacs and don't like to work. However, it will take more than a holiday in Italy to understand its vigorous and remarkably diverse inhabitants. Overall the people remain fiercely protective of their regional customs, including their dialects and cuisine.

ARTS
Architecture, Painting & Sculpture

Italy has often been called a living art museum and certainly it is not always necessary to enter a gallery to appreciate the country's artistic wealth – it is all around you as you walk through Florence or Venice, or a medieval hill-top village in Umbria. In Rome the Forum, the Colosseum and the Pantheon are juxtaposed with churches and palaces of the medieval, Renaissance and baroque periods. Near Rome, at Tarquinia, you can visit 2000-year-old Etruscan tombs to see the vibrant funerary artwork of this ancient civilisation.

In Italy's south and in Sicily, where Greek colonisation preceded Roman domination, there are important Greek archaeological sites such as the temples at Paestum, south of Salerno, and at Agrigento in Sicily. Pompeii and Herculaneum give us an idea of how ancient Romans lived.

Byzantine mosaics adorn churches throughout Italy, most notably at Ravenna, in the Basilica of San Marco at Venice, and in Monreale cathedral near Palermo. There are also some interesting mosaics in churches in Rome. In Apulia, you can tour the magnificent Romanesque churches, a legacy of the Normans (the region's medieval rulers) and their successors, the Swabians.

The Renaissance The 15th and early 16th centuries in Italy saw one of the most remarkable explosions of artistic and literary achievement in recorded history – the Renaissance. Giotto di Bondone (1267-1337),

REGIONS OF ITALY

known simply as Giotto, revolutionised painting by introducing naturalism into his works and was one of the most important precursors of the Renaissance. Among his most noted works are the frescoes of the Scrovegni Chapel in Padua.

Patronised mainly by the Medici family in Florence and the popes in Rome, painters, sculptors, architects and writers flourished and many artists of genius emerged. The High Renaissance (about 1490-1520) was dominated by three men: Leonardo da Vinci (1452-1519), Michelangelo Buonarrotti (1475-1564) and Raphael (1483-1520).

A tour of Renaissance artworks would alone fill an extended trip to Italy. In Florence there is Italy's best known art gallery, the Uffizi. Ten of its rooms trace the development of Florentine and Tuscan painting from the 13th to 16th centuries, and works include Botticelli's *Birth of Venus* and *Primavera* (Spring) and Leonardo da Vinci's *Annunciation*. In the Accademia is Michelangelo's *David*, while the Bargello houses Donatello's bronze *David*. At the Vatican in Rome there is Michelangelo's ceiling and *Last Judgment* in the Sistine Chapel and Raphael's frescoes in Pope Julius II's private apartment. In St Peter's Basilica is Michelangelo's *Pietà* and his *Moses* is in the church of San Pietro in Vincoli.

Baroque The baroque period (17th century) was characterised by sumptuous, often fantastic architecture and richly decorative painting and sculpture.

In Rome there are many works by the great baroque sculptor and architect Gianlorenzo Bernini (1598-1680), including the central fountain in Piazza Navona. Rome's best loved baroque work is the Trevi Fountain. Cities which were literally transformed by baroque architecture include Lecce, Noto in Sicily and Naples.

Later Styles Neoclassicism in Italy produced the sculptor, Canova (1757-1822). Of Italy's modern artists, Amedeo Modigliani (1884-1920) is perhaps the most famous. The early 20th century also produced an artistic movement known as the Futurists, who rejected the sentimental art of the past and were infatuated by new technology, including

modern warfare. Fascism produced its own style of architecture in Italy, characterised by the EUR satellite city and the work of Marcello Piacentini (1881-1960), which includes the *Stadio dei Marmi* at Rome's Olympic Stadium complex.

Music

Few modern Italian singers or musicians have made any impact outside Italy – one exception is Zucchero (Adelmo Fornaciari), who has become well known in the USA and UK as Sugar. Instead, it is in the realms of opera and instrumental music where Italian artists have triumphed. Antonio Vivaldi (1675-1741) created the concerto in its present form. Verdi, Puccini, Bellini, Donizetti and Rossini, composers from the 19th and early 20th centuries, are all stars of the modern operatic era. Tenor Luciano Pavarotti (1935-) is today's luminary of Italian opera.

Literature

Before Dante wrote his *Divina Commedia* (Divine Comedy) and confirmed vernacular Italian as a serious medium for poetic expression, Latin was the language of writers. Among the greatest writers of ancient Rome were Cicero, Virgil, Ovid and Petronius.

A contemporary of Dante was Petrarch (Francesco Petrarca 1304-74). Giovanni Boccaccio (1313-75), author of the *Decameron*, is considered the first Italian novelist.

Machiavelli's *The Prince*, although a purely political work, has proved the most lasting of the Renaissance works. Alessandro Manzoni (1785-1873) worked hard to establish a narrative language which was accessible to all Italians in his great historical novel *The Betrothed*.

The turbulence of political and social life in Italy in the 20th century has produced a wealth of literature. The often virulent poetry of ardent nationalist, Gabriele d'Annunzio, was perhaps not of the highest quality, but his voice was a prestige tool for Mussolini's fascists.

Italy's richest contribution to modern literature has been in the novel and short story. Cesare Pavese and Carlo Levi both endured internal exile in southern Italy during fascism. Levi based *Christ Stopped at Eboli* on his experiences in exile in Basilicata. The works of Italo Calvino border on the fantastical, thinly veiling his preoccupation with human behaviour in society.

Natalia Ginzburg has produced prose, essays and theatre. Alberto Moravia was a prolific writer who concentrated on describing Rome and its people. The novels of Elsa Morante are characterised by a subtle psychological appraisal of her characters. Umberto Eco shot to fame with his first and best known work, *The Name of the Rose*.

Theatre

At a time when French playwrights ruled the stage, the Venetian Carlo Goldoni (1707-93) attempted to bring Italian theatre back into the limelight with the *commedia dell'arte*, the tradition of improvisational theatre based on a core of set characters including Pulcinella and Arlecchino. Luigi Pirandello (1867-1936) threw into question every preconception of what theatre should be with such classics as *Six Characters in Search of an Author*. Pirandello won the Nobel Prize in 1934. Modern Italian theatre's most enduring contemporary representative is actor/director Dario Fo, who won the Nobel Prize in 1998.

Cinema

Born in Turin in 1904, the Italian film industry originally made an impression with silent spectaculars. Its most glorious era began as WWII came to a close in Europe, when the neorealists began making their films. One of the earliest examples of this new wave in cinema was Luchino Visconti's *Obsession*. From 1945 to 1947, Roberto Rossellini produced three neorealist masterpieces, including *Rome Open City*, starring Anna Magnani. Vittorio de Sica produced another classic in 1948, *Bicycle Thieves*.

Schooled with the masters of neorealism, Federico Fellini in many senses took the creative baton from them and carried it into the following decades, with films such as *La Dolce Vita*, with Anita Ekberg and Marcello Mastroianni. The career of Michelangelo Antonioni reached a climax with *Blow-up* in 1967. Pier Paolo Pasolini's films included *Accattone* and *Decameron*.

Bernardo Bertolucci had his first international hit with *Last Tango in Paris*. He made the blockbuster *The Last Emperor* in 1987. Franco Zeffirelli's most recent film was *Jane Eyre*. Other notable directors include the Taviani brothers, Marco Ferreri, Giuseppe Tornatore and actors-directors Massimo Troisi, Roberto Benigni and Nanni Moretti.

Italy's first international film star was Rudolph Valentino. Among Italy's most successful actors since WWII are Totò, Marcello Mastroianni, Anna Magnani, Gina Lollobrigida and Sophia Loren.

SOCIETY & CONDUCT

It is difficult to make blanket assertions about Italian culture, if only because Italians have lived together as a nation for little over 100 years. Prior to unification, the peninsula was long subject to a varied mix of masters and cultures. This lack of unity contributed to the survival of local dialects and customs. Even today many Italians tend to identify more strongly with their region or home town than with the nation. An Italian is first and foremost a Tuscan or Sicilian, or even a Roman or Neapolitan.

In some parts of Italy, especially in the south, women might be harassed if they wear skimpy or see-through clothing. Modest dress is expected in all churches, and even churches that are major tourist attractions, such as St Peter's in Rome, strictly enforce dress codes (no shorts, bare arms or shoulders).

RELIGION

Around 85% of Italians profess to be Catholic. The remaining 15% includes about 700,000 Muslims, 500,000 evangelical Protestants, 140,000 Jehovah's Witnesses and smaller communities of Jewish people, Waldenses and Buddhists.

LANGUAGE

Although many Italians speak some English (it is studied at school), English is more widely understood in the north, particularly in major centres such as Milan, Florence and Venice. Staff at most hotels and restaurants usually speak a little English, but you will be better received if you at least attempt to communicate in Italian.

Italian is a Romance language which is related to French, Spanish, Portuguese and Romanian. The Romance languages belong to the Indo-European group of languages, which include English. Indeed, as English and Italian share Latin roots, you will recognise many Italian words.

Modern literary Italian developed in the 13th and 14th centuries, predominantly through the works of Dante, Petrarch and Boccaccio, who wrote chiefly in the Florentine dialect. The language drew on its Latin heritage and the many dialects of Italy to develop into the standard Italian of today. Although many and varied dialects are spoken in everyday conversation, standard Italian is the national language of schools, media and literature, and is understood throughout the country.

There are nearly 58 million speakers of Italian in Italy, half a million in Switzerland (where Italian is one of four official languages) and 1.5 million speakers in France and former Yugoslavia. As a result of migration, Italian is also widely spoken in the USA, Argentina, Brazil and Australia.

Many older Italians still expect to be addressed by the third person formal, that is, *Lei* instead of *Tu*. Also, it is not polite to use the greeting *ciao* when addressing strangers, unless they use it first; use *buongiorno* and *arrivederci*.

See the Language Section at the back of this book for pronunciation guidelines and useful words and phrases.

Facts for the Visitor

HIGHLIGHTS
Coming up with a Top 10 list for Italy is a little like trying to find the 10 shiniest gold ingots in Fort Knox. Bearing that in mind, you could try the following:

1. Florence
2. Aeolian Islands
3. Amalfi Coast
4. Siena
5. Italian food
6. The Cinque Terre
7. Ancient ruins of Rome, Pompeii & Paestum
8. Venice

9. Parco Naturale di Fanes-Sennes-Braies (in the Dolomites)
10. Carnevale in Ivrea (Piemonte)

SUGGESTED ITINERARIES
Depending on the length of your stay, you might want to see and do the following things:

Two days
    Visit Rome to see the Forum, the Colosseum, St Peter's Basilica and the Vatican museums.
One week
    Visit Rome and Florence, with detours in Tuscany to Siena and San Gimignano. Or visit Rome and Naples, with detours to Pompeii, Vesuvius and the Amalfi Coast.
Two weeks
    As above, plus Bologna, Verona, Ravenna and at least three days in Venice.
One month
    As above, but go to Sicily and perhaps Sardinia for one week. Explore the north, including the Alps and Liguria, and the south, including Matera and Apulia.

PLANNING
Climate & When to Go
Italy lies in a temperate zone, but the climates of the north and south vary. Summers are uniformly hot, but are often extremely hot and dry in the south. Winters can be severely cold in the north – particularly in the Alps, but also in the Po Valley – whereas they are generally mild in the south and in Sicily and Sardinia. The best time to visit Italy is in the off season, particularly April-June and September-October, when the weather is good, prices are lower and there are fewer tourists. During July and August (the high season) it is very hot, prices are inflated, the country swarms with tourists, and hotels by the sea and in the mountains are usually booked out. Note that many hotels and restaurants in seaside areas close down for the winter months.

Books & Maps
For a more comprehensive guide to Italy, pick up a copy of Lonely Planet's *Italy*. If you enjoy hiking, pick up a copy of Lonely Planet's new *Walking in Italy*.

For a potted history of the country, try the *Concise History of Italy* by Vincent Cronin.

A History of Contemporary Italy – Society and Politics 1943-1988 by Paul Ginsborg is well written and absorbing. Luigi Barzini's classic The Italians is a great introduction to Italian people and culture, while Excellent Cadavers: The Mafia and the Death of the First Italian Republic by Alexander Stille is a shocking and fascinating account of the Mafia in Sicily. Interesting introductions to travelling in Italy include A Traveller in Italy by HV Morton, who also wrote similar guides to Rome and southern Italy. A few suggestions on Italian literature are: The Leopard by Giuseppe de Lampedusa, Christ Stopped at Eboli by Carlo Levi, and The Name of the Rose by Umberto Eco.

For maps of cities, you will generally find those provided by the tourist office adequate. Excellent road and city maps are published by the Istituto Geografico de Agostini and are available in all major bookshops.

What to Bring

A backpack is a definite advantage in Italy, but if you plan to use a suitcase and portable trolley, be warned about the endless flights of stairs at train stations and in many of the smaller medieval towns, as well as the petty thieves who prey on tourists who have no hands free because they are carrying too much luggage. A small pack (with a lock) for use on day trips and for sightseeing is preferable to a handbag or shoulder bag, particularly in the southern cities where motorcycle bandits are very active. A money belt is absolutely essential in Italy, particularly in the south and in Sicily, but also in the major cities, where groups of dishevelled-looking women and children prey on tourists with bulging pockets.

In the more mountainous areas the weather can change suddenly, even in high summer, so remember to bring at least one item of warm clothing. Most importantly, bring a pair of hardy, comfortable, worn-in walking shoes. In many cities, pavements are uneven and often made of cobblestones.

TOURIST OFFICES

There are three main categories of tourist office in Italy: regional, provincial and local. Their names vary throughout the country.

Provincial offices are sometimes known as the Ente Provinciale per il Turismo (EPT) or, more commonly, the Azienda di Promozione Turistica (APT). The Azienda Autonoma di Soggiorno e Turismo (AAST) and Informazioni e Assistenza ai Turisti (IAT) offices usually have information only on the town itself. In some of the very small towns and villages the local tourist office is called a Pro Loco.

The quality of service offered varies dramatically throughout the country and don't be surprised if you encounter lethargic or even hostile staff. You should be able to get a map, an elenco degli alberghi (a list of hotels), a pianta della città (map of the town) and information on the major sights. Staff speak English in larger towns, but in the more out-of-the-way places you may have to rely on sign language. Tourist offices are generally open from 8.30 am to 12.30 or 1 pm and 3 to 7 pm Monday to Friday and on Saturday morning. Hours are often extended in summer.

Tourist Offices Abroad

Information about Italy can be obtained at Italian State Tourist Offices throughout the world, including:

Australia
  (☎ 02-9247 1308) Alitalia, Orient Overseas Building, suite 202, 32 Bridge St, Sydney 2000

Canada
  (☎ 514-866 7667; 739145@icam.net) 1 Place Ville Marie, suite 1914, Montreal, Quebec H3B-2C3

UK
  (☎ 0171-408 1254; Enitlond@globalnet.co.uk) 1 Princes Street, London W1R 9AY

USA
  (☎ 212-245 4822; enitnv@bwav.net) 630 Fifth Ave, suite 1565, New York, NY 10111
  (☎ 310-82 0098) 12400 Wilshire Blvd, suite 550, Los Angeles, CA 90025
  (☎ 312-644 0990) 500 North Michigan Ave, suite 2240, Chicago, IL 60611

Sestante CIT, Italy's national travel agency, also has offices throughout the world (known as CIT outside Italy). It can provide extensive information on Italy, as well as book tours and accommodation. It can also make train bookings. Offices include:

ITALY

Australia
(☎ 02-9267 1255; fkernot@cittravel.com.au)
269 Clarence St, Sydney 2000
(☎ 03-9650 5510) 227 Collins St, Melbourne
3000

Canada
(☎ 514-845 4939; citmil@videotron.ca) 1450
City Councillors St, suite 750, Montreal,
Quebec H3A 2E6
(☎ 905-415 1060; cittours@interlog.com) 80
Tiverton Court, suite 401, Markham, Ontario
L3R OG4

UK
(☎ 0181-686 0677; ciao@citalia.co.uk) Marco
Polo House, 3/5 Lansdown Rd, Croydon,
Surrey CR9 1LL

USA
(☎ 212-730 2121; citnewyork@msn.com) 15
West 44th Street, 10th floor, New York, NY
10036
(☎ 310-338 8615; citlax@email.msm.com)
6033 West Century Blvd, suite 980, Los
Angeles, CA 90045

The Centro Turistico Studentesco e Gio-
vanile (CTS) has offices all over Italy and
specialises in discounts for students and
young people, but is also useful for travellers
of any age looking for cheap flights and
sightseeing discounts. It is linked with the International Student Travel Confederation.
You can get a student card here if you have
documents proving that you are a student.

VISAS & EMBASSIES
EU citizens require only a national identity
card or a passport to stay in Italy for as long
as they like and since Italy is now a member
of the Schengen Area, EU citizens can enter
the country without passport controls.

Citizens of many other countries including
the USA, Australia, Canada and New
Zealand do not need to apply for visas before
arriving in Italy if they are entering the
country as tourists only. While there is an official three-month limit on tourist visits,
border authorities rarely stamp the passports
of visitors from western nations. If you are
entering the country for any reason other than
tourism, you should insist on having your
passport stamped. Visitors are technically
obliged to report to a *questura* (police station)
if they plan to stay at the same address for
more than one week, to receive a *permesso di*

soggiorno – in effect, permission to remain in
the country for a nominated period up to the
three-month limit. Tourists who are staying
in hotels, youth hostels etc are not required to
do this since proprietors are need to register
their guests with the police. A permesso di
soggiorno only becomes a necessity (for non-
EU citizens) if you plan to study, work
(legally) or live in Italy.

Foreigners who want to study at a university in Italy must have a student visa.
Australians and New Zealanders also require
a visa to study at a language school. This can
be obtained from the Italian embassy or consulate in your city, but you must have a letter
of acceptance from the university or school
you will be attending. This type of visa is re-
newable within Italy, but you will be required
to continue studying and provide proof that
you have enough money to support yourself
during the period of study. It should be noted
that the process to obtain a student visa can
take some months.

Citizens of EU countries are able to work
in Italy. If you are from another country and
want to work in Italy, you'll need a work
permit. Italian embassies and consulates in
your country can provide information (see
Work in this chapter).

Italian Embassies Abroad
Italian diplomatic missions abroad include:

Australia
(☎ 02-9392 7900) Level 45, The Gateway, 1
Macquarie Place, Sydney 2000
(☎ 03-9867 5744) 509 St Kilda Rd, Melbourne
3004

Canada
(☎ 416-977 2569) 136 Beverley St, Toronto
M5T 1Y5

France
(☎ 01 49 54 03 00) 47 Rue de Varennes,
75343 Paris

New Zealand
(☎ 04-473 53 39) 34 Grant Rd, Thorndon,
Wellington

UK
(☎ 0171-312 2200) 14 Three Kings Yard,
London W1 2EH

USA
(☎ 212-439 8600 or 737 9100) 690 Park Ave,
New York, NY 10021/5044
(☎ 415-931 4924) 2590 Webster St, San
Francisco, CA 94115

Foreign Embassies in Italy

The headquarters of most foreign embassies are in Rome, although there are generally British and US consulates in other major cities. The following addresses and phone numbers are for Rome (area code ☎ 06):

Australia
(☎ 85 27 21) Via Alessandria 215
Austria
(☎ 844 01 41) Via Pergolesi 3
Consulate: (☎ 855 29 66) Via Liegi 32
Canada
(☎ 44 59 81) Via G B de Rossi 27
Consulate: (☎ 44 59 81) Via Zara 30
France
(☎ 68 60 11) Piazza Farnese 67
Consulate: (☎ 68 80 21 52) Via Giulia 251
Germany
(☎ 88 47 41) Via Po 25c
Consulate: (☎ 88 47 41) Via Francesco Siacci 2c
Greece
(☎ 854 96 30) Via Mercadante 36
Consulate: (☎ 808 20 30) Via Stoppani 10
Japan
(☎ 48 79 91) Via Sella 60
New Zealand
(☎ 440 29 28) Via Zara 28
Spain
(☎ 687 81 72) Largo Fontanella Borghese 19
Switzerland
(☎ 808 36 41) Via Barnarba Oriani 61
Consulate: (☎ 808 83 61) Largo Elvezia 15
UK
(☎ 482 54 41) Via XX Settembre 80a
USA
(☎ 467 41) Via Vittorio Veneto 119a-121

For a complete list of all foreign embassies in Rome and other major cities throughout Italy, look in the local telephone book under *ambasciate* or *consolati*, or ask for a list at the tourist office.

CUSTOMS

People from outside Europe can import, without paying duty, two still cameras with 10 rolls of film, a movie or TV camera with 10 cartridges of film, a portable tape recorder with 'a reasonable amount' of tapes, a CD player, a transistor radio, a pair of binoculars, up to 200 cigarettes, two litres of wine and a litre of liquor.

Visitors who are residents of a European country and enter from an EU country can import a maximum of 300 cigarettes, one bottle of wine and half a bottle of liquor. There is no limit on the amount of lire you can import.

MONEY

A combination of travellers cheques and credit cards is the best way to take your money. If you buy travellers cheques in lire there should be no commission charged for cashing them. There are exchange offices at all major airports and train stations, but it is advisable to obtain a small amount of lire before arriving to avoid problems and queues at the airport and train stations.

Major credit cards, including Visa, Master-Card and American Express, are widely accepted in Italy and can be used for purchases for payment in hotels and restaurants (although smaller places might not accept them). They can also be used to get money from ATMs (*bancomats*) or, if you don't have a PIN, over the counter in major banks, including the Banca Commerciale Italiana, Cassa di Risparmio and Credito Italiano. If your credit card is lost, stolen or swallowed by an ATM, you can telephone toll-free (☎ 167-82 20 56) to have it cancelled. To cancel a MasterCard the number in Italy is ☎ 167-86 80 86, or you can make a reverse-charge call to St Louis in the USA (☎ 314-275 66 90). To cancel a Visa card in Italy, phone ☎ 1678-210 01. The toll-free emergency number to report a lost or stolen American Express card varies according to where the card was issued. Check with American Express in your country or contact American Express in Rome (☎ 06-722 82) which has a 24-hour cardholders' service.

The fastest way to have money sent to you is by 'urgent telex' through the foreign office of a large Italian bank, or through major banks in your own country to a nominated bank in Italy. Keep an exact record of all details associated with the money transfer, particularly the exact address of the Italian bank where the money has been sent. This will always be the head office of the bank in the town to which the money has been sent. Urgent telex transfers will take only a few days, while other means, such as by draft, can take weeks. You will be required to produce identification, usually a passport, in order to collect the money.

A more recent and speedy option is to send money through Western Union (☎ 167-01 38 39 toll-free). This service functions in Italy through the Mail Boxes Etc chain of stores, which you will find in the bigger cities. The sender and receiver have to turn up at a Western Union outlet with passport or other form of ID and the fees charged for the virtually immediate transfer depend on the amount sent.

Currency

From January 1, 2002, Italy will have a new currency, the euro, as one of 11 EU countries in the first intake for the European Monetary Union (EMU). The euro becomes a currency in the financial sense (it can be traded on international exchanges) from January 1999. The actual notes and coins will be phased in over the first six months of the year 2002. Italy's present currency is the lira (plural: lire). The smallest note is L1000. Other denominations in notes are L2000, L5000, L10,000, L50,000, L100,000 and L500,000. Coin denominations are L50, L100, L200, L500 and L1000. Note that Italians (like other Continental Europeans) indicate decimals with commas and thousands with points.

Exchange Rates

Australia	A$1	=	L1069
Canada	C$1	=	L1159
euro	€1	=	L1943
France	1FF	=	L294
Germany	DM1	=	L986
Japan	¥100	=	L1227
New Zealand	NZ$1	=	L899
UK	UK£1	=	L2866
USA	US$1	=	L1746

Costs

A *very* prudent traveller could get by on L70,000 per day, but only by staying in youth hostels, eating one meal a day (at the hostel), buying a sandwich or pizza by the slice for lunch and minimising the number of galleries and museums visited, since the entrance fee to most major museums is cripplingly expensive at around L12,000. You save on transport costs by buying tourist or day tickets for city bus and underground services. When travel-

ling by train, you can save money by avoiding the fast Eurostars which charge a *supplemento rapido*. Italy's railways also offer a few cut-price options for students, young people and tourists for travel within a nominated period (see the Getting Around section in this chapter for more information).

Museums and galleries usually give discounts to students, but you will need a valid student card which you can obtain from CTS offices if you have documents proving you are a student.

A basic breakdown of costs during an average day could be: accommodation L20,000 (youth hostel) to L60,000; breakfast (coffee and croissant) L3000; lunch (sandwich and mineral water) L5000; public transport (bus or underground railway in a major town) L6000; entry fee for one museum L12,000; a sit-down dinner L25,000 to L40,000.

Tipping & Bargaining

You are not expected to tip on top of restaurant service charges, but it is common practice among Italians to leave a small amount, say around 10%. In bars they will leave any small change as a tip, often only L50 or L100. You can tip taxi drivers if you wish but it's not obligatory.

Bargaining is common throughout Italy in the various flea markets, but not normally in shops. You can try bargaining for the price of a room in a *pensione*, particularly if you plan to stay for more than a few days or out of season.

Consumer Taxes

Whenever you buy an item in Italy you will pay value-added tax, known as IVA. Tourists who are non-EU residents are able to claim back this tax if the item costs more than a certain amount (around L400,000 at the time of writing). The goods must be for personal use, they must be carried with your luggage and you must keep the receipt. You have to fill in a form at the point of purchase, have the form checked and stamped by Italian customs and then return it by mail within 60 days to the vendor, who will then make the refund, either by cheque or to your credit card. At major airports and border points, there are places where you can get an immediate cash refund.

POST & COMMUNICATIONS

Stamps (*francobolli*) are available at post offices and authorised tobacconists (look for the official *tabacchi* sign: a big 'T', often white on black). Since letters often need to be weighed, what you get at the tobacconist's for international air mail will occasionally be an approximation of the proper rate. Main post offices in the bigger cities are generally open from around 8 am to at least 5 pm. Many open on Saturday morning too.

Post

Postal Rates The cost of sending a letter air mail (*via aerea*) depends on its weight and where it is being sent. Letters up to 20g cost L1350 to Australia and New Zealand, L1250 to the USA and L750 to EU countries (L850 to the rest of Europe). Postcards cost the same. Aerograms are a cheap alternative, costing only L850 to send anywhere. They can be purchased at post offices only. Sending letters express (*espresso*) costs a standard extra L3000, but may help speed a letter on its way. If you want to post important items by registered mail (*raccomandata*) or by insured mail (*assicurata*), remember that they will take as long as normal mail (or you can pay extra to send them express). Raccomandata costs L3400 on top of the normal cost of the letter. The cost of assicurata depends on the weight of the object, and is not available to the USA.

Urgent mail can be sent by Express Mail Service (EMS), also known as CAI Post. A parcel weighing 1kg will cost L37,000 in Europe, L56,000 to the USA and Canada, and L83,000 to Australia and New Zealand. EMS is not necessarily as fast as private services. It will take four to eight days for a parcel to reach Australia and two to four days to reach the USA. Ask at post offices for addresses of EMS outlets.

Sending Mail An air-mail letter can take up to two weeks to reach the UK or the USA, while a letter to Australia will take between two and three weeks. Postcards will take even longer because they are low-priority mail. The service within Italy is no better: local letters take at least three days and up to a week to arrive in another city. Next-day delivery does not exist in Italy. In Rome, use the

Vatican post office in St Peter's Square; it has an excellent record for prompt delivery but doesn't accept poste restante mail.

Receiving Mail Poste restante is known as *fermo posta* in Italy. Letters marked thus will be held at the counter of the same name in the main post office in the relevant town. Poste restante mail should be addressed as follows:

John SMITH
Fermo Posta
37100 Verona
Italy

American Express card or travellers cheque holders can use the free client mail-holding service at American Express offices in Italy. You can obtain a list of these from American Express offices.

Street Addresses In some Italian towns and cities (such as Florence and Genoa) street numbers for commercial premises (shops) often include an 'r' which stands for *rosso* (red). Therefore, in the same street you might find a house numbered 24 and a shop numbered 24r. Don't worry about it too much, there are plenty of other far more confusing matters to occupy your mind in Italy – just wait until you get to Venice.

Telephone

Rates in Italy, particularly for long-distance calls, are among the highest in Europe – although this should change with deregulation. Travellers from countries which offer direct-dial services paid for at home country rates (such as AT&T in the USA and Telstra in Australia) should take advantage of them. Local and long-distance calls can be made from any public phone, or from a Telecom office in larger towns. Emergency numbers such as ☎ 113 (police), ☎ 115 (fire department) and ☎ 118 (ambulance) are free calls: there is no need to use money or a phonecard in public phones.

Local calls cost a minimum of L200 and are timed, so you might have to put in more money if you speak for more than a few minutes. A three-minute call to the USA will cost approximately L2800 (peak) and L2500 (off peak). Most public phones accept only

Changing Phone Numbers

In mid-1998, all telephone numbers in Italy changed in order to bring the country into line with EU norms for the deregulation of the telecommunications industry. All prefixes (including the zero) were incorporated into the actual phone numbers. For example: you should dial 06 as part of Rome phone numbers, whether you are calling from within Rome, from within Italy or from a foreign country. From 29 December 2000, all phone numbers will change again. The zero will be replaced with a 4 for all phone numbers of fixed telephones; and with a 3 for mobile telephones.

phonecards or other credit cards. You can buy L5000, L10,000 and L15,000 phonecards at tobacconists and newsstands, or from vending machines at Telecom offices. Coin-operated phones accept L100, L200 and L500 coins.

To call Italy from abroad, dial the international access code, ☎ 39 (the country code for Italy), the area code (don't forget to include the initial zero until the end of the year 2000) and the number. Important area codes include: ☎ 06 (Rome), ☎ 02 (Milan), ☎ 055 (Florence), ☎ 081 (Naples), ☎ 070 (Cagliari) and ☎ 091 (Palermo).

To make a reverse-charge (collect) call from a public telephone, dial ☎ 170. All operators speak English. Otherwise, you can direct-dial an operator in your own country (from a public phone) and ask to make your collect call. Numbers for this Home Country Direct service are displayed in the first pages of Italian phone books and include: Australia (☎ 172 10 61, Telstra), Canada (☎ 172 10 01, Teleglobe), New Zealand (☎ 172 10 64), UK (☎ 172 01 44, BT Automatic) and USA (☎ 172 10 11, AT&T). Dial ☎ 176 for 24-hour information on international services, fees and numbers (a call costs about L800).

Mobile Phones GSM is the European digital standard for mobile phones. (GSM is also the standard in Australia, New Zealand and many Asian countries, but not Japan). If you want to take your phone with you, check with your carrier on whether or not you need to make any special arrangements.

Fax & Telegraph There are lots of fax offices in Italy, but the country's high telephone charges make faxes an expensive mode of communication. To send a fax within Italy you can expect to pay L3000 for the first page and L2000 for each subsequent page, plus L50 per second for the actual call. International faxes can cost L6000 for the first page and L4000 per page thereafter, and L100 per second for the call. You can send faxes from specialists fax/photocopy shops, post offices and from some tabacchi shops. Some Telecom public phones can also send faxes.

Telegrams can be sent from post offices or dictated by phone (☎ 186) and are an expensive but sure way of having important messages delivered by the same or next day.

INTERNET RESOURCES

There is an Italy page at Lonely Planet's Web site (www.lonelyplanet.com). Italy has a growing number of Internet cafés, where you can send and receive email, surf the Net etc for around L10,000 to L15,000 an hour. To receive email, you need to have a personal mailbox, which requires a subscription for a certain number of hours. It's also possible to log into your own email account in your home country. Get all of the necessary information before leaving home.

NEWSPAPERS & MAGAZINES

The major English-language newspapers available in Italy are the *Herald Tribune*, an international newspaper available Monday to Saturday, and the *European* (available Friday). Major English newspapers, including the *Guardian*, *The Times* and the *Telegraph*, are sent from London, so outside major cities such as Rome and Milan they are generally a few days old. *Time* magazine, *Newsweek* and the *Economist* are available weekly.

RADIO & TV

The Telemontecarlo (TMC) station broadcasts CNN live from about 3 am. On channel 41, known as Autovox, the American PBS McNeill Lehrer News Hour is broadcast nightly at around 8 pm. The Rete A television station broadcasts MTV 24 hours a day. Vatican Radio (526 on the AM dial or 93.3 and 105 on FM) broadcasts the news in English at 7 and 8.30 am, 6.15 and 9.50 pm.

PHOTOGRAPHY & VIDEO

A roll of normal Kodak film (36 exposures, 100 ASA) costs around L8000. It costs around L18,000 to have 36 exposures developed and L12,000 for 24 exposures. Beware of poor quality development. A roll of 36 slides costs L10,000, and L7000 for processing. Tapes for video cameras are often available at film processing outlets, otherwise you can buy them at stores selling electrical goods.

TIME

Italy is one hour ahead of GMT/UTC, and two hours ahead during summer. Daylight-saving time starts on the last Sunday in March, when clocks are put forward an hour. Clocks are put back an hour on the last Sunday in September. Remember to make allowances for daylight-saving time in your own country. Note that Italy operates on a 24-hour clock.

When it's noon in Rome, it's 11 pm in Auckland, 11 am in London, 6 am in New York, 3 am in San Francisco and 9 pm in Sydney. European cities such as Paris, Munich, Berlin, Vienna and Madrid are on the same time as Italy. Athens, Cairo and Tel Aviv are one hour ahead.

ELECTRICITY

The electric current in Italy is 220V, 50Hz. Power points have two or three holes, and do not have their own switches, while plugs have two or three round pins. Some power points have larger holes than others. Italian homes are usually full of plug adapters to cope with this anomaly. Travellers from the USA need a voltage converter (although many of the more expensive hotels have provision for 110V appliances such as shavers).

WEIGHTS & MEASURES

Italy uses the metric system. Basic terms for weight include: un etto (100g) and un chilo (1kg). Note that Italians indicate decimals with commas and thousands with points.

LAUNDRY

Coin laundrettes, where you can do your own washing, are catching on in Italy. You'll find them in most of the main cities and towns. A load will cost around L8000. Camping grounds have laundry facilities.

TOILETS

You'll find public toilets in locations such as train stations, service stations on the autostrade, and in department stores. Bars are obliged to have a toilet, but you might need to buy a coffee before you'll be allowed to use it. Coin-operated, self-cleaning public toilets are being installed throughout the country, but are still a rarity.

HEALTH

The quality of public hospital care in Italy can vary dramatically. Basically, the further north, the better the care.

Residents of EU countries, including the UK, are covered for emergency medical treatment in Italy on presentation of an E111 form. Australia has a reciprocal arrangement with Italy whereby Australian citizens have access to free emergency medical services. Medicare publishes a brochure with the details. The USA, New Zealand and Canada do not have reciprocal health-care arrangements with Italy.

Travellers should seriously consider taking out a travel insurance policy which covers health care; it will give you greater flexibility in deciding where and how you are treated.

For emergency treatment, go straight to the *pronto soccorso* (casualty section) of a public hospital, where you can also get emergency dental treatment. Your own doctor and dentist may be able to give you some recommendations or referrals before you leave your country. Otherwise, embassies can usually be of assistance.

ITALY

WOMEN TRAVELLERS

Italy is not a dangerous country for women, but women travelling alone will often find themselves plagued by unwanted attention from men. Most of the attention falls into the nuisance/harassment category and it is best simply to ignore the catcalls, hisses and whistles. However, women on their own should use common sense. Avoid walking alone in dark and deserted streets and look for centrally located hotels which are within easy walking distance of places where you can eat at night.

Women travelling alone should be particularly careful in the south, Sicily, and Sardinia, especially in Naples, Palermo, Catania, Brindisi and Bari. Women should also avoid hitchhiking alone.

GAY & LESBIAN TRAVELLERS

Homosexuality is legal in Italy and generally well tolerated in major cities, though overt displays of affection might get a negative response in smaller towns and villages. The national organisation for gays (men and women) is AGAL (☎ 051-644 70 54; fax 644 67 22) in Bologna.

DISABLED TRAVELLERS

The Italian travel agency CIT can advise on hotels which have special facilities. The UK-based Royal Association for Disability and Rehabilitation, or RADAR (☎ 0171-250 3222), publishes a useful guide called *Holidays & Travel Abroad; A Guide for Disabled People*.

DANGERS & ANNOYANCES

Theft is the main problem for travellers in Italy. Thieves and pickpockets operate in most major cities. Watch out for groups of dishevelled-looking women and children. They generally work in groups of four or five and carry paper or cardboard which they use to distract your attention while they swarm around and rifle through your pockets and bag. Never underestimate their skill – they are lightning fast and very adept. The best way to avoid being robbed is to wear a money belt. Never carry a purse or wallet in your pockets and hold on tight to your bag. Pickpockets operate in crowded areas, such as markets and on buses. Motorcycle bandits are particularly active in Rome, Naples, Palermo and Syracuse. If you are using a shoulder bag, make sure that you wear the strap across your body and have the bag on the side away from the road.

Never leave valuables in a parked car – in fact, try not to leave anything in the car if you can help it. It is a good idea to park your car in a supervised car park if you are leaving it for any amount of time. Car theft is a major problem in Rome and Naples. Throughout Italy you can call the police (☎ 113) or *carabinieri* (☎ 112) in an emergency.

BUSINESS HOURS

Business hours can vary from city to city, but generally shops and businesses are open Monday to Saturday from 8.30 am to 1 pm and from 5 to 7.30 pm. Banks are generally open Monday to Friday from 8.30 am to 1.30 pm and from 2.30 to 4.30 pm, but hours vary between banks and cities. Public offices are usually open Monday to Saturday from 8 am to 2 pm, although in major cities some open in the afternoon. Large post offices are open Monday to Saturday from 8 am to 6 or 7 pm. Most museums are open to 10 pm but close on Monday, and restaurants and bars are required to close for one day each week. All food outlets close on Sunday and one weekday afternoon, which varies from town to town.

PUBLIC HOLIDAYS & SPECIAL EVENTS

National public holidays include: 6 January (Epiphany); Easter Monday; 25 April (Liberation Day); 1 May (Labour Day); 15 August (Ferragosto or Feast of the Assumption); 1 November (All Saints' Day); 8 December (Feast of the Immaculate Conception); 25 December (Christmas Day); and 26 December (Feast of St Stephen).

Individual towns also have public holidays to celebrate the feasts of their patron saints. Some of these are the Feast of St Mark in Venice on 25 April; the Feast of St John the Baptist on 24 June in Florence, Genoa and Turin; the Feast of St Peter and St Paul in Rome on 29 June; the Feast of St Januarius in Naples on 19 September; and the Feast of St Ambrose in Milan on 7 December.

Annual events in Italy worth keeping in mind include:

Carnevale
During the 10 days before Ash Wednesday, many towns stage carnivals. The one held in Venice is the best known, but there are also others, including at Viareggio in Liguria and Ivrea near Turin.

Holy Week
There are important festivals during this week everywhere in Italy, in particular the colourful and sombre traditional festivals of Sicily. In Assisi the rituals of Holy Week attract thousands of pilgrims.

Scoppio del Carro
Literally 'Explosion of the Cart', this colourful event held in Florence in Piazza del Duomo on Easter Sunday features the explosion of a cart full of fireworks and dates back to the Crusades. If all goes well, it is seen as a good omen for the city.

Corso dei Ceri
One of the strangest festivals in Italy, this is held in Gubbio (Umbria) on 15 May, and features a race run by men carrying enormous wooden constructions called *ceri*, in honour of the town's patron saint, Sant'Ubaldo.

Il Palio
On 2 July and 16 August, Siena stages this extraordinary horse race in the town's main piazza.

ACTIVITIES

If the churches, museums, galleries and sightseeing are not sufficient to occupy your time in Italy, there are various options for those who want to get off the main tourist routes or who have specific interests.

Hiking

It is possible to go on organised treks in Italy, but if you want to go it alone you will find that trails are well marked and there are plenty of refuges in the Alps, in the Alpi Apuane in Tuscany and in the northern parts of the Appennines. The Dolomites in particular provide spectacular walking and trekking opportunities. In Sardinia head for the eastern mountain ranges between Oliena and Urzulei and along the coastal gorges between Dorgali and Baunei (see the Sardinia section for details).

Skiing

The numerous excellent ski resorts in the Alps and the Apennines usually offer good skiing conditions from December to April (see the Alps section).

Cycling

This is a good option if you can't afford a car but want to see the more isolated parts of the country. Classic cycling areas include Tuscany and Umbria. See under Bicycle in the Getting Around section later in this chapter.

COURSES

There are numerous private schools which offer Italian language courses, particularly in Rome, Florence and Siena (see under these cities for more details), but the cheapest option is to study at the University for Foreigners in Perugia. The average cost of a course in Florence is around L800,000 a month, whereas in Perugia it costs around L350,000 a month. Schools in Florence and Rome also offer courses in art, sculpture, architecture and cooking.

Italian cultural institutes and embassies in your country will provide information on schools and courses as well as enrolment forms. The university in Perugia and all private schools can arrange accommodation (see under Perugia for further information).

WORK

It is illegal for non-EU citizens to work in Italy without a work permit, but trying to obtain one can be difficult. EU citizens are allowed to work in Italy, but they still need to obtain a permesso di soggiorno from the main questura in the town where they have found work. Citizens of other countries must have a promise of a job which cannot be filled by an Italian or citizens of EU countries, and must apply for the visa in their country of nationality.

Traditionally, the main legal employment for foreigners is to teach English, but even with full qualifications an American, Australian, Canadian or New Zealander will find it difficult to secure a permanent position. Foreign visitors can still find 'black economy' work in bars and restaurants, or as babysitters and housekeepers. Most people get started by placing or responding to advertisements in local publications such as *Wanted in Rome*, or *Secondomano* in Milan. Another option is au pair work. A useful guide is *The Au Pair & Nanny's Guide to Working Abroad* by S Griffith & S Legg. Also see *Work Your Way Around the World* by Susan Griffith. If you are looking to work legally in Italy for an extended period, you should seek information from the Italian embassy in your country.

ACCOMMODATION

The prices mentioned here are intended as a guide only. There is generally a fair degree of fluctuation throughout the country, depending on the season. Prices usually rise by 5 to 10% each year, although sometimes they remain fixed for years, or even drop.

Note that it is necessary to produce your passport when you register in a hotel or pensione. You will find that many proprietors will want to keep your passport during your stay. This is not a legal requirement; they only need it long enough to take down the details.

Camping

Facilities throughout Italy are usually reasonable and vary from major complexes with swimming pools, tennis courts and restaurants, to simple camping grounds. Average prices are around L8000 per person and L10,000 or more for a site. Lists of camping grounds in and near major cities are usually available at tourist information offices.

The Touring Club Italiano (TIC) publishes an annual book on all camping sites in Italy, *Campeggi e Villaggi Turistici in Italia* (L22,000). The Istituto Geografico de Agostini publishes the annual *Guida di Campeggi in Europa* (L20,000), available in major bookshops in Italy. Free camping is forbidden in many of the more beautiful parts of Italy, although the authorities seem to pay less attention in the off season.

Hostels

Hostels in Italy are called *ostelli per la gioventù* and are run by the Associazione Italiana Alberghi per la Gioventù (AIG), which is affiliated with Hostelling International

(HI). An HI membership card is not always required, but it is recommended that you have one. Membership cards can be purchased at major hostels, from student and youth travel centre (CTS) offices and from AIG offices throughout Italy. Pick up a list of all hostels in Italy, with details of prices, locations etc from the AIG office (☎ 06-487 11 52) in Rome, Via Cavour 44.

Many Italian hostels are located in castles and old villas, most have bars and the cost per night often includes breakfast. Many also provide dinner, usually for around L12,000. Prices, including breakfast, range from L13,000 to L24,000. Closing times vary, but are usually from 9 am to 3 or 5 pm and curfews are around midnight. Men and women are often segregated, although some hostels have family accommodation.

Pensioni & Hotels

Establishments are required to notify local tourist boards of prices for the coming year and by law must then adhere to those prices (although they do have two legal opportunities each year to increase charges). If tourists believe they are being overcharged they can make a complaint to the local tourist office. The best advice is to confirm hotel charges before you put your bags down, since many proprietors employ various methods of bill padding. These include charges for showers (usually around L2000), a compulsory breakfast (up to L14,000 in the high season) and compulsory half or full board, although this can often be a good deal in some towns.

The cheapest way to stay in a hotel or pensione is to share a room with two or more people: the cost is usually no more than 15% of the cost of a double room for each additional person. Single rooms are uniformly expensive in Italy (from around L40,000) and quite a number of establishments do not even bother to cater for the single traveller.

There is often no difference between an establishment that calls itself a pensione and one that calls itself an *albergo* (hotel); in fact, some use both titles. *Locande* (similar to pensioni) and *alloggi*, sometimes also known as *affittacamere*, are generally cheaper, but not always. Tourist offices have booklets listing all pensioni and hotels, including prices, and lists of locande and affittacamere.

Rental Accommodation

Finding rental accommodation in the major cities can be difficult and time-consuming and you will often find the cost prohibitive, especially in Rome, Florence, Milan and Venice. For details on rental agencies, refer to the individual city chapters. If you are planning to study in an Italian city, the school or university will help you to find rental accommodation, or a room in the house of a family. In major resort areas, such as the Aeolian Islands and other parts of Sicily, and in the Alps, rental accommodation is reasonably priced and readily available and many tourist offices will provide information by mail or fax.

One organisation which publishes booklets on villas and houses in Tuscany, Umbria, Veneto, Sicily and Rome is Cuendet. Write to Cuendet & Cie spa, Strada di Strove 17, 53035 Monteriggioni, Siena (☎ 0577-57 63 10; fax 0577-30 11 49; cuende@mbox.vol.it) and ask for a catalogue (US$15). Prices, however, are expensive. CIT offices throughout the world also have lists of villas and apartments for rent in Italy.

Agriturismo

This is basically a farm holiday and is becoming increasingly popular in Italy. Traditionally, the idea was that families rented out rooms in their farmhouses. However, the more common type of establishment these days is a restaurant/small hotel. All establishments are working farms and you will usually be able to sample the local produce. Recommended areas where you can try this type of holiday are Tuscany, Umbria and Trentino-Alto Adige. Information is available from local tourist offices.

For detailed information on all facilities in Italy contact Agriturist (☎ 06-685 23 42; www.agriturist.it), Corso Vittorio Emanuele 89, 00186 Rome. It publishes a book (L29,000) listing establishments throughout Italy which is available at its office and in selected bookshops.

Religious Institutions

These institutions offer accommodation in most major cities. The standard is usually good, but prices are no longer low. You can expect to pay about the same as for a one-star hotel, if not more. Information about the various institutions is available at all tourist offices, or you can contact the archdiocese in the relevant city.

Refuges

Before you go hiking in any part of Italy, obtain information about refuges from the local tourist offices. Some refuges have private rooms, but many offer dorm-style accommodation, particularly those which are more isolated. Average prices are from L18,000 to L40,000 per person for B&B. A meal costs around the same as at a trattoria. The locations of refuges are marked on good hiking maps and most open only from late June to September. The alpine refuges of CAI (Italian Alpine Club) offer discounts to members of associated foreign alpine clubs.

FOOD

Eating is one of life's great pleasures for Italians. Be adventurous and never be intimidated by eccentric waiters or indecipherable menus and you will find yourself agreeing with the locals, who believe that nowhere in the world is the food as good as in Italy and, more specifically, in their own town.

Cooking styles vary notably from region to region and significantly between the north and south. In the north the food is rich and often creamy, and the regional specialities of Emilia-Romagna, including spaghetti bolognese (known in Italy as *spaghetti al ragù*), tortellini, and mortadella are perhaps the best known throughout the world.

In Tuscany and Umbria the locals use a lot of olive oil and herbs, and regional specialities are noted for their simplicity, fine flavour and the use of fresh produce. As you go further south the food becomes hotter and spicier and the *dolci* (cakes and pastries) sweeter and richer. Don't miss the experience of eating a pizza in Naples and don't leave Sicily without trying their *dolce di mandorle* (almond pastries), or the rich and very sweet ricotta cake known as cassata.

Vegetarians will have no problems eating in Italy. Most eating establishments serve a selection of *contorni* (vegetables prepared in a variety of ways), and the further south you go, the more excellent vegetable dishes you'll find.

ITALY

Restaurants

Eating establishments are divided into several categories. A *tavola calda* (literally 'hot table') usually offers inexpensive, pre-prepared meat, pasta and vegetable dishes in a self-service style. A *rosticceria* usually offers cooked meats, but also often has a larger selection of takeaway food. A pizzeria will of course serve pizza, but usually also a full menu. An *osteria* is likely to be either a wine bar offering a small selection of dishes, or a small *trattoria*. Many of the establishments that are in fact restaurants (*ristoranti*) call themselves trattoria and vice versa for reasons best known to themselves. It is best to check the menu, which is usually posted by the door, for prices. Most eating establishments charge a *coperto* (cover charge) of around L1000 to L3000, and a *servizio* (service charge) of 10 to 15%. Restaurants are usually open for lunch from 12.30 to 3 pm, but will rarely take orders after 2 pm. In the evening, opening hours vary from north to south. In the north they eat dinner earlier, usually from 7.30 pm, but in Sicily you will be hard-pressed to find a restaurant open before 8 pm. Very few restaurants stay open after 11.30 pm.

Italians rarely eat a sit-down breakfast. Their custom is to drink a cappuccino, usually *tiepido* (lukewarm) and eat a *brioche*, *cornetto* or other type of pastry while standing at a bar. Lunch is the main meal of the day, and many shops and businesses close for three to four hours each afternoon to accommodate the meal and the siesta which follows.

A full meal will consist of an antipasto, which can vary from *bruschetta*, a type of garlic bread with various toppings, to fried vegetables, or *prosciutto e melone* (ham wrapped around melon). Next comes the *primo piatto*, a pasta dish or risotto, followed by the *secondo piatto* of meat or fish. Italians often then eat an *insalata* (salad) or contorni and round off the meal with dolci and *caffè*, often at a bar on the way home or back to work.

Numerous restaurants offer tourist menus, at an average price of L18,000 to L28,000. Generally the food is of a reasonable standard, but choices will be very limited and you can usually get away with paying less if you want only pasta, salad and wine.

After lunch and dinner, head for the nearest *gelateria* to round off the meal with some excellent Italian gelati (ice cream), followed by a *digestivo* (liqueur) at a bar.

Remember that as soon as you sit down in Italy, prices go up considerably. A cappuccino at the bar will cost around L1500, but if you sit down, you will pay anything from L2500 to L5000 or more, especially in touristy areas such as Piazza San Marco in Venice (L12,000) and the Spanish Steps in Rome.

Self-Catering

If you have access to cooking facilities, you can buy fruit and vegetables at open markets (see the individual towns for information), and salami, cheese and wine at *alimentari* or *salumerie* (a cross between a grocery store and a delicatessen). Fresh bread is available at a *forno* or *panetteria*. Large supermarkets are becoming more common in Italy.

DRINKS

Italian wine is justifiably world-famous. Few Italians can live without it, and even fewer abuse it, generally drinking wine only with meals. Going out for a drink is still considered unusual in Italy. Fortunately, wine is reasonably priced so you will rarely pay more than L10,000 for a bottle of drinkable wine and as little as L5000 will still buy something of reasonable quality. Try the famous chianti and *brunello* in Tuscany, but also the *vernaccia* of San Gimignano, the *barolo* in Piedmont, the *lacrima christi* or *falanghina* in Naples and the *cannonau* in Sardinia. Trentino's wines are excellent, as are those from Sicily. Beer is known as *birra* and the cheapest local variety is Peroni.

ENTERTAINMENT

Whatever your tastes, there should be some form of entertainment in Italy to keep you amused, including opera, theatre, classical music concerts, rock concerts and traditional festivals. Major entertainment festivals are also held, such as the Festival of Two Worlds in June/July at Spoleto, Umbria Jazz in Perugia in July, Rome's Estate Romana in July, and the Venice Biennale every odd-numbered year. Operas are performed in Verona and Rome throughout summer (for details see the Entertainment sections under both cities) and at various times of the year throughout the country, notably at the opera houses in Milan and Rome. There are plenty of clubs and bars in the big cities, including the Italian version of the Irish pub. For up-to-date information on entertainment in each city, buy the local newspaper. Tourist offices will also provide information on important events, festivals, performances and concerts.

SPECTATOR SPORT

Soccer (*calcio*) is the national passion and there are stadiums in all the major towns. If you'd rather watch a game than visit a Roman ruin, check newspapers for details of who's playing where. The Italian Formula One Grand Prix races are held at Monza, just north of Milan in September. The San Marino Grand Prix is held at Imola in May.

THINGS TO BUY

Italy is synonymous with elegant, fashionable and high-quality clothing. The problem is that most of the clothes are very expensive. However, if you happen to be in the country during the summer sales in July and August and the winter sales in January and February, you can pick up incredible bargains.

Italy is renowned for the quality of its leather goods. At markets such as Porta Portese in Rome and the San Lorenzo leather market in Florence you can find some remarkable bargains – but check carefully for quality.

Other items of interest are Venetian glass, and the great diversity of ceramics produced throughout Italy, particularly at Deruta in Umbria, on the Amalfi Coast and in Sicily.

Getting There & Away

AIR

Although paying full fare to travel by plane in Europe is expensive, there are various discount options, including cut-price fares for students and people aged under 25 or 26 (de-

pending on the airline). There are also stand-by fares which are usually around 60% of the full fare. Several airlines offer cut-rate fares on legs of international flights between European cities. These are usually the cheapest fares available, but the catch is that they are often during the night or very early in the morning, and the days on which you can fly are severely restricted. Some examples of cheap one-way fares at the time of writing are: Rome-Paris L197,000 (L300,000 return); Rome-London L259,000 (L296,000 return); and Rome-Amsterdam L350,000 return.

Another option is to travel on charter flights. There are several companies throughout Europe which operate these, and fares are usually cheaper than for normal scheduled flights. Italy Sky Shuttle (☎ 0181-748 1333), part of the Air Travel Group, 227 Shepherd's Bush Rd, London W6 7AS, specialises in charter flights, but also offers scheduled flights.

Look in the classified pages of the London Sunday newspapers for information on other cheap flights. Campus Travel (☎ 0171-730 3402), 52 Grosvenor Gardens, SW1W OAG, and STA Travel (☎ 0171-361 6161), 86 Old Brompton Rd, London SW7 3LH, both offer reasonably cheap fares. Within Italy, information on discount fares is available from CTS and Sestante CIT offices (see the earlier Tourist Offices section).

LAND

If you are travelling by bus, train or car to Italy it will be necessary to cross various borders, so remember to check whether you require visas for those countries before leaving home.

Bus

Eurolines is the main international carrier in Europe, with representatives in Italy and throughout the continent. Its head office (☎ 0171-730 8235) is at 52 Grosvenor Gardens, Victoria, London SW1, and it has representatives in Italy and throughout Europe. In Italy the main bus company operating this service is Lazzi, with offices in Florence (☎ 055-35 71 10) at Piazza Adua and in Rome (☎ 06-884 08 40) at Via Tagliamento 27b. Buses leave from Rome,

Florence, Milan, Turin, Venice and Naples, as well as numerous other Italian towns, for major cities throughout Europe including London, Paris, Barcelona, Madrid, Amsterdam, Budapest, Prague, Athens and Istanbul. Ticket prices are: Rome-Paris L170,000 (L270,000 return); Rome-London L222,000 (L316,000 return); and Rome-Barcelona L180,000 (L324,000 return).

Train

Eurostar (ES) and Eurocity (EC) trains run from major destinations throughout Europe direct to major Italian cities. On overnight hauls you can book a *cuccetta* (known outside Italy as a couchette or sleeping berth).

Travellers aged under 26 can take advantage of Billet International de Jeunesse tickets (BIJ, also known in Italy as BIGE), which can cut fares by around 50%. They are sold at Transalpino offices at most train stations and at CTS and Sestante CIT offices in Italy, Europe and overseas. Examples of one-way 2nd-class fares are: Rome-Amsterdam L216,900 and Rome-London L244,300. Throughout Europe and in Italy it is worth paying extra for a couchette on night trains. A couchette from Rome to Paris is an extra L45,000.

You can book tickets at train stations or at CTS, Sestante CIT and most travel agencies. Eurostar and Eurocity trains carry a supplement (see Costs & Reservations in the Getting Around section).

Car & Motorcycle

Travelling with your own vehicle certainly gives you more flexibility. The drawbacks in Italy are that cars can be inconvenient in larger cities where you'll have to deal with heavy traffic, parking problems and the risk of car theft. Driving in Italy is expensive once you add up the cost of petrol and toll charges on the autostrade.

If you want to rent a car or motorcycle, you will need a valid EU driving licence, an International Driving Permit, or your driving permit from your own country. If you're driving your own car, you'll need an international insurance certificate, known as a Carta Verde (Green Card) which can be obtained from your insurer.

Hitching

Hitching is never safe in any country and we don't recommend it. Your best bet is to enquire at hostels throughout Europe, where you can often arrange a lift. The International Lift Centre in Florence (☎ 055-28 06 26) and Enjoy Rome (☎ 06-445 18 43) might be able to help organise lifts. It is illegal to hitch on the autostrade.

SEA

Ferries connect Italy to Spain, Croatia, Greece, Turkey, Tunisia and Malta. There are also services to Corsica (from Livorno) and Albania (from Bari and Ancona). See Getting There & Away under Brindisi (for ferries to/from Greece), Ancona (to/from Greece, Albania and Turkey), Venice (to/from Croatia) and Sicily (to/from Malta and Tunisia).

LEAVING ITALY

There is a departure tax on international flights, but it is built into the cost of your ticket.

Getting Around

AIR

Travelling by plane is expensive within Italy and it makes much better sense to use the efficient and considerably cheaper rail and bus services. The domestic airlines are Alitalia, Meridiana and Air One. The main airports are in Rome, Pisa, Milan, Bologna, Genova, Torino, Naples, Catania, Palermo and Cagliari, but there are other, smaller airports throughout Italy. Domestic flights can be booked directly with the airlines or through Sestante CIT, CTS and other travel agencies.

Alitalia offers a range of discounts for students, young people and families, and for weekend travel.

BUS

Bus travel within Italy is provided by numerous companies, and services vary from local routes linking small villages to major intercity connections. It is usually necessary to make reservations only for long trips, such as Rome-Palermo or Rome-Brindisi. Otherwise, just arrive early enough to claim a seat.

Buses can be a cheaper and faster way to get around if your destination is not on major rail lines, for instance from Umbria to Rome or Florence, and in the interior areas of Sicily and Sardinia. Some examples of prices for bus travel are Rome-Palermo L65,000; Rome-Siena L22,000; and Rome-Pompeii L25,000.

You can usually get bus timetables from local tourist offices and, if not, staff will be able to point you in the direction of the main bus companies. See Rome's Getting There & Away section for more details.

TRAIN

Travelling by train in Italy is simple, relatively cheap and generally efficient. The Ferrovie dello Stato (FS) is the partially privatised state train system and there are several private railway services throughout the country.

There are several types of trains: Regionale (R) which usually stop at all stations and can be very slow; interRegionale (iR) which run between the regions; and Intercity (IC) or Eurocity (EC) which service only the major cities. The fast train service between major Italian and European cities is called Eurostar Italia (ES) and has both 1st and 2nd class.

Tickets must be validated in the yellow machines at the entrance to all train platforms. The rule does not apply to tickets purchased outside Italy.

Costs & Reservations

To travel on the Intercity, Eurocity and Eurostar Italia trains, you have to pay a *supplemento*, an additional charge determined by the distance you are travelling and the type of train. For instance, on the Intercity train between Florence and Bologna (about 100km) you pay L5500 for the basic supplement or L9500 for the Eurostar supplement. Always check whether the train you are about to catch is an Intercity or Eurostar, and pay the supplement before you get on the train, otherwise you will pay extra. It's obligatory to book a seat on Eurostar trains, since they don't carry standing-room passengers. The difference in 2nd-class fares for the Eurostar and Intercity trains is around L10,000 from

Rome to Florence, but for the extra expense you'll arrive half an hour earlier.

There are left-luggage facilities at most train stations, except for the smallest, throughout Italy. They are usually open seven days a week, 24 hours a day, but if not, they close for only a few hours after midnight.

Discounts

It is not worth buying a Eurail or Inter-Rail pass if you are going to travel only in Italy. The FS offers its own discount passes for travel within the country. These include the Cartaverde for those aged 26 years and under. It costs L40,000, is valid for one year, and entitles you to a 20% discount on all train travel. Children aged four to 12 years pay 50% and those under four travel for free. You can buy a *biglietto chilometrico* (kilometric ticket), which is valid for two months and allows you to cover 3000km, with a maximum of 20 trips. It costs L206,000 (2nd class) and you must pay the supplement if you catch an Intercity or Eurostar train. Its main attraction is that it can be used by up to five people, either singly or together. Some examples of 2nd-class train fares (plus IC or ES supplement) are: Rome-Florence L25,500 (L13,000 IC; L9500 ES) and Rome-Naples L18,000 (L10,500 IC; L9000 ES). A 2nd-class fare on the Eurostar Italia from Rome to Florence (a 1¾-hour journey) is L48,000.

CAR & MOTORCYCLE

The Istituto Geografico de Agostini publishes detailed road maps for all of Italy. Its book entitled *Atlante Stradale Italiano* has road maps as well as town maps. You can also buy individual maps of the regions you plan to visit. Automobile Club d'Italia (ACI) offers roadside assistance (☎ 116).

Roads are generally good throughout the country and there is an excellent system of autostrade (freeways). The main north-south link is the Autostrada del Sole, which extends from Milan to Reggio di Calabria (called the A1 from Milan to Naples and the A3 from Naples to Reggio). The only problem with the autostrade is that they are toll roads. Connecting roads provide access to Italy's major cities from the autostrada system.

ITALY

Road Rules

Italian traffic, particularly in the cities, can appear extremely chaotic, and people drive at high speed on the autostrade (never remain in the left-hand fast lane longer than is necessary to pass a car).

In Italy, as throughout Continental Europe, people drive on the right-hand side of the road and pass on the left. Unless otherwise indicated, you must give way to cars coming from the right. It is compulsory to wear seat belts if they are fitted to the car (front seat belts on all cars and back seat belts on cars produced after 26 April 1990). Most Italians ignore this requirement and generally wear seat belts only on the autostrada. If you are caught not wearing your seat belt, you will be required to pay a L50,000 on-the-spot fine.

You don't need a licence to ride a moped under 50cc, but you should be aged 14 years or over, and a helmet is compulsory up to age 18; you can't carry passengers or ride on the autostrade. To ride a motorcycle or scooter up to 125cc, you must be at least 16 years old and have a licence (a car licence will do). Over 125cc, you need a motorcycle licence. Helmets are now compulsory for all motorcycle and moped riders and passengers.

The limit on blood-alcohol content is 0.08% and random breath tests have now been introduced.

In Rome and Naples you might have difficulty negotiating the chaotic traffic, but remain calm, keep your eyes on the car in front of you and you should be OK. Most roads are well signposted and once you arrive in a city or village, follow the *centro* signs to reach the centre of town. Be careful where you park your car. In the major cities it will almost certainly be towed away and you will pay a heavy fine if you leave it near a sign reading 'Zona di Rimozione' (Removal Zone) and featuring a picture of a tow truck.

Some Italian cities, including Rome, Bologna, Florence, Milan and Turin, have introduced restricted access to both private and rental cars in their historical centres. The restrictions, however, do not apply to vehicles with foreign registrations, to allow tourists to reach their hotels. If you are stopped by a traffic police officer, you will need to name the hotel where you are staying and produce a pass (provided by the hotel) if required.

Motorini (mopeds) and scooters (such as Vespas) are able to enter the zones without any problems.

Speed limits, unless otherwise indicated by local signs, are: on autostrade 130km/h for cars of 1100cc or more, 110km/h for smaller cars and motorcycles under 350cc; on all main, nonurban highways 100km/h; on secondary nonurban highways 90km/h; and in built-up areas 50km/h.

Expenses

Petrol prices are high in Italy – around L1900 per litre. Autostrada tolls are also expensive. Petrol is called *benzina*, unleaded petrol is *benzina senza piombo* and diesel is *gasolio*. If you are driving a car which uses liquid petroleum gas (LPG), you will need to buy a special guide to service stations which have *gasauto*, also known as GPL. By law these must be located in nonresidential areas and are usually in the country or on city outskirts. The guides are available at service stations selling GPL.

Rental

It is cheaper to organise a rental car before you leave your own country, for instance through some sort of fly-drive deal. Most major firms, including Hertz, Avis and Budget, will arrange this and you simply pick up the vehicle at a nominated point when in Italy. Foreign offices of Sestante CIT can also help to organise car or camper-van rental before you leave home.

You will need to be aged 21 years or over (23 years or over for some companies) to rent a car in Italy, and you will find the deal a lot easier to organise if you have a credit card. You'll find that most firms will accept your standard licence or an International Driving Permit.

At the time of writing, Hertz was offering a special weekend rate of L150,000 for a small car from Friday 9 am to Monday 9 am. The cost for a week was L555,000. Other discounts are also offered to tourists. If you need a baby car seat, call one day ahead to ensure the company has one available. They cost an extra L50,000.

Rental motorcycles are usually 50cc mopeds or scooters, but it is also possible to rent big touring motorcycles. The cost for a

50cc scooter is around L60,000 a day or L300,000 a week. A 600cc Honda costs L120,000 a day and L800,000 a week. Note that most places require a sizeable deposit, sometimes around L300,000, and that you could be responsible for reimbursing part of the value of the vehicle if it is stolen. Always check the fine print in the contract.

Rental agencies are listed under the major cities in this chapter. Most tourist offices have information about where to rent a car or motorcycle, or you can look in the Yellow Pages for each town.

Purchase

Car Basically, it is not possible for foreigners to buy a car in Italy, since the law requires that you must be a resident to own and register one. However, if you manage to find a way around this, the average cost of a safe car older than 10 years is L1,500,000 to L3,500,000, ranging up to around L5,000,000 for a decent five-year-old Fiat Uno. The best way to find a car is to look in the classified section of local newspapers in each town or city.

Motorcycle The same laws apply to owning and registering a motorcycle. The cost of a second-hand Vespa ranges from L500,000 to L1,000,000, and a motorino will cost from L200,000 to L1,000,000. Prices for more powerful bikes start at L1,500,000.

BICYCLE

Bikes are available for rent in most Italian towns – the cost ranges up to L20,000 a day and up to L80,000 a week (see the Getting Around section in each city). But if you are planning to do a lot of cycling, consider buying a bike in Italy; you can buy a decent second-hand bicycle for L200,000. See the Activities section earlier in this chapter for some suggestions on places to cycle. Bikes can travel in the baggage compartment of some Italian trains (not on the Eurostars or Intercity trains).

HITCHING

See under Getting There & Away.

BOAT

Navi (large ferries) service the islands of Sicily and Sardinia, and *traghetti* (smaller ferries) and *aliscafi* (hydrofoils) service areas such as Elba, the Aeolian Islands, Capri and Ischia. The main embarkation points for Sicily and Sardinia are Genoa, La Spezia, Livorno, Civitavecchia, Fiumicino and Naples. In Sicily the main points of arrival are Palermo and Messina, and in Sardinia they are Cagliari, Arbatax, Olbia, Golfo Aranci and Porto Torres.

Tirrenia Navigazione is the major company servicing the Mediterranean and it has offices throughout Italy. The FS also operates ferries to Sicily and Sardinia. Further information is provided in the Getting There & Away sections under both islands. Most long-distance services travel overnight and all ferries carry vehicles (you can usually take a bicycle free of charge).

LOCAL TRANSPORT

All the major cities have good transport systems, including buses and, in Rome, Milan and Naples, underground railways. In Venice, however, your only options are to get around by boat or on foot. Efficient bus services also operate between neighbouring towns and villages. Tourist offices will provide information on urban public transport systems, including bus routes and maps of the underground railway systems.

Bus

Urban buses are usually frequent and reliable and operate on an honour system. You must buy a ticket beforehand and validate it in the machine on the bus. Tickets generally cost from L1500 to L1800, although most cities offer 24-hour tourist tickets for around L4000 to L6000.

The trend in the larger cities is towards integration of public transport services, which means the same ticket is used for buses, trams and the underground. Tickets are sold at authorised tobacconists, bars and newspaper stands and at ticket booths at bus terminals (for instance, outside Stazione Termini in Rome where most of the major buses stop).

Think twice before travelling without a ticket, as in most cities the army of inspectors has been increased along with fines. In Rome you will be fined L100,000 on the spot if caught without a validated ticket.

Underground

On the underground railways (Metropolitana) in Rome, Naples and Milan (where they are referred to as the MM), you must buy tickets and validate them before boarding the trains.

Taxi

Try to avoid using taxis in Italy, as they are very expensive, and you can usually catch a bus instead. The shortest taxi ride in Rome will cost around L10,000, since the flag fall is L6400. Generally taxis will not stop if you hail them in the street. Instead, head for the taxi ranks at train and bus stations or you can telephone for one (radio taxi phone numbers are listed throughout this chapter in the Getting Around sections of the major cities).

ORGANISED TOURS

It is less expensive and more enjoyable to do some research and see the sights independently, but if you are in a hurry or prefer guided tours, go to Sestante CIT or American Express offices. Both offer city and package tours (see under Organised Tours in the major cities for further information). CIT offices abroad can also provide information about and organise package tours to Italy.

Rome

☎ 06

A phenomenal concentration of history, legend and monuments coexists in Rome (Roma) with an equally phenomenal concentration of people busily going about everyday life. It is easy to pick the tourists because they are the only ones to turn their heads as the bus passes the Colosseum.

Rome had its origins in a group of Etruscan, Latin and Sabine settlements on the Palatine, Esquiline, Quirinal and surrounding hills (archaeological evidence shows that the Palatine settlement was the earliest). It is, however, the legend of Romulus and Remus which has captured the popular imagination. They were the twin sons of Rhea Silvia and the Roman war god Mars, and were raised by

a she-wolf after being abandoned on the banks of the Tiber (Tevere). The myth says Romulus killed his brother during a battle over who should govern, and then established the city on the Palatine (Palatino), one of the famous Seven Hills of Rome. Romulus, who established himself as the first king of Rome, disappeared one day, enveloped in a cloud which carried him back to the domain of the gods.

From the legend grew an empire which eventually controlled almost the entire world known to Europeans at the time, an achievement described by a historian of the day as being 'without parallel in human history'.

In Rome there is visible evidence of the two great empires of the western world: the Roman Empire and the Christian Church. On the one hand is the Forum and Colosseum, and on the other St Peter's and the Vatican. In between, in almost every *piazza* (square), lies history on so many levels that what you see is only the tip of the iceberg – a phenomenon exemplified by St Peter's Basilica, which stands on the site of an earlier basilica built by the Emperor Constantine over the necropolis where St Peter was buried.

Realistically, at least a week is a fair amount of time to explore Rome, but whatever time you devote to the city, put on your walking shoes, buy a good map and plan your time carefully – the city will eventually seem less chaotic and overwhelming than it first appears.

Orientation

Rome is a vast city, but the historical centre is relatively small. Most of the major sights are within walking distance of the central train station, Stazione Termini. It is, for instance, possible to walk from the Colosseum, through the Forum and the Palatine, up to the Spanish Steps and across to the Vatican in one day, though this is hardly recommended even for the most dedicated tourist. One of the great pleasures of Rome is to allow time for wandering through the many beautiful piazzas, stopping now and again for a caffè and *paste* (pastries). All the major monuments are to the west of the station area.

Plan an itinerary if your time is limited. Many of the major museums and galleries open all day until 5 or 7 pm, and some remain open until 10 pm. Many museums are closed

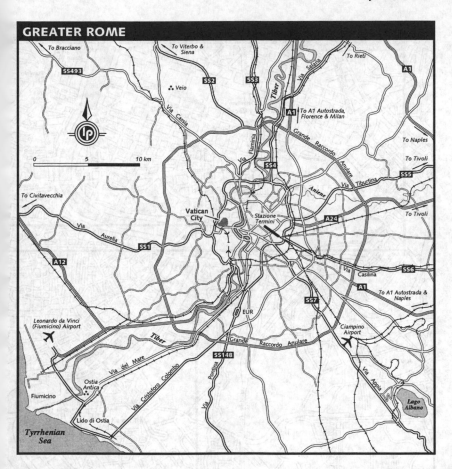

GREATER ROME

To Bracciano
To Viterbo & Siena
To Rieti
SS493
SS2
SS3
Tiber
Via Salaria
A1
Veio
Via Cassia
To A1 Autostrada, Florence & Milan
A1
Grande Raccordo Anulare
To Naples
0   5   10 km
Via Flaminia
SS4
To Tivoli
SS5
Aniene
Via Tiburtina
To Civitavecchia
Vatican City
Stazione Termini
To Tivoli
A24
Via
Aurelia
SS1
Via Casilina
SS6
A12
A1
To A1 Autostrada & Naples
Via
SS7
Leonardo da Vinci (Fiumicino) Airport
EUR
Ciampino Airport
Tiber
Grande Raccordo Anulare
Via del Mare
SS148
Via Cristoforo Colombo
Via Pontina
Via Appia
Ostia Antica
Fiumicino
Lago Albano
Lido di Ostia
Tyrrhenian Sea

on Monday, but it's a good idea to check. Some of the major monuments which open in the afternoon include the Colosseum and St Peter's Basilica.

Most new arrivals in Rome will end up at Stazione Termini, the terminus for all international and national trains. The main city bus terminus is in Piazza dei Cinquecento, directly in front of the station. Many intercity buses arrive and depart from Piazzale Tiburtina, in front of Stazione Tiburtina, accessible from Termini on the Metropolitana Linea B.

The main airport is Leonardo da Vinci at Fiumicino, about 40 minutes by train or an hour by car from the centre. (For more information, see To/From the Airport under Rome's Getting Around section.)

If you are going to be arriving in Rome by car, you should invest in a good road map of the city so you get an idea of the various routes into the city centre (see Rome's Getting There & Away section). Normal traffic is not permitted into the city centre, but tourists are allowed to drive to their hotels.

ITALY

ROME (ROMA)

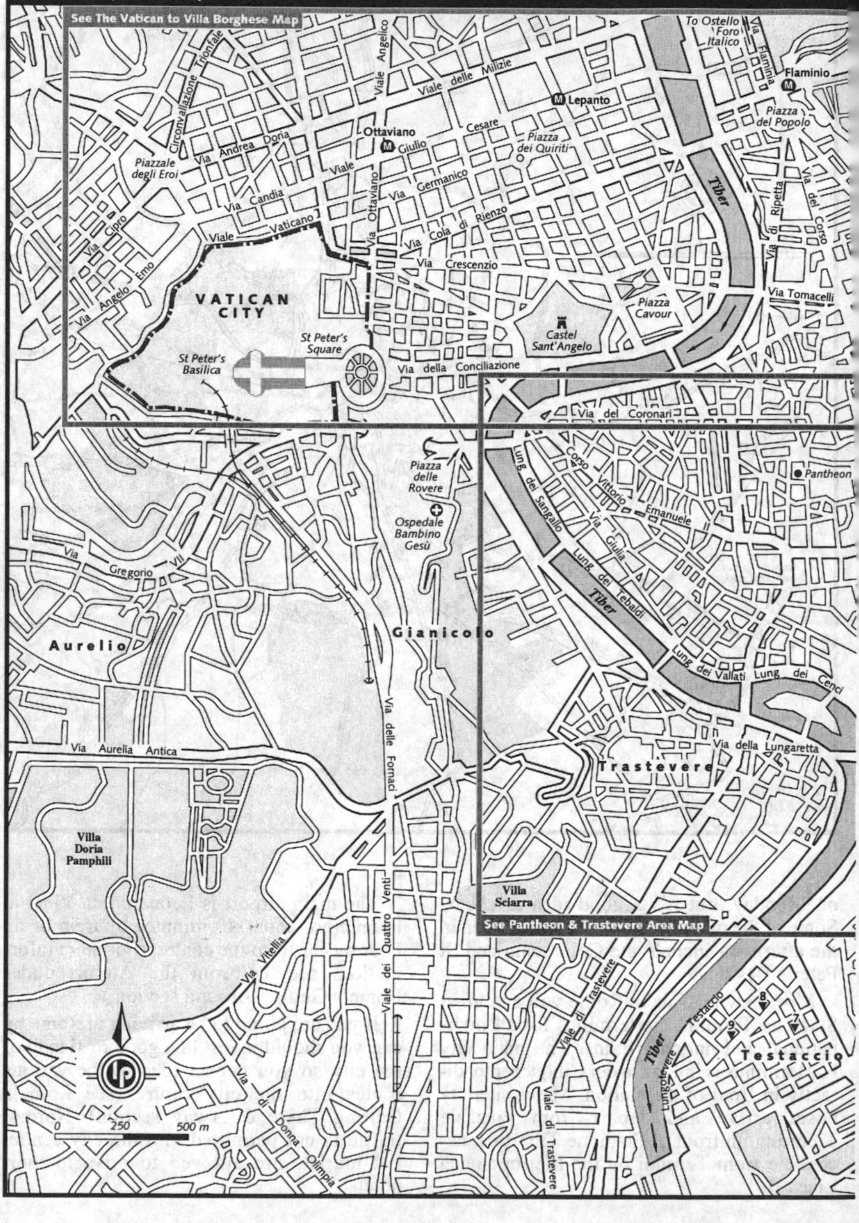

ITALY

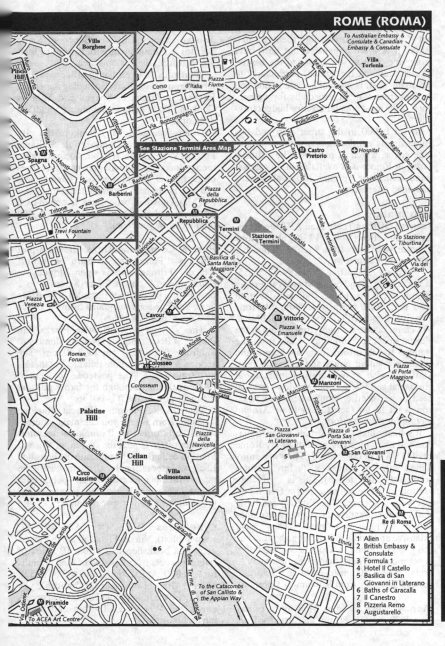

ROME (ROMA)

To Australian Embassy &
Consulate & Canadian
Embassy & Consulate

Villa
Torlonia

Villa
Borghese

Pincio
Hill

Corso d'Italia

Piazza
Fiume

Via Nomentana

Viale Regina Margherita

Via della Trinità dei Monti

Spagna

Via Boncompagni

Viale del Policlinico

Viale Regina Elena

See Stazione Termini Area Map

Via Barberini

Barberini

Via XX Settembre

Piazza
della
Repubblica

Castro
Pretorio

Hospital

Viale dell'Università

Via del Tritone

Trevi Fountain

Repubblica

Termini

Stazione
Termini

To Stazione
Tiburtina

Via dei
Reti

Piazza
Venezia

Basilica di
Santa Maria
Maggiore

Via Cavour

Via C. Alberto

Cavour

Vittorio

Piazza V
Emanuele

Viale del Monte Oppio

Roman
Forum

Colosseo

Piazza
di Porta
Maggiore

Colosseum

Via Labicana

Manzoni

Palatine
Hill

Via di S. Gregorio

Piazza
della
Navicella

Piazza
San Giovanni
in Laterano

Piazza di
Porta San
Giovanni

San Giovanni

Celian
Hill

Villa
Celimontana

Circo
Massimo

Aventino

Via delle Terme di Caracalla

Via Appia Nuova

Re di Roma

Aventino

Via Piram di Cestia

To the Catacombs
of San Callisto &
the Appian Way

Piramide

To ACEA Art Centre

1	Alien
2	British Embassy & Consulate
3	Formula 1
4	Hotel Il Castello
5	Basilica di San Giovanni in Laterano
6	Baths of Caracalla
7	Il Canestro
8	Pizzeria Remo
9	Augustarello

ITALY

The majority of cheap hotels and pensioni are concentrated around Stazione Termini, but if you are prepared to go the extra distance, it is more expensive but definitely more enjoyable to stay closer to the centre. The area around the station, particularly to the south-west, is unpleasant, seedy and can be dangerous at night, especially for women, but it is the most popular area for budget travellers.

Invest L6000 in the street map and bus guide simply entitled *Roma*, with a red-and-blue cover, which is published by Editrice Lozzi in Rome; it is available at any newsstand in Stazione Termini. It lists all streets, with map references.

Information

Tourist Offices There is an APT tourist information office (☎ 487 12 70) at Stazione Termini, open daily from 8 am to 10 pm. It's in the central courseway.

The main APT office (☎ 48 89 92 53/55) is at Via Parigi 5 and opens Monday to Friday from 8.15 am to 7.15 pm and Saturday until 1.30 pm. Walk north-west from Stazione Termini, through Piazza della Repubblica. Via Parigi runs to the right from the top of the piazza, about a five-minute walk from the station. It has information on hotels and museum opening hours and entrance fees. Staff can also provide information about provincial and Intercity bus services, but you need to be specific about where and when you want to go (see the Getting Around section for further information).

It's likely that you'll get all the information and assistance you need at Enjoy Rome (☎ 445 18 43; fax 445 07 34; www.enjoy rome.com), Via Varese 39 (a few minutes north-east of the station). This is a privately run tourist office which offers a free hotel-reservation service. The English-speaking staff can also organise alternative accommodation such as apartments. They have extensive up-to-date information about Rome and good information about accommodation in other cities. The office is open Monday to Friday from 8.30 am to 1 pm and 3.30 to 6 pm and Saturday from 8.30 am to 1 pm.

Money Banks are open Monday to Friday from 8.30 am to 1.30 pm and usually from 2.45 to 3.45 pm. You will find a bank and exchange offices at Stazione Termini. There is also an exchange office (Banco di Santo Spirito) at Fiumicino airport, to your right as you exit from the customs area.

Numerous other exchange offices are scattered throughout the city, including American Express in Piazza di Spagna and Thomas Cook in Piazza della Repubblica 65 and Via del Corso 23.

Otherwise, go to any bank in the city centre. The Banca Commerciale Italiana, Piazza Venezia, is reliable for receiving money transfers and will give cash advances on both Visa and MasterCard. Credit cards can also be used in automatic teller machines (ATMs), known as bancomats, to obtain cash 24 hours a day. You'll need to get a PIN number from your bank.

Post & Communications The main post office is at Piazza San Silvestro 19, just off Via del Tritone, and is open Monday to Sunday from 9 am to 6 pm (Saturday to 2 pm). Fermo posta (poste restante) is available here. You can send telegrams from the office next door (open 24 hours).

The Vatican post office in Piazza San Pietro (St Peter's Square) is open Monday to Saturday from 8.30 am to 7.30 pm. The service is faster and more reliable, but there's no fermo posta. The postcode for central Rome is 00100, although for fermo posta at the main post office it is 00186.

There is a Telecom office at Stazione Termini, from where you can make international calls direct or through an operator. Another office is near the station, in Via San Martino della Battaglia opposite the Pensione Lachea. International calls can easily be made with a phonecard from any public telephone. Phonecards can be purchased at tobacconists and newspaper stands.

Cybercafés Bibli (☎ 588 40 97; www.bibli.it), Via dei Fienaroli 28, in Trastevere, is a bookshop that offers 10 hours of Internet access over a period of three months for L50,000. At Explorer Café (☎ 324 17 57), Via dei Gracchi 85 (near the Vatican), you can pay by the hour (about L12,000) to access email, the Web and CD-Rom and multimedia libraries.

Itaca Multimedia (☎ 686 14 64; fax 689 60 96) at Via delle Fosse di Castello 8, next to Castel Sant'Angelo, allows you to access Internet services, and send and receive email messages. The service costs L15,000 for an hour or L100,000 for a 10-hour subscription, including a personal email box.

Travel Agencies There is a Sestante CIT office (Italy's national tourist agency; ☎ 474 65 55) at Piazza della Repubblica 65, where you can make bookings for planes, trains and ferries. The staff speak English and have information on fares for students and young people. They also arrange tours of Rome and the surrounding areas.

The student tourist centre, CTS (☎ 462 04 31; info@cts.it; www.cts.it), Via Genova 16, off Via Nazionale, offers much the same services and will also make hotel reservations, but focuses on discount and student travel. There is a branch office at Termini. The staff at both offices speak English.

American Express (☎ 676 41 for travel information; ☎ 722 82 for 24-hour client service for lost or stolen cards; ☎ 1678-7 20 00 for lost or stolen travellers cheques), Piazza di Spagna 38, has a travel service similar to CIT and CTS, as well as a hotel-reservation service, and can arrange tours of the city and surrounding areas.

Bookshops Feltrinelli International (☎ 487 01 71), Via VE Orlando 78, has literature and travel guides (Lonely Planet included) in several languages, including Japanese. The Corner Bookshop (☎ 583 69 42) at Via del Moro 48 in Trastevere is very well stocked with English-language books (including Lonely Planet guides). The Anglo-American Book Company (☎ 679 52 22), Via della Vite 102, off Piazza di Spagna, also has an excellent selection of literature, travel guides and reference books. The Lion Bookshop (☎ 32 65 04 37), Via dei Greci 33-36, also has a good range, as does the Economy Book & Video Center (☎ 474 68 77), Via Torino 136, off Via Nazionale, which also has second-hand books. The Libreria del Viaggiatore (☎ 68 80 10 48), Via del Pellegrino 78, close to Campo de' Fiori, is an Italian bookshop specialising in travel books and maps (Lonely Planet included). The staff speak English.

Laundry There is an Onda Blu coin laundrette at Via Principe Amedeo 70b, near the train station.

Medical & Emergency Services Emergency medical treatment is available in the pronto soccorso (casualty sections) at public hospitals including: Ospedale San Giovanni (☎ 77 051), Via dell'Amba Aradam; and Ospedale Fatebenefratelli (☎ 58 731), Isola Tiberina. The Rome American Hospital (☎ 225 51) Via E Longoni 81 is a private hospital and you should use its services only if you have health insurance and have consulted your insurance company. Rome's paediatric hospital is Bambino Gesù (☎ 685 91) on the Janiculum (Gianicolo) Hill at Piazza Sant'Onofrio 4. From Piazza della Rovere (on the Lungotevere near St Peter's) head uphill along Via del Gianicolo. The hospital is at the top of the hill.

For an ambulance call ☎ 118.

There is a pharmacy in Stazione Termini, open daily from 7 am to 11 pm (closed in August). Otherwise, closed pharmacies should post a list in their windows of others open nearby.

The questura (police headquarters; ☎ 468 61) is at Via San Vitale 15. It's open 24 hours a day and thefts can be reported here. Its Foreigners' Bureau (Ufficio Stranieri; ☎ 46 86 29 77) is around the corner at Via Genova 2. For immediate police attendance call ☎ 113.

Dangers & Annoyances Thieves are very active in the areas in and around Stazione Termini, at major sights such as the Colosseum and Roman Forum, and in the city's most expensive shopping streets, such as Via Condotti, although police activity seems to have reduced the problem in recent years. Pickpockets like to work on crowded buses, particularly No 64 from St Peter's to Termini. For more comprehensive information on how to avoid being robbed, see the Dangers & Annoyances section earlier in this chapter.

Things to See & Do

It would take years to explore every corner of Rome, months to begin to appreciate the incredible number of monuments and weeks for a thorough tour of the city. You can, however, cover most of the important monuments in five days, or three at a minimum.

Piazza del Campidoglio Designed by Michelangelo in 1538, the piazza is on the Capitolino (Capitoline Hill), the most important of Rome's seven hills. The hill was the seat of the ancient Roman government and is now the seat of Rome's municipal government. Michelangelo also designed the façades of the three palaces which border the piazza. A modern copy of the bronze equestrian statue of Emperor Marcus Aurelius stands in the centre of the piazza. The original is now on display in the ground-floor portico of the Palazzo del Museo Capitolino. In the two palaces flanking the piazza (Palazzo del Museo Capitolino and Palazzo dei Conservatori) are the **Musei Capitolini**, which are well worth visiting for their collections of ancient Roman sculpture. The museums are slowly being restored and some of the more impressive pieces from their collections have been moved to an unusual temporary location in a former electric power plant in Via Ostiense (see later in this section). They are open Tuesday to Sunday from 9 am to 7 pm. Admission is L10,000.

Walk to the right of the Palazzo del Senato to see a panorama of the Roman Forum. Walk to the left of the same building to reach the ancient Roman **Carcere Mamertino**, where prisoners were put through a hole in the floor to starve to death. St Peter was believed to have been imprisoned there.

The **Chiesa di Santa Maria d'Aracoeli** is between the Campidoglio and the Monumento Vittorio Emanuele II at the highest point of the Capitoline Hill. Built on the site where legend says the Tiburtine Sybil told the Emperor Augustus of the coming birth of Christ, it features frescoes by Pinturicchio in the first chapel of the south aisle.

Piazza Venezia This piazza is overshadowed by a neoclassical monument dedicated to Vittorio Emanuele II, which is often referred to by Italians as the *macchina da scrivere* (typewriter) because it resembles one.

Built to commemorate Italian unification, the piazza incorporates the **Altare della Patria** and the tomb of the unknown soldier,

as well as the **Museo del Risorgimento**. Also in the piazza is the 15th-century **Palazzo Venezia**, which was Mussolini's official residence and now houses a museum.

Roman Forum & Palatine Hill The commercial, political and religious centre of ancient Rome, the Forum stands in a valley between the Capitoline and Palatine (Palatino) hills. Originally marshland, the area was drained during the early republican era and became a centre for political rallies, public ceremonies and senate meetings. Its importance declined along with the empire after the 4th century, and the temples, monuments and buildings constructed by successive emperors, consuls and senators over a period of 900 years fell into ruin, eventually to be used as pasture.

The area was systematically excavated in the 18th and 19th centuries, and excavations are continuing. You can enter the Forum from Via dei Fori Imperiali, which leads from Piazza Venezia to the Colosseum. Entrance to the Forum is free, but it costs L12,000 to head up to the Palatine. The Forum and Palatine Hill open Monday to Saturday from 9 am to 6 pm in summer (to 3 pm in winter), and on Sunday from 9 am to 1 pm year-round.

As you enter the Forum, to your left is the **Tempio di Antonino e Faustina**, erected by the senate in 141 AD and transformed into a church in the 8th century. To your right are the remains of the **Basilica Aemilia**, built in 179 BC and demolished during the Renaissance when it was plundered for its precious marble. The Via Sacra, which traverses the Forum from north-west to south-east, runs in front of the basilica. Towards the Campidoglio is the **Curia**, once the meeting place of the Roman senate and converted into a Christian church in the Middle Ages. The church was dismantled and the Curia restored in the 1930s. In front of the Curia is the **Lapis Niger**, a large piece of black marble which legend says covered the grave of Romulus. Under the Lapis Niger is the oldest known Latin inscription, dating from the 6th century BC.

The **Arco di Settimo Severo** was erected in 203 AD in honour of this emperor and his sons, and is considered one of Italy's major triumphal arches. A circular base stone beside the arch marks the *umbilicus urbis*, the symbolic centre of ancient Rome. To the south is the **Rostrum**, used in ancient times by public speakers and once decorated by the rams of captured ships.

South along the Via Sacra is the **Tempio di Saturno**, one of the most important temples in ancient Rome. Eight granite columns remain. The **Basilica Julia**, in front of the temple, was the seat of justice, and nearby is the **Tempio di Giulio Cesare** (Temple of Julius Caesar), which was erected by Augustus in 29 BC on the site where Caesar's body was burned and Mark Antony read his famous speech. Back towards the Palatine Hill is the **Tempio dei Castori**, built in 489 BC in honour of the Heavenly Twins, or Dioscuri. It is easily recognisable by its three remaining columns.

In the area south-east of the temple is the **Chiesa di Santa Maria Antiqua**, the oldest Christian church in the Forum. It is closed to the public. Back on the Via Sacra is the **Case delle Vestali**, home of the virgins who tended the sacred flame in the adjoining **Tempio di Vesta**. If the flame went out, it was seen as a bad omen. The next major monument is the vast **Basilica di Costantino**. Its impressive design inspired Renaissance architects. The **Arco di Tito**, at the Colosseum end of the Forum, was built in 81 AD in honour of the victories of the emperors Titus and Vespasian against Jerusalem.

From here climb the Palatino, where wealthy Romans built their homes and where legend says that Romulus founded the city. Archaeological evidence shows that the earliest settlements in the area were on the Palatine. Like the Forum, the buildings of the Palatine fell into ruin and in the Middle Ages the hill became the site of convents and churches. During the Renaissance, wealthy families established their gardens here. The Farnese gardens were built over the ruins of the Domus Tiberiana, which is now under excavation.

Worth a look is the impressive **Domus Augustana**, which was the private residence of the emperors, and the **Domus Flavia**, the residence of Domitian; the **Tempio della Magna Mater**, built in 204 BC to house a black stone connected with the Asiatic goddess, Cybele; and the **Casa di Livia**, thought to have been the house of the wife of Emperor Augustus, and decorated with frescoes.

Colosseum Originally known as the Flavian Amphitheatre, its construction was started by Emperor Vespasian in 72 AD in the grounds of Nero's Golden House, and completed by his son Titus. The massive structure could seat 80,000 and featured bloody gladiatorial combat and wild beast shows which resulted in thousands of human and animal deaths.

In the Middle Ages the Colosseum became a fortress and was later used as a quarry for travertine and marble for the Palazzo Venezia and other buildings. Restoration works have been underway since 1992. Opening hours are from 9 am to 6 pm in summer (to one hour before sunset in winter) and to 1 pm Sunday and public holidays. Entry is L10,000.

Arch of Constantine On the west side of the Colosseum is the triumphal arch built to honour Constantine following his victory over his rival Maxentius at the battle of Milvian Bridge (near the present-day Zona Olimpica, north-west of the Villa Borghese) in 312 AD. Its decorative reliefs were taken from earlier structures. A major restoration was completed in 1987.

Circus Maximus There is not much to see here apart from the few ruins that remain of what was once a chariot racetrack big enough to hold 300,000 spectators.

Baths of Caracalla This huge complex, covering 10 hectares, could hold 1600 people and included shops, gardens, libraries and entertainment. Begun by Antonius Caracalla and inaugurated in 217 AD, the baths were used until the 6th century. From the 1930s to 1993 they were an atmospheric venue for opera performances in summer. These performances have now been banned to prevent further damage to the ruins. The baths are open in summer from 9 am to 6 pm and in winter until 3 pm. Sunday and Monday they close at 1 pm. Entry is L8000.

Some Significant Churches Down Via Cavour from Stazione Termini is **Santa Maria Maggiore**, built in the 5th century. Its main baroque façade was added in the 18th century, preserving the 13th-century mosaics of the earlier façade. Its bell tower is Romanesque and the interior is baroque. There are 5th-century mosaics decorating the triumphal arch and nave.

Follow Via Merulana to reach **Basilica di San Giovanni in Laterano**, Rome's cathedral. The original church was built in the 4th century, the first Christian basilica in Rome. Largely destroyed over a long period of time, it was rebuilt in the 17th century.

Basilica di San Pietro in Vincoli, just off Via Cavour, is worth a visit because it houses Michelangelo's *Moses* and his unfinished statues of Leah and Rachel, as well as the chains worn by St Peter during his imprisonment before being crucified.

Chiesa di San Clemente, Via San Giovanni in Laterano, near the Colosseum, defines how history in Rome exists on many levels. The 12th-century church at street level was built over a 4th-century church which was, in turn, built over a 1st-century Roman house containing a temple dedicated to the pagan god Mithras.

Santa Maria in Cosmedin, north-west of Circus Maximus, is regarded as one of the finest medieval churches in Rome. It has a seven-storey bell tower and its interior is heavily decorated with Cosmatesque inlaid marble, including the beautiful floor. The main attraction for the tourist hordes is, however, the **Bocca della Verità** (Mouth of Truth). Legend has it that if you put your right hand into the mouth, while telling a lie, it will snap shut.

Baths of Diocletian
Started by Emperor Diocletian, these baths were completed in the 4th century. The complex of baths, libraries, concert halls and gardens covered about 13 hectares and could house up to 3000 people. After the aqueduct which fed the baths was destroyed by invaders in 536 AD, the complex fell into decay. Parts of the ruins are now incorporated into the Basilica di Santa Maria degli Angeli.

Basilica di Santa Maria degli Angeli
Designed by Michelangelo, this church incorporates what was the great central hall and *tepidarium* (lukewarm room) of the original baths. During the following centuries his work was drastically changed and little evidence of his design, apart from the great vaulted ceiling of the church, remains. An interesting feature of the church is a double meridian in the transept, one tracing the polar star and the other telling the precise time of the sun's zenith. The church is open from 7.30 am to 12.30 pm and from 4 to 6.30 pm. Through the sacristy is an entrance to a stairway leading to the upper terraces of the ruins.

Museo Nazionale Romano
This museum, located in three separate buildings, houses an important collection of ancient art, including Greek and Roman sculpture. The museum is largely located in the restored Palazzo Altemps, Piazza Sant'Apollinare 44, near Piazza Navona. It contains numerous important pieces from the Ludovisi collection, including the *Ludovisi Throne*. Entry is L10,000. Another part of the same museum is located in the Palazzo Massimo, in Piazza dei Cinquecento. It also was recently restored and contains a collection of frescoes and mosaics from the Villa of Livia, excavated at Prima Porta. Entry is L12,000. Opening hours for both are Tuesday to Saturday from 9 am to 9 pm; Sunday to 7 pm. The third seat of the museum, in the former convent buildings next to the Basilica di Santa Maria degli Angeli, is closed for restoration and due to reopen in 1999.

Via Vittorio Veneto
This was Rome's hot spot in the 1960s, where film stars could be spotted at the expensive outdoor cafés. These days you will find only tourists, and the atmosphere of Fellini's *Roma* is long dead.

Piazza di Spagna & Spanish Steps
This piazza, church and famous staircase (Scalinata della Trinità dei Monti) have long provided a major gathering place for foreigners. Built with a legacy from the French in 1725, but named after the Spanish Embassy to the Holy See, the steps lead to the church of Trinità dei Monti, which was built by the French.

In the 18th century the most beautiful men and women of Italy gathered there, waiting to be chosen as artists' models. To the right as you face the steps is the house where Keats spent the last three months of his life, and where he died in 1821. In the piazza is the boat-shaped fountain of the **Barcaccia**, believed to be by Pietro Bernini, father of the famous Gian Lorenzo. One of Rome's most elegant shopping streets, **Via Condotti**, runs off the piazza towards Via del Corso.

Piazza del Popolo This vast piazza was laid out in the 16th century and redesigned in the early 19th century by Giuseppe Valadier. It is at the foot of the **Pincio Hill**, from where there is a panoramic view of the city.

Villa Borghese This beautiful park was once the estate of Cardinal Scipione Borghese. His 17th-century villa houses the **Museo e Galleria Borghese,** a collection of important paintings and sculptures gathered by the Borghese family. It is possible to visit only with a reservation (☎ 32 81 01) so call well in advance. It's open Tuesday to Saturday from 9 am to 10 pm; Sunday to 8 pm. Entry is L10,000, plus a L2000 booking fee. Just outside the park is the **Galleria Nazionale d'Arte Moderna**, Viale delle Belle Arti 131. It's open Tuesday to Saturday from 9 am to 10 pm, Sunday to 8 pm, and closed Monday. Entry is L8000. The important Etruscan museum, **Museo Nazionale di Villa Giulia**, is along the same street in Piazzale di Villa Giulia. It opens Tuesday to Saturday from 9 am to 7 pm (Sunday to 2 pm) and entry is L8000.

Take the kids bike riding in Villa Borghese. You can hire bikes at the top of the Pincio Hill or near the Porta Pinciana entrance to the park, where there is also a small amusement park.

Trevi Fountain The high-baroque Fontana di Trevi was designed by Nicola Salvi in 1732. Its water was supplied by one of Rome's earliest aqueducts. The famous custom is to throw a coin into the fountain (over your shoulder while facing away) to ensure your return to Rome. If you throw a second coin you can make a wish.

Pantheon This is the best preserved building of ancient Rome. The original temple was built in 27 BC by Marcus Agrippa, son-in-law of Emperor Augustus, and dedicated to the planetary gods. Although the temple was rebuilt by Emperor Hadrian around 120 AD, Agrippa's name remains inscribed over the entrance.

Over the centuries the temple was consistently plundered and damaged. The gilded-bronze roof tiles were removed by an emperor of the eastern empire, and Pope Urban VIII had the bronze ceiling of the portico melted down to make the canopy over the main altar of St Peter's and 80 cannons for Castel Sant'Angelo. The Pantheon's extraordinary dome is considered the most important achievement of ancient Roman architecture. In 608 AD the temple was consecrated to the Virgin and all martyrs.

The Italian kings Vittorio Emanuele II and Umberto I and the painter Raphael are buried there. The Pantheon is in Piazza della Rotonda and is open year-round Monday to Saturday from 9 am to 6.30 pm; Sunday and public holidays from 9 am to 1 pm. Admission is free.

Piazza Navona This is a vast and beautiful square, lined with baroque palaces. It was laid out on the ruins of Domitian's stadium and features three fountains, including Bernini's masterpiece, the **Fontana dei Fiumi** (Fountain of the Rivers), in the centre. Take time to relax on one of the stone benches and watch the artists who gather in the piazza to work.

Campo de' Fiori This is a lively piazza where a flower and vegetable market is held every morning except Sunday. Now lined with bars and trattorias, the piazza was a place of execution during the Inquisition.

The **Palazzo Farnese** (Farnese Palace), in the piazza of the same name, is just off Campo de' Fiori. A magnificent Renaissance building, it was started in 1514 by Antonio da Sangallo, work was carried on by Michelangelo and it was completed by Giacomo della Porta. Built for Cardinal Alessandro Farnese (later Pope Paul III), the palace is now the French Embassy. The piazza has two fountains, which were enormous granite baths taken from the Baths of Caracalla.

Via Giulia This elegant street was designed by Bramante, who was commissioned by Pope Julius II to create a new approach to St Peter's. It is lined with Renaissance palaces, antique shops and art galleries.

ITALY

PANTHEON & TRASTEVERE AREA

PANTHEON & TRASTEVERE AREA

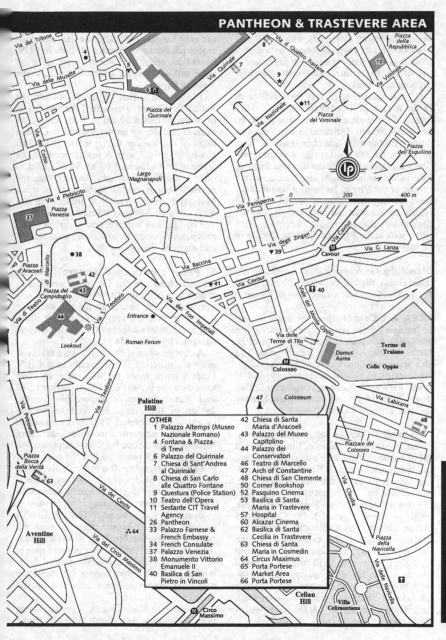

OTHER
1 Palazzo Altemps (Museo Nazionale Romano)
4 Fontana & Piazza di Trevi
6 Palazzo del Quirinale
7 Chiesa di Sant'Andrea al Quirinale
8 Chiesa di San Carlo alle Quattro Fontane
9 Questura (Police Station)
10 Teatro dell'Opera
11 Sestante CIT Travel Agency
26 Pantheon
33 Palazzo Farnese & French Embassy
34 French Consulate
37 Palazzo Venezia
38 Monumento Vittorio Emanuele II
40 Basilica di San Pietro in Vincoli
42 Chiesa di Santa Maria d'Aracoeli
43 Palazzo del Museo Capitolino
44 Palazzo dei Conservatori
46 Teatro di Marcello
47 Arch of Constantine
48 Chiesa di San Clemente
50 Corner Bookshop
52 Pasquino Cinema
53 Basilica di Santa Maria in Trastevere
57 Hospital
60 Alcazar Cinema
62 Basilica di Santa Cecilia in Trastevere
63 Chiesa di Santa Maria in Cosmedin
64 Circus Maximus
65 Porta Portese Market Area
66 Porta Portese

Trastevere You can wander through the narrow medieval streets of this area which, despite the many foreigners who live there, retains the air of a typical Roman neighbourhood. It is especially beautiful at night and is one of the more interesting areas for bar-hopping or a meal.

Of particular note here is the **Basilica di Santa Maria in Trastevere**, in the lovely piazza of the same name. It is believed to be the oldest church dedicated to the Virgin in Rome. Although the first church was built on the site in the 4th century, the present structure was built in the 12th century and features a Romanesque bell tower and façade, with a mosaic of the Virgin. Its interior was redecorated during the baroque period, but the vibrant mosaics in the apse and on the triumphal arch date from the 12th century. Also take a look at the **Basilica di Santa Cecilia** in Trastevere.

Gianicolo Go to the top of the Gianicolo (Janiculum), the hill between St Peter's and Trastevere, for a panoramic view of Rome.

ACEA Art Center This new museum, set up inside a former power plant, houses more than 400 sculptures from the Capitoline Museums and is highly recommended. The idea was to create a setting where art is combined with industrial archaeology and it works very well. It opens Tuesday to Friday from 10 am to 6 pm and Saturday and Sunday to 7 pm. Entry is L12,000.

Catacombs There are several catacombs in Rome, consisting of miles of tunnels carved out of volcanic rock, which were the meeting and burial places of early Christians in Rome. The largest are along the Via Appia Antica, just outside the city and accessible on bus No 218 (from Piazza di Porta San Giovanni – ask the driver when to get off). The **Catacombs of San Callisto** and **Catacombs of San Sebastiano** are almost next to each other on the Via Appia Antica. San Callisto is open from 8.30 am to noon and 2.30 to 5 pm (closed Wednesday and all of February). San Sebastiano is open 8.30 am to noon and 2.30 to 5 pm (closed Sunday and all of November). Admission to each costs L8000 and is with a guide only.

Vatican City After the unification of Italy, the papal states of central Italy became part of the new kingdom of Italy, causing a considerable rift between church and state. In 1929, Mussolini, under the Lateran Treaty, gave the pope full sovereignty over what is now the Vatican City.

The tourist office (☎ 69 88 44 66), in Piazza San Pietro to the left of the basilica, is open daily from 8.30 am to 7 pm, closed on Sunday and during public festivities. Guided tours of the Vatican City gardens (L18,000) can be organised here. A few doors up is the Vatican post office (☎ 69 88 34 06), said to offer a much more reliable service than the normal Italian postal system. It is open Monday to Friday from 8.30 am to 7 pm and until 6 pm on Saturday (closed Sunday).

The city has its own postal service, currency, newspaper, radio station, train station and army of Swiss Guards.

St Peter's Basilica & Square The most famous church in the Christian world, **San Pietro** stands on the site where St Peter was buried. The first church on the site was built during Constantine's reign in the 4th century, and in 1506 work started on a new basilica, designed by Bramante.

Although several architects were involved in its construction, it is generally held that St Peter's owes more to Michelangelo, who took over the project in 1547 at the age of 72 and was particularly responsible for the design of the dome. He died before the church was completed. The cavernous interior contains numerous treasures, including Michelangelo's superb *Pietà*, sculpted when he was only 25 years old and the only work to carry his signature (on the sash across the breast of the Madonna). It has been protected by bulletproof glass since an attack in 1972 by a hammer-wielding Hungarian.

Bernini's huge, baroque *Baldacchino* (a heavily sculpted bronze canopy over the papal altar) stands 29m high and is an extraordinary work of art. Another point of note is the red porphyry disc near the central door, which marks the spot where Charlemagne and later emperors were crowned by the pope.

Entrance to Michelangelo's soaring dome is to the right as you climb the stairs to the atrium of the basilica. Make the entire climb on foot for L5000, or pay L6000 and take the elevator for part of the way (recommended).

The basilica is open daily from 7 am to 7 pm (6 pm in winter) and dress rules are stringently enforced – no shorts, miniskirts or sleeveless tops. Prams and strollers must be left in a designated area outside the basilica.

Bernini's **Piazza San Pietro** (St Peter's Square) is considered a masterpiece. Laid out in the 17th century as a place for Christians of the world to gather, the immense piazza is bound by two semicircular colonnades, each of which is made up of four rows of Doric columns. In the centre of the piazza is an obelisk that was brought to Rome by Caligula from Heliopolis (in ancient Egypt). When you stand on the dark paving stones between the obelisk and either of the fountains, the colonnades appear to have only one row of columns.

The Pope usually gives a public audience at 10 or 11 am every Wednesday in the Papal Audience Hall. You must make a booking, either in person or by fax to the Prefettura della Casa Pontifica (☎ 69 88 30 17; fax 69 88 58 63), on the Monday or Thursday before the audience between 9 am and 1 pm. Go through the bronze doors under the colonnade to the right as you face the basilica.

Vatican Museums From St Peter's follow the wall of the Vatican City (to the right as you face the basilica) to the museums, or catch the regular shuttle bus (L2000) from the piazza in front of the tourist office. The museums are open Monday to Saturday from 8.45 am to 1 pm. At Easter and during summer they are open to 4 pm. Admission is L15,000. The museums are closed on Sunday and public holidays, but open on the last Sunday of every month from 9 am to 1 pm (free admission, but queues are always very long). Guided visits to the Vatican gardens cost L18,000 and can be booked by calling ☎ 69 88 44 66.

The Vatican museums contain an incredible collection of art and treasures collected by the popes, and you will need several hours to see the most important areas and museums. The Sistine Chapel comes towards the end of a full visit, otherwise you can walk straight there and then work your way back through the museums.

The **Museo Pio-Clementino**, containing Greek and Roman antiquities, is on the ground floor near the entrance. Through the tapestry and map galleries are the **Stanze di Rafaello**, once the private apartment of Pope Julius II, decorated with frescoes by Raphael. Of particular interest is the magnificent **Stanza della Segnatura**, which features Raphael's masterpieces *The School of Athens* and *Disputation on the Sacrament*.

From Raphael's rooms, go down the stairs to the sumptuous **Appartamento Borgia**, decorated with frescoes by Pinturicchio, then go down another flight of stairs to the **Sistine Chapel**, the private papal chapel built in 1473 for Pope Sixtus IV. Michelangelo's wonderful frescoes of the *Creation* on the barrel-vaulted ceiling and *Last Judgment* on the end wall have both been recently restored. It took Michelangelo four years, at the height of the Renaissance, to paint the ceiling; 24 years later he painted the extraordinary *Last Judgment*. The other walls of the chapel were painted by artists including Botticelli, Ghirlandaio, Pinturicchio and Signorelli.

Organised Tours

Enjoy Rome (☎ 445 18 43; 167-27 48 19 toll-free), Via Varese 39, offers walking or bike tours of Rome's main sights for L30,000 per person and a shuttle service for Pompeii. ATAC bus No 110 leaves daily at 3.30 pm (2.30 pm in winter) from Piazza dei Cinquecento, in front of Stazione Termini, for a three-hour tour of the city. The cost is L15,000. Vastours (☎ 481 43 09), Via Piemonte 34, operates half-day coach tours of Rome from L48,000 and full-day coach tours of the city from L130,000, as well as tours to Tivoli, the Castelli Romani and other Italian cities. American Express (☎ 676 41) in Piazza di Spagna 38, and the CIT office in Piazza della Repubblica also offer guided tours of the city.

Special Events

Although Romans desert their city in summer, particularly in August when the weather is relentlessly hot and humid, cultural and musical events liven up the place. The Comune di Roma coordinates a diverse series of concerts, performances and events throughout summer under the general title Estate Romana (Roman Summer). The series usually features major international performers. Information is published in Rome's daily newspapers.

A jazz festival is held in July and August in the Villa Celimontana, a park on top of the Celian Hill (access from Piazza della Navicella).

The Festa de' Noantri is held in Trastevere in the last two weeks of July in honour of Our Lady of Mt Carmel. Street stalls line Viale di Trastevere, but head for the backstreets for live music and street theatre.

At Christmas the focus is on the many churches of Rome, each setting up its own nativity scene. Among the most renowned is the 13th-century crib at Santa Maria Maggiore. During Holy Week, at Easter, the focus is again religious and events include the famous procession of the cross between the Colosseum and the Palatino on Good Friday, and the Pope's blessing of the city and the world in St Peter's Square on Easter Sunday.

The Spanish Steps become a sea of pink azaleas during the Spring Festival in April.

Places to Stay

Camping About 15 minutes from the centre by public transport is *Village Camping Flaminio* (☎ 333 26 04) at Via Flaminia 821. It costs L13,000 per person and L12,400 for a site. Tents and bungalows are available for rent. From Stazione Termini catch bus No 910 to Piazza Mancini, then bus No 200 to the camping ground. At night, catch bus No 24n from Piazzale Flaminio (just north of Piazza del Popolo).

Hostel The HI *Ostello Foro Italico* (☎ 323 62 67), Viale delle Olimpiadi 61, costs L24,000 a night, breakfast and showers included. Take Metro Linea A to Ottaviano, then bus No 32 to Foro Italico. The head office of the Italian Youth Hostels Association (☎ 487 11 52) is at Via Cavour 44, 00184 Rome. It will provide information about all the hostels in Italy. You can also join HI here.

B&B This type of accommodation in private houses is a recent addition to Rome's accommodation options for budget travellers.

Bed & Breakfast Italia (☎ 687 86 18; fax 687 86 19; md4095@mclink.it), Corso Vittorio Emanuele II 282, is one of several B&B networks. Central singles/doubles with shared bathroom cost L50,000/95,000, or L70,000/130,000 with private bath.

Hotels & Pensioni There is a vast number of cheap hotels and pensioni in Rome, concentrated mainly to the north-east and south-west of Stazione Termini. The private tourist office, Enjoy Rome (see the earlier Tourist Offices section), will book you a room, but if you want to go it alone, either phone ahead or check your bags in and walk the streets near the station. The area to the north-east is quieter and somewhat safer than that to the south-west.

North-East of Stazione Termini To reach the pensioni in this area, head to the right as you leave the train platforms onto Via Castro Pretorio. *Pensione Giamaica* (☎ 49 01 21), Via Magenta 13, has OK singles/doubles for L50,000/75,000 and triples at L25,000 per person. Nearby at Via Magenta 39 is the excellent *Fawlty Towers* (☎ 445 03 74), which offers hostel-style accommodation at L30,000 per person, or L35,000 with a shower. Run by the people at Enjoy Rome, it offers lots of information about Rome and added bonuses are the sunny terrace and satellite TV.

Nearby in Via Palestro there are several reasonably priced pensioni. *Pensione Restivo* (☎ 446 21 72), Via Palestro 55, has reasonable singles/doubles for L60,000/100,000, including the cost of showers. A triple is L40,000 per person. There's a midnight curfew. *Pensione Katty* (☎ 444 12 16), Via Palestro 35, has basic singles/doubles from L50,000/70,000. Around the corner at Viale Castro Pretorio 25 is *Pensione Ester* (☎ 495 71 23) with comfortable doubles/triples for L75,000/100,000. The recently refurbished *Hotel Positano* (☎ 49 03 60), Via Palestro 49, is a little more expensive. Very pleasant rooms with bathroom, TV and other comforts cost L140,000/160,000.

At Via San Martino della Battaglia 11 are three good pensioni in the same building. The *Pensione Lachea* (☎ 495 72 56) has large, newly renovated doubles/triples for L60,000/80,000. *Hotel Pensione Dolomiti* (☎ 49 10

STAZIONE TERMINI AREA

PLACES TO STAY
1 Hotel Castelfidardo
2 Pensione Katty
4 Pensione Lachea/Hotel
   Pensione Dolomiti
5 Albergo Sandra
7 Pensione Ester
8 Pensione Restivo
9 Hotel Positano
10 Papa Germano
11 Pensione Giamaica
15 Fawlty Towers
22 Hotel Oceania

32 Pensione Everest
35 Hotel Kennedy
37 Hotel Sandy

PLACES TO EAT
13 Trattoria Da Bruno
25 McDonald's
34 McDonald's

OTHER
3 Telecom Office
6 Hospital (Policlinico
   Umberto I)

12 ENIT Tourist Office
14 Enjoy Rome Tourist Office
16 Sestante CIT
   Travel Agency
17 APT Branch Tourist Office
18 Telecom Office
19 Urban Bus Station
20 Baths of Diocletian
21 APT Tourist Office
23 Sestante CIT Travel
   Agency
24 Basilica di Santa Maria
   degli Angeli

26 SAIS Bus Office
27 Eurojet Travel Agency
28 Museo Nazionale Romano
29 Teatro dell'Opera
30 Questura (Police Station)
31 CTS Travel Agency
33 Italian Youth Hostels
   Association Office
36 Basilica di Santa
   Maria Maggiore
38 The Druid's Den
39 Circolo degli Artisti

58) has singles/doubles for L45,000/60,000 (triples for L25,000 per person). *Albergo Sandra* (☎ 445 26 12), Via Villafranca 10 (which runs between Via Vicenza and Via San Martino della Battaglia), is clean, with dark but pleasant rooms for L60,000/80,000, including the cost of a shower.

Papa Germano (☎ 48 69 19) at Via Calatafimi 14a is one of the more popular budget places in the area. It has singles/doubles for L50,000/75,000, or a double with private bathroom for L90,000.

Hotel Castelfidardo (☎ 446 46 38), Via

Castelfidardo 31, off Piazza Indipendenza, is one of Rome's better one-star pensioni. It has singles/doubles for L60,000/75,000 and triples for L95,000/125,000 without/with private bathroom.

Across Via XX Settembre, at Via Collina 48 (a 10-minute walk from the station), *Pensione Ercoli* (☎ 474 54 54) has singles/doubles for L80,000/120,000 and triples for L160,000. In the same building is *Pensione Tizi* (☎ 482 01 28; fax 474 32 66) with singles/doubles for L50,000/70,000. Triples are L120,000 with a shower.

West of Stazione Termini This area is seedier, but prices remain the same. As you exit to the left of the station, follow Via Gioberti to Via G Amendola, which becomes Via F Turati. This street, and the parallel Via Principe Amedeo, harbour a concentration of budget pensioni, so you shouldn't have any trouble finding a room. The area improves as you get closer to the Colosseum and Roman Forum.

At Via Cavour 47, the main street running south-west from the piazza in front of Termini, is **Everest Pensione** (☎ 488 16 29), with clean and simple singles/doubles for L60,000/120,000. **Hotel Sandy** (☎ 445 26 12), Via Cavour 136, has dormitory beds for L30,000 a night. **Hotel Il Castello** (☎ 77 20 40 36), Via Vittorio Amedeo II 9, is close to the Manzoni Metro stop, south of Termini. It has beds in dorm rooms for L28,000.

Better quality hotels in the area include **Hotel Oceania** (☎ 482 46 96), Via Firenze 50, which can accommodate up to five people in a room. It has doubles for up to L230,000.

Hotel Kennedy (☎ 446 53 73), Via F Turati 62, has good quality singles/doubles with bath for up to L120,000/189,000.

City Centre Prices go up significantly in the areas around the Spanish Steps, Piazza Navona, the Pantheon and Campo de' Fiori, but for the extra money you have the convenience and pleasure of staying right in the centre of historical Rome. Budget hotels are few and far between, but there are some pleasant surprises. The easiest way to get to the Spanish Steps is on Metropolitana Linea A to Spagna. To get to Piazza Navona and the Pantheon area, take Bus No 64 from Piazza dei Cinquecento, in front of Termini, to Largo Argentina.

Pensione Primavera (☎ 68 80 31 09), Piazza San Pantaleo 3 on Via Vittorio Emanuele II, just around the corner from Piazza Navona, has immaculate doubles with bathroom for L130,000. A triple is L180,000.

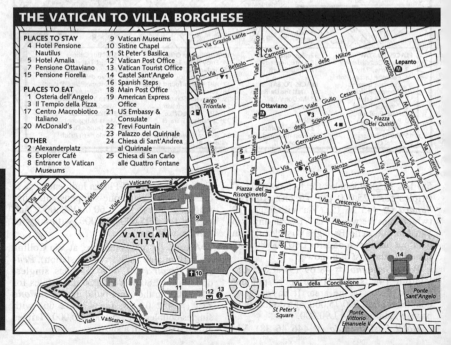

THE VATICAN TO VILLA BORGHESE

PLACES TO STAY
4 Hotel Pensione Nautilus
5 Hotel Amalia
7 Pensione Ottaviano
15 Pensione Fiorella

PLACES TO EAT
1 Osteria dell'Angelo
3 Il Tempio della Pizza
17 Centro Macrobiotico Italiano
20 McDonald's

OTHER
2 Alexanderplatz
6 Explorer Café
8 Entrance to Vatican Museums
9 Vatican Museums
10 Sistine Chapel
11 St Peter's Basilica
12 Vatican Post Office
13 Vatican Tourist Office
14 Castel Sant'Angelo
16 Spanish Steps
18 Main Post Office
19 American Express Office
21 US Embassy & Consulate
22 Trevi Fountain
23 Palazzo del Quirinale
24 Chiesa di Sant'Andrea al Quirinale
25 Chiesa di San Carlo alle Quattro Fontane

ITALY

The *Albergo Abruzzi* (☎ 679 20 21), Piazza della Rotonda 69, overlooks the Pantheon – which excuses, to an extent, its very basic, noisy rooms. You couldn't find a better location, but it's expensive at L87,000/120,000 for singles/doubles and L150,000 for triples. Bookings are essential throughout the year at this popular hotel.

Pensione Mimosa (☎ 68 80 17 53; fax 683 35 57), Via Santa Chiara 61 (off Piazza della Minerva), has very pleasant singles/doubles for L70,000/105,000. The owner imposes a strict no-smoking rule in the rooms.

The *Albergo del Sole* (☎ 68 80 68 73; fax 689 37 87), Via del Biscione 76, off Campo de' Fiori, has expensive singles/doubles with bath/shower for L120,000/170,000, but it's in a great location. Around the corner is *Albergo della Lunetta* (☎ 687 76 30; fax 689 20 28), Piazza del Paradiso 68, which charges L70,000/110,000, or L90,000/150,000 with

private shower. Reservations are essential at both hotels.

The *Albergo Pomezia* (☎/fax 686 13 71) at Via dei Chiavari 12 (which runs off Via dei Giubbonari from Campo de' Fiori) has doubles/triples for L100,000/150,000, breakfast included. Use of the communal shower is free.

Near the Spanish Steps is *Pensione Fiorella* (☎ 361 05 97), Via del Babuino 196, where singles/doubles cost L65,000/105,000, including breakfast.

Near St Peter's & the Vatican Bargains do not abound in this area, but it is comparatively quiet and still reasonably close to the main sights. Bookings are an absolute necessity because rooms are often filled with people attending conferences and so on at the Vatican. The simplest way to reach the area is on the Metropolitana Linea A to Ottaviano. Turn left into Via Ottaviano, and Via

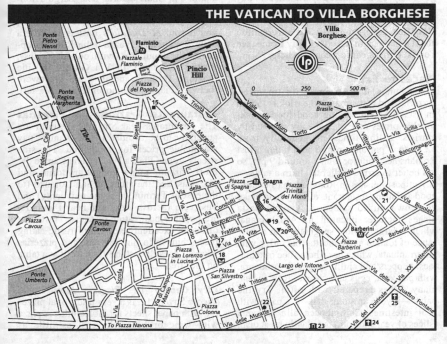

THE VATICAN TO VILLA BORGHESE

Germanico is a short walk away. Bus No 64 from Termini stops at St Peter's – walk away from the basilica along Via di Porta Angelica, which becomes Via Ottaviano after Piazza del Risorgimento, a five-minute walk.

The best bargain in the area is *Pensione Ottaviano* (☎ 39 73 72 53), Via Ottaviano 6, near Piazza Risorgimento. It has beds in dormitories for L28,000 per person. The owner speaks English well. *Hotel Pensione Nautilus* (☎ 324 21 18), Via Germanico 198, offers basic doubles/triples for L100,000/145,000 or L130,000/155,000 with private bathroom (no singles). *Hotel Amalia* (☎ 39 72 33 56; fax 39 72 33 65), Via Germanico 66 (near the corner of Via Ottaviano), has a beautiful courtyard entrance and clean, sunny rooms. Singles/doubles are L95,000/120,000 and include breakfast and use of the communal shower. Triples are L162,000.

Rental Accommodation Apartments near the centre of Rome are expensive, so expect to pay around L2,000,000 a month. A good way to find a shared apartment is to buy *Wanted in Rome,* an English-language fortnightly magazine which publishes both classified advertisements and information about what's on in the city. Enjoy Rome (see Tourist Offices earlier) can also help.

Places to Eat

Rome bursts at the seams with trattorias, pizzerias and restaurants – the trick is to find an establishment serving good food at reasonable prices that isn't already overrun by tourists. Eating times are generally from 12.30 to 3 pm and from 8 to 11 pm. Most Romans head out for dinner around 9 pm, so it's better to arrive earlier to claim a table.

Antipasto dishes in Rome are particularly good and many restaurants allow you to make your own mixed selection. Typical pasta dishes include: bucatini all'Amatriciana, which is large, hollow spaghetti with a salty sauce of tomato and pancetta (bacon); penne all'arrabbiata, which has a hot sauce of tomatoes, peppers and chilli; spaghetti carbonara, with pancetta, eggs and cheese. Romans eat many dishes prepared with offal. Try the paiata – if you can stomach it – it's pasta with veal intestines. Saltimbocca alla Romana (slices of veal and ham) is a classic meat dish,

as is straccetti con la rucola, fine slices of beef tossed in garlic and oil and topped with fresh rocket. In winter you can't go past carciofi alla Romana (artichokes stuffed with garlic and mint or parsley).

Good options for cheap, quick meals are the hundreds of bars, where panini (sandwiches) cost L2500 to L5000 if taken al banco (at the bar), or takeaway pizzerias, usually called pizza a taglio, where a slice of freshly cooked pizza, sold by weight, can cost as little as L2000. Bakeries are numerous and are another good choice for a cheap snack. Try a huge piece of pizza bianca, a flat bread resembling focaccia, costing from around L2000 a slice (sold by weight).

Try *Paladini*, Via del Governo Vecchio 29, for sandwiches, and *Pizza a Taglio*, Via Baullari, between Campo de' Fiori and Corso Vittorio Emanuele II, for takeaway pizza.

There are numerous outdoor markets, notably the lively daily market in Campo de' Fiori. Other, cheaper food markets are held in Piazza Vittorio Emanuele, near the station, and in Via Andrea Doria, near Largo Trionfale, north of the Vatican.

But, if all you really want is a Big Mac, you'll find *McDonald's* outlets in Piazza della Repubblica, Piazza della Rotonda opposite the Pantheon (with outside tables), Piazza di Spagna, in Via Giolitti outside Stazione Termini, and in Viale Trastevere (between Piazza Sonnino and Piazza Mastai).

Restaurants, Trattorias & Pizzerias The restaurants near Stazione Termini are generally to be avoided if you want to pay reasonable prices for good food. The side streets around Piazza Navona and Campo de' Fiori harbour many budget trattorias and pizzerias, and the areas of San Lorenzo (to the east of Termini, near the university) and Testaccio (across the Tiber near Piramide) are popular local eating districts. Trastevere offers an excellent selection of rustic eating places hidden in tiny piazzas, and pizzerias where it doesn't cost the earth to sit at a table on the street.

City Centre The *Pizzeria Montecarlo*, Vicolo Savelli 12, is a very traditional pizzeria, with paper sheets for tablecloths. A pizza with wine or beer will cost as little as

L15,000. The *Pizzeria da Baffetto*, Via del Governo Vecchio 11, is a Roman institution. The pizzas are huge and delicious. Expect to join a queue if you arrive after 9 pm and don't be surprised if you end up sharing a table. Pizzas cost around L9000 to L12,000, a litre of wine costs L9000 and the cover charge (coperto) is only L1500. Farther along the street at No 18 is a tiny, nameless *osteria* run by Antonio Bassetti, where you can eat an excellent, simple meal for around L20,000. There's no written menu, but don't be nervous – the owner/waiter will explain slowly – (in Italian). Back along the street towards Piazza Navona, at Piazza Pasquino 73, is *Cul de Sac 1*, a wine bar which also has light meals at reasonable prices.

Trattoria Pizzeria da Francesco, Piazza del Fico 29, has pasta dishes from L10,000, as well as pizzas for L8000 to L14,000 and a good range of antipasto and vegetables. *Centro Macrobiotico Italiano*, Via della Vite 14, is a vegetarian restaurant which also serves fresh fish in the evenings. It charges an annual membership fee (which reduces as the year goes by), but tourists can usually eat there and pay only a small surcharge.

There are several small restaurants in the Campo de' Fiori. *Hostaria Romanesca* is tiny, so arrive early in winter. In summer there are numerous tables outside. A dish of pasta will cost around L10,000, a full meal around L30,000.

Along Via Giubbonari, off Campo de' Fiori, is *Filetti di Baccalà* in the tiny Largo dei Librari, which serves only deep-fried cod fillets for around L5000 and wine for L7000 a litre. Across Via Arenula, in the Jewish quarter, is *Sora Margherita*, Piazza delle Cinque Scole 30. Open only at lunchtime, it serves traditional Roman and Jewish food and a full meal will cost around L30,000.

Near the Trevi Fountain, in Vicolo Scanderbeg, you'll find *Piccolo Arancio*, which offers reasonable food at around L9000 for a first course and L9000 to L15,000 for a secondo. Most of the restaurants in this area are either high class and very expensive, or tourist traps.

West of the Tiber On the west bank of the Tiber, good-value restaurants are concentrated in Trastevere and the Testaccio district,

past Piramide. Many of the establishments around St Peter's and the Vatican are geared for tourists and can be very expensive. There are, however, some good options. Try *Il Tempio della Pizza*, Viale Giulio Cesare 91, or *Osteria dell'Angelo*, Via G Bettolo 24, along Via Leone IV from the Vatican City, although this place can be difficult to get into.

In Trastevere, try *Frontoni*, on Viale di Trastevere, opposite Piazza Mastai, for fantastic panini made with pizza bianca. *D'Augusto*, Piazza dei Renzi, just around the corner from the Basilica Santa Maria in Trastevere (turn right as you face the church and walk to Via della Pelliccia), is a very popular cheap eating spot. The food might be average, but the atmosphere, especially in summer with tables outside in the piazza, is as traditionally Roman as you can get. A meal with wine will cost around L20,000. *Da Lucia*, Vicolo del Mattinato 2, is more expensive at around L40,000 a full meal, but the food is good and the owners are delightful. In summer you'll sit beneath the neighbours' washing.

Pizzeria San Calisto, Piazza San Calisto, has outdoor tables and serves enormous pizzas. They cost from L10,000 to L14,000. For a Neapolitan-style pizza, try *Pizzeria da Vittorio*, Via San Cosimato 14. You'll have to wait for an outside table if you arrive after 8.30 pm, but the atmosphere is great. A bruschetta, pizza and wine will cost around L20,000.

You won't find a cheaper, noisier, more chaotic pizzeria in Rome than *Pizzeria Remo*, Piazza Santa Maria Liberatrice 44, in Testaccio. *Il Canestro*, Via Maestro Giorgio, Testaccio, specialises in vegetarian food and is relatively expensive. *Augustarello*, Via G Branca 98, off the piazza, specialises in the very traditional Roman fare of offal dishes. The food is reasonable and a meal will cost around L20,000.

Between Termini & the Forum You will find typical local fare and good pizzas at prices students can afford at *Pizzeria l'Economica*, Via Tiburtina 44. Another local favourite is *Formula 1*, Via degli Equi 13, where you'll pay around L15,000 for a bruschetta, pizza and wine.

If you have no option but to eat near Stazione Termini, try to avoid the tourist traps offering overpriced full menus. *Trattoria da Bruno*, Via Varese 29, has good food at reasonable prices – around L8000 for pasta and up to L14,000 for a second course. Home-made gnocchi is served on Thursday. A decent pizzeria is *Alle Carrette*, Vicolo delle Carrette 14, off Via Cavour near the Roman Forum. A pizza and wine will cost around L15,000. Just off Via Cavour in the tiny Via dell'Angeletto is *Osteria Gli Angeletti*, an excellent little restaurant with prices at the higher end of the budget range. You'll pay L10,000 to L14,000 for a pasta and around L16,000 for a second course.

Gelati *Gelateria Giolitti*, Via degli Uffici del Vicario 40, near the Pantheon, and *Gelateria della Palme* around the corner at Via della Maddalena 20 both have a huge selection of flavours. *Fonte della Salute*, Via Cardinale Marmaggi 2-6, in Trastevere, has excellent gelati.

Entertainment

Rome's primary entertainment guide is *Trovaroma*, a weekly supplement in the Thursday edition of the newspaper *La Repubblica*. It provides a comprehensive listing of what's happening in the city, but in Italian only. The newspaper also publishes a daily listing of cinema, theatre and concerts.

Metropolitan is a fortnightly magazine for Rome's English-speaking community (L1500). It has good entertainment listings and is available at outlets including the Economy Book & Video Center, Via Torino 136, and newsstands in the city centre, including at Largo Argentina. Another excellent guide is *Roma C'è*, available at newspaper stands.

Cinema The cinema *Pasquino* (☎ 580 36 22), Vicolo del Piede 19 and around the corner in Piazza Sant'Egidio, in Trastevere, screens films in English. It is just off Piazza Santa Maria in Trastevere. *Alcazar* (☎ 588 00 99), Via Merry del Val 14, Trastevere, shows an English-language film every Monday. *Nuovo Saucer* (☎ 581 81 16) at Largo Ascianghi, in Trastevere, shows films in their original language on Monday and Tuesday.

Nightclubs Among the more interesting and popular Roman live music clubs is *Radio Londra*, Via di Monte Testaccio 67, in the Testaccio area. In the same street are the more sedate music clubs *Caruso Caffè* at No 36 and *Caffè Latino* at No 96, both generally offering jazz or blues. More jazz and blues can be heard at *Alexanderplatz*, Via Ostia 9, and *Big Mama*, Via San Francesco a Ripa 18, in Trastevere. *Circolo degli Artisti*, Via Lamarmora 28, near Piazza Vittorio Emanuele, is a lively club, popular among Rome's 'cool' set.

Roman discos are outrageously expensive. Expect to pay up to L30,000 to get in, which may or may not include one drink. Perennials include: *Alien*, Via Velletri 13; *Piper '90*, Via Tagliamento 9; and *Gilda-Swing*, Via Mario de' Fiori 97. The best gay disco is *L'Alibi*, Via di Monte Testaccio 44.

Exhibitions & Concerts From November to May, opera is performed at the *Teatro dell'Opera*, Piazza Beniamino Gigli (☎ 481 70 03). A season of concerts is held in October and November at the *Accademia di Santa Cecilia*, Via della Conciliazione 4, and the *Accademia Filarmonica*, Via Flaminia 118. A series of concerts is held from July to the end of September at the *Teatro di Marcello*, Via Teatro di Marcello 44, near Piazza Venezia. For information call ☎ 482 74 03.

Rock concerts are held throughout the year. For information and bookings, contact the ORBIS agency (☎ 482 74 03) in Piazza Esquilino near Stazione Termini.

Cafés & Bars Remember that prices skyrocket in bars as soon as you sit down, particularly near the Spanish Steps, in the Piazza della Rotonda and in Piazza Navona, where a cappuccino a tavola (at a table) can cost L5000 or more. The same cappuccino taken at the bar will cost around L1500 – but passing an hour or so watching the world go by over a cappuccino, beer or wine in any of the above locations can be hard to beat!

For the best coffee in Rome head for *Tazza d'Oro*, just off Piazza della Rotonda in Via degli Orfani, and *Caffè Sant'Eustachio*, Piazza Sant'Eustachio 82. Try the granita di caffè at either one.

Vineria in Campo de' Fiori, also known as *Giorgio's*, has a wide selection of wine and beers. In summer it has tables outside, but prices are steep – better to stand at the bar. *Bar della Pace*, Via della Pace 3-7, is big with the young 'in' crowd, but 'cool' always has a price. *Bevitoria Navona*, Piazza Navona 72, has wine by the glass. *Bar San Calisto*, Piazza San Calisto, in Trastevere, has outside tables and you don't pay extra to sit down. The crowd is generally pretty scruffy. *The Druid's Den* is a popular Irish pub, which means you can get Guinness and Kilkenny on tap. It's at Via San Martino ai Monti 28, near Piazza Santa Maria Maggiore.

Things to Buy

It is probably advisable to stick to window-shopping in the expensive Ludovisi district, the area around Via Veneto. The major fashion shops are in Via Sistina and Via Gregoriana, heading towards the Spanish Steps. Via Condotti and the parallel streets heading from Piazza di Spagna to Via del Corso are lined with moderately expensive clothing and footwear boutiques, as well as shops selling accessories.

It is cheaper, but not as interesting, to shop along Via del Tritone and Via Nazionale. There are some interesting second-hand clothes shops along Via del Governo Vecchio.

If clothes don't appeal, wander through the streets around Via Margutta, Via Ripetta, Piazza del Popolo and Via Frattina to look at the art galleries, artists' studios and antiquarian shops. Antique shops line Via Coronari, between Piazza Navona and Lungotevere di Tor di Nona.

Everyone flocks to the famous Porta Portese market every Sunday morning. Hundreds of stalls selling anything you can imagine line the streets of the Porta Portese area parallel to Viale di Trastevere, near Trastevere. Take time to rummage through the piles of clothing and bric-a-brac and you will find some incredible bargains. Catch tram No 8 from Largo Argentina and ask the driver where to get off (it's a 10-minute ride).

The market in Via Sannio, near Porta San Giovanni, sells new and second-hand clothes and shoes at bargain prices.

Getting There & Away

Air The main airline offices are in the area around Via Veneto and Via Barberini, north of Stazione Termini. Qantas, British Airways, Alitalia, Air New Zealand, Lufthansa and Singapore Airlines are all in Via Bissolati. The main airport is Leonardo da Vinci, at Fiumicino (see the Getting Around section).

Bus The main terminal for intercity buses is in Piazzale Tiburtina, in front of the Stazione Tiburtina. Catch the Metropolitana Linea B from Termini to Tiburtina. Buses connect with cities throughout Italy. Numerous companies, some of which are listed below, operate these services. For information about which companies operate services to which destinations and from where, go to the APT office, or Enjoy Rome (see Tourist Offices). At Eurojet (☎ 481 74 55; fax 474 45 21; eurojrt@adv.it), Piazza della Repubblica 54, you can buy tickets for and get information about several bus services. Otherwise, there are ticket offices for all of the companies inside the Tiburtina station. COTRAL buses, which service Lazio, depart from numerous points throughout the city, depending on their destinations.

Some useful bus lines are:

COTRAL (☎ 167-43 17 84) Via Ostiense 131 – services throughout Lazio
Lazzi (☎ 884 08 40) Via Tagliamento 27b – services to other European cities (Eurolines) and the Alps
Marozzi (information at Eurojet) – services to Bari and Brindisi, as well as to Pompeii, Sorrento and the Amalfi Coast and Matera in Basilicata
SAIS & Segesta (☎ 481 96 76) Piazza della Repubblica 42 – services to Sicily
SENA (information at Eurojet) – service to Siena
SULGA (information at Eurojet) – services to Perugia and Assisi

Train Almost all trains arrive at and depart from Stazione Termini. There are regular connections to all major cities in Italy and throughout Europe. An idea of journey times and costs for Eurostar trains from Rome (which require booking and a special supplement) is as follows: Florence (1¾ hours, L48,000); Milan (4½ hours, L79,500) and Naples (two hours, L37,500). For train timetable information phone ☎ 147-88 80 88 (from 7 am to 9 pm), or go to the information office at the station (English is spoken). Timetables can be bought at most newsstands in and around Termini and are particularly

ITALY

useful if you are travelling mostly by train. Services at Termini include telephones, money exchange (see the earlier Information section) and luggage storage (☎ 47 30 62 75; L5000 per piece every six hours, beside track 22). Some trains depart from the stations Ostiense and at Tiburtina.

Car & Motorcycle The main road connecting Rome to the north and south is the Autostrada del Sole A1, which extends from Milan to Reggio di Calabria. On the outskirts of the city it connects with the Grande Raccordo Anulare (GRA), the ring road encircling Rome. If you are entering or leaving Rome, use the Grande Raccordo and the major feeder roads which connect it to the city; it might be longer, but it is simpler and faster. From the Grande Raccordo there are 33 exits into Rome. If you're approaching from the north, take the Via Salaria, Via Nomentana or Via Flaminia exits. From the south, Via Appia Nuova, Via Cristoforo Colombo and Via del Mare (which connects Rome to the Lido di Ostia) all provide reasonable direct routes into the city. The A12 connects the city to Civitavecchia and to Fiumicino airport.

Car rental offices at Stazione Termini in Rome include: Avis (☎ 419 99/98); Hertz (☎ 321 68 31); and Maggiore (☎ 147-86 70 67). All have offices at both airports. Happy Rent (☎ 481 81 85; www.happyrent.com), Via Farini 3, rents scooters and bicycles (with baby seats available), as well as some cars and video cameras. It also offers a free baggage deposit and a free email service to its customers. Another option for scooters and bicycles is I Bike Rome (☎ 322 52 40), Via Veneto 156.

Hitching It is illegal to hitchhike on the autostrade. To head north, wait for a lift on Via Salaria, near the autostrada exit. To go south to Naples, take the Metropolitana to Anagnina and wait in Via Tuscolana. Hitching is not recommended, particularly for women, either alone or in groups. Enjoy Rome might be able to help organise lifts (see under Tourist Offices).

Boat Tirrenia and the Ferrovie dello Stato (FS) ferries leave for various points in Sardinia (see Sardinia's Getting There & Away section) from Civitavecchia. A new Tirrenia fast ferry leaves from Fiumicino, near Rome, and Civitavecchia. Bookings can be made at Sestante CIT, or any travel agency displaying the Tirrenia or FS sign. You can also book directly with Tirrenia (☎ 474 20 41), Via Bissolati 41, Rome, or at the Stazione Marittima (ferry terminal) at the ports. Bookings can be made at Stazione Termini for FS ferries.

Getting Around

To/From the Airport The main airport is Leonardo da Vinci (☎ 65 95 36 40 for flights only) at Fiumicino. Access to the city is via the airport-Stazione Termini direct train (follow the signs to the station from the airport arrivals hall), which costs L15,000. The train arrives at and leaves from platform No 22 at Termini and there is a ticket office on the platform. The trip takes 35 minutes. The first train leaves the airport for Termini at 7.38 am and the last at 10.08 pm. Another train makes stops along the way, including at Trastevere and Ostiense, and terminates at Stazione Tiburtina (L8500). A night bus runs from Stazione Tirburtina to the airport from 12.30 to 3.45 am, stopping at Termini at the corner of Via Giolitti about 10 minutes later. The airport is connected to Rome by an autostrada, accessible from the Grande Raccordo Anulare (ring road).

Taxis are prohibitively expensive from the airport (see Taxi in the main Getting Around section of this chapter).

The other airport is Ciampino, which is used for most domestic and international charter. Blue COTRAL buses (running from 6.50 am to 11.40 pm) connect with the Metropolitana (Linea A at Anagnina), where you can catch the subway to Termini or the Vatican. But if you arrive very late at night you could end up being forced to catch a taxi. A metropolitan train line, the FM4, connects Termini with the Ciampino airport and Albano Laziale. The airport is connected to Rome by Via Appia Nuova.

Bus The city bus company is ATAC (☎ 167-43 17 84 for information in English) and many of the main buses terminate in Piazza Cinquecento in front of Stazione Termini.

Details on which buses head where are available at the ATAC information booth in the centre of the piazza. Another central point for main bus routes in the centre is Largo Argentina, on Corso Vittorio Emanuele south of the Pantheon. Buses run from 5.30 am to midnight, with limited services throughout the night on some routes. A new fast tram service, the No 8, connects Largo Argentina with Trastevere, Porta Portese and the suburb of Monte Verde. ATAC was restructuring many bus routes in 1998. However, at the time of writing, useful bus numbers to remember were No 64 from Stazione Termini to St Peter's; No 75 from Termini to the Colosseum and then Trastevere; No 218 from Piazza di Porta San Giovanni to the catacombs; and No 44 from Piazza Venezia to Trastevere.

Travel on Rome's buses, subway and suburban railways has now been linked, and the same ticket is valid for all three. Tickets cost L1500 and are valid for 75 minutes. They must be purchased *before* you get on the bus and validated in the orange machine as you enter. The fine for travelling without a ticket is L101,500, to be paid on the spot, and there is no sympathy for 'dumb tourists'. Tickets can be purchased at any tobacconist, newsstand, or at the main bus terminals. Daily tickets cost L8500, weekly tickets cost L24,000 and monthly tickets are L50,000 or L70,000 (usable by more than one person).

Metropolitana The Metropolitana (Metro) has two lines, A and B. Both pass through Stazione Termini. Take Linea A for Piazza di Spagna, the Vatican (Ottaviano) and Villa Borghese (Flaminio), and Linea B for the Colosseum, Circus Maximus and Piramide (for Testaccio and Stazione Ostiense). An extension of the Linea A was under construction in 1998. Tickets are the same as for city buses (see under Bus in this section). Trains run approximately every five minutes between 5.30 am and 11.30 pm.

Taxi Taxis are on radio call 24 hours a day in Rome. Cooperativa Radio Taxi Romana (☎ 35 70) and La Capitale (☎ 49 94) are two of the many operators. Major taxi ranks are at the airports, Stazione Termini and Largo Argentina in the historical centre. There are surcharges on Sunday and for luggage (L2000 per item), night service, public holidays and travel to/from Fiumicino airport. The flag fall is L4500 (for the first 150m), then L200 for every 150m. There is a L5000 supplement from 10 pm to 7 am and L2000 from 7 am to 10 pm on Sunday and public holidays. There is a L14,000 supplement on travel to and from Fiumicino airport because it is outside the city limits. This means the fare will cost around L70,000.

Car & Motorcycle Negotiating Roman traffic by car is difficult enough, but you are taking your life in your hands if you ride a motorcycle in the city. The rule in Rome is to watch the vehicles in front and hope that the vehicles behind are watching you.

Most of the historic centre is closed to normal traffic, although tourists are permitted to drive to their hotels. *Vigili* (traffic police) control the entrances to the centre and will let you through once you mention the name of your hotel. Ask at the hotel for a parking permit for the centre, otherwise you might find a brace on your car wheel or, at worst, that the car has been towed away. If your car goes missing after being parked illegally, check with the traffic police (☎ 676 91). It will cost about L180,000 to get it back plus L15,600 for each day it has been in the police deposit.

A major parking area close to the centre is at the Villa Borghese. Entrance is from Piazzale Brasile at the top of Via Veneto. There is a supervised car park at Stazione Termini. There are large car parks at Stazione Tiburtina and Piazza dei Partigiani at Stazione Ostiense (both accessible to the centre of Rome by the Metro). See the preceding Getting There & Away section for information about car, scooter and bike rental.

In Rome, be wary when crossing at traffic lights because most motorcyclists don't stop at red lights. Neither motorcyclists nor motorists are keen to stop at pedestrian crossings, so be extremely careful. The accepted mode of crossing a road is to step into the traffic and walk at a steady pace. If in doubt, follow a Roman.

ITALY

Around Rome

Rome demands so much of your time and concentration that most tourists forget that the city is part of the region of Lazio. There are some interesting places within an easy day trip of the city. In summer, avoid the polluted beaches close to the city and head south to Sabaudia or Sperlonga, or take the train from Ostiense to Lago di Bracciano.

OSTIA ANTICA
☎ 06

The Romans founded this port city at the mouth of the Tiber in the 4th century BC and it became a strategically important centre of defence and trade. It was populated by merchants, sailors and slaves, and the ruins of the city provide a fascinating contrast to a place such as Pompeii. It was abandoned after barbarian invasions and the appearance of malaria, but Pope Gregory IV re-established the city in the 9th century.

The Rome EPT office or Enjoy Rome can provide information about the ancient city or call the ticket office on ☎ 445 18 43.

Things to See & Do

Of particular note in the excavated city are the **Terme di Nettuno**; a **Roman theatre** built by Augustus; the **forum** and **temple**, dedicated to Jupiter, Juno and Minerva; and the **Piazzale delle Corporazioni**, where you can see the offices of Roman merchants, distinguished by mosaics depicting their trades. The site is open from 9 am to about an hour before sunset and entry is L8000.

Getting There & Away

To get to Ostia Antica take the Metropolitana Linea B to Magliana and then the Ostia Lido train (getting off at Ostia Antica).

TIVOLI
☎ 0774

Set on a hill by the Anio River, Tivoli was a resort town of the ancient Romans and became popular as a summer playground for the rich during the Renaissance. It is famous today for the terraced gardens and fountains of the Villa d'Este and the ruins of the spectacular Villa Adriana, built by the Roman emperor Hadrian.

The local tourist office (☎ 31 12 49; fax 33 45 22) is in Largo Garibaldi near the COTRAL bus stop.

Things to See & Do

Hadrian built his summer villa, **Villa Adriana**, in the 2nd century AD. Its construction was influenced by the architecture of the famous classical buildings of the day. It was successively plundered by barbarians and Romans for building materials and many of its original decorations were used to embellish the Villa d'Este. However, enough remains to give an idea of the incredible size and magnificence of the villa. You will need about four hours to wander through the vast ruins.

Highlights include La Villa dell'Isola (the Villa of the Island) where Hadrian spent his pensive moments, the Imperial Palace and its Piazza d'Oro (Golden Square), and the floor mosaics of the Hospitalia. The villa is open daily from 9 am to about one hour before sunset, therefore to around 7.30 pm (last entry at 6.30 pm) in the warmer months. Entry is L8000.

The Renaissance **Villa d'Este** was built in the 16th century for Cardinal Ippolito d'Este on the site of a Franciscan monastery. The villa's beautiful gardens are decorated with numerous fountains, which are its main attraction. Opening hours are the same as for Villa Adriana and entry is L8000. Villa d'Este is closed on Monday.

Getting There & Away

Tivoli is about 40km east of Rome and accessible by COTRAL bus. Take Metro Linea B from Stazione Termini to Ponte Mammolo; the bus leaves from outside the station every 20 minutes. The bus also stops near the Villa Adriana, about 1km from Tivoli. Otherwise, catch local bus No 4 from Tivoli's Piazza Garibaldi to Villa Adriana.

ETRUSCAN SITES

Lazio has several important Etruscan archaeological sites, most within easy reach of Rome by car or public transport. These include Tarquinia (one of the most important cities of the Etruscan League), Cerveteri, Veio and Tuscania. The tombs and religious monuments discovered in the area have yielded the treasures which can now be seen in the large museums, including the Villa Giulia and the Vatican, although the small museums at Tarquinia and Cerveteri are worth visiting.

Tarquinia
☎ 0766

Believed to have been founded in the 12th century BC and to have been the home of the Tarquin kings who ruled Rome before the creation of the republic, Tarquinia was an important economic and political centre of the Etruscan League. The major attractions here are the painted tombs of its *necropoli* (burial grounds). The IAT tourist information office (☎ 0766-85 63 84) is at Piazza Cavour 1.

Things to See & Do The 15th-century Palazzo Vitelleschi houses the **Museo Nazionale di Tarquinia** and an excellent collection of Etruscan treasures, including frescoes removed from the tombs. There are also numerous sarcophagi which were found in the tombs. The museum is open Tuesday to Sunday from 9 am to 7 pm (closed Monday). Entry is L8000 and the same ticket covers entry to the **necropolis**, a 15 to 20-minute walk away (or catch the bus). The necropolis has the same opening hours as the museum. Ask at the tourist office for directions. Only a small number of the thousands of tombs have been excavated and only a handful are open on any given day. You must wait until a group forms and a guide will then take you on a tour of nine tombs. Beware of long waits in summer, when thousands of tourists visit the necropolis daily. The tombs are richly decorated with frescoes, though many are seriously deteriorated. They are now maintained at constant temperatures to preserve the remaining decorations and it is possible to see them only through glass partitions.

Take the time to wander through the streets of medieval Tarquinia and, if you have a car, ask for directions to the remains of Etruscan Tarquinia, on the crest of the Civita Hill nearby. There is little evidence of the ancient city, apart from a few limestone blocks that once formed part of the city walls. However, a large temple, the **Ara della Regina**, was discovered on the hill and has been excavated this century.

Places to Stay & Eat There is a camping ground by the sea, *Tuscia Tirrenica* (☎ 86 42 94), Viale Nereidi. There are no budget options if you want to stay overnight and it can be difficult to find a room if you don't book well in advance. Try the *Hotel all'Olivo* (☎ 85 73 18), Via Togliatti 15, in the newer part of town, about a 10-minute walk downhill from the medieval centre. Singles/doubles with private bath cost L70,000/120,000.

For a good, cheap meal, try *Cucina Casareccia*, at Via G Mazzini 5, off Piazza Cavour, or the *Trattoria Arcadia* opposite at No 6.

Getting There & Away Buses leave approximately every hour for Tarquinia from Via Lepanto in Rome, near the Metropolitana Linea A Lepanto stop, arriving at Tarquinia a few steps away from the tourist office. You can also catch a train from Ostiense, but Tarquinia's station is at Tarquinia Lido (beach), approximately 3km from the centre. You will then need to catch one of the regular local buses.

Cerveteri
☎ 06

Ancient Caere was founded by the Etruscans in the 8th century BC and enjoyed a period of great prosperity as a maritime centre from the 7th to 5th centuries BC. The main attractions here are the tombs known as *tumoli* – great mounds with carved stone bases. Treasures taken from the tombs can be seen in the Vatican Museums, the Villa Giulia Museum and the Louvre. The Pro Loco tourist office is at Piazza Risorgimento 19.

The main necropolis area, **Banditaccia**, is open daily from 9 am to 6 pm, while in winter it closes one hour before sunset. Entry is L8000. You can wander freely once inside the area, though it is best to follow the recommended routes in order to see the best preserved tombs. Banditaccia is accessible by local bus in summer only from the main piazza in Cerveteri, but it is also a pleasant 3km walk west from the town.

There is also a small **museum** in Cerveteri that contains an interesting display of pottery and sarcophagi. It is in the Palazzo Ruspoli and is open from 9 am to 2 pm (closed Monday). Entry is free.

Cerveteri is accessible from Rome by COTRAL bus from Via Lepanto, outside the Lepanto stop on Metropolitana Linea A.

Northern Italy

Italy's northern regions are its wealthiest and offer many and varied attractions to travellers. A tour of the north could take you from the beaches of the Italian Riviera in Liguria, to Milan for a shopping spree, into Emilia-Romagna to sample its remarkable *cucina* (cooking), through countless medieval and Renaissance towns and villages, and into the Alps to ski or trek in the Dolomites, before taking a boat trip down the Grand Canal of timeless Venice.

GENOA
☎ 010

Travellers who think of Genoa (Genova) as simply a dirty port town and bypass the city for the coastal resorts do the city and themselves a disservice. This once-powerful maritime republic, birthplace of Christopher Columbus (1451-1506) and now capital of the region of Liguria, can still carry the title La Superba (The Proud). It is a fascinating city that is full of contrasts. Here you can meet crusty old seafarers in the markets and trattorias of the port area, where some of the tiny streets are so narrow it is difficult for two people to stand together. But go round a corner and you will find young Genoese in the latest Benetton gear strolling through streets lined with grand, black-and-white marble palaces.

Orientation

Most trains stop at both of the main stations in Genoa: Stazione Principe and Stazione Brignole. The area around Brignole is closer to the city centre and offers more pleasant accommodation than does Principe, which is close to the port. Women travelling alone should avoid staying in the port area.

From Brignole walk straight ahead along Via Fiume to get to Via XX Settembre and the historical centre. It is easier to walk around Genoa than to use the local ATM bus service, but most useful buses stop outside both stations.

Information
Tourist Offices IAT tourist information offices are at Stazione Principe and the airport (both open from 8 am to 8 pm Monday to Saturday; the Stazione Principe office also opens on Sunday from 9 am to noon). The main office (☎ 248 71) is on the waterfront at Via del Porto Antico, in the Palazzina Santa Maria. It opens from 9 am to 6.30 pm seven days a week.

Post & Communications The main post office is in Via Dante, just off Piazza de Ferrari. You'll also find public phones here. There is a Telecom office at Piazza Verdi off Stazione Brignole, open from 8 am to 9.30 pm. Genoa's postcode is 16100.

Medical & Emergency Services The Ospedale San Martino (☎ 55 51) is in Via Benedetto XV. In an emergency, call ☎ 118 for an ambulance and ☎ 113 for the police.

Things to See & Do
Start by wandering around the port area, the oldest part of Genoa, to see the 12th-century, black-and-white marble **Cattedrale di San Lorenzo** and the nearby **Palazzo Ducale**, in Piazza Matteotti. In the beautiful, tiny **Piazza San Matteo** are the palaces of the Doria family, one of the most important families of the city in the 14th and 15th centuries. Take a walk along **Via Garibaldi** which is lined with palaces. Some are open to the public and contain art galleries, including the 16th-century **Palazzo Bianco** and the 17th-century **Palazzo Rosso**, where the Flemish painter Van Dyck lived. The **Galleria Nazionale di Palazzo Spinola**, Piazza Superiore di Pellicceria 1, is an important 16th-century mansion housing Italian and Flemish Renaissance works. Ask at the tourist office about its complicated opening hours.

Take the kids to the **aquarium** (Europe's biggest and well worth a visit). It's on the waterfront at Ponte Spinola and is open Tuesday to Friday from 9.30 am to 6.30 pm and on weekends and holidays until 8 pm. In summer it also opens on Monday. Admission is L14,000.

Places to Stay
The HI *Ostello Genova* (☎ 242 24 57; hostelge@iol.it) is at Via Costanzi 120 in Righi, just outside Genoa. B&B costs L22,000 and a meal is L14,000. Catch bus No 40 from Stazione Brignole.

Turn right as you leave Stazione Brignole and walk up Via de Amicis to Piazza Brignole. Turn right into Via Gropallo where there are some good hotels in a lovely old palazzo at No 4. *Pensione Mirella* (☎ 839 37 22) has singles/doubles for L37,000/65,000. A shower costs L2000 extra. On the 3rd floor, the *Carola* (☎ 839 13 40) has pleasant rooms for L45,000/75,000/100,000. *Albergo Rita* (☎ 87 02 07), a few doors up at No 8, has singles/doubles for L35,000/65,000.

Places to Eat
Don't leave town without trying pesto genovese (pasta with a sauce of basil, garlic and pine nuts), torta pasqualina (made with artichokes, cheese and eggs), pansoti (ravioli), farinata (a torte made with chickpea flour) and, of course, focaccia. A good deal in town is at *Da Maria*, Vico Testa d'Oro 14, where a full meal costs L14,000, including wine. Students and old seafarers dine here. *Trattoria Walter*, Vico Colalanza 2r, off Via San Luca, concentrates on Genoese specialities. Pasta dishes cost from L7000. A typical meal at *La Locanda del Borgo*, Via Borgo Incrociati 45, north of the Brignole station (use the pedestrian tunnel) costs around L25,000.

Entertainment
The Genoa Theatre Company performs at the *Politeama Genovese* (☎ 839 35 89) and the *Teatro della Corte* (☎ 534 22 00). Its main season is October to May. *Teatro della Tosse in Sant'Agostino* (☎ 247 07 93), Piazza R Negri 4, has a season of diverse shows from October to May.

Getting There & Away
Air Cristoforo Colombo airport at Sestri Ponente, 6km west of the city, has regular domestic and international connections. An airport bus service, the Volabus (☎ 599 74 14), leaves from Piazza Verdi, just outside Stazione Brignole, and also stops at Stazione Principe.

Bus Buses leave from Piazza della Vittoria for Rome, Florence, Milan and Perugia. Eurolines buses leave from the same piazza for Barcelona, Madrid and Paris. Book at Geotravels (☎ 58 71 81) in the piazza.

Train Genoa is connected by train to major cities. For train information call ☎ 147-88 80 88.

Boat The city's busy port is a major embarkation point for ferries to Sicily, Sardinia and Corsica. Major companies are: Corsica Ferries (☎ 59 33 01) at Piazza Dante 1 (for Corsica); Moby Lines (☎ 25 27 55) at Ponte Asserato (for Corsica); and Tirrenia (☎ 275 80 41) at the Stazione Marittima, Ponte Colombo (for Sicily and Sardinia); and Grandi Navi Veloci and Grandi Traghetti (☎ 26 54 52) at Via Fieschi 17 (for Sardinia, Sicily, Malta and Tunisia). For more information, see the Getting There & Away sections under Sicily and Sardinia, and under Corsica in the France chapter.

RIVIERA DI LEVANTE
☎ 0185
This coastal area of the region of Liguria from Genoa to La Spezia, on the border with Tuscany, rivals the Amalfi Coast in its spectacular beauty. It also has several resorts which, despite attracting thousands of summer tourists, manage to remain unspoiled. The region's climate means that both spring and autumn can bring suitable beach weather.

There are tourist offices in most of the towns, including at Santa Margherita (☎ 28 74 86), Via XXV Aprile, between the station and the sea, and at Camogli (☎ 77 10 66), Via XX Settembre 33, just as you leave the station. They will advise on accommodation.

ITALY

Things to See & Do

Santa Margherita Ligure, a pretty resort town, is a good base from which to explore the area: the resorts of **Portofino**, a haunt of the rich and famous, and **Camogli**, a fishing village turned resort town, are a short bus ride away. The medieval Benedictine monastery of **San Fruttuoso** is accessible either by foot from Camogli or Portofino (2½ hours), or by ferry.

Easily reached by train are the beautiful **Cinque Terre** (Five Lands). These coastal towns (Monterosso, Vernazza, Corniglia, Manarola and Riomaggiore) are linked by walking tracks along the coast.

Places to Stay & Eat

In Santa Margherita a central and relatively cheap place to sleep is *Albergo Annabella* (☎ 28 65 31), Via Costasecca 10, with large rooms for L60,000/80,000. Between the sea and the train station is *Albergo Azalea* (☎ 28 81 60), Via Roma 60, with rooms from L60,000/90,000.

In Camogli try *Albergo la Camogliese* (☎ 77 14 02), Via Garibaldi 55, on the seafront. Some rooms have balconies and views and prices are graded accordingly. The cheapest singles/doubles cost L70,000/100,000. Full board in the high season is L95,000.

In Santa Margherita, try *Trattoria San Siro*, Corso Matteotti 137 (about 15 minutes from the seashore). A full meal costs around L30,000. Try the pansoti (small ravioli in a walnut sauce).

Getting There & Away

The entire coast is served by train and all points are accessible from Genoa. Buses leave from Santa Margherita's Piazza Martiri della Libertà for Portofino.

Boats leave from near the bus stop in Santa Margherita for Portofino (L9000 return), San Fruttuoso (L17,000 return) and the Cinque Terre (L30,000 return).

TURIN
☎ 010

Turin (Torino) is the capital of the Piedmont region. The House of Savoy, which ruled this region for hundreds of years (and Italy until 1945), built for itself a gracious baroque city.

Its grandeur is often compared to that of Paris. Italy's industrial expansion began here with companies like Fiat and Olivetti.

Orientation & Information

The Porta Nuova train station is the point of arrival for most travellers. To reach the city centre walk straight ahead over the main east-west route, Corso Vittorio Emanuele II, through the grand Piazza Carlo Felice and along Via Roma until you come to Piazza San Carlo. The ATL tourist office (☎ 839 45 92) was due to open in mid-1998. Ask at the office at the Porta Nuova train station (☎ 53 13 27) for the latest information.

Things to See & Do

In Piazza San Carlo, known as Turin's drawing room, are the baroque churches of **San Carlo** and **Santa Cristina**, the latter designed by Filippo Juvarra. **Piazza Castello**, the centre of historical Turin, features the sumptuous **Palazzo Madama**, once the residence of Victor Amedeo I's widow Marie Cristina, and the **Museo Civico di Arte Antica**. Nearby is the **Palazzo Reale** (Royal Palace), an austere 17th-century building. Its gardens were designed in 1697 by Louis le Nôtre, whose other works include the gardens at Versailles.

The **Cattedrale di San Giovanni**, west of the Palazzo Reale, off Via XX Settembre, houses the **Shroud of Turin**, the linen cloth which some believed was used to wrap the crucified Christ. Scientists have been able to categorically establish that the shroud is simply not that old – instead it dates from somewhere around the 12th century. The shroud is back on display in the cathedral, in a new disaster-proof shrine, which replaces the **Capella della Santa Sindone** (Chapel of the Holy Shroud), destroyed by fire in 1997. It is only on view at certain times of the year. The **Museo Egizio** (☎ 561 77 76), Via Accademia delle Scienze 6, is considered one of the best museums of ancient Egyptian art after those in London and Cairo. It opens Tuesday to Saturday from 9 am to 7 pm (to 2 pm on public holidays). Admission is L12,000.

Places to Stay & Eat

Cheap rooms can be hard to find. Call the tourist office in advance for some suggestions, although the staff won't make a reservation. *Campeggio Villa Rey* (☎ 819 01 17), Strada Superiore Val San Martino 27, opens March to October. The *Ostello Torino* (☎ 660 29 39), Via Alby 1, on the corner of Via Gatti, is in the hills east of the Po River. Catch bus No 52 from the Porta Nuova station. B&B is L19,000 and a meal is L14,000.

The one-star *Canelli* (☎ 54 60 78), Via San Dalmazzo 5b, off Via Garibaldi, has singles/doubles for L40,000/55,000. The two-star *Albergo Magenta* (☎ 54 26 49), Corso Vittorio Emanuele II 67, has rooms for L90,000/110,000.

One of the better self-service restaurants is *La Grangia*, Via Garibaldi 21, where a full meal costs around L15,000. At *Pizzeria alla Baita dei 7 Nani*, Via A Doria 5, you can have a pizza and a beer for around L12,000. For excellent gelati, head for *Caffè Fiorio*, Via Po 8, and try the gianduia.

Getting There & Away
Turin is serviced by Caselle international airport (☎ 567 63 61), with flights to European and national destinations. The SADEM bus company (☎ 311 16 16) runs a service to the airport every 45 minutes from the corner between Via Sacchi and Corso Vittorio Emanuele II, on the west side of the Porta Nuova train station. Intercity Sadem buses terminate at the main bus station at Corso Inghilterra 1, near Porta Susa train station. Buses serve the Valle d'Aosta, most of the towns and ski resorts in Piedmont and major Italian cities. Regular trains connect with Milan, Aosta, Venice, Genoa and Rome.

Getting Around
The city is well serviced by a network of buses and trams. A map of public-transport routes is available at the station information office.

AROUND TURIN
The main attractions of the Piedmont region are the Alps, including the **Parco Nazionale del Gran Paradiso** and the beautiful natural reserve around **Monte Rosa** in the far north. Walkers can tackle sections of the Grande Traversata delle Alpi, a 200km track through the Alps, running from the Ligurian border to

Lago Maggiore on the border with Lombardy. Information is available at Turin's tourist office. Wine lovers can visit the vineyards around **Asti**, a pleasant town in the Monferrato hills, which gives its name to Italy's best known sparkling wine, Asti Spumante.

MILAN
☎ 02
The economic and fashion capital of Italy, Milan (Milano) has long been an elegant and cultural city. Its origins are believed to be Celtic, but it was conquered by the Romans in 222 BC, and later became an important trading and transport centre. From the 13th century the city flourished under the rule of two powerful families: the Visconti and later the Sforza.

Orientation
From Milan's central train station (Stazione Centrale), it is simple to reach the centre of town on the efficient Milan underground (known as the Metropolitana or MM). The MM3 will take you from the station to the Duomo and the centre of town. The city of Milan is huge, but most sights are in the centre. Use the Duomo and the Castello Sforzesco, at the other end of Via Dante, as your points of reference. The main shopping areas and sights are around and between the two. Note that Milan closes down almost completely in August, when most of the city's inhabitants take their annual holidays. You will find few restaurants and shops open at this time.

Information
Tourist Offices The main branch of the APT (☎ 72 52 43 00/01/02/05) is at Via Marconi 1, in Piazza del Duomo, where you can pick up the useful city guide *Milan is Milano*. It's open Monday to Saturday from 8.30 am to 7 pm and Sunday and public holidays from 9 am to 1 pm and 1.30 to 6 pm. There is a branch office (open the same hours) at the Stazione Centrale.

Milan City Council operates an information office in Galleria V Emanuele II, just off Piazza del Duomo, open Monday to Saturday from 8.30 am to 7 pm.

MILAN (MILANO)

PLACES TO STAY
2   Hotel Italia
3   Albergo Salerno
4   Hotel Verona
5   Hotel Due Giardini
6   Hotel Nettuno
7   Hotel Kennedy;
    Hotel San Tomaso
9   Hotel Tris
14 Albergo Commercio
19 Hotel Nuovo
25 Hotel Speronari

PLACES TO EAT
8   Ciao
10 Bar Assodi Cuori
15 Ciao
17 Luini
18 Ristorante Di Gennaro
20 Ciao
21 Trattoria da Bruno
23 Peck Delicatessan
26 Pizzeria Dogana
27 Ciao
31 Berlin Caffè

OTHER
1   Tourist Office &
    Telecom Telephones
11 Questura (Police Station)
12 Piazza San Marco
13 Palazzo di Brera
16 La Scala Opera House
22 Galleria Vittorio Emanuele II
    (Tourist Office;
    Telecom Telephones)
24 Post Office
28 APT Tourist Office
29 Underground Parking
30 Hospital

Foreign Consulates Foreign consulates include: Australia (☎ 777 04 21) at Via Borgogna 2; Canada (☎ 675 81) at Via Vittorio Pisani 19; France (☎ 655 91 41) at Via Mangili 1; the UK (☎ 72 30 01) at Via San Paolo 7; and the USA (☎ 29 03 51) at Via P Amedeo 2-10.

Money Banks in Milan open Monday to Friday from 8.30 am to 1.30 pm and 2.45 to 3.45 pm. Exchange offices at Piazza Duomo include Banca Ponti at No 19 which is open from 9.10 am to 12.45 pm Saturday. There are also exchange offices open seven days a week at the Stazione Centrale. The American Express office (☎ 167-86 40 46) is at Via Brera 3 and opens Monday to Friday from 9 am to 5 pm.

Post & Communications The main post office is at Via Cordusio 4, off Via Dante, near Piazza del Duomo, and is open 8.15 am to 7.40 pm Monday to Saturday. Fermo posta is here and is open Monday to Saturday from 8.15 am to 12.30 pm. There are also post offices at the station and at Linate airport.

There is a Telecom telephone office at the Stazione Centrale that's open daily from 8 am to 9.30 pm (it has international telephone directories).

Milan's postcode is 20100.

Cybercafés Hard Disk Cafe, Corso Sempione 44 (www.hdc.it) will let you log on to your own email address. Web time costs L10,000 an hour.

Bookshops The American Bookstore (☎ 87 89 20), Via Campiero 16, has a good selection of English-language books.

Medical & Emergency Services For an ambulance call ☎ 118. The public hospital, Ospedale Maggiore Policlinico (☎ 550 31) is at Via Francesco Sforza 35, close to the centre. There is an all-night pharmacy in the Stazione Centrale (☎ 669 09 35). In an emergency call the police on ☎ 113. The questura centrale (police headquarters) for foreigners is at Via Montebello (☎ 62 26 34 00). English is spoken. For lost property call the Milan City Council (☎ 546 52 99) at via Friuli 39.

Dangers & Annoyances Milan's main shopping areas are popular haunts for groups of thieves. They are as numerous here as in Rome and also lightning-fast. They use the same technique of waving cardboard or newspaper in your face to distract you while they head for your pockets or purse. Be particularly careful in the piazza in front of the Stazione Centrale. Don't hesitate to make a racket if you are hassled.

Things to See & Do

Start with the extraordinary **Duomo**, commissioned by Gian Galeazzo Visconti in 1386. The first glimpse of this spiky, tumultuous structure, with its marble façade shaped into pinnacles, statues and pillars, is certainly memorable.

Walk through the graceful **Galleria Vittorio Emanuele II** to **La Scala**, Milan's famous opera house. The theatre's **museum** is open Monday to Saturday from 9.30 am to 12.30 pm and 2 to 5.30 pm. It's also open on Sunday from May to October. Admission is L5000.

At the end of Via Dante is the huge **Castello Sforzesco**, which was originally a Visconti fortress but was entirely rebuilt by Francesco Sforza in the 15th century. Its museums contain an interesting collection of sculpture, including Michelangelo's *Pietà Rondanini*. It's open Tuesday to Sunday from 9.30 am to 5.30 pm. Admission is free.

Nearby in Via Brera is the 17th-century **Palazzo di Brera**, which houses the Pinacoteca di Brera. This gallery's vast collection of paintings includes Mantegna's masterpiece, the *Dead Christ*. The gallery is open Tuesday to Saturday from 9 am to 5.30 pm (Sunday to 12.30 pm). Admission is L8000.

An absolute must is Leonardo da Vinci's *Last Supper*, in the Cenacolo Vinciano, next to the **Chiesa di Santa Maria delle Grazie**, noted for Bramante's tribune. The *Last Supper* was restored in 1995, but centuries of damage from floods, bombing and decay have left their mark. The building is open Tuesday to Sunday from 8 am to 1.45 pm. Admission is L12,000.

Special Events

St Ambrose's Day (7 December) is one of Milan's major festivals, and features a traditional street fair near the Basilica di Sant'Ambrogio, off Via Carducci.

ITALY

Places to Stay

Hostels The HI *Ostello Piero Rotta* (☎ 39 26 70 95), Viale Salmoiraghi 1, is north-west of the city centre. B&B is L23,000. Take the MM1 to the QT8 stop. The place is closed between 9 am and 5 pm and lights out is 12.30 am. *Protezione della Giovane* (☎ 29 00 01 64), Corso Garibaldi 123, is run by nuns for single women aged 16 to 25 years. Beds cost from L35,000 a night. Booking is required.

Hotels Milan's hotels are among the most expensive and heavily booked in Italy, particularly due to trade fairs held in the city, so it's strongly recommended that you book in advance. There are numerous budget hotels around Stazione Centrale, but the quality varies. The tourist office will make bookings, which hotels will hold for one hour.

Stazione Centrale & Corso Buenos Aires One of the nicest places is the *Hotel Due Giardini* (☎ 29 52 10 93), Via Lodovico Settala 46, that has some silent rooms at the back of a cheerful garden and simple but comfortable singles/doubles for L65,000/85,000 (add L20,000 for a bathroom).

In Via Vitruvio, off Piazza Duca d'Aosta (to the left as you leave the station), there are two budget options. The *Albergo Salerno* (☎ 204 68 70) at No 18 has very clean singles/doubles for L50,000/80,000 (add L20,000 for a bathroom). The *Italia* (☎ 669 38 26) at No 44 has less attractive rooms for L50,000/75,000. The *Verona* (☎ 66 98 30 91), at Via Carlo Tenca 12, near Piazza della Repubblica, has rooms for L80,000/120,000 with TV and telephone.

At Viale Tunisia 6, just off Corso Buenos Aires, there are two hotels. The *Hotel Kennedy* (☎ 29 40 09 34) has reasonable singles/doubles for L60,000/80,000. A double with private bathroom is L120,000 and triples with bathroom are L40,000 per person. Bookings are accepted. The *Hotel San Tomaso* (☎ 29 51 47 47) has simple singles/doubles for L60,000/90,000 and triples for L40,000 per person.

Closer to the centre, off Piazza G Oberdan, is the quaint *Hotel Tris* (☎ 29 40 06 74), at Via Sirtori 26. It has appealing singles/doubles/triples with private shower for L50,000/90,000/130,000. The *Nettuno* (☎ 29 40 44 81), Via Tadino 27 (turn right off Via D Scarlatti, which is to the left as you leave the station), is a 10-minute walk away. It has basic singles/doubles with bathroom for L60,000/85,000.

The Centre The *Albergo Commercio* (☎ 86 46 38 80), Via Mercato 1, has basic singles/doubles with shower for L60,000/70,000. From Piazza Cordusio walk down Via Broletto, which becomes Via Mercato. The entrance to the hotel is around the corner on Via delle Erbe.

Very close to Piazza del Duomo is the *Hotel Speronari* (☎ 86 46 11 25), Via Speronari 4, which is eccentrically decorated but comfortable. Singles/doubles without bathroom are L65,000/90,000 and with bath are L80,000/140,000. The *Hotel Nuovo* (☎ 86 46 05 42) at Piazza Beccaria 6 is in a great location just off Corso Vittorio Emanuele II and the Duomo. Singles/doubles cost L60,000/80,000. A double with bathroom costs L120,000.

Places to Eat

In Milan, traditional restaurants are being replaced by fast-food outlets and sandwich bars as the favoured eating places. Try the bar snacks laid in many bars around 5 pm.

Restaurants Avoid the area around the station and head for Corso Buenos Aires and the centre.

Around Stazione Centrale Ciao, Corso Buenos Aires 7, is part of a chain (there are others on Corso Europa and at Via Dante 5), but the food is first-rate and relatively cheap. Pasta dishes cost from L5000 and excellent salads go for around L4000. *Brek* and *Amico* chains are similar but superior alternatives.

City Centre The first time the Milanese tasted pizza it was cooked at *Ristorante Di Gennaro*, Via S Radegonda 14, though today there is not much to set this place above others in the city. The *Trattoria da Bruno*, Via Cavallotti 15, off Corso Europa, has a set-price lunch for L18,000. *Pizzeria Dogana*, on the corner of Via Capellari and

Via Dogana, also near the Duomo, has outside tables. Pasta and pizza each cost around L10,000.

Cafés & Sandwich Bars One of Milan's oldest fast-food outlets is *Luini*, Via S Radegonda 16, just off Piazza del Duomo. A popular haunt of teenagers and students, it sells panzerotti, similar to calzone (a savoury turnover made with pizza dough) but stuffed with tomatoes, garlic and mozzarella (from L3000).

Berlin Caffè, Via G Mora 7 (to the left off Corso Porta Ticinese, near Largo Carrobbio), has a small menu at night (L14,000 for one dish). Otherwise it is a pleasant place for coffee or wine.

A good sandwich bar is *Bar Assodi Cuori* at Piazza Cavour (where you can sit down for no extra charge). *Pattini & Marinoni*, Corso Buenos Aires 55 (not far from Stazione Centrale) and also at Via Solferino 5, sell excellent bread, and pizza by the slice.

The best gourmet takeaway is *Peck*. Its rosticceria is at Via Cesare Cantù 3, where you can buy cooked meats and vegetables. Another outlet is at Via Spadari 9 (near the Duomo).

Entertainment

Music, theatre and cinema dominate Milan's entertainment calendar. The opera season at *La Scala* opens on 7 December. For tickets go to the box office (☎ 72 00 37 44) in the portico in via Filodrammatici, but don't expect a good seat unless you book well in advance. There is also a summer season, which features operas, concerts and ballet.

In March-April and October-November organ concerts are performed at the church of San Maurizio in the Monastero Maggiore, Corso Magenta 15 (the continuation of Via Meravigli). In April-May there is a jazz festival, Città di Milano, and in summer the city stages Milano d'Estate, a series of concerts, theatre and dance performances.

The main season for theatre and concerts starts in October. Full details of all events are available from the tourist office in Piazza del Duomo. For details on cinema, read the listings section in the daily newspaper *Corriere della Sera*.

In summer, locals hang out in Piazza San Marco: in the surrounding area there are plenty of disco-pubs, trendy restaurants and wine bars.

Things to Buy

Every item of clothing you ever wanted to buy, but could never afford, is in Milan. The main streets for clothing, footwear and accessories are behind the Duomo around Corso Vittorio Emanuele II. You can window-shop for high-class fashions in Via Monte Napoleone, Via Borgospesso and Via della Spiga.

The areas around Via Torino, Corso Buenos Aires and Corso XXII Marzo are less expensive. Markets are held in the areas around the canals (south-west of the centre), notably on Viale Papiniano on Tuesday and Saturday morning. A flea market is held in Viale Gabriele d'Annunzio each Saturday and an antique market is in Brera at Via Fiori Chiari every third Saturday of the month.

Getting There & Away

Air International flights use Malpensa airport, about 50km north-west of Milan. Domestic and European flights use Linate airport, about 7km east of the city.

Bus Bus stations are scattered throughout the city, although some major companies use Piazza Castello as a terminal. Check with the APT.

Train Regular trains go from Stazione Centrale to Venice, Florence (and Bologna), Genoa, Turin and Rome, as well as major cities throughout Europe. For timetable information call the green number ☎ 147-88 80 88 or go to the busy office in the Stazione Centrale (English is spoken), open from 7 am to 11 pm. Regional trains stop at Stazione Porta Garibaldi and Stazione Nord in Piazzale Cadorna on the MM2 line.

Car & Motorcycle Milan is the major junction of Italy's motorways, including the Autostrada del Sole (A1) to Rome, the Milano-Torino (A5), the Milano-Genova (A7) and the Serenissima (A4) for Verona and Venice, and the A8 and A9 north to the lakes and the Swiss border.

ITALY

All these roads meet with the Milan ring road, known as the Tangenziale Est and Tangenziale Ovest (the east and west bypasses). From here follow the signs which lead into the centre. The A4 in particular is an extremely busy road, where an accident can hold up traffic for hours. In winter all roads in the area become extremely hazardous because of rain, snow and fog.

Getting Around

To/From the Airports

STAM airport shuttle buses leave from Piazza Luigi di Savoia, on the east side of Stazione Centrale, for Linate airport every 20 to 30 minutes from 5.40 am to 9 pm (20 minutes, L4500). Airpullman Service runs shuttle buses from the same piazza to Malpensa airport every half-hour from 6.30 am to 5.30 pm (no service from noon to 3 pm) and every hour from 5.30 to 8.30 pm (50 minutes, L13,000). A separate service operates between Piazza Castello and Malpensa every hour from 7 to 11 am and every two hours from 11 am to 5 pm. Direct services between Linate and Malpensa operate twice daily (75 minutes, L18,000).

Bus & Metro

Milan's public transport system is extremely efficient. The underground (MM) has three lines. The red MM1 provides the easiest access to the city centre. It is necessary to take the green MM2 from Stazione Centrale to Loreto metro station to connect with the MM1. The yellow MM3 also passes through Stazione Centrale and has a station in Piazza del Duomo. It's the easiest way to get around, but buses and trams are also useful. Tickets for the MM are L1500, valid for one underground ride and/or 75 minutes on buses and trams.

You can buy tickets in the MM stations, as well as at authorised tobacconists and newspaper stands.

Taxi

Taxis won't stop if you hail them in the street – head for the taxi ranks, all of which have telephones. A few of the radio taxi companies serving the city are Radiotaxidata (☎ 53 53), Prontotaxi (☎ 52 51) and Autoradiotaxi (☎ 85 85).

Car & Motorcycle

Entering central Milano by car is a hassle. The city is dotted with ex-pensive car parks (look for the blue sign with a white 'P'). A cheaper alternative is to use one of the supervised car parks at the last stop on each MM line. In the centre there are private garages that charge usually L40,000 for 24 hours. Hertz, Avis, Maggiore and Europcar all have offices at Stazione Centrale.

MANTUA
☎ 0376

Legend, perpetuated by Virgil and Dante, claims that Mantua (Mantova) was founded by the soothsayer Manto, daughter of Tiresias. Virgil was, in fact, born in a nearby village in 70 AD. From the 14th to the 18th centuries the city was ruled by the Gonzaga family, who embellished the town with their palaces and employed artists such as Andrea Mantegna and Pisanello to decorate them with their paintings and frescoes. You can easily see the city on a day trip from Milan, Verona or Bologna.

Information

The APT tourist office (☎ 32 82 53), Piazza Andrea Mantegna 6, is a 10-minute walk from the station along Corso Vittorio Emanuele, which becomes Corso Umberto 1. It is open Monday to Saturday from 8.30 am to 12.30 pm and 3 to 6 pm.

Things to See & Do

Start with the **Piazza Sordello**, which is surrounded by impressive buildings including the **cattedrale**, a strange building that combines a Romanesque tower, baroque façade and Renaissance interior. The piazza is dominated by the **Palazzo Ducale**, a huge complex of buildings, and seat of the Gonzaga family. There is much to see in the palace, in particular the Gonzaga apartments and art collection, and the famous **Camera degli Sposi** (Bridal Chamber), decorated with frescoes by Andrea Mantegna in the 15th century. In the **Sala del Pisanello** (Pisanello's Room) are frescoes by the Veronese painter (discovered in 1969 under two layers of plaster), depicting the cycle of chivalry and courtly love. The palace is open daily from 9 am to 1 pm, and also Tuesday to Saturday from 2.30 to 6 pm. Admission is L12,000.

Don't miss **Palazzo Te**, the lavishly decorated summer palace of the Gonzaga. It's open Tuesday to Sunday from 9 am to 6 pm. Admission is L12,000. Take bus No 5 or 1 from the centre to the palace.

Places to Stay & Eat
The HI *Ostello per la Gioventù* and the nearby *camping ground* were closed at the time of writing. The *Albergo ABC* (☎ 32 33 47), Piazza Don Leoni 25, is the cheapest in town at L70,000/100,000 for singles/doubles with bathroom and breakfast.

Self Service Nuvolari, Piazza Viterbi 11, has good food and cheap prices. *Caà Ramponi*, Piazza Broletto 7, offers pasta and pizza at reasonable prices. *Brek Burger*, Via Broletto 15, is a decent fast-food outlet. There is a fresh produce market in Piazza Broletto.

Getting There & Away
Mantua is accessible by train and bus from Verona (about 40 minutes), and by train from Milan and Bologna with a change at Modena.

VERONA
☎ 045
Forever associated with Romeo and Juliet, Verona has much more to offer than the relics of a tragic love story. Known as La Piccola Roma (Little Rome) for its importance as a Roman city, its golden era was during the 13th and 14th centuries, under the rule of the della Scala (also referred to as Scaligeri) family. This was a period noted for the savage family feuding on which Shakespeare based his play.

Orientation & Information
It's easy to find your way around Verona. Buses leave for the centre from outside the train station; otherwise walk to the right, past the bus station, cross the river and walk along Corso Porta Nuova to Piazza Brà. From there take Via Mazzini and turn left at Via Cappello to reach Piazza delle Erbe.

The main tourist office is at Via Leoncino 61 (☎ 806 86 80), on the corner of Piazza Brà facing the Roman Arena, and is open Monday to Saturday from 9 am to 6 pm (July to September it's open until 8 pm). There is also a branch at the train station.

The main post office is at Piazza Viviani. The Ospedale Civile Maggiore (☎ 807 11 11) is at Piazza A Stefani.

Things to See & Do
The pink-marble Roman amphitheatre, known as the **Arena**, in Piazza Brà, was built in the 1st century and is now Verona's opera house. Walk along Via Mazzini to Via Cappello and **Juliet's House** (Casa di Giulietta), its entrance smothered with lovers' graffiti. Further along the street to the right is **Porta Leoni**, one of the gates to the old Roman Verona; **Porta Borsari**, the other gate to the city, is north of the Arena at Corso Porta Borsari.

In the other direction is **Piazza delle Erbe**, the former site of the Roman forum. Lined with the characteristic pink-marble palaces of Verona, the piazza today remains the lively centre of the city, but the permanent market stalls in its centre detract from its beauty. In the piazza is the **Fountain of Madonna Verona**. Just off the square is the elegant **Piazza dei Signori**, flanked by the Renaissance **Loggia del Consiglio**; the della Scala (Scaligeri) residence now known as the **Governor's Palace** and partly decorated by Giotto; and the medieval town hall. Take a look at the **Duomo**, on Via Duomo, for its Romanesque main doors and Titian's *Assumption*.

Places to Stay & Eat
The HI *Ostello Villa Francescatti* (☎ 59 03 60), Salita Fontana del Ferro 15, should be your first choice. B&B is L20,000 (including sheets) and dinner is L12,000. An HI or student card is necessary. Next door is a *camping ground* (L8000 per person with your own tent) run by the hostel management. To get there catch bus No 73 from the station to Piazza Isolo and follow the signs.

The *Casa della Giovane* (☎ 59 68 80), Via Pigna 7, just off Via Garibaldi, is for women only and costs L22,000 a night for a bed in a small dormitory, while a double is L25,000. Catch bus No 73 and ask the driver where to get off.

Albergo Castello (☎ 800 44 03), Corso Cavour 43, has singles/doubles for L90,000/120,000. *Albergo Ciopeta* (☎ 800 68 43), Vicolo Teatro Filarmonico 2, near Piazza Brà, has singles/doubles for L75,000/120,000.

ITALY

VERONA

PLACES TO STAY
2 Villa Francescatti Ostello
3 Casa della Giovane
12 Albergo Castello
13 Albergo Ciopeta

PLACES TO EAT
15 Pizzeria Liston
16 Brek

OTHER
1 Duomo
4 Governor's Palace
5 Loggia del Consiglio
6 Tourist Office
7 Piazza dei Signori
8 Porta Borsari
9 Post Office
10 Juliet's House
11 Porta Leoni
14 Teatro Filarmonico
17 The Arena
18 Tourist Office
19 Questura (Police Station)

Boiled meats are a local specialty, as is the crisp soave (a dry white wine). In Piazza Brà, with a view of the Arena, is *Brek*, a good bet for cheap meals, with pasta dishes starting from around L7000. The *Pizzeria Liston*, Via dietro Liston 19, has good pizzas for around L9000. A full meal will cost around L25,000.

Entertainment

Verona hosts musical and cultural events throughout the year culminating in a season of opera and drama from July to September at the *Arena* (tickets from around L40,000). There is

a lyric-symphonic season in winter at the 18th-century *Teatro Filarmonico* (☎ 800 28 80), Via dei Mutilati 4, just off Piazza Brà. Information and tickets for these events are available at the Ente Lirico Arena di Verona (☎ 800 51 51), Piazza Brà 28. In the Roman theatre, Shakespeare is performed in summer and there is a jazz festival in June (☎ 807 72 19).

Getting There & Away

The Verona-Villafranca airport (☎ 809 56 66) is just outside the town and accessible by bus and train.

The main APT bus station is in the piazza in front of the station, an area known as Porta Nuova. Buses leave for surrounding areas, including Mantua, Ferrara and Brescia.

Verona is on the Brenner Pass railway line to Austria and Germany. It is directly linked by train to Milan, Venice, Florence and Rome.

The city is at the intersection of the Serenissima A4 (Milan-Venice) and the Brennero A22 autostrade.

Getting Around

The APT airport bus leaves from Porta Nuova and from Piazza Cittadella, off Corso Porta Nuova near Piazza Brà. Bus Nos 2 and 8 connect the station with Piazza Brà and No 32 with Piazza delle Erbe. Otherwise it's a 15-minute walk along Corso Porta Nuova.

If you arrive by car, you should have no trouble reaching the centre. Simply follow the 'centro' signs. There are also signs marking the directions to most hotels. There's a free car park in Via Città di Nimes (near the train station).

PADUA
☎ 049

Although famous as the city of St Anthony and for its university, which is one of the oldest in Europe, Padua (Padova) is often merely seen as a convenient and cheap place to stay while visiting Venice. The city, however, offers a rich collection of art treasures and its many piazzas and arcaded streets are a pleasure to explore.

Orientation & Information

From the train station it's a 10-minute walk to reach the centre of town, or you can take bus No 3 or 8 along Corso del Popolo, which becomes Corso Garibaldi, to the historical centre.

There is a tourist office at the station, open Monday to Saturday from 9 am to 7 pm (9.20 am to 5.45 pm November to March) and Sunday from 8.30 am to 12.30 pm (9 am to noon November to March).

The post office is at Corso Garibaldi 33 and there's a telephone office nearby (open 8.30 am to 12.30 pm and 4 to 7 pm). Padua's postcode is 35100.

Things to See & Do

Thousands of pilgrims arrive in Padua every year to visit the **Basilica del Santo** in the hope that St Anthony, patron saint of Padua and of lost things, will help them find whatever it is they are looking for. The saint's tomb is in the church along with important artworks, including 14th-century frescoes and bronze sculptures by Donatello which adorn the high altar. A bronze equestrian statue, known as the *Gattamelata* (Honeyed Cat), also by Donatello, is outside the basilica.

The **Musei Civici agli Eremitani** and **Cappella degli Scrovegni** are at Piazza Eremitani 8. The interior walls of the chapel were completely covered in frescoes by Giotto between 1303 and 1305. Depicting the life of Christ and ending with the *Last Judgment*, the 38 panels are considered one of the greatest works of figurative art of all time. The museum and the chapel are open daily from 9 am to 7 pm (6 pm in winter). The **Palazzo della Ragione** (Law Courts) is remarkable for its sloping roof and loggias; inside is the enormous, entirely frescoed salon, containing a huge wooden horse built for a joust in 1466.

A special L15,000 ticket (L10,000 for students) allows entry to the city's main monuments and you can buy it at any of the main sights. Since entry to the Scrovegni Chapel alone is L10,000, it's worth the price.

Places to Stay & Eat

Padua has no shortage of budget hotels, but they fill up quickly in summer. The non-HI *Ostello della Città di Padova* (☎ 875 22 19) is at Via A Aleardi 30. B&B is L23,000. Take bus Nos 3, 8 or 12 from the station to Prato della Valle (a piazza about five minutes away) and then ask for directions.

The *Verdi* (☎ 875 57 44), Via Dondi dell'Orologio 7, has basic and clean singles/doubles for L40,000/60,000 and is in the university district off Via Verdi. The *Pavia* (☎ 66 15 58) at Via dei Papafava 11 has slightly dingy singles/doubles for L42,000/57,000. Follow Corso del Popolo until Via Roma and then turn right into Via Marsala.

Daily markets are held in the piazzas around the Palazzo Ragione, with fresh produce sold in Piazza delle Erbe and Piazza della Frutta, and bread, cheese and salami sold in the shops.

ITALY

Trattoria Al Pero, Via Santa Lucia 72, near Piazza dei Signori, serves regional dishes for around L25,000. A real find for a snack is *Dalla Zita*, Via Gorizia 16, off Piazza Pedrocchi, where you can choose from more than 100 freshly prepared sandwiches.

Getting There & Away

Padua is directly linked by train to Milan, Venice and Bologna and is easily accessible from most other major cities. Regular buses serve Venice, Milan, Trieste and surrounding towns. The terminal is in Piazzale Boschetti, off Via Trieste, near the station. There is a large public car park in Prato della Valle, a massive piazza near the Basilica del Santo.

VENICE
☎ 041

Perhaps no other city in the world has inspired the superlatives heaped upon Venice (Venezia) by great writers and travellers through the centuries. It was, and remains, a phenomenon – La Serenissima, the Most Serene Republic.

The secret to seeing and discovering the romance and beauty of Venice is to *walk*. Parts of Dorsoduro and Castello are devoid of tourists even in the high season (July to September). You could become lost for hours in the narrow winding streets between the Accademia and the station, where the signs pointing to San Marco and the Rialto never seem to make any sense – but what a way to pass the time!

After the fall of the Western Roman Empire, as waves of barbarians poured across the Alps, the people of the Veneto cities fled to the islands of the coastal lagoon. The waters that today threaten its existence once protected the city. Following years of Byzantine rule, Venice evolved into a republic ruled by a succession of doges (chief magistrates of the republic), a period of independence which

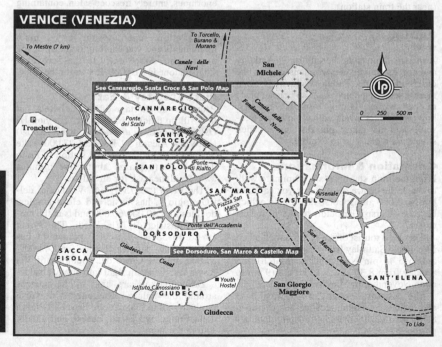

lasted 1000 years. It was the point where east met west, and the city eventually grew in power to dominate half the Mediterranean, the Adriatic and the trade routes to the Levant. It was from here that Marco Polo set out on his voyage to China.

Today, Venice is increasingly being left to the tourists – the regular floods (caused by high tides) and soaring property values make it increasingly unattractive as a place of residence. Most of the 'locals' in fact live in industrial Mestre, which is linked to the city by the 4km-long bridge across the lagoon. A project to install massive floodgates at the main entrances to the lagoon has been approved by the Italian government, but remains stalled. The floodgates would be designed to protect the city from disaster-level floods. This and other projects to 'save' Venice are supported by local and international bodies.

Orientation

Venice is built on 117 small islands and has some 150 canals and more than 400 bridges. Only three bridges cross the Grand Canal (Canale Grande): the Rialto, the Accademia and the Scalzi at the train station. The city is divided into six *sestieri* (sections): Cannaregio, Castello, San Marco, Dorsoduro, San Polo and Santa Croce. The streets are called *calle*, *ruga* or *salizzada*; little side streets can be called *caletta* or *ramo*; a street beside a canal is a *fondamenta*; a canal is a *rio*; and a quay is a *riva*. The only square in Venice called a *piazza* is San Marco – all the others are called a *campo*. On maps, you will find the following abbreviations: Cpo for Campo, Sal for Salizzada, cl for Calle, Mto for Monumento and Fond for Fondamenta.

If all that isn't confusing enough, Venice also has its own style of street numbering. Instead of a system based on individual streets, there is instead a long series of numbers for each sestiere. Ask your hotel for its actual street address. There are no cars in the city and all public transport is via the canals, on *vaporetti* (boats). To cross the Grand Canal between the bridges, use a *traghetto* (basically a public gondola) – a cheaper mode of transport than the tourist gondolas. Signs will direct you to the various traghetto points. The other mode of transportation is *a piedi* (on foot).

To walk from the *ferrovia* (train station) to San Marco along the main thoroughfare, Lista di Spagna (whose name changes several times), will take a good half-hour – follow the signs to San Marco. From San Marco the routes to other main areas, such as the Rialto, the Accademia and the ferrovia, are well signposted but can be confusing, particularly in the Dorsoduro and San Polo areas.

The free map provided by the tourist office (see the following section) provides only a vague guide to the complicated network of streets. Pick up a cheap de Agostini map, simply titled *Venezia*, which lists all street names with map references.

Information

Tourist Offices There is an APT tourist office at the train station, open every day from 8.10 am to 6.50 pm. The main APT office (☎ 522 63 56; fax 529 87 30) is in the Palazzetto Selva in the ex Giardini Reali (former Royal Gardens). From Piazza San Marco, walk to the waterfront then turn right and walk about 100m. It's open Monday to Saturday from 9.40 am to 3.20 pm. People aged between 14 and 29 can buy a Rolling Venice card (L5000) which offers significant discounts on food, accommodation and entry to museums. It is available from tourist offices July to September, and from a number of private offices at other times; check at the tourist office for details.

Foreign Consulates The British Consulate (☎ 522 72 07) is at Palazzo Querini near the Accademia, Dorsoduro 1051. The French Consulate (☎ 522 43 19) is on the Fondamenta Zattere at Dorsoduro 1397.

Money Most of the main banks have branches in the area around the Rialto and San Marco. The American Express office at Salizzada San Moisè (exit from the western end of Piazza San Marco onto Calle Seconda dell'Ascensione) will exchange money without charging commission. Its opening hours are weekdays from 9 am to 5.30 pm (Saturday to 12.30 pm). For card-holders the office also has an ATM.

Thomas Cook, in Piazza San Marco, is open Monday to Saturday from 9 am to 6 pm (Sunday to 2 pm). There is also a bank at the train station, or you can change money at the train ticket office between 7 am and 8.30 pm daily.

Post & Communications The main post office is at Salizzada del Fontego dei Tedeschi, just near the Ponte di Rialto (Rialto Bridge) on the main thoroughfare to the station. You can buy stamps at window Nos 9 and 10 in the central courtyard. There is a branch post office just off the western end of Piazza San Marco.

The Telecom office next to the main post office is open Monday to Friday from 8.30 am to 12.30 pm and 4 to 7 pm.

Venice's postcode is 30100.

Bookshops There is a good selection of English-language guidebooks and general books on Venice at Studium, on the corner of Calle de la Canonica, on the way from San Marco to Castello. San Giorgio, Calle Larga XXII Marzo 2087, west of San Marco, has a good range of English-language books.

Medical & Emergency Services If you need a hospital, the Ospedale Civili Riuniti di Venezia (☎ 529 45 17) is in Campo SS (Santissimi) Giovanni e Paolo. For an ambulance phone ☎ 523 00 00. For police emergencies call ☎ 113. The questura (☎ 271 55 11) is at Marghera, in Via Nicolodi 22. A new emergency service in foreign languages is run by the carabinieri; call ☎ 112.

Things to See & Do

Before you visit Venice's main monuments, churches and museums, catch the No 1 vaporetto along the Grand Canal and then go for a long walk around Venice. Start at **San Marco** and head for the **Accademia Bridge** to reach the narrow, tranquil streets and squares of **Dorsoduro** and **San Polo**. In these sestieri you will be able to appreciate just how beautiful and seductive Venice can be. Remember that most museums are closed on Monday.

Piazza & Basilica di San Marco One of the most famous squares in the world, San Marco was described by Napoleon as the finest drawing room in Europe. Enclosed by the basilica, the old Law Courts and Libreria Vecchia (which houses the Archaeological

Museum and the Marciana Library), the piazza hosts flocks of pigeons and tourists, and both compete for space in the high season. Stand and wait for the famous bronze *mori* (Moors) to strike the bell of the Law Courts' 15th-century **clock tower**, the Torre dell'Orologio.

The basilica, with its elaborately decorated façade, was constructed to house the body of St Mark, which had been stolen from its burial place in Egypt by two Venetian merchants. The saint has been reburied several times in the basilica (at least twice the burial place was forgotten) and his body now lies under the high altar. The present basilica was built in the Byzantine style in the 11th century and richly decorated with magnificent mosaics and other embellishments over the next five centuries. The famous bronze horses which stood above the entrance have been replaced by replicas. The horses were part of Venice's booty from the famous Sack of Constantinople in 1204. The originals are now in the basilica's museum (entry is L3000).

Don't miss the stunning **Pala d'Oro** (L3000), a gold altarpiece decorated with silver, enamel and precious stones. It is behind the basilica's altar.

In the piazza is the basilica's 99m-high freestanding **bell tower**. It was built in the 10th century, but suddenly collapsed on 14 July 1902 and was later rebuilt. It costs L6000 to climb to the top.

Palazzo Ducale The official residence of the doges and the seat of the republic's government, this palace also housed many government officials and the prisons. The original palace was built in the 9th century, and later expanded and remodelled. Visit the **Sala del Maggior Consiglio** to see the paintings by Tintoretto and Veronese. The palace is open daily from 9 am to 7 pm (8.30 am to 5 pm November to March) and the ticket office closes 1½ hours beforehand. Admission is L17,000 and the same ticket allows you to enter the nearby Museo Civico Correr (Piazza San Marco), as well as the Ca' Rezzonico (Dorsoduro area), Palazzo Mocenigo (San Stae area), Burano and Murano Museums.

The **Bridge of Sighs** (Ponte dei Sospiri) connects the palace to the old prisons. This bridge now evokes romantic images, probably because of its association with Casanova, a native of Venice who was incarcerated in the prisons. It was, however, the thoroughfare for prisoners being led to the dungeons.

Galleria dell'Accademia The Academy of Fine Arts contains an important collection of Venetian art, including works by Tintoretto, Titian and Veronese. It's open weekdays from 9 am to 7 pm and Sunday from 9 am to 2 pm. Admission is L12,000. For a change of pace visit the nearby **Collezione Peggy Guggenheim**, once the home of the American heiress. It contains her collection of modern art and is set in a sculpture garden where Miss Guggenheim and her many pet dogs are buried. It is open Wednesday to Monday from 11 am to 6 pm (closed Tuesday). Admission is L12,000.

Churches The **Chiesa del Redentore** (Church of the Redeemer) on Giudecca Island was built in the 16th century by the architect Palladio and is the scene of the annual Festa del Redentore (see the Special Events section). The **Chiesa di Santa Maria della Salute** was built at the entrance to the Grand Canal and dedicated to the Madonna after a plague in the 17th century. It contains works by Tintoretto and Titian. Be sure to visit the great Gothic churches **SS Giovanni e Paolo** and the **Frari**. Entry to each church is L2000, or you can buy a day pass for entrance to six churches (L10,000), or a special Chorus Pass (L22,000) which is valid for three months and allows entry to 13 churches.

The Lido Easily accessible by vaporetto Nos 1, 6, 14 or 82, this thin strip of land, east of the centre, separates Venice from the Adriatic. Once *the* most fashionable beach resort, it is still very popular and it is almost impossible to find a space on its long beach in summer.

Islands The island of **Murano** is the home of Venetian glass. Visit the Glassworks Museum to see the evolution of the famous glassware. **Burano**, despite the constant influx of tourists, is still a relatively sleepy fishing village, renowned for its lace-making. Visit tiny **Torcello** to see the Byzantine mosaics in its cathedral, notably the stunning mosaic of the Madonna in the apse. Excursion boats leave for the three islands from San Marco (L20,000 per hour). If you want to go it alone, vaporetto No 12 goes to all three and costs L4500 one way. It leaves from Fondamenta Nuove.

Gondolas These might represent the quintessential romantic Venice, but at around L120,000 (L150,000 after 8 pm) for a 50-minute ride they are very expensive. It is possible to squeeze up to six people into one gondola and still pay the same price. Prices are set for gondolas, so check with the tourist office if you have problems.

Organised Tours
Shop around the various travel agencies for the best deals, or try Ital-Travel (☎ 522 91 11), San Marco 71G, under the colonnade at Piazza San Marco's western end. It organises tours of the city on foot or by boat and collective gondola rides with serenade for L50,000 per person.

Special Events
The major event of the year is the famous Carnevale, held during the 10 days before Ash Wednesday, when Venetians don spectacular masks and costumes for what is literally a 10-day street party.

The Venice Biennale, a major exhibition of international visual arts, is held every odd-numbered year (for the time being), and the Venice International Film Festival is held every September at the Palazzo del Cinema, on the Lido.

The most important celebration on the Venetian calendar is the Festa del Redentore (Festival of the Redeemer), held on the third weekend in July, which features a spectacular fireworks display. The *regatta storica*, a gondola race on the Grand Canal, is held on the first Sunday in September.

Places to Stay
Simply put, Venice is expensive. The average cost of basic singles/doubles without bath in a one-star hotel is around L70,000/100,000. The hostel and several religious institutions provide some respite for budget travellers. Hotel proprietors are inclined to inflate the

bill by demanding extra for a compulsory breakfast. Prices skyrocket in peak periods (Christmas, Carnevale, Easter etc), but can drop dramatically at other times of the year. It is advisable to make a booking before you arrive. As Venice does not have a traditional street numbering system, the best idea is to ring your hotel when you arrive and ask for specific directions. If you're travelling by car, you can save on car park costs by staying in Mestre.

Camping Litorale del Cavallino, north-east of the city along the Adriatic coast has numerous camping grounds, many with bungalows. The tourist office has a full list, but you could try the *Marina di Venezia* (☎ 530 09 55) Via Montello 6, at Punta Sabbioni, which is open from April to September.

Hostels The HI *Ostello Venezia* (☎ 523 82 11; fax 523 56 89) is on the island of Giudec-

ca, at Fondamenta delle Zitelle 86. It is open to members only, though you can buy a card there. B&B is L24,000 and full meals are available for L14,000. Take vaporetto No 82 (for the Lido) from the station (L4500 one way) and get off at Zitelle. The hostel is closed from 9 am to 2 pm and curfew is at 11.30 pm. *Istituto Canossiano* (☎ 522 21 57; fax 522 21 57) nearby at Ponte Piccolo 428 on Giudecca, has dorm beds for women only at L20,000 per night. Take vaporetto No 82 and get of at Sant'Eufemia. *Foresteria Valdese* (☎ 528 67 97; fax 528 67 97), Castello 5150, has dorm beds for L29,000 a night. It also has doubles for L80,000 per night and two independent apartments at around L180,000 per day – great for families. Take Calle Lunga from Campo Santa Maria Formosa.

Hotels Bargain hotels are few and far between.

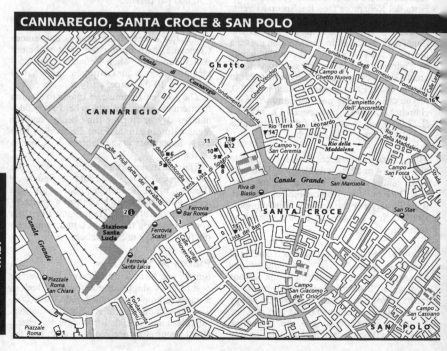

CANNAREGIO, SANTA CROCE & SAN POLO

Cannaregio The two-star *Edelweiss Stella Alpina* (☎ 71 51 79) in Calle Priuli detta dei Cavalletti 99d (first on the left after the Scalzi church) has decent singles/doubles without bathroom for L100,000/130,000. The *Locanda Antica Casa Carettoni* (☎ 762 31) at Rio Terrà Lista di Spagna 130 has basic singles/doubles for L80,000/120,000. Just off Lista di Spagna, at Calle della Misericordia 358, is *Hotel Santa Lucia* (☎ 71 51 80) in a newish building with a strip of garden. The friendly owner offers singles/doubles/triples for L75,000/120,000/150,000 and adds L30,000 for rooms with bathroom. On the same street at No 389, *Hotel Villa Rosa* (☎ 71 89 76) has an internal garden and pleasant well-furnished singles/doubles/triples with bathroom for L100,000/150,000/190,000 including breakfast, TV and telephone. *Albergo Adua* (☎ 71 61 84) is at Lista di Spagna 233a, about 50m past Casa Carettoni on the right. It has slightly shabby but clean singles/doubles for L60,000/90,000 and

triples for L125,000. The *Hotel Minerva* (☎ 71 59 68), Lista di Spagna 230, has modest singles/doubles for L68,000/94,000.

The *Hotel Rossi* (☎ 71 51 64) in the tiny Calle de le Procuratie, through a Gothic arch on the Lista di Spagna, has anonymous rooms with bathroom for L90,000/140,000 a single/double and L175,000/210,000 a triple/quad. At the dark *Al Gobbo* (☎ 71 50 01), Campo San Geremia, sparkling clean doubles are L100,000. In the same piazza at No 283 the pleasant *Casa Gerotto* (☎ 71 53 61), has absorbed the neighbouring *Alloggi Calderan*. Here there's a family-style hostel atmosphere and singles/doubles/triples cost around L50,000/70,000/100,000.

San Marco Although this is the most touristy area of Venice, it has some surprisingly good-quality (relatively) budget pensioni. *Hotel Noemi* (☎ 523 81 44), at Calle dei Fabbri 909, is only a few steps from

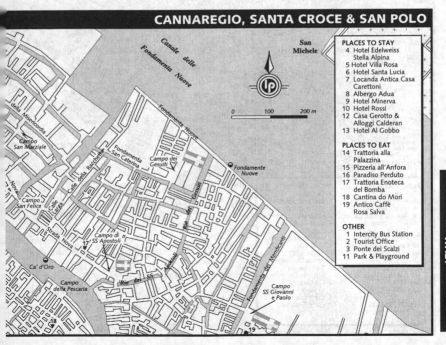

CANNAREGIO, SANTA CROCE & SAN POLO

PLACES TO STAY
4 Hotel Edelweiss Stella Alpina
5 Hotel Villa Rosa
6 Hotel Santa Lucia
7 Locanda Antica Casa Carettoni
8 Albergo Adua
9 Hotel Minerva
10 Hotel Rossi
12 Casa Gerotto & Alloggi Calderan
13 Hotel Al Gobbo

PLACES TO EAT
14 Trattoria alla Palazzina
15 Pizzeria all'Anfora
16 Paradiso Perduto
17 Trattoria Enoteca del Bomba
18 Cantina do Mori
19 Antico Caffè Rosa Salva

OTHER
1 Intercity Bus Station
2 Tourist Office
3 Ponte dei Scalzi
11 Park & Playground

ITALY

the piazza and has basic singles/doubles for L70,000/90,000.

One of the nicest places in this area is **Locanda Casa Petrarca** (☎/fax 520 04 30), San Marco 4394, which has singles/doubles for L70,000/110,000. Extra beds in a room are an additional 35%. Doubles with bath are L135,000. To get there, find Campo San Luca, go along Calle dei Fusari, then take the second street on the left and turn right into the bottom end of Calle delle Schiavine. Just off Piazza San Marco is **Hotel ai Do Mori** (☎ 520 48 17), Calle Larga 658. It has pleas-

ant rooms, some with views of the Basilica. The most expensive double goes for L170,000.

Castello This area is to the east of Piazza San Marco, and although close to the piazza, is less touristy. **Locanda Silva** (☎ 522 76 43), Fondamenta del Rimedio 4423, off Campo Santa Maria Formosa towards San Marco, has quite basic singles/doubles for L65,000/100,000. Next door, **Locanda Canal** (☎ 523 45 38) has simple doubles for L95,000 and doubles with bathroom for

DORSODURO, SAN MARCO & CASTELLO

PLACES TO STAY
2 Hotel Al Gallo
5 Albergo Casa Peron
6 Hotel Dalla Mora
9 Albergo Antico Capon
15 Antica Locanda Montin
18 Hotel Galleria
25 Locanda Casa Petarca
26 Hotel Noemi
33 Locanda Silva; Locanda Canal
34 Foresteria Valdese
36 Hotel Doni
42 Hotel ai Do Mori

PLACES TO EAT
4 Bar ai Nomboli

7 Crepizza
8 Da Silvio
11 Bar Duschamp
12 Gelateria il Doge
13 Ristorante L'Incontro
14 Cicchetti 4 Ferri
16 Gelati Nico
20 Pasticceria Marchini
23 Vino Vino
27 McDonald's
28 Antica Carbonera
29 Trattoria alla Madonna
32 Cip Ciap
37 Al Vecchio Penasa
44 Caffè Quadri
47 Caffè Florian

ITALY

L145,000. *Hotel Doni* (☎ 522 42 67) is a little establishment at Fondamenta del Vin 4656, off Salizzada San Provolo. It has clean, quiet rooms without bathroom for L75,000/110,000/150,000.

Dorsoduro, San Polo & Santa Croce

This is the most authentic area of Venice, in which you can still find the atmosphere of a living city. *Hotel Al Gallo* (☎ 523 67 61), Corte dei Amai 197g, off Fondamenta Tolentini, has excellent doubles with shower for L115,000. The *Casa Peron* (☎ 71 00 21),

Salizzada San Pantalon 84, has clean rooms with shower for L70,000/100,000 including breakfast. To get there from the station, cross the bridge (Ponte Scalzi) and follow the signs to San Marco and Rialto till you reach Rio delle Muneghette, then cross the wooden bridge. *Hotel Dalla Mora* (☎ 71 07 03) is on a lovely small canal just off Salizzada San Pantalon, near the Casa Peron. It has airy rooms, some with canal views and a common open terrace. Singles/doubles/triples with bathroom are L80,000/135,000/170,000. Bookings are a must.

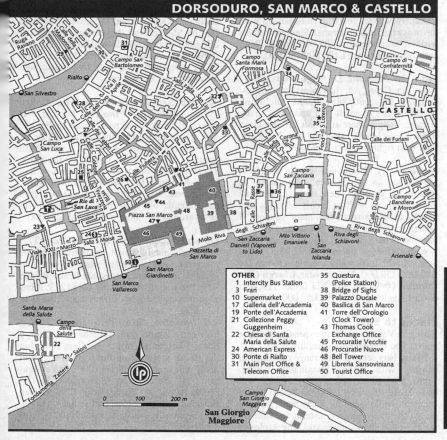

DORSODURO, SAN MARCO & CASTELLO

OTHER
1 Intercity Bus Station
3 Frari
10 Supermarket
17 Galleria dell'Accademia
19 Ponte dell'Accademia
21 Collezione Peggy Guggenheim
22 Chiesa di Santa Maria della Salute
24 American Express
30 Ponte di Rialto
31 Main Post Office & Telecom Office
35 Questura (Police Station)
38 Bridge of Sighs
39 Palazzo Ducale
40 Basilica di San Marco
41 Torre dell'Orologio (Clock Tower)
43 Thomas Cook Exchange Office
45 Procuratie Vecchie
46 Procuratie Nuove
48 Bell Tower
49 Libreria Sansoviniana
50 Tourist Office

ITALY

Albergo Antico Capon (☎ 528 52 92) at Campo Santa Margherita 3004b, one of the nicest squares in Venice, has rooms with bathroom for L120,000/148,000 a single/double and L180,000/240,000 a triple/quad. Ezra Pound and Peggy Guggenheim favoured the *Antica Locanda Montin* (☎ 522 71 51) on the quiet and evocative Fondamenta di Borgo 1147, in Dorsoduro. It's a small and comfortable one-star place where singles/doubles without bathroom cost L60,000/90,000. It also has a popular, but pricey restaurant. *Hotel Galleria* (☎ 520 41 72), Dorsoduro 878a, has elegant rooms facing the Grand Canal at the Accademia Bridge. Located in a 17th-century palace, this is the last remaining affordable hotel on the Grand Canal. However, you'll have to put up with the noisy traffic on the canal. Singles/doubles without bathroom cost L85,00/130,000. With bathroom prices are L120,000/150,000.

Lido The *Pensione La Pergola* (☎ 526 07 84), Via Cipro 15, has pleasant singles/doubles for L60,000/100,000, including breakfast. It's open all year and has a shady terrace. To get there turn left off the Gran Viale Santa Maria Elisabetta into Via Zara, then turn right into Via Cipro.

Mestre Only 15 minutes away on bus No 7, Mestre is an economical alternative to staying in Venice. There are a number of good hotels as well as plenty of cafés and places to eat around the main square. If you're travelling by car, the savings on car-parking charges are considerable. The two-star *Albergo Roberta* (☎ 92 93 55), Via Sernaglia 21, has good-sized, clean rooms for L80,000/130,000. The one-star *Albergo Giovannina* (☎ 92 63 96), Via Dante 113, has decent singles/doubles for L50,000/90,000.

Places to Eat

Eating in Venice can be an expensive pastime unless you choose very carefully.

Many bars serve a wide range of Venetian panini, with every imaginable filling. Tramezzini (three-pointed sandwiches) and huge bread rolls cost L4000 to L6000 if you eat them while standing at the bar. Head for one of the many bacari or osterie, for wine by the glass and interesting snacks. The staples of the Veneto region's cucina are rice and beans. Try the risi e bisi (risotto with peas) and don't miss a risotto or pasta dish with radicchio trevisano (red chicory). The rich mascarpone dessert, tiramisù, is a favourite here.

Restaurants Many restaurants, particularly around San Marco and near the train station, are tourist traps where prices are high and the quality is poor.

Cannaregio The *Trattoria alla Palazzina*, Cannaregio 1509, is just over the first bridge after Campo San Geremia. It has a garden at the rear and serves good pizzas for L8000 to L14,000. A full meal will cost around L50,000. *Trattoria Enoteca del Bomba*, Calle de l'Oca, parallel to Strada Nova near Campo SS Apostoli, has a tourist menu for L30,000. Young people will enjoy *Paradiso Perduto*, Fondamenta della Misericordia 2539, a restaurant/bar with live music, and outside tables in summer.

Around San Marco & Castello At San Marco 2007, *Vino Vino* is a popular bar/osteria at Ponte Veste near Teatro La Fenice. The good-quality menu changes daily. A pasta or risotto costs L10,000, a main dish around L15,000. Wine is sold by the glass. There's a *McDonald's* outlet in Campo San Luca. At *Antica Carbonera*, in Calle Bembo, a continuation of Calle dei Fabbri, you'll find an authentic old trattoria atmosphere. Pasta costs around L15,000; a full meal L50,000.

Dorsoduro, San Polo & Santa Croce This is the best area for small, cheap trattorias and pizzerias. Good pizza and pasta are served at *Pizzeria all'Anfora*, across the Scalzi Bridge from the station at Lista dei Bari 1223. It has a garden at the rear. Pizzas cost L8000 to L14,000.

L'Incontro, Rio Terà Canal 3062a, between Campo San Barnaba and Campo Santa Margherita, offers excellent food, but the prices are a bit on the high side. A full meal will cost around L40,000. The restaurant at the *Antica Locanda Montin*, Fondamenta di Borgo near Campo San Barnaba, has good food and a shady garden, but is quite expensive at around L60,000 for a full meal.

Cantina do Mori, on Sottoportego dei do Mori, off Ruga Rialto, is a small, very popular wine bar which also serves sandwiches. A meal will cost around L30,000. *Trattoria alla Madonna*, Calle della Madonna, two streets west of the Rialto, is an excellent trattoria specialising in seafood. It might be worth splurging here – a full meal of seafood could cost up to L60,000.

Crepizza, Calle San Pantalon 3757, past Campo Santa Margherita, serves pasta, pizza and crêpes for L6000 to L10,000. Around the corner at Crosera San Pantalon 3817 is *Da Silvio*, a good value pizzeria/trattoria with outside tables in a garden setting.

Cafés & Bars If you can cope with the idea of paying L10,000 to L20,000 for a cappuccino, then spend an hour or so sitting at an outdoor table in Piazza San Marco, listening to the orchestra at either *Caffè Florian* or *Caffè Quadri* where you will pay a normal price for a coffee taken on your feet. In the Castello area you can get excellent but cheap panini at *Al Vecchio Penasa*, Calle delle Rasse 4587. Just off Campo Santa Maria Formosa is *Cip Ciap*, at the Ponte del Mondo Novo. It serves fantastic and filling pizza by the slice for L3000 to L5000. In Campo Santa Margherita is *Bar DuChamp*, a student favourite. Panini cost L4000 to L6000 and you can sit outside at no extra charge.

Bar ai Nomboli, between Campo San Polo and the Frari on the corner of Calle dei Nomboli and Rio Terrà dei Nomboli, has a great selection of gourmet sandwiches and tramezzini.

If you're looking for a typical osteria with authentic Venetian cichetti (glasses of wine and finger food) try *4 Ferri* in Calle Lunga San Barnaba off Campo San Barnaba in Dorsoduro.

Gelati & Pastries The best ice cream in Venice is said to be at the *Gelati Nico*, Fondamenta Zattere ai Gesuati 922. You can join the locals taking their evening stroll along the fondamenta while eating gelati, or take a seat at an outside table. *Il Doge*, Campo Santa Margherita, also has excellent gelati. A popular place for cakes and pastries is *Pasticceria Marchini*, just off Campo Santo Stefano, at Calle del Spezier 2769. In the

beautiful Campo SS Giovanni e Paolo, just in front of the equestrian bronze statue of Bartolomeo Colleoni, is *Antico Caffè Rosa Salva*, frequented by locals for its ice creams and special pastries. Try the hot chocolate.

Self-Catering For fruit and vegetables, as well as delicatessens, head for the market in the streets on the San Polo side of the Rialto Bridge. There is a *Standa* supermarket on Strada Nova and a *Mega 1* supermarket just off Campo Santa Margherita.

Entertainment

The weekly booklet *Un Ospite di Venezia*, available at hotels, has entertainment listings. The tourist office also has brochures listing events and performances for the entire year. Concerts of classical and chamber music are often performed in churches and a contemporary music festival is staged at the *Teatro Goldoni* annually in October. Venice lost its opera house, the magnificent Teatro La Fenice, to a fire in January 1996. It was hoped that the building would be reconstructed quickly. Major art exhibitions are held at the *Palazzo Grassi* (at the vaporetto stop of San Samuele), and you will find smaller exhibitions at various venues in the city throughout the year. The city's nightlife is a bit dismal. In summer, try *Paradiso Perduto* in Cannaregio for live music (see under Places to Eat).

Things to Buy

Who can think of Venice without an image of its elaborately grotesque Venetian glass coming to mind? There are several workshops and showrooms in Venice, particularly in the area between San Marco and Castello and on the island of Murano, designed mainly for tourist groups. If you want to buy Venetian glass, shop around carefully because quality and prices can vary dramatically.

The famous Carnevale masks make a beautiful souvenir of Venice. You'll find them in shops throughout the city. Lace is another characteristic product of the Venetian lagoon, produced mainly on the island of Burano. In Venice itself there is a lovely little shop, Annelie Pizzi e Ricami, at Calle Lunga San Barnaba 2748.

The main shopping area for clothing, shoes, accessories and jewellery is in the narrow streets between San Marco and the Rialto, particularly the Merceria and the area around Campo San Luca, although prices tend to be high (for the tourists). Designer wear and luxury items can be found in the area near La Fenice.

Getting There & Away

Air Marco Polo airport (☎ 260 92 60) is just east of Mestre and services domestic and European flights. It is accessible by regular *motoscafo* (motorboat) from San Marco and the Lido (L17,000). From Piazzale Roma there are also ATVO buses (☎ 520 55 30) for L5000 or the ACTV city bus No 5 for L1400. A water taxi from San Marco will cost around L87,000.

Bus ACTV buses (☎ 528 78 86) leave from Piazzale Roma for surrounding areas including Mestre and Chioggia, a fishing port at the southernmost point of the lagoon. Buses also go to Padua and Treviso. Tickets and information are available at the office in the piazza.

Train The Stazione Santa Lucia (☎ 147-88 80 88), known in Venice as the ferrovia, is directly linked by train to Padua, Verona, Trieste, Milan and Bologna and thus is easily accessible from Florence and Rome. You can also leave from Venice for major points in Germany, Austria and the former Yugoslavia. The Venice *Simplon Orient Express* runs between Venice and London, via Verona, Zürich and Paris twice weekly. Ask at any travel agent.

Boat Kompas Italia (☎ 528 65 45), San Marco 1497, operates some ferry and hydrofoil services in summer to Croatia. Kompas also operates day trips to towns on the Istrian peninsula. Minoan Lines (☎ 271 23 45), Porto Venezia, Zona Santa Marta, runs ferries to Greece three times a week in winter and daily in summer. Deck class costs L120,000.

Getting Around

As there are no cars in Venice, vaporetti are the city's mode of public transport.

Once you cross the bridge from Mestre, cars must be left at the car park on the island of Tronchetto or at Piazzale Roma (cars are allowed on the Lido – take car ferry No 17 from Tronchetto). The car parks are not cheap at L25,000 a day. A cheaper alternative is to leave the car at Fusina, near Mestre, and catch the No 16 vaporetto to Zattere and then the No 82 either to Piazza San Marco or the train station. Ask for information at the tourist information office just before the bridge to Venice.

From Piazzale Roma, vaporetto No 1 zigzags its way along the Grand Canal to San Marco and then to the Lido. There is the faster No 82 if you are in a hurry. The No 12 vaporetto leaves from the Fondamenta Nuove for the islands of Murano, Burano and Torcello. A full timetable is available at the tourist office. A single vaporetto ticket costs L4500 (plus L4500 for luggage), even if you only ride to the next station. A 24-hour ticket costs L15,000 for unlimited travel, a 72-hour ticket costs L30,000 (and is probably worth buying) and a one-week ticket costs L55,000. Water taxis are exorbitant, with a set charge of L27,000 for a maximum of seven minutes, then L500 every 15 seconds. It's an extra L8000 if you phone for a taxi, and various other surcharges add up to make a gondola ride seem cheap.

FERRARA
☎ 0532

Ferrara was the seat of the Este dukes from the 13th century to the end of the 16th century. The city retains much of the austere splendour of its heyday – its streets are lined with graceful palaces and in its centre is the Castello Estense, surrounded by a moat.

Information

The tourist information office (☎ 20 93 70; fax 21 22 66; infotur.comfe@fe.nettuno.it) inside the Castello Estense opens Monday to Saturday from 9 am to 1 pm and 2 to 6 pm; Sunday and holidays from 9 am to 1 pm.

Things to See & Do

The historical centre is small, encompassing the medieval Ferrara to the south of the

Castello Estense, and the area to the north, built under the rule of Duke Ercole I during the Renaissance. The castle now houses government offices, but certain areas are open to the public.

Visit the medieval prisons where, in 1425, Duke Nicolò d'Este had his young second wife, Parisina Malatesta, and his son Ugo beheaded after discovering they were lovers, thereby inspiring the poet Robert Browning to write My Last Duchess. The beautiful Romanesque-Gothic Duomo has an unusual pink-and-white marble triple façade and houses some important works of art within its museum. The Renaissance Palazzo dei Diamanti, along Corso Ercole I d'Este, houses the important Pinacoteca Nazionale.

The gallery is open Tuesday to Saturday from 9 am to 2 pm (Sunday to 1 pm). Entry is L8000. The fine 14th-century Palazzo Schifanoia, Via Scandiana 23, another of the Este palaces, houses the Civic Museum and features some interesting frescoes. It is open daily from 9 am to 7 pm; entry is L6000.

Places to Stay & Eat

Ferrara is a cheap alternative to Bologna, and it can even be used as a base for visiting Padua and Venice. The central Tre Stelle (☎ 20 97 48), Via Vegri 15, has very basic singles/doubles for L30,000/40,000. Pensione Artisti (☎ 76 10 38), Via Vittoria 66, has singles/doubles for L30,000/54,000. Better rooms are available at Albergo Nazionale (☎ 20 96 04), Corso Porta Reno 32, for L65,000/100,000 with private bathroom.

A popular budget restaurant is Trattoria da Settimo, Via Cortevecchia 49, where a full meal will cost around L25,000. Pizzeria il Ciclone, Via Vignatagliata 11, has pizzas for around L9000.

Getting There & Away

Ferrara is on the Bologna-Venice train line, with regular trains to both cities. It is 40 minutes from Bologna and 1½ hours from Venice. Regular trains also run directly to Ravenna. Buses run from the train station to Modena (also in the Emilia-Romagna region).

BOLOGNA
☎ 051

Elegant, intellectual and wealthy, Bologna stands out among the many beautiful cities of Italy. The regional capital of Emilia-Romagna, Bologna is famous for its porticoes (arcaded streets), its harmonious architecture, its university (which is the oldest in Europe) and, above all, its gastronomic tradition. The Bolognese have given the world tortellini, lasagne, mortadella and the ubiquitous spaghetti bolognese (known in Bologna as spaghetti al ragù, hence one of the city's nicknames, Bologna la Grassa (Bologna the Fat).

Information

There is an Informazioni e Assistenza Turistica (IAT) office (☎ 23 96 60; fax 23 14 54) in Piazza Maggiore, under the portico of the castle. It is open Monday to Saturday from 9 am to 7 pm and Sunday from 9 am to 2 pm. There are branch offices at the train station and the airport. Pick up a map and the useful booklet A Guest in Bologna, published monthly in English.

The main post office is in Piazza Minghetti. Telecom telephones are at Piazza VIII Agosto 24, and the train station. In a medical emergency call ☎ 118, or Ospedale Maggiore on ☎ 647 81 11. For the police call ☎ 113 or ☎ 112.

Things to See

The beautiful centre of Bologna is formed by Piazza Maggiore, the adjoining Piazza del Nettuno and Fontana di Nettuno (Neptune's Fountain), sculpted in bronze by a French artist who became known as Giambologna, and the Piazza di Porta Ravegnana, with its leaning towers to rival that of Pisa.

In Piazza Maggiore is the Basilica di San Petronio, dedicated to the city's patron saint. The red-and-white marble of its unfinished façade displays the colours of Bologna. It contains important works of art and it was here that Charles V was crowned emperor by the pope in 1530. The Palazzo Comunale (town hall) is a huge building, combining several architectural styles in remarkable harmony. It features a bronze statue of Pope Gregory XIII (a native of Bologna who

ITALY

BOLOGNA

created the Gregorian calendar), an impressive winding staircase and Bologna's collection of art treasures.

The **Basilica di Santo Stefano** is a group of four churches in the Romanesque style. In a small courtyard is a basin which legend says was used by Pontius Pilate to wash his hands after condemning Christ to death. In fact, it is an 8th-century Lombard artefact. The **Basilica of San Domenico**, erected in the early 16th century, houses the sarcophagus of the founder of the Dominican order in a precious chapel with an angel carved by a young Michelangelo. The French Gothic **Basilica of San Francesco**, the **Museo Civico Archeologico** and the **Pinacoteca Nazionale** are other important places to visit.

Places to Stay & Eat

Budget hotels in Bologna are virtually nonexistent and it is almost impossible to find a single room. The city's busy trade-fair calendar means that hotels are often heavily booked, so always book in advance. The best options are the two HI hostels: *Ostello San Sisto* (☎ 51 92 02), Via Viadagola 14, charges L18,000 with breakfast and *Ostello Due Torri* (☎ 50 18 10), in the same street at No 5, charges L20,000. Take bus Nos 93 or 20b from Via Irnerio (off Via dell'Independenza near the station), ask the bus driver where to get off, then follow the signs to the hostel.

Albergo Garisenda (☎ 22 43 69), Galleria del Leone 1, is under the two towers and has decent singles/doubles for L65,000/90,000. The *Apollo* (☎ 22 39 55), Via Drapperie 5, off Via Rizzoli, has singles/doubles for L55,000/92,000 and doubles/triples with bathroom for L120,000/162,000. *Albergo Marconi* (☎ 26 28 32), Via G Marconi 22, has pleasant singles/doubles/triples for L50,000/78,000/105,000.

Fortunately, it is cheaper to eat in Bologna, particularly in the university district north of Via Rizzoli. *Pizzeria D'Amore Bella Napoli* (☎ 55 51 63), Via San Felice 40, serves good pizzas at reasonable prices. *Trattoria da Boni* (☎ 58 50 60), Via Saragozza 88, is another good option. *Pizzeria Altero*, Via Ugo Bassi 10, has good, cheap pizzas by the slice. Try the self-service *Due Torri*, Via dei Giudei 4, under the towers. It opens only for lunch and the food is good value. You can buy panini in most cafés and eat them standing at the bar.

Shop at the **Mercato Ugo Bassi**, Via Ugo Bassi 27, a covered market offering all the local fare. There is also a market in the streets south-east of Piazza Maggiore.

Getting There & Away

Bologna is a major transport junction for northern Italy and trains from virtually all major cities stop here. The only hitch is that many are Eurostar and Intercity trains which means you have to pay a rapido supplement and, for Eurostar, make a compulsory booking.

Buses to major cities depart from the terminal in Piazza XX Settembre, around the corner from the train station in Piazza delle Medaglie d'Oro.

The city is linked to Milan, Florence and Rome by the A1 (Autostrada del Sole). The A13 heads directly for Venice and Padua, and the A14 goes to Rimini and Ravenna.

Getting Around

Traffic is limited in the city centre and major car parks are at Piazza XX Settembre and Via Antonio Gramsci. Bus No 25 will take you from the train station to the historical centre.

RAVENNA
☎ 0544

Ravenna has an ancient and legendary history, but is now best known for its exquisite mosaics, relics of its period as an important Byzantine city. The town is easily accessible from Bologna and is worth a day trip at the very least.

Information

The IAT tourist office (☎ 354 04; fax 350 94) is at Via Salara 8 and is open daily from 8.30 am to 6 pm, and Sunday and holidays from 9.30 am to 12.30 pm and 2.30 to 5.30 pm. The Ospedale Santa Maria delle Croci (☎ 40 91 11) is at Via Missiroli 10. In a police emergency call ☎ 113.

Things to See

The main mosaics are in the Basilica di Sant'Apollinare Nuovo, the Basilica di San Vitale, the Mausoleo di Galla Placidia, which contains the oldest mosaics, and the Battistero Neoniano, also known as the Orthodox Baptistry. These are all in the town centre and an admission ticket to the four, as well as to the **Museo Arcivescovile**, costs L10,000 – a bargain given that a ticket to only one monument costs L5000. The **Basilica di Sant'Apollinare** in Classe is 5km south-east of the city and accessible by bus No 4 from the station.

Special Events

Ravenna hosts a music festival from late June to early August, featuring international artists performing in the city's historical churches and at the open-air Rocca di Brancaleone. An annual theatre and literature festival is held in September in honour of Dante, who spent his last 10 years in the city and is buried there.

Places to Stay & Eat

The HI *Ostello Dante* (☎ 42 11 64), Via Aurelio Nicolodi 12, opens March to November. Take bus No 1 from Viale Pallavacini, to the left of the station. B&B is L20,000 and family rooms are available for L22,000 per person. *Al Giaciglio* (☎ 394 03), Via Rocca Brancaleone 42, has singles/doubles starting at L35,000/50,000. To find it, go straight ahead from the station along Viale Farini and turn right into Via Brancaleone. The two-star *Ravenna* (☎ 21 22 04), near the train station at Via Maroncelli 12, has rooms from L80,000/100,000.

For a quick meal, try *Free Flow Bizantino*, Piazza Andrea Costa, next to the city's fresh-produce market.

Entertainment

In winter, opera and dance are staged at the *Teatro Alighieri*.

Getting There & Away

Ravenna is accessible by train from Bologna, with a change at Castel Bolognese. The trip takes about 1½ hours.

Getting Around

Cycling is a popular way to get around the sights. Rental is L15,000 per day or L2000 per hour from COOP San Vitale, Piazza Farini, in front of the station.

SAN MARINO
☎ 0549

A few kilometres from Rimini in central Italy is the ancient Republic of San Marino, an unashamed tourist trap perched on top of Monte Titano (600m). The world's oldest surviving republic, San Marino was formed in 300 AD by a stonemason said to have been escaping religious persecution. The tiny state (only 61 sq km) strikes its own coins, has its own postage stamps and its own army. Wander along the city walls and drop in at the two fortresses. The main attraction of a visit is the splendid view of the mountains and the coast. The Ufficio di Stato per il Turismo (☎ 88 29 98) is in the Palazzo del Turismo, Contrada Omagnano 20.

The town is accessible from Rimini by bus from the train station (L16,000 return).

The Dolomites

This spectacular limestone mountain range (Dolomiti in Italian) in the Alps stretches across Trentino-Alto Adige into the Veneto. It is the Italians' favoured area for skiing and there are excellent hiking trails.

Information

Information can be obtained at the APT del Trentino (Azienda per la Promozione Turistica del Trentino) in Trent (☎ 0461-83 90 00), Via Rondanini 11; in Rome (☎ 06-36 09 58 42), Via del Babuino 20; or Milan (☎ 02-86 46 12 51), Piazza Diaz 5. The provincial tourist office for Alto Adige (☎ 0471-99 38 08) is at Piazza Parocchia 11, Bolzano. The APT Dolomiti at Cortina (☎ 0436-32 31) can provide information on trekking and skiing in the area.

Skiing

There are numerous excellent ski resorts, including the expensive and fashionable Cortina d'Ampezzo in the Veneto and the less pretentious, more family-oriented resorts, such as those in the Val Gardena in Trentino-Alto Adige. All have helpful tourist offices with loads of information on facilities, accommodation and transport (some are listed in this section).

The high season is generally from Christmas to early January and from early February to April, when prices go up considerably, but actual dates vary throughout the Alps. A good way to save money is to buy a *settimana bianca* (literally, 'white week'), a package-deal ski holiday available through Sestante CIT, CTS or other travel agencies throughout Italy. This covers accommodation, food and ski passes for seven days.

If you want to go it alone, but plan to do a lot of skiing, invest in a ski pass. Most resort areas offer their own passes for unlimited use of lifts at several resorts for a nominated period. The cost in the 1997-98 high season for a six-day pass was around L250,000. The Superski Dolomiti pass (☎ 0471-79 53 98), which allows access to 450 lifts and more than 1100km of ski runs in 12 valleys costs L286,000. The average cost of ski and boot hire in the Alps is from L20,000 to L25,000 a day for downhill and around L15,000 for cross-country.

Trekking

Without doubt, the Dolomites provide the most breathtaking opportunities for walking in the Italian Alps – from a half-day stroll with the kids to demanding treks which combine walking with mountaineering skills. The walking season is roughly from July to late September. Alpine refuges usually close around September 20.

Buy a map of the hiking trails, which also shows the locations of Alpine refuges. The best maps are the Tabacco 1:25,000, which can be bought in newsagents and bookshops in the area where you plan to hike. They are also often available in major bookshops in larger cities. Lonely Planet's new *Walking in Italy* guide outlines several treks in detail and the *Italy* guide also details some suggested treks. Another useful guide is *Walking in the Dolomites* by Gillian Price.

Hiking trails are generally very well marked with numbers on red-and-white painted bands (which you will find on trees and rocks along the trails), or by numbers inside different coloured triangles for the Alte Vie (the four High Routes through the Dolomites – ask for details at the tourist offices listed in this section).

There are numerous organisations offering guided treks, climbs etc, as well as courses. One is the Scuola Alpina Dolomiten (☎ 0471-70 53 43; fax 70 73 89), Via Vogelweidergasse 6, Castelrotto, which has a summer program including week-long treks, expeditions on horseback and mountain bike, and courses in rock climbing. It also has a winter program of ski expeditions and courses. Phone or fax for a program.

Recommended areas to walk in the Dolomites include:

Brenta Group (Dolomiti di Brenta)
    accessible from either Molveno to the east or Madonna di Campiglio to the west
Alpe di Siusi
    a vast plateau above the Val Gardena, at the foot of the spectacular Sciliar
Cortina area
    which straddles Trentino and Veneto and features the magnificent Parco Naturale di Fanes-Sennes-Braies, and, to the south-west, the Marmolada Group, Mt Pelmo and Mt Civetta
Sesto Dolomites
    north of Cortina towards Austria
Pale di San Martino
    accessible from San Martino di Castrozza and Fiera di Primiero

Warning Remember that even in summer the weather is extremely changeable in the Alps and though it might be sweltering when you set off, you should be prepared for very cold and wet weather on even the shortest of walks. Essentials include a pair of good-quality, worn-in walking boots, an anorak or pile/wind jacket, a lightweight backpack, a warm hat and gloves, a waterproof poncho, light food and plenty of water.

Getting There & Away

Trentino-Alto Adige has an excellent public transport network – the two main bus companies for the region are SAD in Alto Adige and Atesina in Trentino. The main towns and many of the ski resorts are also accessible from major cities throughout Italy, including Rome, Florence, Bologna, Milan and Genoa, by a network of long-distance buses operated by various companies including Lazzi, SITA, Sena and STAT. Information about the services is available from tourist offices as well as *autostazioni* (bus stations) throughout Trentino-Alto Adige, or from the following

ITALY

offices: Lazzi Express (☎ 06-884 08 40), Via Tagliamento 27b, Rome, and in Florence at Piazza Adua 1 (055-21 51 55); and SITA (☎ 055-21 47 21), Autostazione, Via Santa Caterina di Siena 17, Florence.

Getting Around

If you are planning to hike in the Alps during the warmer months, you will find that hitch-hiking is no problem, especially near the resort towns. The areas around the major resorts are well serviced by local buses, and tourist offices will be able to provide information on local bus services. During winter, most resorts have 'ski bus' shuttle services from the towns to the main ski facilities.

CORTINA D'AMPEZZO
☎ 0436

The most famous, fashionable and expensive Italian ski resort, Cortina is also one of the best equipped and certainly Italy's most picturesque. If you are on a very tight budget, the prices for accommodation and food will be prohibitive, even in the low season. However, camping grounds and Alpine refuges (open only during summer) provide more reasonably priced alternatives.

Situated in the Ampezzo bowl, Cortina is surrounded by the stunning Dolomites, including the Cristallo, Marmarole, Sorapiss and Tofane groups. Facilities for both downhill and cross-country skiing are first class. The area is also very popular for trekking and climbing, with well-marked trails and numerous refuges. A memorable three-day walk starts at Passo Falzarego and incorporates sections of Alta Via No 1. It takes you through the beautiful Val di Fanes and ends at Passo Cimabanche. Buy a good 1:25,000 map and plan your route.

Information

The main APT tourist office (☎ 32 31) is at Piazzetta San Francesco 8, in the town centre. There is a small Dolomites office at Piazza Roma 1.

Places to Stay

The *International Camping Olympia* (☎ 50 57) is about 5km north of Cortina at Fiames and is open all year. A local bus will take you there from Cortina. If you are trekking in the area, refuges are open July to late September and charge roughly L25,000 to L30,000 per person. There are not many options for cheap accommodation in Cortina. You could try the houses for B&B. *Casa Tua* (☎ 22 78; 0335-656 75 57; casatua@tin.it), Zuel 100, charges L45,000 to L80,000 per person for B&B, depending on the season.

CANAZEI
☎ 0462

Set in the Fassa Dolomites, the resort of Canazei has more than 100km of trails and is linked to slopes in the Val Gardena and Val Badia by a network of runs known as the **Sella Ronda**, which enable skiers to make a day-long skiing tour of the valleys surrounding the Sella Group. Canazei also offers cross-country skiing and summer skiing on the Marmolada glacier. (At 3342m, the Marmolada peak is the highest in the Dolomites.) The Marmolada *camping ground* (☎ 60 16 60) is open all year, or you have a choice of hotels, furnished rooms and apartments. Contact the AAST tourist office (☎ 60 11 13) for full details. The resort is accessible by Atesina bus from Trent and SAD bus from Bolzano.

VAL GARDENA
☎ 0471

This is one of the most popular skiing areas in the Alps, due to its reasonable prices and excellent facilities for downhill, cross-country and alpine skiing. There are excellent walking trails in the Sella group and the Alpi Siusi. The Vallunga, behind Selva, is great for family walks and cross-country skiing.

The valley's main towns are Ortisei, Santa Cristina and Selva, all offering lots of accommodation and easy access to runs. The tourist offices at Santa Cristina (☎ 79 30 46; fax 79 31 98) and Selva (☎ 79 51 22; fax 79 42 45) have extensive information on accommodation and facilities. Staff speak English and will send details on request.

The Val Gardena is accessible from Bolzano by SAD bus. It is connected to major Italian cities by coach services (Lazzi, SITA and STAT).

MADONNA DI CAMPIGLIO
☎ 0465

One of the five major ski resorts in Italy and situated in the Brenta Dolomites, Madonna di Campiglio is a well-equipped place to ski, but also one of the more expensive. The Brenta group offers challenging trails for mountaineers and cross-country skiers, while the nearby, beautiful Val di Genova is perfect for family walks. The resort is accessible by Atesina bus from Trent, and from Rome, Florence and Bologna by Lazzi or SITA coach. More information is available from the helpful APT office (☎ 44 20 00).

SAN MARTINO DI CASTROZZA
☎ 0439

Located in a sheltered position beneath the Pale di San Martino, this resort is popular among Italians and offers good facilities and ski runs, as well as cross-country skiing and a toboggan run. The APT office (☎ 76 88 67) will provide a full list of accommodation, or try the *Garni Suisse* (☎ 680 87), Via Dolomiti 1. Its singles/doubles with breakfast cost L42,000/84,000. Buses travel regularly from Trent and, during the high season, from Milan, Venice, Padua and Bologna.

Central Italy

The landscape in central Italy is a patchwork of textures bathed in a beautiful soft light – golden pink in Tuscany, and a greenish gold in Umbria and the Marches. The people remain close to the land, but in each of the regions there is also a strong artistic and cultural tradition – even the smallest medieval hill town can harbour extraordinary works of art.

FLORENCE
☎ 055

Cradle of the Renaissance, home of Dante, Machiavelli, Michelangelo and the Medici, Florence (Firenze) is overwhelming in its wealth of art, culture and history, and is one of the most enticing cities in Italy.

Florence was founded as a colony of the Etruscan city of Fiesole in about 200 BC and later became the strategic Roman garrison settlement of Florentia. In the Middle Ages the city developed a flourishing economy based on banking and commerce, which sparked a period of building and growth previously unequalled in Italy. It was a major focal point for the Guelph and Ghibelline struggle of the 13th century, which saw Dante banished from the city. But Florence truly flourished in the 15th century under the Medici, reaching the height of its cultural, artistic and political development as it gave birth to the Renaissance.

The Grand Duchy of the Medici was succeeded in the 18th century by the House of Lorraine (related to the Austrian Hapsburgs). As a result of the Risorgimento, the kingdom of Italy was formally proclaimed in March 1861, and Florence was the capital of the new kingdom from 1865 to 1871. During WWII, parts of the city, including all of the bridges except the Ponte Vecchio, were destroyed by bombing, and in 1966 a devastating flood destroyed or severely damaged many important works of art. A worldwide effort helped Florence in its massive restoration works.

Orientation

Whether you arrive by train, bus or car, the central train station, Santa Maria Novella, is a good reference point. Budget hotels and pensioni are concentrated around Via Nazionale, to the east of the station, and Piazza Santa Maria Novella to the south. The main thoroughfare to the centre is Via de' Panzani and then Via de' Cerretani, about a 10-minute walk. You'll know you've arrived when you first glimpse the Duomo.

Once at Piazza del Duomo you will find Florence easy to negotiate, with most of the major sights within easy walking distance. Most important museums stay open until 10 pm (virtually all are closed on Monday). Florence is a living art museum and you won't waste your time by just wandering the streets. Take the city ATAF buses for longer distances such as to Piazzale Michelangelo or the nearby suburb of Fiesole, both of which offer panoramic views of the city (see the Getting Around section later).

ITALY

FLORENCE (FIRENZE)

ITALY

Information

Tourist Offices
The Florence City Council (Comune di Firenze) operates a tourist information office (☎ 21 22 45) just outside the main train station in the covered area where local buses stop, and a new one in Borgo Santa Croce 29r (☎ 234 04 44). During the high season they open Monday to Saturday from 8 am to 7.30 pm. The main APT office (☎ 29 08 32/33) is just north of the Duomo at Via Cavour 1r and opens Monday to Saturday from 8.15 am to 7.15 pm and Sunday from 8.45 am to 1.45 pm. At both offices you can pick up a map of the city, a list of hotels and other useful information. The Consorzio ITA (☎ 28 28 93), inside the station on the main concourse, has a computerised system for checking the availability of hotel rooms and can book you a night for a small fee; there are no phone bookings. A good map of the city, on sale at newsstands, is the one with the white, red and black cover *Firenze: Pianta della Città*, which costs L8000.

Foreign Consulates
The US Consulate (☎ 239 82 76) is at Lungarno Vespucci 38, and the UK Consulate (☎ 21 25 94) is at Lungarno Corsini 2. The French Consulate (☎ 230 25 56) is at Piazza Ognissanti 2.

Money
The main banks are concentrated around Piazza della Repubblica. You can also use the service at the information office in the station, but it has poor exchange rates.

Post & Communications
The main post office is in Via Pellicceria, off Piazza della Repubblica, and is open weekdays and Saturday from 8.15 am to 7 pm. Poste restante mail can be addressed to 50100 Firenze. There is a Telecom office at Via Cavour 21r, open daily from 8 am to 9.45 pm, and another at Stazione Santa Maria Novella, open Monday to Saturday from 8 am to 9.45 pm.

Cybercafés
Libreria Cima (☎ 247 72 45), Borgo degli Albizi 37r, charges L10,000 an hour to access the Internet, or L35,000 for an email address for six months. It's open daily from 9.30 am to 7.30 pm, and on Tuesday, Thursday and Saturday it reopens from 9.30 pm to 1 am.

Bookshops
The Paperback Exchange, Via Fiesolana 31r (closed Sunday), has a vast selection of new and second-hand books. Internazionale Seeber, Via de' Tornabuoni 70r, and Feltrinelli International, Via Cavour 12-20r, also have good selections of English-language books.

Laundry
Onda Blu, Via degli Alfani 24bR, east of the Duomo and at Via Guelfa 22a rosso, is self-service and charges around L6000 for a 6.5kg load.

Medical & Emergency Services
For an ambulance call ☎ 118. The main public hospital is Ospedale Careggi (☎ 427 71 11), Viale Morgagni 85, north of the city centre. Tourist Medical Service (☎ 47 54 11), Via Lorenzo il Magnifico 59, is open 24 hours a day and the doctors speak English, French and German. An organisation of volunteer interpreters (English, French and German) called the Associazione Volontari Ospedalieri (☎ 234 45 67; 40 31 26) will translate free of charge once you've found a doctor. Hospitals have a list of volunteers. All-night pharmacies include the Farmacia Comunale (☎ 28 94 35) inside the station, and Molteni (☎ 28 94 90) in the city centre at Via Calzaiuoli 7r.

Call ☎ 113 for the police. The questura (☎ 4 97 71) is at Via Zara 2. There is an office for foreigners where you can report thefts etc. For information about lost property call ☎ 328 39 42. Towed-away cars (☎ 30 82 49) can be collected from Via dell'Arcovata, 6 (south-west of the centre).

Dangers & Annoyances
Crowds, heavy traffic and summer heat can combine to make Florence unpleasant. Air pollution can be a problem for small children, people with respiratory problems and the elderly, so check with your hotel or the tourist office. Pickpockets are active in crowds and on buses, and beware of the groups of dishevelled women and children carrying newspapers and cardboard. A few will distract you while the others rifle your bag and pockets.

Things to See & Do

Duomo
This beautiful cathedral, with its pink, white and green marble façade and

Brunelleschi's famous dome dominating the Florence skyline, is one of Italy's most famous monuments. At first sight, no matter how many times you have visited the city, the Duomo will take your breath away. Named the Cattedrale di Santa Maria del Fiore, it was begun in 1296 by the Sienese architect Arnolfo di Cambio but took almost 150 years to complete. It is the fourth-largest cathedral in the world.

The Renaissance architect Brunelleschi won a public competition to design the enormous dome, the first of its kind since antiquity. The dome is decorated with frescoes by Vasari and Zuccari and stained-glass windows by Donatello, Andrea del Castagno, Paolo Uccello and Lorenzo Ghiberti. Climb to the top of the dome for an unparalleled view of Florence (open daily from 8.30 am to 6.20 pm, Saturday to 5 pm, Sunday closed; entry L10,000). The Duomo's marble façade was built in the 19th century to replace the original unfinished façade, which was pulled down in the 16th century.

Giotto designed and began building the **bell tower** next to the cathedral in 1334, but died before it was completed. This unusual and graceful structure is 82m high and you can climb its stairs daily between 9 am and 6.50 pm (4.20 pm in winter); entry is L10,000.

The Romanesque-style **baptistry**, believed to have been built between the 5th and 11th centuries on the site of a Roman temple, is the oldest building in Florence. Dante was baptised here. It is famous for its gilded-bronze doors, particularly the celebrated east doors facing the Duomo, the *Gates of Paradise*, by Lorenzo Ghiberti. The south door, by Andrea Pisano, dates from 1336 and is the oldest. The north door is also by Ghiberti, who won a public competition in 1401 to design it, but the *Gates of Paradise* remain his masterpiece. Most of the doors are copies – the original panels are being removed for restoration and are placed in the Museo dell'Opera del Duomo as work is completed. The baptistry is open Monday to Saturday from 1.30 to 6.30 pm and on Sunday from 8.30 am to 1.30 pm; entry costs L5000.

Uffizi Gallery The Palazzo degli Uffizi, built by Vasari in the 16th century, houses the most important art collection in Italy. The vast collection of paintings dating from the 13th to 18th centuries represents the great legacy of the Medici family.

You will need more than one visit to fully appreciate the extraordinary number of important works in the Uffizi, which include paintings by Giotto and Cimabue from the 14th century; 15th-century masterpieces including Botticelli's *Birth of Venus* and *Allegory of Spring*; and works by Filippo Lippi, Fra Angelico and Paolo Uccello. *The Annunciation* by Leonardo da Vinci is also here. There are 16th-century works by Raphael, Michelangelo's *Holy Family* and famous works by Titian, Andrea del Sarto, Tintoretto, Rembrandt, Caravaggio, Tiepolo, Rubens, Van Dyck and Goya. Most of the gallery's second corridor was damaged in a 1993 bomb attack but restoration works should be completed in 1998. The gallery is open weekdays from 8.30 am to 10 pm (Sunday to 8 pm) and is closed Monday. Entry is L12,000.

Piazza della Signoria & Palazzo Vecchio Built by Arnolfo di Cambio between 1299 and 1314, the Palazzo Vecchio is the traditional seat of the Florentine government. In the 16th century it became the ducal palace of the Medici before they moved to the Pitti Palace. Visit the beautiful Michelozzo courtyard just inside the entrance and the lavishly decorated apartments upstairs. It's open weekdays from 9 am to 7 pm (closed Thursday) and Sunday from 9 am to 1 pm. Admission is L10,000. The palace's turrets, battlements and 94m-high bell tower form an imposing and memorable backdrop to Piazza della Signoria, scene of many important political events in the history of Florence, including the execution of the religious and political reformer Savonarola. A bronze plaque marks the spot where he was burned at the stake in 1498. The **Loggia della Signoria**, at right angles to the Palazzo Vecchio, contains important sculptures. Cellini's famous *Perseus* was removed from the Loggia for restorations in April 1997 and is now in the west wing of the Uffizi Gallery.

Ponte Vecchio This famous 14th-century bridge, lined with gold and silversmiths' shops, was the only one to survive Nazi bombing in WWII. Originally, the shops

DUOMO TO PONTE VECCHIO

PLACES TO STAY
5 Albergo Firenze
11 Pensione Maria
   Luisa de Medici
12 Brunori
19 Aily Home

PLACES TO EAT
4 Osteria Il Caminetto
9 Gelateria Perché No?
10 Cantinetta di Verrazzano
14 Gelateria Vivoli
20 Trattoria da Benvenuto
21 Angie's Pub
22 Fiaschetteria

OTHER
1 Baptistry
2 Bell Tower
3 Duomo
6 Internazionale Seeber
  Bookshop
7 Cinema Odeon
8 Post Office
13 Libreria Cima
15 Palazzo del Bargello;
   Museo Nazionale
16 Palazzo Vecchio
17 Loggia della Signoria
18 Uffizi Gallery
23 Comune di Firenze
   Tourist Office

housed butchers. A corridor along the 1st floor was built by the Medici to link the Pitti Palace and the Uffizi Gallery.

Palazzo Pitti The immense and imposing Palazzo Pitti, housing several museums, was originally designed by Brunelleschi. The **Galleria Palatina** (open Tuesday to Saturday 8.30 am to 10 pm, Sunday to 8 pm; entry L12,000) has 16th and 17th-century works by Raphael, Filippo Lippi, Tintoretto, Veronese and Rubens, hung in lavishly decorated rooms. The royal apartments of the Medici,

and later of the Savoy, show the splendour in which these rulers lived. The other museums are the **Museo degli Argenti**, the **Galleria del Costume** (temporarily closed) and the **Galleria d'Arte Moderna**. All are open Tuesday to Sunday from 9 am to 2 pm. After the Pitti Palace, visit the beautiful Renaissance **Giardino di Boboli** (entry L4000).

Palazzo del Bargello & Museo Nazionale del Bargello A medieval palace, also known as the Palazzo del Podestà, the Bargello was the seat of the local ruler and, later, of the chief of police. People were tortured at the site of the well in the centre of the courtyard. The palace now houses Florence's rich collection of sculpture, notably works by Michelangelo, many by Benvenuto Cellini, and Donatello's stunning bronze *David*, the first sculpture since antiquity to depict a fully naked man (open Tuesday to Sunday 8.30 am to 2 pm; entry L8000).

Galleria dell'Accademia Michelangelo's *David* is in this gallery (the one in Piazza della Signoria is a good copy), as are four of his unfinished *Slaves* (or *Prisoners*). The gallery upstairs houses many important works of the Florentine primitives. The gallery, at Via Ricasoli 60, is open Tuesday to Saturday from 8.30 am to 10 pm and Sunday to 8 pm. Entry is L12,000.

Basilica di San Lorenzo & Cappelle Medicee The basilica, rebuilt by Brunelleschi in the early 15th century for the Medici, contains his **Sagrestia Vecchia** (Old Sacristy), which was decorated by Donatello. It's also worth visiting the **Biblioteca Laurenziana**, a huge library designed by Michelangelo to house the Medici collection of some 10,000 manuscripts. Around the corner, in Piazza Madonna degli Aldobrandini, are the Cappelle Medicee (Medici Chapels). The **Cappella dei Principi**, sumptuously decorated with precious marble and semiprecious stones, was the principal burial place of the Medici grand dukes. The graceful and simple **Sagrestia Nuova** was designed by Michelangelo, but he left Florence for Rome before its completion. It contains his beautiful sculptures *Night & Day*, *Dawn & Dusk* and the *Madonna with Child*, which adorn the Medici tombs. The chapels are open Tuesday to Saturday from 8.30 am to 5 pm (Sunday to 1.50 pm). Admission is L10,000.

Other Attractions The Dominican church of **Santa Maria Novella** was built during the 13th and 14th centuries, and its white-and-green marble façade was designed by Alberti in the 15th century. The church is decorated with frescoes by Ghirlandaio (who was assisted by a very young Michelangelo) and Masaccio. The **Cappella di Filippo Strozzi** contains frescoes by Filippo Lippi, and the beautiful cloisters feature frescoes by Uccello and his students.

The **Convento di San Marco** (Monastery of St Mark) is a museum of the work of Fra Angelico, who covered its walls and many of the monks' cells with frescoes and lived here from 1438 to 1455. Also worth seeing are the peaceful cloisters and the cell of the monk Savonarola. It also contains works by Fra Bartolomeo and Ghirlandaio. The monastery is open Tuesday to Sunday from 8.30 am to 2 pm and entry is L8000.

Head up to **Piazzale Michelangelo** for a magnificent view of Florence. To reach the piazzale from the city centre cross the Ponte Vecchio, turn left and walk along the river, then turn right at Piazza Giuseppe Poggi, or take bus No 13 from the station.

Cycling

I Bike Italy (☎ 234 23 71; www.ibikeitaly. com) offers affordable single and two-day guided bike rides in the countryside around Florence with stops at vineyards. It supplies bikes, helmets and English-speaking guides.

Courses

Florence has more than 30 schools offering courses in Italian language and culture. Numerous other schools offer courses in the visual arts, including painting, drawing and sculpture, as well as art history. While Florence might be the most attractive city in which to study Italian language or art, it is also one of the more expensive. Perugia, Siena and Urbino offer good-quality courses at much lower prices. The cost of language courses in Florence ranges from about L450,000 to L900,000, depending on the school and the length of the course (one month is usually the minimum duration). Here are the addresses of some of the language courses available in Florence:

Centro Linguistico Italiano Dante Alighieri
   (fax 234 29 86) Via dei Bardi 12, 50125
   Florence
Istituto di Lingua e Cultura Italiana per Stranieri
   Michelangelo
   (☎ 24 09 75) Via Ghibellina 88, 50122
   Florence
Istituto Europeo
   (☎ 238 10 71) Piazzale delle Pallottole 1,
   50122 Florence

Art courses range from one-month summer workshops (costing from L500,000 to more than L1,000,000) to longer-term professional diploma courses. These can be expensive, some of them costing more than L6,500,000 a year. Schools will organise accommodation for students, upon request, either in private apartments or with Italian families.

Brochures detailing courses and prices are available at Italian cultural institutes throughout the world. You can write in English to request information and enrolment forms – letters should be addressed to the *segretaria*. Some art schools include:

Istituto d'Arte di Firenze Lorenzo de' Medici
(☎ 28 71 43) Via Faenza 43, 50122 Florence
Istituto per l'Arte e il Restauro
(☎ 234 58 98) Palazzo Spinelli, Borgo Santa Croce 10, 50122 Florence

Special Events
Major festivals include the Festa del Patrono (the Feast of St John the Baptist) on 24 June; the Scoppio del Carro (Explosion of the Cart), held in front of the Duomo on Easter Sunday (see Facts for the Visitor at the start of this chapter); and the lively Calcio Storico (Historical Football) on 24 June which features football matches played in 16th-century costume. Italy's oldest music festival, Maggio Musicale Fiorentino, is usually held in June. For information call the Teatro Comunale (☎ 21 11 58, 21 35 35; fax 277 94 10).

Places to Stay
Always ask the full price of a room before putting your bags down. Hotels and pensioni in Florence are becoming increasingly expensive and are notorious for bill-padding, particularly in summer. Many require an extra L6000 to L8000 for a compulsory breakfast and will charge L3000 or more for a shower. Prices listed here are for high season and, unless otherwise specified, are for rooms without private bathroom.

Camping The *Campeggio Michelangelo* camping ground (☎ 681 19 77), Viale Michelangelo 80, is near Piazzale Michelangelo. Take bus No 13 from the train station. *Villa Camerata* (☎ 60 03 15), Viale Augusto Righi 2-4, is next to the HI hostel (see the next section), north-east of the centre (take bus 17b from the station, 30 minutes). There is another camping ground at Fiesole, *Campeggio Panoramico* (☎ 59 90 69), at Via Peramonda 1 which also has bungalows. Take bus No 7 to Fiesole from the station.

Hostels The HI *Ostello Villa Camerata* (☎ 60 14 51), Viale Augusto Righi 2-4, charges L24,000 for B&B, L14,000 for dinner and there is also a bar. Take bus No 17b, which leaves from the right of the station as you leave the platforms. The trip takes 30 minutes. Daytime closing is 9 am to 2 pm. It is open to HI members only and reservations can be made by mail (essential in summer).

The private *Ostello Archi Rossi* (☎ 29 08 04), Via Faenza 94r, is another good option for a bed in a dorm room. *Ostello Santa Monaca* (☎ 26 83 38), Via Santa Monaca 6, is also private. It is a 15 to 20-minute walk from the station. Go through Piazza Santa Maria Novella, along Via de' Fossi, across the Ponte alla Carraia and directly ahead along Via de' Serragli. Via Santa Monaca is on the right. A bed costs L22,000.

Hotels There are more than 150 budget hotels in Florence, so even in peak season, when the city is packed with tourists, you should be able to find a room. However, it is always advisable to make a booking, and you should arrive by late morning to claim your room.

Around the Station The *Pensione Bellavista* (☎ 28 45 28), Largo Alinari 15 (at the start of Via Nazionale), is worth it if you manage to book one of the two double rooms with balconies and a view of the Duomo and Palazzo Vecchio. Single/double rooms cost L70,000/100,000, breakfast included. *Albergo Azzi* (☎ 21 38 06), Via Faenza 56, has helpful management and singles/doubles cost L60,000/110,000 and L100,000/120,000 with bathroom (breakfast included). The same management runs the *Albergo Anna* upstairs.

Across Via Nazionale at Via Faenza 7, is *Pensione Accademia* (☎ 29 34 51). It has pleasant, but expensive, rooms and incorporates an 18th-century palace, replete with magnificent stained-glass doors and carved wooden ceilings; singles cost L110,000 and a double with bathroom is L170,000, breakfast and TV included. Across Via Nazionale, at Via Faenza 20, is *Soggiorno Burchi* (☎ 41 44 54), which has doubles/triples with bathroom for L80,000/100,000. The *Locanda Daniel* (☎ 21 12 93), Via Nazionale 22, has doubles for L65,000 and beds in a large room for L25,000 per person. One of the rooms has a panoramic view of the Duomo. The owner will not take bookings, so arrive very early. In the same building is *Soggiorno Nazionale* (☎ 238 22 03). Singles/doubles are L65,000/95,000, breakfast included.

At No 24 is the *Pensione Ausonia & Rimini* (☎ 49 65 47), run by a young couple who go out of their way to help travellers. Singles/doubles are L70,000/105,000. The price includes breakfast and use of the communal bathroom. The same couple also operates the more expensive *Pensione Kursaal* (☎ 49 63 24) downstairs. *Pensione Mary* (☎ 49 63 10), Piazza della Indipendenza 5, has singles/doubles for L90,000/110,000.

Around Piazza Santa Maria Novella Via della Scala, which runs north-west off the piazza, is lined with pensioni. *La Scala* (☎ 21 26 29) at No 21 is small and has doubles/triples for L90,000/120,000. The *Pensione Margareth* (☎ 21 01 38) at No 25 is pleasantly furnished and has singles/doubles for L80,000/100,000. At No 43 *Pensione Montreal* (☎ 238 23 31) at has singles for L70,000 and doubles with bathroom for L90,000. *La Romagnola* (☎ 21 15 97) at No 40 has large, clean rooms for L48,000/84,000. The same family runs *La Gigliola* (☎ 28 79 81) upstairs.

The *Sole* (☎ 239 60 94), Via del Sole 8, charges L50,000/70,000 for singles/doubles. A double with bathroom costs L90,000. Triples/quads cost L90,000/120,000. The curfew is 1 am. Ask for a quiet room. In the same building is the *Pensione Toscana* (☎ 21 31 56), with singles/doubles with bathroom for L80,000/130,000. The *Ottaviani* (☎ 239 62 23), Piazza Ottaviani 1, just off Piazza Santa Maria Novella, has singles/doubles for L60,000/80,000, breakfast included. In the same building is the *Visconti* (☎ 21 38 77), with a pleasant terrace garden where you can

have breakfast. Singles/doubles are L62,000, 94,000, and a triple is L120,000. Breakfast is included.

The Duomo to the Arno This area is a 15-minute walk from the station and is right in the heart of old Florence. One of the best deals is the small *Aily Home* (☎ 239 65 05), overlooking the Ponte Vecchio at Piazza Santo Stefano 1. It has singles at L35,000 and doubles (three of which overlook the bridge) for L60,000 a night. *Albergo Firenze* (☎ 21 42 03; fax 21 23 70), Piazza dei Donati 4, just south of the Duomo, has singles/doubles with bathroom for L80,000/120,000. The *Brunori* (☎ 28 96 48), Via del Proconsolo 5, has doubles for L80,000, or with private bathroom for L102,000. The *Maria Luisa de' Medici* (☎ 28 00 48), Via del Corso 1, is in a 17th-century palace. It has no singles, but its large rooms for up to five people cater for families. A double is L93,000, a triple L129,000 and a quad L168,000. All prices include breakfast.

Rental If you want an apartment in Florence, save your pennies and start searching well before you arrive. A one-room apartment with kitchenette, in the centre, will cost from L900,000 to L1,500,000 a month. Florence & Abroad (☎ 48 70 04), Via Zanobi 58, handles rental accommodation.

Villa In the hills overlooking Florence is *Bencistà* (☎ 591 63), Via Benedetto da Maiano 4, about 1km from Fiesole. It is an old villa and from its terrace there is a magnificent view of Florence. Half-pension is L135,000 per person in rooms with bathroom, and L115,000 in room without bathroom. It might break the budget, but for one or two days it is well worth it.

Places to Eat
Simplicity and quality best describe the food of Tuscany. Start your meal with fettunta (known elsewhere in Italy as bruschetta), a thick slice of toasted bread, rubbed with garlic and soaked with the rich, green Tuscan olive oil. Try the ribollita, a very filling soup of vegetables and white beans, reboiled with chunks of bread and garnished with olive oil. Another traditional dish is bistecca Fiorenti-

na (steak Florentine) which is big enough for two people; the best come from the Val di Chiana and are called chianine.

Restaurants Eating at a good trattoria can be surprisingly economical, but many tourists fall into the trap of eating at the self-service restaurants which line the streets of the main shopping district between the Duomo and the Arno. Be adventurous and seek out the little eating places in the district of Oltrarno (the other side of the Arno from the centre) and near the Mercato Centrale (the covered market) in San Lorenzo. The market, open Monday to Saturday from 7 am to 2 pm (also Saturday from 4 to 8 pm), offers fresh produce, cheeses and meat at reasonable prices.

City Centre The *Trattoria da Benvenuto*, Via Mosca 16r, on the corner of Via dei Neri, is an excellent trattoria. A full meal will cost around L25,000 and a quick meal of pasta, bread and wine will cost around L12,000. *Angie's Pub*, Via dei Neri 35r, offers a vast array of sandwiches and focaccia (you can design your own) for L4500 to L6500, as well as hamburgers, served Italian-style with mozzarella and spinach, and hot dogs with cheese and mushrooms. There is a good range of beers and no extra charge if you sit down. At *Fiaschetteria*, Via dei Neri 17r, try the excellent ribollita for around L10,000.

Osteria Il Caminetto, Via dello Studio 34, just south of Piazza del Duomo, has a small vine-covered terrace. A pasta dish costs around L9000, and a full meal around L30,000.

Around San Lorenzo Ask anyone in Florence where they go for lunch and they will answer *Mario's*. This small bar and trattoria at Via Rosina 2r, near the Mercato Centrale, is open only at lunchtime. It serves pasta dishes for around L4000 to L6000, and a secondo for L5000 to L9000. A few doors down, at Piazza del Mercato Centrale 20, is *Caffè Za Za*, another favourite with the locals. Prices are around the same as at Mario's. *Bondi*, Via dell'Ariento 85, specialises in focaccia and pizza from L2500.

In the Oltrarno A bustling place popular with the locals is *Trattoria Casalinga*, Via

dei Michelozzi 9r. The food is great and a filling meal of pasta, meat or contorni, and wine will cost you around L15,000 to L20,000. *I Tarocchi*, Via de' Renai 12-14r, serves excellent pizza, ranging from L6000 to L10,000, as well as dishes typical of the region, including a good range of pasta from L7000 to L8000, and plenty of salads and vegetable dishes from L5000 to L8000. The coperto is only L2000. *Angiolino*, Via Santo Spirito 36r, is an excellent trattoria where a full meal will cost around L35,000.

Cafés & Snack Bars *Caffè degli Innocenti*, Via Nazionale 57, near the Mercato Centrale, has a selection of pre-prepared panini and good cakes for around L2500 to L3500. The streets between the Duomo and the Arno harbour many pizzerias where you can buy pizza by the slice to take away for around L2000 to L4000, depending on the weight.

The *Cantinetta da Verrazzano*, Via dei Tavolini 18r, has outdoor tables where you can eat snacks and drink good Chianti wine without paying extra.

Gelati Among the best outlets for gelati are *Gelateria Vivoli* (☎ 29 23 34), Via dell'Isola delle Stinche, near Via Torta, and *Perché No?* (☎ 239 89 69), Via dei Tavolini 19r, off Via Calzaiuoli.

Entertainment
Several publications list the theatrical and musical events and festivals held in the city and surrounding areas. They include the bi-monthly *Florence Today* and the monthly *Firenze Information* and *Firenze Avvenimenti*, all available at the tourist offices. The monthly *Firenze Spettacolo* is the city's definitive entertainment guide. It is L2700 at newsstands, where you could also pick up one of the English-language publications *Vista* and *Events*.

Concerts, opera and dance are performed year-round at the *Teatro Comunale*, Corso Italia 16, with the main seasons running from September to December and January to April. Contact the theatre's box office (☎ 277 92 36).

English films are screened at a number of cinemas: the *Astro Cinema* in Piazza San

Simone, near Santa Croce (every night except Monday); the *Odeon* in Piazza Strozzi (Monday); and the *Goldoni*, Via de' Serragli (Wednesday).

Nightclubs include *La Dolce Vita*, Piazza del Carmine, south of the Arno. *Cabiria* in Piazza Santo Spirito is a bar which is very popular among young people, especially in summer. At *Pongo*, Via Verdi 59r, good jazz is performed on Monday night.

A more sedate pastime is the nightly *passeggiata* (stroll) in Piazzale Michelangelo, overlooking the city (take bus No 13 from the station or the Duomo).

Things to Buy

The main shopping area is between the Duomo and the Arno, with boutiques concentrated along Via Roma, Via dei Calzaiuoli and Via Por Santa Maria, leading to the goldsmiths lining the Ponte Vecchio. Window-shop along Via de' Tornabuoni, where the top designers, including Gucci, Yves Saint Laurent and Pucci, sell their wares.

The open-air market (open Monday to Saturday), held in the streets of San Lorenzo near the Mercato Centrale, offers leather goods, clothing and jewellery at low prices, but quality can vary greatly. Check the item carefully before you buy. You can bargain, but not if you want to use a credit card. The flea market at Piazza dei Ciompi, off Borgo Allegri near the Church of Santa Croce, is not as extensive but there are great bargains. It opens roughly the same hours as retail shops and all day on the last Sunday of the month.

Florence is famous for its beautifully patterned paper, which is stocked in the many *cartolerie* (stationer's shops) throughout the city and at the markets.

Getting There & Away

Air Florence is served by two airports, Amerigo Vespucci and Galileo Galilei. Amerigo Vespucci (☎ 306 17 00/02; 37 34 98), a few kilometres north-west of the city centre at Via del Termine 11, serves domestic and European flights. Galileo Galilei (☎ 21 60 73, Firenze Air Terminal at Santa Maria Novella station), just under an hour away from Florence near Pisa, is one of northern Italy's main international and domestic airports.

Bus The SITA bus station (☎ 21 47 21, 48 36 51, information in English ☎ 478 22 31, in French ☎ 24 47 21), Via Santa Caterina da Siena, is just to the west of the train station. Buses leave for Siena, the Colle Val d'Elsa, Poggibonsi (where there are connecting buses to San Gimignano and Volterra) and Arezzo. Full details on other bus services are available at the APT.

Train Florence is on the main Rome-Milan line and most of the trains are the fast Eurostars, for which you have to book and to pay a rapido supplement. Regular trains also go to/from Venice (three hours) and Trieste. For train information ring ☎ 166-10 50 50.

Car & Motorcycle Florence is connected by the Autostrada del Sole (A1) to Bologna and Milan in the north and Rome and Naples to the south. The motorway to the sea, the so called Firenze-Mare, links Florence with Prato, Pistoia, Lucca, Pisa and the Versilia coast, and a *superstrada* (dual carriageway) joins the city to Siena. Exits from the autostrade into Florence are well signed, and either one of the exits marked 'Firenze nord' or 'Firenze sud' will take you to the centre of town. There are tourist information offices on the A1 both to the north and south of the city.

Getting Around

To/From the Airport Regular trains leave from platform No 5 at Florence's Santa Maria Novella station for Pisa airport daily from 6.47 am to 5 pm. Check your bags in, before 4 pm, at the air terminal (☎ 21 60 73) near platform 5. ATAF bus No 62 leaves every 20 minutes from 6 am to 10.20 pm from the train station for Amerigo Vespucci airport and vice versa. Buy a normal city bus ticket (15 minutes; L1500).

Bus ATAF buses service the city centre and Fiesole. The terminal for the most useful buses is in a small piazza to the left as you go out of the station onto Via Valfonda. Bus No 7 leaves from here for Fiesole and also stops at the Duomo. Tickets must be bought before you get on the bus and are sold at most tobacconists and newsstands or from automatic vending machines at major bus stops (L1500 for one hour, L2500 for three hours, L6000 for 24 hours).

Car & Motorcycle

If you're spending the day in Florence, use the underground parking areas at the train station or in Piazza del Mercato Centrale (L3000 an hour). Less expensive parking is available from November to February at the Fortezza da Basso (L2000 an hour).

To rent a car, try Hertz (☎ 28 22 60), Via M Finiguerra 17r, or Avis (☎ 21 36 29), Borgognissanti 128r. For motorcycles and bicycles try Alinari (☎ 28 05 00), Via Guelfa 85r.

Taxi

You can find taxis outside the station, or call ☎ 4798 or ☎ 4390 to book one.

PISA
☎ 050

Once a maritime power to rival Genoa and Venice, Pisa now seems content to have one remaining claim to fame: its leaning tower. On the banks of the Arno River near the Ligurian Sea, Pisa was once a busy port, the site of an important university and the home of Galileo Galilei (1564-1642). Devastated by the Genoese in the 13th century, its history eventually merged with that of Florence. Today Pisa is a pleasant town focused on the main square, the Campo dei Miracoli, and the old centre.

Information

There are APT tourist information offices at the train station, the airport and at Via Carlo Cammeo 2, near the bus station in Largo Cocco Grifi, west of Campo dei Miracoli. The station and Campo offices open daily from 9.30 am to 1 pm and 2.30 to 6 pm. The office at the station is closed on Sunday. Take bus No 1 from the station to Piazza del Duomo. Pisa's postcode is 56100.

Things to See & Do

The Pisans can justly claim that their **Campo dei Miracoli** (Field of Miracles) is one of the most beautiful squares in the world. Set in its sprawling lawns are the **cathedral**, the **baptistry** and the **leaning tower**. On any day the piazza is teeming with people – students

studying, tourists wandering and Pisan workers eating their lunch.

The Romanesque cathedral, begun in 1064, has a beautiful façade of columns in four tiers and its huge interior is lined with 68 columns. The bronze doors of the transept, facing the leaning tower, are by Bonanno Pisano. The 16th-century bronze doors of the main entrance are by Giambologna and were made to replace the original doors which were destroyed in a fire. It costs L3000 to enter.

The cathedral's marble baptistry, which was started in 1153 and took almost two centuries to complete, contains a beautiful pulpit by Nicola Pisano. Entry to the baptistry is L10,000, which also covers entry to one of the two museums in the Campo.

The famous leaning bell tower was in trouble from the start. Its architect, Bonanno Pisano, managed to complete three tiers before the tower started to lean. The problem is generally believed to have been caused by shifting soil, and the tower has continued to lean by an average 1mm a year. Galileo climbed its 294 steps to experiment with gravity. The tower has been closed for some years while the Italians have been trying to work out how to stop its inexorable lean towards the ground. Today it leans 5m off the perpendicular. Finally, in early 1994, they found a solution – 600 tons of lead ingots which anchor the north foundation. While no one has any intention of turning the leaning tower into a straight tower, many still believe that it will fall down eventually.

After seeing the Campo dei Miracoli, take a walk down Via Santa Maria, along the Arno and into the Borgo Stretto to explore the old city.

Places to Stay & Eat

Pisa has a reasonable number of budget hotels for a small town, but many double as residences for students during the school year, so it can be difficult to find a cheap room. The non-HI *Ostello per la Gioventù* (☎ 89 06 22), Via Pietrasantina 15, is used by students. A bed is L20,000. The place is closed between 9 am and 6 pm. Take bus No 3 from the station. The *Albergo E Gronchi* (☎ 56 18 23), Piazza Arcivescovado 1, just near the Campo dei Miracoli, has modern singles/doubles for L32,000/54,000. *Albergo Giardino* (☎ 56 21 01), Piazza Manin 1, just west of Campo dei Miracoli, has rooms for L40,000/60,000. The *Hotel di Stefano* (☎ 55 35 59), Via Sant'Apollonia 35, offers good-quality rooms for L50,000/70,000.

Near the station is the *Albergo Milano* (☎ 231 62), Via Mascagni 14, with pleasant rooms and a friendly owner. Singles/doubles cost L50,000/95,000 and triples cost L125,000.

Being a university town, Pisa has a good range of cheap eating places. Head for the area around Borgo Stretto and the university. *Pizzeria da Matteo*, Via l'Arancio 46, is a good choice. The restaurant *L'Europeo*, Via Santa Maria 177, near the leaning tower, offers meals for L25,000. There is an open-air food market in Piazza delle Vettovaglie, off Borgo Stretto. Pick up supplies there and head for the Campo dei Miracoli for a picnic lunch.

Getting There & Away

The airport, with domestic and international (European) flights, is only a few minutes away by train, or by bus No 7 from the station. Lazzi (☎ 462 88) buses operate to Florence via Lucca and Prato. CPT (☎ 50 55 11) runs buses to Volterra via Pontedera and to Livorno via Tirrenia. The city is linked by direct train to Florence, Rome and Genoa. Local trains head for Lucca and Livorno.

SIENA
☎ 0577

Italy's best preserved medieval town, Siena is built on three hills and is still surrounded by its historic ramparts. Its historic centre is bristling with majestic Gothic buildings in various shades of the colour known as burnt sienna. According to legend, Siena was founded by the sons of Remus (one of the founders of Rome). In the Middle Ages the city became a free republic, but its success and power led to serious rivalry with Florence. In a famous incident in the 13th century, the Florentines hurled dead donkeys and excrement into Siena, hoping to start a plague.

Painters of the Sienese School produced important works of art and the city was home to St Catherine and St Benedict. Siena is divided into 17 *contrade* (districts) and each year 10 are chosen to compete in the Palio, an extraordinary horse race and pageant held in the shell-shaped Piazza del Campo on 2 July and 16 August.

Orientation

Siena is well geared for tourism. Signs direct you through the modern town to the medieval city, and within the walls there are easy-to-follow signs to all the major sights.

From the train station catch bus No 10 to Piazza Matteotti and walk into the centre along Via dei Termini (it takes about five minutes to reach the Campo). From the bus station in Piazza San Domenico, it's a five-minute walk along Via della Sapienza and then turn right into Via delle Terme to the Campo. No cars, apart from those of residents, are allowed in the medieval centre.

Information

Tourist Office The APT office (☎ 28 05 51; fax 27 06 76) is at Piazza del Campo 56. During July-August it opens Monday to Saturday from 8.30 am to 7.30 pm. During May, June, September and October it also opens on Sunday from 8.30 am to 2.30 pm. At other times of the year it opens weekdays from 8.30 am to 1 pm and 3.30 to 6.30 pm (Saturday to 1 pm).

Post & Communications The main post office is at Piazza Matteotti 1. The Telecom telephone office is at Via dei Termini 40.

Medical & Emergency Services For an ambulance, call ☎ 118. The public hospital (☎ 58 51 11) is in Viale Bracci, just north of Siena at Le Scotte. For police attendance call ☎ 113. The questura is at Via del Castoro 23 and its Foreigners' Bureau is in Piazza Jacopo della Quercia (facing the Duomo)

Things to See & Do

The **Piazza del Campo**, known simply as Il Campo, is a magnificent shell-shaped, slanting piazza, its paving divided into nine sectors. At the lowest point of the piazza is the imposing **Palazzo Pubblico** (also known as Palazzo Comunale or town hall), considered one of the most graceful Gothic buildings in Italy. Inside the town hall are numerous important Sienese works of art, including Simone Martini's *Maestà* and Ambrogio Lorenzetti's frescoes, *Allegories of Good & Bad Government*. There is also a chapel with frescoes by Taddeo di Bartolo. As with all museums and monuments in Siena, the opening hours for the palace vary depending on the time of year. In summer it opens Monday to Saturday from 9.30 am to 6.30 pm and Sunday from 9.30 am to 1.30 pm. Entry is L8000 (L4000 for students).

The spectacular **Duomo** is one of the most

beautiful in Italy. Its black-and-white striped marble façade has a Romanesque lower section, with carvings by Giovanni Pisano. Its upper section is 14th-century Gothic and there are 19th-century mosaics at the top. The interior features an inlaid marble floor, with various works depicting biblical stories. The beautiful **pulpit** was carved in marble and porphyry by Nicola Pisano, the father of Giovanni Pisano. Other important artworks include a bronze statue of St John the Baptist by Donatello and statues of St Jerome and Mary Magdalene by Bernini.

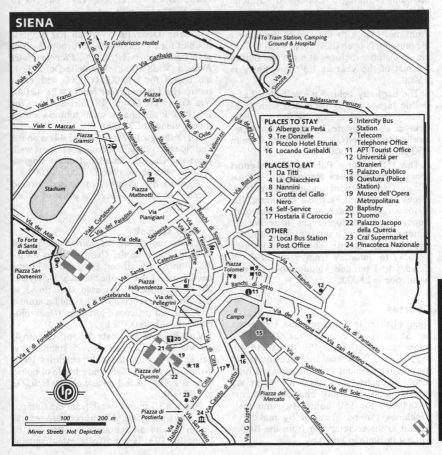

SIENA

PLACES TO STAY
6 Albergo La Perla
9 Tre Donzelle
10 Piccolo Hotel Etruria
16 Locanda Garibaldi

PLACES TO EAT
1 Da Titti
4 La Chiacchiera
8 Nannini
13 Grotta del Gallo Nero
14 Self-Service
17 Hostaria il Caroccio

OTHER
2 Local Bus Station
3 Post Office
5 Intercity Bus Station
7 Telecom Telephone Office
11 APT Tourist Office
12 Universitá per Stranieri
15 Palazzo Pubblico
18 Questura (Police Station)
19 Museo dell'Opera Metropolitana
20 Baptistry
21 Duomo
22 Palazzo Jacopo della Quercia
23 Crai Supermarket
24 Pinacoteca Nazionale

Minor Streets Not Depicted

0   100   200 m

ITALY

Through a door from the north aisle is the **Libreria Piccolomini**, which Pope Pius III (pope during 1503) built to house the magnificent, illustrated books of his uncle, Pope Pius II. It features frescoes by Pinturicchio and a Roman statue of the Three Graces. Entry is L2000.

The **Museo dell'Opera Metropolitana** (Duomo Museum) is in Piazza del Duomo. It houses many important works of art that formerly adorned the cathedral, including the famous *Maestà* by Duccio di Buoninsegna, formerly used as a screen for the cathedral's high altar; and works by artists including Ambrogio Lorenzetti, Simone Martini and Taddeo di Bartolo. The collection also features tapestries and manuscripts. From mid-March to the end of September the museum is open daily from 9 am to 7.30 pm. In October it closes at 6 pm and during the rest of the year at 1.30 pm. Entry is L6000.

The **baptistry** behind the cathedral has a Gothic façade and is decorated with 15th-century frescoes, a font by Jacopo della Quercia, and sculptures by artists such as Donatello and Ghiberti. It is open daily 9 am to 7.30 pm; entry is L3000.

The 15th-century **Palazzo Buonsignori** houses the **Pinacoteca Nazionale** (National Picture Gallery), with innumerable masterpieces by Sienese artists, including the *Madonna dei Francescani* by Duccio di Buoninsegna, *Madonna col Bambino* by Simone Martini and a series of Madonnas by Ambrogio Lorenzetti. The gallery is open Tuesday to Saturday from 9 am to 7 pm (Sunday to 1 pm and Monday to 1.30 pm). Admission is L8000.

Courses

Siena's University for Foreigners, Università per Stranieri (☎ 240 11; fax 28 31 63; info@unistrasi.it) is at Via Pantaneto 45, 53100 Siena. The school is open all year and the only requirement for enrolment is a high school graduation/pass certificate. There are several areas of study and courses cost L1,000,000 for 150 hours (two months). Brochures can be obtained by making a request to the secretary, or from the Italian cultural institute in your city.

Places to Stay

It is always advisable to book a hotel in Siena, particularly in August and during the Palio, when accommodation is impossible to find for miles around the city.

The *Colleverde* camping ground (☎ 28 00 44) is outside the historical centre at Strada di Scacciapensieri 47 (take bus No 8 from Piazza del Sale, near Piazza Gramsci). It opens 21 March to 10 November and costs L13,000 for adults, L6500 for children and L14,000 for a site.

The *Guidoriccio* hostel (☎ 522 12), Via Fiorentina, Stellino, is about 3km out of the centre. B&B is L22,000. Take bus No 15 from Piazza Gramsci.

In town, try the *Tre Donzelle* (☎ 28 03 58), Via delle Donzelle 5, which has singles/doubles for L43,000/71,000. A room for four with bathroom is L150,000. *Piccolo Hotel Etruria* (☎ 28 80 88), Via delle Donzelle 1, has rooms for L65,000/103,000 with bathroom. The *Locanda Garibaldi* (☎ 28 42 04), Via Giovanni Duprè 18, has doubles for L80,000. It also has a small trattoria with a tourist menu at L25,000.

The *Albergo La Perla* (☎ 471 44) is on the 2nd floor at Via delle Terme 25, a short walk from the Campo. Small but clean singles/doubles with shower are L60,000/90,000.

Agriturismo is well organised around Siena. The tourist office has a list of establishments.

Places to Eat

The restaurant *Grotta del Gallo Nero*, Via del Porrione 67, near the Campo, offers a medieval menu for around L35,000. At Piazza del Campo 77 there is the cheap *Self-Service*. Off the Campo, at Via Casato di Sotto 32, is *Hostaria Il Carroccio* with a meal for around L35,000 and bistecca Fiorentina (steak Florentine) for L40,000 a kg.

La Chiacchiera, Costa di Sant'Antonio 4, off Via Santa Caterina, is very small, but it has a good menu with local specialities. Pasta dishes cost from L5000 and a bottle of house wine is L5000. A full meal will cost L20,000 to L25,000.

About a 10-minute walk from the Campo, in a less frenetic neighbourhood, are several trattorias and alimentari. *Da Titti*, Via di Camollia 193, is a no-frills establishment with big wooden bench tables where full meals with wine cost around L23,000.

There are several supermarkets in the town centre, including *Crai* at Via di Città 152-156 and *Consorzio Agrario*, Via Piani Giani. *Nannini*, Banchi di Sopra 22, is one of the city's finest cafés and patisserie.

Getting There & Away
Regular Tra-In buses run from Florence to Siena, arriving at Piazza San Domenico. Buses also go to San Gimignano, Volterra and other points in Tuscany. A daily bus to Rome also leaves from Piazza San Domenico. For Perugia ask at the Balzana travel agency (☎ 28 50 13). Siena is not on a main train line, so from Rome it is necessary to change at Chiusi and from Florence at Empoli, making buses a better alternative.

SAN GIMIGNANO
☎ 0577
Few places in Italy rival the beauty of San Gimignano, a town which has barely changed since medieval times. Set on a hill overlooking the misty pink, green and gold patchwork of the Tuscan landscape, the town is famous for its towers (14 of the original 72 remain), built as a demonstration of power by its prominent families in the Middle Ages.

The town is packed with tourists at weekends, so try to visit during the week. The Pro Loco tourist information office (☎ 94 00 08; fax 94 09 03; prolocosg@mbox.vol.it) is in Piazza del Duomo in the town centre.

Things to See
Climb San Gimignano's tallest tower, **Torre Grossa** (also known as the town hall tower), off Piazza del Duomo, for a memorable view of the Tuscan hills. The tower is reached from within the **Palazzo del Popolo**, which houses the **Museo Civico**, with paintings by Filippo Lippi and Pinturicchio. Also in the piazza is the **Duomo**, with a Romanesque interior, frescoes by Ghirlandaio in the **Cappella di Santa Fina** and a *Last Judgment* by Taddeo di Bartolo. The **Piazza della Cisterna**, with a 13th-century well, is the most impressive piazza in San Gimignano. It is paved with bricks in a herringbone pattern and lined with towers and palaces.

Places to Stay & Eat
San Gimignano offers few options for budget travellers. The nearest camping ground is *Il Boschetto di Piemma* (☎ 94 03 52), about 3km from San Gimignano at Santa Lucia. It costs L8000 a night for adults and L6500 for children, plus L7500 for a tent site. It is open April until mid-October and there is a bus service to the site. The non-HI *hostel* (☎ 94 19 91) at Via delle Fonti 1, opens 1 March to 31 October and charges L20,000 for B&B.

Hotels in town are expensive, but there are numerous rooms for rent in private homes. Agriturismo is well organised in this area. For information on both, contact the tourist office.

Pizzeria Pizzoteca (☎ 94 22 40), Via dei Fossi, outside the walls to the left of Porta San Matteo, has good pizzas, but forget about the pasta. *Trattoria Chiribiri* (☎ 94 19 48), Piazzetta della Madonna, off Via San Giovanni, has pasta at reasonable prices. Nearby is *Pizza a Taglio Lo Sfizio*, with pizza by the slice. There is a fresh-produce market held on Thursday morning in Piazza del Duomo and there are several alimentari in Via San Matteo.

Getting There & Away
Regular buses connect San Gimignano with Florence and Siena, but for both you need to change at Poggibonsi. Buses arrive at Porta San Giovanni and timetables are posted outside the Pro Loco. Enter through the Porta and continue straight ahead to reach the Piazza del Duomo.

CERTALDO
☎ 0571
Located in the Val d'Elsa between Florence and Siena, this small medieval town is definitely worth a visit. Giovanni Boccaccio, one of the fathers of the Italian language, was born in Certaldo in 1313. A real find is *Fattoria Bassetto* (☎ 66 83 42; 66 49 45; bassetto@dedalo.com), 2km east of the town on the road to Siena. A 14th-century Benedictine convent, it was transformed into a farm by the Guicciardini counts. It is surrounded by a garden complete with swimming pool and offers dorm-style accommodation for L30,000 a night.

ITALY

PERUGIA

☎ 075

One of Italy's best-preserved medieval hill towns, Perugia, the capital of the Umbria region, has a lively and bloody past. The city is noted for the internal feuding of its families, the Baglioni and the Oddi, and the violent wars against its neighbours during the Middle Ages. Perugia also has a strong artistic and cultural tradition. It was the home of the painter Perugino, and Raphael, his student, also worked here. Its University for Foreigners, established in 1925, offers courses in Italian language and attracts thousands of students from all over the world. The noted jazz festival, Umbria Jazz, is held here in July.

Orientation & Information

The centre of all activity in Perugia is Corso Vannucci. The IAT tourist office (☎ 572 33 27; fax 573 93 86) is at Piazza IV Novembre 3, opposite the cathedral at one end of the Corso, and is open Monday to Saturday from 8.30 am to 1.30 pm and 3.30 to 6.30 pm (Sunday 9 am to 1 pm). The main post office

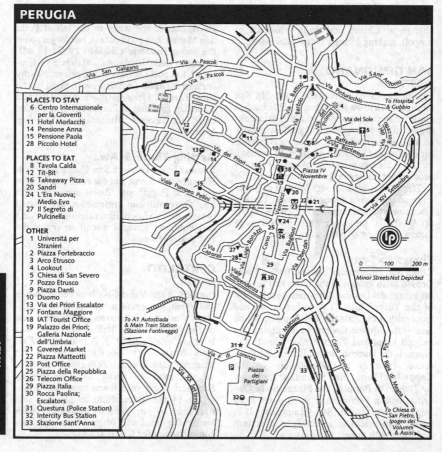

PERUGIA

PLACES TO STAY
6 Centro Internazionale per la Gioventi
11 Hotel Morlacchi
14 Pensione Anna
15 Pensione Paola
28 Piccolo Hotel

PLACES TO EAT
8 Tavola Calda
12 Tit-Bit
16 Takeaway Pizza
20 Sandri
24 L'Era Nuova; Medio Evo
27 Il Segreto di Pulcinella

OTHER
1 Universitá per Stranieri
2 Piazza Fortebraccio
3 Arco Etrusco
4 Lookout
5 Chiesa di San Severo
7 Pozzo Etrusco
9 Piazza Danti
10 Duomo
13 Via dei Priori Escalator
17 Fontana Maggiore
18 IAT Tourist Office
19 Palazzo dei Priori; Galleria Nazionale dell'Umbria
21 Covered Market
22 Piazza Matteotti
23 Post Office
25 Piazza della Repubblica
26 Telecom Office
29 Piazza Italia
30 Rocca Paolina; Escalators
31 Questura (Police Station)
32 Intercity Bus Station
33 Stazione Sant'Anna

To Hospital & Gubbio

To A1 Autostrada & Main Train Station (Stazione Fontivegge)

To Chiesa di San Pietro, Ipogeo dei Volumni & Assisi

0   100   200 m

Minor Streets Not Depicted

ITALY

is in Piazza Matteotti. The monthly *Perugia What, Where, When* (L1000 at newsstands) contains events listings and other useful information.

Things to See & Do

The **Palazzo dei Priori**, on Corso Vannucci, is a rambling 13th-century palace housing the impressively frescoed **Sala dei Notari** and the **Galleria Nazionale dell'Umbria**, with works by Pinturicchio, Perugino and Fra Angelico. Opposite the palazzo is the **Duomo**, with an unfinished façade in the characteristic Perugian red-and-white marble. Inside are frescoes, decorations and furniture by artists from the 15th to 18th centuries.

Between the two buildings, in Piazza IV Novembre, is the 13th-century **Fontana Maggiore**, designed by Fra Bevignate in 1278 and carved by Nicola and Giovanni Pisano. The bas-relief panels represent scenes of the history and trades of Perugia, the sciences and the seasons. At the other end of Corso Vannucci is the **Rocca Paolina** (Paolina Fortress), the ruins of a massive 16th-century fortress built upon the foundations of the palaces and homes of the powerful families of the day, notably the Baglioni. The homes were destroyed and the materials were used to build the fortress under the orders of Pope Paul III, as a means of suppressing the Baglioni. The fortress itself was destroyed by the Perugians after the declaration of the kingdom of Italy in 1860. In the church of **San Severo**, Piazza San Severo, is Raphael's magnificent fresco *Trinity with Saints*, one of the last works by the painter in Perugia and completed by Perugino after Raphael's death in 1520.

Etruscan remains in Perugia include the **Arco Etrusco** (Etruscan Arch), near the university, and the **Pozzo Etrusco** (Etruscan Well), off Piazza Piccinino, near the cathedral.

Courses

Perugia's University for Foreigners offers three-month courses in Italian language and culture for L1,050,000. There are six-month courses for advanced students. Special one-month courses (L350,000) and intensive courses (L500,000 per month) are offered in summer. The quality of the courses is generally good. You may need to apply for a study visa in your own country, and to obtain this you must have confirmation of enrolment in a course (see Visas & Embassies in the Facts for the Visitor section of this chapter). Since obtaining the necessary documentation from the university takes time, ensure that you send your enrolment form at least three months before your intended departure date.

The university will organise accommodation on request – call Pass Agency (☎ 573 29 92). A private room in an apartment with an Italian family will cost around L500,000 a month (L350,000 shared with another student). Course details can be obtained from Italian cultural institutes in your country, or you can write to the secretary at the Università per Stranieri, Palazzo Gallenga, Piazza Fortebraccio 4, 06122 Perugia (☎ 574 62 11; fax 574 62 13).

Places to Stay

Perugia has a good selection of reasonably priced hotels, but if you arrive unannounced in July or during August, expect problems. The non-HI *Centro Internazionale per la Gioventù* (☎ 572 28 80), Via Bontempi 13, charges L16,000 a night. Sheets (for the entire stay) are an extra L2000. Its TV room has a frescoed ceiling and its terrace has one of the best views in Perugia. Lockout is 9.30 am to 4 pm and the hostel closes between mid-December and mid-January.

Pensione Anna (☎ 573 63 04), Via dei Priori 48, off Corso Vannucci, has singles/doubles for L55,000/76,000. The *Pensione Paola* (☎ 572 38 16), Via della Canapina 5, is five minutes from the centre, down the escalator from Via dei Priori. It has pleasant singles/doubles for L43,000/65,000. Just off Corso Vannucci, at Via Luigi Bonazzi 25, is the *Piccolo Hotel* (☎ 572 29 87), where small singles/doubles with bathroom go for L55,000/75,000.

The *Hotel Morlacchi* (☎ 572 03 19), Via Tiberi 2, north-west of Piazza IV Novembre, has singles/doubles/triples for L65,000/90,000/120,000 with bathroom.

The weekly *Cerco e Trovo* (L2500 at newsstands) lists rental accommodation.

Places to Eat

Being a student town, Perugia offers many budget eating options. Good places for pizza are *L'Era Nuova*, just behind the bar *Medio Evo* on Corso Vannucci, and *Tit-Bit*, Via dei Priori 105. Another option is the popular *Il Segreto di Pulcinella*, Via Larga 8. A pizza will cost from L7000 to L14,000 at each restaurant. There is a takeaway pizza place at Via dei Priori 3. The *Tavola Calda* at Piazza Danti 16 has good, cheap food.

Sandri, Corso Vannucci, near the Palazzo dei Priori, is a great meeting place for a quiet coffee and cake, where you don't pay extra to sit down.

Getting There & Away
Perugia is not on the main Rome-Florence railway line. There are some direct trains from both cities, but most require a change, either at Foligno (from Rome) or Terontola (from Florence). Local trains (for towns such as Terni) leave from St Anna station. Intercity buses leave from Piazza Partigiani, at the end of the Rocca Paolina escalators, for Rome, Fiumicino airport, Florence, Siena and cities throughout Umbria including Assisi, Gubbio and nearby Lake Trasimeno. Full timetables for all trains and buses are available at the tourist office.

Getting Around
The main train station is a few kilometres downhill from the historical centre. Catch any bus heading for Piazza Matteotti or Piazza Italia to get to this centre. Tickets cost L1200 and must be bought before you get on the bus.

If you arrive in Perugia by car, be prepared to be confused. Roads leading to the centre wind around a hill topped by the historical centre, and the normal driving time from the base of the hill to the centre is around 10 to 15 minutes. Signs to the centre are clearly marked 'centro' and by following these signs you should arrive at Piazza Italia, where you can leave the car and walk along Corso Vannucci to the tourist office.

Most of the centre is closed to normal traffic, but tourists are allowed to drive to their hotels. It is probably wiser not to do this, as driving in central Perugia is a nightmare because of the extremely narrow streets, most of which are one way. To accommodate other traffic, escalators from the historical centre take you to large car parks

downhill. The Rocca Paolina escalator leads to Piazza dei Partigiani, where there is a supervised car park (L13,000 for the first two days, then L8500 per day), the intercity bus station, and escalators to Piazza Italia nearby. The Via dei Priori escalator leads to two major car parks.

ASSISSI
☎ 075
Despite the millions of tourists and pilgrims it attracts every year, Assisi, home of St Francis, manages to remain a beautiful and tranquil refuge (as long as you keep away from the main tourist drags). From Roman times its inhabitants have been aware of the visual impact of the city, perched halfway up Mt Subasio. From the valley its pink-and-white marble buildings literally shimmer in the sunlight. In September 1997, a strong earthquake rocked the town, causing part of the vault of the upper church of the Basilica di San Francesco to fall in, seriously damaging frescoes by Cimabue.

The APT tourist office (☎ 81 25 34; fax 81 37 27; aptas@krenet.it), Piazza del Comune, has all the information you need on hotels, sights and events in Assisi.

Things to See
Most people visit Assisi to see its religious monuments. **St Francis' Basilica** is composed of two churches, one built on top of the other. The lower church contains the crypt where St Francis is buried and is open to visitors. The upper church (under restoration at the time of writing) was decorated by the great painters of the 13th and 14th centuries, including Giotto and Cimabue. Dress rules are applied rigidly – absolutely no shorts, miniskirts or low-cut dresses/tops are allowed.

The 13th-century **Basilica di Santa Chiara** has an impressive façade. Inside are interesting 14th-century frescoes and the remains of St Clare, friend of St Francis and founder of the Order of Poor Clares. The **Cattedrale di San Rufina** is interesting for its impressive Romanesque façade. Its austere interior was altered in the 16th century, but retains the baptismal font where St Francis and St Clare were baptised. The **Piazza del Comune**, in the town centre, was the site of the Roman

Foro Romano, parts of which have been excavated; access is from Via Portico (entry L4000). The piazza also contains the **Tempio di Minerva.** It is now a church, but retains its impressive pillared façade.

Assisi's 'crown' is the **Rocca Maggiore,** a remarkably well-preserved medieval castle. In the valley below Assisi is the **Basilica di Santa Maria degli Angeli,** a huge church built around the first Franciscan monastery, and the **Cappella del Transito,** where St Francis died in 1226.

Places to Stay & Eat

Assisi is well geared for tourists and there are numerous budget hotels and affittacamere (rooms for rent). Peak periods, when you will need to book well in advance, are Easter, August and September, and the Feast of St Francis on 3 and 4 October. The tourist office has a full list of affittacamere and religious institutions.

The small HI *Ostello della Pace* (☎ 81 67 67), Via Valecchi 177, is open all year. B&B is L20,000. There is a non-HI hostel *Fontemaggio* and camping ground (☎ 81 36 36) just out of the town at Fontemaggio. It has B&B for L22,000 and singles/doubles for L45,000/70,000. From Piazza Matteotti, at the far end of town from St Francis' Basilica, walk uphill less than 2km along Via Eremo delle Carceri till you reach the hostel.

Albergo La Rocca (☎ 81 22 84), Via Porta Perlici 27, has singles/doubles for L48,000/70,000 and half-board for L58,000. The *Albergo Italia* (☎ 81 26 25), Piazza del Comune, has singles/doubles for L45,000/69,000.

For a snack of pizza by the slice, head for *Pizza Vincenzo,* just off Piazza del Comune at Via San Rufina 1a. In the same area a good self-service is *Il Foro Romano* in Via Portico. In the same complex as the camping ground at Fontemaggio is *La Stalla* (☎ 81 23 17), where you can eat a filling meal under an arbour for less than L25,000. In town try *Il Pozzo Romano* (☎ 81 30 57), Via Santa Agnese 10, off Piazza Santa Chiara. The pizzas cost around L10,000. The restaurant at the *Albergo La Rocca* (☎ 81 64 67) has home-made pasta for L5000 to L9000 and a three-course tourist menu for L18,000.

Getting There & Away

Buses connect Assisi with Perugia, Foligno and other local towns, leaving from Piazza Santa Chiara. Buses for Rome and Florence leave from Piazza San Pietro. Assisi's train station is in the valley, in the suburb of Santa Maria degli Angeli. It is on the same line as Perugia and there is a shuttle bus service between the town and the station.

UMBRIA

Umbria is a mountainous region characterised by its many medieval hill towns. After Perugia and Assisi, visit **Gubbio** (north of Perugia) and **Spello, Spoleto, Todi** and **Orvieto** to appreciate the Romanesque and Gothic architecture, particularly Orvieto's cathedral, considered one of the most beautiful in Italy. Try to time your visit to take in the Festival of Two Worlds at Spoleto in late June and early July. These hill towns are accessible by bus or train from Perugia, and the tourist office there has information and timetables.

ANCONA
☎ 071

The main reason to visit Ancona is to catch a ferry to Croatia, Greece or Turkey. This industrial, unattractive port town in the region of the Marches does, however, have an interesting, though small and semi-abandoned, historical centre.

Orientation & Information

The easiest way to get from the train station to the port is by bus No 1. There are tourist information offices at the train station and the stazione marittima (seasonal). The main APT office (☎ 349 38) is out of the way at Via Thaon de Revel 4. The main post office is at Piazza XXIV Maggio, open Monday to Saturday from 8.15 am to 7 pm.

Things to See

Walk uphill to the old town and the **Piazzale del Duomo** for a view of the port and the Adriatic. The town's Romanesque **cathedral** was built on the site of a Roman temple and has Byzantine and Gothic features. The church of **San Francesco delle Scale** has a beautiful Venetian-Gothic doorway, and towards the port are the 15th-century **Loggia dei Mercanti** (Merchants' Loggia) and the Romanesque church of **Santa Maria della Piazza**, which has a remarkable, heavily adorned façade.

Places to Stay & Eat

Many people bunk down at the ferry terminal, although the city has many cheap hotels. *Albergo Fiore* (☎ 433 90), Piazza Rosselli 24, has singles/doubles for L40,000/65,000 and is just across from the train station. The *Pensione Centrale* (☎ 543 88), Via Marsala 10 (near Corso Stamira), has doubles from L55,000.

Trattoria da Dina (☎ 523 39), Vicolo ad Alto 3 in the old town, has full meals for L19,000. For atmosphere and good fare head for *Osteria Teatro Strabacco*, Via Oberdan 2, near Corso Stamira. The *Mercato Pubblico*, off Corso Mazzini, has fresh fruit and vegetables and alimentari.

Getting There & Away

Bus & Train Buses depart from Piazza Cavour for towns throughout the Marches region. Rome is served by Marozzi (☎ 0734-85 91 18). Ancona is on the Bologna-Lecce train line and thus easily accessible from major towns throughout Italy. It is also directly linked to Rome via Foligno.

Boat All ferry operators have information booths at the ferry terminal, off Piazza Kennedy. Remember that timetables are always subject to change and that prices fluctuate dramatically with the season. Most lines offer discounts on return fares. Prices listed are for one-way deck class in the 1998 high season.

Companies include the following: Superfast (☎ 207 02 40) to Patras in Greece (L148,000); Minoan Lines (☎ 567 89) to Igoumenitsa and Patras (L120,000); Adriatica (☎ 20 49 15) to Durrës in Albania (L155,000) and to Split in Croatia (L75,000).

URBINO
☎ 0722

This town in the Marches can be difficult to reach, but it is worth the effort to see the birthplace of Raphael and Bramante, which has changed little since the Middle Ages and remains a centre of art, culture and learning.

The APT tourist information office (☎ 27 88) is at Piazza Duca Federico 35.

Things to See & Do

Urbino's main sight is the huge **Palazzo Ducale**, designed by Laurana and completed in 1482. The best view is from Corso Garibaldi to the west, from where you can appreciate the size of the building and see its towers and loggias. Enter the palace from Piazza Duca Federico and visit the **Galleria Nazionale delle Marches**, featuring works by Raphael, Paolo Uccello and Verrocchio. The palace is open Tuesday to Saturday from 9 am to 7 pm (with plans to extend to 10 pm) and Sunday, Monday and holidays to 2 pm. Entry is L8000. Also visit the **Casa di Rafaello**, Via Raffaello 57, where the artist Raphael was born, and the **Oratorio di San Giovanni Battista**, with 15th-century frescoes by the Salimbeni brothers.

Courses

Urbino's Università degli Studi offers an intensive course in Italian language and culture for foreigners from 3 to 29 August. This one-month courses cost L650,000.

Brochures and enrolment forms can be obtained from Italian cultural institutes in your country or by writing to the secretary, Università degli Studi di Urbino, Via Saffi 2, 61029 Urbino, Pesaro (☎ 30 52 50; fax 30 52 87; corstran@bib.uniurb.it). The university will arrange your accommodation through the Ufficio Alloggi dell'ERSU, Via del Popolo 9, 61029 Urbino (☎ 271 46; fax 27 99). The cost of accommodation is around L250,000 per month.

Places to Stay & Eat

Urbino is a major university town and most cheap beds are taken by students during the school year. The tourist office has a full list of affittacamere. The *Pensione Fosca* (☎ 32 96 22), Via Raffaello 67, has doubles/triples for L59,000/70,000. *Albergo Italia* (☎ 27 01), Corso Garibaldi 32, is next to the Palazzo Ducale and has singles/doubles from L55,000/85,000.

There are numerous bars around Piazza della Repubblica in the town centre and near the Palazzo Ducale which sell good panini. Try **Pizzeria Galli**, Via Vittorio Veneto 19, for takeaway pizza by the slice. **Ristorante Da Franco**, just off Piazza del Rinascimento, next to the university, has a self-service section where you can eat a full meal for around L20,000.

Getting There & Away

There is no train service to Urbino, but it is connected by SAPUM and Bucci buses on weekdays to cities including Ancona, Pesaro and Arezzo. There is a bus link to the train station at the town of Fossato di Vico, on the Rome-Ancona line. There are also buses to Rome twice a day. All buses arrive at Borgo Mercatale, down Via Mazzini from Piazza della Repubblica. The tourist office has timetables for all bus services.

Southern Italy

The land of the *mezzogiorno* (midday sun) will surprise even the most world-weary traveller. Rich in history and cultural traditions, the southern regions are poorer than those of the north, and certainly the wheels of bureaucracy grind more slowly as you travel closer to the tip of the boot. The attractions here are simpler and more stark, the people more vibrant and excitable, and myths and legends are inseparable from official history. Campania, Apulia and Basilicata cry out to be explored and absolutely nothing can prepare you for Naples. Less well known among foreigners, Calabria has beautiful beaches and the striking scenery of the Pollino and Sila Massif.

NAPLES
☎ 081

Crazy and confusing, but also seductive and fascinating, Naples (Napoli), capital of the Campania region, has an energy that is palpable. Beautifully positioned on the Bay of Naples and overshadowed by Mt Vesuvius, it is one of the most densely populated cities in Europe. You will leave Naples with a head full of its classic images – laundry strung across narrow streets, three people and a dog on one Vespa, cars speeding along alleys no wider than a driveway, and the same streets teeming with locals shopping at outdoor markets and drinking wine or caffè with friends.

Naples has its own secret society of criminals, the Camorra, which traditionally concentrated its activities on the import and sale of contraband cigarettes, but has now diversified into drugs, construction, finance and tourist developments.

Orientation

Both the Stazione Centrale (central train station) and the main bus terminal are in the vast Piazza Garibaldi. Naples is divided into *quartieri* (quarters). The main thoroughfare into the historical centre, Spaccanapoli, is Corso Umberto I, which heads south-west from Piazza Garibaldi. West on the bay are Santa Lucia and Mergellina, both fashionable and picturesque and a far cry from the chaotic, noisy historical centre. South-west of Mergellina is Posillipo, where the ultra-wealthy live, and in the hills overlooking the bay is the residential Vomero district.

Information

Tourist Offices The EPT office at the station (☎ 26 87 79) will make hotel bookings, but make sure you give specific details on where you want to stay and how much you want to pay. Some staff speak English. Ask for *Qui Napoli* (Here Naples), published monthly in English and Italian, which lists events in the city, as well as information about transport and other services. The office is open Monday to Saturday from 8.30 am to 8 pm and on Sunday from 9 am to 2 pm.

There's an AAST office in Piazza del Gesù (☎ 552 33 28), near Piazza Dante, open Monday to Saturday from 9 am to 5 pm and Sunday 9 am to 2 pm.

Money There is a branch of the Banca della Comunicazioni in the station, open Monday to Saturday from 8.20 am to 1.20 pm and 2.45 to 3.45 pm.

Post & Communications The main post office is in Piazza G Matteotti, off Via Armando Diaz. It's open weekdays from 8.15 am to 7.30 pm and Saturday to 1 pm.

NAPLES (NAPOLI)

PLACES TO STAY
3 Alloggio Fiamma
4 Hotel Bellini
7 Hotel Primus
8 Hotel Zara

PLACES TO EAT
13 La Brace
14 Trattoria Avellinese
16 Trianon
17 Michele
18 Il Pizzicotto
24 Friggitoria Pizzeria
25 Lo Sfizietto

OTHER
1 Museo Archeologico Nazionale
2 Piazza Cavour
5 Duomo
6 Piazza Principe Umberto
9 EPT Tourist Office
10 All-Night Pharmacy
11 Piazza Garibaldi
12 Urban & Intercity Bus Station
15 Hospital
19 Chiesa di Santa Chiara
20 Piazza del Gesù Nuovo; AAST Tourist Office
21 Chiesa del Gesù Nuovo
22 Piazza Dante
23 Stazione Cumana; Piazza Montesanto
26 Piazza Carità
27 Post Office
28 Piazza G Matteotti
29 Questura (Police Station)
30 Telecom
31 Telephone Office
32 Piazza Municipio
33 Town Hall
34 Galleria Umberto I
35 Castel Nuovo
36 Stazione Marittima (Long-Distance Ferries)
37 Molo Beverello (Local Ferries)
38 Palazzo Reale
39 Piazza Trento e Trieste
40 Piazza del Plebiscito

There is a Telecom office at Via A Depretis 40, open daily from 9 am to 10 pm.
The postcode for central Naples is 80100.

Medical & Emergency Services For an ambulance call ☎ 118. Each city quarter has a Guardia Medica (after hours medical service), check in *Qui Napoli* for details. The Ospedale Loreto Mare (☎ 254 28 40) is near the station, in Largo di Via Vespucci. The pharmacy in the central station is open daily from 8 am to 8 pm.

Call ☎ 113 for the police. The questura (☎ 794 11 11), Via Medina 75, just off Via Armando Diaz, has an office for foreigners where you can report thefts etc.

Dangers & Annoyances The petty crime rate in Naples is extremely high. Carry your money and documents in a money belt and never carry a bag or purse if you can help it. It is a good idea to put your jewellery away too. The city council has started to crack down on bag-snatching thieves on motorcycles, but you should still keep on the alert. Car theft is also a major problem, so think twice before bringing a vehicle to the city.

Women should be careful at night near the station and around Piazza Dante. The area west of Via Toledo and as far north as Piazza Carità can be particularly threatening.

Naples' legendary traffic is less chaotic these days, but you will still need to take care when crossing roads.

Things to See & Do
Start by walking around Spaccanapoli, the historic centre of Naples. From the station and Corso Umberto I turn right into Via Mezzocannone, which will take you to Via Benedetto Croce, the main street of the quarter. To the left is Piazza del Gesù Nuovo, with the Neapolitan baroque **Chiesa di Gesù Nuovo** and the 14th-century **Chiesa di Santa Chiara**, restored to its original Gothic-Provençal style after it was severely damaged by bombing during WWII. The beautiful **Chiostro delle Clarisse** (Nuns' Cloisters) should not be missed.

The **Duomo** (Via Duomo) has a 19th-century façade but was built by the Angevin kings at the end of the 13th century, on the site of an earlier basilica. Inside is the **Cappella di San Gennaro**, which contains the head of St Januarius (the city's patron saint) and two vials of his congealed blood. The saint is said to have saved the city from plague, volcanic eruptions and other disasters. Every year the faithful gather to pray for a miracle, namely that the blood will liquefy and save the city from further disaster (see under Special Events).

Turn off Via Duomo into **Via Tribunali**, one of the more characteristic streets of the area, and head for Piazza Dante, through the 17th-century **Port'Alba**, one of the gates to the city. Via Roma, the most fashionable street in old Naples, heads to the left (becoming Via Toledo) and ends at Piazza Trento e Trieste and the **Piazza del Plebiscito**.

In the piazza is the **Palazzo Reale**, the former official residence of the Bourbon and Savoy kings, now a museum. It is open Tuesday to Sunday from 9 am to 1.30 pm and also from 4 to 7.30 pm on weekends. Admission is L8000. Just off the piazza is the **Teatro San Carlo**, one of the most famous opera houses in the world thanks to its perfect acoustics and beautiful interior.

The 13th-century **Castel Nuovo** overlooks Naples' ferry port. The early-Renaissance triumphal arch commemorates the entry of Alfonso I of Aragon into Naples in 1443. It is possible to visit the **Museo Civico** in the castle. South-west along the waterfront at Santa Lucia is the **Castel dell'Ovo**, originally a Norman castle, which is surrounded by a tiny fishing village, the **Borgo Marinaro**.

The **Museo Archeologico Nazionale** is in Piazza Museo, north of Piazza Dante. It contains one of the most important collections of Graeco-Roman artefacts in the world, mainly the rich collection of the Farnese family, and the art treasures that were discovered at Pompeii and Herculaneum. The museum opens Tuesday to Saturday from 9 am to 10 pm (Sunday to 8 pm). Admission is L12,000.

To escape the noisy city centre, catch the Funicolare Centrale (funicular), in Via Toledo, to the suburb of Vomero and visit the Certosa di San Martino, a 14th-century Carthusian monastery, rebuilt in the 17th century in Neapolitan-baroque style. It houses the **Museo Nazionale di San Martino**. The monastery's church is well worth a visit, as are its terraced gardens, which afford spectacular views of Naples and the bay. The monastery is open Tuesday to Sunday from 9 am to 2 pm. Entry is L8000.

Special Events

Religious festivals are lively occasions in Naples, especially the celebration of St Januarius, the patron saint of the city, held three times a year (the first Sunday in May, 19 September and 16 December) in the Duomo.

Places to Stay

Hostel The HI *Ostello Mergellina Napoli* (☎ 761 23 46), Salita della Grotta 23 in Mergellina, is modern, safe and the best budget option in the city. B&B is L22,000 per person in rooms of four or six beds. Dinner is L14,000 and there's a bar. It's open all year and imposes a maximum three-night stay in summer; it also requires an AIG card (L30,000 for foreigners). Take bus No 152 from the station, or the Metropolitana to Mergellina, and signs will direct you to the hostel from the waterfront.

Hotels Most of the cheap hotels are near the station and Piazza Garibaldi in a rather unsavoury area, and some of the cheaper hotels double as brothels. It is best to ask the tourist office at the station to recommend or book a room.

Station Area The following hotels are safe and offer a reasonable standard of accommodation. The *Hotel Zara* (☎ 28 71 25), Via Firenze 81, is clean with singles/doubles for L35,000/55,000. Via Firenze is off Corso Novara, to the right as you leave the train station. *Albergo Ginevra* (☎ 28 32 10), Via Genova 116, the second street to the right off Corso Novara, is another reliable and well-kept place with singles/doubles for L40,000/60,000 and triples for L90,000. The *Casanova Hotel* (☎ 26 82 87), Corso Garibaldi 333, is quiet and safe. Singles/doubles are L35,000/60,000; triples with shower are L80,000. *Hotel Primus* (☎ 554 73 54), Via Torino 26, has good-standard, renovated rooms with bathroom from L50,000/85,000.

Piazza Dante Area The *Alloggio Fiamma* (☎ 45 91 87), Via Francesco del Giudice 13,

has very very basic rooms for L35,000 a head. Another option is *Hotel Bellini* (☎ 45 69 96), Via San Paolo 44, with singles/ doubles for L40,000/70,000.

Out of the Centre In Santa Lucia, *Pensione Astoria* (☎ 764 99 03), Via Santa Lucia 90, has singles/doubles for L35,000/60,000. In the same building is *Albergo Teresita* (☎ 764 01 05) with rooms for L40,000/ 60,000. At Vomero, just near the funicular station, is *Pensione Margherita* (☎ 556 70 44), Via D Cimarosa 29. This hotel is more upmarket and charges L50,000/90,000. Ask for a room with a bay view. Have a L50 coin on hand for the lift.

Places to Eat

Naples is the home of pasta and pizza. In fact, once you have eaten a good Neapolitan pizza, topped with fresh tomatoes, oregano, basil and garlic, no other pizza will taste the same. Try a calzone, a filled version of a pizza, or mozzarella in carozza (mozzarella deep-fried in bread) which is sold at tiny street stalls. Also sold at street stalls is the misto di frittura (deep-fried vegetables). Don't leave town without trying the sfogliatelle (light, flaky pastry filled with ricotta).

Restaurants There are several inexpensive places to eat in and around Naples' centre.

City Centre According to the locals the best pizza in Naples is served at *Trianon*, Via Pietro Colletta 46, near Via Tribunali. There's a wide selection from L6000. Across the street is *Michele*, another good pizzeria. Nearer the station is *Trattoria Avellinese*, Via Silvio Spaventa 31-35, just off Piazza Garibaldi, which specialises in cheap seafood. Just down the street at No 14 is *La Brace*, a no-nonsense cheap place to eat. *Il Pizzicotto*, Via Mezzocannone 129, has good pizzas and full meals cost around L15,000.

Mergellina & Vomero For a good meal, Neapolitans head for the area around Piazza Sannazzaro, south-west of the centre which is also handy to the HI hostel. *Pizzeria da Pasqualino*, Piazza Sannazzaro 79, has outdoor tables and serves good pizzas and seafood. A meal will cost around L20,000 with wine. *Daniele*, Via A Scarlatti 104, is a bar with a restaurant upstairs. *Cibo Cibo*, Via Cimarosa 150, is another good budget spot.

Food Stalls On the corner of Vico Basilico Puoti and Via Pignasecca is *Lo Sfizietto*. *Friggitoria Pizzeria* is at Piazza Montesanto. Both offer lots of cheap goodies.

Entertainment

The monthly *Qui Napoli* and the local newspapers are the only real guides to what's on. In July there is a series of free concerts called *Luglio Musicale a Capodimonte* outside the Capodimonte Palace. The *Teatro San Carlo* has year-round performances of opera, ballet and concerts. Tickets start at L15,000. Call ☎ 797 21 11 for bookings and information.

Things to Buy

The area around Naples is famous for its ceramic products and many small shops in the city and surrounding areas sell hand-painted ceramics at reasonable prices. Young people shop along Via Roma and Via Toledo. More exclusive shops are found in Santa Lucia, along Via Chiaia to Piazza dei Martiri and down towards the waterfront. Naples is renowned for the work of its goldsmiths and for its *presepi* (nativity scenes). Most artisans are in Spaccanapoli.

The narrow streets of Naples are full of markets, notably in the area off Via Mancinio (off Piazza Garibaldi), near Piazza Carità (which separates Via Roma and Via Toledo) and around Piazza Montesanto.

Getting There & Away

Air The Capodichino airport (☎ 789 62 68), Viale Umberto Maddalena, is about 5km north-east of the city centre. There are connections to most Italian and several European cities. Bus No 14 leaves from Piazza Garibaldi every 20 minutes for the airport (20 minutes).

Bus Buses leave from Piazza Garibaldi, just outside the train station, for destinations including Salerno, Benevento, Caserta (every 20 minutes) and Bari, Lecce and Brindisi in Apulia.

Train Naples is a major rail-transport centre for the south, and regular trains for most major Italian cities arrive and depart from the Stazione Centrale. There are up to 30 trains a day for Rome.

Car & Motorcycle Driving in Naples is not recommended. The traffic is chaotic and car and motorcycle theft is rife. However, the city is easily accessible from Rome on the A1. The Naples-Pompeii-Salerno road connects with the coastal road to Sorrento and the Amalfi Coast.

Boat Traghetti (small ferries), aliscafi (hydrofoils) and new *navi veloce* (fast ships) leave for Capri, Sorrento, Ischia and Procida from the Molo Beverello, in front of the Castel Nuovo. Some hydrofoils leave for the bay islands from Mergellina, and ferries for Ischia and Procida also leave from Pozzuoli. All operators have offices at the various ports from which they leave. Tickets for the hydrofoils cost around double those for ferries, but the trip takes half the time.

Ferries to Palermo and Cagliari (Tirrenia ☎ 720 11 11) and to the Aeolian Islands (Siremar ☎ 761 36 88) leave from the Stazione Marittima on Molo Angioino, next to Molo Beverello (see the Getting There & Away sections under Sicily and Sardinia). SNAV (☎ 761 23 48) runs regular ferries and, in summer, hydrofoils to the islands.

Getting Around

You can make your way around Naples by bus, tram, Metropolitana (underground) and funicular. City buses leave from Piazza Garibaldi in front of the central station bound for the centre of Naples, as well as Mergellina. Tickets, called *GiraNapoli*, cost L1500 for 90 minutes and are valid for buses, trams, the Metropolitana and funicular services. Day tickets cost L4500. Useful buses include: No 14 to the airport; Nos R2 and R1 to Piazza Dante; and No 110 from Piazza Garibaldi to Piazza Cavour and the archaeological museum. Tram No 1 leaves from east of Stazione Centrale for the city centre. To get to Molo Beverello and the ferry terminal from the train station, take bus No R2 or 152, a bus called 'La Sepsa', or the M1.

ITALY

The Metropolitana station is downstairs at central station. Trains head west to Mergellina, stopping at Piazza Cavour, Piazza Amedeo and the funicular to Vomero, and then head on to the Campi Flegrei and Pozzuoli. Another line, now under construction, will eventually connect Piazza Garibaldi and Piazza Medaglie d'Oro, with stops including the Museo Archeologico Nazionale.

The main funicular connecting the city centre with Vomero is the Funicolare Centrale in Piazza Duca d'Aosta, next to Galleria Umberto I, on Via Toledo.

The Ferrovia Circumvesuviana operates trains for Herculaneum, Pompeii and Sorrento. The station is about 400m south-west of Stazione Centrale, in Corso Garibaldi (take the underpass from Stazione Centrale). The Ferrovia Cumana and the Circumflegrei, based at Stazione Cumana in Piazza Montesanto, operate services to Pozzuoli, Baia and Cumae every 20 minutes.

AROUND NAPLES

From Naples it's only a short distance to the **Campi Flegrei** (Phlegraean Fields) of volcanic lakes and mud baths, which inspired both Homer and Virgil in their writings. Today part of suburban Naples, the area is dirty and overdeveloped, but still worth a day trip. The Greek colony of **Cumae** is certainly worth visiting, particularly to see the Cave of the Cumaean Sybil, home of one of the ancient world's greatest oracles. Also in the area is **Lake Avernus**, the mythical entrance to the underworld, and **Baia** with its submerged Roman ruins visible from a glass-bottomed boat.

Reached by ACTC bus from Naples' Piazza Garibaldi or by train from the Stazione Centrale is the **Palazzo Reale** at Caserta (☎ 0823-32 11 37), usually called the Reggia di Caserta. Built by the Bourbon king Charles III, this massive 1200-room palace is set in gardens modelled on Versailles.

Pompeii & Herculaneum
☎ 081

Buried under a layer of lapilli (burning fragments of pumice stone) during the devastating eruption of Mt Vesuvius in 79 AD, **Pompeii** provides a fascinating insight into how the ancient Romans lived. It was a resort town for wealthy Romans, and among the vast ruins are impressive temples, a forum, one of the largest known Roman amphitheatres, and streets lined with shops and luxurious houses. Many of the site's mosaics and frescoes have been moved to Naples' Museo Archeologico Nazionale. The exception is the Villa dei Misteri, where the frescoes remain *in situ*. Many houses and shops are closed, but efforts are underway to open more of Pompeii to the public.

There are tourist offices (AACST) at Via Sacra 1 (☎ 850 72 55) in the new town, and just outside the excavations at Piazza Porta Marina Inferiore 12 (☎ 167-01 33 50 toll-free). Both offer information for visitors, notes on guided tours and a simple map of the ancient city. The ruins are open from 9 am to one hour before sunset and entry is L12,000.

Catch the Circumvesuviana train from Naples and get off at the Pompeii-Villa dei Misteri stop; the Porta Marina entrance is close by.

Herculaneum (Ercolano) is closer to Naples and is also a good point from which to visit Mt Vesuvius. Legend says the city was founded by Hercules. First Greek, then Roman, it was also destroyed by the 79 AD eruption, buried under mud and lava. Most inhabitants of Herculaneum had enough warning and managed to escape. The ruins here are smaller and the buildings, particularly the private houses, are remarkably well preserved. Here you can see better examples of the frescoes, mosaics and furniture that used to decorate Roman houses.

Herculaneum is also accessible on the Circumvesuviana train from Naples. The ruins are open daily from 9 am to one hour before sunset. Entry is L12,000.

If you want to have a look into the huge crater of Mt Vesuvius, catch the Trasporti Vesuviani bus (☎ 739 28 33) from the piazza in front of the Ercolano train station or from Pompeii's Piazza Anfiteatro. The return ticket costs L6000 from Ercolano and L10,000 from Pompeii. The first bus leaves Pompeii at about 9 am and takes 30 minutes to reach Herculaneum. You'll then need to walk about 1.5km to the summit, where you must pay L5500 to be accompanied by a guide to the crater. See Lonely Planet's new *Walking in Italy* guide for detailed information on walking circuits on Vesuvius. The last bus returns to Pompeii from Herculaneum's Quota 1000 car park at 5.45 pm in summer and at 5 pm in winter.

SORRENTO
☎ 081

This major resort town is in a particularly beautiful area, but is heavily overcrowded in summer with package tourists and traffic. However, it is handy to the Amalfi Coast and Capri.

Information

The centre of town is Piazza Tasso, a short walk from the train station along Corso Italia. The AAST tourist office (☎ 807 40 33), Via Luigi de Maio 35, is inside the Circolo dei Forestieri complex. The office is open Monday to Saturday from 8.30 am to 2 pm and 3.30 to 6.30 pm.

The post office is at Corso Italia 210 and the Telecom telephone office is at Piazza Tasso 37. Sorrento's postcode is 80067.

For medical assistance contact the Ospedale Civile (☎ 533 11 11). For the police call ☎ 113.

Places to Stay

There are several camping grounds, including *Nube d'Argento* (☎ 878 13 44), Via Capo 21, which costs L15,000 per person and up to L12,000 for a tent site.

The HI *Ostello Le Sirene* (☎ 807 29 25), Via degli Aranci 160, near the train station, offers B&B for L23,000.

Albergo City (☎ 877 22 10), Corso Italia 221, has singles/doubles with bathroom for L70,000/90,000. *Pensione Linda* (☎ 878 29 16), Via degli Aranci 125, has single/doubles with bathroom for L45,000/75,000.

Places to Eat

You can get a cheap meal at *Self-Service Angelina Lauro*, Piazza Angelino Lauro. *Giardinello*, Via dell'Accademia 7, has pizzas from about L7000. In Via San Cesareo, off Piazza Tasso, there are several alimentari where you can buy food for picnics.

Getting There & Away

Sorrento is easily accessible from Naples on the Circumvesuviana train line. SITA buses leave from outside the train station for the Amalfi Coast. Hydrofoils and ferries leave from the port, along Via de Maio and down the steps from the tourist office, for Capri and Napoli all year round and Ischia in summer only.

In summer, traffic is heavy along the coastal roads to Sorrento.

CAPRI
☎ 081

This beautiful island, an hour by ferry from Naples, retains the mythical appeal which attracted Roman emperors, including Augustus and Tiberius, who built 12 villas here. The town of Capri is packed with tourists in summer, but is more peaceful in the low season. A short bus ride will take you to Anacapri, the town uphill from Capri – a good alternative if rooms are full in Capri. The island is famous for its grottoes, but is also a good place for walking. There are tourist offices at Marina Grande (☎ 837 06 34), where all the ferries arrive, in Piazza Umberto I (☎ 837 06 86; fax 837 09 18; touristoffice@capri.it) in the centre of town, and at Piazza Vittoria 4 in Anacapri (☎ 837 15 24).

Things to See & Do

There are expensive boat tours of the grottoes, including the famous **Grotta Azzurra** (Blue Grotto). Boats leave from the Marina Grande and a round trip will cost about L23,000 (which includes the cost of a motorboat to the grotto, rowing boat into the grotto and entrance fee). It is cheaper to catch a bus from Anacapri (although the rowboat and entrance fee still total around L15,000). It is possible to swim into the grotto before 9 am and after 5 pm, but do so only in company and when the sea is very calm. You can walk to most of the interesting points on the island. Sights include the **Giardini d'Augusto**, in the town of Capri, and **Villa Jovis**, the ruins of one of Tiberius' villas, along the Via Longano and Via Tiberio. The latter is a one-hour walk uphill from Capri. Also visit the **Villa San Michele** at Anacapri.

ITALY

Places to Stay & Eat

The ***Stella Maris*** (☎ 837 04 52), Via Roma 27, just off Piazza Umberto I, is right in the noisy heart of town. Singles/doubles are L80,000/150,000 and triples/quads are an additional 30%. *Villa Luisa* (☎ 837 01 28), Via D Birago 1, and *Vuotto Antonino* (☎ 837 02 30), Via Capo di Teste 2, have nice rooms with great views for around L90,000 a double.

In Anacapri, the *Loreley* (☎ 837 14 40), Via G Orlandi 16, near the town centre, has singles/doubles with bathroom for L100,000/150,000. The *Caesar Augustus* (☎ 837 14 21), Via G Orlandi 4, is a beautiful hotel which becomes a knockout bargain in the off season and when there are empty rooms. It opens from 1 May to the end of October.

In Capri, try *La Cisterna*, Via M Serafina 5, for a pizza. In Anacapri try the *Trattoria il Solitario*, in a garden setting at Via G Orlandi 54. Another good place is *Il Saraceno*, Via Trieste e Trento 18, where a full meal could cost up to L30,000. Try the lemon liqueur.

Getting There & Away

See the Getting There & Away section under Naples.

Getting Around

From Marina Grande, the funicular directly in front of the port takes you to the town of Capri (L1500), which is at the top of a steep hill some 3km from the port up a winding road. Small local buses connect the port with Capri, Anacapri and other points around the island (L1500 for one trip).

AMALFI COAST
☎ 089

The Amalfi Coast swarms with rich tourists in summer and prices are correspondingly high. However, it remains a place of rare and spectacular beauty and if you can manage to get there in spring or autumn, you will be surprised by the reasonably priced accommodation and peaceful atmosphere.

There are tourist information offices in the individual towns, including Positano (☎ 87 50 67; fax 87 57 60) at Via Saracino 2, and Amalfi (☎ 87 11 07) on the waterfront at Marina Grande.

Positano

This is the most beautiful town on the coast, but for exactly this reason it has also become the most fashionable. It is, however, still possible to stay here cheaply.

Villa Nettuno (☎ 87 54 01), Via Pasitea 208, has doubles for L110,000 in the high season, all with private bath, though prices vary according to the length of stay. Half of the rooms are new and have small balconies overlooking the sea. The older rooms are cheaper and open onto a large terrace. Book well in advance for summer.

Villa Maria Luisa (☎ 87 50 23), Via Fornillo 40, has double rooms with terraces for L45,000 per person in the low season and L60,000 per person, breakfast included, in August. The *Villa delle Palme* (☎ 87 51 62), around the corner in Via Pasitea, is run by the same management and charges slightly higher prices. Next door is the pizzeria *Il Saraceno d'Oro*.

Around Positano

The hills behind Positano offer some great walks if you tire of lazing on the beach. The tourist office at Positano has a brochure listing four routes, ranging in length from two to four hours. Visit **Nocelle**, a tiny, isolated village above Positano, accessible by walking track from the end of the road from Positano. Have lunch at *Trattoria Santa Croce* (☎ 81 12 60), which has a terrace with panoramic views. It is open for both lunch and dinner in summer, but at other times of the year it is best to telephone and check in advance. From Nocelle, a walking track leads directly up into the hills overlooking the Amalfi Coast. Nocelle is accessible by local bus from Positano, via Montepertuso.

On the way from Positano to Amalfi is the town of **Praiano**, which is not as scenic but has more budget options, including the only camping ground on the Amalfi Coast. *La Tranquillità* (☎ 87 40 84) has a pensione, bungalows and a small camping ground. It costs L25,000 per head to camp there if you have your own tent. For a double room or bungalow it is L100,000 (with breakfast) and in summer there is compulsory half-pension at L105,000 per head including room, private bathroom, breakfast and dinner. The SITA bus stops outside the pensione. The entire establishment closes down in winter, reopening at Easter.

The *Pensione Aquila* (☎ 87 40 65) at Via degli Ulivi 15 charges L90,000 a double with breakfast and L100,000 in August, L70,000 per person half-board.

Amalfi

One of the four powerful maritime republics of medieval Italy, Amalfi today is a popular tourist resort. Despite this, it manages to retain a tranquil atmosphere. It has an impressive **Duomo**, and nearby is the **Grotta dello Smeraldo**, which rivals Capri's Blue Grotto.

In the hills behind Amalfi is **Ravello**, accessible by bus and worth a visit if only to see the magnificent 11th-century **Villa Rufolo**, once the home of popes and, later, of the German composer Wagner. The **Villa Cimbrone**, built this century, is set in beautiful gardens, which end at a terrace offering a spectacular view of the Gulf of Salerno. There are numerous walking paths in the hills between Amalfi and Ravello. Pick up the book *Walks from Amalfi – The Guide to a Web of Ancient Italian Pathways* (L10,000) in Amalfi.

Places to Stay & Eat The HI *Ostello Beato Solitudo* (☎ 081-802 50 48) is at Piazza G Avitabile, in Agerola San Lazzaro, a village just 16km west of Amalfi. It charges L16,000 for bed only. A bus leaves every 45 minutes from Amalfi, the last at 8.50 pm.

For a room in Amalfi, try the *Albergo Proto* (☎ 87 10 03), Salita dei Curiali 4, which has rooms from L60,000/95,000, breakfast included. The *Hotel Lidomare* (☎ 87 13 32) is at Via Piccolomini 9 (follow the signs from Piazza del Duomo and go left up a flight of stairs). A double costs more than L130,000 in the high season, but rates are affordable at other times of the year.

Cheaper accommodation can be found at Atrani, just around the corner from Amalfi towards Salerno. *A Scalinatella* (☎ 87 14 92), just off Piazza Umberto, has beds in dorms for two, four and six people from L25,000 per person, breakfast included, and half-board for students for L35,000. It also has doubles with bathroom for L100,000.

In Amalfi, *Trattoria Pizzeria al Teatro*, Via Ercolano Marini 19 (follow the signs to the left from Via Pietro Capuana, the main shopping street of Piazza del Duomo), offers good food in very pleasant surroundings. A pizza costs between L7000 and L15,000, pasta costs up to L10,000 and fish up to L15,000. *Trattoria da Maria*, Via Lorenzo d'Amalfi 14, is good value with meals for around L45,000. *A Scalinatella* in Atrani also has a trattoria with meals for L25,000.

Getting There & Away

Bus The coast is accessible by regular SITA buses, which run between Salerno (a 40-minute train trip from Naples) and Sorrento (accessible from Naples on the Circumvesuviana train line). Buses stop in Amalfi at Piazza Flavio Gioia, from where you can catch a bus to Ravello.

Car & Motorcycle The coastal road is narrow and in summer it is clogged with traffic, so be prepared for long delays. At other times of the year you should have no problems. Hire a motorcycle in Sorrento, Salerno or Maiori.

Boat Hydrofoils and ferries also service the coast, leaving from Salerno and stopping at Amalfi and Positano. From Positano in summer you can catch a boat to Capri.

PAESTUM

The evocative image of three Greek temples standing in fields of poppies is not easily forgotten and makes the trek to this archaeological site well worth the effort. The three temples, just south of Salerno, are among the world's best preserved monuments of the ancient Greek world. There is a tourist office (☎ 0828-81 10 16) open from 9 am to 2 pm and an interesting museum (L8000) at the site, open daily (except the first and third Mondays of the month) from 9 am to 6.30 pm (to 10 pm in summer). The ruins are open daily from 9 am to two hours before sunset and entry is L8000.

Paestum is accessible from Salerno by ATACS bus or by train.

MATERA

☎ 0835

This ancient city in the region of Basilicata evokes powerful images of a peasant culture which existed until just over 30 years ago. Its famous *sassi* (the stone houses built in the two ravines which slice through the city) were home to more than half of Matera's population (about 20,000 people) until the 1950s, when the local government built a new residential area just out of Matera and relocated the entire population.

Information

The tourist office (☎ 33 19 83), Via de Viti De Marco 9, off Via Roma (which runs off Piazza V Veneto) can organise a professional tour guide (L,110,000 for three hours, maximum 25 people).

Things to See

The two sassi wards, known as **Barisano** and **Caveoso**, had no electricity, running water or sewerage until well into this century. The oldest sassi are at the top of the ravines, and the dwellings which appear to be the oldest were established in this century. As space ran out in the 1920s, the population started moving into hand-hewn or natural caves, an extraordinary example of civilisation in reverse. The sassi zones are accessible from Piazza Vittorio Veneto and Piazza del Duomo in the centre of Matera. Be sure to see the rock churches, **Santa Maria d'Idris** and **Santa Lucia alla Malve**, both with amazingly well-preserved Byzantine frescoes. The 13th-century Apulian-Romanesque **cathedral**, overlooking Sasso Barisano, is also worth a visit. In Sasso Caveoso you could be approached by young children wanting to act as tour guides.

Some sassi are now being restored and some people have begun to move back into the area. Recent excavations in Piazza Vittorio Veneto have revealed the ruins of parts of Byzantine Matera, including a castle and a rock church decorated with frescoes. Access is restricted, so enquire at the tourist office.

Places to Stay & Eat

There are few options for budget accommodation here and it is best to book in advance. Try the *Albergo Roma* (☎ 33 39 12), Via Roma 62. Singles/doubles are L40,000/60,000. The local fare is simple and the focus is on vegetables. *Da Aulo*, Via Padre Minozzo 21 (☎ 33 24 91), is economical and serves typical dishes of Basilicata. There is a fruit and vegetable market near Piazza V Veneto, between Via Lucana and Via A Persio.

Getting There & Away

SITA buses connect Matera with Potenza, Taranto and Metaponto. The town is on the private Ferrovie Apulo-Lucane train line, which connects with Bari, Altamura and Potenza. There are also three Marozzi buses a day from Rome to Matera. Buses arrive in Piazza Matteotti, a short walk down Via Roma to the town centre.

APULIA

For the dedicated traveller, the Apulia (Puglia) region offers many rich experiences. There are the many beautiful Romanesque churches, notably the cathedrals at Trani, Bari, Bitonto and Ruvo di Puglia. Or visit the beaches and forest of the Gargano peninsula, stopping off at the famous sanctuary of St Michael the Archangel at Monte Sant'Angelo, and making a side trip to the unspoiled Tremiti Islands. Also visit Alberobello to see its *trulli*, which are whitewashed, conical-shaped buildings, and explore the surprising Salento around Lecce, the most elegant town in Apulia.

Brindisi
☎ 0831

As the major embarkation point for ferries from Italy to Greece, the city swarms with travellers in transit. There is not much to do here, other than wait, so most backpackers gather at the train station or at the port in the Stazione Marittima. The two are connected by Corso Umberto I – which becomes Corso Garibaldi – and are a 10-minute walk from each other; otherwise, you can take bus Nos 3 or 9.

The EPT tourist information office (☎ 56 21 26; fax 56 21 49) is at Lungomare Regina Margherita 12. Another information office is inside the ferry terminal.

Dangers & Annoyances Thieves are very active in the area between the station and the port. Carry valuables in a money belt, don't walk alone through the town at night and never leave luggage or valuables unattended.

It is inadvisable to sleep in any of the piazzas between the station and port. If you arrive in Brindisi with a car during summer, allow extra time for the eternal traffic jam around the port.

Things to See & Do From ancient Roman times Brindisi has been Italy's gateway to the east. It was from here that the Crusaders set off for the Holy Land. Tradition has it that Virgil died in a Roman house near the columns marking the end of the **Appian Way** on his return from Greece. In Piazza del Duomo is the 14th-century **Palazzo Balsamo**, with a beautiful *loggetta* (a building open on one or more sides). The town's main monument is the Romanesque church **Santa Maria del Casale**, about 4km from the centre, built by Prince Philip of Taranto in around 1300 AD.

Places to Stay & Eat The non-HI *Ostello per la Gioventù* (☎ 41 31 23) is about 2km out of town at Via N Brandi 4, in Casale. B&B costs L18,000. Take bus No 3 or the longer No 4 from Via Cristoforo Colombo near the train station. *Hotel Venezia* (☎ 52 75 11), Via Pisanelli 4, has singles/doubles for L25,000/45,000. Turn left off Corso Umberto I onto Via S Lorenzo da Brindisi to get there.

There are numerous takeaway outlets along the main route between the train and boat stations, but if you want a meal, head for the side streets. The *Osteria Spaghetti House*, Via Mazzini 57, near the station, has good-value meals for around L25,000. There is a fruit and vegetable market in Via Battisti, off Corso Umberto I, open from 7 am to 1 pm daily except Sunday.

Getting There & Away Marozzi runs several buses a day to/from Rome (Stazione Tiburtina), leaving from Viale Regina Margherita in Brindisi. Appia Travel (☎ 52 16 84), Viale Regina Margherita 8-9, sells tickets (L55,000 or L60,000). Brindisi is directly connected by train to the major cities of northern Italy, as well as Rome, Ancona and Naples.

Boat Ferries leave Brindisi for Greek destinations including Corfu, Igoumenitsa, Patras and Cefalonia. Adriatica (☎ 52 38 25; fax 66 83 32), Corso Garibaldi 85-87, is open from 9 am to 1 pm and 4 to 7 pm; you must check in here until 7 pm (after 8 pm check-in is in front of the ship). Other major ferry companies are Hellenic Mediterranean Lines (☎ 52 85 31; fax 52 68 72), Corso Garibaldi 8; and Med Link Lines (☎ 52 76 67; fax 56 40 70), Corso Garibaldi 49.

Adriatica and Hellenic are the most expensive, but also the most reliable. They are also the only lines which can officially accept Eurail and Inter-Rail passes, which means you pay only the port tax (L10,000) if you travel deck class. For a *poltrona* (airline-type chair) you'll pay L29,000, and L45,000 for a second-class cabin. There is an additional L5000 charge for reservations (see below for normal fares). If you want to use your Eurail or Inter-Rail pass, it is important to reserve some weeks in advance in summer. Even with a booking in summer, you must still go to the Adriatic or Hellenic embarkation office in the Stazione Marittima to have your ticket checked.

Discounts are available for travellers under 26 years of age and holders of some Italian rail passes. Note that fares increase by 40% in July and August. Ferry services are also increased during this period. Average prices in the 1998 high season for deck class were: Adriatica and Hellenic to Corfu, Igoumenitsa, Cefalonia or Patras cost L100,000 (L80,000 return); Med Link to Patras cost L60,000 on deck. Prices go up by an average L20,000 for a poltrona, and for the cheapest cabin accommodation prices jump by L40,000 to L65,000. Bicycles can be taken aboard free, but the average high-season fare for a motorcycle is L50,000 and for a car around L115,000.

The port tax is L10,000, payable when you buy your ticket. It is essential to check in at least two hours prior to departure.

Lecce
☎ 0832

Baroque can be grotesque, but never in Lecce. The style here is so refined and particular to the city that the Italians call it Barocco Leccese (Lecce baroque). Lecce's numerous bars and restaurants are a pleasant surprise in such a small city.

There is an APT information office (☎ 24 80 92) at Via Vittorio Emanuele 24 near Piazza Duomo. Take bus No 2 from the station to the town centre.

Things to See & Do The most famous example of Lecce baroque is the **Basilica di Santa Croce**. Artists worked for 150 years to decorate the building, creating an extraordinarily ornate façade. In the **Piazza del Duomo** are the 12th-century **cathedral** (which was completely restored in the baroque style by the architect Giuseppe Zimbalo of Lecce) and its 70m-high **bell tower**; the **Palazzo del Vescovo** (Bishop's Palace); and the **Seminario**, with its elegant façade and baroque well in the courtyard. In Piazza Sant'Oronzo are the remains of a **Roman amphitheatre**.

Places to Stay & Eat Cheap accommodation is not abundant in Lecce, but camping facilities abound in the province of Salento. *Torre Rinalda* (☎ 38 21 62), near the sea at Torre Rinalda is accessible by STP bus from the terminal in Lecce's Via Adua.

In Lecce try *Hotel Cappello* (☎ 30 88 81), Via Montegrappa 4, near the station. Singles/doubles are L53,000/85,000 with bathroom.

A good snack bar is *Da Guido e Figli*, Via Trinchese 10. A more traditional eating place is *Angiolino*, Via Principi di Savoia, near Porta Napoli. A full meal could cost L15,000.

Getting There & Away STP buses connect Lecce with towns throughout the Salentine peninsula, leaving from Via Adua. Lecce is directly linked by train to Brindisi, Bari, Rome, Naples and Bologna. The Ferrovie del Sud Est runs trains to surrounding areas, including Otranto, Gallipoli and Taranto and major points in Apulia.

Otranto
☎ 0836
Without a car it is difficult to tour the picturesque Adriatic coast of Salento, which extends to the tip of Italy's heel, at Capo Santa Maria di Leuca. However, Otranto is easy to reach by bus and on the Ferrovie del Sud Est train line.

The tourist office (☎ 80 14 36) is at Via Presbitero Pantaleone 10 on the seaside promenade.

Things to See This port town of whitewashed buildings is overrun by tourists in summer, but it is worth a visit if only to see the incredible **mosaic** that covers the floor of the Romanesque **cathedral**. The recently restored 12th-century mosaic, depicting the tree of life, is a masterpiece unrivalled in southern Italy and it's stunning in its simplicity.

The tiny Byzantine **Chiesa di San Pietro** contains some well-preserved Byzantine paintings.

Places to Stay Unfortunately, the town is not geared for budget tourism and has no one-star hotels. *Il Gabbiano* (☎ 80 12 51), Via Porto Craulo 5, has singles/doubles with bath for L55,000/90,000. There are several camping grounds in or near Otranto. The *Hydrusa* (☎ 80 12 55) near the port is basic and cheap.

Getting There & Away A Marozzi bus runs daily from Rome to Brindisi, Lecce and Otranto. Ferries leave from here for Corfu and Igoumenitsa (Greece). For information and reservations for both ferries and the Marozzi bus, go to Ellade Viaggi (☎ 80 15 78; fax 80 27 46) at the port.

CALABRIA
Although the region's beaches have become popular destinations, much of Calabria is still to be discovered by travellers. Tourist development has begun along the region's Ionian and Tyrrhenian coastlines, but in most areas it is minimal compared with Italy's more touristy regions. This is an area with many small villages in picturesque settings where the pace of life is slow and things have remained largely unchanged over the years. Although the fierce feuding of the 'Ndrangheta, Calabria's version of the Sicilian Mafia, continues to cause havoc and atrocious deaths among Calabrians, tourists travelling in the region should not be concerned. Few locals speak English.

Catanzaro & Cosenza
☎ 0961, 0984

The old town of Catanzaro, the region's capital, is strikingly set high on a hill top overlooking the Ionian Sea. Calabria's **riviera**, along the Ionian coast, is overdeveloped and pockmarked with heavy industry, but remains popular among Germans and Italians.

Tropea, to the north of the region on the Tyrrhenian Sea, was an isolated paradise only a decade ago. Today it too has been affected by tourist development, along with nearby **Pizzo** and **Scalea**, further north. For accommodation at Tropea try the *Vulcano* (☎ 0963-6 16 74), Via Campo Superiore. There are camping grounds at Scalea, including *Camping La Pantera Rosa* (☎ 0985-2 15 46), Corso Mediterraneo.

If adventure appeals, the **Parco Nazionale del Pollino** on the border with Basilicata, and **Parco Nazionale di Calabria** in the **Sila Piccola** are places to visit. These beautiful wilderness areas remain on the verge of massive development. The Sila is divided into three areas: the **La Greca**, **La Grande** and **La Piccola**. From **Cosenza**, which is accessible by train from Paola on the Rome-Reggio di Calabria railway line on the west coast, catch a bus or train to **Camigliatello Silano**. (Cosenza has two train stations: the national FS Stazione Nuova, and the Ferrovie della Calabria serving the Sila Massif area. You can get from one to the other on local bus No 5.)

Cosenza has a tourist office at Corso Mazzini 92 in the centre (☎ 274 85) and in Piazza Rossi (☎ 39 05 95) on the road for the A3 highway. For a room try the *Albergo Bruno*(☎ 738 89), Corso Mazzini 27. Rooms are L35,000/50,000.

At Camigliatello Silano you can obtain trekking and tourist information from the Pro Loco (☎ 0984-57 80 91), Via Roma 5. Opening hours are irregular. For accommodation try the *Miramonti* (☎ 0984-57 90 67), Via Forgitelle 87.

Reggio di Calabria
☎ 0965

The port city of Reggio di Calabria on the Strait of Messina is the capital of the province of Reggio di Calabria and was, until 1971, the capital of the region of Calabria. Founded in approximately 720 BC by Greek colonists, this city was destroyed by an earthquake in 1908 (which also razed Messina) and was totally rebuilt. There is a tourist information booth at the station (☎ 271 20) and at Corso Garibaldi 329 (☎ 89 20 12) where you can pick up a map and a list of hotels. The main office is at Via Roma 3 (☎ 211 71).

Things to See The **lungomare** (promenade along the port) overlooks Sicily and, in certain atmospheric conditions, such as at dawn, it is possible to see the fabled **mirage of Morgana**, the reflection of Messina in the sea. Reggio's only really impressive sight is the **Museo Nazionale**, which houses a remarkable collection documenting Greek civilisation in Calabria. Of particular interest are the **Bronzi di Riace** (Bronze Warriors of Riace), two Greek statues found off the coast of Riace in the Ionian Sea in 1972. The museum is open from 9 am to 6.30 pm daily (except the first and third Mondays of the month).

Places to Stay & Eat Try *Albergo Noel* (☎ 89 09 65), Via G Zerbi 13, north of the Stazione Lido, which has singles/doubles for L55,000/75,000.

There are numerous alimentari along Corso Garibaldi, where you can buy cheese, bread and wine. *Ristorante La Pignata*, Via D Tripepi 122, off Corso Garibaldi, has reasonably priced food.

Getting There & Away Reggio is connected by regular train to Naples and Rome, and also to Metaponto, Taranto and Bari (Apulia). Its two stations are the Lido, at the port, and Centrale, in the town centre at Piazza Garibaldi.

Up to 20 hydrofoils run by SNAV (☎ 295 68) leave the port just north of Stazione Lido every day for Messina, some of them proceeding on to the Isole Eolie (Aeolian Islands). The Ferrovie dello Stato (FS) runs several ferries a day from the port to Messina.

It is easier, particularly if you arrive from the north by train, to depart from Villa San Giovanni, 15 minutes north of Reggio by train. Private car ferries cross from here to Messina around the clock. All of the ferry

ITALY

companies have offices in Reggio or at the ferry terminal in Villa San Giovanni. If you arrive at Villa San Giovanni by train, you will most likely have already paid for the ferry passage across the strait. You can stay on your train (which is usually taken aboard the ferry), but the trip is short and it is more pleasant to sit on the boat deck.

Sicily

The largest island in the Mediterranean, Sicily's strategic location made it a prize for successive waves of invaders and colonisers, so that it is now a place of Greek temples, Norman churches and castles, Arab and Byzantine domes and splendid baroque churches and palaces. Its landscape, dominated by the volcano Mt Etna (3330m) on the east coast, ranges from the fertile coast to the mountains of the north and the vast, dry plateau of its centre.

Sicily has a population of about five million. Long neglected by the Italian government after unification, it became a semiautonomous region in 1948, remaining under the control of the central Italian government, but with greater powers to legislate on regional matters. Although industry has developed on the island, its economy is still largely based on agriculture and its people remain strongly connected to the land.

Sicily's temperate climate means mild weather in winter, while summers are relentlessly hot and the beaches swarm with holidaying Italians and other Europeans. The best times to visit are in spring and autumn, when it is hot enough for the beach, but not too hot for sightseeing.

Sicilian food is hotter, spicier and sweeter than that of other parts of Italy. The focus is on seafood, notably swordfish, and fresh produce. Some say that fruit and vegetables taste better in Sicily. Their dolci (cakes and sweets) can be works of art but are very sweet. Try the cassata, both a ricotta cake (traditionally available only in winter) and a rich ice cream, and the *cannoli*, tubes of pastry filled with cream, ricotta or chocolate. Don't miss trying the *dolci di mandorle* (rich almond cakes and pastries) and the *granita*, a drink of crushed ice flavoured with lemon, strawberry or coffee, to name a few flavours.

The Mafia remains a powerful force in Sicily. Since the 1993 arrest of the Sicilian 'godfather', Salvatore 'Toto' Riina, Mafia pentiti (grasses) have continued to blow the whistle on fellow felons, businesspeople and politicians, right up to former prime minister, Giulio Andreotti, who is on trial both in Palermo and Perugia. The 'men of honour' are little interested in the affairs of tourists, so there is no need to fear you will be caught in the crossfire of a gang war while in Sicily.

Getting There & Away

Air There are flights from major cities in Italy and throughout Europe to Palermo and Catania. The easiest way to obtain information is from any Sestante CIT or Alitalia office.

Bus & Train Direct bus services from Rome to Sicily are operated by two companies – SAIS and Segesta. In Rome the buses leave from Stazione Tiburtina. The SAIS bus runs to Catania and Syracuse, with connections to Palermo and Agrigento; it leaves Rome daily at 8 pm. A one-way ticket costs L75,000, but for those under 26 and over 65 it is L65,000. The Segesta bus runs daily directly to Palermo, leaving Rome at 9.30 pm and arriving in Palermo's Piazza Politeama at 9.30 am. It leaves Palermo at 6.30 pm and reaches Rome at 6.30 am. A one-way ticket costs L65,000 (L110,000 return). Be especially wary of pickpockets on the bus and in the bus station.

One of the cheapest ways to reach Sicily is to catch a train to Messina. The cost of the ticket covers the ferry crossing from Villa San Giovanni (Calabria) to Messina. (See the Getting There & Away section under Reggio di Calabria for more details.)

Boat Sicily is accessible by ferry from Genova, Livorno, Naples, Reggio di Calabria and Cagliari, and also from Malta and Tunisia. The main companies servicing the Mediterranean are Tirrenia (☎ 091-33 33 00 in Palermo; 06-474 20 41 in Rome) and Grimaldi (☎ 091-58 74 04 in Palermo; 06-42 81 83 88 in Rome) which runs Grandi

Traghetti and Grandi Navi Veloci. Prices are determined by the season and jump considerably in the summer period (July to September). Timetables can change each year and it's best to check at a travel agency that takes ferry bookings. Be sure to book well in advance during summer, particularly if you have a car.

At the time of writing, high-season fares for a poltrona were: Genoa-Palermo with Grimaldi Grandi Traghetti, L144,000 (20 hours); Naples-Palermo with Tirrenia, L70,600 (13 hours); Palermo-Cagliari (Tirrenia), L66,500 (14 hours); and Trapani-Tunisia (Tirrenia), L92,000 (eight hours). A bed in a shared cabin with four beds costs an additional L25,000 to L30,000. Cars cost upwards of L130,000.

Other ferry lines servicing the island are Grandi Traghetti for Livorno-Palermo and Gozo Channel for Sicily-Malta. For information on ferries going from the mainland directly to Lipari, see the Getting There & Away section under Aeolian Islands.

Getting Around

Bus is the best mode of public transport in Sicily. Numerous companies run services between Syracuse, Catania and Palermo as well as to Agrigento and towns in the interior. See the Getting Around section under each town for more details. The coastal train service between Messina and Palermo and Messina to Syracuse is efficient and reliable.

PALERMO
☎ 091

An Arab emirate and later the seat of a Norman kingdom, Palermo was once regarded as the grandest and most beautiful city in Europe. Today it is in a remarkable state of decay, due to neglect and heavy bombing during WWII, yet enough evidence remains of its golden days to make Palermo one of the most fascinating cities in Italy.

Orientation

Palermo is a large but easily manageable city. The main streets of the historical centre are Via Roma and Via Maqueda, which extend from the central station to Piazza Castelnuovo, a vast square in the modern part of town.

Information

Tourist Offices The main APT tourist office (☎ 58 61 22) is at Piazza Castelnuovo 35 and some of the staff speak English. It's open weekdays from 8 am to 8 pm and Saturday 8 am to 2 pm. There are branch offices at the Stazione Centrale (☎ 616 59 14) and airport (☎ 59 16 98) with the same opening hours as the main office.

Money The exchange office at the Stazione Centrale is open daily from 8 am to 8 pm. American Express is represented by Ruggieri & Figli (☎ 58 71 44), Via Emerico Amari 40, near the Stazione Marittima.

Post & Communications The main post office is at Via Roma 322 and the main Telecom telephone office is opposite the station in Piazza G Cesare, open daily from 8.30 am to 9.30 pm. The postcode for Palermo is 90100.

Medical & Emergency Services For an ambulance call ☎ 118. There is a public hospital, Ospedale Civico (☎ 666 22 07), at Via Carmelo Lazzaro. There is an all-night pharmacy, Lo Cascio (☎ 616 72 98), near the train station at Via Roma 1. For 24-hour medical treatment phone ☎ 703 21 71. Call the police on ☎ 113. The questura (☎ 21 01 11) is at Piazza della Vittoria and is open 24 hours a day.

Dangers & Annoyances Petty crime is rife in Palermo and highly deft pickpockets and motorcycle bandits prey on tourists. Avoid wearing jewellery or carrying a bag and keep all your valuables in a money belt. It is unsafe for women to walk through the streets of the historical centre at night, even in Via Roma or Via Maqueda. At night, travellers should avoid the area north-east of the station, between Via Roma and the port.

Things to See

The intersection of Via Vittorio Emanuele and Via Maqueda marks the **Quattro Canti** (four corners of Palermo). The four 17th-century Spanish baroque façades are each decorated with a statue. Nearby is **Piazza Pretoria**, with a beautiful fountain (**Fontana**

ITALY

PALERMO

PLACES TO STAY
5 Hotel Petit
12 Albergo da Luigi
22 Hotel Sicilia
23 Albergo Orientale
24 Albergo Rosalia
   Conca d'Oro
27 Hotel Villa Archirafi

PLACES TO EAT
3 Osteria Lo Bianc
9 Trattoria Stella
10 Trattoria dei Vespri

OTHER
1 Stazione Marittima
2 Tirrenia Office
4 APT Tourist Office
6 Post Office
7 Vucciria Market
8 AST Bus Station
11 Chiesa di Santa
   Caterina
13 Quattro Canti
14 Fontana Pretoria
15 Palazzo del Municipio
16 La Martorana
17 Chiesa di San Cataldo
18 Cattedrale
19 Questura
   (Police Station)
20 Porta Nuova
21 Palazzo dei Normanni &
   Cappella Palatina
25 All-Night Pharmacy
26 Telecom Telephone
   Office
28 Urban Bus Station
29 Stazione Centrale
30 Intercity Buses
31 Hospital

Pretoria), created by Florentine sculptors in the 16th century. Locals used to call it the Fountain of Shame because of its nude figures. Also in the piazza are the baroque **Chiesa di Santa Caterina** and the **Palazzo del Municipio** (town hall). Just off the piazza is Piazza Bellini and Palermo's most famous church, **La Martorana**, with a beautiful Arab-Norman bell tower and its interior decorated with Byzantine mosaics. Next to it is the Norman **Chiesa di San Cataldo**, which also mixes Arab and Norman styles and is easily recognisable by its red domes.

The huge Norman **cattedrale** is along Via Vittorio Emanuele, on the corner of Via Bonello. Although modified many times over the centuries, it remains an impressive example of Norman architecture. Opposite Piazza della Vittoria and the gardens is the **Palazzo Reale**, also known as the Palazzo dei Normanni, now the seat of the government. Enter from Piazza Indipendenza to see the **Cappella Palatina**, a magnificent example of Arab-Norman architecture, built during the reign of Roger II and decorated with Byzantine mosaics. The **Sala di Ruggero** (King

Roger's former bedroom), is decorated with 12th-century mosaics. It is possible to visit the room only with a guide (free of charge). Go upstairs from the Cappella Palatina.

Take bus No 8/9 from under the trees across the piazza from the train station to the nearby town of **Monreale** to see the magnificent mosaics in the famous 12th-century cathedral of **Santa Maria la Nuova**.

Places to Stay

The best camping ground is *Trinacria* (☎ 53 05 90), Via Barcarello 25, at Sferracavallo by the sea. It costs L7500 per person and L8000 for a site. Catch bus No 616 from Piazzale Alcide de Gasperi, which can be reached by bus Nos 101 or 107 from Stazione Centrale.

In Palermo, head for Via Maqueda or Via Roma for basic, cheap rooms. Women travelling alone would do better to head for the area around Piazza Castelnuovo which, though more expensive, is safer at night and offers a higher standard of accommodation. Catch bus No 7 from the station to Piazza Sturzo. Near the train station try *Albergo Orientale* (☎ 616 57 27), Via Maqueda 26, in an old and somewhat decayed palace. Singles/doubles are L25,000/40,000 and triples are L60,000. Just around the corner is *Albergo Rosalia Conca d'Oro* (☎ 616 45 43), Via Santa Rosalia 7, with very basic singles/doubles/triples at L35,000/50,000/75,000 without bath.

The *Hotel Sicilia* (☎ 616 84 60), Via Divisi 99, on the corner of Via Maqueda, has rooms of a higher standard at L40,000/50,000, or L65,000/75,000 with private shower. Rooms without bath are less expensive. *Albergo da Luigi* (☎ 58 50 85),Via Vittorio Emanuele 284, next to the Quattro Canti, has rooms from L25,000/50,000, or L40,000/60,000 with bathroom. Ask for a room with a view of the fountain.

Near Piazza Castelnuovo is the *Hotel Petit* (☎ 32 36 16), Via Principe di Belmonte 84, where clean and comfortable singles/doubles/triples cost L50,000/65,000/90,000 with private shower. A single without shower is L35,000.

Near central station, close to the orto botanico (botanical garden), the *Hotel Villa Archirafi* (☎ 616 88 27) at Via Lincoln 32 has pleasant singles/doubles with bathroom for L80,000/120,000; triples are L150,000.

Places to Eat

A popular Palermitan dish is pasta con le sarde (pasta with sardines, fennel, peppers, capers and pine nuts). Swordfish is served here sliced into huge steaks. The Palermitani are late eaters and restaurants rarely open for dinner before 8 pm. At *Osteria Lo Bianco*, Via E Amari, off Via Roma at the Castelnuovo end of town, a full meal will cost around L25,000. *Trattoria Stella*, Via Alloro 104, is in the courtyard of the old Hotel Patria. A full meal will come to around L25,000. *Trattoria dei Vespri*, Piazza Santa Croce dei Vespri, off Via Roma past the church of Sant'Anna, has outdoor tables and great food. It costs around L25,000 for a full meal.

At Sferracavallo, the *Trattoria Il Veliero*, Via Torretta 31, offers a full meal based on how much fish you can eat (wine and drinks included) for the fixed price of L35,000.

The *Vucciria*, Palermo's open-air markets, are held daily (except Sunday) in the narrow streets between Via Roma, Piazza San Domenico and Via Vittorio Emanuele. Here you can buy fresh fruit and vegetables, meat, cheese and virtually anything else you want. There are even stalls which sell steaming-hot boiled octopus.

Getting There & Away

Air The airport at Punta Raisi, 32km west of Palermo, serves as a terminal for domestic and European flights. For Alitalia information about domestic flights ring ☎ 147-86 56 41 and for international flights ring ☎ 147-86 56 42.

Bus The main (Intercity) terminal for destinations throughout Sicily and the mainland is in the area around Via Paolo Balsamo, to the right (east) as you leave the station. Offices for the various companies are all in this area. SAIS (☎ 616 60 28), Via Balsamo 16, and Segesta (☎ 616 79 19), Via Balsamo 26, both run a daily bus to Rome.

Train Regular trains leave from the Stazione Centrale for Milazzo, Messina, Catania and Syracuse, as well as for nearby towns such as

Cefalù. Direct trains go to Reggio di Calabria, Naples and Rome. For a one-way ticket to Rome you pay L71,000 in 2nd class plus a L24,000 Intercity supplement, or L117,500 in 1st class plus a L41,000 supplement.

Boat Boats leave from the port (Molo Vittorio Veneto) for Sardinia and the mainland (see the Getting There & Away section under Sicily). The Tirrenia office (☎ 33 33 00) is at the port.

Getting Around

Taxis to/from the airport cost upwards of L70,000. The cheaper option is to catch one of the regular blue buses which leave from outside the station roughly every 45 minutes from 5 am to 9.45 pm. The trip takes one hour and costs L4500. Palermo's buses are efficient and most stop outside the train station. Bus No 7 runs along Via Roma from the train station to near Piazza Castelnuovo and No 39 from the station to the port. You must buy tickets before you get on the bus; they cost L1500 and are valid for one hour.

AEOLIAN ISLANDS
☎ 090

Also known as the Lipari Islands, the seven islands of this archipelago just north of Milazzo are volcanic in origin. They range from the well-developed tourist resort of Lipari and the understated jet-set haunt of Panarea, to the rugged Vulcano, the spectacular scenery of Stromboli (and its fiercely active volcano), the fertile vineyards of Salina, and the solitude of Alicudi and Filicudi, which remain relatively undeveloped. The islands have been inhabited since the Neolithic era, when migrants sought the valuable volcanic glass, obsidian. The Isole Eolie (Aeolian Islands) are so named because the ancient Greeks believed they were the home of Aeolus, the god of wind. Homer wrote of the islands in the *Odyssey*.

Information

The main AAST tourist information office (☎ 988 00 95) for the islands is on Lipari at Corso Vittorio Emanuele 202. Another office is open on Vulcano during summer.

Things to See & Do

On **Lipari** visit the castello, with its archaeological park and museum. You can also go on excellent walks on the island. Catch a local bus from the town of Lipari to the hilltop village of Quattrocchi for a great view of Vulcano. Boat trips will take you around the island – contact the tourist office for information.

Vulcano, with its ever-present smell of sulphur, is a short boat trip from Lipari's port. The main volcano, Vulcano Fossa, is still active, though the last recorded period of eruption was 1888-90. You can make the one-hour hike to the crater, or take a bath in the therapeutic hot muds.

Stromboli is the most spectacular of the islands. Climb the cone (924m) at night to see the Sciara del Fuoco (Trail of Fire), lava streaming down the side of the volcano, and the volcanic explosions from the crater. Many people make the trip (four to five hours) without a guide during the day, but at night you should go with a guided group. The AGAI and GAE official guides (☎/fax 98 62 54; stromboli@iol.it) organise guided tours which depart at around 5 pm and return at 11.30 pm. It's best to contact them in advance to make a booking, since they only depart if groups are large enough. Remember to take warm clothes, wear heavy shoes and carry a torch and plenty of water.

Places to Stay & Eat

Camping facilities are available on Salina and Vulcano. Most accommodation in summer is booked out well in advance on the smaller islands, particularly on Stromboli, and most hotels close during winter.

Lipari provides the best options for a comfortable stay. It has numerous budget hotels, affittacamere and apartments, and the other islands are easily accessible by regular hydrofoil. When you arrive on Lipari you are likely to be approached by someone offering accommodation. This is worth checking out because the offers are usually genuine. The island's camping ground, *Baia Unci* (☎ 981 19 09), is at Canneto, about 2km out of the Lipari township. It costs L20,000 a night per person. The HI *Ostello per la Gioventù* (☎ 981 15 40), Via Castello 17, is inside the walls of the castle. A bed costs L14,000 a night, plus L1000 for a hot shower and L3000 for breakfast. A meal costs L15,000. It's open March to October.

Cassarà Vittorio (☎ 981 15 23), Vico Sparviero 15, costs from L25,000 per person with bathroom, to L40,000, depending on the season. There are two terraces with views, and use of the kitchen is L5000. The owner can be found (unless he finds you first) at Via Garibaldi 78, on the way from the port to the centre.

You can eat surprisingly cheaply on Lipari. For a pizza try *Il Galeone*, Corso V Emanuele 222. For an excellent meal eat at *Trattoria d'Oro*, Corso Umberto I. There is a L30,000 tourist menu.

If you want seclusion, head for Filicudi or Alicudi. However, the hotels aren't exactly cheap. Alicudi's *Ericusa* (☎ 988 99 02/10) costs L105,000 for half-board in summer and Filicudi's *Locanda la Canna* (☎ 988 99 56) charges L110,000 for half-board.

On Stromboli the Mediterranean-style *Tahar Majed Badino* (☎/fax 98 60 30) has rooms for L30,000, or if you want to lash out try the hotel *La Sirenetta* (☎ 98 60 25) which charges from L130,000 for half-board.

On Vulcano, if you can cope with the sulphurous fumes, try *Pensione Agostino* (☎ 985 23 42), Via Favaloro 1 (close to the mud bath), which has doubles with bathroom from L50,000 to L90,000 depending on the season. The *Hotel Arcipelago* (☎ 985 20 02) is beautifully positioned on Vulcano and costs L120,000 for half-board.

Getting There & Away

Ferries and hydrofoils leave for the islands from Milazzo (which is easy to reach by train from Palermo and Messina) and all ticket offices are along Via Rizzo at the port. SNAV runs hydrofoils (L19,700 one way). Siremar also runs hydrofoils, but its ferries are half the price. Both companies have offices at the port. If arriving at Milazzo by train, you will need to catch a bus to the port. If arriving by bus, simply make the five-minute walk back along Via Crispi to the port area. SNAV also runs hydrofoils from Palermo twice a day in summer and three times a week in the off season.

You can travel directly to the islands from the mainland. Siremar runs regular ferries from Naples and SNAV runs hydrofoils from Naples (see the Naples Getting There & Away section), Messina and Reggio di Calabria. Note that occasionally, the sea around the islands can be very rough.

Getting Around

Regular hydrofoil and ferry services operate between the islands. Both Siremar and Aliscafi SNAV have offices at the port on Lipari, where you can get full timetable information.

TAORMINA
☎ 0942

Spectacularly located on a hill overlooking the sea and Mt Etna, Taormina was long ago discovered by the European jet set, which has made it one of the more expensive and touristy towns in Sicily. But its magnificent setting, its Greek theatre and the nearby beaches remain as seductive now as they were for the likes of Goethe and DH Lawrence. The AAST tourist office (☎ 232 43) in Palazzo Corvaja, just off Corso Umberto near Largo Santa Caterina, has extensive information on the town.

Things to See & Do

The **Greek theatre** (entry L4000) was built in the 3rd century BC and later greatly expanded and remodelled by the Romans. Concerts and theatre are staged there in summer and it affords a wonderful view of Mt Etna. From the beautiful **villa comunale** (public gardens) there is a panoramic view of the sea. Along Corso Umberto is the **Duomo**, with a Gothic façade. The local beach is **Isola Bella**, a short bus ride from Via Pirandello or by the *funivia* (cable car) which costs L3000 return.

Trips to Mt Etna can be organised through CST (☎ 233 01), Corso Umberto 101. In nearby Catania *Natura e Turismo,* or *N e T* (☎ 095-33 35 43; fax 095-53 79 10; alexmil@DimTel.nti.it), organises guided walks and excursions on Mt Etna and in surrounding areas.

You can study the Italian language at Babilonia, Centro di Lingua e Cultura Italiana (☎/fax 234 41; babilonia@nti.it), Via Ginnasio 20.

Places to Stay & Eat

You can camp near the beach at *Campeggio San Leo* (☎ 246 58), Via Nazionale, at Capotaormina. The cost is L8000 per person per night, and L12,000 for a tent site.

There are numerous affittacamere in Taormina and the tourist office has a full list. *Il Leone* (☎ 238 78), Via Bagnoli Croce 127, near the public gardens, has singles/doubles for L35,000/70,000. *Pensione Svizzera* (☎ 237 90), Via Pirandello 26, on the way from the bus stop to the town centre, has very pleasant rooms for L70,000/120,000 with private bathroom. *Villa Nettuno* (☎ 237 97; fax 62 60 35) on Via Pirandello, in the front of the funivia, has singles/doubles/triples for L65,000/110,000/130,000 with private bathroom. Breakfast is included.

Ristorante La Piazzetta, Via Paladini 5, has excellent full meals for around L30,000. *Pizzeria Ristorante Porta Messina*, Largo Giove Serapide 4, is a good deal for pizza. *Da Rita*, Via Cala Pitrulli 3, serves pizza, bruschetta and lots of big salads. Typical Sicilian food and wine are served at *La Cantina dei Duchi*, Via Spuches 8, close to Porta Catania. To drink a good Sicilian wine or sangria go to *Arco Rosso*, Via Naumachie 7. Eat a typical Sicilian summer breakfast at *Bambar*, Via Di Giovanni 45. Order a granita of crushed ice with fresh fruit or almonds.

Getting There & Away

Bus is the easiest way to get to Taormina. SAIS buses leave from Messina, Catania and also from the airport at Catania. Taormina is on the main train line between Messina and Catania, but the station is on the coast and regular buses will take you to Via Pirandello, near the centre; bus services are heavily reduced on Sunday.

ETNA
☎ 095

Dominating the landscape in eastern Sicily between Taormina and Catania, Mt Etna (3330m) is Europe's largest live volcano. It has four live craters at its summit and its slopes are littered with crevices and extinct cones. There are also plenty of forested areas which teem with bird life, making the volcano a very special place for walkers and nature lovers. Eruptions of slow lava flows can occur locally, but are not really dangerous. Etna's most recent eruption was in 1992, when a stream of lava threatened the town of Zafferana Etnea. In 1998 it again showed signs of life. To reach the summit, avoid the long, hard climb of about seven hours return, and take the cable car (SITAS ☎ 91 41 41) from *Rifugio Sapienza* on the Nicolosi side of the mountain, or catch a 4WD minibus (STAR ☎ 64 34 30) from Piano Provenzana on the Linguaglossa side of the mountain. Both companies charge L58,000 return.

A better way to enjoy the magic atmosphere of this place is to stay in a refuge and spend the days walking in the pine forests and exploring volcanic caves in summer. In winter there is skiing and even dog sleds available on the north side of Mt Etna at *Rifugio Brunek* (☎ 64 30 15) at 1400m near Piano Provenzana. If you call ahead the friendly staff will pick you up at Linguaglossa. B&B is L35,000 and half-board is L55,000.

Mt Etna is best approached from Catania by AST bus (☎ 746 10 96), which leaves from Via L Sturzo in front of Catania's train station at 8.15 am and goes via Nicolosi to the cable car at *Rifugio Sapienza* (☎ 91 10 62), where it's also possible to stay. The bus returns to Catania at 4 pm. A private Circumetnea train line circles Mt Etna from Giarre-Riposto to Catania. It starts from Catania at Stazione Borgo, Via Caronda 352, accessible by bus Nos 29 or 36 from Catania's main train station. From Taormina, you can take an FS train to Giarre, where you can catch the Circumetnea.

SYRACUSE
☎ 0931

Once a powerful Greek city to rival Athens, Syracuse (Siracusa) is one of the highlights of a visit to Sicily. Founded in 743 BC by colonists from Corinth, it became a dominant sea power in the Mediterranean, prompting Athens to attack the city in 413 BC. In one of the great maritime battles in history, the Athenian fleet was destroyed. Syracuse was conquered by the Romans in 212 BC and, with the rest of Sicily, fell to a succession of invaders through the centuries. Syracuse was the birthplace of the Greek mathematician and physicist Archimedes, and Plato attended the court of the tyrant Dionysius, who ruled from 405 to 367 BC.

The main sights of Syracuse are in two areas: on the island of Ortygia and at the archaeological park 2km across town. There are two tourist information offices. The AAT (☎ 46 42 55), Via Maestranza 33, on Ortygia, opens Monday to Saturday from 8.30 am to 1.45 pm and 4.30 to 7.30 pm (closed afternoons in winter). The APT (☎ 46 14 77), Via San Sebastiano 43, opens Monday to Saturday from 8 am to 7 pm (Sunday to 1 pm). There is a branch office of the APT, with the same opening hours, at the archaeological park.

Things to See

Ortygia On the island of Ortygia the buildings are predominantly medieval, with some baroque palaces and churches. The 7th-century **Duomo** was built on top of the Temple of Athena, incorporating most of the original columns in its three-aisled structure. The **Piazza Duomo** is lined with baroque palaces. Walk down Via Picherali to the waterfront and the **Fonte Aretusa** (Fountain of Arethusa), a natural freshwater spring. According to Greek legend, the nymph Arethusa, pursued by the river god Alpheus, was turned into a fountain by the goddess Diana. Undeterred, Alpheus turned himself into the river which feeds the spring.

Neapolis-Parco Archeologico To get to this archaeological zone, catch bus No 1 from Riva della Posta on Ortygia. The main attraction here is the 5th-century BC **Greek theatre**, its seating area carved out of solid rock. Nearby is the **Orecchio di Dionisio**, an artificial grotto in the shape of an ear which the tyrant of Syracuse, Dionysius, used as a prison. Its extraordinary acoustics led the painter Caravaggio, during a visit in the 17th century, to give the grotto its current name. Caravaggio mused that the tyrant must have taken advantage of the acoustics to overhear the whispered conversations of his prisoners. The 2nd-century **Roman amphitheatre** is impressively well preserved. The park is open daily from 9 am to one hour before sunset. Admission is L4000.

The **Museo Archeologico Paolo Orsi** (☎ 46 40 22), about 500m east of the archaeological zone, off Viale Teocrito, contains the best organised and most interesting archaeological collection in Sicily. The museum is open Tuesday to Saturday from 9 am to 2 pm with the last entry at 1 pm. Entry is L8000. Close to the museum, on Via San Giovanni alle Catacombe, are the church and catacombs of **San Giovanni**. The catacombs were excavated between the 4th and 6th centuries BC. They are open daily except Thursday from 9.30 am to one hour before sunset. Entry is L4000.

Special Events

Since 1914 Syracuse has hosted a festival of Greek classical drama in May and June of every even-numbered year. Performances are given at the Greek theatre. Tickets are available at the APT, at the theatre ticket booth. For information call ☎ 674 15.

Places to Stay

Camping facilities are at *Agriturista Rinaura* (☎ 72 12 24) about 4km from the city near the sea. Camping costs L7000 per person and from L7000 for a site. The *Fontane Bianche* camping ground (☎ 79 03 33), Via dei Lidi 476, has a private beach and charges L7000 per person and L8000 for a site. For both camping grounds catch bus Nos 21, 22 or 24 from Corso Umberto.

The *Gran Bretagna* (☎ 687 65) on Ortygia at Via Savoia 21, just off Largo XXV Luglio, has very pleasant rooms for L62,000/98,000 with bath and L52,000/86,000 without bath. *Hotel Centrale* (☎ 605 28) is less appealing, but close to the train station at Corso Umberto 141. Singles/doubles/triples are L25,000/40,000/55,000.

Places to Eat

On Ortygia, *Ristorante Osteria da Mariano*, Vicolo Zuccalà 9, serves typical Sicilian food. *Pizzeria Trattoria Zsà*, Via Roma 73, serves 65 different kinds of pizza, antipasti and pasta. At both places a full meal will cost under L25,000. A good pizzeria is *Il Cenacolo*, Via del Consiglio Reginale 10.

In the archaeological zone, close to the Greek theatre, try *Ristorante Il Teatro*, Via Agnello 8. At *Pasticceria Cassarino*, Corso

Umberto 86, you can try scrumptious Sicilian sweets including cannoli di ricotta and arancini.

There is an open-air, fresh produce market in the streets behind the Temple of Apollo, open daily (except Sunday) until 1 pm. You will find several alimentari and supermarkets along Corso Gelone.

Getting There & Away
SAIS buses leave from Riva della Posta on Ortygia, for Catania, Palermo, Enna and surrounding small towns. The SAIS service for Rome also leaves from the piazza, connecting with the Rome bus at Catania. AST buses also service Palermo from Piazza della Posta. Syracuse is easy to reach by train from Messina and Catania. Boat services from Syracuse to Malta remain in a state of flux and it is best to check with the tourist offices (see the Malta chapter's Getting There & Away section).

AGRIGENTO
☎ 0922
Founded in approximately 582 BC as the Greek Akragas, Agrigento is today a pleasant medieval town, but the Greek temples in the valley below are the real reason to visit. The Italian novelist and dramatist Luigi Pirandello (1867-1936) was born here, as was the Greek philosopher and scientist Empedocles (circa 490-430 BC). The AAST tourist office (☎ 204 54), Via Cesare Battisti 15, opens Monday to Saturday from 8.30 am to 1.30 pm and 4.30 to 7.30 pm.

Things to See & Do
Agrigento's **Valley of the Temples** is one of the major Greek archaeological sights in the world. Its five main Doric temples were constructed in the 5th century BC and are in various states of ruin because of earthquakes and vandalism by early Christians. The only temple to survive relatively intact is the **Tempio della Concordia**, which was transformed into a Christian church. The **Tempio di Giunone**, a five-minute walk uphill to the east, has an impressive sacrificial altar. The **Tempio di Ercole** is the oldest of the structures. Across the main road which divides the valley is the massive **Tempio di Giove**, one

of the most imposing buildings of ancient Greece. Although now completely in ruins, it used to cover an area measuring 112m by 56m, with columns 18m high. **Telamoni**, colossal statues of men, were also used in the structure. The remains of one of them are in the **Museo Archeologico**, just north of the temples on Via dei Templi (a copy lies at the archaeological site). Close by is the **Tempio di Castore e Polluce**, which was partly reconstructed in the 19th century. The temples are lit up at night and are open until one hour before sunset. To get to the temples from the town, catch bus Nos 1, 2 or 3 from the train station.

Places to Stay & Eat
The *Bella Napoli* (☎ 204 35), Piazza Lena 6, off Via Bac Bac at the end of Via Atenea, has clean and comfortable singles/doubles for L30,000/55,000 (L40,000/75,000 with private bathroom). For a decent, cheap meal try the *Trattoria la Concordia*, Via Porcello 6.

Getting There & Away
Intercity buses leave from Piazza Rosselli, just off Piazza Vittorio Emanuele, for Palermo, Catania and surrounding small towns.

Sardinia

The second-largest island in the Mediterranean, Sardinia (Sardegna) was colonised and invaded by the Phoenicians and Romans, followed by the Pisans, Genoese and finally the Spaniards. But it is often said that the Sardinians, known on the island as Sardi, were never really conquered – they simply retreated into the hills.

The Romans were prompted to call the island's eastern mountains Barbagia (from the word barbarian) because of their views on the lifestyle of the locals. Even today in the island's interior some women still wear the traditional costume and shepherds still live in almost complete isolation as the ancients did. If you venture into the interior, you will find the people incredibly gracious and hospitable, but easily offended if they sense any lack of respect.

The first inhabitants of the island were the

Nuraghic people, thought to have arrived here around 2000 BC. Little is known about them, but the island is dotted with thousands of *nuraghi*, their conical-shaped stone houses and fortresses.

Sardinia became a semiautonomous region in 1948, and the Italian government's Sardinian Rebirth Plan of 1962 made some impact on the development of tourism, industry and agriculture.

The island's cuisine is very varied. Along the coast most dishes feature seafood and there are many variations of *zuppa di pesce* (fish soup). Inland you will find *porcheddu* (roast suckling pig) and kid goat with olives. The Sardi eat *pecorino* (sheep's milk cheese) and the preferred bread throughout the island is the paper-thin *carta musica* (literally, 'music paper'), also called *pane carasau*, often sprinkled with oil and salt.

The landscape of the island ranges from the 'savage, dark-bushed, sky-exposed land' described by DH Lawrence, to the incredibly beautiful gorges and valleys near Dorgali, the rugged isolation of the Gennargentu mountain range and the unspoiled coastline between Bosa and Alghero. Although hunters have been active in Sardinia, some wildlife remains, notably the Sardinian cervo (deer) in the island forests and colonies of griffon vultures on the west coast near Bosa. The famous colony of Mediterranean monk seals at the Grotta del Bue Marino, near the beach of Cala Gonone, has not been sighted for some years.

Try to avoid the island in August, when the weather is very hot and the beaches are overcrowded. Warm weather generally continues from May to October.

Getting There & Away

Air Airports at Cagliari, Olbia and Alghero link Sardinia with major Italian and European cities. For information contact Alitalia or the Sestante CIT or CTS offices in all major towns.

Boat The island is accessible by ferry from Genoa, Livorno, Fiumicino (the port of Rome), Civitavecchia, Naples, Palermo, Trapani, Bonifacio (Corsica) and Tunis. The departure points in Sardinia are Olbia, Golfo Aranci and Porto Torres in the north, Arbatax on the east coast and Cagliari in the south.

The main company, Tirrenia, runs a service between Civitavecchia and Olbia, Arbatax or Cagliari, and between Genova and Porto Torres, Olbia, Arbatax or Cagliari. Tirrenia has recently introduced a new service of fast ships between Fiumicino and Golfo Aranci/ Arbatax; La Spezia and Golfo Aranci; and Civitavecchia and Olbia. The national railway, Ferrovie dello Stato (FS), runs a slightly cheaper service between Civitavecchia and Golfo Aranci. Moby Lines (which also runs Navarma Lines and Sardegna Lines) and Sardinia Ferries (also known as Elba and Corsica Ferries) both operate services from the mainland to Sardinia, as well as to Corsica and Elba. They depart from Livorno, Civitavecchia and arrive at either Olbia or Golfo Aranci. Grandi Navi Veloci runs a service between Genova and Olbia or Porto Torres from late June to late September. Most travel agencies in Italy have brochures on the various companies' services.

Timetables change every year and prices fluctuate according to the season. Prices for a poltrona on Tirrenia ferries in the 1998 high season were: Genoa-Cagliari, L95,500 (21 hours); Genoa-Porto Torres or Olbia, L76,500 (13 hours); Civitavecchia-Cagliari, L70,500 (13½ hours); Civitavecchia-Olbia, L33,900 (seven hours); Naples-Cagliari, L71,500 (16 hours); and Palermo-Cagliari, L66,500 (14 hours). The cost of taking a small car ranged from L121,000 to L170,000, and for a motorcycle from L33,800 to L47,900.

Getting Around

Bus The two main bus companies are ARST, which operates extensive services throughout the island, and PANI, which links the main towns.

Train The main FS train lines link Cagliari with Oristano, Sassari and Olbia. The private railways that link smaller towns throughout the island can be very slow. However, the *trenino* (little train), which runs from Cagliari to Arbatax through the Barbagia, is a relaxing way to see part of the interior (see the Getting There & Away section under Cagliari).

Car & Motorcycle The only way to explore Sardinia properly is by road. Rental agencies are listed under Cagliari and some other towns around the island.

Hitching You might find hitchhiking laborious once you get away from the main towns because of the light traffic. Women should not hitchhike in Sardinia under any circumstances.

CAGLIARI
☎ 070

This attractive city offers an interesting medieval section, the beautiful beach of Poetto, and salt lakes with a population of pink flamingos.

Orientation
If you arrive by bus, train or boat you will find yourself at the port area of Cagliari. The main street along the harbour is Via Roma, and the old city stretches up the hill behind it to the castle. Most of the budget hotels and restaurants are in the area near the port.

Information
Tourist Offices The AAST information booth (☎ 66 92 55), Piazza Matteotti 9, is open daily from 8 am to 8 pm in the high season, and 8 am to 2 pm in other months. There are also information offices at the airport and in the Stazione Marittima.

The Ente Sardo Industrie Turistiche (ESIT) office (☎ 167-01 31 53, 60 23 24; fax 66 46 36), Via Goffredo Mameli 97, is open daily from 8 am to 8 pm in the high season and has information on all of Sardinia.

Post & Communications The main post office is in Piazza del Carmine, up Via La Maddalena from Via Roma. The Telecom telephone office is at Via G M Angioj, north of Piazza Matteotti. The postcode for Cagliari is 09100.

Medical & Emergency Services For an ambulance ring ☎ 28 62 00, and for medical attention go to the Ospedale Civile (☎ 609 22 67), Via Ospedale. Contact the police on ☎ 113, or go to the questura (☎ 602 71), Via Amat 9.

Things to See
The **Museo Archeologico Nazionale**, Piazza Arsenale, in the Citadella dei Musei, has a fascinating collection of Nuraghic bronzes. It's open daily except Monday from 9 am to 2 pm and 3.30 to 8 pm in summer and from 9 am to 7 pm in winter. Entry is L4000.

It's enjoyable enough to wander through the medieval quarter. The Pisan-Romanesque **Duomo** was built in the 13th century, but later remodelled. It has an interesting Romanesque pulpit.

From the **Bastione di San Remy**, which is in the centre of town in Piazza Costituzione and once formed part of the fortifications of the old city, there is a good view of Cagliari and the sea.

The Pisan **Torre di San Pancrazio**, in Piazza Indipendenza, is also worth a look. The **Roman amphitheatre**, on Viale Buon Cammino, is considered the most important Roman monument in Sardinia. During summer opera is performed here.

Spend a day on the **Spiaggia di Poetto** (east of the centre) and wander across to the salt lakes to see the flamingoes.

Special Events
The Festival of Sant'Efisio, a colourful festival mixing the secular and the religious, is held annually for four days from 1 May.

Places to Stay & Eat
There are numerous budget pensioni near the station. Try the *Locanda Firenze* (☎ 66 85 05), Corso Vittorio Emanuele 149, which has comfortable singles/doubles for L40,000/54,000. The *Locanda Miramare* (☎ 66 40 21), Via Roma 59, has rooms for L50,000/70,000. Nearby is *Albergo La Perla* (☎ 66 94 46), Via Sardegna 18, with rooms for L46,000/58,000.

Several reasonably priced trattorias can be found in the area behind Via Roma, particularly around Via Sardegna and Via Cavour. *Trattoria da Serafino*, Via Lepanto 6, on the corner of Via Sardegna, has excellent food at reasonable prices. *Trattoria Gennargentu*, Via Sardegna 60, has good pasta and seafood and a full meal costs around L30,000. *Trattoria Ci Pensa Cannas*, down the street at No 37, is another good choice, with meals for around L25,000. In Via Sardegna there are also grocery shops and bakeries.

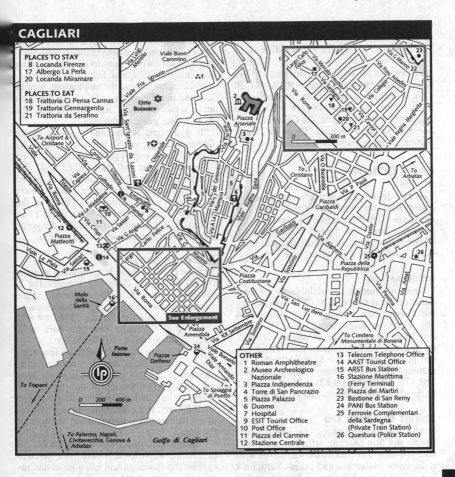

CAGLIARI

PLACES TO STAY
8 Locanda Firenze
17 Albergo La Perla
20 Locanda Miramare

PLACES TO EAT
18 Trattoria Ci Pensa Cannas
19 Trattoria Gennargentu
21 Trattoria da Serafino

OTHER
1 Roman Amphitheatre
2 Museo Archeologico Nazionale
3 Piazza Indipendenza
4 Torre di San Pancrazio
5 Piazza Palazzo
6 Duomo
7 Hospital
8 ESIT Tourist Office
10 Post Office
11 Piazza del Carmine
12 Stazione Centrale
13 Telecom Telephone Office
14 AAST Tourist Office
15 ARST Bus Station
16 Stazione Marittima (Ferry Terminal)
22 Piazza dei Martiri
23 Bastione di San Remy
24 PANI Bus Station
25 Ferrovie Complementari della Sardegna (Private Train Station)
26 Questura (Police Station)

Getting There & Away

Air Cagliari's airport (☎ 24 02 00) is to the north-west of the city at Elmas. ARST buses leave regularly from Piazza Matteotti to coincide with flight arrivals and departures. The Alitalia office (☎ 24 00 79; 147-86 56 43) is at the airport.

Bus & Train ARST buses (☎ 167-86 50 42) leave from Piazza Matteotti for nearby towns, the Costa del Sud and the Costa Rei. PANI buses (☎ 65 23 26) leave from further along Via Roma at Piazza Darsena for towns such

as Sassari, Oristano and Nuoro. The main train station is also in Piazza Matteotti. Regular trains leave for Oristano, Sassari, Porto Torres and Olbia. The private Ferrovie Complementari della Sardegna train station is in Piazza della Repubblica. For information about the *Trenino Verde* which runs along a scenic route between Cagliari and Arbatax, contact ESIT (see Tourist Offices), or the Ferrovie Complementari directly (☎ 58 02 46). The most interesting and picturesque section of the route is between Mandas and Arbatax.

ITALY

Car & Motorcycle For rental cars or motorcycles try Hertz (☎ 66 81 05), Piazza Matteotti 1, or Ruvioli (☎ 65 89 55), Via dei Mille 11.

Boat Ferries arrive at the port just off Via Roma. Bookings for Tirrenia (☎ 06-474 20 41 in Rome) can be made at the port office of Molo della Sanità (☎ 66 60 65) or c/o Agenave (☎ 66 60 65) at Via Campidano 1. See the Sardinia Getting There & Away section for more information.

CALA GONONE
☎ 0784

This fast-developing seaside resort is an excellent base from which to explore the coves along the eastern coastline, as well as the Nuraghic sites and rugged terrain inland. Major points are accessible by bus and boat, but you will need a car to explore.

Information
Tourist information is available at the boat ticket office at the port. At Cala Gonone, try the *Cooperativa Ghivine* (☎ 0348-224 34 36), which organises guided treks. There is a Pro Loco tourist office at nearby Dorgali (☎ 962 43), Via Lamarmora 108, where you can pick up maps, a list of hotels and information to help you while visiting the area. The EPT office (☎ 300 83) in Nuoro, Piazza Italia 19, also has information on the area.

Things to See & Do
From Cala Gonone's port catch a boat to the **Grotta del Bue Marino**, where a guide will take you on a 1km walk to see vast caves with stalagmites, stalactites and lakes. Sardinia's last colony of monk seals once lived here, but have not been sighted in several years. Boats also leave for **Cala Luna**, an isolated beach where you can spend the day by the sea or take a walk along the fabulous gorge called **Codula di Luna**. Unfortunately, the beach is packed with day-tripping tourists in summer. The boat trip to visit the grotto and beach costs L33,000.

A **walking track** along the coast links Cala Fuili, south of Cala Gonone, and Cala Luna (about three hours one way).

For trekking in the nearby Barbagia mountains, contact Barbagia Insolita (☎ 0784-28 81 67), Via Carducci 25, in Oliena; or

Levamus Viaggi (☎ 0784-28 51 90), also in Oliena at Corso Vittorio Emanuele 27. You can choose between demanding treks, relaxing walks, or 4WD tours to places including the Nuraghic village of **Tiscali** in the evocative Lanaittu valley, the impressive **Monte Corrasi** and the gorges of Gola di Gorropu and Codula di Luna. Ask for Murena, the more expert guide of the area.

If you want to descend the impressive **Gorropu Gorge**, ask for information from the team of young expert guides based in Urzulei – Società Gorropu (☎ 0782-64 92 82, 0347-775 27 06). They also offer a wide range of guided walks in the area at good prices. It is necessary to use ropes and harnesses to traverse the Gorropu Gorge; however, when it doesn't rain too much, it is possible to walk into the gorge from its northern entrance for about 1km.

Places to Stay
At Cala Gonone there is a *camping ground* (☎ 931 65) at Via Collodi. It's expensive in summer at up to L20,000 per person. Free camping is forbidden throughout the area.

Hotels include the *Piccolo Hotel* (☎ 932 32), Via C Colombo near the port, with singles/doubles for L50,000/90,000.

Su Gologone (☎ 28 75 12) is a few kilometres east of Oliena, near the entrance to the Lanaittu valley. It's on the expensive side at around L145,000 for half-board, but is in a lovely setting and the owners also organise guided tours, treks and horse-riding expeditions. Its restaurant is renowned throughout the island.

Albergo CiKappa (☎ 28 87 33, 28 80 24) in Oliena is a comfortable base from which to explore the Barbagia and has a good and inexpensive restaurant.

Getting There & Away
Catch a PANI bus to Nuoro from Cagliari, Sassari or Oristano and then take an ARST bus to Dorgali and Cala Gonone. There is also a bus from Olbia's port to Oliena or Dorgali, from where you can catch a bus (only every three hours) to Cala Gonone. If you are travelling by car, you will need a detailed road map of the area. One of the best is published by the Istituto Geografico de Agostini. The tourist office has maps which detail the locations of the main sights.

ALGHERO
☎ 079

One of the most popular tourist resorts in Sardinia, Alghero is on the island's west coast in the area known as the Coral Riviera. The town is a good base from which to explore the magnificent coastline which links it to Bosa in the south, and the famous Grotte di Nettuno (Neptune's Caves) on the Capocaccia to the north.

Information
The train station is on Via Don Minzoni, some distance from the centre, and is connected by a regular bus service to the centre of town.

The AAST tourist office (☎ 97 90 54; fax 97 48 81) is at Piazza Porta Terra 9, near the port and just across the gardens from the bus station. The old city and most hotels and restaurants are in the area west of the tourist office.

The main post office is at Via XX Settembre 108. There is a bank of public telephones on Via Vittorio Emanuele at the opposite end of the gardens from the tourist office. The postcode for Alghero is 07041.

In an emergency ring the police on ☎ 113; for medical attention ring ☎ 93 05 33, or go to the Ospedale Civile (☎ 99 62 33) on Via Don Minzoni.

Things to See & Do
It's worth wandering through the narrow streets of the old city and around the port. The most interesting church is the **Chiesa di San Francesco**, Via Carlo Alberto. The city's **cathedral** has been ruined by constant remodelling, but its bell tower remains a fine example of Gothic-Catalan architecture.

Near Alghero at the beautiful **Capocaccia** are the **Grotte di Nettuno**, accessible by hourly boats from the port (L16,000), or three time a day by the FS bus from Via Catalogna (50 minutes, L3400 one way).

If you have your own transport, don't miss the **Nuraghe di Palmavera**, about 10km out of Alghero on the road to Porto Conte.

The coastline between Alghero and Bosa is stunning. Rugged cliffs fall down to isolated beaches, and near **Bosa** is one of the last habitats of the griffon vulture. It's quite an experience if you are lucky enough to spot one of these huge birds. The best way to see the coast is by car or motorcycle. If you want

to rent a bicycle or motorcycle to explore the coast, try Cicloexpress (☎ 98 69 50), Via Garibaldi, at the port.

Special Events
In summer Alghero stages the Estate Musicale Algherese (Alghero's Summer Music Festival) in the cloisters of the church of San Francesco, Via Carlo Alberto. A festival, complete with fireworks display, is held annually on 15 August for the Feast of the Assumption.

Places to Stay
It is virtually impossible to find a room in August unless you book months in advance. At other times of the year you should have little trouble. Camping facilities include **Calik** (☎ 93 01 11) in Fertilia, about 7km out of town (around L25,000 per person). The HI **Ostello dei Giuliani** (☎ 93 03 53) is at Via Zara 1, Fertilia. Take the hourly bus 'AF' from Via Catalogna to Fertilia. B&B costs L14,000, a shower is L1000 and a meal costs L14,000. The hostel is open all year.

In the old town is the **Hotel San Francesco** (☎ 97 92 58), Via Ambrogio Machin 2, with singles/doubles for L50,000/85,000. **Pensione Normandie** (☎ 97 53 02), Via Enrico Mattei 6, is out of the centre. To get there follow Via Cagliari, which becomes Viale Giovanni XXIII. It has slightly shabby but large singles/doubles for L37,000/65,000.

Places to Eat
A pleasant place to eat is **Trattoria La Singular** (☎ 98 20 98), Via Arduino 45. A full meal will cost around L35,000. A cheaper option is the **pizzeria** just off Via Roma at Vicolo Adami 17. Takeaway pizza by the slice costs about L3000.

Getting There & Away
Alghero is accessible from Sassari by train. The main bus station is on Via Catalogna, next to the public park. ARST (☎ 95 01 79) buses leave for Sassari and Porto Torres. FS buses (☎ 95 04 58) also service Sassari, Macomer and Bosa. The private Turmotravel (☎ 0789-26 101) offers a special service to Olbia to coincide with ferry departures.

Macedonia (Македонија)

The Former Yugoslav Republic of Macedonia (FYROM) is at the south end of what was once the Yugoslav Federation. Its position in the centre of the Balkan Peninsula between Albania, Bulgaria, Serbia and Greece has often made it a political powder keg. The mix of Islamic and Orthodox influences tell of a long struggle which ended in 1913 when the Treaty of Bucharest divided Macedonia among its three neighbours. Serbia got the northern part while the southern half went to Greece. Bulgaria received a much smaller slice. Only in 1992 did ex-Yugoslav Macedonia become fully independent.

In this book, Lonely Planet uses the name Macedonia rather than the Former Yugoslav Republic of Macedonia. This is to reflect what its inhabitants prefer to call their country and is not intended to prejudice any political claims.

For travellers Macedonia is a land of contrasts, ranging from space-age Skopje with its modern shopping centre and timeworn Turkish bazar, to the many medieval monasteries of Ohrid. Macedonia's fascinating blend of Orthodox mystery and the exotic Orient combine with the world-class beauty of Lake Ohrid to make the country much more than just a transit route on the way to somewhere else.

AT A GLANCE

Capital	Skopje
Population	2 million
Area	25,333 sq km
Official Language	Macedonian
Currency	1 Macedonian denar (MKD) = 100 deni
GDP	US$2 billion (1996)
Time	GMT/UTC+0100

Facts about Macedonia

HISTORY

Historical Macedonia (whence Alexander the Great set out to conquer the ancient world in the 4th century BC) is today contained mostly in present-day Greece, a point Greeks are always quick to make when discussing contemporary Macedonia's use of that name. The Romans subjugated the Greeks of ancient Macedonia and the territory to the north in the mid-2nd century BC, and when the empire was divided in the 4th century AD this region became part of the Eastern Roman Empire ruled from Constantinople. Slav

tribes settled here in the 7th century, changing the ethnic character of the area.

In the 9th century the region was conquered by the Bulgarian tsar Simeon (893-927) and later, under Tsar Samuel (980-1014), Macedonia was the centre of a powerful Bulgarian state. Samuel's defeat by Byzantium in 1014 ushered in a long period when Macedonia passed back and forth between Byzantium, Bulgaria and Serbia. After the crushing defeat of Serbia by the Turks in 1389, the Balkans became part of the Ottoman Empire and the cultural character of the region again changed.

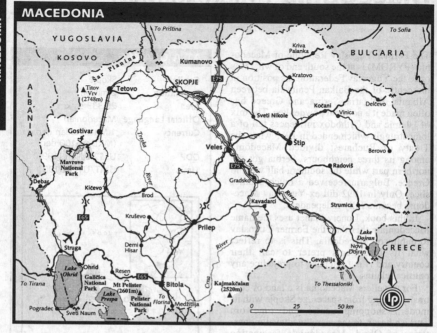

In 1878 Russia defeated Turkey, and Macedonia was ceded to Bulgaria by the Treaty of San Stefano. The Western powers, fearing the creation of a powerful Russian satellite in the heart of the Balkans, forced Bulgaria to give Macedonia back to Turkey.

In 1893 Macedonian nationalists formed the Internal Macedonian Revolutionary Organisation (IMRO) to fight for independence from Turkey, culminating in the Ilinden uprising of May 1903 which was brutally suppressed three months later. Although nationalist leader Goce Delčev died before the revolt he has become the symbol of Macedonian nationalism.

The First Balkan War in 1912 brought Greece, Serbia and Bulgaria together against Turkey. In the Second Balkan War in 1913 Greece and Serbia ousted the Bulgarians and split Macedonia between themselves. Frustrated by this result IMRO continued the struggle against royalist Serbia; the interwar government in Belgrade responded by banning the Macedonian language and even the name Macedonia. Though some IMRO elements supported the Bulgarian occupation of Macedonia during WWII, many more joined Tito's partisans, and in 1943 it was agreed that postwar Macedonia would have full republic status in future Yugoslavia. The first Macedonian grammar was published in 1952 and an independent Macedonian Orthodox Church was allowed to form. By recognising Macedonians as an ethnic group distinct from both Serbs and Bulgarians, the Belgrade authorities hoped to weaken Bulgarian claims to Macedonia.

On 8 September 1991 a referendum on independence was held in Macedonia and 74% voted in favour, so in January 1992 the country declared its full independence from former Yugoslavia. For once Belgrade cooperated by ordering all federal troops present to withdraw and, because the split was peaceful, road and rail links were never broken. In mid-1993, however, about 1000 United Nations troops were sent to Macedonia to monitor the border with Yugoslavia, especially near the potentially volatile province of Kosovo.

Greece delayed diplomatic recognition of Macedonia by demanding that the country find another name, alleging that the term Macedonia implied territorial claims on northern Greece. The concern of Greece is that if the Macedonians use the term Macedonia they may aspire to greater de facto legitimacy to the ambit of ancient Macedonia, which included (and still includes) a large part of Greece. At the insistence of Greek officials, Macedonia was forced to use the absurd 'temporary' title FYROM (Former Yugoslav Republic of Macedonia) for the purpose of being admitted to the UN in April 1993. After vacillating for two years, six of the European Union (EU) countries established diplomatic relations with FYROM in December 1993 despite strong objections from Greece, and in February 1994 the USA also recognised FYROM. At this, Greece declared an economic embargo against Macedonia and closed the port of Thessaloniki to the country's trade. The embargo was lifted in November 1995 after Macedonia changed its flag and agreed to enter into discussions with Greece about the name of the country. Shortly after these decisions were made, president Kiro Gligorov was almost assassinated in a car-bombing. To date, there has been no final resolution of this thorny issue.

Relations with Greece on the trade front nonetheless are looking healthy, though recently introduced visa restrictions for both sides has meant time-wasting visits to embassies in Athens and Skopje for casual travellers, and Macedonians wishing to take a vacation in Greece are often subjected to numbing delays at the border. Macedonians wishing to visit other Western European countries also face many visa requirements.

Macedonia is in the process of seeking possible admission to the EU.

GEOGRAPHY
Much of 25,713-sq-km Macedonia is a plateau between 600 and 900m high. The Vardar River cuts across the middle of the country, passing the capital, Skopje, on its way to the Aegean Sea near Thessaloniki. Ohrid and Prespa lakes in the south-west drain into the Adriatic via Albania. These lakes are among the largest on the Balkan Peninsula, and Lake Ohrid is also the deepest (294m compared to Prespa Lake's 35m). In the north-west the Šar Planina marks Macedonia's border with Kosovo; Titov Vrv (2748m) in this range is Macedonia's highest peak. The country's three national parks are Pelister (west of Bitola), Galičica (between lakes Ohrid and Prespa) and Mavrovo (between Ohrid and Tetovo).

GOVERNMENT & POLITICS
The current government under president Kiro Gligorov is nominally a democratically elected parliament following the American presidential system. However, cronyism and corruption are widely thought to exist and power is still in the hands of the old guard pseudo-communists of the former Yugoslavia and little grass-roots democracy is yet practised.

ECONOMY
Macedonia is a rich agricultural area which feeds itself and exports tomatoes and cucumbers to Western Europe. Cereals, rice, cotton and tobacco are also grown and Macedonian mines yield chromium, manganese, tungsten, lead and zinc. The main north-south trade route from Western Europe to Greece via the valleys of the Danube, Morava and Vardar rivers passes through the country. Tourism is concentrated around Lake Ohrid. At present Macedonia is gradually recovering its economic equilibrium after the lifting of UN sanctions against Yugoslavia which, together with Greece, had provided the ports and land routes for Macedonia's trade. Economic relations with Greece, though not what they once were, are slowly improving.

With the changes in Eastern Europe and especially with the separation of Macedonia from Yugoslavia, a new east-west trading route is developing from Turkey to Italy via Bulgaria, Macedonia and Albania. Over the next decade US$2.5 billion is to be invested in a new railway and motorway corridor linking Sofia, Skopje and Tirana. At present this route is covered only by narrow secondary roads, a legacy of the political policies of former regimes.

Since the late 1960s, tens of thousands of Macedonians have emigrated, and remittances from the 100,000 Macedonians now resident in Germany and Switzerland are a major source of income.

POPULATION & PEOPLE

Of the republic's present population of over two million, 66% are Macedonian Slavs who bear no relation whatsoever to the Greek-speaking Macedonians of antiquity. The Macedonian language is much closer to Bulgarian than to Serbian and many ethnographers consider the Macedonians ethnic Bulgarians. The official position of the Bulgarian government is that Macedonians are Bulgarians, though only a minority of Macedonians support this view.

The largest minority groups are ethnic Albanians (22%), Turks (4%), Serbs (2%), Roma (2%) and others (4%). The birth rate of the mostly rural Albanians is three times the national average. Albanians are in a majority in the region between Tetovo and Debar in the north-west of the republic and there have been demonstrations in defence of the right to education in Albanian.

The 50,000 Macedonians living in northern Greece are subject to assimilatory pressures by the Greek government, which calls them 'Slavophone Greeks'. Education in Macedonian is denied and human rights groups such as Helsinki Watch have documented many cases of police harassment of Greek Macedonians who publicly protested against these policies.

ARTS
Music

The oldest form of Macedonian folk music involves the *gajda* (bagpipes). This is played solo or is accompanied by *tapan* (two-sided drum), each side of which is played with a different stick to obtain a different tone. These are often augmented by *kaval* (flute) and/or *tambura* (small lute with two pairs of strings). Macedonia has also inherited (from the long period of Turkish influence) the *zurla* (double-reed horn), also accompanied by the *tapan*, and the '*Čalgija*' music form

involving clarinet, violin, *darabuk* (hourglass shaped drum) and *džumbuš* (banjo-like instrument).

Bands playing these instruments may be heard at festivals such as the folklore festival in Ohrid in mid-July or the Ilinden festival in Bitola around August 2, and you may catch a stage performance in Skopje or Ohrid at other times. If you're really lucky you may get to see a wedding procession. However, in most restaurants and night spots, synthesiser, drum kit and guitar are the order of the day. Nearly all Macedonian traditional music is accompanied by dancing.

Folk Dancing

The most famous Macedonian folk dance is probably *Teškoto* (The Difficult One). It is a male dance for which music is provided by the *tapan* and *zurla*. It starts very slowly and becomes progressively faster. The finale is dynamic and beautiful to watch. During the dance, a number of symbolic actions take place. At one point, the dance leader climbs on to the tapan, for example. This dance is often included in festivals or concerts, and is always performed by dancers in traditional Macedonian costume.

Other dances often included in performances are *Komitsko*, symbolising the struggle of Macedonian freedom fighters against the Turks and *Tresenica*, a women's dance from the Mariovo region.

SOCIETY & CONDUCT

Macedonians are a proud and hospitable people and welcome visitors. If invited out for a meal, it is assumed that your host will pay for you. Insist on contributing if you must, but don't overdo it. Show respect to your hosts by learning a few words of Macedonian. Be aware that churches and mosques are not built for tourists, but are working places of worship. Dress and behave accordingly. Tread carefully when talking politics, especially about Greeks and Albanians.

RELIGION

Most of the Albanians and Turks are Muslim, while the Slavs are Orthodox.

LANGUAGE

Macedonian is a South Slavic language divided into two large groups, the western and eastern Macedonian dialects. The Macedonian literary language is based on the central dialects of Veles, Prilep and Bitola. Macedonian shares all the characteristics which separate Bulgarian from the other Slavic languages, evidence that it's closely related to Bulgarian.

The Cyrillic alphabet is based on the alphabet developed by two Thessaloniki brothers, St Cyril and St Methodius, in the 9th century. It was taught by their disciples at a monastery in Ohrid, Macedonia, whence it spread across the eastern Slavic world.

The Cyrillic alphabet is used predominantly in Macedonia. Street names are printed in Cyrillic script only, so it is imperative that you learn the Cyrillic alphabet if you don't want to get lost. Road signs use both Cyrillic and Latin scripts.

Lonely Planet's *Mediterranean Europe phrasebook* contains a complete chapter on Macedonian with Cyrillic spellings provided. For a quick introduction to Macedonian, see the Language chapter at the end of this book.

Facts for the Visitor

HIGHLIGHTS

The Byzantine monasteries of Ohrid, particularly Sveti Sofija and Sveti Kliment, are worth a visit. Lake Ohrid itself is simply beautiful. The Čaršija (old Turkish bazar) in Skopje is very colourful.

SUGGESTED ITINERARIES

Depending on the length of your stay, you might want to see and do the following things in Macedonia:

Two days
    Visit Skopje
One week
    Visit Skopje and Ohrid
Two weeks
    As above, plus some hiking in Pelister and Galičica national parks between Ohrid and Bitola

PLANNING
Climate & When to Go

Macedonia's summers are hot and dry. In winter, warm Aegean winds blowing up the Vardar Valley moderate the continental conditions prevailing further north. However, Macedonia receives a lot of snowfall, even if temperatures are warmer than those further north.

Books & Maps

A couple of good background books are *Who Are the Macedonians?* by Hugh Poulton, a political and cultural history of the region, and *Black Lambs and Grey Falcons* by Rebecca West, a between-the-wars Balkan travelogue.

Baedeker's Greece map also covers Macedonia. In Macedonia you should be able to get hold of the excellent *Republic of Macedonia* map, published by GiziMap of Hungary.

What to Bring

You can find most things in Macedonia, but do bring along a universal sink plug since hotels rarely have them.

TOURIST OFFICES

Makedonijaturist (☎ 115 051), based in the Hotel Turist in Skopje, is the state tourist organisation. Private agencies are also appearing on the scene.

VISAS & EMBASSIES
Visas

British and Yugoslav passport-holders do not require visas. Canadians, Americans and Australians need a visa but it's issued free of charge at the border. New Zealanders and South Africans need pre-arranged visas. However, if it is at all feasible, a visa should be obtained beforehand so as to avoid any possible delays or hassles.

Macedonia Embassies Abroad

Macedonian embassies are found in the following countries. There are no embassies as yet in Australia or New Zealand.

France
    (☎ 01-45 77 10 50; fax 01-45 77 14 84) 21 rue Sébastien Mercie 15e, Paris

Netherlands
(☎ 070-427 4464) Laan van Meerdervoort 50/C, 2517 AM, The Hague

UK
(☎ 0171-499 5152) 19a Cavendish Square, London, W1M 8DT 5JJ

USA
(☎ 202-337 3063) 3050 K Street NW, Washington DC, 20007

Foreign Embassies in Macedonia
The following embassies are in Skopje:

Albania
(☎ 614 636; fax 614 200) ul H T Karpoš 94

Bulgaria
(☎ 229 444; fax 116 139) ul Zlatko Šnajder 3 (weekdays from 9 am to noon)

Romania
(☎ 370 114; fax 361 130) ul Londonska 11a

UK
(☎ 116 772; fax 117 555) ul Dimitrija Čupkovski 26 (weekdays from 10 am to 4 pm)

USA
(☎ 116 180; fax 117 103) Bulevar Ilindenska (weekdays from 10 am to 4 pm)

Yugoslavia
(☎ 362 697; fax 361 288) Knez Hacon 2-7-9

Visa requirements and costs for travellers to all nearby countries change frequently, so check with the embassies in question, or see the relevant country chapter.

CUSTOMS
Customs checks are generally cursory. However, if you are carrying photographic or electrical items customs officers may record them in your passport to ensure that you will carry them out when you depart.

MONEY
Colourful Macedonian denar (MKD) banknotes come in denominations of 10, 50, 100, 500, 1000 and 5000 and there are coins of one, two and five denari. The denar is now a stable currency, but outside Macedonia it is worthless.

Travellers cheques can be changed into Macedonian denari at most banks with no commission deducted. Small private exchange offices can be found throughout central Skopje and Ohrid and the rate they offer is generally good.

Exchange Rates
Conversion rates for major currencies in mid-1998 are listed below:

Australia	A$1	=	37 MKD
Canada	C$1	=	40 MKD
France	1FF	=	9.2 MKD
Germany	DM1	=	31 MKD
UK	UK£1	=	89.9 MKD
USA	US$1	=	54.9 MKD

Tipping
It is common practice to round up restaurant bills to the nearest convenient figure and waiters may indeed assume that this is what you intend and keep the expected change anyway. Consequently, don't give the waiter more than you are prepared to part with as a tip.

Taxi drivers will expect a round-up to the nearest convenient figure unless you have agreed on a fee beforehand.

POST & COMMUNICATIONS
Post
Mail addressed c/o Poste Restante, 91000 Skopje 2, Macedonia, can be claimed at the post office next to Skopje train station, weekdays from 8 am to 1 pm. Mail addressed to 91101 can be picked up at the main post office by the river.

Mail addressed c/o Poste Restante, 96000 Ohrid, Macedonia, can be picked up at Ohrid's main post office near the bus station.

Telephone
Long-distance phone calls cost less at main post offices than in hotels. To call Macedonia from abroad dial the international access code, ☎ 389 (the country code for Macedonia), the area code (without the initial zero) and the number. Area codes include ☎ 091 (Skopje), ☎ 096 (Ohrid) and ☎ 097 (Bitola). For outgoing calls the international access code in Macedonia is ☎ 99. Card phones are now available in major centres. You can purchase phonecards, in 100 (75 MKD) or 200-unit (150 MKD) denominations, from post offices.

The approximate cost of a three-minute call to the USA or Australia is about 337 MKD.

While Macedonia has a digital mobile phone network (MOBIMAK), it is unlikely that your own provider has a roaming agreement with Macedonia's domestic network. Check with your own provider to be sure.

INTERNET RESOURCES
A couple of useful World Wide Web sites are www.b-info.com/places/macedonia/republic (*Macedonia Information Almanac*), and www.vmacedonia.com/index2.html (*Virtual Macedonia*). Both sites have useful background and practical information. A number of private Internet service providers operate in Skopje, but the most practical way to access the Net is through Internet cafés.

NEWSPAPERS & MAGAZINES
There are three local Macedonian-language papers, along with an Albanian and a Turkish daily. English-language papers and magazines can be bought at most central kiosks, but *Svet World Press* on the corner of Dame Gruev and Partizanski in Skopje has a wide selection of foreign publications. There is also an English-language monthly called *Skopsko Metro* that you may be able to find at tourist locations.

RADIO & TV
You have a choice of two state TV stations and any number of private and satellite channels, including CBC, Eurosport and Euronews. There are many local FM radio stations. The BBC World Service is found on 104.4, the Voice of America on 107.5 FM.

PHOTOGRAPHY & VIDEO
Film sales and same-day developing services are widespread, at least in Ohrid and Skopje and are reasonably cheap. You are advised to develop your slide film at home. Video paraphernalia is not easy to find, so come supplied with everything you might need.

TIME
Macedonia goes on daylight-saving time at the end of March when clocks are turned forward one hour. On the last Sunday of September they're turned back an hour. Bulgaria

and Greece are always one hour ahead of Macedonia while Yugoslavia and Albania keep the same time as Skopje.

ELECTRICITY
Macedonia uses 220V AC, 50 Hz. A circular plug with two round pins is used.

WEIGHTS & MEASURES
Macedonia uses the metric system.

LAUNDRY
There are currently no self-wash laundry services anywhere in Macedonia. Handwash as you go, or your hotel just might be able to wash your clothes for a fee. Dry cleaning (*chemisko chistenye*) is available, but you'll have to ask around to find an outlet.

TOILETS
Public toilets are invariably of the grotty 'squattie' type and are universally in bad shape. Take toilet paper with you if you must use them, but make use of hotel and restaurant toilets whenever you can.

HEALTH
Basic health services may be available free to travellers from state health centres. Health insurance to cover private health services is recommended.

WOMEN TRAVELLERS
Women travellers should feel no particular concern about travel in Macedonia. Other than possible cursory interest from men, travel is hassle-free and easy.

GAY & LESBIAN TRAVELLERS
Homosexuality in Macedonia is technically legal. However, the profile of gays in the country is so low as to be invisible. Given its tenuous social acceptability, a low profile should always be maintained.

DISABLED TRAVELLERS
Few public buildings or streets have facilities for wheelchairs. Access could be problematic. Newer buildings do provide wheelchair ramps.

DANGERS & ANNOYANCES

Macedonia is a safe country in general. Travellers should be on the lookout for pickpockets in bus and train stations and exercise common sense in looking after belongings.

BUSINESS HOURS

Office and business hours are 8 am to 8 pm weekdays, 8 am to 2 pm on Saturday.

PUBLIC HOLIDAYS & SPECIAL EVENTS

Public holidays in Macedonia are New Year (1 and 2 January), Orthodox Christmas (7 January), Old New Year (13 January), Easter Monday and Tuesday (March/April), Labour Day (1 May), Ilinden or Day of the 1903 Rebellion (2 August), Republic Day (8 September) and 1941 Partisan Day (11 October).

ACTIVITIES

Macedonia's top ski resort is Popova šapka (1845m) on the southern slopes of Šar Planina west of Tetovo. Hiking in any of the three national parks is a good way to get to know the countryside, but there do not seem to be organised outings for visitors.

COURSES

The American Language Company offers 'Survival Courses in Macedonian for Foreigners'. For full details call ☎ 237 614 between 4 and 9 pm. Check also Via Media (☎ 114 669) at Dame Gruev 1/14.

ACCOMMODATION

Macedonia's hotels are very expensive but there are camping grounds and private-room agencies in Ohrid and Skopje. Skopje's convenient HI hostel is open throughout the year, and the Ohrid hostel opens in summer. Beds are available at student dormitories in Skopje in summer. Prices in more expensive hotels are usually quoted in deutschmarks (DM) or US dollars (US$).

FOOD

Turkish-style grilled mincemeat is available almost everywhere and there are self-service cafeterias in most towns for the less adventurous. Balkan *burek* (cheese or meat pie) and yoghurt makes for a cheap breakfast. Look out for a sign sporting *burekdžilnica* if you want burek for breakfast. Watch for Macedonian *tavče gravče* (beans in a skillet) and Ohrid trout, which is priced according to weight.

Other dishes to try are *teleška čorba* (veal soup), *riblja čorba* (fish soup), *čevapčinja* (small skinless sausages), *mešena salata* (mixed salad) and *šopska salata* (mixed salad with grated white cheese).

DRINKS

Skopsko Pivo is the local beer. It's good and reasonably cheap. Other brand name European beers are also available. There is a good number of commercially produced wines of average to better quality and the national firewater is *rakija*, a strong distilled spirit made from grapes. *Mastika*, an ouzo-like spirit, is also popular.

ENTERTAINMENT

Entertainment for Macedonia's hip generation consists of hanging out in smart cafés and bars until the early hours. Movies are popular and all the latest Hollywood blockbusters can be watched at a fraction of the price back home. Live traditional Macedonian music can often be heard in restaurants and Skopje has a couple of bars with live jazz bands.

THINGS TO BUY

Look out for rugs and small textiles, paintings, traditional costumes, antique coins, handmade dolls and, from Ohrid, wood carvings for mementos to take home.

Getting There & Away

AIR

Jugoslavian Airlines (JAT), Macedonian Airlines (MAT), Adria (SLO), Croatia Airlines (HR) and Avioimpex (MK) offer flights from Skopje to a number of European destinations, many via Belgrade. Sample one-way discount prices are: Amsterdam (9765 MKD); Belgrade (3875 MKD); Düsseldorf (8680 MKD); Rome (7000 MKD); and Vienna

(7750 MKD). Return prices are usually a better deal and all prices are usually linked to and quoted in DM.

Any travel agent in Skopje or Ohrid can book these flights. In Skopje, Mata Travel (☎ 239 175), next to the international bus station, or Marco Polo Travel (☎ 222 340), on the corner of ul Maksim Gorki, are two agencies that you may like to approach.

LAND

Bus

The international bus station in Skopje is next to the City Museum. Mata Travel Agency (☎ 239 175; fax 230 269), at the international bus station, has buses to Sofia (twice to three times daily, 6½ hours, 500 MKD), İstanbul (four daily, 16 hours, 1630 MKD), Belgrade (daily, 5½ hours, 1050 MKD) and Munich (once a week, 27 hours, 4300 MKD). Some international buses also leave from a station behind the Stopanska Banka on the Čaršija side of the River and from a parking lot near the Grand Hotel.

To/from Croatia you must head for Belgrade and change for a bus to the Croatian border where you will change to a Croatian bus. Ask about overnight buses from Skopje to Belgrade and Podgorica. Buses between Skopje and Prizren in Kosovo, Yugoslavia (117km), are fairly frequent. To/from Albania you can travel between Skopje and Tirana by bus, or walk across the border at Sveti Naum (see the Ohrid section).

Train

Express trains run three times a day between Skopje and Belgrade (nine hours, 1178 MKD), via Niš. Sleepers are available on the overnight Skopje-Belgrade train. Trains run twice a day between Skopje and Thessaloniki.

Sample 2nd-class international train fares from Skopje are 676 MKD to Thessaloniki (five hours), 1780 MKD to Athens (14 hours), 2762 MKD to Budapest (15 hours) and 4076 MKD to Vienna (20 hours).

Greece-bound, it's cheaper to buy a ticket only to Thessaloniki and get another on to Athens from there. There's no direct rail link between Macedonia and Bulgaria and the train is not recommended for travel between

Sofia and Skopje as you must change trains in Yugoslavia and a visa will be required.

All the timetables and arrivals/departures boards at Skopje train station are in Cyrillic script only. For information in English go upstairs to Feroturist Travel Agency (open daily 7 am to 8.30 pm), which also sells international train tickets and books sleepers to Belgrade.

Note that Thessaloniki in Macedonian is 'Solun'.

Car & Motorcycle

There are several main highway border crossings into Macedonia from neighbouring countries.

Yugoslavia You can cross at Blace (between Skopje and Uroševac) and Tabanovce (10km north of Kumanovo).

Bulgaria The main crossings are just east of Kriva Palanka (between Sofia and Skopje), and east of Delčevo (26km west of Blagoevgrad) and Novo Selo (between Kulata and Strumica).

Greece There are crossings at Gevgelija (between Skopje and Thessaloniki), Dojran (just east of Gevgelija) and Medžitlija (16km south of Bitola).

Albania The crossings are Sveti Naum (29km south of Ohrid), Ćafa San (12km south-west of Struga) and Blato (5km northwest of Debar).

LEAVING MACEDONIA

The airport departure tax at Skopje and Ohrid is 510 MKD (20 DM).

Getting Around

BUS

Bus travel is well developed in Macedonia with fairly frequent services from Skopje to Ohrid and Bitola. Always book buses to/from Ohrid well in advance.

TRAIN

You won't find Macedonia's trains of much use, except perhaps for the overnight train from Skopje to Belgrade and trains to Greece. The local train from Skopje to Bitola takes four hours to cover 229km. There are also local services from Skopje to Kičevo and Gevgelija on the Greek border.

CAR & MOTORCYCLE

Petrol costs are somewhat cheaper than most western European countries, and leaded and unleaded petrol and diesel are widely available. The cost is 36.5 MKD per litre for unleaded and 38.5 MKD for leaded petrol. Diesel is about 27.5 MKD per litre.

Motorway tolls along the main highway between Yugoslavia and Greece work out to approximately 200 MKD per 100km.

Speed limits for cars and motorcycles are 120km/h on motorways, 80km/h on open roads and from 50 to 60km/h in towns. Speeding fines are very high (4000 to 12,000 MKD) and inflexibly enforced by radar-equipped highway police who just love to catch offenders, so never speed! Parking tickets average 2000 MKD and wearing a seatbelt is compulsory.

The Macedonia-wide number for emergency highway assistance is ☎ 987.

HITCHING

Hitching can be undertaken in Macedonia, but you will probably have to wait a long time for a ride. LP does not recommend hitching as a form of transport.

LOCAL TRANSPORT

A quick way of getting around the country if the buses are not convenient is by taxi, especially if there are two or more of you to share the cost. An 88km trip, say from Ohrid to the Greek border at Medžitlija, will work out at around 1500 MKD.

ORGANISED TOURS

Very little in Macedonia is geared to the international visitor market, so you will have to ask around the travel agents for any useful leads. Monthly shopping trips to Thessaloniki and other jaunts are organised by the local expat community. Call ☎ 131 412 for current details.

Around the Country

SKOPJE (СКОПЈЕ)
☎ 091

Macedonia's capital, Skopje (population 600,000), is strategically set on the Vardar River at a crossroads of Balkan routes almost exactly midway between Tirana and Sofia, capitals of neighbouring Albania and Bulgaria. Thessaloniki, Greece, is 260km south-east, near the point where the Vardar flows into the Aegean. The Romans recognised the location's importance long ago when they made Scupi the centre of Dardania Province. Later conquerors included the Slavs, Byzantines, Bulgarians, Normans and Serbs, until the Turks arrived in 1392 and managed to hold onto Uskup (Skopje) until 1912.

After a devastating earthquake in July 1963 killed 1066 people, aid poured in from the rest of Yugoslavia to create the modern urban landscape we see today. It's evident that the planners got carried away by the money being thrown their way, erecting over-sized, irrelevant structures which are now crumbling due to lack of maintenance. The post office building and telecommunications complex next to it are particularly hideous examples of this architectural overkill. Fortunately, much of the old town survived, so you can still get a glimpse of the old Skopje.

Orientation

Most of central Skopje is a pedestrian zone, with the 15th-century Turkish stone bridge (Kamen Most) over the Vardar River linking the old and new towns. South of the bridge is Ploštad Makedonija (the former Ploštad Maršal Tito), which gives into ul Makedonija leading south. The new train station is a 15-minute walk south-east of the stone bridge. The old train station, with its clock frozen at 5.17 am on July 27 the moment the earthquake struck, is now the home of the City Museum and is at the south end of ul Makedonija. The domestic bus station is just over the stone bridge. Further north is Čaršija, the old Turkish bazar.

The left-luggage office at the bus station is open from 5 am to 10 pm. Each item left costs 40 MKD. Left luggage at the train station is open 24 hours.

Information

Tourist Offices The tourist information office is opposite the Daud Pasha Baths on the viaduct between the Turkish bridge and Čaršija. There is also a tourist office inside the Trgovski Centar, the main shopping mall.

The office of the Automoto Sojuz or Automobile Club of Macedonia (☎ 116 011) is at Ivo Ribar Lola 51 just west of the city centre.

Money The Stopanska Banka facing the Turkish bridge opposite the bus station changes travellers cheques on weekdays from 7 am to 7 pm, on Saturday from 7 am to 1 pm. There are many private exchange offices scattered throughout the old and new towns where you can change your cash at a good rate.

There are ATMs on Partizanski Odredi in the Bunjakoveć Shopping Centre; in Trgovski Centar off Ploštad Makedonija; at the SBS Agrobank near Ploštad Makedonija; and at Skopje airport.

Post & Communications Poste-restante mail is held both at the train station post office and the main post office. The telephone centre in the main post office near the city centre is open 24 hours and the post office is open from 7.00 am to 7.30 pm and to 2.30 pm on Sunday.

Cybercafé The Café Astoria (☎ 128 404; astoria@mkinter.net) in the Bunjakoveć Shopping Centre at Partizanska 27a, Skopje, charges 100 MKD per hour for online time. Visit its site at www.astoria.com.mk.

Travel Agencies Mata Travel Agency (☎ 239 175; fax 230 269) is at the international bus station next to the City Museum. Feroturist Travel Agency (daily 7 am to 8.30 pm) is upstairs in the Skopje train station.

Medical & Emergency Services The city hospital (☎ 221 133) is on the corner of ul 11 Oktomvri and Moše Pijade. The Neuromedica private clinic (☎ 215 780) is at ul Partizanski 3-1-4, near the British Embassy.

Things to See

As you walk north from the Turkish bridge you'll see the **Daud Pasha Baths** (1466) on the right, once the largest Turkish baths in the Balkans. The **City Art Gallery** (closed on Monday, 100 MKD) now occupies its six domed rooms. Almost opposite this building is a functioning Orthodox church **Sveta Dimitrija**.

North again is Čaršija, the old market area, which is well worth exploring. Steps up on the left lead to the tiny **Church of Sveti Spas** with a finely carved iconostasis done in 1824. It's half buried because when it was constructed in the 17th century no church was allowed to be higher than a mosque. In the courtyard at Sveti Spas is the tomb of Goce Delčev, a mustachioed IMRO freedom fighter killed by the Turks in 1903.

Beyond the church is the **Mustafa Pasha Mosque** (1492), with an earthquake-cracked dome. The 100-MKD ticket allows you to ascend the 124 steps of the minaret. In the park across the street from this mosque are the ruins of **Fort Kale**, with an 11th-century Cyclopean wall and good views of Skopje. Higher up on the same hill is the lacklustre **Museum of Contemporary Art** (closed Monday; 50 MKD), where temporary exhibitions are presented.

The lane on the north side of Mustafa Pasha Mosque leads back down into Čaršija and the **Museum of Macedonia**. This has a large collection which covers the history of the region fairly well, but much is lost on visitors unable to read the Cyrillic captions and explanations, even though the periods are identified in English at the top of some of the showcases. The museum is housed in the modern white building behind the **Kuršumli Han** (1550), a caravanserai or inn used by traders during the Turkish period. With the destruction of Sarajevo, Skopje's old Oriental bazar district has become the largest and most colourful of its kind left in Europe.

Places to Stay

Camping From April to mid-October you can pitch a tent at *Feroturist Autocamp Park* (☎ 228 246) for 160 MKD per person and tent. Basic camping caravans are for hire year-round at 400 MKD per person. Late-night music from the restaurant can be a problem. This camping ground is between the river and the stadium, just a 15-minute walk

MACEDONIA

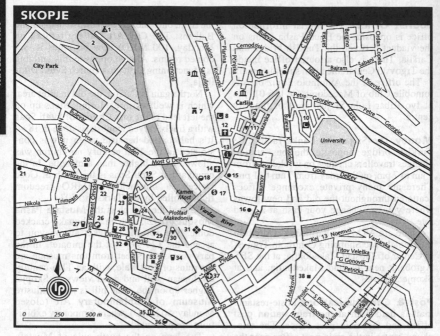

SKOPJE

City Park

Čaršija

University

Kamen Most

Ploštad Makedonija

Vardar River

0   250   500 m

---

upstream from the Turkish stone bridge along the right (south) bank. It's always a good bet.

Hostels The HI *Dom Blagoj Šošolčev Hostel* (☎ 114 849; fax 235 029; mkeuro26@mkinter.net), Prolet 25, is near the train station and is by far the best bet for travellers. The two, three and four-bed dorms are 540 MKD for members, 610 MKD for nonmembers. The newly renovated and air-conditioned double rooms with private bathroom are 830 MKD per person for members, 1350 MKD for nonmembers (including breakfast). Open all year, 24 hours a day, this hostel is often full with groups. Book beforehand if possible.

Private Rooms The tourist information office (☎ 116 854), on the viaduct two blocks north of the Turkish stone bridge, has singles/doubles in private homes beginning at 1050 MKD per person, but they're in short supply and there's no reduction for stays

longer than one night. At this price insist on something in the centre.

Hotels The *Hotel Ambasador* (☎/fax 202 603) at ul Pirinska 38 is an unusual private hotel with pleasant rooms at an approachable price. Single/double rooms go for 2170/3100 MKD. You'll understand why it's unusual after you have spotted the statue on the roof. The central 91-room *Hotel Turist* (☎ 115 051; fax 114 753) just up ul Makedonija charges a hefty 3920/6050 MKD for singles/doubles. There are at least a dozen other hotels in town, but their prices are similar to those above.

Places to Eat

The *Bit Pazar* next to the Čaršija is a colourful and lively market where you can stock up on salad items, and the well-stocked *Kamfood Supermarket* in the basement of the Trgovski Centar is a good place to get your dairy and delicatessen items. There is a

SKOPJE

PLACES TO STAY		5	Bit Pazar	22	JAT & MAT Airline
1	Feroturist Autocamp	6	Kuršumli Han		Offices
	Park	7	Fort Kale	23	Svet World Press
20	Hotel Ambasador	8	Mustafa Pasha Mosque		(Newspaper &
33	Hotel Turist	10	Sultan Murat Mosque		Magazine Shop)
38	HI Youth Hostel	12	Church of Sveti Spas	24	Marco Polo Travel
		13	Tourist Information	25	Neuromedica Clinic
PLACES TO EAT		14	Sveta Dimitrija Orthodox	26	British Embassy
9	Fontana Restaurant		Church	27	Lady Blue 2
11	Pivnitsa An	15	Daud Pasha Baths	28	Colosseum Disco
29	Ischrana Self-Service	16	Macedonian National	31	Trgovski Centar;
30	Dal Met Fu Restaurant		Theatre		Kamfood Supermarket
		17	Stopanska Banka	32	Svet World Press
OTHER		18	Domestic Bus Station	34	Concert Hall; Lady Blue 1
2	Stadium	19	Main Post Office	35	City Museum
3	Museum of	21	Astoria Internet Café;	36	International Bus Station
	Contemporary Art		Bunjakoveć Shopping	37	City Hospital
4	Museum of Macedonia		Centre	39	Train Station

cheap restaurant in the basement of the Youth Hostel (see Places to Stay) which is open to the public.

There are two easy-to-find restaurants in the modern city centre close to Ploštad Makedonija on the south side of Kamen Most. The *Dal Met Fu Restaurant* is fairly obvious across the square at the beginning of ul Makedonija, on the left as you come from the bridge. This place is good for pizza and pasta. The *Ischrana Self-Service* is a no-frills self-service joint half a block away down the next street over to the right. Look for the vertical sign reading 'Restaurant' in large blue letters.

Colourful small restaurants in Čaršija serving *kebabi* and *čevapčinja* reflect a Turkish culinary heritage still dear to the stomachs of many Macedonians. Try the *Fontana* restaurant. It is on a little square with a fountain in the Čaršija. The grills are good and the atmosphere is great. The *Pivnitsa An* nearby is an atmospheric place in an old Turkish inn (*hani*) for a relaxing evening meal.

Entertainment

Check the *Concert Hall*, ul Makedonija 12, for performances. *Club MNT*, downstairs below the Macedonian National Theatre, cranks up around 10 pm and is open in summer. The *Silex Disco* at the stadium is a hot spot as is the unmarked *Coloseum Disco*

a block east of the British Embassy on Dimitri Čupkovski. Live jazz, blues and rock music can be heard at the *Lady Blue 1* and *Lady Blue 2* clubs, the latter on the corner of Ivo Ribar Lola and Sveti Kliment Ohridski and the former in the Concert Hall complex.

Getting There & Away

Bus There are buses to Ohrid, Bitola, Priština, Prizren, Peć, Podgorica and Belgrade. Book a seat on the bus of your choice the day before, especially if you're headed for Lake Ohrid.

There are two bus routes from Skopje to Lake Ohrid: the one through Tetovo (167km) is much faster and more direct than the bus that goes via Veles and Bitola (261km). If you just want to get to the Adriatic from Skopje, catch the overnight bus to Podgorica in Montenegro (382km).

If for some reason you can't take the direct bus to Sofia (see the Getting There & Away section earlier this chapter) there are 12 buses daily to Kriva Palanka (96km), 13km short of the Bulgarian border. Onward hitching should be possible.

Train All trains between central Europe and Greece pass through Skopje. There are two daily trains to/from Thessaloniki (five hours, 676 MKD) and Athens (14 hours, 1780 MKD).

MACEDONIA

Three trains run daily to Belgrade (nine hours, 1178 MKD), and six local trains run to Bitola (four hours, 194 MKD) and, for what it's worth, five trains to Kičevo (two hours, 150 MKD). Couchettes are available to Belgrade. Feroturist Travel Agency upstairs in the Skopje train station sells international tickets and books couchettes and sleepers (800 MKD).

Warning Beware of illegal taxi touts who meet trains. Do *not* get into a taxi that does not have an official taxi sign. You will be ripped off and at worse have your luggage and personal belongings stolen. Official taxis are OK.

Getting Around

To/From the Airport There are 11 special airport buses daily which all pick up at the international bus station as well as major hotels. A ticket costs 100 MKD. A taxi should cost between 800 and 1000 MKD.

Bus Inner-suburban city buses in Skopje cost 10 MKD per trip and outer-suburban buses 30 MKD per trip. Pay as you enter the bus. You can purchase 10-trip tickets for outer suburban buses at major stops for 130 MKD.

OHRID (ОХРИД)
☎ 096

Lake Ohrid, a natural tectonic lake in the south-west corner of Macedonia, is the deepest lake in Europe (294m) and one of the world's oldest. One third of its 450-sq-km surface area belongs to Albania. Nestled amid mountains at an altitude of 695m, the Macedonian section of the lake is the more beautiful, with striking vistas of the water from the beach and hills.

The town of Ohrid is *the* Macedonian tourist mecca and is popular with visitors from Macedonia and neighbouring countries. Some 30 'cultural monuments' in the area keep visitors busy. Predictably, the oldest ruins readily seen today are Roman. Lihnidos (Ohrid) was on the Via Egnatia, which connected the Adriatic to the Aegean, and part of a Roman amphitheatre has been uncovered in the old town.

Under Byzantium, Ohrid became the epis-copal centre of Macedonia. The first Slavic university was founded here in 893 by Bishop Kliment of Ohrid, a disciple of St Cyril and St Methodius, and from the 10th century until 1767 the patriarchate of Ohrid held sway. The revival of the archbishopric of Ohrid in 1958 and its independence from the Serbian Orthodox Church in 1967 were important steps on the road to modern nationhood.

Many of the small Orthodox churches with intact medieval frescos have now been adapted to the needs of ticketed tourists. Neat little signs in Latin script direct you to the sights, but even these tourist touches don't spoil the flavour of enchanting Ohrid.

Orientation
Ohrid bus station is next to the post office in the centre of town. To the west is the old town and to the south is the lake.

Information
Tourist Offices Biljana tourist office (☎ 22 494; fax 24 114) is at Partizanska 3 in front of the bus station.

Automoto Sojuz (☎ 22 338) is on Galičica at Lazo Trpkoski, behind the large 'Mini Market' on the corner of Jane Sandanski and Bulevar Turistička, a major intersection on the east side of town.

Money The Ohridska Banka agency, on Sveti Kliment Ohridski mall (Monday to Saturday from 8 am to 8 pm, Sunday 7 am to 1 pm), changes travellers cheques and cash without commission. Travel agencies often exchange cash as well.

Post & Communications The telephone centre in the modern post office near the bus station is open Monday to Saturday from 7 am to 9 pm, and Sunday from 9 am to noon and 6 to 8 pm. Phonecard phones are located outside the post office.

Note that Ohrid is gradually shifting to six-digit phone numbers, so that some of the numbers listed here may have changed by the time you read this.

Travel Agencies Putnik, Partizanska 4 opposite the bus station, sells train and plane tickets.

Left Luggage The left-luggage office at the bus station is open from 5 am to 8.20 pm daily. Cost is 50 MKD per piece per day.

Things to See

The picturesque old town of Ohrid rises from Sveti Kliment Ohridski, the main pedestrian mall, up towards the Church of Sveti Kliment and the citadel. A medieval town wall still isolates this hill from the surrounding valley. Penetrate the old town on Car Samoil as far as the **Archaeological Museum** in the four-storey dwelling of the Robevu family (1827) at No 62. Admission is 100 MKD. Further along Car Samuil is 11th-century **Sveti Sofija**, also worth the 100/30 MKD (foreigner/student) admission price. Aside from the frescos there's an unusual Turkish *mimbar* (pulpit) remaining from the days when this was a mosque, and an upstairs portico with a photo display of the extensive restoration work. An English-speaking guide is on hand.

From near here ul Ilindenska climbs to the North Gate, then to the right is the 13th-century **Church of Sveti Kliment**, (100 MKD admission), almost covered inside with vividly restored frescos of biblical scenes. An icon gallery is opposite this church with a fine view from the terrace. The walls of the 10th-century **citadel** to the west offer more splendid views.

In the park below the citadel are the ruins of an Early Christian **basilica** with 5th-century mosaics covered by protective sand, and nearby is the shell of **Sveti Pantelejmon**, now a small museum. The tiny 13th-century **Church of Sveti Jovan Bogoslov Kaneo**, on a point overlooking the lake, occupies a very pleasant site. There's a rocky beach at the foot of the cliffs and in summer young men perform death-defying leaps into the water from the clifftop above the lake. All churches and museums at Ohrid are open daily,

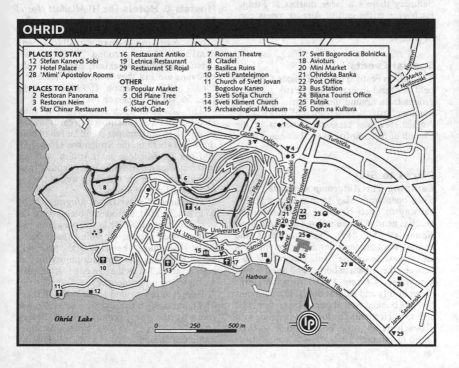

OHRID

PLACES TO STAY	16 Restaurant Antiko	7 Roman Theatre	17 Sveti Bogorodica Bolnička
12 Stefan Kanevči Sobi	19 Letnica Restaurant	8 Citadel	18 Avioturs
27 Hotel Palace	29 Restaurant SE Rojal	9 Basilica Ruins	20 Mini Market
28 'Mimi' Apostolov Rooms		10 Sveti Pantelejmon	21 Ohridska Banka
	OTHER	11 Church of Sveti Jovan	22 Post Office
PLACES TO EAT	1 Popular Market	Bogoslov Kaneo	23 Bus Station
2 Restoran Panorama	5 Old Plane Tree	13 Sveti Sofija Church	24 Biljana Tourist Office
3 Restoran Neim	(Star Chinar)	14 Sveti Kliment Church	25 Putnik
4 Star Chinar Restaurant	6 North Gate	15 Archaeological Museum	26 Dom na Kultura

Ohrid Lake

0   250   500 m

except Monday, from 9 am to 3 pm with a morning break from 10.30 to 11 am.

The better part of a second day at Ohrid could be spent on a pilgrimage to the Albanian border to see the 17th-century **Church of Sveti Naum** on a hill above the lake, 29km south of Ohrid by bus. From here you get a view of the Albanian town of Pogradec across the lake and inside the church is a finely carved iconostasis.

In summer you can also come by boat but it only leaves when a group is present; ask about times at the Putnik office opposite the bus station at the wharf the day before. The fare is around 100 MKD each way. The mountains east of Lake Ohrid, between it and Prespa Lake, are included in Galičica National Park.

There's frequent bus service from Ohrid to **Struga**. This small Macedonian town at the northern end of the lake is divided by the Crni Drim River, which drains Lake Ohrid into the Adriatic near Shkodra, Albania. On Saturday there's a large market at Struga. Each year at the end of August, poets converge on Struga for an international festival of poetry.

Special Events

The Balkan Festival of Folk Dances & Songs, held at Ohrid in early July, draws folkloric groups from around the Balkans. The Ohrid Summer Festival, held from mid-July to mid-August, features classical concerts in the Church of Sveti Sofija as well as many other events.

Places to Stay

Camping The *Autocamp Gradište* (☎ 22 578), open from May to mid-September, is halfway to Sveti Naum. A secluded nudist beach is nearby. There's also *Autocamp Sveti Naum* (☎ 58 811) 2km north of the monastery of the same name. Both camp sites are accessible on the Sveti Naum bus. Just between the Albanian border and Sveti Naum monastery is *Camp Vasko Karandžgleski* (open in July and August only). The caravans here are booked well ahead but you should be able to pitch a tent. The location is good, with a beach nearby and boat service to/from Ohrid in summer.

Private Rooms Private rooms are your best bet at Ohrid as the camping grounds and hostel are far from town and the hotels are pricey. Private rooms from the Biljana tourist office (☎ 22 494; fax 24 114), Partizanska 3, beside the bus station, cost from 250 to 310 MKD per person in a double room, plus 20 MKD per person per day tax. Women who unofficially rent private rooms often wait just outside the Biljana office. Popular with the diplomatic community, *'Mimi' Apostolov Rooms* (☎/fax 31 549) at ul Strašo Pinđura 2 has several comfortable, heated rooms with phone and satellite TV for 800 MKD including breakfast. For real rustic flavour right on the lake the *sobi* (rooms) of Stefan Kanevči (☎ 34 813) in Kaneo are hard to beat. A room goes for 310 MKD plus an extra 150 MKD for a hearty breakfast, if you want it.

Other private rooms are available from Putnik (☎ 32 025; fax 31 606) opposite the bus station or Avioturs (☎/fax 32 110) on Kosta Abraš.

Hostels & Hotels The HI *Mladost Hostel* (☎ 21 626; fax 35 025) is located on the lakeside a little over 2km west of Ohrid, towards Struga. A bed in a dorm or a small four-berth caravan will cost around 200 MKD per person including breakfast. Even if all the caravans are full they'll let you pitch a tent for 80 MKD per person, 150 MKD per tent (and 56 MKD per person tax).

The hostel is open from April to mid-October and YHA membership cards are not essential. In midsummer it will be full of children. Get there on the Struga bus (15 MKD) and ask for Mladost or, if you're walking, turn left after the fifth minaret, counting from the one opposite the old plane tree at the top of Sveti Kliment Ohridski.

Mladinski Centar-Hotel Magnus (☎ 21 671; fax 34 214), a modern hotel next to the hostel, charges 620 MKD per person in two or three-bed rooms, including three meals daily. If you have a hostel card, the price will be 10 to 20% lower. In midsummer they're booked solid, but as they're open all year it's worth trying other months.

Expect to pay around 1560/2400 MKD per night, including breakfast, for a single/double room at the fairly central *Hotel Palace* (☎ 260 440; fax 35 460) on Partizanska, close to the bus station.

Places to Eat

Picnic-minded travellers can stock up on fresh vegetables at the busy *Popular Market* just north of the Old Plane Tree. There is a *mini-market* for meat and dairy produce on Sveti Kliment Ohridski.

There are a number of fast-food and pizza joints in the old town area, but the easiest place to eat at is the *Letnica Self-Service Restaurant* on Bulevar Makedonski Prosvetiteli not far from the little harbour. The food is basic and cheap.

About 100m west of the Old Plane Tree are two low to mid-priced restaurants that warrant a visit. The *Restoran Neim* on the south side of Goce Delčev does some good *musaka* or *polneti piperki* (stuffed peppers) and the *Restoran Panorama* opposite offers similar fare.

A very pleasant mid-range restaurant is the *SE Rojal* at Jane Sandanski 2, about 200m south-east along the lakefront. Despite its smart décor, a meal is very affordable and the owner Sotir speaks English. The *Star Chinar* (Old Plane Tree) is a neat, modern restaurant near the Old Plane Tree and does some tasty local specialities. Try *chulban* – lamb, beef and rice patties in sauce. The smartest and most atmospheric eating place is the *Restaurant Antiko*, Car Samoil 30, in an old house in the old town. It is expensive and ordering Lake Ohrid trout will probably blow your budget.

Entertainment

Ohrid's movie theatre is *Dom Na Kultura* at Grigor Prličev, facing the lakeside park. Various cultural events are also held here. However, entertainment is mainly of the people-watching kind in the many street cafés or night-time bars, though many locals have taken a shine to playing bingo in recent times.

Getting There & Away

Air There is not much choice when it comes to flying to/from Ohrid. MAT and Avioimpex fly from Ohrid to Zürich (320 Sfr); MAT flies to Belgrade (5,890 MKD) and there are occasional summer flights from Ohrid to Amsterdam and one or two cities in Germany, but schedules and prices change too rapidly to rely on. Check with Putnik for current details.

Bus No less than 10 buses a day run between Ohrid and Skopje (167km, three hours, 265 MKD), via Kičevo. Another three go via Bitola and another two via Mavrovo. The first route is much shorter, faster, more scenic and cheaper, so try to take it. It pays to book a seat the day before.

There are six buses a day to Bitola (1¼ hours, 115 MKD). Buses to Struga (7km) leave about every 15 minutes (5 am to 9 pm) from stand No 1 at the bus station. Enter through the back doors and pay the conductor (35 MKD).

Yugoslavia An overnight bus from Ohrid to Belgrade (694km, 1510 MKD), via Kičevo, leaves Ohrid at 5.45 pm, reaching Belgrade 14 hours later. Another two buses go to Belgrade via Bitola, leaving at 5 am and 3.30 pm (1650 MKD).

Albania To go to Albania catch a bus or boat to Sveti Naum monastery, which is very near the border crossing. In summer there are six buses a day from Ohrid to Sveti Naum (29km, 65 MKD), in winter three daily. The bus continues on to the border post. From Albanian customs it's 6km to Pogradec but you may find a taxi to take you if you don't feel like walking.

Greece To get to Greece you can take a bus from Ohrid to Bitola (72km), then hitch or take a taxi 16km to the Medžitlija border crossing. Alternatively, you can try heading for Veles or even Skopje and pick up a train to Thessaloniki from there. Coming from Greece, try to get a cross-border taxi (10,000 drachmas) from Florina to Bitola directly, otherwise you may be stuck on the Macedonian side. Call (☎ 0385-23 851) for one of the cross-border taxi drivers in Florina.

BITOLA (БИТОЛА)
☎ 097

Bitola, the southernmost city of the former Yugoslavia and second largest in Macedonia, sits on a 660m-high plateau between mountains 16km north of the Greek border. The old bazar area (Stara Čaršija) is colourful but the facilities at Bitola are poor.

Private rooms are unavailable and the hotels overpriced. No left-luggage office is provided at either the bus or train stations and the city is useless as a transit point to/from Greece as there's no bus or train to the border (Medžitlija). You must hitch the 16km, or take a taxi. Bus services to Ohrid (72km) and Skopje (181km), on the other hand, are good.

The bus and train station are adjacent to each other, about 1km south of the town centre. It's probably not worth dragging your luggage into town just to see Bitola's Turkish mosques and bazar but the **Heraclea ruins** beyond the old cemetery, 1km south of the

bus/train stations, are recommended (admission 50 MKD, photos 500 MKD and video an exorbitant 1000 MKD extra). Founded in the 4th century BC by Philip II of Macedonia, Heraclea was conquered by the Romans two centuries later and became an important stage on the Via Egnatia. From the 4th to 6th centuries AD it was an episcopal seat. Excavations continue but the Roman baths, portico and theatre can now be seen. More interesting are the two Early Christian basilicas and the episcopal palace, complete with splendid mosaics. There's also a small museum and refreshment stand.

Malta

Malta, Gozo and Comino don't take up much space on the map, but their strategic position in the eastern Mediterranean between Sicily and Tunisia has for centuries made them irresistible to both navigators and invaders. The British were merely the last of a long series of colonisers to leave, but as a result, most Maltese, and most of the tourists who visit the country, speak English. Due to the islands' varied colonial history, the Maltese have developed and retained a unique language and culture in which it is possible to detect Italian, Arabic, English, Jewish, French and Spanish influences.

Malta has long been regarded as an economical and cheerful destination for a beach holiday. The weather is excellent, food and accommodation are good value and the water is clean. However, the coastline is mainly rocky and the few sandy beaches are often crowded. The real highlights are the magnificent 16th-century fortified city of Valletta with its glorious harbour; the bustling Mediterranean life of the city with its lively cafés and bars; the stone villages with their precious baroque churches and exuberant *festas*; the astonishing prehistoric temples and archaeological finds; the beautiful, medieval fortress town of Mdina; and, if you want to get away from it all, the quiet island of Gozo.

Facts about Malta

HISTORY

Malta has a fascinating history, and the island is crowded with physical and cultural reminders of the past. The islands' oldest monuments are the beautifully preserved megalithic temples built between 3800 and 2500 BC, which are the oldest surviving free-standing structures in the world.

From around 800 to 218 BC, Malta was colonised by the Phoenicians and, for the last 250 years of this period, by Phoenicia's principal North African colony, Carthage. The Maltese language (Malti) is Semitic in origin and is believed to be based on Phoenician. With their watchful eyes painted on the prow, the colourful Maltese fishing boats – *luzzu* and *dghajsa* – are scarcely changed from the Phoenician trading vessels that once plied the Mediterranean.

After the Punic Wars between Rome and Carthage and the defeat of the Carthaginian general Hannibal in 208 BC, Malta became part of the Roman Empire. In 60 AD, St Paul – a prisoner en route to Rome – was shipwrecked on the island. According to tradition, he converted the islanders to Christianity.

MALTA

MALTA

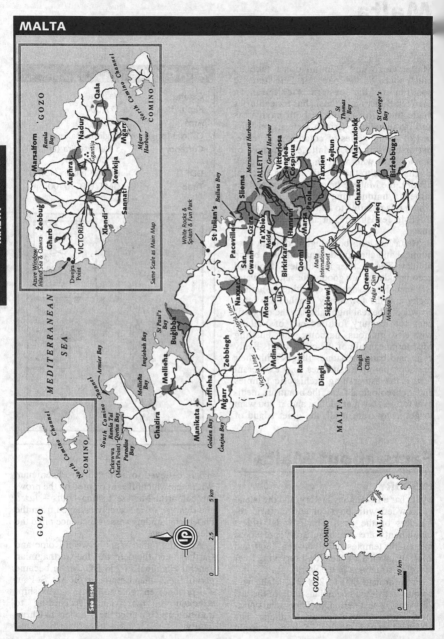

Arabs from North Africa arrived in 870, but tolerated the local Christian population. They introduced citrus fruits and cotton, and had a notable impact on Maltese customs and language. The Arabs were expelled in 1090 by the Norman King Roger of Sicily. For the next 400 years Malta's history was linked to Sicily, and its rulers were a succession of Normans, Angevins (French), Aragonese and Castilians (Spanish). The relatively small population of downtrodden islanders paid their taxes by trading, slaving and piracy, and were repaid in kind by marauding North Africans (Berbers and Arabs) and Turks.

In 1530, the islands were given to the Knights of the Order of St John of Jerusalem by Charles V, Emperor of Spain; their rent was two Maltese falcons a year, one to be sent to the emperor and the other to the Viceroy of Sicily. The 12,000 or so local inhabitants were given no say in the matter.

The Order of St John was founded during the crusades to protect Christian pilgrims travelling to and from the Holy Land, and to care for the sick. The knights were drawn from the younger male members of Europe's aristocratic families; in other words, those who were not the principal heirs. The order comprised eight nationalities or *langues* (languages). In order to preserve their identity, the langues built magnificent palaces, called *auberges*. The eight langues – Italy, Germany, France, Provence, Castile, Aragón, Auvergne and Bavaria – correspond to the eight points of the Maltese Cross. It was a religious order, with the knights taking vows of celibacy, poverty and obedience, and handing over their patrimony. The Order of St John became extremely prestigious, wealthy and powerful as a military and maritime force, and as a charitable organisation which founded and operated several hospitals.

As soon as they arrived in Malta, the knights began to fortify the harbour and to skirmish with infidels. In May 1565, an enormous Ottoman fleet carrying more than 30,000 men laid siege to the island. The 700 knights and 8000 Maltese and mercenary troops were commanded by a 70-year-old grand master, Jean de la Vallette. The Great Siege lasted for more than three months, with continuous and unbelievably ferocious fighting; after enormous bloodshed on both sides,

help finally arrived from Sicily and the Turks withdrew.

The knights were hailed as the saviours of Europe. Money and honours were heaped on them by grateful monarchs, and the construction of the new city of Valletta – named after the hero of the siege – and its enormous fortifications began. Malta was never again seriously threatened by the Turks.

Although the order continued to embellish Valletta, the knights sank into corrupt and ostentatious ways, largely supported by piracy. In 1798 Napoleon arrived, seeking to counter the British influence in the Mediterranean, and the knights, who were mostly French, surrendered to him without a fight.

The Maltese defeated the French in 1800 with the assistance of the British, and in 1814 Malta officially became part of the British Empire. The British decided to develop Malta into a major naval base. In WWII, Malta once again found itself under siege. Considered a linchpin in the battle for the Mediterranean, Malta was subjected to a blockade and, in 1942, to five months of day-and-night bombing raids, which left 40,000 homes destroyed and the population on the brink of starvation.

In 1947 the devastated island was given a measure of self-government. Malta's best known leaders in the postwar period have been the leader of the Nationalist Party and prime minister, Dr George Borg Olivier, who led the country to independence in 1964, and Dominic Mintoff who, as prime minister and leader of the Maltese Labour Party, established the republic in 1974. In 1979 links with Britain were reduced further when Mintoff expelled the British armed services and signed agreements with Libya, the Soviet Union and North Korea. Domestic policy focused on state enterprises.

In 1987 the Nationalist Party assumed power under the prime ministership of Dr Eddie Fenech Adami, and it was returned by a landslide victory in 1992, when one of the party's main platforms was Malta's application to join the EU. However, the 1996 general election saw the Labour Party, led by Dr Alfred Sant, narrowly regain power. One of its main policies was to remove the country's application for full EU membership. In 1998, with the application suspended,

MALTA

Eddie Fenech Adami's Nationalist Party was returned to power.

In recent decades, the Maltese have achieved considerable prosperity, thanks largely to tourism, but increasingly because of trade and light industries.

GEOGRAPHY & ECOLOGY

The Maltese archipelago consists of three inhabited islands: Malta (246 sq km), Gozo (67 sq km) and Comino (2.7 sq km). They lie in the middle of the Mediterranean, 93km south of Sicily and 350km north of Libya.

The densely populated islands are formed of a soft limestone, which is the golden building material used in all constructions. There are some low ridges and outcrops, but no major hills. The Victoria Lines escarpment traverses the island of Malta from the coast near Paceville almost to Golden Bay. The soil is generally thin and rocky, although in some valleys it is terraced and farmed intensively. There are few trees and, for most of the year, little greenery to soften the stony, sun-bleached landscape. The only notable exception is Buskett Gardens, a lush valley of trees and orange groves protected by the imposing southern Dingli Cliffs. There is virtually no surface water and there are no permanent creeks or rivers. The water table is the main source of fresh water, but it is supplemented by several large desalination plants.

The combined pressures of population, land use and development, as well as pollution and the lack of protection of natural areas, have had a significant environmental impact on the islands. In 1990 the Maltese government drew up a plan which designated development zones and identified areas of ecological importance. Hunting, especially of birds, has always been a way of life in Malta but it is now restricted, as the islands lie on three migratory paths between Europe and Africa, migrating birds being protected species.

GOVERNMENT

Malta is an independent, neutral, democratic republic. The president has a ceremonial role and is elected by parliament. Executive power lies with the prime minister and the cabinet, the latter chosen from the majority party in the 65-member parliament.

There are two major parties: the Partit Tal-Haddiema, or Labour Party, and the Partit Nazzjonalista, or Nationalist Party.

ECONOMY

The Maltese enjoy a good standard of living, low inflation and low unemployment. The government's economic strategy is to concentrate on the development of the tourism industry, manufacturing, and financial services. Tourism in particular is rapidly growing in importance.

POPULATION & PEOPLE

Given its history, it's not surprising that Malta has been a melting pot of Mediterranean peoples. Malta's population is around 377,000, with most people living in Valletta and its satellite towns; Gozo has 29,000 inhabitants; while Comino has a mere handful of farmers, six or seven in winter.

ARTS

Malta is noted for its fine crafts – particularly its handmade lace, hand-woven fabrics and silver filigree. Lace-making probably arrived with the knights in the 16th century. It was traditionally the role of village women – particularly on the island of Gozo – and, although the craft has developed into a healthy industry, it is still possible to find women sitting on their doorsteps making lace tablecloths.

The art of producing silver filigree was probably introduced to the island in the 17th century via Sicily, which was then under strong Spanish influence. Malta's silversmiths still produce beautiful filigree by traditional methods, but in large quantities to meet tourist demand.

Other handicrafts include weaving, knitting and glass-blowing; the latter is an especially healthy small industry which produces glassware exported throughout the world.

CULTURE & RELIGION

In Malta, the Mediterranean culture is dominant, but there are quite a few signs of British influence. The Catholic Church is the custodian of national traditions and its enormous churches dominate the villages. Although its influence is waning, Catholicism is a real force in most people's daily lives. Divorce and abortion are illegal; however, the possibility of divorce being legalised is a widely discussed issue.

LANGUAGE

Some linguists attribute the origins of Malti to the Phoenician occupation of Malta and consider it to be a Semitic offshoot of Phoenician. Others consider the Arabic period to be the more significant linguistic force. The Semitic base of Malti grammar has persisted to this day despite the prominence of the Romance languages since the Europeanisation of Malta, which has led to the vocabulary becoming laced with Sicilian, Italian, Spanish, French and English words. The Malti alphabet is a transliteration of Semitic sounds, written in Roman characters.

Nearly all Maltese in built-up areas speak English, and an increasing number speak Italian, helped by the fact that Malta receives Italian TV. French and German are also spoken.

See the Language Guide at the back of the book for pronunciation guidelines and useful words and phrases.

Facts for the Visitor

HIGHLIGHTS

The evocative Ħaġar Qim prehistoric temples are without doubt the highlight of a visit to Malta. The hill-top medieval town of Mdina is another must. On Gozo, visit the imposing megalithic temples of Ggantija and the fascinating Azure Window and nearby Inland Sea at Qawra.

PLANNING
Climate & When to Go

Malta has an excellent climate, although it can get very warm (around 30°C) in midsummer and occasionally in spring and autumn when the hot sirocco winds blow from Africa. The rainfall is low, at around 580mm a year, and it falls mainly between November and February. However, there's still plenty of sun in winter, when temperatures average around 14°C.

The pleasant climate means you can visit Malta at any time. Outside the high season, which is between mid-June and late September, accommodation prices drop by up to 40%. The season of festas (or more correctly *festi*) begins in earnest at the beginning of June and lasts until the end of September.

Books & Maps

There are a number of useful guides to Malta. The best introduction and souvenir is Insight Guides' *Malta* (APA Publications), which has excellent photographs and articles. For detailed information on the historical sights, try the Blue Guide's *Malta* by Stuart Rossiter.

For a fascinating account of life in Malta during its golden period, read *The Great Siege* by Ernle Bradford, who lived in Malta from 1967 to 1977. Bradford's *Siege: Malta 1940-1943* covers the island's second major crisis. *The Kappillan of Malta* by Nicholas Monsarrat tells the story of a priest's experiences during WWII, interwoven with other dramatic historical episodes. Monsarrat lived on Gozo for many years. Malta has many fiction writers; those writing in English include Francis Ebejer and Joseph Attard.

A useful map is the *AA Macmillan Malta & Gozo Traveller's Map*, which shows street names in Malti. This is important, because many street signs give the names in Malti only, though in tourist areas there are increasing numbers of dual-language signs. The Maltese themselves rarely know the English names of streets other than the main thoroughfares. *Triq* means street in Maltese, but is used interchangeably with 'street'. The *Bartholomew Clyde Leisure Map – Malta & Gozo* shows street names in English.

There are several good bookshops which stock guidebooks, maps and general books. Sapienzas Bookshop (☎ 23 36 21), 26 Republic St, Valletta, is recommended.

What to Bring

Summers can get very hot in Malta, so bring light, cool clothing and a hat (one which will not be blown off by the constant wind). Also bring along sunscreen (it's always more expensive in tourist areas) and comfortable shoes if you plan to do some exploring on foot.

TOURIST OFFICES
Local Tourist Offices
The National Tourism Organisation – Malta (NTOM) information offices can provide a range of useful brochures, hotel listings and maps. There are NTOM offices at Malta international airport (☎ 24 96 00), open 24 hours a day; in Valletta (☎ 23 77 47) at 1 City Arcade; and on Gozo at Mgarr Harbour (☎ 55 33 43) and Victoria (☎ 55 81 06) at 1 Palm St.

Maltese Tourist Offices Abroad
The NTOM has its main office in London at Malta House (☎ 0171-292 4900), 36-38 Piccadilly, London W1V OPP. There are also offices in Paris, Frankfurt, Milan, Amsterdam and New York, and representative offices in 16 other cities. Embassies and offices of Air Malta can provide information in other countries (see the following Visas & Embassies section).

VISAS & EMBASSIES
Entry visas are not required for holiday visits of up to three months by Australians, Canadians, New Zealanders, North Americans or Britons.

Maltese Embassies Abroad
Malta has diplomatic missions in the following countries:

Australia
   (☎ 02-6295 1586) 261 La Perouse St, Red Hill, Canberra, ACT 2603
Canada
   (☎ 416-207 0922) The Mutual Group Centre, 3300 Bloor St West, Suite 730, West Tower Etobicoke, Ontario
Italy
   (☎ 06-687 99 47) 12 Lungotevere Marzio, 00186 Rome
UK
   (☎ 0171-292 4800) 36-38 Piccadilly, London W1V OPQ
USA
   (☎ 202-462 3611) 2017 Connecticut Ave, NW Washington, DC 20008

Foreign Embassies in Malta
The following countries have embassies in Malta:

Australia
   (☎ 33 82 01/05) Ta'Xbiex Terrace, Ta'Xbiex MSD 11
Canada
   (☎ 23 31 22) 103 Archbishop St, Valletta
Germany
   (☎ 33 65 31) Il-Piazzetta, Entrance B, 1st floor, Tower Rd, Sliema
Italy
   (☎ 23 31 57/59) 5 Vilhena St, Floriana
Tunisia
   (☎ 43 51 75) Dar Carthage, Qormi Rd, Attard BZN 02
UK
   (☎ 23 31 34/37) 7 St Anne St, Floriana
USA
   (☎ 23 59 60/65) Development House, 3rd floor, St Anne St, Floriana

CUSTOMS
Items for personal use are not subject to duty. One litre of spirits, 1L of wine and 200 cigarettes can be imported duty-free. Duty is charged on any gifts intended for local residents.

MONEY
Currency
The Maltese lira (Lm; a £ symbol is also sometimes used) is divided into 100 cents. There are one, two, five, 10, 25, 50 cent and Lm1 coins; and Lm2, Lm5, Lm10 and Lm20 notes. The currency is often referred to as the pound.

Exchange Rates
Banks almost always offer better rates than hotels or restaurants. There is a 24-hour bureau at the airport available to passengers only. Travellers arriving by ferry should note that there are no exchange facilities at the port. Automatic change machines can be found in most tourist areas.

Australia	A$1	=	Lm0.24
Canada	C$1	=	Lm0.27
euro	€1	=	Lm0.43
France	1FF	=	Lm0.06
Germany	DM1	=	Lm0.22

Italy	L1000	=	Lm0.22
Japan	¥100	=	Lm0.28
New Zealand	NZ$1	=	Lm0.20
UK	UK£1	=	Lm0.65
USA	US$1	=	Lm0.39

Costs

By European standards, Malta is good value, although prices are increasing slowly. If you can budget on around Lm15 per day, you'll get pleasant hostel accommodation, a simple restaurant meal, a decent street-side snack and enough cold drinks to keep you going. If you cook your own meals your costs will be even lower.

Tipping & Bargaining

Restaurants and taxis expect a 10% tip. Bargaining for handicrafts at stalls or markets is essential, but most shops have fixed prices. Hotels will often be prepared to bargain in the off season between October and mid-June. You won't get far bargaining for taxis, but make sure you establish the fare in advance.

POST & COMMUNICATIONS

Post

Post office branches are found in most towns and villages. There is a poste restante service at the main post office, in the Auberge d'Italie, Merchants St, Valletta; it's open from 8 am to 6 pm.

Local postage costs six cents; postcards or letters sent air mail to Europe cost 16 cents, to the USA 22 cents and to Australia 27 cents.

Telephone & Fax

Public telephones are widely available and generally take phonecards only, which you can buy at Maltacom offices, post offices and stationery shops for Lm2, Lm3 or Lm5. There are rows of phones at the offices of Maltacom (the country's phone company). The main office is at Mercury House, St George's Rd, St Julian's (open 24 hours). Other offices are at South St, Valletta (open from 7 am to 6 pm), and Bisazza St, Sliema (open 8 am to 11 pm).

For local telephone enquiries phone ☎ 190; for overseas enquiries phone ☎ 194. Local calls cost five cents. The international direct dialling code is ☎ 00. International calls are discounted by around 20% between 6 pm and midnight and all day Saturday and Sunday (off-peak rate), and by up to 36% between midnight and 8 am (night rate). A three-minute call to the USA costs Lm1.50 (standard rate), Lm1.20 (off-peak) and 96 cents (night).

To call Malta from abroad, dial the international access code, ☎ 356 (the country code for Malta) and the number. There are no area codes in Malta.

Fax and telex services are available at Maltacom offices.

INTERNET RESOURCES

There's a wealth of useful information on the NTOM's official Web site at www.tourism.org.mt and on the Discover Malta Web site at www.discovermalta.com (the latter site provides full details on services from hotel accommodation to leisure activities and childcare facilities).

Internet was introduced into Malta on a commercial basis in 1995 and is growing fast. There are at least 12 service providers, which charge between Lm5 to Lm20 a month for access, and connection reliability is among the best in Europe. See the Valletta, Sliema and St Julian's section for Internet cafés.

NEWSPAPERS & MAGAZINES

The local English-language newspapers are the *Times* (15 cents) and the *Sunday Times* (18 cents), and the more recently established *Independent* (15 cents) and *Independent on Sunday* (18 cents). British, French, German and Italian newspapers are available on the evening of publication.

RADIO & TV

Two local TV stations broadcast in Malti, and all of the main Italian TV stations are received in Malta. Satellite and cable TV are widely available. BBC World Service can be picked up on short-wave radio, and some Maltese radio stations broadcast in English.

TIME

Malta is two hours ahead of GMT/UTC during summer (from the last Sunday in March to the last Sunday in October), and one hour ahead during winter.

MALTA

ELECTRICITY

The electric current in Malta is 240V, 50Hz and plugs have three flat pins. Malta has the same system as the UK, and therefore differs from most other Mediterranean European countries, which tend to run on 220V, 50Hz.

WEIGHTS & MEASURES

The metric system is used in Malta.

TOILETS

Small blocks of public toilets are located throughout Malta.

HEALTH

The water is safe to drink but heavily chlorinated, so stick to the bottled variety. There are no unusual health risks and no inoculations are required. Citizens of Australia and the UK are entitled to free health care because there are reciprocal agreements for the Maltese in both countries. St Luke's Hospital (☎ 24 12 51) in Gwardamanga (on the rounded promontory at the north-western corner of the Valletta defences) is the main general hospital. Gozo General Hospital (☎ 56 16 00), also known as Craig Hospital, is the main hospital on Gozo. For health emergencies phone ☎ 196. Both hospitals have 24-hour emergency services.

WOMEN TRAVELLERS

Malta remains a conservative society by western standards, and women are still expected to be wives and mothers; however, an increasing number of women are now joining the workforce. Young males have adopted the Mediterranean macho style, but they are not usually aggressive. Normal caution should be observed, but problems are unlikely. If you are alone, Paceville – the nightclub zone at St Julian's – is hectic but not particularly unsafe. Walking alone at night in Gzira is not recommended because this is the centre for prostitution.

Dress conservatively, particularly if you intend to visit churches (shorts are out for both sexes in churches). Topless bathing is not acceptable.

DISABLED TRAVELLERS

The Association for the Physically Handicapped (☎ 69 38 63) is a good contact for disabled people wanting to travel to Malta. It is at the Rehabilitation Fund Rehabilitation Centre, Corradino Hill, Paola PLA 07. The NTOM can provide details about hotels which have facilities for the disabled.

TRAVEL WITH CHILDREN

Pharmacies are well stocked with baby needs such as formula, bottles, pacifiers and nappies (diapers). It is always difficult to keep young kids amused, but you could try taking them to see the Malta Experience (see Things to See in the Valletta section), or on a harbour tour (see Organised Tours in the Valletta section). In summer, you can hire snorkelling gear, boats etc at the NSTS Aquacentre Beach Club (see Activities in the Valletta section). There is a Splash & Fun Park (☎ 34 27 24), with water slides and a fairy-tale fun park, at Baħar ic-Cagħaq, White Rocks. Another option for older kids (who are not easily frightened) is a visit to the dungeons at Mdina, which are fitted out with spooky sound-and-light effects and life-size characters (see the Mdina section).

BUSINESS HOURS

Shops are open between 9 am and 1 pm, and open again between 3.30 or 4 and 7 pm. Between 1 October and 14 June, banks are open Monday to Friday from 8.30 am to 12.30 or 12.45 pm (some banks also open in the afternoon). On Saturday they're open from 8.30 am to noon. The summer hours are the same (although few banks are open in the afternoon) except for Saturday, when they close at 11.30 am.

Between 1 October and 30 June, offices are open Monday to Friday from 8 am to 1 pm and from 2.30 or 3 to 5.30 pm, and on Saturday from 8.30 am to 1 pm; from July to September they open Monday to Saturday from 7.30 am to 1.30 pm.

PUBLIC HOLIDAYS & SPECIAL EVENTS

Fourteen national public holidays are observed in Malta: New Year's Day (1 January);

St Paul's Shipwreck (10 February); St Joseph's Day (19 March); Good Friday; Freedom Day (31 March); Labour Day (1 May); commemoration of 1919 independence riots (7 June); Feast of Sts Peter and Paul, and Harvest Festival (29 June); Feast of the Assumption (15 August); Feast of Our Lady of Victories (8 September); Independence Day (21 September); Feast of the Immaculate Conception (8 December); Republic Day (13 December); and Christmas (25 December).

Festi are important events in Maltese family and village life. During the past 200 years they have developed from simple village feast days into extravagant spectacles. Every village has a festa, usually to celebrate the feast day of its patron saint. Most of them are in summer, and for days in advance the island reverberates to the sound of explosions announcing the forthcoming celebration.

The main fireworks display is usually on Saturday night, and is accompanied by one or more local brass bands. On Sunday evening the statue of the patron saint is paraded through the streets accompanied by brass bands, fireworks, petards and church bells. Afterwards, people repair to the bars to drink and chat, or sample savoury snacks or sweets such as *qubbajt* (nougat) from elaborate, temporary stands.

If a festival is held while you are visiting, you should definitely go along. Tourist offices can provide details – check the time for the procession and the main fireworks display. At least one festa is held every weekend from the beginning of June to mid-September.

ACTIVITIES
Diving
Malta offers excellent conditions for diving and competitive rates on courses. There is fantastic clarity (visibility often exceeds 30m) and a dramatic underwater seascape, with caves and enormous drop-offs sometimes only metres from the shore. The water temperature drops to around 14°C in winter and reaches 25°C in summer. It is nearly always possible to find a protected site with easy access, so conditions are ideal for beginners.

Diving is strictly monitored by the Maltese government, and all divers must provide a medical certificate from either their own doctor or a local doctor (Lm3). The minimum age for diving is 14 years. People wanting to dive unaccompanied will also need a local diving permit (Lm1) – this is granted on presentation of the medical certificate, proof of qualification and two passport-sized photos. A PADI open-water dive course will cost Lm125. A package of six accompanied dives including equipment will cost around Lm65. One escorted shore dive with equipment will cost about Lm12. There are around 25 licensed diving schools. Cresta (☎ 31 07 43), Quay Beach Club, St George's Bay, Malta, and Calypso Diving (☎ 56 20 00), Marina St, Marsalforn, Gozo, have been recommended. The NTOM has a list of all diving centres and also produces a useful brochure indicating dive sites.

Horse Riding
There are several registered riding schools – the NTOM can provide a list. Try Darmanin's Riding School (☎ 23 56 49), Stables Lane, Marsa.

Walking
Distances on Malta are relatively small, so you can cover a lot of the islands on foot. The *Bartholomew Clyde Leisure Map – Malta & Gozo* suggests some interesting routes. Unfortunately, the Maltese show little interest in their countryside, so a lot of it is unkempt and littered with rubbish.

Sports Clubs
Sports clubs abound, and most of their facilities are available to visitors through temporary membership. One of the best is the Marsa Sports Club (☎ 23 28 42), 4km south of Valletta, which offers golf, tennis, squash, cricket and swimming.

Beaches
The best sandy beaches on Malta are Gnejna Bay; Tuffieha (bus Nos 47 and 52); Golden Bay (bus Nos 47 and 52); Ċirkewwa and Paradise Bay (bus Nos 45 and 48); Ramla tal-Bir Bay; Ramla tal-Qortin Bay; Armier Bay (bus No 50); Mellieħa Bay (bus Nos 43, 45

and 48); Imgiebah Bay; and St George's Bay (bus No 67).

The best sandy beaches on Gozo are Ramla Bay (bus No 42) and Xlendi Bay (bus No 87). On Comino, the best beaches are Santa Maria Bay and San Niklaw Bay. Where bus numbers are not shown, private transport is necessary.

WORK

It is difficult for foreigners to work legally in Malta. Casual (illegal) work waitering or washing dishes in bars and discos can sometimes be found.

ACCOMMODATION

The NTOM produces a detailed listing of accommodation on Malta, Gozo and Comino. There's a full range of possibilities, from five-star hotels to small guesthouses.

As there are no longer set rates according to class of accommodation, it's best to ring around to get an idea. Prices can be considerably lower in the off season, and two and three-star hotels often work out cheaper than guesthouses. There are hostels on Malta and Gozo (see the Valletta, Sliema and St Julian's section). Camping is not allowed, and apart from hostels the cheapest option is boarding with families for around Lm3 a night. Try the National Student Travel Service (NSTS); see Air in the Getting There & Away section for contact details.

FOOD

Malta is not known as a destination for gourmets, but the food is both good and cheap. The most obvious influence is Sicilian, and most of the cheaper restaurants serve pasta and pizza. English standards (eg grilled chops, sausages and mash, and roast with three veg) are also commonly available, particularly in the tourist areas. Vegetarians are well catered for, with many restaurants offering vegetarian dishes as main courses.

It is definitely worth trying some of the Maltese specialities: *pastizzi* (savoury pasties filled with cheese or peas), which are available from small bakeries and bars; *timpana* (a rich macaroni, cheese and egg pie); and *braģioli* (spicy beef rolls). Two favourite, but

relatively expensive, dishes are *fenech* (rabbit), which is fried or made as a casserole or pie, and *lampuka*, a fish (dorado), which is caught between September and November and usually served grilled, fried or made into a pie.

DRINKS

Local beers are good, with a range of lagers, stouts and pale ales: Hop Leaf (40 cents for a small bottle) is recommended. The local wine industry is continually improving and most table wines are very drinkable. You get what you pay for (from 45 cents to Lm4 a bottle). Imported wines and beers are available at reasonable prices.

ENTERTAINMENT

Paceville is the centre of Malta's nightlife, with lots of bars, clubs and discos.

THINGS TO BUY

Hand-knitted clothing is produced in the villages and can be cheap. Traditional handicrafts include lace, silver filigree, blown glass and pottery. Shop around, though, before you make a purchase; the Malta Crafts Centre, St John's Square, Valletta, is a good place to start. The best bargains are found on Gozo.

Getting There & Away

AIR

Malta is well connected to Europe and North Africa. Scheduled prices aren't particularly cheap, but there are some excellent packages. Some bargains are available through NSTS, the representative in Malta for most student travel organisations (including STA Travel, Campus Holidays, CTS and so on) and an associate member of Hostelling International (HI). NSTS has offices in Valletta (☎ 24 49 83; fax 23 03 30; nststrav@kemmunet .net.mt) at 220 St Paul St and on Gozo (☎ 55 39 77) at 45 St Francis Square, Victoria.

Air Malta (☎ 66 22 11) has scheduled flights to/from Amsterdam, Athens, Berlin, Brussels, Cairo, Catania (Sicily), Damascus,

Dubai, Dublin, Frankfurt, Geneva, Hamburg, London (Heathrow and Gatwick), Lyon, Madrid, Manchester, Munich, Palermo, Paris, Rome, Tunis, Vienna, Zürich and other destinations.

There are weekly direct Air Malta flights from Melbourne and Sydney. Air Malta's sales agents include:

Australia
(☎ 02-9321 9111; fax 02-9290 3641) World Aviation Systems, 403 George St, Sydney, NSW 2000
Canada
British Airways offices throughout Canada
Egypt
(☎ 02-578 2692) Air Malta Office, 2 Tahir Square, Cairo
UK
(☎ 0181-785 3199) Air Malta House, 314-316 Upper Richmond Rd, Putney, London SW15 6TU
USA
(☎ 212-245 7768) Air Malta Office, 630 Fifth Ave, Suite 2662, New York, NY 10111

Other airlines servicing the country include Alitalia, KLM, Lufthansa, Swissair and Tunisavia. Avoid buying tickets in Malta if you can, because prices are higher.

Charter flights, usually for trips of one or two weeks from England or Scotland, offer outstanding value, particularly in winter. Contact a travel agent specialising in budget flights and packages.

SEA

Malta has regular sea links in summer with both Sicily (Palermo, Pozzallo, Syracuse and Catania) and northern Italy (Genoa and Livorno). Cars can be brought by ferry from Sicily and may be imported for up to three months. A Green Card (internationally recognised proof of insurance) for Malta is required.

The Italy-Malta ferry services are constantly changing so it is best to confirm the information given here with a travel agent. SMS Agency (☎ 23 22 11), 311 Republic St, Valletta, has information about all of the services on offer.

In 1998, Virtù Ferries ran a fast catamaran service to Sicily (Catania, Pozzallo and Syracuse) up to five times a week, depending on

the season. The journey to Catania takes three hours and costs Lm21 (one way, all seasons) and as little as Lm14 for same-day return in winter, or Lm21 for same-day return in summer. Virtù Ferries has offices in Ta'Xbiex, near Valletta (3 Princess Elizabeth St; ☎ 34 52 20), and Catania (Piazza Europa 1; ☎ 095-37 69 33).

Other Maltese companies operate regular car-ferry services to Italian ports and to Tunisia. The journey to Catania takes around 12 hours and a deck passenger is charged Lm20. Cars cost around Lm35 to transport. Ferry companies include Meridiana Lines (☎ 23 97 76) and MA.RE.SI Shipping (☎ 32 06 20), both of which have services to Pozzallo and Reggio Calabria, and Grimaldi Group Grandi Traghetti (☎ 24 43 73), with services to Genoa and Tunis.

It is important to note that ferries do not have exchange facilities and there are none available at Malta's port. Nor is there public transport from the port up to the city of Valletta – you either catch a taxi or make the steep 15-minute walk.

LEAVING MALTA

All passengers departing by sea are required to pay a Lm4 departure tax which should be added by the travel agent when you buy your ticket.

Getting Around

HELICOPTER

There is a helicopter service between Malta and Gozo which might be worth the expense if you don't want to spend two hours catching buses and the ferry to reach your destination. Open return tickets cost Lm25 for adults and Lm12.50 for children. Same-day return costs Lm20 and Lm10. There are also helicopter tours of the islands. Contact any travel agency for information and bookings.

BUS

Malta and Gozo are served by a network of buses run by the Malta Public Transport Authority, many of them beautiful and uncomfortable relics of the 1950s. On Malta, fares range from 11 to 30 cents, depending on the number of fare 'stages' you pass through and if it's an express service. Buses run until about 10 or 11 pm, depending on the route. Route numbers change frequently, so check them locally. All buses on Malta originate from the main City Gate bus terminus, which is in a plaza area just outside Valletta's city gates (☎ 22 59 16 for information). The green, white and yellow *Malta Bus Map & Fares Guide* (20 cents) has useful information, including an official timetable. It's available from newsstands.

Bus Nos 45, 48 (summer only), 452 and 453 run regularly from Valletta to Ċirkewwa to connect with the ferry to Gozo. Bus Nos 60, 61, 67 and 68 run from Valletta to Sliema, and bus Nos 68 and 70 go on to St Julian's and Paceville.

On Gozo, the bus terminus is in the main town of Victoria, on Main Gate St just behind Republic St. A flat fare of nine cents will take you anywhere on the island. Note that few buses run after noon (for information phone ☎ 55 60 11). Bus No 25 runs from the ferry port of Mġarr to Victoria, and bus No 21 goes from Victoria to Marsalforn. In the villages, the bus stop is always in or near the church square.

TAXI

Taxis are expensive and should only be used as a last resort or with a group of people. A fare from the airport to Sliema is around Lm6; from Valletta to St Julian's it's around Lm5. Make sure you establish a price in advance. White Taxi Service Amalgamated (☎ 34 39 49) in Gzira offers a 24-hour service.

CAR & MOTORCYCLE

Like the British, the Maltese drive on the left side of the road. Hiring a car in Malta is a good idea, partly because taxis are so expensive. One late-night fare between Paceville and Buġibba could easily cost Lm6, which is nearly the cost of a hire car for a day. All the car-hire companies have representatives at the airport but rates vary, so shop around. In 1998 Alamo was offering a daily rate of Lm8.50 for a small car (Lm8 a day for a week or longer, less in the low season). Its head

office (☎ 23 87 45) is at 38 Villambrosa St, Hamrun. Local garages such as Merlin (☎ 22 31 31) charge slightly less. L'Aronde (☎ 33 40 79), Upper Gardens, St Julian's, hires out motorcycles from Lm3 per day (insurance and delivery included). One litre of petrol costs 26 cents. Call ☎ 24 22 22 for breakdown assistance and towing.

Road rules

You can't drive fast in Malta. If the speed limits (64km/h on highways and 40km/h in urban areas) don't slow you down, the many potholes in the roads definitely will. At intersections where there are no roundabouts, the first to arrive has right of way. Breathalyser tests were introduced in Malta as late as 1998.

BICYCLE

Cycling can be an ideal way to get around Malta because of the small distances, but there are plenty of hills and it can be very hot. The Cycle Store (☎ 44 32 35), 135 Eucharistic Congress St, Mosta, has bikes for Lm1.50 a day. The Marsalforn Hotel (☎ 55 61 47) in Gozo has bikes for Lm2 a day, or less if rented for several days.

HITCHING

Hitchhiking is very unusual in Malta and is frowned upon.

BOAT

Regular ferries link Malta and Gozo, and buses connect with all ferry services (see the Bus information in this section). Ferries depart from Ċirkewwa on Malta and from Mġarr on Gozo. Services are more or less hourly from 6 am to 11 pm. The crossing takes 30 minutes and costs Lm1.75 return for passengers, and Lm4 return for cars. Even if you board at Ċirkewwa, you still pay for your ticket at Gozo on the return leg; this means that car drivers arriving at Ċirkewwa should head straight for the car queue.

Be warned that Maltese families flock to Gozo on Sunday, particularly in summer, which can cause long delays at ferry terminals. Traffic from Ċirkewwa to the main towns is also very heavy on Sunday evening. All ferries are operated by the Gozo Channel Co (☎ 24 39 64, timetable recording ☎ 55 60 16).

There is also a ferry service (☎ 33 56 89) between Valletta's Marsamxett Harbour and Sliema's Tigne seafront (at the end of the Strand) approximately every half-hour from 8 am to 6 pm.

ORGANISED TOURS

A number of companies operate bus tours and they are highly competitive, so shop around the travel agencies. The tours will restrict you to the well-trampled tourist traps, but they can give you a good introduction to the islands nonetheless.

A typical full-day tour of Malta costs Lm3 to Lm6. Tours without lunch are generally cheaper. There are also day tours to Gozo and Comino, and trips to see late-night festa fireworks. Tour guides expect tips.

There are day tours to Sicily (up to Lm30) available through the travel agencies. The journey takes 90 minutes by catamaran and the tour includes a visit to Mt Etna and Taormina. Captain Morgan Cruises (☎ 34 33 73) at Sliema Marina has a great range of cruises, sailing adventures and jeep safaris.

See the Valletta section for information on harbour tours.

Valletta, Sliema & St Julian's

Valletta, the city of the Knights of the Order of St John, is architecturally superb and seemingly unchanged since the 16th century. The city is the seat of Malta's government, and overlooks the magnificent Grand Harbour to the south-east and Marsamxett Harbour to the north-west.

On the south-eastern side of the Grand Harbour lie the fortified peninsulas of Vittoriosa and Senglea and the town of Cospicua (known collectively as the three cities, or the Cottonera). These are older and in some ways more interesting than Valletta itself. They are dominated by their docks, which date from the time of the Phoenicians and were the principal reason for their existence. They are definitely worth exploring.

On the northern side of Marsamxett Harbour lies Sliema, the most fashionable residential area. Restaurants and high-rise hotels line the shores. Farther north-west are the tourist haunts of St Julian's and Paceville.

Orientation

The Maltese think of the suburbs that surround Valletta – Cospicua, Paola, Hamrun, Qormi, Birkirkara, Gzira, Sliema and St Julian's – as separate towns. This may well have been accurate in the relatively recent past, but they now run into one another and effectively create one large city with a population of around 250,000. The entire eastern half of the island is intensively developed, with large suburbs and towns, the airport and numerous industrial sites.

The ferries from Italy dock in the Grand Harbour below Valletta, and it's a steep 15-minute climb up the hill to the main City Gate bus terminus, outside the southern walls.

Information

Tourist Offices The local tourist office (☎ 23 77 47) is at 1 City Arcade, Valletta.

Money There are several banks in Valletta's main street, Republic St, including branches of the Mid-Med Bank at Nos 15 and 233. You can also change money at the American Express office (☎ 23 21 41/42), 14 Zachary St, Valletta, between and parallel to Republic and Merchants Sts.

Cybercafés Internet surfing or email checking can be done at the YMCA (☎ 24 06 80), 178 Merchants St, Valletta, where Internet access costs 75 cents per half-hour. The YMCA is open Monday to Saturday from 10 am to 10 pm. At the Eden Super Bowl Internet Café (☎ 31 98 88), St George's Bay, Paceville, you'll pay 90 cents per half-hour of Internet access. It's open daily from 10 am to midnight.

Laundry The Square Deal laundrette on the Strand, Sliema (opposite the Captain Morgan boats), is one of the few laundries outside the hotels, but it's expensive at Lm2 for one load. Use a sink instead.

VALLETTA, SLIEMA & ST JULIAN'S

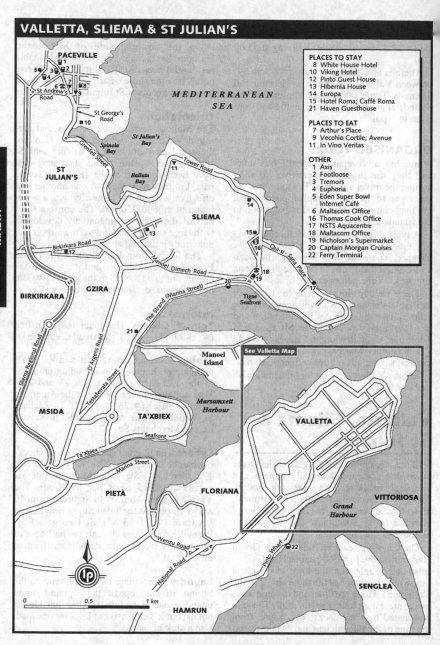

PLACES TO STAY
8 White House Hotel
10 Viking Hotel
12 Pinto Guest House
13 Hibernia House
14 Europa
15 Hotel Roma; Caffé Roma
21 Haven Guesthouse

PLACES TO EAT
7 Arthur's Place
9 Vecchio Cortile; Avenue
11 In Vino Veritas

OTHER
1 Axis
2 Footloose
3 Tremors
4 Euphoria
5 Eden Super Bowl
   Internet Café
6 Maltacom Office
16 Thomas Cook Office
17 NSTS Aquacentre
18 Maltacom Office
19 Nicholson's Supermarket
20 Captain Morgan Cruises
22 Ferry Terminal

Medical & Emergency Services Useful numbers include ☎ 191 for police emergencies and ☎ 196 for health emergencies.

Things to See

The remarkable fortified city of Valletta was built swiftly but with great care and attention paid to town planning and building regulations. Even on a hot day, fresh breezes waft through the streets because the town's layout was designed to take advantage of 'natural' air-conditioning.

Among the city's more impressive buildings is the **Auberge de Castile**, designed by the Maltese architect Girolomo Cassar (who was one of the two architects who designed Valletta). It was once the palace for the knights of the Spanish and Portuguese langue (a division of the main Order of St John of Jerusalem). It is now the office of the prime minister and is not open to the public. The building is on Girolomo Cassar Ave, near its intersection with South and Merchants Sts. The nearby **Upper Barrakka Gardens**, originally the private gardens of the Italian knights, offer a magnificent view of the Grand Harbour and the Cottonera.

The **National Museum of Archaeology** is housed in the Auberge de Provence, which was designed by Cassar for the knights from Provence. The museum is worth visiting for its small collection of relics from the island's Copper Age temples. It's open daily from 7.45 am to 2 pm from 16 June to 30 September, and from 8.15 am to 5 pm (4.15 pm on Sunday) the rest of the year; admission is Lm1.

St John's Co-Cathedral & Museum is the church of the Order of St John of Jerusalem. It's on St John St, and has an austere façade and a baroque interior. Note the patchwork of marble tombstones covering the floor of the church which commemorates the knights. The museum houses a collection of precious tapestries, and there are two works by the Italian painter Caravaggio in the oratory.

The **Grand Master's Palace**, along Republic St, is now the seat of the Maltese president and parliament. It contains an armoury and a fresco depicting the Great Siege. Also of interest is the **Manoel Theatre**, built in 1731, which is one of the oldest theatres in Europe and is appropriate-ly located on Old Theatre St. Apart from performances (generally in winter), entry (Lm1) is by guided tour from Monday to Friday at 10.45 and 11.15 am and on Saturday at 11.30 am.

The **Malta Experience** (☎ 24 37 76) at Valletta's Mediterranean Conference Centre (enter from the bottom of Merchants St) provides a short, painless and interesting audiovisual introduction to Maltese history for those who prefer their information packaged this way. It costs Lm2.50 and starts every hour on the hour Monday to Friday from 11 am to 4 pm, and from 11 am to 1 pm on the weekend. While you're there, check out the adjacent exhibition hall, once the Great Ward of the knights' hospital.

The huge success of the Malta Experience has given rise to the Mdina Experience (see the section on Mdina & Rabat) and the **Malta George Cross: the Wartime Experience** (☎ 24 78 91), Hostel de Verdelin, Civil Service Sports Club, Palace Square, Valletta. Entry is Lm2.

There's a bustling **market** on Merchants St from Monday to Friday until 12.30 pm. On Sunday there's a **flea market** at the City Gate bus terminus from 7 am to 1 pm.

The **Hypogeum** is an important series of underground prehistoric temples at Paola. It was closed to the public at the time of writing.

Activities

The NSTS Aquacentre Beach Club (☎ 24 66 28), Qui-si-Sana Place, Tigne, offers a range of reasonably priced activities. These include the hire of flippers and masks for snorkelling (Lm1 per hour; 75 cents for students); paddle boats (Lm3.50/2.50 an hour); sailboards (Lm2.50/2 an hour; instruction available for Lm1); canoes (Lm1.20/1 an hour); water-skiing (Lm4/2 for five minutes); sailing boats (Lm4/3 an hour); motorboats (Lm5/4 an hour); paragliding (Lm14 single/22 double); and scuba diving (Lm9/7.50 per dive, including equipment).

Organised Tours

Captain Morgan Cruises (☎ 34 33 73) operates short harbour cruises (Lm5.50) throughout the day, and a variety of half and full-day cruises around the islands, priced from Lm9 to Lm20, including a buffet lunch.

MALTA

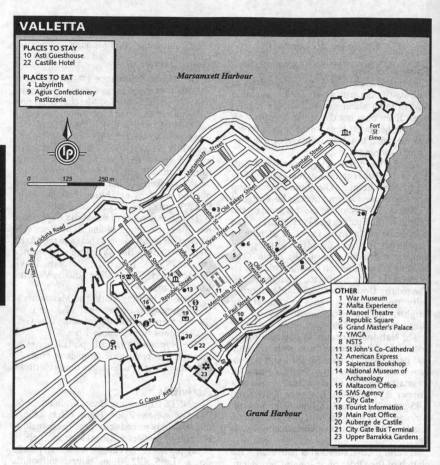

VALLETTA

PLACES TO STAY
10 Asti Guesthouse
22 Castille Hotel

PLACES TO EAT
 4 Labyrinth
 9 Agius Confectionery
    Pastizzeria

Marsamxett Harbour

Grand Harbour

0   125   250 m

OTHER
 1 War Museum
 2 Malta Experience
 3 Manoel Theatre
 5 Republic Square
 6 Grand Master's Palace
 7 YMCA
 8 NSTS
11 St John's Co-Cathedral
12 American Express
13 Sapienzas Bookshop
14 National Museum of
    Archaeology
15 Maltacom Office
16 SMS Agency
17 City Gate
18 Tourist Information
19 Main Post Office
20 Auberge de Castile
21 City Gate Bus Terminal
23 Upper Barrakka Gardens

Boats leave from the Strand in Sliema and tickets can be purchased at any of the travel agencies on the waterfront. They also offer an underwater safari, with passengers seated in a glass observation keel, for Lm4.50.

Places to Stay

Hostels The NSTS is an associate member of Hostelling International (HI). It runs several hostels in Malta and also has agreements with certain guesthouses to provide cheap accommodation to hostellers. An HI membership card is required in order to stay

at any of the hostels in Malta. Cards can be obtained from the NSTS or from the main hostel, **Hibernia House** (☎ 33 38 59; fax 23 03 30) in Depiro St, Sliema, where a bed costs Lm3.55. Take bus No 62 or 67 to Balluta Bay, walk up the hill along Manoel Dimech Rd, then turn left into Depiro St – the hostel is about 100m along on the right. There are other hostels (or places which have hostel-price agreements with the NSTS) at **Lija** (☎ 43 61 68; fax 43 49 63; Lm4.95 per night) and **Buġibba** (☎ 57 30 22; fax 57 19 75; Lm3.55).

The NSTS offers a special hostelling package which includes airport welcome and transfers, seven overnight stays (with breakfast) including at least one night at Hibernia House, a week's bus pass, a phonecard and entry to the Aquacentre Beach Club. The package costs Lm51 for accommodation in eight-bed dorms and Lm73 in two-bed rooms. The NSTS must be notified seven days in advance of arrival date and flight details.

Guesthouses & Hotels The distinction between a large guesthouse and a small hotel is a fine one. In general, though, the guesthouses tend to be family operated and cheaper. Some good ones can be found in and around Paceville and St Julian's. All prices quoted below include breakfast.

The *Pinto Guest House* (☎ 31 38 97), in Sacred Heart Ave, St Julian's, is a steep walk up from Balluta Bay, but worth the hike for the clean, spacious rooms and excellent view. Doubles/singles cost Lm10/7. The *Viking Hotel* (☎ 31 67 02 or 34 09 30), Spinola Rd, St Julian's, just up from Spinola Bay, has doubles for Lm12 and singles for Lm8. In the top rooms you'll be charged extra for the view.

Right in the centre of Paceville is the *White House Hotel* (☎ 37 80 16), in Paceville Ave. Comfortable and clean rooms with bath or shower cost Lm10 per person (dropping to Lm7 in the off season).

The *Europa* (☎ 33 00 80), 138 Tower Rd, Sliema, is well located and has very pleasant rooms with bathroom and TV. It charges Lm14 per person (dropping to Lm8 out of season) in a double room. *Hotel Roma* (☎ 31 85 87), Ghar Il-Lenbi St, Sliema, has rooms with shower for Lm24/16 a double/single, cheaper out of season.

In Gzira, the *Haven Guesthouse* (☎ 33 58 62), 193 The Strand, is spotlessly clean and charges Lm7.70 per person.

In Valletta, there's the *Asti Guesthouse* (☎ 23 95 06), 18 St Ursula St, in a former convent. Rooms are very basic and bathrooms are shared, but prices are good at Lm5.50 per person. The charming three-star *Castille Hotel* (☎ 24 36 77), Castille Square, near the Upper Barrakka Gardens, charges Lm15 per person for a room with shower.

Places to Eat

There are cheap restaurants, bars and cafés on The Strand in Sliema, in Paceville and around St Julian's Bay. Prices tend to be fairly standard – around Lm2 for a pizza, Lm2.50 for pasta and Lm2.50 to Lm4 for a main course.

Arthur's Place, Ball St, Paceville, might look just like any other tourist joint, but it has an interesting range of Maltese dishes. It also offers a children's menu and vegetarian dishes. Starters are in the Lm1 range, and main courses cost from Lm2 to Lm3.50.

You'll pay Lm2.75 for a real Italian risotto alla pescatora at *Vecchio Cortile* in Gort St, Paceville. Pizza costs around Lm2 at the *Avenue*, a few metres along the same street.

There are some other good options on Tower Rd, Sliema. Try *Caffé Roma* (underneath the Hotel Roma) on the corner of Ghar Il-Lenbi St. The pasta is home-made (Lm1.30 to Lm2.50) and pizzas cost Lm1.65 to Lm2. Vegetarians (and others) could try *In Vino Veritas* at 59 Dingli St, on the corner of Tower Rd. The vegetarian lasagne (Lm1.65), vegetarian rice (Lm1.65) and home-made cakes are excellent. The atmosphere is lively and there are many regulars.

For lunch in Valletta, you can't go past *Labyrinth* coffee shop, 44 Strait St, which has generous salads (Lm1.60 to Lm2.50), delicious home-made pies (60 to 70 cents) and great coffee (35 cents). There's a more extensive menu in the basement supper club. Open until midnight or later, often with live jazz, it's one of the few options for dinner or a night out in Valletta. The cheapest lunch is a couple of delicious pastizzi from *Agius Confectionery Pastizzeria* at 273 St Paul St – they're only 15 cents each.

The *Telecell Restaurant Guide Malta & Gozo* (Lm2.95) is widely available and lists restaurants by location and price. It also recommends restaurants that are suitable for vegetarians, those with nonsmoking areas and those with good wheelchair access.

There's a *Nicholson's* supermarket on the top level of the Plaza shopping centre, St Anna Square, Sliema.

Entertainment

Paceville is Malta's nightlife centre. It's quiet from Monday to Thursday but on Friday, Saturday and Sunday the place is jumping.

MALTA

Crowds spill out of the bars onto the street, policemen lounge around, elderly British tourists look bemused and cars crawl around trying to avoid pedestrians' toes. Wander until you find the bar of your choice.

Tremors, a disco club for the young crowd, is opposite *Footloose*, a (loud) rock music pub in St George's Rd. *Euphoria* and *Axis* are other places in Paceville to dance and party till late. Discos cost around Lm2.50 to enter (some are free) and drinks are expensive. Since bus services stop at around 10 pm, most Maltese group together and catch taxis or walk home.

Getting Around

To/From the Airport Bus No 8 leaves from outside the Malta international airport terminal about every half-hour and goes to Valletta City Gate bus terminus. The journey costs 11 cents (you pay the driver). Most arrivals are transferred by courtesy car or coach to their hotels. Taxis operate on official rates; to Sliema or St Julian's it's Lm5.

Local Transport See the preceding Getting Around section in this chapter for more information on transport.

Around Malta

NORTH COAST

Although the north coast is fairly exposed, it's a good place for walking as it's relatively uninhabited. The sandy beach at Mellieha, west of St Paul's Bay, is the best on Malta, although it does get crowded. Catch bus No 43 or 48 from Valletta.

St Paul's Bay & Buġibba

Buġibba, the traditional name for the town on St Paul's Bay, is the main tourist centre – and it's ghastly. There is no reason to stay here unless you're on a very cheap package. However, the nightlife hots up in summer, and there are numerous cheap hotels and restaurants open throughout the year. Catch bus Nos 43, 44, 45 or 49 from Valletta.

Ċirkewwa

This is the port where the Gozo ferry docks. Paradise Bay, one of Malta's best sandy beaches, is a short walk to the south of the town. See the Getting Around section at the beginning of this chapter for information on the ferry to Gozo.

WEST COAST

The west coast is a great place to get away from the crowds. The best access is by private boat. If you're looking for solitude, keep away from the big tourist development and crowded, sandy beach at Golden Bay.

MOSTA

Mosta is famous for its church which has one of the largest unsupported domes in the world, with a diameter of 39.6m. The church was designed by Maltese architect Giorgio Grognet de Vassé whose plan was closely based on the Pantheon in Rome. The foundation stone was laid in 1833 and the church took 27 years to complete. Take bus Nos 53 or 57 from Valletta.

MDINA & RABAT

Until the knights arrived and settled around the Grand Harbour, the political centre of Malta was Mdina. Set inland on an easily defendable rocky outcrop, it has been a fortified city for more than 3000 years. You could spend hours wandering through Mdina's narrow, cobbled streets.

The city is still home to the Maltese aristocracy and is sometimes called the Noble City or the Silent City. Much of it was rebuilt after an earthquake in 1693, but you can still see some original sections which survived the disaster.

Things to See & Do

The best preserved medieval building is the **Palazzo Falzon**, built in 1495, which has Norman architectural features. Mdina has a beautiful main piazza, dominated by the cathedral. The **Cathedral Museum** is open Monday to Saturday from 9 am to 4.30 pm.

The **Mdina Dungeons** (☎ 45 02 67), below the Vilhena Palace, St Publius Square, are medieval dungeons that have been restored to all their dubious glory and have tableaux depicting their victims. The dungeons are unlocked daily between 9.30 am and 5 pm, and entry is Lm1.30.

The **Mdina Experience**, at 7 Mesquita Square, is the local version of Valletta's Malta Experience. It is shown from 11 am to 4 pm, Monday to Friday, and 11 am to 2 pm on Saturday. Entry is Lm1.10.

The adjacent township of Rabat is typically Maltese. **St Paul's Church** and **St Paul's Grotto** lie in the centre of town, both of them classic examples of Maltese baroque. The grotto is believed to be the spot where St Paul lived.

Places to Eat

There are no hotels in Mdina. A great place for lunch or a snack is the *Fontanella Tea Garden*, 1 Bastion St, which is built into the fortifications. If you feel like a splurge, dine at the *Medina*, 7 Holy Cross St. It's one of Malta's best restaurants, and is just off Mdina's main piazza. An excellent meal with wine will come to around Lm12.

There are plenty of bars and a number of restaurants in Rabat. Visit the *Baron* snack bar, 3 Republic St, not so much for the food as for the authentic local atmosphere.

Getting There & Away

Catch bus Nos 80, 81 or 84 from Valletta to reach Mdina and Rabat.

SOUTH COAST

You can enjoy spectacular views from the 200m-high **Dingli Cliffs**. The most interesting and evocative prehistoric temples on Malta are **Ħaġar Qim** and **Mnajdra**, built between 3800 and 2500 BC near the village of Qrendi. The temples are open from 7.45 am to 2 pm in summer and 8.15 am to 5 pm (4.15 pm on Sunday) in cooler weather; entry costs Lm1. These Copper Age megalithic temples are reminiscent of Stonehenge, and a visit is an absolute must.

EAST COAST
Marsaxlokk

This attractive fishing village has a couple of good fish restaurants and a touristy, harbour-side market. Unfortunately, it is now overshadowed by an enormous power station. There are some pleasant swimming spots around **St Thomas Bay**, north-east of the village.

Gozo

Gozo is considerably smaller than the island of Malta and has a distinctive character of its own; the countryside is more attractive, the pace is slower and there are far fewer tourists. It seems to have escaped the worst of the 20th century, so don't come for nightlife and bright lights. The capital is Victoria (also known as Rabat), but most people stay at the small resort town of Marsalforn. You can cram the sights into one day, but the real charm of Gozo is best appreciated at a slower pace.

VICTORIA

Victoria is an interesting, bustling town and the commercial centre of Gozo. There are no hotels in Victoria, but it has a decent range of shops and banks.

There's a wonderful view over the island from the **citadel**, which was constructed by the knights in the 17th century. The archaeological and folklore **museums** are worth a visit, as is the flat-topped **cathedral**. Money ran out when it came to building the cathedral's dome. Its absence is noticeable from the outside but not from within, where there's a magnificent trompe l'oeil painting instead.

The tourist office (☎ 55 81 06), on the corner of Palm and Republic Sts, has a useful brochure and map. It can also supply information about car and bicycle rental on Gozo.

MARSALFORN

Marsalforn is the main resort town on the island and can become crowded on weekends. There's one large hotel, a scattering of smaller places to stay and a dozen restaurants, all built around an attractive bay. Follow the coast road west from the harbour for a fabulous walk past salt pans and spectacular eroded cliffs.

You can change money at the Mid-Med Bank on the harbour front, which is open from 8 am to 12.45 pm (11.30 am on Saturday) from 15 June to 31 October. The diving on Gozo is particularly good (see Activities in the Facts for the Visitor section for further information).

MALTA

MALTA

Places to Stay

Outside the high season, the family-run *Atlantis Hotel* (☎ 55 46 85) in Qolla St offers a poolside room and breakfast for Lm6.60 per person in winter; this jumps to Lm15.50 per person in summer. Lower daily rates can be negotiated for stays of a week or more, and cars and bicycles can be hired. *Calypso Hotel* on the harbour also has good off-season deals. Sea-view rooms cost Lm14.50 per person in summer, dropping to Lm6.50 in winter.

The *Marsalforn Hotel* (☎ 55 61 47), Rabat Rd, is a rather garish green and white hotel in the middle of town. B&B is Lm6 per person. Self-catering flats for four people are Lm10 to Lm12 per day. The hotel also hires out bicycles.

The NSTS recommends *St Joseph Hostel* (☎ 55 64 39) in Ghanjsielem, a 10-minute walk from the ferry dock at Mgarr Harbour.

Places to Eat

The restaurants are clustered around the harbour, and there's not really a great deal to distinguish between them. *Smiley's* is the cheapest, but it's pretty basic: burgers cost 60 cents, fish and chips Lm1.30.

The *Il-Kartell*, on the west side of the bay, is a step up and has good fish, pasta and pizzas; spaghetti is Lm1.20 and main courses and fresh fish are from Lm3 to Lm5. The *Arzella Bar Restaurant Pizzeria*, on a terrace suspended over the east side of the bay, is similarly priced but also offers Maltese specialities such as timpana (Lm1.50) and braġioli (Lm3.20).

Getting There & Away

Marsalforn is a 4km walk from Victoria, or you can catch bus No 21 from the terminus in Main Gate St.

AROUND GOZO

Gozo measures only 14km from east to west and 6km from north to south, so a lot of the island can be covered on foot. The **Ggantija** temple complex near Xaghra village is the most spectacular in Malta – its walls are 6m high. There's a dramatic stretch of coastline around **Dwejra Point**, including the imposing **Azure Window**, a gigantic rock arch in the cliff, only a few metres from the Inland Sea. This is the best area in Malta for walking along the scenic rocky coastline.

Xlendi

Xlendi is a small fishing village on the tip of a deep, rocky inlet on the south-west coast. It's a pretty spot but fast becoming overdeveloped. Some well-marked coastal footpaths start at Xlendi.

The *Serena ApartHotel* (☎ 55 37 19), Upper St, is perched over the town and has great views. A superior suite with a sea view, plus breakfast, costs Lm12 per person. The elegant *St Patrick's Hotel* (☎ 56 29 51) is right on the sea and has rooms from Lm8 per person in the low season, rising to Lm15.50 in summer (rooms with sea views cost a bit more). There are several restaurants in Xlendi. At the St Patrick's Hotel waterfront restaurant, a salad with Gozo cheese (like a peppery feta) costs Lm1.65.

Catch bus No 87 to get to Xlendi from Victoria.

Morocco

Known to the Arabs as *al-Maghreb al-Aqsa*, the 'farthest land of the setting sun', Morocco stands at the western extremity of the Arab and Muslim world. A land saturated with colour and rich in history, it has long held a romantic allure for the westerner. For many, its greatest charm lies in the labyrinths of the imperial cities – Fès, Meknès, Marrakesh and Rabat. The countryside, too, exerts its own fascination. The snowcapped High Atlas Mountains, the great river valleys of the south with their magnificent red-earth kasbahs, the vast expanse of the desert – all offer the visitor a taste of the exotic.

AT A GLANCE

Capital	Rabat
Population	30.4 million
Area	446,550 sq km
Official Language	Arabic
Currency	1 Moroccan dirham (Dr) = 100 centimes
GDP	US$97.6 billion (1996)
Time	GMT/UTC+0000

Also in Fès
Fès-Ville Nouvelle Central p729

Also in Marrakesh
Marrakesh - Central Medina p754

Central Tangier p710
Central Rabat p733
Central Casablanca p736
El-Jadida p741
Essaouira p743
Agadir p746
Marrakesh pp750-1
Meknès p722
Tetouan p715
Chefchaouen p717
Fès pp 726-7

Facts about Morocco

HISTORY

Morocco is largely populated by descendants of the Berber settlers who came to the area thousands of years ago. Their independent spirit has outlived conquerors over the centuries and resulted in one of Africa's most colourful cultures.

The first records of the Berbers recount their control of trans-Saharan trade. Later the Romans gained a tenuous hold in this part of North Africa, only to fade slowly away before the arrival of Islam in the 7th century. The Arab armies swept across Byzantine Egypt and eventually controlled the whole North African coast and much of Spain.

Basic tribal divisions soon reasserted themselves, however, and the Berbers, having adopted Islam, developed their own brand of Shi'ism, known as Kharijism. By 829 the Kharijites had established a stable Idrissid state, with its capital at Fès, which dominated all of Morocco

This unity was short lived. By the 11th century the region had fragmented. Out of the chaos emerged the Almoravids, who overran Morocco and Muslim Spain (Al-Andalus) and founded Marrakesh. They were supplanted by the Almohads, who raised Fès, Marrakesh and Rabat to heights of splendour,

before crumbling as Christian armies regained Spain. The Merenid dynasty revitalised the Moroccan heartland and established Fès el-Jdid (New Fès), but it too collapsed after Granada fell to the Christians in 1492 and Muslim refugees poured into Morocco.

The Merenids were followed by the Saadians but by the 1630s they had succumbed to the 'decadence' of urban living. The Alawites took over and constructed the Imperial City at Meknès during the rule of Sultan Moulay Ismail (1672-1727). It was a last gasp and Morocco increasingly became a neglected

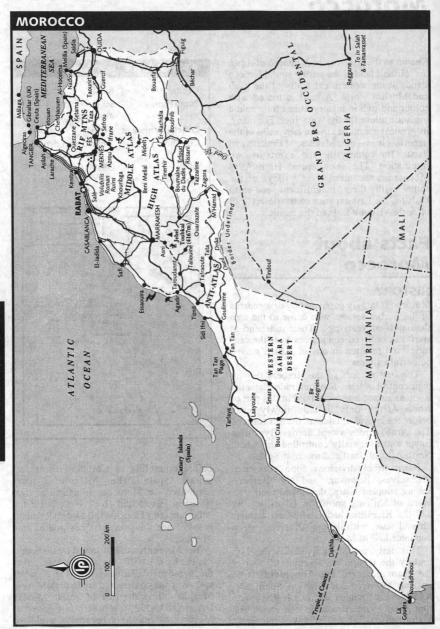

backwater as trans-Saharan trade disintegrated and Europe became industrialised.

Morocco managed to retain its independence as colonialism swept the rest of Africa until, by the 1912 Treaty of Fès, France took over much of the country, handing Spain a zone in the north. Under the enlightened French resident-general, Marshal Lyautey, the colonialists built *villes nouvelles* (new cities) in many of the larger Moroccan cities, thus preserving the traditional medinas.

Rabat was made the capital and Casablanca developed as a major port. By 1934 the last opposition from Berber mountain tribes had been crushed, but Moroccan resistance moved into political channels in the Istiqlal (independence) party. After WWII, opposition again took a more violent turn and in 1953 the French exiled Sultan Mohammed V. This only succeeded in further stoking Moroccan discontent and he was allowed to return in 1955. Independence was granted the following year.

The Spanish withdrew from much of the country at about the same time but have retained the coastal enclaves of Ceuta and Melilla. Sultan Mohammed V became a king and since his death, his son, King Hassan II, despite moves towards democracy and several coup attempts, has retained all effective power.

King Hassan's popularity soared with the 1975 'Green March', when 350,000 unarmed Moroccans marched into the Spanish colony of Western Sahara. Spanish troops left shortly after and the Polisario Front, which had been struggling for years against Spanish rule, turned to fight its new overlords. In 1991, the United Nations brokered a ceasefire on the understanding that a referendum on the territory's future would be held in 1992. By 1997, due to a dispute over who should be eligible to vote, the referendum had still not taken place and the USA, frustrated with the stagnation of affairs, appointed a special envoy to help seek a way forward.

Morocco today suffers from a batch of traditional Third World problems including breakneck population increase, high unemployment and a yawning gap between a wealthy elite and a huge section of the population living below the poverty line.

GEOGRAPHY & ECOLOGY

One of Africa's most geographically diverse areas, Morocco is spectacularly beautiful. It is traversed by four mountain ranges. From north to south, they are the Rif, the Middle Atlas, the High Atlas and the Anti-Atlas. Certain peaks of the High Atlas remain snow-capped all year and are among the highest in Africa.

Between the mountain ranges themselves, and between these ranges and the Atlantic Ocean, are plateaux and plains. Fed by melting snow, they are fertile and well watered. On many of the plains farther south, agriculture is tenuous, except along certain river courses. In the extreme south, at the edge of the Anti-Atlas Mountains, the country is characterised by vast, eroded gorges which, like the rivers that flow at their bases, gradually peter out in the endless sand and stone wastes of the Sahara Desert.

Deforestation and soil erosion are major problems in some areas. Between Ouezzane and Meknès, and Fès and Taza, for instance, vegetation is sparse after a dry winter. Nevertheless, springtime can see blazes of colourful wildflowers and there are still pine and cedar forests in the north and rolling wooded parkland towards the south. The fringes of the desert are graced with verdant *palmeraies* (palm groves).

Wildlife includes little that is truly exotic, although wild boar inhabit the forested areas and a large wild sheep, the *mouflon*, is quite common in the Atlas, as is the macaque monkey. The more arid regions are home to gazelles and fennec foxes but you will be very fortunate to spot either.

Thanks to its relatively mild climate, rich habitat, diversity and importance as a stopover for migratory birds, Morocco has much to offer the birdwatcher. More than 300 species have been recorded, including huge concentrations of migrating storks, hawks and eagles in spring and autumn; colourful bee-eaters and rollers; and the majestic bustards and graceful cranes.

GOVERNMENT & POLITICS

The kingdom of Morocco is ruled by King Hassan II who came to the throne in 1961. During his reign, the country's constitution has been considerably modernised with the introduction of an elected chamber and a system of multiparty politics.

In 1997, Morocco moved closer to becoming a parliamentary democracy with the establishment of a bicameral parliament. In September 1997, national legislative elections for the 325-seat lower house resulted in the formation of a coalition government made up of parties from across the political spectrum. Abderrahmane Youssoufi, the widely respected leader of the left-wing Union Socialiste des Force Populaire (USFP) is prime minister. He has pledged to encourage investment in Morocco and tackle the dire employment situation. (Apart from an unemployment rate of close to 20% of the working population, a recent estimate suggests that some nine million people in Morocco earn less than Dr10 per day.)

Despite these democratic moves, Morocco remains essentially an absolute monarchy. The king retains the right to appoint his prime minister and all ministers subsequently chosen by the prime minister must be approved by the king. The major ministries of justice, foreign affairs and internal affairs remain very firmly in the hands of the king. The 275-seat upper house consists of deputies indirectly elected from local and regional government, professional bodies and trade unions.

ECONOMY

The mainstays of Morocco's economy are agriculture, mining, tourism, manufacturing, and remittances from Moroccans abroad.

Morocco is the world's third-largest exporter of phosphates and this is now a major foreign exchange earner. World prices have recovered from their depression in 1991-93 and look set to continue to rise. Tourism, hard hit by the effects of the Gulf War, picked up in 1992 then recovered strongly again in 1996 after a three-year recession.

Years of IMF-imposed austerity measures, followed by continued public spending cuts and massive privatisation, have made the economy leaner and fitter, but with serious social costs, such as rising unemployment. External debt is still high, but Morocco hopes the free trade zone agreement signed with the European Union (EU) in 1996 will accelerate development. The payoff for Europe could be a tighter clamp on the flow of drugs from Morocco to Europe – a multibillion dollar trade that does neither side much good.

POPULATION & PEOPLE

The population stands at about 30.4 million but, at present growth levels, is expected to double by early next century. The largest city is Casablanca, with a population of around three million. It is followed by Rabat-Salé (1.23 million) and Fès (735,000).

The bulk of the population is made up of Arab and Berber peoples who have intermarried over the centuries. Morocco once hosted a large population of Jews, but the vast majority left after the foundation of Israel in 1948. Trade with trans-Saharan Africa brought a population of black Africans into Morocco – many of whom originally came as slaves.

ARTS

Two things that immediately strike the visitor to Morocco are the music and the architecture. The former is drawn from many traditions, from classics of the Arab-Andalucían heritage through to the more genuinely African rhythms of Berber music. Raï, a fusion of traditional, tribal and modern western popular forms and instruments, began in Algeria and has become very popular in Morocco. Cheap cassettes are easily obtained throughout the country.

With the exception of what the Arabs left behind in Spain, nothing in Europe can prepare you for the visual feast of the great mosques and *medersas* (Koranic schools) that bejewel the major Moroccan cities. Lacking the extravagance of the Gothic or rococo, Moroccan monuments are virtuoso pieces of geometric design and harmony.

SOCIETY & CONDUCT

It is easy to be beguiled by appearances in Morocco. Despite the impact of the west, Morocco remains a largely conservative Muslim society. As a rule, a high degree of modesty is demanded of both sexes in dress as well as behaviour. Women, in particular, are well advised to keep their shoulders and upper arms covered and to opt for long skirts or trousers (beach resorts such as Agadir are an exception).

If invited into a Moroccan home, it is customary to remove your shoes before stepping onto the carpet. Food is served in common dishes and eaten with the right hand. In Muslim countries the left hand is used for personal hygiene after visiting the toilet and should not be used to eat with or to touch any common source of food or water, or to hand over money or presents.

All mosques and religious buildings in active use are off limits to non-Muslims. Cemeteries are pretty much no-go areas, too, and many Muslims don't appreciate westerners taking shortcuts through them.

RELIGION
All but a tiny minority of the population is Sunni Muslim, but in Morocco, Islam is far from strictly orthodox. The main difference lies in the worship of local saints and holy people (*marabouts*) – a sort of resurgence of pre-Islamic traditions. The whitewashed *koubba* (tomb) of the marabout is a common sight all over the Maghreb (north-west Africa).

Where these local saints have accumulated many followers, prosperous individuals have endowed the koubba with educational institutions known as *zawiyyas*, which offer an alternative to the orthodox medersas attached to mosques.

LANGUAGE
Arabic is the official language, but Berber and French are widely spoken. Spanish is spoken in former Spanish-held territory (particularly the north) and some English in the main tourist centres. Arabic and French are taught in schools and French is important in university education and commerce.

Although many Moroccans speak many different languages passably, don't expect much beyond Moroccan Arabic and French outside the main cities and popular tourist spots.

Spoken Moroccan Arabic (*darija*) is considerably different from what you hear in the Middle East. Pick up a copy of Lonely Planet's *Moroccan Arabic phrasebook* by Dan Bacon for more detailed coverage. Various Berber dialects are spoken in the countryside and particularly in the mountains.

See the Language Guide at the back of this book for pronunciation guidelines and useful words and phrases.

Facts for the Visitor

HIGHLIGHTS
Imperial Cities
The four great cities of Morocco's imperial past are Fès, Marrakesh, Meknès and Rabat. Here you will discover Morocco's greatest monuments – mosques and medersas surrounded by the colour of the medina and *souqs* (markets).

High Atlas & the South
In just a few days you can sample the breathtaking heights of the Atlas Mountains, sprinkled with Berber villages, and then head south/for the oases and *kasbahs* (citadels) of the Drâa Valley and the Dadès and Todra gorges to the south-east of Marrakesh.

Coastal Towns & Beaches
The Atlantic coast is dotted with tranquil towns bearing the marks of European occupation. Among the more interesting are Asilah and El-Jadida, which started life as Portuguese settlements, and Essaouira. There are plenty of beaches along the Atlantic coast, and a couple of decent ones on the Mediterranean, too.

SUGGESTED ITINERARIES
Depending on how much time you have, you might want to do the following:

One to two weeks
    Visit the imperial cities (Fès, Meknès, Marrakesh and Rabat).
Two to three weeks
    Visit Marrakesh, the High Atlas, the southern oases and gorges, and finish on the coast at Essaouira.
One month
    At a pinch you could take in the imperial cities, some trekking, the southern oases and gorges, Essaouira and perhaps spend a little time in the Rif Mountains, preferably at Chefchaouen.

Two months
  This should give you time to visit all of Morocco (or a good chunk of it).

PLANNING
Climate & When to Go

In winter the coastal lowlands are pleasantly warm to hot during the day (average 18°C) and cool to cold at night (9°C). In summer, it's very hot during the day (30°C) and warm at night (18°C). A hot, dusty wind from the desert, the *chergui*, can whip temperatures up above 40°C.

Winter in the higher regions demands clothing suitable for Arctic conditions; this is true anywhere in the vicinity of the High Atlas Mountains. In summer it's hot during the day and cool at night.

Passes over the High Atlas can be blocked with snow during winter. Snowploughs usually clear them by the next day, but you may spend a bitter night stuck in an unheated bus.

The main rainy season is between November and April but it usually brings only occasional light rain. Rain rarely falls on the eastern parts of the country, and humidity is generally low.

The most pleasant times to explore Morocco are during spring (April to May) and autumn (September to October). Midsummer can be very enjoyable on the coast but viciously hot in the interior. Likewise, winter can be idyllic in Marrakesh and farther south during the day, but you can be chilled to the bone at night.

Books & Maps

See Lonely Planet's *Morocco* and (if you're planning on travelling farther) *North Africa* for more detailed information on the country.

The Moors: Islam in the West by Michael Brett & Werner Forman details Moorish civilisation at its height, with superb colour photographs. *Histoire du Maroc* by Bernard Lugan is a potted history of the country. *The Conquest of Morocco* by Douglas Porch examines the takeover of Morocco by Paris.

Doing Daily Battle by Fatima Mernissi, translated by Mary Jo Lakeland, is a collection of interviews with 11 Moroccan women giving a valuable insight into their lives and aspirations. A number of western writers

have connections with Morocco, including long-term Tangier resident, Paul Bowles.

The best map is the Michelin No 959 *Morocco* (scale 1:1,000,000). In Rabat, the Cartography Division of the Conservation & Topography Department (☎ 70 53 11; fax 70 58 85), 31 Ave Moulay Hassan, stocks a range of maps, including topographical maps (useful for hiking). Unfortunately, you must make an official request for any maps you want, a process which can take several days.

What to Bring

Bring any special medication you need. Sun protection, including hat, glasses and sunscreen, is a good idea in much of the country for much of the year. You should also bring your own contraceptives. You can get hold of condoms and even the pill, but quality is dubious and availability uncertain.

TOURIST OFFICES

The national tourist body, ONMT, has offices (usually called Délégation Régionale du Tourisme) in the main cities. They have brochures and simple maps of the major places. The head office (☎ 68 15 31) is in Rabat, just off Rue al-Abtal. A few cities also have local offices known as *syndicats d'initiative*. These are in the process of being replaced by a new regional authority, the Groupement Régional d'Intérêt Touristique (GRIT). The first branches to be set up will be in Agadir, Fès, Marrakesh and Tangier.

Tourist Offices Abroad

The ONMT maintains offices in Australia (Sydney), Belgium (Brussels), Canada (Montreal), France (Paris), Germany (Düsseldorf), Italy (Milan), Japan (Tokyo), Portugal (Lisbon), Spain (Madrid), Sweden (Stockholm), Switzerland (Zürich), the UK (London) and the USA (New York and Orlando).

VISAS & EMBASSIES

Most visitors to Morocco need no visa and on entry are granted leave to remain in the country for 90 days. Exceptions include nationals of Israel, South Africa and Zimbabwe. Visa requirements can change, so check with the Moroccan embassy in your country or a reputable travel agent before travelling.

Entry requirements for Ceuta and Melilla are the same as for Spain (see that chapter).

Visa Extensions

If the 90 days you are entitled to are insufficient, the simplest thing to do is leave (eg to the Spanish enclaves) and come back a few days later. Your chances improve if you re-enter by a different route.

People on visas may, however, prefer to try for an extension (this may take up to two weeks). Go to the central police station with your passport, four photos proof of sufficient funds and, preferably, a letter from your embassy requesting a visa extension on your behalf.

Moroccan Embassies Abroad

Algeria
(☎ 02-607408) 8 Rue des Cèdres, Parc de la Reine, Algiers
Australia
(☎ 02-9922 4999) Suite 2, 11 West St, North Sydney, NSW 2060
Canada
(☎ 416-236 7391) 38 Range Rd, Ottawa KIN 8J4
France
(☎ 01-45 20 69 35) 5 Rue Le Tasse, Paris 75016
Germany
(☎ 228 35 50 44) Gotenstrasse, 7-9-5300, Bonn 2
Japan
(☎ 03-478 3271) Silva Kingdom 3, 16-3, Sendagaya, Shibuya-ku, Tokyo 151
Netherlands
(☎ 70-346 9617) Oranjestraat 9, 2514 JB, The Hague
Spain
(☎ 91-563 1090) Calle Serrano 179, 28002 Madrid
Tunisia
(☎ 01-782 775) 39 Avenue du 1er Juin, Mutuelleville, Tunis
UK
(☎ 0171-581 5001) 49 Queen's Gate Gardens, London SW7 5NE
USA
(☎ 202-462 7979) 1601 21st St NW, Washington DC 20009

Foreign Embassies in Morocco

Most embassies are in Rabat but there are also consulates in Tangier, Marrakesh and Casablanca. Embassies in Rabat (telephone code ☎ 07) include:

Algeria
(☎ 76 54 74) 46 Ave Tariq ibn Zayid
Canada
(☎ 67 28 80) 13 bis Rue Jaafar Assadik, Agdal
France
Embassy: (☎ 77 78 22) 3 Rue Sahnoun, Agdal
Consulate (Service de Visas): (☎ 70 24 04) Rue Ibn al-Khattib
Germany
(☎ 70 96 62) 7 Zankat Madnine
Japan
(☎ 67 41 63) 70 Ave Al Oumoum Al Mouttahida
Netherlands
(☎ 73 35 12) 40 Rue de Tunis
Spain
Embassy: (☎ 70 94 81) 3-5 Zankat Madnine
Consulate: (☎ 70 41 47; fax 70 46 94) 57 Ave du Chellah
Tunisia
(☎ 73 06 36; fax 72 78 66) 6 Ave de Fès
UK
(☎ 72 09 05; fax 72 09 06) 17 Ave de la Tour Hassan
USA
(☎ 76 22 65; fax 76 56 61) 2 Ave de Marrakesh

CUSTOMS

You can import up to 200 cigarettes and 1L of spirits duty-free.

MONEY

Currency

The unit of currency is the dirham (Dr), which is equal to 100 centimes. The importation or exportation of local currency is prohibited and there's not much of a black market and little reason to use it. In the Spanish enclaves of Ceuta and Melilla the currency is the Spanish peseta (pta).

Exchange Rates

Australia	A$1	=	Dr5.79
euro	€1	=	Dr10.69
France	1FF	=	Dr1.61
Germany	DM1	=	Dr5.42
Japan	¥100	=	Dr6.67
New Zealand	NZ$1	=	Dr4.90
Spain	100 ptas	=	Dr6.38
UK	UK£1	=	Dr15.79
USA	US$1	=	Dr9.75

Banking services are generally quick and efficient. Branches of BMCE (Banque Marocaine

MOROCCO

du Commerce Extérieur) are the most convenient and often have separate *bureau de change* sections. Avoid them for travellers cheques, as they are one of the few banks to charge commission. Australian and New Zealand dollars are not quoted in banks and are generally not accepted.

Credit Cards

All major credit cards are widely accepted in the main cities and even in many small towns, although their use often attracts a 5% surcharge. American Express is represented by the travel agency Voyages Schwartz, which can be found in Casablanca, Marrakesh and Tangier.

Visa, MasterCard, Access and Carte Bleue are accepted by many banks, but usually only in head branches. The principal banks in all the main cities have automatic teller machines (*guichets automatiques*), but they don't always accept foreign cards.

Costs

Moroccan prices are refreshingly reasonable. With a few small tips here and there plus entry charges to museums and the like, you can get by on US$20 to US$25 a day per person as long as you stay in cheap hotels, eat at cheap restaurants and are not in a hurry. If you'd prefer some of life's basic luxuries, such as hot showers, the occasional splurge at a good restaurant and the odd taxi, plan on US$30 to US$35 a day.

Hostel membership cards are not obligatory for staying in most Moroccan hostels; they'll save a couple of dirham each night. If you're under 31, an international student card can get you a 25% reduction on internal flights.

Tipping & Bargaining

Tipping is a way of life in Arab countries. Practically any service can warrant a tip, but don't be railroaded. The judicious distribution of a few dirham for a service willingly rendered can, however, make your life a lot easier. Between 5% and 10% of a restaurant bill is fine, but if you are waiting for Dr1 change on a Dr4 cup of coffee, don't bother!

Bargaining is also an integral part of Moroccan street life. When souvenir-hunting, decide beforehand how much you are pre-

pared to spend on an item (to get an idea of prices, visit the Ensemble Artisanals in the major cities), offer the vendor around one-third of the asking price and approach your limit slowly.

POST & COMMUNICATIONS
Post

The Moroccan post is fairly reliable, and you shouldn't have any problems receiving letters care of poste restante – although they are sometimes returned to sender a little hastily. Take your passport to claim mail. There's a small charge for collecting letters.

Outgoing parcels have to be inspected by customs (at the post office) before you seal them and pay for postage, so don't turn up with a sealed parcel. Some post offices offer a private packing service, but if you're not sure whether this is available, bring the requirements with you. Post offices are distinguished by the 'PTT' sign or the new 'La Poste' logo.

Telephone & Fax

The telephone system in Morocco is good. Most cities and towns have a phone office attached to the post office – the biggest are open 24 hours, seven days a week. For overseas calls you can either book a call at the office and pay at the counter, or dial direct. Private sector *téléboutiques* are widespread and much quicker than the official phone offices, though fractionally more expensive. The attendant sells phonecards (*télécartes*) and can provide as much change as you might need, which is a lot if you are ringing abroad. Calls are expensive: a three-minute call to the USA will cost about US$6 and a three-minute call to Europe at least US$4. For international calls, there is a 20% reduction between 10 pm and midnight Monday to Friday, and a 40% reduction between midnight and 7 am all week and from 12.30 pm Saturday to 7 am Monday.

Reverse charge (collect) calls to most countries are possible from phone offices – ask to *téléphoner en PCV* (pronounced 'pehseh-veh').

There is one standard phone book for all of Morocco in French – the *Annuaire des Abonnés au Téléphone*. Most phone offices have a copy lying around.

When calling overseas from Morocco, dial ☎ 00, your country code and then the city code and number. To call Morocco from overseas, dial the international access code, then 212 (Morocco's country code), the regional code (minus the zero) and the local number.

Many téléboutiques have fax machines. Prices per page vary but you can expect to pay about Dr50 to Europe and Dr70 to North America and Australia. The better hotels also offer fax services.

INTERNET RESOURCES

There are several Internet providers in Morocco, and cybercafés (though not many offer coffee and chocolate cake) have sprung up in the all the major cities and even in some of the smaller towns. See Post & Communications under each town for addresses.

One hour on the Internet generally costs between Dr30 and Dr50 and sometimes you can just send emails for Dr10 or so. Access is fairly reliable, though you'll be much better off using services in the morning rather than the afternoon or evening.

There is a good site about Morocco at www.maghreb.net/countries/morocco/index .html. Another location, www.i-cias.com /m.s/morocco/index/htm, includes an online course in Arabic.

NEWSPAPERS & MAGAZINES

In the main centres, a reasonable range of foreign press is available at central newsstands and in some of the big hotels. News magazines such as *Newsweek* and *Time* are usually fairly easy to find, along with the *International Herald Tribune* and some UK papers, including the *International Guardian*, and their Continental European equivalents. The French press is the most up-to-date and by far the cheapest.

RADIO & TV

Local radio is in Arabic and French, and you can pick up Spanish broadcasts in most parts of the country. Frequencies change from one part of the country to another. The BBC broadcasts into the area on shortwave frequencies 15,070 and 12,095MHz, from about 8 am to 11 pm.

Satellite television provides several foreign channels, including CNN, NBC and the popular Cartoon Network. The two government-owned stations, TVM and 2M, broadcast in Arabic and French.

PHOTOGRAPHY & VIDEO

Kodak and Fuji colour-negative and slide film, as well as video tapes, are readily available in all large Moroccan cities and towns.

Urban Moroccans are generally easygoing about being photographed but in the countryside you should ask permission beforehand. As a rule, women especially do *not* want to be photographed. Respect their right to privacy and don't take photos.

TIME

Moroccan time is GMT/UTC all year, so when it's summer in Europe, Morocco will be two hours behind Spanish time and one hour behind UK time.

ELECTRICITY

Morocco has 220V and sometimes 110V, depending on which area you are in, so check before plugging in any appliances. Plugs are of the European two-pin type.

WEIGHTS & MEASURES

Morocco uses the metric system. There is a conversion table at the back of this book.

LAUNDRY

You're better off doing it yourself. Some hotels will do it and charge – often you have to wait days to see your clothes again. Establishments called *Pressings* (they look like dry-cleaners) will wash and iron clothes for you. They generally take about 48 hours and prices range from Dr2 for socks up to Dr15 for jackets.

TOILETS

Outside the major cities, public toilets are few and far between (though there will always be a public toilet near a mosque), and usually require your own paper, a tip for the attendant, stout-soled shoes and a nose clip. They are mostly of the 'squatter' variety. If you get caught short, duck into the nearest hotel or café.

HEALTH

The Moroccan health service is largely urban based; almost 50% of all public sector doctors are to be found in Casablanca and Rabat-Salé. Thus, if you're in serious trouble you need to get to one of the bigger towns. The number of rural health centres has, however, increased in recent years and they are quite adequate for dealing with minor complaints. There is also a growing private health sector but, in case of emergency, head for a public hospital outpatients department. Moroccan doctors are, on the whole, reasonably well trained and the top hospitals in the big cities are OK. Pharmacies are widespread and well stocked.

WOMEN TRAVELLERS

Although a certain level of sexual harassment is almost the norm, in some ways Morocco can be less problematic than more overtly macho countries such as Italy and Spain. Harassment is generally of the leering, verbal variety. In the bigger cities especially, female travellers will receive hopeful greetings from every male over the age of 13! Ignore them entirely. Women will save themselves a great deal of grief by dressing modestly – that means keeping shoulders and upper arms covered, opting for long skirts and trousers and avoiding anything skintight. Stricter Muslims consider the excessive display of flesh (whether male or female) offensive; many men will consider it extremely provocative. It's wise not to walk around alone at night – after dark all 'good' Moroccan women are at home.

GAY & LESBIAN TRAVELLERS

Homosexual acts are officially illegal in Morocco, with article 489 of the penal code prohibiting any 'shameless or unnatural act' with a person of the same sex. Penalties are six months to three years imprisonment and a fine of up to Dr1200. Though not openly admitted or shown, male homosexuality remains relatively common. Male homosexuals are advised to be discreet – aggression towards gay male travellers is not unheard of.

DANGERS & ANNOYANCES

Morocco's era as a hippy paradise, riding the Marrakesh Express and all that, is long past. Plenty of fine dope may be grown in the Rif Mountains, but drug busts are common and Morocco is not a good place to investigate local prison conditions. Travellers have reported various drug-related rip-off rackets, including one where tourists are kidnapped and forced to smoke the stuff, photos are taken, and they are told they will be turned over to the police unless they cooperate.

On some of the more popular tourist routes – in particular the road between Marrakesh and Ouarzazate – you may come across professional hitchhikers and people pretending that their cars have broken down. If you assist them, they'll oblige you to accept their thanks with a glass of tea at their house and a heavy duty carpet-sales session.

Morocco has its share of pickpockets and thieves but they're not a major problem.

The police can be reached on ☎ 19 and the highway emergency service on ☎ 177.

Guides

Morocco's notorious *faux guides* (false guides) and hustlers have been dealt a heavy blow in recent years. Following a national policy pursued in the principal cities, a special *Brigade Touristique* (tourist police) has been set up to clamp down on them. Any person suspected of trying to operate as an unofficial guide is liable for a prison sentence of between six months and three years and a fine of between Dr10,000 and Dr20,000.

This has significantly reduced, but not yet eliminated, the problem of the faux guides. You'll still find plenty hanging around the entrances to the big city medinas and outside bus and train stations. They can be persistent and sometimes unpleasant. If you don't want their services, ignore their offers and try not to get your feathers ruffled.

If you do end up with one of these people (you really should not pay an unofficial guide more than Dr25 for two or three hours), remember their main interest is in making a commission from a particular hotel or on articles sold to you in the souqs.

Official guides can be engaged through tourist offices and most hotels at the fixed price of Dr120/150 for a half/full day (plus tip). It's well worth taking a guide when exploring the intricate and confusing medinas of Fès and Marrakesh. Their local knowledge is extensive and they'll save you from being hassled by other would-be guides. If you don't want a shopping expedition included in your tour, make this clear beforehand.

BUSINESS HOURS

Banking hours are Monday to Thursday from 8.30 to 11.30 am and 2.30 to 4.30 pm; on Friday hours are from 8.30 to 11.15 am and 3 to 4.30 pm; and during Ramadan they're 9 am to 3 pm. These times can vary a little. In some of the main tourist cities, the BMCE head branch will have later opening times for currency exchange (often a small separate office). Post offices generally keep similar hours, but don't close until 6 pm or so. Phone offices in the bigger centres are open long hours and seven days a week. Many museums and some monuments are closed on Tuesday.

PUBLIC HOLIDAYS & SPECIAL EVENTS

All banks, post offices and most shops are shut on the main public holidays. The 10 national secular holidays are: New Year's Day, 11 January (Independence Manifesto), 3 March (Feast of the Throne), 1 May (Labour Day), 23 May (National Day), 9 July (Young People's Day), 14 August (Allegiance of Wadi-Eddahab), 20 August (Anniversary of the King's and People's Revolution), 6 November (Anniversary of the Green March), 18 November (Independence Day).

In addition to secular holidays there are many Islamic holidays and festivals, all tied to the lunar calendar. Some are celebrated all over the country but others are local events.

Probably the most important is the Aïd al-Fitr, held at the end of the month-long Ramadan fast, which is fairly strictly observed by most Muslims. The festivities generally last four or five days, during which just about everything grinds to a halt.

Another important Muslim festival is Aïd al-Adha, which marks the end of the Islamic year. It commemorates Abraham's submission to God through the offer of his son Isaac for sacrifice. Again, most things shut down

for four or five days. The third main religious festival, known as Mawlid an-Nabi (or simply Mouloud), celebrates the Prophet Mohammed's birthday.

Local festivals, mostly in honour of marabouts (saints) and known as *moussems* or *amouggars*, are common among the Berbers and usually held in the summer months.

ACTIVITIES
Camel Treks

For many travellers, a camel expedition into the desert is a real highlight of a trip to the south. Though fairly expensive (from Dr300 per person) and hard on the bottom, it's a great way to experience the silence and beauty of the landscape. Most hotels in Zagora can organise trips; in Marrakesh, inquire at the Hôtel Ali.

Surfing & Windsurfing

With thousands of kilometres of ocean coastline, Morocco isn't a bad place to take your board. Places worth investigating include the beaches around Kenitra; Media Beach, a few kilometres north of Rabat; and Anchor Point in Agadir. For windsurfing, Essaouira is the place to head for. There are two places along the beach here where you can hire gear.

Trekking

Trekking the heady heights of the High Atlas is a walking experience unlike anything you will find in Europe. Ascending Jebel Toubkal, the highest peak, takes just a couple of days, but with a guide and mule (from Dr200 per day) you could easily spend a week or more wending your way between welcoming Berber villages. Early spring is the best time to go (for more details see the High Atlas Trekking section).

Other trekking possibilities include the pink Anti-Atlas Mountains and the cedar-forested slopes of the Middle Atlas.

ACCOMMODATION
Camping

You can camp anywhere in Morocco if you have permission from the site's owner. There are also many official sites, where you'll pay

MOROCCO

around Dr10 per person plus Dr10 to pitch a tent. There are extra charges for vehicles, electricity and hot water.

Hostels

There are hostels (*auberges de jeunesse*) at Asni, Azrou, Casablanca, Chefchaouen, Fès, Marrakesh, Meknès, Rabat and Tangier. If you're travelling alone, they are among the cheapest places to stay. They usually cost Dr20 to Dr30 a night. The head office of the Royal Moroccan Federation of Youth Hostels (☎ 47 09 52; fax 22 76 77) is at Parc de la Ligue Arabe, BP 15988, Casablanca.

Hotels

You'll find cheap, unclassified hotels clustered in certain parts of the medinas of the bigger cities. Singles/doubles cost from Dr30/50; showers are often cold, but there are always *hammams* (bath houses) nearby. Some of these places are bright and spotless, others haven't seen a mop for years – it pays to look around a bit if you can.

For a little more, you can often find better unclassified or one-star hotels outside the medinas. In one-star hotels, singles/doubles with shower start at around Dr80/130; rooms in two-star hotels start at around Dr150/200. Prices often include breakfast – around Dr25 compared to the Dr7 to Dr10 you'll pay for a coffee and a croissant in a café.

The additional star in the three-star category (from Dr200/250) gets you a TV and a telephone. Hotels in the five-star category (from Dr1000 for a double) range from rather sterile modern places to former palaces.

FOOD

For those prepared to seek out the best, Moroccan food is superb. Influenced by Berber, Arabic and Mediterranean (particularly Spanish and French) traditions, the cuisine features a sublime use of spices and the freshest of local produce. As everywhere, the best food is to be found in family homes and if you're invited home for lunch or dinner, you're sure to be in for a treat (see Society & Conduct earlier for tips on etiquette).

Restaurant food, particularly in the touristy zones, can be variable. Head for the places full of locals and you won't go far wrong. Typical dishes include *tajine*, a meat and vegetable stew cooked slowly in an earthenware dish and *couscous*, fluffy steamed semolina served with tender meat and vegetables and sometimes a spicy sauce. The preparation of couscous is laborious, so for a really good restaurant couscous you may need to order it ahead. Couscous is traditionally eaten on Friday.

Harira, a thick soup made from lamb stock, lentils, chickpeas, onions, tomatoes, fresh herbs and spices, is usually eaten as a first course in the evening, but is substantial enough to make a meal on its own. In a cheap restaurant a bowl will cost Dr2 or Dr3.

Salads are served everywhere, the nicest being the traditional *salade marocaine* made from finely diced green peppers, tomatoes and red onion. *Brochettes* (skewered meat barbecued over hot coals) or roast chicken served with crispy *frites* (French fries) are other staples.

Pastilla is a very rich and delicious dish made from pigeon meat and lemon-flavoured eggs, plus almonds, cinnamon, saffron and sugar, encased in layer upon layer of very fine *ouarka* pastry. Pastilla is a speciality of Fès.

Vegetarians shouldn't have any major problems – fresh fruit and vegetables as well as a range of pulses, such as lentils and chickpeas, are widely available. When ordering couscous or tajine, simply ask for your dish to be served *sans viande* (without meat).

Coffee and croissant (around Dr7) is a good, cheap breakfast. Even cheaper and really delicious is a breakfast of *bessara* (pea soup with spices and olive oil), fresh bread and sweet mint tea. You'll find bessara stalls near the central markets.

Morocco is full of pâtisseries which produce excellent French and Moroccan pastries – this is where the locals head in the early evening.

If you're on a very tight budget, you can eat for as little as Dr50 per day. A three-course meal in a medium-priced restaurant will cost around Dr80 (without beer or wine). If you want to treat yourself to a meal in a traditional Moroccan palace restaurant or a smart French place, expect to pay upwards of Dr150 per person.

DRINKS

Morocco is bursting at the seams with cafés where sipping mint tea or coffee is a serious occupation. More often than not, the café is an all-male preserve and female travellers may prefer to head for the pâtisseries.

Mint tea is made with Chinese gunpowder tea, fresh mint and vast quantities of sugar. It's usually served in elegant Moroccan teapots and poured into small glasses. In restaurants it may be just served by the glass. English tea is usually served black and is invariably known as *thé Lipton*. Coffee is served in the French style: short black or large milky white. *Qahwa ness-ness* is half coffee, half milk served in a glass.

It's not advisable to drink the tap water in Morocco. Local bottled water is available everywhere and costs Dr5 for a big bottle (more in restaurants). Water taken from streams in the mountains should be treated with purification tablets.

Beer is reasonably easy to find in the villes nouvelles. A bottle of local Stork or Flag beer typically costs from Dr12 to Dr15 in bars (more than double that in fancy hotels). Imported beer is very expensive. Morocco produces some quite palatable wines (the whites and rosés are better than the reds) for as little as Dr35 in liquor stores.

ENTERTAINMENT

Morocco isn't exactly the last word in nightlife. The major cities do have some good cinemas (movies dubbed into French) and there are bars, discos and nightclubs to be found. The latter three tend to be dubious or rather exclusive – or both. Plenty of hotels and restaurants provide traditional music to accompany dinner. The best opportunities to hear music, however, will be at the annual festivals and moussems.

THINGS TO BUY

Moroccan crafts are world-famous for their variety and quality. Items to look for include traditional carpets (Rabat) and flatweave rugs, ceramics (Fès and Safi), chased brass and copperware (Marrakesh, Fès and Tetouan), painted woodwork (Fès), thuya woodcarvings (Essaouira), leather work and silver jewellery (Tiznit and Taroudannt).

Before buying anything, you should look around. All the major cities have a government-run Ensemble Artisanal where you can look at good-quality items in peace and quiet and check the upper-range prices. See the Tipping & Bargaining section earlier.

Morocco has a tradition of perfume making and in the bigger cities you'll find large perfumeries where you can buy excellent copies (Dr49 for 20ml) of all the famous names.

Getting There & Away

AIR

Morocco is well served by air from Europe, the Middle East and West Africa. The main entry point is the Mohammed V airport 30km south-east of Casablanca. International flights also land at Tangier, Agadir, Marrakesh, Fès and Ouarzazate. Air France and Royal Air Maroc (RAM) are the major carriers, but other airlines operating to Morocco include Alitalia, GB Airways (a subsidiary of British Airways), Iberia, KLM, Lufthansa, Swissair and Tunis Air.

Europe & the UK

It is possible to find charter flights to Morocco from some Northern European cities such as Paris, Amsterdam, Brussels and Düsseldorf for the equivalent of around UK£200 or less. Charter tickets are generally return tickets and are usually not valid for more than one month. At the time of writing, the only charter flights from the UK were to Agadir (UK£169 for 14 days).

In the high season, scheduled flights (valid for one month) between London and Casablanca are as much as UK£393. It is much cheaper to fly to Málaga (from as little as £69 one way) in southern Spain, bus it to Algeciras and catch a ferry to Tangier.

There are no cheap flights out of Morocco – a standard one-way fare between Paris and Marrakesh is Dr4315.

North America & Australasia

Royal Air Maroc has a flight from Montreal to Casablanca via New York (C$2800 for a special excursion fare valid for six months), but it would be more economical to fly to Paris or London and continue from there. There are no direct flights between Australia or New Zealand and Morocco. Again, the best bet is to get a flight to Europe.

LAND
Europe

Bus Eurolines and the Moroccan national bus line, CTM (Compagnie des Transports Marocains), operate buses between Morocco and many European cities. A return ticket valid for six months from London to Marrakesh costs UK£200. CTM buses to Paris, other French and Belgian cities run regularly from the major Moroccan cities and cost around Dr1500 to Dr2000 (US$157 to US$210) one way.

For security reasons, the land border between Morocco and Algeria was closed in 1994 and at the time of writing looked set to remain so.

Train Trains give you the option of couchettes and breaking your trip along the way. From London, Rail Europe only sells tickets as far as Algeciras. One-way/return tickets valid for two months cost UK£123/208. The Moroccan rail system is part of the Inter-Rail network. For around UK£300, travellers can purchase an Inter-Rail ticket entitling them to a month of free unlimited 2nd-class travel on trains in up to 28 countries in Europe, including Morocco.

BOAT
Spain

Car ferries are operated by Compañía Trasmediterranea, Islena de Navigación SA, Comarit, Limadet and Transtour. The most popular route is Algeciras-Tangier; others are Algeciras-Ceuta (Spanish Morocco), Almeria-Melilla (Spanish Morocco), Málaga-Melilla (Spanish Morocco) and Tarifa-Tangier. The vessels are mostly car ferries of the drive-on and drive-off type.

Algeciras-Tangier There are nine crossings a day in either direction (more in the high season). Adult one-way fares are 3000 ptas or Dr210 (half-price for children under

12). A car up to 6m long costs 8500 ptas or Dr648. The crossing takes 2½ hours.

Algeciras-Ceuta There are up to 12 crossings a day (ferry and jetfoil) in either direction. The one-way fare is 1700 ptas. Cars cost from 7500 ptas. The ferry trip takes 1½ hours. The jetfoil costs 2700 ptas and takes 30 minutes.

Almeria & Málaga-Melilla Compañía Trasmediterranea has six services a week from Almeria to Melilla and vice versa. The crossing takes 6½ to eight hours. The cheapest one-way fare is 3150 ptas. Cabin space is available from 5000 ptas. Málaga-Melilla operates on a similar schedule and with similar fares but takes around eight hours.

Tarifa-Tangier The Transtour ferry operates once-daily except Sunday in either direction. Fares are the same as those on the Algeciras-Tangier route. The crossing takes one hour.

Gibraltar

The *Idriss II* ferry links Gibraltar with Tangier three times a week. The two-hour crossing costs UK£18 (Dr250) one way. There is an occasional catamaran service between Gibraltar and Restinga Smir, north of Tetouan. When it runs (mainly in summer), it costs around UK£17 one way.

France

The Sète-Tangier and Nador car-ferry service is operated by the Compagnie Marocaine de Navigation and the crossing is usually made once every four to five days. The trip takes 38 hours and the fare, depending on class, is between FF1250 and FF2100 (children half-price). Cars under 4m long cost FF1540. Departures, journey time and fares to Nador (summer only) are similar.

LEAVING MOROCCO

There are no departure taxes from Morocco. If you plan to buy a ferry ticket at the port in Tangier, keep enough dirham handy to do so.

Getting Around

AIR

If time is limited, it's worth considering the occasional internal flight with Royal Air Maroc (RAM). If you're under 22 or a student under 31, you are entitled to 25% off all fares. There are group reductions and children aged two to 12 travel at half-price. The standard one-way fare between Casablanca and Fès is Dr528 (about US$55); between Tangier and Marrakesh it's Dr854 (about US$90).

Internal airports serviced by RAM are at Agadir, Al-Hoceima, Casablanca, Dakhla, Fès, Laayoune, Marrakesh, Oujda, Ouarzazate, Rabat, Smara, Tangier and Tan Tan. There is now an internal airport at Essaouira.

BUS

There is a good network of bus routes all over the country, departures are frequent and tickets are cheap.

CTM (Compagnie des Transports Marocains) is the only national company (privatised in 1994). On most main routes it runs 1st and 2nd-class services. There are more of the former than the latter, so you'll often be paying the higher fare (about 25% more) unless you're very flexible about departure times. Generally, booking is not necessary but it's advisable (where they sell advance tickets) in smaller towns with few services. In some cities, CTM has its own terminal.

The biggest of the remaining companies is SATAS, which covers destinations south of Casablanca. It's just as good as CTM, slightly cheaper and has more services in the south. Some examples of 1st-class CTM fares are:

from	to	fare (Dr)
Casablanca	Agadir	136
	Fès	78
	Marrakesh	63
	Tangier	110
Tangier	Fès	85
	Tiznit	260
Marrakesh	Fès	125
	Ouarzazate	50
Agadir	Laayoune	196
	Tangier	233

There is an official baggage charge on CTM buses – about Dr5 for an average pack. On other lines you'll often be subject to demands for money from baggage handlers. This should rarely be more than Dr3. Theft is generally not a problem.

TRAIN

Morocco has one of the most modern rail systems in Africa and train is the preferred way to travel when you can. You have a choice of 1st and 2nd class in normal and *rapide* trains. The latter are in fact no faster, but have air-con and are more comfortable. The shuttle trains (TNR) between Rabat, Casablanca and Mohammed V international airport are in a class of their own. They are fast (Rabat to Casablanca in 55 minutes) and comfortable. Fares in 2nd class are roughly comparable with bus fares, and there is no need to go 1st class.

Couchettes are available on long-distance night trains between Marrakesh and Tangier. There are refreshment trolleys and sometimes buffet cars on the longer journeys too.

Timetables are prominently displayed in train stations, and a free book of timetables, *Indicateur Horaires,* is sometimes available at stations.

Supratours runs luxury buses in conjunction with trains to some destinations not on the rail network. Useful ones include Tetouan, Agadir and Essaouira. You can buy a bus-rail ticket to any place on the combined network.

CAR & MOTORCYCLE

You drive on the right in Morocco. An International Driving Permit is officially required, but most national licences are sufficient. Main roads are in decent condition, but many secondary roads are not so hot. Some mountain roads can be blocked by snow in winter, and desert roads are sometimes awash with sand drifts.

The traffic accident rate in Morocco is high; night driving can be particularly hazardous since cars, bicycles and donkeys many travel without lights.

There is only one motorway, between Casablanca and Kentira. The speed limit on the motorway is 120km/h. Elsewhere it is

100km/h (40 to 60km/h in built-up areas). When in towns note that you should give way to traffic entering a roundabout from the right when you're already on one. It is compulsory for drivers and passengers to wear seatbelts.

There are frequent police and customs roadblocks, some set up with tyre-shredding traps. Always stop; often you'll be waved through, but have your licence and passport handy.

Most towns have paid parking areas. They give some peace of mind and cost a few dirham for a few hours or Dr10 overnight.

Super (about Dr7.50 a litre) and diesel (Dr4 a litre) are the most widely available types of fuel. Fuel is much cheaper in the Spanish enclaves and the Western Sahara.

Rental

It is worth renting a car for at least a few days, especially to explore the southern oases and kasbah routes.

All the major companies are represented in the main cities, and there are plenty of local companies. The cheapest cars are the Renault 4 and Fiat Uno. Rental for three days with unlimited kilometres starts at around Dr1200. On top comes a 20% tax. You are well advised to take out Collision Damage Waiver insurance (at least Dr50 a day) and personal insurance (around Dr130 a day). You may be asked to leave a deposit of at least Dr3000 if not paying by credit card, and need to be at least 21 years old. It's cheaper if you hire for a week or more (always shop around and always haggle for discounts).

BICYCLE

There's no better way to see some of the country than by bicycle but you need to be fit to cycle in the mountains. Distances are great and you'll need to carry all supplies with you (including any spare parts you may need, food and plenty of drinking water). Many roads are narrow and dusty. You can transport bikes on trains (the minimum charge is Dr20) and buses, although they could take a beating on the latter.

HITCHING

Hitching in Morocco is possible, but demands a thick skin and considerable diplo-

matic expertise in the north because of aggressive hustlers. Women should never hitch alone.

LOCAL TRANSPORT

The big cities all have reasonable local bus networks. A ride costs about Dr2 and can be useful for getting from the ville nouvelle to the medina in places like Marrakesh and Fès.

Petits taxis (city taxis) are equally useful and cheap – provided the driver uses the meter and you have some idea of the fare. Fares around town shouldn't be more than Dr10. Multiple hire is the rule, and fares rise by about 50% after 8 pm.

Grands taxis work a little like buses. Usually ageing Mercedes, they take six passengers to a fixed destination for a standard fare and leave when full. They often leave more frequently than buses, are quicker and up to 50% more expensive.

Grands taxis are a good option where bus services are thin, or on scenic routes that buses might cover partially at night. It is possible to hire these taxis privately, but you must agree on a price with the driver and discuss any stops you might want to make beforehand. They won't stop if you're travelling with other people on a standard run.

The Mediterranean Coast & the Rif

TANGIER
☎ 09

All the peoples who have settled here at one time or another have left their mark on Tangier. The major port of entry for tourists, it was once home to hordes of the world's best hustlers. The Brigade Touristique (see Dangers & Annoyances earlier), however, has cracked down here too and these days Tangier is almost hassle free. Give the place a couple of days and you'll find it a likeable, lively city with a flavour all its own.

Tangier has been coveted for millennia as a strategic site commanding the Strait of Gibraltar. Settled as a trading port by the ancient Greeks and Phoenicians, Tangier has been occupied by the Romans, Vandals,

Byzantines, Arabs, Berbers, Fatimids, Almoravids, Almohads, Merenids, Portuguese, Spanish, British and French.

In the late 19th and early 20th centuries, Tangier (Tanja to the locals) became the object of intense rivalry between the European powers. A final solution was only reached in 1923, when Tangier and the surrounding countryside were declared an 'international zone' controlled by the resident diplomatic agents of France, Spain, Britain, Portugal, Sweden, Holland, Belgium, Italy and the USA. Even the Moroccan sultan was represented by an agent, appointed by the French resident-general.

After independence in 1956, Tangier was reunited with the rest of the country. In the meantime it had become a fashionable Mediterranean resort and haven for freebooters, artists, writers, refugees, exiles and bankers; it was also renowned for its high-profile gay and paedophile scene.

Orientation

Like many larger Moroccan towns, Tangier is divided between the convoluted streets of the old medina and the wide boulevards of the ville nouvelle. The modern shops, offices and services and most of the restaurants and better hotels are in the latter area. The medina has the markets, craft shops, cheaper hotels and smaller restaurants. The square known as the Petit Socco is in the heart of the medina. The larger Grand Socco lies between the medina and the ville nouvelle.

Information

Tourist Offices The tourist office (☎ 93 82 39) at 29 Blvd Pasteur has a very limited range of maps and brochures.

Money There are plenty of banks along Blvd Pasteur and Blvd Mohammed V. The BMCE head office on Blvd Pasteur has ATMs and a change booth which is open seven days a week from 10 am to 2 pm and 4 to 8 pm. The Crédit du Maroc, south of the Hôtel Tanjah-Flandria on Blvd Mohammed V, has taken over from Voyages Schwartz as the agent for American Express.

Post & Communications The main post office is on Blvd Mohammed V, a 20-minute walk from the Grand Socco. There is also a telephone and fax office here.

Internet services (minus the café latte) are available at Cyber Café Mam Net (☎ 94 13 53; fax 34 14 60; mamnet@mamnet.net.ma), 53 Rue du Prince du Moulay Abdallah, and Cyber Espace Pasteur (☎ 33 28 23; fax 33 24 49; pasteur@mamnet.net.ma), 31 Blvd Pasteur. An hour on the Web costs Dr25; to send or receive email costs Dr10.

Bookshops The Librairie des Colonnes (☎ 93 69 55), on Blvd Pasteur, has a good selection of Francophone literature, English novels and international newspapers.

Things to See

In the heart of the medina the **Petit Socco**, with its cafés and restaurants, is the focus of activity. In the days of the international zone this was the sin and sleaze centre and it retains something of its seedy air.

North from the Petit Socco, the Rue des Almohades (ex-Rue des Chrétiens) takes you to the **kasbah**. Built on the highest point of the city, you enter from Bab el-Assa at the end of Rue Ben Raissouli in the medina. The gate opens onto a large open courtyard which leads to the 17th-century **Dar el-Makhzen**, the former sultan's palace and now a museum. The museum is open daily, except Tuesday, from 9 am to 3.30 pm in summer and 9 am to noon and 3 to 6 pm in winter; entry is Dr10.

The **American Legation Museum** is a fascinating reminder that Morocco was the first country in the world to recognise US independence. It's in a fine old house in the medina. Opening hours are erratic, but entry is free. Knock to gain entrance.

Places to Stay

Camping Campers have a choice. The cheaper and more convenient is *Camping Miramonte*, about 3km west of the centre. Though run-down, it is close to the beach. To get there, take bus No 12 or 21 from near the Grand Socco.

Camping Tingis, about 6km east of the centre, has a tennis court and swimming pool. To get there, take bus No 15 from the Grand Socco.

CENTRAL TANGIER

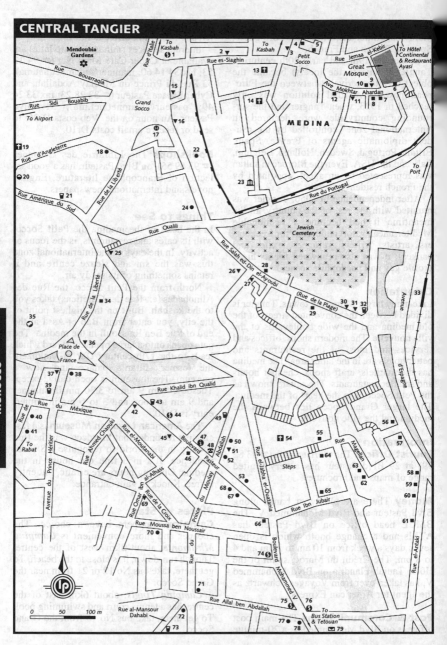

To Kasbah

Mendoubia Gardens

Rue d'Italie

Rue Bouarraqia

Rue Sidi Bouaibb

To Airport

Rue d'Angleterre

Rue Amérique du Sud

Rue de la Liberté

Rue Qualili

Rue Salah ed-Din el-Ayoubi

Grand Socco

Rue es-Siaghin

To Kasbah

Petit Socco

Rue Jemaa el-Kebir

Great Mosque

Ave Mokhtar Ahardan

To Hôtel Continental & Restaurant Ayasi

MEDINA

To Port

Rue du Portugal

Jewish Cemetery

(Rue de la Plage)

Avenue d'Espagne

Rue de la Liberté

Place de France

Rue de Fès

Rue du Méxique

Avenue du Prince Héritier

To Rabat

Rue Ahmed Chaouki

Rue el-Moutanabi

Rue al-Alhass

Rue Khalid ibn Qualid

Boulevard Pasteur

Rue du Moulay

Rue Omar ibn Khattab

Rue de la Croix

Rue Prince

Rue Moussa ben Noussair

Rue du

Rue Allal ben Abdallah

Rue al-Mansour Dahabi

Rue el-Jabha el-Outania

Steps

Rue Ibn Jubair

Boulevard Mohammed V

Rue Magellan

Rue el-Antaki

To Bus Station & Tetouan

0   50   100 m

CENTRAL TANGIER

PLACES TO STAY
4	Pension Mauritania
5	Pension Becerra
6	Pension Tan Tan
7	Hôtel Olid
8	Pension Karlton
10	Hôtel Mamora
12	Pension Palace
28	Pension Atou
29	Pension Miami
34	Hôtel El Minzah
46	Hôtel de Paris
55	Hôtel El Muniria & Tanger Inn
56	Hôtel Biarritz
57	Hôtel Cecil
58	Hôtel Marco Polo
59	Hôtel El Djenina
60	Hostel
61	Hôtel Bristol
62	Hôtel L'Amor
63	Hôtel Magellan
64	Hôtel Ibn Batouta
65	Hôtel Panoramic Massilia
66	Hôtel Tanjah-Flandria; Le Palace Disco

PLACES TO EAT
2	Restaurant Mamounia Palace
3	Café Tingis
9	Restaurant Mamora
11	Restaurant Ahlan
15	Pâtisserie Charaf
16	Restaurant Economique
25	Restaurant Populaire
26	Sandwich Genève
27	Sandwich Cervantes
30	Hassi Baida Restaurant
31	Restaurant Africa
36	Café de Paris
37	Café de France
42	Big Mac
45	Pâtisserie Le Petit Prince
51	Romero's Restaurant
69	Pizza Capri

OTHER
1	BMCE Bank (ATMs)
13	Church of the Immaculate Conception
14	Spanish Church
17	Hammam
18	Cinéma Rif
19	St Andrew's Church
20	Local Bus Terminal
21	Dean's Bar
22	Covered Market
23	American Legation Museum
24	Covered Market
32	Café Bar La Paix
33	Tanger Gare (Train Station)
35	French Consulate
38	Royal Air Maroc
39	Hole-in-the-Wall Bar
40	Pilo Wine Shop
41	Cinéma Le Paris
43	Paname Bar
44	BMCE (Late Bank & ATMs)
47	Tourist Office
48	Telephone & Fax Office; Cyber Espace Pasteur
49	Les Ambassadeurs Bar
50	Budget
52	Limadet Boat Ticket Office
53	Iberia Airlines
54	Church
67	Avis
68	Librairie des Colonnes
70	Paris Pressing (Laundry)
71	Cyber Café Mam Net
72	Cinéma Roxy
73	London's Pub
74	Crédit du Maroc (American Express)
75	Banque Populaire
76	Wafabank
77	Cady & Douka (Car Rental)
78	Hertz
79	Post Office

Hostel The *hostel* (☎ 94 61 27) is at 8 Rue el-Antaki, just past the Hôtel El Djenina. Beds cost Dr25. Another Dr5 will get you a hot shower.

Hotels There are numerous small hotels in the medina around the Petit Socco and along Ave Mokhtar Ahardan (formerly Rue des Postes), which connects the Petit Socco and the port area. If you arrive by ferry, walk out of the port area until you pass through the main gates, turn right into the medina and then left up the steps to Ave Mokhtar Ahardan.

If you prefer the more European-style hotels outside the medina then, once out of the port gates, carry on past the train station and take the first street on your right (Rue de la Plage, also known as Rue Salah ed-Din el-Ayoubi), or Rue Magellan 200m farther on, where there's also a good choice of hotels.

Medina Area There are plenty of cheap pensions here, most of them basic, although some offer hot water for a small extra charge. Singles cost Dr30 to Dr50 and doubles Dr60 to Dr100. They include the pensions *Mauritania*, *Becerra*, *Karlton* and *Tan Tan* (see map).

Two of the best places are the *Pension Palace* (☎ 93 61 28), at 2 Ave Mokhtar Ahardan, and the *Hôtel Olid* (☎ 93 13 10) at No 12. They charge Dr50/100 for singles/ doubles. The Palace's rooms are small but spotless, and many front onto a verdant courtyard. There are shared toilets and hot showers for Dr10. The Olid has seen better days, but the rooms come with own shower.

The two-star *Hôtel Mamora* (☎ 93 41 05), 19 Ave Mokhtar Ahardan, offers clean single/double rooms with shower for Dr197/230.

The pick of the crop is the *Hôtel Continental* perched above the port (☎ 93 10 24; fax 93 11 43). Used for some scenes in the

MOROCCO

film version of Paul Bowles' *The Sheltering Sky*, it is full of character. Singles/doubles cost Dr194/224, including breakfast.

There are several hammams around the Petit Socco and one at 80 Rue des Almohades.

Ville Nouvelle The unclassified hotels and pensions along Rue Salah ed-Din el-Ayoubi are no better than the cheapies in the medina and basic rooms with shared bath and toilet are similarly priced. The *Pension Miami* is popular; the *Pension Atou* is a little run-down but boasts terraces with great views of the city.

A better selection of hotels can be found up the steep and winding Rue Magellan, which starts between the hotels Biarritz and Cecil. The hotels *L'Amor* and *Magellan* (☎ 37 23 19) have reasonable rooms for Dr50/100. The Magellan has hot showers for Dr10.

The front rooms with balcony and shower in the *Hôtel Cecil* (☎ 93 10 87) are good value at Dr80/150. The *Hôtel Biarritz* (☎ 93 24 73) has comfortable, spacious old rooms overlooking the sea for Dr158/178.

Farther up Rue Magellan, you get to the *Hôtel El Muniria* (☎ 93 53 37) and the *Hôtel Ibn Batouta* (☎ 93 93 11; fax 93 93 68), opposite one another just before you reach a flight of steps. They're both one-star hotels offering immaculate rooms. William Burroughs wrote *The Naked Lunch* while staying at the Muniria. Singles/doubles with shower cost Dr100/120 at the Muniria; the Ibn Batouta has comfortable rooms with bathroom and telephone for Dr100 per person.

Close by, with front-room views over the harbour, is the one-star *Hôtel Panoramic Massilia* (☎ 37 07 03), on the corner of Rue Ibn Jubair and Rue Targha. Rooms with shower, toilet and hot water cost Dr80/130 including breakfast.

A good choice of mid-range hotels can be found in the streets off Blvd Pasteur, close to the tourist office. One of the better ones is the two-star *Hôtel de Paris* (☎ 93 18 77), at 42 Blvd Pasteur. Clean, comfortable rooms with shower cost Dr198/240.

There's also a decent trio of places where Rue el-Antaki heads up from Ave d'Espagne on the waterfront. The German-run *Hôtel*

Marco Polo (☎ 32 24 51) has impeccable rooms as well as a restaurant and lively bar. Singles/doubles cost Dr150/200. Next door, the recently refurbished two-star *Hôtel El Djenina* (☎ 94 22 44) has similarly priced rooms and an equally popular bar. A couple of doors up is the two-star *Hôtel Bristol* (☎ 94 29 14). Singles/doubles with shower cost Dr170/250. The hotel also has a restaurant and bar.

Places to Eat

Medina Area There are numerous small cafés and restaurants around the Petit Socco and the Grand Socco offering traditional fare for reasonable prices. At No 7 Rue Dar el-Baroud, just down the hill from the Hôtel Continental, *Restaurant Ayasi* (unsigned) serves excellent bessara in the morning; a filling bowl served with fresh French bread costs Dr5. Fish, chicken and tajines (Dr20) are served after 11 am.

On the east side of the Grand Socco, the tiny stall-like *Restaurant Economique* offers harira, bessara and brochettes all day long.

Restaurant Mamora, on Ave Mokhtar Ahardan, is open seven days a week and offers enormous, well-prepared tajines with fried potatoes and salad for Dr25. Harira is available in the evening. The nearby *Restaurant Ahlan* is also popular.

Just north of the Petit Socco at 7 Rue Commerce, *Restaurant Andalus* is a pleasant hole-in-the-wall place specialising in brochettes. Farther north at 15 Mostafa Doukkali, not far from the Agadir Bazaar, the *Restaurant Sose* (unsigned) serves a range of Moroccan staples and on Thursday specialises in couscous (Dr20). It's closed on Friday.

The *Restaurant Mamounia Palace* (☎ 93 50 99) on Rue es-Siaghin offers full 'Moroccan feasts' in more comfortable surroundings. Two four-course menus are available for Dr100. It's open daily for lunch and dinner, but is often busy with tour groups at lunchtime.

To watch the world go by over coffee or mint tea, try the pleasantly faded *Café Tingis* on the Petit Socco. The *Pâtisserie Charaf*, just off the Grand Socco, serves excellent coffee and a large selection of pastries.

Throughout the medina you'll find plenty of small grocery stores where you can stock up on basic supplies. Hassan's store on Rue

Dar el-Baroud sells everything from French bread to batteries.

Ville Nouvelle Two good, cheap places are *Sandwich Cervantes* and *Sandwich Genève*, close to each other on Rue Salah ed-Din el-Ayoubi. Both have seating and offer rolls filled with meat or fish and salad for Dr7.

Farther down towards Ave d'Espagne, the *Restaurant Africa* (No 83) and, next door, the *Hassi Baida* have set meals for around Dr45 or main courses from Dr25. The Africa is licensed and both places are open daily until 11 pm.

Established in 1925, the low-key and very pleasant *Royal Yacht Club of Tangier* (☎ 93 89 09) sits by the busy fishing quays down near the port (head for the palm tree). Open daily for lunch and dinner, the club offers a selection of fish dishes for around Dr35 as well as couscous and paella. Beer costs Dr12 and a half bottle of wine with tapas is just Dr40.

Restaurant Populaire, down the steps from Rue de la Liberté, is a local favourite serving excellent fresh food at reasonable prices. The house speciality is fish tajine.

If you're desperate for western-style fast food, *Big Mac* on the corner of Blvd Pasteur and Rue Ahmed Chaouki isn't bad. *Pizza Capri* (☎ 93 72 21), 2 Rue de la Croix, makes a decent pizza for around Dr30.

Somewhat more expensive meals can be had in the restaurants and cafés near Place de France (a coffee at the ageing *Café de Paris* is a must). The stretch of Rue du Prince du Moulay Abdallah around the corner from the tourist office is laden with eating possibilities. *Romero's* at No 12 is considered one of the best seafood restaurants in Tangier. Mains start at Dr50 and a half bottle of wine costs from Dr38.

For wonderful cakes, savoury pastries, fruit juice and ice cream, try the *Pâtisserie Le Petit Prince* at 34 Blvd Pasteur.

The *Pilo Wine Shop* at 9 Rue de Fès stocks a huge range of beer and wine and also sells groceries and toiletries.

Entertainment

Bars The nearest bar to the medina is the *Café Bar La Paix* across from the train station on Ave d'Espagne. South of the Grand Socco on Rue Amérique du Sud is the famous *Dean's Bar* – hardly a westerner of any repute did not prop up this bar at one time or another. Satisfyingly seedy and intimate, beer and tapas costs from Dr13.

Some particularly lively and colourful local bars include the *Hole in the Wall* on Ave du Prince Héritier, the *Paname* at 15 Blvd Pasteur, *Les Ambassadeurs* on Rue du Prince du Moulay Abdallah and the *Marco Polo* on Rue el-Antaki.

London's Pub, Rue al-Mansour Dahabi, has live music every night and a happy hour from 7 to 9 pm. Another remnant of Tangier's yesteryear is the tiny *Tanger Inn*, next to the Hôtel El Muniria on Rue Magellan. It's open from 9 pm until late. Knock on the heavy wooden door to get in.

The much-reduced European gay population still frequents some of the beach bars south of town. Popular places include the *Macumba*, *Miami Beach* and *Coco Beach*.

Nightclubs The three most popular nightclubs in town are: *Pasarela*, down by the beach on Ave des FAR; the *Olivia Valere* in the Ahlan Hôtel, about 5km along the road to Rabat; and *Le Palace* disco in the Hôtel Tanjah-Flandria. Entry to all the clubs is Dr100; drinks start at Dr40.

Getting There & Away

Bus Most CTM buses leave from an office near the port entrance. All others leave from the bus station on Place Jamia el-Arabia, a half-hour walk south of the Grand Socco.

Regular CTM departures include Casablanca (Dr110), Rabat (Dr83), Tetouan (Dr13.50) and Fès (Dr85).

Train There are two train stations: Tanger Gare and Tanger Port. The former is more convenient. Trains south from Tangier split at Sidi Kacem to Rabat (five hours), Casablanca (six hours) and Marrakesh (10½ hours), or to Meknès (five hours), Fès (six hours) and Oujda (12 hours). The 2nd-class fare on a normal train to Marrakesh is Dr143; to Fès it is Dr74.

Taxi Grands taxis leave from the bus station; there are frequent departures to Tetouan (Dr20) and Asilah (Dr20).

MOROCCO

Car The following are among the car-rental agencies in Tangier:

Avis
 (☎ 93 89 60) 54 Blvd Pasteur
Budget
 (☎ 93 79 94) 7 Rue du Prince du Moulay Abdallah
Europcar
 (☎ 94 19 38) 87 Blvd Mohammed V
Goldcar
 (☎ 94 01 64, 94 65 68) Hôtel Solazur, Ave des FAR
Hertz
 (☎/fax 32 22 10) 36 Blvd Mohammed V

Boat If you're heading to Spain or Gibraltar by boat, you can buy tickets from virtually any travel agency or at the port itself. Both the Limadet and Trasmediterranea offices are on Rue du Prince du Moulay Abdallah.

Getting Around
The local bus terminal is just up from the Grand Socco, on Rue d'Angleterre. Petits taxis are metered and cost under Dr10 around town.

TETOUAN
☎ 09
Tetouan's flavour is unmistakably Spanish-Moroccan, as a result of its settlement by Arab-Berber and Jewish refugees from Muslim Andalucía in the 16th century and subsequent occupation by the Spanish during the protectorate years. The whitewashed and tiled houses of the medina are dramatically set against the brooding Rif Mountains.

Information The tourist office (☎ 96 19 16; fax 96 19 14) is at 30 Blvd Mohammed V. Some of the staff speak English.

There are plenty of banks along Blvd Mohammed V. The most useful (with ATM) is the BMCE, below the Pension Iberia on Place Moulay el-Mehdi.

The post office is also on Place Moulay el-Mehdi, with the telephone office nearby.

Spain has a consulate at Ave al-Massira (☎ 97 39 41; fax 97 39 46) which is open weekdays from 9 am to noon.

Cybercafés Cyber Mania (☎ 70 49 87; fax 96 58 83), upstairs at 68 Blvd Mohammed V,

provides Internet access for Dr30 per hour and an email service for Dr10.

Things to See
Place Hassan II, the town's showpiece, links the old and new parts of the city. The busiest entrance to the **medina** is Bab er-Rouah. In the area towards the eastern gate, Bab el-Okla, are some fine houses built by the city's residents in the last century. Just inside Bab el-Okla, the excellent **Musée Marocain** is built in an old bastion in the town wall and has well-presented exhibits of everyday Moroccan and Andalucían life. It is open weekdays from 8.30 am to noon and 2.30 to 6 pm; admission is Dr10.

Just outside Bab el-Okla is the **Artisanat School**, where you can see children learning traditional crafts such as leather work, woodwork and the making of enamel (*zellij*) tiles. The building itself is worth a visit. The school is open weekdays from 8.30 am to noon and 2.30 to 5.30 pm; entry is Dr10.

Places to Stay
The nearest *camping ground* is on the beach at Martil, 8km away.

Tetouan has plenty of cheap, basic pensions, some decidedly better than others in terms of facilities, views and character. The *Pension Iberia* (☎ 96 36 79), on the 3rd floor above the BMCE bank on Place Moulay el-Mehdi, has great views over the square. Singles/doubles with shared bathroom cost Dr40/70. Hot showers are Dr5.

The popular *Hôtel Cosmopolita* (☎ 96 48 21), 5 Rue du Prince Sidi Mohammed, has large, spotlessly clean rooms for Dr50/80.

The front rooms with balcony at the *Hôtel Bilbao* (☎ 96 41 14), 7 Blvd Mohammed, are large but a little gloomy. Rooms with cold shower cost Dr51 for one or two people.

The *Hôtel Trebol* (☎ 96 20 18) is close to the long-distance bus station and has singles/doubles with cold shower for Dr50/70.

More expensive is the *Hôtel Oumaima* (☎ 96 34 73), 10 Rue Achra Mai. Singles/doubles with bathroom and telephone cost Dr170/200.

Places to Eat
The best place to get a cheap, nutritious meal is *El Yesfi Snack*, on Rue ben Tachfine. They

TETOUAN

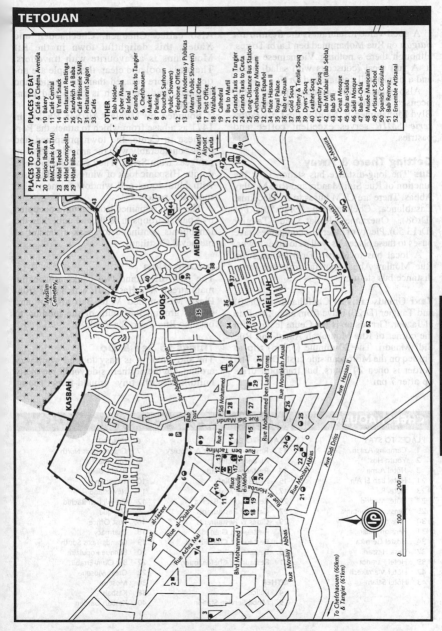

PLACES TO STAY
2 Hôtel Oumaima
20 Pension Iberia &
   BMCE Bank (ATM)
23 Hôtel Trebol
28 Hôtel Cosmopolita
29 Hôtel Bilbao

PLACES TO EAT
4 Café & Cinema Avenida
10 Bakery
11 Café Central
14 El Yesfi Snack
15 Restaurant Restinga
26 Sandwich Ali Baba
27 Café Pâtisserie SMIR
31 Restaurant Saigon
33 Cafés

OTHER
1 Bab Noider
3 Cyber Mania
5 Bar Ideal
6 Grands Taxis to Tangier
   & Chefchaouen
7 Market
8 Parking
9 Douches Sarhoun
   (Public Showers)
12 Telephone Office
13 Duchas Modernas y Publicas
   (Mens' Public Showers)
16 Tourist Office
17 Post Office
18 Wafabank
19 Cathedral
21 Bus to Martil
22 Grands Taxis to Tangier
24 Grands Taxis to Ceuta
25 Long-Distance Bus Station
30 Archaeology Museum
32 Cinema Español
34 Place Hassan II
35 Royal Palace
36 Bab er-Rouah
37 Gold Souq
38 Pottery & Textile Souq
39 Dyers' Souq
40 Leather Souq
41 Carpentry Souq
42 Bab M'Kabar (Bab Sebta)
43 Bab Sfii
44 Great Mosque
45 Bab as-Saida
46 Saïdi Mosque
47 Bab el-Okla
48 Musée Marocain
49 Artisanat School
50 Spanish Consulate
51 Bab Remouz
52 Ensemble Artisanal

MOROCCO

do great baguettes with various meats, potato salad, chips and salad for Dr15.

A good-value restaurant is the *Restaurant Saigon* on Rue Mohammed ben Larbi Torres, although there's nothing Vietnamese about it. A full meal (couscous with salad, bread and a drink) will cost around Dr30.

Also popular and reasonably priced is the licensed *Restaurant Restinga*, set back off Blvd Mohammed V. Nearby, the *Café Pâtisserie SMIR* serves excellent coffee and pastries.

Getting There & Away

Bus The long-distance bus station is at the junction of Rue Sidi Mandri and Rue Moulay Abbas. There are CTM buses to Al-Hoceima, Casablanca, Chefchaouen (Dr16.50), Fès (Dr68), Ouezzane, Rabat and Tangier (Dr13.50). Plenty of other bus companies have buses to these places, as well as to other towns.

A local bus to Martil (Dr3) leaves from Rue Moulay Abbas, not far from the long-distance bus station.

Taxi Grands taxis to Chefchaouen (Dr20) and Tangier (Dr20) leave from a rank on Rue al-Jazeer. Grands taxis for Ceuta leave from the corner of Rue Mourakah Anual and Rue Sidi Mandri. The 20-minute (33km) trip to Fnideq on the Moroccan side costs Dr14. The border is open 24 hours, but transport dries up after 7 pm.

CHEFCHAOUEN
☎ 09

Also called Chaouen, Chechaouen and Xauen, this delightful town in the Rif Mountains is a favourite with travellers. The air is cool and clear, the people are noticeably more relaxed than in Tangier and Tetouan, and the town is small and manageable.

Founded by Moulay Ali ben Rachid in 1471 as a base from which to attack the Portuguese in Ceuta, the town prospered and grew considerably with the arrival of Muslim refugees from Spain. They gave the town its unique Hispanic look of whitewashed houses with blue doors and window frames, tiled roofs and patios.

The town remained isolated until occupied by Spanish troops in 1920, and until then the inhabitants continued to speak a variant of medieval Castilian.

Information

The post office and two banks are on the main street, Ave Hassan II, which runs from Plaza Mohammed V to Bab al-'Ain and curves around the south of the medina to become Rue Tariq Ibn Ziad.

Things to See & Do

The old **medina** is easy to find your way around. On the northern side you'll see many buildings with tiny ground-floor rooms

CHEFCHAOUEN

PLACES TO STAY		PLACES TO EAT			
1	Camping Azilan	13	Restaurants Zouar & Moulay	6	Hospital
2	Youth Hostel		Ali ben Rachid	7	Grands Taxis North
3	Hôtel Asma	14	Restaurant Assada	8	Mosque
21	Hôtel Bab El Ain	15	Pâtisserie Diafa	9	BMCE Bank
23	Hôtel Rif	17	Pâtisserie Magou	10	Telephones
24	Hôtel Madrid	26	Restaurant El-Baraka	11	Newsstand
25	Pension Mauritania	27	Cafés & Restaurants	12	Sidi Ali ben Rachid
30	Pension Znika	29	Cafés & Restaurants		Mosque
31	Pension Valencia	32	Restaurant Granada	16	Post Office
34	Hostel Gernika	33	Restaurant Chez Fouad	18	Pharmacy
37	Casa Hassan	35	Bessara Stall	19	Grands Taxis South
39	Hôtel Parador	41	Restaurant Chefchaouen	20	Banque Populaire
42	Hôtel Marrakech			22	Bar Oum-Errabii
43	Hôtel Salam	**OTHER**		28	Great Mosque
		4	Police	36	Mosque
		5	Mobil Service Station	38	Kasbah
				40	Kasbah Garden

CHEFCHAOUEN

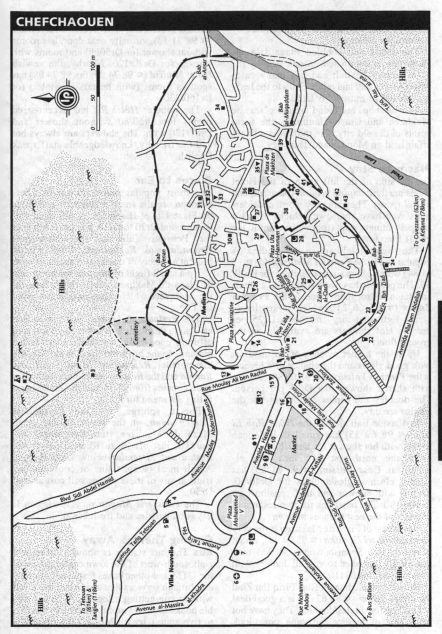

crowded with weaving looms – a legacy of the days when silkworms were introduced by Andalucían refugees.

The shady and cobbled **Plaza Uta el-Hammam** is dominated on one side by the 17th century **kasbah** and has many cafés where you can sit and relax. Entry to the leafy kasbah and its museum is Dr10.

Tourist shops are found around plazas de Makhzen and Uta el-Hammam, the focal points of the old city. The **market** is a lively affair held on Monday and Thursday.

Places to Stay

On the side of the hill north of the Hôtel Asma are the *camping ground* (pleasant) and *hostel* (poor). They are only worth considering if you have your own vehicle, as it's a steep 30-minute walk (follow the signs to the hotel) from town.

The cheap hotels are in the medina. A popular one is the *Pension Mauritania* (☎ 98 61 84) which offers singles/doubles for Dr20/30. The pension has two terraces and a pleasant salon. Also good value is the *Pension Znika* (☎ 98 66 24), which is spotlessly clean, light and airy and costs Dr25 per person. Hot showers are available on the ground floor.

Up in the higher reaches of the medina, with good views and the chance of a breeze, is the *Pension Valencia* (☎ 98 60 88). Rooms with shared shower cost Dr25 per person. The doubles and triples are decent but the singles are tiny.

Just inside Bab al-'Ain the *Hôtel Bab El Ain* (☎ 98 69 35) has smallish but clean rooms with hot shower for Dr51/82.

To the north-east of Plaza Uta el-Hammam, *Casa Hassan* (☎ 98 61 53) has simple, clean singles/doubles for Dr40/60. Rooms with shower and half-pension cost Dr106/190. The hotel has its own restaurant and one of the best terraces in town.

North-east of Plaza de Makhzen is the very pleasant *Hostel Gernika* (☎ 98 74 34), which is run by two Spanish women. It has nine beautifully furnished rooms, all doubles with own shower, for Dr110.

Outside the medina on Rue Tariq Ibn Ziad the *Hôtel Salam* (☎ 98 62 39) is a good deal at Dr40/60 for singles/doubles. They have hot water most of the time and some rooms look

over the valley to the south. The hotel has a terrace restaurant. The *Hôtel Marrakech* (☎ 98 71 13), virtually next door, has rooms without shower for Dr50/80 and rooms with shower for Dr70/120. Nearby, the newish *Hôtel Madrid* (☎ 98 74 96; fax 98 74 98) has spotless rooms (with heaters in winter) for Dr160/230.

The popular *Hôtel Rif* has decent-sized rooms for Dr50/80 without shower and Dr87/120 with. The showers are always hot and the friendly, knowledgeable staff speak English.

Places to Eat

The most popular places to eat in Chefchaouen are the small restaurants and cafés on Plaza Uta el-Hammam. A full meal will cost around Dr20 to Dr30. Farther north near the Pension Valencia, the *Restaurant Granada* and *Restaurant Chez Fouad* present a variety of dishes at reasonable cost.

Up a small flight of steps on the north side of Plaza de Makhzen you'll find a hole-in-the-wall place which offers excellent bessara for Dr5.

The *Restaurant Assada*, just inside Bab al-'Ain to the north, is another tiny local spot offering good-value standards. Outside the medina, up the hill from the Bab al-'Ain, are the popular *Restaurant Moulay Ali ben Rachid* and the *Restaurant Zouar*. Both offer main courses from Dr16 and the Zouar has a filling set menu for Dr25.

For a splurge, try the *Restaurant Chefchaouen*, on the street leading up to Plaza de Makhzen; the *Restaurant El-Baraka*, just off Plaza Kharrazine; or the *Restaurant Tissemlal* below Casa Hassan. A full meal (soup, tajine or couscous and fruit) at any of these places will cost around Dr50.

The *Pâtisserie Magou* on Ave Hassan II has good pastries and fresh bread.

Getting There & Away

Bus The bus station is about a 20-minute walk south-west of the town centre. Many of the CTM and other buses (especially to Fès) are through services that arrive and leave full without you getting a look-in. Where possible book ahead. If you can't get a Fès bus (4½ to five hours), try for Meknès (four hours) –

there are loads of buses and grands taxis between there and Fès.

There are also buses to Tetouan (two hours), Fnideq (for Ceuta), Tangier, Ouezzane (not a bad alternative launch pad for Fès), Rabat, Casablanca and Nador.

Taxi Grands taxis going north to Tetouan (Dr20) and Tangier (Dr80) leave from a lot just off Plaza Mohammed V. Taxis heading south to Ouezzane (Dr25) and beyond leave from Rue Tariq Moulay Driss.

Spanish Morocco

Ceuta and Melilla are Spanish enclaves on the northern Moroccan coast. They came under Spanish control in the 16th and 15th centuries respectively and, although administered as city provinces of Spain, are waiting to be granted full autonomous status on an equal footing with the other provinces.

About 70% of the inhabitants are Spanish. The main function of the cities is to supply Spanish troops stationed there, and as duty-free centres – goods entering the enclaves find their way all over northwestern Africa. Morocco occasionally campaigns half-heartedly for their return to Morocco, but Rabat is not keen to rock the boat as Spain is an increasingly important trading partner.

Travellers come here mainly for the ferry services to and from Spain and the cheap, tax-free petrol. Don't forget that Ceuta and Melilla keep Spanish, not Moroccan, time.

CEUTA
☎ 0956

Known as Sebta in Arabic, Ceuta (pronounced Thayuta) doesn't offer a great deal for visitors and it's not very cheap. If you're heading for Morocco, you may prefer to catch an early ferry from Algeciras and continue straight through to Tetouan or Chefchaouen.

Information
There's a tourist office in the centre of town, not far from the town hall. It is open on weekdays from 8 am to 3 pm.

Plenty of banks (many with ATMs) line the main street, Paseo de Revellín, and its continuation, Calle Camoens. Outside business hours you can change money at the Hôtel La Muralla, on Plaza de Africa. There's no need to buy dirham here, as you can do so at the border as long as you have cash.

The main post office (*correos y telégrafos*) is on Plaza de España, just off Calle Camoens.

Things to See
The **Museo de la Legión** on Paseo de Colón holds a staggering array of military paraphernalia. It is open every day except Wednesday from 10 am to 2 pm (until 1 pm on Sunday; and on Saturday from 4 to 6 pm only). Entry is free.

Opened in May 1995, the Maritime Park (Parque Marítimo del Mediterráneo) is a huge complex on the seafront, complete with manufactured beach, pools, waterfalls, restaurants and bars. Entry costs 500 ptas per adult and 300 ptas per child.

Places to Stay & Eat
There is no shortage of *fondas* (inns) and *casas de huéspedes* (boarding houses), easily identifiable by the large blue-and-white F or CH on the entrance. Cheapest of these is the small *Pensión Charito* (☎ 51 39 82), on the 1st floor at 5 Calle Arrabal, about 15 minutes walk along the waterfront from the ferry terminal. Basic singles/doubles cost 800/1400 ptas. There are no hot showers.

If you can afford a little more, the two best deals in town are the *Casa de Huéspedes Tiuna* (☎ 51 77 56), at 3 Plaza Teniente Ruiz, and the *Pensión La Bohemia* (☎ 51 06 15), 16 Paseo de Revellín. The Casa charges 3000/4000 ptas for singles/doubles; the Bohemia charges 2000/3000 ptas. Both have piping hot showers in shared bathrooms.

There are plenty of cafés that serve snacks, such as bocadillos and pulgas, which are basically rolls with one or two fillings. Things get cheaper as you head east from the town centre along Calle Real.

The restaurant *Club Nautico* (☎ 51 44 40), on Calle Edrisis, has good fish meals for about 1400 ptas, and a couple of vegetarian options.

Getting There & Away

Morocco There are several buses (including the No 7) which run to the border every 15 minutes or so from Plaza de la Constitución for 75 ptas (20 minutes). If you arrive by ferry and want to head straight for the border, there is a stop for the No 7 just up from the port and off to the right opposite the ramparts.

Once through the border, there are plenty of grands taxis to Tetouan (Dr20 a seat). The trip from Ceuta to Tetouan should take no more than two hours.

Mainland Spain The ferry terminal is west of the town centre, and there are frequent departures to Algeciras. You can take the bus marked Puerto-Centro from Plaza de la Constitución.

MELILLA
☎ 0952

Smaller but much more run-down than Ceuta, Melilla (pronounced Melee-ya) retains a lingering fascination because of its medieval fortress. Until the end of the 19th century, almost all of Melilla was contained within these massive walls. This old part of town has a distinctly Castilian flavour with narrow, twisting streets, squares, gates and drawbridges.

The new part of town, west of the fortress, was begun at the end of the 19th century and still vaguely reflects the dictates of the Spanish modernist architecture of the time.

Information

The well-stocked tourist office (☎ 68 40 13) is at the junction of Calle de Querol and Avenida General Aizpuru (signposted from the port). Most of the banks are along the main street, Avenida de Juan Carlos I Rey, and you can buy and sell dirham. Money-changers hang around the cafés on the Plaza de España but they won't offer you better deals than the banks.

Things to See

The fortress of Melilla la Vieja, also known as the Medina Sidonia, offers good views over the town and out to sea. Inside the walls,

don't miss the Iglesia de la Concepción with its gilded reredos and shrine to Nuestra Señora la Virgen de la Victoria (the patron of the city), and the Museo Municipal.

The main entrance to the fortress is through the massive Puerta de la Marina, or you can enter from the west side via the Plaza de Armas and the drawbridges of Puerta de Santiago.

Places to Stay & Eat

Cheapest is the *Pension del Puerto*, a largely Moroccan establishment off Avenida General Macías. A bed should cost less than 1500 ptas.

Easily the best place for those on a budget is the *Hostal Residencia Rioja* (☎ 68 27 09), at 6 Calle Ejército Español. It has decent singles/doubles from 2400/3400 ptas with communal hot showers.

The best area to search for good cheap bocadillos and the like is along Calle Castelar (not far from the Mercado Municipal). A popular place with the locals is the *Antony Pizza Factory*, just off Avenida de Juan Carlos I Rey, which has good pizza from 650 ptas.

For a splurge, try the *Barbacoa de Muralla* at Calle Fiorentina in the southernmost corner of the old town. A three-course set menu costs 4000 ptas.

Getting There & Away

Morocco Local buses go from Plaza de España to the border from about 7.30 am until 10 pm. From where the buses stop, it's about 150m to Spanish customs and another 200m to Moroccan customs. On the other side of Moroccan customs there are frequent buses and grands taxis to Nador until about 8 pm.

Mainland Spain Trasmediterranea has an office on Plaza de España for ferries to the Spanish mainland. Otherwise, buy tickets at the ferry terminal itself. You can book Spanish rail tickets at the RENFE office. It's worth checking out flights to Málaga too.

The Middle Atlas

MEKNÈS
☎ 05

Although a town of considerable size even in the days of the 13th century Merenids, Meknès didn't reach its peak until Moulay Ismail, the second Alawite sultan, made it his capital in 1672. Over the next 55 years an enormous palace complex was built, transforming Meknès out of all recognition.

Under Sultan Sidi Mohammed III, however, Morocco's capital was moved back to Marrakesh. The 1755 earthquake that severely damaged many Moroccan cities also took its toll on Meknès. No restoration was done and the city was allowed to decay until recently, when its tourism potential was recognised and major restoration begun. Oued Boufekrane divides the new town from the old.

Information
The tourist office (☎ 52 44 26) is next to the main post office facing Place de France.

The banks are concentrated in the new city, mainly on Ave Hassan II, Ave Mohammed V and Blvd Allal ben Abdallah. The BMCE operates a bureau de change on Ave des FAR, opposite the Hôtel Volubilis, which is open daily from 10 am to 2 pm and 4 to 8 pm.

Things to See
The focus of the old city is the massive **Bab el-Mansour**, the main entrance to Moulay Ismail's 17th-century **Imperial City**. It is highly decorated and well preserved. The gate faces Place el-Hedim, where storytellers and musicians gather in the evening. On the north side of the square is the **Dar Jamaï Museum**, housed in a beautiful late 19th-century palace. The exhibits consist of traditional ceramics, jewellery, rugs, textiles and woodwork. It is open daily, except Tuesday, from 9 am to noon and 3 to 6.30 pm. Entry costs Dr10.

The **medina** stretches north behind the Dar Jamaï Museum. The easiest access is through the arch immediately to the left of the museum. The covered main street leads to the **grand mosque** and the mid-14th century **Medersa Bou Inania**. Similar in design to the Fès medersas, it is open daily from 9 am to

noon and 3 to 6 pm. Entry costs Dr10 and there's a good view from the roof.

A visit to the Imperial City starts from the Bab el-Mansour. The gate gives onto the *mechouar*, a parade ground where Moulay Ismail reviewed his famed black regiments. Follow the road round to the small, white **Koubbat as-Sufara'**, where foreign ambassadors were once received. Beside it is the entrance to a huge underground granary. Entry to the vaults and the reception hall costs Dr10.

Opposite and a little to the left, through another recently restored gate, you come to the **Mausoleum of Moulay Ismail**, one of the few functioning Islamic monuments in the country open to non-Muslims. The mausoleum is open daily from 9 am to noon and 3 to 6 pm (3 to 6 pm only on Friday) and entry costs Dr5.

From the tomb, the road leads into a long, walled corridor flanking the **Dar el-Makhzen**, once Moulay Ismail's palace and now one of King Hassan's residences (closed to visitors). Follow the road around and, just beyond the camp site, you arrive at the spectacular **Heri es-Souani**, built as a granary, warehouse and water point. The storerooms are impressive in size, and wells for drawing water can still be seen. The stables, which once housed 12,000 horses, stand in partial ruin. The Heri es-Souani is open daily from 9 am to noon and 3 to 6 pm. Entry costs Dr10.

Behind this building is the **Agdal Basin**, once a reservoir for the sultan's gardens and a pleasure lake. Above the granaries is a pleasant rooftop café set in a garden of wild rosemary and geraniums.

Places to Stay
Camping There is a good, shady camp site, *Camping Agdal* (☎ 55 18 28), near the Agdal Basin. It's a long walk to the site, and a taxi from the train, CTM or main bus stations will cost about Dr12. Each person pays Dr17 (children Dr12), plus Dr10 to pitch a tent, Dr17 for a car, Dr7 for a hot shower and Dr10 for electricity.

Hostel The *hostel* (☎ 52 46 98) is close to the Hôtel Transatlantique in the ville nouvelle, about 1km from the centre. It's open from 8 to 10 am, noon to 3 pm and 6 to

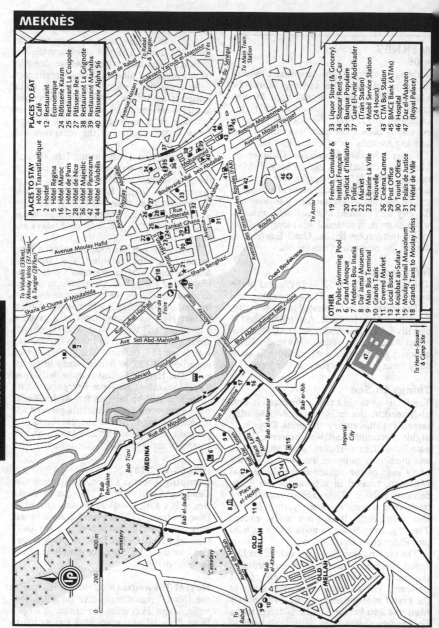

MEKNÈS

PLACES TO STAY

1 Hôtel Transatlantique
2 Hostel
5 Hôtel Regina
16 Hôtel Maroc
17 Hôtel de Paris
28 Hôtel de Nice
36 Hôtel Majestic
42 Hôtel Panorama
44 Hôtel Volubilis

PLACES TO EAT

4 Café
12 Restaurant Économique
24 Rôtisserie Karam
25 Restaurant La Coupole
27 Pâtisserie Rex
38 Restaurant La Grignote
39 Restaurant Marhaba
40 Pâtisserie Alpha 56

OTHER

3 Public Swimming Pool
6 Grand Mosque
7 Medersa Bou Inania
8 Dar Jamaï Museum
9 Main Bus Terminal
10 Grands Taxis
11 Covered Market
14 Local Buses
15 Koubbat as-Sufara'
18 Moulay Ismail Mausoleum
    Grands Taxis to Moulay Idriss

19 French Consulate &
    Institut Français
20 Syndicat d'Initiative
21 Police
22 Market
23 Librairie La Ville
    Nouvelle
26 Cinéma Camera
29 Post Office
30 Tourist Office
31 Palais de Justice
32 Hôtel de Ville

33 Liquor Store (& Grocery)
34 Stopcar Rent-a-Car
35 Banque Populaire
37 Gare El-Amir Abdelkader
    (Train Station)
41 Mobil Service Station
    (24 Hours)
43 CTM Bus Station
45 BMCE Bank (ATMs)
46 Hospital
47 Dar el-Makhzen
    (Royal Palace)

10 pm. A dorm bed costs Dr25. There are family rooms for Dr30 per person.

Hotels Most of the cheapest hotels are in the old city along Rue Dar Smen and Rue Rouamzine. The *Hôtel Maroc* (☎ 53 00 75), on Rue Rouamzine, has quiet rooms gathered around a courtyard. Rooms with washbasin cost Dr50 per person. Farther along, the shabbier *Hôtel de Paris* has singles/doubles for Dr30/60. The *Hôtel Regina* (☎ 53 02 80), 19 Rue Dar Smen, has reasonably clean rooms for Dr60/90. Hot showers are available for Dr5.

In the ville nouvelle, the *Hôtel Panorama* (☎ 52 27 37), a little way from the centre off Ave des FAR, has spacious rooms with bathroom for Dr72/104. A two-minute walk from the train station, the popular *Hôtel Majestic* (☎ 52 20 35; fax 52 74 27), 14 Ave Mohammed V, has spotlessly clean rooms with washbasin and bidet for Dr102/137. Some rooms open onto a pleasant courtyard. The shared showers have piping hot water.

The two-star *Hôtel de Nice* (☎ 52 03 18), 10 Zankat Accra, is a very good deal with comfortable singles/doubles with bathroom for Dr135/166.

Places to Eat

There are some simple restaurants with cheap standard fare in the old town along Rue Dar Smen, between the Hôtel Regina and Place el-Hedim. The *Restaurant Économique*, at No 123, lives up to its name, serving large portions of traditional dishes at very reasonable prices.

There is a mass of cheap eats stalls spilling out in the lanes just outside the Bab el-Jadid. On the west side of Place el-Hedim is a covered market where you can buy nuts, dates, figs and olives.

In the ville nouvelle, there are a few cheap eateries along Ave Mohammed V, including a couple of roast chicken places. You can eat well at any of these for Dr30 to Dr45. *La Coupole* and *Rôtisserie Karam*, on and near Ave Hassan II respectively, offer decent, moderately priced Moroccan cuisine.

The spacious *Restaurant Marhaba*, not far from the Hôtel Majestic on Ave Mohammed V, is a popular place offering tajines (Dr30) and brochettes (Dr18) along with the usual salad and chips. In the evening they serve harira with spicy potato cakes.

More upmarket is the very pleasant *La Grignote*, just off Ave Mohammed V, which offers pizzas (very good though a tad on the small side) and Moroccan dishes from around Dr35. The restaurant is licensed. Watch out for the 20% taxes.

The *Pâtisserie Alpha 56*, across from the Marhaba, is a decent spot for coffee and cake. The *Pâtisserie Rex* has wonderful strawberry tarts and good ice cream.

Getting There & Away

Bus The CTM bus terminal is on Ave Mohammed V near the junction with Ave des FAR. There are daily departures to Fès, Casablanca, Rabat, Tangier, Taza, Ifrane, Azrou and Er-Rachidia.

The main bus terminal is outside Bab el-Khemis on the north side of the new mellah along Ave du Mellah. There are regular departures to most major destinations.

Train All trains stop at the central Gare El-Amir Abdelkader, which is more convenient than the main station on Ave du Sénégal.

Taxi Most grands taxis, including those going to Fès (Dr15) and Rabat (Dr35), leave from a lot outside the main bus station. Grands taxis to Moulay Idriss (for Volubilis, Dr7) leave from a lot just to the north-east of Place de la Foire.

AROUND MEKNÈS

About 33km from Meknès are the best preserved Roman ruins in Morocco. **Volubilis** (Oualili in Arabic) dates largely from the 2nd and 3rd centuries AD, although the site was originally settled by Carthaginian traders in the 3rd century BC. It is noted for its mosaic floors, many of which have been left *in situ*.

The site is open daily from sunrise to sunset and entry is Dr20. To get there, take a grand taxi (Dr7 per person) from Place de la Foire in Meknès and hop out at the turn-off to Moulay Idriss. From there it's a pleasant half-hour walk. Going back, you can hitch or walk to Moulay Idriss and wait for a bus or taxi. If you have a group, you could negotiate to hire a grand taxi for a half-day trip (don't pay more than Dr300).

FÈS
☎ 05

Fès is the oldest of the imperial cities of Morocco, founded shortly after the Arabs swept across North Africa following the death of the Prophet Mohammed. It has been the capital of Morocco on several occasions and for long periods. The city's magnificent buildings reflect the brilliance of Arab-Berber imagination and artistry. Fassis, the people of Fès, justifiably look on their city as the cultural and spiritual capital of Morocco.

The medina of Fès el-Bali (Old Fès) is one of the largest living medieval cities in the world and the most interesting in Morocco. Its narrow, winding alleys and covered bazaars are crammed with craft workshops, restaurants, mosques, medersas, food markets and extensive dye pits and tanneries. The exotic smells, the hammering of the metalworkers, the call of the muezzin, the jostling crowds and the countless 'delivery' donkeys create an unforgettable experience.

Fès was founded in 789 AD by Idriss I on the right bank of the Oued Fès in what is now the Andalus Quarter. His son, Idriss II, extended the city onto the left bank in 809; these two parts of the city constitute Fès el-Bali.

The earliest settlers were mainly refugees from Córdoba (Spain) and Kairouan (Tunisia). Both groups were from well-established Islamic centres of brilliance and their skills laid the groundwork for one of the most important centres of Islamic intellectual and architectural development.

The city reached its height under the Merenids, who took it from the Almohads in 1250 and erected a new quarter, Fès el-Jdid. Fès remained the capital throughout their rule. With the rise of the Saadians in the 16th century, Marrakesh once again gained the ascendancy and Fès slipped into relative obscurity, only to be revived under the Alawite ruler Moulay Abdallah in the 19th century. In 1916, the French began building the ville nouvelle on the plateau to the southwest of the two ancient cities.

Orientation

Fès consists of three distinct parts. The original walled city of Fès el-Bali lies to the east; to the south-west is the French-established ville nouvelle where most of the restaurants and hotels are located; between the two is the Merenid walled city of Fès el-Jdid.

Information

Tourist Offices The ONMT office (☎ 62 34 60) is on Place de la Résistance in the new city. It's open weekdays from 8.30 am to noon and 2.30 to 6 pm.

The syndicat d'initiative, on Place Mohammed V, keeps the same hours as the tourist office and is also open Saturday morning. The syndicat can provide official guides to the medina for the fixed price of Dr120/150 for a half/full day.

Money Most of the banks are in the new city on Blvd Mohammed V and Ave de France. The banks in the medina don't have ATMs and will not change travellers cheques.

Post & Communications The main post and phone offices are on the corner of Ave Hassan II and Blvd Mohammed V. Internet access is available at Cyber C@fé El Boustan (☎ 93 09 09) in the Sheraton Fès Hôtel on Ave des FAR. It's open every day from 10 am to 8 pm, and access costs Dr50 per hour.

Bookshops The English Bookshop at 68 Ave Hassan II, close to Place de la Résistance, has a wide range of books. It's closed at lunchtime and on weekends. There are a number of places for foreign newspapers and magazines along Blvd Mohammed V.

Guides To get the most out of Fès it's worth hiring an official guide (see Tourist Offices above). Not only will you benefit from their extensive local knowledge, but you'll be free to enjoy the city without being hassled by hordes of unofficial guides.

For those intent on saving a few dirham, you'll find plenty of would-be guides hanging around Bab Bou Jeloud in Fès el-Bali, and in the new city. Initially, it's best to feign a lack of interest until you come across someone who seems reliable. If you're not interested in a shopping tour of Fès, make this very clear before setting out.

For more information on hustlers and guides, see Dangers & Annoyances at the beginning of this chapter.

Things to See

Fès el-Bali The old walled **medina** is the area of most interest to visitors. It's an incredible maze of twisting alleys, arches, mosques, medersas, shrines, fountains, workshops and markets. The most convenient entry point is **Bab Bou Jeloud**, the main western gate. Just in from the bab is the **Medersa Bou Inania**, built by the Merenid sultan Bou Inan between 1350 and 1357. The tilework, plasterwork and woodwork are magnificent and it is one of the few functioning religious buildings non-Muslims may enter. The medersa is open from 8 am to 5 pm, except at prayer times and Friday mornings. Entry costs Dr10.

In the heart of the medina is the **Kairaouine Mosque**, one of the largest mosques in Morocco and said to be capable of holding 20,000 people. It was founded between 859 and 862 by Fatma bint Mohammed ben Feheri for her fellow refugees from Tunisia, and its university has one of the finest libraries in the Muslim world. Non-Muslims may not enter, but you can get good views from the main doorways.

Nearby, the **Medersa el-Attarine** was built by Abu Said in 1325 and has some particularly fine examples of Merenid work. It's open from 9 am to noon and 2 to 6 pm, but closed Friday morning and often Thursday afternoon, too. Entry is Dr10.

Near Bab Bou Jeloud, on the boundary between Fès el-Bali and Fès el-Jdid, is the **Dar Batha** (Musée du Batha) on Place de l'Istiqlal. Built as a palace about 100 years ago by moulays al-Hassan and Abd al-Aziz, it houses historical and artistic artefacts from ruined or decaying medersas, Fassi embroidery, tribal carpets, and ceramics. It's open daily, except Tuesday, from 8.30 am to noon and 2.30 to 6.30 pm. Entry costs Dr10.

Fès el-Jdid The other walled city has the old Jewish quarter and a couple of mosques but is far less interesting than Fès el-Bali.

The grounds of the **Dar el-Makhzen** (Royal Palace) on Place des Alaouites comprise 80 hectares of palaces, pavilions, medersas, mosques and pleasure gardens but are not open to the public.

At the northern end of the main street, Sharia Moulay Suleiman (aka Grande Rue de Fès el-Jdid), is the enormous Merenid gate of **Bab Dekkaken**, formerly the main entrance to the royal palace. Between this gate and Bab Bou Jeloud are the **Bou Jeloud Gardens**. Through them flows the Oued Fès, the city's main source of water.

Outskirts For a spectacular view over Fès, walk to the end of Sharia Moulay Suleiman and through the Bab Dekkaken; continue straight on through the mechouar and Bab Segma, across the main road and around behind the Kasbah des Cherarda and cemetery to the Borj Nord fortress. The whole of Fès lies at your feet. The **Borj Nord** was built in the late 16th century by the Saadian sultan Ahmed al-Mansour. It houses the **Arms Museum**. Opening hours are as for the Dar Batha and entry is Dr10.

Places to Stay

Camping The nearest site is *Camping International* (☎ 73 14 30; fax 73 15 54), about 3km south of town on the Sefrou road. Set in large gardens with pool, tennis courts, restaurants and bars, it costs Dr50/20 per adult/child, Dr30 for a tent, and Dr40/30/15 for a caravan/car/motorbike. Bus No 38 from Place Atlas in Fès comes past the site.

Camping Diamant Vert, 6km out of town off the Ifrane road, sits in a valley through which a clean stream passes. There's plenty of shade and facilities include a pool. It costs Dr20/10 per adult/child plus Dr30 for a car and Dr25 to pitch a tent. Bus No 17 to 'Ain Chkef (from Place de Florence) will get you close to the site.

Hostel The cheapest place in the ville nouvelle is the *youth hostel* (☎ 62 40 85), 18 Rue Mohammed el-Hansali. It costs Dr30 per person in dorms and the showers are cold. Simple three-course meals are available for Dr40. It's open from 8 to 9 am, noon to 3 pm and 6 to 10 pm.

Hotels – Fès el-Bali The most colourful places to stay here are the cheapies around Bab Bou Jeloud. They're very basic and the shower situation is grim, but there are hammams all over the medina. The *Hôtel Cascade* (☎ 63 84 42), just inside the gate, has clean singles/doubles for Dr40/60, hot

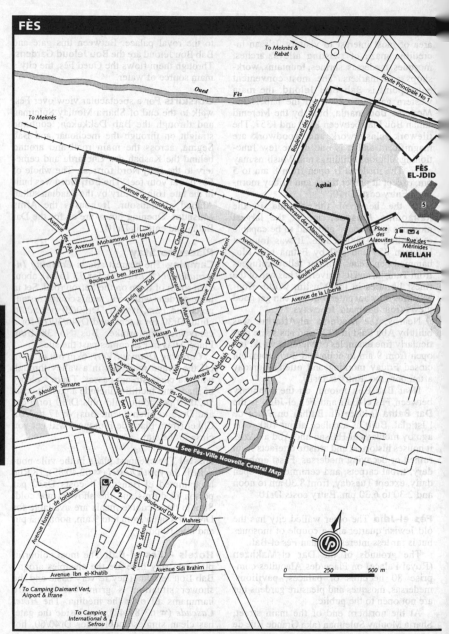

FÈS

To Meknès & Rabat

Route Principale No 1

Oued

Fès

To Meknès

Boulevard des Saadiens

Agdal

Boulevard des Alaouites

FÈS
EL-JDID

5

Avenue des Almohades

Avenue des FAR

Avenue Mohammed el-Hayani

Rue Chenguit

Avenue Mohammed el-Korri

Avenue des Sports

Boulevard Moulay Youssef

Place
des
Alaouites

3 4

Rue des
Mérinides

MELLAH

Boulevard ben Jerrah

Boulevard Tariq Ibn Ziad

Boulevard Lalla Maryam

Avenue Hassan II

Avenue de la Liberté

Avenue Mohammed

Mohammed

Boulevard Abdallah Chefchaouni

Avenue Moulay Slimane

Avenue Youssef ben Tachfine

Boulevard es-Slaoui

See Fès-Ville Nouvelle Central Map

Avenue Hussein de Jordanie

Boulevard Dhar Mahres

C 1
2

Avenue de Sefrou

Avenue Ibn el-Khatib

Avenue Sidi Brahim

To Camping Daimant Vert,
Airport & Ifrane

To Camping
International &
Sefrou

0   250   500 m

MOROCCO

FÈS

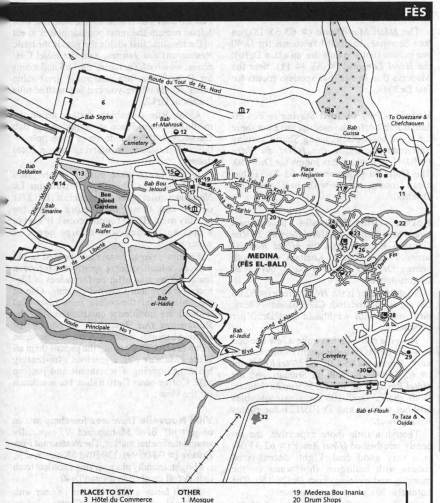

PLACES TO STAY
3 Hôtel du Commerce
10 Hôtel Palais Jamaï
14 Hôtel du Parc
17 Hôtel Cascades &
    Hôtel Mauritania
18 Hôtel Lamrani

PLACES TO EAT
11 Restaurant Dar Jamaï
13 Café Restaurant La Noria
21 Cheap Restaurants
26 Palais de Fès Restaurant

OTHER
1 Mosque
2 Grands Taxis to Ifrane & Azrou
4 Post Office
5 Dar el-Makhzen
   (Royal Palace)
6 Kasbah des Cherarda
7 Borj Nord (Arms Museum)
8 Merenid Tombs
9 Petits Taxis to Ville Nouvelle
12 New Non-CTM Bus Station
15 Place Baghdadi Bus Station
16 Dar Batha (Musée du Batha)

19 Medersa Bou Inania
20 Drum Shops
22 Tanneries
23 Medersa el-Attarine;
   Maison Bebère (Carpet Shop)
24 Zawiyya Moulay Idriss II
25 Kairaouine Mosque & University
27 Bus No 19 to Ville Nouvelle
28 Andalus Mosque
29 Potters' Souq
30 Non-CTM Buses to Taza
31 Grands Taxis to Taza
32 Borj Sud

Map labels:
Route du Tour de Fès Nord
Bab Segma
Cemetery
6
7
8
Bab el-Mahrouk
12
Bab Guissa
To Ouezzane & Chefchaouen
9
Bab Dekkaken
13
14
15
Bab Bou Jeloud
18 19
17
16
Place an-Nejjarine
21
10
11
Bou Jeloud Gardens
At-Talaa al-Kebir
At-Talaa as-Seghir
20
24
23
22
Bab Smarine
Bab Riafer
Sharia-Moulay Suleman
MEDINA (FÈS EL-BALI)
25 26
27
Oued Fès
Ave de la Liberté
Bab el-Hadid
Bab el-Jedid
Mohammed el-Alaoui
28
Route Principale No 1
Cemetery
29
30
31
Blvd
Bab el-Ftouh
To Taza & Oujda
32
Bab Sud

water in the shared showers and great views from the roof.

The *Hôtel Mauritania* (☎ 63 35 18), on Rue Serrajine, has cell-like rooms for Dr40 per person (hot showers are an extra Dr10); the *Hôtel Lamrani* (☎ 63 44 11), near the Medersa Bou Inania, has spotless rooms for just Dr30/60.

Hotels – Fès el-Jdid Staying in Fès el-Jdid doesn't offer the medina buzz but there are some basic places along Sharia Moulay Suleiman, including the *Hôtel du Parc* (☎ 94 16 98), which has rooms for Dr30/50. The *Hôtel du Commerce* (☎ 62 22 31) has clean rooms, some with balconies, for Dr40/60.

Hotels – Ville Nouvelle The cheapest hotels here include the *Hôtel Regina*, 21 Rue Ghassan Kanfani, and the *Hôtel Renaissance*, 29 Rue Abdel el-Khattabi, which both charge Dr40/80 for very basic but clean singles/doubles.

Slightly better is the *Hôtel Savoy* (☎ 62 06 08) on Blvd Abdallah Chefchaouni. Clean, airy rooms with washbasin cost Dr50 per person.

The ville nouvelle has quite a few one and two-star hotels, but the quality does tend to vary. Among the best are the *Hôtel Kairouan* (☎ 62 35 90), 84 Rue du Soudan, and the *Hôtel Royal* (☎ 62 46 56), 36 Rue du Soudan. Both charge Dr85/100 for singles/doubles without shower and Dr105/121 for rooms with shower.

Though a little more expensive, the recently refurbished *Hôtel Amor* (☎ 62 33 04) is a very good deal. Light, decent-sized rooms with bathroom (hot water in the morning and evening) cost Dr128/160. The hotel also has a restaurant and bar.

The three-star *Grand Hôtel* (☎ 93 20 26; fax 65 38 47), on Blvd Abdallah Chefchaouni, still lives up to its name. It has large rooms with all facilities for Dr177/207. The hotel has a pleasant dining salon and basement parking.

The modern *Hôtel Splendid* (☎ 62 21 48; fax 65 48 92), 9 Rue Abdelkrim el-Khattabi, has comfortable rooms with big windows and all facilities for Dr238/287.

Places to Eat

Fès el-Bali The restaurants around Bab Bou Jeloud remain the most popular places to eat in the medina. Just inside the gate is the basic *Restaurant des Jeunes*, near the Hôtel Cascades, which offers harira for Dr5 and mains for Dr30. There are also some great-value snack stands where you can buy stuffed rolls for about Dr12.

Along Rue Achabine, farther inside the medina between Place an-Najjarine and Bab Guissa, you'll find a dozen or more hole-in-the-wall restaurants offering cheap local dishes.

In the north-west corner of the Bou Jeloud Gardens, the *Café Restaurant La Noria* is a quiet place for breakfast (Dr12 for coffee and toast) or a more expensive midday meal (Dr40 for couscous). It's set in a pleasant garden with a large *noria*, or water wheel.

Fès has several restaurants housed in old palaces which offer expensive Moroccan feasts. Many also offer performances of Moroccan music and Oriental dancing. One of the cheapest of the palace restaurants (and without the traditional entertainment) is the *Restaurant Dar Jamaï* (☎ 63 56 85), 14 Funduq Lihoudi, which has a three-course set menu for Dr100. Possibly the pick of them all is the *Palais de Fès*, a gracious 14th-century building housing a restaurant and rooftop café. Coffee costs Dr10 a shot, but is worth it for the views.

Ville Nouvelle There are a few cheap eats on or just off Blvd Mohammed V, especially around the central market. The *Restaurant Fish Friture* (☎ 94 06 99), 138 Blvd Mohammed V, is a bright, friendly place serving excellent fresh fish. A full meal costs around Dr40.

If you fancy a glass of wine or beer with your meal, try the *Café du Centre*, also on Blvd Mohammed V, which offers simple French fare at reasonable prices.

The *Restaurant Sicilia* (☎ 62 65 65), at 4 Blvd Abdallah Chefchaouni opposite the syndicat d'initiative, does decent pizzas from around Dr30.

La Cheminée (☎ 62 49 02), 6 Ave Lalla Asma, is a tranquil little place with air-con and waiters in bow ties. It serves prepared

FÈS-VILLE NOUVELLE CENTRAL

PLACES TO STAY
11 Hôtel Amor
14 Hôtel Royal
15 Hôtel Kairouan
25 Hôtel Savoy
26 Hostel
30 Grand Hôtel
33 Hôtel Renaissance
34 Hôtel Splendid
35 Sheraton Fès Hôtel;
    Cyber C@fe
41 Hôtel Regina

PLACES TO EAT
6 Restaurant La Cheminée
10 Sandwich Venesia
24 Restaurant Fish Friture
31 Restaurant Sicilia
36 Pâtisserie Assouen
39 Café du Centre;
    Pâtisserie L'Epi d'Or

OTHER
1 Train Station
2 Grands Taxis to Meknès;
   Petits Taxis
3 Supermarket La Gare
4 Swimming Pool
5 All-Night Pharmacy
7 Mosque
8 Hertz
9 French Consulate
12 BMCE Bank (ATM)
13 Société Général Bank
16 Budget
17 Tourist Office
18 English Bookshop
19 Europcar
20 Post Office
21 Police
22 Newsstand
23 Kodak Shop
27 American Language
   Center
28 Central Market
29 Wine Shop
32 Goldcar
37 Ensemble Artisanal
38 BMCE Bank (ATM)
40 Syndicat d'Initiative
42 Grands Taxis to Rabat &
   Casablanca
43 Public Showers
44 CTM Bus Station
45 Church

To Merenid Tombs & Chefchaouen
Place de la Gare
Agdal
Boulevard des Alaouites
To Meknès
Avenue Mohammed el-Hayani
Avenue des Almohades
Avenue des Sports
Boulevard Moulay Youssef
To Bab el-Ftouh (& Taza)
Avenue de la Liberté
Ave Lalla Asma
Boulevard ben Jerrah
Avenue Mohammed el-Korri
Place de la Résistance
Rue du Soudan
Boulevard Tariq Ibn Ziad
Ave de France
Rue Saoudite
To Meknès (60km) & Rabat (196km)
Rue Arabie
Place de Florence
Avenue des FAR
Avenue Hassan II
Boulevard Mohammed V
Boulevard Abdallah Chefchaouni
Rue A el-Khattabi
Avenue Mohammed es-Slaoui
Place Mohammed V
Avenue Allal Ben-Abdullah
Avenue Youssef ben Tachfine
To Airport & Azrou

0   100   200 m

MOROCCO

Moroccan and French dishes for Dr60 to Dr75.

The *Pâtisserie L'Epi d'Or*, 83 Blvd Mohammed V, is a good, central place for a quiet breakfast (around Dr12). The swanky *Pâtisserie Assouan*, just down the road from the Sheraton Fès Hôtel, is very popular with well-heeled Fassis.

The *Marché Centrale* (Central Market), just off Blvd Mohammed V, has a wide range of fruit and vegetable stalls as well as several small grocery shops. It's open daily from 9 am to 1 pm. The supermarket *La Gare*, not far

from the train station just off Rue Cheguit, is open from 8.30 am to 12.30 pm and 3 to 9 pm.

Getting There & Away
Bus The CTM bus station is in the ville nouvelle on Blvd Mohammed V, but will shortly move to a new site not far away on Blvd Dhar Mahres. Tickets can be bought up to five days in advance – a good idea as demand is high, especially on the Fès-Tangier and Fès-Marrakesh runs. There are daily departures to Casablanca, Marrakesh, Meknès, Oujda, Tangier and Tetouan.

Most non-CTM buses leave from Place Baghdadi, near Bab Bou Jeloud. Buses depart from here for all destinations and reservations can be made for the most popular runs. CTM also has an office in the complex. Some buses (including a service to Chefchouen) leave from a new bus station at the foot of the cemetery next to the kasbah.

Train The train station is in the ville nouvelle, a 10-minute walk from the centre. Trains are the best bet if you are heading to Meknès (one hour), Casablanca (five hours), Tangier (six hours) or Marrakesh (eight hours). Most trains from Fès to Marrakesh involve a change of trains at either Rabat or Casa-Voyageurs station in Casablanca. All trains between Fès and Casablanca or Marrakesh stop at Meknès and Rabat.

Taxi Grands taxis for Rabat (Dr55) leave from the streets around the CTM station and those for Meknès (Dr15) leave from in front of the train station. Grands taxis for Taza (Dr30) depart from just outside Bab el-Ftouh. For Ifrane (Dr20) or Azrou (Dr25) there's a rank behind the mosque on Blvd Dhar Mahres.

Car The following are among the car-rental agencies located in Fès:

Avis
   (☎ 62 67 46) 50 Blvd Abdallah Chefchaouni
Budget
   (☎ 62 09 19) Corner of Ave Hassan II and Rue Bahrein
Europcar
   (☎ 62 65 45) 41 Ave Hassan II
Hertz
   (☎ 62 28 12) Ave de France

Getting Around

Bus Fès has a fairly good local bus service, although the buses are like sardine cans at certain times of the day. Useful routes include the following:

No 9: Place de l'Atlas, Ave Hassan II, Dar Batha
No 10: Train station, Bab Guissa, Sidi Bou Jidda
No 12: Bab Bou Jeloud, Bab Guissa, Bab el-Ftouh
No 16: Train station, Airport
No 17: Blvd Tariq ibn Ziad, 'Ain Chkef
No 18: Bab el-Ftouh, Dar Batha
No 47: Train station, Bab Bou Jeloud

Taxi The red petits taxis are cheap and plentiful. The drivers generally use the meters without any fuss. Expect to pay about Dr10 from the CTM station to Bab Bou Jeloud. Only grands taxis go out to the airport and although it's only 15km they're virtually impossible to beat down to less than Dr80.

AROUND FÈS
Set against jagged mountain bluffs and rich farmland, the picturesque Berber town of **Sefrou** makes a fine contrast to the intensity of Fès, just 28km away. The town boasts a small walled **medina** and **mellah**. The best points of entry/exit are the Bab Taksebt, Bab Zemghila and the Bab Merba. There's a **waterfall** about 1.5km west of town.

Accommodation options are limited. There's a *camping ground* on the hill overlooking the town; the basic *Hôtel Frenaie* on the road to Fès (Dr70/100 for singles/doubles); and south of the medina, the two-star *Hôtel Sidi Lahcen el-Youssi* (☎ 68 34 28), Rue Sidi Ali Bouserghine, which has rooms with hot shower and balcony for Dr150/179.

Regular buses and taxis between Fès and Sefrou drop you off at Place Moulay Hassan in front of the Bab M'Kam and Bab Taksebt.

TAZA
☎ 05
Overlooking the Taza Gap – the only feasible pass from the east between the Rif Mountains and the Middle Atlas – Taza has been important throughout Morocco's history as a base from which to exert control over the country's eastern extremities.

If you have your own transport, the drive around **Mt Tazzeka**, with a visit to the incredible caverns of the **Gouffre du Friouato**, is superb. Said to be the deepest in North Africa, the caverns have only been partially explored.

In the town itself, the old medina is relaxed and worth a wander, particularly around the ramparts to **Bab er-Rih** (Gate of the Wind), from where there are excellent views over the surrounding countryside.

Places to Stay & Eat
In the medina, the basic but cheerful *Hôtel de l'Étoile* (☎ 27 01 79), on Moulay el-Hassan,

has rooms for Dr35. There is no shower but you'll find a hammam nearby.

The *Hôtel de la Gare* (☎ 67 24 48), near the train station, has simple singles/doubles for Dr48/64, and rooms with shower for Dr75/95.

In the centre of the new town (about 3km from the medina), the *Hôtel Guillaume Tell* (☎ 67 23 47) offers big rooms with double beds for Dr41/62. Showers are cold. The nearby *Hôtel de la Poste* (☎ 67 25 89) has small but comfortable rooms for Dr48/64 but no shower.

The *Hôtel du Dauphiné* (☎ 67 35 67), Place de l'Indépendance, is an attractive colonial-style place with its own restaurant and lively bar. Rooms without bathroom cost Dr70/87; with shower Dr96/120. There's hot water in the evening.

The best of the few eateries in town is the *Restaurant Majestic* on Ave Mohammed V, near the hotels. You can eat well for around Dr30.

Getting There & Away
Buses and grands taxis leave for Fès, Tangier, Al-Hoceima, Nador and Oujda several times a day from a lot on the Fès-Oujda road near the train station. The CTM terminal on Place de l'Indépendance is more convenient for the hotels.

There are daily trains to Casablanca via Fès, Meknès and Rabat as well as regular services to Marrakesh, Tangier and Oujda.

The Atlantic Coast

ASILAH
☎ 09

About 46km south of Tangier, the small port of Asilah has enjoyed a tumultuous history disproportionate to its size. Settled first by the Carthaginians and then the Romans, it came under Portuguese and Spanish control in the 15th and 16th centuries respectively. Early this century, Asilah became the residence of a powerful brigand, Er-Raissouli who, in spite of attempts by the sultan and various European powers to control him, was master of north-eastern Morocco until he was imprisoned in 1925 by a Rif rival, Abd el-Krim.

Things to See
The 15th-century Portuguese **ramparts** are intact, but access is limited. The two prongs that jut into the ocean can be visited at any time and afford the best views.

The **Palais de Raissouli**, a beautifully preserved three-storey building, was constructed in 1909 and includes a terrace overlooking the sea from which Raissouli forced convicted murderers to jump to their deaths. The guardian will expect a tip. Several decent **beaches** stretch north of the town.

In August the town is transformed into an outdoor gallery as local and foreign artists celebrate the **Fine Arts Festival**.

Places to Stay
Camping There are a number of camping grounds along the beaches south of town. They include *Camping As-Saada*, *Camping Echrigui*, *Camping l'Océan*, *Camping Atlas* and *Camping Sahara*. They all have guarded camping facilities, shower and toilet blocks, and restaurants and bars. They fill up in summer.

Hotels The recently refurbished *Hôtel Marhaba* (☎ 91 71 44) overlooks Place Zelaka, in front of the main entrance (Bab Kasaba) to the old town. Rooms cost Dr50 per person. Hot showers are Dr5 extra. The *Hôtel Asilah* (☎ 91 72 86), on Ave Hassan II, has singles/doubles without shower for Dr35/70 and rooms with for Dr100/120.

The *Hôtel Mansour* (☎ 91 73 90; fax 91 75 33), 49 Ave Mohammed V, is a friendly place offering spotless rooms with shower and toilet for Dr146/195.

Places to Eat
There is a string of restaurants and cafés on Ave Hassan II and around the corner on Rue Imam al-Assili. A main course will cost around Dr30. Of the slightly more expensive restaurants across from Bab Kasaba, the *Restaurante Oceano Casa Pepe* (☎ 91 73 95) is the best. Its Spanish-style fish dishes cost around Dr45.

Getting There & Away
The best way to reach Asilah is by bus (Dr10) or grand taxi (Dr20) from Tangier, or bus from Larache (Dr9), south of Asilah. There

MOROCCO

are trains, but the station is 2.5km north of town. There are also buses to Rabat, Casablanca and Meknès.

RABAT
☎ 07

Rabat's history goes back 2500 years to Phoenician exploration. Little remains of their influence or that of the Romans, who came after and built a settlement known as Sala. The Almohad Sultan Yacoub al-Mansour ushered in a brief period of glory for Rabat in the 12th century. He used the kasbah as a base for campaigns in Spain, and built the magnificent Almohad Bab Oudaia and the unfinished Tour Hassan. However, the city rapidly declined after his death in 1199.

Muslims who had been expelled from Spain resettled the city and neighbouring Salé in the early 17th century and the stage was set for the colourful era of the Sallee Rovers. These corsairs set sail from here and plundered thousands of merchant vessels returning to Europe from Asia, West Africa and the Americas throughout the 17th and 18th centuries.

Rabat's role as Morocco's capital dates from the days of the French protectorate. Few of its people are involved in the tourist trade, which means you can walk about town without having to steel yourself against high-pressure sales tactics.

Orientation

Rabat lies on the west bank of the Oued Bou Regreg, and Salé lies on the east bank. The Roman ruins of Sala, later known as Chellah, are immediately south of the town centre, while the relatively small medina area is just north.

Information

Tourist Office The extraordinarily inconvenient location of the ONMT office (☎ 68 15 31) on Rue al-Abtal in the west of the city renders a visit a waste of time unless you desperately want the usual handouts and brochures.

Foreign Embassies See Foreign Embassies in Morocco in the Facts for the Visitor section at the start of this chapter for details of embassies and consulates in Rabat.

Money The banks are concentrated along Ave Mohammed V. The BMCE is open normal banking hours Monday to Friday, on weekends from 10 am to 2 pm and 4 to 8 pm. There is an exchange kiosk in the train station that remains open on weekends and holidays from 9 am to noon and 3 to 6 pm.

Post & Communications The post office, on Ave Mohammed V, is open weekdays from 8.30 am to 6.30 pm. The telephone office, across the road, is open 24 hours a day, seven days a week. Poste restante is in the phone office.

Bookshops The English Bookshop (☎ 70 65 93) is at 7 Rue al-Yamama. The American Bookstore, part of the American Language Center (☎ 76 71 03), is at 4 Rue Tanger.

Things to See

The walled **medina** dates from the 17th century and though only mildly interesting is worth a stroll. There are some excellent carpet shops and many jewellery stores. Follow Rue Souika then head north up Rue des Consuls to get to the **Kasbah des Oudaias**, built on the bluff overlooking the Atlantic Ocean. The main entry is via the impressive **Almohad Bab Oudaia**, built in 1195.

The kasbah houses a palace built by Moulay Ismail that now contains the Museum of Moroccan Arts. The museum is open every day from 9 am to noon and 3 to 5 pm (6 pm in summer). Entry is Dr10.

Rabat's most famous landmark is the **Tour Hassan**, the incomplete minaret of the great mosque begun by Yacoub al-Mansour. The 1755 earthquake finished off the half-built mosque. On the same site, to the south-east of the medina within walking distance of the centre of town, is the **Mausoleum of Mohammed V**, the present king's father.

Beyond the city walls, at the end of Ave Yacoub el-Mansour, are the remains of the ancient Roman city of Sala, which subsequently became the independent Berber city of **Chellah** and then later still the Merenids'

CENTRAL RABAT

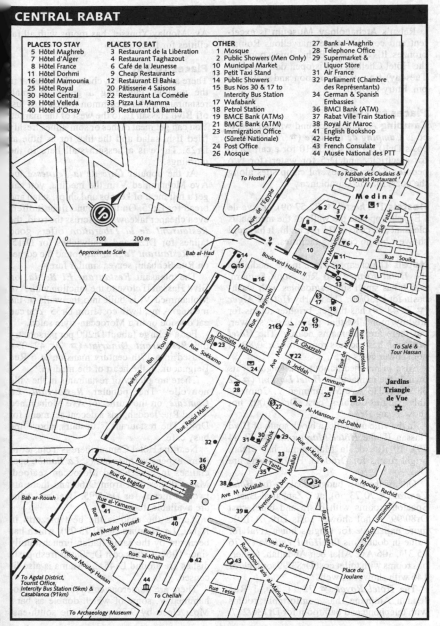

PLACES TO STAY
5 Hôtel Maghreb
7 Hôtel d'Alger
8 Hôtel France
11 Hôtel Dorhmi
16 Hôtel Mamounia
25 Hôtel Royal
30 Hôtel Central
39 Hôtel Velleda
40 Hôtel d'Orsay

PLACES TO EAT
3 Restaurant de la Libération
4 Restaurant Taghazout
6 Café de la Jeunesse
9 Cheap Restaurants
12 Restaurant El Bahia
20 Pâtisserie 4 Saisons
22 Restaurant La Comédie
33 Pizza La Mamma
35 Restaurant La Bamba

OTHER
1 Mosque
2 Public Showers (Men Only)
10 Municipal Market
13 Petit Taxi Stand
14 Public Showers
15 Bus Nos 30 & 17 to
Intercity Bus Station
17 Wafabank
18 Petrol Station
19 BMCE Bank (ATMs)
21 BMCE Bank (ATM)
23 Immigration Office
(Sûreté Nationale)
24 Post Office
26 Mosque

27 Bank al-Maghrib
28 Telephone Office
29 Supermarket &
Liquor Store
31 Air France
32 Parliament (Chambre
des Représentants)
34 German & Spanish
Embassies
36 BMCI Bank (ATM)
37 Rabat Ville Train Station
38 Royal Air Maroc
41 English Bookshop
42 Hertz
43 French Consulate
44 Musée National des PTT

MOROCCO

royal burial ground. It's open daily from 8.30 am until sunset. Entry is Dr10.

Rabat's **Archaeology Museum** is excellent and contains some marvellous Roman bronzes. It's on Rue al-Brihi, almost opposite the Hôtel Chellah, and is open daily (except Tuesday) from 9 am to noon and 2.30 to 6 pm. Entry is Dr10.

Places to Stay

Camping At Salé beach and well signposted is *Camping de la Plage* (☎ 78 23 68). It costs Dr10 per person, Dr10 for a car, Dr10 for electricity and Dr5 for water (for two people). There are several camp sites along the coast road to Casablanca.

Hostels The *hostel* (☎ 72 57 69), at Ave de l'Egypte opposite the walls of the medina, is pleasant and costs Dr31 per night. It has cold showers but no cooking facilities.

Hotels The cheapest place in the medina is the *Hôtel France*, 46 Rue Souk Semara, which has small singles/doubles with washbasin for Dr30/50. The nearby *Hôtel d'Alger* (☎ 72 48 29) has bigger, brighter rooms for slightly more. Neither place has a shower, but there are hammams nearby. The *Hôtel Mahgreb* has spotless rooms for Dr50/80. A hot shower costs Dr5.

Also in the medina, but in a league of its own, is the immaculate *Hôtel Dorhmi* (☎ 72 38 98) at 313 Ave Mohammed V. Comfortable singles/doubles cost Dr80/100; hot showers are Dr7.

In the ville nouvelle, a block south of Blvd Hassan II, the *Hôtel Mamounia* (☎ 72 44 79), 10 Rue de la Mamounia, has clean, bright rooms for Dr60/83. Hot showers are Dr5.

One of the best budget deals is the *Hôtel Central* (☎ 70 73 56), at 2 Zankat al-Basra. Spacious rooms with basin and bidet cost Dr80/99. A hot shower costs Dr9. A little more expensive for singles but a rival for value in doubles is the *Hôtel Velleda* (☎ 76 95 31), 106 Ave Allal ben Abdallah. Generous rooms with toilet cost Dr83/99, or Dr125/146 with shower as well.

The *Hôtel Royal* (☎ 72 11 71), 1 Rue Jeddah Ammane, has comfortable rooms with telephone and bathroom for Dr186/217.

The friendly, three-star *Hôtel d'Orsay* (☎ 2(22 77), just across from the train station on Ave Moulay Youssef, has rooms with all facilities for Dr211/250.

Places to Eat

There are several good, cheap places to eat in the medina, including a group of small restaurants under a common roofed area just off Blvd Hassan II, to the west of the market. You can get meat dishes or sometimes freshly fried fish, salad and the like for as little as Dr25. There is a bessara stall here in the mornings.

At the popular *Café de la Jeunesse*, on Ave Mohammed V in the medina, you can get a full meal of kebabs and chips, salad and bread for Dr25. On the ground floor it offers even cheaper takeaways. Across the road, the *Restaurant de la Libération* offers good tajines for Dr26 and sandwiches for Dr15. The *Restaurant Taghazout*, round the corner on Rue Sebbahi, serves similar fare.

The pleasant *Restaurant El Bahia*, on Blvd Hassan II close to the junction with Ave Mohammed V, is built into the walls of the medina. A meal will cost from Dr35. You can eat outside or in a Moroccan-style salon.

For a splurge (about Dr200 per person) try the *Restaurant Dinarjat* (☎ 70 42 39), housed in a 17th-century mansion at 6 Rue Belgnaoui, in the heart of the medina.

There are plenty of restaurants in the ville nouvelle. The popular *Restaurant La Comédie*, on the corner of Ave Mohammed V and Rue Jeddah, has a decent set menu for Dr40. The restaurant is upstairs, above the busy café.

Near the Hôtel Central there is a cluster of more expensive restaurants. *La Bamba* specialises in French and Moroccan seafood. Mains dishes cost from Dr60 and there are two set menus for Dr65/95. Beer and wine are available, too.

Across the road is the best pizzeria in Rabat, *La Mamma* (☎ 70 73 29), which has been run by the same Italian-French family since 1964. Pizzas cost Dr50 and fresh pasta dishes are around Dr45. La Mama is also licensed.

There are numerous cafés along Ave Mohammed V, some of which double as bars. Most close by 9.30 pm. In the south-east orner of the Kasbah des Oudaias, the quiet and shady *Café Maure* overlooks the estuary to Salé. The café is closed in the evening.

Getting There & Away
Bus The bus station is inconveniently situated 5km from the centre of town. There are local buses (No 30) and petits taxis (Dr15) to the centre.

CTM has buses to most destinations including Casablanca, Tangier, Fès, Tetouan, Tiznit and Marrakesh.

Train The Rabat Ville train station is centrally located on Ave Mohammed V. Don't get off at Rabat Agdal station. There are some 20 daily express trains to Casablanca. They take 50 minutes and cost Dr27 (2nd class) one way.

There are also daily departures to Tangier (five hours), Meknès and Fès (four hours) and Marrakesh (six hours).

Taxi Grands taxis for Casablanca (Dr27) leave from outside the main bus station. Others leave from near the Hôtel Bou Regreg on Blvd Hassan II for Fès (Dr55), Meknès (Dr40) and Salé (Dr3).

Car The following are among the car-rental agencies in Rabat:

Avis
   (☎ 76 97 59) 7 Rue Abou Faris al-Marini
Budget
   (☎ 76 76 89) train station, Ave Mohammed V
Europcar
   (☎ 72 23 28) 25 Rue Patrice Lumumba
Hertz
   (☎ 70 92 27) 46 Ave Mohammed V

Getting Around
To/From the Airport At least 10 shuttle trains run daily between Rabat Ville and Casablanca's Mohammed V international airport with a change at Casa-Port station. The fare is Dr45 in 2nd class and the journey takes about 90 minutes.

Local Transport The main city bus station is on Blvd Hassan II. From here, bus No 16 goes to Salé. Bus Nos 30 and 17 run past Rabat's intercity bus station; they leave from

a stop just inside Bab al-Had. Most of Rabat's petits taxis are metered.

AROUND RABAT
The town of **Salé** is worlds away from Rabat. Largely left to itself since the demise of the corsairs, you can experience the sights, smells and sounds of the Morocco of yesteryear here without the tourist hordes.

In the 13th century the Merenid sultan built the walls and gates that stand today and a canal between the Oued Bou Regreg and the Bab Mrisa to allow safe access for shipping. Salé became the principal seaport through which the sultanate at Fès traded with the outside world until the end of the 16th century.

The main sight inside the walls is the classic Merenid **medersa** built in 1333 next to the grand mosque. Entry costs Dr10.

Grands taxis to Rabat (Dr3) leave from Bab Mrisa. Bus No 16 also links the two, or you could catch the small boats which cross the river below Bab Bou Haja.

CASABLANCA
☎ 02
With a population of at least three million, Casablanca is Morocco's largest city and industrial centre. Although it has a history going back many centuries and was colonised by the Portuguese in the 16th century (who stayed until 1755), it had declined into insignificance by the mid-1880s.

Its Renaissance came when the resident-general of the French protectorate, Lyautey, decided to develop Casablanca as a commercial centre. It was largely his ideas that gave Casablanca its wide boulevards, public parks and fountains, and imposing Mauresque civic buildings (a blend of French colonial and traditional Moroccan styles).

Look for the white, medium high-rise 1930s architecture, the many Art Deco touches and the pedestrian precincts thronged with speedy, fashion-conscious young people. Casablanca is cosmopolitan Morocco and an excellent barometer of liberal Islam.

Information
Tourist Offices The ONMT (☎ 27 11 77) is at 55 Rue Omar Slaoui. It's open from

MOROCCO

CENTRAL CASABLANCA

CENTRAL CASABLANCA

PLACES TO STAY
2 Hostel
10 Cheap Hotels
15 Hôtel Plaza
16 Hôtel du Centre
22 Hôtel Sheraton; Cybercafé
23 Hôtel Safir
26 Hôtel Touring; Restaurant Point Central
27 Hôtels de Foucauld & du Périgord
28 Hyatt Regency Hotel
33 Hôtel Rialto
36 Hôtel Colbert
50 Hôtel de Paris; Swiss Ice Cream Factory
59 Hôtel du Palais

PLACES TO EAT
5 Centre 2000 (Restaurants & Cafés)
8 Taverne du Dauphin
11 Restaurant Widad
25 Restaurant de l'Étoile Marocaine
34 Restaurant Au Petit Poucet
37 Rôtisseries; Restaurant Amine
42 Restaurant Vertigo
43 Glacier Goya
44 Pâtisserie/Boulangerie
45 Restaurant Snack Bar California
56 Restaurant Al-Mounia

OTHER
1 Mosque
3 Post Office
4 Hammam
6 Casa-Port Train Station
9 Great Mosque
12 Mosque
13 Clock Tower
14 Air France
17 German Consulate
18 Royal Air Maroc
19 Avis
20 Budget
21 BMCE Bank (ATMs)
24 CTM Bus Terminal
29 Wafabank
30 Trasmediterranea
31 Crédit du Maroc (ATM)
32 Cinéma Rialto
35 Post Office; Syndicat d'Initiative
38 Central Market
39 Grands Taxis for Rabat
40 Somatt Car Rental
41 Grocery Store
46 Citibank
47 Parcel Post
48 Main Post Office
49 English Bookshop
51 BMCE Bank (ATMs)
52 Voyages Schwartz (American Express)
53 Cathédrale du Sacré Coeur
54 Hôtel de Ville
55 Palais de Justice
57 BMCI Bank
58 Music Shop
60 French Consulate
61 Tourist Office
62 Cinéma Lynx
63 Main Bus Station (Non-CTM)

8.30 am to noon and 2.30 to 6.30 pm Monday to Thursday and on Friday from 8.30 to 11.30 am and 3 to 6.30 pm. The syndicat d'initiative is at 98 Blvd Mohammed V. It keeps the same hours, and is also open from 9 am to noon on Sunday.

Money There are BMCE branches with ATMs on Ave Lalla Yacout and Ave des FAR. The Crédit du Maroc bank on Ave Mohammed V will change travellers cheques. There are also banks with ATMs at Mohammed V international airport.

American Express is represented by Voyages Schwartz (☎ 22 29 46), 112 Rue Prince Moulay Abdallah.

Post & Communications The main post office is on Place Mohammed V. It's open weekdays from 8 am to 6.30 pm and Saturday until noon. The poste-restante counter is in the same section as the international telephone office, which is open 24 hours a day. The entrance is the third door along Blvd de Paris.

Cybercafés Internet access (Dr50 per hour) is available at the cybercafé on the 1st floor of the Hôtel Sheraton (☎ 31 78 78), 100 Ave des FAR. It's open Monday to Friday from 10 am to 10 pm and on Saturday from 10 am to midnight.

The Open Group (☎ 29 34 50), 63 Blvd Moulay Youssef, next to the Pizza Hut, is a busy Internet club open Monday to Saturday from 8.30 am until 7.30 pm. Access costs Dr30 per hour, but the club members have priority.

Things to See
Don't miss the beautiful **Hassan II Mosque**, which overlooks the ocean just beyond the northern tip of the medina. Finished in 1993, it is the biggest religious monument in the world after Mecca. It is also open to non-Muslims. There are guided tours (Dr100 per person; Dr50 for students) every day except Friday at 9, 10 and 11 am and 2 pm (2.30 pm in summer).

The central **ville nouvelle** around Place Mohammed V has some of the best examples of Mauresque architecture. They include the *hôtel de ville* (town hall), the *palais de justice* (law courts), the post office, and the extraordinary but shamefully neglected Cathédrale du Sacré Cœur.

Casablanca's **beaches** are to the west of town along the Blvd de la Corniche and beyond in the suburb of 'Ain Diab. It's a trendy area and very crowded in summer. The beaches are nothing special. Bus No 9 goes to 'Ain Diab from Place Oued al-Makhazine, just to the west of Place des Nations Unies.

Places to Stay

Camping About 9km south-west of town, on the main road to El-Jadida, is *Camping de l'Oasis* (☎ 25 33 67), which charges around Dr10 per person, tent and car. Bus No 31 runs past it.

Hostel The *hostel* (☎ 22 05 51; fax 22 76 77), 6 Place de l'Amiral Philibert, faces a small leafy square in the medina, just off Blvd des Almohades. It's large, comfortable and clean, and costs Dr40 per person, including breakfast. There are also rooms with two beds for Dr100. It's open daily from 8 to 10 am and noon to 11 pm (midnight in summer).

Hotels The hotels in the medina are unclassified and seedy. None have hot showers, but there are hammams around. Several are clustered around Rue Centrale, to the north-west of the clock tower. They all cost about Dr40 per person, but for a little more you can do much better outside the medina.

The *Hôtel du Palais* (☎ 27 61 91), at 68 Rue Farhat Hachad near the French consulate, is one of the cheapest places outside the medina. It has clean, spacious single/double rooms for Dr62/76. The showers are cold.

There's a cluster of cheapies on and around Rue Allal ben Abdallah, near the central market. The *Hôtel Touring* (☎ 31 02 16), 87 Rue Allal ben Abdallah, has big old rooms with desk, washbasin and bidet for Dr62/78 (Dr7 for a hot shower).

The friendly *Hôtel Colbert* (☎ 31 42 41), opposite the market at 38 Rue Chaoui, has simple rooms with washbasin, desk and telephone for Dr68/83. A hot shower costs Dr10. Rooms with bathroom cost Dr84/100.

The *Hôtel du Périgord* (☎ 22 10 85), 56 Rue Araibi Jilali, has clean singles/doubles for Dr62/82. The showers are cold. At No 52, the *Hôtel de Foucauld* (☎ 22 26 66) has decent rooms without shower for Dr75/100 and rooms with for Dr110/140.

The *Hôtel Rialto* (☎ 27 51 22), 9 Rue Salah Ben Bouchaib, is a welcoming place offering spotless rooms with shower for Dr84/112.

The *Hôtel du Centre* (☎ 44 61 80; fax 44 61 78), just off the Ave des FAR, is a decent two-star place with clean rooms (own bathroom and phone) for Dr176/206. Built in 1936, the characterful *Hôtel Plaza* (☎ 29 76 98), 18 Blvd Houphouet-Boigney, has large rooms (some have balconies and sea views) with bathroom for Dr199/237 and rooms without for Dr118/156. The hotel has a bar.

The three-star *Hôtel de Paris* (☎ 27 38 71; fax 29 80 69), in the pedestrian zone off Rue Prince Moulay Abdallah, has comfortable, light-filled rooms with heating, phone, TV and plenty of hot water for Dr293/347.

Places to Eat

There are a few cheap restaurants around the clock tower entrance to the medina. A popular one is the *Restaurant Widad*, which serves decent Moroccan dishes.

Outside the medina, the best place for good, cheap food is along Rue Chaoui. There are several rôtisseries offering roast chicken and an excellent new fish place, *Restaurant Amine*, which serves large portions of freshly cooked seafood (and good pastilla) from Dr25. There are also a couple of cheap restaurants inside the spacious and relatively tranquil central market.

The *Restaurant Point Central*, next to the Hôtel Touring on Rue Allal ben Abdallah, offers a very good midday tajine for Dr25, and couscous on Friday. Also on Rue Allal ben Abdallah is the friendly *Restaurant de l'Étoile Marocaine* (☎ 31 41 00) which serves decent Moroccan dishes (including a delicious pastilla) in pleasant surroundings. Main courses cost around Dr50.

The *Restaurant Snack Bar California*, 19 Rue Tata, is a pleasant, central spot for cheap

Moroccan food. Main courses, including tajine, couscous and brochettes, cost Dr30.

The licensed *Restaurant Au Petit Poucet*, on Blvd Mohammed V, is a relic of the 1920s (the ancient menu in the window offers foie gras, smoked salmon and caviar from the Caspian Sea). Main courses cost around Dr80 and a half bottle of wine from Dr35.

For excellent Moroccan food in traditional surroundings, check out the *Restaurant Al-Mounia* (☎ 22 26 69), 95 Rue du Prince du Moulay Abdallah. Main courses start at Dr80.

The licensed *Taverne du Dauphin* (☎ 22 12 00), 115 Blvd Houphouet-Boigny, is a very popular, reasonably priced seafood restaurant. A big platter of grilled garlic prawns costs Dr46; fish costs from around Dr40. A 20% tax is added.

The licensed *Restaurant Vertigo* (☎ 29 46 39), 110 Rue Chaoui, is an attractive new French restaurant offering very good main courses for around Dr80.

For excellent coffee, head to *Glacier Goya*, on Ave Houmane el-Fetouaki; there's a good pâtisserie across the road. The *Swiss Ice Cream Factory*, next to the Hôtel de Paris, serves home-made ice cream.

Entertainment

Bars & Nightclubs Central Casablanca has a large red-light district and plenty of seedy bars and cabaret places. Women should be particularly mindful of this after dark. The big hotels have decent bars; one of the best is the *Bar Casablanca* in the Hyatt Regency. Beer costs from Dr40, but you do get nibbles as well. Happy hour (the second drink comes free) is from 6.30 to 7.30 pm.

Both the Hyatt and the Sheraton have popular nightclubs. Entry costs Dr120/150 during the week/weekend and drinks cost about the same. The trendiest clubs and bars are to be found in the wealthy beachside suburb of 'Ain Diab to the west of town.

Cinema *Cinéma Lynx* (☎ 22 02 29), 50 Ave Mers Sultan, is considered to be the best in town. Tickets cost from Dr20. The more central Cinéma Rialto, on Rue Salah Ben Bouchaib, is a classic Art Deco building.

Getting There & Away

Bus The CTM bus terminal is on Rue Léon L'Africain at the back of the Hôtel Safir. Most other lines use the chaotic main station just off Rue Strasbourg, two blocks south of Place de la Victoire – it's quite a hike, so a take a petit taxi or local bus No 4 or 5.

There are CTM departures to Agadir (five daily), Essaouira, Fès and Meknès (every half-hour from 7 am), Marrakesh (five daily), Oujda, Rabat, Safi, Tangier (six daily), Taza and Tetouan.

CTM also operates international buses to France and Belgium from Casablanca.

Train Most train departures are from Casa-Voyageurs station, which is 4km east of the city centre. Local bus No 30 runs to Casa-Voyageurs along Ave des FAR and Blvd Mohammed V; a petit taxi costs Dr10.

Trains to Tangier, Fès and Meknès leave from the central Casa-Port station, a short walk north-east of Place des Nations Unies. Additional trains run to these destinations from Casa-Voyageurs as well as to Marrakesh and El-Jadida. All but those to Marrakesh and El-Jadida stop at Rabat. Oujda trains all stop at Fès and Meknès.

For Rabat, take one of the high-speed shuttles which take 50 minutes (Dr27 in 2nd class). They leave from both Casablanca stations.

Taxi Grands taxis to Rabat leave from Blvd Hassan Seghir, near the CTM bus station. The fare is Dr27.

Car The following are among the car-rental agencies in Casablanca:

Avis
  (☎ 31 24 24) 19 Ave des FAR,
  (☎ 33 90 72) Mohammed V airport
Budget
  (☎ 31 37 37) Tour des Habous, Ave des FAR,
  (☎ 33 91 57) Mohammed V airport
Europcar
  (☎ 31 37 37) Complexe des Habous, Ave des FAR, (☎ 33 91 61) Mohammed V airport
Somatt Car
  (☎ 47 39 42) 62 Rue Chaoui

Getting Around

To/From the Airport Shuttle trains (TNR) run from Mohammed V airport to the

Casa-Voyageurs and Casa-Port train stations. They take 24 minutes and cost Dr25 in 2nd class. A grand taxi to Mohammed V airport will cost you Dr150 (Dr200 after 8 pm).

Bus Local buses run from a terminus west of central Casablanca on Place Oued al-Makhazine to 'Ain Diab (No 9) and Place de la Victoire (No 5). Bus No 30 connects the Casa-Voyageurs train station to central Casablanca.

Taxi There's no shortage of metered petits taxis in Casablanca – just make sure the meter is on. Expect to pay Dr10 for a ride in or around the city centre.

EL-JADIDA
☎ 03

The Portuguese founded El-Jadida (which they called Mazagan) in 1513 and held it until 1769, when it was besieged by Sultan Sidi Mohammed bin Abdallah. The massive bastioned fortress, with its enclosed medina, churches and enormous cistern, was rebuilt in 1820 by Sultan Moulay Abd ar-Rahman and is still remarkably well preserved. These days, El-Jadida is also a popular beach resort.

Information
The tourist office (☎ 34 47 88) is on Rue Ibn Khaldoun. It's open Monday to Friday from 8.30 am to noon and from 2.30 to 6.30 pm. There are several banks in the town centre; the BMCE branch near the tourist office has an ATM.

Things to See
The old **Portuguese Fortress** (Cité Portugaise) is the focal point of town. There are two entrance gates to the fortress; the southernmost one, which is more convenient, opens onto the main street through the medina, Rue Mohammed Ahchemi Bahbai. About halfway down this street is the atmospheric **Citerne Portugaise** (Portuguese Cistern), where Orson Welles filmed scenes for *Othello*. It's open daily from 8.30 am to noon and 2.30 to 6 pm. Entry is Dr10.

Entry to the **ramparts**, which you can walk all the way around, is through the large door

at the end of the tiny cul-de-sac on the right after you enter the fortress.

Places to Stay
Camping The nearest site, *Camping Caravaning International* (☎ 34 27 55), is on Ave des Nations Unies, a 15-minute walk southeast of the bus station. It costs Dr12 per person, Dr6.50 per car, Dr10 to pitch a tent, Dr5 for a hot shower and Dr11 for electricity. There's another camp site 5km south of town at Sidi Bouzid.

Hotels Rooms can be scarce in the summer, so you may want to book ahead. The *Hôtel Bordeaux* (☎ 35 41 17), 47 Rue Moulay Ahmed Tahiri, has small but pleasant singles/doubles for Dr40/60. A hot shower costs Dr5.

The *Hôtel du Maghreb* and *Hôtel de France* (☎ 34 21 81), just off Place Hansali, are two hotels knocked into one. Some of the big rooms look out to the sea. Singles/doubles cost Dr40/55, and a hot shower costs Dr4.

The *Hôtel Royal* (☎ 34 11 00) on Ave Mohammed V has comfortable rooms without shower for Dr62/80 and rooms with shower for Dr98/116. The hotel has a restaurant and bar.

El-Jadida's only two-star hotel, the *Hôtel de Provence* (☎ 34 23 47; fax 35 21 15), 42 Ave Fkih Mohammed Errafil, is one of the most pleasant places in town. Rooms with bathroom cost Dr151/190. The hotel has a popular restaurant and bar.

The three-star *Hôtel Palais Andalous* (☎ 34 37 45; fax 35 16 90), Blvd Docteur de la Lanouy, is a converted pasha's residence and a luxurious splurge. Rooms with everything cost Dr274/330.

Places to Eat
The *Restaurant La Broche*, on Place Hansali, is a family-run place offering decent Moroccan dishes from around Dr30. The *Restaurant Chahrazad* serves similar food in plainer surroundings.

For very good, cheap seafood (Dr25 for a meal) try the basic *Restaurant Tchikito*, in a lane a short walk north-west of Place Hansali. The more upmarket *Restaurant du Port* (☎ 34 25 79), which overlooks the fortress,

EL-JADIDA

To Safi (Coastal Route; 160km),
Sidi Bouzid (5km) & Beaches

Cité Portugaise

Rue Mohammed
Ahchemi Bahbal

Place Mohammed
ben Abdallah

Modern
Dock
Area

ATLANTIC
OCEAN

Rue Zerktoun

Place
Hansali
Rue Lescouf

Rue Ibn Khaldoun

Avenue Hassan II

Avenue Mohammed V

To Hôtel
Palais Andalous

Avenue Fkih Mohammed Errafil

Boulevard al-Mouhit

Beach

Avenue
al-Jaich al-Malaki

Avenue et-Jamia al-Arabia

Avenue Feh Mohammed Errafil

0   100   200 m

To Bus & Train Stations,
Camping Caravaning International,
Safi (157km) & Marrakesh (197km)

PLACES TO STAY
17 Hôtel Bordeaux
21 Hôtel du Maghreb;
     Hôtel de France
32 Hôtel de Provence
34 Hôtel Royal

PLACES TO EAT
10 Café
12 Restaurant du Port
14 Restaurant Tchikito
18 Café La Renaissance
19 Restaurant La Broche
20 Restaurant Chahrazad
23 Café La Royale
28 Cafés

OTHER
 1 Bastion St Sebastian
 2 Former Synagogue
 3 Hammam (Women Only)
 4 Bastion St Antoine
 5 Jewellers' Workshops
 6 Mosque
 7 Citerne Portugaise
 8 Porto do Mar
 9 Church of the Assumption
11 Ramparts Entry
13 Parking
15 Mosque
16 Market
22 Bar
24 Petrol Station
25 Municipal Theatre
26 Post Office
27 Night Chemist
29 BMCI Bank
30 Bank al-Maghrib
31 BMCE Bank (ATM)
33 Tourist Office

MOROCCO

also specialises in seafood. Expect to pay
around Dr100 for a meal.

In a similar price range, the popular restaurant at the *Hôtel de Provence* offers a choice
of Moroccan, French and seafood dishes.

The *Café La Royale* is a quiet spot for
coffee and pastries; the *Café La Renaissance*, at the top of Place Hansali, is livelier.
In summer, there are some pleasant seafront
cafés along Blvd al-Mouhit.

Getting There & Away
The bus terminal is south-east of town just off

Ave Mohammed V. It's about a 15-minute
walk from the Portuguese Fortress. There are
several runs to Casablanca, Rabat and Safi,
and frequent departures to Marrakesh.

SAFI
☎ 04

Safi (Asfi) is a modern Atlantic fishing port
and industrial centre in a steep crevasse
formed by the Oued Chabah. It has a lively
walled medina and souq, with battlements
dating from the brief Portuguese era, and is
well known for its pottery.

Things to See
In the walled city the Portuguese built and to which the Moroccans later added, the **Qasr al-Bahr** (Castle on the Sea) is usually the first port of call. There are good views from the ramparts, and a number of 17th-century Spanish and Dutch cannons. It's open from 8.30 am to noon and 2.30 to 6 pm; entry costs Dr10.

Across the street lies the **medina**, which is dominated by the **Kechla**, a massive defensive structure with fine views out to the Qasr al-Bahr. Inside is the **National Ceramics Museum** which features both ancient and contemporary pottery. It's open from 8.30 am to noon and from 2 to 6 pm. Entry costs Dr10.

Safi's famous **potteries**, where traditional wood-fired kilns are still used, are on the hill opposite Bab Chabah, to the north-west of the Kechla. You can purchase pottery here for very reasonable prices.

Places to Stay
About 2km north of town, just off the coast road to El-Jadida, is *Camping International*. It's a shady site with a small swimming pool and costs Dr12 per person, Dr9 per car, Dr9 per tent and Dr10 for a hot shower.

There are some basic cheapies (from Dr30 per person) clustered around the port end of Rue du Souq and along Rue de R'bat.

The *Hôtel Majestic* (☎ 46 31 31), next to the medina wall at the junction of Ave Moulay Youssef and Place de l'Indépendance, is the best value. Well-maintained, pleasant singles/doubles with washbasin and bidet cost Dr40/80. A hot shower is Dr5.

The two-star *Hôtel Anis* (☎ 46 30 78), just off Rue de R'bat to the south of the medina, has comfortable singles/doubles with shower and toilet for Dr122/150. The *Hôtel Assif* (☎ 62 23 11), on Ave de la Liberté near Place Mohammed V, has rooms with shower for Dr190/247. The hotel has a restaurant.

Places to Eat
The hole-in-the-wall seafood restaurants in the alleys off Rue du Souq in the medina offer cheap, excellent food for about Dr20 a head. The *Restaurant de Safi*, on Rue de la Marine, offers reasonably priced brochettes and other Moroccan dishes. Almost next door, the *Restaurant Gegene* serves fish and Italian dishes.

The more expensive *Restaurant Le Refuge* (☎ 46 43 54), a few kilometres north of Safi on the coast road to Sidi Bouzid, has a good reputation for seafood.

Getting There & Away
CTM and other companies share a terminal south-east of the town centre. There are regular departures to Casablanca and several to Marrakesh, Essaouira and Agadir. A couple of buses head north to El-Jadida. Some are through services from elsewhere, but you shouldn't have too much trouble on main runs.

A daily 5 am train connects with services to Marrakesh, Casablanca (Casa-Voyageurs station) and Rabat at Benguerir.

ESSAOUIRA
☎ 04

Essaouira (pronounced Esa-weera) is one of the most popular coastal towns for independent travellers. Not only does it have a long curve of magnificent beach (much appreciated by windsurfers), it also has a pleasantly laid-back atmosphere. It's a favourite with painters, and in summer months the cool sea breezes provide welcome relief from the heat of the interior.

Originally a small Phoenician settlement called Mogodor, it was occupied by the Portuguese in the 16th century. The present town, however, dates largely from 1765, when Sultan Sidi Mohammed bin Abdallah hired a French architect to redesign the town for use as a trade centre with Europe.

The fortifications are thus an interesting mix of Portuguese, French and Berber military architecture, although the walls around the town date mainly from the 18th century. Their massiveness lends a powerful mystique to the town, yet inside the walls it's all light and charm. You'll find narrow, freshly whitewashed streets, tranquil squares, friendly cafés, and artisans in tiny workshops beavering away at fragrant thuya wood.

Information
The helpful syndicat d'initiative (☎ 47 36 30), just inside Bab as-Sebaa on Rue de Caire, is open Monday to Friday from 9 am to noon and 3 to 6.30 pm.

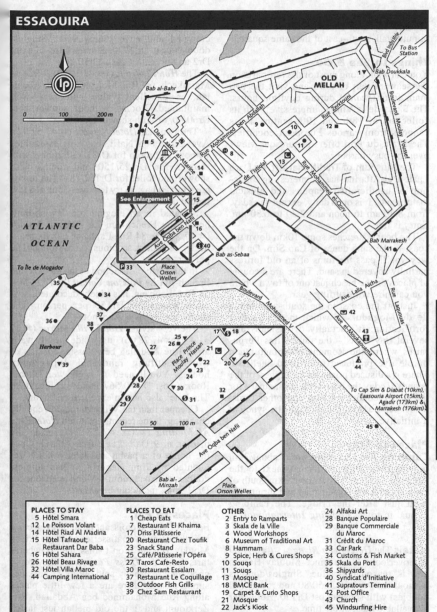

ESSAOUIRA

ATLANTIC OCEAN

To Île de Mogador

Harbour

OLD MELLAH

Bab al-Bahr

Bab Doukkala

To Bus Station

Boulevard Moulay Youssef

Bab Marrakesh

Bab as-Sebaa

Bab al-Minzah

Place Orson Welles

Place Prince Moulay Hassan

Ave Oqba ben Nafti

Boulevard Mohammed V

Ave Lalla Aicha

Ave el-Mouqaouama

To Cap Sim & Diabat (10km),
Eaasouria Airport (15km),
Agadir (173km) &
Marrakesh (176km)

MOROCCO

PLACES TO STAY
- 5 Hôtel Smara
- 12 Le Poisson Volant
- 14 Hôtel Riad Al Madina
- 15 Hôtel Tafraout;
  Restaurant Dar Baba
- 16 Hôtel Sahara
- 26 Hôtel Beau Rivage
- 32 Hôtel Villa Maroc
- 44 Camping International

PLACES TO EAT
- 1 Cheap Eats
- 7 Restaurant El Khaima
- 13 Driss Pâtisserie
- 20 Restaurant Chez Toufik
- 23 Snack Stand
- 25 Café/Pâtisserie l'Opéra
- 27 Taros Cafe-Resto
- 30 Restaurant Essalam
- 37 Restaurant Le Coquillage
- 38 Outdoor Fish Grills
- 39 Chez Sam Restaurant

OTHER
- 2 Entry to Ramparts
- 3 Skala de la Ville
- 4 Wood Workshops
- 6 Museum of Traditional Art
- 8 Hammam
- 9 Spice, Herb & Cures Shops
- 10 Souqs
- 11 Souqs
- 13 Mosque
- 18 BMCE Bank
- 19 Carpet & Curio Shops
- 21 Mosque
- 22 Jack's Kiosk
- 24 Alfakai Art
- 28 Banque Populaire
- 29 Banque Commerciale du Maroc
- 31 Crédit du Maroc
- 33 Car Park
- 34 Customs & Fish Market
- 35 Skala du Port
- 36 Shipyards
- 40 Syndicat d'Initiative
- 41 Supratours Terminal
- 42 Post Office
- 43 Church
- 45 Windsurfing Hire

There are four banks around Place Prince Moulay Hassan. The post office is a 10-minute walk south-east of the same square.

Things to See & Do
You can walk along most of the **ramparts** on the seaward part of town and visit the two main forts (*skalas*) during daylight hours. The **Skala de la Ville** is impressive, with its collection of 18th and 19th-century brass cannons from various European countries. The **Skala du Port** offers picturesque views over the busy harbour.

The **Museum of Traditional Art**, on Darb Laalouj al-Attarine, has an interesting collection of handicrafts, weapons and musical instruments. It is open daily, except Tuesday, from 8.30 am to noon and 2.30 to 6.30 pm. Entry is free.

The **beach** stretches some 10km down the coast to the sand dunes of Cap Sim. On the way you'll pass the ruins of an old fortress partially covered in sand. There are a couple of places on the beach just out of town where you can hire **windsurfing** gear.

Just off the coast to the south-west is the **Île de Mogador**, on which there's another fortification. It's actually two islands and several tiny islets – the famed Îles Purpuraires where the Romans manufactured a purple dye produced from local shellfish. There is a disused prison on the biggest of the islands. Today the islands are a sanctuary for the rare Eleonora's falcon and other birds. Visits can be arranged through the syndicat d'initiative.

Places to Stay
Camping The best *camp site* is about 3km beyond the village of Diabat, next to the Auberge Tangaro. Drive about 5km south of Essaouira on the Agadir road and turn to the right just after the bridge. The camping ground in town, *Camping International*, is rather bare.

Hotels The *Hôtel Beau Rivage* (☎/fax 47 59 25) overlooks Place Prince Moulay Hassan and is reasonable value. Singles/doubles without shower cost Dr50/80 and rooms (all doubles) with shower cost Dr120. Hot water is available most of the time.

The *Hôtel Smara* (☎ 47 56 55) on Rue de la Skala has several good rooms with sea views; some of the others, however, are very cramped and have lumpy beds. Singles/doubles cost Dr50/70. Showers are an extra Dr2 and breakfast costs Dr10.

The *Hôtel Tafraout* (☎ 47 21 20), 7 Rue de Marrakech, off Rue Mohammed ben Abdallah, is excellent value and very well maintained. Rooms without shower cost Dr60/80, or with shower Dr75/90.

The two-star *Hôtel Sahara* (☎ 47 52 92), Ave Oqba ben Nafii, has singles/doubles without bathroom for Dr81/110, rooms with shower for Dr125/150 and rooms with shower and toilet for Dr157/187. The rooms are a mixed bag, so try to have a look at a few before deciding.

Situated in an elegant old Jewish-built home, the French-run *Le Poisson Volant* (☎ 47 21 50), 34 Rue Labbana, has six beautifully decorated, spacious rooms from Dr150 per person.

In the north-east section of the medina, the French-run *Le Poisson Volant* (☎ 47 21 50), 34 Rue Labbana, has nicely decorated, spacious rooms for Dr150 per person. The shared shower is always hot.

The very stylish *Hôtel Villa Maroc* (☎ 47 31 47; fax 47 28 06), just inside the city walls at 10 Rue Abdallah ben Yassin, consists of two beautifully renovated 18th-century houses. You'll need to book well ahead. Rooms cost Dr480/567 including breakfast. The hotel also has an excellent restaurant.

Cheaper than the Villa Maroc, but equally charming, is the recently restored *Hôtel Riad Al Madina* (☎/fax 47 57 27), inside the medina at 9 Darb Laalouj al-Attarin. Once the home of a pasha and later a hotel frequented by Jimi Hendrix, it has singles/doubles with bathroom, TV and telephone for Dr312/544 including breakfast.

Places to Eat
For a coffee and croissant breakfast you can't beat the cafés and pâtisseries on Place Prince Moulay Hassan (don't miss the strawberry tarts from the *Driss Pâtisserie*, they're so good they're usually sold out by 11 am). For simple snacks there are a few little places along Rue Mohammed ben Abdallah, Rue Zerktouni and in the old mellah just inside Bab Doukkala.

On Place Prince Moulay Hassan you'll find two stands where you can get excellent baguettes stuffed with meat, salad and just about anything else you want for about Dr15.

The *Taros Cafe-Resto*, upstairs at 2 Rue de la Skala, is a fabulous new place offering light meals and drinks (including wine and beer) in comfortable rooms filled with books and magazines. There's a great terrace too.

The *Restaurant Essalam*, also on Place Prince Moulay Hassan, is a simple but popular place offering tajines and other Moroccan favourites for around Dr40.

The nearby *Restaurant Chez Toufik* serves more expensive meals in traditional Berber surroundings. There's music in the evenings. The *Restaurant El Khaima* is licensed and has Moroccan specialities and seafood from Dr60. There's a pleasant outdoor patio and two set menus for Dr80 and Dr180.

The *Restaurant Dar Baba*, near the Hôtel Tafraout, does a range of Italian dishes.

For cheap seafood, head to the outdoor fish grills down by the harbour where you can feast for as little as Dr20. For pricier seafood in delightful surroundings, try *Chez Sam* at the far end of the port area. The restaurant is licensed and there are set menus for Dr70 and Dr170. The new *Restaurant Le Coquillage* also specialises in seafood.

For a real splurge, book a table at the restaurant in the *Hôtel Villa Maroc*. Expect to pay around Dr150 per head.

Things to Buy

Essaouira is a centre for thuya carving, and the quality of the work is superb. Most of the carvers have workshops under the Skala de la Ville. Nearby are craft shops with an equally impressive range of goods. Try also Alfakai, on Place Prince Moulay Hassan.

Carpet, bric-a-brac, jewellery and brassware shops are in the narrow street and small square flanking Ave Oqba ben Nafii, between Place Prince Moulay Hassan and the ramparts.

Getting There & Away

The bus terminal is 1km north-east of the town centre along Blvd Industrie. There are regular departures to Safi, Casablanca, Marrakesh and Agadir. Grands taxis to Agadir (or neighbouring Inezgane) leave from a nearby lot. Supratours runs a fast bus to Marrakesh every morning at 6.30 am. The terminal is outside Bab Marrakesh.

AGADIR
☎ 08

Agadir is a modern city, which was completely rebuilt after a devastating earthquake in 1960. Sitting by a vast sweep of protected beach, the town has been specifically developed as a resort for short-stay package tourists from Europe.

Though one of the more expensive and least appealing cities in Morocco, Agadir is a good take-off point for visits farther south along the coast and east into the Atlas mountains.

Information

The ONMT tourist office (☎ 84 63 78) is in the market area just off Ave Prince Sidi Mohammed; there's also a syndicat d'initiative (☎ 84 03 07) on Blvd Mohammed V at the junction with Ave du Général Kettani.

Places to Stay

Camping Agadir's *camping ground* (☎ 84 66 83) is just off Blvd Mohammed V, within walking distance of the beach and town. Campervans tend to predominate.

Hotels Most of the budget hotels and a few of the mid-range ones are around the bus terminal area and along Rue Allal ben Abdallah. In the high seasons you must get into Agadir early to be sure of a room.

The *Hôtel Select*, off Rue Allal ben Abdallah, is a basic place with singles/doubles without shower for Dr63/81. There are public showers next door.

The *Hôtel Amenou* (☎ 84 56 15) and the *Hôtel Aït Laayoune* (☎ 82 43 75), both on Rue Yacoub el-Mansour, have clean rooms without shower for Dr70/90. The *Hôtel La Tour Eiffel* (☎ 82 37 12), on Rue du 29 Février opposite the mosque, has rooms for the same price.

The *Hôtel de Paris* (☎ 82 26 94), Ave du Président Kennedy, is pleasant and has reliable hot water. Rooms without bathroom cost Dr80/120 and rooms with shower and toilet are Dr130/160.

MOROCCO

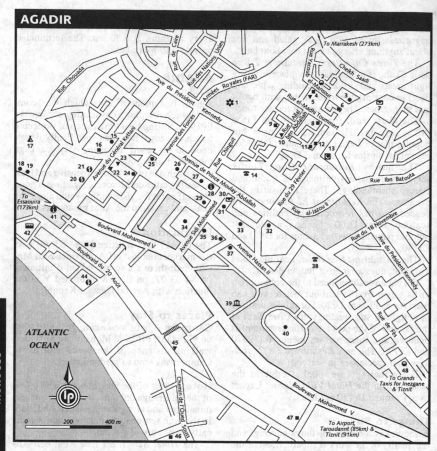

AGADIR

The recently refurbished *Hôtel Petite Suède* (☎ 84 07 79), just off Ave du Général Kettani, has comfortable rooms with bathroom for Dr136/195.

The *Hôtel El Bahia* (☎ 82 27 24), on Rue El-Mahdi ben Toummert, is another good mid-range option. Rooms without shower cost Dr110/130, those with shower go for Dr150/180 and rooms with full bathroom cost Dr180/220.

There are numerous luxury hotels in Agadir, including the *Hôtel Beach Club* (☎ 84 07 91) and the *Hôtel Sahara* (☎ 84 06 60), where you'll pay from Dr800 for a double room. These places are generally block-booked by charter groups.

Places to Eat

You'll find cheap restaurants and sandwich bars on the same street as the bus terminal. Also near here is a small plaza, with the *Restaurant Echabab*, the *Restaurant Mille et Une Nuits*, and the *Café Restaurant Coq d'Or* all next to each other. The food is very good, portions are large and three-course menus are offered for as little as Dr25.

AGADIR

PLACES TO STAY		OTHER		31	Hôtel de Ville
4	Hôtel Aït Laayoune	1	Jardin de Olhâo	32	New Labcolor (Kodak)
6	Hôtel Amenou	2	Bus Terminal	33	Liquor Store
8	Hôtel El Bahia	3	Ensemble Artisanal	34	Place de l'Espérance
9	Hôtel Select	7	Post Office	35	Air France
11	Hôtel de Paris	13	Mohammed V Mosque	36	Car/Motorbike Hire
12	Hôtel La Tour Eiffel	14	Téléboutique (Phones)	37	Travel Agents (Local
16	Hôtel Petite Suède	15	Royal Air Maroc		Excursions & Charter
17	Camp Site	18	Budget		Flights)
43	Hôtel Sheraton	19	Hertz	38	Téléboutique (Phones)
46	Hôtel Beach Club	20	BMCE Bank (ATM)	39	Musée Municipal
47	Hôtel Sahara	21	BMCI Bank (ATM)	40	Stadium
		24	Tour Agents	41	Syndicat d'Initiative
PLACES TO EAT		25	Supratours	42	Public Swimming Pool &
5	Cheap Restaurants	26	Cinéma Rialto		Café
10	Restaurant Select	27	Central Market	44	Banque Populaire
22	Restaurant Darkoum	28	Tourist Office	48	Local Buses
23	Restaurant La Tour de Paris	29	Uniprix Supermarket		
45	Expensive Restaurants	30	Post Office		

The *Restaurant Select*, near the hotel of the same name, is another popular cheapie. For fresh seafood, try the busy stalls near the entrance to the port, just west of town.

There are dozens of more upmarket restaurants to choose from in Agadir, including a whole group clustered near the big hotels down on Blvd du 20 Août.

The *Restaurant La Tour de Paris* (☎ 84 09 06), on Ave Hassan II, serves very good French food. Main courses start at Dr80 and there's a four-course menu for Dr170.

The *Restaurant Darkoum* (☎ 84 06 22), on Ave Général Kettani, serves expensive Moroccan dishes in traditional Moorish surroundings.

Getting There & Away

Bus The buses leaving from Rue Yakoub el-Mansour should be sufficient for most destinations. CTM has daily buses to Casablanca, Dakhla, El-Jadida, Essaouira and Safi, Marrakesh, Smara and Laayoune, Tafraoute, Taroudannt and Tiznit.

SATAS has buses to Casablanca, Essaouira, Marrakesh, Tan Tan, Taroudannt and Tiznit.

The region's main bus terminal is actually in Inezgane, 13km south of Agadir, and you may arrive here. Plenty of local buses and grands taxis run between the two.

Taxi Grands taxis to Inezgane (Dr5) and Tiznit (Dr25) leave from a lot 1km south-east of the centre of town. Grands taxis leave from Inezgane to Essaouira, Taroudannt, Tiznit, Goulimime and Tan Tan.

Car The following are the main car-rental agencies in Agadir:

Avis
  (☎ 84 17 55) Ave Hassan II
  (☎ 83 92 44) airport
Budget
  (☎ 84 46 00) Bungalow Marhaba, Blvd Mohammed V
Europcar
  (☎ 84 02 03) Bungalow Marhaba, Blvd Mohammed V
Hertz
  (☎ 84 09 39) Bungalow Marhaba, Blvd Mohammed V
  (☎ 83 90 71) airport

TAROUDANNT
☎ 08

Taroudannt, with its magnificent, extremely well-preserved red-mud walls, has played an important part in the history of Morocco, and briefly became the capital under the Saadians in the 16th century.

Similar but much smaller and more relaxed than Marrakesh, Taroudannt makes a good

MOROCCO

day trip from Agadir; it's also well placed as a base from which to explore the western High Atlas. You'll find high-quality handicrafts, including Berber silver jewellery, limestone carvings and local carpets, in the souqs.

Things to See

You can explore the **ramparts** of Taroudannt on foot, but it's better to hire a bicycle or take one of the horse-drawn carriages (around Dr35 for half an hour).

The **Arab Souq**, to the east of Place al-Alaouyine, is where most of the quality crafts are to be found. The **Berber Souq**, south of Place an-Nasr, deals mainly in fruit, vegetables, spices and household goods.

Modest **tanneries** are just beyond Bab Taghount, north-west of Place al-Alaouyine. Turn left outside the gate and follow the signs.

Places to Stay

There are many cheap hotels in the centre, around or close to Place al-Alaouyine. On the square, it's a toss-up between the *Hôtel de la Place* and the *Hôtel Roudani*. Prices hover around Dr40/80 for singles/doubles.

The newer *Hôtel Tiout* (☎ 85 03 41), on Ave al-Jama' al-Kabir, has decent, clean rooms with bathroom for Dr100/150.

The best deal by far is the creaky-old *Hôtel Taroudant* (☎ 85 24 16). With rooms gathered around a tranquil, leafy courtyard, it's full of character. Singles/doubles without bathroom cost Dr40/68, with shower Dr64/95, and with shower and toilet Dr84/110. The water is boiling hot, the hotel has one of the few bars in town and the food in the restaurant is good and moderately priced.

Places to Eat

The small cafés that line the street between Place an-Nasr and Place al-Alaouyine serve traditional food such as soup, salads and tajine. Among these small cafés are several with seafood at rock-bottom prices.

Also good are the restaurants on the ground floors of the *Hôtel de la Place* and the *Hôtel Roudani* (Dr30 for generous serves of brochettes, chips and salad). The licensed restaurant at the *Hôtel Taroudant* offers both French and Moroccan dishes. There are set menus for Dr65 and Dr80.

Getting There & Away

CTM and SATAS have terminals on Place al-Alaouyine. SATAS buses run to Agadir and Marrakesh. CTM has a bus to Casablanca via Agadir and Marrakesh and another to Ouarzazate. Several smaller companies operate services from outside Bab Zorgan, the southern gate. Local buses going to Marrakesh over the Tizi n'Test pass leave from here at about 5 am. Grands taxis to Agadir (Inezgane) also leave from Bab Zorgan.

TIZNIT

☎ 08

In an arid corner of the Souss Valley at the end of the Anti-Atlas range, is Tiznit. With its 6km of encircling red-mud walls, it looks old but is actually a recent creation. It makes a pleasant short stop and the silver jewellery is reputed to be some of the best in the south.

Places to Stay

There's a fairly bare *camp site* between Bab Oulad Jarrar and the main roundabout. The budget hotels are mostly on or near Place al-Machouar, the main square within the city walls, and are all pretty similar.

The *Hôtel Belle-Vue* (☎ 86 21 09), off the square on Impasse Idakchouch, has large, sunny rooms for Dr60/70. A hot shower costs Dr5. On Place al-Machouar, the *Hôtel/Café Atlas* has rooms (some overlooking the square) for around Dr40 per person.

The two-star *Hôtel de Paris* (☎ 86 28 65), on Blvd Mohammed V by the roundabout, has clean and comfortable rooms with bathroom for Dr108/135. The hotel also has a restaurant.

Places to Eat

Several of the hotels on Place al-Machouar have restaurants, and there are a few cafés scattered around inside and outside the walls. At the *Restaurant Essaraha*, across Blvd Mohammed V from the main city gates, you can eat well for around Dr25. The market virtually next door is good for fresh food.

The *Café/Restaurant du Carrefour*, opposite the Hôtel de Paris, offers a particularly good breakfast featuring fresh almond and spicy agane oil.

Getting There & Away

Buses (including CTM and SATAS) leave from Place al-Machouar to Agadir, Essaouira, Casablanca, Marrakesh, Tafraoute and Sidi Ifni. Grands taxis to Agadir (Dr25) and Sidi Ifni (Dr25) leave from the main lot opposite the post office.

TAFRAOUTE

Some 107km east of Tiznit is the pretty Berber town of Tafraoute. The reason for visiting is the surrounding countryside. The nearby **Ameln Valley**, with its fields dotted with mud-brick villages, provides days of hiking possibilities. The journey up from Tiznit (or Agadir) into the heart of the Anti-Atlas to Tafraoute is well worth the effort.

Places to Stay & Eat

The cheapest places are the *Hôtel Tanger* (☎ 80 00 33), which offers basic rooms for Dr25 per person, and the *Hôtel Reddouane* (☎ 80 00 66), where singles/doubles cost Dr35/50.

Much better altogether is the *Hôtel Tafraout* (☎ 80 00 60), where you can get clean modern rooms for Dr50 per person. There's steaming hot water in the communal showers.

You can eat fairly well for about Dr25 in either of the two cheap hotels. The pleasant *Restaurant l'Étoile du Sud*, opposite the post office, has a good set menu for Dr70.

Getting There & Away

Transport is scarce. CTM runs a daily service to Tiznit and Agadir and local services run to Tiznit twice a day.

The High Atlas

MARRAKESH
☎ 04

Marrakesh is one of Morocco's most important artistic and cultural centres. It was founded in 1062 AD by the Almoravid sultan Youssef bin Tachfin but experienced its heyday under his son, Ali, who built the extensive underground irrigation canals (*khettara*) that still supply the city's gardens with water. Although Fès later gained in prominence as a result of the Almoravid conquest of Spain, Marrakesh remained the southern capital.

The city was largely razed by the Almohads in 1147, but they soon rebuilt what would remain the capital of the Almohad empire until its collapse in 1269. For the following 300 years the focus of Moroccan brilliance passed to Fès, but the Saadians made Marrakesh the capital again in the 16th century.

The mellah, Mouassine mosque and the mosque of Ali ben Youssef with its adjacent medersa were all built in Saadian times. In the 17th century, Moulay Ismail moved the capital to Meknès, and although Marrakesh remained an important base of central power, it only really came into its own again when the French built the ville nouvelle and revitalised the old town under the protectorate. Tourism has ensured its relative prosperity since then.

Orientation

As in other major Moroccan towns, the ville nouvelle and the medina are separate entities. The Djemaa el-Fna, Marrakesh's atmospheric main square, is the heart of the medina.

Information

Tourist Office On Place Abdel Moumen ben Ali, in the ville nouvelle, the tourist office (☎ 44 88 89) has the usual range of glossy leaflets and hotel lists. Official guides can be arranged here or in the big hotels for Dr150/120 for a full/half day.

Money Most banks are in the ville nouvelle but they can also be found near the Djemaa el-Fna. The BMCE opposite the tourist office and the one on Rue de Moulay Ismail have ATMs and exchange facilities open Monday to Friday.

American Express is represented by Voyages Schwartz (☎ 43 66 00) on the 1st floor of Immeuble Moutaouakil, 1 Rue Mauritania.

Post & Communications The main post office is on Place du 16 Novembre in the ville nouvelle. There is a branch office on the Djemaa el-Fna; the small telephone office downstairs sells phonecards.

MARRAKESH

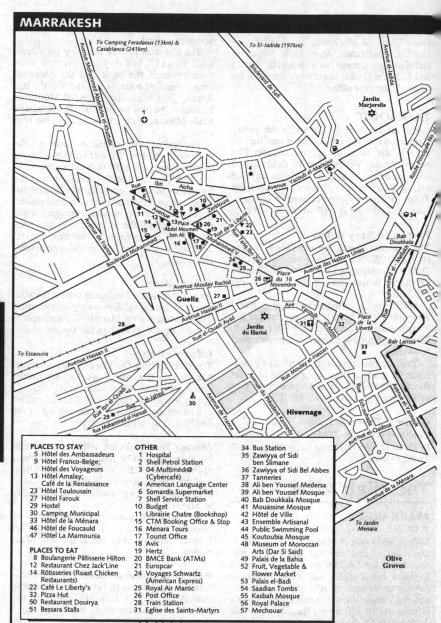

To Camping Feradaous (13km) &
Casablanca (241km)

To El-Jadida (197km)

Jardin
Marjorelle

Rue Ibn Aicha

Avenue Yacoub el-Mansour

Route Principale No 7?

Bab
Doukkala

Avenue Abdel Moumen
ben Ali

Place Abdel Moumen ben Ali

Rue de la Liberté

Avenue des Nations Unies

Rue Moulay el-Mehdi

Boulevard Mohammed

Avenue Moulay Rachid

Gueliz

Avenue Hassan II

Ave Yacoub al-Mansour

Place
de la
Liberté

Jardin
du Hartsi

Bab Larissa

To Essaouira

Avenue Hassan II

Rue el-Quadi Ayad

Rue Moulay el-Hassan

Avenue el-Yamouk

Rue Ibn el-Quadi

Rue el-Jahed

Avenue de France

Avenue du President Kennedy

Rue Echouhada

Hivernage

Avenue el-Qadissa

Rue Mohammed el-Hansali

To Jardin
Menara

Avenue de la Menara

Olive
Groves

PLACES TO STAY
5   Hôtel des Ambassadeurs
9   Hôtel Franco-Belge;
    Hôtel des Voyageurs
13 Hôtel Amalay;
    Café de la Renaissance
23 Hôtel Toulousain
27 Hôtel Farouk
29 Hostel
30 Camping Municipal
33 Hôtel de la Ménara
46 Hôtel de Foucauld
47 Hôtel La Mamounia

PLACES TO EAT
8   Boulangerie Pâtisserie Hilton
12 Restaurant Chez Jack'Line
14 Rôtisseries (Roast Chicken
    Restaurants)
22 Café Le Liberty's
32 Pizza Hut
50 Restaurant Douirya
51 Bessara Stalls

OTHER
1   Hospital
2   Shell Petrol Station
3   04 Multimédi@
    (Cybercafé)
4   American Language Center
6   Somardis Supermarket
7   Shell Service Station
10 Budget
11 Librairie Chatre (Bookshop)
15 CTM Booking Office & Stop
16 Menara Tours
17 Tourist Office
18 Avis
19 Hertz
20 BMCE Bank (ATMs)
21 Europcar
24 Voyages Schwartz
    (American Express)
25 Royal Air Maroc
26 Post Office
28 Train Station
31 Eglise des Saints-Martyrs

34 Bus Station
35 Zawiyya of Sidi
    ben Slimane
36 Zawiyya of Sidi Bel Abbes
37 Tanneries
38 Ali ben Youssef Medersa
39 Ali ben Youssef Mosque
40 Bab Doukkala Mosque
41 Mouassine Mosque
42 Hôtel de Ville
43 Ensemble Artisanal
44 Public Swimming Pool
45 Koutoubia Mosque
48 Museum of Moroccan
    Arts (Dar Si Said)
49 Palais de la Bahia
52 Fruit, Vegetable &
    Flower Market
53 Palais el-Badi
54 Saadian Tombs
55 Kasbah Mosque
56 Royal Palace
57 Mechouar

MOROCCO

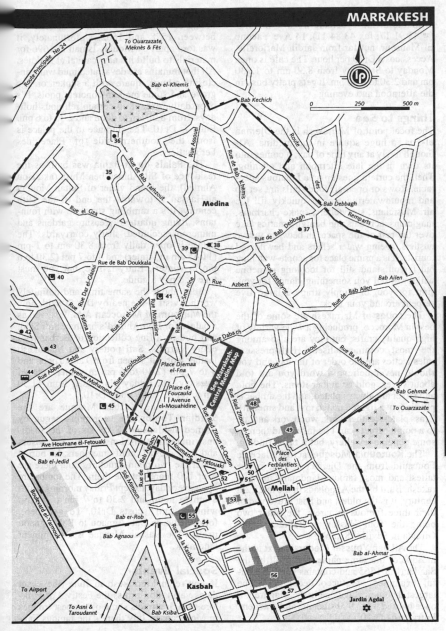

MARRAKESH

Medina

Kasbah

Mellah

Jardin Agdal

To Ouarzazate,
Meknès & Fès

Bab el-Khemis

Bab Kechich

Bab Debbagh

Bab Ailen

Bab Gehmat

To Ouarzazate

Bab al-Ahmar

Bab Ksiba

To Asni &
Taroudannt

To Airport

Bab er-Rob

Bab Agnaou

Bab el-Jedid

Remparts

Route Principale No 24

Rue Assouel

Rue de Bab Khemis

Rue de Bab Tarhzout

Rue el Gza

Rue de Bab Doukkala

Rue Dar el-Ghaoui

Rue Sidi el-Yamani

Fatima Zahra

Rue Mouassine

Rue Souq as-Sma nine

Rue Dabach

Rue Azbezt

Rue Iseddyne

Rue el-Koutoubia

Avenue Mohammed V

Sebti

Rue Abbes

Avenue
el-Mouahidine

Ave Houmane el-Fetouaki

Ave Houmane
el-Fetouaki

Boulevard el-Yarmouk

Rue de la Kasbah

Rue Sidi Mimoun

Rue de Bab Agnaou

Rue Riad Zitoun el-Jedid

Rue Riad Zitoun el-Qdim

Graoui

Rue Ba Ahmad

Place Djemaa
el-Fna

Place de
Foucauld

See Marrakesh:
Central Medina Map

Place
des
Ferblantiers

35
36
37
38
39
40
41
42
43
44
45
46
47
48
49
50
51
52
53
54
55
56
57

0   250   500 m

MOROCCO

Cybercafés Internet access (and coffee!) is available at the cybercafé 04 Multimédi@ (☎ 43 91 17; fax 43 84 11), 14 Ave Yacoub El-Mansour, not far from Jardin Marjorelle. Access costs Dr30 per hour. The café is open Monday to Saturday from 8.30 am to 12.30 pm and 2.30 to 8.30 pm. It gets pretty busy in the afternoon and evening.

Things to See

The focal point of Marrakesh is the **Djemaa el-Fna**, a huge square in the medina. Although lively at any time of day, it comes into its own in the late afternoon and evening. Then the curtain goes up on a fabulous spectacle. Rows of open-air food stalls are set up and mouthwatering aromas quickly fill the air. Musicians, storytellers, snake charmers, magicians, acrobats and benign lunatics take over the rest of the space. In between weave hustlers, ageing water sellers and bewildered tourists. It is a prime place for people-watching but if you stand still for too long someone will try to sell you something, dance for you, sing for you, or simply drape a large live serpent around your neck.

The **souqs** of Marrakesh are some of the best in Morocco, producing a wide variety of high-quality crafts, but they are also among the most commercialised. High-pressure sales tactics are the order of the day and you should never believe a word you are told about silver, gold or amber items. The gold and silver are always plated, and the amber is plastic (put a lighted match to it and smell it). Brass plates, leather work, woodwork and, up to a point, carpets can't be faked and there is some genuine jewellery, but it takes finding.

The **Koutoubia Mosque**, across Place de Foucauld from the Djemaa el-Fna, is the tallest and most famous landmark in Marrakesh. Built by the Almohads in the late 12th century, it is the oldest and best preserved of their three famous minarets, the other two being the Tour Hassan in Rabat and the Giralda in Seville (Spain).

The **Ali ben Youssef Medersa**, next to the mosque of the same name, was built by the Saadians in 1565 and contains some beautiful examples of stucco decoration. The largest theological college in the Maghreb, it once housed up to 900 students and teachers. Entry costs Dr10.

Marrakesh's most famous palace was the **Palais el-Badi**, built by Ahmed al-Mansour between 1578 and 1602. Unfortunately, it was torn apart by Moulay Ismail in 1696 for materials to build his new capital at Meknès. All that remains are devastated mud walls enclosing a huge square with a sunken orange grove and some modern concrete pools. It's open daily, except on certain religious holidays, from 8.30 am to noon and 2.30 to 6 pm. Entry is Dr10. The entrance to the palace is from the southern side of Place des Ferblantiers.

The **Palais de la Bahia** was built as the residence of Si' Ahmed ben Musa (aka Bou Ahmed), the grand vizier of Sultan Moulay al-Hassan I, towards the end of the 19th century. It's a rambling structure with fountains, living quarters, pleasure gardens and numerous secluded, shady courtyards. The palace is open daily from 8.30 am to 1 pm (11.45 am in winter) and 4 to 7 pm (2.30 to 6 pm in winter). Entry is free, but you must take and pay a guide.

Built about the same time and definitely worth a visit is the nearby **Dar Si Said**, now the **Museum of Moroccan Arts**. It served as a palace for Bou Ahmed's brother, Sidi Said, and houses a fine collection of Berber jewellery, carpets, Safi pottery and Marrakesh leather work. It's open from 9 am to noon and 4 to 7 pm (2.30 to 6 pm in winter); closed Tuesday. On Friday it's closed from 11.30 am to 3 pm. Entry costs Dr10.

Next to the Kasbah Mosque are the **Saadian Tombs**, the necropolis begun by Ahmed al-Mansour. Sixty-six of the Saadians, including Al-Mansour, his successors and their closest family members, lie buried under the two main structures, and there are over 100 more outside them. The tombs are open every day, except Friday morning, from 8 am to noon and 2.30 to 7 pm (6 pm in winter). Entry costs Dr10. To get there, follow Rue de Bab Agnaou to Bab Agnaou itself – the Kasbah Mosque is a prominent landmark.

Special Events

If you're in Marrakesh in June (the exact dates vary), don't miss the Festival of Folklore, which attracts some of the best troupes in Morocco. In July there's the famous Fantasia, featuring charging Berber horsemen outside the ramparts.

Places to Stay

Camping The only camp site in Marrakesh is *Camping Ferdaous* (☎ 31 31 67) 13km north of town on the road to Casablanca. There's little shade. It costs Dr12 per person, Dr12 per tent, Dr11 per car and Dr18 for electricity. The site has a swimming pool and a grocery store.

Hostel The *hostel* (☎ 44 77 13) is close to the train station but a long walk from the medina. Beds cost Dr20 a night and hot showers are Dr5. You'll need your membership card. It's open from 8 to 9 am, noon to 2 pm and 6 to 10 pm.

Hotels – Djemaa el-Fna There are plenty of small hotels in the area south of the Djemaa el-Fna. Most of the cheaper ones charge extra for showers. Rooms start at Dr30 per person. The very bright and welcoming *Hôtel Essaouira* (☎ 44 38 05) is a cut above some of its neighbours. Rooms cost from Dr30 to Dr40 per person and a hot shower is Dr5. There's a pleasant roof terrace and space to do laundry.

The *Hôtel Afrique* (☎ 44 24 03) has a courtyard full of orange trees and clean, tiled rooms with washbasin for Dr40/70. A hot shower costs Dr5. The *Hôtel Chellah* (☎ 44 29 77), just off Rue Zitoune el-Qedim, is easier to get to than some of the other cheapies. Spotless rooms with washbasin cost Dr40 per person. A hot shower is Dr10.

The popular *Hôtel Souria* (☎ 44 59 70) has decent rooms for Dr70/90, but the shower is cold. The hotel has a small private terrace.

The *Hôtel Ali* (☎ 44 49 79), just south of the Djemaa el-Fna, is excellent value and a longtime favourite with travellers. Rooms with shower and toilet cost Dr70/90. A bed on the terrace is Dr30. The hotel also has a good restaurant and can help organise High Atlas treks and other excursions. Nearby, the *Hôtel Ichbilia* (☎ 39 04 86) and the *Hôtel La Gazelle* (☎ 44 11 12) have decent rooms with washbasin for Dr60/100.

One of the nicest places in Marrakesh is the *Hôtel Sherazade* (☎/fax 42 93 05), just off Rue Zitoune el-Qedim, a two-minute walk from the Djemaa el-Fna. Housed in two adjoining *riads* (large homes built around central courtyards), the hotel offers a variety of rooms at different prices. The more expensive rooms (from Dr200/250 for singles/doubles with bathroom) look onto the tranquil, tiled courtyards. There's also a mini-apartment with kitchen and two single beds for Dr275/325 for one/two people. An extra bed costs Dr50. Opening onto the pleasant roof terrace are five cheaper rooms without bathroom which cost from Dr120/170. The shared showers are always hot and don't cost any extra. Breakfast is Dr30 and other meals are available on request. It's best to book ahead.

Another comfortable option is the two-star *Hôtel Gallia* (☎ 44 59 13; fax 44 48 53), 30 Rue de la Recette. Singles/doubles without shower cost Dr135/190 and rooms with shower are Dr188/251, including breakfast. The rooms are nicely decorated and have heating and air-conditioning. There's a nice roof terrace, too. Again, it's best to book.

The *Hôtel de Foucauld* (☎ 44 54 99; fax 44 13 44), Ave el-Mouahidine, has some pleasant tiled rooms with full bathroom and air-conditioning for Dr144/174. There's plenty of hot water and the hotel has its own restaurant.

There are a couple of hotels on the Djemaa el-Fna itself. The *Hôtel de France* (☎ 44 23 19) has good-value, spacious rooms with washbasin and desk for Dr60 per person. The *Hôtel CTM* (☎ 44 23 25) has ordinary rooms without shower for Dr68/92 and singles/doubles with shower for Dr92/132. The rooms at the back are quiet.

Hotels – Ville Nouvelle The ville nouvelle has very few cheap hotels. The quiet *Hôtel Toulousain* (☎ 43 00 33; fax 43 14 46), 44 Rue Tariq Ben Ziad, is good value. Pleasant singles/doubles without shower cost Dr90/125; rooms with shower are Dr115/150. The hotel has two shady courtyards, plenty of hot water and space for parking.

The *Hôtel Farouk* (☎ 43 19 89; fax 43 36 09), 66 Ave Hassan II, isn't a bad deal either, with basic but clean rooms with bathroom for Dr80/120. The hotel has a restaurant.

The *Hôtel des Voyageurs* (☎ 44 72 18), 40 Blvd Mohammed Zerktouni, is quite old but

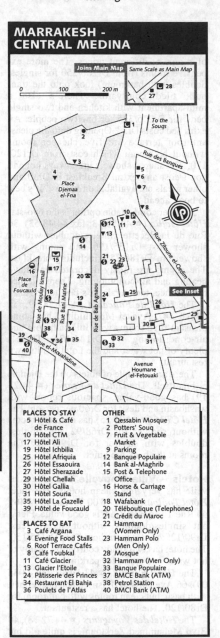

MARRAKESH - CENTRAL MEDINA

Joins Main Map

Same Scale as Main Map

0   100   200 m

To the Souqs

Rue des Banques

Place Djemaa el-Fna

Rue Zitoune el-Qedim

Place de Foucauld

Rue de Moulay Ismail

Rue Bani Marine

Rue de Bab Agnaou

See Inset

Avenue el-Mouahidine

Avenue Houmane el-Fetouaki

PLACES TO STAY
5   Hôtel & Café de France
10 Hôtel CTM
17 Hôtel Ali
19 Hôtel Ichbilia
25 Hôtel Afriquia
26 Hôtel Essaouira
27 Hôtel Sherazade
29 Hôtel Chellah
30 Hôtel Gallia
31 Hôtel Souria
35 Hôtel La Gazelle
39 Hôtel de Foucauld

PLACES TO EAT
3   Café Argana
4   Evening Food Stalls
6   Roof Terrace Cafés
8   Café Toubkal
11 Café Glacier
13 Glacier l'Etoile
24 Pâtisserie des Princes
34 Restaurant El Bahja
36 Poulets de l'Atlas

OTHER
1   Qessabin Mosque
2   Potters' Souq
7   Fruit & Vegetable Market
9   Parking
12 Banque Populaire
14 Bank al-Maghrib
15 Post & Telephone Office
16 Horse & Carriage Stand
18 Wafabank
20 Téléboutique (Telephones)
21 Crédit du Maroc
22 Hammam (Women Only)
23 Hammam Polo (Men Only)
28 Mosque
32 Hammam (Men Only)
33 Banque Populaire
37 BMCE Bank (ATM)
38 Petrol Station
40 BMCI Bank (ATM)

spotlessly clean. Simple rooms cost Dr80 per person and rooms with bathroom are Dr110. The nearby *Hôtel Franco-Belge* (☎ 44 84 72) is clean but overpriced. Singles/doubles without shower cost Dr100/130; rooms with shower are Dr130/150.

Most of the mid-range and top-end hotels are in the ville nouvelle. The *Hôtel des Ambassadeurs* (☎ 44 71 59), on the corner of Rue Ibn Aicha and Ave Mohammed V, has comfortable rooms with full bathroom, heating and air-conditioning for Dr223/260. The *Hôtel Amalay* (☎ 43 13 67; fax 43 15 54), near the Café de la Renaissance, is another decent mid-range choice. Spacious, squeaky-clean rooms with bathroom, TV, phone and air-conditioning, cost Dr260/315.

Closer to the medina is the *Hôtel de la Ménara* (☎ 43 64 78; fax 44 73 86), Ave des Remparts, overlooking Place de la Liberté. The large rooms are self-contained, have balconies and cost Dr316/414 including breakfast. The hotel has a restaurant, bar, swimming pool and tennis courts.

Places to Eat

Medina The cheapest, liveliest place to eat is on the Djemaa el-Fna itself. By the time the sun sets, a good portion of the square is taken over by food stalls, each specialising in a certain type of food. Some offer harira and honey cakes, others specialise in brochettes and salad or fish and chips. Look for the stalls busy with locals. A full meal shouldn't cost more than Dr25 and a bowl of soup is just Dr2. Around the stalls are dozens of orange juice stands where you can down a tall glass of freshly squeezed juice for Dr2.50.

There are several café restaurants around the edge of the Djemaa el-Fna where you can eat well for Dr40 or less. The *Café Toubkal*, in the far south-east corner near Rue Zitoune el-Qedim, is so popular that it's almost always crammed with locals. The salads, brochettes and tajines are all very good. The *Café de France*, on the east side of the square, is a little more expensive (Dr30 for tajine or couscous) but the food is generally good (try the Moroccan salad and couscous with chickpeas) and the restaurant itself is a pleasant, cool place to sit.

There are a few small restaurants along the pedestrianised Rue de Bab Agnaou and Rue

Bani Marine. The *Restaurant El Bahja*, near the Hôtel La Gazelle, serves decent three-course set menus from Dr40. At the southern end of Rue Bani Marine you'll find the tiny *Poulets de l'Atlas* (Chicken of the Atlas!) which does excellent chicken and chips.

Many of the hotels in the medina have restaurants. The *Hôtel Ali* serves a very good-value buffet from 6.30 to 10.30 pm every night. For Dr60 (less for hotel residents) you can load up your plate from various pots of typical Moroccan fare, along with salad, vegetables and fruit or dessert.

For a splurge, you can always try one of the city's palace restaurants. The *Restaurant Douirya* (☎ 40 30 30; fax 40 30 55), 14 Derb Jedid Essalame in the Mellah, has had good reviews. Fixed menus are around Dr200.

For breakfast, there are a couple of decent cafés on Rue de Bab Agnaou. The *Glacier l'Etoile* on the corner serves consistently good coffee (Dr6) and the *Pâtisserie des Princes*, farther down, offers a range of Moroccan and French pastries. For bessara lovers, you'll find a couple of early morning stalls around Place des Ferblantiers in the Mellah.

Ville Nouvelle There are plenty of medium-priced restaurants to choose from in the new city and almost all the hotels have restaurants. For those in need of the familiar, *Pizza Hut*, Ave Mohammed V, offers decent pizzas from Dr50. The *Restaurant Chez Jack'Line* (☎ 44 75 47) is a quirky French-style restaurant presided over by Madame Jack'Line and her 23-year-old parrot. Excellent three-course set menus cost Dr68 (more in the evening); a la carte main courses cost from Dr55. The restaurant is licensed.

Near the Café de la Renaissance are a couple of well-patronised *rôtisseries* offering fresh roast chicken and chips for around Dr20.

For a mouthwatering selection of sweet and savoury things (including pastilla) don't miss the *Boulangerie Pâtisserie Hilton*, opposite the Café de la Renaissance. The café *Le Liberty's*, 23 Rue de la Liberté, is a quiet, shady spot for breakfast or lunch.

Getting There & Away

Bus The bus station is just outside the city walls by Bab Doukkala. This is a 20-minute walk or a Dr10 taxi ride from the Djemaa el-Fna.

Train The train station is on Ave Hassan II and a long way from the Djemaa el-Fna. Take a taxi or bus No 8 into the centre. Trains operate regularly from Marrakesh to Casablanca (four hours) and Rabat (five hours). From there they continue to either Tangier (10½ hours) or Meknès (seven hours) and Fès (eight hours). These trips sometimes involve changes.

Car Car-rental agencies in Marrakesh include:

Avis
 (☎ 43 37 27; fax 44 94 85) 137 Ave Mohammed V
Budget
 (☎ 43 11 87) 68 Blvd Mohammed Zerktouni
Europcar
 (☎ 43 12 28) 63 Blvd Mohammed Zerktouni
Hertz
 (☎/fax 43 46 80) 154 Ave Mohammed V
Novaloc
 (☎/fax 43 24 93) 61 Yougoslavie Passage

Getting Around

A taxi to the airport should be no more than Dr60, but you'll be lucky. Bus No 11 runs irregularly between the airport and Djemaa el-Fna.

A petit taxi between the train station and Djemaa el-Fna should cost Dr10 (with difficulty). Bus No 8 does the same run for Dr2. Taxi trips around town should cost no more than Dr10, but insist that the meter is used.

Horse carriages are an expensive way to get around – the fares are posted in French and Arabic in the cab.

AROUND MARRAKESH

The road between Marrakesh and Taroudannt goes over the spectacular 2092m **Tizi n'Test pass**, one of the highest passes in Morocco. It's a good, if sometimes hairy, road and the views are magnificent. On the way, a worthwhile stop is the partly restored **Tin Mal Mosque**, the launch pad for the Almohad campaign of conquest in the 12th century.

MOROCCO

HIGH ATLAS TREKKING

If you have good shoes or boots, plenty of warm clothes and a sleeping bag, the ascent of Jebel Toubkal (4167m), Morocco's highest mountain, is worth making. It's a beautiful area and on clear days there are incredible views.

You don't need mountaineering skills, as long as you go outside the winter months and take the normal route from Imlil and stay at the Toubkal hut for the night. You can do this trek in two days – up to the Toubkal hut the first day, and up to the summit and back down again the second.

The usual starting point for the trek is the village of Imlil, 17km south of Asni on the Tizi n'Test road from Marrakesh to Agadir. Other possible starting points are the villages of Setti Fatma and Oukaïmeden in the Ourika Valley, but these involve longer treks.

Guides

You don't need a guide for the normal two-day trek, but longer treks will almost certainly require a guide and mule. You can arrange this in Imlil at the CAF Refuge or Bureau des Guides. In Marrakesh, the Hôtel Ali (☎ 44 49 79; fax 43 36 09) and the Hôtel de Foucauld (☎ 44 54 99; fax 44 13 44), both near the Djemaa el-Fna, are good places to track down experienced mountain guides.

Official guides carry ID cards and the official prices for guides, mules and muleteers are published annually in *The Great Trek through the Moroccan Atlas*, a very useful tourist office booklet generally available only in Marrakesh.

Guidebooks

For information beyond the two-day trek, consult the *Great Atlas Traverse – Morocco* by Michael Peyron. Volume I (Moussa Gorges to Aït ben Wgemmez) covers the Toubkal area. Another excellent guide (in French) is *Le Haut Atlas Central* by André Fougerolles. Detailed maps are available in Rabat (see Maps in the Facts for the Visitor section).

Imlil

Most trekkers stay in Imlil for the first night. Stock up here for the trek, as there's nothing available farther up the mountain. The Imlil shops have a wide range of food including bread, canned and packaged goods, mineral water, soft drinks and cigarettes, but no beer.

Places to Stay & Eat The cheapest place to stay in Imlil is the *Club Alpin Français (CAF) Refuge* in the village square. It offers dormitory-style accommodation for Dr20 (CAF members), Dr30 (HI members) and Dr40 (nonmembers), plus there's a common room with an open fireplace, cooking facilities (Dr5 for use of gas), cutlery and crockery. Bookings for *refuges* (huts) farther up cannot be made from here, but instead must go through the CAF (☎ 27 00 90; fax 29 72 92), BP 6178, Casablanca 01, or through CAF, BP 888, Marrakesh.

Good deals in Imlil include the *Hôtel L'Aine*, which charges Dr30 per person in comfortable and bright rooms, and the *Café Soleil* (☎ 31 92 09 in Asni), which has singles/doubles with shower for Dr40/70.

Chez Jean Pierre (☎ 44 91 05 in Marrakesh), just out of Imlil on the road to Ouanesskra, has four simple, spotlessly clean rooms and a recommended restaurant. Demi-pension costs Dr135 per person.

Discovery Ltd, a UK company which specialises in small group trips to the High Atlas, has restored the kasbah on the hill above Imlil. Beds are available in three large rooms which have dorm space above mezzanine floors and comfortable Moroccan-style salons below. Demi-pension costs Dr130/220. The meals are excellent. You can camp for Dr20 per person. Bookings can be made through the Hôtel de Foucauld in Marrakesh.

All the hotels have restaurants offering standard Moroccan meals from around Dr30.

The Two-Day Trek

The first day takes you from Imlil to the Toubkal hut (3207m) via the villages of Aroumd and Sidi Chamharouch. This takes about five hours. Bottled drinks are usually available at both these villages. The Toubkal hut has beds for 29 people in two dorms, but you must provide your own bedding. There's a kitchen with a gas stove and cooking utensils. It costs Dr60 per person for non-CAF members, plus an extra charge if you use the cooking facilities or hot water. There's a resident warden. You must bring all your own food, although the warden may, if given plenty of notice, prepare meals for you. In the high season you may find it full, so book ahead.

The ascent from the hut to the summit should take you about four hours and the descent about two. Carry water with you – any water from the streams on the mountainside should be boiled or treated or there's a fair chance you'll pick up giardia. It can be bitterly cold at the top even in summer.

Other Treks

The five-hour trek north-east from Imlil to Tacheddirt is a good, longer alternative. The walk takes you over a pass at 3000m, above the snow line, then down the other side and up again. There's a good *CAF refuge* here with panoramic views where you can stay for Dr40, plus Dr5 if you use the gas for cooking.

Many other treks are possible from Tacheddirt, including a one or two-day walk to the village of Setti Fatma at the head of the Ourika Valley. There are several cheap hotels here and local buses (Dr10) and taxis to Marrakesh.

The possibilities for even longer treks in the Toubkal area are almost unlimited. A popular seven to 10-day circuit takes in Toubkal, Lake Sidi Ifni, Tacheddirt, Oukaïmeden and Tizi Oussem.

Getting There & Away

There are frequent buses (Dr10) and grands taxis (Dr13) to Asni from Bab er-Rob in Marrakesh. From Asni, trucks operate fairly frequently to Imlil and will take passengers for around Dr15. Grand Taxis cost DR15.

Southern Morocco

OUARZAZATE

☎ 04

Ouarzazate (pronounced War-zazat) was created by the French as a garrison and regional administrative centre in 1928 and now has about 30,000 inhabitants.

The best thing about Ouarzazate is the journey there from Marrakesh over the Tizi n'Tichka pass which offers superb views over the mountains and into the valleys.

Ouarzazate's other draw card is the spectacular **Kasbah of Aït Benhaddou**, 32km north of town off the Marrakesh road.

Information

The helpful tourist office (☎ 88 24 85) is in the centre of town, opposite the post office. The Banque Populaire on Blvd Mohammed V is open for exchange on weekends. For cash advances go to the Crédit du Maroc at the western end of Blvd Mohammed V.

Things to See

The only place worth visiting in Ouarzazate is the partly restored **Taourirt Kasbah** at the eastern end of town. Built in the 19th century by the powerful Glaoui dynasty, the kasbah would have housed family members as well as hundreds of servants and workers. The kasbah is open daily from 8 am to noon and 3 to 6.30 pm. Entry costs Dr10.

Places to Stay & Eat

There's a *camp site* (signposted) next to the so-called Tourist Complex off the main road out of town towards Tinerhir, about 3km from the bus station.

It can be difficult to find a cheap hotel in Ouarzazate if you arrive late in the day. The *Hôtel Royal* (☎ 88 22 58), 24 Blvd Mohammed V, has spotless singles/doubles without shower for Dr51/72 and rooms with shower for Dr81/92. The nearby *Hôtel Atlas* (☎ 88 23 07), 13 Rue du Marché, has rooms with shower for Dr41/75.

The friendly *Hôtel La Vallée* (☎ 85 40 34; fax 85 40 43), about 2km out of town on the Zagora road, has pleasantly furnished rooms from Dr120. The hotel also has a small pool and a good restaurant.

The *Restaurant Essalam*, just off Blvd Mohammed V, offers eight set menus for Dr55. The bright restaurant at the Hôtel Atlas also offers cheap meals. *Chez Dimitri*, next to the Hôtel Royal, serves good French and Moroccan dishes (around Dr170 with wine).

Getting There & Away

CTM has a terminal on Blvd Mohammed V, near the post office. SATAS and other lines depart from a new bus station about 1km north-west of town.

MOROCCO

CTM buses go to Agadir, Casablanca, Er-Rachidia (via Boumalne du Dadès, seven hours), Marrakesh (five hours) and Zagora/ M'Hamid (four hours to Zagora). The other companies have more and slightly cheaper services. Grands taxis leave from the main bus lot to Zagora (Dr80), Boumalne (Dr50) and Marrakesh (Dr100).

Car Since the Drâa Valley makes such a spectacular journey, consider renting a car in Ouarzazate. Some of the main agencies are:

Avis
   (☎ 88 48 70) Corner Blvd Mohammed V & Rue A Sehraoui
Budget
   (☎ 88 35 65) Résidence Al-Warda, Blvd Mohammed V
Europcar
   (☎ 88 20 35) Bureau 4, Place du 3 Mars
Hertz
   (☎ 88 20 84) 33 Blvd Mohammed V

THE DRÂA VALLEY & ZAGORA
☎ 04
The journey through the Drâa Valley, with its crumbling red-mud kasbahs and lush, green palmeraies hemmed in by craggy desert cliffs, is a thoroughly exotic experience.

Zagora, the valley's administrative centre, is fairly dull but it's a good place to stop for a night or two on a tour of the south. It's in Zagora that you'll find the famous sign, 'Timbuktoo 52 jours' – by camel.

All the hotels in Zagora can arrange camel treks.

Places to Stay & Eat
There are a couple of good sites near the palmeraies south of town. *Camping d'Amezrou*, is a pleasant site about 200m past the Hôtel La Fibule. *Camping Montagne* is about 2km away, at the foot of Jebel Zagora. Bring your own food.

The unclassified *Hôtel Vallée du Drâa* (☎ 84 72 10), Blvd Mohammed V, has simple singles/doubles for Dr50/65 and rooms with bathroom for Dr77/100. Nearby, the *Hôtel des Amis* has basic rooms for Dr25 per person.

The refurbished *Hôtel de la Palmeraie* (☎ 84 70 08), Blvd Mohammed V, has

singles/doubles without shower for Dr50 per person and rooms with bathroom for Dr85/ 150. The hotel has a bar and a restaurant.

The relaxing *Hôtel La Fibule* (☎ 84 73 18; fax 84 72 71), on the south side of the Oued Drâa, is built in traditional Berber style. Doubles cost Dr190 with shower and Dr360 with full bathroom and air-con. It has a restaurant, bar and swimming pool.

For cheap eats there are quite a few places along Blvd Mohammed V. The *Restaurant Timbouctou* and the *Café Snak Ennahda* are both popular with the locals. The most pleasant places for a meal are the hotel restaurants, where you'll pay from Dr70.

Getting There & Away
The CTM terminal is at the south-western end of Blvd Mohammed V. There's a daily 7 am service (Dr35) to Ouarzazate (and on to Marrakesh) and a 4 pm departure for M'Hamid. Other buses leave from a separate dirt lot by the market. Grands taxis cost Dr80 per person to Ouarzazate.

SOUTH OF ZAGORA
About 18km south of Zagora is the small town of **Tamegroute** which has a *zawiyya* (religious foundation) containing an old Koranic library with texts dating back to the 13th century. There's also a small pottery factory in the town and a Saturday souq.

The *Restaurant Auberge Jnane-Dar* (☎ 84 86 22), opposite the library, has eight rooms with shared bathroom (hot water) for Dr60/100. It's a quiet relaxing place with a lovely big garden.

At the end of the road, about 95km south of Zagora, is the village of **M'Hamid**. The attraction again is the journey itself which takes you across stony desert and through lush oases. There are several places to stay in M'Hamid, including the friendly *Hôtel Restaurant Sahara* (☎ 84 80 09), which has basic rooms for Dr30 per person. Camel treks can be arranged here.

BOUMALNE DU DADÈS & THE DADÈS GORGE
☎ 04
The Dadès, the first gorge on the road from Ouarzazate to Er-Rachidia, is peppered with

magnificent *ksour* (fortified strongholds), both ruined and lived-in. The rock formations make this valley one of Morocco's most fantastic sites.

A bumpy tarmac road wiggles through this fantasia for about 27km from the main Ouarzazate-Boumalne road, after which it reverts to a dirt track requiring a 4WD.

Places to Stay & Eat

In the Gorge You'll find a cluster of hotels right up where the bitumen road runs out. Just before, in Aït Oudinar, there's the *Auberge des Gorges du Dadès* (☎ 83 17 10) on the river. Simple singles/doubles cost Dr40/60 (communal hot showers) and classier self-contained rooms cost Dr100/140. Breakfast is included. There's also space to camp.

Farther up is the *Hôtel La Gazelle du Dadès* where spotless rooms with two or three beds cost Dr60. The popular *Hôtel La Kasbah de la Vallée* (☎ 83 17 17) has a few double rooms without shower for Dr60 and singles/doubles with bathroom for Dr80/120. At both you can pitch a tent by the river or sleep on the roof for Dr20.

The new *Hôtel Le Vieux Chateaux du Dadès* (☎ 83 17 10) has bright, clean rooms without shower for Dr40/60 and rooms with bathroom for Dr100/140. All the hotels in the gorge have restaurants. Any supplies you might want should be purchased in Boumalne du Dadès.

Boumalne du Dadès There are plenty of accommodation options in town. The *Hôtel Adrar* (☎ 83 03 55) is a popular cheapie with singles/doubles for Dr40/60. Farther up the hill heading east, the new *Hôtel Al Manadire* (☎ 83 01 72) has singles/doubles without shower for Dr30/50 and rooms with shower for Dr60/100.

Built in kasbah style, the comfy *Kasbah Tizzarouine* (☎ 83 06 90; fax 83 02 56) offers double rooms with half-pension for Dr220.

The Hôtel Adrar has its own basic restaurant; the restaurant at the Kasbah Tizzarouine is very good and reasonably priced (about Dr80 for dinner).

Getting There & Away

CTM runs two daily buses to Ouarzazate and one to Er-Rachidia. As is usual in smaller places like this, grands taxis are probably a better bet. The fare is Dr40 to Ouarzazate, Dr14 to Tinerhir and about Dr10 to Aït Oudinar, at the top of the gorge.

TINERHIR & THE TODRA GORGE
☎ 04

The spectacular Todra Gorge is 15km from Tinerhir, at the end of a lush valley of palmeraies and mud-brick villages. It's best visited in the morning, when the sun penetrates to the bottom, turning the rock from rose pink to a deep ochre. The area is becoming increasingly popular with rock climbers and in the high season can get very busy with large tour groups.

Places to Stay & Eat

In the Gorge There are three good camp sites along the road to the gorge, about 9km from Tinerhir: the *Auberge de l'Atlas* (☎ 83 42 09), *Camping Le Lac* and *Camping Auberge*. You'll pay about Dr10 per person and up to Dr15 to pitch a tent. There's a small grocery shop across from the Auberge de l'Atlas.

Within the gorge, the *Hôtel Restaurant les Roches* (☎ 83 48 14) has doubles without/with shower for Dr60/150, including breakfast. A place in the big Berber tent costs Dr20. Next door, the *Hôtel Restaurant Yasmina* (☎ 83 42 07) has rooms with bathroom for Dr83/110. In summer you can sleep on the roof for Dr20 a head.

Just by the gorge entrance, the *Hôtel Le Mansour* and the *Etoile de la Gorge* (☎ 83 51 58) have very basic rooms from Dr30/60.

In Tinerhir The *Hôtel El Fath*, 56 Ave Hassan II, has simple singles/doubles for Dr35/75. They promise hot water in the shared shower. The *Hôtel Al-Qods*, at the end of the block, has bright, basic rooms for Dr30/60.

Behind Ave Hassan II near the central market area is the *Hôtel de l'Avenir* (☎/fax 83 45 99). It has a friendly atmosphere and pleasant rooms for Dr60/100. The restaurant serves a decent paella, too. The *Hôtel Tomboctou* (☎ 83 46 04; fax 83 35 05), off

MOROCCO

Mohammed V on Ave Bir Anzarane, is in an old kasbah which has been carefully restored and beautifully furnished by the Spanish owner Roger Mimó. Very comfortable rooms cost Dr230/300.

There are a few simple restaurants on Ave Hassan II, including the *Café des Amis* which is a popular spot for freshly grilled brochettes. The *Restaurant La Kasbah* and the restaurant in the *Hôtel L'Oasis* both have three-course menus for Dr70.

Getting There & Away

CTM has a couple of buses that pass through on their way east to Er-Rachidia and west to Ouarzazate and on to Marrakesh. Only a few seats are set aside for passengers boarding at Tinerhir. Several other bus lines have services east and west, and there are grands taxis, too. Some taxis head up to the Todra Gorge (stress that you want a place in a shared taxi), and there are trucks to High Atlas villages beyond, especially on Monday after the market.

Portugal

Spirited yet unassuming, Portugal has a dusty patina of faded grandeur; the quiet remains of a far-flung colonialist realm. Even as it flows towards the economic mainstream of the European Union (EU), and basks in the glow of its own Expo '98, it still seems to gaze nostalgically over its shoulder and out to sea.

For visitors, this far side of Europe offers more than beaches and port wine. Beyond the crowded Algarve, one finds wide appeal: a simple but hearty cuisine based on seafood and lingering conversation, an enticing architectural blend that wanders from the Moorish to Manueline to surrealist styles, and a changing landscape that occasionally lapses into impressionism. Like the *emigrantes*, economically inspired Portuguese vagabonds who eventually find their way back to their roots, *estrangeiros* (foreigners) who have had a taste of the real Portugal can only be expected to return.

Facts about Portugal

HISTORY

The early history of Portugal goes back to the Celts who settled the Iberian Peninsula around 700 BC. A subsequent pattern of invasion and reinvasion was established by the Phoenicians, Greeks, Romans and Visigoths.

In the 8th century, the Moors crossed the Strait of Gibraltar and commenced a long occupation which introduced their culture, architecture and agricultural techniques to Portugal. Resistance to the Moors culminated in their ejection during the 12th century.

In the 15th century, Portugal entered a phase of conquest and discovery under the rule of Henry the Navigator. Famous explorers such as Vasco da Gama, Ferdinand Magellan and Bartolomeu Diaz set off to discover new trade routes and helped to create a huge empire that, at its peak, extended to India, the Far East, Brazil and Africa.

This period of immense power and wealth faded towards the end of the 16th century

when Spain occupied Portugal. Although the Portuguese regained their country within a few decades, the momentum of the empire declined over the following centuries.

At the close of the 18th century, Napoleon sent several expeditions to invade Portugal but he was eventually trounced by the troops of the Anglo-Portuguese alliance.

During the 19th century, Portugal's economy fell apart. There was a general muddle of civil war and political mayhem which culminated in the abolition of the monarchy in 1910 and the founding of a democratic republic.

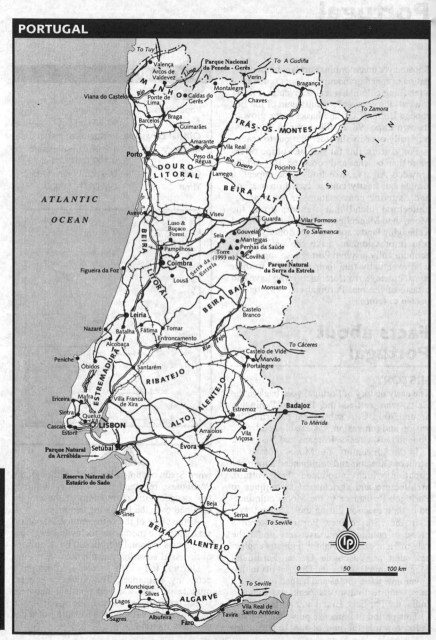

PORTUGAL

The democratic phase was brief, lasting until a military coup in 1926 set the stage for a long period of dictatorship under Antonio de Oliveira Salazar, who clung tenaciously to power until 1968 when he died after falling off a chair! General dissatisfaction with the repressive regime and a pointless and ruinous colonial war in Africa led to the Revolution of the Carnations, a peaceful military coup on 25 April 1974.

During the 1970s and early 1980s, Portugal went through some painful adjustments: the political scene was marked by extreme swings between right and left, and the economy suffered from strikes over government versus private ownership. The granting of independence to Portugal's African colonies in 1974-75 resulted in a flood of nearly a million refugees into the country. Entry into the EU in 1986 secured a measure of stability, buttressed by the acceptance of Portugal as a full member of the European Monetary System in 1992.

Although EU membership has given a tremendous boost to Portugal's development and modernisation, the 1990s have been troubled by recession, rising unemployment, and continuing backwardness in agriculture and education. In the elections of 1995, the electorate showed its dissatisfaction with the scandal-tainted Social Democrat Party by switching back to socialism after 10 years of conservatism.

Expo '98, which attracted some eight million visitors to the country and spurred immense new infrastructure projects, has brought Portugal back into world focus. Its next big challenge is to adjust to monetary union in 1999.

GEOGRAPHY & ECOLOGY

Portugal is one of Europe's smaller countries, about twice the size of Switzerland. It measures 560km from north to south, and 220km from east to west.

The northern and central regions are densely populated, particularly near the coast. The inland region is characterised by lush vegetation and mountains; the highest range is the Serra da Estrela, peaking at Torre (1993m). The south is less populated and, apart from the mountainous backdrop of the Algarve, much flatter and drier.

Portugal has one international-standard national park (the 70,290-hectare Peneda-Gerês), 11 *parques naturais* (natural parks, of which the biggest and best known is 101,060-hectare Serra da Estrela), eight nature reserves and 18 other protected areas. The government's Instituto da Conservação da Natureza (ICN) manages all of them; its information office (☎ 01-352 3317) at Rua Ferreira Lapa 29-A, Lisbon, provides some maps and information, though each park has its own (usually better supplied) information centre as well.

GOVERNMENT & POLITICS

Portugal has a western-style democracy based on the Assembleiada República, a single-chamber parliament with 230 members and an elected president. The two main parties are the ruling Socialist Party (Partido Socialista or PS) and the opposition right-of-centre Social Democratic Party (Partido Social Democrata or PSD). There are several other parties, including the United Democratic Coalition (CDU), which links the Communist Party with the Greens (Partido Ecologista Os Verdes or PEV). The Greens are occasionally referred to as 'watermelons' – green on the outside and red on the inside!

The general election of October 1995 saw the ousting of the PSD after 10 years of rule and the return to power of the Socialist Party under Prime Minister António Guterres. He has reassured many by expressing a strong commitment to budgetary discipline and European monetary unification, but it remains to be seen whether he can fulfil promises to improve health care and education.

ECONOMY

After severe economic problems in the 1980s, Portugal has tamed its rampant inflation rate to around 2.5% and is enjoying a surge of economic expansion, thanks largely to investment in infrastructure and increased privatisation. Agriculture plays a decreasing role in the economy as services (eg real estate, banking and tourism) and industry take over. Portugal looks set to benefit from low labour costs, a young population and traditional trading links with South America and Africa. EU membership has provided vital funding which has already helped to improve the country's infrastructure. Despite competition from within the single European market and a massive budget deficit, the country unexpectedly made the grade for European monetary union in 1999.

POPULATION & PEOPLE

Portugal's population of 9.93 million does not include an estimated three million Portuguese living abroad as migrant workers.

ARTS

Music

The best-known form of Portuguese music is the melancholy, nostalgic songs called *fado*, popularly considered to have originated with the yearnings of 16th-century sailors. Much of what is offered to tourists in Lisbon is overpriced and far from authentic. Amália Rodrigues is *the* star of Portuguese fado, although she no longer gives performances; her recordings can be bought in most record shops in Portugal.

Literature

In the 16th century, Gil Vicente, who excelled at farces and religious dramas, set the stage for Portugal's dramatic tradition. Later in that century, Luís de Camões wrote *Os Lusíadas*, an epic poem celebrating the age of discovery. He is now considered Portugal's national poet. The romantic dramatist Almeida Garrett was one of Portugal's leading literary figures of the 19th century, while Fernando Pessoa is arguably the finest Portuguese poet and dramatist to emerge this century, and one of the few contemporary Portuguese writers to be widely read abroad.

There are translations of Portuguese literature: have a look at Camões' *The Lusiads* and works by Eça de Queiroz (*The Maias*), Fernando Pessoa (*Selected Poems*), Fernando Namora (*Mountain Doctor*) and Mario Braga. For a recent Portuguese 'whodunit' – close to the political bone – pick up *The Ballad of Dog's Beach* by José Cardoso Pires.

Architecture

Of special interest is the development during the 16th century of Manueline architecture, named after King Manuel I (1495-1521). The style represents the zest for discovery during that era and is characterised by boisterous, twisting and spiralling columns and nautical themes.

Crafts

The most striking Portuguese craft is the making of decorative tiles known as *azulejos*, a technique learnt in the 15th century from the Moors. Today, superb examples are to be seen all over Portugal. Lisbon has its own azulejos museum.

SOCIETY & CONDUCT

Despite growing prosperity and influences from abroad, the Portuguese are keeping a firm grip on their culture. Traditional folk dancing is still the pride of villages throughout the land, and local festivals are celebrated with gusto. Soccer is one modern element now ingrained in male Portuguese life; watching matches on TV ensures the continuation of the traditional long lunch break.

The Portuguese tend to be very friendly, but fairly conservative: you'll endear yourself to them more quickly if you avoid looking too outlandish and if you greet and thank them in Portuguese. Skimpy beachwear is tolerated at beach resorts, but shorts (and hats) are considered very offensive inside churches.

RELIGION

The Portuguese population is 99% Roman Catholic. The Protestant community numbers less than 120,000 and there are approximately 5000 Jews.

LANGUAGE

Like French, Italian, Spanish and Romanian, Portuguese is a Romance language, closely derived from Latin. It is spoken by more than 10 million people in Portugal and 130 million in Brazil, and is also the official language of five African nations. In the Algarve and big cities like Porto and Lisbon, it's easy to find Portuguese who speak English, but in remoter areas few locals speak foreign languages unless they are returned emigrants. See the Language Guide at the back of the book for pronunciation guidelines and useful words and phrases.

Facts for the Visitor

HIGHLIGHTS

For scenery, you can't beat the mountain landscapes of the Serra da Estrela and the Peneda-Gerês National Park. Architecture buffs should head for the monasteries at Belém and Batalha, and the palaces of Pena (in Sintra) and Buçaco. Combining the best of both worlds are Portugal's old walled towns such as Évora and Marvão. Not to be missed in Lisbon is the massive Gulbenkian museum and the new Oceanarium, the largest in Europe.

SUGGESTED ITINERARIES

Depending on the length of your stay you might want to see the following places:

Two days
    Stick to Lisbon.
One week
    Spend three days in Lisbon, two in Sintra, and one in Óbidos and Nazaré.
Two weeks
    Spend as above, plus the Algarve, including two days each in Tavira, Lagos and Sagres.
One month
    Spend as above, plus three days each in Porto, Évora, Serra da Estrela Natural Park and Peneda-Gerês National Park, and a day each in Castelo de Vide and Marvão.

PLANNING
Climate & When to Go

Portugal's climate is temperate; it's only searingly hot in midsummer in the Algarve and Alentejo. The Algarve tourist season lasts from late February to November. Peak season extends from June to September; prices for accommodation and museums outside peak season may be discounted by as much as 50%. Prices noted in this chapter are for peak season.

In winter, the north receives plenty of rain and temperatures can be chilly. Snowfall is common in the mountains, particularly the Serra da Estrela, which has basic ski facilities. Tourist season in the north extends from approximately May to September.

You can take advantage of fewer crowds, seasonal discounts and spectacular foliage in spring (late March and April) and late summer (September and early October).

Books & Maps

They Went to Portugal and *They Went to Portugal Too* by Rose Macaulay follow the experiences of a wide variety of visitors from medieval times to the 19th century. For an excellent overview of Portugal and its place in the modern world, read *The Portuguese: The Land and Its People* by Marion Kaplan.

Walkers should pack the *Landscapes of Portugal* series by Brian & Aileen Anderson, with both car tours and walks in various regions, including the Algarve, Sintra/Estoril and the Costa Verde. More detailed is *Walking in Portugal* by Bethan Davies and Ben Cole.

The Michelin map of Portugal is accurate and very useful even if you are not using a car. Maps produced by the Automóvel Club de Portugal (ACP) provide slightly more up to date, but less detailed, coverage.

Topographic maps are published (and sold) by two government mapping agencies in Lisbon: the civilian Instituto Português de Cartográfia e Cadastro (☎ 01-381 96 00; fax 01-381 96 99), Rua Artilharia Um 107, and the military Instituto Geográfico do Exército (☎ 01-852 00 63; fax 01-853 21 19; igeoe@igeoe.pt; www.igeoe.pt), Avenida Dr Alfredo Bensaúde. Another outlet for the (better) military versions is the Porto Editora bookshop (☎ 02-200 76 81), Praça Dona Filipa de Lencastre 42, Porto.

ICN (☎ 01-352 3317), Rua Ferreira Lapa 29-A, Lisbon, the agency that administers national/natural parks, has a few maps. Better information is available at information offices in or near the parks, though little of it is in the kind of detail needed by trekkers.

TOURIST OFFICES
Local Tourist Offices

Known as *postos de turismo* or just *turismos*, local tourist offices are found throughout Portugal and can provide information, maps and varying degrees of assistance.

Tourist Offices Abroad

Portuguese tourist offices operating abroad under the administrative umbrella of ICEP

(Investimentos, Comércio e Turismo de Portugal; www.portugal.org) include:

Canada
Portuguese Trade & Tourism Commission (☎ 416-921 7376; fax 416-921 1353), 60 Bloor Street West, Suite 1005, Toronto, Ont M4W 3B8

Spain
Oficina de Turismo de Portugal (☎ 91-522 44 08; fax 91-522 23 82), Gran Via 27, 1st floor, 28013 Madrid

UK
Portuguese Trade & Tourism Office (☎ 0171-494 1441; fax 0171-494 1868), 22-25a Sackville St, London W1X 1DE

USA
Portuguese National Tourist Office (☎ 212-719 3985; fax 212-764 6137), 590 Fifth Ave, 4th floor, New York, NY 10036-4785

VISAS & EMBASSIES

No visa is required (for any length of stay) for nationals of EU countries. Those from Australia, Canada, Israel, New Zealand and the USA can stay up to 60 days in any half-year without a visa. Others, including nationals of Hong Kong, South Africa and Singapore, need a visa and must produce evidence of financial responsibility, unless they are the spouses or children of EU citizens.

Portugal is a signatory of the Schengen Convention on the abolition of mutual border controls (the others are Austria, Belgium, France, Germany, Greece, Italy, Luxembourg, Netherlands and Spain). You can apply for visas for more than one of these states on the same form, though a visa for one does not automatically grant you entry to the others.

Visa Extensions & Re-Entry Visas

Outside Portugal, visa information is supplied by Portuguese consulates. Inside Portugal, contact the Foreigners' Registration Service (Serviço de Estrangeiros e Fronteiras), Avenida António Augusto de Aguiar 20, Lisbon (☎ 01-346 61 41 or 01-352 31 12), open 9 am to 3 pm on weekdays.

Portuguese Embassies Abroad

Portuguese embassies abroad include:

Australia
(☎ 06-290 1733) 23 Culgoa Circuit, O'Malley, ACT 2606

Canada
(☎ 613-729-0883) 645 Island Park Drive, Ottawa, Ont K1Y OB8

Ireland
(☎ 01-289 4416) Knock Sinna House, Knock Sinna, Fox Rock, Dublin 18

Spain
(☎ 91-261 78 08) Calle del Pinar 1, 28006 Madrid

UK
(☎ 0171-235 5331) 11 Belgrave Square, London SW1X 8PP

USA
(☎ 202-328 8610) 2125 Kalorama Rd NW, Washington, DC 20008

Foreign Embassies in Portugal

Foreign embassies in Lisbon include:

Canada
(☎ 01-347 48 92) Edifício MCB, Avenida da Liberdade 144

Ireland
(☎ 01-396 15 69) Rua da Imprensa à Estrela 1

Spain
(☎ 01-347 23 81) Rua do Salitre 1

UK
(☎ 01-392 40 00) Rua de São Domingos à Lapa 37

USA
(☎ 01-726 66 00) Avenida das Forças Armadas

There are no embassies for Australia or New Zealand in Portugal, though both have honorary consuls in Lisbon. Australian citizens can call ☎ 01-353 07 50 on weekdays between 1 and 2 pm (or their embassy in Paris, ☎ 01-40 59 33 00); New Zealand citizens can call ☎ 01-357 41 34 during business hours (or their embassy in Rome, ☎ 06-440 29 28).

CUSTOMS

There is no limit on the importation of currency. If you leave Portugal with more than 100,000$00 in escudos or 500,000$00 in foreign currency you must provide proof that you brought in at least this much.

The duty-free allowances for travellers coming from non-EU countries include 200 cigarettes (or the equivalent); and 1L of an alcoholic beverage that is over 22% alcohol by volume or 2L of wine or beer.

MONEY

The unit of Portuguese currency is the escudo, further divided into 100 centavos. Prices are written with a $ sign between escudos and centavos; eg 25 escudos 50 centavos is written 25$50.

There are 200$00, 100$00, 50$00, 20$00, 10$00, 5$00, 2$50 and 1$00 coins. Notes currently in circulation are 10,000$00, 5000$00, 2000$00, 1000$00 and 500$00.

From 1 January 1999, when Portugal joined the European Monetary Union, goods and services began to be priced in both escudos and euros. The escudo will be withdrawn on 1 July 2002.

Currency

Portuguese banks can change most foreign cash and travellers cheques but charge a nasty commission of at least 2000$00, plus 140$00 government tax. Eurocheques often draw a 500$00 commission. Better deals for travellers cheques are at private exchange bureaus in Lisbon, Porto and popular tourist resorts.

Better value (and more convenient) are 24-hour Multibanco credit-card machines at nearly all banks. A handling fee of about 1.5% is included and exchange rates are reasonable. Automatic cash-exchange machines are found only in a few major cities.

Major credit cards are widely accepted – especially Visa and MasterCard.

Exchange Rates

Australia	A$1	=	114$72
Canada	C$1	=	118$48
euro	€1	=	202$98
France	1FF	=	30$30
Germany	DM1	=	101$30
Japan	¥100	=	137$00
New Zealand	NZ$1	=	96$60
Spain	100 ptas	=	20$90
UK	UK£1	=	309$00
USA	US$1	=	182$50

Costs

Although costs are rising noticeably, Portugal remains one of the cheapest places to travel in Europe. On a rock-bottom budget – using hostels or camping grounds, and mostly self-catering – you can squeeze by on US$25 a day. With bottom-end accommodation and the occasional cheap restaurant meal, costs will hover around US$30. Travelling with a companion and timing your trip to take advantage of off-season discounts (see the When to Go entry earlier in this section), two can eat and sleep in style for US$70 per day. Outside major tourist areas, prices dip appreciably.

Concessions are often available on admission fees to museums, palaces etc if you're at least 65, under 26 or are the holder of a student card.

Tipping & Bargaining

A reasonable restaurant tip is 10%. For a snack at a *cervejaria*, *pastelaria* (see the Food entry later in this section) or café, a bit of loose change is sufficient. Taxi drivers appreciate 5 to 10% of the fare, and petrol station attendants 30 to 60$00.

Good-humoured bargaining is acceptable in markets but you'll find that the Portuguese are tough opponents! Off season, you can sometimes bargain down the price of accommodation.

Consumer Taxes

A 17% sales tax, called IVA, is levied on hotel and other accommodation, restaurant meals, car rental and some other bills.

If they are resident outside the EU, foreign tourists can claim an IVA refund on goods from shops which are members of Europe Tax-Free Shopping Portugal. The minimum purchase eligible for a refund is 11,700$00 in any one shop. The shop assistant fills in a cheque for the amount of the refund (minus an administration fee). When you leave Portugal you present the goods, the cheque and your passport at the tax-refund counter at customs for a cash, postal-note or credit-card refund.

This service is presently available at the airports in Lisbon, Porto and Faro, and at Lisbon harbour (customs section). If you're leaving overland, contact customs at your final EU border point. Further details are available from Europe Tax-Free Shopping Portugal (☎ 01-840 88 13) in the international departures concourse of Lisbon airport.

PORTUGAL

POST & COMMUNICATIONS
Post
Postal Rates Postcards and letters up to 20g cost 85$00 to EU countries, 100$00 to non-EU European countries and 140$00 elsewhere. For delivery to the USA or Australia, allow eight to 10 days; delivery within Europe averages four to six days.

Sending Mail For parcels, 'economy air' (or surface airlift, SAL) costs about a third less than air mail and usually arrives a week or so later. Printed matter is cheapest (and simplest) to send in batches of under 2kg. Postal regulations for large parcels can tie you and the counter clerk in knots. The post office at Praça dos Restauradores in Lisbon and the main post office in Porto are open into the evening and on weekends.

Receiving Mail Most major towns have a post office with *posta restante* service, but it can take time to learn which branch feels responsible. A charge of 60$00 is levied for each item received, at least in Lisbon and Porto.

Addresses Addresses in Portugal are written with the street name first, followed by the building address and often a floor number with a ° symbol, eg 15-3°. An alphabetical tag on the address, eg 2-A, indicates an adjoining entrance or building. The tag R/C (*rés do chão*) means ground floor.

Telephone
Local calls from public coin telephones start at 20$00. The largest acceptable coin is 50$00, making these impractical for long-distance and international calls. Much handier (and cheaper) are 'Credifones', which accept cards available from newsagents, tobacconists and telephone offices. The card comes in 625$00, 1250$00, 1500$00 and 1875$00 denominations.

All calls, domestic and international, are charged identical rates per time unit (*impulso*), but each destination has a time unit of a different duration. The charge per unit for any call from a public telephone – on the street or at a Portugal Telecom or post office – is 15$00 with coins or 12$50 with a Credifone card, plus three units worth just to make the connection. During economy calling periods (9 pm to 9 am on weekdays and all day Saturday and Sunday) units are longer, ie costs are lower.

A three-minute direct-dial (IDD) call from Portugal, using a Credifone during economy periods, is 320$00 to anywhere in the EU, 396$00 to the USA or Canada, and 565$00 to Australia or New Zealand. Charges are at least 25% higher during peak periods. Hotels typically charge over *three times* the economy/Credifone rate!

To call Portugal from abroad, dial the international access code, ☎ 351 (the country code for Portugal), the telephone code and the number. Important telephone codes include ☎ 01 (Lisbon) and ☎ 02 (Porto). From Portugal, the international access code is ☎ 00. For enquiries, operator help or to make a reverse-charge (collect) call from Portugal, dial ☎ 099 (for Europe and north Africa) or ☎ 098 (for other international destinations); either one should get you an English speaking operator. Many old five-digit telephone numbers in Portugal are now being changed; if those listed in the text no longer work, call the local turismo for help.

Fax
Post offices operate a domestic and international service called CORFAX, costing 850$00 for the first page to Europe or 1000$00 to North America. Some private shops, eg Planet (see Lisbon), offer a much cheaper service.

INTERNET RESOURCES
Useful Web sites on Portugal include EUnet Portugal (www.eunet.pt/portugal/portugal.html) and A Collection of Home Pages about Portugal (www.well.com/user/ideamen/portugal.html). And be sure to have a look at LP's own Portugal 'destinations' page at www.lonelyplanet.com.

In many towns you'll find a branch of the Instituto Português da Juventude or IPJ, a state-funded network of youth centres. Most offer free Internet access, at least during certain hours, and if you have a web-based email account like Hotmail, you're all set. Some will let you send a message or two on their own mail server, but are not enthusiasic about your receiving mail there. Some municipal libraries also have free Internet access, and certain big-city offices of Portugal Telecom, Portugal's biggest Internet provider, offer free or cheap access. A few bigger towns have cybercafés, where you can do the same thing (and get help too) for 200 to 800$00 per hour of online time.

NEWSPAPERS & MAGAZINES

Portuguese-language newspapers include the dailies *Diário de Notícias, Público* and *Jornal de Notícias* and the gossip tabloid *Correio da Manhã*, which may lack finesse but licks the others for circulation. Weeklies include *O Independente* and *Expresso*. For entertainment listings, check the local dailies or the municipality's calendar of events (usually available at tourist offices).

English-language newspapers published in Portugal include *The News*, with various regional editions featuring local news and classified pages, and *Anglo-Portuguese News*. Newspapers and magazines from abroad are widely available in major cities and tourist resorts.

RADIO & TV

Portuguese radio is represented by the state-owned stations *Antenna Um* and *Antenna Dois*, by *Rádio Renascença* and by a clutch of recently established local stations. *Rádio Difusão Portuguesa* transmits daily programs to visitors in English and other languages. The BBC World Service can be picked up on 15.070MHz shortwave.

Portuguese TV has expanded from two state-run channels (RTP-1 or Canal 1, and RTP-2 or TV2) to include two private channels (SIC and TVI). Soaps (known as *telenovelas*) take up the lion's share of broadcasting time.

PHOTOGRAPHY & VIDEO

It's best to bring film with you, especially if you want Kodachrome, which can be very expensive. Other brands of slide film, as well as print film and video cassettes, are widely available for reasonable prices at photo shops in larger towns. Print film processing is as fast and inexpensive as anywhere in Europe.

TIME

Portugal is GMT/UTC in winter and GMT/UTC plus one hour in summer (making it one hour earlier than Spain, year-round). Clocks are set forward by an hour on the last Sunday in March and back on the last Sunday in October.

ELECTRICITY

Electricity is 220V, 50Hz. Plugs are normally of the two-round-pin variety.

WEIGHTS & MEASURES

Portugal uses the metric system; decimals are indicated with commas and thousands with points.

LAUNDRY

There are *lavandarias* everywhere, usually specialising in dry-cleaning (*limpeza à seco*). They'll often do wash-and-dry (*lavar e secar*) too, though it may take a day or two. Figure 1000 to 1500$00 for a 5kg load.

TOILETS

When available (which isn't often), public toilets in towns are of the sit-down variety, generally clean and usually free. Most people, however, go to the nearest café for a drink or pastry and use the facilities there.

HEALTH

For minor matters you can pop into a local chemist (just ask for a *farmácia*). For more serious health problems, ask your embassy, hotel or the tourist office to refer you to the nearest hospital with an English-speaking doctor. The number to dial in any emergency is ☎ 112.

WOMEN TRAVELLERS

In traditionally minded Portugal, especially areas outside Lisbon and Porto, an unaccompanied foreign woman is an oddity. Older people, especially in rural areas, may fuss over you as if you were in need of protection. But women travelling around Portugal on their own or in small groups report few hassles. Nevertheless, Lisbon and Porto are big cities, and women should be cautious

PORTUGAL

there about where they go alone after dark. Hitching is not recommended for solo women anywhere in Portugal.

GAY & LESBIAN TRAVELLERS
In much of this predominantly Catholic country, there is little understanding or acceptance of homosexuality. But Lisbon has a flourishing gay scene: in 1997 it hosted its first Gay Pride Festival (now occurring around June 28 annually) and opened a Gay & Lesbian Community Center (Centro Comunitário Gay e Lésbico de Lisboa, ☎ 01-887 39 18), Rua de São Lazaro 88. It's open daily from 4 to 9 pm.

For information on gay-friendly bars, restaurants, discos and clubs, check out www.ilga-portugal.org.

DISABLED TRAVELLERS
The Secretariado Nacional de Rehabilitação (☎ 01-793 65 17; fax 01-796 51 82), Avenida Conde de Valbom 63, Lisbon, publishes the Portuguese-language *Guia de Turismo* with sections on barrier-free accommodation, transport, shops, restaurants and sights in Portugal. It's only available at their offices.

A private agency called Turintegra, also called APTTO (Associação Portuguesa de Turismo Para Todos; ☎/fax 01-859 53 32), Praça Dr Fernando Amado, Lote 566-E, 1900 Lisbon, keeps a keener eye on developments and arranges holidays for disabled travellers. Lisbon's and Porto's public transport agencies offer dial-a-ride services at costs comparable to those of taxis.

DANGERS & ANNOYANCES
Crime against foreigners usually involves pickpocketing, theft from cars or pilfering from camping grounds (though armed robberies are on the increase), mostly in touristy areas like the Algarve, specific parts of Lisbon and a few other cities. With the usual precautions (use a money belt or something similar and don't leave valuables in cars or tents) there is little cause for worry. For peace of mind take out travel insurance.

Avoid swimming on beaches which are not marked as safe – Atlantic currents are notoriously dangerous (and badly polluted near major cities).

The national emergency number is ☎ 112, for police, fire and other emergencies anywhere in Portugal. For more routine police matters and direct access to the fire brigade there are also numbers for each town or district.

BUSINESS HOURS
Most banks are open weekdays from 8.30 am to 3 pm. Most museums and other tourist attractions are open weekdays from 10 am to 5 pm but are often closed at lunchtime and all day Monday. Shopping hours generally extend from 9 am to 7 pm on weekdays, and from 9 am to 1 pm on Saturday. Lunch is given serious and lingering attention between noon and 3 pm.

PUBLIC HOLIDAYS & SPECIAL EVENTS
Public holidays in Portugal include New Year's Day, Carnival & Shrove Tuesday (February/March), Good Friday, Anniversary of the Revolution (25 April), May Day, Corpus Christi (May), National Day (Camões Day; 10 June), Feast of the Assumption (15 August), Republic Day (5 October), All Saints' Day (1 November), Independence Day (1 December), Feast of the Immaculate Conception (8 December) and Christmas Day.

The most interesting cultural events in Portugal include:

Holy Week Festival
　Easter week in Braga features a series of colourful processions of which the most famous is the Ecce Homo procession, featuring hundreds of barefoot penitents carrying torches.
Festas das Cruzes (Festival of the Crosses)
　Held in Barcelos in May, this festival is known for its processions, folk music and dance performances, and exhibitions of regional handicrafts.
Feira Nacional da Agricultura (National Agricultural Fair) In June, Santarém holds a grand country fair with bullfighting, folk singing and dancing.
Festa do Santo António (Festival of Saint Anthony)
　This street festival is held in Lisbon (mainly in the Alfama district) on June 13.

Festas de São João (St John's Festival)
From 16 to 24 June, Porto parties; the night of the 23rd sees everybody out on the streets amicably bashing each other with leeks or plastic hammers.

Festas da Nossa Senhora da Agónia (Agónia Fair & Festival) This is held in Viana do Castelo on the first Sunday after 15 August and is famed for folk arts, parades, fireworks and a handicrafts fair.

Feira de São Martinho (National Horse Festival)
Equine enthusiasts will want to gallop to Golegã between 3 and 11 November for horses, riding contests and bullfights.

ACTIVITIES
Hiking & Trekking
Despite some magnificent rambling country, walking ranks low among Portuguese passions. There are no national walking clubs or cross-country trails, though some parks (notably Serra da Estrela and Peneda-Gerês) are establishing trails. Small adventure travel agencies now offer walking tours; see Information under Lisbon, Serra da Estrela, Porto and Peneda-Gerês National Park.

Water Sports
Water sports popular in Portugal include white-water rafting, water-skiing, surfing, windsurfing and flat-water boating. For local specialists see the entries for Lagos, Sagres and the Peneda-Gerês National Park.

Cycling
Off-road cycling (called BTT after *bicyclete tudo terrano*, all-terrain bicycle) is booming in Portugal. You'll find operators offering bike trips at many tourist destinations; see Tavira, Setúbal, Évora, Porto and Peneda-Gerês National Park.

Multiactivity & Adventure Programs
Among offerings of the Instituto Português da Juventude (see the Lisbon section for more on the IJP) are holiday programs for 16 to 30-year-olds (visitors too), including BTT, canoeing and rock climbing. Among private organisations assembling multi-faceted programs including these activities as well as trekking, horse riding, caving and hydrospeed (a form of individual white-water

boating, without the boat), are Cabra Montêz (see Lisbon), Montes d'Aventura, Planalto and Trote-Gerês (see Peneda-Gerês National Park) and Trilhos (see Porto).

ACCOMMODATION
Most local tourist offices have lists of accommodation to suit a range of budgets, and can help you find and book it. Although the government uses stars to grade some types of accommodation, criteria seem erratic.

For a room with a double bed, ask for a *quarto de casal*; for twin beds, a *duplo*; and for a single room, a *quarto individual*.

Camping
Camping is popular in Portugal and is easily the cheapest option. The *Roteiro Campista* (800$00), published annually in March and sold in larger bookshops, is an excellent multi-lingual guide with details of Portugal's camping grounds plus regulations for camping outside these sites. Depending on facilities and season, prices per night run about 300-600$00 for an adult (or child over 10 years old), plus 400-500$00 for a car and 200-500$00 for a small tent. Considerably lower prices apply in less touristy regions and in the low season.

Hostels
Portugal has a network of 23 youth hostels (*pousadas da juventude*) and nine accommodation centres (*centros de alojamento*), all part of the Hostelling International (HI) system. Low rates are offset by segregated dorms, midnight curfews and exclusion from the hostel for part of the day at most (but not all) of them.

Rates vary, being higher in more popular hostels such as Lisbon's and Porto's. A dorm bed in high season is 1500-2900$00 at pousadas da juventude, 1700$00 at centros de alojamento; in low season those figures are 1200-1900$00 and 1400$00 respectively. Most hostels also offer private doubles for 2700-3600$00 (without bath) or 3200-6000$00 (with). Bed linen and breakfast are included. Many pousadas da juventude (but not centros de alojamento) have kitchens where you can do your own cooking, as well as TV rooms and other social areas.

Demand is high in summer, so advance reservations are essential. You can book ahead between hostels in Portugal free of charge, or pay 160$00 per set of bookings at Movijovem (☎ 01-313 88 20; fax 01-352 14 66; movijovem@mail.telepac.pt), Avenida Duque d'Ávila 137, Lisbon – Portugal's central HI reservations office (where you can also book hostels abroad).

If you don't already have a card from your national hostel association, you can get HI membership by paying an extra 400$00 (and having a 'guest card' stamped) at each of the first six hostels where you stay.

Cheap Rooms

Another cheap option is a *quarto particular* (private room) or just *quarto*, usually a room in a private house. Home-owners may approach you in the street or at the bus or train station; otherwise watch for 'quartos' signs. Tourist offices sometimes have lists. The rooms are usually clean, cheap (typically 4000-5000$00 for a double in summer), free from the restrictions of hostels and the owners can be interesting characters. A more commercial variant is a *dormida* or rooming house, where doubles are about 4500$00 in high season. You may be able to bargain in the low season.

Guesthouses

The most common types of guesthouse, the Portuguese equivalent of B&Bs, are the *residencial* (plural *residenciais*) and the *pensão* (plural *pensões*). Both are graded from one to three stars, and top-rated establishments are often cheaper and better-run than some hotels clinging to their last star(s). In high season, rates for a double in the cheapest pensão start at around 4500$00; expect to pay slightly more for a residencial, where breakfast is normally included. Many have cheaper rooms with communal bathrooms. In low season, rates can drop by a third or more.

Hotels

The government grades hotels with one to five stars. For a double in high season you'll pay 10,000-15,000$00 at the lower end and 20,000-40,000$00 at the top end. *Estalagem* and *albergaria* are Portuguese terms for up-market inns. Prices drop spectacularly in the low-season, with doubles in a four-star hotel going for as little as 10,000$00. Breakfast is usually included.

Other Accommodation

There is a wide selection of other, opulent accommodation. Pousadas de Portugal are government-run former castles, monasteries or palaces, often in spectacular locations. Details are available from tourist offices, or from Pousadas de Portugal (☎ 01-848 12 21; fax 01-840 58 46), Avenida Santa Joana Princesa 10, 1749 Lisbon.

Private counterparts are operated under a scheme called Turismo de Habitação and smaller schemes called Turismo Rural and Agroturismo (often collectively called 'Turihab'), which allow you to stay in anything from a farmhouse to a manor house as a guest of the owner. Some also have self-catering cottages.

Tourist offices can tell you about local Turihab properties. A hefty book, *Turismo no Espaço Rural*, describing most of these places, is 2500$00 from national (ICEP) tourist offices abroad and in Lisbon and Porto, or from the largest of the Turihab owners' associations, Solares de Portugal (☎ 058-74 16 72; fax 058-74 14 44), Praça da República, 4990 Ponte de Lima, Minho.

Prices are graded by quality and season. For a double in high season you'll pay a minimum of 15,600$00 in a Pousada de Portugal or 16,500$00 in a Turihab manor house, but just 9500$00 in a Turihab farmhouse. Low-season prices can drop significantly and you can literally stay in a palace for the price of an average B&B elsewhere in Europe.

FOOD

Eating and drinking get serious attention in Portugal, where hearty portions and good value for money are the norm. Portugal has steadfastly ignored the fast-food era in favour of leisurely dining and devotion to wholesome ingredients.

The line between snacks and full-scale meals is blurred. Bars and cafés often sell snacks or even offer a small menu. For full-scale meals try a *casa do pasto* (a simple, cheap eatery, popular at lunchtimes), *restaurante*, *cervejaria* (a type of bar and restaurant), or *marisqueira* (a restaurant with an emphasis on seafood). The *prato do dia* (dish of the day) is often a great deal at around 750$00. In touristy regions, restaurants may advertise an *ementa turística* (tourist menu). Unlike the prato do dia, these are rarely bargains.

The titbits offered at the start of a meal, the *couvert*, may include bread, cheese, butter and olives; you'll be charged extra for them. A full portion, ample for two decent appetites, is a *dose*; or you can ask for a *meia dose* (half-portion), usually a quarter to a third cheaper. Lunchtime moves at a leisurely pace from noon to 3 pm; evening meals are taken between 7 and 10.30 pm.

Snacks

Typical snacks include *sandes* (sandwiches), *prego em pão* (a slab of meat with egg sandwiched in a roll), *pastéis de bacalhau* (cod fish cakes) and *tosta mista* (a toasted cheese and ham sandwich). Prices start at around 250$00. Soups are also cheap and filling.

Main Dishes

Seafood in Portugal offers exceptional value, especially fish dishes like *linguado grelhado* (grilled sole), *bife de atúm* (tuna steak) and the omnipresent *bacalhau* (cod) cooked in dozens of different ways. Meat is hit-or-miss, but worth sampling are *presunto* (ham); lamb, usually roasted, and known as *borrego* by the gourmets of Alentejo; and *cabrito* (kid). Prices for main dishes start at around 900$00.

Desserts & Cheeses

In most cafés and *pastelarias* (pastry shops), you can gorge yourself on the sweetest desserts (*sobremesas*) and cakes (*bolos*) imaginable. Cheeses from Serra da Estrela, Serpa and the Azores are worth sampling but pricey at about 2300$00 a kilogram.

Self-Catering

Lively local markets offer excellent fresh seafood, vegetables and fruit. Go early to get the best choice. Big cities have local grocery shops (*minimercadoes*) and many now have vast *hipermercados*.

DRINKS

Nonalcoholic Drinks

Fresh fruit juice is a rarity. Mineral water (*água mineral*) is good, either carbonated (*com gás*) or still (*sem gás*).

Coffee is a hallowed institution with its own convoluted nomenclature. A small black espresso is usually called a *bica*. For coffee with lots of milk, ask for a *galão*. In the north, half coffee and half milk is a *meia de leite*; elsewhere it's *café com leite*. Tea (*chá*) comes with lemon (*com limão*) or with milk (*com leite*).

Alcohol

Local beers (*cerveja*) include Sagres in the south and Super Bock in the north. A draught beer is *um fino* (in the north) or *um Imperial* in Lisbon and the south. *Uma garrafa* is a bottle.

Portuguese wine (*vinho*) offers great value in all its varieties: mature red (*tinto*), white (*branco*) and semi-sparkling young (*vinho verde*), which is usually white but occasionally red. Restaurants often have *vinho da casa* (house wine) for as little as 250$00 for a 350ml bottle or jug. For less than 800$00 you can buy a bottle to please the most discerning taste buds.

Port, synonymous with Portugal, is produced in the Douro Valley near Porto and drunk in three forms: ruby, tawny and white. Dry white port with sardines makes a memorable feast. Local brandy (*aguardente*) is also worth a try. For some rough stuff that tries hard to destroy your throat, ask for a *bagaço* (grape marc). Most bartenders in Portugal have the pleasant habit of serving large measures: a single brandy often contains the equivalent of a triple in the UK or the USA.

ENTERTAINMENT

Cinemas are inexpensive – around 700$00 a ticket – and prices are often reduced once a week to lure audiences from their home videos. Foreign films are usually subtitled, not dubbed.

For dance, music (rock, jazz and classical) and other cultural events, ask at tourist offices for free publications such as Lisbon's monthly *Agenda Cultural*, or pick up a copy of the local newspaper for listings. Discos abound in Lisbon, Porto and the Algarve.

Perhaps the most original forms of entertainment are local festivals (see the earlier Public Holidays & Special Events section).

SPECTATOR SPORT

Football (soccer) dominates the sporting scene – everything stops for a big match. The season lasts from August to May and almost every village and town finds enough players for a team. The three main teams are Benfica and Sporting in Lisbon, and FC Porto in Porto. Ask the tourist office about forthcoming matches.

Bullfighting is still popular in Portugal, despite pressure from international animal-rights activists. If you want to see a *tourada*, the season runs from late April to October. Portuguese rules prohibit a public kill, though the hapless beast must often be dispatched in private afterwards. In Lisbon, bullfights are held at the Campo Pequeno on Thursday. Ribatejo is the region where most bulls are bred; major fights are staged in Vila Franca de Xira and Santarém.

THINGS TO BUY

Leather goods, especially shoes and bags, are good value, as are textiles such as lace and embroidered linen. Handicrafts range from inexpensive pottery and basketwork to substantial purchases like rugs from Arraiolos, filigree gold or silver jewellery, and sets of azulejos made to order.

Getting There & Away

AIR

British Airways and TAP (Air Portugal) have daily direct flights from London to Lisbon and Porto, plus direct services to Faro. On most days there are direct links to Lisbon and Porto from Paris, Frankfurt, Amsterdam, Brussels and Madrid. A discounted London-Lisbon return fare is about £130 in low season, £240-300 in high season, though deals as low as £100 are possible with charter or package return flights to Lisbon or Faro.

From the UK, TAP (☎ 0171-828 0262) and British Airways (☎ 0345-222111) offer discounted youth and student fares, but the best deals are with youth-fare agencies like Campus Travel (☎ 0171-730 3402), STA (☎ 0171-361 6161) and Trailfinders (☎ 0171-937 5400). Portugal specialist agencies in the UK include Abreu (☎ 0171-229 9905) and Latitude 40 (☎ 0171-229 3164). The Portuguese National Tourist Office lists others in its *Tour Operators' Guide: Portugal*.

Since France, and Paris in particular, has a huge population of Portuguese immigrants, frequent flights at reasonable prices link the two countries. From France call Air France (☎ 01 44 08 24 24) or TAP (☎ 01 44 86 89 89). Both offer discounted youth prices.

For prices from Portugal, ask youth travel agencies Tagus Travel (Lisbon ☎ 01-352 55 09, Porto ☎ 02-609 41 46) or Jumbo Expresso (Lisbon ☎ 01-793 92 64, Porto ☎ 02-339 33 20); or Top Tours (Lisbon ☎ 01-315 58 85, Porto ☎ 02-208 27 85). TAP (☎ 0808-21 31 41) and British Airways (☎ 0808-21 21 25) can be contacted at local rates from anywhere in Portugal.

LAND

Bus

Spain InterCentro, Portugal's main Eurolines agent, has services three times a week between Lisbon and Madrid (11 hours) for 6860$00. Eurolines also runs between other Portuguese towns and Spain; call ☎ 91-530 7600 (Madrid) or ☎ 01-357 17 45 (Lisbon). Internorte (Porto ☎ 02-600 42 23) runs coaches to/from northern Portuguese cities, including a service between Porto and Madrid (5230$00) four times a week. In the Algarve, Intersul has express services between Lagos and Seville about four times weekly, via Vila Real de Santo António.

UK & France Intercentro/Eurolines has regular services between central Portugal (Lisbon and other cities) and France, with a bus change in Paris for London, five times a week. Allow 40 hours for the trip from London (Victoria coach station) to Lisbon, which costs UK£75 one way. For more information call Eurolines in the UK at ☎ 0990-143219 or in Portugal at ☎ 01-357 17 45.

Internorte (Porto ☎ 02-609 32 20) has similar services to/from the north (Porto and other cities), with a change in Paris, as well as a once-weekly direct Porto-London coach. A one-way London-Porto ticket is about UK£95.

The private line IASA (Paris ☎ 01 43 53 90 82, Lisbon ☎ 01-793 64 51, Porto ☎ 02-208 43 38) runs coaches five times a week between Paris and Lisbon (695FF one way) and between Paris and Porto (670FF). Both journeys take about 27 hours.

Train

Spain The main rail route is Madrid-Lisbon via Valência de Alcântara; the journey (with an express departure daily) takes about 10 hours. Other popular routes include Vigo-Porto (express trains three times a day) and, in southern Spain, Seville-Ayamonte, across the river from the Portuguese town of Vila Real de Santo António in the Algarve. Also, the daily Lisbon-Paris train (see the following UK and France section) goes via Salamanca, Valladolid, Burgos, Vitória and San Sebastian.

UK & France In general, it's only worth taking the train if you can use under-26 rail passes such as Inter-Rail (see the Getting Around chapter at the beginning of this book for details).

Services from London to Lisbon and other Portugal destinations go via Paris, where you change trains. There are two standard routes. The *Sud Express* runs from Paris via Irún (where you change trains again) and across Spain to Pampilhosa in Portugal (connections for Porto) before continuing to Lisbon. The other route runs from Paris to Madrid, where you can catch the *Lisboa Express* via Entroncamento (connections for Porto) to Lisbon. Allow at least 30 hours for the trip from London to Lisbon. A one-way, 2nd class, under-26 ticket is UK£100. You can cut several hours off the trip (but boost the cost) by taking the Eurostar service to Paris via the Channel Tunnel.

Car & Motorcycle

The quickest routes from the UK are by ferry via northern Spain – from Plymouth to San-

tander with Brittany Ferries (☎ 0990-360360) and from Portsmouth to Bilbao with P&O Stena Line (☎ 0990-980980). Or take the ferry or Channel Tunnel to France, motor down the coast via Bordeaux, through Spain via Burgos and Salamanca to Portugal. One option to reduce driving time on this route is to use Motorail for all or part of the trip from Paris to Lisbon; for information in England call RailEurope's Motorail division (☎ 0171-203 7000); in France, call SNCF (French Railways) at ☎ 08 36 35 35 39.

All border posts are open around the clock.

LEAVING PORTUGAL

An airport departure tax of about 2000$00 for international departures and 800$00 for domestic departures (the exact amount depends on your destination) is usually included in the ticket price.

Getting Around

AIR

Flights inside Portugal are very expensive and not worth considering for the short distances involved, unless you have an under-26 card. PGA Portugália Airlines operates daily flights between Lisbon, Porto and Faro (14,800$00 for the 50-minute Lisbon-Faro flight), with a fat 50% youth discount; call the Lisbon office on ☎ 01-847 20 92. TAP also has domestic connections, including Lisbon-Porto, and daily Lisbon-Faro flights that connect with all international TAP arrivals and departures at Lisbon.

BUS

A host of regional companies together operate a dense network of services of two types: *expressos* which provide comfortable, fast, direct connections between major towns, and *carreiras* which stop at every crossroad. Local weekend services, especially up north, can thin out to almost nothing, especially when school is out in summer. In remote areas, timetables are a rare commodity: stock up on information at tourist offices or bus stations in major towns.

An express coach from Lisbon to Faro takes just under five hours and costs 2200$00

(2550\$00 for the luxury four-hour EVA express); Lisbon-Porto takes 3½ hours and costs about 2000\$00.

TRAIN

Caminhos de Ferro Portugueses (CP), the state railway company, operates three main services: *rápido* or *intercidade* (IC on timetables), *interregional* (IR), and *regional* (R). Tickets for the first two cost at least double the price of a regional service, and reservations are either mandatory or highly recommended. A special intercidade service called Alfa, with fewer stops than usual, operates between selected northern cities (eg Lisbon and Porto). Frequent train travellers may want to buy the *Guia Horário Oficial* (360\$00), containing all domestic and international timetables. It's often out of print but you can try the ticket windows at major stations.

If you can match your itinerary and pace to a regional service, travel by rail is cheaper, if slower, than by bus. Children from four to 12 years old and adults over 65 travel at half-price. Holders of recognised youth cards like Euro<26 get 15% to 30% off regional and interregional services. There are also family discounts. Tourist tickets (*bilhetes turísticos*) are available for seven (18,000\$00), 14 (30,000\$00) or 21 days (42,000\$00), but are only worthwhile if you plan to move around a lot. The same discounts apply for regular tickets.

CAR & MOTORCYCLE

ACP (Automóvel Clube de Portugal) is Portugal's representative for various foreign car and touring clubs. It provides medical, legal and car breakdown assistance for members, but anyone can get road information and maps from its head office (☎ 01-356 39 31; fax 01-357 47 32) at Rua Rosa Araújo 24, Lisbon.

Petrol is pricey – eg 165\$00 and up for 1L of 95-octane unleaded fuel. Unleaded petrol (*sem chumbo*) is readily available in most parts of the country.

Road Rules

There are indeed rules, but the two guiding principles for Portuguese drivers seem to be:

find the fastest route between two points and defy the law of mortality in doing so. Although city driving (and parking) is hectic, minor roads in the countryside have surprisingly little traffic. Recent EU subsidies have ensured that the road system has been upgraded and there are now long stretches of motorway, some of them toll roads.

Speed limits in Portugal are 60km/h in cities and public centres, unless otherwise indicated; 90km/h on normal roads; and 120km/h on motorways. Driving is on the right, and front passengers are required by law to wear seat belts.

Drink-driving laws are strict: the maximum legal blood-alcohol level for anyone behind the wheel is 0.05%.

Car Rental

There are dozens of local car-rental firms in Portugal, but the best deals are arranged from abroad, either in a package with your flight, or through an international car-rental firm. From the UK, for a small car expect to pay about UK£150 for seven days in the high season or UK£65 in low season; in Portugal, figure at least 44,000\$00 in the high season or 31,000\$00 in the low season (including tax, insurance and unlimited mileage). You must be at least 23 years old and have held your licence for over a year.

BICYCLE

Many tourist places have bikes to rent (for 1500-3500\$00 a day). Elsewhere, bike shops and rental outfits are rare; if you're bringing your own machine, pack plenty of spares.

You can take your bike on any regional or interregional train for 1500\$00.

HITCHING

Thumbing a ride takes considerable time because drivers in remote regions tend to be going short distances. You get to meet some interesting characters, but you may only advance from one field to the next! You'll make more progress on major roads.

LOCAL TRANSPORT
Bus

Except in big cities like Lisbon there is little

reason to take a municipal bus. Most areas have regional bus services of some kind, but timetables can be scarce and/or bewildering, with many new private companies operating similar routes – and services can simply disappear on summer weekends, especially in the north.

Metro
Lisbon's recently expanded underground system is handy for getting around the city centre and out to the former Expo site. (See the Lisbon section for more details.)

Taxi
Taxis offer good value over short distances, especially for two or more people, and are usually plentiful in towns. A cross-town trip usually works out at about 500$00. Once a taxi leaves the town or city limits, you may pay a higher fare and possibly the cost of a return trip – whether you take it or not.

Other Transport
Enthusiasts for stately progress should not miss the trams of Lisbon and Porto, an endangered species. Also worth trying are the funiculars and elevators (both called *elevadores*) in Lisbon, Bom Jesus (Braga), Nazaré and elsewhere. Commuter ferries run back and forth across the Rio Tejo all day between Lisbon and Cacilhas (and other points).

ORGANISED TOURS
Gray Lines (☎ 01-352 25 94; fax 01-316 04 04), Avenida Praia da Vitória 12-B, Lisbon, organises three to seven-day bus tours to selected regions of Portugal, normally through local agents or upper-end tourist hotels. The AVIC coach company (☎ 058-82 97 05), Avenida Combatentes 206, Viana do Castelo, offers short tours of the Douro and Lima valleys. Miltours (☎ 089-890 46 00), Verissimo de Almeida 20, Faro, has day trips in the Algarve and elsewhere; they also have offices in Lisbon (☎ 01-313 93 70) and Porto (☎ 02-941 46 71).

Several unusual tours of Portugal are organised by UK agencies eg upmarket art and music tours by Martin Randall Travel (☎ 0181-742 3355; fax 0181-742 1066) and

wine tours by Arblaster & Clarke Wine Tours (☎ 01730-893344). Further listings are available from the Portuguese National Tourist Office. Two UK travel agencies with hiking holidays in Portugal are Explore Worldwide (☎ 01252-319448) and Ramblers Holidays (☎ 01707-331133). See Activities under Facts for the Visitor for information about adventure-travel specialists within Portugal.

Lisbon

☎ 01

Although it has the crowds, noise and traffic of a capital city, Lisbon's low skyline and breezy position beside the Rio Tejo (River Tagus) lend it a small, manageable feel. Its unpretentious atmosphere and pleasant blend of architectural styles conspire with diverse attractions – and a few unique quirks – to make it a favourite with a wide range of visitors. Furthermore, Lisbon (Lisboa to the Portuguese) is one of Europe's most economical destinations. Lovers of Art Deco shouldn't wait: façades are disappearing in a frenzy of redevelopment.

Orientation
Activity centres on the lower part of the city, the Baixa district, focused on Praça Dom Pedro IV, which nearly everyone calls 'the Rossio'. Just north of the Rossio is Praça dos Restauradores, at the bottom of Avenida da Liberdade. West of the Rossio it's a steep climb to the Bairro Alto district where one section, the Chiado, is under renovation after a huge fire in 1988. East of the Rossio, it's another climb to the Castelo de São Jorge and the adjacent Alfama district, a maze of tiny streets. Several kilometres to the west is Belém with its cluster of attractions, while the former Expo '98 site, with its grand Oceanarium, lies on the city's revamped north-eastern waterfront.

Information
Tourist Offices The main tourist office (☎ 346 63 07; fax 346 87 72) in Palácio Foz, Praça dos Restauradores, has free maps and the monthly *Agenda Cultural*, listing current events. It's open daily from 9 am to 8 pm.

PORTUGAL

LISBON

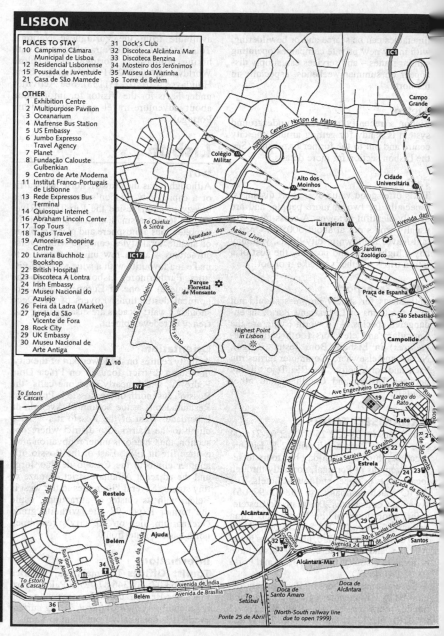

PLACES TO STAY
10 Campismo Câmara
   Municipal de Lisboa
12 Residencial Lisbonense
15 Pousada de Juventude
21 Casa de São Mamede

OTHER
1 Exhibition Centre
2 Multipurpose Pavilion
3 Oceanarium
4 Mafrense Bus Station
5 US Embassy
6 Jumbo Expresso
   Travel Agency
7 Planet
8 Fundação Calouste
   Gulbenkian
9 Centro de Arte Moderna
11 Institut Franco-Portugais
   de Lisbonne
13 Rede Expressos Bus
   Terminal
14 Quiosque Internet
16 Abraham Lincoln Center
17 Top Tours
18 Tagus Travel
19 Amoreiras Shopping
   Centre
20 Livraria Buchholz
   Bookshop
22 British Hospital
23 Discoteca A Lontra
24 Irish Embassy
25 Museu Nacional do
   Azulejo
26 Feira da Ladra (Market)
27 Igreja da São
   Vicente de Fora
28 Rock City
29 UK Embassy
30 Museu Nacional de
   Arte Antiga

31 Dock's Club
32 Discoteca Alcântara Mar
33 Discoteca Benzina
34 Mosteiro dos Jerónimos
35 Museu da Marinha
36 Torre de Belém

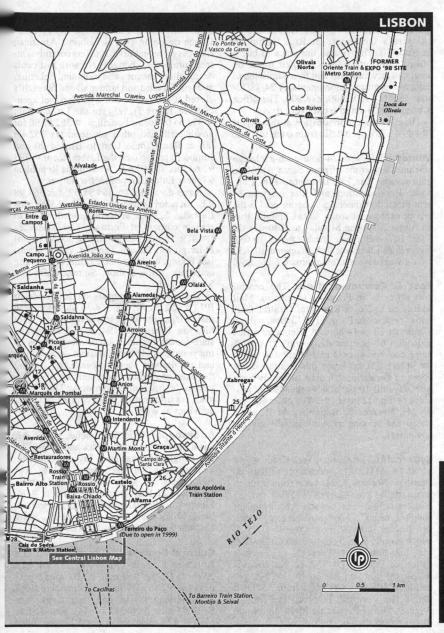

To Ponte de
Vasco da Gama

Olivais
Norte

Oriente Train &
Metro Station

FORMER
EXPO '98 SITE

1

2

Avenida Marechal Craveiro Lopez

Cabo Ruivo

Doca dos
Olivais

3

Avenida Marechal Gomes da Costa

Olivais

Avenida Cidade do Porto

Avenida Almirante Gago Coutinho

Alvalade

Chelas

Avenida do Santo Contestado

rças Armadas

Avenida Estados Unidos da América

Roma

Bela Vista

Entre
Campos

6

Campo
Pequeno

Avenida João XXI

Areeiro

de Berna

Saldanha

7

Olaias

Avenida da República

Alameda

11

Saldanha

12

3

Arroios

Picoas

15

14

Rua Morais Soares

16

Almirante

Reis

arque

17

18

Anjos

Xabregas

Marquês de Pombal

25

Avenida

20

Intendente

Avenida de Liberdade

Avenida

Avenida Infante d'Henrique

Politécnica

Martim Moniz

Graça

Restauradores

Campo de
Santa Clara

Rossio
Train

26

Bairro Alto Station

Rossio

Castelo

27

Baixa-Chiado

Santa Apolónia
Train Station

Alfama

Terreiro do Paço
(Due to open in 1999)

RIO TEJO

28

Cais do Sodré
Train & Metro Station

See Central Lisbon Map

PORTUGAL

0   0.5   1 km

To Cacilhas

To Barreiro Train Station,
Montijo & Seixal

Warmer service is available at the municipal tourist office (☎ 343 36 72; fax 346 33 14) across the square at Rua Jardim do Regedor 50. This is also the place to buy a Lisboa Card, good for unlimited travel on nearly all city transport and free admission to most museums and monuments. A 24/48/72-hour card is 1700/2800/3600$00. The office is open from 9 am to 6 pm every day.

There's also a tourist office at the airport (☎ 849 43 23), open daily from 6 am to 2 am.

Money Banks with 24-hour cash-exchange machines are at the airport; Santa Apolónia train station; Rua 1 de Dezembro 118-A opposite Rossio station; and Rua Augusta 24 near Praça do Comércio. A better deal is the private exchange bureau, Cota Câmbios, Rua do Áurea 283, open Monday to Saturday till 7 pm. Banco Borges e Irmão (☎ 342 10 68), Avenida da Liberdade 9-A, is open until 7.30 pm on weekdays and on alternate Saturdays.

Post & Communications The central post office is on Praça do Comércio. Mail addressed to Posta Restante, Central Correios, Terreira do Paço, 1100 Lisboa, will go to counter 13 or 14 here. A telephone office at Rossio 68 is open daily until 11 pm. A more convenient post and telephone office (☎ 347 11 22), on Praça dos Restauradores opposite the national tourist office, is open weekdays till 10 pm and weekends and holidays to 6 pm. Planet (☎ 343 12 12; fax 793 41 24), Avenida da República 41-B, has a cheap fax service as well as self-service computers.

Cybercafés The pleasant Web Café (☎ 342 11 81; web1@mail.esotérica.pt) at Rua do Diário de Notícias 126 is open from 2 pm to 2 am daily and charges 175$00 per 15 minutes online. The Espaço Ágora student complex, near Cais do Sodré car ferry terminal, has an Internet room (☎ 346 03 90), which is open from 3 pm to 2 am for 300$00 per half-hour. At Portugal Telecom's Quiosque Internet (☎ 352 22 92; email@telepac.pt) you can log on for 180$00 per half-hour. It's open weekdays from 9 am to 5 pm in the Portugal Telecom building at Avenida Fontes Pereira de Melo 38, beside Picoas metro station.

Travel Agencies Top Tours (see the Lisbon map; ☎ 315 58 85; fax 315 58 73), Avenida Duque de Loulé 108, is Lisbon's American Express representative. It offers commission-free currency exchange, help with lost cards or travellers cheques and outbound ticketing, and will forward and hold mail and faxes. It's closed at weekends. Good youth travel agencies are Tagus Travel (see the Lisbon map; ☎ 352 55 09 for air bookings, ☎ 352 59 86 for youth cards and other services; fax 352 06 00) at Rua Camilo Castelo Branco 20 and Jumbo Expresso (see the Lisbon map; ☎ 793 92 64; fax 793 92 67), Avenida da República 97, near Entre Campos metro station.

Rotas do Vento (☎ 364 98 52; fax 364 98 43; rotasdovento@mail.telepac), Rua dos Lusíadas 5, runs weekend guided walks to remote corners of Portugal. Cabra Montêz (☎ 419 53 15; cabramontez@hotmail.com) at Largo Rui Pereira, Linda-a-Velha, organises biking, walking, horse riding and karting activities in the Lisbon, Sintra, Mafra and Setúbal areas.

The Instituto Português da Juventude or IPJ (☎ 352 26 94; fax 314 36 88; ipj.infor@mail.telepac.pt; www.sejuventude. pt), Avenida da Liberdade 194, is a nationwide, state-funded organisation devoted to providing young people with information resources and wholesome social experiences. Among the latter are holiday programs for 16 to 30-year-olds (including visitors). They have stacks of information about courses and other activities as well.

Bookshops Diário de Notícias, Rossio 11, has a modest range of guides and maps. The city's biggest bookseller is Livraria Bertrand, with at least half a dozen shops, the biggest at Rua Garrett 73. Check out classy Livraria Buchholz at Rua Duque de Palmela 4 by Marquês de Pombal metro station. For second-hand books there are several shops along Calçada do Carmo, behind Rossio station.

Cultural Centres The library at the USA's Abraham Lincoln Center (☎ 357 01 02), Avenida Duque de Loulé 22-B, open weekdays from 2 to 5.30 pm, has a massive stock of American books and magazines. The British Council (☎ 347 61 41), Rua de São Marçal 174, also has a good library, open

Monday to Saturday from 2 to 6 pm. At Avenida Luis Bivar 91 is the Institut Franco-Portugais de Lisbonne (☎ 311 14 00).

Maps The national tourist office hands out a free but microscopic city map. The detailed, oblique-perspective *Lisbon City Map – Vista Aérea Geral*, available from kiosks and bookshops, is great for spotting landmarks.

Laundry Self-service Lave Neve Lavandaria (☎ 346 61 05), Rua da Alegria 37, charges 1300$00 for a 5kg load (wash and dry).

Medical & Emergency Services The British Hospital (☎ 395 50 67; after hours ☎ 397 63 29), Rua Saraiva de Carvalho 49, has English-speaking staff and doctors.

Dangers & Annoyances There's no need to be paranoid, but take the usual precautions against theft, particularly in the Rossio, Alfama and Bairro Alto districts. Use a money belt, keep cameras out of sight when not in use, and at night avoid the Alfama and Cais do Sodré districts and unlit or unfamiliar streets. A tourist-oriented, multilingual police office (☎ 346 61 41) is at Rua Capelo 13 in the Chiado district.

Things to See

Baixa The Baixa district, with its orderly streets lined with colourful, crumbling buildings, is ideal for strolling. You can strike out from the Rossio to the hills surrounding the Baixa, ascending at a stately pace by funicular or lift.

Castelo de São Jorge The castle, dating from Visigothic high times, has been tarted up, but still commands a superb view of Lisbon. Take bus No 37 from Praça da Figueira or, even better, tram No 28, which clanks up steep gradients and incredibly narrow streets from Largo Martim Moniz.

Alfama This ancient district is a maze of streets and alleys below the castle, with some superb architecture. The terrace at **Largo das Portas do Sol** provides a great viewpoint, and at No 2 the **Museu-Escola de Artes Decorativas** (Museum of Portuguese Decorative Arts) is worth a look. It's open from 10 am to

5 pm and closed on Tuesday. Restaurants and bars abound in Alfama.

Belém This quarter, about 6km west of Rossio, has several sights which survived the Lisbon earthquake of 1755. **Mosteiro dos Jerónimos** (Jerónimos Monastery) is the city's finest sight – do not miss it. Constructed in 1496, it is a magnificent, soaring extravaganza of Manueline architecture. Admission into the cloisters is 400$00. It's open daily, except Monday and holidays, from 10 am to 5 pm.

A 10-minute walk from the monastery is **Torre de Belém**, a Manueline-style tower which sits obligingly in the river as *the* tourist icon of Portugal. Admission and opening times are as for the monastery.

Beside the monastery, the **Museu da Marinha** (Maritime Museum) houses a collection of nautical paraphernalia. It's open daily, except Monday, from 10 am to 6 pm (to 5 pm in winter); entry is 400$00.

To reach Belém take the train from Cais do Sodré for seven minutes, bus No 28 from Praça do Comércio, or bus No 43 or tram No 15 from Praça da Figueira.

Other Museums One of the most attractive museums in Lisbon is the **Museu Nacional do Azulejo** (National Azulejos Museum) inside the former convent of Nossa Senhora da Madre de Deus, north-east of Santa Apolónia station. Its splendid azulejos are beautifully integrated into the elegant buildings. A restaurant provides light meals in a covered garden. Take bus No 104 from Praça do Comércio or No 105 from Praça da Figueira. It's open Wednesday to Sunday from 10 am to 6 pm and Tuesday from 2 to 6 pm; entry costs 350$00.

The **Fundação Calouste Gulbenkian** has what is considered the finest museum in Portugal. You'll need several hours to view its paintings, sculptures, carpets and more. The most convenient metro station is São Sebastião. In summer it's open Tuesday, Thursday, Friday and Sunday from 10 am to 5 pm, and Wednesday and Saturday from 2 to 7.30 pm; entry costs 500$00 (free to students, children and seniors). The adjacent **Centro de Arte Moderna** exhibits a cross section of modern Portuguese art.

CENTRAL LISBON

Rua Alexandre Herculano
Rua Rosa Araújo
Rua Barata Salgueiro
Rua do Salitre
Avenida da Liberdade
Rua Rodrigues Sampaio
Rua de São José
Rua Gomes Freire
Rua Palmeira
Rua Almirante Reis
Intendente
Rua Andrade

Jardim Botânico (Botanical Gardens)

Campo dos Mártires da Pátria

Largo do Intendente Pina Manique

Rua da Escola Politécnica
da – Alegria
Rua de São Marçal
Rua da Glória
Rua das Portas de Santo Antão
Rua do Passadiço
Rua de S. Lázaro
Rua da Palma

Martim Moniz
Largo Martim Moniz

Rua Dom Pedro V
Rua de São Pedro de Alcântara
Rua dos Condes

Restauradores
Rua Jardim do Regedor
Praça Dom Pedro IV (Rossio)

Calçada do Duque

Rossio
Praça da Figueira

Bairro Alto
Calçada do Combro
Rua do Loreto
Rua Garrett

Chiado
Rua Capelo
Baixa-Chiado

Calçada do Carmo
Rua Nova – Trindade
Rua de Santa Justa
Rua do Carmo
Rua de Santa Justa
Rua da Prata
Rua Áurea
Rua dos Correeiros
Rua dos Fanqueiros
Rua dos Douradores
Rua da Madalena
Rua de São Mamede

Baixa
Rua da Vitória
Rua de São Nicolau
Rua da Conceição
Rua São Julião
Rua do Comércio

do Castelo
Costa do Castelo

Largo das Portas do Sol

Alfama

Rua de São Paulo
Rua do Alecrim
Rua das Remolares
Av Vinte e Quatro de Julho
Ave 24 de Julho
Cais do Sodré

Avenida Ribeira das Naus
Rua do Arsenal
Praça do Comércio

Rua dos Bacalhoeiros
Rua da Alfândega

Terreiro do Paço (Due to open in 1999)

To Cacilhas

RIO TEJO

To Cacilhas

To Barreiro Train Station, Montijo & Seixal

PORTUGAL

0   200   400 m

CENTRAL LISBON

PLACES TO STAY
1 Hotel Presidente
12 Pensão Monumental
13 Pensão Londres
16 Pensão Imperial
19 Pensão Residencial Gerês
23 Pensão Globo
26 Pensão Duque
28 Pensão Henriquez
31 Pensão Residencial Alcobia
32 Pensão Ninho das Aguias
34 Pensão Moderna
35 Pensão Arco da Bandeira
48 Pensão Prata

PLACES TO EAT
10 Restaurante O Brunhal
17 Restaurante Pinóquio
27 Restaurante O Sol
29 Nicola
38 Cervejaria da Trindade
39 Restaurante Sinal Vermelho
40 Adega Machado (Casa de Fado)
41 Restaurante A Primavera
42 Adega do Ribatejo (Casa de Fado)
43 O Cantinho do Bem Estar

45 Lagosta Vermelha
50 Café A Brasileira
55 Martinho da Arcada
57 Leitão do Arco da Conceição
60 Restaurante Porto de Abrigo
61 Pano Mania

OTHER
2 Instituto Português da Juventude
3 Spanish Embassy
4 Canadian Embassy
5 Hot Clube de Portugal
6 British Council
7 Lave Neve Lavandaria
8 Elevador de Lavra
9 Gay & Lesbian Community Centre
11 Banco Borges e Irmão
14 Main Tourist Office
15 Post & Telephone Office
18 Câmara Municipal de Lisboa (CML) Tourist Office
20 24-hour Exchange Machine
21 Rossio Train Station
22 Elevador da Glória
24 Web Café
25 Telephone Office

30 Carris Kiosk
33 Castelo de São Jorge
36 Diário de Notícias Bookshop
37 Cota Câmbios
44 Elevador de Santa Justa
46 Museu de Artes Decorativas
47 Santos Oficios
49 Livraria Bertrand Bookshop
51 Elevador da Bica
52 Fabrica Sant'Ana
53 Tourist Police Office
54 24-hour Exchange Machine
56 Resende, Caima and Frota Azul Bus Terminal
58 Central Post Office
59 Ó Gilíns Irish Pub
62 Mercado da Ribeira
63 Cais do Sordé Train and Metro Station
64 Cais do Sordé Car Ferry Terminal
65 Espaço Ágora
66 Cais de Alfândega Ferry Terminal
67 Terréiro do Paço Ferry Terminal

The **Museu Nacional de Arte Antiga** (Antique Art Museum), Rua das Janelas Verdes, houses the national collection of works by Portuguese painters. Opening times are Wednesday to Sunday from 10 am to 6 pm and Tuesday from 2 to 6 pm. Admission costs 500$00. Take bus No 40 or 60 from Praça da Figueira or tram No 15 from Praça do Comércio.

Oceanarium The centrepiece of Expo '98, this vast Oceanarium – the largest in Europe – hosts 25,000 fish, birds and mammals in a giant two-floor aquarium which recreates the global ocean. Take the metro to Oriente station, an equally impressive Expo project.

Organised Tours
Walking Around Lisbon (☎ 340 45 39) organises guided walks in the Alfama and Castelo areas, Chiado and Bairro Alto for 2500$00 per person. Carris (☎ 363 20 21) offers open-top bus tours (2000$00) and tram tours (2800$00).

Gray Line (☎ 882 03 47) runs two-hour cruises on the Tejo for 3000$00 from the Terreiro do Paço ferry terminal.

Places to Stay
Unless otherwise stated the following entries appear on the Central Lisbon map.

Camping The *Campismo Câmara Municipal de Lisboa* (see the Lisbon map; ☎ 760 20 61) in Parque Florestal de Monsanto is about 6km north-west of Rossio. Take bus No 43 from Praça da Figueira.

Hostels Close to the centre is the *pousada da juventude* (see the Lisbon map; ☎ 353 26 96; fax 353 75 41) on Rua Andrade Corvo 46. It's open 24 hours a day. The closest metro station is Picoas, or take bus No 46 from Santa Apolónia station or Rossio, to the Marquês de Pombal stop. The very pleasant beachside *pousada da juventude de*

PORTUGAL

Catalazete (☎/fax 443 06 38) is on Estrada Marginal (next to Inatel) in Oeiras, 12km west of central Lisbon. Take the train from Cais do Sodré station to Oeiras, a trip of 20 to 25 minutes. Reservations are essential at both hostels.

Hotels & Guesthouses The national tourist office in Restauradores will make enquiries but not reservations for accommodation in Lisbon. During the high season advance bookings are imperative for accommodation near the centre. Prices here are for high season.

Baixa & Restauradores Adequate doubles with shared bath start around 4000$00 at friendly *Pensão Henriquez* (☎ 342 68 86), Calçada do Carmo 31, behind Rossio station; *Pensão Duque* (☎ 346 34 44), farther up at Calçada do Duque 53; and *Pensão Moderna* (☎ 346 08 18), Rua dos Correeiros 205. Slightly more expensive are the top-floor *Pensão Prata* (☎ 346 89 08), Rua da Prata 71, and *Pensão Arco da Bandeira* (☎ 342 34 78), Rua dos Sapateiros 226.

Along seedy Rua da Glória at No 21, *Pensão Monumental* (☎ 346 98 07) has functional but street-noisy doubles from 6000$00. More salubrious, with doubles around 8000$00, are *Pensão Imperial* (☎ 342 01 66), Praça dos Restauradores 78, and old *Pensão Residencial Alcobia* (☎ 886 51 71; fax 886 51 74), Poço do Borratém 15 (prices here include breakfast). Travellers recommend the comfortable (and security-conscious) *Pensão Residencial Gerês* (☎ 881 04 97; fax 888 20 06), Calçada do Garcia 6, with doubles without/with bath for around 8000/9000$00 and triples from 10,000$00.

Bairro Alto & Rato At Rua do Teixeira 37, close to the Elevador da Glória, pleasant *Pensão Globo* (☎ 346 22 79) has doubles without bath from 4500$00. Popular *Pensão Londres* (☎ 346 22 03; fax 346 56 82) at Rua Dom Pedro V 53 has several floors of spacious rooms, the upper ones with great city views. Doubles start at 6700$00. *Casa de São Mamede* (see Lisbon map; ☎ 396 31 66; fax 395 18 96), Rua Escola Politécnica 159, is a stylish hotel in an elegant old house with doubles from 12,000$00.

Marquês de Pombal & Saldahna Bright *Residencial Lisbonense* (see Lisbon map; ☎ 354 46 28), Rua Pinheiro Chagas 1, has doubles from 8000$00. A three-star hotel with the facilities of a four-star, the well-run *Hotel Presidente* (☎ 353 95 01; fax 352 02 72), Rua Alexandre Herculano 13, has doubles for around 11,000$00.

Castelo de São Jorge Below the castle at Costa do Castelo 74, *Pensão Ninho das Aguias* (☎ 886 70 08) offers amazing views after a steep climb. Reservations are essential. Doubles start at around 7000$00.

Places to Eat
Most of the city's good restaurants and cafés are in the Baixa and Bairro Alto districts. A trendy new restaurant and bar zone is riverside Doca de Santo Amaro, near Alcântara-Mar station. The main market, Mercado do Ribeira, is near Cais do Sodré station.

Baixa & Alfama One of several bargain restaurants along Rua dos Correeiros is *Lagosta Vermelha* (☎ 342 48 32), a casual casa de pasto at No 155. *Restaurante Pinóquio* (☎ 346 51 06), Praça dos Restauradores 79, is more expensive, but the seafood is good. *Restaurante O Sol* (☎ 347 19 44), Calçada do Duque 23, is a vegetarian option with set meals for under 1000$00. *Restaurante O Brunhal* (☎ 347 86 34), Rua da Glória 27, is one of several unpretentious places on this street with simple cheap food. Of several restaurants with outdoor seating in lower Alfama we like *Leitão do Arco da Conceição* (☎ 886 98 60), Rua dos Bacalhoeiros 4.

For a coffee or a meal, two turn-of-the-century cafés are *Nicola*, Rossio 24, and *Martinho da Arcada* (☎ 887 92 59), Praça do Comércio 3. The latter was once a haunt of the literary set, including Fernando Pessoa. *Café A Brasileira* (☎ 346 95 47), Rua Garrett 120, is another place with a literary pedigree (a bronze figure of Pessoa sits outside).

Bairro Alto Tiny *Restaurante A Primavera* (☎ 342 04 77), Travessa da Espera 34, has a family ambience complemented by honest, good cooking. Slightly more expensive is *O Cantinho do Bem Estar* (☎ 346 42 65), Rua do Norte 46. You'll have to get here early for a table. Another popular place in the same range is *Restaurante Sinal Vermelho* (☎ 346 12 52) at Rua das Gáveas 89 – make sure you leave room for the yummy desserts.

Cavernous *Cervejaria da Trindade* (☎ 342 35 06), Rua Nova Trindade 20-C, is a converted convent decorated with azulejos. Main dishes start at around 1200$00.

Cais do Sodré A short walk up Rua do Alecrim, at No 47, is the zany *Pano Mania* (☎ 342 24 74) self-service restaurant, offering great salads and cheap daily specials. *Restaurante Porto de Abrigo* (☎ 346 08 73), Rua dos Remolares 18, is recommended for seafood.

Entertainment

For current listings, pick up the free monthly *Agenda Cultural* from the tourist office, or *Público* from a newsstand.

Music In its authentic form, fado is fascinating, but many Lisbon *casas de fado* (which are also restaurants) produce pale tourist imitations at prices which may make you groan like the fado singer. Even the simplest places now have a minimum charge of 2000 to 4500$00. In the Bairro Alto, try *Adega Machado* (☎ 342 87 13), Rua do Norte 91, or the simpler *Adega do Ribatejo* (☎ 346 83 43), Rua Diário de Notícias 23. The tourist offices can suggest others.

Hot Clube de Portugal (☎ 346 73 69), Praça da Alegria 39, is at the centre of a thriving Lisbon jazz scene, with live music three or four nights a week. It's open from 10 pm to 2 am, closed on Sunday and Monday.

Homesick Dubliners can head down to *Ó Gilíns Irish Pub* (☎ 342 18 99) at Rua dos Remolares 8-10, by Cais do Sodré station. It's open daily from 11 am to 2 am and has live Irish tunes most Saturday nights and jazz with Sunday brunch.

Discos boom and bust at lightning speed. Try *Benzina* (see the Lisbon map; ☎ 363 39 59), Travessa de Teixeira Júnior 6 in the Alcântara district, or *Alcântara Mar* (see the Lisbon map; ☎ 363 64 32), down the road at Rua da Cozinha Económica 11, both raving from midnight until 6 or 7 am (though Al-

cântara Mar is open from Thursday to Saturday only). Several other bar-discos are in the nearby riverside areas: *Rock City* (see the Lisbon map; ☎ 342 86 40) on Rua Cintura do Porto de Lisboa has live rock nightly except Monday; *Dock's Club* (see the Lisbon map; ☎ 395 08 56), Rua da Cintura do Porto de Lisboa 226, carries on until 4 am nightly except Sunday.

The African music scene (predominantly Cape Verdean) bops in numerous bars in the area around Rua de São Bento; one of the best known is *Discoteca A Lontra* (see the Lisbon map; ☎ 395 69 68) at No 155, which carries on until 4 am nightly, except on Sunday and Monday.

Cinemas Lisbon has dozens of cinemas. Amoreiras shopping centre has a multi-screen venue (☎ 383 12 75) showing almost a dozen different films each night. Tickets are 800$00 (550$00 on Monday).

Spectator Sport The local football teams are Benfica and Sporting. The tourist offices can advise on match dates and tickets. If you must see one, bullfights are staged at Campo Pequeno between April and October.

Things to Buy

For azulejos, try Fabrica Sant'Ana at Rua do Alecrim 95. The Museu Nacional do Azulejo also has a small shop. Santos Ofícios at Rua da Madalena 87 has an eclectic range of Portuguese folk arts. On Tuesday and Saturday, visit the Feira da Ladra, a huge open-air market at Campo de Santa Clara in the Alfama district.

Getting There & Away

Air Lisbon is connected by daily flights to Porto, Faro and many European centres (see the introductory Getting There & Away and Getting Around sections of this chapter). For arrival and departure information phone ☎ 840 22 62.

Bus The main bus terminal (☎ 354 54 39) – used mainly by Rede Expressos, EVA (from the Algarve) and international coaches – is at Avenida Casal Ribeiro 18 (metro: Saldanha; see the Lisbon map). Renex (☎ 887 48 71), including Resende, Caima and Frota Azul

PORTUGAL

services, operates from Rua dos Bacalhoeiros, a few blocks east of Praça do Comércio. Mafrense (for Mafra and Ericeira) operates from beside Campo Grande metro (see the Lisbon map).

Train Santa Apolónia station (see the Lisbon map; for information ☎ 888 40 25) is the terminus for north and central Portugal, and for all international services. Cais do Sodré station is for Cascais and Estoril. Rossio station serves Sintra and Estremadura. Barreiro station, across the river, is the terminus for the south of Portugal; connecting ferries leave frequently from the pier at Terréiro do Paço, by Praça do Comércio. The new North-South railway line, linking suburban areas across the river (via the Ponte de 25 Abril), is due to open in late 1999 and will eventually link up to lines from Barreiro.

Ferry Ferries cross the Rio Tejo from Praça do Comércio's Terreiro do Praço terminal run to Montijo (280$00) and Seixal (210$00) every hour or so, and to Barreiro (170$00) more frequently; from the adjacent Cais da Alfândega terminal, ferries run all day to Cacilhas (100$00) every 10 minutes. There is also a car ferry (for bikes too) to Cacilhas from Cais do Sodré.

Getting Around
To/From the Airport Bus No 91, the Aero-Bus, runs about every 20 minutes from 7 am to 9 pm and takes 20 to 45 minutes (depending on traffic) between the airport and Cais do Sodré, including a stop right outside the national tourist office. A 430/1000$00 ticket is good for one/three days on all buses, trams and funiculars. Local bus Nos 8, 44, 45 and 83 also run near the national tourist office but are a nightmare in rush hour if you have baggage. A taxi is about 1300$00, plus an extra 300$00 if your luggage needs to go in the boot.

Bus & Tram Individual bus and tram tickets cost 160$00 or half that if purchased beforehand. Prepaid tickets are sold at kiosks with the Carris logo, most conveniently at Praça da Figueira and the Santa Justa *elevador*. If you plan to spend a few days in Lisbon, a tourist pass (Passe Turístico) valid for all

trams and buses and the metro is available for four days (1640$00) or one week (2320$00).

Buses and trams run from about 5 or 6 am to 1 am, with some night services. You might bag a transport map (*Planta dos Transportes Públicas da Carris*) from tourist offices or Carris kiosks, but thanks to the city's building frenzy, route changes are so frequent the map is not always reliable.

Wheelchair users can call Carris on ☎ 363 20 44 for information on its dial-a-ride service. The clattering, antediluvian trams (*eléctricos*) are an endearing component of Lisbon; don't leave without riding No 28 to the old quarter from Rua da Conceiçao.

Metro The newly expanded metro is useful for quick hops across town and to the Oceanarium at the former Expo site (metro: Oriente). Individual tickets cost 80$00; a *caderneta* of 10 tickets is 600$00. A day ticket (*bilhete diário*) is 200$00. The metro operates from 6.30 am to 1 am. Pickpockets can be a nuisance.

Taxi Compared with the rest of Europe, Lisbon's taxis are fast, cheap and plentiful. Flag them down on the street or go to a rank. Some that haunt the airport are less than scrupulous.

Car & Bicycle Car rental companies in Lisbon include Avis (☎ 356 11 76), Europcar (☎ 353 51 15) and Kenning (☎ 354 91 82). Eurodollar (☎ 940 52 47) has good rates. Tejo Bike (☎ 887 19 76) rents bikes for 750$00 an hour from just west of Doca de Santo Amaro, specifically to ride along the dedicated bike lane to Belém.

Around Lisbon

SINTRA
☎ 01
If you make only one side trip from Lisbon, Sintra should get top priority. Long favoured by Portuguese royalty and English nobility (Lord Byron was dotty about it), the thick forests and unusual architecture of Sintra provide a complete change from Lisbon. The efficient tourist office (☎ 923 11 57; fax 923 51 76), Praça da República 23 near the Palácio Nacional, has a good map and photos

of accommodation options. During weekends and the annual music festival in July, expect droves of visitors. In high season it's wise to book ahead.

Things to See

The **Palácio Nacional de Sintra** dominates the town with its twin kitchen chimneys. From Moorish origins, it grew into a synthesis of Manueline and Gothic. It's open daily except Wednesday, from 10 am to 1 pm and 2 to 5 pm; entry is 400$00 (200$00 for students).

One of the best of Sintra's museums is the **Museu do Brinquedo** on Rua Visconde de Monserrate, with over 20,000 toys from around the world. It's open daily except Monday from 10 am to 6 pm for 400$00 (250$00 for children and students).

A steep 3km climb from the centre leads to the ruined **Castelo dos Mouros** with a fine view over town and surroundings. It's open daily from 10 am to 7 pm (5 pm in winter). A further 20-minute climb leads to the **Palácio da Pena**, built in 1839 in an exuberant Romantic style. It's open daily except Monday, from 10 am to 1 pm and 2 to 6.30 pm (4.30 pm in winter); entry is 400$00 (160$00 for students). Cars are not allowed: Stagecoach bus No 434 makes regular runs from the station, via the tourist office, for 500$00.

Rambling and romantic, the **Monserrate Gardens** are a 4km walk from the town, past the brazenly luxurious **Palácio de Seteais** hotel. The gardens are open from 10 am to 7 pm (5 pm in winter), for 200$00. More beguiling is the **Convento dos Capuchos**, a tiny 16th-century hermitage in the forest 9km from Sintra, with cells hewn from rock and lined with cork. It's open daily from 10 am to 7 pm (5 pm in winter) for 200$00. A taxi from town costs about 2000$00 return (20% more at weekends).

Places to Stay

The nearest decent camping ground is *Camping Praia Grande* (☎ 929 05 81), on the coast 11km from Sintra and linked by a frequent bus service. The *pousada da juventude* (☎ 924 12 10) is at Santa Eufémia, 4km from the centre. Reservations are essential.

Casa de Hospedes Adelaide (☎ 923 08 73), Rua Guilherme Gomes Fernandes 11, a 10-minute walk from the station, has reason-able doubles without bath from around 3500$00. Better-value private rooms are around 4000$00 (the tourist office keeps a list). Across the tracks at Rua João de Deus 70, *Piela's* (☎ 924 16 91) has immaculate doubles with bath for around 7000$00.

Places to Eat

The excellent *Tulhas* (☎ 923 23 78) is close to the tourist office at Rua Gil Vicente 4-6. The simple *A Tasca do Manel* (☎ 923 02 15), Largo Dr Vergilio Horta 5 (near the station), serves up standards for around 900$00 a dish, while the pricier *Topico Bar & Restaurant* (☎ 923 48 25) at nearby Rua Dr Alfredo Costa 8, has live music on Friday and Saturday from 11 pm. For something special, try *Orixás* (☎ 924 16 72), an expensive Brazilian restaurant-cum-art gallery at Avenida Adriano Júlio Coelho 7. Near the tourist office, the cavernous *Bistrobar Ópera Prima* (☎ 924 45 18) has live jazz, soul and blues several nights a week.

Getting There & Away

The bus and train stations are together in the north of the town on Avenida Dr Miguel Bombarda, 2km from the Palácio Nacional. Trains from Lisbon's Rossio station take about 45 minutes (190$00). Buses run from Sintra to Estoril, Cascais and Mafra.

Getting Around

A three-hour sightseeing trip by taxi is 6000$00, plus 20% on weekends and holidays (the tourist office has a list of prices). Horse-drawn carriages are a romantic alternative: figure 7500$00 to Monserrate and back. Horse riding is available at Centro Hípico Penha Longa Country Club (☎ 924 90 33) for around 3500$00 an hour. Traditional trams run from Ribeira de Sintra (1.5km from Sintra-Vila) to Praia das Maças, 12km to the west.

CASCAIS
☎ 01

Cascais is the 'in' beach resort on the coast west of Lisbon, and is packed with tourists in summer. The tourist office (☎ 486 82 04; fax 467 22 80), Rua Visconde de Luz 14, has accommodation lists and bus timetables.

Things to See & Do

Two km to the east, **Estoril** is an old-fashioned resort with Europe's biggest **casino**, open daily from 3 pm to 3 am. Estoril's small **Praia Tamariz** beach (beside the train station) has an attractive ocean swimming pool.

Two km west of Cascais is **Boca do Inferno** (literally 'mouth of hell'), where the sea roars into the coast. **Cabo da Roca**, the westernmost point of Europe, is a spectacular and windy spot 16km from Cascais and Sintra (served by buses from both towns); pop into the tiny post office for a commemorative certificate. Those who like their beaches long and wild will appreciate **Guincho**, 3km from Cascais, a popular surfing venue.

Bicycles and motorcycles can be rented from Gesrent at Centro Commercial Cisne (☎ 486 45 66), Avenida Marginal Bloco 3 (near the post office).

Places to Stay

Camping Orbitur do Guincho (☎ 487 10 14; fax 487 21 67), 7km from Cascais near Guincho beach, is useful if you have your own transport. *Residencial Avenida* (☎ 486 44 17), Rua da Palmeira 14, is the most popular budget bet, with doubles without bath for 5000$00. Pretty *Casa da Pergola* (☎ 484 00 40; fax 483 47 91) at Avenida Valbom 13 has doubles with frills from 15,500$00.

Getting There & Away

From Cais do Sodré station in Lisbon it's a 25-minute train trip (190$00) to Estoril and Cascais.

SETÚBAL
☎ 065

Once an important Roman settlement, this refreshingly untouristy city 50km south of Lisbon is an easy hop from Lisbon. It has some fine seafood restaurants and nearby beaches. It's also a suitable base for exploring the nearby Parque Natural da Arrábida and Reserva Natural do Estuário do Sado.

Buses arrive at Avenida 5 de Outubro, five-minutes walk west of the municipal tourist office (☎/fax 53 42 22) on Praça do Quebedo. There's a larger, less helpful regional tourist office (☎ 53 91 20; fax 53 91 27) at Travessa Frei Gaspar 10.

The Instituto Português da Juventude (☎ 53 27 07) at Largo José Afonso has free Internet access for limited periods. It's open weekdays from 9.30 am to 7 pm.

Things to See & Do

The main cultural sight in town is the **Igreja de Jesus** in Praça Miguel Bombarda, a 15th-century creation with some early Manueline decoration inside. The **Galeria da Pintura Quinhentista** around the corner displays a renowned collection of 16th-century paintings. It's open daily except Sunday and Monday from 9 am to noon and 2 to 5 pm (free admission).

A string of good **beaches** west of town, includes Praia da Figuerinha (accessible by bus). Across the estuary at Tróia is a more developed beach, plus the ruins of a Roman settlement. On the ferry trip across you may see some of the 30 or so bottle-nosed dolphins that still live in the estuary.

Activities

Sistemas de Ar Livre (SAL; ☎/fax 2 76 85) organise regular Sunday walks in the region for 1000$00 per person. The tourist office usually has details. For jeep safaris, hiking and biking in the Serra da Arrábida, or canoe trips through the Reserva Natural do Estuário do Sado, contact Planeta Terra (☎ 53 21 40; fax 52 79 21). Mil Andanças (☎ 53 29 96; fax 3 96 63) also offer 4WD tours through the Tróia Peninsula.

Places to Stay & Eat

A municipal *camping ground* (☎ 52 24 75) is 1.5km west of town. A *centro de alojamento* hostel (☎ 53 27 07) in Largo José Afonso has dorm beds for 1700$00. *Residencial Todi* (☎ 2 05 92), Avenida Luísa Todi 244, has doubles without/with bath from 3000/4000$00. *Pensão Bom Regresso* (☎ 2 98 12) overlooking Praça do Bocage has doubles with TV for 5500$00. Up several notches, with doubles in the 8000$00 range, is nearby *Residencial Bocage* (☎ 2 15 98; fax 2 18 09) at Rua São Cristóvão 14.

There are lots of cheap restaurants east of the regional tourist office including *Restaurante A Faca*, Rua Arronches Junqueiro 71. Seafood restaurants line the western end of Avenida Luísa Todi; small, friendly *Casa do*

Chico (☎ 3 95 02) is at No 490. The best grilled fish around is at *Restaurante Verde e Branco* (☎ 52 65 46), Rua Maria Batista 33. It's only open for lunch and serves only fish.

Getting There & Away
Buses leave frequently from Lisbon's Praça de Espanha or from Cacilhas (a quick ferry hop from Lisbon's Cais de Alfândega).

Ferries shuttle across the estuary to Tróia regularly; the tourist office will have the latest timetable.

The Algarve

Loud, boisterous and full of foreigners, the Algarve is about as far from quintessential Portugal as one can get. While sun and sand are the major draw cards, there are some other attractions. West of Lagos are wild and all-but-deserted beaches. The coast east of Faro is dotted with colourful fishing villages. For those who've overdosed on seascapes, there are the forested slopes of Monchique, the fortified village of Silves and the past glory of Estói Palace.

Orientation
The southernmost slice of Portugal, the Algarve divides neatly into five regions: the Costa Vicentina facing west into Atlantic gales, the windward coast (Barlavento) from Sagres to Lagos, the central coast from Lagos to Faro, the leeward coast (Sotavento) from Faro to Vila Real de Santo António, and the interior.

The largest town, and district capital, is Faro. The easternmost town, Vila Real de Santo António, is a border crossing to Ayamonte, Spain – linked to it by a car ferry and a highway bridge across the mouth of Rio Guadiana. The beach, golf, disco and night-club scenes are focused on central Algarve, particularly Albufeira and Lagos. West of Lagos, the shore grows increasingly steep and rocky.

Information
Leaflets describing every Algarve community from tiny Alcoutim to booming Albufeira are available from the district tourist office in Faro. A host of English-language newspapers like the *Algarve News*, *APN* and *Algarve Resident*, aimed primarily at expats, provide entertainment listings and information on coming events.

Dangers & Annoyances
Take extra precautions against theft on the Algarve. Paranoia is unwarranted, but don't leave anything of value in your vehicle or unattended on the beach.

Swimmers should beware of dangerous currents, especially on the west coast. Beaches are marked by coloured flags: red means the beach is closed to bathing, yellow means swimming is prohibited but wading is fine, green means anything goes.

Things to Buy
Few souvenirs are actually made in the Algarve, but Moorish-influenced ceramics and local woollens (cardigans and fishing pullovers) are good value. You may want to try Algarviana, a local *amaretto* (bitter almond liqueur), or the salubrious bottled waters of Monchique, on sale everywhere.

Getting There & Away
Faro airport serves both domestic and international flights (see the introductory Getting There & Away section of this chapter).

It's about four hours by express coach from Lisbon to Faro via Vale Paraíso. Buses also run between Lagos and Seville (Spain) via major Algarve towns (5½ hours).

From Barreiro in Lisbon there are several trains daily to Lagos and Faro (four hours by intercidade train).

For motorists arriving from Ayamonte in Spain, a bridge 4km north of Vila Real de Santo António bypasses the old ferry connection. The most direct route from Lisbon to Faro, on the IP1/E01, takes about four hours.

Getting Around
Rede Expressos and EVA together run an efficient network of bus services throughout the Algarve. The IP1/EO1 superhighway planned to run the length of the coast to Spain, is only partially completed. Bicycles, scooters and motorcycles can be rented all over; see individual town listings.

PORTUGAL

THE ALGARVE

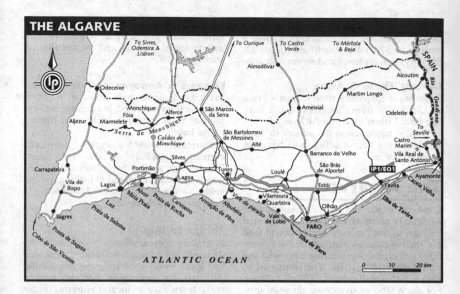

FARO
☎ 089

The capital of the Algarve, Faro is also the main transport hub and a thriving commercial centre, but is otherwise of little interest. The helpful tourism office (☎ 80 36 04; fax 80 04 53), Rua da Misericórdia, can provide a wide range of tourist literature.

Things to See & Do
The waterfront around Praça de Dom Francisco Gomes has pleasant gardens and cafés. Faro's beach, **Praia de Faro**, is 6km southwest of the city on Ilha de Faro. Take bus No 16 from in front of the tourist office; another option between May and September is a ferry from Arco da Porta Nova, close to Faro's port.

At Estói, 12km north of Faro, the wonderful crumbling wreck of **Estói Palace** has a surreal garden of statues, balustrades and azulejos – it's highly recommended. The bus from Faro to São Brás de Alportel goes via Estói.

Places to Stay & Eat
There's a big, cheap *municipal camping ground* on Praia de Faro. A friendly budget place near the centre is *Residencial Adelaide* (☎ 80 23 83; fax 82 68 70) at Rua Cruz dos Mestres 7: singles/doubles without private bath are 2000/3500$00 or 3000/4000$00 with. Close to the bus and train stations is *Residencial Avenida* (☎ 82 33 47), Avenida da República 150. A double is 8000/6000$00 with/without bath. Rooms at nearby *Residencial Madalena* (☎/fax 80 58 06), Rua Conselheiro Bivar 109, are about 5000/7000$00, all with bath.

Sol e Jardim (☎ 2 33 37), Praça Ferreira de Almeida 22, is a lively place serving excellent seafood. A *Garrafeira do Vilaça* (☎ 80 21 50), Rua São Pedro 33, is popular for budget meals. Worth lingering at is *Café Aliança*, a turn-of-the-century gem on Rua Dom Francisco Gomes.

Getting There & Away
The airport is 6km from the city centre. Bus Nos 14 and 16 run into town until around 10 pm in summer. A taxi costs about 1100$00 (1300$00 at weekends).

The bus station is in the centre, close to the harbour. There are at least eight express buses to Lisbon (2200$00) daily, including a deluxe *Alta Qualidade* service (2500$00), and frequent buses to other coastal towns.

The train station is a few minutes on foot west of the bus station. Around six trains go to Lisbon daily, including three intercidade express trains, and a similar number to Albufeira and Portimão.

TAVIRA
☎ 081

Tavira is one of the Algarve's oldest and most beautiful towns. Graceful bridges cross Rio Gilão which divides the town. The excellent tourist office (☎ 32 25 11) is at Rua da Galeria 9. Bicycles and motorcycles can be rented from Loris Rent (☎ 32 52 03, mobile ☎ 0931-27 47 66), Rua Damiao Augusto de Brito 4. For bike tours or a game of paintball, call ☎ 32 19 73 or mobile ☎ 0931-33 08 61.

Pastelaria Anazu (☎ 32 22 59), on the riverfront at Rua Jaques Pessoa 13, has a computer visitors can use for 650$00 an hour.

Things to See & Do
In the old part of town is the **Igreja da Misericórdia**, with a striking Renaissance doorway. From there, it's a short climb to the **castle** dominating the town.

Two km from Tavira is **Ilha da Tavira**, an attractive island beach connected to the mainland by ferry. Walk 2km beside the river to reach the ferry terminal at Quatro Águas or take the bus from the bus station.

For a look at the way the Algarve used to be, take a bus to **Cacela Velha**, an unspoilt hamlet 8km from Tavira. Another worthwhile day trip is to the church and colourful quay at **Olhão**, 22km west of Tavira. Drop in for a delicious seafood lunch at Papy's, Avenida 5 de Outubro 56, opposite the market.

Places to Stay & Eat
There's a *camping ground* on Ilha da Tavira, but the ferry stops running at 11 pm (usually 1 am from July to September). Popular *Pensão Residencial Lagoas* (☎ 32 22 52), Rua Almirante Cândido dos Reis 24, has singles/doubles from 3000/4000$00 without bath. *Pensão Residencial Princesa do Gilão* (☎ 32 51 71), Rua Borda d'Água de Aguiar 10 beside the river, charges 6000/7000$00,

but street-side rooms can be noisy. In the heart of town, *Residencial Imperial* (☎ 32 22 34), Rua José Pires Padinha 24, has rooms with bath and breakfast for 4000/6000$00.

Restaurante O Pátio (☎ 32 30 08), Rua António Cabreira 30, serves excellent Algarve specialties such as *cataplana* (shellfish cooked in a sealed wok). For cheaper fare, try *Restaurante Bica* (☎ 32 38 43), Rua Almirante Cândido dos Reis 24. Both are across the river from the market.

Getting There & Away
Running between Faro and Tavira are 15 trains a day as well as seven buses a day (four at weekends), taking an hour.

LAGOS
☎ 082

Lagos is a major tourist resort with some of the finest beaches on the Algarve. The memorably unhelpful tourist office (☎ 76 30 31) is on Largo Marquês de Pombal in the centre of town.

Things to See & Do
In the old part of town, the **municipal museum** houses an odd assortment of ecclesiastical treasures, handicrafts and preserved animal foetuses. The adjacent **Chapel of Santo António** contains some extraordinarily intricate baroque woodwork.

The beach scene includes **Meia Praia**, a vast strip of sand to the east; and to the west **Praia da Luz** and the more secluded **Praia do Pinhão**.

Espadarte do Sul (☎ 76 18 20) operates **boat trips** from Docapesca harbour, including snorkelling and game fishing. Bom Dia (☎ 76 46 70) has classier outings on a traditional schooner. Local fishermen trawl for customers along the seaside promenade and offer motorboat jaunts to the nearby grottoes.

Landlubbers can go **horse riding** at Tiffany's equestrian centre (☎ 6 93 95), about 10km west on the N125 road; they'll even come and get you in Lagos.

Places to Stay & Eat
Two nearby camping grounds are *Trindade* (☎ 76 38 93), 200m south of the town walls,

and *Imulagos* (☎ 76 00 31), with a shuttle bus from the waterfront road. The *pousada da juventude* (☎ 76 19 70) is at Rua Lançarote de Freitas 50. *Residencial Mara-zul* (☎ 76 97 49), Rua 25 de Abril 13, has smart singles/doubles from around 7000/9000$00. Private rooms are plentiful, for around 5500$00 a double.

For standard food with fado accompaniment, try *Restaurante A Muralha* (☎ 76 36 59), Rua da Atalaia 15. *O Cantinho Algarvio* (☎ 76 12 89), Rua Afonso d'Almeida 17, offers good Algarve specialities. Less touristy is *Adega Ribatejana* (☎ 76 08 06) at Rua dos Peixeiros 1. There's a string of bars in and around Rua 25 de Abril, some serving snacks. Or try *Mullens*, a wood-panelled pub with good food, at Rua Cândido dos Reis 86.

Getting There & Away
Both bus and train services depart up to six times daily to Lisbon.

Getting Around
You can rent bicycles, mopeds and motorcycles from Motoride (☎ 76 17 20) at Rua José Afonso 23 or agents in town. Figure on about 1000$00 a day for a mountain bike or 75000$00 for a motorcycle.

MONCHIQUE
☎ 082
This quiet highland town in the forested Serra de Monchique offers an eco-tourism alternative to the discos and lazy beach life on the coast.

Things to See & Do
In Monchique itself, the Igreja Matriz has an amazing Manueline portal – about the closest you'll get to seeing stone tied in knots! Follow the brown signs which lead pedestrians up above the bus station round the old town's narrow streets.

Six km south is the drowsy hot-spring community of Caldas de Monchique. Have a soak in the spa or try the bottled water. Eight km west is the 902m-high Fóia peak atop the Serra de Monique, the 'rooftop' of the Algarve. If you can ignore the forests of radio masts, the views are terrific.

Monchique's tourist office (☎ 91 11 89) has details of walking, horse riding and mountain-biking trips in the surrounding hills.

Places to Stay & Eat
The central *Residencial Estrela de Mon-chique* (☎ 91 31 11), Rua do Porto Fundo 46, has singles/doubles for 3000/5000$00. *Restaurante A Charrete* (☎ 9 21 42), Rua Samora Gil, is cosy and good value for money. Tiny, eccentric *Restaurante Central*, Rua da Igreja 5, is festooned with visitors' scribbled recommendations. *Barlefante* (☎ 9 27 74), at Travessa da Guerreira, is a long-established bar.

Getting There & Away
Over a dozen buses run daily between Lagos and Portimão, where nine services daily (five at weekends) run to Monchique.

SILVES
☎ 082
Silves was once the Moorish capital of the Algarve and rivalled Lisbon in its influence. Times are quieter now, but the town's huge castle is a reminder of past grandeur and well worth a visit.

The switched-on tourist office (☎ 44 22 55), Rua 25 de Abril, is open weekdays and Saturday morning.

Places to Stay & Eat
Residencial Sousa (☎ 44 25 02), Rua Samoura Barros 17, has singles/doubles for 3500/5000$00. The eye-catching *Residencial Ponte Romana* (☎ 44 32 75) beside the old bridge has doubles for around 6000$00.

Restaurante Rui (☎ 44 26 82), Rua C Vilarinho 27, is the best (and most expensive) fish restaurant in town; it serves a memorable *arroz de marisco* (shellfish rice). For cheaper meals, head for the riverfront restaurants opposite the old bridge.

Getting There & Away
Silves train station is 2km from town; buses meet Faro trains seven times daily (five times daily at weekends). There's a regular bus service to/from Portimão via Lagoa and Albufeira.

PORTUGAL

SAGRES
☎ 082

Sagres is a small fishing port and tourist destination perched on dramatic, windswept cliffs at the south-western extremity of Portugal. The tourist office (☎ 62 48 73) just beyond the central Praça a da República on Rua Comandante Matoso is open weekdays and Saturday morning. Turinfo (☎ 62 00 03) in Praça da República rents cars and bikes, makes hotel bookings and arranges jeep and fishing trips. It's open daily.

Things to See & Do
In the **fort**, on a wide windy promontory, Henry the Navigator established his school of navigation and primed the explorers who later founded the Portuguese empire.

There are several beaches close to Sagres. A particularly pleasant one is at the fishing village of **Salema**, 17km east.

No visit to Sagres would be complete without a trip to precipitous **Cabo de São Vicente** (Cape St Vincent), 6km from Sagres. A solitary lighthouse stands on this barren cape which proclaims itself the south-westernmost point of Europe.

Places to Stay & Eat
The well-maintained *Parques de Campismo Sagres* (☎ 62 43 51) is 2km from town, off the Vila do Bispo road. Many locals in Sagres rent out rooms for around 5000$00 a double. Cheap, filling meals can be had at *Restaurante A Sagres* at the roundabout as you enter the village, and at cafés in Praça da República.

Getting There & Away
There are about a dozen buses daily between Sagres and Lagos, fewer on Sunday and holidays.

Central Portugal

Central Portugal, good for weeks of desultory rambling, deserves more attention than it receives. From the beaches of the Costa de Prata to the lofty Serra da Estrela and the sprawling Alentejo plains dotted with curious megaliths, it is a landscape of extremes.

Some of Portugal's finest wines come from the Dão region, while farther south, the hills and plains are studded with the country's equally famous cork oaks. To literally top it off, the centre is graced with scores of fortresses and walled cities where you can wander along ancient cobbled streets, breathe clean air, and contemplate the awe-inspiring expanses below.

ÉVORA
☎ 066

One of the architectural gems of Portugal, the walled town of Évora (a UNESCO World Heritage Site) is the capital of Alentejo province – a vast district with landscapes of olive groves, vineyards and wheat fields, and in spring brilliant wildflowers. Évora's charm lies in the narrow one-way streets (mind those wing mirrors!) of the remarkably well preserved inner town.

Orientation & Information
The focal point is Praça do Giraldo. From here you can wander through backstreets until you meet the city walls. Poor maps with some walking routes, plus several glossier publications, are available from the tourist office (☎ 2 26 71; fax 74 25 34), Praça do Giraldo 73, while other guides and maps can be found at Nazareth bookshop, Praça do Giraldo 46.

Outside the tourist office is an automatic cash-exchange machine which accepts a wide range of currencies. The hospital (☎ 2 21 32) is on Rua do Valasco. At Ciber Évora (☎ 74 62 00; ciberevora@mail.telepac.pt), Rua Fria 7, you can use the net or send emails for 250$00 per half-hour.

Things to See
On Largo do Marquês de Marialva is the **Sé**, Évora's cathedral, with cloisters and a museum of ecclesiastical treasures, both closed Monday. Admission is 350$00.

Next door, the **Museu de Évora** features Roman and Manueline sculptures, and paintings by 16th-century Portuguese artists. Admission is 250$00. Opposite the museum is the Roman-era **Temple of Diana**, featured in Évora's top-selling postcard.

PORTUGAL

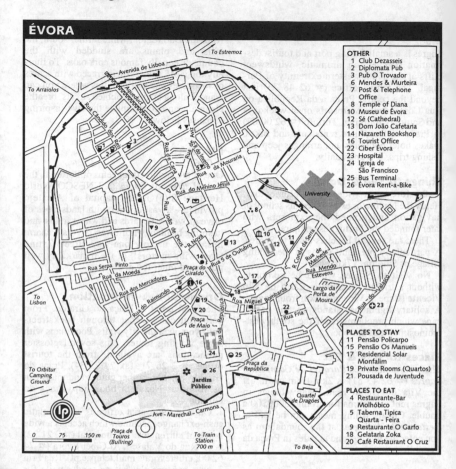

ÉVORA

OTHER
1 Club Dezasseis
2 Diplomata Pub
3 Pub O Trovador
6 Mendes & Murteira
7 Post & Telephone Office
8 Temple of Diana
10 Museu de Évora
12 Sé (Cathedral)
13 Dom João Cafetaria
14 Nazareth Bookshop
16 Tourist Office
22 Ciber Évora
23 Hospital
24 Igreja de São Francisco
25 Bus Terminal
26 Évora Rent-a-Bike

PLACES TO STAY
11 Pensão Policarpo
15 Pensão Os Manueis
17 Residencial Solar Monfalim
19 Private Rooms (Quartos)
21 Pousada de Juventude

PLACES TO EAT
4 Restaurante-Bar Molhóbico
5 Taberna Típica Quarta - Feira
9 Restaurante O Garfo
18 Gelataria Zoka
20 Café Restaurant O Cruz

The **Igreja de São Francisco**, a few blocks south of Praça do Giraldo, includes the ghoulish Capela dos Ossos (Chapel of Bones), constructed with the bones and skulls of several thousand people. Admission is 100$00.

Places to Stay

Accommodation gets very tight in Évora, which is popular with tour groups. The tourist office can help, but in summer you should definitely book ahead.

An *Orbitur* camping ground (☎ 2 51 90) is about 2km south of the town; take a bus towards Alcáçovas or a taxi. There's a new *pousada da juventude* (☎ 74 48 48; fax 74 48 43) at Rua Miguel Bombarda 40.

Among private *quartos* in the streets behind the tourist office, recommended are those at Rua Romão Ramalho 27 (☎ 2 24 53) where doubles are 5000$00. At Rua do Raimundo 35, *Pensão Os Manueis* (☎ 2 28 61) has doubles without/with private bath for 5000/6000$00. *Pensão Policarpo* (☎/fax 2 24 24;), Rua da Freiria de Baixo 16, began as a 16th-century townhouse; doubles are 7000/10,000$00 without/with bath. *Residencial*

Solar Monfalim (☎ 2 20 31; fax 74 23 67), Largo da Misericórdia 1, is a mini-palace with doubles from around 14,000$00.

Places to Eat

Café Restaurant O Cruz (☎ 74 47 79), Praça 1 de Maio 20, dishes out good bacalhau and tasty *carne com ameijoas* (meat with clams). Another good-value place is *Restaurante-Bar Molhóbico* (☎ 74 43 43) at Rua de Aviz 91, which boasts half a dozen versions of *migas* (a traditional bread-based stew).

Jovial *Taberna Tipica Quarta-Feira* (☎ 2 75 30), Rua do Inverno 16, packs in the locals for its specialty creamed spinach and pork dishes. *Restaurante O Garfo* (☎ 2 92 56), Rua de Santa Catarina 13, provides healthy servings at reasonable prices in traditional surroundings.

The town's most popular ice-cream parlour is *Gelataria Zoka* at Largo de São Vicente 14.

Entertainment

Among popular student hang-outs is a cluster of bars north-west of the centre – *Club Dezasseis* (☎ 2 65 59) at Rua do Escrivão da Cámara 16; *Diplomata Pub* (☎ 2 56 75), with frequent live music, at Rua do Apóstolo 4; and *Pub O Trovador* (☎ 2 73 70) at Rua da Mostardeira 4. Another student focal point that stays open late is *Dom João Cafetaria* (☎ 2 04 93), Rua Vasco da Gama 10.

The Feira de São João is Évora's big bash, held from approximately 22 June to 2 July and renowned as one of Alentejo's biggest country fairs.

Getting There & Away

Bus On weekdays there are at least eight buses a day to Lisbon (2 to 2¾ hours), six to Estremoz, and two to Porto; all buses depart from the terminal (☎ 2 21 21) on Rua da República.

Train There are two daily interregional services to Lisbon (three hours), plus slower services. There are also trains to the Algarve (tedious and indirect), Coimbra (changes required) and regional chug-a-lug services to Beja.

Getting Around

Évora Rent-a-Bike (☎ 76 14 53), in the Jardim Público, has mountain bikes for about 2000$00 a day. Mendes & Murteira (☎ 2 74 68; fax 2 36 16 Rua 31 de Janeiro 15-A, can organise tours of the city and nearby mega-lithic monuments.

MONSARAZ
☎ 066

Monsaraz, a magical walled town perched high above the plain, is well worth the effort spent getting there for its eerie medieval at-mosphere, clear light and magnificent views. It's small and easily covered on foot in a couple of hours. Of architectural interest is the **Museu de Arte Sacra**, probably a former tribunal which houses a rare 15th-century fresco of the allegory of justice. Clamber onto the castle's parapets for the best views.

Places to Stay & Eat

There are several places to stay along the main Rua Direita, with doubles around 5000$00. The tourist office (☎ 55 71 36) on the main square can provide details of other Turihab places and a couple of posh estab-lishments just outside town. There are several tourist-geared restaurants and a tiny grocery store near the main gate. Eat before 8 pm, as the town goes to bed early.

Getting There & Away

There are three to four buses daily (weekdays only) from Reguengos de Monsaraz (17km west), which is connected to Évora by three buses daily (more in term-time). The last bus from Monsaraz back to Reguengos currently leaves at 5 pm.

ESTREMOZ
☎ 068

The Estremoz region is dominated by huge mounds of marble extracted from its quarries. The town's architectural appeal lies in its elegant, gently deteriorating buildings, which are liberally embellished with marble.

Information

The welcoming tourist office (☎ 33 35 41; fax 2 44 89), at Largo da República 26, just south of the main square (known as the Rossio), has maps and accommodation lists.

Things to See & Do

The upper section of Estremoz is crowned by the **Torre de Menagem** which affords a fine view of the town and countryside. The former 14th-century palace is now a luxury pousada. Opposite is the **Museu Municipal** which specialises in unique Estremoz pottery figurines. It's open daily except Mondays for 175$00.

The focus of the lower section is the Rossio, where a lively food, pottery and flea **market** takes place every Saturday morning. The nearby **Museu de Ciências da Terra**, all about marble, is housed in the lovely cloisters of the former 16th-century Convento de Maltezas and open daily except Saturday afternoon and Sunday for 300$00.

Vila Viçosa, 17km from Estremoz, is another famous marble town. The major attraction is the **Palácio Ducal** – the ancestral home of the dukes of Bragança – with its horde of carpets, furniture and artworks. It's open daily, except Monday and public holidays, but the admission fee is steep: 1000$00 (plus 500$00 for the armoury museum).

Places to Stay & Eat

Spacious doubles at the friendly *Pensão-Restaurante Mateus* (☎ 2 22 26), Rua Almeida 41, are good value at 4000/5000$00 (without/with bath). The nearby *Adega do Isaias* (☎ 2 23 18) at No 21 is a popular rustic tavern serving great grills.

Getting There & Away

On weekdays about six buses daily (including three expressos) run to/from Évora. Four run to Portalegre and Elvas daily, and around three to Lisbon.

CASTELO DE VIDE & MARVÃO
☎ 045

From Portalegre (near the Spanish border, north-east of Lisbon) it's a short hop to **Castelo de Vide**, noted for its mineral water and picturesque houses clustered around a castle. Highlights are the **Judiaria** (Old Jewish Quarter) in the well-preserved network of medieval backstreets, and the view from the castle.

Try to spend at least one night here or in **Marvão**, a magnificent medieval walled village tucked into a mountaintop 12km from Castelo de Vide. The grand views from its castle encompass large chunks of Spain and Portugal.

Information

The tourist offices at Castelo de Vide (☎ 90 13 61; fax 90 18 27), Rua de Bartolomeu Álvares da Santa 81, and at Marvão (☎ 9 31 04; fax 9 35 26), Rua Dr Matos Magalhães, can both help with accommodation, including private rooms and Turihab places.

Getting There & Away

From Portalegre there are two to four buses daily to Castelo de Vide and one or two to Marvão. Two buses run daily from Lisbon to Castelo de Vide and Marvão. There are two connections daily between Castelo de Vide and Marvão (you may have to change at Portagem, a junction 7km from Marvão). Outside the summer season you may find no buses at all on weekends and holidays.

NAZARÉ
☎ 062

The peaceful 17th-century fishing village of Nazaré was 'discovered' by tourism in the 1970s and dubbed Portugal's most picturesque fishing village. Today, the old fishing skills and distinctive local dress have gone overboard and in the high season the place is a tourist circus. But the beauty of the coastline and fine seafood make it a worthwhile destination.

The tourist office (☎ 56 11 94) is at the funicular end of Avenida da República and open daily from 10 am to 10 pm in high season.

Things to See & Do

The lower part of Nazaré's beachfront has retained a core of narrow streets which now cater to the tourist trade. The upper section, O Sítio, on the cliffs overlooking the beach, is reached by a vintage funicular railway. The cliff-top view along the coast is superb.

The beaches attract huge summer crowds and pollution is an increasing problem. Beware of dangerous currents. The tourist office will tell you which beaches are safe for swimming.

Places to Stay & Eat
There are three nearby camping grounds. The cheap *Camping Golfinho* (☎ 55 36 80) is off the N242 at the top of town. Well-equipped *Vale Paraíso* (☎ 56 15 46), off the Leiria road, and an Orbitur site (☎ 56 11 11) off the Alcobaça road are both 2.5km from Nazaré. Many locals rent private rooms: you will probably be pounced on when you arrive at the bus station. Singles/doubles start around 3000/4500$00. Among several budget pensões is *Residencial Marina* (☎ 55 15 41) at Rua Mouzinho de Albuquerque 6 where doubles range from 3000 to 5000$00. Note that all room prices rocket in August.

A compelling reason to visit is the superb and abundant seafood, though the seafront restaurants are expensive. For cheaper fare in simple surroundings, try *Casa Marques* (☎ 55 16 80) at Rua Gil Vicente 37, run by a troika of Nazarean women. The friendly *A Tasquinha* (☎ 55 19 45) at Rua Adrião Batalha 54 does a superb *carne de porco à Alentejana*. Another attractively priced place is *Casa O Pescador* (☎ 55 33 26) at Rua António Carvalho Laranjo 18-A.

Getting There & Away
The nearest train station, 6km away at Valado, is connected to Nazaré by frequent buses. There are numerous bus connections to Lisbon, Alcobaça, Óbidos and Coimbra.

ALCOBAÇA
☎ 062
Alcobaça's attraction is the immense **Mosteiro de Santa Maria de Alcobaça**, founded in 1178. The original Gothic style has undergone Manueline, Renaissance and baroque additions. Of interest are the tombs of Pedro I and Inês de Castro, the cloisters, the kings' room and the kitchens. It's open from 9 am to 7 pm (5 pm in winter); entry is 400$00.

The tourist office (☎ 58 23 77) is opposite the monastery.

Getting There & Away
Alcobaça is an easy day trip from Nazaré. There are frequent buses to Nazaré, Batalha and Leiria. The closest train station is 5km north-west at Valado dos Frades, from where there are buses to Alcobaça.

BATALHA
☎ 044
Batalha's single highlight is its monastery, the **Mosteiro de Santa Maria de Vitória**, a colossal Gothic masterpiece constructed between 1388 and 1533. Earthquakes and vandalism by French troops have taken their toll, but a full restoration was completed in 1965. Highlights include the Founder's Chapel (with the tomb of Henry the Navigator), the Royal Cloisters, Chapter House and the Unfinished Chapels. It's open from 9 am to 6 pm daily; entry to the Cloisters and Unfinished Chapels is 400$00.

The tourist office (☎ 76 71 80) is in a nearby shopping complex on Largo Paulo VI.

Getting There & Away
There are frequent bus connections to Alcobaça, Nazaré and Leiria, and at least three direct buses to Lisbon daily.

ÓBIDOS
☎ 062
The impressive walled town of Óbidos has preserved its medieval streets and alleys almost too perfectly. The town is easily seen in just a few hours. The efficient regional tourist office (☎ 95 92 31; fax 95 97 70), Rua Direita, has information on Óbidos and the region.

Things to See
Climb onto the town walls and do a circuit for the views and your bearings. Then wander through the back alleys before popping into **Igreja de Santa Maria**, featuring fine azulejos, and the adjacent **museu municipal**.

Places to Stay & Eat
Accommodation isn't cheap but it's plentiful, with residencials and a number of private rooms for around 4500$00 a double. You might fancy dishing out for the romantic *Casa do Poço* (☎ 95 93 58) in Travessa da Mouraria; its four double rooms around a courtyard are 11,500$00 each. A cheaper alternative is *Residencial Martim de Freitas* (☎ 95 91 85), just outside the walls on the Estrada Nacional 8, with doubles from 6000$00.

PORTUGAL

Restaurants are not cheap either. The supermarket inside the town gate would suit self-caterers. *O Conquistador* (☎ 95 95 28), on Rua Josefa de Óbidos, has some imaginative dishes and a pleasant outdoor seating area.

Getting There & Away
There are excellent bus connections to Lisbon, Porto, Coimbra and the surrounding region. From the train station, outside the walls at the foot of the hill, there are five services daily to Lisbon (most with a change at Cacém).

COIMBRA
☎ 039
Coimbra is famed for its university, dating back to the 13th century, and its traditional role as a centre of culture and art, complemented in recent times by industrial development.

The regional tourist office (☎ 83 30 19; fax 82 55 76) at Largo da Portagem has pamphlets and cultural-events information, but a municipal tourist office (☎ 83 25 91) on Praça Dom Dinis by the university, and another (☎ 83 32 02) down in Praça da República, are considerably more helpful. All have the regional office's good city map.

Coimbra's annual highlight is the Queima das Fitas (literally 'burning of ribbons') when students celebrate the end of the academic year by burning their faculty ribbons. This boisterous week of fado and revelry begins on the first Thursday in May.

Things to See
In lower Coimbra, the most interesting sight is **Mosteiro de Santa Cruz** with its ornate pulpit, medieval tombs and intricate sacristy.

In the upper town, the main attractions are the **old university** with its baroque library and Manueline chapel, and the **Machado de Castro Museum**, with a fine collection of sculpture and painting. The back alleys of the university quarter are filled with student hang-outs and an exuberant atmosphere.

At **Conimbriga**, 16km south of Coimbra, are the excavated remains of a Roman city (open daily, in summer from 9 am to l pm and 2 to 8 pm, and in winter to 6 pm), including

impressive mosaic floors, baths and fountains. The site museum (open daily except Monday, from 10 am to l pm and 2 to 6 pm) has a variety of Roman artefacts and a good restaurant. Entry costs 350$00. Buses run frequently to Condeixa, about 2km from the site, or you can take a direct bus at 9.05 or 9.35 am (9.35 am only at weekends) from the AVIC terminal at Rua João de Ruão 18; it returns at 1 and 6 pm (6 pm only at weekends).

Activities
O Pioneiro do Mondego (☎ 47 83 85) rents out kayaks at 3000$00 a day for paddling down the Rio Mondego (a free minibus whisks you 25km upriver to Penacova at 10 am).

Horse riders can trot around Choupal Park by contacting the Coimbra Riding Centre (☎ 83 76 95), Mata do Choupal.

Places to Stay & Eat
The *pousada da juventude* (☎ 82 29 55), Rua António Henriques Seco 12-14, is Coimbra's youth hostel; take bus No 7 from Coimbra A train station. *Hospedaria Simões* (☎ 83 46 38), Rua Fernandes Tomás 69 above Largo da Portagem, has good-value doubles with bath for 4000$00. Near Coimbra A train station, *Pensão Restaurante Vitória* (☎ 82 40 49), Rua da Sota 9 and 19, has bright doubles with shower for the same. Nearby, *Pensão Flôr de Coimbra* (☎ 82 38 65), Rua do Poço 5, has well-tended old rooms with shower for 5000/7000$00 and, in summer, daily vegetarian meals. A block away at Rua das Azeiteiras 55, quiet doubles with bath at *Residência Coimbra* (☎ 83 79 96) start at 7000$00.

At Rua das Flores 18 in the hilltop lanes around the university, Dutch-run *Casa Pombal Guesthouse* (☎ 83 51 75) has everything from bathless ground-floor doubles at 6400$00 to bird's-eye views at 7700$00 with bath, and a huge breakfast.

The lanes off Praça do Comércio and near the Mosteiro de Santa Cruz feature a concentration of cheap, filling fare. *Restaurante Democrática* (☎ 82 37 84) on Travessa da Rua Nova is a low-key venue for Portuguese standards, with some half-portions under 1000$00. *Diligência Bar* (☎ 82 76 67), Rua Nova 30, is also a popular venue for amateur nd professional fadistos. The vaulted *Café Santa Cruz* beside the Mosteiro is an addictive place for coffee breaks. At No 12 in seedy Beco do Forno, *Zé Manel* (☎ 82 37 90) has crazy décor and huge servings; go by 8 pm to beat the crowds.

Rua das Azeiteiras is lined with modest restaurants, including *Adega Funchal* (☎ 82 41 37) at No 18, justifiably proud of its speciality, goat stewed in red wine. Though the food situation is dismal around Praça da República, *Bar-Restaurante ACM* (☎ 82 36 33) at Rua Alexandre Herculano 21A has good, plain fare for under 800$00 per dish.

Getting There & Away

At least a dozen buses and an equal number of trains run daily to Lisbon and Porto and there are frequent express buses to Évora and Faro. Coimbra has three train stations: Coimbra Parque for Lousã; Coimbra A for Figueira da Foz; and the main Coimbra B for all other services (including international). Coimbra A and B are linked by a regular shuttle train service.

Getting Around

Mountain bikes can be rented from O Pioneiro do Mondego (☎ 47 83 85), which has a kiosk in the little park just upriver from Largo da Portagem. Car-rental agencies include Avis (☎ 83 47 86), Hertz (☎ 83 74 91) and Salitur (☎ 82 05 94).

LUSO & BUÇACO FOREST
☎ 031

Walkers will appreciate the Buçaco Forest, which was chosen by monks as a retreat in the 6th century and has escaped serious harm since then. It's a few kilometres from the spa resort of Luso, where the tourist office (☎ 93 91 33) on Avenida Emídio Navarro has a general map of the forest and more detailed leaflets describing trails past wayside shrines and more than 700 species of trees and shrubs.

Places to Stay & Eat

The Luso tourist office has accommodation lists. *Pensão Central* (☎ 93 92 54), Avenida Emídio Navarro, has bright singles/doubles from 2700/4500$00 and a good summer-time restaurant with patio seating.

For a touch of class, try the *Palace Hotel* (☎ 93 01 01; fax 93 05 09), a former royal hunting lodge in the forest and as zany and beautiful an expression of Manueline style as any in Portugal. Figure on at least 2500$00 per dish or 5000$00 for the restaurant's set menu. A stay in this positively elegant five-star establishment will cost you at least 26,000/30,000$00.

Getting There & Away

Five buses a day go to Luso/Buçaco from Coimbra and Viseu (but only two on weekends). Just one train, departing around 10.30 am from Coimbra B, gives you enough time for a day trip.

SERRA DA ESTRELA
☎ 071, 075

Serra da Estrela, Portugal's highest mainland mountain range, stretches between Guarda and Castelo Branco. With steep valleys, forests and streams, it offers superb scope for hiking and is a designated *parque natural*. The highest peak, Torre (1993m), is snow-covered for much of the year.

Orientation & Information

The best sources of general information are at regional tourist offices in Covilhã (☎ 075-32 21 70; fax 075-31 33 64) and Guarda (☎ 071-22 18 17), and the park office in Manteigas (☎ 075-98 23 82; fax 075-98 23 84). Covilhã is an uninteresting industrial hub, but a good base for excursions; another is the nearby hostel at Penhas da Saúde.

The regional tourism administration publishes the walking guide *À Descoberta da Estrela*, with maps and narratives. It is available in an English edition (845$00) from tourist offices and park offices. A more detailed map (1050$00) is also available.

Serious hikers might want to contact the Club Nacional de Montanhismo (☎ 075-32 33 64; fax 075-31 35 14) in Covilhã, which organises weekend walking, camping, skiing and other trips.

Places to Stay

The *pousada da juventude* (☎ 075-33 53 75) at Penhas da Saúde, 10km above Covilhã, has facilities for meals (theirs or you can do them yourself), dormitory accommodation and a few functional doubles. It's open from 8 am to midnight. Buses come up from Covilhã twice a day in August, and hitching is fairly safe and easy; the only other options are your feet or bike, or a taxi (about 2000$00).

Guarda has a *centro de alojamento* hostel (☎ 071-21 22 10) as well.

Getting There & Away

There are several buses a day from Coimbra to Seia, Covilhã and Guarda, as well as some from Porto and Lisbon to Covilhã and Guarda. Twice-daily intercidade trains link Coimbra to Guarda, with twice-daily interregional trains stopping at Gouveia too. Covilhã and Guarda are on the Lisbon-Paris line, with several fast trains a day and connections from Porto.

Getting Around

There are twice-daily buses (and some weekend express services) linking Guarda with Gouveia and with Covilhã. No buses cross the park, though you can go around the north or south end; Seia-Covilhã takes about two hours via Guarda.

The North

Most visitors are surprised by Portugal's northern tier. With quite considerable tracts of forest, rich viticultural country, the peaks of Peneda-Gerês National Park, and a strand of undeveloped beaches, it is Portugal's new tourism horizon. The urban scene focuses on Porto with its magnificent vantage point on the Rio Douro. Within easy reach of Porto are a trio of stately historical cities: Braga, Portugal's religious centre; beautifully situated Viana do Castelo; and Guimarães, which proudly declares itself the country's birthplace.

PORTO

☎ 02

Porto is Portugal's second-largest city. Despite its reputation as a grimy industrial centre, it has considerable charm beyond the imbibing of port wine. Indeed its centre has been declared a UNESCO World Heritage Site.

Orientation

The city clings to the steep north bank of the Rio Douro, spanned here by five bridges. On the opposite bank is Vila Nova de Gaia, a separate town but, with its port wine lodges, Porto's main attraction.

The axis of central Porto is Avenida dos Aliados. Major shopping areas are eastward around the Bolhão Market and Rua de Santa Catarina, and westward along Rua dos Clérigos. Praça da Liberdade marks the southern end of Avenida dos Aliados, close to São Bento station and its cavernous, azulejo-covered booking hall. The picturesque Ribeira district lies along the waterfront, below São Bento and in the shadow of the great Ponte de Dom Luís I bridge.

Information

Tourist Offices The municipal tourist office (☎ 205 27 40; fax 332 33 03) is at Rua Clube dos Fenianos 25, close to the town hall. It's open weekdays from 9 am to 7 pm (to 5.30 pm outside the summer season) and weekends from 10 am to 5 pm. A smaller national tourist office (☎ 205 75 14; fax 205 32 12) is at Praça Dom João I 43. In July-August it's open weekdays from 9 am to 7.30 pm (from 9.30 am the rest of the year) and on weekends from 9.30 am to 7.30 pm (to 3.30 pm the rest of the year).

Foreign Consulates The UK Consulate (☎ 618 47 89; fax 610 04 38) is west of Boavista at Avenida da Boavista 3072. The Spanish Consulate (☎ 56 39 15; fax 510 19 14) is at Rua de Dom João IV 341.

Money Banks with automatic-teller machines (ATMs) and exchange desks are everywhere, including Praça da Liberdade. Automatic cash-exchange machines are at Avenida dos Aliados 21 and 138. Better rates are at the exchange bureaus Portocambios, Rua Rodrigues Sampaio 193, and Intercontinental, Rua de Ramalho Ortigão 8.

Post & Communications The main post office (the place to collect poste-restante mail), with telephone and fax facilities, is across Praça General Humberto Delgado from the municipal tourist office. The main telephone office is at Praça da Liberdade 62.

PORTO

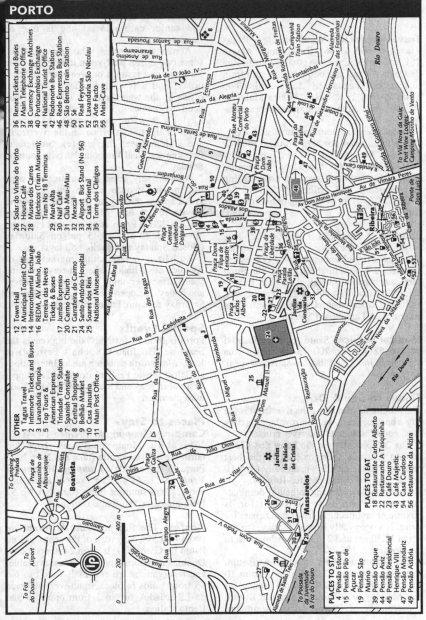

OTHER
1 Tagus Travel
2 Internorte Tickets and Buses
3 Lavandaria Olimpia
5 Top Tours & American Express
6 Trindade Train Station
7 Spanish Consulate
8 Central Shopping
9 Bolhão Market
10 Casa Januário
11 Main Post Office

12 Town Hall
13 Municipal Tourist Office
14 Intercontinental Exchange
16 REDM, AV Minho, João Tickets & Buses
17 Jumbo Bus Station
20 Carmo Church
21 Garrafeira do Carmo
24 Santo António Hospital
25 Soares dos Reis National Museum

26 Solar do Vinho do Porto
27 House Café
28 Museu dos Carros Eléctricos (Tram Museum); Tram No 18 Terminus
29 Maré Alta
30 Naif Café
31 Club Mau-Mau
32 Mexcal
33 Airport Bus Stand (No 56)
34 Casa Oriental
35 Torre dos Clérigos

36 Renex Tickets and Buses
37 Main Telephone Office
38 Currency Exchange Machines
40 Portocambios Exchange
41 National Tourist Office
42 Rodonorte Bus Station
46 Rede Expressos Bus Station
48 São Bento Train Station
50 Sé
51 Real Feytoria
52 Lavandaria São Nicolau
53 Arte Facto
55 Meia-Cave

PLACES TO STAY
4 Pensão Estoril
15 Pensão Pão de Açucar
19 Pensão São Marino
39 Pensão Chique
44 Pensão Aviz
45 Pensão Residencial Henrique VIII
47 Pensão Mondariz
49 Pensão Astória

PLACES TO EAT
18 Restaurante Carlos Alberto
22 Restaurante A Tasquinha
23 Café Douro
43 Café Majestic
54 Casa Cardoso
56 Restaurante da Alzira

Both are open daily (the telephone office until midnight).

Travel Agencies Youth-oriented Tagus Travel (☎ 609 41 46), Rua Campo Alegre 261, and Jumbo Expresso (☎ 339 33 20), Rua de Ceuta 47, sell discounted plane and train tickets, and Tagus sells ISIC cards. Top Tours (☎ 208 27 85), Rua Alferes Malheiro 96, is Porto's American Express representative.

Local adventure-tour operators with experience throughout northern Portugal include Montes d'Aventura (☎ 830 51 57; mobile ☎ 0936-607 37 39; fax 830 51 58; maventura @ip.pt) for trekking, cycling, horse riding and canoeing; and Trilhos (☎ 550 46 04; ☎/fax 52 07 40) for canyoning or hydrospeed trips.

Laundry Lavandaria Olimpia, on Rua Miguel Bombarda in the university area, has laundry and dry-cleaning services, as does Lavandaria 5 à Sec in the Central Shopping centre. A cheaper municipal service, Lavandaria São Nicolau (☎ 208 46 21), is at the west end of the Ribeira district on Rua Infante Dom Henrique. All are closed Sunday.

Medical Services Santo António Hospital (☎ 200 52 41 day; 200 73 54 night), Rua Vicente de José Carvalho, has staff that speak English.

Things to See & Do

The **Ribeira** district along the riverfront is the city's beating heart, with narrow lanes, grimy bars, good restaurants and river cruises.

The 200-plus steps of the **Torre dos Clérigos** on Rua dos Clérigos lead to the best panorama of the city. It's open daily from 10 am to noon and 2 to 5 pm, for 100$00.

The formidable **Sé**, the cathedral dominating central Porto, is worth a visit for its mixture of architectural styles and ornate interior. It's open daily except Sunday, from 9 am to 12.30 pm and 2 to 6 pm. Admission to the cloisters is 250$00.

The **Soares dos Reis National Museum**, Rua Dom Manuel II, is open daily from 10 am to 12.30 pm and 1.30 to 6 pm (except all day Monday and Tuesday morning), with masterpieces of Portuguese painting and sculpture from the 19th and 20th centuries. Admission is 350$00 (half-price for youth and senior card-holders) and is free on Sunday morning.

Across the river in Vila Nova de Gaia, some two dozen **port-wine lodges** are open for tours and tastings on weekdays and Saturday, and a few on Sunday. The tourist office by the waterfront can tell you all you need to know. Some good tours are at Taylor's (up Rua do Choupelo), Ferreira (west of the tourist office on the riverfront) and Calém (near the bridge). Sandeman, Osborne and Real Vinícola also have tours on Sunday.

Alternatively, select from a huge port wine list and sip it on a terrace with excellent views across the city, at the **Solar do Vinho do Porto** (☎ 609 77 93), Rua de Entre Quintas 220 in Porto. It's open until 11.45 pm on weekdays and 10.45 pm on Saturday (closed Sunday and public holidays).

Bolhão is a fascinating market east of Avenida dos Aliados, where cheery strapping ladies offer everything from seafood to herbs and honey. It's open weekdays until 5 pm and Saturday to 1 pm, but mornings are best.

Special Events

Porto is fond of festivals: the big one is the Festa de São João (St John's Festival) in June. Also worth catching are an International Celtic Music Festival in March, a Puppet Festival in May and the Grand Night of Fado in September.

Places to Stay

Camping *Camping da Prelada* (☎ 81 26 16) is at Rua Monte dos Burgos, about 5km north-west of the centre (take bus No 6 from Praça de Liberdade). *Camping Moinho de Vento* (☎ 713 59 48) is at Praia da Madalena, about 12km south of Porto (take bus No 57 from opposite São Bento station).

Hostels The fine *pousada da juventude* (☎ 617 72 57), 5km west of the centre at Rua Paulo da Gama 551, is open 24 hours a day. Doubles and dorm-style quads are available, and reservations are essential. Take bus No 35 from Lóios (a block south-west of Praça da Liberdade), or No 1 from opposite São Bento station.

Guesthouses In the seedy neighbourhood around São Bento station, *Pensão Mondariz* (☎ 200 56 00) at Rua Cimo de Vila 147 is cheap and cheerful, with doubles from 4000$00. *Pensão Residencial Henrique VIII* (☎ 200 65 11), across Praça da Batalha at Rua Duque de Loulé 168, has doubles with bath for 5000$00. A 10-minute walk down towards the river, just outside the old walls at Rua Arnaldo Gama 56, is *Pensão Astória* (☎ 200 81 75) where elegant old doubles, some with river views, are 5000$00 with bath and breakfast.

On the east side of Avenida dos Aliados at No 206 is *Pensão Chique* (☎ 332 29 63), where small doubles are 6500$00 with breakfast. Doubles with bath at *Pensão Aviz* (☎ 332 07 22) at Avenida Rodrigues de Freitas 451, near Praça da Batalha, are 7500$00, with breakfast. Near the municipal tourist office is *Pensão Pão de Açucar* (☎ 200 24 25), Rua do Almada 262, with a pleasant terrace and doubles with shower from 8500$00; bookings are essential.

Near the university, *Pensão Estoríl* (☎ 200 27 51), Rua de Cedofeita 193, offers doubles with shower from 6000$00, but no breakfast. Prim rooms at the nearby *Pensão São Marino* (☎ 332 54 99) at Praça Carlos Alberto 59 are a better deal in the same range, and include breakfast.

Places to Eat
Folksy *Restaurante A Tasquinha* (☎ 332 21 45), Rua do Carmo 23 by the university, is popular with students and families; good regional specialities run about 1000 to 2000$00 per dish. A pleasant option a few blocks away on Praça de Carlos Alberto is small *Restaurante Carlos Alberto* (☎ 200 17 47), with lunch plates under 900$00. A lively student haunt at lunchtime is nearby *Café Douro*, Praça de Parada Leitão 49.

Ribeira is heavy on over-priced, touristy eateries, but a modest back-alley place with prices around 1500$00 per dish is *Restaurante da Alzira* (☎ 200 50 04) at Viela do Buraco 3. Downriver at Rua de Fonte Taurina 58, *Casa Cardoso* (☎ 205 86 44), in an old high-ceilinged house, has a menu including half-portions from 750$00.

Café Majestic at Rua de Santa Catarina 112 is an extravagantly decorated Art Nouveau relic with expensive coffees and afternoon teas.

Entertainment
Several lively pubs in the Ribeira include *Real Feytoria* (☎ 200 07 18), Rua Infante Dom Henrique 20; and *Meia-Cave* (☎ 208 67 02), Praça da Ribeira 6.

A new generation of clubs has sprung up in the riverfront area called Massarelos, about 2km west of the Ribeira. Among them are *Mexcal* (☎ 60091 88) and *Club Mau-Mau* (☎ 607 66 60) along Rua da Restauração; *Naif* and *Maré Alta* (☎ 609 00 01) on Alameda de Basílio Teles; and *House Café* (☎ 609 78 89) at Rua do Capitão Eduardo Romero 1. All are within a few minutes walk of one another, and on the No 1 bus line from opposite São Bento station.

Things to Buy
Port, of course, is a popular purchase. Casa Oriental, Rua dos Clérigos 111, has a good selection interspersed with dangling bacalhau (dried cod). Other good sources are Casa Januário, Rua do Bonjardim 352, and Garrafeira do Carmo, Rua do Carmo 17. Other good buys are shoes and gold-filigree jewellery. For handicrafts, look in on Arte Facto at Rua da Reboleira 37 in the Ribeira (closed Monday).

Getting There & Away
Air International and domestic flights use Francisco Sá Carneiro airport (☎ 948 32 60), 20km north-west of the city centre. Domestic connections include multiple daily Portugália and TAP flights to/from Lisbon. Both TAP and British Airways link Porto with London daily, and on most days there are direct links to Paris, Frankfurt, Amsterdam, Brussels and Madrid.

Bus There are several places to catch long-distance buses. Renex (☎ 208 28 98), Rua das Carmelitas 32, is the choice for long-haul links, including Lisbon and the Algarve, and the ticket office is open 24-hours a day. From Praça Filipa de Lencastre, REDM (☎ 200 31 52) goes to Braga, AV Minho (☎ 200 61 21) to Viana do Castelo and João Terreira das Neves (☎ 200 08 81) to Guimarães. From a terminal at Rua Alexandre Herculano 370, Rede Expressos (☎ 200 69 54) buses go all over Portugal. Rodonorte (☎ 200 56 37) departs from Rua Ateneu Comércial do Porto 19, mainly to Vila Real and Bragança.

Northern Portugal's main international carrier is Internorte (see the introductory Getting There & Away section of this chapter), whose long-distance coaches depart from their booking office (☎ 609 32 20) at Praça da Galiza 96.

Train Porto, a rail hub for northern Portugal, has three major stations. Most international connections, and all intercidade links throughout Portugal, start at Campanhã, east of the centre. Interregional and regional connections depart from either the central São Bento station or from Campanhã (bus No 35 runs frequently between these two stations). Trindade station is for Póvoa de Varzim and Guimarães only.

At São Bento you can book tickets for any destination and any station. For information for all trains and all stations, call ☎ 56 41 41 from 8 am to 11 pm daily.

Getting Around
To/From the Airport
Take bus No 56 from Jardim da Cordoaria (or from Praça da Liberdade after 9 pm). A taxi is around 2500$00 plus a possible baggage charge of 300$00; during peak times allow an hour from the city centre.

Bus An extensive bus system operates from Jardim da Cordoaria (also called Jardim de João Chagas), Praça da Liberdade and Praça Dom João I. Tickets are cheapest from STCP kiosks opposite São Bento and Campanhã stations, on Avenida dos Aliados, at Praça da Batalha and elsewhere. Fares depend on how many zones you cross: a short hop is 80$00, getting to outlying areas is 120$00, and a return ticket for the airport is 310$00. These are also sold in *cadernetas* (books) of 10. A ticket bought on the bus is 160$00. Also available are passes for one (370$00), four (1850$00) or seven days (2400$00).

Wheelchair users can call ☎ 606 68 72 or ☎ 600 63 53 for information on STCP's dial-a-ride service.

Tram Porto's trams used to be one of the delights of the city but only one is left. The No 18 trundles daily from the Tram Museum out to the coast at Foz do Douro and back to Boavista every half-hour all day. Sentimental fans can visit the **Museu dos Carros Eléctricos** (Tram Museum), Cais do Bicalho (look for the STCP building), with dozens of restored old cars in a cavernous tram warehouse. It's open Tuesday to Friday from 2 to 8 pm, and weekends and holidays from 10 am to 8 pm, for 350$00 (half-price for those with youth or senior cards).

Taxi Taxis are good value. For a zip across town, figure on about 500$00. An additional charge is made if you cross the Ponte Dom Luís to Vila Nova de Gaia or leave the city limits.

Car & Motorcycle Driving in the city centre is a real pain, thanks to gridlocked traffic, one-way streets and scarce parking.

Porto's car-rental agencies include Hertz (☎ 205 23 87), Europcar (☎ 205 83 98), Turiscar (☎ 600 84 01) and AA Castanheira (☎ 606 52 56).

ALONG THE DOURO
The Douro Valley is one of Portugal's scenic highlights, with some 200km of bold, expansive panoramas from Porto to the Spanish border. In the upper reaches, port-wine vineyards wrap round every crew-cut hillside, interrupted only by the occasional bright-white port company manor house.

The river, tamed by eight dams and locks since the late 1980s, is now navigable all the way, making boat tours an ideal option. Vistadouro (☎ 02-339 39 50) runs one or two-day cruises throughout the year. Highly recommended, too, is the train trip from Porto to Peso da Régua (about a dozen trains daily, 2½ hours). The last 50km cling dramatically to the river bank. The farther you go, the better it gets: four trains continue daily along the valley to Pocinho (4½ hours).

Bike and car travellers have a choice of river-hugging roads along the south and north banks, but both are wriggly and crowded with Porto escapees at weekends.

The detailed colour map *Rio Douro*

600$00), available from Porto bookshops, is a handy and elegant source of information.

VIANA DO CASTELO
☎ 058

This port, attractively set at the mouth of the Rio Lima, is renowned for its historic old town and its promotion of folk traditions.

The helpful tourist office (☎ 82 26 20) on Praça da Erva has information on festivals and other literature about the region.

In August, the town hosts the Festas de Nossa Senhora da Agónia. (See the Facts for the Visitor section at the start of this chapter for more details).

Things to See & Do
The focal point of the town is splendid Praça da República with its delicate fountain and elegant buildings, including the 16th-century **Misericórdia**.

At the top of Santa Luzia hill, 4km from the centre, is **Igreja de Santa Luzia**, with a grand panorama across the river from its dome lookout. A funicular railway climbs the hill from 9 am to 7 pm (hourly in the morning, every 30 minutes in the afternoon) from behind the train station.

Places to Stay & Eat
For 5000$00 you get a clean double without bath at *Pensão Vianense* (☎ 82 31 18), Avenide Conde de Carreira 79; or one with bath at *Pensão Dolce Vita* (☎ 2 48 60) opposite the tourist office at Rua do Poço 44. Those without/with bath at *Residencial Magalhães* (☎ 82 32 93), Rua Manuel Espregueira 62, are 5500/7000$00. All include breakfast. The tourist office has listings of private rooms.

Most of Viana's pensões have good-value restaurants, open to non-guests too. *A Gruta Snack Bar* (☎ 82 02 14), Rua Grande 87, has a small menu of dishes mostly under 1200$00. *Restaurante Minho* (☎ 82 32 61), Rua Gago Coutinho 103, serves generous portions for modest prices. Seafood is pricey, but good places for it are the cervejaria half of *Os Três Arcos* (☎ 2 40 14), Largo João Tomás da Costa 25, with half-portions from around 1000$00; and *Neiva Mar Marisqueira* (☎ 82 06 69), opposite the fish market at Largo Infante Dom Henrique 1.

Getting There & Away
During the week, over a dozen buses from four companies go daily to Porto, including three express services (1½ hours). At least 10 go daily to Braga (one hour). Daily train services run north to Spain and south to Porto.

BRAGA
☎ 053

Crammed with churches, Braga is considered Portugal's religious capital. During Easter week, huge crowds attend its Holy Week Festival.

The tourist office (☎ 26 25 50), Avenida da Liberdade 1, can help with accommodation and maps.

Things to See & Do
At Bom Jesus do Monte, a pilgrimage site on a hill 5km from the city, is an extraordinary stairway, the **Escadaria do Bom Jesus**, complete with allegorical fountains, chapels and Biblical scenes, and a superb view. Buses run frequently from Braga to the site, where you can either climb the steps or ride a funicular railway to the top.

In the centre of Braga is the **Sé**, an elegant and bewildering cathedral complex. Admission to its rambling treasury museum and several tomb chapels is 300$00.

It's an easy day trip to **Guimarães**, considered the cradle of the Portuguese nation, of interest for its medieval town centre and the palace of the dukes of Bragança.

Places to Stay
The *pousada da juventude* (☎ 61 61 63), Rua de Santa Margarida 6, is a friendly hostel near the city centre. The *Grande Residência Avenida* (☎ 26 29 55), Avenida da Liberdade 738, is good value with doubles from 5500$00. Cheap but not very cheerful is *Casa Santa Zita* (☎ 61 83 31), a hostel for pilgrims (and others) at Rua São João 20, with doubles from 4500$00. Rooms with stunning views at the heavily booked *Hotel Sul-Americano* (☎ 67 66 15) at Bom Jesus start at 6500/8500$00.

Places to Eat
Around the corner from the bus station, at Rua Gabriel Pereira de Castro 100, is *Retiro*

PORTUGAL

da Primavera (☎ 27 24 82) with bargain dishes under 1200$00. Also good value is family-run *Casa Grulha* (☎ 26 28 83), Rua dos Biscaínhos 95, with excellent *cabrito assado* (roast kid, a local specialty). On Praça Velha are two cheerful places with righteous prices: *Taberna Rexío da Praça* (☎ 61 77 01) at No 17 and casa de pasto *Pregão* (☎ 27 72 49) at No 18. For people-watching over coffee or beer, settle down at *Café Astória* or the adjacent *Café Vianna* on Praça da República.

Getting There & Away

The completion of an expressway from Porto has put Braga within easy day-trip reach. Train services connect Braga north to Viana do Castelo and Spain and south to Porto and Coimbra. There are abundant bus services to Porto and Lisbon.

PENEDA-GERÊS NATIONAL PARK
☎ 053, 058, 076

This fine wilderness park along the Spanish border has spectacular scenery and a wide variety of fauna and flora. The Portuguese day-trippers and holiday-makers tend to stick to the main camping areas, leaving the rest of the park to hikers.

The main centre for the park is **Caldas do Gerês** (also called just Gerês), a sleepy, hot-spring village.

Orientation & Information

Caldas do Gerês has a tourist office (☎ 053-39 11 33), in the colonnade at the upper end of Caldas do Gerês. But for park information, go to the nearby park office (☎ 053-39 11 81), others at Arcos de Valdevez or Monta-legre just outside the park, or the head office (☎ 053-600 34 80) in the Quinta das Parretas, Avenida António Macedo in Braga. All sell a useful park map (530$00) with some roads and tracks (but not trails), and a booklet (105$00) on the park's human and natural features; most other information is in Portuguese.

Activities

Hiking An official long-distance footpath is gradually being developed, mostly following traditional roads or tracks between villages where you can stop for the night. Park offices sell map-brochures (300$00) for two major sections so far.

Day hikes around Caldas do Gerês are crowded; avoid the **Miradouro do Gerês** route at weekends when it's packed with car-trippers. A good option is an old Roman road from Albergaria (10km up the valley from Caldas do Gerês by taxi or hitching), past the **Vilarinho das Furnas** reservoir to **Campo do Gerês**. Note that swimming is not allowed in this reservoir (though it's OK in the others in the park). Farther afield, the walks to Ermida and Cabril are excellent, and both have simple accommodation and cafés.

Montes d'Aventura (Porto ☎ 02-830 51 57; mobile ☎ 0936-607 37 39), with a base at the pousada de juventude in Campo do Gerês; Planalto (☎ 053-35 10 05), based at the Cerdeira camping ground in Campo do Gerês; and Trote-Gerês (☎ 053-65 98 60) near Cabril, organise guided walks.

Cycling Mountain bikes can be hired from Água Montanha Lazer (☎ 053-39 17 79) in Rio Caldo; Pensão Carvalho Araújo (☎ 053-39 11 85) in Caldas do Gerês; Cerdeira camping ground (☎ 053-35 70 65) in Campo do Gerês; or Trote-Gerês (☎ 053-65 98 60) in Cabril. All are good sources of cycling information about the park.

Horse Riding The national park operates horse-riding facilities (☎ 053-39 11 81) from beside its Vidoeiro camping ground, near Caldas do Gerês. Two other equine outfits are CasCos (Porto ☎ 02-830 51 57, 02-972 07 75) at Terras de Bouro; and Trote-Gerês (☎ 053-65 98 60) near Cabril.

Water Sports Rio Caldo, 8km south of Caldas do Gerês, is the base for water sports on the Caniçada reservoir. Água Montanha Lazer (☎ 053-39 17 79) rents out kayaks, four-person canoes and pedal, rowing and outboard motor boats. For paddling the Sala-monde reservoir, Trote-Gerês (☎ 053-65 98 60) rents canoes from their camping ground at Cabril.

At Caldas do Gerês' Parque das Termas (150$00 admission) is a swimming pool, open to the public for 700$00 on weekdays or

100$00 on weekends and holidays (cheaper or kids).

Organised Tours

For a spin through the major sights in the park by minibus, Agência no Gerês (☎ 053-39 11 12), at the Hotel Universal in Caldas do Gerês, operates two to five-hour trips in summer for 1000 to 1250$00 per person.

Places to Stay

The *pousada da juventude* (☎ 053-35 13 39) and the good *Cerdeira Camping Ground*, both at Campo do Gerês, make good bases for hikes. One km north of Caldas do Gerês at Vidoeiro is a park-run camping ground (☎ 053-39 12 89). Other camping grounds are at Lamas de Mouro, Entre-Ambos-os-Rios and Cabril.

Caldas do Gerês has plenty of pensões, though many are block-booked by spa patients in summer. Try *Pensão da Ponte* (☎ 053-39 11 21) beside the gushing river, with doubles from 5000/7000$00 without/with bath. At the top of the hill, with the best views, is *Pensão Adelaide* (☎ 053-39 11 88), with doubles with bath from 7000$00. For more rural accommodation, Trote-Gerês (☎ 053-65 98 60) operates the comfortable *Pousadinha de Paradela* cottage in Paradela, with doubles from 4200$00.

Places to Eat

Most pensões at Caldas do Gerês provide hearty meals, usually available to non-guests, too. There are also several restaurants, as well as shops in the main street for picnic provisions. The *pousada da juventude* and *Cerdeira Camping Ground* at Campo do Gerês also offer meals.

Getting There & Away

From Braga at least 10 buses a day run to Caldas do Gerês and at least two a day to Campo do Gerês (plus more on weekdays). Coming from Lisbon or Porto, change at Braga.

Getting Around

Unless you have your own transport, you must rely on infrequent bus connections to a limited number of places in or near the park, or cycle (see Activities in this section), or walk.

Slovenia

Little Slovenia (Slovenija) straddles Western and Eastern Europe. Many of its cities and towns bear the imprint of the Habsburg Empire and the Venetian Republic, while in the Julian Alps you'd think you were in Bavaria. The two-million Slovenes were economically the most well off among the peoples of what was once Yugoslavia, and the relative affluence and the orderliness of this nation is immediately apparent. Slovenia may be the gateway to the Balkans from Italy, Austria or Hungary, but it still has the feel of central Europe.

Slovenia is one Europe's most delightful surprises for travellers. Fairy-tale Bled Castle, breathtaking Lake Bohinj, scenic Postojna and Škocjan caves, the lush Soča Valley, Piran and Koper on the coast and thriving Ljubljana are great attractions, all accessible at much less than the cost of similar places in Western Europe. The amazing variety of settings packed into one small area makes this country truly a 'Europe in miniature'. An added bonus is that Slovenia is a nation of polyglots, and communicating with these friendly, helpful people is never difficult.

AT A GLANCE

Capital	Ljubljana
Population	1.9 million
Area	20,256 sq km
Official Language	Slovenian
Currency	1 tolar (SIT) = 100 stotins
GDP	US$24 billion (1997)
Time	GMT/UTC+0100

Facts about Slovenia

HISTORY

The early Slovenes settled in the river valleys of the Danube Basin and the eastern Alps in the 6th century. Slovenia was brought under Germanic rule in 748, first by the Frankish empire of the Carolingians, who converted the population to Christianity, and then as part of the Holy Roman Empire in the 9th century. The Austro-German monarchy took over in the early 14th century and continued to rule (as the Habsburg Empire from 1804) right up to the end of WWI in 1918 – with only one brief interruption. Over these six centuries, the upper classes became totally Germanised, though the peasantry retained their Slovenian identity. The Bible was trans-

lated into the vernacular during the Reformation in 1584, but Slovene did not come into common use as a written language until the early 19th century.

In 1809, in a bid to isolate the Habsburg Empire from the Adriatic, Napoleon established the so-called Illyrian Provinces (Slovenia, Dalmatia and part of Croatia) with Ljubljana as the capital. Though the Habsburgs returned in 1814, French reforms in education, law and public administration endured. The democratic revolution that swept Europe in 1848 also increased political and national consciousness among Slovenes,

SLOVENIA (SLOVENIJA)

and after WWI and the dissolution of the Austro-Hungarian Empire, Slovenia was included in the Kingdom of Serbs, Croats and Slovenes.

During WWII much of Slovenia was annexed by Germany, with Italy and Hungary taking smaller bits of territory. Slovenian Partisans fought courageously against the invaders from mountain bases, and Slovenia joined the Socialist Federal Republic of Yugoslavia in 1945.

Moves by Serbia in the late 1980s to assert its leading role culturally and economically among the Yugoslav republics was a big concern to Slovenes. When Belgrade abruptly ended the autonomy of Kosovo (where 90% of the population is ethnically Albanian) in late 1988, Slovenes feared the same could happen to them. For some years, Slovenia's interests had been shifting to the capitalist west and north; the Yugoslav connection, on the other hand, had become not only an economic burden but a political threat as well.

In the spring of 1990, Slovenia became the first Yugoslav republic to hold free elections and shed 45 years of communist rule; in December the electorate voted by 88% in favour of independence. The Slovenian government began stockpiling weapons, and on 25 June 1991 it pulled the republic out of the Yugoslav Federation. To dramatise their bid for independence, the Slovenian leaders deliberately provoked fighting with the federal army by attempting to take control of the border crossings, and a 10-day war ensued. But resistance from the Slovenian militia was determined and, as no territorial claims or minority issues were involved, the Yugoslav government agreed to a truce bro-kered by the EC. Slovenia got a new constitution in late December, and on 15 January 1992 the EC formally recognised the country. Slovenia was admitted to the United Nations in May 1992 and has now been invited to begin negotiations for full membership of the EU.

GEOGRAPHY & GEOLOGY

Slovenia is wedged between Austria and Croatia and shares much shorter borders with Italy and Hungary. Measuring just 20,256 sq km, Slovenia is the smallest country in eastern Europe, about the size of Wales or Israel. Much of the country is mountainous, culminating in the north-west with the Julian Alps and the nation's highest peak, Mt Triglav (2864m). From this jagged knot, the main Alpine chain continues east along the Austrian border, while the Dinaric range runs south-east along the coast into Croatia.

Below the limestone plateau of the Karst region between Ljubljana and Koper is Europe's most extensive network of karst caverns, which gave their name to other such caves around the world.

The coastal range forms a barrier isolating the Istrian Peninsula from Slovenia's corner of the Danube Basin. Much of the interior east of the Alps is drained by the rivers Sava and Drava, both of which empty into the Danube. The Soča flows through western Slovenia into the Adriatic.

CLIMATE

Slovenia is temperate with four distinct seasons, but the topography creates three individual climates. The north-west has an Alpine climate with strong influences from the Atlantic as well as abundant precipitation. Temperatures in the Alpine valleys are moderate in summer but cold in winter. The coast and western Slovenia as far north as the Soča Valley has a Mediterranean climate with mild, sunny weather much of the year, though the *burja*, a cold and dry north-easterly wind from the Adriatic, can be fierce at times. Most of eastern Slovenia has a continental climate with hot summers and cold winters.

Slovenia gets most of its rain in March and April and again in October and November. January is the coldest month with an average temperature of -2° C and July the warmest (21° C).

ECOLOGY & ENVIRONMENT

Slovenia is a very green country – more than half its total area is covered in forest – and is home to 2900 plant species; Triglav National Park is especially rich in indigenous flowering plants. Common European animals (deer, boar, chamois) live here in abundance, and rare species include *Proteus anguinus*, the unique 'human fish' that inhabits pools in karst caves.

GOVERNMENT & POLITICS

Slovenia's constitution provides for a parliamentary system of government. The National Assembly, which has exclusive jurisdiction over the passing of laws, consists of 90 deputies elected for four years by proportional representation. The 40 members of the Council of State, which performs an advisory role, are elected for five-year terms by regions and special-interest groups. The head of state, the president, is elected directly for a maximum of two five-year terms. Executive power is vested in the prime minister and the 15-member cabinet.

In the most recent parliamentary elections (November 1996), a centrist alliance of the Liberal Democrats, the People's Party and the Democratic Party of Pensioners of Slovenia garnered more than 55% of the vote, seating 49 MPs. LDS leader Janez Drnovšek, prime minister from the first elections in 1992, was again named head of government. In November 1997 President Milan Kučan was returned for his second term after winning nearly 56% of the popular vote.

ECONOMY

Slovenia has emerged as one of the strongest economies of the former socialist countries of Eastern Europe after a few tough years following independence. Inflation has dropped, employment is on the rise and per-capita GDP – currently 60% of the EU average – is expected to surpass that of Greece and Portugal by 2002.

But for many Slovenes, the economic picture remains unclear. Real wages continue to grow – but faster than inflation, which puts Slovenia's international competitiveness at a disadvantage. Inflation rocketed up to 200% after independence and has steadily decreased since; it is currently at about 9.5%. Unemployment continues to hover around 14.5%.

POPULATION & PEOPLE

Slovenia was the most homogeneous of all the Yugoslav republics; about 87% of the population (estimated at 1,991,000 in 1997) are Slovenes. There are just over 8500 ethnic Hungarians and some 2300 Roma (Gypsies) largely in the north-east as well as 3060 Italians on the coast. 'Others', accounting for 11.5% of the population, include Croats, Serbs, ethnic Albanians and those who identify themselves simply as 'Muslims'.

ARTS

Slovenia's best loved writer is the Romantic poet France Prešeren (1800-49), whose lyric poetry set new standards for Slovenian literature and helped to raise national consciousness. Disappointed in love, Prešeren wrote sensitive love poems but also satirical verse and epic poetry.

Many notable buildings, bridges and squares in Ljubljana and elsewhere in Slovenia were designed by the architect Jože Plečnik (1872-1957), who studied under Otto Wagner in Vienna.

Postmodernist painting and sculpture has been more or less dominated since the 1980s by the multimedia group Neue Slowenische Kunst (NSK) and the five-member artists' cooperative IRWIN. Avante-garde dance is best exemplified by Betontanc, an NSK dance company that mixes live music and theatrical elements (called 'physical theatre' here) with sharp political comment.

Since WWII, many Slovenian folk traditions have been lost, but compilations by the trio Trutamora Slovenica (available at music shops in Ljubljana) examine the roots of Slovenian folk music. Folk groups – both 'pure' and popular – to watch out for include the Avseniki, Ansambel Lojzeta Slaka, the Alpski Kvintet led by Oto Pestner, and the Roma band Šukar.

Popular music runs the gamut from Slovenian *chanson* (best exemplified by Vita Mavrič) and folk to jazz and techno, but it was punk music in the late 1970s and early 1980s, particularly the groups Pankrti, Borghesia and Laibach, that put Slovenia on the world stage.

LANGUAGE

Slovene is a South Slavic language written in the Roman alphabet and closely related to Croatian and Serbian. It is grammatically complex with lots of cases, genders and tenses and has something very rare in linguistics: the dual form. It's one *miza* (table), and three or more *mize* (tables) but two *mizi*.

Virtually everyone in Slovenia speaks at least one other language: Croatian, Serbian, German, English and/or Italian. English is definitely the preferred language of the young. See the Language Guide section at the end of the book for pronunciation guidelines and useful words and phrases. Lonely Planet's *Mediterranean Europe Phrasebook* contains a chapter on Slovene.

Facts for the Visitor

HIGHLIGHTS

Ljubljana, Piran and Koper have outstanding architecture; the hilltop castles at Bled and Ljubljana are impressive. The Škocjan Caves are among the foremost underground wonders of the world. The Soča Valley is indescribably beautiful in spring. The frescoed Church of St John the Baptist is in itself worth the trip to Lake Bohinj.

SUGGESTED ITINERARIES

Depending on the length of your stay, you might want to see and do the following in Slovenia:

Two days
    Visit Ljubljana
One week
    Visit Ljubljana, Bled, Bohinj, Škocjan Caves and Piran
Two weeks
    Visit all the places covered in this chapter

PLANNING
When to Go

Snow can linger in the mountains as late as June, but May and June are great months to be in the lowlands and valleys when everything is fresh and in blossom. (April can be a bit wet though.) In July and August, hotel rates are increased and there will be lots of tourists, especially on the coast. September is an excellent month to visit as the days are long and the weather still warm, and it's the best time for hiking and climbing. October and November can be rainy, and winter (December to March) is for skiers.

Maps

The Geodesic Institute of Slovenia (Geodetski Zavod Slovenije; GZS), the country's principal cartographic agency, produces national (1:300 000), regional (1:50 000) and topographical maps to the entire country (64 1:50 000-scale sheets) as well as city plans. The Alpine Association of Slovenia (Planinska Zveza Slovenije; PZS) has some 30 different hiking maps with scales as large as 1:25 000.

What to Bring

You don't have to remember any particular item of clothing – a warm sweater (even in summer) for the mountains at night, perhaps, and an umbrella in the spring or autumn – unless you plan to do some serious hiking or other sport.

TOURIST OFFICES

The Slovenian Tourist Board (Center za Promocijo Turizma Slovenije; CPTS; tel 061-189 1840; fax 061-189 1841; cpts@ cpts.tradepoint.si) in Ljubljana's World Trade Centre at Dunajska cesta 160 is the umbrella organisation for tourist offices in Slovenia. It can handle requests for information in writing or you can check out its excellent Web site (see Internet Resources later).

The best office for face-to-face information in Slovenia – bar none – is the Ljubljana Tourist Information Centre. Most of the places described in this chapter have some form of tourist office but if the place you're visiting doesn't, seek assistance at a branch of one of the big travel agencies (eg Kompas, Emona Globtour or Slovenijaturist) or from hotel or museum staff.

Tourist Offices & Travel Agencies Abroad

The CPTS maintains tourist offices in the following eight countries:

Austria
   (☎ 0222-715 4010; fax 0222-713 8177) Hilton Center, Landstrasser Hauptstrasse 2, 1030 Vienna
Germany
   (☎ 089-2916 1202; fax 089-2916 1273) Maximilliansplatz 12a, 80333 Munich
Hungary
   (☎ 1-156 8223; fax 1-156 2818) Gellérthegy utca 28, 1013 Budapest
Italy
   (☎ 02-2951 1187; fax 02-2951 0997) Via Lazzaro Palazzi 2a/III, 20124 Milan
Netherlands & Belgium
   (☎ 010-465 3003; fax 010-465 7514) Benthuizerstraat 29, 3036 CB Rotterdam
Switzerland
   (☎ 01-212 6394; fax 01-212 5266) Löwenstrasse 54, 8001 Zurich
UK
   (☎ 0171-287 7133; fax 0171-287 5476) 49 Conduit St, London W1R 9FB
USA
   (☎ 212-358 9686; 212-358 9025) 345 East 12th St, New York, NY 10003

In addition, Kompas has representative offices in many cities worldwide, including:

Australia
   (☎ 07-3831 4400) 323 Boundary St, Spring Hill, 4000 Queensland
Canada
   (☎ 514-938 4041) 4060 Ste-Catherine St West, Suite 535, Montreal, Que H3Z 2Z3
France
   (☎ 01 53 92 27 80) 14 Rue de la Source, 75016 Paris
South Africa
   (☎ 011-884 8555) Norwich Towers, 3/F, 13 Fredman Drive, Santon

VISAS & EMBASSIES

Passport holders from Australia, Canada, Israel, Japan, New Zealand, Switzerland, USA and EU countries do not require visas for stays in Slovenia of up to 90 days; those from the EU as well as Switzerland can also enter on a national identity card for a stay of up to 30 days. Citizens of other countries requiring visas (including South Africans) can get them at any Slovenian embassy or consulate, at the border or Brnik airport. They cost the equivalent of £21/US$35 for single entry and £43/US$68 for multiple entry.

Slovenian Embassies Abroad

Australia
(☎ 02-6243 4830) Advance Bank Centre, Level 6, 60 Marcus Clark St, Canberra, ACT 2601
Austria
(☎ 0222-586 1307) Nibelungengasse 13, 1010 Vienna
Canada
(☎ 613-565 5781) 150 Metcalfe St, Suite 2101, Ottawa, Ont K2P 1P1
Croatia
(☎ 01-612 1503) Savska cesta 41/IX, 10000 Zagreb
Hungary
(☎ 1-325 9202) Cseppkő utca 68, 1025 Budapest
Italy
(☎ 06-808 1272) Via Ludovico Pisano 10, 00197 Rome
UK
(☎ 0171-495 7775) Cavendish Court, Suite One, 11-15 Wigmore St, London W1H 9LA
USA
(☎ 202-667 5363) 1525 New Hampshire Ave NW, Washington, DC 20036

Foreign Embassies in Slovenia

Selected countries with representation in Ljubljana appear below. Citizens of countries not listed here (eg South Africa) should contact their embassies in Vienna or Budapest.

Australia
(☎ 061-125 4252; open weekdays 9 am to 1 pm) Trg Republike 3/XII
Canada
(☎ 061-130 3570; open weekdays 9 am to 1 pm) Miklošičeva cesta 19
UK
(☎ 061-125 7191; open weekdays 9 am till noon) Trg Republike 3/IV
USA
(☎ 061-301 485; open Monday, Wednesday and Friday 9 am till noon) Pražakova ulica 4

CUSTOMS

Travellers can bring in the usual personal effects, a couple of cameras and electronic goods for their own use, 200 cigarettes, a generous 4L of spirits and 1L of wine.

MONEY

Currency

Slovenia's currency, the tolar, is abbreviated SIT. Prices in shops, at restaurants and train and bus fares are always in tolars, but some hotels, guesthouses and even camping grounds still use Deutschmarks (though the government has asked them not to) as the tolar is linked to it.

For that reason, some forms of accommodation listed in this chapter are quoted in DM – though you are never required to pay in the German currency.

There are coins of 50 stotin and one, two and five tolar and banknotes of 10, 20, 50, 100, 200, 500, 1000, 5000 and 10,000 tolars.

Exchange Rates

Australia	A$1	=	104 SIT
Canada	C$1	=	115 SIT
euro	€1	=	184 SIT
France	FF1	=	28 SIT
Germany	DM1	=	94 SIT
Japan	Y100	=	122 SIT
New Zealand	NZ$1	=	105 SIT
South Africa	Rand1	=	35 SIT
UK	UK£1	=	270 SIT
USA	US$1	=	166 SIT

Costs

Slovenia remains much cheaper than neighbouring Italy and Austria, but don't expect it to be a bargain basement like Hungary: everything costs about 50% more here.

If you stay in private rooms or at guesthouses, eat at medium-priced restaurants and travel 2nd class on the train or by bus, you should get by for under US$40 a day.

Those staying at hostels or college dormitories, eating takeaway for lunch and at self-service restaurants at night will cut costs considerably.

Travelling in a little more style and comfort – occasional restaurant splurges with bottles of wine, an active nightlife, staying at small hotels or guesthouses with 'character' – will cost about US$65 a day.

Cash & Travellers Cheques

It is very simple to change cash and travellers cheques at banks, travel agencies, any *menjalnica* (private exchange bureau) and certain post offices.

There's no black market, but exchange rates can vary, so it pays to keep your eyes open. Banks take a commission (*provizija*) of 1% or none at all, but tourist offices, travel agencies, exchange bureaus and hotels have ones of 3% to 5%.

Credit Cards & ATMs

Visa, MasterCard/Eurocard and American Express credit cards are widely accepted at upmarket restaurants, shops, hotels, car-rental firms and some travel agencies; Diners Club less so.

SKB Banka maintains more than 50 Cirrus-linked automated teller machines (ATMs) throughout the country; their locations are noted in the Information sections of the individual towns. At the time of writing, no other ATMs in Slovenia were open to foreign-account holders. Clients of Visa, however, can get cash advances in tolars from any A Banka branch, MasterCard and Eurocard holders from the Nova Ljubljanska Banka (☎ 061-125 0155) at Trg Republike 2 in Ljubljana and American Express customers from Atlas Express (☎ 061-133 2024 or ☎ 061-131 9020) at Trubarjeva cesta 50 in Ljubljana.

Taxes & Refunds

A 'circulation tax' (*prometni davek*) not unlike Value-Added Tax (VAT) covers the purchase of most goods and services here. Visitors can claim refunds on total purchases of 12,500 SIT or more (not including tobacco products or spirits) through Kompas MTS, which has offices at Brnik airport and some two dozen border crossings. Make sure you do the paperwork at the time of purchase.

Most towns and cities levy a 'tourist tax' on overnight visitors of between 150 and 300 SIT per person per night (less at camping grounds).

POST & COMMUNICATIONS
Post

Poste restante is sent to the main post office in a city or town (in the capital, it goes to the branch at Slovenska cesta 32, 1101 Ljubljana) where it is held for 30 days. American Express card holders can have their mail addressed c/o the Atlas Express, Trubarjeva cesta 50, 1000 Ljubljana.

Domestic mail costs 14 SIT for up to 20g

and 26 SIT for up to 100g. Postcards are 13 SIT. For international mail, the base rate is 90 SIT for 20g or less, 186 SIT for up to 100g and 70 to 90 SIT for a postcard, depending on the size. Then you have to add on the air-mail charge for every 10g: 16 SIT for Europe, 21 SIT for North America, 22 SIT for most of Asia and 28 SIT for Australasia. An aerogramme is 120 SIT.

Telephone

The easiest place to make long-distance calls as well as send faxes and telegrams is from a post office or telephone centre; the one at Trg Osvobodilne Fronte (Trg OF) near the train and bus stations in Ljubljana is open 24 hours a day.

Public telephones on the street do not accept coins; they require a phonecard (*telefonska kartica*) or phone tokens (*žetoni*), which are being used less and less these days. Both are available at all post offices and some newsstands.

Phonecards cost 600/900/1500/2600/3300/4000 SIT for 25/50/100/200/300/400 impulses. A local two-minute call absorbs one impulse, and a three-minute call from Slovenia will cost about 292 SIT to neighbouring countries, 357 SIT to Western Europe (including the UK) and 617 SIT to the USA or Australia. Rates are 25% cheaper between 7 pm and 7 am.

The international access code in Slovenia is 00. The international operator can be reached on ☎ 901 and international directory inquiries on ☎ 989. To call Slovenia from abroad, dial the international access code, ☎ 386 (Slovenia's country code), the area code (without the initial zero, eg 61 in Ljubljana) and the number.

INTERNET RESOURCES

The best single source of information on the Internet is the CPTS's SloWWWenia site: www.ijs.si:90/slo/. It has an interactive map where you can click on to more than two dozen cities, towns, ski resorts etc as well as information on culture, history, food and wine, getting to and from Slovenia and what's on.

See the Internet Resources section in the Ljubljana section for more sites.

BOOKS

Books are very expensive in Slovenia so try to buy whatever you can on the country before you arrive. Lonely Planet's *Slovenia* is the only complete and independent English-language guide to the country. *Discover Slovenia*, published annually by Cankarjeva Založba (3300 SIT), is a colourful and easy introduction.

NEWSPAPERS & MAGAZINES

Slovenia counts four daily newspapers, the most widely read being *Delo* (Work) and *Večer* (Evening). There are no English-language newspapers though the *International Herald Tribune*, the *Guardian International*, the *Financial Times* and *USA Today* are available on the day of publication in the afternoon at hotels and department stores in Ljubljana.

RADIO & TV

In July and August both Radio Slovenija 1 & 2 broadcast a report on the weather, including conditions on the sea and in the mountains, in English, German and Italian at 7.15 am. News, weather, traffic and tourist information in the same languages follows on Radio 1 at 9.35 am daily except Sunday. Also during this period Radio 2 broadcasts weekend traffic conditions after each news bulletin from Friday afternoon through Sunday evening. There's a nightly news bulletin at 10.30 pm throughout the year on Radio 1.

You can listen to radio 1 on MHz/FM frequencies 88.5, 90.0, 90.9, 91.8, 92.0, 92.9, 94.1 and 96.4 as well as AM 326.8. Radio 2 can be found on MHz/FM 87.8, 92.4, 93.5, 94.1, 95.3, 96.9, 97.6, 98.9 and 99.9.

PHOTOGRAPHY & VIDEO

Film and basic camera equipment are available throughout Slovenia, though the largest selection is in Ljubljana. Film prices vary but 24 exposures of 100 ASA Kodacolor II, Agfa or Fujifilm will cost about 650 SIT, 36 exposures 750 SIT. Ektachrome 100 (36 exposures) is 1110 SIT. Super 8 (P5-60) film costs about 1300 SIT while an EC45 video cassette is 1300 SIT. Developing print film costs about 2500 SIT for 36 prints. For 36 framed transparencies, expect to pay around 1200 SIT.

TIME

Slovenia is one hour ahead of GMT/UTC. The country goes onto summer time (GMT/UTC plus two hours) on the last Sunday in March when clocks are advanced by one hour. On the last Sunday in October they're turned back one hour.

ELECTRICITY

The electric voltage is 220V, 50 Hz, AC. Plugs are the standard European type with two round pins.

WEIGHTS & MEASURES

Slovenia uses the metric system.

LAUNDRY

Commercial laundrettes are pretty much nonexistent in Slovenia. The best places to look for do-it-yourself washers and dryers are hostels, college dormitories and camping grounds, and there are a couple of places in Ljubljana that will do your laundry reasonably quickly (see Laundry under Information in the Ljubljana section).

HEALTH

Foreigners are entitled to emergency medical aid at the very least; for subsequent treatment entitlement varies. Some EU countries (including the UK) have contractual agreements with Slovenia allowing their citizens free medical care while travelling in the country. This may require carrying a special form so check with your Ministry of Health or equivalent before setting out.

WOMEN TRAVELLERS

The Društvo Mesto Žensk (City of Women Association), part of the Government Office for Women's Affairs (☎ 061-125 112), is at Kersnikova ulica 4 in Ljubljana. It sponsors an international festival of contemporary arts called City of Women usually in October. In the event of an assault ring ☎ 080 124 or any of the following six numbers: ☎ 9780 to ☎ 9785.

GAY & LESBIAN TRAVELLERS

The gay association Roza Klub (☎ 061-130 4740), at Kersnikova ulica 4 in Ljubljana, publishes a quarterly newsletter called *Revolver* and organises a disco every Sunday night at the Klub K4 in Ljubljana. Magnus (☎ same as Rosa Klub) is the gay branch of the Student Cultural Centre (Študentski Kulturni Center; ŠKUC).

Lesbians can contact the ŠKUC-affiliated organisation LL (☎ 061-130 4740) at Metelkova ulica 6 in Ljubljana.

The GALfon (☎ 061-132 4089) is a hotline and source of general information for gays and lesbians. It operates daily from 7 to 10 pm. The Queer Resources Directory on the Internet (www.ljudmila.org/~siqrd) leaves no stone unturned.

DISABLED TRAVELLERS

A group that looks after the interests and special needs of physically challenged people is the Zveza Paraplegikov Republike Slovenije (ZPRS; ☎ 061-132 7138) at Štihova ulica 14 in Ljubljana.

SENIOR TRAVELLERS

Senior citizens may be entitled to discounts in Slovenia on things like transport (eg those over 60 years of age holding an international Rail Europe Seniors (RES) card get from 30% to 50% off on Slovenian Railways), museum admission fees etc, provided they show proof of age.

DANGERS & ANNOYANCES

Slovenia is hardly a violent or dangerous place. Police say that 90% of all crimes reported involve thefts so take the usual precautions. In the event of an emergency, the following numbers can be dialled nationwide:

Police ☎ 113
Fire/first aid/ambulance ☎ 112
Automobile assistance (AMZS) ☎ 987

LEGAL MATTERS

The permitted blood-alcohol level for motorists is 0.5g/kg (0.0g/kg for professional drivers) and the law is very strictly enforced. Anything over that could earn you a fine of 25,000 SIT and one to three points.

BUSINESS HOURS

Shops, groceries and department stores are open from 7.30 or 8 am to 7 pm on weekdays and to 1 pm on Saturday. Bank hours are generally from 8 am to 4.30 or 5 pm on weekdays (often with a lunchtime break) and till noon on Saturday. The main post office in any city or town is open from 7 am to 8 pm on weekdays, till 1 pm on Saturday and occasionally from 9 to 11 am on Sunday.

PUBLIC HOLIDAYS & SPECIAL EVENTS

Public holidays in Slovenia include two days at New Year (1 & 2 January), Prešeren Day (8 February), Easter Sunday & Monday (March/April), Insurrection Day (27 April), two days for Labour Day (1 & 2 May), National Day (25 June), Assumption Day (15 August), Reformation Day (31 October), All Saints' Day (1 November), Christmas (25 December) and Independence Day (26 December).

Though cultural events are scheduled year round, the highlights of Slovenia's summer season (July and August) are the International Summer Festival in Ljubljana; the Piran Musical Evenings; the Primorska Summer Festival at Piran, Koper, Izola and Portorož; and Summer in the Old Town in Ljubljana, with three or four cultural events a week taking place. The Cows' Ball (*Kravji Bal*) at Bohinj is a zany weekend of folk dance, music, eating and drinking in mid-September to mark the return of the cows to the valleys from their high pastures.

ACTIVITIES
Skiing

Skiing is by far the most popular sport in Slovenia, and every fourth Slovene is an active skier. The country has many well-equipped ski resorts in the Julian Alps, especially Vogel (skiing up to 1840m) above

Lake Bohinj, Kranjska Gora (1600m), Kanin (2300m) above Bovec, and Krvavec (1970m), east of Kranj. World Cup slalom and giant slalom events are held at Kranjska Gora in late December, and the current world ski-jumping record (200m) was set at nearby Planica in 1994.

All these resorts have multiple chair lifts, cable cars, ski schools, equipment rentals and large resort hotels.

Hiking

Hiking is almost as popular as skiing, and there are 7000km of marked trails and 165 mountain huts. You'll experience the full grandeur of the Julian Alps in Triglav National Park at Bohinj, and for the veteran mountaineer there's the Slovenian Alpine Trail, which crosses all the highest peaks in the country.

Kayaking, Canoeing & Rafting

The best white-water rafting is on the Soča, one of only half a dozen rivers in the European Alps whose upper waters are still unspoiled. The centre is at Bovec.

Fishing

Slovenia's rivers and Alpine lakes and streams and lakes are teeming with trout, grayling, pike and other fish. The best rivers for angling are the Soča, the Krka, the Kolpa and the Sava Bohinjka near Bohinj. Lake fishing is good at Bled and Bohinj.

Cycling

Mountain bikes are for hire at Bled and Bohinj. You can also rent bikes on the coast and in Ljubljana.

ACCOMMODATION
Camping

In summer, camping is the cheapest way to go, and there are conveniently located camping grounds all over the country. You don't always need a tent as some camping grounds have inexpensive bungalows or caravans, too. Two of the best camping grounds are Zlatorog on Lake Bohinj and Jezero Fiesa near Piran, though they can be very crowded in summer. It is forbidden to camp 'rough' in Slovenia.

Hostels & Student Dormitories

Slovenia has only a handful of 'official' hostels, including two in Ljubljana and one each in Bled and Koper, but not all of them are open year round. Some college dormitories accept travellers in the summer months.

Private Rooms & Apartments

Private rooms arranged by tourist offices and travel agencies can be inexpensive, but a surcharge of up to 50% is usually levied on stays of less than three nights. You can often bargain for rooms without the surcharge by going directly to any house with a sign reading 'sobe' (rooms).

Pensions & Guesthouses

A small guesthouse (called penzion or gostišče) can be good value, though in July and August you may be required to take at least one meal and the rates are higher then.

Farmhouses

The agricultural cooperatives of Slovenia have organised a unique program to accommodate visitors on working farms. Prices go from DM30 per person for a 2nd-category room with shared bath and breakfast in the low season (from September to about mid-December and mid-January to June) to around DM45 per person for a 1st-category room with private bath and all meals in the high season (July and August). Bookings can be made through ABC Farm & Countryside Holidays (☎ 061-576 127) at Ulica Jožeta Jame 16 in Ljubljana or at Brnik airport (☎ 064-261 684). Its British agent is Slovenija Pursuits (☎ 01763-852 646), 14 Hay St, Steeple Morden, Royston, Herts SG8 0PE.

Hotels

Hotel rates vary according to the season, with July and August being the peak season and May/June and September/October the shoulder seasons. In Ljubljana, prices are constant all year. Many resort hotels, particularly on the coast, close in winter.

FOOD

Slovenian cuisine is heavily influenced by the food of its neighbours. From Austria, it's klobasa (sausage), zavitek (strudel) and

Dunajski zrezek (Wiener schnitzel). *Njoki* (potato dumplings), *rižota* (risotto) and the ravioli-like *žlikrofi* are obviously Italian, and Hungary has contributed *golaž* (goulash), *paprikaš* (chicken or beef 'stew') and *palačinke* (thin pancakes filled with jam or nuts and topped with chocolate). And then there's that old Balkan standby, *burek*, a greasy, layered cheese, meat or even apple pie served at takeaway places everywhere.

No Slovenian meal is complete without soup, be it the simple *goveja juha z rezanci* (beef broth with little egg noodles), *zelenjavna juha* (vegetable soup) or *gobova kremna juha* (creamed mushroom soup). There are many types of Slovenian dumplings; the cheese ones called *štruklji* are the most popular. Try also the baked delicacies, including *potica* (walnut roll) and *gibanica*, pastry filled with poppy seeds, walnuts, apple and/or sultanas and cheese and topped with cream. Traditional dishes are best tried at an inn (*gostilna* or *gostišče*).

DRINKS

The wine-growing regions of Slovenia are Podravje in the east, noted for such white wines as Renski Rizling (a true German Riesling), Beli Pinot (Pinot Blanc) and Traminec (Traminer); Posavje in the south-east (try the distinctly Slovenian light-red Cviček); and the area around the coast, which produces a hearty red called Teran made from Refošk grapes.

Žganje is a strong brandy or *eau de vie* distilled from a variety of fruits but most commonly plums. The finest brandy is Pleterska Hruška made from pears.

Getting There & Away

AIR

Slovenia's national airline, Adria Airways (JP; ☎ 061-133 4336 in Ljubljana, ☎ 064-223 555 at Brnik airport; www.kabi.si/~si21/aa), has nonstop flights to Ljubljana from 18 cities, including Amsterdam, Barcelona, Brussels, Copenhagen, Frankfurt, London (LHR), Manchester (May-September), Moscow, Munich, Ohrid (Macedonia), Paris (CDG), Sarajevo, Skopje, Split, Tel Aviv, Tirana, Vienna and Zurich.

Other airlines that serve Ljubljana include Aeroflot (SU) from Moscow, Austrian Airlines (OS) from Vienna, Avioimpex (M4) from Skopje, British Airways (BA) from London, Lufthansa (LH) from Frankfurt and Swissair (SR) from Zurich.

LAND
Bus

Nova Gorica is the easiest exit/entry point between Slovenia and Italy as you can catch up to five buses a day to/from the Italian city of Gorizia or simply walk across the border at Rožna Dolina. Koper also has good connections with Italy: some 17 buses a day on weekdays go to/from Trieste, 21km to the north-east.

From Ljubljana you can catch a bus to Budapest three times a week and there's a weekly service to Lenti. Otherwise take one of up to five daily buses to Lendava; the Hungarian border is 5km to the north. The first Hungarian train station, Rédics, is only 2km beyond the border. From Rédics, there are up to 10 trains a day (1¼ hours) to Zalaegerszeg, from where there are three direct trains (3¾ hours) and five buses to Budapest.

For information about getting to/from other neighbouring countries and ones farther afield, see Getting There & Away in the Ljubljana section.

Train

The main train routes into Slovenia from Austria are Vienna to Maribor and Salzburg to Jesenice. Tickets cost 5615 SIT from Ljubljana to Salzburg (4½ hours) and 7906 SIT to Vienna (six hours). But it's cheaper to take a local train to Maribor (1011 SIT) and buy your ticket on to Vienna from there. Similarly, from Austria only buy a ticket as far as Jesenice or Maribor as domestic fares are much lower than international ones.

There are two trains a day between Munich and Ljubljana (seven hours, 9737 SIT) via Salzburg. The EuroCity *Mimara* travels by day, while the *Lisinski* express goes overnight (sleeping carriage available). A 258 SIT supplement is payable on the

Mimara. Seat reservations (160 SIT) are available on both.

Four trains a day run from Trieste to Ljubljana (three hours, 2464 SIT) via Divača and Sežana. From Croatia it's Zagreb to Ljubljana (2½ hours, 1513 SIT) via Zidani Most, or Rijeka to Ljubljana (2½ hours, 1460 SIT) via Pivka. Most services between Slovenia and Croatia require a change of trains at some point, but connections are immediate. The InterCity *Drava* and *Venezia Express* trains link Ljubljana with Budapest (7½ hours, 6747 SIT) via north-west Croatia and Zagreb respectively.

Car & Motorcycle
Slovenia maintains some 150 border crossings with Italy, Austria, Hungary and Croatia though not all are open to citizens of other countries.

SEA
Between early April and October on Friday, Saturday and Sunday the *Prince of Venice*, a 39m Australian-made catamaran seating some 330 passengers, sails between Portorož and Venice (2½ hours, 6860/9800 SIT one way/return) with an additional sailing on Tuesday from late June to early September. Another catamaran, the *Marconi*, links Trieste with Piran (35 minutes, 2000/4000 SIT return) on Wednesday, Friday and Sunday from mid-May to September.

LEAVING SLOVENIA
A departure tax of DM25/US$14 is levied on all passengers leaving Slovenia by air though this is almost always included in the ticket price.

Getting Around

BUS
Except for long journeys, the bus is preferable to the train in Slovenia and departures are frequent. In some cases you don't have much of a choice; travelling by bus is the only practical way to get to Bled and Bohinj, the Julian Alps and much of the coast from Ljubljana.

In Ljubljana you can buy your ticket with

seat reservation (60 to 120 SIT, depending on the destination) the day before, but many people simply pay the driver on boarding. The one time you really might need a reservation is Friday afternoon, when many students travel from Ljubljana to their homes or people leave the city for the weekend.

Footnotes you might see on Slovenian bus schedules include: *vozi vsak dan* (runs daily); *vozi ob delavnikih* (runs on working days – Monday to Friday); *vozi ob sobotah* (runs on Saturday); and *vozi ob nedeljah in praznikih* (runs on Sunday and holidays).

TRAIN
Slovenske Železnice (SŽ; Slovenian Railways) operates on just over 1200km of track. The country's most scenic rail routes run along the Soča River from Jesenice to Nova Gorica via Bled (Bled Jezero station) and Bohinjska Bistrica (89km) and from Ljubljana to Zagreb (160km) along the Sava River.

On posted timetables in Slovenia, *odhod* or *odhodi vlakov* means 'departures' and *prihod* (or *prihodi vlakov*) is 'arrivals'. If you don't have time to buy a ticket, seek out the conductor who will sell you one for an extra charge of 200 SIT.

CAR & MOTORCYCLE
The use of seat belts in the front seats is compulsory in Slovenia, and a new law requires all vehicles to show their headlights throughout the day outside built-up areas. Speed limits for cars are 50km/h in built-up areas, 90km/h on secondary roads, 100km/h on main highways and 130km/h on motorways.

Tolls are payable on several motorways, but they're not terribly expensive; from Ljubljana to Postojna, for example, it costs 250 SIT for cars and motorcycles. Petrol remains relatively cheap: 100.40/103.50/119.80 SIT per litre for 91/95/98 octane. Diesel costs 100.50 SIT.

Slovenia's automobile club is the Avto Moto Zveza Slovenije (AMZS; tel 987)

Car Rental
Car rentals from international firms like National, Budget, Avis and Kompas Hertz vary widely in price, but expect to pay from about US$57/$287 a day/week with unlimited

mileage for a Renault 5 or Ford Fiesta. Optional collision insurance to reduce the excess/deductible is about US$8 a day extra, theft protection another US$8 and personal accident insurance US$2 to US$5. Smaller agencies like ABC Rent a Car and Avtoimpex in Ljubljana (see Getting Around in that section) have more competitive rates.

Some agencies have minimum-age rules (21 or 23 years) and/or require that you've had a valid licence for one or even two years.

HITCHING

Hitchhiking is legal everywhere except on motorways and some major highways and is generally easy; even young women do it. But hitching is never a totally safe way of getting around and, although we mention it as an option, we don't recommend it.

Ljubljana

☎ 061

Ljubljana (Laibach in German, population 270,000) is by far Slovenia's largest and most populous city. But in many ways the city, whose name almost means 'beloved' (*ljubljena*) in Slovene, does not feel like an industrious municipality of national importance but a pleasant, self-contented town with responsibilities only to itself and its citizens. The most beautiful parts of the city are the Old Town below the castle and the embankments designed by Plečnik along the narrow Ljubljanica River.

Ljubljana began as the Roman town of Emona, and legacies of the Roman presence can still be seen throughout the city. The Habsburgs took control of Ljubljana in the 14th century and later built many of the pale-coloured churches and mansions that earned the city the nickname 'White Ljubljana'. From 1809 to 1814, Ljubljana was the capital of the Illyrian Provinces, Napoleon's short-lived springboard to the Adriatic.

Despite the patina of imperial Austria, contemporary Ljubljana has a vibrant Slavic air all its own. It's like a little Prague without the hordes of tourists but with all the facilities you'll need. More than 25,000 students attend Ljubljana University's 14 faculties and three art academies so the city always feels young.

Orientation

The tiny bus station and renovated train station are opposite one another on Trg Osvobodilne Fronte (known as Trg OF) at the northern end of the centre (called Center). The 24-hour left-luggage office (*garderoba*; 160 SIT per piece) at the train station is on platform No 1. A smaller garderoba (open from 5.30 am to 8.30 pm) is inside the bus station.

Information

Tourist Offices The Tourist Information Centre (TIC; tel 133 0111; fax 133 0244; pcl.tic-lj@siol.net) is in the historical Kresija building south-east of Triple Bridge at Mačkova ulica 1. It's open weekdays from 8 am to 7 pm and on Saturday from 9 am to 5 pm. The branch office (☎ 133 9475) at the train station is open daily (including Sunday) June to September from 8 am to 9 pm (10 am to 6 pm the rest of the year). The TIC is well worth visiting to pick up free maps and brochures.

The Cultural Information Centre (☎ 214 025) next to Trg Francoske Revolucije 7 can answer questions about what's on in Ljubljana and has a free booklet listing all the city's museums, galleries and exhibitions.

The main office of the Alpine Association of Slovenia (☎ 134 3022; www.pzs.si) is at Dvoržakova ulica 9, a small house set back from the street.

Money The currency exchange office inside the train station is open daily from 6 am to 10 pm. It accepts travellers cheques, charges no commission and the rate is good. The best rate anywhere in Slovenia, though, is at Nova Ljubljanska Banka, Trg Republike 2 (open weekdays 8 am to 5 pm, on Saturday 9 am till noon). There's an A Banka branch at Slovenska cesta 50. The Hida exchange bureau in the Seminary building near the open-air market at Pogarčarjev trg 1 is open weekdays from 7 am to 7 pm and on Saturday to 2 pm. Another Hida branch at Čopova ulica 42 is open weekdays from 8 am to 8 pm and on Saturday to 1 pm.

SKB Banka Cirrus-linked ATMs are at Trg Ajdovščina 4, in the very centre of the big shopping mall; outside the Emona Globtour agency in the Maximarket passageway connecting Trg Republike with Plečnikov trg; and in the

Gledališka pasaža connecting Čopova ulica with Nazorjeva ulica. Next to the SKB Banka ATM on Trg Ajdovščina is a currency exchange machine that changes the banknotes of 18 countries into tolar.

Post & Communications Poste restante is held for 30 days at the post office at Slovenska cesta 32 (postal code 1101). It is open weekdays from 7 am to 8 pm and to 1 pm Saturday. You can make international telephone calls or send faxes from here or the main post office at Pražakova ulica 3, which keeps the same hours.

To mail a parcel you must go to the special customs post office at Trg OF 5 opposite the bus station and open round the clock. Make sure you bring your package open for inspection; the maximum weight is about 15kg, depending on the destination.

Internet Resources Useful Web sites for Ljubljana include:

www.ljubljiana.si
  City of Ljubljana
www.uni-lj.si
  Ljubljana University (check out the Welcome chapter with practical information for foreign students)
www.sou.uni-lj/english.html
  Student Organisation of the University of Ljubljana (Študentska Organizacija Univerze Ljubljani; ŠOU)
www.ljudmila/org/
  Ljubljana Digital Media Lab (links with the multimedia group Neue Slowenische Kunst, the MOST-SIC volunteer work organisation etc)

There are two cybercafés with public-access Internet sites in Ljubljana: the Klub K4 Café (☎ 131 7010) at Kersnikova ulica 4 and Club Podhod (☎ 121 4100) in the underpass (subway) between Kongresni trg and Plečnikov trg.

Travel Agencies Backpackers and students should head for the Erazem travel office (☎ 133 1076) at Trubarjeva cesta 7. It can provide information, make bookings and it has a message board. It also sells ISIC cards (800 SIT) and, for those under 26 but not studying, FIYTO cards (700 SIT). Mladi Turist (☎ 125 8260), at Salendrova ulica 4

near the Municipal Museum, is the office of the Slovenian Youth Hostel Association. It sells hostel cards (800 to 1800 SIT, depending on your age), but you're supposed to have resided in the country for six months.

Slovenijaturist (☎ 131 5055), Slovenska cesta 58, sells BIJ international train tickets (one-third cheaper than regular fares) to those under 26 years of age.

The American Express representative is Atlas Express (☎ 133 2024 or tel 131 9020) at Trubarjeva cesta 50 in Ljubljana. It will hold clients' mail but doesn't cash travellers cheques.

Bookshops Ljubljana's largest bookshop is Mladinska Knjiga at Slovenska cesta 29. It also has a branch on Miklošičeva cesta 40, opposite the bus station. Another good chain with a shop at Slovenska cesta 37 is Cankarjeva Založba. Kod & Kam, Trg Francoske Revolucije 7, is excellent for travel guides and maps.

The best places for English and other foreign-language newspapers and magazines are the newsstand in the lobby of the Grand Hotel Union, Miklošičeva cesta 1, and the one in the basement of the Maximarket department store on Trg Republike.

Laundry A couple of the student dormitories, including Dijaški Dom Poljane about 1.5km east of the Old Town at Potočnikova ulica 3 and Dijaški Dom Kam (Building C) at Kardeljeva ploščad 14, north of the centre in Bežigrad, have washing machines and dryers that you can use, as does the Ježica camping ground. Alba at Wolfova ulica 12 near Prešernov trg is an old-style laundry and dry cleaner open weekdays from 8 am to 6 pm.

Medical Services You can see a doctor at the medical centre (*klinični center*; ☎ 133 6236 or ☎ 131 3123) at Zaloška cesta 7, which is in Tabor east of the Park hotel. The emergency unit (*urgenca*) is open 24 hours a day.

Things to See
The most picturesque sights of old Ljubljana are along both banks of the Ljubljanica, a tributary of the Sava that curves around the foot of Castle Hill.

Opposite the TIC in the Kresija building is the celebrated **Triple Bridge**. In 1931, Jože Plečnik added the side bridges to the original central span dating from 1842. On the northern side of the bridge is Prešernov trg with its pink **Franciscan church** (1660), a statue (1905) of poet France Prešeren and some lovely Art Nouveau buildings. A lively pedestrian street, Čopova ulica, runs to the north-west.

On the south side of the bridge in Mestni trg, the baroque **Robba Fountain** stands before the **town hall** (1718). Italian sculptor Francesco Robba designed this fountain in 1751 and modelled it after one in Rome. Enter the town hall to see the double Gothic courtyard. To the south of Mestni trg is **Stari trg**, atmospheric by day or night. North-east are the twin towers of the **Cathedral of St Nicholas** (1708), which contains impressive frescos. Behind the cathedral is Ljubljana's colourful open-air **produce market** (closed Sunday) and a lovely **colonnade** along the riverside designed by Plečnik.

Študentovska ulica, opposite the Vodnik statue in the market square, leads up to **Ljubljana Castle**. The castle has been under renovation for decades, but you can climb the 19th-century **Castle Tower** to the west (daily from 10 am to dusk; 200/100 SIT adults/children) and view the exhibits in a Gothic chapel and the **Pentagonal Tower** (closed Saturday and Monday). Reber ulica between Stari trg 17 & 19 also leads up to the castle.

There's another interesting area worth exploring on the west side of the Ljubljanica River. The **Municipal Museum**, Gosposka ulica 15 (open Tuesday to Saturday from 9 am to 7 pm, Sunday from 2 to 6 pm; 500/300 SIT for adults/seniors, students & children), is a good place to start. The museum has a well presented collection of Roman artefacts, plus a scale model of Roman Emona (Ljubljana). Upstairs rooms contain period furniture and household objects.

At Gosposka ulica 14 near the Municipal Museum is the **National & University Library** (1941) designed by Plečnik, and north on Gosposka ulica at Kongresni trg 12 is the main building of **Ljubljana University** (1902), formerly the regional parliament. The lovely **Philharmonic Hall** (Filharmonija), at No 10 on the south-east corner of the square,

is home to the Slovenian Philharmonic Orchestra. The **Ursuline Church of the Holy Trinity** (1726), with an altar by Robba, faces Kongresni trg to the west.

Walk west on Šubičeva ulica to several of the city's fine museums. The **National Museum**, Muzejska ulica 1 (open Tuesday to Sunday from 10 am to 6 pm, to 8 pm on Wednesday; 300/200 SIT), erected in 1885, has prehistory, natural history and ethnography collections. The highlight is a Celtic situla, a kind of pail, from the 6th century BC sporting a fascinating relief.

The **National Gallery**, Cankarjeva ulica 20, offers Slovenian portraits and landscapes from the 17th to 19th centuries, as well as copies of medieval frescos; the gallery's new wing to the north at Puharjeva ulica 9 (separate entrance) has a permanent collection of European paintings from the Middle Ages to the 20th century and is used for temporary exhibits. It is open Tuesday to Sunday from 10 am to 6 pm, and entry costs 500/300 SIT.

Diagonally opposite the National Gallery, at Cankarjeva ulica 15, is the **Museum of Modern Art**, where the International Biennial of Graphic Arts is held every other summer in odd-numbered years. It is open Tuesday to Saturday from 10 am to 6 pm and on Sunday to 1 pm. Admission costs 300/200 SIT for adults/seniors and children and it's free on Sunday. The Serbian Orthodox **Church of Sts Cyril & Methodius** opposite the Museum of Modern Art is worth entering to see the beautiful modern frescos (open Tuesday to Saturday from 3 to 6 pm). The subway from the Museum of Modern Art leads to Ljubljana's green lung, **Tivoli Park**.

If you have time (or the inclination) for another museum or two, head for the **Museum of Modern History**, Celovška cesta 23 just beyond the Tivoli Recreation Centre, which traces the history of Slovenia in the 20th century via multimedia, or the new **Slovenian Ethnographic Museum** at Metlikova ulica 2. Both are open Tuesday to Sunday from 10 am to 6 pm and cost 400/300 SIT.

Activities
The **Tivoli Recreation Centre**, in the Tivoli Park at Celovška cesta 25, has bowling alleys, tennis courts, an indoor swimming pool, a fitness centre and a roller-skating rink.

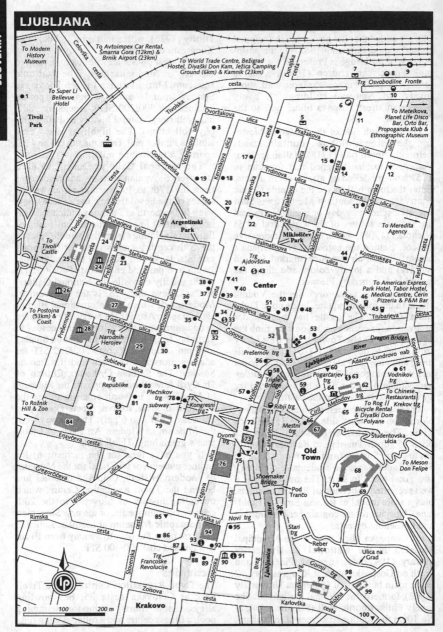

LJUBLJANA

To Modern
History
Museum

To Avtoimpex Car Rental,
Šmarna Gora (12km) &
Brnik Airport (23km)

To World Trade Centre, Bežigrad
Hostel, Diaški Don Kam, Ježica Camping
Ground (6km) & Kamnik (23km)

To Super Li
Bellevue
Hotel

Tivoli
Park

To Metelkova,
Planet Life Disco
Bar, Orto Bar,
Propoganda Klub &
Ethnographic Museum

Trg Osvobodilne Fronte

Celovška cesta

Tivolska cesta

Dunajska cesta

Dvořakova ulica

Pražakova

Dvořakova ulica

Vošnjakova ulica

Kersnikova ulica

Slovenska cesta

Trdinova ulica

Cigaletova ulica

Čufarjeva ulica

Kotnikova

Gosposvetska cesta

Argentinski
Park

Tavčarjeva

Miklošičev
Park

Miklošičeva

To Meredita
Agency

Dalmatinova

Komenskega ulica

Reslijeva cesta

Puharjeva ul

Trg
Ajdovščina

Center

Prešernova ulica

To American Express,
Park Hotel, Tabor Hostel,
Medical Centre, Čerin
Pizzeria & P&M Bar

Trubarjeva cesta

Tivolska cesta

To Tivoli
Castle

Štefanova ulica

Župančičeva

Cankarjeva ulica

Nazorjeva ulica

Čopova

Prešernova

To Postojna
(53km) &
Coast

Beethovnova ulica

Tomšičeva ulica

Trg
Narodnih
Herojev

Slovenska cesta

ulica
Prešernov trg

River

Dragon Bridge

Ljubljanica

Adamič-Lundrovo nab

Šubičeva ulica

Trg
Republike

Plečnikov
trg

subway

Kongresni
trg

Wolfova

Triple
Bridge

Cankarjevo nab

Pogarčarjev
trg

Vodnikov
trg

To Rožnik
Hill & Zoo

Mestni
trg

Metodov

To Chinese
Restaurants

Krekov trg

To Rog
Bicycle Rental
& Diaški Dom
Polyane

Erjavčeva cesta

Ciril

Dvorni
trg

Old
Town

Studentovska
ulica

To Meson
Don Felipe

Gregorčičeva

Igriška ulica

Vegova ulica

Shoemaker
Bridge

Pod Trančo

Rimska

Turjaška ul

Novi trg

River

Stari
trg

Reber
ulica

Ulica na
Grad

Trg
Francoske
Revolucije

Gosposka

Breg

Ljubljanica

Levstikov trg

Gornji trg

Zoisova

Krakovo

Karlovška cesta

Rožna

0   100   200 m

LJUBLJANA

PLACES TO STAY
34 Slon Hotel & Café
44 Turist Hotel & Klub
   Central Disco
50 Grand Hotel Union
86 Pri Mraku Guesthouse

PLACES TO EAT
12 Burek Stand
20 Evropa Café
22 Tavčarjev Hram
36 Daj-Dam
40 Skriti Kot
41 Šestica
42 Super 5 Food Stand
47 Napoli Pizzeria
60 Ribca Seafood Bar
65 Kolovrat
74 Ljubljanski Dvor
85 Foculus Pizzeria
96 Pizzeria Romeo
98 Sichuan
100 Špajza

OTHER
1 Tivoli Recreation Centre,
   Zlati Klub Sauna &
   Klub Manhattan Disco
2 Ilirija Swimming Pool
3 Alpine Association
   of Slovenia
4 Slovenijaturist Travel
   Agency & Burek Stand
5 Main Post Office
6 Canadian Embassy
7 Post Office (Customs)
8 City Airport Buses
9 Train Station & Tourist
   Office Branch
10 Bus Station
11 Kompas Cinema
13 Avis Car Rental
14 Kinoteka Cinema

15 Kompas Hertz Car Rental
16 US Embassy
17 City Bus Ticket Kiosks
18 Klub K4 & University
   Student Centre
19 Adria Airways Office
21 A Banka
23 National Car Rental
24 National Gallery
25 Serbian Orthodox Church
26 Museum of Modern Art
27 Opera House
28 National Museum
29 Parliament Building
30 Gajo Jazz Club
31 Mladinska Knjiga Bookshop
32 Post Office
   (Poste Restante)
33 Hida Exchange Bureau
35 Komuna Cinema
37 Cankarjeva Založba
   Bookshop
38 Skyscraper Building & Café
39 Kompas Travel Agency
   & Holidays' Pub
43 SKB Banka & ATM
45 TrueBar
46 Patrick's Irish Pub
48 Art Nouveau Bank
   Buildings
49 Union Cinema
51 Eldorado Disco
52 Franciscan Church
53 Erazem Travel Agency
54 Urbanc Building/
   Centromerkur Department
   Store
55 Prešeren Monument
56 Ura Building
57 Alba Laundry
58 Horse's Tail Café Pub
59 Tourist Information
   Centre (TIC)

61 Produce Market
62 Cathedral of Saint Nicholas
63 Seminary/Hida
   Exchange Bureau
64 Bishop's Palace
66 Robba Fountain
67 Town Hall
68 Ljubljana Castle
69 Pentagonal Tower
70 Castle Tower
71 River Cruises
72 Delikatesa
73 Filharmonija
75 Burja Delicatessen
76 Ljubljana University
77 Club Podhod
78 Rock Café
79 Ursuline Church
80 Maximarket Shopping
   Arcade & Maxim
   Self-Service Restaurant
81 Emona Globtour
   Travel Agency
82 Nova Ljubljanska Banka
83 UK & Australian
   Embassy
84 Cankarjev Dom
   (Cultural Centre)
87 Ilirija Column
88 Križanke Ticket Office
89 Križanke/Summer
   Festival Theatre
90 Municipal Museum
91 Mladi Turist
92 Kod & Kam Bookshop
93 Cultural Information
   Centre
94 National & University
   Library
95 Academy of Arts
   & Sciences
97 Church of St James
99 Church of St Florian

There's even a popular sauna called **Zlati Klub** that has several saunas, a steam room, warm and cold splash pools and even a small outside pool surrounded by high walls so you can sunbathe in the nude (mixed sexes). Entry costs 1500 SIT at the weekend and 1200 SIT on weekdays and until 1 pm.

The outdoor **Ilirija pool** opposite the Tivoli hotel at Celovška cesta 3 is open in summer from 10 am to 7 pm on weekdays, 9 am to 8 pm at the weekend.

Organised Tours
From June to September, a two-hour guided tour in English (700/500 SIT adults/seniors, students & children) sponsored by the TIC departs daily at 5 pm from the town hall in Mestni trg. During the rest of the year there are tours at 11 am on Sunday only.

In summer a boat called the *Emona II* (☎ 448 112 or mobile ☎ 041-627 857) offers excursions on the Ljubljanica Tuesday to Sunday at 5 and 7 pm from the footbridge just west of Ribnji trg (500 SIT; children under 12 free).

Places to Stay

Camping Some 6km north of Center on the Sava at Dunajska cesta 270 (bus No 6 or 8) is *Camping Ježica* (☎ 168 3913), with a large, shady camping area (860 SIT per person plus 180 SIT for a caravan or tent) and three dozen cramped little bungalows for two costing 6600 SIT. The camping ground is open all year.

Hostels & Student Dormitories Four student dormitories (*dijaški dom*) open their doors to foreign travellers in July and August. The most central by far is the *Dijaški Dom Tabor* (☎ 321 067), opposite the Park hotel at Vidovdanska ulica 7 and affiliated with Hostelling International (HI). It charges 2880 SIT for a single room and 2200 SIT for a bed in a double or triple, including breakfast.

The *Dijaški Dom Bežigrad* (☎ 342 867), another HI member, is at Kardeljeva ploščad 28 in the Bežigrad district 2km north of the train and bus stations. It has doubles/triples with shower and toilet for 3600/4500 SIT and rooms with one to three beds with shared facilities for 1200 SIT per person. An HI card gets you about 10% off. The Bežigrad has 70 rooms available from late June to late August but only about 20 the rest of the year.

Private Rooms & Apartments The TIC has about 40 private rooms on its list, but just a handful are in Center. Most of the others would require a bus trip up to Bežigrad. Prices range from 2500 SIT for singles and 4000 SIT for doubles. It also has eight apartments and two studios – four of which are central – for one to four people costing from 8900 SIT to 16,700 SIT. Reception is at the Meredita agency (☎ 131 1102) in the Ledina shopping centre at Kotnikova ulica 5.

Guesthouse The closest thing to a pension in Ljubljana proper is the *Pri Mraku* pension (☎ 223 412; fax 301 197), west of Trg Francoske Revolucije at Rimska cesta 4, but its 30 rooms are small and quite expensive: 7050 SIT for a single with shower and breakfast and 9900 SIT for a double.

Hotels One of the best deals in town is the 15-room *Super Li Bellevue* hotel (☎ 133 4049) on the northern edge of Tivoli Park at Pod Gozdom 12. There are no rooms with private bath, but bright and airy singles with basins are 3050 SIT, doubles 6000 SIT.

The 122-room *Park* hotel (☎ 133 1306; fax 133 0546) at Tabor 9 is where most people usually end up as it's the city's only large budget hotel close to Center and the Old Town. It's pretty basic, but the price is right: 5500/7000 SIT for singles/doubles with breakfast and shared shower and 6800/8500 SIT with private shower. Students with cards get a 20% discount. The staff are very helpful and friendly.

Places to Eat

Restaurants The *Kolovrat* at Ciril-Metodov trg 14 opposite the cathedral is a renovated Slovenian gostilna with reasonably priced Slovenian meals (lunch menus at 750 and 1300 SIT) or you might try the *Tavčarjev Hram* at Tavčarjev ulica 4. The *Šestica* is a 200-year-old standby with a pleasant courtyard at Slovenska cesta 40. Main courses are in the 600-1200 SIT range and lunch menus are 900 and 1200 SIT. A much more upmarket (and expensive) alternative for Slovenian specialities is the attractive *Špajza* in the Old Town at Gornji trg 28.

The capital abounds in Italian restaurants and pizzerias. Among the best are the *Ljubljanski Dvor* at Dvorni trg 1 on the west bank of the Ljubljanica and *Foculus*, next to the Glej Theatre at Gregorčičeva ulica 3 (small/large pizzas 710/830 SIT, salad bar 390/560 SIT). Other pizza-pasta places include *Pizzeria Romeo* in the Old Town opposite the Café Julija at Stari trg 6, *Napoli* off Trubarjeva cesta at Prečna ulica 7 and the *Čerin* at the eastern end of Trubarjeva cesta at Znamenjska ulica 2.

Meson Don Felipe, south-east of Krekov trg at Streliška ulica 22, is Ljubljana's first – and only – tapas bar (300 to 1000 SIT).

If you've a yen for some Chinese food, the location of the *Sichuan* below the Church of St Florian at Gornji trg 23 is wonderful, but the food is much more authentic at the *Zlati Pav*, Zarnikova ulica 3 (enter from Poljanska cesta 20), and nearby *Shanghai* at Poljanska cesta 14.

Cafés For coffee and cakes you might try the truncated *Evropa* café at Gosposvetska cesta 2 on the corner of Slovenska cesta or the *Slon* café in the Slon hotel at Slovenska cesta 34. Better still (at least for the views) is the *Terasa Nebotičnik*, a café on the top (12th) floor of the Art Deco Skyscraper building at the corner of Slovenska cesta and Štefanova ulica.

Self-Service & Fast Food Among the two cheapest places for lunch are the *Maxim* self-service restaurant in the basement of the Maximarket shopping arcade on Trg Republike, and *Daj-Dam* at Cankarjeva ulica 4, which has a vegetarian menu (750 SIT). But don't expect Cordon Bleu food; it's real school cafeteria stuff. The best self-service restaurant in Ljubljana, according to cognoscenti, is *Skriti Kot*, very much a 'Hidden Corner' in the shopping arcade below Trg Ajdovščina. Hearty main courses go for 350 to 750 SIT.

For a quick and very tasty lunch, try the fried squid (650 to 850 SIT) or whitebait (300 to 450 SIT) at *Ribca*, a basement seafood bar below the Plečnik Colonnade in Pogarčarjev trg.

There are *burek stands* (about 250 SIT) at several locations in Ljubljana and among the best are the one on Pražakova ulica next to Slovenijaturist and the one at Kolodvorska ulica 20 (open 24 hours). If you want something more substantial, head for the outdoor *Super 5*, which faces Slovenska cesta from the shopping mall in Trg Ajdovščina. It serves cheap and cheerful Balkan grills like čevapčiči (700 SIT) and pljeskavica (440 to 540 SIT) as well as sausage (klobasa; 750 SIT) and is open 24 hours.

Self-Catering The *supermarket* in the basement of the Maximarket shopping arcade on Trg Republike has about the largest selection in town (open weekdays 9 am to 8 pm, Saturday 8 am to 3 pm). But the best places for picnic supplies are the city's many delicatessens including *Delikatesa* at Kongresni trg 9 and *Burja* at No 11 of the same square.

Entertainment

Ask the TIC for its monthly programme of events in English called *Where to? in Ljubljana*.

Cinema For first-run films, head for the *Komuna* cinema at Cankarjeva ulica 1 or the *Union* cinema at Nazorjeva ulica 2. They generally have three screenings a day. The *Kompas* cinema, Miklošičeva cesta 38, shows art and classic films as does the *Kinoteka* at No 28 of the same street. Cinema tickets generally cost 400 to 650 SIT, and discounts are usually available at the first performance on weekdays.

Clubs The most popular conventional clubs are *Eldorado* at Nazorjeva ulica 4 and *Klub Central* next to the Turist hotel at Dalmatinova ulica 15. The student *Klub K4* at Kersnikova ulica 4 has a disco on some nights. Other popular venues at present for Ljubljana's young bloods are *Planet Life* in the BTC shopping centre at Šmartinska cesta 152g north-east of the train station (bus Nos 2, 7 & 12) and the *Klub Manhattan* in the Tivoli Recreation Centre in Tivoli Park (Celovška cesta 25).

Gay & Lesbian Ljubljana A popular spot for both gays and lesbians alike on Sunday night is the *Roza Klub* at the Klub K4. It's open from 10 pm to 4 am. At the Metelkova squat, Ljubljana's version of Christiania in Copenhagen between Metelkova ulica and Maistrova ulica, there's a café-pub for gays (Thursday night is reserved for lesbians) called *Club Tiffany*. The *Propaganda Klub* at Grablovičeva ulica 1 has a gay and lesbian night on Friday called 'Does Your Momma Know?'.

Classical Music, Opera & Dance Ljubljana is home to two orchestras. Concerts are held in various locations all over town, but the main venue – with up to 700 cultural events a year – is *Cankarjev Dom* on Trg Republike. The ticket office (☎ 222 815) in the basement of the nearby Maximarket mall is open weekdays from 10 am to 2 pm and 4.30 to 8 pm, Saturday from 10 am to 1 pm and an hour before performances. Tickets cost anywhere between 1500 and 2500 SIT with gala performances as much as 6000 SIT. Also check for concerts at the beautiful *Filharmonija* at Kongresni trg 10.

The ticket office (☎ 125 4840) of the *Opera House*, Župančičeva ulica 1, where ballets are also performed, is open Monday to Friday from 11 am to 1 pm and an hour before each performance.

For tickets to the Ljubljana Summer Festival and anything else staged at the *Križanke*, go to the booking office (☎ 126 4340 or ☎ 226 544) behind the Ilirija Column at Trg Francoske Revolucije 1-2. It is open weekdays from 10 am to 2 pm and from 6 to 8 pm, on Saturday from 10 am to 1 pm and on Sunday one hour before the performance.

Rock & Jazz Ljubljana has a number of excellent rock clubs with canned or live music including *Orto Bar* at Grablovičeva ulica 1 and the *Rock Café*, Plečnikov trg 1. For jazz, you can't beat the *Gajo Jazz Club* at Beethovnova ulica 8 near the Parliament building.

Pubs & Bars Pleasant and congenial places for a *pivo* or glass of *vino* include the outdoor *Konjski Rep* (Horse's Tail) café-pub in Prešernov trg during the warmer months; *TrueBar*, Trubarjeva cesta 53; *Patrick's Irish Pub*, Prečna ulica 6; *Holidays' Pub* next to the Kompas travel agency at Slovenska cesta 36; and *P&M Bar* just off Trubarjeva cesta at Znamenjska ulica 1.

Getting There & Away

Bus You can reach virtually anywhere in the country by bus from the capital. If you're heading for Bled or Bohinj, take the bus not the train. The train from Ljubljana to the former will leave you at the Lesce-Bled station, 4km south-east of the lake. The closest train station to Lake Bohinj is at Bohinjska Bistrica, 6km to the east, and it's on the branch line linking Nova Gorica with Jesenice.

The timetable in the shed-like bus station (☎ 134 3838 for information) on Trg OF lists all routings and times, but here are some sample routings frequencies and one-way fares: Bled (hourly, 790 SIT); Bohinj (hourly, 1190 SIT); Jesenice (hourly, 890 SIT); Koper (nine to 13 a day, 1650 SIT); Maribor (half-hourly, 1660

SIT); Murska Sobota (eight a day, 2430 SIT); Novo Mesto (up to 10 a day, 940 SIT); Piran (six to 10 a day, 1710 SIT); Postojna (half-hourly, 720 SIT).

Buses from Ljubljana serve a number of international destinations including: Belgrade (one daily, 5360 SIT); Berlin (Wednesday at 7.30 pm, 15,821 SIT); Budapest (Tuesday, Thursday and Friday at 10 pm, 4590 SIT); Frankfurt (Wednesday at 7.30 pm, 12,885 SIT); Klagenfurt (Wednesday at 6.15 am, 1310 SIT); Lenti (Thursday at 5.30 am, 3070 SIT); Munich (Tuesday to Thursday at 5.05 or 5.30 am, 5215 SIT); Novigrad (daily at 1.45 pm, 2300 SIT); Prague (Tuesday, Thursday and Saturday at 9 pm, 6940 SIT); Rijeka (daily at 7.40 pm, 1020 SIT); Rovinj (daily at 1.45 pm, 3200 SIT); Split (daily at 7.40 pm, 3620 SIT); Stuttgart (Wednesday and Thursday at 7.30 pm, 10,802 SIT); Trieste (Monday to Saturday at 6.25 am, 1460 SIT); Varaždin (Saturday and Sunday at 6.35 am, 2810 SIT); and Zagreb (four a day, 2030 SIT).

Train All domestic and international trains arrive at and depart from the station (☎ 316 768 for information) at Trg OF 6. Local trains leave Ljubljana regularly for Bled (51km, 486 SIT); Jesenice (64km, 590 SIT); Koper (153km, 1011 SIT); Maribor (156km, 1011 SIT); Murska Sobota (216km, 1356 SIT); Novo Mesto (75km, 651 SIT); and Ptuj (155km, 1011 SIT). Return fares are usually 20% cheaper than double the price, and there's a 160 SIT surcharge on the domestic InterCity train tickets.

For information on international trains to/from Ljubljana, see the introductory Getting There & Away section of this chapter.

Getting Around

To/From the Airport Bus No 28 (350 SIT) makes the run between Ljubljana and Brnik airport, 23km to the north-west, 15 or 16 times a day Monday to Friday and seven times daily at the weekend. A taxi will cost between 4000 and 4500 SIT.

Bus Ljubljana's bus system, run by LPP (☎ 159 4114 for information), is excellent and very user-friendly. There are 22 lines; five of them (Nos 1, 2, 3, 6 and 11) are considered main lines. These start at 3.15 am and run till midnight while the rest operate from 5 am to 10.30 pm. You can pay on board (120 SIT) or use tiny yellow plastic tokens (75 SIT) available at newsstands, tobacconists, post offices and the two kiosks on the pavement in front of Slovenska cesta 55.

Car & Motorcycle Three international car-rental chains are Kompas Hertz (☎ 311 241), Miklošičeva ulica 11; National (☎ 126 3118), Štefanova ulica 13; and Avis (☎ 132 3395), Čufarjeva ulica 2. They also have counters at the airport. Two excellent smaller agencies are ABC Rent a Car (☎ 064-261 684) at Brnik airport and Avtoimpex (☎ 555 025), Celovška cesta 150.

Taxi You can call a taxi on one of 10 numbers: ☎ 9700 to 9709.

Bicycle Two places to rent bicycles are Rog (☎ 315 868), next to Rozmanova ulica 1 (1500 SIT per day; open weekdays 8 am to 7 pm, Saturday till noon) and Kos Damjan (☎ 553 606) at Tugomerjeva ulica 35 (1000 SIT).

Julian Alps

Slovenia shares the Julian Alps in the north-west corner of the country with Italy. Three-headed Mt Triglav (2864m), the country's highest peak, is climbed regularly by thousands of weekend warriors, but there are countless less ambitious hikes on offer in the region. Lakes Bled and Bohinj make ideal starting points – Bled with its comfortable resort facilities, Bohinj right beneath the rocky crags themselves. Most of this spectacular area falls within the boundaries of Triglav National Park, established in 1924.

BLED
☎ 064
Bled (population 5664), a fashionable resort at just over 501m, is set on an idyllic, 2km-long emerald-green lake with a little island and church in the centre and a dramatic castle towering overhead. Trout and carp proliferate in the clear water, which is surprisingly warm and a pleasure to swim in or go boating on. To the north-east, the highest peaks of the Kara-

vanke range form a natural boundary with Austria; the Julian Alps lie to the west. Bled has been a favourite destination for travellers for decades. All in all, it *is* beautiful but it can get very crowded – and pricey – in season.

Orientation
Bled village is at the north-eastern end of the lake below the castle. The bus station is also here on Cesta Svobode, but the main Lesce-Bled train station is about 4km to the south-east. In addition there's Bled Jezero, a branchline train station north-west of the lake, not far from the camping ground.

Information
Tourist Offices The tourist office (☎ 741 122; fax 741 555) is next to the Park hotel at Cesta Svobode 15. Ask for the useful English booklet *Bled Tourist Information*. From April to October the office is open Monday to Saturday from 8 am to 7 pm (to 10 pm in July and August) and from 10 am to 6 pm on Sunday (to 8 pm in July and August). From November to March the hours are 9 am to 5 pm Monday to Saturday and noon to 4 or 5 pm on Sunday. Kompas (☎ 741 515) in the Triglav shopping centre at Ljubljanska cesta 4 sells good hiking maps. The Triglav National Park office information centre (☎ 741 188) is at Kidričeva cesta 2 on the lake's northern shore (open from 8 am to 3 pm on weekdays only).

Money Gorenjska Banka in the Park hotel shopping complex and across from the casino on Cesta Svobode is open from 9 to 11.30 am and 2 to 5 pm on weekdays and 8 to 11 am on Saturday. SKB Banka has a branch with an ATM in the Triglav shopping centre.

Post & Communications The main post office, open weekdays from 7 am to 7 pm and on Saturday till noon, is at Ljubljanska cesta 10.

Things to See
There are several trails up to **Bled Castle** (open daily, 400/200 SIT for adults/children), the easiest being the one going south from behind the hostel at Grajska cesta 17. The castle was the seat of the Bishops of Brixen

(South Tyrol) for over 800 years; set atop a steep cliff 100m above the lake, it offers magnificent views in clear weather. The castle's **museum** presents the history of the area and allows a peep into a small 16th-century chapel.

Bled's other striking feature is tiny **Bled Island** at the western end of the lake. The tolling 'bell of wishes' echoes across the lake from the tall white belfry rising above the dense vegetation. It's said that all who ring it will get their wish; naturally it chimes constantly. Underneath the present baroque church are the foundations of what was a pre-Romanesque chapel, unique in Slovenia. Most people reach the island on a *pletna*, a large gondola hand-propelled by a boatman. The price (1000 to 1200 SIT per person, depending on the season) includes a half-hour visit to the island, church and belfry. If there are two or three of you it would be cheaper and more fun to hire a rowing boat (about 1000/1200 SIT an hour for three/five people) from the Castle Baths on the shore below the castle, in Mlino or at the large beach to the south-west.

You can ride **horses** at the Villa Viktorija, Cesta Svobode 27/a, for 2000 SIT per hour.

Vintgar Gorge An excellent half-day hike from Bled features a visit to this lovely gorge 4.5km to the north-west. Head north-west on Prešernova cesta then north on Partizanska cesta to Cesta v Vintgar. This will take you to Podhom, where signs point the way to the gorge entrance. Or take the bus or train (from Bled Jezero station) to Podhom, from where it's a 1.5km walk westward to the main entrance (open daily from May to October; 300/200 SIT). A wooden footbridge hugs the rock wall for 1600m along the Radovna River, crisscrossing the raging torrent four times over rapids, waterfalls and pools before reaching **Šum Waterfall**. From there a trail leads over Hom Hill (834m) eastward to the ancient pilgrimage **Church of St Catherine**. The trail then leads due south through Zasip and back to Bled. From late June to mid-September an Alpetour bus makes the run from Bled's bus station to Vintgar daily at 9.30 am and returns at about noon.

Places to Stay

Camping *Zaka* camp site (☎ 741 117) is in a quiet valley at the western end of the lake about 2.5km from the bus station. The location is good and there's even a beach, tennis courts, a large restaurant and a supermarket, but Zaka fills up very quickly in summer. The camping ground is open from April to October and costs from 765 to 1080 SIT per person.

Hostel The *Bledec* hostel (☎ 745 250), Grajska cesta 17, is open year round except in November, and has a total of 56 beds in 13 rooms and costs DM20 per person (or DM26 with breakfast). Check in is from 7 am to 10 pm.

Private Rooms Finding a private room in Bled is easy. The travel agencies have extensive lists, and there are lots of houses around the lake with '*sobe*' or '*Zimmer frei*' signs. Kompas has single/double rooms with shared shower from 1800/2600 SIT to 2000/3400 SIT, depending on the category and season, and singles/doubles with shower from 2200/3400 SIT to 3300/5600 SIT. Apartments for two range from 4200 to 6500. The rooms and apartments from Globtour Bled (☎ 741 821) at the Krim hotel, Ljubljanska cesta 7, and ATS (☎ 741 736), at the Vezenine mall at Kajuhova ulica 1, cost about the same.

Hotel Most of Bled's hotels are pretty expensive affairs. Among the cheapest is the 138-bed *Lovec* (☎ 741 500; fax 741 021), Ljubljanska cesta 6, with singles/doubles in the height of summer from 7125/10,450 SIT while the waterfront old-world *Grand Hotel Toplice* (☎ 7910; fax 741 841) at Cesta Svobode 12, charges from a budget-busting 11,500/17,500 SIT at the same time. An affordable (and romantic) alternative is the eight-room *Vila Viktorija* (☎/fax 742 485) at Cesta Svobode 27/a, with singles from 4000 to 5000 SIT and doubles 5000 to 7000 SIT, depending on the season.

Places to Eat

Bled's best choice for an affordable meal is the homy *Gostilna Pri Planincu* at Grajska cesta 8, a stone's throw from the bus station.

BLED

Map labels: To Lesce-Bled Train Station (4km); Želeče; Cankarjeva cesta; Seliška cesta; To Vintgar Gorge (4.5km); Rečica River; Prešernova cesta; Ljubljanska cesta; Partizanska cesta; Grajska cesta; Cesta svobode; Pristava; Riklijeva cesta; Mlinska cesta; Spa Park; Grajska cesta; Grass Beach; Rečica; Lake Bled; Blejski Otok; Viewing Stands; Beach; Kidričeva cesta; Kolodvorska cesta; Prešernova cesta; To Jesenice (10km); To Bohinj (26km); To Selo (1km); Mlino; Strada Hill; Pod na Pod; Cesta svobode

Scale: 0   200   400 m

Excellent mushroom soup and grilled chicken with fries and salad shouldn't cost much more than 1800 SIT. For pizza, try the *Pizzeria Gallus* in the Triglav shopping centre. The *Peking* is a decent Chinese restaurant at Ulica Narodnih Herojev 3 opposite the Krim hotel. There's a small *market* near the bus station and a *supermarket* in the Triglav shopping centre.

Getting There & Around

Buses run at least once an hour to Bohinj as far as the Zlatorog hotel, Kranj, Ljubljana and Podhom-Zasip. One bus a day from July to mid-September goes to Bovec via Kranjska Gora and the heart-stopping Vršič Pass.

Lesce-Bled train station gets up to 15 trains a day from Ljubljana (55 minutes) via Škofja Loka, Kranj and Radovljica. They continue on to Jesenice (15 minutes), where about 10 cross the Austrian border. Up to eight daily trains from Jesenice via Podhom pass through Bled Jezero station on their way to Bohinjska Bistrica (20 minutes) and Nova Gorica (1¾ hours).

Kompas rents bicycles and mountain bikes for 500/1000/1500 SIT for an hour/half-day/day.

BOHINJ
☎ 064

Bohinj is a larger and much less developed glacial lake 26km to the south-west of Bled. It is exceedingly beautiful, with high mountains rising directly from the basin-shaped valley. There are secluded beaches for swimming off the trail along the north shore and many hiking possibilities, including an ascent of Mt Triglav.

Orientation

There is no town called Bohinj; the name refers to the entire valley, its settlements and the lake. The largest town in the area is Bohinjska Bistrica, 6km to the east of the lake. The main settlement right on the lake is Ribčev Laz at the south-east corner. Here, all in a row just up from the bus stop, you'll find the post office, tourist office, a supermarket, a pizzeria, the Club Amor disco and the Alpinum travel agency, which can organise any number of sport activities in Bohinj.

About 1km north across the Sava Bohinjka River and at the mouth of the Mostnica Canyon sits the town of Stara Fužina. The Zlatorog hotel is at Ukanc at the west end of the lake near the camping ground and the cable car up to Mt Vogel (1922m).

Information

Tourist Office The helpful and very efficient tourist office (☎ 723 370; fax 723 330) at Ribčev Laz 48 is open daily from July to mid-September from 7 am to 8 pm. During the rest of the year, the hours are Monday to Saturday from 8 am to 6 pm and on Sunday from 9 am to 3 pm.

Money The tourist office can change money but the rate is not very good, and they take a 3% commission. Gorenjska Banka has a branch in Bohinjska Bistrica at Trg Svobode 2b, about 100m east of the Slovenijaturist office.

Post & Communications The post office at Ribčev Laz 47 is open weekdays from 8 am to 6 pm with a couple of half-hour breaks and on Saturday till noon.

Things to See & Do

The **Church of St John the Baptist**, on the northern side of the Sava Bohinjka across the stone bridge from Ribčev Laz, has exquisite 15th-century frescoes and can lay claim to being the most beautiful and evocative church in Slovenia. The **Alpine Dairy Museum** at house No 181 in Stara Fužina, about 1.5km north of Ribčev Laz, has a small but interesting collection related to Alpine dairy farming in the Bohinj Valley, once the most important such centre in Slovenia (320/160 SIT). If you have time, take a walk over to Studor, a village a couple of kilometres to the east renowned for its *kozolci* and *toplarji*, single and double hayracks that are unique to Slovenia.

The Alpinum travel agency (☎ 723 441), which can organise any number of sport activities in Bohinj, is a couple of doors down from the tourist office at Ribčev Laz 50. The Alpinsport kiosk (☎ 723 486) at Ribčev Laz 53, to the right just before you cross the stone bridge to the church, rents out equipment. **Canoes** and **kayaks** cost from DM6/25 per hour/day. It also organises guided mountain tours and rafting trips on the Sava (DM35 to DM45) and 'canyoning' through the rapids of the Mostnica Gorge safely stuffed into a neoprene suit, life jacket and helmet for DM80.

The **Vogel cable car**, above the camping ground at the western end of Lake Bohinj about 5km from Ribčev Laz, will whisk you 1000m up into the mountains. It runs every half-hour year round except in November, from 7.30 am to 6 pm (till 8 pm in July and August). Adults/children pay 1000/700 SIT for a return ticket. From the upper station (1540m) you can scale **Mt Vogel** in a couple of hours for a sweeping view of the region.

Places to Stay
Camping The large and beautifully situated *Zlatorog* camping ground (☎ 723 441) on the lake near the Zlatorog hotel costs 900 to 1450 SIT per person, depending on the season; it's open from May to September.

Private Rooms The tourist office can arrange private singles/doubles with shower in Ribčev Laz, Stara Fužina and neighbouring villages for 1800/3000 SIT in the low season and up to 2300/3800 SIT in July and August (though there's always a 30% surcharge for stays of less than three days).

Places to Eat
The *MK*, a restaurant and pizzeria next to the Alpinum travel agency (Ribčev Laz 50), is very popular year round. If you've got wheels of any sort, head for *Gostišče Rupa* at house No 87 in Srednja Vas, about 5km north-east of Ribčev Laz. It has some of the best home-cooking in Slovenia. For a truly different lunch, try *Planšar* opposite the Alpine Dairy Museum at Stara Fužina 179. It specialises in homemade dairy products, and you can taste a number of local specialities for about 700 SIT. The *Mercator* supermarket at Ribčev Laz 49 is open weekdays from 7 am to 6.30 pm and to 5 pm on Saturday.

Getting There & Around
Bus services from Ribčev Laz to Ljubljana via Bled, Radovljica, Kranj and Bohinjska Bistrica are very frequent. There are also about six buses a day to Bohinjska Bistrica

via Stara Fužina, Studor and Srednja Vas. All of these buses stop near the post office on Triglavska cesta in Bohinjska Bistrica and in Ribčev Laz before carrying on to the Zlatorog hotel in Ukanc. The closest train station is at Bohinjska Bistrica on the Jesenice-Nova Gorica line.

Alpinum and Alpinsport rent bicycles and mountain bikes for DM7/30 per hour/day.

TREKKING MT TRIGLAV
The Julian Alps are among the finest hiking areas in central and eastern Europe. A mountain hut (*planinska koča* or *planinski dom*) is normally less than five hours' walk away. The huts in the higher regions are open from July to September, and in the lower regions from June to October. You'll never be turned away if the weather looks bad, but some huts on Triglav get very crowded at weekends, especially in August and September. A bed for the night should cost less than 1500 SIT per person. Meals are also available, so you don't need to carry a lot of gear. Leave most of your things below, but warm clothes, sturdy boots and good physical condition are indispensable.

The best months for hiking are August to October, though above 1500m you can encounter winter weather conditions at any time. Keep to the trails that are well marked with a red circle and a white centre, rest frequently and never *ever* try to trek alone. Before you set out, pick up a copy of the 1:20,000 *Triglav* map or the 1:50 000-scale *Julijske Alpe – Vzhodni Del (Julian Alps – Eastern Part)* published by the Alpine Association and available at bookshops and tourist offices.

The Route from Bohinj
An hour's hike west of the Zlatorog hotel at Ukanc is the **Savica Waterfall** (320/160 SIT), the source of the Sava River, which gushes from a limestone cave and falls 60m into a narrow gorge.

From the waterfall a path zigzags up the steep Komarča Crag. From the top of this cliff (1340m) there's an excellent view of Lake Bohinj. Further north, three to four hours from the falls, is the *Koča pri Triglavskih Jezerih* (mobile ☎ 0609-615 235; 1685m), a 104-bed hut at the southern end of the fantastic Triglav Lakes Valley where you'll spend the night. If you want a good overview of the valley and its seven permanent lakes (the others fill up in spring only), you can climb to Mt Tičarica (2091m) to the north-east in about one hour. An alternative – though longer – route from the waterfall to the Triglav Lakes Valley is via *Dom na Komni* (mobile ☎ 0609-611 221; 1520m) and the Komna Plateau.

On the second day, you hike up the valley, past the largest glacial lakes then north-east to the desert-like Hribarice Plateau (2358m). You descend to the Dolič Saddle (2164m) where the *Tržaška Koča na Doliču* (mobile ☎ 0609-614 780; 2152m) has 60 beds. You would have walked about four hours by now from the Koča pri Triglavskih Jezerih and could well carry on to *Dom Planika pod Triglavom* (mobile ☎ 0609-614 773; 2401m), about 1½ hours to the north-east, but this 80-bed hut fills up quickly.

From Dom Planika it's just over an hour to the summit of Triglav (2864m), a well trodden path indeed. Don't be surprised if you find yourself being turned over to have your bottom beaten with a birch switch. It's a long-established tradition for Triglav 'virgins'.

Soča Valley

BOVEC & KOBARID
☎ 065

The Soča Valley, defined by the bluer-than-blue Soča River, stretches from Triglav National Park to Nova Gorica and is one of the most beautiful and peaceful spots in Slovenia. Of course it wasn't always that way. During much of WWI, this was the site of the infamous Soča (or Isonzo) Front, which claimed the lives of an estimated one million people and was immortalised by the American writer Ernest Hemingway in his novel *A Farewell to Arms*. Today visitors flock to the town of **Kobarid** to relive these events at the award-winning **Kobarid Museum** (Gregorčičeva ulica 10; 500/400 SIT adults/students & children) or, more commonly, head for Bovec, 21km to the north, to take part in some of the best white-water rafting in Europe. The season lasts from April to October.

In Bovec, the people to see for the latter are Soča Rafting (☎ 196 200 or mobile ☎ 041-724 472) in the courtyard below the Alp hotel at Trg Golobarskih Žrtev 48 or Bovec Rafting Team (☎ 86 128) in the small kiosk further west on the same street opposite the Martinov Hram restaurant. Rafting trips on the Soča, taking between 1½ and 2½ hours with distances of from 10 to 21km, cost 4500 to 10,800 SIT (including neoprene long john, wind cheater, life jacket, helmet and paddle). A kayak costs from 2880 SIT for the day (3560 SIT with all equipment); a two-person canoe is 5570 SIT. There are kayaking courses on offer in summer (eg a two-day intensive course for beginners costs 9600 SIT).

In Kobarid, the tourist office in the Kobarid Museum (☎ 85 055) and, in Bovec, the Avrigo Tours agency (☎ 86 123) next to the Alp hotel at Trg Golobarskih Žrtev 47 can organise *private rooms* from 1700/3400 SIT for a single/double. There are four camping grounds in Bovec (*Polovnik*, ☎ 86 069, is the closest) and one in Kobarid (*Koren*, ☎ 85 312).

Getting There & Away
There are up to six buses a day between Kobarid and Bovec and to Tolmin. Other destinations include Ljubljana (two to five), Nova Gorica (four to six) and Cerkno (up to five). In July and August there's a daily bus to Ljubljana via the Vršič Pass and Kranjska Gora.

Karst Region

POSTOJNA
☎ 067

Vying with Bled as the top tourist spot in Slovenia, **Postojna Cave** continues to attract the hordes, but many travellers feel they've seen Disneyland after their visit – especially if they've first been to the more natural Škocjan Caves, 33km to the south-west. Visitors get to see about 5.7km of the cave's 27km on a 1½-hour tour in their own language; about 4km are covered by an electric train that will shuttle you through colourfully lit karst formations along the so-called Old Passage and the remaining 1700m is on foot. The tour ends with a viewing of a tank full of *Proteus anguinus*, the unique salamander-like beasties inhabiting Slovenia's karst aves. Dress warmly as the cave is a constant 8°C (with 95% humidity) all year.

From May to September, tours leave daily on the hour between 9 am and 6 pm. In March and April and again in October there are tours at 10 am, noon, 2 and 4 pm with an extra daily one at 5 pm in April and additional tours at the weekend in October at 11 am and 1, 3 and 5 pm. Between November and February, tours leave at 10 am and 2 pm on weekdays with extra ones added at noon and 4 pm at the weekend and on public holidays. Admission costs 1900/950 SIT for adults/ students & children.

If you have extra time, visit **Predjama Castle** (500/250 SIT), the awesome 16th-century fortress perched in the gaping mouth of a hilltop cavern 9km north-west of Postojna. As close as you'll get from Postojna by local bus (and during the school year only), though, is Bukovje, a village about 2km north-east of Predjama. A taxi from Postojna plus an hour's wait at the castle costs 5000 SIT.

Orientation & Information
The cave is about 2km north-west of Postojna's bus centre and bus station. The train station is a kilometre south-east of the centre. The unhelpful tourist office (☎ 24 477), Tržaška cesta 4, is open weekdays from 8 am to 6 pm (7 pm in summer) and till noon on Saturday. Kompas (☎ 24 281) at Titov trg 2a has *private rooms* from 2100 SIT per person.

Getting There & Away
Postojna is a day trip from Ljubljana or a stopover on the way to/from the coast or Croatian Istria; almost all buses between the capital and the coast stop there. There are direct trains to Postojna from Ljubljana (67km, one hour) and Koper (86km, 1½ hours).

ŠKOCJAN CAVES
☎ 067
These caves, near the village of Matavun 4km south-east of Divača (between Postojna and Koper), have been heavily promoted since 1986 when they were entered on UNESCO's World Heritage List. There are seven 1½-hour tours a day from June to September at 10 and 11.30 am and on the hour from 1 to 5 pm. In April, May and October

they leave at 10 am and at 1 and 3.30 pm. From November to March, there's a daily visit at 10 am and an extra one at 3 pm on Sunday and holidays. The entry fee is 1500 SIT for adults and 1000 SIT for children aged six to 12. These caves are in more natural surroundings – some consider a visit the highlight of their stay in Slovenia – than Postojna Cave but tough to reach without your own transport. From the train station at Divača (up to a dozen trains daily to/from Ljubljana), you can follow a path leading south-east through the village of Dolnje Ležeče to Matavun. The driver of any bus heading along the highway to/from the coast will let you off at the access road (there are huge signs announcing the caves) if you ask in advance. From there you can walk the remaining 1.5km to the caves' entrance.

The Coast

KOPER
☎ 066
Koper (population 24,400), only 21km south of Trieste, is the first of several quaint old coastal towns along the north side of the Istrian Peninsula. The town's Italian name, Capodistria, recalls its former status as capital of Istria under the Venetian Republic in the 15th and 16th centuries. After WWII, Koper's port was developed to provide Slovenia with an alternative to Italian Trieste and Croatian Rijeka. Once an island but now firmly connected to the mainland by a causeway, the Old Town's medieval flavour lingers despite the surrounding industry, container ports, high-rise buildings and motorways beyond its 'walls'. This administrative centre and largest town on the Slovene coast makes a good base for exploring the region.

Orientation
The bus and train stations are adjacent about a kilometre south-east of the Old Town at the end of Kolodvorska cesta.

Information
Tourist Office The tourist office (☎ 273 791), opposite the marina at Ukmarjev trg 7, is open June to September Monday to Saturday from 9 am to 10 pm and on Sunday from

10 am to 3 pm. During the rest of the year the hours are 9 am to 2 pm and 5 to 9 pm (till 1 pm on Sunday).

Money Nova Ljubljanska Banka, Pristaniška ulica 45, is open from 8.30 am till noon and from 3.30 to 6 pm on weekdays only. There are also a couple of private exchange offices on Pristaniška ulica, including Maki at No 13 and Feniks in the east wing of the large shopping complex and market across the street at No 2. Both are open from 7 or 7.30 am to 7 pm weekdays and to 1 pm on Saturday.

Post & Communications There's a post office at Muzejski trg 3 near the regional museum open weekdays from 8 am to 7 pm and on Saturday till 1 pm.

Things to See
From the stations you enter Prešernov trg through the **Muda Gate** (1516). Walk past the bridge-shaped **Da Ponte Fountain** (1666) and into Čevljarska ulica (Shoemaker's Street), a narrow pedestrian way that opens onto Titov trg, the medieval central square. Most of the things to see in Koper are clustered here.

The 36m-high **City Tower** (1480), which you can climb daily, stands next to the mostly 18th-century **Cathedral of St Nazarius**. The lower portion of the cathedral's façade is Gothic, the upper part Renaissance. To the north is the sublime **Loggia** (1463), now a café and gallery, and to the south the **Praetorian Palace** (1452), both good examples of the Venetian Gothic style. On the narrow lane behind the cathedral is a 12th-century Romanesque baptistry called the **Carmine Rotunda**. Trg Brolo to the east of the cathedral contains several more old Venetian buildings, including the **Brutti Palace**, now a library, at No 1 and the **Fontico**, a 14th-century granary, at No 4.

The **Koper Regional Museum**, open weekdays from 9 am to 1 pm (in summer also from 6 to 8 pm) and on Saturday till noon, is in the Belgramoni-Tacco Palace at Kidričeva ulica 19. It contains old maps and photos of the port and coast, 16th to 18th-century Italianate sculptures and paintings, and copies of medieval frescoes.

Places to Stay
The closest camping grounds are at Ankaran (*Adria*, ☎ 528 322), about 10km to the north by road, and at Izola (*Jadranka*, ☎ 61 202), 8km to the west.

Both the tourist office and Kompas (☎ 272 346) at Pristaniška ulica 17 opposite the vegetable market have *private rooms* for 1500 to 2260 SIT per person, depending on the category and season. Apartments for two are 4000 to 5170 SIT. Both levy a 30% surcharge if you stay less than three nights. Most of the rooms are in the new town beyond the train station.

In July and August *Dijaški Dom Koper* (☎ 273 252), an official hostel at Cankarjeva ulica 5 in the Old Town east of Trg Brolo, rents 380 beds in triple rooms at DM19 (DM15 after three nights) per person. With breakfast the rate is DM21. The rest of the year only about 10 beds are available. An HI card will get you a 10% discount.

The only hotel in the Old Town, the 80-room *Triglav* (☎ 272 001 or ☎ 274 094; fax 23 598) at Pristaniška ulica 3, is relatively affordable: singles with shower and breakfast are 4400 to 7410 SIT, depending on the season and room category, and doubles 6080 to 11,800 SIT. The 100-room *Žusterna* (☎ 284 385; fax 284 409), the Triglav's sister hotel about 1.5 km west on the main coastal road (Istrska cesta), charges from 4500/6400 SIT to 6200/8200 SIT for singles/doubles.

Places to Eat
For fried dough on the go head for the *burek shop* at Kidričeva ulica 8. The little *Bife Diana* at Čevljarska ulica 36 has čevapčiči, hamburgers and so on. A pizzeria called *Atrij* with a courtyard out the back at Triglavska ulica 2 is open most days till 10 pm.

One of the most colourful places in Koper for a meal is the *Istrska Klet* in an old palace at Župančičeva ulica 39. Main courses are 600 to 1000 SIT and this is a good place to try Teran, the hearty red (almost purple) wine from the Karst and coastal wine-growing areas. The *Taverna*, in a 15th-century salt warehouse at Pristaniška ulica 1 opposite the marina, has some decent fish dishes and lunch menus at 850 and 1000 SIT.

KOPER

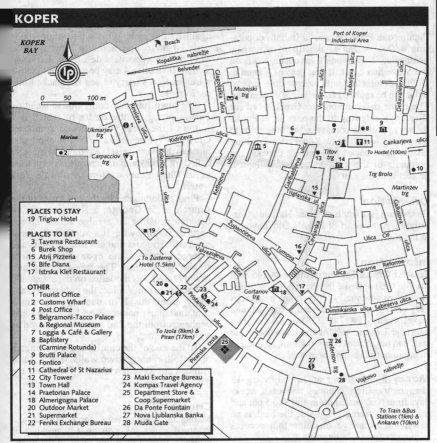

KOPER BAY

Beach

Port of Koper Industrial Area

Kopališka nabrežje

Belveder

Glagoljaška ulica

Verdijeva ulica

Trubarjeva ulica

Dellavalleleva ulica

Muzejski trg 4

Ukmarjev trg 1

Kidričeva ulica

6

7

8 9

12 11 Cankarjeva ulica

Marina

Bešlava ulica

Kolarčeva

5

13 Titov trg 14

To Hostel (100m)

2

Carpaccio trg 3

ulica

Kettejeva ulica

Garibaldijeva ulica

Triglavska ul.

15

10

Trg Brolo

Martinzev trg

Čevljarska ulica

Ulica OF

Gallusova

Župančičeva ulica

Tumova

16

Cevlarska

Ulica Agrarne Reforme

19

To Žusterna Hotel (1.5km)

Valvazorjeva

ulica

Ulica

20 22 23
21 24

Pristaniška

Gortanov trg

18

17

Dimnikarska ulica Sabinjeva ulica

To Izola (8km) & Piran (17km)

Piranska cesta

25

26

27

28

Prešernov trg

Volkovo nabrežje

To Train & Bus Stations (1km) & Ankaran (10km)

PLACES TO STAY
19 Triglav Hotel

PLACES TO EAT
3 Taverna Restaurant
6 Burek Shop
15 Atrij Pizzeria
16 Bife Diana
17 Istrska Klet Restaurant

OTHER
1 Tourist Office
2 Customs Wharf
4 Post Office
5 Belgramoni-Tacco Palace & Regional Museum
7 Loggia & Café & Gallery
8 Baptistery (Carmine Rotunda)
9 Brutti Palace
10 Fontico
11 Cathedral of St Nazarius
12 City Tower
13 Town Hall
14 Praetorian Palace
19 Almerigogna Palace
20 Outdoor Market
21 Supermarket
22 Feniks Exchange Bureau
23 Maki Exchange Bureau
24 Kompas Travel Agency
25 Department Store & Coop Supermarket
26 Da Ponte Fountain
27 Nova Ljubljanska Banka
28 Muda Gate

The large shopping centre and outdoor *market* (open most days from 7 am to 2 pm) on Pristaniška ulica also contains a *supermarket* and various *food shops*. The *Coop* supermarket in the big department store on Piranska cesta is open Monday to Saturday from 9 am to 7.30 pm.

Getting There & Away

There are buses almost every 20 minutes on weekdays to Piran (17km) and Portorož via Izola, and every 40 minutes at the weekend.

Buses also leave every hour or 90 minutes for Ljubljana via Divača and Postojna. You can also take the train to Ljubljana (2¼ hours), which is much more comfortable.

Up to 17 buses a day during the week depart for Trieste. The bus station in Trieste is immediately south-west of the train station in Piazza Libertà.

Destinations in Croatia include Buzet (three or four buses a day); Poreč (two or three); Pula (one or two); Rijeka (one); Rovinj (one); and Zagreb (two).

PIRAN
☎ 066

Picturesque Piran (Pirano in Italian; population 4800), sitting at the tip of a narrow peninsula, is everyone's favourite town on the Slovenian coast. It is a gem of Venetian Gothic architecture with narrow little streets, but it can be mobbed at the height of summer. The name derives from the Greek word for 'fire', *pyr*, referring to the ones lit at Punta, the very tip of the peninsula, to guide ships to the port at Aegida (now Koper). Piran's long history dates back to the ancient Greeks, and remnants of the medieval town walls still protect it to the east.

Orientation
Buses stop just south of Piran Harbour. Tartinijev trg, the heart of Piran's Old Town, is to the north.

Information
Tourist Office The tourist office (☎ 746 382; fax 746 095) opposite the Piran hotel on Stjenkova ulica essentially rents rooms and keeps very brief hours. Instead head for the Maona travel agency (☎ 746 228) at Cankarjevo nabrežje 7 whose helpful and knowledgeable staff can organise accommodation, an endless string of activities and boat cruises.

Money Banka Koper at Tartinijev trg 12 changes travellers cheques and cash weekdays from 8.30 am till noon and 3 to 5 pm and on Saturday morning. Outside the bank is an automatic exchange machine that accepts banknotes from 17 countries.

Post & Communications The post office at Cankarjevo nabrežje 5 is open weekdays from 8 am to 7 pm and till noon on Saturday.

Things to See
The **Maritime Museum**, in a 17th-century harbourside palace at Cankarjevo nabrežje 3, was under renovation at the time of writing. It has exhibits focusing on the three 'Ss' that have been so important to Piran's development over the centuries: the sea, sailing and salt-making (at Sečovlje south-east of Portorož). The museum's antique model ships are very fine; other rooms are filled

with old figureheads, weapons and votive folk paintings placed in church for protection against shipwreck. Piran's **aquarium** (open daily 10 am to 1 pm and 2 to 7 pm; 300/200 SIT) on the opposite side of the marina at Tomažičeva ulica 4 may be small, but there's a tremendous variety of sea life packed into its 25 tanks.

The **town hall** and **court house** stand on Tartinijev trg, in the centre of which is a statue of the local violinist and composer Giuseppe Tartini (1692-1770). A short distance to the north-west is Prvomajski trg (also called trg Maja) and its baroque **cistern**, used in the 18th century to store the town's fresh water.

Piran is dominated by the tall tower of the **Church of St George**, a Renaissance and baroque structure on a ridge above the sea north of Tartinijev trg. It's wonderfully decorated with frescoes and has marble altars and a large statue of the eponymous George slaying the dragon. The free-standing **bell tower** (1609) was modelled on the campanile of San Marco in Venice; the octagonal **Baptistry** from the 17th century next to it contains altars, paintings and a Roman sarcophagus from the 2nd century later used as a baptismal font.

To the east of the church is a 200m stretch of the 15th-century **town walls**, which can be climbed for superb views of Piran and the Adriatic.

Cruises
Maona and other travel agencies in Piran and Portorož can book you on any number of cruises – from a loop that takes in the towns along the coast to day-long excursions to Venice, Trieste or Brioni National Park in Croatia.

From mid-May to October, the large catamaran *Marconi* goes down the Istrian coast in Croatia as far as the Brioni Islands and the national park there (two hours, 8500/8000 SIT return for adults/those over 60 and everyone on Wednesday), with a stop at Rovinj (1¼ hours, 4000/3500 SIT return). The boat leaves at 10 am and returns at about 6.45 pm except in September when it departs and returns 20 minutes earlier. At 8.35 pm (6.50 pm in September) on the same days the *Marconi* heads for Trieste (35 minutes,

PIRAN

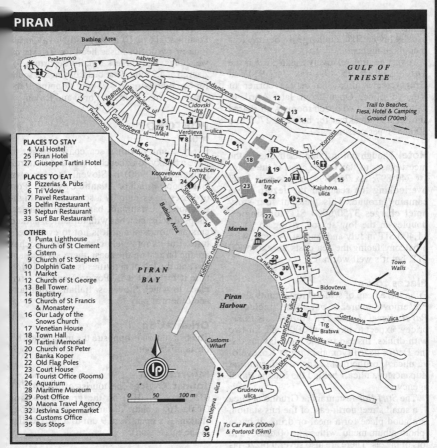

PLACES TO STAY
4 Val Hostel
25 Piran Hotel
27 Giuseppe Tartini Hotel

PLACES TO EAT
3 Pizzerias & Pubs
6 Tri Vdove
7 Pavel Restaurant
8 Delfin Rzestaurant
31 Neptun Restaurant
33 Surf Bar Restaurant

OTHER
1 Punta Lighthouse
2 Church of St Clement
5 Cistern
9 Church of St Stephen
10 Dolphin Gate
11 Market
12 Church of St George
13 Bell Tower
14 Baptistry
15 Church of St Francis
   & Monastery
16 Our Lady of the
   Snows Church
17 Venetian House
18 Town Hall
19 Tartini Memorial
20 Church of St Peter
21 Banka Koper
22 Old Flag Poles
23 Court House
24 Tourist Office (Rooms)
26 Aquarium
28 Maritime Museum
29 Post Office
30 Maona Travel Agency
32 Jestvina Supermarket
34 Customs Office
35 Bus Stops

2000/4000 SIT one-way/return), returning the following morning.

The *Delfin* (mobile ☎ 0609-628 491) boat sails from Piran to the marina at Portorož via the Bernadin tourist complex (one hour, 800 to 1200 SIT) up to five times a day from April to October. In July and August the loop also takes in Fiesa and Strunjan.

Places to Stay

Camping The closest camping ground is *Camping Jezero Fiesa* (☎ 73 150) at Fiesa, 4km by road from Piran (but less than a kilo-

metre if you follow the coastal trail east of the Church of St George). It's in a quiet valley by two small, protected ponds, and close to the beach, but it gets very crowded in summer. It's open from June to September.

Private Rooms & Hostel The tourist offices in Piran and Portorož (☎ 747 015) and the Maona travel agency can arrange *private rooms* and *apartments* throughout the year, but the biggest choice is available in summer. Single rooms are 1880 to 2800 SIT, depending on the category and the season, while doubles are 2460 to 4700 SIT. Apartments for two are 4700 to 6110 SIT. They usually levy a 50% surcharge if you stay less then three nights.

A very central, relatively cheap place is the *Val* hostel (☎ 75 499; fax 746 911) at Gregorčičeva ulica 38a on the corner of Vegova ulica. Open from late April to October, it has two dozen rooms with shared shower and breakfast for between 2700 and 3000 SIT per person.

Hotel Though not in Piran itself one of the nicest places to stay on the coast is the *Fiesa* (☎ 746 897; fax 746 896), a 22-room hotel overlooking the sea near the Jezero Fiesa camping ground. This pleasant four-story hotel charges 3750/6000 SIT for singles/ doubles in the low season, rising to 7125/ 11,400 SIT in July and August. A room with a balcony facing the sea costs an extra 400 SIT, but it's well worth it.

Places to Eat
Piran has a heap of seafood restaurants along Prešernovo nabrežje but most (including *Pavel*, *Pavel 2* and *Tri Vdove*) are fairly pricey; expect to pay about 5000 SIT for two with drinks. Instead try the local favourites: the *Delfin* near Prvomajski trg at Kosovelova ulica 4, or the more expensive *Neptun* at Župančičeva ulica 7 behind the Maona travel agency.

The *Surf Bar* restaurant at Grudnova ulica 1, a small street north-east of the bus station, is a good place for a meal or drink. It has a 'photo-album menu' with some 60 dishes and lots of pizzas. There are also several pizzerias along Prešernovo nabrežje near the Punta lighthouse/Church of St Clement, including *Palma* and *Zeko*. The *Jestvina* supermarket opposite Trg Bratsva 8 is open Monday to Saturday from 7 am to 8 pm.

Getting There & Away
The local bus company I&I (☎ 41 750 in Koper) links Piran with Portorož and Lucija (bus No 1); with Portorož and Fiesa (bus No 2; mid-April to August only); with Strunjan and Portorož (bus No 3); and with Portorož, Sečovlje and Padna (bus No 4). Schedules vary, but bus No 1 runs about every 10 to 15 minutes. The fare is 150 SIT.

Other destinations that can be reached from Piran include Ljubljana via Divača and Postojna (six to 10 a day) and Nova Gorica (one or two). Six buses head for Trieste on weekdays, and there's a daily departure for Zagreb at 4.25 am. One bus a day heads south for Croatian Istria at 4.25 pm, stopping at the coastal towns of Umag, Poreč and Rovinj.

PORTOROŽ
☎ 066
Every country with a sea coast has got to have a honky-tonk beach resort, and Portorož (population 2980) is Slovenia's very own Blackpool, Bondi or Atlantic City. The 'Port of Roses' is essentially a solid strip of high-rise hotels, restaurants, bars, travel agencies, shops, discos, beaches with turnstiles, parked cars and tourists, and it is not to everyone's taste. But its relatively clean, sandy beaches are the largest on the coast, there's a pleasant spa and the list of activities is endless. If you take it for what it is, Portorož can be a fun place to watch Slovenes, Italians, Austrians and others at play.

Orientation
The bus station is opposite the main beach on Postajališka pot.

Information
Tourist Office The tourist office (☎ 747 015; fax 747 013) on the ground floor of Obala 16, a short distance west of the bus station. It's open from 9 am to 7 pm (earlier in the off season).

Money Banka Koper below the Slovenija hotel at Obala 33 is open from 8.30 till noon and 3 to 5 pm on weekdays and on Saturday morning. It has an automatic exchange machine outside which accepts the banknotes of 18 countries. Feniks, a *bureau de change* next to the tourist office gives a good rate and does not charge commission. It's open from 9 am to 10 pm seven days a week. The SKB Banka at Obala 53 has a Cirrus-linked ATM.

Post & Communications The post office is at K Stari cesta 1 opposite the now empty Palace hotel (1891). It is open weekdays from 8 am to 7 pm and on Saturday till noon.

Activities

The beaches at Portorož, including the main one accommodating 6000 bodies, are managed' so you'll have to pay 350 SIT (250 SIT for children) to use them. They are open from 9 am to 7 pm in season. Umbrellas and deck chairs are available for 400 SIT.

The Terme Palace spa complex, just beyond the post office on K Stari cesta, is famous for thalassotherapy (treatment using sea water and its by-products). It is open Monday to Saturday from 7 am to 7 pm. The palatial indoor swimming pool here is open daily from 7 am to 9 pm. It costs 600/800 SIT for two/four hours on weekdays, 900/1200 SIT at the weekend, and 1000/1500 for the period from 1 to 9 pm on weekdays/at the weekend.

Places to Stay

The *Lucija* camping ground (☎ 771 027) has two locations. The 2nd-category site (1000 to 1200 SIT per person) is south-east of the marina at the end of Cesta Solinarjev less than 2km from the bus station, and the 1st-category site (1200 to 1400 SIT), 600km to

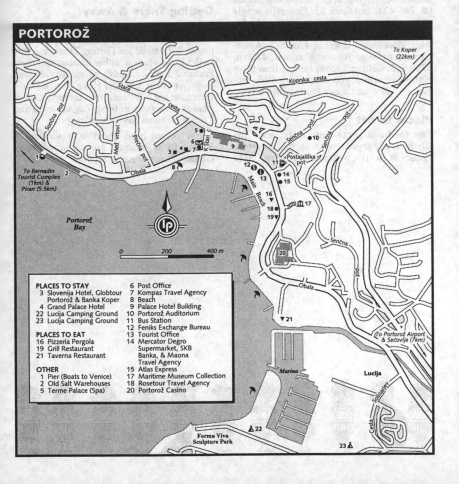

PORTOROŽ

PLACES TO STAY
3 Slovenija Hotel, Globtour Portorož & Banka Koper
4 Grand Palace Hotel
22 Lucija Camping Ground
23 Lucija Camping Ground

PLACES TO EAT
16 Pizzeria Pergola
19 Grill Restaurant
21 Taverna Restaurant

OTHER
1 Pier (Boats to Venice)
2 Old Salt Warehouses
5 Terme Palace (Spa)

6 Post Office
7 Kompas Travel Agency
8 Beach
9 Palace Hotel Building
10 Portorož Auditorium
11 Bus Station
12 Feniks Exchange Bureau
13 Tourist Office
14 Mercator Degro Supermarket, SKB Banka, & Maona Travel Agency
15 Atlas Express
17 Maritime Museum Collection
18 Rosetour Travel Agency
20 Portorož Casino

the west, is on the water. Both camps are open from May to September and get very crowded in summer.

The tourist office's accommodation service (☎ 746 199), on the mezzanine floor of Obala 16, has *private rooms* and *apartments* and is open daily from 9 am to 1 pm and 4 to 7 pm. You can also book them through Atlas Express (☎ 746 772) at Obala 55, just south of the bus station; Kompas (☎ 747 032), Obala 41; Globtour Portorož (☎ 73 356) in the Slovenija hotel at Obala 33; Rosetour (☎ 747 255) opposite the Maritime Museum Collection at Obala 16a; and Maona (☎ 746 423) at Obala 53. Generally single rooms range from 1800 to 2800 SIT, depending on the category and the season, while doubles are 2460 to 4700 SIT. Apartments for two go for a minimum of 4700 to 6700 SIT. Getting a room for less than three nights (for which you must pay a 50% supplement) or a single any time is difficult.

Places to Eat

Fast-food and pizza-pasta restaurants line Obala (eg *Pergola* next to the Rosetour agency at No 16a with pizzas costing 700 to 1000 SIT). But if you want a proper sit-down meal, the terrace at the *Taverna* in the sports field at Obala 22 looks out over the marina and the bay. The *Grill* restaurant, often with something large being roasted on a spit near the entrance, faces the main beach at Obala 20 and has an attractive covered terrace and a menu at 1100 SIT.

The *Mercator Degro* supermarket is a few steps away from the bus station. It is open weekdays from 7 am to 8 pm, Saturdays to 6 pm and Sunday from 8 am to 11 am.

Getting There & Away

Local I&I buses link Portorož with Piran, Strunjan, Fiesa, Lucija, Sečovlje and Podpadna; for details see Getting There & Away in the Piran section. Other destinations from Portorož include Ljubljana via Divača and Postojna (10 a day) and Nova Gorica (two). International destinations include Poreč (three), Pula (one or two), Zagreb (two) and Trieste (seven a day on weekdays).

For information about boat service to Venice from Portorož, see the introductory Getting There & Away section.

Spain

Spaniards approach life with such exuberance that most visitors have to stop and stare. In almost every town in the country, the nightlife will outlast the foreigners. Then just when they think they are coming to terms with the pace, they are surrounded by the beating drums of a fiesta, with day and night turning into a blur of dancing, laughing, eating and drinking. Spain also holds its own in cultural terms with formidable museums like the Prado and Thyssen-Bornemisza art galleries in Madrid, the wacky Dalí museum in Figueres, and Barcelona's Picasso and Miró museums.

Then, of course, you have the weather and the highly varied landscape. From April to October the sun shines with uncanny predictability on the Mediterranean coast and the Balearic Islands. Elsewhere you can enjoy good summer weather in the more secluded coves of Galicia, in the Pyrenees or the mountains of Andalucía, or on the surf beaches of western Andalucía or the País Vasco (Basque Country).

A wealth of history awaits the visitor to Spain: fascinating prehistoric displays at the archaeological museums in Teruel and Madrid; and from Roman times the aqueduct in Segovia, the seaside amphitheatre in Tarragona and the buried streets of Roman Barcelona made accessible via an underground walkway. After Roman times, the Moorish era left perhaps the most powerful cultural and artistic legacy, focused on Granada's Alhambra, Córdoba's mosque and Seville's *alcázar* (fortress) but evident in monuments throughout much of the country. Christian Spain also constructed hundreds of impressive castles, cathedrals, monasteries, palaces and mansions, which still stand across the length and breadth of the country.

Facts about Spain

HISTORY
Ancient History

Located at the crossroads between Europe and Africa, the Iberian Peninsula has always

AT A GLANCE

Capital	Madrid
Population	39 million
Area	504,750 sq km
Official Language	Spanish (Castilian)
Currency	1 peseta (pta) = 100 centimos
GDP	US$593 billion (1996)
Time	GMT/UTC+0100

Also in Madrid Central Madrid p867

Also in Barcelona Central Barcelona p894

Santiago de Compostela p942 · León p884 · San Sebastián p948 · Zaragoza p952 · Barcelona pp890-1 · Salamanca p881 · Madrid pp864-5 · Tarragona p905 · Toledo p886 · Valencia City p915 · Palma de Mallorca p909 · Córdoba p930 · Seville p922 · Granada p927 · Alicante p919 · Gibraltar p935

FRANCE · ANDORRA · PORTUGAL · MOROCCO · ALGERIA

been a target for invading peoples and civilisations. From around 8000 to 3000 BC, people from North Africa known as the Iberians crossed the Strait of Gibraltar and settled the peninsula. Around 1000 BC Celtic tribes entered northern Spain, while Phoenician merchants were establishing trading settlements along the Mediterranean coast. They were followed by Greeks and Carthaginians who arrived around 600 to 500 BC.

The Romans arrived in the 3rd century BC, but took two centuries to subdue the peninsula. Christianity came to Spain during the 1st century AD, but was initially opposed by

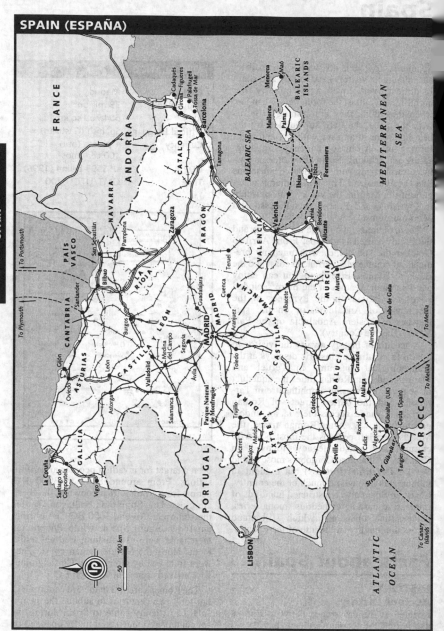

SPAIN (ESPAÑA)

the Romans, leading to persecution and martyrdoms. In 409 AD Roman Hispania was invaded by Germanic tribes and by 419 the Christian Visigoths, another Germanic people, had established a kingdom which lasted until 711, when the Moors – Muslim Berbers and Arabs from North Africa – crossed the Strait of Gibraltar and defeated Roderic, the last Visigoth king.

Muslim Spain & the Reconquista

By 714, the Muslim armies had occupied the entire peninsula, apart from some northern mountain regions. Muslim dominion was to last almost 800 years in parts of Spain. In Islamic Spain – known as al-Andalus – arts and sciences prospered, new crops and agricultural techniques were introduced, and palaces, mosques, schools, gardens and public baths were built.

In 722 a small army under the Visigothic leader Pelayo inflicted the first defeat on the Muslims (known to Christians as Moros, or Moors) at Covadonga in northern Spain. This marked the beginning of the Reconquista, the spluttering reconquest of Spain by the Christians. By the early 11th century, the frontier between Christian and Muslim Spain stretched from Barcelona to the Atlantic.

In 1085, Alfonso VI, king of León and Castile, took Toledo. This prompted the Muslim leaders to request help from northern Africa, which arrived in the form of the Almoravids. They recaptured much territory and ruled it until the 1140s. The Almoravids were followed by the Almohads, another North African dynasty, who ruled until 1212. By the mid-13th century, the Christians had taken most of the peninsula except for the state of Granada.

In the process the kingdoms of Castile and Aragón emerged as Christian Spain's two main powers, and in 1469 they were united by the marriage of Isabel, princess of Castile, and Fernando, heir to the throne of Aragón. Known as the Catholic Monarchs, they united Spain and laid the foundations for the Spanish golden age. They also revived the notorious Inquisition, which expelled and executed thousands of Jews and other non-Christians. In 1492 the last Muslim ruler of Granada surrendered to them, marking the completion of the Reconquista.

The Golden Age

Also in 1492, while searching for an alternative passage to India, Columbus stumbled on the Bahamas and claimed the Americas for Spain. This sparked a period of exploration and exploitation that was to yield Spain enormous wealth while destroying the ancient American empires. For three centuries, gold and silver from the New World were used to finance the rapid expansion and slow decline of the Spanish empire.

In 1516, Fernando was succeeded by his grandson Carlos, of the Habsburg dynasty. Carlos was elected Holy Roman Emperor in 1519 and ruled over an empire that included Austria, southern Germany, the Netherlands, Spain and the American colonies. He and his successors were to lead Spain into a series of expensive wars that ultimately bankrupted the empire. In 1588, Sir Francis Drake's English fleet annihilated the mighty Spanish Armada. The Thirty Years' War (1618-48) saw Spain in conflict with the Netherlands, France and England. By the reign of the last Habsburg monarch, Carlos II (1655-1700), the Spanish empire was in decline.

The 18th & 19th Centuries

Carlos II died without an heir. At the end of the subsequent War of the Spanish Succession (1702-13), Felipe V, grandson of French king Louis XIV, became the first of Spain's Bourbon dynasty. A period of stability, enlightened reforms and economic growth ensued, and was ended by events after the French Revolution of 1789.

When Louis XVI was guillotined in 1793, Spain declared war on the French republic, but then turned to alliance with France and war against Britain, in which the Battle of Trafalgar (1805) ended Spanish sea power. In 1807-08 French troops entered Spain and Napoleon convinced Carlos IV, the Spanish king, to abdicate, in whose place he installed his own brother Joseph Bonaparte. The Spaniards fought a five-year war of independence. In 1815 Napoleon was defeated by Wellington and a Bourbon, Fernando VII, was restored to the Spanish throne.

Fernando's reign was a disastrous advertisement for monarchy: the Inquisition was re-established, liberals and constitutionalists were persecuted, free speech was repressed,

Spain entered a severe recession and the American colonies won their independence. After his death in 1833 came the First Carlist War (1834-39), fought between conservative forces led by Don Carlos, Fernando's brother, and liberals who supported the claim of Fernando's daughter Isabel (later Isabel II) to the throne. In 1868 the monarchy was overthrown during the Septembrina Revolution and Isabel II was forced to flee. The First Republic was declared in 1873, but within 18 months the army had restored the monarchy, with Isabel's son Alfonso XII on the throne. Despite political turmoil, Spain's economy prospered in the second half of the 19th century, fuelled by industrialisation.

The disastrous Spanish-American War of 1898 marked the end of the Spanish empire. Spain was defeated by the USA and lost its last overseas possessions – Cuba won a qualified independence and Puerto Rico, Guam and the Philippines passed to the USA.

The 20th Century

The early 20th century was characterised by military disasters in Morocco and growing instability as radical forces struggled to overthrow the established order. In 1923, with Spain on the brink of civil war, Miguel Primo de Rivera made himself military dictator, ruling until 1930. In 1931 Alfonso XIII fled the country, and the Second Republic was declared.

Like its predecessor, the Second Republic fell victim to internal conflict. The 1936 elections told of a country split in two, with the Republican government (an uneasy alliance of leftist parties known as the Popular Front) and its supporters on one side, and the right-wing Nationalists (an alliance of the army, Church and the fascist-style Falange Party) on the other.

Nationalist plotters in the army rose against the government in July 1936. During the subsequent Spanish Civil War (1936-39), the Nationalists, led by General Francisco Franco, received heavy military support from Nazi Germany and fascist Italy, while the elected Republican government received support only from Russia and, to a lesser degree, from the International Brigades made up of foreign leftists.

By 1939 Franco had won and an estimated 350,000 Spaniards had died. After the war thousands of Republicans were executed, jailed or forced into exile. Franco's 35-year dictatorship began with Spain isolated internationally and crippled by recession. It wasn't until the 1950s and 1960s, when the rise in tourism and a treaty with the USA combined to provide much needed funds, that the country began to recover. By the 1970s Spain had the fastest-growing economy in Europe.

Franco died in 1975, having named Juan Carlos, grandson of Alfonso XIII, his successor. King Juan Carlos is widely credited with having overseen Spain's transition from dictatorship to democracy. The first elections were held in 1977, a new constitution was drafted in 1978, and a failed military coup in 1981 was seen as a futile attempt to turn back the clock. Spain joined the EC in 1986, and celebrated its return to the world stage in style in 1992, with Expo '92 in Seville and the Olympic Games in Barcelona. In 1997 it became fully integrated in the North Atlantic Treaty Organisation and the following year signed up for the EU's single currency.

GEOGRAPHY & ECOLOGY

Spain is probably Europe's most geographically diverse country, with landscapes ranging from the near-deserts of Almería to the green, Wales-like countryside and deep coastal inlets of Galicia, and from the sun-baked plains of Castilla-La Mancha to the rugged mountains of the Pyrenees.

The country covers 84% of the Iberian Peninsula and spreads over nearly 505,000 sq km, more than half of which is high tableland – the *meseta*. This is supported and divided by several mountain chains. The main ones are the Pyrenees along the border with France; the Cordillera Cantábrica backing the north coast; the Sistema Ibérico from the central north towards the middle Mediterranean coast; the Cordillera Central from north of Madrid towards the Portuguese border; and three east-west chains across Andalucía, one of which is the highest range of all, the Sierra Nevada.

The major rivers are the Ebro, Duero, Tajo (Tagus), Guadiana and Guadalquivir, each draining a different basin between the mountains and all flowing into the Atlantic Ocean, except for the Ebro which reaches the Mediterranean Sea.

Flora & Fauna
The brown bear, wolf, lynx and wild boar all survive in Spain, although only the boar exists in healthy numbers. Spain's high mountains harbour the goat-like chamois and Spanish ibex (the latter rare) and big birds of prey such as eagles, vultures and the lammergeier. The marshy Ebro delta and Guadalquivir estuary are important for water-birds, the spectacular greater flamingo among them. Many of Spain's 5500 seed-bearing plants occur nowhere else in Europe because of the barrier of the Pyrenees. Spring wildflowers are spectacular in many country and hill areas.

The conservation picture has improved by leaps and bounds in the past 20 years and Spain now has 25,000 sq km of protected areas, including 10 national parks. But overgrazing, reservoir creation, tourism, housing developments, agricultural and industrial effluent, fires and hunting all still threaten plant and animal life.

GOVERNMENT & POLITICS
Spain is a constitutional monarchy. The 1978 constitution restored parliamentary government and grouped the country's 50 provinces into 17 autonomous communities, each with its own regional government. From 1982 to 1996 Spain was governed by the centre-left PSOE party led by Felipe González. In the 1996 election the PSOE, weakened by a series of scandals and long-term economic problems, was finally unseated by the right-of-centre Partido Popular, led by José María Aznar.

ECONOMY
Spain has experienced an amazing economic turnabout in the 20th century, raising its living standards from the lowest in Western Europe to a level comparable with the rest of the continent. But its booming economy came back to earth with a thud in the early 1990s, and has since recovered only slowly. The official figure for those registered for unemployment benefits has dropped to 12%,

although EU estimates put the real figure at 19.8%. Either way, it is one of the highest rates in Western Europe. Service industries employ over six million people and produce close to 60% of the country's GDP. The arrival of over 50 million tourists every year brings work to around 10% of the entire labour force. Industry accounts for about one-third of both workforce and GDP, but agriculture accounts for only 4% of GDP compared to 23% in 1960, although it employs one in 10 workers.

POPULATION & PEOPLE
Spain has a population of 39 million, descended from all the many peoples who have settled here over the millennia, among them Iberians, Celts, Romans, Jews, Visigoths, Berbers and Arabs. The biggest cities are Madrid (three million), Barcelona (1.5 million), Valencia (750,000) and Seville (715,000). Each region proudly preserves its own unique culture, and some – Catalonia and the País Vasco in particular – display a fiercely independent spirit.

ARTS
Cinema
Early Spanish cinema was hamstrung by a lack of funds and technology, and perhaps the greatest of all Spanish directors, Luis Buñuel, made his silent surrealist classics *Un Chien Andalou* (1928) and *L'Age d'Or* (1930) in France. Buñuel, however, returned to Spain to make *Tierra sin Pan* (Land without Bread, 1932), a film about rural poverty in the Las Hurdes area of Extremadura.

Under Franco there was strict censorship, but satirical and uneasy films like Juan Antonio Bardem's *Muerte de un Ciclista* (Death of a Cyclist, 1955) and Luis Berlanga's *Bienvenido Mr Marshall* (Welcome Mr Marshall, 1953) still managed to appear. Carlos Saura, with films like *Ana y los Lobos* (Anna and the Wolves, 1973), and Victor Erice, with *El Espíritu de la Colmena* (Spirit of the Beehive, 1973) and *El Sur* (The South, 1983), looked at the problems of young people scarred by the Spanish Civil War and its aftermath.

After Franco, Pedro Almodóvar broke away from this serious cinema dwelling on the past with his humorous films set amid the social and artistic revolution of the late 1970s and 1980s – notably *Mujeres al Borde de un Ataque de Nervios* (Women on the Verge of a Nervous Breakdown, 1988). In 1995, Ken Loach produced a moving co-production on the Spanish Civil War, *Tierra y Libertad* (Land and Freedom).

Painting

The golden age of Spanish art (1550-1650) was strongly influenced by Italy but the great Spanish artists developed their talents in unique ways. The giants were the Toledo-based El Greco (originally from Crete), and Diego Velázquez, perhaps Spain's most revered painter. Both excelled with insightful portraits. Francisco Zurbarán and Bartolomé Esteban Murillo were also prominent. The genius of the 18th and 19th centuries was Francisco Goya, whose versatility ranged from unflattering royal portraits and anguished war scenes to bullfight etchings.

Catalonia was the powerhouse of early 20th-century Spanish art, engendering the hugely prolific Pablo Picasso (born in Andalucía), the colourful symbolist Joan Miró, and Salvador Dalí, who was obsessed with the unconscious and weird. Works by these and other major Spanish artists can be found in galleries throughout the country.

Architecture

The earliest architectural relics are the prehistoric monuments on Menorca. Reminders of Roman times include the ruins of Mérida and Tarragona, and Segovia's amazing aqueduct. The Muslims left behind them some of the most splendid buildings in the entire Islamic world, including Granada's Alhambra, Córdoba's mosque and Seville's alcázar – the latter an example of *Mudéjar* architecture, the name given to Moorish work done in Christian-held territory.

The first main Christian architectural movement was Romanesque, in the north in the 11th and 12th centuries, which has left countless lovely country churches and several cathedrals, notably that of Santiago de Compostela. Later came the many great Gothic cathedrals (Toledo, Barcelona, León, Salamanca and Seville) of the 13th to 16th centuries, as well as Renaissance styles, such

as the plateresque work so prominent in Salamanca and the austere work of Juan de Herrera, responsible for El Escorial. Spain then followed the usual path to baroque (17th and 18th centuries) and neoclassicism (19th century) before Catalonia produced its startling modernist (roughly Art Nouveau) movement around the turn of the 20th century, of which Antoni Gaudí's La Sagrada Família church is the most stunning example. More recent architecture is only likely to excite specialists.

Literature

One of the earliest works of Spanish literature is the *Cantar de mío Cid*, an anonymous epic poem describing the life of El Cid, an 11th-century Christian knight. Miguel de Cervantes' novel *Don Quixote de la Mancha* is the masterpiece of the literary flowering of the 16th and 17th centuries, and one of the world's great works of fiction. The playwrights Lope de Vega and Pedro Calderón de la Barca were also leading lights of the age.

The next high point, in the early 20th century, grew out of the crisis of the Spanish-American War that spawned the intellectual 'Generation of '98'. Philosophical essayist Miguel de Unamuno was prominent, but the towering figure was poet and playwright Federico García Lorca, whose tragedies *Blood Wedding* and *Yerma* won international acclaim before he was murdered in the civil war for his Republican sympathies. Camilo José Cela, author of the civil war aftermath novel *The Family of Pascal Duarte*, won the 1989 Nobel Prize for literature. Juan Goytisolo is probably the major contemporary writer; his most approachable work is his autobiography *Forbidden Territory*. There has been a proliferation of women – particularly feminist – writers in the past 25 years, among whose prominent representatives are Adelaide Morales, Ana María Matute and Rosa Montero.

SOCIETY & CONDUCT

Most Spaniards are economical with etiquette but this does not signify unfriendliness. They're gregarious people, on the whole very tolerant and easy-going towards foreigners. It's not easy to give offence. Disrespectful behaviour – including excessively casual dress – in churches won't go down well though.

Siesta

Contrary to popular belief, most Spaniards do not sleep in the afternoon. The siesta is generally devoted to a long leisurely lunch and lingering conversation. Then again, if you've stayed out until 5 am …

Flamenco

Getting to see real, deeply emotional, flamenco can be hard, as it tends to happen semi-spontaneously in little bars. Andalucía is its traditional home. You'll find plenty of clubs there and elsewhere offering flamenco shows; these are generally aimed at tourists and are expensive, but some are good. Your best chance of catching the real thing is probably at one of the flamenco festivals in the south, usually held in summer.

RELIGION

Only about 20% of Spaniards are regular churchgoers, but Catholicism is deeply ingrained in the culture. As the writer Unamuno said: 'Here in Spain we are all Catholics, even the atheists'. Many Spaniards have a deep-seated scepticism of the Church; during the civil war, churches were burnt and clerics shot because they represented repression, corruption and the old order.

LANGUAGE

Spanish, or Castilian (*castellano*) as it is often and more precisely called, is spoken by just about all Spaniards, but there are also three widely spoken regional languages: Catalan (another Romance language, closely related to Spanish and French) is spoken by about two-thirds of people in Catalonia and the Balearic Islands and half the people in the Valencia region; Galician (another Romance language that sounds like a cross between Spanish and Portuguese) is spoken by many in the north-west; and Basque (of obscure, non-Latin origin) is spoken by a minority in the País Vasco and Navarra.

English isn't as widely spoken as many travellers seem to expect. In the main cities and tourist areas it's much easier to find people who speak at least some English, though generally you'll be better received if you at least try to communicate in Spanish.

See the Language Guide at the back of the book for pronunciation guidelines and useful words and phrases.

Facts for the Visitor

HIGHLIGHTS

Beaches

Yes, it's still possible to have a beach to yourself in Spain. In summer it may be a little tricky, but spots where things are bound to be quiet are such gems as the beaches of Cabo Favàritx in Menorca, and some of the secluded coves on Cabo de Gata in Andalucía. There are also good, relatively uncrowded beaches on the Costa de la Luz, between Tarifa and Cádiz. On the Galician coast, between Noia and Pontevedra, are literally hundreds of beaches where even in mid-August you won't feel claustrophobic.

Museums & Galleries

Spain is home to some of the finest art galleries in the world. The Prado in Madrid has few rivals, and there are outstanding art museums in Bilbao, Seville, Barcelona, Valencia and Córdoba. Fascinating smaller galleries, such as the Dalí museum in Figueres and the abstract art museum in Cuenca, also abound. Tarragona and Teruel have excellent archaeological museums.

Buildings

Try not to miss Andalucía's Muslim-era gems – the Alhambra in Granada, the alcázar in Seville and the Mezquita in Córdoba – or Barcelona's extraordinary La Sagrada Família church. The fairy-tale alcázar in Segovia has to be seen to be believed. For even more exciting views, and loads of medieval ghosts, try to reach the ruined castle in Morella, Valencia province.

Scenery

There's outstanding mountain scenery – often coupled with highly picturesque villages – in the Pyrenees and Picos de Europa in the north and in parts of Andalucía such as the Alpujarras. On the coasts, the rugged

SPAIN

inlets of Galicia and stark, hilly Cabo de Gata in Andalucía stand out.

SUGGESTED ITINERARIES

If you want to whiz around as many places as possible in limited time, the following itineraries might suit you:

Two days
Fly to Madrid, Barcelona or Seville, or nip into Barcelona or San Sebastián overland from France.

One week
Spend two days each in Barcelona, Madrid and Seville, allowing one day for travel.

Two weeks
As above, plus San Sebastián, Toledo, Salamanca and/or Cuenca, Córdoba and/or Granada, and maybe Cáceres and/or Trujillo.

One month
As above, plus some of the following: side trips from the cities mentioned above; an exploration of the north, including Santiago de Compostela and the Picos de Europa; visits to Teruel, Mallorca, Formentera, Segovia, Ávila, or some smaller towns and more remote regions such as North-East Extremadura or Cabo de Gata.

PLANNING
Climate & When to Go

For most purposes the ideal months to visit Spain are May, June and September (plus April and October in the south). At these times you can rely on good weather, yet avoid the sometimes extreme heat – and main crush of Spanish and foreign tourists – of July and August, when temperatures may climb to 45°C in parts of Andalucía and when Madrid is unbearably hot and almost deserted.

The summer overflows with festivals, including Sanfermines, with the running of the bulls in Pamplona, and Semana Grande all along the north coast (dates vary from place to place), but there are excellent festivals during the rest of the year too.

In winter the rains never seem to stop in the north, except when they turn to snow. Madrid regularly freezes in December, January and February. At these times Andalucía is the place to be, with temperatures reaching the mid-teens in most places and good skiing in the Sierra Nevada.

Books & Maps

The New Spaniards by John Hooper is a fascinating account of modern Spanish society and culture. For a readable and thorough, but not over-long, survey of Spanish history, *The Story of Spain* by Mark Williams is hard to beat.

Classic accounts of life and travel in Spain include Gerald Brenan's *South from Granada* (1920s), Laurie Lee's *As I Walked Out One Midsummer Morning* (1930s), George Orwell's *Homage to Catalonia* (the civil war), and *Iberia* by James Michener (1960s). Among the best of more recent books are *Homage to Barcelona* by Colm Toíbín, *Spanish Journeys* by Adam Hopkins and *Cities of Spain* by David Gilmour.

Of foreign literature set in Spain, Ernest Hemingway's civil war novel *For Whom the Bell Tolls* is a must.

If you're planning in-depth travels in Spain, get hold of Lonely Planet's *Spain*.

Some of the best maps for travellers are published by Michelin, which produces a 1:1 million *Spain Portugal* map and six 1:400,000 regional maps. The country map doesn't show railways, but the regional maps do.

What to Bring

You can buy anything you need in Spain, but some articles, such as sun-screen lotion, are more expensive than elsewhere. Books in English tend to be expensive and are hard to find outside main cities.

A pair of strong shoes and a towel are essential. A money belt or shoulder wallet can be useful in big cities. Bring sunglasses if glare gets to you. If you want to blend in, don't just pack T-shirts, shorts and runners – Spaniards are quite dressy and many tourists just look like casual slobs to them.

TOURIST OFFICES

Most towns (and many villages) of any interest have a tourist office (*oficina de turismo*). These will supply you with a map and brochures with basic information on local sights, attractions, accommodation, history etc. Some can also provide info on other places too. Their staff are generally helpful and often speak some English.

Tourist Offices Abroad

Spain has tourist information centres in 20 countries including:

Canada
    (☎ 416-961 3131), 102 Bloor St West, 14th floor, Toronto, Ontario M4W 3E2

France
    (☎ 01 45 03 82 50), 43 rue Decamps, 75784 Paris, Cedex 16

Portugal
    (☎ 01-354 1992; fax 01-354 0332), Avenida Fontes Pereira de Melo 51, 4th floor, 1000 Lisbon

UK
    (☎ 0171-493 5760), 22-23 Manchester Square, London W1M 5AP

USA
    (☎ 212-265 8822), 666 Fifth Avenue New York NY 10103

USEFUL ORGANISATIONS

The travel agency TIVE, with offices in major cities throughout Spain, specialises in discounted tickets and travel arrangements for students and young people. Its head office (☎ 91 347 7700) is at Calle de José Ortega y Gasset 71, 28006 Madrid.

VISAS & EMBASSIES

Citizens of EU countries can enter Spain with their national identity card or passport. UK citizens must have a full passport – a British visitor passport won't do. Non-EU nationals must take their passport.

EU, Norway and Iceland citizens require no visa. Nationals of Australia, Canada, Israel, Japan, New Zealand, Switzerland and the USA need no visa for stays of up to 90 days but must have a passport valid for the whole visit.

South Africans are among nationalities who do need a visa for Spain. It's best to obtain the visa in your country of residence to avoid possible bureaucratic problems. Both 30-day and 90-day single-entry, and 90-day multiple-entry visas are available, though if you apply in a country where you're not resident the 90-day option may not be available. Multiple-entry visas will save you a lot of time and trouble if you plan to leave Spain – say to Gibraltar or Morocco – then re-enter it.

The Schengen System

Spain is one of the Schengen Area countries – the others are Portugal, Italy, France, Germany, Austria, the Netherlands, Belgium and Luxembourg (Sweden, Finland, Denmark and Greece are expected to join up soon). They have theoretically done away with passport control on travel between them. (In fact checks have been known to occur at airports and on Lisbon-Madrid trains.) It is illegal to enter Spain without a visa (if you require one) and doing so can lead to deportation.

One good thing about the system is that a visa for one Schengen country is valid for others too. Compare validity periods, prices and the number of permitted entries before you apply, as these can differ between countries.

Stays of Longer than 90 Days

EU, Norway and Iceland nationals planning to stay in Spain more than 90 days are supposed to apply during their first month in the country for a residence card. This is a lengthy, complicated procedure; if you intend to subject yourself to it, consult a Spanish consulate before you go to Spain, as you'll need to take certain documents with you.

Other nationalities are not normally allowed more than one 90-day stay in any six-month period. Visa carriers may be able to get short visa extensions at their local Comisaría de Policía (National Police station), but don't count on it. Otherwise, for stays of longer than 90 days you're supposed to get a residence card. This is a nightmarish process, starting with a residence visa issued by a Spanish consulate in your country of residence; start the process light-years in advance.

Spanish Embassies Abroad

Spanish embassies include:

Australia
    (☎ 02-6273 3555/845), 15 Arkana St, Yarralumla, Canberra 2600, ACT; consulates in Sydney and Melbourne

Canada
    (☎ 613-237 2193/94), 350 Sparks St, suite 802, Ottawa K1R 7S8; consulates in Toronto and Montreal

France
    (☎ 01 44 43 18 00/53), 22 Ave Marceau, 75381 Paris; consulates in Marseille, Bayonne, Hendaye, Pau etc

Portugal
(☎ 01-347 2381/2/3/4), Rúa do Salitre 1, 1200 Lisbon; consulates in Porto and Valença do Minho

UK
(☎ 0171-235 5555), 39 Chesham Place, London SW1X 8SB; consulate (☎ 0171-589 8989) at 20 Draycott Place, London SW3 2RZ and in Edinburgh and Manchester

USA
(☎ 202-265 0190), 2700 15th St, NW, Washington, DC, 20009; consulates in Boston, Chicago, Houston, Miami, Los Angeles, New Orleans, New York and San Francisco

Foreign Embassies in Spain

Some 70 countries have embassies in Madrid, including:

Australia
(☎ 91 441 93 00), Plaza del Descubridor Diego de Ordàs 3-2, Edificio Santa Engracia 120

Canada
(☎ 91 431 43 00), Calle de Nuñez de Balboa 35

France
(☎ 91 435 55 60), Calle de Salustiano Olozoga 9

Germany
(☎ 91 557 90 00), Calle de Fortuny 8

Ireland
(☎ 91 576 35 00), Calle de Claudio Coello 73

Japan
(☎ 91 590 13 21), Calle de Serrano 109

Morocco
(☎ 91 563 79 28), Calle de Serrano 179

New Zealand
(☎ 91 523 02 26), Plaza de la Lealtad 2

Portugal
(☎ 91 561 78 00), Calle del Pinar 1

UK
(☎ 91 319 02 00), Calle de Fernando el Santo 16

USA
(☎ 91 587 22 00), Calle de Serrano 75

CUSTOMS

From outside the EU you are allowed to bring in duty-free one bottle of spirits, one bottle of wine, 50 ml of perfume and 200 cigarettes. From within the EU you can bring 2L of wine *and* 1L of spirits, with the same limits on the rest. Duty-free allowances for travel between EU countries are due to be abolished on 30 June 1999.

MONEY

Currency

Spain's unit of currency is the peseta (pta). The legal denominations are coins of one, five (known as a *duro*), 10, 25, 50, 100, 200 and 500 ptas. There are notes of 1000, 2000, 5000 and 10,000 ptas. Take care not to confuse the 500 ptas coin with the 100 ptas coin.

Exchange Rates

Banks – mostly open Monday to Friday from 8.30 am to 2 pm, Saturday from 8.30 am to 1 pm – generally give better exchange rates than currency-exchange offices, and travellers cheques attract a slightly better rate than cash. ATMs accepting a wide variety of cards are common.

Australia	A$1	=	94.63 ptas
Canada	C$1	=	101 ptas
euro	€1	=	167 ptas
France	1FF	=	25.31 ptas
Germany	DM1	=	84.70 ptas
Japan	¥100	=	108 ptas
Portugal	100$00	=	0.83 ptas
New Zealand	NZ$1	=	79.30 ptas
UK	UK£1	=	248 ptas
USA	US$1	=	151 ptas

Costs

Spain is one of Western Europe's more affordable countries. If you are particularly frugal, it's possible to scrape by on 3000 ptas to 4000 ptas a day; this would involve staying in the cheapest possible accommodation, avoiding eating in restaurants or going to museums or bars, and not moving around too much. Places like Madrid, Barcelona, Seville and San Sebastián will place a greater strain on your money belt.

A more reasonable budget would be 5000 ptas a day. This would allow you 1500 to 2000 ptas for accommodation, 400 ptas for breakfast (coffee and a pastry), 800 to 1000 ptas for a set lunch, 250 ptas for public transport (two metro or bus rides), 500 ptas for a major museum, and 600 ptas for a light dinner, with a bit left over for a drink or two and intercity travel.

Tipping & Bargaining

In restaurants, menu prices include a service

charge, and tipping is a matter of personal choice – most people leave some small change and 5% is plenty. It's common to leave small change in bars and cafés. The only places in Spain where you are likely to bargain are markets and, occasionally, cheap hotels – particularly if you're staying for a few days.

Consumer Taxes & Refunds

In Spain, VAT (value-added tax) is known as IVA (*impuesto sobre el valor añadido*). On accommodation and restaurant prices, there's a flat rate of 7% IVA which is usually – but not always – included in quoted prices. To check, ask if the price is 'con IVA' (with VAT) or 'sin IVA' (without VAT).

On retail goods, alcohol, electrical appliances etc, IVA is 16%. Visitors are entitled to a refund of IVA on any item costing more than 15,000 ptas that they are taking out of the EU. Ask the shop for a Europe Tax-Free Shopping Cheque when you buy, then present the goods and cheque to customs when you leave within three months. Customs stamps the cheque and you then cash it at a booth with the 'Cash Refund' sign. There are booths at all main Spanish airports, the border crossings at Algeciras, Gibraltar and Andorra, and similar refund points throughout the EU.

POST & COMMUNICATIONS

Main post offices in provincial capitals are usually open Monday to Friday from about 8.30 am to 8.30 pm, and Saturday from about 9 am to 1.30 pm. Stamps are also sold at *estancos* (tobacconist shops with the 'Tabacos' sign in yellow letters on a maroon background). A standard air-mail letter or card costs 65 ptas to Europe, 99 ptas to the USA or Canada, and 117 ptas to Australia or New Zealand. Aerogram cost 76 ptas regardless of the destination.

Mail to/from Europe normally takes up to a week, and to North America, Australia or New Zealand around 10 days – but there may be some unaccountable long delays.

Poste-restante mail can be addressed to you at either poste restante or *lista de correos*, the Spanish name for it, in the city in question. It's a fairly reliable system, al-though you must be prepared for mail to arrive late. American Express card or travellers cheque holders can use the free client mail service (see the Facts for the Visitor chapter at the beginning of this book).

Common abbreviations used in Spanish addresses are 1°, 2°, 3° etc, which mean 1st, 2nd, 3rd floor, and s/n (*sin número*), which means the building has no number.

Telephone & Fax

In April 1998, the area codes in Spain became an integral part of the phone number. The result is that all numbers are now nine digits long, without area codes.

Public pay phones are blue, common and easy to use. They accept coins, phonecards (*tarjetas telefónicas*) and, in some cases, credit cards. Phonecards come in 1000 and 2000 ptas denominations and are available at main post offices and estancos. A three-minute call from a pay phone costs 30 ptas within a local area, 80 ptas to other places in the same province, or 190 ptas to other provinces. Calls are around 15% cheaper between 10 pm and 8 am and all day Sunday and holidays.

International reverse-charge (collect) calls are simple to make: from a pay phone or private phone dial ☎ 900 99 00 followed by ☎ 61 for Australia, ☎ 44 for the UK, ☎ 64 for New Zealand, ☎ 15 for Canada, and for the USA ☎ 11 (AT&T) or ☎ 14 (MCI).

A three-minute call to the US at peak rates will cost 350 ptas.

Most main post offices have a fax service, but you'll often find cheaper rates at shops or offices with 'Fax Público' signs.

INTERNET RESOURCES

Cybercafés are beginning to spring up in major Spanish cities. A half-hour online typically costs from 400 to 600 ptas.

An Internet search under 'Spain, Travel' will reveal dozens of sites.

NEWSPAPERS & MAGAZINES

The major daily newspapers in Spain are the solid liberal *El País*, the conservative *ABC*, and *El Mundo*, which specialises in breaking political scandals. For a laugh, have a look at *¡Hola!*, a weekly magazine devoted to the lives and loves of the rich and famous. There's also a welter of regional dailies, some of the best being in Barcelona, the País Vasco and Andalucía.

International press such as the *International Herald Tribune*, *Time* and *Newsweek*, and daily papers from Western European countries reach major cities and tourist areas on the day of publication; elsewhere they're harder to find and are a day or two late.

RADIO & TV

There are hundreds of radio stations, mainly on the FM band – you'll hear a substantial proportion of British and American music. The national pop/rock station, Radio 3, has admirably varied programming.

Spaniards are Europe's greatest TV watchers after the British, but do a lot of their watching in bars and cafés which makes it more of a social activity. Most TVs receive six channels – two state-run (TVE1 and TVE2), three privately run (Antena 3, Tele 5 and Canal+), and one regional channel. Apart from news, TV seems to consist mostly of game and talk shows, sport, soap operas, sitcoms, and English-language films dubbed into Spanish.

PHOTOGRAPHY & VIDEO

Main brands of film are widely available and processing is fast and generally efficient. A roll of print film (36 exposures, 100 ASA) costs around 650 ptas and can be processed for around 1700 ptas – though there are often better deals if you have two or three rolls developed together. The equivalent in slide film is around 850 ptas plus the same for processing. Nearly all pre-recorded videos in Spain use the PAL image-registration system common to Western Europe and Australia. These won't work on many video players in France, North America and Japan.

TIME

Spain is one hour ahead of GMT/UTC during winter, and two hours ahead from the last Sunday in March to the last Sunday in September.

ELECTRICITY

Electric current in Spain is 220V, 50Hz, but some places are still on 125 or 110V. In fact, the voltage sometimes differs in the same building. Plugs have two round pins.

WEIGHTS & MEASURES

The metric system is used. Like other Continental Europeans, the Spanish indicate decimals with commas and thousands with points.

LAUNDRY

Self-service laundrettes are rare. Laundries (*lavanderías*) are common but not particularly cheap. They will usually wash, dry and fold a load for 1000 to 1200 ptas.

TOILETS

Public toilets are not very common in Spain. The easiest thing to do is head for a café. It is polite to buy something in exchange for the loo service.

HEALTH

Apart from the dangers of contracting STDs, the main thing you have to be wary of is the sun – in both cases, use protection. Tap water is safe to drink throughout most of the country – if in doubt ask *¿Es potable el agua?* – although taste-wise it varies from great to blah. Bottled water is available everywhere, generally for around 85 ptas for a 1.5L bottle.

State health care is available for free to EU citizens on provision of an E111 form (available free in your home country – contact your health service before you come to Spain to find out how to get it), but others will have to pay cash, so travel insurance is a must. *Farmacias* (chemists) can treat many ailments. Emergency dental treatment is available at most public hospitals.

WOMEN TRAVELLERS

The best way for women travellers to approach Spain is simply to be ready to ignore stares, cat calls and unnecessary comments. However, Spain has one of the lowest incidences of reported rape in the developed world, and even physical harassment is much less frequent than you might expect. The Asociación de Asistencia a Mujeres Violadas in Madrid (☎ 91 574 01 10, Monday to Friday from 10 am to 2 pm and 4 to 7 pm; recorded message in Spanish at other times) offers advice and help to rape victims, and can provide details of similar centres in other cities, though only limited English is spoken.

GAY & LESBIAN TRAVELLERS

Attitudes towards gays and lesbians are pretty tolerant, especially in the cities. Madrid, Barcelona, Sitges, Ibiza and Cádiz all have active gay and lesbian scenes. A good source of information on gay places and organisations throughout Spain is the Barcelona-based Coordinadora Gai-Lesbiana, Carrer de Buenaventura Muñoz 4, 08018 Barcelona, Cataluña (☎ 93 309 79 97; fax 93 309 78 40; cogailes@pangea.org).

DISABLED TRAVELLERS

Spanish tourist offices in other countries can provide a basic information sheet with some useful addresses, and give info on accessible accommodation in specific places. INSERSO (☎ 91 347 88 88), Calle de Ginzo de Limea 58, 28029 Madrid, is the government department for the disabled, with branches in all of Spain's 50 provinces.

You'll find some wheelchair-accessible accommodation in main centres, but it may not be in the budget category – although 25 Spanish youth hostels are classed as suitable for wheelchair users.

SENIOR TRAVELLERS

There are reduced prices for people over 60, 63 or 65 (depending on the place) at some attractions and occasionally on transport.

DANGERS & ANNOYANCES

It's a good idea to take your car radio and any other valuables with you any time you leave your car. In fact it's best to leave nothing at all – certainly nothing visible – in a parked car. In youth hostels, don't leave belongings unattended – there is a high incidence of theft. Beware of pickpockets in cities and tourist resorts (Barcelona and Seville have bad repu-

tations). There is also a relatively high incidence of mugging in such places, so keep your wits about you. Emergency numbers for the police throughout Spain are ☎ 091 (national police) and ☎ 092 (local police).

Drugs

In 1992 Spain's liberal drug laws were severely tightened. No matter what anyone tells you, it is not legal to smoke dope in public bars. There is a reasonable degree of tolerance when it comes to people having a smoke in their own home, but not in hotel rooms or guesthouses.

BUSINESS HOURS

Generally, people work Monday to Friday from 9 am to 2 pm and then again from 4.30 or 5 pm for another three hours. Shops and travel agencies are usually open these hours on Saturday too, though some may skip the evening session. Museums all have their own unique opening hours: major ones tend to open for something like normal business hours (with or without the afternoon break), but often have their weekly closing day on Monday, not Sunday.

PUBLIC HOLIDAYS & SPECIAL EVENTS

Spain has at least 14 official holidays a year – some observed nationwide, some very local. When a holiday falls close to a weekend, Spaniards like to make a *puente* (bridge) – meaning they take the intervening day off too. The following holidays are observed virtually everywhere:

1 January (New Year's Day)
6 January (Epiphany or Three Kings' Day, when children receive presents)
Good Friday
1 May (Labour Day)
15 August (Feast of the Assumption)
12 October (National Day)
1 November (All Saints' Day)
8 December (Feast of the Immaculate Conception)
25 December (Christmas)

The two main periods when Spaniards go on holiday are Semana Santa (the week leading up to Easter Sunday) and the month of

August. At these times accommodation in resorts can be scarce and transport heavily booked, but other cities are often half-empty.

Spaniards indulge their love of colour, noise, crowds and partying at innumerable local fiestas and *ferias* (fairs); even small villages will have at least one, probably several, during the year. Many fiestas are based on religion but still highly festive. Local tourist offices can always supply detailed info.

Among festivals to look out for are La Tamborada in San Sebastián on 20 January, when the whole town dresses up and goes berserk; *carnaval*, a time of fancy-dress parades and merrymaking celebrated around the country about seven weeks before Easter (wildest in Cádiz and Sitges); Valencia's week-long mid-March party, Las Fallas, with all-night dancing and drinking, first-class fireworks, and processions; Semana Santa with its parades of holy images and huge crowds, notably in Seville; Seville's Feria de Abril, a week-long party in late April, a kind of counterbalance to the religious peak of Semana Santa; Sanfermines, with the running of the bulls, in Pamplona in July; Semana Grande, another week of heavy drinking and hangovers, all along the north coast during the first half of August; and Barcelona's week-long party, the Festes de la Mercè, around 24 September.

ACTIVITIES
Surfing & Windsurfing
The País Vasco has good surf spots – San Sebastián, Zarauz and the legendary left at Mundaca, among others. Tarifa, Spain's southernmost point, is a windsurfers' heaven, with constant breezes and long, empty beaches.

Skiing
Skiing in Spain is cheap and the facilities and conditions are good. The season runs from December to May. The most accessible resorts are in the Sierra Nevada (very close to Granada), the Pyrenees (north of Barcelona) and in the ranges north of Madrid. Contact tourist offices in these cities for information. Affordable day trips can be booked through travel agents.

Cycling
Bike touring isn't as common as in other parts of Europe because of deterrents like the often-mountainous terrain and summer heat. It's a more viable option on the Balearic Islands than on much of the mainland, although plenty of people get on their bikes in spring and autumn in the south. Mountain biking is increasingly popular and areas like Andalucía and Catalonia have many good tracks. Finding bikes to rent is a hit-and-miss affair so if you're set on the idea it's best to bring your own.

Hiking
Spain is a trekker's paradise, so much so that Lonely Planet has published a guide to some of the best treks in the country, *Walking in Spain*. See also the Mallorca and Picos de Europa sections of this chapter.

Walking country roads and paths, between settlements, can also be highly enjoyable and a great way to meet the locals.

Two organisations publish detailed close-up maps of small parts of Spain. The CNIG covers most of the country in 1:25,000 (1cm to 250m) sheets, most of which are recent. The CNIG and the Servicio Geográfico del Ejército (SGE, Army Geographic Service) each publishes a 1:50,000 series; the SGE's tends to be more up to date – the maps were published in the mid-1980s. Also useful for hiking and exploring some areas are the *Guía Cartográfica* and *Guía Excursionista y Turística* series published by Editorial Alpina. The series combines information booklets in Spanish (or sometimes Catalan) with detailed maps at scales ranging from 1:25,000 to 1:50,000, and are well worth their price (around 500 ptas). You may well find CNIG, SCE and Alpina publications in local bookshops but it's more reliable to get them in advance from specialist map or travel shops like La Tienda Verde in Madrid, and Altaïr and Quera in Barcelona.

If you fancy a really long walk, there's the Camino de Santiago. This route, which has been followed by Christian pilgrims for centuries, can be commenced at various places in France. It then crosses the Pyrenees and runs via Pamplona, Logroño and León all the way to the cathedral in Santiago de Compostela. There are numerous guidebooks explaining the route, and the best map is published by CNIG.

COURSES

The best place to take a language course in Spain is generally at a university. Those with the best reputations include Salamanca, Santiago de Compostela and Santander. It can also be fun to combine study with a stay in one of Spain's most exciting cities such as Barcelona, Madrid or Seville. There are also dozens of private language colleges throughout the country; the Instituto Cervantes (☎ 0171-486 4350), 102 Eaton Square, London SW1 W9AN, can send you lists of these and of universities that run courses. Some Spanish embassies and consulates also have info.

Other courses available in Spain include art, cookery and photography. Spanish tourist offices can help with information.

WORK

EU, Norway and Iceland nationals are allowed to work in Spain without a visa, but if they plan to stay more than three months, they are supposed to apply within the first month for a residence card (see Visas & Embassies earlier in this chapter). Virtually everyone else is supposed to obtain, from a Spanish consulate in their country of residence, a work permit and, if they plan to stay more than 90 days, a residence visa. These procedures are even more difficult (see Visas & Embassies). That said, quite a few people do manage to work in Spain one way or another – though with Spain's unemployment rate running at up to 20%, don't rely on it. Teaching English is an obvious option – a TEFL certificate will be a big help. Another possibility is summer work in a bar or restaurant in a tourist resort. Quite a lot of these are run by foreigners.

ACCOMMODATION

Camping

Spain has more than 800 camping grounds. Facilities and settings vary enormously, and grounds are officially rated from 1st class to 3rd class. You can expect to pay around 500 ptas each per person, car and tent. Tourist offices can direct you to the nearest camping ground. Many are open all year, though quite a few close from around October to Easter. With certain exceptions (such as many beaches and environmentally protected areas), it is legal to camp outside camping grounds. You'll need permission to camp on private land.

Hostels

Spain's youth hostels (*albergues juveniles*) are often the cheapest place to stay for lone travellers, but two people can usually get a double room elsewhere for a similar price. With some notable exceptions, hostels are only moderate value. Many have curfews and/or are closed during the day, or lack cooking facilities (if so they usually have a cafeteria). They can be lacking in privacy, and are often heavily booked by school groups. Most are members of the country's Hostelling International (HI) organisation, Red Española de Albergues Juveniles (REAJ), whose head office (☎ 91 347 77 78) is at Calle de José Ortega y Gasset 71, 28006 Madrid. Prices often depend on the season or whether you're under 26; typically you pay 900 to 1700 ptas. Some hostels require HI membership, others don't but may charge more if you're not a member. You can buy HI cards for 1800 ptas at virtually all hostels.

Other Accommodation

Officially, all establishments are either *hoteles* (from one to five stars), *hostales* (one to three stars) or *pensiones*. In practice, there are all sorts of overlapping categories, especially at the budget end of the market. In broad terms, the cheapest are usually *fondas* and *casas de huéspedes*, followed by pensiones. All these normally have shared bathrooms, and singles/doubles for 1000/2000 to 2000/4000 ptas. Some hostales and *hostal-residencias* come in the same price range, but others have rooms with private bathroom costing anywhere up to 6000 ptas or so. Hoteles are usually beyond the means of budget travellers. The luxurious state-run *paradores*, often converted historic buildings, are prohibitively expensive.

Room rates in this chapter are generally high-season prices, which in most resorts and other heavily touristed places means July and August, Semana Santa and sometimes Christmas and New Year. At other times prices in many places go down by 5 to 25%. In many cases you have to add 7% IVA.

SPAIN

FOOD

It's a good idea to reset your stomach's clock in Spain, unless you want to eat alone or only with other tourists. Most Spaniards start the day with a light breakfast (*desayuno*), perhaps coffee with a *tostada* (piece of buttered toast) or *pastel* (pastry). *Churros con chocolate* (long, deep-fried doughnuts with thick hot chocolate) are a delicious start to the day and unique to Spain. Lunch (*almuerzo* or *comida*) is usually the main meal of the day, eaten between about 1.30 and 4 pm. The evening meal (*cena*) is usually lighter and may be eaten as late as 10 or 11 pm. It's common (and a great idea!) to go to a bar or café for a snack around 11 am and again around 7 or 8 pm.

Spain has a huge variety of local cuisines. Seafood as well as meat is prominent almost everywhere. One of the most characteristic dishes, from the Valencia region, is *paella* – rice, seafood, the odd vegetable and often chicken or meat, all simmered up together, traditionally coloured yellow with saffron. Another dish, of Andalucían origin, is *gazpacho*, a soup made from tomatoes, breadcrumbs, cucumber and/or green peppers, eaten cold. *Tortillas* (omelettes) are an inexpensive standby and come in many varieties. *Jamón serrano* (cured ham) is a treat for meat-eaters.

Cafés & Bars

If you want to follow Spanish habits, you'll be spending plenty of time in cafés and bars. In almost all of them you'll find *tapas* available. These saucer-sized mini-snacks are part of the Spanish way of life and come in infinite varieties from calamari rings to potato salad to spinach with chickpeas to a small serving of tripe. A typical tapa costs 100 to 200 ptas (although sometimes they will come free with your drinks), but check before you order because some are a lot dearer. A *ración* is a meal-sized serving of these snacks; a *media ración* is a half-ración.

The other popular snacks are *bocadillos*, long filled white bread rolls. Spaniards eat so many bocadillos that some cafés sell nothing else. Try not to leave Spain without sampling a *bocadillo de tortilla de patata*, a roll filled with potato omelette.

You can often save 10 to 20% by ordering and eating food at the bar rather than at a table.

Restaurants

Throughout Spain, you'll find plenty of restaurants serving good, simple food at affordable prices, often featuring regional specialities. Many restaurants offer a *menú del dia* – the budget traveller's best friend. For around 800 to 1200 ptas, you typically get a starter, a main course, dessert, bread and wine – often with a choice of two or three dishes for each course. The *plato combinado* is a near relative of the menú. It literally translates as 'combined plate' – maybe a steak and egg with chips and salad, or fried squid with potato salad. You'll pay more for your meals if you order à la carte, but the food will be better.

Vegetarian Food

Finding vegetarian fare can be a headache. It's not uncommon for 'meatless' food to be flavoured with meat stock. But in larger cities and important student centres there's a growing awareness of vegetarianism, so that if there isn't a vegetarian restaurant, there are often vegetarian items on menus. A good vegetarian snack at almost any place with bocadillos or sandwiches is a bocadillo (or sandwich) vegetal, which has a filling of salad and, often, fried egg (*sin huevo* means without egg).

Self-Catering

Every town of any substance has a *mercado* (food market). These are fun and great value. Even big eaters should be able to put together a filling meal of bread, chorizo (spiced sausage), cheese, fruit and a drink for 400 ptas or less. If you shop carefully you can eat three healthy meals a day for as little as 600 ptas.

DRINKS

Coffee in Spain is strong. Addicts should specify how they want their fix: *café con leche* is about 50% coffee, 50% hot milk; *café solo* is a short black; *café cortado* is a short black with a little milk.

The most common way to order a beer (*cerveza*) is to ask for a *caña* (pronounced 'can-ya'), which is a small draught beer. *Corto* and, in the País Vasco, *zurrito*, are other names for this. A larger beer (about

300ml) is often called a *tubo*, or in Catalonia a *jarra*. All these words apply to draught beer (*cerveza de barril*) – if you just ask for a cerveza you're likely to get bottled beer, which is more expensive.

Wine (*vino*) comes white (*blanco*), red (*tinto*) or rosé (*rosado*). *Tinto de verano*, a kind of wine shandy, is good in summer. There are also many regional grape specialities such as *jerez* (sherry) in Jerez de la Frontera and *cava* (like champagne) in Catalonia. *Sangría*, a sweet punch made of red wine, fruit and spirits, is refreshing and very popular with tourists.

The cheapest drink of all is, of course, water. To specify tap water (which is safe to drink almost everywhere), just ask for *agua del grifo*.

ENTERTAINMENT

Spain has some of the best nightlife in Europe – wild and *very* late, especially on Friday and Saturday, are an integral part of the Spain experience. Many young Spaniards don't even think about going out until midnight or so. Bars, which come in all shapes, sizes and themes, are the main attractions until around 2 or 3 am. Some play great music that will get you hopping before – if you can afford it – you move on to a disco till 5 or 6 am. Discos are generally expensive, but not to be missed if you can manage to splurge. Spain's contributions to modern dance music are *bakalao* and *makina*, kinds of frenzied (150 to 180bpm) techno.

The live music scene is less exciting. Spanish rock and pop tends to be imitative, though the bigger cities usually offer a reasonable choice of bands. See the earlier Society & Conduct section for info on flamenco.

Cinemas abound and are good value, though foreign films are usually dubbed into Spanish.

SPECTATOR SPORTS

The national sport is *fútbol* (soccer). The best teams to see – for their crowd support as well as their play – are usually Real Madrid and Barcelona, although the atmosphere can be electric anywhere. The season runs from September to May.

Bullfighting is enjoying a resurgence despite continued pressure from international animal-rights activists. It's a complex activity that's regarded as much as an art form as a sport by aficionados. If you decide to see a *corrida de toros*, the season runs from March to October. Madrid, Seville and Pamplona are among the best places to see one.

THINGS TO BUY

Many of Spain's best handicrafts are fragile or bulky – inconvenient unless you're going straight home. Pottery comes in a great range of attractive regional varieties. Some lovely rugs and blankets are made in places like the Alpujarras and Níjar in Andalucía. There's some pleasing woodwork available too, such as Granada's marquetry boxes and chess sets. Leather jackets, bags and belts are quite good value in many places.

Getting There & Away

AIR

Spain has many international airports including Madrid, Barcelona, Bilbao, Santiago de Compostela, Seville, Málaga, Almería, Alicante, Valencia, Palma de Mallorca, Ibiza and Maó (Menorca). In general, the cheapest destinations are Málaga, the Balearic Islands, Barcelona and Madrid.

Australia

In general, the best thing to do is to fly to London, Paris, Frankfurt or Rome, and then make your way overland. Alternatively, some flight deals to these centres include a couple of short-haul flights within Europe, and Madrid or Barcelona are usually acceptable destinations for these. Some round-the-world (RTW) fares include stops in Spain. STA Travel should be able to help you out with a good price. Generally speaking, a return fare to Europe for under A$1700 is too good to pass up.

North America

Return fares to Madrid from Miami, New York, Atlanta or Chicago range from US$780 to US$830 on Iberia or Delta. From the west coast you are usually looking at about US$100 more.

The UK

Scheduled flights to Spain are generally expensive, but with the huge range of charter, discount and low-season fares, it's often cheaper to fly than to take a bus or train. Check the travel sections of *TNT* or *Time Out* magazines or the weekend newspapers. The following are examples of short-notice low-season return fares from London:

Dest'n	Fare (£)	Agent	Phone
Barcelona	127	Charter Flight Centre	☎ 0171-565 6755
Ibiza	119	Connections	☎ 0171-408 4405
Madrid	108	EasyJet	☎ 01582-700047
Málaga	109	Spanish Travel Services	☎ 0171-387 5337

From Spain

For Northern Europe, check the ads in local English-language papers in tourist centres like the Costa del Sol, the Costa Blanca and the Balearic Islands. You may pick up a one-way fare to London for around 12,000 ptas. The youth and student travel agency TIVE, and the general travel agency Halcón Viajes, both with branches in most main cities, have some good fares: generally you're looking at around 13,000 to 15,500 ptas one way to London, Paris or Amsterdam, and at least 30,000 ptas to the USA.

LAND
Bus

There are regular bus services to Spain from all major centres in Europe, including Lisbon, London and Paris. In London, Eurolines (☎ 0990-143219) has services at least three times a week to Barcelona (23 to 25 hours; UK£77 one way), Madrid (at least 27 hours; UK£77 one way) and Málaga (34 hours; UK£79 one way). Tickets are sold by major travel agencies, and people under 26 and senior citizens qualify for a 10% discount. In Spain, services to the major

European cities are operated by Eurolines affiliates such as Linebús and Julià Via. There are also bus services to Morocco from some Spanish cities.

Train

Reaching Spain by train is more expensive than bus unless you have a rail pass, though fares for those under 26 come close to the bus price. Normal one-way fares from London (using the ferry, not Eurostar) to Madrid (via Paris) are UK£112. For more details, contact the International Rail Centre in London (☎ 0990-848848) or a travel agent. See the introductory Getting Around chapter for more on rail passes and train travel through Europe.

Car & Motorcycle

If you're driving or riding to Spain from England, you'll have to choose between going through France (check visa requirements) or taking a direct ferry from England to Spain (see the following section). The cheapest way is one of the shorter ferries from England to France, then a quick drive down through France.

SEA
The UK

There are two direct ferry services. Brittany Ferries (in England ☎ 0990-360360) runs Plymouth-Santander ferries twice weekly from about mid-March to mid-November (24 hours), and a Portsmouth-Santander service (30 hours), usually once a week, in other months. P&O European Ferries (in England ☎ 0990-980980) runs Portsmouth-Bilbao ferries twice weekly almost all year (35 hours). Prices on all services are similar: one-way passenger fares range from about UK£47 in winter to UK£82 in summer (cabins extra); a car and driver costs from UK£152 to UK£275, or you can take a vehicle and several passengers for UK£233 to UK£403.

Morocco

Ferry services between Spain and Morocco include Algeciras-Tangier, Algeciras-Ceuta, Gibraltar-Tangier, Málaga-Melilla, Almería-Melilla and Almería-Nador. Those to/from

Algeciras are the fastest, cheapest and most frequent, with up to 20 ferries and hydrofoils a day to Ceuta (1½ hours/40 minutes) and 14 to Tangier (two hours/one hour). One-way passenger fares on the ferry/hydrofoil are 1801/2945 ptas (Ceuta) and 2960/3440 ptas (Tangier). A car to Ceuta/Tangier costs 9300/8223 ptas. You can buy tickets at Algeciras harbour, but it's more convenient to go to one of the many agencies on the waterfront. The price doesn't vary, so just look for the place with the shortest queue.

Don't buy Moroccan currency until you reach Morocco, as you will get ripped off in Algeciras.

LEAVING SPAIN

Departure taxes on flights out of Spain, which vary, are factored directly into tickets.

Getting Around

AIR

Spain has four main domestic airlines – Iberia (with subsidiary Binter Mediterráneo, both on ☎ 902-40 05 00), Air Europa (☎ 902-24 00 42) and Spanair (☎ 902-13 14 15). They and a couple of smaller airlines compete to produce some fares that can make flying worthwhile if you're in a hurry, especially for longer or return trips.

The return fare between Madrid and Barcelona can be as high as 25,000 ptas. To Palma de Mallorca you are looking at around 28,500 ptas return, 28,000 ptas to Santiago de Compostela and 27,500 ptas to Málaga. All these fares can drop drastically if you comply with certain restrictions.

Among travel agencies, TIVE and Halcón Viajes (see Air under Getting There & Away earlier) are always worth checking for fares. There are some useful deals if you're under 26 (or, in some cases, over 63).

BUS

Spain's bus network is operated by dozens of independent companies and is more extensive than its train system, serving remote towns and villages as well as the major routes. The choice between bus and train depends on the particular trip you're taking;

for the best value, compare fares, journey times and frequencies each time you move. Buses to/from Madrid are often cheaper than (or barely different from) cross-country routes. For instance Seville to Madrid costs 2715 ptas while the shorter Seville-Granada trip is 2700 ptas.

Many towns and cities have one main bus station where most buses arrive and depart, and these usually have an information desk giving info on all services. Tourist offices can also help with info but don't sell tickets.

TRAIN

Trains are mostly modern and comfortable, and late arrivals are now the exception rather than the rule. The main headache is deciding which compartment on which train gives you best value for money.

RENFE, the national railway company, runs numerous types of train, and travel times can vary a lot on the same route. So can fares, which may depend not just on the type of train but also the day of the week and time of day. *Regionales* are all-stops trains – cheap and slow. *Cercanías* provide regular services from major cities to the surrounding suburbs and hinterland, sometimes even crossing regional boundaries.

Among long-distance (*largo recorrido*) trains the standard daytime train is the *diurno* (its night-time equivalent is the *estrella*). Quicker is the InterCity (mainly because it makes fewer stops), while the *Talgo* is the quickest and dearest.

Best of all is the AVE high-speed service that links Madrid and Seville in just 2½ hours. The *Talgo 200* uses part of this line to speed down to Málaga from Madrid. The *Euromed* is an AVE-style train that speeds south from Barcelona to Valencia and Alicante. A Tren Hotel is a 1st-class sleeper-only express.

There's also a bewildering range of accommodation types, especially on overnight trains (fares quoted in this chapter are typical 2nd-class seat fares). Fortunately ticket clerks understand the problem and are usually happy to go through a few options with you. The cheapest sleeper option is usually a *litera*, a bunk in a six-berth 2nd-class compartment.

You can buy tickets and make reservations at stations, RENFE offices in many city centres, and travel agencies that display the RENFE logo.

Train Passes

Rail passes are valid for all RENFE trains, but Inter-Rail users have to pay supplements on Talgo and InterCity services, and full fare on the high-speed AVE service between Madrid and Seville. All pass-holders making reservations for long-distance trains pay a fee of 500 ptas.

RENFE's Tarjeta Turística is a rail pass valid for four to 10 days travel in a two-month period: in 2nd class, four days costs 23,000 ptas, while 10 days is 49,000 ptas.

CAR & MOTORCYCLE

If you're driving or riding around Spain, consider investing 2600 ptas in the *Michelin Atlas de Carreteras España Portugal*. It's a handy atlas with detailed road maps as well as maps of all the main towns and cities.

Spain's roads vary enormously but are generally quite good. Fastest are the *autopistas*, multilane freeways between major cities. On some, mainly in the north, you have to pay hefty tolls (from the French border to Barcelona, for example, it's 1580 ptas). Minor routes can be slow going but are usually more scenic. Petrol is relatively expensive at around 114 ptas for a litre of unleaded.

The head office of the Spanish automobile club Real Automovil Club de España (RACE; ☎ 91 447 32 00) is at Calle de José Abascal 10, 28003 Madrid. For RACE's 24-hour, nationwide, on-road emergency service, call the toll free number ☎ 900-11 81 18.

Road Rules

Although a little hairy, driving in Spain is not too bad and locals show at least some respect for the rules. Speed limits are 120km/h on autopistas, 90 or 100km/h on other country roads and 50km/h in built-up areas. The maximum allowable blood-alcohol level is 0.05%. Seat belts must be worn, and motorcyclists must always wear a helmet and keep headlights on day and night.

Trying to find a parking spot can be a nightmare in larger towns and cities. Spanish drivers park anywhere to save themselves the hassle of a half-hour search, but *grúas* (tow trucks) will tow your car if given the chance. The cost of bailing out a car can be as high as 10,000 ptas.

Rental

Rates vary widely from place to place. The best deals tend to be in major tourist areas, including at their airports. At Málaga airport you can rent a small car for under 20,000 ptas a week. More generally, you're looking at anything up to 7000 ptas for a day with unlimited kilometres, plus insurance, damage waiver and taxes. Hiring for several days can bring the average daily cost down a great deal – a small car for a week might cost 40,000 ptas all up. Local companies often have better rates than the big firms.

BICYCLE

See the Activities section earlier.

HITCHING

It's still possible to thumb your way around parts of Spain, but large doses of patience and common sense are necessary. Women should avoid hitching alone. Hitching is illegal on autopistas and difficult on major highways. Your chances are better on minor roads, although the going can still be painfully slow.

BOAT

For information on ferries to, from and between the Balearic Islands, see that section of this chapter.

LOCAL TRANSPORT

In many Spanish towns you will not need to use public transport, as transport terminals and accommodation are centralised and within walking distance of most tourist attractions.

Most towns in Spain have an effective local bus system. In larger cities, these can be complicated, but tourist offices can advise on which buses you need. Barcelona and Madrid both have efficient underground systems which are faster and easier to use than the bus systems.

Taxis are still pretty cheap. If you split a cross-town fare between three or four people, it can be a decidedly good deal. Rates vary slightly from city to city: in Barcelona, they cost 295 ptas flag fall, plus about 100 ptas per kilometre; in Madrid they're a bit cheaper (170 ptas flag fall). There are supplements for luggage and airport trips.

Madrid

☎ 91

Whatever apprehensions you may have about Madrid when you first arrive, Spain's capital is sure to grow on you. Madrid may lack the glamour or beauty of Barcelona and the historical richness of so many Spanish cities (it was insignificant until Felipe II made it his capital in 1561), but it more than makes up for this with a remarkable collection of museums and galleries, some lovely parks and gardens and wild nightlife.

Orientation

The area of most interest to visitors lies between Parque del Buen Retiro in the east and Campo del Moro in the west. These two parks are more or less connected by Calle de Alcalá and Calle Mayor, which meet in the middle at Puerta del Sol. Calle Mayor passes the main square, Plaza Mayor, on its way from Puerta del Sol to the Palacio Real in front of Campo del Moro.

The main north-south thoroughfare is Paseo de la Castellana, which runs (changing names to Paseo de los Recoletos and finally Paseo del Prado) all the way from Chamartín train station in the north to Madrid's other big station, Atocha.

Information

Tourist Offices The main tourist office (☎ 91 429 49 51) is at Calle del Duque de Medinaceli 2. It opens Monday to Friday from 9 am to 7 pm, and on Saturday from 9 am to 1 pm. The office at Barajas airport (☎ 91 305 86 56) is open Monday to Friday from 8 am to 8 pm and Saturday from 9 am to 1 pm. The one at Chamartín train station (☎ 91 315 9 9 76) keeps the same hours.

Yet another Oficina de Turismo (☎ 91 364 18 76), Ronda de Toledo 1, is located in the Centro Comercial de la Puerta de Toledo. It opens Monday to Friday from 9 am to 7.30 pm and Saturday from 9.30 am to 1.30 pm.

Money Large banks like the Caja de Madrid usually have the best rates, but check commissions first. Banking hours vary but it is generally safe to assume they will be open on weekdays from 9 am to 2 pm (Saturday to 1 pm). American Express (24 hours ☎ 91 527 03 03; ☎ 900-99 44 26 for replacing lost travellers cheques) is at Plaza de las Cortes 2 and has reasonable rates. It's open Monday to Friday from 9 am to 5.30 pm and on Saturday from 9 am to noon.

If you're desperate there are plenty of *bureaux de change* around Puerta del Sol and Plaza Mayor, which offer appalling rates but are often open until midnight. A rare exception is Cambios Uno, Calle de Alcalá 20, which generally offers sporting rates. It's open daily from 9.30 am to 8 pm.

Post & Communications The main post office is in the gigantic Palacio de Comunicaciones on Plaza de la Cibeles. Poste restante (lista de correos) is at window 17 and is open weekdays from 8 am to 9.30 pm and on Saturday from 8.30 am to 2 pm.

The Telefónica *locutorios* (phone centres) at Gran Vía 30 and Paseo de Recoletos 37-41 (near Plaza de Colón) have phone books for the whole country and cabins where you can make calls in relative peace. Both are open daily from 9.30 am to midnight.

Cybercafés Those needing an Internet fix can head to La Casa de Internet, Calle de Luchana 20 (metro: Bilbao). You pay 500 ptas per half-hour online. It is one of several places.

Travel Agencies For cheap travel tickets try Viajes Zeppelin (☎ 91 542 51 54), Plaza de Santo Domingo 2; or TIVE (☎ 91 543 74 12), the student and youth travel organisation, at Calle de Fernando el Católico 88 or in the Instituto de la Juventud (☎ 91 347 77 78) at Calle de José Ortega y Gasset 71. Both open Monday to Friday from 9 am to 1 pm.

Bookshops La Casa del Libro, Gran Vía 29-31, has a broad selection of books on all subjects, including books in English and

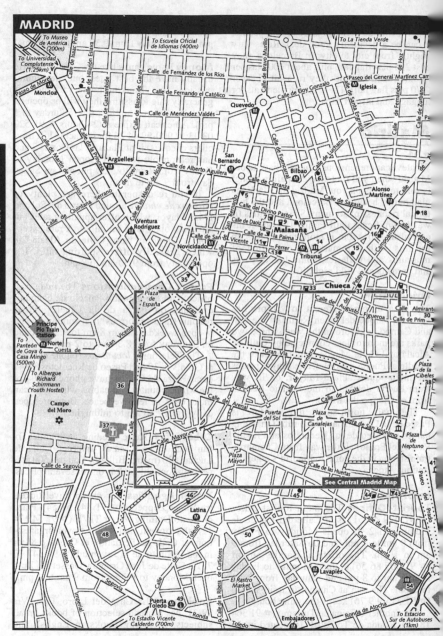

MADRID

SPAIN

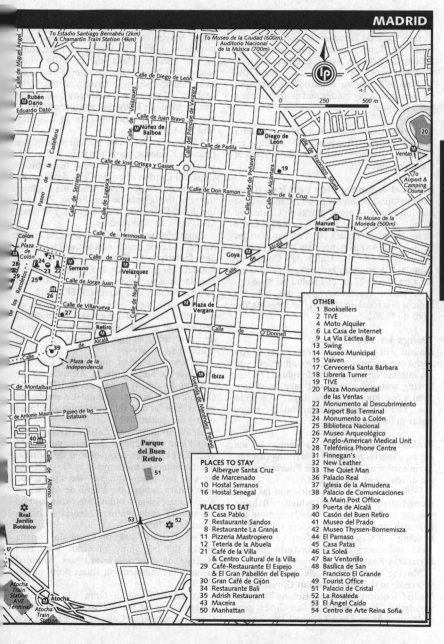

MADRID

To Estadio Santiago Bernabéu (2km)
& Chamartín Train Station (4km)

To Museo de la Ciudad (600m),
Auditorio Nacional
de la Música (700m)

Calle de Diego de León

Rubén Darío
Eduardo Dato

Calle de Juan Bravo

Núñez de Balboa

Calle de José Ortega y Gasset

Diego de León

Calle de Padilla

Ventas

To Airport &
Camping
Osuna

Calle de Don Ramón

Manuel Becerra

To Museo de la
Moneda (500m)

Colón
Plaza de Colón

Serrano

Calle de Goya

Goya

Velázquez

Calle de Jorge Juan

Calle de Villanueva

Retiro

Plaza de Vergara

O'Donnell

Plaza de la
Independencia

Ibiza

C de Montalbán

C de Antonio Maura

Paseo de las Estatuas

Parque
del Buen
Retiro

Real
Jardín
Botánico

Atocha
Train
Station
AVE
Terminal

Atocha

Atocha
Train
Station

OTHER
1 Booksellers
2 TIVE
4 Moto Alquiler
6 La Casa de Internet
9 La Vía Lactea Bar
13 Swing
14 Museo Municipal
15 Vaiven
17 Cervecería Santa Bárbara
18 Librería Turner
19 TIVE
20 Plaza Monumental
de las Ventas
22 Monumento al Descubrimiento
23 Airport Bus Terminal
24 Monumento a Colón
25 Biblioteca Nacional
26 Museo Arqueológico
27 Anglo-American Medical Unit
28 Telefónica Phone Centre
31 Finnegan's
32 New Leather
33 The Quiet Man
36 Palacio Real
37 Iglesia de la Almudena
38 Palacio de Comunicaciones
& Main Post Office
39 Puerta de Alcalá
40 Casón del Buen Retiro
41 Museo del Prado
42 Museo Thyssen-Bornemisza
44 El Parnaso
45 Casa Patas
46 La Soleá
47 Bar Ventorillo
48 Basílica de San
Francisco El Grande
49 Tourist Office
51 Palacio de Cristal
52 La Rosaleda
53 El Ángel Caído
54 Centro de Arte Reina Sofía

PLACES TO STAY
3 Albergue Santa Cruz
de Marcenado
10 Hostal Serranos
16 Hostal Senegal

PLACES TO EAT
5 Casa Pablo
7 Restaurante Sandos
8 Restaurante La Granja
11 Pizzería Mastropiero
12 Tetería de la Abuela
21 Café de la Villa
& Centro Cultural de la Villa
29 Café-Restaurante El Espejo
& El Gran Pabellón del Espejo
30 Gran Café de Gijón
34 Restaurante Bali
35 Adrish Restaurant
43 Maceira
50 Manhattan

SPAIN

other languages. For English-language books, you could also try either Librería Turner, Calle de Zurbano 10, or Booksellers, Calle de José Abascal 48. Librería de Mujeres, Calle de San Cristóbal 17, is a women's bookshop. La Tienda Verde, Calle de Maudes 38 (metro: Cuatro Caminos), specialises in walking guides and maps for many parts of Spain.

Laundry Laundrettes include Lavandería España on Calle del Infante, Lavomatique on Calle de Cervantes, and Lavandería Alba at Calle del Barco 26.

Medical & Emergency Services If you have medical problems pop into the nearest Insalud clinic – often marked 'Centro de Salud'. A handy one in the centre is at Calle de las Navas de Tolosa 10. You can also get help at the Anglo-American Medical Unit (☎ 91 435 18 23), Calle del Conde de Aranda 1. For an ambulance call the Cruz Roja on ☎ 522 22 22 or Insalud on ☎ 061.

In police emergency you can call the Policía Nacional on ☎ 091 or the Guardia Civil on ☎ 062.

Things to See & Do
Madrid will make a lot more sense if you spend some time walking around before you get into the city's cultural delights. The following walking tour could take anywhere from a few hours to a few days – it's up to you. You'll find more detail on the major sights in following sections.

Walking Tour Unless you want to hit the big art galleries first, the most fitting place to begin exploring Madrid is the **Puerta del Sol**, the official centre of Madrid.

Walk up Calle de Preciados and take the second street on the left, which will bring you out to Plaza de las Descalzas. Note the **baroque doorway** in the Caja de Madrid building – it was built for King Felipe V in 1733 and faces the **Monasterio de las Descalzas Reales**.

Moving south down Calle de San Martín you come to the **Iglesia de San Ginés**, one of Madrid's oldest churches. Behind it is the wonderful **Chocolatería de San Ginés**, generally open from 7 to 10 pm and 1 to 7 am.

Continue down to and cross Calle Mayor, and then into Madrid's most famous square, **Plaza Mayor**. After a coffee on the plaza, head west along Calle Mayor until you come to the historic **Plaza de la Villa**, with Madrid's 17th-century *ayuntamiento* (town hall). On the same square stand the 16th-century **Casa de Cisneros** and the Gothic-Mudéjar **Torre de los Lujanes**, one of the city's oldest buildings, dating from the Middle Ages.

Take the street down the left side of the Casa de Cisneros, cross the road at the end, go down the stairs and follow the cobbled Calle del Cordón out onto Calle de Segovia. Almost directly in front of you is the Mudéjar tower of the **Iglesia de San Pedro**. Proceeding down Costanilla de San Pedro you reach the **Iglesia de San Andrés**.

From here you cross Plaza de la Puerta de Moros and head south-west to the **Basílica de San Francisco El Grande**, or east past the market along Plaza de la Cebada – once a popular spot for public executions – to head into the Sunday flea market of **El Rastro**.

Otherwise, head west into the tangle of lanes that forms what was once the **morería** and emerge on Calle de Bailén and the wonderful *terrazas* of Las Vistillas – great for drinking in the views.

Follow the viaduct north to the **Catedral de Nuestra Señora de la Almudena**, the **Palacio Real** (royal palace) and Plaza de Oriente, with its statues, fountains and hedge mazes. The far east side of the plaza is closed off by the **Teatro Real**.

At its northern end, Calle de Bailén runs into **Plaza de España**. Nearby, you could visit the **Ermita de San Antonio de Florida**, which contains a masterpiece by Goya. If you were to continue north past the square you would pass through the Barrio de Argüelles, with some pleasant summer terrazas, and on towards the main centre of Madrid's Universidad Complutense.

The eastern flank of Plaza de España marks the beginning of **Gran Vía**. This Haussmannesque boulevard was slammed through the tumbledown slums north of Sol in 1911.

At the east end of Gran Vía, note the superb dome of the **Metropolis Building**. Continue east along Calle de Alcalá until you

CENTRAL MADRID

PLACES TO STAY
1 Hostal El Pinar
2 Hostal Besaya
5 Hostal Medieval
7 Hostal Odesa
9 Hotel Laris
15 Hotel Regente
22 Pensión Luz
33 Hostal Riesco
35 Hostal Santa Cruz
38 Hostal Tineo & Hostal Gibert
45 Pensión Poza
46 Hostal Lucense & Hostal Prado
51 Hostal Mondragón;
   Hostal León
56 Hostal Dulcinea
57 Hostal Gonzalo;
   Hostal Cervantes
61 Hostal Vetusta
66 Hostal La Macarena
71 Hostal Castro;
   Hostal San Antonio
73 Hostal Casanova
76 Hostal López
79 Hostal Matute

PLACES TO EAT
10 Bar Restaurante Cuchifrito
13 Restaurante Integral Artemisa
18 Taberna del Alabardero
19 Restaurante La Paella Real
21 Café del Real
31 Chocolatería de San Ginés
36 Museo del Jamón

39 La Casa del Abuelo
41 Las Bravas
42 La Trucha
47 La Trucha
50 Mesón La Casolera
52 Restaurante Integral Artemisa
67 Restaurante Sobrino de Botín
72 Restaurante Pasadero
75 Restaurante La Biotika
77 Restaurante La Sanabresa

OTHER
3 Morocco Disco
4 Lavandería Alba (Laundrette)
6 Cruising Bar
8 Rimmel Bar
11 Telefónica Phone Centre
12 Cock Bar
14 La Casa del Libro
16 Centro de Salud
17 Viajes Zeppelin
20 Teatro Real
23 Monasterio de las
   Descalzas Reales
24 El Corte Inglés
   Department Store
25 Police Station
26 Edificio Metropolis
27 RENFE Train Booking Office
28 Police Station
29 Teatro de la Zarzuela
30 Cambios Uno
32 Iglesia de San Ginés
34 Librería de Mujeres

37 La Cartuja Disco
40 Torero Disco
43 Suristán
44 Teatro de la Comedia
48 Viva Madrid
49 La Venencia Bar
53 Carbones Bar
54 American Express
55 Tourist Office
58 Casa de Lope de Vega
59 Lavomatique (Laundrette)
60 La Moderna Bar
62 Mercado de San Miguel
63 Ayuntamiento (City Hall)
64 Casa de Cisneros
65 Torre de los Lujanes
68 Tourist Office
69 Teatro Calderón
70 Lavandería España (Laundrette)
74 Convento de las Trinitarias
78 Café Populart
80 Iglesia de San Pedro
81 Iglesia de San Andrés

SPAIN

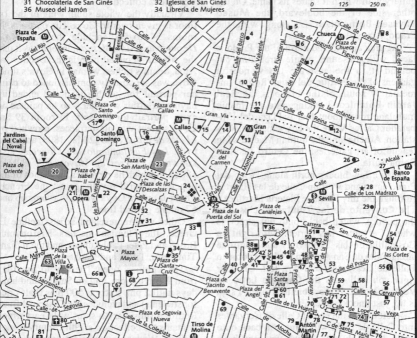

reach **Plaza de la Cibeles**, Madrid's favourite roundabout.

Head north (left) up the tree-lined promenade of Paseo de los Recoletos. On the left you'll pass some of the city's best known cafés, including Gran Café de Gijón, El Espejo and El Gran Pabellón del Espejo. On your right is the enormous **Biblioteca Nacional** (National Library), and a little farther on a statue of Columbus in Plaza de Colón.

From here walk around the back of the National Library, where the **Museo Arqueológico Nacional** is housed. South along Calle de Serrano is Plaza de la Independencia, in the middle of which stands the **Puerta de Alcalá**. The gate was begun at Plaza de la Cibeles to celebrate the arrival of Carlos III in Madrid in 1769, was completed in 1778, and later moved as the city grew.

Turn right and then left at Plaza de la Cibeles to head south down Paseo del Prado, an extension of the city's main tree-lined boulevard, and you'll soon reach the art gallery with which it shares its name. On the other side of the boulevard, the **Museo Thyssen-Bornemisza** is, along with the **Prado**, a must.

The area around and north of the Prado is laced with museums, while stretching out behind it to the east are the wonderful gardens of the **Parque del Buen Retiro**. Immediately south of the Prado is the **Real Jardín Botánico**. Looking onto the manic multilane roundabout that is Plaza del Emperador Carlos V are the city's main railway station, **Atocha**, and the third in Madrid's big league of art galleries, the **Centro de Arte Reina Sofía**.

Head a few blocks north along Paseo del Prado again and west up Calle de las Huertas (through the tiny Plaza de Platería Martínez). The **Convento de las Trinitarias** (closed to the public), which backs onto this street, is where Cervantes lies buried. Turn right up Costanilla de las Trinitarias and continue along Calle de San Agustín until you come to Calle de Cervantes, and turn left. On your right you will pass the **Casa de Lope de Vega** at No 11. If the 'abierto' ('open') sign is up, just knock and enter.

A left turn at the end of Calle de Cervantes into Calle de León will bring you back onto Calle de las Huertas, which you may have

already noticed is one of Madrid's happening streets. Anywhere along here or up on Plaza de Santa Ana will make a great place to take a load off at the end of this gruelling tour! For specific tips, consult the Entertainment section.

Museo del Prado The Prado is one of the world's great art galleries. Its main emphasis is on Spanish, Flemish and Italian art from the 15th to 19th centuries, and one of its strengths lies in the generous coverage given to certain individual geniuses. Whole strings of rooms are devoted to three of Spain's greats – Velázquez, El Greco and Goya.

Of Velázquez's works, it's *Las Meninas* that most people come to see, and this masterpiece – depicting maids of honour attending the daughter of King Felipe IV, and Velázquez himself painting portraits of the queen and king (through whose eyes the scene is witnessed) – takes pride of place in room 12 on the 1st floor, the focal point of the Velázquez collection.

Virtually the whole south wing of the 1st floor is given over to Goya. His portraits, in rooms 34 to 38, include the pair *Maja Desnuda* and *Maja Vestida*; legend has it that the woman depicted here is the Duchess of Alba, Spain's richest woman in Goya's time. Goya was supposedly commissioned to paint her portrait for her husband and ended up having an affair with her – so he painted an extra portrait for himself. In room 39 are Goya's great war masterpieces, crowned by *El Dos de Mayo 1808* (2 May 1808) and, next to it, *Los Fusilamientos de Moncloa*, also known as *El Tres de Mayo 1808* (3 May 1808), in which he recreates the pathos of the hopeless Madrid revolt against the French. There are more Goya works in rooms 66 and 67 on the ground floor.

Other well-represented artists include El Greco, the Flemish masters Hieronymus Bosch and Peter Paul Rubens, and the Italians Tintoretto, Titian and Raphael.

The Prado is open Tuesday to Saturday from 9 am to 7 pm, and on Sunday and holidays until 2 pm. Entry is 500 ptas (half price for students) and includes the Casón del Buen Retiro, a subsidiary a short walk east which contains the collection's 19th-century works. It opens Wednesday to Friday from 11 am to

2.30 pm and 3.30 pm to 8 pm; weekends all day. Tickets costs 500 ptas, but entry is free on Sunday and Saturday afternoon (2.30 to 7 pm), as well as on selected national holidays. A 'Paseo del Arte' ticket for 1050 ptas gives you access to the Prado, Centro de Arte Reina Sofia and Museo Thyssen-Bornemisza. You have a year to use up the three entries.

Centro de Arte Reina Sofia At Calle de Santa Isabel 52, opposite Atocha station, the Reina Sofia museum houses a superb collection of predominantly Spanish modern art. The exhibition focuses on the period 1900 to 1940, and includes, in room 7, Picasso's famous *Guernica*, his protest at the German bombing of the Basque town of Guernica during the Spanish Civil War in 1937. The day of the bombing, 26 April, had been a typical market day in the town of 5000 people. Because of the market there were another 5000 people selling their wares or doing their weekly shopping. The bombs started to drop at 4 pm. By the time they stopped, three hours later, the town and thousands of the people in it had been annihilated.

Guernica was painted in Paris. Picasso insisted that it stay outside Spain until Franco and his cronies were gone and democracy had been restored. It was secretly brought to Spain in 1981, and moved here from the Casón del Buen Retiro in 1992. It's displayed with a collection of preliminary sketches and paintings which Picasso put together in May 1937.

The museum also contains further work by Picasso, while room 9 is devoted to Salvador Dalí's surrealist work and room 13 contains a collection of Joan Miró's late works, characterised by their remarkable simplicity.

The gallery opens Monday to Saturday from 10 am to 9 pm (except Tuesday, when it is closed), and Sunday from 10 am to 2.30 pm. Entry is 500 ptas (half price for students).

Museo Thyssen-Bornemisza Purchased by Spain in 1993 for something over US$300 million (a snip), this extraordinary collection of 800 paintings was formerly the private collection of the German-Hungarian family of magnates, the Thyssen-Bornemiszas. Starting with medieval religious art, it moves on through Titian, El Greco and Rubens to Cézanne, Monet and Van Gogh, then from Miró, Picasso and Gris to Pollock, Dalí and Lichtenstein, thereby offering one of the best and most comprehensive art-history lessons you'll ever have. The museum is at Paseo del Prado 8, almost opposite the Prado, and opens Tuesday to Sunday from 10 am to 7 pm. Entry is 700 ptas (400 ptas for students). Separate temporary exhibitions generally cost more.

Palacio Real Madrid's 18th-century Royal Palace is a lesson in what can happen if you give your interior decorators a free hand. You'll see some of the most elaborately decorated walls and ceilings imaginable, including the sublime Throne Room (and other rooms of more dubious merit). This over-the-top palace hasn't been used as a royal residence for some time and today is only used for official receptions and, of course, tourism.

The first series of rooms you strike after buying your ticket is the Farmacia Real (Royal Pharmacy), an unending array of medicine jars and stills for mixing royal concoctions. The Armería Real (Royal Armoury) is a shiny collection of mostly 16th and 17th-century weapons and royal suits of armour. Elsewhere are a good selection of Goyas, 215 absurdly ornate clocks from the Royal Clock Collection, and five Stradivarius violins, still used for concerts and balls. Most of the tapestries in the palace were made in the Royal Tapestry Factory. All the chandeliers are original and no two are the same.

The palace is open Monday to Saturday from 9.30 am to 5.30 pm, and Sunday and holidays 9 am to 2 pm. Entry costs 850 ptas (350 ptas for students), but is free on Wednesday for EU citizens (bring your passport). The nearest metro station is Opera.

Monasterio de las Descalzas Reales The Convent of the Barefoot Royals, on Plaza de las Descalzas, was founded in 1559 by Juana of Austria, daughter of the Spanish king Carlos I, and became one of Spain's richest religious houses thanks to gifts from noblewomen. Much of the wealth came in the form of art: on the obligatory guided tour you'll be confronted by a number of tapestries based on works by Rubens, and a

SPAIN

wonderful painting entitled *The Voyage of the 11,000 Virgins*. Juana of Austria is buried here. The convent is open Tuesday to Saturday from 10.30 am to 12.30 pm and again (except Friday) from 4 to 5.30 pm. On Sunday and holidays it opens from 11 am to 1.30 pm. Admission costs 650 ptas (250 ptas for students), but is free on Wednesday for EU citizens.

Panteón de Goya Also called the Ermita de San Antonio de la Florida, this little church contains not only Goya's tomb, directly in front of the altar, but also one of his greatest works – the entire ceiling and dome, beautifully painted with religious scenes (and recently restored). The scenes on the dome depict the miracle of St Anthony. The panteón is the first of two small churches 700m north-west along Paseo de la Florida from Príncipe Pío metro station. The chapel opens Tuesday to Friday from 10 am to 2 pm and 4 to 8 pm, and on the weekend from 10 am to 2 pm. Entry is 300 ptas (free on Wednesday and Sunday).

Museo Arqueológico This museum on Calle de Serrano traces the history of the peninsula from the earliest prehistoric cave paintings to the Iberian, Roman, Carthaginian, Greek, Visigothic, Moorish and Christian eras. Exhibits include mosaics, pottery, fossilised bones and a partial reconstruction of the prehistoric Altamira cave paintings. It's open Tuesday to Saturday from 9.30 am to 8.30 pm, and Sunday from 9.30 am to 2 pm. Entry costs 500 ptas (students pay half), but is free on Sunday and from 2.30 pm on Saturday.

Other Museums Madrid almost has more museums than the Costa del Sol has high-rise apartments. They include: the **Museo Municipal**, with assorted art including some Goyas, and some beautiful old maps, scale models, silver, porcelain and period furniture; the **Museo de la Moneda**, which follows the history of coinage in great detail and contains a mind-boggling collection of coins and paper money; the **Museo de América** with stuff brought from the Americas from the 16th to 20th centuries; and even the **Museo de la Ciudad**, perfectly described

by one traveller as 'a must for infrastructure buffs!', which rather drily traces the growth of Madrid. Check the tourist office's *Enjoy Madrid* brochure for more details.

Real Jardín Botánico The perfect answer to an overdose of art and history could be this beautiful botanic garden next door to the Prado. The eight-hectares gardens are open daily from 10 am to 8 pm and entrance costs 200 ptas.

Parque del Buen Retiro This is another great place to escape hustle and bustle. On a warm spring day walk between the flowerbeds and hedges or just sprawl out on one of the lawns.

Stroll along **Paseo de las Estatuas**, a path lined with statues originally from the Palacio Real. It ends at a lake overlooked by a **statue of Alfonso XII**. There are rowing boats for rent at the northern end when the weather is good.

Perhaps the most important, and certainly the most controversial, of the park's other monuments is *El Ángel Caído* (The Fallen Angel). First-prize winner at an international exhibition in Paris in 1878, this is said to be the first statue in the world dedicated to the devil.

You should also visit some of the park's gardens, such as the exquisite **La Rosaleda** (rose garden), and the **Chinese Garden** on a tiny island near the Fallen Angel. The all-glass **Palacio de Cristal** in the middle of the park occasionally stages modern-art exhibitions.

Campo del Moro This stately garden is directly behind the Palacio Real, and the palace is visible through the trees from just about all points. A couple of fountains and statues, a thatch-roofed pagoda and a carriage museum provide artificial diversions, but nature is the real attraction.

El Rastro If you get up early on a Sunday morning you'll find the city almost deserted, until you get to El Rastro. It is one of the biggest flea markets you're ever likely to see, and if you're prepared to hunt around, you can find almost anything. The market spreads along and between Calle de Ribera de Curtidores and Calle de los Embajadores (metro: Latina). It's said to be the place to go if you want to buy your car stereo back – watch your pockets and bags.

Language Courses

The Universidad Complutense offers a range of language and culture courses throughout the year. Contact the Secretaría de los Cursos para Extranjeros (☎ 91 394 53 25; fax 91 394 52 98), Facultad de Filología (Edificio A), Universidad Complutense, Ciudad Universitaria, 28040 Madrid.

Another option is the rather overworked Escuela Oficial de Idiomas (☎ 91 533 00 88, 91 554 99 77), Calle de Jesús Maestro s/n, which has Spanish-language courses at most levels. There are many private language schools too.

Organised Tours

You can pick up a Madrid Vision bus around the centre of Madrid up to 10 times a day. There are only three on Sunday and holidays. A full round trip costs 1700 ptas and you can board the bus at any of 14 clearly marked stops. Taped commentaries in four languages, including English, are available, and the bus stops at several major monuments, including the Prado and near Plaza Mayor. If you buy the 2200 ptas ticket, you can use the buses all day to get around (2900 ptas buys you the same right for two days running).

Special Events

Madrid's major fiesta celebrates its patron saint, San Isidro Labrador, throughout the third week of May. There are free music performances around the city and one of the country's top bullfight seasons at the Plaza Monumental de las Ventas. The Malasaña district, already busy enough (see Entertainment later), has its biggest party on 2 May, and the Fiesta de San Juan is held in the Parque del Buen Retiro for the seven days leading up to 24 June. The few locals who haven't left town in August will be celebrating the consecutive festivals of La Paloma, San Cayetano and San Lorenzo. The last week of September is Chamartín's Fiesta de Otoño (Autumn Festival) – about the only time you would go to Chamartín other than to catch a train.

Places to Stay

Finding a place to stay in Madrid is never really a problem.

Camping There is one camping ground within striking distance of central Madrid. To reach **Camping Osuna** (☎ 91 741 05 10), on Avenida de Logroño near the airport, take metro No 5 to Canillejas (the end of the line), from where it's about 500m. It charges 630 ptas per person, car and tent.

Hostels There are two HI youth hostels in Madrid. The **Albergue Richard Schirrman** (☎ 91 463 56 99) is in the Casa de Campo park (metro: El Lago; bus No 33 from Plaza Ópera). B&B in a room of four costs 950 ptas (under 26) or 1300 ptas.

The **Albergue Santa Cruz de Marcenado** (☎ 91 547 45 32), Calle de Santa Cruz de Marcenado 28 (metro: Argüelles; bus Nos 1, 61 and Circular), has rooms for four, six and eight people. B&B costs the same as in the other hostel. This is one of the few Spanish hostels in HI's International Booking Network.

Hostales & Pensiones These tend to cluster in three or four parts of the city and the price-to-quality ratio is fairly standard. In summer the city is drained of people, thanks to the horrific heat, so if you are mad enough to be here then, you may well be able to make a hot deal on the price. At other times it's only worth trying to bargain if you intend to stay a while.

Around Plaza de Santa Ana Santa Ana is one of Madrid's 'in' districts. Close to Sol and within walking distance of the Prado and Atocha train station, it's also home to countless bars, cafés and restaurants of all classes.

North of the plaza, there's a choice of at least five hostales at Carrera de San Jerónimo 32. **Hostal Mondragón** (☎ 91 429 68 16), on the 4th floor, is pretty good value at 2000/2800 ptas for a biggish single/double without own bathroom. **Hostal León** (☎ 91 429 67 78) in the same building is not bad and has heating in winter. It charges 1800/3000 ptas, although some doubles cost 4000 ptas.

SPAIN

There are a number of very popular places on Calle de Núñez de Arce. *Hostal Lucense* (☎ 91 522 48 88) at No 15 and *Pensión Poza* (☎ 91 232 20 65) at No 9 are owned by the same people (who used to live in Australia). Small, sometimes windowless, rooms start at around 1000 ptas per person, but you can get better ones for 1500/2600 ptas. A hot shower costs 200 ptas extra. In the same building as the Lucense, *Hostal Prado* (☎ 91 521 30 73) on the 2nd floor offers rooms of a similar quality from 1800/3200 ptas.

Hostal Matute (☎ 91 429 55 85), Plaza de Matute 11, has spacious singles/doubles for 2500/4700 ptas without own bath and 3500/5400 ptas with. *Hostal Vetusta* (☎ 91 429 64 04), Calle de las Huertas 3, has small but cute rooms with own shower starting at 2000/3500 ptas; try for one looking onto the street.

Roughly halfway between Atocha train station and Santa Ana, *Hostal López* (☎ 91 429 43 49), Calle de las Huertas 54, is a good choice. Singles/doubles start at 2600/4000 ptas without own bath, or 3800/4800 ptas with.

Hostal Casanova (☎ 91 429 56 91), Calle de Lope de Vega 8, has simple rooms at 2000/3100 ptas. *Hostal Castro* (☎ 91 429 51 47), Calle de León 13, is an attractive place with good, clean rooms at 2300/4000 ptas with own bath. *Hostal San Antonio* (☎ 91 429 51 37), one floor up, also has reasonable rooms with private bath and TV for 3000/4000 ptas.

Hostal Gonzalo (☎ 91 429 27 14), Calle de Cervantes 34, is in sparkling nick. Singles/doubles with private shower and TV are 4000/5200 ptas. The staff will take a few hundred pesetas off the bill if you stay at least three days. If it doesn't satisfy, *Hostal Cervantes* (☎ 91 429 27 45), on the 2nd floor, is OK but more expensive, with rooms ranging up to 4500/6000 ptas.

At No 19, *Hostal Dulcinea* (☎ 91 429 41 71) has well-maintained if simply furnished rooms and is often full. Rooms cost 3800/4800 ptas.

Around Puerta del Sol *You* can't get more central than Plaza de la Puerta del Sol. Generally you'll pay for this privilege, but there are still some good deals in the surrounding streets.

The pick of the bunch is *Hostal Riesco* (☎ 91 522 26 92) at Calle de Correo 2 (3rd floor). Singles/doubles with shower cost 3200/4300 ptas, or 3600/5000 ptas with full bathroom.

Hostal Tineo (☎ 91 521 49 43), Calle de la Victoria 6, charges a standard 2500/3500 ptas for singles/doubles with washbasin only. They range up to 4000/5500 ptas for rooms with private bathroom. In the same building, *Hostal Gibert* (☎ 91 522 42 14) has rooms without bath for the same price, or doubles with private bath for 4000 ptas.

Around Plaza Mayor Plaza Mayor, Madrid's true heart, is not a major accommodation area, but there are a few good options scattered among all the open-air cafés, tapas bars, ancient restaurants and souvenir shops.

Hostal Santa Cruz (☎ 91 522 24 41), Plaza de Santa Cruz 6, is in a prime location. Rooms here start from about 3400/4800 ptas. The more upmarket *Hostal La Macarena* (☎ 91 365 92 21), Cava de la Cava de San Miguel 8, has good rooms with private bath, TV and phone but at 4500/6500 ptas, you pay mainly for the position.

Pensión Luz (☎ 91 542 07 59), Calle de las Fuentes 10, is a friendly place with decent little rooms at 2500/3700 ptas.

Around Gran Vía The hostales on and around Gran Vía tend to be a little more expensive. All the same, it's another popular area.

Hostal El Pinar (☎ 91 547 32 82), Calle de Isabel la Católica 19, has reasonable rooms for 2300/3800 ptas. The stylish *Hostal Besaya* (☎ 91 541 32 07), Calle de San Bernardo 13, has good rooms ranging up to 4500/6200 ptas with private bath.

Hotel Regente (☎ 91 521 29 41), Calle de los Mesoneros Romanos 9, has decent mid-range rooms with private bath, TV, air-con and telephone for 5500/9100 ptas plus IVA. *Hotel Laris* (☎ 91 521 46 80), Calle del Barco 3, is slightly cheaper at 5000/7900 ptas.

Calle de Fuencarral has plenty of options. At No 45, *Hostal Medieval* (☎ 91 522 25 49), Calle de Fuencarral 46, has spacious and bright singles/doubles with shower for 3000/

4000 ptas. Doubles with full private bathroom cost 5500 ptas. *Hostal Ginebra* (☎ 91 532 10 35) at No 17 is a fine choice not far from Gran Vía. All rooms have TV and phone, and singles with shower start at 3600 ptas, while doubles with full bathroom cost 4800 ptas. *Hostal Serranos* (☎ 91 448 89 87), No 95, is spick and span, and rooms with bath and TV are 3000/5000 ptas.

Hostal Odesa (☎ 91 521 03 38), Calle de Hortaleza 38, has straightforward rooms for 2500/4500 ptas – the doubles have private bath and TV. This place caters to a primarily gay clientele.

Hostal Senegal (☎ 91 319 07 71), Plaza de Santa Bárbara 8, is in a pretty spot and has decent rooms with private bath for 4500/5800 ptas.

Rental Many of the hostales mentioned above will do a deal on long stays. This may include a considerable price reduction, meals and laundry. It is simply a matter of asking. For longer stays, check the rental pages of *Segundamano* magazine or notice boards at universities, the Escuela Oficial de Idiomas and cultural institutes like the British Council or Alliance Française.

Places to Eat

Around Santa Ana There are tons of Gallego seafood restaurants in this area, but the best is the newly opened *Maceira*, away from the main tourist hubbub at Calle de Jesús 7. Splash your pulpo a la gallega down with a crisp white Ribeiro.

In *La Casa del Abuelo*, Calle de la Victoria 14, on a back street south-east of Puerta del Sol, you can sip a chato (small glass) of the heavy El Abuelo red wine while munching on heavenly king prawns, grilled or with garlic. Next, duck around the corner to *Las Bravas*, Callejón de Álvarez Gato, for a caña and the best patatas bravas in town. The antics of the bar staff are themselves enough to merit a pit stop and the distorting mirrors are a minor Madrid landmark.

La Trucha, Calle de Núñez de Arce 6, is one of Madrid's great bars for tapas. It's just off Plaza de Santa Ana, and there's another nearby at Calle de Manuel Fernández y González 3. You could eat your fill at the bar or sit down in the restaurant.

Something of an institution is the *Museo del Jamón*. Walk in to one of these places and you'll understand the name. Huge clumps of every conceivable type of ham dangle all over the place. You can eat plates and plates of ham – the Spaniards' single most favoured source of nutrition. There's one on Calle de la Victoria, just east of Sol.

Mesón La Casolera, Calle de Echegaray 3, is an unassuming but popular hang-out with madrileños. Ask for a fritura, a mixed platter of deep-fried seafood.

If it's just plain cheap you want, *Restaurante Pasadero*, Calle de Lope de Vega 9, has a solid set lunch menú for 1100 ptas. Cheaper still and very good is *Restaurante La Sanabresa*, Calle del Amor de Dios 12.

Vegetarians generally do not have an easy time of it Spain, but Madrid offers a few safe ports. *Restaurante La Biotika*, Calle del Amor de Dios 3, is a reliable favourite. It is virtually vegan. *Restaurante Integral Artemisa*, Calle de Ventura de la Vega 4, is excellent. A full meal can cost from 1500 ptas to 2000 ptas, and there is another branch off Gran Vía at Calle de las Tres Cruces 4.

Around Plaza Mayor You know you're getting close to Plaza Mayor when you see signs in English saying 'Typical Spanish Restaurant' and 'Hemingway Never Ate Here'. Nevertheless, when the sun's shining (or rising) there's not a finer place to be than at one of the outdoor cafés in the plaza.

Calle de la Cava San Miguel and Calle de Cuchilleros are packed with mesones that aren't bad for a little tapas hopping. A cut above the rest is *Restaurante Sobrino de Botín*, Calle de Cuchilleros 17, one of Europe's oldest restaurants (established in 1725), where the set menú costs 4165 ptas – it's popular with those who can afford it.

Other Areas Just about anywhere you go in central Madrid, you can find cheap restaurants with good food.

Manhattan, 500m south of Plaza Mayor at Calle de la Encomienda 5, is a busy, no-frills establishment that fills up quickly for its 800 ptas lunch menú. *Bar Restaurante Cuchifrito* at Calle de Valverde 9 is a plain, simple eating house with a set menú for 900 ptas. *Casa Mingo* at Paseo de la Florida 2, near the Panteón de Goya, is a great old place for chicken and cider. A full roast bird, salad and bottle of cider – enough for two – comes to less than 2000 ptas.

If you're after paella at all costs, head for *Restaurante La Paella Real*, Calle de Arrieta 2 near Plaza de Oriente, which does a whole range of rice-based dishes from 1500 ptas. For a really excellent meal in a cosy atmosphere try *Taberna del Alabardero*, nearby at Calle de Felipe V 6. Expect little change from 5000 ptas per person. If this is a bit steep, consider a couple of the mouthwatering tapas at the bar.

In the Malasaña area around Plaza del Dos de Mayo, *Restaurante La Granja* on Calle de San Andrés has a vegetarian menú for 900 ptas. *Restaurante Sandos*, Plaza del Dos de Mayo 8, can do you a cheap outdoor pizza and beer. Better still is the crowded *Pizzeria Mastropiero*, Calle de San Vicente Ferrer 34 (corner Calle del Dos de Mayo), a justifiably popular Argentine-run joint where you can get pizza by the slice. A couple of blocks away, *Casa Pablo*, also known as La Glorieta, Calle de Manuela Malasaña 37, is a rather polished place with good, modestly priced food – the 1050 ptas menú is excellent value.

The Plaza de España area is a good hunting ground for non-Spanish food, though you're looking at 2000 to 2500 ptas for a meal in the better places. *Restaurante Bali*, Calle de San Bernardino 6, has authentic Indonesian fare. The *Adrish*, virtually across the street at No 1, is about Madrid's best Indian restaurant.

Cafés Madrid has so many fine places for a coffee and a light bite that you'll certainly find your own favourites. Ours include: the historic, elegant *Café-Restaurante El Espejo*, Paseo de Recoletos 31 (you could also sit at the turn-of-the-century-style *El Gran Pabellón del Espejo* outside); the equally graceful *Gran Café de Gijón* just down the road; the more down-to-earth *Café de la Villa* in the cultural centre of the same name on Plaza de Colón, a cheery den for arty types and office workers; *Café del Real*, Plaza de Isabel II, with a touch of faded elegance, is good for breakfast and busy at night too. An enchanting teahouse with a hint of the 1960s is the *Tetería de la Abuela*, Calle

del Espíritu Santo 19. Along with the great range of teas you can indulge in scrummy crêpes.

Self-Catering The *Mercado de San Miguel*, just west of Plaza Mayor, is a good place to stock up on food for a cheap lunch.

Entertainment

A copy of the weekly *Guía del Ocio* (125 ptas at newsstands) will give you a good rundown of what's on in Madrid. Its comprehensive listings include music gigs, art exhibitions, cinema, TV and theatre. It's very handy even if you can't read Spanish.

Bars The epicentres of Madrid's nightlife are the Santa Ana-Calle de las Huertas area, and the Malasaña-Chueca zone north of Gran Vía. The latter has a decidedly lowlife element.

Any of the bars on Plaza de Santa Ana makes a pleasant stop, especially when you can sit outside in the warmer months. *La Moderna* attracts a mixed and buzzy crowd. Though it gets very crowded at weekends, you should look into *Viva Madrid*, Calle de Manuel Fernández y González 7. Its tiles and heavy wooden ceilings make a distinctive setting for the earlier stage of your evening. On the same street, *Carbones* is a busy place open till about 4 am with good mainstream music on the jukebox. *La Venencia*, Calle de Echegaray 7, is an ill-lit, woody place that looks as if it hasn't been cleaned in years – perfect for sampling one of its six varieties of sherry.

Café Populart, Calle de las Huertas 22, often has music, generally jazz or Celtic. Just beyond the hubbub of Huertas is *El Parnaso*, a quirky but engaging bar at Calle de Moratín 25. The area around the bar is jammed with an odd assortment of decorative paraphernalia.

In Malasaña, *Cervecería Santa Bárbara* at Plaza de Santa Bárbara 8 is a classic Madrid drinking house and a good place to kick off a night out. Irish pubs are very popular in Madrid: two good ones are *The Quiet Man*, Calle de Valverde 44, and *Finnegan's*, Plaza de las Salesas 9. *La Vía Lactea*, Calle de Velarde 18, is a bright place with thumping mainstream music, a young crowd and a good drinking atmosphere.

Calle de Pelayo Campoamor is lined with an assortment of bars, graduating from noisy rock bars at the north end to gay bars at the south end, where you've reached the Chueca area, the heart of Madrid's gay nightlife. *New Leather* at No 42 is just one of the many gay bars. *Rimmel*, Calle de Luis de Góngora 4, and *Cruising*, Calle de Pérez Galdós 5, are other popular gay haunts.

The quaintly named *Cock Bar*, Calle de la Reina 16, once served as a discreet salon for high-class prostitution. The ladies in question have gone but this popular bar retains plenty of atmosphere.

Live Music & Discos Latin rhythms have quite a hold in Madrid. A good place to indulge is *Vaiven*, Travesía de San Mateo 1 in Malasaña. Entry is free and a beer is about 600 ptas. *Suristán*, Calle de la Cruz 7, near Plaza de Santa Ana, pulls in a wide variety of bands, from Cuban to African, usually starting at 11.30 pm, sometimes with a cover charge up to 1000 ptas. *Swing*, Calle de San Vicente Ferrer 23 in Malasaña, always has something on, including Caribbean music and, on Friday, pop and soul. Entry hovers around 1000 ptas. *Morocco* at Calle del Marqués de Leganés 7 in Malasaña is still a popular stop on the Madrid disco circuit. It gets going about 1 am.

Near Plaza de Santa Ana, Calle de la Cruz has a couple of good dance spaces; try to pick up fliers for them before you go – they may save you queueing. *Torero*, No 26, has Spanish music upstairs and international fare downstairs. *La Cartuja*, No 10, is also pretty popular and is open till 6 am.

La Soleá, Calle de la Cava Baja 27, is regarded by some as the last real flamenco bar in Madrid. *Casa Patas*, Calle de Cañizares 10, hosts recognised masters of flamenco song, guitar and dance. Bigger flamenco names also play some of Madrid's theatres – check listings.

Cinemas Cinemas are very reasonably priced, with tickets around 700 ptas. Films in their original language (with Spanish subtitles) are usually marked VO (*versión original*) in listings. A good part of town for these is on and around Calle de Martín de los Heros and Calle de la Princesa, near Plaza de España. The *Renoir*, *Alphaville* and *Princesa* complexes here all screen VO movies.

Classical Music, Theatre & Opera
There's plenty happening, except in summer. The city's grandest stage, the recently re-opened *Teatro Real* (☎ 91 516 06 06), is the scene for opera. If you can't get into the Teatro Real, the *Teatro Calderón* (☎ 91 369 14 34), Calle de Atocha 18, plays second fiddle. The beautiful old *Teatro de la Comedia*, Calle del Príncipe 14, home to the Compañía Nacional de Teatro Clásico, stages gems of classic Spanish and European theatre. The *Centro Cultural de la Villa*, under the waterfall at Plaza de Colón, stages everything from classical concerts to comic theatre, opera and even classy flamenco. Also important for classical music is the *Auditorio Nacional de Música*, Avenida del Príncipe de Vergara 146 (metro: Cruz del Rayo).

Spectator Sports
Spending an afternoon or evening at a football (soccer) match provides quite an insight into Spanish culture. Tickets can be bought on the day of the match, starting from around 1500 ptas, although big games may be sold out. Real Madrid's home is the huge Estadio Santiago Bernabéu (metro: Santiago Bernabéu). Atlético Madrid plays at Estadio Vicente Calderón (metro: Pirámides).

Bullfights take place most Sundays between March and October – more often during the festival of San Isidro Labrador in May, and in summer. Madrid has Spain's largest bullring, the Plaza Monumental de las Ventas (metro: Ventas), and a second bullring by metro Vista Alegre. Tickets are best bought in advance, from agencies or at the rings, and cost from under 2000 ptas.

Things to Buy
For general shopping needs, start at either the markets or the large department stores. The most famous market is El Rastro (see the section in Things to See earlier). The largest department store chain is El Corte Inglés, with a central branch just north of Sol on Calle de Preciados.

The city's premier shopping street is Calle de Serrano, a block east of Paseo de la Castellana. Calle del Almirante off Paseo de

Recoletos has a wide range of engaging, less mainstream shops. For guitars and other musical instruments, hunt around the area near the Palacio Real. For leather try the shops on Calle del Príncipe and Gran Vía, or Calle de Fuencarral for shoes. For designer clothing, try the Chueca area.

Getting There & Away

Air Scheduled and charter flights from all over the world arrive at Madrid's Barajas airport, 13km north-east of the city. With nowhere in Spain more than 12 hours away by bus or train, domestic flights are generally not good value unless you're in a burning hurry. Nor is Madrid the budget international flight capital of Europe. That said, you *can* find bargains to popular destinations such as London, Paris and New York. For an idea on domestic fares, see the Getting Around section earlier in this chapter. See also Travel Agencies under Information earlier in this Madrid section.

Airline offices in Madrid include:

American Airlines
    Calle de Pedro Teixeira 8 (☎ 91 597 20 68, 901-10 00 01)
British Airways
    Calle de Serrano 60 (☎ 91 577 69 59)
Delta Airlines
    Calle de Goya 8 (☎ 91 577 06 50)
Iberia
    Calle de Velázquez 130 (☎ 91 587 75 36, 902-40 05 00 for bookings)
Lufthansa
    Aeropuerto de Barajas (☎ 902-22 01 01)
Qantas
    Calle de la Princesa 1 (☎ 91 542 15 72)
Singapore Airlines
    Calle de Pinar 7 (☎ 91 563 80 01)

Bus There are eight bus stations dotted around Madrid. Tourist offices can tell you which one you need for your destination. Most buses to the south, and some to other places (including a number of international services), use the Estación Sur de Autobuses (☎ 91 468 42 00), Calle de Méndez Álvaro (metro: Méndez Álvaro). The choice between bus and train depends largely on where you're going – more detail on services to/from Madrid is given in other city sections in this chapter.

Train Atocha station, south of the centre, is used by most trains to/from southern Spain and many destinations around Madrid. Some trains from the north also terminate here, passing through Chamartín, the other main station (in the north of the city), on the way. Chamartín (metro: Chamartín) is smaller and generally serves destinations north of Madrid, although this rule is not cast-iron; some trains to the south use Chamartín and don't pass through Atocha.

The main RENFE booking office (☎ 91 328 90 20) is at Calle de Alcalá 44 and is open Monday to Friday from 9.30 am to 8 pm.

For information on fares, see the Getting There & Away section under the city you are going to.

Car & Motorcycle Madrid is surrounded by two ring-road systems, the older M-30 and the M-40, considerably farther out (a third, the M-50, is also planned). Roads in and out of the city can get pretty clogged at peak hours (around 8 to 10 am, 2 pm, 4 to 5 pm and 8 to 9 pm), and on Sunday night.

Car-rental companies in Madrid include Atesa/Eurodollar (☎ 91 393 72 32), Avis (☎ 91 547 20 48), Budget (☎ 91 393 72 16), Europcar (☎ 91 541 88 92) and Hertz (☎ 900-10 01 11). All these have offices at the airport, in the city centre, and often at the main train stations. Robbery on hire-cars leaving the airport is a problem, so be careful.

You can rent motorbikes from Moto Alquiler (☎ 91 542 06 57), Calle del Conde Duque 13, but it's pricey, starting at 4500 ptas plus 16% IVA per day for a 49cc Vespino. Rental is from 8 am to 8 pm and you have to leave a refundable deposit of 45,000 ptas. Something like a Yamaha 650 will cost you 16,000 ptas a day plus tax and the deposit is 150,000 ptas.

Getting Around

To/From the Airport An airport bus service runs to/from an underground terminal in Plaza de Colón every 12 to 15 minutes. The trip takes 30 minutes in average traffic and costs 380 ptas. A taxi between the airport and city centre should cost around 2000 ptas.

Bus In general, the underground (metro) is faster and easier than city buses for getting around central Madrid. Bus route maps are available from tourist offices. A single ride costs 130 ptas. A 10-ride *Metrobus* ticket (670 ptas) can be used on buses and metro. Night owls may find the 20 bus lines, running from midnight to 6 am, useful. They run from Puerta del Sol and Plaza de la Cibeles.

Metro Madrid has a very efficient, safe and simple underground system. Trains run from 6.30 am to 1.30 am. Fares are the same as on buses.

Taxi Madrid's taxis are inexpensive by European standards. They're handy late at night, although in peak hours it's quicker to walk or get the metro. From Chamartín station to Plaza de Colón costs about 1000 ptas.

Car & Motorcycle There's little point subjecting yourself to Madrid's traffic just to move from one part of the city to another, especially at peak hours. Most on-street parking space in central Madrid is designated for people with special permits, but almost everybody ignores this – also ignoring the 12,000 parking tickets slapped on vehicles every day. But you risk being towed if you park in a marked no-parking or loading zone, or if you double-park. There are plenty of car parks across the city, but they cost about 200 ptas an hour.

Around Madrid

EL ESCORIAL
The extraordinary 16th-century monastery-palace complex of San Lorenzo de El Escorial lies one hour north-west of Madrid, just outside the town of the same name.

El Escorial was built by Felipe II, king of Spain, Naples, Sicily, Milan, the Netherlands and large parts of the Americas, to commemorate his victory over the French in the battle of St Quentin (1557) and as a mausoleum for his father Carlos I, the first of Spain's Habsburg monarchs. Felipe began searching for a site in 1558, deciding on El Escorial in 1562. The last stone was placed in 1584, and the next 11 years were spent on decoration. El Escorial's austere style, reflecting not only Felipe's wishes but also the watchful eye of

architect Juan de Herrera, is loved by some, hated by others. Either way, it's a quintessential monument of Spain's golden age.

Almost all visitors to El Escorial make it a day trip from Madrid. It opens Tuesday to Sunday from 10 am to 6 pm (to 5 pm from October to March).

Information
You can get information on El Escorial from tourist offices in Madrid, or from the tourist office (☎ 91 890 15 54) close to the monastery at Calle de Floridablanca 10. It's open Monday to Friday from 10 am to 2 pm and 3 to 4.45 pm, and Saturday from 10 am to 1.45 pm.

Things to See
Above the monastery's main gateway, on its west side, stands a **statue of San Lorenzo**, holding a symbolic gridiron, the instrument of his martyrdom (he was roasted alive on one). Inside, across the Patio de los Reyes, stands the restrained **basílica**, a cavernous church with a beautiful white-marble crucifixion by Benvenuto Cellini, sculpted in 1576. At either side of the altar stand bronze statues of Carlos I and his family (to the left), and Felipe II with three of his four wives and his eldest son (on the right).

From the basílica, follow signs to the ticket office (*taquilla*), where you must pay 900 ptas (students 450 ptas) to see the other open parts of El Escorial. The price includes an optional guided tour of the *panteones* and one or two other sections.

The route you have to follow leads first to the **Museo de Arquitectura**, detailing in Spanish how El Escorial was built, and the **Museo de Pintura**, with 16th and 17th-century Spanish, Italian and Flemish fine art. You then head upstairs to the richly decorated **Palacio de Felipe II**, in one room of which the monarch died in 1598; his bed was positioned so that he could watch proceedings at the basílica's high altar. Next you descend to the **Panteón de los Reyes**, where almost all Spain's monarchs since Carlos I, and their spouses, lie in gilded marble coffins. Three empty sarcophagi await future arrivals. Backtracking a little, you find yourself in the **Panteón de los Infantes**, a larger series of chambers and tunnels housing the tombs of princes, princesses and other lesser royalty.

Finally, the **Salas Capitulares** in the southeast of the monastery house a minor treasure trove of El Grecos, Titians, Tintorettos and other old masters.

When you emerge, it's worth heading back to the entrance, where you can gain access to the **biblioteca** (library), once one of Europe's finest and still a haven for some 40,000 books. You can't handle them, but many historic and valuable volumes are on display.

Getting There & Away

The Herranz bus company runs up to 30 services a day from the Intercambiador de Autobuses at the Moncloa metro station in Madrid to San Lorenzo de El Escorial (380 ptas one way). Only about 10 run on Sunday and holidays.

Up to 20 sluggish *cercanías* trains (line C-8a) serve El Escorial from Atocha station (via Chamartín) in Madrid (430 ptas; 370 ptas on weekdays). Seven of these go on to Ávila. Local buses will take you the 2km from the train station up to the monastery.

Castilla y León

The one-time centre of the mighty Christian kingdom of Castile, Castilla y León is one of Spain's most historic regions. From Segovia's Roman aqueduct to the walled city of Ávila, and from León's magnificent cathedral to the beautifully preserved old centre of Salamanca, it is crowded with reminders of its prominent role in Spain's past.

SEGOVIA

Segovia is justly famous for its magnificent Roman aqueduct, but also has a splendid ridge-top old city worthy of more than a fleeting visit from Madrid. Originally a Celtic settlement, Segovia was conquered by the Romans around 80 BC. The Visigoths and Moors also left their mark before the city ended up in Castilian hands in the 11th century.

There are two tourist offices, one on Plaza Mayor (☎ 921 46 03 34) and another on Plaza del Azoguejo down beside the aqueduct.

Things to See

You can't help but see the **aqueduct**, stretching away from the east end of the old city – it's over 800m long with 163 arches. The dates are a little hazy, but it was probably built in the 1st century AD.

At the heart of the old city is the 16th-century Gothic **catedral** on the very pretty Plaza Mayor. The austere interior contains an imposing choir in the centre and is ringed by 20-odd chapels. Of these, the Capilla del Cristo del Consuelo houses a magnificent Romanesque doorway preserved from the original church.

Perched on a craggy cliff top at the west end of the old city, Segovia's **alcázar**, with its turrets, towers and spires, is a fairy-tale 15th-century castle. It was virtually destroyed by fire in 1862, but has since been completely rebuilt and converted into a museum (open daily; entry 375 ptas).

Places to Stay

Two km along the road to La Granja is *Camping Acueducto* (☎ 921 42 50 00), open April to September.

Fonda Aragón (☎ 921 46 09 14) and *Fonda Cubo* (☎ 921 46 09 17) both at Plaza Mayor 4 are shabby but among the cheapest in town: 1100/2200 ptas for singles/doubles at the Cubo; 2000/3000 for doubles/triples at the Aragón. More pleasant is *Hostal Plaza* (☎ 921 46 03 03), Calle del Cronista Lecea 11, where rooms start at 2800/4000 ptas without private bath.

Farther from the centre, but about the best deal in town, is the spick-and-span *Hostal Don Jaime* (☎ 921 44 47 87) near the aqueduct at Calle de Ochoa Ondategui 8. Rooms with TV cost 3000/5400 ptas. In the centre, *Hostal El Hidalgo* (☎ 921 46 35 29), Calle de José Canalejas 3-5, has rooms for 4500/5970 ptas.

If you can't find anywhere to stay in Segovia, it may be worth continuing to La Granja (see Around Segovia), which has a few cheap pensiones and considerably better nightlife.

Places to Eat

Bar El Antiguo Buscón, Calle del Marqués del Arco 32, offers breakfast of juice, coffee and toast for 400 ptas. *Bar Yiyo's*, Calle del

Doctor Sánchez 3, has hamburgers and the like and also one of the cheapest set lunches you're likely to find in Segovia – 1000 ptas. *Restaurante Tasca La Posada*, Calle de la Judería Vieja 5, offers various set meals for lunch for up to 2200 ptas. Segovia's speciality is cochinillo asado (roast suckling pig); a set meal featuring this is 2500 ptas at one local favourite, *Mesón José María* at Calle del Cronista Lecea 11.

Getting There & Away
Up to 16 buses run daily to Madrid, and others serve Ávila and Salamanca. The bus station is 500m south of the aqueduct, just off Paseo Ezequiel González. The up to nine daily trains to Madrid (Chamartín or Atocha stations) are pretty slow.

Getting Around
Bus No 3 runs between Plaza Mayor and the train station, passing the bus station on the way.

AROUND SEGOVIA
In the mountain village of San Ildefonso de la Granja, 11km south-east, you can visit the royal palace and glorious gardens of **La Granja**, a Spanish version of Versailles built by Felipe V in 1720. Regular buses run from Segovia to San Ildefonso.

About 50km north-west of Segovia, the **Castillo de Coca** is also well worth a visit. This beautiful all-brick castle dates from the 15th century. It is now a forestry school, but guided tours (☎ 911 58 63 59/66 47) are conducted by the students. Three buses a day run from Segovia.

ÁVILA
Ávila deservedly lays claims to being one of the world's best preserved, and most impressive, walled cities. With its eight monumental gates and 88 towers, the 11th and 12th-century *muralla* (city wall) is one of the best preserved medieval defensive perimeters in the world.

Ávila also is distinguished by being the highest city in Spain (1130m); the birthplace of St Teresa of Ávila, the 16th-century mystical writer and reformer of the Carmelite order; and – less to be boasted about – the

place where Tomás de Torquemada orchestrated the most brutal phase of the Spanish Inquisition, sending off 2000 people to be burnt at the stake in the late 15th century.

Ávila's tourist office (☎ 920 21 13 87) is at Plaza de la Catedral 4.

Things to See & Do
Of the numerous convents, museums and monuments, the **catedral** (open daily) is perhaps the most interesting. It was built into the eastern end of the walls and served as defensive bulwark. Around the west side, the main façade betrays the Romanesque origins of what is essentially the earliest Gothic church built in Spain. Inside, the red and white limestone employed in the columns stands out. Artworks in the small museum include a portrait by El Greco.

Just outside the walls, the Romanesque **Basílica de San Vicente** (open daily) is striking. Gothic modifications in granite contrast with the warm sandstone of the Romanesque original. Work started in the 11th century.

About 500m east of the old town, the **Monasterio de Santo Tomás** is thought to be Torquemada's burial place – built hastily in 1482 as a royal residence, it is formed by three interconnecting cloisters and the church.

The **Convento de Santa Teresa** (open daily) was built over the saint's birthplace in 1636, and in the tiny museum next door are a few bits of memorabilia and relics, including Teresa's ring finger.

Los Cuatros Postes, a lookout point around 2.5km from the city gates on the Salamanca road, has the best view of the city and its perfectly preserved walls.

If you are in the region in October, don't miss the Festival of Santa Teresa (8 to 15 October). Semana Santa in Ávila is also recommended.

Places to Stay & Eat
Hostal Las Cancelas (☎ 920 21 22 49), just south of the cathedral at Calle de la Cruz Vieja 6, has simple singles/doubles from 2500/3500 ptas. *Hotel Jardín* (☎ 920 21 10 74), Calle de San Segundo 38, is a fairly scruffy place with rooms starting at 2600/3600 ptas. Better is the *Hostal Mesón El Rastro* (☎ 920 21 12 18), Plaza del Rastro 1,

which is full of character and has a good restaurant. Rooms start at 3400/4100 ptas.

Restaurante Los Leales, Plaza de Italia 4, has a solid menú for 1000 ptas. At the *Hostal Mesón del Rastro* the 1500 ptas set meal is good value and the comedor exudes Castilian charm.

Getting There & Away

There are up to 17 trains a day between Ávila and Madrid. The two-hour trip costs 835 ptas. Trains to Salamanca cost the same. Buses also connect Ávila with Madrid, Segovia and Salamanca.

The bus and train stations are around 700m and 1.5km east of the old town respectively. Bus No 1 links the train station with the old town.

BURGOS

A mighty chilly place in the depths of winter, Burgos is an ideal setting for the country's greatest Gothic cathedral. Just outside town lie a couple of admirable monasteries.

Information

The regional tourist office (☎ 947 20 31 25) is on Plaza de Alonso Martínez 7. The main post office is on Plaza del Conde de Castro.

Things to See

Work on the massive **Catedral** began in 1221 on the site of a modest Romanesque church. The bulk of the work was completed in 40 years, and the twin towers were added in the 15th century. Inside, the highlight is the Escalera Dorada (gilded staircase) by Diego de Siloé. El Cid lies buried beneath the central dome, and you can visit the cloisters and church treasures for 400 ptas.

Of the two monasteries, the **Monasterio de las Huelgas** is the more interesting. It lies about a half-hour walk west of the town centre on the south bank of the Río Arlanzón. Founded in 1187 by Eleanor of Acquitaine, the convent is still home to 35 Cistercian nuns. Parts of the complex are no-go areas for visitors, but Las Claustrillas, an elegant Romanesque cloister, alone makes a visit worthwhile. Entry is 650 ptas.

About 3.5km east of the centre, the **Cartuja de Miraflores** is a functioning Carthusian

monastery. Bus 26 (summer only) will get you here from Plaza de Miguel Primo de Rivera.

Places to Stay & Eat

Women fancying a stint with the Cistercian nuns can organise to stay for up to eight days at the *Monasterio de las Huelgas* (☎ 947 20 16 30).

The rooms at *Pensión Ansa* (☎ 947 20 47 67), Calle de Miranda 9 (opposite the bus station), are fairly comfortable and cost 3000/4200 ptas. Some of the singles are tiny. Plaza de la Vega is not a bad spot, right by the river. *Pensión Seve* (☎ 947 26 81 05) at No 8 and *Pensión Dallas* (☎ 947 20 54 57), No 6, both have rooms with a view for about 2300/3900 ptas. Closer to the action, *Hostal Las* (☎ 947 20 96 55), Calle del Cardenal Benlloch 1, offers singles/doubles with private bath for 3500/6100 ptas.

La Mejillonera Restaurante, Calle de la Paloma 33, specialises in seafood snacks. Nearer the Catedral, *Restaurante Don Diego*, Calle de Diego Porcelos 7, has a hearty set menú for 950 ptas.

Getting There & Away

Bus Continental Auto runs up to 11 buses a day to Madrid for 1970 ptas. Buses also run to Santander, San Sebastián, Vitoria, and Bilbao.

Train The trains are generally more expensive than the bus. They run through Burgos en route from Madrid to Irún and Bilbao, and east-west between Barcelona and Salamanca and Galicia.

SALAMANCA

Salamanca on a warm, sunny day is a great place to be. The cafés in the beautiful Plaza Mayor fill the square with tables and chairs, and the street artists and musicians come out of their winter hiding places. This is one of Spain's most inspiring cities, both in terms of history and modern life.

Information

The municipal tourist office (☎ 923 21 83 42) on Plaza Mayor, open daily, concentrates on information about the city. For provincial information go to the oficina de turismo (☎ 923 26 85 71) in the Casa de las Conchas, open

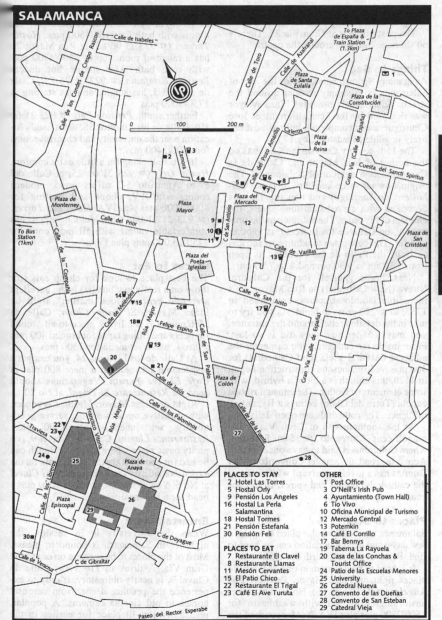

SALAMANCA

To Plaza
de España &
Train Station
(1.3km)

Calle de Isabeles

Calle de los Condes de Crespo Rascon

Calle de Toro

Calle de Azafranal

Plaza
de Santa
Eulalía

Plaza de la
Constitución

Gran Vía (Calle de España)

Caleros

Calle del Pozo Amarillo

Zamora

Plaza
de la
Reina

Cuesta del Sancti Spiritus

Plaza de
Monterrey

Plaza
Mayor

Calle del Prior

Plaza del
Mercado

Plaza del
Poeta
Iglesias

C de San Antonio

Calle de Varillas

Plaza de
San
Cristóbal

To Bus
Station
(1km)

Calle de la Compañía

Calle de San Justo

Ruá Mayor

Felipe Espino

Calle de San Pablo

Gran Vía (Calle de España)

Francisco Vitoria

Ruá Mayor

Travieta

Calle de los Palominos

Plaza de
Colón

Plaza de
Jesús

Calle de la Fuente

Plaza de
Anaya

Plaza
Episcopal

Calle de los Libreros

C de Doyague

C de Gibraltar

Calle de Veracruz

Paseo del Rector Esperabe

PLACES TO STAY
2   Hotel Las Torres
5   Hostal Orly
9   Pensión Los Angeles
16 Hostal La Perla
    Salamantina
18 Hostal Tormes
21 Pensión Estefanía
30 Pensión Feli

PLACES TO EAT
7   Restaurante El Clavel
8   Restaurante Llamas
11 Mesón Cervantes
15 El Patio Chico
22 Restaurante El Trigal
23 Café El Ave Turuta

OTHER
1   Post Office
3   O'Neill's Irish Pub
4   Ayuntamiento (Town Hall)
6   Tío Vivo
10 Oficina Municipal de Turismo
12 Mercado Central
13 Potemkin
14 Café El Corrillo
17 Bar Bennys
19 Taberna La Rayuela
20 Casa de las Conchas &
    Tourist Office
24 Patio de las Escuelas Menores
25 University
26 Catedral Nueva
27 Convento de las Dueñas
28 Convento de San Esteban
29 Catedral Vieja

0   100   200 m

Monday to Friday from 10 am to 2 pm and 5 to 8 pm, and Saturday from 10 am to 2 pm.

The post office is at Gran Vía 25. There's no shortage of banks around the centre.

Things to See

As in many Spanish cities, one of the joys of Salamanca is to simply wander around the streets. Salamanca's beautiful **Plaza Mayor** was designed by the Spanish architect José Churriguera and completed, built almost entirely in golden sandstone, by 1755.

The 15th-century **Casa de las Conchas** on the corner of Rúa Mayor and Calle de la Compañía is a symbol of Salamanca. The original owner was a knight of St James (*caballero de Santiago*) and had the façades decorated with carved-sandstone shells, the emblem of his order. The entrance to the **university**, on Calle de los Libreros, is another wonder. The best place to admire its intricacy from, the **Patio de las Escuelas**, is open from 9.30 am to 1.30 pm and 4 to 7.30 pm.

Next, brace yourself for the **Catedral Nueva** (New Cathedral) on Rúa Mayor. This incredible Gothic structure, completed in 1733, took 220 years to build. As you try to take in the detailed relief around the entrance, you may wonder how they did it so fast. From inside the cathedral, you can enter the adjacent **Catedral Vieja** (Old Cathedral) for 300 ptas. A Romanesque construction begun in 1120, this church is a bit of a hybrid, with some elements of Gothic. The unusual ribbed cupola (Torre del Gallo) betrays a Byzantine influence. The cathedrals are open daily.

At the southern end of Gran Vía is the magnificent **Convento de San Esteban**, where Columbus is said to have once stayed. Across the road, the smaller **Convento de las Dueñas** has a lovely courtyard with views of the cathedrals' domes and spires. Both convents are open daily.

Places to Stay

Salamanca is a very popular place to spend a few days, and accommodation can be hard to find. Persevere as it's worth the effort.

It is hard to beat a room in one of the little places right on Plaza Mayor. *Pensión Los Angeles* (☎ 923 21 81 66), No 10, has rather basic singles/doubles with washbasin for 1500/2800 ptas plus IVA. Not far south of the plaza, *Hostal La Perla Salamantina* (☎ 923 21 76 56) at Calle de Sánchez Barbero 7 has rooms with bath for 2100/4500 ptas. *Hostal Tormes* (☎ 923 21 96 83) at Rúa Mayor 20 has a range of rooms up to 3500/4800 ptas with own bath. The simple but decent *Pensión Estefanía* (☎ 923 21 73 72), Calle de Jesús 3-5, has singles/doubles starting at 1750/3000 ptas.

Farther south, *Pensión Feli* (☎ 923 21 60 10), Calle de los Libreros 58, has a handy location near the university and cheerful rooms for 2400/3400 ptas.

If you're looking for a little extra comfort, *Hostal Orly* (☎ 923 21 61 25) at Calle del Pozo Amarillo 5-7 offers good, modern rooms with TV, phone and heating for 4000/5000 ptas plus IVA. *Hotel Las Torres*, (☎ 923 21 21 00), Calle del Concejo 4, has comfortable rooms with all mod cons for 9750/13,000 ptas plus IVA.

Places to Eat

The best place to look for cheap eats (for those on a really low budget) is the excellent *mercado central* (food market), right by Plaza Mayor. *El Patio Chico*, Calle de Meléndez 13, is a lively place to sit around for beers and filling tapas for around 400 ptas a throw, and a set menú for 1300 ptas.

At Calle de los Libreros 24, you can get a respectable set meal for a mere 800 ptas at *Café El Ave Turuta*. Vegetarians should head for *Restaurante El Trigal*, at No 20.

Right on Plaza Mayor, *Mesón Cervantes*, with attractive upstairs dining, serves good-quality set lunches for 1500 ptas. *Restaurante Llamas*, Calle del Clavel 9, is a pretty basic place where a tasty set lunch can be had for about 1200 ptas. For a walk on the expensive side try the *Restaurante El Clavel* at No 6. You're looking at about 4000 ptas a head for a full meal.

Entertainment

When the university is in session, the nightlife in Salamanca is bound to please. Most of the places to be seen are on or around Gran Vía. A drink in *Tío Vivo*, Calle de Clavel 3, is nearly obligatory, if only to experience the peculiar décor, from carousel horses to old cinema cameras. A popular, pleasantly low-lit place for earlier in the

evening is ***Taberna La Rayuela***, Rúa Mayor
19. ***O'Neill's Irish Pub***, Calle de Zamora 14,
is one of the Irish-style pubs increasingly in
vogue in Spain, and it's always busy. ***Café El
Corrillo*** on Calle de Meléndez is a great
place to have a beer while catching some live
jazz.

Calle de San Justo, Calle de Varillas and
Calle del Consuelo in particular are loaded
with bars. A good little place is ***Bar Bennys***,
Calle del Consuelo 20. Later in the night you
can head for ***Potemkin***, a block north on
Calle del Consuelo, for live music.

Getting There & Away
Bus Salamanca's bus station (☎ 923 23 67
17) is at Avenida de Filiberto Villalobos 85,
about 1km north-west of Plaza Mayor.
AutoRes has 16 express buses daily to
Madrid, taking 2½ hours for 2210 ptas, plus
stopping buses for 1690 ptas.

Among many other destinations served by
regular buses are Santiago de Compostela,
Cáceres, Ávila, Segovia, León and Valladolid.

Train At least four trains leave daily for
Madrid's Chamartín station (3½ hours; 1450
ptas) via Ávila (1¾ hours; 835 ptas). A train
for Lisbon leaves at 4.55 am.

Getting Around
Bus No 4 runs past the bus station and round
the old town perimeter to Gran Vía. From the
train station, the best bet is a No 1, which
heads down Calle de Azafranal. Going the
other way, it can be picked up along Gran
Vía.

LEÓN
León is far too often left off travellers' itineraries. For those who get here, a fresh and
pleasant city awaits, with long boulevards,
open squares, excellent nightlife and one of
Spain's greatest cathedrals. León was at its
mightiest in the 10th to 13th centuries, as
capital of the expanding Christian kingdom
of the same name.

The tourist office (☎ 987 23 70 82) opposite the cathedral at Plaza de la Regla 3 is
open Monday to Saturday from 10 am to 2

pm and 5 to 8 pm, and on Sunday from 11 am
to 2 pm and 4.30 to 8.30 pm.

Things to See
León's **catedral**, built primarily in the 13th
century, is a wonder of Gothic architecture.
Its most outstanding feature is its breathtaking stained-glass windows. Of course, you'll
have to go inside to appreciate their beauty.
Opening hours are 9.30 am to 1 pm and 4 to
6.30 pm (closed Sunday afternoon). At the
northern end of Calle del Cid is a great monument from the earlier Romanesque age, the
Real Basílica de San Isidoro containing the
Panteón Real, burial place of Leonese
royalty with some wonderful 12th-century
frescoes. The panteón can be visited only by
guided tour (300 ptas).

Plaza Mayor in the old town, a short distance south of the cathedral, is a little
rundown, but this is part of its romance. It is
also the heart of León's buzzing nightlife.
Also of interest is the **Casa de Botines** on
Plaza de San Marcelo, designed by the
Catalan genius Antoni Gaudí, although it's
rather conservative by his standards.

Places to Stay
There's plenty of budget accommodation,
mostly on or near Avenida de Ordoño II,
Avenida de Roma and Plaza Mayor in the old
town. ***Pensión Berta*** (☎ 987 25 70 39), Plaza
Mayor 8, has basic singles/doubles for
1800/3000 ptas. The position is unbeatable.

Fonda Roma (☎ 987 22 46 63), Avenida de
Roma 4, is in an attractive old building, with
dirt-cheap rooms at 1100/1700 ptas. More expensive is the ***Hostal Central*** (☎ 987 25 18
06), Avenida de Ordoño II 27, with reasonable
rooms for 1800/2700 ptas. ***Hostal Bayón***
(☎ 987 23 14 46), Calle del Alcázar de Toledo
6, offers clean rooms costing 2700/3500 ptas.
Hostal Orejas (☎ 987 25 29 09), Calle de Villafranca 8, is a pretty good deal; rooms with
TV and phone cost 2900/5000 ptas.

Hotel Paris (☎ 987 23 86 00; fax 987 27 15
72), Calle del Generalísimo Franco 20, is actually two hotels, one with basic singles/
doubles for 3500/5500 ptas, and another next
door with rooms starting at 5600/7500.
Parador Hostal San Marcos (☎ 987 23 73 00;
fax 987 23 34 58), Plaza de San Marcos 7, has
rooms fit for royalty at 21,500 ptas plus IVA.

LEÓN

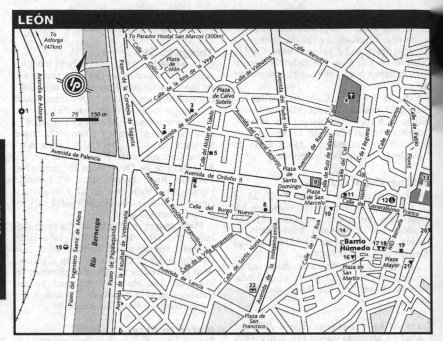

LEÓN

PLACES TO STAY
3   Fonda Roma
5   Hostal Bayón
6   Hostal Central
7   Hostal Orejas
11 Hotel Paris
19 Pensión Berta

PLACES TO EAT
10 Restaurante Bodega Regia

16 Restaurante El Tizón
17 Restaurante El Palomo
18 Restaurante & Sidrería Vivaldi
20 Restaurante Honoré
21 Mesón Leonés del Racimo
    de Oro

OTHER
1   Train Station
2   Pub La Morgue

4   Real Basílica de San Isidoro
    & Panteón Real
8   La Fundación
9   Casa de Botines
12 Tourist Office
13 Catedral
14 Mercado
15 Bus Station
22 Post Office

Places to Eat

There are lots of good places within a short
walk of the cathedral or Plaza Mayor.
Restaurante Honoré, Calle de los Serradores
4, has a good menú for 950 ptas. *Restaurante
El Palomo*, on tiny Calle de la Escalerilla, is
a quality establishment with a lunch menú for
1300 ptas. Next door is the popular *Restaurante & Sidrería Vivaldi*, where you can

wash down your meal with a cider from Asturias.

Restaurante El Tizón, Plaza de San
Martín 1, is good for wine and meat dishes,
and offers an abundant menú for 1600 ptas.
There are a few decent pizzerias and bars on
the same square.

Mesón Leonés del Racimo de Oro, Calle
de Caño Badillo 2, is a long-established

restaurant and reputable place where most mains cost around 1600 ptas. In a similar price league, **Restaurante Bodega Regia**, Calle del General Mola 5, is a good spot for outdoor eating in summer.

Entertainment

León's nocturnal activity flows thickest in the aptly named Barrio Húmedo (Wet Quarter), the crowded tangle of lanes leading south off Calle del Generalísimo Franco. Plaza de San Martín is a particularly pleasant spot for drinks. Calle de Cervantes and Calle de Fernando Regueral north of Calle del Generalísimo Franco, are also lined with bars to suit most tastes.

As the night grows older, the action slides west towards the river. Friday night is the best for dancing till dawn at **Pub La Morgue**, a noisy place for the young bakalao scene on Avenida de Roma. A more mixed crowd and music can be had until 6 am at **La Fundación**, just off Calle del Burgo Nuevo. There are more places on and around Avenida de Lancia.

Getting There & Away

Bus Empresa Fernández has as many as eight buses to Madrid a day. The trip takes 4½ hours. Frequent buses also run to Astorga. Other destinations include Bilbao, Oviedo, Zamora, Salamanca and Valladolid.

Train Up to 10 trains a day leave for Madrid. Plenty of trains head west to Astorga, north to Oviedo and Gijón, and south to Valladolid. There are three to Barcelona and up to five to La Coruña and other destinations in Galicia.

FEVE trains run only as far as Guardo on this private line which links León with the País Vasco. These trains leave from a separate station.

AROUND LEÓN

A more extravagant example of Gaudí's work is in the town of **Astorga**, 47km south-west of Léon. His Palacio Episcopal (1889) is also home to the moderate Museo de los Caminos, with Roman artefacts and religious art. Next door, the cathedral is a hotchpotch of 15th to 18th-century styles. Both are open in summer from 10 am to 2 pm and 4 to 8 pm. The cathe-

dral closes on Sunday, except during August. Note that entry to the Palacio Episcopal and the Museo de la Catedral each cost 250 ptas, or you can pay 400 ptas for both – you must ask specifically for the latter ticket.

Castilla-La Mancha

Best known as the home of Don Quixote, Castilla-La Mancha conjures up images of endless empty plains and lonely windmills. This Spanish heartland is home to two fascinating cities, Toledo and Cuenca.

TOLEDO

The history of this remarkable city stretches back into pre-Roman days. The narrow, winding streets of Toledo, perched on a small hill above the Río Tajo, are crammed with museums, churches and other monumental reminders of a splendid and turbulent past. As the main city of Muslim central Spain, Toledo was the peninsula's leading centre of learning and the arts in the 11th century. The Christians wrested control of it in 1085 and Toledo soon became the headquarters of the Spanish Church. For centuries it was one of the most important of Spain's numerous early capitals. Until 1492, Christians, Jews and Muslims coexisted peaceably here, for which Toledo still bears the label 'Ciudad de las Tres Culturas' (City of the Three Cultures). Its unique architectural combinations, with Arabic influences everywhere, are a strong reminder of Spain's mixed heritage. El Greco lived here from 1577 to 1614 and many of his works can still be seen in the city.

Toledo is quite expensive and packed with tourists and souvenir shops. Try to stay here at least overnight, since you can enjoy the street and café life after the tour buses have headed north in the evening.

Information

The main tourist office (☎ 925 22 08 43) is just outside Toledo's main gate, the Puerta Nueva de Bisagra, at the northern end of town. A smaller, more helpful information office is open in the ayuntamiento (across from the cathedral) from 10.30 am to 2.30 pm and 4.30 to 7 pm (mornings only from Monday to Wednesday).

TOLEDO

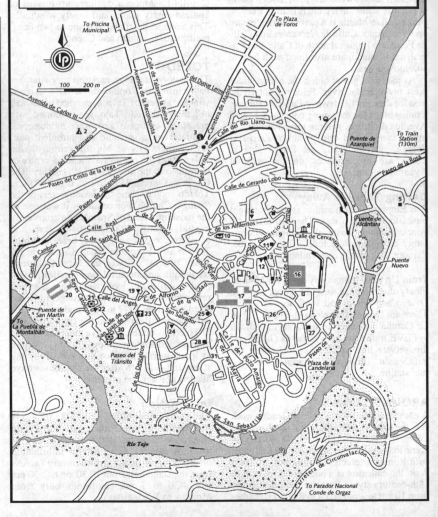

PLACES TO STAY
2 Camping Circo Romano
5 Residencia Juvenil
   de San Servando
7 Pensión Segovia
11 Hotel Maravilla
15 Pensión Lumbreras
27 La Belviseña
28 Hotel Santa Isabel

PLACES TO EAT
6 La Abadía
12 Ludeña
19 Bar La Ría
22 Osiris Bar
24 El Delfin

OTHER
1 Bus Station
3 Main Tourist Office
4 Puerta Nueva de Bisagra
8 Museo de Santa Cruz
9 Plaza de Zocodover
10 Post Office
13 Plaza de la Magdalena
14 Plaza Mayor
16 Alcázar
17 Catedral

18 Plaza del Ayuntamiento
20 San Juan de los Reyes
21 Santa María La Blanca
   Synagogue
23 Iglesia de Santo Tomé
25 Ayuntamiento & Tourist Office
26 Plaza de San Justo
29 Sinagoga del Tránsito &
   Museo Sefardi
30 Casa y Museo de El Greco
31 Plaza de Santa Isabel

SPAIN

Things to See

Most of Toledo's attractions open from about 10 am to 1.30 pm and about 4 to 6 pm (7 pm in summer). Many, including the alcázar, Sinagoga del Tránsito and Casa y Museo de El Greco – but not the cathedral – are closed Sunday afternoon and/or all day Monday.

The **catedral**, in the heart of the old city, is awesome. You could easily spend hours in here, admiring the glorious stone architecture, stained-glass windows, tombs of kings in the Capilla Mayor, and art by the likes of El Greco, Velázquez and Goya. Entry to the cathedral is free, but you have to buy a ticket (500 ptas) to enter four areas – the Coro, Sacristía, Capilla de la Torre and Sala Capitular – which contain some of the finest art and artisanry.

The **alcázar**, Toledo's main landmark, was fought over repeatedly from the Middle Ages to the civil war, when it was besieged by Republican troops. Today it's a military museum, created by the Nationalist victors of the civil war, with most of the displays – which are fascinating – relating to the 1936 siege. Entry is 125 ptas.

The **Museo de Santa Cruz** on Calle de Cervantes contains a large and sometimes surprising collection of furniture, fading tapestries, military and religious paraphernalia, and paintings. Upstairs is an impressive collection of El Grecos including the masterpiece *La Asunción* (Assumption of the Virgin). Entry is 200 ptas (free on Saturday afternoon and Sunday).

In the south-west of the old city, the queues outside an unremarkable church, the **Iglesia de Santo Tomé** on Plaza del Conde, indicate there must be something special inside. That something is El Greco's masterpiece *El Entierro del Conde de Orgaz*. The painting depicts the burial of the Count of Orgaz in 1322 by San Esteban (St Stephen) and San Agustín (St Augustine), observed by a heavenly entourage, including Christ, the Virgin, John the Baptist and Noah. Entry is 150 ptas.

The so-called **Casa y Museo de El Greco** on Calle de Samuel Leví, in Toledo's former Jewish quarter, contains the artist's famous *Vista y Plano de Toledo*, plus about 20 of his minor works. It is unlikely El Greco ever lived here. Entry is 400 ptas (200 ptas for students).

Nearby, the **Sinagoga del Tránsito** on Calle de los Reyes Católicos is one of two synagogues left in Toledo. Built in 1355 and handed over to the Catholic church in 1492, when most of Spain's Jews were expelled from the country, it houses the interesting Museo Sefardi, examining Jewish culture in Spain before 1492. Entry is 400 ptas (free on Saturday afternoon and Sunday).

Toledo's other synagogue, **Santa María La Blanca**, a short way north along Calle de los Reyes Católicos, dates back to the 12th century. Its arches and columns support the roof in a fashion reminiscent of the Mezquita in Córdoba. Entry is 150 ptas.

A little farther north lies one of the city's most visible sights, **San Juan de los Reyes**, the Franciscan monastery and church founded by Fernando and Isabel. The prevalent late Flemish-Gothic style is tarted up with lavish Isabelline ornament and counterbalanced by Mudéjar decoration. Outside hang the chains of Christian prisoners freed after the fall of Granada in 1492.

Places to Stay

The nearest camping ground is *Camping Circo Romano* (☎ 925 22 04 42) at Avenida de Carlos III 19, but better is *Camping El Greco* (☎ 925 22 00 90), well signposted 2.5km south-west of town. Both are open all year.

Toledo's HI hostel, *Residencia Juvenil de San Servando* (☎ 925 22 45 54), is exceptionally well sited in the Castillo de San Servando, a castle that started life as a Visigothic monastery. It's east of the Río Tajo and open all year except Christmas, Easter and mid-August to mid-September.

Cheap accommodation in the city is not easy to come by and is often full, especially from Easter to September. *La Belviseña* (☎ 925 22 00 67), Cuesta del Can 5, is basic but among the best value (if you can get in), with rooms at 1200 ptas per person, plus 100 ptas for a shower. The friendly *Pensión Segovia* (☎ 925 21 11 24), Calle de los Recoletos 2, has spotless doubles from 2100 to 2500 ptas.

Pensión Lumbreras (☎ 925 22 15 71) at Calle de Juan Labrador 9 has reasonable rooms round a pleasant courtyard for 1700/3000/4200 ptas. *Hotel Santa Isabel*

(☎ 925 25 31 36), Calle de Santa Isabel 24, is a good mid-range hotel well placed near the cathedral, yet away from the tourist hordes. Pleasant rooms with TV, bath and air-con are 3673/5720 ptas plus IVA. *Hotel Maravilla* (☎ 925 22 83 17), right in the thick of things at Plaza de Barrio Rey 7, has air-con rooms with private bath for 4000/6500 ptas plus IVA.

Places to Eat

Among the cheap lunch spots, *El Delfín*, Calle del Taller del Moro, has a set menú for 900 ptas. For outdoor dining, the *Osiris Bar* on the shady Plaza del Barrio Nuevo is a decent choice, with set lunches from 1400 ptas.

La Abadía, Plaza de San Nicolás 3, as well as being a popular bar, offers excellent downstairs dining with typical Toledan dishes such as perdiz estofada (stewed partridge). The set lunch menú, at about 1800 ptas, is reliable.

For Toledo's best seafood, *Bar La Ría*, Callejón de los Bodegones 6, is hard to beat. Problem is, it's tiny. A good meal will cost 2000 ptas a head. An excellent little place for a full meal (1200 ptas menú) or simply a beer and tapas is *Ludeña*, Plaza de la Magdalena 13.

Getting There & Away

To reach most major destinations from Toledo, you need to backtrack to Madrid (or at least Aranjuez). Toledo's bus station (☎ 925 21 58 50) is on Avenida de Castilla-La Mancha. There are buses (580 ptas) every half-hour from about 6 am to 10 pm to/from Madrid (Estación Sur). The Aisa line has a service from Toledo to Cuenca at 5.30 pm, Monday to Friday.

Trains from Madrid (Atocha) are more pleasant than the bus, but there are only 10 of them daily (the first from Madrid departs at 7.20 am, the last from Toledo at 9 pm; 630 ptas one way). Toledo's train station is 400m east of the Puente de Azarquiel.

Bus No 5 links the train and bus stations with Plaza de Zocodover.

CUENCA

Cuenca's setting is hard to believe. The high old town is cut off from the rest of the city by the Júcar and Huécar rivers, sitting at the top of a deep gorge. Most of its famous monuments appear to teeter on the edge – a photographer's delight.

The Infotur office (☎ 969 23 21 19) at Calle de Alfonso VIII 2, just before the arches of Plaza Mayor, is especially helpful. It opens from 9.30 am to 2 pm and 4 to 6 pm.

Things to See & Do

Cuenca's **Casas Colgadas** (Hanging Houses) originally built in the 15th century, are precariously positioned on a cliff top, their balconies literally hanging over the gorge. A footbridge across the gorge provides access to spectacular views of these buildings (and the rest of the old town) from the other side. Inside one of the Casas Colgadas is the **Museo de Arte Abstracto Español**. This exciting collection includes works by Fernando Zobel, Sempere, Millares and Chillida. Initially a private initiative of Zobel to unite works by fellow artists of the 1950s Generación Abstracta, it now holds works up to the present day. Entry is 300 ptas, and the museum opens from 11 am to 2 pm and 4 to 6 pm (to 8 pm on Saturday).

Nearby, on Calle del Obispo Valero, is the very different **Museo Diocesano**. Of the religious art and artefacts inside, the 14th-century Byzantine diptych is the jewel in the crown. Entry is 200 ptas. Hours are 11 am to 2 pm and 4 to 6 pm.

On Plaza Mayor you'll find Cuenca's strange **catedral**. The lines of the unfinished façade are Norman-Gothic and reminiscent of French cathedrals, and the stained-glass windows look like they'd be more at home in the abstract art museum.

As you wander the old town's beautiful streets, check the **Torre de Mangana**, the remains of a Moorish fortress in a square west of Calle de Alfonso VIII, overlooking the plain below.

Places to Stay & Eat

Up at the top of the casco is the clean and simple *Pensión La Tabanqueta* (☎ 969 21 12 90) at Calle de Trabuco 13, costing 2000 ptas per person. Ask for a room with views of the Júcar gorge. Just beyond the cathedral,

Posada de San José (☎ 969 21 13 00), Ronda de Julián Romero 4, is a lovely 16th-century residence with doubles for 8900 ptas plus IVA.

Down in the new town, there are several places on Calle de Ramón y Cajal, which runs from near the train station towards the old town, including two no-frills pensiones at No 53: *Pensión Adela* (☎ 969 22 25 33) charging 1250 ptas per person plus 200 ptas for a shower, and *Pensión Marín* (☎ 969 22 19 78) upstairs, which is marginally better value at about the same price.

Just outside the old town is the *Posada de San Julián* (☎ 969 21 17 04), Calle de las Torres 1, a cavernous old place with doubles for 3000 ptas (3800 ptas with own bathroom).

Most of the restaurants and cafés around Plaza Mayor are better for a drink and people-watching than for good-value eating. A decent establishment for solid manchego food is the *Restaurante San Nicolás*, Calle de San Pedro 15. A full meal will come in at around 5000 ptas.

Getting There & Away

There are up to nine buses a day to Madrid (2½ hours, 1305 to 1600 ptas), and daily buses to Barcelona, Teruel and Valencia. There are five trains a day direct to Madrid (Atocha), taking 2½ hours and costing 1355 ptas one way. There are also three trains a day to Valencia.

Bus No 1 or 2 from near the bus and train stations will take you up to Plaza Mayor in the old town.

AROUND CUENCA

A 35km drive north of Cuenca is the bizarre **Ciudad Encantada** (Enchanted City). This 'city', open daily from 10 am to sunset (200 ptas), is a series of fantastically shaped rocks, many now given names that refer somewhat imaginatively to their shapes, such as Crocodile and Elephant Fighting, Mushrooms, and Roller Coaster. If you have a car, it is worth the trip. The scenery on the way is great and the Ciudad Encantada itself makes a wonderful playground – a must if you are with kids. Take food and drink, as the café is expensive.

Catalunya

Catalunya (Cataluña in Spanish; Catalonia in English) is one of the most fiercely independent regions in Spain and also the wealthiest. The Catalans speak a distinct language, Catalan, and many don't consider themselves Spanish. Catalunya's golden age was the 12th to 14th centuries, when it was the leading light in the medieval kingdom of Aragón, and Barcelona was capital of a big Mediterranean seafaring empire. The region has much to offer: Barcelona apart, there's the Costa Brava to its north, Tarragona with its fine Roman remains, Sitges with Spain's most forthright gay community and a vibrant carnaval, and Figueres with the bizarre Dalí museum. Away from the towns and cities, the Pyrenees offer good walking in many areas, especially the Parc Nacional d'Aigüestortes i Sant Maurici, and skiing in winter.

BARCELONA

If you only visit one city in Spain, it probably should be Barcelona. After hosting the Olympic Games in 1992, it has finally taken its place on the list of the world's great cities. Catalonia's modernist architecture of the late 19th and early 20th centuries – a unique melting pot of Art Nouveau, Gothic, Moorish and other styles – climaxes here in the inspiring creations of Antoni Gaudí, among them La Sagrada Família church and Parc Güell. Barcelona also has world-class museums including two devoted to Picasso and Miró, a fine old quarter (the Barri Gòtic) and nightlife as good as anywhere in the country.

Orientation

Plaça de Catalunya is Barcelona's main square, and a good place to get your bearings when you arrive. The main tourist office is right here. Most travellers base themselves in Barcelona's old city (Ciutat Vella), the area bordered by the harbour Port Vell (south), Plaça de Catalunya (north), Ronda de Sant Pau (west) and Parc de la Ciutadella (east).

La Rambla, the city's best known boulevard, runs through the heart of the old city from Plaça de Catalunya down to the harbour. On the east side of La Rambla is the

BARCELONA

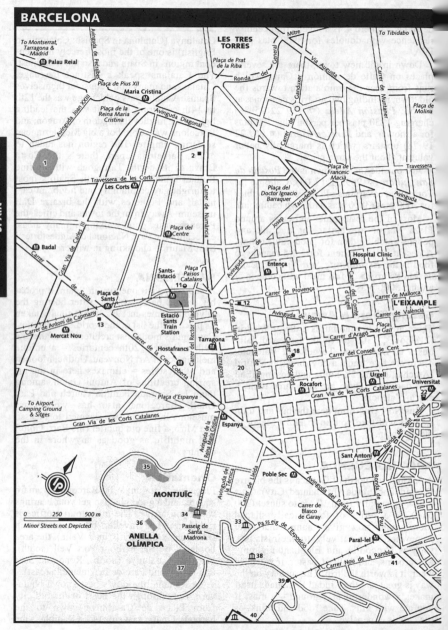

LES TRES TORRES

To Montserrat, Tarragona & Madrid

Palau Reial

Plaça de Pius XII

Maria Cristina

Plaça de la Reina Maria Cristina

Avinguda de Pedralbes

Avinguda Joan XXIII

Avinguda Diagonal

Plaça de Prat de la Riba

Ronda del

Mitre

Via Augusta

General

Carrer de Ganduxer

To Tibidabo

Carrer de Muntaner

Plaça de Molina

1

2

Travessera de les Corts

Les Corts

Carrer de Numància

Plaça de Francesc Macià

Travessera

Avinguda

Gran Via de Carles III

Carrer de Sants

Badal

Plaça del Centre

Plaça de Sants

Sants-Estació

Plaça Paisos Catalans

11

12

Estació Sants Train Station

13

Mercat Nou

Carrer de Antoni de Capmany

Hostafrancs

Carrer de la Creu Coberta

Carrer del Rector Triadó

Tarragona

Tarragona

Carrer de Llança

Plaça del Doctor Ignacio Barraquer

Joseg

Avinguda

Tarradellas

Entença

Carrer de Provença

Avinguda de Roma

Carrer d'Aragó

Hospital Clínic

Carrer de Mallorca

Carrer de València

L'EIXAMPLE

Carrer del Comte d'Urgell

Plaça de Gall

18

Carrer del Consell de Cent

Urgell

20

Carrer de Vilamarí

Carrer de Rocafort

Rocafort

Gran Via de les Corts Catalanes

Universitat

22

To Airport, Camping Ground & Sitges

Plaça d'Espanya

Gran Via de les Corts Catalanes

Espanya

Avinguda de la Reina Maria Cristina

Sant Antoni

Ronda de Sant Antoni

Ronda de Sant Pau

35

MONTJUÏC

34

Avinguda de la Tècnica

Carrer de Lleida

Poble Sec

Avinguda del Paral·lel

Carrer de Blasco de Garay

36

ANELLA OLÍMPICA

33

Passeig de Santa Madrona

Passeig de l'Exposició

Paral·lel

38

37

41

39

Carrer Nou de la Rambla

40

0   250   500 m
Minor Streets not Depicted

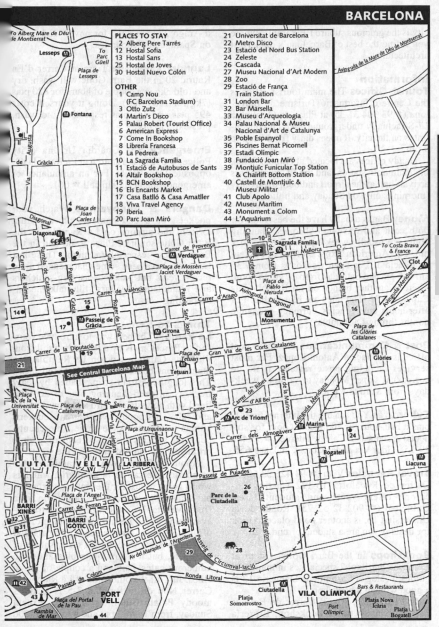

BARCELONA

PLACES TO STAY
- 2 Alberg Pere Tarrés
- 12 Hostal Sofia
- 13 Hostal Sans
- 25 Hostal de Joves
- 30 Hostal Nuevo Colón

OTHER
- 1 Camp Nou (FC Barcelona Stadium)
- 3 Otto Zutz
- 4 Martin's Disco
- 5 Palau Robert (Tourist Office)
- 6 American Express
- 7 Come In Bookshop
- 8 Librería Francesa
- 9 La Pedrera
- 10 La Sagrada Família
- 11 Estació de Autobusos de Sants
- 14 Altaïr Bookshop
- 15 BCN Bookshop
- 16 Els Encants Market
- 17 Casa Batlló & Casa Amatller
- 18 Viva Travel Agency
- 19 Iberia
- 20 Parc Joan Miró
- 21 Universitat de Barcelona
- 22 Metro Disco
- 23 Estació del Nord Bus Station
- 24 Zeleste
- 26 Cascada
- 27 Museu Nacional d'Art Modern
- 28 Zoo
- 29 Estació de França Train Station
- 31 London Bar
- 32 Bar Marsella
- 33 Museu d'Arqueologia
- 34 Palau Nacional & Museu Nacional d'Art de Catalunya
- 35 Poble Espanyol
- 36 Piscines Bernat Picornell
- 37 Estadi Olímpic
- 38 Fundació Joan Miró
- 39 Montjuïc Funicular Top Station & Chairlift Bottom Station
- 40 Castell de Montjuïc & Museu Militar
- 41 Club Apolo
- 42 Museu Marítim
- 43 Monument a Colom
- 44 L'Aquàrium

SPAIN

medieval quarter (Barri Gòtic), and on the west the seedy Barri Xinès. North of the old city is the gracious suburb l'Eixample, where you'll find the best of Barcelona's modernist architecture.

Information

Tourist Offices The main tourist office is the Centre d'Informació Turisme de Barcelona (☎ 93 304 31 35) at Plaça de Catalunya 17-S (actually underground), which concentrates on the city. It opens daily from 9 am to 9 pm.

Handy offices are located at Estació Sants, the main train station, and the EU passengers arrivals hall at the airport and both open daily (mornings only on Sunday and holidays).

Money Banks usually have the best rates for both cash and travellers cheques. Banking hours are usually weekdays from 8 am to 2 pm. The American Express office at Passeig de Gràcia 101 is open weekdays from 9.30 am to 6 pm and Saturday from 10 am to noon. There is another branch on La Rambla dels Capuxtins 74. The rates are reasonable. For after-hours emergencies, currency-exchange booths throng La Rambla.

Post & Communications The main post office is on Plaça d'Antoni López. For most services including poste restante (lista de correos), it's open Monday to Saturday weekdays from 8 am to 8 pm.

Cybercafés You can use the Internet for 600 ptas a half-hour (or 800 ptas an hour for students) upstairs at El Café de Internet (☎ 93 412 19 15), Gran Via de les Corts Catalanes 656.

Travel Agencies Viva (☎ 93 423 33 60) at Carrer de Rocafort 116-122 (metro: Rocafort) offers youth and student fares. Unlimited (☎ 902-32 52 75), Ronda de la Universitat 16, is another good place to look for deals if you are a student or under 26.

Bookshops In the Barri Gòtic, Quera at Carrer de Petritxol 2 specialises in maps and guides; Próleg at Carrer de la Dagueria 13 is a good women's bookshop.

In l'Eixample, Altaïr, Carrer de Balmes 71, is a superb travel bookshop; Librería Francesa at Passeig de Gràcia 91, Come In at Carrer de Provença 203 and BCN at Carrer d'Aragó 277 are good for novels and books on Spain, and dictionaries.

Laundry Lavandería Tigre at Carrer d'En Rauric 20 in the Barri Gòtic will wash, dry and fold 3kg in a couple of hours for 820 ptas (7kg for 1265 ptas). Doing it yourself costs 495 ptas and 745 ptas respectively to wash, plus extra to dry.

Emergency The Guàrdia Urbana (City Police; ☎ 092) has a station at La Rambla 43, opposite Plaça Reial. For an ambulance or emergency medical help call ☎ 061.

Dangers & Annoyances Watch your pockets, bags and cameras on the train to/from the airport, on La Rambla, in the Barri Gòtic south of Plaça Reial and in the Barri Xinès – especially at night. These last two areas have been somewhat cleaned up in recent years but pickpockets, bag-snatchers and intimidating beggars still stalk the unsuspecting.

Things to See

La Rambla The best way to introduce yourself to Barcelona is by a leisurely stroll from Plaça de Catalunya down **La Rambla**, the magnificent boulevard of a thousand faces. This long pedestrian strip, shaded by leafy trees, is an ever-changing blur of activity, lined with newsstands, bird and flower stalls, and cafés. It's populated by artists, buskers, human statues, shoe-shine merchants, beggars, and a constant stream of people promenading and just enjoying the sights.

About halfway down La Rambla is the wonderful **Mercat de la Boqueria**, which is worth going to just for the sights and sounds, but is also a good place to stock up on fresh fruit, vegetables, nuts, bread, pastries – everything you'll need for a park picnic. Just off La Rambla, farther south, **Plaça Reial** was, until a few years ago, a seedy square of ill repute, but it's now quite pleasant, with numerous cafés, bars and a couple of music clubs. Just off the other side of La Rambla at Carrer Nou de la Rambla 3-5 is Gaudí's moody **Palau Güell**, open daily, except Sunday, from 10 to 2 pm and 4 to 8 pm (300 otas; students 150 ptas). This is also where to pick up Ruta del Modernisme tickets, which allow you to see others Gaudí efforts around the city.

Down at the end of La Rambla stands the **Monument a Colom**, a statue of Columbus atop a tall pedestal. A small lift will take you to the top of the monument (250 ptas). Just west is the **Museu Marítim**, in the beautiful 14th-century Royal Shipyards, with an impressive array of boats, models, maps and more. If you like boats and the sea, you won't be disappointed – open Tuesday to Saturday from 10 am to 6 pm; Sunday from 10 am to 2 pm (800 ptas).

Barri Gòtic Barcelona's serene Gothic **catedral** is open daily from 8.30 am to 1.30 pm and 5 to 7.30 pm – be sure to visit the lovely cloister. Each Sunday at noon, crowds gather in front of the cathedral to dance the Catalan national dance, the *sardana*. Just east of the cathedral is the fascinating **Museu d'Història de la Ciutat** (City History Museum) composed of several buildings around **Plaça del Rei**, the palace courtyard of the medieval monarchs of Aragón. From the royal chapel, climb the multitiered Mirador del Rei Martí for good views. The museum also includes a remarkable subterranean walk through excavated portions of Roman and Visigothic Barcelona. It's all open Tuesday to Saturday from 10 am to 2 pm and 4 to 8 pm, and Sunday from 10 am to 2 pm. Entrance is 500 ptas.

A few minutes walk west of the cathedral, **Plaça de Sant Josep Oriol** is a hang-out for bohemian musicians and buskers. The plaza is surrounded by cafés and towards the end of the week becomes an outdoor art and craft market.

Waterfront For a look at the new face of Barcelona, take a stroll along the once-seedy waterfront. From the bottom of La Rambla you can cross the Rambla de Mar footbridge to the **Moll d'Espanya**, a former wharf in the middle of the old harbour, Port Vell. There you'll find **L'Aquàrium**, one of Europe's best aquariums, open daily from 9.30 am to 9 pm, but not cheap at 1400 ptas. North-east of Port Vell, on the far side of the drab La Barceloneta area, the city **beaches** begin. Along the beachfront, after 1.25km you'll reach the **Vila**

Olímpica, site of the 1992 Olympic village, which is fronted by the impressive **Port Olímpic**, a large marina with dozens of rather touristy bars and restaurants (you won't find too many locals here).

La Sagrada Família Construction on Gaudí's principal work and Barcelona's most famous building (metro: Sagrada Família) began in 1882 and is taking a *long* time. The church is not yet half built and it's anyone's guess whether it will be finished by 2082. Many feel that it should not be completed but left as a monument to the master, whose career was cut short when he was hit by a tram in 1926.

Today there are eight towers, all over 100m high, with 10 more to come – the total of 18 representing the 12 Apostles, the four Evangelists and the mother of God, with the tallest tower (170m) standing for her son. Although La Sagrada Família is effectively a building site, the awesome dimensions and extravagant yet careful sculpting of what has been completed make it probably Barcelona's greatest highlight. The north-east Nativity Façade was done under Gaudí's own supervision; the very different north-west Passion Façade has been built since the 1950s.

You can climb high inside some of the towers by spiral staircases for a vertiginous overview of the interior and a panorama to the sea, or you can opt out and take a lift some of the way up. Entry to La Sagrada Família – which is on Carrer de Sardenya, on the corner of Carrer de Mallorca – is 800 ptas for everyone. It's open daily April to the end of August from 9 am to 8 pm; March, September and October from 9 am to 7 pm; and November to February from 9 am to 6 pm.

More Modernism Many of the best modernist buildings are in l'Eixample, including Gaudí's beautifully coloured **Casa Batlló** at Passeig de Gràcia 43 and his **La Pedrera** at No 92, an apartment block with a grey stone façade that ripples round the corner of Carrer de Provença. Next door to Casa Batlló at No 41 is **Casa Amatller**, by another leading modernist architect, Josep Puig i Cadafalch.

Another modernist highpoint is the **Palau de la Música Catalana** concert hall at Carrer de Sant Pere mes alt 11 in the La Ribera area

CENTRAL BARCELONA

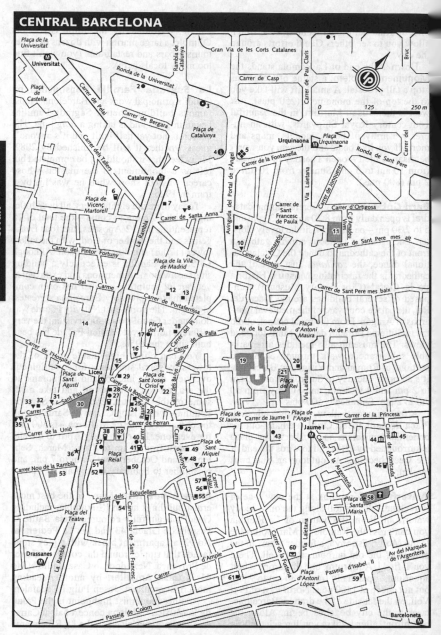

CENTRAL BARCELONA

PLACES TO STAY

7	Hotel Continental
9	Hostal Lausanne
12	Pensión-Hostal Fina
13	Hostal-Residencia Rembrandt
18	Hostal Galerias Maldà
20	Hostal Layetana
24	Pensión Bienestar
25	Pensión Europa
28	Hotel Internacional
29	Hostal Paris
32	Hotel Peninsular
49	Hostal Levante
50	Hotel Roma Reial
52	Youth Hostel Kabul
55	Pensión Alamar
56	Alberg Palau
57	Casa Huéspedes Mari-Luz
61	Abba Youth Hostel

PLACES TO EAT

8	Self-Naturista
10	Els Quatre Gats
15	Juicy Jones
16	Irati

22	Mesón Jesús
31	Bar-Restaurante Romescu
33	Restaurante Els Tres Bots
34	Restaurante Pollo Rico
35	Kashmir Restaurant Tandoori
39	Les Quinze Nits
47	Bar-Restaurant Cervantes
48	El Gallo Kiriko
54	La Fonda Escudellers
59	Restaurante Set Portes

OTHER

1	El Café de Internet
2	Unlimited Travel Agent
3	Catalunya Train Station
4	Main Tourist Office
5	El Corte Inglés Department Store
6	L'Ovella Negra
11	Palau de la Música Catalana
14	Mercat de la Boqueria
17	Quera Bookshop
19	Catedral
21	Museu d'Història de la Ciutat

23	Schilling
26	Cafè de l'Òpera
27	American Express
30	Gran Teatre del Liceu
36	Guàrdia Urbana (Police Station)
37	Barcelona Pipa Club
38	Glaciar Bar
40	Lavandería Tigre
41	Bar Malpaso
42	CIAJ (Youth Information Centre)
43	Próleg Bookshop
44	Museu Textil i d'Indumetària & Museu Barbier-Mueller d'Art Precolombí
45	Museu Picasso
46	El Xampanyet Bar
51	Jamboree & Sala Tarantos
53	Palau Güell
58	Església de Santa Maria del Mar
60	Main Post Office

east of the Barri Gòtic – a marvellous concoction of tile, brick, sculpted stone and stained glass.

The Agència del Paisatge Urbà (Urban Landscapes Agency; ☎ 93 488 01 39) offers four tours (of eight buildings including the Palau Güell, Sagrada Família, Manzana de la Discordia and Palau de la Música Catalana), plus gives you written description of 50 modernista buildings throughout the city (there is also a map *Ruta del Modernisme*, which you can pick up free at the tourist office). The whole lot costs 1600 ptas and you get the ticket (valid for a month) at the Palau Güell. Note that even with this ticket you cannot enter the Manzana de la Discordia buildings.

You can visit La Pedrera, with its giant chimney pots looking like multicoloured medieval knights, independently. It is open daily from 10 am to 8 pm and entry costs 500 ptas (300 ptas for students). Guided visits take place at 6 pm; 11 am on weekends and holidays.

Museu Picasso & Around The Museu Picasso, in a medieval mansion at Carrer de Montcada 15-19 in La Ribera, houses the most important collection of Picasso's work in Spain – more than 3000 pieces, including paintings, drawings, engravings and ceramics. It concentrates on Picasso's Barcelona periods (1895-1900 and 1901-04) early in his career, and shows how the precocious Picasso learned to handle a whole spectrum of subjects and treatments before developing his own forms of expression. There are also two rooms devoted to Picasso's 1950s series of interpretations of Velázquez's masterpiece *Las Meninas*. The museum is open Tuesday to Saturday from 10 am to 8 pm, and Sunday from 10 am to 3 pm. Entry is 600 ptas, but it's 250 ptas on non-holiday Wednesdays and free on the first Sunday of each month.

The **Museu Textil i d'Indumentària** (Textile and Costume Museum), opposite the Museu Picasso, has a fascinating collection of tapestries, clothing and other textiles from centuries past and present. Opening hours are Tuesday to Saturday from 10 am to 5 pm and Sunday from 10 am to 2 pm. Entrance is 400 ptas (or 700 ptas if you combine it with the Museu Barbier-Mueller d'Art Precolombí next door).

The **Museu Barbier-Mueller d'Art Pre-colombí** holds one of the most prestigious collections of pre-Columbian art in the world. It opens Tuesday to Saturday from 10 am to 8 pm and Sunday from 10 am to 3 pm. Admission costs 500 ptas.

At the south end of Carrer de Montcada is the **Església de Santa Maria del Mar**, probably the most perfect of Barcelona's Gothic churches.

Parc de la Ciutadella As well as being a great place for a picnic or a stroll, this large park east of the Ciutat Vella has some more specific attractions. Top of the list are the monumental **cascada** (waterfall), a dramatic combination of statuary, rocks, greenery and thundering water created in the 1870s with the young Gaudí lending a hand; and the **Museu Nacional d'Art Modern de Catalunya**, with a good collection of 19th and early 20th-century Catalan art, open Tuesday to Sunday from 10 am to 7 pm; entry is 300 ptas (students 200 ptas). At the southern end of the park is Barcelona's **zoo**, open daily from 10 am to 7 pm (1400 ptas) and famed for its albino gorilla.

Parc Güell This park, in the north of the city, is where Gaudí turned his hand to landscape gardening. It's a strange, enchanting place where Gaudí's passion for natural forms really took flight – to the point where the artificial almost seems more natural than the natural.

The main, lower gate, flanked by buildings with the appearance of Hansel and Gretel's gingerbread house, sets the mood in the park, with its winding paths and carefully tended flower beds, skewed tunnels with rough stone columns resembling tree roots, and the famous dragon of broken glass and tiles. The house in which Gaudí lived most of his last 20 years has been converted into a museum, open from April to August daily from 10 am to 8 pm; the rest of the year Sunday to Friday from 10 am to 2 pm and 4 to 6 pm (300 ptas). The simplest way to Parc Güell is to take the metro to Lesseps then walk 10 to 15 minutes; follow the signs north-east along Travessera de Dalt then left up Carrer de Larrard. The park is open daily from 9 am: June to September to 9 pm, April, May and October to

8 pm, March and November to 7 pm, and other months to 6 pm (free).

Montjuïc This hill overlooking the city centre from the south-west is home to some of Barcelona's best museums and attractions, some fine parks, and the main 1992 Olympics sites – well worth some of your time.

On the north side of the hill, the impressive **Palau Nacional** houses the **Museu Nacional d'Art de Catalunya**, with a wonderful collection of Romanesque frescoes, woodcarvings and sculpture from medieval Catalonia. Opening hours are Tuesday to Saturday from 10 am to 7 pm (Thursday to 9 pm), Sunday and holidays from 10 am to 2.30 pm (closed Monday and 1 January, 1 May and 25 December). Entry is 600 ptas.

Nearby is the **Poble Espanyol** (Spanish Village), by day a tour group's paradise with its craft workshops, souvenir shops and creditable copies of famous Spanish architecture; after dark it becomes a nightlife jungle, with bars and restaurants galore. It's open from 9 am daily (Monday to 8 pm; Tuesday to Thursday to 2 am; Friday and Saturday to 4 am; Sunday to midnight). Entry is 950 ptas (students and children aged seven to 14 pay 525 ptas). After 9 pm on days other than Friday and Saturday, it's free.

Downhill east of the Palau Nacional, the **Museu d'Arqueologia** (Archaeological Museum) has a good collection from Catalonia and the Balearic Islands. Opening hours are Tuesday to Saturday from 9.30 am to 7 pm, Sunday from 10 am to 2.30 pm (200 ptas, free on Sunday).

Above the Palau Nacional is the **Anella Olímpica** (Olympic Ring), where you can swim in the Olympic pool, the **Piscines Bernat Picornell**, open daily from 7 am until midnight Monday to Friday, 9 pm Saturday, and 7.30 am to 2.30 pm Sunday for 650 ptas, and wander into the main **Estadi Olímpic** (open daily from 10 am to 6 pm; admission free).

The **Fundació Joan Miró**, a short distance downhill east of the Estadi Olímpic, is one of the best modern art museums in Spain. Aside from many works by Miró, there are both permanent and changing exhibitions of other modern art. It's open Tuesday to Saturday from 10 am to 7 pm (Thursday to 9.30 pm), and Sunday and holidays from 10 am to 2.30 pm. Entry is 700 ptas (400 ptas for students).

At the top of Montjuïc is the **Castell de Montjuïc**, with a military museum and great views.

To get to Montjuïc you can either walk or take a bus from Plaça d'Espanya (metro: Espanya). Bus No 61 from here links most of the main sights and ends at the foot of a chairlift (425 ptas) up to the castle. A funicular railway (215 ptas) from Parallel metro station also runs to the chairlift. From November to mid-June, the chairlift and funicular run only on weekends and holidays.

Tibidabo At 542m, this is the highest hill in the wooded range that forms the backdrop to Barcelona – a good place for a change of scene, some fresh air and, if the air's clear, 70km views. At the top are the Temple del Sagrat Cor, a church topped by a giant Christ statue, and the Parc d'Atraccions funfair. A short distance along the ridge is the 288m Torre de Collserola telecommunications tower, with a hair-raising external glass lift (it opens Wednesday to Friday from 11 am to 2.30 pm and 3.30 to 8 pm; weekends all day. Tickets cost 500 ptas).

The fun way to Tibidabo is to take a suburban train from Plaça de Catalunya to Avinguda de Tibidabo (10 minutes), then hop on the *tramvia blau* tram (225 ptas) across the road, which will take you up to the foot of the Tibidabo funicular railway. The funicular climbs to the church at the top of the hill for 300 ptas. All these run every 10 or 15 minutes from at least 9 am to 9.30 pm.

Els Encants Market This good second-hand market by Plaça de les Glòries Catalanes, runs on Monday, Wednesday, Friday and Saturday between 8 am and 6 pm (8 pm in summer).

Language Courses

The Universitat de Barcelona runs one-month Spanish courses about four times a year. Contact its Instituto de Estudios Hispánicos (☎ 93 318 42 66 ext 2084; fax 93 302 59 47) at Gran Via de les Corts Catalanes 585. The main tourist office and the CIAJ youth information centre at Carrer de Ferran 32 in the Barri Gòtic have further information on courses. There are also notice boards with ads for classes at the above-mentioned university building and at Come In bookshop, Carrer de Provença 203. Also advertised at Come In are some jobs for English teachers.

Organised Tours

The Bus Turístic service covers two circuits (24 stops) linking virtually all the major tourist sights. Tourist offices and many hotels have leaflets explaining the system, or you can call ☎ 93 423 18 00. Tickets, available on the bus, are 1700 ptas for one day's unlimited rides, or 2300 ptas for two consecutive days. Service is about every 20 minutes from 9 am to 9.30 pm. Tickets entitle you to discounts of up to 300 ptas on entry fees and tickets to more than 20 sights along the route.

Special Events

Barcelona's biggest festival is the Festes de la Mercè, several days of merrymaking around 24 September including *castellers* (human-castle builders), dances of giants and *correfocs* – a parade of firework-spitting dragons and devils. There are many others – tourist offices can clue you in.

Places to Stay

Camping *Camping Cala Gogó* (☎ 93 379 46 00), 9km south-west, is the closest camping ground to Barcelona and can be reached by bus No 65 from Plaça d'Espanya. Two to 3km farther out in Viladecans, on Carretera C-246, *El Toro Bravo* (☎ 93 637 34 62) and *La Ballena Alegre* (☎ 93 658 05 04) are much more pleasant, and there are several more camping grounds within a few more kilometres on Carretera C-246. To get to any of these, take bus No L95 from the corner of Ronda de la Universitat and Rambla de Catalunya.

Hostels A handful of places in Barcelona provide dormitory accommodation. For two people they're not great value, but they're certainly good places to meet other travellers. All require you to rent sheets, at 150 to 350 ptas for your stay, if you don't have them (or a sleeping bag). Ring before you go as the hostels can get booked up.

Youth Hostel Kabul (☎ 93 318 51 90), at Plaça Reial 17, is a rough-and-ready place but it has no curfew and is OK if you're looking for somewhere with a noisy party atmosphere; it has 150 places and charges 1700 ptas a night (no card needed). Security is slack but there are safes available for your valuables. Bookings are not taken.

Alberg Palau (☎ 93 412 50 80) at Carrer del Palau 6 has just 40 places and is more pleasant. It charges 1300 ptas a night including breakfast and has a kitchen. It's open from 7 am to midnight. No card is needed.

Abba Youth Hostel (☎ 93 319 45 45), Passeig de Colom 9, offers beds in a separate-sex dorm arrangement for 1300 ptas including breakfast. It's handy for the Barri Gòtic and waterfront, but not so much for the metro.

Hostal de Joves (☎ 93 300 31 04), near metro Arc de Triomf at Passeig de Pujades 29, is quite clean and modern, with 68 beds and a kitchen, and charges 1500 ptas including breakfast; there's a 1 or 2 am curfew. A hostel card is only needed during the six peak summer weeks.

Alberg Mare de Déu de Montserrat (☎ 93 210 51 51) is the biggest and most comfortable hostel, but is 4km north of the centre at Passeig Mare de Déu del Coll 41-51. It has 180 beds and charges 1700 ptas if you're under 25 or have an ISIC or IYTC card, 2275 ptas otherwise (breakfast included). A hostel card is needed. It's closed during the day and you can't get in after 3 am. It's a 10-minute walk from Vallcarca metro or a 20-minute ride from Plaça de Catalunya on bus No 28.

Alberg Pere Tarrés, (☎ 93 410 23 09) at Carrer de Numància 149 (about a five-minute walk from Les Corts metro), has 90 beds at B&B costs from 1500 to 2000 ptas, depending on age and whether or not you have a hostel card (rates include breakfast). It has a kitchen, but is closed during the day and you can't get in after 2 am.

Pensiones & Hostales Most of the cheaper options are scattered through the old city, on either side of La Rambla. Generally, the areas closer to the port and on the west side of La Rambla are seedier and cheaper, and as you move north towards Plaça de Catalunya standards (and prices) rise.

Hostal Galerias Maldà (☎ 93 317 30 02) upstairs in an arcade off Carrer del Pi 5 is about as cheap as you'll find. It's a rambling, family-run establishment with basic singles/doubles for 1500/3000 ptas, and one great little single set aside in a kind of tower for 1000 ptas.

Casa Huéspedes Mari-Luz (☎ 93 317 34 63), Carrer del Palau 4, has oppressive dorms and doubles for 3800 ptas (double bed) and 4800 ptas (two beds). *Pensión Bienestar* (☎ 93 318 72 83), Carrer d'En Quintana 3 has 30 clean, ordinary singles/doubles from 1300/2400 or 1500/2600 ptas depending on size. At Carrer de la Boqueria 18, *Pensión Europa* (☎ 93 318 76 20) has small and bare singles for 2000 ptas and better doubles with own bath for 4800 ptas.

Pensión Alamar (☎ 93 302 50 12), Carrer de la Comtessa de Sobradiel 1 (metro: Liceu), has 13 rooms, some with balcony, for 1700/3500 ptas. It's cheap and basic, but you can use the kitchen and washing machine too.

Hostal Paris (☎/fax 93 301 37 85) at Carrer del Cardenal Casañas 4 has 42 mostly large rooms for 3000/4000 ptas, or 4000/5800 ptas with private bathroom.

Hostal Levante (☎ 93 317 95 65), Baixada de Sant Miquel 2, is a good family-run place with singles/doubles for 2500/4000 ptas, or 5000 ptas for doubles with private bath. Up near Plaça de Catalunya is the excellent *Hostal Lausanne* (☎ 93 302 11 39), Avinguda Portal de l'Àngel 24 (1st floor), with good security and rooms from 3500/4900 ptas.

Quiet Carrer Portaferrissa has a couple of good hostales: *Hostal-Residencia Rembrandt* (☎ 93 318 10 11), No 23, charges 2700/4000 ptas, or 3000/5000 ptas with shower. Doubles with full private bathroom cost 5500 ptas. *Pensión-Hostal Fina* (☎ 93 317 97 87), No 11, asks 2750/3750 ptas, or 4750 ptas for a double with private bath.

Hostal Layetana (☎ 93 319 20 12) at Plaça de Berenguer Gran 2 is well kept, with good-sized rooms at 2200/3500 ptas, or 4900 ptas for doubles with bathroom.

Opposite Estació de França, the impressive *Hostal Nuevo Colón* (☎ 93 319 50 77), Avinguda del Marquès de l'Argentera 19, has rooms for 2800/4000 ptas, or 4000/5500 ptas with private bath.

Accommodation near Estació Sants is in-

onvenient for the centre, but if you arrive late
at night, *Hostal Sofía* (☎ 93 419 50 40) at
Avinguda de Roma 1-3 has very good rooms
from 3000/5500 ptas. The modern *Hostal
Sans* (☎ 93 331 37 00) at Carrer de Antoni de
Capmany 82 charges 2200/3200 ptas, or
4200/4900 ptas with private bathroom.

Hotels Higher up the scale, but good value,
is the *Hotel Roma Reial* (☎ 93 302 03 66) at
Plaça Reial 11. Modern singles/doubles with
bath cost 4800/6800 ptas. The once-grand
Hotel Peninsular (☎ 93 302 31 38), Carrer
de Sant Pau 34, has singles/doubles from
5000/6300 ptas in high season, although the
rooms don't quite live up to the impressive
foyer and central atrium.

On La Rambla itself, *Hotel Continental*
(☎ 93 301 25 70) at No 138 and *Hotel Internacional* (☎ 93 302 25 66) at No 78-80 are
among the best value. The Continental has
pleasant, well-decorated rooms starting from
6900/9000 ptas with breakfast in high season;
the Internacional charges 6530/12,000 ptas.

Places to Eat

For quick food, the *Bocatta* and *Pans &
Company* chains, with numerous branches
around the city, do good hot and cold
baguettes with a range of fillings for 300 to
500 ptas.

The greatest concentration of cheaper
restaurants is within walking distance of La
Rambla. There are a few good-value ones on
Carrer de Sant Pau, west off La Rambla.
Kashmir Restaurant Tandoori at No 39 does
tasty curries and biryanis from around 800
ptas. *Restaurante Pollo Rico*, No 31, has a
somewhat seedy downstairs bar where you
can have a quarter chicken or an omelette,
with chips, bread and wine, for 500 ptas; the
restaurant upstairs is more salubrious and
only slightly more expensive. *Restaurante
Els Tres Bots*, No 42, is grungy but cheap,
with a menú for 875 ptas. Just off Carrer de
Sant Pau on Carrer de l'Arc de Sant Agustí,
tiny *Bar-Restaurante Romesco* has good,
home-style food at great prices, with most
main courses around 400 to 700 ptas.

There are lots more places in the Barri
Gòtic. *Self-Naturista*, a self-service vegetarian restaurant at Carrer de Santa Anna 13,
does a good lunch menú for 810 ptas. *Mesón

Jesús, Carrer dels Cecs de la Boqueria 4, and
Bar-Restaurant Cervantes, Carrer de Cervantes 7, do a good lunch menú for 900 ptas.
El Gallo Kiriko at Carrer d'Avinyó 19 is a
friendly Pakistani restaurant that's busy with
travellers. Tandoori chicken and salad, or
couscous with beef or vegetables, is just 450
ptas. A Basque favourite is *Irati*, Carrer del
Cardenal Cassanyes 17. The set menú is 1500
ptas, or you can enjoy the great tapas and a
zurrito of beer or six. A couple of doors down
is the psychedelic *Juicy Jones*, where a vegetarian set menú costs 975 ptas.

For something a bit more upmarket, *Les
Quinze Nits* at Plaça Reial 6 and *La Fonda
Escudellers* on Carrer dels Escudellers are
two stylish bistro-like restaurants, under the
same management, with a big range of good
Catalan and Spanish dishes at reasonable
prices – which can mean long queues in
summer and at weekends. Three courses with
wine and coffee will be about 2500 ptas.
Carrer dels Escudellers also has a couple of
good night-time takeaway felafel joints –
around 300 ptas a serve. Or there's *Restaurante Set Portes* (☎ 93 319 30 33) at Passeig
d'Isabel II 14, which dates from 1836 and
specialises in paella (1200 to 2000 ptas). It's
advisable to book. Another famous institution
is *Els Quatre Gats*, Picasso's former hang-
out at Carrer Montsió 3.

The *Mercat de la Boqueria* on La Rambla
has a great selection of food.

Entertainment

Barcelona's entertainment bible is the weekly
Guía del Ocio (125 ptas at newsstands). Its
excellent listings (in Spanish) include films,
theatre, music and art exhibitions.

Bars Barcelona's huge variety of bars are
mostly at their busiest from about 11 pm to 2
or 3 am, especially Thursday to Saturday.

Cafè de l'Òpera at La Rambla 74, opposite
the Liceu opera house, is the liveliest place
on La Rambla. It gets packed with all and
sundry at night. *Glaciar* on Plaça Reial is
busy with a young crowd of foreigners and
locals. Tiny *Bar Malpaso* at Carrer d'En
Rauric 20, just off Plaça Reial, plays great
Latin and African music. Another hip low-lit
place with a more varied clientele is
Schilling, Carrer de Ferran 23.

SPAIN

El Xampanyet at Carrer de Montcada 22 near the Museu Picasso is another small place, specialising in cava (Catalan champagne, around 500 ptas a bottle), with good tapas too.

West of La Rambla, *L'Ovella Negra*, Carrer de les Sitges 5, is a noisy, barn-like tavern with a young crowd. *Bar Marsella*, Carrer de Sant Pau 65, specialises in absinthe (absenta in Catalan), a potent but mellow beverage with supposed narcotic qualities (500 ptas a shot). If by 2.30 am you still need a drink and you don't want a disco, your best bet (except on Sunday) is the *London Bar*, Carrer Nou de la Rambla 36, which sometimes has live music and opens until about 5 am.

Live Music & Discos Many music places have dance space and some discos have bands on around midnight or so, to pull in some custom before the real action starts about 3 am. If you go for the band, you can normally stay for the disco at no extra cost and avoid bouncers' whims about what you're wearing etc. Women – and maybe male companions – may get in free at some discos if the bouncers like their looks. Count on 300 to 800 ptas for a beer in any of these places.

On Plaça Reial, *Barcelona Pipa Club*, No 3, has jazz Thursday to Saturday around midnight (ring the bell to get in); *Jamboree*, No 17, has jazz nightly and a lively disco later, from about 1.30 am; *Sala Tarantos*, next door, has classy flamenco some nights. *Club Apolo*, Carrer Nou de la Rambla 113, has live world music several nights a week, followed by live salsa or a varied disco.

Otto Zutz, Carrer de Lincoln 15, is for the beautiful people dressed in black. The crowd's cool and the atmosphere's great.

Zeleste, Carrer dels Almogàvers 122, Poble Nou, is a cavernous warehouse-type club, regularly hosting visiting bands. *Mirablau* at the foot of the Tibidabo funicular is a bar with great views and a small disco floor; it's open till 5 am and entry is free.

The two top gay discos are *Metro*, Carrer de Sepúlveda 185, and *Martin's* at Passeig de Gràcia 130. Metro attracts some lesbians and heteros as well as gay men; Martin's is for gay men only.

Cinemas For films in their original language (with Spanish subtitles), check listings for those marked VO (versión original). A ticket is usually 600 to 700 ptas but many cinemas reduce prices on Monday.

Classical Music & Opera The Gran Teatre del Liceu opera house on La Rambla, gutted by fire in 1994, is yet to reopen. Until it does, opera and orchestral music are shared among other theatres, the lovely Palau de la Música Catalana at Carrer de Sant Pere mes alt 11 being the chief venue.

Getting There & Away

Air Barcelona's airport, 14km south-west of the city centre at El Prat de Llobregat, caters to international as well as domestic flights. Always compare the range of available fares. Standard one-way fares to Madrid range from 11,700 ptas to 15,550 ptas, but you can often dig up specials and cheap youth fares.

Iberia (☎ 902-40 05 00) is at Passeig de Gràcia 30; Spanair (24 hours ☎ 902-13 14 15) and Air Europa (☎ 902-24 00 42) are at the airport.

Bus The terminal for virtually all domestic and international buses is the Estació del Nord at Carrer d'Alí Bei 80 (metro: Arc de Triomf). Its information desk (☎ 93 265 65 08) is open daily from 7 am to 9 pm. A few international buses go from Estació d'Autobuses de Sants beside Estació Sants train station.

Several buses a day go to most main Spanish cities. Madrid is seven or eight hours away (2940 ptas), Zaragoza 4½ hours (1640 ptas), Valencia 4½ hours (2900 ptas) and Granada 13 to 15 hours (7830 ptas). Buses run several times a week to London (13,450 ptas), Paris (11,450 ptas) and other European cities.

Train Virtually all trains travelling to/from destinations within Spain stop at Estació Sants (metro: Sants-Estació); most international trains use Estació de Franca (metro: Barceloneta).

For some international destinations you have to change trains at Montpellier or the French border. A 2nd-class seat to Paris is

12,800 ptas sitting or 16,500 ptas in a couchette. Proper sleepers cost more.

Daily trains run to most major cities in Spain. To Madrid there are seven trains a day (6½ to 9½ hours, 4900 ptas); to San Sebastián two (eight to 10 hours, 4600 ptas); to Valencia 10 (as little as three hours on high-speed Euromed train, 4600 ptas) and to Granada (eight hours, 6200 ptas).

Tickets and information are available at the stations or from the RENFE office in Passeig de Gràcia metro/train station on Passeig de Gràcia, open daily from 7 am to 10 pm (Sunday 9 pm).

Car & Motorcycle Tolls on the A-7 autopista add up to 8155 ptas from the French border to Alicante via Barcelona. The N-II from the French border to Barcelona and N-340 southbound are toll-free but slower. The fastest route to Madrid is via Zaragoza on the A-2 (2305 ptas), which heads west off the A-7 south of Barcelona, then the toll-free N-II from Zaragoza.

Getting Around
To/From the Airport Trains link the airport to Estació Sants and Catalunya station on Plaça de Catalunya every half-hour. They take 15 to 20 minutes and a ticket is 305 ptas (350 ptas at weekends). The A1 Aerobús does the 40-minute run between Plaça de Catalunya and the airport every 15 minutes, or every half-hour at weekends. The fare is 475 ptas. A taxi from the airport to Plaça de Catalunya is around 2500 ptas.

Bus, Metro & Train Barcelona's metro system spreads its tentacles around the city in such a way that most places of interest are within a 10-minute walk of a station. Buses and suburban trains are only needed for a few destinations – but note the Bus Turístic under Organised Tours earlier in this section.

A single metro, bus or suburban train ride costs 140 ptas, but a T-1 ticket, valid for 10 rides, costs only 775 ptas, while a T-DIA ticket (575 ptas) gives unlimited city travel in one day.

Car & Motorcycle While traffic flows smoothly thanks to an extensive one-way system, navigating can be frustrating.

Parking a car is also difficult and, if you choose a parking garage, quite expensive. It's better to ditch your car and rely on public transport.

Taxi Barcelona's black-and-yellow taxis are plentiful, reasonably priced and especially handy for late-night transport. From Plaça de Catalunya, it costs around 700 ptas to Estació Sants.

MONESTIR DE MONTSERRAT
Unless you are on a pilgrimage, the prime attraction of Montserrat, 50km north-west of Barcelona, is its setting. The Benedictine Monastery of Montserrat sits high on the side of an amazing 1236m mountain of truly weird rocky peaks, and is best reached by cable car. The monastery was founded in 1065 to commemorate an apparition of the Virgin Mary on this site. Pilgrims still come from all over Christendom to pay homage to its Black Virgin (La Moreneta), a 12th-century wooden sculpture of Mary, regarded as Catalonia's patroness.

Information
Montserrat's information centre (☎ 93 835 02 51, ext 586), to the left along the road from the top cable-car station, is open daily from 9 am to 6 pm. It has a good free leaflet/map on the mountain and monastery.

Things to See & Do
If you are making a day trip to Montserrat, come early. Apart from the monastery, exploring the mountain is a treat.

The two-part **Museu de Montserrat**, on the plaza in front of the monastery's basílica, has an excellent collection ranging from an Egyptian mummy to art by El Greco, Monet and Picasso. It's open weekdays from 10 am to 6 pm (weekends and holidays from 9.30 am to 6.30 pm), for 500 ptas (students 300 ptas).

Daily from 8 to 10.30 am and noon to 6.30 pm (and weekends from 7.30 to 8.30 pm), you can file past the image of the Black Virgin, high above the main altar of the 16th-century **basílica**, the only part of the monastery proper open to the public. The Montserrat Boys' Choir (Escolania) sings in

SPAIN

the basílica every day at 1 and 7 pm, except in July. The church fills up quickly, so try to arrive early.

You can explore the mountain above the monastery on a web of paths leading to small chapels and some of the peaks. The Funicular de Sant Joan (550/875 ptas one way/return) will lift you up the first 250m from the monastery.

Places to Stay & Eat

There are several accommodation options (all ☎ 93 835 02 51) at the monastery. The cheapest rooms are in the *Cel-les de Montserrat*, blocks of simple apartments, with showers, for up to 10 people. A two-person apartment costs 3900 to 5350 ptas in high season. Overlooking Plaça de Santa Maria are the *Hotel El Monestir*, with singles/doubles in high season from 3290/6015 ptas and the comfortable *Hotel Abat Cisneros*, with rooms from 6520/10,755 ptas in high season. The Cisneros has a four-course menú for 2700 ptas.

The *Snack Bar* near the top cable-car station has platos combinados from 875 ptas and bocadillos from about 350 ptas. *Bar de la Plaça* in the Abat Oliva cel.les building has similar prices. *Cafeteria Self-Service* near the car park has great views but is dearer.

Getting There & Away

Trains run from Plaça d'Espanya station in Barcelona to Aeri de Montserrat five to 10 times a day (most often on summer weekdays) – a 1½-hour ride. Return tickets for 1800 ptas include the cable car between Aeri de Montserrat and the monastery.

There's also a daily bus to the monastery from Estació d'Autobuses de Sants in Barcelona at 9 am (plus 8 am in July and August) for a return fare of 1300 ptas. It returns at 5 pm.

COSTA BRAVA

The Costa Brava ranks with Spain's Costa Blanca and Costa del Sol among Europe's most popular holiday spots. It stands alone, however, in its spectacular scenery and proximity to Northern Europe, both of which have sent prices skyrocketing in the most appealing places.

The main jumping-off points for the Costa Brava are the inland towns Girona (Gerona in Castilian) and Figueres (Figueras). Both places are on the A-7 autopista and the toll-free N-II highway which connect Barcelona with France. Along the coast the most appealing resorts are, from north to south, Cadaqués, L'Escala (La Escala), Tamariu, Llafranc, Calella de Palafrugell and Tossa de Mar.

Tourist offices along the coast are very helpful, with information on accommodation, transport and other things; they include Girona (☎ 972 22 65 75), Figueres (☎ 972 50 31 55), Palafrugell (☎ 972 30 02 28), and Cadaqués (☎ 972 25 83 15).

Coastal Resorts

The Costa Brava (Rugged Coast) is all about picturesque inlets and coves. Some longer beaches at places like L'Estartit and Empúries are worth visiting out of season, but there has been a tendency to build tall buildings wherever engineers think it can be done. Fortunately, in many places it just can't.

Cadaqués, about one hour's drive east of Figueres at the end of an agonising series of hairpin bends, is perhaps the most picturesque of all Spanish resorts, and haunted by the memory of the artist Salvador Dalí, who lived here. It's short on beaches, so people spend a lot of time sitting at waterfront cafés or wandering along the beautiful coast. About 10km north-east of Cadaqués is **Cap de Creus**, a rocky peninsula with a single restaurant at the top of a craggy cliff. This is paradise for anyone who likes to scramble around rocks risking life and limb with every step.

Farther down the coast, past L'Escala and L'Estartit, is Palafrugell, itself a few kilometres inland with little to offer, but near three beach towns that have to be seen to be believed. The most northerly of these, **Tamariu,** is also the smallest, least crowded and most exclusive. **Llafranc** is the biggest and busiest, and has the longest beach. **Calella de Palafrugell**, with its picture-postcard setting, is never overcrowded and always relaxed. If you're driving down this coast, it's worth making the effort to stop at some of these towns, particularly out of season.

Other Attractions

When you have had enough beach for a while, make sure you put the **Teatre-Museu Dalí**, on Plaça Gala i Salvador Dalí in Figueres, at the top of your list. This 19th-century theatre was converted by Dalí himself and houses a huge and fascinating collection of his strange creations. From July to September the museum is open from 9 am to 7.15 pm daily. Queues are long on summer mornings. From October to June it's open from 10.30 am to 5.15 pm daily (closed Monday until the end of May, and on 1 January and 25 December). Entry is 1000 ptas (800 ptas October to May).

Historical interest is provided by **Girona**, with a lovely medieval quarter centred on a Gothic cathedral, and the ruins of the Greek and Roman town of **Empúries**, 2km from L'Escala.

For a spectacular stretch of coastline, take a drive north from Tossa de Mar to San Feliu de Guíxols. There are 360 curves in this 20km stretch of road, which, with brief stops to take in the scenery, can take a good two hours.

Among the most exciting attractions on the Costa Brava are the **Illes Medes**, off the coast from the package resort of L'Estartit. These seven islets and their surrounding coral reefs, with a total land area of only 21.5 hectares, have been declared a natural park to protect their extraordinarily diverse flora and fauna. Almost 1500 different life forms have been identified on and around the islands. You can arrange glass-bottom boat trips and diving.

Places to Stay

Most visitors to the Costa Brava rent apartments. If you are interested in renting an apartment for a week or so, contact local tourist offices in advance for information.

Figueres Figueres' HI hostel, the *Alberg Tramuntana* (☎ 972 50 12 13), is two blocks from the tourist office at Carrer Anicet Pagès 2. It charges 1700 ptas if you're under 26 or have an ISIC or IYTC card, 2275 ptas otherwise (breakfast included). Alternatively, *Hotel España* (☎ 972 50 08 69), a block east of the Dalí museum at Carrer de la Jonquera 26, has decent doubles for up to 6600 ptas.

Don't sleep in Figueres' Parc Municipal – people have been attacked here at night.

Girona *Pensión Viladomat* (☎ 972 20 31 76) at Carrer dels Ciutadans 5 has comfortable singles/doubles starting at 2000/4000 ptas.

Cadaqués *Camping Cadaqués* (☎ 972 25 81 26) is at the top of the town as you head towards Cabo de Creus. Two adults with a tent and a car pay 2880 ptas plus IVA. At these prices, a single person is probably better off staying in town near the waterfront. *Hostal Marina* (☎ 972 25 81 99) at Carrer de Frederico Rahola 2, has singles/doubles at 3000/6000 ptas plus IVA, all with private bath.

Near Palafrugell There are camping grounds at all three of Palafrugell's satellites. In Calella de Palafrugell try *Camping Moby Dick* (☎ 972 61 43 07); in Llafranc, *Kim's Camping* (☎ 972 61 67 75); and in Tamariu, *Camping Tamariu* (☎ 972 62 04 22).

Hotel and pensión rooms are relatively thin on the ground here, as many people come on package deals and stay in apartments. In Calella de Palafrugell, the friendly *Hostería del Plancton* (☎ 972 61 50 81) is one of the best deals on the Costa Brava, with rooms at 1800 ptas per person, but it's only open from June to September. *Residencia Montaña* (☎ 972 30 04 04) at Carrer de Cesàrea 2 in Llafranc is not a bad deal if you don't mind taking half-board. This costs 5350 ptas or 6650 ptas from late July to mid-August. In Tamariu, the *Hotel Sol d'Or* (☎ 972 30 04 24), near the beach at Carrer de Riera 18, has doubles with bathroom for 5850 ptas.

Getting There & Away

A few buses daily run from Barcelona to Tossa del Mar, L'Estartit and Cadaqués, but for the small resorts near Palafrugell you need to get to Girona first. Girona and Figueres are both on the railway connecting Barcelona to France. The dozen or so trains daily from Barcelona to Portbou at the border all stop in Girona, and most in Figueres. The fare from Barcelona to Girona is up to 880 ptas, to Figueres 1195 ptas.

SPAIN

SPAIN

Getting Around

There are two or three buses a day from Figueres to Cadaqués and three or four to L'Escala. Figueres bus station (☎ 972 67 42 98) is across the road from the train station.

Several buses daily run to Palafrugell from Girona (where the bus station is behind the train station), and there are buses from Palafrugell to Calella de Palafrugell, Llafranc and Tamariu. Most other coastal towns (south of Cadaqués) can be reached by bus from Girona.

TARRAGONA

Tarragona makes a perfect contrast to the city life of Barcelona. Founded in 218 BC, it was for a long time the capital of much of Roman Spain, and Roman structures figure among its most important attractions. Other periods of history are also well represented, including the medieval cathedral and 17th-century British additions to the old city walls. The city's archaeological museum is one of the most interesting in Spain. Today, Tarragona is a modern city with a large student population and a lively beach scene – and Spain's answer to EuroDisney, Port Aventura, is just a few kilometres south.

Orientation & Information

Tarragona's main street is Rambla Nova, which runs approximately north-west from a cliff top overlooking the Mediterranean. A couple of blocks to the east, parallel to Rambla Nova, is Rambla Vella, which marks the beginning of the old town. To the south-west, on the coast, is the train station.

Tarragona's main tourist office (☎ 977 24 50 64) is at Carrer Major 39. There is also a regional tourist office at Carrer Fortuny 4.

Things to See & Do

The Museu d'Història de Tarragona comprises four separate Roman sites around the city. A single 475 ptas ticket (free for students) is good for all four, along with the modest Museu d'Art Modern, Carrer de Santa Anna 8, and the 14th-century noble mansion now serving as the Museu Casa Castelarnau, Carrer dels Cavallers 14.

From June to September, all these places open Tuesday to Saturday from 9 or 10 am to 8 pm (the Passeig Arqueològic to midnight and Sunday from 10 am to 2 pm. In other months, they tend to open from 10 am to 1.30 pm and at least two afternoon hours (Sunday and holidays 10 am to 2 pm).

A good site to start with is the Museu de la Romanitat on Plaça del Rei, which includes part of the vaults of the Roman circus, where chariot races were held. Nearby, close to the beach, is the well-preserved Roman amphitheatre, where gladiators battled each other, or wild animals, to the death. On Carrer de Lleida, a few blocks west of Rambla Nova, are substantial remains of a Roman forum. The Passeig Arqueològic is a peaceful walkway along a stretch of the old city walls, which are a combination of Roman, Iberian and 17th-century British efforts.

Tarragona's Museu Arqueològic, on Plaça del Rei, gives further insight into the city's rich history. The carefully presented exhibits include frescoes, mosaics, sculpture and pottery dating back to the 2nd century BC. The museum is open Tuesday to Saturday from 10 am to 1 pm and 4.30 to 7 pm, Sunday and holidays 10 am to 2 pm. Entry is 100 ptas, free on Tuesday.

The catedral sits grandly at the highest point of Tarragona, overlooking the old town. Some parts of the building date back to the 12th century AD. It's open for tourist visits Monday to Friday for hours that vary with the season but always include 10 am to 1 pm and (except from mid-November to mid-March) 3 to 6 pm. Entrance is through the beautiful cloister with the excellent Museu Diocesà.

If you're here in summer, Platja del Miracle is the main city beach. It is reasonably clean but can get terribly crowded. Several other beaches dot the coast north of town, but in summer you will never be alone.

Port Aventura

Port Aventura (☎ 902-20 22 20), which opened in 1995 7km west of Tarragona, near Salou, is Spain's biggest and best funfair-adventure park. If you have 4100 ptas to spare (3100 ptas for children aged from five to 12), it makes a fun day out with never a dull moment – although it only opens from Semana Santa to October. There are hair-raising experiences like the Dragon Khan,

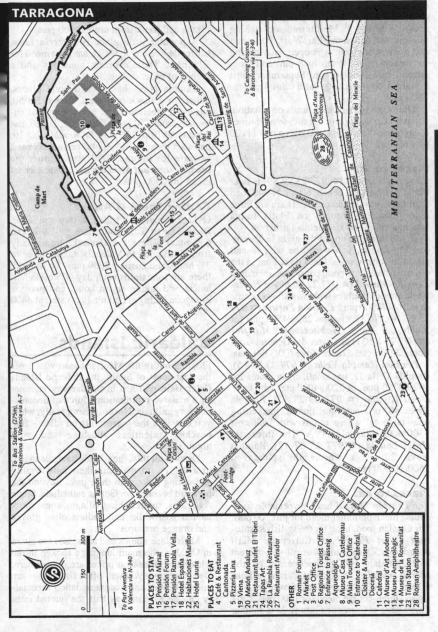

TARRAGONA

SPAIN

MEDITERRANEAN SEA

To Bus Station (275m),
Barcelona & Valencia via A-7

To Port Aventura
& Valencia via N-340

To Camping Grounds
& Barcelona via N-340

Camp de
Mart

0   150   300 m

PLACES TO STAY
15 Pensión Marsal
16 Pensión Forum
17 Pensión Rambla Vella
18 Hotel España
22 Habitaciones Mariflor
25 Hotel Lauria

PLACES TO EAT
4   Café & Restaurant
     Cantonada
5   Pizzeria Lina
19 Viena
20 Mesón Andaluz
21 Restaurant Bufet El Tiberi
24 Tapas Art
26 La Rambla Restaurant
27 Restaurant Mirador

OTHER
1   Roman Forum
2   Market
3   Post Office
6   Regional Tourist Office
7   Entrance to Passeig
     Arqueològic
8   Museu Casa Castelarnau
9   Main Tourist Office
10 Entrance to Catedral,
     Cloister & Museu
     Diocesà
11 Catedral
12 Museu d'Art Modern
13 Museu Arqueològic
14 Museu de la Romanitat
23 Train Station
28 Roman Amphitheatre

SPAIN

claimed to be Europe's biggest roller coaster. The park is divided into five theme areas: China, a Mediterranean fishing village, the American Far West, Polynesia and ancient Mexico. It is open daily during its season from 10 am to 8 pm, and from around mid-June to mid-September until midnight. Night tickets, valid from 7 pm, are 2500 ptas.

Trains run to Port Aventura's own station, about a 1km walk from the site, several times a day from Tarragona and Barcelona (1200 ptas return).

Places to Stay
Camping Tàrraco (☎ 977 23 99 89) is near Platja Arrabassada beach, off the N-340 road 2km north-east of the centre. There are three more camping grounds on Platja Larga beach, a couple of kilometres farther on.

If you intend to spend the night in Tarragona in summer, you would be wise to call ahead to book a room. Plaça de la Font in the old town has a few good pensiones, including *Pensión Marsal* (☎ 977 22 40 69) at No 26. Basic singles/doubles with own shower come in at 1650/3300 ptas. *Pensión Forum* (☎ 977 23 17 18), No 37, charges 2500/4500 ptas for much the same. *Habitaciones Mariflor* (☎ 977 23 82 31) at Carrer del General Contreras 29 has clean rooms for 1700/3300 ptas.

Pensión Rambla Vella (☎ 977 23 81 15), Rambla Vella 31, has small, clean rooms for 1870/3750 ptas, or 2200/4000 ptas with bath. *Hotel España* (☎ 977 23 27 12), Rambla Nova 49, is a well-positioned, unexciting one-star hotel where rooms with bath cost 3300/6000 ptas plus IVA. The three-star *Hotel Lauria* (☎ 977 23 67 12), Rambla Nova 20, is a worthwhile splurge at 5500/10,000 ptas.

Places to Eat
The *Pensión Marsal* has a respectable four-course lunch or dinner menú for just 700 ptas. For Catalan food, head for the stylish *Restaurant Bufet El Tiberi*, Carrer de Martí d'Ardenya 5, which offers an all-you-can-eat buffet for around 1400 ptas per person. Nearby *Mesón Andaluz*, upstairs at Carrer de Pons d'Icart 3, is a backstreet local favourite, with a good three-course menú for 1100 ptas. *Café Cantonada* at Carrer de Fortuny 23 is another popular place and has a lunch menú for 900 ptas; next door, *Restaurant Cantonada* has pizzas and pasta from around 600 ptas.

A popular little place is *Pizzeria Lina*, Carrer de Fortuny 8, which has a set menú for 775 ptas. There's pizza, couscous and a ragbag of other dishes.

Rambla Nova has several good places, either for a snack or a meal. *Viena*, No 50, has good croissants and a vast range of entrepans from 250 ptas. *Tapas Art*, No 26, has good tapas from 200 ptas. *La Rambla*, No 10, has a set menú for 1500 ptas or you can eat à la carte for around 3000 ptas. Across the road, *Restaurant Mirador* has a swankier set menú for 2500 ptas.

Getting There & Away
Over 20 regional trains a day run from Barcelona to Tarragona (one to 1½ hours, 630 ptas). There are about 12 trains daily from Tarragona to Valencia, taking three to 3½ hours and costing 2030 ptas. To Madrid, there are four trains each day – two via Valencia and taking seven hours and two via Zaragoza taking six hours. Fares start at 4400 ptas.

Balearic Islands

Floating out in the Mediterranean waters off the east coast of Spain, the Balearic Islands (Islas Baleares) are invaded every summer by a massive multinational force of hedonistic party animals. Not surprising really, when you consider the ingredients on offer – fine beaches, relentless sunshine and wild nightlife.

Despite all this, the islands have managed, to a degree, to maintain their individuality and strong links with their past. Beyond the bars and beaches are Gothic cathedrals, Stone Age ruins, small fishing villages, some spectacular bushwalks and endless olive groves and orange orchards.

Most place names and addresses are given in Catalan, the main language spoken in the islands. High-season prices are quoted here. Out of season, you will often find things are much cheaper and accommodation especially can be as much as half the quoted rates here.

Getting There & Away
Air Scheduled flights from the major cities on the Spanish mainland are operated by several airlines, including Iberia, Air Europa and Spanair. The cheapest and most frequent flights are from Barcelona and Valencia.

Standard one-way fares from Barcelona are not great value – hovering around 10,000 ptas to Palma de Mallorca and more to the other islands. At the time of writing, however, you could get a return, valid for up to a month, for 13,000 ptas with Spanair. Booking at least four days ahead brought the price down to about 10,000 ptas return. In low season the occasionally truly silly offer, such as 4000 ptas one way, comes up. From Valencia, Ibiza is marginally cheaper by air.

When in the islands keep your eyes peeled for cheap charter flights to the mainland. At the time of writing one-way charters were going for 14,900 ptas to places like Sevilla and Vigo, 9900 ptas for Málaga and 7900 ptas to Alicante.

Interisland flights are expensive (given the flying times involved), with Palma to Maó or Ibiza costing 7800 ptas (return flights cost double).

Boat Trasmediterránea (general information on ☎ 902-45 46 45) is the major ferry company for the islands, with offices in (and services between) Barcelona (☎ 93 295 90 00), Valencia (☎ 96 367 65 12), Palma de Mallorca (☎ 971 40 50 14), Maó (☎ 971 36 60 50) and Ibiza city (☎ 971 31 51 00).

Scheduled services are: Barcelona-Palma (eight hours; seven to nine services weekly); Barcelona-Maó (nine hours; two to six services weekly); Barcelona-Ibiza city (9½ hours, or 14½ hours via Palma; three to six services weekly); Valencia-Palma (8½ hours; six to seven services weekly); Valencia-Ibiza city (seven hours; six to seven services weekly); Palma-Ibiza city (4½ hours; one or two services weekly); and Palma-Maó (6½ hours; one service weekly).

Prices quoted below are the one-way fares during summer; low and mid-season fares are considerably cheaper.

Fares from the mainland to any of the islands are 6660 ptas for a Butaca Turista (seat); a berth in a cabin ranges from 10,960 ptas (four-share) to 16,950 ptas (twin-share)

per person. Taking a small car costs 18,560 ptas, or you can buy a Paquete Ahorro (economy package, which includes a car and four passengers sharing a cabin) for 51,440 ptas.

The exception is Valencia-Ibiza city, for which you pay 5725 ptas for a Butaca Turista, 10,960 ptas (four-share) to 16,950 ptas (twin-share) for a cabin, 15,490 ptas for a small car and 48,370 ptas for a Paquete Ahorro.

Interisland services (Palma-Ibiza city and Palma-Maó) both cost 2895 ptas for a Butaca Turista, 7645 ptas for a small car and 21,580 ptas for a Paquete Ahorro.

During summer, Trasmediterránea also operates the following Fast Ferry services (prices quoted are for a Butaca Turista): Barcelona-Palma (4¼ hours; 8150 ptas; up to three services a week); Valencia-Palma (6¼ hours; 8150 ptas; four services weekly); Valencia-Ibiza city (3¼ hours; 6950 ptas; four services weekly); Palma-Ibiza city (2¼ hours; 5210 ptas; four services weekly).

Another company, Flebasa (☎ 96 578 40 11 in Denia, 971 48 00 12 in Ciutadella), operates a couple of daily ferries from Denia on the mainland (between Valencia and Alicante) to Sant Antoni on Ibiza, and another to Palma de Mallorca via Ibiza city. Flebasa has four daily ferries between Ciutadella on Menorca and Port d'Alcúdia on Mallorca and regular services between Ibiza and Formentera.

Cape Balear (☎ 971 81 86 68) operates three daily fast ferries to Ciutadella (Menorca) from Cala Ratjada (Mallorca) in summer for 7500 ptas (return).

MALLORCA
Mallorca is the largest of the Balearic Islands. Most of the five million annual visitors to the island are here for the three *s* words: sun, sand and sea. There are, however, other reasons for coming. Palma, the capital, is worth exploring and the island offers a number of attractions away from the coast.

Orientation & Information
Palma de Mallorca is on the southern side of the island, on a bay famous for its brilliant sunsets. The Serra de Tramuntana mountain

range, which runs parallel with the north-west coastline, is trekkers' heaven. Mallorca's best beaches are along the north-east and east coasts – so are most of the big tourist resorts.

All of the major resorts have at least one tourist office. Palma has four – on Plaça d'Espanya (☎ 971 71 15 27), at Carrer de Sant Domingo 11 (☎ 971 72 40 90), on Plaça de la Reina and at the airport. Palma's post office is on Carrer de la Constitució.

Things to See & Do

The enormous **catedral** on Plaça Almoina is the first landmark you will see as you approach the island by ferry. It houses an excellent museum, and some of the cathedral's interior features were designed by Antoni Gaudí; entry costs 400 ptas.

In front of the cathedral is the **Palau de l'Almudaina**, the one-time residence of the Mallorcan monarchs. Inside is a collection of tapestries and artworks, although it's not really worth the 400 ptas entry. Instead, visit the rich and varied **Museu de Mallorca** (300 ptas).

Also near the cathedral are the interesting **Museu Diocesà** and the **Banys Àrabs** (Arab baths), the only remaining monument to the Muslim domination of the island. Also worth visiting is the collection of the **Fundació Joan Miró**, housed in the artist's Palma studios at Carrer de Joan de Saridakis 29, 2km west of the centre.

Mallorca's north-west coast is a world away from the concrete jungles on the other side of the island. Dominated by the Serra de Tramuntana mountains, it's a beautiful region of olive groves, pine forests and small villages with stone buildings; it also has a rugged and rocky coastline. There are a couple of highlights for drivers: the hair-raising road down to the small port of **Sa Calobra** and the amazing trip along the peninsula leading to the island's northern tip, **Cap Formentor**.

If you don't have your own wheels, take the **Palma to Sóller train** (see Getting Around later). It's one of the most popular and spectacular excursions on the island. Sóller is also the best place to base yourself for trekking – the easy three-hour return walk from here to the beautiful village of **Deià** is a fine introduction to trekking on Mallorca.

The tourist office's *Hiking Excursions* brochure covers 20 of the island's better walks, or for more detailed information see Lonely Planet's *Walking in Spain*.

Most of Mallorca's best beaches have been consumed by tourist developments, although there are exceptions. There are long stretches of sandy, undeveloped beach south of **Port d'Alcúdia** on the north-east coast. The lovely **Cala Mondragó** on the south-east coast is backed by a solitary hostal, and a little farther south the attractive port town of **Cala Figuera** has escaped many of the ravages of mass tourism. There are also some good quiet beaches near the popular German resort of **Colonia San Jordi**, particularly Ses Arenes and Es Trenc, both a few kilometres back up the coast towards Palma.

Places to Stay

Palma The *Pensión Costa Brava* (☎ 971 71 17 29), Carrer de Ca'n Martí Feliu 16, is a backstreet cheapie with reasonable rooms from 1300/2300 ptas. The cluttered 19th-century charm of *Hostal Pons* (☎ 971 72 26 58), Carrer del Vi 8, overcomes its limitations (spongy beds, only one bathroom); it charges 2000 ptas per person. At Carrer dels Apuntadores 8, *Hostal Apuntadores* (☎ 971 71 34 91) has smartly renovated singles/doubles at 2200/3700 ptas and doubles with bathroom at 4200 ptas. Next door, *Hostal Ritzi* (☎ 971 71 46 10) has good security and comfortable rooms at 2300/4200 ptas with shower, or doubles with shower/bath for 5000 ptas. It offers laundry and kitchen facilities and satellite TV in the lounge.

The superb *Hotel Born* (☎ 971 71 29 42) in a restored 18th-century palace at Carrer de Sant Jaume 3 has B&B at up to 8500/13,000 ptas.

Other Areas After Palma, you should head for the hills. In Deià, the charming *Pensión Villa Verde* (☎ 971 63 90 37) charges 3800/5500 ptas, while *Hostal Miramar* (☎ 971 63 90 84), overlooking the town, has B&B at 3772/7222 ptas. Beside the train station in Sóller, the popular *Hotel El Guía* (☎ 971 63 02 27) has rooms for 5650/8600 ptas, or nearby (go past El Guía and turn right) the cosy *Casa de Huéspedes Margarita* (☎ 971 63 42 14) has singles/doubles/triples for 2000/3000/4000 ptas.

PALMA DE MALLORCA

SPAIN

PALMA DE MALLORCA

PLACES TO STAY		OTHER		19	Post Office
8	Hotel Born	1	Train Stations (To Sóller	20	Main Tourist Office
10	Pensión Costa Brava		& Inca)	21	Ayuntamiento (Town Hall)
12	Hostal Pons	2	Bus Station & Airport Bus	22	Església de Santa Eulàlia
15	Hostal Apuntadores	3	Tourist Office	23	Basílica de Sant Francesc
16	Hostal Ritzi	5	Hospital	24	Palau de l'Almudaina
		6	Església de Santa	25	Catedral
PLACES TO EAT			Magdalena	26	Museu Diocesà
4	Restaurant Celler Sa Premsa	7	Mercat de l'Olivar (Market)	27	Museu de Mallorca
11	Bar Martín	9	Teatro Principal	28	Banys Árabs (Arab Baths)
13	Bon Lloc	17	American Express		
14	Vecchio Giovanni & Abaco	18	Tourist Office		

SPAIN

If you want to stay on the south-east coast, the large *Hostal Playa Mondragó* (☎ 971 65 77 52) at Cala Mondragó has B&B for 3100 ptas per person. At Cala Figuera, *Hostal Ca'n Jordi* (☎ 971 64 50 35) has rooms from 2900/4300 ptas.

If you're camping, *Camping Club Picafort* (☎ 971 53 78 63) on the north coast (9km south of Port d'Alcúdia) has excellent facilities and good beaches opposite. You can also sleep cheaply at several quirky old monasteries around the island – the tourist offices have a list.

Places to Eat

For Palma's best range of eateries, wander through the maze of streets between Plaça de la Reina and the port. Carrer dels Apuntadors is lined with restaurants – seafood, Chinese, Italian – even a few Spanish restaurants! Around the corner at Carrer de Sant Joan 1 is the deservedly popular *Vecchio Giovanni*. Right next door is the amazing *Abaco*, the bar of your wildest dreams (with the drinks bill of your darkest nightmares).

For a simple cheap meal with the locals, head for *Bar Martín*, Carrer de la Santa Creu 2. It has a no-nonsense set menú for 850 ptas.

The rustic *Restaurant Celler Sa Premsa*, Plaça del Bisbe Berenguer de Palou 8, is an almost obligatory stop. The hearty menú costs 1075 ptas (plus IVA). For vegetarian food, try *Bon Lloc*, Carrer de Sant Feliu 7.

Getting Around

Bus No 17 runs every half-hour between the airport and Plaça Espanya in central Palma (30 minutes; 290 ptas). Alternatively, a taxi will cost around 2000 ptas.

Most parts of the island are accessible by bus from Palma. Buses generally depart from or near the bus station at Plaça Espanya – the tourist office has details. Mallorca's two train lines also start from Plaça Espanya. One goes to the inland town of Inca and the other goes to Sóller (760 ptas one way – a highly picturesque jaunt).

The best way to get around the island is by car – it's worth renting one just for the drive along the north-west coast. There are about 30 rental agencies in Palma (and all the big companies have reps at the airport). If you want to compare prices many of them have harbourside offices along Passeig Marítim.

IBIZA

Ibiza (Eivissa in Catalan) is the most extreme of the Balearic islands, both in terms of its landscape and the people it attracts. Hippies, gays, fashion victims, nudists, party animals – this is one of the world's most bizarre melting pots. The island receives over a million visitors each year. Apart from the weather and the desire to be 'seen', the main drawcards are the notorious nightlife and the many picturesque beaches.

Orientation & Information

The capital, Ibiza (Eivissa) city, is on the south-eastern side of the island. This is where most travellers arrive (by ferry or air – the airport is to the south) and it's also the best base. The next-largest towns are Santa Eulària des Riu on the east coast and Sant Antoni de Portmany on the west coast. Other big resorts are scattered around the island.

In Ibiza city, the tourist office (☎ 971 30 19 00) is at Passeig de Vara de Rey 13. There is a Telefónica phone centre on Avinguda de Santa Eulària by the port, and the post office is at Carrer de Madrid 23. You'll find a good laundrette, Lavandería Master Clean, at Carrer de Felipe II 12.

Things to See & Do

Shopping seems to be a major pastime in Ibiza city – the port area of **Sa Penya** is crammed with funky and trashy clothes boutiques and hippy market stalls. From here you can wander up into **D'Alt Vila**, the old walled town, with its upmarket restaurants, galleries and the **Museu d'Art Contemporani**. There are fine views from the walls and from the **catedral** at the top, and the **Museu Arqueològic** next door is worth a visit.

The heavily developed **Platja de ses Figueretes** beach is a 20-minute walk south of Sa Penya – you'd be better off taking the half-hour bus ride (105 ptas) south to the beaches at **Ses Salines**.

If you're prepared to explore, there are still numerous unspoiled and relatively undeveloped beaches around the island. On the north-east coast, **Cala de Boix** is the only black-sand beach in the islands, while farther north are the lovely beaches of **S'Aigua Blanca**. On the north coast near Portinatx, **Cala Xarraca** is in a picturesque, semiprotected bay, and near Port de Sant Miquel is the attractive **Cala Benirras**. On the southwest coast, **Cala d'Hort** has a spectacular setting overlooking two rugged rock-islets, Es Verda and Es Verdranell.

Places to Stay

Ibiza City There are quite a few hostales in the streets around the port, although in midsummer cheap beds are scarce. At Carrer de Vicent Cuervo 14, *Hostal-Residencia Ripoll* (☎ 971 31 42 75) has singles/doubles for 3000/5000 ptas. On the waterfront (officially at Carrer de Barcelona 7), *Hostal-Restaurante La Marina* (☎ 971 31 01 72) has good doubles with harbour views for 3500 ptas. Outside peak season some rooms are let as singles for about half (back rooms are noisy). Another reasonable option is the well-located *Casa de Huéspedes Vara del Rey* (☎ 971 30 13 76), one block along from the tourist office at Passeig de Vara de Rey 7 (3rd floor, no lift!). Rooms with shared bathrooms cost 3000/5200 ptas.

One of the best choices is *Casa de Huéspedes La Peña* (☎ 971 19 02 40) at the far end of Sa Penya at Carrer de la Virgen 76. There are 13 simple and tidy doubles with shared bathrooms ranging from 2500 to 3500 ptas.

Hostal-Residencia Parque (☎ 971 30 13 58), Carrer de Vicent Cuervo 3, is quieter than most of the other hostales. Singles without private bath cost 3800 ptas, while singles/doubles with cost 6000/7900 ptas.

Hotel Montesol (☎ 971 31 01 61), Passeig de Vara de Rey 2, is a comfortable one-star place. Singles/doubles range up to 7500/11,900 ptas. Many of the singles are too pokey for the price.

Other Areas One of the best of Ibiza's half-dozen camping grounds is *Camping Cala Nova* (☎ 971 33 17 74), 500m north of the resort town of Cala Nova and close to a good beach.

If you want to get away from the resort developments the following places are all worth checking out. Near the Ses Salines beach

(and bus stop), *Hostal Mar y Sal* (☎ 971 39 65 84) has doubles at 4700 ptas (plus IVA). The nearby *Casa de Huéspedes Escandell* (☎ 971 39 65 83) has simple doubles with shared bathrooms for 3800 ptas. Near the S'Aigua Blanca beaches, *Pensión Sa Plana* (☎ 971 33 50 73) has a pool and rooms with bath from 4000/4700 ptas. Or you could stay by the island's only true black-sand beach, Cala Boix, at *Hostal Cala Boix* (☎ 971 33 91 24), where B&B costs 2200 ptas per person.

Places to Eat

Bland, overpriced eateries abound in the port area, but there are a few exceptions. The no-frills *Comidas Bar San Juan*, Carrer Montgri 8, is outstanding value with main courses from 400 to 800 ptas. At Carrer de la Cruz 19, *Ca'n Costa* is another family-run eating house with a menú for 900 ptas. If you just want something on the run, the hamburgers at *Mr Hot Dog*, Plaça d'Antoni Riquer, aren't bad and cost from 300 to 500 ptas. If you're looking for somewhere intimate and romantic, head for the candle-lit *La Scala*, Carrer de sa Carrossa 6, up in D'Alt Vila.

Entertainment

Ibiza's nightlife is renowned. The gay scene is wild and the dress code expensive. Dozens of bars keep Ibiza city's port area jumping until the early hours, and after they wind down you can continue on to one of the island's world-famous discos – if you can afford the 3000 to 5000 ptas entry, that is. The big-names are *Pacha*, on the north side of Ibiza city's port; *Privilege* and *Amnesia*, both 6km out on the road to Sant Antoni; and *Kiss* and *Space*, both south of Ibiza city in Platja d'En Bossa.

Getting Around

Buses run between the airport and Ibiza city hourly (115 ptas); a taxi costs around 1700 ptas. Buses to other parts of the island leave from the series of bus stops along Avenida d'Isidoro Macabich – pick up a copy of the timetable from the tourist office.

If you are intent on getting to some of the more secluded beaches you will need to rent wheels. In Ibiza city, Autos Isla Blanca (☎ 971 31 54 07) at Carrer de Felipe II will hire out a Seat Marbella for 13,500 ptas or a scooter for 8100 ptas for three days.

FORMENTERA

A short boat ride south of Ibiza, Formentera is the smallest and least developed of the four main Balearic Islands. It offers fine beaches and some excellent short walking and cycling trails. A popular day trip from Ibiza, it can get pretty crowded in midsummer, but most of the time it is still possible to find a strip of sand out of earshot of other tourists.

Orientation & Information

Formentera is about 20km from east to west. Ferries arrive at La Savina on the north-west coast; the tourist office (☎ 971 32 20 57) is behind the rental agencies you'll see when you disembark. Three kilometres south is the island's capital, Sant Francesc Xavier, where you'll find most of the banks. From here, the main road runs along the middle of the island before climbing to the highest point (192m). At the eastern end of the island is the Sa Mola lighthouse. Es Pujols is 3km east of La Savina and is the main tourist resort (and the only place with any nightlife to speak of).

Things to See & Do

Some of the island's best and most popular beaches are the beautiful white strips of sand along the narrow promontory which stretches north towards Ibiza. A 2km walking trail leads from the La Savina-Es Pujols road to the far end of the promontory, from where you can wade across a narrow strait to S'Espalmador, a tiny islet with beautiful, quiet beaches. Along Formentera's south coast, Platja de Migjorn is made up of numerous coves and beaches – tracks lead down to these off the main road. On the west coast is the lovely Cala Saona beach.

The tourist office's *Green Tours* brochure outlines 19 excellent walking and cycling trails that take you through some of the island's most scenic areas.

Places to Stay

Camping is not allowed on Formentera. Sadly, the coastal accommodation places mainly cater to German and British package-tour agencies and are overpriced and/or

booked out in summer. In Es Pujols you could try *Hostal Tahiti* (☎ 971 32 81 22), with B&B at 5500/9200 ptas. If you prefer peace and quiet you are better off in Es Caló – *Fonda Rafalet* (☎ 971 32 70 16) has good rooms on the waterfront for 4500/8000 ptas in August, or across the road the tiny and simple *Casa de Huéspedes Miramar* (☎ 971 32 70 60) charges 2000/3200 ptas.

Perhaps the best budget bet is to base yourself in one of the small inland towns and bike it to the beaches. In Sant Ferran (1.6km south of Es Pujols), the popular *Hostal Pepe* (☎ 971 32 80 33) has B&B with bath at 3470/5540 ptas. In Sant Francesco Xavier, *Restaurant Casa Rafal* (☎ 971 32 22 05) has doubles without bathroom for 4500 ptas and others with for 6500 ptas. La Savina isn't the most thrilling place, but *Hostal La Savina* (☎ 971 32 22 79) has rooms for up to 5000/7800 ptas.

Getting There & Away

There are 20 to 25 ferries daily between Ibiza city and Formentera. The trip takes about 25 minutes by jet ferry (3800 ptas return), or about an hour by car ferry (2000 ptas return; 9000 ptas for a small car).

Getting Around

A string of rental agencies line the harbour in La Savina. Bikes start at 500 ptas a day (800 ptas for a mountain bike). Scooters start at 1400 and head up to 4000 ptas for more powerful motorbikes. Cars go for 5000 to 7000 ptas. A regular bus service connects all the main towns.

MENORCA

Menorca is perhaps the least overrun of the Balearics. In 1993, it was declared a Biosphere Reserve by UNESCO, with the aim of preserving important environmental areas such as the Albufera d'es Grau wetlands and its unique collection of archaeological sites.

Orientation & Information

The capital, Maó (Mahón in Spanish), is at the eastern end of the island. Its busy port is the arrival point for most ferries, and Menorca's airport is 7km south-west. The main road runs down the middle of the island to Ciutadella, Menorca's second-largest town, with secondary roads leading north and south to the resorts and beaches.

The main tourist office is in Maó (☎ 971 36 37 90) at Plaça de S'Esplanada 40. During summer there are offices at the airport and in Ciutadella on Plaça des Born. Maó's post office is on Carrer del Bon Aire.

Things to See & Do

Maó and Ciutadella are both harbour towns, and from either place you'll have to commute to the beaches. Maó absorbs most of the tourist traffic – while you're here you can take a boat cruise around its impressive harbour and sample the local gin at the **Xoriguer distillery**. Ciutadella, with its smaller harbour and historic buildings, has a more distinctively Spanish feel about it.

In the centre of the island, the 357m-high **Monte Toro** has great views of the whole island, and on a clear day you can see as far as Mallorca.

With your own transport and a bit of footwork you'll be able to discover some of Menorca's off-the-beaten-track beaches. North of Maó, a drive across a lunar landscape leads to the lighthouse at **Cap de Favàritx**. If you park just before the gate to the lighthouse and climb up the rocks behind you, you'll see a couple of the eight beaches that are just waiting for scramblers like yourself to grace their sands.

On the north coast, the picturesque town of **Fornells** is on a large bay popular with windsurfers. Farther west at the beach of Binimella, you can continue (on foot) to the unspoilt Cala Pregonda.

North of Ciutadella is **La Vall**, another stretch of untouched beach backed by a private nature park (600 ptas entry per car). On the south coast are two good beaches either side of the Santa Galdana resort – Cala Mitjana to the east and Macarella to the west.

Menorca's beaches aren't its only attractions. The interior of the island is liberally sprinkled with reminders of its rich and ancient heritage. Pick up a copy of the tourist office's *Archaeological Guide to Minorca*.

Places to Stay

Menorca's two *camping grounds* are near the resorts of Santa Galdana, about 8km south of Ferreries, and Son Bou, south of Alaior. They open in summer only.

Maó and Ciutadella both have a handful of good budget options. In Maó at Carrer de la Infanta 19, *Hostal Orsi* (☎ 971 36 47 51) is run by a Glaswegian and American who are a mine of information. It's bright, clean and well located. Singles/doubles with a washbasin only cost 2500/4300 ptas. *Hostal La Isla* (☎ 971 36 64 92), Carrer de Santa Catalina 4, has excellent rooms with bath at 2300/4100 ptas plus IVA.

In Ciutadella at Carrer de Sant Isidre 33, *Hostal Oasis* (☎ 971 38 21 97) is set around a spacious courtyard and has its own Italian restaurant; doubles with bath and breakfast are 5500 ptas (no singles). *Hotel Geminis* (☎ 971 38 58 96), Carrer Josepa Rossinyol 4, is a friendly and stylish two-star with excellent rooms for 4000/7000 ptas.

In Fornells, *Hostal La Palma* (☎ 971 37 66 34), Plaça S'Algaret 3, has singles (not available in summer) for 3000 and doubles for 6250 ptas (in high season).

Places to Eat

La Dolce Vita, an Italian bistro at Carrer de Sant Roc 25, has great home-made bread, pasta, fresh salads, pizza, and a menú for 1150 ptas. Maó's waterfront road, Andén de Levante, is lined with restaurants with outdoor terraces. For a late night snack, the food at *Texas Bar*, No 65, can't be beat. Generous portions of pollo al curry and tacos cost under 400 ptas.

Ciutadella's port is also lined with restaurants, and you won't have any trouble finding somewhere to eat. After dinner, check out *Sa Clau*, a hip little jazz and blues bar set in the old city walls.

Getting Around

From the airport, a taxi into Maó costs around 1200 ptas – there are no buses.

TMSA (☎ 971 36 03 61) runs six buses a day between Maó and Ciutadella, with connections to the major resorts on the south coast. In summer there are also daily bus services to most of the coastal towns from both Maó and Ciutadella.

If you're planning to hire a car, rates vary seasonally (from around 3500 to 8000 ptas a day) – during summer, minimum hire periods

SPAIN

sometimes apply. In Maó, places worth trying include Autos Valls (☎ 971 36 84 65), Plaça d'Espanya 13, and Autos Isla (☎ 971 36 65 69), Avinguda de Josep Maria Quadrado 28. Hostal Orsi rents bicycles. Motos Rayda (☎ 971 35 47 86) rents mountain bikes (1000 ptas a day) and a range of scooters (2400 to 2900 ptas a day).

Valencia & Murcia

Although perhaps best known for the package resorts of the Costa Blanca, this region also includes Spain's lively third city, Valencia, and a fairy-tale castle at Morella.

VALENCIA
Valencia comes as a pleasant surprise to many. Home to paella and, they claim, the Holy Grail, it is also blessed with great weather and Las Fallas (in March), one of the wildest parties in the country.

Orientation
Plaza del Ayuntamiento marks the centre of Valencia. Most points of interest lie to the north of the train station and are generally within easy walking distance. The Río Turia cuts the central region of the city from the northern and eastern suburbs. This once-mighty river is now almost dry, and has been turned into a city-length park, the Jardines del Turia.

Many Valencian streets now have signs in Catalan as well as the Spanish used in this section. You'll often find Catalan and Spanish signs at opposite ends – or sides – of the street.

Information
Valencia's main tourist office (☎ 96 351 04 17) on Plaza del Ayuntamiento is open weekdays from 8.30 am to 2.15 pm and from 4.15 to 6.15 pm, and Saturday from 9.15 am to 12.45 pm. There's a provincial tourist office (☎ 96 352 85 73) at the train station, open weekdays from 9 am to 6.30 pm.

The post office is on Plaza del Ayuntamiento.

A good selection of English-language novels is available at the English Book Centre at Calle de Pascual y Genis 16. There is a laundrette, Lavandería El Mercat, at Plaza del Mercado 12.

Things to See & Do
Valencia's **Museo de Bellas Artes**, north across the river on Calle de San Pio V, ranks among the very best museums in the country. It contains a beautiful collection including works by El Greco, Goya, Velázquez and a number of Valencian impressionists. It opens Tuesday to Saturday between 9 am and 2.15 pm and 4 and 7.30 pm, and Sunday from 10 am to 2 pm; entry is free. Another museum with works by El Greco is the **Real Colegio del Patriarca** on Plaza del Patriarca (open daily 11 am to 1 pm; entry 100 ptas). The **Instituto Valenciano Arte Moderno (IVAM)**, north-west of the centre at Calle de Guillem de Castro 118, houses an impressive collection of 20th-century Spanish art (open Tuesday to Sunday from 10 am to 7 pm; entry 350 ptas).

Valencia's **catedral** is also worth a visit. Climb to the top of the tower (100 ptas) for a great view of the sprawling city. The cathedral's museum also claims to be home to the Holy Grail (Santo Cáliz), and contains works by Goya.

The baroque **Palacio del Marqués de dos Aguas**, on Calle del Poeta Querol, is fronted by an extravagantly sculpted façade and houses the **Museo Nacional de Cerámica**. It was closed for renovations at the time of writing.

The first stage of what promises to be the city's premier attraction, **L'Hemisfèric**, south-east of the centre at Calle del Arzobispo Mayoral 14, opened in 1998. It will eventually contain art, science museums and an aquarium.

Valencia has OK city beaches east of the centre, but a better bet is to take a bus 10km south to the **Playas del Saler**.

Special Events
Valencia's Las Fallas de San José is one of Spain's most unique festivals, an exuberant and anarchic blend of fireworks, music, festive bonfires (*fallas*) and all-night partying. If you're in Spain between 12 and 19 March, don't miss it.

VALENCIA CITY

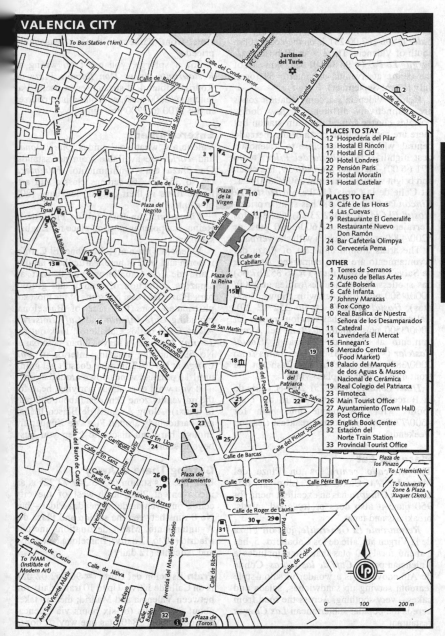

PLACES TO STAY
12 Hospedería del Pilar
13 Hostal El Rincón
17 Hostal El Cid
20 Hotel Londres
22 Pensión Paris
25 Hostal Moratín
31 Hostal Castelar

PLACES TO EAT
3 Café de las Horas
4 Las Cuevas
9 Restaurante El Generalife
21 Restaurante Nuevo
   Don Ramón
24 Bar Cafetería Olimpya
30 Cervecería Pema

OTHER
1 Torres de Serranos
2 Museo de Bellas Artes
5 Café Bolsería
6 Café Infanta
7 Johnny Maracas
8 Fox Congo
10 Real Basílica de Nuestra
   Señora de los Desamparados
11 Catedral
14 Lavendería El Mercat
15 Finnegan's
16 Mercado Central
   (Food Market)
18 Palacio del Marqués
   de dos Aguas & Museo
   Nacional de Cerámica
19 Real Colegio del Patriarca
23 Filmoteca
26 Main Tourist Office
27 Ayuntamiento (Town Hall)
28 Post Office
29 English Book Centre
32 Estación del
   Norte Train Station
33 Provincial Tourist Office

SPAIN

Places to Stay

The nearest camping ground, *Camping del Saler* (☎ 96 183 00 23), is on the coast 10km south of Valencia. There is an HI hostel, *Albergue La Paz* (☎ 96 369 01 52), 3km east of the centre at Avenida del Puerto 69 (open July to mid-September).

Central Valencia's accommodation zones are distinctively different. A few dodgy hostales cluster around the train station but there are better options north of the mercado central, which puts you close to Valencia's best nightlife. *Hospedería del Pilar* (☎ 96 391 66 00), Plaza del Mercado 19, has clean and bright singles/doubles at 1500/2800 ptas. At Calle de la Carda 11, the old *Hostal El Rincón* (☎ 96 391 79 98) has similar prices. *Hostal El Cid* (☎ 96 392 23 23), Calle de los Cerrajeros 13, charges 1600/3000 ptas, or 3200/4000 ptas for doubles with shower/bath.

The areas around and east of Plaza del Ayuntamiento are more upmarket. At Calle de Salva 12, *Pensión Paris* (☎ 96 352 67 66) has spotless singles/doubles/triples at 2000/3000/4500 ptas (doubles with shower 3600 ptas). *Hostal Moratín* (☎ 96 352 12 20), Calle de Moratín 15, has spacious rooms for 2000/3500 ptas. South of Plaza del Ayuntamiento at Calle de Ribera 1, *Hostal Castelar* (☎ 96 351 31 99) has rooms from 2000/3800 ptas – they're not flash but the front ones have good plaza views.

Hotel Londres (☎ 96 351 22 44), Calle de la Barcelonina 1, has well-worn but cosy rooms with TV, phone and bath for 4500/7700 ptas including breakfast (less on weekends).

Places to Eat

The *mercado central* is on Plaza del Mercado. At Calle d'En Llop 2, *Bar Cafetería Olimpya* has an excellent menú for 950 ptas; it also does pretty good salads, breakfasts and tapas.

Restaurante El Generalife, just off Plaza de la Virgen at Calle de los Caballeros 5, has a menú for 1100 ptas that often includes a Valencian paella. *Café de las Horas*, Conde de Almodóvar 1, is a wonderful salon-style tearoom serving up sandwiches, salads and cakes – very soothing. Across the road from here is the popular subterranean *Las Cuevas* restaurant.

Cervecería Pema, Calle de Mossén Femádes 3, has good food, some cooked on a street-front barbecue, that is reasonably priced.

For a splurge, you can't go wrong at *Restaurante Nuevo Don Ramón*, Plaza de Rodrigo Botet 4. It specialises in paella Valenciana (2500 ptas), with other main courses in the 1100 to 2200 ptas range.

Entertainment

Valencia's 'what's on' guides, *Que y Donde* and *Turia*, are available from newsstands. On Plaza del Ayuntamiento, *Filmoteca* (☎ 96 351 23 36) screens classic and arthouse films in their original language (200 ptas entry!).

Finnegan's, an Irish pub on Plaza de la Reina, is a popular meeting place for English speakers.

Valencia's main nightlife zone, El Carme, is north and west of here. Particularly around Calle de los Caballeros, you'll find an amazing collection of grungy and groovy bars. Plaza del Tosal has some of the most sophisticated bars this side of Barcelona, including *Café Infanta* and *Café Bolsería*. Along Calle de los Caballeros, look out for *Johnny Maracas*, a suave Cuban salsa bar at No 39, and the amazing interior of *Fox Congo* at No 35. This zone doesn't get going until 11 pm, and winds down around 3 am.

If you want to continue partying, head for the university zone 2km east (about 600 ptas in a taxi). Along Avenida de Blasco Ibáñez and particularly around Plaza de Xuquer are enough bars and discos to keep you busy beyond sunrise.

Getting There & Away

Bus The bus station (☎ 96 349 72 22) is an inconvenient 2km north-west of the city centre on Avenida de Menéndez Pidal – bus No 8 runs between the station and Plaza del Ayuntamiento. Major destinations include Madrid (10 to 12 daily), Barcelona (six daily) and Alicante (12 daily).

Train Estación del Norte (☎ 96 352 02 02), is on Calle de Játiva. Up to 10 trains daily run between Valencia and Madrid; the trip takes about four hours (or six hours via Cuenca) and costs from 2840 ptas one way. A dozen daily trains make the three-five hour haul north to Barcelona (via Tarragona), including the high-speed Euromed. Seven trains head daily to Alicante.

Getting Around
Points of interest outside the city centre can generally be reached by bus, most of which depart from Plaza del Ayuntamiento. Bus No 19 goes to Valencia's beach, Malvarrosa, as well as the Islas Baleares terminal. No 81 goes to the university and No 11 will drop you off at the Museo de Bellas Artes. No 8 runs to the Estación Central de Autobuses (bus station).

MORELLA
The fairy-tale town of Morella, in the north of Valencia province, is an outstanding example of a medieval fortress. Perched on a hill top, crowned by a castle and completely enclosed by a wall over 2km long, it is one of Spain's oldest continually inhabited towns.

Morella's tourist office (☎ 964 17 30 32) is at Puerta de San Miguel, just inside the main entrance gate to the old town.

Things to See & Do
Although Morella's wonderful castle is in ruins, it is still most imposing. You can almost hear the clashing of swords and clip-clop of horses that were once a part of everyday life in the fortress. A strenuous climb to the top is rewarded by breathtaking views of the town and surrounding country-side. The castle grounds are open daily from 10.30 am until 6.30 pm (until 7.30 pm between May and August). Entry costs 200 ptas.

The old town itself is easily explored on foot. Three small museums have been set up in the towers of the ancient walls, with displays on local history, photography and the 'age of the dinosaurs'. Also worth a visit are the **Basílica de Santa María la Mayor** and attached **Museo Arciprestal**.

Places to Stay & Eat
Hostal El Cid (☎ 964 16 01 25), Puerta San Mateo 2, has reasonable if drab singles/doubles from 1300/2200 ptas (doubles with bath 3500 ptas) – the front rooms at least

have decent views. A better bet is the friendly *Fonda Moreno* (☎ 964 16 01 05), Calle de San Nicolás 12, with rustic, quaint doubles only for 2150 ptas.

At Cuesta Suñer 1 is *Hotel Cardenal Ram* (☎ 964 17 30 85), set in a wonderfully transformed 16th-century cardinal's palace. Rooms start from 5000/7000 ptas (plus IVA).

Restaurante Casa Roque, Calle de Segura Barreda 8, is one of the best restaurants in town. Regional dishes range from 950 ptas up to 2500 ptas for the house speciality, cordero relleno trufado (lamb rolled with truffles).

Getting There & Away
Buses run to Castellón de la Plana, Vinaròs and occasionally to Alcañiz (Aragón).

Morella is beside the N-232 highway – drivers beware in winter as the town is sometimes snowed in for days.

INLAND VALENCIA
Guadalest
A spectacular route runs west from just south of Calpe (see below) to the inland town of **Alcoy**, famous for its Moros y Cristianos fiesta in April. If you were only to make one excursion deep into Valencia, this should be it. About halfway to Alcoy, stop at the old Muslim settlement of **Guadalest**, dominated by the Castillo de San José. You walk to the castillo through a natural tunnel.

Elche (Elx)
Just 20km south-west of Alicante, Elche combines the historic with the industrial and is famed for its extensive palm groves, planted by the Muslims. Visit the **Huerto del Cura**, a lovely private garden with tended lawns, colourful flowerbeds and a freakish eight pronged palm tree in the centre. The gardens, east of the centre at Calle de la Puerta de la Morera, open daily from 9 am to 6 pm; entry costs 300 ptas for adults, 150 ptas for children.

The major festival is the Misteri d'Elx, a two-act lyric drama that dates from the Middle Ages. It is performed in the Basílica de Santa María on 14 and 15 August (with rehearsals the three previous days).

Budget accommodation options are limited. *Pensión Juan* (☎ 96 545 86 09),

Calle del Puente de los Ortissos 15 (3rd floor), is grim but cheap at 1000 ptas per person.

Elche is on the Alicante-Murcia train line, with 17 to 24 trains daily to Alicante. AM Molla has up to 30 buses a day to Alicante.

ALICANTE (ALACANT)

Alicante is a refreshing town with wide boulevards, long white beaches, an interesting old centre and frenetic nightlife. The main tourist office (☎ 96 520 00 00) is at Explanada de España 2.

Things to See & Do The most obvious of Alicante's attractions is the **Castillo de Santa Bárbara**, a 16th-century fortress overlooking the city. There is a lift shaft deep inside the mountain which will take you right to the castle (400 ptas return) – the lift entrance is opposite Playa del Postiguet. The castle opens daily from 10 am to 8 pm (9 am to 7 pm from October to March); entry is free.

The **Colección de Arte del Siglo XX** on Plaza de Santa María houses an excellent collection of modern art including a handful of works by Dalí, Miró and Picasso. It opens daily from 10.30 am to 1.30 pm and 6 to 9 pm (October to April, 10 am to 1 pm and 5 to 8 pm), and closes Monday, Sunday afternoon and public holidays. Entry is free.

Kontiki (☎ 96 521 63 96) runs boat trips most days to the popular **Isla de Tabarca**. The island has quiet beaches and good snorkelling and scuba diving, plus a small hotel. Return fares are 1700 ptas.

Playa del Postiguet is Alicante's city beach, but you are better off heading north to the cleaner and less-crowded beaches of San Juan or Campello.

Places to Stay At Calle de Monges 2, the outstanding *Pensión Les Monges* (☎ 96 521 50 46) is more like a boutique hotel than a pensión. Its eight rooms start at 1900/3500 ptas (2200/3800 ptas with shower or 2800/4500 ptas with bathroom). At Calle de Villavieja 8, *Pensión La Milagrosa* (☎ 96 521 69 18) has clean and bright rooms and a small guest kitchen; it charges 1500 ptas per person. At Calle Mayor 5, *Hostal Mayor*

(☎ 96 520 13 83) has singles/doubles/triples with bath for 2800/4500/6000 ptas.

The three-star *Hotel Palas* (☎ 96 520 93 09), Plaza de la Puerta del Mar, is a rambling, semigrand hotel with a weird collection of artworks, furniture and mirrors. Rooms with mod cons (and a few odd ones) cost 5400/8500 ptas (plus IVA).

Places to Eat At Calle de Maldonado 25, *Restaurante El Canario* is a no-frills local eatery with a hearty menú for 900 ptas. How long since you had goulash? You can across the road at *Restaurante Csárda*.

Restaurante Mixto Vegetariano, Plaza de Santa María 2, is a simple low-ceilinged place with vegetarian and carnivorous menús at 1000 ptas – you can choose or combine dishes from both menús.

Real carnivores could try *Restaurante Casa Ibarra*, Calle de Rafael Altamira 19, which has a set menú for 1100. It is one of several budget places around Plaza del Ayuntamiento.

It is unusual to strike good Italian food in Spain, but a rare exception is *Restaurante Don Camillo*, Plaza del Abad Penalva 2. Pasta dishes range up to 845 ptas.

Entertainment Alicante's El Barrio nightlife zone clusters around the cathedral – look out for *Celestial Copas*, *La Naya*, *Potato-Bar Café*, and *Jamboree Bar*.

During summer the disco scene at Playa de San Juan gets thumping. There are dozens of discos along the coast from Alicante to Denia, and FGV's 'night trains' ferry party-goers along this notorious section of *la ruta bakalao*.

Getting There & Away Alicante is the gateway to the Costa Blanca; the airport is 12km west of the town centre.

There are daily services from the bus station (☎ 96 513 07 00) on Calle de Portugal to Almería (2550 ptas), Valencia (1890 ptas), Barcelona (4590 ptas), Madrid (2895 ptas) and the towns along the Costa Blanca.

The train station (☎ 96 521 02 02) is on Avenida de Salamanca. Services include Madrid (seven daily, 4400 ptas), Valencia (five daily, 2500 ptas) and Barcelona (five daily, 4600 ptas).

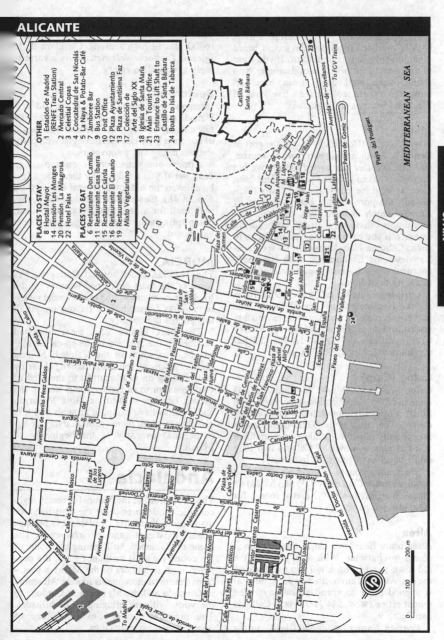

ALICANTE

PLACES TO STAY
8 Hostal Mayor
14 Pensión Les Monges
20 Pensión La Milagrosa
22 Hotel Palas

PLACES TO EAT
6 Restaurante Don Camillo
11 Restaurante Casa Ibarra
15 Restaurante Csárda
16 Restaurante El Canario
19 Restaurante
  Mixto Vegetariano

OTHER
1 Estación de Madrid
  (RENFE Train Station)
2 Mercado Central
3 Celestial Copas
4 Concatedral de San Nicolás
5 La Naya & Potato-Bar Café
7 Jamboree Bar
9 Bus Station
10 Post Office
12 Plaza Ayuntamiento
13 Plaza de Santísima Faz
17 Colección de
  Arte del Siglo XX
18 Iglesia de Santa María
21 Main Tourist Office
23 Entrance to Lift Shaft to
  Castillo de Santa Bárbara
24 Boats to Isla de Tabarca

SPAIN

AROUND ALICANTE

The Costa Blanca is one of Europe's most heavily touristed regions. Who hasn't heard of nightmares such as Benidorm? If you want to find a secluded beach in midsummer, you should keep well away from here. If, however, you are looking for a lively social life, good beaches and a suntan ...

Jávea

Jávea (Xábia), 10km south-east of the port of Denia, is worth a visit early in the season, when the weather has started to improve but the masses haven't arrived yet. This laid-back place is in three parts: the old town (3km inland), the port and the beach zone of El Arenal, which is lined with pleasant bar-restaurants that stay open late during summer. If you have wheels, you might try to get to **Cabo La Nao**, known for its spectacular views, or **Granadella**, with its small, uncrowded beach – both are a few kilometres to the south of Jávea.

Camping El Naranjal (☎ 96 579 10 70) is about a 10-minute walk from El Arenal. The port area is pleasant and has some reasonably priced pensiones. *Fonda del Mar* (☎ 96 579 01 17) at Calle del Cristo del Mar 12 has singles/doubles for 2000/4000 ptas.

Calpe (Calp)

Calpe (22km north-east of Benidorm) is dominated by the Gibraltaresque **Peñon de Ilfach**, a towering monolith that juts out into the sea. The climb to the 332m-high summit is especially popular – while you're up there you can choose which of Calpe's two long sandy beaches to visit later in the day.

There are a couple of good places to bed down. *Pensión Centrica* (☎ 96 583 55 28) on Plaza de Ilfach has cosy, pretty rooms for 1600 ptas per person.

Altea

Altea beats Benidorm hands down when it comes to character. With what's left of the old town perched on a hill top overlooking the sea, Altea (11km north-east of Benidorm) is a good place to spend a few days. The tourist office (☎ 96 584 41 14) is at Calle de San Pedro 9.

Pensión Fornet (☎ 96 584 01 14), in the old town at Calle de Beniarda 1, is open all year. Rooms start at 4500 ptas for a double (6300 ptas in high season). On Plaza de la Iglesia, *Trattoria dels Artistes* is a surprisingly good Italian eatery.

Benidorm

Infamous Benidorm is every bit as bad as it is made out to be: 5km of white beaches (the place's only saving grace) backed by a jungle of concrete high-rise and thronged with pasty tourists toting tacky souvenirs.

Almost everyone here is on a package deal, but if you need to stay there are a few hostales in the old town. *Hostal Calpi* (☎ 96 585 78 48), Costera del Barco 6, has rooms with bath for around 3000 ptas per person, but in spring and summer obliges you to take half-board.

MURCIA

The Murcian coast beyond Cartagena has some of the least developed beaches on the Mediterranean coast, and towns in the interior, such as Lorca, have a flavour unique to this part of the country.

The best known and most touristed beaches in the area are in the so-called Mar Menor, just south of the Valencia-Murcia border. You are better off passing them by and heading on to **Mazarrón** to the west of Cartagena, or even farther south-west to the golden beaches at **Águilas**. Both Mazarrón and Águilas have camping grounds and it is possible to swim there (without dying of hypothermia) as early as the beginning of March.

Andalucía

The stronghold of the Moors for nearly eight centuries and the pride of the Christians for many years thereafter, Andalucía is perhaps Spain's most exotic and colourful region. The home of flamenco, bullfighting and some of the country's most brilliant fiestas, it's peppered with reminders of the Moorish past – from treasured monuments like the Alhambra in Granada and the Mezquita in Córdoba to the white villages clinging to its hillsides. The regional capital, Seville, is one of Spain's most exciting cities.

Away from the main cities and resorts, Andalucía is surprisingly untouristed and makes for some great exploring. Its scenery ranges from semideserts to lush river valleys, from gorge-ridden mountains to the longest coastline of any Spanish region. The coast stretches from the quiet beaches of Cabo de Gata, past the mayhem of the Costa del Sol, to come within 14km of Africa at the windsurfing centre Tarifa, before opening up to the Atlantic Ocean on the Costa de la Luz, where long beaches sweep by Cádiz and the famous wetlands of Doñana National Park to the Portuguese border.

SEVILLE

Seville (Sevilla) is one of the most exciting cities in Spain, with an atmosphere both relaxed and festive, a rich history, some great monuments, beautiful parks and gardens, and a large, lively student population. Located on the Río Guadalquivir, which is navigable to the Atlantic Ocean, Seville was once the leading Muslim city in Spain. It reached its height later, in the 16th and 17th centuries, when it held a monopoly on Spanish trade with the Americas. Expo '92, in 1992, once again plunged Seville into the international limelight.

Seville is an expensive place, so it's worth planning your visit carefully. In high summer, the city is stiflingly hot and not a fun place to be. It's best during its unforgettable spring festivals, though rooms then (if you can get one) are expensive.

Information

The main tourist office at Avenida de la Constitución 21 (☎ 95 422 14 04) is open Monday to Saturday from 9 am to 7 pm and Sunday 10 am to 2 pm (closed on holidays). It's often extremely busy, so you might try the other offices – at Paseo de las Delicias 9 (☎ 95 423 44 65), open Monday to Friday from 8.30 am to 6.30 pm, and on Calle de Arjona (☎ 95 421 36 30), open weekdays from 9 am to 8.45 pm, and weekend mornings. There's also a tourist office (☎ 95 444 91 28) at the airport.

Librería Beta at Avenida de la Constitución 9 and 27 has guidebooks and novels in English. Tintorería Roma at Calle del Caste-

lar 4 will wash, dry and fold a load of washing for 1000 ptas.

Things to See & Do

Cathedral & Giralda Seville's immense cathedral – the biggest in the world, says the *Guinness Book of Records* – was built on the site of Moorish Seville's main mosque between 1401 and 1507. The structure is primarily Gothic, though most of the internal decoration is in later styles. The adjoining tower, La Giralda, was the mosque's minaret and dates from the 12th century. The climb up La Giralda affords great views and is quite easy as there's a ramp (not stairs) all the way up inside. One highlight of the cathedral's lavish interior is Christopher Columbus' supposed tomb inside the south door (no one's 100% sure that his remains didn't get mislaid somewhere in the Caribbean). The four crowned sepulchre-bearers represent the four kingdoms of Spain at the time of Columbus' sailing. The entrance to the Catedral and Giralda is beside the Giralda, on Plaza de la Virgen de los Reyes – open Monday to Saturday from 10.30 am to 6 pm, Sunday 2 to 5 pm, with last entry one hour before closing time (600 ptas; students 200 ptas).

Alcázar Seville's alcázar, a residence of Muslim and Christian royalty for many centuries, was founded in the 11th century as a Moorish fortress. It has been adapted by Seville's rulers in almost every century since, which makes it a mish-mash of styles, but adds to its fascination. The highlights are the **Palacio de Don Pedro**, exquisitely decorated by Moorish artisans for the Castilian king Pedro the Cruel in the 1360s, and the large, immaculately tended **gardens** – the perfect place to ease your body and brain after some intensive sightseeing. The Alcázar is open Tuesday to Saturday from 9.30 am to 7 pm (to 5 pm from October to March), Sunday and holidays 9.30 am to 5 pm (to 1.30 pm October to March). Entry is 600 ptas (free for students).

Walks & Parks If you're not staying in the **Barrio de Santa Cruz**, the old Jewish quarter immediately east of the cathedral and alcázar, make sure you take a stroll among its quaint streets and lovely plant-bedecked plazas.

SPAIN

SEVILLE (SEVILLA)

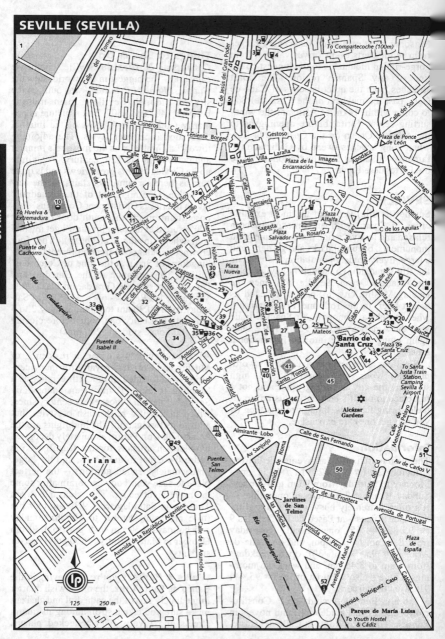

To Compartecoche (100m)

To Huelva &
Extremadura

Puente del
Cachorro

Río
Guadalquivir

Puente de
Isabel II

Triana

Puente
San
Telmo

To Youth Hostel
& Cádiz

Río
Guadalquivir

Jardines
de San
Telmo

Alcázar
Gardens

Barrio de
Santa Cruz

Plaza de
Santa Cruz

To Santa
Justa Train
Station,
Camping
Sevilla &
Airport

Plaza
de
España

Parque de María Luisa

Plaza de Ponce
de León

Plaza de la
Encarnación

Plaza
Alfalfa

Plaza
Salvador

Plaza
Nueva

0   125   250 m

SEVILLE (SEVILLA)

PLACES TO STAY
5   Hostal Duque
6   Hotel Sevilla
7   Hostal Pino
11   Hostal Londres
12   Hotel Zaida
13   Hostal Lis II
15   Hostal Lis
18   Huéspedes La Montoreña
19   Hostal Bienvenido
22   Pensión Fabiola
23   Pensión San Pancracio
24   Hostal Toledo
31   Hotel La Rábida

PLACES TO EAT
8   Bodegón Alfonso XII
14   Patio San Eloy
20   Bar Casa San Fernando
21   Alta-Mira Café-Bar
25   Cervecería Giralda
29   Bodega Paco Góngora

42   Hostería del Laurel
44   El Rincón de Pepe

OTHER
1   Expo '92 Site
2   La Farándula
3   Fun Club
4   La Bruja
9   Museo de Bellas Artes
10   Plaza de Armas Bus
     Station
16   El Mundo
17   La Carbonería
26   La Giralda
27   Catedral
28   Librería Beta
30   American Express
     (Laundry)
32   Mercado del Arenal
33   Tourist Office
34   Plaza de Toros de la
     Maestranza (Bullring)

35   Habana
36   A3
37   Arena
38   Bar Populus
39   Tintorería Roma
40   Main Post Office
41   Archivo de Indias
43   Los Gallos
45   Alcázar
46   Main Tourist Office
47   Librería Beta
48   Torre del Oro & Museo
     Marítimo
49   Alambique, Mui d'Aqui &
     Big Ben
50   University
51   Prado de San Sebastián
     Bus Station
52   Tourist Office

Another enjoyable walk is along the **riverbank**, where the 13th-century Torre del Oro contains a small, crowded maritime museum.

South of the centre, large **Parque de María Luisa** is a pleasant place to get lost in, with its maze of paths, tall trees, flowers, fountains and shaded lawns.

Museums The **Archivo de Indias**, beside the cathedral, houses over 40 million documents dating from 1492 through to the decolonisation of the Americas. Most can only be consulted with special permission, but there are rotating displays of fascinating maps and documents. Entry is free, and it's open Monday to Friday from 10 am to 1 pm.

The **Museo de Bellas Artes**, on Calle de Alfonso XII, has an outstanding, beautifully housed collection of Spanish art, focusing on Seville artists like Murillo and Zurbarán. It's open Tuesday to Sunday (250 ptas, free for EU citizens).

Expo '92 Site The Expo '92 site is west of the Guadalquivir across the Puente del Cachorro. Here **Puerta de Triana** has exhibits on sea exploration in the Pabellón de la Navegación (500 ptas). The **Conjunto Monumental de la Cartuja**, a 15th-century monastery where

Columbus used to stay, was later converted into a china factory (300 ptas). Both sites are closed Monday. You can wander round the rest of the Expo grounds and admire the pavilions, but it's rather lifeless.

Special Events

The first of Seville's two great festivals is Semana Santa, the week leading up to Easter Sunday. Throughout the week long processions of religious brotherhoods (*cofradías*), dressed in strange penitents' garb with tall pointed hoods, accompany sacred images through the city, watched by huge crowds. The Feria de Abril, a week in late April, is a kind of release after this solemnity – the festivities involve six days of music, dancing, horse riding and traditional dress on a site in the Los Remedios area west of the river, plus daily bullfights and a general city-wide party.

Places to Stay

The summer prices given here can come down substantially from October to March, but during Semana Santa and the Feria de Abril they can rise by anything up to 200%.

Seville's 188-place HI hostel *Albergue Juvenil Sevilla* (☎ 95 461 31 50) was closed

SPAIN

for renovation but may be open by the time you get there. It's at Calle de Isaac Peral 2, about 10 minutes by bus No 34 from opposite the main tourist office. A bed costs 1300/1600 ptas for under/over 26s in high season.

Barrio de Santa Cruz has a few good-value places to stay. *Hostal Bienvenido* (☎ 95 441 36 55) at Calle de los Archeros 14 has singles/doubles for 1700/3200 ptas. *Huéspedes La Montoreña* (☎ 95 441 24 07), Calle de San Clemente 12, has clean, simple singles/doubles at 1500/3000 ptas. *Pensión San Pancracio* (☎ 95 441 31 04) at Plaza de las Cruces 9 has small singles for 1800 ptas and bigger doubles for 3200 ptas, or 4000 ptas with bath. The friendly *Hostal Toledo* (☎ 95 421 53 35), Calle de Santa Teresa 15, has good singles/doubles with bath for 2500/5000 ptas. *Pensión Fabiola* (☎ 95 421 83 46) at Calle de Fabiola 16 has simple, well-kept rooms from 2000/4000 ptas.

The area north of Plaza Nueva, only a 10-minute walk from all the hustle and bustle, has some good value too. *Hostal Pino* (☎ 95 421 28 10), Calle de Tarifa 6, is one of the cheapest at 1700/2700 ptas or 2200/3500 ptas with shower. *Hostal Lis II* (☎ 95 456 02 28) in a beautiful house at Calle de Olavide 5 charges 1700 ptas for singles and 3500 ptas for doubles with toilet. The same family owns *Hostal Lis* (☎ 95 421 30 88) at Calle de Escarpín 10 where singles/doubles with shower are 2000/3500 ptas.

Hotel Zaida (☎ 95 421 11 38), Calle de San Roque 26, occupies an 18th-century house with a lovely patio. The 27 rooms are plain but decent, with bath, for 3000/5000 ptas plus IVA.

Hostal Londres (☎ 95 421 28 96), Calle de San Pedro Mártir 1, has plain, clean rooms with private bath at around 3500/5000 ptas.

The 36 varied rooms at friendly *Hostal Duque* (☎ 95 438 70 11), Calle de Trajano 15, are 1800/3500 ptas or 3000/5000 ptas with private bath. *Hotel Sevilla* (☎ 95 438 41 61), Calle de Daóiz 5, has 30 clean, plain, medium-sized rooms with bath for 3745/5885 ptas.

The impressive *Hotel La Rábida* (☎ 95 422 09 60), Calle del Castelar 24, has rooms with bath at 5700/8750 ptas plus IVA.

Places to Eat

In central Seville, Barrio de Santa Cruz is the best area for decent-value eating. Near the Alcázar, *El Rincón de Pepe*, Calle de la Gloria 6, has pretty folksy décor and does a lunch menú of gazpacho or salad, paella and dessert for 1050 ptas. *Hostería del Laurel*, Plaza de los Venerables 5, has an atmospheric old bar with a wide range of good media-raciones (550 to 1450 ptas) and raciones.

Cervecería Giralda, Calle de Mateos Gago 1, is a great spot for breakfast. Tostadas are from 95 to 275 ptas, or there's bacon and eggs for 450 ptas.

Calle de Santa María La Blanca has several good-value places: at the *Alta-Mira Café-Bar*, No 6, a media-ración of tortilla Alta-Mira (with potatoes and vegetables) is almost a meal for 600 ptas, while the busy little *Bar Casa Fernando* round the corner has a decent 800 ptas lunch menú.

West of Avenida de la Constitución, *Bodega Paco Góngora* at Calle del Padre Marchena 1 has a huge range of good seafood at decent prices – media-raciones of fish a la plancha (grilled) are mostly 600 ptas. Farther north, *Patio San Eloy* at Calle de San Eloy 9 is a bright, busy place with lots of good tapas for 110 to 185 ptas. *Bodegón Alfonso XII* at Calle de Alfonso XII 33 is good value with deals like scrambled eggs with mushrooms, ham and prawns for 475 ptas and a menú for 800 ptas.

Mercado del Arenal on Calle de Pastor y Landero is the only food market in the central area.

Entertainment

Seville's nightlife is among the liveliest in Spain. On fine nights throngs of people block the streets outside popular bars, while teenagers and students just bring their own bottles to mass gathering spots such as the Mercado del Arenal. Seville also has some great music bars, often with dance space. As everywhere in Spain, the real action is on Friday and Saturday nights.

Drinking & Dancing Until about midnight, Plaza del Salvador is a popular spot for an open-air drink, with a student crowd and a couple of little bars selling carry-out drinks.

The east bank of the Guadalquivir is busy into the early hours – in summer it's dotted with temporary bars.

There are some hugely popular bars just north of the cathedral, but the crowds from about midnight around Calle de Adriano, west of Avenida de la Constitución, have to be seen to be believed. Busy music bars on Adriano itself include *A3*, *Habana*, *Bar Populus* and *Arena*. Nearby on Calle de García de Vinuesa and Calle del Dos de Mayo are some quieter bodegas (traditional wine bars), some with good tapas, that attract a more mature crowd.

The *Fun Club*, Alameda de Hércules 86, is a small, busy dance warehouse, open Thursday to Sunday from 11.30 pm (9.30 pm on live-band nights) till late. At Calle de la Cruz de la Tinaja 5, *La Farándula* has live music Tuesday to Thursday. It's open daily from 10 pm till late. At *La Bruja* on little Plaza de Europa, the long-haired heavy-rock crowd sits around on the floor rolling joints.

Across the river, *Alambique*, *Mui d'Aqui* and *Big Ben*, side by side on Calle de Betis two blocks north of the Puente de San Telmo, all play good music and attract an interesting mix of students and travellers.

Flamenco Seville is Spain's flamenco capital but even here it can be hard to find authentic flamenco unless you're present for the Feria de Abril, or the Bienal de Arte Flamenco festival, held in September and/or October in even-numbered years. Bars which put on fairly regular flamenco, of erratic quality, include *La Carbonería*, Calle de Levies 18, and *El Mundo*, Calle de las Siete Revueltas 5 (usually Tuesday at midnight). There are also several tourist-oriented venues with regular shows, and some of these, though hardly spontaneous, are good. The best is *Los Gallos* on Plaza de la Santa Cruz, with two shows nightly; entry is 3000 ptas.

Spectator Sport

The bullfighting season runs from Easter to October, with fights most Sundays about 6 pm, and almost every day during the Feria de Abril and the week or two before it. The bullring is on Paseo de Cristóbal Colón. Tickets start around 3000 ptas.

Getting There & Away

Air Seville airport (☎ 95 451 25 78) has quite a range of domestic and international flights. Air Europa flies to Barcelona for 19,200 ptas.

Bus Buses to Extremadura, Madrid, Portugal and Andalucía west of Seville leave from the Plaza de Armas bus station (☎ 95 490 80 40). Buses to other parts of Andalucía use the Prado de San Sebastián bus station (☎ 95 441 71 11).

Daily services include around 10 buses each to Córdoba (two hours, 1200 ptas), Granada (four hours, 2710 ptas), Málaga (3½ hours, 2245 ptas) and Madrid (six hours, 2715 ptas). To Lisbon there are five direct buses a week (eight hours, 4350 to 4510 ptas), and daily buses with a transfer at the border (nine hours, 2875 ptas). For the Algarve you need to change buses at Huelva, or Ayamonte on the border.

Train Seville's Santa Justa train station (☎ 95 454 02 02) is about 1.5km north-east of the city centre on Avenida de Kansas City.

To/from Madrid, there are up to 14 superfast AVE trains each day, covering the 471km in just 2½ hours and costing from 8100 to 9500 ptas in the cheapest class (turista); a couple of Talgos taking 3½ hours for 7000 to 7900 ptas in 2nd class; and the evening Tren Hotel, taking 3¾ hours for 5400 ptas in a seat.

Other daily trains include about 20 to Córdoba (45 minutes to 1¼ hours, 1050 to 2700 ptas); and three each to Granada (four hours, 2280 ptas) and Málaga (three hours, 1825 ptas). For Lisbon (16 hours, 6800 ptas), there's one train a day with a change in Cáceres.

Car Pooling Compartecoche (☎ 95 490 75 82), Calle de González Cuadrado 49, is an intercity car-pooling service. Its service is free to drivers, while passengers pay an agreed transfer rate. Ring for details.

Getting Around

The airport is about 7km from the centre, off the N-IV Córdoba road. Airport buses (750 ptas) run up to 12 times daily – tourist offices have details.

Bus Nos C1 and C2, across the road from the front of Santa Justa train station, follow a circular route via Avenida de Carlos V, close to Prado de San Sebastián bus station and the city centre, and Plaza de Armas bus station. Bus No C4, south on Calle de Arjona from Plaza de Armas bus station, goes straight to the centre.

GRANADA

From the 13th to 15th centuries, Granada was capital of the last Moorish kingdom in Spain, and the finest city on the peninsula. Today it's home to the greatest Moorish legacy in the country, and one of the most magnificent buildings on the continent – the Alhambra. South-east of the city, the Sierra Nevada mountain range (Spain's highest), and the Alpujarras valleys, with their picturesque, mysterious villages, are well worth exploring if you have time to spare.

Information

Granada's main tourist office (☎ 958 22 66 88), on Plaza de Mariana Pineda, opens on weekdays from 9.30 am to 7 pm, Saturday 10 am to 2 pm. There's another office on Calle de Mariana Pineda, open the same hours but busier.

Librería Urbano, Calle de las Tablas 6, south-west off Plaza de la Trinidad, stocks books in English.

Things to See

La Alhambra One of the greatest accomplishments of Islamic art and architecture, the Alhambra is simply breathtaking. Much has been written about its fortress, palace, patios and gardens, but nothing can really prepare you for what you will see.

The Alcazaba is the Alhambra's fortress, dating from the 11th to the 13th centuries. The views of the city from the tops of the towers are great. The Casa Real (Royal Palace), built for Granada's rulers in its 14th and 15th-century heyday, is the centrepiece of the Alhambra. The intricacy of the stonework, epitomised by the Patio de los Leones (Patio of the Lions) and Sala de las Dos Hermanas (Hall of the Two Sisters), is stunning. Finally, there is the Generalife, the summer palace of the sultans, set in soul-soothing gardens. This is a great spot to relax

and contemplate the rest of the Alhambra from afar.

Cuesta de Gomérez leads up to the Alhambra from Plaza Nueva in the city. From April to September, the Alhambra and Generalife are open Monday to Saturday from 9 am to 8 pm, Sunday 9 am to 6 pm; the Palacio Nazaríes is also open Tuesday, Thursday and Saturday from 10 pm to midnight. Hours from October to March are 9 am to 6 pm daily, with the Palacio Nazaríes also open on Saturday from 8 to 10 pm. You can buy your ticket (725 ptas; free for the disabled and children under eight) from 8.30 am until one hour before closing time.

Other Attractions Simply wandering around the narrow streets of the Albayzín Moorish district, across the river from the Alhambra (not too late at night), or the area around Plaza de Bib-Rambla is a real pleasure. On your way, stop by the Casa del Castril (archaeological museum) and El Bañuelo (Arab baths), both on Carrera del Darro in the Albayzín, and the Capilla Real (Royal Chapel) on Gran Vía de Colón in which Fernando and Isabel, the Christian conquerors of Granada in 1492, are buried along with their daughter and son-in-law. Next door to the chapel is Granada's catedral, which dates in part from the early 16th century. The Gypsy caves of Sacromonte, in the north of the city, are another popular attraction.

Places to Stay

Granada's youth hostel, *Albergue Juvenil Granada* (☎ 958 27 26 38), is at Calle de Ramón y Cajal 2, just off Camino de Ronda, 1.7km west of the centre and a 600m walk south-west of the train station. It charges 1300/1600 ptas for under/over 26s in high season. An alternative budget option is the *Posada Doña Lupe* (☎ 958 22 14 73), on Avenida del Generalife, just above the Alhambra car park, which has plentiful singles/doubles from 1000/1950 ptas including a light breakfast.

On the east side of Plaza Nueva (well placed for the Albayzín and Alhambra), *Hostal Gomérez* (☎ 958 22 44 37), Cuesta de Gomérez 10, is cheap and cheerful with rooms for 1400/2300 ptas. *Hostal Britz*

GRANADA

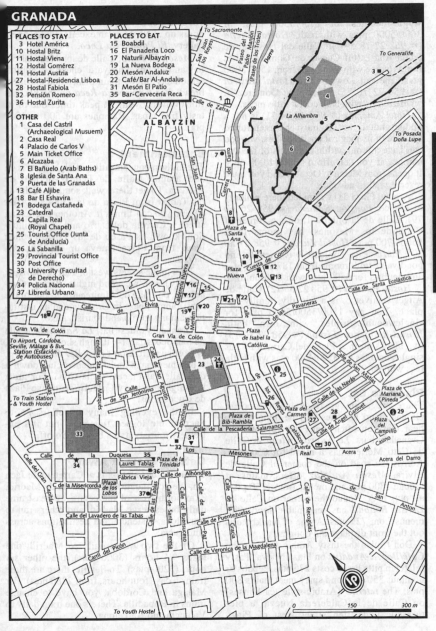

PLACES TO STAY
3 Hotel América
10 Hostal Britz
11 Hostal Viena
12 Hostal Gomérez
14 Hostal Austria
27 Hostal-Residencia Lisboa
28 Hostal Fabiola
32 Pensión Romero
36 Hostal Zurita

OTHER
1 Casa del Castril
(Archaeological Musuem)
2 Casa Real
4 Palacio de Carlos V
5 Main Ticket Office
6 Alcazaba
7 El Bañuelo (Arab Baths)
8 Iglesia de Santa Ana
9 Puerta de las Granadas
13 Café Aljibe
18 Bar El Eshavira
21 Bodega Castañeda
23 Catedral
24 Capilla Real
(Royal Chapel)
25 Tourist Office (Junta
de Andalucía)
26 La Sabanilla
29 Provincial Tourist Office
30 Post Office
33 University (Facultad
de Derecho)
34 Policía Nacional
37 Librería Urbano

PLACES TO EAT
15 Boabdil
16 El Panadería Loco
17 Naturii Albayzín
19 La Nueva Bodega
20 Mesón Andaluz
22 Café/Bar Al-Andalus
31 Mesón El Patio
35 Bar-Cervecería Reca

ALBAYZÍN

La Alhambra

To Sacromonte

To Generalife

To Posada
Doña Lupe

Plaza de
Santa Ana

Plaza
Nueva

Gran Vía de Colón

To Airport, Córdoba,
Seville, Málaga & Bus
Station (Estación
de Autobuses)

To Train Station
& Youth Hostel

Plaza
de Isabel la
Católica

Plaza del
Carmen

Plaza de
Mariana
Pineda

Plaza
del
Campillo

Plaza de
Bib-Rambla

Puerta
Real

Acera del Casino

Acera del Darro

Plaza de la
Trinidad

Plaza
de los
Lobos

To Youth Hostel

0   150   300 m

SPAIN

(☎ 958 22 36 52) at No 1 has clean, adequate singles/doubles for 2300/3500 ptas, or 3600/5000 ptas with bath. *Hostal Viena* (☎ 958 22 18 59), in Calle del Hospital de Santa Ana 2 (off Cuesta de Gomérez), has rooms (some with own bath) from 1500/3000 ptas. The same owners run *Hostal Austria* (☎ 958 22 70 75), Cuesta de Gomérez 4, where rooms with bath cost a little more.

Hotel América (☎ 958 22 74 71) is not a budget hotel, but it must be mentioned because of its magical position. Yes, you too can have a room within the walls of the Alhambra, if you can afford 6500/11,000 ptas. It opens from March to October and you must reserve well in advance.

Around Plaza de la Trinidad there's plenty of choice. *Pensión Romero* (☎ 958 26 60 79), Calle de la Sillería 1, on the corner of Calle de los Mesones, has rooms from 1500/2700 ptas. *Hostal Zurita* (☎ 958 27 50 20), Plaza de la Trinidad 7, is friendly and good value with rooms from 1875/3750 ptas and doubles for 4500 ptas with bathroom.

Hostal Fabiola (☎ 958 22 35 72), Calle de Ángel Ganivet 5, is a friendly, family-run place. You pay 1800/3500/5000 ptas for singles/doubles/triples with own bath. *Hostal-Residencia Lisboa* (☎ 958 22 14 13) two blocks north at Plaza del Carmen 27 has singles/doubles for 3300/4700 ptas with bath, less without.

Places to Eat

There are some great deals on food in Granada, and bar flies will be delighted to hear that you often don't pay for tapas in Granada's bars. *La Nueva Bodega* in Calle de Cetti Meriém has a menú for 850 ptas. Across the road on the corner of Calle de Elvira, *Mesón Andaluz* offers mains at around 1300 ptas and menús from 1250 ptas, all plus IVA. Round the corner on Calle de Elvira, *Boabdil* has reasonable food with menús from 725 ptas. A line of blackboards out the front displays the options.

Don't miss the tasty Arabic food at the *Café/Bar Al-Andalus* on Plaza Nueva. Tasty felafel in pitta bread costs 275 ptas, kebabs or hummus 350 ptas, and spicy meat mains 800 ptas. The *teterías* (Arabic-style tea houses) on Calle de la Calderería Nueva, a picturesque pedestrian street west of Plaza Nueva, are expensive. *Naturii Albayzín*, No 10, is a good vegetarian restaurant. A few doors up at No 14 is an excellent wholemeal bakery, *El Panadería Loco*.

Mesón El Patio, Calle de los Mesones 50 has an outdoor courtyard, cheap bocadillos, reasonably priced main dishes and excellent bread. *Bar-Cervecería Reca* on the plaza is full to overflowing at peak times due to its tasty free tapas. Raciones are 500 to 1000 ptas.

Entertainment

The highest concentration of nightspots is on and around Calle de Pedro Antonio de Alarcón. To get there, walk south on Calle de las Tablas from Plaza de la Trinidad. After 11 pm, you can't miss it. Another interesting street is Carrera del Darro and its continuation, known as Paseo de los Tristes, which leads from Plaza Nueva up into the Albayzín.

Bars in the streets west of Plaza Nueva get very lively on weekend nights. *Bodega Castañeda*, on Calle de Almireceros, is one of the most famous bars in Granada and an institution among locals and tourists alike.

Granada's oldest bar, *La Sabanilla*, Calle de San Sebastían 14, though showing its age, is worth a visit. Don't miss *Bar El Eshavira*, a basement jazz and flamenco club down a dark alley at Placeta de la Cuna. For great late-night music try *Café Aljibe*, above Plaza de Cuchilleros.

In the evening many travellers go to Sacromonte to see flamenco, but it's extremely touristy and a bit of a rip-off.

Getting There & Away

Granada's bus station is at Carretera de Jáen s/n, the continuation of Avenida de Madrid, 3km north-west of the centre. At least nine daily buses serve Madrid, and others run to Barcelona, Valencia and destinations across Andalucía.

Of the two trains daily to Madrid, one takes 9½ hours (3000 ptas), the other six hours (3200 ptas). To Seville, there are three trains a day (four hours, from 2280 ptas). For Málaga and Córdoba, you have to change trains in Bobadilla. There's one train daily to Valencia and Barcelona.

CÓRDOBA

n Roman times Córdoba was the capital of Hispania Ulterior province and then, after a reorganisation, of Baetica province. With the building of the Mezquita (mosque) in the 8th century it became the most important Moorish city in Spain and the most splendid city in Europe, a position it held for 200 or so years until the Córdoban Caliphate broke up after the death of its great ruler Al-Mansur in 1002. Thereafter Córdoba was overshadowed by Seville and in the 13th century both cities fell to the Christians in the Reconquista.

Orientation

Immediately north of the Río Guadalquivir is the old city, a warren of narrow streets focused on the Mezquita. The area north-west of the Mezquita was the Judería (Jewish quarter). The main square of the modern city is Plaza de las Tendillas, 500m north of the Mezquita.

Information

The Junta de Andalucía tourist office (☎ 957 47 12 35) faces the Mezquita at Calle de Torrijos 10. In summer it's open Monday to Saturday from 9 am to 8 pm, Sunday and holidays 10 am to 2 pm. The municipal tourist office (☎ 957 20 05 22) is on Plaza de Judá Leví, a block west of the Mezquita.

The main post office is on Calle de José Cruz Conde. There are plenty of telephones on Plaza de las Tendillas.

Things to See & Do

After Granada and Seville, Córdoba seems almost provincial. It is quite a laid-back town and a pleasant place to spend a couple of days just relaxing. Its most important attraction is the Mezquita. Built by the Emir of Córdoba, Abd al-Rahman I, in the 8th century AD, and enlarged by subsequent generations, it became the largest mosque in the Islamic world. In 1236 it was converted into a church and in the 16th century a cathedral was built in the centre of the mosque. Opening hours are Monday to Saturday from 10 am to 7.30 pm (October to March, to 5 pm), Sunday 2 to 7 pm (October to March, 3.30 to 5.30 pm). Entry is 750 ptas. You can enter free during mass from 9 to 10 am.

South-west of the Mezquita stands the **Alcázar de los Reyes Cristianos** (Castle of the Christian Monarchs). It is undergoing long-term renovations, but the extensive gardens are open to the public. Entry is 300 ptas (free on Friday). The **Museo de Bellas Artes** on Plaza del Potro houses a collection of works by Córdoban artists and others, including Zurbarán, Ribera and Goya (250 ptas, free for EU residents). Across the courtyard from here is the **Museo Julio Romero de Torres**, with a wonderful collection of his dark, sensual portraits of Córdoban women (425 ptas, free on Friday).

The **Museo Arqueólogico** on Calle del Marqués del Villar is also worth a visit (250 ptas, free for EU citizens). On the other side of the river, across the **Puente Romano**, is the **Torre de la Calahorra** which houses the Museo Vivo de Al-Andalus. Although some aspects of the museum are rather kitsch, it contains excellent models of the Mezquita and Granada's Alhambra; some of the commentary in the sound-and-light display is interesting. Entry is 500 ptas.

Places to Stay

Most people look for lodgings in the area around the Mezquita. Córdoba's ultramodern youth hostel, *Albergue Juvenil Córdoba* (☎ 957 29 01 66), is perfectly positioned on Plaza de Judá Leví, has excellent facilities and no curfew. Beds are 1300/1600 for those under/over 26.

Huéspedes Martínez Rücker (☎ 957 47 25 62), Calle de Mártinez Rücker 14, with singles/doubles from 1750/3500 ptas, is particularly friendly. At Calle del Cardenal González 25, *Hostal Santa Ana* (☎ 957 48 58 37) has one single at 1750 ptas and doubles at 3000 to 4500 ptas. *Hostal Rey Heredia* (☎ 957 47 41 82), Calle del Rey Heredia 26, has singles/doubles around a plant-filled patio for 1500/3000 ptas.

There are some good hostales to the east, farther from the tourist masses. *Pensión San Francisco* (☎ 957 47 27 16), Calle de San Fernando 24, has one small single at 2000 ptas and doubles from 4500 ptas. *Hostal La Fuente* (☎ 957 48 78 27), Calle de San Fernando 51, has compact singles at 2000 ptas and doubles with bath at 5500 ptas; its café serves a decent breakfast. *Hostal Los Arcos*

CÓRDOBA

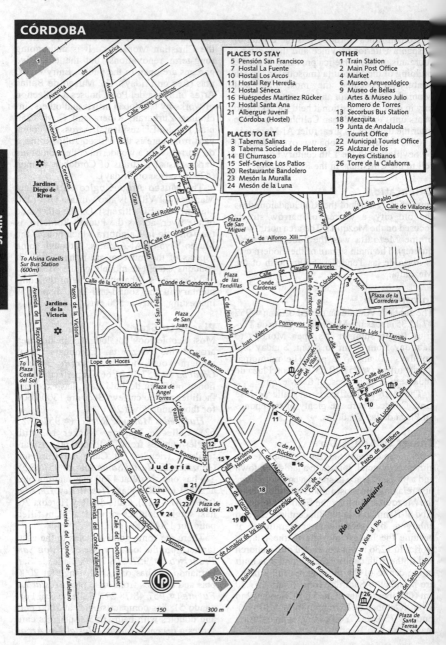

PLACES TO STAY
5 Pensión San Francisco
7 Hostal La Fuente
10 Hostal Los Arcos
11 Hostal Rey Heredia
12 Hostal Séneca
16 Huéspedes Martínez Rücker
17 Hostal Santa Ana
21 Albergue Juvenil
   Córdoba (Hostel)

PLACES TO EAT
3 Taberna Salinas
8 Taberna Sociedad de Plateros
14 El Churrasco
15 Self-Service Los Patios
20 Restaurante Bandolero
23 Mesón la Muralla
24 Mesón de la Luna

OTHER
1 Train Station
2 Main Post Office
4 Market
6 Museo Arqueológico
9 Museo de Bellas
   Artes & Museo Julio
   Romero de Torres
13 Secorbus Bus Station
18 Mezquita
19 Junta de Andalucía
   Tourist Office
22 Municipal Tourist Office
25 Alcázar de los
   Reyes Cristianos
26 Torre de la Calahorra

☎ 957 48 56 43), Calle de Romero Barros 4, has singles/doubles around a pretty courtyard for 2000/3500 ptas, and doubles for 4500 ptas with bath.

Just north of the Mezquita, the charming *Hostal Séneca* (☎ 957 47 32 34), Calle del Conde y Luque 7, boasts a traditional courtyard and a breakfast room; rooms with shared bath cost 2450/4600 ptas, with attached bath 5600 ptas, including breakfast.

Places to Eat

You shouldn't have too much trouble finding somewhere to eat in Córdoba. *Self-Service Los Patios*, right by the Mezquita on Calle del Cardenal Herrero, has a good choice of functional main courses and desserts with nothing over 800 ptas. The two restaurants in the city walls on Calle de la Luna, *Mesón de la Luna* and *Mesón la Muralla*, both have pretty courtyards and menús from 1200 to 1900 ptas.

For a first-class meal try *Restaurante Bandolero*, Calle de Torrijos 6 by the Mezquita. It has platos combinados from 975 to 1100 ptas; if you order à la carte expect to pay around 4000 ptas per person. *El Churrasco* in the Judería at Calle de Almanzor Romero 16 is one of Córdoba's best restaurants. The food is rich and service attentive. The set menú costs 3000 ptas.

If you'd rather try somewhere less touristy, *Taberna Sociedad de Plateros*, Calle de San Francisco 6, is a popular local tavern with a good range of tapas and raciones to choose from. Likewise *Taberna Salinas* at Calle de los Tundidores 3 offers good, cheap, local fare. Raciones cost around 700 ptas.

There is an excellent market in Plaza de la Corredera, another part of town beyond the tourist precinct. The *market* opens from Monday to Saturday and gets going at around 9.30 am – Saturday is the busiest day. There are lots of good bakeries with pastries, cakes and bocadillos in both the old and new parts of town; try Calle de la Concepción off the south end of the Avenida del Gran Capitán pedestrian mall.

Entertainment

Córdoba's lively bars are scattered around the north and west of town. One lively street is Calle de los Reyes Católicos, off Plaza de Colón; there are more bars in Calle de Córdoba de Veracruz and Calle de Alonso de Burgos, south of Avenida de Ronda de los Tejares. A third nightlife area is the Ciudad Jardín suburb around Plaza de la Costa del Sol, 350m west of Avenida de la República Argentina; and finally there's the northern El Brillante suburb, especially along Avenida del Brillante.

Getting There & Away

Buses to cities around Andalucía leave from the Alsina Graells Sur bus station (☎ 957 23 64 74) at Avenida de Medina Azahara 29. Long-distance buses to Barcelona and other cities on the Mediterranean coast, operated by Bacoma (☎ 957 45 65 14), also leave from this bus station. Buses to Madrid are run by Secorbus (☎ 957 46 80 40), Camino de los Sastres 1, on the corner of Avenida de la República Argentina.

The station (☎ 957 40 02 02) is on Avenida de América, 1km north-west of Plaza de las Tendillas. About 20 trains a day run to/from Sevilla, taking 45 minutes to 1¼ hours for 1050 to 2700 ptas. The numerous services to/from Madrid range from a single InterCity (4¼ hours, 3700 ptas) to several AVEs (1¾ hours, 5900 to 7000 ptas).

COSTA DE ALMERÍA

The Costa de Almería in south-east Andalucía, running from the Golfo de Almería round Cabo de Gata to the border of Murcia, is perhaps the last section of Spain's Mediterranean coast where you can have a beach completely to yourself. In high summer forget it, but this is Spain's hottest region, so even in late March it can be warm enough to take in some rays and try out your new swimsuit.

Orientation & Information

The most useful tourist offices are in Almería (☎ 950 27 43 55), San José (☎ 950 38 02 99) and Mojácar (☎ 950 47 51 62). Change money before going to Cabo de Gata as there are no banks there.

Things to See & Do

The **Alcazaba**, an enormous 10th-century Moorish fortress, is the highlight of Almería city. In its heyday the city it dominated was more important than Granada. In the desert 25km inland on the N-340 is **Mini-Hollywood** (☎ 950 36 52 36), where *A Fistful of Dollars* and other classic Westerns were shot. It's fun to drop in; the Western town set is preserved and shoot-outs are staged daily (entry 995 ptas). From Almería you can get there on a Tabernas bus.

The best thing about the region is the wonderful 50km coastline and semidesert scenery of **Cabo de Gata**. All along the coast from Cabo de Gata village to Agua Amarga, some of the most beautiful and empty beaches on the Mediterranean alternate with precipitous cliffs and scattered villages. At Las Salinas, 3km south of Cabo de Gata village, is a famous **flamingo colony**. The main village is laid-back **San José**, from where you can walk or drive to some of the best beaches such as **Playa de los Genoveses** and **Playa de Mónsul**. Some other beaches can only be reached on foot or by boat.

Mojácar, 30km north of Agua Amarga, is a white town of Moorish origin, perched on a hill 2km from the coast. Although a long resort strip, Mojácar Playa, has grown up below, Mojácar is still a pretty place and it's not hard to spend some time here, especially if you fancy a livelier beach scene than Cabo de Gata offers.

Places to Stay & Eat

A good cheapie in Almería is *Hostal Universal* (☎ 950 23 55 57), in the centre at Puerta de Purchena 3, with singles/doubles for 1500/3000 ptas. *Restaurante Alfareros*, nearby at Calle de Marcos 6, has a good three-course lunch and dinner menú for 950 ptas.

In high summer it's a good idea to ring ahead about accommodation on Cabo de Gata, as some places fill up. There are several camping grounds: *Camping Los Escullos* (☎ 950 38 98 11) and *Camping Cabo de Gata* (☎ 950 16 04 43) are open year-round. San José's *albergue juvenil* (youth hostel; ☎ 950 38 03 53), on Calle de Montemar s/n, opens from late Easter to 1 October, plus holidays, and charges 1000 to 1300 ptas depending on season. In San José village centre, *Fonda Costa Rica* (☎ 950 38 01 03) has doubles with bath for 5500 ptas. *Hostal Bahía* (☎ 950

38 03 07) nearby on Calle de Correo ha lovely singles/doubles for 5000/7500 ptas *Restaurante El Emigrante* across the roac does good fish and meat dishes for 850 o 1100 ptas, and big salads and tortillas for 35C to 500 ptas. There's accommodation in othe villages too.

In Mojácar, the cheaper places are mostly up in the town. *Pensión Casa Justa* (☎ 95C 47 83 72), Calle de Morote 7, is good value with singles/doubles from 2000/4000 ptas *Hostal La Esquinica* (☎ 950 47 50 09), nearby at Calle de Cano 1, charges 1750/3500 ptas. *Pensión La Luna* (☎ 950 47 80 32), Calle de la Estación Nueva 15, is more comfortable, with 10 doubles with bath for 6000 ptas including breakfast, and other good meals available.

Restaurante El Viento del Desierto on Plaza del Frontón is good value with main courses such as beef Bourguignon for 600 to 750 ptas. *Café Bar El Rincón de Embrujo*, Calle de la Iglesia 4, does platos combinados and seafood raciones from only 500 ptas. *Hotel Mamabel's*, Calle de los Embajadores 3, serves up some of the best food in Mojácar, with main dishes from 1250 ptas.

Getting There & Away

Almería has an international and domestic airport and is accessible by bus and train from Madrid, Barcelona, Granada and Seville, and by bus from Málaga and Murcia. Buses run from Almería to Cabo de Gata village and (except on Sunday) to San José. Mojácar can be reached by bus from Almería, Murcia, Granada and Madrid.

MÁLAGA & THE COSTA DEL SOL

The Costa del Sol, a string of tightly packed high-rise resorts running south-west from Málaga towards Gibraltar, is geared for – and incredibly popular with – package tourists from Britain and Germany and the time-share crowd. The main resorts are Torremolinos (which has such a bad reputation that it has been dubbed 'Terrible Torre'), Fuengirola and Marbella. From Marbella onwards, you can see the Rif Mountains in Morocco on a clear day.

Things to See & Do

The Costa del Sol pulls in the crowds because of its weather, beaches, warm Mediterranean water and cheap package deals. The resorts were once charming Spanish fishing villages, but that aspect has all but disappeared in most cases. If you're more interested in Spain than in foreign package tourists, **Málaga** itself is a better place to stop over. It has a bustling street life, a 16th-century cathedral and a Moorish palace/fortress, the Alcazaba, from which the walls of the Moorish castle, the Gibralfaro, climb to the top of the hill dominating the city.

Torremolinos and **Fuengirola** are a concrete continuum designed to squeeze as many paying customers as possible into the smallest conceivable area. You'll be surprised if you hear someone speak Spanish. **Marbella** is more inviting; the old town has managed to retain some character and has a well-preserved 15th-century castle. **Puerto Banús**, 4km west, is the only town on the Costa del Sol that could be called attractive. Consequently it's also exorbitant. Its harbour is a port of call for yachts that moor in Monte Carlo at other times of the year. A lot of the money here is rumoured to be on the crooked side, but nobody asks any questions.

Probably the only reason to stay long on the Costa del Sol is to work. If you go about it the right way, you may get work on one of the yachts in Puerto Banús. Some young travellers make good money in Marbella, Fuengirola and Torremolinos, touting for time-share salespeople.

Places to Stay

In Málaga the friendly *Pensión Córdoba* (☎ 95 221 44 69), Calle de la Bolsa 9, has singles/doubles at 1300/2500 ptas. *Hostal Chinitas* (☎ 95 221 46 83), Pasaje de Chinitas 2 off Plaza de la Constitución, is run by a friendly family and has clean, basic singles/doubles for 1700/3400 ptas plus IVA.

Rooms down the coast are expensive in July, August and maybe September but prices usually come down sharply at other times from the levels given here. In Terrible Torre, *Hostal Micaela* (☎ 95 238 33 10), Calle de Bajondillo 4 near Playa del Bajondillo, has doubles with bath for 4000 ptas plus IVA. *Hostal Prudencio* (☎ 95 238 14 52), Calle

del Carmen 43, at 3000/6000 ptas, is a stone's throw from the beach.

At Fuengirola, the British-run *Pensión Coca* (☎ 95 247 41 89), Calle de la Cruz 3, has decent rooms at 3600/5800 ptas. The friendly *Hostal Italia* (☎ 95 247 41 93), Calle de la Cruz 1, has doubles for 4580 ptas plus IVA.

Marbella's modern *Albergue Juvenil Marbella* youth hostel (☎ 95 277 14 91), above the old town at Calle del Trapiche 2, has good rooms at 1300/1600 ptas for under/over 26s and a pool. The British-run *Hostal del Pilar* (☎ 95 282 99 36) in the old town at Calle de Mesoncillo 4 is popular with backpackers and charges up to 2000 ptas a person.

Places to Eat

Near the cathedral in Málaga, *Bar Restaurante Tormes*, Calle de San Agustín 13 (closed Monday), and the slightly fancier *El Jardín* on Calle del Cister both have good menús for 1100 ptas. For local flavour, sample fish dishes at outdoor tables at the reasonably priced marisquerías on Calle del Comisario. In Torremolinos and Fuengirola, it's just a matter of going for a walk along the beachfront – you'll find plenty of places with menús for well under 1000 ptas.

In Marbella, *Bar El Gallo* at Calle de Lobatos 44 in the old town does great-value burgers and fish and meat dishes for 300 to 500 ptas. *El Patio Andaluz* is a charming old coaching inn on Calle de San Juan de Dios; sardines, boquerones and chips with wine will set you back just 800 ptas.

Getting There & Away

Málaga is the main landing and launching pad for the Costa del Sol and its airport has a good range of domestic as well as international flights. Málaga is linked by train and bus to all major Spanish centres, including Madrid, Barcelona, Seville, Granada and Algeciras. Málaga's bus and train stations are round the corner from each other, 1km west of the centre.

Getting Around

Trains run every half-hour from Málaga airport to the city centre and west to Torremolinos and Fuengirola. There are even more frequent buses from Málaga to Torremolinos, Fuengirola and Marbella.

SPAIN

RONDA

One of the prettiest and most historic towns in Andalucía, Ronda is a world apart from the nearby Costa del Sol. Straddling the savagely deep El Tajo gorge, the town stands at the heart of some lovely hill country dotted with white villages and ripe for exploring.

The main tourist office (☎ 95 287 12 72) is at Plaza de España 1.

Things to See & Do

Ronda is a pleasure to wander around, but during the day you'll have to contend with bus loads of day-trippers up from the coast.

The **Plaza de Toros** (1785) is considered the home of bullfighting and is something of a mecca for aficionados; inside is the small but fascinating **Museo Taurino**. Entry is 275 ptas.

To cross the gorge to the originally Moorish old town, you have a choice of three bridges. The 18th-century **Puente Nuevo** (New Bridge) is an amazing feat of engineering and the views from here are great. The old town itself is littered with ancient churches, monuments and palaces. The **Palacio de Mondragón** houses a rather inconsequential museum, but is almost worth the 200 ptas entry (students 100 ptas) for the views alone. You can walk down into the gorge from nearby Plaza de María Auxiliadora. Also of interest are the **Iglesia de Santa María la Mayor**, a medieval church whose tower was once the minaret of a mosque, and the **Baños Arabes** (Arab Baths), also dating from the 13th century.

Places to Stay & Eat

Camping El Sur (☎ 95 287 59 39) is in a pleasant setting 2km south-west of town and has a swimming pool and restaurant.

The bright *Pensión La Purísima* (☎ 95 287 10 50), Calle de Sevilla 10, has nine rooms at 2000/3000 ptas. *Hostal Morales* (☎ 95 287 15 38), Calle de Sevilla 51, is reasonable value at 1200/2400 ptas.

For good eating check out Plaza del Socorro. *Marisquería Paco* here does good seafood and jamón tapas. *El Molino* is popular for its pizzas and pasta at 500 to 700 ptas and platos combinados from 600 ptas. The old-fashioned *Restaurante Doña Pepa* has menús for 1300 and 1750 ptas.

Getting There & Away

There are several buses daily to Seville (2½ hours, 1235 ptas) and Málaga (two hours 1075 ptas, some via the Costa del Sol), and one (except Sunday) to La Línea (Gibraltar) for 990 ptas. The bus station is on Plaza de Concepción García Redondo.

Daily trains go to Seville (three hours, 1860 ptas), Málaga (two to 2½ hours, 1130 ptas), Granada and Córdoba, mostly with a change at Bobadilla, and there are direct trains to Algeciras. The station is on Avenida de Andalucía.

Gibraltar

The British colony of Gibraltar occupies a huge lump of limestone, 5km long and 1km wide, at the mouth of the Mediterranean Sea. It's a curious and interesting port of call if you're in the region. Gibraltar has certainly had a rocky history; it was the bridgehead for the Moorish invasion of Spain in 711 AD and Castile didn't finally wrest it from the Moors until 1462. Then in 1704 an Anglo-Dutch fleet captured Gibraltar after a one-week siege. Spain gave up military attempts to regain it from Britain after the failure of the 3½-year Great Siege in 1779-83, but during the Franco period Gibraltar was an extremely sore point between Britain and Spain, and the border was closed for years.

Gibraltar is self-governing and depends on Britain only for defence. An overwhelming majority of Gibraltarians – many of whom are of Genoese or Jewish ancestry – want to remain with Britain. Spain has offered Gibraltar autonomous-region status within Spain, but Britain and the Gibraltarians reject any compromise over sovereignty.

Information

EU, US, Canada, Australia, New Zealand, Israel, South Africa and Singapore passport-holders are among those who do *not* need visas for Gibraltar, but anyone who needs a visa for Spain should have at least a double-entry Spanish visa if they intend to return to Spain from Gibraltar.

Gibraltar has helpful tourist offices at the border. The main office (☎ 45000) is in Duke of Kent House, Cathedral Square, open

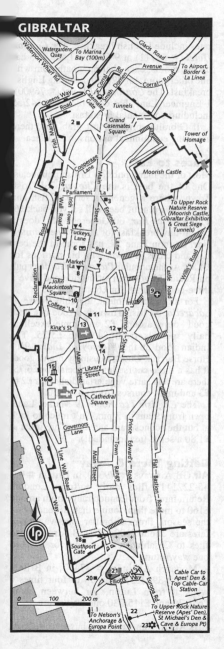

GIBRALTAR

PLACES TO STAY
2 Emile Youth Hostel
3 Continental Hotel
11 Cannon Hotel
18 Toc H Hostel
20 Queen's Hotel

PLACES TO EAT
4 House of Sacarello
5 The Clipper
7 Viceroy of India
8 The English Tea Room
12 Three Roses Bar
14 Cannon Bar
21 Piccadilly Gardens

OTHER
1 Bus No 9
6 Post Office
9 St Bernard's Hospital
10 Tourist Office
13 Roman Catholic Cathedral
15 Gibraltar Museum
16 Bus No 3
17 Anglican Cathedral
19 Trafalgar Cemetery
22 Bottom Cable-Car Station
23 Alameda Botanical Gardens

Monday to Friday from 9 am to 5.30 pm; another is at The Piazza (☎ 74982), Main St, open Monday to Friday from 9 am to 5.30 pm, Saturday 10 am to 2 pm.

The currency is the Gibraltar pound or pound sterling. You can use pesetas but currency conversion rates aren't in your favour. Exchange rates for buying pesetas are, however, a bit better than in Spain. Change any unspent Gibraltar pounds before you leave.

To phone Gibraltar from Spain, the telephone code is ☎ 9567; from the UK dial ☎ 00, then ☎ 350 (the code for Gibraltar) and the local number. To phone Spain from Gibraltar, just dial the nine-digit Spanish number.

Things to See & Do

Central Gibraltar is nothing special – you could almost be in Bradford or Bletchley – but the **Gibraltar Museum**, at 18-20 Bomb House Lane, has a very interesting historical architectural and military collection and includes a Moorish bathhouse. It's open the same hours as the main tourist office. Entry is UK£2. Many graves in the **Trafalgar Cemetery** are of those who died at Gibraltar from wounds received in the Battle of Trafalgar (1805).

The large **Upper Rock Nature Reserve**, covering most of the upper rock, has spectacular views and several interesting spots to visit. It's open daily from 9.30 am to sunset. Entry, at UK£5 a person and UK£1.50 a vehicle, includes all the following sites, which are open to 6.15 pm. Cable-car tickets (see Getting Around later) include entry to the reserve, the Apes' Den and St Michael's Cave.

The rock's most famous inhabitants are its colony of **Barbary macaques**, the only wild primates (apart from *Homo sapiens*) in Europe. Some of these hang around the **Apes' Den** near the middle cable-car station, others can often be seen at the top station or Great Siege Tunnels.

From the top cable-car station, there are views as far as Morocco in decent weather. **St Michael's Cave**, a 20-minute downhill walk south from here, is a big natural grotto renowned for its stalagmites and stalactites. Apart from attracting tourists in droves, it's used for concerts, plays and even fashion shows. The **Great Siege Tunnels**, a 30-minute walk north (downhill) from the top cable-car station, are a series of galleries in the rock hewn out by the British during the Great Siege to provide new gun emplacements. Worth a stop on the way down to the town from here are the **Gibraltar, a city under siege** exhibition and a **Muslim castle** (aka the Tower of Homage).

Places to Stay

The *Emile Youth Hostel* (☎ 51106) at Montagu Bastion, Line Wall Rd, is a step up from Gibraltar's other budget options. It has 43 places in two to eight-person rooms for £10 including continental breakfast. The *Toc H Hostel* (☎ 73431), a ramshackle old place tucked into the city walls at the south end of Line Wall Road, has beds at £5 a night and cold showers.

The *Queen's Hotel* (☎ 74000) at 1 Boyd St has a restaurant, bar, and singles/doubles at £16/24 (£20/36 with private bath or shower).

Reduced rates of £14/20 and £16/24 are offered for students and young travellers. Al rates include English breakfast. The *Cannor Hotel* (☎ 51711) at 9 Cannon Lane also ha decent rooms, each sharing a bathroom with one other room, for £20/30 including English breakfast. The *Continental Hotel* (☎ 76900) 1 Engineer Lane, has cosy rooms at £42/55 including continental breakfast.

If Gibraltar prices don't grab you, there are some economical options in La Línea.

Places to Eat

Most of the many pubs do British pub meals. One of the best is the *Clipper*, 78B Irish Town, where a generous serve of fish and chips and a pint of beer will set you back £6. *Three Roses Bar*, 60 Governor's St, does a big all-day breakfast for £2.80. The *Cannon Bar*, Cannon Lane 27, has some of the best fish and chips in town, with big portions for £4.50. At the popular *Piccadilly Gardens* pub on Rosia Rd you can sit outside and have a three-course lunch for £6.

For a restaurant meal, the chic *House of Sacarello*, 57 Irish Town, is a good bet, with good soups around £2 and some excellent daily specials from £4.95 to £5.75. The Indian food at the *Viceroy of India*, 9/11 Horse Barrack Court, is usually pretty good. It has a three-course lunch special for £6.75; there are à la carte vegetarian dishes for £2 to £3 and main courses from £6 to £10.

The *English Tea Room*, 9 Market Lane, open from 9 am to 7 pm, isn't much to look at but the scones, jam and cream are great at £1.80 a serve (tea included!).

Getting There & Away

Air GB Airways (☎ 79300, in Britain ☎ 03-45-222111) flies daily to/from London. Return fares from London range from around £160 to more than double that, depending on the season. From Gibraltar, one-way/return fares are about £100/180. GB Airways also flies to Casablanca most days for £99/146 one way/return.

Monarch Airlines (☎ 47477, in Britain ☎ 01582-398333) flies up to four times a week to/from Luton, for between about £65/130 and £115/230 one way/return.

Bus Apart from excursion buses from Costa

del Sol resorts, there are no regular buses to Gibraltar, but the bus station in La Línea is only a five-minute walk from the border.

Car & Motorcycle Vehicle queues at the border often make it less time-consuming to park in La Línea, then walk across the border. To take a car into Gibraltar you need an insurance certificate, registration document, nationality plate and driving licence.

Ferry There are normally three ferries a week each way between Gibraltar and Tangier, taking two hours for £18/30 one way/return per person and £40/80 per car. In Gibraltar, buy tickets at Tourafrica (☎ 77666), ICC Building, Main St.

Getting Around

Bus Nos 3 and 9 run direct from the border into town. On Sunday there's only a limited service – but the 1.5km walk is quite interesting, as it crosses the airport runway.

All of Gibraltar can be covered on foot, but there are other options. The cable car leaves its lower station on Red Sands Rd from Monday to Saturday every few minutes, weather permitting, from 9.30 am to 5.15 pm. One-way/return fares are £3.45/4.90. For the Apes' Den, disembark at the middle station. If you're in a hurry, you can take a taxi tour of the rock's main sights for around £20 plus.

Extremadura

Extremadura, a sparsely populated tableland bordering Portugal, is far enough from the most beaten tourist trails to give you a genuine sense of exploration – something that *extremeños* themselves have a flair for. Many epic 16th-century *conquistadores* including Francisco Pizarro (who conquered the Incas) and Hernán Cortés (who did the same to the Aztecs) sprang from this land.

Trujillo and Cáceres are the two not-to-be-missed old towns here, while a spot of hiking, or just relaxing, in the valleys of north-east Extremadura makes the perfect change from urban life. Elsewhere, Mérida has Spain's biggest collection of Roman ruins, and the Parque Natural de Monfragüe, famous for its birds of prey, is a great stop for drivers north

of Trujillo. If you can, avoid June, July and August, when Extremadura is *very* hot.

TRUJILLO

With just 9000 people, Trujillo can't be much bigger now than in 1529, when its most famous son Francisco Pizarro set off with his three brothers and a few local buddies for an expedition that culminated in the bloody conquest of the Inca empire three years later. Trujillo is blessed with a broad and fine Plaza Mayor, from which rises its remarkably preserved old town, packed with aged buildings exuding history. If you approach from the Plasencia direction you might imagine that you've driven through a time warp into the 16th century. The tourist office (☎ 927 32 26 77) is on Plaza Mayor.

Things to See

A **statue of Pizarro**, done by an American, Charles Rumsey, in the 1920s, dominates the Plaza Mayor. On the plaza's south side, the **Palacio de la Conquista** (closed to visitors) sports the carved images of Francisco Pizarro and the Inca princess Inés Yupanqui. Their daughter Francisca lived in this house with her husband Hernando, the only Pizarro brother to return alive to Spain. Two noble mansions you *can* visit are the 16th-century **Palacio de los Duques de San Carlos**, also on the Plaza Mayor, and the **Palacio de Orellana-Pizarro**, through the alley in the plaza's south-west corner.

Up the hill, the **Iglesia de Santa María la Mayor** is an interesting hotchpotch of 13th to 16th-century styles, with some fine paintings by Fernando Gallego of the Flemish school. Higher up, the **Casa-Museo de Pizarro** has informative displays (in Spanish) on the lives and adventures of the Pizarro family. At the top of the hill, Trujillo's **castillo** is an impressive though empty structure, primarily of Moorish origin.

Places to Stay & Eat

Camas Boni (☎ 927 32 16 04), Calle Domingo de Ramos 7, is good value with small but well-kept singles/doubles from 2000/3000 ptas, and doubles with bathroom for 4500 ptas. *Casa Roque* (☎ 927 32 23 13), Calle Domingo de Ramos 30, has singles at

1500 ptas, and doubles with bath at 3500 ptas. *Hostal Nuria* (☎ 927 32 09 07), Plaza Mayor 27, has nice singles/doubles with bath for 3000/5000 ptas. The friendly eight-room *Hostal La Cadena* (☎ 927 32 14 63), Plaza Mayor 8, is also good, at 4500/5500 ptas.

The menú at *Restaurante La Troya* on Plaza Mayor costs 1990 ptas, but if you're a meat-eater it will save you from eating much else for the next couple of days. Portions are gigantic and they also give you a large omelette and a salad for starters, and an extra main course later on! If you're not quite that hungry there are great tapas here too. Elsewhere on Plaza Mayor *Cafetería Nuria* has various dished from 500 to 900 ptas. *Café-Bar El Escudo* up the hill on Plaza de Santiago is also moderately priced.

Getting There & Away
The bus station (☎ 927 32 05 00) is 500m south of Plaza Mayor, on Carretera de Badajoz. At least six buses daily run to/from Cáceres (45 minutes, 400 ptas), Badajoz and Madrid (2½ to four hours, 1985 ptas), and four or more to/from Mérida (1¼ hours, 830 ptas).

CÁCERES
Cáceres is larger than Trujillo and has an even bigger old town, created in the 15th and 16th centuries and so perfectly preserved that it can seem lifeless at times – but if things seem a bit quiet, the student-led nightlife around Plaza Mayor, on the north-west side of the old town, more than makes up for that on weekends. The tourist office (☎ 927 24 63 47) is on Plaza Mayor.

Things to See
The old town is still surrounded by walls and towers raised by the Almohads in the 12th century. Entering it from Plaza Mayor, you'll see ahead the fine 15th-century **Iglesia de Santa María**, Cáceres' cathedral. Any time from February to September, Santa María's tower will be topped by the ungainly nests of the large storks which make their homes in every worthwhile vertical protuberance in the old city.

Many of the old city's churches and imposing medieval mansions can only be admired from outside, but you *can* enter the good **Museo de Cáceres** on Plaza de Veletas, housed in a 16th-century mansion built over a 12th-century Moorish cistern (*aljibe*) which is the museum's prize exhibit. It's open daily except Monday, from 9 am to 2.30 pm (200 ptas, free for EU citizens). Also worth a look is the **Casa-Museo Árabe Yussuf Al-Borch** at Cuesta del Marqués 4, a private house decked out with oriental and Islamic trappings to capture the feel of Moorish times. The **Arco del Cristo** at the bottom of this street is a Roman gate.

Places to Stay
The best area to stay is around Plaza Mayor, though it gets noisy at weekends. *Pensión Márquez* (☎ 927 24 49 60), just off the low end of the plaza at Calle de Gabriel y Galán 2, is a friendly family-run place with clean singles/doubles at 1500/3000 ptas. *Hostal Castilla* (☎ 927 24 44 04), one block west at Calle de los Ríos Verdes 3, has adequate rooms for 2000/4000 ptas. *Hostal Plaza de Italia* (☎ 927 24 77 60), away from the hustle and bustle at Calle Constancia 12, has clean, pleasant rooms with shower and TV for 3500/5000 ptas.

Places to Eat
Cafetería El Puchero, Plaza Mayor 33, is a popular hang-out with a huge variety of eating options, from good bocadillos (around 400 ptas) and raciones to solid platos combinados (675 to 900 ptas) or à la carte fare. *Cafetería El Pato*, a block down the arcade, has excellent coffee and an upstairs restaurant with good three-course menús, including wine, for 1200 and 1800 ptas plus IVA.

Restaurante El Figón de Eustaquio, Plaza de San Juan 12, is a good bet for a traditional extremeño meal. The three-course menú de la casa, with wine, is 1650 ptas plus IVA.

Getting There & Away
Bus Minimum daily services from the bus station (☎ 927 23 25 50) include at least six to Trujillo (400 ptas) and Madrid (3½ hours, 2385 ptas); five each to Mérida (1¼ hours, 650 ptas) and Plasencia; three each to Salamanca (three to four hours, 2000 ptas), Zafra and Sevilla (four hours, 2170 ptas) and two to Badajoz (825 ptas).

Train Three to five trains a day run to/from Madrid (3½ to five hours; from 2300 ptas) and Mérida (one hour) and two or three each to/from Plasencia (1¼ hours), Badajoz (two hours) and Barcelona. The single daily train to Lisbon (six hours; from 4400 ptas) leaves in the middle of the night.

MÉRIDA

Once the biggest city in Roman Spain, Mérida is home to more ruins of that age than anywhere else in the country. The tourist office (☎ 924 31 53 53) is at Avenida de José Álvarez Saenz de Buruaga, by the gates to the Roman theatre.

Things to See

For 750 ptas (half price for students and EU citizens) you can get a ticket that gives you entry to the **Teatro Romano**, **Anfiteatro**, the **Casa del Anfiteatro**, the **Casa Romana del Mithraeo** and the **Alcazaba**, all open daily from 9 am to 1.45 pm and 5 to 7.15 pm (4 to 6.15 pm in winter). Entry to just the Teatro Romano and Anfiteatro is 600 ptas. The theatre was built in 15 BC and the gladiators' ring, or Anfiteatro, seven years later. Combined they could hold 20,000 spectators. Various other reminders of imperial days are scattered about town, including the **Puente Romano**, at 792m one of the longest the Romans ever built.

Places to Stay & Eat

Pensión El Arco (☎ 924 31 83 21), Calle de Miguel de Cervantes 16, is great value and deservedly popular with backpackers; spotless singles/doubles cost 1800/3500 ptas with shared bathroom. *Hostal Bueno* (☎ 924 30 29 77), Calle del Calvario 9, is also good at 2500/4500 ptas.

Casa Benito on Calle de San Francisco is a great old-style wood-panelled bar and restaurant, decked with bullfighting photos and posters, doing meat, sheep cheese and other local fare at reasonable prices as tapas, raciones or main dishes.

Three good eateries line up on Calle de Felix Valverde Lillo. *Restaurante El Briz*, at No 5, does a great montado de lomo (pork loin sandwich) for 350 ptas and has a restaurant at the back with a menú for 1350 ptas.

Next door, the upmarket *Restaurante Nicolás* has a 2000 ptas menú. *Restaurante Antillano*, No 15, is popular with locals and has a menú for just 1200 ptas.

Getting There & Away

From the bus station (☎ 924 37 14 04) at least seven daily buses run to Badajoz (665 ptas), Sevilla (1575 to 1690 ptas) and Madrid (from 2720 ptas), and at least four to Cáceres (650 ptas) and Trujillo (830 ptas).

At least four trains run a day to Badajoz, and two or more to Cáceres, Ciudad Real, Madrid (five to six hours, 2840 to 4000 ptas).

NORTH-EAST EXTREMADURA

From Plasencia, the green, almost Eden-like valleys of La Vera, Valle del Jerte and Valle del Ambroz stretch north-east into the Sierra de Gredos and its western extensions. Watered by rushing mountain streams called *gargantas*, and dotted with medieval villages, these valleys offer some excellent walking routes and attract just enough visitors to provide a good network of places to stay.

Information

The Editorial Alpina booklet *Valle del Jerte, Valle del Ambroz, La Vera* includes a 1:50,000 map of the area showing walking routes. Try to get it from a map or bookshop before you come; if not, the tourist office in Cabezuela del Valle may have copies.

There are tourist offices at Plasencia (☎ 927 42 21 59), Jaraíz de la Vera (☎ 927 17 05 87), Jarandilla de la Vera (☎ 927 56 04 60) and Cabezuela del Valle (☎ 927 47 21 22). Most sizeable villages have banks.

Things to See & Do

La Vera About halfway up the valley, **Cuacos de Yuste** has its share of narrow village streets with half-timbered houses leaning at odd angles, their overhanging upper storeys supported by timber or stone pillars. Up a side road, 2km north-west, is the **Monasterio de Yuste**, to which in 1557 Carlos I, once the world's most powerful man, retreated for his dying years. The simple royal chambers and the monastery church are open Tuesday to Saturday from 9.30 am to 12.30 pm and 3.30 to 6 pm, Sunday 9.30 to

SPAIN

11.30 am, 1 to 1.30 pm and the same afternoon hours. Entry is by guided tour in Spanish for 100 ptas.

The road continues past the monastery to **Garganta la Olla**, another typically picturesque village, from where you can head over the 1269m **Puerto del Piornal** pass into the Valle del Jerte.

Jarandilla de la Vera is a bigger village, with a 15th-century fortress-church on the main square (below the main road), and a parador occupying a castle-palace where Carlos I stayed while Yuste was being readied for him. A Roman bridge over the Garganta Jaranda below the village makes a focus for short rambles. Of the longer hikes, the Ruta de Carlos V (see Valle del Jerte, below) is one of the most enticing. If you want to do it in reverse, ask for directions at Camping Jaranda.

Valle del Jerte This valley grows half of Spain's cherries and turns into a sea of white at blossom time in April. **Piornal**, high on the south flank, is a good base for walks along the Sierra de Tormantos. In the bottom of the valley, **Cabezuela del Valle** has a particularly medieval main street. A 35km road crosses from just north of here over the 1430m Puerto de Honduras pass to Hervás in the Valle del Ambroz. For hikers, the PR-10 trail climbs roughly parallel, to the south. From **Jerte** you can walk into the beautiful **Parque Natural de la Garganta de los Infiernos**.

Tornavacas, near the head of the valley, is the starting point of the **Ruta de Carlos V**, a 28km marked trail following the route by which Carlos I (who was also Carlos V of the Holy Roman Empire) was carried over the mountains to Jarandilla on the way to Yuste. It can be walked in one long day – just as Carlos' bearers did it back then.

Valle del Ambroz Towards the head of the valley **Hervás**, a pleasant small town, has the best surviving 15th-century Barrio Judío (Jewish quarter) in Extremadura, where many Jews took refuge in hope of avoiding the Inquisition. About 22km west by paved roads across the valley, **Granadilla** is a picturesque old fortified village that was abandoned after the Embalse de Gabriel y Galán reservoir

almost surrounded it in the 1960s. Now it's restored as an educational centre and you can visit, free, from 10 am to 1 pm and 4 to 6 pm daily, except Sunday afternoon and Monday.

Places to Stay & Eat
There are *camping grounds* – many with fine riverside positions – in several villages including Cuacos de Yuste, Hervás, Jarandilla de la Vera and Jerte. Most are only open from March/April to September/October. There are free zonas de acampada, camping areas with no facilities, at Garganta la Olla and Piornal.

In Plasencia, *Hostal La Muralla* (☎ 927 41 38 74), Calle de Berrozana 6, charges from 1700/3000 to 3350/3950 ptas plus IVA for a range of rooms. On the main road in Cuacos de Yuste, *Pensión Sol* (☎ 927 17 22 41) has good rooms for 1900/2700 ptas, and a restaurant. In Jarandilla de la Vera, *Hostal Jaranda* (☎ 927 56 02 06), on the main road at Avenida de Soledad Vega Ortiz 101, has big, bright rooms with bath for 3250/6500 ptas, and an excellent-value three-course menú with wine for 1000 ptas. In Piornal, *Casa Verde* (☎ 927 47 63 95), Calle de la Libertad 38, is a friendly hostel-style place charging 2500 ptas a person, including breakfast, in decent doubles with private bath. Book ahead, especially in spring.

In Cabezuela del Valle, the good *Hotel Aljama* (☎ 927 47 22 91), Calle de Federico Bajo s/n, almost touching the church across the street, has nice rooms for 3000/4900 ptas plus IVA. There are numerous places to eat and drink on nearby Calle del Hondón. *Hostal Puerto de Tornavacas* (☎ 927 17 73 13), a couple of kilometres up the N-110 from Tornavacas, is an inn-style place with rooms for 2500/4600 ptas, and a restaurant specialising in extremeño food.

Getting There & Away
Your own wheels are a big help but if you do use the buses, you can at least walk over the mountains without worrying about how to get back to your vehicle! The following bus services run Monday to Friday, with much reduced services on weekends.

Mirat runs a bus from Cáceres and Plasencia to Madrigal de la Vera, stopping at the villages on the C-501 in La Vera. One or two

Mirat buses run from Plasencia as far as Garganta la Olla, Losar de la Vera and Robledillo de la Vera. From Madrid's Estación Sur de Autobuses, the Doaldi line runs daily buses to La Vera.

From Plasencia, a daily bus heads for Piornal, and four a day run up the Valle del Jerte to Tornavacas.

Los Tres Pilares runs two buses between Plasencia and Hervás. Enatcar has a few services between Cáceres, Plasencia and Salamanca via the Valle del Ambroz, stopping at the Empalme de Hervás junction on the N-630, 2km from the town.

Galicia, Asturias & Cantabria

Galicia has been spared the mass tourism that has reached many other parts of Spain. Its often wild coast is indented with a series of majestic inlets – the Rías Altas and Rías Bajas – which hide some of the prettiest and least known beaches and coves in Spain. Inland, potholed roads cross rolling green hills dotted with picturesque farmhouses. In winter, Galicia can be freezing, but in summer it has one of the most agreeable climates in Europe – although you must expect a little rain.

Highlights of the still greener and at least as beautiful Asturias and Cantabria regions, east of Galicia, are the Picos de Europa mountains and coastal towns like Santillana del Mar.

SANTIAGO DE COMPOSTELA

This beautiful small city marks the end of the Camino de Santiago, a collective name for several major medieval pilgrim routes from as far away as France, still followed by plenty of the faithful today. Thanks to its university, Santiago is a lively city almost any time, but is at its most festive around 25 July, the Feast of Santiago (St James). Its tourist office (☎ 981 58 40 81) at Rúa do Vilar 43 is open Monday to Friday from 10 am to 2 pm and 4 to 7 pm, and Saturday 10 am to 2 pm.

Things to See & Do

The goal of the Camino de Santiago is the **catedral** on magnificent **Praza do Obradoiro**. Under the main altar lies the supposed tomb of Santiago Apóstol (St James the Apostle). It's believed the saint's remains were buried here in the 1st century AD and rediscovered in 813, after which he grew into the patron saint of the Christian Reconquista, and his tomb attracted streams of pilgrims from all over Western Europe. The cathedral is a superb Romanesque creation of the 11th to 13th centuries, with later decorative flourishes, and its masterpiece is the Pórtico de la Gloria inside the west façade.

Santiago's compact old town is a work of art, and a walk around the cathedral will take you through some of its most inviting squares. It's also good to stroll in the beautifully landscaped **Carballeira de Santa Susana** park south-west of the cathedral. Just north-east of the old city, off Porta do Camino, an impressive old convent houses the **Museo do Pobo Galego**, covering Galician life from fishing through music and crafts to traditional costume (open Monday to Saturday, free).

Places to Stay

Santiago is jammed with cheap pensiones, but many are full with students. A quiet and cheap central option with decent rooms is **Hospedaje Forest** (☎ 981 57 08 11), Callejón de Don Abril Ares 7, where singles/doubles start at 1300/2400 ptas. **Hostal Real** (☎ 981 56 66 56), Rúa da Calderería 49, has good-sized rooms for 2200/3300 ptas. The attractive **Hostal Pazo de Agra** (☎ 981 58 90 45), Rúa da Calderería 37, is a spotlessly kept old house. Singles/doubles without private bath start at 2000/4000 ptas – a little more for private bath. Inquire at Restaurante Zingara, Rúa de Cardenal Payá. The popular little **Hostal Suso** (☎ 981 58 66 11), Rúa do Vilar 65, has amiable hosts; comfortable modern rooms with bath cost 3000/4200 ptas.

Places to Eat

For a full and solid meal with wine and dessert for less than 1000 ptas, try **Restaurante Cuatro Vientos**, Rúa de Santa Cristina 19. Popular with readers of travel guides is **Casa Manolo**, Rúa Travesa 27, which has a good-value set meal for 700 ptas without drinks.

SANTIAGO DE COMPOSTELA

1 Restaurante Cuatro Vientos
2 Museo do Pobo Galego
3 Hospedaje Forest
4 Casa Manolo
5 Paraíso Perdido
6 Café das Crechas
7 Catedral
8 Restaurante El Hispano
9 Mercado Plaza de Abastos (Food Market)
10 Post Office
11 Police Station
12 Tourist Office
13 Hostal Pazo de Agra
14 University
15 Hostal Real
16 Restaurante Zingara
17 Hostal Suso
18 Restaurante Entre Rúas & Restaurante A Tulla

A couple of modestly priced places that come up with some good dishes are *Restaurante Entre Rúas* and *Restaurante A Tulla*, next to each other in the tiny square on Entrerúas, a laneway linking Rúa do Vilar and Rúa Nova. You should get away with around 1500 ptas. For a fresh fish grill (parrillada de pescados), head for *Restaurante El Hispano*, Rúa de Santo Agostiño, just opposite the market.

Entertainment

For traditional Celtic music, Galician style, head for *Café das Crechas*, Via Sacra 3. Some-

times it's live. *Paraíso Perdido* on the tiny square of Entrealtares, is one of Santiago's oldest bars. The local drinking and dancing scene is centred in the new town, especially around Praza Roxa. *Black*, Avenida de Rosalía de Castro s/n, is a popular disco. For more of a Latin American touch, have a look in at *Makumba*, Rúa de Frei Rodendo Salvado 16.

Getting There & Away

Lavacolla airport, 11km south-east of Santiago, caters to international flights, plus flights to Madrid, Barcelona and Málaga.

Santiago's bus station is just over 1km north-east of the cathedral, on Rúa de Rodriguez Viguri. City bus No 10 runs to Praza de Galicia, on the south edge of the old town. Castromil runs regular services to Vigo via Pontevedra, south-east to Orense and north to La Coruña. For Costa da Morte, Transportes Finisterre runs buses to Finisterre. Enatcar has three buses to Barcelona (8½ hours). Dainco has three a day to Salamanca, two to Cádiz and one to Algeciras.

The train station is 600m south of the old town at the end of Rúa do Horreo. Bus Nos 6 and 9 from near the station go to Praza de Galicia. Up to four trains a day run to Madrid (eight to 11 hours), and frequent trains head to La Coruña (1½ hours, 475 ptas), Pontevedra (one hour, 490 ptas) and Vigo.

RÍAS BAJAS

The grandest of Galicia's inlets are the four Rías Bajas, on its west-facing coast. From north to south these are the Ría de Muros, Ría de Arousa, Ría de Pontevedra and Ría de Vigo. All are dotted with low-key resorts, fishing villages and plenty of good beaches.

Tourist offices in the region include one at Calle del General Mola 3, Pontevedra (☎ 986 85 08 14) and several in Vigo (☎ 986 43 05 77).

Things to See & Do

On Ría de Arousa, **Isla de Arousa** is connected to the mainland by a long bridge. Its inhabitants live mainly from fishing (and, it appears, smuggling). Some of the beaches facing the mainland are very pleasant and protected and have comparatively warm water. **Cambados**, a little farther south, is a peaceful seaside town with a magnificent plaza surrounded by evocative little streets.

The small city of **Pontevedra** has managed to preserve intact a classic medieval centre backing on to the Río Lérez and is ideal for simply wandering around. Along the coast between **Cabo de Udra**, on the south side of the Ría de Pontevedra, and Aldán village are cradled a series of pretty, protected beaches, among them **Praia Vilariño** and **Areacova**. There are more good beaches around little **Hío**, a few kilometres south-west of Aldán.

Vigo, Galicia's biggest city, is a disappointment given its wonderful setting, although its small, tangled old town is worth a wander.

The best beaches of all in the Rías Bajas are on the **Islas Cíes** off the end of the Ría de Vigo. Of the three islands, one is off limits for conservation reasons. The other two, Isla del Faro and Isla de Monte Agudo, are linked by a white sandy crescent – together forming a 9km breakwater in the Atlantic. You can only visit the islands from mid-June to the end of September, and numbers are strictly limited. A return boat ticket from Vigo costs 1700 ptas; the frequency of services depends largely on the weather.

Places to Stay & Eat

A couple of *camping grounds* are open in summer on Isla de Arousa. In Cambados, *Hostal Pazos Feijoo* (☎ 986 54 28 10), Calle de Curros Enríquez 1, near the waterfront in the newer part of town, has singles/doubles for 2500/4000 ptas. The *Café-Bar* on Rúa Caracol does reasonable seafood meals for about 1000 ptas.

In Pontevedra, *Casa Alicia* (☎ 986 85 70 79), Avenida de Santa María 5, and *Casa Maruja* (☎ 986 85 49 01) over the road are good. The former has homy doubles for around 2700 to 3000 ptas, while the latter charges 3000/4000 ptas for spotless rooms. You can eat cheaply on Calle de San Nicolás at *Casa Fidel O' Pulpeiro* at No 7 (an unbeatable 1000 ptas menú), or *O' Noso Bar* at No 5.

Hostal Stop (☎ 986 32 94 75) in Hío has rooms for as little as 1200/2300 ptas in winter, but more like 3000/5000 ptas in summer.

In Vigo, *Hostal Madrid* (☎ 986 22 55 23), Rúa de Alfonso XIII 63, near the train station, has doubles for 2500 ptas with shower or 4500 ptas with full private bathroom. *Hotel Pantón* (☎ 986 22 42 70), Rúa de Lepanto 18, can give you a room with private bathroom and TV for 2800/4800 ptas. Old Vigo is laced with tapas bars and eateries of all descriptions. *Restaurante Fay-Bistes*, Rúa Real 7, has a set lunch for 950 ptas and good tapas.

Camping is the only option if you want to stay on the Islas Cíes. You must book the camp site (485 ptas per person and per tent, plus IVA) at the office in the estación marítima in Vigo – places are limited. You can then organise a round-trip boat ticket for the days you require.

Getting There & Away

Pontevedra and Vigo are the area's transport hubs, with a reasonable network of local buses fanning out from them. Both are well served by buses and trains from Santiago de Compostela and La Coruña, and Vigo has services from more distant places like Madrid and Barcelona, as well as Iberia flights from those cities. Three trains a day run from Vigo to Porto in Portugal (3½ hours).

LA CORUÑA

La Coruña (A Coruña in Galician), Galicia's capital, is an attractive port city with decent beaches and a wonderful seafront promenade, the Paseo Marítimo. The older part of town, the Ciudad Vieja, is huddled on the headland east of the port, while the most famous attraction, the Torre de Hércules lighthouse, originally built by the Romans (open daily from 10 am to 7 pm), caps the headland's northern end. The north side of the isthmus joining the headland to the mainland is lined with sandy beaches, more of which stretch along the 30km sweep of coast west of the city.

Places to Stay & Eat

Calle de Riego de Agua, a block back from the waterfront Avenida de la Marina on the southern side of the isthmus, is a good spot to look for lodgings. *Pensión La Alianza* (☎ 981 22 81 14), Calle de Riego de Agua 8, charges 2000/3500 ptas for average singles/doubles. *Hostal Roma* (☎ 981 22 80 75) nearby at Rúa Nueva 3 offers basic doubles for 2100 ptas.

Calle de la Franja has several good places to eat. *Casa Jesusa* at No 8 offers a tasty seafood set lunch for 1200 ptas.

Getting There & Away

There are daily trains and buses to Santiago de Compostela, Vigo, Santander, León, Madrid and Barcelona.

RÍAS ALTAS

North-east of La Coruña stretches the alternately pretty and awesome coast called the Rías Altas. This has some of the most dramatic scenery in Spain, and beaches that in good weather are every bit as inviting as those on the better known Rías Bajas. Spots to head for include the medieval towns **Betanzos**, **Pontedeume** and **Viveiro** (all with budget accommodation), the tremendous cliffs of **Cabo Ortegal** and the **beaches** between it and Viveiro. Buses from La Coruña and Santiago de Compostela will get you into the area – after that you'll need local buses and the occasional walk or lift.

PICOS DE EUROPA

This small mountainous region straddling Asturias, Cantabria and Castilla y León is some of the finest walking country in Spain. Spectacular scenery, combined with unique flora and fauna, ensures a continual flow of visitors from all over Europe and beyond.

The Picos are 25km from the coast, and only around 40km long and 40km wide. They are comprised of three limestone massifs. In the south-east is the Andara Massif, with a summit of 2441m, and in the west the Cornión Massif, with a summit of 2596m. In the centre is the best known and largest, the Uriello Massif, soaring to 2648m.

Books & Maps

Serious trekkers are advised to buy a copy of Lonely Planet's *Walking in Spain*. If you want detailed topographical maps of the area before coming to Spain, Edward Stanford, 12-14 Long Acre, London WC2E 9LP, can send you a list of those available. Try getting hold of the *Mapa Excursionista del Macizo Central de los Picos de Europa* by Miguel Andrade (1:25,000) and *Mapa del Macizo del Cornión* by José Ramón Lueje (1:25,000).

Things to See & Do

Trekkers should allow plenty of time for the Picos. If you're not quite that adventurous, perhaps the least strenuous way to get a feel for the area is to drive up to **Lago de la Ercina** from Covadonga in the west of the Picos or to **Sotres** in the east. From either of these places you can set out on well-marked walking trails into the heart of the mountains.

Places to Stay & Eat

Right on Lago de Enol, the *refugio* (☎ 98 584 85 76) is a simple stone mountain hut where you can also get meals and camp. Camping is also possible a little farther on at Lago de la Ercina. In Sotres, *Pensión La Perdiz* (☎ 98 594 50 11) charges 3000/3900 ptas for singles/doubles with private bath (less without). *Casa Cipriano* (☎ 98 594 50 24), across the road, is a little more expensive.

In Espinama (for a southern approach), *Hotel Máximo* (☎ 942 73 66 03) has rooms for 3300/5300 ptas and is possibly the pick of the crop; it has a good restaurant.

The main access towns – Cangas de Onís, Arenas de Cabrales and Potes – all have a wide range of hostales.

Getting There & Away

A series of roads almost encircles the Picos and off these three main routes lead into the heart of the mountains: from Cangas de Onís to Covadonga and Lago de Enol; from Arenas de Cabrales to Sotres; and from Potes to Fuente Dé.

Buses from Santander, León, Oviedo and Gijón serve the three main access towns, although outside summer you'll find precious few. Others run from Potes to Fuente Dé, and from Cangas de Onís to Covadonga and (in summer only) Lago de Enol.

SANTANDER

Santander, capital of Cantabria, is a modern, cosmopolitan city with wide waterfront boulevards, leafy parks and crowded beaches. Semana Grande in August is a pretty wild party, but you won't find any accommodation here, or anywhere else on the north coast at that time, without booking well in advance.

The main tourist office (☎ 942 36 20 54) is in the harbourside Jardines de Pereda, and another is not far off in the north-eastern corner of Plaza de Velardo (aka Plaza Porticada).

Things to See & Do

Santander's main attractions are the nightlife (see Entertainment later) and El Sardinero

beach. As you come round to El Sardinero on bus Nos 1 or 2, you may notice an uncanny resemblance to Bondi Beach in Australia, with surfers out in force by mid-March, despite the cold. The streets back from the sea near El Sardinero are lined with beautiful houses. This is some of Spain's most expensive real estate.

Places to Stay

Camping Bellavista (☎ 942 39 15 30), Avenida del Faro, out by the lighthouse on Cabo Mayor at the far end of Playa del Sardinero, charges 1500 ptas per person.

Rooms are expensive in high summer, but the rates given here come down substantially from October to May. *Pensión La Porticada* (☎ 942 22 78 17), down by the waterfront at Calle de Méndez Núñez 6, has reasonable rooms for 3000/4000 ptas. Try for one overlooking the bay.

Hospedaje Botín (☎ 942 21 00 94), Calle de Isabel II 1, has some spacious rooms kept in an impeccable state of cleanliness. They start at 2000/3200 ptas. A few steps away, *Pensión Real* (☎ 942 22 57 87), Plaza de la Esperanza 1, is a little pricey with rooms starting at 3500/4000 ptas, more if you want a private bath.

Pensión La Corza (☎ 942 21 29 50), Calle de Hernán Cortés 25, is nicely located on a pleasant square. Sizeable if rather quirkily furnished rooms with shower (loo down the hall) come in at 2000 ptas per person.

Places to Eat

A good area for cheap eats is around Plaza de Cañadio, three blocks back from the municipal tourist office. On the plaza itself the stylish *Restaurante Cañadio* serves first-class seafood and local specialities, with a lunch menú for 1550 ptas.

Bodega del Riojano, Calle del Río de la Pila 5, is stacked with floor-to-ceiling wine racks and serves tasty but simple dishes, particularly of the day's catch. *Bodega Mazón*, Calle de Hernán Cortés 57, is another good choice. *Sidrería Recino*, Calle de Santa Lucía 20, has a set lunch for 1100 ptas and you can down a cider with such rarities as Hungarian goulash. *Cervecería Las Anclas*, Calle de Casimiro Sainz, has a set lunch for 800 ptas.

Entertainment

Check out Calle del Río de la Pila and the immediate neighbourhood – it is teeming with bars of all descriptions. In summer, there is also quite a good scene in El Sardinero along the main drag.

Getting There & Away

Santander is one of the major entry points to Spain, thanks to its ferry link with Plymouth in England (see Getting There & Away at the start of this chapter).

The ferry terminal and train and bus stations are all in the centre of Santander, within 300m of each other. Six buses a day go to Madrid (3225 ptas) via Burgos. Frequent services run south to Reinosa, and less frequently on to destinations in Castilla y León. Turytrans buses run to San Sebastián (1790 ptas) and Irún in the east and Gijón/Oviedo (1970 ptas) in the west.

Trains to Bilbao (one to three daily, 2½ hours, 910 ptas) and Oviedo are run by FEVE, a private line which does not accept rail passes. From Oviedo you can continue around into Galicia. Trains to Madrid (via Ávila) and Galicia are run by RENFE, so rail passes are valid. To Madrid there are three trains daily (5½ to nine hours, from 3550 ptas).

SANTILLANA DEL MAR

The beautiful village of Santillana del Mar, 30km west of Santander, has a wonderful feeling of timelessness. Cobbled streets lined with well-preserved old houses give it a character all its own.

Things to See & Do

Santillana's fame lies as much in the **Cueva de Altamira**, 2km west, as in the town itself. The 14,000-year-old animal paintings in the Altamira cave reduce many people to tears, and all those lucky enough to gain entry are deeply moved by what they see. A maximum of 20 people a day are allowed into the cave and if you want to be one of them, you must ask permission at least a year in advance, listing three or four preferred dates, by writing to: Centro de Investigación Altamira, 39330 Santillana del Mar, Cantabria, Spain. If you're one of the lucky ones, admission is

400 ptas. There's a small museum, open to all, at the cave; its hours are Tuesday to Sunday from 9.30 am to 2.30 pm.

Places to Stay & Eat

In the old town, *Posada Octavio* (☎ 942 81 81 99) at Plaza de las Arenas 4, has charming rooms with timber-beam ceilings for 2500/3500 ptas with own bathroom, or less without. There are a couple more such places on, and also just off, Plaza de Ramón Pelayo.

Casa Cossío, about the nearest restaurant to the Colegiata, serves a good range of seafood. The *Restaurante Altamira*, attached to the hotel of the same name, has a reliable set lunch for 1100 ptas. There are several snack and burger places too if you want to keep it simple.

Getting There & Away

Several buses call in at Santillana en route between Santander and other destinations farther west. More frequent services connect the town with Torrelavega, itself easily reached by FEVE train from Santander.

País Vasco, Navarra & Aragón

The Basque people have lived for thousands of years in Spain's País Vasco (Basque Country, or Euskadi in the Basque language) and the adjoining Pays Basque across the border in France. They have their own ancient language (Euskara), a distinct physical appearance, a rich culture and a proud history. Along with this strong sense of identity has come, among a significant minority of Basques in Spain, a desire for independence. The Basque nationalist movement was born in the 19th century. During the Franco years the Basque people were brutally repressed and Euskadi ta Askatasuna (ETA), a separatist movement, began its terrorist activities. With Spain's changeover to democracy in the late 1970s, the País Vasco was granted a large degree of autonomy, but ETA has pursued its violent campaign.

ETA terrorism may be a deterrent to tourism but the País Vasco is a beautiful region. Although the Bilbao area is heavily industrialised, the region has a spectacular coastline, a green and mountainous interior and the elegance of San Sebastián and the Guggenheim art gallery in Bilbao itself. Another great reason to visit is to sample the delights of Basque cuisine, considered the best in Spain.

South-east of the País Vasco, the Navarra and Aragón regions reach down from the Pyrenees into drier, more southern lands. Navarra has a high Basque population and its capital is Pamplona, home of the Sanfermines festival with its running of the bulls. The Aragonese Pyrenees offer the best walking and skiing on the Spanish side of this mountain range. Serious walkers should head for the Parque Nacional de Ordesa (the park entrance is at Torla) but note – especially in the peak Spanish holiday period, mid-July to mid-August – that a maximum 1500 visitors are allowed in at any time. Weatherwise the best months up there are late June to mid-September. Aragón has half a dozen decent ski resorts – the regional tourist office in Zaragoza has information.

SAN SEBASTIÁN

San Sebastián (Donostia in Basque) is stunning. Famed as a ritzy resort for wealthy Spaniards who want to get away from the hordes in the south, it has also been a stronghold of Basque nationalist feeling since well before Franco. The surprisingly relaxed town, of 180,000 people, curves round the beautiful Bahía de la Concha. Those who live here consider themselves the luckiest people in Spain, and after spending a few days on the beaches in preparation for the wild evenings, you may begin to understand why.

Information

The municipal tourist office (☎ 943 48 11 66), Calle de la Reina Regente s/n, is open in summer from Monday to Saturday from 8 am to 8 pm, and 9 am to 2 pm on Sunday. Otherwise it opens from 9 am to 2 pm and 3.30 to 7 pm, but is closed on Sunday afternoon. The regional tourist office (☎ 943 42 62 82) is at Paseo de los Fueros 1.

The main post office is on Calle de Urdaneta, behind the cathedral.

Lavomatique, Calle de Iñigo 14, is a rarity in Spain – a good self-service laundrette.

Things to See

The **Playa de la Concha** and **Playa de Ondarreta** make up one of the most beautiful city beaches in Spain. You can get out to **Isla de Santa Clara**, in the middle of the bay, by boat from the port – but it's more exciting to swim. In summer, rafts are anchored about halfway from Ondarreta to the island to serve as rest stops.

If you intend to spend your evenings as the locals do, you won't be up to much more than sitting on the beach during the day. However, there is some worthwhile sightseeing to be done in and around San Sebastián.

The **Museo de San Telmo**, in a 16th-century monastery on Plaza de Zuloaga, has a bit of everything – ancient tombstones, a good art collection and the squeakiest floors in Spain. It's open Tuesday to Saturday from 10.30 am to 1.30 pm and 4 to 8 pm and is free.

Overlooking Bahía de la Concha from the east is **Monte Urgull**, with a statue of Christ on the top and wonderful views. It only takes half an hour to walk up; a stairway starts from Plaza de Zuloaga in the old town. At the base of the hill, San Sebastián's **aquarium** is also well worth a visit. It's open daily, except Monday from mid-September to mid-May, and costs 700 ptas. The nearby **Museo Naval** is interesting too but you need to read Spanish to fully appreciate the displays (200 ptas).

The views are even better from **Monte Igueldo**, on the far side of the bay. A funicular runs from the base up to the top-end Hotel Monte Igueldo, an amusement park and the Ku disco.

Places to Stay

As in much of northern Spain, July and August can be trying months for searching out accommodation in San Sebastián. Arrive early or call ahead, and be aware that summer prices often rise sharply. Rates given here for singles/doubles tend to jump up about 1000/1500 ptas in peak periods, unless otherwise noted. They may also drop significantly in winter (try bargaining).

SAN SEBASTIÁN (DONOSTIA)

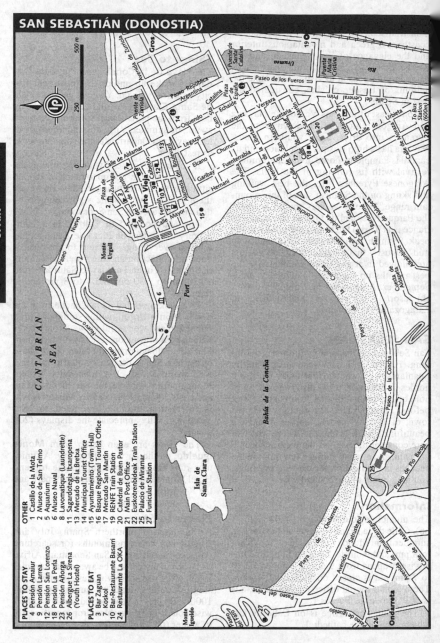

PLACES TO STAY
4   Pensión Amaiur
9   Pensión Larrea
12 Pensión San Lorenzo
18 Pensión La Perla
23 Pensión Añorga
26 Albergue La Sirena
    (Youth Hostel)

PLACES TO EAT
3   Bar Zaguan
7   Koskol
10 Bar-Restaurante Basari
24 Restaurante La OKA

OTHER
1   Castillo de la Mota
2   Museo de San Telmo
5   Aquarium
6   Museo Naval
8   Lavomatique (Laundrette)
11 Sagardotegia Itxaropena
13 Mercado de la Bretxa
14 Municipal Tourist Office
15 Ayuntamiento (Town Hall)
16 Basque Regional Tourist Office
17 Mercado San Martin
19 RENFE Train Station
20 Catedral de Buen Pastor
21 Main Post Office
22 Euskotrenbideak Train Station
25 Palacio de Miramar
27 Funicular Station

Albergue de la Juventud La Sirena (☎ 943 31 02 68), Paseo de Igueldo 25, is San Sebastián's HI hostel. It's 1550 ptas for a bunk bed and breakfast (1850 ptas if you're over 26). Curfew is midnight during the week, 2 am on weekends.

In the Parte Vieja, *Pensión San Lorenzo* (☎ 943 42 55 16), Calle de San Lorenzo 2, has a kitchen that guests can use. Singles/doubles start at 2500/3500 ptas. *Pensión Amaiur* (☎ 943 42 96 54), Calle del 31 de Agosto 44 (2nd floor), is as pretty as a picture and has rooms ranging from 2800 to 4800 ptas, although you may be able to bargain them down a little. *Pensión Larrea* (☎ 943 42 26 94), Calle de Narrika 21, has been recommended by travellers. It is simple but pleasant and singles/doubles start at 2500/3500 ptas.

The area down near the cathedral is a little more peaceful than the Parte Vieja. *Pensión La Perla* (☎ 943 42 81 23), Calle de Loyola 10 (1st floor), has excellent rooms with private shower, and some look over the cathedral. Singles/doubles range from 2750/3750 ptas to 3000/5000 ptas plus IVA. *Pensión Añorga* (☎ 943 46 79 45) at Calle de Easo 12, has a range of rooms with or without private bath/shower. Singles/doubles are 2000/3000 ptas plus IVA.

Places to Eat

Eating in San Sebastián is a pleasure. It's almost a shame to sit down in a restaurant when the bars have such wonderful tapas, or pinchos, as they are known here. The Parte Vieja and the eastern suburb of Gros are jammed with great restaurants, though most are not cheap. If you want to construct your own meals, there are excellent *food markets* on Alameda del Boulevard in the Parte Vieja (Mercado de la Bretxa), and on Calle de San Marcial (Mercado San Martín).

Bar Zaguan, Calle del 31 de Agosto 31, does one of the town's cheapest lunch menús for 950 ptas, and platos combinados from 650 ptas. Even better is the delicious lunch deal offered by the tiny *Koskol*, Calle de Iñigo 5. For 1000 ptas you get exceedingly generous portions. *Bar-Restaurante Basarri*, Calle de Fermín Calbetón 17, has a very plain dining room but the 1400 ptas menú is worth every peseta.

A fun self-service vegetarian place is *Restaurante La OKA*, Calle de San Martín 43.

Entertainment

San Sebastián's nightlife is great. The Parte Vieja comes alive at around 8 pm nearly every night. The Spanish habit of bar-hopping has been perfected here and one street alone has 28 bars in a 300m stretch! Typical drinks are a zurrito (beer in a small glass) and txacolí (a Basque wine, not to everyone's liking). If you'd like to have a swig of Basque cider (sidra), head for *Sagardotegia Itxaropena*, Calle de Embeltran 16.

Once the Parte Vieja quietens down, the crowd heads for the area behind the cathedral. Things are usually pretty quiet here until a couple of hours after midnight.

Getting There & Away

Bus The bus station is a 20-minute walk south of the centre on Plaza de Pío XII, with ticket offices along the streets to its north. Buses leave for all over Spain. Those to Bilbao along the autopista go every half-hour (one hour; 1060 ptas). Via Zarauz and the coast the trip takes about three hours. The bus to Pamplona takes over two hours (750 ptas).

Train The RENFE train station is across the river on Paseo de Francia, on a line linking Paris with Madrid. Six a day go to Madrid (six to nine hours, from 4400 ptas), and a few to Barcelona (nine to 10½ hours, from 4600 ptas) via Pamplona and Zaragoza. To Paris (six to eight hours, from 11,000 ptas), there's one direct train a day and several others with a change at Hendaye. Other destinations include Salamanca, La Coruña and Algeciras.

Trains to Bilbao, and some to Hendaye, are run by a private company, Euskotrenbideak, from a separate station on Calle de Easo.

COSTA VASCA

Spain's often ruggedly beautiful Costa Vasca (Basque Coast) is one of its least touristed coastal regions. A combination of cool weather, rough seas and terrorism tends to put some people off.

Things to See & Do

Between the French border and San Sebastián, **Fuenterrabia** (Hondarribia) is a picturesque fishing town with good beaches nearby, while **Pasajes de San Juan** (Pasaia

Donibane) has a pretty old section and some good-value fish restaurants.

West of San Sebastián, the coast extends to Bilbao, passing through some of the finest **surfing** territory in Europe. Keep your wet suit handy though, as the water here can be pretty chilly. **Zarauz** (Zarautz), about 15km west of San Sebastián, stages a round of the World Surfing Championship each September, when all the big names turn up for one of Europe's greatest surfing spectacles. Slightly west, the picturesque village of **Guetaria** (Getaria) has a small beach, but the main attraction is just in wandering around the narrow streets and the fishing harbour.

Mundaca (Mundaka), 12km north of Guernica (Gernika), is a surfing town. For much of the year, surfers and beach bums hang around waiting for the legendary 'left-hander' to break. When it does, it's one of the longest you'll ever see! If you're interested in renting a surfboard or stocking up on Aussie surf gear, ask the locals to direct you to Craig's shop (Craig is an Australian who came here to surf some years ago and never managed to leave). *Camping Portuondo* (☎ 94 687 63 68) is on the riverfront about 1km south of town, on the road to Guernica. For food, you will be pretty much limited to sandwiches or do-it-yourself fare, as anything else is prohibitively expensive.

Getting Around

The coastal road is best explored by car. If you don't have your own transport, there are buses from San Sebastián to Zarauz and Guetaria, and from Bilbao to Guernica. From Guernica you can take a bus to Bermeo which will drop you in Mundaca. Hitching can be painfully slow.

BILBAO

Long the industrial heart of the north (and it shows), Bilbao has spruced itself up and, since 1997, created for itself a tourist gold mine – the US$100 million **Museo Guggenheim de Arte Contemporáneo**. Frank Gehry's fantastical titanium-and-glass structure, all swirling lines in symbolic imitation of fish and boats, contains a top flight exhibition of modern art, largely extracted from the New York Guggenheim's treasure chest.

Among the works are Picasso's *Mandolin and Guitar*, a Modigliani nude, paintings by Braque, Ernst, Schiele, Kandinsky, and Miró, and a fat Botero statue. It is open Tuesday to Sunday from 11 am to 8 pm, and admission costs 700 ptas (half price for students).

On a more old-fashioned note, the excellent **Museo de Bellas Artes** in Parque de Doña Casilda de Iturriza has works by El Greco, Velázquez and Goya, and an important collection of Basque art.

The Iniciativas Turísticas office (☎ 94 416 00 22) is in the Teatro Arriaga.

Places to Stay & Eat

Pensión Méndez (☎ 94 416 03 64), Calle de Santa María 13, is about as central as you can get, and it's cheap too, at 2000/3000 ptas for singles/doubles. Be prepared to sleep little for all the street noise. *Hostal La Estrella* (☎ 94 416 40 66), Calle de María Múñoz 6, is a charming, brightly painted little place also right in the heart of the old town. Rooms without bath go for 2500/3750 ptas and those with bath are 3100/5000 ptas.

Gure Talo, Calle del Príncipe 1, is an earthy place serving up good Basque food and it's popular with bilbaínos. The set lunch meal costs 950 ptas.

Getting There & Away

Bus Most buses use one of two main stations. Long-distance services to Madrid (up to 12 daily; 3245 ptas), Barcelona (four daily; 4750 ptas), and other cities depart from the bus station at Calle de la Autonomía 17. Most other buses use the new Termibus lot in the south-west corner of town (metro: San Mamés).

Train RENFE's Abando station in the city centre sends out three trains daily to Madrid (4300 ptas), and two to Barcelona (4800 ptas), Alicante and Galicia.

Boat P&O ferries leave for Portsmouth from Santurtzi, about 14km north-west of Bilbao's city centre. The voyage takes about 36 hours from England and 28 hours the other way.

PAMPLONA

The madcap festivities of Sanfermines in

Pamplona (Iruñea in Basque) run from 6 to 14 July and are characterised by nonstop partying and, of course, the running of the bulls. The safest place to watch the *encierro* (running) is on TV. If this is too tame for you, see if you can sweet-talk your way on to a balcony in one of the streets where the bulls run. The bulls are let out at 8 am, but if you want to get a good vantage point you will have to be there around 6 am.

If you visit at any other time of year, you'll find a pleasant and modern city, with lovely parks and gardens, and a compact, partly walled old town. The tourist office (☎ 948 22 07 41) is just south of the old town at Calle del Duque de Ahumada 3.

Places to Stay & Eat
The nearest camping ground is *Camping Ezcaba* (☎ 948 33 03 15), 7km north of the city. To get there, take an Arre or Oricain bus from Calle de Teovaldos near the bullring. The camping ground fills up a couple of days before Sanfermines.

If you want to stay in a pensión or hostal during Sanfermines, you'll need to book well in advance (and pay a substantial premium). During the festival, beds are also available in private houses (casas particulares) – check with the tourist office or haggle with the locals at the bus and train stations. Otherwise, you'll have to do what everyone else does and sleep in one of the parks, plazas or shopping malls. You can leave your bags in the consigna at the bus station. Alternatively, you could make day trips here from San Sebastián or other towns.

Fonda La Montañesa (☎ 948 22 43 80), Calle de San Gregorio 2, has clean and basic rooms for 1500 ptas per person. *Camas Escaray Lozano* (☎ 948 22 78 25), Calle Nueva 24, has small but clean singles/doubles for 2000/4000 ptas, and is probably the best value in this range.

Calle de San Nicolás is densely packed with tapas bars, and *Bar Ulzama* is particularly good for snacking. The popular *Bar San Nicolás*, at No 13, does a Basque set meal for 1500 ptas.

Getting There & Away
The bus station is on Avenida de Yanguas y Miranda, a five-minute walk south of the old

town. There are up to 12 buses a day to San Sebastián (2½ hours, 700 ptas) and daily services to Madrid, Zaragoza and Bilbao.

Pamplona is on the San Sebastián-Zaragoza line, but the station is awkwardly situated north of town. If you arrive this way, catch bus No 9 to Paseo de Sarasate.

ZARAGOZA
Zaragoza, capital of Aragón and home to half its 1.2 million people, is often said to be the most Spanish city of all. Once an important Roman city, under the name Caesaraugusta, and later a Muslim centre for four centuries, it is today relatively untouched by tourism. The old town is full of lively bars and restaurants.

Information
The city tourist office (☎ 976 20 12 00) is in a surreal-looking glass cube on Plaza del Pilar. From Monday to Saturday it's open from 9.30 am to 1.30 pm and 4.30 to 7.30 pm, and Sunday from 10 am to 2 pm. There's also a regional tourist office (☎ 976 39 35 37) in the Torreón de la Zuda, a Mudéjar tower on Plaza de César Augusto.

Things to See
Zaragoza's focus is the vast 500m-long main square, **Plaza de Nuestra Señora del Pilar** (or Plaza del Pilar for short). Dominating the north side is the **Basílica de Nuestra Señora del Pilar**, a 17th-century church of epic proportions. People flock to kiss a piece of marble pillar – believed to have been left by the Virgin Mary when she appeared to Santiago (St James) in a vision here in AD 40 – in the church's Capilla Santa.

At the south-east end of the plaza is **La Seo**, Zaragoza's brooding 12th to 16th-century cathedral. Its north-west façade is a Mudéjar masterpiece. The inside is closed for restoration.

The odd trapezoid thing in front of La Seo is the outside of a remarkable structure housing the **Roman forum** of ancient Caesaraugusta. Well below modern ground level you can visit the remains of shops, porticos and a great sewerage system, all brought to life by an imaginative show of slides, music and Spanish commentary. The forum is open

ZARAGOZA

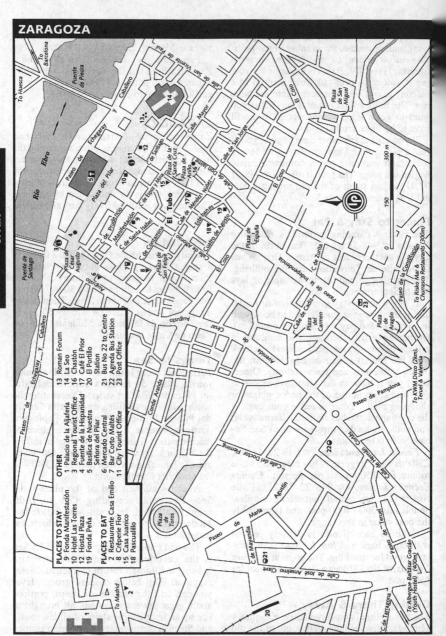

PLACES TO STAY
9 Fonda Manifestación
10 Hotel Las Torres
12 Hostal Plaza
19 Fonda Peña

PLACES TO EAT
2 Restaurante Casa Emilio
8 Crêperie Flor
15 Casa Juanico
18 Pascualillo

OTHER
1 Palacio de la Aljafería
3 Regional Tourist Office
4 Fuente de la Hispanidad
5 Basílica de Nuestra
  Señora del Pilar
6 Mercado Central
7 Bar Corto Maltés
11 City Tourist Office

13 Roman Forum
14 La Seo
16 Chastón
17 Café El Prior
20 El Portillo
   Station
21 Bus No 22 to Centre
22 Agreda Bus Station
23 Post Office

Tuesday to Saturday from 10 am to 2 pm and 5 to 8 pm (mornings only on Sunday). Entry costs 400 ptas (half price for students).

A little over 1km west of the plaza, the **Palacio de la Aljafería**, today housing Aragón's *cortes* (parliament), is Spain's greatest Muslim building outside Andalucía. It was built as the palace of Zaragoza's Muslim rulers, who held the city from 714 to 1118, and the inner Patio de Santa Isabel displays all the geometric mastery and fine detail of the best Muslim architecture. The upstairs palace, added by the Christian rulers Fernando and Isabel in the 15th century, boasts some fine Muslim-inspired Mudéjar decoration. The Aljafería is open Monday to Saturday from 10 am to 2 pm and 4 to 8 pm (4.30 to 6.30 pm in winter), and on Sunday from 10 am to 2 pm. Entry is free.

Places to Stay

Zaragoza's HI hostel, the *Albergue de la Juventud Baltasar Gracián* (☎ 976 55 13 87), Calle de Franco y López 4, is open all year.

The cheapest rooms elsewhere are in El Tubo, the maze of busy lanes and alleys south of Plaza del Pilar. An excellent choice is *Fonda Peña* (☎ 976 29 90 89), Calle de Cinegio 3, with rooms for 1200/1800 ptas. It has a decent little comedor (dining room) too. Another reasonable cheapie is *Fonda Manifestación* (☎ 976 29 58 21), Calle de la Manifestación 36, with singles/doubles for 1500/3000 ptas.

Hostal Plaza (☎ 976 29 48 30), perfectly positioned at Plaza del Pilar 14, has reasonable singles/doubles for 3000/3900 ptas – the rooms overlooking the square are the best value in town. At Plaza del Pilar 11, *Hotel Las Torres* (☎ 976 39 42 50) has modern rooms with air-con, private bath and TV for 4500/7000 ptas plus IVA.

Places to Eat

In El Tubo, *Pascualillo*, Calle de la Libertad 5, does a good menú for under 1000 ptas. *Casa Juanico*, Calle de la Santa Cruz 21, is a popular old-style tapas bar with a comedor out the back. The solid menú costs 1500 ptas. A great dessert of crêpes can be had in the *Crêperie Flor*, just off Plaza de San Felipe.

Near the Palacio de la Aljafería, *Restaurante Casa Emilio*, Avenida de Madrid 5, is a simple place with wholesome, low-priced home-cooked meals.

For a higher class of eating, head for Calle de Francisco Vitoria, 1km south of Plaza del Pilar. *Risko Mar* at No 16 is a fine fish restaurant – an excellent set meal for two will cost 5000 ptas. Across the road, *Churrasco* is another Zaragoza institution, with a wide variety of meat and fish dishes. You'll be up for 3000 ptas.

Entertainment

There's no shortage of bars in and around El Tubo. *Bar Corto Maltés*, Calle del Temple 23, is one of a string of rather cool places in this lane. All the barmen sport the corto maltés (sideburns). *Chastón*, Plaza de Ariño 4, is a relaxing little jazz club.

Café El Prior, near Plaza de la Santa Cruz on Calle de Contamina, is a good place for a little dancing in the earlier stages of a night out. Farther south, *KWM* at Paseo de Fernando el Católico 70 is a popular disco open until about 5 am.

Getting There & Away

Bus stations are scattered all over town – tourist offices can tell you what goes where from where. The Agreda company runs to most major Spanish cities from Paseo de María Agustín 7. The trip to Madrid costs 1750 ptas and to Barcelona 1640 ptas.

Up to 14 trains daily run from El Portillo station to both Madrid (three to 4½ hours, 3000 to 3700 ptas) and Barcelona (3½ to 4½ hours, from 3000 ptas). Some Barcelona trains go via Tarragona. Trains also run to Valencia via Teruel, and to San Sebastián via Pamplona.

TERUEL

Aragón's hilly deep south is culturally closer to Castilla-La Mancha or the backlands of Valencia than to some other regions of Aragón itself. A good stop on the way to the coast from Zaragoza, or from Cuenca in Castilla-La Mancha, is the town of Teruel, which has a flavour all its own thanks to four centuries of Muslim domination in the middle ages and some remarkable Mudéjar architecture dating from after its capture by the Christians in 1171.

SPAIN

The tourist office (☎ 978 60 22 79) is at Calle de Tomás Nogués 1.

Things to See

Teruel has four magnificent Mudéjar towers, on the cathedral of **Santa María** (12th and 13th centuries) and the churches of **San Salvador** (13th century), **San Martín** and **San Pedro** (both 14th century). These, and the ceiling inside Santa María, are among Spain's best Mudéjar architecture. Note the complicated brickwork and colourful tiles on the towers, so typical of the style. A further example of Mudéjar work is **La Escalinata**, the flight of stairs leading down to the train station from Paseo del Óvalo, on the edge of the old town.

The **Museo Provincial de Teruel** on Plaza del Padre Polanco is well worth a visit, mainly for its fascinating, well-presented archaeological collection going back to the days of *Homo erectus*.

Places to Stay & Eat

Fonda El Tozal (☎ 978 60 10 22) at Calle del Rincón 5 is great value. It's an amazing rickety old house run by a wonderful, friendly family, and most of the rooms have cast-iron beds, enamelled chamber pots and exposed ceiling beams. Singles/doubles cost 1500/3000 ptas. In winter, you might prefer *Hostal Aragón* (☎ 978 60 13 87), Calle de Santa María 4, which is also charming but has mod cons such as heating. Doubles are 2900 ptas, and 4500 ptas with private bath. Both these places are just a couple of minutes walk from the main square, Plaza de Carlos Caste.

Teruel is famed for its jamón. If you can't fit a whole leg of ham in your backpack, at least sample a tostada con jamón, with tomato and olive oil. One of the best places for hamming up is *La Taberna de Rokelin* at Calle de Tozal 33, a narrow bar with a beautiful rack of smoked pig hocks.

Getting There & Away

The bus station (☎ 978 60 20 04) is on Ronda de Ambeles. There are daily buses to Barcelona (six hours), Cuenca (2¾ hours), Valencia (2½ hours) and Madrid (4½ hours, 2330 ptas).

By rail, Teruel is about midway between Valencia and Zaragoza, with three trains a day to both places.

Tunisia

Despite being the smallest country in North Africa, Tunisia boasts a rich cultural and social heritage – Phoenician, Roman, Byzantine, Arab, Ottoman and French empires have all come and gone in this part of the world.

Facts about Tunisia

HISTORY

The ancient city-state of Carthage, arch rival of Rome, was only a few kilometres from the centre of the modern capital, Tunis. Carthage began life in 814 BC as one of a series of Phoenician staging posts. It remained relatively unimportant until Phoenicia (situated on what is now coastal Lebanon and Syria) was overrun by the Assyrians in the 7th century BC. As a result, Carthage rapidly grew into the metropolis of the Phoenician world, recording a population of about half a million at its peak.

By the 6th century BC, it had become the main power in the western Mediterranean, bringing it into inevitable conflict with the emerging Roman Empire. The two fought each other almost to a standstill in the course of the 118-year Punic Wars, which began in 264 BC. Carthage's legendary general Hannibal appeared to have brought the Romans to their knees after his invasion of Italy in 216 BC, but the wars ended in total victory for Rome. The Romans showed no mercy after the fall of Carthage in 146 BC. The city was razed and the population sold into slavery.

Carthage was rebuilt as a Roman city and became the capital of the province of Africa, an area roughly corresponding to modern Tunisia. Africa's main attraction for the Romans was the grain-growing plains of the Medjerda Valley, west of Carthage, which became known as the bread basket of the empire. The remains of the cities they built on these plains, such as Dougga, are among Tunisia's best known attractions.

The Vandals captured Carthage in 439 AD and made it the capital of their North African empire until they were ousted by the Byzantines in 533. The Byzantines never managed

AT A GLANCE

Capital	Tunis
Population	9 million
Area	164,150 sq km
Official Language	Arabic
Currency	1 Tunisian dinar (TD) = 1000 millimes
GDP	US$43.3 billion (1996)
Time	GMT/UTC+0100

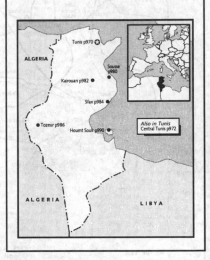

more than a shaky foothold, and put up little resistance when the Arabs arrived from the east in 670, ruling from the holy city of Kairouan, 150km south of Carthage. They proved to be the most influential of conquerors, introducing both Islam and the social structure which remains the basis of Tunisian life today.

After the political fragmentation of the Arab empire, Tunisia became the eastern flank of a Moroccan empire belonging to the group of Islamic Berbers known as the Almohads. The Moroccans appointed the Hafsid family as governors and they ruled,

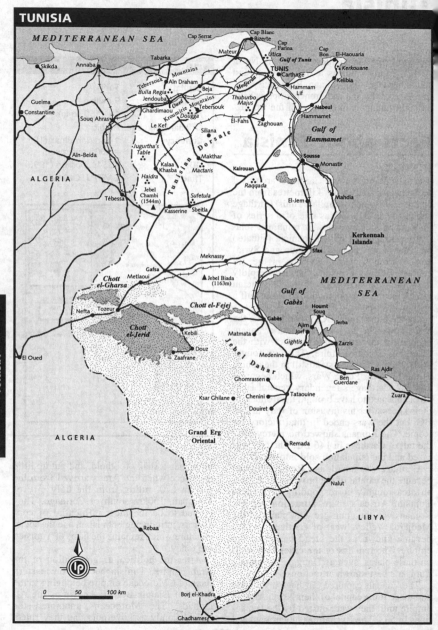

TUNISIA

eventually as an independent monarchy, from 1207 until 1574 – a period of stability and prosperity.

The Hafsids were defeated by the Ottoman Turks and Tunisia came to be ruled by a local elite of Turkish janissaries (the professional elite of the Ottoman armies). By the 18th century, this elite had merged with the local populace and produced its own national monarchy, the Husseinid beys.

In the 19th century, the beys were careful not to provoke the expansionist French. They managed to delay colonisation for some years by outlawing piracy, westernising their administration and, in 1857, adopting a constitution. However, serious financial mismanagement finally gave the French an excuse to invade from Algeria in 1881, and Tunisia became a French protectorate in 1883.

In the 1930s, the Néo-Destour movement for national liberation grew under the leadership of Habib Bourguiba, a Sorbonne-educated lawyer. The French banned the movement and jailed Bourguiba, though it flourished briefly during the German occupation of Tunis in WWII when Bourguiba was released and the beys appointed ministers from the Néo-Destour movement. This came to an end with the Allied victory in North Africa, and Bourguiba went into exile. He orchestrated two years of guerilla warfare from Egypt, eventually forcing the French to grant autonomy in 1955. Bourguiba returned to head the new government, and Tunisia was granted independence a year later.

In 1957, the bey was deposed and Bourguiba became the first president of the new republic. In 1975, the national assembly made him president for life. Bourguiba consolidated his power in 1981 at the country's first multiparty elections.

However, as the 1980s progressed, Bourguiba began to loose touch with his people and became isolated from the rest of the Arab world. In November 1987, the interior minister, Zine el-Abidine ben Ali, orchestrated Bourguiba's downfall and was installed as president.

Tunisia remains one of the most stable and moderate Arab countries. It has developed close ties with both the USA and Germany, which supply the bulk of its foreign aid.

In recent years, the country has become one of the Mediterranean's major tourist attractions, drawing millions of Europeans to its shores each year.

GEOGRAPHY & ECOLOGY

Tunisia occupies an area of about 164,150 sq km, bordered by Algeria to the west, Libya to the south-east, and the Mediterranean to the east and north. The mountainous northern third of the country is dominated by the eastern extensions of the Atlas Mountains.

The north coast is Tunisia's green belt, with a fertile coastal plain backed by the densely forested Kroumirie Mountains. The forests are home to large numbers of wild boar, as well as jackals, mongooses and genets. The country's main mountain range is the rugged central Dorsale, farther south. It runs from Kasserine in the west and peters out into Cap Bon in the east, and includes the country's highest peak, Jebel Chambi (1544m). Between these ranges lies the fertile Medjerda Valley, fed by the Oued Medjerda, country's only permanent river. South of the Dorsale, a high plain falls away to a series of salt lakes (*chotts*) and then to a sandy desert on the edge of the Sahara known as the Grand Erg Oriental.

The east coast is remarkable for the vast areas under olive cultivation, particularly around Sfax.

GOVERNMENT & POLITICS

The republic of Tunisia is governed by a president and a chamber of deputies of 163 members. Political reforms since the ousting of Bourguiba in 1987 have legalised some opposition parties, although they hold only a token number of seats. President ben Ali won 99% of the vote at the presidential elections in March 1994.

ECONOMY

Tunisia's oil is running out fast. Petroleum, which once contributed 25% of export income, now generates less than 10%. The economy relies heavily on tourism to bridge the gap. Leather and textiles are the biggest income earners, followed by phosphates, olive oil, fertilisers and chemicals. Food, raw materials and capital goods are the chief imports.

The main problem is unemployment, estimated at between 15% and 20%. Living standards, however, are high compared to other developing countries. Education is free during primary and secondary school, but universities are now charging fees. Health care is no longer free for everyone.

POPULATION & PEOPLE

Tunisia has an estimated population of almost nine million, although no census has been taken since 1984. Most people are of Arab/Berber stock. The original Berbers make up only 1% of the population and are confined mainly to the south of the country. Before the creation of Israel, Tunisia had a Jewish population of around 150,000. Only 2000 remain, mainly in Tunis and on Jerba. The major cities and their estimated populations are Tunis and suburbs (1.89 million), Sfax (275,000), Sousse (230,000) and Bizerte (135,000).

ARTS

Artistic activity is heavily focused on Tunis, which has a large number of galleries – these are listed on the inside back page of the *Tunisia News*.

Tunisia has long been a popular location for international film-makers. Major films shot in Tunisia include *The Life of Brian*, *The English Patient*, *Star Wars* and *Star Wars IV*.

SOCIETY & CONDUCT

Tunisia is easy-going by Muslim standards, especially in Tunis and the major tourist areas. You'll find many western trappings, such as fast food, pop music and women dressed in the latest European fashions. However, traditional life has changed little in rural areas, where the mosque, the *hammam* (bathhouse) and the café remain the focal points of life.

You can avoid problems by erring on the side of modesty in what your wear. Women are advised to keep shoulders and upper arms covered and to opt for long skirts or trousers, while men should avoid shorts – which are looked on as underwear – outside resort areas.

Thanks largely to the efforts of their secular, socialist, former president, Habib Bourguiba, conditions for women in Tunisia are better than just about anywhere in the Islamic world – to western eyes, at least. His 1956 Personal Status Code banned polygamy and ended divorce by renunciation. He called the *hijab* (veil) an 'odious rag', and banned it from schools as part of a campaign to phase out a garment he regarded as demeaning. He didn't quite succeed, although it is very unusual to find a woman under 30 wearing one. You will encounter some interesting mother-daughter combinations wandering around: mother wrapped in hijab, and daughter adorned in the latest western fashions.

Women make up about 20% of the paid workforce.

RELIGION

Islam is the state religion and 99.75% of the population are Sunni Muslims. There are about 20,000 Roman Catholics and 2000 Jews.

Ramadan is the ninth month of the Muslim calendar, when all Muslims must abstain from eating, drinking, smoking and having sex between dawn and dusk. It commemorates the month when the Koran was revealed to Mohammed.

For the traveller it can be an interesting, though frustrating, time to travel. During the day it's often difficult to find a restaurant open, although the big tourist hotels usually function normally. Be discreet about where you drink and smoke – don't do it openly during the day. When the sun goes down, things get really busy, and restaurants and shops stay open late. It's a great contrast to the normal routine, when very little happens in towns after about 9 pm.

LANGUAGE

Tunisia is virtually bilingual. Arabic is the language of education and government, but almost everyone speaks some French. You are unlikely to come across many English, German or Italian-speakers outside the main tourist centres. You'll get a good reception if you try to speak Arabic rather than French. It's a good idea to learn the basic greetings. Tunisian Arabic is essentially the same as Moroccan Arabic (see the Language Guide at

he back of the book for pronunciation guide-
ines and useful words and phrases).

Facts for the Visitor

HIGHLIGHTS
Most of the highlights are in the south. The
oasis towns of Tozeur and Nefta are full of
surprises – the *palmeraie* (palm groves) are
veritable gardens of Eden. Both towns are
also famous for the intricate brickwork of
their traditional quarters.

Other highlights include staying in the fine
old *funduqs* (caravanserai) of Houmt Souq;
early morning visits to the ksour around
Tataouine; and camel trekking in the desert
around Douz. Three Roman sites stand out
among the crowd: El-Jem, Dougga and Bulla
Regia.

SUGGESTED ITINERARIES

One Week
  Arrive in Tunis (one day) and visit Sousse (one
  day), Tozeur/Nefta (two days), Douz (one day)
  and Jerba (one day); fly back to Tunis.
Two Weeks
  Spend three days in Tunis, including a day trip
  to Dougga; then visit Sousse (two days); travel
  to Sfax via El-Jem (one day); visit Tozeur/Nefta
  (two days), Douz (two days), Jerba (two days)
  and Tataouine (one day); return to Tunis via
  Kairouan (one day).
Four Weeks
  Arrive in Tunis (three days); visit Bizerte (two
  days), Tabarka (two days) and Ain Draham (one
  day); travel to Le Kef via Bulla Regia (two
  days); travel to Tunis via Dougga (one day);
  head south to Sousse (two days) and Mahdia
  (one day); travel to Sfax via El-Jem (two days);
  continue to Tozeur/Nefta (two days) and Douz
  (two days); hang out on Jerba (four days); visit
  Tataouine (two days); return to Tunis via
  Kairouan (one day).

PLANNING
Climate & When to Go
Northern Tunisia has a typical Mediterranean
climate, with hot, dry summers and mild, wet
winters. The farther south you go, the hotter
and drier it gets. Some Saharan areas go
without rain for years.

Summer is the most popular time to visit,
mainly because this is the European holiday
season, but it is not the ideal time because it's
so hot – hovering at around 40°C for days on
end. Transport during this period is also
stretched to the limit and hotel rooms are hard
to find after noon.

The best time to visit is in spring, when the
north is still green, the south is pleasantly
warm and the summer hordes have yet to
arrive. Autumn is the next best time.

Books & Maps
Lonely Planet's *Tunisia* provides detailed information about the country, while Freytag &
Berndt produces the best map. The tourist
office in Tunis hands out a perfectly adequate
road map.

What to Bring
Essential items for the summer visitor
include a broad-brimmed hat, good sunglasses and a sunscreen. If you're planning on
visiting the Sahara, a light sweater will come
in handy even in summer because it gets surprisingly cold at night. In winter, you will
need a warm sweater and – in the north – a
raincoat. An alarm clock is important for
catching early morning buses. Unless you're
happy with a diet of expensive foreign
papers, bring a supply of books.

TOURIST OFFICES
Don't hold your breath waiting for a tidal
wave of information. There are offices of the
government-run Office National du Tourisme
Tunisien (ONTT) in all major towns and
tourist centres, as well as local offices called
syndicats d'initiative – a serious misnomer.

Tourist Offices Abroad
There are Tunisian tourist offices in the following countries:

Belgium
  (☎ 02-511 11 42) Galerie Ravenstein 60, 1000
  Brussels
Canada
  (☎ 514-397 11 82) 1253 McGill College,
  Montreal, Quebec H3A 3B6
France
  (☎ 78 52 35 86) 12 Rue de Séze, 69006 Lyon
  (☎ 01 47 42 72 67) 32 Ave de l'Opéra, 75002
  Paris

TUNISIA

Germany
(☎ 030-885 0457) Kurfuerstendamm 171, 10707 Berlin
(☎ 0211-84 218) Steinstrasse 23, 40210 Dusseldorf
(☎ 069-23 18 91/2) Am Hauptbahnhof 6, 6329 Frankfurt Main 1
Italy
(☎ 02-86 45 30 26) Via Baracchini 10, 20123 Milan
Netherlands
(☎ 020-622 49 71) Muntplein 2, 1012 WR Amsterdam
Sweden
(☎ 08-678 06 45) Stureplan 15, 11145 Stockholm
Switzerland
(☎ 01-211 48 30) Bahnhofstrasse 69, 8001 Zürich
UK
(☎ 0171-224 5561) 77A Wigmore St, London W1H 9LJ

VISAS & EMBASSIES

Nationals of most Western European countries can stay up to three months without a visa – you just roll up and collect a stamp in your passport. Americans, Canadians, Germans and Japanese can stay up to four months. The situation is a bit more complicated for other nationalities. Most require no visa if arriving on an organised tour.

Australians, New Zealanders and South Africans can obtain a one-week visa at the airport for TD3, or a one-month visa for TD6. Those wanting to stay longer can get a three-month visa (TD6) before they arrive – available wherever Tunisia has diplomatic representation.

Israeli nationals are not allowed into the country.

Visa Extensions

It is unlikely that you will need to extend your visa because a month in Tunisia is ample for most people. Applications can be made only at the Interior Ministry on Ave Habib Bourguiba in Tunis. They cost TD3 (payable only in revenue stamps), take up to 10 days to issue, and require two photographs, bank receipts and a *facture* (receipt) from your hotel. It may sound simple, but the process is more hassle than it's worth.

Tunisian Embassies Abroad

Australia
Honorary Consulate: (☎ 02-9363 5588) GPO Box 801, Double Bay, Sydney 2028 – for visa application forms
Canada
(☎ 613-237 0330) 515 O'Connor St, Ottawa K1S 3P8
France
(☎ 01 45 53 50 94) 17-19 Rue de Lubeck, 75016 Paris
(☎ 78 93 42 87) 14 Ave du Maréchal Foch 69412 Lyon
(☎ 04 91 50 28 68) 8 Blvd d'Athènes, 13001 Marseille
Germany
(☎ 030-472 20 64/7) 110 Esplanade 12, 1100 Berlin
(☎ 0211-371 007) 7-9 Graf Adolf Platz, 4000 Dusseldorf
(☎ 040-220 17 56) Overbeckstrasse 19, 2000 Hamburg 76
(☎ 089-55 45 51) Adimstrage 4, 8000 Munich 19
Greece
(☎ 01-671 7590) Ethnikis Antistasseos 91, 15231 Halandri, Athens
Italy
(☎ 06-860 42 82) Via Asmara 5, 00199 Rome;
(☎ 091-32 89 26) 24 Piazza Ignazio Florio, 90100 Palermo
Japan
(☎ 03-3353 4111) 1-18-8 Wakaba Cho, Shinjuku-ku, 160 Tokyo
Morocco
(☎ 07-73 05 76) 6 Rue de Fés, Rabat
Netherlands
(☎ 070-351 22 51) Gentestraat 98, 2587 HX The Hague
South Africa
(☎ 012-342 6283) 850 Church St, Arcadia, 0007 Pretoria
Spain
(☎ 1-447 35 08) Plaza Alonzo Martinez 3, 28004 Madrid
UK
(☎ 0171-584 8117) 29 Prince's Gate, London SW7 1QG
USA
(☎ 202-862 1850) 1515 Massachusetts Ave NW, Washington DC 20005

Foreign Embassies in Tunisia

Countries with diplomatic representation in Tunis include:

Australia
Australian affairs are handled by the Canadian Embassy in Tunis

Canada
(☎ 01-796 577) 3 Rue du Sénégal
France
(☎ 01-347 838) Place de l'Indépendance,
Ave Habib Bourguiba
Germany
(☎ 01- 786 455) 1 Rue el Hamra
Greece
(☎ 01-288 411) 9 Impasse Antelas
Italy
(☎ 01-341 811) 3 Rue de Russie
Japan
(☎ 01-791 251) 10 Rue el-Matri
Morocco
(☎ 01-782 775) 39 Rue du 1 Juin
Netherlands
(☎ 01-799 442) 8 Rue Meycen
UK
(☎ 01-341 444) 5 Place de la Victoire
USA
(☎ 01-782 566) 144 Ave de la Liberté

DOCUMENTS

People planning to hire a car or motorbike of more than 50cc will need their national driving licence. It must be valid for a year.

Although there are no advertised discounts for students, it never hurts to ask, so bring your ID.

CUSTOMS

The duty-free allowance is 400 cigarettes, 2L of wine, 1L of spirits and 250mL of perfume. It is advisable to declare valuable items (such as cameras) on arrival to ensure a smooth departure.

MONEY

The Tunisian dinar is a nonconvertible currency, and it's illegal to import or export it. All the major European currencies are readily exchangeable, as well as the US and Canadian dollars and the Japanese yen. Australian and New Zealand dollars and South African rand are not accepted. It is not necessary to declare your foreign currency on arrival. Foreign currency can be exchanged at banks, post offices and major hotels.

When leaving the country, you can exchange up to 30% of the amount you changed into dinar, up to a limit of TD100. You need to produce bank receipts to prove you changed the money in the first place.

Major credit cards such as Visa, American Express and MasterCard are widely accepted throughout the country at large shops, tourist hotels, car-rental agencies and banks. Maestro-Cirrus cards can also be used, but in a limited number of places.

Cash advances are given in local currency only.

Currency

The unit of currency is the Tunisian dinar (TD), which is divided into 1000 millimes (mills). There are five, 10, 20, 50, 100 and 500-mill coins and one-dinar coins. There are five, 10, 20 and 30-dinar notes. Changing the larger notes is not a problem.

Exchange Rates

Exchange rates are regulated, so the rate is the same everywhere. Banks charge a standard 351 mills commission per travellers cheque, and the larger hotels take slightly more. Post offices will change cash only.

Australia	A$1	=	TD0.66
Canada	C$1	=	TD0.73
euro	€1	=	TD1.27
France	1FF	=	TD0.19
Germany	DM1	=	TD0.64
Italy	L1000	=	TD0.65
Japan	¥100	=	TD0.82
New Zealand	NZ$1	=	TD0.56
UK	UK£1	=	TD1.37
USA	US$1	=	TD1.13

Costs

Tunisia is a cheap country to travel in, especially for Europeans. It's usually possible to find a clean room for about TD5 per person, main meals in local restaurants are seldom over TD3.500, and transport is cheap. If you're fighting to keep costs down, you can get by on TD20 a day. You'll have more fun with a budget of about TD30 per day and you can be quite lavish for TD50.

Tipping & Bargaining

Tipping is not a requirement. Cafés and local restaurants put out a saucer for customers to throw their small change into, but this is seldom more than 50 mills. Waiters in tourist restaurants are accustomed to tips – 10% is

TUNISIA

plenty. Taxi drivers do not expect tips from locals, but they often round up the fare for foreigners.

Handicrafts are about the only items you may have to bargain for in Tunisia. To be good at bargaining, you need to enjoy the banter. If you don't, you're better off buying your souvenirs from one of the government-run craft shops (see Things to Buy) where prices are fixed. It's a good idea to go there anyway just to get an idea of prices.

POST & COMMUNICATIONS
Post
The Tunisian postal service is slow but reliable. Letters from Europe generally take about a week to arrive; letters from farther afield take about two weeks. Delivery times are similar in the other direction, although it can take three weeks for a letter to reach Australia. Air-mail letters cost 650 mills to Europe, and 700 mills to Australia and the Americas; postcards cost 100 mills less. You can buy stamps at post offices, major hotels and some general stores and newsstands.

Post offices are open in summer (1 July until 30 September) from 7.30 am to 1.30 pm, Monday to Thursday, and from 7.30 am to 12.30 pm on Friday. In winter, opening hours are 8 am to 6 pm, Monday to Saturday. During Ramadan, they open from 8 am to 3 pm, Monday to Saturday. The main post office in Tunis, on Rue Charles de Gaulle, is open seven days a week. Post office hours vary from town to town.

You can receive mail at any post office in the country. It should be addressed clearly, with your surname first.

Parcel Post Parcels should be taken along unwrapped for inspection. Parcels weighing less than 2kg can be sent by ordinary mail. Larger parcels should be taken to the special parcel counter. Indicate clearly if you want to send something surface mail.

Telephone
The telephone system is efficient and modern. Public telephones, known as Taxiphones, are everywhere and it's rare to find one that doesn't work. Most places have Taxiphone offices, readily identified by the yellow sign, with about a dozen booths and attendants to give change. Local calls cost 100 mills, and long-distance calls cost a maximum of 200 mills per minute. The number for directory information is ☎ 120.

International Calls The same phones can also be used for international direct dialling, except that you will need to feed them one-dinar and half-dinar coins. International calls are not cheap: 980 mills per minute to most European countries, TD1.500 per minute to the USA and TD1.750 per minute to Australia and New Zealand. (A three-minute call to the US costs TD4.500). To dial out, phone the international access code ☎ 00, followed by the country code, then the local code and number.

If you're calling Tunisia from abroad, the country code is ☎ 216.

INTERNET RESOURCES
The Internet was launched in Tunisia in the middle of 1997, but the amount of information about the country that can be gleaned from the Web is still fairly limited. Many sites visited were still under construction at the time of writing. The Tunisian National Tourist Organisation's site (www. tourism tunisia.com) is more advanced than most, but offers little more than you'll find in their glossy brochures.

A more interesting site to explore is www.tunisiaonline.com, where you can read the Tunisian newspapers. You'll find La Presse and Le Temps in French, and the Arabic dailies Essahafa and Assabah, all available on the day of publication.

There is no public access to the Internet in Tunisia. The only way to gain access, or email, is through friends.

NEWSPAPERS & MAGAZINES
You will need to speak French or Arabic to make much sense of the Tunisian press. The weekly Tunisian News is the only local publication in English, but it's not much to get excited about. La Presse and Le Temps are the main French-language papers. They both have a couple of pages of international news as well as local service information such as

train, bus and flight times. In the main centres you can buy two-day-old European newspapers.

RADIO & TV
There is a French-language radio station broadcasting on (or around) FM 98MHz. It broadcasts in English from 2 to 3 pm, German from 3 to 4 pm and Italian from 4 to 5 pm. A much better source of English-language radio is the BBC World Service, which can be picked up on 15.07MHz and 12.095MHz.

The French-language TV station has half an hour of news at 8 pm every night, which includes foreign news and sport.

PHOTOGRAPHY & VIDEO
Kodak and Fuji film are widely available in Tunis and resort areas, but cost a good deal more – especially at resorts. All main towns have quick processing labs which can develop any type of print film.

Always ask before taking photographs of people. Although Tunisia is a relatively liberal country, photographing women is still a no-no in parts of the country. Photographing anything to do with the military or police is forbidden – and they mean it.

TIME
Tunisia is one hour ahead of GMT/UTC from October to April, and two hours ahead of GMT/UTC from May to September.

ELECTRICITY
The power supply is 220V and plugs have two round pins, as in Europe.

WEIGHTS & MEASURES
Tunisia uses the metric system. For readers more familiar with the imperial system, there's a conversion table at the back of this book.

LAUNDRY
Laundrettes don't exist in the western sense, although there is a place in Tunis (see the Tunis section) with washing machines where you can pay for washing to be done by the

kilogram. You just drop off the load and collect it later. Most hotels offer a laundry service, although it tends to be expensive. Most towns have dry-cleaning shops. Typical prices are TD1.500 for a shirt, TD1.800 for jeans and TD2 for a cloth jacket.

TOILETS
Public toilets are a rarity. About the only places you'll find them are at bus and train stations. Otherwise, cafés are the best option – although you will be expected to buy a coffee or something for the privilege. Most are equipped with a hose for washing yourself; if you like to use paper, carry your own.

HEALTH
You will need to show a yellow-fever vaccination certificate if you have visited an infected area in the six days prior to arrival. The telephone number for an ambulance is ☎ 190.

WOMEN TRAVELLERS
Women should encounter few problems. It's advisable to dress more conservatively outside Tunis and the resort towns. A headscarf may come in handy in remote areas as proof of modesty. Cosmetics, tampons etc are widely available.

GAY & LESBIAN TRAVELLERS
While the lifestyle is liberal by Islamic standards, society has yet to come to terms with homosexuality. All forms of homosexual activity are illegal under Tunisian law.

DANGERS & ANNOYANCES
Probably the worst hassles you will encounter are the carpet touts of Kairouan, but they don't hold a candle to their Moroccan counterparts. There have been isolated reports of beach thefts, but crimes such as mugging are very rare.

BUSINESS HOURS
Government offices and businesses are open Monday to Thursday from 8.30 am to 1 pm and 3 to 5.45 pm. They're also open on Friday and Saturday from 8.30 am to

1.30 pm. In July and August, offices don't open in the afternoon.

Banks are open from 8 to 11 am and 2 to 4 pm Monday to Thursday, and 8 to 11 am and 1 to 3 pm Friday. Some banks in Tunis extend opening times beyond these hours. Banks are not open in the afternoon in July and August.

Most shops are open Monday to Friday from 8 am to 12.30 pm and 2.30 to 6 pm, and from 8 am to noon on Saturday. Summer hours are usually 7.30 am to 1 pm.

PUBLIC HOLIDAYS & SPECIAL EVENTS

Public holidays and festivals are either religious celebrations or festivities marking the anniversary of historic events. The Islamic holidays fall 10 days earlier every western calendar year because the Gregorian (western) and Islamic calendars are of different lengths. Ramadan is the main one to watch out for, because opening hours and transport schedules are disrupted for an entire month.

Other public holidays in Tunisia are: New Year's Day (1 January); Independence Day (20 March); Youth Day (21 March); Martyrs' Day (9 April); Labour Day (1 May); Republic Day (25 July); Public Holiday (3 August); Women's Day (13 August); Evacuation Day (15 October); and Ben Ali's Presidential Anniversary (7 November).

Some of these holidays, such as Women's Day and Evacuation Day, pass without notice. On other holidays, everything except transport comes to a halt. Avoid travel before Eid al-Fitr (celebrating the end of Ramadan) when everyone is trying to get home for the festivities.

The capital stages the annual Carthage Festival in July and August, with performances of classical theatre at Carthage's Roman theatre. It also hosts the biennial Carthage Film Festival (October, in odd-numbered years).

Other cultural events of note are the El-Jem Symphonic Music Festival, held every July in El-Jem's spectacular floodlit colosseum, and the Dougga festival of classical theatre at the site's fine Roman theatre.

Almost every tourist town stages an annual festival, usually a week-long line-up of parades and fairly tacky folkloric events. The best of them is the Sahara Festival in Douz and Tozeur during December/February. The main festivals are:

Sahara Festival – Held in December/January in Douz and Tozeur, this festival has everything from camel races and saluki dog trials to traditional marriages

Nefta Festival – Held in April, this festival features parades and folkloric events

Monastir Festival – This is held in May

Siren Festival – Held in July/August, this festival takes place on the Kerkennah Islands

Hammamet Festival – Held in July/August, this festival features music and cultural events

Tabarka Festival – This festival held in July/August features music, theatre and a coral exhibition

Ulysses Festival – Held in July/August on Jerba, this festival is strictly for the tourists, right down to the Miss Ulysses competition

Baba Aoussou Festival – This is held in July/August in Sousse

ACCOMMODATION

You'll find everything in Tunisia, from camping grounds and basic hotels to five-star luxury resorts.

Camping

Most of the official camping grounds have only basic facilities and charge about TD2.500 per person. It's technically possible to camp anywhere as long as you get the landowner's permission.

There are good camping sites – complete with electricity and hot water – at Aghir (Jerba), Douz, Gabès, Nabeul, Remel Plage (near Bizerte) and Tozeur.

Hostels

Hostels in Tunisia fall into two categories: the government-run maisons des jeunes and the auberges de jeunesse, affiliated to Hostelling International (HI) – and they couldn't be more different.

The auberges de jeunesse are thoroughly recommended; most have prime locations, such as a converted palace in the Tunis medina and a fascinating old funduq at Houmt Souq, Jerba. They charge TD4.500 per night for bed and breakfast, with other meals available for TD3 each. You need an

HI card to use the hostels. The address for HI in Tunisia is 25 Rue Saida Ajoula, Tunis medina (☎ 567 850).

Almost without exception, maisons des jeunes are characterless, concrete boxes with all the charm of army barracks. Almost every town has a maison des jeunes, normally stuck way out in the boondocks and used primarily to house visiting sporting teams and for school-children's holiday camps. The only reason to mention them is that sometimes they represent the only available budget accommodation. They all charge TD4 for a dormitory bed.

There are a couple of places where the maisons des jeunes concept has been expanded into a scheme called *centres des stages et vacances*. These are holiday camps which combine hostels and camp sites. There is one on the beach at Aghir, and another in the oasis at Gabès. Camping charges are TD2 per person and 500 mills per tent. Electricity and hot showers are available.

Hotels

Tunisian hotels are generally clean, if a little shabby. All hotels must display the tariff by the reception desk, so you can always see what the price should be. In most places, you can find a clean room with shared bathroom for TD5 to TD8 per person, and TD18 to TD25 will get you a comfortable double with bathroom. Prices for all but the most basic places usually include breakfast, which means coffee, French bread, butter and jam.

FOOD

The national dish is couscous (semolina granules). There are apparently more than 300 ways of preparing the stuff – sweet as well as savoury. A bowl served with stew costs about TD2.500 in local restaurants. A curiosity in Tunisian cuisine is the *briq*, a crisp, very thin pastry envelope which comes with a range of fillings always including egg.

Other dishes include:

harissa
  fiery red chilli paste that comes as a side serve
kammounia
  meat stew made with lots of cumin
lablabi
  spicy chickpea broth which is doled out on a bed of broken bread

mloukhia
  similar to kammounia, except that it's made with a blend of dried herbs; cuts of lamb or beef are simmered until they almost disappear into the rich, green sauce
salade mechouia
  very spicy mixture of mashed roast vegetables, often predominantly eggplant, which is served as an accompaniment to dishes such as roast chicken
salade tunisienne
  finely diced salad vegetables mixed with a dressing of lemon juice and olive oil
shakshuka
  thick vegetable soup based on onions and green peppers; unfortunately for vegetarians, it's normally made with a meat stock
tajine
  the Tunisian version is no relation to its Moroccan namesake; it's similar to quiche and is normally served cold with chips and salad

Restaurants

Restaurants can be divided into three broad categories.

You'll find most of the food mentioned above in *gargottes*. They vary from very basic to slightly upmarket. Generally a main dish and salad won't cost much over TD3.500; many serve fish, lamb cutlets and kebabs.

Rotisseries are easy to spot because they normally have a rotating spit of roast chickens outside; that's about all they serve, usually with chips and salad. Prices start at TD1.700 for a quarter of a chicken.

Tourist restaurants serve what they like to call Franco-Tunisienne cuisine. If you can avoid lobster, most meals will cost under TD10. Tourist restaurants sell alcohol – unlike the others.

Fast Food

Almost every town has a shop selling *casse-croûtes*, half a French loaf stuffed with a choice of fillings – fried egg, chips and harissa is a favourite known as *khaftegi*. Western-style fast food is also becoming popular. Pizza parlours and hamburger joints can be found in most of the major towns.

DRINKS

Mineral water is cheap and available everywhere, as are soft drinks such as Coca-Cola.

TUNISIA

Alcohol is readily available. The Monoprix chain of supermarkets sells a good range of local wines. Supermarkets sell alcohol only from midday to 6.30 pm, and not on Friday.

The only local spirit is a fiery number called *boukha*, which is produced from figs.

Whisky drinkers are advised to bring a bottle as part of their duty-free allowance – a bottle costs at least TD60 locally.

Bars

Bars can be found in all the major towns. They are generally hard-drinking, smoke-filled, male preserves. Beer is the most popular drink and Celtia is the only beer. It sells for TD1.400 per bottle in Tunis and for as little as TD1.200 outside the capital. It is possible for accompanied foreign females to stop for a beer at these places, but don't be surprised by the attention levels. Most foreigners, particularly women, feel more comfortable drinking at the resort hotels.

ENTERTAINMENT

Nightlife is not promising outside Tunis and the resort areas. The favourite local entertainment is coffee and cards at the café, but that's strictly for the blokes. Almost every town has a cinema, although the posters don't look auspicious. If you like discos, stick to the resorts.

THINGS TO BUY

The most popular items to buy in Tunisia are rugs and carpets, jewellery, pottery, beaten copper and brass items, leather and straw goods, and *chechias* (small, red, felt hats worn by Tunisian men).

Although they're not cheap, rugs and carpets are among the most readily available and beautiful souvenirs. The main carpet-selling centres are Tunis, Kairouan, Tozeur and Jerba. Look out for carpets which have been inspected by the Office National de l'Artisanat Tunisien (ONAT). It classifies the carpets by quality and affixes a label and seal on the back. Carpets not classified by ONAT are cheaper, but their quality may be suspect.

Jewellery, particularly gold, is very ornate. The Hand of Fatima (daughter of the Prophet) is a traditional Arabic design, usually made of silver.

Sand roses are sold all over the country. They are formed of gypsum, present in the desert sand, which crystallises into beautiful patterns.

Markets

Town and village life revolves around the weekly market. Market day is a good day to be in a town because it's far livelier than usual and the markets attract both itinerant merchants and people from outlying districts.

Getting There & Away

AIR

Tunisia has four international airports: Tunis, Jerba, Monastir and Tabarka. Tunis handles most of the scheduled flights, while Jerba and Monastir are the main charter airports.

Europe

British Airways flies to Tunis three times a week and does a 30-day return for UK£215, dropping as low as UK£160 at times. Most of the flights using Jerba and Monastir are charters. These can be incredibly cheap – as low as UK£99 return – if you don't mind minimum and maximum-stay restrictions; you get the biggest discounts at the last minute.

Overseas branches of the ONTT have lists of charter operators. In the UK, Horizon Holidays (☎ 0181-200 8733) and Thomson Holidays (same number) are the two biggest operators.

The USA & Canada

There are no direct flights between Tunisia and the USA or Canada. The cheapest way to travel between North America and Tunisia is to get a cheap fare to London and a charter flight or bucket-shop deal from there. One-month Apex fares from New York start at around US$1200.

Australia

There are no direct flights to/from Australia either, although several of the major European airlines serving Australia have good connections with Tunis. The cheapest and quickest route is with Alitalia, who can get you to Tunis from Sydney or Melbourne via Rome for as little as A$1650 return.

Morocco

Royal Air Maroc and Tunis Air fly regularly between the two countries. An Apex ticket, valid for one month, costs TD335.800 return.

LAND
Algeria

It's years now since the last recorded crossing of this border by a tourist. The problems in Algeria have prompted the cancellation of bus and train services between Tunis and Annaba, leaving *louages* (shared taxis) as the only option. They operate from Place Sidi Bou Mendil in the Tunis medina to Annaba (TD28) and Constantine (TD35).

Libya

The border crossing between Tunisia and Libya on the coast at Ras Ajdir is open, but tourist visas are still as scarce as hen's teeth. There are regular buses (TD17.350) and louages (TD20) from Sfax to Tripoli, as well as a daily bus from Tunis to Tripoli for TD26.420.

SEA
Italy

There are ferries between Tunis and the Italian ports of Genoa and Trapani (Sicily). The shortest crossing is the weekly Tirrenia Lines service to Trapani (eight hours, TD65 one way). It leaves Trapani at 8 am on Monday morning and Tunis at 8 pm the same day.

Boats to Genoa are run by the Compagnie Tunisienne de Navigation (CTN). Services to Genoa vary between four a month in winter and 11 a month at the height of summer. The trip takes 24 hours and costs TD140 one way.

You can get tickets for both services from the CTN office (☎ 322 802) at 122 Rue de Yougoslavie.

France

CTN also operates regular ferries from Tunis to Marseille (24 hours, TD180 one way). There are at least seven ferries a month even in winter, and daily sailings in August. The service is packed in summer, so visitors taking cars will need to book ahead.

LEAVING TUNISIA

There is no departure tax to be paid when leaving the country. A TD8 airport tax is included in the price of an air ticket, and a similar TD2 port tax is included in the price of ferry tickets.

Getting Around

Tunisia has a well-developed transport network, and just about every town in the country has daily bus connections with Tunis. For most of the year public transport copes easily with demand, but things get pretty hectic during August and September and on public holidays. Book ahead if possible.

AIR

Tunisia's domestic air network is fairly limited because it's such a small country. The domestic airline, Tuninter, operates the following services: Tunis to Jerba (six flights per day); Tunis to Tozeur (every day except Tuesday and Wednesday); Tunis to Sfax (Monday to Thursday); Monastir to Jerba (Saturday); and Tozeur to Jerba (Monday, Tuesday and Saturday).

BUS

SNTRI, the national bus company, runs daily air-con buses to most towns in the country. These green-and-yellow buses are fast, comfortable, not too expensive, and run pretty much to schedule. Many of the long-distance buses run at night to avoid the heat, which means you won't see much of the country you're travelling through. It's especially important to book in advance when leaving Tunis in summer.

There are also regional bus companies, which are reliable and cheap, but slow and without air-con. Booking in advance is both impossible and unnecessary. The only way to be sure of bus schedules is to go to the bus station and ask. Most stations do not have timetables displayed; those that do, have them in Arabic only – with the exception of

Houmt Souq in Jerba. Departures tend to be early in the day. If you're seeking directions to the bus station, ask for the *gare routière*.

Some towns are served by two or three regional companies. These competing companies generally share stations, but in some cases, such as Tabarka, each company has its own station. Officials from one company never know about the schedules of another, so always ask if there is more than one company operating in town.

TRAIN

Tunisia's rail network is modern and efficient, but hardly comprehensive. There are passenger services from Tunis to Bizerte, El-Jem, Gabès, Ghardimaou, Kalaa Khasba, Mahdia, Metlaoui, Monastir, Nabeul, Sfax and Sousse. The best service is on the main line south from Tunis to Sousse and Sfax.

Passenger trains offer three classes: second, first and *confort*. Second class costs about the same as a local bus, and is normally packed with people, produce and livestock. First-class carriages have reclining, upholstered seats, and cost about 40% more than 2nd class. Confort costs a bit more again, but doesn't offer much extra. Prices quoted in this chapter are for 2nd class.

LOUAGE

Louages are long-distance taxis offering a parallel service to the buses. Whereas buses leave to a timetable, louages leave when they're full. Most are station wagons with an extra bench seat in the back, designed to take five passengers. Drivers stand by their vehicles and call out their destinations. They seldom take long to fill up. Louages are the fastest way to get around, and the fares are only slighter higher than the buses. Most louages are white with a red stripe.

In most towns, the louage 'station' is close to, or incorporated with, the bus station, enabling you to choose between the services.

CAR & MOTORCYCLE

Tunisia has an excellent road network. All but the most minor roads are tar sealed and well maintained. Potholes are almost unheard of. Many of the roads which are marked as

unsealed on older maps have now been sealed.

There are still a lot of unsealed roads in the desert areas of the south, but these too are graded regularly and can usually be negotiated easily enough with a conventional vehicle. The worst road you are likely to encounter is the back road from Matmata to Medenine. People will tell you it's for 4WDs only, but it can be negotiated with caution in even the smallest Fiats and Citroëns.

Although the short distances and good road conditions make motorcycling an ideal way to travel, you hardly see a bike bigger than 90cc. If you're bringing your own motorbike, make sure you have basic spare parts; they're virtually impossible to find because of the scarcity of motorbikes.

Road Rules

The road rules in Tunisia are basically the same as in Continental Europe. You drive on the right, and overtake on the left. The speed limits are 50km/h in built-up areas and 90km/h on the open road. The only exception is on the toll road from Tunis to Sousse, where the speed limit is 110km/h.

The regulation that causes the most problems for tourists concerns giving priority to traffic coming from the right in built-up areas. This also extends to roundabouts, where you are obliged to give way to traffic approaching from the right even if you are already on the roundabout.

Clubs

The Touring Club de Tunisie has reciprocal rights arrangements with many European automobile clubs, including Britain's Automobile Association (AA). If your car conks out, they can supply you with the name of the nearest affiliated breakdown service. The club's address is 15 Rue d'Allemagne, Tunis 1000 (☎ 01-323 114; fax 324 834).

Rental

Hiring a car can be a great way to see the country, but unless you have a fat wallet or are part of a small group, it's not a realistic option. All the major international operators have offices in the larger towns. Rental conditions are fairly straightforward. If you are paying by cash, you will be required to leave a deposit roughly equivalent to the rental charge. Credit cards don't have the same restriction.

Typical rental charges for the smallest cars (Renault Esp or Citroën 15) are about TD24 per day plus 220 mills per kilometre. It's cheaper to take an unlimited-kilometre deal; these start at about TD350 per week. On top of these rates, you'll have to pay 17% tax, insurance at about TD10 per day, contract fees etc. By the time you've filled the petrol tank at 603 mills per litre, your wallet will be a lot lighter.

When you hire a vehicle car, make sure there is an accident report form with the car's papers. If you have an accident, both parties involved must complete the form. If the form is not completed, you may be liable for the costs, whether you've paid for insurance or not.

Rental companies require that drivers be aged over 21 and hold a driver's licence valid for at least a year.

There are military checkpoints all over the country, and although officials are not too bothered about checking foreigners, make sure you have your passport handy.

BICYCLE

Cycling is an excellent way to see the country in spring or autumn. It's too hot to cycle in summer and a little bleak in winter, though it is possible to put a bike on the train if you get too exhausted or want to skip a long stretch.

A few places hire out bikes, normally for about TD8 per day. If there's no hire facility in town, it's worth asking at a local bike-repair shop to see if they'll rent a spare bike for a few hours. Make sure that the brakes work.

HITCHING

The following information is intended solely as an explanation of how hitching works in Tunisia, not as a recommendation. Although many people do hitch, it is not an entirely safe method of transport, and you do so at your own risk. It is strongly recommended that women do not attempt to hitch without a male companion.

Conditions for hitching vary throughout the country. The south is the easiest because there is a great deal more tourist traffic – either people who hire cars in Jerba or overlanders heading for Tozeur and the Sahara. You shouldn't have to wait long for a lift. In the north, people seem less inclined to pick up hitchers, particularly in the summer when there are so many tourists.

Between small towns in the south, hitching is a standard way of getting around, although you will normally be expected to pay the equivalent of the bus fare. See the introductory Getting Around chapter for more information on hitching.

SEA

There are two scheduled ferry services in the country. The first connects Sfax with the Kerkennah Islands. There are up to eight crossings a day in summer, dropping to four in winter. The trip takes 1-1/2 hours and costs 570 mills. The second service runs from Jorf on the mainland to Ajim on Jerba. The crossing takes only a few minutes and the ferries run 24 hours.

LOCAL TRANSPORT

You'll find orange, metered taxis in almost every town. Flag fall is 280 mills, followed by 370 mills per kilometre. In the south, *camionnettes* (small trucks) operate between towns and outlying villages, such as Douz and Zaafrane. They charge by the place, and leave when there are enough passengers to make it worthwhile.

Tunis

☎ 01

Tunisia's capital is a cosmopolitan modern city with a population of about 1.9 million. It's an easy place to spend two or three days. The main attractions are the ancient medina, the ruins of Carthage and the Bardo Museum.

Orientation

The medina, the original city of Tunis, was built on a narrow strip of land between Lake Tunis and the Sebkhet Sejoumi salt lake. When the French arrived, they built a new city, the *ville nouvelle*, on land reclaimed from Lake Tunis to the east of the medina.

TUNIS

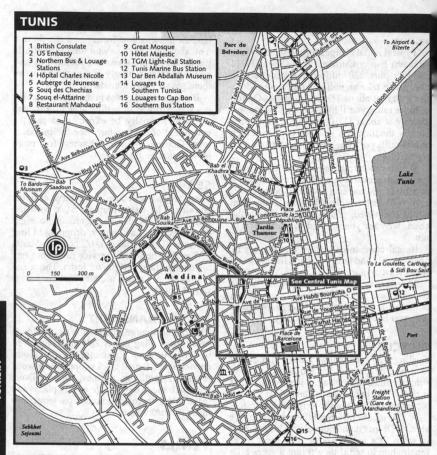

1	British Consulate	9	Great Mosque
2	US Embassy	10	Hôtel Majestic
3	Northern Bus & Louage Stations	11	TGM Light-Rail Station
4	Hôpital Charles Nicolle	12	Tunis Marine Bus Station
5	Auberge de Jeunesse	13	Dar Ben Abdallah Museum
6	Souq des Chechias	14	Louages to Southern Tunisia
7	Souq el-Attarine	15	Louages to Cap Bon
8	Restaurant Mahdaoui	16	Southern Bus Station

The main thoroughfare of the ville nouvelle is Ave Habib Bourguiba, which runs from Lake Tunis to the Bab Bhar, the medina's eastern gate – also known as the Porte de France.

Most of the budget hotels are in the area around the Bab Bhar and to the south of Ave Habib Bourguiba. A causeway at the eastern end of Ave Habib Bourguiba carries road and light-rail traffic across Lake Tunis to the port suburb of La Goulette, and north to the affluent beach suburbs of Carthage, Sidi Bou Said and La Marsa.

Information

Tourist Offices The tourist office (☎ 341 077) is on Place du 7 Novembre at the eastern end of Ave Habib Bourguiba. It has a good free map of Tunis and useful brochures on Carthage and the medina.

Money The major banks are on Ave Habib Bourguiba. The Banque de l'Habitat and the UIBC bank have 24-hour automatic exchange machines. American Express (☎ 347 381) is represented by Carthage Tours, 59 Ave Habib Bourguiba.

Post & Communications The main post office is on Rue Charles de Gaulle. Telephone calls can be made from any of the many Taxiphone offices around the city centre (see the Central Tunis map for a couple of the most convenient).

Laundry The Lavarie Tahar at 15 Rue d'Allemagne charges TD5.500 to wash and dry 5kg.

Medical & Emergency Services The telephone number for the police and fire brigade is ☎ 197 (nationwide); the number for the ambulance service is ☎ 190. There is an antipoison centre in Tunis (☎ 245 075).

Things to See

Medina The Tunis medina is a veritable treasure trove of Islamic architecture dating back to the beginning of the 8th century. The major monuments are all marked and explained in the medina brochure available from the tourist office.

The main entry to the medina is along Rue Jamaa Ez Zitouna, which runs from the Bab Bhar to the **Zitouna Mosque**, also known as the great mosque. Built by the Aghlabids at the beginning of the 8th century, it is the oldest surviving building in Tunis and features many columns salvaged from the ruins of Roman Carthage. It is open from 8 am to noon every day except Friday. Admission is TD1.600.

The other major attraction is the **Dar Ben Abdallah Museum**, a splendid old Turkish palace housing traditional costumes and local artefacts. It is open Tuesday to Sunday from 9 am to 5 pm. Admission is TD1.600.

Two souqs to check out are the **Souq el-Attarine** (the perfume souq) and the **Souq des Chechias**, where the traditional, red, felt caps are made. They are worn mainly by older men these days.

Bardo Museum Housed in an old palace 3km north-west of the city centre, the Bardo is home to one of the world's finest collections of Roman mosaics. It is open from 9 am to 5 pm in summer and 9.30 am to 4.30 pm in winter; closed on Monday. Entry costs TD3.100, plus TD1 to take photos. *Métro léger* (tram) line 4 has a stop (Le Bardo) near

the museum, or catch bus No 3 from opposite the Hôtel Africa Meridien on Ave Habib Bourguiba.

Carthage The ruins of Punic and Roman Carthage are spread along the coast about 10km north of the city centre. Before you head out there, stop at the tourist office in town to pick up a copy of the Carthage brochure. It has a good map of the area and information on the major sites.

The Romans did such a thorough job of destroying Carthage in 146 BC that virtually nothing remains of the original city apart from the Punic ports. Excavation work has uncovered a small area of streets and houses in the grounds of the **National Museum** on top of the **Byrsa Hill**, the focal point of the ancient city.

The ruins of Roman Carthage are far more extensive. They include villas, a heavily restored theatre and the enormous **Antonine Baths**.

Entry to all the sites at Carthage is by a multiple ticket (TD4.100), which can be bought only at the Antonine Baths, the Roman villas and the museum.

The best way to visit Carthage is to take the TGM light rail from Tunis Marine bus station at the eastern end of Ave Habib Bourguiba to Carthage Hannibal station and wander from there.

Sidi Bou Said A few stops farther along the TGM line from Carthage is the beautiful, whitewashed, cliff-top village of **Sidi Bou Said**. It's really an outer suburb of Tunis, and is considered one of the city's most upmarket residential areas. Although it's on every tour group's itinerary, it remains very relaxed, especially late in the afternoon after the tour buses have left. There are no specific attractions, but it's a delight to wander through the old cobbled streets.

Places to Stay

Camping isn't really an option. The nearest camping ground is 15km south of the city near Hammam Lif.

Fortunately, Tunis has an excellent *auberge de jeunesse* (☎ 567 850). It occupies an old palace, the Dar Saida Ajoula, right in the heart of the medina on Rue Es Saida

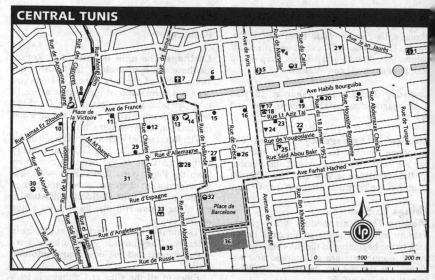

CENTRAL TUNIS

CENTRAL TUNIS

PLACES TO STAY		25	Restaurant Le Bolero		15	National Theatre
8	Hôtel Medina				16	SOCOPA
10	Hôtel Marhaba	**OTHER**			18	Taxiphone Office
19	Hôtel Africa Meridien	1	Tourist Office		20	Tunis Air
23	Hôtel Bristol	3	Buses to Airport & Bardo		21	Interior Ministry
26	Hôtel Salammbô		Museum		28	Taxiphone Office
27	Hôtel Maison Doree	5	Banque de l'Habitat		29	Lavarie Tahar
35	Hôtel Cirta	6	Carthage Tours (American		30	Louages to Algeria &
			Express)			Libya
PLACES TO EAT		7	Cathedral		31	Central Market
2	Restaurant Istambul	9	UK Embassy		32	Place de Barcelone Buses &
4	Restaurant La Mamma	11	Magasin Général			Trams
17	Café de Paris	12	Monoprix Supermarket		33	Post Office
22	Gaston's Restaurant	13	UIBC		34	Second-Hand Bookshop
24	Restaurant Carcassonne	14	French Embassy		36	Train Station

Ajoula. Rates range from TD5 for a dormitory bed and breakfast up to TD11 for full board. Hot showers are free.

There are lots of cheap hotels in the medina charging TD3 for a bed in a shared room, but they are impossible to recommend. They are totally unsuitable for women. There are a couple of possibilities around Place de la Victoire. The *Hôtel Medina* (☎ 255 056) has basic doubles for TD10, while the *Hôtel*

Marhaba (☎ 343 118), on the opposite side of the square at 5 Rue de la Commission, has singles/doubles for TD8/10.

Most travellers opt to stay outside the medina in the area south of Ave Habib Bourguiba. A popular choice is the *Hôtel Bristol* (☎ 244 836) on Rue Lt Mohamed Aziz Taj. It has singles/doubles with breakfast for TD6/8. The alternative is the *Hôtel Cirta* (☎ 321 584), 42 Rue Charles de Gaulle, which charges TD7/11. Hot showers cost an extra TD1.

There are plenty of good mid-range hotels. They don't come any better than the two-star *Hôtel Maison Doree* (☎ 332 401), an old-style French hotel on Rue el-Koufa, just north of Place de Barcelone. It is immaculately clean and well kept, the staff are friendly and efficient, and it even has a lift. Singles/doubles with shower cost TD23.800/30.500, including breakfast.

If those prices sound too steep, try the *Hôtel Salammbô* (☎ 334 252; fax 337 498), a block to the east at 6 Rue de Grèce. It's a one-star version of the Maison Doree – a huge old timber staircase instead of a lift, for example. It offers a wide choice of rooms, starting with a couple of basic singles without facilities for TD12. Singles/doubles with shower and toilet are TD16/25, including breakfast.

The *Hôtel Majestic* (☎ 332 848; fax 336 908), 36 Ave de Paris, is a splendid piece of fading grandeur with one of the finest French colonial façades in town. It has huge singles/doubles with bathroom and TV for TD35/48, including breakfast.

Places to Eat

There's a host of good places in the streets south of Ave Habib Bourguiba, particularly around Ave de Carthage and Rue Ibn Khaldoun. It's hard to beat the *Restaurant Carcassonne*, 8 Ave de Carthage, for value. It turns out a four-course menu for TD3.800, supplemented by as much bread as you can eat.

The Carcassonne is not the cheapest place around. That title goes to the *Restaurant Istambul*, just north of Ave Habib Bourguiba on Rue Pierre Coubertin. It charges an amazing TD2.900 for four courses.

The *Restaurant Mahdaoui*, opposite the great mosque in the medina, is a good place to stop for lunch. It's the oldest restaurant in Tunis and has a daily blackboard menu featuring dishes like couscous with lamb (TD2.200).

The *Restaurant La Mamma*, 11 Rue de Marseille, has a range of pizzas from TD4.200 and pasta dishes starting at TD2.800.

If you want to enjoy a wine with your meal, check out the *Restaurant Le Bolero*, on a small side street off Rue de Yougoslavie. It's always packed with locals at lunchtime and a hearty meal for two with wine will cost about TD20.

Entertainment

There are a few restaurants that put on entertainment. The *Restaurant le Bleuet*, 23 Rue de Marseille, is something of an institution among the night owls of Tunis. It has music every night, and a belly dancer makes a brief appearance around 1 am. The action here doesn't kick off until 10 pm and then continues until about 5 am. Reckon on spending around TD25 per person. The restaurant is about 250m north of Ave Habib Bourguiba.

Gaston's, 73 Rue de Yougoslavie, has folk music and dance on Friday and Saturday night for a TD5 surcharge.

Things to Buy

The SOCOPA store on the corner of Ave Habib Bourguiba and Ave de Carthage has the best selection of handicrafts in the country.

Another place worth checking out is Mains des Femmes, above the Banque de l'Habitat at 47 Ave Habib Bourguiba. It is run by Association Essalem, which promotes handicrafts produced by women in disadvantaged rural areas. It stocks some beautiful stuff – and the money goes to a good cause.

Getting There & Away

Air Domestic airline Tuninter has at least six flights a day to Houmt Souq as well as four flights a week to Sfax and three a week to Tozeur. Tickets can be bought from the Tunis Air office (☎ 330 100) on the corner of Ave Habib Bourguiba and Rue 18 Janvier 1952. Tuninter has a special reservations service (☎ 701 111).

Most of the international airline offices are along Ave Habib Bourguiba and Ave de Paris.

Bus Tunis has two bus stations, one for departures to the north (Gare Routière Nord de Bab Saadoun) and the other for buses heading south or to international destinations (Gare Routière Sud de Bab el Alleoua).

TUNISIA

The northern station is on the north-western side of Bab Saadoun. You can get there by métro léger line Nos 3 or 4 from Place de Barcelone or République stations. Get off at Bab Saadoun station and keep following the line away from Tunis for 250m and you'll see the louages in front of the station on the right.

The southern bus station is an easy 10-minute walk south of Place de Barcelone, east of the flyover at the end of Ave de la Gare. The nearest métro léger station is Bab Alloua, the first stop south of Place de Barcelone on line No 1.

Train The train station is close to the centre of town on Place de Barcelone. All scheduled departures and arrivals are displayed on an electronic board in the terminal building. There are services to Bizerte, El-Jem, Gabès, Ghardimaou, Kalaa Khasba, Mahdia, Met-laoui, Monastir, Nabeul, Sfax and Sousse.

Louage Louages to Cap Bon leave from opposite the southern bus station, and services to other southern destinations leave from the station at the eastern end of Rue Al Aid el-Jebbari, off Ave Moncef Bey. Louages to the north leave from outside the northern bus station.

Car All the major car-rental companies have offices both at the airport and in town (most of them are on Ave Habib Bourguiba).

Ferry Ferries from Europe arrive in Tunis at La Goulette, at the end of the causeway that crosses Lake Tunis. The cheapest way to reach the city is by TGM light rail. From the port, walk straight out to the kasbah, turn left and walk about 500m until you come to a railway crossing; La Goulette station is 100m to the right. A taxi from the port to Ave Habib Bourguiba shouldn't cost more than TD5.

The CTN office (☎ 322 802) at 122 Rue de Yougoslavie handles tickets for all the ferries.

Getting Around

To/From the Airport Tunis-Carthage airport is 8km north-east of the city. Yellow city bus No 35 runs to the airport from the Tunis Marine bus station every 20 minutes from 6 am to 9 pm and costs 620 mills. The bus leaves the airport from just outside the terminal building, to the right of the exit. A taxi to the city centre from the airport costs about TD5.

Bus The yellow city buses operate to all parts of the city, but apart from getting to the airport, the Bardo Museum or the northern bus station, you should have little cause to use them. Fares are cheap – 330 mills to the Bardo, for example. Most conductors are happy to help by telling you where to disembark.

There are three main bus terminals: Tunis Marine, which is next to the TGM station at the causeway end of Ave Habib Bourguiba; Place de Barcelone; and Jardin Thameur, 500m north of Ave Habib Bourguiba, off Ave Habib Thameur.

Light Rail The TGM light-rail system connects central Tunis with the beachside suburbs of La Goulette, Carthage, Sidi Bou Said and La Marsa. Trains run from 4 am until midnight.

Tram The efficient, modern métro léger has four routes. The most useful line is No 4, which has a new station right next to the Bardo Museum. Lines 3 and 4 stop at Bab Saadoun, close to the northern bus and louage stations, and Line 1 stops at Bab Alloua, close to the southern bus and louage stations.

Taxi Taxis are a cheap and easy way to get around. Flag fall is 280 mills and the meter then ticks over at about 380 mills per kilometre. Sample fares from the city centre include TD3.500 to the airport and TD4 to the Bardo Museum. Taxis can be booked by phone, which is very handy if you're going to the airport with a mountain of baggage; ask at your hotel.

Cap Bon Peninsula

HAMMAMET
☎ 02

The fact that a third of all Tunisia's foreign visitors wind up here doesn't make it a great place to stay. The building of more than 80 huge resort hotels has transformed this part of Tunisia into a monument to the package-tourism industry. Don't even consider coming here in summer unless you want to rub shoulders with thousands of other foreigners.

NABEUL
☎ 02

These days Nabeul has virtually merged with its boomtown southern neighbour, Hammamet, although it's not quite as over the top. Nabeul is the major service town of the Cap Bon region, and its economy is not entirely dependent on tourism.

The helpful tourist office (☎ 286 800) is at the beach end of Ave Taieb Mehiri.

Places to Stay & Eat

Nabeul does at least have some decent budget accommodation. There's an *auberge de jeunesse* (☎ 285 547) right on the beach at the end of Ave Mongi Slim. Dormitory accommodation and breakfast costs TD4.500, half-board is TD7 and full board is TD10. The *Hôtel Les Jasmins* (☎ 285 343), a couple of kilometres towards Hammamet, has a good, shady camping ground which is only a short walk from the beach.

The *Pension Les Roses* (☎ 285 570) is a friendly place offering spotless rooms for TD8 per person. It's right next to the main mosque in the middle of town. The *Restaurant du Bonheur*, next to the Pension Les Roses, specialises in couscous. Prices start at TD3 for couscous with lamb stew.

Getting There & Away

There are frequent buses from Nabeul to Tunis (one hour, TD2.700) as well as regular louages (TD3). The bus and louage stations are about 400m from the town centre on Ave Habib Thameur – the road to Hammamet. There's a train to Tunis every morning at the impossible time of 5.45 am. It leaves Tunis at a more respectable 2.20 pm. Louages to Kelibia and buses to other parts of Cap Bon leave from Ave Farhat Hached on the far side of the town centre.

KELIBIA
☎ 02

Kelibia, 58km north of Nabeul, remains relatively untouched by the ravages of mass

tourism. There are a few big hotels at Mansourah Beach, just north of town, but it's still fairly low-key. The nicest part of Kelibia is the old fishing port, 2km from the town centre. The port is overlooked by a 16th-century Spanish fort. It's worth clambering up for the commanding views along the coast.

Places to Stay

Camping (TD2.500 per person) is permitted in the grounds of the *maison des jeunes* hostel (☎ 296 105), for once conveniently located. It's between the fort and the port on the road to Mansourah Beach. The *Hôtel Florida* (☎ 296 248), on the beach near the fort, charges TD20.500 for singles with breakfast and TD34 for doubles. It turns out a good three-course dinner for TD5.500.

Getting There & Away

All forms of public transport leave from the main intersection in the middle of town. There are regular buses (one hour, TD2.650) and louages to Nabeul, and less frequent services to El-Haouaria.

AROUND KELIBIA

The small town of **El-Haouaria** sits under the mountainous northern tip of Cap Bon, 25km from Kelibia. The **Roman caves** near the cape were cut when stone was quarried for the building of Roman Carthage. The 3km walk from town takes about 45 minutes. There is also a good beach at **Ras el-Drek**, on the southern side of the cape.

Halfway between Kelibia and El-Haouaria there's a signpost to **Kerkouane**, the country's best preserved Punic site. It's about 1.5km from the road, closed Monday.

Northern Tunisia

BIZERTE
☎ 02

Bizerte, 66km north-west of Tunis, was the scene of a post-independence conflict between the French and Tunisian governments which resulted in the death of 1000 Tunisian soldiers in the early 1960s. The French fought to retain their naval base in the town after Tunisia was granted independence, and it was not until 1963 that they finally withdrew.

Orientation & Information

The centre of Bizerte is the ville nouvelle, built on the compact grid favoured by the French. It is flanked by a shipping canal connecting Lake Bizerte with the Mediterranean to the south-east and Ave Habib Bourguiba to the north-west. The old town – the kasbah and medina – is just north of Ave Habib Bourguiba.

The tourist office (☎ 432 897) is on the corner of Ave Taieb Mehiri and Quai Tarak ibn Ziad, close to the shipping canal. The post office is on Ave d'Algérie. The banks are mostly grouped around the main square; one bank is rostered to be open on Saturday morning (ask at the tourist office for details).

Things to See & Do

Beaches are the main attraction. The best beach is at **Remel Plage**, about 3km east of town off the road to Tunis. Buses to Ras Jebel can drop you off at the turn-off, 1km from the beach. There are more beaches along the Corniche, which begins about 2km north-west of the city centre and runs up to Cap d'Afrique – the northernmost point of the African continent.

Places to Stay & Eat

Campers can head for the *Centre de la Jeunesse* (☎ 02-440 819) at Remel Plage. The facilities are fairly basic, but there are good shady sites beneath the pine trees and the beach is only five minutes walk away. It charges TD2 per person for camping, and TD3 for dorm beds. The centre is signposted at the turn-off to Remel Plage. To get there, take a bus to Ghar el-Melh or Ras Jebel and get off at the Remel Plage turn-off. Phone first to check that it's open outside summer.

The budget hotels are all in and around the city centre. The best of the bunch is the *Hôtel Saadi* (☎ 422 528), opposite the soccer stadium on Rue Salah ben Ali. It has clean singles/doubles with shared bathroom for TD7.500/13.

The *Restaurant du Bonheur*, on Ave Thaalbi, specialises in traditional soups and stews and is worth seeking out. It also serves alcohol.

There is a cluster of upmarket hotels along the Corniche, the best of which is the *Hôtel Petite Mousse* (☎ 432 185), 2km west of the city centre. It charges TD40/64 in summer for comfortable singles/doubles with breakfast. The main reason to come here is the restaurant, which rates as one of the best in the country. Reckon on spending TD30 for two, plus wine.

Getting There & Away

Most public transport leaves from the south-eastern edge of town near the shipping canal. The bus station is at the end of Ave d'Algérie. There are buses to Tunis (1¼ hours, TD2.510) every 30 minutes. SRT Jendouba operates buses to Tabarka (2½ hours, TD5.300) and Aïn Draham (3¼ hours, TD6.030) at 6 am and 12.15 pm.

The train station is 300m from the bus station at the end of Rue de Russie. There are four trains a day to Tunis (1½ hours, TD2.550). Louages do the trip in 45 minutes for TD3, leaving from under the shipping bridge.

Getting Around

Local buses depart from the train station. Buses to the Corniche beaches can be caught at the corner of Ave Habib Bourguiba and Blvd Hassan en Nouri.

TABARKA
☎ 08

The densely forested Kroumirie Mountains provide a dramatic backdrop to the small coastal town of Tabarka, 170km west of Tunis, near the Algerian border.

Most of the tourist development is just east of town, leaving the town itself relatively unspoiled. The small bay to the north is watched over by an impressive Genoese fort. There's not much to do except hang out at the beach, but the atmosphere is right for it.

Information

There is a small tourist office on the main street, Ave Habib Bourguiba. If it's closed, contact the regional tourist office (☎ 643 496) on Rue de Bizerte, near the roundabout at the southern edge of town. There's a choice of banks along Ave Habib Bourguiba, and the post office is on Ave Hedi Chaker, diagonally opposite the Hôtel de France.

Places to Stay & Eat

The cheapest rooms in town are at the *Hôtel Corail* (☎ 643 082), right in the middle of town at the junction of Ave Habib Bourguiba and Rue de Tazarka. It has basic doubles (no singles) for TD10.

Most travellers head for the friendly *Pension Mamia* (☎ 671 058), on Rue de Tunis, which has spotless rooms built around a central courtyard. It charges TD13.500 per person, including breakfast. Hot showers cost an extra TD1.500. Next best is the *Hôtel la Plage* (☎ 670 039), 11 Ave du 7 Novembre, which has singles/doubles for TD21/26 or TD23/26 with private bathroom.

There are lots of small restaurants around the town centre serving delicious grilled fish for TD2.500. You'll see the small *charcoal grills* out in the street around the junction of Rue du Peuple and Rue Farhat Hached. The restaurant at the *Hôtel de France* does a good three-course meal for TD7.

Getting There & Away

The SNTRI bus office and louage station for Tunis are on Rue du Peuple. SNTRI has nine buses a day to Tunis (3¼ hours, TD7.120). The SRT Jendouba office, east of the town centre on Ave Habib Bourguiba, has regular buses to Jendouba via Aïn Draham. Louages to these towns leave from the eastern end of Ave Habib Bourguiba.

DRAHAM
☎ 08

Aïn Draham is Tunisia's hill station, nestled among the cork forest of the Kroumirie Mountains at an altitude of about 900m. The climate is markedly cooler than on the coast in summer, and snow is quite common in winter. Other than walking, there's not much to do. The 25km drive from Tabarka takes in some of the prettiest scenery in Tunisia.

Places to Stay & Eat

There is a *maison des jeunes* hostel at the top end of town on the road to Jendouba. The

only hotel in town is the pleasant *Hôtel Beauséjour* (☎ 655 0363; fax 655 527). Singles/doubles cost TD17.500/29 with breakfast. Full board is good value – two three-course meals for an extra TD7.500. The porcine trophies on the walls are evidence of the hotel's past popularity as a hunting lodge in colonial times.

Getting There & Away

SNTRI has three buses a day to Tunis (four hours, TD7.350) from the bus station at the foot of the hill. SRT Jendouba has regular buses to Tabarka and Jendouba, and an 8.15 am service to Le Kef.

BULLA REGIA
☎ 08

Bulla Regia, 160km west of Tunis near the town of Jendouba, is famous as the town where the Romans went underground to escape the summer heat in much the same way as the Berbers did around Matmata.

They built their villas with one level below ground, usually with a small courtyard open to the sky. They lived in some style, if the three underground homes on display are anything to go by. They are named after the mosaics that were found inside them: the Palace of Fishing; the House of Amphitrite (in Greek mythology, a sea goddess and wife of Poseidon); and the Palace of the Hunt. A few mosaics have been left *in situ*, but the best examples are now in the Bardo Museum in Tunis. The site is open from 8 am to 7 pm in summer, and 8.30 am to 5.30 pm in winter. Admission is TD2.100.

Places to Stay

There is nowhere to stay near the site. The closest accommodation is in the nearby town of Jendouba, a dull administrative centre that most people avoid. If you get stuck, the only budget option is the grotty *Pension Saha en Noum*, west of the main square on Blvd Khemais el-Hajiri, with beds for TD3 per person. The alternative is the *Hôtel Simitthu* (☎ 08-634 043; fax 632 595), a clean, modern two-star hotel on the western edge of town charging TD31/46 for singles/doubles with breakfast.

Getting There & Away

The turn-off to Bulla Regia is clearly sign-posted 6km from Jendouba on the road to Aïn Draham. If you're coming by bus or louage from Aïn Draham, you can get off at the junction and walk the last 3km. Much of the walk is along an avenue of eucalypts. Coming from Jendouba, the simplest solution is to catch a cab for about TD4. You can arrange to be picked up later or take your chances; there's a fair amount of passing traffic.

Jendouba is a regional transport hub with a good range of options. Train is the most comfortable way to get to Tunis (2½ hours, TD5.050). The last of five daily services leaves at 5 pm. There are also frequent buses and louages to Tunis, as well as to Le Kef, Aïn Draham and Tabarka.

DOUGGA

☎ 08

Dougga is an excellent Roman ruin in a commanding position on the edge of the Tebersouk Mountains, 110km south-west of Tunis. The site is home to the country's most photographed Roman monument, the imposing **Capitol of Dougga**. This huge monument is dedicated to the gods Jupiter, Juno and Minerva. Fragments of the enormous statue of Jupiter are now housed in the Bardo Museum in Tunis, along with the best mosaics from the site. Next to the capitol is the **Square of the Winds**. In the centre is an enormous circular inscription listing the names of the 12 winds. On the southern edge of the site is **Trifolium House**, once the town's brothel. Dougga's well-preserved **theatre** makes a spectacular setting for performances of classical drama during the Dougga Festival in July and August. The site is open from 8 am to 7 pm in summer, and from 8.30 am to 5.30 pm in winter. Admission is TD2.100.

Places to Stay

Tebersouk is the closest town to the site, and the only hotel is the *Hôtel Thugga* (☎ 465 713). The place caters almost exclusively to tour groups and charges TD27/38 for singles/doubles with breakfast. It's easy to visit the site on a day trip from Tunis or Le Kef.

Getting There & Away

SNTRI's frequent buses between Tunis and Le Kef stop at Tebersouk, ensuring a steady flow of departures in both directions until about 6 pm. At the bus stop you'll find locals asking about TD5 per person to take you the remaining 7km to the site and pick you up at a time of your choice. You can also walk to the site from Nouvelle Dougga, a village on the Tunis-Le Kef road just west of Tebersouk. It's a solid 3km uphill hike to the site.

LE KEF

☎ 08

The ancient fortress city of Le Kef, 170km south-west of Tunis, dominates the region from its spectacular setting on the slopes of Jebel Dyr. At an altitude of more than 1000m, the temperatures here are a welcome few degrees cooler than on the surrounding wheat-growing plains. The city centre, Place de l'Independance, is a 10-minute walk uphill from the bus and louage station.

Things to See

The city's crowning glory is its mighty **kasbah**, which overlooks the city from a spur running off Jebel Dyr. The structure that stands today is the latest of a string of fortresses that have occupied the site since the 5th century BC. After years of neglect, it was in the middle of a major face-lift at the time of writing.

The regional **museum** occupies a beautifully restored old *zaouia* (shrine) on the edge of the medina on Place ben Aissa – a short walk from the kasbah along Rue de la Kasbah. It has put together a good display on the lifestyle of the area's nomads.

Places to Stay & Eat

The *Hôtel Medina* (☎ 220 214), 18 Rue Farhat Hached, is a safe choice with clean doubles for TD8, but no singles. There are good views from the rooms at the back, which are also much quieter. Hot showers are 500 mills. The *Hôtel de la Source* (☎ 224 397), on Rue de la Source, improves once you make it past the mustard-yellow lobby. It has basic singles/doubles for TD8/10.

The best rooms in town are at the *Résidence Venus* (☎ 224 695), nestled beneath he walls of the kasbah on Rue Mouldi Khamessi. It's a small, family-run pension with comfortable rooms for TD20/32, including breakfast. All rooms come with private bathroom and central heating – important in winter.

The *Restaurant el-Andalous*, diagonally opposite the post office on Rue Hedi Chaker, serves tasty local food. A bowl of spicy chorba (700 mills) is perfect on a cold day.

Getting There & Away

SNTRI has regular buses to Tunis (2½ hours, TD6.850) via Tebersouk. Louages do the journey in two hours for TD7. There are local buses to Jendouba and Kasserine.

Central Tunisia

SOUSSE
☎ 03

Sousse, 142km south of Tunis, is the country's third-largest city and a major port. The huge medina and impressive fortifications are the main pointers to the city's long history as a commercial centre. It began life as the Phoenician town of Hadrumète, and later became Roman Hadrumetum, capital of the province of Byzacée. The Vandals renamed it Hunericopolis in honour of their chief's son.

The latest invaders are package tourists, who rule from their custom-built tourist village of Port el-Kantaoui, 14km to the north. The coastline here is one long line of giant hotel complexes.

Orientation & Information

Everything of importance in Sousse happens around the enormous Place Farhat Hached, the town's main square. The medina is on its south-western corner, the port lies to the south-east and Ave Habib Bourguiba runs north to the beaches. The Tunis-Sfax railway line runs right through the centre of the square.

The efficient tourist office (☎ 225 157) is on the corner of Place Farhat Hached and Ave Habib Bourguiba. There's also a syndicat d'initiative, dispensing smiles from a small, white-domed building across the square, near the medina. The post office and main train station are close by.

Things to See

The main monuments of the medina are the **ribat**, a sort of fortified monastery, and the **great mosque**. Both are in the north-eastern part of the medina, close to Place Farhat Hached, and were built in the 9th century.

The ribat was primarily a fort, but the men could study the Koran in the small cells surrounding the courtyard when they weren't fighting. The *nadour* (watchtower) offers excellent views over the medina and the courtyard of the great mosque below. It's open every day from 8 am to 5.30 pm. Admission is TD2.100.

The great mosque is open from 9 am to 2 pm every day.

The **kasbah museum**, at the south-western corner of the medina, houses a fine collection of mosaics from the area. It's open Tuesday to Sunday from 8 am to 5.30 pm; admission is TD2.100. Note that there is no access to the kasbah from inside the medina.

Places to Stay

The best budget place in town is the spotless *Hôtel de Paris* (☎ 220 564; fax 219 038), just inside the medina's north wall at 15 Rue du Rempart Nord. It has small singles for TD8, and larger singles/doubles for TD10/16. There are free hot showers and laundry facilities.

Other budget possibilities include the *Hôtel Gabès* (☎ 226 977), 12 Rue de Paris, and *the Hôtel Ezzouhour* (☎ 228 729), 48 Rue de Paris. Both have singles/doubles for TD6/12.

A step up from these is the *Hôtel Hadrumete* (☎ 226 291; fax 226 863), overlooking the port on Place Ibn el-Fourat. It has singles/doubles with bathroom and breakfast for TD20/31.

The *Hôtel Medina* (☎ 225 157; fax 224 262), right next to the great mosque, has good doubles with bathroom and breakfast for TD28, but no singles in the high season.

If you want to go more upmarket, the tourist office can supply information about the dozens of big hotels that line the beaches to the north of the city centre.

Places to Eat

The medina is the place to look for cheap local food. The *Restaurant Populaire*, at the

TUNISIA

SOUSSE

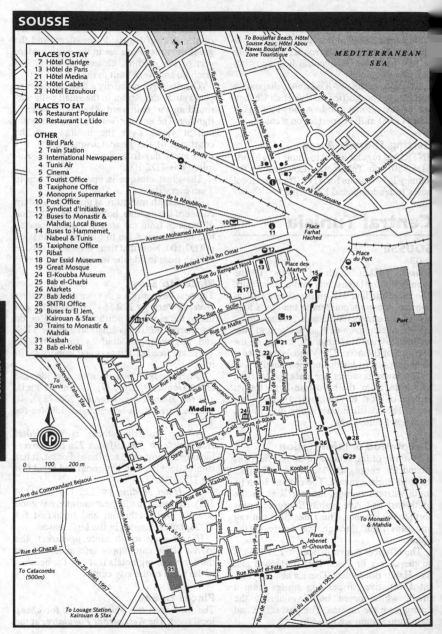

PLACES TO STAY
7 Hôtel Claridge
13 Hôtel de Paris
21 Hôtel Medina
22 Hôtel Gabès
23 Hôtel Ezzouhour

PLACES TO EAT
16 Restaurant Populaire
20 Restaurant Le Lido

OTHER
1 Bird Park
2 Train Station
3 International Newspapers
4 Tunis Air
5 Cinema
6 Tourist Office
8 Taxiphone Office
9 Monoprix Supermarket
10 Post Office
11 Syndicat d'Initiative
12 Buses to Monastir &
   Mahdia; Local Buses
14 Buses to Hammemet,
   Nabeul & Tunis
15 Taxiphone Office
17 Ribat
18 Dar Essid Museum
19 Great Mosque
24 El-Koubba Museum
25 Bab el-Gharbi
26 Markets
27 Bab Jedid
28 SNTRI Office
29 Buses to El Jem,
   Kairouan & Sfax
30 Trains to Monastir &
   Mahdia
31 Kasbah
32 Bab el-Kebli

MEDITERRANEAN SEA

To Boujaffar Beach, Hôtel
Sousse Azur, Hôtel Abou
Nawas Boujaffar &
Zone Touristique

Rue de Carthage
Rue d'Alger
Rue Remada
Avenue Habib Bourguiba
Rue Sadi Carnot
Rue du Caire
Rue de l'Independance
Rue Avicenne

Ave Hasouna Ayachi

Avenue de la République

Avenue Mohamed Maarouf

Place Farhat Hached

Boulevard Yahia Ibn Omar

Rue du Rempart Nord

Place des Martyrs

Place du Port

Rue de Sicilie

Rue de Malte

Rue Najjar

Rue d'Angleterre

Rue Aghlaba

Rue Sidi Saïd

Rue Sidi Bouraoui

Medina

Rue Souq el-Caïd

Souq el-Ribaa

Rue de la Kasbah

Rue Kobgar

Rue el-Maar

Boulevard Tahar Star

To Tunis

Avenue Maréchal Tito

Avenue Mohamed Ali

Avenue Mohammed V

Port

To Monastir
& Mahdia

Ave du Commandant Bejaoui

Rue el-Ghazali

Ave 25 Juillet 1957

To Catacombs
(500m)

Rue Ibn Rachid

Rue Sidi Baazizi

Place Jebenet
el-Ghourba

Rue el-Hajra

Rue Khalef el-Fata

Ave du 18 Janvier 1952

Rue de Esk ka

To Louage Station,
Kairouan & Sfax

0   100   200 m

entrance to the medina, is always packed. You pay for your meal before you sit down and hand the receipt to the waiter. The extensive menu includes an enormous serving of couscous with chicken for just TD2.100.

There's keen competition for the tourist trade from the countless restaurants that line Ave Habib Bourguiba and Place Farhat Hached. You can get a good meal for TD10, plus wine at most places. *Le Lido*, opposite the port on Ave Mohamed V, is well known for its seafood.

Getting There & Away

Train is the way to travel. There are eight trains a day to Tunis (2¼ hours, TD4.850), and four to Sfax (two hours, TD4.400) via El-Jem. One train a day continues south to Gabès. Regular trains for Monastir and Mahdia leave from Bab Jedid station at the southern end of Ave Mohamed V. Buses leave from a variety of locations. Northbound SNTRI buses leave from the port side of Place Farhat Hached. Southbound SNTRI buses and regional buses to Kairouan (1½ hours, TD2.550) are to be found farther south on Ave Mohamed Ali, near the medina's Bab Jedid gate.

Buses to Monastir and Mahdia leave from Place Sidi Yahia, on the northern edge of the medina.

Catching a louage from Sousse has become a hassle since the louages were moved to a new station at the Souq el-Ahad, 2km south-west of the city centre.

KAIROUAN
☎ 07

The old, walled city of Kairouan is historically the most important town in Tunisia. To Muslims, it ranks behind only Mecca, Medina and Jerusalem. The city, situated 150km south of Tunis, is also famous for its carpets, its carpet salesmen and its orchards.

Orientation & Information

The medina is the focal point of Kairouan. Its busy main street, Ave Ali Belhouane, runs from Bab Tunis on the western side to Bab ech Chouhada in the south. It's packed with carpet shops – and with bogus guides trying to get you into them.

The tourist office (☎ 231 897) is inconveniently on the northern edge of town, next to the Aghlabid Basins. A collective ticket (TD4.200) covering the main sites can be bought here, as well as at the great mosque and at the Zaouia of Sidi Sahab.

Things to See

The city's main monument, the outwardly plain **great mosque**, is in the north-eastern corner of the medina. Much of the mosque dates from the 9th century, although the lowest level of the minaret is thought to have been built early in the 8th century, making it the oldest standing minaret in the world. The mosque is open from 8 am to 2.30 pm every day except Friday, when it closes at noon.

Other places of interest include the **Zaouia of Sidi Sahab**, also known as the Mosque of Barber because Sidi Sahab always carried with him three hairs from the Prophet's beard; the **Mosque of the Three Doors**, famous for the rare Arab inscriptions carved on its façade; the **Zaouia of Sidi Abid el-Ghariani**; and the tourist trap known as **Bir Barouta**, which features a blindfolded camel drawing water from a well whose waters are said to be connected to Mecca.

Places to Stay & Eat

Most travellers head for the *Hôtel Sabra* (☎ 230 263), opposite the Bab ech Chouhada on the southern side of the medina. The staff are used to dealing with budget travellers and the rooms are good value at TD10/16 for singles/doubles with breakfast and free hot showers.

An interesting alternative is the friendly *Hôtel Les Aghlabites* (☎ 220 880), a converted funduq off Place de Tunis to the west of the medina. The rooms here open out onto a splendid tiled courtyard. It charges TD6/12 for clean singles/doubles with hot showers.

The two-star *Tunisia Hôtel* (☎ 231 855) is a good older-style hotel about 400m south of the medina on Ave de la République. It has large singles/doubles with bathroom for TD18/30, including breakfast.

The *Restaurant de la Jeunesse*, on Ave Ali Belhouane, has excellent couscous, while the friendly *Restaurant Sabra*, next to the Tunisia Hôtel, has a choice of set menus priced from TD6. Stalls everywhere sell

TUNISIA

KAIROUAN

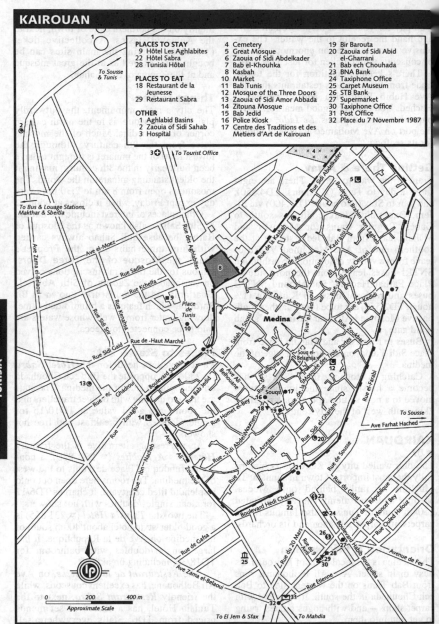

PLACES TO STAY
9 Hôtel Les Aghlabites
22 Hôtel Sabra
28 Tunisia Hôtel

PLACES TO EAT
18 Restaurant de la Jeunesse
29 Restaurant Sabra

OTHER
1 Aghlabid Basins
2 Zaouia of Sidi Sahab
3 Hospital

4 Cemetery
5 Great Mosque
6 Zaouia of Sidi Abdelkader
7 Bab el-Khouhka
8 Kasbah
10 Market
11 Bab Tunis
12 Mosque of the Three Doors
13 Zaouia of Sidi Amor Abbada
14 Zitouna Mosque
15 Bab Jedid
16 Police Kiosk
17 Centre des Traditions et des Metiers d'Art de Kairouan

19 Bir Barouta
20 Zaouia of Sidi Abid el-Gharrani
21 Bab ech Chouhada
23 BNA Bank
24 Taxiphone Office
25 Carpet Museum
26 STB Bank
27 Supermarket
30 Taxiphone Office
31 Post Office
32 Place du 7 Novembre 1987

To Sousse & Tunis

To Tourist Office

To Bus & Louage Stations, Makthar & Sbeitla

Ave el-Moez

Ave Zama el-Belaoui

Rue des Aghlabites

Rue Sadia

Rue Kchelfa

Rue Sidi Sfir

Rue Kenaha

Place de Tunis

Rue de -Haut Marché

Rue Sidi Gaïd

Boulevard Sadika

Rue Bab Jedid

Rue- el- Ghadroui

Rue - Zouabi

Rue Sidi Abdelkader

Boulevard Brahim ben Lagheb

Rue de la Kasbah

Rue- el- Kadi-aoui

Rue de Jerba

Rue el- Kadi aoui

Rue Sidi Bou Omrani

Rue Dar - el- Bey

Rue el-Kadraoui

Rue el- Kedil

Rue Zoukbar

Rue Salah J Soussi

Medina

Souq el-Belaghja

Rue des ferailleurs

Mosque des Trois Portes

Rue el-Farabi

Ave Ali Behouaine

Rue des Souqs

Rue de la Mosquée des Trois Portes

Rue Homet el-Bey

Rue Sidi el-Ghuztani

Rue de Sousse

To Sousse

Ave Farhat Hached

Rue- Ibn- Nicheb

Ave Ali Zouaoui

Rue Sidi Abdelwazen

Rue des Arcaux

Rue de la République

Rue du Gabal

Rue Moncef Bey

Rue Ouled Haltouz

Boulevard Hedi Chaker

Rue Gafsa

Rue de Gafsa

Ave Zama el-Belaoui

Rue du 20 Mars

Rue du 9 Avril

Boulevard Habib Bourguiba

Ave de la République

Avenue de Fes

Rue Etienne

To El Jem & Sfax

To Mahdia

0   200   400 m
Approximate Scale

nakhroud, a local speciality comprising
money-soaked pastry stuffed with dates.

Getting There & Away
The bus and louage stations are next to each
other about 2km north-west of the medina on
the road to Sbeitla, signposted off Ave Zama
el-Belaoui near the Zaouia of Sidi Sahab.

MONASTIR
Monastir, 24km south-east of Sousse, is
another town that has surrendered lock, stock
and barrel to the tourist trade. There's a nice
sheltered **beach** – packed in summer – and
scenes from Monty Python's *The Life of
Brian* were shot at the small, heavily restored
ribat, but both can easily be visited on a day
trip from Sousse.

MAHDIA
☎ 03
Mahdia, 60km south of Sousse, is one of the
few towns on this section of coast that has
managed to escape being turned into a total
tourist trap. Founded by the Fatimids in 916,
it's a beautifully relaxed place with an unspoiled old medina stretched out along a
narrow peninsula.

There is a small tourist office (☎ 681 098)
just inside the medina.

Things to See
The main gate to the old medina, **Skifa el-
Kahla**, is all that remains of the 10m-thick
wall which once protected the city. The un-
adorned **great mosque** is a 20th-century
replica of the mosque built by the Mahdi in
the 10th century.

Places to Stay & Eat
The *Hôtel el-Jazira* (☎ 681 629) is the only
medina hotel. It has a great location, with
rooms overlooking the sea for TD10/16.
Don't miss a meal at the *Restaurant el-Moez*,
on the edge of the medina near the market.

Getting There & Away
The bus, louage and train stations are about
500m from the town centre, past the fishing
port. There are eight trains a day to Sousse
(1½ hours, TD2).

EL-JEM
This small town in the middle of Tunisia's
olive-growing region is dominated by a well-
preserved **Roman amphitheatre** – arguably
the most impressive Roman monument in
North Africa.

The amphitheatre suffered badly in the
17th century when one side was blown up to
flush out rebels hiding inside. There is a good
museum housing mosaics and local artefacts;
it's about 500m south of the train station on
the road to Sfax. Both amphitheatre and
museum are open daily from 7 am to 7 pm in
summer and from 8 am to 5.30 pm in winter.
Admission to both is covered by a joint ticket
costing TD4.100.

Places to Stay
The *Hôtel Julius* (☎ 690 044), right next to
the train station, is the only hotel and bar in
town. It has single/double rooms for
TD21.500/30.

Getting There & Away
All forms of transport leave from around the
train station, so just grab the first service that
comes by – bus, louage or train.

SFAX
☎ 04
The unglamorous, eastern coastal town of
Sfax is Tunisia's second-largest city. It has
two big things going for it – its unspoiled old
medina and the fact that there's hardly a
package tourist in sight.

Orientation & Information
Sfax is a big, sprawling city. The only parts
of interest to the visitor are the medina and
the ville nouvelle, built on reclaimed land
between the medina and the port.

The tourist office (☎ 211 040) is out by the
port on Ave Mohammed Hedi Khefecha. The
post office occupies most of a block at the
north-eastern end of Ave Habib Bourguiba,
near the train station. There are plenty of
banks, mostly along Ave Habib Bourguiba
and Ave Hedi Chaker.

Things to See & Do
It's easy to spend hours wandering around the
medina's maze of narrow streets. This is still

TUNISIA

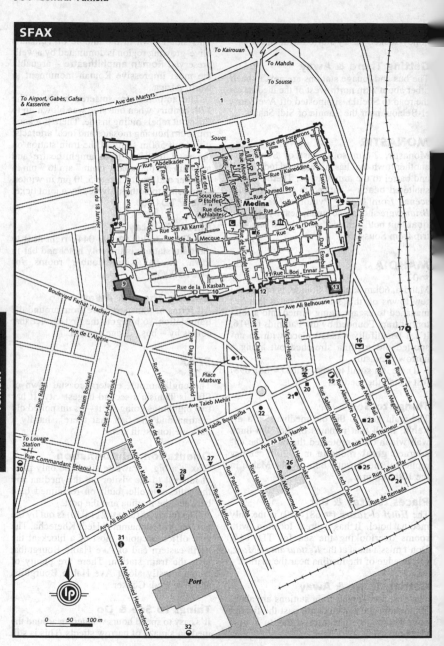

SFAX

To Kairouan

To Mahdia

To Sousse

To Airport, Gabès, Gafsa & Kasserine

Ave des Martyrs

1

Souqs

3 Rue des Forgerons

2

Rue Abdelkader

Rue Sidi Belhassen

Rue des Notaires

Rue Cheikh Tijani

Rue ben Kaddour

Rue el-Kasrar

Ave du 18 Janvier

8

Rue Mongi Slim

Rue des Teinturiers

Rue el-Caïd

Rue Kaireddine

Ahmed Bey

Rue Essouar

Souq des Étoffes

Rue des Aghlabites

Medina

Rue

Sidi el-Khelil

4

7

5

Rue de la Driba

6

Rue Sidi Ali Karra

Rue de la Mecque

Rue de la Grande Mosquée

Rue Dag la Esseba

Ave de l'Armée

11 Rue Borj Ennar

13

Rue de la Kasbah

10

12

Ave Ali Belhouane

9

Boulevard Farhat Hached

Ave de L'Algérie

Ave Hedi Chaker

Rue Victor Hugo

17

16

Rue Dag Hammarskjold

14

Place Marburg

15

18 Rue de Tazarka

Rue Cheikh Magdich

Rue Imam Boukhari

Rue el-Arbi Zarrouk

Rue Hafrouz

Ave Taieb Mehiri

19 Rue Alexandre Dumas

Rue Salem Harrablah

Rue Mongi Bali

20

21

Rue Rabat

22

Ave Habib Bourguiba

23

Rue Habib Thameur

To Louage Station

Rue Commandant Bejaoui

Rue Mohsen Kallel

Rue de Kairouan

27

Rue Patrice Lumumba

Rue Habib Maazoun

Ave Ali Bach Hamba

Ave Hedi Chaker

Ave Mohammed Ali

26

Rue Abdulacen ech Chabbi

25

Rue Tahar Sfar

24

Rue de Remada

30

28

29

31

Ave Ali Bach Hamba

Rue de Hafrouz

Port

32

Ave Mohammed Hedi Khefacha

0   50   100 m

lp

SFAX

PLACES TO STAY		3	Bab Jebli	18	SNTRI Buses
6	Hôtel Medina	4	Bab el Chergui	19	French Embassy
20	Hôtel Sfax Centre	5	Dar Jellouli Museum of	21	Monoprix Supermarket
23	Hôtels Alexander &		Popular Traditions	22	Town Hall
	De la Paix	7	Great Mosque	24	Libyan Consulate
		8	Bab el Gharbi	25	ONAT
PLACES TO EAT		9	Kasbah	26	Park
10	Café Diwan	12	Bab Diwan	28	Bar
11	Restaurant Tunisien	13	Borj Ennar	29	Market
27	Restaurant l'Opéra	14	International	30	Soretras Bus Station
			Newspapers	31	Tourist Office
OTHER		15	Taxiphone Office	32	Ferries to Kerkennah
1	Market	16	Post Office		Islands
2	Bab Jedid	17	Train Station		

a working medina, without the glitz and wall-to-wall tourist shops of the medinas in Tunis and Sousse. The **Souq des Etoffes**, just north of the 9th century **great mosque**, was used as the location for the market scenes in the film *The English Patient*.

It's also worth checking out the **Dar Jellouli Museum of Popular Traditions**, signposted off Rue de la Driba, a small street east off Rue Mongi Slim. It's open Tuesday to Saturday from 9.30 am to 4.30 pm.

No visit to the medina would be complete without a stop for coffee at the **Café Diwan**, built into the medina wall west of the Bab Diwan.

Places to Stay

The cheap hotels are in the medina. Most charge about TD3.500 per person. The *Hôtel Medina* (☎ 220 354), on Rue Mongi Slim, is the best of them with clean rooms for TD4 per person.

There are a couple of good mid-range places on Rue Alexandre Dumas in the ville nouvelle. The *Hôtel Alexander* (☎ 221 911) has large, comfortable rooms with bath for TD15/20, including breakfast. The *Hôtel de la Paix* (☎ 296 437), a few doors up from the Alexander, has rooms for TD10/12.

Places to Eat

The *Restaurant Tunisien*, inside the medina east of Bab Diwan, has good cheap local food. Couscous with vegetables costs TD1.200, and couscous with lamb costs TD2.

The *Restaurant l'Opéra*, next to the port

on Rue de Haffouz, does a good three-course meal for TD3.300. It also has a range of pizzas from TD3.300 and fast food such as humburgers (sic) for TD1.500.

Getting There & Away

Sfax has direct flights to Tunis (45 minutes, TD42.500 one way) from Monday to Thursday. Tickets can be bought from the Tuninter office at the Hôtel Sfax Centre on Ave Habib Bourguiba.

The city is well served by the national bus line, SNTRI, which is conveniently central on Rue de Tazarka, opposite the train station. There are regular buses to Tunis (four hours, TD10.260) via Sousse (two hours, TD5.560); three a day to Jerba (four hours, TD9.300) via Gabès; and two a day to Tataouine (four hours, TD10.350). Regional bus services are operated by local company Soretras and leave from the bus station at the junction of Rue Rabat and Rue Commandant Bejaoui. The louage station is 100m further west along Rue Commandant Bejaoui.

There's also a daily train to Gabès at 11.10 am, and four trains a day to Tunis via El-Jem and Sousse.

The ferry port for the Kerkennah Islands is a 10-minute walk south-west of the city centre.

KERKENNAH ISLANDS

The Kerkennah Islands are a couple of depressing, flat, featureless islands 21km from Sfax. The islands are linked by a causeway built in Roman times. Long used as a place of

TUNISIA

exile, they have a general air of abandonment. Even the palm trees appear to be turning up their toes. There is a cluster of low-budget resort hotels at Sidi Fredj.

There are between four and eight ferries a day to Sfax (1½ hours, 570 mills) depending on the season. All ferries are met by buses, at least one of which goes via Sidi Fredj. Bicycles are the best way of getting around; they can be rented at the resorts.

Southern Tunisia

TOZEUR
☎ 06

Tozeur is a thriving town on the edge of the Chott el-Jerid, the largest of Tunisia's salt lakes. The place has a relaxed atmosphere and is a popular destination for travellers.

The tourist office on Ave Abdulkacem Chebbi (☎ 454 088) and the syndicat d'initiative at Place ibn Châabat (☎ 462 034) have

nothing to offer that you couldn't discover by asking the first person you met on the street. There are several banks on Ave Habib Bourguiba, which is also lined with souvenir shops selling the area's famous rugs. Bargain hard if you're buying.

Things to See
The impressive **Museum Dar Charait** is 1km west of the tourist office at the western end of Ave Abdulkacem Chebbi. It's open every day from 8 am until midnight; admission is TD3.

The enormous **palmeraie** is best explored by bicycle, which can be hired from Location de Velos, opposite the Hôtel La Palmeraie near the Museum Dar Charait.

The **Ouled el-Hadef**, the town's labyrinthine old quarter, is well worth exploring for its striking architecture and brickwork; enter by the road past the Hôtel Splendid.

Ballooning
Aeation (☎ 452 361), opposite the Hôtel

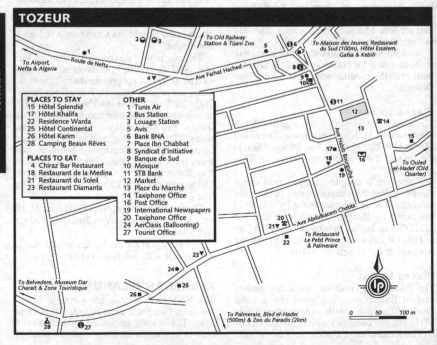

TOZEUR

To Old Railway Station & Tijani Zoo

To Maison des Jeunes, Restaurant du Sud (100m), Hôtel Essalem, Gafsa & Kebili

To Airport, Nefta & Algeria
Route de Nefta

Ave Farhat Hached

Ave Habib Bourguiba

To Ouled el-Hadef (Old Quarter)

Ave Abdulkacem Chebbi

To Restaurant Le Petit Prince & Palmeraie

To Belvedere, Museum Dar Charait & Zone Touristique

To Palmeraie, Bled el-Hader (500m) & Zoo du Paradis (2km)

0   50   100 m

PLACES TO STAY	OTHER
15 Hôtel Splendid	1 Tunis Air
17 Hôtel Khalifa	2 Bus Station
22 Residence Warda	3 Louage Station
25 Hôtel Continental	5 Avis
26 Hôtel Karim	6 Bank BNA
28 Camping Beaux Rêves	7 Place Ibn Chabbat
	8 Syndicat d'Initiative
	9 Banque de Sud
PLACES TO EAT	10 Mosque
4 Chiraz Bar Restaurant	11 STB Bank
18 Restaurant de la Medina	12 Market
21 Restaurant du Soleil	13 Place du Marché
23 Restaurant Diamanta	14 Taxiphone Office
	16 Post Office
	19 International Newspapers
	20 Taxiphone Office
	24 AerOasis (Ballooning)
	27 Tourist Office

Continental on Ave Abdulkacem Chebbi, is a small French-run company that organises balloon rides at a range of locations around Tozeur. Flights are timed to catch either the sunrise or sunset and cost TD80 for an hour. They will travel as far as Douz in search of the right conditions.

Places to Stay

Near the tourist office on Ave Abdulkacem Chebbi, *Camping Beaux Rêves* (☎ 453 331) is a good, shady site that backs onto the palmeraie. It charges TD4 per person, either in your own tent or one of the communal nomad-style tents. Hot showers are 900 mills.

The *Hôtel Khalifa* (☎ 454 858), opposite Place du Marché in the centre of town, has basic rooms for TD5 per person and singles/doubles with showers for TD8/13.500.

Most travellers head for the excellent *Residence Warda* (☎ 452 597) on Ave Abdulkacem Chebbi. It has rooms with shared bathroom for TD11/17, and with private bathroom for TD12/19. Prices include breakfast. If it's full, try the *Hôtel Karim* (☎ 454 574) farther along Ave Abdulkacem Chebbi at No 69, with almost identical prices.

Places to Eat

The *Restaurant du Soleil*, opposite Residence Warda, is a popular place that does a delicious thick, spicy chorba for TD1 and couscous with lamb for TD2.500. It is one of the few places in the country to acknowledge the existence of vegetarians.

Other good places are the *Restaurant de la Medina*, just off Ave Habib Bourguiba, and the *Restaurant Diamanta*, 200m west of the Restaurant du Soleil.

Getting There & Away

Tozeur has three flights a week to Tunis (70 minutes, TD48.500 one way), and three a week to Jerba (50 minutes, TD27 one way). The airport is 4km from town off the road to Nefta. Tunis Air (☎ 450 038) has an office in town on Route de Nefta, about 200m beyond the bus and louage stations.

SNTRI has five buses a day to Tunis (eight hours, TD16.550). The buses travelling inland via Gafsa and Kairouan are quicker than those going via Gabès and the coast. It also has one bus a day to Douz (2½ hours,

TD4.300). There are local buses to Nefta (30 minutes, 950 mills). The louage station is opposite the bus station.

NEFTA
☎ 06

Nefta is a sleepy oasis town close to the Algerian border. The palmeraie is worth exploring, and there are some beautiful examples of traditional brickwork in the old quarter. If you want to stay the night, check out the *Hôtel Marhala* (☎ 430 027). It occupies a converted brickworks and charges TD11/18 for singles/doubles with breakfast. To get there, follow the signs to the Zone Touristique and you'll find the Marhala on the way. It's worth considering half-board or full board at TD2.500 per meal because the town isn't exactly brimming with good restaurants.

The bus station is on the main road into town. SNTRI has two buses a day to Tunis, and there are regular local buses and louages to Tozeur.

DOUZ
☎ 05

Right on the fringe of the Grand Erg Oriental (Great Eastern Desert), Douz promotes itself as the 'gateway to the Sahara'. The town centre is tiny, and everything of importance is within five minutes walk. You can change money at the bank on the Kebili road, and there's a post office on Ave des Martyrs.

Things to See & Do

Most people come to Douz to organise **camel trekking**. Trekking touts can now be found as far afield as the bus station in Gabès, and the offers are flying thick and fast by the time you reach Douz. Most of the time they are touting for a couple of big operators at Zaafrane – which is the place to go to get the best deals. There are regular camionnettes and louages (both 500 mills) to Zaafrane from opposite the louage station in Douz. In Zaafrane you will be dropped at a huge vacant lot dotted with hundreds of camels. Among the camels are two small palm-thatch huts, bases for the rival organisations. Both offer trekking for as long as you care to nominate – from an hour (TD3.500) upwards. It's a good idea to sit on a camel for an hour before signing up for an adventure like an eight-day, oasis-hopping trek to Ksar Ghilane. You'll pay about TD30 a day for an experience like this, including all meals. Meals are cooked on a campfire, and you'll sleep in basic nomad-style tents.

Douz is well known for its colourful Thursday market.

Places to Stay

There's a good choice of budget accommodation, starting with the *Desert Club* camping ground (☎ 470 575) in the palmeraie at the southern end of Ave 7 Novembre.

The friendly *Hôtel 20 Mars* (☎ 470 269), in the centre of town, has rooms around a small courtyard. Basic rooms with shared bathroom are TD5 per person and singles/doubles with private bathroom are TD9/14.

Another good choice is the nearby *Hôtel Essaada* (☎ 470 824). It has basic rooms downstairs for TD3 per person, and better rooms upstairs for TD5 per person.

Getting There & Away

Buses leave from around the clock tower in the middle of town. SNTRI has two buses a day to Tunis (nine hours, TD19.640). There's a local bus to Tozeur (2½ hours, TD4.300) and Gabès (three hours, TD5.110) at 6.45 am.

There are frequent louages to Kebili and occasional services to Gabès – but none to Tozeur.

GABÈS
☎ 05

There is little reason to stay in this industrial city on the Gulf of Gabès. Its only attraction is a mediocre palmeraie which tour groups get trotted through in *calèches* (horse carts). If you get stuck overnight, the *Hôtel Ben Nejima* (☎ 271 591) is a spotless place charging TD7 per person. It's close to the bus station at the junction of Ave Farhat Hached and Rue Haj Djilani Lahbib.

The bus and louage stations are at the western end of Ave Farhat Hached. Three bus companies operate from here and can take you just about anywhere in Tunisia. SNTRI has regular departures to Tunis for TD14.700. There are two trains a day to Tunis.

MATMATA
☎ 05

It's easy to work out why the makers of *Star Wars* picked Matmata, 45km south-west o Gabès, as the home planet of Luke Skywalker. Set amid a bizarre lunar landscape, the Berbers of Matmata went underground centuries ago to escape the summer heat.

Although conventional modern buildings are now in the majority, the town still boasts dozens of the troglodyte pit homes that are its main attraction. Each of the many mounds represents a home. They are all built along the same lines: a large central courtyard, usually circular, is dug out of the soft sandstone, and the rooms are then tunnelled off the perimeter.

Fascinating though Matmata might be, it's hard not to feel sorry for the long-suffering residents. The first tour buses roll up at 9 am every day, and they just keep on coming – day after day. The residents are sick of being stared at like goldfish. Many holes are surrounded by barbed wire to keep the tourists out.

Places to Stay

Three troglodyte homes have been transformed into interesting budget hotels. The *Sidi Driss* (☎ 230 005), setting for the bar scene in *Star Wars*, is the best of them – and the cheapest at TD7.200 per person for B&B.

MEDENINE
☎ 05

Medenine, 75km south-east of Gabès, is the main town of the ksour (plural of *ksar*, a fortified Berber granary) area of the country's south. Medenine itself has a small ksar, which is something of a tourist trap, but the best examples are farther south, near Tataouine.

There's no reason to stay in Medenine, but the *Hôtel Essaada* (☎ 640 300) on Ave Habib Bourguiba is OK if you get stuck. It asks TD4.500/7 for clean singles/doubles. The hotel is just a short walk from the bus and louage stations on Rue 18 Janvier. There are regular departures for Gabès, Jerba and Tataouine.

'ATAOUINE

☎ 05

'ataouine is a fairly dull administrative entre 50km south of Medenine, but it's a good base for visiting the surrounding Berber villages.

The *Hôtel La Medina* (☎ 860 999), on Rue Habib Mestaoui, charges TD6.500 per person for B&B and has the best budget restaurant in Tataouine.

Buses and louages both leave from the city centre. There are frequent departures to Medenine, and occasional buses continuing to Jerba, Gabès and Tunis (nine hours, TD19.380).

AROUND TATAOUINE
Chenini

This is a spectacular Berber village perched on the edge of an escarpment 18km west of Tataouine. There are occasional camionnettes (TD1) to Chenini from Rue 2 Mars in Tataouine – otherwise you'll have to hitch or hire a taxi, which will cost about TD20 for the return journey. It's worth the effort, but get there early to avoid the tourist buses.

Douiret

The hill-top village of Douiret, 22km south-west of Tataouine, is every bit as spectacular as Chenini but far less visited. It's a maze of crumbling abandoned houses rising above a gleaming white mosque. The top of the hill is crowned by the ruins of an ancient kasbah – inaccessible unless you possess the nerve and agility of a mountain goat. A taxi to Douiret from Tataouine costs about TD20 return.

Jerba

Jerbans, especially those involved in the tourist industry, like to claim that their island is the legendary Land of the Lotus Eaters visited by Ulysses in the course of Homer's *Odyssey*. Whatever the story, there's something about the place that keeps drawing the tourists in ever increasing numbers – over a million in 1997.

The island now boasts a tourist strip covering more than 20km of prime beachfront in the north-east. The island's main town and transport hub is Houmt Souq, in the middle of the north coast.

The island is linked to the mainland by a causeway which was built in Roman times, and by 24-hour car ferries between Ajim and Jorf.

HOUMT SOUQ

☎ 05

Jerba's main town is a tangle of whitewashed houses, narrow alleys and attractive café-lined squares. There are a couple of tourist offices, but the syndicat d'initiative (☎ 650 915) in the middle of town is the only one worth visiting. There are several banks, a post office and countless souvenir shops.

Places to Stay

Houmt Souq has some of the most interesting places to stay in the country – old funduqs that have been converted into a range of accommodation to suit every budget.

They start with the excellent *auberge de jeunesse* (☎ 650 619) on Rue Moncef Bey. It's great value at TD4.500 for a dorm bed and breakfast, or TD7.500 with dinner as well. The other funduq hotels are the *Arischa* (☎ 650 384), the *Marhala* (☎ 650 146) and the *Erriadh* (☎ 650 756). Prices for singles/doubles range from TD11/16 at the Arischa to TD19.500/30 at the Erriadh.

Places to Eat

The *Restaurant Les Palmiers*, at the northern end of Rue Mohamed Ferjani, is a popular place with an extensive menu of local dishes. These include mloukhia (TD2.200) and kammounia (TD2.200) as well as grilled fish, chips and salad (TD3.500).

The *Restaurant La Mama (Petit Repas)*, on Rue Habib Bougatfa, is always packed with locals tucking into dishes like chorba (800 mills) or couscous with lamb (TD1.800).

Getting There & Away

Tuninter flies to Tunis (one hour, TD50.500 one way) up to six times a day, depending on the season. There are also three flights a week to Tozeur (50 minutes, TD27 one way). The airport is 8km from Houmt Souq – about TD3 by taxi.

HOUMT SOUK

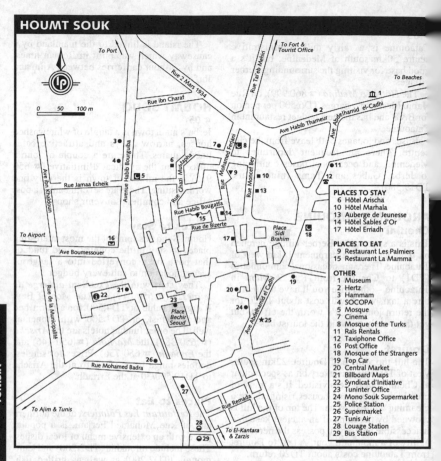

To Port
To Fort &
Tourist Office
To Beaches
Rue 2 Mars 1934
Rue Taïeb Mehiri
Rue ibn Charaf
Ave Habib Thameur
Ave Abdelhamid el-Cadhi
Rue Jamaa Echeik
Rue Ibn Khaldoun
Avenue Habib Bourguiba
Rue Ghazi Mustapha
Rue Mohamed Ferjani
Rue Moncef Bey
Rue Habib Bougatfa
Rue de Bizerte
Place Sidi Brahim
To Airport
Ave Boumessouer
Rue de la Municipalité
Place Bechir Seoud
Rue Mohamed Badra
To Ajim & Tunis
Rue Remada
To El-Kantara & Zarzis

0   50   100 m

PLACES TO STAY
6 Hôtel Arischa
10 Hôtel Marhala
13 Auberge de Jeunesse
14 Hôtel Sables d'Or
17 Hôtel Erriadh

PLACES TO EAT
9 Restaurant Les Palmiers
15 Restaurant La Mamma

OTHER
1 Museum
2 Hertz
3 Hammam
4 SOCOPA
5 Mosque
7 Cinema
8 Mosque of the Turks
11 Raïs Rentals
12 Taxiphone Office
16 Post Office
18 Mosque of the Strangers
19 Top Car
20 Central Market
21 Billboard Maps
22 Syndicat d'Initiative
23 Tuninter Office
24 Mono Souk Supermarket
25 Police Station
26 Supermarket
27 Tunis Air
28 Louage Station
29 Bus Station

The bus and louage stations are side by side at the southern end of the main street. SNTRI has three buses a day to Tunis (eight hours, TD17.760), and there are also daily buses to Gabès and Tataouine. Gabès is the main louage destination.

JERBA ISLAND
☎ 05

Although Jerba is famous for its **beaches**, the only decent beaches are in the north-eastern corner of the island – and they are monopo-

lised by the residents of the big hotels. There's nothing to prevent nonresidents from using them, and you'll find every conceivable form of water sports from windsurfing to parasailing.

Scattered among the big hotels are numerous places offering **horse riding** for about TD10 per hour.

Other activities include **scenic flights**, which are operated by Air Tropic (☎ 09-723 344) from the sand flats 5km south of Aghir on the east coast. It charges TD30 for a 30-

inute flight. The same company also hires
it land yachts (TD10 per hour).

laces to Stay

here are a couple of camping grounds on the
ast coast near Aghir – at the *Auberge Centre
ghir* and attached to the *Hôtel Sidi Slim*.
'he bus to Club Med from Houmt Souq goes
ight past both sites.

The hotels of the Zone Touristique are
riced beyond the means of most backpack-
rs. The cheapest rooms are at the *Hôtel*

Beau Rivage (☎ 757 130; fax 758 123), signposted off the main road about 12km east of
Houmt Souq. It charges TD21/32 for singles/
doubles with breakfast.

Getting Around

Most of Jerba is flat, which makes it a good
place to explore by bicycle or moped, both of
which can be hired from Raïs Rentals (☎ 650
303) on Ave Abdelhamid el-Cadhi in Houmt
Souq. The island's bus network is centred on
Houmt Souq.

Turkey

Turkey is usually considered Asia's foothold in Europe, the country that bridges two continents. There is no denying that it's a Mediterranean country, with over 4000km of warm-water coastline. A tourism boom in the 1980s put it on the travel map for everyone from package tourers to villa-renters. Holiday villages now share shore space with the hundreds of ruined Greek and Roman cities. The Turks are mostly quite friendly, especially when you escape the resorts and head into the heartland, and prices are very low compared to Western Europe.

AT A GLANCE

Capital	Ankara
Population	63.5 million
Area	780,580 sq km
Official Language	Turkish
Currency	Turkish lira (TL)
GDP	US$379.1 billion (1996)
Time	GMT/UTC+0200

Facts about Turkey

HISTORY

The Mediterranean region was inhabited as early as 7500 BC, and by 7000 BC a Neolithic city had grown up at Çatal Höyük, near Konya. The greatest of the early civilisations in Anatolia (Asian Turkey) was that of the Hittites. Long believed to be a purely mythical people, they were in fact a force to be reckoned with from 2000 to 1200 BC.

After the collapse of the Hittite empire, Anatolia broke up into a number of small states, and not until the Graeco-Roman period were parts of the country reunited. Later, Christianity spread through Anatolia, carried by the apostle Paul, a native of Tarsus (near Adana).

Byzantine Empire

In 330 AD the Roman emperor Constantine founded a new imperial city at Byzantium (modern İstanbul). Renamed Constantinople, this strategic city became the capital of the Eastern Roman Empire and was the centre of the Byzantine Empire for 1000 years. During the European Dark Ages, when the glories of Greece were just a memory and Rome had been overrun by barbarians, the Byzantine Empire kept alive the flame of western culture. Through the centuries it was threatened by the powerful empires of the east (Persians, Arabs, Turks) and west (the Christian powers of Europe).

The beginning of the Byzantine Empire's decline came with the arrival of the Seljuk Turks – they had previously conquered Persia and were beginning to encroach on Byzantine territory. The threat posed by the Seljuks precipitated the election of a new Byzantine emperor, Romanus IV Diogenes.

Romanus assembled an army to battle the Seljuks, but in August 1071 he was defeated at Manzikert, near Lake Van, and taken prisoner. The Seljuks took over most of Anatolia, and established a provincial capital at Konya. Their domains included today's Turkey, Iran and Iraq.

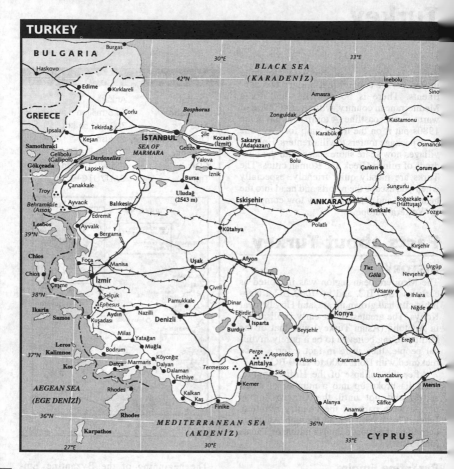

With significantly reduced territory, the Byzantines, under their new emperor, Alexius I Comnenus, endeavoured to protect Constantinople and reclaim Anatolia.

The Crusades

In 1095 Pope Urban II called for crusaders to fight in a holy war. To reach the Holy Land it was necessary for the First Crusade to pass through Constantinople. In return for this right of passage, Alexius Comnenus struck a deal with the crusade leaders, demanding that any territories won from the Turks by the cru-

saders be returned to the Byzantines. Although the crusaders failed to cooperate totally with the terms of the pact, in 1097 the Byzantines were able to win back the city of Nicaea from the Seljuks and reoccupy western Anatolia, with the Seljuks maintaining their power in the rest of Anatolia. The Fourth Crusade (1202-04) proved less fruitful for the Byzantines, with a combined Venetian and crusade force taking and plundering the city of Constantinople. The ravaged city was eventually regained by the Byzantines in 1261.

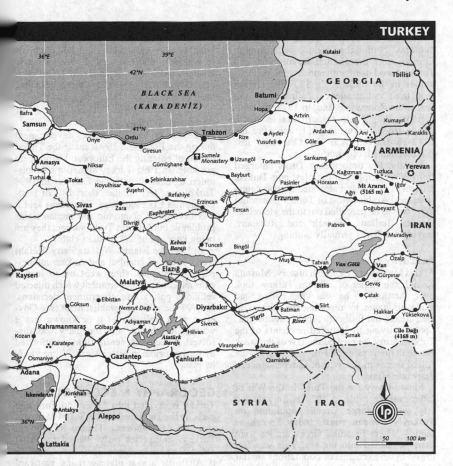

TURKEY

Ottoman Empire

A Mongol invasion of the late 1200s put an end to Seljuk power, but new small Turkish states were born soon after in western Anatolia. One, headed by Osman (1258-1326), grew into the Ottoman Empire, and in 1453 (just under 40 years before Columbus sailed for America), Constantinople fell to the Ottoman sultan Mehmet II (the Conqueror).

A century later, under Süleyman the Magnificent, the Ottoman Empire reached the peak of its cultural brilliance and power, spreading deep into Europe, Asia and North

Africa. The janissaries, members of the sultan's personal guard and the first modern standing army, gave the Turks an advantage, as the European nations had to raise armies anew for each war. The Turks tolerated minority groups, including Christians and Jews.

Ottoman success was based on military expansion. When the march westwards was stalled at Vienna in 1683, the rot started. A succession of incompetent sultans hardly helped, especially when combined with discontent among the janissaries, who by now had become totally unreliable.

By the 19th century the great European powers had begun to covet the sultan's vast domains. Nationalist ideas swept through Europe after the French Revolution, and Turkey found itself with unruly subject populations in the Balkans. In 1829 the Greeks won their independence, followed by the Serbs, the Romanians and, in 1878, the Bulgarians. Italy took Tripolitania in North Africa from Turkey in 1911, and after the 1912-13 Balkan War the Ottomans lost Albania and Macedonia.

Finally, the unfortunate Turks emerged from WWI stripped of their last non-Turkish provinces – Syria, Palestine, Mesopotamia (Iraq) and Arabia. Most of Turkey (Anatolia) itself was to be parcelled out to the victorious Greeks, Italians, French and Russians, leaving the Turks virtually nothing.

Atatürk

At this low point in Turkish history, Mustafa Kemal, the father of modern Turkey, took over. Atatürk, as he was later called, had made his name by repelling the Anzacs in their heroic but futile attempt to capture Gallipoli. Rallying the tattered remnants of the Turkish army, he pushed the last of the weak Ottoman rulers aside and out-manoeuvred the Allied forces in the War of Independence, a desperate affair.

Final victory for the Turks in the War of Independence came in 1923 at Smyrna – a city with a large Greek population on Turkey's Aegean coast, today known as İzmir – where invading Greek armies were literally pushed into the sea. This was followed by an exchange of populations similar to that which took place in India at the time of the India-Pakistan partition. Well over a million Greeks left Turkey and nearly half a million Turks moved in. Relations with Greece improved markedly in 1930, but were soured again after WWII by the conflict over Cyprus, particularly after the Greek-led anti-Makarios coup, and subsequent Turkish invasion of the island, in 1974.

With Turkey reduced to smaller but more secure boundaries, Atatürk embarked on a rapid modernisation program that centred around establishing a secular democracy, de-emphasising religion, introducing the Roman alphabet and European dress, and moving towards equal rights for women. In 1923 the country's capital was moved from 'decadent' İstanbul to Ankara, which was laid out anew to a modern plan. Naturally, such sweeping changes did not come easily, but Turkey is certainly more progressive in these areas than most of its neighbours.

Modern Turkey

Turkey's rapid economic development during the 1980s and 1990s made the Turks' dream of entering the European Union seem possible. In 1995 Turkey signed a customs-union agreement with the EU, but in 1998 Turkey was left off the 'short list' of next-generation EU candidates. Europeans said it was because of economic and human rights problems, but Muslim Turks suspect they are being kept out of a 'Christian club'.

In 1994 the Islamic Welfare Party (Refah) won control of İstanbul and Ankara municipal governments, then went on to lead a national coalition government which injected religious policy into government decisions. In 1997 the military establishment (see Government & Politics) let it be known that it wanted Refah out, and the party was dissolved. A secularist centre-right coalition led by former prime minister Mesut Yılmaz took its place.

GEOGRAPHY & ECOLOGY

Turkey is divided into Asian and European parts by the Dardanelles, the Sea of Marmara and the Bosphorus. Thrace (European Turkey) comprises only 3% of the total 780,580 sq km land area. The remaining 97% is Anatolia, a vast plateau rising eastward towards the Caucasus Mountains. Turkey's coastline is over 6000km long and includes many popular resort areas.

Turkey is ecologically conscious with admirable environmental protection laws. Unfortunately, weak government enforcement and strong commercial pressures often retard ecological progress.

GOVERNMENT & POLITICS

Turkey is a multiparty parliamentary democracy, with the military establishment acting as an unofficial – but effective – guarantor of democracy and secularism. The president is ne head of state, with limited constitutional powers. The prime minister is the head of government.

About half of the Turkish electorate is right-of-centre in its sympathies, voting for the Motherland (Anavatan) and True Path (Doğru Yol) parties, which are virtually identical in beliefs but separated by incompatible leaderships. About a fifth of the electorate sympathises with Islamicist politicians. The rest of the electorate is split among smaller socialist, social democratic, Kurdish and neofascist parties. This fragmented political landscape produces unstable coalition governments which spend most of their time jockeying for position and votes, and much less time making effective government policy.

In 1960, 1970 and 1980, the army stepped in to 'correct' what it saw as an undemocratic drift away from the principles set forth by Atatürk. In 1997 the military expressed its distrust of the government headed by Refah, the Islamic Welfare Party, and charges were brought that Refah had engaged in unconstitutional antisecularist activities. The party was disbanded, though many of its members went on to found a new, less radical religious party.

ECONOMY

Turkey has a strong agricultural sector, being a net exporter of food. Wheat, cotton, sugar beet, sunflowers, hazelnuts, tobacco, fruit and vegetables are abundant. Sheep are the main livestock, and Turkey is the biggest wool producer in Europe. However, manufactured goods now dominate the economy. Turkey builds motor vehicles, appliances, consumer goods and large engineering projects, and exports them throughout the region. Tourism brings in billions of dollars each year. Many Turks send home money from jobs in Europe, particularly from Germany.

POPULATION & PEOPLE

Turkey's population of 63.5 million is made up predominantly of Muslim Turks, with a significant minority (perhaps eight to 10 million) of Muslim Kurds and small groups of Jews, Greeks, Armenians, Laz (a Black Sea people) and Arabs. Its five biggest cities are İstanbul (12 million people), Ankara (3.2 million), İzmir (2.7 million), Adana (1.9 million) and Bursa (1.6 million).

ARTS

Islam discourages images of any being 'with a soul' (ie animal or human), so there was little sculpture or portraiture in Ottoman times (though there was Turkish miniature painting). Instead, Turkish artists pursued calligraphy, architecture, textile design (especially carpets and apparel), jewellery, faïence, glass-making and many crafts.

Ottoman literature and court music were mostly religious, and both sound pompous and lugubrious to western ears. Folk music was (and is) sprightly; troubadours were highly skilled and very popular, although TV and cassettes have largely wiped them out.

As with all else, Atatürk changed Turkey's cultural picture overnight, encouraging painting, sculpture, western music (he loved opera), dance and drama. In recent days, Ottoman arts such as paper-marbling and the Karagöz shadow-puppet plays are enjoying a resurgence, and are seen as valuable traditions worthy of preservation. Carpet-weaving is, was and always will be a Turkish passion.

SOCIETY & CONDUCT

Ottoman Turkey was ruled by the sharia (Islamic religious law), but republican Turkey – thanks to Atatürk – has largely adapted to a modern, westernised lifestyle. Although many Turks drink alcohol (and don't mind if others drink), they still revere the moral and spiritual teachings of their religion, and observe its customs, if sometimes loosely.

Liberal western attitudes born of Atatürk's reforms are strongest in the urban centres of the west and along the coasts – among the middle and upper classes. You will feel quite comfortable among these Turks; they look to western culture as the ideal, and accept the validity of other religious beliefs.

The working and farming classes, particularly in the east, are more conservative, traditional and religious. There is a small but growing segment of 'born-again' Muslims, fervent and strict in their religion but otherwise modern. Though always polite, these Turks may give you the feeling that east is east and west is west, and that the last echo of 'crusaders versus Saracens' has not yet died away.

RELIGION

Turkey is 99% Muslim, predominantly Sunni, with Shias in the east and south-east. When you visit mosques, dress conservatively (no 'revealing' clothing like shorts or sleeveless shirts), remove your shoes, don't take flash photographs and be respectful. Women should cover their head, shoulders and arms to the elbow.

LANGUAGE

Ottoman Turkish was written in Arabic script, but Atatürk decreed a change to Roman script in 1928. In big cities and tourist areas, many locals know at least some English and/or German. See the Language Guide at the back of this book for pronunciation guidelines and useful words and phrases.

Facts for the Visitor

HIGHLIGHTS

In İstanbul, don't miss Topkapı Palace, Aya Sofya (Hagia Sofia), the Blue Mosque and the Kariye Museum. The battlefields of Gallipoli, on the Dardanelles, are particularly moving. Many visitors find Troy disappointing, but not so Ephesus, the best-preserved classical city on the Mediterranean.

Seljuk Turkish architecture, earlier than Ottoman, is particularly fine. Alanya, Konya, Sivas and Erzurum have good Seljuk buildings.

Turkey's beaches are best at Pamucak (near Ephesus), Ölüdeniz, Bodrum, Patara, Antalya, Side and Alanya. The improbable 'lunar' landscapes of Cappadocia are perhaps the single most visually impressive feature in all Turkey. Farther east near Malatya, the great Commagenian heads on Nemrut Dağı certainly repay an early start to the day.

SUGGESTED ITINERARIES

İstanbul, the Aegean and Mediterranean coasts, and Cappadocia are the areas most people come to see. The Black Sea coast can be travelled in a day or a week, as you wish. If your time is limited, consider these itineraries:

Two days
Explore İstanbul or Selçuk/Ephesus.
One week
See İstanbul and the Aegean coast to Bodrum or Marmaris, with a quick trip to Pamukkale.
Two weeks
Travel from İstanbul south and east along the coasts to Antalya or Alanya, then return to İstanbul via Cappadocia.
Three weeks or more
Travel from İstanbul to İznik, Bursa, the Aegean coast and the Mediterranean coast to Silifke, then inland to Konya, Cappadocia and Ankara, and back to İstanbul.

PLANNING
Climate & When to Go

The Aegean and Mediterranean coasts have mild, rainy winters and hot, dry summers. In İstanbul, summer temperatures average around 28 to 30°C; the winters are chilly but usually above freezing, with rain and perhaps a dusting of snow. The Anatolian plateau is cooler in summer and quite cold in winter. The Black Sea coast is mild and rainy in summer, and chilly and rainy in winter.

Mountainous eastern Turkey is very cold and snowy in winter, and only pleasantly warm in high summer. The south-east is dry and mild in winter and very hot in summer, with temperatures above 45°C not unusual. In general, spring (April/May) and autumn (September/October) have the most pleasant weather.

Books & Maps

Lonely Planet publishes the more detailed *Turkey* guide, the *Turkish phrasebook* and the *Turkey Travel Atlas*.

For a short cut to an understanding of Turkey, read *Atatürk* by Lord Kinross (JPD Balfour). *Lords of the Golden Horn* by Noel Barber is an absolutely gripping account of the decline of the Ottoman Empire from its peak under Süleyman the Magnificent. Freya Stark's *Alexander's Path* retraces Alexander the Great's route across southern Turkey; it's good on the pre-tourist-boom south, if sometimes a little too learned. An easier read is

Mary Lee Settle's *Turkish Reflections*, which casts a novelist's eye over the whole country.

Inspect locally produced maps carefully to assess their probable accuracy and usefulness before you buy.

What to Bring
You'll find the following items useful in Turkey: prescription medicines (refills *may* be available in Turkey), mosquito repellent (from April to September), sunscreen (it's expensive in Turkey), a universal sink plug, a towel and reading matter. Women should bring tampons or sanitary pads.

TOURIST OFFICES
Local Tourist Offices
Ministry of Tourism (Turizm Bakanlığı) offices exist in every tourist-oriented town. There may be provincial or local offices as well. The enthusiasm and helpfulness of the staff vary widely. Most offer regional brochures and local maps of at least minimal usefulness; the big town maps, however, are excellent. Ask for the *Youth Travel Guide Book*, which has lots of advice for budget travellers.

Turkish Tourist Offices Abroad
Turkey has tourist offices in the following countries:

Australia
(☎ 02-9223 3055; fax 02-9223 3204; turkish@ ozemail.com.au) Suite 101, 280 George St, Sydney NSW 2000
Canada
(☎ 613-230 8654; fax 613-230 3683) Constitution Square, 360 Albert St, Suite 801, Ottawa ON 1R 7X7
UK
(☎ 0171-629 7771; fax 0171-491 0773; eb25@ cityscape.co.uk) 170-173 Piccadilly, 1st floor, London W1V 9DD
USA
(☎ 212-687 2194; fax 212-599 7568; www .turkey.org/turkey) 821 UN Plaza, New York, NY 10017

VISAS & EMBASSIES
Have a passport valid for at least three months beyond your date of entry into Turkey. Nationals of most Western European countries may enter free for visits of up to three months,

others must pay a visa fee: UK subjects pay UK£10, Netherlands citizens NF120, US citizens US$45, for a visa on arrival. Embassies are in Ankara; many nations have consulates in İstanbul, and some have them in İzmir and resort towns (Antalya etc) as well.

Turkish Embassies Abroad
Turkey has embassies in the following countries:

Australia
(☎ 02-6295 0227; fax 02-6239 6592) 60 Mugga Way, Red Hill 2603 ACT
Bulgaria
(☎ 02-980 2270; fax 02-981 9358) Blvd Vasil Levski No 80, 1000 Sofia
Canada
(☎ 613-789 4044; fax 613-789-3442) 197 Wurtemburg St, Ottawa, Ontario KIN 8L9
Greece
(☎ 01-724 5915; fax 01-722 9597) Vasilissis Georgiou B 8, 10674 Athens
UK
(☎ 0171-393 0202; fax 0171-393 0066) 43 Belgrave Square, London SW1X 8PA
USA
(☎ 202-659 8200; fax 202-659 0744) 1714 Massachusetts Ave NW, Washington, DC, 20036

Foreign Consulates in Turkey
Countries with diplomatic representation in Turkey include:

Australia
(☎ 212-257 7050; fax 212-257 7054) Tepecik Yolu 58, 80630 Etiler, İstanbul; open from 8.30 am to 12.30 pm weekdays
Canada
(☎ 212-272 5174) Büyükdere Caddesi 107/3, Bengün Han, 3rd floor, Gayrettepe, İstanbul
France
(☎ 212-243 1852; fax 212-249 9168) İstiklal Caddesi 8, Taksim, İstanbul
Greece
(☎ 212-245 0596; fax 212-252 1365) Turnacıbaşı Sokak 32, Ağahamam, Beyoğlu, İstanbul
New Zealand
(☎ 212-275 2989; fax 212-275 5008) Maya Akar Center, 24th floor, Büyükdere Caddesi 100/102, 80280 Esentepe, İstanbul
UK
(☎ 212-293 7540; fax 212-245 4989) Meşrutiyet Caddesi 34, Tepebaşı, Beyoğlu, İstanbul
USA
(☎ 212-251 3602; fax 212-252 3218) Meşrutiyet Caddesi 104-108, Tepebaşı, Beyoğlu, İstanbul

CUSTOMS

You may import, duty-free, two cartons of cigarettes (that's 400), 50 cigars or 200g of smoking tobacco, and 5L of liquor. Duty-free items are on sale in both arrival and departure areas of Turkey's international airports.

Turkey is full of antiquities: ancient coins, figurines, pots and mosaics. *It is illegal to buy, sell or export antiquities!* Penalties are severe – if caught, *you may go to jail.* Customs officers spot-check the luggage of departing passengers. For information on bringing a motor vehicle into Turkey, see Car & Motorcycle in the Getting Around section of this chapter.

MONEY

Currency

The Turkish lira (TL) comes in coins of 5000, 10,000, 25,000 and 50,000 liras, and notes (bills) of 20,000, 50,000, 100,000, 250,000, 500,000, one million and five million liras, with higher denominations added regularly as inflation (close to 100% per annum) devalues the currency. It's well past time for a number of zeros to be dropped from the currency. Prices in this chapter are quoted in more-stable US dollars.

Turkey has no black market; you can often spend US dollars or Deutschmarks in place of liras. Exchanging cash in major currencies is fast and easy in most banks, exchange offices, post offices, shops and hotels. Cashing major travellers cheques is less easy (some places resist) and the exchange rate is usually slightly lower. Many places charge a commission (*komisyon*); ask first. At the time this guide went to press Turkey had +100% inflation/devaluation – the following rates will be way out of date by the time you read them:

Exchange Rates

Australia	A$1	=	164,000TL
Canada	C$1	=	177,000TL
euro	€1	=	303,000TL
France	1FF	=	46,000TL
Germany	DM1	=	153,000TL
Japan	¥100	=	187,000TL
New Zealand	NZ$1	=	140,000TL
UK	UK£1	=	442,000TL
USA	US$1	=	271,000TL

Costs

Turkey is Europe's budget destination, and you can travel on as little as US$15 to US$20 per person per day using buses, staying in pensions and eating one restaurant meal daily. For US$20 to US$35 per day you can travel more comfortably by bus and train, staying in one and two-star hotels with private baths, and eating most meals in average restaurants. For US$30 to US$70 per person per day you can move up to three and four-star hotels, take the occasional airline flight and dine in restaurants all the time. Costs are highest in İstanbul and the big coastal resorts, and lowest in small eastern towns off the tourist track.

Tipping

In middle-range restaurants, waiters appreciate a tip of 5 to 10% (15% in expensive places) of the bill; hotel porters, 50 cents to US$1; barbers, hairdressers and Turkish-bath attendants, 10 to 15%; and cinema ushers, a few coins or a small lira note. Porterage at airports, and train and bus stations is set and should be posted (50 cents to US$1 per bag). Except for special service, don't tip taxi drivers; rather, round up the fare. Minibus (*dolmuş*) drivers are not tipped.

Bargaining

In some shops prices are set, but in others – and in all markets – use your *pazarlık* (bargaining) skills. You *must* bargain for souvenirs. Even if the establishment has set prices, bargain if you are buying several items or are shopping in the off season. For hotel rooms, bargain if you visit any time between October and late May, or if you plan to stay more than a single night.

Consumer Taxes

A value-added tax (KDV, Katma Değer Vergisi) of 15 to 20% is included (KDV *dahil*) in the price of most items and services. A few hotels and shops give discounts if you agree not to request an official receipt (*fatura*); this way, they (and you) don't pay the tax. It's illegal but not unusual.

If you buy an expensive item (eg carpet, leather apparel) for export, ask the shopkeeper for a KDV *iade özel fatura* (special VAT refund receipt). Get the receipt stamped as you

:lear customs, then get your refund at a bank
branch in the airport departure lounge; or you
:an mail the receipt and be sent a cheque.

POST & COMMUNICATIONS
Post
Turkish post offices are called 'Posta Telgraf'
or 'PTT'; look for the black-on-yellow signs.
If you have mail addressed to you care of
poste restante in a major city, the address
should include Merkez Postane (central post
office) or the name of the neighbourhood post
office at which you wish to retrieve it.

Telephone & Fax
Turkey's public telephones, now separated
from the PTT and operated by Türk Telekom,
take a *telekart* (phonecard), sold at telephone
centres, at shops and by street vendors. A few
older phones use *jeton* (tokens). Turkey's
country code is ☎ 90.

To call from one city to another, dial ☎ 0
(zero), then the city code and number. To call
abroad, dial ☎ 00, then the country and area
codes, and number. A three-minute telekart
call to the USA costs US$6 peak, US$4.50
off peak.

It's easiest to send and receive faxes at
your hotel for a fee (ask in advance). Türk
Telekom telephone centres have faxes but
require more paperwork.

In theory, you can call one of the numbers
below toll-free from Turkey to access your
home telephone company, which may have
cheaper rates. In practice, the call often
doesn't go through:

Australia	☎ (00-800) 61 1177
Canada (Teleglobe)	☎ (00-800) 1 6677
France (Telecom)	☎ (00-800) 33 1177
Germany (PTT)	☎ (00-800) 49 1149
Ireland	☎ (00-800) 353 1177
Italy	☎ (00-800) 39 1177
Japan (IDC Direct)	☎ (00-800) 81 0086
(IDC)	☎ (00-800) 81 0080
(KDD)	☎ (00-800) 81 1177
Netherlands (PTT)	☎ (00-800) 31 1177
UK (BTI)	☎ (00-800) 44 1177
USA (AT&T)	☎ (00-800) 1 2277
(MCI)	☎ (00-800) 1 1177
(SPRINT)	☎ (00-800) 1 4477

INTERNET RESOURCES
Cybercafés are appearing in the major cities
and tourist centres. Many small hotels and
pensions have an Internet service which you
can use for a fee to send and receive email.
CompuServe has nodes (9600 bps) in Ankara
(modem 312-468 8042) and İstanbul (modem
212-234 5168). America Online's İstanbul
node is at 212-234 5158 (28,800 bps).

NEWSPAPERS & MAGAZINES
The *Turkish Daily News* is the local English-
language paper. In major tourist areas you'll
find many day-old European and US newspapers and magazines.

RADIO & TV
Broadcasting is by the government-funded
TRT (Turkish Radio & Television) and numerous independent stations. TRT offers
short news broadcasts in English each
morning and evening on radio, and late each
evening on TV.

PHOTOGRAPHY & VIDEO
Colour print film costs about US$8, plus de-
veloping, for 24 exposures. It's readily
available and easily processed in city photo
shops, as are E-6 process slide films such as
Ektachrome, Fujichrome and Velvia; Kodachrome slide film is rarely found, and
cannot be developed in Turkey.

Still cameras are subject to an extra fee in
most museums; in some they are not allowed
at all. For use of flash or tripod, you must
normally obtain written permission from the
staff or the appropriate government ministry
(not easy). Video fees are usually even
higher.

Don't photograph anything military. In
areas off the tourist track, it's polite to ask
'*Foto/video çekebilir miyim?*' (May I take a
photo/video?) before shooting close-ups of
people.

TIME
Turkey is on Eastern European Time, two
hours ahead of GMT/UTC. When it's noon in
Turkey, it's 11 am in Paris and Frankfurt, 10
am in London, 5 am in New York and 2 am
in Los Angeles. In summer/winter it's 5/7 pm

in Perth and Hong Kong, 7/9 pm in Sydney and 9/11 pm in Auckland. From late March to late September, Turkey observes daylight-saving time and clocks are turned ahead one hour.

ELECTRICITY

The electric current in Turkey is 220V, 50Hz. Cheap hotel rooms (up to two-star) usually have one power point/outlet. Most camp sites, however, are very rudimentary, and power may not be easily available.

WEIGHTS & MEASURES

Turkey uses the metric system.

LAUNDRY

Attended laundrettes are beginning to appear in the larger cities, but most tourist laundry (*çamaşır*) is done in hotels. Talk to the staff; the cost may be negotiable. Dry cleaners (*kuru temizleme*) are readily found in the cities; ask at your hotel.

TOILETS

The word is *tuvalet*. All mosques have toilets, often basic and smelly. Major tourist sites have better ones. Almost all public toilets require payment of a small fee (10 to 30 cents).

Though most hotels and many public toilets have the familiar raised bowl commode, Turkey also has flat toilets, which are simply a hole in the floor with footrests on either side. Squatting gets easier with experience. Watch out for stuff falling from your pockets into the hole. Traditionally, one cleans up not with toilet paper but with water (from a spigot, jug or little pipe attached to the toilet), using the left hand. When not in your hotel, carry toilet paper with you.

HEALTH

Travellers in Turkey may experience 'traveller's diarrhoea', so take precautions. Drink bottled water; make sure fruit is washed in clean water or peeled with clean hands; avoid raw or undercooked seafood and meat; and don't eat food which has been standing unrefrigerated.

Pharmacists can advise you on minor problems and dispense on the spot many drugs for which you would need a prescription at home. Emergency medical and dental treatment is available at simple dispensaries (*sağlık ocağı*), clinics and government hospitals (*hastane*). Look for signs with a red crescent or big 'H'. Payment is required, but is usually low.

WOMEN TRAVELLERS

In traditional Turkish society, men and women have lives apart: the husband has his male friends, the wife has her female friends. Younger Turks are shedding these roles, and women now hold some positions of authority.

Still, foreign women are often hassled while travelling in Turkey. Men pinch, grab and make strange noises, which can become very tiresome; more serious assault is uncommon but possible. Travelling with a male improves matters, as does travelling with another female, or preferably two.

Turkish women completely ignore men who speak to them in the street. Wearing a headscarf, a skirt which comes below the knees, a wedding ring and sunglasses makes you less conspicuous. Away from beach resorts you should certainly avoid skimpy tops and brief shorts.

STUDENT TRAVELLERS

The International Student Identity Card (ISIC) gets you reductions at some museums and archaeological sites (20 to 50%), for train travel (30%), on Turkish Maritime Lines ships (10%) and sometimes on private bus lines and Turkish Airlines.

GAY & LESBIAN TRAVELLERS

Homosexuality is illegal in Turkey, though it exists openly at a small number of gay bars and clubs in major cities and resorts. Be discreet. For more information, www.qrd.org /qrd/world/europe/turkey is worth a surf.

DISABLED TRAVELLERS

Turkey is not well prepared for disabled travellers. Steps and obstacles are everywhere; ramps, wide doorways and properly equipped lodgings and toilets are rare. Crossing most streets is for the young and agile; all others are in peril. You must plan each hour of your

...rip carefully, and usually patronise luxury-level hotels, restaurants and transport.

SENIOR TRAVELLERS

Seniors (altın yaş, literally 'golden-agers') are welcomed and respected in Turkey, and sometimes receive discounts at hotels, museums and other touristic sites.

DANGERS & ANNOYANCES

Although Turkey is considered one of the safest countries in the region, you must still take precautions. Wear a money belt under your clothing. Be wary of pickpockets and purse-snatchers in buses, markets and other crowded places.

In İstanbul, single men have been victims of a thinly veiled form of robbery: after being lured to a bar or nightclub (often one of those along İstiklal Caddesi) by new Turkish 'friends', the man is then made to pay an outrageous bar bill whether he drank or not.

On intercity buses, there have been isolated incidents of theft by drugging: a person (or persons) who has befriended you buys you a beverage (often ayran in a sealed container) at a rest stop, injects a drug into it and, as you sleep, makes off with your luggage. More commonly, the hard-sell tactics of carpet sellers can drive you to distraction; be warned that 'free' lifts and suspiciously cheap accommodation often come attached to nearly compulsory visits to carpet showrooms.

BUSINESS HOURS

Banks and offices are open Monday to Friday, generally from 8.30 am to noon and from 1.30 to 5 pm; shops are open Monday to Saturday from 9.30 am to 6 or 7 pm, some taking a lunch break from 1 to 2 pm. Food shops open early (6 or 7 am) and close late (7 or 8 pm). One food shop in each neighbourhood opens on Sunday.

PUBLIC HOLIDAYS & SPECIAL EVENTS

National public holidays include: 1 January; 23 April (National Sovereignty and Children's Day); 19 May (Youth & Sports Day); 30 August (Victory Day); 29 October (Republic Day, biggest patriotic holiday).

The official Turkish calendar is the western Gregorian one used in Europe, but religious festivals are celebrated according to the Muslim Hijri lunar calendar. The lunar calendar is 11 days shorter than the Gregorian, so Muslim festivals take place around 11 days earlier each year.

Kurban Bayramı – Sacrifice Holiday
This four-day holiday is the most important religious holiday of the year. Commemorating Abraham's near-sacrifice of Isaac, millions of families sacrifice rams and have a feast, donating most of the meat to charity. It starts on 28 March 1999, 16 March 2000, 5 March 2001 and 22 February 2002. Plan ahead – almost everything closes.

Kırkpınar Oiled Wrestling Competition
In late June or early July, amateur wrestlers gather in Edirne for an annual event which has been going on for six and a half centuries. Huge men clad only in leather breeches slather themselves with olive oil and wrestle Turkish-style for three days (Friday to Sunday).

International İstanbul Music Festival
From early June to early July, world-class performers of all types of music gather in İstanbul to give concerts. A highlight is the performance of Mozart's Abduction from the Seraglio staged right in Topkapı Palace.

Anniversary of Atatürk's Death
Although not a public holiday, the national hero's death on 10 November 1938 is commemorated each year on that date with special ceremonies.

Mevlana Festival
The Mevlevi dervishes whirl in Konya from 14 to 17 December to commemorate their spiritual leader, the great mystic poet and philosopher Celaleddin Rumi (1207?-1273), called Mevlana. Celebrations culminate on the 17th, the anniversary of Mevlana's death, or 'wedding night with God'. Reserve your hotel room well in advance.

Ramazan – Ramadan
During the holy month of Ramazan, observant Muslims fast during daylight hours, feast after sunset and go to mosque often. The month-long observance is followed by the three-day Şeker Bayramı (Sweets Holiday), a public holiday when children go door-to-door requesting treats. Ramazan runs from 19 December 1998 to 17 January 1999, 8 December 1999 to 6 January 2000, 27 November to 26 December 2001 and 16 November to 15 December 2002.

ACTIVITIES

Archaeology

Turkey abounds with ancient sites. You may have some of the remote ones all to yourself.

Water Sports

The Aegean and Mediterranean coasts are the places to go; the Black Sea is too chilly, and most lakes are too salty or undeveloped. The big resort hotels have windsurfing, snorkelling, scuba-diving and rowing gear for hire.

Yacht Cruising

Turkey has lots of opportunities for yacht cruising, from day trips to two-week luxury charters. Antalya, Bodrum, Fethiye, Kuşadası and Marmaris are the main centres. You can hire crewless bareboats or flotilla boats, or take a cabin on a boat hired by an agency. Ask near the docks for information.

Hiking

Hiking and mountain trekking are becoming popular in Turkey, particularly in the northeast. *The Mountains of Turkey* by Karl Smith (Cicerone Press, 1994) is a good guide.

Turkish Baths

The pleasures of the Turkish bath are famous: soaking in the steamy heat, getting kneaded and pummelled by a masseur, then being scrubbed squeaky clean and lathered all over by a bath attendant, before emerging swaddled in puffy Turkish towels for a bracing glass of tea.

Traditionally, men and women bathe separately, but in popular tourist areas baths often accept foreign men and women at the same time for higher than usual prices. For safety's sake, women should know at least some of the men in the bath with them, and females might want to avoid male masseurs (a Turkish woman would only accept a masseuse). Not all baths accept women.

WORK

You must have residence and work permits to be legally employed; your employer can help you with these. Some people work illegally (as waiters, English teachers or journalists) and cross the border to Greece every three months to keep their visas current. If you're thinking of doing this, remember that after a while the immigration officer checking your passport is going to question all those exit and entry stamps. Job opportunities for English-speakers are listed in the classified of the *Turkish Daily News*.

ACCOMMODATION

You'll find camping facilities here and there throughout Turkey. Some hotels and pensions let you camp in their grounds and use their toilets and washrooms for a small fee. Well-equipped European-style camp sites are rare.

Turkey has plenty of cheap hotels, although the very cheapest are probably too basic for many tastes and often not suitable for women travelling without men. The cheaper places (up to US$20 a night) are usually subject to rating by municipalities. Above this level, ratings are by the national Ministry of Tourism.

The very cheap hotels are just dormitories where you're crammed into a room with whoever else fronts up. To avoid this, negotiate a price where you (and yours) have the whole room. Women travellers will get less unwanted attention in hotels by asking for *aile* (family/women's) accommodation.

There are a few very basic student hostels in the cities, available only in summer when they're not being used by Turkish students, and a couple of accredited Hostelling International (HI) youth hostels which differ little in price from cheap hotels.

In tourist areas look for small *ev pansiyonu* (home pensions), which sometimes offer kitchen facilities too.

One and two-star hotels (US$20 to US$45 for a double) offer reasonable comfort and private bathrooms at excellent prices; three-star places can be quite luxurious.

FOOD

Turkish food is similar to Greek but more refined. It has been called the French cuisine of the east – and with good reason. *Şiş kebap* (shish kebab), lamb grilled on a skewer, is a Turkish invention. You'll find the *kebapçı*, a cheap eatery specialising in roast lamb, everywhere. Try the ubiquitous *döner kebap* – lamb packed onto a vertical revolving spit and sliced off when done.

The best cheap and tasty meal is *pide*, Turkish pizza. Fish, though excellent, is often expensive – be sure to ask the price before you order. A proper meal consists of a long procession of dishes. First come the *meze* (hors d'oeuvres), such as:

beyaz peynir – white sheep's-milk cheese
börek – flaky pastry stuffed with white cheese and parsley
cacık – yoghurt, cucumber and garlic
(*kuru*) *fasulye* – (dried) beans
kabak dolması – stuffed zucchini
patlıcan salatası – puréed aubergine salad
patlıcan tava – fried aubergine
pilaki – beans vinaigrette
taramasalata – fish-roe dip
yaprak dolması – stuffed vine leaves

Dolma are vegetables (aubergine, zucchini, peppers, cabbage or vine leaves) stuffed with rice, currants and pine nuts, and served cold, or hot with lamb. The aubergine (eggplant) is the number one vegetable to the Turks. It can be stuffed as a dolma (*patlıcan dolması*), served puréed with lamb (*hünkar beğendi*), stuffed with minced meat (*karnıyarık*) or appear with exotic names like *imam bayıldı* – 'the priest fainted' – which means stuffed with ground lamb, tomatoes, onions and garlic. Well might he!

For dessert, try *fırın sütlaç* (baked rice pudding), *kazandibi* (caramelised pudding), *aşure* (fruit and nut pudding), baklava (flaky pastry stuffed with walnuts or pistachios, soaked in honey), or *tel kadayıf* or *burma kadayıf* (shredded wheat with nuts in honey).

Finally, Turkish fruit is terrific, particularly the melons.

DRINKS

Good bottled water is sold everywhere. Beers, such as Tuborg lager or Efes Pilsen, the sturdy Turkish pilsener, supplement the familiar soft drinks. There's also good Turkish wine – red or white – and fierce aniseed *rakı*, which is like Greek ouzo (the Turks usually cut it half-and-half with water). Turkish coffee (*kahve*) is legendary; order your first cup *orta* (with middling sugar). Turkish tea (*çay*), grown on the eastern Black Sea coast, is served in tiny glasses, sweet and without milk. A milder alternative is apple tea (*elma çay*).

ENTERTAINMENT

İstanbul, Ankara and İzmir have opera, symphony, ballet and theatre. Many smaller towns have folk-dance troupes. Every Turkish town has at least one cinema and one nightclub with live entertainment. In summer the seaside resorts throb to the sounds of innumerable loud clubs and discos.

THINGS TO BUY

Clothes, jewellery, handicrafts, leather apparel, carpets, coloured tiles and crockery, carved meerschaum, brass and copperware are all good buys. Bargaining usually pays off.

Getting There & Away

You can get in and out of Turkey by air, sea, rail and bus, across the borders of seven countries.

AIR

International airports are at Adana, Ankara, Antalya, Dalaman, İstanbul and İzmir. Turkish Airlines has direct flights from İstanbul to two dozen European cities, New York and Chicago, as well as the Middle East, North and South Africa, Central Asia, Bangkok, Karachi, Singapore, Tokyo and Osaka.

Major European airlines such as Aeroflot, Air France, Alitalia, Austrian Airlines, British Airways, Finnair, KLM, Lufthansa, SAS and Swissair fly to İstanbul; British Airways, Lufthansa and the independent airline İstanbul Airlines have flights to Ankara, Antalya, İzmir and Dalaman as well. One-way full-fare tickets from London to İstanbul can cost as much as US$450, so it's usually advisable to buy an excursion ticket (US$250 to US$425) even if you don't plan to use the return portion.

Turkish Airlines flies nonstop to İstanbul from New York and Chicago, Delta nonstop from New York. The European airlines also fly one-stop services from many North American cities to İstanbul. Return fares range from US$500 to US$1200.

There are no direct flights from Australia or New Zealand to Turkey, but you can fly Qantas or British Airways to London, or Olympic to Athens, and get a connecting flight from these cities. You can also fly Qantas or Singapore Airlines from most Australian cities, or from Kuala Lumpur, to Singapore to connect with Turkish Airlines' thrice-weekly flights to İstanbul. Excursion fares start from around US$2200, which is almost as much as you would pay for a more versatile round-the-world (RTW) ticket.

LAND
Europe
The daily İstanbul Express train links Munich, Slovenia, Croatia, Yugoslavia and Bulgaria to İstanbul's Sirkeci train station, but the going is slow, the trains are barely comfortable and theft is a problem.

Several Turkish bus lines, including Ulusoy and Varan/Bosfor, offer service between İstanbul and some Central European cities such as Frankfurt, Munich and Vienna. One-way tickets range from US$85 to US$140 – so there's little savings over a cheap air ticket.

Greece There are daily bus connections (Varan charges US$65) between Athens and İstanbul via Thessaloniki.

SEA
Turkish Maritime Lines (TML) runs car ferries between İzmir and Venice weekly year round. The fare is US$200 to US$225 one way with reclining seat, or US$310 to US$380 per person in a mid-price cabin; all meals included. The Brindisi-Çeşme service is 40% cheaper. There are daily services to Turkish Cyprus from Taşucu (near Silifke).

Private ferries run between Turkey's Aegean coast and the Greek islands, which are in turn linked by air or boat to Athens. Services are frequent (usually daily) in summer, several times weekly in spring and autumn, and infrequent (perhaps once a week) in winter. The most reliable winter services are Chios-Çeşme, Rhodes-Marmaris and Samos-Kuşadası; the warm-season services are Lesvos-Ayvalık, Lesvos-Dikili, Kos-Bodrum, Rhodes-Bodrum and Kastellorizo-Kaş.

LEAVING TURKEY
Don't carry any antiquities in your luggage. If you're caught smuggling them out, you'll probably go to jail. The departure tax of about US$12 is included in the price of your air ticket.

Getting Around

AIR
Turkish Airlines (Türk Hava Yolları, THY) links all the country's major cities, including the busy İstanbul-Ankara corridor (50 minutes, US$90), and flies to most neighbouring countries. Domestic flights tend to fill up, so book a few days in advance. İstanbul Airlines competes with Turkish Airlines on a few routes with lower fares but less frequent flights. Smoking is prohibited on domestic flights.

BUS
Big, modern buses go everywhere frequently, cheaply (around US$2 to US$3 per hour or 100km) and usually very comfortably. Kamil Koç, Metro, Ulusoy and Varan are premium lines, and have better safety records than most. Traffic accidents take a huge number of lives on Turkish roads each year.

The bus station (*otogar*) is often on the outskirts of a city, but the bigger bus companies often have free şehiriçi servis (shuttle minibuses) between the city-centre ticket office and the otogar. Many of the larger otogars have left-luggage rooms called *emanet*; there is a small charge. Don't leave valuables in unlocked luggage. If there's no emanet, leave luggage at your bus line's ticket office.

All buses are by law nonsmoking, though the driver may (and usually does) smoke, as might a few rebels.

TRAIN

The ageing rolling stock of the Turkish State Railways (Türkiye Cumhuriyeti Devlet Demiryolları, TCDD or DDY) has a hard time competing with the best long-distance buses for speed and comfort. Only on the special İstanbul-Ankara express trains such as the *Fatih* and *Başkent* can you get somewhere faster and more comfortably than by bus, at a comparable price.

Ekspres and *mototren* services sometimes have one class only. If they have 2nd class it costs 30% less than 1st. Student fares are 20% less, return fares 10% less. These trains are somewhat slower and often a bit cheaper than buses. On *yolcu* and *posta* trains you could grow old and die before you got to your destination. Trains east of Ankara are not as punctual or comfortable as those to the west.

Sleeping-car trains linking İstanbul and Ankara (US$25 a single, US$35 a double, all in) are good value; the cheaper *örtülü kuşetli* carriages have four simple beds per compartment.

Major stations have emanet (left-luggage rooms).

CAR & MOTORCYCLE

Turkey has a very high motor vehicle accident rate. Drive defensively, avoid driving at night, don't drink and drive, and never let emotion affect your driving.

An International Driving Permit may be handy if your licence is from a country likely to seem obscure to a Turkish police officer.

Türkiye Turing ve Otomobil Kurumu (TTOK), the Turkish Touring & Automobile Association (☎ 212-282 8140; fax 212-282 8042), Oto Sanayi Sitesi Yanı, Seyrantepe, 4 Levent, İstanbul, can help with questions and problems.

Carnets are not required if you're staying for less than three months, but details of your car are stamped in your passport to ensure it leaves the country with you.

Mechanical service is easy to find, reason-

ably competent and cheap. The most easily serviced cars are Fiat, Mercedes, Renault and Toyota.

If you plan to spend time in a major city, park your car and use public transport: traffic is terrible and parking impossible. Your hotel will advise you on parking. Multilevel car parks are called *katotopark*.

BICYCLE

The countryside is varied and beautiful, and the road surfaces are acceptable (if a bit rough), though often narrow. Turkish drivers regard cyclists as a curiosity and/or a nuisance.

HITCHING

Because of the extensive, cheap bus system, hitching is not popular in Turkey. If you ask for a ride, the driver will expect you to offer the bus fare for the privilege. They may politely refuse to accept it, but if you don't offer, you will be considered a freeloader.

Women should not hitchhike, especially alone; if you absolutely must hitch, do it with another woman or (preferably) a man, don't accept a ride in a vehicle which has only men in it, and expect some hassles.

BOAT

A car-ferry service departs from İstanbul on Friday (all year round) and arrives the next morning in İzmir. It departs Sunday afternoon for the return trip to İstanbul, arriving Monday morning. Fares, including meals, are US$25 (reclining seat) to US$80 (luxury cabin bed), and US$50 for a car.

A daily ship/train service called the *Marmara Ekspresi* links İstanbul and İzmir via Bandırma, costing US$10 one way for the 10-hour trip.

LOCAL TRANSPORT

The big towns all have local bus services, and also private dolmuş (shared taxi or minibus) services. İstanbul has a growing metro system of trains, trams and underground. Ankara has an excellent if limited metro, with more lines being built.

In the big cities, taxis have digital meters

TURKEY

and are required by law to run them. The greatest risk of taxi rip-offs (drivers refusing to run the meter, taking the long way etc) is in İstanbul. Service is usually fairly honest and efficient in the other big cities. In smaller places, where taxis have no meters, fares are set by the town, but you'll be at a loss to know what they are. Agree on a fare before you get in the car.

ORGANISED TOURS
Most independent travellers find tours in Turkey expensive. Almost all tours park you in a carpet shop for an hour or two (the guide gets a kickback of up to 30%). In general, it's faster and cheaper to make your own travel arrangements.

İstanbul

İstanbul, formerly Constantinople, is a treasure trove of fine buildings, intriguing streets and glittering bazars. After a day of wandering around tangled streets, mosques and ruins where empires have risen and fallen, you'll realise what is meant by the word 'Byzantine'. Nor should it be forgotten that it was here, five and a half centuries ago, that the final fragment of the Roman Empire crumbled, and that through Europe's Dark Ages this city carried European civilisation on from its Greek and Roman origins.

History
In the late 2nd century AD, Rome conquered the small city-state of Byzantium, and in 330 Emperor Constantine moved the capital of his empire there from Rome and renamed the city Constantinople.

The city walls kept out barbarians for centuries as the western part of the Roman Empire collapsed before Goths, Vandals and Huns. When Constantinople fell for the first time it was to the misguided Fourth Crusade in 1204. Bent on pillage, the crusaders abandoned their dreams of Jerusalem and ravaged Constantinople's churches, shipping out the art and melting down the silver and gold. When the Byzantines regained the city in 1261 it was a shadow of its former glory.

The Ottoman Turks laid siege in 1314, but withdrew. Finally, in 1453, after a long and bitter siege, the walls were breached at Topkapı Gate on the west side of the city. Mehmet the Conqueror marched to Hagia Sofia (Aya Sofya) and converted the church to a mosque. The Byzantine Empire had ended.

As capital of the Ottoman Empire, the city entered a new golden age. During the glittering reign of Süleyman the Magnificent (1520-66), the city was graced with many new buildings of great beauty. Even during the empire's long and celebrated decline, the capital retained many of its charms. Occupied by Allied forces after WWI, it came to be thought of as the decadent capital of the sultans, just as Atatürk's armies were shaping a new republican state.

The Turkish Republic was proclaimed in 1923, with Ankara as its capital. But İstanbul, the much beloved metropolis, is still the centre of business, finance, journalism and the arts.

Orientation
The Bosphorus strait between the Black and Marmara seas divides Europe from Asia. On its western shore, European İstanbul is further divided by the Haliç (Golden Horn) into the 'newer' quarter of Beyoğlu in the north and Old İstanbul in the south.

Sultanahmet is the heart of Old İstanbul, with the ancient Hippodrome, the Sultan Ahmet Camii (Blue Mosque), Aya Sofya, Topkapı Palace and many cheap hotels and restaurants. West of Sultanahmet, the boulevard called Divan Yolu runs past the Kapalı Çarşı (Grand Bazar) and İstanbul University to Aksaray, a major traffic intersection and heart of a chaotic shopping district. South of Aksaray at Yenikapı, fast catamarans (*deniz otobüsü*) and car ferries (*feribot*) head for Yalova and the southern shore of the Sea of Marmara.

İstanbul's bus terminal (otogar) is at Esenler, about 10km west of Sultanahmet on the metro tram line (*hızlı tramvay*) from Aksaray.

Eminönü, north of Sultanahmet at the southern end of the Galata Bridge, is a major transport point, and the terminus of a tram and many bus lines. Ferries and catamarans depart from Eminönü up the Bosphorus and to the Asian shore, including to the Asian bus station at Harem. Sirkeci train station, the terminus for the European railway line, is 100m south of Eminönü.

Beyoğlu, on the north side of the Golden Horn, is considered the 'new' or 'European' city, although there's been a city here since Byzantine times. Karaköy, formerly Galata, is where cruise ships dock at the *yolcu salonu* (maritime terminal). Ferries depart from Karaköy for the Asian shore at Haydarpaşa (the Asian train terminus) and Kadıköy, and fast catamarans head for more-distant Asian points. There's another Asian ferry and catamaran dock at Kabataş, 1km north-east of Karaköy.

A short underground railway (Tünel) runs up the hill from Karaköy to the southern end of Beyoğlu's main street, İstiklal Caddesi, now a pedestrian way. At the northern end of the street is Taksim Meydanı (Taksim Square), heart of 'modern' İstanbul with its luxury hotels and airline offices.

Information

Ask at Sirkeci train station about trains. Budget travel agencies in Sultanahmet can get you bus, train and plane tickets, but may put high mark-ups on the tickets. The bus companies have ticket offices near Taksim Square on Mete Caddesi and İnönü Caddesi.

Tourist Offices The Ministry of Tourism has offices in the international arrivals hall at Atatürk airport (☎ 573 4136); in the yolcu salonu (maritime terminal; ☎ 249 5776) at Karaköy; in Sirkeci train station (☎ 511 5811); at the north-east end of the Hippodrome in Sultanahmet (☎ 518 8754); near the UK Consulate in Beyoğlu at Meşrutiyet Caddesi 57, Tepebaşı (☎ 243 2928); in Taksim Square (☎ 245 6876) on İstiklal Caddesi; and in the İstanbul Hilton arcade on Cumhuriyet Caddesi (☎ 233 0592), four long blocks north of Taksim Square.

Money Ubiquitous ATMs spit out Turkish liras upon insertion of your credit or bank cash card; Yapı Kredi seems best. Exchange offices (*döviz Bürosu*) are cheapest outside the Kapalı Çarşı (Grand Bazar), but are also plentiful in Sultanahmet, Sirkeci and Taksim. Most are open from 9 am to 9 pm.

Post & Communications The main post office (*merkez postane*) is just south-west of Sirkeci station. Go here for poste-restante mail. There are branch post offices in Aksaray and the Grand Bazar, and in Beyoğlu at Galatasaray and Taksim, as well as in the domestic and international departure areas at Atatürk airport.

İstanbul has two telephone codes: ☎ 212 for the European side and ☎ 216 for the Asian. Assume that phone numbers given here are ☎ 212 unless stated otherwise.

Travel Agencies Sultanahmet has many small travel agencies, all of them selling air and bus tickets and tours, sometimes at a big mark-up; shop around for the best deals. Most also offer speedy (but expensive) foreign-exchange facilities and can arrange minibus transport to the airport.

Bookshops Aypa (☎ 516 0100), Mimar Mehmet Ağa Caddesi 19, Sultanahmet, just down the hill from Aya Sofya and the Blue Mosque, has guides, maps and magazines in English, French and German.

The best stores are on İstiklal Caddesi near Tünel, including Robinson Crusoe (☎ 293 6968), İstiklal Caddesi 389; Dünya Aktüel (☎ 249 1006), İstiklal Caddesi 469; ABC Kitabevi (☎ 279 6610), İstiklal Caddesi 461; and Metro Kitabevi (☎ 249 5827), İstiklal Caddesi 513.

Laundry In the Sultanahmet area try the Hobby Laundry (☎ 513 6150), Caferiye Sokak 6/1, in the Yücelt Interyouth Hostel; or Active Laundry, Dr Emin Paşa Sokak 14, off Divan Yolu beneath the Arsenal Youth Hostel.

Emergency Try the tourist police (☎ 527 4503), Yerebatan Caddesi 6, Sultanahmet, across the street from Yerebatan Saray (Sunken Palace Cistern). The ordinary police (☎ 155 in an emergency) are less experienced in dealing with foreigners.

As for hospitals, the American Hospital (☎ 231 4050), at Güzelbahçe Sokak, Nişantaşı (2km north-west of Taksim Square), and the International (☎ 663 3000), Çınar Oteli Yanı, İstanbul Caddesi 82, in Yeşilköy near the airport, do good work.

İSTANBUL

Eyüp
To Eyüp Sultan
Camii

Balıkhane

Old Galata
Bridge

Balat

To International İstanbul
Bus Terminal (Otogar)
& Edirne

16

17

Draman

15

Edirnekapı

Karagümrük

Fener

14
Fethiye

Çarşamba   13

18

Ulubatlı

Fatih
20

Zeyrek

To Atatürk
Airport

Topkapı

Aqueduct of Valens
(Bozdoğan Kemeri)

19

Pazar Tekke

Baruthane   Cad   Guraba Hastanesi Cad

Emniyet

Saraçhane   22

Çapa

21

Şehremini

Çapa

Mevlanakapı

Fındıkzade

Aksaray

Haseki

Yusuf
Paşa

Aksaray

Laleli

Haseki

Nişanca

Hayriye – Tüccan

Cerrahpaşa

Yenikapı

Yenikapı

Fast Car Ferry to Bandırma
İzmir Train

Belgradkapı
To Yedikule

A Nafiz Gürman

Sahil   Yolu

Kennedy

PLACES TO STAY	
5 Marmara Hotel	17 Kariye Müzesi
10 Pera Palas Oteli	(Chora Church)
	18 Mihrimah Camii
OTHER	19 Topkapı
1 Dolmabahçe Palace	(Cannon Gate)
2 German Consulate	20 Fatih Camii
3 Turkish Airlines	21 Belediye Sarayı
(THY) Office	(City Hall)
4 PTT (Post Office)	22 Şehzade Camii
6 French Consulate	23 Süleymaniye Camii
7 Balık Pazar & Çiçek	24 Rüstem Paşa Camii
Pasajı	25 Yeni Cami
8 UK Consulate	26 Mısır Çarşısı
9 PTT (Post Office)	(Egyptian Bazaar)
11 US Consulate	27 Merkez Postane
12 Galata Tower	(Central Post Office)
13 Selimiye Camii	28 Çemberlitaş Hamamı
14 Fethiye Camii	(Turkish Bath)
15 St Stephen	29 Kapalı Çarşı
(Cast Iron) Church	(Covered Market/
16 Constantine's Palace	Grand Bazar)
(Tekfur Saray)	30 Beyazıt Camii

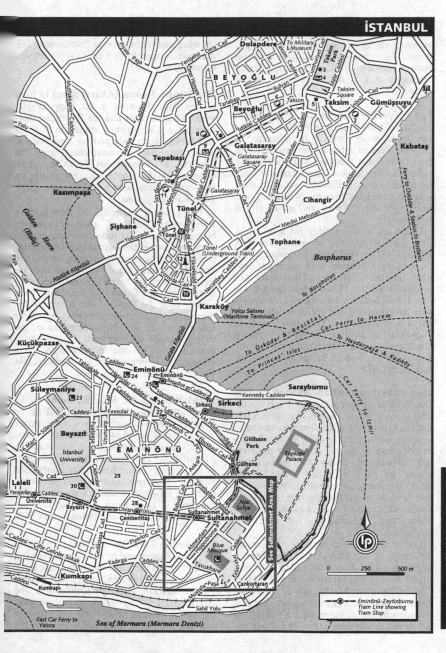

Things to See & Do

Sultanahmet is the first place to go, with all the major sights arranged around the Hippodrome. There is a sound-and-light show on summer evenings – different nights, different languages. Ask at the Hippodrome tourist office.

Aya Sofya The Church of the Holy Wisdom (Hagia Sofia in Greek, Aya Sofya in Turkish) was begun under Emperor Justinian in 532 and was intended to be the grandest church in the world. For a thousand years it was the largest in Christendom. The interior reveals the building's magnificence; stunning even today, it must have been overwhelming centuries ago when it was covered in gilded mosaics.

Climb up to the gallery for a different view, and to see the splendid surviving mosaics. After the Turkish conquest the mosaics were covered over, as Islam prohibits images of beings. They were not revealed until the 1930s, when Atatürk declared Aya Sofya a museum. The minarets were added during the centuries when Aya Sofya was a mosque. The church is open from 9.30 am to 4 pm daily, till 5 pm in summer (closed on Monday); note that the gallery closes from 11.30 am to 1 pm. Admission is US$5.

Blue Mosque (Sultan Ahmet Camii)

The Mosque of Sultan Ahmet I, just southwest of Aya Sofya, was built between 1609 and 1619. It's light and delicate compared to its squat, massive, ancient neighbour. The exterior is notable for its six slender minarets and cascade of domes and half-domes. Inside, the tiled walls and painted dome create the luminous overall impression of blue which earns the mosque its name. You're expected to make a small donation when visiting the mosque – and leave your shoes outside.

On the north side of the Blue Mosque, up the ramp, is the **Carpet & Kilim Textile Museum** (open from 9.30 am to 4.30 pm, closed Sunday and Monday; entry US$1).

Rents from the **Arasta** (row of shops) on the street behind the Blue Mosque to the east provide support for the mosque's upkeep. In the Arasta is the entrance to the newly re-

stored **Great Palace Mosaic Museum**, with portions of ancient Byzantine pavements showing marvellous scenes from nature. The museum is open from 9 am to 4 pm (closed Monday) for US$1.

The Hippodrome (Atmeydanı) In front of the Blue Mosque is the Hippodrome, where chariot races and the Byzantine riots took place. Construction started in 203 AD and it was later enlarged by Constantine. Today, three ancient monuments remain. The **Obelisk of Theodosius** is an Egyptian column from the temple of Karnak, resting on a Byzantine base, with perfectly clear, 3500-year-old hieroglyphs.

The 10m-high **Obelisk of Constantine Porphyrogenitus** was once covered in bronze (the crusaders stole the bronze plates). The base rests at the former level of the Hippodrome, now several metres below the ground. Between these two monuments are the remains of the Spiral Column. Erected at Delphi by the Greeks to celebrate their victory over the Persians, the bronze sculpture of three intertwined snakes was later transported to the Hippodrome and the snakes' heads disappeared. At the north-eastern end of the Hippodrome is a ceremonial fountain built to commemorate Kaiser Wilhelm's visit in 1901.

Turkish & Islamic Arts Museum On the west side of the Hippodrome, the Türk ve İslam Eserleri Müzesi is housed in the former palace (built in 1524) of İbrahim Pasha, grand vizier and son-in-law of Süleyman the Magnificent. The exhibits run the gamut of Islamic history, from beautifully illuminated Korans to carpets and mosque furniture, crafts and Turkish miniature paintings. The museum is open from 9 am to 4.30 pm (closed on Monday); admission costs US$2.

Yerebatan Saray Across Divan Yolu from the north-eastern end of the Hippodrome is a small park; on the north side of the park is the entrance to Yerebatan Saray, the **Sunken Palace Cistern**. Built by Constantine and later enlarged by Justinian, this vast, columned cistern held water not only for summer use but also for times of siege. It's open daily from 9 am to 4.30 pm (5.30 pm in summer); admission costs US$4.

Topkapı Palace Just north-east of Aya Sofya is the fortified, sprawling Topkapı Sarayı, the palace of the sultans from 1462 until they moved to Dolmabahçe Palace, across the Golden Horn, in the 19th century. Topkapı is not just a palace but a collection of gardens, houses and libraries, and a 400-room harem. In the vast outer courtyard, where the crack troops known as janissaries once gathered, is the **Aya İrini** or Church of Divine Peace, dating from around 540. Entrance is through the Ortakapı (middle gate).

Within the park-like Second Court are exhibits of priceless porcelain (in the former palace kitchens), silverware and crystal, arms and calligraphy. Right beside the Kubbealtı, or Imperial Council Chamber, is the entrance to the **harem**, a succession of sumptuously decorated rooms which served as the sultan's family quarters.

In the Third Court are the sultan's ceremonial robes and the fabulous **treasury**, which contains an incredible wealth of gold and gems. The **Shrine of the Holy Relics** holds a solid-gold casket containing the Prophet Mohammed's cloak and other Islamic relics. The beautiful little tiled kiosks have fine views of the city.

Topkapı is open daily from 9 am to 4.30 pm but is closed on Tuesday; admission costs US$6, with an extra US$2.50 payable to visit the harem, which is open from 9.30 am to 3.30 pm.

Archaeological Museums Down the hill from the outer courtyard, to the west of Topkapı Palace, are the Arkeoloji Müzeleri, a complex of three museums. The **Archaeological Museum** has an outstanding collection of Greek and Roman statuary, and what was once thought to be Alexander the Great's sarcophagus (stone coffin). The **Museum of the Ancient Orient** (Eski Şark Eserleri Müzesi) is dedicated to the pre-Islamic and pre-Byzantine civilisations. The **Çinili Köşk** (Tiled Pavilion), built by order of Sultan Mehmet the Conqueror in 1472, is among the oldest Turkish buildings in the city. It is now a museum of Turkish tile work.

The museums are open from 9 am to 4.30 pm (they're all closed on Monday; the Museum of the Ancient Orient only opens Tuesday through Friday, and the Tiled Pavilion opens on Tuesday afternoon); admission to all three costs US$3. Down the slope and west from the museums is **Gülhane Park**, the former palace park, now with a small zoo, restaurants and amusements. It's open from 7 am to 6 pm daily for free.

Divan Yolu Walk westward up Divan Yolu from Sultanahmet. Near the top of the slope, on the right, is a complex of **tombs** of several 19th-century sultans, including Mahmut II (1808-39), Abdülaziz (1861-76) and Abdülhamid II (1876-1909).

A bit farther along, on the right, is the **Çemberlitaş** (Banded Stone), a monumental column erected by Constantine the Great some time during the 4th century. Within a century it had to be strengthened with iron bands. During a storm in 1105 Constantine's statue toppled off the top, killing several people sheltering below. In 1779 the column was badly damaged by a fire, and it was further strengthened with the iron hoops you see today.

Grand Bazar (Kapalı Çarşı) This covered market is a labyrinthine medieval shopping mall. Most of the old stalls have been converted into modern, glassed-in shops. Still, it's fun to wander among the 65 streets and 4400 shops, and a great place to get lost – which you certainly will.

Some streets are given over to selling one item: carpets for example, or jewellery, clothing or silverware and so on. West of the bazar proper, across Çadırcılar Caddesi, beside the Beyazıt Camii mosque, is the **old book market** (*sahaflar çarşısı*) with many stalls selling second-hand books, most of them in Turkish. The bazar is open Monday to Saturday from 8 am to 7 pm.

Beyazıt & Süleymaniye Beyazıt takes its name from the graceful mosque **Beyazıt Camii**, built in 1506 on the orders of Sultan Beyazıt II, son of Mehmet the Conqueror. In Byzantine times this plaza was the **Forum of Theodosius**, laid out in 393 AD. The great portal on the north side of the square is that of

SULTANAHMET AREA

İstanbul University. The portal, enclosure and buildings behind it date mostly from Ottoman times, when this was the Ministry of War.

Behind the university to the north-west rises İstanbul's grandest mosque complex, the **Süleymaniye**. Construction was completed in 1557 on orders of Süleyman the Magnificent; he and his foreign-born wife Roxelana (Hürrem Sultan) are buried in **mausolea** behind the mosque to the south-east. The buildings surrounding the mosque were originally seminaries, a hospital, soup kitchen, baths and hospice.

Theodosian Walls Stretching for 7km from the Golden Horn to the Sea of Marmara, the walls date back to about 420 AD, but many parts have been restored during recent decades.

At **Yedikule**, close to the Sea of Marmara, you can visit a Byzantine-Turkish fortress where obstreperous diplomats and 'inconvenient' princes were held in squalor and despair. The fortress is open daily from 9 am to 4.30 pm (closed on Monday); admission costs 75 cents. Get there on a *banliyö* (suburban) train from Sirkeci to Yedikule, or on İETT bus No 80 from Eminönü.

SULTANAHMET AREA

PLACES TO STAY
4   Hotel Anadolu
5   Hotel Ema
6   Yücelt Interyouth Hostel &
    Hobby Laundry
14 Arsenal Youth Hostel &
    Active Laundry
22 Four Seasons Hotel
23 Mavi Guesthouse
24 Troy Hostel
26 İlknur Pansiyon
27 Konya Pansiyon
28 Orient Youth
    Hostel
29 Hotel Side Pension
36 Can Pansiyon

PLACES TO EAT
11 Pudding Shop

12 Can Restaurant &
    Sultanahmet Köftecisi
13 Vitamin Restaurant
35 Yeni Birlik Lokantası
37 Doy Doy Restaurant

OTHER
1   Cağaloğlu Hamamı (Turkish
    Bath)
2   Gülhane Park
3   Aya İrini (Hagia Eirene
    Church)
7   Imperial Gate (Entrance to
    Topkapı Palace)
8   Aya Sofya (Hagia Sofia)
9   Tourist Police
10 Yerebatan Saray (Sunken
    Palace Cistern)
15 Imperial Tombs

16 Tourist Office
17 Kaiser Wilhelm's Fountain
18 Law Courts
19 Turkish & Islamic Arts
    Museum
20 Obelisk of Theodosius
21 Haseki Hürrem Hamamı
    (Carpet Shop)
25 Cankurtaran (Sultanahmet)
    Banliyö Railway Station
30 Aypa Bookshop
31 Carpet & Kilim Textile
    Museum
32 Great Palace Mosaic
    Museum
33 Blue Mosque (Sultan Ahmet
    Camii)
34 Spiral Column

Near the **Edirnekapı** (Adrianople Gate) is the marvellous **Kariye Müzesi** (Chora Church), a Byzantine building with the best 14th-century mosaics east of Ravenna. Built in the 11th century, it was later restored, then converted to a mosque, and is now a museum. It's open daily from 9 am to 4 pm (closed on Wednesday), and admission costs US$3. To get there, take an Edirnekapı bus or dolmuş along Fevzipaşa Caddesi to Edirnekapı.

Turkish Baths İstanbul's most interesting historical baths are now very touristy. However attractive, the **Cağaloğlu Hamamı**, Yerebatan Caddesi 34, has priced itself out of most pockets.

Instead, you could try **Çemberlitaş Hamamı**, off Divan Yolu at the Sultanahmet end, which was designed by the great Ottoman architect Sinan in 1584. Both the men's and women's sections are open from 6 am to 12 pm daily. Prices here would be outrageous anywhere else in Turkey: about US$10 for an assisted bath with massage, supposedly inclusive of tips.

Eminönü At Galata Bridge's southern end looms the large **Yeni Cami** (New Mosque), built between 1597 and 1663. Beside it is the **Mısır Çarşısı** (Egyptian Bazaar), full of spice and food vendors. To the west, in the fragrant market streets, is the **Rüstem Paşa Camii**, a small, richly tiled mosque also designed by Sinan.

Beyoğlu Cross the Galata Bridge and head uphill towards the **Galata Tower**. In its present form this tower dates from 1216, when Galata was a Genoese trading colony. Later it served as a prison, an observatory, then a fire lookout before it caught fire itself in 1835. In 1967 it was completely restored as a supper club. The observation deck, perfect for views and photos, is open daily from 9 am to 6 pm in winter and 7 pm in summer; admission costs US$2. Inside, a small sign announces that during the 17th century an intrepid local flier made the first intercontinental flight clear across to Asian İstanbul from the top of the Galata Tower.

At the top of the hill is **İstiklal Caddesi**, once called the Grand Rue de Péra, now a pedestrian way served by a restored tram. The famed Pera Palas Oteli (rooms for US$180 a double) is off to the west; huge consulates line the avenue. In Galatasaray are the colourful **Balık Pazar** (Fish Market) and **Çiçek Pasajı** (Flower Passage), and an assortment of fish restaurants. **Taksim Meydanı** (Taksim Square), with its huge hotels, park and Atatürk Cultural Centre, is the hub of modern İstanbul.

TURKEY

The Bosphorus North from İstanbul, towards the Black Sea, are some beautiful old Ottoman buildings, including the imposing **Dolmabahçe Palace** and several big mosques; **Rumeli Hisar**, the huge castle built by Mehmet the Conqueror on the European side to complete his stranglehold on Constantinople; and many small and surprisingly peaceful villages that are now the city's dormitory suburbs. Towns on the Asian side in particular have charm, open space and good food. A ferry ride up the Bosphorus is *de rigueur* for all visitors to İstanbul.

The Princes' Isles Once the site of monasteries and a haven for pirates, this string of nine small islands is a popular summer getaway for İstanbul's middle class. With a few tiny beaches, some open woodland and transport by horse-drawn carriages, they make a pleasant escape from İstanbul's noise and hustle. Ferries (US$1.75) depart from Sirkeci's Adalar İskelesi dock.

Organised Tours
The standard 1¾-hour tourist cruise from Eminönü (departs at 10.35 am from 'Boğaz Hattı' dock) to Sarıyer on a normal ferry costs US$6 round trip (half-price on Saturday and Sunday). Ignore the scalpers; pay your fare at the ticket window, and count your change.

Alternatively, you can take the shorter 'budget cruise' across the Bosphorus by boarding any boat from Eminönü for Üsküdar, or from Karaköy for Haydarpaşa or Kadıköy, then just come back (50 cents each way).

A long-established, reputable travel agency and tour operator that has English-speaking staff is Orion-Tour (☎ 248 8437; fax 241 2808), Halaskargazi Caddesi 284/3, Marmara Apartımanı, Şişli, about 2km north of Taksim. Orion (pronounced 'OR-yohn') sells tickets to just about anywhere and has tours all over Turkey.

Special Events
Celebration of the capture of Constantinople from the Byzantines (1453) are held on the anniversary, 29 May, near Edirnekapı in the city walls. The İstanbul International Music Festival is held each year from early June to early July, with top-name artists from around the world.

Places to Stay
Camping In this big city, camping is not particularly convenient and costs almost as much as staying in a cheap hotel (US$8 to US$10 for a tent site). *Londra Camping* (☎ 560 4200) is a truck stop with a large camping area behind it; you'll find it on the south side of the Londra Asfaltı between Topkapı otogar and the airport (coming east from the airport, follow the *servis yolu* signs). *Ataköy Tatil Köyü* (☎ 559 6000), on the shore south-east of the airport, and *Florya Turistik Tesisleri* (☎ 663 1000) are holiday beach-hotel-bungalow complexes with camping facilities. To get to the Ataköy, take bus No 81 from Eminönü; to get to Florya, take the banliyö (suburban) train from Sirkeci train station.

Hostels & Hotels South-east of Sultanahmet is Cankurtaran, an area of quiet streets and good, cheap and moderate hotels. For four and five-star hotels, go to Taksim. Most cheap hotels have carpet shops attached, so beware of being pressured – gently or tediously – to buy.

Sultanahmet The *Yücelt Interyouth Hostel* (☎ 513 6150), Caferiye Sokak 6/1, has dorm beds for US$6, beds in three or four-bed rooms for US$8 and doubles with toilet for US$18.

Arsenal Youth Hostel (☎ 513 6407), Dr Emin Paşa Sokak 12, off Divan Yolu by the Tarihi Park Hamamı, has similar prices, but fewer services.

Yerebatan Caddesi runs west from Aya Sofya. A block past the Sunken Palace Cistern, turn right on Salkım Söğüt Sokak to find *Hotel Ema* (☎ 511 7166) and *Hotel Anadolu* (☎ 512 1035). The Anadolu is old, cheap and quiet at US$20 for a double with sink (free hot showers), or US$30 for a double with private shower. The Ema is newer, and almost as cheap.

Cankurtaran Incredibly, many budget hotels are clustered around the deluxe Four Seasons Hotel Istanbul (US$350+ per night), south-east of the fountain park between Aya Sofya and the Blue Mosque.

Opposite the Four Seasons' front door is the *Hotel Side Pansiyon* (☎/fax 517 6590),

GREATER İSTANBUL

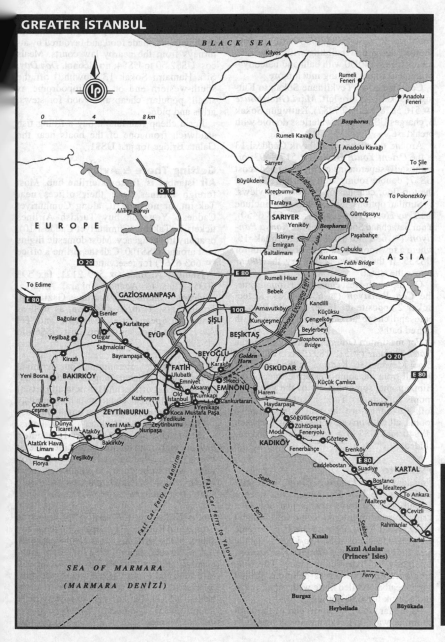

Utangaç Sokak 20. It has two buildings, an older one with rooms for US$20/25 a single/double with sink, US$30/35 with private shower; and a new building with quite nice rooms for US$40/50 with bath and balcony – as good as rooms costing much more.

Continue down Tevkifhane Sokak to Kutlugün Sokak and turn left. *Mavi Guesthouse* (☎ 516 5878; fax 517 7287), Kutlugün Sokak 3, charges US$20 for a waterless double with breakfast.

Around the corner at Akbıyık Caddesi 13 is the *Orient Youth Hostel* (☎ 517 9493; ori enthostel@superonline.com); dorm beds cost US$7, double rooms with sink US$20, and the top-floor café has marvellous sea views.

Similar options farther downhill include the *Troy Hostel* (☎ 516 8757; fax 638 6450), Yeni Saraçhane Sokak 6; and the *Konya Pansiyon* (☎ 638 3638), Terbıyık Sokak 15, where a few rooms also have private bath for US$35. If the Konya is full, try the *İlknur* across the street.

Off the south-west end of the Hippodrome, the *Can Pansiyon* (☎ 638 6608), Kaleci Sokak 2 opposite the Hotel Sokullu Paşa, is bare and cheap at US$5 per person, with shared baths.

For maximum Ottoman ambience, try the *Hotel Turkuaz* (☎ 518 1897; fax 517 3380), Cinci Meydanı 36, Kadırga, at the bottom of the hill from the south-western corner of the Hippodrome, somewhat out of the way. The rooms, furnishings, Turkish bath and Turkish folk-art lounge are the real thing. The 14 rooms, all with private shower, cost between US$40 and US$80 a double, breakfast included.

Places to Eat

Nowadays, the *Pudding Shop*, officially known as the Lale Restaurant and once a legend amongst travellers, is just one of a string of medium-priced *lokanta* (restaurants) along Divan Yolu opposite the Hippodrome – typical meals cost US$4 to US$6. Try the *Can Restaurant*, or the *Vitamin Restaurant*, a brightly lit, hyperactive place. The *Sultanahmet Köftecisi* serves delicious grilled lamb meatballs called köfte with salad, bread and a drink for US$3 or less.

At the far (south-western) end of the Hippodrome, walk up Peykhane Sokak one short block to the *Yeni Birlik Lokantası* (☎ 517 6465), at No 46, a large, light restaurant serving ready-made food and favoured by attorneys from the nearby law courts. Meals cost US$2.50 to US$4; no alcohol. *Doy Doy*, Şifa Hamamı Sokak 13, downhill off the south-western end of the Hippodrome, is small, popular, cheap and good for stews, grills and pide.

For a cheap fish lunch, buy a filling fish sandwich from one of the boats near the Galata Bridge for just US$1.

Getting There & Away

Air İstanbul is Turkey's airline hub. Most foreign airlines have their offices near Taksim, or north of it, along Cumhuriyet Caddesi. You can buy Turkish Airlines tickets in Taksim (Cumhuriyet Caddesi 10), or at any travel agency. Most domestic flights cost around US$100. Call the airline's office (☎ 663 6363) for reservations.

İstanbul Airlines (☎ 509 2121; fax 593 6035) flies to Adana, Ankara, Antalya, Bodrum, Dalaman, Erzurum, Gaziantep, İzmir, Kars, Trabzon and Van, as well as many European cities, Moscow and Tel Aviv. Most domestic flights cost US$65 to US$90.

Bus İstanbul's international bus terminal (Uluslararası İstanbul Otogarı, ☎ 658 0505) has 168 ticket offices and buses to all parts of Turkey and beyond. Get to it via hızlı tramvay (fast tram) from Aksaray; get out at Otogar.

Buses depart for Ankara (seven hours, US$15 to US$24) roughly every 15 minutes, day and night, and to most other cities at least every hour. Heading east to Anatolia, you might want to board at the smaller otogar at Harem, north of Haydarpaşa on the Asian shore, reachable by car ferry from Sirkeci.

Train Sirkeci is the station for trains to Edirne and Europe. Haydarpaşa, on the Asian shore, is the terminus for trains to Anatolia. Ask at Sirkeci station (☎ 527 0050) or Haydarpaşa station (☎ 216-336 0475) for rail information. From Sirkeci there are four express trains daily to Edirne (five to seven hours, US$3), but the bus is faster (three hours, US$5). The nightly *İstanbul Express* goes to Munich.

From Haydarpaşa there are seven express trains daily to Ankara (seven to eight hours, US$6 to US$12); the *Ankara Ekspresi* (nine hours, US$25) is all sleeping cars.

See Boat, below, for the Marmara Express to İzmir.

Boat From Yenikapı, just south of Aksaray, fast car ferries depart daily for Bandırma (2½ hours, US$6), whence you may continue to İzmir on the *Marmara Ekspresi* train (6½ hours, US$4), or by bus to Çanakkale. Another fast car ferry goes to Yalova (50 minutes, US$5), whence you can continue to İznik or Bursa by bus. Also, fast catamarans (deniz otobüsü) run from Kabataş, just south of Dolmabahçe, to Yalova five times on weekdays, 11 times on Saturday and Sunday.

Reserve your space on the weekend car ferry to İzmir at the Turkish Maritime Lines (Denizyolları) office (☎ 249 9222 for reservations, ☎ 244 0207 for information), Rıhtım Caddesi, Karaköy, just east of the Karaköy ferry dock.

Getting Around
To/From the Airport Havaş airport buses depart from the domestic terminal about every 30 minutes for Taksim Square (30 to 45 minutes, US$3.50). To get from the international terminal to the domestic terminal, take the infrequent Havaş shuttle, or a rip-off taxi for US$3, or make the eight-minute walk. City buses from the airport to Sultanahmet are infrequent and slow.

An airport taxi costs about US$12 to US$14 for the 23km to Old İstanbul, and US$13 to US$15 to Beyoğlu; it costs 50% more at night. Many of the Divan Yolu travel agencies and Sultanahmet hostels and hotels book minibus transport from your hotel to the airport for about US$5 or US$6. For more than two people, a taxi is cheaper unless it's after midnight and before 7 am.

Bus Destinations and intermediate stops on city bus routes are shown on a sign on the right (kerb) side of the bus. IETT buses are run by the city, and you must have a ticket (50 cents) before boarding; some long routes require that you stuff two tickets into the box. You can buy tickets from the white booths near major stops or from nearby shops. Stock

up in advance. *Özel Halk Otobüsü* are private buses regulated by the city; they accept either city bus tickets or cash.

Dolmuş Minibuses called dolmuş run on fixed routes around the city and up the Bosphorus, charging a bit more than the bus fare.

Train To get to Sirkeci train station, take the tramvay (tram) from Aksaray or Sultanahmet, or any bus signed for Eminönü. Haydarpaşa train station is connected by ferry to Karaköy (at least every 30 minutes, 50 cents). Banliyö (suburban) trains (40 cents) run every 20 minutes along the southern walls of Old İstanbul and westward along the Marmara shore, stopping at Cankurtaran, Kumkapı, Yenikapı etc.

Underground The Tünel (İstanbul's underground train) mounts the hill from Karaköy to Tünel Square and İstiklal Caddesi (every 10 or 15 minutes, 35 cents). An underground line running north from Taksim should be operational soon.

Tram The hızlı tramvay (50 cents), runs west from Aksaray via Adnan Menderes Bulvarı through the city walls to the otogar. A street tram (50 cents) runs from Eminönü to Gülhane and Sultanahmet, then along Divan Yolu to Çemberlitaş, Beyazıt (for the Covered Bazar) and Aksaray, thence south-west to Zeytinburnu. A restored turn-of-the-century tram (30 cents) trundles along İstiklal Caddesi, which runs between Tünel and Taksim.

Taxi İstanbul has 60,000 yellow taxis, all with digital meters; some are driven by lunatics who will really take you for a ride. From Sultanahmet to Taksim costs US$3 to US$4; to the otogar costs around US$10.

Around İstanbul

EDİRNE
☎ 284
European Turkey is known as Thrace (Trakya). If you pass through, stop in Edirne, a pleasant, undervisited town with decent

cheap hotels and several striking mosques. The best is the **Selimiye Camii**, the finest work of Süleyman the Magnificent's master architect Sinan. The impressive **Beyazıt II Camii** is well worth a walk across the river. Both the **Üçşerefeli Cami** and the **Eski Cami** are currently undergoing restoration, but are still impressive.

The tourist office (☎ 225 1518), Hürriyet Meydanı 17, is in the town centre. Around the corner from the tourist office on Maarif Caddesi are the cheap but threadbare *Anıl* (☎ 212 1482) with US$4 beds and, down the street, the better *Efe Hotel* (☎ 213 6166) at US$18/26. The comfortable *Park Hotel* (☎ 213 5276), also on Maarif, charges US$22/30 a single/double. The *Otel Şaban Açıkgöz* (☎ 213 1404), near the Eski Cami, is good value for US$16/23 with shower, TV and breakfast. Buses run very frequently to İstanbul (three hours, US$5) and five times daily south to Çanakkale.

BURSA
☎ 224

Sprawled at the base of Uludağ mountain, Turkey's biggest winter sports centre, Bursa was the Ottoman capital prior to İstanbul's conquest. It retains several fine mosques and pretty neighbourhoods from early Ottoman times, but Bursa's big attraction, now and historically, is its thermal springs. Besides healthy hot water, Bursa produces lots of succulent fruit and most of the cars made in Turkey. It's also famous for its savoury kebabs.

Orientation & Information

The city centre, with its banks and shops, is along Atatürk Caddesi between the Ulu Cami (Grand Mosque) to the west and the main square, Cumhuriyet Alanı, commonly called Heykel (*heykel* means 'statue'), to the east. The post office is on the south side of Atatürk Caddesi across from the Ulu Cami. Çekirge, with its hot springs, is about 6km west of Heykel. Bursa's bus station ('terminal') is 10km north on the Yalova road, reached by special grey buses marked 'Terminal' which leave from Heykel (35 cents).

You can get maps and brochures at the tourist office (☎ 251 1834) in the Orhangazi

Altgeçidi subway, Ulu Cami Parkı, opposite the Koza Han (silk market).

Things to See & Do

The largest of Bursa's beautiful mosques is the 20-domed **Ulu Cami** (Grand Mosque), built in 1399; it's on Atatürk Caddesi in the city centre. About 1km east of Heykel in a pretty pedestrian zone are the early-Ottoman **Yeşil Cami** (Green Mosque, built in 1424), its beautifully tiled **Yeşil Türbe** (Green Tomb; open from 8 am to noon and 1 to 5 pm; entry free) and the **Turkish & Islamic Arts Museum**, or Türk İslam Eserleri Müzesi (open 8.30 am to noon and 1 to 5 pm; closed Monday; entry US$1.50).

A few hundred metres farther east is the **Emir Sultan Camii** (1805). To get there, take a dolmuş or bus No 18 (marked Emir Sultan) from Heykel.

Uphill and west of the Grand Mosque, on the way to Çekirge, are the beautifully situated **Tombs of Osman & Orhan**, which house the remains of the first Ottoman sultans. A kilometre beyond is the **Muradiye Mosque Complex**, with its decorated tombs dating from the 14th and 15th centuries.

The **mineral baths** are in the suburb of Çekirge.

On a clear day it's worth going up **Uludağ**. From Heykel take bus 3/B, 3/C etc or a dolmuş east to the *teleferik* (cable car) up the mountain (US$5 one way), or take a dolmuş (US$6) from Orhangazi Caddesi for the entire 22km to the top.

Places to Stay

In Tahtakale, south of the Ulu Cami, the *Otel Güneş* (☎ 222 1404), İnebey Caddesi 75, has useable waterless rooms for US$8/12. The neighbouring *Otel Çamlıbel* (☎ 221 2565), İnebey Caddesi 71, is fancier at US$20/30. Better value is the *Hotel İpekçi* (☎ 221 1935), Çancılar Caddesi 38, in the market north of Heykel, with singles/doubles at US$12/18. The tidy, quiet *Hotel Çeşmeli* (☎ 224 1511), Gümüşçeken Caddesi 6, just north of Heykel, is good but pricey at US$26/40, with breakfast.

Staying in Çekirge, you get free mineral baths. The *Öz Yeşil Yayla Oteli* (☎ 236 8026), Selvi Sokak 6, is straight from the 1950s, with matching prices: US$22 a

ouble. The nearby *Boyugüzel* (☎ 233 3850)
s similar. Four and five-star hotels abound.

Places to Eat

Bursa is renowned for İskender kebap (döner
kebap topped with savoury tomato sauce and
browned butter). Competition for patrons is
fierce among kebapçıs. *Kebapçı İskender*,
Ünlü Caddesi 7, just east of Heykel, dates
back to 1867 and has a posh dining room but
decent prices – about US$6 with a soft drink.
Adanur Hacıbey, opposite, charges the same
but is less fancy.

Çiçek Izgara, Belediye Caddesi 15, just
north of the half-timbered belediye (town
hall) in the flower market, is bright and
modern, good for women travellers, and open
every day from 11 am to 3.30 pm and from
5.30 to 9 pm.

For cheaper eats, head for Tahtakale and
the *Şehir* and *Ümit* restaurants on İnebey
Caddesi. Sakarya Caddesi, downhill from the
Great Mosque off Altıparmak Caddesi, has
numerous tavernas for a jolly evening of
seafood and drinks.

Getting There & Away

The fastest way to İstanbul is by bus to
Yalova (every half-hour, 70 minutes, US$3),
then the fast (one hour) Yalova-İstanbul
(Yenikapı) deniz otobüsü (catamaran; five a
day), or the 'jet feribot' to Yenikapı, either
for US$6.

Buses to İstanbul designated *feribot ile* use
the Topçular-Eskihisar ferry, which is
quicker (2½ hours) than the land route
(*karayolu ile*) round the Marmara (four
hours, US$9).

An airport is under construction at
Yenişehir, 40km east of Bursa.

Getting Around

Buy BOI city bus tickets (40 cents) at kiosks
and shops. Most routes stop on Atatürk
Caddesi. Bursa dolmuş with little 'D' plates
on top charge 45 cents or more for a seat.
Those marked 'SSK Hastanesi' go to
Çekirge, 'Dev(let) Hast(anesi)' go to the
Orhan & Osman tombs, and those marked
'Yeşil' go to the Yeşil Cami (Green Mosque)
area. Special grey 'Terminal' buses shuttle
the 10km north to the bus station.

The Aegean Coast

Olive groves and a unique history distinguish
this gorgeous but rapidly developing coast.
Gallipoli, Troy and Pergamum are only a few
of the famous places to be visited.

ÇANAKKALE
☎ 286

Laid-back Çanakkale is a hub for transport to
Troy and across the Dardanelles to Gallipoli.
It was here that Leander swam across what
was then called the Hellespont to his lover
Hero, and here too that Lord Byron did his
romantic bit and duplicated the feat. The
defence of the straits during WWI led to a
Turkish victory over Anzac forces on 18
March 1916, now a major local holiday.

The helpful tourist office (☎ 217 1187) and
many cheap hotels and cafés are within a few
blocks of the ferry pier, near the landmark
clock tower.

The Ottoman **castle** built by Sultan
Mehmet the Conqueror in 1452 is now the
Army & Navy Museum. Just over 2km south
of the ferry pier, the **Archaeological Museum**
holds artefacts found at Troy and Assos.

Places to Stay

Camping is at Güzelyalı Beach, 15km south
by dolmuş off the road to Troy; try *Mocamp
Trova* (☎ 232 8025). Most of the small
Çanakkale hotels and pensions have identical
city-regulated prices (singles/doubles for
US$6/10, or US$7/11 with shower). All are
heavily booked in summer; the town is in-
sanely crowded around Anzac Day, 25 April.

Anzac House (☎ 217 1392), Demiricioğlu
Caddesi, has dorm beds for US$4, singles/
doubles for US$6/10. Look at the room first.

Hotel Efes (☎ 217 4687), behind the clock
tower at Aralık Sokak 5, is bright and cheerful. *Hotel Akgün* (☎ 217 3049), across the
street, is similar, as are the *Hotel Erdem*
(☎ 217 4986) and *Hotel Umut* (☎ 217 6473),
nearer to the clock tower. *Yellow Rose
Pension* (☎ 217 3343), Yeni Sokak 5, is passable, though it could be friendlier. By the
clock tower, the *Kervansaray* (☎ 217 8192),
an attractive old house with a garden, is a
good option, as is the more up-to-date *Konak*
(☎ 217 1150).

TURKEY

Otel Aşkın (☎/fax 217 4956), Hasan Mevsuf Sokak 53, less than a block north of the bus station, charges US$16 a double with shower and breakfast. The nearby Aşkın Pansiyon (same phone), has waterless doubles for US$8.

The Hotel Temizay (☎ 212 8760; fax 217 5885), Cumhuriyet Meydanı 15, is central, clean and new, with singles/doubles/triples for US$20/30/45. The one-star Hotel Kestanbol (☎ 217 0857; fax 217 9173), Hasan Mevsuf Sokak 5, inland a few blocks and across the street from the Emniyet Sarayı (police station), has 26 rooms, all with bath, costing US$20/30 a single/double including breakfast.

Places to Eat

The Gaziantep Aile Kebap ve Pide Salonu, behind the clock tower, serves good cheap pide and more substantial kebabs, while Trakya Restaurant, on the main square, always has lots of food ready and waiting 24 hours a day. If you eat at the waterfront fish restaurants, ask for all prices in advance.

GALLIPOLI

Although the Dardanelles had always been İstanbul's first line of defence, it was in WWI that they proved their worth. Atop the narrow, hilly peninsula, Mustafa Kemal (Atatürk) and his troops fought off a far superior but badly commanded force of Anzac and British troops. A visit to the battle-grounds and war graves of Gallipoli (Gelibolu), now a national park, is a moving experience.

Several companies run four-hour minibus tours (US$14 to US$20) of Gallipoli from Çanakkale, Eceabat and Gelibolu. Most companies are allied with hotels or pensions, which may put pressure on you to take their tour. Ask other travellers which tour they've liked. If you're a hiker, take a ferry from Çanakkale to Eceabat and a dolmuş to Kabatepe, and follow the trail around the sites described in a booklet sold at the visitor centre (Kabatepe Tanıtma Merkezi) there.

Turkish Maritime Lines' car ferries cross the straits hourly from Lapseki to Gallipoli and from Çanakkale to Eceabat (50 cents per person). Small private 'dolmuş' ferries cross more frequently, more cheaply and mor quickly (15 to 20 minutes) from Çanakkal (in front of the Hotel Bakır) to Kilitbahi Buses make the five-hour trip to Gallipol from İstanbul's Esenler otogar.

TROY

There's not much of the historic 'Trojar Horse' Troy (Truva) to be seen, because it' estimated that nine successive cities have been built on this same site. Troy I goes righ back to the Bronze Age. Legendary Troy is thought to be Troy VI. Most of the ruins you see are Roman ones from Troy IX. Still, it' nice to say you've been there.

Dolmuş run the 30km from Çanakkale frequently for US$1.50. Walk straight inland from the ferry pier to Atatürk Caddesi, and turn right towards Troy; the dolmuş station is at the bridge.

Tevfikiye, the farming village 1km before the site, has a few small pensions charging US$12 a double, or you can camp at the Priamos Restaurant for US$2 a head. Troy is open daily from 8 am to 5 pm; admission is US$2.

BEHRAMKALE (ASSOS)

Nineteen kilometres west of Ayvacık, Behramkale, once known as Assos, has the hill-top Temple of Athena looking across the water to Lesvos (Greece), and was considered one of the most beautiful cities of its time. It is still beautiful, particularly the tiny port (iskele) 2km beyond the village.

Dost provides camping at the port for US$5.50; or camp in the olive groves east of the town for US$2. On the heights, Halıcı Han and other pensions can put you up for US$12 a double, and the Kale Restaurant will feed you. Port hotels (Behram, Kervansaray, Şen, Yıldız) are more expensive (US$60 a double with two meals), but also more comfy and atmospheric. Visit in low season (US$25 a double) if you can.

AYVALIK

☎ 266

Once inhabited by Ottoman Greeks, this popular beach resort is packed with Turkish holiday-makers in summer. The main street, İnönü Caddesi, links the otogar, 1.5km north

f the town centre, and the tourist office
☎ 312 2122), 1km south, opposite the marina.

Offshore is **Alibey Island**, with open-air
restaurants, linked by ferries and a causeway
to the mainland (take the red 'Ayvalık
Belediyesi' bus north). Six kilometres south
on a blue 'Sarımsaklı Belediyesi' bus is the
2km-long **Sarımsaklı Plaj** (beach), also
called Plajlar.

Turkish boats make the two-hour trip to
Lesvos in the morning, Greek boats in the
evening, for an outrageous US$50 one way
and US$65 same-day return. Boats operate at
least three days per week from late May to
September.

Places to Stay & Eat
Several camping grounds are on Alibey Adası
outside the village. *Taksiyarhis Pansiyon*
(☎ 312 1494), Mareşal Çakmak Caddesi 71,
is a beautiful renovated Ottoman house charging US$5 a head, plus US$2 for breakfast; it's
often full in summer. The *Çiçek Pansiyon*
(☎ 312 1201), 200m south of the town centre
and one street in from the water (follow the
signs), rents basic, badly faded rooms for
US$4 a head; the *Biret* and *Melisa* round the
corner take the overflow. *Motel Kıyı* (☎ 312
6677), Gümrük Meydanı 18, charges US$8 a
head for small rooms with shower.

Off İnönü Caddesi are several good, cheap
restaurants such as the *Ayvalık* and the
Anadolu Pide ve Kebap Salonu. The ones in
the market, east of the main road, are more atmospheric. The *Öz Canlı Balık Restaurant*
on the waterfront is pricier but good for
seafood.

BERGAMA
☎ 232
From the 4th to the 2nd centuries BC,
Bergama (Pergamum) was a powerful and
cultured kingdom. A line of rulers beginning
with a general under Alexander the Great
ruled over this small but wealthy kingdom,
whose **asclepion** (medical school; 3.5km
from the city centre; entry US$2.50) grew
famous and whose library rivalled that of
Alexandria in Egypt. The star attractions here
are the city's ruins, especially the **acropolis**
(a hill-top site 6km from the city centre; entry
US$2), and an excellent **archaeology &**

ethnography museum (in the city centre,
entry US$2).

The tourist office (☎ 633 1862) is at
Cumhuriyet Meydanı in the town centre.
Taxis wait here and charge US$4.50 to the
acropolis, US$10 total if they wait an hour
and bring you back down. If you're a walker,
follow the path down through the ruins
instead. A tour of the acropolis, the asclepion and the museum costs US$20.

Places to Stay & Eat
Hotel Berksoy (see following) and, just west
of it, *Karavan Camping* have sites.

The spotless, family-run *Böblingen
Pension* (☎ 633 2153), Asklepion Caddesi 2,
has doubles with shower and breakfast for
US$12. The *Pension Athena* (☎ 633 3420),
İmam Çıkmazı 5 (follow the signs from the
Meydan Restaurant), is in a 160-year-old
stone house and a newer building. Rooms
with/without shower cost US$7/5, breakfast
another US$2.

Cross the nearby bridge and turn left to
find the *Nike Pension* (☎ 633 3901), Tabak
Köprü Çıkmazı 2, with bigger rooms in a
300-year-old Ottoman Greek house for US$8
including breakfast.

For luxury, there's the *Hotel Berksoy*
(☎ 633 2595) east of the town, charging
US$45/65 a single/double amid well-kept
gardens with a pool.

About 150m south-west of the old red
basilica on the main street is a square where
you'll find the *Meydan Restaurant* charging
about US$5 or US$6 for a three-course meal
on vine-shaded terraces. The simpler
Sarmaşık Lokantası has no outdoor seating,
but is cheaper. Heading south-west towards
the museum and pensions, the *Şen Kardeşler*
and *Çiçek Sever Kebap Salonu* are good,
cheap options.

The *Sağlam Restaurant*, on the left as you
head into town from the otogar, with another
branch near the Meydan Restaurant, specialises in Urfa-style kebaps.

Getting There & Away
Buses shuttle between Bergama and İzmir
every half-hour in summer (1¾ hours, US$4).
Four buses connect Bergama's otogar and
Ayvalık daily; or you can hitch out to the
highway and catch a bus.

ESKİ FOÇA

☎ 232

The ancient Phocaea, founded in 600 BC, is now one of the Aegean's nicer resort towns. The otogar is near the town centre, as is the tourism office (☎ 812 1222).

Enjoy a meal at a seaside restaurant, poke around the two old **castles**, take a boat trip to nearby islands, or head north along the coast toward Yeni Foça (New Foça, 25km north), stopping at any of several decent **beaches**.

Foça's many small pensions charge US$8 to US$12 for double rooms with breakfast. Try the *Ensar Aile Pansiyonu* (☎ 812 1777), 161 Sokak 15, or the adjoining *Siren Pansiyon* (☎ 812 2660). Small hotels may charge up to US$25 for doubles with private bath, as do the nice *Hotel Melaike* (☎ 812 2414), 32 Sokak 4, and the *Sempatik Hotel Güneş* (☎ 812 2195), 206 Sokak No 11.

Walk from the main square to the small bay (Küçük Deniz) to find the cheap restaurants including the *Zümrüt*, *Julianna's* and *İmren*, with meals for US$2 or US$3. Along the waterfront, the *Celep*, *Gemici*, *Foça* etc charge US$12 to US$20 for full fish dinners.

Buses run to and from İzmir (1½ hours, US$1.75) hourly in summer.

İZMİR

☎ 232

Turkey's third-largest city, once named Smyrna, is said to be the place where Homer was born in 700 BC. Today it's a transport hub, but otherwise a good place to skip. İzmir is spread out and baffling to find your way around, and its hotels are overpriced. If you stay, you can enjoy the good **bazar**, the 2nd-century Roman agora, the hill-top Kadifekale **fortress**, and the **archaeological and ethnographic museums**. Other than that there is not much to see here because of the great fire of 1922. You can get to the Greek island of Chios from Çeşme, 90km (two hours) west of İzmir.

Orientation

Central İzmir is a web of plazas linked by streets that aren't at right angles to each other. Instead of names, the back streets have numbers. Luckily, the tourist office hands out detailed maps.

Budget hotels are clustered near the Basmane train station. South-west, Anafartalar Caddesi twists and turns through the labyrinthine bazar to the waterfront at Konak, the commercial and government centre. Atatürk Caddesi, also called Birinci Kordon, runs north-east from Konak along the waterfront 1.4km to Cumhuriyet Meydanı (and its equestrian statue of Atatürk), where you'll find the main post office, luxury hotels, and tourist and airline offices.

At Atatürk Caddesi's northern end is the harbour (Alsancak Yeni Limanı) and the smaller, mostly suburban Alsancak train station. İzmir's otogar is 2km east of Alsancak train station.

Information

The tourist office (☎ 484 2147) is in the Büyük Efes Oteli at Gaziosmanpaşa Bulvarı 1/C, Cumhuriyet Meydanı, with another at Adnan Menderes airport. There's a good city information desk in the Belediye (Municipality) building in Konak.

Places to Stay

From Basmane train station, walk south along Anafartalar Caddesi. Turn right on 1296 Sokak, a quiet street lined with cheap hotels charging about US$8 a double, or US$12 with private shower.

Anafartalar Caddesi winds into the bazar. Near the Hatuniye (or Kuşlu) Camii (mosque) is the *Otel Saray* (☎ 483 6946), at Anafartalar Caddesi 635, which has been popular with backpackers for years. Get a room on the upper floor (it's quieter there) for US$12 a single/double with sink. Up 945 Sokak at No 26 is the cleaner, cheaper, more comfortable *Otel Hikmet* (☎ 484 2672), which charges US$3/6 for waterless rooms, US$7.50/14 a single/double with private shower.

For other hotels, walk straight down Fevzipaşa Bulvarı from Basmane station and turn right (north). 1368 Sokak and its westward continuation, 1369 Sokak, have good, clean, quiet and cheap hotels such as the *Çiçek Palas*, *Divan*, *Kamioğlu*, *Ova*, *Gönen Palas* and *Akgün*, charging about US$12 to US$18 for a double room with a private shower. The *Otel Antik Han* (☎ 489 2750), Anafartalar Caddesi 600, in a restored house

İZMIR

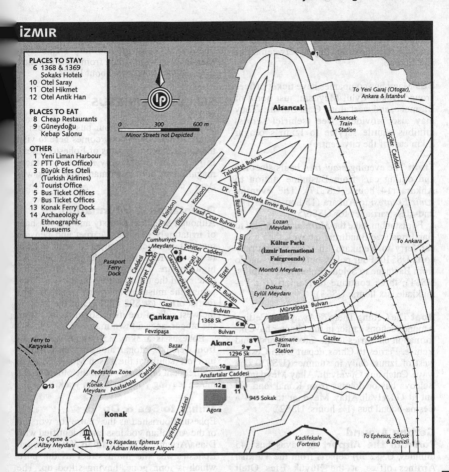

PLACES TO STAY
6 1368 & 1369
   Sokaks Hotels
10 Otel Saray
11 Otel Hikmet
12 Otel Antik Han

PLACES TO EAT
8 Cheap Restaurants
9 Güneydoğu
   Kebap Salonu

OTHER
1 Yeni Liman Harbour
2 PTT (Post Office)
3 Büyük Efes Oteli
   (Turkish Airlines)
4 Tourist Office
5 Bus Ticket Offices
7 Bus Ticket Offices
13 Konak Ferry Dock
14 Archaeology &
   Ethnographic
   Musuems

right in the bazar, has character and costs US$20/30 with baths, TVs and ceiling fans.

Places to Eat

Immediately opposite Basmane station, the *Ankara*, *Karaca Birtat*, *Ödemis Azim* and *Aydın-Denizli-Nazili* restaurants offer quick, cheap meals in noisy surroundings. Little eateries are also scattered along the budget-hotel streets.

On 1296 Sokak is the cheap *Güneydoğu Kebap Salonu*, where a kebab plate and a drink cost US$4 or less. But the restaurants on 1368 and 1369 sokaks, just across Fevzipaşa Bulvarı, are much more pleasant. The *Dört Mevsim Et Lokantası*, 1369 Sokak No 51/A, specialises in meats, and will fill you up for US$5.

The upmarket restaurants are along Ata-türk Caddesi, by the sea.

Getting There & Away

Air Turkish Airlines (☎ 484 1220), Gazios-manpaşa Bulvarı 1/F, in the Büyük Efes Oteli at Cumhuriyet Meydanı, has flights to İstanbul (50 minutes, US$90) and Ankara, with connections to other places.

TURKEY

İstanbul Airlines (☎ 489 0541), Gaziosmanpaşa Bulvarı 2/E, has some flights to İstanbul, and numerous flights between İzmir and Europe.

Bus Many bus companies have ticket offices around Dokuz Eylül Meydanı, just north of Basmane, and west along Gazi Bulvarı. They may also provide a free (şehiriçi servis) minibus shuttle service to İzmir's otogar (3km east of the city centre).

Train The evening *mavi tren* hauls sleeping and dining cars from Basmane station to Ankara (14 hours, US$17). The evening *İzmir Ekspresi* to Ankara (15 hours) has 1st/2nd-class carriages for US$6/5.

For İstanbul, take the *Marmara Ekspresi* to Bandırma (see Bandırma, above), then a fast car ferry to Yenikapı; in total the journey costs US$10. Four pokey but cheap trains go from Basmane to Selçuk/Ephesus (2½ hours, US$1); three continue to Denizli (for Pamukkale, six hours, US$3).

Boat The Getting There & Away and Getting Around sections earlier in this chapter have information on ferries to the Greek Islands and Venice. Ferries to Chios depart from Çeşme, west of İzmir, daily in summer (US$30 one way). Catch any Güzelyalı, Altay Meydanı or Balçova bus or dolmuş from Konak and get out at Güzelyalı/Altay Meydanı to board a Çeşme-bound bus (1½ hours, US$2).

Getting Around
To/From the Airport A Havaş bus (45 minutes, US$2.50) departs from the Turkish Airlines office at the Büyük Efes Oteli several times daily for the 25km trip to Adnan Menderes airport. Trains (50 cents) run hourly from Alsancak train station to the airport, and *some* southbound trains from Basmane also stop at the airport, but a dolmuş is faster and more reliable. From Montrö Meydanı, 700m north of Basmane, southbound 'Adnan Menderes Belediyesi' buses go to the airport during the day for US$1. A taxi costs US$18 to US$20 if you can get the driver to run the meter.

Local Transport City buses 50, 51 and 52 ('Yeni Garaj-Konak') go from the otogar via Alsancak Garı and Çankaya (for Basmane) to Konak for 70 cents; buy your ticket before boarding. There are dolmuş ('Çankaya-Mersinli') as well. A taxi from the city centre to the bus station costs about US$4.

SELÇUK & EPHESUS
☎ 232

Selçuk is an easy 1¼-hour bus trip south of İzmir. Almost everybody comes here to visit the splendid Roman ruins of Ephesus (Efes). In its Ionian heyday only Athens was more magnificent, and in Roman times this was Asia's capital.

Orientation & Information
Although Selçuk is touristy and has its share of irritatingly persistent carpet and pension touts, it is modest compared with coastal resorts like Kuşadası. On the east side of the highway are the otogar, restaurants, some hotels and the train station; on the west side, behind the museum, are many pensions. The tourist office (☎ 892 1328) is in the park on the west side of the main street, across from the otogar, as is a town map.

Ephesus is a 3km, 35-minute walk west from Selçuk's otogar along a shady road – turn left (south) at the Tusan Motel. Or there are frequent minibuses from the otogar to the motel, leaving you just a 1km walk.

Things to See & Do
Ephesus flourished as the centre for worship of the Anatolian goddess later identified with Diana/Artemis. The **Arcadian Way** through Ephesus was the main street to the port, which is long gone, having silted up. The immense **Great Theatre** holds 24,000 people. The **Temple of Hadrian**, the **Celsus Library**, the **Marble Way** (where the rich lived) and the **Fountain of Trajan** are still in amazingly good shape, or under painstaking restoration. The site, permanently swamped with coach groups, is open daily from 8.30 am to 5.30 pm (7 pm in summer). Entry fees are US$6, plus US$1.25 to park a car.

The excellent **Ephesus Museum** in Selçuk (open from 8.30 am to noon and 1 to 5 pm; closed Monday; entry $3.50) has a striking collection of artefacts from the Roman period. The foundations of the **Temple of**

Artemis, between Ephesus and Selçuk, are all that is left of one of the Seven Wonders of the World. Ephesus was later a centre of early Christianity. It was visited by St Paul, who wrote a famous letter to the Ephesians. Above Selçuk is the **Basilica of St John**, said to be built over his tomb. The Virgin Mary is said to have lived her last years at **Meryemana**, on a nearby mountain top.

Places to Stay

Garden Motel & Camping (☎ 892 6165) is west of Ayasoluk, the hill bearing the citadel and Basilica of St John; walk past the basilica, down the hill, then turn right at the İsabey Camii. Quiet tent and caravan sites amidst fruit orchards cost US$7, dorm beds US$3. Other sites are at Pamucak, 7km west of town.

There are many pensions up the hill behind the Selçuk Museum, charging about US$6 to US$8 per person. Good choices are the *Barım*, at Turgutreis Sokak 34, on the first street back from the museum, and the *Australia & New Zealand Pension* (☎ 892 6050) at Profesör Mitler Sokak 17, on the second street back. Also worth seeking out are the *Homeros* (☎ 892 3995), Asmalı Sokak 17; *Abasız* (☎ 892 1367), Turgutreis Sokak 13, with nine rooms (some with views); and the 10-room *Outback Pansiyon* (☎ 891 4039), Turgutreis Sokak 5, some with showers.

The family-run *Vardar Pension* (☎ 891 4967), close to the market at Sahabettin Dede Caddesi 9, has 16 small, clean rooms, most with bath, and a nice dining terrace.

For luxury, the best place is the atmospheric, 50-room *Otel Kalehan* (☎ 892 6154), on the main road just north of the Shell station. Rooms with showers, minifridges and air-con cost US$30/50/60 a single/double/triple, simpler bungalows only US$20. There's a pool as well.

Cengiz Topel Caddesi, a pedestrian street between the Cybele fountain at the highway and the town square by the train station, has several decent hotels charging US$18 to US$25 a double with private bath.

Places to Eat

Cengiz Topel Caddesi has many outdoor restaurants and cafés. For cheap pide, try the *Artemis Pide Salonu*, a half-block south of the tea garden at the eastern end of Cengiz Topel, where Turkish-style pizza goes for US$1.50 to US$2.50. *Okumuşlar Pide Salonu* on Namık Kemal Caddesi is similar. The *Kodalak Restaurant* at the otogar serves cheap stews, but ask for prices before you order.

Getting There & Away

Minibuses leave frequently for Kuşadası (30 minutes, 80 cents) and Pamucak (10 minutes, 70 cents), passing the Ephesus turn-off (five minutes, 50 cents). Taxis to Ephesus charge US$4; ask for the *güney kapısı* (southern gate) so you can walk downhill. A dolmuş to Pamucak leaves at 8 am daily from the otogar.

You can make a day trip to Pamukkale (three hours, US$7 one way) on direct buses leaving before 9 am and returning by 5 pm. Frequent buses and three cheap trains (US$2) go daily to Denizli, where you can get a dolmuş to Pamukkale. Hourly buses go to Bodrum and to Marmaris. Buses to İzmir leave regularly from 6.30 am to 7 pm (1¼ hours, US$1.75); the six daily trains are slower (2½ hours) but cheaper (US$1).

KUŞADASI
☎ 256

This is a cruise-ship port and a cheerfully shameless tourist trap. The main reason to visit is to catch a boat to the Greek island of Samos, although Kuşadası is a good base for visits to the ancient cities of **Priene**, **Miletus** and **Didyma** to the south. Tours are pricey at US$18 to US$25, so you might want to try a combination of local buses and hitching instead. There are also good beaches and a national park at **Güzelçamlı**, 25 minutes south by dolmuş.

The tourist office (☎ 614 1103) is right by the pier and the otogar 1.5km south-east of the town centre on the highway. Boats to Samos (Sisam) sail daily in summer for US$30 one way, US$35 same-day return, or US$55 open return, including Turkish port tax; ticket offices are close to the tourist office.

Places to Stay

The *Önder* and *Tur-Yat Mocamp* camping grounds, north of town on the waterfront near the marina, charge US$8 for two people in a tent.

Decent cheap hotels and pensions (US$8 to US$12 per person with shower) are uphill behind the Akdeniz Apart-otel. *Düsseldorf Pansiyon* (☎ 613 1272), on Yıldırım Caddesi, is an excellent choice with spotless rooms arrayed in front of a secluded garden. Up Aslanlar Caddesi (follow the signs), *Pension Golden Bed* (☎ 614 8708) is quiet and family-run, with a terrace café. Follow Aslanlar Caddesi to Bezirgan Sokak and turn right to find the *Pansiyon Dinç* (☎ 614 4249), Mercan Sokak, which is small, simple and cheap at US$16 for a waterless double, breakfast included; the nearby *Enişte* and *Hasgül* are similar. *Stella* (☎ 614 1632) costs more (US$60 a double) but boasts stunning harbour views.

The historic *Hotel Kervansaray* (☎ 614 4115) in the centre of town costs US$50/80 for singles/doubles including breakfast, but the nightclub noise will keep you up; you're better off just enjoying a drink in the courtyard bar. The hotels *Köken*, *Çidem* or *Akman* on İstiklal Sokak, 1km north-east of the centre, offer more comfort for less money (US$22/36 a single/double).

Places to Eat

Good seafood places along the waterfront close to the wharf charge US$15 to US$25 for a fish dinner, depending on the fish and the season. The exception is the much cheaper *Ada Restaurant* on Güvercin Adası (the little fort-topped island). Cheap meals (US$3 to US$6) are also served on Sağlık Caddesi between Kahramanlar Caddesi and İnönü Bulvarı. Try the *Konyalı* at No 40.

The Kaleiçi district shelters several charming cafés, a million miles in atmosphere from the crass offerings of so-called Pub Lane.

PAMUKKALE
☎ 258

Three hours east of Selçuk by bus, this fascinating site is famous for the hot, calcium-rich waters that flowed over a plateau edge and cooled to form a series of water-filled, brilliant white ledges, or **travertines**. Above and behind this natural wonder lie the extensive ruins of the Roman city of **Hierapolis**, an ancient spa.

There are tourist offices on the ridge at Pamukkale (☎ 272 2077) and in Denizli train station. You pay admission (US$3) to the ridge as you climb the hill. Most of the travertine pools are now closed and dry as the site is being restored. The most famous (and most expensive, at US$4 for two hours), complete with sunken Roman columns, is at the Pamukkale Motel on top of the ridge. Some of the pensions in the village at the bottom of the ridge have pools too.

A worthwhile but time-consuming detour on your way back to Selçuk or Kuşadası would be to the beautiful ruined city of **Aphrodisias**, south of Nazilli near Karacasu. Many think it rivals Ephesus.

Places to Stay

The bargain pensions and hotels (over sixty of them) are in the village below – the farther from the highway, the cheaper they are. For cheerful service and decent rooms, try the *Kervansaray Pension* (☎ 272 2209), where rooms cost US$12/18 a single/double, and the nearby *Aspawa* (☎ 272 2094). The friendly, tidy *Koray Otel* (☎ 272 2300), a few streets south, has a restaurant, bar and pool; doubles cost US$18, including breakfast. Posh lodgings are next to the nearby village of Karahayıt.

Places to Eat

Taking meals in your pension or hotel is usually best here – but ask for prices in advance! Of the restaurants in the town, the *Gürsoy*, opposite the Yörük Motel in the village centre, has the nicest terrace, but the *Han*, around the corner facing the square, offers the best value for money. Meals at either cost US$4 to US$6.

BODRUM
☎ 252

Bodrum, formerly Halicarnassus, is the site of the **Mausoleum**, the monumental tomb of King Mausolus, which was another of the Seven Wonders of the World. Little now remains of the Mausoleum, which was probably partially destroyed by an earthquake and then demolished by the Knights of St John.

Placed between Bodrum's perfect twin bays is the medieval **Castle of St Peter**, built in 1402 and rebuilt in 1522 by the knights, using stones from the tomb. It's now a **museum of underwater archaeology** and contains finds from the oldest shipwreck ever discovered. The museum is open from 8.30 am to noon and from 1 to 5 pm; entry costs US$3.50, with another US$1 each to visit the ancient wreck and a model of a Carian princess' tomb.

Walk west past the marina and over the hill to **Gümbet**, which has a nicer beach than Bodrum proper, though it's a bit polluted. **Gümüşlük**, to the far west of the Bodrum peninsula, is the best of the many smaller villages nearby. Dolmuş run there every hour.

The otogar is 500m inland along Cevat Şakir Caddesi from the Adliye Cami, a small mosque at the centre of the town. The post office and several banks are on Cevat Şakir Caddesi. The tourist office (☎ 316 1091) is at Barış Meydanı, beside the castle.

Places to Stay

Some of the smaller villages on the peninsula, such as Bitez Yalısı and Ortakent Yalısı, have camp sites. There are more on the peninsula's north shore.

Bodrum is full of pensions and hotels charging US$9 to US$13 per person; prices rise steeply as you approach the waterfront, but they drop in the off season.

Behind the belediye (town hall) on Türkkuyusu Sokak, try the friendly *Şenlik Pansiyon* (☎ 316 6382) at No 115, charging US$12 a double. Behind it is the family-run *Sedan* (☎ 316 0355), Türkkuyusu 121. Newer double rooms with shower go for US$24; older, waterless doubles for US$16. *Otel Espri* (☎ 316 1129), Türkkuyusu 98, has a swimming pool, and 40 rooms with bath costing US$38 a double, breakfast included.

Right on the seafront the small *Öykü Pansiyon* (☎ 316 4604), Neyzen Caddesi 200, has slightly cramped rooms but lovely views from its rooftop terrace. Beds cost US$10 including breakfast. The *Alias Pansiyon* (☎ 316 3146) nearby has small, rather crowded cabins set around a pool and rose garden for US$20 per person.

Best of all is the wonderful *Su Otel* (☎ 316 6906), Turgutreis Caddesi, 1201 Sokak (follow the signs), with a charming flower-filled courtyard, a swimming pool, and rooms decorated in local crafts; doubles with bath cost US$40 to US$55 in summer.

Places to Eat

For very cheap eats, buy a dönerli sandviç (sandwich with roast lamb) for less than US$2 at a streetside *büfe*. Look for the words in the window.

In July and August the cheapest food is at simple local eateries well inland – without menus in English or German. Most serve no alcohol.

In the grid of small market streets just east of the Adliye Camii are several restaurants. *Babadan* and *Ziya'nin Yeri* are patronised by locals as well as foreigners, and serve plates of döner for about US$3 and beer for US$1.50. For cheaper fare, continue eastward to a little plaza filled with open-air restaurants serving pide and kebab. The *Nazilli* and *Karadeniz* serve pide (US$3 to US$4), pizzas and kebaps.

In warm weather, inspect Meyhaneler Sokak, off İskele Caddesi. Wall-to-wall tavernas serve food and drink to happy crowds nightly for US$12 to US$18, more for fish.

Of the upmarket places, *Amphora* (☎ 316 2368), on the western bay, is the best, with meals for around US$15 a head.

More expensive, but quite pleasant, is *Kocadon* (☎ 316 3705), back toward the centre a bit.

Getting There & Away

Bodrum has a fast and frequent bus service to all points in the region and some beyond, including Antalya (11 hours, US$12), Fethiye (4½ hours, US$6), İzmir (four hours, US$10), Kuşadası and Selçuk (three hours, US$5), Marmaris (three hours, US$4) and Pamukkale (five hours, US$6).

Hydrofoils and boats go to Kos (İstanköy) frequently in summer for US$20 one way and US$25 return. In summer there are also boats to Datça, Didyma, Knidos, Marmaris and Rhodes; check with the tourist office.

The Mediterranean Coast

Turkey's Mediterranean coastline winds eastward for more than 1200km from Marmaris to Antakya on the Syrian border. East of Marmaris, the 'Turquoise Coast' is perfect for boat excursions, with many secluded coves and quiet bays all the way to Fethiye. The rugged coastline from Fethiye east to Antalya – immortalised by Homer as Lycia – and the Taurus Mountains east of Antalya are wild and beautiful. Farther east you pass through fewer seaside resorts and more workaday cities. The entire coast is liberally sprinkled with impressive ruins, studded with beautiful beaches and washed by clear water ideal for sports.

MARMARIS
☎ 252

Even more than Kuşadası and Bodrum, Marmaris, situated on a beautiful bay at the edge of a hilly peninsula, has yielded to mass tourism. Nevertheless, the sculptured coastline and crystalline waters explain why it's

become Turkey's premier yachting port. The Greek island of Rhodes (Rodos) is a short voyage south. Marmaris is not as pretty as Bodrum, although the swimming in the surrounding bays is probably safer. They're both overcrowded and noisy in summer.

Orientation & Information
Marmaris has a small castle overlooking the town centre. İskele Meydanı (the main square) and the tourist office (☎ 412 1035) are near the ferry pier just north-east of the castle. The centre is mostly a pedestrian precinct. New development stretches many kilometres to the south-east around the bay

The otogar is north of the yacht harbour Hacı Mustafa Sokak, otherwise known as Bar Street, runs down from near the otogar to the bazar; action here keeps going until the early hours of the morning.

Things to See & Do
The **castle** has a few unexciting exhibition rooms, resident peacocks and fine views of Marmaris. It's open from 8 am to noon and 1 to 5.30 pm daily for US$1.

There are daily boat trips in summer to nearby **Paradise Island** (about US$15 a head)

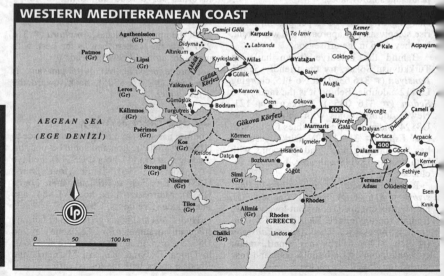

WESTERN MEDITERRANEAN COAST

AEGEAN SEA
(EGE DENİZİ)

Patmos (Gr)
Agathenission (Gr)
Lipsi (Gr)
Leros (Gr)
Gümüşlük
Kálimnos (Gr)
Psérimos (Gr)
Kos (Gr)
Strongili (Gr)
Nissiros (Gr)
Tilos (Gr)

Camiçi Gölü
Karpuzlu
To İzmir
Didyma
Labranda
Altınkum
Kıyıkışlacık
Milas
Yatağan
Göktepe
Bayır
Güllük
Güllük Körfezi
Yalıkavak
Karaova
Muğla
Turgutreis
Bodrum
Ören
Gökova
Ula
Gökova Körfezi
Körmen
Marmaris
İçmeler
Köyceğiz Gölü
Dalyan
Knidos
Datça
Bozburun
Hisarönü
Söğüt
Dalaman
Simi (Gr)
Tersane Adası
Fethiye
Ölüdeniz
Chálki (Gr)
Allmiá (Gr)
Rhodes (GREECE)
Rhodes
Lindos

Kemer Barajı
Kale
Acıpayam
Köyceğiz
Dalaman
Ortaca
Göcek
Çameli
Arpacık
Kargı
Kemer
Esen
Kınık
Çay
Dalaman

0 50 100 km

nd farther afield to **Dalyan** and **Caunus** about US$30 a head). The beach at **İçmeler**, 0km away by minibus, is marginally better han that at Marmaris.

Datça, a village two hours drive away, out on the peninsula, has now been 'discovered' out is still a great place to visit; less spoilt are **Bozburun**, not as far west, and **Aktaş**, 4km east of Marmaris. At the tip of the peninsula are the ruins of the ancient port of **Knidos**, accessible by road or excursion boat.

Places to Stay

Marmaris has hundreds of lodgings, but few are cheap. Ask at the tourism office about *ev pansiyonları* (home pensions), renting double rooms for US$8 to US$12.

For lodgings and camping on the beach, take a 'Siteler-Turban' minibus along the waterfront road to the last stop (Şirinyer) at the Turban Marmaris Tatil Köyü holiday village, 4km south-west of the main square. Besides **Berk Camping**, with tent sites for US$6 and cabins for US$18, there are several small pension-like hotels renting double rooms for around US$24 to US$40: the *Birol* (☎ 412 1054), *Yüzbaşı* (☎ 412 2762), *Sembol* (☎ 412

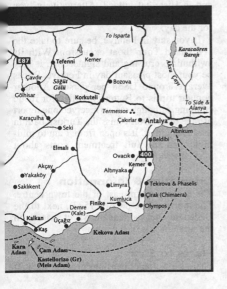

1356), *Panorama* (☎ 413 1958) and *Tümer* (☎ 412 4413).

The *Interyouth Hostel* (☎ 412 6432) at Kemeraltı Mahallesi, İyiliktaş Mevkii 14, has been joined by a second hostel deep in the bazar at Tepe Mahallesi, 42 Sokak No 45, which has the same *Interyouth Hostel* (☎ 412 3687) name. Neither is ideal – the original is stranded in Marmaris' rear wastelands, its newer rival in the noisy bazar. Both charge US$6 for a dorm bed, US$8 per person in a double.

Pricier but charming, quiet and set in nice gardens is the *Hotel Halıcı* (☎ 412 1683), Hacı Cem Sokak 1, inland from Abdi İpekçi Park. A double room with breakfast costs US$58 in summer.

Places to Eat

The 'resort rule' applies: the farther you go inland from the water, the higher the quality and the lower the price. Have some Marmaris honey while you're here – it's famous.

Of the open-air restaurants along 51 Sokak (the street with the PTT), the *Marmaris Lokantası* is one of the best, offering İskender kebap for US$4. The *Yeni Liman Restaurant* is also good and cheap, with full meals for US$8 to US$10.

Hacı Mustafa Sokak (Bar Street) harbours many possibilities for cheap eating, from filled baked potatoes (kumpir) to pizzas. *Beyoğlu Café-Bar* sometimes has cheap fish meals for US$10. *Pizza Napoli* offers tasty, filling pizzas for around US$6.

For fancier surroundings, the *Birtat Restaurant* south of the castle on the waterfront is tried and true, with meals for US$6 to US$10, and to US$18 for fish.

The best place for a sundowner is *Panorama Bar*; follow the signs from the castle end of the bazar. Drinks cost US$3.25 or US$4.

Getting There & Away

Marmaris otogar, north of the yacht marina, has frequent direct buses and minibuses to all places in the region, including Antalya (seven hours, US$9), Bodrum (three hours, US$4.50), Dalyan (via Ortaca, two hours, US$3), Datça (1¾ hours, US$3) and Fethiye (three hours, US$6). Bozburun minibuses run at least once daily (1½ hours, US$2), more frequently in summer. Small car ferries run to

TURKEY

Rhodes daily, except Sunday, in summer (less frequently in the off season) for US$41 one way or US$56 return (plus US$13 port tax at Rhodes and US$10 to re-enter Turkey).

KÖYCEĞİZ & DALYAN
☎ 252

Köyceğiz, 75km east of Marmaris, stands on the edge of a great, placid lake. Although a pleasant, peaceful farming town with a few pensions and hotels, it's overshadowed by its smaller but more touristy neighbour, the town of Dalyan.

Set in lush river-delta farming country, Dalyan has it all: fertile soil, a river meandering by, excellent fishing and, to the south at İztuzu, beautiful **beaches** which are the natural nesting ground of the *Carretta carretta*, or ancient sea turtle.

As if that were not enough, Dalyan has ruins: dramatic rock-cut **Lycian tombs** in the cliff facing the town, and the ruined city of **Caunus** easily visited by boat excursion downriver. Upriver on the shores of Köyceğiz Lake are **hot springs** at Sultaniye Kaplıcaları.

The local boaters' cooperative sets rates for river excursions to points of interest. Daily tours taking in the mud baths, the ruins at Caunus and Turtle Beach cost about US$4.50 a head. Forty-minute runs just to the beach cost US$2.

Dozens of pensions and small but comfortable hotels are spread north and south of Dalyan's town centre. Cheapest are those nearest to the bus stop, but those farther south along Maraş Caddesi, like the *Dipdağ* (☎ 284 4572) and *Kilim* (☎ 284 2253), offer more for your money. Camp (US$4 per person) at *Dalyan Camping*, south of the centre.

The *Körfez* and *Köşem* restaurants off the main square on the water are the favourites, but the inland *Café Natural* is cheaper.

DALAMAN & GÖCEK
Dalaman, 23km south-east of Dalyan, is another farming community, but with an international airport (*hava limanı*). A few scheduled flights supplement the holiday charters. The town has hotels and pensions in all price brackets. Buses run to all points along the coast and beyond.

Göcek, 23km east of Dalaman through fragrant pine forests, is a small yachting port with a small but varied collection of lodgings from posh boutique hotels to simple family pensions. It's a pleasant, laid-back hamlet even though it lacks good beaches.

FETHİYE
☎ 252

Fethiye has superb beaches and cheap lodgings; it's crowded in summer but worth the diversion off the road. This is the site of ancient **Telmessos**, with giant Lycian stone **sarcophagi** from 400 BC littered about, and the rock-cut **Tomb of Amyntas** looming from a cliff above the town. There's a marked hiking trail over the hills to the Ottoman Greek ghost town of **Kayaköy**.

Four kilometres north, the beach at **Çalış** is many kilometres long, and backed by hotels and pensions. To the south, 12km over the mountains, is the gorgeous lagoon of **Ölüdeniz** (Dead Sea), too beautiful for its own good and now one of the Mediterranean's most famous beach spots. Inland from the beach are moderately priced bungalows and camping areas, as well as some hotels. There are some even cheaper pensions several kilometres inland on the Fethiye road at Ovacık and in Hisarönü village. Alternatively, you can sleep in Fethiye and minibus to Ölüdeniz for the day.

If you stay in Fethiye, be sure to take the '12 Island Tour' boat excursion. With its swimming, cruising and sightseeing, it may be your most pleasant day in Fethiye. Prices average around US$8 per person. Another popular trip is to Butterfly Valley for rustic camping, although we've received one report of rape there. Don't miss the Turkish bath in the bazar either. It's open from 7 am to midnight and the full treatment costs about US$10.

Orientation & Information
The otogar is 2km east of the town centre. The tourist office (☎ 614 1527), next to the Dedeoğlu Otel, is near the yacht marina on the western side of the town.

Places to Stay
There's a cluster of pensions near the stadium

TURKEY

ust west of the otogar. To find them walk straight down the road heading north from the minibus station.

North of the stadium, 450m off Atatürk Caddesi, *Göreme Pansiyon* (☎ 614 6944), Dolgu Sahası, Stadyum Yanı 25, has spotless singles/doubles for US$10/16, and is run by a lady who lived in London.

Other pensions are uphill from the yacht marina along Fevzi Çakmak Caddesi. The *Yıldırım* (☎ 614 3913), the *Pınara* (☎ 614 2151), the *Derelioğlu* (☎ 614 5983), the *Polat* (☎ 614 2347) and the *İrem* (☎ 614 3985) all charge US$9 to US$11 per person; breakfast costs another US$1 or US$2.

Up the hill behind these it's less noisy. The *İdeal Pension* (☎ 614 1981), Zafer Caddesi 1, has superb views from its terrace, but is a bit more expensive. Even farther uphill, the *İnci Pansiyon* (☎ 614 3325) has marvellous views and blissful quiet at similar prices, as does the *Cesur Pansiyon* (☎ 614 3398) across the street.

Hotel Mara (☎ 614 6722), Kral Caddesi, Yalı Sokak 2, north of the hospital, offers fine comfort for US$30/46 a single/double, with central air-con, private bath and breakfast.

Places to Eat

The market district is packed with open-air restaurants, where you should watch out for bill fiddling. The *Özlem Pide ve Kebap Salonu* on Çarşı Caddesi (the main market street) is good and cheap; the *Çakıroğlu* across the street is bigger and slightly nicer.

Around the corner on Tütün Sokak is the *Sedir Lokantası*, serving pizzas (US$2 to US$3), soups and mezes (US$1.25), and main courses (US$3 to US$4), including a 'vegetarian surprise'.

Pricier but with a wonderful choice of appetisers is *Restaurant Güneş* at Likya Caddesi 4 in the bazar. A good meat-based meal should cost between US$8 and US$12, fish is more expensive.

Getting There & Away

The coastal mountains force long-haul bus services to travel east and west – to Marmaris, Muğla and Antalya – before going anywhere else. If you're heading directly for Antalya, note that the *yayla* (inland) route is shorter (3½ hours) and cheaper (US$5) than the *sahil* (coastal) route (eight hours, US$6).

Buses from the otogar also serve Kalkan (US$2) and Kaş (US$2.50). Minibuses depart from their own terminal, 1km west of the otogar toward the centre, on short hops to other points along the coast, like Patara (US$2), Kınık (for Xanthos, US$1.50) and Ölüdeniz (US$1).

RUINS NEAR FETHİYE

Lycia was heavily populated in ancient times, as shown by the large number of wonderful old cities, which can be reached by minibus from Fethiye. **Tlos** is 40km up into the mountains near Kemer on the inland route to Antalya. **Pınara**, south of Fethiye, is an undervisited mountainous site.

Letoön, 4km off the highway in a fertile valley filled with tomato greenhouses, has excellent mosaics, a good theatre and a pool sacred as the place of worship of the goddess Leto. **Xanthos**, a few kilometres south-east of Letoön above the village of Kınık, is among the most impressive sites along this part of the coast, with its Roman theatre and Lycian pillar tombs.

At **Patara**, 7km farther south (turn at Ovaköy), the attraction is not so much the ruins as the incredible 20km-long beach. Lodgings in Patara village, 2.5km inland from the beach, range from camping through cheap pensions and hotels to the three-star *Otel Beyhan Patara* (☎ 242-843 5098).

KALKAN

☎ 242

Kalkan, everybody's idea of what a small Turkish fishing village should be, is 11km east of the Patara turn-off. It tumbles down a steep hillside to a yacht marina (in ancient times, the port).

Kalkan's old stone and wood houses have been restored as lodgings – some expensive, some moderate, some still fairly cheap. The streets above the marina are chock-a-block with atmospheric open-air restaurants. There are no good beaches to speak of, but the inevitable excursion boat tours (or minibuses) can take you to Patara Beach and secluded coves along the coast.

TURKEY

Places to Stay

If you decide to stay, look for cheap pensions (US$10/15 a single/double) at the top of the town.

On the main shopping street, *Özalp Pansiyon* (☎ 844 3486) charges US$9/13 for good, modern rooms with shower and balcony. Not far away, the *Çelik Pansiyon* (☎ 844 2126), Yalıboyu 9, is a standard simple pension charging US$9/16 for a single/double, breakfast included. Continue along the road to the end for the *Holiday Pension*, or go up the hill across the street for the *Gül Pansiyon* (☎ 844 3099); both are more primitive and slightly cheaper.

Farther down towards the harbour, the *Akın Pansiyon* (☎ 844 3025) has some waterless rooms on the top floor priced at US$12 a double; rooms lower down with private showers cost US$16, breakfast included. The *Akgül* (☎ 844 3270) around the corner is similar.

Çetin Pansiyon (☎ 844 3094), in the southern part of town, is quieter and cheaper at US$16 a double.

Zinbad Hotel (☎ 844 3404), Yalıboyu Mahallesi 18, is quiet and friendly, with fine sea views, for US$30/36 a single/double, breakfast included.

Places to Eat

Kervan Han has a *pide salonu* serving good, fresh cheap Turkish pizza for US$1.25 to US$2. The *Alibaba Lokantası* and the *Doyum*, west of the PTT at the entrance to the town, are patronised mostly by locals, not tourists. The *Steps Terrace Cafe-Bar* has a varied menu and sandwiches to go for US$1 to US$2.50. For fancier meals, head down to the harbour to the *İstanbul Boğaziçi*, *Pala'nın Yeri*, *Yakamoz* and *Patara*, where a full meal costs US$8 to US$12, US$16 to US$20 for fish.

KAŞ
☎ 242

Kaş, called Antiphellus in ancient times, has a picturesque quayside square, friendly people, a big Sunday **market**, Lycian stone **sarcophagi** dotted about its streets and rock-cut **tombs** in the cliffs above the town – it's a fine, laid-back place.

The Greek island of Kastellorizo (Meis i Turkish) is visible just a short distance across the water and can be reached by daily boat.

Aside from enjoying the town's ambienc and a few small pebble beaches, you ca walk west a few hundred metres to the ver well preserved **theatre**, then take a boat ex cursion to Kalkan, Patara, the Blue Cave Saklıkent Gorge, Üçağız (see the Kekova & Üçağız section) or Demre.

The tourist office (☎ 836 1238) is on the main square.

Places to Stay

Kaş has everything from camp sites to cheap pensions and four-star hotels. *Kaş Camping*, in an olive grove 1km west of town past the theatre, has tent sites and simple bungalows.

At the otogar you'll be accosted by pension-pushers. Yenicami Caddesi (or Recep Bilgin Caddesi), just south of the otogar, has lots of places, including the *Orion Hotel* (☎ 836 1286), with tidy rooms and sea views for US$11/18, breakfast included, which is the typical price. Farther along the street, or just off it, are the *Anıl Motel* (☎ 836 1791), the *Hilal* (☎ 836 1207) and the *Melisa* (☎ 836 1068). At the southern end of the street by the mosque is the *Ay Pansiyon* (☎ 836 1562), where the front rooms have sea views.

Turn right at the Ay Pansiyon and follow the signs to the quieter *Korsan Karakedi Motel* (☎ 836 1887) with a lovely roof terrace with bar.

On the other (eastern) side of town many more pensions offer similar accommodation. Try the *Koştur* (☎ 836 1264).

For more comforts and services, try the two-star *Hotel Kayahan* (☎ 836 1313) above Küçük Çakıl Plaj, where rooms with wonderful sea views cost US$24/30; or the three-star *Hotel Club Phellos* (☎ 836 1953), the fanciest place in town, with a swimming pool and comfortable rooms for US$40/55, including breakfast. There are at least 40 similar hotels here.

Places to Eat

On the main square, the *Noel Baba* is a favourite café-restaurant for breakfast and light meals (US$1.50 to US$4). The *Corner Café*, at the PTT end of İbrahim Serin

Caddesi, serves juices or a vegetable omelette or US$1, and yoghurt with fruit and honey or US$1.50. The *Café Merhaba* across the street is good for cakes.

The *Eriş*, behind the tourist office, is a favourite, as much for its setting as for its food. Also popular is *Smiley's Restaurant* nearby, where pizza or main course plates cost around US$2 to US$3. The *Bahçe Restaurant*, father inland, is even better.

The town's classiest is the *Mercan*, right on the water in the centre. Prices are posted for most things; haggle over fish. A fish dinner with drinks may cost US$12 to US$20.

KEKOVA & ÜÇAĞIZ

Up in the hills 14km east of Kaş, a road goes south to Kekova and Üçağız, two villages amid partly sunken ancient ruins. Üçağız, 20km from the highway, is a farming and fishing hamlet with a handful of very basic pensions and a few simple waterfront restaurants built on top of the ruins of ancient Teimiussa.

Boat owners will try to cajole you into taking a tour (US$10 to US$16 per person) of the bay, including a look at the picturesque little village of **Kale** (not to be confused with the other Kale, which is also known as Demre/Myra), and the sunken ruins (Batık Şehir) on **Kekova Adası** island. A swim near the ruins is included.

KAŞ TO ANTALYA

Hugging a coast backed by pine-clad mountains, the main road goes east from Kaş and then north to Antalya, passing a dozen ruined cities. From ancient times until the 1970s, virtually all transport to this region was by sea. The modern towns built over or near the ancient ones are still deeply involved in maritime life.

Demre
☎ 242

Demre (ancient Myra, also known as Kale), set in a rich alluvial plain covered in greenhouses, is interesting because of its generous 4th-century bishop, later canonised as St Nicholas, the original Father Christmas or Santa Claus.

For a lofty US$3 you can visit the restored 12th-century **Church of St Nicholas** (Noel Baba), which was built to hold his tomb; save your money, there's little to see inside. Two kilometres inland from the church at Demre there is a rock face honeycombed with ancient **tombs**, right next to a large **Roman theatre**. Both are open from 7.30 am to 7 pm in summer; entry is cheap at US$1.

Few people stay overnight here, but if you do, try the *Hotel Kıyak* (☎ 871 2092), İlkokul Caddesi 38, 800m south of the main square past the otogar towards the beach, where singles/doubles with good bathroom facilities go for US$12/18. The neighbouring *Otel Topçu* (☎ 871 4506) is much cheaper. Across the highway, the *Hotel Andriake* (☎ 871 2249) is the town's best at US$35 a double.

The *Hotel Şahin* (☎ 871 5686), on Müze Caddesi just west of the main square on the way to the St Nicholas Church, charges US$20 for a double with shower and breakfast, which is a bit high; haggle with them. For only slightly more (US$14 a single, US$25 a double) you can stay at the much newer *Grand Hotel Kekova* (☎ 871 4515), 300m east of the main square opposite the PTT.

As for meals, the *Şehir* in the main square, and the *Çınar* and *İnci Pastanesi* on the way to the St Nicholas Church, are serviceable. The *Simena* serves beer with your food. In summer, try dining 5km west at *Çayağzı*, the ancient Andriake, Demre's harbour, where the beach, the views and the food are fine.

Finike

Known as Phoenicus in ancient times, Finike, 30km east of Demre past wide beaches and along twisting mountain roads, is an attractive little town living on a mixture of farming, fishing and tourism. Small pensions and hotels provide for travellers, some of whom come to enjoy the vast 15km-long pebble beach at **Sahilkent**, east of the town.

Olimpos & the Chimaera
☎ 242

After climbing into the mountains, you reach the turn-off for Olimpos. From here it's just over 8km down a winding, unpaved road to the village, and a farther 3.5km along an ever-worsening road to the site of ancient

Olimpos. Wild and abandoned, the Olimpos ruins peek out from forest copses, rock outcrops and river banks. The pebble beach is magnificent. *Kadir's Yörük Top Tree House* (☎ 892 1250) has beds in funky tree houses and an Internet café for US$10 per person, breakfast and dinner included.

Çavuşköy/Adrasan, a cove to the east, has half a dozen hotels and pensions, ranging from very simple to quite comfortable.

According to legend, the Chimaera (Yanartaş), a natural eternal flame, was the hot breath of a subterranean monster. Easily sighted by mariners in ancient times, it's a mere glimmer of its former self today. Even so, it is a wonder, a flame which, when extinguished, always reignites.

Turn off the highway less than 1km east of the eastern Olimpos turn-off; the road is marked for **Çıralı**, 7km towards the sea. To see the Chimaera, go 3km east from Çıralı down a neighbouring valley. If you're driving, park at the end of the valley, then follow the signs for the half-hour climb.

Çıralı has lots of good camping grounds and cheap pensions (US$20 for a double room with private shower and breakfast), including the *Emin* (☎ 825 7155), *Fehim* (☎ 825 7250) and *Sima Peace* (☎ 825 7245), all right down by the beach in a grove of lofty pines. Inland from the beach are many other pensions such as the *Orange Home* (☎ 825 7128) and the *Aygün* (☎ 825 7146), not to be confused with the Grand Aygün.

Phaselis

Two kilometres from the highway, Phaselis is a collection of ruins framing three small, perfect bays. It's a good place for a swim and a picnic. The ruins are open from 7.30 am to 7 pm in summer; entry costs US$1.

Kemer
☎ 242

Built to the specifications of resort planners and architects, Kemer was custom-made for the package-holiday traveller. Its white buildings and straight streets seem sterile, but there's a nice little beach in **Moonlight Park** by the marina and, above it, **Yörük Park** (Nomad Park), showing aspects of the region's traditional life.

The place to stay here is the *King' Garden Pension* (☎ 814 1039), on the north side of town, 400m north-east of the minibus station. From June to September double rooms with compulsory full board cos US$40 (US$20 for B&B at other times). You can camp in the grounds of the King's Garden for US$4 a tent. Too much? There cross the canal and look for the *Portakar Pansiyon* (☎ 814 4701), opposite, which charges about US$15 for a double room with breakfast.

ANTALYA
☎ 242

The main town along the coast, Antalya has one of the most attractive harbour settings in the Mediterranean. It's fun to kick around in **Kaleiçi**, the old restored Ottoman town by the Roman harbour – now the yacht marina. The **bazar** is interesting and the archaeological museum outstanding. The **beaches** are out of town: Konyaaltı Plajı, a long pebble beach, to the west, and Lara Plajı, a sand beach crowded by high-rise development, to the east.

Orientation & Information

The otogar is 4km north of the centre on the D650 highway to Burdur, reached by dolmuş along Güllük (Anafartalar) Caddesi. The city centre is at Kalekapısı, a major intersection right next to Cumhuriyet Meydanı, with its dramatic equestrian statue of Atatürk. Kaleiçi, the old town, is south of Kalekapısı down the hill.

Atatürk Caddesi, 100m east of Kalekapısı, goes south past Hadriyanüs Kapısı (Hadrian's Gate). A bit farther along is the pleasant Karaalioğlu Park.

The tourist office (☎ 241 1747) is located at Cumhuriyet Caddesi 2, 250m west of Kalekapısı (look for the sign 'Antalya Devlet Tiyatrosu' on the right-hand side; it's in this building). The Turkish Airlines office (☎ 241 0558) is in the same building. The central post office is around the corner on Güllük Caddesi.

Owl Bookshop, Akarçeşme Sokak 21 in Kaleiçi, offers a rare (for Turkey) chance to buy or exchange books in English.

KALEİÇİ (OLD ANTALYA)

PLACES TO STAY
16 Adler Pension
17 Atelya Pension
18 Erkal Pansiyon
20 Erken Pansiyon
22 Frankfurt Pansiyon
24 Senem Family Pansion

PLACES TO EAT
1 01 Güneyliler
3 Parlak Restaurant & Plaza Fast Food
6 Hisar Restaurant
9 Eski Sebzeciler İçi Sokak (Meat Restaurants)

OTHER
2 PTT (Post Office)
4 Government House
5 Atatürk Statue
7 Yivli Minare (Grooved Minaret)
8 Saat Kulesi (Clock Tower)
10 Tekeli Ali Paşa Camii
11 Tourist Police
12 Post Office
13 Hadriyanüs Kapısı (Hadrian's Gate)
14 Sefa Hamamı (Turkish Bath)

15 Mosque
19 Owl Bookshop
21 Tourist Office
23 Kesik Minare & Korkut Camii
25 Hıdırlık Kulesi (Tower)
26 Belediye (Town Hall)
27 Police

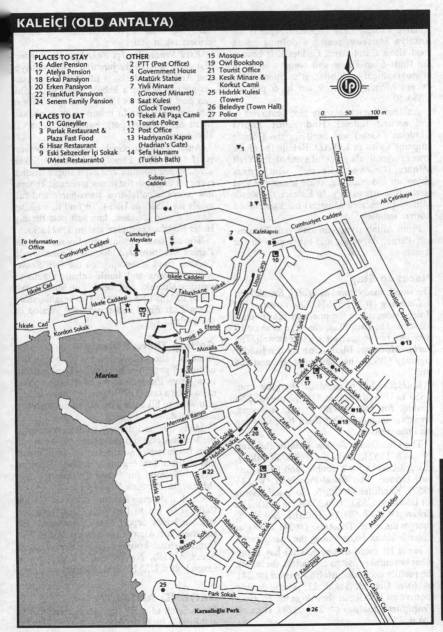

0   50   100 m

TURKEY

Things to See & Do

Antalya's single most important sight is the **Antalya Museum** (catch a dolmuş going west along Cumhuriyet Caddesi). It houses the finds from Perge and some wonderful ethnographical exhibits; it's open daily except Monday from 9 am to 6 pm for US$3.50.

Ancient monuments are also scattered in and around Kaleiçi. **Hadriyanüs Kapısı** (Hadrian's Gate) was built for the Roman emperor's visit in 130 AD. Behind the clock tower is Antalya's graceful symbol, the **Yivli Minare** (Grooved Minaret), which rises above an old building, once a mosque and now a fine-arts gallery. In Kaleiçi, the **Kesik Minare** (Truncated Minaret) marks a ruined Roman temple.

From Antalya you can also visit Termessos, Perge, Aspendos and other sites in the region.

Places to Stay

The small, shady *Bambus Motel, Restaurant & Camping* (☎ 321 5263), 300m west of the Hotel Dedeman on the one-way (eastbound) coast road to Lara Plajı, can take nine or 10 caravans, but you can pitch a tent as well. The *Parlar Mocamp*, 14km north on the Burdur highway (D650), has unshaded tent and van sites.

Kaleiçi is full of pensions charging from US$8 to US$18 a single, US$12 to US$22 a double, for rooms with private showers, breakfast included; find them by following the little signs.

The clean, safe *Senem Family Pansion* (☎ 247 1752), Zeytin Geçidi Sokak 9, charges US$18 for a double, and has a fine roof terrace. The *Erkal Pansiyon* (☎ 241 0757), Kandiller Geçidi 5, has good rooms for US$12 to US$22 (No 304 is the best). The *Erken* (☎ 247 9801), Hıdırlık Sokak 5, charges the same. The *Adler* (☎ 241 7818), at Civelek Sokak 16, is among the cheapest.

For a bit more money Kaleiçi has many other beautiful pensions and hotels, including the prettily decorated *Atelya Pension* (☎ 241 6416) at Civelek Sokak 21, where double rooms cost US$30, as they do at the spotless *Frankfurt Pansiyon* (☎ 247 6224), Hıdırlık Sokak 25.

Places to Eat

Many pensions serve good meals at decent prices; ask at yours.

Eski Sebzeciler İçi Sokak, a short street just south-west of the junction of Cumhuriyet and Atatürk caddesis, is filled with open-air restaurants where a kebab, salad and drink can cost as little as US$4. The speciality is Antalya's own tandır kebap (mutton cooked in an earthenware pot), but döner kebap is also served.

Antalya's most popular kebapçı, however, is *01 Güneyliler*, Elmalı Mahallesi, 4 Sokak 12/A, where families and even single women come for the fresh flat bread, authentic kebaps, low prices, alcohol-free atmosphere and full meals for US$3 or US$4. To find it, walk up Kazım Özalp Caddesi, turn left past the big Hotel Kışlahan complex and go 1½ blocks.

The old-time bar-and-grill favourite is the *Parlak Restaurant*, a block up Kazım Özalp Caddesi from Kalekapısı on the left. Skewered chickens and lamb kebabs sizzle as patrons sip rakı and beer. Full meals cost US$8 to US$12 a person. The neighbouring *Plaza Fast Food* is the sanitised version of the Parlak.

Getting There & Away

Antalya's shiny new airport is busy with lots of daily flights from İstanbul and Ankara, and many from Europe and the Middle East. You must take a taxi (US$10) to the centre unless you want to hike the 2km out to the highway and flag down a dolmuş.

Many bus and dolmuş routes go through the Vatan Kavşağı (intersection of Vatan and Gazi boulevards), so it serves as an informal bus station for regional traffic. Take an 'Aksu' dolmuş for Perge (75 cents), or a 'Manavgat' for Side (US$1.75).

Catch a dolmuş heading north on Güllük Caddesi to get to the Yeni Garaj (otogar), whence buses depart every 20 minutes (in summer) for Alanya (two hours, US$3.25), Denizli (four hours, US$6), Konya (four hours, US$8), Nevşehir (for Cappadocia, seven hours, US$12) and other towns.

AROUND ANTALYA

This stretch of coast has plenty more Greek and Roman ruins if you can take them. **Perge,**

15km east of Antalya, just north of Aksu, includes a 12,000-seat stadium and a theatre for 15,000. **Aspendos**, 47km east of Antalya, has Turkey's best-preserved ancient theatre, dating from the 2nd century AD; it is still used for performances during the Antalya Festival in September. **Termessos**, high in the mountains off the Korkuteli road, has a spectacular setting and demands some vigorous walking and climbing if you want to see it all.

SİDE
☎ 242

Once an idyllic seaside village, Side (pronounced 'SEE-deh') has been overrun by tourists and by carpet and leather shops. Once the main slave market at this end of the Mediterranean and a base for pirates, it's now a tawdry, overcrowded caricature of its former self which you might prefer to visit as a day trip. Its impressive ancient structures include a **Roman bath** (now an excellent museum, open from 8 am to noon and 1 to 5 pm daily; admission US$2.50), the old **city walls**, a huge **amphitheatre** (closed for restoration) and seaside marble **temples** to Apollo and Athena. Its excellent beaches are packed in summer.

The village is 3km south of the highway from Manavgat; minibuses (70 cents) will run you between the two. Heading for Antalya or Alanya it's usually best to travel via Manavgat. The tourist office (☎ 753 1265) is on the road into town, 1.5km from the village centre.

The village itself is packed willy-nilly with pensions and hotels which fill up quickly in summer. Most attractive are the ones near the sea behind the Apollo temple, but there are cheaper offerings near the theatre and, less conveniently, on the road into town from Manavgat. The larger hotels and motels are east and west of the town along the beaches.

ALANYA
☎ 242

Dominated by the ruins of a magnificent Seljuk fortress perched high on a promontory, Alanya is second only to Antalya as a Turkish Mediterranean resort. Indeed, it was a resort in the 13th century, when the Seljuk sultans came down from Konya for sun and fun. Once a pretty, easy-going place, it has grown in recent years into a big, bustling and noisy city. The good beaches to the east and west are now lined with hotels.

The otogar is 3km west of the centre; you can get to town in a dolmuş or a municipal bus – disembark at the roundabout by the little mosque. Downhill towards the big mosque is the old waterfront area with trendy shops, good food and a few cheap hotels. The tourist office (☎ 513 1240) is on Kalearkası Caddesi, on the western side of the promontory.

Things to See & Do
If you stop here, visit the Seljuk Turkish **Kızıl Kule** (Red Tower, built in 1226), down by the harbour. It's open from 8 am to noon and from 1.30 to 5.30 pm (closed on Monday) for US$1.50. Also worth checking out is the **fortress** (*kale*, also built in 1226) atop the promontory. It's open from 8 am to 7 pm daily and entry is US$2.50. The hyper-touristy **Damlataş Mağarası** (Dripping Stones Cave, US$1.50), good for asthma sufferers, is on the western side of the promontory, near the tourist office and the museum. Take a boat (US$5.50 to US$8 per person) for an excursion to other caves beneath the promontory.

Places to Stay
In high season your best bet may be to go with a private pension owner who approaches you at the otogar, but find out how far from the centre the pension is. Try the *Alaiye Pansiyon* (☎ 247 5731), Elmalı Mahallesi, Milli Egemenlik Caddesi, 4. Sokak 42.

Hürriyet Meydanı (square), in the centre, has some shabby old hotels which rent rooms for less than US$20 a double. As you head down İskele Caddesi from the highway the first you'll come to is the *Baba Hotel* (☎ 513 1032), İskele Caddesi 6, where mundane rooms cost US$6/12 a double without shower, cash on arrival. If it's open, the *Alanya Palas* (☎ 513 1016) next door is similar.

More expensive but infinitely preferable is the 24-room *Hotel Temiz* (☎ 513 1016), İskele Caddesi 12, a few steps farther along towards the Red Tower. Comfortable singles/doubles with showers cost US$12/18.

TURKEY

A little farther along and upstairs on the right is the *Yili Hotel* (☎ 513 1017), with the most basic of waterless rooms for US$6 a head.

At the southern end of Bostancı Caddesi near the Kuyularönü mosque is the *Çınar Otel* (☎ 512 0063), where faded rooms rent for US$8/11 a single/double with shower. *Günaydın Otel* (☎ 513 1943), Kültür Caddesi 26/B, one long block inland towards the Damlataş Cave, is similar.

Hotel Kaptan (☎ 513 4900), on İskele Caddesi, is quite comfy, charging US$40/55 for modern singles/doubles with TVs, mini-bars, air-con and spotless bathrooms. Singles/doubles at the back are cheaper.

Places to Eat
The best area for cheap food is between the first two waterfront streets, near the big mosque, where the alleys are filled with tables and chairs. Look for signs saying 'İnegöl Köftecisi', and snap up grilled meatballs and salad for US$4 or so. The *Yönet* and *Mahperi* along the waterfront promenade are worth visiting for evening meals (around US$8 to US$12).

THE EASTERN COAST
East of Alanya the coast sheds some of its touristic freight. Seven kilometres east of **Anamur** there is a wonderful castle (Mamure Kalesi, built by the emirs of Karaman in 1230); there are pensions and camping grounds nearby. The ghostly ruins of Byzantine **Anamurium** are 8.5km west of the town.

Silifke has a crusader castle and a ruined Roman temple, but is mostly a transport hub. At **Taşucu**, 11km south-west of Silifke, boats and hydrofoils depart daily for Girne (Kyrenia) in Turkish Cyprus. **Kızkalesi** (Maiden's Castle) is a small holiday town with a striking crusader castle offshore. **Mersin** is a modern city of no great interest. **Tarsus**, just east of Mersin, was the birthplace of St Paul and the place where Antony first ran into Cleopatra. Little is left to testify to these events, however. Smoky industry prevails.

Adana is the country's fourth-largest city, an important agricultural centre and a major bus interchange for eastern Turkey.

HATAY
South-east of Adana, a tongue of Turkish territory licks at the mountains of north-western Syria: the land is called Hatay. You'll pass several impressive castles on the way to the port city and pipeline terminus of İskenderun (formerly Alexandretta), where Alexander the Great defeated the Persians and Jonah is thought to have been coughed up by the whale.

Antakya
☎ 326

This is the biblical Antioch, where St Peter did a spell of converting. It was said to be the Roman Empire's most depraved city. You can see St Peter's church, the **Senpiyer Kilisesi**, 3km north-east of the town centre, for free. **Antakya Museum** boasts some of the world's best Roman mosaics (open from 8 am to noon and 1.30 to 5 pm, closed on Monday; entry costs US$2.50). Buses run from here to Aleppo and Damascus in Syria.

The provincial tourist office (☎ 216 0610) is 1km north of the museum.

Cheap hotels are south of the otogar. The *Jasmin Hotel* (☎ 212 7171), İstiklal Caddesi 14, has decent double rooms with shared baths for US$6. *Hotel Güney* (☎ 214 9713), İstiklal Sokak 28, is one narrow street east of İstiklal Caddesi. The big, bright, bare rooms suffer from dampness but it's friendly enough for US$8/12 with shower, US$6/10 without. The *Divan Oteli* (☎ 215 1518), İstiklal Caddesi 62, is good for US$10/16.

Hotel Orontes (☎ 214 5931), İstiklal Caddesi 58, is the best mid-range choice, with air-con singles/doubles at US$31/44, some with river views.

Central Anatolia

İstanbul may be exotic and intriguing, the coasts pretty and relaxing, but it's the Anatolian plateau which is Turkey's heartland. Atatürk acknowledged this when he moved the capital to Ankara in 1923. Don't think of this area as a great central nothingness; cruise across the undulating steppe to Cappadocia and you'll be amazed by a region that looks as if it belongs in another world.

ANKARA

☎ 312

There was a Hittite settlement on the site of Ankara nearly 4000 years ago. Today it is the capital of Turkey but not an especially exciting city. Nevertheless, because of its central location there's a good chance you'll at least pass through here.

Orientation

Atatürk Bulvarı is the city's north-south axis. AŞTİ, Ankara's mammoth otogar, is 6.5km south-west of Ulus, the historic centre, and 6km west of Kızılay, the modern centre. Turkish Airlines city buses stop at the train station (*gar*), 1.4km south-west of Ulus, and at AŞTİ otogar.

The Ankaray underground train connects AŞTİ, Tandoğan and Kızılay; a metro is under construction.

The diplomatic area is Çankaya, 5km south of Kızılay, and the adjoining districts of Gaziosmanpaşa and Kavaklıdere.

Information

The tourist office (☎ 231 5572) is at Gazi Mustafa Kemal Bulvarı 121, opposite the Maltepe Ankaray station. The main post office is on Atatürk Bulvarı just south of Ulus, although there's a handy branch beside the train station where you can also change cash and travellers cheques. In an emergency, you could try the tourist police at Boncuk Sokak 10/2, but the tourist office is probably a better bet.

Things to See

The **Anatolian Civilisations Museum** (Anadolu Medeniyetleri Müzesi), on Hisarparkı Caddesi, is Ankara's most worthwhile attraction. With the world's richest collection of Hittite artefacts, it's an essential supplement to visiting central Turkey's Hittite sites. It's uphill (south-west) from Ulus, and is open from 8.30 am to 5.15 pm, 'closed' on Monday in winter unless you pay twice the entry fee of $2.50. When you're done at the museum, go to the top of the hill and wander among the castle's old streets.

The **Ethnographic Museum** is uphill from the junction of Atatürk Bulvarı and Talatpaşa Caddesi.

North of Ulus, east of Çankırı Caddesi (the continuation of Atatürk Bulvarı north of Ulus), are some Roman ruins, including the **Jülyanüs Sütunu** (Julian's Column, erected in 363 AD) and the **Temple of Augustus & Rome**. Right next to the temple is the **Hacı Bayram Camii**, a sacred mosque commemorating the founder of a dervish order established in 1400. On the west side of Çankırı Caddesi are the **Roma Hamamları** (Roman Baths).

The **Anıtkabir** (Mausoleum of Atatürk), 2km west of Kızılay, is a monumental tomb and memorial to the founder of modern Turkey. It's open daily from 9 am to 5 pm, for free.

Places to Stay

Along the east side of Opera (or İtfaiye) Meydanı, on Sanayi Caddesi and Tavus Sokak near the Gazi Lisesi high school, try the *Otel Devran* (☎ 311 0485), Tavus Sokak 8, with doubles for US$15 with shower, US$18 with bath. *Otel Fuar* (☎ 312 3288), a block away at Kosova Sokak 11, charges the same, or US$5/10 for a decent single/double room with sink, with showers down the hall.

For more comfort, the *Otel Mithat* (☎ 311 5410), Tavus Sokak 2, has shower-equipped doubles for US$17, and is a better choice than the adjoining *Otel Akman* (☎ 324 4140), Tavus Sokak 6, which charges more.

North of Ulus and one street west of Çankırı Caddesi, the three-star *Hotel Oğultürk* (☎ 309 2900), Rüzgarlı Eşdost Sokak 6, has singles/doubles with TV and minibar for US$26/40, breakfast included. The nearby *Yıldız* (☎ 312 7584) is similar.

In 'new' Ankara south of Kızılay, the one-star *Hotel Ergen* (☎ 417 5906), Karanfil Sokak 48, near Olgunlar Sokak, charges US$30/42 a single/double with bath.

Places to Eat

At the south-eastern corner of Ulus at Atatürk Bulvarı 3 is the *Akman Boza ve Pasta Salonu*, in the courtyard of a huge block of offices and shops. Order a pastry, omelette, sandwich or snack, and consume it at terrace tables around a tinkling fountain. Overlooking this place, on the upper storey, is *Kebabistan*, a kebab place with good food

TURKEY

ANKARA

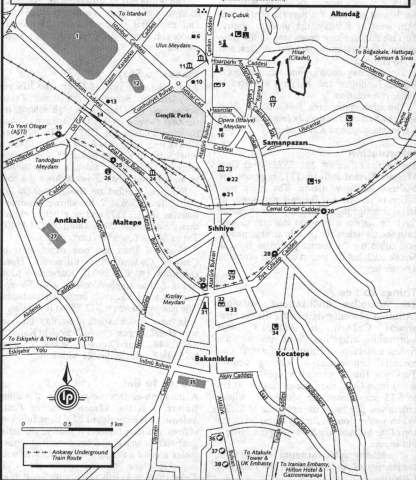

nd low prices – about US$3 to US$5 for a full meal of roast lamb, or less for just pide.

Çankırı Caddesi north of Ulus also has numerous restaurants. *Çiçek Lokantası* is quite attractive and serves drinks with meals US$6 to US$9).

For a memorable meal at a very reasonable price (US$9 to US$16 per person), try the *Zenger Paşa Konağı* (☎ 311 7070), Doyran Sokak 13, in Ankara's *hisar* (castle). It's an old house with wonderful crafts and ethnographic displays, as well as good Ottoman-style food. *Kınacılar Evi* (☎ 312 5601), Kalekapısı Sokak 28, straight uphill from the castle entrance, is an imposing place with airy rooms and some traditional dishes such as mantı (Turkish ravioli).

Getting There & Away

Air Turkish Airlines (☎ 309 0400), at Atatürk Bulvarı 167/A, Bakanlıklar, has flights daily to most Turkish cities. Most international routes require a connection in İstanbul. İstanbul Airlines (☎ 432 2234), Atatürk Bulvarı 83, Kızılay, serves several Turkish cities, but more foreign ones.

Bus Ankara's huge otogar (AŞTİ) is the vehicular heart of the nation, with coaches to all places day and night. For İstanbul (six hours, US$9 to US$12 to US$15) they go at least every 15 minutes. Other coaches go to Antalya (eight hours, US$15), Bodrum (10 hours, US$17), Erzurum (13 hours, US$18), İzmir (eight hours, US$13) and Ürgüp/Cappadocia (five hours, US$9).

Train Seven express trains, two of them with sleeping cars, connect Ankara and İstanbul (7½ to 11 hours, US$12 to US$15). The *Fatih* and *Başkent* express trains are the fastest and most expensive.

The *İzmir Mavi Tren* (14 hours) hauls sleeping (US$24) and dining cars. The evening *İzmir Ekspresi* (15 hours) has 1st/2nd-class carriages (US$9/7) and couchettes (US$11).

Trains heading east of Ankara are not as comfortable or as punctual as those travelling westward. The *Yeni Doğu Ekspresi* to Erzurum and Kars (21 hours, US$11, or US$19 in a sleeper) is faster and better than the *Doğu Ekspresi*.

Getting Around

To/From the Airport Ankara's Esenboğa airport is 33km north of the city centre. Havaş buses (US$3.50) depart about every 30 minutes from AŞTİ otogar, stopping at Ankara Garı train station; allow two hours to get to the airport. A taxi costs US$25 or more. Cheaper shared taxis run from the train station to the airport as well.

Local Transport The Ankaray underground train is useful (see Orientation). For the train station, use the Maltepe Ankaray station and the long underground walkway. Many city buses run the length of Atatürk Bulvarı. Buy a *bilet* (ticket, 50 cents) from kiosks by bus stops, or from a shop with the sign 'EGO Bilet(i)'.

City bus No 198 departs from the otogar headed for the train station and Ulus; bus No 623 goes via Kızılay to Gaziler.

Taxis are multitudinous, suicidal and metered, charging about US$3 for an average ride, or US$4 to US$6 from one end of the city to the other.

BOĞAZKALE
☎ 364

The Hittites ruled central Anatolia from about 2000 to 1180 BC. To see where they lived, visit Boğazkale, 29km off the Ankara-Samsun road. Called Hattuşaş in Hittite, this was the ancient capital of the Hittites until it was destroyed by the Phrygians.

Today there's little left apart from the walls and foundations of buildings. But what walls! Crumbling though they are, they stretch for over 10km and have five entrances, including the **Kral Kapı** (King's Gate), the **Aslanlı Kapı** (Lion Gate) and an underground tunnel, **Yer Kapı**.

The massive, imposing foundations are also inspiring. Largest is the site of the **Büyük Mabed** (Great Temple of the Storm God), which has no fewer than 70 storerooms. The natural rock temple of **Yazılıkaya**, 2km from the main site, has bas-reliefs of Hittite deities carved into the rock face.

Alacahöyük, 36km from Boğazkale near the main road, is a pre-Hittite site, probably 6000 years old. The remains, however, including the **Sphinx Gate**, are Hittite.

Buses run to Boğazkale from Ankara, or take a bus to Sungurlu, from where there should be minibuses to Boğazkale and Alacahöyük. Both these villages have small **museums**.

Boğazkale's small hotels – the *Hattusas* (☎ 452 2013), *Başkent* (☎ 452 2037) and *Aşikoğlu* (☎ 452 2004) – may fill up in summer; all have camping grounds.

KONYA
☎ 332

Known as Iconium in Roman times, Konya is a humourless, religiously conservative place, but it's one of the oldest continually occupied cities in the world, and a showplace for some striking Seljuk architecture. This was the capital of the Seljuk Turks, and it was here, in the 13th century, that the poet Celaleddin Rumi (Mevlana) founded the whirling dervishes, one of Islam's major mystical orders. Atatürk put a stop to the whirling except as 'folk dance'; you can see it here in May and during the **Mevlana Festival** every December.

Mevlana's **tomb** is topped by the brilliant green-tiled tower near the tourist office (☎ 351 1074) and hotel area; it's now the **Mevlana Müzesi**, open from 9 am to 5.30 pm daily (10 am to 5.30 pm Monday), for US$1. Other fine Seljuk buildings include the **Karatay Müzesi**, once a Muslim theological seminary and now a ceramics museum, and the **İnce Minare Medresesi**, now a wood and stone-carving museum.

If you're staying, the best lodging bargain is the *Yeni Köşk Otel* (☎ 352 0671), Yeni Aziziye Caddesi, Kadılar Sokak 28, where tidy rooms with private bath and TV cost US$19. For food, try the *Şifa Lokantası*, Mevlana Caddesi 30. The otogar is 3.5km north of the city centre, linked by Konak-Otogar minibus (30 cents).

CAPPADOCIA

South-east of Ankara, almost in the centre of the country, the Cappadocia (Kapadokya in Turkish) region is famous for the fantastic natural **rock formations** of its valleys. Over the centuries people have carved rooms, houses, churches, fortresses and even complete underground cities into the soft, eeril eroded volcanic stone.

Attractions include the Göreme, Zelve an Soğanlı valleys with their scores of rock-cu chapels (early Christian monastics sough refuge throughout the region); the fortres. towns of Uçhisar and Ortahisar; the huge un derground cities at Kaymaklı and Derinkuyu (open from 8 am to 5 pm, to 6.30 pm in summer; US$1.25 entry); and rugged Ihlara Valley (south of Aksaray) dotted with ancien churches.

Nevşehir is the biggest town. Ürgüp has a good selection of hotels, but the pensions in Göreme village are more attractive to budget travellers.

Transport is easy between Nevşehir and everywhere else, and buses run on the hour between Avanos and Ürgüp, stopping in Göreme.

Nevşehir
☎ 384

A loud, unattractive provincial capital, Nevşehir is good for information and for transport connections. Catch minibuses here for the astonishing underground cities of **Derinkuyu** and **Kaymaklı**, and for the rock-carved monasteries and churches, Hittite traces and interesting mosques much farther south at **Niğde**.

Nevşehir's tourist office (☎ 213 3659) is sympathetic to budget travellers.

Göreme
☎ 384

The Göreme Valley is one of the most amazing sights in Turkey. Over the centuries a thick layer of volcanic tufa has eroded into fantastic shapes. Early Christians carved cross-shaped churches, stables and homes into the cliffs and cones. Painted **church murals** date from as early as the 8th century, though the best are from the 10th to 13th centuries; unlit for many centuries, they've hardly faded at all, although vandals have left their indelible mark. The best are those in the **Göreme Open-Air Museum** (Göreme Açık Hava Müzesi), which is open from 8 am to 5.30 pm (4.30 pm in winter) daily; entry is US$5.

Less crowded is the **Zelve Valley**, east of the Göreme-Avanos road.

Three kilometres south-west of Göreme village is picturesque **Uçhisar**, a town built around, and into, a prominent peak. A room-to-room scramble through its rock citadel (US$1) leads to fine views from the summit.

Good, reasonably priced tours of the region are offered by Turtle Tours (☎ 271 2388) across the road from Göreme otogar; and Hiro Tour (☎ 271 2542), in the otogar.

Places to Stay & Eat You can camp in the gardens of many pensions, or at the *Dilek* or *Berlin* camping grounds, side by side amid wonderful rock formations on the road leading from Göreme village to the open-air museum. *Kaya Camping*, above the museum entrance, is even better.

The many pensions in Göreme village charge similar rates of around US$4 per bed in a dorm, US$5.50 in a waterless private room or US$7 to US$10 per bed with private facilities. One of the most popular is *Köse* (☎ 271 2294), on the right-hand side of the flood channel, with a good café and a book-exchange scheme. Other favourites are the *Tan* (☎ 271 2445), *Rock Valley* (☎ 271 2153), *Paradise* (☎ 271 2248), *Ufuk* (☎ 271 2157) and *Peri* (☎ 271 2136). The *Cave Hotel Melek* (☎ 271 2463), high on the valley wall, has rock-cut double rooms with private bath and breakfast for US$25. The prominent *Ottoman House* (☎ 271 2616) offers luxury at affordable prices: US$20/30 a single/double, but breakfast is another US$5.

Restaurants offering standard fare at slightly above average prices, such as the *Asena Kafeteryası*, are clustered around the central spindle of rock called the Roma Kalesi. The ones along the Uçhisar road (*Sultan*, *Sedef*, *Ufuk II*) are more expensive except for the *SOS* at the main intersection. *Cafedoci@*, uphill on the Uçhisar road, is the local Internet café.

Avanos
☎ 384

On the north bank of the Kızılırmak (Red River), Avanos is known for its pottery, onyx and carved alabaster. Good value is *Kirkit Pansiyon* (☎ 511 3148), where beds cost US$10 a double with shower, breakfast included; from the northern end of the bridge, walk east and bear left at the first alley.

Other cheapies in the old town up behind the main square include the basic *Nomade* and the slightly cheerier *Panorama* and *Kervan*, all with doubles for US$8 to US$12. Moving up the price and comfort scale, the *Sofa Motel* (☎ 511 4489), across the bridge from the tourist office, has tastefully decorated rooms in a group of old houses for US$15/20 a single/double with private bath.

Ürgüp
☎ 384

In spite of heavy tourist traffic (Ürgüp seems to be the base for tour groups in Cappadocia), this low-rise town is still very appealing, with its old sandstone buildings, cobbled streets and a stone hill carved full of rooms and passages. You can go **wine-tasting** here; Cappadocia's best is bottled at wineries on Mustafapaşa Caddesi and at the top of the hill on the Nevşehir road.

The helpful tourist office (☎ 341 4059) is in the park, downhill from the main square.

Places to Stay & Eat The *Göreme Pansiyon* (☎ 341 4022), on Kayseri Caddesi near the posh Hotel Büyük Almira, has the lowest rates, at US$7 per person without bath. *Hotel Kilim* (☎ 384-341 3131), a block from the otogar at Dumlupınar Caddesi 47, charges US$20 for a double with shower. The *Elvan* (☎ 384-341 4191), west of the otogar past the Dutlu Cami, has great doubles with shower for US$20 to US$30.

Alfina Hotel (☎ 341 4822), İstiklal Caddesi 27, has both cave and regular rooms for US$36/53 a single/double with private bath and breakfast.

The *Şölen* and *Kardeşler* restaurants above the otogar have good, cheap food. The *Şömine*, right in the centre, is good for grills and fresh bread.

Ihlara Valley
☎ 382

Ihlara is a remote canyon full of carved and painted **Byzantine churches** – a must for walkers.

The village of Ihlara Köyü is 85km south-west of Nevşehir and 40km south-east of Aksaray. *Akar Pansiyon* (☎ 453 7018), on the Aksaray road, is a simple hotel offering doubles with shower for US$15, breakfast included.

The similar *Anatolia Pansiyon* (☎ 453 7128), at the intersection, has basic rooms with showers for US$18, or camping for US$3. There are more pensions and a camp site in the gorge itself at the village of Belisırma.

Ihlara Belediyesi buses run several times daily from Aksaray's otogar, charging US$1 one way.

Kayseri & Sivas

Sitting in the shadow of snowy Mt Erciyes, Kayseri, known as Caesarea in Roman times, was the provincial capital of Cappadocia. Thankfully, its once notoriously persistent carpet merchants are learning the art of soft sell.

A religiously conservative town, it's full of mosques, tombs and old seminaries (*medrese*). Near the tourist office (☎ 352-222 3903) is the beautiful **Hunat Hatun** mosque, tomb and seminary. The nearby Güpgüpoğlu Konağı is a 19th-century mansion which now serves as the **Ethnography Museum**.

Opposite, behind the massive 6th-century city walls, are the **bazar** and the **Ulu Cami** (Great Mosque), begun by the Seljuks in 1136. Pride of place goes to the fine decorations on the **Döner Kümbet** (Revolving Tomb), 1km south of the tourist office on Talas Caddesi.

Sivas, on the central route through Turkey, has many marvellous Seljuk buildings to prove its past importance as a crossroads on the caravan route to Persia and Baghdad. In 1919 it was the starting point for Atatürk's War of Independence.

The Black Sea Coast

This region is dramatically different from the rest of Turkey – steep and craggy, damp and lush, and isolated by the Pontic Mountains along most of its length. It's the country's dairy belt, and the area's hazelnuts make Turkey the world's biggest exporter of them. The tea you drink in İstanbul probably comes from east of Trabzon; the cigarette smoke you endure probably comes from tobacco grown west of Samsun.

Legend has it that the coast was first settled by a tribe of Amazons. Its kingdoms have tended to be independent-minded; Trabzon was where the last Byzantines held out against the Ottomans. Even tourism hasn't penetrated far, though you'll find plenty of cheap hotels and camping grounds. Prices are lower than on the Mediterranean coast, and get even lower in the off season. With the exception of Samsun and Trabzon, less English is spoken than in other areas of Turkey.

Partly because of heavy industry around Zonguldak, the coast west from Sinop to the Bosphorus is almost unknown to tourists, though the fishing port of **Amasra**, with its Roman and Byzantine ruins, and **Safranbolu** and **Bartın**, with their traditional timber houses, are worth a look.

Good long-distance bus lines here are Ulusoy and Aydın, but there's plenty of much cheaper town-to-town dolmuş transport. On your way to the coast, stop at **Amasya**, an old Ottoman town in a dramatic mountain setting.

SİNOP

This fishing and boat-building town, three hours by bus west of Samsun, was the birthplace of Diogenes, the Cynic philosopher. Thanks to the development of Samsun's harbour, Sinop is a fine little backwater now. There are miles of **beaches** on both sides of the peninsula.

SAMSUN

Under the Seljuks, Samsun was a major trading port and had its own Genoese colony. When the Ottomans looked set to capture it in the 15th century, the Genoese burned the city to the ground before fleeing. There's little of interest here now, but it's a good starting point for travel along the coast and a port of call for the ferry from İstanbul.

Atatürk landed here on 19 May 1919 to begin the Turkish War of Independence. The otogar is 3km east of town by dolmuş.

SAMSUN TO TRABZON

There are good beaches (but chilly water) around the cheerful resort town of **Ünye**, on a wide bay 85km east of Samsun. Beaches are the only reason to stop in the glum town of **Ordu**, 80km east of Ünye. There is a tourist office (☎ 452-223 1607) half a block east of the central Atatürk statue and mosque.

Europe's first cherry trees came from **Giresun** courtesy of Lucullus, the Roman general and famous epicure, and the town is still surrounded by cherry orchards.

Dramatic remains of a big Byzantine fortress are on a headland beside the friendly village of **Akçakale**, 22km west of Trabzon.

TRABZON
☎ 462

Trabzon is certainly the most interesting place on the Turkish Black Sea coast, with mild weather, good-natured people, lots of Byzantine architecture, beaches and the amazing Sumela Monastery. Known as Trebizond in Byzantine times, this town was the last to fall to the Ottoman Turks, and earlier was a stronghold against the Seljuks and Mongols as well.

Orientation & Information
Modern Trabzon is centred on Atatürk Alanı (Atatürk Square), on a steep hill above the harbour. Uphill from it are Ulusoy and Metro bus ticket offices. Turkish Airlines is on the west side of the square. The long-distance otogar is 3km east of the port. The helpful government tourist office (☎ 321 4659) is temporarily down at the port.

Things to See
The dark walls of the Byzantine city are a half-hour walk west from Atatürk Alanı. The **old town**, with its timber houses and stone bridges, still looks medieval.

Trabzon has many **Byzantine churches**. Best-preserved is the 13th-century Aya Sofya, now a museum (open from 8.30 am to 5 pm daily but closed on Monday in winter; entry US$1); take a minibus from Atatürk Alanı. Among its more beautiful Ottoman mosques are the **Gülbahar Hatun Camii** west of the city walls and the **Çarşı Camii** (or Osmanpaşa Camii) in the bazar. For a look at a beautiful 19th-century villa, visit the **Atatürk Köşkü** high above the town.

Some travellers come to Trabzon just to visit the 14th-century **Sumela Monastery**, built into a cliff face like a swallow's nest. It was inhab-

ited until 1923, and has many fine murals (much damaged by vandals, but being restored) and amazing views. In summer, Ulusoy runs an 11 am bus (returning at 2 and 3 pm) from the town-centre terminal just uphill from Atatürk Alanı. The 40-minute trip costs US$4.

Taxis depart from Atatürk Alanı and charge US$22 to US$30 for a carload of five to the monastery, a two-hour wait, and back. Entry to Sumela National Park and the monastery is US$1.50.

Places to Stay
Many of the hotels east of Atatürk Alanı on Güzelhisar Caddesi and adjacent streets are filled with traders and prostitutes from the former Soviet states.

The **Anıl** (☎ 326 7282), Güzelhisar Caddesi 10, has a flashy lobby and fairly clean rooms with bath and TV for US$11/18 a single/double. The lobby at the **Gözde Aile Oteli** (☎ 321 9579), just off Güzelhisar Caddesi, is dingy but the rooms are better, and well priced at US$12 a double with shower. The **Sankta Maria Katolik Kilisesi Hostel** (☎ 321 2192), Sümer Sokak 26, was built by French Capuchins in 1869 when Trabzon was a cosmopolitan trading port. The hostel offers clean, simple rooms and the use of hot showers in exchange for a donation. You needn't be Catholic to stay here.

Hotel Toros (☎ 321 1212), Gençoğlu Sokak 3/A, has clean doubles with/without showers for US$12/10. Rooms at the **Hotel Benli** (☎ 321 1022), behind the belediye at Cami Çıkmazı Sokak 5, are old and drab but useable, for US$13 a double with shower. The newer **Nur** (☎ 321 2798), opposite, has clean cell-like rooms with sinks for slightly more.

Probably the best bet, if you can afford it, is the **Otel Horon** (☎ 321 1199), Sıramağazalar 125, where clean singles/doubles with shower cost US$30/40, breakfast included.

Places to Eat
Derya Restaurant, across from the belediye on the north-east corner of Atatürk Alanı, has a good selection of ready-made food and serves a tasty İskender kebap for US$3. Look also for the **Volkan 2** a few steps to the west. Close by is the **Tad Pizza ve Hamburger**, a US-style pizza parlour. Pizzas cost US$2.25 to US$3; burgers, half that.

TURKEY

Çardak Pide Salonu, behind the Turkish Airlines office (enter from Uzun Yol), serves fresh, good, cheap Turkish pizza for US$1.50 to US$2.

On the south side of Atatürk Alanı are the *İnan Kebap Salonu* and the *Çınar Lokantası*, both with a good selection of ready-made meals, best eaten fresh at lunchtime.

At the *Kıbrıs Restaurant* on the east side of the square you can get alcoholic drinks with your meal (US$6 to US$10).

Getting There & Away

Air Turkish Airlines (☎ 321 1680), on the south-west corner of Atatürk Alanı, has daily flights to Ankara and İstanbul. An airport bus (US$1) leaves from outside the office 1½ hours before flights. İstanbul Airlines (☎ 322 3806), Kazazoğlu Sokak 9, Sanat İşhanı, on the north-west corner of Atatürk Alanı, also flies daily to İstanbul for a lower fare.

Bus Dolmuş taxis to the otogar (Garajlar – Meydan) leave from Taksim Caddesi, just up the hill from Atatürk Alanı.

From the otogar, minibuses go every half-hour to Rize (1½ hours, US$1.25), Hopa (three hours, US$2.50) and Artvin (five hours, US$5). A dozen buses a day head for Erzurum (six hours, US$8), a beautiful but slow ride via Gümüşhane, or an equally beautiful and slow route via Artvin.

Boat See the Getting Around section at the beginning of this chapter for information about car ferries to İstanbul.

KAÇKAR MOUNTAINS

The eastern end of the coastal mountain range is dominated by 3937m Kaçkar Dağı, inland from Rize. Around it are excellent opportunities for camping and wilderness treks, and even white-water rafting on the Çoruh River. There are many small villages with cheap accommodation.

At **Uzungöl**, 50km east of Trabzon and 50km inland, is an alpine lake, with camping, bungalows and a few small hotels. A good base for day hikes and trekking towards Kaçkar Dağı is **Ayder**, 40km east of Rize and 40km inland, with hot springs as a bonus.

Eastern Turkey

Turkey's eastern region is the harshest and hardest part of the country to travel in, but it rewards visitors with dramatic landscapes – like majestic views of the 5165m Mt Ararat (the legendary resting place of Noah's Ark) – and some unusual historical relics. In the winter, bitterly cold weather is imported direct from the Russian steppes, so unless you're well equipped and something of a masochist, avoid travelling here from October to April. For full coverage of this region see Lonely Planet's *Turkey* guide.

Warning

In recent years, the terrorist Kurdistan Workers' Party (PKK) has carried out terrorist raids throughout Turkey, but particularly in the east, in pursuit of its goal of an independent Kurdistan.

At the time of writing, the region was still unstable, though Turkish government forces have the upper hand. Check with your consulate before travelling east, especially to Diyarbakır, Mardin or any points east of them. If you do travel here, stick to the main roads and large towns, and travel only in daylight on recognised train, bus and air lines.

ERZURUM

☎ 442

Eastern Turkey's main transport hub and a military centre, Erzurum is a fairly drab town famous for its harsh climate, although it has some striking Seljuk buildings that justify staying for a day or so.

Orientation & Information

The tourist office (☎ 218 5697) is on Cemal Gürsel Caddesi, the main street, just west of the Atatürk statue, although you may not find anyone there. The otogar is inconveniently located on the edge of town on the airport road, but the town centre itself is compact, with all the main sites within walking distance.

Things to See & Do

From the well-preserved walls of a 5th-century **Byzantine fortress**, you get a good view of the town's layout and the bleak plains that surround it. The **Çifte Minareli Medrese** (built in 1253) is a seminary famous for its Seljuk architecture. It's beautifully symmetrical, with a classic carved portal flanked by twin minarets which frame a conical dome behind.

The oldest mosque, **Ulu Cami**, built in 1179, is next door. Farther west along Cumhuriyet Caddesi, an open square marks the centre of town, with an Ottoman mosque and, at the western corner, another seminary, the **Yakutiye Medresesi**, built by the local Mongol emir in 1310. It's now the Turkish and Islamic Arts and Ethnography Museum, which is open from 8 am to noon and 12.30 to 5 pm (closed Monday) for US$1.

Take an excursion to **Yusufeli**, north of Erzurum, and neighbouring **Georgian Valleys** to see the ancient churches and to go white-water rafting on the Çoruh River.

Places to Stay

Erzurum has lots of cheapies, although showers and winter heating may cost extra, and some of the places are pretty dismal. *Örnek Otel* (☎ 218 1203), Kazım Karabekir Caddesi 8, has basic rooms for US$8/12/14 a single/double/triple. The neighbouring *Otel Polat* (☎ 218 1623), Kazım Karabekir Caddesi 3, is better, with singles/doubles from US$11/16. Both are well situated between the train station and the town centre.

Round the corner the *Hotel Sefer* (☎ 218 6714), İstasyon Caddesi, charges US$16/22/28 a single/double/triple with bath and TV, including breakfast.

Opposite the Yakutiye Medresesi, the *Kral Hotel* (☎ 218 7783) at Erzincankapı 18 has much nicer rooms than the lobby might suggest for US$15 to US$18 a single, US$21 to US$25 a double, with shower, TV and breakfast.

The best in town is the three-star *Hotel Dilaver* (☎ 235 0068), Aşağı Mumcu Caddesi, Pelit Meydanı, but it costs a hefty US$60/85, including breakfast.

Places to Eat

There are a number of reasonable options along Cumhuriyet Caddesi near the Yakutiye Medresesi. *Güzelyurt Restorant*, although tarted up with tablecloths and uniformed waiters, is not that expensive. Try the house speciality mantarlı güveç, a delicious lamb stew. Meals cost US$7 to US$10. The *Salon Çağın* and *Salon Asya* on Cumhuriyet are a bit cheaper. *Sultan Sekisi Şark Sofrası*, opposite the Çifte Minareli Medrese, serves local fare in traditional décor for US$3 to US$5.

Getting There & Away

Air Turkish Airlines (☎ 218 1904), on 50. Yıl Caddesi, has two flights daily (US$65) to Ankara, with connections to İstanbul and İzmir. A taxi to the airport costs US$3.50.

Bus Catch a No 2 bus into town from the otogar, which is 3km north-east of the town centre.

There are plenty of bus company offices uphill from the train station.

Train See the Ankara section for train information. The bus is faster.

KARS

About 260km north-east of Erzurum, this frontier town was much fought over and has a suitably massive fortress. The main reason to come here now is to see the ruins of ancient Ani and look across the border at Armenia. You'll need official permission to visit Ani; ask at the tourist office (☎ 474-223 3568), at Ordu Caddesi 241, but be wary of schemes to charge too much for transport to Ani.

There's not much to do in Kars, although there's a **museum** (closed on Monday), north-east of the train station on Cumhuriyet Caddesi, with exhibits dating from the Bronze Age.

Ani, 44km east of Kars, was completely deserted in 1239 after a Mongol invasion, but before that it had been a major city and a capital of both the Urartian and Armenian kingdoms. Surrounded by huge walls, the ruins lie in fields overlooking the Arpaçay River, which forms the border with Armenia. The ghost city is extremely dramatic and there are several notable churches, including a cathedral built between 989 and 1010 that was the seat of the Armenian prelate.

TURKEY

DOĞUBEYAZIT

Known jocularly as 'dog biscuit', this drab town, dramatically situated at the far side of a sweeping grass plain that runs to the foot of Mt Ararat, is the departure point for people going to Iran. It doesn't take long to find your bearings, as everything is within a five-minute walk. Apart from spectacular views of **Mt Ararat**, there's an interesting palace-fort, the **İshak Paşa Sarayı** (open from 7 am to 5 pm; entry US$2), 5km east of town. Perched romantically among rocky crags, it overlooks the town and the plains. The occasional dolmuş passes nearby, but unless you want to walk you'll probably have to negotiate for a taxi (about US$5 there and back).

Until recently Doğubeyazıt was also a base for climbing Mt Ararat, but because of the Kurdish revolt the area is now out of bounds to trekkers. Instead, there are excursions to the **meteor crater, Diyadin hot springs** and the supposed resting-place of **Noah's Ark**.

If you decide to stay, the *Hotel İsfahan* (☎ 472-311 5159), Emniyet Caddesi 26, has serviceable rooms (some with real bathtubs) for US$25/38 a single/double. Several smaller hotels nearby provide rooms for US$5 to US$7 a bed.

VAN
☎ 432

The town of Van, on the south-east shore of the vast salt lake of the same name, has a 3000-year-old **citadel** at Van Kalesi (Rock of Van) and a small **museum**. Tourists are beginning to return to Van after years of being scared off by the Kurdish revolt.

The tourist office is at Cumhuriyet Caddesi 19 (☎ 216 2018). The otogar is several kilometres north-west of the centre.

There's a 10th-century church on **Akdamar Island** in the lake. The church is a fascinating piece of Armenian architecture in a beautiful setting, with frescos inside and reliefs outside depicting biblical scenes.

Dolmuş (US$1) from Beş Yol in Van take you to the dock for boats to Akdamar. Unless you can rustle up a group to share costs, expect to pay US$18 to US$20 for a boat.

Places to Stay
Cheap hotels in the bazar (*çarşı*) charge US$4.50 per person in rooms with sink and/or private shower. Among the better ones are the *Otel İpek* (☎ 216 3033) and the more basic *Aslan Oteli* (☎ 216 2469), Eski Hal Civarı. The 63-room *Hotel Kent* (☎ 216 2404) charges the same for less.

For more comfort, try the *Otel Güzel Paris* (☎ 216 3739), next to the government building (Van Valiliği), which charges US$15/19 a single/double for big, comfy rooms with bath, breakfast included. The two-star *Büyük Asur Oteli* (☎ 216 8792), Cumhuriyet Caddesi, Turizm Sokak 5, has 48 clean rooms with shower, a lift and a restaurant, for US$18/25 a single/double with plentiful hot water.

Erzurum's supposed best is the 75-room, three-star *Büyük Urartu Oteli* (☎ 212 0660), near the Devlet Hastanesi hospital, overpriced at US$65/78 a single/double.

SOUTH-EASTERN TURKEY

Turkey's south-east corner, along the border with Syria and Iraq, is the region once known as Upper Mesopotamia; it is drained by the historic Tigris (Dicle) and Euphrates (Fırat) rivers. It's the area with the largest Kurdish population and thus the area worst affected by PKK terrorism and government reprisals. If you do mean to travel here, it's vital to take heed of the warning given at the start of this section.

Nemrut Dağı

North of Şanlıurfa and south of Malatya, pretty much in the middle of nowhere, is Nemrut Dağı (Mt Nimrod), on whose summit is a 2000-year-old **memorial sanctuary** for an obscure Commagene king. It has huge statues of gods and kings, their heads toppled by earthquakes and scattered on the ground.

Malatya tourist office (☎ 422-323 3025), on the first floor of the Vilayet Binası in the main square, arranges minibus trips almost daily for around US$30 per person, including one night in a hotel near the summit. On the south side of the mountain in **Kahta**, the tourist office (☎ 416-725 5007) can help with minibus tours. All hotels in Kahta, including the *Kommagene* (☎ 416-715 1092), *Mezopotamya* (☎ 416-725 5112) and *Zeus Camping* (☎ 416-725 5695), arrange tours.

Yugoslavia (Југославија)

The new Federal Republic of Yugoslavia (SRJ), made up of Serbia and Montenegro, occupies the heart of the Balkan Peninsula astride the main road, rail and river routes from Western Europe to Asia Minor.

Since the withdrawal of Croatia, Slovenia, Bosnia-Hercegovina and Macedonia in 1991, Yugoslavia (Jugoslavija) seems to have become a mere 'Greater Serbia', with oppressed Hungarian, Slavic Muslim and Albanian minorities.

This tragic outcome and the continuing ethnic strife have cast a pall over a country still rich in mountains, rivers, seascapes, cultures, customs, cuisines and peoples. Now shorn of most of its coastal tourist resorts, rump Yugoslavia seems destined to be forgotten by the world of mass tourism. However, awaiting those visitors who do stray beyond the transit corridors to Turkey and Greece are the glorious gorges and beaches of Montenegro, the mystical Orthodox monasteries of southern Serbia and Kosovo, the imposing fortresses along the Danube, and hundreds of other tangible traces of a tumultuous history stretching back thousands of years.

United Nations (UN) sanctions have come and gone and seem to have barely dented Yugoslavia's pride, though the country's recent ventures against Kosovar Albanians have yet again tainted its reputation and brought renewed sanctions against the country.

Yugoslavia's tourist economy, though severely compromised as a result of internal upheavals and to a lesser degree by sanctions, is suffering and while the security of travellers in lesser volatile areas is guaranteed, travellers should avoid potential political and military hotspots and undertake travel in the country with a certain spirit of adventure.

AT A GLANCE

Capital	Belgrade
Population	11.3 million (Serbia 10.5 million Montenegro 680,000)
Area	102,350 sq km (Serbia 88,412 sq km Montenegro 13,938 sq km)
Official Language	Croatian/Serbian
Currency	1 Yugoslav Novi Dinar (DIN) = 100 paras
GDP	US$21 billion (1997)
Time	GMT/UTC+0100

Facts about Yugoslavia

HISTORY
The original inhabitants of this region were the Illyrians, followed by the Celts, who arrived in the 4th century BC. The Roman conquest of Moesia Superior (Serbia) began in the 3rd century BC and under Augustus the empire extended to Singidunum (Belgrade) on the Danube. In 395 AD Theodosius I divided the empire and what is now Serbia passed to the Byzantine Empire, while Croatia remained part of the Western Roman Empire.

In the middle of the 6th century, Slavic tribes (Serbs, Croats and Slovenes) crossed

YUGOSLAVIA (JUGOSLAVIJA)

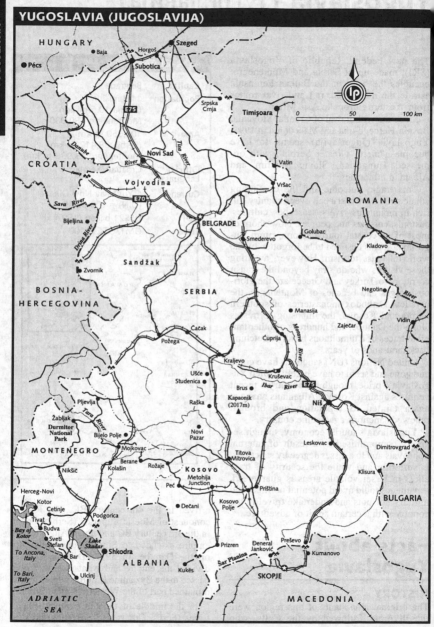

he Danube in the wake of the Great Migra-
on of Nations and occupied much of the
Balkan Peninsula. In 879 the Serbs were con-
erted to the Orthodox Church by Sts Cyril
nd Methodius. In 969 Serbia broke free from
Byzantium and established an independent
tate; however, Byzantium re-established its
authority in the 11th century.

An independent Serbian kingdom returned
n 1217 and during the reign of Stefan Dušan
1346-55) Serbia was a great power including
much of present Albania and northern Greece
within its boundaries. Numerous frescoed Orthodox monasteries were erected during this
Serbian 'Golden Age'. After Stefan's death
Serbia declined, and at the Battle of Kosovo
on 28 June 1389 the Serbian army was defeated by the Ottoman Turks, ushering in 500
years of Islamic rule. The Serbs were pushed
north as the Turks advanced into Bosnia in
the 15th century and the city-state of Venice
occupied the coast. By 1459 Serbia was a
Turkish *pashalik* (province) and the inhabitants had become mere serfs. In 1526 the
Turks defeated Hungary at the Battle of
Mohács, expanding their realm north and
west of the Danube.

The first centuries of Turkish rule brought
stability to the Balkans but, as the power of
the sultan declined, local Turkish officials
and soldiers began to oppress the Slavs. After
their defeat at Vienna in 1683, the Turks
began a steady retreat.

By 1699 they had been driven out of
Hungary and many Serbs moved north into
Vojvodina, where they enjoyed Habsburg
protection. Through diplomacy the sultan regained northern Serbia for another century,
but a revolt in 1815 led to de facto Serbian independence in 1816.

Serbia's autonomy was recognised in
1829, the last Turkish troops departed in
1867, and in 1878, after Russia's defeat of
Turkey in a war over Bulgaria, complete independence was achieved. Montenegro also
declared itself independent of Turkey in
1878. Macedonia remained under Turkish
rule into the 20th century.

The 20th Century

Tensions mounted after Austria's annexation
of Bosnia-Hercegovina in 1908, with Russia
backing Serbia. There was more overt trouble

in Macedonia; in the First Balkan War
(1912), Serbia, Greece and Bulgaria combined against Turkey for the liberation of
Macedonia. The Second Balkan War (1913)
saw Serbia and Greece join forces against
Bulgaria, which had claimed all of Macedonia for itself. At about this time Serbia
wrested control of Kosovo from Albania with
the help of the Western powers.

WWI was an extension of these conflicts
as Austria-Hungary used the assassination of
Archduke Ferdinand by a Serb nationalist on
28 June 1914 as an excuse to invade Serbia.
Russia and France came to Serbia's aid,
while Germany backed Austria. Thus began
'the war to end all wars'. In the winter of
1915-16 a defeated Serbian army of 155,000
retreated across the mountains of Montenegro to the Adriatic from where it was
evacuated to Corfu. In 1918 these troops
fought their way back up into Serbia from
Thessaloniki, Greece.

After WWI, Croatia, Slovenia and Vojvodina were united with Serbia, Montenegro
and Macedonia to form the Kingdom of
Serbs, Croats and Slovenes under the king of
Serbia. In 1929 the name was changed to Yugoslavia. The Vidovdan constitution of 1921
created a centralised government dominated
by Serbia. This was strongly opposed by the
Croats and other minorities, forcing King
Alexander to end the political turmoil by declaring a personal dictatorship in 1929. The
1934 assassination of the king by a Macedonian terrorist with links to Croat separatists
brought to power a regent who continued the
Serbian dictatorship. Corruption was rampant
and the regent tilted towards friendship with
Nazi Germany.

On 25 March 1941, Yugoslavia joined the
Tripartite Alliance, a fascist military pact,
after being promised Greek Macedonia and
Thessaloniki by the Germans. This sparked
mass protest demonstrations and a military
coup that overthrew the profascist regency.
Peter II was installed as king and Yugoslavia
abruptly withdrew from the alliance. Livid,
Hitler ordered an immediate invasion and the
country was carved up between Germany,
Italy, Hungary and Bulgaria. In Croatia, a
fascist puppet state was set up which massacred hundreds of thousands of ethnic Serbs
and Jews.

Almost immediately the Communist Party, under Josip Broz Tito, declared an armed uprising. There was also a monarchist resistance group, the Četniks, but they proved far less effective than Tito's partisans, and after 1943 the British gave full backing to the communists. A 1943 meeting of the Antifascist Council for the National Liberation of Yugoslavia (AVNOJ) at Jajce, in Bosnia, laid the basis for a future communist-led Yugoslavia.

The partisans played a major role in WWII by tying down huge Italian and German armies, but Yugoslavia suffered terrible losses, especially in Croatia and Bosnia-Hercegovina, where most of the fighting took place. According to the Serbian author Bogoljub Kočović some 487,000 Serbs, 207,000 Croats, 86,000 Muslims, 60,000 Jews, 50,000 Montenegrins, 32,000 Slovenes, 7000 Macedonians and 6000 Albanians died in the war. The resistance did, however, guarantee Yugoslavia's postwar independence.

Postwar Communism

In 1945 the Communist Party (which had been officially banned since 1920) won control of the national assembly, which in November abolished the monarchy and declared Yugoslavia a federal republic. Serbia's size was then greatly reduced when Bosnia-Hercegovina, Montenegro and Macedonia were granted republic status within this 'second' Yugoslavia. The Albanians of Kosovo and Hungarians of Vojvodina were denied republics of their own, however, on the pretext that they were not nations because their national homelands were outside the boundaries of Yugoslavia. Under Tito's slogan *bratstva i jedinstva* (brotherhood and unity), nationalist tendencies were suppressed.

Tito broke with Stalin in 1948 and, as a reward, received US$2 billion in economic and military aid from the USA and UK between 1950 and 1960. For the West this was a cheap way of protecting NATO's southern flank, but for Yugoslavia the Western subsidies alleviated the need for reform, contributing to the economic problems of today.

After the break with the USSR, Yugoslavia followed its own 'road to socialism' based on a federal system, self-management, personal freedom and nonalignment. The decentralisation begun in 1951 was to lead to the eventual 'withering away of the state' of classical Marxism. Yugoslavia never became member of either the Warsaw Pact or NATO and in 1956 the country played a key role in the formation of the nonaligned movement.

The 1960s witnessed an economic boom in the north-west accompanied by liberalisation throughout the country, and in July 1966 Tito fired his hardline secret police chief Alexander Ranković. Growing regional inequalities led, however, to increased tension as Slovenia, Croatia and Kosovo demanded greater autonomy within the federation. In 1971 Tito responded with a 'return to Leninism', which included a purge of party reformers and a threat to use military force against Croatia.

With the most talented members of the leadership gone, Yugoslavia stagnated through the 1970s while borrowing billions of recycled petrodollars from the West. A 1970 constitutional amendment declared that the federal government would have control of foreign policy, defence, trade, the national economy and human rights, and all residual powers were vested in the six republics (Croatia, Bosnia-Hercegovina, Macedonia, Montenegro, Serbia and Slovenia) and two autonomous provinces of Serbia (Kosovo and Vojvodina). The 1974 constitution strengthened the powers of the autonomous provinces.

After Tito

Tito died in 1980 and the presidency then became a collective post rotated annually among nine members who were elected every four years by the national assembly, the six republics and the two autonomous provinces. This cumbersome system proved unable to solve either Yugoslavia's deepening economic problems or its festering regional and ethnic antagonisms.

In 1986 a working group of the Serbian Academy of Sciences prepared a memorandum calling on Serbia to reassert its hegemony in Yugoslavia. A year later Slobodan Milošević took over as party leader in Serbia by portraying himself as the champion of an allegedly persecuted Serbian minority in Kosovo. Milošević hoped to restore the flagging popularity of the League of Communists by inciting the Serbs' latent ti-Albanian sentiments. When moves by erbia to limit Kosovo's autonomy led to massive protest demonstrations in the rovince in late 1988 and early 1989, the erbian government unilaterally scrapped osovo's autonomy. Thousands of troops ere sent to intimidate Kosovo's 90% Albanian majority, and in direct confrontations vith the security forces dozens of civilians vere shot dead.

Milošević's vision of a 'Greater Serbia' orrified residents of Slovenia and Croatia, vho elected non-communist republican governments in the spring of 1990. These called or the creation of a loose Yugoslav 'confederation' which would allow Slovenia and Croatia to retain most of their wealth for hemselves, and both republics threatened to secede from Yugoslavia if such reforms were not forthcoming. In the Serbian elections of December 1990, however, Milošević's policies paid off when the communists won 194 of 260 seats (the Albanians boycotted the election). In the other republics communists managed to hold on to Montenegro but lost Bosnia-Hercegovina and Macedonia.

In March 1991 Serbia's state-controlled media broadcast false reports of a massacre of ethnic Serbs in Croatia in an attempt to precipitate a crisis leading to a military takeover. This outraged prodemocratic Serbian students who, led by Serbian Renewal Movement leader Vuk Drašković, massed outside the TV studios in Belgrade demanding that those responsible be sacked.

Civil War

On 25 June 1991 Slovenia and Croatia declared themselves independent of Yugoslavia. This soon led to fighting as the federal army moved into Slovenia. Fearing a tidal wave of refugees, the European Community (EC), now known as the European Union (EU), rushed a delegation of foreign ministers to Yugoslavia to negotiate a truce, which soon broke down. In Belgrade, Milošević went on TV to reaffirm his support for Yugoslavia and the right of people to continue to live in it. He said the Yugoslav People's Army would intervene to defend Serbs wherever they lived.

On 7 July, federal and republican leaders met on Brijuni Island off Istria in the hope of preventing a full-scale civil war, while the EC imposed a weapons embargo on Yugoslavia and froze US$1 billion in aid and credits. It soon became clear that the matter would be decided in Croatia; on 18 July the Yugoslav government announced that all federal troops would be withdrawn from Slovenia within three months.

Intervention by the federal army on the side of Serb separatists in Croatia led to months of heavy fighting, with widespread property damage and thousands of casualties. The EC sent unarmed cease-fire monitors to the trouble areas in September and organised a peace conference in the Netherlands but this failed, and in November the EC applied economic sanctions against Serbia and Montenegro. On 20 December 1991 the federal prime minister, Ante Marković (a Croat), resigned after the army demanded 81% of the 1992 budget.

In December it was agreed that a UN peacekeeping force would be sent to Croatia and from 3 January 1992 a cease-fire generally held. On 15 January the EC recognised the independence of Croatia and Slovenia, whereupon both Macedonia and Bosnia-Hercegovina demanded recognition of their own independence. Montenegro alone voted to remain in Yugoslavia. The secession of Bosnia-Hercegovina, with its large Serb population, sparked bitter fighting as Serb militants with army backing again used force to seize territory, as they had done in Croatia.

The Third Yugoslavia

On 27 April 1992 a 'third' Yugoslav federation was declared by Serbia and Montenegro in a rushed attempt to escape blame for the bloodshed in Bosnia-Hercegovina. The rump state disclaimed responsibility for the federal army in Bosnia-Hercegovina and announced that all soldiers hailing from Serbia and Montenegro would be withdrawn.

In May 1992, with Sarajevo under siege and the world losing patience with what was seen as Serbian aggression, the UN Security Council passed a sweeping package of economic and diplomatic sanctions against Yugoslavia. In mid-July US and Western European warships began patrolling the Adriatic off Montenegro to monitor the embargo. Yugoslavia was denied its old seat at the UN in

September 1992 and in November a UN naval blockade was imposed. Sanctions against Yugoslavia were greatly strengthened in April 1993 after the Serb side rejected a peace plan for Bosnia-Hercegovina. Yet, despite severe economic hardship, the socialists won the December 1993 elections.

With the division of Bosnia into Serb and Croat-Muslim states in late 1995, the dream of a 'Greater Serbia' seemed close to reality, stained with the blood of tens of thousands of unfortunate people and soiled by the ashes of their burned homes.

Meanwhile, five years of hostile relations with Croatia officially ended in August 1996, with the signing of a landmark treaty which recognised national borders and normalised relations between the two countries.

In the winter of 1996/97 the Milošević government clumsily attempted to overturn local elections, leading to widespread and daily street marches fronted by a coalition grouping called *Zajedno* (Together). Zajedno ultimately hoped to topple the Milošević government, but after he backtracked and reinstated the election results the street marches fizzled out

The new constitution of rump Yugoslavia had made no mention of 'autonomous provinces', and the Albanian majority in Kosovo, long brutally repressed by Serbia, finally erupted in January 1998 with the Serb military and police machine moving in to systematically wipe out Albanian Kosovar resistance leaders in Kosovo, provoking a storm of protest from the West but no reaction other than a re-imposition of an arms embargo. By May 1998 the situation was volatile and still threatened to disrupt peace in the wider region. (See the Kosovo section later in this chapter for background information).

GEOGRAPHY

Mountains and plateaus account for the lower half of this 102,173-sq-km country (the size of the US state of Virginia), the remainder being the Pannonian Plain, which is drained by the Sava, Danube and Tisa rivers in the north-east. Yugoslavia's interior and southern mountains belong to the Balkan range, and the coastal range is an arm of the Alps. Most of the rivers flow north into the Danube, which runs through Yugoslavia for 588km. In the south many smaller rivers have cut deep canyons in the plateau, which make for memorable train rides.

When the country split up in 1991, most of the Adriatic coast went to Slovenia and Croatia, though the scenically superb 150km Montenegrin coast remains in Yugoslavia. The Bay of Kotor here is the only real fjord in southern Europe, and Montenegro's Durmitor National Park has ex-Yugoslavia's largest canyon. Between Ulcinj and Albania is one of the longest beaches on the eastern Adriatic.

GOVERNMENT & POLITICS

Yugoslavia has nominally at least a presidential parliamentarian system, with regular multi-party elections. Power, however, has remained firmly in the hands of Serb nationalist Slobodan Milošević, two-term president of Serbia and now president, in the largely ceremonial post, of Yugoslavia. Opposition parties are largely divided and fragmented, thus providing little opportunity for a change in political direction in the foreseeable future.

ECONOMY

After WWII, Yugoslavia was a war-torn land of peasants. From 1948 to 1951 a concentrated attempt was made to form agricultural cooperatives. This failed, however, and most of the land continued to be worked privately by small farmers. In 1953 individual private holdings were reduced to a maximum of 10 hectares.

During the 1950s, state property was handed over to the workers in a reaction against Stalinist state socialism. The economy was thus reorganised on the basis of 'self-management', and elected workers' councils began running the factories and businesses, with coordination from producers' councils on a regional level. State control was limited to the broadest economic planning.

This system soon led to inefficiencies and an expensive duplication of services without the full benefits of open competition. Since collectively owned property had no clear owner, it was impossible to enforce economc efficiency or to guarantee profits. Initiative was stifled and employees often used self-management to improve their own financial standing without feeling any responsibility towards their property. Income was spent on higher wages and, with little or no capital left for development, companies turned to the banks. The cycle of inefficiency and dependency deepened as companies borrowed with little hope of ever paying off the loans.

The crisis of 2000% inflation in 1989 shattered the self-management ideal and led reformers to believe that a return to private property was inevitable. At the beginning of 1990 the government attempted to halt inflation by stopping the printing presses of the Belgrade mint and declaring a wage freeze. Prices still jumped by 75% but by mid-1990 inflation had levelled off to 13% a year. However, in 1992 hyperinflation returned as the government again turned to printing money to finance government operations and the war in Bosnia-Hercegovina. UN economic sanctions did the rest.

In 1993 incomes were a tenth of what they had been three years previously, industrial output had dropped 40% from that of a year before and 60% of factory workers were unemployed. Over 80% of Yugoslav property is still collectively owned and if normal bankruptcy procedures were applied most firms would go broke. Many people get by on remittances from relatives overseas or by subsisting on their gardens and livestock.

The end of the Cold War has greatly reduced the strategic importance of the entire Balkan region and Western countries are unlikely to rush in with 1950s-style aid or 1970s-style loans, even assuming that peace and stability do somehow return. Yugoslavia owes foreign governments and banks about US$16 billion, most of it dating back to the 1970s.

After a period of relative currency stability with the novi dinar holding its own against the mighty deutschmark, Yugoslavia was finally forced, following the Kosovo débâcle, to devalue the dinar in April 1998 by about 45% bringing the value of the DM up to six dinars from the previous level of 3.3. While a boon for travellers, its effect on the long-suffering Yugoslav is bound to be negative.

POPULATION & PEOPLE

The 11 million people of the 'third' Yugoslavia include Serbs (62.3%), Albanians (16.6%), Montenegrins (5%), Hungarians (3.3%) and Slavic Muslims (3.1%), plus a smattering of Croats, Romas, Slovaks, Macedonians, Romanians, Bulgarians, Turks and Ukrainians. The Montenegrins are officially considered ethnic Serbs. In 1991 an estimated 170,000 Romas lived in Yugoslavia, 100,000 of them in Kosovo. There are about 500,000 war refugees from Croatia and Bosnia-Hercegovina in Serbia and another 64,000 in Montenegro.

Nearly a quarter of Vojvodina's population is Hungarian and 90% of Kosovars are Albanian. Around 200,000 Serbs also live in Kosovo and there are large Slavic Muslim and Albanian minorities in Montenegro. In total there are 1.8 million ethnic Albanians in present-day Yugoslavia, a large number considering that the population of Albania itself is only 3.2 million. Some 250,000 Slavic Muslims live in the Sandžak region of Serbia and Montenegro between Novi Pazar and Berane (part of Bosnia until 1918). The human rights of all minorities are challenged by an increasingly nationalistic Serbia.

Yugoslavia's largest cities are Belgrade (population 1.5 million), Novi Sad (250,000), Niš (230,000), Priština (210,000) and Subotica (160,000).

ARTS

The artistic group FIA (☎ 011-347 355), at Hilandarska 4, 11000 Belgrade, founded in 1989 by Stavislav Sharp and Nada Rajičić, uses art to explore Serbia's tumultuous present through 'Phobjects' – suggestive images juxtaposed against folk art, political symbols and provocative quotations.

At exhibitions, group members dress in black paramilitary uniforms and show videos of skits in which FIA 'conspiracies' are acted out. Their 1992 Belgrade exhibition was visited by over 50,000 people in two weeks before being suddenly closed by force.

Phobjects have been exhibited in the ruins of the railway station in Sarajevo and at the bombed-out zoo in Osijek (Croatia). Surrealist 'posters of conscience' bring the FIA message to the streets. Their works are often prophetic.

Film

The award-winning film *Underground*, by Sarajevo-born director Emil Kusturica, is worth seeing. Told in a chaotic, colourful style, the film deals with the history of former Yugoslavia over the last 50 years.

Literature

Nobel Prize winner Ivo Andrić is Serbia's most respected and most translated writer. His novel *Na Drini Ćuprija* (Bridge over the Drina), which is about the gap between religions, accurately foresaw the disasters that befell the Balkans in the early 1990s. Respected writer Milorad Pavić's novel *Hazarski Rečnik* (Hazar Dictionary) is a historical narrative, interlaced with fact and fiction, which has also been translated into English.

An excellent source of rare and out-of-print books on Serbia is Eastern Books (☎/fax 0181-871 0880; info@easternbooks.com), 125a Astonville St, Southfields, London SW18 5AQ. View their web page at www.easternbooks.com.

Music

Serbia's vibrant dances are similar to those of neighbouring Bulgaria. Serbian folk musicians use the *caraba* (small bagpipes), *gajde* (larger bagpipes), *frula* (small flute), *duduk* (large flute) and the fiddle.

The gajde employed in much Balkan music probably dates back to 4th-century Celtic invasions; unlike Scottish sheepskin bagpipes, the gajde is made from goatskin. The music of the Albanians of Kosovo bears the deep imprint of five centuries of Turkish rule, with the high whine of an Arab *zorna* (flute) carrying the tune above the beat of a goatskin drum. The *kolo* (round dance) is often accompanied by Gypsy musicians.

Blehmuzika, or brass music, has become the national music of Serbia. Though documented as far back as 1335, blehmuzika evolved under the influence of Turkish and, later, Austrian military music.

For popular modern music check out Momčilo Bajagić, who often appears on CD together with his group Bajaga & Instruktori. His music fuses traditional elements with street poetry and jazz and he is very popular

with the younger generation. Đorđe Balašević, equally if not more popular, appeals to wider listening audience, combining onc again traditional folkloric elements wit modern musical motifs.

SOCIETY & CONDUCT

The Serbs are a proud and hospitable people, despite their newly-tarnished reputation. Visitors are a source of pride and are made to feel welcome. As in Macedonia, respect for all religious establishments and customs should be shown; these should not be treated as tourist entertainment. Dress appropriately at all times – look at what locals are wearing. Learning some basic Serbian, Hungarian or Albanian will open doors and create smiles.

RELIGION

The Serbs and Montenegrins are Orthodox, the Hungarians are Roman Catholic and the Albanians are predominantly Muslim.

LANGUAGE

Ordinary Yugoslavs are most likely to know German as a second language, though educated people in Kosovo and Serbia can often speak French. Serbian is the common language, and Albanian is spoken in Kosovo.

Serbian and Croatian are almost the same language, although Serbian is written in Cyrillic and Croatian is written in Latin characters (see the Croatian & Serbian language section at the end of the book). Before the break-up of the Yugoslav Federation, the language was referred to as Serbo-Croatian, but this term is now obsolete. Serbs in Yugoslavia call their language Serbian.

The Latin alphabet is used by the Albanians in Kosovo and the Hungarians in Vojvodina. In Montenegro you'll encounter a mixture of Latin and Cyrillic, but in Serbia most things are written only in Cyrillic. It's advisable to spend an hour or two studying the Cyrillic alphabet if you want to be able to read street and travel destination signs. (See the Macedonian language section at the back of this book for an explanation of the alphabet.)

Facts for the Visitor

HIGHLIGHTS

Yugoslavia has a wealth of castles, such as Smederevo Castle on the Danube, which is Serbia's last medieval fortress. Petrovaradin Citadel at Novi Sad is one of Europe's great baroque fortresses and Belgrade's Kalemegdan Citadel must be mentioned for its historic importance. The old Montenegrin capital of Cetinje will please romantics. Of the beach resorts, Budva is chic but Ulcinj has more atmosphere and is much cheaper. Montenegro's Tara Canyon is good for nature lovers and river rafters and is on a par with any similar location in the world.

SUGGESTED ITINERARIES

Depending on the length of your stay, you might want to see and do the following things in Yugoslavia:

Two days
    Visit Novi Sad and Belgrade
One week
    Visit Novi Sad, Belgrade, Ulcinj, Budva and Cetinje
Two weeks
    Visit all areas covered in this chapter except Kosovo
One month
    Visit all areas covered in this chapter

PLANNING
Climate & When to Go

The interior has a more extreme continental climate than the Adriatic coast of Montenegro. Belgrade has average daily temperatures above 17°C from May to September, above 13°C in April and October and above 7°C in March and November. In winter a cold wind (koshava) often blows across Belgrade.

Books & Maps

Rebecca West's *Black Lambs & Grey Falcons* is a classic portrait of prewar Yugoslavia. Former partisan and leading dissident Milovan Djilas has written many fascinating books about history and politics in Yugoslavia, most of them published in English. Any good library will have a couple of them.

The disintegration of former Yugoslavia has produced a wealth of reading material. A highly recommended recent book (updated to July 1991) on the region's political upheaval is *Remaking the Balkans* by Christopher Čilić (Pinter Publishers). The precise background information contained in this slim volume offers a clear explanation of events. *The Destruction of Yugoslavia* by Branka Magaš (Verso Publishers) offers many insights into the period from the death of Tito in 1980 to the end of 1992. Other titles dealing with the turbulence of the 1990s include *Yugoslavia: Death of a Nation* by Laura Silber and Allan Little, based on the 1995 BBC documentary series of the same name, and *Yugoslavia's Bloody Collapse,* a 1996 publication by Christopher Bennett.

Current Hallwag or Baedeker maps of Yugoslavia are hard to find or non-existent. Older maps show the former borders. The *Savezna Republika Jugoslavija Autokarta,* showing the new borders and a few regional town maps, and the detailed Belgrade city map *Plan Grada Beograd,* are both available for 15 and 10 DIN respectively from the Tourist Organisation of Belgrade.

What to Bring

You should plan on bringing your own film and video requirements, to be on the safe side. Bring a universal bath plug, since hotels rarely supply them.

TOURIST OFFICES

All overseas offices of the Yugoslav National Tourist Office closed in 1991 but should gradually be reopening. Municipal tourist offices still exist in Belgrade, Novi Sad and Podgorica. Commercial travel agencies such as Montenegroturist and Putnik will often provide general information on their area.

VISAS & EMBASSIES

Most visitors require visas and these are issued at Yugoslav consulates for a set fee depending on your nationality. Australian passport holders are charged A$5 – UK passport holders as much as £30 for a double entry visa. You will most likely need a confirmed travel itinerary and an invitation from a Yugoslav citizen, or a confirmed hotel reservation before a visa will be issued.

Before the troubles of the early 90s you could get a Yugoslav visa at the border, but this is no longer possible; you *must* obtain your Yugoslav visa in advance at an embassy or consulate. As a result of the US-led re-imposition of sanctions on Yugoslavia in April 1998, US travellers in particular are being given a hard time obtaining a visa and may be subject to considerable questioning by consular authorities.

If you plan on entering Yugoslavia more than once, ask for a double or triple-entry visa, otherwise you'll have to apply for a visa again.

Yugoslav Embassies Abroad

In addition to those listed below, Yugoslav consulates or embassies are found in Bucharest, Budapest, Prague, Skopje, Sofia, Timişoara, Tirana and Warsaw. Try to avoid the chaotic Tirana consulate.

Australia
(☎ 02-9362 3003; fax 02-9362 4555; yugcon@rosebay.matra.com.au) 12 Trelawney St, Woollahra, NSW 2025

Canada
(☎ 613-233 6289) 17 Blackburn Ave, Ottawa, Ontario, K1N 8A2

France
(☎ 01 40 72 24 24; fax 01 40 72 24 10) 54 rue Faisanderie 16e, Paris

Greece
(☎ 01-777 4344) Vasilisis Sofias 106, Athens
(☎ 031-244 266) Komninon 4, Thessaloniki

Netherlands
(☎ 070-363 2397) Groot Hertoginnelaan 30, 2517 EG, The Hague

UK
(☎ 0171-370 6105; fax 0171-370 3836) 5 Lexham Gardens, London, W8 5JJ

USA
(☎ 202-462 6566) 2410 California St NW, Washington DC, 20008

Foreign Embassies in Yugoslavia

Most consulates and embassies are on or near Belgrade's Kneza Miloša, a 10-minute walk south-east from the train station. Visas are payable in cash only, specifically US$ or DM, and vary in price considerably, depending on how long you are prepared to wait. Opening times may vary.

Albania
(☎ 646 864; fax 642 941) Kneza Miloša 5 (weekdays, 9 to 11 am)

Australia
(☎ 624 655; fax 628 189) Čika Ljubina 13 (8.30 am to 4.30 pm)

Bulgaria (Consulate)
(☎ 646 422) Birčaninova 26 (weekdays, 8 am to 3 pm)

Canada
(☎ 644 666; fax 641 343) Kneza Miloša 75 (weekdays, 8 am to noon and 1 to 4 pm)

Czech Republic (Consulate)
(☎ 323 0133) Bulevar Revolucije 22 (Monday to Thursday from 9 to 11 am)

Hungary (Consulate)
(☎ 444 0472) Ivana Milutinovića 75 (weekdays, 9 to 11 am)

Poland (Consulate)
(☎ 644 866) Kneza Miloša 38 (weekdays, 10 am to noon)

Romania (Consulate)
(☎ 646 071) Kneza Miloša 70 (weekdays, 8 am to 3 pm)

Slovakia (Consulate)
(☎ 311 1052) Bulevar Umetnosti 18, Novi Beograd (weekdays except Wednesday, 8 to 11 am)

UK
(☎ 645 055; fax 659 651) Generala Ždanova 46 (weekdays, 8.30 to 11 am)

USA
(☎ 645 655; fax 644 053) Kneza Miloša 50 (weekdays, 8 to 11 am)

MONEY
Currency

Since 1991 the Yugoslav dinar has suffered repeated devaluations. In December 1993 Yugoslavia experienced the highest inflation in the history of Europe (higher even than the monthly 32,000% record set by Weimar Germany in 1923). To most of us, such a situation is inconceivable but the Yugoslavs are experienced at dealing with inflation.

In 1990 four zeros were knocked off the Yugoslav dinar, so 10,000 old dinars became one new dinar, and in mid-1993 another six zeros were dropped. When this currency in turn inflated into obsolescence, a 'super dinar' was issued in January 1994 with a value of one to 12 million old dinars. By mid-1996 a new currency, the 'novi dinar', was holding its own against harder currencies, but it, in turn, was devalued by 45% in April

998. There are coins of five, 10 and 50 para
and one novi dinar and notes of five, 10, 20,
0 and 100 dinars.

Note: Travellers are now *supposed* to fill
in a currency declaration form listing all hard
currency being brought into the country. This
form should theoretically be provided at all
entry points, but is more often than not
ignored unless you ask for it. Beware: if you
fail to produce a declaration form upon
leaving the country, you *may* run the risk of
having any hard currency in your possession
confiscated. (see Leaving Yugoslavia in the
Getting There & Away section of this
chapter).

Exchange Rates

Australia	A$1	=	7.10 DIN
Canada	C$1	=	7.60 DIN
euro	€1	=	11.79 DIN
France	1FF	=	1.78 DIN
Germany	DM1	=	6.00 DIN
Switzerland	Sfr1	=	7.21 DIN
UK	UK£1	=	18.25 DIN
USA	US$1	=	0.90 DIN

Changing Money

All banks, travel agencies and hotels will
change cash hard currency into Yugoslav
dinars at the official rate; unlike in Western
Europe, you won't be given a worse rate at
the fancy hotels or on Sunday.

Bring cash, preferably Deutschmarks, as
you can spend or change them almost anywhere. A few people in Yugoslavia still
change money on the street and unlike Budapest, Bucharest and Prague, it's fairly
straightforward to do so and you probably
won't be ripped off (but still take care). It's
technically illegal and in any case you would
be better advised not to flash your cash out in
the open.

Only change what you're sure you'll need,
as it's difficult to change dinars back into
hard currency. Conversion rates for major
currencies in mid 1998 are listed below:

Tipping

It is common practice to round up restaurant
bills to the nearest convenient figure and
waiters may indeed assume that this is what
you intend and keep the expected change
anyway. Consequently, don't give the waiter

more than you are prepared to part with as a
tip. Taxi drivers will expect a round-up to the
nearest convenient figure unless you have
agreed on a fee beforehand.

POST & COMMUNICATIONS
Post

To mail a parcel from Yugoslavia, take it unwrapped to a main post office where the staff
will inspect it before dispatch. Allow plenty
of time to complete the transaction.

Mailing a letter to Europe will cost you
1.60 DIN and to Australia or the USA 2.30
DIN.

Receiving Mail You can receive mail addressed to poste restante in all towns for a
small charge per letter.

Mail addressed c/o Poste Restante, 11101
Belgrade 1, Yugoslavia, will be held for one
month at window No 2 in the main post
office, Takovska 2.

Telephone

To place a long-distance phone call in Yugoslavia you usually go to the main post office.
Avoid weekends as the office may be
jammed with military personnel waiting to
call home. International calls made from
hotels are much more expensive. Calls from
post offices go straight through and cost 19
DIN a minute to the USA and Australia, with
no minimum.

Telephone cards purchased at post offices
or news kiosks are an inexpensive, easy way
of making international calls, but only in Belgrade as card phones are hard to find
elsewhere. Cards can be bought in units of
100 (19 DIN), 200 (31 DIN), 300 (44 DIN)
and 400 (56 DIN). The international access
code for outgoing calls is ☎ 99. To call
another town within Yugoslavia dial the area
code with the initial zero and the number.

To call Yugoslavia from Western Europe
dial the international access code, ☎ 381 (the
country code for Yugoslavia), the area code
(without the initial zero) and the number.

Fax

Faxes can be sent from the main post office
in Belgrade, or from any large hotel.

INTERNET RESOURCES

A useful Web site for general information on Yugoslavia is www.yugoslavia.com. The Tourist Organisation of Belgrade has a Web site at www.beograd.com/belgrade–guide.

While Yugoslavia is connected to the Internet, access from within the country for the majority of Yugoslavs is fairly limited at present. See the Belgrade section for information on Internet cafes there.

NEWSPAPERS & MAGAZINES

There is a wide selection of Serbian newspapers and magazines, as will be obvious by the displays at street kiosks. Not so useful if you do not read Serbian. *Politika* is the main daily for serious reading.

Until publication was suspended in 1993 as a consequence of UN sanctions, the English-language *International Weekly* carried the best stories of the week from *Politika*. To date it has not made a reappearance.

Also before UN sanctions, many foreign-language publications were widely available in Yugoslavia. At the moment there is a healthy selection of foreign-language magazines, though not a very wide variety of foreign-language newspapers.

RADIO & TV

There are some 11 local TV stations in Belgrade, including two from Novi Sad. Satellite TV stations such as CNN, Eurosport and MTV are also available if the receiver is suitably equipped. There are fewer stations in regional areas. Many FM and AM radio stations cater to all tastes.

PHOTOGRAPHY & VIDEO

Bring all your own film, as that sold locally is expensive and may be unreliable outside Belgrade. Keep your camera stowed away while crossing the border and be careful about taking pictures of anything other than obvious tourist attractions, as you could arouse unwelcome curiosity. Taking photos from a train or bus is not advisable and photographing soldiers or military facilities will cause serious problems if you're caught. The funny little signs with a camera crossed out should be taken seriously.

Video paraphernalia – tapes and batterie – are available in Belgrade, but you ar advised to bring your own since these thing are generally more expensive in Yugoslavia

TIME

Yugoslavia is one hour ahead of GMT/UTC The country goes on summer time at the enc of March when clocks are turned forward ar hour. At the end of September they're turned back an hour.

ELECTRICITY

The current is 220V, 50Hz. Plugs are of the standard European two-pronged type.

WEIGHTS & MEASURES

Yugoslavia uses the metric system.

TOILETS

Public toilets outside Belgrade are probably better avoided as they tend to be unsanitary and smelly. Make full use of the facilities at restaurants and hotels. A 1 DIN charge is common for use of public toilets in Belgrade.

HEALTH

The cost of medical treatment in Yugoslavia is very low and if you're covered at home by a regular health insurance plan which includes treatment abroad, special travel medical insurance is unnecessary and a waste of money. Conditions, however, in state-run services may not be up to your expectations. Private clinics offer a more presentable level of service and will normally be covered by your travel insurance.

WOMEN TRAVELLERS

Women travellers should feel no particular concern about travel in Yugoslavia. Other than cursory interest shown by men towards solo women travellers, travel is hassle-free and easy. Dress more conservatively than usual in Albanian Muslim areas of Kosovo.

GAY & LESBIAN TRAVELLERS

Homosexuality has been legal in Yugoslavia since 1932. For more information, contact Arkadia, Brace Baruh 11, 11000 Belgrade.

DISABLED TRAVELLERS
Few public buildings or streets have facilities or wheelchairs. Access could be problematic in Belgrade with its numerous inclines.

DANGERS & ANNOYANCES
Belgrade is a remarkably safe city, even late at night. Even around the seedy train station area there's no particular danger. Throughout Yugoslavia theft is rare.

Many Yugoslavs are chain-smokers who can't imagine that anyone might be inconvenienced by their habit, so choose your seat in trains, restaurants, bars and other public places carefully. Buses are supposed to be smoke-free and there are no-smoking sections on trains but this is sometimes ignored by other passengers.

If the subject turns to politics, it's best to listen to what Yugoslavs say rather than to tell them what you think, as nationalist passions can be unpredictable. It's striking the way Serbs who seem to be reasonable, amenable people suddenly become tense and defensive as soon as the subject of Kosovo comes up.

Don't give the police the impression you are anything but a tourist, otherwise you may be in for a searching interrogation. Avoid Kosovo for now unless you have a very good reason for going there.

BUSINESS HOURS
Banks in Yugoslavia keep long hours, often from 7 am to 7 pm weekdays and 7 am to noon on Saturday. On weekdays many shops close for lunch from noon to 4 pm but stay open until 8 pm. Department stores, supermarkets and self-service restaurants generally stay open throughout the day. On Saturday most government offices are closed, though shops stay open until 2 pm; many other businesses close at 3 pm.

PUBLIC HOLIDAYS & SPECIAL EVENTS
Public holidays include:

1 and 2 January
New Year
6 and 7 January
Orthodox Christmas

27 April
Day of the FR of Yugoslavia
1 and 2 May
International Labour Days
9 May
Victory Day
29 and 30 November
Republic Days

In addition, 28 March (Constitution Day) and 7 July (Uprising Day) are holidays in Serbia and 13 July is a holiday in Montenegro. If any of these should fall on a Sunday, then the following Monday or Tuesday is a holiday.

Orthodox Easter falls from anywhere between one and three weeks later than regular Easter. Most institutions close down at this time, so check the dates before you plan to visit Yugoslavia at Orthodox Easter time.

Belgrade hosts a film festival in February, an international theatre festival in mid-September, a festival of classical music in October and a jazz festival in November. The Novi Sad Agricultural Fair is in mid-May. Budva has a summer festival in July and August.

ACTIVITIES
Skiing
Serbia's largest ski centre is Kopaonik (2017m), south of Kraljevo, with 26 different runs covering a total of 54km. Get there from Belgrade by taking a bus to Brus (246km, five hours), then a local bus to the resort at Brzeče (18km). Otherwise take a bus from Belgrade to Kruševac (194km) and another from there to Brus (52km). Kopaonik has a 150-bed hostel (☎ 037-833 176) with three, four and five-bed rooms at 100 DIN per person, open year-round.

On the north side of the Šar Planina, which separates Kosovo from Macedonia, is Brezovica (1750m), Kosovo's major ski resort. Montenegro's main ski resort is at Žabljak. The ski season is from about December to March.

White-Water Rafting & Hiking
White-water rafting is offered on the Tara River in Montenegro's Durmitor National Park. See Travel Agencies in the Belgrade section for a contact address. For high-altitude lakes and one of the world's deepest canyons, Durmitor can't be beaten. This is also a popular hiking and skiing area.

LANGUAGE COURSES

Courses for linguists, or Slavists who wish to learn Serbian, are run in September each year by the International Slavic Centre (MSC) in Belgrade. For further details write to the MSC at Studenski trg 3, Belgrade.

ACCOMMODATION

You won't find any really inexpensive hotels in Yugoslavia, though the 1998 devaluation has had a beneficial levelling effect for travellers. Prices are often quoted in US dollars or DM, although payment in dinars is OK and hotel room prices are normally linked to the value of the dinar against these two foreign currencies. Be aware that the cost of accommodation may change considerably if the dinar slips further against the DM or the greenback. Foreigners still pay up to three times as much as locals at state-owned hotels – a legacy of the old socialist days when foreigners were supposed to be able to afford higher rates. Food prices are fortunately the same for everyone.

In summer you can camp along the Montenegrin coast; organised camping grounds are few and many of those that do exist are closed due to the absence of tourists. There's a hostel in Belgrade but it's far from the centre, overcrowded and overpriced. Other HI hostels exist at Kopaonik and Ulcinj (summer only). The hostel prices for foreigners are fixed in DM and thus staying in hostels could be more expensive and often less convenient than taking a private room.

Private rooms are usually available along the coast but seldom inland. They are hard to find in Belgrade and there are steep surcharges if you stay less than three nights. If you plan to stay that long, Budva and Bar make good central bases from which to make side trips to Cetinje and Ulcinj.

An overnight bus or train can sometimes get you out of an accommodation jam.

FOOD

The cheapest breakfast is Balkan *burek*, a greasy layered pie made with cheese *(sir)* or meat *(meso)*, and it's available everywhere. *Krompirusa* is potato burek. Food is cheaper in the interior than along the coast and meat dishes can be very cheap in Turkish-influenced areas.

Regional Dishes

Yugoslavia's regional cuisines range from spicy Hungarian goulash in Vojvodina to Turkish kebab in Serbia and Kosovo. A speciality of Vojvodina is *alaska čorba* (fiery riverfish stew). In Montenegro try the pastoral fare such as boiled lamb or *kajmak* (cream from boiled milk which is salted and turned into cheese).

Serbia is famous for grilled meats such as *čevapčići* (kebabs of spiced, minced meat, grilled), *pljeskavica* (a large, spicy hamburger steak) and *ražnjići* (a pork or veal shish kebab with onions and peppers). If you want to try them all at once, order *mešano meso* (a mixed grill of pork cutlet, liver, sausage, and minced meat patties with onions). Serbian *duveč* is grilled pork cutlets with spiced stewed peppers, zucchini and tomatoes in rice cooked in an oven – delicious.

Other popular dishes are *musaka* (aubergine and potato baked in layers with minced meat), *sarma* (cabbage stuffed with minced meat and rice), *kapama* (stewed lamb, onions and spinach served with yoghurt), *punjena tikvica* (zucchini stuffed with minced meat and rice), and peppers stuffed with minced meat, rice and spices, cooked in tomato sauce.

Most traditional Yugoslav dishes are based on meat so vegetarians will have problems, though every restaurant menu will include a Serbian salad *(Srpska salata)* of raw peppers, onions and tomatoes, seasoned with oil, vinegar and chilli. Also ask for *gibanica* (a layered cheese pie) and *zeljanica* (cheese pie with spinach). *Švopska salata* is also very popular, consisting of chopped tomatoes, cucumber and onion and topped with grated soft white cheese.

DRINKS

Beer *(pivo)* is always available. Nikšićko pivo brewed at Nikšić in Montenegro is terribly good when imbibed ice-cold at the beach on a hot summer day. Its taste has a smoky flavour in comparison with the Bip

eer served around Belgrade, which tends to
e on the flat side.

Yugoslav cognac (grape brandy) is called
injak. Coffee is usually served Turkish-
tyle, boiled in a small individual pot, 'black
s hell, strong as death and sweet as love'.
lotel breakfast coffee is universally un-
drinkable. Drink tea instead. Superb espresso
and capuccino, however, can be found at
Belgrade's many cafés.

Getting There & Away

AIR

Since the lifting of UN sanctions in November 1995, JAT has recommenced services and
provides for a limited but growing number of
domestic and international destinations. As at
mid-1998, services to the US and Australia
had not resumed but that may change.

LAND

In mid-1991, all rail and road links between
Croatia and Serbia were cut, making it necessary to do a loop through Hungary to travel
from Zagreb to Belgrade. Five years later the
border was reopened. The main vehicle and
rail crossing is at Batrovci, near the town of
Šid, on the main Belgrade-Zagreb *autoput*.
Other border crossings at Bačka Palanka,
Bogojevo and Bezdan were still under the
control of UNPROFOR in mid-1998. The
southern border between Croatia and Montenegro had not reopened as of mid-1998.

A couple of bus services use the main
crossing instead of transiting through
Hungary. You cross the border on foot and
change to a Croatian/Serbian bus accordingly. At the time of going to press there were no
train links between Yugoslavia and Croatia.

Private-vehicle crossings should be possible without too much difficulty.

Bus

Buses travelling to/from Slovenia and Macedonia can use the main Yugoslavia-Croatia
border crossing instead of going through
Hungary. Buses to/from Croatia require a
change of bus at the border. Two agencies in
Belgrade currently organise these itineraries.

In Belgrade, the travel agencies Basturist,
Turist Biro Lasta and BS Tours all sell tickets
for international buses (see Travel Agencies
in the Belgrade section for addresses and
contact numbers). Sample fares from Belgrade, payable in DM only, are:

Destination	Cost
Munich	DM107
Paris	DM155
Thessaloniki	DM22
Vienna	DM70
Zürich	DM174

Train

Only buy a ticket as far as your first stop in
Yugoslavia, as domestic fares are much
cheaper than international fares. Consider
breaking your journey in Subotica, Niš or
even Skopje for this purpose alone. A student
card will get you a reduction on train fares
from Yugoslavia to other Eastern European
countries.

All the international 'name trains' mentioned here run daily all year unless otherwise
stated.

Hungary & Beyond Since mid-1991,
trains between Western Europe and Belgrade
have run via Budapest, Subotica and Novi
Sad. About six trains a day cover the 354km
between Budapest and Belgrade (six hours,
410 DIN). The *Hunyadi* and the *Ivo Andrić*
link just the two capitals. The *Hellas Express*
runs between Thessaloniki (Solun) and Budapest, the *Balkan Express* between Istanbul
and Budapest, and the *Avala* and *Beograd*
express trains run between Belgrade and
Vienna (Beč). Belgrade is 11 hours from
Vienna (627km, 700 DIN) and 17 hours from
Munich. Reservations are usually required on
these trains.

An unreserved local train runs four times a
day between Subotica and Szeged in
Hungary (45km, 1¾ hours, 35 DIN).

Croatia You can take a direct train from
Zagreb to Budapest then change to another
train for Belgrade. Otherwise take the daily
train from Zagreb to Pécs (Hungary), a bus
from Pécs to Szeged and a train from Szeged
across the border to Subotica in Vojvodina.

You would have to spend at least one night somewhere along the way. (See the relevant chapters for ticket prices).

Romania From Romania the overnight *Bucureşti* express train runs between Bucharest and Beograd station (693km, 13 hours, 380 DIN) via Timişoara and there is also a day service, the *Banat* that departs Bucureşti at 10.55 am each day. Reservations are required on both trains. Two daily unreserved local trains on this route connect Timişoara to Vršac (76km).

Bulgaria & Turkey The most reliable service to/from Bulgaria and Turkey is the *Balkan Express* train, which connects Budapest with Istanbul and runs through Belgrade. From Istanbul the train goes via Sofia, Niš, Belgrade and Novi Sad. If bound for Bulgaria you can board this train in Novi Sad.

From Belgrade it's nine hours to Sofia (417km, 250 DIN) and 21½ hours to Istanbul (1051km, 560 DIN). The *Balkan Express* departs from Belgrade each morning at 10 am and reservations are required.

Greece The southern main line between Belgrade and Athens (1267km, 22 hours, 400 DIN) is through Skopje and Thessaloniki, with two trains a day. Reservations are recommended.

Car & Motorcycle
Following are the main highway entry/exit points around Yugoslavia (travelling clockwise), with the Yugoslav border post named.

Hungary There are crossings at Bački Breg (32km south of Baja), Kelebija (11km northwest of Subotica) and Horgoš (between Szeged and Subotica).

Romania You may cross at Sprska Crnja (45km west of Timişoara), Vatin (between Timişoara and Belgrade), Kaluđerovo (120km east of Belgrade) and Kladovo (10km west of Turnu Severin).

Bulgaria You have a choice of Negotin (29km north-west of Vidin), Zaječar (45km

south-west of Vidin), Gradina (at Dimitrovgrad between Sofia and Niš) and Klisur (66km west of Pernik).

Macedonia You can cross at Preševo (10km north of Kumanovo) and Đeneral Janković (between Uroševac and Skopje).

Albania There are crossings at Vrbnica (18km south-west of Prizren) and Božaj (24km south-east of Podgorica).

SEA
A ferry service operates between Bari or Ancona (Italy), and Bar in Montenegro. The Belgrade agent is Yugoagent at Kolarčeva 3. There are a couple of agents in Bar.

LEAVING YUGOSLAVIA
The airport departure tax on international flights is 90 DIN.

Travellers should be prepared to furnish the currency declaration that they were supposed to have completed upon entering the country. Failure to do so could mean confiscation of any hard currency you are carrying.

Getting Around

AIR
JAT domestic flights operate from Belgrade to Tivat (Montenegro) four to six times daily and to Podgorica (also in Montenegro) twice daily. Both fares cost about 500 DIN, plus 20 DIN domestic departure airport tax. These flights are heavily booked.

Only 15kg of checked baggage is allowed on domestic flights. JAT runs inexpensive buses between airports and city centres.

BUS
Though present-day Yugoslavia depends on railways far more than the other four countries of ex-Yugoslavia, there are also many buses. You'll depend on buses to travel along the Montenegrin coast from Bar to Budva and Ulcinj, to go from Montenegro to Kosovo and to get to Durmitor National Park. On long hauls, overnight buses can be exhausting but they do save you time and money.

TRAIN

The Jugoslovenske Železnice (JŽ) provides adequate railway services along the main interior line from Subotica to Novi Sad, Belgrade, Niš, Priština and Skopje and here's a highly scenic line from Belgrade down to the coast at Bar, especially between Kolašin and Bar. There are four classes of train: *ekspresni* (express), *poslovni* (rapid), *brzi* (fast) and *putnicki* (slow). Make sure you have the right sort of ticket for your train.

The train is cheaper than the bus and you don't have to pay for luggage. It is, however, slower and can get very crowded. The quality of the rolling stock varies enormously from OK to dilapidated and dirty. The international 'name' trains are usually of good quality. It's more reliable to make reservations in the train's originating station, unless reservations are mandatory from the in-between stations, in which case try to book the day before. Most trains have 'no smoking' compartments. Inter-Rail passes are valid in Yugoslavia, but Eurail passes are not.

All train stations (except in Kosovo) have left-luggage offices where you can dump your bag (passport required).

CAR & MOTORCYCLE

Yugoslavia's motorways *(autoput)* run southeast through Belgrade, Niš and Skopje towards Greece. Yugoslavs pay low tolls in dinars but foreign-registered vehicles pay much higher prices. Toll charges are posted at the motorway exit, not at the entrance. All other roads are free and, with a little time and planning, you can avoid the motorways.

Speed limits for private cars and motorcycles are 120km/h on motorways, 100km/h on 1st-class roads, 80km/h on 2nd-class roads and 60km/h in built-up areas.

Members of foreign automobile clubs get a reduced rate on towing services provided by the Automoto Savez Jugoslavije (AMSJ). It has branches in almost every town, with repair facilities available. Call ☎ 987 for AMSJ emergency assistance.

Petrol is available in regular (86 octane), super (98 octane) and unleaded or *bezolovni* (95 octane) varieties. In mid-1998 the cost was about 6 DIN for a litre of super.

Driving around Yugoslavia should present no particular problems these days. The hoards of transiting tourists have backed off and the roads are relatively untravelled and in good repair. All borders are open, including the one with Croatia (although at the time of writing, train and air routes had not been fully restored), and the large towns and the coast are quiet. The police are ever-vigilant and always on the lookout to fine unwary motorists on the spot for some minor infringement, so beware. Kosovo should be avoided because of the Serb-Albanian clashes and the continuing possibility of trouble. Take reasonable security precautions when parking – an alarm or steering wheel lock is a good idea.

HITCHING

While technically possible in Yugoslavia, you are more than likely to be hampered by drivers only covering short distances. By hitching you are also opening yourself up to unscrupulous opportunists and in any case, LP does not recommend hitching as a form of transport.

LOCAL TRANSPORT

Public transport strip tickets and tokens are available from newsstands in Belgrade. Punch your ticket as you board the vehicle.

ORGANISED TOURS

Day trips along the Danube and further afield are available. Check with the Tourist Organisation of Belgrade (☎ 011-324 8404) in the city centre for details. Ski Centar Durmitor organises one-week skiing packages and Putnik Tours in Belgrade has various tailored packages for visitors.

Belgrade (Београд)

☎ 011

The dominant role of Serbia (Srbija) in the former Yugoslav Federation was underlined by the inclusion within its boundaries of two formerly 'autonomous provinces', Vojvodina and Kosovo, and the national capital, Belgrade.

Belgrade (Beograd) is strategically situated on the southern edge of the Carpathian basin where the Sava River joins the Danube. Just east of the city is the Morava Valley, route of the famous 'Stamboul Road' from Turkey to Central Europe. At this major crossroads developed a city which has long been the flashpoint of the Balkans. It's an interesting place to look around for a few days, but accommodation is absurdly expensive.

Until WWI Belgrade was right on the border of Serbia and Austria-Hungary, and its citadel has seen many battles. Destroyed and rebuilt 40 times in its 2300-year history, Belgrade has never quite managed to pick up all the pieces. It is nonetheless a lively, vibrant city with fine restaurants and street cafés and a rhythm that reminds you more of northern Europe than the Balkans.

History

The Celtic settlement of Singidunum was founded in the 3rd century BC on a bluff overlooking the confluence of the Sava and Danube rivers. The Romans arrived in the 1st century AD and stayed till the 5th century. The present Slavic name Beograd (White City) first appeared in a papal letter dated 16 April 878.

Belgrade became the capital of Serbia in 1403, when the Serbs were pushed north by the Turks. In 1456 the Hungarians, under János Hunyadi, succeeded in defeating a Turkish northward advance, but in 1521 the Turks finally took Belgrade. In 1842 the city again became the capital of Serbia and in 1918, the capital of Yugoslavia. In April 1941, 17,000 lives were lost in a Nazi bombing raid on Belgrade. Soon after, on 4 July 1941, Tito and the Communist Party's central committee, meeting at Belgrade, decided to launch an armed uprising. Belgrade was liberated on 20 October 1944, and since then the population has grown six-fold to over 1.7 million.

Orientation

You'll probably arrive at the train station on the south side of the city centre or at one of the adjacent bus stations. The left-luggage office at the train station (open 24 hours) is just past the kiosks at the end of track No 9. Left luggage costs 5 DIN per piece. The left-luggage room at the main (BAS) bus station is open from 6 am to 10 pm and costs 6 DIN

per piece. A passport is required at both o these. Allow enough time to pick up you bag. For information on other facilities at th train station, see Getting There & Away a the end of the Belgrade section.

To walk into town from the train station go east along Milovanovića for a block, ther straight up Balkanska to Terazije, the heart o modern Belgrade. Kneza Mihaila, Belgrade's lively pedestrian boulevard, runs north-west through Stari Grad (the old town) from Terazije to Kalemegdan Park, where you'll find the citadel. The crowds are surprisingly chic, the cafés well patronised and the atmosphere bustling and businesslike.

Information

The friendly, helpful Tourist Organisation of Belgrade (☎ 635 622; fax 635 343; tob@beograd.com), open weekdays from 9 am to 8 pm and Saturday from 9 am to 4 pm, has an office in the underpass at the beginning of Terazije, on the corner of Kneza Mihaila. (Note the public toilets down there for future reference.) There's also a tourist office at the airport open daily from 8 am to 8 pm.

Information on HI hostels around Yugoslavia is available from Ferijalni Savez Beograd (☎ 324 8550; fax 322 0762), Makedonska 22, 2nd floor.

Motorists are assisted by the English-speaking staff at the special Informativni Centar (☎ 419 822) around the corner from the Automoto Savez Jugoslavije, Ruzveltova 16a, a little south-east of Tašmajdan Park.

Money The JIK Banka is across the park in front of the train station (open from 8 am to 8 pm weekdays and 8 am to 3 pm Saturday). The exchange window in the train station gives a slightly less favourable rate.

American Express travellers cheques can only be changed at the Karić Banka on the corner of Maršala Birjuzova and Pop Lukina, at the airport branch which is also open on weekends and at the Komercijalna Banka on trg Nikole Pašića. The Hyatt Regency and Inter Continental hotels accept credit cards and travellers cheques from guests. American Express is represented by Atlas Tours, Kosovska 8, 6th floor. Although the office is functioning they cannot yet provide any

BELGRADE (BEOGRAD)

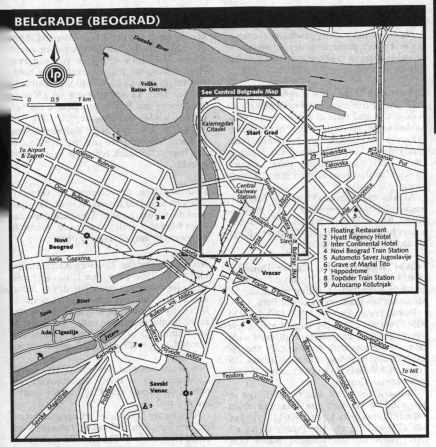

Danube River

Veliko
Ratno Ostrvo

See Central Belgrade Map

Kalemegdan
Citadel

Stari Grad

0   0.5   1 km

To Airport
& Zagreb

Lenjinov Bulevar

Drug Bulevar

29 Novembra
Takovska

Partizanski Put

Central
Railway
Station

Spojn.

Mike Kovačevica

Nemanjina

Mitić.

Makedonska

Takara

Kneza

Trg
Slavija

Bulevar JNA

Novi
Beograd

Jurija Gagarina

Gazela

Vracar

Bulevar Franše D'Eperea

Bulevar Mira

Sava River

Ada Ciganlija

Jezero

Bulevar voj. Mišića

Vojvode Mišića

Radnička

Teodora Drajzera

Neznanog Junaka

Vojvode Strpe

JNA

Stevana Prvovenčanog

To Niš

Savska Magistrala

Požeška

Savski
Venac

1	Floating Restaurant
2	Hyatt Regency Hotel
3	Inter Continental Hotel
4	Novi Beograd Train Station
5	Automoto Savez Jugoslavije
6	Grave of Maršal Tito
7	Hippodrome
8	Topčider Train Station
9	Autocamp Košutnjak

American Express services nor cash travellers cheques.

There are a few private exchange offices in Belgrade. One very central office is VODR (open weekdays from 9 am to 7 pm and Saturday from 9 am to 3 pm). You may occasionally come across black marketeers angling for 'devize', but the difference between bank and black market rates nowadays is not great.

There are currently no ATM machines operating anywhere in Belgrade. Come prepared with cash.

Post & Communications The main post office, at Takovska 2, holds poste-restante mail (postcode 11101) at window No 2 for one month. International telephone calls can be placed here from 7 am to 10 pm daily. This is the only place in Belgrade where you can send a fax (one page to the USA or Australia costs 78 DIN, to Europe 60 DIN). A more convenient telephone centre (open 24 hours a day) is in the post office at Zmaj Jovina 17 in the centre of town.

The telephone centre in the large post office on the right (south) side of the train station opens weekdays from 7 am to midnight and weekends from 7 am to 10 pm.

Note that Belgrade is gradually introducing seven-digit phone numbers, so beware of probable changes to phone numbers listed in this section.

Cybercafés There are a couple of Internet cafés within five minutes of each other. One is on the ground floor of the *Bioskop Doma Omladine* cinema on the corner of Makedonska and Moše Pijade, but the six terminals are nearly always in use. The other is *Café Sezam* (☎ 322 7231; info@sezampro.yu) at Skadarska 40c (2nd floor) and is open from 10 am to 11 pm.

Also try the American Center (☎ 630 011; teachers@classroom.opennet.org) in the middle of Kneza Mihaila which offers public access from 10 am to 6 pm. All three charge around 15 DIN per hour.

Travel Agencies Ski Centar Durmitor (☎ 634 944), Kralja Petra 70, has information on white-water rafting, skiing and hiking in Montenegro's Durmitor National Park.

Putnik Travel Agency (☎ 330 669; fax 334 505), Terazije 27, is the largest and oldest travel agency in Yugoslavia. It offers a wide range of services both domestically and internationally, including tickets to Croatia. BS Tours (☎ 558 347) at Gavril Principa 46 also runs buses to Croatia.

Basturist (the office with the JAT sign in the window between the bus and train station), Turist Biro Lasta (☎ 641 251; fax 642 473) and the adjacent Putnik office all sell tickets for international buses (see Getting There & Away for fare prices).

Beograd Tours (☎ 641 258; fax 687 447) at Milovanovića 5, a block up the hill from the train station, will book couchettes and sleepers within Yugoslavia and tickets to other countries. The English-speaking staff provide reliable train information and sell tickets at the same prices charged in the station, but without the crowds.

Bookshops A good place to get your favourite magazine and possibly newspaper is at the Plato Bookshop, Vasina 17. Another option is at Jugoslovenska Knjiga above the Tourist Organisation of Belgrade office.

Libraries If you plan on spending any time in Belgrade, you can pay the 70 DIN membership fee to join the British Council Library (☎ 622 492; BCLib@britcoun.org.yu) at Kneza Mihailova 48. Here you can read English-language magazines, borrow books and videos and access CD-ROM archives. It is open from 11 am to 4 pm on Monday, Wednesday and Friday and from 2 pm to 7 pm on Tuesday and Thursday.

The City Library is at the Kalemegdan end of Kneza Mihaila. Here you can have a coffee or a beer in the snack bar, or do some photocopying.

Laundry The dry cleaners at Generala Ždanova 6, just off Bulevar Revolucije (open weekdays from 7 am to 8 pm and Saturday from 8 am to 3 pm), can do your laundry in 24 hours but they charge per item.

Medical Services The Boris Kidrič Hospital (☎ 683 755), Pasterova 1, has a special clinic for foreigners open Tuesday to Saturday from 7 am to 1 pm (consultations 20 DIN). It's also possible to consult the doctors in the regular clinic here until 7 pm daily. At other times go to the Klinički Centar just across the street at Pasterova 2, which is open 24 hours.

A dental clinic for foreigners (Stomatološka Služba) is at Ivana Milutinovića 15, behind the Slavija Hotel (open daily from 7 am to 7 pm).

Two handy pharmacies are open 24 hours: the Prvi Maj, Srpskih Vladara 9 and the Sveti Sava, Nemjanina 2. The first aid emergency phone number is ☎ 94.

Things to See

From the train station take tram No 1, 2 or 13 north-west to **Kalemegdan Citadel**, the strategic hill-top fortress at the junction of the Sava and Danube rivers. This area has been fortified since Celtic times and the Roman settlement of Singidunum was on the flood plain at the foot of the citadel. Much of what is seen today dates from the 17th century, including medieval gates, Orthodox churches, Muslim tombs and Turkish baths. Ivan Meštrović's *Monument of Gratitude to France* (1930) is at the citadel's entrance, and on the ramparts overlooking the rivers stands is 1928 statue *The Winner*. The large **Miliary Museum** on the battlements of the citadel presents a complete history of Yugoslavia in 53 rooms. The benches in the park around the citadel are relaxing and on summer evenings lots of people come strolling past.

Next to Kalemegdan Citadel is Stari Grad, the oldest part of Belgrade. The best museums are here, especially the **National Museum**, trg Republike, which has archaeological exhibits downstairs and paintings upstairs. The collection of European art is quite good. A few blocks away at Studentski trg 13 is the **Ethnographical Museum**, with an excellent collection of Serbian costumes and folk art. Detailed explanations are provided in English. Not far away, at Cara Uroša 20, is the **Gallery of Frescoes**, with full-size replicas of paintings from remote churches in Serbia and Macedonia. Belgrade's most memorable museum is the **Palace of Princess Ljubice**, on the corner of Svetozara Markovića and Kralija Petra, an authentic Balkan-style palace (1831) complete with period furnishings.

The **Skupština**, or Yugoslav parliament (built 1907-32), is at the beginning of Bulevar Revolucije, just before the main post office. East again, behind the main post office, is **Sveti Marko Serbian Orthodox Church** (built in 1932-39), with four tremendous pillars supporting a towering dome. There's a small Russian Orthodox church behind it.

If you'd like to visit the white marble **grave of Maršal Tito** (open from 9 am to 4 pm), it's within the grounds of his former residence on Bulevar Mira, a few kilometres south of the city centre (take trolleybus No 40 or 41 south from Kneza Miloša 64). The tomb and all of the museums are closed on Monday.

Escape the bustle of Belgrade on **Ada Ciganlija**, an island park in the Sava River just upstream from the city. In summer you can swim in the river (naturists walk 1km upstream from the others), rent a bicycle or just stroll among the trees. The many small cafés overlooking the beach sell cold beer at reasonable prices.

Places to Stay

Accommodation in Belgrade is generally expensive, compounded by the fact that foreigners can pay up to three times as much as Yugoslavs. Budget places are hard to come by and private rooms almost impossible to find. The 1998 devaluation of the dinar has in effect brought prices down, but how long the hotel prices will stay at the current level is anyone's guess. Prices listed here may change considerably.

A valuable tip which will save a day's travelling time, a night's hotel bill and a lot of aggravation, is to book a sleeper or couchette out of Belgrade. This is easily done and costs from 14 to 63 DIN extra. Just try getting a room for that! Don't forget that a train ticket is required in addition to the sleeper/couchette ticket.

If for some reason you can't get a sleeper or couchette, consider taking an overnight bus to your next destination. It's cheaper than the train and advance tickets are easily purchased at the bus station, but a bus trip is much more tiring.

Camping *Autocamp Košutnjak* (☎ 555 127), Kneza Višeslava 17, is about 8km south-west of the city centre. Camping is possible from May to September only, but there are expensive new bungalows open all year (180 DIN per person with private bath). The older, cheaper bungalows are permanently occupied by locals. Camping will cost about 60 DIN for two persons and a tent. It's a fairly pleasant wooded site with lots of shade, but pitch your tent far from the noisy restaurant. To get there take tram No 12 or 13 south from beside the train station to Kneza Višeslava, the next stop after you see the horse-racing track (hippodrome) on the left. From the tram stop it's 1km up the hill.

Private Rooms Private rooms have become more or less nonexistent in Belgrade. You will not be approached by anyone as you leave the bus or train station and finding one will be a challenge. It's better to opt for one of the cheaper hotels (if there is a room available), or fork out a bit extra for a room at a mid-range hotel in the centre.

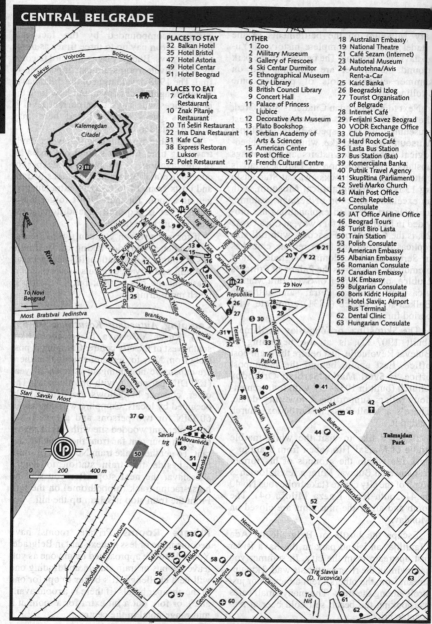

CENTRAL BELGRADE

PLACES TO STAY
32 Balkan Hotel
35 Hotel Bristol
47 Hotel Astoria
49 Hotel Centar
51 Hotel Beograd

PLACES TO EAT
7 Grčka Kraljica Restaurant
10 Znak Pitanje Restaurant
20 Tri Šeširi Restaurant
22 Ima Dana Restaurant
31 Kafe Car
38 Express Restoran Luksor
52 Polet Restaurant

OTHER
1 Zoo
2 Military Museum
3 Gallery of Frescoes
4 Ski Centar Durmitor
5 Ethnographical Museum
6 City Library
8 British Council Library
9 Concert Hall
11 Palace of Princess Ljubice
12 Decorative Arts Museum
13 Plato Bookshop
14 Serbian Academy of Arts & Sciences
15 American Center
16 Post Office
17 French Cultural Centre

18 Australian Embassy
19 National Theatre
21 Café Sezam (Internet)
23 National Museum
24 Autotehna/Avis Rent-a-Car
25 Karić Banka
26 Beogradski Izlog
27 Tourist Organisation of Belgrade
28 Internet Café
29 Ferijalni Savez Beograd
30 VODR Exchange Office
33 Club Promocija
34 Hard Rock Café
36 Lasta Bus Station
37 Bus Station (Bas)
39 Komercijalna Banka
40 Putnik Travel Agency
41 Skupština (Parliament)
42 Sveti Marko Church
43 Main Post Office
44 Czech Republic Consulate
45 JAT Office Airline Office
46 Beograd Tours
48 Turist Biro Lasta
50 Train Station
53 Polish Consulate
54 American Embassy
55 Albanian Embassy
56 Romanian Consulate
57 Canadian Embassy
58 UK Embassy
59 Bulgarian Consulate
60 Boris Kidrič Hospital
61 Hotel Slavija; Airport Bus Terminal
62 Dental Clinic
63 Hungarian Consulate

Hotels Belgrade is full of state-owned B-category hotels charging 250/375 DIN and up for a single/double. The cheapest central place is *Hotel Centar* (☎ 644 055; fax 657 838), Savski trg 7, opposite the train station. It's 180 DIN for a basic single or 210 DIN for a single room with bath.

A reasonably cheap and handy state-run hotel is the *Hotel Bristol* (☎ 688 400; fax 637 453) at Karađorđeva 50, close to the bus stations. It's a bit run-down, but OK and the 180/260 DIN single/double rooms shouldn't be sneezed at.

If you are prepared to fork out more, the B-category *Hotel Beograd* (☎ 645 199; fax 643 746) at Nemanjina 6, visible from the main entrance to the train station, has time-worn singles/doubles for 220/310 DIN including breakfast. The *Hotel Astoria* (☎ 645 422; fax 686 437), nearby at M. Milovanovića 1, has singles/doubles with breakfast for 235/360 DIN.

The *Balkan Hotel* (☎ 687 466; fax 687 543) on the corner of Terazije and Prizrenska is very central and fine if you want that extra bit of comfort without going too overboard. A single/double will work out at around US$50/65.

For the record, and if you want to give your credit card a real workout, the *Inter Continental* (☎ 311 3333) and the *Hyatt Regency* (☎ 311 1234) over in dull Novi Beograd will charge you between US$150 and US$190 for the privilege of sleeping there.

Places to Eat

The *Expres Restoran Luksor*, at Balkanska 7, is the cheapest self-service place in town. Further up the street, the *Leskovac* takeaway window sells authentic Balkan-style hamburgers. A great place for breakfast burek near the train station is the *Burek i Pecivo* shop at Nemanjina 5, just below Hotel Beograd (open weekdays from 5 am to 1 pm and Saturday from 5 to 11 am). The *Kafe Car*, at Terazije 4 near the tourist office, is perfect for an espresso and a croissant.

For inexpensive seafood try the *Polet Restaurant*, Njegoševa 1. The attractive maritime décor is designed to resemble the interior of a large ship. The menu is only in Serbian but all prices are clearly listed. On weekdays between 1 and 6 pm there's a special set menu of spicy fish soup (čorba), salad, bread and a main dish of fish and vegetables. The portions are large and the service is good.

The *Znak Pitanje* (Question Mark) restaurant, Kralja Petra 6 opposite the Orthodox church, is in an old Balkan inn serving traditional meat dishes, side salads and flat draught beer. You sit at low tables on low wooden stools. Look for the question-mark sign above the door. Prices are mid-range and the food is very good.

The *Grčka Kraljica*, at the Kalemegdan end of Kneza Mihaila, is a would-be Greek restaurant with vivid blue and white décor and Greek background muzak. The food is actually quite good, though heavy on the Serbian influence, and you can have Greek wine to accompany it. The location is particularly pleasant, situated as it is on a busy pedestrian mall. Prices are mid-range.

For local colour and if the budget is up to it, try the folkloric restaurants in the Bohemian quarter along Skadarska. In the evening, open-air folkloric, musical and theatrical performances are often staged here. There are a clutch of restaurants lining this atmospheric cobbled street among which the *Tri Šeširi* and *Ima Dana* stand out, but for more economical dining with all the atmosphere there are three good outdoor hamburger stands at the bottom end of Skadarska.

Finally, there are some even more atmospheric floating restaurants along the Danube river bank opposite the wooded island of Veliko Ratno Ostrovo, if you feel like a walk across the Brankov Most bridge towards Novi Beograd.

Entertainment

During the winter season, opera is performed at the elegant *National Theatre* (1869) on trg Republike. Their box office opens Tuesday to Sunday from 10 am to 1 pm, and from 3 pm on performance days. The Yugoslavs aren't pretentious about theatre dress – jeans are OK even at the opera.

Concerts are held at the concert hall of *Kolarčev University*, Studentski trg 5 (box office open daily from 10 am to noon and 6 to 8 pm). In October a festival of classical music is held here. The *Belgrade Philharmonia* is hidden at the end of the passageway at Studentski trg 11, directly across the street from the Ethnographical Museum.

Concerts also take place in the hall of the **Serbian Academy of Arts & Sciences**, Kneza Mihaila 35. The **French Cultural Centre**, Kneza Mihaila 31 (closed weekends), often shows free films and videos. In the evening throngs of street musicians play along Kneza Mihaila.

The British Council's Cultural Centre (☎ 323 2441; fax 324 9013; director.EA@britcoun.org.yu) has some captivating events each month from seminars to concerts and from talks to films. Contact the centre for details, or visit their Web site: www.britcoun.org/yugoslavia/yugeven.htm.

The Bilet Servis, trg Republike 5, has tickets to many events and the friendly English-speaking staff will search happily through their listings for something musical for you. Ask them about the **Teatar T**, Bulevard Revolucije 77a, which stages musicals several times a week (but is closed Wednesday and Thursday).

Belgrade has a growing number of discos, though most people do their socialising in the many fashionable cafés around trg Republike. One disco called **Club Promocija** is reached through a dark lane at Nušićeva 8 just off Terazije (open from 11 pm to 5 am daily except Sunday). If you really must add yet another HRC T-shirt to your collection, visit Belgrade's **Hard Rock Café** in a basement of an alleyway leading from Terazije. There is usually some live music on.

Things to Buy
There are thankfully – for the moment at least – few tacky tourist souvenirs on display to tempt you to part with your dollars or dinars. On trg Republike there is *Beogradski Izlog* (Belgrade Window), next to Bilet Servis, where you may find some tasteful local art and craftwork. Pottery features prominently, though you may also find souvenir sweaters and T-shirts emblazoned with 'Beograd' in Cyrillic.

Getting There & Away
Bus The two bus stations have computerised ticketing and there are overnight buses to many places around Yugoslavia. Buy your ticket as far ahead as you can to be assured of

a good seat. Posted destinations are in Cyrillic only. It is easier to buy your ticket from a ticket agency.

Train Belgrade is on the main railway lines from Istanbul and Athens to Western Europe. International trains on these routes are covered in the Getting There & Away section earlier in this chapter. Overnight domestic trains with couchettes or sleepers run from Belgrade to Bar (524km, 8½ hours), Peć (490km, 9½ hours) and Skopje (472km, nine hours). All trains depart from the main station on Savski trg.

Sample fares from Belgrade to Bar are as follows: 103 DIN in 2nd class in a three-bed compartment, 93 DIN in a four-bed compartment, 83 DIN in a six-bed compartment; 1st-class sleepers are 153 DIN. These prices are all-inclusive. Regular train tickets for the Belgrade-Bar journey (524km, 7½ hours) cost 69 DIN in 2nd class, or 90 DIN in 1st class.

Train Station At the main train station, the ticket counters are numbered 1 to 26. International tickets are sold at window Nos 3 and 4 and regular tickets at window Nos 7 to 20. Sleeper and couchette reservations are made in a separate office just off platform 1. Look for the blue and white 'bed' sign. Timetable and departure information is posted in Cyrillic only in the ticket hall. There is a currency-exchange window, a souvenir shop and Wasteels travel office in the smaller building facing the end of the tracks. Toilets and left luggage are next to platform 9.

Getting Around
To/From the Airport The JAT bus (15 DIN) departs from the street next to Hotel Slavija, trg Slavija (D. Tucovića), roughly every hour. This bus also picks up from the forecourt of the main train station. Surčin airport is 18km west of the city. If you're stuck at the airport waiting for a flight, visit the nearby Yugoslav Aviation Museum (closed Monday).

Public Transport Because Belgrade lacks a metro, the buses, trams and trolleybuses are tremendously overcrowded. Six-strip public transport tickets costing 8 DIN are sold at tobacco kiosks and you validate your own ticket by punching a strip once on board. If you pay a city bus or tram driver directly it will be about double the fare. Fold the top of the strip over each time you use it. Local bus riders usually have monthly passes, so don't be surprised if they do not seem to use tickets.

Taxi A motley bunch of old and new vehicles all in different colours, Belgrade's taxis are in plentiful supply. Flag fall is 4 DIN. A trip around the centre should cost between 10 and 20 DIN. Check that the taxi meter is running. If not, point it out to the driver.

Car Rental Autotehna/Avis (☎ 629 423), Obilićev Venac 25, and Putnik Hertz (☎ 641 566; fax 627 638) have cars from an expensive 915 DIN per day. A cash bond equivalent to US$500 must be paid in advance, or a credit card will suffice. Their cars are only for use within Yugoslavia.

Vojvodina
(Војволина)

Vojvodina (21,506 sq km) was an autonomous province until 1990 when Serbia scrapped this arrangement and annexed Vojvodina to the Republic of Serbia. Slavs settled here in the 6th century, followed by Hungarians in the 10th century. Following their defeat at the hands of the Turks in 1389, many Serbs fled north but they and the Hungarians were later swamped by the 16th-century Turkish conquest. When the Habsburgs drove the Turks back across the Danube in the late 17th century the Vojvodina region again became a refuge for the Serbs, who had moved into this Hungarian-controlled area to escape unbroken Ottoman rule in the lands further south. The region remained a part of Hungary until 1918.

Today ethnic Serbs make up most of the population. Minorities include Hungarians (24%), Croats (8%), Slovaks (4%) and Romanians (3%). Some 170,000 ethnic Germans were expelled from Vojvodina after WWII and large numbers of Serbs immigrat-

ed here to occupy the areas the Germans formerly inhabited. As a result, the percentage of Serbs in the total population of Vojvodina increased from 37% in 1921 to 57.2% in 1991.

This low-lying land of many rivers merges imperceptibly into the Great Hungarian Plain and Romania's Banat. The Tisa River cuts southward through the middle of the region, joining the Danube midway between Novi Sad and Belgrade. The Sava and Danube rivers mark Vojvodina's southern boundary with Serbia; the Danube also separates Vojvodina from Croatia in the west. Numerous canals crisscross this fertile plain which provides much of Yugoslavia's wheat and corn. Most of Yugoslavia's crude oil comes from wells here.

NOVI SAD (НОВИ САД)
☎ 021

Novi Sad (Hungarian: Újvidék), capital of Vojvodina, is a friendly, modern city situated at a strategic bend of the Danube. The city developed in the 18th century when a powerful fortress was constructed on a hill-top overlooking the river to hold the area for the Habsburgs. Novi Sad remained part of the Austro-Hungarian empire until 1918 and it still has a Hungarian air about it today. The main sights can be covered in a couple of hours or you can make a leisurely day of it.

Novi Sad's attractions are simply wandering the pedestrian streets with their smart boutiques and outdoor cafés and visiting the Petrovaradin Citadel.

Orientation & Information
The adjacent train and bus stations are at the end of Bulevar Oslobođenja, on the northwest side of the city centre. There is a tourist agency to the right as you come out of the train station.

It's a brisk 40-minute walk from the train station to the city centre, otherwise catch bus No 4 (pay the conductor 3 DIN) from the station to Bulevar Mihajla Pupina, then ask directions to the tourist office at Dunavska 27, in a quaint old part of town. It has brochures and maps of Novi Sad.

The Automoto Klub Vojvodine is at Arse Teodorovića 15 off Pap Pavla.

YUGOSLAVIA

Post & Communications The telephone centre next to the main post office is open 24 hours. The postcode for Novi Sad is 21101.

Travel Agencies KSR Beograd Tours on Svetozara Miletića sells both domestic and international train tickets without the possible communication problems that you may have at the train station.

Things to See

There are two **museums** on Dunavska near the tourist office: both are part of the **Muzej Vojvodine**, one building is at No 35 and the other at No 39. The museums have exhibits on everything about Vojvodina and are worth a visit. They are open from Tuesday to Friday (9 am to 5 pm) and on weekends (9am to 2 pm). Entry is 3 DIN.

Walk across the old bridge to majestic **Petrovaradin Citadel** (built 1699-1780), the 'Gibraltar of the Danube', designed by French architect Vauban. The stairs beside the large church in the lower town lead up to the fortress. Today the citadel contains an expensive hotel, a restaurant and two small museums (closed Monday), but the chief

pleasure is simply to walk along the walls enjoying the splendid view of the city, river and surrounding countryside. There are up to 16km of underground galleries and halls below the citadel, but these can only be visited by groups.

Other sights in Novi Sad include three substantial **art galleries** (closed Monday and Tuesday) side by side on Vase Stajića, not far from trg Slobode, and the ultramodern **Serbian National Theatre** (1981).

Places to Stay

Camping There's a large *autocamp* (☎ 368 400) near the Danube at Ribarsko Ostrvo, with bungalows (158/163 DIN for a single/double) available all year. There is no free camping. Bus No 4 runs frequently from the train station to Liman via the city centre. From the end of the line walk towards the river. If you walk all the way from the centre of town, it will take about an hour.

Hotels The most appealing and oldest of Novi Sad's six hotels is *Hotel Vojvodina* (☎ 622 122; fax 615 445), right on trg Slobode. It has an attractive pastel façade and

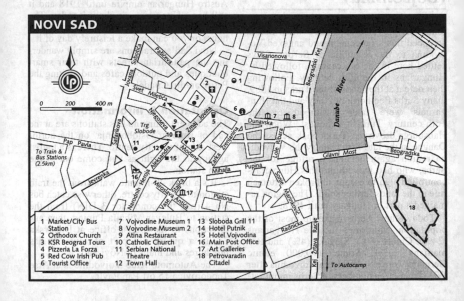

NOVI SAD

0   200   400 m

To Train &
Bus Stations
(2.5km)

Visarionova

Danube River

Glavni Most

To Autocamp

1 Market/City Bus Station
2 Orthodox Church
3 KSR Beograd Tours
4 Pizzeria La Forza
5 Red Cow Irish Pub
6 Tourist Office
7 Vojvodine Museum 1
8 Vojvodine Museum 2
9 Atina Restaurant
10 Catholic Church
11 Serbian National Theatre
12 Town Hall
13 Sloboda Grill 11
14 Hotel Putnik
15 Hotel Vojvodina
16 Main Post Office
17 Art Galleries
18 Petrovaradin Citadel

is very conveniently located. The 62 rooms with private bath are 180/220 DIN for a single/double, breakfast included.

The even more pricey *Hotel Putnik* (☎ 615 555; fax 622 561), round the corner from the Vojvodina on Ilije Ognjanocića has singles/ doubles for 480/600 DIN.

Places to Eat & Drink

The *Sloboda Grill 11*, on Modene in the centre, is cheap and unassuming. Take your pick and pay the cashier. The *Atina Restaurant*, next to the catholic church on trg Slobode, has a self-service section for a quick lunch and a full-service restaurant at the back. It's nothing special but at least there's a menu with prices clearly listed.

The *Pizzeria La Forza,* round the corner from the Atina at Katolička Porta 6, is a bright and cheery spot for a quick bite and if you really need a Big Mac, there's even a *McDonald's* cheek to jowl with the Town Hall.

The *Red Cow* Irish pub is a trendy spot for Guinness (cans only) and for an evening out. Enter via an arched alleyway off Zmaj Jovina or from an alleyway off Dunavska.

Getting There & Away

Novi Sad is on the main railway line between Budapest, Belgrade, Thessaloniki, Sofia and Istanbul. In the morning you can easily pick up the *Balkan Express* train to Istanbul (via Sofia; 1118km, 23 hours) or the *Hellas Express* to Thessaloniki (844km, 16 hours) in the afternoon. Trains to Subotica (99km, 1½ hours) and Belgrade (89km, 1½ hours) run every two hours. There are six trains daily to Budapest (274km, 6¼ hours) and one direct to Vienna (547 km, 9¼ hours).

SUBOTICA (СУБОТИЦА)
☎ 024

Subotica (Hungarian: Szabadka) is a large predominantly Hungarian-speaking city 10km from the Hungarian border at Kelebija. Over half the 180,000 inhabitants are of Hungarian origin and another quarter are Croats. Subotica is a useful transit point to/from Szeged (Hungary) and the train station is just a short walk from the centre of town.

The left-luggage office at the train station

is open 24 hours (passport required). You pay when you collect your luggage later. The cost is 5 DIN per item.

Information

Putnik (☎ 525 400), Borisa Kidriča 4, is helpful with information and sells train tickets.

Money Vojvođanska Banka has a currency exchange office in the old town hall (open weekdays from 7.30 am to 7 pm and Saturday from 7.30 am to 1 pm). Other exchange offices are at the train station and at the Hotel Patria.

Things to See

The imposing Art Nouveau **town hall** (1910) contains an excellent **historical museum** (closed Sunday and Monday) on the 1st floor (captions in Serbian and Hungarian). Entry to the museum is through the rear entrance to the town hall. Check to see whether the exquisitely decorated council chambers on the same floor as the museum are open.

Palić, 8km east of Subotica on the railway line to Szeged, is the city's recreation centre, with a zoo, lake, sporting facilities, restaurants and pleasant walks. The attractive park was laid out in 1912 and the pointed water tower is visible from the train.

Places to Stay & Eat

The only hotel in Subotica is the sevenstorey, B-category *Hotel Patria* (☎ 554 500; fax 551 762), on Đure Đakovića, three blocks left as you exit the train station. The Singles/doubles are 238/376 DIN with bath and breakfast.

There is a noticeable dearth of regular restaurants in the immediate town centre area, but the *Boss Pizzeria*, Engelsova 7 off Borisa Kidriča, is a relaxing spot for a decent pizza and a beer.

There are three hotels at Palić. The best is the *Park* near the train station. The *Jezero* is also near the station, while the less expensive *Sport* is close to the camping ground, about 10 minutes walk away. In winter only the Park is open. The train to/from Szeged stops near these hotels. You can also get there on bus No 6 from the main bus station near Hotel Patria in Subotica.

Getting There & Away

There are four local trains a day to/from Szeged, Hungary (45km, 1¾ hours, 35 DIN). Several daily buses also shuttle between Szeged and Subotica (DM4), but the train is more convenient. A daily bus links Subotica to Budapest (216km, DM25). Buses to Hungary must be paid for in either DM or Hungarian forints.

Subotica shares the same international train connections as Novi Sad with a 1½ hour time difference. (See Getting There & Away for Novi Sad).

Montenegro
(Црна Гора)

The Republic of Montenegro (Crna Gora) occupies a corner of south-western Yugoslavia directly north of Albania, close to where the Dinaric Alps merge with the Balkan range. The republic's Adriatic coastline attracts masses of Serbian sunseekers, but there are also the spectacular Morača and Tara canyons in the interior.

Between Podgorica and Kolašin a scenic railway runs right up the Morača Canyon, with fantastic views between the countless tunnels. West of Mojkovac, the next station after Kolašin, is the 100km-long Tara Canyon, thought to be the second-largest in the world. Other striking features of this compact, 13,812-sq-km republic are the winding Bay of Kotor (the longest and deepest fjord in southern Europe) and Lake Skadar (the largest lake in the Balkans), which Montenegro shares with Albania. There are no major islands off the Montenegrin coast but the sandy beaches here are far longer than those further north in Croatia. Now cut off from northern Europe by the closed border with Croatia and the troubles in Bosnia-Hercegovina, Montenegro is a bit of a backwater these days.

History

Only tiny Montenegro kept its head above the Turkish tide which engulfed the Balkans for over four centuries. Medieval Montenegro was part of Serbia, and after the Serbian defeat at Kosovo Polje in 1389 the inhabitants of this mountainous region continued to resist the Turks. In 1482 Ivan Crnojević established an independent principality at Cetinje ruled by *vladike* (bishops) who were popularly elected after 1516. Beginning in 1697 the succession was limited to the Petrović Njegoš family (each bishop being succeeded by his nephew), who forged an alliance with Russia in 1711.

Intermittent wars with the Turks and Albanians continued until 1878, when the European portion of the Ottoman Empire largely collapsed and Montenegrin independence was recognised by the Congress of Berlin. Nicola I Petrović, Montenegro's ruler from 1860, declared himself king in 1910. In 1916 the Austrians evicted the bishop-king and in 1918 Montenegro was incorporated into Serbia. During WWII Montenegrins fought valiantly in Tito's partisan army and after the war the region was rewarded with republic status within Yugoslavia. In 1946 the administration shifted from Cetinje to Podgorica (known until 1991 as Titograd), a modern city with little to interest the visitor.

The history of Montenegro is hard to follow unless you remember that, like the Albanians, the Montenegrins were divided into tribes or clans, such as the Njegoš clan west of Cetinje and the Paštrović clan around Budva. While blind obedience to the clan leader helped Montenegrins resist foreign invasions, it has not made the transition to democracy easy.

Getting There & Away

In the past, most visitors to Montenegro arrived from Dubrovnik by car or bus. The 1991 fighting closed this route and until the situation normalises the easiest way to get there is by train from Belgrade to Bar. You can also fly directly to Tivat or Podgorica airports from Belgrade. Regular ferries also run from Bari and Ancona in Italy.

BAR (БАР)
☎ 085

Backed by a barren coastal range, Bar (Italian: Antivari) is a would-be modern city whose architects seemed to have graduated from the socialist cement school of thought. It is not a terribly attractive city, punctuated as it is with white apartment blocks surrounding a socialist kitsch commercial centre with its obligatory flying saucer-style buildings. It is however a strategically important city to Yugoslavia and is the terminus of the railway from Belgrade and Yugoslavia's only port.

The development of Bar as an Adriatic port for landlocked Serbia was first proposed in 1879, yet it was not until 1976 that the dream became a reality, with the opening of the train line. In Summer a daily ferry connects Bar with Bari and three times a week with Ancona in Italy. As long as the border between Croatia and Yugoslavia remains closed, Bar will probably be your gateway to Montenegro. Bar is a convenient transport centre and if you find a cheap private room it makes a good base for day trips to Ulcinj, Cetinje, Kotor and Budva.

Orientation

The ferry terminal in Bar is only a few hundred metres from the centre of town, but the bus and train stations are side by side about 2km south-east of the centre. The rather pebbly beach is north of the port.

Information

The tourist office next to Putnik near the port has a few brochures and the adjacent Montenegro Express office can answer questions in English.

Money There are a number of banks in the port area and you can change money at the post office. You may encounter touts asking to change your money illegally.

Places to Stay & Eat

Autocamp Susanj, 2km north of the ferry landing along the beach, is once again open for business during summer. However, it's a basic camp with fairly rundown facilities.

Putnik Turist Biro opposite the ferry terminal, open from 7 am to 9 or 10 pm in summer, arranges private rooms for around 60 DIN per person, depending on facilities. Putnik is normally open to meet boat arrivals and is the best bet for accommodation in Bar.

Hotel Topolica (☎ 11 244; fax 12 731), a crumbling four-story socialist relic on the beach a few hundred metres north of the port, is the only hotel as such in town. It offers hyperinflated singles/doubles for 432/960 DIN, including a paltry breakfast. Avoid it if you can.

The *Pizzeria Napoletana*, just up from the Putnik office, is handy if you are waiting for a ferry, and the *Grill Holiday*, between the bus and train stations, is convenient for a tasty hamburger if you are waiting for a bus or a train.

Getting There & Away

Four trains a day (two with couchettes) travel to/from Belgrade (524km, nine hours, 69 DIN). The left-luggage office at the train station is open from 7 am to 9 pm. There are buses to all destinations along the coast. In summer there is a daily ferry linking Bar to Bari (Italy) which leaves at either 9 or 10 pm, and another ferry to Ancona three times a week. Fares on most ferries must usually be paid for in hard currency. Out of season there are only three ferries a week to Bari. In midsummer all transport to/from Bar is very crowded as all of Serbia heads for the beach.

ULCINJ (УЛЦИЊ)
☎ 085

A broad highway tunnels through hills between olive groves for 26km from Bar to Ulcinj (Ulqin in Albanian, Dulcigno in Italian), near the Albanian border.

Founded by the Greeks, Ulcinj gained notoriety when it was used as a base by North African pirates from 1571 to 1878. There was even a slave market from which the few resident black families are descended.

The Turks held Bar and Ulcinj for over 300 years, and today there are many Muslim Albanians in Ulcinj. You'll notice the difference in people right away: the characteristic white headshawls of the women, the curious direct looks you get, the lively bazar atmosphere in the many small shops, and the sound of Albanian on the streets. Many older women in Ulcinj still wear traditional Islamic dress, especially on market day (Friday). It's a popular holiday resort for Serbs, who arrive en masse via the Belgrade-Bar train. In July and August it can get very crowded, although accommodation is always available.

Orientation

Ulcinj's bus station is about 2km south of Mala Plaža, the small beach below the old town. You will most likely be dropped off nearer the main drag, 26 Novembar, rather than at the bus station proper. Walk uphill along 26 Novembar to Mala Plaža and you'll pass several buildings with *sobe* and *zimmer* signs where you can rent a room.

Velika Plaža (Great Beach), Ulcinj's famous 12km stretch of unbroken sand, begins about 5km south-east of town (take the bus to Ada).

Information

Adriatours, at 26 Novembar 18, is about 500m from the bus station on the way into town on the right (see Places to Stay).

Money There are several banks in town. Room proprietors and restaurant owners will often change hard cash for you.

Post & Communications The telephone centre in the main post office, at the foot of 26 Novembar near the bus station, is open Monday to Saturday from 7 am to 9 pm and Sunday from 9 am to noon.

Things to See

The ancient **ramparts** of old Ulcinj overlook the sea, but most of the buildings inside were shattered by earthquakes in 1979 and later reconstructed. The **museum** (closed Monday) is by the upper gate. You can walk among the houses and along the wall for the view.

Places to Stay

Camping There are two camping grounds on Velika Plaža: *Milena* and *Neptun*. On Ada Island, just across the Bojana River from Albania, is *Camping Ada Bojana FKK*, a nudist camping ground accessible by bus (guests only).

Private Rooms *Adriatours* (☎ 52 057), 26 Novembar 18, is a private travel agency with helpful English-speaking staff who will find you a private room for about 60 DIN per person a night. They're open all year. If you arrive outside business hours knock on the door of the adjacent house with the *zimmer frei* signs (owned by the same family) and if they can't accommodate you they'll suggest someone else who can.

If you continue into town towards Mala Plaža, you'll pass *Olcinium Travel Agency* (more private rooms) nearly opposite Kino Basta (Basta Cinema). Facing Mala Plaža itself is *Turist Biro 'Neptun' Montenegroturist*, with another selection of private rooms (60 DIN per person).

Hotels The cheapest hotel is the 240-room *Mediteran* (☎ 81 411), a pleasant modern hotel five minutes walk uphill from Mala Plaža. Singles/doubles with private bath and breakfast are 210/300 DIN and most have a balcony overlooking the sea. It's only open in the summer season.

Places to Eat

There are some chic eating places in the old town if your budget can stand a blowout. There are also numerous inexpensive restaurants around town offering cheap grilled meat or more expensive seafood. Try the *Dubrovnik Restaurant* next to the unfinished cultural centre on 26 Novembar.

Getting There & Away

Buses to/from Bar (26km, 10 DIN) run every couple of hours.

BUDVA (БУДВА)

☎ 086

Budva is Yugoslavia's top beach resort. A series of fine beaches punctuate the coastline all the way to Sveti Stefan, with the high coastal mountains forming a magnificent backdrop. Before the troubles, Budva used to cater mostly to people on package tours from northern Europe, but its main clientele these days is domestic. Although Budva is not cheap, you may find some good deals just outside the main tourist season of July and August. Though Bar is better positioned transport-wise as a base for making coastal day trips, Budva is far more beautiful and worth the extra effort and expense if you're not in a hurry.

Orientation & Information

The modern bus station is located in a new part of town about 1km from the old town. Upon exiting the bus station turn left, walk for about 150m before heading right until you hit the main road. Turn right and follow this road to the traffic lights. Turn left here and follow the road round until you come to the main square, trg Republike. There's no left-luggage office at Budva bus station.

The people at Montenegro Express on trg Republike near the old town are good about answering questions.

Money There are two banks on trg Republike: Montenegro Bank and Jugobank. Hotels will normally exchange cash without any problem.

Things to See

Budva's big tourist-puller is its old **walled town**. This was levelled by two earthquakes in 1979, after which the residents were permanently evacuated. Since then it has been completely rebuilt as a tourist attraction and the main square with its three churches, museum and fortress (there's a great view from the ramparts) is so picturesque it seems almost contrived. It's possible to walk three-quarters of the way around the top of the town wall. Start from near the north gate.

Budva's main beach is pebbly and fairly average. A better beach is **Mogren Beach**, reached by following a coastal path northwards for 500m or so. The path starts in front of the Grand Hotel Avala.

Only a few kilometres south-east of Budva is the former village of **Sveti Stefan**, an island now linked to the mainland. During the 1960s the entire village was converted into a luxury hotel but unlike Budva, which you may enter free, you will be charged to set foot on the hallowed soil of Sveti Stefan during the summer months. Settle for the long-range picture-postcard view and keep your money.

Places to Stay

Camping If you have a tent, try *Autocamp Avala* (☎ 51 205), behind Hotel Montenegro, 2km south-east along the shore (through a small tunnel). It's crowded with caravans, but at least it's near the beach. No bungalows are available but the manager may help you find a private room nearby. Avala is open from June to September. Right next to Avala is *Autokamp Boreti*, which has less in the way of security (fences and gates especially).

Private Rooms *Maestral Tours* (☎ 52 250) at Mediteranska 23, just down from the post office, rents private rooms at around 60 to 70 DIN per person in July and August only. *Emona Globetour* nearby may also have private rooms, and a third place to try is *Montenegro Express* (☎ 51 443) on trg Republike, closer to the old town. You may be able to find your own room by looking for signs, but during the October to May low season finding a private room may take some searching out.

Hotels The easiest and most convenient option is the modern *Hotel Mogren* (☎ 51 780; fax 51 750) just outside the north gate of the old town. Rates are a fairly pricey 480/720 DIN for singles/doubles in July and August, but this place is open all year and prices out of season are 360/552 DIN.

Maestral Tours runs the *Hotel Mediteran* (☎ 51 423), about 2km south along the coast at Bečići. Prices here range from 280 to 375 DIN per person. Check with Maestral Tours for room availability first.

In the high season try asking for room-filler deals from the other resort hotels, but don't be too optimistic since room prices tend to be fixed by the government and demand is usually high.

Places to Eat

For a cheap feed without the frills, the *Restoran Centar* is upstairs beside the supermarket (above the vegetable market) just inland from the post office. At the bus station there is a reasonable *self-service restaurant* if you are in transit or waiting for a bus.

Budva has no shortage of expensive bars and restaurants along the seafront and in the old town. Unfortunately these bars and restaurants don't often display their prices outside, so always ask to see a menu before ordering. Locals tend to avoid these restaurants. Check out instead the *Restaurant Jadran* about 800m south along the waterfront. It is a popular local eating place and specialises in fish dishes at quite affordable prices.

Getting There & Away

There are almost hourly buses to Podgorica (74km) via Cetinje (31km) and 16 a day to Bar (38km). There are also buses to Belgrade and other parts of Yugoslavia.

If coming by train from Belgrade, get off at Podgorica and catch a bus from there to Budva. In the other direction it's probably best to take a bus from Budva to Bar and pick up the train to Belgrade there, since many people board the train at Podgorica.

If you choose to fly to Tivat, a JAT bus (15 DIN) will take you to Budva and drop you off at trg Republike.

Getting Around

From May to September a small tourist train shuttles up and down the beach from Budva to Bečići for 10 DIN a ride. Ask around the harbour for tourist boats to the little island of Sveti Stefan just across the bay.

CETINJE (ЦЕТИЊЕ)
☎ 086

Cetinje, perched on top of a high plateau between the Bay of Kotor and Skadar Lake, is the old capital of Montenegro, subject of songs and epic poems. The open, easily defended slopes help to explain Montenegro's independence, and much remains of old Cetinje, from museums to palaces, mansions and monasteries. At the turn of the century all the large states of Europe had embassies here. Short hikes can be made in the hills behind Cetinje Monastery. It's well worth spending the night here if you can find an inexpensive place to stay.

Orientation & Information

The bus station is 500m from the main square, Balšića Pazar. From the station turn left and the first right and you will find it easily. There is a big wall map in the square to help you get oriented with the main sights and reference points.

Things to See

The most imposing building in Cetinje is the **State Museum**, the former palace (1871) of Nicola I Petrović, the last king. Looted during WWII, only a portion of its original furnishings remain, but the many portraits

and period weapons give a representative picture of the times.

Nearly opposite is the older 1832 residence of the prince-bishop Petar II Petrović Njegoš, who ruled from 1830 to 1851. This building, now a museum, is also known as **Biljarda Hall** because of a billiard table installed in 1840.

Around the side of Biljarda Hall is a large glass-enclosed pavilion containing a fascinating relief map of Montenegro created by the Austrians in 1917 for tactical planning purposes. Ask one of the Biljarda Hall attendants to let you in.

Beyond the map is **Cetinje Monastery**, founded in 1484 but rebuilt in 1785. The monastery treasury contains a copy of the *Oktoih* or 'Octoechos' (Book of the Eight Voices) printed near here in 1494 – it's one of the oldest collections of liturgical songs in a Slavic language. Vladin Dom, the former Government House (1910) and now the National Gallery, is not far away.

Twenty km away at the summit of **Mt Lovčen** (1749m), the 'Black Mountain' which gave Montenegro its Italian name, is the mausoleum of Petar II Petrović Njegoš, a revered poet as well as ruler. The masterful statue of Njegoš inside is by Croatian sculptor Ivan Meštrović. There are no buses up Lovčen and taxis want 160 DIN return; the building is visible in the distance from Cetinje. From the parking lot you must climb 461 steps to the mausoleum and its sweeping view of the Bay of Kotor, mountains and coast. The whole of Mt Lovčen has been declared a national park.

Places to Stay & Eat

For a private room ask at *Intours* (☎ 21 157), the place marked 'Vincom Duty Free Shop' next to the post office. Chances are they'll send you to Petar Martinović, who lives a block away at Bajova Pivljanina 50, next to Belveder Mini Market.

If this fails you have a problem as the only hotel is the *Grand Hotel* (☎ 21 104), a modern so-called five-star hotel that would barely rate two stars anywhere else. Singles/doubles are 220/310 DIN with bath and breakfast. It's a five-minute walk from the centre.

There is not a glut of eating places in Cetinje. The *Restoran Cetinje* next to the post office and the *Mlječni Restoran* on the main square are usually closed out of season, but open in summer. Failing these two, you might opt for passable pasta or pizza at the *Spoleto* pizzeria further down from the post office.

Getting There & Away

There are 19 buses a day between Cetinje and Podgorica (45km), and a similar number back to Budva (31km).

You can easily make Cetinje a day trip from Bar by catching an early train to Podgorica, where you'll connect with a bus to Cetinje. An early afternoon bus down to Budva will give you some time at the beach and a chance to look around the reconstructed old town before taking a late afternoon bus back to Bar.

DURMITOR NATIONAL PARK

Montenegro's Durmitor National Park is a popular hiking and mountaineering area just west of **Žabljak**, a ski resort which is also the highest town in Yugoslavia (1450m). A chair lift from near Hotel Durmitor towards Mt Štuoc (1953m) operates in winter. Žabljak was a major partisan base during WWII, changing hands four times.

Some 18 mountain lakes dot the slopes of the Durmitor Range south-west of Žabljak. You can walk right around the largest lake, **Crno jezero** (Black Lake), 3km from Žabljak, in an hour or two, and swim in its waters in summer. The rounded mass of Međed (2287m) rises directly behind the lake, surrounded by a backdrop of other peaks, including Savin kuk (2313m). You can climb Savin kuk in eight hours there and back. The national park office next to Hotel Durmitor sells good maps of the park.

Durmitor's claim to fame is the 1067m-deep **Tara Canyon**, which cuts dramatically into the mountain slopes and plateau for about 100km. The edge of the Tara Canyon is about 12km north of Žabljak, a three-hour walk along a road beginning near Hotel Planinka. Yugoslav tourist brochures maintain that this is the second-largest canyon in the world after the Grand Canyon in the USA, a claim other countries such as Mexico and Namibia also make for their canyons, but any way you look at it, it's a top sight.

White-Water Tours

Travel agencies sometimes offer rubber-raft trips on the clean green water, over countless foaming rapids, down the steep forested Tara Gorge. These begin at Splavište near the Đurđevića Tara bridge. Three-day raft expeditions go right down the Tara River to the junction with the Piva River at Šćepan Polje (88km), near the border with Bosnia.

For advance information on white-water rafting on the Tara River contact Ski Centar Durmitor, (☎ 011-629 602; fax 011-634 944) Kralja Petra 70, Belgrade. At last report two-day, one-night raft trips departed from Žabljak every Monday from June to August; they cost about 500 DIN per person including transfers, meals and gear. There's a 10-person minimum to run a trip, so inquire well ahead. In winter the same Belgrade office will know all about ski facilities at Žabljak.

Places to Stay

The *tourist office* in the centre of Žabljak is not much help – it arranges expensive private rooms at 80 DIN for a single and hands out brochures written in Serbian.

Žabljak has four hotels owned by Montenegroturist. The *Planinka* (☎ 083-88 344) and *Jezera* (☎ 083-88 226) are modern ski hotels charging 132 DIN per person with half-board in summer. The *Hotel Žabljak* (☎ 083-88 300) right in the centre of town also offers rooms with half-board for 210 DIN per person.

The cheapest of the bunch is the old four-storey wooden *Hotel Durmitor* (☎ 083-88 278), past Hotel Jezera at the entrance to the national park, a 15-minute walk from town. Singles/doubles with shared bath here are 120 DIN, with half-board. Although the Durmitor seems to have the reputation of being run-down and unfit for foreigners, some of the rooms are quite pleasant, with balconies facing the mountains. Just be aware that there's no hot water or showers in the building.

On a hill-top five minutes' walk beyond the national park office is *Autocamp Ivan-do* which is little more than a fenced-off field. People around here rent *private rooms* at rates far lower than those charged in town and you'll get an additional discount if you have a sleeping bag and don't require sheets. Set right in the middle of the forest, Ivan-do is a perfect base for hikers.

Places to Eat

The *Restoran Sezam* next to the small market just below the Turist Biro bakes its own bread and is one of the only places apart from the hotels that serves meals.

Getting There & Away

The easiest way to get to Žabljak is to take a bus from Belgrade to Pljevlja (334km), then one of the two daily buses from Pljevlja to Žabljak (57km). On the return journey, these buses leave Žabljak for Pljevlja at 5 am and 5 pm, connecting for Mojkovac and Podgorica at Đurđevića Tara, where there's a spectacular bridge over the canyon. If you have to change buses at Pljevlja, hurry as they don't wait long.

As soon as you arrive at Žabljak inquire about onward buses to Belgrade, Pljevlja, Mojkovac and Podgorica at the red kiosk marked 'Turist Biro' beside the bus stop. Seats should be booked the day before.

Another jumping-off point is Mojkovac on the Belgrade-Podgorica line. About four trains daily run from Bar to Mojkovac (157km, two hours); catch the earliest one for the best connections. At Mojkovac you must walk 2km from the train station to the bus station, where you can pick up buses running from Podgorica to Pljevlja. They'll usually drop you at Đurđevića Tara and from there you may have to hitch the remaining 22km to Žabljak.

Coming from Bar, take a train to Podgorica and then take the afternoon bus from there direct to Žabljak.

Kosovo (KOCOBO)

A visit to Kosovo (Kosova in Albanian) can be a traumatic experience, if it is at all possible. Probably nowhere in Europe are human rights as flagrantly and systematically violated as they are here. The people have an uninhibited friendliness and curiosity which sets them apart from other Yugoslavs and the direct looks you get are at first disconcerting. The region's poverty and backwardness are apparent, as is the watchful eye of the Serbian government. Police posts have taken the place of left-luggage facilities in the region's bus and train stations. Your presence may not be welcome.

Until recently an autonomous province, Kosovo is now an integral part of the Republic of Serbia. Just under two million people occupy Kosovo's 10,887 sq km, making it the most densely populated portion of Yugoslavia; it also has the highest birth rate. The Albanians adopted Islam after the Turkish conquest and today the region has a definite Muslim air, from the inhabitants' food and dress to the ubiquitous mosques. The capital, Priština, is a depressing, redeveloped city with showplace banks and hotels juxtaposed against squalor, but in the west the Metohija Valley between Peć and Prizren offers a useful transit route from the Adriatic to Macedonia, or Belgrade to Albania, plus a chance to see another side of this troubled land.

History

Isolated medieval Serbian monasteries tell of an early period which ended in 1389 with the Serbs' crushing defeat at the hands of the Turks at Kosovo Polje, just outside Priština (Prishtinë in Albanian). After this disaster the Serbs moved north, abandoning the region to the Albanians, descendants of the ancient Illyrians, who had inhabited this land for thousands of years.

In the late 19th century the ethnic Albanians, who make up 90% of the population today, struggled to free themselves of Ottoman rule. Yet in 1913, when the Turkish government finally pulled out, Kosovo was handed over to Serbia. Over half a million ethnic Albanians emigrated to Turkey and elsewhere to escape Serbian rule and by 1940 at least 18,000 Serb families had been settled on the vacated lands. During WWII, Kosovo was incorporated into Italian-controlled Albania and in October 1944 it was liberated by Albanian communist partisans to whom Tito had promised an autonomous republic within Yugoslavia. The area came under Tito's forces in early 1945, not without force.

After the war Tito wanted Albania itself included in the Yugoslav Federation as a seventh republic, with Kosovo united to it. This never came to pass and thus began two decades of pernicious neglect. Between 1954 and 1957 another 195,000 Albanians were coerced into emigrating to Turkey. After serious rioting in 1968 (and with the Soviet invasion of Czechoslovakia pushing Yugoslavia and Albania closer together), an autonomous province was created in 1974 and economic aid increased. Due to these concessions Kosovo is one of the only parts of ex-Yugoslavia where Tito is still warmly remembered. You see his portrait in restaurants and cafés everywhere and the main street in Peć is still named after him.

Yet the changes brought only cosmetic improvements and the standard of living in Kosovo (which has some of the most fertile land in the Balkans) remained a quarter the Yugoslav average. Kosovo was treated as a colony, its mines providing raw materials for industry in Serbia. In 1981, demonstrations calling for full republic status were put down by military force at a cost of over 300 lives. The 7000 young Albanians subsequently arrested were given jail terms of six years and up. This brutal denial of equality within the Yugoslav Federation sowed the seeds which led to the violent break-up of the country a decade later.

State of Emergency Trouble began anew in November 1988 as Albanian demonstrators protested against the sacking by Belgrade of local officials, including the provincial president Azem Vllasi, who was later arrested. A Kosovo coal miners' strike in February 1989 was followed by new limits imposed by Serbia on Kosovo's autonomy, a curfew and a state of emergency. This resulted in serious rioting, and 24 unarmed Albanian civilians were shot dead by the Yugoslav security forces.

On 5 July 1990 the Serbian parliament cancelled Kosovo's political autonomy and dissolved its assembly and government. The only Albanian-language daily newspaper, *Rilindja*, was banned and TV and radio broadcasts in Albanian ceased. In a process termed 'differentiation' some 115,000 Albanians suspected of having nationalist sympathies were fired from their jobs and Serbs installed in their places. At Priština University, 800 Albanian lecturers were sacked, effectively ending teaching in Albanian and forcing all but 500 of the 23,000 Albanian students to terminate their studies. Albanian secondary-school teachers were forced to work without salaries, otherwise the schools would have closed. All Albanians working in state hospitals were sacked, creating a growth industry in private clinics where most Albanian women now give birth. (This happened after rumours that the survival rate for male Albanian babies born in hospitals had suddenly dropped.)

Large numbers of Albanians went abroad after losing their jobs and a third of adult male Kosovars now work in Western Europe. Ironically, with Yugoslavia now in an economic tailspin, the families of the émigrés are fairly well off thanks to the hard currency their men send home, while the Serbs who took their government jobs are paid in supersoft Yugoslav dinars. The 20% of ethnic Albanians who do have jobs in Kosovo work almost exclusively in private businesses.

In September 1991, Serbian police and militia mobilised to block a referendum on independence for Kosovo, turning voters away and arresting election officials. The vote went ahead anyway and, with a 90% turnout, 98% voted in favour of independence from Serbia. In further elections on 24 May 1992, also declared illegal by Serbia, the writer Ibrahim Rugova was elected president of Kosovo. The unrecognised parliament of the Republic of Kosovo, elected at the same time as Mr Rugova, is attempting to create a parallel administration that can offer passive resistance to Serbia and has requested UN peacekeeping troops for Kosovo.

The Spectre of War An Albanian national uprising would certainly unleash the bloodiest of ex-Yugoslavia's latest series of civil wars and the Kosovars are intensely aware of the way Western countries stood by and tolerated ethnic genocide in Bosnia, so they have attempted to resist Serb aggression with non-violence. Yugoslavia stationed an estimated 40,000 troops and police in Kosovo and nobody doubted its readiness to use them. Serb nationalists are firmly convinced they have a historic right to Kosovo as part of a 'Greater Serbia' and a plan exists to colonise Kosovo with Serbs. In December 1992, Kosovo Serbs elected to parliament a thuggish militia leader named Arkan whose troops have been accused of murdering 3000 Muslims in northern Bosnia.

Early in 1998, however, the Serbian army clamped down on Albanians in Kosovo with a series of clinical attacks on so-called

'Kosovar terrorists' principally in and around the village of Dečani near Peć. Officially only 40 or so Albanians were killed, including women and children, but the true number is likely to have been much higher. Condemned widely by most international governments, the Milošević regime ignored protests and continued the clampdown throughout the first half of 1998, attracting a US-led arms embargo on Serbia for its intransigence. A national referendum in Yugoslavia in April 1998 on whether foreign powers should be allowed to interfere in the internal matters of Yugoslavia was firmly rejected by the Serb majority and Yugoslavia's isolation from the international community was once again assured. As this chapter was being updated, arms were being covertly supplied to the Kosovars by Albanians in Albania and the Yugoslavia/Albania border region became one of high alert with the threat of all-out war between the two countries a strong possibility.

Warning As of mid-1998 it was almost impossible to visit Kosovo without a very good reason. Tourism was certainly not one of them. Tourist information on the area was only cursorily checked for this edition and may not be totally accurate should the situation ease and safe travel to the area be possible once more. Should you seek to cross into Kosovo you will almost certainly be stopped and questioned at the internal border. Whether you will be allowed into Kosovo will depend entirely on the prevailing political and military situation.

Getting There & Away
Getting to Kosovo from Serbia and Macedonia is technically easy as there are direct trains from Belgrade to Peć (490km, 9½ hours), and buses from Skopje to Prizren (117km).

Getting from the Adriatic coast to Kosovo, on the other hand, takes a full night or day. From Budva or Cetinje catch a bus to Podgorica and look for a direct bus to Peć from there. The buses usually go via Berane, though some may go via the 1849m Čakor pass. If you're leaving from Ulcinj, take an early bus to Bar, then a train to Podgorica. Try to get as far as Peć or Prizren on the

first day since accommodation between the coast and Kosovo is either nonexistent or dire. If you do get stuck, *Autocamp Berane* (☎ 084-61 822) is less than 1km from Berane bus station. If you are in a real bind, you could stop at Rožaje (32km from Berane) and spend the night at the truly dreadful *Rožaje Hotel* (☎ 0871-54 335), which charges 170 DIN for a dingy single. An early bus will carry you the 37km from Rožaje to Peć the next morning. There's nil to see or do in Rožaje. For the route to/from Albania, see the later Prizren section.

PEĆ (ПЕЋ)
☎ 039
Peć (Peja in Albanian), below high mountains between Podgorica and Priština, is a friendly, untouristed town of picturesque dwellings with some modern development. Ethnic Albanian men with their white felt skullcaps and women in traditional dress crowd the streets, especially on Saturday (market day). The horse wagons carrying goods around Peć share the streets with lots of beggars.

Orientation
The bus and train stations are about 500m apart, both in the east part of Peć about 1km from the centre. Neither station has a left-luggage room. Follow Rruga Maršal Tito west from the bus station into the centre of town.

Information
Try Kosmet Tours at Nemanjina 102; Putnik, Nemanjina 64; and Metohija Turist, Nemanjna 20.

Post & Communications The main post office and telephone centre is opposite the Hotel Metohija.

Things to See
There are eight well-preserved, functioning mosques in Peć, the most imposing of which is the 15th-century **Bajrakli Mosque**. Its high dome rises out of the colourful **bazar** (*čaršija*), giving Peć an authentic Oriental air.

By the river 2km west of Peć is the **Patri-jaršija Monastery**, seat of the Serbian

Orthodox patriarchate in the 14th century, from 1557 to 1766 and again after 1920. The rebirth of the patriarchate in 1557 allowed the Serbs to maintain their identity during the darkest days of Ottoman domination, so this monastery is of deep significance to Serbs. Inside the high-walled compound are three mid-13th century churches, each of which has a high dome and glorious medieval frescoes. There is a detailed explanation in English in the common narthex (admission 20 DIN). Two km west of the monastery along the main highway is the **Rugovo Gorge**, an excellent hiking area.

Peć's most impressive sight, however, is 15km south and accessible by frequent local bus. The **Visoki Dečani Monastery** (1335), with its marvellous 14th-century frescoes, is a 2km walk from the bus stop in Dečani (Dečan in Albanian) through beautiful wooded countryside. This royal monastery, built under kings Dečanski and Dušan, survived the long Turkish period intact. From Dečani you can catch an onward bus to Prizren.

Places to Stay

Camping Over the bridge and 1km up the hill from the Metohija Hotel is the quiet and rather pleasant *Kamp Karagač* (☎ 22 358), with lots of shade. This camping ground has been privatised and its main business is now the restaurant. It doesn't really cater to campers any more, though this could change, so ask.

Hotels The B-category *Hotel Park* (☎ 21 864), just beyond Kamp Karagač, is your best bet. Prices here vary but it's not too expensive.

The A-category *Metohija Hotel* (☎ 22 611), Nemanjina 60, is a budget-breaker at 280/360 DIN for a single/double with private bath and breakfast. Also consider the private *Hotel Dypon* (☎ 31 593) which charges around 300 DIN for a single/double room.

None of the travel agencies in town offers private rooms.

Getting There & Away

Bus Services from Prizren (73km) and Skopje (190km) are good and there's a night bus to/from Belgrade (388km). In July and August buses run direct to Peć from Ulcinj (279km).

Train Express trains going between Belgrade and Peć stop at Kosovo Polje, a junction 8km west of Priština. From here, Peć is 91km away (two hours) while a separate line runs to Prizren (125km, three hours). There's an overnight train with couchettes to/from Belgrade.

PRIZREN (ПРИЗРЕН)
☎ 029

Prizren, which is the most Albanian-looking city in Yugoslavia, is midway between Peć and Skopje. The road from Shkodra reaches the Albanian border at Vrbnica, 18km west of Prizren.

Prizren was the medieval capital of 'Old Serbia' but much of what we see today is Turkish. Colourful houses climb up the hillside to the ruined citadel *(kalaja)*, from which the 15th-century Turkish bridge and 19 minarets are visible.

The Bistrica River emerges from a gorge behind the citadel and cuts Prizren in two on its way into Albania. East up this gorge is the Bistrica Pass (2640m), once the main route to Macedonia. Wednesday is market day, when the city really comes alive.

Orientation

The bus and train stations are adjacent on the west side of town, but there's no left-luggage facility in either. From the bus station follow Rruga Metohjska towards the mountains, then take Rruga Vidovdanska up the riverside into town.

Information

Try the Tourist Association of Prizren, Rruga Vidovdanska 51, or Putnik on trg Cara Dušana in the centre of town.

Post & Communications The main post office and telephone centre is adjacent to the Theranda Hotel.

Things to See

On your way into town from the bus station you'll see the huge white-marble Bankos Prizren building facing the river. On a backstreet behind the bank is the **Church of Bogorodica Ljeviška** (1307), which has an open bell tower above and frescoes inside. Nearby, a tall square tower rises above some

Turkish baths, now the **Archaeological Museum** (usually closed).

The **Sinan Pasha Mosque** (1561) beside the river in the centre is closed, as are the **Gazi Mehmed Pasha Baths** (1563) beyond the Theranda Hotel. A little back from these is the large dome of the beautifully appointed 16th-century **Bajrakli (Gazi Mehmed) Mosque**, which is still in use. Behind this mosque, on the side facing the river, is the **Museum of the Prizren League**, a popular movement which struggled for Albanian autonomy within the Ottoman Empire from 1878 to 1881. In 1881 Dervish Pasha suppressed the League, killing thousands of Albanians and exiling thousands more to Asia Minor.

The largest Orthodox church in Prizren is **Sveti Georgi** (1856) in the old town near the Sinan Pasha Mosque. Higher up on the way to the **citadel** is **Sveti Spas**, with the ruins of an Orthodox monastery.

Places to Stay & Eat

Unfortunately, no private rooms are available in Prizren. The B-category *Theranda Hotel* (☎ 22 292), by the river in the centre of town charges 160/220 DIN for a single/double with private bath and breakfast.

Motel Putnik (☎ 43 107; fax 41 552), near the river three blocks from the bus station (ask directions), charges similar prices for foreigners and locals, which makes it relatively cheap (prices vary). The camping ground behind the motel has been officially closed for years but they'll probably let you pitch a tent there at no cost.

Several good *čevapčiči* places lie between Sveti Georgi and Sinan Pasha.

Getting There & Away

Bus service is good from Priština (75km), Peć (73km) and Skopje (117km). Only slow local trains to Metohija junction (64km, 1½ hours) and Kosovo Polje (125km, three hours) leave from Prizren, so you're much better off coming and going by bus.

Buses to the Albanian border used to leave from the street beginning at Rruga Vidovdanska 77.

Appendix I – Climate Charts

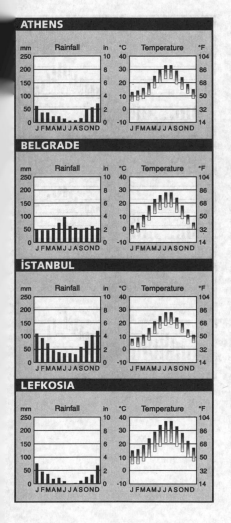

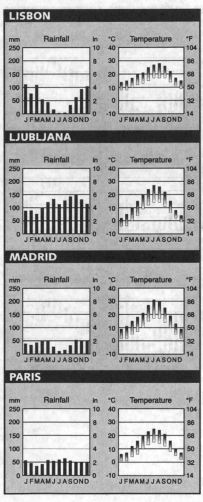

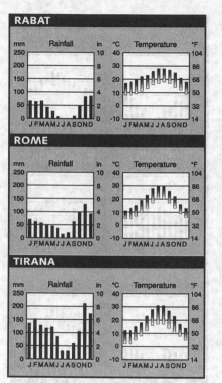

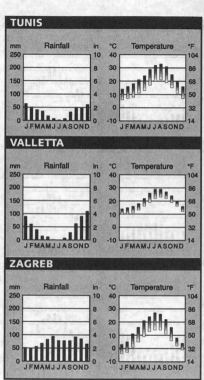

Appendix II – Telephones

Dial Direct

You can dial directly from public telephone boxes from almost anywhere in Europe to almost anywhere in the world. This is usually cheaper than going through the operator. In much of Europe, public telephones accepting phonecards are becoming the norm and in some countries coin-operated phones are difficult to find.

To call abroad you simply dial the international access code (IAC) for the country you are calling from (most commonly 00 in Europe but see the following table), the country code (CC) for the country you are calling, the local area code (usually dropping the leading zero if there is one) and then the number. If, for example, you are in Italy (international access code 00) and want to make a call to the USA (country code 1), San Francisco (area code 212), number ☎ 123 4567, then you dial ☎ 00-1-212-123 4567. To call from the UK (00) to Australia (61), Sydney (02), number ☎ 123 4567, you dial ☎ 00-61-2-1234 5678.

Home Direct

If you would rather have somebody else pay for the call, you can, from many countries, dial directly to your home country operator and then reverse charges; you can also charge the call to a phone company credit card. To do this, simply dial the relevant 'home direct' number to be connected to your own operator. For the USA there's a choice of AT&T, MCI or Sprint Global One home direct services. Home direct numbers vary from country to country – check with your telephone company before you leave, or with the international operator in the country you're ringing from. From phone boxes in some countries you may need a coin or local phonecard to be connected with the relevant home direct operator.

In some places (particularly airports), you may find dedicated home direct phones where you simply press the button labelled USA, Australia, Hong Kong or whatever for direct connection to the operator. Note that the home direct service does not operate to and from all countries, and that the call could be charged at operator rates, which makes it expensive for the person paying. Placing a call on your phone credit card is more expensive than paying the local tariff.

Dialling Tones

In some countries, after you've dialled the international access code, you have to wait for a second dial tone before dialing the code for your target country and the number. Often the same applies when you ring from one city to another within these countries: wait for a dialling tone after you've dialled the area code for your target city. If you're not sure what to do, simply wait three or four seconds after dialling a code – if nothing happens, you can probably keep dialling.

Phonecards

In major locations phones may accept credit cards: simply swipe your card through the slot and the call is charged to the card, though rates can be very high. Phone-company credit cards can be used to charge calls via your home country operator.

Stored-value phonecards are now almost standard all over Europe. You usually buy a card from a post office, telephone centre, newsstand or retail outlet and simply insert the card into the phone each time you make a call. The card solves the problem of finding the correct coins for calls (or lots of correct coins for international calls) and generally gives you a small discount.

Call Costs

The cost of international calls varies widely from one country to another: a US$1.20 call from Britain could cost you US$6 from Turkey. The countries in the table opposite are rated from * (cheap) to *** (expensive), but rates can vary depending on which country you are calling to (for example, from Italy it's relatively expensive to call North America, but more expensive to call Australia). Reduced rates are available at certain times, usually from mid-evening to early morning, though it varies from country to country – check the local phone book or ask the operator. Calling from hotel rooms can be very expensive.

Telephone Codes & Costs

	CC	cost (see text)	IAC	IO
Albania	355	***		
Andorra	376	**	00	821111
Austria	43	*	00	09
Belgium	32	**	00	1224 (private phone)
				1223 (public phone)
Bosnia	387	**	00	901
Bulgaria	359	***	00	
Croatia	385	**	99	901
Cyprus	357	***	00	
Cyprus (Turkish)	905		00	
Czech Republic	420	***	00	0149
Denmark	45	**	00	141
Estonia	372	***	8(w)00	007
Finland	358	**	990	020222
France	33	*	00(w)	12
Germany	49	*	00	00118
Gibraltar	350	***	00	100
Greece	30	*	00	161
Hungary	36	*	00(w)	09
Iceland	354	**	90	09
Ireland	353	*	00	114
Italy	39	**	00	15
Latvia	371	***	00	115
Liechtenstein	41 75	***	00	114
Lithuania	370	***	8(w)10 8(w)	194/195
Luxembourg	352	**	00	0010
Macedonia	389	***	99	
Malta	356	**	00	194
Morocco	212	***	00(w)	12
Netherlands	31	**	00	0800-0410
Norway	47	**	095	181
Poland	48	**	0(w)0	901
Portugal	351	*	00	099
Romania	40	***	40	071
Russia	7	***	8(w)10	
Slovakia	421	**	00	0149/0139
Slovenia	386	**	00	901
Spain	34	**	00(w)	025
Sweden	46	**	009(w)	0018
Switzerland	41	**	00(w)	114
Tunisia	216	**	00	
Turkey	90	***	00	115
UK	44	*	00	155
Yugoslavia	381	***	99	901

CC – Country Code (to call *into* that country)
IAC – International Access Code (to call abroad *from* that country)
IO – International Operator (to make enquiries)
(w) – wait for dialling tone

Other country codes include: Australia 61, Canada 1, Hong Kong 852, India 91, Indonesia 62, Israel 972, Japan 81, Macau 853, Malaysia 60, New Zealand 64, Singapore 65, South Africa 27, Thailand 66, USA 1

Appendix III – European Organisations

Membership of Political & Economic Organisations

	Council of Europe	EU	EFTA	NATO	Nordic Council	OECD	WEU
Albania	✓	–	–	–	–	–	–
Andorra	✓	–	–	–	–	–	–
Austria	✓	✓	–	–	–	✓	–
Belgium	✓	✓	–	✓	–	✓	✓
Bosnia-Hercegovina	◆	–	–	–	–	–	–
Bulgaria	✓	–	–	–	–	–	–
Croatia	✓	–	–	–	–	–	–
Cyprus	✓	–	–	–	–	–	–
Czech Republic	✓	–	–	–	–	✓	–
Denmark	✓	✓	–	✓	✓	✓	–
Estonia	✓	–	–	–	–	–	–
Finland	✓	✓	–	–	✓	✓	–
France	✓	✓	–	✓	–	✓	✓
Germany	✓	✓	–	✓	–	✓	✓
Greece	✓	✓	–	✓	–	✓	✓
Hungary	✓	–	–	–	–	✓	–
Iceland	✓	–	✓	✓	✓	✓	–
Ireland	✓	✓	–	–	–	✓	–
Italy	✓	✓	–	✓	–	✓	✓
Latvia	✓	–	–	–	–	–	–
Lithuania	✓	–	–	–	–	–	–
Luxembourg	✓	✓	–	✓	–	✓	✓
Macedonia	✓	–	–	–	–	–	–
Malta	✓	–	–	–	–	–	–
Netherlands	✓	✓	–	✓	–	✓	✓
Norway	✓	–	✓	✓	✓	✓	–
Poland	✓	–	–	–	–	✓	–
Portugal	✓	✓	–	✓	–	✓	✓
Romania	✓	–	–	–	–	–	–
Slovakia	✓	–	–	–	–	–	–
Slovenia	✓	–	–	–	–	–	–
Spain	✓	✓	–	✓	–	✓	✓
Sweden	✓	✓	–	–	✓	✓	–
Switzerland	✓	–	✓	–	–	✓	–
Turkey	✓	–	–	✓	–	✓	–
UK	✓	✓	–	✓	–	✓	✓
Yugoslavia	–	–	–	–	–	–	–

✓ full member   ◆ special guest status

Council of Europe

Established in 1949, the Council of Europe is the oldest of Europe's political institutions. It aims to promote European unity, protect human rights and assist in the cultural, social and economic development of its member states, but its powers are purely advisory. Founding states were Belgium, Denmark, France, Ireland, Italy, Luxembourg, the Netherlands, Norway, Sweden and the UK. It now counts 40 members. Its headquarters are in Strasbourg.

European Union (EU)

Founded by the Treaty of Rome in 1957, the European Economic Community, or Common Market as it was once known, broadened its scope far beyond economic measures as it developed into the European Community (1967) and finally the European Union (1993). Its original aims were to develop and expand the economies of its member states by abolishing customs tariffs, coordinating transportation systems and general economic policies, establishing a common economic policy towards non-member states, and promoting the free movement of labour and capital within its borders. Further measures included the abolishment of border controls and the linking of currency exchange rates. Since the 1991 Maastricht treaty, the EU is committed to establishing a common foreign and security policy and close cooperation in home affairs and the judiciary. A single European currency called the euro came into effect in January 1999.

The EEC's founding states were Belgium, France, West Germany, Italy, Luxembourg and the Netherlands – the Treaty of Rome was an extension of the European Coal and Steel Community (ECSC) founded by these six states in 1952. Denmark, Ireland and the UK joined in 1973, Greece in 1981, Spain and Portugal in 1986 and Austria, Finland and Sweden in 1995. Five more countries – Czech Republic, Estonia, Hungary, Poland and Slovenia – are expected to be granted full membership by 2002. The main EU organisations are the European Parliament (elected by direct universal suffrage, with growing powers), the European Commission (the daily government), the Council of Ministers (ministers of member states who make the important decisions) and the Court of Justice. The European Parliament meets in Strasbourg; Luxembourg is home to the Court of Justice. Other EU organisations are based in Brussels.

European Free Trade Association (EFTA)

Established in 1960 as a response to the creation of the European Economic Community, EFTA aims to eliminate trade tariffs on industrial products between member states, though each member retains the right to its own commercial policy towards nonmembers. Its four members (Iceland, Liechtenstein, Norway and Switzerland) cooperate with the EU through the European Economic Area agreement. Denmark and the UK left EFTA to join the EU in 1973 and others have since followed suit, leaving EFTA's future in doubt. Its headquarters are in Geneva.

North Atlantic Treaty Organisation (NATO)

The document creating this defence alliance was signed in 1949 by the USA, Canada and 10 European countries to safeguard their common political, social and economic systems against external threats (read: against the powerful Soviet military presence in Europe after WWII). An attack against any member state would be considered an attack against them all. Greece and Turkey joined in 1952, West Germany in 1955, and Spain in 1982; France withdrew from NATO's integrated military command in 1966 and Greece did likewise in 1974, though both remain members. NATO's Soviet counterpart, the Warsaw Pact founded in 1955, collapsed with the democratic revolutions of 1989 and the subsequent disintegration of the Soviet Union; most of its former members are now NATO associates. NATO's headquarters are in Brussels.

Nordic Council

Established in Copenhagen in 1952, the Nordic Council aims to promote economic, social and cultural cooperation among its member states (Denmark, Finland, Iceland, Norway and Sweden). Since 1971, the Council has acted as an advisory body to the Nordic Council of Ministers, a meeting of ministers from the member states responsible for the subject under discussion. Decisions taken by the Council of Ministers are usually binding, though member states retain full sovereignty. Environmental, tariff, labour and immigration policies are often coordinated.

Organisation for Economic Cooperation & Development (OECD)

The OECD was set up in 1961 to supersede the Organisation for European Economic Cooperation, which allocated US aid under the Marshall Plan and coordinated the reconstruction of postwar Europe. Sometimes seen as the club of the world's rich countries, the OECD aims to encourage economic growth and world trade. Its member states include most of Europe, as well as Australia, Canada, Japan, Mexico, New Zealand and the USA. Its headquarters are in Paris.

Western European Union (WEU)

Set up in 1955, the WEU was designed to coordinate the military defences between member states, to promote economic, social and cultural cooperation, and to encourage European integration. Social and cultural tasks were transferred to the Council of Europe in 1960, and these days the WEU is sometimes touted as a future, more 'European', alternative to NATO. It counts 10 full members and many more associate members and partners. Its headquarters are in Brussels.

Appendix IV – Alternative Place Names

The following abbreviations are used:

(A) Albanian	(Gr) Greek
(Ar) Arabic	(I) Italian
(B) Basque	(P) Portuguese
(C) Catalan	(S) Serbian
(Cr) Croatian	(Sle) Slovene
(E) English	(S) Spanish
(F) French	(T) Turkish
(G) German	

ALBANIA
Shgipëi
Durrës (A) – Durazzo
Korça (A) – Koritsa (Gr)
Lezha (A) – Allessio (I)
Saranda (E) – Sarandë (A)
Shkodra (E) – Shkodër (A), Scutari (I)
Tirana (E) – Tiranë (A)

CYPRUS
Kípros (Gr)
Kibris (T)
Gazimağusa (T) – Famagusta (Gr),
  Ammochostos (Gr)
Girne (T) – Kyrenia (Gr), Keryneia (Gr)
Lefkoşa (T) – Nicosia (Gr)
Limassol (Gr) – Lemessos (Gr)

CROATIA
Hrvatska
Brač (Cr) – Brazza (I)
Brijuni (Cr) – Brioni (I)
Cres (Cr) – Cherso
Dalmatia (E) – Dalmacija (Cr)
Dubrovnik (Cr) – Ragusa (I)
Hvar (Cr) – Lesina (I)
Korčula – Curzola (I)
Krk (Cr) – Veglia (I)
Kvarner (Cr) – Quarnero (I)
Losinj (Cr) – Lussino (I)
Mljet Island (Cr) – Melita (I)
Poreč (Cr) – Parenzo (I)
Rab (Cr) – Arbe (G)
Rijeka (Cr) – Fiume (I)
Rovinj (Cr) – Rovigno (I)
Split (Cr) – Spalato (I)
Trogir (Cr) – Trau (G)

Zadar (Cr) – Zara (I)
Zagreb (Cr) – Agram (G)

FRANCE
Bayonne (F, E) – Baiona (B)
Basque Country (E) – Euskadi (B),
  Pays Basque (F)
Burgundy (E) – Bourgogne (F)
Brittany (E) – Bretagne (F)
Corsica (E) – Corse (F)
French Riviera (E) – Côte d'Azur (F)
Dunkirk (E) – Dunkerque (F)
Channel Islands (E) – Îles Anglo-Normandes (F)
English Channel (E) – La Manche (F)
Lake Geneva (E) – Lac Léman (F)
Lyons (E) – Lyon (F)
Marseilles (E) – Marseille (F)
Normandy (E) – Normandie (F)
Rheims (E) – Reims (F)
Rhine (River) (E) – Rhin (F), Rhein (G)
Saint Jean de Luz (F) – Donibane Lohizune (B)
Saint Jean Pied de Port (F) – Donibane Garazi (B)
Sark (Channel Islands; E) – Sercq (F)

GREECE
Hellas (or Ελλας)
Athens (E) – Athina (Gr)
Corfu (E) – Kerkyra (Gr)
Crete (E) – Kriti (Gr)
Patras (E) – Patra (Gr)
Rhodes (E) – Rodos (Gr)
Salonica (E) – Thessaloniki (Gr)
Samothrace (E) – Samothraki (Gr)
Santorini (E, Gr, I) – Thira (Gr)

ITALY
Italia
Aeolian Islands (E) – Isole Eolie (I)
Apulia (E) – Puglia (I)
Florence (E) – Firenze (I)
Genoa (E) – Genova (I)
Herculaneum (E) – Ercolano (I)
Lombardy (E) – Lombardia (I)
Mantua (E) – Mantova (I)
Milan (E) – Milano (I)
Naples (E) – Napoli (I)
Padua (E) – Padova (I)
Rome (E) – Roma (I)

Sicily (E) – Sicilia (I)
Sardinia (E) – Sardegna (I)
Syracuse (E) – Siracusa (I)
Tiber (River) (E) – Tevere (I)
Venice (E) – Venezia (I)

MOROCCO
Ceuta (S) – Sebta (Ar)
Casablanca (F) – Dar al-Beida (Ar)
Marrakesh (E) – Marrakech (F)
Tangier (E) – Tanger (F), Tanja (Ar)

PORTUGAL
Cape St Vincent (E) – Cabo de São Vicente (P)
Lisbon (E) – Lisboa (P)
Oporto (E) – Porto (P)

SLOVENIA
Slovenija
Koper (Sle) – Capodistria (I)
Ljubljana (Sle) – Laibach (G)
Piran (Sle) – Pireos (Gk)
Postiojna Caves (Sle) – Adelsberger Grotten (G)
Vintgar Gorge (E) – Soteska Vintgar (Sle)

SPAIN
España
Andalusia (E) – Andalucía (S)
Balearic Islands (E) – Islas Baleares (S)
Basque Country (E) – Euskadi (B), País Vasco (S)
Catalonia (E) – Catalunya (C), Cataluña (S)
Cordova (E) – Córdoba (S)
Corunna (E) – La Coruña (S)

Majorca (E) – Mallorca (S)
Minorca (E) – Menorca (S)
Navarre (E) – Navarra (S)
San Sebastián (E, S) – Donostia (B)
Saragossa (E) – Zaragoza (S)
Seville (E) – Sevilla (S)

TURKEY
Türkiye
Cappadocia (E) – Kapadokya (T)
Ephesus (E) – Efes (T)
Euphrates River (E) – Firat (T)
Gallipoli (E) – Gelibolu (T)
İzmir (T) – Smyrna (G)
Mt Ararat (E) – Ağri Daği (T)
Mt Nimrod (E) – Nemrut Daği (T)
Thrace (E) – Trakya (T)
Tigris River (E) – Dicle (T)
Trebizond (E) – Trabzon (T)
Troy (E) – Truva (T)

YUGOSLAVIA
Jugoslavija
Bar (Se) – Antivari (I)
Belgrade (E) – Beograd (Se)
Deçan (A) – Dećani (Se)
Kotor (Se) – Cattaro (I)
Montenegro (E) – Crna Gora (Se)
Novi Sad (Se) – Neusatz (G)
Peć (Se) – Pejë (A)
Priština (Se) – Prishtinë
Serbia (Se) – Serbija (Se)
Ulcinj (Se) – Ulqin (A), Dulcigno (I)

Appendix V – International Country Abbreviations

The following is a list of official abbreviations that you may encounter on motor vehicles in Europe. Other abbreviations are likely to be unofficial ones, often referring to a particular region, province or even city. A vehicle entering a foreign country must carry a sticker identifying its country of registration, though this rule is not always enforced.

A	–	Austria
AL	–	Albania
AND	–	Andorra
B	–	Belgium
BG	–	Bulgaria
BIH	–	Bosnia-Hercegovina
BY	–	Belarus
CDN	–	Canada
CH	–	Switzerland
CY	–	Cyprus
CZ	–	Czech Republic
D	–	Germany
DK	–	Denmark
DZ	–	Algeria
E	–	Spain
EST	–	Estonia
ET	–	Egypt
F	–	France
FIN	–	Finland
FL	–	Liechtenstein
FR	–	Faroe Islands
GB	–	Great Britain
GE	–	Georgia
GR	–	Greece
H	–	Hungary
HKJ	–	Jordan
HR	–	Croatia
I	–	Italy
IL	–	Israel
IRL	–	Ireland
IS	–	Iceland
L	–	Luxembourg

LAR	–	Libya
LT	–	Lithuania
LV	–	Latvia
M	–	Malta
MA	–	Morocco
MC	–	Monaco
MD	–	Moldavia
MK	–	Macedonia
N	–	Norway
NGR	–	Nigeria
NL	–	Netherlands
NZ	–	New Zealand
P	–	Portugal
PL	–	Poland
RL	–	Lebanon
RO	–	Romania
RSM	–	San Marino
RUS	–	Russia
S	–	Sweden
SK	–	Slovakia
SLO	–	Slovenia
SYR	–	Syria
TN	–	Tunisia
TR	–	Turkey
UA	–	Ukraine
USA	–	United States of America
V	–	Vatican City
YU	–	Yugoslavia
ZA	–	South Africa

OTHER

CC	–	Consular Corps
CD	–	Diplomatic Corps
GBA	–	Alderney
GBG	–	Guernsey
GBJ	–	Jersey
GBM	–	Isle of Man
GBZ	–	Gibraltar

Language

This language guide contains pronunciation tips and basic vocabulary to help you get around Mediterranean Europe. For background information about each language see the individual country chapters. For more extensive coverage of the languages included here, see Lonely Planet's *Mediterranean Europe* and *Western Europe phrasebooks*.

Albanian

Pronunciation

Written Albanian is phonetically consistent and pronunciation shouldn't pose too many problems for English speakers. The Albanian 'rr' is trilled and each vowel in a diphthong is pronounced. However, Albanian possesses certain letters that are present in English but rendered differently. These include:

c	as the 'ts' in 'bits'
ç	as the 'ch' in 'church'
dh	as the 'th' in 'this'
gj	as the 'gy' in 'hogyard'
j	as the 'y' in 'yellow'
q	between 'ch' and 'ky', similar to the 'cu' in 'cure'
th	as the 'th' in 'thistle'
x	as the 'dz' in 'adze'
xh	as the 'j' in 'jewel'
zh	as the 's' in 'pleasure'

Basics

Hello.	*Tungjatjeta.*
Goodbye.	*Lamtumirë.*
	Mirupafshim. (informal)
Yes.	*Po.*
No.	*Jo.*
Please.	*Ju lutem.*
Thank you.	*Ju falem nderit.*
That's fine.	*Eshtë e mirë.*
You're welcome.	*S'ka përse.*
Excuse me.	*Me falni.*
Sorry. (excuse me, forgive me)	*Më vjen keq. (më falni, ju lutem)*
Do you speak English?	*A flisni anglisht?*

How much is it?	*Sa kushton?*
What's your name?	*Si quheni ju lutem?*
My name is ...	*Unë quhem ... /Mua më quajnë*

Getting Around

What time does the ... leave/arrive?	*Në ç'orë niset /arrin ...?*
boat	*barka/lundra*
bus	*autobusi*
tram	*tramvaji*
train	*treni*

I'd like ...	*Dëshiroj ...*
a one-way ticket	*një biletë vajtje*
a return ticket	*një biletë vajtje-ardhje*

1st/2nd class	*klas i parë/i dytë*
timetable	*orar*
bus stop	*stacion autobusi*

Where is ...?	*Ku është ...?*
Go straight ahead.	*Shko drejt.*
Turn left.	*Kthehu majtas.*
Turn right.	*Kthehu djathtas.*
far/near	*larg/afër*

Around Town

a bank	*një bankë*
the ... embassy	*... ambasadën*
my hotel	*hotelin tim*

Signs

HYRJE	ENTRANCE
DALJE	EXIT
PLOTSKA VENDE TË	FULL/NO VACANCIES
INFORMACION	INFORMATION
HAPUR/MBYLLUR	OPEN/CLOSED
E NDALUAR	PROHIBITED
POLICIA	POLICE
STACIONI I POLICISË	POLICE STATION
NEVOJTORJA BURRA/GRA	TOILETS MEN/WOMEN

Emergencies

Help!	Ndihmë!
Call a doctor!	Thirrni doktorin!
Call the police!	Thirrni policinë!
Go away!	Zhduku!/Largohuni!
I'm lost.	Kam humbur rrugë

the post office	postën
the market	pazarin
chemist/pharmacy	farmaci
newsagency	agjensia e lajmeve
the telephone exchange	centrali telefonik
the tourist office	zyra e informimeve turistike

What time does it open/close?	Në ç'ore hapet/mbyllet?

Accommodation

hotel	hotel
camping ground	vend kampimi

Do you have any rooms available?	A keni ndonjë dhomë të lirë?

a single room	një dhomë teke
a double room	një dhomë më dy krevatë

How much is it per night/per person?	Sa kushton një natë/për person?
Does it include breakfast?	A e përfshin edhe mëngjesin?

Time, Days & Numbers

What time is it?	Sa është ora?
today	sot
tomorrow	nesër
yesterday	dje
morning	mëngjes
afternoon	mbasdite

Monday	e hënë
Tuesday	e martë
Wednesday	e mërkurë
Thursday	e enjte
Friday	e premte
Saturday	e shtunë
Sunday	e diel

1	një	7	shtatë
2	dy	8	tetë
3	tre	9	nëntë
4	katër	10	dhjetë
5	pesë	100	njëqind
6	gjashtë	1000	njëmijë

one million	një milion

Bosnian, Croatian & Serbian

Pronunciation

The writing systems of Bosnian, Croatian and Serbian are phonetically consistent: every letter is pronounced and its sound will not vary from word to word. With regard to the position of stress, only one rule can be given: the last syllable of a word is never stressed. In most cases the accent falls on the first vowel in the word.

Serbian uses the Cyrillic alphabet so it's worth familiarising yourself with it (see the Macedonian section in this chapter). Bosnian and Croatian use a Roman alphabet; many letters are pronounced as in English – the following are some specific pronunciations.

c	as the 'ts' in 'cats'
ć	as the 'cu' in 'cure'
č	as the 'ch' in 'chop'
đ	as the 'gu' in 'legume'
dž	as the 'j' in 'just'
j	as the 'y' in 'young'
lj	as the 'lli' in 'million'
nj	as the 'ny' in 'canyon'
š	as the 'sh' in 'hush'
ž	as the 's' in 'pleasure'

The principal difference between Serbian and Croatian is in the pronunciation of the vowel 'e' in certain words. A long 'e' in Serbian becomes 'ije' in Croatian (eg reka, rijeka, 'river'), and a short 'e' in Serbian becomes 'je' in Croatian (eg pesma, pjesma, 'song'). Sometimes, however, the vowel 'e' is the same in both languages, as in selo, 'village'. Bosnian shares some of its vocab with both Serbian and Croatian. There are also a number of variations in vocabulary. In the following

phraselist these are indicated with 'B' for
Bosnian, 'C' for Croatian and 'S' for Serbian.

Basics

Hello.
   Zdravo.   Здраво.
Goodbye.
   Do viđenja.   До виђења.
Yes.
   Da.   Да.
No.
   Ne.   Не.
Please.
   Molim.   Молим.
Thank you.
   Hvala.   Вала.
That's fine/
You're welcome.
   U redu je/   У реду јеју/
   Nema na čemu. Нема на чему.
Excuse me.
   Oprostite.   Опростите.
Sorry. (excuse me,
forgive me)
   Pardon. (izvinite) Пардон. (опростите
                   извините)
Do you speak
English?
   Govorite li   Говорите ли
   engleski?   енглески?
How much is it ...?
   Koliko košta ...? Колико кошта ...?
What's your name?
   Kako se zovete? Како се зовете?
My name is ...
   Zovem se ...   Зовем се ...

Getting Around

What time does
the ... leave/arrive?
   Kada ...   Када ...
   dolazi (C)/   долазиюполази?
   polazi (S)?

boat
   brod   брод
bus (city)
   autobus   аутобус
   (gradski)   (градски)
bus (intercity)
   autobus   аутобус
   (međugradski) (међуградски)

train
   voz (S, B)/   воз
   vlak (C)
tram
   tramvaj   трамвај

one-way ticket
   kartu u jednom карту у једном
   pravcu   правцу
return ticket
   povratnu kartu повратну карту
1st class
   prvu klasu   прву класу
2nd class
   drugu klasu другу класу

Where is the bus/tram stop?
   (Gde/Gdje) je autobuska/tramvajska
   stanica (S/B, C)/postaja (C)?
   Где је аутобуска/грамвајска станица?

Signs

ENTRANCE/EXIT
   УЛАЗ/ИЗЛАЗ
   ULAZ/IZLAZ
FULL/NO VACANCIES
   СВЕ ЈЕ ЗАУЗЕТО/НЕМА СЛОСО
   SVE JE ZAUZETO/
   NEMA SLOBODNE SOBE
INFORMATION
   ИНФОРМАЦИЈЕ
   INFORMACIJE
OPEN/CLOSED
   ОТВОРЕНО/ЗАТВОРЕНО
   OTVORENO/ZATVORENO
POLICE
   МИЛИЦИЈА
   MILICIJA (S)/POLICIJA (B, C)
POLICE STATION
   СТАНИЦА МИЛИЦИЈЕ
   STANICA MILICIJE (S)/POLICIJA (B, C)
PROHIBITED
   ЗАЊЕНО
   ZABRANJENO
ROOMS AVAILABLE
   СЛОСО
   SLOBODNE SOBE
TOILETS
   ТОАЛЕТИ
   TOALETI (S, B)/ZAHODI (C)

Can you show me (on the map)?
Možete li mi pokazati (na karti)?
Можете ли ми показати (на карти)?
Go straight ahead.
Idite pravo napred (S)/*naprijed* (B, C)
Идите право напред.
Turn left.
Skrenite lijevo. (B, C)/*Skrenite levo.* (S)
Скрените лево.
Turn right.
Skrenite desno.
Скрените десно.
near
blizu
близу
far
daleko
далеку

Around Town
bank
banka   банка
... embassy
... ambasada   амбасада
my hotel
moj hotel   vjå отел
post office
pošta   пошта
market
tržnica (C)/   пијаца
pijaca (B, S)
telephone centre
telefonska   телефонска централа
centrala
tourist office
turistički   туристички
informativni biro информативни ьиро

Accommodation
hotel
hotel   отел
guesthouse
privatno   приватно
prenoćište   преноћиште
youth hostel
omladinsko   омладинско
prenoćište   преноћиште
camping ground
kamping   кампинг

Do you have any rooms available?
Imate li slobodne sobe?
Имате ли слоьодне соье?

How much is it per night/per person?
Koliko košta za jednu noć/po osobi?
Колико кошта за једну ноћ/по особи?
Does it include breakfast?
Dali je u cenu (S)/*cijenu* (B, C)
uključen i doručak?
Дали је у цену укључен и доручак?

I'd like ...
Želim ...
Желим ...

a single room
sobu sa jednim krevetom
собу са једним креветом
a double room
sobu sa duplim krevetom
собу са дуплим креветом

Time, Days & Numbers
What time is it?
Koliko je sati?   Колико је сати?
today
danas   данас
tomorrow
sutra   сутра
yesterday
juče (S, B)   јуче
jučer (C)

Emergencies

Help!
Upomoć!
Упомоћ!
Call a doctor!
Pozovite lekara! (B, S)
Pozovite liječnika! (C)
Позовите лекара!
Call the police!
Pozovite miliciju! (S)
Pozovite policiju! (C)
Позовите милицију!
Go away!
Idite!
Идите!
I'm lost.
Izgubio sam se. (m)
Izgubina sam se. (f)
Изгубљен/Изгубљена сам се.

n the morning		
ujutro	ујутро	
n the afternoon		
popodne	поподне	

Monday		
ponedeljak	понедељак	
Tuesday		
utorak	уторак	
Wednesday		
sreda (S)	среда	
srijeda (B, C)		
Thursday		
četvrtak	четвртак	
Friday		
petak	петак	
Saturday		
subota	субота	
Sunday		
nedelja (S)	недеља	
nedjelja (B, C)		

1	*jedan*	један
2	*dva*	два
3	*tri*	три
4	*četiri*	четири
5	*pet*	пет
6	*šest*	шест
7	*sedam*	седам
8	*osam*	осам
9	*devet*	девет
10	*deset*	десет
100	*sto*	сто
1000	*hiljada* (B, S)	иљада
	tisuća (C)	

one million *jedan milion* (S) један милион
jedan milijun (B, C)

French

Pronunciation

French has a number of sounds which are difficult for Anglophones to produce. These include:

- The distinction between the 'u' sound (as in *tu*) and 'oo' sound (as in *tout*). For both sounds, the lips are rounded and projected forward, but for the 'u' the tongue is towards the front of the mouth, its tip against the lower front teeth, whereas for the 'oo' the tongue is towards the back of the mouth, its tip behind the gums of the lower front teeth.
- The nasal vowels. During the production of nasal vowels the breath escapes partly through the nose and partly through the mouth. There are no nasal vowels in English; in French there are three, as in *bon vin blanc*, 'good white wine'. These sounds occur where a syllable ends in a single 'n' or 'm'; the 'n' or 'm' is silent but indicates the nasalisation of the preceding vowel.
- The 'r'. The standard 'r' of Parisian French is produced by moving the bulk of the tongue backwards to constrict the air flow in the pharynx while the tip of the tongue rests behind the lower front teeth. It's similar to the noise made by some people before spitting, but with much less friction.

Basics

Hello.	*Bonjour.*
Goodbye.	*Au revoir.*
Yes/No.	*Oui/Non.*
Please.	*S'il vous plaît.*
Thank you.	*Merci.*
That's fine, you're welcome.	*Je vous en prie.*
Excuse me.	*Excusez-moi.*
I'm sorry.	*Pardon*
Do you speak English?	*Parlez-vous anglais?*
How much is it?	*C'est combien?*
What's your name?	*Comment vous appelez-vous?*
My name is ...	*Je m'appelle ...*

Getting Around

When does the next ... leave/arrive?	*À quelle heure part/ arrive le prochain ...?*
boat	*bateau*
bus (city)	*bus*
bus (intercity)	*car*
tram	*tramway*
train	*train*
1st class	*première classe*
2nd class	*deuxième classe*

left luggage (office)	*consigne*
timetable	*horaire*
bus/tram stop	*arrêt d'autobus/ de tramway*
train station/ ferry terminal	*gare/gare maritime*

I'd like to hire a car/bicycle.	*Je voudrais louer une voiture/un vélo.*
Where is ...?	*Où est ...?*
Go straight ahead.	*Continuez tout droit.*
Turn left.	*Tournez à gauche.*
Turn right.	*Tournez à droite.*
far/near	*loin/proche*

I'd like a ... ticket.	*Je voudrais un billet ...*
one-way	*aller simple.*
return ticket	*aller retour.*

Around Town

a bank	*une banque*
the ... embassy	*l'ambassade de ...*
my hotel	*mon hôtel*
post office	*le bureau de poste*
market	*le marché*
chemist/pharmacy	*la pharmacie*
newsagency/ stationers	*l'agence de presse/ la papeterie*
a public telephone	*une cabine téléphonique*
the tourist office	*l'office de tourisme/ le syndicat d'initiative*
What time does it open/close?	*Quelle est l' heure de ouverture/fermeture?*

Signs

ENTRÉE	ENTRANCE
SORTIE	EXIT
COMPLET	FULL/ NO VACANCIES
RENSEIGNEMENTS	INFORMATION
OUVERT/FERMÉ	OPEN/CLOSED
INTERDIT	PROHIBITED
(COMMISSARIAT DE) POLICE	POLICE STATION
CHAMBRES LIBRES	ROOMS AVAILABLE
TOILETTES, WC	TOILETS
HOMMES	MEN
FEMMES	WOMEN

Emergencies

Help!	*Au secours!*
Call a doctor!	*Appelez un médecin!*
Call the police!	*Appelez la police!*
Leave me alone!	*Fichez-moi la paix!*
I'm lost.	*Je me suis égaré/ée*

Accommodation

the hotel	*l'hôtel*
the youth hostel	*l'auberge de jeunesse*
the camping ground	*le camping*
Do you have any rooms available?	*Est-ce que vous avez des chambres libres?*
How much is it per night/ per person?	*Quel est le prix par nuit/ par personne?*
Is breakfast included?	*Est-ce que le petit dé- jeuner est compris?*
for one person	*pour une personne*
for two people	*deux personnes*

Time, Days & Numbers

What time is it?	*Quelle heure est-il?*
today	*aujourd'hui*
tomorrow	*demain*
yesterday	*hier*
morning/afternoon	*matin/après-midi*

Monday	*lundi*
Tuesday	*mardi*
Wednesday	*mercredi*
Thursday	*jeudi*
Friday	*vendredi*
Saturday	*samedi*
Sunday	*dimanche*

1	*un*
2	*deux*
3	*trois*
4	*quatre*
5	*cinq*
6	*six*
7	*sept*
8	*huit*
9	*neuf*
10	*dix*
100	*cent*
1000	*mille*
one million	*un million*

Greek

Alphabet & Pronunciation

Pronunciation of Greek letters is shown using the closest-sounding English letter.

Greek	English	Pronunciation
A α	a	as in 'father'
B β	v	as the 'v' in 'vine'
Γ γ	gh, y	like a rough 'g', or as the 'y' in 'yes'
Δ δ	dh	as the 'th' in 'then'
E ε	e	as in 'egg'
Z ζ	z	as in 'zoo'
H η	i	as the 'ee' in 'feet'
Θ θ	th	as the 'th' in 'throw'
I ι	i	as the 'ee' in 'feet'
K κ	k	as in 'kite'
Λ λ	l	as in 'leg'
M μ	m	as in 'man'
N ν	n	as in 'net'
Ξ ξ	x	as the 'ks' in 'looks'
O o	o	as in 'hot'
Π π	p	as in 'pup'
P ρ	r	slightly trilled 'r'
Σ σ	s	as in 'sand' ('ς' at the end of a word)
T τ	t	as in 'to'
Y υ	i	as the 'ee' in 'feet'
Φ φ	f	as in 'fee'
X χ	kh, h	as the 'ch' in Scottish *loch*, or as a rough 'h'
Ψ ψ	ps	as the 'ps' in 'lapse'
Ω ω	o	as in 'lot'

Letter Combinations

ει, οι	i	as the 'ee' in 'feet'
αι	e	as in 'bet'
ου	u	as the 'oo' in 'mood'
μπ	b	as in 'be'
	mb	as in 'amber' (or as the 'mp' in 'ample')
ντ	d	as in 'do'
	nd	as in 'bend' (or as the 'nt' in 'sent')
γκ	g	as in 'go'
γγ	ng	as the 'ng' in 'angle'
γξ	ks	as in 'yaks'
τζ	dz	as the 'ds' in 'suds'

Certain pairs of vowels are pronounced separately if the first has an acute accent (eg ά), or the second has a dieresis (eg ï).

All Greek words of two or more syllables have an acute accent which indicates where the stress falls. The suffix of some Greek words depends on the gender of the speaker, eg, *asthmatikos* (m) and *asthmatikya* (f), or *epileptikos* (m) and *epileptikya* (f).

Basics

Hello.	*yasu* (inf)/ *yasas* (polite, plural)
Goodbye.	*andio*
Yes.	*ne*
No.	*okhi*
Please.	*sas parakalo*
Thank you.	*sas efkharisto*
That's fine/ You're welcome.	*ine endaksi/parakalo*
Excuse me. (forgive me)	*signomi*
Do you speak English?	*milate anglika?*
How much is it?	*poso kani?*
What's your name?	*pos sas lene/ pos legeste?*
My name is ...	*me lene ...*

Getting Around

What time does the ... leave/arrive?	*ti ora fevyi/apo horito ...?*
boat	*to plio*
bus (city)	*to leoforio (ya tin boli)*
bus (intercity)	*to leoforio (ya ta proastia)*
tram	*to tram*
train	*to treno*

Signs

ΕΙΣΟΔΟΣ	ENTRANCE
ΕΞΟΔΟΣ	EXIT
ΠΛΗΡΟΦΟΡΙΕΣ	INFORMATION
ΑΝΟΙΚΤΟ	OPEN
ΚΛΕΙΣΤΟ	CLOSED
ΑΣΤΥΝΟΜΙΚΟΣ ΣΤΑΘΜΟΣ	POLICE STATION
ΑΠΑΓΟΡΕΥΕΤΑΙ	PROHIBITED
ΤΟΥΑΛΕΤΕΣ	TOILETS
ΑΝΔΡΩΝ	MEN
ΓΥΝΑΙΚΩΝ	WOMEN

I'd like a ... ticket.	*tha ithela isitirio ...*
one-way	*horis epistrofi*
return	*met epistrois*

1st class	*proti thesi*
2nd class	*dhefteri thesi*
left luggage	*horos aspokevon*
timetable	*dhromologhio*
bus stop	*i stasi tu leoforiu*

Go straight ahead.	*pighenete efthia*
Turn left.	*stripste aristera*
Turn right.	*stripste dheksya*

Around Town

a bank	*mia trapeza*
the ... embassy	*i ... presvia*
the hotel	*to ksenodho khio*
the post office	*to takhidhromio*
the market	*i aghora*
pharmacy	*farmakio*
newsagency	*efimeridhon*
the telephone centre	*to tilefoniko kentro*
the tourist office	*to ghrafio turistikon pliroforion*

What time does it open/close?	*ti ora aniyi/klini?*

Accommodation

a hotel	*ena xenothohio*
a youth hostel	*enas xenonas neoitos*
a camp site	*ena kamping*

I'd like a ... room.	*thelo ena dhomatio ...*
single	*ya ena atomo*
double	*ya dhio atoma*

How much is it ...?	*poso kostizi ...?*
per night	*ya ena vradhi*
per person	*ya ena atomo*

Time, Days & Numbers

What time is it?	*ti ora ine?*
today	*simera*
tomorrow	*avrio*
yesterday	*hthes*
in the morning	*to proi*
in the afternoon	*to apoyevma*

Monday	*dheftera*
Tuesday	*triti*

Wednesday	*tetarti*
Thursday	*pempti*
Friday	*paraskevi*
Saturday	*savato*
Sunday	*kiryaki*

1	*ena*	7	*epta*
2	*dhio*	8	*okhto*
3	*tria*	9	*enea*
4	*tesera*	10	*dheka*
5	*pende*	100	*ekato*
6	*eksi*	1000	*khilya*

one million	*ena ekatomirio*

Italian

Pronunciation

Italian pronunciation isn't difficult once you learn a few basic rules. Although some of the more clipped vowels and stress on double letters require careful practice for English speakers, it's easy enough to make yourself understood.

Vowels Vowels are generally more clipped than in English.

a	as the second 'a' in 'camera'
e	as the 'ay' in 'day', but without the 'i' sound
i	as the 'ee' in 'see'
o	as in 'dot'
u	as the 'oo' in 'too'

Consonants The pronunciation of many Italian consonants is similar to that of English. The following sounds depend on certain rules:

c	as 'k' before a, o and u; as the 'ch' in 'choose' before e and i
ch	a hard 'k' sound
g	as in 'get' before a, o
gh	as in 'get'
gli	as the 'lli' in 'million'
gn	as the 'ny' in 'canyon'
h	always silent
r	a rolled 'rrr' sound
sc	as the 'sh' in 'sheep' before e and i; a hard sound as in 'school' before h, a, o and u
z	as the 'ts' in 'lights' or as the 'ds' in 'beds'

Note that, unless it's accented, the i in 'ci', 'gi' and 'sci' isn't pronounced when followed by a, o or u. Thus the name 'Giovanni' is pronounced 'joh-VAHN-nee' – the 'i' sound after the 'G' is not pronounced.

Stress Stress often falls on the next to last syllable, as in 'spaghetti'. When a word has an accent, the stress is on that syllable, as in *città* (city). Double consonants are pronounced as a longer, often more forceful sound than a single consonant.

Basics

Hello.	*Buongiorno.* (pol)/ *Ciao.* (inf)
Goodbye.	*Arrivederci.* (pol)/ *Ciao.* (inf)
Yes/No.	*Sì/No.*
Please.	*Per favore/Per piacere.*
Thank you.	*Grazie.*
You're welcome.	*Prego.*
Excuse me.	*Mi scusi.*
Sorry. (forgive me)	*Mi scusi/Mi perdoni.*
Do you speak English?	*Parla inglese?*
How much is it?	*Quanto costa?*
What's your name?	*Come si chiama?*
My name is ...	*Mi chiamo ...*

Getting Around

What time does the ... leave/arrive?	*A che ora parte/ arriva ...?*
boat	*la barca*
bus	*l'autobus*
ferry	*il traghetto*
train	*il treno*
tram	*il tram*

I'd like to hire a car/bicycle.	*Vorrei noleggiare una macchina/bicicletta.*
I'd like a one-way/ return ticket.	*Vorrei un biglietto di solo andata/ di andata e ritorno.*

1st class	*prima classe*
2nd class	*seconda classe*
left luggage	*deposito bagagli*
timetable	*orario*
bus stop	*fermata dell'autobus*
train station	*stazione*
ferry terminal	*stazione marittima*

Where is ...?	*Dov'è ...?*
Go straight ahead.	*Si va sempre diritto.*
Turn left.	*Giri a sinistra.*
Turn right.	*Giri a destra.*
far/near	*lontano/vicino*

Around Town

a bank	*una banca*
the ... embassy	*l'ambasciata di ...*
my hotel	*il mio albergo*
post office	*la posta*
market	*il mercato*
chemist/pharmacy	*la farmacia*
newsagency	*l'edicola*

Signs	
INGRESSO/ ENTRATA	ENTRANCE
USCITA	EXIT
COMPLETO	FULL/ NO VACANCIES
INFORMAZIONE	INFORMATION
APERTO/CHIUSO	OPEN/CLOSED
PROIBITO/ VIETATO	PROHIBITED
POLIZIA/ CARABINIERI	POLICE
QUESTURA	POLICE STATION
CAMERE LIBERE	ROOMS AVAILABLE
GABINETTI/BAGNI	TOILETS
UOMINI	MEN
DONNE	WOMEN

Emergencies

Help!	*Aiuto!*
Call a doctor!	*Chiama un dottore/*
	un medico!
Call the police!	*Chiama la polizia!*
Go away!	*Vai via!* (informal)
I'm lost.	*Mi sono perso/*
	persa. (m/f)

stationers	*il cartolaio*
telephone centre	*il centro telefonico*
the tourist office	*l'ufficio di turismo*

What time does it open/close?	*A che ora (si) apre/chiude?*

Accommodation

hotel	*albergo*
guesthouse	*pensione*
youth hostel	*ostello per la gioventù*
camping ground	*campeggio*

Do you have any rooms available?	*Ha delle camere libere/ C'è una camera libera?*
How much is it per night/per person?	*Quanto costa per la notte/ciascuno?*
Is breakfast included?	*È compresa la colazione?*

a single room	*una camera singola*
a double/twin room	*una camera matrimoniale/doppia*
for one night	*per una notte*
for two nights	*per due notti*

Time, Days & Numbers

What time is it?	*Che ora è?/ Che ore sono?*
today	*oggi*
tomorrow	*domani*
yesterday	*ieri*
morning	*mattina*
afternoon	*pomeriggio*

Monday	*lunedì*
Tuesday	*martedì*
Wednesday	*mercoledì*

Thursday	*giovedì*
Friday	*venerdì*
Saturday	*sabato*
Sunday	*domenica*

1	*uno*
2	*due*
3	*tre*
4	*quattro*
5	*cinque*
6	*sei*
7	*sette*
8	*otto*
9	*nove*
10	*dieci*
100	*cento*
1000	*mille*
one million	*un milione*

Macedonian

Pronunciation

The spelling of Macedonian is more or less phonetic: almost every word is written exactly the way it's pronounced and every letter is pronounced. With regard to the position of the stress accent, only one rule can be given: the last syllable of a word is never stressed. There are 31 letters in the Cyrillic alphabet. The pronunciation of the Roman or Cyrillic letter is given to the nearest English equivalent.

Basics

Hello.
   Zdravo.   Здраво.
Goodbye.
   Priatno.   Приатно.
Yes/No.
   Da/Ne.   Да/Не.
Please.
   Molam.   Молам.
Thank you.
   Blagodaram.   благодарам.
You're welcome.
   Nema zošto/   Нема зошто/
   Milo mi e.   мило ми е.
Excuse me.
   Izvinete.   Извинете.
Sorry. (forgive me)
   Oprostete ve   Опростете ве молам.
   molam.

The Cyrillic Alphabet

Cyrillic	Roman	English Pronunciation
А а	a	as in 'rather'
Б б	b	as in 'be'
В в	v	as in 'vodka'
Г г	g	as in 'go'
Д д	d	as in 'do'
Ѓ ѓ	gj	as the 'gu' in 'legume'
Е е	e	as the 'e' in 'bear'
Ж ж	zh	as the 's' in 'pleasure'
З з	z	as in 'zero'
Ѕ ѕ	zj	as the 'ds' in suds
И и	i	as the 'i' in 'machine'
Ј ј	j	as the 'y' in 'young'
К к	k	as in 'keg'
Л л	l	as in 'let'
Љ љ	lj	as the 'lli' in 'million'
М м	m	as in 'map'
Н н	n	as in 'no'
Њ њ	nj	as the 'ny' in 'canyon'
О о	o	as the 'aw' in 'shawl'
П п	p	as in 'pop'
Р р	r	as in 'rock'
С с	s	as in 'safe'
Т т	t	as in 'too'
Ќ ќ	ć	as the 'cu' in 'cure'
У у	u	as the 'oo' in 'room'
Ф ф	f	as in 'fat'
Х х	h	as in 'hot'
Ц ц	c	as the 'ts' in 'cats'
Ч ч	č	as the 'ch' in 'chop'
Џ џ	dz	as the 'j' in 'judge'
Ш ш	š	as the 'sh' in 'shoe'

Do you speak English?
Zboruvate li angliski? — Зборувате ли англиски?

What's your name?
Kako se vikate? — Како се викате?

My name is ...
Jas se vikam ... — Јас се викам ...

How much is it?
Kolku čini toa? — Колку чини тоа?

Getting Around

What time does the next ... leave/arrive?
Koga doagja/zaminuva idniot ...?
Кога доаѓаю/заминува идниот ...?

boat
brod — брод

bus (city)
avtobus (gradski) — автобус (градски)

bus (intercity)
avtobus (megjugradski) — автобус (меѓуградски)

train
voz — воз

tram
tramvaj — трамвај

I'd like ...
Sakam ... — Сакам ...

a one-way ticket
bilet vo eden pravec — билет во еден правец

a return ticket
povraten bilet — повратен билет

1st class
prva klasa — прва класа

2nd class
vtora klasa — втора класа

timetable
vozen red — возен ред

bus stop
avtobuska stanica — автобуска станица

train station
eleznička stanica — железничка станица

Where is ...?
Kade je ...? — Каде је ...?

Go straight ahead.
Odete pravo napred. — Одете право напред.

Turn left/right.
Svrtete levo/desno. — Свртете ево/десно.

far/near
daleku/blisku — далеку/блиску

I'd like to hire a car/bicycle.
Sakam da iznajmam kola/točak.
Сакам да изнајмам колаю/точак.

Around Town

bank
banka — банка

the embassy
ambasadata — амбасадата

my hotel
mojot hotel — мојот отел

the post office
poštata — поштата

Signs

ENTRANCE
 ВЛЕЗ
 VLEZ
EXIT
 ИЗЛЕЗ
 IZLEZ
FULL/NO VACANCIES
 ПОЛНО/НЕМА МЕСТО
 POLNO/NEMA MESTO
INFORMATION
 ИНФОРМАЦИИ
 INFORMACII
OPEN/CLOSED
 ОТВОРЕНО/ЗАТВОРЕНО
 OTVORENO/ZATVORENO
POLICE
 ПОЛИЦИЈА
 POLICIJA
POLICE STATION
 ПОЛИЦИСКА СТАНИЦА
 POLICISKA STANICA
PROHIBITED
 ЗАБРАНЕТО
 ZABRANETO
ROOMS AVAILABLE
 СОЗА ИЗДАВАЊЕ
 SOBI ZA IZDAVANJE
TOILETS (MEN/WOMEN)
 КЛОЗЕТИб (МАШКИ/ЖЕНСКИ)
 KLOZETI, (MAŠKI/ENSKI)

the market
 pazarot пазарот
chemist/pharmacy
 apteka аптека
newsagency/
stationers
 kiosk za vesnici/ киоск за весници/
 knižarnica ryb;fhybwf
the telephone centre
 telefonskata телефонската
 centrala централа
the tourist office
 turističkoto biro туристичкото биро

What time does it
open/close?
 Koga se otvora/ Кога се отвора/
 zatvora? затвора?

Accommodation
Do you have any rooms available?
 Dali imate slobodni sobi?
 Дали имате слободни соби?
How much is it per night/per person?
 Koja e cenata po noć/po osoba?
 Која е цената по нокюпо особа?
Does it include breakfast?
 Dali e vključen pojadok?
 Дали е вклучен ројадок?

hotel
 hotel
 отел
guesthouse
 privatno smetuvanje
 приватно сметување
youth hostel
 mladinsko prenokevalište
 младинско преноќевалиште
camping ground
 kamping
 кампинг

a single room
 soba so eden krevet
 соба со еден кревет
a double room
 soba so bračen krevet
 соба со брачен кревет
for one/two nights
 za edna/dva večeri
 за еднаюдва вечери

Time, Days & Numbers
What time is it?
 Kolku e časot?
 Колку е часот?

Emergencies

Help!
 Pomoš! Помош!
Call a doctor!
 Povikajte lekar! Повикајте лекар!
Call the police!
 Viknete policija! Викнете полиција!
Go away!
 Odete si! Одете си!
I'm lost.
 Jas zaginav. Јас загинав.

today		
denes	денес	
tomorrow		
utre	утре	
yesterday		
včera	вчера	
morning		
utro	утро	
afternoon		
popladne	попладне	

Monday		
onedelnik	понеделник	
Tuesday		
vtornik	вторник	
Wednesday		
sreda	среда	
Thursday		
chetvrtok	четврток	
Friday		
petok	петок	
Saturday		
sabota	сабота	
Sunday		
nedela	недела	

1	*eden*	еден
2	*dva*	два
3	*tri*	три
4	*četiri*	четири
5	*pet*	пет
6	*šest*	шест
7	*sedum*	седум
8	*osum*	осум
9	*devet*	девет
10	*deset*	десет
100	*sto*	сто
one million	*eden milion*	еден милион

Maltese

The following is a brief guide to Maltese pronunciation, and includes a few useful words and phrases.

Pronunciation

ċ	as the 'ch' in child
ġ	as in good
ġ	'soft' as the 'j' in job
għ	silent; lengthens the vowel following it
h	silent, except when preceded by 'g'

ħ	as the 'h' in hello
j	as 'y'
ij	as the 'igh' in high
ej	as the 'ay' in say
q	a very faint 'kh' sound
x	as the 'sh' in shop
z	as the 'ts' in 'bits'
ż	'soft' as in 'buzz'

Basics

Good morning/ Good day.	*Bonġu.*
Goodbye.	*Saħħa.*
Yes/No.	*Iva/Le.*
Please.	*Jekk jogħġobok.*
Thank you.	*Grazzi.*
Excuse me.	*Skużani.*
Do you speak English?	*Titkellem bl-ingliż?* (informal)
How much is it?	*Kemm?*
What's your name?	*X'ismek?*
My name is ...	*Jisimni ...*

Getting Around

When does the boat leave/arrive?	*Meta jitlaq il-vapur?*
When does the bus leave/arrive?	*Meta titlaq il-karozza?*
I'd like a ... ticket. one-way/return 1st/2nd class	*Nixtieq biljett ...* *'one-way/return'* *'1st/2nd class'*
left luggage	*bagalji*
bus/trolleybus stop	*xarabank/coach*
I'd like to hire a car/bicycle.	*Nixtieq nikri karozza/rota.*

Signs

DHUL	ENTRANCE
HRUG	EXIT
INFORMAZJONI	INFORMATION
MIFTUH	OPEN
MAGHLUQ	CLOSED
TIDHOLX	NO ENTRY
PULIZIJA	POLICE
TOILETS	TOILETS
RGIEL	MEN
NISA	WOMEN

Where is a/the ...?	*Fejn hi ...?*
Go straight ahead.	*Mur dritt.*
Turn left.	*Dur fuq il-lemin.*
Turn right.	*Dur fuq il-ix-xellug.*
far/near	*il-boghod/viċin*

Around Town

the bank	*il-bank*
the ... embassy	*l'ambaxxata ...*
the hotel	*il-hotel/lakanda*
the post office	*il-posta*
the market	*is-suq*
chemist/pharmacy	*l-ispiżerija*
a public telephone	*telefon pubbliku*
What time does it open/close?	*Fix'hin jiftah/jaghlaq?*

Accommodation

Do you have a room available?	*Ghandek kamra jekk joghoġbok?*
Do you have a room for one person/ two people?	*Ghandek kamra ghal wiehed/ tnejn?*
Do you have a room for one/two nights?	*Ghandek kamra ghal lejl/zewgt iljieli?*
Is breakfast included?	*Il-breakfast inkluż?*

Time, Days & Numbers

What's the time?	*X'hin hu?*
today	*illum*
tomorrow	*ghada*
yesterday	*il-bierah*
morning/afternoon	*fil-ghodu/nofs in-nhar*

Monday	*it-tnejn*
Tuesday	*it-tlieta*
Wednesday	*l-erbgha*
Thursday	*il-hamis*
Friday	*il-gimgha*
Saturday	*is-sibt*
Sunday	*il-hadd*

Emergencies

Help!	*Ajjut!*
Call a doctor.	*Qibghad ghat-tabib.*
Police!	*Pulizija!*
I'm lost.	*Ninsab mitluf.*

1	*wiehed*
2	*tnejn*
3	*tlieta*
4	*erbgha*
5	*hamsa*
6	*sitta*
7	*sebgha*
8	*tmienja*
9	*disgha*
10	*ghaxra*
100	*mija*
1000	*elf*

one million	*miljun*

Moroccan Arabic

Pronunciation

Arabic is a difficult language to learn, but even knowing a few words can win you a friendly smile from the locals.

Vowels There are at least five basic vowel sounds that can be distinguished:

a	as in 'had' (sometimes very short)
e	as in 'bet' (sometimes very short)
i	as in 'hit'
o	as in 'hot'
u	as the 'oo' in 'book'

A stroke over a vowel ('macron') gives it a long sound. For example:

ā	as in 'far'
ē	as in 'ten', but lengthened
ī	as the 'e' in 'ear', only softer (often written as 'ee')
ō	as in 'for'
ū	as the 'oo' in 'food'

Combinations Certain combinations of vowels with vowels or consonants form other vowel sounds (diphthongs):

aw	as the 'ow' in 'how'
ai	as the 'i' in 'high'
ei, ay	as the 'a' in 'cake'

Consonants Many consonants are the same as in English, but there are some tricky ones:

j	more or less as the 'j' in 'John'
H	a strongly whispered 'h', almost like a sigh of relief
q	a strong guttural 'k' sound
kh	a slightly gurgling sound, like the 'ch' in Scottish 'loch'
r	a rolled 'r' sound
s	as in 'sit', never as in 'wisdom'
sh	as in 'she'
z	as the 's' in pleasure
gh	called 'ghayn', similar to the French 'r', but more guttural

Glottal Stop (') The glottal stop is the sound you hear between the vowels in the expression 'oh oh!'. It can occur anywhere in the word – at the beginning, middle or end. When the (') occurs before a vowel (eg 'ayn), the vowel is 'growled' from the back of the throat. If it's before a consonant or at the end of a word, it sounds like a glottal stop.

Basics

Hello.	as-salām 'alaykum
Goodbye.	ma' as-salāma
Yes.	īyeh
No.	la
Please.	'afak
Thank you (very much).	shukran (jazilan)
You're welcome.	la shukran, 'ala wajib
Excuse me.	smeH līya
Do you speak English?	wash kat'ref neglīzīya?
I understand.	fhemt
I don't understand.	mafhemtsh
How much (is it)?	bish-hal?
What's your name?	asmītak?
My name is ...	smītī ...

Getting Around

What time does the ... leave/arrive?	emta qiyam/wusūl ...
boat	al-babūr
bus (city)	al-otobīs
bus (intercity)	al-kar
train	al-mashīna
1st/2nd class	ddarazha llūla/ttanīya
train station	maHattat al-mashīna/ al-qitar
bus stop	mawqif al-otobis

Where can I hire a car/bicycle?	fein yimkin ana akra tomobīl/beshklīta?
Where is (the) ...?	fein ...?
Go straight ahead.	sīr nīshan
Turn right.	dor 'al līmen
Turn left.	dor 'al līser

Around Town

the bank	al-banka
the embassy	as-sifāra
the market	as-sūq
the police station	al-bolīs
the post office	al-bōsta, maktab al-barīd
a toilet	bayt al-ma, mirHad

Accommodation

hotel	al-otēl
youth hostel	dar shabbab
camp site	mukhaym

Is there a room available?	wash kayn shī bīt xawīya?
How much is this room per night?	bshaHal al-bayt liyal?
Is breakfast included?	wash lftor mHsūb m'a lbīt?

Time, Dates & Numbers

What time is it?	shHal fessa'a?
today	al-yūm
tomorrow	ghaddan
yesterday	al-bareh
in the morning	fis-sabaH
in the evening	fil-masa'

Monday	(nhar) al-itnēn
Tuesday	(nhar) at-talata
Wednesday	(nhar) al-arba'
Thursday	(nhar) al-khamīs
Friday	(nhar) al-juma'
Saturday	(nhar) as-sabt
Sunday	(nhar) al-ahad

Emergencies

Help!	'teqnī!
Call a doctor!	'eyyet at-tabīb!
Call the police!	'eyyet al-bolīs!
Go away!	sīr fHalek!

Arabic numerals are simple enough to learn and, unlike the written language, run from left to right. In Morocco, European numerals are also often used.

1	*wāHid*
2	*jūj* or *itnīn*
3	*talata*
4	*arba'a*
5	*khamsa*
6	*sitta*
7	*saba'a*
8	*tamanya*
9	*tissa'*
10	*'ashara*
100	*miyya*
1000	*alf*
one million	*melyūn*

Portuguese

Portuguese pronunciation can be tricky for the uninitiated; like English, vowels and consonants have more than one possible sound depending on position and stress. Moreover, there are nasal vowels and diphthongs in Portuguese with no English equivalents.

Vowels Single vowels should present relatively few problems:

a	short, as the 'u' in 'cut' or long, as the 'ur' in 'hurt'
e	short, as in 'bet' or longer, as in French *été* or English 'heir'. Silent at the end of a word and in unstressed syllables.
é	short, as in 'bet'
ê	long, as the 'a' in 'gate'
i	short, as in 'ring' or long, as the 'ee' in 'see'
o	short, as in 'pot'; long as in 'note'; as the 'oo' in 'good'
ô	long, as in 'note'
u	as the 'oo' in 'good'

Nasal Vowels Nasalisation is represented by an 'n' or an 'm' after the vowel, or by a tilde over it, eg ã. The nasal 'i' exists in English as the 'ing' in 'sing'. For other

vowels, try to pronounce a long 'a', 'ah', or 'e', 'eh', holding your nose, as if you have a cold.

Diphthongs Vowel combinations are relatively straightforward:

au	as the 'ow' in 'now'
ai	as the 'ie' in 'pie'
ei	as the 'ay' in 'day'
eu	as 'e' followed by 'w'
oi	similar to the 'oy' in 'boy'

Nasal Diphthongs Try the same technique as for nasal vowels. To say *não*, pronounce 'now' through your nose.

ão	nasal 'ow' (owng)
ãe	nasal 'ay' (eing)
õe	nasal 'oy' (oing)
ui	similar to the 'uing' in 'ensuing'

Consonants The following consonants are specific to Portuguese:

c	hard, as in 'cat' before a, o or u
c	soft as in 'see' before e or i
ç	as in 'see'
g	hard, as in 'go' before a, o or u
g	soft, as the 's' in 'treasure' before e or i
gu	hard, as in 'guest' before e or i
h	never pronounced when word-initial
nh	as the 'ni' in 'onion'
lh	as the 'lli' in 'million'
j	as the 's' in 'treasure'
m	not pronounced when word-final – it simply nasalises the previous vowel, eg *um* (oong), *bom* (bõ)
qu	as the 'k' in 'key' before e or i
qu	as the 'q' in 'quad' before a or o
r	at the beginning of a word, or **rr** in the middle of a word, a harsh, guttural sound similar to the French *rue*, Scottish *loch*, or German *Bach*. In some areas of Portugal this **r** isn't guttural, but strongly rolled.
r	in the middle or at the end of a word it's a rolled sound stronger than the English 'r'
s	as in 'so' when word-initial and when doubled (**ss**) within a word
s	as the 'z' in 'zeal' when between vowels

s   as the 'sh' in 'ship' when before another consonant, or at the end of a word

x   as the 'sh' in 'ship', as the 'z' in 'zeal', or as the 'x' in 'taxi'

z   as the 's' in 'treasure' before a consonant or at the end of a word

Word Stress Word stress is important in Portuguese, as it can affect meaning. In words with a written accent, the stress always falls on the accented syllable.

Note that Portuguese uses masculine and feminine word endings, usually '-o' and '-a' respectively – to say 'thank you', a man will therefore use *obrigado*, a woman, *obrigada*.

Basics

Hello/Goodbye.	*Bom dia/Adeus.*
Yes/No.	*Sim/Não.*
Please.	*Se faz favor.*
Thank you.	*Obrigado/a.* (m/f)
You're welcome.	*De nada.*
Excuse me.	*Com licença.*
Sorry. (forgive me)	*Desculpe.*
Do you speak English?	*Fala Inglês?*
How much is it?	*Quanto custa?*
What's your name?	*Como se chama?*
My name is ...	*Chamo-me ...*

Getting Around

What time does the ... leave/arrive?	*A que horas parte/ chega ...?*
boat	*o barco*
bus (city)	*o autocarro*
bus (intercity)	*a camioneta*
tram	*o eléctrico*
train	*o combóio*
I'd like a ... ticket.	*Queria um bilhete ...*
one-way	*simples/de ida*
return ticket	*de ida e volta*
I'd like to hire ...	*Queria alugar ...*
a car	*um carro*
a bicycle	*uma bicicleta*
1st class	*primeira classe*
2nd class	*segunda classe*
timetable	*horário*
bus stop	*paragem de autocarro*
train station	*estação ferroviária*

Signs

ENTRADA	ENTRANCE
SAÍDA	EXIT
ENTRADA GRÁTIS	FREE ADMISSION
INFORMAÇÕES	INFORMATION
ABERTO	OPEN
ENCERRADO (OR FECHADO)	CLOSED
O POSTO DA POLÍCIA	POLICE STATION
PROÍBIDO	PROHIBITED
EMPURRE/PUXE	PUSH/PULL
QUARTOS LIVRES	ROOMS AVAILABLE
LAVABOS/WC	TOILETS
h, HOMENS	MEN
s, SENHORAS	WOMEN

Where is ...?	*Onde é ...?*
Go straight ahead.	*Siga sempre a direito/ Siga sempre em frente.*
Turn left.	*Vire à esquerda.*
Turn right.	*Vire à direita.*
near	*perto*
far	*longe*

Around Town

a bank	*um banco*
the ... embassy	*a embaixada de ...*
my hotel	*o meu hotel*
the post office	*os correios*
the market	*o mercado*
the chemist/ pharmacy	*a farmácia*
the newsagency	*a papelaria*
the stationers	*a tabacaria*
the telephone centre	*a central de telefones*
the tourist information office	*o turismo/o posto de turismo*
What time does it open/close?	*A que horas abre/ fecha?*

Accommodation

hotel	*hotel*
guesthouse	*pensão*
youth hostel	*pousada da juventude*
camping ground	*parque de campismo*

Do you have any rooms available?	*Tem quartos livres?*
How much is it per night/per person?	*Quanto é por noite/ por pessoa?*
Is breakfast included?	*O pequeno almoço está incluído?*

a single room	*um quarto individual*
a double room	*um quarto duplo/de casal*
for one/two night/s	*para uma/duas noite/s*

Time, Days & Numbers

What time is it?	*Que horas são?*
today	*hoje*
tomorrow	*amanhã*
yesterday	*ontem*
morning	*manhã*
afternoon	*tarde*

Monday	*segunda-feira*
Tuesday	*terça-feira*
Wednesday	*quarta-feira*
Thursday	*quinta-feira*
Friday	*sexta-feira*
Saturday	*sábado*
Sunday	*domingo*

1	*um/uma*
2	*dois/duas*
3	*três*
4	*quatro*
5	*cinco*
6	*seis*
7	*sete*
8	*oito*
9	*nove*
10	*dez*
11	*onze*
100	*cem*
1000	*mil*
one million	*um milhão*

Emergencies

Help!	*Socorro!*
Call a doctor!	*Chame um médico!*
Call the police!	*Chame a polícia!*
Go away!	*Deixe-me em paz!/ Vai-te embora!* (inf)
I'm lost.	*Estou perdido/a.*

Slovene

Pronunciation

Slovene pronunciation isn't difficult. The alphabet consists of 25 letters, most of which are very similar to English. It doesn't have the letters 'q', 'w', 'x' and 'y', but the following letters are added: ê, é, ó, ò, č, š and ž. Each letter represents only one sound, with very few exceptions, and the sounds are pure and not diphthongal. The letters l and v are both pronounced like the English 'w' when they occur at the end of syllables and before vowels. Though words like *trn* (thorn) look unpronounceable, most Slovenes add a short vowel like an 'a' or the German 'ö' (depending on dialect) in front of the 'r' to give a Scot's pronunciation of 'tern' or 'tarn'. Here is a list of letters specific to Slovene.

c	as the 'ts' in 'its'
č	as the 'ch' in 'church'
ê	as the 'a' in 'apple'
e	as the 'er' in 'opera' (when unstressed)
é	as the 'ay' in 'day'
j	as the 'y' in 'yellow'
ó	as the 'o' in 'more'
ò	as the 'o' in 'soft'
r	a rolled 'r' sound
š	as the 'sh' in 'ship'
u	as the 'oo' in 'good'
ž	as the 's' in 'treasure'

Basics

Hello.	*Zdravo.*
	Živio. (informal)
Good day.	*Dober dan!*
Goodbye.	*Nasvidenje!*
Yes/No.	*Ja/Ne.*
Please.	*Prosim.*
Thank you (very much).	*Hvala (lepa).*
You're welcome.	*Prosim/Ni za kaj!*
Excuse me.	*Oprostite.*
My name is ...	*Moje ime je ...*
Where are you from?	*Od kod ste?*
I'm from ...	*Sem iz ...*

Getting Around

| one-way (ticket) | *enosmerna (vozovnica)* |
| return (ticket) | *povratna (vozovnica)* |

What time does ...	Ob kateri uri ...
leave/arrive?	odpelje/pripelge?
boat/ferry	ladja/trajekt
bus/tram	avtobus/tramvaj
train	vlak

Around Town

bank/exchange	banka/menjalnica
embassy	konzulat, ambasada
post office	pošta
telephone centre	telefonska centrala
tourist office	turistični informacijski urad

Accommodation

hotel	hotel
guesthouse	gostišče
camping ground	kamping

Do you have a ...?	Ali imate prosto ...?
bed	posteljo
cheap room	poceni sobo
single room	enoposteljno sobo
double room	dvoposteljno sobo

for one/two nights	za eno noč/za dve noči

How much is it per	Koliko stane na noč/
night/per person?	na osebo?

Time, Days & Numbers

today	danes
tonight	danes zvečer
tomorrow	jutri
in the morning	zjutraj
in the evening	zvečer

Monday	ponedeljek
Tuesday	torek
Wednesday	sreda

Signs

VHOD	ENTRANCE
IZHOD	EXIT
POLNO/	FULL/
NI PROSTORA	NO VACANCIES
INFORMACIJE	INFORMATION
ODPRTO/ZAPRTO	OPEN/CLOSED
PREPOVEDANO	PROHIBITED
STRANIŠČA	TOILETS

Emergencies

Help!	Na pomoč!
Call a doctor!	Pokličite zdravnika!
Call the police!	Pokličite policijo!
Go away!	Pojdite stran!

Thursday	četrtek
Friday	petek
Saturday	sobota
Sunday	nedelja

1	ena	7	sedem
2	dve	8	osem
3	tri	9	devet
4	štiri	10	deset
5	pet	100	sto
6	šest	1000	tisoč

one million	milijon

Spanish

Pronunciation

Spanish pronunciation isn't difficult, given that many Spanish sounds are similar to their English counterparts and there's a clear and consistent relationship between pronunciation and spelling. If you stick to the following rules you should have very few problems making yourself understood.

Vowels Unlike English, each of the vowels in Spanish has a uniform pronunciation which doesn't vary. For example, the Spanish 'a' has one pronunciation rather than the numerous pronunciations we find in English, such as 'cat', 'cake', 'cart', 'care', 'call'. Many Spanish words have a written accent. The acute accent (as in *días*) generally indicates a stressed syllable and doesn't change the sound of the vowel. Vowels are pronounced clearly even if they are in unstressed positions or at the end of a word.

a	as the 'u' in 'nut', or a shorter sound than the 'a' in 'art'
e	as in 'met'

i	somewhere between the 'i' in 'marine' and the 'i' in 'flip'
o	similar to the 'o' in 'hot'
u	as the 'oo' in 'hoof'

Consonants Some Spanish consonants are the same as their English counterparts. The pronunciation of other consonants varies according to which vowel follows and also according to which part of Spain you happen to be in. The Spanish alphabet also contains three consonants that are not found within the English alphabet: **ch**, **ll** and **ñ**.

b	softer than in English; sometimes as in 'be' when word-initial or preceded by a nasal
c	a hard 'c' as in 'cat' when followed by a, o, u or a consonant; as the 'th' in 'thin' before e and i
ch	as in 'church'
d	as in 'do' when initial; elsewhere as the 'th' in 'then'
g	as in 'get' when initial and before a, o and u; elsewhere much softer. Before e or i it's a harsh, breathy sound, similar to the 'h' in 'hit'
h	silent
j	a harsh, guttural sound similar to the 'ch' in Scottish 'loch'
ll	as the 'lli' in 'million'; some pronounce it rather like the 'y' in 'yellow'
ñ	a nasal sound, as the 'ni' in 'onion'
q	as the 'k' in 'kick'; q is always followed by a silent u and is combined only with the vowels e (as in *que*) and i (as in *qui*)
r	a rolled 'r' sound; longer and stronger when initial or doubled
s	as in 'see'
v	the same sound as b
x	as the 'ks' sound in 'taxi' when between two vowels; as the 's' in 'see' when preceding a consonant
z	as the 'th' in 'thin'

Semiconsonant Spanish also has the semi-consonant **y**. When at the end of a word or when standing alone as a conjunction it's pronounced like the Spanish **i**. As a consonant, it's somewhere between the 'y' in 'yonder' and the 'g' in 'beige', depending on the region.

Basics

Hello.	*¡Hola!*
Goodbye.	*¡Adiós!*
Yes/No.	*Sí/No.*
Please.	*Por favor.*
Thank you.	*Gracias.*
You're welcome.	*De nada.*
Excuse me.	*Perdón/Perdoneme.*
I'm sorry. (forgive me)	*Lo siento/Discúlpeme.*
Do you speak English?	*¿Habla inglés?*
How much is it?	*¿Cuánto cuesta?/ ¿Cuánto vale?*
What's your name?	*¿Cómo se llama?*
My name is ...	*Me llamo ...*

Getting Around

What time does the next ... leave/arrive?	*¿A qué hora sale/ llega el próximo ...?*
boat	*barco*
bus (city)	*autobús, bus*
bus (intercity)	*autocar*
train	*tranvía*
I'd like a ...	*Quisiera un billete ...*
one-way	*sencillo/de sólo ida*
return ticket.	*de ida y vuelta*
1st/2nd class	*primera/segunda clase*
left luggage	*consigna*
timetable	*horario*
bus stop	*parada de autobus*
train station	*estación de ferrocarril*

Signs	
ENTRADA	ENTRANCE
SALIDA	EXIT
OCUPADO, COMPLETO	FULL/ NO VACANCIES
INFORMACIÓN	INFORMATION
ABIERTO	OPEN
CERRADO	CLOSED
PROHIBIDO	PROHIBITED
COMISARÍA	POLICE STATION
HABITACIONES LIBRES	ROOMS AVAILABLE
SERVICIOS/ASEOS	TOILETS
HOMBRES	MEN
MUJERES	WOMEN

I'd like to hire ...	Quisiera alquilar ...
a car	un coche
a bicycle	una bicicleta

Where is ...?	¿Dónde está ...?
Go straight ahead.	Siga/Vaya todo derecho.
Turn left.	Gire a la izquierda.
Turn right.	Gire a la derecha/recto.
near/far	cerca/lejos

Around Town

a bank	un banco
the ... embassy	la embajada ...
my hotel	mi hotel
the post office	los correos
the market	el mercado
chemist/pharmacy	la farmacia
newsagency/	papelería
stationers	
the telephone centre	el locutorio
the tourist office	la oficina de turismo

| What time does it open/close? | ¿A qué hora abren/ cierran? |

Accommodation

hotel	hotel
guesthouse	pensión/casa de huéspedes
youth hostel	albergue juvenil
camping ground	camping

Do you have any rooms available?	¿Tiene habitaciones libres?
How much is it per night/per person?	¿Cuánto cuesta por noche/por persona?
Is breakfast included?	¿Incluye el desayuno?

a single room	una habitación individual
a double room	una habitación doble
for one/two night/s	para una/dos noche/s

Emergencies

Help!	¡Socorro!/¡Auxilio!
Call a doctor!	¡Llame a un doctor!
Call the police!	¡Llame a la policía!
Go away!	¡Váyase!
I'm lost.	Estoy perdido/a.

Time, Days & Numbers

What time is it?	¿Qué hora es?
today	hoy
tomorrow	mañana
yesterday	ayer
morning	mañana
afternoon	tarde

Monday	lunes
Tuesday	martes
Wednesday	miércoles
Thursday	jueves
Friday	viernes
Saturday	sábado
Sunday	domingo

1	uno, una	10	diez
2	dos	11	once
3	tres	12	doce
4	cuatro	13	trece
5	cinco	14	catorce
6	seis	15	quince
7	siete	16	dieciéis
8	ocho	100	cien/ciento
9	nueve	1000	mil

| one million | un millón |

Turkish

Pronunciation

The new Turkish alphabet is phonetic and thus reasonably easy to pronounce, once you've learned a few basic rules. Each Turkish letter is pronounced, there are no diphthongs, and the only silent letter is ğ.

Vowels Turkish vowels are pronounced as follows:

A, a	as the 'ar' in 'art' or 'bar'
E, e	as in 'fell'
İ, i	as 'ee'
I, ı	as 'uh'
O, o	as in 'hot'
U, u	as the 'oo' in 'moo'
Ö, ö	as the 'ur' in 'fur'
Ü, ü	as the 'ew' in 'few'

Note that both ö and ü are pronounced with pursed lips.

LANGUAGE

Consonants Most consonants are pronounced as in English, with a few exceptions:

Ć, ç	as the 'ch' in 'church'
C, c	as English 'j'
Ğ, ğ	not pronounced; draws out the preceding vowel a bit – ignore it!
G, g	hard, as in 'gun'
H, h	as the 'h' in 'half'
J, j	as the 's' in 'treasure'
S, s	hard, as in 'stress'
Ş, ş	as the 'sh' in 'shoe'
V, v	as the 'w' in 'weather'

Basics

Hello.	*Merhaba.*
Goodbye.	*Allahaısmarladık/ Güle güle.*
Yes/No.	*Evet/ Hayır.*
Please.	*Lütfen.*
Thank you.	*Teşekkür ederim.*
That's fine/ You're welcome.	*Bir şey değil.*
Excuse me.	*Affedersiniz.*
Sorry/Pardon.	*Pardon.*

Do you speak English?	*İngilizce biliyor musunuz?*
How much is it?	*Ne kadar?*
What's your name?	*Adınız ne?*
My name is ...	*Adım ...*

Signs

GİRİŞ	ENTRANCE
ÇIKIŞ	EXIT
DOLU	FULL/ NO VACANCIES
DANIŞMA	INFORMATION
AÇIK/KAPALI	OPEN/CLOSED
POLİS/EMNİYET	POLICE
POLİS KARAKOLU/ EMNİYET MÜDÜRLÜĞÜ	POLICE STATION
YASAK(TIR)	PROHIBITED
BOŞ ODA VAR	ROOMS AVAILABLE
TUVALET	TOILET

Getting Around

What time does the next ... leave/arrive?	*Gelecek ... ne zaman kalkar/gelir?*
ferry/boat	*feribot/vapur*
bus (city)	*şehir otobüsü*
bus (intercity)	*otobüs*
tram	*tramvay*
train	*tren*

I'd like ...	*... istiyorum*
a one-way ticket	*gidiş bileti*
a return ticket	*gidiş-dönüş bileti*
1st/2nd class	*birinci/ikinci mevkii*

left luggage	*emanetçi*
timetable	*tarife*
bus/tram stop	*otobüs/tramvay durağı*
train station	*gar/istasyon*
boat/ship dock	*iskele*

I'd like to hire a car/bicycle.	*Araba/bisiklet kiralamak istiyorum.*

Where is a/the ...?	*... nerede?*
Go straight ahead.	*Doğru gidin.*
Turn left.	*Sola dönün.*
Turn right.	*Sağa dönün.*
far/near	*uzak/yakın*

Around Town

a bank	*bir banka*
the ... embassy	*... büyükelçiliği*
my hotel	*otelimi*
the post office	*postane*
the market	*çarşı*
a chemist/pharmacy	*bir eczane*
the telephone centre	*telefon merkezi*
the tourist office	*turizm danışma bürosu*

What time does it open/close?	*Ne zamam açılır/kapanır?*

Accommodation

hotel	*otel(i)*
guesthouse	*pansiyon*
student hostel	*öğrenci yurdu*
camping ground	*kampink*

Do you have any rooms available?	*Boş oda var mı?*
How much is it per night/per person?	*Bir gecelik/Kişibaşına kaç para?*

Is breakfast included? *Kahvaltı dahil mi?*

a single room   *tek kişilik oda*
a double room   *iki kişilik oda*

Time, Days & Numbers

What time is it?	*Saat kaç?*
today	*bugün*
tomorrow	*yarın*
yesterday	*dün*
morning	*sabah*
afternoon	*öğleden sonra*

Monday	*Pazartesi*
Tuesday	*Salı*
Wednesday	*Çarşamba*
Thursday	*Perşembe*
Friday	*Cuma*
Saturday	*Cumartesi*
Sunday	*Pazar*

January	*Ocak*
February	*Şubat*
March	*Mart*
April	*Nisan*
May	*Mayıs*
June	*Haziran*
July	*Temmuz*
August	*Ağustos*
September	*Eylül*
October	*Ekim*
November	*Kasım*
December	*Aralık*

1	*bir*
2	*iki*
3	*üç*
4	*dört*
5	*beş*
6	*altı*
7	*yedi*
8	*sekiz*
9	*dokuz*
10	*on*
11	*on bir*
12	*on iki*
13	*on üç*
100	*yüz*
1000	*bin*

one million   *bir milyon*

Emergencies

Help!/Emergency!	*İmdat!*
There's been an accident!	*Bir kaza oldu!*
(There's a) fire!	*Yangın var!*
Call a doctor!	*Doktor çağırın!*
Call the police!	*Polis çağırın!*
Could you help us please?	*Bize yardım edebilirmisiniz lütfen?*
Go away!	*Gidin/Git!/Defol!*
I'm lost.	*Kayboldum.*

Acknowledgements

THANKS

Many thanks to the travellers who used the last edition and wrote to us with helpful hints, useful advice and interesting anecdotes:

Rod Allan, Kelly Anderson, Philip Anthony, Christine Aquilina, Phoenix Arrien, Catherine Ashford, Jerry Azevedo, Kate Baker, Ramon Baker, Dr RJ Barnes, Jacqueline & Deon Barnes, Peggy Bendall, Javier Betancourt, Dane Birdseye, Ulrika & Jan Bjorkman, Richard Bluett, RS Boylen, David Browning, Gayle Brownlee, Jonathan Bryan, Helene Budinski, Sid Cara, Richard Carnell, Joel Chusid, Christopher Clarke, Bruce & Julie Cook, Cliff Cordy, David Critics, R Curran, Zelko Cvitkovic, Pat Daniel, Kevin Davies, John Deacon, Katja Diezel, Rob Dighton, Juan Gonzalez Dominguez, Rob Duncan, Sarah Dunlop, Richard Eardley, Veronica Egron, Sara Elison, Phillip Elrod, Zeyda Erol, Diane Fahey, Andrea Fechter, Mrs M Foster, Jan Frith, Dave Fuller, Andy Ganner, Jenny Garcia, Donatella Gatti, Josef Gaug, Anne Geange, Johnny Ghanem, Dave & Louise Giles, Luke Gillian, David Glasson, Joel Goldsmith, Gorrit Goslinga, Rene Granacher, Pauline Gummer, Kathy Hagen, Sharyn Hammond, Bjarne Stig Hansen, F Harmelin, Philip Harper, Jonathan Harris, John Harrison, Steve Harrison & Friend, Susie Hartmann, Maria Heritage, NG Hetterley, Frank Higginson, Timothy Hill, Trev Hill, Kate Hill, Melanie Hoods, Mary Hutchings, Dr Ing, Sabahattin Ismail, Peter James, Chris James, Anton Jansen, J Jarman, Sonja Sun Johnsen, Arthur Jones, AJ Julicher, Alfie Kaech, Melita Khawly, Buket Kop Robin Kortright, AH & J Koutsaplis, Ralph Kuehn John Lea, Debbie Lelek, Christoph Lenssen, Len Levine, Paul Lewtas, Matthew Low, Peter Lyon, H Martin, LD Mathews, Graeme Mawson, Sarah McLellan, Andrew McMahon, Jodi McMillan, George Meeker, Kathy Meredith, George Miller, Barbara Molin, Robert Moon, Heico Neumeyer, Sara Newhall, Scott Newman, Christine Newtown, Ippolito Nievo, Stephen O'Neil, Rick Owen, Anne Palmer, Pasco Panconcelli, Sarah Papali'i, Paula Park, Clinton Parkes, Antoine Pecoud, Craig Peers, Renee Petry, Vanessa Pollett, Scott Reardon, Sergio Rebelo, Annette Reeves, F Risi, F Roberts, Dr A Robertson, Maureen Roult, JD Rowe, Karen Sackler-Novick, Robert Saltzstein, M & V Sarubin, Markku Sarubin, Julien Scaife, Rachel Scanlon, Etienne Scheeper, Peg Schlekat, Jacqueline Schliebs, Pushparcy Shetty, Brian Shunamon, Dragan Simic, Anica Siric, Greg Slade, Brendan Smith, Mackay Smith, Kate Smith, Andrew Sneddon, Gary Spinks, Sheila Stephenson, Phini Strati, Johnny Sundberg, Terry Sustig, Flemming Svenningsen, Oscar Szanto, Kiri Tan, Peter Thayer, Sarah Thompson, Anthony Thompson, Michael Tracy, Liesl Trotter, Sharda Ugra, Dorothea Vafiadis, Rimas Valaitis, Maarten van Galen, S van der Donck, Constant van der Heijden, Wikke van Dijk, Nigel Varey, Colin Viney, Dean Vuletic, P Walsh, Jim & Beryl Walter, Pat & John Webb, Peter Wheelan, Lance Williams, Jason Williams, Betty Wilson, Jean-Philippe Wispelaere, Andrew Wyss

LONELY PLANET

Phrasebooks

Lonely Planet phrasebooks are packed with essential words and phrases to help travellers communicate with the locals. With colour tabs for quick reference, an extensive vocabulary, use of script, these handy pocket-sized language guides cover day-to-day travel situations.

- handy pocket-sized books
- easy to understand Pronunciation chapter
- clear & comprehensive Grammar chapter
- romanisation alongside script to allow ease of pronunciation
- script throughout so users can point to phrases for every situations
- full of cultural information and tips for the traveller

'...vital for a real DIY spirit and attitude in language learning'
– Backpacker

'the phrasebooks have good cultural backgrounders and offer solid advice for challenging situations in remote locations'
– San Francisco Examiner

Arabic (Egyptian) • Arabic (Moroccan) • Australia *(Australian English, Aboriginal and Torres Strait languages)* • Baltic States *(Estonian, Latvian, Lithuanian)* • Bengali • Brazilian • Burmese • Cantonese • Central Asia • Central Europe *(Czech, French, German, Hungarian, Italian and Slovak)* • Eastern Europe *(Bulgarian, Czech, Hungarian, Polish, Romanian and Slovak)* • Egyptian Arabic • Ethiopian (Amharic) • Fijian • French • German • Greek • Hill Tribes • Hindi/Urdu • Indonesian • Italian • Japanese • Korean • Lao • Malay • Mandarin • Mediterranean Europe *(Albanian, Croatian, Greek, Italian, Macedonian, Maltese, Serbian, Slovene)* • Mongolian • Nepali • Papua New Guinea • Pilipino (Tagalog) • Quechua • Russian • Scandinavian Europe *(Danish, Finnish, Icelandic, Norwegian and Swedish)* • South-East Asia *(Burmese, Indonesian, Khmer, Lao, Malay, Tagalog Pilipino, Thai and Vietnamese)* • Spanish (Castilian) *(Also includes Catalan, Galician and Basque)* • Spanish (Latin American) • Sri Lanka • Swahili • Thai • Tibetan • Turkish • Ukrainian • USA *(US English, Vernacular Talk, Native American languages and Hawaiian)* • Vietnamese • Western Europe *(Basque, Catalan, Dutch, French, German, Greek, Irish)*

Lonely Planet Journeys

JOURNEYS is a unique collection of travel writing – published by the company that understands travel better than anyone else. It is a series for anyone who has ever experienced – or dreamed of – the magical moment when they encountered a strange culture or saw a place for the first time. They are tales to read while you're planning a trip, while you're on the road or while you're in an armchair, in front of a fire.

These outstanding titles explore our planet through the eyes of a diverse group of international writers. JOURNEYS books catch the spirit of a place, illuminate a culture, recount a crazy adventure, or introduce a fascinating way of life. They always entertain, and always enrich the experience of travel.

MALI BLUES
Traveling to an African Beat
Lieve Joris (translated by Sam Garrett)

Drought, rebel uprisings, ethnic conflict: these are the predominant images of West Africa. But as Lieve Joris travels in Senegal, Mauritania and Mali, she meets survivors, fascinating individuals charting new ways of living between tradition and modernity. With her remarkable gift for drawing out people's stories, Joris brilliantly captures the rhythms of a world that refuses to give in.

THE GATES OF DAMASCUS
Lieve Joris (translated by Sam Garrett)

This best-selling book is a beautifully drawn portrait of day-to-day life in modern Syria. Through her intimate contact with local people, Lieve Joris draws us into the fascinating world that lies behind the gates of Damascus. Hala's husband is a political prisoner, jailed for his opposition to the Assad regime; through the author's friendship with Hala we see how Syrian politics impacts on the lives of ordinary people.

THE OLIVE GROVE
Travels in Greece
Katherine Kizilos

Katherine Kizilos travels to fabled islands, troubled border zones and her family's village deep in the mountains. She vividly evokes breathtaking landscapes, generous people and passionate politics, capturing the complexities of a country she loves.

'beautifully captures the real tensions of Greece' – *Sunday Times*

KINGDOM OF THE FILM STARS
Journey into Jordan
Annie Caulfield

Kingdom of the Film Stars is a travel book and a love story. With honesty and humour, Annie Caulfield writes of travelling in Jordan and falling in love with a Bedouin with film-star looks.

She offers fascinating insights into the country – from the tent life of traditional women to the hustle of downtown Amman – and unpicks tight-woven Western myths about the Arab world.

LONELY PLANET

Lonely Planet Online
www.lonelyplanet.com *or* **AOL keyword: lp**

Whether you've just begun planning your next trip, or you're chasing down specific info on currency regulations or visa requirements, check out Lonely Planet Online for up-to-the minute travel information.

As well as mini guides to more than 250 destinations, you'll find maps, photos, travel news, health and visa updates, travel advisories, and discussion of the ecological and political issues you need to be aware of as you travel. You'll also find timely upgrades to popular guidebooks which you can print out and stick in the back of your book.

There's also an online travellers' forum where you can share your experience of life on the road, meet travel companions and ask other travellers for their recommendations and advice.

And of course we have a complete and up-to-date list of all Lonely Planet travel products including travel guides, diving and snorkelling guides, phrasebooks, atlases, travel literature and videos, and a simple online ordering facility if you can't find the book you want elsewhere.

Lonely Planet Diving & Snorkelling Guides

Known for indispensible guidebooks to destinations all over the world, Lonely Planet's Pisces Books are the most popular series of diving and snorkelling titles available.

There are three series: **Diving and Snorkelling Guides**, **Shipwreck Diving** series, and **Dive Into History**. Full colour throughout, the **Diving & Snorkelling Guides** combine quality photographs with detailed descriptions of the best dive sites for each location, giving divers a glimpse of what they can expect both on land and in water. The **Dive Into History** series is perfect for the adventure diver or armchair traveller. The **Shipwreck Diving** series provides all the details for exploring the most interesting wrecks in the Atlantic and Pacific Oceans. The list also includes underwater nature and technical guides.

LONELY PLANET

Guides by Region

L onely Planet is known worldwide for publishing practical, reliable and no-nonsense travel information in our guides and on our web site. The Lonely Planet list covers just about every accessible part of the world. Currently there are nine series: travel guides, shoestring guides, walking guides, city guides, phrasebooks, audio packs, travel atlases, diving and snorkelling guides and travel literature.

AFRICA Africa – the South • Africa on a shoestring • Arabic (Egyptian) phrasebook • Arabic (Moroccan) phrasebook • Cairo • Cape Town • Central Africa • East Africa • Egypt • Egypt travel atlas • Ethiopian (Amharic) phrasebook • The Gambia & Senegal • Kenya • Kenya travel atlas • Malawi, Mozambique & Zambia • Morocco • North Africa • South Africa, Lesotho & Swaziland • South Africa, Lesotho & Swaziland travel atlas • Swahili phrasebook • Trekking in East Africa • Tunisia • West Africa • Zimbabwe, Botswana & Namibia • Zimbabwe, Botswana & Namibia travel atlas
Travel Literature: The Rainbird: A Central African Journey • Songs to an African Sunset: A Zimbabwean Story • Mali Blues: Travelling to an African Beat

AUSTRALIA & THE PACIFIC Australia • Australian phrasebook • Bushwalking in Australia • Bushwalking in Papua New Guinea • Fiji • Fijian phrasebook • Islands of Australia's Great Barrier Reef • Melbourne • Micronesia • New Caledonia • New South Wales & the ACT • New Zealand • Northern Territory • Outback Australia • Papua New Guinea • Papua New Guinea (Pidgin) phrasebook • Queensland • Rarotonga & the Cook Islands • Samoa • Solomon Islands • South Australia • Sydney • Tahiti & French Polynesia • Tasmania • Tonga • Tramping in New Zealand • Vanuatu • Victoria • Western Australia
Travel Literature: Islands in the Clouds • Sean & David's Long Drive

CENTRAL AMERICA & THE CARIBBEAN Bahamas and Turks & Caicos • Bermuda • Central America on a shoestring • Costa Rica • Cuba • Eastern Caribbean • Guatemala, Belize & Yucatan: La Ruta Maya • Jamaica • Mexico • Mexico City • Panama
Travel Literature: Green Dreams: Travels in Central America

EUROPE Amsterdam • Andalucia • Austria • Baltic States phrasebook • Berlin • Britain • Central Europe • Central Europe phrasebook • Czech & Slovak Republics • Denmark • Dublin • Eastern Europe • Eastern Europe phrasebook • Estonia, Latvia & Lithuania • Finland • France • French phrasebook • Germany • German phrasebook • Greece • Greek phrasebook • Hungary • Iceland, Greenland & the Faroe Islands • Ireland • Italian phrasebook • Italy • Lisbon • London • Mediterranean Europe • Mediterranean Europe phrasebook • Paris • Poland • Portugal • Portugal travel atlas • Prague • Romania & Moldova • Russia, Ukraine & Belarus • Russian phrasebook • Scandinavian & Baltic Europe • Scandinavian Europe phrasebook • Slovenia • Spain • Spanish phrasebook • St Petersburg • Switzerland • Trekking in Spain • Ukrainian phrasebook • Vienna • Walking in Britain • Walking in Italy • Walking in Switzerland • Western Europe • Western Europe phrasebook
Travel Literature: The Olive Grove: Travels in Greece

INDIAN SUBCONTINENT Bangladesh • Bengali phrasebook • Bhutan • Delhi • Goa • Hindi/Urdu phrasebook • India • India & Bangladesh travel atlas • Indian Himalaya • Karakoram Highway • Nepal • Nepali phrasebook • Pakistan • Rajasthan • South India • Sri Lanka • Sri Lanka phrasebook • Trekking in the Indian Himalaya • Trekking in the Karakoram & Hindukush • Trekking in the Nepal Himalaya
Travel Literature: In Rajasthan • Shopping for Buddhas

LONELY PLANET

Mail Order

Lonely Planet products are distributed worldwide. They are also available by mail order from Lonely Planet, so if you have difficulty finding a title please write to us. North and South American residents should write to Embarcadero West, 150 Linden St, Suite 251, Oakland CA 94607, USA; European and African residents should write to 10a Spring Place, London, NW5 3BH; and residents of other countries to PO Box 617, Hawthorn, Victoria 3122, Australia.

ISLANDS OF THE INDIAN OCEAN Madagascar & Comoros • Maldives • Mauritius, Reunion & Seychelles

MIDDLE EAST & CENTRAL ASIA Arab Gulf States • Central Asia • Iran • Israel & the Palestinian Territories • Israel & the Palestinian Territories travel atlas • Istanbul • Jerusalem • Jordan & Syria • Jordan, Syria & Lebanon travel atlas • Lebanon • Middle East on a shoestring • Turkey • Turkish phrasebook • Turkey travel atlas • Yemen
Travel Literature: The Gates of Damascus • Kingdom of the Film Stars: Journey into Jordan

NORTH AMERICA Alaska • Backpacking in Alaska • Baja California • California & Nevada • Canada • Florida • Hawaii • Honolulu • Los Angeles • Miami • New England USA • New Orleans • New York City • New York, New Jersey & Pennsylvania • Pacific Northwest USA • Rocky Mountain States • San Francisco • Seattle • Southwest USA • USA phrasebook • Washington, DC & the Capital Region
Travel Literature: Drive Thru America

NORTH-EAST ASIA Beijing • Cantonese phrasebook • China • Hong Kong • Hong Kong, Macau & Guangzhou • Japan • Japanese phrasebook • Japanese audio pack • Korea • Korean phrasebook • Kyoto • Mandarin phrasebook • Mongolia • Mongolian phrasebook • North-East Asia on a shoestring • Seoul • South West China • Taiwan • Tibet • Tibet phrasebook • Tokyo
Travel Literature: Lost Japan

SOUTH AMERICA Argentina, Uruguay & Paraguay • Bolivia • Brazil • Brazilian phrasebook • Buenos Aires • Chile & Easter Island • Chile & Easter Island travel atlas • Colombia • Ecuador & the Galapagos Islands • Latin American (Spanish) phrasebook • Peru • Quechua phrasebook • Rio de Janeiro • South America on a shoestring • Trekking in the Patagonian Andes • Venezuela
Travel Literature: Full Circle: A South American Journey

SOUTH-EAST ASIA Bali & Lombok • Bangkok • Burmese phrasebook • Cambodia • Ho Chi Minh City • Indonesia • Indonesian phrasebook • Indonesian audio pack • Jakarta • Java • Laos • Lao phrasebook • Laos travel atlas • Malay phrasebook • Malaysia, Singapore & Brunei • Myanmar (Burma) • Philippines • Pilipino (Tagalog) phrasebook • Singapore • South-East Asia on a shoestring • South-East Asia phrasebook • Thailand • Thailand's Islands & Beaches • Thailand travel atlas • Thai phrasebook • Thai audio pack • Thai Hill Tribes phrasebook • Vietnam • Vietnamese phrasebook • Vietnam travel atlas

ALSO AVAILABLE: Antarctica • Brief Encounters: Stories of Love, Sex & Travel • Chasing Rickshaws • Not the Only Planet: Travel Stories from Science Fiction • Travel with Children • Traveller's Tales

LONELY PLANET

FREE Lonely Planet Newsletters

We love hearing from you and think you'd like to hear from us.

Planet Talk

Our FREE quarterly printed newsletter is full of tips from travellers and anecdotes from Lonely Planet guidebook authors. Every issue is packed with up-to-date travel news and advice, and includes:

- a postcard from Lonely Planet co-founder Tony Wheeler
- a swag of mail from travellers
- a look at life on the road through the eyes of a Lonely Planet author
- topical health advice
- prizes for the best travel yarn
- news about forthcoming Lonely Planet events
- a complete list of Lonely Planet books & other titles

To join our mailing list, residents of the UK, Europe and Africa can email us at go@lonelyplanet.co.uk; residents of North and South America can email us at info@lonelyplanet.com; rest of the world can email us at talk2us@lonelyplanet.com, or contact any Lonely Planet office

---

Comet

Our FREE monthly email newsletter brings you all the latest travel news, features, interviews, competitions, destination ideas, travellers' tips & tales, Q&As, raging debates and related links. Find out what's new on the Lonely Planet Web site and which books are about to hit the shelves.

Subscribe from your desktop: www.lonelyplanet.com/comet

Index

Abbreviations

Text

Bold indicates maps

Bold indicates maps

MAP LEGEND

BOUNDARIES

International
State
Disputed

HYDROGRAPHY

Coastline
River, Creek
Lake
Intermittent Lake
Salt Lake
Canal
Spring, Rapids
Waterfalls
Swamp

ROUTES & TRANSPORT

Freeway
Highway
Major Road
Minor Road
Unsealed Road ========
City Freeway
City Highway
City Road
City Street, Lane

Pedestrian Mall
Tunnel
Train Route & Station
Metro & Station
Tramway
Cable Car or Chairlift
Walking Track
Walking Tour
Ferry Route

AREA FEATURES

Building
Park, Gardens
Cemetery

Market
Beach, Desert
Urban Area

MAP SYMBOLS

CAPITAL	National Capital		Airport
CAPITAL	State Capital		Ancient or City Wall
CITY	City		Archaeological Site
Town	Town	$	Bank
Village	Village		Beach
o	Point of Interest		Castle or Fort
■	Place to Stay		Cave
Å	Camping Ground		Church
ᗏ	Caravan Park		Cliff or Escarpment
Ç	Hut or Chalet	O	Embassy
▲	Place to Eat	O	Hospital
☐	Pub or Bar		Mosque

血	Museum
▲	Mountain or Hill
血	Stately Home
☷	Swimming Pool
☎	Telephone
盒	Temple
☻	Toilet
☺	Tourist Information
☺	Transport
🐾	Zoo

☐	Post Office
❖	Shopping Centre
✳	Police Station
)(	Pass
🅿	Parking
→	One Way Street

Note: not all symbols displayed above appear in this book

LONELY PLANET OFFICES

Australia
PO Box 617, Hawthorn 3122, Victoria
tel: (03) 9819 1877 fax: (03) 9819 6459
e-mail: talk2us@lonelyplanet.com.au

USA
150 Linden St, Oakland, CA 94607
tel: (510) 893 8555 TOLL FREE: 800 275-8555
fax: (510) 893 8572
e-mail: info@lonelyplanet.com

UK
10a Spring Place, London, NW5 3BH
tel: (0171) 428 4800 fax: (0170) 428 4828
e-mail: go@lonelyplanet.co.uk

France
1 rue du Dahomey, 75011 Paris
tel: 01 55 25 33 00 fax: 01 55 25 33 01
e-mail: bip@lonelyplanet.fr

World Wide Web: www.lonelyplanet.com *or* **AOL keyword: lp**
Lonely Planet Images: lpi@lonelyplanet.com.au